Germany

THE ROUGH GUIDE

There are more than one hundred Rough Guide titles
covering destinations from Amsterdam to Zimbabwe

Forthcoming titles include
Brussels • Central America
Japan • Maya World • New England

Rough Guide Reference Series
Classical Music • European Football • The Internet • Jazz
Opera • Reggae • Rock Music • World Music

Rough Guide Phrasebooks
Czech • Egyptian Arabic • French • German • Greek • Hindi & Urdu
Hungarian • Indonesian • Italian • Japanese • Mandarin Chinese
Mexican Spanish • Polish • Portuguese • Russian • Spanish
Swahili • Thai • Turkish • Vietnamese

Rough Guides on the Internet
http://www.roughguides.com

ROUGH GUIDE CREDITS

Text editor: Chris Schüler
Series editor: Mark Ellingham
Editorial: Martin Dunford, Jonathan Buckley, Samantha Cook, Jo Mead, Kate Berens, Amanda Tomlin, Ann-Marie Shaw, Paul Gray, Sarah Dallas, Julia Kelly, Helena Smith, Caroline Osborne, Kieran Falconer, Judith Bamber, Olivia Eccleshall, Orla Duane (UK); Andrew Rosenberg (US)
Production: Susanne Hillen, Andy Hilliard, Judy Pang, Link Hall, Nicola Williamson, Helen Ostick

Picture research: Eleanor Hill
Cartography: Melissa Flack, Maxine Burke
Online editors: Alan Spicer (UK); Geronimo Madrid (US)
Finance: John Fisher, Celia Crowley, Neeta Mistry
Marketing & Publicity: Richard Trillo, Simon Carloss, Niki Smith (UK); Jean-Marie Kelly, SoRelle Braun (US)
Administration: Tania Hummel, Alexander Mark Rogers

ACKNOWLEDGEMENTS

Special thanks are due on this edition to Chris Schüler for careful and attentive editing of the much-altered text; to Ulf Schiefer for updating the entry on Bremen, and the whole of Chapter 7; to Andrew Roth for updating Berlin and Potsdam; and to Janice and Steve Hopwood for their ever-generous hospitality in Munich.

Thanks also to all the dozens of tourist offices in Germany who provided so much information and help and in particular to Astrid Ganssen and her press office colleagues (Munich), Ute Meesmann (Würzburg) and Johannes Kempter (Rothenburg ob der Tauber); to Agatha Suess of the German National Tourist Office in London for introductory letters; to Helen McLachlan, Birgit Lang, Marianne Rombach and Wilfried Renkel for help, encouragement and advice; to Link Hall for typesetting; Derek Wilde for proofreading; and to Stratigraphics, and Maxine Burke, for the cartography. We are also grateful to Richard Mead for the Beatles box on p.665; to

Natascha Norton, for her contributions to previous editions; and to all the readers who have written in, with honourable mention to Günter Hartmann for recommendations in Kassel and to regular correspondent Dr Stephan v. Paczynski for so many useful tips about a host of places, notably Mainz, the Rheingau and Tübingen. A full list appears on p.v.

the author

Gordon McLachlan first became fascinated by Germany while studying modern European history at school and university in his native Edinburgh. Over the past decade, while researching this guide and its three predecessors, plus books on Berlin and the Romantic Road, he has visited every corner of the country, monitoring closely its transition from a divided to a unified nation. He has also written parts of several other Rough Guides, including Edinburgh, Scotland, Britain and Poland.

PUBLISHING INFORMATION

This fourth edition published March 1998 by Rough Guides Ltd, 62–70 Shorts Gardens, London WC2H 9AB. Reprinted in January 1999.
Distributed by the Penguin Group:
Penguin Books Ltd, 27 Wrights Lane, London W8 5TZ
Penguin Books USA Inc., 375 Hudson Street, New York 10014, USA
Penguin Books Australia Ltd, 487 Maroondah Highway, PO Box 257, Ringwood, Victoria 3134, Australia
Penguin Books Canada Ltd, 10 Alcorn Avenue, Toronto, Ontario, Canada M4V 1E4
Penguin Books (NZ) Ltd, 182–190 Wairau Road, Auckland 10, New Zealand
Typeset in Linotron Univers and Century Old Style to an original design by Andrew Oliver.
Printed in England by Clays Ltd, St Ives PLC
Illustrations in Part One and Part Three by Edward Briant.

Illustration on p.1 by Simon Fell & on p.983 by David Loftus
1072pp - Includes index
A catalogue record for this book is available from the British Library
ISBN 1-85828-309-4

Germany

THE ROUGH GUIDE

written and researched by

Gordon McLachlan

with additional contributions by

John Gawthrop, Jack Holland, Andrew Roth and Ulf Schiefer

THE ROUGH GUIDES

THE ROUGH GUIDES

TRAVEL GUIDES • PHRASEBOOKS • MUSIC AND REFERENCE GUIDES

 We set out to do something different when the first Rough Guide was published in 1982. Mark Ellingham, just out of university, was travelling in Greece. He brought along the popular guides of the day, but found they were all lacking in some way. They were either strong on ruins and museums but went on for pages without mentioning a beach or taverna. Or they were so conscious of the need to save money that they lost sight of Greece's cultural and historical significance. Also, none of the books told him anything about Greece's contemporary life – its politics, its culture, its people, and how they lived.

So with no job in prospect, Mark decided to write his own guidebook, one which aimed to provide practical information that was second to none, detailing the best beaches and the hottest clubs and restaurants, while also giving hard-hitting accounts of every sight, both famous and obscure, and providing up-to-the-minute information on contemporary culture. It was a guide that encouraged independent travellers to find the best of Greece, and was a great success, getting shortlisted for the Thomas Cook travel guide award,

and encouraging Mark, along with three friends, to expand the series.

The Rough Guide list grew rapidly and the letters flooded in, indicating a much broader readership than had been anticipated, but one which uniformly appreciated the Rough Guide mix of practical detail and humour, irreverence and enthusiasm. Things haven't changed. The same four friends who began the series are still the caretakers of the Rough Guide mission today: to provide the most reliable, up-to-date and entertaining information to independent-minded travellers of all ages, on all budgets.

We now publish 100 titles and have offices in London and New York. The travel guides are written and researched by a dedicated team of more than 100 authors, based in Britain, Europe, the USA and Australia. We have also created a unique series of phrasebooks to accompany the travel series, along with an acclaimed series of music guides, and a best-selling pocket guide to the Internet and World Wide Web. We also publish comprehensive travel information on our web site:

http://www.roughguides.com

HELP US UPDATE

We've gone to a lot of effort to ensure that this new edition of The Rough Guide to Germany is accurate and up-to-date. However, things change — places get "discovered", opening hours are notoriously fickle, restaurants and rooms raise prices or lower standards, extra buses are laid on or off. If you feel we've got it wrong or left something out, we'd like to know, and if you can remember the address, the price, the time, the phone number, so much the better.

We'll credit all contributions, and send a copy of the next edition (or any other Rough Guide if you prefer) for the best letters. Please mark letters: "Rough Guide Germany Update" and send to:
Rough Guides, 62–70 Shorts Gardens, London WC2H 9AB, or Rough Guides, 375 Hudson St, 9th floor, New York NY 10014. Or send email to: mail@roughguides.co.uk
Online updates about this book can be found on Rough Guides' website at http://www.roughguides.com

READERS' LETTERS

Thanks to the readers of the last edition who wrote in with helpful comments and suggestions:

John R. T. Bailey, S. Barton, A.C. Berridge, Paul T. Bryant, John Buttery, Liz Cooke, Nigel Cox, Barry Creevy, Nicola Davenport, Richard Drew, E. Durban, Doris Eddelbüttel, Maurice Fairall, Katharina Füllenbach, M.D. Grieve, Ellen Harland, Günter Hartmann, Kay Hatfield, John Haeussler, Martin M. Hill, David & Greeba Hughes, David Isherwood, Anton Jansen, Ken Kimber, Matt Kingsland, Martin Kirby, Dr Martin Kraatz, Gary Lancet, Sarah Lane, Emily Lewis, M.W. Lloyd, Edgar Locke, June Lowery-Kingston, Julie MacPherson, Kirsty Martin, Lisa O'Sullivan, James Peters & Michelle Continho, Dr Stephan v. Paczynski, G. Parker, Ben Pollard, Sarah Price, Sally & Mark Ramsey, Christof Schatz, H. Schleef, Susan Tamlyn, Ray Tarling, Catherine Taylor, Robert Thorne & Liz Robinson, Anna Vaughn & Sophie van Wingerden, Mary Wharmby, Tim Yates.

Apologies to any reader whose name has been omitted inadvertantly or spelt incorrectly.

CONTENTS

Introduction x

PART THREE CONTEXTS 983

LIST OF MAPS

MAP SYMBOLS			
———	Railway	▲	Peak
═══	Road	⌃⌃	Mountains
- - - - -	Path	ⓘ	Tourist office
– – –	Ferry route	⊠	Post office
———	Waterway	■	Building
▬ ▬ ▬	Chapter division boundary	✛	Church
■■■■	International boundary	₊†₊	Cemetery
⚊	Campsite	▨	Park
Ⓤ	U-Bahn	▨	National park
Ⓢ	S-Bahn		

INTRODUCTION

Germany has always been the problem child of Europe. For over a millennium it was no more than a loose confederation of separate states and territories, whose number at times topped the thousand mark. When unification belatedly came about in 1871, it was achieved almost exclusively by military might; as a direct result of this, the new nation was consumed by a thirst for power and expansion abroad. Defeat in World War I only led to a desire for revenge, the consequence of which was the Third Reich, a regime bent on mass genocide and on European, indeed world, domination. It took another tragic global war to crush this system and its people. When the victors quarrelled over how to prevent Germany ever again becoming dominant, they divided it into two hostile states; the parts held by the western powers were developed into the **Federal Republic of Germany**, while the eastern zone occupied by the Soviets became the **German Democratic Republic**.

The contest between the two was an unequal one – the GDR, never able to break free from being a client state of the Soviet Union and forced to adopt a Communist system at odds with the national character, had fallen so far behind its rival in living standards that in 1961 the authorities constructed the notorious electrified barbed wire frontier, with the **Berlin Wall** as its lynchpin, to halt emigration – the first time in the history of the world that a fortification system had been erected by a regime against its own people. Thereafter, the society settled down, but the GDR was a grey, cheerless place whose much trumpted economic success was a mirage, and bought at the price of terrible pollution problems.

On the other hand, the Federal Republic – which was seen as the natural successor to the old Reich, if only on account of its size – had not only picked itself up by the boot-straps, but developed into what many outsiders regarded as a **model modern society**. A nation with little in the way of a liberal tradition, and even less of a democratic one, quickly developed a degree of political maturity that put other countries to shame. In atonement for past sins, the new state committed itself to providing a haven for foreign refugees and dissidents. It also became a multiracial and multicultural society – even if the reason for this was less one of penance than the self-interested need to acquire extra cheap labour to fuel the economic boom. A delicate balance was struck between the old and the new. Historic town centres were immaculately restored, while the corporate skyscrapers and well-stocked department stores represented a commitment to a modern consumer society. Vast sums of money were lavished on preserving the best of the country's cultural legacy, yet equally generous budgets were allocated to encouraging all kinds of contemporary expression in the arts.

Officially, the Federal Republic was always a "provisional" state, biding its time before national re-unification occurred. Yet there was a realization that nobody outside Germany was really much in favour of this. "I love Germany so much I'm glad there are two of them", scoffed the French novelist François Mauriac, articulating the unspoken gut reactions of the powers on both sides of the Iron Curtain. German division may have been cruel, but at least it had provided a lasting solution to the German "problem". Such thinking was rendered obsolete by the unstoppable momentum of events in the wake of the **Wende**, the peaceful revolution that toppled the Communist regime in the GDR in 1989, leading to the full union of the two Germanys less than a year later. Yet initial euphoria has been quickly replaced by concern about the myriad problems facing the new nation as it attempts to integrate the bankrupt social and economic system of the GDR into the successful framework of the Federal Republic. While Germany may officially be one again, it will certainly continue to look and feel like two separate countries until the end of the century – and probably well beyond. Moreover, international pressure has ensured that, far from being a re-creation of the old Reich, it can be no more than the nineteenth-century concept of a *Kleines Deutschland* ("little Germany"), excluding not only Austria but also the "lost" Eastern Territories, which are now part of Poland, the Czech Republic and the Russian Federation.

In total contrast to Germany's intrinsic fascination as the country which has played such a determining role in the history of the twentieth century, is its otherwise predominantly **romantic image**. This is the land of fairy-tale castles, of thick dark forests, of the legends collected by the Brothers Grimm, of perfectly preserved timber-framed medieval towns, and of jovial locals swilling from huge foaming mugs of beer. As always, there *is* some truth in these stereotypes, though most of them stem from the southern part of the country, particularly **Bavaria**, which, as a predominantly rural and Catholic area, stands apart from the urbanized Protestant north which engineered the unity of the nation last century and thereafter dominated its affairs.

Regional characteristics, indeed, are a strong feature of German life, and there are many hangovers from the days when the country was a political patchwork, even though some historical provinces have vanished from the map and others have merged. More detail on each of the current Länder, as the constituent states are now known, can be found in the chapter introductions. **Hamburg** and **Bremen**, for example, retain their age-old status as free cities. The Imperial capital, **Berlin**, also stands apart, as an island in the midst of the erstwhile GDR where the liberalism of the West was pushed to its extreme, sometimes decadent, always exciting. In polar opposition to it, and as a corrective to the normal view of the Germans as an essentially serious race, is the **Rhineland**, where the great river's majestic sweep has spawned a particularly rich fund of legends and folklore, and where the locals are imbued with a Mediterranean-type sense of fun. The five **new Länder** which have supplanted the GDR, and in particular the small towns and rural areas, are in many ways the ones which best encapsulate the feel and appearance of Germany as it was before the war and the onset of foreign influences which were an inevitable consequence of defeat.

Where and when to go

There's enough variety within all but the smallest Länder to fill several weeks of travel, and you may prefer to confine your trip to just one or two regions. Among the **scenic highlights** are the Bavarian Alps, the Bodensee, the Black Forest, the valleys of the Rhine and Mosel, the Baltic island of Rügen, the Harz, and Saxon Switzerland. However, you may prefer one of the many less spectacular areas of natural beauty, which can be found in every province – these are the places the Germans themselves love the most, and where they spend their holidays and weekends. Several of the cities have the air of capitals, though **Bonn** has lost the role it "temporarily" carried for fifty years. Nearby **Cologne**, on the other hand, is one of the most characterful cities in the country, and the richest in historic monuments. Bavaria's capital, **Munich**, is another obvious star and boasts of having the best the country has to offer – whether in museums, beer, fashion or sport. **Nürnberg** reflects on its bygone years of glory, while **Frankfurt** looks on itself as the "real" capital of the country and **Stuttgart** and **Düsseldorf** compete for the title of champion of German postwar success. In the east, **Dresden** is making a comeback as one of the world's great cultural centres, while **Leipzig** is returning to its role as one of the continent's main trading centres. However, as all these cities have suffered to a considerable extent from bomb damage and ugly postwar redevelopment, the smaller places in many respects offer a more satisfying experience. Chief among these is the university city of **Heidelberg**, star and guiding light of the Romantic movement. Trier, Bamberg, Regensburg, Rothenburg and Marburg in the west, and Potsdam, Meissen and Quedlinburg in the east, are some of the many towns which deserve to be regarded among the most outstanding in Europe.

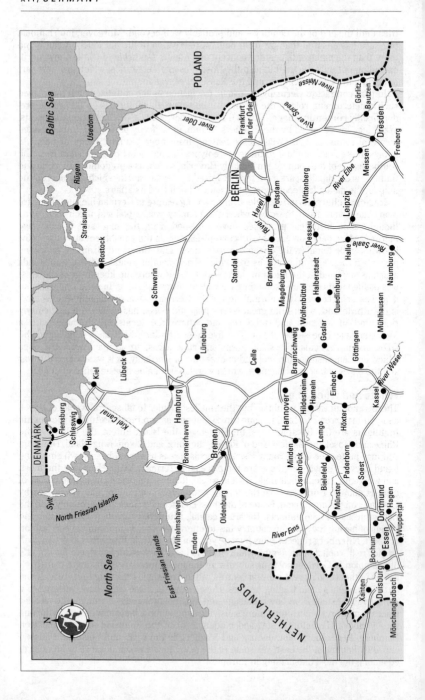

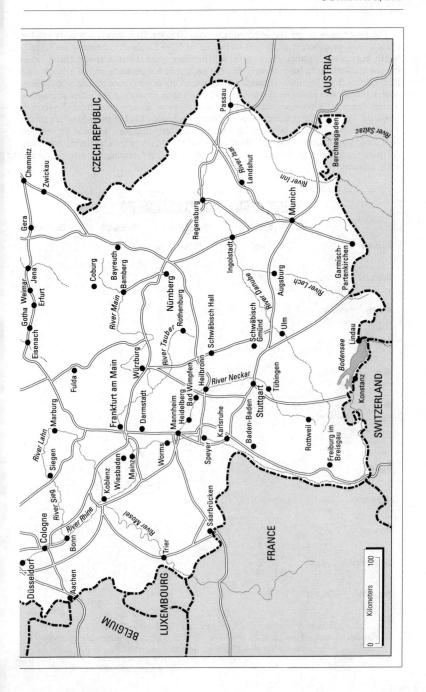

The best **times to go** are between April and October. Germany has a fairly volatile climate, not so different from that of Britain or New England. Summers are usually warm, but not overpoweringly so; good weather may come at an unexpected time, while it's not uncommon to have several abrupt changes in temperature within a single day. Rain occurs fairly regularly throughout the year. Unless you're intending to go skiing, winter travel can't really be recommended, other than for seeing the cities stripped of tourist hordes. Otherwise, there's a chance of snow at any time from November onwards. In the really popular areas, the claustrophobic effect of masses of organized tour groups is a factor to be taken into account between mid-June and mid-September: best avoid such places altogether then, and head for the many less spoiled alternatives. All things considered, however, the ideal times for visiting Germany are late spring and early autumn.

AVERAGE TEMPERATURES (°F)		Berlin	Frankfurt	Hamburg	Munich
January	Max	48	50	36	35
	Min	10	14	28	23
February	Max	52	54	37	38
	Min	10	16	28	23
March	Max	63	66	44	48
	Min	19	25	31	30
April	Max	72	75	55	56
	Min	28	32	38	38
May	Max	82	84	64	64
	Min	36	37	46	45
June	Max	86	88	69	70
	Min	43	45	51	51
July	Max	90	91	73	74
	Min	48	50	55	36
August	Max	88	90	72	73
	Min	46	48	54	55
September	Max	82	82	66	67
	Min	39	41	49	54
October	Max	70	70	55	62
	Min	30	32	43	48
November	Max	55	59	45	56
	Min	25	27	37	40
December	Max	50	52	39	44
	Min	16	19	31	33

To convert °Fahrenheit into °Centigrade, subtract 32 and multiply by 5/9
Rainfall is consistent throughout the year for all the above cities, at 2–3 inches per month; only Munich exceeds this, with an average 4–6 inches per month in summer

PART ONE

THE
BASICS

GETTING THERE FROM BRITAIN

The most convenient and usually best-value way to get to Germany is to fly – flights from London Heathrow to Frankfurt take 65 minutes, compared with a minimum of 9 hours by train. Taking the train and driving has become even easier now that Le Shuttle cross-Channel services are operating. There are also two direct ferry services to Hamburg, from Harwich and Newcastle.

BY PLANE

Most major west German cities have numerous daily links with London (Heathrow and Gatwick), as well as with several regional UK airports. Flight times are around sixty to ninety minutes. Often you'll find that the lowest fares and the most frequent flights are to **Frankfurt**, very much at the centre of German air routes. To fly to other German cities costs slightly more, while **Berlin** and the former GDR cities are the most expensive of all to reach.

SCHEDULED FLIGHTS

A **scheduled flight** is the most obvious option, with *British Airways* and *Lufthansa* being the main carriers. They are rarely the cheapest option but can give you the flexibility you may need, and some of their special promotional offers can be highly competitive. Also available are **open-jaw flights** (fly into one airport, back from another) which are expensive but ideal if you want to cover a lot of the country; fly-drive deals; and inexpensive connections from most regional airports.

The **cheapest tickets** go by various, constantly changing names at different times of the year, but they are usually valid for seven to ninety days, require you to stay at least one Saturday night, and don't allow for change or cancellation. From London, expect prices of around £119 to Frankfurt, £129 to Hamburg or Munich and £159 to Berlin. From Birmingham, British Airways flies direct to Frankfurt for £139, Hamburg for £149 and Berlin for £209; from Glasgow or Edinburgh you're looking at £155, £204 and £234 respectively.

You can usually cut costs by booking through a discount agent who will often be able to sell you a scheduled seat cheaper or find you a direct charter flight.

DISCOUNTED FLIGHTS

For **discounted flights**, the widest selection of ads for London departures is invariably found in the classified pages of the London listings magazine *Time Out*. For departures from other British airports check the travel supplements of local evening papers and the *Sunday Times*, the *Independent on Sunday* or the *Observer*. The agents and operators listed in the box on p.4 make a good start. The *German Travel Centre* is particularly worth trying as they deal solely in flights to Germany. You should be able to find fares more around £99 to Frankfurt, £115 to Hamburg or Munich, £150 to Berlin, although remember that discounted tickets do carry restrictions. Often, these flights will be short hops with airlines on long-haul routes to the Gulf states or the USA, and all leave from London.

Charters are usually blockbooked by package holiday firms, but even in the middle of August spare seats are often sold off at discounts. For an idea of current prices and availability, contact any high street travel agent, or a specialist operator. The major disadvantage with charter flights is the fixed return date – a maximum of four weeks from the outward journey.

Students and anyone **under 26** can also take advantage of special discount flights, most frequently to Frankfurt. The best firms for these are independent travel specialists *STA Travel* and *Campus Travel* (see box for addresses). Student-union travel bureaux can usually fix you up with flights through one of these operators, and they are also worth calling whether you are a student

AIRLINES AND OPERATORS IN BRITAIN

British Airways 156 Regent St, London W1R 6LB; 146 New St, Birmingham B2 4HN; 19–21 St Mary's Gate, Market St, Manchester M1 1PU; 66 Gordon St, Glasgow G1 3RS; 32 Frederick St, Edinburgh EH2 2JR (all enquiries ☎0345/222111).

Lufthansa 10 Old Bond St, London W1X 4EN; 78 St Vincent St, Glasgow G2 5UB (all enquiries ☎0345/737747).

AGENTS AND OPERATORS

Bents The Blue Cross, Orleton, Ludlow, Shrops (☎01568/780800).*Cycle and walking tours.*

Campus Travel 52 Grosvenor Gardens, London SW1 (☎0171/730 3402); 541 Bristol Rd, Selly Oak, Birmingham (☎0121/414 1848); 39 Queen's Rd, Clifton, Bristol (☎0117/929 2494); 5 Emmanuel St, Cambridge (☎01223/324283); 53 Forest Rd, Edinburgh (☎0131/668 3303); 166 Deansgate, Manchester (☎0161/833 2046); 105–6 St Aldates, Oxford (☎01865/242067); also in YHA shops and on university campuses throughout Britain. *Youth/student specialist.*

DER Travel Service 18 Conduit St, London W1R 9TD (☎0171/290 1111). *The national German travel agency offering a full range of tours as well as accommodation service and rail passes.*

German Travel Centre German House, 403–9 Rayners Lane, Pinner, Middlesex HA5 5ER (☎0181/429 2900). *Discount flight specialist.*

Moswin's 21 Church St, Oadby, Leicester (☎0116/271 4982). *A specialist in Germany, with a wide variety of package holidays.*

Ramblers Holidays PO Box 43, Longcroft House, Frethern Rd, Welwyn Garden City, Herts AL8 6PQ (☎01707/320226). *Long-established and reputable walking holiday specialist offering organized trips to the Black Forest and Allgäu Alps.*

STA Travel 86 Old Brompton Rd, London SW7, 117 Euston Rd, London NW1; 38 Store St, London WC1 (☎0171/361 6161); 25 Queen's Rd, Bristol BS8 1QE (☎0117/929 4399); 38 Sidney St, Cambridge CB2 3HX (☎01223/66966); 36 George St, Oxford OX1 2OJ (☎01865/792800); 75 Deansgate, Manchester M3 2BW (☎0161/834 0668). *Independent travel specialists; discounted flights.*

Taber Holidays 126 Sunbridge Rd, Bradford (☎01274/735611). *Another German specialist.*

Waymark Holidays 44 Windsor Rd, Slough SL1 2EJ (☎01753/516477). *Walking holidays in the Black Forest and winter cross-country skiing trips to Oberammergau.*

or not as they offer a good range of budget fares. Current student fares begin at £96 to Frankfurt, and it should be possible to get a ticket to most other major German cities for a similar outlay.

PACKAGE AND CITY BREAKS

Most travel agents have brochures detailing the many **package holidays** to Germany. For the most part, you'll pay more than would be the case if you arrange everything yourself. But if you're in a rush or just can't be bothered with the donkey work, they do represent a reliable and well-organized alternative.

The most common type of package, and also the best value, are **motoring holidays**, where you drive your own car to Germany and have pre-arranged accommodation (and sometimes meals) in hotels or guest houses in several locations. The price also includes the ferry crossing

and insurance. The pick of these are operated by *DER Travel Service* (see box above), who have a wide selection of packages all over Germany and whose prices include ferry travel from a choice of five UK ports. Typical charges per person are around £300 for a week for two people sharing in the Rhineland or Black Forest; this rises by £98–129 if you go by rail instead. The same company offers **fly-drive packages**, where you fly to a German city and pick up a rental car there.

Short **city breaks** are offered by most major travel agents. If you don't want the hassle of booking the flight and finding accommodation yourself, these can be very convenient and, especially out of season, you can get some good bargains. Prices start at £169 for three days (two nights) in Cologne or Düsseldorf, £199 in Berlin, Leipzig, Hamburg, Bremen or Munich. Adding extra nights or upgrading your hotel is possible. The prices always include return flights, transfers and bed and breakfast in a centrally located hotel. Again, ask your travel agent for the best deal, and check the specialists in the box opposite. If you want an all-inclusive trip to the **Oktoberfest** arranged for you, you're looking at around £335 for three nights and again DER are the best operators to try. They also offer an eight-day **Romantic Road** route with bed and breakfast accommodation along the way for £715. Other companies with a good choice of holidays throughout Germany are *Moswin's* and *Taber* (see box). Organized **cruises** on the Rhine and Mosel, Danube or Elbe are offered by several operators, but are always expensive, starting at just over £1000 for seven nights.

Several companies offer guided **walking tours**. *Ramblers Holidays* take small groups to Bonndorf in the Black Forest for £398 for a week, and around the mounain huts in the Allgäu Alps for £494 for nine days, both including flights. *Waymark Holidays* do a ten-day walking trip in the Black Forest for £585, as well as a week-long **cross-country skiing** holiday based in Oberammergau for £525. *Bents* offers ten-day **cycle tours** of the Bavarian Alps for £599, Franconia for £719 and the Black Forest for £749, as well as a couple of eight-day walking tours (one strenuous, the other not) of the Bavarian Alps for £619.

BY TRAIN

Unless you qualify for one of the discounts listed below, there are no major savings to be made travelling to Germany **by train** – you'll usually be paying more than travelling by plane or bus.

Most **routings** from London are daily and cross the Channel from Victoria via Dover to Ostend (taking 1hr 40min) or from Liverpool Street via Harwich to the Hook of Holland (3hr 40min). If you take the **Eurostar train** through the Channel Tunnel you can greatly reduce your travelling time on the London–Paris or London–Brussels leg of the journey, but you will probably pay a bit more for the convenience. High-speed trains operate from London Waterloo via Folkestone and Calais to Paris Gare du Nord in three hours and to Brussels in two and a half hours.

Once you have crossed the Channel, connections are simple and speedy – getting you to Frankfurt in six hours and to Berlin in ten.

TICKETS AND PASSES

A **standard return** rail ticket from London to the main German cities costs: Cologne £94, Frankfurt £131, Hamburg £166, Munich £197, Berlin £187, Leipzig £184 and Dresden £201. It's worth enquiring about the different routes across the Channel as this can affect prices: it's often cheaper to go via the Hook of Holland rather than the short Ostend crossing. Tickets are bookable through some travel agents or at London's Victoria Station.

The alternative for under-26s is a discounted **BIJ ticket** from Eurotrain (through *Campus Travel*) or *Wasteels*. These can be booked for journeys from any British station to any major station in Europe; like full-price tickets they are valid for two months and they allow as many stopovers as you want along a pre-specified route (which can be different going out and coming home). The return fare from London to Frankfurt is £107, to Hamburg £147, to Munich £148 and to Berlin £148.

Tickets for the **Channel Tunnel** crossing are available at the terminal toll booths, or in advance from travel agents and *Eurostar*. Return fares to Brussels start at £65 if booked a minimum of three days in advance (£79 otherwise), and to Paris start at £69 and £89 respectively.

If you plan to travel extensively in Europe by train, there are better-value options than simply buying a return ticket. Under-26s can invest in an **InterRail** pass from Rail Europe or a travel agent; the only restriction is that you must have been resident in Europe for at least six months. This comes in two forms: either an *InterRail Global* pass, valid for one month's unlimited travel in 26 European countries including Germany (£279), or an *InterRail Zonal* pass, whereby the 26 countries are split into seven zones and you choose which countries you want the pass to be valid for. A fifteen-day pass for any one zone costs £189; any two contiguous zones, valid for one month, £224; any three, also for one month, £249. In addition all InterRail passes offer discounts on rail travel in the UK and on cross-Channel ferries.

Since Germany has an extensive rail network, this is basically a bargain, though be prepared to pay extra supplements, especially on InterCity services. There are also some private lines (including east Germany's narrow-gauge steam rail lines) on which passes are not valid. Germany is in the same zone as Austria, Switzerland and Denmark. If you want to add another zone,

TRAIN INFORMATION

Eurostar
Eurostar House, Waterloo Station, London SE1
☎0345 303030; http://www.eurostar.com/

Eurotrain
52 Grosvenor Gardens, London SW1
☎0171/730 3402

German Rail
23 Oakhill Grove, Surbiton, Surrey
☎0181/390 8833

Rail Europe
European information line
☎0990 848848

Wasteels
Victoria Station, London SW1
☎0171/834 7066

BUS INFORMATION

Eurolines
52 Grosvenor Gardens, London SW1
☎0990/808080 for enquiries (*National Express*),
☎0990/143219 for credit card bookings.

perhaps to include ferry services from Britain, the two adjoining zones are France, Belgium, Netherlands and Luxembourg; or the Czech Republic, Slovakia, Poland, Hungary, Bulgaria and Croatia.

If you are over 26, you can buy an **InterRail 26 Plus** pass which covers all of Europe excluding France, Belgium, Switzerland, Spain, Italy and Portugal. It costs £215 for 15 days, and £275 for one month.

If you're 60 or over, the **Rail Europe Senior Card** brings you approximately 30 percent discounts on cross-border rail and sea travel in most of Western Europe, including Germany. To obtain this card, you must first have a Senior Citizen Railcard (£5 from any train station).

BY BUS

Travelling to Germany by bus won't bring any major savings over the cheapest air fares, and the journey will be long and uncomfortable, interrupted every 3–4 hours by stops at highway services. The one advantage is that you can have an open return at no extra cost.

Summer frequencies, timings and return fares to the major cities are: to Cologne (daily, 13hrs)

£69; Frankfurt (3 a week, 18hrs) £79; Hamburg (5 a week, 22hr 30min) £83; Berlin (4 a week, 26hr) £91; Munich (3 a week, 23hrs 30min) £94. Winter departures are only slightly fewer and fares are usually the same as during the summer. There are small reductions (£2–10) for students, youths and senior citizens, slightly more substantial ones for children.

All these routes are operated by *Eurolines* (see box left for details). Tickets are bookable through most major travel agents; *Eurolines* sells tickets and through transport to London at all *National Express* bus terminals.

BY CAR, FERRY AND LE SHUTTLE

If you're driving to Germany, the hardest choice you'll have to make is where to cross the Channel, a decision dependent on which part of Germany you're heading for. In addition to the time-honoured French and Belgian ferry services and the new service though the Channel Tunnel, there are also two direct ferries to Hamburg. For northern Germany or Berlin and the former GDR, you'll save time by taking a boat to Holland (or, of course, directly to Hamburg), but for anywhere else you're best off landing in Belgium or France.

Once across, particularly if you drive through Holland or Belgium – less so in France – you'll rarely be travelling on anything but highways all the way to any German city (and international border formalities are virtually non-existent – you'll be waved straight through unless you or your vehicle look highly suspicious). From the Channel ports allow about 3 hours to Cologne or Düsseldorf, 6–7 to Hamburg or Frankfurt, and 12 to Munich or Berlin. For practical details on driving in Germany see pp.30–31.

THE FERRY TO HAMBURG

Scandinavian Seaways have two **ferries** which ply directly from the UK to Hamburg. From Harwich, they run (with the occasional break in the cycle) every other day throughout the year. Between early May and early September there are also sailings every fourth day from North Shields near Newcastle. The former crossing takes around 19 hours, the latter 23 hours, and passengers are required to book at least a couchette berth. Fares on the two routes are identical. Cheapest is the excursion fare, which is for a return journey of 6 nights or less, including those on the ship. It must be booked 21 days in

FERRY COMPANIES

Hoverspeed International Hoverport, Dover, Kent (☎01304/240241); also in London (☎0181/554 7061). *To Boulogne and Calais.*

North Sea Ferries King George Dock, Hedon Rd, Hull HU9 5QA (☎01482/377177). *To Zeebrugge and Rotterdam.*

P&O European Ferries Channel House, Channel View Rd, Dover, Kent CT17 9TJ (☎0990 980980). *To Calais.*

Sally Lines Argyle Centre, York St, Ramsgate, Kent (☎0990/980980). *To Ostend.*

Scandinavian Seaways (☎0990 333000 for reservations); Parkeston Quay, Harwich, Essex CO2 4QG (☎01255/243456 for bookings); International Ferry Terminal, Royal Quays, North Shields, NE29 6EE (☎0191/293 6262); 15 Hanover St, London W1 (☎0171/409 6060). *To Hamburg.*

Stena Sealink/Line Charter House, Park St, Ashford, Kent TN24 8EX (☎01233/647047). *To Calais, Cherbourg and Dieppe.*

advance and costs the same as a standard single: £57 in the low season (Jan–March & Oct–Dec), rising to £99 in the peak period from mid-July to mid-August. The excursion rate for a car is £59 in the low season, rising to a maximum of £80 in summer (as opposed to the standard single fares of £42 and £64 respectively). For longer stays in Germany, the best option is usually the *Seapex* return, which likewise needs to be booked 21 days in advance; moreover, it does not allow you to travel on a Friday or Saturday. The cheapest rates are £64 per person and £69 for a car in the low season, rising to £124 and £119 respectively in the high season. If travelling in a group, the *All in a Car* ticket is even better value. Covering up to four people plus a car, prices range from £250 on weekdays in winter to £550 on weekends in high summer.

CROSS-CHANNEL SERVICES

If you're aiming for the Rhineland and the south, it's a far better bet to take one of the much **shorter Channel crossings** by boat or hovercraft from Dover, Folkestone or Ramsgate to Boulogne or Calais in France, or to Ostend or Zeebrugge in Belgium, or from Harwich to the Hook of Holland – any of which will leave you with a drive of only 2–3 hours to the German border.

The *Sally Lines* service to Ostend costs £48 return for foot passengers (£25 if you return within 5 days), while car fares start from £113. *Hoverspeed* operates a hovercraft service from Dover to Calais taking just 35 minutes, and a Seacat service from Folkestone to Boulogne which takes 55 minutes. Both cost £50 return for foot passengers (£25 if you return within 5 days)

and £150 standard return for a car (with various reductions for short periods, the cheapest being a 72-hour return on the Seacat for £45). From the **north of England**, there's a routing from Hull to Zeebrugge or Rotterdam with *North Sea Ferries*, whose summer passenger fares are £64 return, with a further £106 for a car. There are also five-day excursion fares, which must include a Saturday night away; these are £40 per person, £66 for a car.

Any travel agent in the UK should be able to provide details and make ferry bookings for you, which should be done well in advance especially if you're travelling during the summer or over holiday periods.

Probably the most convenient way of taking your car across to the Continent is to drive down to the **Channel Tunnel**, load your car on the train shuttle, and be whisked under the Channel in 35 minutes. The tunnel entrance is off the M20 at Junction 11A, just outside Folkestone, and *Le Shuttle* aims to operate services round the clock, 365 days a year. At present, there are two trains an hour – this will increase to four at peak times. You don't have to buy a ticket in advance; just arrive and pay at the terminal, where there is a promised loading time of ten minutes. While you're inside the carriages, you can get out of your car to stretch your legs during the crossing.

Tickets are available through *Le Shuttle* Customer Service Centre (☎0990 353535) or from your local travel agent. Fares are charged per car, irrespective of the number of passengers. A day return is currently £29 (£39 on Sat), a five-day return £89, a standard return £149.

GETTING THERE FROM IRELAND

Only *Aer Lingus* has direct flights to Germany from Dublin. Alternatives via London are unlikely to prove attractive, considering the additional time factor and the cost of a flight from Ireland to Britain. Package holidays and city breaks will often be routed via London.

Aer Lingus flies direct to Frankfurt for £IR205, to Munich via Amsterdam for £IR236. British Airways takes you to London first for a connection to Germany and flights are much more expensive, currently £IR343 to Frankfurt and £IR414 to Berlin.

Students and anyone under 31 should contact USIT, which generally has the best discount deals on flights and train tickets. For InterRail details see "Getting There from Britain" (pp.5-6).

If you want to take your car, Irish Ferries runs services from Cork and Rosslare to Le Havre and Cherbourg, with summer prices starting at £IR390 return for a car and two passengers. It's a long crossing, 21 hours to Le Havre and 17 to Cherbourg. Brittany Ferries operates a weekly summer crossing from Cork to Roscoff which takes 14 hours.

USEFUL ADDRESSES IN IRELAND

AIRLINES

Aer Lingus Northern Ireland reservations ☎0645/737 747; 40–41 O'Connell St, Dublin 1; 13 St Stephen's Green, Dublin 2; 12 Upper St George's St, Dun Laoghaire (centralized reservations at Dublin airport ☎01/705 3333); 2 Academy St, Cork (☎021/327 155); 136 O'Connell St, Limerick (☎061/474 239); Minicom/Text telephone ☎01/705 3994.

British Airways 1 Fountain Centre, College St, Belfast BT1 6ET (reservations ☎0345/222 111, bookings and travel agency services ☎0345/326 566). BA doesn't have a Dublin office; *Aer Lingus* acts as their agents (reservations ☎1800/626 747).

Lufthansa Reservations in the Republic ☎01/844 5544.

AGENTS AND OPERATORS

Brittany Ferries Tourist House, 42 Grand Parade, Cork (☎021/277 801, reservations and information ☎021/277 705, fax 021/277 262). *Routes: Cork to Roscoff (March–Oct only).*

Irish Ferries (in conjunction with P&O European Ferries), reservations in Northern Ireland ☎0345/171 717; 2–4 Merrion Row, Dublin 2 (☎01/661 0511, 24hr information ☎01/661 0715); St Patrick's Bldgs, Cork (☎021/551 995). *Ferries Cork–Le Havre and Rosslare–Cherbourg.*

Joe Walsh Tours 34 Grafton St, Dublin 2 (☎01/671 8751); 69 Upper O'Connell St, Dublin 2 (☎01/872 2555); 8–11 Baggot St, Dublin 2 (☎01/676 3053); 117 St Patrick St, Cork (☎021/277 959). *General budget fares agent.*

Thomas Cook 11 Donegall Place, Belfast (☎01232/24 23 41); 118 Grafton St, Dublin 2 (☎01/677 1721). *Package holiday and flight agent, with occasional discount offers.*

USIT Fountain Centre, College St, Belfast BT1 6ET (☎01232/324 073); 10–11 Market Parade, Patrick St, Cork (☎021/270 900); 33 Ferryquay St, Derry (☎01504/371 888); 19 Aston Quay, Dublin 2 (☎01/602 1777 or 677 8117, Europe and UK ☎01/602 1600 or 679 8833, long-haul ☎01/602 1700); Victoria Place, Eyre Square, Galway (☎091/565 177); Central Buildings, O'Connell St, Limerick (☎061/415 064); 36–37 Georges St, Waterford (☎051/872 601). *Student and youth specialists for flights and trains.*

GETTING THERE FROM NORTH AMERICA

Partly as a result of the presence of US military forces, German cities, especially those in the west, are well served by US airlines. Fares between North America and Germany are among the cheapest trans-Atlantic crossings. Frankfurt, Germany's largest airport, handles most international flights, with connections plentiful to other cities such as Munich, Hamburg, Berlin, Stuttgart and Düsseldorf. *Lufthansa*, the German national airline, currently has the most direct flights from the US or Canada to what used to be East Germany, serving Dresden, East Berlin and Leipzig via Frankfurt.

Though it may be more interesting, it's not usually cheaper to stop over in **another European country** and make your way to Germany from there. You may find cheap flights to **Paris** or **Amsterdam**, but the most common deals available through the seat consolidators are on scheduled airlines plying long-haul routes to the Gulf states, almost all of which stop in **London**. From mainland Europe, **trains** are the cheapest and easiest way to make the final leg to Germany – a *Eurail* pass (see pp.12–13) is useful, especially if you are on a longer European trip, as you can use it to get from any part of Europe to Germany. From England, flying is often as cheap if not cheaper than ground travel.

SHOPPING FOR TICKETS

On busy routes, discount ticket outlets – advertised in the Sunday newspaper travel sections such as the *New York Times* – are usually your best bet for cheap tickets. They come in several forms. Consolidators buy up blocks of tickets that airlines don't think they'll be able to sell at their published fares, and unload them at a discount. Many advertise fares on a one-way basis, enabling you to fly into one city and out from another without penalty. **Consolidators** normally don't impose advance purchase requirements (although in busy times you should book ahead just to be sure of getting a ticket), but they do often charge very stiff fees for date changes. Also these companies' profit margins are pretty tiny, so they make their money by dealing in volume – don't expect them to entertain lots of questions. **Discount agents** also deal in blocks of tickets offloaded by the airlines, but they typically offer a range of other travel-related services like insurance, rail passes, youth and student ID cards, car rentals and tours. These agencies tend to be most worthwhile for students and under-26s, who can benefit from special fares and deals. **Travel clubs** are another option – most charge an annual membership fee, which may be worth it for their discounts on air tickets and car rental. Some agencies specialize in **charter flights**, which may be even cheaper than anything available on a scheduled flight, but again there's a trade-off: departure dates are fixed, and withdrawal penalties are high (check the refund policy).

For destinations not handled by discounters you'll have to deal with airlines' published fares. The cheapest way to go is with an **APEX** (Advance Purchase Excursion) ticket. This carries certain restrictions: you have to book – and pay – at least 21 days before departure and spend at least 7 days abroad (maximum stay 3 months), and you're liable to penalties if you change your schedule. There are also winter **Super APEX** tickets, sometimes known as "Eurosavers" – slightly cheaper than an ordinary APEX, but limiting your stay to between 7 and 21 days. Some airlines also issue **Special APEX** tickets to those under 24, often extending the maximum stay to a year.

Note that fares are heavily dependent on **season**, and are highest from early June to the end of September; they drop during the "shoulder" seasons, April/May and October, and you'll get the best deals during the low season, November to the end of March (excluding Christmas). Note that flying on weekends ordinarily adds $60 to the return fare; **prices quoted in the sections below assume midweek travel.**

FLIGHTS FROM THE US

You can usually find **direct flights** from the major gateway cities of New York JFK, Newark, Atlanta, Boston, Washington DC, Miami, Chicago and Los Angeles to either **Frankfurt** or **Berlin**, with connections to Hamburg, Stuttgart, Munich and Düsseldorf.

FARES

There are constant fare wars raging between the airlines on flights to Germany. On average, the European airlines offer some of the lowest fares and best connection possibilities, and many nonstop flights have been added lately.

Out of **New York JFK**, flights to Frankfurt can be as low as $358 with restrictions during low season, and up to $1070 during high season. To fly to Berlin from the East Coast with a regular inexpensive fare you'll be looking at around $650 low season and close to $1100 high season. Out of **Atlanta**, flights to Frankfurt run $404 low season, $1184 high season; to Munich, $760 low season, $1180 high season. From the **Midwest**, *Northwest* flies nonstop from Detroit to Frankfurt for $428 low season and $1135 high season, while *Sabena* flies from Chicago to Frankfurt for $339 low season, $1227 high season, with summer fare specials plentiful.

Flying direct from the **West Coast** isn't that much more expensive than flying out of New York, with average fares to Frankfurt being around $418 in low season and $1300 in high season. You can usually get direct flights from the main gateways of Los Angeles, San Francisco and Seattle.

DISCOUNT TRAVEL COMPANIES IN NORTH AMERICA

Air Brokers International 150 Post St, Ste 620, San Francisco, CA 94108-4707 (☎800/883-3273; *http://www.airbrokers.com*). *Consolidator.*

Council Travel Head Office: 205 E 42nd St, New York, NY 10017 (☎212/822-2600; for reservations ☎800/226-8624; http://www.ciee.org). *Student travel organization with branches (among others) in San Francisco, Washington DC, Boston, Austin, Seattle, Chicago and Minneapolis.*

Educational Travel Center 438 N Frances St, Madison, WI 53703 (☎800/747-5551; *http://www.edtrav@execpc.com*). *Student/youth discount agent.*

Encore Travel Club 4501 Forbes Blvd, Lanham, MD 20706 (☎800/444-9800; *http://www.travelfare.com/encorehtm*). *Discount travel club.*

Interworld Travel 800 Douglass Rd, Miami, FL 33134 (☎800/468-3796; 305/443-4929; *http://www.itravel@compuserve.com*). *Consolidator.*

Last Minute Travel 100 Sylvan Rd, Woburn, MA 01801 (☎800/LAST MIN). *Offers discount air packages.*

Moment's Notice 7301 New Utrecht Ave, Brooklyn, NY 11201 (☎212/486-0503; *http://www.moments-notice.com*). *Discount travel club.*

New Frontiers/Nouvelles Frontières Head offices: 12 E 33rd St, New York, NY 10016 (☎800/366-6387); 1001 Sherbrook East, Suite 720, Montréal, H2L 1L3 (☎514/526-8444). *French discount travel firm. Other branches in Los Angeles, San Francisco and Québec City.*

STA Travel 10 Downing St, New York, NY 10014, with 150 offices worldwide (☎800/777-0112; http://www.sta-travel.com). *Discount travel agency for students and youth.*

Travac Head office: 989 Sixth Ave, New York, NY 10018 (☎800/872-8800; *http://www.travac.com*). *Consolidator; has another branch in Orlando.*

Travel CUTs Head office: 187 College St, Toronto, ON M5T 1P7 (☎800/667-2887 [Canada only]; ☎416/979-2406; http://www.travelcuts.com). *Canadian student travel organization specializing in student fares, IDs and other travel services.*

Travelers Advantage 3033 S Parker Rd, Suite 900, Aurora, CO 80014 (☎800/548-1116; TravelerAdvantage.com). *Full-service discount travel club.*

UniTravel 1177 N Warson Rd, St Louis, MO 63132 (☎800/325-2222; air4less.com). *Consolidator.*

Worldwide Discount Travel Club 1674 Meridian Ave, Miami Beach, FL 33139 (☎305/534-2082). *Discount travel club.*

AIRLINES IN NORTH AMERICA

Air Canada (☎800/776-3000; *http://www.air-canada.ca/*). *Flies nonstop from Toronto to Frankfurt, with direct flights from Vancouver and Montréal, with connections to other German cities.*

Air France (☎800/237-2747; in Canada, ☎800/667-2747; *http://www.airfrance.com*). *Miami, Chicago, Houston, Los Angeles, San Francisco, New York and Washington Dulles to Paris, with connections to major German cities, including Berlin.*

American Airlines (☎800/433-7300). *Flies nonstop from Chicago and Dallas to Frankfurt.*

British Airways (in US, ☎800/247-9297; in Canada, ☎800/668-1059; *http://www.us.british-airways.com*). *Flies from most major North American cities to London, with extensive connections to 10 German cities including Frankfurt, Munich, Stuttgart, Berlin and Hamburg.*

Canadian Airlines (in Canada, ☎800/665-1177; in US, ☎800/426-7000; *http://www.cdnair.ca*). *Flies from Montréal and Vancouver to London then Frankfurt, and from Toronto to Chicago, Paris, then Frankfurt.*

Continental Airlines (☎800/231-0856; *http://flycontinental.com*). *Newark to Frankfurt and Düsseldorf, with connections to other German cities.*

Delta Airlines (☎800/241-4141; *http://www.delta-air.com*). *Nonstop flights from New York, Cincinnati and Atlanta to Frankfurt; from New York to Berlin and Munich; from Atlanta to Munich and Stuttgart; and connecting flights through Brussels to Stuttgart and Düsseldorf.*

KLM (in US, ☎800/374-7747; in Canada, ☎1-800/361-5073; *http://www.klm.nl*).

Numerous gateways in both the US and Canada (partners with Northwest Airlines*) to Amsterdam, with connections to most major German cities.*

LTU (☎800/888-0200; *http://www.ltu.com*). *Flights from Miami, Orlando, Ft. Myers, Los Angeles, Phoenix, Denver, San Francisco and JFK to most major German cities.*

Lufthansa (☎800/645-3880; *http://www.lufthansa.com*). *Flies from ten North American gateways to all major German cities.*

Northwest Airlines (☎800/447-4747; *http://www.nwa.com/*). *Flies nonstop from Detroit to Frankfurt. Through partner* KLM, *flies through Amsterdam to Germany from many US cities.*

Sabena (☎800/955-2000; *http://www.sabena.com*). *Flies to Germany through Brussels from Chicago, New York, Boston, Cincinnati and Atlanta, with connections on* Delta *from other cities.*

Singapore Airlines (☎800/742-3333; *http://www.singaporeair.com*). *Flies nonstop from New York to Frankfurt four times a week.*

Swissair (☎800/221-4750; *http://www.swissair.com*). *Daily service to several German cities from several North American cities, transferring in Zurich or Geneva.*

United Airlines (☎800/538-2929; *http://www.ual.com*). *Chicago and Washington Dulles direct to Frankfurt with connections to Berlin.*

US Air (☎800/622-1015; *http://www.usairways.com*). *Flies nonstop from Pittsburgh and Philadelphia to Frankfurt and from Philadelphia to Munich, with connections to other German cities.*

FLIGHTS FROM CANADA

Canadians have fewer direct options than Americans, though again European carriers such as *British Airways, Lufthansa, KLM* and *Swissair* offer the most choices. The best selections are out of **Toronto** and **Montréal**, with fares to Frankfurt ranging from $CDN729 (low season) and $CDN1387 (high season), and to Berlin from $CDN789 (low season) to $CDN1496 (high).

The main carrier, *Air Canada*, is a good bet for a nonstop service and flies to Frankfurt from Toronto. *Canadian*'s flight from Vancouver direct to Frankfurt is $CDN979 in low season and close to $CDN1789 in high season. However, you'll often do best travelling to **New York** and buying a flight from there. With reduced options, Canadians will find it worth while to think about getting a discount fare to a city like London, Amsterdam or Paris and travelling on from there.

PACKAGES AND ORGANIZED TOURS

Package tours may not sound like your kind of travel, but don't dismiss the idea out of hand. If

TOUR OPERATORS IN NORTH AMERICA

Abercrombie & Kent 1520 Kensington Rd, Oak Brook, IL 60523 (☎800/323-7308; *http://www.abercrombiekent.com*). *General tour operator.*

Adventure Tours 815 North Rd, Westfield, MA 01085 (☎800/628-9655; *http://www.advonskis.com*). *Ski tour company.*

Angersbach International Tours 170 Main St, Manasquan, NJ 08736 (☎800/526-2358; *http://www.angersbach.com*). *Specialty tours to Germany including Oktoberfest and Christmas.*

Bergen Line, Inc 405 Park Ave, New York, NY 10022 (☎800/323-7436; *http://www.BergenLine.com*). *Cruises to Germany from other European destinations.*

Brendan Tours 15137 Califa St, Van Nuys, CA 91411-3021 (☎800/421-8446). *Escorted tours to Germany's main cities.*

CBT College Bicycle Tours Inc 415 W Fullerton Parkway, Suite 1003, Chicago, IL 60614 (☎800/736-BIKE). *Affordable tours, spring and summer only ranging from one to nine weeks.*

Danube Cruises Inc 5250 W Century Blvd, Suite 304, Los Angeles, CA 90045 (☎800/999-0226; *http://www.NNSDCA@aol.com*). *Cruises in Germany.*

Delta Vacations PO Box 1525, Fort Lauderdale, FL 33302 (☎800/221-6666; *http://www.DeltaVacations.com/*). *Fly/drives and city packages.*

DER Tours 9501 W Devon Ave, Rosemont, IL 60018 (☎800/782-2424; *http://www.dertravel.com*). *Wide variety of packages including* Oktoberfest.

Euro Bike Tours PO Box 990, De Kalb, IL 60115 (☎800/252-1990). *Cycling tours to southern Germany.* Euro-Connection 7500 212 SW, Ste 103, Admonds, WA 98026 (☎800/645-3876). *Tour specialists.*

EuroCruises 303 W 13th St, New York, NY 10014 (☎800/688-EURO; *http://www.eurocruises.com*). *Cruises on the Rhine and Danube rivers.*

European Tours Inc 7605 Saratoga, Lubbock, TX 79424 (☎800/722-3679). *General tour operator.*

KD River Cruises of Europe 2500 Westchester Ave, Purchase, NY 10577 (☎800/346-6525; *http://www.rivercruises.com*). *German cruise specialists.*

Maupintour 1515 St Andrews Drive, Lawrence, KS 66047(☎800/255-6162). *General tour operator.*

Sno Search Ski Tours 13700 Alton Pkwy, Ste 158, Irvine, CA 92618 (☎800/628-8884; *http://www.snowsearch@prodigy.com*). *Ski tour operator.*

Swan Hellenic 581 Boylston St, Boston, MA 02116 (☎800/426-5492). *Major European cruise operator.*

United Vacations 106 Calvert St, Harrison, NY 10528 (☎800/678-0949). *A wide range of packages including fly/drives.*

---

your trip is geared around special interests, packages can work out cheaper than the same arrangements made on arrival. A package trip can also be great for your peace of mind, if only to ensure a worry-free first week while you're finding your feet on a longer tour. The **German National Tourist Office** is your best starting-off point for gathering information and the airlines are all good sources for deals. *Delta* and some other airlines have city and fly/drive packages. *Delta*, for example, can arrange hotel stays in Munich, Frankfurt, Berlin, Heidelberg, Dresden, Cologne and Nürnberg. Most of the tour operators listed in the box arrange similar city packages and fly/drives as well as **trips to the Oktoberfest.** Other specialist companies offer skiing, cycling and river cruises. **Cruises** are generally around the $1000–2000 mark.

RAIL PASSES

A *Eurail* **pass** is not likely to pay for itself if you're planning to stick to Germany. The pass, which must be purchased before arrival in Europe, allows unlimited free train travel in Germany and sixteen other countries. Several options are available. For example, for adults over 26, you can have a *Eurail Flexipass* for $616, allowing 10 travel days in two months; for youths, the cost is $431. A *Eurail* pass costs $522 for 15 days of travel, $365 for youths. With a *Euro Adult* pass or *Euro Youth* pass, you pay $316 or $210 for five days' travel in two months, respectively, and up to $736 and $500 for 15 days' travel in two months to five countries. Look into discounts for a second traveller. A further alternative is to attempt to buy an *InterRail* pass in Europe (see "Getting There From Britain" pp.5–6) – most

RAIL CONTACTS IN NORTH AMERICA

CIT Tours 15 W 44th St, 10th Floor, New York, NY 10036 (☎800/223-7987). *Eurail, German, Italian passes.*

DER Tours/GermanRail 9501 W Devon Ave, Suite 301, Rosemont, IL 60018 (☎800/782-2424; http://www.dertravel.com). *Eurail, German, Italian, Benelux and Central Europe passes.*

Rail Europe 226 Westchester Ave, White Plains, NY 10604 (☎800/438 7245; http://www.raileurope.com). *Official Eurail Pass agent in North America; also sells the widest range of European regional and individual country passes.*

agents don't check residential qualifications, but once you're in Europe it'll be too late to buy a *Eurail* pass if you have problems.

You may wish to remember that North Americans are also eligible to purchase more spe-

cific passes valid for travel in Germany only, for details of which see "Getting Around", p.25. The more common European passes can be purchased through most travel agents or try the agents listed in the box above.

GETTING THERE FROM AUSTRALIA & NEW ZEALAND

There is a good choice of flights to German destinations chiefly via Southeast Asian cities and Frankfurt. Some stopovers will be only a few hours while with other flights you have to change planes or break your journey en route.

As destinations in Europe are "common rated" – you pay the same fare whatever your destination – some airlines offer free flight coupons, car rental or accommodation if you arrange these extras with your ticket. Choose carefully, though, as these perks are impossible to alter later.

Alternatively, you could buy the cheapest possible flight to anywhere in Europe and make your way to Germany by stand-by flight, train or bus, but this rarely works out as cheaply as buying a discounted airfare all the way; however, if you intend to take in Germany as part of a wider European trip it's worth checking out the many rail passes that are available.

For extended trips, a **round-the-world** (RTW) ticket can work out very good value – especially from New Zealand, where airlines offer fewer bonuses to fly with them. Currently the best deals on offer are *Cathay Pacific/United*'s "Globetrotter", *Air New Zealand/KLM/ Northwest*'s "World Navigator", *Qantas/BA*'s "Global Explorer" tickets – all allow six stopovers worldwide with limited backtracking and open-jaw travel, from A$2499 to NZ$3089.

Fares are seasonally adjusted with high season mid-May to end-August (the European summer) and December to mid-January, shoulder seasons March to mid-May and September, and low season the rest of the year. Seasons vary slightly depending on the airline. Tickets purchased direct from the airlines tend to be expensive. Travel agents offer much better deals and have the latest information on limited specials and stopovers, with the best discounts being through Flight Centres and STA, who can also advise on visa regulations. Students

AIRLINES IN AUSTRALIA AND NEW ZEALAND

☎ *800 numbers are toll-free, but only apply if dialled outside the city in the address.*

Aeroflot 24/44 Market St, Sydney (☎02/9262 2233). No NZ office. *Twice weekly flights from Sydney to Moscow, with connections to Berlin, Munich and Frankfurt.*

Air France 12 Castlereagh St, Sydney (☎02/9321 1000); 2/143 Nelson St, Auckland (☎09/303 3521). *Sydney to Paris daily via Tokyo or Singapore, with connections to several destinations in Germany.*

Air New Zealand 5 Elizabeth St, Sydney (☎13 2476); 139 Queen St, Auckland (☎09/357 3000). *Auckland to Frankfurt via Los Angeles 3 times a week.*

Alitalia, 32 Bridge St, Sydney (☎02/9247 1308); 6/229 Queen St, Auckland (☎09/379 4457). *Sydney to Rome 3 times a week, with connections to Frankfurt, Düsseldorf, Berlin, Hamburg and Cologne.*

British Airways 26/201 Kent St, Sydney (☎02/9258 3300); 154 Queen St, Auckland (☎09/356 8690). *Daily from major Australasian cities to London via Singapore or Hong Kong, onward connections to other destinations in Germany.*

Canadian Airlines 8/80 Clarence St, Sydney (☎02/9299 7843 & 1800/251 321); 15/44 Emily Place, Auckland (☎09/309 0735). *Daily from Sydney to Frankfurt via a transfer in Vancouver and Munich via Toronto.*

Garuda 55 Hunter St, Sydney (☎02/9334 9944 & 1-800/800 873); 120 Albert St, Auckland (☎09/366 1855). *Sydney to Frankfurt 3 times a week, and to Berlin and Munich once a week via either a transfer or stopover in Jakarta or Denpasar.*

Japan Air Lines 14/201 Sussex St, Sydney (☎02/9272 1111); 12/120 Albert St, Auckland (☎09/379 9906). *Daily from Sydney to Frankfurt with a night's accommodation in either Tokyo or Osaka included in the fare.*

KLM 5 Elizabeth St, Sydney (☎02/9231 6333 & 1800/505 747). No NZ office. *Sydney to Amsterdam via Singapore twice a week, with connections to various German cities.*

Lauda Air 143 Macquarie St, Sydney (☎02/9251 6155). *Sydney or Melbourne to destinations in Germany via Vienna and Bangkok twice weekly.*

Lufthansa (☎02/9367 3888); 109 Queen St, Auckland (☎09/303 1529). *Sydney to Frankfurt 3 times a week via a transfer in Bangkok, with connections to all German airports.*

Malaysia Airlines 16 Spring St, Sydney (☎13 2627); 12/12 Swanson St, Auckland (☎09/373 2741). *Several flights weekly from Sydney, Melbourne, Brisbane, Perth and Auckland to Frankfurt and Munich via Kuala Lumpur.*

Philippine Airlines 49 York St, Sydney (☎02/9262 3333). No NZ office. *Brisbane or Sydney three times a week to Frankfurt via either a transfer or stopover in Manila.*

Qantas 70 Hunter St, Sydney (☎13 1211); 154 Queen St, Auckland (☎09/357 8900 & 800/808 767). *Daily flights from major Australasian cities to Frankfurt via Bangkok.*

Singapore Airlines 17 Bridge St, Sydney (☎13 1011); cnr Albert St & Fanshawe St, Auckland (☎09/379 3209). *Several flights a week to Frankfurt and twice a week to Berlin from major Australian and New Zealand cities via Singapore.*

Thai International 17 Bridge St, Sydney (☎13 1011); cnr Albert St & Fanshawe St, Auckland (☎09/379 3209). *Sydney, Brisbane, Perth and Auckland to Frankfurt several times a week via Bangkok, with onward connection to other destinations in Germany.*

United 10 Barrack St, Sydney (☎13 1777); 7 City Rd, Auckland (☎09/379 3800). *Sydney to Frankfurt via Los Angeles and either Chicago, Washington or New York, with onward connections to Hamburg, Munich and Stuttgart.*

and under-26s are usually able to get at least ten percent off published prices.

FROM AUSTRALIA

Most of the major airlines quote the same fare from all the eastern cities (ie they are commonly rated), with flights from Perth via Asia and Africa around $200 less and via the Americas about $400 more. The cheapest **scheduled** flights via Asia (these generally involve a transfer in the carrier's Asian hub city) are with *Philippine Airlines* and *Garuda* for around $1500 in low season and $1900 in high season, while *Aeroflot*'s lowest fare starts at $1750, In the mid range, *JAL*, *Malaysia Airlines*, *Thai Airways*, *Cathay Pacific* and *Singapore Airlines* all fly to Frankfurt for around AUS$1899–2510. If you're after a bit more comfort, *British Airways* and *Qantas* both quote published fares from AUS$2399 in low season up to AUS$3199 in high season.

Flights are pricier **via North America**, with *United Airlines* offering the cheapest deal via LA and either New York, Washington or Chicago for AUS$2299–2899, while *Air New Zealand* via Auckland and LA and *Canadian Airlines* via

Toronto or Vancouver are both around AUS$2499–3099.

FROM NEW ZEALAND

From Auckland fares are all similar so it depends on which route you prefer. The lowest are to Frankfurt with *Garuda* NZ$1899 low season, NZ$2400 high season and *Thai Airways* NZ$2099–2499, while *Malaysia Airlines*, *Cathay Pacific*, *Singapore Airlines*, *Air New Zealand*, *Lufthansa* and *JAL* charge around NZ$2199–2999. *United Airlines* fly via LA from NZ$2599.

DISCOUNT AND SPECIALIST AGENTS AND OPERATORS

There is very little in the way of organized tours to Germany from Australia or New Zealand, and you are better off making arrangements once you're in Europe.

Anywhere Travel 345 Anzac Parade, Kingsford, Sydney (☎02/9663 0411).

Brisbane Discount Travel 260 Queen St, Brisbane (☎07/3229 9211).

Budget Travel 16 Fort St, Auckland, plus branches around the city (☎09/366 0061 & 0800/808 040).

Destinations Unlimited 3 Milford Rd, Auckland (☎09/373 4033).

European Travel Office 122 Rosslyn St, West Melbourne (☎03/9329 8844); 133 Castlereagh St, Sydney (☎02/9267 7727); 407 Great South Rd, Auckland (☎09/525 3074). *Tourist – five star accommodation, city stays, car hire and cultural tours throughout Germany.*

Flight Centres Australia: 82 Elizabeth St, Sydney, plus branches nationwide (☎13 1600); New Zealand: 205 Queen St, Auckland (☎09/309 6171), plus branches nationwide. *Good fare discounts worldwide.*

Northern Gateway 22 Cavenagh St, Darwin (☎08/8941 1394).

STA Travel Australia: 702 Harris St, Ultimo, Sydney; 256 Flinders St, Melbourne; other offices in state capitals and major universities (nearest branch ☎13 1776, fastfare telesales ☎1300/360 960); New Zealand: 10 High St, Auckland (☎09/309 0458, fastfare telesales ☎09/366

6673), plus branches in Wellington, Christchurch, Dunedin, Palmerston North, Hamilton and at major universities. World Wide Web site: *www.statravelaus.com.au*; email: *traveller@sta-travelaus.com.au Discounts for students and under-26s.*

Thomas Cook Australia: 175 Pitt St, Sydney; 257 Collins St, Melbourne; plus branches in other state capitals (local branch ☎13 1771, Thomas Cook Direct telesales ☎1800/063 913); New Zealand: 96 Anzac Ave, Auckland (☎09/379 3920). *Travellers cheques, bus and rail passes as well as general travel arrangements.*

Walkabout Gourmet Adventures PO Box 52, Dinner Plain, Melbourne (☎03/5159 5556). *Classy food, wine and walking tours from Kassel and Munich.*

YHA Travel Centre Australia: 422 Kent St, Sydney (☎02/9261 1111); 205 King St, Melbourne (☎03/9670 9611); 38 Stuart St, Adelaide (☎08/8231 5583); 154 Roma St, Brisbane (☎07/3236 1680); 236 William St, Perth (☎08/9227 5122); 69a Mitchell St, Darwin (☎08/8981 2560); 28 Criterion St, Hobart (☎03/6234 9617). New Zealand: 36 Customs House, Auckland (☎09/379 4224). *Organizes budget accommodation and travel throughout Germany for YHA members.*

RED TAPE AND VISAS

GERMAN EMBASSIES ABROAD

Australia 119 Empire Circuit, Yarralumla, Canberra, ACT (☎02/6270 1911).

Britain 23 Belgrave Square, London SW1X 8PZ (☎0171/235 5033).

Canada 1 Waverly St, Ottawa, Ont. K2P 0T8 (☎613/232-1101; *http://www.100566.2620 @compuserve.com*).

Ireland 31 Trimelston Ave, Booterstown, Blackrock, Co. Dublin (☎01/693011).

New Zealand 90–92 Hobson St, Thordon, Wellington (☎04/736 063).

US 4645 Reservoir Rd NW, Washington 20007 (☎202/298 8140).

Citizens of most EU countries (and of Norway and Iceland) need only a valid national identity card to enter Germany for up to ninety days. Since Britain has no identity card system, however, British citizens do have to take a passport.

US, Canadian, Australian and New Zealand passport holders can also enter the country for ninety days (in any one year) for a tourist visit without a visa. However, you're strongly advised, if you know your stay will be longer than this, to apply for an extension visa from the local German embassy before you go. In order to extend a stay once in the country, all visitors should contact the *Ausländeramt* (Alien Authorities) in the nearest large town: addresses are in the phone books.

EU nationals are also entitled to **work in Germany**, but anyone else has to have secured a job **before** arrival in order to get a work permit, for which they should apply to their local German consulate or embassy. For casual labour jobs during harvests or in the hotel and catering trades, nobody is going to ask too many questions, but wages are accordingly low and the work tough.

CUSTOMS

Customs and duty-free restrictions vary throughout Europe, with subtle variations even within the European Union.

Since the inauguration of the EU Single Market, travellers entering Germany from another EU country do not have to make a declaration to Customs at their place of entry. You can effectively bring in as much duty-paid wine or beer as you can carry (the legal limits being 90 litres of wine or 110 of beer), though there are still restrictions on the volume of tax- or duty-free goods you can bring into the country. The current duty-free allowance for EU citizens is 200 cigarettes, one litre of spirits and five litres of wine; for non-EU residents the allowances are usually 200 cigarettes, one litre of spirits and two litres of wine.

Residents of the USA and Canada can take up to 200 cigarettes and one litre of alcohol home, as can **Australian** citizens, while **New Zealanders** must confine themselves to 200 cigarettes, 4.5 litres of beer or wine, and just over one litre of spirits.

COSTS, MONEY AND BANKS

Despite the cost of unification, Germany is still one of the world's most industrialized and wealthiest consumer societies, and its currency, the *Deutschmark*, is one by which international financial standards are set. This will, however, shortly be superseded by the *Euro* if the European single currency – a pet German project – goes ahead as planned. Another point to note is that Germany is a cash society: people carry money with them, rather than rely on credit cards. In the face of these facts, it's surprising that this can be a country that's easily affordable to travel in, with the reasonable price of food and accommodation in popular holiday areas helping keep costs down.

COSTS

If you're prepared to cut every corner by staying in youth hostels or campsites, and never eating out, you could get by on upwards of DM60 (just over £20/$30) per day, though DM100–150 is a more realistic budget on which to enjoy yourself properly. Should you have the means to spend a bit more than that, you will be able to live really well. Bear in mind that visiting cities will cost far more than staying in the countryside – a gap that is widening – and that a trip to Berlin is guaranteed to knock a large hole in any budget. If you intend to base yourself mainly in one or two rural areas – even ones as famous as the Alps or Black Forest – as opposed to travelling around a lot, you should be able to reduce the above figures by a quarter.

Accommodation costs per person can be confined to an average of about DM20–25 per day for youth hostels, around DM25–30 for rooms in private houses, and around DM30–60 for guest houses, pensions and the more basic hotels: double rooms cost on average a bit less than twice the above rates. **Food** prices in shops are slightly lower than in Britain, and eating out is markedly cheaper at every level – except for the scarcity of bargain lunches. North Americans, however, will find prices slightly higher. Snack bars abound, and for around DM10-15 you can put together a very filling meal. DM25–30 should buy a hearty German meal plus drink in a traditional *Gaststätte*, while a decent dinner in a classy restaurant can be had for around DM35–40. Drink is marginally more expensive than in Britain or the US, but the quality, especially of the beer, is significantly higher.

Public transport is the one area where prices are likely to present a problem. A single fare within a city, for example, is generally DM2–3, while a sample single train fare from Munich to Frankfurt would be DM124. The only ways in which you can soften these costs are to use rail and other passes, confine your travel to a limited area, or make use of the organized alternative, the *Mitfahrzentralen* (see p.31).

CURRENCY AND THE EXCHANGE RATE

German currency is the *Deutschmark*, which comes in **notes** of DM5 (now rarely encountered), DM10, DM20, DM50, DM100, DM200, DM500 and DM1000; and **coins** of DM0.01 (one *Pfennig*), DM0.02, DM0.05, DM0.10, DM0.50, DM1, DM2 and DM5.

The exchange rate for the Deutschmark is currently around DM2.80 to the pound sterling, DM1.75 to the US dollar. You can bring as much currency as you wish into Germany.

TRAVELLERS' CHEQUES AND CREDIT CARDS

Travellers' cheques are the safest way of carrying the majority of your money. Theoretically, they can be cashed in any bank or exchange office, and used in flashier shops in larger cities. Unfortunately, banks in small towns can be very choosy about which travellers' cheques they will accept, often refusing even some of the best-known names. **Eurocheques** (issued by most British banks with a Eurocheque card) can be used without any problems everywhere, both in banks and shops or restaurants. If you're using them to get cash you pay a 1.6 percent fee to the bank, plus a small handling fee chargeable to your UK bank account.

Unusually, for such a consumer-orientated society, credit cards are little used in Germany, at least by British or American standards. They are growing in popularity, though plenty of shops and restaurants still do not accept them.

Should you need cash on your plastic, the *Reisebank* (see below) will give a cash advance against *Visa* and *Master Card (Access)* cards, subject to a DM150–200 minimum. Various other banks offer cash advance facilities – look for stickers in their windows to find out which credit card they're associated with. Many have automatic machines, usually with computerized instructions in English, which can be used in conjunction with a Personal Identification Number (PIN). Surprisingly, *Visa* is the hardest card of all on which to obtain an advance, with *Citibank*

being the only bank apart from *Reisebank* to accept it. *American Express* card holders can use that company's facilities in the major cities.

CHANGING MONEY

Banking hours are Monday to Friday 9am–noon and 1.30–3.30pm, with late opening on Thursday until 6pm. In the cities, these hours are often extended and you'll always find at least one bank open on a Saturday morning, as well as the *Postbank* in the main post office. If you're on a tight budget, it may be worth shopping around several banks (including the savings banks or *Sparkassen*), as the amount of commission deducted varies. Commission tends to be charged at a flat rate, meaning that small-scale transactions are not cost-effective.

Exchange facilities for cash and travellers' cheques can be found in virtually all banks as well as in commercial exchange shops called *Wechselstuben*, usually located near stations and airports, though often also in city centres, on the main shopping street. The *Reisebank* has branches in the train stations of most main cities; these are generally open seven days a week, and until quite late in the evening.

INSURANCE AND HEALTH

Some form of travel insurance is highly recommended. Besides medical emergencies and the cost of any drugs prescribed, poli-cies also cover loss or theft of luggage, tickets and money. Any claims for theft must be supported by a report made to the local police within 24 hours of the incident.

EUROPEAN INSURANCE COVER

In **Britain and Ireland**, travel insurance schemes, from around £25 per month, are sold by almost every travel agent and bank, or you can consider a specialist insurance firm. Policies issued by any of the firms listed below are good value; *Columbus* also does an annual multi-trip policy which offers twelve months' cover for £125. If you're going skiing in the Alps, or engaging in any other high-risk outdoor activity, you'll probably have to pay an extra premium; check carefully that your policy will cover you in case of an accident.

INSURANCE COMPANIES AND AGENTS

NORTH AMERICA

Access America PO Box 90315, Richmond, VA 23230 (☎800/284-8300).

Carefree Travel Insurance PO Box 9366, Garden City, NY 11530 (☎800/323-3149).

Desjardins Travel Insurance (Canada only) 200 Avenue des Commanders, Lavis, Québec G6V 6R2 (800/463-7830).

STA Travel Insurance has several branches in the US (head office is 10 Downing St, New York, NY 10014; ☎800/777-0112; http://www.sta-travel.com). Offers insurance with and without medical coverage.

Travel Assistance International 1133 15th St NW, Suite 400, Washington, DC 20005 (☎800/821-2828; http://www.wassist@aol.com).

Travel Guard 1145 Clark St, Stevens Point, WI 54481 (☎800/826-1300; http://www.noelgroup.com).

Travel Insurance Services 2930 Camino Diablo, Suite 200, Walnut Creek, CA 94596 (☎800/937-1387).

BRITAIN AND IRELAND

Campus Travel 52 Grosvenor Gardens, London SW1 (☎0171/730 3402).

Columbus Travel Insurance 17 Devonshire Square, London EC2M 4SQ (☎0171/375 0011).

Endsleigh Insurance 97–107 Southampton Row, London WC1B 4AG (☎0171/436 4451).

Frizzell Insurance Frizzell House, County Gates, Bournemouth BH1 2NF (☎01202/292 333).

STA Travel 86 Old Brompton Rd, London SW7 3LH; 117 Euston Rd, London NW1 (☎0171/361 6161).

USIT Dublin ☎01/679 8333; Belfast ☎01232/324073; see p.8 for full list of addresses.

AUSTRALASIA

Ready Plan 141 Walker St, Dandenong, Melbourne (☎03/9791 5077 & 1800/337 462); 10/63 Albert St, Auckland (☎09/379 3208).

NORTH AMERICAN INSURANCE

In the **US and Canada**, insurance tends to be much more expensive, and may be medical cover only. Before buying a policy, check that you're not already covered by existing insurance plans. **Canadians** are usually covered by their provincial health plans; holders of **ISIC cards** and some other student/teacher/youth cards are entitled to $3000 worth of accident coverage and sixty days ($100 per day) of hospital in-patient benefits for the period during which the card is valid. **Students** will often find that their student health coverage extends during the vacations and for one term beyond the date of last enrolment. Bank and credit cards (particularly *American Express*) often have certain levels of medical or other insurance included, and travel insurance may also be included if you use a major credit or charge card to pay for your trip. **Homeowners' or renters'** insurance often covers theft or loss of documents, money and valuables while overseas, though conditions and maximum amounts vary from company to company.

After exhausting the possibilities above you might want to contact a **specialist travel insurance company**. Your travel agent can usually recommend one or see the box above for a listing of some of the bigger ones. Policies are quite comprehensive (accidents, illnesses, lost luggage, delayed or cancelled flights etc) but maximum payouts tend to be meagre. The best deals are usually to be had through student/youth travel agencies – *Isis* policies, for example, cost $48–69 for fifteen days (depending on coverage), $80–105 for a month, $149–207 for two months, and up to $510–700 for a year. If you're planning on doing any **skiing** or other **high-risk outdoor activities**, figure on a surcharge of 20–50 percent.

Most North American travel policies apply only to items lost, stolen or damaged while in the custody of an identifiable, responsible third party – hotel porter, airline, luggage consignment, etc. Even in these cases you will have to contact the local police to have a complete report made out so that your insurer can process the claim. Note also that very few insurers will arrange on-the-spot payments in the event of a major expense or loss; you will usually be reimbursed only after going home.

If you are travelling via London, it might be better to take out a **British policy**, available instantly and easily (though making the claim may prove more complicated).

AUSTRALASIAN COVER

Travel insurance is available from most travel agents (see p.15) or direct from insurance companies (see box on p.19), for periods ranging from a few days to a year or even longer. Most policies are similar in premium and coverage – but if you plan to indulge in high-risk activities such as mountaineering, bungee jumping or scuba diving, check the policy carefully to make sure you'll be covered.

A typical policy for Germany will cost: A$100/NZ$110 for 2 weeks, A$170/NZ$190 for 1 month, A$250/NZ$275 for 2 months.

HEALTH

Citizens of all EU countries are entitled to free medical care in Germany on production of a **form E111**, available over the counter from main post offices. Without this form you'll have to pay in full for all medical treatment, which is expensive – currently a minimum of DM40 for a visit to the doctor. The scheme does not cover you for dental charges. Whether or not you are eligible for an E111, it's sensible to take out some form of **health insurance** and remember that to make claims you will need to keep copies of receipts and prescriptions.

DOCTORS AND PHARMACISTS

In the case of an **emergency**, such as a broken leg, phone ☎110 for the police, who will get you an ambulance, or go straight to the casualty unit of the nearest hospital. For minor ailments, you'll need to visit a GP (*Arzt für Allgemeinmedizin*) in his surgery; these are usually open on weekday mornings, and on afternoons other than Wednesday. German **doctors** usually speak English, but if you want to be certain, your consulate can provide a list of English-speaking doctors in the major cities, which also have a GP on call for out-of-hours emergencies (*Ärztlicher Notdienst*).

To get a prescription made up, go to a pharmacy (*Apotheke*): German pharmacists are well-trained and often speak English. *Apotheken* serving **international prescriptions** can be found in most large cities, and a rota of late-opening or 24-hour places in larger towns is posted on all *Apotheken* doors.

TRAVELLERS WITH DISABILITIES

You'll find that ease of access and facilities are good in Germany and plenty of information is available. ICE, IC and EC trains (see p.24) are adapted for wheelchair access and there's a mandatory right to a free seat reservation. Help within stations is available if requested in advance. Museums and public buildings are usually equipped with ramps.

The **Touristik Union International** (*TUI*), 3000 Hannover 61 (☎0511/5670), has a centralized information bank on many German hotels, pensions and resorts that cater to the needs of dis-

abled travellers or those with specific dietary requirements – not in specially designed and separate establishments, but within the mainstream of German tourist facilities. The *TUI* can book you onto a package tour or organize rooms according to individual itineraries, taking into account each customer's needs, which are gauged from a questionnaire filled out before booking arrangements commence. Their services also include such details as providing suitable wheelchairs for train travel, the transportation of travellers' own wheelchairs, and the provision of transport at airports and stations.

CONTACTS FOR TRAVELLERS WITH DISABILITIES

BRITAIN

Holiday Care Service 2nd Floor, Imperial Building, Victoria Rd, Horley, Surrey RH6 9HW (☎01293/774535). *Information on all aspects of travel.*

Mobility International 228 Borough High St, London SE1 1JX (☎0171/403 5688). *Information, access guides, tours and exchange programmes.*

RADAR 12 City Forum, 250 City Rd, London EC1V 8AS (☎0171/250 3222). *A good source of advice on holidays and travel abroad.*

Tripscope The Courtyard, Evelyn Rd, London W4 5JL (☎0181/994 9294). *A national telephone information service offering free transport and travel advice.*

IRELAND

Disability Action Group 2 Annadale Ave, Belfast BT7 3JH (☎01232/491 011).

Irish Wheelchair Association Blackheath Drive, Clontarf, Dublin 3 (☎01/833 8241, fax 833 3873; email: *iwa@iol.ie*

NORTH AMERICA

Directions Unlimited 720 N Bedford Rd, Bedford Hills, NY 10507 (☎800/533-5343). *Travel agency specializing in custom tours for people with disabilities.*

Jewish Rehabilitation Hospital 3205 Place Alton Goldbloom, Montréal, Québec H7V 1R2 (☎514/688-9550, ext.226). *Guidebooks and travel information.*

Kéroul 4545 Ave Pierre de Coubertin, CP 1000 Station M, Montréal H1V 3R2 (☎514/252-3104;

http://www.craph.org/keroul). *Organization promoting travel for mobility-impaired people. Annual membership $10.*

Mobility International USA Box 10767, Eugene, OR 97440 (Voice and TDD; ☎541/343-1284). *Information and referral service, access guides, tours and exchange programs. Annual membership $25.*

Society for the Advancement of Travel for the Handicapped (SATH) 347 Fifth Ave, Ste 610, New York, NY 10016 (☎212/447-7284; *http://www.sittravel.com*). *Non-profit travel industry referral service; allow plenty of time for a response.*

Travel Information Service Moss Rehabilitation Hospital, 1200 West Tabor Rd, Philadelphia, PA 19141 (☎215/456-9600). *Telephone information and referral service.*

Twin Peaks Press Box 129, Vancouver, WA 98666 (☎360/694-2462 or 800/637-2256). *Publisher of the Directory of Travel Agencies for the Disabled, listing more than 370 agencies worldwide; Travel for the Disabled; the Directory of Accessible Van Rentals, and Wheelchair Vagabond, loaded with personal tips.*

AUSTRALIA

ACROD (Australian Council for Rehabilitation of the Disabled) PO Box 60, Curtin, ACT 2605 (☎02/6282 4333).

NEW ZEALAND

Disabled Persons Assembly 173–175 Victoria St, Wellington (☎04/811 9100).

INFORMATION AND MAPS

Before you leave, it's worth contacting the German National Tourist Office, who have extensive information on campsites, youth hostels, hotels, train timetables and many glossy brochures besides.

TOURIST OFFICES

In **Germany**, you'll find **tourist offices** everywhere, even in tiny villages – addresses are listed in the *Guide*. They're almost universally friendly and very efficient, providing large amounts of free literature, maps and glossy bumph in a selection of languages. Most publish an annual accommodation price list (which becomes a glossy prospectus in resort towns); many also produce a monthly programme of events. The German word for a tourist office is *Fremdenverkehrsamt* (or just *Verkehrsamt*) though many sport a sign saying *Tourist Information*. Another useful facility is that they can book a room for you, for which there's normally a small fee (see "Accommodation" p.33). An increasing number of tourist offices, particularly in major cities and resorts, have an after-hours computer-based service.

Opening hours are given throughout the *Guide*, except for resorts whose hours vary drastically according to season. Beware that a weekend shutdown from Friday lunchtime is quite common during the off-season. In major cities, offices are open virtually every day of the year from early morning until late at night – which can be invaluable in tracking down accommodation.

The **German National Travel Agency** is universally represented by the *DER* offices, generally to be found near train stations or next to tourist offices. They'll book your national and international train tickets, as well as provide general information about travel onwards from Germany. There is a *DER* office in London at 18 Conduit St, W1R 9TD (☎0171/408 0111) and in the States at 11933 Wiltshire Blvd, Los Angeles, CA 90025 (☎800/421-4343).

MAPS

German **maps** set international standards, and there's no shortage of excellent regional, motoring and hiking maps in most bookshops,

GERMAN NATIONAL TOURIST OFFICES

Australia Level 2, St Andrews House, Sydney Square, Sydney 2000 (☎02/9267 8148). *Open Mon–Fri 9am–noon.*

Belgium Rue A. de Boeckstraat 54–6, Brussels (☎02/245 9700).

Britain 65 Curzon Street, London W1Y 7PE (☎0891/600 100).

Canada 175 Bloor Street East, North Tower, 6th Floor, Toronto, Ontario (416/968 1570); Place Bonaventure, Montréal, Québec H5A 1B8 (☎514/8778 9885).

Denmark Vesterbrogade 6 D III, Copenhagen (☎33/127095).

Holland Hoogoorddreef 76, Amsterdam (☎020/697 8066).

New Zealand PO Box 80079 Green Bay, Auckland 1 (☎09/620 0601). *Appointment needed as there are no specific opening times.*

Sweden Birger Jarlsgatan 11, Stockholm (☎08/679 5095).

US 747 Third Ave W, New York, NY 10017 (☎212/308 3300); 44 S Flower St, Suite 220, Los Angeles, CA 90017 (☎213/668 7332).

MAP OUTLETS

BRITAIN

London *Daunt Books*, 83 Marylebone High St, W1 (☎0171/224 2295); *National Map Centre*, 22–24 Caxton St, SW1 (☎0171/222 4945); *Stanfords*, 12–14 Long Acre, WC2 (☎0171/836 1321); *The Travel Bookshop*, 13–15 Blenheim Crescent, W11 (☎0171/229 5260).

Glasgow *John Smith and Sons*, 57–61 St Vincent St (☎0141/221 7472).

Maps are available by **mail or phone order** from Stanfords; ☎0171/836 1321.

IRELAND

Easons Bookshop 40 O'Connell St, Dublin 1 (☎01/873 3811).

Fred Hanna's Bookshop 27–29 Nassau St, Dublin 2 (☎01/677 1255).

Hodges Figgis Bookshop 56–58 Dawson St, Dublin 2 (☎01/677 4754).

Waterstone's Queens Bldg, 8 Royal Ave, Belfast BT1 1DA (☎01232/247 355); 7 Dawson St, Dublin 2 (☎01/679 1415); 69 Patrick St, Cork (☎021/276 522).

UNITED STATES

New York *The Complete Traveller Bookstore*, 199 Madison Ave, NY 10016 (☎212/685-9007).

Santa Barbara *Map Link, Inc*, 30 S. La Petera Lane, Unit #5, Santa Barbara, CA 93117 (805/692-6777).

Seattle *Elliott Bay Book Company*, 101 S Main St, WA 98104 (☎206/624-6600; 800/962-5311; http://www.elliottbaybook.com).

CANADA

Toronto *Open Air Books and Maps*, 25 Toronto St, Toronto, Ontario M5R 2C1 (☎416/363-0719).

Montréal *Ulysses Travel Bookshop*, 4176 St-Denis (☎514/843-9447).

Vancouver *World Wide Books and Maps*, 736 Granville St, Vancouver, BC V6Z 1E4 (☎604/687-3320).

Note *Rand McNally* now has stores in two dozen North American cities. (Mail order 800/333-0136; http://www.randmcnally.com)

Amazon.com (http://www.amazon.com) online bookstore has thousands of titles.

AUSTRALIA

Sydney *Travel Bookshop*, 20 Bridge St (☎02/9241 3554).

Melbourne *Bowyangs*, 372 Little Bourke St (☎03/9670 4383).

Adelaide *The Map Shop*, 16a Peel St (☎08/8231 2033).

Perth *Perth Map Centre*, 891 Hay St (☎08/9322 5733).

Brisbane *Worldwide Maps and Guides* 187 George St, Brisbane (☎07/3221 4330).

NEW ZEALAND

Auckland *Specialty Maps*, 58 Albert St (☎09/307 2217).

---

newsagents and tourist offices. The best general maps are those printed by *RV* or *Kümmerly and Frey*, whose 1:500,000 map is the most detailed single sheet of the country available.

Specialist maps marking cycling routes or alpine hikes can be bought in the relevant regions and information on German **alpine climbs and hikes** can be obtained from the *Deutscher*

Alpenverein, Prater Insel 5, Munich. Other useful reference guides available are: *Fahrrad-Atlas*, the best for cycle routes in Germany; and *Mitfahrzentralen in Europa*, which is in three languages and lists all hiking agencies, their fees and regional accommodation options. If you'd like to order these books before starting your journey write to *DJH-Hauptverband*, 32754 Detmold.

GETTING AROUND

While it may not be cheap, getting around Germany is spectacularly quick and easy. Barely a square kilometre of the country is untouched by an unfailingly reliable public transport system, and it's a simple matter to jump from train to bus on the integrated network. Driving is also a straightforward affair on what's probably the best road network on the continent. Costs can be offset by various discounts and passes available to visitors, and it's worth studying all the options outlined below before committing yourself.

TRAINS

By far the best means of public transport in Germany is the train. The **rail network**, operated by the privatized national company *Deutsche Bahn (DB)* – formed in 1994 from the union of the old West and East German networks – covers most of the country. Where natural obstacles or a sparse population make rail routes unrealistic, the *DB*-associated buses, *Bahnbusse*, take over. North–south travel is particularly straightforward, while east–west journeys are likely to be less direct and require a change of train (or bus) along the way. Everywhere services are very efficient, but expensive at DM26 second class, DM39 first class (DM24 and DM36 respectively in the former GDR), per 100km.

On all intercity routes, even from one end of the country to another, the minimum **frequency** of service from early morning till late evening is one per hour. Between smaller towns, it's seldom

worse than every two hours, and even the most isolated lines have several trains per day, although these are liable to cease in the early evening and be much reduced at weekends.

There are several **types of train**: most luxurious is the 250km-per-hour *InterCityExpress (ICE)*, which only operates on the most popular intercity routes. On top of the normal fare, there's a supplement to be paid, increasing according to the distance travelled up to a maximum of DM50. Otherwise, the fastest and most comfortable trains, and the best option between major cities, are the *InterCity (IC)* and *EuroCity (EC)* trains (identical except that the *EC*s cross international borders). With these you can travel from one end of the country to the other – Hamburg to Munich, for example, takes six and a half hours. The only drawback is the supplement (*Zuschlag*) of DM8 (or DM6 if you buy it at the station before boarding the train), which is compulsory unless you've already invested in a rail pass (see opposite).

Slightly downscale from the *IC*s and *EC*s are the *InterRegio (IR)* trains offering a swift cross-country service along less heavily used routes – and charging a DM4 supplement for journeys of under 50km. This also applies to the relatively cumbersome *D-Zug* or *Schnellzug*, which is used on most overnight routes. Of the more localized services, the *RegionalExpress (RE)* covers the most ground in the shortest time; the *RegionalBahn (RB)* and the misleadingly named *StadtExpress (SE)* are prone to stop just about everywhere.

Around major cities, the **S-Bahn** is a commuter network on which all rail passes are valid; though these cannot be used on the underground **U-Bahn** system, or on municipally owned trams and buses.

The colossal national **timetable** (*Kursbuch*), which is published annually, can be bought from stations for DM25, though it's too bulky to be easily portable. A condensed version of it (*Städteverbindungen*), concentrating on routes between cities, is free of charge. Otherwise, you can easily plan your route by picking up the many free leaflets detailing intercity services, available at any main train station.

TICKET TYPES

Regular tickets (*Fahrkarten*) permit you to break the journey as often as you wish. For distances of up to 100km, they're valid for a day, and for further distances, for four days. Return tickets are valid for one month. Where automatic vending machines exist, tickets for journeys up to 50km can only be bought from them, and not from the counter. Prices are based on distance travelled and therefore a return will cost the same as two singles. One useful bargain offer is the *Guten-Abend-Ticket*, which allows a one-way journey of any length to be made between 7pm and 2am for DM59 second class, DM99 first class (DM69 and DM109 respectively if an *ICE* train is used). If you're making a lot of rail journeys, it's extremely sensible to buy a **rail pass**.

RAIL PASSES

InterRail (see pp.5–6) and **Eurail** (see pp.12–13) passes, and BIJ tickets are valid on all trains but you will have to pay supplements on intercity services. If you're using the trains extensively in Germany, there are other passes which can make train travel much cheaper.

The broadest-ranging pass is the *EuroDomino*, which entitles the holder to unlimited travel on all trains and *Bahnbusse*, on the buses which ply the tourist-orientated "scenic routes" such as *Burgenstrasse* (Castle Road), Rhine-Mosel, *Romantische Strasse* (Romantic Road) and *Schwarzwald Hochstrasse* (Black Forest Highway), and the *K-D Linie* steamers on the Mosel and on the Rhine between Cologne and Mainz (see "Boats" on p.29). Valid for three, five or ten days (not necessarily consecutive) within the period of a month, it can be excellent value particularly as no further supplements are payable, except on *ICE* trains.

More localized but still temptingly priced, the **DB Regional Rail Rover** (*Regionaltourenkarte*) gives unlimited travel on trains and *Bahnbusse* for 5 or 10 days out of 21 in a specific area of Germany – 15 different regions in all, including all the main holiday spots. These are quite large – certainly big enough for two or three weeks' touring – and it's often possible to cover the cost of the ticket with just one return journey. In addition to the standard single pass, there are twin passes for two adults travelling together and family passes for two adults travelling with any number of children; see box below for current prices.

You must buy the above passes **before entering Germany** and they are available from agents throughout Europe (for British addresses see box on p.6). You can also buy them from *DER* offices; see p.4 and 12 for addresses.

Should you be staying in Germany for an extended period it's worth considering the *Bahncard* which gives half-price travel for a full year on all trains. This costs DM240 for standard second class, half that for over-60s, under-22s and students up to 26. In all cases, the price is double for first class.

RAIL PASSES			
	3 days	5 days	10 days
EuroDomino			
1st class	£209	£229	£309
2nd class	£109	£159	£209
youth pass	£119	£139	£159
Regional pass			
1st class	–	£94	£142
2nd class	–	£59	£94
Regional twin pass			
1st class	–	£141	£211
2nd class	–	£94	£141
Regional family pass			
1st class	–	£167	£251
2nd class	–	£111	£167

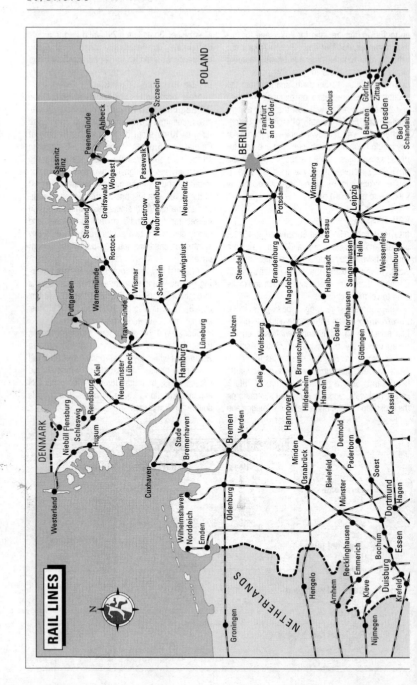

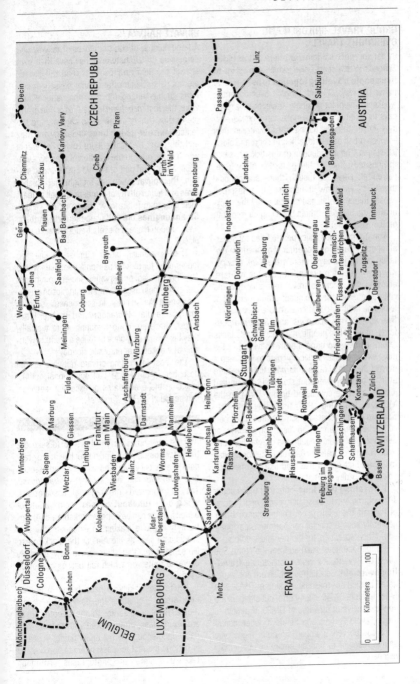

GROUP TRAVEL, CHILDREN AND OVERNIGHT TRAVEL

By far the best bargain *DB* offers is the DM35 *Schönes-Wochenend-Ticket*, which allows **up to five people travelling together** to use any local trains (*RE, RB, SE* and *S-Bahn*) over an entire weekend. Even for a single traveller, this soon pays for itself, and it can make astronomical savings if used to make a long cross-country journey – which it can easily do, albeit in short and slowish stages. The introduction of this ticket has had the desired effect of filling up previously little-patronized services, though there are periodic threats to withdraw it because of widespread abuses (many people sell or give away their ticket after the first day, others tag along for free with perfect strangers).

There are various other possibilities for several people travelling together. For medium-distance return journeys, there's the *Mini-Gruppe-Karte*, whereby the first adult pays the full fare, allowing the others to travel half-price and the children quarter-price. To qualify, there must be at least one adult and one child, and a maximum of five adults. The *Sparpreis* and *Supersparpreis* fares for up to five people making a long-distance return journey can bring massive savings, in the most extreme cases reducing costs to less than a third of the normal rates. *Sparpreis* tickets require at least a Friday overnight stay and the outward journey must be completed before 10am on the Monday following the first day of use. *Supersparpreis* tickets (which are around 20 percent cheaper) cannot be used on Fridays or Sundays after 10am, require the outward journey to be completed before 10am on Friday or Sunday following first day of use, and likewise have an obligatory Friday night stay.

If **travelling with kids**, note that those under 4 travel free, while those between 4 and 11 travel for half the adult price. Long-distance trains generally have a special compartment, designated a *Kinderabteilung*, for mother and toddlers.

On long journeys, such as from the North Sea coast to Bavaria, it's worth considering **travelling overnight**. Couchettes (which are not segregated by sex) are reasonable value at DM30 in a 6-berth cabin, DM40 in a 4-berth, but sleepers are very expensive at upwards of DM90. If aiming to sit up, avoid Fridays and Sundays, when conditions can be very cramped; on other nights you should manage to find an empty or near-empty compartment.

PRIVATE RAILWAYS

A large number of short stretches of railway line lie outside the *DB* network. They have their own special ticketing arrangements, and rail passes are not valid. Some offer regular passenger services supplementing those of the national network; the *Tegernseebahn* in the Alps is one example of this. Others in the same category are the famous **narrow-gauge lines** in Saxony, the Harz and the coast of Mecklenburg-Lower Pomerania which were, prior to the creation of the new *DB* in 1994, an integral part of the old East German system. Their privatization has brought much higher fares and led to plenty of protests, though at least their long-term future now seems totally secure. **Steam engines** are still used regularly on these lines, though modern diesels frequently take their place.

There's a much larger number of lines no longer used for regular passenger services where *DB* allows a local preservation society to run special excursions, usually with historic locomotives, throughout the summer. In some cases, such as the spectacular *Wutachtalbahn* in the Black Forest, these are quite frequent; more typically, they take place only once or twice a month, invariably at weekends or on public holidays.

The most interesting private railways are all described in the *Guide*. Full operational details, including the exact dates of excursion services, can be found in *DB*'s *Kursbuch*.

BUSES

At such rare times as you have to forsake the trains for **buses**, you'll find no decline in the standard of efficiency. Most buses are run in association with *DB* and are known as *Bahnbusse*. They're organized into regional associations, which offer **runabout passes** for a variety of periods; these can be quite remarkable value, particularly if you're making an extended stay in a scenic area such as the Alps or the Black Forest. Note, however, that there are a few privately operated routes on which rail passes cannot be used.

You're most likely to need buses in remote rural areas – or along the designated "scenic routes" mentioned earlier. On these routes buses are luxury-class, often packed with tourists, and pause long enough by the major points of scenic or historic interest for passengers to hop out and take a couple of photographs. Although expensive to use without a railcard (*EuroDomino* holders travel free and *InterRail* cards get a 50 percent reduction), these buses are usually the only way to visit certain locales if you don't have your own transport or the patience to zigzag around on the slow local buses. Trains sometimes whizz through the same areas but seldom is there a convenient station to get off at or a chance to see much of the landscape through the windows.

A point to watch out for in the remoter country areas is punctuality. Unlike trains, buses are allowed to run ahead of their timetable – and often do if they have few passengers to pick up. It's therefore prudent to be at the stop at least ten minutes before the bus is due to arrive.

Finally, Germany does not have long-distance bus companies undercutting the rail lines. Indeed, the only – and very limited – opportunities for intercity bus travel are on stretches of the long-haul international routes.

BOATS

Travelling by **boat** is another option, though more for relaxation than covering large distances. All along the **Rhine** and **Mosel** rivers, and on various Bavarian lakes, there are innumerable local boats waiting to ferry you across or around the waters. For a longer trip, *K-D Linie* steamers sail on the Rhine between Cologne and Mainz, and on the Mosel between Koblenz and Cochem, every day from April to October inclusive. On these routes, possession of a *EuroDomino* or *Eurail* pass will get you free passage, while *InterRail* brings a 50 percent reduction.

The steamers call at many riverside villages and you can get on or off wherever you want. The fare, as you'd expect, depends on how far you travel; Cologne to Koblenz, for example, costs DM74.20 (DM105.20 by fast boat), although you can make savings by opting for a return journey along a shortish section, such as Koblenz to St Goarshausen and back for DM29.80. Several smaller companies also operate short-haul services along both the Rhine and Mosel, and along most other main navigable rivers as well. In the former GDR, there are particularly beautiful cruises to be had on the Elbe, particularly the stretch from Dresden south into the Czech Republic.

Germany's biggest lake, an enormous bulge in the Rhine called the **Bodensee**, is also a prime spot for water-borne travel, either for a lazy cruise or to explore the nooks and crannies of its shoreline, which spans Austria and Switzerland as well as Germany; full details are on p.258.

TRAMS AND OTHER MUNICIPAL TRANSPORT

Municipal transport in most German cities is still centred on **trams**. In the west, these are usually sleek modern vehicles capable of moving at a fair speed between stops. They often have an underground stretch in the city centre, where they're known as the **U-Bahn**. This is often a source of confusion; it's important to remember that Berlin, Hamburg, Munich and Nürnberg have a much more extensive U-Bahn system using tube trains as distinct from trams, while in cities with trams only you may have to look both above and below ground in the central area to find the stop for the service you want. In some eastern German cities, old boneshaker trams are still the mainstay of the public transport system, though these are gradually being replaced. Wherever the trams and U-Bahns do not go, you can be sure that there will be a bus to fill the void.

Tickets, which can be bought from automatic vending machines or the driver, are valid on all the different forms of transport (which include the S-Bahn and mainline trains in all the major conurbations) and you can change from one to another, with no supplement for transfers. **Single** fares are usually expensive – DM3 is the standard rate in many cities, although it's normally a bit less in the former GDR. There's generally a special lower tariff for short journeys (*Kurzstrecke*).

If you're planning to make several journeys, it's advisable either to buy in **blocks** (usually offering a total saving of around 30 percent), or invest in a **fixed time period** (generally 24 hrs) ticket. The latter, which can be bought for the city itself or the whole of the regional network, can be a tremendous bargain – in some cities, up to two adults and two children are covered by the ticket, for an outlay of around DM8 or DM15 respectively. Even better value are the cards recently introduced in many cities which, for a minimal extra outlay, include admission to the main municipal museums.

PLANES

While **domestic flights** are numerous and quick between the major cities, they are also expensive. Single fares are available in business class

CAR RENTAL AGENCIES

BRITAIN
Avis ☎0181/848 8733.
Budget ☎0800/181181.
Eurodollar ☎01895/233300.
Europcar/InterRent ☎01345/222525.
Hertz ☎0990/996699.
Holiday Autos ☎0171/491 1111 or
0990/300400.

IRELAND
Avis
Northern Ireland ☎0990/900 500;
Republic ☎01/874 5844.
Budget Rent-A-Car
Northern Ireland ☎0800/181 181;
Republic ☎0800/973 159.
Europcar
Northern Ireland ☎0345/222 525;
Republic ☎01/874 5844.
Hertz
Northern Ireland ☎0990/996 699;
Republic ☎01/676 7476.
Holiday Autos
Northern Ireland ☎0990/300 400;
Republic ☎01/872 9366; freefax 1800/729 366;
email: *info@holidayautos.ie*

NORTH AMERICA
Alamo ☎800/522-9696;
http://www.goalamo.com/
Auto Europe ☎800/223-5555;
http://www.world.com/ae
Avis ☎800/331-1084; *http://www.avis.com/*
Budget ☎800/527-0700;
http://www.budgetrentacar.com
Europe by Car ☎800/223-1516;
http://www.ebcar.com
Hertz ☎800/654-3001; *http://www.hertz.com*
Canada ☎800/263-0600
Holiday Autos ☎800/422 7737;
http://www.kemwel.com

AUSTRALIA
Avis ☎1800/225 533.
Budget ☎13 2727.
Hertz ☎13 3039.

NEW ZEALAND
Avis ☎09/526 2847.
Budget ☎09/375 2222.
Hertz ☎09/309 0989.

only, and are far more expensive than the cheapest returns, which include Frankfurt–Berlin for DM220, Frankfurt–Hamburg for DM260. If you're in a desperate rush, it's worth trying to obtain one of these tickets, even if it means destroying the return portion. Student and youth fares are 25 percent less than normal rates. Any tourist office or *Lufthansa* agent will be able to provide full details of the current offers. If you definitely want to fly between German cities and are starting and finishing your journey in the UK, it's cheaper to book all the flights together, although this usually means that dates of travel cannot be changed.

DRIVING AND VEHICLE RENTAL

Foreigners may drive in Germany for one year with a national or international driving licence (for more than a year you must have a German licence). At least third party **insurance** is mandatory (normal third party insurance in Britain doesn't cover foreign travel, although more extensive

policies do). It's not necessary to carry a green card, but some other form of proof of insurance is essential.

Seatbelts are compulsory for all passengers as well as the driver, and **children under 12** years must sit in the back. Right of way can be problematic. Main roads have a yellow diamond indicating who has priority but it's sometimes necessary in built-up areas to give way to vehicles coming from the right. There are **on-the-spot fines** for speeding and other offences. For speeding these are charged on a sliding scale from about DM20–50; after a cut-off point of roughly 25km above the limit, you're charged and taken to court.

In cities be aware that **trams** always have the right of way. Unfamiliarity with the traffic system means that unwary visiting drivers are prone to cut in front of turning trams at junctions – a frightening and potentially lethal error. Also, when trams halt at their designated stops it's forbidden to overtake until the tram starts moving, to allow passengers time to cross the road and board.

Germany's highways, or *Autobahnen*, are the most extensive and efficient network in Europe, though those in the north can sometimes be only two lanes. Fuel stations, roadside restaurants and motels are located every 30–40km, and every city and virtually all the towns are within simple striking distance, using equally high-quality secondary roads to link them to the *Autobahnen*. A huge amount of work has been done in the former GDR to bring its road system up to western standards, though many minor routes still remain in a poor state of repair.

There are no legally enforced **speed limits** on the *Autobahnen* although there is a recommended limit of 100–130kmph. The official speed limit on country roads is 80–100kmph, and in built-up areas 50kmph.

CAR RENTAL

Car rental (*Autovermietung*) is available at most airports and major train stations, and regional tourist offices will always be able to inform you of the nearest car rental firm. Although the major companies like *Avis*, *Budget* or *Hertz* are easy to find, smaller local companies often offer better rates. Rates tend to be higher than in the UK and markedly higher than in the US (upwards of DM400 for a small hatchback for a week). You'll need to be 21 or over to rent a car in Germany.

Fly-drive deals can be good value if you know in advance that you want to rent a car, but you'll often get a better deal through someone who deals with local agents. *Holiday Autos* (see box opposite for number) is one of the best, substantially undercutting the large companies – weekly rates for a small car in Germany (including the collision damage waiver and unlimited mileage) start at £155 between April and October, £132 from November to March. If you're going in high season, book well in advance.

TAXIS

In cities and towns, taking into account the high cost of local public transport, several people sharing a cab may actually save money over using a local bus or train. Taxis (nearly all of which are Mercedes) have a sign on the roof which is illuminated if they are free. Hail one from the street, or wait at the taxi stands – alternatively there are always plenty hovering around train stations and big hotels.

MITFAHRZENTRALEN

As in most other countries today, casual hitching in Germany is not recommended as a safe method of getting around.

However, the Germans have developed an institutionalized form called **Mitfahrzentralen**, located in most large cities and listed throughout the *Guide*. (Beware that their addresses and phone numbers tend to change rapidly, so it's always worth checking the local directory.) These are agencies that put drivers and travellers in touch with each other for a nominal fee, and then it's up to the participants to work out an agreeable fuel contribution, usually a simple two-way split, although the agency does suggest a reasonable sum. There's a valuable safety factor in this system, since all drivers have to notify the agencies of their addresses and car registration numbers. There are also a few **women-only agencies**, known as *Frauenmitfahrzentralen*.

CYCLING

Cyclists are well catered for in Germany – at least in comparison with the UK or US – though sensibly they're banned from the *Autobahnen*. Many smaller roads have marked cycle-paths, and bike-only lanes are a common sight in cities and towns. Fairly hassle-free **long-distance cycling** is possible all over the country, but obviously you'll need a strong pair of legs and a sturdy, reliable machine to get much joy out of the Bavarian Alps. To take your own **bike on a train** (not permitted on *ICEs*, *ICs*, *ECs* or small local trains), you need to purchase a *Fahrrad-Karte* (bicycle ticket). This costs DM6 for up to 100km, DM12 otherwise, and you have to take the bike to the luggage van yourself.

Between April and October, the best place to **rent a bike** is from a train station participating in the *Fahrrad am Bahnhof* scheme (most of the main stations), whereby a bike costs from DM10–20 per day. You can return it to any other participating station and *EuroDomino* or InterRail card holders get a 50 percent discount. This is obviously perfect for splitting train travel with pedalling as and when the mood, terrain or weather takes you. During the rest of the year, or in an area where there's no suitable station, simply look in the phone book under *Fahrradverleih* to find the address of a local bike rental outlet. Renting this way, however, means you'll have to leave a deposit, usually around DM50.

WALKING AND HIKING

The German countryside is laced with colour-coded **hiking trails**, most of which are suitable for a Sunday afternoon stroll, though many trails are actually sections of much longer hikes. Very few hikes pass through remote or isolated areas and there's always a village, campsite or youth hostel fairly close by so you can make a trek of just a few hours or of several days' duration without much trouble. The best of the trails are described in the *Guide* and the local tourist offices have masses of **information and maps** (*Wanderkarten*) relating to the walks in their area. Because the hikes are so easy, you won't need any specialist equipment, but take a comfortable day-pack for carrying picnic provisions.

There are some **potential frustrations**, however. The prevalence of trees in all the scenic areas (with the exception of the Swabian Jura and the upper reaches of the Bavarian Alps) not only means that you're only occasionally rewarded with long-range views, but also ensures that there's seldom much chance to deviate from the regimentation of the marked paths. Don't let this rigidity fool you into skimping on proper maps: at times the trails can peter out or become confused, particularly when signs have become weather-worn or have been vandalized.

ACCOMMODATION

Be it high-rise city hotels or half-timbered guest houses in the country, accommodation of all types is easy to find in Germany and can often be good value – especially in the growing number of rooms available in private houses. For those on a really tight budget, the youth hostels and campsites which proliferate over the entire country are a sound, cost-cutting alternative.

HOTELS

Accommodation in Germany is subject to a somewhat complicated categorization system. The official classification of **Hotel** is not applied as widely as in many other countries, being confined in the main to mid-range and expensive establishments which have a manned reception desk and offer a full range of services, including a restaurant. Those of similar standing which serve no meals other than breakfast are classified as **Hotel garni**. The designation **Gasthof** signifies a uniquely German institution, one roughly equivalent to the traditional English inn. More often than not, you have to ask for a room at its bar-cum-restaurant. The latter almost invariably has a

ACCOMMODATION PRICE CODES

All the pensions and hotels in this book have been graded according to the following price categories. The prices quoted are for the cheapest available double room, although many of the budget places will also have more expensive rooms. Youth hostels are graded under separate categories. See p.34 for more details.

① less than DM50	④ DM81–100	⑦ DM151–200
② DM51–65	⑤ DM101–125	⑧ DM201–250
③ DM66–80	⑥ DM126–150	⑨ more than DM250

regular local clientele, and forms the mainstay of the business, with accommodation playing a secondary role.

Despite these different categories, the bedrooms on offer tend not to vary much: they're normally clean, comfortable and functional with conveniences like TV, phone and *en-suite* bathroom usually taken for granted in the medium-range establishments upwards. Note that in the former GDR most hotels are either new or recently refurbished, and hence tend to be more expensive than their western counterparts. The listings in the *Guide* concentrate on the best options in all price categories from the points of view of convenience, character and value for money. However, you should always call into the nearest **tourist office** to check any special deals which they may have with local establishments. This can result in you spending less than the figures quoted on the official **hotel lists** which every tourist office provides. Many tourist offices charge DM3–10 for finding you a room, but others perform the service free. You should take care not to find yourself stuck in a large town or city when there's a trade fair, or *Messe*, taking place – at such time hotels often double their rates and are booked solid.

In budget and medium-priced hotels, there's rarely any great saving to be made by two people sharing as opposed to one person travelling alone. In country areas, the least you'll have to spend is about DM30 for a single, DM50 for a double – at least DM10–20 extra for something similar in a city. Remember that any savings on accommodation costs that can be made by staying on the outskirts of a city may be offset by the price of public transport into the centre.

cities have private rooms on offer other than to relieve congestion when there's a trade fair on; rates are then comparable with those of hotels.

In the former GDR, on the other hand, thousands of householders have opened up their **homes** to guests, in order to earn a bit of extra cash. This helped plug the huge shortfall in accommodation for travellers that would otherwise have existed in the years immediately following the *Wende*, and nowadays provides a budget alternative to the hotel sector, which in eastern Germany is now dominated by expensive business-class ventures. In the cities, many of the rooms are in high-rise apartment blocks, and thus impossible to locate under your own steam. You therefore need to go to the local tourist office or one of the **private agencies** (*Zimmervermittlung*), which are often open until late in the evening, to book a room. Usually, there's a charge similar to that made for booking hotels, but beware of any tourist office or agency which wants to levy a daily fee: in such cases, book for one night and then try to negotiate a longer stay with your hosts.

Farmhouse holidays (*Ferien auf dem Bauernhof*) are increasingly popular in Germany, and in many ways are the best bargains of all, with full board rates from as little as DM30 per day. Full lists are available from local tourist offices; the major snag is that this option is really only feasible if you have your own transport. Even more ubiquitous are holiday homes (*Ferienhäuser*) which you rent by the week, and these can be the cheapest option if you are with a family or a group. Full lists are available from tourist offices in all main holiday areas.

PENSIONS AND PRIVATE ROOMS

The official designation of **Pension** is applied to less formal establishments than hotels, though in some holiday areas – particularly in Bavaria – the term **Gästehaus** (guest house) is used instead. In such places, the rooms are usually within a private house or apartment block. Prices tend to be quite a bit lower than in hotels, though this is less marked in cities than in the countryside.

In busy holiday areas, an increasingly prevalent budget option is **bed and breakfast** accommodation in a private house (look for signs saying *Fremdenzimmer* or *Zimmer frei*): prices vary but are usually around DM25–35 for a single, DM50–60 for a double. Very few west German

YOUTH HOSTELS

In Germany, you're never far away from a **youth hostel** (*Jugendherberge*) – the YH movement was born here, in fact, in 1909 – and these are likely to form the backbone of genuine budget travelling. Note, however, that at any time of the year they're liable to be block-booked by school groups – this is particularly likely on weekdays during the summer, and at weekends out of season. It's therefore advisable to make a reservation by phoning or writing to the hostel as far in advance as possible to be sure of a place – and be prepared to put up with marauding adolescents. Though most **wardens** and their staff are courteous and helpful, there's an unfortunate minority

YOUTH HOSTEL PRICE CODES

Germany's *HI* hostels divide into a number of categories according to facilities and size of room, which determines their price per night (which always includes breakfast) and these grades are listed for each hostel in the Guide. Junior prices apply to anyone under 27. You can expect the following facilities:

	Junior	Senior
❶ Basic affairs with large dormitories, sometimes even lacking heating and hot water.	DM16–18	DM18–20
❷ Slightly better equipped than grade ❶ hostels, usually with eight-bedded rooms.	DM18–20	DM20–22
❸ Four- and six-bedded rooms, more communal leisure rooms and washing facilities.	DM20–22	DM22–24
❹ Usually located in busier regions than the lower grades, with leisure and sports facilities.	DM22–24	DM24–27
❺ City-based versions of grade 4 hostels.	DM24–27	DM27–30
❻ Also known as youth guest houses, and containing two- and four-bedded rooms; the fee includes full bedlinen.	DM27-45 regardless of age	DM27-45 regardless of age

who seem to be leftovers from the leadership of the Hitler Youth, insisting on rigid regimentation and pedantic enforcement of the rules. You should be wary, too, of **age restrictions** (see below) and the fact that prices are slightly cheaper if you're under 27 years of age.

Apart from a few privately owned ventures, all hostels are run by the German Youth Hostel Association (*Deutsches Jugendherbergswerk*) and indicated by signs reading *DJH*. **Prices** are inclusive bed and breakfast rates (see box above for details), and apply to *HI* members; non-members, if admitted at all, will be charged an extra DM4 per night. If you're not a member and intend to use hostels for more than a couple of nights, it's wise to buy a year's *HI* **membership** from your own national association, before leaving home. You can buy the same thing at larger hostels in Germany but it's slightly more expensive.

Only **sheet sleeping bags** or sheets are permitted (you may be asked to show them to the warden), and if you don't have either, you can **rent a sleeping bag** for up to 10 days for DM2.

German youth hostels do carry a number of other **rules** and restrictions. **Reservations** will only be held until 6pm unless you've informed the warden that you'll be arriving late. When things are busy, **priority** is given to people under 18, or hiking families travelling with children. Those **over 27**, if they've not made a reservation, are only supposed to get a place if the hostel is not fully booked at 6pm – though this is by no means strictly applied. A more serious restriction for this age group is that they can't use the hostels in **Bavaria** at all, unless they are accompanying children.

All hostels have a **curfew**, which can be as early as 10pm (and usually is in rural areas) but may be later, as is the case in all the big cities. 10pm is usually the latest time you are able to check in. **Length of stay** is officially limited to three days unless a longer period has been booked in advance. You can, however, stay longer – provided you're not going to deprive new

YOUTH HOSTEL ASSOCIATIONS

Australia *Australian Youth Hostels Association,* 422 Kent St, Sydney (☎02/9261 1111); 205 King St, Melbourne (☎03/9670 9611); 38 Stuart St, Adelaide (☎08/8231 5583); 154 Roma St, Brisbane (☎07/3236 1680); 236 William St, Perth (☎08/9227 5122); 69a Mitchell St, Darwin (☎08/8981 2560); 28 Criterion St, Hobart (☎03/6234 9617).

Canada *Canadian Hostelling Association,* Room 400, 205 Catherine St, Ottawa, ON K2P 1C3 (☎613/237-7884 or 800/663-5777).

England and Wales *Youth Hostel Association (YHA),* Trevelyan House, 8 St Stephen's Hill, St Albans, Herts AL1 2DY (☎01727/45047). London shop and information office: 14 Southampton St, London WC2 (☎0171/836 1036).

Germany *Deutsches Jugendherbergswerk-Hauptverband,* 32704 Detmold (☎05231/74010).

Republic of Ireland *An Oige,* 39 Mountjoy St, Dublin 1 (☎01/830 4555).

New Zealand *Youth Hostels Association of New Zealand,* PO Box 436, Christchurch (☎03/379 9970).

Northern Ireland *Youth Hostel Association of Northern Ireland,* 22–32 Donegal Rd, Belfast, BT12 5JN (☎01232/324733).

Scotland *Scottish Youth Hostel Association,* 7 Glebe Crescent, Stirling, FK8 2JA (☎01786/451181).

US *Hostelling International-American Youth Hostels (HI-AYH),* 733 15th St NW, Suite 840, PO Box 37613, Washington, DC 20005 (☎202/783-6161).

arrivals from getting in. In **winter** many hostels close altogether; many more shut every other weekend. Very few German hostels offer self-catering facilities, but most do provide meals.

The *Naturfreundehaus* association offers a variant on the hostel theme. Its establishments, often located in rural countryside close to towns and cities, are designed more for older people, with accommodation in singles, doubles or very small dorms.

CAMPING

Big, well-managed **campsites** are a feature of Germany, and they're located almost anywhere anybody could even think about wanting to camp. It's significant that sites are officially graded on a scale beginning at "good" and working up to "excellent". Even the lowest grade have toilet and washing facilities and a shop nearby on the site, while the grandest are virtually open-air hotels with swimming pools, supermarkets and various other comforts – though it must be said that camping purists find German sites rather too regimented. **Prices** are based on facilities and location, comprising a fee per person (DM3–10) and per tent (DM3–6). There are extra fees for cars,

caravans, etc, so you could easily spend quite a bit more than you might in other countries if there are several of you travelling in a car.

Bear in mind, too, that many sites, especially those in popular holiday areas, are nearly always full from June to September, and you should arrive early in the afternoon for a good chance of getting in. Most campsites close down in the winter, but those in popular skiing areas remain open all year.

All the most useful sites are listed in the *Guide,* and you can also pick up the highly condensed **list of sites** which is available free from German National Tourist Offices. The complete official guide is available direct from the *German Camping Club,* the *DDC,* at Mandlestr. 28, Munich. The motoring organization, *ADAC,* also produces a similar guide which includes Germany and much of northern and central Europe.

Rough camping on communally owned land is illegal in the interests of protecting the environment, though a blind eye seems to be turned to camper vans: indeed stays ranging from 24 hours to 3 days are sometimes officially sanctioned. You can camp on private farmland by obtaining permission – which is often freely granted – from the owner.

EATING

German food is, as a rule, both good value and of high quality. However, it does help if you share the national penchant for solid, fatty food accompanied by compensatingly healthy fresh vegetables and salad. The pig is the staple element of the German menu – it's prepared in umpteen different ways, and just about every part of it is eaten. It also forms the main ingredient for sausages, which are not only the most popular snack, but are regarded as serious culinary fare – in Bavaria, there are even specialized *Wurstküchen* (sausage kitchens) which have gained Michelin ratings.

BREAKFAST

The vast majority of German hotels and guest houses, and all youth hostels, include breakfast in the price of their accommodation. Although some places go in for the spartan French affair of rolls, jam and coffee, the normal German breakfast lies midway between this and the elaborate Scandinavian-style cold table, but the latter is catching on, particularly in middle- and upper-range hotels. Typically, you'll be offered a small platter of **cold meats** (usually sausage-based) and **cheeses**, along with a selection of marmalades, jams and honey. Muesli or another cereal is sometimes included as well, or as an alternative to the meats and cheeses. You're generally given a variety of **breads**, which are among the most distinctive features of German cuisine. Both brown and white rolls are popular; these are often given a bit of zap by the addition of a condiment, such as caraway, coriander, poppy or sesame seeds. The rich-tasting black rye bread, known as *Pumpernickel*, is a particular national favourite, as is the salted *Brezel*, which tastes nothing like any foreign imitation. **Coffee** (which is normally freshly brewed) is the usual accompaniment, but tea – whether plain or herbal – is gaining popularity, while drinking chocolate is another common alternative. Fruit juice – almost invariably orange – is sometimes included as well.

If breakfast isn't included in your accommodation costs, you can usually do quite well by going to a local **baker's shop**, which generally opens from 7am, if not before. Most chain bakeries have an area set aside for breakfast, known as a *Stehcafé* (standing café), a practice taken up by some family establishments as well. The coffee and chocolate on offer tend to be of high quality, and there's the added bonus of being able to choose from the freshly made bakery on display; DM4–5 should cover an adequate breakfast.

SNACKS AND FAST FOOD

Just as the English have their morning and afternoon tea, so the Germans have *Kaffee und Kuchen* (coffee and cakes). Though the elegant type of **café** serving a choice of espresso, cappuccino and mocha to the accompaniment of cream cakes, pastries or handmade chocolates is indelibly associated with Austria, it's every bit as popular an institution in Germany. This hardly constitutes a cheap snack but is unlikely to be a rip-off – except in the most obvious tourist traps. An almost equally ubiquitous institution is the **ice-cream parlour** (*Eiscafé*). Almost invariably, these are run by Italian émigrés and offer a huge range of flavours and concoctions to choose from, which can either be eaten on the premises or taken away.

More substantial food is available from **butcher's shops**. Even in rural areas, you can generally choose from a variety of freshly roasted meats to make up a hot sandwich. It's also worth going to the open-air **markets** which are held anything from once to six times a week in the central square of most towns. With a bit of judicious shopping round the stalls, you should be able to make up an irresistible picnic for an outlay of a few

FOOD GLOSSARY

Basics

Abendessen	supper, dinner	*Gabel*	fork	*Öl*	oil
Belegtes Brot	open sandwich	*Gemüse*	vegetables	*Pfeffer*	pepper
		Glas	glass	*Rechnung*	bill
Biertieg	batter	*Hauptgericht*	main course	*Reis*	rice
Brot	bread	*Honig*	honey	*Salz*	salt
Brötchen	bread roll	*Joghurt*	yoghurt	*Senf*	mustard
Butter	butter	*Käse*	cheese	*Sosse*	sauce
Butterbrot	sandwich	*Löffel*	spoon	*Spätzle*	shredded pasta
Ei	egg	*Marmelade*	jam		
Eintopf	a soup-stew hybrid	*Maultaschen*	form of ravioli	*Speisekarte*	menu
		Messer	knife	*Tasse*	cup
Essig	vinegar	*Mittagessen*	lunch	*Teller*	plate
Fisch	fish	*Nachspeise*	dessert	*Trinkgeld*	tip
Fleisch	meat	*Nudeln*	noodles	*Vorspeise*	starter
Frühstück	breakfast	*Obst*	fruit	*Zucker*	sugar

Soups and Starters

Bohnensuppe	bean soup	*Lachsbrot*	smoked salmon on bread
Erbsensuppe	pea soup	*Leberknödelsuppe*	clear soup and liver dumplings
Flädlesuppe, Pfannkuchensuppe	clear soup with pancake strips	*Leberpastete*	liver paté
Fleischsalat	sausage salad with onions	*Linsensuppe*	lentil soup
Fleischsuppe	clear soup and meat dumplings	*Melone mit Schinken*	melon and ham
		Ochsenschwanzsuppe	oxtail soup
Grüner Salat	mixed green salad	*Schnittlauchbrot*	chives on bread
Gulaschsuppe	thick soup in imitation of goulash	*Sülze*	jellied meat loaf
		Suppe	soup
Gurkensalat	cucumber salad	*Würzfleisch*	supreme of pork
Hühnersuppe	chicken soup	*Zwiebelsuppe*	onion soup

Meat and Poultry

Aufschnitt	mixed slices of cold sausage	*Herz*	heart
Bockwurst	chunky boiled sausage	*Hirn*	brains
Bratwurst	grilled sausage	*Hirsch, Reh*	venison
Broiler	chicken	*Huhn, Hähnchen*	chicken
Currywurst	sausage served with piquant sauce	*Innereien*	innards
		Jägerschnitzel	cutlet in wine and mushroom sauce
Eisbein	boiled knuckle of pig		
Ente	duck	*Kanninchen*	rabbit
Fasan	pheasant	*Kassler Rippchen*	smoked and pickled pork chops
Fleischpflanzerl	meatball (in Bavaria)		
Frikadelle	meatball	*Kotelett*	cutlet (cheapest cut)
Froschschenkel	frogs' legs	*Krautwickerl*	cabbage leaves filled with mincemeat
Gans	goose		
Geschnetzeltes	shredded meat, usually served with rice	*Lamm*	lamb
		Leber	liver
Gyros	kebab	*Leberkäse*	baked meatloaf served hot or cold
Hackbraten	mincemeat roast		
Hackfleisch	mincemeat	*Lunge*	lungs
Hammelfleisch	mutton	*Nieren*	kidneys
Hase	hare	*Ochsenschwanz*	oxtail

Meat and Poultry (continued)

Rahmschnitzel	cutlet in cream sauce	*Schweinehaxe*	grilled knuckle of pig
Rindfleisch	beef	*Spanferkel*	suckling pig
Sauerbraten	braised pickled beef	*Speck*	bacon
Saure Lunge	pickled lungs	*Truthahn*	turkey
Schaschlik	diced meat with piquant sauce	*Weisswurst*	white herb sausage made with veal and pork
Schinken	ham	*Wiener Schnitzel*	thin cutlet in breadcumbs
Schlachtplatte	mix of cured meats, including blood	*Wienerwurst*	standard boiled pork sausage
Schnecke	snail	*Wild*	wild game
Schnitzel Natur	uncoated cutlet (usually pork)	*Wildschwein*	wild boar
		Wurst	sausage
Schweinebraten	roast pork	*Zigeunerschnitzel*	cutlet in paprika sauce
Schweinefleisch	pork	*Zunge*	tongue

Fish

Aal	eel	*Kaviar*	caviar	*Schellfisch*	haddock
Forelle	trout	*Krabben*	prawns	*Scholle*	plaice
Goldbarsch	redfish	*Lachs*	salmon	*Schwertfish*	swordfish
Hecht	pike	*Makrele*	mackerel	*Seezunge*	sole
Hering, Matjes	herring	*Muscheln*	mussels	*Skampi*	scampi
Hummer	lobster	*Rotbarsch*	rosefish	*Thunfisch*	tuna
Kabeljau	cod	*Sardellen*	anchovies	*Tintenfisch*	squid
Karpfen	carp	*Sardinen*	sardines	*Zander*	pike-perch

Vegetables

Blumenkohl	cauliflower	*Paprika*	green or red peppers
Bohnen	beans	*Pellkartoffeln*	jacket potatoes
Bratkartoffeln	fried potatoes	*Pilze*	mushrooms
Champignons	button mushrooms	*Pommes frites*	fries
Erbsen	peas	*Reibekuchen*	potato cake
Grüne Bohnen	green beans	*Rosenkohl*	brussels sprouts
Gurke	cucumber	*Rote Rübe*	beetroot
Karotten, Möhren	carrots	*Rotkohl*	red cabbage
Kartoffelbrei	mashed potatoes	*Rübe*	turnip
Kartoffelpuree	creamed potatoes	*Salat*	salad
Kartoffelsalat	potato salad	*Salzkartoffeln*	boiled potatoes
Knoblauch	garlic	*Sauerkraut*	pickled cabbage
Knödel, Kloss	dumpling	*Spargel*	asparagus
Kopfsalat	lettuce	*Tomaten*	tomatoes
Lauche	leeks	*Weisskohl*	white cabbage
Maiskolben	corn on the cob	*Zwiebeln*	onions

Fruits

Ananas	pineapple	*Feigen*	figs
Apfel	apple	*Himbeeren*	raspberries
Aprikose	apricot	*Johannisbeeren*	redcurrants
Banane	banana	*Kirschen*	cherries
Birne	pear	*Kompott*	stewed fruit or mousse
Brombeeren	blackberries	*Mandarine*	tangerine
Datteln	dates	*Melone*	melon
Erdbeeren	strawberries	*Obstsalat*	fruit salad

Orange	orange	*Schwarze*	blackcurrants
Pampelmuse	grapefruit	*Johannisbeeren*	
Pfirsich	peach	*Stachelbeeren*	gooseberries
Pflaumen	plums	*Trauben*	grapes
Rosinen	raisins	*Zitrone*	lemon

Cheeses and Desserts

Emmentaler	Swiss Emmental	*Kaiserschmarrn*	shredded pancake
Käseplatte	mixed selection of		served with
	cheeses		powdered sugar,
Schafskäse	sheep's cheese		jam and raisins
Weichkäse	cream cheese	*Käsekuchen*	cheesecake
Ziegenkäse	goat's cheese	*Keks*	biscuit
Apfelstrudel mit Sahne	apple strudel with	*Krapfen*	doughnut
	fresh cream	*Nüsse*	nuts
Berliner	jam doughnut	*Nusskuchen*	nut cake
Dampfnudeln	large yeast dumplings	*Obstkuchen*	fruitcake
	served hot with	*Pfannkuchen*	pancake
	vanilla sauce	*Schokolade*	chocolate
Eis	ice cream	*Schwarzwälder Kirschtorte*	Black Forest gateau
Gebäck	pastries	*Torte*	gateau, tart

Common Terms

Art	style of	*Geräuchert*	smoked
Blau	rare	*Gutbürgerliche Küche*	traditional German
Eingelegte	pickled		cooking
Frisch	fresh	*Hausgemacht*	home-made
Gebacken	baked	*Heiss*	hot
Gebraten	fried, roasted	*Kalt*	cold
Gedämpft	steamed	*Spiess*	skewered
Gefüllt	stuffed	*Topf (Eintopf)*	stew, casserole
Gegrillt	grilled	*Vom heissen Stein*	raw meats you cook
Gekocht	cooked		yourself on a red hot
			stone

Deutschmarks. Larger cities tend to have a daily indoor version of this, known as the *Markthalle*.

The easiest option for a quick snack, however, is to head for the ubiquitous **Imbiss** stands and shops. In the latter you have the option of eating in or taking away; the price is the same. These indigenous types of snack bar tend to serve a range of sausages, plus meat-balls, hamburgers and chips; the better ones have soups, schnitzels, chops and salads as well. Spit-roasted chicken is usually recommendable and very cheap, at around DM4-6 for half a bird. Mustard is usually available at no extra cost with all dishes, whereas small supplements are levied for mayonnaise or ketchup. Most *Imbiss* places sell beer, but as many are unlicensed you may be forbidden from consuming it on the premises.

Among the fast-food **chains**, *Kochlöffel* stands out for cleanliness and good food. The speciality here is spit-roast chicken; prices compare very favourably with the many American-owned hamburger joints. Another chain with acceptable food is *Wienerwald*, but its menu, set-up and price structure are more comparable to a restaurant than a snack bar. The Bavarian butcher's chain *Vincenz Murr* sells full main courses to be eaten on your feet, costing DM5–12; many smaller concerns throughout the country offer a similar service. Virtually the only places outside northern Germany where you can regularly find salt-water **fish** are in the shops of the *Nordsee* chain. These vary a lot in quality, but unfortunately the standard of the fish prepared for consumption on the premises is seldom equal to that sold for home cooking. By far the most innovative and original chain is that run by *Mövenpick* under the *Restaurant Marché* logo. Here, fresh market ingredients are the watchwords, whether in the enormous cold buffet selection from which you help yourself, or in the hot grill dishes cooked to order before your eyes. Because of the sheer scale of each operation, they're only to be found in the centres of major cities, though the company is expanding.

Ethnic snack bars are predominantly Italian, Greek or Turkish. The **pizzerias** are a major boon if you're on a tight budget. Either taking away or eating standing up, prices start at around DM5 for a simple tomato and cheese pizza. Most pizzerias also serve pasta dishes, though these are usually less of a bargain. As always, the **kebab** houses adapt their technique to suit the national taste. The *Gyros* or *Döner* is based on real lamb meat and fat and served in bread, generally with tsatziki as a sauce, and costs DM4–6.

MEALS AND RESTAURANTS

All **restaurants** display their menus and prices by the door, as well as which day is their *Ruhetag*, when they're closed. Hot meals are usually served throughout the day, but certainly where it says *durchgehend warme Küche*. The *Gaststätte*, *Gasthaus, Gasthof, Brauhaus* or *Wirtschaft* establishments, which are the nearest equivalents to old-fashioned English inns, mostly belong to a brewery and function as social meeting points, drinking havens and cheap restaurants combined. Their style of cuisine is known as **gutbürgerliche Küche**; this resembles hearty German home cooking (hence the comparatively low prices), and portions are almost invariably generous. Most of these places have a hard core of regular customers who sit at tables marked *Stammtisch*; unless invited to do so, it's not the done thing to sit there. The bulk of the menu is the same all day long, though some establishments offer two- or three-course lunches at a bargain price. **Standards** in west German restaurants are amazingly high: you're far less likely to be served a dud meal than in almost any other country. In the east, erratic restaurant performances, once commonplace, are becoming ever rarer.

Choice for **soup** is fairly restricted, and tends to be based on an adaptation of foreign fare; prices are usually in the range of DM3–8. Among the most popular are *Gulaschsuppe*, a liquidized

version of the staple Magyar dish (despite often being dignified as *Ungarische*, it's not something a Hungarian would recognize); *Bohnensuppe*, which is often quite spicy, and derived from the Serbian model; and *Zwiebelsuppe*, which is a direct copy of the famous French brown onion soup, usually with floating cheese and croutons. In east Germany, *Soljanka* is a spicy Ukrainian soup with sliced sausages. More authentically German are the clear soups with dumplings, of which the Bavarian *Leberknödelsuppe* is the best known. Other **starters** tend to be fairly unsophisticated – either a salad, pâté or cold meat dish; prices are similar to those for soups.

Main courses in all German restaurants are overwhelmingly based on **pork**. As a rule, this is of noticeably higher quality than in Britain, and the variety in taste wrought by using different sauces (it's quite common to find a choice of up to 20 different types) and unexpected parts of the animal means that the predominance of the pig is far less tedious than might be supposed. As an alternative to the ubiquitous *Schnitzel*, try *Schweinehaxe* or *Eisbein*, respectively the grilled (or roasted) and boiled versions of pig's knuckles. **Sausages** regularly feature on the menu, with distinct regional varieties.

Whereas a main course pork-based dish is likely to cost DM20 or less, one with **beef** will cost a fair bit more. As is the case with snack bars, **chicken** dishes are comparatively cheap. Many restaurants have a **game** menu, with more exotic poultry such as duck or goose, along with venison, rabbit and hare; prices then tend to be DM25 or more.

Outside northern Germany, where a wide variety of newly caught salt-water **fish** is readily available, you'll probably have to be content with fresh-water varieties; trout is by far the most popular, though there's obviously a greater choice in places close to lakes and rivers. Where salt-water fish is available, the unfamiliar rosefish (*Rotbarsch*) is generally the most reliable. Oddly enough, you're far more likely to encounter a choice of fresh fish in east Germany, where there are many privatized survivors from the long-established *Gastmahl des Meeres* chain.

The main course price invariably includes **vegetables**. Potatoes are usually roasted, fried or made into a cold salad; boiled potatoes are becoming increasingly popular, but they are rarely baked or mashed. Dumplings made from potatoes and flour are a common alternative. Cabbage is the other popular accompaniment – the green variety is pickled as *Sauerkraut*, whereas the red is normally cooked with apple as *Apfelrotkohl*. Salads of lettuce, cucumber, beetroot, carrots and gherkins are often included as a side-dish. In May and June, when **asparagus** is in season, many restaurants have a special menu (*Spargelkarte*) of dishes - both vegetarian and carnivore - with this vegetable as a key ingredient. The noodles known as *Spätzle* and *Maultaschen* are a distinctive component of Swabian cuisine, occasionally adopted elsewhere.

Because so many Germans go to cafés (see above) for their daily helping of cakes, **desserts** in restaurants are an anti-climax, where they exist at all. The Bavarian *Dampfnudel* is one of the few distinctive dishes; otherwise there's just the usual selection of fresh and stewed fruits, cheeses and ice creams.

Germany has a wide variety of **ethnic restaurants**. The density of these is very much in line with the general *Gastarbeiter* influx, and there's a heavy southern European bias. Of these, the Italian are generally the best recommendations; there are also plenty offering Balkan and Greco-Turkish cuisines. Chinese restaurants are also ubiquitous and usually very consistent, with most offering good-value set lunches. On the other hand, Indian and Thai food is often toned down, largely because few Germans care for hot spices.

VEGETARIAN FOOD

Vegetarians will find Germany less than ideal – most menus are almost exclusively for carnivores, and even an innocent-sounding item like tomato soup might have small chunks of bacon floating around in it. However, it's usually easy enough to find such staples as salads, omelettes, pancakes, pasta and pizzas. Most cities also tend to have at least one specialist vegetarian and wholefood restaurant, and these are listed throughout the *Guide*. Many have self-service buffets where you pay for the items chosen according to their weight.

Ich bin Vegetarier	I am a vegetarian
Haben Sie etwas	Do you have
ohne Fleisch?	anything without meat?

DRINKING

The division between eating and drinking establishments in Germany is less demarcated than in the English-speaking world. Despite their inevitable connotations with **beer** and **wine**, the *Brauhäuser* and *Weinstuben* inevitably double as restaurants, though there are some purely drinking dens, generally known as *Kneipen*. Apart from beer and wine, there's nothing very distinctive about German beverages, save for *Apfelwein*, a variant of cider. The most popular spirits are the fiery *Korn* and after-dinner liqueurs, which are mostly fruit-based. Both hot and soft drinks are broadly the same as in Britain.

BEER

For serious beer drinkers, Germany is the ultimate paradise. Wherever you go, you can be sure of getting a product made locally, often brewed in a distinctive style. The country has around 40 percent of the world's breweries, with some 800 (about half the total) in Bavaria alone. All voluntarily adhere to the *Reinheitsgebot* (Purity Law) of 1516, which lays down stringent standards of production, including a ban on chemical susbtitutes. The current outlook is very rosy: although a few breweries bite the dust each year, there has been a revival of long-forgotten techniques, often put into practice in new small *Hausbrauereien*. These are springing up all the time, and are deservedly very hip, often being the trendiest spot in town.

More generally, there's an encouraging continuation of old-fashioned **top-fermented** brewing styles. Until the nineeenth century, all beers were made this way, but the interaction of the yeasts with a hot atmosphere meant that brewing had to be suspended during the summer. It was the Germans who discovered that the yeast sank to the foot of the container when stored under icy conditions; thereafter, brewing took on a more scientific nature, and yeast strains were bred so that beer could be **bottom-fermented,** thus allowing its

DRINKS GLOSSARY

Apfelsaft	apple juice	Mineralwasser	mineral water
Apfelwein	apple wine	Orangensaft	orange juice
Bier	beer	Roséwein	rosé wine
Federweisser	new wine	Rotwein	red wine
Glühwein	hot mulled wine	Sekt	sparkling wine
Grog	hot rum	Tee	tea
Herrengedeck	cocktail of beer and *Sekt*	Tomatensaft	tomato juice
Kaffee	coffee	Traubensaft	grape juice
Kaffee mit Milch	coffee with milk	Trinkschokolade	drinking chocolate
Kakao	cocoa	Wasser	water
Korn	rye spirit	Weinbrand	brandy
Kräutertee, Pflanzentee	herbal tea	Weinschorle	spritzer
Likör	liqueur	Weisswein	white wine
Milch	milk	Zitronenlimonade	lemonade
Milchshake	milk shake	Zitronentee	lemon tea

production all year round. The top-fermentation process, on the other hand, allows for a far greater individuality in the taste (often characterized by a distinct fruitiness), and can, of course, now be used throughout the year, thanks to modern temperature controls. All wheat beers use this process.

A quick beer tour of Germany would inevitably begin in **Munich**, which occupies third place in the world production league table. The city's beer gardens and beer halls are the most famous drinking dens in the country, offering a wide variety of premier products, from dark lagers through tart *Weizens* to powerful *Bocks*. Nearby **Freising** boasts the oldest brewery in the world, dating back to the eleventh century. In Franconia, distinctive traditions are found in **Bamberg** (national champion for beer consumption per resident), **Kulmbach** and **Bayreuth**.

In Baden-Württemberg, the local brews are sweeter and softer, in order to appeal to palates accustomed to wine; **Stuttgart** and **Mannheim** are the main production centres. Central Germany is even more strongly wedded to wine, though there are odd pockets of resistance. Indeed, **Frankfurt**, the German cider metropolis, also has the largest brewery in the country, *Binding*.

Further north, where it's too cold to grow grapes, the beer tradition returns with a vengeance. **Cologne** holds the world record for the number of city breweries, all of which produce the jealously guarded *Kölsch*. **Düsseldorf** again has its own distinctive brew, the dark *Alt*. **Dortmund** even manages to beat Munich for the title of European capital of beer production, and is particularly associated

with *Export*. Less well known, but equally good, are the delicate brews of the **Sauerland** and **Siegerland**, made using the soft local spring water.

Hannover, **Bremen** and **Hamburg** all have long brewing pedigrees, with many of their products widely available abroad. The most distinctive beers of the northernmost Länder, however, are those of **Einbeck** (the original home of *Bock*) and **Jever**. In contrast to these heady brews is the acidic *Weisse* of **Berlin**, which is completely transformed into a refreshing summer thirst-quencher by the addition of a dash of syrup.

East German brews are far less exciting, with the notable exception of *Köstrizer*, an outstanding black beer made in **Bad Köstritz** in the outskirts of Gera. **Magdeburg** has a long and varied brewing tradition, but elsewhere there's seldom anything other than the standard fare of light beers and local variations of *Pils*, of which the best are from **Radeberg** near Dresden and those made from the soft water of the **Vogtland**.

WINE

Many people's knowledge of German wine starts and ends with *Liebfraumilch*, the medium sweet easy-drinking wine. Sadly, its success has obscured the quality of other German wines, especially those made from the *Riesling* grape, and it's worth noting that the *Liebfraumilch* drunk in Germany tastes nothing like the bilge swilled back abroad.

The vast majority of German wine is white since the northern climate doesn't ripen red grapes regularly. If after a week or so you're pining for a glass of red, try a *Spätburgunder* (the *Pinot Noir* of Burgundy).

BEER GLOSSARY

Alt — Literally, any beer made according to an old formula; particularly associated with the dark brown top-fermented barley malt beer of Düsseldorf (also made in Mönchengladbach and Münster).

Altbierbowle — Glass of *Alt* with addition of a fresh fruit punch.

Berliner Weisse — Wheat beer from Berlin, usually served in a bowl-shaped glass, and with addition of woodruff (*mit Grün*) or raspberry essence (*mit Schuss*).

Bock — Light or dark strong beer, originally from Einbeck, but particularly popular in Bavaria, containing at least 6.25 percent alcohol.

Dampfbier — "Steam beer" from Bayreuth, a fruity brew top-fermented in its own yeast.

Doppelbock — Extra-strong Bock, usually made specially for festivals.

Dunkel — Generic name for any dark beer.

Eisbock — "Ice beer", particularly associated with Kulmbach; the freezing process concentrates the alcohol.

Export — Originally, beers made to be exported. Now used to describe a premium beer, or in association with the brewing style of Dortmund, stronger than a *Pils* and lying midway between dry and sweet in taste.

Hausbrauerei — 'House brewery', or pub where beer is brewed on the premises.

Hefe-Weizen — Wheat beer given strong yeast boost.

Hell, Helles — Generic names for light beers.

Hofbräu — Brewery formerly belonging to a court; that in Munich is the most famous.

Klosterbräu — Brewery attached to a monastery.

Kölsch — Top-fermented pale coloured beer peculiar to Cologne, invariably served in small glasses.

Kristall-Weizen — Sparkling brew made from wheat: the beer answer to champagne.

Maibock — Pale, high premium *Bock*, specially made to celebrate spring.

Malz — Unfermented black malt beer, similar to sweet stout.

Märzenbier — Strong beer made in March, but stored for later consumption; particularly associated with Munich's Oktoberfest.

Münchener — Brown-coloured lager, a style pioneered in Munich.

Pils — Bottom-fermented golden-coloured beer; very high hop content.

Radler/ Alsterwasser — Shandy.

Rauchbier — Aromatic beer from Bamberg made from smoked malt.

Spezial — Name given by breweries to their premium product, or to that made for special events.

Starkbier — Generic name for strong beers.

Steinbier — Beer made with the help of hot stones, an old technique recently revived.

Urquell — Name used to identify the original of a particular brewing style.

Vollbier — Standard (as opposed to premium) type of beer.

Weihnachts-bier — Special strong beer made for Christmas.

Weisse — Pale coloured wheat beer.

Weizen — Light or dark wheat beer.

Zwickelbier — Unfiltered beer.

First step in any exploration of German wine should be to understand what's on the label: the predilection for Gothic script and gloomy martial crests makes this an uninviting prospect, but the division of categories is intelligent and helpful – if at first a little complex.

Like most EU wine, German wine is divided into two broad categories: *Tafelwein* ("table wine", for which read "cheap plonk") and *Qualitätswein* ("quality wine"), equivalent to the French *Appellation Contrôlée*.

TAFELWEIN

Tafelwein can be a blend of wines from any EU country; *Deutscher Tafelwein* must be 100 percent German. *Landwein* is a superior *Tafelwein*, equivalent to the French *Vin de Pays* and medium dry. Like all German wines, *Tafelwein* can be *trocken* (dry) or *halb-trocken* (medium dry).

QUALITÄTSWEIN

There are two basic subdivisions of *Qualitätswein*:
Qba (*Qualitätswein eines bestimmten Anbaugebietes*) and **Qmp** (*Qualitätswein mit Prädikat*). "Qba" wines come from eleven delimited regions and must pass an official tasting and analysis. "Qmp" wines are further divided into six grades:

Kabinett The first and lightest style.

Spätlese Must come from late-picked grapes, which result in riper flavours.

Auslese Made from a selected bunch of grapes, making a concentrated medium-sweet wine. If labelled as a *Trocken*, the wine will have lots of body and weight.

Beerenauslese Wine made from late-harvested, individually picked grapes. A rare wine, made only in the very best years, and extremely sweet.

Trockenbeerenauslese Trocken here means dry in the sense that the grapes have been left on the vine until some of the water content has evaporated. As with *Beerenauslese*, each grape will be individually picked. This is a very rare wine which is intensely sweet and concentrated.

Eiswein Literally "ice wine", this is made from *Beerenauslese* grapes – a hard frost freezes the water content of the grape, concentrating the juice. The flavour of an *Eiswein* is remarkably fresh tasting, due to its high acidity.

GRAPE VARIETIES

These often appear on wine labels and are a handy guide to judging a wine's flavour.

Riesling Germany's best grape variety. It can have a floral aroma when young, is often "honeyed" when ripe, and develops interesting bouquets after 5–7 years in the bottle.

Gewürztraminer Gewürz means spicy, and the wine has an intense aromatic nose, likened by some people to lychees and by others to Turkish delight.

Müller-Thurgau The most widely planted grape in Germany. Its flavour is less distinguished than *Riesling* but is generally fruity, has less acidity and a grapey, Muscat taste.

Silvaner A fairly neutral wine, quite full-bodied and often blended with more aromatic varieties.

WINE REGIONS

Particularly at the Qualitätswein level, regional variations in climate produce markedly differing styles of wine.

Mosel-Saar-Ruhr The steep banks of the river Mosel and two of its tributaries enable the vines to catch long hours of sun, thus allowing grapes to ripen in one of the world's most northerly plantations. Much *Riesling* is grown in the slatey soil, producing elegant wines in the best years.

Rheingau On the sloping northern bank of the Rhine as it flows between Hochheim and Assmanshausen, this is a small, prestigious region that produces wines slightly fuller than those from the Mosel region. They're considered to be among the country's finest.

Nahe Both geographically and stylistically between the Mosel-Saar-Ruhr and the Rheingau, this is a relatively small region whose wines are often underrated.

Rhein-Hessen (Rhine-Hesse) Germany's main producer of *Liebfraumilch* from large plantations of *Müller-Thurgau* and *Silvaner* grapes.

Rheinpfalz (Palatinate) A southern wine region that produces full-bodied, ripe wines, chiefly *Liebfraumilch* and *Riesling*.

Franken (Franconia) Produces high-quality wines which are easy to identify, as they always come in a distinctively dumpy, round-shouldered bottle known as a *Bocksbeutel*.

Baden The most southerly wine-growing region, extending as far as the Bodensee. The warm climate allows French grape varieties to be grown here, and the majority of the wines are dry in flavour.

COMMUNICATIONS

POST OFFICES

Post offices (*Postämte*) are normally open Monday–Friday 8am–6pm and Saturday 8am–noon. A restricted range of services is available beyond these hours at offices in or beside main train stations in large cities. Outbound mail should reach the UK within a few days, North America in one to two weeks and Australia, over two weeks. In the major cities, there's a separate **parcels office** (marked *Pakete*), either within the same building or a block or so away.

Poste restante services are available at the main post offices in any given town (see listings in the *Guide* for addresses in the major cities): collect it from the counter marked *Postlagernde Sendungen* (always remember to take your passport). It's worth asking anyone writing to you to use this designation as well as, or instead of, poste restante. Incredible as it may seem in view of the country's reputation for super-efficiency,

many German post offices don't understand the international term and are likely to return a letter to the sender marked "address unknown". Bear in mind also that mail is usually only held for a couple of weeks. **Telegrams** can be sent either by ringing ☎01131, or from any post office. **Fax** services are available at large post offices, usually at more favourable rates than in copy shops. If you want your mail to be **registered**, ask for it to be sent *einschreiben*.

TELEPHONES

Telephoning is simple and most kiosks are equipped with basic instructions in several languages, including English. You can **call abroad** from all but those clearly marked "National". Coins of DM0.10, DM1 and DM5 are accepted; only wholly unused ones are returned. Calling **rates** vary according to the time of day: there are five different periods, which are progressively cheaper. The first cheap period begins at 6pm, the next at 9pm, the last at 2am. Some boxes are equipped with a ringing symbol to indicate that you can be called back on that phone. The major international codes are given in the box below; remember then to omit the initial zero from the subscriber's number.

For **local calls**, you need to insert a minimum of DM0.20, which will last for a minimum of 90 seconds at the peak daytime rate. In the *Guide*, local codes are included with each telephone number, except in major cities, where they're given in a box towards the start of each account.

The number of **card phones** is on the increase. A card, available from post offices for DM12 or DM50, is worth buying, especially if you're intending to call home. Another option is to use the **direct phone service** facility of the

---

PHONING ABROAD

From Germany dial ☎00 + IDD country code + area code minus first 0 + subscriber number
From Britain to Germany dial ☎00 49 + area code minus first 0 + number
From the USA to Germany dial ☎011 49 + area code minus first 0 + number

IDD CODES

Australia ☎ 61   Britain ☎44   Canada ☎ 1   Ireland ☎ 353   New Zealand ☎ 64   USA ☎1

USEFUL NUMBERS WITHIN GERMANY	
Operator	☎03
Directory enquiries	☎01188
International directory enquiries	☎00118
Operator wake-up call	☎01141
Ambulance	☎112
Fire	☎112
Police	☎110

main post office (*Hauptpost*): a phone booth will be allocated to you from the counter marked *Fremdgespräche*, which is also where you pay once you've finished.

The German **phone network** has expanded enormously since unification, and many numbers have changed – particularly in the east, where some towns have gone through repeated upheavals in this field. Hopefully, the system will become more stable over the coming years, but if the number you require turns out to be unobtainable, it's always worth checking the appropriate telephone directory (which is updated annually) to see if it has changed. Main post offices, and those in or near main stations, usually have a complete set of German directories for public consultation.

MEDIA

Germany is well supplied with **British newspapers**: in the larger cities it's relatively easy to pick up most of the London-printed editions on the same day. Some **US papers**, especially the *International Herald Tribune* are also readily obtainable.

With a few exceptions, **German newspapers** tend to be highly regionalized, mixing local and international news. Only the liberal *Frankfurter Rundschau* and Munich's *Süddeutsche Zeitung* are distributed much outside their own areas. Berlin produces two reputable organs: the *Tagespiegel*, a good left-wing read, and the Greenish/alternative *Tageszeitung*, universally known as the *Taz*. Of the national daily papers, the two best-sellers come from the presses of the late, unlamented Axel Springer: *Die Welt* is a right-wing heavyweight, and the tabloid *Bild* a reactionary, sleazy and sensationalist rag. The *Frankfurter Allgemeine* is again conservative, appealing particularly to the business community, but follows a politically independent line.

Germany has more **magazines** than any other country in Europe. The leftish weekly news and current affairs magazine *Der Spiegel* is the most in-depth magazine for political analysis and investigative journalism. Unless your German is fluent, though, it's a heavy and often difficult read. Though further to the right, *Die Zeit*, the weekly magazine of the newspaper of the same name, is a wider-ranging (and to learners of the language, easier-to-read) alternative. *Stern* is the most popular current affairs magazine, though no longer in the same league as *Die Zeit* or *Der Spiegel* since its prestige took a tumble following its publication of the forged Hitler diaries a few years ago.

German **television** is stuck in something of a time warp, its ads and presentation style generally still reminiscent of the 1960s and early 1970s. There are two main national channels, *ARD* and *ZDF*, plus the *Drittes Programm*, which features separate regional and educational programmes. Additionally, there a number of commercial channels, while the Austrian and Swiss networks can be picked up in some areas. Many houses and hotels are equipped with **satellite** or **cable TV**; in such cases, you'll have access to a choice of British and American channels.

The only **English-speaking radio** channels are the *BBC World Service* (90.2FM), the British Forces station *BFBS* (98.8FM) and the dire American Armed Forces radio station *AFN* (87.6FM), which combines American music charts with military news. These should continue broadcasting for at least as long as the troops remain.

BUSINESS HOURS

Shopping hours in western Germany were strictly curtailed by a law passed in the 1950s in a bid to counter national workaholic tendencies. This measure remains in force, modified only by a limited reform, allowing slightly longer opening times, introduced in 1996.

All shops must close at 8pm on weekdays and at 4pm on Saturdays. In practice, many still adhere to the old deadlines of 6.30pm and 2pm, extending the latter only on the first Saturday of the month, the so-called *Langer Samstag*. Shops are closed all day Sunday (except for bakers, who may open between 11am and 3pm). Pharmacists can extend their opening hours on a strict basis of rotation. The only other exceptions are shops in and around train stations, which generally do stay open late and at weekends. These are for bona fide travellers only, and you could be asked to show a ticket, though in practice you're most unlikely to find this absurd restriction applied.

MUSEUMS AND MONUMENTS

Museums and **historic monuments** such as castles and palaces are, with very few exceptions, closed all day Monday. Otherwise, opening times (which are detailed in the *Guide*) are usually more generous than in other countries, with lunchtime closures rare. Many major civic museums are additionally open on at least one evening per week. However, many museums and monuments in the former GDR still close two days a week, and they have been joined in this plight (though hopefully only temporarily) by a number of cash-strapped institutions in the west.

In range and diversity, German museums far surpass those of most other European countries, a legacy of the nation's long division into a plethora of separate states, and of the Romantic movement, which led to a passion for collecting. **Admission charges** for the museums vary enormously, and tend to reflect whether the relevant authority regards them as a social service or an exploitable asset, rather than their intrinsic quality. Historic monuments tend to charge around DM2–7, comparing favourably with similar places in Britain and the US. In east Germany, however, admission prices can be at the top end of the scale, as a result of the shortage of municipal funds. The overall costs of German unification have also led to many western German museums introducing charges, with others considering doing so. Indeed, the free museum may well soon be a thing of the past in Germany. Wherever you go, a **student card** nearly always brings a reduction in admission costs, often substantial. It's always worth asking about combination tickets or museums passes to several sights in the same city, which bring substantial savings. Note that most larger cities now offer public transport tickets (see p.29) which also give admission to the local museums.

There's rarely any difficulty gaining access to **churches**; hence opening times are only listed in the *Guide* for ancillary attractions such as treasuries or towers, or when set times are both limited and rigidly enforced. Bear in mind that churches used for Protestant worship (predominantly in Swabia, Hesse, northern Germany and the former GDR) tend to keep office hours, whereas those in Catholic areas usually open earlier and close later.

FESTIVALS AND PUBLIC HOLIDAYS

Germany probably has more annual festivals than any other European country, with almost every village having its own summer fair, as well as a rich mixture of religious and pagan festivals that have merged over the ages to fill the whole calendar.

These tend to flourish most in Bavaria, Baden-Württemberg and the Rhineland. In the former GDR, there are far fewer festivals – Communism is by no means entirely to blame for this, the roots lying in the puritanism which has long characterized the area. Since the *Wende*, a fair number of festivals have been initiated (or reinstated), though only time will tell whether any of these gain more than a local following.

The most famous German festival is undoubtedly the **Oktoberfest** in Munich, but **Carnival** and the **Christmas fairs** are other annual highlights, and take place all over the country. There's also a wealth of **music festivals**, ranging from opera seasons to open-air jazz and rock concerts. Main events are listed in the *Guide*, but below is a general overview.

January is a quiet month, though there are various events associated with the **Carnival season**, particularly the proclamation of the "Carnival King". Climax of the season comes in **February** or **March**, seven weeks before the date nominated for Easter. The Rhenish *Karneval* tends to have rather more gusto than its Bavarian counterpart, known as *Fasching*. Cologne has the most spectacular celebrations (detailed in the *Guide* on p.497), followed by those of Mainz and

Düsseldorf; the *Rosenmontag* parades are the highlight. Baden-Württemberg's *Fastnet* is a distinctive, very pagan, Carnival tradition, best experienced in Rottweil. Another old pagan rite is the *Schäfertanz* held in Rothenburg in March. This time of year sees things hotting up for **Easter**, and colourful church services are held throughout the country, particularly in rural Catholic areas. Another important **April** festival is the witches' sabbath of *Walpurgisnacht*, celebrated throughout the Harz region on the 30th of the month.

May marks the start of many **summer festivals**. Costume plays such as the *Rattenfängerspiele* in Hameln begin regular weekend performances, while there are classical concerts in historic buildings, notably the Schlosstheater in Schwetzingen. Every ten years (next in 2000), the famous *Passionspiele* in Oberammergau begins its run. On a lighter note, there's the *Stabenfest* in Nördlingen. **Whitsun**, which usually falls towards the end of the month, sees distinctive religious festivals in many towns. On the same weekend, there are two celebrated reconstructions of historic events – the *Meistertrunk* drama in Rothenburg and the *Kuchen- und Brunnenfest* in Schwäbisch Hall. Shortly afterwards, *Corpus Christi* is celebrated in Catholic areas, and is best experienced in Cologne.

June sees important **classical music festivals**, with the *Bach-Woche* during the second weekend of the month in Lüneburg, the *Händel-Festspiele* in Göttingen and Halle, the *Schumann-Woche* in Zwickau and the *Europäische Wochen* in Passau, while there's a big festival of all kinds of music held under canvas in Freiburg. Throughout northern Germany, the shooting season is marked by *Schützenfeste*, the largest being Hannover's. Bad Wimpfen's *Talmarkt*, which begins at the end of the month, is a fair which can trace its history back a thousand years.

July is a particularly busy festival month, with summer fairs and both **wine** and **beer festivals** opening up every week; pick of the latter is that in Kulmbach. Dinkelsbühl's *Kinderzeche* and Ulm's *Schwörmontag* are the most famous folklore events at this time. The Bayreuth *Opernfest*, exclusively devoted to Wagner, is held during late July, but note that all tickets are put on sale a year in advance and immediately snapped up.

PUBLIC HOLIDAYS

New Year's Day Jan 1
Epiphany Jan 6 and only honoured in Bavaria and Baden-Württemberg
Good Friday
Easter Monday
May Day May 1
Ascension Day
Whit Monday
Corpus Christi early or mid-June and honoured only in Baden-Württemberg, Bavaria, Hesse,

Rhineland-Palatinate, North Rhine-Westphalia and Saarland
Feast of the Assumption Aug 15, honoured only in Bavaria and Saarland
Day of German Unity Oct 3
All Saints Day Nov 1, honoured only in Bavaria, Baden-Württemberg, Rhineland-Palatinate, North Rhine-Westphalia and Saarland
Christmas Day
Boxing Day

August is the main month for colourful displays of fireworks and illuminations, such as the *Schlossfest* in Heidelberg and *Der Rhein in Flammen* in Koblenz. There are a host of *Weinfeste* during the month in the Rhine-Mosel area, notably those in Rüdesheim and Mainz, while Straubing's *Gäubodenfest* is one of the country's largest beer festivals. Other important events at this time are the *Plärrer* city fair in Augsburg, the *Mainfest* in Frankfurt and the *Zissel* folk festival in Kassel.

Paradoxically, Munich's renowned *Oktoberfest* actually takes place mostly in **September** – it usually starts on the second last Saturday, but can be the third last (see p.80). This month sees many of the most bacchanalian festivals, such as Heilbronn's *Weindorf* and Bad Cannstatt's *Volksfest*. **October** sees things qui-

etening down, though there's still the odd *Weinfest* in the Rhineland, along with the *Freimarkt* folk festival in Bremen, while in the Alpine region there are a number of religious festivals with an equestrian component; the *Colomansfest* in Schwangau is the most famous of these. In **November**, there's the month-long *Hamburger Dom* fair in Hamburg, while the *Martinsfest* on the 10th/11th of the month is celebrated in northern Baden and the Rhineland, most notably in Düsseldorf.

Finally, **December** is the month of Christmas markets (variably known as *Christkindelsmarkt* or *Weihnachtsmarkt*), and, if you were to choose just one, it should be Nürnberg's, which swells with traditional stalls selling everything from toys and trinkets to delicious sweets and biscuits.

SPORTS

Sports occupy a central position in German life: indeed it was the Germans who were chiefly responsible for developing sport towards its present key role in modern international society. This began with the introduction of gymnastics into schools as a means of pre-military training during the Napoleonic Wars. It continued in an overtly political way with Hitler's exploitation of the 1936 Olympic Games and the GDR's nurturing – at great cost and by dubious means – of a sporting elite as a means of gaining international prestige. Facilities for both

spectators and participants remain excellent in both parts of the united Germany, which seems likely to maintain its current leading position in a wide variety of sports, while doing its utmost to shed sinister undertones of the past.

FOOTBALL

Football is the nearest Germany comes to having a national sport. The West German team's victory in the 1990 World Cup equalled the record (since surpassed by Brazil) of three wins in the competition while marking the end of separate represen-tation for the two German states. Failure to pro-duce a successful national team was always rec-ognized as the biggest failure of the GDR's sports policy, though on the one occasion the two German states met in a tournament – in the 1974 World Cup – the East Germans scored what proved to be a hollow victory, as their victims sub-sequently went on to lift the trophy.

The *Bundesliga* elite division of 18 clubs is fiercely competitive. The German style of play, mirroring the national character, tends to be based on well-organized, methodical teamwork, rather than on the individual brilliance favoured in Latin countries. League matches are held on Saturday afternoons; European cup games are usually on Wednesday evenings.

By far the most famous team is *Bayern München*, whose record down the years entitles it to be ranked among the world's top clubs. Given the game's working-class roots, it's not surprising that many of the other leading clubs – *Borussia Mönchengladbach, Borussia Dortmund* and *Schalke 04* – are based in industrial towns. Others which have enjoyed recent success are *Werder Bremen, Hamburger SV, FC Köln and VfB Stuttgart.* Erstwhile GDR teams have struggled badly since unification, with only the hitherto unfashionable *Hansa Rostock* managing to hold down a regular place in the top flight. Those which have been reduced to amateur status include *Dynamo Berlin* (now *FC Berlin*), the Stasi-sponsored team whose connections were a sig-nificant factor in their ten consecutive champi-onship triumphs.

TENNIS

Tennis has been a real German obsession ever since 1985, when the 17-year-old **Boris Becker** blasted all his opponents off the court to become the first unseeded and youngest-ever men's sin-gles champion at Wimbledon. He did not quite fulfil his early promise, winning just five further Grand Slam tournaments before his retirement from major competitions in 1997 – a smaller haul than someone of his talent and longevity might have expected. Nonetheless, he inspired a whole new generation of German players, one of whom, **Michael Stich**, became Wimbledon champion in 1991, but was thereafter persistently dogged by injury, retiring from the game altogether at the same time as Becker withdrew from further par-

ticipation in Grand Slam events. Even more sig-nificant has been the steamrolling success of **Steffi Graf**, who won all four Grand Slam tourna-ments at the age of 19 in 1988. For two years she carried an "invincible" tag, and although her form then fluctuated for several years, she was virtual-ly unbeatable in 1996, by which time her career total of Grand Slam singles titles had risen to 21, the second highest on the all-time list. However, a spate of injuries in 1997 set her world ranking, never lower than no. 2 over the previous decade, into freefall, giving rise to the fear that she would never recover and that Germany would be left without a tennis player of the front rank.

Despite the leading position Germany has enjoyed in the game in recent years, the **tourna-ments** staged there are only second-string events on the international circuit. In early May, the Citizens' Cup for women is held in Hamburg; the German Open for men is held in the same city the next week, with the women's version following later that month in Berlin. The German Masters for women takes place in Leipzig in late September, while Stuttgart hosts a men's event in October. At the very end of the season are Germany's two most important tournaments, both male-only: the ATP World Championships in Hannover in November, and the Grand Slam Cup in Munich in early December.

ATHLETICS

The sport of **athletics** has had more than its share of controversy in recent years, and nowhere has that been more manifest than in Germany. Though West Germany did once in a while pro-duce an outstanding individual athlete, it could never match the consistency of the GDR, which reaped a massive crop of golds at every Olympics; in women's events especially, it often ranked as the best team in the world. This con-sistency was always dogged by allegations of drug-taking, and it is now absolutely indubitable that the athletes were indeed specially "manu-factured" by sports scientists using every means at their disposal. This huge state-sponsored scheme was in an altogether different league from the many cases of individual drug cheats (many of whom were never caught) in the free world. It has since come to haunt the combined German team, as witnessed by the disgrace of the star ex-GDR sprinter Kathrin Krabbe and oth-ers. To add to German discomfiture, there has been a growing demand from aggrieved rivals for all athletes who competed under the GDR flag to be stripped of their medals, with these being awarded instead to whoever finished immediately behind them.

The main annual grand prix **events** are all in the former West, with meets in early September in Cologne, Berlin and Koblenz.

OTHER SPORTS

Main venues for **motor sports** are Hockenheim near Heidelberg (where the German Formula 1 Grand Prix is held each July) and the venerable Nürburgring (which has recently returned to eminence as the site of the Luxembourg Grand Prix in September). The leading **equestrian events** are held consecutively in Hamburg and Aachen in June, while the celebrated dressage displays in Celle take place in September and October. Germany's **horse racing** calendar is dominated by the spring and autumn season at Iffezheim near Baden-Baden, and by the Derby week in Hamburg in late June.

WINTER SPORTS

From December to February, **winter sports** competitions, many associated with the skiing World Cup, are held in the southern part of the country. The main venues are **Garmisch-Partenkirchen** and Oberstdorf in Bavaria, and the Black Forest resorts of Todtmoos, Todtnau, Furtwangen and Schonach.

The German Alps offer some very attractive ski resorts, often overlooked in the rush to get to Austria, Switzerland and France. Everyone has heard of **Garmisch-Partenkirchen** (720–2966m), if only because of the 1936 Olympic runs still used by many professionals. Unfortunately it's an expensive – though well-equipped – resort. For equally excellent facilities, plenty of runs and lifts, affordable prices and a beautiful setting, **Oberstdorf** (700–2224m) is undoubtedly the all-round winner. Other, smaller resorts, which are high on picturesque views and ideally suited to novice and medium skiers, are **Bayrischzell** (800–1724m), **Mittenwald** (750–2385m), **Berchtesgaden** (550–1800m) and **Schliersee** (800–1693m). These are all traditional resorts, each with quite a few runs, good accommodation and plenty of activities other than skiing available. Families are especially well catered for, with resident ski schools to take care of the kids.

Travel to the German resorts is normally by plane to Munich, where trains connect with most skiing areas, the journey taking less than two hours in all cases. If you go on a package tour, a coach will normally pick you up from the airport, but check with your travel agent.

POLICE AND TROUBLE

The German police (*Polizei***) are not renowned for their friendliness, but they usually treat foreigners with courtesy. It's important to remember that you are expected to carry ID (your passport, or at least a student card or driving licence) at all times. Failure to do so could turn a routine police check into a drawn-out and unpleasant process.**

Traffic offences or any other misdemeanours will result in a rigorous checking of documentation, and on-the-spot fines are best paid without argument. The police are generally very correct, and shouldn't subject you to any unnecessary chicanery.

Reporting thefts at local police stations is straightforward, but inevitably there'll be a great deal of bureaucratic bumpf to wade through. All **drugs** are illegal in Germany, and anyone caught with them will face either prison or deportation: consulates will not be sympathetic towards those on drug charges. **Jaywalking** is illegal in Germany and you can be fined if caught.

The **GDR**'s claim that it was a crime-free state was a myth: there were always unsafe areas in the main cities, and particular problems with skinheads and football hooligans; these have, if anything, increased since unification. Bear in mind that the level of **theft** in this part of Germany has – inevitably – increased dramatically in line with unemployment and the dashed hopes of the many who have found their dreams of quick riches unfulfilled. However, provided you take the normal precautions, there's certainly no particular cause for alarm.

> Throughout Germany the number to ring for the police is ☎110.

WOMEN'S GERMANY

Women have traditionally been confined to a very subordinate role in German society, and this improved only relatively amid the postwar prosperity of the Federal Republic.

Few women reach senior positions in the main **political parties**; indeed, Chancellor Kohl has been chauvinistic enough to woo the female vote by referring to "our pretty women" as "one of Germany's natural resources". To some extent, the situation changed with the arrival of the Greens as a credible political force, with the late Petra Kelly the best known of several women in its corporate leadership. Many commentators, however, see this merely as a natural extension of the tendency for women to be at the forefront of German radicalism, continuing the tradition established by the early Communist leader Rosa Luxemburg, and continuing via the terrorist groups of the 1970s.

There are no effective laws against sex discrimination. Few women manage to get to the top in the **professions** and civil service, even though they now account for around half the total of university undergraduates. The situation has improved somewhat in medicine, with 20 percent of doctors being women, and in the Protestant churches, which allow women to become pastors. In the latter case, they've been quick to make an impact and a woman was appointed Bishop of Hamburg in 1993.

Officially, the **GDR** claimed to have established sexual equality, and it earned extravagant praise from many western feminists who accepted this at face value. The reality was very different. Dictator Erich Honecker's (often estranged) wife, Margot, was the only woman who reached a senior governmental position, and, in spite of the obligation placed on women to work, they fared little better elsewhere. In addition, because of the declining population, women were encouraged to have as large a family as possible; they were also expected to take the brunt of the shopping (involving much patient queuing) and household chores. This added up to a well-nigh intolerable burden on many, and it was small wonder that two out of every three marriages – the highest national percentage in the world – ended in divorce.

If you want to find out about grass-roots feminism, your best bet would be to contact the local **women's centre** (*Frauenzentrum*). These can be found in most cities, and are listed in the *Guide*. They're run with the usual German sense of organization and efficiency; they usually have a café and discussion groups and workshops. Additionally, there are plenty of **women's book-shops** (the best of which are listed in the *Guide*), as well as women-only *Mitfahrzentralen* (see p.31).

The level of **sexual harassment** is fortunately very low in Germany, and single women in restaurants, bars and cafés are nothing unusual and don't generally get bothered. People will come and sit at your table if there's limited space, but that doesn't automatically mean you're about to get chatted up.

GAY GERMANY

Germany is one of the best countries in Europe in which to be gay (in German, *schwul*). The only real legal restriction is that the male age of consent is 18, and on the whole it's a tolerant place as far as attitudes go.

However, to this rosy picture it's necessary to add a serious **caveat**. In rural areas people are often hostile towards gays and this intensifies in the Catholic southern part of the country, particularly in ultra-conservative **Bavaria**. Here small-town prejudice was given a judicial edge by the local parliament which, in 1987 under the late and fairly unlamented Franz-Josef Strauss, introduced mandatory AIDS testing for people who were suspected of being HIV-positive. Not content with this draconian measure they also formulated a law whereby HIV-positive people who don't follow official guidelines on "proper behaviour" can be arrested and held indefinitely. But although both these measures remain on the statute books, **Munich** has a flourishing and very visible gay scene.

Fortunately saner attitudes prevail in the rest of Germany, particularly in the **big cities**, all of which have thriving gay scenes, as do many medium-sized and even relatively small towns. The listings sections in the *Guide* give a run-down of the gay scene in the larger cities and towns.

The main gay centres are Berlin, Hamburg, Cologne, Munich and Frankfurt. Berlin in particular has, despite the horrors of the past, a good record for tolerating an open and energetic gay and lesbian scene. As far back as the 1920s Christopher Isherwood and W.H. Auden both came here, drawn to a city where, in sharp contrast with oppressive London, there was a gay community which did not live in fear of harassment and legal persecution.

The national gay organization is the *Bundesverband Homosexualität*, PO Box 120 630, 5300 Bonn 12 and there's a also a national AIDS help organization: the *Deutsche AIDS-Hilfe e.V* (*D.A.H.*) at Nestorstr. 8–9, 1000 Berlin 31 (☎030/896 9060). The most widely-read gay magazine is *Männer*, which comes out bi-monthly.

Many of the attitudes described above apply equally to **lesbians**. Outside of major cities, Germany's lesbian community is perforce more muted; being openly out in rural areas is impossible. Most of the women's centres listed in the *Guide* have details of local bars and meeting places. Alternatively, *GAIA's Guide*, available from bookstores in Britain and Germany, lists lesbian bars and contact addresses throughout the country. Worth scanning while you're in Germany is *UKZ-Unsere Zeitung*, the monthly lesbian magazine.

DIRECTORY

ADDRESSES The street name is always written before the number. Strasse (street) is commonly abbreviated as Str., and often joined on to the end of the previous word. Other terms include *Allee* (avenue), *Damm* (embankment), *Gasse* (alley), *Platz* (square), *Ring* (ring road), *Ufer* (quay), and *Weg* (way). Note that when a town or village has been incorporated into the municipality of a larger neighbour, it assumes a double-barrelled name: thus Babelsberg appears in addresses as Potsdam-Babelsberg, Bad Godesberg as Bonn-Bad Godesberg, Hohenschwangau as Schwangau-Hohenschwangau.

AIRPORT TAX A charge of DM12–15 is usually made for both domestic and international flights.

ELECTRIC CURRENT The supply is 220 volts, and anything requiring 240 volts (all UK appliances) will work. Sockets are of the two-pin variety, so a travel plug is useful.

EMBASSIES AND CONSULATES are listed under the relevant cities. Bear in mind that the level of help, other than in Berlin or Bonn, is likely to be variable – some cities keep up a fantasy diplomatic life, in which the honorary consul is a local businessman who has bought the title for the kudos it confers on him.

KIDS Travelling with youngsters shouldn't be a problem. Kids under 4 travel free on trains; those between 4 and 11 qualify for half-fare. On many municipal public transport tickets, kids travel free if accompanied by an adult. Similarly reduced rates are offered by hotels and guest houses. Most towns have crèche facilities: contact tourist offices for details. The best entertainments for kids are listed in the *Guide*.

LAUNDRY Laundries are not a very common sight in Germany west or east, but they do exist – look under *Wäscherei* in the local Yellow Pages to find the nearest. Dry cleaners (*Reinigung*) are more frequent, but also quite expensive. Many youth hostels have washing machines in their basements.

LEFT LUGGAGE All main stations have a vast number of left luggage lockers. The smallest and cheapest are large enough to hold all but the bulkiest rucksack or suitcase, and at DM2 for 24 hours they make humping heavy luggage around town a false economy. Most lockers take any combination of DM0.50, DM1 and DM2 pieces, though occasionally there's a specific requirement: sometimes this is for two DM1 pieces, at other times for one DM2 piece. Leaving bags with the station attendants costs DM4 per item, but this is often the only option in small towns, where the hours of service are often very restricted.

RACISM Thanks to the massive influx of *Gastarbeiter*, mainly from southern Europe, Germany is now firmly multicultural. However, there's no effective law against racial discrimination, and it's far from unknown for crankish pub landlords or nightclub proprietors to refuse entry on simple colour grounds.

STREET NAMES The vast majority of streets in the former GDR have been stripped of their Communist names, though a number survive, with Karl Marx, in particular, hanging on in there in a surprising number of towns.

STUDENT CARDS are worth carrying for the substantial reductions on entry fees they bring.

TIME GMT plus one hour. 9 hours ahead of US Pacific Standard Time and 6 hours ahead of Eastern Standard Time. Clocks are turned an hour forward at the end of March, and an hour back in late October.

TIPPING This is seldom necessary in restaurants, as prices are almost invariably inclusive, but rounding up to at least the next mark is expected, particularly in the former GDR – and even if you omit to say so, this will often be taken as read when change is given. In taxis, add a mark or two to the total.

CHAPTER ONE

BAVARIA

Bavaria (*Bayern*) is the original home of many of Germany's best-known clichés: beer-swilling *Lederhosen*-clad men, sausage dogs, cowbells and Alpine villages, *Sauerkraut* and *Wurst* and the fairy-tale castle of Neuschwanstein. Yet all this is only a small part of the Bavarian picture, and one that's restricted to the areas of the south in and around the Alps.

Historically and **politically**, Bavaria has always occupied a special position within Germany. Although a wealthy duchy within the Holy Roman Empire, its rulers preferred artistic patronage to the territorial expansionism and dynastic feuding characteristic of the rest of the nation. A fundamental change in status occurred at the beginning of the nineteenth century, when it profited from Napoleon's decision to re-order the map of Germany: Bavaria was doubled in size, and promoted to the rank of a kingdom. Thereafter, it retained much of its independence and its own monarch, even after the union of Germany in 1871. When the monarchy abdicated at the end of World War I, Bavaria briefly became a free state, but quickly degenerated into a hotbed of rightwing extremism – Hitler had his first successes there. This reputation for reactionary politics continues to the present day: Bavaria has long been ruled by the ultra-conservative CSU.

Bavaria is made up of four distinct regions, each with its own identity and culture, and its cities are equally varied in character. In **Munich** Bavaria has a cosmopolitan, if conservative, capital, that ranks as one of Germany's star attractions. The city lies at the centre of **Upper Bavaria**, the state's heartland, a region that ranges from the snow-capped peaks of the **Alps** to gentle hop-growing farmland. It's a traditional, deeply Catholic area whose rural traditions continue in spite of the inroads of mass tourism.

West of here is **Bavarian Swabia**. Detached by Napoleon from the rest of its traditional province (thereafter known as Württemberg), it remains stubbornly Swabian in culture – most obviously in its distinctive pasta-based cuisine. Even so, it is home to the most outrageous of the Romantic castles which form such a crucial part of the Bavarian stereotype. Outside of the mountainous **Allgäu** area in the south, this is a region of undulating agricultural country, ideal for walking and cycling holidays, dotted with medieval towns along the route of the **Romantic Road** – one of Germany's major tourist routes – and the upper reaches of the **River Danube**. The pristine local capital of **Augsburg** has been a place of importance since the days of the Romans, and its resplendent Renaissance buildings give it a highly distinctive appearance.

To the north lies **Franconia**, which was likewise not absorbed into Bavaria until 1803. The most obvious evidence of Franconia's separateness can be seen in the wine-growing area around **Würzburg** in the northwest, where a culture quite at odds with the beer-loving rest of Bavaria exists. In the northeast of Franconia the difference can be seen most obviously in the elegantly plain Baroque architecture of the Lutheran strongholds of **Ansbach** and **Bayreuth** – the Reformation left Franconia more or less split down the middle along religious lines. **Nürnberg**, a place risen from the rubble of wartime destruction and restored to the splendour of its Middle Ages heyday, was another city which quickly embraced Protestantism. Yet nearby **Bamberg**, whose magnificently varied architectural legacy is unsurpassed in all of Germany, remained staunchly Catholic.

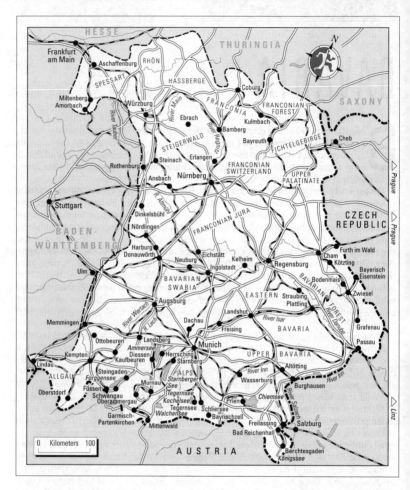

Eastern Bavaria, incorporating the old provinces of Lower Bavaria and the Upper Palatinate, is the state's backwater: a rustic, relatively poor region where life in the highlands revolves around logging and workshop industries like traditional glass production. However, the region also has a number of urban attractions, most notably the wonderfully well-preserved medieval cities of **Regensburg** and **Landshut,** and the border town of **Passau**, notable for its harmonious Baroque layout.

Travel is made easy by a generally good network of trains and regional buses, though public transport is sometimes a little thin on the ground in Bavarian Swabia and Eastern Bavaria – having a car makes life easier here. Cycling is an excellent and very popular way to get around, and is facilitated by a great many marked cycling paths throughout the state. **Accommodation** is uniformly good; it's normally not too difficult to find a bed, though problems may be experienced in the mountain resorts and some of the more popular tourist towns. An unfortunate **restriction for travellers over 27**

is that they're barred from using youth hostels, though reasonably priced private rooms in most places should compensate.

MUNICH (MÜNCHEN)

Pending Berlin's full recovery from its long period of division, **MUNICH** is the German city which most has the air of a capital about it. Even though it has never ruled over a territory any larger than the present-day Land, the grandiose palaces from Bavaria's era as an independent kingdom give it the appearance of a metropolis of great importance. When this is added to a remarkable postwar economic record (courtesy of such hi-tech giants as the car manufacturer BMW, the aerospace company MBB and the electronics group Siemens), and to its hard-won status as the national trendsetter in fashion matters, it's easy to see why Munich is often presented as a German Paris. Students flock here to study; the rich and jet-set like to live here, as do writers, painters, musicians and film-makers. Munich's other, more familiar face is of a homely city of provincially minded locals whose zest for drinking, seen at an extreme during the annual **Oktoberfest**, is kept up all year round in cavernous beer halls and spacious gardens.

Munich is something of a late developer in German terms. It was founded in 1158 by Henry the Lion, the powerful Saxon duke who for a short time also ruled Bavaria, as a monastic village (*Mönchen* means monks) and toll-collection point on the River Isar, a Danube tributary. In 1180, it was allocated to the **Wittelsbachs**, who ruled the province continuously until 1918 – the longest period achieved by any of the nation's dynasties. Munich was initially overshadowed by Landshut, though it became the capital of the upper part of the divided duchy in 1255. Only in 1503 did it become capital of a united Bavaria, and it remained of relatively modest size until the nineteenth century, when it was expanded into a planned city of broad boulevards and spacious squares in accordance with its new role, granted by Napoleon, as a royal capital. Hitler began an even more ambitious construction programme in accordance with Munich's special role as *Hauptstadt der Bewegung* "Capital city of the (Nazi) Movement"; thankfully, only a part of it was built, surviving to this day as a reminder of this inglorious chapter in the city's history.

Despite its cosmopolitanism, Munich is small enough to be digestible in one visit, and has the added bonus of a great setting, the snow-dusted mountains and Alpine lakes just an hour's drive away. The best time of year to come is from June to early October, when all the beer gardens, street cafés and bars are in full swing.

Arrival, information and getting around

Munich's spanking new **airport**, *Franz-Josef-Strauss-Flughafen*, lies some 30km north of the city centre, to which it's linked by S-Bahn #8, with departures every twenty minutes or so. Within the main hall is a **tourist office** (Mon–Fri 10am–9pm, Sat & Sun noon–8pm; ☎9759 2815), which performs all the usual services, including booking accommodation.

The **Hauptbahnhof** lies in a slightly seedy area at the western edge of the city centre. On its eastern side, at Bahnhofplatz 2, is another **tourist office** (Mon–Sat 10am–8pm, Sun 10am–6pm; ☎233 30256). Although long queues are the norm in sum-

---

The **telephone code** for Munich is ☎089

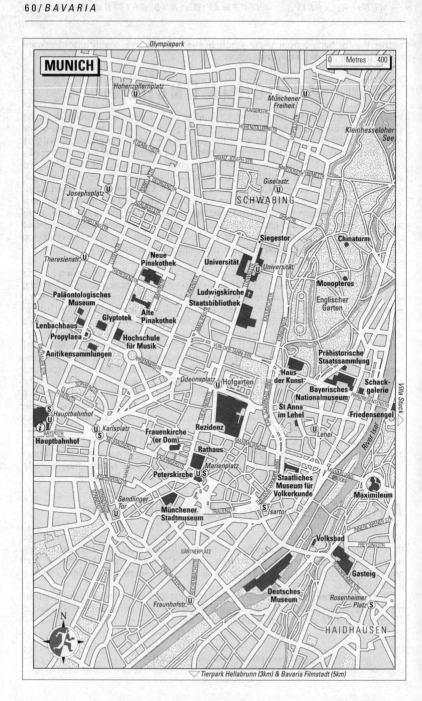

mer and during Oktoberfest, the staff are extremely helpful and will always help find a room for a DM5 fee. Within the station, alongside platform 11, is another very useful information office, *EurAide* (May–Oktoberfest daily 7.30–11.30am & 1–4.30/6pm). This office provides free train information to English-speaking travellers, preparing schedules and helping with itineraries and accommodation. Also within the station are plenty of shops plus a bank and a post office, all of which stay open until late evening.

A third **tourist office** can be found in the heart of the city, in the Rathaus on Marienplatz (Mon-Fri 10am–8pm, Sat 10am–4pm; ☎233 30272). The monthly English-language **magazine**, *Munich Found*, available from newsagents for DM4, has useful listings and information, as well as articles about the city and Germany in general.

City transport

Munich's public transport system, an integrated network of **buses**, **trams** and **U- and S-Bahn trains**, is good, though the fare and ticketing system, despite attempts at simplification, remains by far the most complicated in Germany. **Prices** vary according to how many zones are crossed: the city is divided up into a series of concentric circles, clearly displayed on the transport maps at any station, tram or bus stop.

Travel passes

If intending to stay for a week or more, your best bet is to buy a **travel pass**, for which you'll need your passport and two photos. The most convenient office for buying this is in the Hauptbahnhof – to reach it go down to the U-Bahn level and follow signs to the *Zeitkartenstelle* (Mon–Fri 7am–6pm, Sat 8am–noon). There are also *Zeitkarten* offices at the Poccistrasse U-Bahn station (Mon–Fri 8am–6pm), and at the Ostbahnhof and various other S-Bahn stations.

The cheapest pass, covering the city centre and most of Schwabing, costs DM13.40 for a week or DM52.50 for a month. For the whole city, a weekly pass is DM35, its monthly equivalent DM132; the charges rise to DM55.40 and DM216 respectively if you also want to cover neighbouring places on the network, such as Dachau and the Ammersee. Note that weekly passes are only valid from Monday to Monday, so buying mid-week means losing out; similarly monthly passes are for calendar months.

Tickets

Other tickets for city transport are available from ticket machines in all U-Bahn stations, at some bus and tram stops, and inside trams. This is where it gets particularly complicated: if you're going longer distances across the city it's not worth buying single tickets. Instead you will need to buy a **strip ticket** (*Streifenkarte*), costing DM13 (DM8.50 for children) for ten strips. You then stamp two strips for every zone crossed except for journeys of up to four bus or tram stops or two S- or U-Bahn stops, when only one has to be cancelled. It's not necessary to cancel every strip: only the last needs to be punched. Alternatively, various **day tickets** are available. The *Single-Tageskarte* for individual travellers costs DM8 for journeys within Munich, or DM16 for the city and S-Bahn region. These charges rise to DM12 and DM24 respectively for the *Partner-Tageskarte*, which covers two adults and up to three children (though this limit is waived in the case of verifiable offspring).

Accommodation

You'll find a good range of **accommodation** in the city. There are abundant **hotels** in every category from the basic to the hyper-luxury, and you'll even find several **hostels** in which the normal Bavarian restriction on those over 27 does not apply. Beware, however, that without advance booking it can be virtually impossible to find budget accommodation during the Oktoberfest beer festival/fair that runs from the last Saturday in September to the first Sunday in October: to be in with a chance, turn up very early in the day at the tourist office, and be prepared to queue for hours. On each of the three weekends, the only places likely to have free rooms are the most expensive hotels. If you're planning on an extended stay in Munich, contact one of the competing *Mitwohnzentralen* for a room or a flat.

ACCOMMODATION PRICE CODES

All the pensions and hotels in this book have been graded according to the following price categories. The prices quoted are for the cheapest available double room, although many of the budget places will also have more expensive rooms. Youth hostels are graded under separate categories. See p.34 for more details.

① less than DM50	④ DM81–100	⑦ DM151–200
② DM51–65	⑤ DM101–125	⑧ DM201–250
③ DM66–80	⑥ DM126–150	⑨ more than DM250

Hotels and pensions

There are well over 300 **hotels** and **pensions** scattered all over Munich. By far the densest concentration is around the Hauptbahnhof, particularly its southern side. Unfortunately, although there are many good-value establishments here, this area can feel a little rough after dark, despite being well policed. There are also plenty of places – mostly homely-type pensions – in Schwabing and the area around the University just to the south; these have the advantage of proximity to many of the best bars and restaurants. Provision in the city centre is sparser, but still adequate: most of the luxury establishments are located in this area.

Around the Hauptbahnhof

Alfa, Hirtenstr. 22 (☎545 9530, fax 592301). Located in one of the quieter streets to the north of the Hauptbahnhof. ⑤

Eder, Zweigstr. 8 (☎554660, fax 550 3675). On a quiet road, but very central between the Hauptbahnhof and Marienplatz. ③

Europäischer Hof, Bayerstr. 31 (☎551510, fax 515 1222). Directly facing the Hauptbahnhof, and offering a very high overall standard; it's also one of the few hotels in the area with a restaurant. ⑤

Excelsior, Schützenstr. 11 (☎551370, fax 5513 7121). The most upmarket hotel in the vicinity of the Hauptbahnhof, with a renowned wine bar-restaurant, *Vinothek*. ⑨

Haberstock, Schillerstr. 4 (☎557855, fax 550 3634). Right beside the Hauptbahnhof with basic, no-frills facilities, but it's good value nonetheless. ⑤

Helvetia, Schillerstr. 6 (☎554745, fax 550 2381). Next door to the *Haberstock*; similar in style and marginally less expensive. ④

Jedermann, Bayerstr. 95 (☎533617 or 533639, fax 536506). Located well away from any noise and seediness, five minutes' walk from the Hauptbahnhof in the opposite direction from the centre. Has a friendly English-speaking management, a wide choice of rooms of various degrees of luxury and an excellent breakfast buffet. Guests can surf the Internet and send e-mail from the hotel computer free of charge. ⑤

Stachus, Bayerstr. 7 (☎592881, fax 550 3833). Conveniently situated halfway between the Hauptbahnhof and Karlsplatz, the gateway to the city centre. ④

The city centre

Am Markt, Heiliggeiststr. 6 (☎225014, fax 224017). Pension with a fine setting overlooking the Viktualienmarkt. ⑤

Bayerischer Hof, Promenadeplatz 6 (☎21200, fax 212 0906). An internationally celebrated hotel which has been run by four generations of the same family. The public rooms are beautifully furnished, while the facilities include a roof garden swimming pool with sun terrace, sauna, solarium and massage. There are three restaurants: the moderately priced *Palais Keller*, the *Garden-Restaurant* with terrace and winter garden, and the renowned *Trader Vic's* (evenings only). ⑨

Blauer Bock, Sebastiansplatz 9 (☎231780, fax 2317 8200). A recommended central hotel right beside the Stadtmuseum. ⑤

Diana, Altheimer Eck 15/3 (☎260 3107, fax 263934). Pension on the third floor of an old mansion, just one block south of the main pedestrian street, Neuhauser Strasse. ③

Königshof, Karlsplatz 25 (☎551360, fax 5513 6113). Fine old privately-owned hotel which has been going strong since the 1860s. Its restaurant, which boasts an outstanding wine list, is among the best in the city. ⑨

Rafael, Neuturmstr. 1 (☎290980, fax 222539). Super-luxury establishment in a neo-Renaissance building of the 1880s. The bedrooms are individually decorated with antiques; there's also a roof terrace with swimming pool and a highly exclusive restaurant. ⑨

Schlicker, Tal 8 (☎227941, fax 296059). This hotel has as an ideal setting just off Marienplatz. ⑦

Vier Jahreszeiten, Maximilianstr. 17 (☎21250, fax 2125 2000). Grand hotel built at royal request in 1858 as an essential adornment to the latest showpiece boulevard. Now part of the *Kempinski* group, and fully refurbished a few years back, it maintains its reputation as one of the world's leading hotels. The facilities include a rooftop swimming pool, a massage, a nightclub and three restaurants. ⑨

Schwabing and the university area

Am Kaiserplatz, Kaiserplatz 12 (☎349190). Very friendly, good location and big rooms. Wacky decor, with each room done in a different style – ranging from red satin to Bavarian rustic. ③

Am Siegestor, Akademiestr. 5 (☎399550, fax 343050). Well-regarded pension just a stone's throw from the Siegestor and the main university building. ④

Englischer Garten, Liebergesellstr. 8 (☎392034, fax 391233). Occupies a fine old villa on the edge of the Englischer Garten, by the Kleinhesseloher See. ⑥

Excelsior, Kaulbachstr. 85 (☎380 1480, fax 380 14872). Opposite the *Irish Pub*, close to Leopoldstrasse and hard by the Giselastrasse U-Bahn stop. ④

Frank, Schellingstr. 24 (☎281451, fax 280 0910). Located midway between Ludwigstrasse and the Neue Pinakothek. Mainly frequented by young travellers. Lovely big rooms, and there's a fridge available to keep food in. ④

Hauser, Schellingstr. 11 (☎286 6750, fax 2866 7599). Unassuming hotel with a good location just off Ludwigstrasse and right beside the university. ⑥

Isabella, Isabellastr. 35 (☎271 3503, fax 271 2903). Tiny pension with just 12 beds with one bathroom on the landing. ④

Lettl, Amalienstr. 53 (☎286 6970, fax 2866 9797). Friendly hotel midway between Ludwigstrasse and the Neue Pinakothek. ⑦

Steinberg, Ohmstr. 9 (☎331011). Nice atmosphere and a good location right by the university. ④

Strigl, Elisabethstr. 11 (☎271 3444). Rather gruff management, but well situated with reasonable prices. ③

Elsewhere in the city

Adria, Liebigstr. 8a (☎293081, fax 227015). Just two blocks south of the Englischer Garten and Prinzregentenstrasse museums. ⑦

Galleria, Plinganserstr. 142 (☎723 3001, fax 724 1564). Set in a handsome Jugendstil villa in the suburb of Thalkirchen. ⑥

Habis, Maria-Theresia-Str. 6a (☎470 5071, fax 470 5101). Just over the Isar and to the rear of the Maximileum, this is among the most characterful of the city's upper bracket hotels. It also has a reasonably priced restaurant (evenings only). ⑦

Kriemhild, Guntherstr. 16 (☎170077, fax 1777478). Although far from the centre, it's only a short walk from Schloss Nymphenburg and its beautiful park, and is good value at the price asked. ⑤

Krone, Theresienhöhe 8 (☎504052, fax 506706). Classy hotel overlooking the Theresienwiese, setting of the Oktoberfest. ⑥

Obermaier, Truderinger Str. 304b (☎429021, fax 426400). Way out in the eastern suburbs, this is a country-style *Gasthaus*, with beer garden and a restaurant serving its own homegrown produce. ⑦

Stadt Rosenheim, Orleansplatz 6a (☎448 2424, fax 485987). Right by the Ostbahnhof and convenient for the bars and restaurants of Haidhausen, nowadays Munich's liveliest area by night. ⑤

Mitwohnzentralen

City Mitwohnzentrale, Lämmerstr. 4 (☎19422). Located conveniently close to the Hauptbahnhof.

Mit-Wohn-Börse, Georgenstr. 45 (☎19445). Part of a national network, this can find accommodation for any period from two nights upwards.

Mitwohnzentrale Mr Lodge, Ligsalzstr. 30 (☎503838). Deals only in stays of a month or longer.

Wohnen auf Zeit, in Universität S-Bahn station (☎339493). Located by the Adalbertstrasse exit, this is staffed by native English-speakers.

Hostels

CVJM-Jugendgästehaus, Landwehrstr. 13 (☎5521 410). The local YMCA hostel, located a couple of blocks from the Hauptbahnhof and open to everyone. Beds in dorms DM38, singles from DM48, doubles from DM82.

4 you münchen ökologisches Jugendgästehaus, Hirtenstr. 18 (☎5521 660). Brand-new, environmentally conscious hostel with vegetarian restaurant. Dorm beds DM27-32, singles DM57, doubles DM84.

Haus International, Elisabethstr. 87 (☎120060). A no-age-limit youth hotel in Schwabing, complete with disco and swimming pool. Beds in small dorms from DM40; also regular singles from DM55, doubles from DM104.

Jugendgästehaus München, Miesingstr. 4 (☎723 6550). Recently remodelled, this is the nicest and most expensive of the 3 IYHF establishments (see also the 2 following entries): all require a membership card, and are open only to those under 27, except for parents travelling with children. Take either U-Bahn #3 to Thalkirchen and then walk, or U-Bahn #6 or S-Bahn #7 or #27 to Harras then tram #16 to Boschetsriederstrasse. 🏠

Jugendherberge München, Wendl-Dietrich-Str. 20 (☎131156). This is the largest and most basic hostel, with beds in large, spartan dormitories. Take U-Bahn #1 to Rotkreuzplatz, then walk down Wendl-Dietrich-Strasse. 🏠

Jugendherberge Pullach, Burg Schwaneck, Burgweg 4–6, Pullach (☎793 0643). Atmospherically housed in an old castle by the River Isar, but a long way from downtown Munich. Take S-Bahn #7 to Pullach, then follow the signs. 🏠

Jugendhotel Marienherberge, Goethestr. 9 (☎555805). Roman Catholic-run hostel near the Hauptbahnhof for women aged up to 25 only. Beds in small dorms cost DM25-30; there are also singles for DM35, doubles for DM60.

Kolpinghaus St Theresia, Hanebergstr. 8 (☎126050). Another Catholic hostel, this time open to everyone. Beds in dorms DM32, singles DM48, doubles from DM68. Take U-Bahn #1 to Rotkreuzplatz; it's then a five-minute walk.

Campsites

Kapuzinerhölzl, Frank-Shrank-Strasse (☎141 4300). Known as "The Tent" and municipally run, this is the cheapest place to stay during its period of operation (late June to end Aug), and is a fun place to be, despite the lack of privacy. Officially for under-23s only (though older boy- or girl-friends aren't usually turned away) and for a maximum stay of three nights. Take U-Bahn #1 to Rotkreuzplatz, then tram #12 to Botanischer Garten, walk down Frank-Schrank-Strasse and turn left at the end of the road. Check whether it's open before setting out, as its future is far from secure.

Langwieder See, Eschenrieder Str. 119 (☎864 1566). Small site in a quiet lakeside setting on the western fringe of the city. Open year-round, though notification must be given in advance from Nov 1 to March 14. Being off the U- and S-Bahn routes, it's really only practical if you've got your own transport.

Obermenzing, Lochhausener Str. 59 (☎811 2235). In a posh suburb, close to Schloss Nymphenburg, and open March 15 to Oct 31. Take S-Bahn #2 to Obermenzing, then bus #75 to Lochhausener Strasse.

Thalkirchen, Zentralländstr. 49 (☎723 1707). Set in an attractive part of the Isar valley and open March 15 to Oct 31. Very popular during Oktoberfest because of its proximity to the fairground. Take U-Bahn #3 to Thalkirchen.

The city

Heart of the city and its Altstadt is the **Marienplatz**; the pedestrian centre fans out from here in an approximate circle of one square kilometre. This is tourist and shopping land, with all the city's major department stores, the central market, the royal palace and the most important churches. North of Marienplatz, Ludwigstrasse and Leopoldstrasse run straight through the heart of **Schwabing**, Munich's entertainment quarter, full of *Schickies* (German yuppies) who frequent the many bars and pose in the street cafés. It's also close to the city's main park, known as the **Englischer Garten**, with one of the city's most famous beer gardens, the *Chinesischer Turm*. West of the Marienplatz–Schwabing axis is the main **museum quarter**, with many of the most important of Munich's three dozen or so museums, including the world-famous Alte Pinakothek. Running the length of the eastern part of town is the River Isar, while **Nymphenburg**, with its palace and gardens, is the most enticing of the outer districts.

The Altstadt

Relatively little is left of medieval Munich, but three of the **gateways** remain to mark today's city centre. Bounded by the **Odeonsplatz** and the **Sendlinger Tor** to the north and south, and the **Isartor** and **Karlstor** to the east and west, it's only a fifteen-minute walk from one end to the other. This doesn't mean you can see everything in one day: there is so much packed into this area that you will need at least two or three days to explore it thoroughly.

Marienplatz and around

Marienplatz marks the most central spot in the city and the heart of the U-Bahn system below. There's something almost cosy about it: street musicians and artists entertain the crowds and local youths lounge around the central fountain. At 11am and noon, the square fills with tourists as the carillon in the **Rathaus** jingles into action, displaying two events that happened on this spot: the marriage of Wilhelm V to Renata von Lothringen in 1568, and the first *Schäfflertanz* (coopers' dance) of 1517, intended to cheer people up during the plague. This dance is still held every seven years, next in 1998.

The Rathaus itself is a late nineteenth-century neo-Gothic monstrosity; its redeeming features are the view from the **tower** (ascent by elevator May–Oct Mon–Fri 9am–4pm, Sat & Sun 10am–7pm; Nov–April Mon–Thurs 9am–4pm, Fri 9am–1pm; DM3) and the open-air café in the cool and breezy courtyard, perfect for having a drink away from the crowds. To the right is the plain Gothic tower of the **Altes Rathaus**, which was rebuilt to its original fifteenth-century form after being destroyed by lightning. Today it houses the **Spielzeugmuseum** (Mon–Sat 10am–5.30pm, Sun 10am–6pm; DM5), a fascinating collection of historic toys.

Just to the south is the slightly elevated **Peterskirche** (popularly known as *Alter Peter*), the oldest church within the bounds of the old city walls. Its distinctive **tower** (Mon–Sat 9am–5/8pm, Sun 10am–5/7pm according to season; DM2.50) offers an even higher and better view than that from the Rathaus, and is far less busy. Originally a pillared Romanesque basilica, the church owes its present form to a fourteenth-century

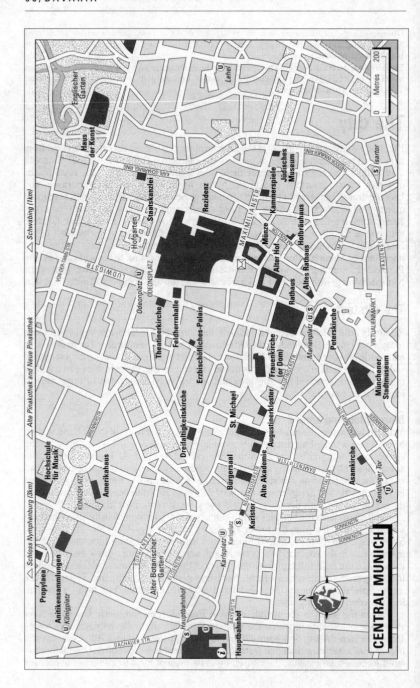

CENTRAL MUNICH

△ Schloss Nymphenburg (3km)   △ Alte Pinakothek and Neue Pinakothek   △ Schwabing (1km)

Englischer Garten

Haus der Kunst

Staatskanzlei

Hofgarten

Rezidenz

Jüdisches Museum

Kammerspiele

Münze

Hochschule für Musik

Amerikahaus

Propyläen

Antikensammlungen
U *Königsplatz*

KÖNIGSPLATZ

Theatinerkirche

Feldherrnhalle

Odeonsplatz U
ODEONSPLATZ

LUDWIGSTR.

MAXIMILIANSTR.

Alter Hof

Hofbräuhaus

Altes Rathaus

Rathaus

Erzbischöfliches-Palais

Dreifaltigkeitskirche

St. Michael

Augustinerkloster

Frauenkirche (or Dom)

Marienplatz U S

Peterskirche

VIKTUALIENMARKT

Münchener Stadtmuseum

Bürgersaal

Alte Akademie

Karlstor

Karlsplatz U
Karlsplatz S

Asamkirche

Sendlinger Tor U

Alter Botanischer Garten

Hauptbahnhof S U

Hauptbahnhof

DACHAUER STR.

BAYERSTR.

SONNENSTR.

Lehel U

Issartor S

Metres
0   200

N

Gothic rebuilding following a fire. The original **high altar**, a collaboration between Erasmus Grasser and Jan Polack, respectively Munich's leading sculptor and painter in the fertile late Gothic period, is split up and distributed throughout the chancel with the statue of Saint Peter centre stage in a theatrical Rococo extravaganza. However, your attention is most likely to be caught by the grizzly **shrine to Saint Munditia**, the patron saint of single women. Her skeletal relics are poised in a glass box on a side altar, including the skull wrapped in netting with two glass eyes gazing out from a deathly face.

Following Burgstrasse or Sparkassenstrasse from the Altes Rathaus, you soon come to the **Alter Hof**, a shady medieval courtyard which was the original palace of the Wittelsbachs. To the north lie the **Postamt**, a Baroque palace transformed last century to serve as the post office, and the Renaissance **Münze** (Mint). However, the prime attraction in this area is the **Hofbräuhaus** just to the east. This describes itself as "the most famous pub in the world", and is the epitome of the Munich beer hall, with its spacious chambers, hard benches, well-worn tables, crowds of revellers and traditional oompah music. Originally the court brewery, it boasts an uninterrupted tradition dating back to 1589, though the present building is some three centuries younger. A favourite haunt of Hitler in the days when he was struggling to establish the Nazi Party, it still has a large hard-core local clientele, though in summer it is often overrun by tourists.

The Frauenkirche

The other great symbol of Munich is the **Frauenkirche** (or **Dom**), whose copper onion-domed **towers** (ascent by elevator April–Oct Mon–Sat 10am–5pm; DM4) dominate the skyline. It stands in its own small square, just to the west of the Rathaus. Close up, the building, built as a parish church but now the seat of an archbishop, isn't really seen to its best advantage: its redbrick Gothic architecture is unrelievedly spare. The lofty whitewashed interior, however, has inspired the **legend of the Devil's footprint**. Apparently the architect Jerg von Halspach (who also built most of the other surviving medieval monuments in the city) made a pact with the Devil. In order to get enough money to complete this church, he had to construct it without a single visible window. When the Devil came to inspect the completed church, he saw the high Gothic windows from a distance and thought he'd get the builder's soul. Once inside, he was led to a certain point from which not one window was visible, since all were hidden by pillars. Stamping his foot in rage the Devil stormed off, leaving his black hoofed footprint in the pavement by the entrance hall. Rebuilding following war damage has meant the trick no longer quite works, but the footprint is still there.

In the first nave chapel to the south is the huge Mannerist **tomb of Ludwig IV**, a belated tribute, made over a hundred years after his death, to the first of only two Wittelsbachs who managed to get elected as Holy Roman Emperor. Many of the figures are by Hubert Gerhard, a Dutch-born sculptor whose work is still a ubiquitous feature of the city. Some of the church's other artistic treasures have been destroyed, among them Erasmus Grasser's **choir stalls**, though the arresting wooden statues were saved and placed on the modern replacements. There also remain beautiful stained-glass windows in the ambulatory chapels, notably the central Sakramentskapelle, which also has a fine painted **altar**, *The Virgin of the Protecting Cloak*, by Jan Polack.

West of Marienplatz

The almost straight line between Marienplatz and the Hauptbahnhof is the hub of the city's commercial activity; alongside the numerous department stores, many of the city's most famous beer halls are to be found, as well as a series of contrasting churches. At the point where the pedestrianized Kaufingerstrasse changes its name to Neuhauser Strasse, you'll find the deconsecrated **Augustinerkloster** whose ornate Rococo interior now houses the **Deutsches Jagd- und Fischerei Museum** (Mon &

Thurs 9.30am–9pm, Tues, Wed, Fri–Sun 9.30am–5pm; DM5), an array of hunting and fishing trophies and dioramas of animals in their natural environments.

A little further down the street, the Mannerist facade of **St Michael** stands unassumingly in line with the street's other buildings. Built between 1583 and 1597 under the auspices of Wilhelm V, this Jesuit church – the first in northern Europe – was intended to symbolize the local victory of Catholicism over Lutherism. Hubert Gerhard's large bronze statue between the two entrances shows the Archangel Michael fighting for the Faith and killing Evil in the shape of a satyr. The interior, with a barrel vault second only in size to St Peter's in Rome, is decorated in elegant white stucco. A huge Neoclassical monument to Eugène de Beauharnais by Bertel Thorwaldsen can be seen in the transept. In the **crypt** (Mon–Fri 10am–1pm and 2–4.30pm, Sat 10am–3pm; DM1) below are the tombs of the Wittelsbach dynasty, among them the famous castle-builder Ludwig II, whose coffin is permanently draped with flowers, a candle burning at its foot.

Alongside the church, forming a continuous architectural unit with it, is the **Alte Akademie**, the college where the Jesuits instilled their burning missionary ideals in the hearts and minds of their pupils. In front is the **Richard-Strauss-Brunnen**, a fountain in honour of the Munich-born composer. The reliefs show scenes from his opera *Salomé*, based on Oscar Wilde's play of the same name.

Continuing westwards, you soon arrive at the **Bürgersaal**, which was built for a Marian student congregation in the early eighteenth century. Pride of the upstairs **oratory** (Mon–Fri 11am–3pm) is a set of guardian angels under the organ gallery, carved by Ignaz Günther, Bavaria's greatest Rococo sculptor. However, it's the crypt at entrance level that is most visited, since **Rupert Mayer**, one of the city's main opponents of Nazism, is buried here and his grave has become something of a pilgrims' centre, particularly since his beatification in 1987. Father Mayer was the parish priest during the war and became such a nuisance to the authorities that he was shipped off to Sachsenhausen concentration camp. Because of his immense popularity and the bad press his death would have caused, he was transferred to house arrest in the Alpine Ettal monastery. He survived to return to the Bürgersaal after the war, but died later the same year.

South of Marienplatz

Immediately south of Peterskirche is the **Viktualienmarkt**, the city's main marketplace for the last 200 years. Bossy women sell delicious-looking fruit and veg, as well as all kinds of cheeses, meats and delicatessen; if you get talked into buying, be warned it's not cheap, though the quality is excellent. Right in the middle of all the bustle is a small beer garden, a good place to have a snack.

On St Jakobsplatz to the rear is the **Münchner Stadtmuseum** (Tues & Thurs–Sun 10am–5pm, Wed 10am–8pm; DM5). This has fascinating permanent displays about the history of the city, supplemented by changing special exhibitions. On the ground floor are the Waffenhalle, containing a magnificent array of historic weapons, and the wonderfully contorted set of *Morris Dancers*, carved as adornments for the ballroom of the Altes Rathaus by **Erasmus Grasser**. The upper floors house specialist displays on photos and films, brewing, musical instruments, and one of the largest collections of puppets in the world, from Indian and Chinese paper dolls to the large mechanical European variety.

To the west is Sendlinger Strasse, where at no. 62 you can see the small **Asamkirche** (officially known as **St-Johann-Nepomuk**), one of the most enchanting examples of a Rococo church in Bavaria. Built between 1733 and 1746, it's the crowning effort of the partnership of the two Asam brothers, who here successfully achieved their goal of a building whose architecture was completely integrated with all aspects of its interior decoration. The younger brother, Egid Quirin Asam (who was the sculptor and stuccoist), bought the land and underwrote the cost of the whole enterprise, which was intended to serve as his private family church, and therefore one where he had the rare luxury of being able to put his artistic ideals into effect without the intervention of a patron. He added a Rococo facade to the sixteenth-century house next door and lived there for the rest of his life.

North of Marienplatz

The smartest part of the city centre lies north of Marienplatz, where ritzy shops and expensive cafés line Theatinerstrasse, Maffeistrasse and Kardinal-Faulhaber-Strasse. At Theatinerstr. 15 is the **Kunsthalle der Hypo-Kulturstiftung** (Mon-Wed & Fri-Sun 10am–6pm, Thurs 10am–9pm; variable admission charge), which puts on a programme of international-class temporary exhibitions on artistic and archaeological themes. Kardinal-Faulhaber-Strasse has the most ostentatious buildings of the lot, mostly palaces of the earlier rich which have been turned into banks and insurance houses. One which is still lived in is François Cuvilliés' **Erzbischöfliches-Palais**, the residence of the local archbishop. West of here, on Parcellistrasse, a Carmelite church, the **Dreifaltigkeitskirche**, was one of the few historic buildings in Munich to come through the last war unscathed. It's a copybook example of Italianate Baroque by the Swiss architect Giovanni Antonio Viscardi (who was also responsible for the design of the Bürgersaal), with a vivacious dome fresco of *The Adoration of the Trinity* by Cosmos Damian Asam.

The Residenz

In the late fourteenth century, the Wittelsbachs moved their seat from the Alter Hof in the heart of the Altstadt to a new site at what was then the northeastern periphery of the town. Between 1570 and 1620, this fortress was replaced by a splendid Mannerist **Residenz**, constructed by a team of mostly Netherlandish architects and designers led by **Friedrich Sustris**. It was modified and expanded in the Baroque and Rococo periods, though the most significant additions were made, in accordance with its new function as a royal palace, by **Leo von Klenze**, the architect primarily responsible for giving Munich its nineteenth-century face: he added the rusticated Königsbau facing Max–Joseph-Platz to the south and the Festsaalbau on the garden side to the north. Extensively damaged in the last war, the Residenz was reconstructed in the 1950s and 1960s – and is still the subject of restoration work.

The Residenzmuseum

About half the palace, including all the most significant historical apartments, is open to the public as the **Residenzmuseum** (Tues–Sun 10am–4.30pm; DM6), entered from Max–Joseph-Platz. To see it all you have to go round twice, as part of it is open mornings only, with a different section open in the afternoons.

On both tours, you see the **Ahnengalerie** (Ancestors' Gallery), decorated in the richest Rococo style, which looks for all the world like a Hall of Mirrors, except that the glass is replaced by 121 (mostly imaginary) portraits of the Wittelsbachs, who tried to give their line the most prestigious roots possible by including tenuously linked predecessors like Charlemagne. The morning tour then procedes to the Mannerist **Grottenhof** (Grotto Court), whose centrepiece is a fountain with a statue of Perseus. Under the loggia is the grotto of tufa, crystal and coloured shells, framing a statue of Mercury. Alongside is the **Antiquarium**, the oldest and most original part of the palace. This long, cavernous chamber was built in 1571 to house the family's famous collection of antiquities. A generation later, its austere architecture was sharply modified in accordance with the new Mannerist craze to serve as a festive hall, and its tunnel vault covered with humanist-inspired frescos. In the **Kurfürstenzimmer** (Rooms of the Elector), look out for three paintings by Bernardo Bellotto, who here applied to Munich the technique his uncle Canaletto had used so successfully to immortalize the Venice of his day. Other highlights are a passageway hung with a cycle of 25 views of Italy by the Munich Romantic painter Carl Rottmann, and a suite of rooms containing extensive collections of fourteenth- to nineteenth-century Chinese, Japanese and European porcelain.

The last stage of the morning tour can also be seen in the afternoon. This includes the eight appropriately named **Reiche Zimmer** (Rich Rooms) in the sumptuous Rococo style of François Cuvilliés, and the five **Nibelungen Säle** (Halls of the Nibelungs), in which medieval Germany's most famous epic is depicted in a series of paintings by the Nazarene artist Julius Schnorr von Carolsfeld. Other rooms can be seen in the afternoon only, and include further displays of ceramics, along with the silverware collection and the sumptuous early Baroque **Goldener Saal** (Golden Hall). You can also see the ecclesiastical treasury and the two chapels, which were both built in the early years of the seventeenth century. The larger **Hofkapelle**, closely modelled on the town church of St Michael, was for general use, while the more lavish **Reichekapelle** was built for the private meditations of one of the most famous of the Wittelsbachs, Maximilian I. Another memento of Maximilian comes with the **Steinzimmer**, a suite of profusely furnished rooms with a complicated set of allegories illustrating the Elector's personal vision of the world and the after-life.

The Schatzkammer

Sharing the same entrance but requiring a separate ticket is the **Schatzkammer** (same times; DM6), which houses a really fabulous collection of treasures. Among the early items, look out for the late ninth-century **miniature ciborium** that belonged to King Arnulf of Carinthia, and the **cross** of Queen Gisela of Hungary. There's a spectacular array of **crowns** too, including that of Princess Blanche of England (daughter of Henry IV), but the star piece of the whole display, kept in a room of its own, is the **statuette of St George**, made in Munich around 1590 for Wilhelm V. This has a base of gold, silver and enamel, and is encrusted with diamonds, rubies, sapphires, emeralds and rock crystal. The outstanding German Renaissance tradition in the decorative arts can be seen in a host of chalices, tankards, caskets, pendants, clocks and portable altars; look out for the rock crystal dish with gold mount designed by Holbein. Faced with such competition, the Bavarian **crown jewels**, made in the early nineteenth century soon after the duchy was promoted to a kingdom, seem rather tame.

The rest of the complex

From the entrance on Residenzstrasse, you pass through the Kapellenhof into the elongated **Brunnenhof**, in the middle of which stands a large fountain in honour of the Wittelsbachs, replete with allegorical figures of the Elements, river gods, tritons and dragons. At the far end is the entrance to the **Cuvilliéstheater** (Mon–Sat 2–5pm, Sun 10am–5pm; DM3), a perfectly intact Rococo gem, dripping in gold and bristling with intricate carvings and delicate stucco. Formerly the Wittelsbachs' private theatre, it's now the jewel in the crown of the city's performing arts venues. It's deservedly named after the man who built it, **François Cuvilliés**, a tenacious little Walloon who began his career in the debilitating role of court dwarf to the Elector Max Emanuel, but proved that he was capable of greater things by designing defensive systems for the army he was precluded from joining. As a result, he was sent to Paris to study the latest architectural theories, and on his return developed the new Rococo style to its most extravagant limits in a series of stunningly original buildings.

The northwestern part of the Residenz, entered from Hofgartenstrasse, houses the **Staatliche Sammlung Ägyptischer Kunst** (Tues 9am–4pm & 7–9pm, Wed–Fri 9am–4pm, Sat & Sun 10am–5pm; DM5). As well as objects from all periods of Egyptian antiquity, this features displays of Coptic art and monumental reliefs from Assyria. Highlights include the statue of Amenemhets III, a masterpiece of royal portraiture from about 1800 BC; the gold treasure of the Queen of Meroë; and Egyptian statues from the palace of Emperor Hadrian. The **Hofgarten** to the north, formerly the royal park, is an ideal place for a quiet stroll. At the far end, the bombed-out Armeemuseum was until recently left as an anti-war memorial, its contents having been transferred to Ingolstadt. It has since been rebuilt with modern wings as the **Staatskanzlei**, the Bavarian State Chancellery.

The nineteenth-century city

The additions to the Residenz were merely one aspect of the changing face of Munich in line with its new royal status; the city was greatly expanded, particularly to the north, with a series of broad boulevards and spacious squares lined by grandiosely self-confident Neoclassical buildings.

Odeonsplatz

In 1817, Leo von Klenze began the project to link Munich with the outlying village of Schwabing to the north by constructing the **Odeonsplatz** at the far end of the Residenz. The southwest corner of this square, however, was already occupied by the Baroque **Theatinerkirche** (or **St Catejan**), which ranks as one of Munich's most regal churches, its golden-yellow towers and green copper dome adding a welcome splash of colour to the city skyline. It was designed in the 1660s by the Bolognese Agostino Barelli, on the model of St Andrea della Valle in Rome, though many alterations to the original plan were made by Enrico Zuccalli, his successor as court architect, and it was only completed by Cuvilliés over a century later – hence the Rococo bravura of the facade.

Although other buildings in the square, including the **Odeon** itself (originally a music college, now a government office), are by Klenze, the building which finished it off, the **Feldherrnhalle** on the southern side, is by his rival **Friedrich von Gärtner**. The hall, closely modelled on the Loggia dei Lanzi in Florence, shelters statues of Bavaria's two greatest military heroes: Johann Tilly, the Imperial Field Marshal in the Thirty Years' War, and Karl Philipp von Wrede, the commander of the Bavarian corps originally allied with Napoleon, which changed sides in time to help defeat the French at the Battle of the Nations. Between the two is a memorial to the Bavarian dead of the Franco-Prussian War. It was here on November 9, 1923 that armed police stopped Hitler's Beer Hall Putsch in its tracks, opening fire on the future dictator's band of would-be revolutionaries as they stood at the head of the narrow Residenzstrasse, in the shadow of the Feldherrnhalle.

Ludwigstrasse

From Odeonsplatz, the dead straight **Ludwigstrasse** leads to Schwabing. Its name comes from King Ludwig I, who commissioned it; though it remained unfinished when he was forced to abdicate as a result of a scandal caused by his affair with a dancer, he continued to fund it from his private resources – a decision which later proved to have been a shrewd business investment, as he was able to let the buildings at enormous rates. The most southerly palaces, up to and including the **Bayerisches Hauptstaatsarchiv**, are in a style imitating the Italian Renaissance. Immediately to the north, and in a broadly similar style, is the **Bayerische Staatsbibliothek** (Mon–Fri 9am–7.30pm, Sat 9am–4.30pm): it houses one of Europe's richest libraries, the most famous treasure being the original of the great monastic collection of medieval songs and poems, *Carmina Burana*. There's usually a thematic exhibition on display, and you can always see the late sixteenth-century globes of the earth and the heavens made for Duke Albrecht V, which stand at the top of the stairway.

Beyond stands one of the country's most significant nineteenth-century churches, the inevitably named **Ludwigskirche**. It's an example of the peculiarly German architectural style known as *Rundbogenstil*, which took its cue from any previous form of building – whether Classical, early Christian, Romanesque or Renaissance – using rounded arches; this appears to have been the invention of Ludwig as much as Gärtner. The chancel fresco of *The Last Judgment* by the Nazarene painter Peter Cornelius is one of the largest paintings in the world, and is a self-conscious (if ultimately unsuccessful) attempt to rival Michelangelo.

Further north is the main building of the **Ludwig-Maximilian-Universität**, which is now the biggest university in Germany. Although it's relatively young, only establishing itself in Munich in 1826, it has a distinguished academic record. The philosopher Friedrich Wilhelm von Schelling was an early luminary, while later professors have included such celebrated scientists as Georg Simon Ohm (discoverer of the law of magnetic resistance which bears his name), Justus von Liebig (father of scientific agriculture) and Wilhelm Conrad Röntgen (inventor of the x–ray). Linking the university with the **Priesterseminar** (Seminary) opposite is a circular plaza known as Geschwister-Scholl-Platz. This is one of a large number of places in Germany dedicated to the memory of Hans Scholl and his sister Sophie, the Munich students who launched the *Weisse Rose* resistance movement to Hitler – an act of defiance which cost them their lives.

The final building on Ludwigstrasse, before it passes into Schwabing and becomes known as Leopoldstrasse, is the **Siegestor**, a triumphal arch balancing the Feldherrnhalle, this time exclusively dedicated to commemorating the Bavarian army's part in the wars against Napoleon between 1813 and 1815.

Königsplatz

West of Ludwigstrasse, a planned town was laid out on a strict geometrical pattern of huge squares. The focus of this is **Königsplatz**, which was intended as a sort of Bavarian Acropolis, with a grassy middle surrounded by showpiece public buildings. In the Nazi period, it was paved over to serve as a parade ground, and it has only recently been returned to its original form.

On the north side of the square is the **Glyptothek** (Tues, Wed & Fri–Sun 10am–5pm, Thurs 10am–8pm; DM6), built by Klenze to house Ludwig I's collection of Greek and Roman sculptures. At the heart of the display are the surviving parts of the front of the **Aphaia temple of Aegina**, whose sculptures rank among the supreme masterpieces of Hellenistic art. As these were acquired under decidedly dubious circumstances, the Greeks would like them back: indeed they rank alongside the British Museum's Elgin Marbles at the top of Greece's shopping list in appeals for the return of the country's "looted" heritage. Other highlights of the museum are the tomb relief of Mnesarete, the daughter of Socrates; the famous *Barberini Faun*, a surpassingly beautiful carving of a sleeping satyr from about 220 BC; and a large collection of Roman busts, including one of the finest of more than 200 extant portraits of Emperor Augustus.

Across the square, a later building contains the **Staatliche Antikensammlungen** (Tues & Thurs–Sun 10am–5pm, Wed 10am–8pm; DM6, DM10 for joint ticket with the Glyptothek), whose displays include Greek vases from the fifth and sixth centuries BC, as well as jewellery and small statues from Greek, Etruscan and Roman antiquity.

On the west side of the square is the **Propylaeum**, a severe twin-towered structure in an unashamedly derivative Grecian style. The reliefs show the Greek War of Independence against the Turks, whose successful conclusion led to the western powers forcing Prince Otto of Bavaria on the victors as their king. This didn't prove to be a happy match: Otto's authoritarian methods went down badly with his subjects, and he was eventually forced to abdicate. Before that had happened, however, this Propylaeum had already been built in his honour.

Just off Königsplatz, facing the Glyptothek in a picturesquely manicured garden, is the **Lenbachhaus** (Tues–Sun 10am–6pm; DM8), the villa of the nineteenth-century Bavarian painter **Franz von Lenbach**, an enormously successful high society portraitist. Many of his paintings are displayed inside, in rooms furnished as he knew them. Works by other Munich painters down the centuries are also featured, with the highlight being those by *Der Blaue Reiter* (see p.1019), whose members included **Kandinsky**, **Klee**, **Marc** and **Macke**; the Kandinsky collection here is particularly outstanding. In recent years the museum has also concentrated on important contemporary German art, and is worth checking for special exhibitions.

Immediately to the north, at Richard-Wagner-Str. 10, you'll find the **Paläontologisches Museum** (Mon–Thurs 8am–4pm, Fri 8am–2pm, Sun 10am–4pm; free). Kids will love the display of prehistoric animal skeletons in the entrance hall, which include a sabre-toothed tiger from California, a giant deer from Ireland, and an elephant found in Upper Bavaria which is calculated to be ten million years old. However, these are mere striplings in comparison to some of the skeletons upstairs, such as a fish and a crocodile found in Baden-Württemberg, both of which date back 190 million years.

The most sinister building in Munich stands on Arcisstrasse, opposite the Glyptothek. Now serving as a music academy known as the Hochschule für Musik, it was formerly the **Braunhaus**, the local Nazi headquarters, and the place where Neville Chamberlain made the infamous agreement to force Czechoslovakia to cede Hitler the Sudetenland, thereby making the very name of Munich synonymous in the English language with treachery.

The Alte Pinakothek

The Alte Pinakothek closed in 1994 for major structural repairs. Its re-opening, originally due in 1997, has been re-scheduled for May/June 1998; in the interim, its most important works are on display in part of the Neue Pinakothek. The description given here is of the arrangement of the museum prior to its closure; it's likely that most or all of this will be re-adopted.

The **Alte Pinakothek** (new opening hours and prices are likely to be the same as those for the Neue Pinakothek), a Florentine-style palazzo by Klenze at Barer Str. 27, is one of the largest art galleries in Europe, housing an outstanding collection of paintings spanning the period from the fourteenth to eighteenth centuries, including the finest representation of the German School to be found anywhere in the world (for more information on these artists, see Contexts). The ground floor covers fifteenth-century German painting in the left wing, and sixteenth- to seventeenth-century German and Dutch painting in the right, while the first floor begins with fifteenth-century Netherlandish painting in the left wing, and then proceeds to German, Italian, Flemish, Dutch, French and Spanish art.

THE GERMAN SCHOOL

German painting of the fifteenth century has predominantly religious themes, and, in keeping with an age that believed art was for the greater glory of God, the names of many of the artists have not survived. Look out for the beautifully observed narrative cycle which has provided the nickname of **Master of the Life of the Virgin** for an unknown Cologne painter, and the idiosyncratic *trompe l'oeil* scenes of a Bavarian contemporary, **Master of the Tegernsee Altar**, whose panels are executed as if in imitation of a carved retable. From the following generation, the works of the Tyrolean

Michael Pacher stand out. Though better known as a sculptor, his luxuriant *Altarpiece of the Four Fathers of the Church*, an early attempt at fusing the rich late Gothic style of southern Germany with the new approach of the Italian Renaissance, shows he was no less talented with the brush than the chisel.

Under the impact of the Renaissance, portraiture became increasingly popular, and **Dürer**'s *Self-Portrait* is one of the most famous paintings from this time, the artist looking out with a self-assured poise, his face framed by shoulder-length golden locks and his torso clad in a fur coat. The famous panels of *The Four Apostles* come from the very end of Dürer's career and are generally held to be his greatest achievement. Originally, they were meant as wings of an altarpiece dedicated to the Virgin, but the project was scrapped when the city of Nürnberg – with the artist himself an enthusiastic supporter – went over to Protestantism.

Another painting with a Reformation connection is **Grünewald**'s *Disputation of SS Erasmus and Maurice*. This was commissioned by the leading member of the conciliatory Catholic party, Cardinal Albrecht von Brandenburg. The gorgeously attired Saint Erasmus, who is shown arguing for the peaceful conversion of the world against the armed struggle favoured by the black warrior Saint Maurice, represents a double allusion to the contemporary approach favoured by the Cardinal and his great friend, Erasmus of Rotterdam. As can be seen in the early *Mocking of Christ*, Grünewald himself was of a far more impassioned nature, and he became a supporter of the extreme wing of Protestantism. Strange as it seems, Cardinal Albrecht also patronized Luther's very own propagandist, **Lucas Cranach the Elder**, who took advantage of the new liberties of the age to introduce sensually explicit nudes – such as the full-lengths of *Lucretia* and *Venus and Cupid* – into German art for the first time. This approach was soon taken up and developed by **Hans Baldung**, as in the pair of allegorical female figures, perhaps representing *Prudence* and *Music*.

Albrecht Altdorfer's *Battle of Alexander*, depicting the victory of Alexander the Great over the Persian king Darius III in 333 BC, is a masterpiece of another new genre, that of history painting. Literally hundreds of soldiers are painted individually in minute detail, but at the same time represented as a heaving mass, dramatically giving the sense of a momentous battle. The artist often used identifiable landscapes in the Danube valley as backgrounds for his paintings; indeed, in *St George and the Dragon* the ostensible subject is really an excuse for a masterly nature study of the lush foliage of the beech trees which are a feature of the region.

THE FLEMISH AND DUTCH SCHOOLS

Among the fifteenth-century Flemish works, **Rogier van der Weyden**'s *Adoration of the Magi*, which was commissioned for St Kolumba in Cologne, is regarded as one of the greatest portrayals of this classic, Christmas-card subject. It makes a fascinating contrast with the tiny house altar of the same scene (known as *The Pearl of Brabant* because of its highly polished sheen), by **Dieric Bouts**. Equally outstanding is **Memling**'s lyrical *Seven Joys of the Virgin*, which integrates all the scenes into a single dream-like fantasy of architecture and landscape. From the following century comes **Pieter Bruegel the Elder**'s *Land of Cockaigne*, depicting a seemingly utopian scene of plenty, where food cooks itself and pigs come ready-roasted. It's full of entertaining details, but, for all its humour, the real purpose of the work was actually to condemn gluttony and idleness.

Centrepiece of the entire museum, and the main consideration in its architectural design, is the collection of works by the seventeeth-century Flemish painter **Rubens**. Sixty-two paintings display a wide range of the artist's prodigious output, including everything from the *modellos* the master made for the guidance of his large workshop to such massive finished altarpieces as *The Fall of the Rebel Angels* and *The Last Judgment* (which was commissioned for the Hofkirche in Neuburg an der Donau); from intimate portraits such as *Rubens and Isabella Brandt in the Honeysuckle Bower* (painted to celebrate his first marriage) to such boisterous mythological scenes as *Drunken Silenus*, and from the quiet beauty of *Landscape with a Rainbow* to the horrors of *The Massacre of the Innocents*.

Van Dyck, Rubens' most distinguished pupil, is also extensively represented, with portraits and religious scenes drawn from the main phases of his career. The small cabinet rooms beyond contain the largest collection of works in existence by **Adriaen Brouwer**, the most trenchant observer of the seamier side of life in seventeenth-century Flanders. There's also a haunting *Passion Cycle* by **Rembrandt**, commissioned by the House of Orange as Reformed Protestant visions of Holy Week. In both *The Raising of the Cross* and *The Deposition*, the familiar figure of Rembrandt himself appears as a leading witness to the events.

THE ITALIAN, FRENCH AND SPANISH SCHOOLS
The Italian section begins with three little panels from a dispersed altarpiece by **Giotto**; other highlights include **Fra Filippo Lippi**'s classically inspired *The Annunciation*, **Botticelli**'s theatrical *Pietà*, **Raphael**'s tender *Holy Family*, and a rare authenticated example of the young **Leonardo da Vinci**, *Madonna of the Carnation*. However, works by **Titian** steal the show here, notably the *Seated Portrait of Charles V*, which perfectly captures the self-confident poise of a man of destiny, and *Christ Crowned with Thorns*, dating from the end of the artist's very long life. The French display includes **Poussin**'s *Lamentation over the Dead Christ* and several classical landscapes by **Claude**. There's also a room of seventeenth-century Spanish painting, including a *Portrait of a Young Man* by **Velázquez**, and genre pictures by **Murillo**; the latter were to have an enormous influence on French and English art of the following century.

The Neue Pinakothek
The **Neue Pinakothek** (Tues & Thurs 10am–8pm, Wed & Fri–Sun 10am–5pm; DM7) immediately to the north houses collections of eighteenth- and nineteenth-century painting and sculpture. After the wealth and variety of its neighbour, it can't help but seem a little thin on the ground, but it does have good examples of Neoclassical, Romantic and Realist art.

Cool, detached and precise, the portrait of the *Marquise de Sourcy de Thélusson* by the French painter **David** is a beautiful example of the Neoclassical style. Of all the works from the mid-nineteenth century Romantic period, those by the Munich painter **Carl Spitzweg** are among the best. He painted scenes from everyday life, depicting human emotions and frailties with a wry sense of humour and cartoon-like style. *The Poor Poet*, *The Bookworm* and *The Childhood Friend* cover just some of his themes, which are always subtly observed and with a dig against pretension.

More controversial are the heroic visions of the city's mid-nineteenth century history painters. The sketches by **Wilhelm von Kaulbach** for the frescos of the Neue Pinakothek's exterior are the only reminders left of this grandiose scheme, which was completely destroyed in the war. A monumental *Destruction of Jerusalem by Titus* by the same artist is remarkable for its scale and attention to detail, though the most celebrated example of this style is the far less bombastic *Seni with the Corpse of Wallenstein* by his pupil **Karl von Piloty**.

Of the works by French Impressionists and Post-Impressionists, **Manet**'s *Breakfast in the Studio* is probably the most famous; other highlights are one of **van Gogh**'s *Sunflowers* and **Gauguin**'s *Breton Farmwomen*. The main German exponent of this phase is **Liebermann**, whose *Boys by the Beach* beautifully captures a scene from turn-of-the-century life. The museum rounds off with a small selection of Symbolism and Art Nouveau. **Franz von Stuck**'s *Sin* is the most striking piece, the vice represented as a lascivious woman exposing herself. Much more romantic and stylized is **Klimt**'s portrait of *Margarethe Stonborough-Wittgenstein*.

Maximilianstrasse

Maximilian II, who succeeded his disgraced father in 1848, also wanted to have a showpiece boulevard named in his own honour; indeed, he had begun planning for it long before he came to the throne. The resultant **Maximilianstrasse** runs east from Max-Joseph-Platz in front of the Residenz, forming Munich's answer to the Champs-Elysées.

As with Odeonsplatz, there was already an extant building at the beginning of the street, this time Klenze's **Nationaltheater**, which maintains its reputation as one of Europe's most prestigious opera houses; almost completely destroyed by bombs in World War II, it was re-created for a little matter of DM63 million. In many ways, it sets the tone for the rest of the street, which is a real theatre quarter, an almost equally prestigious venue being the Jugendstil **Münchener Kammerspiele** at no. 26. A little further along, at no. 36, is the **Jüdisches Museum** (Tues & Wed 2–6pm, Thurs 2–8pm; free) which is claimed to be the smallest Jewish museum in the world; space is so restricted that all exhibitions are temporary. Across the road is the city's most exclusive address, the *Hotel Vierjahreszeiten*, while elsewhere are some two dozen commercial galleries and a seemingly endless number of luxury shops selling the latest fashions and trendiest designer goods.

Over the hideous ring road, at no. 42 on the street, is the **Staatliches Museum für Völkerkunde** (Tues, Wed & Fri 9am–5pm, Thurs 10am–9pm, Sat 10am–5pm; variable charge), illustrating the art and history of non-European cultures in a series of excellently presented changing exhibitions. Further east is a huge bronze monument to Maximilian II. To the north, St-Anna-Strasse leads to the Franciscan church of **St Anna im Lehel**, designed by Johann Michael Fischer and decorated by the Asam brothers.

Prinzregentenstrasse

The last of Munich's three great boulevards is **Prinzregentenstrasse**, which runs east from the Prinz-Carl-Palais at the far end of the Hofgarten. Laid out at the end of the nineteenth century and the beginning of the twentieth, its name comes from Prince Luitpold, who ruled as regent after the deposition of his nephew Ludwig II. Nowadays, it's the city's second main museum quarter.

The **Haus der Kunst**, the first building on the northern side, was built by the Nazis as a showcase for the sort of art they favoured. By a pleasing irony, the building now houses the **Staatsgalerie Moderner Kunst** (Tues, Wed & Fri–Sun 10am–5pm, Thurs 10am–8pm; DM6), which in large part is devoted to the "degenerate" Expressionist and abstract art they ridiculed and destroyed. Alongside examples of all the main German artists of the century are works by foreign big names such as Picasso, Braque, Matisse, Dalí, Magritte, Mondrian and de Chirico; it's also worth checking on the regular special exhibitions.

Next door is the rambling pile of the **Bayerisches Nationalmuseum** (Tues–Sun 9.30am–5pm; DM5). On the first floor, the exhibition halls are pastiches of the architectural style contemporary with the artefacts they display. The medieval sections feature the surviving sculptures from the original Kloster Wessobrunn and *Der Kleine Dom*, a gorgeous miniature cathedral made by a fourteenth-century goldsmith, along with a superb display of German wood sculpture at its fifteenth- and sixteenth-century peak. In particular, there are examples of **Tilman Riemenschneider**'s art drawn from all phases of his career, ranging from the early *St Mary Magdalene Surrounded by Angels*, via a magnificently characterized set of Apostles made to adorn the Marienkapelle in Würzburg, to the serene late *St Barbara*. Many of his most talented contemporaries – Hans Multscher, Michel and Gregor Erhart, Hans Leinberger and Erasmus Grasser – are also well represented.

From the following generation is a statuette of *Judith with the Head of Holofernes* by **Conrad Meit**, one of the few major German sculptors to work in an Italianate style. There's also a miniature *Portrait of a 27-year-old Man* by **Hans Holbein the Younger**; this probably depicts Harry Maynert, a painter-colleague at the English court of Henry

VIII and is one of only a dozen or so miniatures by Holbein to have survived. Look out also for the map of Bavaria drawn by the great geographer Philipp Apian in the 1560s and, from a decade later, the lovingly crafted models by Jacob Sandtner of the province's five courtly capitals. Despite the focus on Bavarian art, there's a decent Italian Renaissance section, which includes six magnificent bronze reliefs of *The Passion* by **Giambologna**, plus sculptures by Luca della Robbia and Antonio Rossellino. The museum's basement features Bavarian folk art and a really outstanding collection of **Christmas cribs**, while the second floor has stained glass, crystal, ceramics from Bavaria, Austria and Italy and clocks.

Just behind at Lerchenfeldstr. 2, is the **Prähistorische Staatssammlung** (Tues, Wed & Fri–Sun 9am–4pm, Thurs 9am–8pm; DM5). This makes a good attempt at bringing alive Bavarian prehistory, the Roman occupation and early medieval life. Lots of models, drawings and artefacts are presented in an accessible and interesting manner. Look out in particular for the Bronze Age golden cone from Ezelsdorf, the Roman treasure from Eining, the jewellery from tribal graves, the Carolingian choir screen and the surprising wheel-shaped Byzantine chandelier.

Further along the street from the Bayerisches Nationalmuseum is the former Prussian embassy, now housing the **Schackgalerie** (10am–5pm, closed Tues; DM4). Count Schack was Munich's most important art patron during the nineteenth century, supporting struggling painters such as Franz von Lenbach, Marées, Böcklin and others until they achieved public acclaim. The museum, which preserves his collection intact, contains important examples of all those artists, plus other Romantic painters such as Feuerbach and Spitzweg.

Schwabing

Just north of the city centre lies the stylish district of **Schwabing**. During the Second Reich and the Weimar Republic it gained a reputation as a centre for radical bohemian chic. Its habitués included outcast revolutionary politicians, the young Lenin and Hitler among them, the artists of *Der Blaue Reiter*, and writers such as Ibsen, the Mann brothers, Rilke, Brecht and Wedekind. Today, in contrast, Munich's real Latin Quarter has moved to Haidhausen, leaving Schwabing as the favourite haunt of the city's *Schickies*.

A much larger area than the city centre, Schwabing spreads untidily to the left and right of **Leopoldstrasse**, the northern continuation of Ludwigstrasse. The **Englischer Garten** makes up one pleasant border. Schwabing divides into three distinct areas. West of Leopoldstrasse, residential streets mix with wacky shops, student bars and restaurants. Along the centre line and to its right, trendy shops and café-bars ensure permanent crowds, day and night. Nightclubs are thick on the ground here too, especially around the Wedekindplatz near Münchener Freiheit. The far north of Schwabing is a tidily bourgeois residential area, uninteresting for visitors apart from the **Olympiapark**, which is way out, at the end of the U-Bahn line. For listings of the area's bars, restaurants and clubs see pp.82–88.

The Englischer Garten

The **Englischer Garten** takes its name from the eighteenth-century landscaping fashion which tried to create parks resembling untouched nature. Occupying what was formerly marshland, it was created at the instigation of Bavaria's most unlikely statesman, the American-born Benjamin Thompson, who was a leading minister under the garden-loving Elector Carl Theodor (see p.308).

When you've had enough of the city, the Eisbach meadow opposite the **Monopteros,** a Neoclassical temple by Klenze, is a good place to relax. The city's main playground, people come here to sunbathe, picnic, swim in the aptly named *Eisbach* (ice-stream) or ride horses. Visitors often find the large-scale nudity a little unnerving – and it certainly wouldn't be acceptable in any other German city. Even "respectable" businessmen will pop over in the lunch hour, fold their suits in a neat pile and read the paper stark naked. There are rules on where exactly nude sunbathing is allowed, but the police have given up trying to enforce them.

One of the city's most famous beer gardens is around the **Chinesischer Turm** (known locally as the **Chinaturm**) just to the north of the Monopteros, though its days as the best in town are long gone. What used to be *the* place to meet in Munich has become sadly over-commercialized, with expensive food and uniformed guards to watch over propriety, though it's still worth seeing and remains one of the city's most famous landmarks. It's at its best (or worst) on Sunday afternoons, when a Bavarian band blares across the crowd from the heights of the Chinaturm itself. Two, more peaceful, beer gardens are not far off by the **Kleinhesseloher See**. Heading north from here, you get the feeling of being in the countryside rather than in a city park.

The Olympiapark

During the summer months of July and August the **Olympiapark** is the setting for open-air rock and pop concerts every weekend. Usually it's local bands of varying standards, but it doesn't cost anything and is worth checking out; the venue is a modern-day version of a Greek theatre, known as the **Theatron**, right next to the park's lake. The stadia all around were built for the 1972 Olympics and still have a somewhat futuristic look about them. In particular, the main **Olympiastadion** is a strange construction of steel poles and plexiglass expanses, looking rather like an overgrown tent. From the 290-metre-high **tower** (daily 9am–midnight; DM5), there's a wonderful view over Munich and the Alps.

Just to the west rises another of Munich's most arresting modern buildings, the **BMW-Gebäude**, symbolically shaped as four tightly clustered cylindrical towers. The separate structure alongside houses the **BMW-Museum** (daily 9am–5pm; DM5.50). This has a certain novelty value in being laid out along a gently sloping ramp which you gradually ascend on your way round. A fair number of vintage models are on view, but essentially the presentation is a flash – and often none-too-subtle – advert for the company and its products. If you'd like to see round the works, ask at the reception (or better still, phone ☎3895 3306 as far in advance as possible); tours (in English as well as German) are held regularly, but are often booked up weeks in advance.

South along the River Isar

Following Prinzregentenstrasse across the Isar over the Luitpoldbrücke, you come to the **Friedensengel**, a nineteenth-century monument to peace shining in gold splendour. There's a good view of Munich from there, and on New Year's Eve people come up to watch the fireworks across the city. Past the Europaplatz at Prinzregentenstr. 60 is Munich's most eccentric nineteenth-century building, the **Villa Stuck** (Tues, Wed & Fri–Sun 10am–5pm, Thurs 10am–9pm; DM2). This was the house of Franz von Stuck, the leader of the Munich Secession, and was designed by him – using a decidedly eclectic mix of styles, though showing distinct echoes of the city's Neoclassical palaces built earlier in the century – in his only attempt at architecture. Inside is a large collection of his paintings, plus other examples of turn-of-the-century art, with Jugendstil predominating. South of the Friedensengel, the **Maximileum**, a grandiose palace by the Dresden architect Gottfried Semper, finishes off Maximilianstrasse; intended as a cultural establishment, it's now home to the Bavarian parliament.

Just to the east, Wienerplatz marks the beginning of **Haidhausen**. Around here it's still more or less the working-class quarter that it always was, with its own market and the large and shady beer garden of the *Hofbräukeller*. Until the early 1980s, Haidhausen was a run-down part of town that had become something of a Turkish ghetto. The peeling squares and prewar houses have since been rediscovered, and now trendy little health-food stores, alternative craftshops and hip bars have sprouted like mushrooms. It's become *the* place to live, and spiralling rents have forced out most of the original inhabitants.

Down towards the Isar on the Rosenheimer Strasse is hidden one of Munich's real gems, the **Volksbad** (Mon 10am–8pm, Tues, Thurs & Fri 8am–8pm, Wed 6.45am–8pm, Sat 8am–7pm, Sun 9am–6pm; prices range from DM3.50 for a swim to DM17 for the full treatment of a Roman-Irish bath), a beautifully restored Jugendstil indoor swimming hall. High stuccoed ceilings arch over two pools, with mahogany changing cubicles surrounding each, and the sound of splashing water issuing from sculptured fountains makes the atmosphere perfect. There are a couple of saunas and a traditional Turkish bath.

On an island spanned by Ludwigsbrücke is the **Deutsches Museum** (daily 9am–5pm; DM10). Covering every conceivable aspect of technical endeavour, from the first flint tools to the research labs of modern industry, this is the most compendious collection of its type in Europe. The sheer scale of the place is in itself impressive and some of the examples of innovative engineering – biplanes, cars and boats – are ranged in rooms the size of hangars. Part of the second floor of the building has been converted into a replica of the Altamira caves while in the basement there's a convincingly gloomy mock-up of a coalmine. Meticulously constructed large-scale models are featured, and the use of interactive displays makes them as absorbing for kids as adults. Check the noticeboards for the times of the daily demonstrations given by museum staff; that of the historical musical instruments on the first floor is particularly worth catching. Make sure you arrive in the morning – come later on and you'll regret leaving too little time. As a supplement, visit the **Forum der Technik** (daily 9am–11pm) next door: this boasts the world's most modern Planetarium (various programmes from DM11.90) and a 400-square-metre screen for *Audi-Max* films (DM11.90), shown throughout the day.

From the Reichenbachbrücke onwards, paths follow the course of the Isar all the way to the city's zoo, **Tierpark Hellabrunn** (daily April–Sept 8am–6pm; Oct–March 9am–5pm; DM10), which can be reached from the city centre by taking U-Bahn #3 to Thalkirchen. The east bank rises steeply around here and the river and canals are completely hidden by thick woodland. Finally, if you want to see Bavaria's equivalent of Hollywood, and Europe's largest film-making centre, there are guided tours through **Bavaria Filmstadt** (March–Oct daily 9am–4pm; DM15). It's 2km further south from the zoo and reached by tram #25: this can be picked up on Grünwalder Strasse a block to the east of the zoo or at the Silberhorn U-Bahn station (lines #1 and #2 from the centre).

The Theresienwiese

Southwest of the Hauptbahnhof, reached by U-Bahn #4 or #5, lies the inevitable trade fair quarter. In addition to the functional exhibition halls, Munich also has a large egg-shaped fairground, known as the **Theresienwiese**. For most of the year, this is an unremarkable meadow, but for sixteen days it's home to Germany's biggest annual event, the world-famous beer festival-cum-fair, the **Oktoberfest**.

At other times, the only points of note are those overlooking the field to the west. The colonnaded **Ruhmeshalle** (Hall of Fame) is a Bavarian counterpart to the earlier Walhalla near Regensburg, and was likewise paid for by Ludwig I and built by Leo von Klenze. In front stands the colossal bronze **Bavaria statue** (Tues–Sun 10am–noon, 2–4pm; DM3), a very Germanicized derivative of the art of Classical Greece, which was designed by Ludwig von Schwanthaler, and took six years to cast.

THE OKTOBERFEST

Munich's **Oktoberfest** has its origins in the marriage between the Bavarian Crown Prince Ludwig (the future King Ludwig I) and Princess Thérèse of Saxe-Hildburghausen on October 17, 1810. A massive fair was held on the fields now named after the princess, and it was such a popular event that it has been repeated annually ever since, and has spawned innumerable smaller imitations throughout Germany. Nowadays, it's quite simply an orgy of beer-drinking, with upwards of 50,000 hectolitres consumed, ensuring fabulous profits for the brewers – and the publicans lucky enough to be chosen as landlords. Each of the seven Munich breweries (*Hacker-Pschorr* dividing back into two for this purpose) has its own huge **tent**, where in addition to beer, bretzels, chicken halves, sausages and pork knuckles are sold. Visitors sit ten to a bench, and after a few litres of beer half the hall is singing and dancing on the tables. There are also a number of smaller tents, which tend to be far less boisterous and not so overcrowded. The accompanying **fair** offers some great rides to churn your guts, some so hairy that they're banned in countries like the US.

Despite its name, the Oktoberfest actually begins in September: it lasts for sixteen days, always ending on the first Sunday of October. The traditional **opening ceremonies** on the first Saturday revolve around the great horse-drawn brewery wagons arriving at the fairground at 11am to the sound of brass bands and much pomp and speech-making. That evening, a **folklore concert** is held in the *Circus Krone*, Marsstr. 43, involving a selection of those taking part in the big **procession** the following day. It leaves from the centre of town at 10am, this time made up of hundreds of traditional folklore groups, marching bands, musicians, jesters, commercial floats and decorated horsemen that slowly converge on the fairground. A week later, a concert of all the Oktoberfest bands is held on the steps of the Bavaria statue at 11am, though this is postponed for a week if the weather is poor.

The proportions of the fair are so massive that the grounds are divided along four main **avenues**, creating a boisterous city of its own, heaving with revellers from morning till night. Ostensibly a family affair, with rides and stalls of every description jostling for customers, it attracts around seven million visitors. Over seventy percent of these come from Bavaria and its immediate vicinity; the rest are drawn from all over the world, with Australians, New Zealanders and Italians forming the largest foreign contingents. Things are fairly relaxed during daylight hours, and it's advisable to visit at lunchtime if you want to eat and drink in comfort, or to avoid long queues for the rides. However, the atmosphere gets increasingly wild as the evening wears on: many of the big tents are packed to overflowing, and at closing time (around 11pm) staff have the unenviable task of trying to eject hundreds of fighting drunks.

For **information** on the opening ceremonies and pageants, read the *Monatsmagazin* or contact the tourist office; advance **tickets** for the folklore concert are available from the organizers, *Münchner Festring*, Pestalozzistr. 3a (☎260 8134). Even though entrance to the grounds is free, expect to spend lots of money. Accommodation during this time is often hiked up price-wise; on any of the three weekends you'll have trouble finding anything at all if you haven't booked in advance, while on weekdays only middle- and upper-range hotels are likely to have vacancies. Many Munich women choose to avoid the Oktoberfest altogether, and it's probably wise for unaccompanied women to proceed with caution after dark, avoiding the more raucous tents. **Dates** for forthcoming years are: September 19 to October 4 1998; September 18 to October 3 1999; September 16 to October 1 2000; September 22 to October 7 2001.

Nymphenburg

Schloss Nymphenburg (April–Sept Tues–Sun 9am–12.30pm & 1.30–5pm; Oct–March Tues-Sun 10am–12.30pm & 1.30–4pm; DM4, or DM8 including the Marstallmuseum and pavilions), which is reached by taking U-Bahn #1 to Rotkreuzplatz and then tram #12, was the summer residence of the Wittelsbachs. Its kernel is a small Italianate palace begun in 1664 by Agostino Barelli for the frivolous Electress Adelaide, who dedicated it to the pastoral pleasures of the goddess Flora and her nymphs – hence the name. Her son Max Emmanuel commissioned an ingenious extension, whereby four pavilions were built to the side of the palace and connected to it by arcaded passages. Later, the palace itself was modified and further buildings added, resulting in a remarkably unified whole, despite having been nearly a century in the making. By this time, an extensive French-style park had been laid out as an appropriate backdrop. In 1761 the famous porcelain factory was transferred to the site, but plans to establish a planned town on the model of Ludwigsburg in Württemberg came to nothing.

The approach to the palace is either side of a tree-lined canal stretching nearly a kilometre, and when it freezes over in winter it makes a favourite spot for ice-skaters. Through the palace gates, the first hundred metres continue the Schloss's strict symmetry with manicured lawns and straight paths lined with marble statues. The park then opens up into a country landscape, with two lakes and a number of small royal lodges. As you'd expect, the interior of the palace is high Baroque, with rich gold-plated stucco ornamentation and ceiling frescoes. The most famous room is the **Schönheitengalerie** – a collection of 36 portraits of Munich beauties who caught King Ludwig I's eye between 1827 and 1850. In the south wing you can visit the **Marstallmuseum** (same hours; DM3) which houses the elaborate coaches and sleighs of the Wittelsbachs, including several made for the ill-fated Ludwig II.

The Schlosspark

More enticing than the palace itself is the wonderful **Schlosspark**. Three of the four pavilions, which are all of a markedly different character, were designed by Joseph Effner, the innovative court architect who was also responsible for the harmonization of the palace. Immediately behind the northern wing is the **Magdalenenklause** (April–Sept 10am–12.30pm & 1.30–5pm; DM2), deliberately built to resemble a ruined hermitage, with a grotto and four simple cell-like rooms within. It's a very early example of the Historicism which was later to become a German obsession, borrowing elements from Roman, Gothic and even Moorish architecture. The Elector would come here when he wished to meditate – and he hadn't far to go if he tired of its peace and asceticism. Westwards through the park is the **Pagodenburg** (same times; DM2), which was used for the most exclusive parties thrown by the court. Effner's third building, the **Badenburg** (same times; DM3), lies on the opposite side of the canal. It reflects contemporary interest in chinoiserie, though both the bathing room and the two-storey banqueting hall are in the richest Baroque tradition.

For all their charm, Effner's pavilions are overshadowed by the stunning **Amalienburg** (same hours as the Schloss; DM3), the hunting lodge built behind the south wing of the Schloss by his successor as court architect, **François Cuvilliés**. This is among the supreme expressions of the Rococo style, marrying a cunningly thought-out design – which makes the little building seem like a full-scale palace – with extravagant decoration. The entrance chamber, with its niches for the hunting dogs, must be the most tasteful kennel ever built. However, the showpiece is the circular **Spiegelsaal** (Hall of Mirrors), best seen on a bright day when the light casts magical reflections on the silvery-blue walls, the rocaille console tables, the panelled garlands and the rich stucco nymphs and putti.

To the north of the Schloss, the **Botanischer Garten** (daily 9am–4.30/7pm, hothouses closed 11.45am–1pm; DM3) hides all manner of plants in its steamy hothouses and landscaped herbarium.

Eating and drinking

Munich is awash with places to eat and drink, and you can find somewhere open at any time of the day or night. Though best known for its cavernous beer halls and leafy beer gardens, it also has a host of ethnic eateries as well as a lively café-bar culture which carries on well into the early hours. It's not difficult to eat well for relatively little money, with generous portions of heavy food being the norm in establishments which specialize in Bavarian cuisine.

If you're on a very tight budget, **mensas** are the cheapest places to get a good basic meal: you're supposed to have a valid student card to eat in them, but no one seems to check. The most central is at Leopoldstr. 13a; another is at the Technical University, Arcisstr. 17 (both 11am–2pm). Most **butchers' shops** sell bread rolls with various hot and cold fillings from as little as DM3. Good places for this type of snack are the shops of the*Vinzenz Murr* chain, which can be found all over the city; they usually also serve hot daily specials which can be eaten within the shop. The city's classiest **Imbiss** is *Zerwirk-Gewölbe*, Ledererstr. 1, which offers the products of the game butcher's shop in which it is located.

Restaurants

Munich has a wide selection of **restaurants**, and plenty of places offer good food at reasonable prices. For traditional **Bavarian cooking**, the *Gaststätten* are good value and friendly, often with music, providing meals to a mixed clientele.

Gaststätten

Alter Ofen, Zieblandstr. 41. Although a little worn about the edges this is still immensely popular with its student crowd.

Andechs am Dom, Weinstr. 7a. Despite its short menu, this restaurant is very "in"; it's also the only place in Munich serving the products of the monastic brewery at Andechs.

Baal, Kreittmayrstr. 26. Good for relaxed socializing in the evening.

Braunauer Hof, Frauenstr. 40. Slightly more formal atmosphere than most places but still offers local cuisine at middle-of-the-range prices.

Burg Pappenheim, Baaderstr. 46. Fine old *Gaststätte* that's hugely popular with just about everyone.

Donisl, Weinstr. 1. A lively yet traditional establishment, dating back to the early eighteenth century.

Fraunhofer, Fraunhoferstr. 9. For a bit of theatre with your beer – usually gets packed early in the evening.

Haxnbauer, Münzstr. 6. Specializes in the delicious roasted pork knuckles that are such a high-point of German cuisine; the lamb version is no less tasty. Curiously, the beers come not from Munich but from *Dinkelacker* in Stuttgart.

Hundskugel, Hotterstr. 18. Munich's oldest surviving inn, established in 1440. The dishes are lighter than in most rival establishments – which many will rate a positive advantage.

Nürnberger Bratwurst-Glöckl, Frauenplatz 9. Standing in the shadow of the Dom, this is a transplant of the famous gourmet sausage restaurants of Nürnberg.

Schlosswirtschaft zur Schwaige, Eingang 30, Schloss Nymphenburg. A highly recommendable restaurant in its own right, and an ideal place to break for a meal when visiting Nymphenburg.

Zum Spöckmeier, Rosenstr. 9. Large and popular three-storey *Gaststätte* just off Marienplatz.

Other restaurants

Adria, Leopoldstr. 19, Schwabing. Popular late-night joint with excellent pizzas at reasonable prices.

Antalya, Bergmannstr. 50. West-end location and excellent Anatolian dishes.

Bernard & Bernard, Innere Wiener Str. 32, Haidhausen. Great place for crêpes, next to Wienerplatz. Closed Sat.

Bodega Dalí, Augustenstr. 46. One of the best Spanish places in town, despite lower than average prices.

Bombay, Kurfürstenstr. 47, Schwabing. Classic Indian dishes at reasonable prices.

Dalmatiner Grill, Geibelstr. 10, Haidhausen. The best bet in the district for affordable Balkan specialities.

Le Fleuron de l'Isar, Erhardstr. 27. Small, welcoming French restaurant, with realistic mid-range prices.

Friulana, Zenettistr. 43. A genuine, homely local much patronized by Italian expatriates; it's way off the tourist track, yet not too far from Theresienwiese.

Hammadan, Augustenstr. 1. Well placed for the Königsplatz museums, this is one of several Persian restaurants in the city, with bargain lunchtime menus and buffets.

Klein Bukarest, Thalkirchner Str. 186. Offers a rare chance to sample Romanian cuisine.

Kyklos, Wilderich-Lang-Str. 10. One of the oldest Greek restaurants in the city; better than average, with excellent *gyros*.

La Marmite, Lilienstr. 8. Munich's most popular French restaurant. Reservations essential (☎482242).

Matoi, Hans-Sachs-Str. 10. Japanese restaurant offering bargain sushi dishes on Mon and Wed.

Opatija, Viktualienmarkt 13 and Briennerstr. 14. Long-established Balkan favourites; the former has the benefit of a summertime patio, the latter is handy for the Königsplatz museums.

Tai Tung, Prinzregentenstr. 60. Located in the basement of the Villa Stuck, Munich's oldest Chinese restaurant is still the best. The set lunches are excellent value.

Vegetarian

Gollier, Gollierstr. 83. Excellent vegetarian food with organically produced drinks available.

Ignaz, Georgenstr. 67, Schwabing. Thanks to its location, this has a large student clientele.

Prinz Myshkin, Hackenstr. 2. Offers creative vegetarian special dishes plus wholemeal pizzas.

Vierjahreszeiten, Sebastianplatz 9. Light and airy vegetarian restaurant with reasonable prices.

Beer halls and beer gardens

The **beer cellar** (*Bierkeller)* and **beer garden** (*Biergarten*) are Munich's most characteristic institutions. Generally speaking the former are roomy halls (rather than cellars); often standing in leafy gardens, they serve strong, heady beer produced in a local brewery, plus hearty traditional Bavarian food. Although a few have become tainted by excessive tourism, they remain an essential and unmissable feature of the city.

City centre

Altes Hackerhaus, Sendlinger Str. 75. The city-centre beer hall of the *Hacker-Pschorr* brewery.

Augustinerbräu, Neuhauser Str. 27. One of Munich's most celebrated beer halls, with an unusually long menu and wonderfully evocative turn-of-the-century decor.

Franziskaner Fuchsenstuben, Perusastr. 5. A good choice for either a full meal or a snack: it's said to serve Munich's best *Weisswurst*, the white sausage which traditionally should only be eaten before noon.

Hofbräuhaus, Platzl 9. The most famous one – which is consequently on the itinerary of just about every visitor to the city. Nonetheless, it's perfectly genuine, with plenty of regular customers, and the food and drink are fairly priced.

Löwenbräukeller, Nymphenburger Str. 2. Located a short distance west of Königsplatz, this serves excellent food and has a beer garden.

Spatenhaus, Residenzstr. 12. The most upmarket of *Spaten's* hostelries, with an interior decked out in traditional Alpine style.

Spatenhofkeller, Neuhauser Str. 39. Offers hearty Bavarian cooking at lower than average prices, with bargain midday menus which sometimes feature quite innovative dishes.

Weisses Bräuhaus, Im Tal 10. This is the flagship of the *Schneider* brewery, a *Weissbier* specialist which moved its production base after the war from this site to Kelheim in Eastern Bavaria. Though it has a full menu, it's best known for its *Weisswurst*, which should preferably be eaten to the accompaniment of a *Weissbier*.

Englischer Garten

Aumeister, Sondermeierstr. 1. At the far northern end of the Englisher Garten, this one is a good place for daytime breaks.

Chinesischer Turm, Englischer Garten 3. Though worth a visit, this famous beer garden has become a real tourist trap.

Seehaus, Kleinhesselohe 2. This has an excellent setting on the shores of the Kleinhesseloher See – you can feed the swans while you enjoy your drink.

Theresienwiese

Hackerkeller, Theresienhöhe 4. On the heights above the Theresienwiese, with a laid-back atmosphere and live music in the evenings.

Pschorrkeller, Theresienhöhe 7. Just along the street from the cellar of its sister brewery, thus making for an easy change of scene.

Elsewhere in the city

Augustinerkeller, Arnulfstr. 52. Near the S-Bahn stop Hackerbrücke, in one of Munich's grottier quarters, with a large, shady garden and hardly a tourist in sight.

Hirschgarten, Hirschgartenallee 1, Nymphenburg. Near Schloss Nymphenburg, this one, notwithstanding its seating capacity of over 2000, is rather civilized.

Hofbräukeller, Innere Wiener Str. 19, Haidhausen. Nestling under ancient chestnut trees, this is a very popular evening destination.

MUNICH'S BEER CULTURE

Munich's **beer halls** have their origins in the Middle Ages, when brewers stored barrels indoors, planting chestnut trees around their premises to shade them from the heat of the sun. These days beer gardens remain popular with natives and visitors alike, really coming into their own in summer when tables and chairs are set up in the open. Beer is served in litre *Maas* measures, and the enduring image is that of the traditionally clad waitress sailing from table to table clutching several enormous, foaming glasses in each hand while the resident brass band plays an endless succession of oompah tunes. Many beer gardens serve up roasted half chickens (always well salted to ensure a healthy customer thirst) with side orders of potato salad, while some have more extensive menus, and others allow you to bring your own food. Beer garden **etiquette** can be a little hard to grasp for outsiders: don't sit at a *Stammtisch* (regular's table) as you won't be served and the staff won't bother to tell you, preferring to let you figure it out for yourself.

Munich ranks as the third largest producer of beer in the world, and it can legitimately claim to be both the most influential and the most varied in output: it pioneered wheat-based and brown-coloured beers, and adapted the original *Bock* of Einbeck to the form in which it's generally known today. Nowadays six major breweries operate in the city. Largest is *Paulaner*, which produces a full range of styles, generally with a drier flavour than those of its competitors; the dark and extremely powerful *Salvator-Doppelbock* is its star product. *Paulaner* has a controlling stake in *Hacker-Pschorr*, which has had a complicated history, having begun as one company before splitting then re-uniting; its product lines include the copper-coloured *Hubertusbock* and *Pschorr-Weisse*, a very pale wheat beer. *Löwenbräu*, better known abroad through being a bigger exporter, produces a similarly wide variety of generally maltier beers, among which the *Pils* enjoys the highest reputation. *Hofbräu*, the oldest of the breweries, makes the classic *Maibock* plus the unfiltered *Kindl Weissbier*, though its standard line is an *Export*. The main strength of *Augustiner* is its pale (*Hell*) beer, but it produces several prestigious dark brews as well. *Spaten* has the best amber and black beers, known respectively as *Ur-Märzen* and *Ludwig-Thoma-Dunkel*, though it's equally known for its *Franziskaner Weissbier* (available in both light and dark versions) and *Maibock*.

Menterschwaige, Menterschwaigestr. 4, Harlaching. One of Munich's best beer gardens. On the edge of the Isar valley, out in a southern suburb, it's the place to bring a picnic to go with your beer.

Paulanerkeller (or **Salvatorkeller**), Hochstr. 77, Au. High up on the Nockherberg, in the district immediately south of Haidhausen, this is the venue for the spring *Starkbierfest*, and one of the oldest havens for serious beer drinkers.

Zum Erdinger Weissbräu, Heiglhofstr. 13, Grosshaidern. Beer hall and garden, reached by U-Bahn #6, which serves the products of the eponymous brewery in the small town of Erding northeast of Munich. It's well known for its wide range of wheat beers.

Zum Flaucher, in the Flaucherpark, Thalkirchen. Hiding amid the tall trees of the park on an island in the Isar, it does excellent fish dishes in summer.

Hausbrauereien

Predictably, Munich has taken the national lead in the current craze for new *Hausbrauereien*, which represent a return to traditional methods by having a boutique brewery in or alongside the bar-restaurant where it is served, thereby ensuring the utmost freshness.

Bamberger Haus, Brunnerstr. 2, Schwabing. Occupies a lovely Rococo mansion with terrace in the Luitpoldpark, just east of the Olympiapark. Makes several different beers, and also serves high-class meals.

Braustübl der Forschungsbrauerei, Unterhachinger Str. 76, Altperlach. In a southeastern suburban setting with garden, producing a fine dark beer. Reached by U-Bahn #8 or S-Bahn #2; open mid-March to mid-Oct only, closed Mon.

Flieger-Bräu, Sonnenstr. 2, Feldkirchen. In an eastern suburb, reached by S-Bahn #6, this is a sister establishment of the better-known *Isar-Bräu*.

Isar-Bräu, Kreuzeckstr. 23, Grosshesselohe. Located within the Grosshesselohe Isartalbahnhof on S-Bahn line #7, it makes a *Weissbier* and a dark *Spezial*, and also serves the products of its parent, the out-of-town *Hofbräuhaus Traunstein*.

Paulaner Bräuhaus, Kapuzinerplatz 5. *Paulaner* have opened this in the old *Thomasbräu*, whose name lives on in its non-alcoholic beer. Very trendy, particularly on Thurs, the day the new *Weissbier* is brewed.

Unionsbräu, Einsteinstr. 42, Haidhausen. The cellar has huge communal benches where you sit to sip the fine *Helles* made on the premises.

Bars

The city's social life revolves around its bars. Beer, coffee and snacks are served in most places, and while the list of "in" and "out" bars is ever-changing, the ones listed below are of proven worth. *Schickies* hang out in **Schwabing** and hipsters head for **Haidhausen**, though things are pretty provincial in both areas. The city's bars suffer from limiting licensing laws (midnight closing at most places).

City centre

Café an der Uni, Ludwigstr. 24. Very popular with students from the nearby university, and nearly always packed to the gills.

Café Giesing, Bergstr. 5. Friendly place, often with live music.

Havana Club, Herrenstr. 30. Great place for cocktails; so packed it's normally standing room only.

Jodlerwirt, Altenhof 4. There's a typical *Gaststube* on the ground floor, but the draw is the cramped little bar above, which is always jam-packed for the yodelling sessions: come along in the late evening and you'll immediately be sucked into the arm-linking singalong, a harmless piece of kitsch that's great fun.

Nachtcafé, Maximiliansplatz 5 (7pm–5am). Haunt of the true night owls, this is the place to see and be seen in the early hours of the morning.

Ruffini, Orffstr. 22. Friendly bar with a good roof terrace.

THE GAY SCENE

Deeply conservative Bavaria is not the best part of Germany in which to be gay. Nonetheless, Munich has one of Germany's most active and visible gay scenes, centred on the bars in and around Gärtnerplatz. The widely available *Columbia Fun Map* shows the main gay meeting-places; there's also a free newsheet for gays entitled *Our Munich* (despite it's name, it's in German only). For further information, contact the *Schwules Kommunikations- und Kulturzentrum*, Müllerstr. 38 (☎260 3056).

The Women's Centre, *Frauenzentrum*, Güllstr. 3 (Mon–Fri 6–11pm; ☎725 4271) runs a series of workshops and a café for all women, not just lesbians. On Tuesday between 1pm and 8pm, women from 13 to 20 years meet in the café, with Friday evenings specifically for lesbians. Cafés that cater predominantly for lesbians are *Karotte*, Baaderstr. 13; *Frauencafé im Kofra*, Baldestr. 8; and *Mädchenpower-Café*, Baldestr. 16. The only nightclub is *Mylord*, Ickstättstr. 2a (daily 6–9pm, 6pm–3am weekends), which gets mixed reviews.

Among the many gay men's bars, the following are the best known: *Colibri*, Utzschneiderstr. 8; *Juice*, Buthelmelcherstr. 2a; *Klimperkasten*, Maistr. 28; *Nil*, Hans-Sachs-Str. 2 and *Teddybar*, Hans-Sachs-Str. 1. *New York*, Sonnenstr. 25 (10pm–4am), is a gay disco offering chart and dance sounds, while *Ochsengarten*, Müllerstr. 47, is a leather bar.

Schumann's, Maximilianstr. 36. Munich's movers and shakers congregate here, so this is the place to head for if you're looking to make contacts.

Schwabing

Alter Simpl, Türkenstr. 57. Famous literary café-bar which spawned the satirical magazine *Simplicissimus*; after a long period in the doldrums, it has become fashionable again. Open daily 5pm till 3am, 4am at weekends.

Ayinger Extra, Herzogstr. 14. This small *Kneipe* is a good place to sample the diverse product lines of the "country" brewery of Aying, just outside Munich.

Drugstore, Feilitzschstr. 12. Lively place that manages to avoid the usual Schwabing excess.

Extrablatt, Leopoldstr. 7. Ritzy café-bar that's worth visiting at least once.

Haus der 111 Biere, Franzstr. 3. As the name suggests, there are 111 different sorts of beer on sale, with 25 different countries represented.

Palmengarten, Herzogstr. 93. Though not too bad in the early evening, this place fills with an obnoxiously affluent crowd as the night wears on.

Reitschule, Königinstr. 34. Place to be seen if you aspire to Munich high life, but it's expensive and the service is off-hand.

Haidhausen

Grössenwahn, Lothringerstr. 11. Well-known bar frequented by the Munich in-crowd.

Hinterhof Caféhaus, Sedanstr. 29. Also a health-food café for times when the beer and schnapps become too much.

Julep's, Breisacher Str. 18. Recommended cocktail bar with a popular happy hour.

Paris Bar, Gravelottestr. 7. Very trendy yuppie hangout.

Traditional cafés

These are the traditional *Kaffee und Kuchen* places, seemingly favoured mainly by ladies with lapdogs. They're great places to load up on cakes, cream and strong coffee. All these cafés are only open during normal shopping hours, which usually means from 8.30am to 6pm.

Café Frischhut, Prälat-Zeistl-Str. 7–11. A good place to sample a *Schmalznudel*, a kind of large deep-fried doughnut, eaten either plain or sprinkled with sugar.

Café Kreuzkamm, Maffeistr. 4. Delicious cakes and sweets make this one of the best in town.

Café Luitpold, Briennerstr. 11. Elegant café with a mixed clientele.

Café Schneller, Amalienstr. 59, Schwabing. A university location makes this popular with students rather than the antique lady contingent.

Wine bars

There isn't a great deal of choice in this beer haven, but the following are all worth a visit.

Pfälzer Weinprobierstuben, Residenzstr. 1. Wines and food from the Rhineland served in a pleasant atmosphere in this wine bar in the Residenz.

Rolandseck, Viktoriastr. 23, Schwabing. Has the best selection of Baden wines in town.

St Georg, Prinzregentenplatz 13. Recommended cellar wine bar.

Weinhaus Neuner, Herzogspitalstr. 8. Nineteenth-century wine bar known for its gourmet food.

Weinstadl, Burgstr. 6. This unpretentious place, serving excellent wines, is housed in one of the city's oldest buildings. There's a terrace in summer.

Weintrödler, Briennerstr. 10 (5pm–6am). Open after everywhere else has closed, and consequently always full.

Music, nightlife and entertainment

Munich has a great deal to offer **musically**, whether you're into classical concerts or more modern stuff. There's everything you'd expect to find in a cosmopolitan capital, and during the summer a glut of open-air music festivals takes place in or around the city. Three orchestras of international repute are based here, and the annual opera festival in July ranks with the Salzburg and Bayreuth festivals. Not that it's all highbrow: there's plenty of trash and tinsel as well, though perhaps the bars are more interesting than the discos. Best sources for **listings** are the *Münchener Stadtmagazin* or *In München*, available at any kiosk.

Rock and pop

During the summer the **free rock concerts** by the lake in the Olympiapark, at the purpose-built stage known as the *Theatron*, usually get going around 2pm. Several **venues** have regular music programmes throughout the year:

Flughafen Riem, Töginger Landstr. 400, Riem. The old airport terminal, reached by S-Bahn #6, has been given a new lease of life as a major live music venue.

Kaffee Giesing, Bergstr. 5. Run by the singer Konstantin Wecker, and usually featuring small bands or solo artists.

Rockclub, Frankfurter Ring 226, Schwabing. Newish venture, already very popular.

Jazz

Munich has a monthly jazz magazine called *Münchener Jazz-Zeitung*, available in music shops and jazz venues. The city is corporate headquarters of the avant-garde jazz record label *ECM*, and club dates are accordingly more exciting than the German norm, attracting many big names on tour. The following venues play predominantly jazz, but check programmes:

Alabamahalle, Domagkstr. 33. As you'd expect, this plays predominantly Dixieland fare.

Feierwerk, Hansastr. 39. Has jazz, blues or rock every evening from 9pm.

Jam, Rosenheimer Str. 4, Haidhausen. A good bet for solid, reliable jazz, though don't expect any musical surprises.

Max–Emanuel, Adalbertstr. 33, Schwabing. The clientele takes its music just a little bit too seriously here, though the place is open until 1am.

Schwabinger Podium, Wagnerstr. 1, Schwabing. If watching earnest German jazzers sweating their way through Dixieland tunes is your idea of a good time then this is the place you should head for. Rock music is also featured.

Unterfahrt, Kirchenstr. 96, Haidhausen. Munich's modern jazz venue. Big names and unknowns play here, and the music is nearly always excellent. Closed Mon.

Folk

Predictably, the Munich folk scene is dominated by Germany's two favourite foreign imports – Irish and country and western.

The Dubliner, Candidplatz 9. Sometimes rings the changes over the normal Irish fare by having Scottish music or reggae instead.

Oklahoma, Schäftlarnstr. 156. Has live country and western music Wed–Sun from 7pm.

Rattlesnake Saloon, Schneeglöckchenstr. 91. There's either live country and western or blues every evening Thurs–Sun from 7pm.

Shamrock Irish Pub, Trautenwolfstr. 6. Live music, usually Irish folk, is played from 9pm each evening.

Shananigins, Ungererstr. 19. There are ceilidhs on Tuesdays, folk music or karaoke on other evenings.

Discos and nightclubs

Munich has a thriving nightclub scene, though in this city where money and appearances are everything, the snooty attitudes of many places can be rather off-putting. Most places are open 10pm–4am and entrance is about DM10.

Crash, Ainmillerstr. 10. Heavy metal mecca and headbanger's delight (Mon–Thurs 8pm–1am, Fri–Sat 8pm–3am).

Far Out, Am Kosttor. Central venue where chart stuff, hip-hop and techno are the order of the evening.

Jackie O, Rosenkavalierplatz 12. Just about the strictest door policy in town, so unless you're loaded and look it, forget it (10pm–4am).

Liberty, Rosenheimer Str. 30, Haidhausen. Funk and black dance sounds.

Nachtwerk, Landsberger Str. 189. One of the city's best and most affordable nightlife possibilities. They put on occasional indie gigs here too.

Oly, Helene-Meyer-Ring 9. Located in the Olympia-Dorf and particularly popular with students. Opens at 9pm, with no cover charge during the first hour.

Parkcafé, Sophienstr. 7. Ranks among Munich's most popular nightclubs (10pm–3am).

Sugar Shack, Herzogspitalstr. 6. Standard central disco, but fun nevertheless (11pm–4am).

Classical music

A number of resident orchestras and two opera houses cater to a very spoilt audience. The *Bayerisches-Rundfunk-Sinfonie-Orchester* is conducted by the American Lorin Maazel, who was lured here by what was probably the most lucrative contract ever made to a conductor. For a quarter of a century, the *Münchner Philharmoniker* was directed by Sergiu Celibidache, one of the great conductors of the century, a man who developed an aura by his stubborn refusal to make records. His recent death means that the orchestra faces an uphill struggle to maintain its prestige. A third full-sized body, the *Bayerischer Staatsorchester*, plays for the opera under the baton of Peter Schneider. Hans Stadlmair's *Münchener Kammerorchester* has gained international standing for its interpretations of Baroque music and the Viennese classics. Among several distinguished choirs, Hanns-Martin Schneidt's *Münchener-Bach-Chor* has long been renowned for its performances of Bach's church cantatas, notwithstanding the irony of its championing such overtly Protestant music in this stoutly Catholic city.

Best way to find out what's on and for how much is to buy the city's **official monthly programme** (*Monatsprogramm*), which costs DM2.50, from the tourist office. Advance tickets for concerts can be bought at the relevant box offices or commercial ticket shops, such as the one located in the Marienplatz U-Bahn station. The **Münchener Opernfest**, which takes place from the middle of July to the beginning of August, has a very high reputation. Classical concerts are also held at Schloss Nymphenburg and in the courtyard of the Residenz at this time of year.

Venues

Bayerische Staatsoper (or **Nationaltheater**), Max-Joseph-Platz 1; advance booking office at Maximilianstr. 11 (☎2185 1920). One of the world's most beautiful and distinguished opera houses, presenting both grand opera and ballet. Unsold and cheap standing tickets can be bought an hour before performance within the theatre itself.

Gasteig, Rosenheimer Str. 5 (☎480980 or 5481 8181). Modern concert hall complex in Haidhausen. In addition to the main *Philharmonie*, where symphony orchestras perform, there's the *Carl-Orff-Saal* for chamber orchestras, and the *Kleiner Konzertsaal* for soloists and small ensembles.

Hochschule für Musik, Arcisstr. 12 (☎5591 589). The one-time Nazi Party headquarters, nowadays the local music academy, often stages high-quality solo instrumental and chamber music concerts, many of them free.

Olympiahalle, in the Olympiapark (☎3067 2424). The huge sports hall is frequently used for blockbuster all-star operas and concerts. High prices for even the worst seats.

Prinzregententheater, Prinzregentenplatz 12; advance booking at Maximilianstr. 13 (☎2916 1414). Munich's main ballet venue, though other types of music are also featured.

Residenz, Residenzstr. 1 (☎29067 263). There are two concert halls within the palace – the tapestry-lined *Herkulessaal* for orchestral music, and the *Max-Joseph-Saal* for chamber performances.

Staatstheater am Gärtnerplatz, Gärtnerplatz 3 (☎201 6767); advance booking office as for Staatsoper. Presents operettas and the lighter fare of the operatic repertoire.

Cinema and theatre

Non-German **films** are usually dubbed into German, but the following places specialize in showing films with the original soundtrack: *Broadway*, Feilitzischstr. 7 (☎337022); *Cinema*, Nymphenburger Str. 31 (☎555255); *Türkendolch*, Türkenstr. 74 (☎271 8844). Entrance prices vary according to where you sit, but range between DM10 and DM14.

Theatre

Munich has a host of theatres and cabaret venues, all of which are listed in the official programmes and the local press. Almost all productions are exclusively in German.

Cuviliéstheater (or Altes Residenztheater), Residenzstr. 1 (☎2185 1940). Munich's star venue for drama, this Rococo building saw the premiere of Mozart's *Idomeneo*.

Deutsches Theater, Schwanthalerstr. 13 (☎55234 360 or 5523 4444). Features both home-grown and imported spectaculars.

Münchener Kammerspiele, Maximilianstr. 26 (☎2372 1328). An excellent venue, offering a wide variety of productions.

Münchner Lach- und Schiessgesellschaft, corner of Haimhauser Strasse and Ursulastrasse (☎391997). The best known of a host of cabaret venues in the city.

Münchner Marionettentheater, Blumenstr. 29a (☎265712). A puppet theatre – mainly for kids, though once a week the marionettes are put to more serious use in the performance of an opera or drama classic.

MUNICH'S FESTIVALS

Inevitably, all local **festivals** stand in the shadow of the Oktoberfest (see p.80), but there are plenty of other annual events. **Fasching**, Munich's Carnival, begins in earnest immediately after Epiphany with a week-long series of costume parades. Fancy-dress balls are held regularly up to and including Carnival Week, whose festivities come to a climax on Ash Wednesday with a ceremony of washing money bags at the Fischerbrunnen in Marienplatz. A couple of weeks later begins **Starkbierzeit**, the period when strong beer is served in the taverns to help make the stringencies of Lent bearable. More specially brewed strong beer can be sampled at the **Maibock-Anstich** in May.

The **Auer Dult** is a traditional market that takes place on the Mariahilfplatz during the last weeks of April, July and October each year. It has a combination of hardware, crafts and antiques, as well as a fairground for the kids. An annual **Christmas market**, known as the *Christkindlmarkt*, is held on the Marienplatz during the month of December, though the ones at the Münchener Freiheit, and around the Pariser Platz in Haidhausen are less commercialized with more hand-made crafts.

Münchner Theater für Kinder, Dachauer Str. 46 (☎595454). Speciality children's venue.

Münchner Volkstheater, Am Stiglmaierplatz (☎523 4655). Plays predominantly modern drama, whether new works or classics.

Residenztheater, Max-Joseph-Platz 1 (☎2185 1940). Traditional dramatic fare in high quality productions.

Schauburg am Elisabethplatz, Franz-Joseph-Str. 47 (☎237 21365). Youth theatre venue.

Theater im Marstall, Marstallplatz; advance tickets from Max-Joseph-Platz 1 (☎2185 1940). An offshoot of the Residenztheater, specializing in experimental drama.

Zirkus Krone, Marsstr. 43 (☎558166). Germany's only permanent circus tent, located close to the Hackerbrücke S-Bahn station.

Listings

Airlines *British Airways*, Promenadeplatz 10 (☎292121); *Lufthansa*, Lenbachplatz 1 (☎545599).

Airport information ☎9752 1313.

American Express Promenadeplatz 6 (Mon–Fri 9am–5.30pm, Sat 9.30am–12.30pm; ☎290900).

Bike rental The cheapest place is *Aktiv-Rad*, Hans-Sachs-Str. 7, while the most convenient is *Radius Touristik*, located opposite platform 31 in the Hauptbahnhof. You can also rent bikes at many of the outlying *S-Bahn stations*, such as Aying, Dachau, Freising, Herrsching, Holzkirchen, Starnberg and Tutzing.

Bookstores *Anglia English Bookshop*, Schellingstr. 3, and *Wordsworth*, Schellingstr. 21, have a good selection of paperbacks and English-language newspapers. *Geobuch*, Rosental 6, has the best selection of maps and guides, and there's a women's bookstore at Arccistr. 57.

Car rental *Avis*, Nymphenburger Str. 61 (☎60000); *Hertz*, Nymphenburger Str. 81 (☎129 5001)); there are also many competing offices in both the Hauptbahnhof and airport.

Consulates *British*, Bürkleinstr. 10 (☎211090); *Canadian*, Tal 29 (☎219 9570); *Dutch*, Nymphenburger Str. 1 (☎545 9670); *Irish*, Mauerkircherstr. 1a (☎985723); *US*, Königinstr. 5 (☎28880).

Cultural institutes *Amerikahaus*, Karolinenplatz 3 (☎552 5370); *British Council*, Rumfordstr. 7 (☎290 0860).

Cultural societies The following run social functions advertised in the local press: *Deutsch-Englische Gesellschaft*(☎280 2077); *Deutsch-Kanadische Gesellschaft* (☎307 3345 or 314 8410); *Munich Scottish Association*(☎391253).

Medical emergencies ☎551771.

Mitfahrzentralen Amalienstr. 87 (☎19444) and Lämmerstr. 4 (☎194440).

Pharmacy At the *Internationale Apotheke*, Neuhauser Str. 11, you can get your prescription no matter which country it comes from.

Post office The main post office is at Residenzstr. 2 (Mon-Fri 8am–6pm, Sat 8am–1pm; the longest hours are kept by the branch in the Hauptbahnhof (Mon–Fri 7am–8pm, Sat 8am–4pm, Sun 9am–3pm).

Sports *FC Bayern München*, Germany's most consistent football club, winner of many European trophies down the years, play at the *Olympiastadion* in the Olympiapark, which is also the venue for major athletics meetings.

Taxis ☎21610.

Travel agents *Studiosus Reisen*, Oberanger 6 (☎235 0520); *Thomas Cook*, Kaiserstr. 45 (☎3838 830).

UPPER BAVARIA

The name of **Upper Bavaria** (*Oberbayern*), Munich's own traditional province, is associated above all with the **Alps**. Quite simply, this is the most spectacular scenery Germany has to offer, a wonderfully contrasting array of glacial lakes and peaks commanding stunning panoramic views, with many dramatic castles and churches thrown in for good measure. Amid this picture-book scenery you'll find the Bavarian folklore and customs that are the subject of so many tourist brochures: men still wear leather *Lederhosen* and checked shirts, and women the traditional *Dirndl* dresses. Superficially it can all seem very kitsch, but beyond the packaged culture lies a fascinating mixture of Catholic and pagan rites that dominate the annual calendar – events usually accompanied by large amounts of eating and drinking.

Head for **Oberammergau** where the world-famous Passion Play is staged every ten years. From here it's only a few kilometres to the international ski resort of **Garmisch-Partenkirchen**, above which towers the **Zugspitze**, Germany's highest and most famous peak. The most dramatic heights of all are in the Berchtesgadener Land, an area that includes the town of **Berchtesgaden** as well as the marvellous peak of the **Watzmann** and the high ridges forming the border with Austria. The area is intensely geared towards tourism, as are the **Upper Bavarian lakes**, most of which lie in the glacial valleys of the Alpine foothills.

In contrast, other parts of the province are relatively little known, yet offer plenty of varied attractions. Between the Alps and the capital lie some equally enticing lakes and monasteries; to the east are the valleys of the **Inn** and **Salzach** rivers with the pilgrimage site of **Altötting** and the medieval towns of **Wasserburg** and **Burghausen**; while north of Munich are several wonderful old towns, most notable of which are the old metropolitan see of **Freising**, the former university and ducal capital of **Ingolstadt**, and the planned residential seat of **Neuburg**.

As if the scenery wasn't enough, manifold culinary delights are available in the wonderful old *Gaststätten*, often with beer gardens, where traditional Bavarian menus and innumerable regional beers are served. There are rail links to many destinations, and a network of connecting bus services between the Alpine towns, the only snag being that some of these only operate once or twice a day. **Accommodation** shouldn't be a major problem, except during July and August in the most sought-after destinations. There's a huge choice of rooms in private houses (identified by the *Zimmer frei* signs; contact the local tourist office if you want to make an advance booking) where prices are surprisingly reasonable (①–③) – even in major resorts such as Garmisch. Youth hostels (for the under-27s) and campsites are also plentiful.

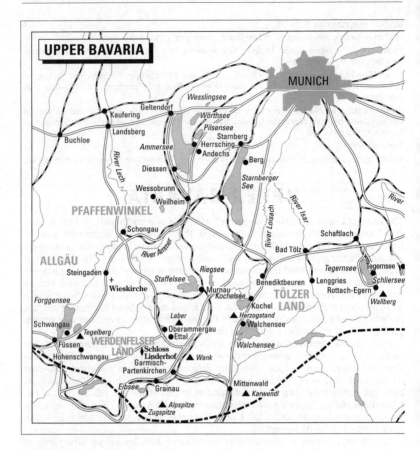

North from Munich

North of Munich, making easy day-trips by the city's excellent S-Bahn network, are two sharply contrasting excursion possibilities. A visit to **Dachau** concentration camp is a harrowing experience, while **Freising** is one of Bavaria's most venerable and attractive towns.

Dachau

Situated on the S-Bahn #2 line, 17km north of Munich, **DACHAU** is a picturesque provincial town. But whatever its charms may be, the place and word itself have associations with horrors that have been indelibly stamped on the consciousness of twentieth-century Europe. Dachau was Germany's first **concentration camp**, built in 1933, and the model for all others. Though not itself an extermination camp, many thousands were murdered here, and the motto that greeted new arrivals at the gates has taken its own chilling place in the history of Third Reich brutality: *Arbeit Macht Frei* – "Work

Brings Freedom". The camp was mainly for political prisoners, and numbered among its inmates Pastor Martin Niemöller, the former French premier Léon Blum, and Johann Elser, who tried to assassinate Hitler in 1939.

To reach the camp or **Konzentrationslager** (Tues–Sun 9am–5pm; free), take bus #722 from Dachau's Bahnhof to Robert-Bosch-Strasse. The rows of huts where prisoners lived were all torched by the Allies after the war, and neat windswept patches of rectangular gravel mark their former outlines. A replica of one of these huts gives some idea of the cramped conditions prisoners were cooped up in, but the only original buildings still standing are the gas chambers, never used, since the war ended before they could be set to work. Open ovens gape at you, and bright whitewashed walls almost distract from the ominous gas outlets set in the ceilings of the shower rooms. The stark wire perimeter fencing and watchtowers also remain. A permanent **exhibition**, with photographs and accompanying text in several languages including English, speaks for itself. Turn up at 11.30am or 3.30pm and you can also view the short, deeply disturbing documentary *KZ-Dachau* in English. Three small memorial churches – Catholic, Protestant and Orthodox – have been built within the complex, and the first two are normally kept open for visits.

Freising

FREISING, the terminus of S-Bahn #1, lies some 35km north of Munich, about halfway towards Landshut, and only 8km from the airport, to which it's linked by bus #635. One of Bavaria's oldest towns, it was the province's spiritual capital during its period as an episcopal see from 739 to 1803, and its name is retained in the title of the local archbishop, who now resides in Munich. Despite its proximity to the state capital, it gives no impression of belonging to commuter-belt land, retaining instead the very distinct atmosphere of a country town, particularly in the centre, where the picturesque Markt and Hauptstrasse, overlooked by the handsome Baroque tower of the Gothic **Stadtpfarrkirche St Georg**, are lined by colourful mansions of varying dates.

The hill between the River Isar and the centre, known as the Domberg, is a self-contained episcopal quarter centred on the twin-towered Romanesque **Dom**, whose exterior is covered with a startling coat of whitewash. After this, the interior comes as another surprise, the original architecture masked by a lavish decoration scheme carried out by the Asam brothers in an idiom which belongs to the final phase of Baroque. A few older furnishings, such as the late Gothic choir stalls with busts of the local prince-bishops and the *Lamentation* group by Erasmus Grasser in the apse of the north aisle, look rather incongruous amid this theatricality. Thankfully, the Asams didn't tamper with the **crypt**, the resting place of Saint Korbinian, founder of the bishopric. Among the pillars supporting the vault of this beautiful chamber is the amazing *Bestiensäule*, which is festooned with carvings of fantastic animals. The **cloisters** built onto the east end of the Dom have Rococo decoration by Johann Baptist Zimmermann, as does François Cuvilliés' **Bibliotheksaal** (May–Oct Mon-Fri 2-3pm) alongside.

At the far end of the cloisters is the Gothic **Benediktuskirche**. A second and much larger church of the same period, the **Johanniskirche**, is built right against the front end of the Dom, and is in turn linked to the former **Residenz** of the prince-bishops, thereby creating a truly monumental complex of interconnected buildings. Occupying a former seminary at the western end of the Domberg is the **Diözesanmuseum** (Tues–Sun 10am–5pm; DM3), the largest ecclesiastical museum in Germany. It features works by many of the leading Baroque and Rococo artists of Bavaria, though its most valuable treasure, gleaming in a dimly lit room, is a Byzantine icon known as the *Lukasbild*. There are also two magnificent paintings by **Rubens** of *The Adoration of the Shepherds* and *The Assumption*, which originally adorned the side altars of the Hofkirche in Neuburg an der Donau.

West of the town centre is another hill, on which stands **Kloster Weihenstephan**, a former monastery which is now home to the agricultural and brewing faculties of the Technical University of Munich. Its main claim to fame is the **Weihenstephan-Brauerei**, which has been in operation since 1040, and is thus generally accepted as the oldest brewery in the world. Guided tours (DM3) are run through the present ultra-modern premises from Monday to Thursday, but it's necessary to phone ahead (☎08161/5360) to join a group. Otherwise, you can content yourself with sampling the products – of which the wheat beers are the best known – in the *Bräustüberl* or its beer garden.

Ingolstadt

Even by German standards, **INGOLSTADT**, 60km due north of Munich, reeks of prosperity, courtesy of its four oil refineries, fed by pipelines from France and Italy, and the Audi car factory which migrated from Zwickau when the Iron Curtain went up. At least some of the wealth generated is used wisely, for the town spends more money on the upkeep of its historic monuments than anywhere else in Bavaria. For centuries one of

Germany's most redoubtable fortresses, Ingolstadt is compact enough to be seen in a day, and has the benefit of being unspoiled by mass tourism.

The fortifications

The old city snuggles within its medieval horseshoe-shaped **Stadtmauer** on the north bank of the Danube, safely away from the industrial quarters. In the nineteenth century, an additional set of fortifications in a stern Neoclassical style was designed by Leo von Klenze to encase them, and to protect both sides of the bridgehead. Those on the south bank, centred on the **Reduit Tilly**, have been converted into a grandiose park; from here there's a marvellous view of the whole skyline.

Crossing over Konrad-Adenauer-Brücke, the most impressive stretch of the medieval walls lies just to the left; it's made yet more picturesque by the houses which were built directly on to it. This section is pierced by the **Taschenturm** (Pocket Tower), whose tall, whitewashed and gabled silhouette has a fairty-tale look about it, for all that it's perfectly genuine. Even it is eclipsed, however, by the **Kreuztor** which now stands like a pint-sized castle in splendid isolation further north. Nowadays, it seems hard to believe that such a lovingly crafted masterpiece of brickwork was built for purely military purposes.

Beyond, a green belt has been laid out round the huge polygonal fragments of the Neoclassical fortifications. One of these, the **Kavalier Hepp** (Tues–Sat 9am–noon & 1–5pm, Sun 10am–5pm; DM3, free Sun) to the northwest now contains a historical museum whose exhibits range from a Celtic silver hoard via sculptures from the medieval city gates and the teaching stool of Johannes Eck, the Ingolstadt theologian who provided the (none-too-successful) frontline Catholic defence against Luther, to a stuffed horse said to have been King Gustavus Adolphus's mount during the Swedish siege in the Thirty Years' War.

The Neues Schloss

From here, you can continue all the way round the walls to the strongest point of the defences, the **Neues Schloss**, which sits in gleaming white spendour at the far end of the waterfront. The original structure with its distinctive angular towers was built in the fifteenth century during the short period when Ingolstadt was capital of an independent duchy; the imposing battlements were added a hundred years later. Built for the Francophile Duke Ludwig the Bearded, it looks completely un-German, resembling instead a French château. Part of the Schloss now houses the **Bayrisches Armeemuseum** (Tues–Sun 8.45am–4.30pm; DM4), the most comprehensive collection of arms and armour in Germany. On the ground floor, the **Dürnitz**, the great banqueting hall, forms an appropriately grand setting for an outstanding section on the Thirty Years' War. Highlight of the displays upstairs is the booty, including a magnificent golden helmet, captured from the Turks in 1682; here also is the finest room in the building, the **Schöner Saal**, whose vault springs from a graceful central pillar.

The town centre

The pedestrianized shopping streets lie west of the Neues Schloss. Along Hallstrasse, and now very much in the shadow of the huge modern Stadttheater, is the modestly sized **Altes Schloss**, built in the thirteenth century as a second residence for the Landshut dukes. Later prettified by the addition of ornate gables, it was demoted to serving as a granary when the new Schloss was built, but has found a new lease of life as the public library. Further along is the **Altes Rathaus**, created at the end of last century by knocking several old burghers' houses together. Behind rise the massively severe towers of the Gothic **Stadtkirche St Moritz**, whose interior was tarted up in the eighteenth century with extravagant stucco. On Ludwigstrasse, a block to the north, is the **Ickstatthaus**, the most ornate of the town's many Rococo mansions.

From the Stadtkirche, Dollstrasse and Hoher Schulstrasse lead westwards to the **Hohe Schule**, built as a prebendary, but from 1472 until 1800 the main building of the University of Bavaria, one of the most famous in Germany and a leading centre of Counter-Reformation theology. Ingolstadt's academic tradition lay dormant until 1989, when an economics faculty was opened, but several reminders of its pre-eminence survive in this quarter. One of these is the **Alte Anatomie** at the end of Griesbadgasse to the southeast, a dignified, classically inspired Baroque building whose courtyard once again serves as a herb garden. The interior contains the **Deutsches Medizinhistorisches Museum** (Tues–Sun 10am–noon & 2–5pm; DM3, free Sun), which shows the evolution of medical instruments from the ancient Egyptians to the present day.

The Liebfrauenmünster

To the north, and just east of the Kreuztor, is the huge **Liebfrauenmünster**, begun by Duke Ludwig as a sacred counterbalance to the Neues Schloss at the opposite end of town. The unfinished towers, set at startlingly oblique angles, are reminiscent of those of the castle, but otherwise this is a copybook German hall church, the plain brickwork outside brilliantly offset by the sweeping elevation of the whitewashed interior. As work neared completion in the early sixteenth century, the masons created for the six nave chapels the most spectacularly ornate **vaults** in the entire history of European architecture. Here the delicately coloured filigree stonework has been twisted into such shapes as a crown of thorns, a giant insect and great flowering plants, which seem to sprout from the ceiling like huge jewels. The church served as the parish of the University, whose centenary was commemorated by the commissioning of Hans Mielich's **high altar**: look out for the scenes on the reverse, showing cameos of the different faculties at work. On the north side of the ambulatory is the bronze epitaph to Johannes Eck; also of special note are the brilliantly coloured **stained-glass windows** of the east end, made from designs by Dürer and his followers.

The Maria-de-Victoria-Kirche

A very different but equally dazzling church is the **Maria-de-Victoria-Kirche** (Tues–Sun 9am–noon & 1–5/6pm; DM3) immediately to the north on Konviktstrasse, an oratory built by the Asam brothers for the Jesuit-run Marian student congregation. Egid Quirin's simple little hall is little more than a stage-set for Cosmas Damian's colossal **ceiling fresco**, which was executed in just eight weeks. Its subject – a complicated allegory on the mystery of the Incarnation – hardly seems to matter, as you're likely to be completely mesmerized by its illusionistic tricks, in which everything appears to be in correct perspective, no matter what your vantage point. Ask the caretaker to let you see the **monstrance** depicting the Battle of Lepanto, another display of Rococo pyrotechnics, this time by an Augsburg goldsmith.

The Tillyhaus and the Franziskanerkirche

Directly opposite, at the corner of Johannesstrasse, stands the **Tillyhaus**, where Field Marshal Johann Tilly, the Catholic hero of the Thirty Years' War, died in 1632. By then his awesome military reputation was in tatters, his once-invincible troops having been unequal to the challenge posed by the new fighting techniques of the Swedish army. The wounds of which he died were sustained in a vain attempt at preventing the Swedes crossing the Lech in their sweeping advance on Munich, though at least there was the compensation that Ingolstadt's fortifications proved strong enough to withstand the enemy siege. At the end of the street is a square dominated by the

Franziskanerkirche, whose plain architecture is enlivened by a magnificent set of Renaissance and Baroque epitaphs.

Practicalities

Ingolstadt's **Hauptbahnhof**, a junction of the Munich–Nürnberg and Ulm–Regensburg lines, lies 2km south of the old city, to which it's connected by regular buses. The **tourist office** (Mon–Fri 8am–5pm, Sat 9am–noon; ☎0841/305 1098) is in the Altes Rathaus, Rathausplatz 2.

There are a couple of **pensions** fairly close to the Hauptbahnhof: *Bauer*, Hölzlstr. 2 (☎0841/66099 or 67086; ③) is to the northeast, *Eisinger*, Dorfstr. 17a (☎0841/973660; ④) to the southwest. In the Altstadt there are just three **hotels**: *Adler*, Theresienstr. 22 (☎0841/17099 or 35107; ⑤); *Bayerischer Hof*, Münzbergstr. 12 (☎0841/1403; ⑥); and *Rappensberger*, Harderstr. 3 (☎0841/3140; ⑦). The **youth hostel** is close to the Kreuztor at Friedhofstr. 4½ (☎0841/34177; ⍟). **Camping** facilities are available at Auwaldsee in the outskirts (April–Sept only; ☎0841/961 1616); take bus #60.

All the hotels listed above have **restaurants**, though the best place to eat is *Im Stadttheater*, Schlossländle 1. Also of special note is the flagship of the local brewery, *Weissbrauhaus zum Herrnbräu*, Dollstr. 3, a true old Bavarian tavern. Ingolstadt's main **festival** is the *Bürgerfest* on the first or second weekend of July.

Neuburg an der Donau

NEUBURG AN DER DONAU, 22km upstream from Ingolstadt on the rail line to Ulm, makes an enjoyable afternoon's outing or restful overnight stop. It is a rarity for Bavaria: medieval towns are two a penny, but Neuburg is characterized by Renaissance architecture and dreamy cobbled streets that give it the feeling of a forgotten town. Perched on a chalk promontory overlooking the Danube, the town was a strategic trading post in Roman times, but its real moment of glory was in 1505, when it became the capital of the House of Pfalz-Neuburg, a junior branch of the Counts Palatine of Heidelberg.

Throughout the sixteenth century, Neuburg was redesigned and built up into an elegant town with an imposing castle and beautiful Renaissance and Baroque buildings on leafy squares. The **Karlsplatz** in particular is a perfect picture of stylish sixteenth-century design, and the facade of the **Hofkirche** forms a fine base to the square's symmetry. This church was intended as a Protestant answer to the Jesuits' St Michael in Munich, but the ruling family converted back to Catholicism during its construction, so it was finished off in a rather more elaborate manner than originally intended. The interior has wonderfully plain white stucco, with just a lick of gold and sparing use of black veined marble-effect to create a light and harmonious whole.

Neuburg's most significant and dominant building is the **Residenzschloss** (Tues–Sun 10am–5pm; DM4), built between 1530 and 1545 by order of Ottheinrich, the future Elector of the Palatinate, who was later to transform the great Schloss in Heidelberg. The displays concentrate on presenting the history of the duchy of Pfalz-Neuburg, the region's paleolithic origins, and its religious art and garments – a strange combination, but interesting nevertheless.The **Schlosskapelle** is one of the earliest custom-built Protestant churches, adorned with a cycle of frescoes by the Salzburg artist Hans Bocksberger, illustrating the Bible in line with the tenets of the new faith. It's worth strolling in the **Schlossgarten**, where a number of Baroque grottoes, notably the startling blue *Muschelgrotte*, have recently been the subject of a highly successful restoration programme.

Practicalities

Neuburg's **Bahnhof** lies at the southern edge of town. The **tourist office** (May–Oct Mon–Fri 8am–noon & 2–5.30pm, Sat & Sun 10am–noon & 2–5pm; Nov–April Mon–Thurs 8am–noon & 2–4pm, Fri 8am–noon; ☎08431/55240) is at Residenzstr. A65. Here you can ask about rooms in **private houses** (②–③), which are in plentiful supply.

Among the **hotels**, *Kieferl*, Eybstr. 239 (☎08431/2014; ③), is particularly good value, and has the bonus of an excellent restaurant serving wholefood as well as *bürgerlich* cuisine. Other possibilities include *Neuwirt*, Färberstr. 88 (☎08431/2078; ③); *Am Schrannenplatz*, Schrannenplatz C153 (☎08431/67210; ③); and *Bergbauer*, Fünfzehnerstr. 11 (☎08431/47095; ⑤). The **campsite** is at Oskar-Wittmann-Str. 5 (☎08431/9473).

In odd-numbered years, there's a folklore **festival**, the *Schlossfest*, on the last weekend of June and the first weekend of July.

The Five Lakes Region

The **Five Lakes Region** (*Fünf-Seen-Land*) is a popular playground of the people of Munich, and it can easily be explored in day-trips from the city by S-Bahn. Three of the lakes are small and of minor interest, but the **Starnberger See** and **Ammersee**, which both offer boat trips, bear comparison with their Alpine counterparts.

The Starnberger See

Lying just to the southwest of the city and reached by S-Bahn #6, the largest lake of the group, the **Starnberger See**, is predominantly the domain of the city's rich and their weekend villas. The main resort is **STARNBERG** at the northernmost tip; here you'll find the local **tourist office** at Wittelsbacher Str. 9 (Mon–Fri 8am–6pm; July–Sept also Sat 9am–1pm; ☎08151/90600), which will help with accommodation. The most bracing way to explore the lake is by **boat**; *Staatliche Schiffhart Starnberger See* (☎08151/12023) charges DM22.50 for a three-hour round trip, while journeys from one stop to the next cost DM7.

The S-Bahn continues down the west coast as far as its terminus at Tutzing. This is the more commercialized side of the lake, with cafés and restaurants vying for your money; the main public beach is at **Possenhofen**. The eastern shore is lined with private properties and it's not always possible to get at the water, though there are some small public stretches between the villages of Berg, Leoni and Ammerland. The **Schloss** of the first (still a private residence of the Wittelsbachs and not open for visits) was where the ill-starred King Ludwig II was staying at the time of his mysterious death. Just to the south, a small **Votivkapelle**, modelled on the Church of the Holy Sepulchre in Jerusalem, has been erected in his memory.

Another tribute comes in the form of Germany's most popular long-distance footpath, the **King Ludwig Way** (König-Ludwig-Weg), covering the 120km between Starnberg and Füssen. It's easy to follow, being marked by signposts showing a blue K with a crown; although the scenery is magnificent, the terrain is undemanding and is easily covered in a four- or five-day hike.

The Ammersee

The S-Bahn #5 line goes from Munich to the resort of **HERRSCHING** on the **Ammersee**; its three previous stops cover the remaining lakes of the group – Wessling is by the minute lake of the same name; Steinebach is on the west side of the deep blue

Wörthsee; while Seefeld lies on the peaceful Pilsensee. Herrsching is a favourite place to go swimming and sailing and can get very crowded, particularly on summer weekends. There's a footpath along the water's edge to the west, where a few public beaches are slotted in between stretches of private property. The **tourist office** is at Bahnhofsplatz 3 (Mon–Fri 8.30am–noon & 2–5pm, Sat 10am–noon; ☎08152/5227). Boat trips are run by *Staatliche Schiffahrt Ammersee* (☎08143/229); three-hour cruises cost DM22, though there are various cheaper options.

The village of **ANDECHS** sits atop the hill of the same name, Bavaria's "Holy Mountain". There's an attractive if strenuous walking trail from Herrsching; the alternative is to take bus #951 or #956, which continue to the western shore of the Starnberger See. A Gothic **Kloster** was built in the late fourteenth century to celebrate the rediscovery of some relics brought to Andechs from Jerusalem by the local count in 952. Its church is the one you see today, though the interior has been remodelled in Rococo style. An additional enticement for the modern pilgrim is the delicious beer brewed by the monks, a strong dark *Doppelbock* available, with hearty local dishes and homemade cheese, in the *Bräustüberl* attached to the monastery.

Across the lake lies **DIESSEN**, a village whose population includes a sizeable artistic colony, with potters pre-eminent. Here you'll find a **tourist office** at Mühlstr. 4a (Mon–Wed 8am–noon & 2–5pm, Thurs 8am–noon & 2–6pm, Fri 8am–noon; ☎08807/1048), plus a **campsite** (☎08807/7305). On the hill above is an Augustinian **Kloster**, which boasts one of Bavaria's finest Rococo churches: the design is by J.M. Fischer, the high altar by Cuvilliés, the ceiling frescoes by Johann Georg Bergmüller, while among the side altars is a theatrical *Martyrdom of St Sebastian* by Tiepolo.

Landsberg am Lech and the Pfaffenwinkel

A staging-post on the Romantic Road (see p.176), **LANDSBERG** lies less than 40km up the River Lech from Augsburg, and about 55km west of Munich. Like the latter, it was founded by Henry the Lion, and until the Napoleonic period it was Bavaria's westernmost outpost. It later became the site of a jail for high-profile political prisoners, and has the misfortune to have gone down in history as the place where Hitler, imprisoned there following the botched Beer Hall Putsch, dictated to Rudolf Hess the insidious rantings of *Mein Kampf*. This unfortunate connection notwithstanding, it's a highly attractive town with easy access to the pre-Alpine countryside to the south. Known as the **Pfaffenwinkel** (literally, "Clerics' Corner"), this has no major towns, but – as the name suggests – is dotted with religious foundations. Be aware that the public transport network in this area is based primarily on buses, which operate very infrequently at weekends, particularly out-of-season. However, the Pfaffenwinkel is ideal walking country, and the King Ludwig Way (see opposite) cuts all the way through it.

The town

As befits its long status as a border town, Landsberg was equipped with a formidable **Stadtmauer**, and its southern, eastern and western ranges still survive. The most impressive part, situated high above the town centre, is the fifteenth-century **Bayertor** (May–Sept daily 10am–noon & 2–5pm; DM2), a mighty gateway consisting of an outer barbican and a 36-metre-high tower whose outer face is adorned with a monumental carving of the Crucifixion. On a clear day, the Alps can be seen from the top, though much of the Altstadt is out of view.

In spite of being sandwiched among a row of mansions, the **Rathaus** ((May–Oct Mon–Fri 8am–6pm, Sat & Sun 10am–noon & 2–5pm; Nov–April Mon–Wed 8am–noon & 2–5pm, Wed 8am–noon & 2–5pm, Thurs 8am–noon & 2–5.30pm, Fri 8am–12.30pm;

DM2) dominates the Hauptplatz, in large part because of its exuberant stuccowork facade. Together with the decoration of the main **Ratsstube** on the second floor, this was the only major secular commission undertaken by the great Rococo church-builder Dominikus Zimmermann, who did a stint as burgomaster of the town. He also created the **Johanniskirche** a short distance north on Vorderer Anger. Despite the minute size of the site, this is a wonderfully original design, with an oval nave preceding a horseshoe-shaped chancel filled with a theatrical high altar of the Baptism of Christ. The choir of the large Gothic **Stadtpfarrkirche Mariä Himmelfahrt** diagonally opposite contains another work by Zimmermann, a Rosary altar made to shelter a beautiful *Madonna and Child* by the fifteenth-century Ulm sculptor Hans Multscher.

On the left bank of the Lech is the curious **Mutterturm** (Mother Tower; April–Jan Tues–Sun 2–5pm; DM2), built by the Anglo-German artist Hubert von Herkomer as his Landsberg studio. Although now neglected, Herkomer was a leading light of Victorian society; a successful painter, film pioneer, early racing car promoter and occasional composer who was friendly with many of the greatest musicians of the day. The tower contains examples of his graphic work; portraits, landscapes and drawings can be seen in the adjacent **Herkomer-Museum** (same times and ticket), formerly the home of his parents.

Practicalities

Landsberg is now a dead-end terminus for passenger trains; the **Bahnhof** is on the west side of the Lech, not far from the Mutterturm. The **tourist office** is in the Rathaus, Hauptplatz 1 (same hours as above; ☎08191/128246). This is the best source for information about one of the biggest and most colourful **children's festivals** in Germany, the *Ruethenfest*, which takes place over a weekend in July every four years (1999, 2003), and features two big processions plus recreations of military camps, a handicrafts market, street theatre and concerts.

Budget accommodation is in short supply: there are only a few **private rooms** (②–③) plus one small guest house, *Christine*, Galgenweg 4 (☎08191/5210; ④). Otherwise, there are three good hotels to choose from: *Landsberger Hof*, Weilheimer Str. 5 (☎08191/32020; ④); *Gasthof Zum Mohren*, Hauptplatz 148 (☎08191/42210; ⑤); and *Goggl*, Herkomerstr. 19–20 (☎08191/3240; ⑤). There's also a campsite, *Romantik am Lech*, in a woodland setting by the Lech to the south of the Altstadt at Am Pössinger Wald (☎08191/47505). All the hotels listed above have restaurants, though strong competition comes from *Zederbräu*, Hauptplatz 155.

Steingaden

STEINGADEN, another stop on the Romantic Road, can be reached by bus from either Landsberg (this sometimes involves a change at Schongau) or Füssen (see p.196). The little town is centred on the **Welfenmünster**, the church of a former Premonstratensian monastery. It encompasses virtually the entire history of Bavarian ecclesiastical architecture: the exterior is one of the area's rare Romanesque survivors, while the interior was remodelled to celebrate its sixth hundreth anniversary, with refined stuccowork, a showy pulpit, and an outstanding set of ceiling frescoes of the life of the order's founder, St Norbert, by Johann Georg Bergmüller.

There are three **hotels**: *Gasthof Zur Post*, Marktplatz 1 (☎08862/200; ③); *Gasthof Graf*, Schongauer Str. 15 (☎08862/246; ③); and *Gasthof Lindenhof*, Schongauer Str. 35 (☎08862/6011; ④). Each has a **restaurant** serving homely Bavarian fare at moderate prices.

The Wieskirche

Within Steingaden's municipality, albeit tucked away in the countryside 5km southeast, is the **Wieskirche** (Meadow Church), the best-known pilgrimage church in Germany, and a UNESCO World Heritage Site. When the Steingaden monks discarded a statue of the suffering Christ which they formerly carried in their Holy Week processions, a farmer's wife found the figure crying. So many pilgrims flocked to the simple shrine her husband built that the monks asked **Dominikus Zimmermann** to erect a worthy temple for the image. His carefully thought-out design, based on his earlier pilgrimage church in Steinhausen (see p.254), has an almost umbilical relationship with the mountains in the background.

The plain exterior belies the extravagance of the interior, which is crammed with furnishings displaying craftsmanship of the highest class. In a symbolic reference to the contrast between earth and heaven, the plain white pillars are offset by the gold-plated stucco ornamentation of the arches above and the bravura ceiling **fresco** by Johann Baptist Zimmermann (Dominikus's elder brother). Executed in glowing, pastel-like colours, this presents a radiant vision of the afterlife: the resurrected Christ sits on a rainbow in the centre, with the still unoccupied Throne of Judgment and the as yet unopened Gate to Eternity at either end.

Dominikus Zimmermann, a deeply pious man, built a house for himself alongside the church, and lived out his retirement there. Nowadays, it's a restaurant, *Schweiger*, serving marvellous Bavarian cuisine; *Moser*, which is down by the car park, also offers good food. The latter may have **rooms** if you fancy a quiet night in the countryside; a couple of the nearby farmhouses also offer accommodation (①–②). Note that there are only three or four **buses** a day to and from Steingaden, though there's a very pleasant walking trail.

Oberammergau and around

OBERAMMERGAU, the terminus of a branch rail line at the western end of the Upper Bavarian Alps, is world-famous for the **Passion Play** (see box) that the local villagers have been performing since 1634; the next performances will take place in the year 2000. The huge **Passionspielhaus** (May–Oct daily 9.30am–noon & 1–4pm; Nov, Dec & Feb–April Tues–Sat 10am–noon & 1.30–4pm; DM4), custom-built just north of the central axis, Dorfstrasse, in the 1930s to ensure every member of the audience has a good view of the performance, can be visited, along with the backstage museum.

Without the tradition of the play, it's likely that Oberammergau would be stuck in total obscurity, instead of being the tourist trap it has become, crammed with souvenir shops selling examples of the local **woodcarving** to the choking busloads of organized tour parties who roll up every summer. To find out about the historical background to this, visit the **Heimatmuseum** (mid–May to mid–Oct Tues–Sun 2–6pm; rest of year Sat 2–6pm only; DM3) at Dorfstr. 8, which has an especially notable collection of cribs. At the **Pilatushaus** (June–Oct Mon–Fri 1–6pm, Sat 10.30am–12.30pm; free), on Verlegergasse just to the south, you can see the craftsmen at work.

Despite the crowds, Oberammergau does preserve features genuinely characteristic of small Alpine communities. In particular, many of the houses have the traditional **frescoes**, which you can see as either quaint or kitsch. This style of decoration, known as *Lüftlmalerei*, is a uniquely Catholic art, dating from the period of the Counter-Reformation, which successfully fostered an increased religious zeal. Thus the scenes depicted are usually based on biblical stories, making a highly distinctive transfer of a sacred art form to secular buildings. The modest **Pfarrkirche** on Pfarrplatz at the southern end of Dorfstrasse is a typical example of Bavarian Rococo, with a fine set of frescoes by the Augsburg artist, Matthäus Günther.

For the best view of Oberammergau and its surroundings take the cable car (DM13 single, DM19 return) from the eastern end of the village to the **Laberjoch** (1683m).

THE PASSION PLAY

In 1632, **the plague**, whose spread was greatly facilitated by the famines caused by the Thirty Years' War, struck the area around Oberammergau. So many people had died by the following July that the surviving inhabitants gathered and made a pledge that they and their descendants would forever stage a play on the Passion of Jesus if they would be rid of the plague. Even though some were already suffering from the first stages of the disease, there were to be no more deaths from it. In honour of the pledge, the first performance was staged; it has been revived (with few exceptions) every ten years since then, though it was quickly decided to change the year of the performances to the one at the beginning of each decade.

The cast is always exclusively made up of local villagers, who vie for the honour of a role, but with up to 200 players on stage in some scenes, most get a chance to participate, and all the leading roles are now alternated between two actors. Even the props have to be made locally, displaying a shrewd sense for combining piety with business. Performances last five and a half hours, with a two-hour break for lunch, and visitors are forced to move on after two nights. Controversy has long been a feature of the play, and the text has had to be revised for various reasons: the original came to be seen as too bawdy and had to be toned down, while the virulent anti-Semitic stance, which was only recently watered down, was for long a source of protests. In the most recent production, traditionalists were offended by the granting of a key part to a Protestant for the first time ever, and by the choice of a mother-of-two for the role of Mary.

Practicalities

The **tourist office** at Eugen-Papst-Str. 9a (Mon–Fri 8.30am–6pm, Sat 8.30am–noon; ☎08822/1021) can help with finding **private rooms** (①–③). If you want to visit during the next performances of the Passion Play, you should sort out tickets and accommodation well in advance; note that you will only be allowed to stay for two nights.

One of the best-value **hotels** is *Enzianhof*, Ettaler Str. 33 (☎08822/215; ④). There are several slightly more expensive alternatives on Dorfstrasse: *Alte Post* at no. 19 (☎08822/9100; ⑤); *Wolf* at no. 1 (☎08822/3071; ⑤); and *Wittelsbach* at no. 21 (☎08822/1011; ⑥). There's also a **youth hostel** at the southwestern edge of town at Mahlensteinweg 10 (☎08822/4114; ✿).

As usual in resorts of this kind, the best **restaurants** are attached to hotels, and those in *Alte Post* and *Wolf* are as good as any.

Ettal and Schloss Linderhof

ETTAL, 4km down the road, is a little less touristy. It's a small health resort, but is mainly notable for the Benedictine **Kloster**, whose church has a twelve-cornered nave design, based on the Church of the Holy Sepulchre in Jerusalem. The original fourteenth-century structure was rebuilt in the Baroque style by Enrico Zuccalli, embellished with rich stucco decorations. The monastery produces a variety of wonderful fruit liqueurs and brandies, plus some fine beers. A fine hotel with restaurant, *Ludwig der Bayer*, occupies the old monasic guest house at Kaiser-Ludwig-Platz 10–12 (☎08822/6601; ④).

Schloss Linderhof (guided tours daily April–Sept 9am–5.30pm; DM9; Oct–March 10am–4pm; DM7) is one of King Ludwig's more restrained fantasies, and the only one that was actually completed. About 10km west of Ettal, and connected by a regular bus service, it was built as a private residence rather than a statement in royal architecture, and from the garden terraces its creamy white walls and square shape make it look like a sparkling wedding cake. As you enter, it's impossible to miss a large bronze statue of one of Ludwig's heroes, Louis XIV, and, though this was a private retreat, Ludwig still had a reception room with gold-painted carvings, stucco ornamentation and a throne canopy draped in ermine curtains.

However, the top attraction is the delightful **Schlosspark**. The palace forms the axis of a cross design, which is built on the Italian Renaissance model of terraces, cascades and pools rising up in front and behind, while the shorter gardens to the right and left have strictly manicured lawns, hedges and flowerbeds. Initially, it's hard to tell that the surrounding "wild" scenery is actually a clever English garden design that gradually blends into the forests of the mountain beyond. A number of romantic little buildings are dotted around the park, the most remarkable of which is the **Venus-Grotte**. It's supposed to be based on the set from the first act of Wagner's opera *Tannhäuser* and has an illuminated lake with an enormous golden conch floating on it in which the king would sometimes take rides. Equally outrageous is the **Maurischer Kiosk**, a mock-Moorish pavilion in which stands a throne with a backdrop of three huge peacocks crafted out of enamel and coloured glass. Also in the grounds is the *Schlosshotel* (☎08822/3014; ⑥), which offers **rooms** with balconies and a restaurant specializing in game dishes.

Garmisch-Partenkirchen and Mittenwald

GARMISCH-PARTENKIRCHEN, some 19km south of Oberammergau by road, is the most famous resort in the German Alps, partly because it's at the foot of the highest mountain – the **Zugspitze** – and also because it hosted the fourth Winter Olympics back in 1936. The location is marvellous, placed between the gentle Ammer mountains and the imposing peaks of the Wetterstein chain which form the frontier with Austria. During the winter months Garmisch is one of the foremost **skiing** bases, and it has excellent facilities for **skating** and other winter sports too. In summer, mountaineers and **hiking** enthusiasts come to explore the craggy heights, while there are cable cars for the less energetic. What were two separate villages have merged to form one town, but there are still distinct identities, with Garmisch aspiring to ritzy shops and trendy brasseries, while Partenkirchen retains its Alpine village feel with traditional painted houses.

The peaks

From Garmisch, there are two possibilities for ascending the **Zugspitze** (2966m) by public transport; each costs DM40 single, DM72 return in summer, DM34 single, DM59 return in winter. The electric train, the *Zugspitzbahn*, travels westwards to a forest lake, the **Eibsee**. Here you can either continue by the rack rail line, which goes up a winding tunnel carved through the interior of the mountain, or transfer to the *Eibseebahn* cable car. Whereas the latter goes straight to the summit, the former deposits you at the *Hotel Schneefernhaus* (2645m), which commands a huge skiing area. You can then ascend to the summit by the *Gipfelbahn* cable car, or walk via the tunnel to the customs point, the *Zugspitzkamm* (2805m), from where yet another cable car, the *Tiroler Zugspitzbahn*, runs to Ehrwald in Austria. The **views** from the top are all you'd expect, stretching from the Tyrolean High Alps to the Allgäu and the Bavarian lowlands.

Closer to Garmisch, the **Alpspitze** (2628m) is the highest peak in a range popular with serious hikers. In this case, there's no cable car to the summit, though one runs to the nearby **Osterfelderkopf** (2050m) for DM24 single, DM36 return. Three more summits further north, **Kreuzeck** (1652m), **Eckbauer** (1236m) and **Hausberg** (1350m) also have their own (correspondingly less expensive) cable cars, so it's easy enough to devise your own itinerary according to how much walking you want to do. Close to the last-named is the magnificent gorge known as **Partnachklamm** (a DM3 admission is levied throughout most of the day), which can be traversed by a circular path hewn out of the rock. East of Garmisch, the **Wank** (1780m) offers the best view of the basin in which the town is set, as well as a complete panorama of the Wetterstein chain. A cable car goes to the summit for DM18 single, DM26 return.

Practicalities

Garmisch-Partenkirchen's **Bahnhof** is handily placed between the two constituent villages; immediately to its rear is the **Zugspitzbahnhof**, terminus of the mountain rail line. At the latter you can buy passes for most cable cars, something well worth considering if you're planning on doing a lot of hiking here. These are available between June and October inclusive and cost DM64 for adults, DM35 for under-16s for three days; DM105 and DM61 for a week. Three-day winter ski passes for the region cost DM136 (DM90 for under-16s), while a weekly pass will set you back DM277 (DM183). The **tourist office** (Mon–Sat 8am–6pm, Sun 10am–noon; ☎08821/1806) is on Richard-Strauss-Platz, five minutes' walk south of the Bahnhof.

Among the town's **hotels** *Ohlsenhof*, Von-Brug-Str. 18 (☎08821/2168; ③) is a particular bargain. If it's a room with a view you're after, *Berggasthof Panorama*, up from the Wank cable car station at St Anton 3 (☎08821/2515; ⑤) should fit the bill. More centrally located medium-range choices include *Zum Rassen*, Ludwigstr. 45 (☎08821/2089; ⑤); and *Mirabell*, Hindenburgstr. 20 (☎08821/93050; ⑥). There are many enticing luxury options, notably *Posthotel Partenkirchen*, Ludwigstr. 49 (☎08821/51067; ⑦), a marvellous old inn decked out in rustic style; *Reindl's Partenkircher Hof*, Von-Brug-Str. 24 (☎08821/53096; ⑦), which is furnished with antiques, has a swimming pool, fitness room, garden terrace and balconies with panoramic views; and *Grand Hotel Sonnenbichl*, Burgstr. 97 (☎08821/7020; ⑦), which offers similar facilities, though if anything is even grander in style.

Private rooms (①–④), while generally more expensive than elsewhere in the Alps, are still wonderful value. Unfortunately, the **youth hostel**, Jochstr. 10 (☎08821/2980; ⚑; bus #6 or #7 from the Bahnhof) isn't very central. A much friendlier place in the same price range and without an age restriction is the *Naturfreundehaus*, Schalmeiweg 21 (☎08821/4322). There's also a **campsite**, *Zugspitze* (☎08821/3180), ideally placed for the peaks, by the village of Grainau to the west.

Mittenwald

Just 20km southeast of Garmisch by road or rail, **MITTENWALD** could hardly be more different. Goethe said in 1786 that Mittenwald was like a "living picture book", and so it remains. A large village with traditional frescoes on many houses, it still feels like a community and not just a resort. This is reflected in the **Pfarrkirche St-Peter-und-Paul**, which has beautifully carved seats and each family's nameplate attached to their special section on the benches. The statue outside honours **Mathias Klotz**, who brought the highly specialized craft of violin-making to Mittenwald in the seventeenth century and saved the village from being an impoverished backwater. Since then local violin-makers have achieved international fame and examples of some of their finest work can be seen in the little doll's house of a museum, the **Geigenbaumuseum** (May–Oct Mon–Fri 10–11.45am & 2–4.45pm, Sat & Sun 10–11.45am; DM2.50) in the Ballenhausgasse. Not far away, on Im Gries, stand the oldest Mittenwald houses, with faded frescoes decorating their frontages.

Walks around town

Towering above Mittenwald is the **Karwendl** (2244m), one of the most popular climbs in Germany. The view from the top is exhilarating; a cable car will take you up for DM17 single, DM28 return. There are plenty of enticing but less demanding walks in the Isar valley below, including the **Leutaschklamm** (daily 9.30am–5.30pm; DM2) 2km south of Mittenwald. Though technically in Austria, this dramatic narrow gorge is inaccessible from that side of the border. To the west of town, two small lakes, the **Lautersee** and the **Ferchensee**, stand in the shadow of the mighty Wetterstein mountains; there are boats for rent and a good country *Gasthof* at each. The path from Mittenwald, which starts just beyond the Kurpark, passes via a pretty waterfall, the **Laintalschlucht**.

Practicalities

The **tourist office** is located at Dammkarstr. 3 (Mon–Sat 9am–5pm; ☎08823/33981). There are many good-value **guest houses**, such as *Bergfrühling*, Dammkarstr. 12 (☎08823/8089; ③); *Franziska*, Innsbrucker Str. 24 (☎08823/5051; ④); and *Somnenbichl*, Klausnerweg 32 (☎08823/92230; ⑤), the last of which is the place for a view. **Hotels** in the town centre include *Alpenrose*, Obermarkt 1 (☎08823/505557; ⑥); and *Post*, Karwendelstr. 14 (☎08823/1094; ⑥). For an isolated setting, with the bonus of wonderful panoramas, there's *Berggasthof Gröblalm* (☎08823/9110; ⑥), 2km north. The **youth hostel** at Buckelwiesen 7 (☎08823/1701; ❸) is an hour's walk from the Bahnhof, so isn't a very practical option. However, the tourist office can fix you up with a room in a **private house** (①–③).The nearest **campsite** *Am Isarhorn*(☎08823/5216) is 3km north, on the road to Garmisch and open all year. The three hotels mentioned above all have good **restaurants**. *Postkeller*, Innsbrucker Str. 13 is also recommendable, while *Arnspitze*, Innsbrucker Str. 68, is the best and most expensive in town.

The Tölzer Land

To the north of Mittenwald, the **Tölzer Land** offers altogether gentler scenery. Nonetheless, the area embraces two major lakes – the **Walchensee** and the **Kochelsee** – as well as the plush spa town of **Bad Tölz** on the River Isar. It also has a rich folklore tradition of riflemen's festivals and costumed parades.

The Walchensee

Of the Tölzer Land's two lakes, the **Walchensee**, some 25km southwest of Bad Tölz, and 19km north of Mittenwald, is by far the more dramatic. Its depth is unknown and the water is so cold in the lower reaches that the many trees fallen from the mountainous shores haven't been able to sink completely; instead they've formed an impenetrable false bottom to the lake. Many people believe that that the Nazis dumped their hoarded treasures here in the last days of the war. Plenty of divers have tried their luck and some have died, tangled in the branches.

This is a good place to come if you're into **boats** and **windsurfing**, since it's never as crowded as the lowland lakes, and is cheaper too. A popular tour around here is the two-hour walk from Urfeld at the northern tip of the lake to the summit of the **Herzogstand** (1731m). From here you can see both the region's lakes plus the snow-capped Austrian peaks to the south and the Bavarian plateau to the north. Alternatively, take the cable car from the village of Walchensee on the western shore (DM8 single, DM13 return). You won't have trouble finding a **hotel** here, and there's also a **campsite** in Walchensee (☎08858/237) and a **youth hostel** at Mittenwalder Str. 17 (☎08851/230; ❸) in Urfeld.

The Kochelsee

A wonderful twisting nine-kilometre-long road links Urfeld with the **Kochelsee**. This lake combines lowland and highland attractions: to the north lies marshland while the Benediktenwand, the first slopes in the Alpine chain, rise immediately from its southern shore. The shoreline has an agreeably empty feel to it, but a good deal of the immediate surrounding area is flat and rather dull. The village of **KOCHEL** on the northeastern side is the largest settlement; it's the terminus of a branch rail line which links up with the Munich S-Bahn network at Tutzing on the Starnberger See.

The Expressionist painter **Franz Marc** lived around here from 1908 until 1916, when he died in World War I at the age of 36. Unlike his friends in the *Blaue Reiter* group such as Kandinsy and Macke, he preferred country life, and his pictures of horses and other animals are his most famous works. The **Franz-Marc-Museum** at Herzogstandweg 43 (April–Oct Tues–Sun 2–6pm; DM3.50) contains a representative collection of his work, comprising about a hundred paintings, as well as examples of other members of *Der Blaue Reiter*.

Kochel's **tourist office** is at Kalmbachstr. 11 (☎08851/338), and **cruises** are run between June and September by *Motorschiffahrt Kochelsee* (☎08851/416). Accommodation possibilities include a **youth hostel** at Badstr. 2 (☎08851/5296; ✿) and the **campsites** *Kesselberg* (☎08851/464) and *Renken* (☎08851/5776), as well as a vast number of **hotels**; the most enticing are *Zur Post*, Schmied-von-Kochel-Platz 6 (☎08851/1526; ⑤); and *Seehotel Grauer Bär*, Mittenwalder Str. 82–6 (☎08851/861; ⑥), both of which have **restaurants**.

The Tegernsee

The **Tegernsee**, some 15km east of Bad Tölz, is among the most beautiful lakes in Bavaria. It has long been a favourite with the rich, who have built weekend homes along its privately owned sections, and a couple of the leading Alpine resorts can be found on its banks. To the east and southeast lies countryside that is far less well known, including two more lakes and the most isolated section of the Bavarian Alps.

Tegernsee

The little town of **TEGERNSEE** is on the east bank of the lake, at the end of the *Tegernseebahn*, a privately owned railway (DM4 single, DM7, rail passes not valid) which runs from Schaftlach on the main line to Munich. By the waterside towards the southern end of the resort is the former Benedictine **Kloster**, which was founded in 746 and flourished for over a millennium. A major centre for manuscript illumination and calligraphy, it once had a library considered superior to that of the Vatican. Following the Napoleonic secularization, Leo von Klenze converted the monastic buildings into a summertime **Schloss** for the Bavarian kings. He also added a twin-towered facade to the Baroque **Klosterkirche**, whose main body was designed by Enrico Zuccalli and frescoed by Hans Georg Asam.

The **tourist office** is in the *Haus des Gastes*, Hauptstr. 2 (Mon–Fri 8am–6pm, Sat & Sun 9am–noon & 3–5pm; ☎08022/180140). Here you can pick up a list of **private rooms** and **guest houses** (①–④). There are several lakeside **hotels**, including *Fischerstüberl am See*, Seestr. 51 (☎08022/4672; ④); and *Guggemos*, Hauptstr. 23 (☎08022/3915; ⑤). *Leeberghof*, on a hillside to the south of town at Ellingerstr. 10 (☎08022/3966; ⑧) only has three bedrooms, but also has a superb restaurant with a panorama terrace. Tegernsee's top address is *Bayern*, uphill from the Bahnhof in the north of town at Neureuthstr. 23 (☎08022/1820; ⑧).

The north wing of the Schloss contains the *Bräustüberl* of the local **brewery**, the *Herzogliches Bayerisches Brauhaus*, which is still owned by the Wittelsbach family. This is an extraordinary sight in the evening, when it's crammed full of local farmers trying to drink each other under the table. Only basic snacks are served there; for a full meal and a quieter atmosphere, go instead to the adjacent cellar **restaurant**, the *Herzoglicher Schlosskeller*. Alternative places to eat can be found in all the hotels listed above. **Boat trips** around the southern part of the lake are run by *Staatliche Schiffahrt Tegernsee* (☎08022/4760); an hour-long cruise costs DM12.50.

Rottach-Egern

At the southern end of the lake, reached by bus or boat (DM4) from Tegernsee, is the double village of **ROTTACH-EGERN**. From there, you can take a cable car (DM11 single, DM19 return) up the **Wallberg** (1722m) for a grandstand view over the lake and the surrounding hills. There's a pleasant terrace **restaurant**, *Alpenwildpark*, at the valley station. Rottach-Egern has a few reasonably priced **hotels**, including *Reuther*, Salitererweg 6 (☎08022/24024; ⑤); and *Café Sonnenhof*, Sonnenmoosstr. 20 (☎08022/5812; ⑥). However, no matter how incongruous it may seem in this country setting, it's best known as a hangout of the chic, who favour such super-luxury establishments as *Park-Hotel Egerner Hof*, Aribostr. 19 (☎08022/6660; ⑨); and *Bachmair am See*, Seestr. 47 (☎08022/2720; ⑨); the latter is one of the most expensive hotels in Bavaria, and comes complete with a high-fashion boutique.

The Chiemsee and Chiemgau

The **Chiemgau** is a large Alpine and pre-Alpine region, stretching eastwards from the industrial town of Rosenheim, a major railway junction, all the way to the border with Austria along the River Salzach. At its western edge is the **Chiemsee**, Bavaria's largest lake, which is usually regarded as a separate region in its own right.

Prien

The Chiemsee's main resort, well placed for visiting all the local beauty spots, is **PRIEN**, at the southwestern edge of the lake: it's easily accessible, as it lies on the main Munich–Salzburg rail line. In the town centre, set back 1.5km from the lake, is the Baroque **Pfarrkirche Mariä Himmelfahrt**, which has a spectacular illusionist ceiling **fresco** by Johann Baptist Zimmermann depicting the Christian naval victory over the Turks at the Battle of Lepanto. Though it's a pleasant enough walk down Seestrasse to the harbour district of **Stock**, it's far more fun to take the **narrow-gauge railway**, the *Chiemseebahn* (Easter–Sept only; DM3 single, DM5 return), which has been running since 1887 from its own little terminal alongside the Bahnhof, and is pulled by a steam engine at weekends and on public holidays. Stock is the hub of the watersports activities and of the **ferry** connections to the islands and the other resorts on the lake run by the *Chiemseeschiffahrt* (☎08051/6090).

The **tourist office** is in the *Kurverwaltung* at Alte Rathausstr. 11 (Mon–Fri 8.30am–6pm, Sat 9am–noon; ☎08051/69050). **Private houses** (①–④) with rooms to let can be found all over town; otherwise, the main concentration of accommodation is in and around Stock. Among the **guest houses** here are *Neuer*, Seestr. 104 (☎08051/2410; ⑤); and *Drexler*, Seestr. 95 (☎08051/4802; ⑤); **hotels** include *Seehotel Feldhütter*, Seestr. 101 (☎08051/4321; ⑥); *Luitpold am See*, Seestr. 110 (☎08051/609100; ⑥); and *Reinhart*, Seestr. 117 (☎08051/6940; ⑥). There are a few other hotels in the town centre, such as

Lindenhof, Alte Rathausstr. 24 (☎08051/1525; ④); and *Bayerischer Hof*, Bernauer Str. 3 (☎08051/6030; ⑦). Just west of Stock and north of Seestrasse, at Carl-Braun-Str. 46 (☎08051/2972; ⓐ), is one of the local **youth hostels**; the other, reachable by bus, is by the moor lakes in the nature reserve to the north, in the hamlet of Hemhof (Haus 84; ☎08053/509; ⓐ). Two of the lake's many **campsites** are at the extreme southern edge of Prien: *Hofbauer* (☎08051/4136) is off the main road out of town, while *Harras* (☎08051/2515) is by the lakeside. All the hotels listed above have **restaurants**; another good place to eat and drink is *Weissbräu-Bräustuben*, Höhenbergstr. 6.

The Chiemsee islands

Just a few minutes by boat (DM10 return) from Prien is the Chiemsee's largest island, **Herreninsel**, site of King Ludwig II's final monument to glorious absolutism and isolation: **Schloss Herrenchiemsee** (guided tours April–Sept daily 9am–5pm; Oct–March 10am–4pm; DM7). After saving the island – previously occupied by a monastery – from deforestation, Ludwig II set about building a complete replica of Versailles. Funds ran out in 1885 with only the central section – including a faithful copy of the Hall of the Mirrors – complete. For all the money squandered, the king only ever lived there for one week. The guided tours through the state apartments are very rushed, whereas you can see the **König-Ludwig-II-Museum** (same times; DM4, or DM9 combined ticket) at leisure. This contains a fascinating collection of Ludwig memorabilia, including portraits, photographs, his christening and coronation robes, plans for unexecuted buildings and model backdrops for Wagner's operas. Herreninsel itself is a great place for walks, and by the landing stage there's a beer garden with a good view of the lake.

The neighbouring **Fraueninsel** (DM12 return from Prien, which allows the journey to be broken at Herreninsel) is a much smaller island, built up with holiday homes, restaurants, cafés and an ancient, still-functioning Benedictine nunnery – hence the name. Its **Klosterkirche** still preserves its original Romanesque form save for the fancy late Gothic vault and the onion dome crowning the freestanding belfry. An even rarer survival is the Carolingian gatehouse or **Torhalle** (late May to early Oct daily 11am–6pm; DM3), which features an upstairs chapel with ninth-century frescoes; reproductions of the church's Romanesque ceiling paintings – now concealed above the vaulting – are also on display.

Aschau and Ruhpolding

A small railway, the *Chiemgaubahn*, runs from Prien up towards the Chiemgau Alps. It terminates at the mountain resort of **ASCHAU**, directly below the **Kampenwand** (1669m), one of the most popular hiking areas in the Alps. From the northern end of the village, a cable car (DM14 single, DM22 return) ascends to the summit; otherwise, it's a walk of about three and a half hours. Just east of the cable car station, the immense **Schloss Hohenaschau** (guided tours April & Oct Thurs at 9.30am, 10.30am & 11.30am; May–Sept Tues–Fri at same times; DM3) rises above a hilltop. The interior includes a fine Baroque **Schlosskapelle** and the **Preysingsaal**, an extraordinary reception room covered in white stuccowork, with gigantic statues of the local dynasty's ancestors.

Aschau's **tourist office** is in the *Kurverwaltung*, Kampenwandstr. 38 (May–Sept Mon–Fri 8am–noon & 2–6pm, Sat 9am–noon, Sun 10am–noon; Oct–April Mon–Fri 8am–noon & 1.30–5pm; ☎08052/904937). There are plenty of **private rooms** (①–③) and **hotels**; *Alpengasthof Brucker*, Schlossbergstr. 12 (☎08052/4987; ③) is a particular bargain, and also has a good restaurant. *Residenz Heinz Winkler*, Kirchplatz 1 (☎08052/17990; ⑨), a supremely elegant modern hotel within a historic coaching inn, is one of the top gourmet addresses in the whole of Germany.

East of Aschau are several more resorts, of which the most attractive is **RUH-POLDING**, at the end of a branch rail line from the junction of Traunstein. Following the Weisse Traun 3km upstream brings you to the **Taubensee**, a secluded lake which is the valley station of the cable car (DM15 single, DM25 return) up the **Rauschberg** (1645m). The summit commands a marvellous view over the Chiemgau Alps, south into Austria and north to the Chiemsee. Ruhpolding's **tourist office** is in the *Kurverwaltung*, Hauptstr. 60 (Mon–Fri 8am–noon & 2–6pm; Easter–Sept also Sat 9am–noon; ☎08663/9687), and the town is choc-a-bloc with **private houses** and **guesthouses** (①–④), and good **hotels**.

Bad Reichenhall

At the far eastern end of the Chiemgau, just 19km from Salzburg, the old salt-producing town of **BAD REICHENHALL** lies in a majestic mountain-framed setting in the valley of the River Saalach. Its saline springs are the most concentrated in Europe, with a salt content of 24 percent. Their curative properties led to its nineteenth-century development into one of the country's classiest spas – a status it still holds – and the town is full of grand villas from this period.

The old saltworks, the **Alte Saline** (guided tours April–Oct daily 10–11.30am & 2–4pm; Nov–March Tues & Thurs 2–4pm; DM7), is at the southern edge of the town centre. It was established in the sixteenth century, but remodelled in the 1830s by King Ludwig I according to the mock-medieval tastes then in vogue. All the equipment – including a pair of water wheels 13 metres in diameter and 15 tonnes in weight – is in good working order and can be seen in action, but production has long since moved to larger and more practical premises a few blocks away.

Just to the north the elegant Ludwigstrasse, the town's main street, is lined with exclusive shops and spa hotels. At its far end is the **Kurpark**, a carefully tended park with mountain views and the principal spa buildings, the **Kurhaus** and the **Trinkhalle**; the latter regularly hosts concerts by the forty-strong *Philharmonisches Orchester*, the largest spa orchestra in Germany. The focal point of the park is the huge wooden **Gradierwerk**, whose function is to ensure that the air is kept as fresh and healthy as possible. Still further north, beyond Karlspark, is the basilica of **St Zeno**, built in the early thirteenth century in the Lombard Romanesque style. Although remodelled down the centuries, it preserves some of its original features, including the peaceful cloisters and the magnificent, very Italianate coloured-marble entrance portal complete with crouching lions and a tympanum showing the Madonna and Child adored by the church's patron and Saint Rupert, the Irish monk who became the first Bishop of Salzburg.

Walks around town

Just south of the town centre, in the district of Kirchberg on the opposite side of the Saalach, is the valley station for the cable car (DM17 single, DM27 return) to the **Predigtstuhl** (1613m). From the upper station, follow the signs to the *Aussichtskanzel* belvedere, which gives a fine northwards view. For more extensive panoramas of the region, take the hiking trail to the nearby summits of **Hochschlegel** (1688m), **Karkopf** (1738m) and **Dreisesselberg** (1680m); a round trip will last about three hours.

Immediately north of Bad Reichenhall is a small massif whose main peak is **Hochstaufen** (1771m). The direct way up is not for the faint-hearted, as it involves ascents by fixed ladders, but there's also a normal path which swings round towards the summit from the west. For gentler walks, take bus #2 4km west to its terminus at **Thumsee**, a pretty little lake circumnavigated by a path. It has a couple of country *Gaststätten*, while at the roadside immediately to the east is an even smaller and equally picturesque stretch of water, the **Seerosen-Anlage**.

Practicalities

Bad Reichenhall's **Hauptbahnhof** lies west of St Zeno on the main outer axis. A second station, **Bahnhof Kirchberg**, is at the extreme southern end of town, on the opposite side of the river from the cable car. The **tourist office** is just to the south of the Hauptbahnhof, in the *Kurgastzentrum* at Wittelsbacherstr. 15 (Mon–Fri 8am–5.30pm, Sat 9am–noon; ☎08651/3003).

There are plenty of rooms in **private houses** and **guesthouses** (①–③); among the cheapest, a short walk north of St Zeno, are *Haus Rachl*, Salzburger Str. 44 (☎08651/3641; ①); and *Landhaus Kirchholz*, Salzburger Str. 44c (☎08651/5582; ①). The town has **hotels** to suit all tastes: the environmentally conscious *Hansi am Kurpark*, Rinckstr. 3 (☎08651/98310; ⑤) occupies a town centre villa, and has a vegetarian restaurant for guests; *Hofwirt*, Salzburger Str. 21 (☎08651/98380; ⑤) is a renovated sixteenth-century inn; while *Bürgerbräu*, Waaggasse 2 (☎08651/6089; ⑦) is the grand *Wirtshaus* of the local brewery. The two leading spa hotels are *Parkhotel Luisenbad*, Ludwigstr. 33 (☎08651/6040; ⑨); and the *Axelmannstein*, Salzburger Str. 2–6 (☎08651/7770; ⑨). There's a **campsite** (☎08651/2134; April–Oct only) at the north end of town, by the Saalach. The hotels above all have excellent **restaurants**, though the top gourmet address is *Kirchberg-Schlössl*, Thumseestr. 11. Among the many fine **cafés**, pride of place goes to *Café Reber*, Ludwigstr. 10, whose home-made chocolates, sold in the adjoining shop, are among the best known in Germany.

The Berchtesgadener Land

Almost entirely surrounded by mountains, the area south of Bad Reichenhall, the **Berchtesgadener Land**, gives the impression of being a separate little country. In fact this is exactly what it used to be. For centuries it was one of the smallest states in the Holy Roman Empire, ruled by an Augustinian prior. There's a magical atmosphere here, especially in the mornings, when mists rise from the lakes and swirl around lush valleys and rocky mountainsides. Not surprisingly the area is steeped in legends, often featuring the spiky peaks of the **Watzmann** (2713m), Germany's second highest mountain. A popular one has it that they're really the family of a tyrant king who ruled so mercilessly that God punished its members by turning them to stone. The entire southern half of the region has been declared the **Berchtesgaden National Park**, and is thus under stricter environmental protection than any other part of the Bavarian Alps.

Berchtesgaden

The town of **BERCHTESGADEN** itself is 18km from Bad Reichenhall by rail or by either of two magnificent scenic roads, both of which are serviced by bus. At its heart is an attractive triangular square dominated by the **Schloss** (May–Sept 10am–1pm & 2–5pm, closed Sat; Oct–April Mon–Fri 10am–1pm & 2–5pm; DM7), which was originally the Augustinian priory. Following the Napoleonic secularization, when Berchtesgaden was incorporated into Bavaria, the complex was transformed into a sumptuous royal residence. After World War I, the deposed King Ludwig III fled here, and it remains the property of the family. Inside you can see the art treasures collected by his son, Crown Prince Ruprecht – medieval religious wood carvings, sixteenth- and seventeenth-century Italian furniture, and a fearsome collection of weaponry. Some parts of the medieval architecture still survive, notably the Romanesque cloister with its beautiful columns, and the graceful Gothic dormitory. Alongside the Schloss is the **Stiftskirche**, another Romanesque and Gothic mix, with its elaborate choir stalls.

In the north of town, a twenty-minute walk from the centre along the valley of the Berchtesgadener Ache, is the salt mine or **Salzbergwerk** (guided tours, lasting 90min,

May 1–Oct 15 daily 8.30am–5pm; Oct 16–April 30 Mon–Sat 12.30–3.30pm; DM20), which has been the region's source of wealth since 1515. Donning the traditional protective clothing (don't wear a skirt), you're taken deep into the mountain astride a wooden train. Once underground, the tour passes all the machinery and processes of salt-mining in disused shafts connected by wooden shoots, which everyone descends in groups, rather like at the fairground. There follows a raft trip across an underground salt lake, a ride back up towards the surface in the miners' elevator, before a final train journey to the exit. It's all great fun, so don't be deterred by the high entrance cost and the inevitable commercial trappings of the place. Be sure to arrive early, or else be prepared to queue.

Practicalities

Berchtesgaden's **Bahnhof** and **bus station** are at the southern end of town. The regional **tourist office** for the Berchtesgadener Land is directly opposite, in the *Kurdirektion* at Königsseer Str. 2 (late June to mid-Oct Mon–Fri 8am–6pm, Sat 8am–5pm, Sun 9am–3pm; rest of year Mon–Fri 8am–5pm, Sat 9am–noon; ☎08652/9670). In the same building, there's an information point on *Berchtesgaden Mini Bus Tours* (☎08652/64971), which offers a variety of English-language trips, including a detailed exploration of the nearby Nazi sites. An **information centre** on the Berchtesgaden National Park is in the heart of town at Franziskanerplatz 7 (Mon-Sat 9am-5pm; ☎08652/64343).

There are plenty of remarkably good value **guest houses**. The very friendly *Haus am Hang*, Göllsteinbichl 3 (☎08652/4359; ①) has bedrooms with balconies offering grandstand views of the surrounding mountains. Other inexpensive possibilities are *Hansererhäusl*, Hansererweg 8 (☎08652/2523; ②); *Gästehaus Alpina*, Ramsauer Str. 6 (☎08652/2517; ③); and *Haus Achental*, Ramsauer Str. 4 (☎08652/4549; ③). **Hotels** include *Watzmann*, Franziskanerplatz 2 (☎08652/2055; ③); *Vier Jahreszeiten*, Maximilianstr. 20 (☎08652/5026; ⑥); and *Fischer*, Königsseer Str. 51 (☎08652/9550; ⑦). The top address is *Geiger*, set in its own park at the western edge of town at Berchtesgadener Str. 103-115 (☎08652/9653; ⑦). All these hotels have **restaurants**, though there are plenty of other recommendable places to eat and drink. In the centre, *Neuhaus*, Marktplatz 1, is a good traditional *Gaststätte*, while *Da Noi*, Kälbersteinstr. 4, is an Italian restaurant in a villa built for King Maximilian II. On the way to the Salzbergwerk, at Bräuhausstr. 13, the *Bräustübl* of the adjoining brewery, the *Hofbräuhaus Berchtesgaden*, serves hearty Bavarian fare.

The only official **youth hostel** is in the village of Strub, 2.5km west of Berchtesgaden on the road to Ramsau, at Gebirgsjägerstr. 52 (☎08652/2190; **⑧**). There are several **campsites** in the region, the nearest to town being *Allweglehen* (☎08652/2396) in Untersalzberg.

The Königssee

The focal point of the Berchtesgaden National Park is the **Königssee**, Germany's highest lake, which lies 5km south of town and can be reached by bus. This bends around the foot of the Watzmann, rather like a Norwegian fjord, and the surrounding rock faces rise steeply and dramatically straight from the water. The northern tip of the lake, which is outside the National Park, is crammed with cafés, restaurants and snack bars; to escape the crowds, follow the marked path to the *Malerwinkel* belvedere for an overall view. For a far more extensive panorama of the lake and the surrounding peaks, take the cable car up the **Jenner** (1874m); this costs DM24 single, DM31 return. This summit is also a useful starting point for an extended hike in the mountains.

Ferries, run by *Motorschiffahrt Königssee*, Seestr. 55 (☎08652/4026), make round trips to the far end of the Königssee and back. Although likewise rather expensive at

DM21.50 return, it's money well spent; the boats have been electric-powered since 1909, so the deep green waters are refreshingly clean and healthy. The boats stop at the lakeside church of **St Bartholomä**, whose appearance is familiar from its pictures in all the tourist brochures to the region. Romanesque by origin, it was remodelled in Baroque at the end of the seventeenth century by the addition of the projecting apses and onion-domed towers. Alongside is the former **Jagdschloss** of the Bavarian kings, which was converted into a restaurant almost immediately after the fall of the monarchy. There are some wonderful mountain hikes to be made from St Bartholomä; another good starting point is **Salet** at the far end of the Königssee, the only other place where the boats make a scheduled stop. This lies just a few minutes' walk from another, much smaller lake, the **Obersee**.

Obersalzberg

High above Berchtesgaden to the east is the scattered village of **OBERSALZBERG**, which can be reached from the town by cable car (DM7 single, DM11 return), or by a steep winding road. Hitler rented a home here which was later enlarged into the **Berghof**, a stately retreat where he could meet foreign dignitaries. With a final dramatic sweep of steps, its setting was expressly designed to awe visitors. Here, in 1938, British Prime Minister Neville Chamberlain journeyed to dissuade Hitler from attacking Czechoslovakia, the first in a series of meetings that ended with Chamberlain returning from Munich clutching the infamous piece of paper that would ensure "peace in our time" at the expense of Czechoslovakia. "He seemed a nice old man," smirked Hitler, "so I thought I would give him my autograph." Today the remains of the Berghof are almost entirely overgrown; what was left after wartime bombing was blown up by US troops in 1952 to avoid its becoming an object of pilgrimage for future Nazi generations. The only intact part of the complex is a **hotel**, *Zum Türken*, Hintereck 2 (☎08652/2428; ⑤), which pre-dated Hitler's appropriation of the site, and was afterwards returned to its rightful owners. Underneath it is the Nazi-era **Bunker** (daily 9am–5.30pm; DM5).

One of the very few legacies of the Third Reich still looked upon with a large amount of pride is the 6.5-kilometre-long **Kehlsteinstrasse**, which rises from Obersalzberg in a series of curves before making a bold ascent up the northwest side of the **Kehlstein** (1834m). The road – generally considered the most spectacular in the country – is impassable because of snow for most of the year and permanently closed to normal traffic, but regular local buses (DM20 return) make the ascent from the Hintereck stop between early May and mid-October. From the bus terminus, there's a long tunnel through the mountain to a lift (included in the ticket price), which covers the final 124m to the summit. Here is the **Kehlsteinhaus**, nowadays a restaurant, but originally Hitler's tea house, which became known as the "Eagle's Nest". The views across the Alps are stunning, and there's an enjoyable short trail round the summit which leads to very different vantage points, one offering a close-range perspective of the mighty **Hoher Göll** (2522m) to the southeast.

Another magnificent road from Obersalzberg, this time one on which you can take your own transport, is the 21-kilometre-long **Rossfeld-Höhen-Ringstrasse**. This circular route passes through glacier country below the Hoher Göll, climbing to a height of 1604 metres, then for a time hugs the Austrian frontier, before making a return loop to Obersalzberg through the wooded Oberau valley. The bus journey costs DM11.30 return; private cars are charged a DM10 toll.

Elsewhere in the Berchtesgadener Land

Two of the finest yet least demanding walks in the region are along gorges reachable from Berchtesgaden in just a few minutes by bus. The larger and more dramatic is the **Almbachklamm** (DM4 admission levied throughout most of the day) 6km to the northeast, just off the road to Marktschellenberg. At the entrance to the gorge is the **Kugelmühle**, a mill for grinding marble which has been in operation since the seventeenth century.

The **Wimbachklamm** (DM2 admission), a similar distance to the southwest, has the advantage of being a jumping-off point for various longer hikes in the region. It's certainly well worth continuing as far as the refreshment hut known as the *Wimbachschloss*, as the path passes through a dramatic rocky valley, where the Wimbach follows an underground course. The northern end of the Wimbachklamm is the starting point for the main **trail up the Watzmann**. After 3–4 hours of walking, there's the *Watzmannhaus* refuge (☎08652/1310) at 1930m, where you can break the journey for the night; note that the final push to the summit requires mountaineering skills and has claimed many lives.

Some 3km west of the Wimbachklamm is the small resort of **RAMSAU**, the most popular base after Berchtesgaden for exploring the region. Continuing westwards through the enchanted forest of the **Zauberwald** brings you to the **Hintersee**, a beautiful lake commanding views towards the rugged precipices of the **Reiteralpe** and the icy blue **Hochkalter** (2608m), the most northerly glacier in the Alps.

The Inn-Salzachgau

The **Inn-Salzachgau** is the name given to the triangular area north of the Alps whose western and eastern boundaries are defined respectively by the mighty River Inn and its tributary, the Salzach. Inevitably, the landscapes of this rich farming country can't compete with those further south, but it's an unspoiled area preserving several fine old towns which well merit a detour from the established tourist circuits.

Wasserburg am Inn

The region's gateway is **WASSERBURG**, dramatically set on a promontory on a loop of the River Inn, 55km east of Munich. In the fifteenth and sixteenth centuries, the town became prosperous through shipping and its position on key salt trade routes, but it fell into decay, never to recover. Today, it's a sleepy, somewhat dowdy little place of narrow streets and crooked medieval houses whose vaguely Italianate appearance is a direct consequence of the old trading links. You'll get the best **views**, showing the buildings rising abruptly from the Inn, by crossing over the river and walking uphill to the *Schöne Aussicht* belvedere.

Heart of the town is Marienplatz, dominated by the tall step gables of the **Rathaus** (guided tours Tues–Fri 10am, 11am, 2pm, 3pm & 4pm, Sat & Sun 10am & 11am; DM1.50), whose first-floor **Ratssaal** is decorated with richly carved woodwork and painted panels. The disparate assortment of houses which complete the square makes a picturesque group, with arcades and oriels prominent; they range from the old toll-house, the **Altes Mauthaus**, which is Gothic with a Renaissance facade, to the fripperies of the **Kernhaus**, a Rococo patrician mansion designed by Johann Baptist Zimmermann. On the nearby Kirchplatz rises the parish church of **St Jakob**, whose nave is by Hans von Burghausen, an inspired Gothic architect who left a profound mark on the eastern regions of Bavaria. The chancel and tower were added later in the fifteenth century and show a somewhat abrupt change in building materials from brick to stone. Inside, the highlight of the furnishings is the elaborate late Renaissance pulpit.

Practicalities

Wasserburg's **Bahnhof**, on the Inn valley rail line linking the junctions of Mühldorf and Rosenheim, is 5km west of the town centre, to which it's connected by a regular bus service. The **tourist office** in the Rathaus (Mon–Fri 9am–12.30pm; ☎08071/10522) can supply a list of **private houses** (①–②) with rooms to let. There are three central **hotels**: *Gasthof Hubertwirt*, on the south side of the Inn at Salzburger Str. 25 (☎08071/7433; ③); *Paulaner-Stuben*, in the aforementioned Kernhaus, Marienplatz 9 (☎08071/3903; ④); and *Fletzinger*, diagonally opposite at Fletzingergasse 1 (☎08071/90890; ⑥). All of these have **restaurants**; other good places to eat are *Herrenhaus*, occupying a fine Gothic mansion at Herrengasse 17, and *Weisses Rössl*, Herrengasse 1, which does bargain lunches.

Cruises on the Inn (☎08071/4793) depart daily at 2.15pm in summer; there are occasional off-season sailings as well.

Altötting

At Mühldorf, the rail line splits, with one branch line continuing eastwards to **ALTÖTTING**. This small town of spires and domes is one of the most venerable in Germany, having been a favourite residence of both the Carolingian emperors and the early Bavarian dukes, but for the past five hundred years it has chiefly been famous as the site of one of the most visited **shrines** in the country.

The town

An immaculately tended square lined by dignified buildings, **Kapellplatz** forms the centre of the town. Its outsized dimensions really come into play at the time of the big pilgrimages: the most important is to celebrate the Feast of the Assumption (Aug 15); Corpus Christi (variable date in May/June) is next in order of rank, but there are many others throughout the year. The goal of the believers is the **Gnadenkapelle** (or **Heilige-Kapelle**) in the centre of the square, a tiny octagonal chapel which offers a tantalizing reminder of Altötting's distinguished early history as it dates back to Carolingian times and may once have served as the baptistry of the imperial palace. In 1489, a three-year-old local child who had drowned in the Inn was cured when her grief-stricken mother placed her in front of the **wooden statue** of the *Black Madonna* at the high altar. News of the miracle quickly spread, and the chapel was immediately extended by the erection of a nave and covered walkway. The sculpture seems to have been working cures relentlessly ever since, to judge from the thousands of **ex–votos** – many of them outstanding examples of folk art – which now completely cover the walls. Since the seventeenth century, it has been housed in an elaborate silver shrine and is now generally to be seen draped in gorgeous robes which stand in stark contrast to the simplicity of the original carving. Opposite the altar are appropriately shaped **urns** containing the hearts of many of the Bavarian dukes, who thereby commended the most precious part of themselves to the special care of the Virgin.

Across from the Gnadenkapelle is the twin-towered **Stiftskirche**, a fine late Gothic church erected in the early years of the sixteenth century in order to cater for the ever-growing influx of pilgrims. Its **Schatzkammer** (April–Oct Tues-Sun 10am–noon & 2–4pm; DM2.50) contains an excellent collection of treasury items. Particularly outstanding is the *Goldenes Rössl* (Golden Steed), a masterpiece by a Parisian goldsmith of the turn of the fifteenth century, commissioned by Isobel of Bavaria as a present for her husband, King Charles VI of France. Another exceptional piece is the *Füllkreuz*, a late sixteenth-century crucifix adorned with nineteen miniatures of the Passion painted on lapis lazuli. From the church's cloisters you can descend to the **Tilly-Gruft** (May–Oct daily 8–10am & 2–4pm) where you can peer into the coffin containing the gruesome skeleton of Field Marshal Johann Tilly, the Catholic hero of the Thirty Years' War.

As the Stiftskirche eventually proved insufficiently large for the number of people who flocked here, a monstrous neo-Baroque **Basilika**, capable of accommodating 6000 worshippers at a time, was erected just off the square at the beginning of the present century. Also from this period is the **Panorama** (daily March 15 to Sept 30 9am-5/6pm; Oct 9am-4pm; DM4), a few minutes' walk to the east at Gebhard-Fugel-Weg 10. Housed in a custom-built rotunda, this monumental circular painting was a co-operative venture between Gebhard Fugel, who painted the figurative passages, notably the main scene of the Crucifixion, and Josef Krieger, who was responsible for the lovingly detailed background depiction of Jerusalem. Nearby, at Kreszentiaheimstr. 18, is the **Mechanische Krippe** (Mechanical Crib; daily 9am-5pm; DM2), which was made in the 1920s by woodcarvers from Oberammergau.

Practicalities

Altötting's **Bahnhof** is just south of the centre. The **tourist office** (May–Oct Mon–Fri 8am–noon & 2–5pm, Sat 9am–noon; Nov–April Mon–Thurs 8am–noon & 2–5pm, Fri 8am–noon; ☎08671/8068) is in the Rathaus, Kapellplatz 2a. Here you can book to stay in one of the many **private houses** (①–③) with rooms to let.

There are also plenty of **hotels** in the heart of town, most of them very good value for what they offer. They include *Weissbräustuben*, Kapuzinerstr. 3b (☎08671/5511; ③); *Altöttinger Hof*, Mühldorfer Str. 1 (☎08671/5422; ④); *Zwölf Apostel*, Bruder-Konrad-Platz 3–4 (☎08671/96960; ⑤); *Plankl*, Schlotthamer Str. 4 (☎08671/85151; ⑤); and *Scharnagl*, Neuöttinger Str. 2 (☎08671/6983; ⑤). *Zur Post*, Kapellplatz 2 (☎08671/5040; ⑥), which has wonderful bathing facilities, is the best hotel in town. These hotels all have good **restaurants**. For **drinking**, there are the taps of the two local breweries: *Hell-Bräu* is just to the north of the centre at Herrenmühlstr. 15, while *Weissbräu* is south of the Bahnhof at Graming 79; both have beer gardens and serve basic meals.

Burghausen

At the terminus of the branch rail line 15km southeast of Altötting lies **BURGHAUSEN**, which for centuries ranked alongside Munich, Landshut, Ingolstadt and Straubing as one of the five residential cities of the Bavarian dukes. Nowadays, it's a modest-sized border town and an affluent centre for computer-based industries.

A tightly packed Altstadt nestles along the bank of the river and most of the buildings of note are found on the elongated **Stadtplatz**. On the eastern side are the colourful former ducal administrative buildings and the Rathaus. The south side is closed by the Gothic parish church of **St Jakob**, while at the opposite end stands the **Gymnasium** established by the Jesuits, now serving once more as a school. An alley leads from the middle of the east side of the square to the finest local vantage point, the bridge over the Salzach to Austria.

From here, you get a great view of the **Burg**, which stands on a ridge high above the old town and between two stretches of water, the Salzach and the Wöhrsee. Measuring 1030m from end to end, it ranks as the longest castle in Europe. With no fewer than six courtyards, it has the appearance of a complete upper town, rather than simply a fortress. The oldest surviving section of the fortifications dates back to the mid-thirteenth century, but much of what can be seen today is due to the expansion carried out at the end of the fifteenth century when there was fear of a Turkish invasion. Steps lead up from Stadtplatz to the main residential part of the palace, set in the last of the courtyards, but it's more fun to circle round and go up from the Wöhrsee side, entering via the massive double gateway known as the **Georgstor** facing would-be attackers.

The former ducal apartments contain the **Staatliche Sammlungen** (April–Sept daily 9am–noon & 1–5pm; Oct–March Tues–Sun 10am–noon & 1–4pm; DM4), a collection of German paintings and furniture contemporary with the Burg itself. Included in the ticket is entrance to the observation platform, which commands a splendid view over the fortress and the town. The **Kemenate**, the chambers of the duchess, now house the **Historisches Stadtmuseum** (daily March, April, Oct & Nov 10am–4.30pm; May–Sept 9am–6.30pm; DM2.50), featuring the usual local history displays, but well worth visiting for the sake of the late Gothic interiors.

Practicalities

Burghausen's **Bahnhof** is situated just over 1km north of the town centre, which is reached by following Marktler Strasse straight ahead. The **tourist office** (Mon–Wed 8am–noon & 2–4pm, Thurs 8am–noon & 2–6pm, Fri 8am–noon; ☎08677/2435) is in the Rathaus at Stadtplatz 112.

There are a couple of **pensions**: *Kaffeemühle*, Wöhrgasse 265 (☎08677/61965; ④); and *Salzburger Hof*, In den Grüben 190 (☎08677/911000; ④). **Hotels** include *Post*, Stadtplatz 39 (☎08677/3043; ⑤); *Glöcklhofer*, Ludwigsberg 4 (☎08677/7024; ⑥); and *Bayerische Alm*, Robert-Koch-Str. 211 (☎08677/9820; ⑥). The **youth hostel** is at Kapuzinergasse 235 (☎08677/911318; ⑫). All three hotels mentioned above have **restaurants** with beer gardens. Hottest nightspot is the *Jazzkeller* in the Mautnerschloss on Mautnerstrasse at the southern edge of the old town, which attracts the big names for periodic **jazz festivals**.

EASTERN BAVARIA

Eastern Bavaria (*Ostbayern*), which incorporates **Lower Bavaria** and the **Upper Palatinate** (two of the three provinces into which the medieval duchy was divided), is the least well-known region of the whole state, among Germans as well as visitors. Part of the reason for this is that its eastern boundary is the Czech border, which was effectively a dead-end until a few years ago. Misconceptions about remote forests populated by bumpkins have kept almost everyone except hiking enthusiasts away, so while tourists crowd each other out in the south and Alpine regions, the east remains an insider's tip even during the busy months of July and August.

Curiously enough, the region includes both of the cities that preceded Munich as capital of Bavaria. **Regensburg**, the main seat of power in the tribal days of the Dark Ages and nowadays capital of the Upper Palatinate, survived World War II almost unscathed, the most complete and one of the most beautiful medieval cities in Germany. In the region's southwestern corner is the wonderfully preserved city of **Landshut**. The capital of Lower Bavaria, it rivalled Munich in wealth and status during the fifteenth and sixteenth centuries. Downstream along the Danube are enticing ancient towns like **Straubing** and **Passau**.

Most of the southeastern part of the region is taken up by the **Bavarian Forest**, the largest forested area in Central Europe and one that still retains much of its primeval character, especially in the **National Park** between Frauenau and Mauth. A couple of train routes make it relatively accessible, and campsites, hostels and private rooms abound. In addition, the Bavarian Forest has an unexpectedly vibrant cultural life, especially during summer, when **festivals** take place throughout the region.

Landshut

Picturesquely set below wooded hills on the banks of the Isar 70km northeast of Munich lies **LANDSHUT**. The Wittelsbachs established it as their capital at the beginning of the thirteenth century, and the town consistently outshone Munich, even when the latter became capital of the separate duchy of Upper Bavaria. However, when the local dukes died out in 1503 and Bavaria became a united province again, it lost its status as a capital; following a brief flowering as the second residence, it went into decline, never to recover. As a result, its showpiece centre was subject to few later alterations and remains wonderfully evocative of its fifteenth- and early sixteenth-century heyday. Nowadays, it's put to good use as the perfect backdrop for Germany's largest costumed festival.

THE LANDSHUT WEDDING

The original **Landshut Wedding** (*Landshuter Hochzeit*) of Georg, son of Duke Ludwig the Rich, and Princess Jadwiga of Poland, was a spectacular society affair: the Archbishop of Salzburg conducted the ceremony, while all the leading German and Polish nobles were present, including the Holy Roman Emperor Friedrich III and his son, the future Maximilian I. Afterwards, the people of Landshut celebrated for a week at the expense of the bridegroom's father, and it is recorded that 40,000 chickens, 11,500 geese, 2700 lambs, nearly 700 pigs, 400 calves and over 300 oxen were consumed.

Needless to say, there is no such munificence in the modern re-creations of the event, which, with eyes firmly on the tourist market, have been moved from the original November date to high summer and go on for four weeks. **Weekends** are the best times to come: each Saturday at 9pm, the gathering of the guests is re-enacted, while at 2.30pm on Sundays, the **wedding procession** makes its way through the streets of the town, with a medieval-style **tournament** following at 4.30pm. Some 2000 participants are involved, each decked out in authentic reproductions of the costumes of the period. In addition to various impromptu events, there are also concerts of fifteenth-century music in the Stadtresidenz and Burg Trausnitz, while entertainments are held in the Rathaus; the latter are repeated on the evenings of Wednesday, Thursday and Friday.

The next **performances** will occur in June and July 2001. **Tickets** for the tournament and indoor events, and grandstand seats for the procession are available in advance from Landshut's tourist office

The town

Most of Landshut's sights are concentrated on its main street, whose magnificence is immediately suggested by its name – **Altstadt**, the term normally used for the entire central part of a German city. Starting from the banks of the Isar, it ascends towards Burg Trausnitz, the old feudal fortress dominating the town, by means of a majestically sweeping curve. Of an unusual width and spaciousness, it's lined with a resplendent series of colourful high-gabled mansions of widely varying design.

Altstadt

Two very different hall churches stand at either end of Altstadt; both were designed by **Hans von Burghausen**, one of the most brilliant late Gothic architects. Overlooking the river is the **Heiliggeistkirche** (or **Spitalkirche**), which uses the same architectural methods as its earlier counterpart at the opposite end, but with each detail cleverly modified: the tower, for example, stands over the transept. The hospital buildings it served are across the road, but these were rebuilt in the Baroque period. About halfway down Altstadt is the **Rathaus**, an assemblage of several burghers' mansions. Under the patronage of King Ludwig II, this was given a neo-Gothic facelift last century, starting with a new facade. A team of Romantic artists was then asked to decorate the main reception hall, the **Prunksaal** (Mon–Fri 2–3pm; free). They painted it with colourful scenes showing the 1475 wedding between the last Duke of Lower Bavaria and Princess Jadwiga of Poland. Such a stir was caused by this work that the people of Landshut decided to re-enact the event – and have done so every four years throughout this century (see box).

Across from the Rathaus is the **Stadtresidenz** (guided tours April–Sept daily 9am–noon & 1–5pm; Oct–March Tues–Sun 9am–noon & 1–4pm; DM3). Modelled on the Palazzo Tè in Mantua, this was begun in 1537 as the first palace in the Italian Renaissance style to be built north of the Alps. Though the wing facing the street was later given a somewhat Germanic Neoclassical facade, the rest of the building – and in particular the magnificent courtyard – immediately evokes a sunny Mediterranean atmosphere. The local museum is housed inside, but it's completely eclipsed by the apartments themselves. Most notable is the **Italienischer Saal**, with its carved medallions of the Labours of Hercules and ceiling frescoes juxtaposing biblical and mythological scenes.

Dominating Altstadt from the far end is Landshut's proudest adornment, the tower of **St Martin**. In design alone, it's extraordinarily ingenious, beginning as a square shape, then narrowing and changing into an octagon. With a height of 133m, it's also the tallest brick structure in the world. The walls of the main body of the church are pierced by five portals bearing rich terracotta sculptures. The interior, with slender pillars sweeping up to the lofty network vault, is hardly less impressive than the tower, the spareness of effect enhanced by the relative lack of furnishings. Nonetheless there are some fine works, such as Michel Erhart's impassioned *Triumphal Cross*, the elaborate choir stalls and the high altar. Best of all is the larger-than-life polychrome wood *Madonna and Child* in the south aisle, carved around 1520 by the local sculptor Hans Leinberger.

The rest of the town

From St Martin, you can climb up to the romantically dilapidated **Burg Trausnitz** (guided tours same hours as for the Stadtresidenz; DM4); the long haul up hundreds of steep steps is worth the effort for the view alone, stretching over Landshut's red-tiled roofs and church steeples and along the Isar valley. Parts of the old fortress (which predated the town) remain, including a double Romanesque chapel and a Gothic hall, but the bulk of the surviving complex results from the Renaissance rebuilding, which is a generation later than the Stadtresidenz. A highlight is the **Narrentreppe** (Buffoons' Staircase), decorated with vivacious portrayals of characters from the *commedia dell'arte*. To the east lies the expansive **Hofgarten**,which offers more belvederes with fine panoramic views.

Practicalities

Landshut's **Hauptbahnhof**, a major rail junction, is 2km to the northwest of the centre, which is reached by bus #2. The **tourist office** at Altstadt 315 (Mon–Fri 9am–1pm & 2–5pm, Sat 10am–noon; ☎0871/922050) is the best place for details of the *Landshuter Hochzeit*.

Within walking distance of the Hauptbahnhof, but some distance from the historic part of town, is an inexpensive **guest house**, *Bayerwald*, Bayerwaldstr. 43 (☎0871/12536; ②). The cheapest central **hotel** is *Weinstube Heigl*, Herrngasse 385 (☎0871/89132; ④). Good middle-range places are *Gasthof Ochsenwirt*, south of the centre at Kalcherstr. 30 (☎0871/23439; ⑤), and *Goldene Sonne*, Neustadt 520 (☎0871/92530; ⑥). An enticing alternative in this price category is *Schloss Schönbrunn* (☎0871/95220; ⑥), a Historicist castle in the incorporated village of Schönbrunn at the northeastern edge of town. Landshut's most expensive hotel is *Fürstenhof*, which is a short distance southeast of the Hauptbahnhof at Stethaimer Str. 3 (☎0871/92550; ⑦). The **youth hostel** is just south of Burg Trausnitz at Richard-Schirmann-Weg 6 (☎0871/23449; ❶), while the **campsite** (☎0871/53366) is on the banks of the Isar in the northeastern district of Mitterwöhr.

All the hotels mentioned above have recommendable **restaurants**; the *Herzogstüberl* and *Fürstenzimmer* in the *Fürstenhof* are the best and priciest. Formidable competition comes from *Stegfellner*, Altstadt 71, which does moderately priced set lunches. *Bernlocher Pizzeria*, Ländtorplatz 2–5, serves good cheap food, while *Hofreiter*, Neustadt 505, has a beer garden.

Regensburg (Ratisbon)

"Regensburg surpasses every German city with its outstanding and vast buildings," drooled Emperor Maximilian I in 1517, and the centre of **REGENSBURG** has changed remarkably little since then. Founded as the military camp *Castra Regina* by the Romans, the city remained of importance during the Frankish period and was capital of the earliest Bavarian duchy. Most of the surviving architecture originates from the glory days between the thirteenth and sixteenth centuries, when Regensburg was a Free Imperial City, rich from trade with Europe, the Balkans and the Orient. Although other cities may have a more spectacular cathedral or town hall as a focal point, none

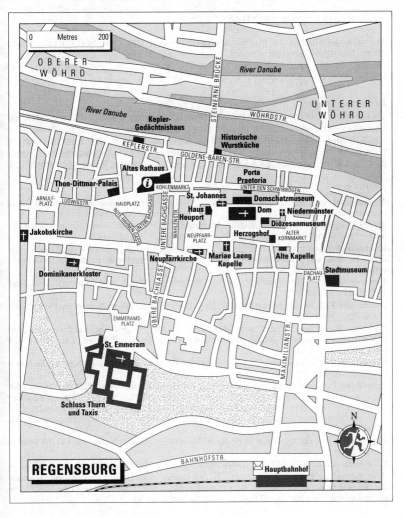

> The **telephone code** for Regensburg is ☎0941

can match the satisfyingly integrated nature of the Regensburg townscape, which gives a unique insight into the size and feel of a prosperous community of the Middle Ages.

Regensburg is today a prosperous centre for hi-tech industries. Train connections into the Bavarian Forest and south to Passau are fast and efficient from here, while its *Gaststätten* and beer gardens – the favoured haunts of the large student population – along with its stunning location on the banks of the Danube make it a great place to spend a couple of days.

Arrival and accommodation

The **Hauptbahnhof** is at the southern end of the city. From here, follow Maximilianstrasse straight ahead to reach the centre. Regensburg's **tourist office** is located in the Altes Rathaus (Mon–Fri 8.30am–6pm, Sat 9am–4pm, Sun 9.30am–2.30/4pm; ☎507 4410).

Accommodation

There are plenty of good choices for **accommodation** in Regensburg, with several atmospheric places on islands in the Danube. Most of the top hotels are in the Altstadt. The **youth hostel**, Wöhrdstr. 60 (☎57402; ⚑) is about five minutes' walk from the heart of town, on an island in the Danube, while the **campsite**, *Azur-Camping*, is about twenty minutes' walk from the centre, pleasantly situated next to the river at Weinweg 40 (☎270025).

HOTELS

Altstadthotel Arch, Am Haidplatz 4 (☎58660, fax 5866 168). One of Regensburg's very best hotels, occupying an eighteenth-century mansion: there's also a vaulted cellar restaurant. ⑦

Apollo, Neuprüll 17 (☎91050, fax 910570). Moderately priced hotel with restaurant in a village-like setting close to the University at the southernmost end of the city; take bus #6. ④

Bischofshof, Krautermarkt 3 (☎59086, fax 53508). Housed in the former episcopal palace right beside the Dom, with a fine restaurant and shady beer garden serving the products of the brewery of the same name. ⑦

Karmeliten, Dachauplatz 1 (☎54658, fax 561751). Upmarket Altstadt establishment with an excellent Spanish restaurant. ⑦

Münchener Hof, Tändlergasse 9 (☎58440, fax 561709). Comfortable mid-range hotel with restaurant in the Altstadt. ⑥

Parkhotel Maximilian, Maximilianstr. 28 (☎56850, fax 52942). Regensburg's most prestigious and expensive hotel, occupying palatial premises just north of the Hauptbahnhof. It also has a well-regarded restaurant. ⑨

Peterhof, Fröhliche-Türken-Str. 12 (☎57514, fax 57561). Basic budget hotel charging the lowest rates in the Altstadt. ④

Prösslbräu, Dominikanerinnenstr. 2, Adlersberg (☎09404/1822, fax 09404/5233). Occupying a former convent in the northwestern outskirts and reached by bus #12, this is the epitome of a country *Gasthof*. As well as inexpensive rooms, it has a large shady beer garden serving the products of the small adjoining brewery (light and dark beers plus a powerful *Doppelbock*) and good, sensibly priced food. ④

Roter Hahn, Rote-Hahnen-Gasse 10 (☎595090, fax 560993). Another budget place in the heart of the city. ④

Schildbräu, Stadtamhof 24 (☎85724). A good medium-priced hotel and restaurant on a Danube island. ⑤

Spitalgarten, St-Katharinen-Platz 1 (☎84774). This *Gasthof*, located just across from *Schildbräu*, has the cheapest rooms in Regensburg. Its beer garden, which serves the products of the *Spital* brewery and commands a fine view of the city, is a great local favourite. ③

Wiendl, Universitätsstr. 9 (☎920270, fax 920 2728). Pleasant middle-range hotel with restaurant, sited immediately to the rear of the Hauptbahnhof. ⑤

The Altstadt

Most of what you're likely to want to see in Regensburg is crowded within a relatively small area; the medieval centre is only about twice the size of the original Roman fort, so exploration on foot is an easy business. With no fewer than 1300 buildings listed as being of historical interest, you'll find treasures at every turn.

Around the waterfront

The best **view** of Regensburg's medieval skyline is from the twelfth-century **Steinerne Brücke** (Stone Bridge). Legend has it that the builder made a pact with the Devil to give him the first soul that crossed the finished bridge. In return the builder was able to complete his project in just eleven years and so beat the cathedral builder, who'd bet him he'd be finished first. The bridge builder didn't only trick his competitor, he also tricked the Devil – the first living thing that was sent across the bridge was a donkey.

At the time the bridge was built, it was the only safe and fortified crossing along the entire length of the Danube and had tremendous value for the city as a major international trading centre. Of the three original watchtowers, the one above the bridge's town gate is the only survivor. On the left, just past the medieval salt depot, the **Historische Wurstküche** (daily 8am–7pm) originally functioned as the bridge workers' kitchen. It's been run by the same family for generations and serves nothing but delicious Regensburger sausages with sweet mustard and sauerkraut. Have a look at the watermark on the outside wall and you'll see that the whole place was almost washed away in 1988.

Along the road known as Unter den Schibbögen, remains of the Roman fort are still visible at the corner of one of the houses. The **Porta Praetoria**, once the northern watchtower, was discovered during restoration work in 1887.

The Domstadt

Immediately to the south lies a dense complex of ecclesiastical buildings, known as the **Domstadt**. The **Dom** itself is Bavaria's most magnificent example of the Gothic building period. It replaced an earlier Romanesque church, of which the **Eselsturm** (Donkey Tower) is the only remaining part above ground; this takes its name from the fact that donkeys were used to carry building materials up a ramp inside. If you look up to the top from the Dom's back courtyard, a man holding a jug sticking out from the upper ledge becomes visible: he's supposed to be the architect, who threw himself off the tower when he lost his bet with the bridge builder.

The Dom took almost 300 years to build, from 1250 to 1525, and the two spires weren't erected until the mid-nineteenth century; the main reason for the delay in completion was the Reformation, during which the bishop remained Catholic, while the secular leadership went Lutheran. Highlights of the interior include the expressive late thirteenth-century statues of *The Annunciation* in the transept and the medieval **stained-glass windows** in the chancel. According to local legend, Judgment Day will be heralded when the real human hair on the late sixteenth-century wooden *Crucifix* on the south transept wall grows to knee-length. Another quirky feature is the pair of fourteenth-century figures in the niches either side of the western nave entrance: on the left is the **Devil's grandmother** and on the right the **Devil** himself. They were intended to remind the congregation that as soon as they left the safety of the church evil and temptation awaited. It's well worth trying to hear a concert or sung service (generally at 9am on Sunday) featuring the *Domspatzen* (Cathedral Sparrows), the most famous Catholic choir in Germany.

The **cloisters**, which are only accessible during **guided tours** (May–Oct Mon–Sat 10am, 11am & 2pm, Sun noon & 2pm; Nov–April Mon–Sat 11am, Sun noon; DM3), have two interesting chapels, of which the **Allerheiligenkapelle** is a Romanesque gem, with many of the original twelfth-century frescoes surviving. Nearby, the eleventh-century **Stephanskapelle** was the bishop's private chapel, and though the frescoes have been lost, the altar is from the original building period. The hollowed-out section of the altar indicates that it used to contain the relics of a martyr, generally believed to have been Saint Florian, and the openings at the base were for the faithful to insert intercessory notes to him.

Housed in the former bishop's palace on the north side of the Dom is the **Domschatzmuseum** (April–Oct Tues–Sat 10am–5pm, Sun noon–5pm; Dec–March Fri & Sat 10am–4pm, Sun noon–4pm; DM3), a collection of ecclesiastical vestments and gold and silver ceremonial ware ranging from the eleventh century to the present day. Further treasures, including paintings and sculptures, are contained in the **Diözesanmuseum** (April–Oct Tues–Sun 10am–5pm; DM3, DM5 for joint ticket) occupying the church of **St Ulrich** at the rear of the Dom. Constructed in the Transitional style between Romanesque and Gothic, the building itself is one of the most remarkable in the city, featuring an unusual vaulted gallery at the west end.

Previously, St Ulrich was the Dom's parish church, but this function has passed to the **Niedermünster** further east, a Romanesque collegiate foundation remodelled internally in Baroque style. At the opposite end of the Domstadt, adjoining the northwestern end of the Dom, is the Gothic church of **St Johannes**, the former baptistery. Inside is an altarpiece of *The Fair Virgin* by Altdorfer.

South of the Dom

On the corner of the Pfauengasse leading off the Domplatz, there's a very nondescript door just past the corner shop which leads to an interesting place of folkloric worship. Dedicated to the Virgin Mary, it's the town's smallest chapel, known as the **Mariae-Laeng-Kapelle** after the seventeenth-century belief that the best way to get one's prayers heard was to write out prayer notes the same length (*laeng*) as Mary herself. The Church never accepted this idea, but people have come here ever since to pray to Mary and leave notes and gifts. Occasions when help has appeared are recorded by the faithful in little framed cards or pictures, crowding the back of the chapel.

At the far end of the Domstadt lies the Alter Kornmarkt, whose northwestern corner is defined by the so-called **Römerturm**, though its earliest masonry is Carolingian rather than Roman. A covered passageway links it to the Romanesque ducal palace, the **Herzogshof**, now a cultural centre. On the south side of the square stands the **Alte Kapelle**, whose sober medieval exterior hardly prepares you for the riotous fricassee of Rococo decoration inside.

The **Historisches Museum** (Tues–Sun 10am–4pm; DM4) lies just to the southeast, on Dachauplatz. This encompasses over 100 rooms spread out on four floors of the former Minorite monastery, and charts the town's cultural and artistic history over the past 2000 years. Not surprisingly the wealth of exhibits and information is rather overwhelming, but the layout is clear, with each floor related to a different subject or era. Of particular interest is the section on **Albrecht Altdorfer**, who, apart from being one of Germany's greatest artists, was also a leading local politician, being involved in the decisions which saw the expulsion of the Jews and the introduction of the Reformation. Among his etchings shown here are two of the beautiful Romanesque–Gothic synagogue he helped destroy, which make a fascinating documentary record. The remains of the frescoes he painted for the *Kaiserbad* are also here, along with a panel showing *The Two St Johns*, which is set in a typically luxuriant Danube landscape.

A few minutes' walk to the east, the **Neupfarrkirche** stands rather forlorn in the middle of a car park, occupying the site of the old synagogue. Originally, it was intended to be a vast pilgrimage church dedicated to the Virgin as thanksgiving for deliverance from the Jewish "peril"; the model for this ambitious design can be seen in the Stadtmuseum. However, the city council's cynical attempts to foster the bogus cult met with such apathy that it was hastily dropped. When the council decided to adopt the Reformation a few years later, the church was completed in a much reduced form to serve as the city's Protestant flagship. Notwithstanding its unfortunate history and situation, the interior is very dapper, with an unusual little hexagonal nave. In the entrance of Neupfarrplatz 7 you'll see a pilfered Jewish tombstone – the ultimate status symbol for medieval Christians – set into the wall.

The merchant quarter

The streets west of the Dom were where the merchants who made Regensburg so prosperous in the Middle Ages had their homes. Unique for a German medieval town are the many **towers** built in the style of Italian fortified palaces; about twenty of these survive. Unlike their southern counterparts, however, they had no real defensive function; instead they were a statement of the competitive ethos that ruled their owners' lives: the higher the tower, the richer and more prestigious the occupier.

Directly facing the Dom is the **Haus Heuport**, which boasts another of the city's jokey sculptures in the form of a stone relief at the left-hand corner of the courtyard staircase representing the seduction of a careless virgin. One of the most beautiful of the fortified towers with high balconies is the **Baumburgerturm** in Watmarkt, just west of here. The **Goldener Turm** in the Wahlenstrasse is the town's highest remaining tower, and on its top floor there's a very cosy wine bar.

Apart from the Dom, the town's most important Gothic structure is the **Altes Rathaus** on the Kohlenmarkt. From the outside it's difficult to get an idea of its grand scale. To appreciate this you need to take a guided tour of the **Reichstagsmuseum** within (Mon–Sat 9.30am–noon & 2–4pm, Sun 10am–noon; May–Sept tours in English Mon–Sat 3.15pm; DM5), which is worth it to see, among other things, the beautiful Renaissance panelling and fittings in the **Kurfürstliches Nebenzimmer** (Electors' Ante-chamber) and the **Blauer Saal** (Blue Hall) with its glittering star-studded ceiling. All the original furnishings remain, including the torture chamber in the basement with some pretty gruesome instruments. The largest and most significant room is the **Beratungszimmer der Reichsstände**, where the Perpetual Imperial Diet met from 1663 to 1806. The seating order was strictly defined by status, and the different colouring of the benches indicates individual groups – red for Electors, green for lesser princes.

Outside, on the right-hand side of the Rathaus entrance, a little alleyway twists around the back, known as **Zum Roten Herzfleck** (Red Heart Patch), a polite name that barely admits its origin, since for many years the house in the corner here was the town's brothel. Meanwhile, on the left-hand side of the Rathaus steps, the town's official measurements, cast in iron and mounted on the wall, were used in medieval times to sort out rows between merchants and customers if someone thought they'd been cheated. People would take their cloth or shoe, for example, and compare it to the fixed measures on the Rathaus.

To the west lies **Haidplatz**, a square which was built to be seen. Its largest building is the **Haus zum Goldenen Kreuz** which was the town's main hotel between the sixteenth and nineteenth centuries and the site of one of Regensburg's biggest scandals, when Emperor Charles V fell in love with a local girl called Barbara Blomberg. They used to meet in this house, and their son Juan de Austria was born here in 1547. In the grand tradition of royal illegitimates, he became a great naval commander, winning the Battle of Lepanto against the Turks, and died Governor of the Netherlands in 1578. Less scandalous, but fun in passing, is the little stone mouse hidden in the right-hand corner outside the shop window on the ground floor. The locals say that if you rub it your purse will never be empty. Also on the square is the **Thon-Dittmer-Palais**, nowa-

THE THURN AND TAXIS DYNASTY

The Thurn and Taxis family is generally accepted as being the richest in Germany, with a fortune estimated at five billion *Deutschmarks*. Originally known as Daxis and based in the Dolomite region between Austria and northern Italy, they came to prominence in the sixteenth century by developing a European-wide postal system, of which they held a monopoly within Germany itself for some 250 years. In the process, they were raised to the title of Prince, moving their base to Regensburg in 1748 when they became the Holy Roman Emperor's personal representatives at the Perpetual Imperial Diet. When this ratified Napoleon's dissolution of the empire, including the secularization of the monasteries and an end to the independence of nearly all the city states, the family seized the opportunity to acquire a new home for themselves and to build up control over the local economy. Currently they're reckoned to own nearly a fifth of Regensburg – a real irony, given the city's long independence from any kind of aristocratic control – as well as extensive tracts of land in the Bavarian Forest. The most visible sign of their varied business interests is the eponymous brewery, the largest one in Bavaria still in private hands, though locally its beer is known as *Tod und Teufel* (Death and the Devil). Much of the wealth is currently being held in trust for the heir to the title, who inherited his fortune at the age of seven.

days one of the main cultural venues; during the summer concerts and plays are held in its courtyard.

On Keplerstrasse to the north, the **Kepler-Gedächtnishaus** (guided tours Tues–Sat 10am, 11am, 2pm & 3pm, Sun 10am & 11am, also at 2pm & 3pm April–Oct only; DM4) is dedicated to the famous astronomer who lived and worked in Regensburg during the early seventeenth century – on the occasions when he was not wasting his talents dabbling in astrology in order to earn his keep from the superstitious monarchs of the day. Compiler of the *Rudolphine Tables* and author of *The Mystery of the Universe*, Kepler achieved major advances in the study of both astronomy (proving the elliptical path of planetary movements) and optics (being the first to understand how the eye works). His family actually lived in no. 2 Keplerstrasse, but he died at no. 5 while visiting a merchant friend, and it's this house that's been turned into a museum of his life and times.

The southwestern quarter

The southwestern part of Regensburg was formerly something of a monastic quarter, and although the monks have long gone, their buildings survive. Particularly intriguing is **St Jacob** just off Bismarckplatz. It was first settled by Irish Benedictines, but is still generally known as the *Schottenkirche* in honour of the Scottish community which lived there from the sixteenth century until its dissolution in 1878, when the monks returned to Fort Augustus on Loch Ness. Pollution from the busy road in front of the church has blackened the exterior, and the profusion of sandstone figures is badly eroded, but the main **portal** is still as eye-catching as ever, with its mixture of pagan and Christian images and delicate patterns carved on the pillars.

On Beraiterweg to the east stands the **Dominikanerkloster**, one of the first Gothic buildings in Germany; its church likewise has a fine portal, adorned with a statue of its patron, Saint Blasius. One of the priors during the period the monastery was under construction in the thirteenth century was Saint Albertus Magnus, later the city's bishop. Among the most highly regarded scholars and philosophers of medieval Europe, he was a man of unusually broad sympathies, being steeped in the works of his Jewish and Arab contemporaries.

At the extreme southern end of the old city is the former Benedictine monastery of **St Emmeram**, another great centre of learning in days gone by. The Romanesque architecture of the church is smothered inside by the exuberant decorative scheme created by the Asam brothers, but the grandiose double portal with its eleventh-century figures of Christ between Saints Emmeram and Dionysius survives, while under the apse is a crypt dating back to the eighth century. More fine sculptures can be seen among the pantheon of monuments to leading figures in early Bavarian history: most notable are the grief-stricken Gothic tombstone to the executed Queen Hemma and its idealized counterpart to the legendary Blessed Aurelia.

Following the Napoleonic secularization, the monastic buildings were acquired by the Thurn and Taxis family (see box) and converted into the most modern residence of the day, with hot and cold running water, flushing toilets, central heating, and most luxurious of all, electricity. The resultant **Schloss Thurn und Taxis** (guided tours April–Oct Mon–Fri at 11am, 2pm, 3pm & 4pm, Sat & Sun at 10am, 11am, 2pm, 3pm & 4pm; Nov–March Sat & Sun at 10am, 11am, 2pm & 3pm; DM12) isn't open to the public when the family is in residence, but at all other times you will be shown the state rooms, still regularly in use, with some wonderful Brussels tapestries on the walls recording the family's illustrious history.

In the former **cloisters** (included in the tour, otherwise DM6) you get a fascinating visual record of the stylistic development of the Gothic style from the twelfth to the fourteenth century. It's easy to tell how far each abbot progressed with the building programme by the number of arches along the ceiling before his portrait is hewn into the stone at the crossover. Highlight of this section is the *Normannisches Portal*, its zigzag patterns around the arch indicating the Norman origins of the first monks to settle here. The **Marstallmuseum** (April–Oct Mon–Fri 11am–5pm, Sat & Sun 10am–5pm; DM4; Nov–March guided tours Sat & Sun 11.30am–2pm; DM7) holds an enormous collection of Thurn and Taxis coaches down the ages, ranging from those used during the centuries when they held the imperial postal franchise to ceremonial carriages, travelling coaches and winter sleighs.

Eating and drinking

You're spoilt for places to eat and drink in Regensburg, which has a bewildering variety of restaurants (including several of real curiosity value), bars, beer gardens and cafés, both traditional and modern. See the hotels section (p.120) for further recommendations.

Restaurants

Alte Münz, Fischmarkt 8. Top-class, moderately priced traditional restaurant with a special line in small delicacies of the Upper Palatinate known as *Schmankerlküche*.

Dampfnudel-Uli, Watmarkt 4. Eccentric little restaurant serving mainly dumplings, housed in the Baumburger Turm. Open Tues–Fri 10am–6pm, Sat 10am–3pm.

Fischerhaus, Untere Regenstr. 7. Speciality fish restaurant which also has a beer garden. Closed Mon.

Gänsbauer, Keplerstr. 10. Cosy and fairly pricey restaurant with a pretty inner courtyard.

Goldene Ente, Badstr. 32. Inexpensive restaurant which is popular with students and has the benefit of a beer garden shaded by chestnut trees.

Historische Wurstküche, An der Steinernen Brücke. The famous sausage restaurant which has become one of the essential sights of Regensburg.

Historisches Eck, Watmarkt 6. Regensburg's most renowned and expensive gourmet restaurant. Closed Sun & Mon.

Kneitinger, Arnulfsplatz 3. Excellent traditional *Gaststätte* of the eponymous local brewery.

Zur Brauschänke, Galgenbergstr. 3. The main *Gaststätte* of the *Thurn und Taxis* brewery.

Zur Goldenen Krone, Keplerstr. 3. Offers a huge choice of reasonably priced schnitzels with temptingly varied fillings; as an added attraction there's a beer garden in a quaint medieval courtyard, overgrown with vines. Evenings only, closed Sun.

Cafés and bars

Alt-Regensburger Weinkeller, Fischgässel 4. One of a group of wine bars clustered around Fischmarkt, which are particularly pleasant in summer when tables are set up outside.

Ambrosius, Brückstr. 5. Best choice for breakfast; open till 1am.

Brauhaus Johann Albrecht, Schwarze-Bären-Str. 6. *Hausbrauerei* with a predominantly young clientele which brews both light and dark beers and serves full meals.

Jenseits, Steinergasse 4. A leading late-niter, open daily 8pm–2/3am.

Kneitinger Keller, Galgenbergstr. 18. With 1200 seats, this is Regensburg's largest beer garden; it's up by the University and is accordingly popular with students.

Orphée, Untere Bachgasse 8. Self-consciously trendy; open evenings only.

Palletti, Pustet Passage, Gesandtenstr. 9. Currently the favourite haunt of the in-crowd.

Prinzess, Rathausplatz 2. The oldest coffee house in Germany, founded in 1686, and still the best choice for hand-made chocolate and cakes.

Roter Löwe, Rote Löwengasse 10. Atmospheric bar with good music.

Schwedenkugel, Haaggasse 15. Another student favourite.

Nightlife and festivals

Regensburg's main **theatre**, featuring a varied programme of drama, opera and musicals, is the *Stadttheater*, Bismarckplatz 7 (☎59156). Other venues include the *Freilichtheater*, the open-air courtyard of the Thon–Dittmer-Palais (☎59156); the *Turmtheater* in one of the medieval towers, the Goliathhaus at Watmarkt 5 (☎562223); and the marionette *Figurentheater* in the Stadtpark (☎28328).

The *Kulturzentrum Alte Mälzerei*, Galgenbergstr. 20 (☎75749), presents all kinds of **live music** as well as cabaret and theatre, while the main **jazz** venue is *Leerer Beutel*, Bertoldstr. 9 (☎563375). Among the many **discos**, the most enduringly popular are *Sudhaus*, Untere Bachgasse 8, and *Scala*, Gesandtenstr. 6.

Two big beer **festivals**, each lasting two weeks, take place annually – the *Frühjahrsdult* at Whitsun, and the *Herbstdult* at the end of August and beginning of September. Held on alternate years are a couple more folk events – the *Altstadtfest* in June and the *Oberpfalzwoche* in September. There is also a contrasting pair of music festivals each summer: the *Bach-Woche* in June and the *Bayerisches Jazz-Weekend* in July.

Listings

Bike rental *Park and Bike*, Am Donaumarktplatz.

Car rental *Europcar*, Straubinger Str. 8 (☎799680); *Hertz*, Bahnhofstr. 24 (☎51515); *Sixt*, Gewerbepark C38 (☎401035).

City river trips Easter to late Oct hourly 10am–4pm; DM10, including going through the rapids under the Steinerne Brücke. Tickets can be bought at the landing stage beside the Historische Wurstküche.

Danube cruises run regularly Easter to late Oct to Walhalla (DM10 single, DM15 return); there are also occasional summer trips to Straubing, Passau and the Altmühl valley via the Rhine-Main-Danube Canal. All departures are from Werftstrasse on the island of Unterer Wöhrd.

Medical emergencies ☎19222.

Mitfahrzentrale Prüfeninger Str. 13 (☎19440 or 22022).

Post office The main office with poste restante service is on Bahnhofstrasse immediately to the left on leaving the Hauptbahnhof.

Women's centre Badstr. 6 (☎81644).

The Danube country around Regensburg

Within easy reach of Regensburg are some wonderful Danube landscapes, together with several spectacular historic monuments. While all the places described in this section are readily accessible by road, the cruise ships which run in summer are a far more atmospheric way to travel.

Kelheim and the Donaudurchbruch

At the confluence of the Altmühl and the Danube about 20km southwest of Regensburg is **KELHEIM**, a little medieval town unusual for its time in having been laid out as a planned grid. Crowning the Michelsberg above is the **Befreiungshalle** (Liberation Hall; daily April–Sept 9am–5pm; Oct–March 10am–noon & 1–4pm; DM3), one of two grandiose constructions on either side of Regensburg funded by King Ludwig I and built by Leo von Klenze. Designed in the manner of an early Christian rotunda, it commemorates the Bavarian dead in the wars against Napoleon.

Kelheim is home to *Schneider*, one of Bavaria's best-known **breweries**, which decamped from Munich after World War II. It makes two classic bottled wheat beers, *Schneiderweisse* and *Aventinus-Doppelbock*; these can be sampled in the *Weisses Bräuhaus* (a smaller version of its Munich namesake), located just off the central Ludwigsplatz at Emil-Ottl-Str. 3. Among the town's several **hotels**, two are attached to the other local breweries: *Ehrnthaller*, Donaustr. 22 (☎09441/3333; ④); and *Aukoferbräu*, Alleestr. 27 (☎09441/2020 or 202120; ⑤).

From Easter until the beginning of November, daily cruises (DM5.50 single, DM9.50 return) run from Kelhiem's Danube jetty through the famous **Donaudurchbruch** gorge. Here the river washes past some very attractive wooded hillsides, and then dramatically cuts through white cliffs, becoming a fast current only 80 metres wide. The Danube took an estimated 4000 years to force its way through these rocks; once past the obstacle, it widens out into a broad sweep.

Situated here on a bend of the river is the goal of the excursion boats, **Kloster Weltenburg**, Bavaria's oldest monastery, founded in the seventh century by Benedictine monks. The complex was completely rebuilt in Baroque style, and the **Klosterkirche**, an early example of the collaborative skills of the Asam brothers, has as its focal point an illusionistic high altar depicting the fight between Saint George and the dragon. In the *Klosterschenke*, a bar-restaurant with beer garden, you can sample the dark **beers** made in the monastery's own brewery, the oldest of its type in the world.

Walhalla

Ludwig I's **Walhalla** monument (daily April–Sept 9am–5.45pm; Oct 9am–4.45pm; Nov–March 10–11.45am & 1–3.45pm; DM3) stands high above the Danube 11km east of Regensburg. Self-consciously modelled on the Parthenon in Athens, the building takes its name from the Nordic mythological resting place for warriors' souls, and contains busts of 118 famous Germans, along with 64 plaques for older celebrities whose likenesses are unknown. The qualification adopted for being a German is decidedly generous, as Swiss and Austrians are included, as well as men such as Erasmus and Copernicus who would probably have considered themselves outsiders; yet there are several unfathomable omissions along with others whose claim to fame is decidedly dubious. If the whole idea behind this project now seems slightly sinister, the view across the Danube valley is magnificent, and the surrounding park and forests are good places for picnics.

Straubing

About 30km downstream from Regensburg, **STRAUBING** is the main market town of the fertile Gäuboden region, one of the country's main granaries. Every August, it hosts Bavaria's second largest **fair**, the *Gäubodenvolksfest*, which began in the early nineteenth century as an occasion for the farmers of the region to meet, do business and celebrate. These days it has expanded into a scaled-down Oktoberfest – though one that still attracts over a million visitors. Check ahead with the tourist office (see below) for exact dates of the festival, and don't expect to find cheap accommodation available during this time.

The town

Straubing's pedestrian heart, which is lined with the medieval and Baroque facades characteristic of Bavarian country towns, is dominated by its symbol, the **Stadtturm**, a picturesque Gothic tower crowned with five steeples. Alongside is the **Rathaus**, which consists of two originally separate fourteenth-century houses with various eighteenth-century extensions.

Rising just to the north, **St Jakob** was built by the great late Gothic architect Hans von Burghausen, though the profusion of side chapels - each sponsored by a different family and all trying to outshine one another - and Baroque altars mask the puritanical aspect of the original. The **Schusterkapelle**, which boasts an altarpiece by Holbein the Elder, is the most prestigious of the chapels.

A couple of blocks east of here, on Fraunhoferstrasse, is the **Gäubodenmuseum** (Tues–Sun 10am–4pm; DM4), which holds one of the most important collections of **Roman treasures** ever found on German soil. It includes everything from iron and bronze tools and domestic ware to beautifully crafted armour and masks for both soldiers and horses. The ornamental quality of the horse masks, which shows Oriental as well as Hellenistic influence, suggests they were used for parades and exhibition games rather than war.

A further block to the east is the **Karmelitenkirche**, another impressive design by Hans von Burghausen, albeit one given a heavy Baroque interior overlay. To its rear is the sumptuous **St Ursula**, the last church the prolific Asam brothers built and decorated together. Immediately to the north of here, overlooking the Danube, stands the **Schloss**, which was begun in the mid-fourteenth century as the seat of the short-lived Duchy of Straubing-Holland. It's currently used as offices, though part has recently been converted to house an outstation of the **Bayerisches Nationalmuseum** (Tues–Sun 10am–4pm; DM4).

Every four years (1998, 2002) a **theatrical festival** held in the Schloss courtyard relates the death of a local girl called Agnes Bernauer. In the best tradition of tragedy, the story revolves around the love between two people from separate worlds destroyed by bigotry and self-interest. In the fifteenth century, the heir to the local duchy fell in love with the beautiful commoner Agnes and they got married in secret. When the old duke found out about this, he tricked his son into leaving town for a while, then had Agnes tried for witchcraft and drowned in the Danube. She's been a favourite character in local songs and storytelling ever since, and the play about her life and death is taken from a ballad written last century. The guilty duke erected a chapel to Agnes' memory in the cemetery of the church of **St Peter**, just east of the town centre; nearby stands an ossuary painted with the Dance of Death.

Practicalities

Straubing's **Bahnhof** lies at the southern end of the Altstadt. The **tourist office** is at Theresienplatz 20 (Mon–Wed & Fri 9am–noon & 1.30–5pm, Thurs 9am–noon & 1.30–6pm, Sat 9.30am–noon; ☎09421/944307).

For the cheapest rooms in town, head for *Fürst*, a **pension** in the heart of the Altstadt at Theresienplatz 32 (☎09421/10792; ②); note that it does not serve breakfast. South of the Bahnhof are a couple of budget **hotels**: *Weisses Rössl*, Landshuter Str. 65 (☎09421/32581; ③) and *Landshuter Hof*, Landshuter Str. 36 (☎09421/30366; ③). More upmarket options include *Villa Wittelsbach*, Stadtgraben 25 (☎09421/9430; ⑥); *Seethaler*, Theresienplatz 25 (☎09421/12022; ⑥); and *Theresientor*, Theresienplatz 41 (☎09421/8490; ⑥).

Straubing's **youth hostel** is at Friedhofstr. 12 (☎09421/80436; ⍾), just east of the Bahnhof and there's a **campsite** at Dammweg 17 on the north side of the Danube, near the Gstütt bridge (May 1–Oct 15; ☎09421/12912).

The best **restaurants** are in the last two hotels listed above, while beer drinkers should head for the *Erstes Straubinger Weissbierhaus*, Theresienplatz 29.

Passau

"In all of Germany I never saw a town more beautiful" is how the marauding Napoleon Bonaparte is said to have reacted to **PASSAU**. Tucked away by the Austrian border, 90km downstream from Straubing, it's a place that the tourist brochures hail as the "Bavarian Venice". While that's a piece of hyperbole, the city does have a certain magic, and its character is very much defined by water, standing as it does at the confluence of the Danube, Inn and Ilz. For centuries, Passau was the seat of a powerful prince-bishopric, the largest in the Holy Roman Empire, and it was probably for this court that the national epic, the *Nibelungenlied* (see p.410), was written at the turn of the thirteenth century. Nowadays, it's a bustling town given a youthful edge by a university founded in 1978.

> The **telephone code** for Passau is ☎0851

The city

Passau's **Altstadt** is crammed along the peninsula between the Danube and Inn. Even in medieval times, the city spilled across the rivers to form suburbs on each bank, the most important being **Oberhaus**, north of the Danube and west of the Ilz, and the **Innstadt** south of the Inn.

The Altstadt

Virtually the whole of the Altstadt burnt down in the seventeenth century, so the architectural picture features predominantly Baroque, Rococo and Neoclassical facades, which give the town a pleasingly elegant feel in spite of the tight squeeze of buildings. The enormous **Dom** is suitably enthroned at the highest point. Nearly all the original Gothic structure was destroyed by fire, to be replaced by a Baroque building designed by the Italian architect Carlo Lurago. His fellow-countrymen, the stuccoist Giovanni Battista Carlone and the fresco painter Carpoforo Tencalla, were entrusted with the interior decoration, which is sumptuous in the extreme. The most notable furnishing is the world's largest church **organ**, which has no fewer than 17,300 pipes and 231 separate registers. Recitals are given every weekday from May to October at noon (DM4); longer ones on Thursdays at 7.30pm (DM8).

The **Residenzplatz**, which is lined by the mansions of wealthy burgher families, is one of the very few open spaces in the tightly packed centre, and offers a fine view of the Dom's resplendent east end, the only significant section remaining from the Gothic period. It's named after the **Neue Residenz**, the Baroque town palace of the prince-bishops. Part of this houses the valuable treasures of the **Domschatz-und-**

Diözesanmuseum (May–Oct Mon–Sat 10am–4pm; DM2); the ticket also gives admission to the **Bibliotheksaal**, which is festooned with *trompe l'oeil* frescoes, and the magnificent main staircase.

Down towards the Danube is the **Rathaus**, a Gothic building with neo-Gothic accretions, notably the tall tower, where you can see the marks from the alarmingly high floods that have plagued the town. The main reception room, the **Rathaussaal** (Easter–Oct daily 10am–4/5pm; DM2), is lined with heroic nineteenth-century paintings illustrating key events in Passau's history. Directly opposite, the **Glasmuseum** (daily March–Oct 10am–4pm; Nov–Feb 2-4pm; DM5) in the *Hotel Wilder Mann* has a huge collection of glass – 30,000 exhibits in 35 rooms – ranging in style from Baroque to modern via Neoclassical, Empire, Biedermeier, Jugendstil and Art Deco. Products from the nearby huts in the Bavarian and Bohemian Forests feature prominently.

To the east, alleys and streets intertwine in picturesque disorder, offering a tantalizing reminder of how the medieval town must have looked. A restored patrician mansion at Bräugasse 17 contains the **Museum Moderner Kunst** (Tues–Sun 10am–6pm; DM8), which has no permanent collection, staging instead highly ambitious temporary exhibitions, often of big names in the international art world. The tip of the peninsula is known as the **Dreiflusseck** (Three Rivers Corner), being the point where the Ilz, Danube and Inn all come together. Since the days of antiquity, the great combined river which flows east from here through three European capitals to the Black Sea has been known as the Danube. However, as can be seen clearly from this vantage point, the Inn is actually the major river: it is deeper, broader and faster-flowing, and has also travelled further to reach the place of convergence.

The Veste Oberhaus

High above the north bank of the Danube is the former castle of the prince-bishops, the **Veste Oberhaus**. The steep walk up by the path along the southern side of the ramparts is enjoyable in its own right; alternatively, take one of the buses from Rathausplatz, which run every thirty minutes from 11.30am to 5pm between Easter and October. Much of the fortress is given over to the **Kulturhistorisches Museum** (Tues–Thurs & Sat & Sun 9am–5pm, Fri 9am–7pm, closed Feb; DM5), which contains displays on local and regional history, with informative sections on the medieval salt trade and on local sculptors and painters, the latter including Altdorfer's most talented follower, Wolf Huber. The museum circuit includes access to a section of the medieval fortifications, from where there's a wonderful picture-postcard view over the city and the confluence of the three rivers.

The Innstadt

Itself a fine vantage point, the Innbrücke links the Altstadt with the **Innstadt** on the opposite side of the Inn. This suburb is dominated by the **Wallfahrtskirche Mariahilf**, a pretty twin-towered Baroque pilgrimage church approached via an extraordinary covered stairway with 321 steps. From the terrace, there's yet another wonderful panoramic view. A short walk west of the Innbrücke, at Ledergasse 43, is the **Römermuseum Kastell Boiotro** (March–Nov Tues–Sun 10am–noon & 1/2–4pm; DM2). Outdoors, you can see the excavations of the eponymous Roman fort; the medieval house in the grounds contains archeological finds from the Passau region.

Practicalities

Passau's **Hauptbahnhof** is immediately west of the Altstadt. Outside, at Bahnhofstr. 36, is one of the **tourist offices** (Easter to mid-Oct Mon-Fri 9am–5pm, Sat & Sun 10am–2pm; rest of year Mon-Thurs 9am–5pm, Fri 9am–4pm; ☎955980); the other is at

Rathausplatz 3 (Easter to mid-Oct Mon–Fri 8.30am–6pm, Sat & Sun 10am–2pm; rest of year Mon–Thurs 8.30am–5pm, Fri 8.30am–4pm; ☎955980).

Accommodation

Passau has a good choice of **hotels** in all categories. The **youth hostel** (☎41351; ☷) is within the Veste Oberhaus, while there's a **campsite** next to the River Ilz at Halserstr. 34 (☎41457).

HOTELS AND PENSIONS

Altstadthotel, Bräugasse 23–29 (☎3370, fax 337100). Hotel and restaurant with a marvellous location at Dreiflusseck. ⑤

Gambrinuskeller, Haibach 20. *Gasthof* with beer garden lying directly on the Danube cycle route, on the south bank of the river at the far eastern end of the city. Take bus #7 from the centre. ③

Passauer Wolf, Rindermarkt 6 (☎34046, fax 36757). Elegant hotel in the central part of the Altstadt. Its restaurant (closed Sun) is among the very best in Passau. ⑦

Rosencafé, Donaustr. 23 (☎42811, fax 41072). Very good value *Gasthof* on the north bank of the Danube, at the extreme eastern edge of the city. It can be reached from the centre by bus #1 or #3, though the walk is very pleasant. ②

Rössner, Bräugasse 19 (☎931350, fax 32391). An immaculately maintained pension in a restored mansion in the eastern part of the Altstadt. All rooms have private facilities. ④

Rotel Inn, Donaulände (☎95160, fax 951 6100). Directly overlooking the Danube, just a stone's throw from the Hauptbahnhof, this building in the shape of a sleeping man is a patented hotel idea based on the sort of transportable accommodation used on long-haul safaris. The "rooms" are cabins measuring just 4m by 1.5m. May–Sept only. ①, ② with optional breakfast.

Schloss Ort, Im Ort 11 (☎34072, fax 31817). Recently renovated hotel overlooking the Inn near the Dreiflusseck. Its restaurant has a pleasant garden terrace. ⑥

Weisser Hase, Ludwigstr. 23 (☎92110, fax 9211 100). Historic hotel and restaurant in the very heart of the Altstadt, completely refurbished to a very high standard a few years back. ⑦

Wienerwald 2000, Grosse Klingergasse 17 (☎& fax 33069). Offers good value at the price asked, particularly in view of its convenient Altstadt setting. ③

Wilder Mann, Am Rathausplatz (☎35071, fax 31712). Passau's best-known hotel, occupying a former patrician mansion. Its accommodation ranges from basic rooms to exquisitely furnished suites named after two former guests, King Ludwig II and Empress Susi. The latter also gives her name to the evenings-only gourmet restaurant, which draws on the world's largest collection of German-language cookery books for inspiration. The rooftop café-restaurant is open throughout the day. ⑤

Eating and drinking

There's a wide range of enticing places to eat and drink in Passau, quite apart from the many fine hotel restaurants listed above.

Bräustüberl Hacklberg, Bräuhausplatz 7. A highly atmospheric *Gaststätte*, complete with Passau's biggest beer garden. It's located alongside its brewery, a handsome Baroque building on the north side of the Danube (cross by the eastern of the two bridges, the Schanzlbrücke). As well as a good range of beers, it serves highly innovative meals.

Chesa Pressl, Römerplatz 3. Offers Swiss cuisine and fish specialities. Closed Tues.

Goldener Schiff, Unterer Sand 8. A good old-fashioned *Gaststätte* of the *Peschl* brewery, popular with students and seasoned drinkers alike. The food is tasty and cheap.

Heilig-Geist-Stift-Schenke, Heilggeistgasse 4. Wonderful fourteenth-century *Weinstube* with garden, serving some of the best meals in Passau, including fish dishes and Austrian pastries. Closed Wed.

Innstadt Bräustüberl, Schmiedgasse 23. The *Gaststätte* of the nearby *Innstadt* brewery, offering good-value poultry dishes and other traditional fare.

Kalinka, Schrottgasse 5. Inexpensive Russian speciality restaurant. Closed Mon.

Oberhaus, Veste Oberhaus. Café-restaurant in the castle grounds, with a terrace offering a grandstand view over the city.

Stadtschreiber, Schustergasse 1. Popular student *Kneipe*, offering some twenty different beers.

Cruises, festivals and entertainment

An excellent way to get an overall impression of the city is to take the 45-minute *Dreiflüsse-Rundfahrt* **cruise** (DM10) offered by *Wurm & Köck*, Höllgasse 26 (☎929292). From March to early November there are daily sailings from the quay at Rathausplatz, with departures every 20 to 30 minutes at the height of the season. Between May and mid-October, the same company also runs cruises (DM36 return) to Linz, the capital of Upper Austria, daily except Wednesdays.

The *Maidult* is a large and colourful market and beer **festival**, while during the *Europäische Wochen* in June, July and August, **concerts** are played by internationally renowned orchestras and musicians, and there's also ballet and opera. Passau's star **venue**, worth checking on throughout the year, is the eighteenth-century *Theater im Fürstbischöflichen Opernhaus*, Gottfried-Schäffer-Str. 2–4 (☎929 1910). *Scharfrichterhaus*, Milchgasse 2 (☎35900), has live music and cabaret, plus a cinema and a relaxed bar.

The Bavarian Forest

Poor, provincial and a bit out of the way, the **Bavarian Forest** (*Bayerischer Wald*) is part of Central Europe's largest woodland region, which also includes the Bohemian Forest on the other side of the Czech border. It's an area that retains a great deal of wilderness, plus much of its traditional culture. The craggy earth is full of rocks and barely fertile, and the inhabitants had to develop means of survival other than farming. Easy availability of firewood made **glass-blowing** a natural industry, and workers still tend to be employed in huts, working by hand in the heat of the furnaces. It's superb **hiking** country, with well-marked paths of varying length and difficulty throughout the region. There are also some wonderful **popular festivals**; see the box opposite for details of two of these.

Generally, **prices** are very low, and even during the height of summer finding accommodation is never a problem. Private **rooms** and small guest houses (①–②) are everywhere and there are often rooms available in farmhouses. **Public transport** is a bit fiddly. From Plattling, which lies between Straubing and Passau, a rail line cuts through the heart of the forest and on into the Czech Republic. Along the way, at Zwiesel, there are short branch lines running northwest to Bodenmais and southeast to Grafenau. Another line travels from Schwandorf on the main route north of Regensburg along the northern fringe of the forest to Furth im Wald. En route, at Cham, there are again two short branch lines, including one to Lam via Kötzting. Buses fill in the gaps in this network, though there are only a few services per day on most routes.

Frauenau

FRAUENAU, which lies on the Zwiesel–Grafenau rail line, is the best place to see the living crafts of glass-blowing and cutting. Just off Bahnhofstrasse is the **Freiherr von Poschinger Kristallglasfabrik** (guided tours Mon–Sat 10am–1.15pm; free), the oldest glass-making factory in the world, which offers the opportunity to watch workers transform red molten lumps into glasses, plates and ornaments. For a technical history of glass production and representative work of each age, visit the **Glasmuseum** at Am Museumspark (daily mid-May to Oct 9am–5pm; Nov to mid-May 10am–4pm; DM3). Highlights of the collection are exquisite seventeenth- and eighteenth-century Venetian pieces, and some anarchic Jugendstil vases. Local specialities, such as heavy cut crystal and delicate snuff bottles, are also included.

The **tourist office** (Mon–Fri 8am–noon & 1.30–5pm; mid-May to mid-Oct also Sat 9.30–11.30am; ☎09926/710) is at Hauptstr. 12. Here you can pick up a list of private rooms and guest houses (①–②). **Hotels** include *Büchler*, Dörflstr. 18 (☎09926/350; ④)

and *Eibl-Brunner*, Hauptstr. 18 (☎09926/9510; ⑤), both of which have restaurants. The tiny **youth hostel** is at Hauptstr. 29a (☎09926/735; ✿).

The Bavarian Forest National Park

Frauenau is the northern gateway to the **Bavarian Forest National Park** (*Nationalpark Bayerischer Wald*), some 130 square kilometres of strictly protected countryside bounded to the east by the Czech frontier. The highest peak, the **Rachel** (1453m), is in the far north of the park, almost due east of Frauenau. Below it, the **Rachelsee** adds an isolated splash of blue to the landscape. Further south, stretches of moorland open out the forest.

An excellent **information centre** about the park is located in the *Hans-Eiesenmann-Haus* at Böhmstr. 35 (Mon–Sat 9am–5pm; ☎08558 1300) in the village of **NEUSCHÖNAU**, which lies at its southwestern edge and can be reached by bus from Grafenau. Some buses continue onwards to a **youth hostel**, *Waldhäuser* (☎08553/300; ✿), located right in the heart of the National Park. An ideal hiking base, this is the only accommodation available within the park itself.

Bodenmais

BODENMAIS, terminus of the other branch railway from Zwiesel, is the most popular resort in the Bavarian Forest, and can get quite busy in summer, though nothing like as crowded as its counterparts in the Alps. It stands below the **Grosser Arber** (1456m), the highest peak in the region and, together with the nearby **Arbersee**, the only part prone to be overrun by tourist coaches. There's an exhilarating hiking trail up the mountain from Bodenmais, passing through the **Risslochschlucht**, a gorge with waterfalls, on the way.

The **tourist office** is in the *Kurverwaltung*, Bahnhofstr. 56 (Mon–Fri 8am–5pm, Sat 8am–noon, Sun 10am–noon; ☎09924/77835). As well as the usual extensive provision of private rooms and pensions (①–③), there are numerous high-quality **hotels**, including *Kurparkhotel*, Amselweg 1 (☎09924/1094; ⑥); *Hofbräuhaus*, Marktplatz 5 (☎09924/7770; ⑥); and *Andrea*, Hölzlweg 10 (☎09924/386 or 7480; ⑦). The **youth hostel** (☎09924/281 ✿) is situated on the trail up the Arber, a good ninety minutes' walk from town.

FESTIVALS IN THE BAVARIAN FOREST

FURTH IM WALD, at the extreme northeastern edge of the Bavarian Forest, is home to one of Bavaria's largest and oldest popular festivals, the *Drachenstich* (literally, "Dragon Sticking"). This event, which goes back as far as 1431, begins on the second Sunday in August and ends a week later. Its central theme, the story of a maiden rescued by a gallant knight from the clutches of a wicked dragon, is clearly rooted in the legend of Saint George, though is also thought to have a symbolical reference to the Magyar invasions the area once suffered. A play based on this story is performed in the open air on several occasions throughout the duration of the festival. Lasting for about 75 minutes, it culminates in the grand and gory finale of the dragon's death, where the skewered monster spews blood over the street during its death throes. Tickets can be ordered in advance from *Drachenstichfestausschuss*, Stadtplatz 4 (☎09973/9308).

KÖTZTING, which lies at the foot of the Kaitersberg, one of the best hiking areas in the Bavarian Forest, hosts the *Pfingstritt* each Whit Monday. Although a religious festival, it probably has its origins in an ancient Germanic fertility rite; it involves the menfolk riding their richly adorned horses to a nearby pilgrimage church, and a symbolic wedding of a young couple elected as Whit bride and groom.

FRANCONIA

Geographically the largest part of Bavaria, **Franconia** (*Franken*) makes up the north of the state, bordering on Thuringia, Hesse and Baden-Württemberg. About half of it is covered by highland forest ranges, which span the entire width of the province, but the chief attractions are urban. **Nürnberg**, Bavaria's second city, is a particularly evocative place, with its heady reminders of the very best and the very worst of German culture. Within easy reach are **Erlangen**, with its famous university, and the courtly town of **Ansbach**, while to the north lie Wagner's **Bayreuth**, **Coburg**, the town from which the British royal family originally descended, and the artistic treasure chest of **Bamberg**. Further west are the old episcopal residential cities of **Aschaffenburg** and **Würzburg**. The latter is the starting point of Germany's most popular tourist route, the **Romantic Road**, whose highlights include the magnificently well-preserved medieval towns of **Rothenburg ob der Tauber** and **Dinkelsbühl**.

Franconia takes its name from the Frankish tribes of whose territory it formed a major part. In the tenth century it was made into a duchy which stretched all the way to the Rhine, but this was later split into two and the name retained only for the eastern half. Emperor Maximilian I's decision to restructure the Empire into ten confederate regions in the sixteenth century helped establish Franconia as a distinctive cultural entity. This lasted until 1803, when most of the historic province was absorbed into the new Bavarian kingdom.

Today, even after nearly 200 years of being part of Bavaria, the people still cling to their **regional heritage** and often only grudgingly see themselves as Bavarian. Certainly their dress, food and dialect are quite different. No one wears *Lederhosen* here and Nürnberg is one of a very few cities to have a Socialist mayor in this conservative state. On the other hand, the regions along the border with Thuringia (formerly the virtually impermeable border with the GDR) harbour some of the most fanatically nationalist and right-wing people in the country. This **political divide** has been closely linked to a religious one, created by the adoption of the Reformation in Nürnberg and the margraviates of Ansbach and Bayreuth. It is also reflected in architecture, where the plain lines and more sombre colours of Lutheran Baroque make a potent contrast to the sometimes overrich Catholic style. Even drinking habits are different, with central and western Franconia a staunch beer zone, while the district around Würzburg is very much a wine area.

Nürnberg (Nuremberg)

Nothing more magnificent or splendid is to be found in the whole of Europe. When one perceives this glorious city from afar, its splendour is truly dazzling. When one enters it, one's original impression is confirmed by the beauty of the streets and the comeliness of the houses. The burghers' dwellings seem to have been built for princes. In truth, the kings of Scotland would be glad to be housed so luxuriously as the ordinary citizen of Nürnberg.

This mid-fifteenth-century eulogy, written by the future Pope Pius II, shows the esteem in which medieval **NÜRNBERG** was held. As the favourite royal residence and seat of the first Diet called by each new emperor, the city then functioned as the unofficial capital of Germany. It was a status which had been achieved with remarkable speed, as Nürnberg was only founded in the eleventh century; thereafter, its position at the intersection of the north–south and east–west trading routes led to economic prosperity, and, as a corollary, political power. The arts flourished, too, though the most brilliant period was not to come until the late fifteenth and early sixteenth centuries, when the roll-call of citizens was led by **Albrecht Dürer**, Germany's most complete personification of Renaissance Man.

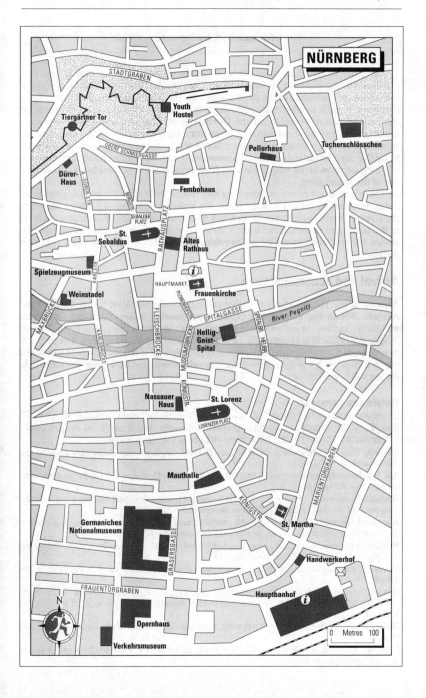

NÜRNBERG

STADTGRABEN

Tiergärtner Tor

Youth Hostel

OBERE SCHMIEDGASSE

Pellerhaus

Tucherschlösschen

Dürer-Haus

A. DÜRER STR

BERGSTR

Fembohaus

SEBALDER PLATZ

St. Sebaldus

RATHAUSSTR

Altes Rathaus

Spielzeugmuseum

KARLSTR

HAUPTMARKT

Frauenkirche

Weinstadel

MAXBRÜCKE

KARLSBRÜCKE

FLEISCHBRÜCKE

FÜRBERGSTR

SPITALGASSE

SPITALBR

River Pegnitz

HEUBR

MUSEUMSBRÜCKE

Heilig-Geist-Spital

KÖNIGSTR

Nassauer Haus

St. Lorenz

LORENZER PLATZ

MARIENTORGRABEN

Mauthalle

KÖNIGSTR

St. Martha

Germaniches Nationalmuseum

GRASERGASSE

Handwerkerhof

FRAUENTORGRABEN

Hauptbahnhof

N

Opernhaus

Verkehrsmuseum

0   Metres   100

> The **telephone code** for Nürnberg is ☎0911

Like other wealthy European cities, Nürnberg went into gradual decline once the maritime trading routes to the Americas and Far East had been established; moreover, the official civic adoption of the Reformation cost the city the patronage of the Catholic emperors. It made a comeback in the nineteenth century, when it became the focus for the Pan-German movement, and the **Germanisches Nationalmuseum** – the most important and extensive collection of the country's arts and crafts – was founded at this time. This symbolic status was given a horrifying twist during the Third Reich; even today the city's image is marred by its association with the regime, a tangible reminder of which survives in the weather-beaten **Nazi architecture** of suburban Luitpoldhain, site of the mass rallies.

There's so much to see in Nürnberg that two or three days are probably the minimum necessary to get to know the place. It's especially enticing in the summer, when the Altstadt is alive with street theatre and music, and there are open-air pop concerts in the parks and stadiums; but there's always a wide and varied range of nightlife. In winter, the renowned month-long **Christkindlesmarkt** (Christmas market) is held in the city.

Arrival and accommodation

Arriving at the **Hauptbahnhof**, you're just outside the medieval fortifications of the Altstadt. Within the central hall is the main **tourist office** (Mon–Sat 9am–7pm; ☎233632); another branch (Mon–Sat 9am–6pm, May–Sept also Sun 10am–1pm & 2–4pm; ☎233635) is at Hauptmarkt 18 in the Altstadt. **Public transport,** though hardly necessary for the compact city centre, is provided by U-Bahns (this is the smallest city in Europe with a genuine tube train network), trams, and buses, and the same tickets are valid on all three.

Hotels and pensions

There are plenty of mid-range hotels within the the Altstadt and this is also where you'll find Nürnberg's many excellent upmarket addresses. The majority of budget establishments are situated in the immediate vicinity of the Hauptbahnhof.

Altstadt, Hintere Ledergasse 4 (☎226102, fax 221806). Small pension on an alley close to the Hauptmarkt. ③

Am Jakobsmarkt, Schottengasse 5 (☎20070, fax 200 7200). Upmarket hotel at the southwestern corner of the Altstadt. ⑧

Brendel, Blumenstr. 1 (☎& fax 225618). Very pleasant pension in a quiet location a few minutes' walk north of the Hauptbahnhof and just to the east of the Altstadt. ③

Burghotel Grosses Haus, Lammsgasse 3 (☎204414, fax 223882). Luxury hotel situated just below the Kaiserburg, offering fine views plus an indoor swimming pool. ⑦

Burghotel Kleines Haus, Schildgasse 14–16 (☎203040, fax 226503). A smaller version of its sister, with similar facilities and slightly lower rates. ⑥

Fischer, Brunnengasse 11 (☎226189). Good-value pension on a quiet street in the heart of the Altstadt. ③

Grand, Bahnhofstr. 1–3 (☎23220, fax 232 2444). Nürnberg's leading hotel, now part of the *Forte* chain, is a large and stylish Art Deco building directly opposite the Hauptbahnhof. It also has one of the city's leading restaurants. ⑨

Melanchthon, Melanchthonplatz 1 (☎412626). Small pension just a few blocks further west of *Vater Jahn*. ③

Pillhofer, Königstr. 78 (☎& fax 226322). Reasonably priced *Gasthof* at the southern end of one of the main pedestrian streets. ③

Vater Jahn, Jahnstr. 13 (☎ & fax 444507). Decent basic pension situated just west and to the rear of the Hauptbahnhof. ③

Weinhaus Steichele, Knorrstr. 2–8 (☎204377, fax 221914). Probably Nürnberg's most atmospheric hotel, occupying an old wine house. Also serves good and fairly priced meals. ⑥

Zum Schwänlein, Hintere Sterngasse 11 (☎225162, fax 241 9008). Inexpensive and basic Altstadt *Gasthof.* ②

Hostels and campsite

Jugendgästehaus, Burg 2 (☎221024 or 241352). A top-class youth hostel located in part of the Kaiserburg, the castle overlooking the Altstadt. It's a 20min walk from the Hauptbahnhof; otherwise, take the U-Bahn to Plärrer and then tram #4 to Vestnertor. ⑥

Jugendhotel, Rathsbergstr. 300 (☎529092). A privately owned hostel without age restrictions, situated to the north of the city. The journey from the Hauptbahnhof by U-bahn #2 to Herrenhütte and then bus #21 to Felsenkeller takes 20min. Dorm beds cost DM28.50–DM32.50.

Campingplatz am Stadion, Hans-Kalb-Str. 56 (☎811122). The campsite is beside the football stadium; take the U-Bahn #1 to Messezentrum. May–Sept only.

The city centre

On January 2, 1945 a storm of bombs reduced ninety percent of Nürnberg's city centre to ash and rubble. Yet walking through the **Altstadt** today, you'd never guess this had ever happened, so loving and effective was the postwar rebuilding. Covering about four square kilometres, the reconstructed medieval core is neatly spliced by the River Pegnitz and surrounded by the ancient **Stadtbefestigung** which is guarded by eighty towers and pierced by four massive gateways. To walk from one end to the other takes about twenty minutes, but much of the centre, especially the area around the castle (known as the **Burgviertel**), is on a steep hill, and speedy walking is impractical. This makes wandering around all the more pleasurable, the rise and fall of the streets creating lopsided views and houses squeezing together as if for comfort. The atmosphere is pleasantly relaxed as well; most of the area is pedestrianized, and there's little in the way of city rush within the fortifications. It's not all medieval pictures, however. Significant areas of modern architecture and open spaces are also prominent, thus ensuring a refreshing (and deliberate) mix of old and new.

The Kaiserburg

On one of the highest points of the city, and offering the best views, the **Kaiserburg** (guided tours of the interior daily 9.30–11.55am & 12.45–3.25pm, Oct–March 3.25pm; DM5) sits chunkily above all else. Scene of many imperial meetings from the eleventh to the sixteenth century, this castle was the "treasure chest of the German Empire", and, despite innumerable modifications and war damage down the centuries, it remains a key feature of the city's silhouette.

The earliest surviving part of the castle is the **Fünfeckturm** (Pentagonal Tower) on the eastern side, which dates back to the eleventh-century Salian epoch. A century later, Frederick Barbarossa decided to extend the castle to the west, using the Salian buildings as the first line of defence. From this period there remain several examples of the smooth ashlar structures characteristic of the Hohenstaufens. The **Sinwellturm** (Round Tower), built directly on the rock, can be ascended for the best of all the views. Another survivor is the two-storey **Kaiserkapelle**, a chapel whose high and airy upper level was reserved for the use of the emperor, with the courtiers confined to the squat and heavy lower tier. In a most unusual architectural arrangement, the bizarrely named **Heidenturm** (Heathens' Tower) was built over its chancel. At the extreme east end is the fourteenth-century **Luginslandturm**, which was erected by the city council to protect Nürnberg from the ambitious Hohenzollern family, who had acquired the old

Salian part of the fortress and aimed to take control over local affairs. After a long war of attrition, the city emerged victorious, but most of the original castle was destroyed in the process.

Apart from the east wall, the Hohenstaufen residential quarters were demolished in the mid-fifteenth century and replaced by the late Gothic **Palais**, which retains its suite of halls. These now look rather plain and soulless, redeemed only by two eye-catching painted wooden ceilings, which were added the following century. At the end of the fifteenth century, the local authorities joined their Luginslandturm to the formerly hostile Fünfeckturm by building the vast **Kaiserstallung**, which today makes the perfect setting for a youth hostel. During the sixteenth century the covered Tiefer Brunnen (Deep Well) was built and the defences strengthened by the erection of huge bastions on the north side.

The northwestern quarter

The area around the **Tiergärtner Tor** next to the Kaiserburg is one of the most attractive parts of the old town centre, and the open space inside the city gate is the main meeting point for summertime street vendors, artists and musicians. On warm evenings the surrounding pubs spill out on to the cobblestoned piazza and the half-timbered houses form a picturesque backdrop for relaxed summer drinking.

A few minutes' walk away along Johannisstrasse lies the **Johannisfriedhof** (daily April–Sept 7am–7pm; Oct–March 8am–5pm). This medieval cemetery, set outside the confines of the old city, is one of the country's most fascinating graveyards. The tombstones lie lengthwise above the graves, like so many coffins lined side by side, each simply decorated with a bowl of red-flowering plants. Look carefully on the "lids" – some show little scenes from the deceased person's life or trade chiselled into the stone.

Among the worthies buried in the graveyard is Albrecht Dürer. The **Albrecht-Dürer-Haus** (March–Oct Tues–Sun 10am–5pm; Nov–Feb Tues–Fri 1–5pm, Sat & Sun 10am–5pm; DM4), where the versatile painter, engraver, scientist, writer, traveller and politician lived from 1509 to 1528, is virtually next door to the Tiergärtner Tor. It's one of the very few original medieval houses still standing in the city, though there are many skilful reconstructions in the streets round about. Much of the furniture and decor dates back to the fifteenth century, giving a real sense of how people lived in the late Middle Ages. At present, there are only copies of Dürer's paintings on display, plus works by other artists paying homage to the great man, though plans are afoot to exhibit some of his graphic work here.

Southeast from here runs Bergstrasse, where at no.19 you'll find the **Altstadthof**, a late sixteenth-century courtyard. Here you can visit the **Felsengänge** (guided tours hourly Mon–Fri 2–7pm, Sat & Sun 11–7pm; DM4), a series of sandstone storage cellars four floors deep which were used as shelters in World War II. There's also a museum-piece brewery, the **Altstadthof-Hausbrauerei**, which was put back into production a few years ago. Its main line is a wonderful unfiltered dark beer which can be bought in bottles at the end of the tour, or sampled on draught in the adjoining bar (see p.145).

Proceeding southwards past the Weinmarkt, you come to the **Spielzeugmuseum** (Toy Museum; Tues & Thurs–Sun 10am–5pm, Wed 10am–9pm; DM5) at Karlstr. 15. This celebrates Nürnberg's continuing role as the world metropolis of toy production by means of a thorough historical presentation of the craft. It's a must for kids – but is just as enjoyable for adults, who can enjoy a sentimental wallow in nostalgia. Further south, the huge half-timbered **Weinstadel**, a medieval wine depot, overlooks a particularly picturesque stretch of the Pegnitz, lined with weeping willows and spanned by the covered wooden walkway known as **Henkersteg** (Hangman's Bridge).

St Sebaldus

Nürnberg's oldest and most important church, the twin-towered **St Sebaldus**, lies just to the east of the Spielzeugmuseum via the quaint Weissgerbergasse. It was erected in the thirteenth century in the Transitional style, with choirs at each end of the building. A century later, the eastern choir was replaced by a soaring hall design. The exterior of the church drips with sculpture: on the south side are early fourteenth-century portals dedicated to the Last Judgment and to the Virgin Mary, while to the north is the slightly later Bridal Doorway, with its carvings of the Wise and Foolish Virgins.

An even more astonishing array of works of art can be found inside the church. Particularly striking is the bronze **shrine of St Sebald**, an early sixteenth-century masterpiece which combines late Gothic and Renaissance decoration and is heavy with religious symbols. **Peter Vischer the Elder**, aided by his two sons, took eleven years to complete this project; look out for the self-portrait of the master founder at work, dressed in skullcap and apron. On the pillar behind is an expressive *Crucifixion* scene (whose figures are taken from two separate groups, made two decades apart) by Nürnberg's most famous sculptor, **Veit Stoss**. The same artist also made the *St Andrew* and the three stone *Passion* reliefs on the end walls of the chancel.

The northeastern quarter

Immediately to the east of St Sebaldus is the **Altes Rathaus**, a self-confident late Renaissance building in the style of a Venetian *palazzo* which incorporates two older houses. If you're into the gorier side of medieval times, visit the torture chambers in the **Lochgefängnisse** underneath (mid-April to mid-Sept Tues–Sun 10am–5pm; DM3). On a lighter note, go through to Rathausgasse to see one of the finest of the city's many fountains, the Renaissance **Gänsemännchen Brunnen**, which shows a farmer carrying two water-spouting geese to market.

Up the road at Burgstr. 15 is the **Fembohaus** (temporarily closed for reconstruction; otherwise March–Oct Tues–Sun 10am–5pm; Nov–Feb Tues–Fri 1–5pm, Sat & Sun 10am–5pm; DM4), now containing the municipal museum. Originally built at the end of the sixteenth century for a rich silk merchant, it has truly startling interior decoration, featuring lurid colour schemes of pastel pink, yellow and green, with riotously ornate white stuccoed ceilings forming the icing on top. A number of interiors from other houses which failed to make it through the war have also been transferred here.

To the east is Egidienplatz, on the north side of which stands the **Pellerhaus**. Originally the finest patrician house in the city, it was almost totally destroyed in the war, but the stately arcaded late Renaissance courtyard has been painstakingly reconstructed. Further along, in the shadow of the modern university buildings, is the earlier **Tucherschlösschen** (currently closed for reconstruction). This home of another (and, thanks to their beer, still prominent) Nürnberg dynasty survived in better shape, enabling it to be fully restored to serve as an illuminating illustration of the lifestyle enjoyed by its former owners.

The Hauptmarkt and around

Commercial heart of the city and main venue for the normal daily markets and the famous Christmas market, the **Hauptmarkt** lies just south of the Altes Rathaus, occupying the site of the Jewish quarter, which was razed to make way for it in a fourteenth-century pogrom. In the centre of the square stands a brightly coloured replica of the celebrated Gothic **Schöner Brunnen** (Beautiful Fountain). A tall stone pyramid chiselled out in filigree style and adorned with statues of the Electors accompanied by pagan, Jewish and Christian heroes, prophets, evangelists and church fathers, it has the dimensions of a great church spire rather than a mere fountain.

The Hauptmarkt's east side is bounded by the **Frauenkirche**. This little jewel of a church, commissioned by Emperor Charles IV as his court chapel, was one of the first buildings by the celebrated Parler family. Its facade, sheltering a porch with a delicately carved doorway dedicated to the Nativity, was enlivened in the early sixteenth century by the addition of a gable, an oriel and a clockwork mechanism known as the

Männleinlaufen, which tinkles away each day at noon. The rather recondite story it tells is of the **Golden Bull** of 1356, whereby the church's founder established the identities of the seven Electors (here shown honouring him) on a permanent basis, as well as designating Nürnberg as the city in which every new emperor had to hold his first Imperial Diet. Among the works of art inside, pride of place goes to the *Tucher Altar* in the chancel, a late Gothic *Crucifixion* **triptych** painted by an unknown but highly expressive artist – now dubbed the Master of the Tucher Altar as a result – who was Nürnberg's finest painter of the period prior to Dürer.

Walking southwards from Hauptmarkt, you cross the River Pegnitz by Museumsbrücke, which gives you a good view of the **Fleischbrücke** to the right (modelled on the Rialto Bridge in Venice) and the **Heilig-Geist-Spital** on the left. The latter – one of the largest hospitals built in the Middle Ages – stands on an islet, with two graceful arches spanning the water. Now a restaurant, it has an old-world inner courtyard with wooden galleries.

The southern quarter

Following Königstrasse south from the river, you shortly come to the parish church of **St Lorenz**. At first sight, it's remarkably similar in appearance to St Sebaldus; the reason for this is that Nürnberg grew out of two separate settlements either side of the Pegnitz, which competed with each other for the most imposing church. In fact it soon becomes apparent that, notwithstanding the near-identical shape and ground plan, the churches are actually quite different, with the constituent parts of St Lorenz built about fifty years after those of its counterpart. Thus the nave, complete with a majestic main portal and a resplendent rose window, is modelled on the High Gothic cathedrals in France, while the hall chancel, lit by a gleaming set of stained-glass windows, is in the Flamboyant style. Look out for the graceful late fifteenth-century **tabernacle** some 20m high, worked out of local sandstone by **Adam Kraft**, who depicted himself as a fiery, pensive figure crouching at the base. Equally spectacular is the larger-than-life polychrome wood *Annunciation* by **Veit Stoss** which is suspended from the ceiling above the high altar.

Outside the church is another wonderful fountain, the Mannerist **Tugendbrunnen**, in which water gushes from the breasts of the Seven Virtues and from the trumpets of the putti. Diagonally opposite is the oldest house in the city, the thirteenth-century **Nassauer Haus**. If you follow Karolinenstrasse west from here, you can see two notable modern additions to the city's tally of fountains. The **Peter-Henlein-Brunnen** on Hefnersplatz honours the local inventor who produced the first-ever pocket watch in the early sixteenth century. On Ludwigsplatz further west is the **Ehekarussell Brunnen**; illustrating a poem by the cobbler Hans Sachs (see box opposite), it displays six scenes from marriage, humorously alternating between bliss and nightmare.

Returning to Nassauer Haus and continuing down Königstrasse in the direction of the Hauptbahnhof you come to the massive and austere Renaissance **Mauthalle**, whose sloping roof is pierced by six tiers of windows. Formerly a granary and later a customs house, it now houses various stores plus another *Hausbrauerei* (see p.145). Beyond is the Gothic church of **St Martha**, the former hall of the Mastersingers.

The **Handwerkerhof** (March 20–Dec 23 Mon–Fri 10am–6pm, Sat 10am–4pm; restaurants open till 10pm) by the Königstor, is an enclosed "medieval" village that brings to life historic Nürnberg trades such as handmade tin soldiers, dolls, brass objects and the famed *Lebkuchen* spice-cakes. Hot *Apfelstrudel* or the local delicacy of *Nürnberger Bratwürste* for sale in old-style taverns are very tasty. Just outside the Altstadt to the west of here, at Lessingstr. 6, is the **Verkehrsmuseum** (Transport Museum; Tues–Sun 9am–5pm; DM5). This concentrates on German railways and has many ancient locomotives parked in its showrooms. These include a copy of the country's first train (named the *Adler* after Germany's eagle symbol) and the original of King Ludwig II's state train

THE MASTERSINGERS OF NÜRNBERG

Nürnberg was only one of many homes of the distinctive form of lyric poetry known as *Meistergesang*, which flourished from the fourteenth century onwards, practised mainly by members of the skilled artisan class. The rules were highly pedantic, with words having to be fitted to *Töne* composed by thirteenth-century minstrels, and by the sixteenth century it had become a rather moribund art, despite a relaxation of the restrictions placed on the introduction of new *Töne*.

Nonetheless, it had a glorious final fling in Nürnberg, thanks above all to **Hans Sachs**. For a man who had to fit his literary activities into his spare time away from his trade of shoemaking, Sachs was unbelievably prolific, producing some 6000 works, including well over 100 full-length plays which do not, however, show him at his best. Apart from some of the most accomplished *Meistergesänge*, Sachs wrote *Schwänke* (humorous stories told in doggerel verse) and *Fastnachtspiele* (dramatic interludes performed at Shrovetide). He was also a propagandist for the Reformation, coining Luther's proudly borne nickname of "the Nightingale of Wittenberg". That grandest of grand operas, Wagner's *The Mastersingers of Nürnberg*, is a celebration of the art of Sachs and his cronies; though historically rather wayward, it ranks as the most spectacular of the many tributes paid to the city by the Romantic movement.

which really does look like a miniature version on wheels of one of his fantasy castles. An instructive section on the role of rail during the Third Reich is also featured.

The Germanisches Nationalmuseum

The **Germanisches Nationalmuseum** (Tues & Thurs–Sun 10am–5pm, Wed 10am–9pm; DM6) on Kartäusergasse, which concentrates almost exclusively on the German cultural tradition, is one of the largest and most varied collections in the country. It occupies the late fourteenth-century **Karthaus** (Charterhouse) which is itself of considerable interest as the most complete example of this type of monastery in Germany, though the modern galleries which have been added to provide badly needed extra display space seriously mar the effect.

THE GROUND FLOOR

On the **ground floor**, the first rooms contain the earliest items, ranging from a golden cone from the Bronze Age to the tenth-century *Echternach Gospels*. Immediately following is the section devoted to medieval **stone sculptures** from some of Nürnberg's most famous buildings (notably the Schöner Brunnen and the two parish churches), brought here for conservation, and replaced *in situ* with copies. You next enter the **Karthauskirche**, which still preserves the simple Gothic form favoured by the silent Carthusian monks. Exhibited here are the reliefs of *The Seven Stations of the Cross* by Adam Kraft, which originally lined the road to the Johannisfriedhof.

In the adjoining cloister are carvings by **Veit Stoss**, including an anguished *Crucifixion*, a light-hearted pair of *Tobias and the Archangel Raphael*, and the *Rosenkranztafel*, a large wooden panel graphically portraying the drama of Judgment Day. A few sculptures by the other great woodcarver of the period, **Tilman Riemenschneider** – notably a noble figure of *St Elizabeth* – can be seen in the gallery beyond, which is chiefly devoted to fifteenth-century painting. The most important work here is *The Annunciation*, one of the best of the few surviving works of **Conrad Witz**, who played a crucial role in moving German painting towards a greater sense of realism: the perspective attempted in this panel is a world away from the flat backgrounds found in most of the other paintings here. Next comes an outstanding collection of historical **musical instruments**, which occupies the whole of the south wing.

THE FIRST FLOOR

German painting at its Renaissance peak dominates the **first floor**, where you can see some **Dürer** originals. *Hercules Slaying the Stymphalian Birds* is a fairly early work, and the only mythological painting by the artist to have survived. The pair of imaginary portraits of *The Emperor Charlemagne* and *The Emperor Sigismund* were commissioned to adorn the room in which the imperial treasury (now in Vienna) was kept during the

NÜRNBERG UNDER THE NAZIS

As the present city council is eager to point out, the Nazis' choice of Nürnberg as the backdrop for their *Reichsparteitage* had little to do with local support of the "brown" ideology. Indeed, in marked contrast to Munich, the votes cast for them here in each of the elections before their assumption of power were derisory. The crucial factor was what the medieval city represented in German history: not only had it been the *de facto* capital, its rapid rise to prominence was seen as showing the nation's dynamism at its very peak. Also, the local police made it very easy for the NSDAP to gain the upper hand here, since they resented centralized Bavarian control and hoped to gain more independence if the Nazis took over.

The first of the **Nürnberg rallies** was held in 1927; between 1933 and 1938 they were an annual event, Hitler using the 1938 rally to raise world tension during the Munich crisis. As the most important display of Nazi power for home and foreign consumption, they were highly organized and ritualized mass demonstrations. Hitler's speeches formed the climax of the show, the intention being to underline his own unquestioned status as *Führer* and the total unity of purpose existing between the leadership and the led. Up to 250,000 people took part in these events, which were expertly stage-managed and totally hypnotic for the mass of participants. The sheer organizational skills which had to be brought to bear were themselves a form of preparation for war – and intended as a further warning to potential enemies. Leni Riefenstahl's film *Triumph of the Will*, a lyrical hymn to Nazism, is the best record of the week-long rallies.

There was no more fanatical proponent of the Nazis' anti-Semitic policies than the Franconian party chief, **Julius Streicher**, who strode around the city administering instant "justice" with his whip, and whose depravities reached such depths that even fellow party members felt sickened. His odious anti-Semitic newspaper *Der Stürmer* was specifically designed to stir up hysteria against the Jews, with its stories of their alleged child sacrifices and sexual perversities. The highlight of his career came with the passing of the so-called **Nürnberg Laws** in 1935, which deprived Jews of their citizenship and forbade relations between Jews and Gentiles. It was through these laws that the Nazis justified their extermination of six million Jews, 10,000 of whom came from Nürnberg – where the Jewish population was reduced to single figures by the end of the war.

So great was Nürnberg's identification with the proudest demonstrations of power of the Third Reich that it was deliberately chosen by the victorious Allies as the place for the **war-crime trials**, which are graphically recounted in Rebecca West's book *A Train of Powder*. The surviving leading players of the "Thousand Year Reich", before whom an entire nation had trembled for twelve years, now mostly appeared as broken men – and were shown up publicly as the ragbag of fanatics and misfits they had in reality always been. Ten of the most important Nazis – Ribbentrop, Keitel, Kaltenbrunner, Rosenberg, Frank, Frick, Streicher, Seyss-Inquart, Sauckel and Jodl – were successively hanged here at short intervals in the early hours of October 16, 1946. Ex-Field Marshall Hermann Göring committed suicide by swallowing a concealed cyanide pill two hours before his appointed execution. Of the rest, Hess, Funk and Raeder were confined to prison for life, while Speer, Schirach, Dönitz and Neurath were all given long-term sentences. Three men were acquitted: the propaganda officer Hans Fritzsche; Franz von Papen, the bungling ex-Chancellor who was more responsible than anyone else for Hitler's initial assumption of power; and Hjalmar Schacht, the financial guru who had managed the economic affairs of the Third Reich with the same enthusiasm, shrewdness and lack of political concern as he had shown when running the national economy in the days of the Weimar Republic.

years it was displayed in Nürnberg; the actual crown, orb and sceptre are accurately depicted in the paintings. In contrast, *Emperor Maximilian I* and *Michael Wolgemut* are portraits made from life; the latter is a touching yet unsentimental portrayal of the artist's former teacher, by then a wrinkled old man of 82. Three panels from a dispersed series of *The Life of St Florian* by **Altdorfer** use the landscapes of the Danube valley to impressive effect; this same backdrop also occurs in **Baldung's** *Rest on the Flight into Egypt*. Most interesting of several works by **Cranach** is *King Christian II of Denmark*; the monarch had by then been deposed and had fled to Wittenberg, where he stayed as the artist's house guest.

The following rooms focus on the diversity of Nürnberg's achievements during the Renaissance. There was a strong **goldsmith** tradition, shown to best effect in the superbly fashioned model of a three-masted ship. The city also played a leading role in the fast-developing science of geography, and you can see the first globe of the earth, made by **Martin Behaim** in 1491 – just before the discovery of America. From three-quarters of a century later is a globe of the heavens by another local man, Wenzel Jamnitzer. This floor's south wing is entirely devoted to German **folklore** and in particular religious traditions which show the roots of customs still alive in rural areas.

Luitpoldhain

In virtually everyone's mind the word Nürnberg conjures up thoughts of Nazi rallies and the war-crime trials: in most peoples' memories are the scratchy black-and-white newsreels of fanatical crowds roaring *Sieg Heil*, and of Göring, Ribbentrop and other leaders standing in the dock a few years later. Nürnberg has the unenviable task of facing up to its historical role (see box opposite) more closely and openly than other cities, and the authorities, to their credit, have made a positive move towards helping visitors get to grips with the events of that time. The park known as the **Luitpoldhain** in the southeastern suburbs of the city, where many of the Nazi buildings still stand, has been dedicated to the memory of their victims, though it is also used for commercial and recreational purposes. If this seems a somewhat incongruous mix, it is in reality a case of history turning full circle, as the Luitpoldhain was originally laid out for the Bavarian Jubilee Exhibition of 1906, and was later a memorial for the dead of World War I before being commandeered by the Nazis.

At the northern entrance to the park, reached from the city centre by tram #9, is the **Luitpoldarena**, where parades of Nazi groups such as the SA and SS were held. Its grounds contained the former exhibition hall where the party conferences were held, but this was completely destroyed by bombing in 1945. The custom-built but unfinished **Kongressbau** behind, however, remains standing, and is the most chilling surviving visual reminder of the pretensions of the Third Reich. Built in the debased Neoclassical style beloved of modern totalitarian dictators, it self-consciously tries to present an updated, upstaging version of Rome's Colosseum. Appropriately enough, all attempts to find a suitable use for this monstrosity have come to nothing; part of it is used as a store, while it's pressed into occasional service for crowd-pulling pop concerts.

To the rear, the **Grosse Strasse** leads over the artificial lake down to another parade ground, the **Märzfeld**. The dimensions of this road – 2km long and 60m wide – are awesome; the vista it opens up includes a distant view of the Kaiserburg, thus creating a visual reference to the symbolic union the Nazis wished to have with the medieval city. Nowadays, part of it is used as a car park by visitors to the modern trade fair buildings nearby. You can return to the Kongressbau by taking the path to the east. This passes firstly the **Stadion**, used for meetings of the Hitler Youth but now returned to its original purpose as a sports venue as home of the football club *FC Nürnberg*. Further north is the **Zeppelinfeld**, which was transformed by Albert Speer (Hitler's favourite architect, and subsequently armaments minister) into a stadium for the most important parades. The colonnaded tribunes, so familiar from old films, had to be dismantled for safety reasons, but the towers and terraces remain. Nowadays, the complex is used as a sports centre and for the celebrated **Norisring car races** in late June. (Information and tickets are available from *MCN Motorsport-Club Nürnberg*, Spittlertorgraben 47, ☎267990.) At the back is the entrance to a multi-media presentation on the city's Nazi legacy, **Faszination und Gewalt** (Fascination and Force; May–Oct Tues–Sun 10am–6pm; DM2). By the year 2000, it will be replaced by a more permanent documentation centre on the northern face of the Kongressbau. It's also worth asking at the tourist office for the useful leaflet *Nürnberg 1933–1945*.

Eating, drinking and nightlife

Nürnberg is the liveliest Bavarian city next to Munich, with a wealth of watering-holes and nightspots to suit all tastes and pockets. If the Bavarian's favourite snack is a *Weisswurst*, the Franconian's is the *Bratwurst*. These are slim pork sausages, roasted over wood fires and served with a choice of accompaniments: sauerkraut, potato salad, onions or radishes. The most curious culinary feature of Nürnberg is that these sausages have been turned into an item of serious cuisine, best sampled in the highly rated speciality restaurants to the accompaniment of a glass of one of the wide variety of beers produced by the local *Tucher* or *Patrizier* breweries. Equally ubiquitous are Nürnberger *Lebkuchen*, delicious spice-cakes made from flour, nuts, honey, eggs and spices. Usually they're only eaten around Christmas: this is the only place you can buy them all year round.

While many of the obviously recommendable places are in or near the Altstadt, it's also worth taking the U-Bahn to the grand nineteenth-century inner suburbs to the west, where there are some enticing alternatives.

Restaurants

SAUSAGE RESTAURANTS

Bratwurst-Friedl, Hallplatz 21. Offers a full, moderately priced menu in addition to the sausage specialities. Closed Sun.

Bratwurst-Glöcklein, Im Handwerkerhof. Despite its commercialized position in the crafts market, the food here can rival that of any of its competitors. Closed Sun.

Bratwurst-Häusle, Rathausplatz 1. With its huge chimney for grilling the sausages smoking over the main square, this is the most famous of the group: in spite of the restricted menu and frequent tourist hordes, it really shouldn't be missed. Closed Sun.

Bratwurst-Röslein, Obstmarkt 1. Has a fairly upmarket menu in addition to the traditional sausage fare. Closed Mon.

Historische Bratwurstküche, Zirkelschmiedsgasse 26. Housed in a renovated fifteenth-century tavern, with a truly *gemütlich* atmosphere. Closed Sun.

OTHER RESTAURANTS

Böhms Herrenkeller, Theatergasse 19. Popular old wine bar-cum-restaurant. Closed Sun.

Essigbrätlein, Weinmarkt 3. One of the city's top restaurants for both international and traditional German cuisine. Very expensive; closed Sun & Mon.

Frankenstube, Pilotystr. 73. Situated just north of the Altstadt, this combines reasonably priced food with a good atmosphere.

Goldenes Posthorn, Glöckleinsgasse 2. A *Gaststätte* which has been on the go since the time of Dürer, and is still among the best in the city.

Heilig-Geist-Spital, Spitalgasse 12. Occupying the medieval hospital, this is arguably the city's most atmospheric restaurant; the food is outstanding too.

Kettensteg, Maxplatz 35. Traditional *Gasthaus* with picturesque beer garden by the River Pegnitz.

Mount Lavinia, Jakobsplatz 22. The one and only Sinhalese restaurant in Germany; also serves Thai dishes. Evenings only.

Nassauer Keller, Karolinenstr. 2. Highly rated restaurant in the cellars of Nürnberg's oldest house.

Pele-Mele, Grossweidenmühlstr. 17. Bistro just west of the Altstadt which presents a choice of riverside beer garden or cool vaulted cellar in which to have your meal.

Zig-Zag, Rohledererstr. 6. Serves excellent Spanish meals in a bar-type setting by the Pegnitz, a short distance northwest of the Altstadt.

Zum Schuldturm Heubrücke, Vordere Insel Schütt 4. *Gaststätte* with the nicest beer garden in the Altstadt, directly overlooking the Pegnitz.

Zum Sudhaus, Bergstr. 20. Well-regarded, fairly pricey restaurant with engagingly rustic decor.

Bars

Barfüsser, Hallplatz 2. *Hausbrauerei* in the cavernous cellars of the Mauthalle, whose walls are lined with pictures of film stars of the Fifties and Sixties. It brews a *Weisse* as well as light and dark beers; the food is inexpensive and typically hearty.

Freudenpark, Kilianstr. 125. This bar immediately north of the Altstadt has a 30-page drinks list that should keep you busy.

Landwehrkeller, Innere-Laufer-Gasse 11. Good choice for late-night drinking (and eating); also has occasional live music.

Lederer-Bräu, Sielstr. 12. Another *Hausbrauerei*, occupying a modern glass palace. Its main product is a dark beer known as *Krokodil*, and it also serves full meals. It's in the western part of the city, reached by U-Bahn to Bärenschanze.

O'Neill's, Bärenschanzstr. 121. The pick of the local Irish pubs is situated well off the beaten track; take the U-Bahn to Bärenschanze.

Palais Schaumburg, Kernstr. 46. Reached by taking the U-Bahn to Gostenhof, this has a beer garden, and also serves inexpensive meals, including an extensive vegetarian menu.

Schwarzer Bauer, Bergstr. 19. This small *Kneipe* is attached to the *Altstadthof-Hausbrauerei* mentioned on p.138. It also serves the products of its parent, the out-of-town *Lammsbräu*.

Werkstatt, Adam-Klein-Str. 87. A real oddity: features spare car parts for interior design, and beer served out of a petrol pump. Take the U-Bahn to Maximilianstrasse.

Cafés and café-bars

Balazzo Brozzi, Hochstr. 2. Located just west of the Altstadt, this is a good place to start the day if you want a choice of cheap and decent breakfast dishes.

Café Dampfnudel-Bäcker, Johannisstr. 34. Traditional café specializing in steamed dumplings.

Meisengeige, Am Laufer Schlagturm 3. Tiny café-bar catering for a mixed and unpretentious crowd; there's also a small cinema attached that runs an off-beat selection of films you won't find in the commercial venues.

Mohr, Färberstr. 3. Candlelit café-bar handy for the Germanisches Nationalmuseum.

Ruhestörung, Tetzelgasse 21. One of the main young and trendy watering-holes, with raucous music.

Wiener Spezialitäten Café, Kaiserstr. 1. As its name suggests, this is a Viennese-style coffee house.

Entertainment and nightlife

The main **theatre** venue, with the *Opernhaus* and the *Schauspielhaus*, is at Richard-Wagner-Platz 2 (☎231 3808), just a few minutes' walk to the west of the Hauptbahnhof. Another leading drama venue is *Die Bühne im Altstadthof*, Bergstr. 19 (☎224327). **Concerts**, notably those by the *Nürnberger Symphoniker*, are held at the *Meistersingerhalle*, some 2km southeast of the centre at Münchener Str. 21 (☎492011). For details of all events, consult either the *Monatsmagazin* (DM2), available from the tourist office, or the *Plärrer* magazine (DM4), on sale at any kiosk.

Music bars

Rock-Café Brown Sugar, Königstorgraben 3. A couple of minutes' walk north of the Hauptbahnhof, this is the best of the city's seemingly endless number of heavy metal bars, with pinball machines and videos among the heady attractions.

Schmelztiegel, Bergstr. 21. Jazz bar which plays predominantly Dixieland.

Starclub, Maxtorgraben 33. Combination of a music bar and traditional beer haven, complete with garden.

Zabo-Linde, Zerzabelshofer Hauptstr. 28, Zerzabelshof. Both a traditional *Gaststätte* with beer garden and a regular venue for live music, ranging from rock to disco. Worth making the trip out for, if the evening's music programme appeals. Check in the *Plärrer*, Nürnberg's listings magazine (see p.145). It's in an eastern suburb, reached by bus #43 or #44 to Zerzabelshof/Mitte.

Nightclubs

Amico, Köhnstr. 53. Gay disco-bar just to the rear of the Hauptbahnhof, with a tiny dance floor. Mon–Wed & Sun 9pm–2am, Fri–Sat 9pm–3am.

Bezirk 40, Humboldstr. 116. Cosy place offering TV, video games and pinball machines, which is popular with people who like going to nightclubs without having to make too much of an effort. Also serves food. Daily 7pm–1am.

Mach 1, Kaiserstr. 1–9. Currently the city's trendiest nightspot; the four different bars ensure variety, and there are some good lighting effects. Thurs–Sat 10pm–4am.

NÜRNBERG'S FESTIVALS

Nürnberg really comes alive in the summer when open-air music festivals and concerts abound. The season starts off in late May with Musica Franconia, a week-long series of concerts of old music played on period instruments. For a fortnight in June, the Kulturzirkus, an international theatre festival, is held. Towards the end of the same month begins the three-week-long Internationale Orgelwoche, featuring organ recitals in the city's churches and in the *Meistersingerhalle*; the office for information and tickets is at Bismarckstr. 46 (☎163528). The Bardentreffen in the last week of July or first week of August is a popular annual event where singers and songwriters from Europe come together in free open-air concerts all over the city. An equally high status is enjoyed by the Ost-West Jazzfestival in the last week of October, which encompasses every jazz style and brings together musicians from around the world.

Prominent among folklore festivals is the Altstadtfest at the end of September, a local fair celebrating Franconian culture, with lots of food and drink, as well as river tournaments and a procession in traditional costumes. Finally, with a 400-year tradition, the Nürnberg Christkindlesmarkt (Christmas market) held on the Hauptmarkt from November 25 until December 24, is the largest and most popular in Germany, as well as being the founder of what has become very much a national institution, with derivatives found in every town of any size. It stands apart from its imitators by the wealth of handmade quality goods on sale, such as toys, brass utensils and tin soldiers, glass objects of all kinds, and, of course, the delicious *Lebkuchen*.

Listings

Airport ☎3506 200 for flight information.

Car rental *Avis*, Allersberger Str. 139 (☎49696); *Europcar*, Scharrorstr. 5 (☎946270); *Hertz*, Untere Grasersgasse 25, (☎209086). There are also many offices at the Hauptbahnhof and airport.

Medical emergencies Kesslerplatz (☎533771).

Mitfahrzentrale Aussere-Laufer-Gasse 26 (☎19440); Strauchstr. 1 (☎19444).

Post office The main post office is situated at Bahnhofsplatz 1 with poste restante services.

Taxis ☎19410.

Erlangen

Just 20km north of Nürnberg, and regarded as an integral part of its conurbation, **ERLAN-GEN** is nevertheless itself a major city, with its own history, traditions and appearance. On the revocation of the Edict of Nantes in 1683, ending religious toleration in France, a large number of Huguenots settled here at the invitation of Margrave Christian Ernst of Bayreuth. A **planned town** of regular streets and squares in the sober Baroque style then current in Protestant circles was built to accommodate them; this was extended to cover the whole of the city when the medieval Altstadt was destroyed by fire twenty years later. The Huguenots, skilled in textiles and leather crafts, established Erlangen's reputation as a major industrial centre, a tradition maintained today by electro-technics and power engineering. Indeed, Erlangen might be regarded almost as a company town of Siemens, were it not for the presence of the university, founded in 1743 and now shared with Nürnberg. The presence of so many students ensures an almost continuously lively atmosphere, and makes what might otherwise seem a place of specialist appeal into one seriously worth considering as an alternative base to its famous and more expensive neighbour.

The town

Arriving at the **Hauptbahnhof**, at the western side of town, you're immediately confronted with the quarter of the original refugees. Across Bahnhofplatz stand the parish administration buildings of the **Hugenottenkirche**, which fronts the eponymous square on the far side. Outside, it appears as a plain box, enlivened only by the tower which was added a generation after the main body of the building. Inside, the wooden galleries have been arranged to give the illusion that the church is round in shape; otherwise, the pulpit provides the only decorative touch. Across Hugenottenplatz is the **Universitätskirche**, which has a similar tower but is otherwise less austere, its double-galleried hall interior, in which pulpit and altar are combined in a single unit, being enlivened with rich stucco work. A fine group of eighteenth-century houses, including the old pharmacy, stand around the church.

A couple of blocks to the north, divided by the pedestrian section of the central Hauptstrasse, are two more important squares. To the west is Marktplatz, on whose southern side is the **Stutterheimsches Palais**, formerly the Rathaus, now the public library and main local cultural centre. Across the road is Schlossplatz, in the centre of which stands a statue to Margrave Friedrich, the founder of the university. The **Schloss** itself, which takes up the entire eastern side of the square, now serves as the university's administrative headquarters. Despite Erlangen's association with technology, its academic tradition has been strongest in the humanities. Three of Germany's best-known nineteenth-century philosophers – Fichte, Schelling and Feuerbach – taught here. However, the most famous professor was the Orientalist **Friedrich Rückert**, who introduced poetry based on Persian, Sanskrit and Chinese models into the German language. Schubert and Brahms were among the composers who set his texts, while Mahler's kaleidoscopic song cycles *Rückert-Lieder* and *Kindertotenlieder* have raised his artistic standing to a level far beyond its purely literary merit.

Some compensation for the fact that the Schloss' original interiors were lost in a fire last century is the **Schlosspark** to the rear. The first part of this is a formal French garden, closed off by the horseshoe-shaped **Orangerie** to the north, and with the **Hugenottenbrunnen**, a large allegorical fountain, as centrepiece. Further reaches of the park are laid out in the English manner; tucked away in the middle is an equestrian memorial to Margrave Christian Ernst.

Immediately north of the Schloss is the **Wasserturm**, which served as the student prison for most of last century. Northeast of here is Theaterplatz, whose south side is lined by the three buildings primarily responsible for Erlangen's continued high standing in the dramatic field. The **Markgrafentheater**, indeed, is the town's finest feature, a part-Baroque part-Rococo jewel worthy of Bayreuth itself and still put to regular use. Alongside it stand the **Redoutensaal**, built as the main festival hall of the local Margraves, and the **Marstall** (stables), now the home of the experimental *Theater in der Garage*. North of here, at the top end of Hauptstrasse, the **Dreifaltigkeitskirche** was originally the parish church of the Altstadt, but rebuilt in the Lutheran Baroque style of its two counterparts in the new town. Once again the pulpit and altar blend seamlessly into one.

Beyond the built-up area are the ample open spaces of the **Burgberg**, the main public park. For eleven days up to and including Pentecost (variable date in May/June) each year, this is the site of the **Bergkirchweih**, one of Bavaria's leading folk festivals. It's rather like a smaller version of Munich's Oktoberfest, with orgies of beer drinking in massive tents, hairy funfair rides, and performances of traditional and rock music. However, it is less blatantly commercialized and thus more authentically German, and all the attractions are concentrated in a manageable area.

Practicalities

The **tourist office** (May–Oct Mon–Fri 8am–6pm, Sat 10am–noon; Nov–April Mon–Thurs 8am–4.30pm, Fri 8am–12.30pm; ☎09131/89510) is beyond the southern end of Hauptstrasse at Rathausplatz 1.

Erlangen really scores in its range of accommodation. Budget **hotels** in the centre include *Gasthof Schwarzer Bär*, just south of the Hauptbahnhof at Innere-Brucker-Str. 19 (☎09131/22872; ③), and *Gasthof Oppelei*, Halbmondstr. 4 (☎09131/21562; ③). There are plenty of more upmarket options, including *Grauer Wolf*, Hauptstr. 80 (☎09131/81060; ⑥); *Altmann's Stube*, Theaterplatz 9 (☎09131/89160; ⑥); and *Rokokohaus*, Theaterplatz 13 (☎09131/7830; ⑦).

The **youth hostel** is right in the heart of town at Südliche Stadtmauerstr. 35 (☎09131/862555; ❷), while the **campsite** (☎09131/28499), which is open all year round, is at the same address as the *Regnitz-Stuben*, near the Hauptbahnhof.

All the hotels listed above, except for *Rokokohaus*, have **restaurants**. Good alternatives are *Grüner Markt*, just off Marktplatz at Einhornstr. 9; *Weinstube Kach*, Kirchenstr. 2; and *Bärengarten*, below the Burgberg at Rathsberger Str. 2. Plenty of **student bars** and **discos** can also be found dotted all over the town centre.

Eichstätt

EICHSTÄTT, in the far south of Franconia, can be reached via a short branch line from the main rail route linking both Nürnberg and Würzburg with Munich. Nowadays, it's best known as the gateway to Germany's largest *Naturpark*, the **Altmühl valley**, a Jurassic region first inhabited by humans 100,000 years ago, whose soils have produced many yields of prehistoric fossils and minerals in a quite remarkable state of preservation. The town itself was for centuries a prince-bishopric at the junction of the three historic provinces of Bavaria, Franconia and Swabia, and was sufficiently prestigious for one of its rulers to gain election as Pope Victor II. Having been almost completely destroyed in the Thirty Years' War, it was rebuilt by Italian Baroque architects, giving it an incongruously Mediterranean appearance. Since it was incorporated into Bavaria in the Napoleonic reforms, it seems to have gone to sleep, though in 1980 it became the seat of a new Catholic university – the only one in the German-speaking world.

The city

The main part of Eichstätt lies on the right bank of the Altmühl, on the opposite side of the river from the **Stadtbahnhof**, which is connected by diesels to the mainline Bahnhof 5km away.

The Dom

As you'd expect, the **Dom** is the focal point of the Altstadt. Essentially, it's a fourteenth-century Gothic structure with a number of Baroque accretions, of which the facade is the most jarring. The Dom is especially notable for a number of outstanding works of art. Prominent among these is the **Pappenheim altar** in the north transept, a virtuoso carving by an unknown late Gothic master of the Crucifixion, with each of the myriad figures carefully characterized. In the chancel, look out for the extraordinarily realistic **seated statue of St Willibald**, a memorial to the first Eichstätt bishop. Though dating from just a couple of decades after the altar, it is fully Renaissance in style and is by one of the few German sculptors to master this idiom, **Loy Hering**, who also carved the *Wolfsteinaltar* on the west wall and the *Crucifix* in the Sakramentskapelle. Off the west side of the cloisters is the **Mortuarium**, which is anything but the grim chamber its name suggests: it's a stately Gothic hall divided by a row of differently shaped columns, one of which is known as the Schöne Säule (Beautiful Pillar) from its profuse carvings. There's also a brilliantly coloured stained-glass window of *The Last Judgment*, designed by Holbein the Elder, and a *Crucifixion* group by Hering.

The rest of the Altstadt

South of the Dom is **Residenzplatz**, one of Germany's most harmonious squares, lined with magnificent Baroque and Rococo palaces of the local knights and canons, and with the cheerful Marienbrunnen in the centre. The **Residenz** (guided tours Mon–Thurs 10am, 11am, 2pm & 3pm, Fri 10am & 11am, Sat and Sun every 30min 10–11.30am 2–3.30pm; DM2), formerly the home of the prince-bishops, is now occupied by offices, which seems a rather unworthy use of a building with such decorous features as the monumental staircase and the second-floor **Spiegelsaal**. At no. 7 on the same square is the **Diözesanmuseum** (April–Oct Tues–Sat 9.30am–1pm & 2–5pm, Sun 11am–5pm; DM2.50), containing the Dom's treasury and a collection of sacred art.

Continuing south, you pass the handsome Jesuit **Schutzengelkirche** en route to the stately Hofgarten, one of whose borders is taken up by the long frontage of the **Sommerresidenz**, formerly the second residence of the bishops, now the administrative headquarters of the Catholic University. Just beyond is the **Kapuzinerkirche**, which houses a twelfth-century Holy Sepulchre, one of the earliest and most accurate reproductions of the Jerusalem original, constructed with the help of descriptions supplied by Crusaders who had been there.

On the opposite side of the Dom, the commercial life of the city is centred on **Marktplatz**, another Baroque square whose central fountain bears another statue of St Willibald. Further north is the convent of **St Walburg**, a popular pilgrimage place, as it contains the tomb of the eponymous saint, Willibald's sister. There's the bonus of the best view of the town and the valley from the balcony in front of the church.

The Willibaldsburg

Occupying a dominant position high above the left bank of the Altmühl, and reached via Burgstrasse from the rear of the Stadtbahnhof, is the **Willibaldsburg**. The earliest parts of this huge fortress date back to the mid-fourteenth century, but the most prominent part is the sumptuous palatial wing designed in the early seventeenth century by the great Augsburg architect, Elias Holl. This section now houses the **Jura Museum** and the **Historisches Museum** (both April–Sept Tues–Sun 9am–noon & 1–5pm; Oct–March Tues–Sun 10am–noon & 1–4pm; DM5). Here you can see some of the many finds made in the region; don't be put off by the subject matter, as hi-tech display techniques make this a fascinating experience. The rarest object is the skeleton (one of only five in the world) of a prehistoric bird known as the archeopteryx, while the most imposing is the four-metre-high, sixty-thousand-year-old mammoth.

Practicalities

Eichstätt's **tourist office** (May–Oct Mon–Fri 9am–noon & 1–6pm, Sat 10am–noon & 1–5pm, Sun 10am–noon; Nov–April Mon–Fri 8am–noon & 1–4pm only; ☎08421/7977) is at Kardinal-Preysing-Platz 14. In addition, there's a separate information centre for the Altmühl valley at Notre Dame 1 (April–Oct Mon–Sat 9am–5pm, Sun 10am–5pm; ☎08421/6733).

There's a good range of central **hotels**, including *Gasthof Zum Griechen*, Westenstr. 17 (☎08421/2640; ③); *Gasthof Ratskeller*, Kardinal-Preysing-Platz 8 (☎08421/1258; ④); *Gasthof Sonne*, Buchtal 17 (☎08421/6791; ④); and *Adler*, which occupies a Baroque mansion at Marktplatz 22–24 (☎08421/6767; ⑥). An excellent alternative is the *Burgschänke* in the Willibaldsburg, Burgstr. 19 (☎08421/80444; ⑤). There are also plenty of **private houses** offering rooms (①–②): the tourist office can supply a list. You'll find the **youth hostel** to the west of town at Reichenaustr. 15 (☎08421/4427; ✿).

All the hotels listed above, with the exception of *Adler*, have **restaurants**, and all are good and reasonably priced. Another enticing choice for a meal is *Krone*, Domplatz 3, which also has a beer garden; though the top cuisine is at the pricey *Domherrenhof*, which occupies a Rococo mansion at Domplatz 5.

Ansbach

ANSBACH, 50km southwest of Nürnberg, wears a grand air which is quite disproportionate to its small size. Having chosen the town as their home, the local margraves (members of the Hohenzollern dynasty) were keen to have a seat of suitable splendour, and over the centuries Ansbach became quite polished, its streets characterized by Renaissance and Baroque buildings. Alongside its architecture, Ansbach has gone down in the annals of German history as the site of the unsolved murder of **Kaspar Hauser**, the notorious foundling.

The town centre

The **Residenzschloss** (guided tours April–Sept Tues–Sun 9am–noon & 2–5pm; Oct–March Tues–Sun 10am–noon & 2–4pm; DM4) is situated just on the edge of the old town centre, and is best known for its Rococo interior. Highlights are the high-ceilinged ballroom, the **Spiegelkabinett** (Cabinet of Mirrors), and the **Fayencenzimmer** (Porcelain Gallery), which displays thousands of delicately designed tiles made in the local factory. Just across the road the **Hofgarten** and **Orangerie** form a pleasant setting for walks along paths lined by centuries-old trees. It was in this park in 1833 that poor Kaspar Hauser received fatal stab wounds, and just next to the Orangerie is a stone memorial with the inscription: "Here died a man unknown by means unknown". The local **Markgrafenmuseum** on Schaitbergerstrasse (Tues–Sun 10am–noon & 2–5pm; DM2) documents the story of his life and times in a comprehensive fashion, though you'll need to have some German to get the most from the exhibition.

Right in the middle of the old town centre is the church of **St Gumbertus**. Originally it was part of a Romanesque Benedictine monastery, but the only remainder from that period is the **crypt** (Fri–Sun 11am–noon & 3–5pm). Its Gothic chancel was converted to

THE MYSTERY OF KASPAR HAUSER

One day in 1828, a plainly dressed, bewildered-looking youth turned up in the streets of Nürnberg, carrying two letters addressed to the authorities. One was from a labourer who claimed to have guarded him for the past sixteen years, albeit in conditions of close confinement; the other purported to be from his natural mother, stating that his deceased father had been a cavalry officer. The boy gave his name as **Kaspar Hauser**, but he was unable to tell anyone where he came from, shunned all nourishment except for bread and water, and seemed to lack all knowledge of external objects. His appearance caused an immediate sensation in the local press; this soon spread across Germany and beyond, fuelled by the burgeoning interest in psychology and the abnormal. There were all kinds of wild speculations as to his origins: one theory that was particularly popular was that he was the eldest son of Grand Duke Carl Ludwig of Baden, who had been kidnapped by order of his step-mother, though this seemed to be disproved by evidence that the child in question had died in infancy. In due course Kaspar was educated and proved to be highly intelligent and creative. He moved to Ansbach in 1831, becoming clerk to the president of the court of appeal. Two years later, just as he seemed to be falling out of the limelight, he met his violent death there. His murderer was never found, adding a final unsettling mystery to his life story: many suspected that he had died by his own hand. Much has been written about him since, little of it conclusive.

A highly effective fictionalization of the story by the Jewish author, Jakob Wassermann, which was once among the most widely read German novels, is the most rewarding book on the subject.

serve as the **Schwannenritterordenkapelle**, sheltering the elaborate tombs of members of the Order of the Swan, a lay foundation of the local margraves. The **nave** was remodelled in the eighteenth century into a vast preaching hall according to the restrained Lutheran tastes of the day. It's a classic among German Protestant churches – all slate grey and cream, without paintings or side altars, it presents a cool clarity. The focus is the small marble altar, and above it the pulpit marks the only splash of gold in the whole interior.

Practicalities

Ansbach's **Bahnhof**, the junction of the Nürnberg–Stuttgart and Munich–Würzburg lines, is a few minutes' walk south of the centre. The **tourist office** is at Johann-Sebastian-Platz 1 (Mon–Fri 8.30am–12.30pm & 2–5pm; ☎0981/51243).

The cheapest centrally sited **hotel** is *Gasthof Augustiner*, Karolinenstr. 30 (☎0981/2432; ④), while *Christl*, Richard-Wagner-Str. 39–41 (☎0981/8121; ⑤) is a good middle-range choice. There are four excellent upmarket options: *Der Platengarten*, Promenade 30 (☎0981/971420; ⑥); *Schwarzer Bock*, Pfarrstr. 31 (☎0981/95111; ⑥); *Am Drechselgarten*, Am Drechselgarten 1 (☎0981/89020; ⑦); and *Bürger-Palais*, Neustadt 48 (☎0981/95131; ⑦), a beautifully renovated Baroque mansion. All but the last of these have **restaurants**, which rank as the best in town; that of *Der Platengarten* also has the benefit of a beer garden.

A number of **festivals** take place in Ansbach, of which the best known is the *Bach-Woche*, which occurs every two years at the end of July. Concerts are held in St Gumbertus, which has excellent acoustics. The *Ansbacher Rokokospiele* are period plays performed in the Residenzschloss and the local parks at the beginning of July each year. Held every four years (1998, 2002), the *Heimatfest* is a grand occasion where eighteenth-century music and dance play the most important part, but there's also a fair with plenty of regional delicacies.

Bayreuth

Situated about 80km northeast of Nürnberg within easy reach of several of Franconia's most scenic areas, polished and respectable **BAYREUTH** enjoys its reputation as one of the great cultural centres of Europe. Except for the festival period during late July and the first three weeks in August, it's a quiet provincial town, whose fame is due to a series of imported creative spirits. First of these was the eighteenth-century **Margravine Wilhelmine**. One of Frederick the Great's sisters, she was intended for the English royal throne, but her father was diplomatically inept and messed up her chances, so she got stuck with her kinsman, the notoriously boring Margrave Friedrich. Instead of settling down to obscurity, however, Wilhelmine set about creating a lively court, employing Europe's best architects, artists and musicians to transform her surroundings into something more elegant and sophisticated. A century later, **Richard Wagner** decided to settle in Bayreuth because the town offered to build him a stage large enough to put on his grand-scale opera productions. The impetus generated by him was tremendous, and Bayreuth's **opera festival**, the *Richard-Wagner-Festspiele*, has been rightly famous ever since. Although the festival – like everything else to do with Wagner – was tarnished by association with Hitler's patronage and exploitation for propaganda purposes, it continues to flourish as one of the great annual events of the music world.

Arrival and accommodation

Bayreuth's **Hauptbahnhof** is a short walk north of the town centre. The **tourist office** is at Luitpoldplatz 9 (Mon–Fri 9am–6pm, Sat 9am–1pm; ☎88560).

Accommodation

If visiting Bayreuth for the festival, you should take care to reserve accommodation well in advance, preferably as soon as you receive your tickets. At other times there should be no problem in finding somewhere to stay, as there are plenty of **hotels** in all categories. The **youth hostel**, Universitätsstr. 28 (☎25262; 🏠) isn't particularly central, but the bus service (#4 from the town centre) is regular since it's almost next door to the University.

HOTELS

Bayerischer Hof, Bahnhofstr. 14 (☎24094, fax 12264). One of several swanky hotels around the Hauptbahnhof; it also has a fine restaurant. ⑦

Eremitage, Eremitage 6 (☎799970, fax 799 9711). Located in the former stables of the Eremitage (see p.155), this only has six rooms, so should be booked well in advance. Its restaurant, *Cuvée* (closed Sun & Mon), is among the very best in Bayreuth.

Goldener Anker, Opernstr. 6 (☎65051, fax 65500). Old-fashioned hotel with restaurant; it's close to the Festspielhaus and was once much patronised by singers and conductors. ⑥

Goldener Löwe, Kulmbacher Str. 30 (☎746060, fax 47777). Cosy *Gasthof* of the adjoining *Maisel* brewery. Its restaurant (closed Sun evening) serves the full range of beers as well as excellent food. ④

Hirsch, St Georgen 26 (☎26714). Inexpensive *Gasthof* located a short distance west of the Altstadt. ③

Königshof, Bahnhofstr. 23 (☎24094, fax 12264). A direct competitor to the nearby *Bayerischer Hof* in every respect. ⑦

Kropf, Tristanstr. 8 (☎26298). Good-value *Gasthof* in the north of town, near the Festspielhaus. ③

The **telephone code** for Bayreuth is ☎0921

Schlosshotel Thiergarten, Oberthiergärtner Str. 36, Wolfsbach (☎9840, fax 98429). This former hunting lodge, which only has eight bedrooms, is 6km southeast of town near the terminus of bus #11. Its *Kaminrestaurant* (closed Sun evening & Mon) is one of Franconia's leading gourmet haunts; alternatively, there's the more affordable *Jägerstüberl*.

Spiegelmühle, Kulmbacher Str. 28 (☎41091, fax 47320). Good medium-range choice right alongside *Goldener Löwe*. It likewise has a recommendable restaurant (evenings only, closed Sun). ⑤

Zum Brandenburger, St Georgen 9 (☎20570, fax 852396). Another inexpensive *Gasthof*, with the benefit of a beer garden. ③

Zum Herzog, Herzog 2 (☎41334). Located just off Kulmbacher Strasse, this *Gasthof* serves good-value meals and beer from both the *Maisel* and *Bayreuther* breweries. ④

Zur Lohmühle, Badstr. 37 (☎53060, fax 58286). Located in an old mill at the extreme east of the Altstadt, this has a top-notch restaurant (closed Sun evening) offering Franconian and international dishes plus fish specialities. ⑦

The town

Bayreuth is a small place with all but two of its main sights closely grouped together in the Altstadt and the Hofgarten just beyond. On the Wagner trail you can visit his home, now a musuem, and the Festspielhaus, site of the summer festival.

The town centre

Margravine Wilhelmine's proudest legacy is the **Markgräfliches Opernhaus** (guided tours April–Sept Tues–Sun 9–11.30am & 1.30–4.30pm; Oct–March Tues–Sun 10–11.30am & 1.30–4.30pm; DM3) on Opernstrasse in the heart of town. Erected in the 1740s by Giuseppe and Carlo Galli da Bibiena of the great Bolognese dynasty of theatre-designers, it keeps its glamour for the interior, which is entirely of wood and painted in dusky greens, blues, browns and gold, not just a mark of Wilhelmine's influence,

---

RICHARD WAGNER (1813–83)

As the annual crowds to Bayreuth testify, no composer – with the possible exception of Mozart – has a more loyal, not to say adoring, following than **Richard Wagner**. His influence on musical history is also unsurpassed: his operas were revolutionary in their approach, using a recurring theme, or *leitmotiv*, for programmatic purposes, and varying it to depict psychoanalytical developments. He expanded the orchestral palette (including the invention of the Wagner tuba) to create a more sumptuous sound than had ever previously been heard, and developed a new harmonic language in which rich chromaticism predominates. Apart from a few early works and occasional pieces, Wagner's output consists of lengthy "music dramas", all but one of them based on heroic love themes drawn from Germanic mythology. In these, he attempted to fuse all the arts: not only did he compose the music, he chose the plots and the associated symbolism, wrote the libretti, and took an active role in staging.

Representing the Romantic approach to the arts at its most extreme, Wagner was a dreamer whose ambitions were only realized courtesy of the patronage of his equally unworldly soul-mate, King Ludwig II of Bavaria. For all his accomplishments, he was always a controversial figure, and even today he remains a composer whose stature is disputed far more than any other: despite the legions of adulators, many music lovers of otherwise catholic tastes listen only to fragments of his works, if they listen to them at all. This is not simply a question of Wagner's excessive nationalism and virulent anti-Semitism, which made the appropriation of his music by the Nazis inevitable. To all but the most initiated, his texts are mere doggerel, while his music is long-winded and repetitive, a point encapsulated in one of the famous asides made by the conductor Sir Thomas Beecham: "We've been playing for two solid hours and we're playing this bloody tune still!"

but also of the prevailing Lutheran taste which had established itself in Bayreuth in the sixteenth century. Although Wagner found it too small, it makes an ideal venue for eighteenth-century opera, of which there's a separate annual **festival**, the *Fränkische Festwoche*, at the end of May.

Immediately to the west stands the **Schlosskirche**, a Baroque hall church erected in the following decade. Painted in a delicate pink and adorned with tasteful stuccowork, it contains, in an oratory beneath the organ, the tombs of Wilhelmine and her husband. Alongside, dominated by its octagonal Renaissance tower, is the **Altes Schloss**. Much of this palace was accidentally burnt down in 1753 by the unfortunate Margrave Friedrich with a misplaced candle.

On Kirchplatz just to the south is the **Stadtmuseum** (Tues–Sun 10am–4pm; DM2). Its displays concentrate mainly on the eighteenth century, with collections of fine local porcelain and glazed beer mugs, rustic furniture and weapons, as well as exhibits relating to the Bayreuth margraves. From here, a short detour can be made to the **Maisel-Brauerei** (guided tours Mon–Thurs at 10am; DM5 including a glass of beer) at Kulmbacher Str. 40, a steam-powered brewery of 1887 still in perfect working order, though production has been moved to a modern plant next door. Its highly individual steam beer (*Dampfbier*) is its main line; it also makes several fine wheat beers.

The Hofgarten

At the northwestern end of the Hofgarten, which lies south of the Altes Schloss, is the replacement **Neues Schloss** (guided tours Tues–Sun 10am–noon & 1.30–3.30/5pm; DM4). Wilhelmine succeeded here in creating something all her own and each room is different, ranging from the ballroom in white, gold and blue, to the **Japanisches Zimmer** (Japanese Room), grottoes and a striking wood-panelled dining-room. Best of all is the **Spiegelzimmer** (Mirror Room), lined from top to bottom with broken and uneven shapes, as if put together from several broken mirrors. Based on a design by Wilhelmine, it's thought to be her comment on the false glamour of her age. Her other personal stamp is the split-tailed dragon motif, which was her favourite emblem and appears throughout the palace in different sizes and materials.

To the east stands the sternly Neoclassical **Villa Wahnfried**, now the **Richard-Wagner-Museum** (daily 9am–5pm; DM4). Wagner had this built to his own designs as his Bayreuth home: its enigmatic name literally means "peace from delusion". The interior was well tuned to cosy middle-class life, centred around a large sitting-room-cum-concert-room for the composer. This was the setting for Wagner's famed soirées, attended by intellectuals, musicians and royalty alike. His wife Cosima was the daughter of another famous composer, Franz Liszt, and the combination of the couple's backgrounds and interests made the household an important focus of German cultural life. Theirs was also one of the most famous love stories of the nineteenth century (he lured her from her first husband, the conductor Hans von Bülow, who was sufficiently stoic about the affair to maintain his role as the leading contemporary interpreter of Wagner's music), and they lie buried together in the villa's garden.

Likewise in the Hofgarten is the **Deutsches-Freimaurer-Museum** (Tues–Fri 10am–noon & 2–4pm, Sat 10am–noon; DM2), an intriguing museum dedicated to the Freemasons. They're represented here as a sort of collective peace movement rather than anything sinister, and the library of some 12,000 volumes is an important centre for research. It's revealing to see just how many well-known people were Freemasons, including Harry S. Truman, Churchill, Frederick the Great, Dickens, Goethe, Haydn and Mozart.

The Festspielhaus

Set on a little hill at the far northern end of town (from the Hauptbahnhof, go along Bürgerreuther Strasse in the opposite direction from the town centre) is the **Festspielhaus** (guided tours at 10am, 10.45am, 2.15pm & 3pm; 10am & 10.45am only during the festival; closed Nov; DM3), the custom-built theatre for the performance of Wagner's music dramas. Designed by Gottfried Semper, the leading German architect of the day, it's remarkable for its unique acoustics – one reason people are prepared to pay silly prices to attend the annual summer festival. The theatre was inaugurated in 1876, when the *Ring* cycle was performed in its entirety for the first time; ever since, nothing but Wagner's operas has been performed. After the composer's death in 1882, his widow Cosima ensured that the annual festival continued, and various family members have been in charge ever since. It was during his English daughter-in-law Winifred's "reign" from 1931 to 1944 that the festival had the unfortunate honour of Hitler's patronage, and he stayed as her house-guest whenever he came to Bayreuth. Wagner buffs still argue over the extent to which she should be blamed for the misappropriation of Wagner's music during the Nazi era, and bitter quarrels within the Wagner family continue to fuel the flames.

The demand for **tickets** is so great that you need to write the year before you wish to visit to *Kartenbüro, Festspielleitung Bayreuth*, 95402 Bayreuth, but this only ensures entry into the lottery which is heavily oversubscribed. The various Wagner societies around the world receive special allocations, but the only other way you will realistically get to see a performance at the festival is to take an expensive package tour from abroad (see p.4 & 12 for tour operators).

The Eremitage

Lying 4km east of town, and reached by bus #2 from Marktplatz, is the curious **Eremitage**, which has its origins in the eighteenth-century fad of the nobility for playing at asceticism by occasionally staying in sparse monks' cells and eating nothing but soup. When the original hermitage or **Altes Schloss** (guided tours March & Oct Tues–Sun 10–11.30am & 1–2.30pm; April–Sept Tues–Sun 9–11.30am & 1–4.30pm; DM4) was given to Wilhelmine as a birthday present, she proceeded to enlarge it into a glamorous summer hideaway in line with her own quirky vision of retreat as perfect indulgence. Thus some splendid Rococo chambers, notably the **Musikzimmer** and **Japanisches Kabinett**, are juxtaposed with the original bare cells. Additionally, a brand-new palace, the **Neues Schloss**, was built a short distance away. This is designed in a horseshoe shape, with mosaic-encrusted arcades flanking a central rotunda known as the **Sonnentempel** after the gilded sculptural group of Apollo and his sun chariot on its roof. Wilhelmine also commissioned a romantic landscaped garden dotted with **fountains** (which play hourly May to mid-Oct 10am–5pm) and numerous follies, including a grotto and an open-air theatre built in the shape of a ruin, where she herself took to the stage, often with her friend Voltaire.

Eating, drinking and entertainment

Bayreuth is awash with quality restaurants, many of the best choices being in the hotels (see pp.152–153). As the home of several breweries, it's also a good place for a pub crawl.

Restaurants and cafés

Becher-Bräu, St-Nikolaus-Str. 25. Bayreuth's oldest brewery-owned *Gaststätte*, with a tradition going back more than two centuries. These days, however, the *Becher* label products (a *Pils*, a *Bock* and a *Dunkel*) are made under contract by the *Schinner* brewery. Closed Tues.

Brauereischänke am Markt, Maximilianstr. 56. A fairly genteel pub-restaurant on the main square, serving the beers of the *Bayreuther* brewery.

Braunbierhaus, Kanzleistr. 15. Occupying Bayreuth's oldest surviving building, this is the flagship of the *Schinner* brewery, and is named after the brown beer which is its principal product. There's a bar on the ground floor, a pricey restaurant upstairs. Closed Mon.

Götschel, St Georgen 25. The *Gaststätte*, complete with beer garden, of the eponymous brewery, whose amber *Beck'nbier* is brewed under licence by *Schinner*. Closed Mon.

Jean-Paul-Café, Friedrichstr. 10. A good choice for *Kaffee und Kuchen*. Closed Mon.

Podium, Gerberhaus, Gerberplatz 1. Bayreuth's jazz and blues bar.

Schützenhaus, Am Schiesshaus 2. Serves inexpensive Franconian specialities; also has a beer garden. Closed Thurs.

Zur Sudpfanne, Oberkonnersreuther Str. 6, Oberkonnersreuth. Situated in an incorporated village 3km southeast of town, and reached by bus #11, this is the *Gaststätte* of the small *Schaller* brewery. It serves exquisite food and has a large beer garden. On Sat, it's only open in the evening.

Culture and festivals

Advance tickets for **concerts** and **theatre**, other than the *Richard-Wagner-Festspiele*, can be had from the box office on Jean-Paul-Platz (☎69001). Musical **festivals** by no means begin and end with the Wagner jamboree; in addition, there's the *Musica Bayreuth* in early May and the aforementioned *Fränkische Festwoche* at the end of the same month. Folklore events include *Maisels Weissbierfest* in mid-May, the *Volksfest* in early June and the *Bürgerfest* at the beginning of July.

Around Bayreuth

Not the least of Bayreuth's attractions is its proximity to three of Franconia's most scenic areas. Parts of each of these are relatively little known, and make a refreshing alternative to the province's more obvious tourist attractions, particularly if you fancy a spot of hiking.

Franconian Switzerland

The pear-shaped area bounded by the rivers Regnitz, Pegnitz and Main is popularly known as **Franconian Switzerland** (*Frankische Schweiz*): as well as Bayreuth, Erlangen and Bamberg are possible jumping-off points for its exploration. More sparsely forested than the ranges surrounding it because of the infertile Jurassic ground, Franconian Switzerland has an abundance of varied natural attractions such as strange rock formations, lonely high plateaux and stalactite caves. While poor quality soil also accounts for the low population, the region nevertheless has a plethora of castles, usually perched on conical hills above tightly packed villages or overlooking picturesque valleys.

From Bayreuth, the easiest approach by public transport is to take a train south to Pegnitz, then continue westwards by bus. A good base for exploring the region is the health resort of **POTTENSTEIN**, some 20km away, where there's a **youth hostel** at Jugendherbergsstr. 20 (☎09243/1224; ☎), along with a **campsite** (☎09243/206), and numerous good-value hotels. The village is crowned by a **Burg** (guided tours May–Oct Tues–Sat 10am–5pm; DM4.50), while a couple of kilometres to the southeast are the most impressive of the region's caves, the **Teufelshöhle** (guided tours April–Oct daily 9am–5pm; Nov–March Tues & Sat 10am–noon; DM4.50).

The star of the region is **GÖSSWEINSTEIN**, another small resort health resort, which is perched high above the valley of the River Wiesent 9km to the west. It's also a pilgrimage centre, and the **Wallfahrtskirche** is a masterly creation by Balthasar Neumann, given a distinctive note by the pyramidal high altar. The **Burg** (April–Oct daily 10am–6pm; DM3) provides a second focus to the town; from there you can follow the paths to the **Marienfelsen**, a series of cliffs punctuated by belvederes offering wonderful views over the valley and beyond. There are several inexpensive hotels in the village, while at the extreme western edge, at Etzdorfer Str. 142 (☎09242/259; ☎), is another **youth hostel**.

From Gössweinstein, you can follow the Wiesent towards its confluence with the Regnitz at the somewhat larger market and brewery town of **FORCHHEIM**, some 20km north of Erlangen on the main rail line to Bamberg. Here the **Pfarrkirche St**

Martin, which contains a Gothic altarpiece illustrating the life of its patron saint, and the moated **Pfalz** both date back to the fourteenth century, while there are many half-timbered houses. A few kilometres east is the **Walberla**, a flat-topped hill which is the region's main "peak". It's traditionally dedicated to Saint Walpurgis, and, on the first Sunday of May, is the site of one of Franconia's best festivals, when thousands gather for the annual *Volksfest* and an orgy of beer and food.

The Fichtelgebirge

The **Fichtelgebirge** (Spruce Mountains) just east of Bayreuth are not really as mountainous as their name would imply, but rather a craggy landscape of crumbling granite hills, wildly romantic and full of bubbling streams and large areas of forest interspersed with highland moors. Three trains run daily from Bayreuth to Warmensteinach. The **youth hostel** at Haus no. 42 (☎09277/249; 🏠) in the adjacent village of **OBERWAR-MENSTEINACH** would be a good base for hiking. Other accommodation in local farms and guesthouses in the region can be arranged at the regional **tourist office** at Bayreuther Str. 4 (☎09272/6255) in **FICHTELBERG**, a further 6km west, while just to the north of this village, on the banks of the Fichtelsee, is the **campsite** (☎09272/270). All these places offer easy access to the most popular of the "mountains", the **Ochsenkopf** (1024m). Unfortunately, this is marred by a huge television tower on top, along with a cable car and the attendant commercial trappings.

To see the best of the Fichtelgebirge, you really have to head further west. The strangest landscape the range has to offer is what's known as the **Luisenburg** near Wunsiedel, 12km from Fichtelberg. Again the name is misleading, as there's no castle here but instead a kind of rocky sea of granite blocks, eroded over the years to look like some giant child's pebbles left strewn untidily across the countryside. Its natural drama makes it a perfect open-air theatre, whose possibilities are put to full use in an annual summer season of plays.

The Franconian Forest

Until 1989, the **Franconian Forest** (*Frankenwald*), the extreme northeastern corner of the province, was one of the least-known corners of western Germany. Hemmed in on three sides by the GDR and deprived of access to neighbouring communities, it wore an air of neglect and consequently saw few tourists. Now that the border has reopened, the area is being regenerated and will profit from its proximity to the well-developed Thuringian Forest.

Kulmbach

Situated on the extreme southwestern fringe of the forest, **KULMBACH** was sufficiently far from the border to escape the blight from which the rest of the region suffered. It predated Bayreuth, which is only 25km distant, as the seat of the local margraves, and their vast fortified castle, the **Plassenburg** (guided tours April–Sept Tues–Sun 10am–5pm; Oct–March 10am–3pm; DM3) still rises high above the town. Given the feudal austerity of its outline, the main courtyard, known as the **Schöner Hof**, comes as a complete surprise. One of the richest creations of the German Renaissance, it bristles with intricate carvings, including medallion portraits of the Hohenzollerns. Because the Plassenburg was used as a prison throughout the nineteenth century, very little of the original interior remains, though some state rooms have been restored. The castle also houses the **Zinnfigurenmuseum** (same times; DM3), thought to be the world's largest collection of tin figurines, comprising some 300,000 individual pieces.

Back down in the town, the main attraction is the **beer**: in medieval times, everyone who became a citizen of Kulmbach automatically received the right to brew their own beer, and the town remains a major brewery centre, with an astonishing variety of products. The *Eisbock* of the *Reichelbräu* is a powerful ice beer; the *Schwarzbier* of the old monastic *Mönchshof* is one of Germany's best dark beers; while *EKU*'s *Kulminator 28* claims to be the strongest brew in the world. A major **festival** is held annually in late July/early August, but the beers can be sampled all year round at the *Gaststätten* of the breweries, of which *Stadtschänke*, Holzmarkt 3 (which belongs to *Mönchshof*), and *EKU-Fässle*, Sutte 18, are in the town centre.

Kulmbach's **Bahnhof** is a few minutes' walk northwest of the Altstadt and the town is connected by rail to both Bamberg and Bayreuth. The **tourist office** (Mon–Fri 9am–1pm & 1.30–5.30pm; May–Oct also Sat 9.30–11.30am; ☎09221/958840) is in the Stadthalle, Sutte 2. Though there are plenty of **hotels**, only *Weisses Ross*, Marktplatz 12 (☎09221/95650; ④) and *Kronprinz*, Fischergasse 4 (☎09221/84031; ⑤) are central. The **youth hostel** is 3km south of the Altstadt at Mangersreutherstr. 43 (☎09221/7243; ❶).

Coburg

COBURG, which lies about 50km northwest of Kulmbach, was one of the towns most affected by the postwar division of Germany, as it lay close to the border, cut off from much of its former hinterland. During the four centuries when it was capital of an independent duchy, the ruling house of Saxe-Coburg was masterly at self-promotion: in the nineteenth century its clever dynastic marriage policy created ties with the royal families of Belgium, Bulgaria and Portugal as well as Britain. This was achieved when **Albert of Saxe-Coburg-Gotha** married his first cousin, Queen Victoria, thus establishing the present ruling dynasty of Britain, tactfully renamed the House of Windsor during World War I. When the last duke abdicated in 1920, the locals voted for union with Bavaria. This proved to be a fortuitous choice, as it saved Coburg from the fate of all the other old Saxon-Thuringian principalities, which were incorporated into the GDR after World War II. However, refugees flocked over the border to the town which, almost inevitably, became one of the main rallying points of neo-Nazism and a place noted for its disquieting atmosphere and backward economy. This unsavoury situation has noticeably improved since the demise of the GDR.

The town

Despite Coburg's modest size, its attractions are well spaced out: the great feudal castle which gives the town its name lies to the east of the compact Altstadt, while there's also an important palace in the far outskirts.

Veste Coburg

The **Veste Coburg** is one of the largest remaining medieval fortresses in Germany. Towering high above the valley, it dates back in part at least as far as the twelfth century, though most of the present massive structure of twin walls and inner courts was built when the independent duchy was created in the sixteenth century. From the town centre, it can be reached by a steep thirty-minute walk through the Hofgarten; alternatively, bus #8 stops nearby.

Of the buildings lining the inner courtyard, the most imposing is the **Fürstenbau** (guided tours April–Oct Tues–Sun 9.30am–noon & 2–4pm; Nov–March Tues–Sun at 2pm & 3pm; DM4), which contains the apartments of the ruling family plus the Schlosskapelle, which was remodelled in the nineteenth century. The neighbouring edifices house the **Kunstsammlungen** (April–Oct Tues–Sun 9.30am–1pm & 2–5pm;

Nov–March Tues–Sun 2–5pm; DM4). In addition to displays of paintings, sculptures, glassware and decorative arts, there's a selection drawn from a 300,000-strong collection of graphics which includes work by Rembrandt, Dürer and Cranach. Of similar note are one of Germany's most important collections of medieval arms and armour, and a marvellous array of historic coaches, two of which date back to the sixteenth century. You can also see the room Luther occupied in 1530, the year of his heresy trial, when he took refuge in the Veste and found time to write no fewer than sixteen works on the issues arising from the Reformation.

The Altstadt

In the late sixteenth century, the local dukes, in accordance with the fashion of the time, moved their residence from the Veste to **Schloss Ehrenburg** (guided tours Tues–Sun at 10am, 11am, 1.30pm, 2.30pm & 3.30pm; also at 4.30pm in summer; DM4) at the eastern edge of the Altstadt. Only one wing of the original Renaissance palace survives: the rest was destroyed by fire and rebuilt in Baroque style, while the present facade is neo-Gothic and clearly inspired by the Tudor architecture of England. For all its diversity, the palace is incredibly rich and sumptuous in its interior design, with precious tapestries lining walls and intricate parquet floors made to different designs in each room. The furnishings too are priceless pieces collected from all over Europe, and there are even modern gadgets such as Germany's first flushing toilet in the room in which Queen Victoria used to stay. Also of special note is the **Schlosskapelle**, a fine example of Lutheran Baroque whose no-frills interior has been beautifully restored.

Just to the west of here is the central **Marktplatz**, lined with handsome Renaissance buildings erected in the early years of the duchy, and with a statue of Prince Albert, paid for by his widow, in the middle. The **Rathaus** on the southern side was extensively rebuilt in Rococo style, but retains the characteristic two-storey oriel, plus the main hall on the second floor. Opposite stands the **Stadthaus**, the former government building, still in all its original splendour. Leading off the square are several streets of half-timbered houses: look out for the grandiose **Münzmeisterhaus** on Ketschengasse. Further down the same street is the most imposing of the town's Renaissance buildings, the **Gymnasium Casimirianum**, founded with the intention of developing into a university, but which never rose beyond the status of a school.

Across from the Gymnasium is the Gothic church of **St Moritz**, which is given a distinctive appearance by its two very dissimilar towers, both capped by Baroque helmets. The chancel houses superb funerary monuments to the local sixteenth- and early seventeenth-century dukes, notably the huge alabaster memorial to Johann Friedrich II and his wife.

Schloss Rosenau

Prince Albert was born in 1819 at **Schloss Rosenau** (guided tours Tues–Sun 10–11.30am & 1.30–3.45/4.30pm; DM3), near the village of Rödental 7km to the northeast. He spent much of his youth playing around this romantic little castle based on plans drawn up by Karl Friedrich Schinkel and set in a wonderful park designed in the English fashion to imitate nature. There's an attractive path leading from the Veste to the park of Rosenau and back to Coburg, which is worth following if you've got the time; otherwise, the Schloss can be reached by bus.

Practicalities

Coburg's **Bahnhof** is situated on the northwestern side of town; the quickest way to the centre is by going sharp right along Lossaustrasse. The **tourist office** is just off the Marktplatz at Herrngasse 4 (April–Oct Mon–Fri 9am–6.30pm, Sat 9am–1pm; Nov–March Mon–Fri 9am–5pm, Sat 9am–1pm; ☎09561/74180).

There are a fair number of **private houses** (①–③) with rooms to rent, bookable via the tourist office. Reasonably priced **hotels** include *Gasthof Juliusturm*, about ten minutes' walk east of the centre at Pilgramsroth 45 (☎09561/29968; ③); and *Goldenes Kreuz*, on the corner of the Markt at Herrengasse 1 (☎09561/90473; ④). Among the more upmarket alternatives are *Goldener Anker*, Rosengasse 14 (☎09561/95027; ⑥); *Goldene Traube*, Am Viktoriabrunnen 2 (☎09561/8760; ⑥); and *Coburger Tor*, south of the centre at Ketschendorfer Str. 22 (☎09561/25074; ⑦). The **youth hostel**, Schloss Ketschendorf, Parkstr. 2 (☎09561/15330; ⑧) is located in a redbrick mock-castle 2km south of the centre.

Schaller, in the *Coburger Tor*, is Coburg's leading **restaurant**; its counterpart in *Goldene Traube* is also of high quality, while the *Ratskeller* in the Rathaus is a reliable cheaper alternative. Northeast of the Altstadt, at Rosenauer Str. 98, the *Scheidmantel* brewery has a *Gaststätte* with beer garden on its premises.

Bamberg

There can be no doubt about the status of **BAMBERG** as one of the most beautiful small towns in Europe. Its relative geographical isolation, some 60km north of Nürnberg, was a key factor in preserving its magnificent **artistic heritage** from the ravages of war. More can be learned about architectural history in a couple of days here than from weeks of studying textbooks: every single European style from the Romanesque onwards has left its mark on Bamberg, each bequeathing at least one outstanding building. For art lovers, there's the added bonus of the most marvellous array of sculpture to be found in the country.

Not the least of Bamberg's attractions is that, in contrast to Franconia's other picturesque old cities, it hasn't been mothballed into a museum-piece. It's an animated city

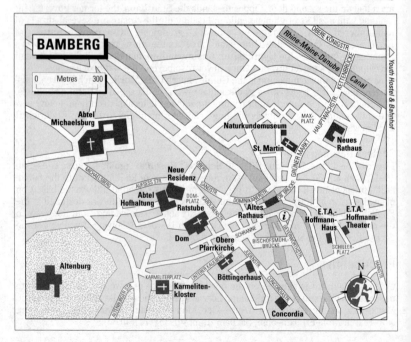

> The **telephone code** for Bamberg is ☎0951

of modern industries which profits from the youthful presence of a university. It's also one of the country's great **beer** centres: Bambergers knock back proportionately more booze than the inhabitants of any other town, being served by no fewer than nine breweries which together produce thirty different kinds of beer. Most notable is the appropriately named *Rauchbier* (smoky beer): made from smoked malt according to a formula developed in the sixteenth century, it's as distinctive a local brew as you'll find in Germany, leaving its own very special lingering aftertaste.

Bamberg was brought to prominence by the saintly eleventh-century **Emperor Heinrich II**, who wanted to turn it into a German metropolis on a scale and of an importance to rival Rome. Though the city has in fact never grown particularly big, it nonetheless has a sense of spacious grandeur which belies its actual size. Like the Italian capital, Bamberg is built on seven hills, pocked with belvederes which each offer a different perspective on the city. The Dom and related structures take up the entire crown of the main hill, towering high above the town to form the **Domstadt**. Unique in Germany, it was headquarters of the prince-bishopric which ruled until the Napoleonic suppression, whereupon it gave way to the purely spiritual archbishopric still based here. Clinging to the lower slopes of the valley of the River Regnitz are the residential districts which constitute an unusually complete Baroque townscape of picturesque corners, with the play of light on the river lending an extra sense of magic to the scene.

Arrival and accommodation

Bamberg's **Bahnhof** is about fifteen minutes' walk to the northeast of the historic centre. From here, follow Luitpoldstrasse straight ahead, before turning into the third street on the right, Obere Königstrasse, cross the bridge over the Rhein-Main-Donau-Kanal and you're right in the heart of the lower town. The **tourist office** (April–Oct Mon–Fri 9am–7pm, Sat 9am–5pm; Nov–March Mon–Fri 9am–6pm, Sat 9am–2pm; ☎0951/871161) is on an island in the River Pegnitz at Geyerswörthstr. 3.

Accommodation

Bamberg offers an exceptionally good choice of **hotels**, ranging from inexpensive brewery-owned *Gasthöfe* to upmarket establishments in characterful historic buildings. The **youth hostel** is pleasantly situated on the bank of the Regnitz 2km south of the centre, at Oberer Leinritt 70 (☎56002; 🅱); take bus #1, #7 or #11 from the Bahnhof to ZOB Promenade, then change to bus #18 to Regnitzufer. Another 2km further down the river is the local **campsite** (☎56320).

HOTELS

Bamberger Weissbierhaus Zum Maisel-Bräu, Obere Königstr. 38 (☎& fax 25503). One of a trio of brewery-owned *Gasthöfe* on Obere Königstrasse; it only has seven rooms so is best booked in advance. There's a wider range of beers available than in any of its competitors. ③

Barockhotel am Dom, Vorderer Bach 4 (☎54031, fax 54021). An aptly named hotel, offering good value at the price asked. ⑥

Bergschlösschen, Am Bundleshof 2 (☎52005, fax 59454). Situated high up on the Michaelsberg, this is the place to come if you want a grandstand view. ⑥

Fässla, Obere Königstr. 21 (☎22998 or 26516, fax 201989). Another brewery *Gasthof*, offering typically homely fare and its own *Rauchbier*. ④

Hospiz, Promenadestr. 3 (☎981260, fax 981 2660). A good budget alternative to the brewery *Gasthöfe* on Obere Königstrasse. ③

ERNST THEODOR AMADEUS HOFFMANN (1776–1822)

A native of the Prussian university city of Königsberg (today called Kaliningrad, a stranded enclave of the Russian Federation), **Theodor Hoffmann** was a man of extraordinarily varied talents. For most of his life, he was employed by the civil service, but for the years he lived in Bamberg (1808–13) he tried to establish himself as a composer, conductor and theatre director, having previously failed as a painter. Music was his greatest interest, but, notwithstanding the fact that he was arguably the first truly Romantic composer, he came to realize that his genius lay with words. He developed into an unusually perspicacious music critic, then increasingly devoted himself to his real forte as an author of weird short stories that reflected his own rather schizophrenic nature. Appropriately enough, he was a constant source of inspiration to later composers: Offenbach portrayed his bizarre personality in the opera *The Tales of Hoffmann*, while his stories formed the basis for two of the great Romantic ballets, Delibes' *Coppélia* and Tchaikovsky's *The Nutcracker*. His finest works are the chillingly supernatural *The Golden Pot*, and the later *Mademoiselle de Scudéry*, which is now generally regarded as the first detective story.

Kaiserdom-Stuben, Urbanstr. 18 (☎980730, fax 202378). Hotel and restaurant of the eponymous brewery. ⑤

Messerschmitt, Lange Str. 41 (☎27866, fax 26141). Part of the *Romantik* chain, this hotel and restaurant occupy a fine old *Weinhaus* with inner courtyard. ⑦

Residenzschloss, Untere Sandstr. 32 (☎60910, fax 6091 701). Bamberg's leading hotel, a member of the *Treff* chain, occupies a monumental Baroque hospital building. The facilities include a fitness centre, sauna, solarium, steam bath, whirlpool and two restaurants: *Orangerie* and *Fürst Bischof von Erthal*. The beautiful house chapel is a popular venue for weddings. ⑨

St Nepomuk, Obere Mühlbrücke 9 (☎98420, fax 984 2100). Classy hotel and restaurant occupying a picturesque old mill in the Regnitz. ⑦

Spezial, Obere Königstr. 10 (☎24304). Cosy brewery-owned place with restaurant. ④

Weierich, Lugbank 5 (☎54004, fax 55800). Moderately priced hotel with a top-notch restaurant serving Franconian specialities in a rustic setting. ⑤

Wilde Rose, Kesslerstr. 7 (☎981820, fax 22071). Good middle-range hotel with restaurant, located east of the centre. ⑥

The lower city

Heart of the lower city is the **Maxplatz**, dominated by Balthasar Neumann's **Neues Rathaus**, which was originally built as a seminary. Your best bet is to use this square as a focal point for wandering around the centre and gradually head towards the Domstadt across the river. A market is held every day on Maxplatz, and the adjoining Grüner Markt stands in the shadow of **St Martin**, a huge Jesuit church designed by the Dientzenhofer brothers, who were responsible for many of the best Baroque buildings in the city. Just off the square, at Fleischstr. 2, the **Naturkundemuseum** (April–Sept Tues–Sun 9am–5pm; Oct–March Tues–Sun 10am–4pm; DM3) is of rather specialized appeal, though an added attraction is that the collections of rare and exotic birds and other animals are displayed in beautiful Neoclassical exhibition rooms.

On an islet anchoring the Obere Brücke and Untere Brücke together is the **Altes Rathaus**, which is almost too picturesque for its own good. Except for the half-timbered section overhanging the rapids, the original Gothic building was transformed into Baroque and Rococo, and its walls are busily tattooed with exuberant frescoes. It now contains the **Sammlung Ludwig** (Tues–Sun 9.30am–4.30pm; DM6), a collection of Baroque porcelain and faience. The famous **Klein-Venedig** (Little Venice) of fishermen's houses is best seen from the Untere Brücke and presents one of the very few medieval scenes you'll find in the lower parts of town.

Elsewhere, the architectural character is almost completely Baroque. Walking around town the facades glow in rich ochre and russet tones, their elaborate stucco and intricate frescoes unashamedly exuding the wealth of their former residents. Grandest, but perhaps a little vulgar too, is the **Böttingerhaus** at no. 14 in the Judengasse, on the western side of the Regnitz. Built by the Franconian chargé d'affaires in the early eighteenth century, it now houses an art gallery. The nearby **Concordia** water-palace on the banks of the river belonged to the same man: the best time to see it is in the evenings from the opposite river bank, when the effect is heightened by its glittering reflection in the water. Further east, at Schillerplatz 26, is the tiny **E.T.A.-Hoffmann-Haus** (May–Oct Tues–Fri 4–6pm, Sat & Sun 10am–noon; DM2), which was the home of one of the foremost figures of the Romantic movement (see box opposite).

The Domplatz

The spacious, sloping **Domplatz** is lined with such a superb variety of buildings that it has no possible rival for the title of Germany's finest square. It unfolds like a great picture-book of architecture: with no more than a turn of the head you can see how Romanesque evolved into Gothic; and how the latter developed through various phases before giving way to the Renaissance, which in turn was supplanted by Baroque.

The Dom

Consecrated in 1012, the **Dom** (often dignified as the **Kaiserdom**) was burnt down twice in the following two centuries, and the present sandstone structure is the result of a slow rebuilding process that continued throughout the thirteenth century. During this period architectural tastes were beginning to change, but the ground plan follows the precedent of the imperial cathedrals of the Rhineland in having a choir at both ends of the building, each of which is flanked by twin towers. The east chancel is dedicated to the warrior Saint George, symbolizing the Empire, while its western counterpart bears a dedication to Saint Peter, representing the Papacy. These were the first and last parts of the Dom to be completed, and you can see that the rounded Romanesque arches and heavy vaults of the eastern choir had given way to the tall pointed windows and graceful ribs characteristic of early Gothic by the west end. In between, the nave was erected in the so-called Transitional style, offering insight into the way the original masons were experimenting with the new techniques.

What makes the Kaiserdom one of Europe's greatest cathedrals is the astonishing array of **sculptural decoration**. As with the architecture, this was initially executed in an orthodox Romanesque style, the best example being the *Fürstenportal* on the nave's north side, facing the main slope of the square. Its tympanum warns of *The Last Judgment*, while the progressively receding arches are each adorned with the figure of an Apostle standing on the shoulders of an Old Testament prophet. Carvings in a similar style can be found on the *Marienportal* on the right-hand door to the east chancel, which shows the Madonna and Child adored by the Kaiserdom's patrons, founders and builders, and on the choir screen panels, also placing Apostles and prophets in juxtaposition.

THE BAMBERG RIDER

Created by an unknown French-trained artist, the most famous of all this sculpture is the enigmatic **Bamberg Rider** (*Bamberger Reiter*) just inside the entrance doorway, one of the few equestrian statues which had been made since the days of classical antiquity. Nobody knows for sure who this noble figure is; the Romantics imagined it was an idealized portrait of a German emperor of the Hohenstaufen line. This was eagerly seized on by the Nazis, and during the Third Reich the statue was the national symbol of Germanic perfection, adorning every public hall and classroom. Two other statues to look out for are *Ecclesia* and *Synagogue*, the female personifications of the Christian and Jewish faiths, now placed at the southeast end of the nave. The victory of Christianity over Judaism is highlighted by the women's contrasting countenances: the Christian is a beautiful woman clad in rich cloth, while the Jewess stands blindfolded holding a broken rod and wearing a plain tunic that emphasizes the outline of her fallen breasts. Even finer are the two figures of *The Visitation* directly opposite. The Virgin Mary is young and bright, draped in a swirling dress; Saint Elizabeth is an ancient, haggard old crone whose expression speaks of an overwhelming sense of pathos.

OTHER SCULPTURE

As a perfect complement to the carvings associated with its construction, the Dom also contains a masterpiece by each of the two most famous sculptors of the early sixteenth century. Focus of the nave is the white limestone **tomb** of the canonized imperial couple, Heinrich II and Kunigunde, which stands slightly elevated as a result of the crypt built below. **Tilman Riemenschneider** laboured away for fourteen years on this sarcophagus, whose reliefs depict scenes taken from the life and times of the couple. The south transept contains **Veit Stoss**' dark limewood *Nativity Altar*, made when the artist was about eighty years old, as a result of a commission from his son, who was a Carmelite prior in Nürnberg. It was meant as a sort of artistic testament, executed without the usual studio assistance. Unfortunately, it's unfinished – the younger Stoss, a virulent anti-Protestant, was kicked out of Nürnberg when the city council adopted the Reformation, and the sculptor received no payment for his retable, which was soon afterwards moved to Bamberg.

Although it's not accessible to the public, it's worth knowing that the western choir holds the only **papal grave** in Germany, namely that of Pope Clement II. He was the local bishop before becoming pope, but died in 1047 after having ruled for a mere twelve months. **Tomb slabs** to the Dom's other bishops can be found scattered throughout the church. The most impressive, artistically speaking, is the *Monument to Friedrich von Hohenlohe* in the south aisle, just before the transept. Dating from the latter half of the fourteenth century, it conveniently represents the period midway between the Bamberg Rider and the works of Riemenschneider and Stoss.

The Diözesanmuseum

The **Diözesanmuseum** (Tues–Sun 10am–5pm; DM3) is in the chapterhouse off the cloisters on the south side of the Dom, and is entered from the adjacent aisle. Highlight is the collection of **ecclesiastical vestments**, the vibrant colours and intricate designs amazingly well preserved. Also kept here are the six original **statues** from the *Adamportal*, the dogtooth doorway to the left of the east choir. Here the ubiquitous Emperor and his wife turn up in the company of the Dom's two patrons, plus Adam and Eve. The last two are unashamedly sensual; covered only by fig-leaves, they come as near to erotic art as was ever dared in the Middle Ages.

The rest of the square

The **Ratstube** opposite the Dom is a Renaissance gem, with elegantly tapering gables and an ornate oriel window. It now contains the **Historisches Museum** (May–Oct Tues–Sun 9am–5pm; DM4), which covers local and regional history from the Stone Age to the twentieth century, as well as Bamberg's rich art history. Adjoining it is the **Reiche Tor**, in which Heinrich and Kunigunde appear once more; the model they carry is recognizably the Kaiserdom. This gate leads into the huge fifteenth-century courtyard of the **Alte Hofhaltung**, the former episcopal palace, which incorporates the remains of the eleventh-century hall of the Imperial Diet. The overhanging eaves of the huge sloping roof shelter two tiers of wooden galleries, and there's an unusual perspective on the towers of the Dom.

Across the street is the building which supplanted it in the eighteenth century, the **Neue Residenz** (daily 9am–noon & 1.30–4/5pm; DM4). It's an early example of the passion for building huge new palaces in the Baroque style that was to sweep across the German principalities, built in a massive L-shape and standing in sumptuous splendour overlooking the town below. Inside, the richly decorated state rooms culminate in the grandiloquent imperial ballroom. Also housed in the palace is the **Staatsgalerie Bamberg**, with medieval and Baroque paintings by German masters. Look out for *The Great Flood*, a typically idiosyncratic work by **Hans Baldung Grien**, who here tackled with relish a subject most painters shied away from; there are also several examples of Lucas Cranach the Elder. While you're here, have a glance into the reading room of the **Staatsbibliothek** too, for a glimpse of a delicate white and pink stucco ceiling in the best tradition of Baroque interior design.

The hills

From the rose garden at the back of the Neue Residenz there's a view of the **Michaelsburg**, which is crowned by the huge **Abtei**. Much of the original Romanesque shell of the church remains, though it was modified in the Gothic and Baroque periods. The interior is an amazing hotchpotch, its ceiling depicting over six hundred medicinal herbs. Housed in the cellars of the monastic buildings is the **Fränkisches Brauereimuseum** (Thurs–Sun 1–4pm; DM3), which shows just how those famous local brews are made, and displays all the old gear that used to be necessary for traditional brewing. Even if you're not interested in this, it's worth coming up here for the wonderful panorama of Bamberg's skyline and surrounding hills.

Yet another place for a great view is the **Altenburg**, a ruined castle at the end of the very steep Altenburger Strasse. Walk up to it via the Unterer Kaulberg and past Karmelitenplatz, and you'll find the **Karmelitenkloster**. The Romanesque **cloister** (daily 8.30–11.30am & 2.30–5.30pm; free), the largest in Germany, has been preserved, and its sculptured thirteenth-century columns each have their own individual patterns, revealing just how rich the imagination of early medieval craftsmen could be. Along with the depiction of biblical scenes on the capitals, there's a fabulous bestiary, ranging from fearsome dragons to weird creepy-crawlies.

Eating, drinking and entertainment

Many of Bamberg's best restaurants are in the hotels (see pp.161–162). The brewery-owned restaurants, the **Brauereigaststätten**, are the obvious places for solid, good-value food accompanied by locally made beer; note that, as well as those listed below, there are four others included in the hotels section.

Brauereigaststätten

Greifenklau, Laurenziplatz 20. Beer cellar and garden of Bamberg's smallest brewery, offering the bonus of a fine view over the city. Closes at 2pm on Sun.

Keesmann, Wunderburg 5. A traditional *Hausbrauerei* serving good food and Bamberg's best *Pils* in a large beer garden. Closed Sun.

Klosterbräu, Obere Mühlbrücke 3. This riverside *Hausbrauerei* with inner courtyard is Bamberg's oldest functioning brewery; its main product is a dark beer. Closed Wed.

Mahrs-Bräu-Keller, Oberer Stephansberg 36. Beer garden and restaurant of the eponymous brewery. Evenings only, except on Sun; closed Mon.

Mahrs-Bräu-Stübla, Wunderburg 10. Located right alongside its brewery, this cosy little pub is a genuine "local".

Schlenkerla, Dominikanerstr. 6. Not to be missed: the seventeenth-century tavern of the *Heller* brewery, which makes what's generally regarded as the best smoky beer, *Aecht Schlenkerla Rauchbier*. Also does good basic meals. Closed Tues.

Spezial-Keller, Oberer Stephansberg 47. Large and popular beer cellar-cum-garden, run by another of the breweries which produces *Rauchbier*.

Other restaurants

Alte Hofreit, Dominikanerstr. 10. Restaurant combining a traditional beer hall atmosphere with wholefood dishes.

Bassanese, Obere Sandstr. 32. High quality Italian restaurant. Closed Sun evening and Mon lunchtime.

Polarbär, Judenstr. 7. A popular student rendezvous: it serves salads, vegetarian dishes and biologically produced wine, and has a large beer garden.

Würzburger Weinstube, Zinkenwörth 6. Classy wine restaurant in a half-timbered building.

Cafés, bars and café-bars

Café Abseits, Pödeldorfer Str. 39. Music bar frequented by a young clientele.

Café Michaelsberg, Michaelsberg 10e. Has the benefit of a wonderful view over Bamberg. Closed Tues.

Café Rosengarten, Domplatz 1. Another good terrace café; open April–Oct only.

Downstairs, Lange Str. 16. Bamberg's best nightclub. Daily 10pm–3am.

Live-Club, Obere Sandstr. 7. Bar with live bands. Closed Wed.

Entertainment

For its size, Bamberg is an amazingly vibrant cultural centre, especially for **classical music**. The *Bamberger Symphoniker* was actually the old *Deutsches Orchester* of Prague, which fled over the border at the time the Iron Curtain was going up. They're especially known for their candle-lit concerts in the Neue Residenz. The principal **theatre**, not surprisingly, is the *E.T.A. Hoffmann-Theater*, Schillerplatz 7 (☎871431); the resident company also holds an open-air season in June and July in the Alte Hofhaltung.

Bamberg's main **festivals** are *Corpus Christi* (variable date in May/June) and the *Sandfest* in August, with colourful church processions and fishermen's jousts.

Around Bamberg

Bamberg is a good base for excursions into the surrounding countryside. To the east is Franconian Switzerland (see pp.156–157), while westwards lies another popular hiking area, the **Steigerwald**, which also has a couple of major setpiece attractions. However, the most popular outing from the city is to a pair of isolated Baroque churches in the Main valley to the north.

Kloster Banz and Vierzehnheiligen

Kloster Banz is perched high above the River Main, midway between Bamberg and Coburg. This former Benedictine monastery was begun by Leonhard Dientzenhofer in 1695. After his death, his brother Johann took over, designing the elongated church, which is richly decorated with frescoes, altars and fancy woodwork. The monastic buildings now belong to the CSU who've turned the place into a grand venue for conferences and training courses for their party faithful.

Much more rewarding to visit is the pilgrimage church known as **Vierzehnheiligen** (Fourteen Saints), which faces Banz from the opposite bank. One of the most important and original Baroque churches in the country, it's generally considered to rival the Würzburg Residenz as Balthasar Neumann's supreme accomplishment. It takes its name from the legend that a shepherd had recurring visions here of Christ with the fourteen Saints of Intercession. The centrepiece of the basilica is an altar dedicated to the fourteen saints, known as the *Gnadenaltar*, around which the entire interior is designed. This gives it the unusual shape of an oval nave and short transept, with the altar taking up the central point of the transept crossing. The marble and stucco altar is built to a pyramid design, rich in Rococo curls and cherubs as well as the white marble figures of the the fourteen saints.

Without your own transport, the churches are slightly tricky to reach; the best bet is to take a train to the rail junction of Lichtenfels, then cover the remaining 5km by the irregular buses, a taxi or on foot.

The Steigerwald

The best way to see a cross-section of the **Steigerwald** is to take a trip through the heart of the forest along the *Steigerwald Höhenstrasse*. This begins at Eltmann, on the south bank of the Main 19km northwest of Bamberg, and describes a roughly semicircular course towards its terminus at Schlüsselfeld. En route you pass through **EBRACH**, which grew out of a twelfth-century Cistercian **Abtei**. The church's exterior is one of the finest German examples of the order's distinctive early Gothic building style, but the inside was radically changed in the eighteenth century, with pink stuccoed marble pillars and golden yellow ornamentations.

Pommersfelden

At the edge of the Steigerwald, about 15km east of Schlüsselfeld and 20km south of Bamberg, the village of **POMMERSFELDEN** is dominated by **Schloss Weissenstein** (guided tours April–Oct Tues-Sun 9am–4pm; DM7), the jewel in the crown of the enormous building programme Prince-Bishop Lothar Franz von Schönborn funded from the sizeable fortune he assured himself by masterminding the election of Emperor Charles VI in 1711. Built around the same time as Germany's other great Baroque palaces such as Nymphenburg, Würzburg and the Neue Residenz in Bamberg itself, Weissenstein was designed by Johann Dientzenhofer in equally ostentatious proportions. The entrance hall of the central pavilion takes up the full height of the three-storey palace, and the showpiece **double staircase** swings up to upper galleries that encase the hall rather like great Italian courtyards. The ceiling fresco uses clever perspective and elegantly rounds off a perfect whole. Elsewhere, you'll find richly decorated mirror cabinets, state rooms and the obligatory ballroom, known as the **Marmorsaal** because of the stuccoed marble pillars that line its walls. From mid-July to mid-August each year, it's used for the classical concerts of the *Collegium Musicum*, an international festival of young musicians. For information and tickets, contact the *Schlossverwaltung* (☎09548/203). It's worth knowing that there's a fine **hotel** (☎09548/680; ⑥) with restaurant in the Schloss.

Aschaffenburg and the Odenwald

King Ludwig I called **ASCHAFFENBURG**, which is situated on the River Main at the extreme northwestern corner of the state, his "Bavarian Nice". Although the city has lost some of its charm since those days, the well-preserved historic centre and pleasant parks make it an agreeable place to spend a day or two, and it's also the obvious jumping-off point for exploring the unspoiled highland countryside of the **Odenwald** to the south. Once the second residence of the Archbishop-Electors of Mainz, Aschaffenburg is now mainly a dormitory town for Frankfurt.

The town

Aschaffenburg's compact centre is dominated by **Schloss Johannisburg**, a very French-looking late Renaissance red sandstone pile. Although its appearance would suggest otherwise, it served the archbishops as a palace rather than filling any defensive role. Today the first and second floors are home to the **Schlossmuseum** (April–Sept Tues–Sun 9am–noon & 1–5pm; Oct–March Tues–Sun 11am–4pm; DM4), which houses over 400 paintings from the fifteenth to the eighteenth century, with the emphasis on devotional works by Lucas Cranach the Elder and his contemporaries, along with Dutch and Flemish landscapes. Also of note is the **Schlosskirche** which contains fine alabaster reliefs and a magnificent doorway.

A few minutes' walk downstream along the Main is **Das Pompejanum** (March 15 to Oct 15 Tues–Sun 10am–12.30pm & 1.30–5pm; DM3), a replica of the house of Castor and Pollux in Pompeii, built by Friedrich Gärtner for King Ludwig I. Its gardens of Mediterranean trees and plants and its vineyard sloping down to the River Main make for an enjoyable stroll; the interior has only recently been restored following war damage.

A walk down Pfaffengstrasse from Schloss Johannisburg takes you through the heart of the Altstadt, with its narrow streets of half-timbered houses, and leads to Stiftsplatz and Aschaffenburg's other main sight, the **Stiftskirche**. Founded in 957, the church combines Romanesque, Gothic and Baroque styles and it's this architectural identity crisis that gives it real visual impact. The church boasts late Romanesque cloisters, a crucifix dating from 1120 and a small panel of *The Lamentation* by Grünewald.

Also worth visiting is **Park Schöntal**, on the eastern edge of the old city centre, with a lake, a ruined monastery and the **Fasanerie** (Pheasantry). Walk up Lindenallee, cross the rail bridge and up Bismarckallee, popular in summer with its restaurants and beer gardens. **Park Schönbusch**, on the western bank of the Main (best reached by bus #3 from Freihofplatz) is an eighteenth-century English-style garden, featuring a labyrinth of paths leading through woods and gardens past miniature temples and mazes. Here also is the pretty **Schlösschen Schönbusch** (guided tours March 15 to Oct 15 Tues–Sun 9am–12.30pm & 1.30–5pm; DM4).

Finally, on the southern edge of town at Obernnauer Str. 125 (reached by bus #1 from Schweinheimer Strasse), the **Rosso Bianco Collection** (April–Oct Tues–Sun 10am–6pm; Nov–March Sun 10am–6pm; DM10) has the biggest collection of racing cars in the world – some 200 gleaming Porsches, Ferraris, Alfa Romeos and the like.

Practicalities

Aschaffenburg's **Hauptbahnhof** is just north of the Altstadt. The **tourist office** is located in the Stadthalle, Schlossplatz 1 (Mon–Fri 9am–noon & 1.15–4.30pm, Sat 9am–noon; ☎06021/395800).

Budget **hotels** with a central location include *Café Central*, Steingasse 5 (☎06021/23392; ③); *Gasthof Zum Goldenen Karpfen*, Löherstr. 20 (☎06021/23946; ④); and *Syndikus*, Löherstr. 40 (☎06021/23588; ④). The town has two highly appealing upmarket choices in *Hofgut Fasanerie*, a former wine-producing estate at Bismarckallee 1 (☎06021/91006; ⑥); and *Schönbusch*, which occupies the court gardener's residence in Park Schönbusch (☎06021/80005; ⑦). The **youth hostel** is at Beckerstr. 47 (☎06021/930763; 🄰) and is best reached by bus #5 or #15. **Camping** is possible at Mainparksee (☎06021/278222) and in the suburb of Mainaschaff (☎06021/278222), fifteen minutes away by bus #44 from the Hauptbahnhof.

Each of last two hotels listed above has a fine **restaurant** with adjoining beer garden. *Zeughaus*, Bismarckallee 5, is also worth visiting in summer, when you can drink locally produced ciders in the shade of chestnut trees. Within Schloss Johannisburg is a recommendable wine bar-restaurant, *Schlossweinstuben*. *Klimperkasten* at Rossmarkt 21 is a lively, friendly bar with regular live music, while *Engelsberg* at Dalbergstr. 66 is a traditional but arty pub. The Neoclassical *Stadttheater*, Schlossgasse 8 (☎06021/27078) hosts **drama** and **concerts**.

The Odenwald

The Bavarian section of the **Odenwald**, a forest which straddles across into both Baden-Württemberg and Hesse (see also p.358–360) includes two small towns well worth making the object of a day-trip: they are easily combined, as both lie on a rail line from Aschaffenburg.

Miltenberg

MILTENBERG, due south and 45km upstream, is a particularly good example of the half-timbered towns so characteristic of central Germany. Its picturesque triangular **Marktplatz** features many of the finest houses, along with the Gothic church of St Jakob and a Renaissance fountain. The square slopes up to the **Mildenburg** (Tues–Sun 10.30am–5.30pm; DM2), a restored medieval castle in whose courtyard stands an enigmatic five-metre-high monolith dating back to Roman times, if not before; there's also a good view of the town from up here. On Hauptstrasse are several notable buildings: *Zum Riesen* at no. 97 is an inn with an uninterrupted tradition since the fifteenth century (see below); the **Altes Rathaus** at no. 137 is a likeable example of fifteenth-century architecture; while at no.199, behind the *Kalt-Loch-Bräuerei*, is the **Alte Synagoge**, one of the few medieval Jewish temples left in Germany.

The **tourist office** at Engelplatz 69 (Mon–Fri 9am–noon & 2–5pm; May–Sept also Sat 9.30am–noon; ☎09371/40019) can book private **rooms** (①–②). There are some lovely old **hotels** on Hauptstrasse: *Zum Riesen* at no. 97 (☎09371/3644; ⑥); *Brauerei Keller* at no. 66 (☎09371/5080; ⑥); *Altes Bannhaus* at no. 211 (☎09371/3061; ⑥); and *Jagdhotel Rose* at no. 280 (☎09371/40060; ⑦). With the exception of the first-named, each has a **restaurant**.

Amorbach

A further 10km south is **AMORBACH**, like Aschaffenburg a former possession of the Archbishops of Mainz. In the mid-seventeenth century the court architect Maximilian von Welsch was commissioned to transform its Romanesque **Abtei** into something more in keeping with the times. He responded with a design which is restrained by Bavarian standards – he went as far as preserving the original towers – yet which is none the worse for that, being a masterly exercise in late Baroque grandeur. Outstanding features of the Abteikirche are the ceiling frescoes, the wrought-iron screen dividing the nave from the transept and the sweet-toned organ. **Guided tours** (March Mon–Sat 9.40–11.40am & 1.40–5pm, Sun 1–5pm; April & Oct Mon–Sat 9.20am–noon & 1.20–5.20pm, Sun 11.20am–5.20pm; May–Sept Mon–Sat 9.20am–noon & 1.20–6pm, Sun 11.20am–6pm; DM4) are run through the slightly later monastic buildings, which give a foretaste of the emergent Neoclassical style in such lovely interiors as the **Bibliotheksaal** and the **Grüner Saal**.

The **tourist office** (May–Oct Mon–Fri 9am–12.30pm & 3–6pm, Sat & Sun 10am–noon; Nov–April Mon–Fri 9am–noon & 3–5pm; ☎09373/20940) is in the Altes Rathaus on Marktplatz. Private **rooms** (①–②) can be booked here; otherwise there are several **hotels**, including *Weinstube Amorstüble*, Johannesturmstr. 6 (☎09373/1292; ④) and *Badischer Hof*, Am Stadttor 4 (☎09373/9505; ⑦). The **youth hostel** is well to the northwest of the centre at Am der Kniebrecht 2 (☎09373/1366; ☎).

Würzburg

Capital of Franconian wine and northern terminus of the **Romantic Road** (see box on p.176), Germany's most famous tourist route, **WÜRZBURG** spans the River Main some 80km upstream from Aschaffenburg and 110km northwest of Nürnberg. During the night of March 16, 1945 it got the same treatment from Allied bombers that Nürnberg had received two months earlier. The 1200-year-old city had no important war industries but the presence of a busy rail junction provided a tenuous rationale for its destruction. Unfortunately, Würzburg has been less successful in rebuilding itself: gone is much of the Altstadt, leaving individual surprises of Baroque and Gothic beauty sandwiched between modern supermarkets and the new town. For all that, the city's location on the banks of the River Main, a number of really outstanding sights and a marvellous range of places to eat and drink easily justify a visit of several days.

Würzburg has been one of Germany's most influential episcopal cities for many centuries, and some of the greatest architects and artists were employed by the prince-

The **telephone code** for Würzburg is ☎0931

bishops, bequeathing an exceptionally rich legacy. Prominent among them was the sculptor **Tilman Riemenschneider**, whose hauntingly characterized carvings, executed in the heady years leading up to the Reformation, decorate so many churches throughout Franconia. A later period saw the patronage of **Balthasar Neumann**, who was then totally unknown and untried, but who duly developed here into the most inventive and accomplished architect of eighteenth-century Europe.

Arrival and accommodation

Just outside the **Hauptbahnhof** at the northern end of the city centre there's a **tourist office** (Mon–Sat 10am–6pm; ☎37436). Two other branches are near the centre of town, at the *Haus zum Falken* on the Markt (Mon–Fri 9am–6pm, Sat 10am–2pm; April–Oct also Sun 10am–2pm; ☎37398), and opposite the *Congress-Centrum* near the Friedensbrücke (Mon–Thurs 8.30am–5pm, Fri 8.30am–noon; ☎37335).

Accommodation

Though budget options are fairly thin on the ground, Würzburg has plenty of good middle- and upper-range **hotels**. The **youth hostel**, Burkarderstr. 44 (☎42590; 🏠) is situated on the left bank of the Main below the Marienberg fortress; take tram #3 to Ludwigsbrücke from the Hauptbahnhof. There are several **campsites** in the outskirts, the most convenient being at Winterhäuser Str. 160 (☎65598) in Heidingsfeld, about 4km south of Würzburg and best reached by taking bus #16 from Barbarossaplatz.

HOTELS AND PENSIONS

Alter Kranen, Kärrnergasse 11 (☎35180, fax 50010). Middle-range hotel with a lovely location right by the Main. ⑥

Amberger, Ludwigstr. 17–21 (☎35100, fax 351 0800). High-class hotel and restaurant, situated just north of the Residenz. ⑦

Goldener Hahn, Marktgasse 7 (☎51941, fax 51961). *Gasthof* located just off the Markt. It has basic singles which cost less than half the price of the doubles. ⑥

Rebstock, Neubaustr. 7 (☎30930, fax 309 3100). A splendid Rococo mansion in the university quarter, completely modernized inside. It serves wonderful buffet breakfasts, while full meals are available at either the reasonably priced *Fränkische Weinstube* (evenings only, closed Tues) or the pricey main restaurant (closed Sun evening). ⑨

Russ, Wolfahrtsgasse 1 (☎50016, fax 50969). Hotel with a well-regarded restaurant, handily located in the Altstadt. ⑤

Schloss Steinburg, Auf dem Steinberg (☎97020, fax 97121). Occupies a Romantic-era castle built on the foundations of its medieval predecessor on a hill 6km northwest of the centre. The facilities include a sauna, a swimming pool, a garden terrace commanding a grandstand view of the city, and a high-class wine restaurant. ⑦

Schönleber, Theaterstr. 5 (☎12068, fax 16012). Pleasant, moderately priced hotel in the heart of the city. ⑤

Siegel, Reisgrubengasse 7 (☎52941 or 52964, fax 52967). Würzburg's cheapest pension, with a convenient location between the Hauptbahnhof and the centre of the city. ④

Spehnkuch, Röntgenring 7 (☎54752, fax 54760). Good pension in a grand tenement directly facing the Hauptbahnhof. ④

Till Eulenspiegel, Sanderstr. 1a (☎355840, fax 355 8430). Non-smoking hotel in the heart of the university quarter. It has a pleasant *Weinstube* plus a *Bierkeller* which is one of the liveliest nightspots in the district. ⑥

Walfisch, Am Pleidenturm 5 (☎35200, fax 352 0500). Upmarket hotel with restaurant commanding a wonderful view over the Main at its most picturesque spot. ⑧

Zur Stadt Mainz, Semmelstr. 39 (☎53155, fax 58510). This is a real gem, a Franconian inn dating back to the fifteenth century, albeit with fully modern bedrooms. Its restaurant serves wonderful local dishes, including a couple from its own recipe book of 1850. The gargantuan breakfast buffet (which non-residents can enjoy for DM20) is surely the best in all of Germany. ⑦

The city

The heart of the old city lies between the Main and the Residenz, roughly encompassed by the Juliuspromenade to the north and Neubaustrasse to the south. Most of the sights lie within this compact area, though you need to cross over to the right bank for a couple of major attractions – and the best views.

The Residenz

The **Residenz** (April–Sept Tues–Sun 9am–5pm; Oct–March Tues–Sun 10am–4pm; DM7) on the eastern edge of the town centre is a truly marvellous palace set in a park to match. It was intended to symbolize all the wealth and status of the Würzburg bishops, and to show they could hold their own with such great European courts as Versailles and Vienna – which, in artistic terms, they more than succeeded in doing. Construction was left largely in the hands of the prolific **Balthasar Neumann**, who had started off as a humble craftsman of churchbells and weapons before working his way into the fine art of architecture. The palace is built in a great U-shape made up of a central pavilion and four equally proportioned two-storey courts. In themselves, the external proportions are impressive, but they're rather overshadowed by the overwhelming magnificence of the interior.

As you enter the palace via the central wing, you're almost immediately confronted with the famed **staircase** which is covered by a single unsupported vault of audacious design. In response to jealous rivals who claimed this was bound to collapse, Neumann offered to have a battery of artillery fired under it. This experiment was never carried out, but full vindication of Neumann's faith in his design came in 1945, when the vault held firm against aerial bombardment. Its **fresco**, the largest in the world, thus miraculously survived unscathed. An allegory extolling the fame of the prince-bishops in the most immodest way imaginable, it was painted by the greatest decorator of the age, the Venetian **Giovanni Battista Tiepolo**. The four continents then known are depicted paying their respects to the ruler of Würzburg, Carl Philipp von Greiffenklau, who is transported to Heaven in triumph in the centre of the composition. Each continent is personified as a representative female character, Europe being a Greek goddess enthroned above a globe to symbolize this continent's status as ruler of the world. To her right, sitting on an old cannon, a reference to his original trade, Balthasar Neumann surveys the scene; behind him are Tiepolo and his fellow-decorators.

The **Weisser Saal**, whose plain white stucco is a tasteful contrast to the staircase, gives the visitor a break before being hit by the opulence of the **Kaisersaal**, which is the centrepiece of the palace and the room reserved for the use of the emperor whenever he happened to be in the area. The marble, the gold-leaf stucco and the sparkling chandeliers combine to produce an effect of dazzling magnificence, but finest of all are more frescoes by Tiepolo, which dovetail with the architecture to absolute perfection. This time they glorify the concept of the Holy Roman Empire and Würzburg's part within it. On the ceiling, Beatrix of Burgundy is brought to the city as Frederick Barbarossa's betrothed: on the southern wall, the couple are married by the prince-bishop, who is invested with the title of Duke of Franconia in the scene opposite. To the left and right are an array of **state rooms**, painstakingly re-created from the ashes with the help of photographs and old etchings. Look out in particular for the recently restored **Spiegelkabinett**, a unique work of its kind, the walls consisting entirely of glass panels decorated on the back.

Built discreetly into the southwest corner of the palace in order not to spoil the symmetry, the **Hofkirche** (which you visit independently) is a brilliant early example of the spatial illusionism that was to become a Neumann speciality – the interior, based on a series of ovals, appears to be much larger than is actually the case. Both the side altars of *The Fall of the Rebel Angels* and *The Assumption* are by Tiepolo. Entered from within the main courtyard is the **Martin-von-Wagner-Museum** (Tues–Sat 9.30am–12.30pm & 2–5pm, Sun 9.30am–12.30pm; free). In the mornings and on alternate Sundays you see the gallery, featuring works by Riemenschneider and Tiepolo; at other times the collection of Classical antiquities is on view. To the rear of the Residenz is the **Hofgarten**, a series of delightful terraced gardens enlivened by playful Rococo sculptures.

The episcopal and academic quarters

From the Residenz, it's only a short walk along Hofstrasse to the city's episcopal centre, in which the two main churches nestle side by side. The more northerly is the **Neumünster**, a Romanesque basilica partly rebuilt in the Baroque period, whose perfect symmetry is highlighted by a twin set of steps leading up to the elevated entrance from either side. In the **crypt**, a modern shrine contains the remains of Saint Kilian, an Irish missionary martyred on the spot in 689, together with his assistants St Kolonat and St Totnan, for trying to convert Franconia. The busts of the three martyrs on the church's high altar are copies of the originals by Riemenschneider, which were destroyed in 1945, but the statue of the Madonna and Child under the dome is a genuine work by the same sculptor.

If you leave the Neumünster by its northern exit, you'll come to the tiny **Lusamgärtchen** and the remains of the twelfth-century cloister. These days it's a romantically overgrown square, and at its centre is a commemorative block to the famous medieval minstrel **Walther von der Vogelweide**. He was the most popular poet and singer of the early thirteenth century, but also a valued political commentator of the Staufen rulers, which is why he was given a pension from the estate of this church and is assumed to have been buried in the cloister in 1230. His popularity still holds, and local residents always ensure that fresh flowers decorate his memorial stone, over 750 years after his death. To the northeast stand several fine old mansions, including the Renaissance **Hof Conti**, the present-day home of Würzburg's bishop.

The **Dom**, again consecrated to Saint Kilian, was one of the largest Romanesque churches in Germany, but was completely burnt out in 1945, and only the exterior is true to the original. Inside, the rich stucco embellishments of the eighteenth century have only been restored in the transept and chancel, and for the rest the walls are left plain white, with surviving **tombstones** of canons and prince-bishops lining the pillars: look out for those on the seventh and eighth bays of the north side, which are both by Riemenschneider. At the end of the northern transept, Balthasar Neumann's **Schönbornkapelle** holds the remains of four bishops from the House of Schönborn, the dynasty which specialized in collecting episcopal appointments and then building great palaces as spin-offs – Bamberg, Pommersfelden, Bruchsal and Würzburg itself being among their legacies.

A couple of blocks south of here, the eastern end of Neubaustrasse is dominated by the huge Renaissance frontage of the **Alte Universität**, built in the late sixteenth century by order of one of the city's most enlightened prince-bishops, Julius Echter. The attached church also dates from this period, but the tower was added by Antonio Petrini, the seventeenth-century Italian architect who was responsible for transforming Würzburg into one of Germany's first Baroque cities.

Marktplatz, the hospitals and the waterfront

To the west of the episcopal quarter is the city's commercial heart, centred on **Marktplatz**, whose daily food market ensures that there's always a lively bustle. Just off the northeast side is the **Haus zum Falken**, the city's prize example of a Rococo mansion, bristling with white stucco decorations and perfectly restored to the very last curl. It now houses one of the city's tourist offices and the municipal library.

Overlooking Marktplatz is the **Marienkapelle**, an exceptionally graceful Gothic church of the fourteenth century, whose most interesting feature is the arch above the northern portal. The scene represented is *The Annunciation*, and if you look closely, you'll see that the artist has chosen to be very literal in his interpretation. There's the usual archangel with his scripted band indicating his speech to Mary, but another band leads from God the Father above to Mary's ear, and tucked away in the folds of this band, a little baby is sliding down towards her. Inside, is the touching sandstone tomb of the knight Conrad von Schaumberg by Riemenschneider.

Eichhornstrasse leads eastwards from the Markt to Theaterstrasse, where you'll find the **Bürgerspital**, a charitable institution for the poor, old and sick established in the early fourteenth century by the wealthier citizens of the city. Its good works were funded from its vineyards, still among the largest in Germany; in accordance with the wishes of the founders, residents get a quarter of a litre of wine each day and double on Sundays. The Gothic chapel remains from the initial complex, though other parts were rebuilt in the Baroque period. A short walk away on Juliuspromenade is the **Juliusspital**, a second and much larger institution of the same kind. It takes its name from its benefactor, Bishop Julius Echter, but again it was rebuilt in the Baroque period, partly by Petrini, who added the beautiful little pharmacy, which survives as an intact period-piece. It's best to visit the hospitals when you're in the mood for something to eat and drink, as they each incorporate a *Weinstube* (see opposite) where the products of their vineyards can be sampled. While walking between the two, it's worth making a short detour down Hauger Pfarrgasse to see Petrini's strikingly Roman-looking **Stift Haug**, which contains a large painting of *The Crucifixion* by Tintoretto.

At the western end of Juliuspromenade, the eighteenth-century **Alte Kranen** (old cranes), used to unload shipping, stand guard over the Main. Further south stands the **Alte Mainbrücke**, the oldest bridge spanning this river. Built in 1133, it was often damaged over the centuries, most recently in 1945 when the Allies toppled the eighteenth-century statues of the town's bishops and saints into the river. However, some of the originals have been reinstated, joining with a number of copies to oversee the traffic once again. Just to the east is the **Grafeneckart** or **Rathaus**, a thirteenth-century Romanesque-Gothic building with a Renaissance extension.

The Marienberg

Towering high above the left bank of the Main, the **Festung Marienberg** was home to the prince-bishops from 1253 to 1719. Over this period, it evolved from a medieval castle into a Renaissance palace, which was fortified in the Baroque period, following its sacking at the hands of the Swedes, by the addition of a ring of bastions. At the entrance to the complex, the seventeenth-century **Zeughaus** houses the large **Mainfränkisches Museum** (April–Oct Tues–Sun 10am–5pm; Nov–March Tues–Sun 10am–4pm; DM3.50). Pride of place among the collections is taken by a magnificent array of **Riemenschneider sculptures**, including the original stone carvings from the Marienkapelle; there's also an impressive display of old wooden wine presses.

Within the courtyard is the round **Marienkirche**, Würzburg's original cathedral. This dates back to the eighth century and is claimed to be the oldest intact church in Germany, though it has been remodelled on several occasions. Another structure of special note is the Renaissance **Brunnenhaus**, an ornate octagonal structure sheltering the 105-metre well which was chiselled through rock in the early fourteenth century to ensure self-sufficiency in water. The eastern palace wing or **Fürstenbau** (April–Sept Tues–Sun 9am–12.30pm & 1–5pm; Oct–March Tues–Sun 10am–12.30pm & 1–4pm; DM4) contains a historical museum whose exhibits include the thirteenth-century battle standard, the St Kilian banner, and the treasury of the prince-bishops. On the terrace below the palace is the **Fürstengarten**, a formal Baroque garden seen at its best when the roses are in bloom in summer, but always worth visiting for the sake of the wonderful view over the city.

St Burkhard and the Käppele

Returning to the waterfront and heading south towards the youth hostel, you pass **St Burkhard**, whose late Gothic choir picturesquely straddles the street, forming a covered walkway. It's also worth a quick look inside to see a tender polychromed Madonna and Child by Riemenschneider.

During work on the Residenz, Balthasar Neumann took time off to build the **Käppele**, a twin-towered pilgrimage church crowned with onion domes, imperiously perched on the heights at the southwestern end of the city. Apart from the opportunity to see the interior, lavishly covered with frescoes and stucco, it's well worth visiting for the **view** from the terrace, which offers a frontal panorama of the Marienberg surrounded by its vineyards, with the city nestling in the valley below.

Eating and drinking

Würzburg is a place for gourmets and those who simply enjoy good food. Although meals here aren't necessarily cheap, they're certainly value for money. The best places to sample the local wines and traditional Franconian cooking are the famous *Weinstuben*, but the city is amply endowed with a wide range of restaurants (see the hotels section on pp.171–172 for more recommendations) and bars.

Weinstuben

Bürgerspital, Theaterstr. 19. The obvious place to sample the wines from the vineyards of the famous old hospital. Produces very dry *Riesling*, *Silvaner* and *Müller-Thurgau*; the food is almost equally excellent and surprisingly reasonably priced. Closed Tues.

Fränkischer Weinkeller, Marienplatz 5. Wonderful vaulted cellar. Open from 2pm, closed Sun.

Haus des Frankenweins, Kranenkai 1. A modern building by the Main with a shop selling the full range of Franconian wines, plus a restaurant, terrace and garden.

Hofkeller, Residenzplatz 1. The former court vineyards maintain a modern rivalry to those of the two hospitals; their wide variety of wines can be enjoyed here in the splendid cellars of the Residenz itself. Closed Mon.

Juliusspital, Juliuspromenade 19. Full-bodied wines, with *Silvaner* being the most common type, are characteristic of this hospital's vineyards; they're matured in old oak casks to give a particularly strong flavour. Meals are also very good value here. Closed Wed.

Weinhaus Stachel, Gressengasse 1. The city's oldest wine-drinking inn, it has a particularly picturesque courtyard for *al fresco* meals and does river fish specialities, but is pricier than its rivals. Closed Sun.

Other restaurants

Backöfele, Ursulinergasse 2. Top-class traditional *Gaststätte* right in the heart of the city.

Burggaststätten, Festung Marienberg. The restaurant complex in the Marienberg includes a *Weinstube* (featuring wines from the *Hofkeller*), a beer garden (selling the local *Hofbräu* beers) and a traditional café; any of these is well worth patronizing when you're visiting the fortress. Closed Mon.

Hofbräukeller, Höchberger Str. 28. In this wine stronghold, it's appropriate that the leading *Bierkeller*, whose garden can seat 1000 people, is way out of the centre on the western side of the city. An adventurous menu includes many vegetarian options as well as the expected Franconian dishes.

WÜRZBURG'S FESTIVALS

Würzburg hosts several **wine festivals** throughout the year. The series begins with the *Würzburger Weindorf* in late May and early June, held in some forty little huts set up throughout the city centre. The Bürgerspital holds its *Weinfest* in late June; the Hofkeller has a similar event in the Hofgarten soon after. In September, the season ends with the *Würzburger Weinfest*, which is held in a huge tent.

The main **musical** event is the *Mozartfest* throughout June, in which Mozart concerts are held outdoors in the Hofgarten and indoors by candlelight in the opulent settings of the Weisser Saal and Kaisersaal of the Residenz. There's also a shorter festival devoted to Bach, the *Bachtage*, in late November and early December. At the beginning of July is the most important **popular** and **religious** festival, the fortnight-long *Kilianifest*. This consists for the most part of a huge funfair at the Talavera, a fairground on the left bank of the Main opposite the Congress-Centrum. However, it begins on a Saturday afternoon with a costumed pageant through the city; the following morning, there's a solemn religious procession followed by high mass in the Dom.

Mal was anderes, Herzogenstr. 13. Würzburg's main vegetarian and wholefood specialist.

Ratskeller, Langgasse 1. Serves both Franconian and international dishes, and has an extensive wine list.

Schiffbäuerin, Katzengasse 7. Top choice for local fish specialities, with a fine selection of wines. Closed Sun evening & Mon.

Schützenhof Gutsschänke, Mainleitenweg 48. Terrace restaurant offering a beautiful view over the Main from its lofty position near the Käppele. Serves fruit wines and home-made cakes as well as Franconian dishes.

Bars and cafés

Brückenbäck, Alte Mainbrücke. Coffee house which also serves light meals, and has the benefit of wonderful riverside views.

THE ROMANTIC ROAD

Glibly named, but with many beautiful spots along it, the **Romantic Road** (*Romantische Strasse*) runs for 350km between Würzburg and Füssen in the Allgäu. The road gets its name from the fact that it passes gently rolling countryside, which is never very dramatic but instead pleasantly unspoilt and tranquil.

If pushed for time, taking the *Europabus* along the whole or part of the route is a good way to get a quick impression; both *Eurail* and *EuroDomino* passes are valid, but note that services run just once a day in each direction, and only during the summer. One snag is that stops are very short, which means that you only get a superficial impression unless you break your journey for a day or trust to the infrequent local buses. (Many places on the route are not served by rail.) It's essential to detour from the main drag to get a full impression of the area and to escape the tourists – exploring the regions alongside becomes much more rewarding with your own transport. A bike is an especially appropriate means of transport, as there's a waymarked cycling route, the *Radroute Romantische Strasse*, which utilizes a mixture of pre-existing and specially laid tracks, plus some minor roads. There's a fully comprehensive guide to this: *Germany's Romantic Road* by Gordon McLachlan (Cicerone Press).

For the first section of the Road after Würzburg – Bad Mergentheim, Weikersheim and Creglingen – see Chapter Two. The stage after that, including Rothenburg and Dinkelsbühl, is described below, followed immediately by the first part of the Bavarian Swabia section, that between Nördlingen and Augsburg. For the next stretch, along the Lech valley via Landsberg and Steingaden, see pp.99-101. The southernmost staging posts, Schwangau and Füssen, are described on pp.196-98.

Café Uni, Neubaustr. 2. Trendy café-bar popular with local students.
Gehrings, Neubaustr. 24. Café-bistro right by the Alte Universität.
Kult, Landwehrstr. 10. Student *Kneipe* serving a variety of breakfasts and vegetarian dishes.
Victoria, Neubaustr. 8. A good choice for *Kaffee und Kuchen*.

Listings

Bike rental At the Hauptbahnhof.
Car rental *Avis*, Nürnberger Str. 107 (☎200 3939); *Europcar*, Am Hauptbahnhof (☎12060); *Hertz*, Höchberger Str. 10 (☎415221); *Sixt*, Rottendorfer Str. 46 (☎72093).
Cruises Information and tickets by the *Alte Kranen* on the riverbank at the bottom of Juliuspromenade; two different firms operate cruises in summer. Downstream, the destination is Veitshöchheim, with its Rococo Schloss and gardens (April–Sept Tues–Sun 9am–noon & 1–5pm; DM3). Upstream, you can sail to the fortified towns of Ochsenfurt and Sulzfeld.
Mitfahrzentrale Bahnhofsvorplatz-Ost (☎19448).
Post office The main post office is at Bahnhofplatz 2 with poste restante service.

Rothenburg ob der Tauber

ROTHENBURG OB DER TAUBER, which is some 60km south of Würzburg, is the most famous and most visited medieval town in Germany, and although it's very beautiful, it has been reduced to the ultimate museum-piece, with nearly half its working population employed in the tourist trade. Nonetheless, it should still merit at least one overnight stop: the only way to get this place to yourself is to stay the night and go out, either early in the morning or in the evening, when the crowds are absent.

Perched on a promontory 90 metres above the River Tauber, Rothenburg was a prosperous Free Imperial City in medieval times, but suffered a spectacular slump in its fortunes as it found itself cut off from the new trading routes and reduced to a very provincial market town. Without money to expand or erect new buildings, it vegetated until the nineteenth century, when its self-evident attraction for the Romantic movement led to the enforcement of preservation orders. In 1945, part of the town suffered severe damage in an American air raid. Thankfully, a civilian working for the US army, J.J. McCloy (later the High Commissioner to Germany), knew and loved Rothenburg, and lobbied successfully for it to be spared from further bombing. Money to pay for its restoration subsequently poured in from almost every quarter, and it was soon returned to its former appearance. Nowadays, its conservation policies are the strictest in Germany: even the biggest international chains are obliged to use traditional wrought-iron shop signs instead of corporate logos.

> The **telephone code** for Rothenburg ob der Tauber is ☎09861

Inside the walls

The best way to get your bearings and a first impression is to walk round the fourteenth-century **Stadtmauer**, most of whose sentry walk survives. Tightly packed within the walls, the town's houses get larger towards the middle where the local patricians and merchants lived. Nearer the wall, tradesfolk and peasants lived in crooked little dolls' houses, half-timbered and with steeply pointed roofs. The plan of the town is also highly distinctive, having a shape like a question mark, with an elongated southern stalk. For a more elevated view, climb the eastern gateway, the **Rödertor** (April–Oct daily 9am–5pm; DM2).

Marktplatz

The sloping central Marktplatz is dominated by the **Rathaus**, which is in two clearly defined parts. To the rear is the surviving half of the original Gothic building, the rest of which was destroyed by fire and replaced in the 1570s by a splendid new Renaissance structure, which was adorned with Baroque arcades a century later. Access to both parts of the Rathaus is via the stair turret which leads up to the wood-beamed **Kaisersaal** on the first floor, where festive events are held. From the landing above, a narrow staircase goes up to the top of the slender 60-metre **tower** (April–Oct daily 9.30am–12.30pm & 1–4pm; Nov–March Sat & Sun noon–3pm only; DM1) of the Gothic Rathaus. It's the highest point in Rothenburg and provides the best view of the town and surrounding countryside. Back at street level, the inner courtyard between the two parts of the Rathaus gives access to the dungeons or **Historiengewölbe** (mid-March to Oct daily 9am–5/6pm; DM3) below, which were said to be more dreadful than any others of the day.

The other main tourist attraction on the Marktplatz is the pair of figures looking out from the windows on either side of the three clocks on the gable of the **Ratsherrntrinkstube** (Councillors' Tavern). Every day at 11am, noon, 1pm, 2pm, 3pm, 8pm, 9pm and 10pm, they re-enact a famous but apocryphal event. The story goes that in 1631, during the Thirty Years' War, the imperial army, led by the fearsome Johann Tilly, captured the town and intended to destroy it as a punishment for its support of the Protestant cause. In a gesture of peace, the general was brought the huge civic tankard known as the *Meistertrunk*, which was filled with wine to its capacity of 3.25 litres, and was persuaded to accept the wager that Rothenburg should be spared if one of the councillors could down the contents in one go. The former burgomaster Georg Nusch duly obliged, taking ten minutes to accomplish the feat, after which he needed three days to sleep off the effects.

To the opposite side of the Marktplatz is Rothenburg's largest building, the Gothic parish church of **St Jakob** (daily Easter–Oct 9am–5pm; rest of year 10am–noon & 2–4pm; DM2.50), whose main body and two towers rise above the sea of red roofs like a great ship, visible for miles around. The elevated west choir, built over an archway straddling the street, contains **Riemenschneider**'s *Holy Blood Altar*, which is exquisitely carved in limewood, with a centrepiece showing the Last Supper. Also of note is the church's high altar, the *Zwölfbotenaltar*, by the Nördlingen artist Friedrich Herlin. The outer wings illustrate *The Legend of St James*; the scene where the saint's dead body is carried to a medieval town features a depiction of fifteenth-century Rothenburg.

North of Marktplatz

Just to the northwest of St Jakob is the **Reichstadtmuseum** (daily April–Oct 10am–5pm; Nov–March 1–4pm; DM4) on Klosterhof. This occupies the former Dominican convent and is most interesting for the building's original medieval workrooms, which include the oldest surviving kitchen in Germany. Other highlights are the *Rothenburg Passion*, a cycle of twelve pictures painted at the end of the fifteenth century by Martinus Schwarz, the abbot of the Franciscan monastery, and the decorated glass vessel which inspired the *Meistertrunk* legend. Also of note is the collection on Jewish local history. In the thirteenth century Rothenburg had a large settlement of Jews, but their synagogue and ghetto were destroyed in the fifteenth-century pogroms. You can see one surviving feature of their heritage, however, by going eastwards from here along Judengasse. At the end, built up against the twelfth-century **Weisser Turm** (White Tower), is the former Jewish dance hall, whose walls are embedded with gravestones.

At the extreme northwestern end of town stands the late Gothic church of **St Wolfgang** (daily March–Oct 10am–noon & 2–6pm; DM2), whose austere northern wall, pierced only by embrasures, forms part of the Stadtmauer. Now deconsecrated, it was traditionally the parish of the local shepherds, and the sentry's house above the adjoin-

Linderhof, Bavaria

Munich: the Rathaus

Passau: view of the city from the River Inn

Munich: Oktoberfest

Zugspitz in the Bavarian Alps

Munich: the Dom

Ruhpolding: the view from Raschberg

Ulm: the Dom

C. BOWMAN

The Black Forest

STEVE BENBOW

Bamberg: the Altes Rathaus

N. SETCHFIELD

The Neue Staatsgalerie, Stuttgart

C. BOWMAN

Neuschwanstein, Bavaria

G. MCLACHLAN

Heidelberg: the Schloss

ing gateway appropriately contains a display on the *Schäfertanz* (see p.180). You can also descend to the casemates below the church, which have dungeons and gun emplacements.

West of Marktplatz

Herrngasse, which leads west from Marktplatz, is the widest street in Rothenburg. At its top end is **Käthe Wohlfahrt**, Europe's largest all-year-round Christmas store and the most obviously over-the-top of the many tourist-orientated shops which have lumbered the town with a reputation for kitsch. However, the street also has many outstanding patrician mansions, notably the **Staudtsches Haus**, where you can ring for a short guided tour (DM2) which also takes in the lobby, the kitchen, and the remarkable wooden stairwell. Opposite is the severe early Gothic **Franziskanerkirche**, which still preserves the rood screen which divided the monks from the laity. Its walls and floor are covered with funerary monuments to local families, and there's a startlingly realistic retable, believed to be an early work by Riemenschneider, showing *The Stigmatization of St Francis*.

At the far end of Herrngasse is the tiny **Figurentheater**, which has gained international acclaim for the gentle humour and artistic integrity of its puppet shows. These take place at 8.30pm from Monday to Saturday; from June to September, there are also shorter performances at 3pm on the same days. Alongside is the **Burgtor**, the tallest of the town's gateways, which gives access to the immaculately tended **Burggarten**, from where there are wonderful views of the town's skyline and the Tauber valley below. In the early Middle Ages there was a castle belonging to the Hohenstaufen emperors here, but it was destroyed by a violent earthquake in 1356. Some of its masonry was used to construct the **Blasiuskapelle**, which is now a memorial to the dead of the two World Wars.

South of Marktplatz

At no. 13 on Hofbronnengasse, which leads off the southern side of Marktplatz, is the **Puppen- und Spielzeugmuseum** (daily Jan & Feb 11am–5pm; March–Dec 9.30am–6pm; DM5), Germany's largest private collection of toys and dolls. The exhibits date from 1780 to 1940 and are all beautifully displayed. Facing you across Burggasse at the end of the street is the fascinating **Mittelalterisches Kriminalmuseum** (daily April–Oct 9.30am–5.30pm; Nov, Jan & Feb 2–3.30pm; Dec & March 10am–3.30pm; DM4), which contains extensive collections of torture instruments and punishment devices – for example the beer barrels that drunks were forced to walk around in. An added attraction is that all exhibits are fully labelled and explained in English.

Schmiedgasse, which leads off the southeastern corner of Marktplatz, is lined with the most prestigious of all the mansions in town. The **Bauermeisterhaus**, the finest house, was built by the same architect who designed the Rathaus, Leonhard Weidmann. The first floor is adorned with statues of the Seven Virtues; on the next level, the Seven Deadly Sins sound their warning notes. Burgomaster Nusch of *Meistertrunk* fame lived at no. 21, now a hotel called **Roter Hahn**. For an insight into how the medieval tradesfolk lived, it's worth making a short detour east along Alter Stadtgarten to see the **Alt-Rothenburger Handwerkerhaus** (April–Oct daily 9am–6pm; Nov–March Sat & Sun 10am–4pm; DM3), which is believed to be the oldest surviving house in town, dating back to 1270. Its eleven rooms are decked out in the style of centuries past.

At the far end of Schmiedgasse is the **Plönlein**, an outrageously picturesque little triangular square. Beyond lies the narrow southern stem of the town, which functioned as the hospital quarter. The **Spital** itself is a complex of various dates: the chapel is Gothic, the main building is by Weidmann. One of the town's two youth hostels occupies its former bakery; another is in the nearby **Rossmühle**, a sixteenth-century mill

ROTHENBURG'S FESTIVALS AND FOLKLORE

If you can stand the crowds and a certain sense of tweeness, it's worth trying to make your visit coincide with one of Rothenburg's many **festivals**. Each Whit Monday, the **Meistertrunk drama** is re-enacted – albeit with no more than a pretence at matching Nusch's feat. The preceding day sees one of the renditions of the historic **Schäfertanz** (Shepherds' Dance) in front of the Rathaus; this is repeated on selected Sundays in spring and summer. According to one tradition, the dance began as a thanksgiving for Rothenburg's deliverance from the plague; another theory asserts that it derives from the celebration of a discovery of hidden treasure by one of the shepherds. Also at Whitsun, and throughout July and August, there are costume performances of **plays by Hans Sachs**. The second weekend in September sees the **Freiereichstadtfest**, featuring pageants, historical tableaux and a fireworks display, as well as performances of the *Meistertrunk* and the *Schäfertanz*. Rothenburg, like neighbouring Dinkelsbühl and Nördlingen, is among the last towns in Europe still employing a **nightwatchman**. From April to October, he leads tours round the town, starting from the Rathaus; the 8pm tour is in English, the one at 9.30pm in German.

formerly powered by sixteen horses. To the east is the **Spitalbastei**, the strongest as well as most modern part of the fortification system, dating from the turn of the seventeenth century.

Outside the walls

From either Plönlein or the Spitalbastei, you can descend to the **Doppelbrücke**, a Gothic viaduct faithfully reconstructed after the war. From here, there's a superb long-range view of Rothenburg. More fine panoramas can be had by following the S-bend in the Tauber downstream to the **Topplerschlösschen** (Fri–Sun 1–4pm; DM3), the summer and weekend retreat of Burgomaster Heinrich Toppler. This late fourteenth-century tower house has a bizarre top-heavy effect, with the upper storeys jutting out well over the stumpy base.

From here it's a 2km walk down the Tauber to **DETWANG**, a village which is actually older than Rothenburg, but has been part of its municipality since the thirteenth century. The Romanesque **Pfarrkirche** (April–Oct daily 8.30am–noon & 1.30–5/6pm; Nov–March Tues–Sun 10am–noon & 2–4pm; DM1) contains another masterpiece by Riemenschneider, the *Kreuzaltar*, featuring a central *Crucifixion* by the master, with wing reliefs of *The Agony in the Garden* and *The Resurrection* by his assistants.

Practicalities

Rothenburg is the terminus of a branch **rail line** from Steinach on the stretch between Würzburg and Ansbach; buses sometimes supplant the trains on this route. From the **Bahnhof**, it's no more than a five-minute walk to the Rödertor. The **tourist office** is in the Ratsherrntrinkstube on Marktplatz (Mon–Fri 9am–noon & 2–6pm, Sat 9am–noon, also 2–4pm May–Sept only; ☎40492).

Accommodation

Rothenburg offers a huge choice of accommodation, ranging from remarkably cheap **pensions** to luxurious historic **hotels**. Despite the volume of tourism, there's rarely any problem finding somewhere with vacancies. **Private rooms** (①–③) are also in reasonable supply – look out for *Zimmer frei* signs. The two **youth hostels** are in beautifully restored half-timbered houses off the bottom of the Spitalgasse: *Rossmühle*, Mühlacker 1 (☎94160; **ⓖ**), is the main building; the *Spitalhof* is its rather more spartan annex. Both **campsites** are in Detwang: *Tauber-Romantik* (☎6191) and *Tauber-Idyll* (☎3177).

HOTELS AND PENSIONS

Altfränkische Weinstube, Klosterhof 7 (☎6404, fax 6410). Small hotel attached to a wine bar-restaurant. The local English Conversation Club meets in the latter every Wednesday at 8pm, and invites all English-speaking visitors to the town to join them for a chat. ④

Café Gerberhaus, Spitalgasse 25 (☎94900, fax 86555). Named after the old tannery it occupies, this offers modern hotel comforts at moderate prices. The buffet breakfasts are outstanding. ④

Eisenhut, Herrengasse 3–7 (☎7050, fax 70545). Rothenburg's leading hotel occupies four patrician mansions on its most prestigious street. It is beautifully decorated with furniture and antiques, has a garden terrace and a first-rate restaurant. ⑦

Glocke, Am Plönlein 1 (☎3025, fax 86711). Fine old inn, now part of the *Ringhotel* chain, situated at one of Rothenburg's most famous corners. Its restaurant, *Wirtshaus in Franken*, has a strong line in fish dishes. ⑥

Goldene Rose, Spitalgasse 28 (☎4638, fax 86417). Typical Franconian *Gasthof*, with a variety of rooms, including tiny singles which are among the cheapest in town. ③

Goldener Greifen, Obere Schmiedgasse 5 (☎2281, fax 86374). *Gasthof* with a choice of rooms in various categories, a quiet garden, and a good restaurant serving inexpensive Franconian specialities. ③

Goldener Hirsch, Untere Schmiedgasse 16 (☎7080, fax 708100). One of the town's most luxurious hotels, with a renowned restaurant, *Die Blaue Terrasse*, commanding a wonderful view over the Tauber valley. ⑦

Markusturm, Rödergasse 1 (☎94280, fax 2692). Tastefully furnished hotel with restaurant, part of the *Romantik* chain. Located at one of the town's most picturesque corners, it takes its name from the adjoining tower, a survivor of the original twelfth-century Stadtmauer. ⑦

Pöschel, Wenggasse 22 (☎3430). Small family-run pension with immaculate, comfortable bedrooms. ②

Raidel, Wenggasse 3 (☎3115). Another good-value pension, located in a six–hundred-year-old half-timbered house. ②

Roter Hahn, Obere Schmiedgasse 21 (☎5088, fax 5140). A famous old hotel, formerly the home of Burgomaster Nusch. It has a good and reasonably priced restaurant. ⑥

Then, Johannitergasse 8a (☎5177, fax 86014). Friendly pension with English-speaking owners, located down a quiet sidestreet between the Bahnhof and the Rödertor. ②

Eating and drinking

The distinctive local **snowball** (*Schneebällchen*) is Rothenburg's best-known culinary speciality; this is made of dough, twisted into shape, then dipped in any one of several different coverings. For the best selection, visit *Diller* at Hofbronnengasse 16 or Hafengasse 4. Most of the town's many excellent **restaurants** are attached to hotels (see above), though there are a few other eateries worth a visit.

Altstadt-Café Alter Keller, Alter Keller 8. Offers Franconian food and wines, plus home-made cakes and gateaux. Closed Sun evening & Tues.

Baumeisterhaus, Obere Schmiedgasse 5. Provides a strong rivalry to its hotel counterparts for traditional German dishes. It's located in one of the town's most important Renaissance buildings, with a charming covered inner courtyard.

Café Toppler-Felsenkeller, Taubertalweg. Located near the Doppelbrücke, this café has a garden terrace commanding a spectacular view of the town.

Landsknechtstübchen, Galgengasse 21. Pleasant *Gaststätte* serving hearty Franconian cuisine.

Louvre, Klingengasse 15. Rothenburg's most creative restaurant, serving French-inspired cuisine and hosting changing art exhibitions. At weekends, it's open evenings only.

Dinkelsbühl

Some 40km southwards along the Romantic Road from Rothenburg is **DINKELSBÜHL**, which presents another immaculately preserved townscape from the Middle Ages. In contrast to its neighbour, it has managed to avoid being overrun by tourists and thus has a rather more authentic air.

The town

The **Stadtmauer** survives almost intact, except for the sentry walk, of which only a small section remains. It's therefore best to begin your tour by walking round the outside of the walls via the pathway known as the Alte Promenade. Of the four gateways, the eastern **Wörnitz Tor** is part of the original thirteenth-century fortification system, though it was later prettified by the addition of a clock gable and a coating of orange paint. Proceeding southwards, you pass the most photogenic of the towers, the **Bäuerlinsturm**, whose projecting half-timbered upper storey was added when it passed into residential use. Beyond stands the late fourteenth-century **Nördlinger Tor**, again embellished with a Renaissance gable.

Alongside it is the **Stadtmühle**, perhaps the most formidable-looking mill ever built; because it lay outside the walls, it had to be fortified with corner towers and gun loops. It now houses the **Museum 3 Dimension** (April–Oct daily 10am–6pm; Nov–March Sat & Sun 11am–4pm; DM10), an unexpected yet fascinating series of hands-on displays about three-dimensional effects. The western section of the Stadtmauer is pierced by a series of round towers, but its gateway, the **Segringer Tor**, is a decorative Baroque replacement for the one destroyed in the Thirty Years' War. However, the northern **Rothenburger Tor** still preserves most of its medieval form, including a sturdy gatehouse.

Within the walls, the dominant monument is the church of **St Georg** on Weinmarkt. From the top of its **tower** (Easter–Sept Mon–Fri 9am–noon & 2–6pm, Sat 10am–noon & 1–5pm, Sun 1–5pm; DM3), which survives from the original Romanesque church, there's a marvellous view of the town. The rest of the building is a textbook Gothic hall church from the second half of the fifteenth century, with an airily light interior of slen-

---

DINKELSBÜHL FOLKLORE

In common with Rothenburg and Nördlingen, Dinkelsbühl still has a paid **nightwatchman**. Decked out in cloak, breeches and felt hat, and carrying a halberd, horn and lantern, he sets out from St Georg at 9pm each evening from April to October (9.30pm in July and August), and does the rounds of the town's hotels. At each, he performs his song, and is thereupon presented with a glass of wine, which is passed round the tourists accompanying him.

The most famous piece of local folklore is the **Kinderzeche**, a ten-day-long festival held each July, the pivotal date being the third Monday of the month. This commemorates an event in the Thirty Years' War which has obvious parallels with Rothenburg's *Meistertrunk*. This time it was the Swedes who were bent on destruction. According to legend, when the town finally capitulated after a long siege, the Swedish commander was dissuaded from ransacking it by a deputation of local children. The events are re-enacted in plays performed in the Schranne, while on the Monday and each of the two Saturdays and Sundays there are costumed pageants through the streets. Music is provided by the *Knabenkapelle*; perhaps the best-known boys' band in Germany, its members are kitted out like little soldiers in red and white eighteenth-century uniform. In line with Bavarian taste, there are side-shows of open-air theatre, fireworks and the inevitable beer tents.

der pillars and elaborate network vaults. In the north walk of the ambulatory is a didactic *Panel of the Ten Commandments*, which pairs each scene with the consequences of failure to obey.

Facing the church are five magnificent mansions, of which the most notable are the half-timbered **Deutsches Haus**, now a hotel-restaurant, and the resplendently gabled **Schranne**, which contains the town's main festive hall. More fine houses can be seen down Segringer Strasse to the west: nos. 3 and 5 share a single gable, while no. 7 has a lovely arcaded, flower-strewn courtyard. In the opposite direction, the Altrathausplatz in the shadow of the Wörnitz Tor is another of the most picturesque corners, with the **Löwenbrunnen** (Lion Fountain) as its focal point.

Practicalities

Dinkelsbühl lies on a rail line which used to provide a useful link with Nördlingen, the next stop on the Romantic Road some 30km south, but this has been superseded, except for occasional excursion steam trains in summer, by a **bus** service. Most departures are from the **Bahnhof**, a few minutes' walk east of the Altstadt, though the *Europabus* coaches travelling the Romantic Road leave from Schweinemarkt in the heart of town. The **tourist office** is on Marktplatz (April–Oct Mon–Fri 9am–noon & 2–6pm, Sat 10am–noon & 2–5pm, Sun 10am–1pm; Nov–March Mon–Fri 9am–noon & 2–6pm, Sat 10am–1pm; ☎09851/90240). Ask here if you're interested in staying in either a **private house** (①–②) or a neighbouring **farm** (①); provided you've got your own transport, the latter can be a tremendous bargain, particularly for stays of four days or more.

Otherwise, the cheapest rooms are at a small and homely Altstadt **pension**, *Lutz*, Schäfergässlein 4 (☎09851/9454; ③). There are numerous **hotels**, all of them in characterful old buildings; they include *Gasthof Sonne und Palmengarten*, Weinmarkt 11 (☎09851/57670; ③); *Gasthof Goldenes Lamm*, Lange Gasse 26–28 (☎09851/2267; ④); *Eisenkrug*, Dr-Martin-Luther-Str. 1 (☎09851/57700; ④); *Goldene Rose*, Marktplatz 4 (☎09851/57750; ⑤); *Weisses Ross*, Steingasse 12 (☎09851/2274 or 7840; ⑥); *Blauer Hecht*, Schweinemarkt 1 (☎09851/5810; ⑥); and *Deutsches Haus*, Weinmarkt 3 (☎09851/6059; ⑥).

The **youth hostel** is housed in an old granary at Koppengasse 10 (☎09851/9509; ❷), while there's a **campsite** (☎09851/7817) to the northeast of the old town, just off the road from Rothenburg.

Nearly all the hotels in the town centre have **restaurants**, which are surprisingly good value: even *Deutsches Haus* serves affordable meals. *Eisenkrug's* renowned gourmet restaurant, *Zum kleinen Obristen,* is the only really expensive place, though it serves reasonably priced food in its evenings-only *Weinkeller*.

BAVARIAN SWABIA

Approximately bordered by the rivers Iller and Lech, the southwestern part of Bavaria has a small-scale landscape of rolling farmland dotted with quiet villages and picturesque medieval towns. The region is called **Bavarian Swabia** (*Bayerisch-Schwaben*) and used to form part of the medieval Duchy of Swabia, the rest of which became the separate state of Württemberg. Its capital is **Augsburg**, one of the greatest metropolises of sixteenth-century Europe and still an elegant city full of fine Renaissance architecture, largely unspoilt by later building.

North of here is the stretch of the **Romantic Road** immediately following on from Dinkelsbühl the initial Franconian section; its main draws are **Nördlingen**, a well-preserved medieval walled town in a truly extraordinary natural setting, and fortified **Harburg**. South of Augsburg is the **Allgäu** region. The hilly pre-Alpine section includes the pretty town of **Kaufbeuren** and the health resort of **Ottobeuren**, whose Benedictine abbey should stun even the most jaded visitor of Baroque churches. Beyond here, everything is played against the dramatic backdrop of snow-capped mountains and sparkling lakes: highlights are the pair of fantasy castles near **Füssen**; **Oberstdorf**, a top-class resort set amid challenging peaks; and the island town of **Lindau** on the Bodensee.

An added pleasure of travelling through this region is the distinctive and excellent **food**: delicate handmade pasta and rich sauces quite different from the Italian kind, followed by sweets with irreverent names like *Nonnenfürzle* (Nun's Fart) and *Versoffene Jungfern* (Drunken Virgins).

Nördlingen and around

NÖRDLINGEN, together with 99 villages, lies in an enormous crater, known as the **Ries**, which was formed about 15 million years ago by a meteor which crashed to earth at a speed of about 100,000 kilometres per hour, and with a velocity 250,000 times that of the Hiroshima bomb. The initially transient crater spread to cover an almost circular area with a diameter of about 25km, in the process bringing a new type of rock, known as suevite, into existence. It's among the largest craters on earth, and presents one of the main locations for scientists to study stone formations similar to those on the moon; it also provided ideal terrain for the Apollo 14 team to prepare for their lunar mission.

The town

Along with Rothenburg and Dinkelsbühl, Nördlingen makes up the trio of towns on the Romantic Road which have almost completely retained their fortified medieval character. Of the three, it's the one which has made the most concessions to the modern commercial world, but the illusion remains. The fourteenth-century **Stadtmauer** forms an almost perfect circle, guarded by five gates, eleven towers and one bastion. You can traverse the covered sentry walk, the only one in Germany to survive intact, all the way round the 3km circuit. There are also limited opportunities for ascending the eastern gateway, the **Löpsinger Tor** (May to mid-Oct Fri–Sun 10am–noon & 1.30–4.30pm; DM2).

However, the best view – which shows clearly the distinctive shape and topography of the Ries – is from the 90-metre **Danielturm** (daily 9am–sundown; DM2.50), the town's symbol, its highest building – and also the bull's-eye of the circular urban plan. The tower illustrates a gradual shift in architectural tastes from the late Gothic of its lower storeys to the full-blooded Renaissance of its cupola. A watchman still lives at the top of the tower, and sounds out the watch every half-hour from 10pm until midnight. The Danielturm actually forms part of the hall church of **St Georg**, the largest suevite building in the world, whose design closely resembles that of its namesake in Dinkelsbühl. At the high altar is an emotional polychrome wood *Crucifixion* by the great fifteenth-century Dutch sculptor Nicolaus Gerhaert von Leyden.

On the opposite side of the spacious Marktplatz lies the **Rathaus**, which has an entertaining little detail beside its ritzy outdoor stairway. The space underneath the steps used to hold the town's prisoners, and just by the wooden entrance is a medieval fool carved into the wall with an inscription saying *Nun sind unser zwey* – "Now there are two of us". Directly across is the half-timbered **Tanzhaus** (Dance Hall), bearing a statue of Emperor Maximilian I who had a special affinity with the town; he's depicted in the guise by which he most wanted to be remembered, that of a chivalrous knight. Walking northwards from Marktplatz, you reach the curious building known as the **Klösterle** (Little Monastery), which has had a decidedly chequered history. Once the

---

NÖRDLINGEN'S FESTIVALS

On the second Monday of May, the *Stabenfest* (Staff Festival) celebrates the arrival of spring with a children's procession. Trumpets sound the festival's beginning from the heights of the Danielturm and boys gather holding flags and poles decorated with flowers, the girls wearing costumes and crowns of flowers around their heads. At around 9am, the procession moves off accompanied by music and song until it reaches the Kaiserwiese, the fairground just to the north of the Stadtmauer, where the usual trappings of a Bavarian fair are set up around the beer tent. Another popular annual event is the *Scharlachrennen* in mid-July, whose origins lie in a horse race first held in 1438, with a piece of red cloth as a prize. Today, carriage events are also featured.

---

church of the bare-footed Franciscan friars, it was converted into a grain store after the Reformation, and is now the town's main festive hall.

Beyond, on Vordere Gerbergasse, is the **Spital**, an extensive medieval hospital complex complete with its own church, mill and stores. It now houses the **Stadtmuseum** (Easter to mid-Oct Tues–Sun 10am–noon & 1.30–4.30pm; DM4), whose main treasure is a colourful cycle of paintings of *The Legend of St George* by the fifteenth-century local master Friedrich Herlin. The local history section features terrible exhibits from the torture chambers used during the sixteenth-century witch-hunts: in Nördlingen alone, 35 women were put to death. There's also a diorama of the Battle of Nördlingen of 1634, the worst Protestant reverse in the Thirty Years' War. On nearby Hintere Gerbergasse, a fifteenth-century barn has been converted to house the snazzy **Reiskrater-Museum** (Tues–Sun 10am–noon & 1.30–4.30pm; DM5) which gives detailed information on the Ries crater's formation and geological history.

Practicalities

Nördlingen's **Bahnhof**, which lies on the slow route between Augsburg and Stuttgart via Schwäbisch Gmünd, is just to the east of the Altstadt. The **tourist office** is at Marktplatz 2 (Easter–Oct Mon–Thurs 9am–6pm, Fri 9am–4.30pm, Sat 9.30am–12.30pm; rest of the year Mon–Thurs 9am–5pm, Fri 9am–3.30pm; ☎09081/4380 or 84116).

There are plenty of budget **hotels** within or beside the Stadtmauer, including *Gasthof Walfisch*, Hallgasse 15 (☎09081/3107; ②); *Gasthof Drei Mohren*, Reimlinger Str. 18 (☎09081/3113; ③); *Café Altreuter*, Marktplatz 11 (☎09081/4319; ③); *Gasthof Zum Engel*, Wemdinger Str. 4 (☎09081/3167; ③); and *Gasthof Goldenes Lamm*, Schäfflesmarkt 3 (☎09081/28749; ④). Two good upmarket choices are *Sonne*, Marktplatz 3 (☎09081/5067; ⑤) and *Klösterle*, Beim Klösterle 1 (☎09081/88054; ⑥). There's also a **youth hostel**, just to the northwest of the Stadtmauer at Kaiserwiese 1 (☎09081/84109; ②).

The **restaurants** of the last two hotels listed above are the best in town, while all the aforementioned *Gasthöfe* serve good and inexpensive Swabian cuisine. For a trendier atmosphere, try *Café Radlos*, Löpsinger Str. 8, which serves bistro-type food and has a wide range of guest beers on tap.

Harburg

From Nördlingen, it's only about 15km by road or rail to the next stop on the Romantic Road, the picturesquely sited little town of **HARBURG**. High above, dominating the valley of the River Wörnitz, is a huge **Schloss** (guided tours mid-March to Sept Tues-Sun 9am–5pm; Oct Tues-Sun 9.30am–4.30pm; DM5), which was founded in the twelfth century by the Hohenstaufen emperors, before passing to the Counts of Oettingen, whose descendants still own it. Never taken in battle, its fortifications and residential buildings – which date from a variety of periods – survive in pretty good condition. The Renaissance Fürstenbau houses the **Kunstsammlung** (mid-March to Oct Tues–Sun 10am–noon & 2–5pm; DM5), whose prize exhibit is a poignant, almost monumental ivory Crucifix of the eleventh-century Ottonian period, a unique work of its kind. There are also several outstanding treasury items, notably a jewelled reliquary cross bearing the figures of the donor, Count Ludwig XII of Oettingen, and his family.

Gasthof Zum Straussen, Marktplatz 2 (☎09080/1398; ②) is one of the best-value **hotels** anywhere in Germany, and its **restaurant** serves king-sized portions of superb Swabian cuisine. If it's full, there are a couple of other places to stay on the same square.

Augsburg

Only 60km northwest of Munich, and a quarter of the size, **AUGSBURG** certainly doesn't suffer from any inferiority complexes. Founded in 15 BC as *Augusta Vindelicorum* by two stepsons of Augustus, the city is one of the oldest in Germany. A Free Imperial City from 1276 and a frequent choice for meetings of the Diet, Augsburg had its heyday between the fifteenth and seventeenth centuries, when the **Fugger** and **Welser** dynasties made it Europe's most important centre of high finance. As a result it grew into one of the largest cities on the continent. It was the one place in Germany to take the Renaissance style to its heart, and the stylish buildings of **Elias Holl** still dominate the cityscape.

Local people have gone to vast expense to restore the numerous palaces and civic buildings to their original splendour. In fact civilian municipal life is the key to Augsburg's history. Trade and banking riches spawned a social conscience – in 1514 Augsburg built the world's first housing estate for the poor, the **Fuggerei**, an institution still in use today. Here too the revolutionary reforms of Martin Luther found their earliest support, as the city played a pivotal role in the Reformation and its aftermath. It became the model example of how different faiths could co-exist, making this visible by the curious practice of building new Protestant churches alongside existing Catholic ones.

Despite these associations, Augsburg is far from being a museum-piece. It has long been a leading centre for **new technologies**: here, for example, Rudolf Diesel invented the engine which has put his name into languages all round the world. There's also a lively cultural scene ranging from Mozart festivals to jazz and cabaret, and the local university means you'll find plenty of student bars and a thriving alternative culture.

Arrival and accommodation

The **Hauptbahnhof** lies just to the west of the Altstadt and is itself a remarkable sight, a mock *palazzo* of the 1840s which ranks as the longest-serving main station of any city in the world. Just down the road, at Bahnhofstr. 7, is the **tourist office** (Mon–Fri 9am–6pm; ☎502070). This has a small branch on Rathausplatz (Mon–Fri 9am–6pm, Sat 10am–1pm; May to mid-Oct Sun 10am–1pm; ☎502070). A day ticket on the public transport network is a good investment; it costs DM7 for the city, DM16 for the whole circuit - which stretches as far as Donauwörth.

The **telephone code** for Augsburg is ☎0821

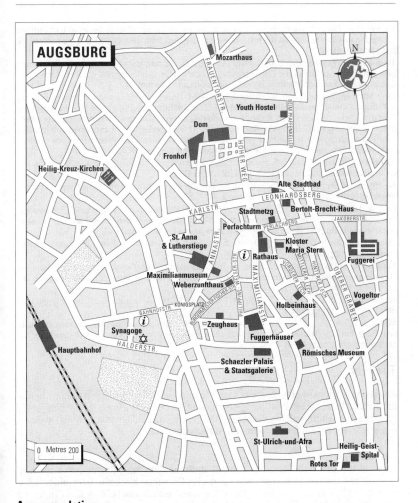

Accommodation

Augsburg has a wide choice of **hotels** and pensions, with a surprisingly large number of eminently good budget options for such a major city. The **youth hostel** is centrally located, three minutes' walk from the Dom, at Beim Pfaffenkeller 3 (☎33909; **🏠**); if you're coming from the Hauptbahnhof, take tram #2 to *Stadtwerke*. The nearest **campsite** is at highway exit *Augsburg-Ost*, next to the Autobahnsee (☎707575) reachable by bus #75.

HOTELS AND PENSIONS

Altstadthotel Ulrich, Kapuzinergasse 6 (☎33077, fax 33081). Excellent middle-range hotel handily placed just off Maximilianstrasse. ⑥
Augsburger Hof, Auf dem Kreuz 2 (☎314083, fax 38322). Part of the *Romantik* chain, this classy hotel and restaurant occupies a historic building in the northern Altstadt. ⑥

Bayerischer Löwe, Linke Brandstr. 2, Lechhausen (☎702870, fax 706194). Good budget pension, situated in an inner suburb on the opposite side of the Lech from the city centre, a ten-minute ride away on tram #1. ③

Dom-Hotel, Frauentorstr. 8 (☎153031, fax 510126). Attractive hotel occupying the former *Domprobstei*, the palace of the Dom's provost, in heart of the quiet episcopal quarter. It has a garden terrace and an indoor swimming pool with sauna and solarium. ⑥

Drei Mohren, Maximilianstr. 40 (☎50360, fax 157864). Run by the *Steigenberger* chain, this is one of Germany's most famous hotels, founded in 1723 and with an illustrious guest list which includes Mozart, Goethe, Napoleon and Wellington. Following wartime damage, it was rebuilt in a predominantly modern style, but is still very luxurious, with a lovely garden terrace and a moderately priced bistro as an alternative to the main restaurant. Substantial reductions in room rates are available from early July to mid-Sept, and at weekends throughout the year. ⑧

Fischertor, Pfärrle 16 (☎34583, fax 345 8395). One of the most appealing hotels in Augsburg, run as an adjunct to the top restaurant in the city centre. ⑥

Georgsrast, Georgenstr. 31 (☎502610). In the northwestern quarter of the Altstadt and one of the few inexpensive places you'll find in this area. ④

Gregor, Landsberger Str. 62, Haunstetten (☎80050, fax 800569). Country-style hotel 7km south of the Altstadt. Its expensive gourmet restaurant, *Cheval Blanc* (closed Sun, Mon & all Aug) is one of the two best in Augsburg; the *Lindenstube* serves more affordable meals. ⑤

Jakoberhof, Jakoberstr. 39–41 (☎510030, fax 150844). Good-value hotel with restaurant, located close to the Fuggerei. ⑤

Lenzhalde, Thelottstr. 2 (☎520745, fax 528761). Greek-run *Gasthof* sited immediately behind the Hauptbahnhof, though it's a circuitous walk or drive to get here. In summer, its taverna spills out onto the shady beer garden in front. ③

Linderhof, Aspernstr. 38, Lechhausen (☎713016, fax 716766). Across the Lech, but only ten minutes from the centre; take tram #1. ③

Märkl, Schillstr. 20, Lechhausen (☎791499, fax 716766). This pension has the cheapest rooms in Augsburg, but is perfectly comfortable, with showers in every room. It's on the first street over the Lechbrücke; take tram #1. ②

The city

Augsburg is a remarkably easy city to get to grips with. The Altstadt is defined by the old fortifications, substantial parts of which still survive. Virtually everything you'll want to see is within walking distance of the central Maximilianstrasse, which makes a ready reference point for exploring the various quarters.

Rathausplatz

Heart of the city is the spacious cobbled **Rathausplatz**, which turns into a massive open-air café during the summer and a glittering Christmas market in December. At the baseline of this great semicircle stands the massive **Rathaus** built by Elias Holl, and generally regarded as Germany's finest example of a secular Renaissance building. The proportions and style of the elegantly plain exterior topped by two octagonal towers recall a Florentine palace rather than a town hall, a likeably overstated symbol of Augsburg's wealth and influence. What stands today is a painstaking reconstruction; only the shell survived a 1944 air raid targeting the city's Messerschmidt aircraft factories. Not that you'd guess this from looking at the showpiece **Goldener Saal** (daily 10am–6pm; DM2), which is once more resplendent with its gold-leaf pillars, marble floor and painted cedarwood ceiling.

Next to the Rathaus stands the **Perlachturm** (daily mid-May to mid-Oct 10am–6pm; DM2), which was remodelled by Holl to its present height of just over 70m. A climb to the top gives a good vantage point from which to take in the whole city and get your bearings on Augsburg's main axis, neatly formed between the Dom to the north and the church of St-Ulrich-und-Afra at the far end of Maximilianstrasse to the south. The

THE FUGGER DYNASTY

The Fugger family settled in Augsburg in the fourteenth century, and were originally active in the linen trade. They gradually moved into the even more profitable business of money-lending, which they established throughout Germany and beyond, becoming the biggest banking outfit in Europe and reputedly five times richer than the Medici, their Italian counterparts. Although the youngest of seven brothers, **Jacob Fugger II** (1459–1525) became the head of the firm, and can legitimately be regarded as the first modern business tycoon.

He established the family interests as a public company, expanding its activities by gaining mining rights for copper and silver in the Tyrol and Silesia and entering the profitable spice trade. In addition, he safeguarded his prosperity by spreading his assets across a wide range of investments, including the acquisition of land – which brought the family into the ranks of the nobility. He also moved into big-time politics by initiating the long-running funding of the Habsburgs, whose goal of European domination seemed to have been achieved when Charles I of Spain won election in 1519 as the Holy Roman Emperor Charles V through outright bribes to the seven Electors with money largely supplied by the Fuggers.

The Reformation dealt a severe blow to the family, who lost key markets by remaining faithful to Catholicism, though the Habsburg connection was put to good use in the establishment of business interests in the burgeoning Spanish empire. Some 4 million ducats lent to the Habsburgs have never been repaid, but the Fuggers were able to sit back on the income from their landed holdings. To this day, the three branches of the family retain a high position in the German league table of wealth – and they still own their own bank.

tower forms part of the Romanesque church of **St Peter am Perlach**, the oldest brick building in southern Germany, which preserves life-sized thirteenth-century murals of four saints. Opposite is the Mannerist **Augustusbrunnen**, by the Dutchman Hubert Gerhard, one of many grandiose fountains dotting the centre of the city, bearing symbolic figures representing Augsburg's four rivers.

Maximilianstrasse

Maximilianstrasse is a true showpiece thoroughfare, lined with the headquarters of the leading corporate and municipal bodies, and the palatial residences of the richest merchant families who dominated their affairs. It's named in honour of the Habsburg Maximilian I, the last Holy Roman Emperor to preside over a unified empire and the man who set in motion his family's plans for European-wide domination. Augsburg was his favourite residence – no doubt partly because his political scheming was dependent on the backing of the city's bankers.

The first building of note is the fourteenth-century **Weberzunfthaus**, the guild hall of the linen weavers. Beyond, in the centre of the street, is the resplendent **Merkurbrunnen** by another Dutch-born Mannerist, Adrian de Vries, court sculptor to the Habsburgs. Soon after, the **Fuggerhäuser** stand proudly to the right. Built in 1515 by Jacob Fugger "the Rich", these mansions remain in family hands (see box above), but you can walk through the main door to see the arcaded **Damenhof**, designed in Italian Renaissance style and often used for plays in the summer. In 1518 this courtyard was the venue for the meeting between Martin Luther and Cardinal Tommaso Cajetan, in which the great reformer attempted to justify his 95 theses against Catholic orthodoxy.

Continuing south down Maximilianstrasse, you come to Adrian de Vries' heroic **Herkulesbrunnen**, the most arresting of all the city's fountains. To the right is the **Schaezlerpalais** (Wed–Sun 10am–4pm; DM4), the town's foremost Rococo building. Its sumptuous ballroom is in its original condition – right down to the candle-lit chandeliers that are still used during the annual Mozart concerts held in June and July. There's also a collection of sixteenth- to eighteenth-century German and Austrian paintings, plus a few works by foreigners, including Veronese and Tiepolo. Through the courtyard and included on the same entrance ticket is the old Dominican nunnery, now housing the **Staatsgalerie**. This displays the work of the fifteenth- and sixteenth-century school of local painters – notably Hans Holbein the Elder and Hans Burgkmair – as well as Dürer's portrait of Jacob Fugger "the Rich", looking every bit the king-maker that he was.

Towards its end, Maximilianstrasse widens and sweeps up to the late Gothic basilica of **St-Ulrich-und-Afra**, whose Renaissance tower is crowned by the most famous of the city's characteristic onion domes. In the airily light interior are the tombs of the city's two patrons. Saint Afra, a Roman virgin martyr, is interred in a simple sarcophagus, whereas Saint Ulrich, the local prince-bishop whose army helped save the empire by turning back the rampaging Magyars at the Battle of Lechfeld in 955, is honoured by an ornate Rococo shrine. The three monumental gilded altars by Hans Degler in the choir are late Renaissance masterpieces belonging to the same brilliant artistic period as Holl's buildings. In the early eighteenth century, as a symbol of the religious tolerance of the time, the preaching hall on the north side of the basilica was rebuilt as the Lutheran church of **St Ulrich**, its cheerful Baroque facade making an effective foil to its much grander neighbour.

East of Maximilianstrasse

Just to the southeast of St-Ulrich-und-Afra is another distinctive landmark, the **Rotes Tor**, a fortified tower strengthened by Holl at the time of the Thirty Years' War, whose courtyard is now put to effective use as an open-air theatre. The same architect's **Heilig-Geist-Spital** alongside is home to the celebrated *Puppenkiste* marionette theatre.

Following Bäckergasse and then Dominikanergasse back towards the city centre, you come to the former Dominican monastery, which now houses the **Römisches Museum** (Wed–Sun 10am–4pm; DM4), the city's collection of prehistoric and Roman remains. The richly stuccoed interior of the church makes an excellent setting for the artefacts, including a life-sized second-century bronze horse's head, which was probably part of a statue honouring Emperor Marcus Aurelius.

East of here is the most impressive surviving part of the medieval **Stadtmauer**, dominated by the fifteenth-century **Vogeltor**. Beyond lies the picturesque old artisans' quarter, laid out along the narrow canals of the Vorderer, Mittlerer and Unterer Lech. These back streets must have looked very similar a few hundred years ago, when they were populated with the tradesfolk and craftspeople who serviced the grand houses on Maximilianstrasse. At Vorderer Lech 20 the **Holbeinhaus** (Tues–Sun 11am–5pm; free) stands on the site of the original, which was destroyed in 1944. Here Hans the Younger, portraitist of the brilliant English court of Henry VIII, spent his childhood, his father having established himself as the city's leading painter. Changing exhibitions complement documentary material on the artists' lives.

Continuing northwards, you come to Elias-Holl-Platz to the rear of the Rathaus, on which stands a convent, **Kloster Maria Stern**. Originally built in the 1570s in late Gothic style by Johannes Holl, father of Elias, it was remodelled inside in the Baroque period. The slender brick belfry is crowned by the earliest example of the *Welsche Haube*, the distinctive onion dome that is a recurrent feature of the Augsburg skyline. A few paces on, fronting Schachthausgasse, is one of Elias Holl's finest buildings, the **Stadtmetzg**, the former guild hall and market of the butchers. Though its rusticated facade is the most visually impressive feature, it was also a technical tour-de-force in its day, harnessing the waters of the Lech canals which lie directly underneath for the cooling of meats and disposal of waste.

At Auf dem Rain 7 just to the north is the **Bertolt-Brecht-Haus** (Wed–Sun 10am–4pm; DM2.50), the birthplace of the great poet and playwright whose relationship with the city is far more problematic than that of any of its other famous sons. The embarrassing fact is that the people of Augsburg couldn't stand Brecht when he was alive – but then neither could he stomach his bourgeois home city. Today, however, all is forgiven, and the house presents a mainly photographic record of the writer, predictably concentrating on his early life in Augsburg.

The Fuggerei

One "Our Father", one "Hail Mary" and one "Credo" daily, plus DM1.72 per annum, and good Catholics can retire to the **Fuggerei** at the age of 55. It's the world's oldest housing estate for the poor and must be one of the cleverest ploys ever devised for a place in Heaven – even if it now appears that Jacob Fugger's seeming generosity was at least partly inspired by the opportunities it offered for laundering part of his fortune. Entered via a gate which, in accordance with the still-enforced original regulations, is kept locked between 10pm and 5am, it's a town within a town, with two-storey ivy-covered houses lining six car-less streets. Originally intended for families with children, it has gradually evolved into a retirement colony, though residents must still be Roman Catholic, needy, free of a criminal record, and citizens of Augsburg.

Behind the main gateway is the the Fuggerei's modest little church, the **Markuskirche**, which was built by Johannes Holl. The only other interior open to the public is that of Mittlere Gasse 13, which has been designated the **Fuggereimuseum** (March–Oct daily 9am–6pm; Nov & Dec Sat & Sun 9am–6pm; DM1), with furnishings vividly illustrating the lifestyle of the community's inhabitants of the seventeenth and eighteenth centuries. Another house from the time of the first settlement is no. 14 in the same street, which is where Mozart's great-grandfather lived in the late seventeenth century.

West of Maximilianstrasse

Exactly the other side of town, in the Annastrasse, stands the unassuming church of **St Anna**; judging from its outside appearance, you'd never guess that it's one of the most important monuments in Augsburg. In 1509, Ulrich and Jacob Fugger endowed a memorial chapel here for themselves and their deceased brother Georg. The clout they wielded is shown by the fact that, against all convention, this formed an extension of the nave, instead of taking the humbler normal position off an aisle. The sumptuous **Fuggerkapelle** which resulted marks the belated German debut of the full-blooded Italian Renaissance style. An integrated, no-expenses-spared decorative scheme – marble pavement, an organ with painted shutters, stained glass, choir stalls, balustrade with putti, a monumental sculptural group of *The Lamentation over the Dead Christ*, and memorial relief tablets made after woodcuts designed by Dürer – creates an effect of overwhelming richness. No one knows for sure whether the chapel was created by German or Italian craftsmen, but its influence on Augsburg was profound, inspiring all subsequent building there for over a century.

St Anna is also celebrated for its role in the Reformation, when Luther found refuge with its Carmelite monks when he was summoned to meet the Pope's legate Cardinal Cajetan, and today part of the monastery has been turned into the **Lutherstiege** (Tues–Sun 10am–noon & 3–5pm; free), a museum of the reformer's life and times. Along with extensive documentation on the events, you can see the **Lutherkammer**, the actual room where he stayed in 1518; the *Empore*, the old gallery for the Carmelite monks, shows the excommunication bull which resulted from his refusal to retract his views.

Across from the monastery, in a Renaissance mansion with *sgraffito* decoration at Philippine-Welser-Str. 24, is the **Maximilianmuseum** (Wed–Sun 10am–4pm; DM4), whose displays illustrate the city's historic and cultural development. Here you can see Elias Holl's building plans, exquisite book illustrations, and the wonderful Baroque and

Rococo creations of the goldsmiths, silversmiths and watchmakers who made Augsburg one of Europe's leading producers of luxury goods. A couple of blocks further south, dominating the square named after it, is the **Zeughaus**, the first structure designed by Holl in his capacity as municipal architect. It's a brilliantly original composition whose facade is uncannily anticipatory of the Baroque style to come. Above its doorway is a striking monumental bronze group of *St Michael overcoming Satan*, the masterpiece of Hans Reichle, one of the few native German Mannerists.

North of Maximilianstrasse

Dominating the northern part of the old city is the **Dom**. Architecturally, it's a bit of a hotchpotch: in the fourteenth century, Gothic aisles were added to the original eleventh-century structure; a hundred years later, a lofty hall choir replaced its predecessor altogether. Nonetheless, it contains many outstanding features. The Romanesque **bronze doors**, decorated with 35 endearingly simple panels depicting Old Testament scenes and allegorical figures and animals, have been moved inside for conservation reasons. They make a fascinating contrast with the **portals** on the north and south sides of the chancel, which are dedicated to the Virgin Mary, and crowded with richly decorative Gothic sculptures. On the southern side of the nave's clerestory are five **stained-glass windows** showing the Old Testament figures of Moses, David, Hosea, Daniel and Jonah. The freshness of colour and the vibrancy of the design make it hard to believe they were made in the eleventh century: they're the oldest windows remaining in situ in any church in the world. Another Romanesque survivor is the **bishop's throne** in the west choir, imperiously perched on crouching lions. Look out also for the eight fine **altarpieces** by Hans Holbein the Elder, fixed to the pillars of the nave, of scenes from the life of the Virgin.

Facing the Dom's facade is the **Fronhof**, the former palace of the prince-bishops. Only the tower remains of the medieval building where the Confession of Augsburg, the basic creed of Protestantism, was presented in 1530. The rest was rebuilt in Baroque style, and has served since 1817 as the regional government of Bavarian Swabia; the frescoed staircase and the main Festsaal are freely accessible, except when an official function is taking place. Further west are the **Heilig-Kreuz-Kirchen**, another of the paired Catholic and Protestant churches. Both contain fine religious paintings, with the star being the former's altarpiece of *The Assumption* by Rubens.

North of the Dom, at Frauentorstr. 30, is the **Mozarthaus** (Wed-Sun 10am–4pm; DM2.50), which documents the lives of Leopold and Wolfgang Amadeus and contains a number of bits and pieces of the original furnishings. Actually, this modest little house was the birthplace of Leopold, who moved to Salzburg long before his famous son was born; nonetheless, you can't really blame Augsburg for wanting to claim a place in the Mozart biography. In any case, Leopold himself, notorious even in his day as a Svengali figure, is now recognized as a highly competent composer in his own right, whose works include one of the best trumpet concertos ever written and two effective comic pieces, *A Musical Sleigh Ride* and the *Toy Symphony*.

Outside the Altstadt

Just beyond the confines of the Altstadt is the **Synagoge** (Tues–Fri 9am–4pm, Sun 10am–5pm; DM3) at Halderstr. 8, a few minutes' walk from the Hauptbahnhof. This imposing Jugendstil complex, grouped round an open courtyard, was built during World War I as the main place of worship for what was one of Germany's largest and most liberal Jewish communities. Nowadays, the tiny orthodox sect that remains uses only the small prayer hall; the domed main temple (which you can only view from the gallery) and ancillary buildings (which house a surprisingly rich treasury) now serve as a museum of Swabian and Bavarian Jewish culture. Just beyond the southwestern fringe of the Altstadt, housed in the Industrie und Handelskammer at Stettenstr. 1–3, is the **Lettl-Atrium** or **Museum für Surreale Kunst** (daily 11am–5pm; free). This contains well over a hundred canvases by the Augsburg Surrealist artist **Wolfgang Lettl**; his work provides a refreshing corrective to the idea that Germans lack a sense of humour.

Eating and drinking

In the food and drink field, Augsburg's main strengths are a wide range of restaurants offering hearty traditional fare, plus a large number of student pubs. In addition to the places listed below, it's worth knowing about the market and meat halls off Annastrasse, where you'll find several *Imbiss* stands which are the best bet for on-your-feet snacks.

Restaurants

Blaues Krugle, Vorderer Lech 8. Features traditional Bavarian specialities. Closed Mon.

Bräustüble Goldene Gans, Weite Gasse 11. The beer hall and garden of the eponymous brewery, which is located alongside. It serves good-value meals, including plenty of vegetarian and wholefood dishes. Closed Sun.

Caruso, Karlstr. 9. Good, reasonably priced Italian restaurant.

Die Ecke, Elias-Holl-Platz 2. Famous old restaurant in the shadow of the Rathaus; among the most expensive, but also one of the best in the city.

Fuggerei-Stube, Jakoberstr. 26. The "local" of the Fuggerei, serving some of the best food in town. Closed Mon.

Fuggerkeller, Maximilianstr. 38. Typically hearty German fare at reasonable prices is served up in the cellars of the Fuggerhäuser. Closed Sun.

Kaiser-Augustus-Weinstuben, Frauentorstr. 51. Historic wine cellar-cum-restaurant with summer terrace. Evenings only, closed Sun.

Oblinger, Pfärrle 14. A true gourmet paradise, universally regarded as the best in central Augsburg. Very small, so you must book (☎345830); closed Sun & Mon.

Welser-Kuche, Maximilianstr. 83. Extremely gimmicky, but nonetheless a true original, this restaurant does nothing but Renaissance-style banquets using recipes from the cookery book of Philippine Welser. Meals start at 8pm and last for 3 hours; reservations essential (☎96110).

Wirtshaus am Lech, Leipziger Str. 50, Lechhausen. Traditional *Gasthaus* with beer garden serving really excellent Swabian cooking. It's situated just over the Lechbrücke, and can be reached by tram #1.

Zeughaus-Stuben, Zeughausplatz 4. Another good choice for local cuisine, in the historic setting of the Zeughaus itself; there's also a beer garden. Closed Sun evening.

Zum Weissen Hasen, Unter dem Bogen 4. The city centre *Gaststätte* of Hasenbräu, one of the big local breweries, offering cheap lunchtime specials.

Bars and cafés

Café Drexl, Maximilianstr. 18. Extremely elegant city centre coffee house.

Café Stadler, Bahnhofstr. 30. Another good choice, complete with winter garden, for *Kaffee und Kuchen* – and conveniently placed to while away the time waiting for a train. Closed Sun.

Charly-Bräu, Ulmer Str. 43, Oberhausen. *Hausbrauerei* with a predominantly young clientele, located near the Oberhausen S-Bahn station. It makes an amber-coloured *Weizen* and a very dark *Braunbier*.

Kappeneck, Kappeneck 30. Friendly, youthful café-bar with a wide range of drinks and snacks.

Kerosin, Gögginger Str. 26–28. Popular live music bar. Tues–Sat 9pm–1am.

König von Flandern, Karolinenstr. 12. Basement *Hausbrauerei* producing very mild-tasting light and dark beers. Also does basic meals, including cheap daily specials.

Lailos, Kleines Katharinengässchen 8. Tapas bar regularly featuring all kinds of live music.

Sputnik, Stettenstr. 32. The leading late-nighter; open 9pm till 3am, 4am at weekends.

Striese, Kirchgasse 1. A student favourite, sometimes featuring theatre and live music. Daily 7pm–1am, also Sun 10am–1pm for breakfast.
Thorbräukeller, Heilig-Kreuz-Str. 20. Beer garden and *Kneipe* of the brewery of the same name.
Underground, Kapuzinergasse 1. Jazz bar with good atmosphere; open daily 9pm–3am.

Nightlife and entertainment

There's a surprising dearth of **discos** and nightclubs, but try *Spectrum-Club*, Ulmer Str. 234; *Circus*, Ludwigstr. 36 (Sun–Thurs 9pm–3am, Fri 9pm–5am, Sat 9pm–4am); or *Ostwerk*, Partnachweg 2 (Thurs–Sat from 10pm). Heavy rock fans should check out *Rockfabrik*, Riedinger Str. 24 (Mon–Wed 8pm–3am, Thurs 9pm–3am, Fri 9pm–4am, Sat 9pm–5am), north of the city centre on bus route #26 from Königsplatz.

Augsburg's most famous **theatre** is the *Puppenkiste* – even with the language barrier, kids will love the marionette shows, but tickets are hard to come by. Contact the box office at Spitalgasse 15 (☎434440) well in advance. The *Freilichtbühne* in the adjoining Rotes Tor mounts its open-air season of plays – with Brecht now featuring regularly – in June and July. Drama and opera are performed at the *Stadttheater*, Kennedyplatz 1 (☎36604), while *Spielküche*, Henisiusstr. 1 (☎155777) is a youth theatre. Orchestral **concerts** are held at the *Kongresshalle*, Göppinger Str. 10 (☎502 8425), chamber and instrumental recitals at a variety of smaller venues, including the *Mozarthaus*, Frauentorstr. 30 (☎518588). It's also worth checking on events at a couple of **arts centres**: *Kresslesmühle*, Barfüsserstr. 4 (☎37170) and *abraxas*, Sommestr. 30 (☎324 6355).

AUGSBURG'S FESTIVALS

The main local **festival** is *Plärrer*, which is rather like a smaller version of Munich's Oktoberfest, except that it takes place twice annually, lasting for a fortnight on each occasion. The spring version, the *Frühjahrsplärrer*, begins on the Sunday after Easter; its autumn counterpart, the *Herbstplärrer*, takes place on the last week in August and the first in September. Other annual events are the *Jakober Kirchweih* at the end of July and beginning of August; the *Friedensfest* (Peace Festival) on August 8; the *Mozartsommer* in late August and early September; and the *Christkindlesmarkt*, whose opening on November 23 is marked by a colourful pageant, and which features live Christmas music each subsequent weekend.

Listings

Bike rental Available at the Hauptbahnhof.
Bookshop *Probuch*, Gögginger Str. 34, specializes in contemporary German literature and alternative books.
Craft workshops Augsburg is a flourishing centre of traditional crafts, and the tourist office has devised a trail round over a dozen different workshops, mostly concentrated in the vicinity of the Lech canals. Get hold of the leaflet *Augsburg and its Sights*, which details the exact times of visiting hours and demonstrations.
Mitfahrzentrale Barthof 3 (☎157019).
Post office The main post office is on Karlstrasse, northwest of Rathausplatz; there's a branch with extended opening hours beside the Hauptbahnhof.
Swimming The luxuriant Jugendstil Altes Stadtbad (Mon & Tues 8am–7pm, Wed–Fri 8am–9pm, Sat 8am–8pm, Sun 8am–noon) on Leonhardsberg (just north of the Bertolt-Brecht-Haus) is one of Germany's finest bathing halls. Prices start at DM5 for a swim, DM17 for a full Roman-Irish bath.
Women's centre Mauerbergstr. 31 (☎153307).

The Allgäu

The southwesternmost part of Bavaria is known as the **Allgäu**, and is as famed for its cheeses – which are the finest produced in Germany – as for its magnificent scenery. There are four constituent parts to the region. Closest to Augsburg is the **Lower Allgäu** (*Unterallgäu* or *Allgäuer Voralpenland*), a rolling pre-Alpine landscape punctuated by a few towns and villages, among which **Kaufbeuren** and **Ottobeuren** are particularly worth visiting. Prime attractions of the **Eastern Allgäu** (*Ostallgäu*) are the frivolous and extravagant but irresistible castles of **Hohenschwangau** and **Neuschwanstein**, which rather overshadow the neighbouring towns of **Füssen** and **Schwangau**. Jutting into Austria is the **Upper Allgäu** (*Oberallgäu*), a classic Alpine area dominated by the resort of **Oberstdorf**. Finally, there's the **Western Allgäu** (*Westallgäu*), part of which lies in Baden-Württemberg, though the Bavarian section includes the island town of **Lindau** on the shores of the **Bodensee**.

Ottobeuren

The star attraction of the Lower Allgäu is the small health resort of **OTTOBEUREN**, or more specifically the **Reichsabtei**, which stands on a gentle incline above the rest of the village. This still-functioning Benedictine abbey founded in 764 is one of the most imposing and grandiose monasteries north of the Alps. Its patron Charlemagne gave the abbot important rights, elevating him to the status of a prince of the Holy Roman Empire.

Architecturally the abbey has undergone many changes since its foundation. The present Baroque **Basilika** was created, after several false starts by other architects, by the Munich master Johann Michael Fischer in the eighteenth century. It's huge: physical details such as the 90-metre nave and 60-metre transept hardly convey the bombastic impression you get on entering. The wealth of altars, frescoes, paintings and stuccoed embellishments needs time to be appreciated fully, and yet there's nothing busy about the whole effect. Among the many treasures, a twelfth-century Romanesque *Crucifixion* is the most precious, but also special are the elaborate choir stalls and the three **organs**, considered among the most beautiful instruments in the world. At least one of them can be heard at the recitals held at 4pm every Saturday between February and November.

Apart from the church, there's also the **Museum der Benediktinerabtei** (daily 10am–noon & 2–5pm; DM3), which is housed in a part of the abbot's palace. Highlights are the amazingly delicate seventeenth- and eighteenth-century inlaid furniture pieces and the beautiful Baroque library, which looks more like a ballroom than a place for contemplation, so rich is the decor of marble pillars and frescoed ceiling. Note also the theatre, which was an important element of arts teaching in any eighteenth-century Benedictine monastery.

Ottobeuren is not on a rail line, but has a regular **bus** link with Memmingen, a junction on the Munich-Lindau and Ulm-Oberstdorf lines, 11km to the northwest. Should you want to stay, there's a **youth hostel** at Kaltenbrunnweg 11 (☎08332/368; ⓕ), along with plenty of **rooms** in private houses (①–③). Other than sanatoria, the only **hotels** in the village proper are *Hirsch*, Marktplatz 12 (☎08332/7990; ⑤), which also administers *Post*, Luitpoldstr. 7 (⑤); and *Am Mühlbach*, Luitpoldstr. 57 (☎08332/7072; ⑥). *Hirsch* also has the village's best **restaurant**, and is the main tap of the local brewery. The **tourist office** is in the *Kurverwaltung*, Marktplatz 14 (Mon–Fri 8am–noon & 2–5pm; May–Oct also Sat 10am–noon; ☎08332/6817).

Kaufbeuren

KAUFBEUREN, a former Free Imperial City some 55km southwest of Augsburg by road or rail, is in many ways reminiscent of the better-known and more heavily touristed medieval towns further north. The key difference is that it is larger and more industrialized, largely as a result of the creation of the suburb of **Neugablonz**, the only community set up after World War II by refugees from a single area of Eastern Europe (Gablonz in the Sudetenland) from which Germans had been expelled. An intact **Stadtmauer**, part of whose sentry walk survives, still surrounds the cobblestoned Altstadt. At its highest point, the northwestern corner, are a terrace commanding a bird's-eye view and the impressive fortified church of **St Blasius**, whose round tower has a decidedly military rather than ecclesiastical appearance. Ironically, the interior is a graceful Gothic hall, with an outstanding high altar featuring carvings by Jörg Lederer. The best time to visit the town is on the third Sunday of July when the highpoint of the main local **festival**, the *Tänzelfest*, occurs. This features a costumed procession performed by 1600 children, re-enacting a visit to the town by Emperor Maximilian I in 1497.

Kaufbeuren's **tourist office** is in the Rathaus, Kaiser-Max-Str. 1 (Mon–Fri 9am–6pm, Sat 9.30am–noon; ☎08341/40405). If you need a **hotel**, one of the lowest priced is *Gasthof Leitner*, Neugablonzer Str. 68 (☎08341/3344; ③). In the Altstadt itself, there are three good places to choose from: *Hasen*, Ganghoferstr. 7–8 (☎08341/8941; ④); *Am Turm*, Josef-Landes-Str. 1 (☎08341/93740; ⑤); and *Goldener Hirsch*, Kaiser-Max-Str. 39 (☎08341/43030; ⑤). Both *Leitner* and *Goldener Hirsch* also have good **restaurants**; otherwise the best place to eat is *Wärmflasch*, Am Hofanger 33.

Füssen

FÜSSEN, the southern terminus of the Romantic Road (see p.176), lies in a beautiful setting close to the Austrian border between the **Forggensee** reservoir and the **Ammer** mountains. Although used by most visitors merely as a jumping-off point for the two royal castles situated some 4km to the southeast, it's of far more than passing interest. Dominating the Lech valley from a position high above the Altstadt is the **Hohes Schloss**, which assumed its present late Gothic appearance at the turn of the sixteenth century, when the old fortress was rebuilt as a summer residence of the Augsburg prince-bishops. In an ingenious cost-saving device, the inner courtyard is adorned with illusionistic paintings showing elaborate door and window frames and oriels. Part of the north wing houses a branch of the **Bayerische Staatsgalerie** (April–Oct Tues–Sun 11am–4pm; Nov–March Tues–Sun 2–4pm; DM4). Paintings by fifteenth- and sixteenth-century south German masters and members of the nineteenth-century Munich School are on view, but the chief attraction is the **Rittersaal**, which has a magnificent coffered vault.

Below the Schloss is the former **Kloster St Mang**, named in honour of the eighth-century "Apostle of the Allgäu". The present complex is almost entirely Baroque, but below the church, nowadays designated the **Stadtpfarrkirche**, is a Carolingian crypt containing the grave of the saint. This is only accessible on Sunday mornings, or by occasional guided tours, the times for which are posted in the porch. The monastic buildings house the **Museum der Stadt Füssen** (April–Oct Tues–Sun 11am–4pm; Nov–March Tues–Sun 2–4pm; DM3), though the exhibits are overshadowed by the splendid Baroque interiors themselves, including the sumptuous **Festsaal**, which is still regularly used for concerts; the domed colloquium; and the oval refectory, which has an aperture in its ceiling looking up into the library above. Also of special note is the **Annakapelle**, the original monastic church, which was converted to serve as a funerary chapel and has a remarkable early seventeenth-century mural of *The Dance of Death*.

Practicalities

Füssen's **Bahnhof**, a dead-end terminus, is linked directly with Munich and Augsburg, with services departing on alternate hours. From outside, **buses** marked *Königsschlösser* leave at regular intervals for the castles. A couple of minutes' walk to the east, at Kaiser-Maximilian-Platz 1, is the **tourist office** (June–Aug Mon–Fri 8am–noon

& 2–6pm, Sat 9.30am–12.30pm, Sun 10am–noon; Oct–May Mon–Fri 8am–noon & 2–6pm, Sat 10am–noon; ☎08362/7077). Ask here about **private rooms** (①–③), which can be surprisingly good value, though a stay of three nights may be required.

There are plenty of **hotels** in town, including *Elisabeth*, Augustenstr. 10 (☎08362/6275; ③); *Zum Hechten*, Ritterstr. 6 (☎08362/91600; ④); *Sonne*, Reichenstr. 37 (☎08362/9080; ⑤); and *Hirsch*, Kaiser-Maximilian-Platz 7 (☎08362/5080; ⑥).

The **youth hostel** is at the western edge of town at Mariahilferstr. 5 (☎08362/7754; ✿), while there's a **campsite** (☎08362/7431) by the Hopfensee to the north.

Füssen's best **restaurants** are *Zum Schwanen*, Brotmarkt 4, and *Pulverturm* in the *Kurhaus* at the eastern edge of the town centre.

Schwangau

SCHWANGAU, 3km northeast of Füssen, to which it's connected by a frequent bus service, combines the roles of a traditional agricultural community and health resort. Its name literally means "Swan Country", and the presence of a sizeable colony of these aloof birds has cast a spell on rulers of the area down the centuries. As the decoration of their fantasy castles testifies, the nineteenth-century Bavarian kings Maximilian II and his son Ludwig II were obsessed by the swan motif and the medieval Grail legends associated with it.

The only historical monument of note in Schwangau itself is the Baroque **Wallfahrtskirche St Coloman**, which is set in isolation in the meadows north of town. Dedicated to an eleventh-century Irish martyr, it was designed and decorated by Johann Schmutzer. On the second Sunday of October, it's the setting for one of Germany's most picturesque and moving religious festivals, the **Colomansfest**. This features around three hundred horses and some beautifully decorated carriages, which process from the town centre to the surroundings of the church, where an open-air mass is held. The horses are then ridden round the church three times for good luck, after which beer and food, the essential accompaniments to any Bavarian festival, are dispensed from the nearby tents.

Hohenschwangau

Within the Schwangau muncipality is the village of **HOHENSCHWANGAU**, 2km to the southeast. Consisting in the main of hotels, guest houses, restaurants, snack bars and souvenir shops, not to mention five enormous car parks, it's the most rampantly commercialized place in the whole of Germany – though it's only fair to add that it's set in close proximity to some of the most spectacular scenery the country has to offer. To escape from the worst of the crowds, it's well worth taking a stroll along the footpaths encircling the two beautiful lakes which lie directly to the east. In summer, you can swim or sail in the larger lake, the **Alpsee**, whereas the **Schwansee** (literally, "Swan Lake") is a strict nature reserve surrounded by an English-style park offering wonderful framed vistas of the two royal castles.

The smaller of these, the golden yellow **Schloss Hohenschwangau** (guided tours daily April–Oct 9am–5.30pm; Nov–March 10am–4pm; DM10), rises directly above the Alpsee; note that there's free access to its lovely terraced garden, which commands wonderful views. Built in mock-Tudor style in the 1830s for Crown Prince Maximilian to replace a ruined feudal fortress, the Schloss still belongs to the Wittelsbach family, and feels like a lived-in private residence, crammed full of gifts from grateful subjects and fellow rulers. Several rooms are decorated with heroic **fresco cycles** illustrating German history and legends (including that of Lohengrin, the Swan Knight) painted from cartoons by Moritz von Schwind. In the **Hohenstaufensaal** is a square piano where Wagner would entertain **King Ludwig II** with themes from operas in progress. The latter's main contribution to the castle was to have the **ceiling** of his bedroom changed from a daytime to a night sky which could be illuminated by concealed spotlights.

Ludwig's own personal fantasy, the grey granite **Schloss Neuschwanstein** (guided tours same hours as Schloss Hohenschwangau; DM10), is a steep twenty-minute walk from the village. The ultimate story-book castle and Germany's most ubiquitous tourist icon, Neuschwanstein has become famous the world over through posters, cards and Disney films, not to mention the innumerable theme park castles directly inspired by it. Begun in 1869 but never finished, it was intended as a tribute to medieval German chivalry and to Wagner, who had evoked this past so intoxicatingly in his vast music dramas; and as a symbol of Ludwig's belief in himself as a divinely chosen king. Plans were drawn by the theatre designer Christian Jank, working in close collaboration with the king; professional architects were used only for supervising the actual construction. It undoubtedly looks far better from a distance than close up or inside. The architecture and decoration draw freely from different historical styles: Byzantine for the **Thronsaal**, Romanesque for the private apartments, Gothic for the showpiece **Sängersaal**. Note that the guides are forced to rush round in 35 minutes, and that it is often necessary to queue for much longer than this to gain admission: it's best to come as early as possible, and to avoid weekends.

Practicalities

Schwangau's **tourist office** is in the *Kurverwaltung*, Münchener Str. 2 (Mon–Fri 7.30am–12.30pm & 1.30–5pm; ☎08362/81980). There's a reasonale supply of **private rooms** (①–②), as well as a few similarly inexpensive **pensions**, the most attractive being *Schlossblick*, Füssener Str. 48 (☎08362/8355; ②), with a view across to the castles. Among the **hotels** are *Gasthof Hanselewirt*, Mitteldorf 13 (☎08362/8237; ③); *Gasthof Zur Post*, Münchener Str. 5 (☎08362/98218; ⑤); and *Weinbauer*, Füssener Str. 3 (☎08362/9860; ⑤), all of which have good, reasonably priced **restaurants**.

If you'd prefer to be based in Hohenschwangau, there are several **pensions**, including *Haus Magdalena*, Schwangauer Str. 11 (☎08362/81126; ②) and *Weiher*, Hofwiesenweg 11 (☎08362/81161; ③). Alternatively, you can stay in style at one of the classy **hotels**, such as *Meier*, Schwangauer Str. 37 (☎08362/81152; ⑤); *Müller*, Alpseestr. 16 (☎08362/81990; ⑧); or *Schlosshotel Lisl und Jägerhaus*, Neuschwansteinstr. 1–3 (☎08362/8870; ⑨). Each of these has a top-notch **restaurant**; more basic fare is available at the *Schlosswirtschaft* just below Neuschwanstein. The only ready way of seeing any of Schloss Neuschwanstein at leisure is to attend one of the **concerts** in the *Sängersaal*; these are held over a week in mid- to late September, and tickets can be ordered in advance from the tourist office.

Oberstdorf

Imagine your ideal mountain resort and **OBERSTDORF** will almost certainly fit the picture. Tucked away about 50km southwest of Kaufbeuren by road or rail, amid magnificent Alpine mountains and valleys, the old village has grown discreetly, without any high-rise aberrations, but with excellent modern sports facilities, including swimming pools, a skating rink and an Olympic ski-jump. These co-exist with traditional farming life: there are open fields right on the outskirts of town.

The valleys and peaks

The higher mountain valleys beyond Oberstdorf take you to lonely Alpine huts and the sort of views that give a surge of energy. Serious mountaineers will find the **Nebelhorn** (2224m) to the east of town the most challenging, while for less strenuous Alpine walking the **Fellhorn** (2039m) and **Söl60lereck** (1706m) to the south make good alternatives – the latter is especially gentle. All three peaks are also accessible by cable car (various rates, the maximum being DM39 return to the Nebelhorn summit), and in winter form the heart of an excellent skiing range. Another worthwhile excursion is to the gorges of the **Breitachklamm**, some 6km southwest of Oberstdorf; these are best seen in late winter, when draped with ice.

A bit further south, the valley known as **Kleinwalsertal** is a real novelty. Once one of the most isolated corners of the Alps, it was settled by a hardy people known as the Walsers who gave their allegiance to the House of Habsburg. Today, it remains officially part of Austria, although it uses the *Deutschmark* as its currency, and is only accessible by the road from Oberstdorf, which is serviced by regular buses.

Practicalities

There are any number of reasonably priced **private rooms** (①–③) and **guest houses** near the town centre. The latter include *Amman*, Weststr. 23 (☎08322/2961; ③); *Alpenglühn*, Wittelsbacherstr. 4 (☎08322/4692; ③); and *Buchenberg*, Lorettostr. 6 (☎08322/2315; ③). Among many excellent **hotels**, *Kurpark*, Prinzenstr. 1 (☎08322/96560; ⑥), has a fine setting, while *Haus Wiese*, Stillachstr. 4a (☎08322/3030; ⑦) and *Waldesruhe*, Alte Walserstr. 20 (☎08322/4061; ⑦) both offer outstanding views.

At Haus no. 8 in the neighbouring village of Kornau, which can be reached by bus, you'll find the nearest **youth hostel** (☎08322/2225; ⓕ), while the all-year-round **campsite** (☎0832/4022) is just north of the Bahnhof. If you need help with finding somewhere to stay, contact the **tourist office** (Mon–Fri 8.30am–noon & 2–6pm, Sat 9.30am–noon; ☎08322/7000), Marktplatz 7, or its *Zimmervermittlung* branch across from the Bahnhof (same times; ☎08322/700217).

The best and most expensive **restaurant** is *Maximilians*, Freibergstr. 21; *Bacchus-Stuben*, Freibergstr. 4 is a far more moderately priced alternative.

Lindau

At their most westerly point the Alps descend to the waters of the **Bodensee** and the tiny island town of **LINDAU**, which is nowadays linked to the mainland by a road bridge and rail causeway. It's the starting point of the **German Alpine Road**, (*Deutsche-Alpenstrasse*), a tourist route that runs the length of the German Alps, terminating 250km away in Berchtesgaden. In the Middle Ages, Lindau was a bustling trading post and city-state, and rich merchants built grand gabled houses on town squares that have a distinct Italian flavour. The half-timbered buildings lean over like stacks of dominoes, and narrow streets like Zitronengasse lead to quiet nooks and crannies.

At the southern end of the island is the **Hafen** (harbour), which, with its hazy views across the lake to the Alps, is the most popular spot in town. Its narrow entrance is guarded by two tall pillars, one a lighthouse, the other bearing the defiant Lion of Bavaria. The previous lighthouse, the **Mangturm** (variable opening hours; DM2), stands in the middle of the sheltered port and was originally part of the medieval fortifications. Around it stand large hotels from an age when nineteenth-century travellers resided here in splendour. As soon as the summer sun comes out, the harbour promenade fills with coffee tables, giving a Mediterranean feel to the bustling waterfront. Several **ferries** operate on the lake (for full information, see p.258). All sorts of boats, canoes and windsurfers can be rented from the yacht marina east of the harbour.

On Reichsplatz, in the centre of the island, stands the Gothic **Altes Rathaus**; unfortunately the elaborate murals have made it seem overdressed in comparison with the buildings around it. From here, you can walk west along the Maximilianstrasse, before turning north to see the **Diebsturm** (Brigands' Tower), the other surviving part of the fortifications. Alongside, Romanesque **St Peter**, now a war memorial, is the sole church in Lindau still in its medieval state. Hans Holbein the Elder's faded *Passion Cycle* in the apse is his only surviving fresco.

The most stylish building in Lindau is the **Haus zum Cavazzen** (April–Oct Tues–Sun 9am–noon & 2–5pm; DM4) on Marktplatz towards the eastern end of the island, whose three-storey Baroque facade is painted in subtle sandy-red tones, and which contains one of the most attractive local history museums of any town in Bavaria. There's an intriguing collection of seventeenth-century family trees painted on wooden panels that open up like a photo-album, to reveal little portraits and dates for each member. A particular rarity are the seventeenth- and eighteenth-century paintings mocking Luther, known as *Spottbilder*. On the second and third floors are fine displays of furniture, ranging from items from the workshops of Lindau's former artisan guilds to beautifully inlaid Biedermeier furniture.

Should you only have time for one trip outside the island, take bus #7 to the suburb of Hoyren and walk up the **Hoyrenberg** for a stunning view of the lake and the Austrian and Swiss Alps. The villages and apple orchards around here seem very quiet after Lindau: Oberreitnau, Unterreitnau and Bodolz are especially pretty.

Practicalities

The **Hauptbahnhof** is at the southwestern corner of the island, right beside the harbour. Just across from the entrance, at Am Hauptbahnhof, is the **tourist office** (April–Oct Mon–Fri 9am–6pm, Sat 9am–1pm; Nov–March Mon–Fri 9am–noon & 2–5pm; ☎08382/26000).

Among the **guest houses** and **pensions** on the island are *Ladine*, In der Grub 25 (☎08382/5326; ②); *Limmer*, In der Grub 16 (☎08382/5877; ②); and *Seerose*, Auf der Mauer 3 (☎08382/24120; ④). The many medium-range **hotels** include *Inselgraben*, Hintere Metzgergasse 4–6 (☎08382/5481; ⑤); *Alte Post*, Fischergasse 3 (☎08382/93460; ⑦); and *Insel-Hotel*, Maximilianstr. 42 (☎08382/5017; ⑦). Along Seepromenade are the four swankiest hotels, the most exclusive being *Bayerischer Hof* (☎08382/9150; ⑨). There are plenty of **rooms** in private houses (①–②), but most are on the mainland. The **youth hostel** is at Herbergsweg 11 (☎08382/5813 or 96710; ✿) on mainland Lindau; take bus #1, #3 or #6 from the Hauptbahnhof. Lindau's **campsite** *Lindau-Zech* (☎08382/72236), by the lakeside to the east of the island, is open from April to September.

Inevitably, the leading **restaurants** are in the waterfront hotels, but there are plenty of excellent and far less expensive alternatives. *Zum Sünfzen*, Maximilianstr. 1, and *Weinstube Frey*, Maximilianstr. 15 are both eminently recommendable, as is the restaurant in *Alte Post*. Even cheaper restaurants, plus a few bars, can be found in the suitably named In der Grub, a block north of Maximilianstrasse.

travel details

Munich to: Augsburg (every 20min; 30min); Cologne (12 daily; 5hr 20min); Düsseldorf (6 daily; 6hr 30min); Frankfurt (frequent; 4hr); Garmisch-Partenkirchen (frequent; 1hr 15min); Hamburg (hourly; 8hr); Ingolstadt (frequent; 45min); Innsbruck (16 daily; 2hr 25min); Nürnberg (hourly; 1hr); Regensburg (hourly; 2hr); Rosenheim (hourly; 40min); Salzburg (hourly; 1hr 30min); Strasbourg (6 daily; 5hr); Stuttgart (10 daily; 2hr 15min); Ulm (hourly; 2hr 15min); Würzburg (hourly; 2hr 20min); Zurich (5 daily; 4hr 20min).

Nürnberg to: Ansbach (every 30min; 45min); Augsburg (hourly; 1hr); Bamberg (every 30min; 45min); Bayreuth (every 30min; 1hr 10min); Coburg (hourly; 1hr 35min); Frankfurt (hourly; 2hr); Passau (hourly; 2hr 20min).

Würzburg to: Cologne (hourly; 3hr 40min); Frankfurt (hourly; 1hr 20min); Stuttgart (10 daily; 2hr).

CHAPTER TWO

BADEN-WÜRTTEMBERG

Baden-Württemberg only came into existence in 1952 as a result of the merger, approved by plebiscite, of three relatively small provinces established by the American and French occupying forces. Theodor Heuss, the first Federal President, saw it as "the model of German possibilities", and it hasn't disappointed, maintaining its ranking as the most prosperous part of the country. Being weak in natural resources, the area has had to rely on ingenuity to provide a spur to its industrial development, and ever since the motor car was invented here last century, it has been at the forefront of the world technology scene.

Ethnically, culturally and historically, the Land has two separate roots. The people of **Baden**, the western part of the province, are predominantly Catholic, and are generally seen as being of a relaxed, almost carefree disposition. Their neighbours in **Württemberg** (or **Swabia**, as the locals still prefer to call it), on the other hand, are renowned for being hard-working, thrifty and house-proud, values instilled in them since the Reformation they embraced so openly. This stark division, however, has been much modified by the extensive influx of refugees from the Eastern Territories after World War II: along with their descendants, they now account for about a quarter of the total population.

For variety of scenery, Baden-Württemberg is rivalled only by Bavaria. The western and southern boundaries of the province are defined by the River Rhine and its bulge into Germany's largest lake, the **Bodensee**. Immediately beyond lies the **Black Forest**, one of Europe's main holiday areas. Here rises another of the continent's principal waterways, the **Danube**, which later forms a grandly impressive gorge at the foot of the **Swabian Jura**, the range in which the Neckar begins its increasingly sedate northerly course. At the eastern end of the province there's an even gentler valley, that of the **Tauber**.

Each of Baden-Württemberg's three largest cities – **Stuttgart, Mannheim** and **Karlsruhe** – was formerly a state capital (of Württemberg, the Palatinate and Baden respectively). All were extensively damaged in World War II and none could be called beautiful, though all have excellent museums and Stuttgart offers a wide variety of nightlife. Unfortunately, the historical centres of **Freiburg im Breisgau** and **Ulm** were also bombed, but both their Münsters, which rank among Germany's greatest buildings, were spared. Other than this, Baden-Württemberg's lack of a heavy industrial base meant that it escaped the war relatively lightly. Germany's two most famous university cities, **Heidelberg** and **Tübingen**, were hardly touched, enabling the former to maintain its cherished role as the most romantic place in the entire country.

Almost equally enticing is the wealth of towns which stand as period pieces of different epochs. **Bad Wimpfen** and **Schwäbisch Hall** each preserve the form and appearance of the Middle Ages, whereas **Rottweil** has medieval survivals amid streets which bridge the gap between Renaissance and Baroque, and **Haigerloch** is a varied confection enhanced by a superb natural setting. **Bruchsal**, **Ludwigsburg** and **Rastatt** are proud courtly towns in the full-blown Baroque manner, while **Schwetzingen** is a creation of pure Rococo fantasy and **Baden-Baden** remains wonderfully evocative of its nineteenth-century halcyon years as the favourite playground of European aristocracy. Another special historical feature of the province is the number of monasteries

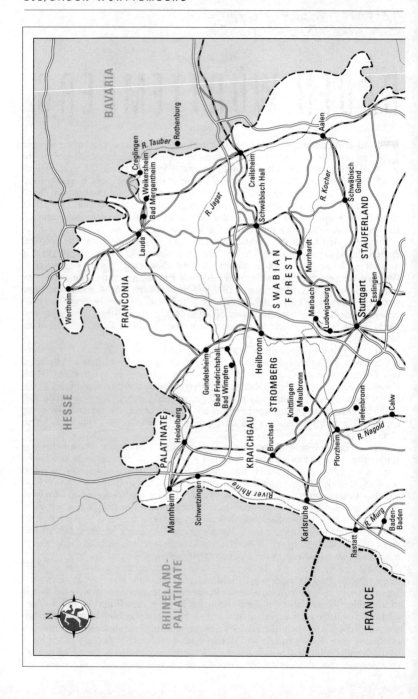

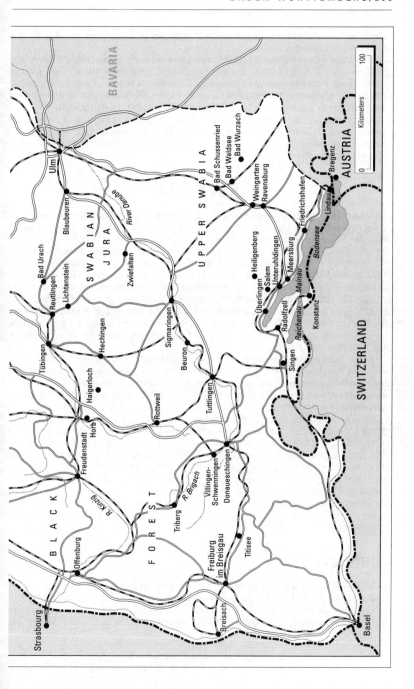

which have survived intact, among which **Maulbronn** ranks as the most complete and impressive in northern Europe.

A typically comprehensive **public transport** network means there's never any problem moving around, though waiting periods in rural areas not served by trains may be longer than is normal in Germany. Travelling is rendered particularly enjoyable by the profusion of scenic routes, of which the *Schwarzwalder-Hochstrasse* and the rail lines known as the *Schwarzwaldbahn*, the *Höllentalbahn* and the *Donautalbahn* are the most outstanding. There's the usual provision of **accommodation** in youth hostels and campsites, while the availability of lodgings in private houses is well above the national average. Only in the larger cities are you likely to encounter high prices.

SWABIA

Swabia (*Schwaben*) has long ceased to exist as any form of political entity, yet such is the emotional attachment to the name that it stubbornly refuses to vanish from the map, far less from local consciousness. The rugged plateaux cutting right through the middle of the province continue to be known as the **Swabian Jura**, and two of many former Free Imperial Cities, **Schwäbisch Gmünd** and **Schwäbisch Hall**, have adopted their present forenames in order to show where their loyalties lie. Certainly, the name is far more popular than that of Württemberg, taken from the aristocratic family who established dominance over most of rural Swabia in the Middle Ages from their capital of **Stuttgart**. It remains something of a sore point that the Land of Baden-Württemberg was not designated as Swabia, on the grounds that to do so would have offended the people of Baden, with their very different ethnic and historical background.

At the Reformation, the extreme wing of Protestantism – here known as **Pietism** – took firm root, bringing with it a commitment to the work ethic and a burning sense of individualism, tempered only by communal loyalties. There's no doubt that the intellectual rigour fostered in the province has led to its nurturing a gallery of inventors, philosophers and poets out of all proportion to its size.

If you despair of mastering the horrendous complexities of the German language, it's worth bearing in mind that the ingenious Swabians have developed a partial solution to the problem, put to everyday use in their own **dialect**. By adding -le to most nouns, they don't have to worry about genders (which immediately become neuter), while they omit the cumbersome ge- prefix from past participles, and regularize the declension of verbs. The local **cuisine** is no less distinctive, with noodles as ubiquitous as in Italian or Chinese cooking. Nearly every savoury dish comes with either *Spätzle*, a shredded pasta made from eggs and flour, or *Maultaschen*, which, with the exception of the sauces used to cover it, is broadly similar to ravioli. Equally popular are *Flädle* (pancakes) which turn up in both soups and desserts.

Stuttgart

STUTTGART breathes modern-day success. Düsseldorf and Hamburg may have more millionaires, but Baden-Württemberg's capital has the highest general standard of prosperity of any city in Germany, or, indeed, in Europe. Beaming out imperiously from its lofty station above the city centre is the local trademark, the three-pointed white star

The **telephone code** for Stuttgart is ☎0711

STUTTGART'S FESTIVALS

The main annual event is the sixteen-day **Cannstatter Volksfest**, held in the last week in September and the first in October. Founded in 1818 by King Wilhelm I of Württemberg, it's the second biggest beer festival in the world. In fact, most of the features are direct imitations of the larger Oktoberfest in Munich, although the beers on tap are all Swabian. A more fundamental difference is that whereas Oktoberfest is relentlessly Bavarian, this festival has a wider outlook, with two recurrent features being the *Scwarzwalderlebniszelt* celebrating Black Forest culture, and the *Französische Dorf*, a group of French-style brasseries.

If wine is your tipple, the **Stuttgarter Weindorf**, held in the city centre from the last Friday in August until the first Sunday in September, has over 300 varieties available for tasting. Another big wine festival is the **Fellbacher Herbst**, held on the second weekend of October in Fellbach, which adjoins Bad Cannstatt to the east. The **Weihnachtsmarkt**, beginning in late November, has existed since the seventeenth century and is thus one of the oldest in the country, but the harlequins and tightrope walkers have unfortunately long gone, to be replaced by the standard offerings. Other notable events are the **Frühlingsfest**, lasting for a fortnight in late April/early May, and a **Sommerfest** in mid-August.

of Daimler-Benz. Stuttgart is also home to the Porsche factory and, together, they have made the city into a car production centre to rival Detroit. Along with the almost equally celebrated electronics giant Robert Bosch, these companies have given the city a place at the world forefront of the hi-tech industrial scene.

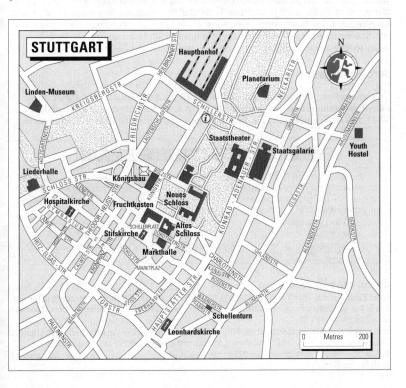

For all Stuttgart's present self-confidence, it was initially slow to develop. Founded around 950 as a stud farm (*Stutengarten* – hence the city's name), it only became a town in the fourteenth century, and lay in the shadow of its more venerable neighbours right up to the early nineteenth century, when Napoleon raised Württemberg to the status of a kingdom and placed the former Free Imperial Cities under its control. Though Stuttgart's standing as a royal capital was only to last for a century, the city has never looked back.

From the point of view of conventional sights, Stuttgart has relatively little to offer. On the other hand, it has a range of superb **museums** to appeal to all tastes, and a varied cultural and nightlife scene. It also has an enviable **setting** in a hollow surrounded by hills, which enables the cultivation of vineyards within a stone's throw of the centre, and the liberal endowment of parks and gardens successfully soften what would otherwise be a drab and unappealing cityscape.

Arrival and information

The **Hauptbahnhof** – an impressive example of railway architecture, built during the Weimar Republic – is plumb in the centre of the city. Immediately behind is the **bus station**. Line #A departs every 20 minutes between 5am and midnight for the **airport**. In front of the Hauptbahnhof is the underground Klett-Passage, whose shops stay open until late into the evening. Across the road at Königstr. 1a is the **tourist office**, *i-Punkt* (Mon–Fri 9.30am–8.30pm, Sat 9.30am–6pm, Sun 11am–6pm, 1–6pm out of season; ☎2228 240 or 241). The integrated **public transport** network, which covers nearby towns as well as the Stuttgart metropolitan area, enables you to switch among buses, trams, the U-Bahn, and mainline and S-Bahn trains. Given that the sights are very scattered, it's worth investing in a day ticket which covers the whole of the surrounding region. This costs DM18.50 for an adult and child, but at weekends and after 9am on weekdays can be used by up to four adults travelling together, or by two adults and four children.

Accommodation

To some extent, the astronomical cost of rented accommodation in Stuttgart is reflected in **hotel** rates. However, there are bargains to be had, often with a decent location. The tourist office will always book you a room, and there's no charge for this service.

ACCOMMODATION PRICE CODES

All the pensions and hotels in this book have been graded according to the following price categories. The prices quoted are for the cheapest available double room, although many of the budget places will also have more expensive rooms. Youth hostels are graded under separate categories. See p.34 for more details.

① less than DM50	④ DM81–100	⑦ DM151–200
② DM51–65	⑤ DM101–125	⑧ DM201–250
③ DM66–80	⑥ DM126–150	⑨ more than DM250

Hotels and pensions

Alter Fritz, Feuerbacher Weg 101 (☎135650, fax135 6565). By the Killesberg in the north of the city, this is one of Stuttgart's more characterful upmarket hotels; there's also an innovative restaurant. Take bus #43 or #50. ⑦

Am Schlossgarten, Schillerstr. 23 (☎20260, fax 2026 888). The pick of the luxury city-centre hotels, located just across from the Hauptbahnhof, witha terrace facing Oberer Schlossgarten. ⑨

Eckel, Vorsteigstr. 10 (☎290995, fax 223 8123). Small pension just west of the centre; take tram #2 to Hölderlinplatz. ③

Ketterer, Marienstr. 3 (☎20390, fax 2039 600). City centre business hotel in a relatively quiet street; has a very reasonably priced restaurant in the form of a traditional beer hall. ⑧

Krehl's Linde, Obere Waiblinger Str. 113, Bad Cannstatt (☎5277567, fax 548370). Located just to the southeast of the Kurpark, this boasts a really outstanding restaurant. ⑦

Lamm, Karl-Schurz-Str. 7 (☎262 2354, fax 262 2374). Located east of the centre, close to the Neckar and below Rosensteinpark. ④

Märklin, Friedrichstr. 39 (☎291315). Small pension in the very heart of Stuttgart, offering some of the cheapest rooms in the city. ④

Schwarzwaldheim, Fritz-Elsar-Str. 20 (☎296988). Traditional *Gasthof* just southwest of the centre. ③

Solitude, Hohewartstr. 10 (☎85554919). *Gasthof* in the suburb of Feuerbach, north of the centre; take U-Bahn #6 or tram #13 to Feuerbach Krankenhaus. ③

Sphinx, Neckarstr. 215a (☎261924, fax 261149). Egyptian-run hotel and ethnic restaurant, just west of Rosensteinpark; take U-Bahn #1, #11 or #14 or tram #2 to Metzstrasse. Note that it no longer serves breakfast. ④

Waldhotel Schatten, Magstadter Str. (☎68670, fax 6867 999). Upmarket hotel in peaceful woodland setting within easy reach of the city centre. Also has a fine restaurant. Bus #92 to Schattengrund goes nearest. ⑧

Wörtz zur Weinsteige, Hohenheimer Str. 30 (☎2367000, fax 236 7007). Popular hotel and *Weinstube* with garden terrace at the southeastern end of the city centre; take U-Bahn #5 or #7 to Dobelstrasse. ⑦

Youth hostels and campsites

Cannstatter Wasen, Mercedesstr. 40 (☎556696). The campsite is on the banks of the River Neckar in Bad Cannstatt. Open year round.

IYHF Jugendherberge, Haussmannstr. 27 (☎241583). Stuttgart's youth hostel is only about a 15-min walk east of the Hauptbahnhof. ▣

Jugendgästehaus Stuttgart, Richard-Wagner-Str. 2–4a (☎241132). Beds in dorms cost DM30; there are also singles at DM50; tram #15 or #16 to Budenbad.

Tramper Point, Wiener Str. 317 (☎817 7476 or 237 2815). At DM10 for a mattress, this offers rock bottom accommodation for young people between 16 and 27 only. Open late June to early Sept; take U-Bahn #6 or tram #13 to Sportpark Feuerbach.

The city centre

One consequence of having been a late developer is that Stuttgart has one of the most manageable centres of any large German city, and one which has a spacious feel in spite of its compact size.

Schlossplatz

Königstrasse leads straight from the Hauptbahnhof past the modern Dom (a strong contender for the title of the dullest cathedral in Europe) to **Schlossplatz**. The vast open space here comes as a welcome relief after the hectic bustle of the neighbouring streets, but it does mean that it's the favourite spot of the tramps and alcoholics who form a noticeable sub-class amid the prosperity. On the eastern side of the square is the colossal Baroque **Neues Schloss**, now used for various state purposes by the government of Baden-Württemberg, and out of bounds to visitors except for the cellars which contain the **Römisches Lapidarium** (Sat & Sun 10am–5pm; free), a collection of stone fragments from Roman times. Particularly impressive are the surviving parts of a massive Jupitersäule erected around 200 AD in a settlement near Heilbronn. Opposite is the **Königsbau**, lined with shops all along its 135-metre facade and built in the late Neoclassical style much favoured in the city. Another example of this is the **Jubileumssäule**, erected in the centre of Schlossplatz to commemorate the twenty-fifth anniversary of the accession of King Wilhelm I of Württemberg.

On the north side of the square lies the Kunstgebäude, containing the **Galerie der Stadt Stuttgart** (Tues & Thurs–Sun 11am–6pm, Wed 11am–8pm; free). This houses seminal works by **Otto Dix**: the luridly coloured *Grosstadt* triptych is one of his finest canvases, perfectly conjuring up the Weimar Republic's false sense of values and its smoky, decadent nightclub scene. The rest of the gallery is an anticlimax, but there are a number of small works by the three leading Stuttgart painters of this century – Adolf Hölzel, Oskar Schlemmer and Willi Baumeister.

The Altes Schloss

At the southern end of Schlossplatz is the **Altes Schloss**. A fortress was first built on this site in the tenth century to protect the stud farm; one wing survives of the fourteenth-century moated castle which succeeded it. In the 1550s, the rest of the building was replaced by a resplendent Renaissance palace with a majestic triple-tiered courtyard, designed by Aberlin Tresch. This forms the perfect setting for nominally priced concerts of classical music throughout the summer. Ask at the porter's desk for the key to the **Schlosskapelle**, which disputes with its counterpart in Torgau the right to be regarded as the earliest-ever example of Protestant religious architecture. The interior was specially designed in accordance with the tenets of the new faith, with its emphasis on preaching rather than the sacraments: it's a simple rectangular hall with galleries on three sides, and the elevated pulpit is given the same prominence as the altar.

THE LANDESMUSEUM

Badly damaged in the war, much of the Schloss is given over to the **Württemburgisches Landesmuseum** (Tues 10am–1pm, Wed–Sun 10am–5pm; DM5). Highlight of this richly varied museum is the **Kunstkammer** of the House of Württemberg, displayed in one of the corner towers. The first floor has small bronze sculptures of predominantly Italian origin, while the second is laid out in the manner of a Renaissance curio cabinet, with the star exhibit being a beautiful set of Gothic playing cards. On the top storey are the nineteenth-century crown jewels, including a necklace with the 22-carat *Harlequin* diamond.

The Baroque sleighs of the dukes can be seen on the ground floor of the main part of the building, while upstairs is a large and important collection of Swabian devotional wood sculptures, arranged thematically rather than chronologically, thus offering inviting comparisons. Displayed alongside are fine examples of stained glass. On the same floor, the **archeology** section includes finds from the excavations at Troy, varied Roman antiquities (notably a stunning third-century cameo of Jupiter), the intact grave of a Celtic prince, and jewellery from the Frankish period. The top floor features a wonderful array of **clocks.**

Schillerplatz and the Stiftskirche

To the west, the Altes Schloss overlooks **Schillerplatz**, Stuttgart's sole example of an old-world square. A pensive statue of Schiller himself by Bertel Thorwaldsen presides in the middle. Also here are three more Renaissance buildings – the **Prinzenbau**, the **Alte Kanzlei** (Old Chancellery) and the gabled **Fruchtkasten** (Granary; same hours and ticket as Landesmuseum). Behind its facade, the last-named preserves its original fourteenth-century core; this has now been converted to house the Landesmuseum's collection of historical musical instruments.

At the back of Schillerplatz is the **Stiftskirche**. Its present form is due to the prolific late fifteenth-century Stuttgart architect Aberlin Jerg, whose special skill, shown here to good effect, lay in welding old and new parts of buildings into a coherent whole. The western tower, an octagon on a square base, is Jerg's own work; unfortunately, the planned openwork steeple was never built. Inside the church, the choir is lined with one of the most important pieces of German Renaissance sculpture, an **ancestral gallery** of the counts and dukes of Württemberg. Each of the eleven swarthy figures is brilliantly characterized – a considerable feat of imagination on the part of the sculptor, Sem Schlör. Look out also for the gilded late Gothic pulpit, and the relief of *Christ Sheltering Humanity*.

The eastern boundary

A large modern boulevard, Konrad-Adenauer-Strasse, forms the eastern boundary of the city centre. At the southern end is the **Leonhardskirche**, another church reworked by Aberlin Jerg, containing the funerary monument to the celebrated Renaissance humanist and Hebrew scholar, Johannes Reuchlin. To the north is the Neoclassical **Wilhelmspalais**, used by the last kings of Württemberg as their main residence; it's now the main municipal archive and library.

Across the road, at the back of the Neues Schloss, lies the **Akadamiegarten**. This forms a southerly extension of the **Schlossgarten**, which stretches for 4km all the way to the banks of the Neckar. On the right is the straggling complex of the **Staatstheater** (see p.215) and, further on, close to the Hauptbahnhof, you'll find the **Carl-Zeiss-Planetarium** (sessions Tues & Thurs 10am & 3pm, Wed & Fri 10am, 3pm & 8pm, Sat & Sun 2pm, 4pm & 6pm; DM9), whose projection equipment, made by Carl Zeiss, the famous Stuttgart optics company, ranks among the most modern in Europe.

The Staatsgalerie

Facing the Staatstheater from the other side of Konrad-Adenauer-Strasse is the **Staatsgalerie** (Tues & Thurs 10am–8pm, Wed & Fri–Sun 10am–5pm; DM5). It's not often that an art gallery ranks as one of the most imposing buildings in a major city, but this is an exception. James Stirling – internationally regarded as Britain's most accomplished postwar architect – was commissioned to build an extension to the solid Neoclassical home of the city's magnificent collection of paintings, which was no longer big enough to accommodate the ever-growing acquisition of modern works. The result, completed in 1984, is an original masterpiece.

THE ALTE STAATSGALERIE

The displays begin upstairs in the old building. Of the medieval works, the earliest and most important is a **Bohemian School** altarpiece made in 1385 for a chapel on the outskirts of Stuttgart. You'll either see the inner part, in which Good King Wenceslas is flanked by St Vitus and Emperor Sigismund, or else the Biblical scenes on the wings; the position is changed every fortnight. Among many examples of the fifteenth-century Swabian School, those by the Ulm painters **Bartolomäus Zeitblom** and the **Master of the Sterzing Altar** stand out, particularly the latter's courtly *Journey of the Magi*. The most startling work in the gallery is the huge, violently expressive *Herrenberg Altar* by **Jerg Ratgeb**, a man who knew all about violence himself in his other calling as a radical political leader. His reputation rests almost entirely on this single work, which cleverly compresses the Passion scenes into four panels and has an unusual reverse side, showing the Apostles going out to preach the Word to all the corners of the earth.

The Italian section begins with two wonderfully stylized panels of *The Apocalypse* by a mid-fourteenth-century **Neapolitan** master, and continues with some excellent examples of the Venetian Renaissance, including works by Bellini, Carpaccio and Tintoretto. However, the gems of the display are several sketches by **Tiepolo**, notably a superbly compressed study for the central section of the great staircase fresco in Würzburg's Residenz. **Memling**'s sensual *Bathsheba at her Toilet* kicks off the Low Countries section. The rare Mannerist **Joachim Wtewael** is represented by an animated cycle of portraits of *The Four Evangelists* and by an enamel-like *Adoration of the Shepherds*. There are two masterpieces by **Michael Sweerts**, another long-forgotten artist who has recently come to the fore: the pendants *Taste* and *Sight*, each characterized by an allegorical figure of a child. **Rembrandt** also treated the theme of sight in the tender *Tobit Healing his Father's Blindness*. It forms a sort of unofficial counterpart to the horrific *Blinding of Samson* in Frankfurt, which was painted the same year. One of his earliest works, *St Paul in Prison*, is also on show, along with important examples of Hals, Rubens and Ter Brugghen.

The biggest surprise of the gallery is a whole room devoted to **Edward Burne-Jones**'s cycle of *The Legend of Perseus*. Commissioned by Arthur Balfour, the future British prime minister, this constitutes one of the finest achievements of the Pre-Raphaelite movement. Three of the eight scenes were never completed, but the full-scale cartoons shown here make ample substitutes. Other nineteenth-century highpoints are *Bohemian Landscape* and *The Cross in the Woods* by **Friedrich**, an impressive group of works by a local Neoclassical sculptor, **Johann Heinrich Dannecker**, and a decent cross-section of French Impressionism.

THE NEUE STAATSGALERIE

The modern extension features the seven vibrant figures made by **Oskar Schlemmer** for the kaleidoscopic *Triadschen Ballett* in 1922. Displayed high up on pedestals, they're arguably his most original creations. There are also monumental bronzes by **Matisse**, while examples of many of the century's leading sculptors can be found in the sculpture court downstairs or scattered throughout the galleries. A wooden group entitled *The Bathers* constitutes one of the main items in what's one of the two best **Picasso** collections in Germany. **Modigliani** is represented by *Portrait of Chaim Soutine* (the Russian-born painter) and *Reclining Nude*. The entire progress of German art this century is copiously traced: particularly outstanding are **Kirchner**'s *Friedrichstrasse, Berlin*; **Dix**'s *Matchstick Seller*; and **Beckmann**'s *Ascension* and *Self-Portrait with Red Scarf*. Avant-garde works occupy the end halls, while important temporary exhibitions are regularly featured downstairs.

The western quarters

The streets in the grid-plan western half of the city centre are given over almost entirely to shopping. Almost the only building of note is the **Hospitalkirche**, which is a rare example of Aberlin Jerg being allowed to design his own building from scratch. Unfortunately only the chancel has survived intact; it houses a monumental *Crucifixion* by the Heilbronn sculptor Hans Syfer.

Further west, on Hegelplatz at the opposite end of the Stadtgarten, is the **Linden-Museum** (Tues & Thurs–Sun 10am–5pm, Wed 10am–8pm; free). This well-presented ethnology museum has displays covering the full gamut of non-European cultures, with Peru, Melanesia, Benin and the Congo being particularly well represented. A full-scale reproduction of an Islamic bazaar, using many original exhibits, is one of the most eye-catching features.

Outside the centre

If Stuttgart's centre is one of the easiest to come to terms with, the exact opposite is true of the city as a whole, several of the main attractions being dotted all over the suburbs. However, everything is readily accessible with a bit of forward planning and proper use of the excellent integrated municipal transport network.

The Weissenhofsiedlung and the Rosensteinpark

Below the Killesberg hill to the northwest of the centre, reached by bus #43, is the **Weissenhofsiedlung**. This settlement was laid out in 1927, in conjunction with an exhibition of the *Deutscher Werkbund*. Sixteen well-known architects contributed to this Bauhaus scheme, among them Le Corbusier, Gropius and Mies van der Rohe. Badly bombed in the war, the houses have been restored, but with variable success, and it's only worth making a special trip here if you're passionately keen on modern architecture. The **Höhenpark Killesberg** immediately behind is a large, remarkably peaceful recreation area. It's equipped with scented gardens, a flamingo park, and fields with donkeys, rabbits and sheep, making it a good place to take kids.

More generally enticing is the **Rosensteinpark** at the far end of the Schlossgarten; take U-Bahn #1, #2 or #14 to Mineralbäder. At the bottom end of the park is an artificial lake; a little way up the hill you'll find the ritzy **Schloss Rosenstein** (Tues–Fri 9am–5pm, Sat & Sun 10am–6pm; DM4), the former country house of the Kings of Württemberg, complete with rose garden, fountains and heroic statues. The interior now houses a natural history museum; the fossil part of the collection is separately housed at the western end of the park in the **Museum am Löwentor** (same times and ticket). At the northern extremity is the superbly landscaped **Wilhelma** (daily 8.15am–4, 5 or 6pm according to season; DM12, kids DM6), originally laid out as a Moorish garden for King Wilhelm I. Nowadays, it is both a botanical garden and a zoo with some 8000 animals.

Bad Cannstatt

From the Rosensteinpark, it's just a hop across the Neckar to the old spa town of **BAD CANNSTATT**, whose favourable situation at a bend in the river meant that it initially outstripped Stuttgart. It gradually declined in importance and was incorporated into its erstwhile rival in 1905. If you're coming from the city centre, take either a mainline train, or S-Bahn #1, #2 or #3.

Nowadays, Cannstatt is best known as the home of a huge beer festival (see p.205), and as the main sports and recreation area of the Stuttgart conurbation. However, it also preserves some of the faded elegance of a once-fashionable spa, and a great deal of self-confident turn-of-the-century architecture remains. There are a few older buildings, too, such as the **Stadtkirche**, another Aberlin Jerg confection, retaining parts of earlier Romanesque and Gothic structures. The **Kurpark**, with its mineral water springs and shady willow paths, is the most restful spot in Stuttgart. Cruises on the Neckar are run by *Neckar-Personen-Schiffahrt*, Anlegestelle Wilhelma (☎541073 or 541074).

Overlooking the park at Taubenheimerstr. 13 is the **Gottlieb-Daimler-Gedenkstätte** (Tues–Sun 10am–4pm; free). In 1882, Daimler, who was consumed by the dream of developing a new means of mechanical propulsion, gave up his highly successful corporate career, acquired a villa in Cannstatt (destroyed during the war), and carried out his top-secret experiments in an expanded version of its greenhouse, which somehow managed to escape the bombs. This humble, unpromising setting was where Daimler toiled away in obscurity for four years, aided only by his protégé Wilhelm Maybach. In their quest to create a light, fast-moving internal combustion engine which could power a moving vehicle, Daimler and Maybach invented the motorbike by 1885; the following year, the motorboat and four-wheeled motorcar had been added to their achievements. A year later, they established a factory in the town.

The Mercedes-Benz-Museum

By an extraordinary coincidence, another German inventor, **Carl Benz**, invented a motorcar in the same year as Daimler, though neither was aware of the other's work. Both went on to run highly successful factories producing their inventions; these were united in 1926 (long after Daimler's death and Benz's retirement) and are now based at **Untertürkheim**, immediately south of Bad Cannstatt. In 1986, the **Mercedes-Benz-Museum** (Tues–Sun 9am–5pm; free) was set up to celebrate the centenary of the inventions. Unless you positively rue the day the car was invented, this museum is an absolute must. Even entering here is an experience – take S-Bahn #1 to Neckarstadion, then walk straight ahead at the exit to the works entrance, or else go by bus #56 to Stadion. In accordance with the company's obsession about industrial espionage, you then have to wait for a special sealed minibus to take you through the Daimler-Benz factory complex to the museum doors which are opened only in conjunction with these arrivals.

Over seventy **historical vehicles** are on display, all with their bodywork restored to pristine condition. The earliest exhibit is the *Daimler Reitwagen* of 1885, the first-ever motorbike, which was capable of 12kmph. Benz's patent *Motorwagen* (a tricycle whose engine and bodywork are both his own design) from January the following year just beats the Daimler-Maybach *Motorkusche* (which was fitted into a four-wheeled horse-carriage) for the title of the world's first car. Both used one-cylinder engines and had a maximum speed of 16kmph. The Daimler company's first *Mercedes* dates from 1902. This Spanish-sounding name was borrowed from the daughter of the firm's principal foreign agent, Emil Jellinek; it proved so successful a trademark that it replaced the recently deceased founder's name on all products.

The exhibits also include a fire engine, a motorboat, an aeroplane and a bus, but it's the **luxury cars** that steal the show – look out for the elite handmade *Grand Mercedes* models of the 1930s, including one used by the Japanese royal family, the official *300d* limousine of Konrad Adenauer, and the first of the "Popemobiles", the *Landaulet* of Paul VI. Equally impressive are the space-age vehicles specially designed for **world record attempts**; these look so futuristic it's hard to believe they were made more than half a century ago. In 1938, the *W125* achieved 437.7kmph on the Frankfurt–Heidelberg *autobahn*, still the fastest speed ever registered on a public road. The *T80* was designed for travel at 600kmph – but World War II killed off this project, which was never subsequently revived.

The Porschewerk

Based right beside the Bahnhof of the northern suburb of **Neuwirtshaus** (served by S-Bahn line #6), Porsche is considerably more relaxed about visitors than Mercedes-Benz. Not only can you wander at will around the factory, there are free **guided tours of the production lines** every working day. These are generally booked solid weeks in advance, but a few extra visitors are allowed to tag on at short notice, though it's best to phone first (☎827 5685).

The Bohemian-born **Ferdinand Porsche** had already had a brilliant career when he set up in Stuttgart after World War II. As Austrian director of Daimler-Benz, he was responsible for the design of the handsome if underpowered *Pullman* saloons, and led the technical team involved with the world record attempts. His services had also been acquired by Hitler for the creation of the original *Volkswagen*. For his own enterprise, Porsche concentrated on the opposite end of the market. The fifty vehicles on show in the **Porsche-Museum** (Mon–Fri 9am–4pm, Sat & Sun 9am–5pm; free) at Porschestr. 42 illustrate all the company's models from the *356 Roadster* of 1948 to those currently in production.

The southern suburbs

In the hills due south of the city centre, reached by tram #15, is the 217-metre-high **Fernsehturm** (daily 9am–midnight; DM5 including ascent by lift). Completed in 1956, this was the first such television tower ever built and has been much imitated round the world, most of all in Germany itself, where it often became a civic obsession to acquire such an amenity. The view from the observation platform is much the best Stuttgart can offer, stretching over the Swabian Jura to the Black Forest and the Odenwald, with the Alps visible on clear days.

In the former ice cellar of the *Schwabenbräu* brewery at Robert-Koch-Str. 12 in the southwestern suburb of **Vaihingen** (reached from the centre by S-Bahn #1, #2 or #3) is the **Schwäbisches Brauereimuseum** (Tues–Sun 10.30am–5.30pm; free). This charts the history of beer-making from the third century BC right up to the present day; exhibits include a complete experimental brewery from the 1930s, a collection of drinking vessels and pieces of old equipment. Not surprisingly, there's an enticing selection of beers on sale at the bar.

Schloss Solitude

On a ridge in the hills to the west of the city centre, reached by bus #92, sits the appropriately named **Schloss Solitude** (April–Oct Tues–Sun 9am–noon & 1.30–5pm; Nov–March Tues–Sun 10am–noon & 1.30–4pm; DM4). This exquisite oval pleasure palace, built in the 1760s, was the main summer residence of the Württemberg court. It ranks as the masterpiece of Pierre Louis Philippe de la Guêpière, one of the prime movers behind the introduction of the Louis XVI style (which marks the transition from Rococo to Neoclassicism) into Germany. A bonus here is that you're free to wander round its marbled and panelled apartments without being subject to the ubiquitous guided tour.

Eating and drinking

Stuttgart's expensive reputation thankfully doesn't entirely extend to food and drink; though fancy restaurants abound, there are also any number of places offering traditional Swabian dishes at low cost, as well as plenty of ethnic eateries. Local **wines** are almost equally divided between *Riesling* (white) and *Trollinger* (red) varieties. Demand for these within Stuttgart itself is often so high that they can't be obtained elsewhere. The best and safest recommendations for sampling these vintages are the many **Weinstuben**; these cosy, homely establishments are archetypally German, and are as well known for their solid cooking as for wine, but note that they're usually open evenings only and are all closed on Sundays. A wide variety of **beers** is produced in Stuttgart as well. The *Hofbräu*'s gentle, sweetish *Herren-Pils* is probably the most popular brew locally; the rival *Schwaben-Bräu*'s *Meister-Pils* has a far more bitter taste. Outside the city, *Dinkelacker*'s products are the best known: these include the classic *CD-Pils*, plus both light and dark varieties of *Weizen*.

Weinstuben

Bäcka-Metzger, Aachener Str. 20, Bad Cannstatt. A genuine local, serving superb food.

Kachelofen, Eberhardstr. 10. The preferred haunt of the local bigwigs and in-crowd.

Klösterle, Marktstr. 71, Bad Cannstatt. Another great favourite of the spa town, occupying a medieval almshouse.

Schellenturm, Weberstr. 72. Housed in an old prison tower, with an appropriately cosy atmosphere.

Vetter, Bopserstr. 18. In summer this spills over into the square outside.

Weinhaus Stetter, Rosenstr. 32. Offers the largest choice of wines: some 600 in all. The meals are extraordinarily good value.

Zur Kiste, Kanalstr. 2. The most famous of Stuttgart's *Weinstuben*, so it's fairly pricey and prone to get very crowded.

Other restaurants

Alt Cannstatt, Königsplatz 1, Bad Cannstatt. Excellent traditional restaurant in the elegant setting of the spa town's *Kursaal*, with a large beer garden outside. Closed Mon.

Délice, Hauptstätter Str. 61. The leading gourmet restaurant in the city centre, housed in a cellar and featuring modern art exhibitions. Open Mon–Fri, evenings only.

Dinckelacker, Tübinger Str. 48. The *Gaststätte* of the eponymous brewery, decked out in rustic style. Closed Sun.

Fernsehturm, Jahnstr. 120. There are two high-class restaurants in the TV tower: *Skyline* (closed Mon) at the top is very expensive; *Landhaus am Turm* at the foot is rather less so.

Iden, Schwabenzentrum, Eberhardstr. 1. The most interesting of the city's vegetarian restaurants.

Kiche, Jakobstr. 19. Japanese restaurant and sushi bar.

La Scala, Friedrichstr. 41. One of many fine Italian restaurants in Stuttgart. Closed Sun.

Litfass, Eberhardstr. 37. Serves both Swabian and Turkish dishes; very popular with students.

Max-und-Moritz, Geiss Str. 5. Pizzeria mainly patronized by students.

Ochsen, Markgräflerstr. 6. Popular Swabian *Gasthaus* that has been run by the same family for well over a century. It's in the suburb of Uhlbeck, east of Untertürkheim, and reached by bus #62. Closed Mon & Tues.

Russische Datscha, Aachener Str. 23, Bad Cannstatt. Both Russian and Georgian dishes are on the menu in this restaurant, whch is tastefully furnished with antiques. Closed Mon.

Schloss Restaurant, Haus no. 2, Schloss Solitude. Out to the west of the centre and a good place to eat if you're visiting the Schloss. It specializes in *Neue Deutsche Küche* and is fairly expensive. Closed Mon.

Speisemeisterei, Am Schloss Hohenheim. Located in the far south of the city, this is generally regarded as Stuttgart's best restaurant. Very expensive; reservations advisable (☎456 0037). Closed Sun evening & Mon.

Tauberquelle, Torstr. 19. Fine Swabian *Gaststätte* in the city centre. Evenings only, closed Sun.

Taverne Mimis, Waiblinger Str. 44, Bad Cannstatt. The best Greek restaurant in the whole Stuttgart conurbation. Closed Sun.

Zum Paulaner, Calwer Str. 45. A Bavarian *Bierkeller* may seem an anomaly in Swabia, but this has been in existence since 1879.

Bars, cafés and café-bars

Academie der Schönen Künste, Charlottenstr. 5. Trendy artists' café with regular exhibitions. Has good wine list, serves full meals and has the benefit of a courtyard garden. Closed Sat & Sun evenings.

Amadeus, Charlottenplatz 17. Situated in the former orphanage, this serves bistro-style dishes and has space for 700 in its beer gardens.

Café Königsbau, Königstr. 28. One of the best places in Stuttgart for *Kaffee und Kuchen*.

Café KönigX, Esslinger Str. 22. *Szene* bar in the city centre.

Café Stella, Hauptstätter Str. 57. Popular café-bar that makes a good choice for breakfast.

Exil di Nuovo, Filderstr. 61. Trendy bar which doubles as an Italian restaurant.

Haus im Glück, Geiss Str. 8. Cocktail bar which also serves bistro food.

Jenseitz-Schwulencafé, Bebelstr. 25. Stuttgart's main gay café; predominantly male, and prone to become very crowded.

Merlin, Augustenstr. 72. Alternative café and arts centre which serves vegetarian food and organically produced beers, wines and fruit juices.

Stuttgarter Lokalbrauerei, Calwer Str. 31. *Hausbrauerei* serving good-value meals.

Teehaus, Im Weissenburgpark. Outdoor city centre venue that's predictably popular during hot summer days.

Entertainment

Local prosperity helps fund a highbrow cultural scene which is arguably richer and more diverse than that of any other city of comparable size in Europe. The tourist office produces a monthly programme of events, *Stuttgarter Monatsspiegel*, for DM2.80. "Alternative" listings can be found in both *Stuttgart Live* and *Ketchup*, available from newsagents. There's also a lively nightlife which takes place in a various pockets throughout the city. To find out what's on, consult the listings magazines *Prinz* (DM5) or *Lift* (DM4.50).

Nightclubs and live music

Classic Rock Café, Eberhardstr. 22. Plays both live and recorded rock music. German, American and vegetarian food available. Open daily from 5pm until 2 or 4am.

Dixieland Hall, Marienstr. 3b. Leading trad jazz venue, though modern styles are also featured. Entrance upwards of DM6, but drinks and food are reasonably priced.

Jazzothek Roers Kiste, Hauptstäter Str. 35. Jazz bar featuring live music every evening Sun–Thurs.

Laboratorium, Wagenburgstr. 147. Live music and cabaret venue that's been a favourite with Stuttgart's alternative set for the past two decades.

Perkins Park, Stresemannstr. 39. Stuttgart's most popular disco, particularly with those in their 20s and 30s (Wed & Thurs 9pm–4am, Fri & Sat 9pm–5am, Sun 7pm–2am).

Röhre, Wagenburgtunnel, Willy-Brandt-Str. 2/1. The celebrated "tunnel" nightclub occupies what was originally designed as a new rail line. Live bands play everything from jazz to punk; it's also a disco (Thurs–Sun 11pm–5am) patronized mainly by the most fashion-conscious locals.

Classical music

The three halls of the *Liederhalle* on Schloss Strasse (☎221795) serve for concerts of all kinds. Pick of the city's five **orchestras** is the *Stuttgarter Kammerorchester,* which is currently directed by the American Dennis Russell Davies. The smaller halls often feature performances by the local *Melos-Quartett,* one of Europe's finest string quartets. Stuttgart is, after Leipzig, the main centre for research into Bach performance practice, so any concerts by Helmut Rilling's *Bach Collegium* are worth looking out for. The city has more top-class **choirs** than anywhere else in Germany, the most celebrated being the *Hymnus Chorknaben.* Free concerts are often held in the churches – the Stiftskirche has a series at 7pm during the winter months. Every four years (next in August/September 2001), Stuttgart is host to an international *Musikfest,* with orchestras from all round the world.

Theatres

Stuttgart's leading highbrow venue is the **Staatstheater**, Oberer Schlossgarten 6 (☎202090), a complex of three separate houses. The resident **ballet** and **opera** companies alternate in the *Grosses Haus*; the former is one of the most famous in the world, with the great tradition established in the 1960s by the South African-born John Cranko (many of whose choreographies remain in the repertoire), continued by his protégé, the Brazilian Marcia Haydée, and now in the hands of Reid Anderson. **Plays** are performed in the *Kleines Haus*, while the James Stirling-designed *Kammertheater* is equipped with a moveable stage and seating, and puts on more experimental work. The city's other theatres include:

Altes Schauspielhaus, Kleine Königstr. 9 (☎226 5505). Specializes in nineteenth- and twentieth-century classics.

FITS Figuren Theater, Eberhardstr. 61d (☎241541). A great place to take kids, this is the home of several puppet companies.

Friedrichsbau-Varieté, Friedrichstr. 24 (☎225700). Stuttgart's spectacular new variety theatre.

Komödie in Marquardt, Bolzstr. 4–6 (☎227 7022). A theatre specializing in comedies of all kinds.

Kruschteltunnel, Möhringer Str. 56 (☎282534). Shows for the under-12s.

Makai-City-Theater, Marienstr. 12 (☎626208). Mime is the predominant fare here.

Renitenz-Theater, Eberhardstr. 65 (☎297075). The place to go for satirical cabaret; good German is obviously needed for an appreciation.

SI-Centrum, Plieninger Str. 100 (☎2228 243 or 54444). New venue for blockbuster musicals, it opened in 1994 with *Miss Saigon*, which was still running in 1997. A second theatre (due to open in 1998 with *Beauty and the Beast*) is under construction just across the road, along with a new cinema complex.

Theater der Altstadt, Charlottenplatz 1 (☎244332). Contemporary plays and forgotten older works are performed here.

Theaterhaus Stuttgart, Ulmer Str. 241 (☎402070). This is the big venue for alternative events, including feminist work and visiting foreign groups.

Listings

Airlines *American Airlines*, Charlottenstr. 44 (☎236 9412); *British Airways* Kriegsbergstr. 28 (☎299471); *Lufthansa*, Lautenschlagerstr. 20 (☎227140); *TWA*, Sophienstr. 38 (☎058183).
Airport information ☎948 3388.

Bookshops *Weises Hofbuchhandlung* and *Wittwer*, both on Obere Königstrasse, are the main general shops. There's a women's bookshop, *Frauenbuchladen*, at Olgastr. 75.

Car rental *Avis*, Katharinenstr.18 (☎239320); *Europcar*, Im Hauptbahnhof (☎223 7136); *Hertz*, Im Hauptbahnhof (☎226 2921); *Schlosstein*, Hegelstr. 12 (☎293844).

Consulates British, Breite Str. 2 (☎162690); USA, Urbanstr. 7 (☎210080).

Dentist ☎780 0266.

Doctor ☎280211.

Markets The daily markets in the Jugendstil *Markthalle* on Schillerplatz are ideal for putting a picnic together. On Saturday mornings, a flower market is held on Schillerplatz itself, while there's also a flea market on Schlossplatz.

Mitfahrzentralen Hauptstätter Str. 144 (☎603606), Lerchenstr. 65 (☎636 8036), Tübinger Str. 20 (☎221210).

Pharmacies ☎224310 for information on late-opening pharmacies.

Post office Main office, with poste restante, is at the rear of the Königsbau on Schillerplatz.

Sports The *Neckarstadion* in Bad Cannstatt is the main stadium for outdoor events, including the matches of the leading local football team, *VfB Stuttgart*, one of the most consistent in Germany in recent seasons. Indoor events, including an international tennis tournament in November, are held at the Martin-Schleyer-Halle alongside it (☎561565).

Women's centre Kernerstr. 31 (☎296432).

Esslingen

If Stuttgart seems rather thin on historic monuments, ample compensation is provided by **ESSLINGEN**. Nowadays, this is virtually a southeastern suburb of the state capital, reached in 15 minutes by S-Bahn #1, but for centuries it was a Free Imperial City and jealously guards its municipal independence. In the nineteenth century, it became an important centre of machine tool manufacturing and is still ringed by ugly factories which provide a sharp contrast to the vineyard-clad hills above the town. However, the old centre has been preserved almost intact. With its winding streets, narrow alleys, spacious squares and dramatic views, it's one of the most visually pleasing – and most unexpected – parts of this otherwise hi-tech dominated part of Baden-Württemberg.

The town

The centre of town is separated from the Bahnhof by the Neckar canal. From the Bahnhof, go straight up the street of the same name and cross over the bridge. Two more bridges can be seen down to the right; the second of these, the fourteenth-century **Innere Brücke**, is outstanding, incorporating a graceful chapel which now serves as a memorial to the victims of the Third Reich.

Marktplatz

Heart of the town is **Marktplatz**, scene of markets on Wednesday and Saturday mornings. Dominating the square is the Romanesque-Gothic **Stadtkirche St Dionys**, whose two towers are linked by a covered passageway, which served as a defensive look-out post. The church preserves its late Gothic rood screen, along with a soaring tabernacle and a font from the same period. In the chancel are glittering stained-glass windows, made in the late thirteenth and early fourteenth centuries. If you're keen on archeology, it's well worth coming here on a Wednesday between 2.30pm and 5pm, when you can view the extensive underground **excavations** for DM1.50. These include Roman finds, plus the foundations of two previous churches on this spot – the first was erected around 720, the second throughout the first half of the following century.

Facing the back of the church is the **Speyrer Zehnthof**, a mid-sixteenth-century tithe barn. Since 1826, this has served as the headquarters of the oldest *Sekt* cellar in Germany; production of high-quality sparkling wines remains a local speciality. The **Spitalkelter**, a half-timbered structure on the north side of Marktplatz, is an earlier relic of the city's wine tradition, having been built as a wine-pressing factory, before later becoming a hospital.

Rathausplatz

Adjoining Marktplatz to the east is Rathausplatz. The **Altes Rathaus** began life in the early fifteenth century as a merchants' trading hall and tax collection point, but was taken over for municipal purposes at the end of the following century. It was then given a cheerful pink facade, much influenced by Dutch buildings of the time, and adorned with an astronomical clock. Opposite is the Baroque **Neues Rathaus**, originally a patrician palace. Beyond are a number of picturesque old streets, along with the Hafenmarkt, where you'll find the thirteenth-century **Gelbes Haus** (Yellow House), probably Germany's oldest surviving and most architecturally distinguished brothel. However, it hasn't served its original purpose since a fire devastated the town in 1701.

West of Marktplatz

Just west of Marktplatz is **St Paul**, a Dominican monastery consecrated by Albertus Magnus in 1268. It's of particular significance in marking the debut on German soil of the sober, unadorned Gothic architecture characteristic of the mendicant religious orders. In total contrast is the **Frauenkirche** on the brow of the hill behind, which represents the Gothic style at its most elaborate. The marked resemblance, albeit on a reduced scale, to the great Münster in Ulm is no coincidence: it shared the same master masons, members of the Ensinger and Böblinger families. There are two exquisite portals, showing the *Life of the Virgin* and *The Last Judgment*, while the hall church interior has lovely stained-glass windows made a generation after those in the Stadtkirche. However, as at Ulm, it's the highly decorated **tower**, crowned with an openwork spire, which provides the most memorable feature.

At the east end of the Frauenkirche is the **Blaubeurer Pfleghof**, the most impressive of about a dozen such institutions in Esslingen, which served as town headquarters and charitable institutions of rural monasteries. From here, you can ascend to the **Burg** along its own covered ramparts. Most of the thirteenth-century defensive system has disappeared, save for the walls themselves, the bulky Hochwacht (the corner tower where the fortifications stop climbing) and the Dicker Turm (Fat Tower) at the summit. This was restored last century in the Romantic manner, and is now an excellent, upmarket restaurant. From here, there's a good **view** over the Neckar Valley towards the Swabian Jura.

Practicalities

The **tourist office** (Mon–Fri 8am–6pm, Sat 9am–noon; ☎0711/3512 2703) is at Marktplatz 16. There's one cheap **pension**, *Zora*, Bahnhofstr. 4 (☎0711/350 8564; ①) plus a few **hotels**, the best and most convenient being *Am Schillerpark*, Necharstr. 60 (☎0711/931330, fax 0711/9313 3100; ⑤) and *Am Schelztor*, Schelztorstr. 5 (☎0711/396 96640, fax 0711/359887; ⑦). The **youth hostel** is a long way to the north of town at Neuffenstr. 65 (☎0711/381848; ⓐ).

The town centre abounds with places to **eat** and **drink**. *Palm'scher Bau*, Innere Brücke 2, has a beer garden, while *Zum Schwanen*, Franziskanergasse 3 has a tiny house brewery and specializes in *vom heissen Stein* dishes.

Ludwigsburg and Marbach

The creation of **LUDWIGSBURG** began in 1697, when French troops destroyed an isolated hunting lodge of the House of Württemberg which lay some 15km north of Stuttgart and 35km south of Heilbronn. When Duke Eberhard Ludwig decided to rebuild the lodge, he found himself desiring something rather grander. By 1704, he hit on the idea of a planned town (named, needless to say, in his own honour); five years later, he had decided to make this his main residence and the duchy's new capital. To entice people to come to live there, he provided free land and building materials, plus exemption from taxes for fifteen years – an offer which duly found plenty of takers. Ludwigsburg makes a good day-trip from the state capital and can be combined with a visit to the **Schiller museum** at Marbach.

The town centre

In contrast to Mannheim and Karlsruhe, the Schloss is not the epicentre of the Ludwigsburg plan; that distinction belongs to the **Marktplatz**. As in the Schloss, there are churches for both the Catholic and Protestant faiths, facing each other across the square. One of Ludwigsburg's main claims to fame is that it has nurtured rather more than its fair share of literary celebrities, and an obelisk in **Holzmarkt** immediately to the north commemorates four nineteenth-century writers who were born in the town – the Romantic poets Eduard Mörike and Justinus Kerner, and the realist philosophers Friedrich Theodor Vischer and David Friedrich Strauss. Schiller went to school in the town, while the revolutionary writer Friedrich Schubart did a six-year stint as organist of the Protestant church.

The palaces

Ludwigsburg's complex of palaces and parks lies to the east of the town centre. The Baroque **Schloss** (guided tours in German mid-March to mid-Oct daily 9am–noon & 1–5pm; mid-Oct to mid-March Mon–Fri at 10.30am & 3pm, Sat & Sun 10am–noon & 1–4pm; guided tours in English Mon–Sat at 1.30pm, Sun 11am, 1.30pm & 3.15pm; DM8) took thirty years to build under the direction of a whole team of architects, and was only completed in the year of the patron's death. By then, funds had completely dried up and much of the lavish interior decoration was put in place by his successors, who preferred to live in Stuttgart. There are 432 rooms in all, grouped in eighteen separate buildings arranged round three courtyards; some sixty of these are included in the compulsory tour. Among the highlights are two chapels, one each for the Protestants and Catholics, and a theatre, the first in the world to be equipped with a revolving stage. The **Ordenshalle** serves as an opulent venue for the concerts which take place throughout the summer festival season. Also housed in the Schloss, and included in the entrance ticket, is a branch of the **Württemburgishes Landesmuseum**. Appropriately enough, this concentrates on the decorative arts produced in Baroque courts, including plenty of examples of the local porcelain.

The **Schlosspark** (daily 7.30am–8.30pm; DM11, DM4.50 after 6.30pm) is the scene of a huge floral festival, *Blühendes Barock*, held between April and October each year. In front of the Schloss, the formal Baroque section has been re-created from old plans. To the east are various modern additions to the facilities, including a Japanese garden, an aviary and the *Märchengarten*. The last-named is a kitsch playground with huge model giants, witches and other fairy-tale figures, complete with sound effects. Kids will love it, but otherwise it's not worth paying the hefty entrance fee.

A better destination for a stroll is **Schloss Favorite** (guided tours mid-March to mid-Oct daily 9am–noon & 1.30–5pm; mid-Oct to mid-March Tues-Sun 10am–noon & 1.30–4pm; DM4) in the grounds immediately to the north, which was built as a resting place for Ludwig and his cronies on their hunting trips. Even if you don't want to see yet another Baroque interior, it's still worth coming to enjoy the grounds, to which there's free access. It's then a walk of about 30 minutes to the third and last of Ludwig's palaces, **Monrepos**. This has a tranquil lakeside setting which is perfect for a picnic, but the building itself is in private hands and there's no admission. Within the grounds is the town's top luxury hotel, *Schlosshotel Monrepos* (see below).

Practicalities

Ludwigsburg's **Bahnhof** is just a short walk to the west of the town centre. As well as being on the main line between Stuttgart and Heilbronn, it's linked to the state capital by S-Bahn #4 and #5. The **tourist office** (Mon–Fri 8.30am–noon & 2–5.30pm, Sat 9–11.30am; ☎07141/910252) is at Wilhelmstr. 10.

If you want to stay the night, there are hotels in all price categories. At the lower end of the scale are *Kepler*, Keplerstr. 2 (☎07141/923887; ③), *Mignon*, Solitudestr. 43 (☎07141/903501; ⑤) and *Pfauter*, Stresemannstr. 25 (☎07141/950 6010; ⑤). Pick of the upmarket options are *Westend*, Friedrich-List-Str. 26 (☎07141/462312; ⑦), *Nestor*, Stuttgarter Str. 35 (☎07141/9670; ⑦) and the aforementioned *Schlosshotel Monrepos* (☎07141/3020; ⑨). The **youth hostel** is at Gemsenbergstr. 21 (☎07141/51564; ❶); take bus #422 from the Bahnhof to its terminus.

Most young inhabitants of Ludwigsburg confine their nightlife to Stuttgart, but the town has several good, inexpensive **restaurants**. The obvious choices are *Roter Ochsen* and *Margherita* on Holzmarkt, along with the pricier *Weinhaus Schnepple* on Marktplatz. Even better is *Württemberger Hof*, Bismarckstr. 24, which offers a comprehensive vegetarian menu, alongside standard Swabian fare. The last three hotels mentioned above all have excellent restaurants which are a good deal less expensive than the town's two gourmet citadels: *Alte Sonne*, Bei der Katolische Kirche 3, and *Le Carat*, Schwieberdinger Str. 60. *Jahnkes*, Bahnhofstr. 17, is a *Hausbrauerei* with a large beer garden.

Marbach

A few kilometres northeast of Ludwigsburg, at the terminus of S-Bahn #4, is **MARBACH**. This small town of half-timbered houses is indelibly associated with **Friedrich Schiller**, who was born in the house at Niklastorstr. 20, which is now a small museum (daily 9am–5pm; DM3). It's a modest building, entirely typical of Marbach – the writer's mother had also been born in the town, and the family moved back to this rented property when his father retired from the army. As space is restricted here, a much grander memorial was created early this century in the shape of the **Schiller Nationalmuseum** (daily 9am–5pm; DM4), which is housed in a huge mock-Baroque castle perched above the Neckar Valley. If you're at all into literary memorabilia, this is a must, with mementoes of Schiller and the other leading Swabian writers.

The *Stadthalle* near the museum has one of the best **restaurants** in town, offering the bonus of fine panoramic views from its terrace; *Goldener Löwe*, Niklastorstr. 39, is another good choice occupying a nicely furnished seventeenth-century house. There's no hostel or campsite, but there are several **hotels**, including *Gasthof zum Bären*,

Marktstr. 21 (☎07144/5455; ④), *Schillerhof*, Marktstr. 19 (☎07144/12381; ⑤) and *Parkhotel*, Schillerhöhe 14 (☎07144/9050; ⑦).

The Stromberg

The northwestern part of Swabia is known as the **Stromberg**. A large portion of its area is designated the **Naturpark Stromberg-Heuchelberg** and is cut by two deep valleys, the Kirbach and the Metter, which provide fertile agricultural land and on whose slopes grapes have been cultivated since at least the eighth century. Much of the area, however, is taken up by the two separate mountain ranges after which the park is named. These are actually fairly gentle, with even the highest peaks being under 500m. A footpath, laid out in the seventeenth century for military use, crosses right through the middle of the park, linking Mühlacker with Eppingen directly to the north; it makes a good day's hike, offering a mixture of forest and upland scenery.

Maulbronn

MAULBRONN, whose famous Cistercian Kloster is the best-preserved medieval monastery north of the Alps, lies in the heart of the Stromberg region. In 1557, just a couple of decades after the last monks had left, a Protestant school was established here under the protection of the Dukes of Württemberg; this meant that Maulbronn never suffered as a target for iconoclasts and revolutionaries, and stands today as a complete monastic complex giving a unique insight into a way of life which exercised such enormous power and influence throughout the medieval period. A wonderfully evocative description of the monastery (thinly disguised as Mariabronn) in its heyday can be found in the picaresque novel *Narziss and Goldmund* by Hermann Hesse, one of the school's most famous old boys.

The Kloster

A characterless modern town has grown up on the slopes above the Kloster, but that is forgotten as soon as you enter the walled precincts. The **Kloster** (April–Oct daily 9am–5.30pm; Nov–March Tues–Sun 9.30am–5pm; DM8) was founded in 1147 in what was then the isolated valley of the River Salzach. This was exactly the sort of location favoured by the reforming Cistercian order, whose rule stressed both spirituality and the importance of manual labour. According to legend, the site was chosen when the monks stopped to water their mules – hence the name Maulbronn, meaning "Mule Well".

THE OUTBUILDINGS

Entry to the complex is through the Romanesque **Klostertor**. Immediately to the right is a ruined chapel, in which early masses were said; facing it is the priest's house, now converted into the **Klostermuseum** (April–Oct daily 9.30am–noon & 2–5pm; free).

Beyond here, you pass into the spacious main **Klosterhof**, the first part of which is taken up by a jumble of predominantly late Gothic half-timbered buildings. These served as the storerooms and workshops, which were the province of the lay brothers of the monastery. They're now put to a variety of uses: the forge has been converted into a restaurant; the stables serve as the Rathaus. The stone-built mill, the oldest of the buildings, is linked to the passageway along the ramparts, at the end of which is the thirteenth-century **Haspelturm** ("Witches' Tower").

At the southeast corner is the **Faustturm**, so called from having been the residence of the original Dr Faust (see p.222), whose claim to be able to manufacture gold gained him employment for a time by an unscrupulous abbot who was willing to try anything to bolster the monastery's sagging finances. Within the corresponding corner to the north, the Dukes of Württemberg built a Renaissance **Jagdschloss** with fairy-tale corner turrets; it now forms the girls' section of the school they founded.

THE CHURCH AND CLOISTERS

Facing the Klosterhof is the core of the monastery. The **Klosterkirche** was the first part to be built; it's in the severe, unadorned style laid down in the tenets of the order, with no tower and no decoration. Later generations were less enthusiastic about asceticism; in order to enliven their church they replaced the wooden roof with a lofty net vault, added a row of chapels with elaborate traceried windows to the south side, and commissioned works of art. The fathers reserved the eastern part of the church for their own exclusive use, confining the lay brothers to the nave by the erection of a stone screen; members of the public weren't allowed into the church at all.

Instead, a **porch** (or "Paradise"), enabling visitors to look in on the services, was built onto the facade of the church in 1220. This seems to be the earliest building in Germany to show awareness of the new Gothic style pioneered in France. The same anonymous mason then began building the cloister, completing the southern wing plus the **monks' refectory** on the opposite side. Appropriately, the refectory is a masterpiece; it was the Cistercian custom to make the dining hall particularly splendid and luminous, in order to draw thoughts away from the frugality of the meals. The rest of the cloister, including the graceful **chapter house** on the east side, dates from around a century later; the use of elaborate tracery is the first visible sign of the dilution of the early Cistercian ideal of austerity. As a culmination, a striking polygonal **well-house** was added to house the fountain where the monks washed before each meal. Buildings continued to be added periodically – the long, narrow **parlatorium** (the room where conversations were held) beside the chapter house was built by a lay brother at the end of the fifteenth century, while the cloister was given a picturesque half-timbered upper storey soon after.

THE FRESCOES

In the early sixteenth century, as the original Cistercian ideal of plain and unadorned architecture held ever less appeal, the most violently expressive of German artists, **Jerg Ratgeb**, was commissioned to execute a series of fresco cycles. He made a series of preliminary red chalk drawings, which can still be seen; these include the depiction of the legend of the monastery's foundation in the well-house, and a number of allegorical subjects (incorporating a stern self-portrait) in the refectory. Completion of the project was interrupted by the Reformation when the painter abandoned art in favour of politics, serving as "War Councillor" and "Chancellor" of the Peasants' War in 1525. The failure of this rebellion led to Ratgeb's arrest; he was quartered in the Markt in Pforzheim a decade before his erstwhile patrons became very different casualties of the Reformation.

Practicalities

Maulbronn is slightly tricky to reach by **public transport**. It's best to come by bus from Mühlacker, which is a regular stop for trains between Stuttgart and Karlsruhe. There is a stop, *Maulbronn West*, on the branch rail line to Bruchsal, but it's some 3km from the Kloster. The **tourist office** (Mon & Thurs 8am–noon & 1–5.30pm, Tues & Wed 8am–noon & 1–4.30pm, Fri 8am–1.30pm, Sat & Sun 11am–5pm; ☎07043/10312) is in the Rathaus, Klosterhof 31.

As an alternative to the excellent but expensive **restaurant** *Klosterkeller*, Klosterhof 32, *Scheffelhof*, just outside the gates at Frankfurter Str. 9, serves homely and hearty fare, including imaginative vegetarian dishes. There are a few **private rooms** (①–③) and a few **hotels**: *Ochsen*, Stuttgarter Str. 54 (☎07043/7314; ❺), *Birkenhof*, Birkenplatz 1 (☎07043/6763; ⑤) and *Klosterpost*, Frankfurter Str. 2 (☎07043/10080; ⑥); all have good restaurants.

Knittlingen

KNITTLINGEN, 6km northwest of Maulbronn, is notable for only one reason – it was the birthplace of the notorious necromancer **Johannes Faust**. Inevitably, a **museum** charting his impact has been set up in the half-timbered house where he is believed to have been born (Tues–Fri 9.30am–noon & 1.30–5pm, Sat & Sun 10am–6pm; DM2).

JOHANNES FAUST AND THE FAUST LEGEND

Surprisingly little is known about the real-life Johannes Faust, though he seems to have been a celebrity in his day and the leading intellectuals of the time took him seriously, while regarding his practices as wholly evil. Unlike other leading practitioners of the occult, such as Nostradamus and Paracelsus, Faust left no tangible legacy, and his name would certainly have passed into oblivion had it not been for an unknown author who in 1587 published the *Faustbuch*, a pot-boiling collection of tales allegedly told by the magician, who had died nearly half a century before; this quickly became a bestseller, despite the crudity of the text. It was the English playwright Christopher Marlowe who, just a few years afterwards, first realized the dramatic possibilities of the story, endowing the hero with a tragic dignity.

Ever since, the Faust legend – with its themes of absolute knowledge, absolute power and the relationship between the two – has ranked as one of the great subjects of the European literary tradition, one capable of a vast variety of interpretations and a convenient backdrop for the discussion of all kinds of issues. Lessing provided a happy ending, a lead followed by Goethe, whose vast two-part drama is the unchallenged summit of all German literature. It took him the best part of sixty years to write; in it, he explored the entire European cultural heritage. In the present century, the Faust themes are equally relevant, and Thomas Mann provided an appropriately updated version of the story in his novel of 1950, thus following in the footsteps of his son Klaus, whose *Mephisto*, a *roman à clef* about the Third Reich, was banned in Germany for several decades.

Heilbronn

HEILBRONN, which lies in the Neckar Valley just to the east of the Stromberg, 50km due north of Stuttgart, is deemed to mark the boundary of the mystical concept of Swabia – no true *Schwob* would live any further north. Today, it still boasts one of the richest folklore traditions in Germany and is also a leading centre for **wine** production – some five million litres, mostly *Riesling* and *Trollinger* varieties, are produced each year by the surrounding vineyards. Sadly, however, the old streets were almost razed

---

HEILBRONN'S FESTIVALS

Foremost of the many local festivals is the **Heilbronner Herbst**, which begins with a procession through the streets on the first Saturday in September, and continues with a parade of lantern-bearing children and a fireworks display the next day. Later in the week, the *Weindorf* (Wine Village) is set up for nine days in the town centre, with the inevitable oompah bands to enliven the atmosphere. Nearly two hundred vintages are on offer at the various booths; in contrast to the inflated prices normally charged at German festivals, the rates are surprisingly reasonable – usually DM1 per glass.

Heilbronn's other big event is the **Neckarfest**, featuring historical boat pageants, a flotilla of bizarre home-made "water transport" contraptions, aquatic tournaments and a serenade of lights. This takes place during June, but in even-numbered years only, as it alternates with the more orthodox *Stadtfest*. Other festivals are the huge *Pferdemarkt* (Horse Fair) in February and the *Unterländer Volksfest* in late July/early August; the latter sees beer take a rare centre-stage role in this wine stronghold.

---

to the ground in an air raid at the end of 1944. The rebuilding programme was unusual in that it concentrated on providing housing in the town centre, with most commercial activity banished to the suburbs. Only a few first class monuments now remain, and it's best to time your visit to coincide with one of the many **festivals** which dot the calendar.

The town

The surviving monuments are conveniently grouped closely together in the town centre. By far the most imposing is the Gothic hall church of **St Kilian**, on Kilianplatz, with its amazing later adjunct, the sixteenth-century **belfry** (daily 9.30am–4/5pm; DM1), which can be climbed for a view of the town.. One of the few examples of ecclesiastical architecture in northern Europe directly inspired by the Italian High Renaissance, its lower parts are richly decorated, much in the manner of the late Gothic style then still popular elsewhere in Germany, while the upper storeys are built in the manner of a miniature Classical temple. At the summit, the *Männle* (a statue of an infantryman bearing the municipal coat of arms) lords it over the town. Inside the church is a wonderful retable of *The Virgin and Child with Saints* by a local man, **Hans Syfer**, one of the seemingly endless number of virtuoso carvers active in late fifteenth-century Germany. Underneath the building is the *Heiliger Brunnen*, a well with supposedly miraculous properties, from which the town's name is derived.

Directly opposite St Kilian is the **Rathaus**, another amalgam of Gothic and Renaissance, whose facade is enlivened by a graceful balcony used for making public pronouncements and by an astronomical clock. The latter, which tells the day and the month as well as the time, was considered the ultimate municipal status symbol when it was installed in 1580. Its construction was entrusted to Isaak Habrecht, the finest horologist of the day, who was responsible for the clock inside Strasbourg Cathedral.

Also on Marktplatz is the **Käthchenhaus**, a Gothic patrician mansion embellished with a Renaissance oriel. It takes its name from the legend of Käthchen of Heilbronn, best known through the play by Heinrich von Kleist. Käthchen was the product of a one-night stand between a German emperor and the wife of the blacksmith of Heilbronn. Her true identity was only revealed when, as a fifteen-year-old, she developed a mystical attraction to a count who had a premonition that he was going to marry an emperor's daughter. The town still gets a lot of mileage out of the story – every two years, a pretty local girl is designated as "Käthchen", to preside over all the festivals and to adorn the front cover of all the glossy promotional brochures.

In the pedestrian precinct south of Marktplatz is the **Deutschhof**, formerly belonging to the Teutonic Knights, which contains a Gothic church and Baroque administrative buildings. The **Städtisches Museum** (Tues 10am–7pm, Wed–Sun 10am–noon & 2–5pm; free) is now housed in the latter, though its natural history and archeology departments are in the Renaissance **Gerichtshaus** (Law Courts) across the street. There's also a third section, devoted to shipping on the Neckar, in its own building on Frankfurter Strasse, not far from the river itself. Up Obere Neckarstrasse from the Gerichtshaus is one of the few surviving parts of the medieval fortifications, the tower known as the **Götzenturm**. It's so called as a result of the daring escape made from it by the great adventurer Götz von Berlichingen, who was held prisoner there in 1519.

Practicalities

The **Hauptbahnhof** is situated just to the west of the town centre; follow Bahnhofstrasse straight ahead. The **tourist office** (Mon–Fri 9am–5.30pm, Sat 9am–12.30pm; ☎07131/562270) is on Marktplatz. Reasonably priced hotels include *Armida*, Frankfurter Str. 14 (☎07131/80013; ④) and *Allee-Post*, Titostr. 12 (☎07131/81656; ④). Among the upmarket options are *Stadthotel*, Neckarsulmer Str. 36 (☎07131/95220; ⑥) and *Insel-Hotel*, Friedrich-Ebert-Brücke (☎07131/6300; ⑦). The **youth hostel** is at Schirrmannstr. 9 (☎07131/72961; ❶): take bus #1 to the Trappensee terminus.

Recommendable **restaurants** include that in the *Insel-Hotel*, plus *Am Stadtgarten*, Allee 28, *Haus des Handwerks*, Alle 76, and the *Ratskeller*, Marktplatz 7. *Vegiday*, Querschulgasse 5, is a good vegetarian café. *Dachpavilion*, on top of a row of shops at Kaiserstr. 25, is one of the most enticing **bars** in Heilbronn. Another lively hangout is *Bukowski*, Hafenstr. 36, which never seems to close at the weekend.

Classical music can be heard at the *Harmonie* concert hall on Allee; look out for performances by the *Württemberger Kammerorchester*, one of the best chamber orchestras in Europe. On the same street, the spanking-new *Stadttheater* presents all forms of **drama**. The booking office for **Neckar cruises** is beside Friedrich-Ebert-Brücke. There are generally at least a couple of sailings each day in summer to Gundelsheim; trips round the harbour are occasionally offered as an alternative.

The Swabian Forest

The **Swabian Forest** (*Schwäbischer Wald*) stretches over a neat, almost square geographical area between Heilbronn and Stuttgart in the west, and Schwäbisch Gmünd and Schwäbisch Hall in the east. To the north, it enters Franconia where it gives way to the flat plain of Hohenlohe, while its southern extremity borders the Stauferland. Stretching over some 900 square kilometres, the whole area is designated a *Naturpark*. Thickly wooded, it consists of three separate forest areas, plus two ranges of hills. Though there's little that's tremendously dramatic, the region offers the opportunity of escaping from the crowds, on weekdays at least. The old Roman **Limes-Wall**, some of whose towers have been restored to serve as vantage points, traverses the forest from north to south; and there's a marked trail along the entire route.

At the heart of the forest is the town of **MURRHARDT**, which lies on the rail line between Ludwigsburg and Schwäbisch Hall, and makes an obvious base from which to plan your explorations. The town boasts an outstanding monument in the **Walterichskapelle**, a tiny, highly ornamented late Romanesque chapel adjoining the fifteenth-century Stadtkirche. A number of half-timbered houses and a section of the town walls also survive.

If you want to stay, there are a couple of **hotels**: *Gasthof Engel* (☎07192/5232; ②), Hauptstr. 15, and *Sonne-Post*, Walterichsweg 1 (☎07192/8081; ⑥). The only **youth hos-**

tel in the region is at Karnsberger Str. 1 (☎07192/7501; **❸**) at the northern end of town, while there's a **campsite**, *Am Waldsee*, in the incorporated village of Fornsbach (☎07192/6436).

Schwäbisch Hall

SCHWÄBISCH HALL, which lies just beyond the Swabian Forest and south of the Hohenlohe plain, 55km east of Heilbronn, was an important centre of minting, making the silver *Häller* (or *Heller*), the smallest unit of currency used in the Holy Roman Empire. Though now long out of circulation, the *Heller*'s name lives on as a simile for worthlessness in many idiomatic expressions in modern German. Ultimately, the coin's name derives from the industry on which the local economy was originally based: *Hall* means "Place of Salt". Excavations show that the salt springs attracted Celtic tribes to establish a permanent settlement here; following the medieval revival, they served as the keystone of local prosperity, only going into decline in the nineteenth century with discoveries of richer deposits elsewhere. Subsequent attempts to develop a more modern industrial base failed, as did a bid to make Hall a bathing and health resort on the lines of so many other German spas. Coupled with the fact that bombing in World War II caused little more than superficial grazing, this means that the town preserves an unusually intact reminder of its medieval self, complete with tantalizing insights into the social and political preoccupations of the time.

Marktplatz

The central, steeply sloping **Marktplatz** is lined by a series of handsome buildings which form an encyclopedia of German architecture. Its present character was largely determined during the late medieval period, at a time when the rampantly successful bourgeoisie had ousted the aristocracy from control of the council, forcing many of the latter to leave town. As a symbol of the self-confident spirit, it was decided to build a spectacular new church, to be approached by a monumental flight of 42 (now 54) steps. The dramatic possibilities of this backdrop were immediately evident, and the space was used for jousting and tournaments.

Today, the Marktplatz is put to use as an **open-air theatre**. This is one of the most impressive you're ever likely to come across, with magical staging effects in a dense, rapt atmosphere. The season lasts from mid-June to early August, and usually features a play by Shakespeare, a European classic and a twentieth-century work. Performances start at 8.30pm, but the scramble for the best seats begins as early as 6pm. Tickets cost DM10 for standing room and from DM20 for seats and are available from the theatre headquarters at no. 8 on the square.

The Münster

The late Gothic **Münster** has a nave in the hall church style with slender pillars and wide vaults, contrasting with the much higher choir, which was only completed in 1525, the year that the authorities of Hall decided to go over to Protestantism. Luther's youthful protégé **Johannes Brenz** – a far more tolerant figure than most of the leading lights of the time – came from Heidelberg to be the new preacher. His portrait can be seen on one of the epitaphs in the nave. Another particularly interesting memorial tablet is in the fourth chapel from the left in the ambulatory; this was made for his own tomb by the sixteenth-century artist and calligrapher Thomas Schweiker, who painted with his feet, having been born without hands or arms. The most striking work of art, however, is Michel Erhart's impassioned *Crucifixion*, placed above the Netherlandish *Retable of the Passion* at the high altar. For the best view of the town, climb the **tower**

(March 15–Nov 1 Mon 2–5pm, Tues–Sat 9am–noon & 2–5pm, Sun 11am–noon & 2–5pm; Nov 2 –March 14 Tues–Sat 11am–noon & 2–3pm, Sun 11am–noon; DM1).

Elsewhere on Marktplatz

Another embellishment to the square, erected at the same time as the Münster's chancel, is the **Marktbrunnen**, showing St Michael in the company of two other warriors against evil, Samson and St George. Rather bizarrely, the structure also incorporates the pillory, still preserving the manacles which bound the wrong-doers. The north side of the square is lined with a picturesque jumble of buildings, including what are now two of the best (and most expensive) hotel-restaurants in town, the graceful half-timbered *Goldener Adler*, an inn since the sixteenth century, and the gaunt stone *Ratskeller*. Opposite are a series of houses which traditionally belonged to various religious and charitable bodies. The west side of the square seems to be jinxed – the church which formerly stood there was destroyed by fire in the eighteenth century, to be replaced by the **Rathaus**, which was in turn a rare casualty of the last war. However, it's been successfully restored, its ritzy curved facade and stately belfry giving it the look of a sumptuous Baroque palace.

The rest of the centre

South of Marktplatz run a series of alleys – Untere Herrngasse, Obere Herrngasse and Pfargasse – which are all lined with superb old buildings often linked to one another by stairways. They all lead to the Stadtbefestigung (fortifications), which survives in part all round the town, unfortunately shorn of most of the towers which were demolished when Hall became part of the Kingdom of Württemberg in the early nineteenth century. Rising high above the weakest part of the defensive system is the massive **Neubau**, which, in spite of its name, dates back to the time of the Reformation. It served as an arsenal and granary, and is now a concert hall. The other dominant building at this side of town is the eight-storey **Keckenburg**, a tower-house from the Staufer period. Along with a diverse series of historic buildings nearby, it houses the **Hällisch-Fränkisches Museum** (Tues & Thurs–Sun 10am–5pm, Wed 10am–8pm; free). Well above average for a regional collection, the museum has displays on local history and industry, archeology, geology, crafts and sacred sculpture, including a fine group by Leonhard Kern, Germany's most accomplished carver of the late Renaissance period.

A short walk from here brings you to the banks of the sedate River Kocher, lined with weeping willows and with a picturesque group of stone and wooden bridges reaching out to three islets. From the quays on the opposite side, you have an outstanding **view** of the main part of the town, rising majestically in tiers. The left bank, which had its own set of walls and towers, was the artisans' district; it clusters around St Katharina, a Gothic church with gorgeous fourteenth-century stained-glass windows. At the northern end is a reproduction of the oldest of the bridges, **Henkersbrücke** (Hangman's Bridge), named after the house on it, in which the holder of the least coveted municipal office was forced to live.

The northern part of Hall presents another characterful old quarter, beginning at the **Säumarkt** (Pig Market), a couple of minutes' walk due north of Marktplatz, which features a sixteenth-century tower and weigh-house, behind which is the late seventeenth-century tannery, whose arcades were used for drying skins until 1972. Leading off the square is Gelbinger Gasse, the longest and arguably the finest street in Hall, whose buildings cover the full gamut of styles from Gothic to Jugendstil. Look out in particular for no. 25, the **Engelhardbau**, the Baroque mansion of a town councillor; and for no. 47, the late Renaissance **Gräterhaus**, whose beam decoration includes the scraping tools of the tanners, an indication that the house was built by a prosperous member of that guild.

Comburg

Perched magisterially on its hill a couple of kilometres south of the centre of Hall via the banks of the Kocher is the awesome **Klosterburg Gross Comburg**. Fortress-monasteries are common enough in Spain and the Middle East, but such blatant expressions of the Church Militant are extremely rare in Western Europe. In 1079 this collegiate foundation was endowed by the Count of Comburg, Burkhard II, who, as a cripple, felt unable to perform the normal aristocratic duties and decided to retire to a monastic life. Much of the original Romanesque architecture survives intact, including the mighty ring wall with its defensive towers. The extensive additions to the complex made down the years included the progressive strengthening of the entrance, and you now pass through the Baroque Bastion and the Renaissance Zwingertor before arriving at the Romanesque **Michaelstor**, guarding a twelve-metre-long tunnel which served as the last line of defence. As the Baroque monastic buildings are now used as a college, there's normally unrestricted entry to the courtyard. Here you can see another Romanesque survival, the hexagonal **Ebehardskapelle**, which is ornamented with a graceful dwarf gallery. Its function is disputed, but it probably served as an ossuary.

The **Klosterkirche** (April–Oct Tues–Sat 10am–noon & 1.30–5pm, Sun 1.30–5pm; DM2) retains the three imperious towers of the first church, but was otherwise rebuilt in the Würzburg Baroque style. Although the exterior retains much of the austerity of its predecessor, the interior, with its gleaming white stuccowork, comes in complete contrast. It still preserves, however, two stunning twelfth-century treasures made in the monastery's once-celebrated workshop: an enormous golden wheel-shaped **chandelier** (which is even larger and more impressive than those in Aachen and Hildesheim, the only others to have survived) and the gilded beaten-copper **antependium** (altar front), which has engravings of Christ surrounded by his disciples. A number of masterly tombs, including that of the founder, can be seen in the **chapter house**, which still preserves its Romanesque form.

It's also worth crossing over to the hill directly opposite, crowned by the **Klein Comburg**. This was founded as a convent about thirty years after its big brother and was also used for some time as a hospice. The church here was always very much the poor relation, but scores in the fact that it preserves its simple original form.

Wackershofen

Some 5km northwest of the centre of Hall is **WACKERSHOFEN**, where you'll find the **Freilandmuseum** (April & Oct daily 9am–5pm; May–Sept daily 9am–6pm; DM7). This brings together redundant rural buildings from throughout the north of Baden-Württemberg, including the Tauber Valley and the eastern Jura but concentrating on the Hohenlohe region. Ceramics, furniture-making and textiles are among the crafts demonstrated, while there's a *Backofenfest* on the last weekend in September. A historic inn, *Roter Ochsen*, is among the reconstructed buildings, providing a handy stopping-off point for lunch.

Practicalities

Schwäbisch Hall's **Hauptbahnhof**, which lies on the branch line from Heilbronn, is on the western bank of the Kocher; it's a fifteen-minute walk to the centre straight ahead via Bahnhofstrasse, then over the river. **Bahnhof Hessental**, on the fast Stuttgart–Nürnberg line, is 3km southeast of the centre, to which it's linked by bus #4. The **bus station** is by the bank of the Kocher just outside the northern quarter. The **tourist office** (May–Oct Mon–Fri 9am–6pm, Sat & Sun 10am–3pm; Nov–April Mon–Fri 9am–5pm; ☎0791/751246) is at Am Markt 9. If you want to make a detailed exploration of the old streets, ask for their *Walking Tour* brochure, which has a good map and extensive historical information in English.

For centrally located accommodation, the best-value **hotels** are *Gästehaus Sölch*, Hauffstr. 14 (☎0791/51807; ③), *Gasthof Krone*, Klosterstr. 1 (☎0791/6022; ④) and *Gasthof Dreikönig*, Neue Str. 25 (☎0791/7473; ③). More upmarket, and located in wonderful historic buildings, are *Goldener Adler*, Am Markt 11 (☎0791/6168; ⑦), *Der Adelshof*, Am Markt 12–13 (☎0791/75890; ⑦) and *Hohenlohe*, Weilertor 14 (☎0791/75870; ⑧). There's a **youth hostel** at Langenfelderweg 5 (☎0791/41050; ☎); from the rear of Marktplatz, follow Crailsheimer Strasse (the ring road) in an easterly direction, then turn left into Blutsteige. The **campsite** is south of town at Steinbacher See (April to mid-Oct only; ☎0791/2984).

The best **restaurants** are in the three luxury hotels listed above but you'll find cheap, homely Swabian cooking at *Zum Dorle*, Blockgasse 14 and *Salzsiedler*, Schulgasse 4. There's also a widely varied clutch of ethnic restaurants along Gelbinger Gasse. The local *Haller Löwenbräu* **beer** (not to be confused with its Munich namesake) is available as both *Pils* and *Weizen*.

Entertainment possibilities are headed by the open-air theatre, but **kids** will prefer the *Marionettentheater* near the left-bank quay at Im Lindbach 9, which has both historical and modern puppets.

Festivals

Schwäbisch Hall's salt heritage is celebrated each Whit weekend in one of Baden-Württemberg's most famous **festivals**, the *Kuchen und Brunnen Fest der Haller Salzsieder* (Cake and Fountain Festival of the Salt-Simmerers of Hall). This commemorates the occasion when the salt workers quenched a fire at the town mill. It features dancing and music on the Grasbödele (one of the islets) by the simmerers in their red, black and white historical costume. There's also a simulation of the blaze and a tattoo, both held on the Marktplatz.

Schwäbisch Gmünd and the Stauferland

SCHWÄBISCH GMÜND is 45km south of Schwäbisch Hall, and a similar distance east of Stuttgart on an almost dead straight rail line. The town lies in the heart of the **Stauferland**, a countryside of gentle slopes, lush meadows and juniper heathland straddling the northern end of the Swabian Jura and the southern edge of the Swabian Forest, and is a good base for hikes in the area.

The town

The town was founded by the first of the emperors of the local Hohenstaufen dynasty (see pp.229–30), Conrad III, but after the family died out, it became a Free Imperial City. Known in the Middle Ages for the luxury goods produced by its goldsmiths, silversmiths, jewellers, glass-blowers and watchmakers, today it's a lively provincial town with a compact Altstadt dominated by one of Germany's seminal churches, the **Heiligkreuzmünster**.

The Heiligkreuzmünster

Around 1310, the citizens began the construction of the **Heiligkreuzmünster** as the centrepiece of their town. Some time later, Heinrich Parler arrived from Cologne and took charge of operations; he was later aided by his son Peter, who was soon after called to Prague, where he developed into one of the most brilliant and imaginative architects Europe ever produced. The Parler style – of which this church is recognized as the prototype – soon usurped France's long-standing architectural leadership and made its mark on a host of cities throughout central Europe. The celebrity status of the family is confirmed by the fact that, in contrast to the general anonymity of most of the masons who designed the great medieval cathedrals, they are relatively well documented. In spite of the lack of a tower, the Münster, whose exterior bristles with highly elaborate pinnacles, gables and gargoyles, floats high above the town. Its five entrance **portals** introduce the characteristic Parler sculpture, which aimed at a far greater sense of realism than had hitherto been in vogue. The figures are short and stocky, and are often placed in dramatic relationships to each other; they have lifelike facial expressions and wear contemporary dress, with heavy horizontal drapery folds.

However, there's no doubt that it's the **interior** which is the real show-stopper; it was the first hall church to be erected in southern Germany, and triumphantly gives the lie to the theory that this form of building is inherently dull and unvaried. Standing just inside the main western entrance, you're confronted by the majestic spectacle of 22 huge rounded pillars marching towards the choir. They support a coloured vault which grows ever richer, moving from a fanciful pattern of ribs in the nave to a rich tapestry of network and star shapes in the chancel which, contrary to normal practice, was the last part to be built. The ring of side-chapels, cleverly placed between the buttresses so that their presence is not immediately apparent from outside, contains a wealth of late Gothic altarpieces, notably a *Tree of Jesse* in the baptistery. Above the seats of the Renaissance stalls stand animated figures of the Apostles (on the left) and Old Testament prophets; a peculiarity is that each figure is carved twice and placed back-to-back, so that it faces the ambulatory as well as the choir.

The Johanniskirche, Prediger and Marktplatz

The original parish church, the octagonal-towered **Johanniskirche** on the central Bocksgasse, is overshadowed by the Münster but is nevertheless a highly unusual building. It dates from the very end of the Romanesque period in the mid-thirteenth century and is extravagantly adorned all round its exterior with delicate reliefs of fantastic animals, fables, hunting scenes, flowers and foliage. The interior (May–Oct Tues–Thurs 10am–noon & 2–4pm, Fri 10am–noon & 2–5pm, Sat 2–4pm, Sun 10am–noon & 2–4pm; DM1) has nineteenth-century pastel murals and also serves as a repository for original lapidary fragments from the Münster and elsewhere.

Facing the west end of the Johanniskirche is the **Prediger**, a former Dominican monastery which has been converted into a cultural centre, including the **Predigermuseum** (Tues–Fri 2–5pm, Sat & Sun 10am–noon & 2–5pm; free) which contains good collections of medieval and Baroque sculpture, in addition to examples of the town's expertise in jewellery-making and the usual local history displays. On the opposite side of the Johanniskirche, the **Marktplatz**, now largely Baroque in character, has several cheerful mansions and a rather saccharine fountain bearing a double-sided statue of the Madonna and Child. However, there are also a number of half-timbered houses from earlier periods, notably the **Amtshaus Spital** at the far end. A bit further east are four of the five remaining towers of the fourteenth-century city wall, with the highest of the group, the **Königsturm**, a short walk to the south.

Behind the Hauptbahnhof, there's a wonderful wooded uphill walk along Taubentalstrasse, past shrines dating as far back as the fifteenth century, to the dark, secret **St-Salvator-Kapelle** at the top. This former hermit's cave and its adjoining stone-walled rooms are bedecked with candles, icons, statues and other religious paraphernalia.

The Stauferland

The **Stauferland** is ideal country for hiking if you prefer routes which aren't too strenuous. The area is named after its former overlords, the **Hohenstaufen dynasty**, who were one of the dominant forces of early medieval Germany and Italy. Their leading member was the great crusader **Frederick Barbarossa**, later to become one of the heroes of the nineteenth-century Romantic movement.

Just south of Gmünd the landscape is characterized by three conical wooded hills, the **Kaiserberge**, each commanding an extensive view and each formerly crowned by a feudal castle; to walk around them makes for the best day-trip in the region. Most westerly is **Hohenstaufen** (684m) itself, lying mid-way between Gmünd and Göppingen. Unfortunately, the ancestral home of the family was completely destroyed in the 1525 Peasants' Revolt War, leaving little more than the foundations. A few kilometres on is the holiday resort of Rechberg, nestling below **Hohenrechberg** (707m), whose Romanesque **Burg** (daily 10am–dusk; DM2) survived largely intact until being burnt out last century. It's an impressive ruin nonetheless, and is definitely the one to visit if you haven't time to see all three. The area has been a place of pilgrimage since the fifteenth century. The present Baroque church is approached uphill via a set of Stations of the Cross. Further east is **Stuifen** (757m), the highest but least atmospheric of the hills.

Practicalities

The **Hauptbahnhof** is just to the northwest of the centre, which is reached by following Uferstrasse straight ahead, before turning into Bocksgasse. The **tourist office** (Mon–Fri 9am–5.30pm, Sat 9am–noon; ☎07171/603455) is at Kornhausstr. 14.

Among the centrally placed **hotels**, cheapest are *Gasthof Weisser Ochsen*, Parlerstr. 47 (☎07171/2812; ②) and *Gasthof Goldener Stern*, Vordere Schmiedgasse 41 (☎07171/66337; ③). *Patrizier*, Kornhausstr. 25 (☎07171/927030; ⑤) is a good medium-priced choice, while the upper range is well served by *Einhorn*, Rinderbucher Gasse 10 (☎07171/63023; ⑦) whose restaurant occupies a vaulted medieval cellar. The **youth hostel** is at Taubentalstr. 46 (☎07171/2260; ❷), in a peaceful hilly location to the rear of the Hauptbahnhof and you can **camp** to the west of town at *Schurrenhof* (☎07165/8190).

There are plenty of other good places to **eat** and **drink** in the centre; best for traditional Swabian fare is the historic *Fuggerei*, Münstergasse 2, though it's on the expensive side. *Kübele*, Engelgasse 2, is a good, less pricey alternative. Gmünd has some superb **cafés** including *Margrit*, Johannisplatz 10 which has delicious cakes, the long-established *Zieher*, Marktgässle 3, and *Spielplatz* at Münsterplatz 12, which often features exhibitions of contemporary international artists. Alternatively, try the restaurant in the *Stadtgarten* (between the Hauptbahnhof and the centre) which offers quality dishes at low cost, with the added bonus of views across the park; in the halls here **concerts** of all kinds take place. The local **beer** is *Aloisle*, made with the soft spring water of the Swabian Jura. For serious drinking, head for *Bierakademie*, Ledergasse 50 which serves what it claims are the fifteen best brews in the world. *Taverne*, Kornhausstr. 13, is the main concession to the American community, fitted out to resemble a saloon bar of the Fifties.

If you want your visit to coincide with a **festival**, come on the second Saturday in June, when *Schwabenalter* celebrates those who have passed their fortieth birthday – the watershed year for the acquisition of true wisdom, according to Swabian custom. Otherwise, *Fastnet* is the main event, reaching a climax on Shrove Tuesday.

Tübingen

"We have a town on our campus," runs a local saying in TÜBINGEN. No irony is intended – the **University** dominates the life of this city to an extent unparalleled even in Germany's other world-famous centres of learning, such as Heidelberg, Marburg and Göttingen. Over half the population of 70,000 is in some way connected with the University, and the current size of the town is due entirely to the twentieth-century boom in higher education – it was not until a hundred years ago that the number of

> The **telephone code** for Tübingen is ☎07071.

inhabitants reached five figures, having remained static since the time of the University's foundation in 1477.

Tübingen's **setting**, on the gentle slopes above the willow-lined banks of the Neckar, some 30km south of Stuttgart, immediately sets the tone of the place. Upstream, the river follows a turbulent course, but here it's serene and placid, the perfect backdrop for the unhurried and unworldly groves of academe. With its students punting on the river on a balmy summer evening, the town is often described as a German counterpart of Oxford or Cambridge. Study is a very serious business here, however, with no nostalgic wallowings in ancient traditions – other than the small and discredited duelling *Verbindungen*. High jinks by the students are kept firmly in check and the prevailing atmosphere is of peace and quiet and of scholarly contemplation.

Arrival, information and accommodation

The **Hauptbahnhof** and **bus station** are side by side just five minutes' walk from the old town – turn right and follow Karlstrasse straight ahead. At the edge of Eberhardsbrücke is the **tourist office** (Mon–Fri 9am–8pm, Sat 9am–4pm; ☎91360). Mitfahrzentrale is at Münzgasse 6 (☎19440 or 5081).

Accommodation

The tourist office has details of **private rooms** (②–④). There are **hotels** in all categories, though they are thin on the ground in the centre. The **youth hostel** is on the bank of the Neckar, a short walk to the right on the far side of the bridge at Gartenstr. 22/2 (☎23002; ⌂). To reach the **campsite**, also with a riverside setting, at Rappenberghalde (☎43145), it's quicker to turn left from the Hauptbahnhof, and cross at Alleenbrücke.

HOTELS AND GUESTHOUSES

Am Bad, Am Freibad 2 (☎73071, fax 75336). Hotel backing onto the huge open-air swimming pool in a quiet park setting in the southwest of town, reached by bus #18. Its restaurant serves evening meals to guests only. ⑥

Am Schloss, Burgsteige 18 (☎92940, fax 929410). Characterful hotel in a half-timbered building immediately below Schloss Hohentübingen. No fewer than 25 different kinds of Maultaschen are among the many different Swabian specialities on the menu of its restaurant *Mauganeschtle*. ④

Barbarina, Wilhelmstr. 94 (☎26048, fax 550839). Fine middle-range hotel in the northeast of town, reached by bus #1, #2 or #7. It also has a good restuarant, though this is open Mon–Fri evenings only. ⑤

Krone, Uhlandstr. 1 (☎13310, fax 133132). Tübingen's top hotel, situated just south of Eberhardsbrücke, has been in existence for well over a century, and remains strongly traditional. It has a similarly high-class restaurant. ⑦

Kupferhammer, Westbahnhofstr. 57 (☎4180, fax 418299). Another medium-price hotel, situated just west of the Altstadt on the route of bus #9. ⑥

Kürner, Weizsäckerstr. 1 (☎22735, fax 27920). Moderately priced hotel with restaurant in the northeastern quarters; take bus #1 or #7. ⑤

Landhotel Hirsch, Schönbuchstr. 28, Bebenhausen (☎68027, fax 600803). Country house-style hotel and restaurant. ⑧

Marianne, Johannesweg 14 (☎93740, fax 937499). Small guesthouse in the south of town, a 10-minute walk from the Hauptbahnhof. ③

Sonne, Schönbuchstr. 15, Bebenhausen. Good value *Gasthof*. ④

Spracheninstitut Tübingen (SIT), Eugenstr. 71 (☎93540, fax 38457). This modern languages centre has a guesthouse geared mainly at students taking their courses, but normally has rooms available for other visitors. ③

The town

The Altstadt, having been spared the ravages of war, is a visual treat, a mixture of brightly painted half-timbered and gabled houses ranging from the fifteenth to the eighteenth century, grouped into twisting and plunging alleys. There are few truly outstanding buildings, but the whole ensemble is much more than the sum of its parts. Two large squares – **Holzmarkt** and the **Markt** – provide a setting for communal activities. The best **view** is from the Eberhardsbrücke over the Neckar, which embraces the Altstadt, the waterfront and the Platanenallee, the celebrated promenade along the man-made island in the river.

Holzmarkt

Dominating Holzmarkt is the **Stiftskirche St Georg**, an outwardly gaunt late Gothic church erected at the end of the fifteenth century, with a contrastingly stunning interior. Under the extravagant stellar vault of the nave, the pulpit is adorned with reliefs of the Madonna and the Four Doctors of the church, and crowned by a tapering canopy.

A triple-arched rood screen sheltering a painted retable by Hans Schäufelein, a pupil of Dürer, leads to the **chancel** (daily Easter–Oct 11am–5pm; DM1). Here an outstanding series of stained-glass lancet windows, dating from the same period as the church's construction, cast their reflections on the pantheon of the House of Württemberg. In 1342 this family bought Tübingen, then no more than a village, from the local grandee; on the promotion of their territory to a duchy in 1495, they made the town their second residence. The thirteen tombs show the development of Swabian sculpture in the Gothic and Renaissance periods; finest is that of Countess Mechthild, made in the workshop of Hans Multscher of Ulm. Look out also for the monument to Duke Eberhard the Bearded, founder of the University. The **tower** (same hours and ticket) can be ascended for a view over the red roofs of Tübingen to the Neckar and the Swabian Jura.

Also on the square are the **Georgsbrunnen**, a fountain with a statue of St George, and the *Buchhandlung Heckenhauer*, where Hermann Hesse spent a four-year apprenticeship as a bookbinder and bookseller at the end of the last century, having dropped out of formal education.

On the far corner of Holzmarkt, which doubles as part of Munzgasse, is the original home of the University, the **Alte Aula**, rebuilt in Baroque style for celebrations marking the 300th anniversary of its foundation. Also here, at no. 15, is **Cottahaus**, the former headquarters of the famous company, now based in Stuttgart, which represented the high point of Tübingen's publishing tradition, begun soon after the foundation of the University. **Johann Friedrich Cotta**, who took over an ailing family company set up five generations previously, was an extremely astute and successful publisher; through friendship with Schiller, he came to know and publish all the leading figures of the German Enlightenment, and also set up the *Allgemeine Zeitung*, whose independence and liberal views came as a blast of fresh air in the context of the censored and despotically controlled press of the time. The **Studentenkarzer** (Students' Prison) at no. 20 in the same street is older than the one in Heidelberg and has more varied graffiti, but unfortunately isn't so accessible (guided tours April–Oct Sat, Sun & holidays at 2pm; DM1).

The Hölderlinturm and Evangelisches Stift

Overlooking the banks of the Neckar on Bursagasse, the street immediately below Holzmarkt, is the **Hölderlinturm** (Tues–Fri 10am–noon & 3–5pm, Sat & Sun 2–5pm; DM3). Originally part of the medieval fortifications, it's now named after one of Tübingen's most famous alumni, **Friedrich Hölderlin**, who lived here in the care of a carpenter's family, hopelessly but harmlessly insane, from 1807 until his death 36 years later. There's a collection of memorabilia of the poet, largely ignored in his lifetime, but now regarded as one of the greatest Germany ever produced. Just before the onset of his madness, he produced his most striking work, grandiose apocalyptic visions couched in complex language and original imagery, showing the anguished state of his own existence – "A son of earth I seem, born to love and suffer."

At the end of Bursagasse is the **Evangelisches Stift**, a Protestant seminary established in a former Augustinian monastery in 1547 as the theological faculty of the University. The great astronomer Johannes Kepler studied here at the end of the sixteenth century and Hölderlin, who never managed to find the sense of belief to accompany his essentially religious outlook, was another of its students; he was joined by his classmates, Hegel and Schelling, subsequently the dominant figures of German philosophy. From here you can continue down Neckarhalde; at no. 24 is the birthplace of **Christoph Uhland**, the lyric poet and chronicler of old German legends.

The Markt, the Schloss and around

The **Markt**, heart of old Tübingen, is just a short walk uphill from the Stift. It preserves many of its Renaissance mansions, along with a fountain dedicated to Neptune, round which markets are held on Mondays, Wednesdays and Fridays. The **Rathaus**, originally fifteenth-century but much altered down the years, is covered with historical frescoes, though these are hardly more than a hundred years old; other eye-catching features are the pulpit-like balcony for public announcements and the gabled pediment housing an astronomical clock made in 1511.

Burgsteige, one of the oldest and most handsome streets in town, climbs steeply from the corner of the Markt to **Schloss Hohentübingen**, the Renaissance successor to the original eleventh-century feudal castle. Entry is via a superb **gateway** in the form of a triumphal arch, made in 1604. It's adorned with the arms of the House of Württemberg and the riband of the Order of the Garter; the latter had recently been bestowed on Duke Friedrich by Queen Elizabeth I. A second, less ornate doorway leads to the heavily restored courtyard. One wing of this has recently been given over to the **Schausammlungen der Universität** (Wed–Sun 10am–5pm; DM4). One of the largest university mueums in the world, it features important archeology displays, notably from the Ice Age and ancient Egypt, as well as the collections of the history and ethnology departments. Only by taking a **guided tour** (April–Sept Sat 5pm, Sun 11am & 3pm; DM3) can you see the Schloss **prison**, and the **cellars** with a vat capable of holding 85,000 litres.

The northwestern part of town, immediately below the Schloss, has traditionally been reserved for the non-academic community, particularly the *Gogen* or vine-growers who are renowned for their rich fund of earthy humour. Here are some of the city's oldest and most spectacular half-timbered buildings, such as the municipal **Kornhaus** (Tues–Sat 3–6pm, Sun 11am–1pm & 3–6pm; free) on the alley of the same name, which now contains the local history museum, and the **Fruchtschranne**, the storehouse for the yields of the ducal orchards, on Bachgasse.

The northeastern quarters

The quarter to the northeast of the Markt is once more dominated by the University. Down Collegiumsgasse is the **Wilhelmstift**, built in the late sixteenth century as the Collegium Illustre, an academy for members of the Protestant nobility, but since 1817 the site of the Catholic seminary. This building became the focus of worldwide media attention in the early 1970s when its leading theologian, the Swiss **Hans Küng**, published a series of articles and books attacking cherished doctrines, notably papal infallibility. The upshot was that he was stripped of his sacral offices, but he has remained in Tübingen as a professor (now with emeritus status), a celebrity, an ecumenical leader – and a Catholic. Crossing Langegasse and continuing along Metzgergasse, you come to the **Nonnenhaus**, most photogenic of the half-timbered houses, with its outside stairway and *Sprachhaus*.

Just outside the northeastern boundary of the old town is the former **Botanischer Garten**. This has been replaced by another complex (Mon–Fri 7.30am–4.45pm, Sat & Sun 10am–noon & 1.30–4.30pm), complete with arboretum and hothouses, located, along with most of the modern buildings of the University, a kilometre or so north by the ring road. The gardens serve as a reminder that botany has long been one of Tübingen's strong subjects. One of the leading lights in the academic life of the sixteenth century, Leonhard Fuchs (after whom the fuchsia is named), published an exhaustive and practical encyclopedia on plants and their medicinal properties. To the east, at Philosophenweg 76, the **Kunsthalle** (Tues–Sun 10am–8pm; variable charges) hosts tempting art exhibitions, sometimes of international standing.

Bebenhausen

Immediately to the north of the built-up area of Tübingen are the former hunting grounds of the dukes and kings of Württemberg, now re-stocked with deer and designated as the **Naturpark Schönbuch**. The main road to Stuttgart cuts right through this protected landscape, but its 150 square kilometres are virtually uninhabited – a welcome break from the urban area which encircles it. Within the park is the village of **BEBENHAUSEN**, just 5km north of the centre of Tübingen, of which it's now officially a part. It can be reached by frequent bus #7600 or #7955, but it's far more fun to sample the park's scenery on foot. There's a choice of **trails** – you can either follow the course of the Goldersbach, parallel to the main road, or else set out from the Botanical Gardens in Tübingen and continue via Heuberger Tor and the path beside the Bettelbach. In 1190, a group of Cistercian monks arrived in Bebenhausen, taking over from a Premonstratensian congregation who had settled there just a decade before.

The Abtei

The **Abtei** (Tues–Fri 8.30am–noon & 1.30–5pm, Sat & Sun 9.30am–noon & 1.30–5pm; DM3) is set in a walled enclosure with many half-timbered outbuildings matching those in the village; the main complex presents a cross-section of medieval European architecture. That the buildings survive in remarkably complete condition is due to the fact that they were converted into a (now defunct) Protestant seminary after the Reformation.

The best place to begin a tour is the **Abteikirche**. Built in the Transitional style between Romanesque and Gothic characteristic of the Cistercians, it was completed in 1228, but modernized a century later with the addition of the huge, airy east window, still with the original stained glass in between the tracery. At the beginning of the fifteenth century an eccentric crown-shaped tower topped with a miniature openwork steeple was built over the crossing. Unfortunately, the nave was truncated to a third of its original size after the suppression of the monastery, so the dimensions are now more those of a chapel. A suite of rooms – the chapter house, parlatorium and lay brothers' hall – was built along the east walk of the present cloister in a pure early Gothic style after work had finished on the church.

In the middle of the fourteenth century, the **summer refectory** was added to the southern side. Not only is this Bebenhausen's great glory, it's one of the finest Gothic buildings in Germany, a dining room like no other. Three central pillars stand like palm trees sprouting out their branches to form a vault of consummate grace and precision, which is painted with motifs of plants and birds. Later, the outer walls of the cloister were built, including a pretty **well-house**. This isn't quite symmetrical, as the mason himself realized, playfully confessing his guilt by adding a corbel of a fool holding up a mirror to show him where he had gone wrong.

The Jagdschloss

Also in the monastery grounds is the **Jagdschloss** of the kings of Württemberg (guided tours Tues–Fri at 9am, 10am, 11am, 2pm, 3pm, 4pm, Sat & Sun 10am, 11am, 2pm, 3pm, 4pm; DM4). This was adapted from the monastery's former guest house and is luxuriantly furnished in nineteenth-century style, with many souvenirs of the chase. The building later did improbable service as a parliament, being the headquarters of the Land of Südwürttemberg-Hohenzollern, which was set up by the French in 1945, but merged into the more viable province of Baden-Württemberg seven years later.

Eating, drinking and entertainment

Predictably, Tübingen is awash with student **bars**, **cafés** and **discos**, and also has plenty of good **restaurants**. For highbrow **culture**, there's a choice between the traditional fare of plays and concerts at *Landestheater*, Eberhardstr. 6 (☎93131), and the experimental productions of the tiny *Zimmertheater*, Bursagasse 16 (☎92730). **Bikes** can be rented at Fahrradlager, Lazarettgasse 19–21, or Fahrradladen am Rathaus, Haaggasse 3. **Rowing boats** are available at Neckarbrücke; if you want to try **punting**, ask at the tourist office or take the piloted trip which leaves from the Hölderlinturm at 4pm on Saturdays.

RESTAURANTS

Forelle, Kronenstr. 8. *Gemütlich* old *Weinstube* in a listed building, serving good fish and game specialities. Closed Mon, also Sun in summer.

Krumme Brücke, Kornhausstr. 17. Tiny restaurant with kitsch decor and a varied menu including plenty of vegetarian options.

Museum, Wilhelmstr. 3. Well-regarded if somewhat pricey restaurant at the corner of Alter Botanischer Garten.

Ratskeller, Haaggasse 4. Cellar restaurant whose speciality is giant pancakes.

Rosenau, Rosenau 15. Pricey gourmet restaurant on the heights above the northern end of town, close to the Botanischer Garten. Closed Mon.

Waldhorn, Schönbuchstr. 49, Bebenhausen. An even more prestigious restaurant, generally agreed to be the best in Tübingen. Serves both *Neue Deutsche Küche* and traditional local dishes. Closed Mon & Tues.

Wurstküche, Am Lustnauer Tor 8. Cosy restaurant serving good Swabian fare.

BARS AND CAFÉS

Bären, Schmiedtorstr. 3. Opens at 6am Mon–Sat and is consequently popular with both early risers and night owls finishing off the previous evening.

Café Lieb, Karlstr. 6. Traditional coffee house serving the best cakes in town.

Marktschenke, Markt 11. Lively student bar with jukebox.

Neckarmüller, Gartenstr. 4. *Hausbrauerei* with a big beer garden on the north bank of the Neckar by Eberhardsbrücke. Makes light and dark *Weizen* beers; also serves full meals including bargain lunches.

Neckartor, Neckargasse 22. Modern-style bistro serving good breakfasts and snacks.

Piccolo Solo d'Oro, Metzgergasse 39. Italian café which is one of the places to be seen. In summer you can sit outside on the so-called "Plaza Tübingen".

DISCOS AND LIVE MUSIC PUBS

Cinderella, Düsseldorfer Str. 4. Big disco which plays chart and techno; particularly popular with younger punters. Wed–Sun.

Foyer an der Blauen Brücken, Friedrichstr. 12. Student disco in former French army cafeteria. Fri & Sat only.

Jazzkeller, Haaggasse 15. Discos on Mon, Wed & Fri, live jazz or blues Thurs.

Zentrum Zoo, Schleifmühleweg 86. Hugely popular live music pub with beer garden which features regular disco sessions. Closed Mon.

The Swabian Jura

The **Swabian Jura** (*Schwäbische Alb*) is the name given to the series of limestone plateaux forming the watershed between the valleys of the rivers Rhine, Neckar and Danube. It's a harsh, craggy landscape, with poor soils and a severe climate, though its appearance has mellowed thanks to the plantation of forests. Geological faults have meant that individual mountains have become detached from the main mass; these formed ideal natural defensive fortresses for feudal overlords, and many are still crowned by castles. The Jura has few towns and even less in the way of major sights; the area is primarily of note for its **hiking** possibilities. As usual in Germany, marked trails cross the countryside, and the views on offer have a majestic sweep, even if they're often rather monotonous. It's an area rich in **flora**, with thistles, daphnes, anemones and lady's slippers being particularly prominent. Highlights of the region are the beautiful little town of **Haigerloch**, the old ducal capital of **Bad Urach**, the relaxing resort of **Zwiefalten** and the fantasy castles outside **Lichtenstein** and **Hechingen**.

The following section describes the western and central parts of the Jura. For the southern and eastern border (which has much the grandest scenery of all), see p.244; to the north the Jura merges imperceptibly into the Stauferland (see p.229). **Public transport** in the area is slightly complicated. The rail lines tend to run parallel to each other, involving circuitous connections, while some of the bus companies are entirely in private hands, meaning that (most unusually) rail passes are not always valid.

Bad Urach

BAD URACH, some 30km east of Tübingen, is serviced by buses which have replaced the branch rail line. It's primarily a health resort and has the standard, predictable spa facilities. Nevertheless, it also has many half-timbered houses (otherwise a rarity in the Jura), with the most impressive being the sixteenth-century group on **Marktplatz**, which also boasts a Renaissance fountain with a statue of St Christopher.

In 1442, when the county of Württemberg was partitioned, Urach was made joint capital with Stuttgart and a new **Residenzschloss** (guided tours April–Oct Tues–Sun at 10am, 11am, 2pm, 3pm, 4pm & 5pm; Nov–March Tues–Sun at 11am, 2pm, 3pm & 4pm; DM4) was built. The most impressive rooms are the Gothic **Türnitz** on the ground floor, and the **Goldener Saal** upstairs, originally built by Eberhard the Bearded who was born in the town and later re-united Württemberg as a duchy. These rooms were sumptuously transformed at the end of the Renaissance epoch. Likewise associated with Eberhard is the **Stiftskirche** opposite, erected in late Gothic style by his court architect, Peter von Koblenz; the octagonal tower was, however, only completed last century.

Just to the west of town is the **Uracher Wasserfall**, set in beautiful secluded surroundings. Further into the hills are more waterfalls, a nature reserve and the ruins at **Burg Hohenurach**, the original feudal castle. Continuing westwards, towards the tiny village of Glems, the scenery gets more and more luxuriant, brimming with wild flowers and foliage.

Practicalities

Bad Urach's **tourist office** is in the *Kurverwaltung*, Bei den Thermen 4 (☎07125/94320). There are more than a score of **private houses** (①–④) with rooms to let. Among the **hotels**, several small *Gasthöfe* offer similarly low rates; these include *Weberbleiche*, Weberbleiche 11 (☎07125/7339; ①), *Schöneck*, Neue Str. 26 (☎07125/70337; ②); *Krone*, Marktplatz 17 (☎07125/8148; ③) and *Fanfarenhof*, Ulmer Str. 1 (☎07125/40663; ④). More comfortable are *Ratstube*, an old guild house at Kirchstr. 7 (☎07125/1844; ⑤), *Buck*, Neue Str. 5–7 (☎07125/94940; ⑤) and the spa hotel *Graf*

Eberhard, Bei den Thermen 2 (☎07125/1480, fax 07125/8214; ⑦). The **youth hostel** is at Burgstr. 45 (☎07125/8025; ❷) on the southwestern side of town.

Bad Urach has many elegant **cafés**, while there are good **restaurants** in each of the last three hotels. The **beers** of the local *Olpp* brewery are among the finest made in Swabia.

Lichtenstein

LICHTENSTEIN is the designation given to a federation of villages 12km south of Reutlingen, a large industrial town on the Stuttgart–Tübingen rail line, just 10km east of the latter. The name is taken from the **Schloss** (guided tours Feb, March & Nov Sat, Sun & holidays 9am–noon & 1–5pm; April–Oct Mon–Sat 9am–noon & 1–5pm; Sun 9am–5.30pm; DM4), set on a high, narrow peak, and familiar through its appearance on the covers of all the tourist brochures to the region. Like many other castles in the area, it's a Romantic fantasy, erected in the 1840s as a replacement for one demolished in 1802. In the rebuilding, the architects were strongly influenced by the imaginary descriptions of its predecessor contained in the historical novel *Lichtenstein*, which was published in 1826. This was written by a remarkable author, Wilhelm Hauff, who died at the age of 25 but bequeathed a very considerable output, including many fairy stories which are still popular in Germany today. Inside the Schloss there's an excellent collection of arms and armour, while the chapel has Gothic stained-glass windows and a beautiful fifteenth-century altarpiece. It's a good thirty minutes' walk from Lichtenstein to the castle, but worth doing for the fantastic views across the Jura.

About the same distance further up, and reached by marked footpath, is the **Nebelhöhle** (Misty Cave; March–Nov daily 8.30am–5.30pm; DM3), an impressive stalactite grotto, some 380m in length. Although its full extent was only discovered this century, it had long been used as a refuge by the Württemberg dukes. You're allowed to wander around at leisure, instead of being subjected to a guided tour. A similar formation, the **Bärenhöhle** (Bears' Cave; same hours; DM3) is 3km south of Lichtenstein near the village of Erpfingen.

Zwiefalten

Continuing southeast, the peaceful health resort of **ZWIEFALTEN** lies in a valley at the edge of the Swabian Jura, just a few kilometres north of the Danube. Its name, meaning "duplicate waters", refers to the two streams which converge at this point. In the late eleventh century, a daughter church of Hirsau was established here. The huge Romanesque monastic complex survived until 1738 when, in preparation for its change in status to an Imperial Abbey, and in accordance with the passion for all things Baroque, it was demolished to make way for an entirely new set of buildings. This arrangement lasted for only a few decades. After the Napoleonic suppression, the church was given to the local Catholic parish and the outbuildings were converted into an asylum – a situation which persists to this day.

The **Münster**, the former monastic church, is a worthy rival to the great pilgrimage churches of Bavaria. Its highly original design, largely the work of **Johann Michael Fischer**, is already apparent from the outside, with its identical white towers and their green onion domes. Standing by the entrance grille, your eye is drawn down the enormous length of the church, yet is also diverted to the wavy lines of the side chapels; to the grey and rose marble columns with their gold-leaf capitals which shine like jewels against the pristine white walls; to the huge vault paintings glorifying the Virgin; and to the confessionals shaped like fantastic grottoes. The monks' choir is the most extravagantly sumptuous part of all, featuring a virtuoso set of walnut **stalls**, adorned with gilded limewood reliefs illustrating the life of the Virgin. Note that the entrance grille is generally closed between 11am and 1pm during the summer and all day through the week in winter, leaving you only with the sweeping initial view.

Following the Ach, one of Zwiefalten's rivers, for a couple of kilometres north of town, brings you to the **Friedrichshöhle** (or **Wimsener Höhle**), where it disappears underground. This is the only subterranean river in Germany which is readily accessible to the public; it's possible to penetrate a short way along the crystal-clear waters into the cave by **boat** (daily April–Oct 9am–6pm; DM3) before the passage becomes too narrow.

Practicalities

If you want to use Zwiefalten as a base for exploring the Jura, the **tourist office**, Marktplatz 3 (☎07373/20520) can book **private rooms** (①–③). There is also a largish **pension**, *Münsterblick*, Gustav-Werner-Str. 1 (☎07373/369; ③) and a couple of good-value **hotels**: *Gasthof zum Hirsch*, Hauptstr. 2 (☎07373/318; ③) and *Gasthof Zur Post*, Hauptstr. 44 (☎07373/302; ③).

The *Gasthof Zur Post* has the best restaurant in town; the *Gaststätte* of the *Klosterbräu* is also a good bet for food and makes an excellent variety of beers from its premises opposite the Münster at Hauptstr. 24.

From Zwiefalten, it's only 13km to Riedlingen on the Danube and regular buses run there, connecting with the trains of the *Donautalbahn* (see pp.244–247).

Hechingen

The market town of **HECHINGEN** lies on and around a hill some 20km southwest of Tübingen on the rail line which travels across the western Jura, eventually linking up with the *Donautalbahn*. The main reason for visiting is to see the fabulous Romantic **Burg Hohenzollern**.

In the lower part of town, close to the Bahnhof, a pilgrims' route, complete with wayside shrines, leads to the **Franziskanerkirche St Luzen**. This late sixteenth-century church is rather plain-looking from the outside, but lusciously ornate within, containing richly decorated half-columns and pilasters, an elaborate vault with large polychrome keystones, and shell-shaped niches with statues of the Apostles.

The upper town, which preserves a number of quaint, twisting streets, is entered via the bulky **Unterer Turm**. Built at the same time as St Luzen, this is now the only surviving part of the fortifications. Crowning the highest point of the hill is the **Stiftskirche**, erected in the grandly sombre Neoclassical Louis XVI style by the French architect Michel d'Inxard. Look out for the grave slab of Count Eitelfriedrich von Zollern, made by the doyen of German bronze-casters, Peter Vischer of Nürnberg. In the nearby Goldschmiedstrasse, which plunges back down the hill, is the Baroque **Synagoge**, immaculately restored to serve as a cultural centre.

There's no hostel or campsite in the vicinity, but there are a couple of **hotels**: *Mohren*, Schloss Str. 18 (☎07471/2393; ②) and *Klaiber*, Obertorplatz 11 (☎07471/2256; ⑥); the latter has the best **restaurant** in town. You'll find the **tourist office** (☎07471/940114) in the Rathaus at Marktplatz 1.

Burg Hohenzollern

Rearing high above Hechingen, some 4km south of town on the most prominent of all the isolated rocks of the Swabian Jura, is **Burg Hohenzollern** (daily April–Oct 9am–5.30pm; Nov–March 9am–4.30pm; DM7), the ancestral seat of the most powerful family in Germany. From afar, the fortress, girded with intact battlements and bristling with a varied assortment of soaring towers, looks like the perfect incarnation of a vast medieval castle. Close up, however, it's soon apparent that the present complex is almost entirely a Romantic dreamland. It was commissioned by the most heritage-conscious of the clan, King Friedrich Wilhelm IV, and built by August Stüler, a pupil of the

Even in a country whose entire history is dominated by the rise and fall of powerful dynasties, there's nothing quite comparable to the story of the **Hohenzollerns**. Their path to national leadership seems like a carefully hatched master-strategy which took centuries to achieve, yet which had a certain remorseless inevitability about it. The barren, windswept territories they ruled in their capacity as Counts of Zollern from the thirteenth century hardly seemed an auspicious beginning, while their first attempt at aggrandizement, in their capacity as Burgraves of Nürnberg – then the effective capital of the Holy Roman Empire – was soundly defeated by that city's independently minded council.

Frustrated in their quest for power at the heart of the empire, the Hohenzollerns turned to its periphery. In 1415, they were put in charge of the March of Brandenburg and were thus responsible for securing the country's eastern frontier; they also gained one of the seven seats on the imperial electoral college. The big breakthrough came in 1525, when Albrecht von Hohenzollern, Grand Master of the Teutonic Knights, converted to Protestantism and secularized the order's holdings as the Duchy of Prussia, which paid nominal homage to the Polish crown; this gave the family a power-base beyond the jurisdiction of the emperor.

By 1701, the Hohenzollerns had wrested Prussia from dependency on Poland; they conferred royal status on themselves and merged their territories. In time, they built up a centralized military state which, by skilful warfare and diplomacy, became one of the great powers of Europe. The nineteenth century saw the completion of the jigsaw – as the Habsburgs increasingly turned their attentions towards the Balkans, the Hohenzollerns ousted them from German leadership, eventually excluding them from the unified nation they created by 1871. However, the family's reign was brief – Germany's defeat in World War I led to the collapse of the old aristocratic order and the abolition of the monarchy.

great Schinkel. Only the fifteenth-century **St-Michael-Kapelle** survives from the previous fortress; it has been retained for the use of the Roman Catholic branch of the family and preserves beautiful Gothic stained-glass windows, along with Romanesque reliefs from its own predecessor.

The **Schatzkammer** contains valuable heirlooms, notably the crown of Prussia, reconstructed in 1889 after the original was destroyed. There's also the snuffbox that saved the life of Frederick the Great at the Battle of Kunersdorf by absorbing a bullet, which is still embedded in it.

Haigerloch

Unchallenged star of the western part of the Swabian Jura is **HAIGERLOCH**. Buses run from Hechingen, which is 17km east, and from Tübingen via Rottenburg, but the rail line is now used only for occasional steam train jaunts in the summer months. One of the most outstanding small towns in Germany, Haigerloch's isolation means it's considerably less self-conscious than most of its rivals. Here there's a perfect blend of landscape and architecture, with an unorthodox setting, on rocks high above an S-bend on the River Eyach, playing a crucial role. The surrounding countryside is at its most luxuriant in May, when the **lilac** is in full, riotous bloom, but it's hard to be disappointed by the picture at whatever time of year you come.

The Schloss

The northern side of the river is dominated by the **Schloss**, a photogenic jumble of mostly Renaissance buildings which replaced a medieval fortress. Until a few years ago, it was in the possession of the Hohenzollern family, who were probably based in

Haigerloch in the eleventh century. Nowadays, the Schloss serves as a hotel and arts centre. The **Schlosskirche**, lower down the hill, has an outwardly Gothic appearance, in spite of being built at the turn of the seventeenth century. The interior was given the full Rococo treatment 150 years later, with the addition of elaborate altars, frescoes and stuccowork. It's also worth walking eastwards through the woods from the Schloss courtyard; after a few minutes, you come to the **Kapf**, a belvedere with a large cross which commands a superb view over both parts of Haigerloch.

The rest of town

Underneath the Schloss' rock is the **Atomkeller-Museum** (May–Sept daily 10am–noon & 2–5pm; March, April, Oct & Nov same times Sat & Sun only; DM2). Here, in March and April 1945, a distinguished group of German scientists carried out a series of experiments in nuclear fission. Throughout the war, the Allies had trembled at the prospect that Germany would be first to develop atomic weapons; thankfully, Hitler never took the project very seriously, while Himmler, who was nominally in charge of the scientists, constantly diverted the researchers into absurd pet projects of his own. When the Americans captured Haigerloch on April 23, they made a point of rounding up the scientists; the reactor was dismantled and shipped to the USA in order to help with the successful testing of the atomic bomb just three months later.

Ironically, the American victory in this particular race owed a lot to Albert Einstein, who, as a Jew, had been forced to leave Germany in 1933. Haigerloch itself had been something of a Jewish stronghold until 1941. The **ghetto** can be seen at the western edge of the upper town; the synagogue and the rabbi's house still survive, though neither is used for its original purpose. There's also a Jewish cemetery, which (most unusually) is located well inside the municipal boundaries.

Further up is the pilgrimage church of **St Anna**, erected in the 1750s as an integrated ensemble with the monumental garden enclosure and the facing curate's house. The interior of the church has a sense of spaciousness out of all proportion to its small size and is filled with examples of Rococo workmanship of the highest class.

Outside the church is a belvedere offering the directly opposite panorama to that from the Kapf. Another fine view can be had from the **Römerturm** (April–Oct Sat & Sun 9am–6pm, variably on other days; DM1) which dominates the centre of town. In spite of its name, it's of Romanesque, not Roman origin, and formed part of the citadel of the Counts of Zollern. The nineteenth-century Protestant **Pfarrkirche** contains a meticulous copy of Leonardo da Vinci's *Last Supper*. If you see a busload of excited Italian tourists in town, the reason is that they've come specially to see this painting, which is in far better condition than the original.

Practicalities

The **tourist office** (Mon–Wed & Fri 8am–noon, Thurs 8am–noon & 4–6pm; ☎07474/69727) is in the Rathaus at Oberstadtstr. 11. Haigerloch, like so many places in the Jura, has no hostel or campsite. There are, however, a couple of cheapish **hotels**: *Gasthof Römer*, Oberstadtstr. 41 (☎07474/1015; ③); and *Krone*, Oberstadtstr. 47 (☎07474/95440; ④). At the opposite end of the scale, there are two special places to stay: the seventeenth-century *Schwanen*, Marktplatz 5 (☎07474/7575; ⑦) and the aforementioned *Gastschloss Haigerloch* in the Schloss (☎07474/6930; ⑦). All these hotels have **restaurants**; that of *Schwanen* is a true gourmet paradise renowned throughout southern Germany.

The chimney of the *Schlossbräu* brewery on the banks of the Eyach is the only sign of industry for miles around. An adventurous range of **beers** is made here – *Pils*, three varieties of *Weizen* and *Spezial*. The best place to sample these is their own *Gaststätte Schlössle*, Hechinger Str. 9, which also does good meals at reasonable prices.

Rottweil

In spite of the fact that the dog has put **ROTTWEIL**'s name into many foreign languages, this unhurried provincial market town is itself relatively little known. Lying between the Black Forest and the Swabian Jura, it's way off the beaten tourist track, with nothing of interest nearby and no overwhelming set-piece of its own to draw the crowds, yet the town is a visual marvel. Its isolation spared it from the horrors of modern warfare, and it has changed very little since the seventeenth century. Add to this highly original townscape a dramatic **setting**, a history as remarkable as that of any epic, one of the most impressive arrays of sculpture in Germany and a rich tradition of festivals, and you have what deserves to be considered one of the most enticing small towns in the country.

The town

Rottweil is built on a strategically secure spur high above the still young River Neckar. This restricted area means that the buildings had to be packed tightly together, with no room for expansion. The town is approached via the **Hochbrücke**, which spans a deep gully. The site of *Arae Flaviae* lies just over 1km to the left down Königstrasse, and **Roman baths** have been excavated at the corner of what is now the cemetery.

Hochbrücktorstrasse

Immediately over the bridge, and named after the tower which once guarded it, is **Hochbrücktorstrasse**, the town's north–south axis. Here you'll see the brilliantly colourful **old houses** characteristic of Rottweil. These are mostly late Renaissance or Baroque in style, and are adorned with three-sided oriel windows, sometimes reaching up several storeys. Each balcony tries to outdo its neighbour in the profusion of carvings. These often illustrate the coat of arms of the original family or the emblem of the guild to which they belonged; others bear the Imperial Eagle, proud symbol of a Free Imperial City (a status this little town held for nearly six centuries). At the end of Hochbrücktorstrasse is the slender red sandstone **Marktbrunnen**, the most elaborate of the town's four Renaissance fountains. Built in tiers like a wedding cake, it's decorated with delicate statuettes made after woodcuts by Hans Burgkmair, and is crowned by a figure of a Swiss soldier, in commemoration of the "perpetual bond" between Rottweil and the Confederation of Switzerland.

The Kapellenkirche

Standing in a cramped square just behind is the **Kapellenkirche**, Gothic successor to an old pilgrimage chapel. It was begun in the early fourteenth century as a miniature version of the Münster in Freiburg, but money ran out with only the square lower part

---

ROTTWEIL'S DOGS

With its characteristic mixture of black and tan markings, stocky frame and stubby tail, the **Rottweiler** dog is now a familiar sight all over the world. When the Romans came on a road-building mission to southwestern Germany around 73 AD, they brought with them dogs to drive the livestock and defend the camp; in time, these were successfully bred with local species. The resultant crossbreed has survived down the centuries, named after Rottweil, the town which developed from the Roman settlement of *Arae Flaviae*, which stood at the intersection of the two main highways linking Strasbourg with Augsburg, and the Aargau region of Switzerland with the Middle Neckar. Local butchers trained the Rottweiler to pull their carts – hence its alternative name of *Metzgerhund* (butcher's dog) – but it's now used by the German police, army, customs and mountain rescue services, and as a guide for the blind.

of the tower completed. Some 150 years later, the Duke of Württemberg's architect, Aberlin Jerg, added a double octagonal storey to the tower, providing Rottweil with the dominant central monument it needed. The church's outstanding **sculptural decoration** is by several identifiable masters, with the mystical and gentle style of the so-called "Marienmeister" perfectly contrasting with the lively narrative approach of his successor, the "Christusmeister". These works have been replaced *in situ* by copies; the originals are now in the Lorenzkapelle (see opposite).

Hauptstrasse

From the northern side of the church, you pass into the resplendent main street, **Hauptstrasse**, which runs uphill by constantly changing gradients. It's lined by an even more impressive group of houses than those on the perpendicular Hochbrücktorstrasse. The oldest of these, no. 62, dates back to the thirteenth century, while the next two buildings, including the historic inn *Gasthaus zum Sternen*, are in late Gothic style. To see the backs of these houses, whose half-timbering is uncharacteristic of Rottweil, go down to the massive viaduct, a notable piece of nineteenth-century engineering which carries the road out of town high over the valley. From here, there's also a sweeping view over the Swabian Jura.

In the upper half of Hauptstrasse, at no. 20, is the **Stadtmuseum** (Mon–Thurs & Sat 9am–noon & 2–5pm, Fri 9am–noon, Sun 10am–noon; free), whose star exhibit is the extraordinary **Pürschgerichtskarte** of 1564 – a *tour de force* of detail – proving how little Rottweil's overall appearance has altered. An adjoining room is devoted to the town's **Fastnet** celebrations (see opposite), with wooden masks of the principal characters and a painstakingly executed cardboard cut-out of the *Narrensprung* – which makes an acceptable substitute if you don't manage to see the real thing.

Directly across the street, the **Apostelbrunnen**, with its figures of SS Peter, James and John, has been re-erected in front of the **Altes Rathaus**, whose simple Gothic architecture gives the street a rare touch of sobriety.

The top of Hauptstrasse is closed by the formidable **Schwarzes Tor** (Black Tower). Its lower section, with its rough masonry, dates back to 1230; the upper storeys were added around 1600 as a prison. Continuing uphill, you come to the **Hochturm** via the alley of the same name. This also belongs to the Staufian period and is a watchtower guarding Rottweil's vulnerable western flank, the only one to lack a natural defensive barrier. In the late eighteenth century, an octagon was added to the top to serve as a look-out gallery; it commands a superb view of the town and surrounding countryside. A plaque on the door tells you which family currently holds the key; otherwise, ask for it at the tourist office.

North of Hauptstrasse

Rathausgasse leads from the Rathaus to Münsterplatz, and its **Heilig-Kreuz-Münster**, a late Gothic basilica with a tall tower. Its most important work of art is an anguished *Crucifixion* at the high altar which is an early work by Veit Stoss. Proceeding down Bruderschaftsgasse at the eastern side of the Münster, you pass the **Dominikanerkirche**, a Gothic church with a sumptuous Baroque interior, and the last of the Renaissance fountains, the **Christophorusbrunnen**, with a relief of the city's coat of arms as well as a statue of St Christopher carrying the Christ child.

Further north is the gleaming new building of the **Dominikanermuseum** (Tues–Sun 10am–1pm & 2–5pm; DM3), a joint venture between the town and the Land of Baden-Württemberg in order that the former's remarkable collection of Swabian wood sculpture could be exhibited in its entirety. The museum also contains important excavations from *Arae Flaviae*, dominated by the second-century **Orpheus mosaic**. Made of some 570,000 coloured stones, this shows the god playing his lyre to the enchantment of the birds and beasts around him – among them a dog, who is doubtless an early Rottweiler.

The Lorenzkapelle

At the end of Lorenzgasse is the **Lorenzkapelle** (Tues–Sat 10am–noon & 2–5pm, Sun 2–5pm; DM2), a late Gothic funerary chapel which is devoted to an array of **stone sculpture**. Pride of place here is given to the original carvings from the Kapellenkirche, including two reliefs by the "Marienmeister": *The Opening of the Book* symbolizes Knowledge, while the tender *Betrothal of the Knight* is an allegory of the marriage of Jesus to the Christian soul. A humorous figure, the *Weckenmännle*, probably served as the basis of the pulpit: it's thought to be a self-portrait of Anton Pilgram, who later became master mason at the Dom in Vienna. Outside the Lorenzkapelle is the **Pulverturm** (Powder Tower), one of the remaining vestiges of the fortifications.

Practicalities

Rottweil lies on the main rail line between Stuttgart and Tuttlingen, with onward connections to Switzerland; even international trains stop here. It can also be reached from various points in the Black Forest via the junction of Horb, 35km north. Arriving at the **Bahnhof**, turn right and walk straight uphill to the Hochbrücke. The **tourist office** (Mon–Fri 9.30am–12.30pm & 2–6pm, May–Oct Sat 9.30am–12.30pm; ☎0741/494280) is on Rathausgasse, off Hauptstrasse.

The **youth hostel** has an ideal location in the centre of town at Lorenzgasse 8 (☎0741/7664; 🄑), but there's no campsite. There's a large concentration of **hotels** on Hauptstrasse, including three cheap **Gasthöfe**. Currently the lowest rates are at *Goldenes Rad* at no. 38 (☎0741/7412; ②); the alternatives are *Löwen* at no. 66 (☎0741/7640; ④) and *Hasen* at no. 69 (☎0741/7798; ④). More upmarket are *Lamm* at no. 45 (☎0741/45015; ④) and the aforementioned *Haus zum Sternen* at no. 60 (☎0741/53300; ⑦) which is part of the *Romantik* chain. Other recommendable hotels are *Bären*, Hochmaurenstr. 1 (☎0741/22046; ④), *Parkhotel*, Königstr. 21 (☎0741/534330; ⑦) and *Johanniterbad*, Johannsergasse 12 (☎0741/530700; ⑦).

Each of the hotels mentioned above has a **restaurant**; that in *Haus zum Sternen* is particularly good with plenty of vegetarian options. However, the best place to eat is *Villa Duttenhofer*, Königstr. 1, which has an expensive restaurant, *L'Etoile* (evenings only) and a reasonably priced bistro. There's also a wide choice of genteel cafés around the town centre.

Festivals

All **festivals** stand in the shadow of Fastnet (see below), but other folklore events include the week-long *Volksfest* in mid-August and the *Stadtfest* on the second weekend

---

THE ROTTWEIL FASTNET

Rottweil is at its most animated during the Carnival season, and its **Fastnet celebrations** – which are fifteenth-century in origin and very different from those in the Rhineland – are arguably Baden-Württemberg's top popular festival. The action begins on the evening of the Thursday before Carnival Sunday (variable date Feb/March) with the *Schmotzige*, in which groups perform satirical revues of the previous year's events. On the Sunday, the mayor hands over control of the town for the duration of the festival, and the afternoon features a children's procession. The high point comes at 8am sharp the following morning with the *Narrensprung* (Parade of Fools), which is repeated on Shrove Tuesday at both 8am and 2pm. This features a cast of colourfully dressed characters in wooden masks. Their names are untranslatable; among them are the friendly *Gschell*, who represents the promise of summer, the fiery *Biss* and the vampire-like *Federahannes*, who both appear to symbolize the winter months, and *Fransenkleid*, a haughty aristocratic woman.

in September. On a more highbrow note, there's a series of **concerts** of Renaissance and Baroque music in late April/early May, and of chamber recitals later in the month, while for a fortnight in October a mixed programme of drama, cinema, exhibitions, jazz and classical music takes place.

The Upper Danube valley

For much of its course through Germany, the **Danube** gives little hint of the great river it is to become. Most of the famous landscapes with which it's associated lie in the Balkans, yet there's a short stretch early in its course which is equal to anything downstream. Known as the **Bergland Junge Donau** (Mountain country of the young Danube), this begins just beyond Donaueschingen and continues as far as Sigmaringen. The **rail** line to Ulm, the *Donautalbahn*, closely follows the mazy path of the river and ranks as one of the finest scenic routes in the country. There are services every couple of hours or so; the only snag is that there are relatively few stops.

The river valley forms the centrepiece of the **Naturpark Obere Donau**, which stretches northwards to the Heuberg, the highest range of the Swabian Jura; about half the area is forest, though a large amount is used for farming. It's superb country for **hiking**, particularly above the valley, where there are any number of belvederes offering wonderful views of the river's meandering course. If you've an interest in **flora**, note that springtime sees the countryside awash with snowdrops, narcissi and daphnes, while orchids and the tall Turk's Cap Lily blossom at the end of the season. Autumn is if anything even more beautiful; the white limestone rocks of the valley are perfectly offset by the golden tones of the trees and shrubs lower down. Plenty of inexpensive accommodation makes the region ideal for a break away from the crowds.

Beuron and around

BEURON lies right in the heart of the Junge Donau at the point where the scenery is at its most dramatic, about 15km beyond Tuttlingen, where there's a junction between the *Donautalbahn* and the rail line between Stuttgart and Switzerland. It's immediately obvious that religion has loomed large in this place – one of the tall, seemingly impenetrable rocks on the opposite bank of the Danube is crowned by a large cross.

The village itself, laid out on a terrace above the river, nestles round the enormous **Kloster**. Completely rebuilt in the Baroque period, its size belies the fact that very few monks (sometimes no more than 15) ever actually lived there. Architecturally, the late seventeenth-century monastic buildings are superior to the church, which dates from forty years later. By south German standards, it's fairly restrained, though the nave vaults are decorated with colourful frescoes; the legend of the monastery's foundation is sandwiched between scenes from the lives of its patron saints, Martin and Augustine. Try to catch one of the main services (High Mass Mon–Sat 11.15am, Sun 10am; Vespers Mon–Sat 6pm, Sun 3pm) to hear the stark, ethereal beauty of the monks' **Gregorian chant**.

Practicalities

Information on the walks in the *Naturpark* is available during normal working hours from the **tourist office** (☎07466/214) in Beuron's Rathaus. Here you can also obtain a list of private houses with **rooms** to let (①–③). Otherwise, the cheapest place to stay is the pilgrims' *St-Gregorius-Haus* (☎07466/202; ④) opposite the Kloster at Wolterstr. 9; the only **hotel** as such is *Pelikan*, Abteistr. 12 (☎07466/406, fax 07466/408; ④). The nearest **campsite** (☎07579/559) is in the incorporated village of Hausen im Tal to the north; and the youth hostel is located 6km out of town (see below).

Hikes around Beuron

Among the many wonderful **hikes** which can be made around Beuron, two stand out. Back in the direction of Tuttlingen (but reached via the Holzbrücke, at the opposite side of town from the Bahnhof), you come after 6km to **Knopfmacherfelsen**, the finest of all the belvederes overlooking this stretch of the Danube. To the east, a similar distance away, is **Burg Wildenstein**, a feudal castle-stronghold dating back to the eleventh century in a stunningly precarious situation overlooking the Danube; part of it now houses a **youth hostel** (☎07466/411; ☎).

Sigmaringen

Just beyond Hausen is the last stretch of high cliffs; between Thiergarten and Gutenstein, they are replaced by jagged rock needles. Thereafter the landscape is tamer, though there are exceptions, notably at **SIGMARINGEN**, next stop on the train line to Ulm, 20km from Beuron. This pint-sized princely capital came into the hands of the **Hohenzollern** dynasty in 1535, having at one time belonged to their rivals, the Habsburgs. The branch of the family who lived here remained Catholic and supplied the last ill-fated kings of Romania. They were very much junior relations of their Berlin cousins, but provided a useful south German foothold for the Prussians during their predatory takeover of the country last century.

Sigmaringen's main **festivals** are *Fastnet* and the *Donaufest*; the latter is held at the end of July and features a small-scale version of the fishermen's jousts made famous in Ulm.

The town

The little town is completely dominated by its photogenic **Schloss** (guided tours daily Feb–April & Nov 9.30am–4.30pm, May–Oct 9am–4.45pm; DM6). However, the Schloss is essentially a product of the final phase of the Romantic movement, a sort of Swabian counterpart to "Mad" Ludwig's castles in Bavaria, which moves abruptly from one pastiche style to another. Only the towers remain from the medieval fortress, which was sacked in the Thirty Years' War, then ravaged by fire in 1893. The *Waffenhalle*, with over 3000 pieces of arms and armour, is one of the best private collections in Europe; it's also a reminder of just how much the Hohenzollerns' rise to national leadership owed to their militarism. A dream-like neo-Gothic hall contains a good collection of south German paintings and sculptures of the fifteenth and sixteenth centuries, including works by the so-called **Master of Sigmaringen**, who was actually two people: the brothers Hans and Jacob Strüb. The entry ticket also covers admission to the **Kutschenmuseum**, a collection of historic coaches housed in the former stables.

Beside the Schloss is the Rococo **Johanniskirche**, containing the shrine of Saint Fidelio, a local man who became the first Capuchin martyr when he was murdered in 1622 by the fiercely Calvinist inhabitants of the Grisons region of Switzerland. In the town itself, there's nothing much to see, other than the usual array of half-timbered houses, mostly dating from the Baroque period.

Practicalities

The **tourist office** (Mon–Fri 9am–12.30pm & 2–5.30pm, Sat 9am–noon; ☎07571/106233) is at Schwabstr. 1, between the Bahnhof and the Schloss. If you want to use Sigmaringen as a base for touring the Danube valley and the Swabian Jura, there are a few **hotels** in town: *Eichamt*, Donaustr. 15 (☎07571/14918; ④), *Traube*, Fürst-Wilhelm-Str. 19 (☎07571/12227; ④) and *Jägerhof*, Wentelstr. 4 (☎07571/2021; ⑤) are worth trying. The **youth hostel** is at Hohenzollernstr. 31 (☎07571/13277; ☎) on the northeastern side of town and there's a **campsite** (☎07571/5479) by the Danube. The local *Zoller* **beer** is widely available.

Blaubeuren

Between the next two train stops, Mengen and Riedlingen, there's an extensive stretch of marshland on the right bank of the Danube, frequented by many species of waterfowl. After Ehingen, the *Donautalbahn* leaves the Danube and loops towards Ulm via **BLAUBEUREN**, which lies in a wonderful amphitheatre-like setting at the edge of the Swabian Jura. With its mix of natural and artistic attractions, this ranks as one of the most enticing places in the region and a good choice as a **hiking** base. The rocky hills above not only afford marvellous views over the red roofs of the spaciously laid-out little town and the wilder landscape beyond; they also offer constant surprises, such as labyrinths, caves, grottoes and ruined castles.

The Blautopf and Hammerschmiede

At the opposite end of town from the Bahnhof is the **Blautopf**, a shady pool formed during the glacial period; it's the source of the River Blau, the Danube tributary from which the town derives its name. In spite of its small size, the Blautopf is 20m deep, and its waters have a constant temperature of 9°C. The best time to see it is on a sunny or showery day. In bright weather, the pool is a deep rich blue, but the rain turns this successively to a lighter shade, then green, then a yellowish brown. Alongside is the **Hammerschmiede** (daily 9am–6pm; DM2), a remarkable piece of industrial archeology. Built in the mid-eighteenth century as a water-mill, it was converted into a smithy at the beginning of the following century, before doing service as a mechanical workshop up until 1956, when it was finally retired – though the clanking machinery is still in full working order.

The Kloster

To the side of the Blautopf is the extensive complex of the former **Kloster**. Just 25 years after it had been completely rebuilt in late Gothic style, Württemberg went over to the Reformation; the monastery was disbanded and the buildings were put to use as a Protestant school. As in Maulbronn, with whose seminary Blaubeuren is now united, there's a remarkably complete picture of a monastic community, with a series of picturesque half-timbered workshops lining the courtyard. You can wander around and also in the cloister with its abutting lavabo and chapter house with tombs of the patrons.

The **Klosterkirche** (Palm Sunday–Oct 31 daily 9am–6pm; rest of year Mon–Fri 2–4pm, Sat & Sun 10am–noon & 2–5pm; DM3) ingeniously preserves the tower of its Romanesque predecessor as a barrier separating the monks' choir from the nave. Only the former is kept open: it bristles with flamboyant works of art, among which the **high altar** – the only one of its kind to have escaped the iconoclasts – stands out. It's a co-operative work by at least two major Ulm studios – that of the sculptor **Michel Erhart** and his son **Gregor**, and of the painter **Bartholomäus Zeitblom**, who was assisted by **Bernhard Strigel** and at least one other pupil. When closed, it illustrates the Passion; the first opening shows scenes from the life of St John the Evangelist, patron of the Kloster. The carved heart of the retable has figures of the Virgin and Saints flanked by reliefs of *The Adoration of the Shepherds* and *The Adoration of the Magi*. Originally, this part was only shown on the major feast days of the church calendar. Nowadays, it can be seen any time a tour group is passing through, though the only guaranteed times are Sundays at 2.30pm and 3.30pm.

Also within the monastery walls is another survivor which is unique of its kind, the **Badhaus**, which was added to the amenities in 1510. It now houses the local museum (April–Oct Tues–Fri 10am–4pm, Sat & Sun 10am–5pm; DM1.50), but the main interest is in the building itself – on the ground floor, you can see the baths and heating system, while upstairs is a room decorated with hunting frescoes. The archeological part of the collection is housed in the **Spital** (same times and ticket), the most imposing of the half-timbered houses in the town centre.

Practicalities

There's a **youth hostel** at Auf dem Rucken 69 (☎07344/6444; ②) on a hill at the eastern side of town, between the Bahnhof and the Blautopf. Alternatively, there are several **hotels** including *Gasthof zum Waldhorn*, Klosterstr. 21 (☎07344/6342; ②), *Adler*, Karlstr. 8 (☎07344/5027; ④), *Löwen*, Marktstr. 1 (☎07344/96660; ④) and *Ochsen*, Marktstr. 4 (☎07344/6265; ⑤). All of these have **restaurants**, with that in *Ochsen* having the edge over the others. Tourist **information** is available at the Rathaus, Karlstr. 2 (☎07344/1317) during office hours.

Ulm

Right on the border with Bavaria, **ULM** lies on the Danube, 18km downstream from Blaubeuren, and 85km southeast of Stuttgart. The city is famous for having the highest church spire in the world, and for being the birthplace of one of the all-time giants of science, **Albert Einstein**. Hermann Hesse, on a prewar visit, was entranced by its "ancient fishermen's homes tilted at an angle in the water, tiny houses on the city ramparts, stately burghers' residences in the alleys, an unusual gable here, a majestic doorway there".

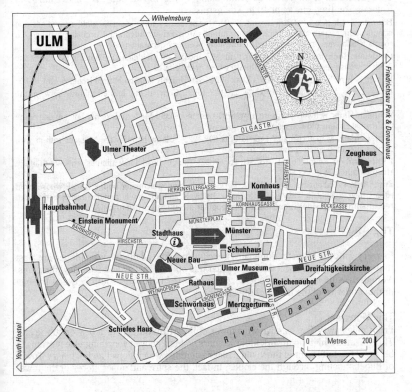

> The **telephone code** for Ulm is ☎ 0731

Regrettably, some perseverance is now necessary for enjoyment of Ulm; a single air raid at the end of 1944 caused one of the worst devastations suffered by any German city, wiping out the vast majority of the historic centre. Much of this had to be rebuilt quickly. Try not to let this put you off; many of the finest streets escaped lightly and many painstaking restoration projects have been undertaken in recent years. Moreover, only superficial damage was inflicted on Ulm's magnificent centrepiece, the **Münster**.

Arrival, information and accommodation

The **Hauptbahnhof** lies to the west of the town centre and an unprepossessing shopping precinct leads straight to Münsterplatz. The **tourist office** (Mon–Fri 9am–6pm, Sat 9am–12.30pm; ☎161 2830) is housed in the Stadthaus, an audacious new building in front of the Münster. There are **motorboat trips** on the Danube every afternoon (May to early Oct; DM9) departing from the Metzgerturm.

Accommodation

There's a good choice of **hotels** right in the city centre, while Ulm's **youth hostel** is 4km southwest of the centre at Grimmelfinger Weg 45 (☎384455; ❷); take tram #1 to Ehinger Tor, then bus #4 or #9 to Königstrasse.

Bäumle, Kohlgasse 6 (☎62287, fax 602 2604). One of the few hotels in an old building, and one that is outstanding value at the price. Its restaurant (Mon–Fri evenings only) occupies two fine old rooms which have preserved their late nineteenth-century decoration. ③

Goldener Bock, Bockgasse 25 (☎28079, fax 921 7668). Good middle-range hotel in the east of the Altstadt whose restaurant is one of the very best in the city. ⑤

Rösch, Schwörhausgasse 18 (☎65718, fax 602 2584). Homely pension in the Fischerviertel. ③–⑤

Roter Löwe, Ulmer Gasse 8 (☎62031, fax 602 1502). Conveniently located midway between the Hauptbahnhof and the Münster. ⑥

Schiefes Haus, Schwörhausgasse 6 (☎967930, fax 967 9333). Modern designer hotel in one of the city's most famous old houses. ⑧

Ulmer Spatz, Münsterplatz 27 (☎68081, fax 602 1925). Classy hotel by the Münster with its own garden and a top-notch restaurant. ⑦

Ulmer Stuben, Zinglerstr. 11 (☎67041, fax 67027). Budget hotel a few minutes' walk south of the Hauptbahnhof. ③

Zum Anker, Rabengasse 2 (☎63297). Very friendly and welcoming budget hotel, whose front rooms have a fantastic view of the Münster. Its lively and absolutely genuine Spanish wine bar-restaurant (closed Mon) is one of the most popular meeting places in town. ③

The city

In every way, the Münster dominates the city, dwarfing all the other buildings, not least those on Münsterplatz, the setting for markets on Wednesday and Saturday mornings. Nonetheless there are atmospheric quarters to the north and south between the natural boundaries of the hills and the Danube.

The Münster

From miles away, the massive west tower of the **Münster** acts as a beacon to the city. The 161-metre-high openwork **steeple** soars so high above everything else it seems to be a real-life fulfilment of those old master paintings which depict an imaginary Tower of Babel shooting through the clouds. In fact, the spire and upper storey of the tower

THE BUILDING OF THE MÜNSTER

Work on the Münster began in the last quarter of the fourteenth century under the direction of the most famous master mason of the day, **Heinrich Parler**, and was continued by his descendants. Credit for its ultimate appearance, however, must go to the head of the succeeding dynasty, **Ulrich von Ensingen**, who altered the plans to make the church wider and loftier, and designed the lower part of the great tower. Despite the Münster's huge size, it was built as, and remains, no more than a parish church. An expression of a vain civic pride, its capacity of 20,000 was more than twice the population of the city, then one of the largest in Germany. At the end of the fifteenth century, when the structure was substantially complete, the architect **Matthäus Böblinger** made a drawing (which can be seen in the Ulmer Museum) for the completion of the tower, reaching to a height that had never previously been attempted. When he tried to build it, however, cracks appeared in the masonry and he fled in disgrace. As his successor's main problem was to repair the existing building, no more work was done on the tower, and the project was abandoned altogether when the city formally adopted the Reformation in 1530. It was only when the Romantic movement re-awakened interest in the Middle Ages that steps were taken to finish it.

were for centuries no more than a seemingly impossible dream and were only finished in 1890, faithfully following drawings made four hundred years before.

As you might expect, the tower offers a stupendous **view** from its platform (daily June–Aug 8am–6.45pm; times reduce seasonally to 9am–3.45pm; DM3.50). A fair amount of puff is needed to climb the 768 steps, but you're rewarded with a panorama which stretches over the city and the Danube to the Swabian Jura and Black Forest, with the Swiss Alps visible on a clear day. On the final stage, there's also the rare opportunity to see the filigree architecture of an openwork spire at close quarters.

In accordance with Ulm's great sculptural tradition, there are no fewer than five superb **portals** to the Münster; that under the tower is appropriately the grandest. Above the doorway are depictions of the *Book of Genesis*, while the pillars have masterly statues of saints in the "Soft Style" of **Master Hartmann**, the first Ulm sculptor known by name. The ensemble is completed by a poignant *Man of Sorrows* (now replaced by a copy; the original can be seen inside), an early work by **Hans Multscher**, the founding father of the remarkable group of late Gothic and early Renaissance German sculptors.

THE INTERIOR

The sense of massive space in the **interior** is as overwhelming as the tower's great height; the impression is aided by the simplicity of the design, which comprises a wide nave of five aisles culminating in a single chancel, with no intervening transept. The best time to come here is on a bright morning, when the sun's rays filter through the stained-glass windows onto the magnificent set of **choir stalls**: "a bold oaken outburst of three dimensional humanism" was how Patrick Leigh Fermor described them. Made between 1469 and 1474 under the direction of two local men, **Jörg Syrlin the Elder** and **Michel Erhart**, the sheer profusion and originality of their carvings – particularly the vibrant life-sized busts – immediately grab your attention. They're a hymn of praise to the achievements of the antique as well as of the Christian world, with women, for once, given the same recognition as men.

Ulm's obsession with the steeple motif can be seen in the huge canopy covering the **font**, and in the sounding board added to the **pulpit** which includes, high up above the column capitals, a second pulpit inaccessible to a human preacher – a symbol that the sermon was really delivered by the Holy Ghost. It's seen even more spectacularly in the slender, tapering **tabernacle**, a structure of gossamer delicacy for all its towering height. In spite of its figurines of popes and bishops, this somehow survived the iconoclasm which denuded the Münster following the introduction of the Reformation. Over the triumphal arch leading to the chancel is a colossal crowded **fresco** of *The Last Judgment*, placed so that every member of the congregation could see it. As an antidote to the massiveness of the Münster, the **Besserer-Kapelle** to the right of the chancel is a small family chapel still retaining its beautifully drawn and coloured fifteenth-century stained glass windows.

The Rathaus

That other self-conscious symbol of civic pride, the **Rathaus**, is situated just a block away from the Münster across Neue Strasse, the central arterial road. Even in a country as rich in picturesque town halls as Germany, there's none quite so photogenic as this disparate jumble of buildings, which has been restored to a pristine approximation of how it looked in 1540. In this year, the northern front was rebuilt in the Renaissance style and equipped with an arcaded passageway; the local painter **Martin Schaffner** was then let loose on the exterior walls, covering them with a series of brilliantly coloured **frescoes** of religious subjects, plus allegories of the Vices and Virtues. On the southern side of the building he painted battle scenes, along with a barge (symbolizing Ulm's dependence on the Danube), plus the coats of arms of the city's trading partners. Between the windows here are polychrome statues of six of the Electors, carved the previous century by Master Hartmann. Even more luxuriant is the eastern facade, with figures by Multscher of Charlemagne, the Kings of Hungary and Bohemia, and two pages; there's also an elaborate astronomical clock made in 1520.

Inside the Rathaus, you can see a replica of the equipment used in 1811 by **Albrecht Berblinger**, "The Tailor of Ulm", in an ill-fated attempt to fly across the Danube; widely regarded in his own day as an eccentric fool, he's since been elevated to the status of a local hero. In 1944, the Rathaus formed an appropriately grand backdrop for the notorious state funeral of Field Marshal Erwin Rommel, who accepted this consolation prize, along with a draught of poison, rather than face trial and certain public execution for his alleged involvement in the July Plot against Hitler.

Marktplatz

To the rear of the Rathaus is the **Marktplatz**, preserving a few old houses but dominated by the brightly coloured **Fischkasten** (Fish Crate), finest of the many old fountains in the city. Made during the late fifteenth century in the workshop of Syrlin the Elder, it features statues of three saints attired as knights, bearing the coats of arms of city and Empire. In Taubenplätzle, just off the eastern end of the square, is the bronze **Delphinbrunnen**; a century younger, it was formerly part of a water-tower.

Behind stands a Renaissance mansion which has been adapted to house the **Ulmer Museum** (Tues–Sun 11am–5pm; DM5). On the ground floor are choice examples of the city's artistic heritage; the **original figures** from the Rathaus and several of the fountains have been moved here. Alongside further works by Multscher and Erhart are carvings by **Daniel Mauch**, whose Italianate style represents the last flourish of Ulm's great sculptural tradition. The city's heritage in painting is far less rich, but Schaffner's *Eitel Besserer* (a descendant of the family who endowed the chapel in the Münster) is a masterpiece of Renaissance portraiture, and there are several works by an influential master of the previous generation, **Bartholomäus Zeitblom**. Highlight of the archeology department is a weird *Statuette of a Woman with the Head of a Lioness*, which dates back to 30,000 BC. Upstairs, Ulm's history is extensively documented, with an illuminating section on the construction of the Münster.

The Neuer Bau and Schwörhaus

Westwards down Neuestrasse is the vast bulk of the **Neuer Bau**, a municipal warehouse built in the sixteenth century; its pentagonal courtyard contains a graceful staircase tower and a fountain with a statue of Hildegard, one of Charlemagne's wives.

Turning left into Sattlergasse, you come to Weinhof, whose main building is the early seventeenth-century **Schwörhaus** (Oath House). Each year, the mayor addresses the citizens from the balcony, taking an oath according to the constitution of 1397 by which he must be "the same man to rich and poor alike in all common and honourable matters without discrimination or reservation". This was an advanced statement for its time, and is often taken as evidence that medieval Ulm was a democratic state. In fact, what the document signified was a passing of power from the patrician class to the guilds, who established an inbuilt majority for themselves on the council.

The Fischerviertel and southern quarters

One of the most interesting features of Ulm is the way the old patterns of settlement can still be clearly discerned. Between the Schwörhaus and the Danube is the celebrated **Fischerviertel** (Fishermen's Quarter), whose quaint scenes of half-timbered houses, waterways, courtyards and tiny bridges so delighted Hermann Hesse. This was actually the area where the artisan classes lived – the island on the Blau and the streets alongside were inhabited by tanners and millers, while on Fischergasse you can see a boatman's house at no. 18, a baker's at no. 22, and a fisherman's at no. 23. Look out for the **Schiefes Haus** (Crooked House), a hefty half-timbered building from about 1500 standing beside a remnant of the twelfth-century fortifications; it takes its name from its pronounced tilt over the river, into whose bed it's fastened by stilts. Another picturesque vista is on Fischerplätzle, which looks towards Häuslesbrücke and boasts the late fifteenth-century **Zunfthaus** (the fishermen's guildhall) and the seventeenth-century **Schönes Haus**, adorned with a scene of shipping on the Danube.

From here, you can walk high above the Danube along the medieval ramparts, now laid out as a shady promenade with a view over the backs of the Fisherviertel. Parallel with the Rathaus is the most impressive surviving gate, the **Metzgerturm** (Butchers' Tower), locally dubbed "The Leaning Tower of Ulm" because it slants a good 2m from the vertical. Beyond Herdbrücke is the patrician **Reichenau Hof**, while Grünen Hof just to the north has the oldest intact buildings in Ulm – the Romanesque **Nikolauskapelle** (whose interior has Gothic frescoes), and a stone house of similar date. Nearby is the **Dreifaltigkeitskirche**, a plain Lutheran preaching house in the late Renaissance style, incorporating the Gothic chancel of the monastery which previously stood on the site. For a really superb **view** of Ulm, with the Münster rearing high up behind the houses of the Fishermen's Quarter, cross over to the quays of Neue-Ulm, the city's southern extension but actually in neighbouring Bavaria.

The northern quarters

The merchants and craftsmen of medieval Ulm tended to live in the streets north of Neue Strasse. These aren't nearly so well preserved, but some fine buildings remain. Just behind the Münster's east end is the sixteenth-century **Schuhhaus**, the guildhall of the shoemakers; it's now used for art exhibitions. Beyond is the Judenhof, the former ghetto; no. 10 seems to pre-date the pogrom of 1499. The streets immediately north of the Münster contain rows of simple houses once inhabited by skilled craft workers, along with several stores, finest of which is the **Kornhaus**. In spite of its self-confident look and its current function as a concert hall, this was built as a panic measure at the end of the sixteenth century in the belief that there would soon be a famine. Look out also for Herrenkellergasse 12, whose turret served as an observation post for fathers trying to keep an eye on the evening jaunts of their eligible daughters.

Further north on Frauengrabben and Seelengrabben are terraces of soldiers' houses from the early seventeenth century, beyond which is the **Zeughaus** with a monumental Renaissance gateway and other surviving parts of the medieval fortifications. Ulm's military role reached a peak in the mid-nineteenth century with its transformation into a fortress of the German Confederation. This citadel was seventeen years in the making, but never once had to withstand a siege; the crumbling buildings are dotted all round the outer perimeter of the city. Finest is the **Wilhelmsburg**, an intact fort crowning the commanding heights of the Michelsberg at the extreme north of the city; it's well worth climbing up for the **view**. If you walk up via Frauenstrasse, you can see the **Pauluskirche**; built to serve the Protestant members of the garrison, it ranks as one of the finest Jugendstil churches in Germany.

Wiblingen

WIBLINGEN, 5km south of central Ulm and reached by bus #3 or #8, is now a large dormitory suburb but for centuries was no more than a hamlet clustered round the Benedictine **Abtei**. The present extensive complex was erected in a leisurely fashion throughout the eighteenth century. Only twenty years after completion, the abbey was secularized; the monastic quarters are now used by the University of Ulm.

Left of the entrance is the **Bibliothek** (April–Oct Tues–Sun 10am–noon & 2–5pm; Nov–March Sat & Sun 2–4pm; DM3), lavishly adorned with stuccowork of shells, leaves and putti, columns painted pink and blue to resemble marble, large allegorical statues representing the Virtues and a colossal ceiling fresco glorifying wisdom, with subjects from the Bible and pagan mythology freely mixed together. The **Basilika St Martin**, which is later in date, shows a shift from Rococo self-indulgence towards the solemnity of Neoclassicism. On the flattened domes are masterly, highly theatrical *trompe l'oeil* frescoes by **Januarius Zick**, with a foreshortened *Last Supper* and a cycle illustrating *The Legend of the Cross*.

Eating, drinking and entertainment

Ulm has a wide range of good places to eat and drink, with the Fischerviertel and the streets north of the Münster both ideal areas for a pub crawl. There's also a decent choice of good entertainment.

Restaurants

Allgäuer Hof, Fischergasse 12. Pancakes are the main line here, with 41 varieties to choose from, but the usual hearty German fare is available as well.

Drei Kannen, Hafenbad 31/1. Traditional *Gaststätte* housed in an old *Brauhaus* with an adjoining Renaissance loggia and beer garden.

Gerberhaus, Weinhochberg 9. Reasonably priced choice for high-quality Swabian fare. Closed Fri.

Herrenkeller, Herrenkellergasse 4. *Gaststätte* with a pedigree dating back to the seventeenth century, serving both Swabian and Bavarian dishes. Closed Sun pm.

Kornhäusle, Kornhausgasse 8. Small place specializing in salads and crepes.

Pflugmerzler, Pfluggasse 6. High quality restaurant offering regional cuisine.

Weinkrüger, Weinhofberg 7. Excellent wine bar-cum-restaurant.

Zunfthaus der Schiffleute, Fischergasse 31. The old fishermen's guildhall, decked out as a cosy restaurant offering an excellent range of Swabian cuisine.

Zur Forelle, Fischergasse 25 (☎63924). Arguably the best restaurant in Ulm, particularly for fish dishes. Limited capacity, so booking is advisable. Closed Sun.

Zur Lochmühle, Gerbergasse 6. Occupies an old water mill with a big beer garden, and serves both local and international cooking.

Bars and cafés

Barfüsser, Lautenberg 1. *Hausbrauerei* serving its own beer plus a good range of food.

Café Tröglen, Münsterplatz 5. One of a number of excellent traditional cafés grouped around the Münster. Closed Sun.

Rebstöckle, Rebengasse 6. Tiny *Weinstube* offering wines drawn from vats. Closed Sun.

Ulmer Brettle, Rabengasse 10. Lively student bar.

Ulmer Weizenbierhaus, Kronengasse 12. Popular bar that's a mecca for all lovers of the tart and refreshing *Weizenbier*, with over 20 varieties to choose from. Open daily 4pm–3am.

Entertainment

In 1641, Ulm became the first city in Germany to establish a permanent civic **theatre**; its modern successor, the *Ulmer Theater*, Olgastr. 73 (☎161 4444) presents drama, opera and operetta; it also has a small cinema. For cabaret, there's *Theater im Fundus*, Deinselsgasse 11 (☎602 4560). **Concerts** and large-scale spectaculars are featured at the *Congress Centrum*, Basteistr. 40 (☎922990); more intimate highbrow musical events are held in the *Kornhaus* on Kornhausplatz (☎161 7670). Choral music is performed in the Münster every other Saturday, while the five-manual organ can be heard daily between 11am and noon. There's jazz most evenings at *Sauschsdall*, Prittwitzstr. 36 (☎23077), and there are live rock bands and alternative film programmes at *Charivari*, Stuttgarter Str. 13 (☎36333).

Festivals

The main annual **popular festival** is *Schwörmontag* on the penultimate Monday of July; this begins at 11am in the Weinhof with the mayor's taking of the oath, and continues in the afternoon with a barge procession down the Danube. On the preceding Saturday evening there's the *Lichterserenade*, with thousands of illuminations. Each June, the *Stadtfest* is held in Münsterplatz. However, the most spectacular local tradition, *Fischerstechen* (Fishermen's Jousting), a colourful tournament with boats in place of horses, is only held at four-year intervals (next in July 2001). Prior to the competitions, there are processions and dances in the streets.

The Upper Swabian spas

Upper Swabia (*Oberschwaben*) is a triangular-shaped area of rich farmland to the south of the Danube; this is one of the least urbanized parts of the country, with no major cities and only a few medium-sized towns. In the heart of Upper Swabia is a group of health resorts, each specializing in mud bath (*Moorheilbad*) cures, and lying on both of the area's two tourist routes, the **Baroque Road** (*Barockstrasse*) and the **Spa Road** (*Bäderstrasse*). Any one of these is a good choice for a relaxing break, or as a base for exploring the whole region. Although the spa resorts and magnificent Baroque and Rococo monasteries are well known to the Germans themselves, they're little visited by foreigners.

Bad Schussenried

BAD SCHUSSENRIED lies some 60km southwest of Ulm on the rail line to the Bodensee; alternatively, it can be reached by bus from Riedlingen in the Danube valley via Bad Buchau, the least interesting of the four Upper Swabian spa towns. Ultra-modern clinics now form a large part of its overall appearance, but the Baroque buildings of the huge former Premonstratensian **Kloster** at the northeastern edge of town retain their pre-eminence.

The monastic church, now the **Pfarrkirche St Magnus**, was built by a whole team of architects, including several members of the prolific Beer and Thumb families. Save for the single tower with its distinctive onion dome, it's rather plain on the outside, but the interior, set beneath Januarius Zick's **ceiling frescoes** of scenes from the life of St Norbert, the order's founder, is far more arresting. Highlight of the furnishings is the set of **choir stalls**, whose backs have limewood reliefs providing a complete illustrated Bible. However, the church is rather overshadowed by the **Bibliotheksaal** (April–Oct daily 10am–noon and 2–5pm; Nov–March Mon–Fri 2–4pm, Sat & Sun 10am–noon & 2–4pm; DM2.50) in the former conventual buildings. There's no library in all of

Germany to compare with this luxuriant creation, designed by **Dominikus Zimmermann** at the same time as he was working on the famous Wieskirche in Bavaria. It's a masterly balance of colour, light and shade, with the white porcelain statues contrasting with the pink marble columns and the ethereally blue bookcases with their *trompe l'oeil* volumes. The ceiling fresco, appropriately enough, is a glorification of Wisdom in both heavenly and earthly guises.

Bad Schussenried's **Bahnhof** is in Kürnbach, an incorporated village 1.5km south. To the rear of the station is the **Freilichtmuseum** (April & Oct Mon–Sat 10am–5pm, Sun 11am–5pm; May–Sept Tues–Sat 9am–6pm, Sun 11am–6pm; DM3), a collection of redundant rural buildings from the surrounding area, though the centrepiece, a large seventeeth-century farmhouse, is original to the spot.

Practicalities

There are about thirty houses with **rooms** to let (①–③); the main concentrations are at the southern end of the main part of town, on Welfenstrasse, Blasius-Erler-Weg and Mozartstrasse. The best **hotels** are *Barbara,* Schulstr. 9 (☎07583/26503; ③) and *Amerka,* Zeppelinstr.13 (☎07583/94250; ④). A full list of places to stay is available from the **tourist office** (Mon–Fri 9am–noon & 2–5pm, Easter–Sept also Sat 10am–noon; ☎07583/940171) in the *Kurverwaltung,* Georg-Kuess-Str. 10.

Steinhausen

STEINHAUSEN, 5km northeast of Bad Schussenried, but always an integral part of the town, is well connected by bus. The settlement clusters round the **Wallfahrtskirche**, a building of the highest artistic importance, being generally accepted as the earliest church in the full-blown Rococo style where architecture, painting and decorations are all fused into an indivisible whole. This unity was made possible by the close collaboration between the **Zimmermann brothers**: Dominikus as architect, Johann Baptist as painter. The church consists of a large nave and a tiny chancel, both oval in shape; pristine white pillars, which look as if they're made of china, shoot up to the vault, whose **fresco**, an evocation of Heaven in limpid pastel colours, seems to be a continuation of the architecture. No less remarkable is the **stuccowork**, with its superbly crafted depictions of the animal, bird and plant kingdoms.

The main **pilgrimages** are on Good Friday and on the day of the patron saints, Peter and Paul (29 June). Across from the church is a **hotel**, *Landgasthof Linde* (☎07583/2381; ③) with a good restaurant; an even better place to eat is *Zur Barokkirsche,* Dorfstr. 6.

Bad Waldsee

Some 15km southeast of Bad Schussenried, and reached either by bus or by a looping branch rail line, is **BAD WALDSEE**, which enjoys a pretty setting on an isthmus between two lakes, and which benefits from a rather more animated market-town feel than its soporific neighbour.

From just outside the Bahnhof, you get a fine view of the town over the Stadtsee, the larger of the lakes and a popular boating centre. Rising above everything else is the Baroque **Stiftskirche**, whose twin-facade towers are set at startling angles to one another. It's yet another church in which Dominikus Zimmermann had a hand: he created the multicoloured high altar, plus the smaller ones to the side. However, the greatest treasure is a resplendent early Renaissance bronze epitaph in the northern aisle, nicknamed *Der eiserne Mann* (The Iron Man), to a local noble.

In the medieval town centre are a number of half-timbered houses and step-gabled public buildings; the most notable are the **Kornhaus** and the **Rathaus**. Further west is the Renaissance and Baroque **Schloss** of the local grandees, the House of Waldburg-

Waldsee. It's closed to the public, but you get a good view of the exterior by walking round the rustic-looking Schloss See, the smaller of the town's lakes.

Practicalities

The **tourist office** (Mon–Fri 8am–noon & 2–5pm, May–Sept also Sat 10am–noon; ☎07524/941342) is in the *Kurverwaltung* at Ravensburger Str. 1 beside the Rathaus and can provide a complete list of all the rooms available in **private houses** (①–③). There are also several **hotels**, including *Altes Tor,* Hauptstr. 49 (☎07524/97190; ⑥) and *Grüner Baum,* Hauptstr. 34 (☎07524/97900; ⑥); the latter has one of the best **restaurants** in a town which is noticeably better off for places to eat and drink than the other spas in the region. The main local **festival** is the *Altstadt-und Seenachtfest* in August, featuring a fireworks display over the Stadtsee.

Bad Wurzach

The last of the spas, **BAD WURZACH**, 12km further southeast, is very similar in feel to Bad Waldsee and there are regular bus services between the two towns. The best time to visit is on the second Friday in July, when Upper Swabia's most distinctive **festival**, the *Heilig-Blut-Fest*, takes place. Here this takes the form of a mounted pilgrimage to the Baroque church on the **Gottesberg**, the hill to the south; over 1500 horses take part, with their riders decked out in colourful costumes.

Dominating the main Marktstrasse is the dignified white **Schloss**, now a school run by Jesuits. Although the castle is mostly closed to the public, the main entrance is generally kept open to enable visitors to see the resplendent Baroque **staircase** and its gloriously profane ceiling fresco of *The Apotheosis of Hercules*. On Schulstrasse, the eastern continuation of the street, is the **Kloster Maria Rosengarten**, a functioning convent whose ornate Rococo chapel can be visited. However, the most intriguing monument is the half-timbered **Leprosenhaus** (Easter–Oct Fri, Sun & holidays 2–5pm; free) at the edge of town on the road southwest to Ravensburg; a leper colony existed there from the mid-fourteenth century until the end of the eighteenth century.

North of town is the **Wurzacher Ried**, 14 square kilometres of moorland punctuated by woods and tarns with an extraordinarily rich indigenous flora and fauna. The whole area is a nature reserve and is listed by the Council of Europe as a landscape of outstanding botanical and geological importance.

Practicalities

The **tourist office** (Mon–Fri 9am–noon & 2–5pm, Easter–Nov Sat 9am–noon; ☎07564/302150) is in the *Kurverwaltung* at Mühltorstr. 1. A generous number of **private rooms** (①–②) are available as in the other spas; prices if anything are slightly lower. Bad Wurzach is also the only one of the towns with a **campsite** (☎07564/3482); it's by the outlying village of Wiesen about a kilometre to the southeast. There are a couple of excellent **hotels**, both with restaurants, in the centre: *Adler*, Schloss Str. 8 (☎07564/93030; ⑤), and *Rössle*, Schulstr. 12 (☎07564/2055; ⑥).

Weingarten and Ravensburg

Just over 30km south of Bad Schussenried on the main rail line to the Bodensee are two adjacent towns which are so close together as to be virtually one unit, yet which are very different in appearance and jealously guard their own municipal independence. Both are foundations of the Welf dynasty, one of the two most powerful families of early medieval Germany, and one which held sway in its later base in Lower Saxony right up to the twentieth century.

Weingarten

The town of **WEINGARTEN**, nowadays quite a bustling place, was originally no more than an adjunct to the huge hilltop Benedictine **Kloster** of the same name, which remains the sole monument of note. At the end of the seventeenth century, plans were drawn up to transform this, one of Germany's most famous medieval monasteries, into the principal centre of monasticism north of the Alps. Such an ambitious project was never fully realized, but the Baroque complex which was built is nonetheless the largest monastery in the country and an active centre of Roman Catholic education.

The **Basilika** is strikingly reminiscent of St Peter's in Rome and is a colossal structure, even if, both in its length and the height of its central dome, it's only about half the size of its great model. Inside, the vivacious **ceiling frescoes** by Cosmas Damian Asam glorify Christ, the Virgin and St Benedict; no less eye-catching are the **choir stalls**, Josef Anton Feichtmayr's first major commission. However, the most impressive feature of the furnishings is the **organ** by Josef Gabler, a particularly ingenious design, with the pipes housed in a series of towers specially constructed so as not to obscure the facade windows.

As in Bad Wurzach, the *Heilig-Blut-Fest* is the main **festival**; the monastery's most treasured relic is the focus of the procession. If you want to stay, there are several good **hotels,** including *Baren,* Kirchstr. 3 (☎0751/561200; ⑤) and *Alt Ochsen,* Ochsengasse 5 (☎0751/561040; ⑤), both of which have recommendable restaurants. Liveliest **bar** in town is *Schwinderhannes,* Liebfrauenstr. 37, which has a beer garden.

Ravensburg

If most of Upper Swabia seems too provincial and too relentlessly Baroque, then the regional "metropolis" of **RAVENSBURG** offers a refreshing antidote. This former Free Imperial City became, courtesy of the linen trade, one of the richest towns in Germany in the fifteenth century. Even if it lacks a spectacular centrepiece, its medieval core presents an unusually satisfying and well-preserved townscape, dominated by the towers and gates of the former fortifications, now laid out as a promenade encircling the heart of the old city.

The town

Marienplatz, which is really a broad street rather than a square but which is used for outdoor markets, lies at the heart of the city, with a whole series of public buildings from the period when Ravensburg was at the height of its prosperity. An indication of the importance of commerce to the city is the fact that the **Rathaus** is overshadowed by the **Waaghaus** alongside; the latter had the weigh house and mint (Ravensburg was long a major centre for coin production) on the ground floor, with the trading hall upstairs. It was adorned in the mid-sixteenth century with the **Blaserturm**, a watchtower crowned by a Renaissance octagon which has become the symbol of the town.

Not far from the Bahnhof, on the corner of Charlottenstrasse and Untere Breite Strasse, is the **Vogthaus** (April–Oct Tues–Sat 3–5pm, Sun 10am–noon & 3–5pm; July & Aug also Mon 10am–noon; free), a half-timbered patrician residence of the fifteenth century. It's now the local museum, but the house itself, which includes rooms in Gothic, Renaissance and Baroque styles, is the main attraction. Further down the street is the **Zehntscheuer**, a large timber-framed building of the previous century which looks for all the world like a farmhouse; previously part of the leper hospital, it's now an arts centre. Behind it is part of the Stadtmauer, including the round **Wehrturm** and the tall square **Gemalter Turm** (Painted Tower), which preserves the jazzy decoration which was once a feature of all of Ravensburg's towers.

A few minutes' walk east is another corner of the wall, with the round **Grüner Turm** (Green Tower) and the step-gabled **Frauentor**. Another tower here doubles as the belfry of the **Liebfrauenkirche**, the town's parish church. From the original fourteenth-century building, there remains the beautiful portal tympanum with scenes from the life of the Virgin. The interior has often been remodelled but preserves some fine stained-glass windows in the chancel. It formerly contained one of the masterpieces of fifteenth-century German sculpture, Michel Erhart's *Ravensburg Madonna* (a haunting carving showing the Virgin sheltering humanity under her cloak), but this has been replaced by a copy, the original now being in the Skulpturensammlung at Dahlem in Berlin.

Bachstrasse leads southwest from Marienplatz to the **Untertor**, while Marktstrasse snakes up to the other main gateway, the **Obertor**. Continuing upwards, and therefore out of the boundaries of the old city, you come to the **Mehlsack** (Sack of Flour), a cylindrical tower erected by the independently minded city council in the sixteenth century as an extra line of defence against the expansionist designs of the aristocratic owners of the **Veitsburg**. A path climbs up steeply to this fortress, imperiously perched on the hill above; on the way you pass through the half-timbered **Burghaldentorkel**, the only surviving example of twenty buildings in the town where grapes were stored and pressed. The original Veitsburg has completely disappeared, leaving only some later workshop buildings, now modernized as the youth hostel, and a small Baroque pavilion which houses a restaurant. However, it's well worth going up for the sake of the wonderful **views** of the town you get on the way.

Practicalities

The **tourist office** (Mon 8am–12.30pm, Tues–Fri 8am–12.30pm & 2–5.30pm, Sat 9am–noon; ☎0751/82324) is at Kirchstr. 16. Centrally sited **hotels** include *Gasthof Ochsen*, Eichelstr. 17 (☎0751/25480; ③), *Café Baur*, Marienplatz 1 (☎0751/25616; ⑤), *Obertor*, Marktstr. 67 (☎0751/36670; ⑦) and *Waldhorn*, Marionplatz 15 (☎0751/36120; ⑧). The **youth hostel** has an atmospheric location in the Veitsburg (☎0751/25363; ⑧). Good choices for **food** and **drink** are *Räuberhöhle*, Burgstr. 14, *Ratstube*, Marienplatz 19, *Altes Lädele*, Seebruckstr. 2, *Brotlaube*, Gaspinstmarkt 25 and the restaurant in the Veitsburg. Best of all are the restaurants in the *Hotel Waldhorn*, one of these, the *Weinstube Rebleubehaus*, occupies a medieval guildhall. *Fastnet* and the *Rutenfest* in July are the main **festivals.**

THE BODENSEE

The **Bodensee** (also know as Lake Constance, or the *Schwäbisches Meer* – the "Swabian Sea") is in reality an enormous bulge in the River Rhine, which enters it from the Austrian side to the east and leaves it again on the Swiss border to the west. It's the largest lake in Germany, 14km across at its widest point and about 65km long, and one of its most popular holiday destinations. Its main, eastern part is known as the Obersee, while the northern of the western forks is the Überlinger See, the southern the Untersee. Thanks to its balmy, dry climate the Bodensee has developed into the nearest the country comes to having a Riviera, though thankfully the shorelines have been preserved from high-rise developments. **Meersburg** and **Überlingen** on the northern side are two of Germany's most picturesque towns; across the water are **Konstanz**, the most cosmopolitan centre in this whole region, and the contrasting islands of **Mainau** and **Reichenau**.

The north shore

Of the three countries bordering the Bodensee, Germany has the lion's share of the shoreline, including the entire northern side. Although the warm climate means that the sweep-

BOAT TRIPS ON THE BODENSEE

By far the largest operator of passenger ships on the lake is the *DB*-affiliated *Bodensee-Schiffsbetriebe (BSB)*, whose main offices are: Seestr. 22, Friedrichshafen (☎07541/201389); Hafenstr. 6, Konstanz (☎07531/281398); and Am Hafen, Lindau (☎08382/6099). *DB* rail passes are valid; there's also a special Bodensee Pass available for various periods (eg DM33 for 3 days, DM57 for 7 days), which allows half-price travel by ship, train or bus. However, normal fares are very reasonable, being calculated at similar rates to other forms of public transport. Bikes can be taken on board without extra charge. Frequency of services is very seasonal, but free current timetables are available at all the harbours. Excursion cruises are run in summer, though these offer few advantages over the main scheduled routes, which are:

- Friedrichshafen–Romanshorn (Switzerland). The only car ferry operated by the company.
- Kreuzlingen (Switzerland)–Konstanz–Reichenau–Schaffhausen (Switzerland). The most scenic of the routes, continuing along the Rhine and terminating at the Rheinfall.
- Konstanz-Reichenau–Rudolfzell
- Konstanz–Meersburg–Friedrichshafen–Lindau–Bregenz (Austria).
- Konstanz–Meersburg–Mainau–Überlingen.

Perhaps the most useful crossing of all, however, is the car ferry across the very heart of the lake between Konstanz and Meersburg. Run by the *Stadtwerk Konstanz* (☎07531/8030), it operates throughout the day and night, with frequencies ranging from fifteen minutes to one hour. In addition, various smaller companies offer excursions on the lake; check locally for the best deals.

ing views across to the Alps are often lost in haze, this is nevertheless one of the most beautiful parts of Germany, with a couple of the country's most outstanding small towns as added attractions. A **corniche road**, served by regular buses, runs all the way along the shore from the eastern end at Lindau (see p.190). This is far preferable to the rail line, which deviates inland, though the ferries (see above) offer the best means of seeing the lake.

ZEPPELINS AND DORNIERS

Count Ferdinand von Zeppelin, a native of Konstanz, was intrigued by the use of hot-air balloons in the American Civil War, which he witnessed as an official observer. He developed the idea to build a rigid airship with a cigar-shaped trussed frame supported by gas cells; the first model, the LZ-1, was tested in Friedrichshafen (which thereafter became both the manufacturing and launch base) in 1900. These strange, silent machines, capable of going at no more than 35 kilometres per hour, were turned from their original peaceful purpose to undertake bombing missions in World War I. Afterwards, however, their potential for long-distance travel was realized, and in 1928 the new, specially built *Graf Zeppelin* made the first transatlantic passenger flight, then a round-the-world trip the following year. By 1937 it had made 590 flights, including 114 ocean crossings. Disaster then struck when the huge new airship *Hindenburg* crashed while landing in New Jersey, killing 36 passengers. No more flights were undertaken, and production was not resumed after the factory's destruction in the war, although by then a safe, non-inflammable gas had been developed.

Claude Dornier, originally an employee of Zeppelin, used the Bodensee to test his "flying boats", but eventually moved into the production of fighter aircraft. His planes were deployed extensively in the Blitz, something which seems to have been a sore point with the French occupying forces in 1945, who systematically looted the factory. Unlike its counterpart, this was revived and is still in operation under the management of Daimler-Benz.

Friedrichshafen

Situated at the widest part of the Bodensee, 22km west of Lindau and 19km south of Ravensburg, **FRIEDRICHSHAFEN** is best known for its distinguished place in aviation history (see opposite), Despite being the only industrial blot on the lake, it manages a decidedly curious double existence, taking full advantage of its setting to serve as a rather flashy resort.

The eastern part of the waterfront has been laid out as an attractive promenade with gardens. At the far end is the one historical monument of any note, the Baroque onion-towered **Schlosskirche**, built at the very end of the seventeenth century by Christian Thumb. Its monastic buildings were converted into a palace for the Kings of Württemberg last century and are still in private hands.

At the opposite end of town in part of the Bauhaus-style Hafenbahnhof at Seestr. 22, is the new **Zeppelin-Museum** (Tues–Sun 10am–5/6pm; DM10). This contains a number of original aircraft, a reconstruction of a section of the famous *Hindenburg* (which can be boarded for inspection) and fascinating archive film (English soundtrack available) of the Zeppelins. There's also an art gallery, dominated by the works of the folksy school of painters based in the Bodensee in the fifteenth century.

Practicalities

Friedrichshafen has two train stations: the **Stadtbahnhof** near the promenade and the **Hafenbahnhof** further east by the commercial harbour. The **tourist office** (May–Sept Mon–Fri 8am–noon & 2–5pm; Oct–April Mon–Thurs 8am–noon & 2–5pm, Fri 8am–1pm; ☎07541/30010) is just across from the former at Bahnhofplatz 2.

Good budget **hotels** include *Pension Wurster*, Georgstr. 14 (☎07541/726940; ③), and *Ailinger Hof*, Ailinger Str. 49 (☎07541/22788; ③). If you want something more upmarket, try *City-Krone*, Schamstr. 7 (☎07541/7050; ⑤) or *Buchhorner Hof*, Friedrichstr. 33 (☎07541/2050; ⑥). The **youth hostel** is in the eastern part of town at Lindauer Str. 3 (☎07541/72404; ❷) and there are two **campsites** (☎07541/73421 and ☎07541/42059) on the other side of town. The best place to **eat** is the classy *Kurgartenrestaurant* in the *Graf-Zeppelin-Haus,* Olgastr. 20, which has a terrace overlooking the lake.

Meersburg

MEERSBURG, which clings to a steeply sloping site 16km from Friedrichshafen, is one of those places which perfectly fits the tourist-board image of Romantic Germany. It therefore usually swarms with an uncomfortably large number of day-trippers, but it's an atmospheric and picturesque little town well worth braving the hordes to see.

The town

Arriving by the corniche road, which at this point passes high above the Bodensee, you enter the historic quarter via the dignified **Obertor**. It's then just a short walk down to the riotously picturesque **Marktplatz**, where three streets converge. Steigstrasse, lined on both sides with half-timbered houses, then plummets towards the lake; its west side, with a sloping ramp giving access to the houses, is particularly eye-catching.

All over town, you get tantalizing glimpses of its great pride and joy, the **Altes Schloss** (daily March–Oct 9am–6pm, Nov–Feb 10am–5pm; DM7), whose round corner towers and gabled central block produce a distinctive silhouette. Founded by the Merovingian King Dagobert, it boasts of being the oldest surviving castle in Germany, a claim recently substantiated by the discovery that some sections of the masonry do actually appear to date back as far as the seventh century. For most of its history, it was a seat of the Prince-bishops of Konstanz, who extensively rebuilt it throughout the medieval period, making it their main residence when they were bundled out of their city at the Reformation; since secularization, it has been in private ownership. Germany's greatest woman poet, **Annette von Droste-Hülshoff**, came to live here during the 1840s as guest of the then-owner, her brother-in-law, Baron von Lassberg. Her rooms, whose period furnishings are in stark contrast to the austerity of the medieval chambers, are still as they were in her day, and many of her most famous poems are exhibited on the walls.

The **Neues Schloss** above was built under the direction of Balthasar Neumann in the mid-eighteenth century, when the Prince-bishops decided they warranted a more comfortable and modern residence. It now houses a cultural centre and local museum (April–Oct daily 10am–1pm & 2–6pm; DM4), which includes displays on Claude Dornier and the fifteenth-century Cologne painter Stefan Lochner, who is thought to have been a native of the town. There's a wonderful view over the Bodensee from the gardens in front; an even better one can be had from the belvedere known as the **Känzele** a short walk to the east.

Practicalities

The Seepromenade below the Altes Schloss, lined with cafés and restaurants, many specializing in fresh fish from the lake, is the most popular rendezvous point. Here also is the **harbour** for the *BSB* ships; the terminal for the **car ferry** to Konstanz is some 700m west. **Buses** stop near the latter, as well as near the Obertor; Meersburg is not on the rail line. The **tourist office** (Mon–Fri 8am–noon & 1.30–5pm; April–Sept also Sat 10am–2pm; ☎07532/82383) is at Kirchstr. 4 at the top of the town.

If you want to base yourself in only one resort while touring the Bodensee, Meersburg is probably the best choice, as its central location means that everywhere is within easy reach. There is no youth hostel or campsite, but otherwise there's ample accommodation. Cheapest options are the **guesthouses**: there's a cluster on Stettener Strasse near the eastern entrance to town, such as *Gästehaus Irmgard* at no. 39 (☎07532/9494; ④), and *Haus Mayer-Bartsch* at no. 53 (☎07532/6050; ⑤). Another concentration can be found further west and uphill on Von-Lassberg-Strasse, the view compensating for the steep climb up; at no. 1 is *Säntisblick* (☎07532/9277; ③). It usually costs far more to stay in the old part of town; an exception, with an excellent situation in the street behind the waterfront, is *Pension Klingenstein*, Unterstadtstr. 14 (☎07532/6630; ②). Among a host of enticing upmarket hotels are the two historic inns on Marktplatz: the seventeenth-century *Gasthof Zum Bären* at no. 11 (☎07532/43220; ⑤) and the fifteenth-century *Löwen* at no. 2 (☎07532/43040; ⑥). Pick of the lakeside hotels are *Café Off,* Uferpromenade 51 (☎07532/333; ⑦) and *Residenz am See,* Uferpromenade 11 (☎07532/80040; ⑦), which boasts a rose garden as well as a terrace. The best views of all can be had from *Terrassenhotel Weisshaar,* Stefan-Lochner-Str. 24 (☎07532/45040; ⑦). All these upmarket hotels have excellent restaurants.

Unteruhldingen and Birnau

Next resort along the lake, 7km away, is Uhldingen-Mühlhofen, a federation of several previously separate villages. Shoreside **UNTERUHLDINGEN** has the most unusual open-air museum in Germany, the **Pfahlbauten** (guided tours daily April–Sept 8am–6pm; Oct daily 9am–5pm; March & Nov Sat & Sun 9am–5pm; DM6), containing conjectural re-creations of Stone Age dwellings, remains of which were found here, built on huge wooden stilts driven into the bed of the lake. Come early as the queues are usually horrendous.

About twenty minutes' walk uphill is the Cistercian **Basilika Birnau**, whose wonderful, isolated setting is now marred by the proximity of the main road. Built in just four years, it's a collaboration by three of the finest Rococo artists – the architect Peter Thumb, the fresco painter Gottfried Bernard Göz and the sculptor Josef Anton

Feichtmayr. The dazzling interior is a paean of praise to the Virgin Mary; its illusionistic tricks reach a climax in the cupola which incorporates a mirror to enhance its effects. Look out for the famous statuette known as the *Honigschlecker* (a cherub sucking the finger that has just been inside a bee's nest); it's placed beside an altar dedicated to St Bernard of Clairvaux, in honour of the claim that his words were as sweet as honey.

Überlingen

A further 5km on, the former Free Imperial City of **ÜBERLINGEN**, nowadays a specialist *Kneipp* health resort, rises gently above the lake. For sheer good looks and polished appearance, it has few rivals in all of Germany: with its magnificent public buildings of a distinctive pale green stonework, picturesque alleys of half-timbered houses, glorious lakeward vistas and luxuriant gardens, it seems almost indecently favoured for a place whose population has never numbered more than a few thousand.

Among the town's **festivals**, the most important is the *Schwedenprozession*, commemorating this Catholic town's successful defence of its independence against the Swedes in the Thirty Years' War. This is performed twice annually: on the Sunday after May 16, and on the second Sunday in July. *Fastnacht* is also a big annual event and bizarrely features Bengali costumes.

Münsterplatz

Dominating the town is the **Münster**, a huge Gothic structure which was constructed over a period of two hundred years. Its two towers make a fascinating pairing. The tall square clock tower to the south, which provides a landmark visible from far off, was specially heightened to serve as a watchtower, and crowned with an octagonal Renaissance lantern. In contrast, its stumpy northern counterpart which houses the huge *Osanna* bell, nestles under a steeply pitched wooden roof which looks as though it should belong on a barn rather than a church. The sobriety of the rest of the exterior sharply contrasts with the majestic interior, whose intricately vaulted nave of five aisles, built in the second half of the sixteenth century, shows the by then archaic Gothic style bowing out with a bang. Also marking the end of an era is the tiered main **altarpiece**, carved by Jörg Zürn in the early seventeenth century, which was the last of the great series of wooden retables illustrating Biblical stories which adorn so many German churches; soon after, these were completely supplanted by more florid Baroque altars. Zürn also made the graceful tabernacle alongside, while he or members of his family carved four of the altars which adorn each of the fourteen nave chapels.

Across Münsterplatz, and backing onto Hofstatt, the market square, is the **Rathaus** (Mon–Fri 9am–noon & 2.30–5pm, Sat 9am–noon; free). Its first-floor **Ratsaal,** complete with panelled walls, projecting arches and a ribbed ceiling, is a masterpiece of late fifteenth-century design.

The rest of town

Climbing up either Krummebergstrasse or Luitzengasse on the northern side of Münsterplatz brings you to the **Reichlin-von-Meldegg-Haus** (Tues–Sat 9am–12.30pm & 2–5pm, Sun 10am–3pm; DM4), another late fifteenth-century building, named after the wealthy doctor whose home it was. The interiors include a chapel and an ornate Rococo **Festsaal**, but most of the space is taken up by a surprisingly good **Heimatmuseum**, including the largest collection of dolls' houses in Germany, ranging from Renaissance to Jugendstil. From the balcony at the end of the gardens is the best **view** in Überlingen, showing the town etched out against the background of the Bodensee and Swiss Alps.

Above the northwest side of Münsterplatz is the **Franziskanerkirche**, with a spare, gaunt exterior typical of the mendicant orders. Its interior, however, was given the full Baroque treatment. More striking than the church is the late Gothic **Franziskanertor**, the northern entrance to the town. This is one of seven surviving gateways and towers of the **Stadtmauer**, which has now been laid out as a shady promenade.

The waterfront is dominated by the Neoclassical **Greth**, crowned with a huge slanting roof. Just to the west is the gabled Gothic **Zeughaus** (May–Sept Mon–Sat 10am–noon; DM2), containing a private collection of arms and armour. At the end of the promenade are the *Kurpark* and spa quarters.

Practicalities

The **Bahnhof** lies at the extreme western end of town, but **buses** stop on the one-way streets immediately south of the Münster. The **tourist office** (Mon–Fri 8am–noon & 2–6pm, Sat 9am–noon, Sun 10am–noon; ☎07551/991122) is housed in the Greth, Landungsplatz 14.

Hotels are plentiful, though mostly pricey by Bodensee standards, being geared to the lucrative spa market. Among the less expensive options are *Haus Klemm*, Zum Hecht 66 (☎07551/63749; ③), and *Gästehaus Mainamblick*, Zum Stichling 6 (☎07551/63474; ④). Among many fine upmarket choices, those with lakeside views include *Reichent*, Seepromenade 3 (☎07551/63857; ⑥), *Bad-Hotel*, Christophstr. 2 (☎07551/8370; ⑥), *Seegarten*, Seepromenade 7 (☎07551/63498; ⑦) and *Parkhotel St Leonhard*, Obere-St-Leonhard-Str. 71 (☎07551/808100; ⑧). Each of these has a recommendable **restaurant**. There's a large modern **youth hostel** at the eastern end of the waterside at Alte Nussdorfer Str. 26 (☎07551/4204; ✆), and four separate **campsites** in the vicinity: one (☎07551/64583) in the town itself, close to the Bahnhof, the others in Nussdorf a couple of kilometres down the lake.

Salem

SALEM, a group of villages 11km east of Überlingen, is centred on the great **Reichsabtei** (guided tours April–Oct Mon–Sat 9am–6pm, Sun 11am–6pm; DM8) of that name. Formerly a Cistercian monastery, and the mother house of Birnau, it was taken over on secularization by the Grand Dukes of Baden and remains in the possession of their descendants. Part of the complex is now occupied by one of Germany's most exclusive schools, founded by Kurt Hahn who later emigrated to Britain and established Gordonstoun. There's also a **hotel**, *Schwanen* (☎07553/283; ⑥), which has an excellent restaurant.

The **Münster** is rarely used for public worship and hence has an inevitable coldness about it. Nonetheless, it's an outstanding example of the grandly sober Gothic architecture of the Cistercians, with their favoured characteristics of a large chancel terminating in a flat east end. In the eighteenth century, the church was littered with a series of altars and monuments in a very early Neoclassical style; the marriage of two very different kinds of artistic austerity works surprisingly well. Although originally the conventual part of the monastery, the **Schloss** indeed seems more like a palace, having been built in a luxuriant Baroque style following the destruction of the medieval buildings in a fire. The **Kaisersaal**, a richly decorated reception hall to accommodate any visiting Imperial entourage, is particularly impressive.

Heiligenberg

Commanding a grandstand view over the whole Bodensee area on the heights above Salem and some 7km away by road, is the little *Kurort* of **HEILIGENBERG**; unfortunately, there's no bus directly linking the two, though both have services to Überlingen. Its enormous **Schloss** (guided tours daily April to early July & mid-Aug to Oct

9am–noon & 1–6pm; DM7) came into the possession of the House of Fürstenberg in the sixteenth century; they had the existing medieval castle radically rebuilt, creating a fine Renaissance palace. The **Rittersaal** is outstanding, especially its intricately carved coffered ceiling (which is suspended from the vault on steel rods to support its weight), and the glass paintings of coats of arms. Only marginally less impressive is the brightly painted **Schlosskapelle**, which is arranged more like a theatre than a chapel and has beautiful stained-glass windows brought from the former Dominican monastery in Konstanz. You're allowed up into the family oratory to inspect the vault, with its seemingly inexhaustible series of angels in different guises, at close range.

Between the Schloss and the village is the graceful **Glockenturm** (Bell Tower), built by Jerg Schwartzenberger, the principal architect of the Schloss. There are plenty of **hotels**, including *Bayerischer Hof*, Röhrenbacher Str. 1 (☎07554/217; ③), *Haus Alpenblick*, Betenbrunner Str. 14 (☎07554/355; ③) and *Berghotel Bunden,* Salemer Str. 5 (☎07554/802100; ⑤). The last-named has a renowned gourmet restaurant, but even this faces strong competition from *Restaurant de Weiss im Hohenstein* at Postplatz 5, which doubles as an art gallery.

Konstanz (Constance)

By any standards, **KONSTANZ** has a remarkable geographical position. It's split in two by the Rhine, which re-emerges here from the Obersee (the main part of the Bodensee) as a channel for a brief stretch, before forming the Untersee, the arm from which it finally re-emerges as a river. The Altstadt is a tiny enclave on the otherwise Swiss side of the lake, a fact which was of inestimable benefit during the war when the Allies desisted from bombing it for fear of hitting neutral Switzerland. Curiously

---

THE COUNCIL OF 1414–18

In 1409, the Council of Pisa elected Alexander V pope in an attempt to end the **Great Schism**, which had left rival claimants to the papacy in Rome and Avignon since 1378. Far from solving the problem, however, this left the world with three competing popes. Eventually, Emperor Sigismund forced Alexander's successor, John XXIII, to call an ecumenical council of ecclesiastical and secular rulers in Konstanz in 1414. This became one of the largest and most extraordinary gatherings in world history: the sittings lasted four years, during which time 72,000 visitors (more than seven times the number of the permanent population) flocked to the town. As well as re-uniting the Church, the intention was also to reform it, as its institutions and practices, notably the rite of confession, apostolic supremacy and the granting of indulgences, had come under attack from **Jan Hus**, the first Czech Rector of Prague University, who had gained a large popular following in the process. Hus was guaranteed a safe return passage in order to defend his views, but was imprisoned, tried and condemned as a heretic, and handed over to the secular authorities for burning at the stake.

John XXIII, who realized he was likely to lose his position as pope, attempted to sabotage the council by withdrawing from it, whereupon it issued the highly dubious *Sacrosancta*, affirming its own superiority over the papacy. In 1417, both John and Gregory XII, his Roman rival, agreed to step down in favour of a compromise candidate; although the Avignon pope, Benedict XIII, stubbornly refused to do likewise, he found himself deserted by his supporters and was deposed. The way was therefore cleared for the election of Cardinal Oddo Colonna as Pope Martin V and an end to the schism. Various reforms, primarily financial, were then enacted, but the failure to undertake anything more radical – symbolized by the treatment of Hus – eventually led to a far more serious and lasting split in the Church with the Reformation exactly a century later.

enough, the latter is one country to which Konstanz has never belonged: probably founded by the Romans, it has been a Prince-bishopric and a Swabian Free Imperial City, then Austrian, before finally being allocated to Baden. Between 1414 and 1418, when the conclave met here to resolve the Great Schism, the city was the nerve-centre of European power politics.

Nowadays, it contents itself with more modest roles as a resort town, frontier post and seat of a new university whose students help to give it a relaxed and lively air all year round. The main annual **festival** is the *Seenachtsfest* in August, with a spectacular display of fireworks over the Bodensee, and classical music concerts, the *Konstanzer Internationale Musiktage*, are held throughout the summer.

The town centre

Nearly everything of interest in Konstanz lies in the **Altstadt** which stretches from the southern bank of the Rhine to the very abrupt border with Switzerland about 1km to the south.

The Münster

The famous conclave met in the **Münster**, suitably set on the highest point of the Altstadt. Its subsequent history has been less glorious: once the Reformation had taken hold, the local bishop was driven out of town, and after the see (which dated back at least as far as the seventh century) was dissolved in 1821, the church sank into insignificance. Begun as a Romanesque pillared basilica – whose outline is still obvious – building continued for 600 years, so there are marked differences in style, particularly in the interior: the aisles and their chapels are Gothic, while the organ-case and gallery were built during the Renaissance, and the original ceiling was replaced by a vaulted Baroque one. The spot on which Hus is said to have stood during his trial is marked in the central aisle, by the twenty-fourth row.

Of the furnishings, the most remarkable are the vigorously carved fifteenth-century **choir stalls** designed by Nicolaus Gerhaert, and the broadly contemporary and equally ornate **Schnegg**, a staircase in the northern transept. From here you descend to the **Konradikapelle**, named in honour of Saint Konrad, a tenth-century bishop of Konstanz, who is commemorated by a Gothic funerary slab and a golden shrine. The saint would probably still recognize the tiny **crypt** further on, the oldest surviving part of the building, whose walls are hung with remarkable gilded enamel medallions. Beyond are the Gothic cloisters, off which are several imposing chambers, notably the rotunda known as the Mauritiuskapelle, which houses a magnificent late thirteenth-century **Holy Sepulchre**, inspired by the original in Jerusalem. Next door is the Sylvesterkapelle, with a complete cycle of fifteenth-century frescoes of the life of Christ.

For a fine view of the town, climb up the **tower** (mid-April to mid-Oct Mon–Sat 10am–5pm, Sun 1–5pm; DM1.50). The central lantern and openwork spire of this are nineteenth-century additions to the massive Gothic facade, whose three sections were, unusually, all of similar height, giving it a decidedly forbidding and unecclesiastical look.

Münsterplatz and the Niederburg

On Münsterplatz are a number of fine old mansions, including the **Haus zur Katz**, a fifteenth-century guildhouse which is the earliest example of rusticated stonework in Germany, and the **Haus zur Kunkel** (Tues–Fri 10am–noon & 2–4pm, Sat 10am–noon; free), formerly the residence of the sacristan. Behind the latter's Baroque exterior lurk some original thirteenth-century rooms, one of which features some beautiful early Gothic frescoes showing linen weavers at work; a sign tells you at which door to ring in order to see them.

Between here and the Rhine is the best-preserved part of town, the **Niederburg**, a quarter of twisting little alleys lined by old houses. Overlooking the river are two fragments of the fortifications – the **Pulverturm** and the **Rheintorturm**. The latter, hard by the modern Rheinbrücke which carries the main road and rail line into the heart of Konstanz, is particularly impressive; it dates back to the late twelfth century and preserves some scanty frescos. Across the bridge is **Seestrasse**, a promenade of grandiosely elegant villas, one of which contains the **casino**, a particular magnet to the Swiss.

At the southeast corner of the Rheinbrücke is the exclusive **Inselhotel**, occupying the old Dominican monastery. Its cellars were used to imprison Hus, and it was also the birthplace of Ferdinand von Zeppelin, a statue to whom can be seen overlooking the main **harbour** – a bustle of colourful sails in the summer – just to the south. Behind it is the **Konzilgebäude**, a fourteenth-century storehouse with a prominent hipped roof. It owes its name to the disputed contention that it was the scene of the election of Pope Martin V; nowadays it has been restored to serve as a festival hall and a restaurant.

The Rosgartenmuseum

Konstanz's two market squares, Fischmarkt and Marktstätte, are respectively west and southwest of the Konzilgebäude. South of the latter, along the street of the same name, is the **Rosgartenmuseum** (Tues–Thurs 10am–5pm, Fri–Sun 10am–4pm; DM3), which has a good collection of local archeological finds, in particular from the paleolithic period, and also art and craft exhibits from the Middle Ages. The museum was designed in 1871, and everything, including the original display cabinets, is as it was then, creating a pleasantly musty atmosphere. You might think from the name that the building must originally have had something to do with roses, but it's an old euphemism for the local horse abattoir: the German for horse was traditionally *Ross*, but by omitting one letter people could say *Rosgarten* and ignore its sorry purpose.

At the end of the same street is the **Dreifaltigkeitskirche**, the church of the old Augustinian monastery. It was frescoed during the time of the Council with scenes from the history of the order, plus portraits of various personalities, among them Emperor Sigismund.

The rest of the centre

Returning to Marktstätte, Kanzleistrasse leads west past the Renaissance **Rathaus**, whose facade was jollied up by the addition of Romantic murals. At the end of the street is **Obermarkt**, which is lined with more colourful mansions; here, in 1417, the Hohenzollerns were invested with control over the March of Brandenburg, a crucial step in their drive, achieved four and a half centuries later, to unite the German nation under their control.

Hussenstrasse leads south from here to the **Schnetztor**, a fourteenth-century fortified gateway complete with outer courtyard. On the way you pass, at no. 64, the **Hus-Museum** (June–Sept Tues–Sun 10am–5pm; Oct–May Tues–Sun 10am–noon & 2–4pm; free). This half-timbered house, where the reformer stayed on his arrival in Konstanz, was bought by the Prague Museum Society in 1923 to turn it into a memorial to one of the Czechs' most important national heroes. Apart from his importance as a religious thinker, Hus had a major influence on the Czech sense of nationhood and almost single-handedly established his country's national literature.

Practicalities

The *DB* **Bahnhof**, the terminus of the line from the Black Forest, is right beside the Konzilgebäude; immediately south is its Swiss counterpart, which is the departure point for most **bus** services beyond the urban area. In front of the former, at

Bahnhofplatz 13 is the **tourist office** (Jan–March, Nov & Dec Mon–Fri 9am–noon & 2–6pm; April & Oct Mon–Fri 9am–noon & 2–6pm, Sat 9am–1pm; May–Sept Mon–Fri 9am–6.30pm, Sat 9am–1pm (☎07531/133030/284376). For information on **boat trips**, see the box on p.258. Note that the car ferry to Meersburg is in the suburb of Staad; all other services leave from the harbour behind the Bahnhof.

Accommodation

There are **private rooms** (①–⑤) all over town. Many of the more central **hotels** are in historic buildings and therefore somewhat expensive, though arguably worth it for the atmosphere. At the lower end of the scale are *Pension Gretel*, Zollenstr. 6–8 (☎07531/23283; ④), *Sonnenhof*, Otto-Raggenbass-Str. 3 (☎07531/22257; ④) and *Germania*, Konradigasse 2 (☎07531/23735; ⑤). More upmarket choices include *Barbarossa*, Obermarkt 8–12 (☎07531/22021; ④), *Stadthotel*, Bruderturmgasse 2 (☎07531/90460; ⑥) and *Bayrischer Hof*, Rosgartenstr. 30 (☎07531/22075; ⑦). At the top of the range are the aforementioned *Inselhotel*, Auf der Insel (☎07531/1250; ⑨) which is part of the *Steigenberger* chain and *Seehotel Silben*, which is at Seestr. 25 (☎07531/63044; ⑨) in a modernized Jugendstil villa.

Konstanz's **youth hostel** is at Zur Allmannshöhe 18 (☎07531/32260; **2**; bus #4 from the Bahnhof to *Jugendherberge*, or bus #1 to *Post Allmannsdorf*). There's a **campsite** near the car ferry at Fohrenbühlweg 50 in the suburb of Staad, 4km north of the centre (☎07531/31388), and a couple more further north in the incorporated fishing village of Dingelsdorf: *Klausehorn* (☎07533/6372) and *Fliesshorn* (☎07533/5262); all three can be reached by bus #4. Dingelsdorf also has a couple of competitively priced lakeside hotels: *Gasthaus Seeschau*, Zur Schiffslände 11 (☎07533/5190; ④) and *Gasthaus Anker*, Zur Schiffslände 5 (☎07533/6220; ⑤).

Eating and drinking

Konstanz's best and most expensive restaurant is in the *Seehotel Silben*. Its closest rivals are the nearby *Casino-Restaurant*, Seestr. 21 and the two in the *Inselhotel*, among which the *Dominikanerstube* is a bit less pricey than the showpiece *Seerestaurant*. The *Konzilgebäude*, Hafenstr. 2, also deserves a special mention for both quality and setting. Other good choices are the wine bar-restaurant *St Stephanskeller*, St-Stephans-Platz 43; and *Bürgerstuben*, Bahnhofplatz 7, which features Bodensee fish specialities.

The Bodensee islands

There are only two islands of any size in the Bodensee, and, notwithstanding the fact that both put their rich soils to good use, they could hardly be more different: **Mainau** is an exotic, scented floral isle which seems to have been wafted up from the Mediterranean, while **Reichenau**, which is mostly given over to the cultivation of fruit and vegetables, retains its three ancient monasteries as vivid reminders of its status as one of the cradles of German civilization. Ironically enough, the easiest way to reach either of the islands is by bus (causeways having been constructed to link them to the mainland), though it's obviously far more atmospheric to arrive by boat.

Mainau

Mainau (Easter to mid-Oct daily 7am–8pm; DM16.50, DM5.50 kids; rest of year daily 9am–5pm; DM8, kids free), which lies in the Überlinger See, possesses an aura of immense grandeur, thanks to the riotous colours of the flowers and shrubs which bedeck it, and the exhilarating long-distance views over the lake across to the opposite shore, which are particularly spectacular at sunset. It's like a little tropical paradise – or it would be were it not for the relentless presence of thousands of visitors every day for at least six months of the year. With this in mind, try to come as early as possible: the crowds start to build up by mid-morning. Local bus #4 from the centre of Konstanz stops at the end of the causeway at the western approach to Mainau; ferries between Meersburg and Unteruhldingen call at the landing stage at the opposite side of the island.

For over 500 years Mainau belonged to the Teutonic Knights, and the **Schloss** at the highest point of the island is a typical example of the Baroque architecture they favoured during the time they were based in Bad Mergentheim. It's now the residence of the island's flamboyant Swedish owner, Count Bernadotte, a descendant of the grand dukes of Baden who took possession of Mainau last century. Only the *Schlosskapelle*, with its frothy ceiling paintings and elaborate woodwork, can be visited, though that hardly seems to matter as the carefully manicured gardens, which occupy almost every available part of the island, are what everyone comes to see.

The gardens

A combination of the freak micro-climate and the utilization of scientific techniques means that at least part of the garden is in bloom for half of the year; a unique feature is the presence of three-dimensional **floral sculptures**, which were specially created as diversions for the youngest visitors. **Spring** is the most delightful season here, with a big display of orchids in the Palmenhaus, along with an array of tulips, hyacinths, narcissi and primroses outside; azaleas and rhododendrons appear later. **Summer** sees the rose walk at its best, while palm trees, bananas, lemons and oranges also ripen then. **Autumn** features a dahlia show, whereafter the colour disappears, leaving only the year-round greenery of the cedars, sequoias and cypresses until the cycle starts again.

As well as various snack bars, there are a couple of places where you can have a full **meal**: the *Comturey-Keller*, which has special lunchtime menus, and the classy *Schwedenschenke* uphill by the Schloss. Note that, although you can stay on past the official closing time, you have to be off the island by midnight.

Reichenau

Reichenau, set in the Untersee 8km west of Konstanz, has a history almost as venerable as the city itself. Monastic life was established here in 724, and three monasteries, which all survive, were in place by the end of the ninth century. Many of the early abbots also held high positions in the Holy Roman Empire, and the island was a famous centre of scholarship, literature and painting, with the two arts combined in the great local speciality of manuscript illumination. However, by the twelfth century the monasteries were already in decline, and there was no more than a token monastic presence for several hundred years before the dissolution in 1803. Nowadays, two-thirds of the island's area is devoted to market gardens, giving it a character not dissimilar to the tulip-growing regions of Holland. Very quiet and sedate, it's a popular holiday resort with pensioners and families, who rent apartments around its coast.

The monasteries

Just 4.5km long and 1.5km wide, the layout of Reichenau is easy to grasp. There are three villages, each centred on a monastery. First up is **OBERZELL**, with the church of **St Georg**, the only one of the trio not completely reconstructed at a later date. The dignified Romanesque entrance hall was the sole significant addition made to the original, one of the most complete examples of Carolingian architecture to have survived anywhere in Europe. Inside is a wonderful set of Ottonian **frescoes**, which are about a century younger than the building and show the same style as the famed Reichenau miniatures, albeit on a monumental scale. The eight main scenes, whose colours have been vividly brought out in a recent restoration, illustrate the miracles of Christ – subjects which were mostly eschewed by later artists.

Just over a kilometre further on is **MITTELZELL**, whose large **Münster** is the mother-church of Reichenau. Its present form, apart from the Gothic chancel, dates from the very beginning of the eleventh century and is an impressive sight, particularly when viewed from across the garden on its northern side. The **Schatzkammer** (May–Sept Mon–Sat 11am–noon & 3–4pm; DM1) on the northern side of the chancel contains a carved fifth-century ivory pyx and a poignant Romanesque *Crucifix* from St Georg, along with the usual array of reliquaries.

Towards the far end of the island is **NIEDERZELL**, with the twin-towered twelfth-century Romanesque church of **St-Peter-und-Paul**. This is the least distinctive of the three and is further marred by a fair amount of frivolous Baroque interior decoration, but a fresco of *The Last Judgment*, the final expression of the Reichenau school of painting, can be seen in the apse.

The Wollmatinger Ried

Located between Reichenau and its inconvenient train station (see below) is the **Wollmatinger Ried**, a protected landscape of reedy marsh, islets and flowery meadows inhabited by a rich variety of birdlife which is recognized as being of exceptional importance. An **information centre** (Mon–Fri 9am–noon & 2–5pm, April–Sept also Sat & Sun 1–5pm; ☎07531/78870) has been set up in the Reichenau Bahnhof; **guided visits** (the only permitted method of entry) are usually made daily, except on Sundays and Mondays, throughout the summer.

Practicalities

Reichenau's **tourist office** (May–Sept Mon–Fri 8.30am–noon & 2–6pm, Sat 9am–noon; March, April & Oct Mon–Fri 8.30am–noon & 2–5pm; Nov–Feb Mon–Fri 9am–noon; ☎07534/276) is at Ergat 5 in Mittelzell. There's a **campsite** (☎07534/7384) on the shore in Niederzell, plus a score of **private houses** (①–③) with rooms to let. The most inexpensive **hotel** is *Kaiserpfalz*, Abt-Berno-Str. 1 (☎07534/275; ③), in Mittelzell. If you want to treat yourself, *Seeschau*, An der Schiffslände 8 (☎07534/257; ⑦), overlooking the harbour in Mittelzell, is superb and has one of the best restaurants in the Bodensee area. Of high quality is the nearby *Strandhotel Löchnerhaus*, An der Schiffslände 12 (☎07534/8030; ⑦). Not far away, at Untere Rheinstr. 21, is *Reichenauer Salatstuben*, offering a huge self-service cold buffet.

Ferries between Konstanz and the Swiss city of Schaffhausen call at Reichenau. Otherwise, regular *DB* **buses** leave from outside the Bahnhof in Konstanz; less conveniently, there's a station near the island on the main rail line to the Black Forest.

THE BLACK FOREST REGION

Even in a country where woodland is so widespread as to exert a grip over such varied aspects of national life as folklore, literature and leisure activities, the **Black Forest** or *Schwarzwald* stands out as a place with its own special mystique. Stretching 170km north to south, and up to 60km east to west, it's by far the largest German forest – and the most beautiful. Geographically speaking, it's a massif in its own right, but forms a pair with the broadly similar French Vosges on the opposite side of the Rhine valley, which demarcates the borders with both France and Switzerland. The name of the forest comes from the dark, densely packed fir trees on the upper slopes; oaks and beeches are characteristic of the lower ranges. With its houses sheltering beneath massive

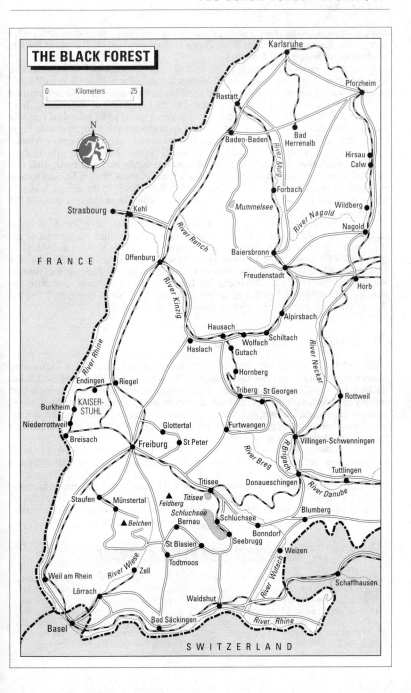

sloping straw roofs, its Black Forest gateau, its cuckoo clocks and its colourful, often outrageous traditional dress, the Black Forest ranks second only to Bavaria as the font of stereotyped images of the country.

Even as late as the 1920s, much of this area was a rarely penetrated wilderness, forming a refuge for everything from boars to bandits. Romantics were drawn here by the wild beauty of watery gorges, dank valleys and exhilarating mountain views. Nowadays, most of the villages have been opened up as spa and health resorts, full of shops selling tacky souvenirs, while the old trails have become manicured gravel paths smoothed down for ramblers and strollers. Yet, for all that – and in spite of fears about the potentially disastrous effects of *Waldsterben*, which may have affected as many as half the trees – it remains a landscape of unique character, and by no means all the modernizations are drawbacks.

Accommodation, for example, is plentiful and generally excellent value. **Rail** fans will find several of the most spectacular lines in Europe, some of them brilliant feats of engineering. Note, though, that the trains tend to stick closely to the valleys, **bus services** are much reduced outside the tourist season, and that **walking** is undoubtedly the most satisfying way to get around.

Most of the Black Forest is associated with the Margraviate (later Grand Duchy) of **Baden**, whose old capital of **Baden-Baden** – once the ultimate playground of the mega-rich – is at the northern fringe of the forest, in a fertile orchard and vineyard-growing area. This was later usurped by custom-built **Karlsruhe**, which is technically outside the Black Forest but best visited in conjunction with it. The only city actually surrounded by the forest is **Freiburg im Breisgau**, one of the most distinctive and enticing in the country. Nestling in the far southeastern corner of Germany, it lies just 30km from the French border and the gateway town of Breisach.

Freiburg im Breisgau

FREIBURG IM BREISGAU, "capital" of the Black Forest, basks in a laid-back atmosphere which seems completely un-German. As the seat of a university since 1457, it has an animated, youthful presence which, unlike so many other academic centres, is kept up all year round, with the help of a varied programme of festivals. It's a city of music, of street theatre and buskers, and a haunt of colourfully clad gypsies. Furthermore, the sun shines here more often, and there are more vineyards within the municipal area than in any other city in the country.

Freiburg's singularity is often attributed to the fact that they aren't Germans at all, but Austrians. Between 1368 and 1805, when it was allocated to the buffer state of Baden, it was almost continuously under the protection of the House of Habsburg. It's often claimed that the Austrians brought a touch of humanity to the German character, and that it was their eventual exclusion from the country's affairs which led to the triumph of militarism. The persistence here of the relaxed multicultural climate characteristic of Austria suggests that there's a grain of truth in this cliché.

FREIBURG'S FESTIVALS

The **Fastnet** celebrations are among the best in Baden-Württemberg; there are burning ceremonies on the evening of Shrove Tuesday, as well as parades of jesters the day before. Both the *Frühlingsfest* in May and the *Herbstsfest* in October last for ten days, and include spectacular fairground amusements. In June, the two-week *Internationales Zeltmusikfest* features all varieties of music, performed under canvas. Later in the month, five days are given over to a wine market known as the *Weintagen*. Mid-August has the nine-day-long *Weinkost*, a sampling session for wines produced in the Freiburg region.

Freiburg makes the most obvious base for visiting the Black Forest, with fast and frequent public transport connections to all the famous beauty spots. In its own right, it warrants a couple of days' exploration at least, and is renowned for its excellent mix of lively bars and restaurants. Even if you're only passing through, you should make a point of visiting Freiburg's lovely **Münster**. Although the city was extensively destroyed in a single air raid in 1944, no modern building has been allowed to challenge the supremacy of its magisterial tower, which the doyen of art historians, Jacob Burckhardt, described as "the greatest in Christendom".

Arrival, information and accommodation

Freiburg's **Hauptbahnhof**, with the **bus station** on its southern side, is about ten minutes' walk from the centre; follow Eisenbahnstrasse straight ahead. The **tourist office** is en route at Rotteckring 14 (June–Sept Mon–Fri 9.30am–8pm, Sat 9.30am–5pm, Sun 10am–noon; Oct–May Mon–Fri 9.30am–6pm, Sat 9.30am–2pm, Sun 10am–noon; ☎388 1880). **Mitfahrzentrale** is at Belfortstrasse 55 (☎19444). The main **post office** at Eisenbahnstr. 58–62 has a poste restante service.

The **telephone code** for Freiburg is ☎0761.

ACCOMMODATION PRICE CODES

All the pensions and hotels in this book have been graded according to the following price categories. The prices quoted are for the cheapest available double room, although many of the budget places will also have more expensive rooms. Youth hostels are graded under separate categories. See p.34 for more details.

① less than DM50   ④ DM81–100   ⑦ DM151–200
② DM51–65   ⑤ DM101–125   ⑧ DM201–250
③ DM66–80   ⑥ DM126–150   ⑨ more than DM250

The tourist office will find you a room free of charge; if you arrive after closing time, there's an electronic noticeboard equipped with a phone telling you which places have vacancies, though this is not an exhaustive service. For the best **budget hotels** you'll need to head out a little way from the centre, although if you are looking for a medium-priced place, Freiburg is one German city where a **luxury hotel** right in the centre of town might well be within your range. There are also plenty of **private houses** with rooms to let (①-⑤).

Freiburg has an excellent **youth hostel** and four **campsites**, although some of these are a bit out of the city. If you're staying far out, it makes sense to invest in a **rover ticket** on the public transport system. Prices for 24 hours are DM7.50 for the city, DM15 for the whole circuit; these rise to DM10 and DM20 respectively for two people travelling together.

Hotels and Pensions

Colombi, Am Colombi-Park (☎21060, fax 31410). The city's leading hotel, well located at the western edge of the Altstadt and boasting all the luxuries including a swimming pool, steam baths, a sauna, solarium, fitness centre and a renowned gourmet restaurant. ⑨

Dionysos, Hirschstr. 2 (☎29353, fax 29138). Greek-run hotel and ethnic restaurant in the south of the city, halfway towards Schauinsland; take tram #4. ③

Haus Gisela, Am Vogelbach 27 (☎82472, fax 81152). Homely, good value pension in the north-western suburbs, reached by bus #10. ④

Markgräfler Hof, Gerberau 22 (☎32540, fax 37947). Occupies a fine fifteenth-century town palace. Its restaurant (closed Sun & Mon), one of the best in town, has a truly amazing wine list. ⑤

Oberkirchs Weinstuben, Münsterplatz 22 (☎31011, fax 31031). Has an ideal location overlooking the Münster, and one of the city's best wine bar-restaurants. ⑦

Rappen, Münsterplatz 12 (☎31353, fax 382252). Another hotel with many rooms overlooking the Münster; also has an excellent restaurant and a cosy *Weinstube*. ④

Schemmer, Eschholzstr. 63 (☎272424, fax 22010). The lowest-priced central hotel, just south of the Hauptbahnhof on the opposite side of the tracks from the Altstadt. ④

Schwarzwälder Hof, Herrenstr. 43 (☎38030, fax 380 3135). Hotel-cum-*Weinstube* in the heart of the Altstadt. ⑤

Waldheim, Schauinslandstr. 20 (☎290494). Pension in the south of the city en route to Schauinsland; take tram #4. ③

Zum Roten Bären, Oberlinden 12 (☎387870, fax 387 8717). Germany's longest-functioning inn, now run by the *Ringhotel* chain, is in a house dated 1120. Nonetheless it offers everything that would be expected of a comfortable modern hotel, including a fine if expensive restaurant (closed Sun pm & Mon). ⑦

Youth hostel and campsites

Breisgau, Seestr. 20 (☎07665/2346). Way to the north in the village of Hochdorf, this site is the cheapest of the five. Open all year.

Hirzberg, Kurtäuserstr. 99 (☎35054). Not far from the youth hostel on the eastern outskirts of the city. Open all year.

IYHF Jugendherberge, Karthäuserstr. 151 (☎67656). Freiburg's luxurious youth hostel is at the extreme eastern end of the city, ideally placed for walks in the hills or along the banks of the River Dreisam. Take tram #1 to Hasemannstrasse. ☎

Mösel-Park (☎72938). South of the houses on the opposite side of the river and reached by tram #1. Open mid-March to Oct.

Tunisee (☎07665/2249 or 1249). An enormous site also located in Hochdorf. Open April–Oct.

The city

As so often, most of what you'll want to see is in the Altstadt, and even here the main sights are concentrated on Münsterplatz and in the museum quarter to the south. However, it's also well worth venturing into the nearby hills for some wonderful views over the city and the Black Forest.

The Münster

Crafted out of a dark red sandstone quarried in one of the surrounding hills, the **Münster** (or **Dom**) is so magnificent and overpowering that it puts the rest of the city in the shade. Not the least remarkable fact about it is that, though it rivals any of the great European cathedrals, it was built as a mere parish church. No funds from the well-lined coffers of the ecclesiastical top brass were forthcoming for its construction – the costs were met entirely from the pockets of local citizens, to whom it was the ultimate symbol of municipal pride. In 1827, on the suppression of the Prince-bishopric of Konstanz, the Münster's artistic standing was given due recognition when it became the seat of the Upper Rhenish archbishopric.

THE EXTERIOR

Work on the Münster began in about 1200, to replace a much simpler church dating from the time of the town's foundation eighty years before. The **transepts** were built first, in the picturesque late Romanesque style then still popular in Germany. However, there was an abrupt change when the masons became aware of the structural advantages of Gothic, which the French had already mastered. At first, the same masons began building in this unfamiliar idiom; later, one of the architects of Strasbourg Cathedral took over. He created a masterly **nave**, resplendent with flying buttresses, gargoyles and statues, already diverging from French models.

Further originality is evident in the west **porch**, begun around 1270. The figures, which still bear traces of colouring, are much the most important German works of their time. A sweetly carved *Madonna and Child* guards the door; above, the tympanum illustrates the entire New Testament. On the end walls, the Wise and Foolish Virgins confront each other, while deliberately shrouded on the west wall (at the point where the natural light is weakest) are the most striking figures: Satan as Prince of Darkness, beguilingly disguised as a youthful knight, and Sensuality, who has toads and serpents writhing on her back.

FREIBURG'S DRAINS

A peculiarity of Freiburg is the continuous visible presence throughout the old part of the city of its **sewage system**, known as the *Bächle*. These are rivulets, fed by the River Dreisam, which run in deep gulleys, serving as a trap for the unwary pedestrian or motorist. Formerly used for watering animals and as a sure precaution against the fire hazard which accounted for so many medieval towns, they have their purpose even today, helping to keep the city cool.

The single **tower** (March–Nov Mon–Sat 9.30am–5pm, Sun 1–5pm; DM2) above the porch was a unique design for its time, but was subsequently much imitated, most notably at Ulm. Though it seems to be an organic unity, it wasn't planned as a whole. The square plan of the lower storeys supports a soaring octagon, bearing animated statues of prophets and angels, which forms the stage above the bells. From the platform, you're rewarded with a fine panorama over the city and the Black Forest. However, the best view is of the lace-like tracery of the **openwork spire**, which rounds off the tower with a bravura flourish. The first of its kind, it was inspired by the mysticism of the time and symbolizes the human soul stretching out to receive divine knowledge. Many similar spires were planned for subsequent German churches, though most remained unbuilt until the nineteenth century. Exceptions are the two miniature versions which were immediately placed on Freiburg's own **Hahnentürme** (Cock Towers).

For the **chancel**, begun in the mid-fourteenth century (about 25 years after the completion of the spire), the authorities again struck it lucky with their choice of architect, a man named Johannes of the famous Parler dynasty. His regular geometric layout marked a major advance on French models, and his two **portals**, particularly the northern one dedicated to the Creation, are adorned with superbly expressive sculptures – look out for the unusual depiction of God resting on the seventh day.

THE INTERIOR

Inside, the transept is lit by luminous **stained-glass** windows of the early thirteenth century. Most of those in the nave date from a hundred years later and were donated by the local trades and guilds, who incorporated their coats of arms. Other items to look out for are a delicate late thirteenth-century *Madonna* on the west wall, a poignant fourteenth-century *Holy Sepulchre* in the south aisle, and the pulpit, an archaic Gothic work of the mid-sixteenth century with depictions of Freiburg personalities of the day. At the entrance to the chancel is a fine *Adoration of the Magi* by the leading local woodcarver of the late Gothic period, Hans Wydyz. This artist sometimes collaborated with the mercurial **Hans Baldung**, Dürer's most talented follower, whose high altar triptych of *The Coronation of the Virgin* – arguably his masterpiece – can be glimpsed from this point.

To see the chancel, and to get a better view of the Baldung triptych, you have to take a **guided tour** (daily departure times posted at the south transept entrance; DM2). In the Universitätskapelle, there are two wings of a curious **Holbein** retable. The portraits of the donor family are by Hans the Elder, but the main scenes of *The Nativity* and *Epiphany* are youthful works by his son, whose superior gifts are already in evidence. A *Rest on the Flight into Egypt* in the Kaiserkapelle has sculptures by Wydyz and a painted background by Baldung, who also designed many of the stained-glass windows in the chapels, though some of these have been replaced by copies. Hans Sixt von Staufen, another talented local sculptor of the time, carved the *Madonna of Mercy* in the Locherer Kapelle. In the Villinger Kapelle is a rare relic of the first Münster, a silver *Crucifix*.

Münsterplatz

Until the war, the spacious **Münsterplatz** formed a fitting setting for the great church in its midst. However, the north side was flattened by bombs (which miraculously hardly touched the Münster itself) and only the late fifteenth-century **Kornhaus**, the municipal granary, has been rebuilt. The rest of the square has survived in much better shape and hosts an excellent daily market. There are also a couple of pretty **fountains** directly in front of the Münster – the *Georgsbrunnen* and the *Fischbrunnen* – along with three tall columns that bear statues of the local patron saints.

The south side of the square is dominated by the blood-red **Kaufhaus**, a sixteenth-century merchants' hall; its arcaded facade bears four statues by Sixt von Staufen of members of the House of Habsburg. On either side of the Kaufhaus are handsome Baroque palaces – to the west is the **Erzbischöfliches Palais** while the

Wentzingerhaus (Tues–Fri 9.30am–5pm, Sat & Sun 10.30am–5pm; DM4) stands to the east. The latter is named after the sculptor Christian Wenzinger who built it as his own residence; it features a resplendent Rococo staircase, complete with frescoed ceiling. In the back courtyard are huge allegorical statues of the Four Seasons by Wentzinger himself. The rest of the house is given over to displays on the history of Freiburg. Münsterplatz is closed on the far side by the canons' residences and the former **Hauptwache** (Guard House). The latter is now home to the *Haus der Badischen Wein* where local vintages can be sampled and bought.

South of Münsterplatz

Following the main channel of the *Bächle* southwards, you come to the **Schwaben Tor**, one of two surviving towers of the medieval fortifications. On Oberlinden, just in front, is **Zum Roten Bären**, which is said to be Germany's oldest inn – a function it has held since 1311, although the building itself is two centuries older. The parallel **Konviktstrasse** has won conservation prizes for the restoration of its old houses.

Just to the west is Salzstrasse, which is lined with Baroque and Neoclassical mansions. Also here is the **Augustinermuseum** (Tues–Sun 10am—5pm; DM4), which takes its name from the former monastery whose buildings it occupies. One of the most pleasing smaller collections in Germany, it makes an essential supplement to a visit to the Münster, containing as it does many works of art, such as gargoyles, statues and stained glass, which have been replaced *in situ* by copies to prevent further erosion. Also on show are examples of the religious art of the Upper Rhine, along with folklore displays on the Black Forest. There are also a few top-class old masters. Three panels of a *Passion Altar*, including the central *Crucifixion*, constitute the most important surviving paintings by the great but mysterious draughtsman known as **Master of the Housebook**. *The Miracle of the Snow* by **Grünewald** is one of the wings of the altarpiece now in Stuppach: it depicts Pope Liberius laying the foundation stone of Santa Maria Maggiore in Rome, following a miraculous fall of snow on Midsummer's Day. As well as his stained glass, **Baldung** is represented by three typically unorthodox paintings, notably a *Cupid in Flight*, while there's a brightly coloured *Risen Christ* by **Cranach**.

South of here, on Marienstrasse, is the **Museum für Neue Kunst** (same hours as Augustinermuseum; free). Though it can't rival the richness of the parent collection, it does have a good cross-section of twentieth-century German painting. Beside it stands the Baroque **Adelhauserkirche**, retaining important works of art from its predecessor, notably a fourteenth-century *Crucifix*. The former convent buildings now house the **Museum für Naturkunde**, which has a dazzling display of gems, and the **Museum für Völkerkunde,** with exhibits drawn from all non-European cultures (both same times as the other museums; free). From here, follow Fischerau, the former fishermen's street, and you come to the other surviving thirteenth-century tower, the **Martinstor**, which now stands in the middle of Freiburg's central axis, Kaiser-Joseph-Strasse.

The western quarters

Immediately west of here is the **Uni-Viertel** (University quarter), the liveliest part of the city during term-time and the best place to check out Freiburg's nightlife (see p.277). Alongside the inevitable modern buildings are several interesting older structures, including two Rococo mansions and a large Jugendstil lecture hall. On Bertoldstrasse, to the north, are the **Universitätskirche**, formerly a Jesuit college, and the Baroque **Alte Universität.**

The **Neues Rathaus**, formed out of two separate Renaissance houses, one of which has an oriel adorned with a noble relief of *The Lady and the Unicorn*, was an earlier home of the University. It forms part of a shady chestnut tree-lined square whose other buildings include the **Altes Rathaus**, itself a fusion of several older buildings, and the plain Gothic Franciscan monastery church of **St Martin**. A few minutes' walk to the west, in the Columbipark opposite the tourist office, is the **Columbischlössle**, a nineteenth-century villa built for a Spanish countess, which served after the war as parliament for the short-lived Land of South Baden (Südbaden). It now houses the **Museum für Ur- und Frühgeschichte** (Tues–Sun 10am–5pm; DM3.50 donation requested), which has important archeological collections on the Black Forest region, particularly from the times of the Alemanni and the Franks; the treasury items in the basement are particularly worth seeing.

In the alley behind St Martin is the cheerful late Gothic facade of the **Haus zum Wallfisch**. For two years, this was the home of the great humanist **Desiderius Erasmus**, the most conciliatory and sympathetic of the leading figures of the Reformation period, who was forced to flee from his residence in Basel in the light of the turbulent religious struggles there. A late fifteenth-century palace nearby, on the main Kaiser-Joseph-Strasse, is known as the **Baseler Hof** as it served for nearly a century as the residence of the exiled cathedral chapter of the Swiss city.

Views of the city

It's well worth climbing one of the hills surrounding the city for the wonderful views they offer. The **Schlossberg** immediately to the east of the city centre is easily reached by a path from the Schwabentor; there's no need to take the cable car. This summit also has the benefit of including close-range views of the Münster. For photography, it's best to come in the morning. To the south, the **Lorettoburg** (where the stone for the Münster was quarried) makes a good afternoon or evening alternative. Far higher, and thus with more spectacular panoramas than either of these, is the **Schauinsland** (1284m), still within the city boundaries but a good 15km southeast, reached by tram #4 to Günterstal, then bus #21. A series of marked nature trails comb the area, which is still inhabited by chamois, or you can ascend by a fifteen-minute cable car ride.

Eating, drinking and entertainment

Freiburg is a wonderful place for food and drink, with **restaurants** and **bars** to cater for all tastes and pockets, the liveliest concentration, as you'd expect, clustered around the University quarter. Some of the best restaurants are in the hotels (see p. 272); for snacks the *Markthalle*, Kaiser-Joseph-Str. 237 is the best place to go. The city has a similarly eclectic choice of other entertainments.

Restaurants

Dattler, Am Schlossberg 1. First choice for *al fresco* eating, with a terrace on top of the Schlossberg commanding a superb view of Freiburg and the Kaiserstuhl.

Exil, Jan-von-Weerth-Str. 9. The best place for vegetarian specialities with bargain lunch menus.

Greiffenegg-Schlössle, Schlossbergring 3. Another good terrace restaurant with a much closer view of the city than from Schlossberg.

Grosser Meyerhof, Grünwälderstr. 7. Top quality south German fare at eminently reasonable prices. Closed Mon & Tues.

Kleiner Meyerhof, Rathausgasse 27. Small and select south German restaurant with good value set lunches.

Le Marrakech, Waldkircher Str. 1. Speciality Moroccan restaurant, located a short walk north of the Hauptbahnhof.

Milano, Schusterstr. 7. Bargain-priced trattoria.

Tessiner Stuben, Bertoldstr. 17. Restaurant-cum-wine bar, complete with garden. Closed Sun.

Wolfshöhle, Konviktstr. 8. One of the best Italian restaurants in the country. Closed Sun.

Zur Traube, Schusterstr. 17. Quieter alternative to the wine bars on nearby Münsterplatz. Closed Sun.

Bars, cafés and discos

Altstadt-Café, Gerberau 12. Good traditional café.

Blue Monday, Waldseestr. 86. Live music pub with beer garden.

Café Atlantik, Schwabentorring 7. Run-down music pub serving very cheap food in the evenings.

Café Journal, Universitätsstr. 3. Popular if fairly expensive student hangout.

Dampfross, Löwenstr. 7. Another student favourite, serving inexpensive meals.

Feierling, Gerberau 46. In addition to the fruity *Inselhopf* beer brewed on the premises, imaginative meals are also served.

Irish Pub, Münsterplatz 11. Regular live music sessions are featured here in the historic setting of the Kornhaus.

Martins Bräu, Fressgässle 1. Another *Hausbrauerei* which makes a blond beer and also has a short but eclectic menu.

Parabel Club, Universitätsstr. 3. Tiny disco. Thurs–Sun 11pm–3am.

Salatstuben, Schieffstr. 5–7 and Löwenstr. 1. Vegetarian cafés with self-service salad bars. Both closed Sun.

Schlappen, Löwenstr. 2. Currently Freiburg's hippest pub.

Subway, Kaiser-Joseph-Str. 248. One of Freiburg's most popular discos, with a predominantly young clientele.

Uni-Café, Niemensstr. 7. The trendiest café with the Freiburg in-crowd; serves a wide selection of coffees and has good snacks.

Theatre and concert venues

Freiburger Theater, Bertoldstr. 46 (☎34874). The city's main theatre venue featuring drama, dance and opera; there are three auditoria plus the *Theatercafé* where late-night cabaret and variety shows are held.

Jazzhaus, Schnewlinstr. 1 (☎34973). Freiburg now ranks as one of the leading German cities for jazz, thanks to this venue which has concerts every evening at 8.30pm.

Kaufhaus, Münsterplatz (☎36890). Hosts small-scale concerts.

Konzerthaus, Konrad-Adenauer-Platz 1 (☎34506). Brand-new state-of-the-art concert hall. It regularly features performances by the renowned radio orchestra, the *SWF Sinfonieorchester*, as well as by the *Freiburger Philharmonisches Orchestrer* and the period-instrument *Freiburger Barockorchester.*

Musikhochschule, Schwarzwaldstr. 141. Often features recitals by high-calibre classical soloists and groups.

Paulussaal, Dreisamstr. 3 (☎23749). Another regular venue for instrumental recitals.

Theater in Marienbad, Marienstr. 4 (☎31470). Children's and youth theatre, housed in a converted Jugendstil swimming pool.

Wallgrabentheater, Rathausgasse 48 (☎25656). An intimate stage in the Altes Rathaus specializing in modern classics and the theatre of the absurd.

Breisach

BREISACH, whose historic heart is perched high above the Rhine on a promontory about 30km west of Freiburg, is an archetypal frontier post in what has been one of the most heavily disputed parts of Europe. Even if the river is now firmly established as a natural border and the town regarded as being indisputably German, the turbulent legacy of its past is still clearly visible. Breisach stands in the shadow of the **Kaiserstuhl**, an isolated volcanic mass in which Frederick Barbarossa, who died on his way to the Holy Land, is said to rest, waiting for his second coming – hence its name, which means "Emperor's Seat".

The town

The lower town (*Unterstadt*) by the Rhine is modern – all the sights are located in the spacious, half-deserted upper town (*Oberstadt*), which is surrounded by the

Some 25km west of Breisach, and served by five buses per day, is the beautiful old Alsatian city of **COLMAR**. French since 1918, Colmar was German for much of its history, as is abundantly clear from its general appearance, and from the fact that most inhabitants are bilingual. It was the home town of medieval artist Martin Schongauer, and a good deal of his work can be seen there; it also possesses Grünewald's titanic *Isenheim Altar*, generally regarded as the supreme masterpiece of Grünewald painting. A short train journey to the north is cosmopolitan **STRASBOURG**, specially chosen as home of the European Parliament in honour of its mixed Franco-German history. It was a free city of the Holy Roman Empire for three centuries and its magnificent cathedral is mostly the work of German masons.

Stadtbefestigung, dating from the thirteenth century. The ramparts visible today bear the unmistakable stamp of the greatest of all military engineers, the Frenchman Sébastien Vauban, who was also responsible for laying out the town of Neuf Brisach on the opposite bank. Indeed, the monumental **Rheintor** at the northwest end of Breisach itself is as purely French a building as can be seen in Germany. Yet, just above it, the gabled medieval **Kapftor** could hardly be more German in feel, and the same applies to the earlier **Hagenbachtor** on the brow of the hill further south. Just beyond this is one of Breisach's many belvederes, offering grandstand views of France.

The Münster

Looming high above all else is the **Münster**. From outside, it's no beauty, fashioned out of rough, diffuse stonework, and truncated on the southern side in order to squeeze into an irregular, constricted space. It was originally built in the late Romanesque period on the foundations of a Roman fortress; the nave, transept and the two "Cock" towers survive from this time. The upper parts of the southern tower were re-fashioned in Gothic style in the early fourteenth century, a period which also saw the construction of a new chancel (under which is an open crypt – apparently the only one of its kind in the world) and the stumpy facade, whose tympanum illustrates the life of the Münster's patron, St Stephen. At the end of the fifteenth century, it was decided to commission new decorations for the interior of the Münster rather than rebuild it; as a result, it came to acquire one of the most impressive arrays of **works of art** of any church in Germany, all created at the transitional point between Gothic and Renaissance.

Filling the three walls of the west end is a huge **fresco cycle** of *The Last Judgment*, sadly very faded, by **Martin Schongauer**, the father-figure of the golden age of German art. Contemporary with the frescoes is the filigree **rood screen**. In the chapel beside it is a silver **shrine** containing the relics of the early martyr-saints Gervase and Protase, which were swiped from Milan at the same time as those of the Three Magi (which were taken to Cologne), and allegedly arrived in Breisach by miraculous means, whereupon they became the joint patrons of the town. The reliefs on the lid include an illustration of this journey, complete with a depiction of fifteenth-century Breisach.

SS Gervase and Protase turn up again on the right wing of the main **retable**, while on the opposite side of the central *Coronation of the Virgin* are the martyred deacons, SS Stephen and Lawrence. This altarpiece is an astonishing piece of wholly eccentric yet hyper-skilled woodcarving. It may be late Gothic, but the entwined mass of cherubs, the swirling hair and drapery folds of the figures are uncannily anticipatory of the Baroque style of over a century later. Many attempts have been made to unmask the identity of the mysterious sculptor, known as **Master HL** after his cryptic signature, but to no conclusive effect. The sinuous upper part of the retable is by a more orthodox carver, but is still remarkable for the fact that it's actually higher than the ceiling, a trick achieved by means of a subtle slant.

Practicalities

Breisach's **Bahnhof** is at the southern end of town; from there follow Neutorplatz and Rheinstrasse and you come to Werd, where you'll find the **tourist office** (Mon–Fri 8.30am–12.30pm & 1.30–5.30pm, Sat 8.30am–noon; ☎07667/83227) at no. 9. Ask here about **Rhine cruises** and visits to **wine cellars** – the town is the headquarters of the largest winery in Europe, the *Zentralkellerei Badischer Winzergenossenschaften* (☎07667/82270).

Breisach makes an excellent base for exploring the Kaiserstuhl. If you want to stay, good, reasonably priced **hotels** include *Gasthof Bayrischer Hof*, Neutorstr. 25 (☎07667/289; ③), *Schlüssel*, Neutorstr. 17 (☎07667/402; ③) and *Breisacher Hof*, Neutorplatz 16 (☎07667/392; ④). Pick of the upmarket establishments are *Kapuzinergarten*, Kapuzinergasse 26 (☎07667/93000; ④–⑧) and *Am Münster*, Münsterbergstr. 23 (☎07667/8380; ⑦). The spanking-new **youth hostel** is by the river at Rheinuferstr. 12 (☎07667/7665; ⑫). Alternatively, there's a **campsite**, *Münsterblick* (☎07667/285), in the village of Hochstetten 2km south. The best **restaurants** are in the last two hotels listed above; there are plenty of cheaper places to eat scattered all over the lower town.

The Southern Black Forest

The southern part of the Black Forest is a mountainous region encompassed by the French border to the west and the Swiss border to the south, and gradually petering out towards the southeast, somewhat before the shores of the Bodensee. At the southern fringe of the region is a beautiful stretch of the Rhine, here dividing Germany from Switzerland. Its landscape of forested hills is especially wonderful around the high points of the **Belchen** and the **Feldberg**. At 1414m and 1493m respectively, they're hardly mountains in the Alpine sense, but on clear days you get vast panoramas from their summits, reaching as far as the Swiss Alps and the western Rhine valley. While there are only two main highways heading from west to east (one following the Swiss border on the southern side of the region, and the road connecting Freiburg to Konstanz on the northern side), **travel** along the fringes of this area is easy and efficient by train. The interior, on the other hand, involves circuitous connections by infrequent bus services.

St Peter and Glottertal

Some 20km east of Freiburg, and connected by regular bus services, **ST PETER** is a tiny health resort clustering round a Benedictine **Kloster**. This was founded in the eleventh century, but the present complex belongs to a rebuilding begun in 1724. Peter Thumb built the striking twin-towered church, a classically inspired Baroque design of unusual width and spaciousness. The monastic buildings, now used as a seminary, are Rococo in style, dating from a generation later. Particularly eye-catching is the galleried library, the **Bibliotheksaal** (guided tours Sun–Wed at 11.30am, Thurs at 2.30pm; DM5), gleaming with white stuccowork and frescoes. Colourful costumed **festivals** are held in the village on Corpus Christi and on the Sunday after the feast day of SS Peter and Paul (June 29).

A few kilometres northwest is **GLOTTERTAL**, reached via the gentle wine-growing valley of the same name. This has gained national fame as a result of the hospital perched above the village, which forms the setting for the soap opera *Black Forest Clinic*, Germany's answer to *Coronation Street* and *Dallas*.

Around Belchen

Belchen, surrounded by deep gorges some 20km south of Freiburg, is the most beautiful of the southern peaks, with wonderful views and quiet little villages in the valleys. The highlight of the region is the serene **Kloster St Trudpert**.

Münstertal

The **Münstertal** is a valley dotted with the characteristic low shingle roofs of traditional Black Forest farms, set among lush pastures clinging to the steep hillsides of the northern Belchen reaches. On the southwestern outskirts, near the village of Neuenweg, you'll find the **Nonnenmattweiher**, which is one of the oldest lakes of the region, formed during the receding Ice Age and an excellent place to combine hiking with fishing or simply picnicking. Be prepared for a lot of steep paths and deep furrows.

Some time in the seventh century, Irish missionaries came to Christianize this area: the most famous, Saint Trudpert, was murdered in 607 after only three years of missionary work. The **Kloster St Trudpert** in the upper Münstertal was founded about 250 years later, and the large Baroque complex you see today is the visual centre of the whole upper valley. It was a Benedictine monastery until secularization in 1806, but now it's home to the *Josephschwestern* order of nuns. The refreshingly plain Baroque interior of the church is considered architect Peter Thumb's masterpiece: white stucco decorations predominate, with only the ceiling frescoes and side altars adding discreet colour.

The Münstertal is awash with accommodation possibilities: look out for the *Zimmer frei* signs or you can book through the tourist office in Freiburg (see p.271). There's a **youth hostel** at Wieden (☎07673/538; **2**): take the train from Freiburg to Münstertal, then bus to Wieden.

Staufen

Following the Münstertal west, the foothills sink into the Rhine valley, the landscape quickly changing into gently rolling hills that make up some of Germany's most famous vineyards and provide a lucrative living to many small and ancient towns. Of these, **STAUFEN** is particularly attractive. Situated at the bottom of the Münstertal and surrounded by its vineyards, its idyllic location makes it a great base for relaxed hiking tours, while the cobbled streets and medieval houses mean it's worth a visit in its own right. The place also harbours a murky past in the shape of **Doktor Faustus** (Johannes Faust – see also p.222). He came here in 1539 at the behest of Count Anton von Staufen, who was in serious debt and hoped to extricate himself by using the great necromancer's alleged ability to manufacture gold. However, Faust accidentally blew himself into small pieces when an experiment exploded in his room in the *Gasthaus zum Löwen*.

The **tourist office** is in the Rathaus (☎07633/80536). You can stay in the *Zum Löwen*, Hauptstr. 47, (☎07633/7078; ⑤) including Faust's room, no. 5 on the third floor. Less expensive is *Zum Bahnhof,* Bahnhofstr. 6 (☎07633/6190; ②). A few rooms in private houses are also available (①–②) and you can book these at the tourist office.

The annual *Sommerfest* is held during the last week in June, while the local *Weinfest* takes place on the first weekend in August. Star vineyards of the area are on the **Batzenberg** just north of town, and wine connoisseurs come from all over to go winetasting in the surrounding cellars. An even bigger *Weinfest* is held in nearby Schönberg in late April and early May.

Around Feldberg

Feldberg, the highest peak in the Black Forest, was, until last century, the heart of a remote and wild region, far away from human habitation. Nowadays, in contrast, the area is one of the most popular holiday destinations containing some spectacular scenery, notably the Höllental and the Wutachschlucht.

Höllental

The most atmospheric approach to Feldberg is by train from Freiburg. For the first leg of this, you pass through the narrow and formerly almost inaccessible **Höllental** (Hell Valley) gorge, which lies between Himmelreich and Hinterzarten. The track was first laid in 1887 by Robert Gerwig, who had earlier constructed the *Schwarzwaldbahn* (see p.286), and was an amazing technical achievement for the time, using a network of tunnels and viaducts. To appreciate both the scenery and the engineering, however, you really need to get out and walk along the footpath on the gorge's northern side; it takes about four hours to make a one-way trip.

Titisee, Schluchsee and Seebrugg

TITISEE, the next stop after Hinterzarten, lies on the glacial lake of the same name which is encircled by a footpath. It's a highly commercialized and inordinately popular summer resort, particularly with holidaymakers around retirement age. Far preferable is **SCHLUCHSEE**, which lies on a larger glacial lake directly to the south. From Titisee, trains crawl up the side of the Feldberg towards Germany's highest station, **Feldberg-Bärental**, which is the place to alight if you want to walk all the way up the mountain. They then descend to Schluchsee, terminating a couple of kilometres further on at the hamlet of **SEEBRUGG**, which has a decent beach with sailing and windsurfing facilities. Motorized boats aren't allowed on the lake, a fact that makes for pleasant (and clean) swimming.

Titisee is awash with **accommodation** of all types, and you won't have trouble finding a hotel in Schluchsee either. There's also a **youth hostel** at Im Wolfsgrund 28 in Schluchsee (☎07656/329; ⚑), plus a **campsite** (☎07656/7739). Seebrugg also has a hostel, at Haus 9 (☎07656/494; ⚑).

Feldberg and the mountain resorts

In the eighteenth and nineteenth centuries, the rounded heights of the **Feldberg** itself (which can be reached more directly by bus from Freiburg than by the train connection) were denuded of forest and turned into highland pastures, so today the peak stands treeless above a sea of forest and isn't in itself particularly attractive. The TV tower and radio dishes plus the chairlift (DM5 return) and gravel path to the top don't do the place any favours either, and the hotel and souvenir shop just about ruin it. Nonetheless, the area around is still an excellent hiking region, with many beautiful trails through uninhabited forests and gorges laced with a couple of romantic waterfalls and streams along the way. Even near the Feldberg, you'll find unspoilt and quiet places like the **Feldbergsee**, only accessible on foot, and the **Windgfällweiher**, another lake near the village of Altglasshütten a few kilometres southeast.

For keen hikers, **BERNAU**, 5km south of Feldberg, is a good place to stay. It's actually a collection of small villages and farms, ideal for groups looking for farmhouse accommodation or private holiday flats. Contact the **tourist office** in the *Kurverwaltung* at Rathausstr. 18 (☎07675/160030) for accommodation lists.

The picturesque village of **TODTMOOS** is another centre for walking enthusiasts, offering all the facilities of Alpine villages. Its **tourist office** (☎07674/90600) in the *Kurverwaltung*, Wehratalstr. 19, provides accommodation lists. There's no official youth hostel here, but there are cheap beds at the *Europäisches Jugendgästehaus* (☎07674/410) instead. Todtmoos is also an ideal base from which to explore the rarely visited **Hotzenwald**, which seamlessly extends south from the Black Forest, until dropping sharply towards the Rhine valley that marks the Swiss border.

St Blasien

The most famous monastery of the Southern Black Forest is in **ST BLASIEN**, some 20km southeast of the Feldberg. Burnt down a number of times, the **Klosterkirche** was given its present shape in 1768, when the local prince-abbot hired the Frenchman Michel d'Ixnard to design one of Germany's grandest classically inspired buildings; the great dome, carried by twenty Corinthian pillars, was modelled after St Peter's in Rome. Inside, the great rotunda is a blaze of white marble, shining oppressively new and creating an atmosphere reminiscent of a cold, oversized bathroom.

For brochures and accommodation lists contact the **tourist office**, Am Kurgarten (Mon–Fri 9.30am–noon & 2.30–5pm, Sat 10am–noon; ☎07672/41430). The nearest **youth hostel** is in Menzenschwand, at Vorderdorferstr. 10 (☎07675/326; ☎); take a bus from Seebrugg. This is a particularly beautiful hostel, located in one of the all-wood traditional farmhouses, 8km up the road from St Blasien.

Bonndorf and the Wutach valley

BONNDORF, on the eastern edges of the Black Forest, is an excellent hiking base, set among rich orchards. It's very close to the so-called "Grand Canyon" of the Black Forest, the **Wutachschlucht**, which is a small riverine gorge, very narrow in places, with gushing white-water shooting over mossy rocks and lined by ancient forest. About 10km long, it has been declared a nature reserve; a map of it is available from the **tourist office** (☎07703/7607), Schloss Str. 1. The local **youth hostel** is at Waldallee 19 (☎07703/359; ☎) and the best budget hotel is *Haus Schüler*, Lindenstr. 9 (☎07703/7164; ②).

Some 15km east of Bonndorf is **BLUMBERG**, departure point for another of the Black Forest's amazing rail lines, the *Wutachtalbahn* to **WEIZEN**. Although the two termini are less than 10km apart as the crow flies, the rail track stretches for a meandering 26km along the side of the River Wutach, and features numerous horseshoe curves, a bridge, three large viaducts and five tunnels, including the only spiral tunnel in Germany. The line closed as part of the normal network a couple of decades ago, and is now used for excursion services only, invariably pulled by steam engines. These run every Saturday and Sunday from May to September, and variably on Wednesdays to Fridays as well. Check locally, or in the *DB* timetable, for the current times.

The Upper Rhine valley

The **Upper Rhine valley** forms the southern boundary of the Black Forest, and – most of the time – the frontier with Switzerland as well. Though less famous than the Middle Rhine, it's a grandly beautiful landscape, easily appreciated from the train which close-

---

INTO SWITZERLAND

It's easy enough to hop over into Switzerland from the Upper Rhine valley. In the case of the towns along the latter stretch, you simply need to walk over the appropriate bridge to the town on the opposite bank; customs officials often do not bother to check passports. However, the big draw is undoubtedly **BASEL**, Switzerland's second city, which straddles both sides of the Rhine at the point where the river makes a sharp north turn away from its previous east–west course. It's far more attractive than most of its German counterparts of similar size, Swiss neutrality having ensured it has not suffered in war. The **Öffentliche Kunstsammlung**, one of the oldest public museums in the world, has by far the largest collection of extant paintings by two of Germany's greatest artists, Conrad Witz and Hans Holbein the Younger.

One of Basel's two main stations, the Deutscher Bahnhof, is run by *DB*, using the *Deutschmark* as currency. It's a junction of the lines south from Freiburg and east to the Bodensee and is also an official frontier crossing point.

ly follows the course of the river upstream towards the Bodensee. Along the way are many pretty small towns, usually directly facing their Swiss counterparts on the opposite bank.

Bad Säckingen

The most attractive of the Upper Rhenish towns is **BAD SÄCKINGEN**, 30km upstream from Basel. Its name gained a certain international renown last century courtesy of the verse epic *The Trumpeter of Säckingen* by Joseph Victor von Scheffel, a work that is unjustly neglected nowadays. With a neat little Altstadt beside the Rhine and a plush modern spa quarter in the foothills to the north, Bad Säckingen is able to present two faces to visitors. By far the most impressive monument is the extraordinary **Rheinbrücke**, a covered wooden bridge which still provides a pedestrian link over the Rhine to the Swiss town of Stein. Thirteenth-century by origin, it was rebuilt in the seventeenth and eighteenth centuries, and restored only a few years back. In the quiet shady park overlooking the river is the seat of the one-time local lords, **Schloss Schönau**, a miniature Renaissance palace with distinctive polygonal corner towers. It now houses the **Hochrheinmuseum** (Tues, Thurs & Sun 2–5pm; DM3), the regional museum of the Upper Rhineland, featuring archeology finds, an array of Black Forest clocks and, in continued homage to the town's literary fame, what's claimed as the largest collection of historic trumpets in the world.

The **Bahnhof** lies between the Altstadt and the spa quarters; directly opposite, at Waldshuter Str. 20, is the **tourist office** (Mon–Fri 8am–noon & 2–5pm, Sat 9am–noon; ☎07761/56830).

Private rooms (①–②) can be booked at the tourist office. There are a couple of enticing **hotels** in the Altstadt – *Kater Hiddigeigei*, Tanzenplatz 1 (☎07761/4055; ⑥) and *Goldener Knopf*, Rathausplatz 9 (☎07761/5650; ⑦). Best **restaurant** is *Fuchshöhle*, Rheinbrückstr. 9, while *Margaretenschlössle*, Baltherplatz 1, is another good choice, whether for a full meal or *Kaffee und Kuchen*.

The Central Black Forest

The central part of the Black Forest is the one most enshrined in popular imagination. This is the land of cuckoo clocks, of huge balconied farmsteads with hipped roofs, and of some of the world's most outrageous headgear: the *Schäppelkrone*, a "crown" made from hundreds of coloured glass beads and ribbons, and the *Bollenhut*, the woollen pom-pom hat whose colour indicates the wearer's marital status (red for unmarried, black for married). As a result, it's hardly surprising that this is the part of the forest which has gone in most for the tourist hard-sell, and is consequently the most spoiled, with an abundance of accommodation, a highly developed network of trains and buses, and a surfeit of tacky souvenir shops. Nonetheless, it's easy enough to escape from the organized tour groups, while the good communications make travel by public transport a pain-free experience.

Donaueschingen

Gateway to the Central Black Forest is the rail junction of **DONAUESCHINGEN**, which lies some 50km northwest of the Bodensee on the windswept Baar Plateau. Both its name and fame are due to its status as the official source of one of the world's most celebrated rivers, the **Danube** (*Donau*), though it's also of note as a well-preserved example of a tinpot princely capital. Initially, the harsh climate militated against its growth – it was no more than a hamlet until the 1720s when Prince Joseph Wilhelm Ernst of the **Fürstenberg** dynasty descended from his feudal castle in the hills above to begin the planning of a new courtly town.

The town

Between the Bahnhof and the town centre is the Schlosspark, site of the source of the Danube. The **Schloss** (guided tours April–Sept daily except Tues 9am–noon & 2–5pm; DM5) itself is actually a fairly unassuming Baroque building at the far end of its park; much of the interior was modernized at the end of the nineteenth century. Its trappings are typical: Brussels tapestries, assorted objets d'art and family portraits. Among the last-named, there's one surprise – *Max Egon* was painted by the English artist Graham Sutherland. The sitter kept up the family tradition of musical patronage (Mozart and Liszt had both been guests) by establishing a **festival** now known as the *Donaueschinger Musiktage*. Held each October in the modern Donauhalle at the western end of town, this focuses on the work of contemporary composers. Many of the century's leading musicians – Stravinsky, Hindemith, Boulez and Stockhausen – have had works premiered there.

The main family treasures, known as the **Fürstenberg-Sammlungen** (March–Oct Tues–Sun 9am–noon & 1.30–5pm, Dec–Feb Tues–Sun 9am–noon & 1.30–4pm; DM5), are housed in a building on Karlsplatz, a Baroque square situated over the main road directly behind the Schloss. Here various zoological and mineralogical collections are set out in the old-fashioned manner of cabinets of curiosities. There's also a room devoted to the history of the Fürstenbergs, complete with their ceremonial coach and sleighs. However, the main attraction is the outstanding second-floor display of south German and Swiss paintings and sculptures of the fifteenth and sixteenth centuries. Highlight is **Hans Holbein the Elder**'s *Grey Passion*, an expressive cycle of twelve pictures formerly in SS Ulrich und Afra in Augsburg. It takes its name from the idiosyncratic device of showing all the participants dressed in grey – until halfway through, when they change into white. There's also an important array of works by the enigmatic **Master of Messkirch**, one of Dürer's most distinctive followers, including parts of his eponymous work, and the jewel-like *Wildensteiner Altar*.

On a terrace to the side of the Schloss is the twin-towered **Johanniskirche**, whose restrained Baroque style is reminiscent of the churches then being built in Bohemia, rather than elsewhere in southern Germany. In the nave there's a wooden *Madonna* by the eccentric **Master HL** which predates the building by over 200 years.

Other than these obvious attractions, all closely grouped together, Donaueschingen doesn't have much in the way of sights. However, several **streets** are good examples of period pieces. An example is Josefstrasse, linking the Bahnhof with the town centre, which is lined by stately Baroque and Neoclassical mansions. The outbuildings of the court are found on Haldenstrasse; the library here possesses one of the three original

---

THE SOURCE OF THE DANUBE

In Donaueschingen's Schlosspark a grandiose early nineteenth-century fountain has been erected round the *Donauquelle*, a very unassuming spring. This flows eastwards through the grounds (at times invisibly below the surface), before joining the **Brigach**, a headstream which rises in the Black Forest and which has become a substantial river by the time it reaches this point. At the edge of town a couple of kilometres further on is the more substantial confluence with another and bigger Black Forest headstream, the **Breg**; from then on, the combined waters are known as the **Danube**. It's the longest river in Europe after the Volga, and the only important one to flow from west to east, following a course of some 2840km through seven different countries, eventually forming a labyrinth-like delta in Romania which feeds into the Black Sea. Whether or not the *Donauquelle* is really the ultimate source of this great river is a matter for dispute – the spring which feeds the Breg has a far better geological claim. However, given that the crucial merger occurs at Donaueschingen, it's easy to see why the town has been blessed with official recognition.

thirteenth-century manuscript versions of *The Nibelungenlied*. Though this street is now tucked away between the town centre and the Brigach, it's easily located by the chimneys of the *Fürstenberg* **brewery**, one of the most famous in Germany. In its present form it dates back to 1705, but the family's initial beer-making rights were granted in the thirteenth century.

Practicalities

The obvious place to sample the products of the brewery (the *Pils* is one of Germany's best) is the *Bräustüble*, housed in a pink Baroque palace on Postplatz. Plenty more places to **eat** and **drink**, including several classy cafés, can be found on Karlstrasse, the town's main shopping street, which runs west from the Johanniskirche. At no. 58 is the **tourist office** (Mon–Fri 8am–noon & 2–5/6pm, Sat 9am–noon; ☎0771/857221). They have a list of private houses with **rooms** (①–③). The cheapest **hotel** in town is *Bären*, Josefstr. 7–9 (☎0771/2518; ③); more expensive alternatives include *Zur Sonne*, Karlstr. 38 (☎0771/83130; ⑤) and *Linde*, Karlstr. 18 (☎0771/83180; ⑥), both of which have good restaurants. The **campsite** (☎0771/5511) is 8km away on the banks of the Riedsee.

Villingen-Schwenningen

Created as recently as 1972, the double town of **VILLINGEN-SCHWENNINGEN**, some 15km north of Donaueschingen, is a decidedly curious union, as its two constituent parts belonged for centuries to different countries: Villingen, on the very fringe of the Black Forest, was Austrian before being allocated by Napoleon to Baden, while Schwenningen, set on the Baar plateau, was part of Württemberg. Villingen, much the more attractive of the two, really comes to life during the Shrovetide celebrations of **Fastnet**, which rival Rottweil's as the best in southern Germany.

At other times, Villingen is a busy enough market town, its pristine houses set behind the medieval **Stadtmauer**, of which several sections, including three towers and three impressive gates, survive. The huge **Münster** provides a central focus, particularly the two tall flamboyant towers of the late Gothic chancel, which was tacked on to the Romanesque nave when its predecessor burned down. Unfortunately the interior was completely redecorated – none too successfully – in the eighteenth century, but compensation comes in the variety of colourful mansions which form the Münsterplatz. These include the Romanesque **Rabenscheuer** to the north and the gabled Gothic **Altes Rathaus** (Tues–Sun 10am–noon, Thurs also 3–5pm; DM2) to the west, where you can see both the main council chamber on the first floor and the former prison and torture room above, as well as a collection of fine medieval tapestries.

Also worth a visit is the **Franziskaner-Museum** (Tues, Wed & Fri 3–5pm, Thurs 10am–noon & 3–5pm, Sat & Sun 10am–noon; DM2) at Rietstr. 39 on the western edge of the old town, which has comprehensive collections of material on the prehistory, folklore and crafts of the Black Forest. The adjoining buildings of the old monastery, the **Franziskaner-Klosteranlage** (Tues–Fri 10am–noon & 3–5pm, Sat & Sun 10am–noon; DM1), give a good idea of the severely functional Gothic architecture that was favoured by the mendicant friars, and contain displays of sacred art.

Practicalities

The **tourist office** (Mon–Fri 8.30am–12.30pm & 1.30–5.30pm, Sat 8.30am–1.30pm; ☎07721/822340) is at Rietstr. 8 and has a list of **private rooms** (①–③) in the town. There's an official **youth hostel** in the very north of Villingen at St Georgener Str. 36 (☎07721/54149; 🏠), along with the YMCA's *CJVM-Hüttle* (☎07720/5315) in a secluded wooded setting on the road between Schwenningen and Weilersbach. Among **hotels**, *Gasthof Bären*, Bickenstr. 19 (☎07721/55541; ④) is particularly worth trying; it also has one of the best **restaurants** in town, with an extensive vegetarian menu. Alternatives include *Im Klosterring,* Klosterring 3 (☎07721/89940; ④) and *Gasthaus Zum Schlachthof,* Schlachthamsstr. 11 (☎07721/22584; ⑤). Another good choice for eating is the *Ratskeller* in the Oberes Tor, which also has a beer garden.

Triberg

Heart of the central part of the Black Forest is the little town of **TRIBERG**, which lies at an altitude of 1000m, 25km northwest of Villingen. It's a renowned health resort, with the forest acting as a dust filter, ensuring particularly pure air. Some of the most imposing scenery in the region is nearby, and Triberg itself makes a good base for a day or two's relaxation. If you're travelling by train, arriving at the **Bahnhof** is a strange experience. As there's nothing but cliffs on either side of the narrow tracks it's easy to understand the derivation of the town's name, a corruption of "three mountains", after the peaks which surround it. It's a fifteen-minute walk uphill to the centre.

Prime attraction is the **Gutacher Wasserfall** at the top end of town. At 162m, it ranks as the highest waterfall in Germany and is undeniably impressive, even though it plunges in seven separate stages instead of a single dramatic dive. Unfortunately, in a reverse of the normal German penchant for unrestricted access to nature, it's sealed off, with a DM2.50 levy for admission.

The **Schwarzwald-Museum** (daily May–Sept 9am–6pm; Oct–April 10am–noon & 2–5pm; DM5) on Wallfahrtstrasse offers fascinating insights into the rural culture of the Black Forest as it was – and, to some extent, still is. There's a fine group of woodcarvings by the rustic local artist Karl Josef Fortwängler, who depicted the thick-set country bumpkins of the area in an idiosyncratic yet highly sympathetic manner. In addition, there's a large model of the *Schwarzwaldbahn,* while music boxes, clocks and examples of the traditional dress for carnivals and everyday wear complete the display. Further up the hill is the Baroque **Wallfahrtskirche St Maria in den Tannen**, whose painting of *The Virgin of the Pines* draws pilgrims for its allegedly miraculous qualities.

Practicalities

The **youth hostel** is high in the hills at Rohrbacher Str. 35 (☎07722/4110; ☎); a bus will take you as far as the waterfall and then it's a very steep twenty-minute climb. Otherwise, try one of the **hotels**, such as *Gasthaus Krone,* Schulstr. 37 (☎07722/4524; ③) which also serves excellent food, *Central,* Hauptstr. 64 (☎07722/4360; ④) or *Adler,*

THE SCHWARZWALDBAHN

Villingen is the terminus for one of the most spectacular rail lines in Europe, the *Schwarzwaldbahn* to Offenburg in the Rhine valley. Laid out between 1863 and 1873, this line successively follows the valleys of the Brigach, Gutach and Kinzig rivers, cutting through what had hitherto been impenetrable countryside, and was intended as a major prestige project by the Grand Duchy of Baden, which was always keen to present itself at the forefront of German progressiveness. It was built by the nation's most celebrated railway engineer, Robert Gerwig, who later went on to construct the St Gotthard route over the Alps, as well as another Black Forest line, the *Höllentalbahn.* The nature of the terrain posed technical problems which had never previously been tackled, notably the need to climb a gradient of 448m in the short distance of 11km. To achieve this, Gerwig built 36 tunnels through the mountains, plus a series of daring hairpin bends. Two of these – the narrow, deep and rocky stages between St Georgen and Triberg, and between Triberg and Hornberg – involve the rail line virtually doubling back on itself to traverse the gradient.

Hauptstr. 52 (☎07722/4574; ⑤). Top of the range is *Parkhotel Wehrle,* Garbanstr. 24 (☎07722/86020; ⑦), which is set in its own park. It has a gourmet **restaurant** plus the more affordable *Alta Schmieke.* A full accommodation list is available from the **tourist office** (Mon–Fri 8am–noon & 2–5pm, May–Sept also Sat 10am–noon; ☎07722/953230) in the *Kurverwaltung,* Luisenstr. 10.

The Gutach valley

The **Gutach valley** north of Triberg is best known as the home of the traditional *Bollenhut* hat. At **HORNBERG**, the *Schwarzwaldbahn* emerges into a light and airy landscape again and traverses a huge viaduct. There's a fine view of the ensemble of town and rail line from the ruined Burg set high on a hill to the west.

A few kilometres north is the town of **GUTACH** itself, outside which is the **Schwarzwälder Freilichtmuseum** (April–Oct daily 8.30am–6pm; DM4), a collection of buildings from the region. Centrepiece is what's probably the most famous house in the Black Forest, the late sixteenth-century *Vogtsbauernhof.* With its huge sloping roof and tiered facade, it's an outstanding example of the characteristic vernacular building style of the region. This was the original farmhouse on the site, whereas the various other exhibits have been removed from other locations. There are four more farmsteads, along with a wooden chapel and all kinds of workshops – smithies, granaries, a bakehouse, a distillery and various types of mills. Displays on the folklore and lifestyle of the region are also featured, and there are demonstrations of old crafts.

CLOCKMAKING IN THE BLACK FOREST

The first clocks to be seen in the Black Forest were mechanical contraptions brought by pedlars from Bohemia in the 1640s. Someone must have had the idea of reproducing them in wood, as a couple of decades later the first workshops had appeared. Originally, clockmaking was an adjunct to farming and forestry, and was normally a co-operative venture involving several families, each of whom specialized in a different part of the business, such as woodcarving, painting, or making the mechanism. The products were sold by itinerant hawkers, who gradually began to expand their operations abroad; by the end of the eighteenth century, demand was so great that clockmaking became a lucrative full-time trade for many families and the single largest local industry. It has remained of key importance to the local economy to this day.

Although the cuckoo clock (*Kuckucksuhr*) is what most tourists want to buy, the alternative *Schilderuhr,* which has a hand-painted clockface, has a far longer and more prestigious tradition. Beautiful models designed to the customer's specification can be ordered throughout the Central Black Forest region; these contrast dramatically with the junk sold in the tackier souvenir shops.

The Kinzig valley

At the next stop along the rail line, Hausach, the Gutach merges with the **Kinzig valley**; similarly, there's the junction of the *Schwarzwaldbahn* with the *Kinzigtalbahn.* **HASLACH**, an old market town and health resort just 8km from Hausach, is the most striking place on the *Schwarzwaldbahn's* stretch along the Kinzig towards the terminus at Offenburg. Its Rathaus is tweely painted with depictions of locals in traditional dress, while the former **Kapuzinerkloster** (April–Oct Tues–Sat 9am–5pm, Sun 10am–5pm; Nov–March Tues–Fri 10am–5pm; DM2) has a huge collection of Black Forest costumes and folklore displays.

Following the *Kinzigtalbahn* eastwards from Hausach, the first stop is **WOLFACH**, situated at the point where the river after which the village is named joins the Kinzig.

SCHILTACH, a pretty, flower-lined place of half-timbered houses a further 10km east, is likewise set at the confluence of its river with the Kinzig.

ALPIRSBACH, 19km northeast of Schiltach, is grouped round the former **Kloster**, now a Protestant parish church. Begun in the late twelfth century, it preserves much of the simple, pure Romanesque form characteristic of the style of building championed at Hirsau (see p.291). The east end is especially notable – later Gothic masons ingeniously perched the chancel above the existing storey. Only one tower was built, however, and this was not finished until the Renaissance period, when it received an unusual gabled top. **Guided tours** (March 15–Nov 1 Mon–Sat at 10am, 11am, 2pm, 3pm & 4pm, Sun 11am, 2pm, 3pm & 4pm; DM4) are run round the monastic buildings and the late Gothic cloisters which are often used for open-air concerts in summer.

Handsome half-timbered buildings decorate the centre of Alpirsbach, most notably the Rathaus; the town also makes a good centre for walks in the Kinzig valley. There are plenty of reasonably priced **pensions** (①–③), a **youth hostel** high on the Sulzberg at Reinerzauer Steige 80 (☎07444/2477; **⌷**) and two **campsites**. **Hotels** include *Löwen-Post,* Marktplatz 12 (☎07444/2393, fax 07444/955944; ⑤), *Rüssle*, Aischbachstr. 5 (☎07444/2281, fax 07444/2368; ⑤) and *Gasthof Waldhorn,* Kranzgasse 4 (☎07444/95110, fax 07444/951155; ⑤). A full accommodation list is available from the **tourist office** in the *Kurverwaltung,* Hauptstr. 20. Alpirsbach's brewery, the *Klosterbräu*, produces a wide variety of excellent **beers**.

The Northern Black Forest

To non-Germans, the northern stretch of the Black Forest, most of which belonged to Württemberg rather than Baden, is the least familiar part. Yet here are some of the most imposing landscapes – the forest really does look at its blackest and is cut by several deep, dark valleys which provide the strongest possible contrast to the long panoramic views from the hills. There are three main **touring routes**, each offering a widely varying choice of scenery: the Black Forest Highway, the Black Forest Valley Road and the circuitous Black Forest Spa Road. Walking or cycling are the best ways of **getting around**, but superb scenic rail lines, closely hugging the river valleys, enable all of the second and part of the third of these routes to be followed by even the most sedentary. Buses fill in the gaps, though the frequency of these varies considerably according to season, often drying up altogether in the winter months.

Freudenstadt

The hub of the transport system of the Northern Black Forest is **FREUDENSTADT**, situated at high altitude on a plateau bordered by the rivers Murg and Kinzig. It's a polished, spick and span town and coupled with its extreme climate and arcaded streets, it has a feel reminiscent more of Switzerland than Germany. Its regularly built streets look gleamingly new, but it's new only in one sense, its history being dogged by an ill luck than contradicts its name, which means "town of joy".

The town

Freudenstadt is still sufficiently singular to justify a look round, even if you aren't attracted to the leisure facilities or the excellent hiking opportunities in the neighbourhood. The **Marktplatz** must have seemed extraordinary when it was first built; it's an impressive sight even to the modern eye which is far more attuned to the large-scale, and it still ranks as much the biggest square in Germany. At diagonally opposite corners are the two main public buildings, the **Rathaus** and the **Stadtkirche**.

THE CURIOUS HISTORY OF FREUDENSTADT

Freudenstadt was founded in 1599 by **Duke Friedrich I of Württemberg**. He had three main aims in establishing the new community: to give a much-needed boost to his ever-empty state coffers by exploiting the silver mines in the nearby Christophstal; to provide a home, at a time of high religious rivalry, for Protestant refugees from Austria; and to have a new, "secret" capital for Württemberg, which he dreamed of building up as an effective counterweight to France on the one hand and the Habsburg-dominated Holy Roman Empire on the other.

A highly talented Italian-trained architect, **Heinrich Schickhardt**, was accordingly charged with designing the first planned town in the province. He laid it out in the manner of a vast Roman camp, centred on a spaciously grandiose central square. In the middle, there was meant to be an even bigger Schloss than the one in Stuttgart but it was never built – the silver mines proved to be a **mirage**, and the town was devastated by **epidemic and fire** within 35 years of its birth, whereupon it lost all sense of importance. Something of a comeback was made in the nineteenth century with its development into one of the leading spas in the Black Forest. Two weeks before the end of World War II, **disaster struck again** – French artillery bombarded the town, and when it fell, the victors ran amok; only two streets survived the blaze intact. Within five years, however, Freudenstadt had been completely **rebuilt** to the old plans. This was regarded as a stunning achievement, even by the standards of German postwar reconstruction, but the undeniable effect – avoided in more painstaking restoration projects – is that the historic buildings look anachronistically modern.

The Stadtkirche is particularly intriguing, built in an L-shape so that the men and women of the congregation could be segregated. Indeed, the arrangement meant they could not even see each other – the better to keep their minds on the sermon. The church houses a magnificent polychrome wooden **lectern** made around 1150, which bears large statues of the Four Evangelists and their symbols. It's unique of its kind and one of the most important pieces of Romanesque church furniture to have survived. Along with the **font**, made half a century earlier and adorned with carvings of symbolical animals, it presumably came from one of the Black Forest monasteries.

Practicalities

There are two train stations: the **Stadtbahnhof**, on the *Murgtalbahn*, is just a few minutes' walk north of Marktplatz and has the **bus terminus** just outside, whereas the **Hauptbahnhof** is at the eastern edge of town, at a much lower altitude. The **tourist office** (April–Oct Mon–Fri 9am–6pm, Sat & Sun 9am–noon; Nov–March Mon–Fri only 9am–noon & 2.30–5pm; ☎07441/8640) is in the *Kurverwaltung* at Promenadeplatz 1.

Hotels and **pensions** are scattered all over town; for the lowest rates, try the concentration on Lauterbadstrasse. For something a bit more upmarket there's *Adler*, Forstr. 15–17 (☎07441/91520; ④), *Jägerstüble*, Marktplatz 12 (☎07441/2387, fax 07441/51543; ⑤), *Zum Warteck*, Stuttgarter Str. 14 (☎07441/7418; ⑤), *Alte Kanzlei*, Strassburger Str. 6 (☎07441/88860; ⑤) and *Bären*, Lange Str. 33 (☎07441/2729; ⑥). Alternatively, the **youth hostel** is at Eugen-Nägele-Str. 69 (☎07441/7720; ❶), not far from the Stadtbahnhof, and a **campsite**, *Langenwald* (☎07441/2862), 3km to the west.

All the hotels listed above have recommendable **restaurants**: *Jägerstüble* is perhaps the best value, while *Zum Warteck* scores for quality.

The Black Forest Highway

The **Black Forest Highway** (*Schwarzwald-Hochstrasse*), linking Freudenstadt with Baden-Baden, is one of Germany's most famous roads. Up to five buses daily run in each direction in summer along this 60km stretch, which has no villages to speak of. However, there are plenty of **hotels**, many with spa facilities and nearly all on the expensive side. One of the most reasonably priced is *Berghotel Mummelsee* (☎07842/1088; ④). In addition, there's a single **youth hostel**, *Zuflucht* (☎07804/811; ☎), located at a particularly scenic part just off the main road 19km north of Freudenstadt. It makes an excellent base for hiking in summer and for skiing in winter. Walking along the accompanying trail is really much the best way to see the area, which is pocked with belvederes offering vast panoramas towards the Rhine and the French Vosges.

Just beyond the hostel is the **Buhlbachsee**, the first of several tiny natural lakes along the highway. Before this, however, is a by-road leading west to Oppenau which joins with another fine scenic road running north to the coomb of **Allerheiligen**, rejoining the *Hochstrasse* at Ruhestein. Allerheiligen has the ruins of a former Premonstratensian **Kloster**, the first Gothic building in southwest Germany, probably built by the same team of masons as Strasbourg Cathedral. There's also an impressively curling stepped **waterfall** and a good restaurant, the *Klosterhof*, which makes its own fruit wines and liqueurs.

East of Ruhestein is the **Wildsee**, but the most celebrated of the lakes is the **Mummelsee** a further 8km north. It stands at the foot of the Hornigsrinde (1164m), the highest point in the Northern Black Forest, offering a particularly outstanding view. The Mummelsee itself, now a popular boating centre, is allegedly haunted by water-sprites and by the luckless King Ulmon, who was condemned by a sorceress to live for 1000 years, in spite of his continuous pleas to be released to join his friends in the after-life. This legend has proved a potent inspiration for many German writers and formed the subject of one of Eduard Mörike's most evocative poems. It's often necessary to change buses here, particularly out of season when there are no through services.

The Murg valley

The **Murg valley** north of Freudenstadt is the second stage of the Black Forest Valley Road (*Schwarzwald-Tälerstrasse*). This is the only one of the three scenic routes which doesn't officially begin at Freudenstadt, its first stretch being the Kinzig valley from Alpirsbach.

What is arguably the most scenic of all the region's rail lines, the 60km *Murgtalbahn* line to Rastatt, follows a parallel course to the road. Though never more than a modest stretch of water, the River Murg cleaves an impressively grand valley in its downward journey towards its confluence with the Rhine. One of the best hikes which can be made from **BAIERSBRONN** (the first stop, 6km north of Freudenstadt) is west along the course of the young river towards its source in the shadow of the 1055-metre-high **Schliffkopf**.

All the little towns along the Murg have impressive settings, and make good bases for exploring an underrated part of the Black Forest. Particularly worthy of mention is **FORBACH**, about halfway down the line, which has a wonderful sixteenth-century single-span covered wooden bridge, the largest of its type in Europe. West of town is some fine countryside, with the artifical **Schwarzenbach Stausee**, a watersports centre, and the tiny **Herrenwieser See**. The latter lies below the **Badener Höhe**, whose TV tower commands an extensive view of the region. There's a **youth hostel** just to the north of Forbach at Birket 1 (☎07228/2427; ☎) and another out in the sticks at Haus no. 33 in Herrenwies (☎07226/257; ☎). **Campsites** are also to be found in both locations, as well as a good number of cheap **pensions** (①–③).

The Nagold valley

Much the most impressive stretch of the Black Forest Spa Road (*Schwarzwald-Bäderstrasse*) is the wonderfully dark, secret **Nagold valley**. The *Nagoldtalbahn*, which runs most of the way alongside it, begins at the rail junction of Horb, which has connections to Stuttgart, Tübingen and Rottweil, but there's also a branch line to Freudenstadt which links up 6km further north, at Eutingen.

Calw

"The most beautiful town of all that I know," was how Hermann Hesse described **CALW**, the old textile centre which is the focal point of this valley. The eulogy needn't be taken too seriously – his judgement was more than a little bit coloured by the fact that he happened to have been born and bred there, though he eventually chose to reside in Switzerland. Fans of Hesse's novels will certainly want to come here to see his **birthplace** at Marktplatz 30, now designated the **Hermann-Hesse-Museum** (Tues–Sat 2–5pm, Sun 11am–5pm; DM3), containing memorabilia of the writer.

Other than this, Calw boasts an impressive array of half-timbered houses, mostly dating from the late seventeenth and early eighteenth centuries, just after a fire had destroyed the medieval town. One of the few older monuments is the **Nikolausbrücke** from around 1400, which incorporates a picturesque little votive chapel. Hesse, true to form, considered the bridge and the square on its west bank to form an assemblage superior to the Piazza del Duomo in Florence.

If you want to stay, good **hotels** include *Alte Post*, Bahnhofstr. 1 (☎07051/2196; ③), *Rössle*, Hermann-Hesse-Platz 2 (☎07051/79000; ⑤) and *Ratsstube,* Marktplatz 12 (☎07051/1864; ⑤). Each of the last two has a **restaurant.** There's a **youth hostel** right in the centre of town at Im Zwinger 4 (☎07051/12614; ☎). **Campsites** are located at Eiselstätt (☎07051/12131 or 13437) in the eastern part of town, and in the outlying villages of Stammheim (☎07051/4844) and Altburg (☎07051/50788).

Hirsau

HIRSAU, 2km downstream, is now a small health resort and officially part of Calw, but actually has a far longer history. Its Benedictine **Kloster**, indeed, was once the most powerful monastery in Germany, serving as mother-house to a host of dependent congregations and initiating a highly influential reform movement whose main effect was to free religious houses from the clutches of secular patrons, placing them instead under the direct control of the pope. The simple, original monastic church is tucked away in among a number of much later buildings, not far from the bridge over the Nagold. A ninth-century Carolingian structure, it was rebuilt in the mid-eleventh century, and now serves as the Catholic parish church of St Aurelius.

The eleventh-century complex, built in warm red sandstone, was directly modelled on the most famous and powerful European monastery of the day – that of Cluny in Burgundy – on sloping ground above the west bank of the Nagold. Almost completely destroyed by the French in the War of the Palatinate Succession, only the **Eulenturm** (Owl Tower), originally one of a pair, survives from this epoch. However, there are also fragments from later building periods, notably the late fifteenth-century **cloisters**, the early sixteenth-century **Marienkapelle** (now restored to serve as the Protestant church), and the Renaissance **Jagdschloss** of the dukes of Württemberg, who expelled the monks after the Reformation, taking over the land as pleasure and hunting grounds.

Tiefenbronn

TIEFENBRONN, an unassuming-looking village situated at the extreme edge of the Black Forest in the peaceful valley of the River Würm 12km southeast of Pforzheim, has two claims to fame. Firstly, it's a renowned gastronomic centre; people come from Stuttgart and beyond in order to eat at the *Ochsen-Post*, Franz-Josef-Gall-Str. 13 (☎07234/8030; ⑥), a **hotel** in a seventeenth-century timber-framed building. The main restaurant, one of the best in southern Germany, is expensive, but the *Bauernstuben*, open evenings only, is more affordable.

From the outside, there's little to suggest that there's anything remarkable about the steep-roofed fourteenth-century Gothic church of **St Maria Magdalena**. Architecturally, it's very ordinary indeed, yet it contains a magnificent array of **works of art** which put to shame those in most cathedrals. Jewel-like stained-glass windows, made in Strasbourg around 1370, illuminate the choir, and there are fifteenth-century wall-paintings throughout the church, including a depiction of *The Last Judgment*, a frieze of coats of arms, and portraits of the family who provided the endowments. The high altar tells the story of the Passion and has panels of the Nativity on the reverse.

However, this is outclassed by the altar dedicated to the local patron saint, which is housed in the southern aisle. One of the most beautiful of all European Gothic paintings, it bears a curious inscription: "Weep, Art, weep and lament loudly, nobody nowadays wants you, so alas, 1432. Lucas Moser, painter of Wyl, master of this work, pray God for him." Nothing is known about the embittered **Lucas Moser**, whose style seems oddly modern for its day. The first German painting to try a realistic approach, including a sense of perspective, it still has all the grace and delicacy characteristic of the earlier Soft Style. It shows Mary Magdalene washing Christ's feet, her miraculous journey in a ship without sail or rudder to Marseille, her stay there and her last communion in the Cathedral of Aix-en-Provence.

Baden-Baden

It is an inane town, full of sham, and petty fraud, and snobbery, but the baths are good . . . I had had twinges of rheumatism unceasingly during three years, but the last one departed after a fortnight's bathing there, and I have never had one since. I fully believe I left my rheumatism in Baden-Baden. Baden-Baden is welcome to it. It was little, but it was all I had to give. I would have preferred to leave something that was catching, but it was not in my power.

Mark Twain, *A Tramp Abroad*

Mark Twain's ambivalent reactions to **BADEN-BADEN** – he actually seems to have revelled in the snob aspect, delighting in the fact that the little old woman he sat behind in church and had decided to foster, turned out to be the Empress of Germany – mirror the contrasting reactions of late nineteenth-century visitors to this town, then the glittering rendezvous of the wealthy and famous.

In the present century, the idle rich classes who made Baden-Baden the "summer capital of Europe" have been almost entirely wiped out. The Bolshevik Revolution accounted for the Russian landowners, while World War II took care of their counterparts in Prussia and the Balkans. Yet, if Baden-Baden isn't quite what it was, it has still maintained its image remarkably well; like Bath in England, it has a sense of style that no other spa in the country can quite match. This is in large measure thanks to the German infatuation with the concept of the spa cure, which is underpinned by an incredibly lenient health insurance system. Buoyed by the postwar economic prosperity, people flock here to enjoy a taste of a lifestyle their parents could only have dreamed about. It remains a place you're likely to either love or hate, but is somewhere which definitely should be experienced at first hand.

The **telephone code** for Baden-Baden is ☎07221

THE HISTORY OF THE SPA

The discovery of hot springs in the Florintinerberg, on the east side of the River Oos, was made by the Romans, who found in them cures for arthritis and rheumatism. They established a settlement at this point, known simply as *Aquae* (Waters). The vernacular form of this was later used not only for the town, but also for the margraviate established by the **Zähringen** family, who moved here in the eleventh century to rule their combined territories at the western frontiers of the Holy Roman Empire. In the sixteenth century, the Swiss alchemist and doctor Paracelsus utilized the springs to save the life of Margrave Philipp I. However, Baden-Baden's rise to international fame only came about as a result of Napoleon's creation of the buffer state of Baden in 1806, 35 years after it had lost its role as ducal capital to Karlsruhe. The grand dukes promoted their ancestors' old seat as a resort and began embellishing it with handsome new buildings, many designed by the Neoclassical architect Friedrich Weinbrenner.

A casino formed an integral part of the facilities from the beginning, though it only took off with the arrival from Paris in 1836 of the flamboyant impresario **Jacques Bénazet**, *Le Roi de Bade*. With gambling outlawed in France, he devoted all his energies to building up Baden-Baden as the gambling capital of Europe. Among the famous visitors was Dostoyevsky, who became a compulsive addict, a theme he treated in his novella *The Gambler*. In 1872 Kaiser Wilhelm I – a faithful annual visitor to Baden-Baden over a period of forty years – abolished gambling throughout his newly united empire, forcing the town to concentrate on its spa facilities once more. However, the gaming tables were licensed again by Hitler in 1933, and have remained in operation ever since, save for the break caused by World War II.

The town

Although it's a relatively small town with a population of no more than 50,000, Baden-Baden is not a place to be seen in a hurry. The sights are spread out all over the valley of the River Oos and the hills around, while time is needed to bask in the varied spa attractions.

The Kurhaus and casino

The **Kurhaus** was built in the 1820s by Weinbrenner as the focal point of the new spa quarter on the west side of the Oos. Its solemn, stately facade of eight Corinthian columns is now approached via an elegant shopping arcade of expensive shops. Bénazet's son Edouard, *Le Duc de Zéro*, added an opulent suite of gaming rooms to the Kurhaus, employing the same team of designers as had worked on the Paris Opéra; they married the contemporary style of *La Belle Epoque* to the extravagant type of decor found at Versailles. Highlight is the **Wintergarten**, with its glass cupola, Chinese vases and pure gold roulette table, which is used only on Saturdays or for special guests. Almost equally striking is the **Roter Saal**, covered from top to bottom in red silk damask from Lyon, and with a glorious marbled fireplace and raised oval ceiling.

The easiest way to see these is to take a **guided tour** (daily April–Sept 9.30am–noon; Oct–March 10am–noon; DM4). However, it's far more fun to go when the action is on. A **day-ticket** costs DM5, with no obligation to participate. Formal dress (ie any kind of jacket and tie for men, skirt or dress for women) is a precondition of entry; access is officially forbidden to residents of Baden-Baden, anyone under 21 and students. Roulette is played daily 2pm–2am (until 3am on Saturday), black jack from 5pm–1am Monday–Thursday, 4pm–1am Friday and Sunday, 4pm–2am Saturday, while baccarat is for the real night owls, running daily 3pm–6am. Minimum stake is DM5; maximum is DM50,000 though this limit is waived for baccarat.

Around Lichtentaler Allee

South of the Kurhaus runs Baden-Baden's most important thoroughfare, the **Lichtentaler Allee**. This was originally lined with oaks, but was transformed at the instigation of Edouard Bénazet into a landscape in the English style, with the addition of exotic trees and shrubs. It requires little effort of the imagination to visualize the procession of aristocratic carriages along this route; at Kettenbrücke, at the far end, an attempt was made on the life of Wilhelm I in 1861.

First of the buildings on Lichtentaler Allee is the Parisian-style **Theater** which opened in 1862 with the premiere of Berlioz's opera *Béatrice et Bénédict*. Next in line comes the **International Club**, built by Weinbrenner for a Swedish princess but now the headquarters of the big flat races which are held in Iffezheim, 12km northwest of Baden-Baden. There's a meeting in May, and a *Grosse Woche* in late August, which is the most important in the German calendar and now ranks as the high point of the Baden-Baden season. Further along is the **Kunsthalle** (Tues & Thurs–Sun 10am–6pm, Wed 10am–8pm; DM8), which has no permanent collection but regularly hosts major loan exhibitions of twentieth-century art.

Immediately north of the Kurhaus, the **Trinkhalle** (Pump Room; daily 10am–4.30/5.30pm; free) was built by a follower of Weinbrenner, Heinrich Hübsch. There are fourteen large frescoes by the Romantic painter Jakob Götzenberger, illustrating legends about the town and the nearby countryside. Different varieties of spring water are dispensed from a modern mosaic fountain.

The Michaelsberg, which rises behind the spa quarter, is named after the last Romanian Boyar of Moldavia, Michael Stourdza, who settled in Baden-Baden after he had been expelled from his homeland. In 1863, his teenage son was murdered in Paris; as a memorial, he commissioned the **Stourdza Mausoleum** to be built on the hill. Construction of this domed chapel, the most distinguished of the three nineteenth-century churches in Baden-Baden built for expatriate communities, was entrusted to the aged Leo von Klenze who had created so much of nineteenth-century Munich, but he died before it was complete. It's normally kept locked but the priest, who lives in the house alongside, will open it on request.

The Altstadt

Little remains of the old town of Baden-Baden, which was almost completely destroyed in a single day in 1689, the result of a fire started by French troops. However, halfway up the Florintinerberg is the Marktplatz, where you'll find the **Rathaus**, formerly a Jesuit college but partially remodelled by Weinbrenner to serve as the original casino. Opposite is the **Stiftskirche**, a Gothic hall church whose tower is an amalgam of the Romanesque lower storeys of the first church, a Gothic octagon and a Baroque cap.

It may seem unexpected that Baden-Baden possesses one of the all-time masterpieces of European sculpture, but the Stiftkirche's 5.4-metre-high sandstone *Crucifixion*, depicting Christ as a noble giant triumphant over his suffering, certainly warrants such a rating. Carved in 1467, it stood for nearly five centuries in the Alter Friedhof, before being moved inside for conservation reasons. The work is signed by **Nicolaus Gerhaert von Leyden**, a mysterious, peripatetic sculptor of Dutch origin who pioneered a realist approach to art which was to have a profound influence on the German carvers of the next generation. The tabernacle was made about twenty years later by a mason who had clearly come under Gerhaert's spell, while there are also several impressive **tombs** of the Margraves of Baden lining the chancel; particularly eye-catching is the Rococo monument to "Türkenlouis" (see also p.298 and p.302), replete with depictions of his trophies.

From Marktplatz you can climb the steep steps to the **Neues Schloss** whose terrace commands the best view over Baden-Baden, a dramatic mixture of rooftops, church spires and the Black Forest surroundings. The site served as the seat of the margraves

THE NAMING OF BADEN-BADEN

The division of the Margraviate into Catholic and Protestant lines in 1525 is the source of the town's curious double-barrelled name. The Protestants moved to Durlach and founded the House of Baden-Durlach; the Catholic branch therefore became known as the House of Baden-Baden, following the usual practice, on the division of a state, of modifying the original name by adding that of its capital. Although this is also what the town itself has commonly been called ever since, the name was only officially adopted in 1931, more out of snobbery than anything else, in order to distinguish it from lesser spa towns named Baden in Austria and Switzerland.

of Baden from 1437, and of the Catholic line of Baden-Baden when the House divided in 1525. Still the property of the Zähringen family, the main Renaissance and Baroque apartments can only be seen by **guided tour** (subject to change, but normally May–Sept Mon–Fri at 3pm; DM3). However, another wing contains part of the local history displays of the **Stadtgeschichtliche Sammlungen** (Tues–Sun 10am–12.30pm & 2–5pm; DM2).

The Römerbad, Friedrichsbad and the Caracalla Therme

Hidden underneath the Stiftskirche are the remains of the Roman Imperial Baths; the more modest **Römerbad** (Easter–Oct daily 10am–noon & 1.30–4pm; DM2.50) just to the east on Römerplatz was probably for the use of soldiers. If you don't fancy paying the entrance fee, you can still see the ruins through the glass-fronted windows.

Above the ruins is what must rank as one of the most magnificent bathing halls in the world, the **Friedrichsbad** (Mon–Sat 9am–10pm, Sun noon–10pm). Begun in 1869, it's as grandly sumptuous as a Renaissance palace. This elaborateness is at least partly due to the fact that, as gambling was outlawed while the building was under construction, the medicinal springs became even more crucial to local prosperity than they had been before. The red and white sandstone facade is crowned with sea-green cupolas, while inside the pools are surrounded by pillars, arches and classical-style tiles, giving a truly exotic atmosphere. Speciality of the house is a "Roman-Irish Bath", which consists of a two-hour programme of showers, hot air and steam baths, soap and brush massage, thermal bathing, and a half-hour snooze in a specially designed rest room. The entire treatment is nude, with mixed bathing all day Wednesday and Friday. It will set you back all of DM36, upwards of DM46 with massage treatment.

The **Caracalla Therme** (daily 8am–10pm) on the same square is a vast complex, completed in 1985, as a replacement for the former *Augustabad*. There are seven pools, both indoors and out, which are all at different temperatures, along with a sauna, solarium and massage facility. In reality, it's no more than an upmarket swimming hall with thermal water springs, though it makes an ideal complement to the Friedrichsbad. Its humbler status is reflected in the considerably cheaper prices: it costs DM19 for a two-hour swim, DM25 for three hours, DM33 for four hours.

The Südstadt and Lichtental

The Südstadt, immediately south of the Florintinerberg, was traditionally the home of foreigners. Just off Bertholdsplatz is the onion-domed **Russische Kirche** (daily 10am–5/6pm), while the neo-Gothic **Johanneskirche** on Bertholdstrasse was the place where Mark Twain had his encounter with the empress. Beyond the church is the **Gönneranlagen**, a fine park with pergolas, fountains and a rose garden – a real highlight of the town.

Further south is the old village of **LICHTENTAL**, which can be reached by bus #201. The tranquil thirteenth-century **Kloster** (Tues–Sat 2.30–5pm, Sun 3–5pm, closed first Sun in month; DM3) is still occupied by Cistercian nuns, who keep up a long tradition of handicrafts, and also make several fiery liqueurs, which can be bought at their shop. There are two Gothic chapels: the larger one is used for services, while the other, the **Fürstenkapelle**, served as the pantheon of the margraves of Baden prior to the Stiftskirche. Particularly outstanding is the tomb of the foundress Irmengard, carved by a Strasbourg mason in the mid-fourteenth century.

Just down the road from here, at Maximilianstr. 85, is the **Brahms-Haus** (Mon, Wed & Fri 3–5pm, Sun 10am–1pm; DM3), a tiny attic crammed with memorabilia, left exactly as when the great composer lived in it periodically during the years 1865 to 1874. This was the time when Brahms, ever conscious of his mantle as Beethoven's successor, was struggling to establish himself as a symphonist, only publishing his first, tormented essay in this form after he had passed his fortieth birthday. Its elegiac successor was largely written during a later visit to Lichtental, while part of the massive *Ein Deutsches Requiem*, his most important choral work, was also composed here.

Other suburbs

The original castle of the Margraves, **Burg Hohenbaden** (Tues–Sun 10am–10pm; free), is situated on the wooded slopes of the Battert, some 3km from the Neues Schloss, from which it's reached via Alter Schlossweg; alternatively, bus #215 goes there from the town centre. At one time, it boasted over a hundred rooms but is now ruinous, albeit still very much worth visiting for the sake of the sweeping views; there's also a good and reasonably priced restaurant. To the east, on the same bus route, lies the wine-growing village of **EBERSTEINBURG**, likewise dominated by a ruined fortress of the local rulers. Further south and reached from Ebersteinburg by footpath, or from the Bahnhof or centre by bus #205, is the **Merkur**, at 668 metres the highest hill in the Baden-Baden range. There's a choice of trails along it, or you can ascend to the summit by an unusually steep rack rail line (daily 10am–6pm; DM7 return). To obtain much of a view, you then need to climb the Jugendstil **Aussichtsturm**.

Practicalities

The **Bahnhof**, on the fast Freiburg to Karlsruhe line, is in the suburb of Oos, 4km northwest of the centre, which is reached by bus #201, #205 or #216. As the sights are scattered, it's well worth investing in a 24-hour ticket on the public transport network. This costs DM8 for Baden-Baden or DM15 for the whole region including Karlsruhe and covers two adults and two children travelling together. The **tourist office** is in the *Kurverwaltung* at Augustaplatz 8 (daily 9.30am–6pm; ☎275200).

Accommodation

Baden-Baden has **hotels** to suit every pocket, from the plain and serviceable to the super-luxury establishments frequented by aristocrats and oil sheiks. There are a fair number of **private rooms** (②–⑤); the tourist office has a list but is unlikely to help with bookings. The **youth hostel** is between the Bahnhof and the centre at Hardbergstr. 34 (☎52223; ⑧); take bus #201, #205 or #216 to Grosse-Dollen-Strasse, from where the way is signposted. **Camping** presents more of a problem, with no sites in the immediate vicinity. Nearest is in a large pleasure park named Oberbruch (☎07223/23194) in the outskirts of Bühl, 10km southwest and three stops away by slow train.

HOTELS

Altes Schloss, Alter Schlossweg 10 (☎26948, fax 391775). A tiny hotel is run as an adjunct to the restaurant in Burg Hohenbaden. It only has two doubles and one single, so is best booked well in advance. ③
Am Friedrichsbad, Gernsbacher Str. 31 (☎271046, fax 38310). Located directly opposite the Friedrichsbad, this has a Czech speciality restaurant, *Prager Stuben,* extravagantly decorated in the distinctive Art Nouveau style of Prague. ⑤

Am Markt, Marktplatz 18 (☎22747, fax 391887). Well-regarded family-run hotel in the heart of the Altstadt. It serves evening meals to house guests only. ⑤

Bad-Hotel Zum Hirsch, Hirschstr. 1 (☎9390, fax 38148). Altstadt hotel in a three-hundred-year-old building with some splendid public rooms, notably the *Ballsaal*. The bedrooms are nicely furnished, and some are supplied directly with thermal water. Evening meals are served to residents only. ⑧

Badischer Hof, Lange Str. 47 (☎9340, fax 934470). Now part of the *Steigenberger* chain, this luxury hotel was founded in 1809 in the premises of a suppressed Capuchin monastery. As well as sauna and massage facilities, it has its own thermal swimming pool, and some of the rooms have thermal water supplies. The restaurant is among the town's best. ⑨

Bratwurstglöckle, Steinstr. 7 (☎90610, fax 906161). Historic hotel in a very quiet Altstadt street, just up from the Friedrichsbad. Its restaurant is worth seeking out in its own right for its inexpensive traditional fare. ⑥

Brenner's Park-Hotel, An der Lichtentaler Allee (☎9000, fax 38772). Baden-Baden's most exclusive address is an enduring reminder of its halcyon years. Set in its own manicured private park, it boasts an extensive bathing complex with swimming pool, steam baths, sauna and solarium. Each room is individually decorated with chintz fabrics and antiques. There are two restaurants – the gourmet and very formal *Park Restaurant* and the more relaxed and slightly less expensive *Schwarzwald-Stube*. ⑨

Der Kleine Prinz, Lichtentaler Str. 36 (☎3464, fax 38264). A flagship of the *Romantik* chain, exquisitely furnished and decorated throughout; a chief source of inspiration is Antoine de Saint Exupéry's illustrated children's novel *Le Petit Prince*, after which it is named. The restaurant is outstanding, albeit among the most expensive in town. ⑨

Goldener Stern, Ooser Haupstr. 16 (☎61509). An archetypal German hotel and restaurant which offers the best value of the concentration near the Bahnhof in the suburb of Oos. ④

Greiner, Lichtentaler Allee 88 (☎71135). A very competitively priced option, especially in the light of its prestigious location. ④

Holland Hotel Sophienpark, Sophienstr. 14 (☎3560, fax 356121). One of the least expensive of the town's luxury hotels, notwithstanding its setting in its own fine park. Set-price buffet lunches are served in its *Parkrestaurant,* an à la carte menu in the evening in the *Bauernstuben*. ⑨

Waldhorn, Beuerner Str. 54 (☎72188 or 72288, fax 73488). Two-hundred-year old *Wirtshaus* in the suburb of Oberbeuern, just beyond Lichtental. Its restaurant (closed Mon & Tues) is generally regarded as being among Baden-Baden's best. ⑥

Wolfsschlucht, Ebersteinburgstr. 2 (☎22382, fax 22309). This hotel with café-restaurant is a good choice if you'd like to stay out of town. It's located by the main road on the outskirts of Ebersteinburg, at the junction of several hiking trails, one leading in a couple of minutes to the "Wolf's Glen" from which it takes its name. ④

Zur Nest, Rettigstr. 1 (☎23076, fax 28672). The cheapest rooms in central Baden-Baden are now available at what was previously solely a restaurant (closed Tues). This serves some of the best-value meals in town, offering authentic Magyar cooking as well as local dishes and plenty of vegetarian options. ③

Eating and drinking

Most of the best restaurants in Baden-Baden are in the hotels (see above), though there are plenty of other enticing places to eat and drink.

Baden-Badener Weinkeller, Maria-Viktoria-Str. 2. Small wine bar-restaurant in the town centre. Evenings only, closed Sun.

Böckeler's Café, Lange Str. 40–42. Traditional café with a wonderful selection of cakes and sweets; also does light meals.

Eckberg, Eckhöfe 12. Baden-Baden's only *Weingut,* situated in the northern part of Lichtental, has an adjoining wine bar where you can sample its products. Full meals are also served. Open Mon, Wed, Thurs & Sat 3–10pm, Sun 10am–10pm.

Kurhaus-Betriebe, Kaiserallee 1. Predictably classy restaurant attached to the casino.

Leo's, Luisenstr. 10. Trendy café-bar and, as such, something of a rarity in Baden-Baden.

Molkenkur, Quettigstr. 19. *Gaststätte* specializing in local dishes.

Münchner Löwenbräu, Gernsbacher Str. 9. This is like a little piece of Munich successfully transplanted to alien surroundings; it serves typically solid and inexpensive Bavarian fare, and is fronted by a small beer garden.

Papalangi, Lichtentaler Str. 13. Smart designer-style bistro with a courtyard terrace serving high-quality if pricey Italianate dishes.

Stahlbad, Augustaplatz 2. An extremely elegant and expensive restaurant with garden terrace. In both cuisine and decor it rivals any of the hotel restaurants.

Warsteiner Brasserie, Kaiserallee 4. A popular rendezvous, particularly with the young. It serves a whole gamut of functions throughout the day, ranging from breakfast café to evening cocktail bar.

Entertainment

Baden-Baden maintains a prestigious highbrow cultural scene. It is the smallest town in the world to have two distinguished **symphony orchestras,** namely the recently retitled *SWF Sinfonieorchester* (which is now shared with Freiburg) and the *Baden Badener Philharmonie.* Concerts by both, and by visiting orchestras and soloists, regularly feature at the *Weinbrennersaal* and the *Benazetsaal* in the *Kurhaus.* Tickets for these, and for the **drama** and **opera** at the nearby *Theater* on Goetheplatz, can be had from the *Kurhaus* box office (☎932751 or 932791).

Rastatt

In 1698, Margrave Ludwig, nicknamed "Türkenlouis" on account of his victories over the Turks, decided to shift his seat from Baden-Baden to **RASTATT**, then an insignificant village 15km to the north, just before the point where the River Murg flows into the Rhine. This move was partly precipitated by the dilapidated condition of the Neues Schloss after the War of the Palatinate Succession. However, it was also influenced by the courtly culture of the time, which had decided that hilltop fortresses were redundant and should be replaced by planned palatial towns on the model of Versailles.

The town centre

Rastatt's town centre was planned in conjunction with its great Schloss but only finished in the mid-eighteenth century. Centrepiece is the elliptical Marktplatz, with several fountains, the **Rathaus** and the **Stadtkirche St Alexander**, the last-named already showing Neoclassical influence. Between here and the Schloss are a number of handsome courtiers' houses. One of these, Herrenstr. 11, houses the **Heimatmuseum** (Wed, Fri & Sun 10am–noon & 3–5pm; free), which traces the history of the town and includes displays of medieval art and souvenirs of Türkenlouis.

The Schloss and Schlossgarten

The massive red sandstone **Schloss** was built in just ten years to plans by an Italian architect, Domenico Rossi. It's approached via a spacious U-shaped courtyard, guarded by a balustrade with writhing Baroque statues, while the central wing is topped by a glistening figure of Jupiter, dubbed the *Goldener Mann.* The main reception rooms of the interior are under long-term restoration, but some are now accessible by **guided tour** (Tues–Sun 10am–4/5pm; DM6). In addition you can see the **Wehrgeschichtliches Museum** (same times; free) and the **Freiheitsmuseum** (Tues–Fri 10am–5pm, Sat & Sun 10am–noon & 2–5.30pm; free) on the ground floor. The former shows weapons, uniforms and other military memorabilia from medieval times to the present day. The latter traces the history of German liberalism – a slender theme. Rastatt was chosen as the venue for this museum because it was the last stronghold of the rebels in the revolutions of 1848–49, one of the few occasions when the authoritarian nature of German society was seriously challenged. In the north wing of the building, entered from Lyzeumstrasse, is the sumptuous **Schlosskirche**; it's generally kept locked but a notice will tell you where to get the key.

The most imposing part of the Schlossgarten is now unfortunately cut off by an arterial road to the south, though at least it does leave a peaceful corner at the edge of town. Here is the graceful **Einsiedelner Kapelle**, a miniaturized version of the great Swiss church of the same name. Türkenlouis' widow, Margravine Augusta Sibylla, went on pilgrimage there to pray for her son Ludwig Georg, who, at the age of six, was still unable to speak; needless to say, her faith worked the trick. Later, the **Pagodenburg** was made as a play-house for the prince and his brother. This was modelled on its counterpart in Nymphenburg on the outskirts of Munich; like the chapel, it was built by the new court architect, Johann Michael Ludwig Rohrer. Behind is the Jugendstil **Wasserturm**, now a café.

Schloss Favorite

Some 5km from the centre of Rastatt, on the way to Baden-Baden, is **Schloss Favorite** (guided tours mid-March to Sept 9am–5pm; Oct to mid-Nov 9am–4pm; DM8), the summer residence of Augusta Sibylla in her years as regent. Here, J.M.L. Rohrer attempted to create the smaller-scale opulence characteristic of the Central European courts which the margravine preferred to the French-inspired grandeur favoured by her husband. The interiors are often riotously ornate, notably the **Spiegelkabinett** with its 330 mirrors, and the **Florentiner Zimmer,** lavishly adorned with coloured marbles, stucco, rare woods and semi-precious stones.

Practicalities

Rastatt's **Bahnhof** is at the eastern end of town; here the scenic *Murgtalbahn* from Freudenstadt connects with the express line down the Rhine. The **tourist office** is in the Rathaus on Marktplatz (Mon 8.30am–6pm, Tues–Fri 8.30am–4.30pm; ☎07222/972462).

Reasonably priced **hotels** include *Zum Löwen*, Kaiserstr. 9 (☎07222/34556; ③) and *Kehler Hof,* Kehler Str. 43 (☎07222/ 32938; ③). For something more upmarket try *Zum Engel,* Kaiserstr. 65 (☎07222/77980; ④), *Schiff,* Poststr. 2 (☎07222/7720; ⑤) or *Schwert,* in a Baroque mansion at Herrenstr. 3a (☎07222/7680; ⑥).

As can be seen from the smoking chimneys, Rastatt is a **beer** town in the middle of a wine region. The *Bräustübl* of *Hofbräu Hatz* is at Poststr. 12; the food here is very reasonably priced. Among the best restaurants are *Sigi's* in *Hotel Schwert* and *Zum Storchennest,* Karlstr. 24.

Karlsruhe

KARLSRUHE is the baby of German cities. It didn't exist at all until 1715, when **Carl Wilhelm**, Margrave of Baden-Durlach, began the construction of a retreat at the edge of the Hardter Wald. There he could escape from a wife who bored him, in order to pursue his cultural interests – and to enjoy the company of several mistresses. The planned town which subsequently grew up around the palace was given an appropriate appellation – "Carl's Rest". Initially modest in size, its growth was stimulated by its establishment as the capital of the re-united state of Baden in 1771 and by the subsequent elevation of its rulers to the title of Grand Dukes under Napoleon's re-organization of the European political map. Karlsruhe flourished throughout the nineteenth century, enjoying what was, by German standards, a remarkably liberal atmosphere and becoming a major centre for both science and art. In 1945, however, it finally lost its status as a regional capital; Baden was divided between the American and French occupation zones, and Stuttgart made the obvious choice as seat of government for the embryonic province of Baden-Württemberg. As if by way of compensation, Karlsruhe was nom-

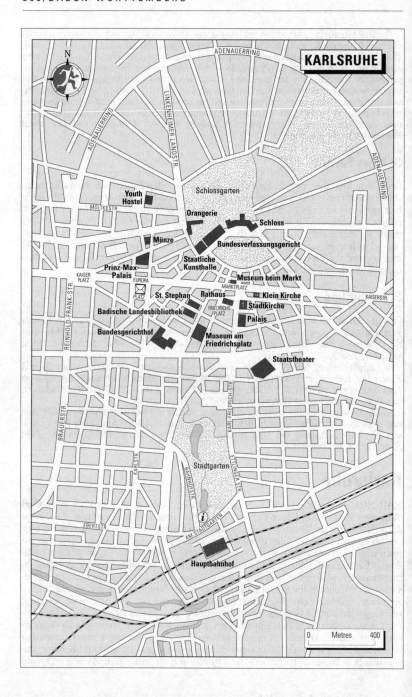

N

KARLSRUHE

ADENAUERRING

LINKENHEIMER LANDSTR.

ADENAUERRING

ADENAUERRING

Schlossgarten

Youth
Hostel

MOLTKESTR.

Orangerie

Schloss

Münze

Bundesverfassungsgericht

Prinz-Max-
Palais

Staatliche
Kunsthalle

KAISER
PLATZ

Museum beim Markt

EUROPA

REINHOLD-FRANK-STR.

PLATZ

MARKTPLATZ

KAISERSTR.

St. Stephan

Rathaus

Klein Kirche

Badische Landesbibliothek

FRIEDRICHS
PLATZ

Stadtkirche

Palais

Bundesgerichthof

Museum am
Friedrichsplatz

Staatstheater

BRAUERSTR.

KARL-FRIEDRICH-STR.

KARLSTR.

BAHNHOFSTR.

Stadtgarten

ETTLINGER STR.

EBERTSTR.

AM STADTGARTEN

Hauptbahnhof

0   Metres   400

THE FAN TOWN

Looking at a map or an aerial photograph, Karlsruhe appears as an extraordinarily hand-some city, thanks to its striking fan-shaped plan. As in an earlier purpose-built princely town, Mannheim, the hub of the system is the Schloss, here placed in isolation to the extreme north. Again this building is U-shaped, but thereafter the geometric patterns become far more imaginative and complex. The Schloss gardens are circular, with the outer half left in a natural state, while the inner is closed by a crescent of regular build-ings; this forms a triangle with the Schloss which takes up exactly a quarter of the grounds. From here radiate nine dead-straight avenues (representing each of the Muses); the central axis, Karl-Friedrich-Strasse, runs in a vertical line from the palace's central pavilion, while the two end ones shoot outwards at angles of 45° from the wings, with the others placed at regular intervals in between.

inated as the home of the two highest courts of the Federal Republic, a role which has saved it from sinking to the status of a provincial backwater.

As a standard large industrial city, Karlsruhe is by no means the central target of any-one's travels, but it nonetheless has much to offer – to discerning eggheads at least. The city's own propaganda baldly proclaims that it occupies fifth place in the hierarchy of the country's cultural centres. Whether or not this self-estimation is accurate, the **museums** (which are among the oldest public collections in Germany) are undeniably top class, the **Kunsthalle** alone being sufficient reason to justify a visit. In June of even-numbered years, Karlsruhe hosts the *Internationales Trachten-und-Folklorefest,* a colourful **festival** featuring folk groups from all over Europe and beyond.

The city

At ground level, the streets of the fan-shaped plan are rather less impressive than on a map, due largely to the fact that most of the original buildings have been supplanted by undistinguished successors, something for which war damage is partly, but by no means entirely, responsible. Nonetheless, outstanding architecture survives – includ-ing some of the finest **Neoclassical buildings** in Germany – though the Kunsthalle and the Landesmuseum are undoubtedly the city's prime attractions.

The Schloss and Schlosspark

Although the oldest surviving building, the **Schloss** is actually the second on the site, built in the French-influenced Baroque style of the 1750s. Sadly, it was completely gutted in the last war; the interior has now been modernized to house the **Badisches Landesmuseum** (Tues & Thurs–Sun 10am–5pm, Wed 10am–8pm; DM5). To the left of the entrance is the **archeology** section. Highlights are the ivory treasure from the Assyrian city of Arslan Tash; a relief of two horsemen from Nineveh; a Sicilian statuette of the goddess *Nike*; and a carving of a gift bringer from Xerxes' palace in Persepolis. Further on are some impres-sive pieces of Roman sculpture, notably *Hanging Marsyas* from a villa near Rome; *Mithras Killing the Bull,* which came from near Heidelberg; and a relief of two underwater gods from a settlement not far from Karlsruhe. In the corresponding wing to the right of the entrance is the medieval and Renaissance section, which includes four stunningly bold stained-glass windows designed by **Baldung** for the Carthusian monastery in Freiburg and a polychrome limewood *Madonna and Child* by **Riemenschneider**.

The **telephone code** for Karlsruhe is ☎0721

Upstairs is a re-creation of the Schloss' **Thronsaal** and the crown jewels of the Grand Duchy of Baden. However, these are completely overshadowed by the **Turkish booty** (*Türkenbeute*), captured by the Margrave Ludwig of Baden-Baden in his seventeenth-century campaigns against the Turks. Unique in Western Europe, this includes embroidery, illuminated books, cutlery, jewellery, leather, woodwork, saddles and weapons of all types. From this floor a staircase leads up to the balcony of the **tower** which has recently been made accessible again following decades of closure. This is the only public place from which the city's famous fan shape can be seen to proper effect.

In a building immediately to the left of the Schloss is housed the highest judicial authority in the country, the **Bundesverfassungsgericht** (Federal Constitutional Court). This is, in theory, an essential bulwark against the rise of any would-be Hitler, whose accession to power was greatly facilitated by the excessively liberal constitution of the Weimar Republic, which gave full rights to groups pledged to its destruction. The German "Basic Law" has been made much tougher; all political parties must now pledge themselves to the democratic process, or else be outlawed by this court.

The Staatliche Kunsthalle

At Hans-Thoma-Str. 2, the left side of the circular road round the Schlosspark, is the **Staatliche Kunsthalle** (Tues–Fri 10am–5pm, Sat & Sun 10am–6pm; DM5), housed in the mid-nineteenth century Academy of Art.

EARLY GERMAN PAINTING

The magnificent collection of old masters on the first floor is reached via a monumental staircase adorned with a huge fresco by **Moritz von Schwind**, *The Consecration of Freiburg Münster*. Focal point of the gallery is one of the world's greatest pictures, *The Crucifixion* by **Grünewald**. The last and most powerful of his four surviving versions of this scene, it conveys an almost unbearable feeling of tragic intensity. One of the most baffling aspects of Grünewald's art is its inconsistency, and *The Fall of Jesus*, which came from the same altarpiece, has far less emotional impact. Two small monochrome pictures, *St Elizabeth* and *St Lucy*, give a good idea of his early style.

A tiny *Christ with Symbols of the Passion* is a recently discovered **Dürer**; near it hangs a painted version of his famous woodcut *Knight, Death and the Devil* by one of his pupils. Other German paintings to look out for are **Burgkmair**'s *Portrait of Sebastian Brant* (the satirist), **Cranach**'s *Frederick the Wise Adoring the Virgin and Child*, and several works by **Baldung**, among which is *Margrave Christoph I of Baden in Adoration*; Moritz von Schwind included a cameo of the artist painting this work in the stairway fresco. Among the gallery's rarities is *The Raising of Lazarus* by **Wendel Dietterlin**, author of a book of fantastical Mannerist engravings which was immensely influential with late sixteenth-century architects and decorators.

FLEMISH, DUTCH AND FRENCH PAINTING

The representation of Flemish, Dutch and French painting is equally good. *St Jerome in the Desert* by **Patinir** is one of the few paintings definitely from the hand of this elusive Antwerp master of landscapes with fantastic rock formations. There are also important examples by three other rare painters – **Lucas van Leyden**'s *St Andrew*, **Wtewael**'s *Chicken Inspection*, and **Sweerts**' *Roman Wrestling Match*. **Rembrandt** is represented by a middle-period oval *Self-Portrait*, while there are several examples of **Rubens**. One of **Claude**'s largest canvases, *Adoration of the Golden Calf*, is the star of the seventeenth-century French section, which also includes a diptych of *The Annunciation*, perhaps the only surviving painting by the great Mannerist engraver **Jacques Bellange**, and canvases by Poussin, Le Brun, and the Le Nain brothers. From the following century are four still lifes by **Chardin**.

NINETEENTH-CENTURY GERMAN PAINTING
A notable array of nineteenth-century German painting is dominated by the work of **Hans Thoma**, who served as director of this gallery for twenty years. He was accomplished at both landscape and portraiture but had an unfortunate tendency to drift into sentimentality. **Menzel** and **Feuerbach** are represented by important works, but the gem of this section is **Friedrich**'s tiny *Rocky Reef by a Beach*.

The Orangerie

The **Orangerie** (same hours and ticket) next door houses paintings by many of the established names of twentieth-century European art, along with a cross-section of nineteenth-century French schools, ranging from Delacroix and Courbet to the Impressionists and their followers. There's a good representation of the *Blaue Reiter* group, notably a couple of fine animal paintings by **Marc**. Another Expressionist masterpiece is **Kokoschka**'s *View of Mont Blanc from Chamonix*, while **Beckmann**'s *Transport of the Sphynxes* is an allegorical canvas alluding to France's liberation from Nazism.

Marktplatz and around

Few buildings from the same generation as the Schloss remain; an exception is the sole place of worship the town then possessed, the **Kleine Kirche** (Little Church) on the main horizontal street, Kaiserstrasse. The next phase of the building of Karlsruhe only occurred with Baden's promotion to an independent Grand Duchy. During the following 25 years, a remarkable local architect, **Friedrich Weinbrenner**, completely transformed the city into a worthy capital. As a young man, he had travelled to Rome; having assimilated the style of the ancient world, he employed its grand style in the creation of the great public buildings required by a modern city. Between the Schloss and the start of the central axis, he laid out the rectangular Marktplatz, at the far end of which is an austere red sandstone **Pyramid** containing the grave of Carl Wilhelm. The western side of the square is dominated by the long pink range of the **Rathaus**. Opposite, the Corinthian facade of the **Stadtkirche** looks like an updated version of a Roman temple. Its present interior is modern and functional, the dignified galleried original having been a casualty of wartime bombs.

Just off the northern side of the square at Karl-Friedrich-Str. 6 is the **Museum beim Markt** (Tues & Thurs–Sun 10am–5pm, Wed 1.30–8pm; DM2, but included in price of Landesmuseum entrance). It's devoted to the applied and industrial arts of the twentieth century, featuring a good Art Nouveau/Jugendstil section, as well as works by members of the Bauhaus and other big names in international design.

Immediately south of Marktplatz is another square, Rondellplatz, this time circular in shape. It contains the **Palais** (now a bank), whose forms are almost identical to those of the Stadtkirche. In the centre of the square rises an **Obelisk** in honour of the Grand Duke Carl, celebrating his granting of a constitution to the citizens of Baden. West along Erbprinzstrasse is the **Museum am Friedrichsplatz** (Tues–Sat 10am–4pm, Sun 10am–6pm; DM4), the original late Neoclassical home of the Grand Ducal collections. It's now entirely given over to natural history, mostly stuffed animals, but has a good prehistoric section, which includes the only complete skeleton of a hipparion (a forerunner of the horse) yet discovered. Alongside is the **Badische Landesbibliothek** (Mon–Wed & Fri 9am–6pm, Thurs 9am–8pm, Sat 9.30am–12.30pm; free), which displays its treasures – including many wonderful medieval illuminated manuscripts – in a series of temporary exhibitions.

St Stephan and the Bundesgerichthof

Further evidence of the enlightened, tolerant nature of the young state of Baden is provided by the Catholic church of **St Stephan** directly opposite the Landesbibliothek.

This was built by Weinbrenner, himself a Protestant, at the same time as he was working on the Stadtkirche for members of his own faith. The main body of the church is circular while the portico is Doric, the whole being a conscious re-interpretation of the great Pantheon in Rome. Down Ritterstrasse is a heavy late nineteenth-century palace formerly used by the heir to the grand duchy; it now houses the second most important law court in Germany, the **Bundesgerichthof** (Federal Supreme Court). This is where the most important postwar criminal trials have been held, including those of several of the Baader-Meinhof gang.

The Münze and Prinz-Max-Palais

Karlsruhe's third Federal institution is the **Münze** (Mint) on Stephanienstrasse just to the west of the Kunsthalle. Weinbrenner's last building, this is still serving its original purpose, albeit on a much larger scale. Just down Karlstrasse is the **Prinz-Max-Palais** (Tues & Thurs–Sun 10am–5pm, Wed 11am–8pm; free), a stolid Wilhelmine mansion now named after one of its former owners, who served a heady five-week stint in the autumn of 1918 as last Chancellor of the Second Reich. In that time, he democratized the constitution, dismissed the military dictator Erich Ludendorff, began peace negotiations, and announced the abdication of the Kaiser before the latter had consented; whereupon he himself resigned and vanished from the national stage. The top floor of the building now contains the local history museum, with maps and prints, plus a model of how the city looked in 1834, when it was at its most splendid. Also exhibited is the *Draisienne*, first exhibited in Paris in 1818 by the Karlsruhe inventor **Karl von Drais**: decide for yourself whether or not it deserves its disputed title as the world's first bicycle.

Durlach

DURLACH, 5km east of the city centre, can be reached by train, or by tram #1 or #2. It was the original seat of the local Margraves, and is hence described as the "mother town" of Karlsruhe, of which it now forms a part, while retaining its own quiet atmosphere. The focal point of Durlach is **Schloss Karlsburg,** an unfinished Baroque rebuild of the Gothic-Renaissance castle destroyed by the French in the War of the Palatinate Succession. Part of it now houses the **Pfinzgaumuseum und Karpatendeutsches Museum** (Tues 4–7pm, Wed 10am–noon, Sat 2–5pm, Sun 10am–5pm; free), the former focusing on the region, the latter on the folklore of the German communities in the Carpathians. A short walk to the east is the lower station of Germany's oldest functioning **rack railway,** the *Turmbergbahn,* which ascends to the summit of the Turmberg (mid-May to late Sept daily 10am–6/7pm, reducing gradually to weekends only in winter; DM1.50 each way).

Practicalities

Karlsruhe's **Hauptbahnhof** is situated well to the south of the city centre. Directly facing the entrance at Bahnhofplatz 6 is the **tourist office** (Mon–Fri 8am–6/7pm, Sat 8am–1pm; ☎35530). Ask here if you're interested in a **Rhine cruise**; there's a varied choice of routes from Easter to November, departing from the port at the western extremity of the city. The 24-hour ticket on the **public transport** system is a bargain at DM8 for the city, DM15 for the whole circuit (including Baden-Baden and Bruchsal). Note that the regional S-Bahn is unique in Germany, being serviced by trams which run both on the main rail tracks and through the streets of the city. This can cause confusion, as their numbers duplicate those of normal trams serving completely different routes, except that they are also marked with the letter S. To reach the centre, you can either go from the eastwards-pointing stop with tram #3 or #6 (the latter is circuitous) to Marktplatz, or from the westward-pointing stop with tram #3 or #4 to Europaplatz. **Mitfahrzentrale**'s office is at Rankestr. 14 (☎33666).

Accommodation

Centrally sited **hotels** are plentiful, but cater overwhelmingly for the business market; there are, however, a few bargains to be found. The **youth hostel** has a good location just five minutes' walk from the Schloss at Moltkestr. 2b (☎28248; 🏠). You can stay for much less in the outlying villages; there's a **campsite**, *Turmbergblick*, Tiengerer Str. 40 (☎44060) 5km east in the incorporated town of Durlach.

HOTELS AND PENSIONS

Am Markt, Kaiserstr. 76 (☎20921, fax 28066). Of all the many business-class hotels in the city centre, this is the one with the best location. ⑥

Am Zoo, Ettlinger Str. 33 (☎33678). Pleasant small pension located a short walk north of the Hauptbahnhof. ⑤

Beim Schupi, Durmersheimer Str, 6, Grünwinkel (☎55940, fax 559480). Highly characterful hotel in a western inner suburb which doubles as the headquarters of a dialect theatre, the *Volkstheater d'Badisch Bühn*. The rooms are furnished in Black Forest style, while the restaurant serves traditional local dishes and has a beer garden. ⑦

Eden, Bahnhofstr. 15–19 (☎18180, fax 181 8222). Large hotel just off the western side of the Stadtgarten, midway between the Hauptbahnhof and the city centre. Among the facilities are a good restaurant and a pleasant garden terrace. ⑦

Residenz, Bahnhofplatz 14–16 (☎37150, fax 371 5113). Part of the *Ringhotel* chain, this fine hotel with restaurant is situated directly opposite the Hauptbahnhof. ⑧

Schlosshotel, Bahnhofplatz 2 (☎38320, fax 38322). Very grand and traditional hotel right beside the Hauptbahnhof. In addition to the expensive main restaurant, there's the more reasonably priced *Schwarzwaldstube*. ⑨

Schwannen, Augustenburgstr. 10, Grötzingen (☎463496, fax 463496). This is located in an incorporated town immediately east of Durlach, and is easily reached by S-Bahn or mainline train. The rooms here, which form an adjunct to an Italian restaurant, are the cheapest in Karlsruhe but nonetheless perfectly adequate. ②–③

Stadtmitte, Zähringerstr. 72 (☎389637). Pension handily located in a city centre apartment block. ⑤

Steuermann, Hansastr. 13, Daxlanden (☎503201, fax 574020). Good medium-range hotel and restaurant right by the Rhine harbour in the far west of the city. ⑦

Zum Ochsen, Prinzstr. 64, Durlach (☎943 8643, fax 943 8643). Seventeenth-century inn which has been refurbished in French country house style. It only has six rooms, so is best booked well in advance. The gourmet restaurant, which continues the Gallic theme, is generally considered to be the best in Karlsruhe. ⑧

Eating and drinking

Karlsruhe has many fine restaurants in addition to those in the hotels (see above). For a university city, it's surprisingly quiet come the evening, though a few pockets – notably around Ludwigsplatz – do spring to life.

RESTAURANTS

Africa, Kaiserpassage 18. Has a varied menu of North African food, and sometimes features live music.

Dudelsack, Waldstr. 79. Well known for its game and fish dishes, and has a pleasant terrace courtyard.

Goldenes Kreuz, Karlstr. 21a. *Gaststätte* of the local *Hoepfner* brewery, occupying an eighteenth-century building. Good-value set lunches are available.

Hansjakob Stube, Ständehausstr. 4. Cellar restaurant offering excellent *Gutbürgerliche Küche*. Closed Sun evening & Wed.

Künsterlerkneipe zur Krone, Pfarrstr. 18, Daxlanden. A lovely old *Weinstube* with half-timbered courtyard located on a quiet suburban street. Its walls are hung with paintings by turn-of-the-century Black Forest artists; the food served is among the very best in the city. Closed Sun & Mon.

Oberländer Weinstube, Akademiestr. 7. Karlsruhe's oldest wine bar-restaurant has a truly *gemütlich* interior and garden courtyard; it also serves the best meals in the town centre. Closed Sun.

Rosa Bianca, Akademiestr. 23. Small, extremely popular Italian restaurant.

Schützenhaus, Jean-Ritzert-Str. 8, Durlach. Good *Gaststätte* with beer garden on top of the Turmberg. Closed Mon & Tues.

BARS AND CAFÉS

Alta Natura, Kaiserstr. 229. Vegetarian café attached to a wholefood shop.

Café Feller, corner of Marktplatz and Kaiserstrasse. Traditional café which spills out into the square in summer.

Café Salmen, Ludwigsplatz. Animated café-bar much patronized by students.

Das Krokodil, Waldstr. 63. Café-bar which offers a good selection of salads and sometimes features live music.

Stephanie, Stephanienstr. 92. Trendy bar which is particularly popular with artists and art students.

Vogelbräu, Kapellenstr. 50. Hausbrauerei serving a cloudy unfiltered beer.

Theatre and live music

The main **theatre** is the *Badisches Staatstheater*, Baumeisterstr. 11 (☎35570 or 380300) which presents opera, operetta, musicals, ballet and concerts in its main auditorium, plays in the smaller hall. Other venues for drama include *Kammertheater*, Karl-Friedrich-Str. 24 (☎23111) and *Die Insel*, Wilhelmstr. 14 (☎365330) while *Marotte Figurentheater*, Kaiserallee 11 (☎841555) has puppet shows. Other concerts are held at the *Stadthalle* at Festplatz 4 (☎37200) and **live jazz** is performed at *Jubez*, Am Kronenplatz (☎33048).

NORTHERN BADEN-WÜRTTEMBERG

The northern part of Baden-Württemberg consists of various territories which were only incorporated into the Grand Duchy of Baden and the Kingdom of Württemberg as a result of the Napoleonic redistribution of the map of Europe, and whose very different history and geography mean that they're best considered separately.

The fertile **Kraichgau** region, between the Rhine and the Neckar north of Karlsruhe, was particularly associated with the Prince-bishops of Speyer, who established their resplendent new palatial headquarters at **Bruchsal** in the eighteenth century. Further north is the heart of the **Palatinate** (*Pfalz* or *Kurpfalz*), which was ruled by the Count Palatine of the Rhineland, the most senior official in the Holy Roman Empire and one of the seven Electors. The name of the old state lives on in the Land of Rhineland-Palatinate, but its original boundaries were very different. For five hundred years its capital was **Heidelberg** – a huge favourite with visitors, and a place which definitely warrants several days' stay. The planned town of **Mannheim**, now Baden-Württemberg's second city, was built as the new Palatine capital in the early eighteenth century, with **Schwetzingen** and its fantastical gardens used by the court in the summer months. Down the Neckar from Heidelberg is the well-preserved medieval town of **Bad Wimpfen**, for centuries a Free Imperial City.

Like Swabia, **Franconia** (*Franken*) was one of the five great provinces of medieval Germany. Under Napoleon, nearly all of this was incorporated into Bavaria, but the northwestern part – consisting of the **Hohenlohe** plain and part of the **Tauber valley** – was split off and used to beef up both Baden and Württemberg. This includes a section of the famous **Romantic Road**, which mostly lies in Bavaria.

Bruchsal

It was the first time I had seen such architecture. The whole of next day I loitered about the building; hesitating half-way up shallow staircases balustraded by magnificent branching designs of wrought metal; wandering through double doors that led from state room to state room; and gazing with untutored and marvelling eyes down perspectives crossed by the diminishing slants of winter sunbeams.

Patrick Leigh Fermor, *A Time of Gifts*

On his walk to Constantinople, Patrick Leigh Fermor struck it lucky at **BRUCHSAL**, staying as guest of the burgomaster in the resplendent Baroque **Schloss**. His description reflects the fact that this is no ordinary palace; indeed, it's a complete courtly town, comprising over fifty different buildings, which stands as an oasis in the midst of the ugly modern community which now surrounds it.

The town

Other than the magnificent Schloss, Bruchsal has very little to offer in the way of sights. Bruchsal's **Bahnhof** is a junction on the rail lines linking Stuttgart, Karlsruhe and Heidelberg. To reach the Schloss from there, turn left and continue straight on; you'll reach the gardens within a few minutes. Alternatively, turn right on arriving at Kaiserstrasse; this soon brings you to the end of Schönbornstrasse.

The Schloss

Construction of the **Schloss** began in 1720 by order of the newly enthroned Prince-bishop of Speyer, Cardinal Hugo Damian von Schönborn, who had fallen out with the local burghers and so decided to move his seat across the Rhine to what was then no more than a hamlet in the heart of the Kraichgau region. Several talented architects were recruited to carry out the work, and the great **Bathasar Neumann** was occasionally seconded from his employment at Würzburg to supply the bravura touches needed to lift the project into the artistic first division.

The Schloss complex, whose cheerful yellow, red and white buildings have been restored to pristine condition following devastation in an air raid at the end of the war, stands on Schönbornstrasse, which leads north to Heidelberg. Along the eastern side of the street are a series of offices, with the chancellery centre-stage; an army of lackeys lived in the large edifice to the south. At the northern end of the street is the **Damianstor**, while a smaller triumphal arch gives access to the main courtyard. To the left is the **Hofkirche**, whose haughty onion-domed belfry towers over all the other buildings; the interior has unfortunately been modernized. On the opposite side is the **Kammerflügel** where prestigious international **concerts** are often held.

THE INTERIOR
The great reception rooms are all in the central **Corps de Logis** (Tues–Sun 9am–5pm; DM5). Facing you on entry is Neumann's ingenious monumental **staircase**. The lower section is laid out as a dark grotto, covered with antique-style frescoes; you then ascend via walls richly covered with stucco to the airily bright oval landing. Here a brilliant *trompe l'oeil* fresco – an integral part of the overall design – apparently reaches the height of the dome, extending a perspective into the open heavens. Painted by **Januarius Zick**, the most accomplished German decorative artist of the day, it eulogizes the history of the Speyer diocese. Neumann and Zick also collaborated on the two rooms off the staircase.

THE MUSEUM MECHANISCHER MUSIKINSTRUMENTE
It's definitely worth paying the extra money to visit the **Museum Mechanischer Musikinstrumente** (Tues 10am–5pm, Wed–Sun 9.30am–5pm; DM7 including Schloss admission) which has recently been installed in some of the vacant rooms. Short demonstrations are given on a cross-section of the 200-odd exhibits, which were regarded as scientific miracles in their own time. Earliest of these are the musical clocks which were much in favour in eighteenth-century courts such as Bruchsal itself, and for which even the greatest composers were forced to prostitute their talents – Haydn wrote a delightful set of miniatures, while Mozart created several profound masterpieces, which have to be played on a full-sized organ for maximum effect. From the turn of the present century are examples of the piano-roll system pioneered by the German *Firma Welte*, which enables the accurate play-back of performances by famous pianists. This technique was later ambitiously adapted for the organ, and there's a marvellous instrument here which was formerly used to entertain guests in the *Hotel Excelsior* in Berlin.

Practicalities
The **tourist office** (Mon–Wed & Fri 8am–noon & 2–4pm, Thurs 8am–noon & 2–5pm; ☎07251/72771) is in the huge modern shopping centre called *Bürgerzentrum* at Am Alten Schloss 2. The cheapest **hotels** are *Gasthof Graf Kuno*, Württemberger Str. 97 (☎07251/2013; ④) and *Trautwein*, Amalienstr. 6 (☎07251/2138; ⑤). More expensive options are *Ratskeller*, Kaiserstr. 68 (☎07251/71230; ⑥), *Brauhaus Wallhall*, Kübelmarkt 8 (☎07251/72130; ⑥) and *Scheffelhöhe*, Adolf-Bieringer-Str. 20 (☎07251/8020; ⑦). There's a **campsite** and *Naturfreundehaus* at Karlsruher Str. 215 (☎07251/15106) to the south of the centre. For a meal or just a drink, try *Zum Bären*, within the Schloss complex at Schönbornstr. 28; it serves the best food in town and has a beer garden.

Schwetzingen

There's nothing quite like the gardens of **SCHWETZINGEN**. This town, which lies on the rail line between Karlsruhe and Mannheim, some 12km west of Heidelberg, was of very minor significance until the 1740s, when the **Jagdschloss** (guided tours April–Oct Tues–Sun 9am–4pm; Nov–March Sat & Sun 11am–3pm; DM8) was constructed as a summer residence for the Electors Palatine by the Heidelberg architect Johann Adam Breunig. The building itself is low-key; it's the **gardens** which get all the praise and all the visitors.

ELECTOR CARL THEODOR (1724–99)

Schwetzingen's stunning transformation from its long history of mediocrity was due to the Elector Carl Theodor, who inherited the Palatinate from his childless uncle and later became a somewhat reluctant Elector of Bavaria as well, when another branch of the Wittelsbachs died out. As if by compensation, Carl Theodor started several aristocratic lines, ennobling such of his many mistresses as were not high-born; even today, there's a standing joke in the region that his bastard descendants can immediately be identified through having his distinctive nose. If Carl Theodor's ambitious political goals ultimately ended in failure (the Palatinate was carved up just two years after his death), his track record as a patron of the arts has proved far more enduring. The most important decision he took, alongside opening the great art treasures of the Alte Pinakothek in Munich to the public, was to make Schwetzingen his summer residence and to embellish it with the pleasure park he craved yet was unable to have in his fortified seat at Mannheim.

The Schlossgarten

The **Schlossgarten** (daily during official summertime 8am–8pm; rest of year 9am–5/6pm; DM3.50, but included in Schloss entrance) is a supreme triumph of the art of landscaping and of the Rococo style, representing a highly original escape into a world of pure fantasy. It took some thirty years to lay out the gardens and adorn them with a series of whimsical buildings. These aimed at capturing the atmosphere of various far-off civilizations; this fascination with the exotic marks out Schwetzingen as one of the precursors of the budding Romantic movement. Best time to see the gardens is late spring – the lilac, ivy and chestnut trees are a riot of colour in May, while the linden trees are at their most fragrant during June. High summer can be uncomfortably crowded; off-season, you might have the park to yourself, but, in addition to the absence of bloom, the pavilions are then kept locked.

The Schlosstheater and around

The **Schlosstheater** (daily guided tours June–Sept at 11.30am, 2pm, 3pm & 3.30pm; DM2) was added to the main building by **Nicolas de Pigage**, an ingenious architect from Lorraine who arrived in Schwetzingen in 1750 and spent much of the next three decades constructing its garden buildings. In an individual confection, mixing Rococo with Neoclassicism, Pigage built a triple-tiered auditorium in the shape of a lyre, facing a deep stage harbouring complicated machinery underneath. It was originally intended for the performance of French comedies, and Voltaire, a personal friend of the Elector, was a regular visitor. With its grand dimensions, long vistas, straight avenues and symmetrical layout, the French-style **formal garden** is very much a product of the Age of Reason. It's richly endowed with fountains (which play daily in summer), mock-antique urns and a host of statues.

Just west of here is the **Tempel Apollos**, which served as an open-air auditorium. A sunken garden with sphinxes leads to an artificial mound crowned by a temple in the style of Classical Rome housing a statue of the god. This is the first in a row of buildings by Pigage; alongside is one of his finest works, the **Badhaus** (daily in summer 10am–12.30pm & 1–6pm). Its nine rooms are adorned with rosewood panellings, sculptures, landscape paintings, and Chinese tapestries and silks. The marble bath repeats the elliptical shape of the central drawing room; its water pipes are artistically decorated, and the chamber itself adorned with mirrors and jewels. Next to the Badhaus is an arbour with a fountain of water-spouting birds; it's nicknamed "The End of the World" because of the *trompe l'oeil* perspective, which terminates in a painted diorama. Crossing the moat and continuing northwards, you come to the **Tempel der Botanik**, supposedly representing the trunk of an oak tree, and the **Römischer Wasserweg**, a spectacular fake of a fort and aqueduct, deliberately built as an ivy-covered ruin to enhance its illusory effect. Beyond here are the outer reaches of the park, laid out in the contrastingly untamed style of an English garden. By following the path traversing this section, you can return to the main part of the park via the humpbacked **Chinesische Brücke**.

The Tempel Merkurs, the Moschee and the Tempel Minervas

Pigage's remaining buildings are at the opposite end of the park. The **Tempel Merkurs** is reached via either of the paths along the side of the artificial lake. Originally, this monument was intended to be redolent of ancient Egypt, but ended up as a pastiche of the clifftop ruin of a European Romanesque castle, anachronistically adorned with scenes of the life of Mercury. From here, there's a spectacular vista over a pond to the pink cupola and minarets of the **Moschee** or Mosque (daily in summer 10am–12.30pm & 1–6pm), the most original structure in the gardens and the last to be built. It's a unique translation of Oriental forms into the language of eighteenth-century

European architecture. Returning in the direction of the circular section of the garden, you come to the sixteen-columned **Tempel Minervas**, which goes back to the favourite source of inspiration, Classical Rome. The goddess of wisdom is seated inside; she also appears in a frieze above the entrance, poring over a plan of the gardens of Schwetzingen, to which she gives her seal of approval.

Practicalities

The **tourist office** (Mon–Fri 9am–noon & 2–5pm, Sat 9–11am; ☎06202/4933) is at Schlossplatz 2, in one of the few imposing buildings in the town itself, the eighteenth-century **Palais Hirsch**. This is also where you can book for performances in the Schlosstheater. The **Bahnhof** is five minutes' walk from here down Carl-Theodor-Strasse. **Buses** to and from Heidelberg stop on Schlossplatz; services run every half-hour for most of the day. Although there's no particular reason for staying in Schwetzingen, it makes a good alternative base if Heidelberg is booked solid. Among the many **hotels** are *Gasthof Zum Ritter,* Schlossplatz 1 (☎06202/93300; ⑤) and *Löwe,* Schloss Str. 4 (☎06202/26066, fax 06202/10726; ⑦).

Asparagus has been cultivated in Schwetzingen for more than three centuries; in season (April–June) it can be sampled in any of the town's **restaurants**, including those in the hotels listed above. Each April and May, the Schlosstheater is the setting for an international **music festival**, often focusing on the works of Gluck. Another festival in September is devoted solely to Mozart; there are also regular musical and theatrical performances of all kinds throughout the year.

Mannheim

MANNHEIM was formerly considered one of the most beautiful cities in Germany. Writing in 1826, William Hazlitt called it "a splendid town, both from its admirable buildings and the glossy neatness of the houses. They are too fine to live in, and seem only made to be looked at." A mere stripling among German cities, it was founded in 1606 as a fortress at the strategically important intersection of the rivers Rhine and Neckar. Its meteoric rise to prominence came with the return of the Counts Palatine to Catholicism; unable to establish a satisfactory relationship with the burghers of Heidelberg, Carl Philipp decided in 1720 to make Mannheim the main seat of his court. A daringly original **planned town** was laid out, which served as capital of the Palatinate for the next 57 years, becoming one of Europe's most celebrated centres of the performing arts. The nineteenth century saw heavy industrialization, centred on the harbour trade and shipbuilding, though its most prestigious feature was the automobile factory established by Carl Benz, who demonstrated his first vehicle here in 1886. Alas, the continued prominence of industry, coupled with heavy damage in the last war, means that the city's former glory has long since vanished. However, the highly esteemed **grid-plan** still survives.

The city

Most of Mannheim's obvious sights are situated within or near the original grid. However, several notable technical attractions are a bit further afield in the green area adjacent to the Neckar.

The **telephone code** for Mannheim is ☎0621

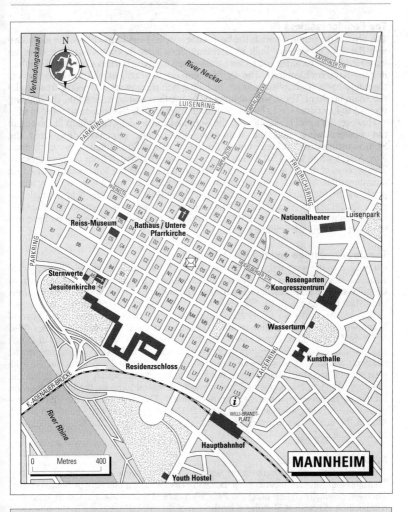

THE CHESSBOARD TOWN

The construction of Mannheim was based on a **chessboard layout** on the strip of land between the Rhine and Neckar. Streets to the west of the central axis are designated A to K, moving northwards; proceeding in the same direction, those to the east are L to U. The street number indicates proximity to the axis, so that D7, for example, is to the far west, whereas R7 is at the extreme east. Obviously, each house then bears a second number, which indicates its position on the square. At first the system can be confusing, particularly when you arrive at the Hauptbahnhof, which is at the extreme southeast corner of the grid, at a point where the blocks are of widely varying sizes. However, once you get the hang of it, there's really no other European city which it's so simple to find your way around.

The Residenzschloss

The pivot of the planned town is the horseshoe-shaped **Residenzschloss**, the most massive Baroque palace ever built in Germany. Soon after its completion, it became an expensive white elephant – the court transferred to Munich when Carl Theodor inherited the Bavarian Electorate. The dignified exterior is heavily indebted to Palladianism; the interior was far more sumptuous, including rich stuccowork and ceiling frescoes by the Asam brothers. These were obliterated by wartime bombs; afterwards, the building was put to functional use to house the university, with only the outside restored in full.

However, as a real labour of love, the **Schlosskirche** (daily 9am–5pm) at the end of the western wing, plus the main reception rooms, nowadays designated the **Schlossmuseum** (guided tours April–Oct Tues–Sun 10am–1pm & 2–5pm; Nov–March same hours Sat & Sun only; DM4) were re-created from old photographs. The success of this project is highly debatable, but at least the **Rittersaal**, reached via a monumental staircase, provides an effective concert hall, which is particularly appropriate as the Mannheim court's greatest achievements were in the field of music. Its orchestra, which pioneered the mellow tones of the clarinet, was regarded in the eighteenth century as the best in the world, while the symphony was developed here into the chief form of instrumental music.

The Jesuitenkirche and the Reiss-Museum

On A5, just to the west of the Residenzschloss, is the **Jesuitenkirche**, deliberately constructed as the largest church in town to symbolize the Palatinate court's return to Catholicism; the grandiose facade and the central dome are the most striking features. Immediately to its rear is the **Sternwarte**, an observatory tower now used by artists.

Just to the north on C5 is the **Zeughaus**, erected in the penultimate year of Mannheim's period as Palatine capital. It now houses the **Reiss-Museum** (Tues, Wed & Fri–Sun 10am–5pm, Thurs noon–5pm; DM4, free Thurs), with collections of Dutch and Flemish cabinet pictures, of decorative arts and of local history – look out for the old maps and prints which give an idea of the original dignified appearance of the grid-plan streets, something hardly even hinted at today. On the square directly in front of the Zeughaus is a brand-new building specially designed to house the most important section of the museum, the archeology department. This originated as the Elector's private cabinet of antiquities, and ranges from the Stone Age to the early medieval period. Also in the new museum are ethnological displays from Africa, the Islamic countries, India, China and Japan.

Around the Marktplatz

The **Marktplatz**, which occupies the square G1, is the scene of markets on Tuesday, Thursday and Saturday mornings. In the centre rises a large monument presented by Carl Theodor; originally representing the Four Elements, it was re-worked into an allegorical composition in praise of Mannheim by the son of the original sculptor. On the south side of the square is a curious Siamese twin of a building, erected just before Mannheim became the seat of the court. Sharing a central tower, the eastern part serves as the **Rathaus**, while the western is the **Untere Pfarrkirche**; their physical union is supposed to symbolize the concord between Justice and Piety, between secular and sacred authority.

The fringe of the grid

The other main square, the Jugendstil **Friedrichsplatz**, is due east from here, just outside the central grid. It was laid out around the **Wasserturm**, which is some fifteen years older, and is the main example of a style which left a considerable mark all over the city. Another fine Jugendstil building is the **Kunsthalle** (Tues, Wed & Fri–Sun 10am–5pm, Thurs noon–5pm; DM4) on Moltkestrasse, the next street to the south. This contains one of the best collections of nineteenth- and twentieth-century painting and sculpture in Germany, and is now the city's most obvious single draw. Highlight of the collection is one of the great masterpieces of Impressionism, **Manet**'s *Execution of Emperor Maximilian of Mexico*, the largest and most complete of the four versions he painted of this subject. Other notable works in the same room are **Cézanne**'s *Pipe Smoker*, and still lifes by Renoir and van Gogh. The German section was brutally pruned in the Nazi purges against "degenerate art", but there's a room devoted to Romanticism, including several important examples of **Feuerbach**. *Portrait of the Writer Max Herrmann-Neisse* is one of **George Grosz**'s best canvases, while there's an outstanding array of modern German sculpture, with **Barlach** and **Lehmbruck** strongly represented, along with a host of avant-garde works. Major temporary exhibitions are frequently held in the gallery.

On the banks of the River Neckar

At the northernmost end of the grid-plan the central axis road continues over the Neckar by the Kurpfälzbrücke. Moored close to the bridge is the 1920s passenger steamer *Mainz*, now designated the **Museumsschiff Mannheim** (Tues–Sun 10am–5pm; free). Nearby is the departure point for **harbour cruises** (Easter & June–Aug; 40min trip DM5.50; 90min voyage along the Neckar DM11).

Eastwards along the river is the city's playground, the **Luisenpark** (May–Aug 9am–9pm; rest of year 9am–dusk; DM5). This boasts various flower gardens, hothouses, an aquarium, a menagerie of farmyard animals and waterfowl, an open-air stadium for concerts, a gondola course and a watersports centre. There's also the **Fernmeldeturm** (Mon–Thurs & Sun 10am–9pm, Fri–Sat 10am–10pm; DM3.50) offering the best view of the city.

Just south of the park on Wilhelm-Varnholt-Platz is the **Planetarium** (showings Tues–Sun 3pm, also Tues 10am, Wed & Fri 8pm, Sat & Sun 5pm & 7pm; DM8). Nearby, at Museumsstr. 1, you'll find the **Landesmuseum für Technik und Arbeit** (Tues & Thurs 9am–5pm, Wed 9am–8pm, Sat & Sun 10am–5pm; DM4) housing a spectacular collection of historic machinery, including a steam locomotive which transports visitors through the grounds.

Practicalities

The **tourist office** (Mon–Fri 8.30am–6pm, Sat 8.30am–noon; ☎101011) is just across from the Hauptbahnhof at Willy-Brandt-Platz 4. **Mitfahrzentrale** have an office at L14, 11 (☎19444).

Accommodation

Hotels are overwhelmingly geared to the expense-account market, but there are a few budget choices as well. The **youth hostel** is at Rheinpromenade 21 (☎822718; ☎); take the underground passageway at the back entrance of the Hauptbahnhof, then turn left; it's only a few minutes' walk away. This convenient location makes it a good base for touring the surrounding area. **Camping** is possible (April–Sept only) on the banks of either of the city's two great rivers. The larger and cheaper site is at Neuostheim (☎416840) on the Neckar to the east; the other is to the south on Strandbad in Neckarau (☎856240); in spite of its name, it's located on a bend of the Rhine.

HOTELS AND PENSIONS

Arabella, M2, 12 (☎23050). The cheapest rooms in the city centre are in this apartment block pension. ③

Basler Hof, Tattersallstr. 27 (☎28816, fax 153292). One of several reasonably priced hotels on the street, a couple of minutes' walk north of the Hauptbahnhof. ④

Goldene Gans, Tattersallstr. 19 (☎105277 or 422020, fax 422 0260). Good value *Gasthaus* with *Weinstube* which includes wonderful buffet breakfasts in the price of a room. ④

Mannheimer Hof, Augusta-Anlage 4 (☎40050, fax 400 5190). Classy hotel with restaurant, part of the *Steigenberger* chain, at the eastern edge of the city centre. ⑨

Maritim Parkhotel, Friedrichsplatz 2 (☎15880, fax 158 8800). Although now part of the eponymous chain, this deluxe turn-of-the-century hotel with restaurant is nonetheless a place of real character. ⑨

Rosenstock, N3, 5 (☎27343). Centrally located *Gasthof* offering moderately priced rooms and meals. ④

Zum Ochsen, Haupststr. 70, Feudenheim (☎799550, fax 799 5533). This seventeenth-century *Gasthof,* the oldest in Mannheim, is situated north of the Neckar, 5km east of the city centre. Its restaurant is among the best in the city for solid German fare, and it also has a shady beer garden. ⑦

Eating and drinking

Although Mannheim has no obvious concentration of good places to eat and drink, there's a varied assortment of recommendable establishments scattered throughout the city.

Augusta, Augusta-Anlage 40. Moderately priced Italian restaurant.

Da Gianni, R7, 34. One of Germany's most highly regarded Italian restaurants, the cooking showing *nouvelle* touches. Predictably, it's very expensive.

Eichbaum, Käfertalerstr. 168. Located just north of the Neckar, this is the *Gaststätte* of the eponymous brewery, the largest in Mannheim. Its *Weizen* beers, both light and dark, are its most highly regarded products.

Flic Flac, B2, 12. Arty pub which features regular exhibitions and live music.

Heller's, N7, 13. Specialist vegetarian restaurant.

Henninger's Gutsschänke, T6, 28. Excellent and fairly priced wine bar-restaurant.

Martin, Lange Rötterstr. 53. This restaurant to the north of the Neckar is best known for its fish dishes, though it has a varied menu, including vegetarian options.

Zum Habeereck, Q4, 13. *Hausbrauerei* which also serves full meals.

Theatre and concerts

Mannheim has a vibrant **theatre** tradition; the *Nationaltheater* on Goetheplatz (☎24844) is the successor to the now-destroyed building near the Schloss which was associated with Schiller's youthful *Sturm und Drang* phase. Performances of plays, opera, ballet and musicals are presented, along with special shows for kids. Other venues are *Klapsmühl' am Rathaus* at D6, 3 (☎22488) for cabaret and pantomime, and *Puppenspiele,* Collinistr. 26 (☎24949) for puppets, while **concerts** are held at *Kongresszentrum Rosengarten* on Friedrichsplatz (☎410 6303).

Heidelberg

When the Romantic movement discovered **HEIDELBERG** in the late eighteenth century, the city was very much a fallen star. Capital of the Palatinate for five hundred years, it had never fully recovered from two sackings at the hands of French troops in the previous century; its rulers had abandoned their magnificent, crumbling Schloss in favour of the creature comforts of their new palace in Mannheim. Yet this wistful feeling of decay only enhanced the charms of the city, majestically set on both banks of the swift-flowing River Neckar between two ranges of wooded hills – a real-life fulfilment of the ideal German landscape, and a site known to be one of the earliest inhabited places in the world. To many of the rushed Grand Tour of Europe coach parties of today, Heidelberg *is* Germany, the only place in the country they see – or, perhaps, want to see.

For English-speaking visitors, the distinguished roll-call of predecessors gives Heidelberg special claims on the attention. Earliest of these was the Scots-born princess, **Elizabeth Stuart**, daughter of the first monarch of the United Kingdom, James I. She arrived in 1613 as the seventeen-year-old bride of the Elector Palatine and presided over

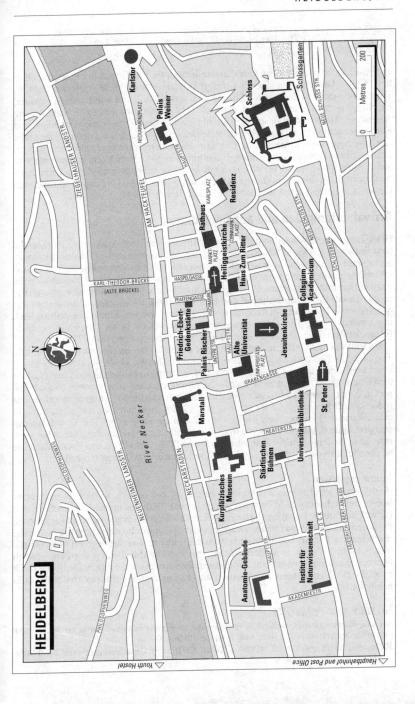

a spectacular court life for five years, before leaving for Prague and her ill-fated spell as the "Winter Queen". Heidelberg's greatest painter is also Britain's greatest: **J.M.W. Turner** first came to the city in 1836, and, in a series of oils and watercolours, captured its changing moods and magical plays of light in his own inimitable way. Among Americans, **Mark Twain** deserves pride of place: he began the hilarious travels round Europe recounted in *A Tramp Abroad* in Heidelberg in 1878, and his descriptions of the city have never been surpassed. By this time, Heidelberg was already a popular sojourn for Americans visiting Europe, though the numbers were a trickle in comparison with today. After World War II (in which, significantly, the city was spared from aerial bombardment), Heidelberg was chosen as the headquarters of the US Army in Europe, with the soldiers housed in the purpose-built Patrick Henry Village, to the south.

Arrival, information and accommodation

Heidelberg is best avoided in high summer: the students, who make such an essential contribution to the life of the city, clear out then and are replaced by hordes of tourists. Surprisingly, it's possible to cover all the essential sights fairly quickly, but you should certainly plan on staying for several days, in order to soak up the city's atmosphere. Be warned that first impressions of Heidelberg are likely to make you wonder what all the fuss is about: the **Hauptbahnhof** and **bus terminus** are situated in an anonymous quarter some 1.5km west of the centre, with a dreary avenue, Kurfürsten-Anlage, leading towards town. The rather harassed **tourist office** is on the square outside (Mon–Sat 9am–7pm, March 16–Nov 15 also Sun 10am–6pm; ☎21341 27735).

It's well worth investing in one of the rover tickets on the **public transport** network. The *Ticket 24 Plus* costs DM9 for 24 hours, or DM17.50 for the whole weekend. Provided it is not used before 9am on weekdays it can be used by up to two adults and three children travelling together. Alternatively, there's the *Heidelberg Card* which covers public transport in the city, free entry to nearly all the museums and sights and a host of miscellaneous reductions. Prices are DM25 for one day or DM34 for three days for one adult, rising to DM35.50 and DM48 respectively if up to two children are taken along. The Altstadt is mostly pedestrianized; tram #1 takes you from the Hauptbahnhof to Bismarckplatz, at the western end of the long, straight Hauptstrasse. Alternatively, bus #11 goes to Universitätsplatz on the southern side of the old city, bus #34 to Kornmarkt at the eastern end.

Accommodation

Heidelberg's popularity as a convention centre, as well as with tourists means that its **hotels** can be booked solid even out of high season. With this in mind it's worth reserving well in advance, or paying the tourist office's booking fee. If you want to look yourself, the board outside tells you where vacancies exist. The **youth hostel** is near the Zoo on the north bank of the Neckar, about 4km from the centre at Tiergartenstr. 5 (☎412066; 🏠); take bus #32. If it's full, as is often the case, the hostel in Mannheim is also close enough to make commuting cost-effective. Both **campsites** are east of the city by the river – *Heide* (☎06223/2111) is between Ziegelhausen and Kleingemünd; *Neckartal* (☎802506) is in Schlierbach.

HOTELS AND PENSIONS

Astoria, Rahmengasse 30 (☎402929). Very pleasant guesthouse in a quiet setting on the northern side of the Neckar, yet only a short walk from the Altstadt. ④

Ballmann, Rohrbacher Str. 28 (☎24287 or 25320, fax 182035). Capacious, good-value hotel situated just south of the Altstadt. ④

HEIDELBERG VIEWPOINTS

It's the long-range views which have made Heidelberg so famous, and the city is a ready-made subject for picture-postcard **photography**; with its hilly setting, there are plenty of angles to choose from. If you take the trouble to go to the same vantage point at different times of day, you'll see the reason for Heidelberg's hold on painters: the red sandstone buildings change their hue with the movement of the sun, and the shafts of light make magical effects as they illuminate and cast into shadow different parts of the scene. "One thinks Heidelberg by day the last possibility of the beautiful," wrote Mark Twain, "but when he sees Heidelberg by night, a fallen Milky Way. . . he requires time to consider upon the verdict."

The best-known view is from the northern quays of the Neckar, where you get a full-frontal panorama of the Altstadt nestling snugly below the Schloss, itself sharply etched against the background of the wooded Königstuhl. The spectacle from street level is surpassed by climbing up the slopes of the Heiligenberg via the celebrated **Philosophenweg** (Philosopher's Walk), so called because of the stimulus it offered to the meditation of Heidelberg thinkers. As an alternative, start from the town centre, and follow Neue Schloss Strasse and Molkenkurweg to the *Molkenkur* hotel, whose terrace gives a very different perspective. Further up, the Königstuhl is crowned by the **Fernsehturm** (Television Tower; March–Oct daily 10am–6/7pm; DM2), commanding a sweeping panorama over the Neckar valley and Odenwald. Both the *Molkenkur* and the Königstuhl are accessible by funicular (DM7.40 return).

Elite, Bunsenstr. 15 (☎25734, fax 163949). A much smaller hotel in the same part of town as *Ballmann*. ④

Goldener Hecht, Steingasse 2 (☎166025 or 53680, fax 536899). Thanks to its location beside the Alte Brücke, this historic hotel with restaurant occupies a prominent position in the famous view of Heidelberg from across the Neckar. ⑦

Hackteufel, Steingasse 7 (☎27162, fax 165379). Another good-quality hotel and restaurant on the same alley as *Goldener Hecht*. ⑦

Hirschgasse, Hirschgasse 3 (☎4540, fax 454111). This five-hundred-year-old *Gasthaus* is one of Heidelberg's poshest hotels. It possesses the oldest dwelling hall in Germany, one which features in Mark Twain's *A Tramp Abroad*. The bedrooms are decorated in modern designer style, and the restaurant (evenings only, closed Sun) is among the best in the city. ⑨

Jeske, Mittelbadgasse 2 (☎23733). Basic pension in the heart of the Altstadt with what are by far the cheapest rooms in Heidelberg. It's regularly full, and is reluctant to take reservations, so the best strategy is to turn up as early as possible. Breakfast is not included. ①

Molkenkur, Klingenteichstr. 31 (☎10894, fax 26872). Stands on the site of the original Schloss, high above its successor, and is directly accessible by the funicular. The terrace commands a grand-stand view of the city; there's also a fine restaurant. ⑦

Perkeo, Hauptstr. 75 (☎14130, fax 141337). Comfortable hotel named in honour of the dwarf who was the custodian to the predecessor of the Grosses Fass. It has an ideal location in the heart of the pedestrianized precinct. ⑦

Schnookeloch, Haspelgasse 8 (☎14460, fax 22377). Heidelberg's oldest surviving inn, dating back to 1407. Its tavern, which has a beer garden, is one of those which has long been associated with the students' corps. ⑦

Schönberger Hof, Untere Neckarstr. 54 (☎14060, fax 22377). Upmarket hotel in a handsome Baroque palace facing the Neckar. ⑦

Zum Ritter St George, Hauptstr. 178 (☎1350, fax 135230). Heidelberg's most magnificent mansion is now home to one of its most attractive hotels, a member of the *Romantik* group. It has a recommendable though fairly expensive restaurant. ⑦

The Schloss

Centrepiece of all the famous views of Heidelberg is the **Schloss**. A series of disparate yet consistently magnificent buildings of various dates, it somehow hasn't been diminished by its ruined condition; if anything, it has actually grown in stature. Enough remains (with the help of the plentiful pictorial records which exist) to give a clear idea of what it looked like in its prime, yet a new dimension has been added by the destruction, which reveals otherwise hidden architectural secrets and magnifies its relationship with the surrounding landscape.

The fortifications

The Schloss can be reached by funicular from the Kornmarkt for DM4.70 return, but it's more fun to walk up via the Burgweg: that way, you can make a complete circuit of the exterior before entering. At the northwest corner is the sixteenth-century **Dicker Turm** (Fat Tower), now a semicircular shell, its outer wall, along with its top, having been blasted away. Behind the northern fortifications you get a glimpse of the Renaissance buildings and pass the **Zeughaus**, before coming to the **Redoute**, built just a few years before the Schloss was destroyed. Behind it stands the **Glockenturm** (Bell Tower), originally a single-storey defence tower, to which six residential levels were later added.

Continuing along the eastern side, you see the protruding **Apothekerturm**, an old defensive tower which was later converted into the apothecary's plus residential quarters. Between it and the Glockenturm is a superb oriel window, part of a now-vanished banqueting hall. At the southeastern corner you'll find the most romantic of the ruins, the **Pulver Turm** (Powder Tower), now generally know as the **Gesprengter Turm** (Blown-up Tower). Originally a gunpowder store, it was destroyed by miners who tunnelled underneath and blew it up from the centre. This left a clean break in the now-overgrown masonry; the collapsed section still lies intact in the moat, leaving a clear view into the chambers of the interior, with their once-elegant central column supports.

From here, it's best to proceed to the western side of the Schloss, an artificial plateau formerly used as a gun battery but converted by Friedrich V into a pleasure garden. At its entrance is the graceful Roman-inspired **Elizabethpforte**, a gateway said to have been erected in a single night in 1615 as a surprise for the princess; the sober **Englischer Bau** adjoining the Dicker Turm was also built in her honour. At the western end of the garden is the semicircular **Rondell**, commanding a view over the rooftops of the city.

The Schlosshof

The **Schlosshof** (daily 9am–5pm; DM2, but free access outside these hours; guided tours of interiors daily April–Oct 9am–5pm; Nov–March 9am–4pm; check on noticeboard for times of departures in English; DM4) is reached by a series of sixteenth-century defensive structures – the Brückenhaus, the bridge itself and the severe **Thorturm** (Gate Tower), the only part of the Schloss not blown up. Immediately to the left of the entrance is the Gothic **Ruprechtsbau**, where you can see two restored chambers, one with an elaborate chimneypiece. After the ruined library comes the **Frauenzimmerbau**, where the women of the court resided; its colossal ground-floor hall has been restored as a venue for concerts. Looking anti-clockwise from the entrance gate, you first of all see the Gothic **Brunnenhaus** (Well House), a loggia with a graceful star vault. Its marble columns were brought here from Charlemagne's palace, and had previously adorned a Roman building. This is followed by a series of functional buildings – the **Kaserne** (Barracks) and the **Oekonomiebau**, which housed offices and workshops; part of it has been converted to the *Weinstube Schloss Heidelberg*, one of the best restaurants in town, and one surprisingly reasonable in price.

THE OTTHEINRICHSBAU AND DEUTSCHES APOTHEKENMUSEUM

What really catches your eye in the courtyard, however, is the group of Renaissance palaces on the north and east sides. Next to the Oekonomiebau is the mid-sixteenth-century **Ottheinrichsbau**, now just a shell but preserving its vigorous horizontal facade. The magnificent sculptural decoration has successive tiers of allegorical figures

THE HISTORY OF THE SCHLOSS

The Schloss originally dates back to the first quarter of the thirteenth century. It was then that the title of **Count Palatine**, the most senior office under the Holy Roman Emperor and one carrying the status of an Elector, was bestowed on a Wittelsbach, Duke Ludwig of Bavaria, whose family retained the office right to the end of the Holy Roman Empire. The earliest significant portions of what can be seen today date from the following century, as the castle evolved into a sturdy medieval fortress capable of withstanding the most powerful siege weapons of the day. In the sixteenth century, the inner courtyard of the Schloss began to be embellished with sumptuous palatial buildings, as its role as a princely residence became of increasing importance; this gathered momentum in mid-century when the Electors converted to Protestantism and began the construction of the most splendid **Renaissance buildings** in Germany.

Lutheranism was later jettisoned in favour of Calvinism, and the **Heidelberg Catechism** of 1562 remains the basic creed for many Reformed churches. This took on an increasingly militant aspect when Elizabeth Stuart's youthful husband, **Friedrich V**, became nominal leader of the Calvinist League, which aimed to establish the irreversible supremacy of Protestantism in Germany and to topple the Habsburgs from their position of pre-eminence in the country's affairs. Friedrich's ham-fisted attempt was not only a personal disaster (he was defeated, exiled and stripped of his titles), but also led to the Thirty Years' War, which devastated the country. However, it was French designs on the Palatinate in 1689 which led to the destruction of Heidelberg and its Schloss; although their claim on the territory was eventually withdrawn, the Electorship passed to a Catholic branch of the family. Unable to establish a rapport with the locals, they moved their seat; the planned rebuilding of the Schloss never occurred, and Heidelberg was left to vegetate.

representing Strength, the Christian Virtues and the Planetary Deities. In the basement is the **Deutsches Apothekenmuseum** (March 15–Oct 31 daily 10am–5pm; Nov–March 14 Sat & Sun only 11am–5pm; DM3), an offbeat but worthwhile collection. Among the displays are several complete Baroque and Rococo workshops, an early seventeenth-century travelling pharmacy and a herbarium. You can also descend to the bowels of the Apothekenturm, which has been rigged out with a furnace and distilling apparatus in an attempt to re-create its old appearance.

THE FRIEDRICHSBAU

The triple loggia of the earlier **Saalbau** forms a link to the celebrated late sixteenth-century **Friedrichsbau** built by Alsatian architect Johannes Schoch. A series of bucolic, larger-than-life statues is a pantheon of the House of Wittelsbach, beginning with Charlemagne (the alleged founder of the dynasty) and continuing right up to the ruling Elector. Those now on view are copies, but the originals can be seen inside, along with a number of restored rooms which have been decked out in period style. On the ground floor is the intact **Schlosskapelle**, which, in total contrast to the facade, harks back to the Gothic period; not surprisingly, in view of the photo opportunities outside, it's now a popular venue for weddings.

THE FASSBAU

The **Fassbau** is reached down a passageway in front of the Schlosshof. It contains the celebrated **Grosses Fass** (Great Vat), said to be the largest wine barrel in the world with a capacity of over 50,000 gallons; this is crowned with a platform which did service as a dance floor. Made in the late eighteenth century, the vat is the third in a spectacular line; though a folly and long out of service, it's reputed to have been filled on at least one occasion, when there was a particularly good grape harvest in the Palatinate (whose Elector was entitled to claim a tithe). Facing the entrance, as a ploy to elicit a gasp from visitors when they turn the corner and see the real thing, is the so-called **Kleines Fass** (Little Vat), itself of ample proportions.

The Altstadt

The Altstadt, the historic centre of Heidelberg, is a largely pedestrianized area between the Schloss and the Neckar, bisected by an unusually long main street, Hauptstrasse. In comparison with the Schloss, its monuments can seem prosaic: although the old lay-out of the medieval city survives, the French devastation means that nearly all the buildings are eighteenth-century or later, and are excessively sober in style. To many people, these are familiar from the Hollywood version of *The Student Prince* by the Hungarian-American composer Sigmund Romberg.

Marktplatz and the eastern quarters

The finest surviving buildings in the Altstadt are grouped on Marktplatz. In the middle is the Gothic red sandstone **Heiliggeistkirche**, founded just after the University at the end of the fourteenth century; its lofty tower, capped by a Baroque dome, is one of the city's most prominent landmarks. Note the tiny shopping booths between its buttresses, a feature ever since the church was built – this was a common practice in medieval times but has been frowned upon for so long that examples are now rare. Inside, it's light, airy and uncluttered, but was not always so, as the church was built to house the mausoleum of the Palatinate Electors. Only one tomb now remains – that of Ruprecht III, who became King of Germany in 1400, and his wife, Elizabeth von Hohenzollern. Furthermore, the triforium gallery once housed one of the great libraries of the world, the *Bibliotheca Palatina*; this was confiscated by Field Marshal Johann Tilly as war booty and presented to the pope. Some items were returned last century, but the finest books remain in the Vatican.

Facing the church is the only mansion to survive the seventeenth-century devasta-tion of the town, the **Haus zum Ritter**, so called from the statue of St George dressed as a knight which crowns the pediment. Built for a Huguenot refugee cloth merchant, it was clearly modelled on the Ottheinrichsbau in the Schloss to which, with its extrav-agant decoration of caryatids, scrollwork and fancy gables, it stands as a worthy com-petitor. Now an expensive hotel and restaurant, it completely outclasses its Baroque neighbours, among which is the **Rathaus** on the eastern side of the square.

Plenty more Baroque mansions can be found dotted all over the Altstadt; most notable is the **Residenz** of the Grand Dukes of Baden on Karlsplatz, which now houses the German Academy of Sciences and Letters. Further east, at Hauptstr. 235, is the **Palais Weimar**, now containing the **Völkerkunde Museum** (Tues–Fri 3–5pm, Sun 1–5pm; DM3), which has good African collections. At the end of the street is the Neoclassical **Karlstor**, a triumphal arch in honour of the Elector Carl Theodor, designed by his court architect, Nicolas de Pigage. However, the most important structure this great artistic patron gave to his ancestors' capital is the **Alte Brücke** downstream. Dating from the 1780s, it's at least the fifth on this site. In the last war, it suffered the inevitable fate of being blown up but has been painstakingly rebuilt, including its fairy-tale gateway.

The University quarter

Much of the western half of the Altstadt is occupied by buildings of the **University**, offi-cially known as the *Ruperto-Carola*, in honour of its two founders. It was established in 1386 by the Elector Ruprecht I: this makes it the oldest in Germany.

One side of Universitätsplatz, the Altstadt's second main square, is occupied by the **Alte Universität**; like so many of the city's buildings, it dates back to the first quarter of the eighteenth century, and was designed by the local architect Johann Adam Breunig. To its rear on Augustinergasse is the most celebrated University building, the former **Studentenkarzer** (Student Prison; April–Oct Tues–Sat 10am–noon & 2–5pm, Nov–March Tues–Fri 10am–noon & 2–5pm, Sat 10am–1pm; DM1.50), which is now a protected monument. Between 1712 and 1914, it was used to detain students (a sizeable proportion, by all accounts) who had been convicted of an offence. Every available square centimetre of the walls of the otherwise spartan cells is covered with graffiti, with a black silhouette self-portrait of the prisoner the most popular motif.

HEIDELBERG UNIVERSITY

Initially, Heidelberg University's fortunes were closely tied to that of the Palatinate electors; it became a great centre of humanism and the Reformation, but fell into decline in the eighteenth century, to be revived in 1803 by Grand Duke Karl Friedrich as the first state university of Baden. One of its most lasting achievements came soon after: while still a student, Clemens Brentano and his brother-in-law Achim von Arnim put together the collection of folk poetry known as *Des Knaben Wunderhorn* (The Boy's Magic Horn) in the years 1805–8. This was to be a key influence on the future evolution of Romanticism, directly inspiring the researches of the Brothers Grimm, whose prose folk tales (being more amenable to translation) have gained a far wider international fame. However, the work of Arnim and Brentano has been spread by the composer Gustav Mahler, who gave the verses idiomatic tunes and cloaked them in succulent orchestral colours, with several finding their way into his symphonies.

In spite of the vicissitudes of German history in the last two centuries, Heidelberg has managed to preserve its academic reputation. It's one of the few universities largely exempted in criticism of the modern German higher educational system, which is generally seen as something of a failure. Heidelberg is particularly renowned in the natural sciences, where it has nurtured a stream of Nobel Prize winners. It was also here, under Max Weber, that sociology was developed as an academic discipline.

Of the many traditions associated with the University, the oddest was the fact that, until the present century, its students were not subject to civil jurisdiction. When a crime or breach of the peace was committed, the offender had to be dealt with by the university authorities. Moreover, when found guilty, the student did not need to serve his punishment immediately; he could do so at his leisure. Nor was there any stigma attached to imprisonment – indeed, it was seen as an essential component of the university experience. Nobody knows how this system came into being, but it presumably dates back to the times when most alumni were aristocratic and subject to the mores of *noblesse oblige*.

A second Heidelberg tradition – this time one which spread throughout Germany – was the Mensur, or fencing match. Students were divided into confraternities (*Verbindungen*) according to the region of their birth; the members wore a distinguishing cap and were forbidden from socializing with those belonging to other groups. At least three (in practice, far more) duels were held on two days of every week. Each bout lasted for fifteen minutes, excluding stoppages, unless it became dangerous to proceed; if the outcome was inconclusive, it had to be re-staged at a later date. The combatants wore goggles and every vital organ was padded, so that the risk of death was minimal. They were placed at arm's length from each other and fought by moving their wrists alone; to flinch or to step back were the ultimate disgraces. Wounds were frequent, particularly on the top of the head and left cheek; these were treated immediately by a surgeon or medical student. What was really bizarre was that the wounds became highly prized badges of courage; for optimum prestige, salt was rubbed into them, leaving scars which would remain for life.

Another tradition associated with the fencing corps was the *Kneipe*, a stag party where competition was confined within the group. The idea was to down as many mugs of beer as possible in a given space of time; the winner became the *Bierkönig*. As the rules were concerned solely with emptying the contents of the glass down the throat, and not about retaining the alcohol in the system, those who didn't mind the discomfort of consistently spewing up were able to accomplish prodigious totals of close to one hundred pints in an evening. Several taverns which were the scene of these bouts still exist (see p.322).

The **Universitätsbibliothek** is down Grabengasse to the south of Universitätsplatz, with the entrance for temporary exhibitions round the corner on Plöck. In summer (normally 10am–7pm; free) there's generally a display centred on the treasures of the collection. Outstanding is the fourteenth-century *Codex Manesse*; apart from containing 137 beautiful miniatures, it ranks as the most important collection of Middle High German poetry.

The **Jesuitenkirche**, tucked away just to the east of Universitätsplatz on Schulgasse, is in the sombre, classically inspired style favoured by this evangelizing order, who came here with the intention of recapturing Heidelberg for Catholicism, a mission which doesn't seem to have been particularly successful. Housed in its gallery and the adjoining monastery is a rather moderate **Museum für Sakralkunst** (June–Oct Tues–Sat 10am–5pm, Sun 1–5pm; Nov–May Sat 10am–5pm, Sun 1–5pm only; DM2.50).

Following Plöck in a westerly direction, you come to the former **Institut für Naturwissenchaften** at the junction with Akadamiestrasse. Heidelberg's most famous scientist, **Robert Wilhelm Bunsen**, was based there for four decades. His name is familiar to school pupils all over the world for popularizing that staple gadget of the laboratory, the "Bunsen burner"; he was also the first to separate the colours of the spectrum.

The Kurpfälzisches Museum

Housed in the **Palais Morass** at Hauptstr. 97, an early eighteenth-century mansion built for a law professor, is the **Kurpfälzisches Museum** (Tues & Thurs–Sun 10am–5pm, Wed 10am–9pm; DM5). It's best kept until the end of your stay, as it provides an effective summing-up of what you have seen. The archeology section includes a cast of the jawbone of *Homo heidelbergiensis* (the original is owned by the University); this is estimated to come from the inter-glacial period 500,000 years ago, making it one of the oldest human bones ever discovered. On the first floor is a room devoted to the history of the Palatinate. The intact Schloss can be seen in a large documentary picture from the early seventeenth century; it also turns up in the background of Jan Brueghel's exquisite *Allegory of Summer*. The museum's prize possession is the limewood *Altar of the Twelve Apostles* by **Tilman Riemenschneider**. For centuries masked under a thick coat of polychrome, it was only recognized as the work of the master about a generation ago; it has since been returned to its original unpainted state.

Eating, drinking and entertainment

Hauptstrasse and the adjacent side streets are jammed with places of entertainment to suit all tastes; there's no better place for a pub crawl in all of Germany. The much-trumpeted **student taverns** (see also *Hotels* above) are a must; they're perfectly genuine and are still patronized by the leftovers of the old fraternities, even if parties of tourists now make up the bulk of the clientele, particularly in summer. They're sights in themselves, with their faded photos and daguerreotypes, their trophies, swords, pads, helmets and miscellaneous paraphernalia.

Historic student taverns

Roter Ochsen, Hauptstr. 217. One of the two most famous of the historic student taverns, its U-shaped interior has been patronized by the confraternities since it was built at the beginning of the eighteenth century. Reasonably priced food, but open evenings only, except Sun.

Schnizelbank, Bauamtsgasse 7. The only one of the student taverns where the emphasis is on wine rather than beer.

Zum Sepp'l, Hauptstr. 213. Along with *Roter Ochsen*, the tavern every tourist wants to visit; having been used by the student corps continuously since 1634, it has the longest uninterrupted tradition. More commodious than any of the others, and with the cheapest food.

Other restaurants

Abel's, Hauptstr. 133. Relaxed wine bar-cum-restaurant where you can sit outside.

Da Mario, Rohrbanler Str. 3. The best Italian restaurant in the city.

Essighaus, Plöck 97. Inexpensive *Gaststätte* serving traditional German food; also has a small beer garden.

Güldenes Schaf, Hauptstr. 115. The place to come for an extensive menu of game dishes.

Kurpfälzisches Museum, Hauptstr. 97. This wine bar is situated in the museum courtyard and serves excellent food.

Schlossquell-Bräustübl, Bergheimer Str. 91. The beer hall and restaurant of the main local brewery, whose products are made from spring water and have a soft, delicate flavour.

Schlossweinstube, Im Schlosshof. Classy and expensive wine bar-restaurant in the Schloss.

Simplicissimus, Ingeimstr. 16. High-class French restaurant. Very small, so reservations are obligatory (☎183336). Evenings only, closed Tues.

Waves, Kurfürsten-Anlage 9. Vegetarian restaurant with a wide selection of dishes. Closed Sun.

Wilhelmsplatz, Kaiserstr. 30. This is well off the beaten tourist track, and a good place to meet locals; serves large, cheap meals. Closed Sun & Mon.

Wirtshaus zum Spreissel, Neckarstalden 66. Serves huge portions of traditional German food.

Zur Herrenmühle, Hauptstr. 239. Heidelberg's best restaurant, occupying a fine seventeenth-century building with an inner courtyard. The cooking is innovative and therefore expensive; it's advisable to book in advance (☎12909). Evenings only, closed Sun.

Cafés and bars

Biermuseum, Hauptstr. 143. Here you'll find the largest selection of beers in Heidelberg, with 101 varieties to choose from, 10 of them on draught.

Café Journal, Hauptstr. 162. Best of the bistro-type cafés which are all the rage among present-day Heidelberg students. Has a wide selection of newspapers, and makes a good choice for breakfast.

Café Knösel, Haspelgasse 20. Heidelberg's oldest and most elegant café; their speciality is the *Heidelberger Studentenkuss*, a dark chocolate filled with praline and nougat. Full meals also available. Closed Mon.

Café Schaftheutle, Hauptstr. 94. Another old-world café, with its own garden and celebrated for its marzipan fancies. Closed Sun.

Café 7 do Brazil, Marktplatz 7. Serves good cakes and ice cream, plus Brazilian food.

Goldener Reichsapfel, Untere Str. 35. Popular student bar.

Hard Rock Café, Hauptstr. 142. Very American in feel, this café has huge pop video screens, and serves delicious baguettes.

Hemingway, Fahrtgasse 1. Student pub that sees very few tourists.

Max Bar, Marktplatz 5. French-style bistro that puts tables out onto the square in summer.

Palmbräuhaus, Hauptstr. 18. A modern re-creation of palm court days, with resident pianist.

Trinidad, Friedrich-Ebert-Anlage 62. The place to come for exotic cocktails.

Vetters Alt-Heidelberger Brauhaus, Steingasse 9. *Hausbrauerei* which makes *Pils*, *Weizen* and an extremely powerful *Bock*; also does good-value meals.

Discos and live-music pubs

Cave 54, Krämergasse 2. Normally a nostalgic-style disco, except on Tues, when it's live jazz.

Doctor Flotte, Hauptstr. 130. Raucous bar playing both rock and jazz.

Fischerstübchen, Obere Neckarstr. 2. The favourite disco of the local students.

Mata Hari, Oberbadgasse 10. Gay men's disco.

Regenbogen, Fahrtgasse 18. Women-only disco.

Schwimmbad Musik-Club, Tiergartenstr. 13. Has regular live gigs and discos Wed–Sat.

Ziegler, Bergheimer Str. 18. Varied late-night spot, featuring a varied programme of jazz and rock concerts, cabaret and theatre.

Zigarillo, Bergheimer Str. 147. Crowded disco housed in an old factory.

Classical music and theatre

Classical music concerts are held in the modern *Kongresshaus Stadthalle* overlooking the Neckar. The *Heidelberger Kammerorchester* is a Mozartean-sized orchestra of good standing, even if their programmes tend to be conservative. At the main **theatre**, the *Städtischen Bühnen*, Theaterstr. 4 (☎583520), there's a varied mixture of plays, opera, operetta, and performances by an experimental corps de ballet. Straight drama is also offered at the tiny *Zimmertheater*, Hauptstr. 118 (☎21069), and the *Landfriedhaus*, Bergheimer Str. 147 (☎163333). Productions for **kids** are performed at the *Heidelberger Kinder und Jugendtheater*, Zwingerstr. 3–5 (☎583546). The *Kulturzentrum Karlsterbahnhof*, Am Karlsterbahnhof 1, is a new cultural centre with theatre, cinema and café.

Festivals

Heidelberg's most spectacular **festivals** are those using the Schloss as a backdrop. On the first Saturdays of June and September, and the second in July, there are firework displays and historical pageants; these attract horrendously large crowds, but are highly enjoyable all the same. From late July until the end of August, there are open-air concerts and opera performances (inevitably, *The Student Prince* is included) in the Schlosshof at 8pm on most evenings (☎58976 for tickets and information); in bad weather, they're transferred indoors. Throughout the year, various **fairs** are held on Karlsplatz – *Heidelberger Frühling* (early June); *Weindorf* (mid-Sept); *Heidelberger Herbst* (late Sept). The climax of **Carnival** (variable Feb/March) is the Rose Monday parade; there's another procession through the streets on the third Sunday before Easter.

Listings

Bike rental *Per Bike,* Bergheimer Str. 125 (☎181108).

Bookshops The best ones are located around Sofienstrasse and Universitätsplatz.

Car breakdown (☎19211) for 24-hour service.

Car rental *Avis*, Karlsruher Str. 43 (☎22215); *Hertz*, Kurfürsten-Anlage 1 (☎23434); *InterRent*, Bergheimer Str. 159 (☎20845).

Kids *Märchenparadies* on top of the Königstuhl (March–Oct daily 10am–6/7pm; DM5, kids DM4) is an adventure playground featuring fairy-tale characters and a miniature railway.

Markets Wed and Sat on Marktplatz, Tues and Fri on Friedrich-Ebert-Platz.

Mitfahrzentrale Kurfürsten-Anlage 57 (☎24646).

Neckar cruises leave from the quay beside the Stadthalle mid-May to mid-Sept, run by *Rhein-Neckar-Fahrgastschiffahrt* (☎20181) and *Personenschiffahrt Hornung* (☎480064). A 45min local journey costs DM6; the round trip to Neckarsteinach, DM16.50.

Post office Main branch with poste restante is beside the Hauptbahnhof; another is at Sofienstr. 6.

Shopping Untere Strasse is the trendiest street, featuring some amazing second-hand clothes shops, with quality ballgowns and hats available at knock-down prices. *Flic-Flac*, Untere Str. 12, is one of the best.

Sports The main swimming pool is beside the Zoo on Tiergartenstrasse. Tennis has become a Heidelberg mania, as two German superstars, Boris Becker and Steffi Graf, both come from villages just outside the city. The German Grand Prix motor race takes place at nearby Hockenheim each July.

Travel agencies *American Express*, Brückenkopfstr. (☎91270); *HS Reisebüro*, Hauptstr. 23 (☎97700),does student deals.

Zoo, Tiergartenstr. 3. (April–Sept daily 9am–7pm; Oct–March daily 9am–5pm; DM7, kids DM3).

Bad Wimpfen

The prefix "Bad", used by hundreds of German towns as a free advert for the presence of spa facilities, immediately conjures up the image of geriatrics and hypochondriacs pottering around the manicured lawns of soulless, white-walled sanatoria, with only the chirping of birds to disturb the deathly hush. **BAD WIMPFEN** has a spa quarter at its northern extremity which conforms to this stereotype, but is otherwise so totally different it seems strange the authorities want to use such a misleading designation. It certainly shouldn't be needed to draw visitors, as this pocket-sized town with a population of just a few thousand, built high above a bend in the Neckar, is a real visual treat, preserving a wonderful array of monuments as testament to its richly varied history. The site has been inhabited since prehistoric times; Romans, Frankish kings and the Bishops of Worms were later rulers, prior to its choice, from around 1200, as a favourite **residence of the Staufian emperors**. Some 150 years later Wimpfen was made a Free Imperial City, an independence it retained, courtesy of the lucrative salt trade, until the advent of Napoleon.

The **skyline** is immediately impressive, one of the most dramatic in Germany: it's best seen from the right bank of the Neckar, where the imperious towers, illuminated by night, give it the appearance of a miniature medieval Manhattan. The town is divided into two parts, the upper town, **Wimpfen am Berg**, and the lower town, **Wimpfen in Tal**. Wimpfen am Berg was actually built within the ruins of the Imperial Palace and has more sights, but the dominant surviving monument is the **Ritterstift** in Wimpfen in Tal.

Wimpfen am Berg

Hauptstrasse is the central street of the upper town, known as Wimpfen am Berg. About halfway up is the **Schwibbogen Tor**, which formerly gave access to the **Kaiserpfalz** (Imperial Palace). Substantial portions of the palace remain to this day, ranking among the most important of the relatively few surviving examples of Romanesque civil architecture in Europe. The austere riverside wall, which had the advantage of a formidable natural barrier behind, survives largely intact. At its southern end, it's guarded by the **Nürnberger Türmchen** and the **Roter Turm**, a gaunt box-like structure which was the last line of defence. From here, there's a fine view over the town and valley.

Further along is the **Kaiserkapelle** (daily April–Oct 10am–noon & 2–4.30pm; DM1), now containing a small museum of religious art. The gallery was reserved for the emperor who could, if necessary, make a quick getaway through a passageway to the haven of the Roter Turm. Adjoining the chapel is the sole surviving part of the **Palast** itself – a weather-worn but still elegant row of arcades, each of whose paired columns is carved in a different manner.

The Steinhaus and the Blauer Turm

Also from the Staufian epoch is the large **Steinhaus** (Stone House), which stands out among the later predominantly half-timbered buildings. Originally the home of the castle commandant, it was modernized in the sixteenth century by the addition of Gothic gables. It's currently fitted out as the **Museum des Mittelalters** (April–Oct Tues–Sun 10am–noon & 2–4.30pm; Nov–March 10am–noon; DM2), with exhibits from prehistoric times to the period of the Staufian emperors. Diagonally opposite is the symbol of Wimpfen and the most potent reminder of its days of power and glory, the **Blauer Turm** (Blue Tower; same hours as Museum des Mittelalters; DM2). Named after the tints of the limestone used in its construction, this watchtower was all but destroyed in a fire in 1848 and was only recently made fully secure. At noon on Sundays from April to September, the resounding strains of a trumpeter playing chorales from the top can be heard throughout the streets.

Around the Stadtkirche

The twin towers of the **Stadtkirche** are the last main features of the Romanesque part of Wimpfen's skyline; the rest of the building is a late Gothic hall church. Behind can be seen an emotional *Crucifixion*, similar to the one its sculptor, Hans Backoffen, made for his own tomb in Mainz. Close by is the **Wormser Hof**, part of which is also Staufian; it was the residence of the administrator in the service of the Bishop of Worms, with a barn to store the tithe of agricultural produce he collected. Nowadays, it's home to the 250 historic dolls of the **Puppenmuseum** (Wed, Sat & Sun 2–5pm; DM3).

It's worth sauntering round the streets of the old town, which curve and plunge their way past half-timbered houses, Baroque mansions and quiet squares with Renaissance fountains. Among the many surprising vistas, that from the **Adlerbrunnen** (Eagle Fountain) at the junction of Hauptstrasse and Salzgasse is particularly fine. The best-preserved street is **Klostergasse**, several of whose buildings have exterior galleries which formerly served as bath houses. Down Bollwerkgasse is the artillery bastion, built in the sixteenth century to designs by Dürer, no less. Nearby, the monumental half-timbered fifteenth-century **Spital** on Hauptstrasse has recently been restored to house the **Reichstädtisches Museum** (April–Oct Tues–Sun 10am–noon & 2–4.30pm; Nov–March Tues–Sun 10am–noon; DM2). This takes up the story of Wimpfen from the Middle Ages through to the nineteenth century, though the wonderful original interiors are the best reason for a visit.

Wimpfen in Tal

The lower town, known as Wimpfen in Tal, is built round the great **Ritterstift St Peter** (Mon–Sat 10am–noon & 3–5pm, Sun 10.30am–noon & 3.30–5pm) which, after a break of five centuries, was repopulated in 1947 by Benedictine monks who had fled from Silesia. Try and catch a service to hear their wonderful Gregorian chant.

The fortress-like facade of the **Stiftskirche**, with a huge porch and a pair of octagonal towers, dates from the tenth century; the rest of the building is a masterly French-inspired Gothic design. This is generally attributed to the near-legendary mason **Erwin von Steinbach** who built part of Strasbourg Cathedral. Superb original sculptures can be seen on the south doorway and inside the chancel; the latter group includes the then-recently-deceased St Francis of Assisi. Access to the **cloister**, which has sections in each of the three phases of the Gothic style, is only allowed to groups who have booked in advance, but you can tag along with one of these (which are frequent during the summer) if you ask at the shop.

Practicalities

The **Bahnhof**, on one of the lines between Heidelberg and Heilbronn, is by the river in the lower part of town. Within the station building is the **tourist office** (Mon–Fri 9am–noon & 2–4/5pm, April–Sept also Sat & Sun 10am–noon & 2–4pm; ☎07063/97200. Turn right outside to reach Hauptstrasse, or follow the main road to the left for ten minutes to reach Wimpfen in Tal. **Neckar cruises**, which run both upstream and down throughout the summer months, depart from the jetty beside the Neckarbrücke.

Provided you're not looking for swinging nightlife, Bad Wimpfen makes a good place to stay, particularly as budget **accommodation** is plentiful and inexpensive, with over twenty private houses – scattered all over town – offering **rooms** (①–③). **Hotels** include *Gasthof Traube,* Hauptstr. 1 (☎07063/266; ④), *Weinmann,* Marktplatz 3 (☎07063/8582; ④), *Grüner Baum,* Hauptstr. 84 (☎07063/294; ⑤), *Blauer Turm,* Burgviertel 5–7, (☎07063/225 or 7884; ⑤), *Neckarblick,* Erich-Sailer-Str. 48 (☎07063/7002; ⑤) and the superb *Sonne,* Hauptstr. 87 (☎07063/245; ⑤). The **youth hostel**, run by a very hospitable family, has an unbeatable location at Burgviertel 21–23

(☎07063/7069; ☎) – it's in an old half-timbered house built against the ramparts beside the ruins of the Palast.

There's a clutch of **restaurants** serving hearty *bürgerlich* cuisine all down Hauptstrasse; those attached to the hotels *Traube* and *Sonne* are the best. Alternatively, try *Kräuterweible*, Marktrain 5, popular with locals for its chicken dishes.

Festivals

Wimpfen in Tal is the scene of one of Germany's oldest **popular festivals**: it's claimed the week-long *Talmarkt* in honour of SS Peter and Paul (June 29–July 5) has been celebrated every year since 965. Nowadays, the end is marked by a spectacular fireworks display. Two more fairs dating back to the Middle Ages are held in the centre of Wimpfen am Berg – the *Hafenmarkt* for handicrafts at the end of August, and the *Weihnachtsmarkt* in December, which is a cut above the imitative versions found in practically every German town. *Fasching* also has a long tradition here; highlights are the Sunday parade and the evening celebrations on Ash Wednesday.

Burg Guttenberg

In a gentle landscape of vineyards and market gardens, some 15km down the Neckar from Bad Wimpfen, the small medieval town of **GUNDELSHEIM** is set in the shadow of **Schloss Horneck**, Baroque successor to a fortress of the Teutonic Knights. The Bahnhof here is close to the most interesting castle of the region, **Burg Guttenberg** (daily March–Nov 9am–6pm; DM4); to reach it, you have to cross the bridge to the other side of the river and walk uphill for 2km. This building, with a tall, narrow keep and an impressive curtain wall, dates back to the Staufian epoch, but has been much altered inside. Among its many curiosities are the wooden library, and a herbarium in which the plants are stored in a series of trick compartments.

However, the castle's main claim to fame is for having Europe's largest collection of **birds of prey** – over a hundred in all. Each day at 11am and 3pm (DM10, DM13 including admission to the Burg), there's an exhilarating demonstration of several of these birds in free flight. Yet all this is not just for show – there has been a highly successful programme for breeding endangered species, and an average of fifty birds per year are released back into the wild. There's also a good restaurant, the *Burggaststätte*, set on a terrace commanding an extensive view over the valley.

The Tauber valley

At the extreme northeastern corner of Baden-Württemberg, the gentle **River Tauber** cuts through a lush, verdant landscape of undulating hills, often dotted with vineyards, which stands in sharp contrast to the rugged contours of the neighbouring Swabian Jura. It manages to preserve an agreeable atmosphere of rustic peace and quiet, at least outside those towns which are staging posts on the famous tourist route known as the **Romantic Road** (see p.176), which closely follows the entire length of the Tauber valley, with the exception of its northernmost stretch. Bad Mergentheim, Weikersheim and Creglingen all lie on the route while the equally popular Wertheim is just to the north. All except Creglingen are on the same rail line.

Wertheim

Situated at the point where the Tauber joins the westward-flowing Main, **WERTHEIM** is the most northerly town in Baden-Württemberg. It's nicknamed "Little Heidelberg", and with some justification, as there are clear similarities between the two – the setting between the riverside and wooded slopes, the prevalence of superb and varied panoramic viewpoints, the twisting alleyways, the ruined castle looming high above. The original town was situated on the northern bank of the Main for fear of flooding, but it moved in the twelfth century when the local counts, realizing the strategic importance of the spit of land between the two rivers, used it as the basis for building up a territory between the two ecclesiastical principalities of Mainz and Würzburg. A precarious independence was maintained down the centuries from the prying hands of the bishops, whose unwelcome advances were a major factor in Wertheim becoming one of the earliest bastions of Protestantism.

The town

The town is an ideal place in which to wander simply at leisure. On the right bank of the Tauber, the quays are lined with old fishermen's houses; on the **Kittstein Tor** there's a scale recording the water-mark of each flood since 1595. Further up towards the Main is the **Spitzer Turm** (Pointed Tower), the original corner point of the fortifications erected around 1200. The streets immediately behind housed a large Jewish population right up until the days of the Third Reich. At the heart of Wertheim is the **Marktplatz**, lined with half-timbered houses; colourful markets are held here on Wednesdays and Saturdays. Behind is the **Kilianskapelle**, an unusual fifteenth-century double chapel; the lower storey served as an ossuary. Opposite is an earlier Gothic building, the **Stiftskirche**, in whose choir are a series of ornate Renaissance tombs, the pantheon of the House of Wertheim.

Wertheim's museums are a short walk down Mühlenstrasse. In a half-timbered house you'll find the **Glas-Museum** (April–Oct Tues–Sun 10am–noon & 2–4pm; DM1), a surprisingly comprehensive collection. Across the street is the **Historisches Museum** (April–Dec Mon–Fri 10am–noon & 2–4pm, Sat & Sun 2–4pm; free), with wide-ranging displays of Franconian sacred art, traditional costumes, ceramics and local history. There are also a number of paintings of Wertheim by Otto Modersohn, the leading light of the artistic community at Worpswede (see "Bremen and Lower Saxony"). The building housing the museum is a Baroque palace built to replace the **Schloss**, a casualty of the Thirty Years' War. From the twelfth-century fortress, the tall watchtower and part of the walls survive; later additions include the twin-towered barbican and the residential quarters. In spite of its condition, it's well worth climbing up for the outstanding view over the two rivers, with the vast stretch of the Odenwald to the west and the wooded Spessart hills to the north.

Bronnbach

BRONNBACH, 7km upstream and officially now part of Wertheim, is built round its **Kloster** (guided tours Easter–Oct Mon–Sat 9.15–11.45am & 2–5pm, Sun 1–5pm; DM3), a daughter foundation of Maulbronn. The bulk of the architecture is in the severe Transitional style favoured by the Cistercians, with just a nod towards the Gothic in the church. Whereas Maulbronn became Protestant at the Reformation, Bronnbach remained Catholic. This accounts for significant differences in their present appearances: in the early eighteenth century, the passion for Baroque led to a desire to transform the face of the old monastery. The church was adorned with a cluster of ornate altarpieces and the *Josephsaal*, a sumptuous refectory used during the summer, was added.

Practicalities

Wertheim's **Bahnhof** is on the left bank of the Tauber, only a few minutes' walk from the centre. In the town itself there's an inexpensive **pension**, *Hofgarten*, Untere Heeg 1 (☎09342/6426; ③). Additionally, there are several **hotels**: *Löwensteiner Hof*, Bahnhofstr. 11 (☎09342/1259: ③), *Bronnbacher Hof*, Mainplatz 10 (☎09342/7797; ④) and *Schwan*,

Mainplatz 8 (☎09342/92330; ⑤). The **tourist office** on Am Spitzen Turm (Mon–Fri 9am–12.30pm & 2–5pm, Sat 9am–noon; ☎09342/1066) can find cheaper rooms, free of charge, in outlying villages. There's a **youth hostel** in the hills at Alte Stiege 16 (☎09342/6451; ❷), and also a **campsite** (☎09342/5719). The best **restaurant** is in *Hotel Schwan*; otherwise try *Bach'sche Brauerei*, Marktplatz 11; or *Zum Zepfhahn*, Hämmelsgasse 28.

Bad Mergentheim

BAD MERGENTHEIM, some 36km up the river from Wertheim, is one of the most celebrated spas in the country. Judging from the evidence of excavations, which have led to the uncovering of a Celtic well, the presence of hot salt springs at this point was known to Bronze Age tribes. However, they lay forgotten for over two millennia, until their rediscovery in 1826 by a shepherd who noticed his flock crowding round a trickle of water close to the north bank of the Tauber. Three years later, the first hotel opened and the town has never looked back. The timing of the finding of the springs was fortuitous, as seventeen years before Mergentheim had lost the prestigious role it had held since 1525 – as seat of the **Order of Teutonic Knights** (see p.330). Even if you normally find spas a turn-off, it's worth coming to see the old part of town, on which the Knights left a characteristic stamp. This is sharply differentiated from the cure facilities, and situated on the opposite side of the river.

The town centre

The whole of the eastern part of town is taken up by a gargantuan complex of buildings, most of it now used as offices. The Knights originally established themselves in the former Hohenlohe castle, which was expanded and rebuilt to form this enormous **Deutschordensschloss**. The **Schlosspark** beyond, laid out in the English style, forms a south-bank counterpart to the manicured **Kurpark** opposite. In accordance with the tenets of the order, the architecture is severely ascetic, with only the occasional touch of frivolity, as in the bright orange **Torbau** which forms the main entrance. At the corner of the main courtyard is the handsome Rococo **Schlosskirche**, in part the work of the two greatest German architects of the day – Balthasar Neumann designed the twin towers, and François Cuvilliés provided plans for the white stuccoed interior, whose vault is covered by a huge fresco glorifying the Holy Cross.

Opposite the facade of the church is the main range of the Schloss, approached by two Renaissance **staircases**: the northern one has an ingenious corkscrew shape and leads up to the **Deutschordensmuseum** (Tues–Sun 10am–5pm; DM6). Apart from the Neoclassical **Kapitelsaal**, the rooms are surprisingly unostentatious and are used for displays on the history of the Order, including valuable treasury items and portraits of all the Mergentheim Grand Masters.

The spacious central Markt is divided in two by the step-gabled sixteenth-century **Rathaus**; the arms of the Grand Master who built it are borne by the hero Roland in the fountain in front. A colourful array of houses of various dates erected by vassals of the order lines the rest of the square. Immediately to the north of the square is the Gothic **Stadtkirche,** which was founded by another Order of Crusaders, that of St John of Jerusalem. Beside it is the **Spital**, with a tiny Rococo chapel. South of Marktplatz is the **Marienkirche,** a former Dominican monastery. On the north wall of its nave is a magnificent Renaissance funerary monument to Grand Master Walter von Cronburg by Hans Vischer of Nürnberg. The chapel opposite has fourteenth-century frescoes of mystical scenes.

The outskirts

Now officially part of Bad Mergentheim, the village of **STUPPACH**, 8km southwest and serviced by occasional buses, possesses one of the supreme masterpieces of

Originally founded as a hospitaller community in Palestine in 1190, the Order of Teutonic Knights (*Deutschritterorden*) quickly took on a religious and military character. It increasingly turned its attention towards the Christianization of Eastern Europe, pushing Germany's frontiers eastwards. By the early fourteenth century the Knights had exterminated the heathen Prussians, appropriating their name and controlling a powerful Baltic state from the fortress-headquarters at Marienburg. They repopulated the territories with German peasants, and grew rich from the grain trade. Prosperity bred complacency; in 1410 the Knights were defeated at the Battle of Grunwald by the Poles and Lithuanians. As a result of the Thirteen Years' War of 1454–66, in which the German settlers joined the alliance against them, they had to cede half their lands and re-establish themselves at Königsberg in East Prussia.

In 1525, the Grand Master Albrecht von Hohenzollern converted to Protestantism and turned the territory into a secular duchy. Those of the Order still loyal to Catholicism moved to Mergentheim. Although broken as a military force, the Order retained great prestige, and its Grand Master belonged to the highest rank of the German nobility. Mergentheim remained the Knights' base until they were disbanded by order of Napoleon in 1809; however, the order was reconstituted in Vienna 25 years later, where it remains active as a charitable body.

German Renaissance painting, **Grünewald**'s *St Mary of the Snows*, in its otherwise unremarkable Pfarrkirche (daily March & April 10am–5pm, May–Oct 9am–5.30pm, Nov–Feb 11am–4pm; DM2). This is part of a triptych, one wing of which also survives and can be seen in the Augustinermuseum in Freiburg.

In the Katzenwald (Cats' Forest) 5km southeast of Bad Mergentheim on the main road to Crailsheim is the **Wildpark** (March–June, Sept & Oct daily 9am–6pm, July & Aug daily 9am–7pm, Nov–Feb Sat & Sun 10.30am–5pm; DM9.50), the largest zoo in Europe where animals are kept in conditions close to their natural habitats. The best time to visit is in the afternoon, when there are successive feeding sessions, culminating in that of the pack of thirty wolves, which emerges and disperses with lightning speed.

Practicalities

Bad Mergentheim's **Bahnhof** is conveniently situated between the medieval and spa parts of the town, on the same side of the Tauber as the former. The pavilion at Markt 3 contains the **tourist office** (Mon–Fri 9am–noon & 2.30–5pm, Sat 9am–noon; ☎07931/57135).

If you're looking for budget accommodation, the tourist office can supply a list of **private rooms** and small **pensions** (②–④). Otherwise, the cheapest **hotels** are *Gasthof Zum Wilden Mann,* Reichengasse 6 (☎07931/7638; ③) and *Gasthof Johanniter,* Deutschordensplatz 5 (☎07931/7502; ④). There are several good middle-range options: *Deutschmeister,* Ochsengasse 7 (☎07931/9620; ⑤), *Alte Münze,* Münzgasse 10 (☎07931/5660; ⑥) and *Bundschu,* Cronbergstr. 15 (☎07931/9330; ⑥). Top of the range is *Victoria,* Poststr. 2–4 (☎07931/5930; ⑧). The last-named has a gourmet **restaurant**, *Zirbelstuben,* along with a more affordable *Weinstube*. All the other hotels also have recommendable restaurants. There's a **youth hostel** at Erlenbachtalstr. 44 (☎07931/6373; ⓑ) in the outlying village of Igersheim (which has its own Bahnhof) to the northeast. The **campsite** is 2km south of town at Willinger Tal (☎07931/2177). The main **festival** is the *Stadtfest* in late June.

Weikersheim

WEIKERSHEIM, 11km due east of Bad Mergentheim, is the ancestral seat of the **House of Hohenlohe**, which first came to local prominence in the twelfth century and whose various branches ruled for centuries over tiny tracts of territory between the Free Imperial Cities of Schwäbisch Hall, Heilbronn and Rothenburg ob der Tauber. The planned central **Marktplatz** was laid out at the beginning of the eighteenth century as a processional way linking the **Stadtkirche**, which contains tombs of members of the Hohenlohe family, with the Schloss. Also on the square is the **Tauberländer Dorfmuseum** (April–Oct Tues–Sun 10am–noon & 2–5pm; DM3), with folklore displays on rural life throughout Franconia.

The Schloss

A particular touch of swagger is provided by the arcaded buildings immediately fronting the main entrance to the **Schloss** (guided tours daily April–Oct 9am–6pm; Nov–March 10am–noon & 1.30–4.30pm; DM6). In 1586, when Count Ludwig II re-established Weikersheim as the family's main residence, he decided to replace the old moated castle with a magnificent new Renaissance palace. The Dutch architect Georg Robin chose a daringly original ground-plan based on an equilateral triangle. Only one wing of this, characterized by six magnificent scrollwork gables, was built, as the Hohenlohes turned their money and attention to supporting the Protestant cause in the Thirty Years' War. In the early eighteenth century the complex was completed in the Baroque style, though still retaining some parts of the medieval fortress.

Unquestionably the highlight of the reception rooms is the **Rittersaal**, the most sumptuous banqueting hall ever built in Germany, whose decorations are a hymn of praise to the dynasty and its preoccupations. The huge coffered ceiling is painted with depictions of the glories of the hunt, the entrance doorway is carved with a scene of a battle against the Turks, and the colossal chimneypiece is adorned with a complicated allegory which illustrates the family motto, "God gives Luck". Flanking the fireplace are the reclining stucco figures of Count Ludwig and his wife, sister of William the Silent, above which are their respective family trees. Even more eye-catching are the life-sized stuccos of deer parading along the main walls, joined by an elephant, a beast the craftsmen had clearly never seen.

The **Schlossgarten**, which is contemporary with the later parts of the Schloss, is exceptionally well preserved. On the terrace immediately behind the palace is a series of sixteen caricature statues of members of the court, the only surviving set of the many inspired by the engravings of the Lorraine artist Jacques Callot. In the central pond is a representation of *Hercules Fighting the Hydra*: like many other petty German princes, the Hohenlohes fondly saw analogies between themselves and the great hero. Further evidence of their megalomania comes with the **Orangerie** at the end of the garden, which provides a theatrical backdrop to the Tauber valley beyond. Among the figures represented are the emperors of ancient Assyria, Persia, Greece and Rome whom they imagined to be their spiritual ancestors.

Practicalities

Weikersheim's **Bahnhof** is just a few minutes' walk northeast of Marktplatz. The **tourist office** (Mon–Fri 9am–noon & 2.30–5pm, April–Sept also Sat 9am–noon & 2–4pm; ☎07934/10255) is at Marktplatz 7. If you want to stay, there are a fair number of **private rooms** (①–④). The lowest-priced **hotel**, *Gasthof Krone,* Hauptstr. 14 (☎07934/8314; ③) is an excellent bargain. The more expensive alternatives include *Grüner Hof,* Am Schlosseingang (☎07934/252; ④), *Deutschherren-Stuben,* Marktplatz 9 (☎07934/8376; ④) and *Laurentius*, Marktplatz 5 (☎07934/7007; ⑤). There's also a **youth hostel** on the bank of the Tauber at Im Heiligen Wöhr (☎07934/7025; ☎).

You can indulge in a spot of **wine-tasting** of the local vintages at the *Gutskellerei* (Mon–Fri 8am–5pm, Sat 9am–5pm, Sun 11am–5pm), just beside the entrance to the Schloss. Each of the **hotels** listed above has a restaurant; *Krone* is the best value, *Laurentius* has the most ambitious standards.

Creglingen

CREGLINGEN, 13km upstream from Weikersheim, and on the border with Bavaria, is an old-world village with half-timbered houses. Some of these are built directly over the former ramparts; another, the recently restored **Römschlössle** has the dimensions of a Renaissance palace and now serves as a conference centre. After Creglingen, the Romantic Road crosses into Bavaria, the next stops being Detwang and Rothenburg ob der Tauber (see p.177 and p.180).

The village's renown is based on the isolated **Herrgottskirche** (April–Oct daily 9.15am–5.30pm; Nov–March Tues–Sun 10am–noon & 2–4pm; DM2), a Gothic pilgrimage chapel founded in the fourteenth century after a ploughman had dug up a miraculous holy wafer in a nearby field. If you're travelling by *Europabus*, a stop is made here; otherwise the quickest and most pleasant way to come from Creglingen is via the path running alongside the brook named after the church.

The Herrgottskirche is architecturally unremarkable but houses the magnificent limewood *Altar of the Assumption*, carved by **Tilman Riemenschneider** in about 1510. Set in a filigree shrine specially constructed in order to catch the day's changing light effects, the main scene ranks as the artist's masterpiece. The four reliefs of the life of the Virgin are of markedly lower quality and are presumably not the work of the master, who employed as many as twenty assistants in order to fulfil the flood of commissions which came his way. However, Riemenschneider certainly made the exquisite predella scenes of *Epiphany* and *Christ Among the Doctors*; the calm, pensive central figure in the group of scholars is probably a self-portrait. A couple of decades after the retable was made, the chapel was given over to the Lutherans; its excellent state of preservation is due to the fact that, as the main scene was anathema to Protestant doctrine, it was closed off and not re-opened until the nineteenth century.

Practicalities

Creglingen is no longer on a rail line; **buses** to Weikersheim and Rothenburg leave from the terminal on the town centre side of the Tauber. There are three **hotels** in the town proper: *Gasthof Grüner Baum,* Torstr. 20 (☎07933/618; ③), *Gasthof Herrgottstal,* Herrgottstal 13 (☎07933/518; ④) and *Gasthof Krone,* Hauptstr. 12 (☎07933/558; ⑤). Additionally, there are a few **private rooms** (①–③) and also a number of **farmhouses** offering bargain deals, the wackiest being the *Heuhotel Stahl* (☎07933/378; ④) in the incorporated hamlet of Weidenhof to the northeast, where you can sleep on hay in the loft for DM28, evening meal included. For more information about these, contact the **tourist office** (Mon–Fri 9am–5pm; ☎07933/631), by the roadside on the main route out of town to the north, at An der Romantischen Str. 14. Beside the Münstersee some 3km away is a **campsite** (☎07933/321), while there's a **youth hostel** on a hillside at the eastern end of Creglingen itself at Erdbacher Str. 30 (☎07933/336; ☎).

travel details

Trains

Heidelberg to: Bad Wimpfen (hourly; 50min); Bonn (hourly; 2hr 20min); Bruchsal (every 30min; 20min); Cologne (hourly; 2hr 25min); Mainz (hourly; 1hr 5min); Mannheim (hourly; 10min).

Karlsruhe to: Baden-Baden (every 20min; 20min); Freiburg (every 30min; 1hr); Freudenstadt

(hourly; 2hr); Mannheim (frequent; 30min); Schwetzingen (every 30min; 40min).

Stuttgart to: Cologne (hourly; 3hr 45min); Donaueschingen (hourly; 2hr); Esslingen (every 30min; 10min); Frankfurt (hourly; 2hr 5min); Freiburg (hourly; 2hr 45min); Hamburg (8 daily; 6hr 45min); Hannover (9 daily; 5hr 30min); Heidelberg (hourly; 1hr 10min); Heilbronn (hourly; 45min);

Karlsruhe (every 30min; 1hr 10min); Konstanz (hourly; 2hr 40min); Ludwigsburg (frequent; 10min); Mainz (hourly; 2hr); Mannheim (hourly; 1hr 30min); Marbach (every 30min; 25min); Rottweil (hourly; 1hr 30min); Schwäbisch Gmünd (every 30min; 40min); Schwäbisch Hall (hourly; 1hr); Tübingen (every 30min; 1hr); Ulm (every 20min; 1hr).

Ulm to: Blaubeuren (hourly; 10min); Heidelberg (hourly; 2hr 15min); Mainz (hourly; 3hr 5min); Mannheim (hourly; 2hr 25min).

CHAPTER THREE

HESSE

O ccupying the geographical centre of Germany and manifesting elements of both north and south German culture, **Hesse** (*Hessen*) claims to be the very heart of the nation. Although one of the parts of the country least visited by foreigners, it's also, paradoxically, one which has created preconceived images of Germany more than any other. This is because of the worldwide familiarity of the folk tales collected by the most famous Hessians, the **Brothers Grimm**, which are set in the darkly forested highlands, feudal castles and half-timbered towns so characteristic of the province.

Modern Hesse – flung together by the Americans as an administrative unit after World War II – represents an approximate revival of a territory founded in the thirteenth century which reached the height of its power and influence during the Reformation. Its ruler, Landgrave Philipp the Magnanimous, was the undisputed champion of **political Protestantism**. On his death in 1567, however, Hesse was divided into four separate states. Within a short period, they had crystallized into two – Hesse-Kassel and Hesse-Darmstadt – and these formed the main basis of the region's division until modern times, though there were many other later fragmentations. The division proved to be particularly destructive during the Thirty Years' War, in which much of Hesse was devastated.

During the eighteenth century the region's main export was mercenary soldiers, and a large press-ganged contingent helped Britain to lose the American War of Independence. The nineteenth century was a period of more conventional commercial activity, with the arrival of the Industrial Revolution and the founding of big concerns like Opel (originally a sewing machine factory) along the banks of the River Main. It was also a period of political wheeling and dealing as the local princes attempted to play Prussia and Austria off against each other. Hesse-Kassel, hitherto regarded as the senior province, backed the wrong side and was absorbed by the expanding Kingdom of Prussia in 1866. The wilier rulers of Hesse-Darmstadt were able to remain as independent Grand Dukes, and in this capacity joined the Second Reich five years later.

Today Hesse is one of the most prosperous of the German Länder, focused on the American-style dynamism of **Frankfurt**. Although traditional heavy industry still exists around the confluence of the Rhine and the Main, it's the serious money generated by banking and modern communications-related industries in Frankfurt which provides the region's real economic base. The two former capitals, **Kassel** and **Darmstadt**, are likewise industrial. Both suffered heavily in the war, though both are worth visiting for the sake of their many reminders of past periods of artistic patronage. Otherwise, apart from occasional light industrial pockets, most of Hesse's inhabitants live from farming or tourism. By far the most beautiful city is modest-sized **Marburg**, Hesse's first capital and home to one of Germany's most prestigious universities; in conjunction with the other towns of the **Lahn** valley, it's a great place to spend a few days. The same can be said of the Baroque city of **Fulda**, still a major episcopal centre, which offers easy access to the **Vogelsberg** and **Rhön** hills. From a tourist point of view, the most popular part of Hesse is the **Rheingau**, a scenic stretch on the right bank of the Rhine, west of the Land capital **Wiesbaden**, a money-oriented playground and gambling centre.

Hesse is very accessible: Frankfurt has the busiest international airport in Europe and is easily reached by **rail** and **road** from the rest of Germany. There are good rail

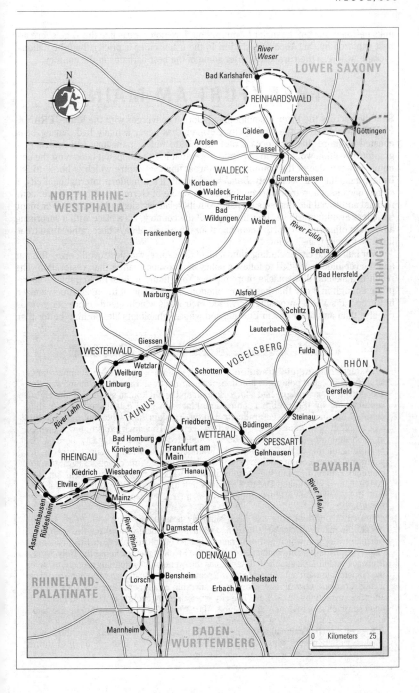

links between most of the major towns, although remoter areas like the Vogelsberg are best explored by car. **Accommodation** in the major cities is pricier than the national average, whereas the rural areas offer some of the best bargains in the country.

FRANKFURT AM MAIN

Straddled across the River Main not long before it converges with the Rhine, **FRANKFURT AM MAIN** is the capital city Germany has never actually had, having been cheated on more than one occasion of the role to which its history and central geographical position would seem to entitle it. Yet that hasn't stopped it becoming the economic powerhouse of the country, a cut-throat financial centre which is home to 388 banks, including the all-mighty *Bundesbank* itself. It's a modern international city, a communications and transport centre for the whole of Germany, with a frenetic commercial and social life that sets it apart from its relatively sleepy hinterland. For many travellers Frankfurt will be their first taste of the country; it's a place with a surprising amount to offer and it's worth spending at least a couple of days here rather than treating it as a mere transit point.

Over half of the city, including almost all of the centre, was destroyed during the war and the rebuilders decided to follow a policy of innovation rather than restoration. The result is a skyline that smacks more of New York than the Federal Republic – appropriate enough in a city that has the reputation of being one of the most Americanized in Europe. It's also a surprisingly civilized metropolis which spends more per year on the arts than any other city in Europe, and whose inhabitants like nothing better than

THE CAPITAL CITY THAT NEVER WAS

Frankfurt's **commercial tradition** goes back to Roman times, when its importance as a river crossing point and junction between north and south Germany was first recognized. Charlemagne had a fortress built on the old Roman site during the eighth century, and by the twelfth century Frankfurt was well established as a trading centre. This market evolved gradually into the Frankfurt fair which flourishes to this day, albeit in new premises just outside the centre. The stock exchange was opened in 1585 and Meyer Amschel Rothschild founded a financial dynasty here at the beginning of the nineteenth century. Frankfurt was also the main centre of the postwar German economic recovery. It was here that the Americans set in motion the currency reform that put the shattered nation back on its feet – overnight, on June 20, 1948, they introduced DM10.7 billion worth of new currency, printed in the USA and delivered to Frankfurt under armed guard, to replace the vastly inflated *Reichsmark*.

The city's **political role** has been similarly prominent, albeit with more variable results: its failure to establish itself as the nation's capital symbolizes the tragedy of German history, in which authoritarianism has so often triumphed. In 1356, Frankfurt gained permanent status as the place where the Electors met to choose the Holy Roman Emperor, and in 1562 supplanted Aachen as the scene of the imperial coronations. After the Napoleonic wars it was chosen as the seat of the National Assembly, but hopes that it might provide neutral, liberal-minded leadership of a united Germany were dashed after the revolutions of 1848–49. The city was seized by Prussia in 1866 and has never been so much as a regional capital since. After World War II, it seemed to be the natural choice as capital of West Germany, but lost out on the casting vote of Chancellor Adenauer, who had campaigned in favour of Bonn, the city nearest his own home, in an alliance with Berliners who feared that Frankfurt would be strong enough to thwart Berlin's chances of ever regaining capital status.

The **telephone code** for Frankfurt is ☎069

to spend an evening knocking back a few jugs of the local apple wine in the open-air taverns of the **Sachsenhausen** suburb.

Frankfurt has an energetic nightlife and is a thriving recreational centre for the whole of Hesse, with a good selection of theatres and galleries, and an even better range of museums, mostly concentrated along the south bank of the River Main. It comes across as a confident and tolerant city, and in the **Bockenheim** district there's a healthy "alternative" scene, not self-consciously institutionalized in the way that Berlin's has become.

Arrival and accommodation

Frankfurt **airport** (☎690 30511 for flight information) is one of the world's busiest, and is a major point of entry into Germany from abroad. There are regular rail departures from the airport **Bahnhof** which will enable you to reach most of Germany's cities fairly easily. Trains leave approximately once every ten minutes for Frankfurt's **Hauptbahnhof** (journey time 11min) from where there are even more comprehensive services covering Germany and beyond.

The airport is also linked to the Hauptbahnhof by two S-Bahn lines, run by the regional transport company (*RMV*), which is also responsible for bus, tram and U-Bahn services. A curiosity of the Frankfurt system is that single tickets are more expensive from 6.30–8.30am and 4–6.30pm on Mondays to Fridays (currently DM3.30 as opposed to DM2.80 at other times). The 24-hour rover ticket costs DM8.80, though it's usually better to invest in the Frankfurt Card (DM10 for one day, DM15 for two days), which includes half-price entry to virtually all the city's museums. (Bear in mind that these are free on Wednesdays.) From the Hauptbahnhof you can take tram #11, which goes right through the heart of the historic city centre; it takes about fifteen minutes to walk the same distance. Frankfurt has two main **tourist offices**. There's one in the Hauptbahnhof, opposite track 23 (Mon–Fri 8am–9pm, Sat & Sun 9am–6pm; ☎2123 8849), and another in the heart of the city at Römerberg 27 (Mon–Fri 9.30am–5.30pm, Sat & Sun 10am–4pm; ☎2123 8708).

Accommodation

Accommodation is predictably pricey, thanks to the expense-account business people who come for the various *Messen* or trade fairs. It can also be quite difficult to find, and it's best to try and sort it out in advance – especially if you're arriving when one of the major fairs is on, such as the Book Fair, at the end of September/beginning of

ACCOMMODATION PRICE CODES

All the pensions and hotels in this book have been graded according to the following price categories. The prices quoted are for the cheapest available double room, although many of the budget places will also have more expensive rooms. Youth hostels are graded under separate categories. See p.34 for more details.

① less than DM50	④ DM81–100	⑦ DM151–200
② DM51–65	⑤ DM101–125	⑧ DM201–250
③ DM66–80	⑥ DM126–150	⑨ more than DM250

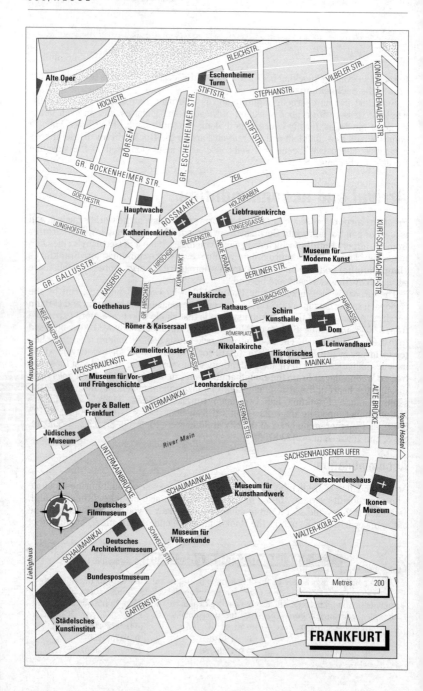

FRANKFURT

October. To do this via the tourist board, write to the administrative headquarters at Kaiserstr. 52. Information, but no booking facility, is available on ☎2123 6869. If you're planning on staying for a while, contact one of the **Mitwohnzentralen**, at Klingerstr. 9 (☎284340) or Wiesenstr. 32b (☎462030), who will arrange the let of an apartment.

Hotels and pensions

Predictably, budget hotels and pensions are scant, especially in the city centre. If you don't mind the sleazy environs, most of the few reasonably priced hotels cluster around the Hauptbahnhof, close to the Kaiserstrasse red-light district. There's also a clutch in the more enticing location of the Westend district by the University. Expensive business-class hotels, on the other hand, are thick on the ground, though they still get booked out at busy times, and only a few have real character.

Admiral, Hölderlinstr. 25 (☎448021, fax 439402). For Frankfurt this is a good reasonably priced hotel, a little bit east of the Altstadt. ⑥

Am Dom, Kannengiessergasse 3 (☎282141, fax 283237). Scores heavily for its location in a quiet Altstadt alley, with the museums and nightspots of Sachsenhausen only a short walk away over the Alte Brücke. ⑦

Atlas, Zimmerweg 1 (☎723946, fax 723946). Small, homely hotel in an apartment block within easy walking distance of the Hauptbahnhof, yet away from the sleazier streets. ④

Backer, Mendelssohnstr. 92 (☎747992). Basic pension located just round the corner from the U-Bahn Westend station. ③

Bruns, Mendelssohnstr. 42 (☎748896). Another no-frills pension featuring large, light rooms with wooden floors in the Westend neighbourhood. ③

Diana, Westendstr. 83 (☎747007, fax 747079). Very pleasant Westend hotel on a quiet residential street. ⑦

Frankfurter Hof, Am Kaiserplatz (☎21502, fax 215847). A flagship of the *Steigenberger* chain, this is the grandest of Frankfurt's grand hotels, occupying a palatial edifice from the time of the Second Reich. Of its four restaurants, *Français* is a gourmet paradise ranking among the most prestigious in the country, *Hofgarten* is a grill room, *Kaiserbrunnen* serves lighter meals, while *Frankfurter Stubb* has traditional German fare at reasonable prices. ⑨

Glockshuber, Mainzer Landstr. 120 (☎742628, fax 742629). Basic hotel near the Hauptbahnhof. ④

Goldener Stern, Karlsruher Str. 8 (☎233309). Close to the Kaiserstrasse red-light district, by the Hauptbahnhof. ④

Gölz, Beethovenstr. 44 (☎746735, fax 716142). A good Westend pension, situated near the University. ⑥

Hessischer Hof, Friedrich-Ebert-Anlage 40 (☎75400, fax 754 0924). Super-luxury hotel directly opposite the *Messe* buildings. It's beautifully furnished throughout, with a valuable porcelain collection in the restaurant. ⑨

Life, Weserstr. 12 (☎231014, fax 231014). Another of the low-cost options near the Hauptbahnhof. ④

Maingau, Schifferstr. 38–40 (☎617001, fax 620790). A good choice if you fancy staying in Sachsenhausen, which has surprisingly few hotels. There's the bonus of an outstanding restaurant. ⑥

Terminus, Münchener Str. 59 (☎242320, fax 237411). Virtually facing the Hauptbahnhof and one of the best value in this price range. ⑤

Turm, Eschenheimer Landstr. 20 (☎154050, fax 553578). Situated just to the north of the Altstadt and very comfortable. ⑦

Youth hostel and campsite

Campingplatz Heddernheim, An der Sandelmühle 35 (☎570332). In the northern suburb of Heddernheim; take U-Bahn #1, #2 or #3.

Haus der Jugend, Deutschherrnufer 12 (☎619058). The youth hostel is in Sachsenhausen, reached by bus #46 from the Hauptbahnhof, and is the best budget deal in Frankfurt. ☎

The city

Most of central Frankfurt can be covered on foot; almost all the main sights lie within the bounds of the old city walls, which have been turned into a stretch of narrow parkland describing an approximate semicircle around the city centre. From here it's an easy matter to cross the Main into Sachsenhausen, where most of the museums are conveniently located along the southern river bank.

The Altstadt

Until it was devastated in two massive air raids in 1944, Frankfurt had the largest and most complete Altstadt of any important German city. After the war, the most important monuments were carefully restored; other parts were hastily rebuilt in a modern manner. Even so, large gaps remained until the 1970s, when, after much debate, they were filled with a mixture of pastiche medieval buildings and ultra-modern public commissions.

The Römerberg

As good a point as any to begin your explorations is the **Römerberg**, the historical and, roughly speaking, geographical centre of the city. Charlemagne built his fort on this low hill, on the site of earlier Roman and Alemannic settlements, to protect the ford which gave Frankfurt its name – *Frankonovurd* (Ford of the Franks). Throughout the Middle Ages the Römerberg was Frankfurt's focal point, serving as market place, fairground, venue for every imaginable kind of *Volksfest* and, less frequently, for the celebrations associated with an Imperial coronation. At the start of this century the Römerberg was still the heart of the city, an essentially medieval quarter ringed by half-timbered houses built by the rich merchants and bankers who had made Frankfurt one of Germany's richest centres – its "secret capital", according to Goethe.

At the western end of the Römerberg is the **Römer** building itself, which formerly served as the Rathaus. Its distinctive Gothic facade, with its triple-stepped gables, was more or less all that remained after the war, but the building has been restored with consummate skill. Its two upper storeys house the **Kaisersaal** (daily 10am–1pm & 2–5pm; DM3), the former imperial coronation hall, which contains 52 bombastic nineteenth-century portraits of the German emperors. The building fronts the Römerplatz, the market square, with the Mannerist **Gerechtigkeitsbrunnen** (Justice Fountain) in the middle. Facing the Römer, a row of seven half-timbered houses was built in the late 1970s using original plans and traditional construction methods.

On the southern side of Römerplatz stands the Gothic **Nikolaikirche**, originally the court chapel, now a Protestant parish church. It's a highly distinctive and lovingly restored little building, built on a virtually square ground plan. Opposite is the **Steinernes Haus**, a postwar reconstruction of one of the few stone-built houses of the Frankfurt Altstadt; it now houses a commercial art gallery (Tues 11am–6pm, Wed 11am–8pm, Thurs–Sat 11am–6pm).

Off the northern side of Römerplatz is the Neoclassical **Paulskirche** (daily 11am–3pm), built in the late eighteenth century as a Lutheran preaching hall. However, it was soon taken over for secular purposes, and it was here that the ill-fated German National Assembly met during the revolutionary upheavals of 1848–49. The church still functions as a meeting hall and looks totally unecclesiastical inside. On the northern wall there's a monument to the victims of the Nazis.

Around the Römerberg

East of Römerplatz is the most controversial of the inner-city developments. At its core is the **Schirn Kunsthalle** (Tues & Fri–Sun 10am–7pm, Wed & Thurs 10am–10pm; variable entrance charges), a cultural centre consisting of a glass tunnel for exhibitions (which regularly attracts prestigious shows, particularly of archeological subjects, old master paintings and modern art) and a rotunda with more display space and a café. The centre also houses the **Struwwelpeter-Museum** (Tues & Thurs–Sun 10am–5pm, Wed 10am–8pm; free), which has displays of international editions of the eponymous children's classic, and documentary material on its creator, the nineteenth-century physician, psychiatrist and liberal politician, Heinrich Hoffmann. Locals have dubbed the Schirn the "Federal Bowling Alley", or, in their more fanciful moments, "Murder at the Cathedral", due to its proximity to the Dom. Whether you like it or not will probably depend on how you feel about Post-Modernism, but in many ways it represents a brave attempt to re-create a sense of the Römerberg as the centre of Frankfurt. Running roughly parallel with it, and bounded to the south by Saalgasse, is a row of gabled townhouses which, though essentially modern in design and construction, echo the medieval past of the Römerberg.

Beyond is the **Historischer Garten**, where the foundations of some of the Roman, Carolingian and medieval buildings which previously occupied the site have been laid bare to form a little park. Diagonally opposite is the Gothic **Leinwandhaus** (Tues & Thurs–Sun 11am–6pm, Wed 11am–8pm), formerly a cloth hall. It now contains three galleries, one of which is used for international photography exhibitions. Just to the north, in Domstrasse, looms the **Museum für Moderne Kunst** (Tues & Thurs–Sun 10am–5pm, Wed 10am–8pm; DM7, free Wed), looking like a hi-tech slice of cake. This has attracted a fair amount of criticism on the grounds that the collection is as yet unworthy of its setting, though it does include examples of such famous postwar artists as Beuys, Warhol and Lichtenstein.

The Dom

The most significant building in the Altstadt is the red sandstone church of **St Bartholomäus**, popularly if inaccurately referred to as the **Dom**, a courtesy title granted it by virtue of the fact that, being the venue for the election and coronation of the Holy Roman Emperors, it was far more important than most cathedrals. In essence, it's a Gothic hall church built in the thirteenth and fourteenth centuries. The two **portals** – and particularly that on the south side, which retains most of its original sculptures – are the finest features from this period. However, the outstanding part of the Dom is its 95-metre **tower** (April–Oct 9am–1pm & 2.30–6pm; DM3), added in the early fifteenth century by the brilliantly idiosyncratic municipal architect **Madern Gerthener**, whose quirky genius left a profound mark on the city. The pinnacled summit is one of the most original creations of German Gothic and is a clear attempt to re-think earlier spires, such as those of Freiburg's Münster, in a more modern idiom. Before the construction of the modern skyscrapers, the tower was the tallest structure in the city, and even today, strict planning rules are enforced to preserve its dominance over the Altstadt, of which there's a marvellous **view** from the top.

The treasures of the spacious, light-filled interior include a monumental *Crucifixion* group on the west wall by the Mainz sculptor Hans Backoffen; the poignant fifteenth-century *Maria-Schlaf-Altar* in the north transept chapel; the nearby tomb of the royal pretender Günther von Schwarzburg, rival of Emperor Charles IV; and an intricately carved set of mid-fourteenth-century choir stalls. To the right of the choir is the relatively simple and unadorned **Wahlkapelle**, where the seven Electors used to make their final choice as to who would become emperor. Housed in the cloister is the **Dommuseum** (Tues–Fri 10am–5pm, Sat & Sun 11am–5pm; DM2), which contains treasury items and historic ecclesiastical garments, plus precious artefacts recently unearthed from royal Merovingian graves during restoration work.

The southern Altstadt

Immediately south of Römerberg is the **Saalhof**, an amalgam of several architecturally diverse Imperial buildings which also incorporates the Rententurm, one of the few surviving towers from the old city defences, and a Romanesque chapel, the Saalkapelle.

The complex and its modern extensions house the excellent **Historisches Museum** (Tues & Thurs–Sun 10am–5pm, Wed 10am–8pm; DM5, free Wed). Look out for the magnificent coloured woodcut, exhibited with part of the original block, showing a bird's-eye view of Frankfurt as it was in 1552; it's the masterpiece of one of the city's finest artists, Conrad Faber von Kreuznach. There's also an intriguing section on the seventeenth-century Merian family, who were responsible for the detailed topographic engravings of German cities which are such a ubiquitous feature of museums all over the country. Frankfurt's greatest painter, Adam Elsheimer, is represented by a tiny panel of *Tobias and the Angel*, displayed alongside a strong showing of the city's many highly accomplished still-life specialists. Another section of the museum offers belated homage to Anne Frank, the young Frankfurt-born Jewess who died at Belsen but who gained posthumous international fame through her intensely moving diaries.

A short distance to the west is the **Leonhardskirche**, originally a pilgrimage station on the well-trodden route to Santiago de Compostela in northern Spain. Surviving from this Romanesque church are the octagonal east towers and two beautiful portals, but the latter are now indoors as a Gothic aisle was built over them. At the end of this is the *Salvatorchörlein*, a chapel whose amazing pendant vault was considered the great sight of Frankfurt in the early days of tourism. The replacement chancel, built by Madern Gerthener, preserves most of its luminous stained-glass windows; to the side is a magnificent gilded altar from Antwerp.

A little to the northwest, entered from Münzgasse, is the **Karmeliterkloster** (Tues & Thurs–Sun 11am–6pm, Wed 11am–8pm; DM3, free Wed), a secularized late Gothic monastery renowned for its marvellously idiosyncratic murals by the sixteenth-century painter and revolutionary leader **Jerg Ratgeb**. These were badly damaged in the war, but have been painstakingly restored: their faded condition is due in large part to their having been executed in tempera. The cycle in the cloisters forms a complete illustrated Bible; that in the refectory – which is nowadays used for temporary exhibitions of works by living artists – narrates the life of the prophet Elijah and the mission and martyrdom of Carmelite monks in the Holy Land.

The rest of the monastery contains the **Museum für Vor- und Frühgeschichte** (Tues & Thurs–Sun 10am–5pm, Wed 10am–8pm; DM5, free Wed), and has a separate entrance on Karmelitergasse. This features archeological finds from the Near East and Classical Greece and Rome, but is mainly dedicated to material excavated locally. In the transept of the former church are finds from a wide variety of prehistoric sites, the most notable being the contents of an Iron Age warrior's grave. The nave is entirely devoted to the Roman period, with stone monuments, glass, ceramics, weapons and jewellery, much of it dug up in the settlement of Nida, which lies within the present-day boundaries of Frankfurt. Finally, the chapel alongside has rich hoards of valuables from Alemannic and Frankish graves, plus early medieval artefacts found underneath the city centre.

Further west, at Untermainkai 14–15, is the **Jüdisches Museum** (same hours; DM5, free Sat), which recounts the history of Frankfurt's once powerful and wealthy Jewish community, the largest in Germany after that of Berlin.

The northern Altstadt

A few minutes' walk north of the Karmeliterkloster, at Grosser Hirschgraben 23, is the **Goethehaus und Goethe-Museum** (April–Sept Mon–Sat 9am–6pm, Sun 10am–1pm; Oct–March Mon–Sat 9am–4pm, Sun 10am–1pm; DM4), the interior of which has been immaculately restored after being completely burned out during the war. This is where Goethe was born and raised, and the house has been made to look as much as possible like it did when he lived here. There are a few original objects which survived the war, while the well-stocked library has some autographed examples of his writings.

The **Katharinenkirche**, a little further along on Kleiner Hirschgraben, is where Goethe was baptized and confirmed. Opposite is the **Hauptwache**, an eighteenth-century Baroque building which used to be Frankfurt's biggest police station. These days it's a pricey city-centre café, while the station of the same name is a junction on nearly all of Frankfurt's S- and U-Bahn lines.

Nearby on the Liebfrauenberg stands the **Liebfrauenkirche**, a fifteenth-century church now belonging to a Capuchin monastery. Look inside for the unusual Baroque altar, a huge alabaster and gilt affair which sits well in the dusky pink sandstone interior. Even finer is the original south doorway, now only visible from the inside; its gorgeous and still brightly coloured tympanum of *The Adoration of the Magi* is a masterpiece of the "Soft Style", and is thought to be the work of Madern Gerthener.

The **Markthalle** just behind the church is a hive of activity and sells the best fresh fruit and veg in town as well as fresh imported produce from Turkey. To the north, **Zeil** is one of Germany's most expensive and exclusive shopping streets, though the area around Konstablerwache has become notorious for its drugs pedlars: one downside of Frankfurt's prosperity is that it has become the undisputed drugs capital of Germany.

A little to the northwest of the Hauptwache is the **Börse**, Frankfurt's stock exchange. It's open to the public on application (Mon–Fri 10am–noon). Appropriately enough two of the most expensive shopping streets in the city are just around the corner. **Goethestrasse** sells expensive jewellery and designer clothes, while **Grosse Bockenheimer Strasse**, known to the natives as *Fressgasse* (Guzzle Lane), is home to upmarket delicatessens and smarter restaurants. Look out for *Stefan Weiss*, a butcher's shop that's sometimes described as a "meat boutique", owing to its immaculate interior and high prices.

Both of these streets lead into Opernplatz, home of the grandiose **Alte Oper**, built in 1880 in imitation of, and as a rival to, the opera houses of Paris and Dresden. The present structure is the result of years of work to restore the damage of 1945 – the vestibule and first-floor café, all fake marble and colonnades, recapture something of the late nineteenth-century ambience. With its excellent acoustics, the Alte Oper is often used as a congress hall as well as playing host to classical musicians and stars of stage and screen. Oddly enough you won't see much opera here, apart from the occasional production which doesn't need elaborate staging.

The fringes of the Altstadt

For one of the best **views** of Frankfurt old and new, it's worth taking a walk through the **Taunusanlage** and the **Gallusanlage**, two narrow stretches of parkland running into each other that begin south of Opernplatz and curve round to the Main, following the line of the old city wall. With the Alte Oper to the north, the Hauptbahnhof to the west, the Römerberg to the southeast and all around you the ultra-modern high-rise office buildings which give the city its distinctive skyline, it's a great place to capture a view of the city. But – and it's a big but – this area is the favourite hangout of the city's junkies, and it's best to steer clear of the area at night.

A much more pleasant stroll from Opernplatz is in the opposite direction through the **Bockenheimer Anlage** and past a small lake to the **Nebbienisches Gartenhäuschen**, a playful little villa built in 1810 by a local publisher to mark his third marriage. At the end of the Bockenheimer Anlage rises the **Eschenheimer Turm**, the highest defensive tower in Germany. There were once 42 towers ringing the city and this is the most imposing of the survivors; its fantastical shape, peppered with oriels and turrets and looking like it was designed in the Hollywood dream factory, marks it out as the handiwork of the ever-resourceful Madern Gerthener. Look out for the nine holes in the shape of a figure 9 on the weather vane which, according to legend, were shot into it by a local poacher.

Nearby in Stephanstrasse is the **Petersfriedhof**, which for years was Frankfurt's most fashionable cemetery. In the adjacent school courtyard you can see the grave of Goethe's mother, "Frau Aja". About ten minutes' walk to the south, just off Fahrgasse, is a surviving stretch of the **Staufenmauer**, the twelfth-century city wall which was the grand daddy of all Frankfurt's subsequent defences. Just beyond here, a left turn into Berliner Strasse leads to Battonstrasse and the **Jüdischer Friedhof**, which was in use from 1462 to 1828 and contains the Rothschild family vault.

Sachsenhausen

If you want to escape from the centre of Frankfurt, or have a laid-back evening out, then head for **Sachsenhausen** on the south bank of the Main. Although it has been part of Frankfurt since 1318, this city-within-a-city retains a distinctive atmosphere. It's best known as the "apple wine quarter", in honour of its most famous product, which is served in practically every bar in the area, and it's here that you'll find Frankfurt's most civilized nightlife. In **Schweizer Strasse** there's every imaginable kind of speciality shop, while in the old *Schlachthaus* (slaughterhouse) on Deutschherrnufer (opposite the Flösserbrücke) there's a *Flohmarkt* (flea market) every Saturday morning.

The heart of the quarter

The best way to approach Sachsenhausen is over the **Eiserner Steg**, an iron footbridge which runs from just outside the Historisches Museum. Lazy alternatives, which cross via the Alte Brücke further to the east, are bus #46 from the Hauptbahnhof or, if you're feeling in the mood for a bit of tourist tack, the *Ebbelwei-Express*, an old-time tram with on-board apple wine and pretzels (Sat & Sun at 1.30pm & 5.30pm; DM4 inclusive). However you decide to get there, you'll be doing a lot of walking when you arrive as most the attractions are well spread out.

Just over the Alte Brücke is the **Deutschordenshaus**, a triple-winged eighteenth-century building formerly belonging to the Teutonic Knights, whose Baroque facade cunningly hides a Gothic church. A section of the conventual buildings has been adapted to house the **Ikonen-Museum** (Tues & Thurs–Sun 10am–5pm, Wed 10am–8pm; DM2, but included on Museum für Kunsthandwerk ticket, free Wed), a collection of icons concentrating on the eighteenth and nineteenth centuries. Overlooking the river just a couple of minutes' walk away is the **Kuhhirtenturm** (Cowherds' Tower): built in 1490 as part of the Sachsenhausen fortifications, it looks like an elongated fortified barn.

Most people go to Sachsenhausen to eat, drink and be merry in the restaurants and bars of **Alt-Sachsenhausen**, the network of streets around Affentorplatz to the south. The main attractions are the apple wine houses – recognized by the pine wreath or *Fichtekränzi* hanging outside – where drinkers sit at long wooden benches in an atmosphere that makes it easy to get into conversation (see p.351).

At the southernmost end of the quarter looms the 120-metre **Henninger Turm** (Mon–Sat 3–11pm, Sun 11am–11pm; DM3.50) of the eponymous Frankfurt brewery. The entrance fee includes access to a museum (open until 7pm) illustrating the history of beer in the city from the Middle Ages to the present day, and to the observation platform, which commands a fine view over Frankfurt. There are also a couple of top-notch restaurants, which are pricey, though not unreasonably so.

Along Museumsufer

Between the Eiserner Steg and the Friedensbrücke to the west is Schaumainkai, popularly known as the **Museumsufer**, as the best museums in Frankfurt, seven in all, are straddled along its bank. First up, at no. 15, is the **Museum für Kunsthandwerk** (Tues & Thurs–Sun 10am–5pm, Wed 10am–8pm; DM6, free Wed), which has one of the largest and best collections of applied art in Germany. It's housed in a discreetly innovative building designed by the American architect Richard Meier: all sloping ramps in place of stairs and glassless internal windows framing *objets d'art*. The museum is divided into four sections: European, featuring furniture, glassware and ceramics; Islamic, with some fine carpets; Far Eastern, with lots of jade and lacquerwork plus a liberal sprinkling of porcelain and sculptures; and finally a section devoted to books and writing. In a nineteenth-century villa at no. 29, the **Museum für Völkerkunde** (same hours; DM4, free Wed) is a small ethnographical museum with an extensive collection of masks and totems.

The **Deutsches Filmmuseum** (Tues, Thurs, Fri & Sun 10am–5pm, Wed 10am–8pm, Sat 2–8pm; DM5, free Wed) at no. 41 is Germany's biggest and best on the subject, featuring a huge collection detailing the development of films and the film industry. A distinctly "hands-on" approach encourages visitors to get to grips with the various film-related items on display, which range from early bioscopes to modern movie cameras. On a larger scale, there's a reconstruction of the *Grand Café* in Paris where the Lumière brothers showed the first-ever public film, and of a Frankfurt cinema from 1912. There's also a good collection of film posters and a very extensive section on film music. Not surprisingly the museum has its own cinema (entry DM8, DM9 for a combined ticket with the museum).

A passage leads from the Filmmuseum café to the **Deutsches Architektur-museum** (Tues & Thurs–Sun 10am–5pm, Wed 10am–8pm; DM8, free Wed) at no. 43, installed in a self-consciously avant-garde conversion of a nineteenth-century villa. The high point of the interior, which has been gutted and restyled in dazzling white, is the "house within a house", which dominates the museum like an oversized doll's house. Most of the space is given over to changing exhibitions on architectural themes, though the top floor has a permanent display of miniature theatre sets presenting a potted history of world architecture. More conventional in layout is the **Bundespostmuseum** (same hours; free) at no. 53, a big collection of anything remotely connected with postal matters. The museum is also big on telephones, as Frankfurt calls itself the birthplace of the telephone, irrespective of the claims of Alexander Graham Bell.

The Städelsches Kunstinstitut

Very much the star of the Museumsufer, the **Städelsches Kunstinstitut** or **Städel** (Tues & Thurs–Sun 10am–5pm, Wed 10am–8pm; DM8, free Wed) at no. 63 ranks as one of the most comprehensive art galleries in Europe. Unlike the galleries of Munich and Berlin, it is not rooted in a royal collection – it was founded in the early nineteenth century by a local banker as an art college, with an assembly of old masters from which students could learn.

MEDIEVAL AND RENAISSANCE GERMAN PAINTING

Chronologically, the layout begins on the top floor. Highlights of the **German section** include a naive but surpassingly beautiful *Garden of Paradise* by an unknown Middle Rhenish master of the early fifteenth century, the squeamish *Martyrdom of the Twelve Apostles* by the normally placid **Lochner**, *The Resurrection* by **Master of the Housebook**, *Job on his Dungheap* by **Dürer**, and two grisailles from a lost altarpiece by **Grünewald**. Holbein the Elder's large *Passion Altar*, painted for the city's Dominican monastery, is one of his finest works, with no quarter given in the representation of gruesome detail. **Cranach**'s *The Holy Kinship*, which incorporates portraits of some of the leading personalities of the day, is another major altarpiece from the eve of the Reformation. The idiosyncratic art of **Baldung** is represented by a *Baptism of Christ* triptych and *Two Weather Witches*, while in **Altdorfer**'s opulent *Adoration of the Magi* the artist typically indulges his love of rich and elaborate detail. The outstanding *Portrait of Simon George of Cornwall* by **Holbein the Younger** is particularly intriguing for the fact that the subject was clean-shaven when the sittings began; the artist had to carry out a skilful modification in order to show the beard his patron subsequently grew.

NETHERLANDISH AND EARLY ITALIAN WORKS

One of the main strengths of the gallery is its wealth of paintings from the early **Netherlandish School**, dominated by the gem of the whole collection, **Jan van Eyck**'s *Lucca Madonna*, which shows his legendary precision at its finest. The first great painter of the School, now generally identified as **Robert Campin** but labelled here as the Master of Flémalle, is represented by several works, while his pupil **Rogier van der Weyden** features with a magnificent *Virgin and Child with SS Peter, John the Baptist, Cosmas and Damian*. Also in the room are superbly observed male portraits by Memling and Massys, and one of **Bosch**'s earliest known works, *Christ Presented to the People*; though restrained by his standards, it already shows his penchant for caricature and facial distortions. The Madonna and Child, a frequent subject in the Netherlandish section, also dominates the **Italian**, where the outstanding treatment is the ethereal image by **Fra Angelico**. Versions by Verrocchio, Moretto da Brescia, Perugino, Bellini, Cima and Carpaccio make fascinating comparisons. Other highlights here are an *Annunciation* by **Carlo Crivelli**, *St Mark* by **Mantegna**, *Portrait of Simonetta Vespucci* by **Botticelli** and **Pontormo**'s *Lady with Lap-Dog*.

SEVENTEENTH- & EARLY EIGHTEENTH-CENTURY PAINTING

Pride of place among **seventeenth-century** paintings goes to Frankfurt's own **Adam Elsheimer**. The largest work ever painted by this master of the small-scale is the *Altarpiece of the Cross*, the seven panels of which have been patiently accumulated over the years. Also here are *The Great Flood* – a miracle of compression – and *The Dream of Joseph*. Poussin, Claude and Rubens, all admirers of Elsheimer, are on display in the next section, which also includes the most purely Baroque work in **Rembrandt**'s entire output, the violent *Blinding of Samson* – a striking contrast with the quiet dignity of his very early *David Playing the Harp before Saul*. There's a gloriously luminous **Vermeer**, *The Geographer*, and examples of most of the lesser artists of seventeenth-century Holland. Representation of the early eighteenth century is sparser, but there are two scenes from a *Horrors of War* series by **Goya**, and examples of Tiepolo, Canaletto and Chardin. A recent acquisition is a newly discovered **Watteau**, the frothy *Isle of Cythera*.

LATE EIGHTEENTH- & NINETEENTH-CENTURY PAINTING

Paintings from the **late eighteenth century onwards** occupy the first floor. Of the big French names, **Courbet** (a *View of Frankfurt*), **Degas** and **Monet** are the ones to look out for. However, German artists predominate. *Goethe in the Roman Campagna* by **Johann Heinrich Tischbein** is the most celebrated of the many Romantic portrayals of the writer. The Nazarene Brotherhood figures strongly, notably with a huge detached fresco of *The Introduction of the Arts into Germany*, painted by **Philip Veit**, once director of the Städel. If this isn't to your taste, you might prefer the realism of **Wilhelm Leibl**, whose *Unlikely Couple* is an update of a favourite Renaissance theme – mercenary love.

TWENTIETH-CENTURY WORK

Until the days of the Third Reich, the Städel had perhaps the finest array of modern painting in Germany. However, over 500 paintings were removed in the measures against "degenerate art", and the collection has never recovered, although it now has the benefit of being able to display loans from local industrialists and financial institutions. German highlights include **Beckmann**'s *The Synagogue*, **Dix**'s unflattering *The Artist's Family*, **Ernst**'s spooky *Nature in Morning Light* and **Kirchner**'s *Nude Wearing a Hat*; the most notable foreign paintings are **Matisse**'s *Still Life* and **Picasso**'s *Portrait of Fernance Olivier*. The new extension features avant-garde work, including several huge canvases by **Anselm Kiefer**.

The Liebieghaus

Last but by no means least of the museums is the **Liebieghaus** (same hours; DM5, free Wed) at no. 71. The villa which houses it can easily be identified by the bits and pieces of statuary on display in the garden, including *Ariadne on the Panther* by Johann Heinrich Dannecker. The collection is a step-by-step guide to the history of sculpture, and as such is the most important in the country. Sumerian, Egyptian, Greek, Roman and Coptic examples give a comprehensive overview of the Classical world. German works predictably predominate in the later periods; look out in particular for the late fifteenth- and early sixteenth-century golden period, featuring important carvings by Nicolaus Gerhaert, Hans Multscher and Tilman Riemenschneider. There's also an illuminating section on Baroque altarpieces.

Westend and Bockenheim

Frankfurt's financial district, the **Westend**, developed as home to the commercial class during the nineteenth century. Until the Nazis came to power many of the wealthier members of Frankfurt's Jewish community (the second largest in Germany) lived here – for example huge swathes of land between Bockenheimer Landstrasse and Reuterweg were owned by the Rothschild family until the city bought them out in 1938, for a "bargain" price. In the 1960s the property speculators moved in, forcing ordinary people out of their homes so the old buildings could be converted into offices or the sites used for skyscrapers. Scant attention was paid to planning laws as the developers fell over themselves to grab every available inch of land, and from 1970 onwards there was a rash of house occupations and squattings in protest. Fierce clashes with the police ensued, but caused only temporary delays to the process of redevelopment.

Ugliest building in the area is undoubtedly the **Hochhaus am Park** in Fürstenberger Strasse, a totally incoherent structure designed by a succession of architects. The most impressive of the high-rises is the sleek **Deutsche Bank**, a little to the west of the Alte Oper, which dominates the Frankfurt skyline. At **Siesmayerstrasse 6** you can take a look at a piece of very recent history; this elegant upper-middle-class villa (now fallen on very hard times) was the last squatted house in the Westend to succumb.

Westend has its own stretch of greenery too. In the northwest of the area is the **Grüneburgpark**, a nineteenth-century English-style park which these days is popular with joggers and weekend footballers. On the northeastern edge is the **Botanischer Garten**, a good place to go for a walk as it has a sort of cultivated wildness to it. It incorporates the manicured **Palmengarten** (daily 9am–4/5/6pm; DM7), which is planted with tropical and sub-tropical trees, plants and flowers.

Bockenheim

Bockenheimer Landstrasse, once Frankfurt's millionaires' row, will take you from Westend to **Bockenheim**, a predominantly working-class district which since the 1960s has been turned into the centre of Frankfurt's alternative scene by a big influx of students and arty types. The area also has a large *Gastarbeiter* population and is best thought of as a Frankfurt version of Berlin's Kreuzberg. Leipziger Strasse is the main shopping drag (on U-Bahn line #6) and there are a lot of good bars and restaurants around – the Italian ones are best from a culinary viewpoint but the Greek places are usually best value for money.

The University complex is at the southeastern edge of Bockenheim, which partly accounts for its popularity with students. In the vicinity is the **Senckenbergmuseum**, Senckenberganlage 25 (Mon, Tues, Thurs & Fri 9am–5pm, Wed 9am–8pm, Sat & Sun 9am–6pm; DM7, free Wed), a massive natural history museum. Even if you're not normally attracted by this subject, it's well worth coming to see the remarkable paleontology collection, dominated by an awe-inspiring array of dinosaur skeletons.

Höchst

Nowadays a western suburb of Frankfurt, **HÖCHST**, which can be reached by S-Bahn line #1 or #2 from the Hauptbahnhof or Hauptwache, is an ancient town in its own right, as well as being the home of the famous Hoechst chemical company. Although very much in the shadow of the chemical works, the small Altstadt rewards a quick look round. The **Balongaropalast** at Balongarostr. 109 is a slightly over-the-top Baroque townhouse, in whose gardens open-air theatre performances are occasionally held. A little further down the same street, in the **Dalberghaus** (no. 186), Höchst porcelain is once again being manufactured – replica eighteenth-century shepherdess figurines and the like are for sale at unhealthy prices. On Schlossplatz to the south there's a Renaissance **Schloss** and the old **Zollturm** (Customs Tower). The latter houses the local museum (daily 10am–4pm; free), which, having been sponsored by Hoechst, tends to dwell on the history of that company. East of here is the **Justiniankirche**, by far the oldest church in the Frankfurt conurbation. It preserves its Carolingian nave intact, though the chancel was replaced in the Gothic period.

Bus #54 from the Altstadt takes you down Höchster Farben Strasse and to your left you'll see the huge chemical complex stretching out down to the Main. The cathedral-like administrative offices of the factory were designed by the Jugendstil architect Peter Behrens and must be among the most aesthetically balanced factory buildings anywhere. The bus then goes on to Zeilsheim, which in the immediate postwar years was the black market centre of Germany and where, around **Coburger Strasse**, you can still see the little cottages of the **Arbeiter Kolonie Zeilsheim**, a turn-of-the-century model housing development for Hoechst workers.

Eating, drinking and nightlife

Not surprisingly, given its status as one of Germany's main urban centres, Frankfurt has a wealth of gastronomic possibilities. Whether it's vegan breakfast, Japanese afternoon tea or a gourmet Italian dinner you're after, you'll be able to find it somewhere. As for drink, the city is situated close to several famous wine-producing regions, and is itself an important beer centre. *Binding* is the largest brewery in the country, while *Henninger* is one of the biggest exporters, and both produce a wide range of products. However, the city's favourite beverage is apple wine (*Apfelwein*; known as *Ebbelwei* or *Ebbelwoi* in the local dialect), a cider variant best sampled in the specialist taverns in Sachsenhausen.

Restaurants

Many of the restaurants in the city centre are fast-food joints or credit-card rip-offs for unwary lunching business people, but you will find some of the best Thai, Mexican, Greek and Italian food here too. Sachsenhausen is very popular for eating and you'll usually need to book, especially if there's a trade fair on.

The centre

Aubergine, Alte Gasse 14. Good French food, good service, reasonable prices (by central Frankfurt standards). Open for both lunch and dinner during the week, evenings only at the weekend.

Avocado-Le Bistro, Hochstr. 27. Fine bistro fare, complemented by a carefully selected wine list. Closed Sun.

Bistro Rosa, Grüneburgweg 25. The walls hung with pictures of pigs lend an element of kitsch, but the food is excellent. Evenings only, closed Sun.

Buffalo, Kaiserhofstr. 18. City-centre steakhouse, much favoured by the American community. Also does good enchiladas and tacos. Closed Sun.

Fisch-Franke, Domstr. 9. Offers fresh fish dishes, with a choice of waitress- or self-service. Closed Sun.

Gaylord, Elbestr. 24. Excellent Indian food, friendly and helpful staff.

Haus Wertheym, Fahrtor 1. A medieval *Gaststätte* on the Römerberg with *Bockbier*, traditional food and a friendly atmosphere. Closed Tues.

Iwase, Vilbeler Str. 31. Reasonably priced Japanese, with seating at the counter or the few tables. Tues–Sun 6.30–10.30pm.

Kutscher Kneipe, Eschenheimer Anlage 40. Home-style cooking in a cosy setting; good for night owls; excellent schnitzels. Sun–Thurs 10pm–4am, Fri & Sat 10pm–6am.

Lalibela, Klingerstr. 2. An Ethiopian restaurant with finger eating only, low prices and plenty of vegetarian options. Closed Mon.

Madrid, Habsburger Allee 43. Serves all the classic Spanish dishes, along with a good selection of wines. Evenings only, except on Sun, when it's also open for lunch.

Nibelungenschänke, Nibelungenallee 55. Typical Greek food at reasonable prices. The clientele is young and the place is usually open until 1am. Take U-Bahn #5 to Nibelungenallee.

Sawadi, Grosse Friedberger Str. 34. Probably the best Thai place in Frankfurt; very popular, so you're not encouraged to linger. Closed Mon.

Tse-Yang, Kaiserstr. 67. Frankfurt's leading Chinese restaurant, located just a stone's throw from the Hauptbahnhof. The business lunches are especially good value.

Westend and Bockenheim

Al Arischa, Leipziger Str. 108. A small family-run Lebanese place serving lamb and vegetarian dishes at reasonable prices. Daily 6pm–midnight.

Ban Thai, Leipziger Str. 26. Good, reasonably priced Thai restaurant, which also has a cheap *Imbiss* section.

Erno's Bistro, Liebigstr. 15. Sublime mix of French and German cuisine that regularly wins top awards in the international dining guides. Closed Sat & Sun, except when there's a *Messe* on. Expensive; best book in advance (☎721997).

Gargantua, Friesengasse 3. One of Bockenheim's best, with a 4-course "international" menu. Closed Sun. Expensive; reservations advisable (☎720718).

Golfo di Napoli, Leipziger Str. 16. Pricey Italian, popular with the Westend yuppies, but the food and atmosphere are good. Closed Sun.

Isoletta, Feldbergerstr. 23. One of the more affordable Italian restaurants, popular with the nearby ad agency types during the day.

Knoblauch, Staufenstr. 39. Friendly, intimate little place where everything comes liberally laced with garlic. Closed Sat & Sun.

Peking, Schloss Str. 55. Frankfurt's oldest Chinese restaurant, now in a new postmodern setting. Good value.

Sachsenhausen

Alt Prag, Klappergasse 14. Czech speciality place with *Budweiser* (the original) on tap. Evenings only.

Bistrot 77, Ziegelhüttenweg 1–3. French restaurant with strong lines in game and fish. Has an outstanding selection of French wines, including some from the family's own vineyard in Alsace. Closed Sun; must book (☎614040).

Maaschanz, Färberstr. 75. Small, congenial restaurant specializing in French cuisine at affordable prices. Good fish dishes. Closed Mon; best book ahead (☎622886).

Taj Mahal, Schweizer Str. 28. Popular Pakistani-run restaurant which has won an award as the city's best curry house. Evening reservations essential (☎620240).

Wolkenbruch, Rotlintstr. 47. No-smoking vegetarian serving everything from tofu burgers to wholemeal pizzas.

Bars, cafés and café-bars

Sachsenhausen with its cobbled streets and lively atmosphere is the place to head for, above all for its famous apple wine taverns. As home to a large student population, Bockenheim has plenty of youthful, inexpensive cafés. In the city centre, there are a few gems which are well worth seeking out in preference to the many overcrowded and overpriced alternatives.

The centre

Bar Central, Elefantengasse 11. A long-established pillar of the Frankfurt *Szene*. Happy hour 8–9pm, and good music at all times.

Club Voltaire, Kleine Hochstr. 5. An eclectic clientele: political activists, artists, musicians, Greens, gays – you'll find them all here in one of Frankfurt's best-established meeting places. Also serves good food at good prices.

Dominicus Weinkeller, Brückhofstr. 1. A vaulted cellar establishment with live music at weekends, whose good wines and free *Schmalzbrot* (black bread) draw a young crowd.

Eckstein, An der Staufenmauer 7. Arty meeting point with obligatory exhibitions on the walls and occasional live music in the basement. Stylish and highly recommended.

Gegenwart, Bergerstr. 6. Spacious and very trendy hangout whose walls are a forum for avant-garde art. The best coffee in town and imaginative breakfasts, lunches and dinners.

Harvey's, Bornheimer Landstr. 64. Slick, high-ceilinged colonnaded bar which in the evening hosts a mainly gay and lesbian crowd. Excellent breakfasts and daily specials.

Helium, Bleidenstr. 7. Trendy bar which stays open late and serves night-time snacks. Daily 11am–4am.

Vinum, Kleine Hochstr. 9. Traditional German wine bar, serving some food, but it's expensive. Gets crowded, so arrive early to secure a table. Closed Sun.

Zu den Zwölf Aposteln, Rosenberger Str. 1. Frankfurt's first *Hausbrauerei*, producing organically brewed *Pils* and dark beer. The ground floor restaurant serves Balkan cuisine.

Westend and Bockenheim

Café au Lait, Am Weingarten 12. Among Bockenheim's trendiest meeting places, with a great selection for breakfast.

Laumer, Bockenheimer Landstr. 67. One of Frankfurt's oldest cafés, halfway up the Westend's main thoroughfare, now enjoying a new lease of life with a young arty clientele.

Plazz, Kirchplatz 8. Fun café offering a full repertoire of international breakfasts: English, French, German and Russian. Attracts a mixed crowd.

Stattcafé, Grempstr. 21. Another place which does good breakfast. The emphasis is on healthy eating in an informal atmosphere – popular with the Bockenheim arty crowd. A real focal point, with work from Frankfurt artists on the walls.

Sachsenhausen

Achter Kontinent, Frankensteiner Platz 25. Trendy bar with a wide choice of snacks and breakfasts at weekends. Open till 1am.

An Sibin, Wallstr. 9. One of Frankfurt's main Irish bars, popular with local expats and with Kilkenny, Guinness and Murphys on tap. Live music at weekends.

Café Bar, Schweizer Str. 14. Despite an unimaginative name, this is the trendiest café in Sachsenhausen, all black (it's also known as the *Schwarzes Café*) and mirrored decor with a very hip clientele.

Gaggia, Schwanthaler Str. 16. Cheap and cheerful student hangout. Breakfast here or linger over a few beers.

Das Lesecafé, Diesterwegstr. 7. Popular with would-be intellectuals, the gimmick here is that you read as you eat and drink. You can select a book from the neighbouring bookshop – or just admire the art on the walls.

Tannenbaum, Brückenstr. 19. Friendly English pub-style place with tasty food.

APPLE WINE

There's a theory that Europe has a cider belt separating the areas producing wine and beer, and that Frankfurt is the hub of this. This seems tenuous at best, as the apple wine tradition here is historically a relatively recent one, having started in 1750. Made by the same process used in the production of ordinary wine, apple wine is bought in blue-grey stone jugs called *Bembel* and drunk from a *Schobbeglas*. There are four types: *Süsser*, sweet and fresh from the presses in autumn, and relatively weak; *Rauscher*, which will blow your head off if you don't treat it with respect; *Heller*, which is clear and smooth; and the hazy and golden *Altar*. Those in the know order *Handkäs mit Musik* (cheese served with onions and vinaigrette) or *Rippchen mit Kraut* (smoked pork chop with *Sauerkraut*) as a culinary accompaniment to their *Ebbelwei*.

APPLE WINE TAVERNS

Buchscheer, Schwarzsteinkautweg 7. Set amidst the rose gardens on the southeastern edge of Sachsenhausen and very popular with walkers. Good home cooking and home-produced apple wine. Open from 3pm on weekdays, from 11am at weekends. Take tram #14 or bus #35 from the city centre, or tram #16 from the centre of Sachsenhausen.

Klaane Sachsehäuser, Neuer Wall 11. A family place favoured by native Sachsenhauseners. Open from 4pm; closed Sun.

Wagner, Schweizer Str. 71. One of the best of the taverns, with a lively clientele ranging from young to middle-aged. Frequently packed out; open daily from 11am.

Zu den Drei Stuebern, Dreieichstr. 28/Klappergasse. Mainly patronized by locals; has a small bar-room and pleasant terrace at the rear. Open from 3.30pm; closed Sat & Sun.

Zum Eichkatzerl, Dreieichstr. 29. An excellent traditional apple wine tavern with a very popular and low-priced restaurant. Open from noon; closed Sun & Mon.

Zum Gemalten Haus, Schweizer Str. 67. A bit kitschy with its oil-painted facade and stained-glass windows, yet quite lively, with long rows of tables outside. Open from 10am; closed Mon & Tues.

Zur Germania, Textorstr. 16. Best of the many traditional taverns on the street; nearly always crowded. Open from 4pm Mon-Thurs, from 11am Fri-Sun.

Nightlife

Not surprisingly Frankfurt's nightlife is pretty eclectic, and many of the clubs are very expensive. The following is a selective rundown of the more affordable venues. Worth knowing about is Kleine Bockenheimer Strasse, aka *Jazzgasse* (Jazz Alley), the centre of Frankfurt's lively jazz scene. Many leading German jazzers cut their musical teeth playing in the bars around here and there's live music going on most nights.

Live music

Batschkapp, Maybachstr. 24. Live music or fairly up-to-the-minute DJ dance sounds. Daily 9pm–1am.

Brotfabrik, Bachmannstr. 2–4. One of the most innovative venues in the city, featuring live and disco music from all over the world, with salsa, African and Asian sounds particularly featured. Also has a café and a Spanish restaurant.

Irish Pub, Kleine Rittergasse 11–13. Every big German city has its Irish pub; Frankfurt's is very popular, with good Irish music. Daily until 1am or 2am.

Jazzkeller, Kleine Bockenheimer Str. 18. This atmospheric cellar is Frankfurt's premier jazz venue. Open 9pm–3am; closed Mon.

Sinkkasten, Brönnerstr. 5. This place has everything – pool room, cabaret stage, disco and, most importantly, a concert hall where they put on everything from jazz to avant-garde and indie stuff. Daily 9pm–2am.

Discos

Frankfurt's disco scene is heavily dance music-oriented, with most venues serving up house/techno beats for predominantly young crowds. Places tend to stay open until 4am during the week and 5am or 6am at weekends. Entry starts at about DM10.

Cooky's, Am Salzhaus 4. Frankfurt's best-known and most popular disco. Dance music and chart stuff draws in a youthful crowd. On Mon there are usually live bands. Daily 10pm–4/6am.

Dorian Gray, Airport C, level 0. Oddly located at the airport, one of the largest discos in Germany, and not always so easy to get into. Open until 6am; closed Mon & Tues.

Funkadelic, Brönnerstr. 11. Mainly hard-core dance music which attracts a lot of GIs.

Maxim's, Karlstr. 17. Rough-and-ready atmosphere with varied DJs playing to a youthful crowd. Near the Hauptbahnhof.

Omen, Junghofstr. 14. More heavy-duty dance music, dished up by the leading lights of the local DJ scene.

Gay Frankfurt

Blue Angel, Brönnerstr. 17. Popular gay men's dance bar.

Central Park, Holzgraben 9. One of a number of gay hangouts in the area.

Madame, Allerheiligenstr. 25. Relatively laid-back lesbian bar.

Zum Schwejk, Schäfergasse 20. Relaxed and unpretentious – a good way into the Frankfurt gay scene.

Entertainment

Frankfurt has a predictably lively performing arts scene, with a wide range of choice in both music and theatre, and an established tradition of productions in English. For details of events, the best magazine is *Prinz*, which costs DM3.50 from newsagents. Free magazines such as *Fritz*, which also covers other towns in central Hesse, are also useful, as is the tourist office's *Frankfurter Woche*, which theoretically costs DM3 but can often be obtained without payment.

Venues

Alte Oper, Opernplatz (☎134 0400). There are 3 halls here, of which the largest is used for orchestral concerts (the *Radio-Sinfonie-Orchester-Frankfurt* is the pick of the local bands), while the other two host chamber, instrumental and vocal recitals.

English Theater, Kaiserstr. 52 (☎2423 1620). Flourishing company which performs only in English.

Gallus-Theater, Krifteler Str. 55 (☎7580 6020). Long-established *Gastarbeiter* theatre and the most distinguished cultural institution of the immigrant community in the whole of Germany.

Jahrhunderthalle, Pffafenwiese, Höchst (☎360 1240). Modern concert hall offering similar fare to the Alte Oper.

Oper, Untermainanalge 11 (☎2123 7333). Presents top-class performances of opera and ballet.

Schauspielhaus, Willy-Brandt-Platz (☎2123 7999). The main civic theatre, offering drama old and new.

Die Schmiere, Seckbächer Gasse 2 (☎281066). Satirical cabaret, housed in the Karmeliterkloster.

Theater am Turm, Eschenheimer Landstr. 2 (☎2123 7999). Trendy *Szene* theatre.

Tiger-Palast, Heiligkreuzgasse 16–20 (☎920 0220). The place to come for good old-fashioned variety shows, which are making something of a comeback in Germany.

Volkstheater, Grosser Hirschgraben 21 (☎288598). Presents performances in the local dialect.

Listings

Airlines *Air Canada*, Friedensstr. 11 (☎2711 5233); *Air New Zealand*, Friedrichstr. 10 (☎971 4030); *British Airways*, Düsseldorfer Str. 1–7 (☎232441); *Lufthansa*, Am Hauptbahnhof 2 (☎255255); *Qantas*, Bethmannstr. 56 (☎2990 0236); *TWA*, Hamburger Allee 2–10 (☎7950 4200).

Bike rental *Per Pedale*, Falkstr. 28, Bockenheim (☎707 2363).

Book Fair Held annually in Sept/Oct at the *Messe* in the centre, this is the largest book fair in the world. On the last day you can often pick up great bargains from the English and American stalls.

Bookstore *British Bookshop*, Börsenstr. 17 (☎281492).

Car rental *Mini Rent*, Eckenheimer Landstr. 91 (☎596 2038); all the big companies have offices at the airport and the Hauptbahnhof.

Consulates *Australian*, Gutleutstr. 85 (☎273 9090); *British*, Bockenheimer Landstr. 42 (☎170 0020); *US*, Siesmayerstr. 21 (☎75350 or 7535 2441).

Cultural institute *Amerika-Haus,* Staufenstr. 1 (☎971 4480).

Doctor ☎7950 2200.

Festivals Main folklore events are the *Waldchestag* at Whit weekend and the *Mainfest* in early August.

Mitfahrzentralen Baseler Str. 7 (☎236444); Homburger Str. 36 (☎19444).

Pharmacy ☎19292 for details of late-opening pharmacies.

Post offices The main post office with poste restante is at Zeil 110; the longest hours as kept by the branch on the first floor of the Hauptbahnhof (Mon-Fri 6am-10pm, Sat & Sun 8am-9pm).

Women's centre and bookstore Consult the bi-monthly *Frankfurter Frauenblatt* for information. There's a women's centre at Hamburger Allee 45 (☎707 4157), a women's *Mitfahrzentrale* at Konrad-Brosswitz-Str. 11 in Bockenheim (☎771777), and a women's bookstore at Kiesstr. 27.

Zoo, Alfred-Brehm-Platz 16 (daily 8am–5/7pm; DM11). Take U-Bahn #6 or #7.

SOUTHERN HESSE

The southern part of Hesse offers a wide variety of scenery, ranging from the wooded heights of the **Odenwald** at the extreme tip of the province and the highland regions of the **Taunus** and **Spessart**, to the famous vine-growing **Rheingau** on the east bank of the Rhine. Although there are plenty of outstanding small towns in the area, including Michelstadt, Bad Homburg and Gelnhausen, there are only two cities: the staid spa of **Wiesbaden** and the former ducal residence of **Darmstadt**, which is a place with more than a few surprises in store.

Darmstadt

A cursory inspection of **DARMSTADT**, some 30km south of Frankfurt, at the end of S-Bahn line #12, is unlikely to leave you with much of an impression. The only way it differs from any other prosperous German city rebuilt after the war is in the survival of the planned Neoclassical layout, with broad streets and spacious squares. Don't be discouraged, though; Darmstadt has a rich cultural heritage, traces of which have survived both the bombs and the planners.

During the second half of the eighteenth century the *Darmstädter Kreis* (Darmstadt Circle) flourished under the protection of Landgravine Karoline, numbering among its members Goethe, Martin Wieland and Johann Herder. The playwright Georg Büchner spent much of his short life in the city and wrote his great drama *Danton's Death* here in 1834, while under police observation for suspected revolutionary activities. It was at the turn of the present century, however, that the arts flourished most freely in Darmstadt when Grand Duke Ernst Ludwig (a grandson of Queen Victoria) supported the first and finest flowering of **Jugendstil**, the German form of Art Nouveau. The surviving monuments of this period are the most lasting and visible symbol of the city's support for artistic innovation.

The **telephone code** for Darmstadt is ☎06151

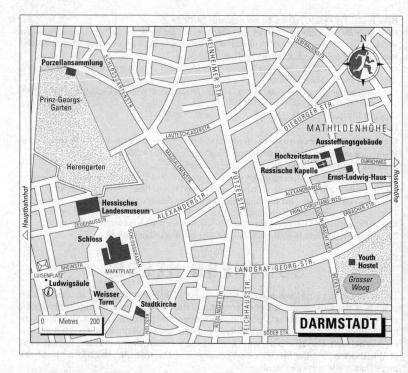

Arrival, information and accommodation

If you arrive at the **Hauptbahnhof**, which is about 1km west of the city centre, you'll immediately get your first taste of the local Jugendstil heritage, as the station was a key part of the style's second phase in the second decade of the century.

In a pavilion immediately outside is one of the **tourist offices** (Mon–Fri 9am–6pm, Sat 9am–noon; ☎132782), but the main branch is in the Neues Rathaus, Luisenplatz 5 (Mon–Fri 9am–6pm, Sat 10am–1pm; ☎132781). **Mitfahrzentrale**'s office is at Im Niederfeld 8 (☎897564).

Accommodation

The cheapest options are out in the suburbs, while the city centre has plenty of mid- and upper-range hotels. Darmstadt's **youth hostel** is at Landgraf-Georg-Str. 119 (☎45293; 🏠), right beside the open-air swimming pool at the Grosser Woog lake and also handily placed for visiting the Jugendstil buildings on Mathildenhöhe.

Bockshaut, Kirchstr. 7–9 (☎99670, fax 996767). Good old-fashioned German inn with a convenient position in the very heart of the city. ④

Hornung, Mornewegstr. 43 (☎9266, fax 891892). Located a couple of minutes' walk from the Hauptbahnhof, on the way to the city centre. ⑦

Mathildenhöhe, Spessartring 53 (☎48046, fax 498450). Part of the *Akzent* chain, it's on the eastern side of the eponymous hill, ideally placed for visiting the city's Jugendstil heritage. ⑦

Prinz Heinrich, Bleichstr. 48 (☎899888, fax 895901). On the western edge of the centre, with tasteful furnishings and a high-quality restaurant. ⑦

Waldfriede, Friedrich-Naumann-Str. 8, Eberstadt. Occupies a large old villa in the northern part of an incorporated town which lies due south of Darmstadt proper. Take tram #1, #6, #7 or #8. ⑤
Weinmichel, Schleiermacherstr. 10–12 (☎29080, fax 23592). One of the best of the upmarket places and an adjunct to a celebrated wine restaurant. ⑧
Zentral, Schuhardstr. 6 (☎26411, fax 26858). As central as its name suggests, located on a pedestrianized shopping street just off the east side of Luisenplatz. ④
Zur Sonne, Heidelberger Landstr. 246, Eberstadt (☎55754, fax 592872). Worth the 7km journey south to the centre of Eberstadt for very reasonably priced rooms. Take tram #1, #6, #7 or #8. ④

The city

Between 1567 and 1918, the city was capital of the state of Hesse-Darmstadt, which was promoted to a Grand Duchy, with control over a large chunk of the Rhineland, during the Napoleonic period. The subsequent flurry of building activity to create a worthy capital meant that Darmstadt had its fair share of grand streets and squares, but most were destroyed on the night of September 11, 1944 when it was hit by 300,000 incendiary bombs and 700 high explosive bombs. The resulting fire-storm, deliberately created following the tried and tested Hamburg pattern, killed 12,000 people. Darmstadt made a remarkably quick recovery, particularly in the cultural arena, but most of its historic quarter was gone forever.

The centre

At the centre of modern Darmstadt sprawls **Luisenplatz**, a windswept shopping plaza criss-crossed by tram and bus lines and notable only for the **Ludwigsmonument**, a 33-metre-high column bearing a statue of Grand Duke Ludwig I. From here, Rheinstrasse leads east to Ernst-Ludwig-Platz, on which stands the **Weisser Turm**, a fifteenth-century defensive tower which was later restyled in fashionable Baroque. Beyond is the spacious triangular Marktplatz, on whose southern side stands the gabled Renaissance **Rathaus**. Round the corner, the much-altered fourteenth-century **Stadtkirche** is mainly of note for the colossal Renaissance funerary monument to Landgrave Georg I and his wife Magdalena zur Lippe.

On the north side of Marktplatz is the **Schloss**, an extensive complex which developed gradually over seven hundred years. Reduced to a shell in the 1944 bombing raid, it has been diligently restored. The Baroque *Neuschloss* houses a library and the town archive, while the predominantly Renaissance *Altschloss* is home to a technical university and the **Schlossmuseum** (guided tours Mon–Thurs 10am–1pm & 2–5pm, Sat & Sun 10am–1pm; DM3.50). Basically this is another example of the dreaded German *Heimatmuseum*, but it's redeemed by **Hans Holbein the Younger**'s *Madonna of Jacob Meyer*, painted in 1526, one of the supreme masterpieces of Renaissance painting. It's particularly intriguing in being the last Catholic altarpiece by any of the great German masters of the period, all of whom (including Holbein himself) became Protestant. The picture shows the former Burgomaster of Basel, accompanied by his living and deceased wives, asking the Virgin to intercede on behalf of his sickly baby son, whose features – bizarrely – duplicate those of the Christ child.

The Hessisches Landesmuseum

Slightly to the north of the Schloss is the **Hessisches Landesmuseum** (Tues–Sat 10am–5pm, Wed also 7–9pm, Sun 11am–5pm; DM5), one of the best general museums in the country. Though there's a small **archeology** section, featuring an impressive Roman floor mosaic and jewellery from Frankish graves, most of the ground floor is given over to **applied art**. The medieval section is outstanding, highlights being a beautiful pair of tenth- or eleventh-century brooches found under the Dom in Mainz, and several masterly twelfth-century reliquaries from Cologne, including the domed *Darmstädter Kuppelreliquar*. In the basement, there's a glittering array of stained glass, notably a complete cycle from the Ritterstiftskirche in Bad Wimpfen, and a fragmentary ninth-century *Head of a Saint* from Kloster Lorsch. There's also an excellent Art Nouveau/Jugendstil section which sets Darmstadt's contribution in an international perspective.

The first floor is devoted to **natural history**: a redundant open-cast shale pit near Darmstadt has proved fruitful ground for excavations, and remains of prehistoric crocodiles, fish and horses recently dug up there are now on view.

THE PICTURE GALLERY

Undoubtedly, the Landesmuseum's main claim to fame is as a picture gallery. The east wing of the ground floor contains one of the best collections of German Primitives, going back as far as the mid-thirteenth-century altar-table from Worms. **Lochner's** gorgeous *Presentation in the Temple* shows the Cologne School at its mid-fifteenth-century peak, while the **Master of St Bartholomew's** *Madonna and Child with SS Adrian and Augustine* belongs to the final flowering of this movement a couple of generations later. Mid-Rhenish painters closely followed Cologne's lead, and two of the finest products of this region are the works from which the **Master of the Ortenberg Altar** and the **Master of the Darmstadt Passion** derive their names. Several pictures by **Cranach** dominate the Renaissance section, including one of his greatest canvases, *Cardinal Albrecht von Brandenburg as St Jerome*.

Among the old masters on the second floor, the most important is the enigmatic *Magpie on the Gallows*, one of **Pieter Bruegel the Elder's** last works. The evil-looking contraption for public executions strikes a menacingly discordant note in the sunny landscape, which forms the backdrop to a peasant dance. Highlights from the seventeenth century include pieces by Rubens, Domenichino and Domenico Feti, and a touching *Lamentation over the Dead Christ* by **Mathieu Le Nain**.

A number of canvases by the Swiss **Arnold Böcklin** dominate the Romantic section, which also includes *Iphigenia*, one of **Feuerbach's** finest works. The rest of the floor is designated the **Beuys-Block** and contains some 300 works by the iconoclastic sculptor **Joseph Beuys**, the largest collection of his work in existence. The German avant-garde gets precedence in the galleries of the new extension, though many of the country's best-known twentieth-century artists, such as Corinth, Kirchner, Beckmann and Dix, are also represented.

The Herrngarten

Just behind the Landesmuseum is the **Herrngarten**, a spacious English-style park which contains the tomb of Landgravine Karoline and a Jugendstil monument to Goethe. At the northeastern end is the **Prinz-Georgs-Garten**, a formal Rococo garden. Its pavilion, the Prinz-Georg-Palais, houses the **Grossherzogliche Porzellansammlung** (previously Mon–Thurs 10am–1pm & 2–5pm, Sat & Sun 10am–1pm; DM2.50, but currently closed for structural repairs), an extensive porcelain museum featuring examples from the local Kelsterbach factory, other leading German centres, and major pieces from England and Russia.

The Mathildenhöhe

The **Mathildenhöhe**, a unique artists' colony on the eastern edge of the city centre, is a living monument to Jugendstil. It's only a fifteen-minute walk along Erich-Ollenhauer-Promenade from just behind the Schloss. Alternatively, take tram #4 from Luisenplatz; get off at Grosser Woog, and from there head up Eugen-Bracht-Weg to Europa Platz.

At the centre of the Mathildenhöhe stands a building which fits in well with the Jugendstil buildings but pre-dates the colony itself – the **Russische Kapelle** (daily 9am–5/6pm; DM1). This heavily ornamented Russian Orthodox chapel crowned by two gilded domes was built in 1898 at the behest of the last czar of Russia, Nicholas II, who often spent the summer in Darmstadt with his Hessian wife. Serbian Orthodox services are regularly held here for Darmstadt's Balkan community.

Work on the Mathildenhöhe colony began in 1901 with the construction of the **Ernst-Ludwig-Haus**, designed by the Viennese architect Joseph Maria Olbrich for the *Dokument Deutscher Kunst 1901*, an exhibition whose aim was to encapsulate all aspects of the Jugendstil movement. Approached via a broad flight of steps, the building has something of the mausoleum about it, with its imposing portal flanked by monumental figures of Adam and Eve carved by Ludwig Habig. The **Museum Künstlerkolonie Darmstadt** (Tues–Sun 10am–5pm; DM5) now occupies the interior, showing products made by the colony – ranging from stained-glass windows to jewellery, silverware and porcelain.

To complement the Ernst-Ludwig-Haus, Olbrich built seven houses as artists' residences immediately below on Alexandraweg and Mathildenhöhweg, also in 1901. Five survive in reasonably authentic shape: they vary in style from the slightly subverted villa look of the **Olbrich-Haus**, where the architect spent the last years of his life, to the angular southern European appearance of the **Kleines Glückert-Haus**, and all have unique and intricate design features which differentiate them from each other. The smallest of the group, the **Haus Deiters** (Tues–Sun 10am–5pm), a striking re-interpretation of the English cottage style, was restored a few years ago to serve as a space for small exhibitions. It's also possible to enter the **Grosses Glückert-Haus**, which best represents the ethos of the original project; you can try ringing at the gate, but it's advisable to ask the tourist office to arrange a visit for you. Next door to it is the **Behrens-Haus**, designed by the Hamburg architect Peter Behrens, also in 1901. Its brick-framed white facade and red-tiled roof inject an element of Hanseatic sobriety into the colony, in deliberate contrast with Olbrich's more playful Mediterranean efforts. Only the door, decorated with swirling bronze appliqué work and flanked by rippling turquoise columns, has much in common with the neighbouring houses.

In 1908 work on the huge and gleaming **Austellungsgebäude** (Exhibition Hall; Tues–Sun 10am–5pm) at the top of the Mathildenhöhe was completed. It's still in use, and the first-floor café is equipped with Jugendstil furnishings. Look out for the Olbrich-designed mosaic in the roof of the pavilion halfway up the entrance steps. Next to the Austellungsgebäude rises the **Hochzeitsturm** (Wedding Tower), a 48-metre-high brick tower with a distinctive roof which, when seen head-on, looks like a hand facing palm outwards. It was presented to Grand Duke Ernst Ludwig and his bride by the city three years after their 1905 wedding and has become so popular that it's now Darmstadt's official emblem. A lift takes visitors to the top (March-Oct Tues–Sun 10am–6pm, DM3).

Rosenhöhe

Because most of the Mathildenhöhe buildings are now used by various design institutes and cultural organizations, Darmstadt's practising artists have moved to the nearby **Rosenhöhe** area. This is reached in about ten minutes from the Olbrich-Haus by following Alexandraweg, turning right into Fiedlerweg, left into Seitersweg and then crossing the rail bridge. During the late 1960s a new artists' colony was established here in the **Rosenhöhe-Park**, whose original purpose was to provide a last resting place for members of the ruling family of Hesse-Darmstadt. At the entrance to the park is the **Löwentor**, a gate comprising six Jugendstil lions standing on top of decorative brick pillars. Nearby is the **Ostbahnhof**, built in the style of a Russian country station at the request of Czar Nicholas II.

Eating, drinking and nightlife

Darmstadt's **nightlife** is somewhat fragmented. There is, however, a good cluster of **bars** and **restaurants** just west of the Herrngarten, while most of the *Apfelwein* places are to the east of the same park. The latter area is where many of the students live, and it makes a good starting point for a pub crawl.

Restaurants

Alt-Hamburg, Landgraf-Georg-Str. 17. Speciality game, fish and seafood restaurant.

Burg Frankenstein, Mühltal. Way out on top of a 370m hill in the southern suburb of Eberstadt, but the reasonably priced food is among the best in Darmstadt, and the views alone make the trip worthwhile. Bus #N goes closest.

Las Palmas, Dieburger Str. 22. Good, cheap Spanish restaurant; also serves German food.

Lokales, Dieburger Str. 50. Specializes in cheap, mouth-watering Italian pizzas.

Oberwaldhaus, Dieburger Str. 257. This picturesque large house in the woods at the eastern edge of the city might have come straight out of a German fairy tale. It offers an international menu and has a large beer garden. Take bus #F.

Orangerie, Bessunger Str. 44. One of Darmstadt's best restaurants, set in a fine eighteenth-century park 1.5km south of Luisenplatz.

Ratskeller, Marktplatz 8. Located on the ground floor of the Rathaus, rather than the usual cellars. It has its own *Hausbrauerei*, which makes light, dark and *Weizen* beers, plus a seasonal *Bock*.

Bars and café-bars

Café Chaos, Mühlstr. 36. Popular café-bar which also serves good pizzas and light meals.

Grohe, Nieder-Ramstädter Str. 1. *Hausbrauerei* with beer garden.

Kronenbräugarten, Dieburger Str. 97. Beer garden worth checking out if the weather is good.

Petri, Ahrheilger Str. 50. Favourite haunt of hip youngsters.

Rem, Beckerstr. 22. Best place in town for exotic cocktails.

Sumpf, Kasinostr. 105. Studenty pub which does fairly cheap snacks.

Live music pubs, clubs and discos

Eledil, Adelungstr. 9. Serves heavy-duty wholefood meals and features live music and discos.

Goldene Krone, Schustergasse 18. An amazing warren of a place, with several bars, games rooms and stages presenting live acts ranging from cabaret to various kinds of music. Entry is DM5.

Jagdhofkeller, Bessunger Str. 84. Jazz bar featuring live sessions Wed–Sun at 9pm.

Kulturcafé, Hermannstr. 7. Vegetarian café featuring occasional theatre or live music.

Oktave, Landwehrstr. 13. Upmarket jazz bar.

Studentenkeller, Im Schlosshof. Enduringly popular student meeting place, situated in the Schloss courtyard. Open daily from 9pm.

Tanzclub Huckebein, Heidelberger Str. 89a. Currently the city's hippest disco.

Worschtküsch, Erbacher Str. 5–7. Excellent jazz bar and bistro housed in a converted butcher's shop near the Mathildenhöhe – it advertises itself as "a pub without standards".

Culture

The main venue for **drama**, **opera** and formal **concerts** is the *Hessisches Staatstheater* on Georg-Büchner-Platz (☎281 1211), which maintains Darmstadt's reputation for artistic innovation with three-quarters of its performances per season likely to be new productions. **Cabaret** is performed at *halbNeun-Theater*, Sandstr. 32 (☎233 3330) and *Tap*, Bessunger Str. 125 (☎33555), while adult **puppet** shows feature at *Kikeriki*, Heidelberger Str. 131 (☎964266).

Local **festivals** include the *Frühlingfest* in March or April, the *Heinerfest* for five days in early July, and the *Herbstfest* in late September.

The Odenwald

The **Odenwald** is a large upland forest area – which is designated as the *Naturpark Bergstrasse-Odenwald* – occupying almost all of the southernmost part of Hesse and stretching into both Bavaria and Baden-Württemberg. On its westernmost fringe is the misleadingly named **Bergstrasse** (Mountain Road): nowadays it's a tourist route running from Darmstadt to Heidelberg, but to the Romans – who called it the *Strata Montana* – it was a major military road. During the Middle Ages it developed as a trading route, and numerous castles sprang up along it to protect the merchants from outlaws lurking in the marshland around the Rhine. These days the area is known primarily for the fact that spring starts here earlier than anywhere else in Germany, and the best time to visit is in late March or early April, when the fruit trees that line it all suddenly come into bloom. Further east, the hilly countryside of the heart of the Odenwald is punctuated by postcard-pretty half-timbered towns where traditional craft industries continue to flourish.

Along the Bergstrasse

Although the Bergstrasse is best explored by car, it's easy enough to follow it by public transport, with most places lying on a rail line, and buses filling the gaps. In any case, the towns along the Hessian part of the route virtually run into one another, and are never more than a few kilometres apart. If pressed for time, the monastery at **Lorsch** and the palaces at **Auerbach** are the undoubted highlights.

Auerbach and Bensheim

First up is the little health resort of **AUERBACH**, now officially incorporated into the much larger town of **BENSHEIM**, which has a typical half-timbered centre. Set high above Auerbach is a thirteenth-century **Schloss** (Tues–Sun 10am–5pm or dusk; free), which was blown up by the French in the seventeenth century but which remains an impressive ruin. Immediately to the south is the **Fürstenlager**, a beautiful landscaped park planted with exotic trees and dotted with whimsical eighteenth-century pavilions which served as summer retreats for members of the Hesse-Darmstadt court.

The local **tourist office** (Mon–Fri 9am–noon & 2–5pm, Sat 10am–noon; ☎06251/14117) is at Rodensteinstr. 19 near Bensheim's Bahnhof. If you've the money to spare, Auerbach makes a wonderful overnight stop, as it has a couple of top-notch **hotels**: *Poststuben*, Schloss Str. 28–30 (☎06251/72987; ⑤) and *Parkhotel Herrnhaus* (☎06251/72274; ⑦) in the Fürstenlager's main building. Both of these have classy **restaurants**, though they face strong competition from *Burggraf-Bräu*, Darmstädter Str. 231, which offers a varied menu including plenty of vegetarian specialities, and also has its own *Hausbrauerei*.

Lorsch

From Bensheim, the Bergstrasse takes a short detour west to **LORSCH**, which lies on a small branch rail line linking the two parallel main lines between Frankfurt and Mannheim. Once again, the centre is half-timbered, but everything is completely overshadowed by the former Benedictine **Kloster** (free access at all times; guided tours of the interiors Tues–Sun 10am–4/5pm; DM6), a UNESCO-listed World Heritage Site. Founded in 764, the monastery was once among the most powerful in Germany, its abbot ranking as a secular prince answerable directly to the emperor. The extraordinary **Torhalle** (or **Königshalle**), which probably dates back to the ninth century, is the best-preserved monument to have survived from the Carolingian period. Its outline was clearly inspired by Roman triumphal arches, while the patterned stonework, arranged in the manner of a mosaic, is of outstanding quality. Inside, the upper storey, which functioned as a chapel, has a lively series of fourteenth-century frescoes. The only other intact part of the monastery is the austere mid-twelfth-century **Vorkirche** which, despite its dimensions, was no more than the narthex of the main church, of which nothing other than the foundations can be seen.

Lorsch's **hotels** include *Gasthof Schillereck*, Schillerstr. 27 (☎06251/52301; ④); and *Jäger*, Bahnhofstr. 79 (☎06251/52244; ⑤). *Zum Schwannen,* Nibelungenstr. 52, is a renowned but expensive **restaurant**.

The **tourist office** is in the finest of the half-timbered buildings, the Rathaus, Marktplatz 1 (Mon–Thurs 9am–noon & 2–4pm, Fri 9am–noon; ☎06251/596570).

The heart of the forest

The central part of the Odenwald is serviced by a branch rail line from Darmstadt, on which trains run nearly every hour. It's an easy target for day trips, though the provision of abundant cheap accommodation makes it a good place to spend a restful few days.

Michelstadt

MICHELSTADT, which celebrated its 1250th birthday in 1991, is the undoubted star of the Odenwald. The late fifteenth-century **Rathaus**, which dominates the central Marktplatz, features on every tourist brochure to the region. With its characteristic half-timbering and spooky corner oriels crowned with sharp spires, it perfectly encapsulates the Romantic image of medieval Germany. Just to the west is the **Kellerei**, a courtyard formed by the half-timbered store buildings of the former castle; it now houses the folklore collections of the **Odenwaldmuseum** (Easter–Oct Tues–Sun 10am–12.30pm & 2–5pm; Nov Sat & Sun 10.30am–12.30pm & 2–4pm; DM2).

At the northern end of town, about 1km from the centre, is the **Einhardsbasilika** (March–Oct Tues–Sun 10am–noon & 1–5pm; Nov–Feb Tues–Sun 11am–3pm; DM2), a church dating back to 827, the year of its foundation by the local grandee Einhard, courtier to Charlemagne, and author of a fascinating biography of the emperor. Just to the east, **Schloss Fürstenau**, a moated thirteenth-century castle, is privately owned, but you're allowed to go into the courtyard and stroll in the extensive park.

Michelstadt's **Bahnhof** is midway between the Altstadt and Schloss Fürstenau. The **tourist office** is at Marktplatz 1 (Mon–Fri 8am–noon & 2–4pm; ☎06061/74146). You can pick up a list of the dozen or so private houses with **rooms** (①–③) to let here. Alternatively, there are plenty of **hotels** in the centre, often with excellent **restaurants** attached. Among the best are the seventeenth-century *Gasthaus Zum Grünen Baum*, Grosse Gasse 17 (☎06061/2409; ④); *Gasthof Burgschänke*, Kallereibergstr. 3 (☎06061/3185 or 71022; ⑤); and *Drei Hasen*, Braunstr. 5 (☎06061/71017; ⑤). There's also the *Odenwaldparadies* **campsite** (May–Sept only) at Am Waldstadion (☎06061/3256).

The town hosts a number of **festivals**, the most important being the ten-day *Bienenmarkt* at Whit.

Erbach

Adjoining Michelstadt to the south is **ERBACH**. The town is completely dominated by its huge Baroque **Schloss** (March–Oct Tues–Sun 8.30am–noon & 1.30–5pm; DM5), which incorporates part of its medieval predecessor and contains a more interesting than average local museum. Since the eighteenth century, Erbach has been the main German centre for ivory carving, an art celebrated in the **Deutsches Elfenbeinmuseum** (daily 10am–5pm; DM8) at Otto-Glenz-Str. 1.

The **tourist office** is situated at Marktplatz 1 (☎06062/6439) and offers the usual provision of private **rooms** (①–③). Good-value **hotels** include *Gebhardt*, Jahnstr. 32 (☎06062/3286; ④) and *Gasthof Odenwälder Bauern-und-Wuppenstube*, Am Schlossgraben 30 (☎06062/2236; ⑤). The latter has one of the town's best restaurants; its main rival is *Zum Hirsch*, Bahnstr. 2. Erbach's **youth hostel** is at Eulbacher Str. 33 (☎06062/3515; ❶), while the **campsite**, *Camping Safari* (☎06062/3159), is in the suburb of Bullau to the southeast.

Wiesbaden

WIESBADEN, 40km west of Frankfurt, is the modern capital of Hesse, a role bestowed on it by the American occupying forces, in large part because – in contrast to all its possible rivals – it came through World War II virtually unscathed. Historically speaking, it does not even belong to the province and – its Roman origins notwithstanding – is very much a late developer. Indeed, it still had little more than two thousand inhabitants when, under the Napoleonic reforms, it became sole capital of Nassau, which was re-unified and raised to the status of a duchy.

Strolling through the centre, with its grandiloquent Historicist architecture, it's not difficult to imagine how the city must have looked during its glory days as a nineteenth-century *Kurstadt*, when the aristocracy of Europe flocked to take the waters at the numerous thermal spas and to gamble away their fortunes in the famous casino. Today the Russian nobles who were once the main patrons have been replaced by wealthy Arabs and tanned, nouveau riche Germans. Wiesbaden bears little resemblance to any other major German city and is a place you'll either love or loathe, but it's certainly worth coming to get at least a taste of the atmosphere.

> The **telephone code** for Wiesbaden is ☎0611

Arrival, information and accommodation

Wiesbaden's **Hauptbahnhof** is about fifteen minutes' walk south of the city centre, which can be reached by bus #1 or #8. The **tourist office** is at Marktstr. 6 (Mon–Fri 9am–6pm, Sat & Sun 10am–4pm; ☎172 9780 or 19433).

Accommodation

Hotels in Wiesbaden are predictably pricey, but if you're prepared to splash out a bit, there are some excellent upmarket choices. Most of the budget options are out in the suburbs; the **youth hostel** is at Blücherstr. 66 (☎48657; ❸), best reached by bus #14 from the Hauptbahnhof.

HOTELS

Am Landeshaus, Moritzstr. 51 (☎373041, fax 373044). Good medium-range city centre hotel. ⑥

Ambrosius, Alfred-Schumann-Str. 9, Schierstein (☎22324). One of several possibilities in this incorporated village, a train stop between Biebrich and Eltville. ③

Bären, Bärenstr. 3 (☎301021, fax 301024). One of the least outrageously priced of the upmarket hotels in the city centre, nothwithstanding the fact that it has its own thermal baths. ⑦

Domäne Mechtildshausen, An der Airbase (☎737460, fax 737479). Wiesbaden's most unexpected hotel is an organic farm 4km southeast of the city centre. Its highly creative restaurant (closed Sun evening & Mon) is a popular excursion destination with locals. Take bus #28. ⑦

Hansa, Bahnhofstr. 23 (☎39955, fax 418 6123). Part of the *Inter Europe* chain, this classy hotel with restaurant is conveniently close to the Hauptbahnhof. ⑥

Hubertus, Wasserrolle 17, Schierstein (☎25824). Another good value option in this easily accessible suburb. ④

Landhaus Diedert, Am Kloster Klarenthal 9 (☎461066, fax 461069). Country house-style hotel with gourmet restaurant 5km northwest of the city centre. Take bus #12 or #A14. ⑦

Meuser, Stettiner Str. 13, Biebrich (☎69360). Inexpensive hotel in Wiesbaden's most attractive suburb. ③

Nassauer Hof, Kaiser-Friedrich-Platz 3 (☎1330, fax 13362). This is not only Wiesbaden's grandest hotel, but also among the most renowned and expensive in Germany, boasting every conceivable luxury, thermal baths included. Its principal restaurant, *Die Ente von Lehel*, is no less celebrated, while the *Orangerie* is a leading exponent of *Neue Deutsche Küche*. ⑨

Nassauer Hof, Rheingaustr. 2, Schierstein (☎22771). Very different from its namesake, a good value budget hotel just a short train ride from the centre. ③

Oranien, Platter Str. 2 (☎525025, fax 525025). Excellent, fully modernized nineteenth-century hotel with restaurant in the pedestrian zone. ⑦

Ring, Bleichstr. 29 (☎403021, fax 451573). The nearest there is to a budget option in the city centre. ⑤

The city centre

At the heart of Wiesbaden is the **Kurhaus**. Completed in 1906 in a Neoclassical style which would have been fashionable a hundred years previously, it's the self-conscious symbol of a city where appearances are everything. The building also houses the **Spielbank** (casino), opened in 1949. However, gambling first started in earnest in 1771 and Wiesbaden's original casino was the inspiration for "Roulettenburg", in Dostoyevsky's novel *The Gambler*. Gambling was suspended between 1872 and 1949 as a result of a ban imposed by Kaiser Wilhelm I after his son, Crown Prince Friedrich III, had formed an "unsuitable" attachment to a woman gambler. The **Kurhauskolonnade** to the north, the longest pillared hall in Europe, contains the slot machine section of the casino complex and a space for exhibitions. Opposite, the **Theaterkolonnade**, with its luxury boutiques, forms a front to the lavish neo-Rococo **Hessisches Staatstheater**, which was built at the end of the nineteenth century by Viennese architects. To the rear of the Kurhaus is the **Kurpark**, an English-style park. From there you can walk up into the wooded slopes of the Taunus, which rise to the north of the city.

Wilhelmstrasse, the main shopping street, runs past the Kurhaus into Friedrich-Ebert-Strasse and is full of expensive antique shops and glitzy designer stores. On Schlossplatz stands the **Stadtschloss**, built in the 1840s as the town residence of the Dukes of Nassau. Nowadays, it's the Hesse state parliament. Facing the Stadtschloss is the seventeeth-century **Altes Rathaus**, the oldest building in the city. In front of it, on Marktplatz, where markets are held on Wednesdays and Saturdays, there's a small fountain topped by a playful-looking lion, one of the symbols of the city. The brick **Marktkirche** (Tues, Wed, Fri & Sat 10.30am–12.30pm, Thurs 3.30–5.30pm), which bristles with towers, steeples and turrets, bears the hallmarks of the pervasive influence of the English Gothic Revival style.

A few minutes' walk to the northwest, at Langgasse 38–40, is the most atmospheric and expensive of the city's thermal baths, the mock-Roman **Kaiser-Friedrich-Bad** (May–Sept Tues–Fri 9am–10pm; Oct–April Mon 1–10pm, Tues–Fri 9am–10pm, Sat & Sun 10am–7pm; DM20), which dates back to 1913. The entry ticket is valid for three hours and includes a full Roman-Irish steam bath plus the use of the solarium. Note that Tuesdays and Thursdays are for women only, Wednesdays for men; the other days are mixed. On Kranzplatz, not much more than a stone's throw to the north, is the **Kochbrunnen**, which has no fewer than 15 different hot springs. You can sample the waters at the taps in the little Neoclassical temple. Despite their much-vaunted healing properties, you're advised to limit your intake to one litre per day.

Many of finest of the grand villas so characteristic of Wiesbaden can be seen in the streets immediately south of the Kurhaus. Particularly notable is the **Villa Clementine** at the head of Frankfurter Strasse. Nowadays a cultural centre, it was the scene in 1888 of the abduction of Crown Prince Alexander of Serbia, who was forceably repatriated by his captors. Alongside is the mid-nineteenth-century Anglican church of **St Augustine of Canterbury**, which is still in regular use, thanks to the continued presence of a sizeable American community. Just to the south, at the top end of Friedrich-Ebert-Allee, is the **Museum Wiesbaden** (Tues noon–8pm, Wed–Fri 10am–4pm, Sat & Sun 11am-5pm; DM5). This possesses a large number of paintings by the Russian artist Alexej Jawlensky, a member of the Expressionist *Der Blaue Reiter* group who was a Wiesbaden resident for the last two decades of his life, and a valuable collection of Roman antiquities.

The outskirts

On the northern edge of Wiesbaden looms the **Neroberg**, a 245-metre Taunus foothill commanding good views of the city. To get there take bus #1 to Nerotal and from there ascend by the water-powered funicular railway, the *Nerobergbahn* (April & Sept Wed & Sat noon–7pm, Sun 10am–7pm; May–Aug daily 9.30am–7pm; Oct Wed, Sat & Sun noon–6pm; DM2 single, DM3 return), whose technology has remained unchanged since its inauguration in 1888. On the summit stand the Neoclassical **Neroberg-Tempel** and the **Opelbad** (May–Sept daily 9am–8pm), a Bauhaus-style open-air swimming pool. A short distance downhill is the **Russische Kapelle**, a nineteenth-century Russian-style chapel instantly recognizable by its five gilded cupolas. It was built as a mausoleum for the Russian-born Duchess Elisabeth of Nassau, who died in childbirth at the age of nineteen. Nearby is the **Russischer Friedhof**, with the elaborate tombs of many Russian aristocrats and soldiers.

Northeast of the city centre, reached by bus #18 or #A32, is the **Kurzentrum Aukammtal**, the hub of the modern-day spa facilities. In addition to several clinics, there's the city's principal public baths, the **Thermalbad Wiesbaden** (Mon 12.30–10pm, Tues–Thurs 7.30am–10pm, Fri 7.30am–11pm, Sat & Sun 7.30am–7pm; DM10 for up to 4hr, DM 18 for up to 6hr including sauna and solarium).

It's also worth making a trip south to **Schloss Biebrich**, set on the Rhine in the suburb of the same name (take bus #3, #4, #13, #A3 or #A13). This eighteenth-century Baroque palace, the original Wiesbaden home of one of the lines of the Nassau dynasty, has a restrained elegance which puts the showy city centre to shame. Though the building itself is only open to the public for the occasional concert, you can stroll in the fine park. It's also the first embarkation point after Mainz for **cruises** down the Rhine (for more details on these, see p.437).

Eating, drinking and entertainment

Predictably enough, **eating** and **drinking** in Wiesbaden can be an expensive business. There are plenty of upmarket restaurants (see also the Accommodation section above), but good cheaper places do exist and there are some excellent centrally located pubs too.

Restaurants

Centro Italia, Wörthstr. 18. One of several notable Italian restaurants, distinguished by its range of Sicilian wines and speciality dishes. Closed Tues.

Estragon, Wilhelmstr. 12. Highly innovative restaurant which combines classic French cooking with African and Asian influences. Closed Tues.

Käfer's Bistro, Kurhausplatz 1. One of the best of Wiesbaden's upmarket restaurants, located in the Kurhaus. The cooking has a German accent, even though the decor is reminiscent of a Parisian bistro.

La Maree, Adolfstr. 3. High-class fish speciality restaurant.

Rathsbräu, Schlossplatz 6. This is Wiesbaden's version of the inevitable *Ratskeller*, occupying the cellars of the Neues Rathaus. Its new name is a result of the addition of a *Hausbrauerei*, which produces organically brewed light and dark beers. Closed Sun.

Rheingold, Saalgasse 30. This is reckoned to be *the* place in Wiesbaden for *gutbürgerliche Küche*. Evenings only.

Schlossweinstube, Am Schlosspark, Biebrich. Wine bar-restaurant, the only part of Schloss Biebrich regularly open to the public.

Sir Winston Churchill, Taunusstr. 23. Long-established restaurant-cum-bistro-cum-café which starts serving breakfast at 8.30am and remains open till 4am. It aims to combine high culinary standards with the atmosphere and style of a British club.

Trüffel, Marktstr. 9. Located in one of the city's best delicatessens, this serves Italianate bistro food and is a lunchtime favourite with shoppers and office workers. Open Mon-Fri 10am–8pm, Sat 9am–4pm.

Viva, Schützenhofstr. 3. Vegetarian and wholefood restaurant on a terrace above its own shop. It has a huge selection of dishes which you pay for by weight. Open Mon–Fri 11am–7pm, Sat 11am–4pm.

Weihenstephan, Armenruhstr. 6, Biebrich. A successful transplant of a Bavarian *Bierkeller*, serving good food (particularly fish dishes) and having the obligatory beer garden. Closed Sat.

Zum Dortmunder, Langgasse 34. Excellent traditional *Gaststätte* serving hearty cuisine and Dortmund beers.

Bars and cafés

Bebop, Saalgasse 11. Trendy bar which sometimes features blues and jazz. Closed Fri; opens at 7pm every other day.

Café Blum, Wilhelmstr. 44–46. The most prestigious of the many elegant coffee houses in the city centre.

Café Cicero, Citypassage. Tucked away on the first floor of a shopping centre, this *Kulturcafé* features regular artistic events, especially live jazz.

Domi, Moritzstr. 52. An alternative bar with a good atmosphere which also serves cheap meals.

Irish Pub, Michelsberg 15. One of the better and more original of the new wave of Irish pubs which have sprung up all over Germany. There's often live music, and it's generally packed out by mid-evening.

Park-Café, Wilhelmstr. 36. Extremely chic nightspot patronized by the beautiful set. Open Tues–Sun 9pm–4am.

Sächsische Konditorei, Langgasse 43. The café is an adjunct to the shop, which makes what are reckoned to be the best cakes and sweets in Wiesbaden.

Sherry & Port, Adolfsallee 11. The name of this bar, which combines English and Irish influences, is due to the large selection of sherries and ports on offer. Live jazz, folk and classical music sessions take place several times a week.

Weisbadener Bub, Nerostr. 33. A favourite student bar.

Wirtshaus, Nerostr. 24. Another good student bar, still patronized by leftovers of the Sixties generation. Open daily from 8pm.

Culture

The *Hessisches Staatstheater* on Kurhausplatz (☎1321) is the principal cultural venue; it presents **opera**, **operetta** and **ballet** in the plush main auditorium, **drama** on the two smaller, plainer stages. Classical **concerts** take place in the ornate *Friedrich-von-Thiersch-Saal* (☎172 9930) in the *Kurhaus*. The main **cabaret** venues are *Pariser Hoftheater*, Spiegelgasse 9 (☎300607) and *Hinterhaus*, Karlsruher Str. 15 (☎379548). The *Internationales Maifestspiel* throughout May is Wiesbaden's most important cultural **festival**, while the top popular event is the *Theatrium*, a huge street fair on Wilhelmstrasse on a weekend in early June.

The Rheingau

The Hessian side of the Rhine, running from Wiesbaden to the border with Rhineland-Palatinate at Lorchhausen, is known as the **Rheingau**. Sheltered from the elements by the gentle slopes of the Taunus, the region has developed into one of Germany's foremost wine-producing districts, and its vineyards, ruined castles and drowsy little villages make it a favourite destination for coach parties and package tourists. Road B42, running from Wiesbaden to the Rhineland-Palatinate border and taking in all the little wine villages, has been designated the *Rheingauer-Riesling-Route*, a special-interest stretch for wine fans, enabling them to stop off and do a spot of tasting and buying. There's also a walking route, the *Rheingauer-Riesling-Pfad*, which runs through the lower slopes of the **Rheingau-Gebirge** – the part of the Taunus which rises from the banks of the Rhine. Classical music buffs should make a point of visiting during the three months in summer when the *Rheingau-Musik-Festival* takes place, as it features of dozens of concerts by international musicians of the highest rank. Though some performances are in Wiesbaden, the vast majority take place in the region's smaller towns and villages.

Eltville

The first stop out of Wiesbaden, just beyond its suburbs, is **ELTVILLE**, which lies on the main rail line north, and has plenty of bus connections into the surrounding countryside. It's famous for its sparkling wines, for its 20,000 rose bushes which burst into a riot of colour in summer, and for being the place where the urbane conman, Felix Krull, hero of Thomas Mann's comic novel, spent his youth. Overlooking the Rhine is the ruined **Burg** of the Archbishop-Electors of Mainz, now a shady promenade with rose garden. There are plenty of cute half-timbered houses, plus a Gothic **Pfarrkirche** with a fifteenth-century fresco of *The Last Judgment* and a font made in the workshop of the Mainz sculptor Hans Backoffen.

However, Eltville is above all a place for **eating** and, especially, **drinking**. Many of its **Weingüte** can be visited and most serve food and drink. *Koegler*, at Kirchgasse 5, is of special note: it occupies the fifteenth-century Bechtermünzhof, the home and printing workshop of Gutenberg in his final years. Others to head for are *Diefenhardt'sches Weingut*, Hauptstr. 11 and *Krone*, Am Rheinufer. There are also plenty of **wine-restaurants** where you can sample the local vintages – the best are *Weinhaus Weinpump*, Rheingauer Str. 3, and *Gelbes Haus*, Burgplatz 3. The town also has its own boutique brewery, *Kleines Eltviller Brauhaus*, Schwalbacher Str. 41–43, with an adjoining beer garden.

Eltville's **Bahnhof** is at the northern end of the town centre, while the **tourist office** is at Schmittstr. 2 (Mon–Thurs 9.30am–noon & 2–5pm, Fri 9.30am–noon & 2–6pm, Sat 9am–noon; ☎06123/697154). Accommodation is in rather short supply, with only a few **private rooms** (②–③), plus three **hotels**: the tiny *Rheingauer Winzerhaus*, Wilhelmstr. 7 (☎06123/2370; ④); *Café Glockenhof*, Marktstr. 3 (☎06123/61141; ⑤); and *Frankenbach-Mainzer Hof*, Wilhelmstr. 13 (☎06123/5056; ⑦). The big local **festival** is the *Biedermeier- und Sektfest* over five days in early July.

Kiedrich

From Eltville, it's only a 3km bus journey inland to **KIEDRICH**, a wine-growing village of half-timbered houses. Dominating it from the north is **Burg Scharfenstein**, a ruin since the seventeenth century, which commands a fine view over the region. In the centre of town is a walled close containing two imposing late Gothic churches. The smaller of these, the fifteenth-century **St Michaelskapelle**, has a tall lantern turret crowned with an openwork spire, an indication of its function as a funerary chapel. There are actually two chapels, the lower serving as the ossuary. Its counterpart above, which is generally kept open, is light and airy, with a graceful altar recess (or *Chörlein*) and an elaborate candelabra bearing a double-sided sculpture of the *Madonna and Child*. The external pulpit was used to address the epilepsy sufferers who once flocked to Kiedrich on pilgrimage.

Although it preserves parts of its predecessor, the **Pfarrkirche St Valentin** (March–Oct Mon–Sat 10.30am–12.30pm, Sun 2.30–4pm; Nov–Feb Sat 10.30am–12.30pm, Sun 2.30–4pm) is likewise predominantly fifteenth-century in date. Entry is via the main portal, which has an exquisite "Soft Style" polychromed **tympanum** with a combined scene of *The Annunciation* and *Coronation of the Virgin*. The interior is an extraordinary evocation of the Middle Ages, preserving as it does virtually all the original furnishings including the rood screen, pulpit, tabernacle, altars, choir stalls and the pews with their remarkable carved and painted vine motifs and Gothic script. Even more precious are the *Kiedrich Madonna*, a gorgeous fourteenth-century statue showing strong French influence, and the oldest church **organ** in the world still in working order. The latter, which preserves around eighty percent of its original pipework from around 1500, can be heard every Sunday morning at 9.30am, along with the local **choir**, the *Chorbuben*, who since 1333 have practised a unique form of singing Gregorian chant in Germanic dialect. Immediately after the service, their illuminated missals can be viewed in the parish house opposite.

Kiedrich has one large **pension**, *Ankermühle*, Eltviller Str. 6 (☎06123/90570; ⑥), and a couple of **hotels**, both with **restaurants**: *Goldene Krone*, Oberstr. 5 (☎06123/90560; ⑤); and *Nassauer Hof*, Bingerpfortenstr. 17 (☎06123/2476; ⑦). Also recommended, whether for a meal or a glass of wine, is *Gutsschänke Schloss Groenesteyn*, Oberstr. 36; other possibilities are *Weinstube Zum Bur*, Oberstr. 3, and *Winzerhaus*, Kammstr. 3.

Kloster Eberbach

Several buses per day continue 5km westwards from Kiedrich to **Kloster Eberbach** (April–Sept daily 10am–6pm; Oct–March Mon–Fri 10am–4pm, Sat & Sun 11am–4pm; DM5), one of the best-preserved medieval monasteries in Germany. It's situated at the lower end of the valley of the Kisselbach directly below the Taunus: exactly the sort of secluded setting favoured by the Cistercian order, who founded it in 1135. The Romanesque **Klosterkirche** is grandiosely austere, and devoid of decoration save for a few aristocratic tombs, the most notable being that in the chancel to a fourteenth-century Archbishop of Mainz, Gerlach von Nassau. Behind the church are the leafy cloisters, surrounded by the former living quarters of the monks. Particularly outstanding is the upstairs **dormitory**, an immense vaulted room divided into two aisles, with a slight incline in its floor-level to make it seem even longer than it actually is. Built in the 1240s, it ranks among the masterpieces of early Gothic architecture. Below it is the **Fraternei**, another impressive hall, which formerly contained the monastic workshops. In the **lay brothers' refectory** the huge wine presses once used by the monks are on display; some date back to the seventeenth century.

Wine production continued after the dissolution of the monastery in 1803, and the outbuildings are now used to press, ferment and store the produce of the *Eberbacher Steinberg*, the former monastic vineyard. Tasting sessions for groups are held in the **Hospital**, a magnificent Transitional-style building which is the only medieval monastic infirmary anywhere in Europe to have survived in its original form. Otherwise, you can buy the products at the shop, or drink them in the **restaurant** of the *Gästehaus Kloster Eberbach* (☎06723/9930; ⑦), an upmarket **hotel** which has recently been set up in the monastery.

Rüdesheim

RÜDESHEIM claims the dubious distinction of being the most visited town in the region, attracting over three million sightseers a year. It's a favourite stopping-off point for coach parties and Rhine cruisers as it conforms pretty well to the general conception of what a typical Rhine town should look like – all crooked narrow streets, half-timbered houses and souvenir shops, sloping down gently from the wooded hills and terraced vineyards above.

The big local attraction is the **Drosselgasse**, a street comprised entirely of taverns offering "traditional" German entertainment, which is crowded all day long with tourists being ripped off. The twelfth-century **Brömserburg**, a squat and angular fortress a few minutes' walk to the west, now houses the **Weinmuseum** (mid-March to mid-Nov daily 9am–6pm; DM5). It contains 21 old presses and a vast collection of wine vessels, including some fine examples of vases that were used to store and transport wine from Roman times through to the Middle Ages. There's the bonus of a marvellous view over the town and the Rhine from the top of the keep.

The twelfth-century defensive tower called the **Boosenburg** just to the north and the circular late Gothic **Adlerturm** at the eastern end of the waterfront are further reminders of an era when this stretch of the Rhine was a turbulent and contested area. Lining Oberstrasse to the east of the Boosenburg are a number of nobles' houses, notably the **Brömserhof**, which has a picturesque half-timbered tower. It now houses **Siegfried's Mechanisches Musikkabinett** (guided tours March 1 to Nov 15 daily 10am–6pm; DM9), one of the largest collections of mechanical musical instruments in the country. Just off the central Marktplatz is another fine mansion, the **Klunkardshof**, which has a particularly well-preserved half-timbered facade.

The much-restored **Pfarrkirche Eibingen** at the extreme northeastern edge of Rüdesheim was formerly part of a convent established by the great mystic, poet and composer **Hildegard of Bingen** (see also p.436). In the early years of the twentieth century, a new, considerably larger **Abtei St Hildegard** was built in neo-Romanesque style on the heights above. Wines from its vineyard, plus a couple of powerful spirits, can be purchased at its shop. To commemorate Hildegard's 900th anniversary, the abbey will host a full programme of events throughout 1998, culminating in the *Hildegardisfest* on September 17.

The main road just west of the abbey continues up to the **Niederwalddenkmal**, a bombastic statue of *Germania* built to mark the unification of Germany in 1871. This immense monument 225m above the town can be reached more directly by foot or by gondola (DM6.50 single, DM10 return) over the vineyards which swarm up the slopes behind Rüdesheim. Lower down, by one of the footpaths to Assmannshausen, are the undeniably romantic ruins of the thirteenth-century **Burg Ehrenfels**. This one-time toll castle was used in conjunction with the Mäuseturm, a tower built on a mid-river island, by the Archbishops of Mainz to control traffic on the Rhine.

Practicalities

Ferries dock right by the town centre, whereas the **Bahnhof** lies a short distance further west. The **tourist office** (Mon–Fri 8.30am–6.30pm, May–Sept also Sat 10am–5.30pm, Sun 11.30am–3.30pm; ☎06722/19433) is at Rheinstr. 16.

There are plenty of **private rooms** (②–④) and **hotels** but they tend to be booked up during the high summer. A couple of inexpensive possibilities are *Gasthof Zur Guten Quelle*, Katharinenstr. 3 (☎06722/2757; ③) and *Weinstube zur Lindenau*, Löhrstr. 10 (☎06722/3327; ④). If you want more luxury, try *Felsenkeller*, Oberstr. 39–41 (☎06722/2094; ⑥); *Zum Bären*, Schmidtstr. 31 (☎06722/1091; ⑥); *Central*, Kirchstr. 6 (☎06722/9120; ⑦); or *Rüdesheimer Schloss*, Steingasse 10 (☎06722/90500; ⑨). The local **youth hostel** is set amidst the vines, a long walk from the town, at Am Kreuzburg (☎06722/2711; ❶). There are two **campsites** in Rüdesheim: *Campingplatz am Rhein* (☎06722/2528 or 2582) and *Ponyland* (☎06722/2518) near the Niederwalddenkmal.

All the hotel listed above have **restaurants**. Good **wine bars** include *Weingut Jakob Christ*, Grabenstr. 17, and *Weinhaus Fendel*, Marienthalerstr. 46. For something not so obviously typical of the region, try *Schlossberg*, Grabenstr. 8, which does bistro cooking, or *Rüdesheimer Brauhaus*, Oberstr. 49, a *Hausbrauerei* which makes light, dark and *Weizen* beers.

At the beginning of July there's a firework display and in mid-August Rüdesheim has its *Weinfest*. During the latter it seems like all of those three million visitors have hit town at once and accommodation is impossible to find unless booked a very long time in advance.

Assmannshausen

Just out of Rüdesheim proper, the Rhine suddenly bends through ninety degrees to flow more or less south–north, and there follows a treacherous stretch of river called the **Binger Loch**, where most of the barges which ply the Rhine normally take a pilot on board to negotiate the channel through the rapids and reefs. After 5km (one stop on the train or an enticing hour-long walk along the marked footpath) you arrive at **ASS-MANNSHAUSEN**, a smaller and less touristy version of Rüdesheim, of which it now forms a part. In the terraced vineyards round about some of Germany's best red wines are produced from Spätburgunder grapes. A chairlift (DM6.50 single, DM10 return) runs up to **Jagdschloss Niederwald**, an eighteenth-century hunting lodge turned hotel (☎06722/1004; ⑨) near the Niederwalddenkmal, and commanding similarly good views of the Rhine.

Milberg, Am Rathaus 2 (☎06722/2945; ④) is a centrally located **pension**. One of the most enticing **hotels** is the sixteenth-century *Altes Haus*, Lorcher Str. 8 (☎06722/2051; ④) which has a really excellent **restaurant**. Likewise from the sixteenth century is *Krone*, Rheinuferstr. 10 (☎06722/4030; ⑨), which ranks among the most exclusive hotels in the whole of the Rhineland, with a restaurant renowned for its fish and game specialities - and a remarkable wine list.

CENTRAL HESSE

The attractions of the central part of Hesse are diverse. To the west is the valley of the Lahn, a Rhine tributary, on whose banks stand two of Germany's most famous university towns, **Marburg**, a truly beautiful place, and **Giessen**, now rather a shadow of its prewar self. Further downstream are three very contrasting destinations: **Wetzlar**, with its distinguished legal and literary traditions, the *Residenzstadt* of **Weilburg** and the small cathedral city of **Limburg**. In the very heart of Hesse is the volcanic **Vogelsberg** range, with a number of pretty towns, most notably **Alsfeld**. Further east, at the edge of the Rhön, is **Fulda**, one of Germany's leading episcopal centres.

The Taunus

The favourite playground of the citizens of Frankfurt, the **Taunus** is a hilly forest area bordered on three sides by the rivers Rhine, Main and Lahn. Much of it, notably the **High Taunus**, is unspoiled landscape ideal for hiking, though the undoubted high point is the spa town of **Bad Homburg** in the southern foothills.

The High Taunus

The thickly wooded slopes of the **High Taunus** (*Hochtaunus*) have been designated a *Naturpark*. On the whole, they're atmospheric and invigorating rather than breathtaking, and the most attractive part can be explored in a day's outing. The main peak, the **Grosser Feldberg** (880m), is the highest of any of the Rhineland schist massifs: from the summit there's a marvellous panorama of the region. In the nearby village of **OBERREIFENBERG**, the **youth hostel** at Limesstr. 14 (☎06082/2440; ⓐ) is the main local hiking base.

The area's principal town is **KÖNIGSTEIN IM TAUNUS**, which can be reached by train from Frankfurt or from Wiesbaden via Höchst. It boasts a striking ruined **Burg** (daily March 9am–4.30pm; April–Sept 9am–7pm; Oct–Feb 9.30am–3/4pm; DM3), whose keep commands a sweeping panorama over the region, with the main landmarks of Frankfurt visible on even a half-decent day. If you want to stay, there are plenty of **hotels**, ranging from *Haus der Begegnung*, Bischof-Kaller-Str. 3 (☎06174/3061; ④) to the super-luxury *Sonnenhof*, Falkensteiner Str. 9 (☎06174/29080; ⑧). For a list of **private rooms** (②–⑤), contact the **tourist office**, Hauptstr. 21 (Mon, Tues, Thurs & Fri 8.30am-12.30pm & 2.30-5.30pm, Wed 8.30am-12.30pm, Sat 9am-1pm; ☎06174/202251).

Bad Homburg vor der Höhe

BAD HOMBURG, reached by S-Bahn #5 from Frankfurt or bus #917 from Königstein, ranks second only to Baden-Baden as Germany's classiest spa. Following nearly two centuries as capital of the tiny state of Hesse-Homburg, it was annexed by Prussia in 1866 and quickly established itself as the favourite summer retreat of the Kaisers. It's very much a place of two faces: the historic centre, with its market-town air, is built on a steeply pitched hill, while the somnolent spa quarter is laid out on the low ground to the north.

The town centre

At the very top of the town, set in an extensive landscaped park, is the **Schloss** (guided tours Tues–Sun 10am–4/5pm; DM6). The predominantly Baroque exterior of the palace is largely due to Friedrich II, the hero of Kleist's play *Prince Friedrich of Homburg*. His **bust**, a masterly portrait by the Berlin sculptor Andreas Schlüter, stands in the entrance hall, while his famous wooden leg, known as the "Silver Leg" because of its silver joints, is one of the highlights of the tour. For the most part, the interiors are nineteenth-century and reflect the taste of the Empress Augusta: among the adornments she ordered is one of the world's first telephone kiosks.

A second guided tour, currently run on Sundays only (at 11am, noon, 1pm, 2pm & 3pm; DM6) goes round the so-called **Englischer Flügel** (or **Elisabethenflügel**), which is named in honour of Princess Elizabeth, daughter of King George III of Great Britain, who married Landgrave Friedrich VI in 1818. She was a talented amateur artist, and many of her own creations, including some striking works in lacquer, are displayed throughout her apartments. This tour also takes in the galleried **Schlosskirche**, which contains the burial vault of the House of Hesse-Homburg. The tall **Weisser Turm** (White Tower; Tues–Sun 10am–4/5pm; DM1) in the Schloss courtyard is the only reminder of the previous medieval castle. It can be ascended for an extensive panorama over the Taunus.

Opposite the Schloss, at the corner of Löwenstrasse and Dorotheenstrasse, is the **Sinclair-Haus** (Tues–Fri 3–7pm, Sat & Sun 10am–5pm; free), a Baroque mansion named after a prominent Homburg courtier. It's used for temporary art exhibitions, a mixture of ephemera and international blockbusters. Across the road is the **Erlöserkirche** (Church of the Redeemer), an extravagant Historicist building funded by Kaiser Wilhelm II.

The **Kurpark** is a huge and beautiful landscaped park designed by Peter Joseph Lenné. Along its main axis of Brunnenallee are no fewer than seven mineral springs, the most prestigious being the **Elisabethenquelle**, over which stands a handsome Neoclassical pavilion. At the heart of the park is the stolidly Wilhelmine building of the **Kaiser-Wilhelm-Bad**, which is still the main centre for therapeutic cures. Alongside, the **Spielbank** (daily 3pm–2.30am; DM5) is the oldest casino in the world, founded in 1841 by the Frenchman François Blanc, who decamped to Monte Carlo when gambling was outlawed throughout Germany in 1872. It's essential to be respectably dressed in order to gain admission; minimum stakes are DM5 for roulette, DM10 for black jack.

Further east are the two main bathing complexes. The **Taunus-Therme** (Mon, Tues, Thurs & Sun 9am–11pm, Wed, Fri & Sat 9am–midnight; DM23 for 2hr, DM45 for the whole day, rising to DM26 and DM49 at weekends) occupies a Japanese-style building with garden, and includes a Roman-Irish steam bath and a Finnish sauna among its facilities. Its more conventional neighbour, the **Seedammbad** (Mon 2–9pm, Tues–Fri 7am–9pm, Sat & Sun 8.30am–8pm; DM6 for a 2hr swim, DM15 for a sauna) likewise has indoor and outdoor sections. Also worth seeking out are a couple of exotic little turn-of-the century buildings: the **Russische Kirche** at the southern end of the park and the **Siamesischer Tempel** at the northwestern corner, which was donated to the spa by one well-satisfied partaker of the waters, the King of Siam.

Practicalities

Bad Homburg's **Bahnhof** is on the south side of town. The **tourist office** (Mon–Fri 8.30am–7pm, Sat 9am–1pm; ☎06172/675110) is in the *Kurhaus* building in the heart of the town centre at Louisenstr. 58.

There's a huge range of accommodation to suit all pockets, including a **youth hostel** just south of the Schloss at Meiereiberg 1 (☎06172/21315; ✿) and plenty of **private rooms** (②–⑤). Several of the city-centre **hotels** are surprisingly reasonable: try *Johannisberg*, Thomasstr. 5 (☎06172/21315 or 24806; ④); *Zur Brücke*, Ritter-von-Marx-Brücke 2 (☎06172/22295; ⑤); or *Haus Fischer am Park*, Landgrafenstr. 12 (☎06172/867927; ⑤). *Villa Kisseleff*, Kisseleffstr. 19 (☎06172/21559; ⑥) is a good medium-range choice, while a couple of the less outrageously priced upmarket options are *Haus Dalheim*, Elisabethenstr. 42 (☎06172/677350; ⑦) and the Jugendstil *Villa am Kurpark*, Kaiser-Friedrich-Promenade 57 (☎06172/26047; ⑧). At the very top of the range is the *Steigenberger Bad Homburg*, Kaiser-Friedrich-Promenade 69–75 (☎06172/1810; ⑨), an Art Deco-style glass palace offering every conceivable luxury. There's an equally wide variety of places to **eat** and **drink**, quite apart from the hotel restaurants. These include a vegetarian place, *Kartoffelküche*, Audenstr. 4. *Schreinerei Pfeiffer*, Audenstr. 6, has Hessian specialities, while *Isoletta*, Louisenstr. 80, is a good and not too expensive Italian. *Kofler* is a café-restaurant in the Schloss which does themed eat-as-much-as-you-can buffets on Thursday evenings. If you've plenty of money to spare, *Assmanns*, Kisseleffstr. 27, is a renowned exponent of *Neue Deutsche Küche*, while *Sänger's*, Kaiser-Friedrich-Promenade 85, is a gourmet restaurant with a national reputation.

Antidotes to the peace and quiet of the spa quarter are provided by Germany's oldest **dance-bar**, the *Tennis Bar* (Tues–Thurs 9pm–4am, Fri & Sat 9pm–5.45am, Sun 3pm–4am) on Kisseleffstrasse opposite the Spielbank, and by *Gambrinus* in the Fürstenbahnhof, the former royal terminal beside the Bahnhof, which has a **disco** or live music each evening. The *Kulturzentrum Englische Kirche* in the deconsecrated Anglican Christ Church on Ferdinandplatz (☎06172/100310), presents a varied programme of **cabaret**, **jazz** and **classical** music. Bad Homburg's churches host an international **organ** festival, *Fugato*, in the second half of September.

The Spessart

The **Spessart**, which is divided between Hesse and Bavaria, forms Germany's largest continuous upland forest area. Most of it has been dedicated a *Naturpark*, though strung along the valley of the River Kinzig, which separates it from the Vogelsberg, are a number of towns, the most notable being **Gelnhausen**, a long-time Free Imperial City, and **Steinau**, of Brothers Grimm fame.

Gelnhausen

GELNHAUSEN lies 40km east of Frankfurt on the fast road and rail routes to Fulda, and is also the starting point for a branch rail line through the Vogelsberg to Giessen. One of the most atmospheric and picturesque small towns in Germany, it was a city-state for most of its history and exudes a grandeur which belies the fact that its population has never numbered more than a few thousand. It likes to call itself *Barbarossastadt*, a reference to its foundation in the twelfth century by **Frederick Barbarossa**, the emperor who was primarily responsible for moulding the feudal structure of the Holy Roman Empire. However, it's equally proud of being the birthplace of the seventeenth-century writer **Johann Jacob Christoffel von Grimmelshausen**, whose semi-autobiographical *Simplicissimus* is the first great German novel and one of the leading tragi-comedies of European literature.

The town

The ruins of Barbarossa's palace, the **Kaiserpfalz** (Tues–Sun 10am–5/6pm; DM3), stand in what was formerly an island in the Kinzig, midway between the Bahnhof and the Altstadt, which clings to the steep hillside above. Substantial sections of the red sandstone masonry survive, including parts of the gateway, the tower and the chapel, though the most notable feature is a wall of the royal residence itself, featuring arcades adorned with beautifully carved Romanesque capitals. Above the palace portal is an enigmatic grotesque sculpture of a man, traditionally presumed to depict the red-bearded emperor himself.

The upper town is centred on two market squares, the Untermarkt and the Obermarkt., but the main feature of the skyline is the **Marienkirche** between the squares. Although built at various stages, it's a magnificent structure which graphically illustrates the transition from Romanesque to Gothic. Especially worthy of note are the four **towers**, which form an irresistibly photogenic ensemble, and the elaborately decorated interior of the chancel. This features a **rood screen** bearing highly expressive sculptures illustrating *The Last Judgment*, a gleaming set of stained-glass windows, and a carved and painted high altar. In the vestry are two precious fifteenth-century tapestries, which the caretaker will show for a DM1 donation. Immediately below the church, and nowadays serving as its hall, is the **Romanisches Haus**, which was built for the officials of Barbarossa's court.

Half-timbered buildings are otherwise predominant in the upper town, with the **Rathaus** on Obermarkt ranking as the most imposing. On Brentanostrasse, just west of Untermarkt, the **Synagoge**, now used as a cultural centre, retains some of its original Baroque decoration and furnishings, notably the Torah shrine. Much of the **Stadtbefestigung** enclosing the town also survives, including the picturesque **Hexenturm** on the southeast side, where supposed witches were imprisoned. It's well worth continuing uphill from here to the **Halbmondturm**, which commands a breath-taking view over the town and the valley.

Practicalities

Gelnhausen's **tourist office** (Mon–Fri 8am–noon & 2–4.30pm, Sat 9am–noon & 2–4.30pm, Sun 2–4.30pm; ☎06051/830300) is on the northern side of Obermarkt. The **youth hostel** is a couple of blocks to the west at Schützengraben 5 (☎06051/4424; ❷). Likewise in the historic centre are one small **guest house**, *Kapellenweg*, Kapellenweg 23 (☎06051/2044; ④), and five **hotels**: *Schelm von Bergen*, Obermarkt 22 (☎06051/2755; ③); *Zur Burgschänke*, Burgstr. 19 (☎06051/2915; ④); *Grimmelshausen*, Schmidtgasse 12 (☎06051/92420; ④); *Stadt-Schänke*, Fürstenhofstr. 1 (☎06051/16051; ⑤); and *Burg-Mühle*, Burgstr. 2 (☎06051/82050; ⑤). Each of the hotels, except *Grimmelshausen*, has a **restaurant**; another good choice for a meal is the historic tavern *Zum Löwen*, Langgasse 28, which also has the benefit of a beer garden.

Steinau an der Strasse

The little half-timbered town of **STEINAU**, some 25km northeast of Gelnhausen on the main transport routes to Fulda, was the childhood home of the Brothers Grimm (see box on p.391), a connection resulting in a considerable volume of tourism these days. Focal point of the town is a large Renaissance **Schloss** (Tues–Sun 10am–4/6pm; DM3.50 museum only, DM5.50 including guided tour of the interiors), which contains period furnishings plus extensive documentation on the work of the brothers. There's more on the Grimms in the nearby **Amtshaus** (daily April–Oct 2–5pm; DM3) at Brüder-Grimm-Str. 80, where they lived during the period of their father's service as the local magistrate. Puppet performances of some of their most famous stories are regularly performed at the **Marionettentheater**, Am Kumpen 4 (☎06663/245).

Steinau's **Bahnhof** is at the northwestern fringe of town, a 15-minute walk from the centre. The **tourist office** is in the Rathaus, Brüder-Grimm-Str. 47 (☎06663/97355). There are numerous **hotels**, including *Gasthaus Bayrischer Hof*, Am Bayrischen Hof 2 (☎06663/1522; ②); *Gasthaus Weisses Ross*, Brüder-Grimm-Str. 48 (☎06663/5804; ③); and *Grüner Baum*, Leipziger Str. 45 (☎06663/9740; ⑤).

The Lahn valley from Limburg to Giessen

The **River Lahn** forms a natural boundary dividing the upland forest areas of the Taunus and the Westerwald. Most of it lies within Hesse, but a small downstream stretch, shortly before it flows into the Rhine just south of Koblenz, is in Rhineland-Palatinate. A series of historic towns, each conveniently separated by intervals of approximately 20km, punctuate the Hessian section. Exploration is made easy by the road and rail line which closely follow the river for all but its uppermost stretch.

Limburg an der Lahn

The little episcopal city of **LIMBURG**, which lies hard by the Land border some 50km north of Wiesbaden, is beautifully situated on a rocky spur on the south bank of the Lahn. Compact enough to be seen in a short time, it's deservedly a popular destination with day-trippers from the Rhineland.

The city

Limburg's **Dom** is built right at the top of the town and might at first sight appear to be a sacred counterpart to the fantasy castles erected all over Germany in the Romantic period. In fact, it's a perfectly genuine church from the first half of the thirteenth century, with an orange, white and yellow colour scheme and an exotic roofline comprising seven towers and spires. In essence the Dom belongs to the last phase of Romanesque, and, despite using some elements of the newly emerging Gothic style, it seems that the builders were unaware of the structural advantages of pointed arches and the rib vault, using them merely for novelty value and decorative effects. Just before the church was consecrated, it was endowed with a series of naive but vigorous **frescoes**, most of which survive; look out in particular for the striking depiction of Samson in the south transept. Two other furnishings from the same period can also be seen — the elaborate stone **font** in a south aisle chapel, and the **tomb** of the founder Conrad Kurzbold in the northern transept.

To the rear of the Dom, the **Schloss** of the local lords is another very picturesque jumble of buildings now used to house offices and the municipal archives. Down Domstrasse is the **Diözesanmuseum** (mid-March to mid-Nov Tues–Sat 10am–1pm & 2–5pm, Sun 11am–5pm; DM2). This contains some stunning treasury items, notably the *Staurothek*, a Byzantine reliquary in the shape of a cross, which was brought back from the Crusades by a local knight; the jewelled *Staff of St Peter*, made by a tenth-century goldsmith from Trier; and the eleventh-century lead reliquary from the high altar of the previous church on the site of the Dom.

The venerable houses of the Altstadt at the foot of the hill are predominantly half-timbered, with the cluster around **Fischmarkt** ranking among the oldest in the country. Here also is the **Historisches Rathaus**, which served as the town hall for exactly six centuries. To end your visit, cross over the **Alte Lahnbrücke**, a fourteenth-century bridge which preserves its original defensive tower. From here, or better still the opposite bank, you're rewarded with a wonderful **view** of the skyline.

Practicalities

Limburg's **Bahnhof** is just south of the Altstadt. The **tourist office** (April–Oct Mon–Fri 8am–12.30pm & 2–6pm, Sat 10am–noon; Nov–March Mon–Thurs 8am–12.30pm & 2–5pm, Fri 8am–12.30pm; ☎06431/6166) is a couple of minutes' walk to the north at Hospitalstr. 2.

The cheapest **hotels** with a decent location are *Gasthaus Schwarzer Adler*, Barfüsserstr. 14 (☎06431/6387; ②) and *Gasthaus zum Weissen Ross*, Westerwaldstr. 2 (☎06431/8776; ④). More upmarket choices include a group around the Bahnhof – *Huss*, Bahnhofsplatz 3 (☎06431/25087; ⑥); *Martin*, Holzheimer Str. 2 (☎06431/41001 or 94840; ⑥); and *Zimmermann*, Blumenröder Str. 1 (☎06431/4611; ⑦) – plus a couple in the Altstadt – *Nassauer Hof*, Brückenstr. 1 (☎06431/25050; ⑦); and *Dom-Hotel*, Grabenstr. 57 (☎06431/24077; ⑦). There's a **youth hostel** at the extreme southern edge of town at Auf dem Guckucksberg (☎06431/8776; ❸; take bus #3) and a **campsite** (☎06431/22610) at the northern end, on the opposite side of the Lahn.

Both *Nassauer Hof* and *Dom-Hotel* have excellent **restaurants**; otherwise the best place to eat in Limburg is *St Georgsstube* in the *Stadthalle*, Hospitalstr. 4.

Weilburg

What **WEILBURG** lacks in size, it makes up for in visual appeal. Standing on a promontory surrounded on three sides by the River Lahn, its compact centre is grouped around the elegant sixteenth-century **Schloss** (guided tours Tues–Sun 10am–4/5pm; DM6) which, together with its outbuildings and grounds, almost forms a town in itself. Once the residence of an offshoot line of the House of Nassau, the Schloss has a particularly beautiful central courtyard, offering an almost rustic interpretation of the Renaissance style. In the eighteenth century, the complex was greatly expanded by the addition of the **Marstall** (stables) on the northern side, and by the laying out of the **Schlossgarten** as a series of terraces leading down to the Lahn. Within the latter is the curvaceous **Obere Orangerie** (same hours as Schloss; DM2), which is used for temporary exhibitions of *objets d'art*, and the **Untere Orangerie**, now a café-restaurant. Alongside is the **Schlosskirche**, one of the finest Baroque churches in Hesse – its elaborate pillared altar, decorated with cherubs and sunbursts, has an almost Rococo feel to it.

Directly opposite the main entrance to the Schloss is the **Stadt- und Bergbaumuseum** (April–Oct Tues–Sun 10am–noon & 2–5pm; Nov–March Mon–Fri 10am–noon & 2–5pm; DM4), whose main attraction is the *Tiefe Stollen*, a full-sized mock-up of a local mine. Upstairs, there's an early nineteenth-century pharmacy and the *Weilburger Herbarium* of 1842, which is still in its original display cabinets. In the middle of the adjacent Marktplatz is a heavily ornamented Renaissance fountain, the **Neptunbrunnen**.

North of the Schloss, the Lahn is crossed by the five-arched **Steinerne Brücke**, first erected in the 1760s. On either side of the peninsula, you can see the two entrances to the **Schiffstunnel**, the only such construction in Germany, which was dug in the middle of the nineteenth century to save ships from having to sail all the way round the town. It cuts underneath the **Kalvarienberg**, a hill with an unfinished sixteenth-century attempt at re-creating the Holy Places of Jerusalem.

Practicalities

Weilburg's **Bahnhof** is beside the Lahn, on the opposite bank from the Schloss. You'll find the **tourist office** to the south of the Schloss at Mauerstr. 6 (Mon–Fri 9am–noon & 2–4.30pm, Sat 10am–noon; ☎06471/7671 or 31467).

There are two conveniently central **pensions**: *Zur Altstadt*, Schulgasse18 (☎06471/39186; ④) and *Jägerhof* on Neugasse (☎06471/7161; ④). Additionally, there are four **hotels**: *Weilburger Löwe*, Frankfurter Str. 23–27 (☎06471/7671; ④); *Lindenhof*, Frankfurter Str. 23 (☎06471/7685; ⑤); *Villa im Park*, Frankfurter Str. 12 (☎06471/93830; ⑥); and *Schlosshotel*, which occupies the Marstall, Langgasse 25 (☎06471/39096; ⑧). The **youth hostel** is at Am Steinbühl (☎06471/1542; ⚑) in the outlying village of Odersbach, 4km to the west, along with a riverside **campsite** (☎06471/7620).

Weilburg has an abundance of good places to **eat** and **drink**. Predictably, the *Schlosshotel* has the best and most expensive restaurant. *Weilburger Hof*, Schwannengasse 14, is another good choice for traditional German dishes; *La Lucia*, Marktplatz 10, is a fine Italian restaurant; while *Zur Turmschmiede* on Turmgasse has a shady beer garden.

Wetzlar

The long-time city-state of **WETZLAR** occupies a hallowed place in the annals of German literature (see box below), which in turn was a consequence of its role from 1693 to 1803 as seat of the *Reichskammergericht*, the highest civil court of the Holy Roman Empire. These days it's a light industrial town, and is centred on a well-preserved Altstadt of half-timbered, grey-roofed houses precipitously clinging to the hillside above the Lahn.

THE SORROWS OF YOUNG WERTHER

While working at the *Reichskammergericht* as a legal clerk, **Goethe** fell in love with Lotte Buff, the fiancée of a close friend. His response to this awkward situation was to run away from it. However, when another friend there, Karl Wilhelm Jerusalem, committed suicide over an unrequited love affair, he was inspired to fuse the two episodes by writing an epistolary novella, *The Sorrows of Young Werther*. It was an immediate sensation; before his twenty-fifth birthday, Goethe had become the most celebrated literary figure in Europe, inspiring a Romantic reaction against the Age of Reason and creating a continent-wide phenomenon of young men wearing blue coats and yellow breeches, suffering from melancholy and contemplating suicide.

The Altstadt

Of the many steeply plunging squares in Wetzlar's Altstadt, the largest is Domplatz, named after the so-called **Dom**, a former collegiate church used for both Catholic and Protestant worship. It offers a fascinating insight into medieval building practices, as the Romanesque structure was demolished piece by piece to make way for a Gothic hall design. However, money ran out before completion, with the result that the old north tower and main entrance (the Heathens' Portal) still survive, the latter marooned behind its partly completed successor. The Gothic **south tower**, later capped with a Baroque belfry, is the symbol of the town and its most prominent landmark.

Just off the south side of Domplatz is the small Fischmarkt, on which stands the former **Rathaus**, later the seat of the *Reichskammergericht*, and now a café. Following Pfaffengasse uphill from Domplatz brings you to the **Hof des Deutschen Ritterordens** (Court of the Teutonic Knights). Within the courtyard is the **Lottehaus** (Tues–Sun 10am–1pm & 2–5pm; free), the house where Lotte Buff lived with her parents and siblings. A must for Goethe aficionados, it has been turned into a small museum containing period furniture, pictures and books – with lots of first editions and translations of *Werther*. Next door is the **Stadt- und Industriemuseum** (same hours; free), which details Wetzlar's history as a Free Imperial City and the development of its iron and optical industries. It was here that Oskar Barnack pioneered today's standard 35mm camera, and the town is home to Leitz, a leading camera manufacturer.

At the southeastern corner of the Altstadt, reached via the picturesque squares of Kornmarkt and Eisenmarkt, are three more small museums each well worth a visit. The pick of these is the **Sammlung Dr Irmgard von Lemmers-Danforth** (Tues–Sun 10am–1pm & 2–5pm; free) at Kornblumengasse 1, which has a really lovely collection of Renaissance and Baroque furniture and decorative art from all over Europe, displayed in a handsome town mansion. A few paces away, at Hofstatt 19, is the **Reichskammergerichtsmuseum** (same hours; free), detailing the history of the institution that brought Wetzlar its fame. Finally, just to the south at Schillerplatz 5 is the half-timbered **Jerusalemhaus** (Tues–Sun 2–5pm; free), which has been restored to give a period feel of the time when it was the home of the lovelorn youth who was the inspiration for Goethe's Werther.

Practicalities

Wetzlar's **Bahnhof** is about 1km north of the Altstadt and on the opposite side of the Lahn. The **tourist office** is at Domplatz 8 (Mon–Wed & Fri 8am–noon & 2–4.30pm, Thurs 8am–noon & 2–5pm, Sat 9.30–11.30am; ☎06441/99338).

Hotels with a central location include *Niedergirmes*, Kirchstr. 1 (☎06441/32158; ⑤); *Domblick*, Langgasse 64 (☎06441/90160; ⑤); *Wetzlarer Hof*, Obertorstr. 3 (☎06441/48021; ⑥); *Bürgerhof*, Konrad-Adenauer-Promenade 20 (☎06441/9030; ⑦); and *Mercure*, Bergstr. 41 (☎4170; ⑦). There are cheaper alternatives in the outlying villages and the tourist office can help with these. Wetzlar's **youth hostel** is in a lovely secluded setting southeast of the Altstadt at Richard-Schirmann-Str. 3 (☎06441/71068; ✿); take bus #12 to Sturzkopf. Within walking distance of town are two **campsites** – the first of these, *Niedergirmes*, is north of the Bahnhof (☎06441/34103), the other is at *Dutenhofener See* (☎0641/21245), about halfway to Giessen, near the Bahnhof Wetzlar-Ost.

The best **restaurants** are in the last three hotels listed above. Otherwise, try *Zur Domtreppe*, Domplatz 5, which has a secluded beer garden, or head north of the Altstadt to *Häusler's*, Garbenheimer Str. 18, the *Gaststätte* of the local *Euler* brewery.

Giessen

Before the war **GIESSEN** was as famous for its half-timbered houses as it was for its university, founded in the early seventeenth century. Unfortunately, it was severely battered by bombs, and the centre is now a bland postwar reconstruction. Giessen is also a US army garrison town and supply centre, but it's a lively place and, as a major rail junction, you may well find yourself passing through.

The town

The skyline of the Altstadt is dominated by the disembodied Gothic tower that is all that remains of the **Stadtkirche**. Directly opposite, at Georg-Schlosser-Str. 2, is one of the few timber-framed buildings to have survived, the fourteenth-century **Burgmannenhaus.** Together with the adjoining building, it now contains the **Oberhessisches Museum** (Tues–Sun 10am–4pm; free), featuring the extensive archeology collections of the university, together with displays of regional history and folklore.

The other main concentration of historic sights is just to the east around Brandplatz. Here the **Neues Schloss**, a picturesque late Gothic half-timbered palace, is dwarfed by the adjacent **Zeughaus**, a Renaissance arsenal which houses part of the University. Opposite is the heavily restored fourteenth-century **Altes Schloss** (Tues–Sun 10am–4pm; free), now home to the art collection of the Oberhessisches Museum. Behind it is the **Botanischer Garten** (Mon–Fri 8am–3.30/8pm, Sat & Sun 8am–4/6pm; free), the oldest such institution in Germany, founded in 1609 for the purposes of scientific research. It's also a much-loved recreation spot, an oasis of calm in the heart of the city.

Just to the southwest of the Altstadt, at Liebigstr. 12, is the **Liebig-Museum** (Tues–Sun 10am–4pm; DM3). Originally a guard house, it was specially converted to serve as the teaching and research laboratory of the hugely influential nineteenth-century scientist Justus von Liebig (after whom the university is named) and is still preserved almost exactly as he knew it. Here Liebig pioneered a systematic approach to the study of chemistry, attracting students from all over Europe.

Some 6km southeast of the town centre is the **Schiffenbergkloster**, a walled monastery which began life as an Augustinian collegiate foundation, before being taken over by the Teutonic Knights. The rough-hewn Romanesque church is substantially intact, though it's open on the cloister side, which is now a huge beer garden. It's a favourite excursion goal at the weekends: all kinds of live music are performed on both days, while students conduct "secret" fencing matches at the crack of dawn on Sunday. Bus #6 runs out regularly from Berliner Platz, just beyond the southern edge of the Altstadt, on Sundays only.

Practicalities

Giessen's **Hauptbahnhof**, a grandly self-confident product of the golden era of the railways, is a short walk southwest of the town centre. The **tourist office** (Mon–Wed & Fri 9am–1pm & 2–5pm, Thurs 9am–1pm & 2–8pm, Sat 9am–noon; ☎0641/306 2489) is at Berliner Platz 2.

Budget **hotels** include *Möbus*, Marburger Str. 146 (☎0641/51337; ②) and *Gasthaus zum Strümpfchen*, Wetzlarer Str. 42 (☎0641/21124; ②). For something more upmarket (and central) try *An der Lahn*, Lahnstr. 21 (☎0641/73516; ⑤); *Am Ludwigsplatz*, Ludwigsplatz 8 (☎0641/33082; ⑦); or *Steinsgarten*, Hein-Heckroth-Str. 20 (☎0641/38990; ⑧). The **youth hostel** is at the western side of town at Richard-Schirmann-Weg 53 (☎0641/65879; ❷); take bus #4 or #7.

If you happen to find yourself in Giessen at night, head for Ludwigstrasse, which is known as *Kneipenstrasse* by the locals because it's full of **pubs**. Also worth checking out for occasional live music is *Ulenspiegel*, Seltersweg 53–55. The best **restaurants** are that in *Hotel Steinsgarten* and the *Schlosskeller* in the cellars of the Altes Schloss, Brandplatz 2. A varied **cultural** programme, including opera, ballet, musicals, concerts and drama, is performed at the Jugendstil *Stadttheater* on Berliner Platz (☎0641/795760).

Marburg

The cradle of Hesse and its original capital, **MARBURG** clusters up the slopes of the Lahn valley some 30km upstream from Giessen in a maze of narrow streets and medieval buildings. There are distinctive lower and upper towns, dominated respectively by two of Germany's greatest buildings, the Elisabethkirche and the Schloss. However, the whole ensemble is in many ways the most remarkable feature, as the town has been touched by war less than almost any other city in the country.

Marburg was one of the major pilgrimage centres of northern Europe on account of its patron **St Elisabeth** – a thirteenth-century princess of Thuringia who had devoted herself to the poor – until the cult was abolished by her descendant, **Landgrave Philipp the Magnanimous**, at the time of the Reformation. In 1527 he established the university, the first in the world to be subject to the new Protestant faith. Nowadays, nearly a quarter of the population is in some way associated with the university, and the presence of 15,000 students gives it a relaxed and lively atmosphere. Marburg has good rail and road links with Frankfurt, Kassel and Koblenz, and is one place in Hesse worth going far out of your way to visit.

The **telephone code** for Marburg is ☎06421

The lower town

Although much of it is now taken up with functional modern buildings of the university, the kernel of the lower town (*Unterstadt*) survives from the thirteenth century. It
was then the property of the **Order of Teutonic Knights** (see p.330). Given their bel-
licosity, it's all the more ironic that they showed such dedication to Saint Elisabeth,
whose life could hardly have presented a greater contrast.

The Elisabethkirche

No sooner had Elisabeth gained papal recognition as a saint in 1235, than the Teutonic
Knights began the construction of the **Elisabethkirche** (April–Sept Mon–Sat
9am–6pm, Sun 12.30–6pm; Oct Mon–Sat 9am–5pm, Sun 12.30–5pm; Nov–March
Mon–Sat 10am–4pm, Sun 12.30–4pm; DM3) on the site of her hospice, encasing her
tomb in the process. The first purely Gothic building on German soil, it's also one of
the most original and most beautiful, with the hall church format (which necessitated
heavy wall buttresses), and the trefoil or "clover leaf" plan for the east end adapted to
the new style of architecture for the first time. The twin **towers**, with their relentless
upward movement and tall pointed steeples, are also very Germanic and noticeably different from their more varied and elaborate French counterparts.

Inside, the church is full of statues and frescoes, mainly celebrating Elisabeth's piety.
Curiously enough, her cult underwent a major revival just before the Reformation, and
five magnificent winged **altars** were created by the local master carver Ludwig Juppe
and the painter Johann von der Leyten. On the right as you enter is one of these, the
Elisabeth-Altar, which vividly relates the saint's life. In an alcove to the other side is the
tomb of **Paul von Hindenburg**, the *Reichspresident* who appointed Hitler Chancellor
in 1933. His body was brought to this decidedly unsuitable location after the war by the
Americans. At the opposite end of this aisle, a curvaceous **statue of Elisabeth** from
about 1470 depicts her in a pose she would have despised – as a richly robed, crowned
princess clutching a model of her church.

Just around the corner is the *Elisabeth-Chor*, as the northern part of the clover leaf
plan is known. Its centrepiece is the towering **mausoleum** containing her coffin in its
original location. Look out for the reliefs on the pedestal, which show her being
mourned by beggars and cripples instead of the kings and bishops who normally occupied such a position. Among the **altars**, pride of place goes to that dedicated to the
Virgin, in which Juppe skilfully incorporated a much-venerated older sculpture of *The
Pietà* into the predella. A number of **murals** illustrating the saint's life, long covered up
and only rediscovered this century, can also be seen.

The main choir or *Hochchor* still preserves its original thirteenth-century adornments – a
curious high altar shaped like the narthex of a church, a complete set of stalls and stained-
glass windows. Some of the windows have been mutilated, although an engagingly stylized
series illustrating the Crucifixion remain. On the north side, the former sacristy now
contains the church's most spectacular treasure, the resplendent mid-thirteenth-century
golden shrine which contained the relics of Elisabeth until Philipp the Magnanimous had
them re-interred. Elisabeth's life is illustrated yet again on the reliefs on the lid..

Finally, the *Landgrafen-Chor*, the southern arm of the trefoil plan, serves as the **pantheon**
of the rulers of Hesse. The first tomb in the eastern row is to Elisabeth's brother-in-law
Conrad, while the fourth, artistically the finest of the group, commemorates Heinrich I, the
first Landgrave of Hesse. The only alabaster intruder among the stone tombs is Philipp the
Magnanimous' father Wilhelm II, who is gruesomely depicted as a decaying corpse.

The rest of the quarter

Grouped around the Elisabethkirche are several other buildings formerly belonging to
the Teutonic Knights. Forming a sort of close around the church's east end are the thir-

teenth-century **Brüderhaus** and **Herrenhaus**, the fifteenth-century **Deutsch-Orden-Haus** and the sixteenth-century **Kornspeicher**. All are now used by the University: the Kornspeicher, formerly a corn store and bakehouse, now houses the **Mineralogisches Museum** (Wed 10am–1pm & 3–6pm, Thurs & Fri 10am–1pm, Sat & Sun 11am–3pm; free), which is more interesting than it sounds, with a glittering array of precious stones. Up a little hill to the west of the Elisabethkirche is the **Michaelskapelle**, a funerary chapel for the Knights and pilgrims to the shrine. Saint Elisabeth herself was buried in its peaceful little cemetery once the ban on her cult had been imposed.

Following Deutschhausstrasse southeastwards, then turning right into Biegenstrasse, at no. 11 you'll find the **Universitätsmuseum für bildende Kunst** (Tues–Sun 11am–1pm & 2–5pm; free), which has a Lucas Cranach the Elder portrait of Luther, a Klee, a Kandinsky and a Picasso, and works by German artists, notably the local painter Karl Bantzer.

The upper town

Other than its one supreme monument, the most remarkable feature of the upper town (*Oberstadt*) is its atmospheric appearance, with plunging streets, steep stairways, narrow alleys, secluded corners and surprising vistas. The most enticing way up is to follow the **Steinweg**, an old stepped street hemmed in by half-timbered buildings, from the Elisabethkirche.

Marktplatz

Heart of the Altstadt is the **Marktplatz**, with its St-Georg-Brunnen and an appealing line-up of golden half-timbered houses. During term-time the square is the focal point of Marburg's nightlife, but out of term it's very peaceful, except for the twice-weekly markets. Here you might see older women in the traditional costumes still sometimes worn in the area, a hangover from the days when Protestant and Catholic had to be able to tell each other apart – the Protestants wore black, dark brown, blue or green, while the Catholics wore bright colours with plaited hair. The **Rathaus** is a sixteenth-century Gothic building with a gabled Renaissance staircase tower featuring another statue of Elisabeth by Ludwig Juppe, holding the arms of the Landgraves of Hesse. The heraldic symbol is supposed to be a lion, but the sculptor mischievously made it look like a monkey.

South of Marktplatz

South of the Markt is the **Kiliankirche**, Marburg's oldest church, but one which has been secularized since the sixteenth century. In the Nazi period it was appropriated for use as the local SS headquarters, and was also the final place to which Marburg's Jews were taken before deportation. Nowadays, it's the head office of the German Green Cross. Further south is the **Alte Universität**, which took over a Gothic Dominican monastery, of which only the church (9am–6pm, closed Wed) now remains. The rest of the complex was rebuilt in a grandiose neo-Romanesque style, with the centrepiece being the **Aula**, a ceremonial hall adorned with frescoes depicting the history of the city.

The Marienkirche and the Kanzlei

Nicolaistrasse leads west from Marktplatz to the thirteenth-century **Marienkirche**, from whose terrace there's a good view out over Marburg and the Lahn. Just past here is a stairway called the Ludwig-Bickell-Treppe which provides the shortest route up to the top of the town. Alternatively, you can ascend the slower way to the northeast via the Renaissance **Kanzlei**, which now houses another University collection, the **Religionskundliche Sammlung** (Mon, Wed & Fri 10am–1pm; free), with material on the history of religions.

The Schloss

Towering above Marburg at a height of 102m above the Lahn is the **Schloss** (April–Oct Tues–Sun 10am–6pm; Nov–March Tues–Sun 11am–5pm; DM3). There was a castle on this site as far back as the twelfth century, but the present structure was begun by order of Sophie of Brabant, daughter of St Elisabeth, to serve as the seat of the Landgraves of the new state of Hesse. Marburg lost its role as capital to Kassel at the beginning of the fourteenth century, but before then a substantial portion of the present Schloss had been built. This included the south wing, at the end of which is the **Schlosskapelle**. Inside, the lurid rose-coloured interior is quite striking; some original murals and part of the mosaic pavement also survive.

From the same period is the **Saalbau** on the northern side. This is notable for illustrating that this Schloss was primarily a residential palace, as opposed to the then standard fortified castle. Although the magnificent great hall, the largest structure of its kind in Germany, is known as the **Rittersaal**, it actually had no military function, instead being a venue for feasts and receptions. The most famous of these was the **Marburg Colloquy** of 1529, when Philipp the Magnanimous failed to unite Protestantism.

The hall's two spectacular Renaissance inlaid-wood doorways are among the many additions and embellishments made to the Schloss during the fifteenth and sixteenth centuries, when Marburg periodically regained its position as capital of all or part of Hesse. At the eastern side of the complex, the **Wilhelmsbau**, linked to the main courtyard by a covered bridge, was the last significant part to be built. It now contains miscellaneous archeology, applied art and local history displays of the **Museum für Kulturgeschichte**. From the terrace outside there's a wonderful aerial **view** over the Elisabethkirche and the lower town.

Practicalities

Marburg's **Hauptbahnhof** is on the right bank of the Lahn at the northern end of town, just five minutes' walk from the Elisabethkirche. Immediately outside, at Neue Kasseler Str. 1, is the **tourist office** (Mon–Fri 9am–6pm, April–Sept also Sat 9.30am–1pm; ☎201262 or 201249).

Accommodation

There's a surprising lack of **hotels** with a convenient location and it might be a good idea to enquire at the tourist office about places in outlying villages if you're after a budget deal. The **youth hostel** is at Jahnstr. 1 (☎23461; 🖬), a little to the southeast of the Altstadt; the *Lahnaue* **campsite** (☎21331) is a bit further down the river at Trojedamm 47.

HOTELS AND GUESTHOUSES

Dammühle, Dammühlenstr. 1, Wehrshausen (☎93560, fax 36118).Well worth considering if you've got your own transport, this occupies an old half-timbered watermill, 5km west of the centre, and has a café-restaurant. ⑦

Einsle, Frankfurter Str. 2a (☎23410). Small guesthouse with large comfortable rooms, located south of the upper town. ④

Europäischer Hof, Elisabethstr. 12 (☎6960, fax 66404). Marburg's top hotel has been in existence since 1834. It has rooms of varying degrees of luxury and offers a good breakfast buffet. The restaurant, *Atelier*, has a predominantly Italianate menu. ⑦

Hesse-Stübche, Untergasse 10 (☎25887, fax 162947). Typically German hotel with pub-restaurant in the heart of the upper town. ⑥

Hostaria del Castello, Markt 19 (☎25884, fax 123225). Italian restaurant with a few rooms for rent. ⑥

Müller, Deutschhausstr. 29 (☎65659). Good-value guesthouse in the lower town, close to the Elisabethkirche. ④

Quellehaus, Bahnhofstr. 14 (☎65644, fax 65644). Medium-priced hotel by the Hauptbahnhof. ⑤

Schneider, Gladenbacher Weg 37 (☎34236, fax 34236). Good-value pension in the far southwestern part of town. ④

Tusculum, Gutenbergerstr. 25 (☎22778, fax 15304). Guesthouse located just south of the upper town, with brightly painted rooms. ⑤

Zur Sonne, Markt 14 (☎26036, fax 161348). This pretty half-timbered building, a *Gasthaus* since the sixteenth century, is the most atmospheric of the expensive options. It also has a superb restaurant. ⑦

Eating and drinking

There's no shortage of places for eating and drinking in this student-dominated town. The best bars are among the half-timbered buildings on Hirschberg, the street leading off from the Markt, and on Untergasse.

Café Barfuss, Barfüsserstr. 33. Café-bar with an excellent selection of tacos and pasta.

Café Vetter, Reitgasse 4. One of the most trendy café-bars, with its own panorama terrace.

Hinkelstein, Markt 18. Cellar tavern with occasional live music, popular with students.

Kalimera, Lingelgasse 13a. The best vegetarian restaurant in town.

Milano, Biegenstr. 19. Highly regarded upmarket Italian restaurant.

Piscator, Stadthalle, Biegenstr. 15. A good traditional German restaurant and a worthy rival to *Zur Sonne* (see above).

Quodlibet, Am Grün 37. Good bar with billiard tables.

Roter Stern, Am Grün 28. Housed in a bookshop, this is where Marburg's coolest crowd hang out. Well known for its superb Nicaraguan coffee.

Rustica, Untergasse 18. A good cheap pizzeria which also does Italian-style breakfasts.

Weinlädele, Schlosstreppe 1. A cosy wine bar in a half-timbered building. Evenings only.

Entertainment

It's always worth checking up on **events** held on the Schlosspark's open-air stage. Otherwise, the principal highbrow **drama** and **concert** venue is the *Stadthalle*, Biegenstr. 15 (☎25608); *KFZ*, Schulstr. 6 (☎13898) is an alternative cultural centre featuring all kinds of live music, theatre and cabaret. The only **disco** as such is *Kult-Lager*, in the south of town at Terminstr. 9. Marburg's main **festival** is the bucolic *Marktfrüschoppen* on the first Sunday in July, while the *Elisabethmarkt* in mid-October is another good time to visit. **Boats** can be rented from *Bootsverleih*, Auf dem Wehr (☎26864).

The Vogelsberg

The **Vogelsberg** is a quiet region of gently rolling hills, forests and small villages which has long been known to the weekend trippers of Hesse but remains relatively undiscovered by outsiders. A massive extinct volcano about 50km in diameter, the Vogelsberg rises to a maximum altitude of 774m at the **Taufstein** – not a dramatic landscape, but a good place for a bit of rustic recuperation. The heart of the range, the area known as the **High Vogelsberg** (*Hoher Vogelsberg*), has been designated a *Naturpark*. There are rail lines along the western and northern fringes of the range. Elsewhere bus connections run regularly between the small towns and villages on weekdays, but tend to dry up by midday on Saturdays.

Büdingen

BÜDINGEN lies at the southwestern edge of the Vogelsberg, on the rail line linking Giessen with Gelnhausen. Like the latter, which is little more than a ten-minute journey away, it dates back to the time of the Hohenstaufen emperors, and is chiefly worth visiting for its medieval survivals, though it's also a popular health resort. The Altstadt shelters behind a completely intact **Stadtmauer**, which is pierced with decorated Gothic gateways. There's also a **Schloss** (guided tours mid-March to mid-Dec Tues–Sun at 11.30am, 2pm, 3pm & 4pm; DM6.50), which still serves as the seat of the Prince of Yburg-Büdingen. This is in two parts, with a Gothic *Vorburg* protecting the main *Kernburg*, a truly remarkable structure with thirteen sides. It was continuously rebuilt down the ages, so the component parts run the full gamut of architectural styles from the twelfth to seventeenth centuries. The late Gothic **Schlosskapelle**, with its elaborate network vaulting and richly carved stalls, is particularly outstanding.

Büdingen's **tourist office** is at Marktplatz 7 (☎06042/96370). There are several **hotels**, including *Stadt Büdingen*, Jahnstr. 16 (☎06042/96290; ⑥); and *Haus Sonnenberg*, Sudetenstr. 4–6 (☎06042/3051; ⑥). Additionally, there's a **youth hostel**, but it's on top of a hill 3km from the town centre at Auf dem Berge (☎06042/3697; ✿).

Schotten

Some of the buses from Giessen continue southeast for a further 10km to **SCHOTTEN**, which lies in the middle of the High Vogelsberg. It's a quiet little town, notwithstanding the fact that its *Schottenring* is the oldest motor-racing track in Germany. The Gothic **Liebfrauenkirche** is unexpectedly grand for such a rural community; it boasts a delicately carved entrance portal of the Adoration of the Magi and a magnificent late fourteenth-century painted altar depicting both the Passion and the Life of the Virgin. Schotten makes the obvious starting point for exploring the Taufstein's wooded slopes or the nearby **Nidda-Stausee**, a watersports and angling centre with **camping** facilities. There are several **hotels**: *Sanssoucci*, Parkstr. 2 (☎ 06044/2254; ②); *Adler*, Vogelsbergstr. 160 (☎06044/1017; ④); *Haus Sonnenberg*, Laubacher Str. 25 (☎06044/96210; ⑤); and *Parkhotel*, Parkstr. 9 (☎06044/9700; ⑥). The **tourist office** is at Vogelbergstr. 184 (☎06044/6651).

Alsfeld

The 30km route from Schotten to **ALSFELD** at the northern fringe of the Vogelsberg takes you through the core of the *Naturpark*, along a stretch of the German Holiday Road (*Deutsche Ferienstrasse*), and under the shadow of the Taufstein. Alsfeld itself, which also lies on the looping rail line between Giessen and Fulda, is the undoubted star of the region, and is so postcard-pretty that it once won a designation as a model town in a European-wide competition.

Its buildings conform in the main to the half-timbered blueprint of the area, and many of them are so old that they seem ready to pitch forward into the cobbled streets. The slightly spooky-looking late Gothic **Rathaus**, one of the finest in the country, stands on the northern side of the Marktplatz, focal point of the Altstadt. Its arcaded lower storey formerly served as a covered market. On the eastern side of the square is the Renaissance **Hochzeitshaus**, a rare stone building originally constructed for the celebration of weddings and festivals. Just off the southwest corner of Marktplatz, at Rittergasse 3–5, two showy Baroque mansions have been combined to house the **Regionalmuseum** (Mon–Fri 9am–5pm, Sat 9am–noon & 2–4pm, Sun 10am–noon & 2–4.30pm; DM2), with the usual displays on local archeology, history, trades, costumes and folklore. To the rear of the Rathaus is the **Walpurgiskirche**, a grey, geometrical church dating from the thirteenth century, but partly rebuilt in late Gothic style. Its Renaissance galleries are adorned with paintings illustrating Protestant doctrines, though plenty of pre-Reformation furnishings survive, notably the Romanesque font and the Gothic frescoes and high altar.

Practicalities

Alsfeld's **Bahnhof** lies a few minutes' walk to the west of the Altstadt. The **tourist office** is at Obergasse 6 (Mon–Fri 9am–6pm, Sat 10am–1pm; ☎06631/182165).

There are four **hotels**, all capacious, centrally located and offering high standards in relation to the prices charged: *Krone*, Schellengasse 2–4 (☎06631/4041; ⑤); *Zur Erholung*, Grünberger Str. 26 (☎06631/2023; ⑤); *Zum Schwalbennest*, Pfarrwiesenweg 12–14 (☎06631/5061; ⑤); and *Klingelhöffer*, Hersfelder Str. 47 (☎06631/2073; ⑤). Each of these has a recommendable **restaurant**: otherwise the most appealing places to eat are a trio of old wine bars – *Marktkeller*, which is in the Hochzeitshaus, Marktplatz 7; *Ramsbeck's Weinkeller*, Marktplatz 9; and *Zum Brünnchen*, Untergasse 10.

The main **festivals** are *Pfingstenfest* over the long Whit weekend and the *Stadt- und Heimatfest* on the first Saturday in August.

Schlitz

SCHLITZ, which boasts a well-preserved and strongly fortified Altstadt, is 10km north-east of Lauterbach and 15km northeast of Fulda, and can be reached from either by bus. The **Stadtmauer** is pierced by just two small gateways, yet ringed by no fewer than four castles of varying dates. At the highest part of town is the oldest and largest of these, the **Vorderburg**, which now houses the **Heimatmuseum** (April–Oct Tues–Sun 2–4pm; Nov–March Sat & Sun 2–4pm; DM2), with displays of weapons, costumes and handicrafts. The thirteenth-century keep of the **Hinterburg** (daily April–Oct 9am–noon & 2–5/7pm; DM2) can be ascended by lift for a fine panorama over the region. Neither of the other castles – the half-timbered **Schachtenburg** alongside the Hinterburg and the **Ottoburg**, a Baroque residential palace – had any defensive function. Within the Stadtmauer are many fine half-timbered houses, but the dominant monument is the **Stadtkirche**. Apart from the fifteenth-century steeple, the church is largely thirteenth-century in date, though some masonry survives from the original ninth-century basilica.

The **tourist office** is in the Rathaus, An der Kirche 4 (☎06642/80560). Two of the budget **hotels**, *Braustübchen*, Brauhausstr. 18 (☎06642/1018; ③) and *Gasthof Zum Auerhahn*, Untergasse 1 (☎06642/5031; ④) are named after the nearby *Auerhahn-Bräu*, which makes light and dark beers in its half-timbered nineteenth-century premises. Other hotels include *Guntrum*, Otto-Zinsser-Str. 5 (☎06642/5093; ④) and *Vorderburg*, An der Vorderburg 1 (☎06642/5041; ⑤). The main **festival** is the colourful *Schlitzerländer Heimat- und Trachtenfest*, held every other year on the second weekend of July.

Fulda

Lying in a narrow valley between the Vogelsberg and the Rhön, **FULDA** was best known throughout the Cold War as the weak point in NATO's front line (the so-called "Fulda Gap") through which the massed tanks of the Warsaw Pact were supposedly most likely to pour into Western Europe. With that dubious threat now gone, the city can concentrate once more on its role as a major episcopal centre, the venue for the annual meetings of both the Catholic Bishops' Conference and the German Protestant Convention. Church

The **telephone code** for Fulda is ☎0661

affairs have dominated Fulda's history. Its roots go back to the eighth century when a small town grew up around the abbey founded by Saint Boniface, a monk sent from England to convert the Germans. After his martyrdom in 754, Fulda became a pilgrimage site, and over the years its abbey grew into one of the most important monasteries in Germany. It was here that a couple of monks transcribed the *Lay of Hildebrand*, one of the first recorded pieces of German literature. For centuries, the abbots doubled as secular princes, and on their promotion to the rank of bishops they transformed their seat into a Baroque vision of golden towers and crosses.

The city

The city centre, dotted with open squares and areas of greenery, is still predominantly Baroque. There are very few older buildings and not too many modern eyesores either. Outside the centre are several other attractions well worth the detour including the heights of the Petersberg and the magnificent Schloss Fasanerie.

The episcopal quarter

Fulda's imposing **Dom**, on the western edge of the town centre, is a classic early Baroque structure by Johann Dientzenhofer, the most accomplished member of a dynasty of architects, and is totally unlike any other German cathedral. The glory of the spacious and stuccoed interior is the high altar, depicting the Assumption of the Madonna in full-blown gilded splendour and flanked by six marble columns. Behind is a small and austere chapel where the monks used to assemble for prayer. St Boniface's tomb is in the slightly oppressive crypt beneath the high altar – it's incorporated into a sepulchral black marble altar with carved reliefs depicting the saint's martyrdom and his resurrection on Judgment Day.

The **Dommuseum** (April–Oct Tues–Sat 10am–5.30pm, Sun 12.30–5.30pm; Nov, Dec, Feb & March Tues–Sat 10am–12.30pm & 1.30–4pm, Sun 12.30–4pm; DM4) occupies the Dechanei (deanery) adjoining the northern transept. It contains Boniface's relics, which include his sword, his head and the book with which he vainly tried to fend off his murderers.

Next to the Dom is the Romanesque **Michaelskirche** (daily April 1–Oct 15 10am–6pm; Oct 16–March 31 2–4pm; DM1), built in the shape of a Greek cross as a copy of the Church of the Holy Sepulchre in Jerusalem. It's among the very few significant buildings to have survived the wholesale conversion of Fulda to the Baroque. In comparison to the mighty Dom it's quite inconspicuous, but in some ways is more impressive than its larger neighbour, incorporating as it does the rotunda of an earlier church – although this has been much altered; two of its eight columns date back to 822. Inside, look out for the fourteenth-century **stone tablet** in the Baroque chapel built onto the northern transept: it illustrates the Passion in an unusual graphic code for the benefit of the illiterate of the time, with symbolic images such as lips to signify Judas' kiss.

Across from the Dom stands the former episcopal palace, the cream-coloured **Stadtschloss** (Mon–Thurs, Sat & Sun 10am–6pm, Fri 2–6pm; DM4). Again the work of Johann Dientzenhofer, it's a huge building with several wings which has housed the municipal offices ever since it was acquired by the city last century. The most imposing chambers are the small **Spiegelsaal** (Mirror Room) and the main **Daalbergsaal**, which is painted with a quirky representation of the Four Seasons, with winter in the guise of a harlequin. There are also extensive displays of locally produced porcelain.

It's well worth taking a stroll in the **Schlossgarten**, a geometrical ornamental park which leads to the **Orangerie**, the best-looking of Fulda's secular Baroque buildings, nowadays a café. Inside, look out for the *Sauerkrautbild*, a ceiling painting showing Greek deities eating sausages. The **Floravase** in front of the Orangerie, named after the floral goddess whose statue crowns it, is a masterpiece of the art of garden sculpture. Opposite the Schlossgarten are two more Baroque showpieces, the **Paulustor**, an ornamental gateway, and the **Hauptwache**, the former guard house.

Elsewhere in the centre

In the heart of the pedestrianized town centre, reached from the Hauptwache via Friedrichstrasse, is the **Stadtpfarrkirche**, which pretty much conforms to Fulda house style, and the **Altes Rathaus**, which breaks the mould by having a half-timbered facade. Just to the south is the Jesuit Alte Stadtschule, now housing the **Vonderau-Museum** (Tues–Sun 10am–6pm; DM4), a collection covering archeology, natural history, and the arts. Among the exhibits is the *Fuldamag*, a locally produced three-wheeled car which was once a familiar sight on the streets of Britain as well as Germany. A short distance to the west is the **Abtei St Maria**, a seventeeth-century convent built in an archaic Gothic style. It's still active, and indeed is a flourishing centre of contemporary religious art. Finally, on Heinrich-von-Bibra-Platz, the eastern continuation of Schloss Strasse, the **Hessische Landesbibliothek** (Mon–Thurs 10am–noon & 2–4pm, Fri 10am–noon; free) has a permanent exhibition featuring a Gutenberg Bible and some beautiful illuminated manuscripts.

Outside the centre

The **Petersberg**, a four-hundred-metre-high hill about 4km to the east of the centre and reached by bus #3, commands wonderful views of Fulda itself and across to the Vogelsberg and Rhön. The hill is crowned by the **Peterskirche** (daily 9.30–11.30am & 2.30–4.30pm), the most significant of the four monastic churches grouped round the town in the symbolic shape of a cross. Its **crypt**, the burial place of Saint Lioba, a kinswoman of Saint Boniface, survives from the first building on the spot, and has precious if rather ghostly ninth-century frescoes. The main part of the church was rebuilt in the fifteenth century but preserves six outstanding **Romanesque reliefs** on and around its triumphal arch. On the western bank of the River Fulda, much closer to town, is another of the monasteries, the **Andreaskirche**, which has some more or less intact tenth- or eleventh-century frescoes in the crypt; these are currently the subject of a painstaking restoration programme.

Further delights await at **Schloss Fasanerie** (guided tours April–Oct Tues–Sun 10am–noon & 1–5pm; DM8), about 6km southwest of the centre, and about fifteen minutes' walk beyond the Engelhelms terminus of bus #3. It was built at enormous expense in the eighteenth century as a hunting lodge and summer residence for the local Prince-bishops. However, its original Baroque character was modified after it came into the possession of the Electors of Hesse-Kassel, with several of the main reception rooms refurbished to suit their penchant for the Neoclassical style. A stud farm occupies the subsidiary buildings, while the landscaped **Schlosspark** features Chinese and Japanese pavilions.

Practicalities

Fulda's **Hauptbahnhof** is at the northeastern end of the town centre. You'll find the **tourist office** within the Stadtschloss at Schloss Str. 1 (Mon–Fri 8.30am–noon & 2–4.30pm, Sat 9.30am–noon; ☎102345). The main venue for **cultural** events is the *Schlosstheater*, Schloss Str. 5 (☎102326).

Accommodation

Fulda is quite well off for **hotels** in all price categories. There's a **youth hostel** at the southwestern edge of town at Schirmanstr. 31 (☎73389; ✿); the easiest way there is by bus #12 to Stadion.

HOTELS AND PENSIONS

Brauhaus Wiesenmühle, Wiesenmühlenstr. 13 (☎928680, fax 928 6839). Occupies a converted fourteenth-century mill. It has both an upmarket restaurant and a hugely popular bar and beer garden serving a range of inexpensive food. The *Hausbrauerei* brews a wide range of seasonally appropriate beers. ⑥

Goldener Karpfen, Simpliziusbrunnen 1 (☎70044, fax 73042). Now a member of the *Romantik* chain, and equipped with plenty of mod cons such as a sauna and solarium, this has long been Fulda's top hotel: Goethe was once a patron, writing much of the *Ost-West Divan* there. It has a distinguished wine bar-restaurant. ⑨

Hodes, Peterstor 14 (☎72862, fax 241179). Bargain-price pension at the edge of the Altstadt. ③

Wenzel, Heinrichstr. 38–40 (☎75335). Another very homely pension, conveniently close to the Hauptbahnhof. ③

Zum Kronhof, Am Kronhof 2 (☎74147, fax 74147). *Gasthof* just to the rear of the Dom, offering some of the cheapest rooms in town. ②

Zum Kurfürsten, Schloss Str. 2 (☎70001, fax 77919). Hotel and restaurant occupying an eighteenth-century palace opposite the Stadtschloss. It's very good value at the price asked. ⑤

Zum Ritter, Kanalstr. 18–20 (☎8165, fax 71431). Grand nineteenth-century hotel modernized a few years back to a very high standard. Its restaurant is quite reasonably priced. ⑦

Eating and drinking

Some of the best places to eat and drink are in the hotels (see above), but there's a wide variety of other options.

Café Thiele, Mittlestr. 2. Perhaps the pick of several good traditional cafés in the town centre.

Da Mario, Bonifatiusplatz 2. Moderately priced Italian restaurant in the Hauptwache, serving tasty pizzas made in a wood-fired oven.

Dachsbau, Pfandhausstr. 7–9. Upwardly mobile types gravitate here to sample what's arguably the most creative cooking in Fulda. The restaurant is fairly pricey, the bistro and wine bar on the opposite side of the street a little less so.

Felsenkeller, Leipziger Str. 12. *Gaststätte* of the *Hochstift* brewery, which is located alongside. It makes a fine dark beer, *Schwarzer Hahn*, as well as a *Pils*.

Krokodil, Karlstr. 31. Fairly upmarket café-bar, much favoured by the alternative set, which stays open until 1am.

Löhertor, Gerberstr. 9. A large complex which has several bars and restaurants plus a disco and cinema.

Schoppenkeller, Paulustor 6. *Weinkeller* with a very mixed clientele and quiet atmosphere.

Waidesgrund, Esperantostr. 10. Vegetarian and wholefood restaurant, situated just to the rear of the Hauptbahnhof.

Wirtshaus Zum Schwarzen Hahn, Friedrichstr. 18. A good choice for typical German cooking.

Zur Windmühle, Karlstr. 17. Popular traditional pub in a half-timbered building.

The Rhön and the Hessian Forest

East of Fulda stretches the **Rhön**, a volcanic region a little more wild and threatening than the Vogelsberg. It's split between Hesse, Bavaria and Thuringia, but Hesse has the highest and most attractive parts. These hills have become a big hang-gliding centre and there are plenty of good walking and cycling routes, best explored by using the small health resort of **Gersfeld** as a base. Immediately to the north of the Rhön is the **Hessian Forest** (*Waldhessen*), a low-lying rural area. This suffered throughout the Cold War era as a result of being a dead-end right up against the barbed wire frontier, but the principal town, the spa resort of **Bad Hersfeld**, successfully avoided any sense of blight.

Gersfeld

GERSFELD is the terminus of the *Rhönbahn*, a branch rail line from Fulda. In the Baroque **Pfarrkirche** in the town centre the altar, pulpit and organ are piled on top of one another in the approved Lutheran manner to great dramatic effect. The other dominant monument, situated in the nearby park, is the **Schloss**, which is likewise Baroque. Until recently it was a museum but, in a reversal of the normal process, it has been turned back into a private residence and can now only be viewed from outside.

The **Bahnhof** is a few minutes' walk south of the centre, while the **tourist office** is in the *Kurverwaltung* just off the Markt at Brückenstr. 1 (Mon–Fri 9am–12.30pm & 1.30–5.30pm, Sat 10am–noon; ☎06654/1780). There's a **youth hostel** at Jahnstr. 6 (☎06654/340; **2**), but most of the other accommodation in town costs little more: it includes **pensions** such as *Rhönlerche*, Hochstr. 34 (☎06654/348; ②) and *Simon*, Am Kreuzgarten 12 (☎06654/523; ②), as well as the **hotels** *Krone Post*, Marktplatz 30 (☎06654/622; ③) and *Zur Sonne*, Amelungstr. 1 (☎06654/96270; ④).

Within the municipality of Gersfeld is the **Wasserkuppe** (950m), the highest peak in the Rhön. It can be reached by road, or by the 7km-long footpath running almost due north from Fliegerstrasse. On the summit, which commands extensive views, are two **hotels**: *Deutscher Flieger* (☎06654/381 or 7007; ②) and *Peterchens Mondfahrt* (same phone; ⑤). The latter has a fine restaurant, and bedrooms decorated in the styles of different countries.

Bad Hersfeld

BAD HERSFELD, which is situated some 45km north of Fulda and easily reached by train, acted decisively to counter the threat of isolation posed by the proximity of the GDR border. In 1951 it inaugurated an annual **drama festival**, the *Bad Hersfelder Festspiele*, which quickly established itself as one of the leading permanent fixtures in the German cultural calendar and remains so to this day. Lasting from mid-June to early August, it normally features five different plays, taking in both classical theatre (this is Germany's most celebrated Shakespeare stage) and modern works (typically one serious drama and one musical). A series of **concerts** of classical music runs concurrently with the drama festival, which is succeeded by a short **opera** season filling out the month of August.

All performances take place against the stirring backdrop of the **Stiftsruine** (March–Oct Tues–Sun 10am–noon & 2–5pm; DM2), the remains of a Romanesque monastery which is the largest surviving example of its period anywhere in Europe. Although destroyed by French soldiers in 1761, its awesome proportions are still evident, and it retains impressive fragments, in particular the single-towered facade. The **Katharinenturm**, a detached belfry at the northeastern corner of the complex, houses the oldest bell in Germany, the nine-hundred-year-old *Lullusglocke*, named in honour of Archbishop Lullus of Mainz, who founded Hersfeld in 736. During the festival, the Stiftsruine can normally only be visited in conjunction with a performance; admission is also curtailed both beforehand and afterwards, to allow for the installation and dismantling of all the attendant apparatus. Only in spring and autumn is it possible to see the monument to full advantage, or to climb the west tower for a view over the town.

To the northeast of the Stiftsruine is the Altstadt, which presents the familiar half-timbered spectacle. There's a particularly fine group of houses on Kirchplatz, clustered around the Gothic **Stadtkirche**, whose tall tower dominates the skyline. A few paces away is the **Rathaus**, with an exterior in the cheery Weser Renaissance style. The peaceful **Kurpark** is on the opposite side of the Stiftsruine.

Practicalities

Bad Hersfeld's **Bahnhof** lies just outside the northeastern confines of the Altstadt, about fifteen minutes' walk from the Stiftsruine. The **tourist office** is at Am Markt 1 (Mon–Fri 9am–12.30pm & 3–6pm; May–Sept also Sat 10.30am–12.30pm; ☎06621/201274 or 3782). A pavilion in the middle of the same square houses the drama festival's **box office** (☎06621/72066), which should be contacted as far in advance as possible for tickets. Its counterpart for concerts and opera is at Nachtigallenstr. 7 (☎06621/64355 or 506730). Another big annual event, the *St-Lullus-Fest*, which claims to be the longest-established **popular festival** in the country, takes place in the week which includes October 16.

The **youth hostel** is towards the northern fringes of town at Wehneberger Str. 29 (☎06621/2403; ☎). **Private rooms** (②–④) can be booked via the tourist office, which has a separate phone number (☎06621/19433) for this service. The main concentration of **hotels** is just south of the Stiftsruine and west of the Kurpark. In this area, the lowest rates are at *Hakehaus*, Gerwigstr. 4 (☎06621/74561; ④) and *Haus Tanneck*, Stresemannallee 4 (☎06621/50350; ④). Excellent mid-range alternatives in the same district include *Wenzel*, Nachtigallenstr. 3 (☎06621/92200; ⑤) and *Schönewolf*, Brückenmüllerstr. 5 (☎06621/92330; ⑥), while the top address in town is the historic *Zum Stern*, Linggplatz 11 (☎06621/1890; ⑦). Each of the last three hotels has a recommendable **restaurant**, with *Wenzel* offering the unexpected pleasure of Swedish fare. Also worth a visit, whether for Hessian specialities or vegetarian dishes, is the half-timbered *Marktschänke*, Am Markt 22.

NORTHERN HESSE

Northern Hesse is, relatively speaking, well off the beaten tourist track. The only city is **Kassel**, which has one of the dullest centres in Germany, yet also boasts wonderful parks and fabulous art treasures. To the north lies the Reinhardswald, with the Baroque Huguenot settlement of **Bad Karlshafen**, while to the south is the outstanding medieval town of **Fritzlar**. Much of the western part of the area, known as the Waldeck, was for centuries a principality completely independent of Hesse. Here are the elegant spa of **Bad Wildungen**, the planned courtly town of **Arolsen** and the **Edersee** reservoir of Dambusters fame, and, as a recent adjunct to the region, the half-timbered town of **Frankenberg**.

Kassel

Although nowadays chiefly famous for the *documenta*, the huge modern art exhibition held here once every five years, **KASSEL** is basically an industrial city. Its big armaments industry ensured four-fifths destruction of its centre during the war, and consequently most of the buildings there are functional products of the 1950s. Despite the unenticing appearance of most of the centre, the city is one of the greenest in Germany, primarily due to the enormous **Wilhelmshöhe**. It also preserves plenty of reminders of its period of glory, which began in the late seventeenth century with the arrival of Huguenots expelled from France, continued throughout the following century with the acquisition of all the trappings of a capital city, and culminated in the years 1806–13, when it was the royal seat of the Kingdom of Westphalia.

The **telephone code** for Kassel is ☎0561

Arrival and accommodation

Kassel has two main train stations. Express services tend to use **Bahnhof Wilhelmshöhe**, which is about 1km east of the Wilhelmshöhe park. The increasingly overshadowed **Hauptbahnhof**, 2.5km away at the northern edge of the city centre, is a dead end. To reverse its descent into seediness, it has recently been revamped as the *Kulturbahnhof*, with cinemas, bars and the *Caricatura* art gallery, while Jonathan Borofsky's *Man Walking to the Sky*, the most famous work from the 1992 *documenta*, has been re-erected in front of the main entrance. There are **tourist offices** in Bahnhof Wilhelmshöhe (Mon–Fri 9am–1pm & 2–6pm, Sat 9am–1pm; ☎34054) and in the city centre at Königsplatz 53 (Mon–Thurs 9.15am-6pm, Fri 9.15am–4.30pm; ☎707707). Among several competing **Mitfahrzentralen** are *Mitfahrzentrale des Westens*, Friedrich-Ebert-Str. 107 (☎773 3057), and *ADM Cityline*, Friedrichstr. 18 (☎19440).

Given the spread-out nature of the city, it's worth investing in the DM8 **public transport** ticket, which covers any 24-hour period, or the entire weekend. An alternative to this is the *Kassel Card*, which also gives admission to the museums; it costs DM12 for one day, DM19 for three days.

Accommodation

It's probably best to base yourself in Wilhelmshöhe, which has a wide variety of **hotels** – the budget end of the market is particularly well served here. There's another handy concentration on the southern half of Frankfurter Strasse (reached by tram #5 or #7), just beyond the far end of the Karlsaue park; those in the city centre itself are mostly geared towards expense-account travellers. Kassel's **youth hostel** is a fifteen-minute walk west of the Hauptbahnhof at Schenkendorfstr. 18 (☎776455; 🏠), and there are **camping** facilities at Giesenallee 7 (☎22433), on the banks of the Fulda just south of Karlsaue.

HOTELS AND GUESTHOUSES

Am Rathaus, Wilhelmsstr. 29 (☎978850, fax 978 8530). One of the more reasonably priced hotels in the city centre. ⑤

Deutscher Hof, Lutherstr. 3–5 (☎91800, fax 776666). Excellent rooms right in the centre of Kassel. ⑥

Elfbuchen, Habichtswald (☎62041, fax 62043). Country house hotel with café-restaurant in a peaceful woodland setting north of the Herkules. It has been run by the same family for well over a century. ⑧

Gude, Frankfurter Str. 299 (☎48050, fax 480 5101). By some way the classiest of the concentration of hotels on the street, with a highly regarded restaurant, *Pfeffermühle*. ⑦

Kö 78, Kölnische Str. 78 (☎71614, fax 17982). The most obviously attractive of the city centre hotels, a family-run concern in a late nineteenth-century building. ⑥

Kurparkhotel, Wilhelmshöher Allee 336, Wilhelmshöhe (☎31890, fax 318 9124). One of the city's best hotels, with a fine restaurant and a health centre complete with swimming pool, sauna and solarium. It's on the route of tram #1. ⑧

Lenz, Frankfurter Str. 176 (☎43373, fax 43373). Has some basic rooms which are among the cheapest in Kassel, along with some which are more luxurious. ④

Neu Holland, Hüttenbergstr. 6, Wilhelmshöhe (☎33229). Small guesthouse at the extreme western edge of Kassel, a short distance south of the Herkules; take bus #43. ⑤

Neue Drusel, Im Drusetal 42, Wilhelmshöhe (☎32056, fax 32057). Budget hotel at the edge of the Habichtswald, not far from a path leading up to the Herkules. ④

Palmenbad, Kurhausstr. 27, Wilhelmshöhe (☎32691, fax 32691). A good budget choice in the residential part of Wilhelmshöhe. Take tram #3 or bus #23. ④

Schlosshotel Wilhelmshöhe, Am Schlosspark 2 (☎30880, fax 308 8428). Luxurious modern hotel immediately north of the Schloss. The facilities include a high-class restaurant, a casino, a swimming pool, sauna and solarium. ⑨

Stock, Harleshäuser Str. 60 (☎64798). Located just beyond the northeastern fringe of the Wilhelmshöhe quarter; take bus #10 or #41. ④

Wilhelmshöhe

It was Landgrave Carl, the same ruler who invited the Huguenots to settle in Kassel, who began the laying-out of the **Wilhelmshöhe**, a huge upland forest park which is the largest urban example of its kind in Europe. Situated at the western edge of the city, and reached by tram #1, it remains its most enduring permanent attraction. Although originally intended as a formal garden in the Italian Baroque manner, it was modified by Carl's successors in line with the eighteenth-century preference for the English approach to landscaping, with a predominantly "natural" appearance mingled with an assortment of hidden follies.

The Schloss and the Gemäldegalerie Alte Meister

Curiously enough, the gargantuan **Schloss Wilhelmshöhe** was something of an after-thought, only begun in the 1780s. One of the finest Neoclassical buildings in Germany, it was designed and partly built by Simon-Louis du Ry, the last and most distinguished of a dynasty of local architects of Huguenot extraction. Its **Weissensteinflügel** is now designated the **Schlossmuseum** (guided tours Tues–Sun 10am–4/5pm; DM6), and is decked out with opulent furniture, glassware, porcelain and other *objets d'art*, many from the time when Napoleon's brother Jérôme held court here as king of the puppet state of Westphalia. On the ground floor of the central block of the Schloss is the **Antikensammlung** (Tues–Sun 10am–5pm; DM3, free Sat), a collection of Classical antiquities. Its prize possession is the *Kassel Apollo*, a Roman copy of an archetypal Classical Greek bronze.

THE GEMÄLDEGALERIE ALTE MEISTER

The rest of the building is normally occupied by the **Gemäldegalerie Alte Meister** (Old Masters Picture Gallery), which originated in the collection of Landgrave Carl's successor Wilhelm VIII, whose spell as Governor of Breda and Maastricht fuelled a passion for the painting of the Dutch Golden Age. He accumulated what remains one of the world's finest collections of this period, supplemented by seventeenth-century paintings from elsewhere in Europe. Because of structural repairs, it is probable that the gallery will be closed until 2000. In the interim, nearly all the most important Dutch and Flemish works are on view in the Neue Galerie, those of other schools in the Hessisches Landesmuseum.

There are eleven masterpieces by **Rembrandt**, most notably the profoundly touching *Jacob Blessing his Grandchildren*. This rarely depicted subject shows the patriarch choosing to bless Joseph's second son Ephraim first, on the grounds he was destined for greater things – namely, to be the ancestor of the Gentiles. Rembrandt accordingly showed Ephraim as a fair-haired Aryan-type, in contrast to the dark features of the first-born, Manasseh. From roughly the same period comes one of his greatest portraits, *Nicolaes Bruyningh*, vividly conveying the sitter's animated personality. Two paintings from a decade earlier are unique in Rembrandt's oeuvre. *Winter Landscape* is his only nature study executed in bright colours, while the intimate *Holy Family with the Curtain* presents the scene in the manner of a tiny theatre set. *Profile of Saskia* is a demonstration of the young artist's virtuosity, with his first wife, gorgeously decked out in velvet and jewellery, depicted as an icon of idealized womanhood.

Hals' *Man in a Slouch Hat* is a late work, clearly showing the influence of Rembrandt married to his own talent for caricature, which can be seen more plainly in the earlier *Merry Toper*. Other pieces from seventeenth-century Holland on show include paintings by Ter Brugghen and Jan Steen, and more than twenty works by **Philips Wouwerman**. In spite of Landgrave Wilhelm's strict Calvinism, which drew him to the Dutch School above all others, he assembled a magnificent group of Flemish paintings of the same period. There are some choice canvases by **Rubens**, notably *The Crowning* *of the Hero, The Madonna as a Refuge for Sinners*, the highly unflattering *Nicolas de Respaigne as a Pilgrim to Jerusalem*, and a beautiful nocturnal *Flight into Egypt*. **Van Dyck** is represented by portraits drawn from all phases of his career, while the examples of **Jordaens** show his taste for the exotic on a large scale.

The seventeenth-century Dutch and Flemish collection takes up most of the first and second floors, but the end cabinets are devoted to small-scale fifteenth- and sixteenth-century paintings, mostly from Germany. **Cranach's** early *Resurrection Triptych* is one of a number of highlights, others being **Dürer's** *Elsbeth Tucher*, **Baldung's** *Hercules and Antaeus*, and an impassioned *Crucifixion*, set in a Danube landscape, by **Altdorfer**. On the top floor a group of Italian Renaissance pictures is dominated by a magnificent full-length *Portrait of a Nobleman* by **Titian**. However, once again it was the seventeenth-century masters who most appealed to the Hessian taste, and there are some spectacular examples of Italian Baroque, finest of which is **Preti's** *Feast of Herod*. From Spain come outstanding pieces by **Murillo** and **Ribera**, while **Poussin's** *Cupid's Victory over Pan* represents French art of this same period. **Schönfeld's** *The Great Flood* is one of the finest of all seventeenth-century German paintings, while there are a couple of examples of the brilliant but short-lived **Johann Liss**: the enigmatic *Scene with Soldiers and Courtesans* and the effervescent *Game of Morra*, a work anticipatory of the Rococo style of a century later.

The rest of the park

Immediately to the north of the Schloss is the **Ballhaus** (April–Oct Tues–Sun 10am–5pm; DM3, free Sat), a neat little Neoclassical building which King Jérôme, Napoleon's brother, had built as a theatre in 1808 to plans by the young Leo von Klenze, who went on to design so much of Munich. Twenty years later it was turned into a ballroom with rich mock-Pompeian decoration and is nowadays used for temporary exhibitions. On the other side of the lake is the **Löwenburg** (Tues–Sun 10am–4/5pm; DM6), built in the late eighteenth century as a medieval-style ruin, complete with artifical portcullis and drawbridge.

The **Bergpark**, the original Baroque ornamental garden, features a 250-metre-long, 885-tiered cascade. It's overlooked by the famous **Herkules** (mid-March to mid-Nov Tues–Sun 10am–5pm; DM2), which might look like an eighteenth-century Michelin Man, but which commands a sweeping panoramic view, as well as being a source of great pride to the burghers of Kassel, who have made it the symbol of their town. The statue lounges on top of a bizarre pyramidal structure, which is in turn set into a purely decorative castle called the **Oktogon**. At 2.30pm on Wednesdays, Sundays and holidays in summer, the floodgates at the foot of Herkules are opened and water pours down the cascade and over a series of obstacles, culminating some 75 minutes later in a 52-metre-high jet of water spurting from the fountain in front of the Schloss.

Finally, at the park's eastern entrance, at Wilhelmshöher Allee 361, the Japanese-style **Kurhessen-Therme** (Mon, Tues, Thurs & Sun 9am–11pm, Wed, Fri & Sat 9am–midnight; DM19 for 90min or DM44 for the day) is an ultra-modern, open-plan spa complex complete with indoor and outdoor thermal pools, saunas, jacuzzis, cinema and restaurant.

The city centre

In the centre of Kassel, the few remaining historic monuments are rather marooned among the postwar buildings, but there are several **museums** well worth taking the trouble to see.

Museums on Brüder-Grimm-Platz and Schöne Aussicht

Starting from the west, the **Hessisches Landesmuseum** (Tues–Sun 10am–5pm; DM3, free Sat) on Brüder-Grimm-Platz contains several collections, the most important being

THE BROTHERS GRIMM

One of the great inseparable partnerships, **Jacob Grimm** (1785–1863) and **Wilhelm Grimm** (1786–1859) were of an impeccable Hessian background. Born in Hanau, they were brought up in Steinau and educated in Marburg, before moving to Kassel, where they spent the longest part of their careers, working principally as court librarians. It was at Kassel that they put together the collection of tales, which they first published in 1812 under the title *Kinder- und Hausmärchen*. This was primarily a work of scholarship; the stories were all of folk origin and were taken straight down from oral sources. The book went through many editions, culminating in the definitive version of 1857, which contained two hundred tales. In the process, the desire of Jacob (the more gifted scholar of the two) to preserve the original unadorned version of the stories underwent increasing modification at the hands of Wilhelm, who had superior literary talents and favoured a certain amount of stylization and embroidering of the folk idiom.

The collection made the brothers celebrities, and such characters as Cinderella, Rumpelstiltskin, Hansel and Gretel, Snow White and Little Red Riding Hood became familiar to children all over the world. Yet this popular success did not interfere with their dedication to serious scholarship, particularly in their later years as professors at Göttingen (where they were expelled for their liberal views) and Berlin. In 1854, they began to compile *Das Deutsche Wörterbuch* – the German equivalent of the Oxford English Dictionary – a task taken up by several subsequent generations of scholars and only finally completed in 1961.

of applied arts. This features the exotic treasures accumulated by the Counts of Katzenelnbogen, the *Kunstkammer* of the Landgraves of Hesse-Kassel, some notable Gothic sculptures and a fine array of sixteenth-century Venetian glass. The museum also has displays illustrating the pre- and early history of the province, and shows its extensive ethnological holdings in a series of changing exhibitions. It also incorporates the **Deutsches Tapetenmuseum** (German Wallpaper Museum), which is far better than it sounds, adopting a generous interpretation of the word to cover all kinds of hangings, with exhibits from all eras and continents.

Only a couple of minutes' walk to the southeast, the **Neue Galerie** (same hours; DM3, free Sat) at Schöne Aussicht 1 takes up the history of art where the Schloss Wilhelmshöhe collection leaves off. It contains a large number of works by the Tischbeins – in particular Johann Heinrich the Elder, the Kassel-based member of the dynasty – and by the members of the Willingshausen artists' colony, the first such in Germany. There's also a room devoted to the omnipresent Joseph Beuys.

Next door, in Schloss Bellevue, the **Brüder-Grimm-Museum** (daily 10am–5pm; DM3) tells all about the famous fairy tale tellers and philologists (see box); the highlight is their own annotated manuscript version of the *Fairy Tales* – and is a must if you have any interest in their work.

Friedrichsplatz and around

Along Frankfurter Strasse is the vast open space of Friedrichsplatz, on which stands the oldest purpose-built museum building in Europe, the **Museum Fredericianum**, built by Simon-Louis du Ry before he began work on Schloss Wilhelmshöhe. Nowadays, it's used for temporary exhibitions, and is also the headquarters of the *documenta*, a retrospective of contemporary art inaugurated in 1955 which has become a multi-media event embracing everything from painting to video art. In effect, the whole city has become its venue, and many of the spectacular sculptures you see dotted throughout Kassel are leftovers from *documenta* events of previous years. The next will be held from June to September 2002.

Across from the museum, at Steinweg 2, is the **Ottoneum**, constructed in the first decade of the seventeenth century as the first permanent theatre in Germany. Today it is home to the **Naturkundemuseum** (Tues–Fri 10am–4.30pm, Sat & Sun 10am–1pm, free), itself one of the oldest natural history collections in Europe. Among its curiosities are the sixteenth-century *Ratzenberger Herbarium* and the eighteenth-century *Schildbach'sche Holzbibliothek*, whose boxes are made from the wood of different trees and contain a leaf, fruit and flower from each. If you follow Oberste Gasse or Mittelgasse north from here, you come to the **Martinskirche**. Like all the churches in the city centre, this was devastated during the war, and it has been rebuilt in a compromise style which makes no attempt to restore it to its original form. However, it's worth a quick visit to take a look at the huge Renaissance memorial to Landgrave Philipp the Magnanimous, champion of Luther and founder of Marburg University.

Along the River Fulda

The southeastern edge of the city centre, by the banks of the River Fulda, is taken up by another large Baroque park, the **Karlsaue**. In it stands the **Orangerie**, a long, orange-coloured Baroque palace, which now houses the **Museum für Astronomie und Technikgeschichte** (Tues–Sun 10am–5pm; DM3, free Sat). This contains a valuable collection of historic scientific instruments, notably those used in the then revolutionary observatory set up in the former Schloss in 1560 by Landgrave Wilhelm IV. There's also a **Planetarium** (introductory shows Tues, Thurs & Sat at 2pm, Wed & Fri at 3pm; DM6 including museum; full programmes Thurs at 8pm, Sun at 3pm; DM6). Alongside is the **Marmorbad**, an ornate bathing hall adorned with mythological statues and reliefs. Further south, the **Blumeninsel Siebenbergen** (daily April–Oct 10am–7pm; DM1) is a lovely island strewn with flowers, trees, and exotic plants and shrubs.

Eating, drinking and entertainment

As with everything else in Kassel, the best places to eat and drink are scattered throughout the city. See also the hotels section above for some of the leading restaurants.

Restaurants

Boccaccio, Querallee 36. Though prices are low and the decor may not amount to much, this serves some of the best Italian food in the city.

Calvados, Im Drusetal 12. Located just south of the Herkules, this offers both local specialities and international cuisine, with fish dishes prominent.

El Meson, Oberste Gasse 2–8. Spanish restaurant with good food and wines located in one of Kassel's oldest buildings, the thirteenth-century Elisabeth-Hospital.

Holomed, Kurfürstenstr. 10. The main vegetarian and wholefood specialist, located just opposite the Hauptbahnhof. Open Mon-Fri 11am–6pm.

La Frasca, Jordanstr. 11. The best restaurant in central Kassel, serving Gallic and Italianate dishes. Very expensive; reservations advisable (☎14494).

Odysseus, Mergellstr. 33. Greek restaurant in a half-timbered house with summertime courtyard.

Park Schönfeld, Bosestr. 13. Classy restaurant in an eighteenth-century Schloss near the Botanischer Garten in the south of the city. Take tram #5 or #7 or bus #27.

Bars and café-bars

Barranquilla, Friedrich-Ebert-Str. 14. Latin-American dance bar which gets very crowded on Fri and Sat, yet is quiet at other times.

FEZ, Karthäuserstr. 17. A favourite meeting place with the younger crowd.

Gleis 1, Im Hauptbahnhof. Popular bar within the revamped *Kulturbahnhof*.

Irish Pub, Bürgermeister-Brunner-Str. 1. Features live music each evening, often with visiting foreign musicians.

Lohmann, Königstor 8. A long-standing Kassel institution; the bar itself is very small, but it has a summertime beer garden.

Mr Jones, Goethestr. 31. Currently Kassel's hippest spot, a place for those who want to be seen. It serves good food, including late breakfasts and full meals.

Schalander Bräu, Mauerstr. 21. *Hausbrauerei* with a roof garden which also serves basic meals.

Festivals and entertainment

There are several worthwhile **festivals** in addition to the *documenta*. The *Zissel* in early August is a folklore event centred on the River Fulda, with processions, jousting and live music. On the first Saturday of September, the *Lichtfest* sees Wilhelmshöhe lit by a fireworks display and thousands of torchlights, with a large fair held earlier in the day. The beginning of November marks the *Kasseler Musiktage*, one of Europe's oldest festivals of classical music.

Most **concerts** are held in the *Stadthalle*, Friedrich-Ebert-Str. 152 (☎78820). The main **theatres** are the *Hessisches Staatstheater*, Friedrichsplatz 15 (☎109 4222), which features **opera** as well as **drama**, and the *Komödie*, Friedrich-Ebert-Str. 39 (☎18383).

Fritzlar

Some 30km southwest of Kassel, the market town of **FRITZLAR** presents one of the best-preserved medieval cityscapes in Germany. With its 450 half-timbered houses, it might seem at first sight to be archetypally Hessian, but it's actually very untypical of the province: having spent much of its history as an enclave of the Archbishop-Electors of Mainz, it has far more in common with the Rhineland. This is not only manifested in the architecture, but also in religious observance (about half the population is Catholic) and a vibrant tradition of popular festivals.

The town

Built on a gentle slope on the north bank of the River Eder, Fritzlar's historic core is enclosed by the thirteenth-century **Stadtmauer**. This was actually built as a protection against the predatory designs of the Landgraves of Hesse; the fabric remains substantially intact, with nine watchtowers and five bastions, though these are in varying states of repair. The wall encloses the Altstadt, with a separate extension around the tiny riverside Neustadt. A fine view of the ensemble can be had from the **Alte Brücke**, which you cross when approaching the town from the Bahnhof. An even better view is from the top of the **Grauer Turm**, the largest surviving watchtower in Germany, guarding the western entrance to the Altstadt. Though it doesn't have set opening times, it's generally accessible in summer; otherwise the key can be obtained from the tourist office (see p.394).

The Dom

Built at the securest point of the town's defences, the **Dom** has always been Fritzlar's principal building. The present building, a successor to one founded by the Englishman St Boniface, was begun in the picturesque late Romanesque style of the Rhineland. From this period belongs the mighty west end, with its twin towers and graceful "paradise" porch, though most of the rest of the church was constructed in the Gothic style.

The **Dommuseum und Domschatz** (Mon–Sat 10am–noon & 2–4/5pm; DM4) occupies the buildings around the cloisters. There are some stunning treasury items, notably the reliquary of St Boniface, the jewelled cross of Emperor Heinrich IV, and the oldest monstrance in Germany, dating back to 1320. Also included in the ticket is entrance to the two **crypts**, the larger of which contains the fourteenth-century tomb of St Wigbert, Fritzlar's first abbot, featuring an imaginary statue of him clasping a model of his church. Upstairs is the **Bibliothek**, with a valuable collection of printed books and manuscripts, and the festive **Musikzimmer**, whose walls are decorated with a lively cycle of fourteenth-century frescoes.

The rest of the town

Directly opposite the Dom is the **Rathaus**, one of the oldest town halls in Germany still used as such. Originally, it was in the style characteristic of Fritzlar's secular buildings – with a lower storey of stone and an upper one of half-timbering – but the latter was replaced last century with a tiled mansard roof. A block further north is **Marktplatz**, on which stand some of the finest half-timbered mansions in town, the most imposing being a fifteenth-century guildhall, the **Gildehaus der Michaelsbruderschaft**, on the eastern side. In the middle of the square is the Renaissance **Rolandsbrunnen**, a rather more modest counterpart to the statues of the legendary hero found in the Hanseatic towns of the German coast.

On Burggraben west of Marktplatz is the most impressive of Fritzlar's half-timbered buildings, the **Hochzeitshaus** (10am–noon & 3–5pm, closed Sat; DM3), built in the late sixteenth century to host weddings and civic receptions. Together with the patrician residence next door, it contains an unusually engrossing regional museum, which, in addition to the standard displays on archeology, history and folklore, has some nicely offbeat sections, including a collection of the painted roof tiles which are characteristic of the area, and a roomful of unusual inventions, many (including a sort of aerial bicycle) the brainchildren of a talented but totally eccentric local engineer.

Outside the perimeters of the Altstadt, there are only a couple of setpiece attractions. The Neustadt clusters around the **Ursulinenkloster**, a still-inhabited fourteenth-century convent whose church can be visited. It's also worth following Fraumünsterstrasse for about 1km east of the town centre to the recently renovated **Fraumünster**, Fritzlar's oldest building, which stands in a walled garden just north of the Eder. Its stone walls date back to the Carolingian period, while the upper part adopts the Gothic half-timbering so typical of the town's mansions; inside is a cycle of Romanesque frescoes.

Practicalities

Fritzlar's **Bahnhof** is southeast of the centre, whereas the **bus station** is just outside the Stadtmauer, at the top end of Kasseler Strasse. If travelling by train, note that it's often necessary to change at Wabern, 6km to the east, which lies on the main Kassel–Marburg line. The **tourist office** is in the Rathaus (Mon–Thurs 10am–1pm & 2–4.30pm, Fri 10–11.30am; ☎05622/988643), Zwischen den Krämer 7.

There are surprisingly few **hotels**, though nearby Bad Wildungen (see opposite) more than compensates in this department. If you do want to stay over, there's one place between the Bahnhof and the centre: *Zur Post*, Giessener Str. 25 (☎05622/2263; ④) – and two in the Altstadt itself – *Zur Spitze*, Marktplatz 25 (☎05622/4545; ④) and *Kreta*, Neustädter Str. 9 (☎05622/6530; ④). The best **restaurants** are those in *Zur Spitze* and *Zur Post*.

Festivals include a Rhenish-style *Karneval* which reaches its climax on Rose Monday (see p.498); the *Pferdemarkt*, a four-day-long horse fair beginning on the second Thursday in July; and the *Stadtfest* and *Mittelalterisches Fest*, held in alternate years on the third weekend of August.

The Waldeck

For more than seven centuries, the **Waldeck** (or *Waldecker Land*) was an independent territory within the German Empire, firstly as a county, then as a principality. Despite its reputation as a rural backwater, it came to national prominence just before World War I with the construction of the huge **Edersee**, a reservoir created by flooding a large stretch of the valley of the Eder, the river flowing through the middle of the province. The Waldeck, however, did not long outlast the demise of the German aristocracy in 1918, being incorporated into Prussia eleven years later. It now forms an administrative region of Hesse and incorporates the area around the beautiful medieval town of **Frankenberg**. The two former capitals of the province make a fascinating pair: feudal **Waldeck** is now a popular recreation resort, while **Arolsen** is a proud Baroque *Residenzstadt*. No less attractive is **Bad Wildungen**, one of Germany's leading spas.

Bad Wildungen

BAD WILDUNGEN, which was formed this century from the union of two previously separate communities, is set in wooded countryside just 10km west of Fritzlar. The present-day centre, originally the town of Niederwildungen, was a fortified settlement tightly packed on a small hill. Its skyline is dominated by the **Stadtkirche**, whose winged altar by the Westphalian artist **Conrad von Soest** ranks among the loveliest and best preserved of fifteenth-century German paintings, and one of the supreme masterpieces of the courtly International Gothic style. The thirteen panels narrate the life of Jesus in a markedly individual way, and are full of (often humorous) anecdotal detail. Likewise in the chancel are two swaggering Baroque **memorial monuments** to rulers of the House of Waldeck.

Immediately west of the centre is **Brunnenallee**, the spa quarter's main promenade. It terminates at the palatial **Fürstenhof**, an extremely self-confident Jugendstil building which has, throughout its history, maintained its position as the town's top sanatorium. Beyond is the **Kurpark**, a landscaped park merging seamlessly with the wooded hills above, with the **Wandelhalle**, a late Neoclassical pump room, at its far end.

On a much higher hill north of the centre is the former town of Altwildungen, dominated by one of the secondary residences of the Waldeck princes, **Schloss Friedrichstein** (April–Oct Tues–Sun 10am–1pm & 2–5pm; Nov–March Tues–Sun 2–4pm; DM3, free Sat). A Baroque rebuild of the original medieval castle, it's now a museum of hunting and weapons, including booty captured in the seventeenth- and eighteenth-century wars against the Turks, though equally of note for the wonderful view it commands over the surrounding countryside.

Practicalities

Bad Wildungen's **Bahnhof**, a dead-end terminus, lies at the eastern end of town, a ten-minute walk from the centre. The **tourist office** is in the *Kurverwaltung*, just beyond the end of Brunnenallee at Langemarckstr. 2 (Mon–Thurs 7.30am–noon & 1.30–4.15pm, Fri 7.30am–noon & 1.30–5pm, Sat 11am–noon; ☎05621/704113); information can also be had from the Rathaus on Marktplatz (☎05621/7901) during normal working hours.

Both places can book **private rooms** (①–③), of which there's an abundant supply. There are also plenty of good-value **hotels**, often in atmospheric old villas in the spa quarter. Look in particular on Hufelandstrasse, a block south of Langemarckstrasse, where you'll find *Villa Hügel* at no. 17 (☎05621/2514; ③); *Villa Heilquelle* at no. 15 (☎05621/2392; ⑤); and *Wildquelle* at no. 9 (☎05621/5061; ⑤). The two top hotels are

Quellenhof, Brunnenallee 54 (☎05621/8070; ⑧) and *Maritim Badehotel*, Dr-Marc-Str. 4 (☎05621/7999; ⑨).

There are plenty of **cafés** and **restaurants** all along Brunnenallee, though the best place for a meal, other than the two luxury hotels mentioned above, is the *Neues Kurhaus* in the Kurpark.

Frankenberg an der Eder

FRANKENBERG, which lies above the River Eder some 35km west of Bad Wildungen and a similar distance north of Marburg, is an archetypal Hessian town, with a well-preserved half-timbered centre. The Altstadt is centred on two market places, Untermarkt and Obermarkt, each of which is a wide rectangular space rather than the customary square. Between the two is the early sixteenth-century **Rathaus**, a cunning piece of design bridging the slope separating the two markets: indeed its lower storey serves both as a hall and a covered walkway linking them together. Partly half-timbered and partly slate-clad, the Rathaus boasts no fewer than ten spires, a German record. The humorous polychromed console carvings, showing fools sitting on the shoulders of burghers, are intended to proclaim the building's festive function.

Situated on the heights above the west end of the two markets is the **Liebfrauenkirche**, a thirteenth-century hall church modelled on Marburg's Elisabethkirche. It had to be partially rebuilt in the fifteenth century following a fire which destroyed most of the town, and many of the furnishings, plus the decorative paintings on the vault featuring the emblems of the guilds, date from this time. Built onto the south transept, but only accessible from outside, is the **Marienkapelle**, a tiny pentagonal pilgrimage chapel. A gem of fourteenth-century German architecture, it preserves some marvellous carvings, including the presumed self-portrait of master mason Tyle von Frankenburg in the tympanum, and irreverent console figures – the inspiration for those on the Rathaus – inside.

Below the northern side of the Altstadt, at Bahnhofstr. 8–10, is the **Zisterzienserinnenkloster** (Tues, Thurs, Sat & Sun 10am–noon; DM1), a thirteenth-century Cistercian convent whose chapel, refectory and dormitory have been adapted to house the local museum, a surprisingly entertaining array of folklore and religious artefacts. Continuing west from here brings you to the **Museum Thonet** (Mon 10am–noon & 2–5pm, Wed & Fri 2–5pm; free) in the eponymous furniture company's headquarters on Michael-Thonet-Strasse. The display ranges from the mould-breaking bow-shaped chairs of the early years via the luxuriant Jugendstil adornments for Viennese coffee houses and the designs produced in collaboration with the staff of the original Bauhaus, to the very latest avant-garde models.

Practicalities

Frankenberg's **Bahnhof** is just to the northwest of the Altstadt; there's a regular bus connection with Bad Wildungen, but nowadays the only passenger rail link is with Marburg. The **tourist office** (Mon–Thurs 8.30am–noon & 2–4pm, Fri 8.30am–12.30pm; ☎06451/505113) is in the Stadthaus, Obermarkt 13.

There are a few **private rooms** (②–④), but only two excellent and pricey **hotels** – *Rats-Schänke*, Marktplatz 7 (☎06451/72660; ⑦) and *Sonne*, Marktplatz 2 (☎06451/9019; ⑧). These have the best **restaurants** in town; alternatively, try the *Steinhaus*, which occupies a gabled thirteenth-century mansion at Pferdemarkt 20.

The Edersee

In the English-speaking world, the **Edersee**, a long, narrow artifical lake stretching for some 27km east to west, is best known because of its role in the Dambusters operation in World War II (see p.545) To Germans, however, it's a major holiday area, above all for watersports. From mid-May to late September, the **ferries** of the *Personenschiffahrt Edersee* (☎05623/5415) ply the lake, linking all the main resorts.

Waldeck

High above the northeastern end of the Edersee, some 15km northeast of Bad Wildungen and reached by regular buses, is the little town of **WALDECK**, the original home of the Waldeck dynasty. The hilltop **Schloss**, although set below the present-day town, still commands the valley below in much the same way as it did in feudal times. It was abandoned in the seventeenth century and left to fall into ruin, but was later drastically restored, with one wing now serving as the area's plushest hotel. The most notable feature is the exhilarating **view** from the terrace of the Edersee and the surrounding hills. However, it's well worth visiting the **Schlossmuseum** (daily April–Oct 9.30am–5pm; DM3), in which the spartan main chambers look only relatively more comfortable than the dungeons below. There are displays on the history of Waldeck, including a fascinating photographic record of the construction of the Edersee and the drowning of villages that this entailed. Just to the north of the Schloss is the upper terminus of the *Waldecker Bergbahn*, a **cable lift** with open gondolas, which transports you down to the Edersee (DM5 return). Just west of here, at Am Klippenberg, is the **youth hostel** (☎05623/5313; ✿).

There are plenty of **hotels**, and even quite upmarket establishments in rustic surroundings with a view are not too prohibitively priced: *Belvedere*, Bahnhofstr. 2 (☎05623/5390, fax 05623/999199; ⑥) and *Seeschlösschen*, Kirschbaumweg 4 (☎05623/5113; ⑦) especially. Highest rates are at the aforementioned *Schloss Waldeck* (☎05623/5890; ⑨). **Private rooms** (①–③), which are plentiful, can be booked via the **tourist office** in the town centre at Sachsenhäuser Str. 10 (April–Oct Mon–Fri 8.30am–noon & 2–4.30pm; Nov–March Mon–Thurs 8.30am–noon, Fri 1–5pm; ☎05623/99980).

Elsewhere on the lake

The famous dam, the **Edertalsperre**, is 2km south of Waldeck by the village of **EDERSEE** at the eastern end of the reservoir. Capable of storing 202 million cubic metres of water, it remains an enormously important resource, and a major restoration project has only recently been completed. **HEMFURTH**, a further 1km south, stands at the head of a smaller lake, the Affolderner See. From here, an electric **rack rail line** (DM5) ascends to the Peterskopf, which offers another stunning panorama.

Arolsen

In the early eighteenth century, the Princes of Waldeck began laying out a new courtly town at **AROLSEN** in the north of their territory, 45km west of Kassel. This was intended as a miniature Versailles, though implementation of the project was forever dogged by a shortage of funds. Arolsen is, in most respects, the complete antithesis of Waldeck – except that it, too, is now a popular holiday resort and watersports centre, thanks to the creation a couple of decades ago of the **Twistesee** reservoir just to the east of town.

Towards the far eastern end of Arolsen proper is the horseshoe-shaped **Residenzschloss** (guided tours daily April 11am–3pm; May–Sept 10am–5pm; DM5), where the descendants of the former ruling family still live. Outwardly, the debt to Versailles is obvious, though the interiors are far more modest in scale. Because of the financial constraints, these were created over a period of more than a hundred years, with the result that they form a virtual encyclopedia of changing tastes in interior design. The **Gartensaal** has rich Rococo stuccowork, whereas the main **Grosser Saal** exudes a stern Neoclassicism. Many of the private chambers are in the French Empire style, whereas the **Alhambrasaal**, which mimicks the famous Granada palace, is a piece of Romantic kitsch.

The rest of the town centre bears all the hallmarks of having been planned in conjunction with the Schloss. Key buildings are the crescent-shaped **Marstall** (stables) across from the Schloss, and the **Stadtkirche**, which closes off the western end of Schloss Strasse.

Practicalities

Arolsen has lost its rail link to Kassel, though **buses** regularly ply this route: they stop on Schloss Strasse as well as at the former Bahnhof, which is at the opposite end of town. To get there from elsewhere in the Waldeck, you have to change at Korbach, which has supplanted it as the regional capital. The **tourist office** is in the *Kurverwaltung*, just south of the Schloss at Landauer Str. 1 (☎05691/2030).

There's a good reasonably priced **hotel**, *Robitsch*, a few minutes' walk east of the Schloss at Wetterburgstr. 15 (☎05691/3744; ④), but if you've the money to spare, there are two special places to stay – *Brauhaus*, a couple of blocks west of the Schloss at Kaulbachstr. 33 (☎05691/2028; ⑥) occupies the old court brewery; while *Residenzschloss*, Königin-Emma-Str. 10 (☎05691/8080; ⑦) is in part of the Schloss itself. Each of these last two has a top-class **restaurant**.

The Reinhardswald

The northernmost tip of Hesse lying immediately beyond Kassel is known as the **Reinhardswald** after the forest which covers much of its area. It has two major attractions in the Rococo **Schloss Wilhelmsthal** and the Baroque harbour town of **Bad Karlshafen**.

Schloss Wilhelmsthal

Just 10km north of Kassel, close to the village of Calden and reached by bus #46, is **Schloss Wilhelmsthal** (guided tours Tues–Sun 10am–4/5pm; DM6), the summer residence of the Landgraves, and later King Jérôme. It was designed by François Cuvilliés, the great Rococo architect of Munich, and modelled closely on his earlier Amalienburg. However, he was not involved in the actual building, which was entrusted to Simon-Louis du Ry, whose first major commission it was, and who added the two side pavilions to the original plan. The most notable feature of the sumptuously decorated interior is the **Schönheitsgalerie**, a gallery of court beauties painted by Johann Heinrich Tischbein the Elder, the Kassel-based member of the painting dynasty. There's also a fine English-style park, replete with fountains.

Bad Karlshafen

BAD KARLSHAFEN, which can be reached by frequent buses from Kassel, or by train from either Göttingen in Lower Saxony or Paderborn in Westphalia, is a Baroque town straddling the River Weser at the very northern tip of Hesse. Now a spa and a popular tourist destination, it was founded in 1699 by Landgrave Carl, who planned to build a canal from here to Kassel which would enable Hessian merchant ships to avoid the customs toll imposed at nearby Hann. Münden. Carl encouraged many of the Huguenot refugees to come and run the new harbour town, and Paul du Ry, grandfather of Simon-Louis, was responsible for drawing up the original plans. Although the scheme never came to fruition, the town retains a unique ambience as a result of its intended role.

The most atmospheric part of town is the showpiece centre, the **Hafenbecken** (Harbour Basin), which is surrounded by delicately coloured gabled Baroque houses. Prominent among these is the arcaded **Rathaus**, built as Landgrave Carl's hunting lodge. Just to the north, occupying an old cigar factory, is the **Deutsches Hugenotten-Museum** (Tues–Sat 2–6pm, Sun 11am–6pm; DM3), which provides comprehensive documentation on the role of the Huguenot immigrants in the development of the town and on their contribution to German culture. Set back from the Weser, about ten minutes' walk north of the harbour, is the **Kurpark**, which still preserves the remarkable wooden structure of the **Gradierwerk**, a simple but highly effective piece of technology which had the dual function of extracting salt from the town's saline springs and providing a healthy atmosphere for spa visitors, who today still stand underneath and breathe in the air.

Practicalities

The **tourist office** (May–Sept Mon–Fri 9.30am–noon & 2–5pm, Sat 9.30am–noon; Oct–April Mon–Fri 9.30am–noon & 2–4pm; ☎05672/999924) is in the Rathaus, Hafenplatz 8. Ask here about **cruises**, which are run regularly in summer, both around the town and down the Weser to Hann. Münden and Bodenwerder.

There are any number of **rooms** (①–③) available in private houses and small guest houses. Several of the town's **hotels** occupy wonderful old buildings: *Landgraf Carl*, Hafenplatz 2 (☎05672/373; ③); *Hessischer Hof*, Carlstr. 13 (☎05672/1059; ⑥); *Alt Carlshaven*, Weserstr. 23 (☎05672/925100; ⑤) *Zum Weserdampfschiff*, Weserstr. 25 (☎05672/2425; ⑥); and *Zum Schwann*, Conradistr. 3–4 (☎05672/1044; ⑦). All of these also have good **restaurants**.

The **campsite** (☎05672/1770) is located by the bend in the Weser directly opposite the town centre, and the **youth hostel**, on the same side of the river, is just to the rear of the Bahnhof at Winnefelder Str. 7 (☎05672/338; **②**).

travel details

Trains

Frankfurt to: Bremen (hourly; 4hr 20min); Cologne (hourly; 2hr 20min); Darmstadt (every 20min; 15min); Fulda (every 30min; 1hr); Giessen (hourly; 40min); Hannover (hourly; 3hr 15min); Kassel (every 30min; 2hr); Koblenz (hourly; 1hr 40min); Marburg (every 30min; 1hr); Trier (hourly; 2hr 45min); Wiesbaden (every 30min; 30min).

Kassel to: Freiburg (hourly; 1hr 35min); Fulda (hourly; 40min); Marburg (hourly; 1hr).

Wiesbaden to: Rudesheim (hourly; 35min).

CHAPTER FOUR

RHINELAND-PALATINATE AND SAARLAND

O f all the German Länder, the **Rhineland-Palatinate** (*Rheinland-Pfalz*) is the one most overlaid by legend. The **River Rhine** is seen here at its majestic best, and there's hardly a town, castle or rock along this stretch which hasn't made a distinctive contribution to its mythology. This is the land of the national epic, the *Nibelungenlied*, an extraordinary tale of heroism, chicanery, dynastic rivalry, vengeance and obsession, which bites deep into the German soul. It's also the land of the deceptively alluring Lorelei, of the robber barons who presided over tiny fiefs from lofty fortresses, and of the merchant traders who used the natural advantages of the river to bring the country to the forefront of European prosperity.

Nowadays, the Rhine's once treacherous waters have been tamed, enabling pleasure cruisers to run its length, past a wonderful landscape of rocks, vines, white-painted towns and ruined castles. Everything conforms perfectly to the image of Germany promoted by the tourist office; visitors swarm in, and people living on the trade do very nicely. Although the Rhine gorge is the bit most people want to write home about, the rest of the Land has plenty to offer. The **Mosel valley**, running all the way from France to its confluence with the Rhine at **Koblenz**, scores highly for scenic beauty and is not quite as over-subscribed and spoilt. Further north, the valley of the **River Ahr** flows into the Rhine near **Remagen**, rivals both of the larger rivers for spectacular scenery. Only in the **Hunsrück** and the **Eifel**, the Rhineland-Palatinate's "mountain" ranges, do the otherwise ever-present vines give way to bare heathland and forest, creating landscapes that are at times almost desolate.

Industry exists only in isolated pockets, and **Mainz**, the state's capital and chief city, only just ranks among the forty largest in Germany. Its monuments, though, together with those of the two other Imperial cathedral cities of **Worms** (the font of Germany's once-rich Jewish culture) and **Speyer**, do their bit for the historic side of things, the wealth of their architectural heritage equalling the natural beauty of the surrounding countryside. However, the number one city from the point of view of sights is **Trier**, which preserves the finest buildings of Classical antiquity this side of the Alps.

Trier's Roman survivals are a potent reminder of the area's illustrious **history**. The Rhine itself marked the effective limit of Roman power, and from that period onward the settlements along its western bank dominated national development. Throughout the duration of the Holy Roman Empire, the importance of this area within Germany can be gauged by the fact that two of the seven Electors were the Archbishops of Mainz and Trier, while another was the *Pfalzgraf*, or Count Palatine of the Rhine. Like the Romans, the French have often regarded the Rhine as the natural limit of their power, and their designs on the region – ranging from the destructive War of the Palatinate Succession launched in 1689, via the Napoleonic grand design, to the ham-fisted attempts to foster an independent state there after World War I – have had a profound impact on European history.

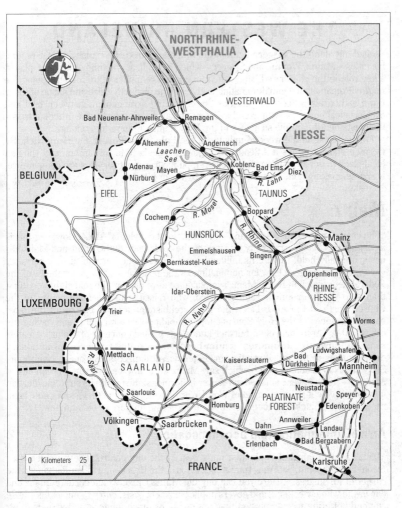

Adjoining Rhineland-Palatinate to the southwest is the miniature province of the **Saarland**. Long disputed between Germany and France because of its natural mineral wealth, it's predominantly an industrial region. From a tourist point of view, it's the least rewarding of all the German Länder, though it does have a few beauty spots, and a vibrant capital in **Saarbrücken**.

As far as **getting around** is concerned, this is one part of Germany where having your own transport is a definite benefit. Otherwise, buses tend to have the edge over trains for seeing the best of the scenery. Despite their associations with over-organized tour groups, the pleasure steamers which glide down the great rivers throughout the summer are certainly worth sampling. **Accommodation**, whether in hotels, youth hostels or campsites, is plentiful, but is best reserved in advance during the high season in the most popular areas.

THE WESTERN RHINELAND

Spaced out along the western bank of the Rhine are three of Germany's most venerable cities – **Mainz**, **Worms** and **Speyer** – which have all, at one time or another, played a key role in the country's history, the most potent reminder of their status being the mighty Romanesque Dom dominating each city. The distinctive size and shape of these three cathedrals reflects the curious power-sharing arrangement between civil and ecclesiastical powers – with each having an unusually large say in the other's affairs – that sustained the fragile structure of the Holy Roman Empire for so long.

Further west lie the wooded uplands of the **Palatinate Forest** and **Hunsrück**. By German standards, it's a little-known region, particularly to foreigners, and thus an ideal place to get away from it all. However, public transport services are comparatively sparse, making it an area best explored by car or bike.

Mainz

"The capital of our dear Fatherland" was how Goethe styled **MAINZ**. However, this is a position this 2000-year-old city, situated by the confluence of the Rhine and Main, has never officially held, though its influential role throughout German history certainly gave it a far stronger claim for nomination as the postwar seat of government of the Federal Republic than Bonn. Mainz's importance developed in the mid-eighth century, thanks to the Englishman Saint Boniface, who raised it to the main centre of the Church north of the Alps. Later, the local archbishop came to be one of the most powerful princes in the Holy Roman Empire, holding Electoral status and having the official title of Archchancellor. Further kudos was gained courtesy of Mainz's greatest son, the inventor **Johannes Gutenberg** (see p.405), whose revolutionary developments in the art of printing made a colossal impact on European civilization. Since the Napoleonic period – which saw Mainz for a time become the French city of *Mayence* – it has never managed to recover its former status, while its strategic location inevitably made it a prime target of World War II bombers. Nonetheless, it's now Land capital of the Rhineland-Palatinate and is an agreeable mixture of old and new.

Arrival, information and accommodation

Mainz's **Hauptbahnhof** is situated northwest of the city centre. The **tourist office** (Mon–Fri 9am–6pm, Sat 9am–1pm; ☎286210) is in the Brückenturm am Rathaus at the corner of Rheinstrasse. Here you can buy the **Mainz Card**, which costs DM10 for one day or the whole weekend, and covers public transport costs, entry to museums (those currently offering free admission may not do so for much longer), and various other discounts, including a 10 percent rebate at selected hotels. If you're flying in or out of Frankfurt, Mainz makes a good alternative place to stay as the **airport** lies on the S-Bahn line between the two cities, with several services every hour and a journey time of less than thirty minutes.

The stretch of the Rhine between Mainz and Koblenz is the most popular with tourists and **steamers** depart from in front of the Rathaus (March–Oct only). You'll also find the *K-D Linie* offices here (☎24511).

The **telephone code** for Mainz is ☎06131

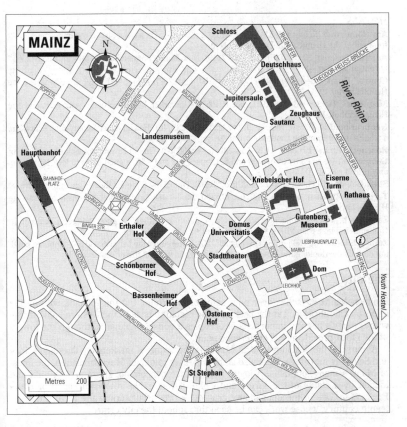

Accommodation

Mainz is a relatively expensive city for accommodation. There's a concentration of **hotels** around the Hauptbahnhof, but you may have to stay some distance out if you're looking for budget rates. The **youth hostel** (☎85332; ☎/☎) is situated 2km east of the centre at Otto-Brunfels-Schneise 4 in the wooded heights of Am Fort Weisenau; catch bus #1 or #22.

ACCOMMODATION PRICE CODES

All the pensions and hotels in this book have been graded according to the following price categories. The prices quoted are for the cheapest available double room, although many of the budget places will also have more expensive rooms. Youth hostels are graded under separate categories. See p.34 for more details.

① less than DM50	④ DM81–100	⑦ DM151–200
② DM51–65	⑤ DM101–125	⑧ DM201–250
③ DM66–80	⑥ DM126–150	⑨ more than DM250

HOTELS

Am Römerwall, Römerwall 51–55 (☎232135, fax 237517). On a quiet street, but only a 5min walk from either the Hauptbahnhof or the city centre. ⑦

Austria, Kaiserstr. 20 (☎270270, fax 2702 7110). New and recommendable hotel with a conveniently central location. ⑥

Central Hotel Eden, Bahnhofsplatz 8 (☎2760, fax 276276). Fine old hotel directly facing the Hauptbahnhof. ⑦

Moguntia, Nackstr. 48 (☎671041, fax 671058). Upmarket hotel, a 10min walk north of the Hauptbahnhof. ⑤

Neubrunnenhof, Grosse Bleiche 26 (☎232237, fax 232240). Has an excellent city-centre location, a stone's throw from the Landesmuseum. ⑦

Roseneck, An der Bruchspitze 3, Gonsenheim (☎680368). One of several hotels in the suburb of Gonsenheim (reached by trams #10 and #11, buses #22 and #23), a good place to look for reasonably priced rooms. ④

Stadt Coblenz, Rheinstr. 49 (☎227602, fax 223307). One of the few good deals right in the centre. ⑤

Terminus, Alicenstr. 4 (☎229 8760, fax 227408). Moderately priced hotel diagonally opposite the Hauptbahnhof. ⑤

Zarewitsch, Kurt-Schumacher-Str. 20, Gonsenheim (☎42404). A good budget place out in Gonsenheim; take tram #10 or #11 or bus #22 or #23. ③

Zum Schildknecht, Heliggrabgasse 6 (☎225755). Hotel-cum-wine bar in an old half-timbered building directly overlooking the Dom. It's remarkably good value at the price asked. ④

The city

Modern Mainz stretches over both sides of the Rhine, but the Altstadt, with all the important sights as well as the best bars and restaurants, is on the western bank. In line with the city's historic importance it occupies a considerable area, though the towers of the **Dom** provide a ready reference point.

Alongside, the spacious central **Markt** is the scene of markets on Tuesday, Friday and Saturday mornings. Here also is the riotously colourful **Marktbrunnen**, the finest of Mainz's many fountains. A joyful Renaissance concoction, adorned with putti and topped by a statue of the Virgin and Child, it was made in the workshop of **Hans Backoffen**, one of the outstanding crop of German sculptors at the turn of the sixteenth century, whose work can be seen throughout the city centre.

The Dom

Rearing high above all the other buildings in the centre of Mainz are the six towers of the massive red sandstone **Dom** (or **Kaiserdom**). A few years ago it celebrated its thousandth anniversary, though little remains from this epoch other than the ground plan, some of the lower masonry and the bronze doors by the north entrance. Most of what can be seen today is twelfth-century Romanesque.

One of the Dom's most singular features – which is a deliberate ploy to emphasize its mass – is that it's completely surrounded by buildings, stuck right up against its walls. The present picturesque group of houses dates from the eighteenth century, but the **St-Gothard-Kapelle**, two storeys high and of a contrasting grey stone, is from the first half of the twelfth century. Once the archbishops' own chapel, it's now the area set aside for private prayer and is entered from the north transept. The Dom's status as an Imperial cathedral, with a special area required for the emperor as well as the clergy, is apparent in the **choirs** at both ends of the building, each flanked by one large and two small towers. What's perhaps less immediately obvious, but a further emphasis of its historical importance, is that it follows the precedent of St Peter's in Rome in being orientated from east to west, the reverse of normal.

The solemn and spacious **interior** for the most part preserves its architectural purity. Above the nave's arcades is a cycle of murals of the life of Christ. Painted in the gentle Nazarene style – which aimed at recapturing the freshness and faith of medieval painting – they're a far more successful adornment than most such well-meaning nineteenth-century attempts at "improving" old churches. However, the interior is remarkable above all for serving as a very superior cemetery for the archbishops. These men were no shrinking violets, commissioning grandiose monuments to themselves which adorn the piers of the nave, forming an unrivalled panorama of sculpture from the thirteenth to nineteenth centuries.

Among the finest is the poignant late fifteenth-century *Monument to Adalbert von Sachsen*, third from the end on the north side; its youthful subject died before his consecration and is thus not shown in ecclesiastical robes. The same sculptor made the touching *Holy Sepulchre* in the Magnuskapelle. From early the following century are the most grandiose of all the tombs, those carved by **Hans Backoffen**. His masterpiece is the *Monument to Uriel von Gemmingen*, on the last but one pillar of the north side of the nave; two others by him are directly opposite.

The **Dom- und Diözesanmuseum** (Mon–Wed & Fri 10am–4pm, Thurs 10am–5pm, Sat 10am–2pm; free), laid out in rooms opening off the cloisters, houses the greatest sculptures of all. These are fragments from the demolished rood screen, created around 1240 by the anonymous mason – one of the supreme artistic geniuses of the Middle Ages – known as the **Master of Naumburg** from his later work in the eastern German cathedral of that name. In his carvings here, such as the scenes of the Elect and the Damned, and above all in the *Head with Bandeau*, his uncanny realism and characterization are far in advance of any other sculpture of the time.

The Gutenberg Museum

Dominating the Liebfrauenplatz, adjoining the Markt, is the resplendent pink Renaissance facade of the **Haus zum Römischen Kaiser**, which houses the offices of the **Gutenberg Museum** (Tues–Sat 10am–6pm, Sun 10am–1pm; DM5, free Sun); the actual displays are in a modern extension behind. It's a fitting tribute to a great inventor, making amends for the abysmal treatment he received at the hands of the authorities of his own day. Until 1978, Mainz had only the second volume of Gutenberg's most famous work, the **42-line Bible**. Made in the 1450s, it's a gravely beautiful production employing magisterial Gothic lettering. The city then managed to repatriate from America the last of the forty-odd surviving complete versions still in private hands, and this has pride of place in the strong room on the second floor. The basement contains a mock-up of Gutenberg's workshop and printing machines of later dates.

Across Schöfferstrasse from the Dom is Gutenbergplatz, with the red sandstone **Staatstheater Mainz** and a **statue** to the inventor by the Danish Neoclassical sculptor, Bertel Thorwaldsen.

JOHANNES GUTENBERG (c. 1400–68)

An illegitimate son of a canon of Mainz, Gutenberg dreamed of being able to reproduce manuscripts to the same standard of beauty and quality as that achieved by copyists, but without the painstaking physical labour that was involved. Although it's a myth that he invented printing as such – the Chinese had been able to do it for centuries – it was only through his pioneering development of moveable type that the mass-scale production of books became possible. His inventions were of tremendous significance, and were to survive without appreciable technological advancement right up to the present century. However, they led to Gutenberg's personal ruin – his short-sighted creditors, interested only in making a quick profit, wrested his inventions from him by means of a lawsuit. Totally destitute, he thereafter had to rely on charitable handouts to continue his researches.

The rest of the centre

Despite war damage, the centre of Mainz, especially around the Dom, contains many fine old streets and squares lined with examples of vernacular building ranging from half-timbered Gothic to Rococo. North of the Dom, the magnificent **Knebelscher Hof** is reminiscent of the Weser Renaissance style of northern Germany, while Kirschgarten and Augustinerstrasse to the south are particularly well preserved. Just off the end of the latter is the sumptuous church of **St Ignaz**, marking the transition from Rococo to Neoclassicism. Outside, a monumental *Crucifixion* group by Hans Backoffen stands over the sculptor's own tomb, which is even more imposing than those he had made for the archbishops. This marks the end of the historic quarter – beyond is a particularly sleazy red-light district, one of the largest vice centres in the Frankfurt conurbation. The former Markthalle on Holzhofstrasse a little further on is home to the **Museum für Antike Schiffahrt** (Tues–Sun 10am–6pm; free). Here you can watch ongoing restoration work on six Roman warships found under the city some years ago, and also see full-sized conjectural reconstructions.

Ludwigstrasse leads west from the Dom to Schillerplatz and Schillerstrasse, which are lined with impressive Renaissance and Baroque palaces, now offices. Here too is the elaborate modern **Fastnachtsbrunnen**, honouring the annual Carnival festivities, whose celebration here ranks for spectacle second only to Cologne's. Up the hill by Gaustrasse is the fourteenth-century Gothic church of **St Stephan** (daily 10am–noon & 2–5pm). Although a pleasant enough building with a pretty cloister, it's chiefly remarkable for its impressive postwar windows. In 1976, the parish priest persuaded **Marc Chagall**, the great Russian Jewish artist long resident in France, to make a series of stained-glass windows. The theme chosen was reconciliation, symbolizing that between France and Germany, Christian and Jew. There are nine windows in all, luminously brilliant in their colouring and quite astonishingly vibrant for an artist in his nineties; they were finished in November 1984, just a few months before Chagall's death.

Along the Rhine

Most of Mainz's remaining monuments of interest are situated in close proximity to the **Rhine**. The quayside is dominated by the stark black and white lines of the 1970s **Rathaus**, designed by Arne Jacobsen and another impressive modern addition to the city's heritage. Across the road is the so-called **Eiserner Turm** (Iron Tower), once part of the medieval fortifications, now a commercial art gallery; the other surviving city gate, the **Holzturm** (Wooden Tower), is south down Rheinstrasse. Continuing northwards up the same street, you come to the Baroque **Zeughaus** and **Deutschhaus**; behind is the gabled Renaissance facade of the old arsenal, the **Sautanz**. Near here, a copy of the **Jupitersäule** – whose original is in the Landesmuseum (see below) – has been set up.

Further on is the **Schloss**, the enormous former palace of the Archbishop-Electors, a superbly swaggering late Renaissance building with a Baroque extension. The once-famous interiors were completely destroyed in the war; in their place is the **Römisch-Germanisches Museum** (Tues–Sun 10am–6pm; free), a rather confusing collection in which copies of famous antiquities mingle with original pieces.

The Landesmuseum Mainz

The **Landesmuseum** (Tues 10am–8pm, Wed–Sun 10am–5pm; DM5, free Sat) occupies the old imperial stables directly down Grosse Bleiche from the Schloss. Its outstanding **archeology** department includes a hall full of Roman sculptural remains, dominated by the original Jupitersäule, the most important Roman triumphal column in Germany. Also here are fragments from demolished medieval buildings, especially the fourteenth-century **Kaufhaus**, one of only two German secular facades of the era to have survived. The most important paintings are at the very end of the ground-floor gallery. They include a series of nine canvases of the *Life of the Virgin* from the studio of the mysterious, highly original fifteenth-century Middle Rhenish draughtsman known as **Master of the Housebook**; the two Nativity scenes are by the Master himself. Also of note are copies of Dürer's celebrated *Adam* and *Eve* by his pupil **Baldung**, *St Jerome* by **Cranach**, and an altar wing by the **Master of St Bartholomew**, whose companion is in London's National Gallery. Upstairs are seventeenth-century Dutch cabinet pictures, and a modern section whose main pull, an array of colourful drawings by Chagall, is unfortunately only occasionally on view. There's also a glittering collection of Jugendstil glass.

Eating, drinking and nightlife

Mainz is unashamedly a **wine** rather than a beer city, boasting more vineyards within its boundaries than any other German city. If you fancy a wine crawl, you don't need to stray far from the vicinity of the Dom: there's an abundance of traditional **Weinstuben**, most of them serving meals, on Liebfrauenplatz, Grebenstrasse, Augustinerstrasse, Kartäuserstrasse and Jakobsbergstrasse. **Nightlife** is especially lively due to the large number of students in the city.

Weinstuben

Alt-Deutsche-Weinstube, Liebfrauenplatz 7. The oldest *Weinstube* in Mainz, popular with a good mixture of locals. Serves cheap daily dishes, but open evenings only.

Geberts Weinstuben, Frauenlobstr. 94. Family-run restaurant with excellent German cooking and a great choice of wines. On Sat & Sun, it's open evenings only.

Haus des Deutschen Weines, Gutenbergplatz 3. High quality if pricey restaurant, serving a huge range of wines from all over Germany.

Löschs Weinstube, Jakobsbergstr. 9. Tiny *Weinstube* offering bargain menus, open evenings only.

Rats- und Zunftstuben Heilig Geist, Rentengasse 2. The city's classiest and most expensive *Weinstube*, housed in the vaulted chambers of the thirteenth-century hospital.

Weinhaus Schreiner, Rheinstr. 38. Best of the *Weinstuben* for top-notch food at reasonable prices.

Other restaurants and cafés

Altstadtcafé, Schönbornstr. 9. A favourite with local students, and a good choice for breakfast.

Café Korfmann, Am Markt 11–13. Elegant café in a decorative Rococo mansion; also a good choice for breakfast or lunch.

Drei Lilien, Ballplatz 2. Highly rated citadel of French *nouvelle cuisine*. Reservations advisable (☎225068). Expensive.

Incontro, Augustinerstr. 57. Good Italian restaurant in the heart of the Altstadt.

Zum Backblech, Nackstr. 16. Offers huge cheap portions of *gutbürgerliche Küche*.

Zum Goldstein, Kartäuserstr. 3. Housed in a former brewery, so it's appropriate that it has the best beer garden in the city.

Zum Kartäuser Hof, Kartäuserstr. 14. Mainz's oldest inn, dating back to the twelfth century, serving German and international dishes.

Zum Salvator, Grosse Langgasse 4. Excellent brewery-owned restaurant.

Bars and clubs

Caveau, Schillerstr. 11. Entered from the back of the Institut Français on Münsterstrasse, this friendly pub has live music on Tues and discos at the weekend.

Doctor Flotte, Kirschgarten 1. Exotic cocktails are the speciality, though hot and cold meals are also available.

Eisgrub-Bräu, Weissliliengasse 1a. *Hausbrauerei* serving its own light and dark unfiltered beers; also does full meals.

Kamin, Kapuzinerstr. 8. Features an unusually wide choice of drinks, including no fewer than 23 Scotch whiskies.

KUZ, Dagobertstr. 20b. Popular concert venue with a disco on Wed and at weekends.

L'Escalier, Am Winterhafen 19. Popular chart music disco.

Pieter van Amstel, An der Theodor-Heuss-Brücke, Kastel. Bar in a three-masted sailing ship moored to the right bank of the Rhine, offering a great view of the city centre skyline.

Pomp, Grosse Bleiche 29. A favourite haunt of the in-crowd.

Terminus, Industriestr. 13. Sparsely decorated warehouse, attracting clubbers from miles around.

Entertainment and festivals

The main **theatre** venue is the *Staatstheater Mainz* (☎285122) on Gutenbergplatz; with alternative productions at the *Forum Theater Unterhaus*, Münsterstr. 5 (☎232121). *KUZ*, Dagobertstr. 20b (☎228 6860), also hosts concerts and theatre. A cultural centre, *Frankfurter Hof*, Augustinerstr. 55 (☎220438), is also worth checking out for music, dance and theatre. On the **classical music** front, look out for concerts by the *Mainzer Kammerorchester*, whose Mozart performances are particularly renowned.

Other than **Carnival** (here known as *Fastnacht* and using a far more intelligible dialect than in Cologne), the principal **popular festivals** are the *Johannisnacht* in mid-June, which includes fishermen's jousts and firework displays; and the *Weinmarkt* jamboree on the last weekend in August and the first in September.

Rhine-Hesse and the German Wine Road

Between Mainz and the Land's southern border are two of Germany's most prestigious **wine** regions. **Rhine-Hesse** (*Rheinhessen*), the immediate hinterland of the city, is given a distinctive appearance by the *Trullos*, small conical white shelters for vineyard workers in among the vines. These are of a type only normally found in Apulia in Italy, and are said to have been built by Italian immigrants 150 years ago. In the **Palatinate** (*Pfalz*) further south there are around 230 square kilometres of vineyards and in some places the climate becomes almost sub-tropical, enabling farmers to grow lemons, figs and tobacco as well as vines.

Oppenheim

Rhine-Hesse's leading wine town is **OPPENHEIM**, midway along the rail line between Mainz and Worms. It has a hilly setting just back from the river, and is full of half-timbered houses set in narrow little streets. At its highest point is the **Katharinenkirche**, a grandiose church built over more than two centuries: the towers are Romanesque, the east end and transept early Gothic, the nave high Gothic. As an afterthought, the west chancel, which has the appearance and dimensions of a self-contained church in its own right, was added in late Gothic style. Inside, look out for the *Oppenheimer Rose*, a fourteenth-century stained-glass window with elaborate tracery, and for the many epitaphs to members of prominent local families. Immediately north of the church is the **Michaelskapelle**, which incorporates a charnel house containing the bones of some 20,000 citizens.

Oppenheim's **tourist office** (Mon–Fri 8am–noon; ☎06133/70699) is in the Rathaus, Merianstr. 2. There are several **hotels**, including *Kurpfalz*, Wormser Str. 2 (☎06133/94940; ⑤); and *Oppenheimer Hof*, Friedrich-Ebert-Str. 84 (☎06133/2032; ⑥). The latter has the best **restaurant** in town; there are also plenty of *Weinstuben* where you can sample the local vintages.

The German Wine Road

The **German Wine Road** (*Deutsche Weinstrasse*), Germany's oldest designated tourist route, travels right through the heart of the Palatinate. Starting at Bockenheim, a small town about 50km south of Mainz and 14km west of Worms, it runs to Schweigen-Rechtenbach on the French border, some 80km away. As with most German tourist routes, it's meant for cars (look out for the bunch of grapes signposts), though you can follow most of it by train, resorting to buses to cover the occasional gap. All the towns and villages along the way have a plentiful supply of reasonably priced **accommodation** in pensions and private houses; the larger places also have hotels of every category.

The first main stop is **BAD DÜRKHEIM**, a little too touristy but worth visiting on the second and third Sundays in September when it hosts a gargantuan wine festival called the **Wurstmarkt** (Sausage Fair). The **tourist office** is in the Rathaus at Mannheimer Str. 24 (☎06322/935156), and there's plenty of **accommodation**, including pensions (②–③) and some very classy hotels. The **campsite** is at *Azur-Knaus*, Am Badesee (☎06322/61356), and there's a small **youth hostel** at Schillerstr. 151 (☎06322/63151; ✿).

Some 15km south at the foot of the Haardt hills (a branch of the Vosges) is the bustling commercial town of **NEUSTADT**, its well-preserved half-timbered centre peppered with inviting little *Weinstuben*. The town's sixteenth-century university building, the **Casimirianum**, is on Ludwigstrasse; on Marktplatz to the east is the handsome Gothic **Stiftskirche**, partitioned between Protestants and Catholics since 1708 by an internal wall. Neustadt has swallowed up the village of **HAMBACH** just to the south, whose neo-Gothic **Schloss** (daily March–Nov 9am–6pm; DM4) sprang to fame in 1832 when a group of students, protesting against Germany's continued political fragmentation, raised the black, red and gold tricolour for the first time.

Buses run from Hambach to the **Kalmit** (673m) about 4km east, which commands incredible views across the plain as far as Speyer. From here head for **ST MARTIN**, a small village with narrow streets and vine-covered restaurants which makes a good place to break your journey. It's dominated by the **Kropsburg**, a ruined thirteenth-century fortress. A couple of kilometres to the south is **EDENKOBEN**. Signs direct you to **Schloss Villa Ludwigshöhe** (Tues–Sun 9am–5/6pm; DM5), a nineteenth-century castle built for King Ludwig I of Bavaria, with some good wall and ceiling frescoes. Nearby is **RHODT**, a typical small wine town full of half-timbered *Winzerhäuser* (winehouses); look out for the arches of vines which grow on frames across some of the streets.

The last main stop is **BAD BERGZABERN**, which can be reached circuitously by train, or directly by bus from Landau, the next town south of Edenkoben. It was formerly the seat of the Dukes of Zweibrücken, though their Schloss – Renaissance with Baroque additions – is completely overshadowed by their smaller residence, the **Gasthaus zum Engel**, unquestionably one of the finest Renaissance buildings in the Palatinate. Accommodation options are good, with lots of pensions (②–③) and a **youth hostel** on Altenbergweg (☎06343/8383; ✿).

Worms

Here is one of the most memorable places in the West, here was the holy temple of the Romans, the royal fortress of the Niebelung, the palace of Charlemagne, the court of the Prince-bishop of Worms.

Inscription on the Dom in Worms

A rich web of fact and myth has been spun around **WORMS**, which lies on the left bank of the Rhine some 40km south of Mainz. Originally settled by Celtic tribes and then by the Romans, the city became the heart of the short-lived fifth-century Burgundian kingdom described in the *Nibelungenlied* (see box on p.410). It was a favoured seat of various subsequent royal dynasties, the scene of the weddings of both Charlemagne and

The **telephone code** for Worms is ☎06241

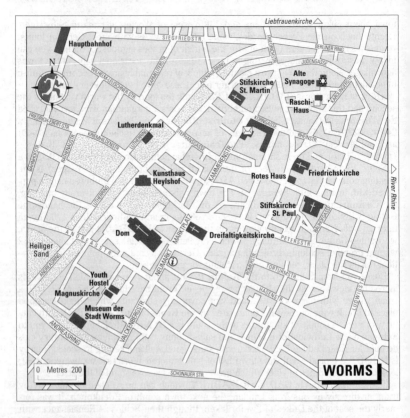

Liebfrauenkirche

Hauptbahnhof

N

Stifskirche
St. Martin

Alte
Synagoge

Raschi-
Haus

Lutherdenkmal

Kunsthaus
Heylshof

Rotes Haus

Friedrichskirche

Stiftskirche
St. Paul

Dom

Dreifaltigkeitskirche

Heiliger
Sand

Youth
Hostel

Magnuskirche

Museum der
Stadt Worms

0 Metres 200

River Rhine

WORMS

Frederick Barbarossa and of the Concordat of 1122 which settled the power struggle between the papacy and the empire. In the Middle Ages Worms achieved great prosperity and was for a while a venue for sittings of the Imperial parliament or **Diet**, most famously that of 1521 at which Luther was declared an outlaw. Unfortunately, much of

THE NIBELUNGENLIED – GERMANY'S NATIONAL EPIC

Written at the end of the twelfth century, the *Nibelungenlied* describes the fall and virtual genocide of the Burgundian nation at the hands of King Etzel (Attila) the Hun. This was the culmination of the long vengeance planned by Etzel's wife, the Burgundian princess Kriemhild, in retribution for the murder of her first husband Siegfried, the famed dragon-slayer. The saga is actually a brilliant fusion, with a great deal of imaginative embroidering, of two quite separate episodes in Worms' colourful early history. The Burgundians, originally allies of the declining Roman Empire, settled in Worms in 413, but were driven out by Attila in 436 shortly after they had established their independence from Rome. At the turn of the seventh century, Worms was the residence of the Visigoth princess Brunichildis (the inspiration for Kriemhild's rival Brunnhild), one of two sisters who married kings of different parts of the Merovingian Empire; a subsequent quarrel led to a fratricidal war which claimed the lives of all four leading participants.

its magnificence was destroyed in successive wars against the French, but several out-standing monuments remain in the midst of the functional modern city centre which has grown up since World War II. As Worms was formerly home to a large **Jewish community**, earning the nickname "Little Jerusalem", it's appropriate that it preserves the most important reminders to be found in Germany of this once-rich heritage.

The city

Given the present size of the city, the Altstadt is surprisingly extensive. The main Jewish monuments are at opposite ends, with the Dom providing the expected centre-piece. There are also a few places worth visiting outside the centre, notably the famous Liebfraumilch vineyards.

The Dom

Foremost among the survivors of Worms' bygone days of glory are the seven city-cen-tre churches, not one of them built later than 1744. Best of the bunch is the **Dom** (or **Kaiserdom**), a huge twelfth-century building which dominates the skyline even from a distance. From outside, it's highly distinctive in appearance, with its two domed choirs and four corner towers; it also displays great unity, with only a few Gothic addi-tions having been made to the original late Romanesque structure.

The **east choir**, the first part to be built, was the prototype for what was to become a distinctive trick of the local school of architecture – although the exterior walls are straight, they are rounded inside. Peering out from the arcades are statues of lions devouring their prey, their terrifying looks apparently intended to frighten off the devil; look out also for the enigmatic figure of a workman (thought to be a self-portrait of the master mason) with a monkey on his shoulder. Even more decorative is the **west choir**, the culmination of the building programme half a century later; with its rose win-dows, zigzag arcades and rich mouldings it ranks among the most imposing examples of all Romanesque architecture.

On the north side of the nave is the **Kaiserportal**, according to the *Nibelungenlied* the site where Kriemhild and her sister-in-law Brunnhild had a quarrel about just who had the right to enter the building first; this led to the murder of Siegfried and the even-tual collapse of the Burgundian nation. These days, however, it's the richly decorated Gothic **Südportal** – a veritable Bible in stone – which is the main entrance. Most unusually, the sculptures from its Romanesque predecessor weren't wasted, being placed on the wall immediately indoors.

As you enter the Dom, the sight of Balthasar Neumann's huge Baroque **high altar** is truly stunning. It's a Technicolor extravaganza in gilded wood and marble, featuring awe-inspired statues of SS Peter and Paul with two angels pointing at the Madonna and Child, who seem to be coming straight towards you. There's an austere stained-glass window backdrop which offsets the altar superbly. Otherwise the Dom is relatively spartan, no more so than in the dark and eerie **crypt**, the last resting place of five gen-erations of the Salian dynasty, whose eight plain sarcophagi sit in oppressive silence. In the south transept a **model** showing the centre of Worms before its destruction by the French is worth a look.

The Museum der Stadt Worms and the Heiliger Sand

From the Dom, Dechaneigasse leads south to the **Magnuskirche**, the first church in this part of Germany to go over to Protestantism. It dates back to Carolingian times but has been heavily extended and altered. Across the square stands the former **Andreasstift**, now housing the **Museum der Stadt Worms** (Tues–Sun 10am–noon & 2–5pm; DM3). The Romanesque church forms an appropriate setting for a collection of medieval sacred art; the monastic buildings contain Roman and Frankish antiquities

LITTLE JERUSALEM

Jews are known to have settled in Worms by the year 1000, and quickly established what was to be one of their largest settlements in Germany for the next 940 years. A synagogue was built in 1034 and a Talmudic school was also established. The latter's leading luminary was Rabbi Salomo ben Isaak, known as **Raschi**, whose commentaries on the Torah and Talmud are works still cited by Hebrew scholars today. In 1096, the community suffered the first of its many trials when fanatical Crusaders destroyed the entire Jewish quarter. Germany's most respected rabbi, **Meir von Rothenburg**, was imprisoned by King Rudolf von Habsburg in order to stifle the zeal for resettlement in Palestine; he died seven years later, without regaining his freedom. During the Great Plague of 1390 the Jews were attacked by their fellow townspeople who accused them of having poisoned local wells; and in 1615 social unrest among the rest of the populace once again meant persecution.

By the nineteenth century, matters had greatly improved. The ghetto to which the Jews had been restricted was opened up and from 1849 to 1852 Worms had a Jewish mayor, Friedrich Eberstadt. It wasn't until the Nazis came to power that Worms' ancient Jewish community was finally destroyed. In 1933 there were 1100 Jews in the city; by 1945 the Jews had ceased to exist here – all were either dead or had fled the country. Despite the rebuilding of the leading Jewish monuments as an act of postwar contrition, nobody returned, and the city's Jewish population currently consists of just two newcomers.

plus the Lutherzimmer, which details the events of the 1521 Diet and includes some of Luther's original writings. Just behind the Andreasstift is a surviving section of the **Stadtmauer**, with the still-intact **Andreastor**.

A modern ring road parallels the course of the wall. At its extreme southwest corner is the **Heiliger Sand**, the oldest Jewish cemetery in Europe and the most poignant reminder, in its leafy tranquillity, of the influential Jewish community of Worms (see box above). The **tombstones**, which have many beautiful inscriptions and carvings, date back as far as 1076. For reasons which have never been explained, they do not have the customary orientation to Jerusalem, the sole exception being that of the martyr Rabbi Meir von Rothenburg at the lowest point of the grounds. Although it's nothing less than a miracle that the cemetery survived the Third Reich, its situation outside the old walls, and the neglected appearance of the twisted and sunken tombstones, are not as sinister as they appear. Jewish tradition believed that contact with the dead, who should be allowed to rest in peace, caused impurity; hence they themselves chose to locate their cemetery at the opposite end of town from where they lived and to eschew the Gentile fashion for tending graves. The absence of tombstones later than 1940 likewise has nothing to do with Nazi depredations: by 1911, the cemetery had become so full that a new burial ground was created elsewhere, with only long-established families allowed to use the Heiliger Sand.

The Heylshofgarten and the Lutherdenkmal

On the north side of the Dom, just up Lutherring from the Heiliger Sand, is the **Heylshofgarten**, occupying the site of the now-vanished Imperial palace. In April 1521 this was the scene of the Diet at which Luther refused to renounce his views; he was forced to go into exile and the Reformation was set in motion. Within the park is the **Kunsthaus Heylshof** (May–Sept Tues–Sun 10am–noon & 2–5pm; Oct–April Tues–Sat 2–4pm, Sun 10am–noon & 2–4pm; DM3), a foundation established by the leading family in Worms' nineteenth-century leather trade. Their exquisite collection of fine and applied arts includes a colourful array of medieval stained glass; a tender *Madonna and Child* by Rubens, along with several modellos by the same artist; a large number of seventeenth-century Dutch cabinet pictures; and a statue of *Adam* by the sixteenth-century Worms sculptor Conrad Meit, one of the few German artists to adopt the full-blooded Italian Renaissance style.

Across the Lutherring directly opposite is the nineteenth-century **Lutherdenkmal**, the largest-ever monument in honour of the Reformation. The bronze figure of Luther is flanked by Frederick the Wise of Saxony and Philipp the Magnanimous of Hesse, the two powerful princes whose support made the Reformation a practical reality; behind stand the two scholars, Johannes Reuchlin and Philipp Melanchthon. The remaining male figures are the main precursors of Protestantism – Petrus Waldus, John Wycliffe, Jan Hus and Girolamo Savonarola; the seated women represent the first German cities to adopt the new faith.

North along the central axis

On the eastern side of the Dom on Neumarkt is the **Adlerapotheke**, a Baroque town house and pharmacy which is one of the few surviving examples of the Baroque architecture which blossomed in Worms following its destruction in the War of the Palatinate Succession. Also from this period is the nearby **Dreifaltigkeitskirche**, but, although it preserves its handsome frontage, the interior was modernized after being burnt out in World War II. Following Kammerer Strasse northwards, you come to the Romanesque **Stiftskirche St Martin**, whose whitewashed walls and angular tower give it a decidedly singular appearance. Saint Martin was supposedly once imprisoned in a dungeon underneath this church.

The old Jewish quarter

Just east of here, centred on Judengasse, is the old Jewish quarter. The **Alte Synagoge** (daily 10am–noon & 2–4/5pm; free) was reduced to ruins on *Kristallnacht* and further damaged by World War II bombing, but was rebuilt using the old stones and rededicated in 1961; it's occasionally used for worship, mostly by the American army's Jewish personnel. The main part of the synagogue, in a late Romanesque style, was built in 1174–75, probably by the same masons as were then working on the Dom, and was for the use of men only. An extension for the use of women, featuring the new pointed arch, was added in 1212, at right-angles to the existing structure. Adjoining the synagogue is the Talmudic teaching room known as the **Raschi-Kapelle**, while in the precincts is the underground **Tauchbad** or ritual bath house (both same times; free). In the **Raschi-Haus**, a former school, meeting house and dance hall, is the **Jüdisches Museum** (Tues–Sun 10am–noon & 2–5pm; DM3), with an extensive collection detailing the history of the Jews of Worms.

South to the Stiftskirche St Paul

Further along Judengasse is another well-preserved section of the city wall, with the **Raschiturm** and the **Friesenspitze**. South of here, Karolingerstrasse leads to the junction of Rheinstrasse and Römerstrasse, on which is the dignified Lutheran Baroque **Friedrichskirche**. Beside it stands the **Rotes Haus**, the only surviving Renaissance town house in Worms; when you see its pink curlicued gables you might suspect that the destruction of the others was no accident. A couple of minutes' walk southwest brings you to the **Stiftskirche St Paul**, a rough sandstone Romanesque church. Although the present nave was rebuilt in the Baroque era, the building as a whole, and in particular the chancel and triple-towered westwork, is self-evidently a miniaturized version of the Dom. Other surviving parts of the city walls, including the **Burgerturm**, the **Torturm** and **Lutherpförtchen**, are located just to the east.

Outside the centre

Because the centre lies about a kilometre inland, visitors to Worms often fail to realize that the city is actually on the banks of the Rhine. It's well worth walking along

Rheinstrasse to the **Torturm**, a massive gateway which straddles the **Nibelungenbrücke** over the river. This Historicist extravaganza was built as recently as 1900, but coming into town by the B46 road gives the impression of entering some mysterious medieval world. Below the gateway, the bronze **Hagenstandbild** illustrates the scene from the *Nibelungenlied* when the villainous Hagen hurls the cursed treasure of the Nibelungen into the Rhine just after he has murdered Siegfried.

Just ten minutes' walk from the centre in the northern suburbs is the Gothic **Liebfrauenkirche**. The church, of cathedral-like dimensions, with multi-coloured stonework and fantastical towers, is set in the **vineyards** which produce *Liebfraumilch*. The German version of this wine isn't anything like the sickly syrup found on foreign supermarket shelves, but a quality product which has to pass through a control centre: *Blue Nun* and *Madonna* are the best-known labels.

Practicalities

Worms' **Hauptbahnhof**, on the main line between Mainz and Mannheim, is northwest of the old city; follow Wilhelm-Leuschner-Strasse straight ahead and you arrive in a few minutes at the Lutherdenkmal. The **tourist office** is at Neumarkt 14 (Mon–Fri 9am–6pm; April–Oct also Sat 9am–noon; ☎25045). For nine days in late August and early September, the city celebrates the *Backfischfest*, a wine **festival** where fried fish is the culinary speciality.

Accommodation

Worms is quite well off for **hotels**; most are reasonably priced for what they offer, but those in the city centre can get oversubscribed. There's a **youth hostel** handily located between the Dom and the Andreasstift at Dechaneigasse 1 (☎25780; ❻). **Camping** facilities are on the eastern bank of the Rhine near the Nibelungenbrücke (☎24355).

HOTELS

Asgard, Gutleutstr. 4 (☎86080, fax 860 8100). Classy hotel in the southern part of the city. It serves good breakfast buffets, though no other meals. ❻

Bechtel, Pfälzer Waldstr. 98, Heppenheim (☎3142, fax 34745). Occupies a large converted farmhouse with balconies in an incorporated village on the western side of the city. ③

Boos, Mainzer Str. 5 (☎947639, fax 947638). Budget hotel a short walk north of the centre. ④

Dom-Hotel, Obermarkt 10 (☎6913, fax 24515). Typical modern business-class hotel with restaurant. ⑦

Faber, Martinspforte 7 (☎920900, fax 920909). Good medium-range hotel with restaurant at the northern edge of the Altstadt. ⑤

Hüttl, Petersstr. 5–7 (☎87874). Pleasant, centrally sited hotel with an adjoining bar-restaurant, *Marktstübchen*. ⑤

Kraft-Hotel, An der Weidenmühle, Gundersheim (☎06244/57632, fax 06244/57432). This new and inexpensive American-style motel, 12km northeast of the city centre near the E31 exit on the A61 Autobahn, is well worth considering if you're travelling by car. It serves big breakfast buffets and hearty German and international meals in its restaurant, *Truck-Centre*. ③

Kriemhilde, Hofgasse 2–4 (☎6278, fax 6277). Good-value hotel and restaurant in a quiet location immediately north of the Dom. ⑤

Römischer Kaiser, Römerstr. 72 (☎6936, fax 22953). Solid, somewhat old-fashioned hotel with an Asian speciality restaurant. ⑤

Weinhaus Weis, Färbergasse 19 (☎23500). This small, no-frills hotel attached to a wine bar on an alley just east of the Dom charges the lowest rates in the city centre. ③

Eating and drinking

From a gastronomic point of view, Worms does not quite match Mainz or Speyer. Nonetheless, there's a wide choice of places to eat and drink.

Café Jux, Judengasse 3. Trendy café-bar.

Hagenbräu, Am Rhein 3. *Hausbrauerei* with restaurant directly overlooking the Rhine.

Kolb's Biergarten, Am Rhein 1. Cosy *Gaststätte* with beer garden located right alongside the above.

Kutscherschänke, Judengasse 2. Another lively bar in the old Jewish quarter.

O'Shea, Rheinstr. 54. An absolutely genuine Irish pub, housed in a grand Romantic-era building between the centre and the Rheinbrücke.

Rôtisserie Dubs, Kirchstr. 6, Rheindürkheim. Worms' most creative restaurant, showing a strong French influence. It's located in an incorporated village by the Rhine, 9km north of the centre.

Stadtschänke, Kranzbühlerstr. 1. The best and most expensive restaurant in the city centre.

Tivoli, Adenauer-Ring 4. First-rate and not too expensive Italian.

Speyer

SPEYER, the final member of the triumvirate of Imperial cathedral cities, is some 50km up the Rhine from Worms: it lies on a relatively minor rail line, and you'll probably have to change trains at the sprawling industrial city of Ludwigshafen. In 1990, Speyer celebrated the 2000th anniversary of its foundation as a Roman infantry camp and it's one of the few Rhenish towns to have come through World War II unscathed. Even though its role was once much grander, it stands today as an archetypal episcopal and market town, lively enough never to seem staid, yet not to the extent of spoiling its atmosphere of restrained dignity.

Speyer is a great culinary city with a really marvellous choice of restaurants. It also claims to have invented the *Brezel*, the crispy salted bread which is such a German favourite, and the main local **festival**, the *Brezelfest*, is held on the second weekend of July.

The city

The city itself is easily seen on foot as it has never grown very large; the focal point, as it always has been, is the Dom.

The Dom

Speyer rocketed to a prominent position in the second quarter of the eleventh century, when the Salian dynasty of emperors chose it, alongside Goslar, as their favourite seat. They ordered the construction of a huge new **Dom** (or **Kaiserdom**) as their burial place. This regal building, in the purest Romanesque style, has dominated Speyer ever since; indeed, when it was finished, it was the largest church in the West. At the turn of the twelfth century it was partially rebuilt, notably with the erection of a new stone vault which was far higher than any ever previously attempted. The **towers** were also added, as were the **dwarf galleries** round the exterior which were to become such an essential feature of Rhineland churches. It's easy enough to distinguish the two building phases, as the smooth ashlar of the embellishments contrasts with the rough-hewn stonework of the original. The Dom was badly damaged by French troops in 1689, when Speyer was almost entirely destroyed; half the nave was left in ruins, but it was later brilliantly restored. Only the **westwork**, a romanticized nineteenth-century replacement for the one destroyed by the French, is a let-down, having taken its inspiration from the decorative late Romanesque style of Worms rather than the austere purity which is the hallmark of the rest of the building.

The **telephone code** for Speyer is ☎06232

The interior has been all but stripped of furnishings, in order to focus attention on its awesome proportions. Its great glory is the **crypt**: although the earliest part to be built, it remains the largest in Germany, and is justifiably claimed as the most beautiful in the world. With its alternately coloured sandstone pillars and slabbed marble floor, it has an almost Middle Eastern quality. It's divided into three connected spaces and contains the coffins of four emperors and four kings, among them Rudolf von Habsburg (the first of the dynasty to become German king), who is depicted in a magnificently carved sepulchral slab displayed on the west wall of the burial vault.

Last century, an English-style park, the **Domgarten**, was laid out around the Dom, meaning that there's an uninterrupted view of the great building from all sides. Particularly fetching is that from the **Heidentürmchen** (Heathens' Tower) to the east, one of the rare surviving sections of the medieval city wall; this formerly overlooked the Rhine, but the river has since been diverted to the east. Occupying the centre of the former cloisters on the south side is the sixteenth-century shrine of *Christ on the Mount of Olives*; however, the sculptures are pastiches of the originals, the sole survivors of which are kept under the northwest tower.

The Historisches Museum der Pfalz

Diagonally across Domplatz, housed in a triple-towered mock-medieval palace from the early years of the twentieth century, is the **Historisches Museum der Pfalz** (Tues & Thurs–Sun 10am–6pm, Wed 10am–8pm; DM8). Highlights of the outstanding archeology department are the so-called *Golden Hat of Schifferstadt*, a gold-plated Bronze Age cone named after the nearby town where it was found, and the contents of a Celtic prince's grave excavated in Bad Dürkheim. The Roman section includes the *terra sigillate* vessels from Rheinzabern, the largest surviving pieces of pottery of the period from north of the Alps, and a Mithras altar from Neustadt which was dedicated in 325, not long before the introduction of Christianity. Lapidary fragments from churches and Jewish buildings illustrate the medieval history of the region, while the paintings of the Speyer artists Anselm Feuerbach and Hans Purrmann dominate the section devoted to the modern Palatinate.

The building houses two other collections, both covered by the same ticket. In the **Weinmuseum**, every conceivable wine-related object is featured, including several old presses and what is claimed to be the oldest bottle of wine in the world, dating from around 300 AD. The **Domschatzkammer** contains a wonderful array of treasures, the oldest being the Phrygian *Omphaloschale* from the sixth or seventh century BC, which is still used on special occasions. Other highlights are the burial crowns of four Salian monarchs; a Romanesque holy water vessel from Mainz; the robe and shoes of King Philipp of Swabia; and the jewelled Gothic staff of Bishop Johannes von Dalberg.

The rest of the city

Across Grosse Pfaffengasse, on the northern side of the museum, lies the enclosed heart of the former Jewish quarter, which can be entered from Judengasse. The east wall of the **Synagoge** still stands, but the main surviving monument is the **Judenbad** (April–Oct Mon–Fri 10am–noon & 2–5pm, Sat & Sun 10am–5pm; DM1.50), a twelfth-century ritual bath-house for women. Seemingly built by the same masons who had recently completed the Dom, it's the oldest and best-preserved example in Germany and a poignant reminder of a vanished culture.

On the northern side of the Dom are the fourteenth-century **Sonnenbrücke**, Speyer's only remaining old bridge, and the **Wirtschaft zum Halbmond**, a seventeenth-century half-timbered inn with a strange polygonal oriel window. On the other side of Hasenpfulstrasse is the **Kloster St Magdalena**, a Carmelite convent whose church has a tastefully understated Baroque interior. The Jewish-born philosopher

Edith Stein, whom the Nazis gassed at Auschwitz, was a nun here from 1923 to 1931; she was beatified in 1987.

Following Grosse Himmelsgasse from the Dom brings you to the **Dreifaltigkeitskirche**, a Protestant example of the many Baroque buildings built in Speyer after the devastation of 1689. Further west, along Korngasse, is **St Ludwig**, the church of a thirteenth-century Dominican monastery. It contains the only surviving medieval altar front in the Palatinate and the winged late Gothic *Bossweiler Altar*.

Speyer's main street, **Maximilianstrasse**, forms a dead-straight processional way right across the heart of the city to the Dom, widening towards the end to form a spacious square. Among the colourful Baroque and Rococo buildings which line it are the **Rathaus** (whose interior can usually be visited during normal working hours) and the **Alte Münze**, the former mint. Closing off the western end of the street is the **Altpörtel** (April–Oct Mon–Fri 10am–noon & 2–4pm, Sat & Sun 10am–5pm; DM1.50), a craggy thirteenth-century gateway which is the only other surviving part of the city walls. A graceful arcaded gallery was built on top in the early sixteenth century, while the steep hip roof which finishes it off was added a couple of hundred years later. From the top, there's a wonderful **view** over Speyer and the Palatinate.

Down Gilgenstrasse and across Bartholomäus-Weltz-Platz is the **Gedächtniskirche der Reformation** (or **Retscherkirche**), a heavy neo-Gothic church built at the turn of the century in honour of the 1529 Diet of Speyer, at which supporters of Luther made their formal protest against the Edict of Worms, thus gaining the name "Protestants" for the first time. A large statue of the reformer dominates the porch; the interior blazes with a complete set of stained-glass windows. A few minutes' walk east at Allerheiligenstr. 9 is the **Feuerbachhaus** (Mon–Fri 4–6pm, Sun 11am–1pm; donation expected), the birthplace of the Romantic painter Anselm Feuerbach, who is chiefly remembered for his sweeping Italianate canvases of mythological scenes. The house is now a wine bar, but upstairs is an exhibition of his paintings and drawings.

Practicalities

Speyer's **Hauptbahnhof** and **bus station** are about ten minutes' walk northwest of the centre, but most buses continue down Bahnhofstrasse to drop you opposite the Altpörtel. The **tourist office** is at Maximilianstr. 11 (Mon–Fri 9am–5pm, Sat 10am–noon; ☎14392).

Accommodation

There's a good choice of hotels in the heart of Speyer, some in attractive old buildings. The **youth hostel** is at Leinpfad (☎75380; ❷), on the banks of the Rhine a little south of the centre.

HOTELS

Deutscher Kaiser, Allerheiligenstr. 37 (☎75630, fax 28617). *Gasthof* in the southern part of the city centre, offering the cheapest rooms in Speyer. ②

Domhof, Im Bauhof 3 (☎13290, fax 132990). Stylishly designed new hotel in an old courtyard building just in front of the Dom. ⑦

Goldener Engel, Mühlturmstr. 1a (☎13260, fax 132695). A modern designer touch has been applied to this historic hotel at the western edge of the city centre, creating a wonderfully distinctive environment. ⑥

Graf's Löwengarten, Schwerdtstr. 14 (☎6270, fax 26452). Fine middle-range hotel just to the southwest of the city centre. Its wine bar-restaurant (closed Sun) serves both local and international dishes. ⑥

Grüne Au, Grüner Winkel 28 (☎& fax 72196). Rustic-looking, ivy-covered *Gasthof* in the north of the city centre. ③

Kutscherhaus, Fischmarkt 5a (☎70592, fax 620922). Half-timbered old coaching inn with a top-notch restaurant (closed Wed) and a huge beer garden. ③

Schlosser, Maximilianstr. 10 (☎76433). Small budget hotel run in tandem with a café on Speyer's main street. ④

Trutzpfaff, Webergasse 5 (☎60120, fax 601230). Has a central but quiet location, and an excellent *Weinstube* (closed Mon) which serves specialities of the Palatinate and vegetarian dishes. ⑤

Eating and drinking

Few small German cities offer such a variety of places to **eat** and **drink**, with the excellent hotel restaurants mentioned above rivalled by several other establishments.

Altpörtel-Café, Postplatz 2. Café with rooftop garden in the shadow of the eponymous gateway.

Backmulde, Karmeliterstr. 11. Very classy restaurant offering innovative cooking. Closed Sun & Mon.

Café Schumacher, Wormser Str. 23. This long-established family-run concern is a good choice for *Kaffee und Kuchen* or a light meal.

Domhof-Brauerei, Grosse Himmelgasse 6. *Hausbrauerei* run in association with the nearby hotel of the same name. It serves Palatinate speciality dishes and has a large beer garden.

Pfalzgraf, Gilgenstr. 26b. Fine traditional and quite moderately priced *Gaststätte*. Closed Wed & Thurs.

Wirtschaft zum Alten Engel, Mühlturmstr. 1a. Wonderfully atmospheric restaurant in a vaulted cellar decked out with antique furniture. The food is outstanding, and includes Alsatian as well as local dishes. Closed Sun.

Zum Domnapf, Domplatz 1. Historic *Gasthaus* named after the old stone trough in front of the Dom. Its four dining rooms are all tastefully furnished; the food is of a high standard, the fish dishes especially, and the set lunch is a particular bargain. Closed Sun evening & Mon.

Zum Halbmond, Nikolausgasse 4. Authentic Hungarian dishes and wines are served up in Speyer's most picturesque half-timbered building.

The Palatinate Forest

Stretching north from the French border as far as the large industrial town of Kaiserslautern, and bounded to the east by the Weinstrasse and to the west by the border with Saarland, the **Palatinate Forest** (*Pfälzer Wald*) is one of the most compelling and unspoiled parts of the province. A sparsely populated, heavily wooded stretch of countryside, it's dotted with castles and half-forgotten villages, and most of it is designated a *Naturpark*. It's popular with walkers and climbers; if you're in more of a hurry, the best way to get around is by car as local bus services are a little sparse.

Annweiler

From Landau on the Weinstrasse (see pp.408–9), it's a twenty-minute train journey to **ANNWEILER** from where there are regular bus services to **Burg Trifels** (Tues–Sun 9am–5/6pm; DM5). Imperiously set on a jagged crag, this is a rebuild of a typical Hohenstaufen palace. To get here you have to walk up a steep hill, but it's well worth the trek. The Schloss is one of the most venerable in Germany, dating back to the eleventh century, and was supposedly one of Frederick Barbarossa's favourite haunts. In 1193 Richard the Lionheart was imprisoned here and only released on payment of an enormous ransom. It subsequently served as an Imperial treasury and then gradually fell into ruin after its abandonment in 1635; the rebuild (which is surprisingly effective) was carried out between 1938 and 1966. The chapel houses copies of the Imperial crown jewels, while from the **Kapellenturm** there's a tremendous panoramic view of the surrounding area, including the ruins of **Burg Anebos** and **Burg Scharfenberg** to the south.

In Annweiler itself there are several cheap **pensions**, including *Haus Bergterrasse*, Trifelsstr. 8 (☎06346/7219; ③), as well as a **youth hostel** at Turnerweg 60 (☎06346/8438; ❷).

Erlenbach

At **ERLENBACH**, 15km southwest of Annweiler, the main attraction is **Schloss Berwartstein** (March–Nov Mon–Sat 9am–6pm, Sun 1–5pm; Dec–Feb Sun only 1–5pm; DM5), a castle with a chequered past. It started life in 1152 when Frederick Barbarossa gave it to the Bishop of Speyer. By 1314 it had become a hideout for local bandits, who caused so much trouble in the area that the authorities had the Schloss destroyed. It was then rebuilt, only to be burned down in 1591. At the end of the nineteenth century it was again reconstructed; looking like an archetypal fairy-tale castle, it now houses a restaurant. You can still see some of the old rooms which were carved out of the rock on which the castle was built. Just to the north of Erlenbach is the ruined **Burg Drachenfels**, which suffered a similar fate to Schloss Berwartstein, but escaped being turned into a restaurant. It too has rooms hewn out of the rock and similarly constructed stone staircases.

Dahn

Northwest at **DAHN,** reached by bus #6840 from Erlenbach, are the ruins of three castles within one outer wall, set on top of a long, rocky ridge. The biggest and best preserved is **Altdahn**, which features watch-posts, rooms cut out of the rock face and some semi-intact towers. Only a few rock chambers and the remains of the walls are left of **Grafendahn**, and practically nothing is left of **Tanstein** apart from a few broken stones. Just outside town are the **Braut und Bräutigam** (Bride and Groom), two immensely tall pillars of limestone, one slightly higher than the other.

Dahn has a few small **pensions** (②–④), plus a first-rate **hotel**, *Pfalzblick*, Goethestr. 1 (☎06391/4040; ⑥). There's also a **youth hostel** at Am Wachtfelsen 1 (☎06391/1769; ❷), and a **campsite** at Im Büttelwoog (☎06391/5622).

The Hunsrück

The **Hunsrück**, which rises up between the rivers Mosel and Nahe, is one of the three huge volcanic schist massifs (the others are the Eifel and the Vosges) to the west of the Rhine. It's not too well served by the rail network and the bus services are meagre in some places – once again this is a region best explored by car. Most of the Hunsrück is forested and dotted with small villages, with the occasional incongruous small industrial town rearing up out of the woods. In the past it was a big source of precious stones and metals, and even today quarrying and related industries are still important to the economic life of the area.

One way of gaining a brief taste of the area is to take a ride on the *Hunsrückbahn*, Germany's **steepest standard-gauge** rail line. This departs from the Rhenish town of Boppard (see p.440), passing through five tunnels and over two viaducts in the spectacular ascent to Buchholz, climbing 300m in 8km. The train then continues for just one more stop, terminating at Emmelshausen.

Idar-Oberstein

IDAR-OBERSTEIN, in the Nahe valley on the southern edge of the range, should definitely be on your itinerary. (It has good rail links with Bingen and the Saarland towns.) Formerly a mining centre for precious stones and minerals, Idar-Oberstein has remained, even with the exhaustion of the old lodes, a centre for stone-cutting and polishing, and for the manufacture of jewellery. In reality, it's two towns joined together: Oberstein, crammed into the steeply wooded Nahe valley, is the historic part, while Idar, sprawling northwards up the narrow Idarbach valley, is more commercial in character.

From Oberstein's Marktplatz, 214 steps lead up to the late fifteenth-century **Felsenkirche** (daily April–June & Sept 10am–6pm; July & Aug 9am–6pm; DM2) set into the rocky northern face of the Nahe valley. Inside, look out for the graphic five-panelled altar painting, dating from 1410, of scenes from the life of Christ, and for the fine stained-glass windows, some of which are as old as the church itself. Above the Felsenkirche are the **Schloss** ruins, the jagged remains of two medieval fortresses, from where there's a good view of Oberstein and the Nahe valley.

On Marktplatz itself is the **Museum Idar-Oberstein** (daily 9am–5.30pm; DM5), which details the development of the local precious stone and jewellery industry. It shows how stones were once cut and polished using *Schleifmühlen*, huge sandstone wheels powered by the waters of the River Nahe. Look out too for the translucent flakes of *Landschaftsachat*, fragments of agate on which patterns seem to take the form of ghostly landscapes.

In Idar an ugly 22-storey office building in Schleiferplatz houses the **Diamant-und-Edelsteinbörse**, Europe's only diamond and precious stone exchange. On the first floor of the same building is the **Deutsches Edelsteinmuseum** (daily 9am–5/6pm; DM7), which is full of precious stones with "before and after" examples of the stonecutters' art. On the outskirts of Idar in Tiefensteiner Strasse you can visit the **Historische Weierschleife** (mid-March to early Nov Mon–Fri 9am–5pm, Sat & Sun 10am–4pm; free), the last surviving water-powered jewel-cutting shop – there used to be over a hundred of these in the area. Here craftsmen still finish stones in the traditional way, lying on wooden beams and pressing the stones against sandstone grinding wheels.

A little to the west of Idar itself, reached by bus #6435, is the **Edelsteinminen Steinkaulenberg** (daily March 15–Nov 15 9am–5pm; DM5), Europe's only precious stone mine. Not for the claustrophobic, this is a huge network of underground tunnels and chambers which have been mined since Roman times and are still a source for the agates you'll see in all the ritzy jewellery shops in town. Between Fischbach and Berschweiler (reached by bus #6455), there's the **Kupferbergwerk**, a similar type of complex, but this time a copper mine. Waxwork figures are used to show how copper ore was mined in days gone by (guided tours daily March 1–Nov 15 10am–5pm; rest of year Sat, Sun & holidays 10am–noon & 1–3pm; DM5).

Practicalities

The **Bahnhof** is in the middle of Oberstein, while the **tourist office** is at Georg-Maus-Str. 1 (☎06781/64421). There are quite a few reasonable **pensions** in Oberstein including *Trarbach*, Wüstlautenbachstr. 11 (☎06781/25677; ①–③); and *Beim Ännchen*, Am Hessenstein 11a (☎06781/6109; ④). Good **hotels** are plentiful: try *Edelstein*, Hauptstr. 302 (☎06781/23058; ⑤) in Oberstein or *Zum Schwann*, Hauptstr. 25 (☎06781/94430; ⑥) in Idar.

The **youth hostel** is on the east side of Oberstein at Alte Treibe 23 (☎06781/24366; ❶). You'll find **camping** facilities in the suburb of Tiefenstein (☎06781/35551; take bus #6443, #6445 or #6446).

At the end of June the *Spiessbratenfest* takes place, with pork and steak cooked over an open fire, garnished according to a recipe brought back from South America by German agate miners during the last century.

THE MOSEL VALLEY

The **River Mosel** (better known in English under its French name, *Moselle*) rises in the foothills of the Vosges in France. In its German stretch, it flows between the Eifel and Hunsrück massifs, entering the Rhine at Koblenz. It's best known as a **wine-producing** area, and vineyards crowd the south-facing slopes, with more rugged terrain elsewhere. The combination of wine and scenery, plus castles and history, attracts a lot of visitors – making it the kind of place that most Germans under the age of thirty wouldn't be seen dead in. That said, there's a great deal to recommend it – though not in high season, when hordes of tourists turn the most popular destinations – such as **Cochem** – into real hellholes.

There are still a few corners which have managed to fend off coach-trip attacks and retain some of the atmosphere which so impressed the **Romans**, on the edge of whose world the Mosel valley was. They've left their mark all along the valley, particularly in **Trier**, which has some of the best-preserved remains of Classical antiquity in northern Europe. You'll be able to cover the ground described here in a rushed four to five days; reckon on at least twice as long to see it in detail.

Trier

"Trier existed 1300 years before Rome" exclaims the inscription on one of the city's historic buildings. In fact, this is a piece of hyperbole: although **TRIER** is the oldest city in Germany, it was actually founded by the Romans themselves. Once the capital of the Western Empire, Trier was also an important early centre of Christianity. This helped give it political clout throughout the Middle Ages and beyond, its archbishop ranking as one of the seven Electors.

Nowadays, Trier has the less exalted role of regional centre for the upper Mosel valley, its relaxed air a world away from the status it formerly held. Despite a turbulent history, an amazing amount of the city's past has been preserved: it presents a veritable encyclopedia of European architectural styles, with pride of place going to the most impressive group of **Roman monuments** north of the Alps. These alone would be enough to put Trier in the rank of "must-see" German cities, and it's one place in the Rhineland-Palatinate deserving an unqualified recommendation.

Arrival, information and accommodation

The **Hauptbahnhof** is northeast of the centre, and it's about ten minutes' walk along Theodor-Heuss-Allee to the main entry of the old city. Here, at An der Porta Nigra, you'll find the **tourist office** (Jan & Feb Mon–Sat 9am–5pm; March Mon–Sat 9am–6pm, Sun 9am–3.30pm; April–Nov 15 Mon–Sat 9am–6.30pm, Sun 9am–3.30pm; Nov 16–Dec 31 Mon–Sat 9am–6pm, Sun 9am–1pm; ☎978080). Here you can buy the **Trier-Card**, which costs DM17 for one person, DM32 for two adults and three children, and covers entrance to the museums and various other discounts over a three-day period. There's also the **Trier-Card-Plus** which additionally includes use of the public transport network; this costs DM25 for one, DM44 for a family. For news of **events**, pick up the free monthly news sheet, *Der Kleine Dicke*. **Mosel cruises** operate from Zurlaubener Ufer in both directions (see box on p.429). **Mitfahrzentrale** is at Kaisterstr. 13 (☎47447).

The **telephone code** for Trier is ☎0651

Trier has plenty of **accommodation** to suit all tastes and pockets. Although many of these are in the centre, the most enticing choices are in the outskirts.

Hotels

Alte Villa, Saarstr. 133 (☎938120, fax 938 1212). Baroque villa, only recently converted into a hotel, in the southern part of the centre. It has a high-quality restaurant, and a pleasant garden terrace. ⑥

Berghotel Kockelsberg, Kockelsberg 1 (☎824 8000, fax 824 8290). An attractive option if you've got your own transport. The hotel commands a wonderful view over Trier from its position atop a hill on the left bank of the Mosel, 5km from the Altstadt. Its well-regarded restaurant is as reasonably priced as its rooms. ③

Blesius-Garten, Olewiger Str. 135, Olewig (☎36060, fax 360633). Capacious hotel in the eighteenth-century premises of a former wine-producing estate. The facilities include mineral baths, a sauna, a solarium, and a shady terrace with old trees and a spring water fountain. The restaurant offers a predominantly French menu and a distinguished wine list. ⑤

Klosterschenke, Klosterstr. 10, Pfalzel (☎6089, fax 64313). Small hotel in a converted medieval convent in an incorporated village on the north bank of the Mosel, 7km east of the Altstadt. It has a fine restaurant with garden terrace. ⑥

Maximin, Ruwerer Str. 12, Ruwer (☎& fax 52577). One of two very cheap hotels side by side in the northern suburb of Ruwer, a couple of kilometres beyond the Altstadt. ②

Villa Hügel, Bernhardstr. 14 (☎33066, fax 37958). Occupies a 1914 villa set in a park above the Kaiserthermen. There's a panorama terrace with a fine view over the city. ⑦

Warsberger Hof, Dietrichstr. 42 (☎975250, fax 975 2540). Just off the Hauptmarkt and part of the *Kolpinghaus* complex, this offers cell-like but perfectly adequate rooms. ③

Weinhaus Becker, Olewiger Str. 206, Olewig (☎938080, fax 938 0888). Another of the *Weinhäuser* in this wine-producing suburb. There are often opportunities for cellar visits and wine tasting. ⑥

Weinhaus Haag, Am Stockplatz 1 (☎975750, fax 975 7531). Budget hotel, centrally located in a pleasant square between the Porta Nigra and the Hauptmarkt, with a decent pizzeria on the ground floor. ④

Weinhaus Thiel, Ruwerer Str. 10, Ruwer (☎& fax 52233). The other budget option in this northern suburb. Products from its own *Weingut* can be drunk at the bar. ②

Zum Christoffel, Simeonstr. 1 (☎74041, fax 74732). An old-fashioned hotel right beside the Porta Nigra with an excellent restaurant specializing in game and lamb dishes. ⑤

Zur Glocke, Glockenstr. 12 (☎73109). Traditional inn right in the heart of the Altstadt. The rooms are unmodernized and inexpensive; the restaurant serves gargantuan portions of hearty food. ③

Youth hostels and campsites

Jugendgästehaus, An der Jugendherberge 4 (☎146620). Trier's official youth hostel is situated on the bank of the Mosel, near the lower station of the cable car. ☎

Kolpinghaus Jugendhotel, Dietrichstr. 42 (☎75131). Just off the Hauptmarkt and charging DM23-27 for dormitory accommodation.

Trier-City, Luxemburger Str. 81 (☎86921). Campsite situated on the western bank of the Mosel.

URANUS (☎35730). This is a ship which is moored in the Mosel between April and Oct; DM22 for a dorm bed.

The city

Despite being relatively small in modern terms, some of Trier's sights are fairly far out, and two days is the minimum amount of time required to see everything, though there's a handy concentration in the centre if you've only a day to spare.

The Porta Nigra and Simeonstift

The **Porta Nigra** (Black Gate) retains its historic function as the main entry point to the old city. By far the most imposing Roman building in northern Europe, it's also the biggest and best-preserved city gate of the Classical period anywhere in the world and dates from the end of the second century. The massive sandstone blocks are held together by iron rods set in lead, and it has been weathered black by the passage of time (hence the name, bestowed in medieval times). Towering above the surrounding streets and buildings, it's an awesome symbol of Roman architectural skill and military might. Would-be attackers were trapped between inner and outer gates, enabling defenders to pour boiling oil and molten lead down from above; the gateway served its purpose well and was never breached.

The Porta Nigra owes its survival to the fact that, during the eleventh century, Saint Simeon, a Greek hermit who was a friend of the powerful Archbishop Poppo, chose the gloomy ground floor of the east tower as a refuge from the world. After his death in 1035 the Porta Nigra was transformed into a **church** in his honour. Various further additions were made, but in 1804 Napoleon ordered their removal, so that only the twelfth-century Romanesque choir and some slightly frivolous Rococo carvings remain from the post-Roman period.

Adjoining the western side is the **Simeonstift**, the collegiate foundation attached to the church. Its cloister, the *Brunnenhof*, is the oldest double cloister in Germany, and unusual in that the main walk is on the upper floor, which is supported by massive arcades below. Today the ground floor houses a restaurant (see p.428), with the **Städtisches Museum** (Easter–Oct daily 9am–5pm; rest of year Tues–Fri 9am–5pm, Sat & Sun 9am–1pm; DM3) above. This version of the inescapable *Heimatmuseum* is vastly better than usual, thanks to an anarchic layout and some outstanding exhibits, notably the original sculptures of some of the prominent structures on the Hauptmarkt:

TRIER UNDER THE ROMANS

Augusta Treverorum was founded, probably in 16 BC, as a crossing point on the junction between the imperial frontier along the Rhine and the Gallic-Belgic provinces. Its name, later shortened to *Treveris* (and the French form *Trèves*), signifies that it lay in the territory of the conquered Treveri tribe. The new settlement quickly developed into a major city, and remained so until it was sacked around 275 AD by the Alemanni. However, it was rebuilt shortly afterwards under **Emperor Diocletian**, who made it the headquarters of the western provinces stretching from Britain to Spain. Trier's prestige reached its height under **Emperor Constantine**, who lived there from 306 to 316: the time when he adopted Christianity, with Trier as the premier bishopric north of the Alps. The city then had 80,000 inhabitants – almost as many as it has today – and was adorned with spectacular new buildings. Decline began with the establishment of Constantinople as the overall imperial capital, though emperors continued to spend some of their time in Trier until the middle of the fourth century, when the administration of the western provinces was moved to Arles. Only its position as a major ecclesiastical centre saved it from falling into irreversible decline.

TRIER'S ROMAN MONUMENTS

Opening times for the Porta Nigra and the rest of Trier's Roman monuments, other than the Konstantinbasilika, are as follows: daily April–Sept 9am–6pm; Oct, Nov & Jan–March 9am–5pm; Dec 10am–4pm. The Barbarathermen are closed 1–2pm, all Dec, and on Mon throughout the year. Entry to individual sites is DM4, DM2 students and pensioners, or you can save by buying a ticket valid for all of them for DM9, DM4.50 students and pensioners.

---

the Marktkreuz, the Steipe and the Petrusbrunnen. Also here is a good ancient history section, with Egyptian grave masks and paintings, hundreds of Roman terracotta lamps, a lot of Greco-Roman statuary and an important collection of Coptic textiles.

Simeonstrasse and the Hauptmarkt

From here, Simeonstrasse runs down to the Hauptmarkt, roughly following the route of an old Roman street. Today it's a busy shopping area, but boasts several medieval monuments. The most notable is the **Dreikönigenhaus** (House of the Magi), whitewashed but with garishly painted highlighting, which dates from the first half of the thirteenth century. An early Gothic dwelling tower of the kind found in Regensburg, this was a secure home in uncertain times for a rich merchant family. Then, the ground floor would not have opened onto the street at all: the original front door can be seen at first-floor level, high above the street. It was reached by a wooden staircase which could easily be dismantled in times of trouble, or by a ladder which could be pulled up from the street.

The **Hauptmarkt** remains a real focal point of the city, especially in summer: there are always a few stalls selling fruit and flowers, and Trier's kids and punks like to loll around the brightly coloured **Petrusbrunnen**, with its ornate replica Renaissance figures of the Four Cardinal Virtues. Alongside, atop a slender column, is a copy of the **Marktkreuz**, the original of which was placed here in the mid-tenth century. On the western side of the square is the late Gothic **Steipe**, the former banqueting hall of the town councillors, nowadays appropriately housing a café and pricey *Ratskeller*. Behind it is the stately Renaissance **Rotes Haus** (Red House), which bears the inscription about Trier being older than Rome. A few paces down Dietrichstrasse stands the **Frankenturm**, a Romanesque tower-house whose austere, unadorned stonework contrasts sharply with the tarted-up appearance of the Dreikönigenhaus.

At the southern end of Hauptmarkt a Baroque portal leads to the Gothic church of **St Gangolf**, which was built in the fifteenth century by the burghers of Trier in an attempt to outdo the Dom and wind up the archbishops, from whose temporal power they hoped to break free. The tower, added in 1507, actually made the church higher than the Dom, which angered the archbishop so much that he had one of the towers of his cathedral specially heightened to restore episcopal superiority. From here Fleischstrasse leads southwest to the Kornmarkt, in the centre of which is the ornate Baroque **Georgenbrunnen**.

Karl-Marx-Haus

On Brückenstrasse, at no. 10, you'll find the **Karl-Marx-Haus** (April–Oct Mon 1–6pm, Tues–Sun 10am–6pm; Nov–March Mon 3–6pm, Tues–Sun 10am–1pm & 3–6pm; DM3). In this archetypally bourgeois Baroque mansion the famous revolutionary theoretician and economist (see box below) was born in 1818 to parents of Jewish extraction: his father was a respected lawyer who had converted to Protestantism, his mother a Dutchwoman who never mastered the German language. Unfortunately the displays here neglect the human angle, concentrating instead on detailed expositions of Marx's political theory. The museum is run by the SPD – something of an irony, as Marx did his best to scupper the party in its early days.

The Domfreihof

Up Sternstrasse from the Hauptmarkt is the **Domfreihof** (Cathedral quarter), which has a history as illustrious as that of Trier itself. Saint Helena, the mother of Constantine, supposedly donated the site of her palace for the creation of an immense double church, which was begun in 330 AD. It was one of the quartet of great churches founded more or less simultaneously by the emperor as the showpieces of the new imperial religion, the others being Old St Peter's in Rome, the Holy Sepulchre in Jerusalem and the Church of the Nativity in Bethlehem.

Some of the basilica's masonry survives in the present quadruple-towered **Dom**, which was started in 1030, though not finished until a couple of centuries later. However, the most tangible reminders of the original church are two granite pillars:

KARL MARX (1818–83)

The revolutions in Eastern Europe in 1989 and the collapse of central government in the Soviet Union in 1991 have dealt a crushing blow to the reputation of **Karl Marx**, a man who had been elevated to the status of a god throughout the Communist world. Yet, in his own lifetime, there were few hints of the heights to which he would posthumously rise. His career as a campaigning journalist in the Rhenish province of Prussia ended with his expulsion after the revolutionary failure of 1849; thereafter he lived in London and Paris, his subsequent writing activity – notably the vast tract *Das Kapital* – dependent on the charity of his well-heeled co-author Friedrich Engels.

Despite the fact that he rarely attended political meetings, disliked public speaking, was intellectually arrogant, and usually expressed himself in prose of mind-numbing turgidity and verbosity, Marx held what Engels described as a "peculiar influence" on working-class and socialist movements – though at the time he was regarded as only one revolutionary prophet among many. His deification only came as a result of Lenin's adaptation of his theories before and after the Bolshevik Revolution of 1917, though there was a double irony here: not only had Marx predicted that the revolution would first occur in the industrialized West, he himself had what almost amounted to a racial prejudice against Russians, most manifest in his bitter struggles in the International against Mikhail Bakunin. Yet for seven decades attempts were made in Russia and its satellites to engineer Marx's prophecies of the classless society; it was only when these supposedly revolutionary regimes were themselves overthrown by popular revolutions that his powers as a seer finally became discredited.

one, the *Domstein*, can be seen in front of the southern portal, the other in the court-yard between the Dom and the Liebfrauenkirche. Save for the extension made to the southern tower to make it higher than St Gangolf, the Dom's austerely impressive facade has changed little since the eleventh century.

Inside, there's an incredible sense of space, much enhanced by the ribbed vaulting of the ceiling. The most eye-catching items, such as the pulpit and the densely peopled *All Saints' Altar* on the third pillar on the south side of the nave, were carved by **Hans Ruprecht Hoffmann**, an inventive local sculptor who was also responsible for the Petrusbrunnen on Hauptmarkt. The Dom's most important relic is the *Seamless Robe*, supposedly the garment worn by Christ when he was crucified: only rarely displayed for veneration, it's kept in the raised **Heiltumskammer** at the east end, whose over-the-top Baroque decoration adds a rare jarring note. Also upstairs is the **Schatzkammer** (Mon–Sat 10am–noon & 2–4/5pm, Sun 2–4/5pm; DM2). This has examples of local goldsmiths' work, notably a bizarre tenth-century portable altar to hold a relic of the sandal of St Andrew.

From the airy **cloisters** you get a wonderful view of the ensemble of the Dom and the adjoining **Liebfrauenkirche** next door. The latter occupies the site of the southern section of Constantine's great double church, and thus continues the original idea of there being two separate places of worship in the complex. Begun in 1235, it was only the second church to be built in Germany in the Gothic style, of which it's a wonderfully pure example. The ground plan is highly original, taking the form of a rotunda with a cross superimposed on it; the vault is supported by twelve pillars representing each of the Apostles. Now darkened by the insertion of modern stained-glass windows, the interior contains the Baroque marble tomb of the warlike Karl von Metternich.

Facing the north side of the Dom on Windstrasse is the **Bischöfliches Museum** (Mon–Sat 9am–1pm & 2–5pm, Sun 1–5pm; DM2). The most important exhibit is the quite stunningly fresh-looking fourth-century ceiling painting from the palace which preceded the Dom. Also of special note is the ninth-century fresco from the vanished Carolingian church of St Maximin, although it has worn its years less successfully. Upstairs is an important collection of **sculptures**, including most of the original statues from the facade of the Liebfrauenkirche, fragments of the Dom's rood screen and the refined *Monument to Archbishop Jakob von Sierck* by Nicolaus Gerhaert von Leyden.

The Konstantinbasilika and around

From the Liebfrauenkirche, Liebfrauenstrasse leads past the ritzy Baroque Palais Kesselstadt to the **Konstantinbasilika** or **Aula Palatina** (April–Oct Mon–Sat 9am–6pm, Sun 11am–6pm; Nov–March Tues–Sat 11am–noon & 3–4pm, Sun 11am–noon; free) on Konstantinplatz. This huge brick structure, once Constantine's throne hall, dates back to 310 AD, and is the most impressive of Trier's Roman remains after the Porta Nigra. Its dimensions are awe-inspiring: although 30m high and 75m long, it's completely self-supporting. Now a Protestant church and comparatively spartan, in Roman times it was richly decorated in accordance with its (albeit short-lived) role as seat of the Roman Empire. At 3pm on most days in summer, there are guided visits to the excavations below.

Next door is the seventeenth-century **Kurfürstliches Schloss**, once the residence of the Archbishop-Electors but now, more mundanely, a local government office. It's rather overshadowed by the adjoining **Rokoko-Palais der Kurfürsten**, which was built in 1756 for an archbishop who felt that the old Schloss wasn't good enough for him. Although it took some knocks over the next two hundred years, particularly in World War II, the facade survives and now sits in shockingly pink glory overlooking the **Palastgarten**, which is populated by Rococo statues.

The Rheinisches Landesmuseum

At the southern end of the garden is the **Rheinisches Landesmuseum** (Tues–Fri 9.30am–5pm, Sat & Sun 10.30am–5pm; DM5), which houses a fantastic collection of Roman relics – one of the best outside Italy. Prize exhibit, kept in the entrance hall, is the *Neumagener Weinschiff*, a stone sculpture found at Neumagen-Dhron in the Mosel valley, depicting a wine ship complete with crew. The following rooms have superb mosaics – among which the third-century *Rennführer Mosaik*, showing the charioteer Polydus and his four horses, is particularly outstanding. The *Igeler Säule*, the magnificent 23-metre-high column in the courtyard, however, is only a copy: the original can be seen in the centre of the village of Igel, 8km up the Mosel. An important recent addition to the collections is a hoard of gold coins unearthed in 1993, the largest ever found in the Roman Empire. Trier's illustrious post-Roman history is illustrated in the following rooms by jewellery and weapons from Merovingian graves, and by sculptural and architectural fragments from the early Middle Ages.

As a supplement to the Landesmuseum, you can visit the **Schatzkammer der Stadtbibliothek** (Easter–Oct Mon–Fri 10am–5pm; free), a couple of minutes' walk to the west at Weberbach 25. Displayed here are two of the world's most beautiful books: the ninth-century *Ada Evangelistary* with an antique cameo of Constantine on the cover, and the tenth-century *Codex Egberti*, partly illuminated in Trier by the Master of the Registrum Gregorii.

The Kaiserthermen and the Amphitheater

Behind the Landesmuseum are the **Kaiserthermen**, the imperial baths built in the reign of Constantine. Although they haven't survived intact, the scale of what was once one of the largest bathing complexes in the Roman world is still apparent. Today only the ruined *Caldarium* (hot bath), with its distinctive strips of brick among the stonework, is visible above ground. The extensive underground heating system has also survived, and you can walk among the service channels and passages. By the Middle Ages local lords had turned the baths into a castle, which was incorporated into the **Stadtmauer**, surviving sections of which can still be seen nearby. An earlier ruined set of Roman baths, the **Barbarathermen**, lie at the opposite end of Südallee from the Kaiserthermen. Built in the second century, only the subterranean sections retain their original shape, a seemingly endless maze of passages, channels and chambers.

From the Kaiserthermen the route to the **Amphitheater** is well signposted. It was built into the slopes of the Petrisberg above the city in around 100 AD and is the oldest of the surviving Roman buildings in Trier. The structure has been exposed in most of its original glory, and you can sense the grandeur of the original, which had a seating capacity of 20,000. It's still possible to see some of the arched cage rooms where the animals were kept and take a look under the arena itself, which is partly supported by timber blocks and has an elaborate – and still functioning – drainage system cut into its base.

Outside the centre

The hills around Trier provide many marvellous panoramic views of the city and the Mosel valley. Easiest of access is the **Weisshaus**, which can be reached by **cable car** (Easter to mid-Nov Mon–Fri 9am–6pm, Sat & Sun 9am–7pm; DM4.50 single, DM8 return), leaving from Zurlaubener Ufer.

Two contrasting churches are also worth short walks out from the centre. On the southern edge of town, about fifteen minutes' walk down Saarstrasse from Südallee, is the **Basilika St Matthias**. In 1127 Crusaders brought back from the Holy Land relics of St Matthias (the apostle who replaced Judas Iscariot); this huge church was then built on the site of an existing one to provide sufficient space for the pilgrims who came here to venerate the only one of Jesus' followers to be buried north of the Alps. The whitewashed facade is startling, the original Romanesque modified by the addition of

Baroque and Neoclassical features to create a truly sumptuous fricassee. The tomb of Saint Matthias is found at the intersection of the nave and transept; those of the first two bishops of Trier, SS Eucharius and Valerius, to whom the previous church was dedicated, are in two Roman sarcophagi in the crypt.

At the other end of town is **St Paulin**, designed by Balthasar Neumann. From the outside it looks quite restrained, sober even, but the interior is an all-singing, all-dancing Rococo extravaganza of colour and light. The eye is assaulted by the complex ceiling frescoes and the ornate pillars, dripping with cherubs and scrollwork. It's all just as Neumann intended: his idea was that entering a church should be like entering heaven. Look out for the carvings on the high altar and the choir stalls by Ferdinand Tiez, which are some of the best Rococo decoration in the Rhineland-Palatinate.

Eating and drinking

Alongside several high-class traditional **restaurants** are plenty of central **bars** where you can get good and inexpensive food, thanks to the presence of a large and hungry student population. There are also numerous opportunities for wine tasting, if you want to sample the full range of the superb local vintages.

Restaurants

Bagatelle, Zurlaubener Ufer 78. Although overshadowed by the neighbouring *Pfeffermühle*, this is nevertheless one of the best restaurants in Trier, particularly for *neue Deutsche Küche*.

Da Paolo, Neue Str. 17. A reasonably priced trattoria.

Hong-Kong-Haus, Georg-Schmitt-Platz 2. The best of the city's Chinese restaurants.

Lenz Weinstuben, Viehmarkt 4. A classy wine bar serving French and regional dishes. Closed Mon.

Löwenbrauerei, Bergstr. 46. Situated behind the Amphitheater, with a shady beer garden, you'll get homely German food here.

Palais Kesselstatt, Liebfrauenstr. 10. Trier's most famous and upmarket restaurant, housed in a magnificent Baroque palace, and with a huge choice of local wines as accompaniment to your meal. Advance booking advisable (☎40204); closed Sun & Mon.

Pfeffermühle, Zurlaubener Ufer 76. Another celebrated, very intimate restaurant, serving French *haute cuisine*. Reservations usually necessary (☎26133); closed Sun & Mon.

Weisshaus, Weisshaus 1. Located right by the cable-car terminus with a wonderful view of Trier, though the food alone is worth the journey. Closed Mon.

Zum Brunnenhof, Im Simeonstift. Prone to be mobbed by tourists, but the food is of high quality, with the bonus of being able to sit outside in the historic cloister in fine weather.

Zum Domstein, Hauptmarkt 5. Trier's most innovative restaurant, offering an adventurous vegetarian menu in addition to the standard *gutbürgerliche Küche*, while Roman-style dishes are served in the cellar. Bargain menus at lunchtime.

WINE TASTING

The *Weininformationen Mosel-Saar-Ruwer*, Konstantinplatz 11 (daily 11am–5pm) is the most convenient place for a spot of wine tasting: you can sample six different vintages for DM6. However, it's more fun to head out to **Olewig** (east of the Amphitheater, and reached by bus #6), where eight different cellars (daily 10am–6pm except in early autumn & Christmas) are open for a week at a time on a rotational basis; you can sample four wines for DM6, or eight for DM10. To find out which one is open during your stay, check first with the tourist office, who also have information about the many wine-related events held throughout the year.

Bars and cafés

Abwärts, Judengasse 2. Cellar bar cum Irish pub.

Astarix, Karl-Marx-Str. 11. Big, relaxed student bar serving an eclectic range of mountainous piles of cheap grub.

Blaues Blut, Corner of Pferdemarkt and Moselstrasse. Bar where the "punk's not dead" crew congregate.

Café Bley, Simeonstr. 19. Elegant traditional café in the Dreikönigenhaus.

In Flagranti, Viehmarkt 13. One of the most popular student haunts; also serves light meals.

La Vazza, Dietrichstr. 3. The favourite watering-hole of successful local yuppies.

Mephisto, Kalenfelsstr. 3. Pub serving good-value food. There's a huge beer garden which gets packed out in summer.

Zapotex, Pferdemarkt 1a. Hangout of the local fashion victims.

The Mosel Wine Road

From Trier you can follow the **Mosel Wine Road** (*Mosel Weinstrasse*) by bus or car to Koblenz where the Mosel flows into the Rhine. You can also do the stretch by rail as there are plenty of trains throughout the day – both express services, which run directly from Trier to Koblenz in about ninety minutes, and slower local services, which stop off at many of the small towns. The river meanders through innumerable wine villages and towns in a series of tortuous curves, the slopes of its valley lined with vineyards. If possible do this trip by road, since the rail line leaves the valley for substantial stretches and crosses relatively nondescript countryside. However, if you follow the B53 as it criss-crosses the Mosel you won't miss any of the splendid scenery which lines the route. Alternatively you can travel by **boat** – see box below for details.

Neumagen-Dhron

Bus #6246 will take you from Trier to Schweich and from here you can take bus #6230 as far as Bullay. **NEUMAGEN-DHRON**, the first town you'll hit en route, is best known for its Roman remains and for being the oldest wine-producing town in Germany. During

---

BOAT TRIPS ALONG THE MOSEL

Between May and early October, you can travel the length of the River Mosel from Trier to Koblenz, or just make short local trips; Eurail and EuroDomino passes allow you to travel on the *K-D Linie* steamers without charge. The same company runs luxury cruises allowing you to see the best of both the Mosel and the Rhine: a three-day trip from Frankfurt to Trier or a two-day one from Trier to Cologne both cost upwards of DM400, meals included.

Ferry Companies and Routes

K-D Linie Rheinwerft, Koblenz (☎0261/31030)	Koblenz–Cochem
Collée–Hölzenbein Rheinzollstr. 4, Koblenz (☎0261/37744)	Koblenz–Cochem
Gebruder Kolb Briedern (☎02673/1515); offices in Cochem (☎02671/7387) and Trier (☎0651/263170)	Cochem–Trier
Hans Michelis Goldbachstr. 52, Bernkastel-Kues (☎06531/8222)	Bernkastel-Kues–Traben-Trarbach
Gerhard Voss Goethestr. 15, Bernkastel-Kues (☎06531/6316)	Bernkastel-Kues–Leiwen

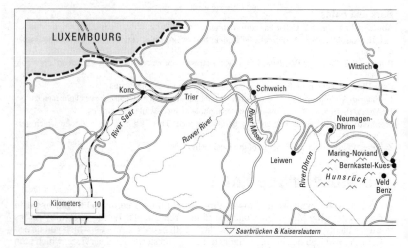

the fourth century it was the summer residence of the Emperor Constantine and you can still see the remains of his castle, which originally covered the size of a football pitch. Fronting the **Peterskapelle** is a replica of the *Neumagener Weinschiff*, the original of which is now in the Landesmuseum in Trier. The **Heimatmuseum**, Römerstr. 137 (April 16 to Oct 31 Tues–Sun 10am–noon & 2.30–5pm; Nov 1 to April 15 Tues–Sun 2.30–5pm; DM1) is marginally more interesting than average, with finds from Constantine's castle and local wine-related exhibits, including a huge wooden press.

Neumagen-Dhron's **tourist office** is at Hinterburg 8 (☎06507/6555). **Hotels** include *Café am Römerweinschiff*, Römerstr. 123 (☎06507/2188; ②); *Zur Post*, Römerstr. 79 (☎06507/2114; ④); *Zum Anker*, Moselstr. 14 (☎06507/6397; ④); and *Gutshotel Reichsgraf von Kesselstatt*, in a former wine-producing estate at Baldiunstr. 1 (☎06507/203; ⑦). **Camping** facilities are at Römerstr. 100 (☎06507/3212).

From Neumagen-Dhron to Bernkastel-Kues

Beyond Piesport the scenery becomes much more enthralling and there's a succession of tiny wine-producing villages on each side of the river. On the southern bank you'll pass through half-timbered Wintrich, backed by steep cliffs, and Filzen with its Franciscan monastery. It's worth taking a little diversion off the beaten track to **VELDENZ**, where a twelfth-century ruined Schloss towers over a village that was once the centre of a medieval dukedom. In the village an uninspiring modern church has been tagged onto a thirteenth-century bell tower, with slightly bizarre results. There's a *Weinfest* here on the last Sunday in July. Also meriting a detour is the little town of **MARING-NOVIAND**, in the Eifel foothills on the north side of the river. Just outside town is the **Klosterhofgut Siebenborn**, featuring a dank, vaulted wine cellar and Roman foundations. The local *Weinfest* is celebrated in the streets with much gusto over the fourth weekend in June.

Bernkastel-Kues

A few kilometres downstream, straddling the river, is the double town of **BERNKAS-TEL-KUES**. This attracts its fair share of coach-tripping tourists and can get pretty busy in summer, but it's worth a visit, particularly out of season or if you just stop off for a couple of hours in the early morning.

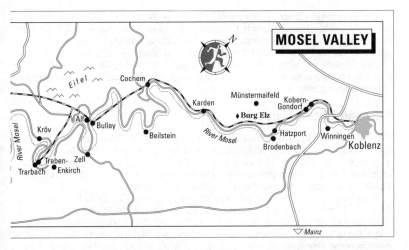

In Bernkastel, on the south side of the Mosel, the main attraction is the half-timbered, gently sloping **Marktplatz**, which for once actually lives up to tourist brochure hyperbole. The coffee-and-cream-coloured Renaissance **Rathaus** looks suitably stately in a municipal sort of way. Next door is the **Spitzhäuschen**, an absurdly narrow half-timbered building with a steep grey slate-pitched roof, which now houses a tiny *Weinstube*. In the middle of the vineyards above Bernkastel stands **Burg Landshut**, a thirteenth-century castle which went up in flames in 1693 and has been a ruin ever since, but from which you get panoramic views of the town and around.

In Kues, on the other side of the river, the bank is lined with the houses and villas of nineteenth-century vineyard owners. Fronting the river is the **St Nikolaus-Hospital**, also known as the **Cusanusstift**, a poorhouse founded by a local fifteenth-century theologian, Nikolaus Cusanus. These days the Gothic riverside buildings are home to 33 destitute old men – a symbolic figure representing each year of Christ's life. In its heavily ornate **Kapelle** there's a vivid mid-fifteenth century *Crucifixion* triptych by the Cologne narrative painter known as the Master of the Life of the Virgin. Next door, the **Mosel-Weinmuseum** (mid-April to Oct Tues–Sun 10am–5pm; Nov to mid-April Tues–Sun 2–5pm; DM2.50) features a large collection of wine presses, vessels and other related objects.

Practicalities

The **tourist office** in Bernkastel-Kues is at Am Gestade 5 (May–Oct Mon–Sat 8.30am–12.30pm & 1–5pm; Nov–April Mon–Fri 8.30am–12.30pm & 1–5pm; ☎06531/4023). Bernkastel-Kues has dozens of **hotels** but can get full up because of the volume of summer traffic. A particularly enticing selection on the Bernkastel side includes *Kapuzinerstübchen*, Römerstr. 35 (☎06531/2353; ②); *Binz*, Markt 1 (☎06531/2225; ④); *Römischer Kaiser*, Markt 29 (☎06531/3038; ④); *Doctor-Weinstuben*, in a seventeenth-century house with inner courtyard at Hebegasse 5 (☎06531/6081; ⑤); and *Zur Post*, Gestade 17 (☎06531/2022; ⑥). In Kues try *Weinhaus St Maximilian*, Saarallee 12 (☎06531/96500; ④); or *Drei Könige*, Bahnhofstr. 1 (☎06531/2035; ⑦). There's a **youth hostel**, Jugendherbergstr. 1 (☎06531/2395; ❶), uphill from Burg Landshut, and a **campsite** at Am Hafen 2 (☎06531/8200) in Kues.

Not surprisingly, there are dozens of **cafés** and **restaurants** in Bernkastel-Kues and the general rule is that the ones in the quieter streets are less likely to be full of tourists being ripped off. All the Bernkastel hotels listed above can also be recommended as places to eat and drink, while the *Ratskeller*, Am Markt, is also particularly good. During the first weekend in September the biggest *Weinfest* on the Mosel takes place here, when consumption of gallons of the most famous local vintage, *Bernkasteler Doctor*, brings plenty of life to the streets.

Kröv and Traben-Trarbach

From Bernkastel-Kues the Mosel snakes round to **KRÖV**. Here there's a vineyard called *Nacktarsch* – literally "Naked Arse" – which, according to local dialect experts, is a corruption of "nectar". The town has the standard array of half-timbered houses, including the mid-seventeenth-century **Dreigiebelhaus** (Three Gable House), and a *Weinfest* which takes place on the first weekend in October.

Round one more bend in the river is another double town, **TRABEN-TRARBACH**. In days of old Traben (on the northern bank) was a prime strategic site, which didn't go down too well with the locals, who soon tired of seeing their town destroyed every time one of the two fortresses above the town was besieged. Sighs of relief went up all round when **Schloss Grevenburg**, now reduced to a couple of walls, was blown up in 1697 in accordance with the terms of a recently signed peace treaty. In 1734 **Mont Royal**, built just 44 years previously by Louis XIV, suffered similar treatment, leaving the citizens free to get on with more peaceful pursuits like building half-timbered houses.

Most of these are actually in Trarbach on the opposite bank, where they rub shoulders with more substantial upper-middle-class villas from the nineteenth century. Also on the Trarbach side of the connecting bridge is the **Brückentor**, a monumental gateway designed by the Jugendstil architect Bruno Möhring, who created several other buildings in town in the same style, including the **Haus Huesgen**, Am Bahnhof 20, and the **Haus Breucker**, An der Mosel 7, both on the river bank in Traben.

Practicalities

Traben's **Bahnhof** is the terminus a branch railway which connects with the main Trier–Koblenz line at Bullay. The **tourist office** is nearby at Bahnstr. 22 (July–Oct Mon–Fri 8am–noon & 2–5pm, Sat 10am–noon; Nov–June Mon–Fri 8am–noon & 2–5pm; ☎06541/9011); pick up their useful map of walks in the surrounding hills.

On Wildbadstrasse, the road wending upwards from Trabach to Kautenbach, are several cheap **pensions**, including *Haus Jutta* at no. 227 (☎06541/9544; ②–③). Traben itself has a good choice of **hotels**, including *Gasthof Germania*, Kirchstr. 101 (☎06541/9398; ②); *Krone*, An der Mosel 93 (☎06541/6004; ⑥); *Oase Moselschlösschen*, Neue Rathausstr. 12–16 (☎06541/8320; ⑥); and *Bellevue*, in a large Jugendstil building at Am Moselufer (☎06541/2065; ⑧).

The **youth hostel** is at Am Letzten Hirtenpfad (☎06541/9278; ⓐ), about 15 minutes' walk from the Bahnhof on the same side of the river. Also in Traben are **camping** facilities at Rissbacher Str. 165 (☎06541/3111), while there's another site 2km down the road at Wedenhofstr. 25 (☎06541/9174 or 1033) in Wolf.

All the hotels listed above have good **restaurants**, with that in *Krone* being particularly renowned. Traben-Trarbach's *Weinfest* is held during the last weekend in July; there's another on the last Sunday in June in Wolf.

From Enkirch to Cochem

Following the southern bank of the Mosel eastwards from Traben-Trarbach will bring you to the village of **ENKIRCH**. This was founded by the Romans, but there's nothing exceptional to see, apart possibly from the sixteenth-century **Drehkäfig**, a cell which was built to house young men who had been leading local girls astray. The *Weinfest* here is on the first Sunday in August and there are plenty of places where you can sample the product. Further north, on the opposite bank, is **ALF**. From here it's an easy ascent to the ruins of **Burg Arras**, a tenth-century castle with a semi-renovated tower reached by rickety wooden stairs. There's a fine panoramic view from its hotel restaurant and luxury rooms are on offer (☎06542/22275; ⑧). The village has a good choice of **pensions**, while nearby are two **campsites** – one at Moselufer 1 (☎06542/22921) in Bullay, and the other just outside the half-timbered village of Ediger-Eller (☎02675/701) further north.

BEILSTEIN is a relatively undiscovered and sleepy little place crowded into a tributary valley on the south bank of the Mosel, with plenty of reasonable **hotels**. Try *Burg*, Moselstr. 2 (☎02673/1424; ②); *Haus Burgfrieden*, Im Mühlental 62 (☎02673/93639; ⑤); or *Haus Lipmann*, Marktplatz 3 (☎02673/1573; ⑥). The last-named serves the best food and drink in town in its old *Weinkeller* and garden terrace. As far as actual sights go, there's only the **Burg** (daily April–Oct 8.30am–7pm; DM2), a romantic ruin built between the thirteenth and fifteenth centuries and owned by the Metternich family until shortly before its destruction in 1689.

Cochem

Next town of any size is **COCHEM**, on the northern bank of the river, and back on the main rail line. It's a place which has sold its soul to tourism and should be avoided like the plague in summer. The main attraction is the **Burg** (daily March 15 to Oct 31 9am–5pm; DM6), one of the Rhineland-Palatinate's more famous replica castles. If it weren't a complete fake (the eleventh- to fourteenth-century original went up in smoke in 1689, assisted by enthusiastic French soldiers), the Burg, which dominates the town with its cluster of towers and implacable walls, would be quite impressive. Inside, it has been decorated in mock medieval style, though there are some fine pieces of Renaissance furniture.

As for the rest of Cochem, there's a half-timbered **Marktplatz** with a sober Baroque **Rathaus**. Behind stands the **Martinskirche**, with a tower that looks like a Rococo soldier's helmet. It's a postwar rebuild of an original which dated back to the ninth century. Parts of the Stadtmauer are also still intact, including three chunky city gates. From one of them, **Enderttor**, you can take a chairlift ride (daily 9am–6pm; DM7) to the top of the **Pinnerkreuz** hill for the best view of the town and its environs.

Cochem's **tourist office** is at Endertplatz 1 (June–Oct Mon–Fri 9am–1pm & 2–5pm; Sat 10am–3pm; Nov–May Mon–Fri 9am–1pm & 2–5pm; ☎02671/3971). Accommodation is plentiful, and includes some **private rooms** (①–②), but can get booked out at the height of the season. Among more than two dozen **pensions** are *Haus Karina*, Zehnthausstr. 48 (☎02671/3482; ②); *Lange*, Endertstr. 52 (☎02671/7173; ②); and *Café Becker*, Oberbachstr. 20–22 (☎02671/7224; ③). An even larger number of **hotels** includes *Zur Weinhexe*, Hafenstr. 1 (☎02671/8482; ③); *Am Hafen*, Uferstr. 4 (☎02671/8474; ⑤); *Karl Müller*, Moselpromenade 9 (☎02671/1333; ⑤); and *Lohspeicher*, Obergasse 1 (☎02671/3976; ⑥). All of these have good **restaurants**, with the palm going to the last-named. There's a **youth hostel** at Klottener Str. 9 (☎02671/8633; ⚑) on the south side of the Mosel. The town has four **campsites**, the most accessible of which are *Freizeitzentrum*, Klottener Str. 17 (☎02671/1212) and *Schausten-Reif*, Endertstr. 124 (☎02671/7528).

Karden, Burg Eltz and around

From Cochem it's another 11km to **KARDEN**, which preserves houses dating back as far as the twelfth century. The **Stiftskirche St Kastor** was under construction for over three hundred years, marking the full transition from Romanesque to Gothic. Although small, its simple white lines make it one of the most visually appealing churches of the

Mosel. Inside, there's a fine early seventeenth-century side altar of *The Martyrdom of St Stephen*, and a slightly faded wall painting of Christ which looks startlingly modern. Built into the cliffs behind the town on the south bank of the Mosel are two castles: the restored twelfth-century **Wildburg**, and **Burg Treis**, an eleventh-century ruin.

Beyond Karden the Mosel valley starts to lose its specialness, but you might care to stop briefly in the riverside town of **HATZENPORT**, which is clustered around a pair of Romanesque stone churches and the old restored **Fährturm** (Ferry Tower). In **BRODENBACH** on the far shore there's a **youth hostel** at Moorkamp 7 (☎02605/3389; 🏠) and a **campsite** at Rhein-Mosel-Str. 63 (☎02605/1437).

Burg Eltz

In any event, make sure you don't miss **Burg Eltz** (daily April–Oct 9.30am–5pm; DM8), one of only three intact medieval castles in the Rhineland-Palatinate (the others are the Pfalzgrafenstein and the Marksburg – see p.438 and p.441). To get there, catch bus #6039 from Hatzenport to Münstermaifeld, from where you can take another bus to Burg Eltz; alternatively, hike the steep 3km-long path from Moselkern, a stop on the rail line midway between Karden and Hatzenport. This castle really is something else: it seems to rise vertically straight out of the woods of the Elzbach valley and bristles with conical towers. It goes back at least as far as the twelfth century, developing over the next four hundred years as a defensive home for the various branches of the Eltz family, who managed to live there peacably for a couple of hundred years until a run-in with Balduin, the Elector of Trier. This resulted in a two-year siege, during which **Burg Trutzeltz** was built by Balduin directly in front in order to lob rocks at the castle. After Burg Eltz fell the Eltz family were allowed to remain in possession as vassals of Balduin and peace returned. Most of what you see today was built during the fifteenth century: inside the walls are a number of residential towers crammed together round an inner courtyard, which escaped destruction by the French in 1689 only because a member of the Eltz family happened to be an officer in the French army.

The **interior** of the castle, which you can only see by guided tour, is more or less as it was during medieval times, complete with original furnishings, wall hangings and paintings. Particularly impressive is the **Rübenach Untersaal**, with sixteenth-century Flemish tapestries of unlikely-looking exotic animals and plants, and a number of panel paintings, including Cranach's *Madonna with Grapes*. The **Schatzkammer** (DM2.50 extra), which can be visited at leisure, is full of silver- and gold-ware, glass, porcelain, weapons and armour, including a suit of armour which belonged to Emperor Maximilian I.

Be warned that Burg Eltz is snarled up with tourists in summer; make sure you arrive early, or visit it out of season. It's best to bring your own picnic as the snack bar is tacky and overpriced.

Kobern-Gondorf and Winningen

KOBERN-GONDORF is a double town trailing out along the Mosel bank 10km east of Hatzenport. The most unusual local attraction is the **Goloring**, a prehistoric circular tomb complex dating from 1200 to 600 BC. In Kirchstrasse (in Kobern) you can see the **Abteihof**, the oldest half-timbered house in the Rhineland-Palatinate: built in 1321, it looks in suspiciously good shape for its age. Also worth visiting is the castle complex. The **Niederburg** is an extensive pile of crumbling masonry with a more or less intact tower, while the **Oberburg** has the almost perfectly symmetrical Romanesque **Matthiaskapelle**, which once housed the remains of the Apostle Matthias (later transferred to the Matthiaskirche in Trier). In Gondorf there's also an **Oberburg**, but it's been cut in half by the road and rail line, which hasn't done a lot for it aesthetically.

The **tourist office** is on the Marktplatz (☎02607/1055). **Hotels** include *Gasthof Kastorschänke*, Bahnhofstr. 18 (☎02607/1259; ③); and *Simonis*, Marktplatz 4 (☎02607/203; ⑤). For **eating** and **drinking**, try *Weingut Thomas Höreth*, housed in an old mill, complete with wine museum. To get there, take the road up to the Matthiaskapelle, then turn down the road opposite the cemetery. Kobern-Gondorf is big on *Weinfeste*; there's one in late June and early July, another during the second weekend in September and a third in the second weekend in October.

Weinfeste also figure in **WINNINGEN**, the last town of any interest before Koblenz, a half-timbered place which holds the oldest wine festival in Germany at the end of August and beginning of September. At this time, wine flows from the town fountain instead of water. A grisly attraction here is the **Hexenhugel** (Witches' Hill), a popular picnic spot where, during the Thirty Years' War, 21 women were burned alive as witches. Just outside the town is the huge bridge which carries the E31 European highway over the Mosel valley; fortunately, it hasn't destroyed the local atmosphere.

THE RHINE GORGE

Beyond Mainz, the **Rhine** bends westwards and continues its hitherto stately but unspectacular journey. Suddenly, there's a dramatic change – the river widens and swings back to a northerly course, threatening the low banks on either side, while long wooded islands block the view ahead.

This marks the entry to the spectacular **gorge**, which, though it's only a small part of the river's total length of 1320km, is the Rhine of popular imagination. The combination of the treacherous waters, whirlpools and rocky banks lining the sharp twists of the river poses a severe test of navigational skill. Nowadays, this has been considerably eased by the digging of channels to control the movement of the river, but it has inevitably thrown up legends of shipwrecks, sirens and mermaids. The lure of the castles of the medieval robber barons, the raw elemental beauty of the landscape itself and the famous wines made from the vines which somehow cling to the lower slopes make for one of Europe's major tourist magnets. Yet the pleasure steamers are still greatly outnumbered by the long, narrow commercial barges, a reminder of the crucial role the river has played in the German economy down the centuries.

The Rhine from Bingen to Koblenz

The first stretch of the gorge, up to the confluence with the Mosel, is undoubtedly the finest, lined with cute half-timbered towns and an extensive range of castles in various states of repair. In high season, this means a flood of organized tour parties, particularly from the UK, this being the one part of Germany the British have really taken to their hearts. If you must do this part of the Rhine in summer and are on a tight budget, then try and book your accommodation well in advance, or be prepared to commute from elsewhere. In addition to the hotels mentioned in the text, there's a reasonable - if not especially extensive - provision of **private rooms** (①–④), bookable via the appropriate local tourist office. Bearing in mind that the true identity of the region has been sacrificed to hard sell, you could do worse than take the **train** through this stretch and admire the best feature – the scenery – in comfort, but it's undeniably more fun to go by **boat**.

Spring and autumn are the best times to visit the area, and you could easily spend several days meandering around. Rail and road links lie on either side of the river and, although there are no bridges between Bingen and Koblenz, fairly frequent ferry links for passengers should enable you to hop from one side of the river to the other without too much difficulty.

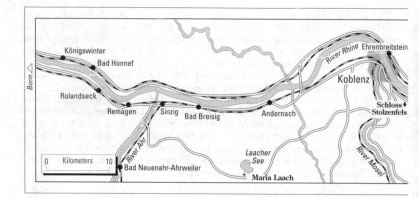

Bingen

Despite its imposing setting at the point where the Nahe joins the Rhine, **BINGEN** is very much the poor relation of Rüdesheim on the latter's opposite bank. Nonetheless, its star has been in the ascendant of late because of the burgeoning interest in one of the great female figures of the European Middle Ages, Abbess Hildegard of Bingen (see box), whose 900th anniversary is being celebrated in 1998 with an extensive programme of events.

Although rarely accessible to visitors, Bingen's best-known monument is the **Mäuseturm**, a former customs tower on an island in the Rhine in which, according to grisly legend, Archbishop Hatto of Mainz was devoured alive by mice after having burned all the local beggars during a famine. Towering above the town centre and commanding a wonderful view out over the Rhine to the Taunus is **Burg Klopp**, a former castle of the Archbishop-Electors of Mainz. The original fortress was destroyed in 1689 and the ruins were blown up in 1711, so that what you see today is a nineteenth-century replica. Housed within its tower is the **Heimatmuseum** (April–Oct Tues–Sun 9am–noon & 2–5pm; DM2), whose prize exhibit is a brutal-looking set of Roman doctor's instruments. Another good vantage point is the **Rupertsberg** above Bingerbrück, the suburb on the opposite side of the Nahe. This is the site of the **Kloster** where Hildegard was abbess, but unfortunately only the cellars plus scanty remains of the church still survive.

ABBESS HILDEGARD OF BINGEN (1098–1179)

The astonishing career of the multi-talented Hildegard of Bingen is quite unlike that of any other woman of her time. Born into a noble family, she was placed in the convent of Disibodenburg in the Nahe valley at the age of eight, becoming abbess in 1136. She went on to found two convents of her own – the Rupertsberg above Bingen in 1150 and Eibingen on the outskirts of Rüdesheim in 1165 – and is the only medieval woman who is known to have undertaken preaching tours, addressing clergy as well as laity. Between 1141 and 1151 she wrote her literary masterpiece *Scivias*, visionary descriptions of the world and the relationship between God and mankind. She also produced a two-volume tract on natural sciences and the art of healing. Yet it is arguable that her most lasting achievement was as a composer. Her legacy consists of the music drama *Ordo Virtutum*, the earliest-known morality play, plus 77 canticles, sequences and songs, in which she deploys a variety of devices, ranging from simple melodies to impassioned declamation, to enrich the vivid imagery of her own poetry.

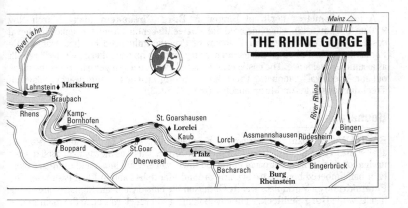

Bingen's **Hauptbahnhof** adjoins the huge rail yards in Bingerbrück; the **Stadtbahnhof** is at the southern edge of the town centre. Close to the latter, at Rheinkai 21, is the **tourist office** (April–Nov Mon–Fri 9am–6pm, Sat 9am–1pm; Dec–March Mon–Fri 9am–4pm; ☎06721/184205). A good range of **hotels** includes *Römerhof*, Rupertsberg 10 (☎06721/32248; ④); *Krone*, Rheinkai 19–20 (☎06721/17016; ④); *Martinskeller*, Martinstr. 1 (☎06721/13475; ⑤); and *Atlantis-Rheinhotel*, Hindenburganlage 1 (☎06721/7960; ⑧). There's a **youth hostel** at Herterstr. 51 (☎06721/32163; ❷) in Bingerbrück and **camping** facilities (☎06721/17160) near the Hindenburgbrücke in the suburb of Kempten. The town's leading **restaurants** are those in the hotels *Atlantis* and *Krone*, plus *Brunnenkeller*, Vorstadt 60.

BOAT TRIPS ALONG THE RHINE

The imperious white vessels of the **K-D Linie** (Rheinwerft, Koblenz; ☎0261/31030; see also listings in Mainz, Bonn and Cologne) have several sailings each way during the June to September high season; the services thereafter progressively run down, and stop altogether at the end of October, to resume in a skeleton format at Easter or the beginning of April, whichever is the earlier. Although prices are lower than they used to be, they're still far from cheap (Bingen to Koblenz costs DM43.40; Mainz to St Goar DM54.80). However, day returns are available for the same price as a single, and you travel free of charge if you can prove that it's your birthday. Both *EuroDomino* and *Eurail* (though not *InterRail*) passes are valid. In addition, a number of smaller companies offer much cheaper sailings along shorter stretches:

Ferry Companies and Routes

Bingen-Rüdesheimer Fähr- und Schiffahrtgesellschaft Rheinkai 10, Bingen (☎06721/14140)	Bingen–St. Goar
Hebel Linie Rheinallee 35, Boppard (☎06742/2420)	Boppard–Koblenz–Kobern–Gondorf
Josef Hewel Bayerhofgasse 11, Boppard (☎06742/2223)	Boppard–Braubach
Collée-Hölzenbein Rheinzollstr. 4, Koblenz (☎0261/37744)	Koblenz–Bingen
Merkelbach Emster Str. 57, Koblenz (☎0261/76810)	Koblenz–Braubach

A few kilometres north of Bingen is **Burg Rheinstein** (daily March–Nov 9.30am–5/7pm; DM6), which inspired the nineteenth-century trend for replica medieval castles when Prince Friedrich Wilhelm of Prussia, influenced by then fashionable Romanticism, had a ruined thirteenth-century fortress he had inherited in 1823 rebuilt as a summer residence. The castle is now owned by an opera singer who rents the place out for "medieval" banquets. There are **camping** facilities in the nearby village of Trechtinghausen at Am Morgenbach 1 (☎06721/6133).

Bacharach

BACHARACH, 10km downstream, was called *Baccaracum* by the Romans after an altar stone to Bacchus which once stood in the Rhine. This was blown up in 1850 to ease navigation of the river, but parts of the old town wall are still intact and there are plenty of half-timbered houses, particularly around Marktplatz and in Blücherstrasse. The **Peterskirche** on Marktplatz is early Gothic on the outside and late Romanesque on the inside, while **Burg Stahleck**, a chunky-looking castle which was once the main seat of the Counts Palatine of the Rhine, now houses the local **youth hostel** (☎06743/1266; ❷). From the overgrown and half-timbered Posthof square there's a good view of the **Wernerkapelle**, the red sandstone frame of a never-completed Gothic chapel.

The **tourist office** is at Oberstr. 1 (Mon–Fri 8.30am–noon & 2–5pm, Sat 10am–noon; ☎06743/2968). A wide choice of **hotels** includes *Im Malerwinkel*, Blücherstr. 41–45 (☎06743/1239; ②); *Gelber Hof*, Blücherstr. 26 (☎06743/1017; ④); *Altkölnischer Hof*, Blücherstr. 2 (☎06743/1339; ⑤); and *Parkhotel*, Marktstr. 8 (☎06743/1422; ⑤). All except the first of these have **restaurants**. The local **campsite** is at Strandbadweg (☎06743/1752).

Kaub

KAUB, a few kilometres north on the opposite bank of the Rhine, was another stronghold of the Counts Palatine, who in 1277 purchased **Burg Gutenfels** above the town, together with the right to levy tolls on passing ships. The castle as you see it today is a late nineteenth-century rebuild of the original, and nowadays functions as a hotel. Though you can't even enter the grounds unless you're a guest, it's worth following the footpath round the back, which leads to a vantage point offering a magnificent view over the Rhine.

It was at Kaub that Field Marshal Blücher, the Prussian general who saved the day with his late arrival at the battle of Waterloo, crossed the Rhine during an earlier campaign against Napoleon by ordering the construction of a spectacular pontoon bridge. He's commemorated in the **Blüchermuseum** (April–Oct Tues–Sun 10am–noon & 2–4pm; Nov–March Tues–Sat 10am–noon, Sun 10am–noon & 2–4pm; DM4) at Metzgergasse 6, the Baroque town house he used as his headquarters. The rooms are decorated in grand Empire style and are full of military memorabilia from the Napoleonic Wars and old Prussia.

From Kaub's waterfront promenade you get a great view of one of the most famous symbols of the Rhineland, the **Pfalzgrafenstein** or **Pfalz** (Easter–Sept Tues–Sun 9am–1pm & 2–6pm; Oct, Nov & Jan–Easter Tues–Sun 9am–1pm & 2–5pm; DM4 plus DM3 for the ferry; note that access is suspended when the river's water level is high). Construction of this white-walled toll fortress, which stands on an islet in the river like a permanently moored ship, was begun in 1326 by order of the Count Palatine Ludwig the Bavarian. Brought up to date in the seventeenth century by the provision of gun emplacements and look-out oriels, the Pfalzgrafenstein continued to serve as a toll-levying station until 1867.

Kaub's **tourist office** (Mon–Fri 8am–noon; ☎06774/222) is in the Rathaus, Metzgergasse 26. The cheapest of several reasonably priced **hotels** are *Deutsches*

Haus, Schulstr. (☎06774/266; ②), which also has a good restaurant, and *Weinhaus Zur Pfalz*, Bahnstr. 10 (☎06774/258; ③). There are **camping** facilities at *Am Elsleinband* on Blücherstrasse (☎06774/560).

Oberwesel

OBERWESEL, back on the left bank just to the north, is overlooked by the huge **Schönburg**, now a ruin but still impressive. There's a hotel, *Auf Schönburg* (☎06744/93930; ⑧) within the castle complex. In town, the Gothic **Liebfrauenkirche** is known to the locals as "the red church", after the huge red sandstone blocks used to build it. In the airy interior, look out for the *Niklausaltar*, on which Saint Nicholas is shown helping three knights who have been sentenced to death for crimes they didn't commit, saving three sisters who have been forced into prostitution by their father, and protecting passengers on board a ship. The town also possesses the best set of fortifications on the Rhine, with eighteen defensive towers still surviving.

Oberwesel's **tourist office** is at Rathausstr. 3 (☎06744/1521). Good **hotels** include *Weinhaus Weiler*, Marktplatz 4 (☎06744/7003; ④) and *Römerkrug*, Marktplatz 1 (☎06744/7091; ⑥); both also have recommendable restaurants. There's a **campsite** (☎06744/245) just off the B9 road to the north of town, while the **youth hostel** is by the castle at Auf dem Schönberg (☎06744/7046; ⑩).

The Lorelei and St Goarshausen

Next stop is **ST GOARSHAUSEN**, which trails along the eastern bank of the Rhine for a couple of kilometres. Just before the entrance to the town is the **Lorelei** (or **Loreley**), the famous outcrop of rock where, according to legend, a blonde woman used to sit combing her hair while she lured passing sailors to watery graves with her eerily compelling song. There's a naff statue at the water's edge to commemorate the legend. The rock itself has been over-hyped – it's impressive, but no more so than dozens of other cliffs in the Rhine gorge. However, there are outstanding views from the top (you can reach it via St Goarshausen itself on bus #6147 or by following the signs marked *Loreley Felsen* if you're travelling under your own steam). Apart from a viewing platform, the summit has a **campsite** (☎06771/7519) and a privately owned **youth hostel** (☎06771/2619). Also up here is the *Loreley Freilichtbühne*, an open-air stage that is frequently used for rock concerts.

Above St Goarshausen itself is **Burg Katz** (Cat Castle), the partially reconstructed fourteenth-century fortress of the Counts of Katzenelnbogen. It was built to rival another castle a few kilometres downstream, which belonged to the Archbishops of Trier and earned the inevitable nickname **Burg Maus** (Mouse Castle) because of its relative puniness. Today Burg Maus is an eagle and falcon station, giving daily displays of bird flight at 11am, 2.30pm and 4.30pm (April–Sept only; DM10).

St Goarshausen's **tourist office** is at Bahnhofstr. 8 (☎06771/427). There's an inexpensive **guesthouse**, *Winzerschänke*, on the way to the Lorelei at Forstbachstr. 38 (☎06771/337; ②). **Hotels** include *Deutsches Haus*, Wellmicher Str. 7 (☎06771/2617; ③); *Colonius*, Am Rheinufer (☎06771/2604; ④); and *Pohl's Rheinhotel Adler*, Bahnhofstr. 6 (☎06771/2613; ⑥). The *Weinwoche* is during the second and third weeks in September, and there are other *Weinfeste* at the end of September and during the third weekend in October.

St Goar

A ferry will take you back across to the west bank of the Rhine and **ST GOAR**, which is slightly prettier and more touristy than its counterpart. Looming above town is one of the best Rhine castles, the enormous **Burg Rheinfels** (daily April–Sept 9am–6pm;

Oct 9am–5pm; DM5) which, until the French blew it up in 1797, was one of the most powerful fortresses on the Rhine. It was founded in 1245 by Count Dieter von Katzenelnbogen, who wanted to look after his Rhine toll-collecting racket, and just ten years later withstood a 9000-man siege by soldiers of the Alliance of Rhenish Towns. During the sixteenth and seventeenth centuries the Landgraves of Hesse extended what was already a formidable castle into an enormous fortification complex which was to prove virtually impregnable: it was the only Rhineland castle that the French were unable to take during the War of the Palatinate Succession. In 1796 the castle surrendered to the troops of Napoleon without a shot being fired, and over the next three years the French did their best to demolish it. Today, the medieval outline can still be seen and you can walk through the underground passages of the later battlements. Models in the **Heimatmuseum** (April–Sept 9.30am–noon & 1–5pm; admission included in Burg entrance fee), which is housed in a rebuilt section, show how the place looked before it was destroyed.

St Goar's **tourist office** is at Heerstr. 86 (May–Sept Mon–Fri 8am–12.30pm & 2–5pm, Sat 9.30am–noon; Oct–April Mon–Fri 8am–12.30pm & 2–4.30pm; ☎06741/383). There are plenty of **hotels** in the town centre, including *Germania*, Heerstr. 47 (☎06741/1610; ③); *Zur Post*, Bahnhofstr. 3 (☎06741/339; ③); *Zum Goldenen Löwen*, Heerstr. 82 (☎06741/1674; ④); and *Montag*, Heerstr. 128 (☎06741/1629; ⑥). If you want to splash out, try the *Schlosshotel* in the Burg Rheinfels complex (☎06741/8020; ⑧-⑨). All of these hotels also have **restaurants**. The **youth hostel** is at Bismarckweg 17 (☎06741/388; ⓘ), just north of the town centre, while you can **camp** at *Friedenau*, Gründelbachstr. 103 (☎06741/368), and *Loreleyblick*, An der Loreley 29–39 (☎06741/2066), neither of which is too far out of town.

Boppard

At **BOPPARD**, a couple of kilometres downstream from Kamp-Bornhofen, but this time on the left bank, the Rhine gorge starts to level out and the valley landscape becomes a gentler one of rounded, vine-covered slopes. The town benefits enormously from a Rhine promenade running along its entire length, having forced the rail authorities to lay the tracks on the opposite side of the centre, instead of their customary position by the river.

Boppard's dominant building is the late Romanesque **Severuskirche** on Marktplatz. A twin-towered structure, brightly painted in white and yellow, it was built during the thirteenth century to house the remains of Saint Severus, Bishop of Ravenna. Contemporary with the church are the wall paintings illustrating the life of the saint, and the poignant triumphal cross.

The squat Gothic **Karmelitenkirche**, near the Rhine quay, has elaborate fifteenth-century choir stalls, a couple of seventeenth-century altars and various tombs of local bigwigs. At the east entrance is a recess which houses the fourteenth-century *Traubenmadonna*. Traditionally, local vine growers place the first ripe bunch of grapes of the year by the statue and leave it there until it withers away.

At the end of Kirchgasse, which is just off Oberstrasse (Boppard's main street), are the remains of the Roman **Stadtmauer**, which has weathered the years remarkably well. Four watchtowers survive of the 28 which guarded the military camp of Baudobirga, laid out in the fourth century, on the site of present-day Boppard.

At the end of Bingergasse stand the remains of more recent fortifications. The **Binger Tor** was built during the Middle Ages and has survived more or less intact, bar the odd bit of crumbling here and there. Between Burgplatz and Rheinallee is the **Alte Burg**, a castle and residence built by the Archbishops of Trier to consolidate their grip in the area. The central keep, with its apertures for the pouring of boiling oil, molten lead and the like, was built around 1327, while the more civilized-looking wings were added during the seventeenth century. These days the building houses the **Museum der Stadt Boppard** (April–Oct Tues–Sun 10am–noon & 2–5pm; free). Part of this is devoted to the furniture of Michael Thonet, a son of Boppard, who, during the early nineteenth century, perfected the technique of laminating wood and earned himself a fortune in the process. At the northern end of town, a **chairlift** (DM7 single, DM10 return) ascends to the **belvedere** known as *Vierseenblick* (Four Lakes View) because the only parts of the Rhine which are visible are four seemingly separate stretches of water. A short waymarked walk away is another viewpoint, the *Rheinschleife*, which commands a magnificent panorama over the Rhine's most spectacular bend.

Practicalities

Boppard's **tourist office** is in the Rathaus on Marktplatz (Mon–Fri 8am–5.30pm; April–Oct also Sat 10am–1pm; ☎06742/3888). There are several inexpensive **hotels** in the town centre, the most recommendable being the Anglo-German *Ohm Patt*, Steinstr. 30 (☎06742/2366; ③); and *Weinhaus Sonnenhof*, Kirchgasse 8 (☎06742/3223; ④), which also has a good restaurant. Of the more upmarket waterfront hotels, best value is the American-owned *Günther*, Rheinallee 40 (☎06742/2335; ④), many of whose rooms have balconies offering grandstand views of the river. Next door, at nos. 41–42, is the *Bellevue Rheinhotel* (☎06742/1020; ⑦) – although it's the most luxurious and expensive in town, this is the place to come for innovative bargain lunches. There are **camping** facilities at *Sonneck*, just north of town on the B9 right next to the Rhine (☎06742/2121).

Braubach

On the right bank of the Rhine 12km downstream from Boppard is **BRAUBACH**. It's a typical Rhenish village, with one outstanding **hotel** in *Zum Weissen Schwanen*, Brunnenstr 4 (☎02627/559 or 9820; ⑤), a seventeenth-century *Weinhaus* with an attached fourteenth-century mill; note that the restaurant is open evenings only.

Set in the hills a good half-hour's walk above the town, the **Marksburg** (guided tours daily Easter–Oct 10am–5pm; Nov–Easter 11am–4pm; DM7) is the only medieval castle on this stretch of the Rhine, other than the Pfalzgrafenstein, to escape destruction by the French. The fact that this one is an original makes it a lot more impressive than the reconstructions you'll already have seen. Most of the building, including the turreted sandstone keep, was built between the twelfth and fourteenth centuries with a few additional defensive features added in the seventeenth century. Inside there's a big collection of weapons from the Middle Ages, including some extremely unpleasant instruments of torture. The Marksburg also has the only preserved medieval botanic garden in Germany.

Lahnstein and Rhens

Next stop is **LAHNSTEIN**, which is remarkable above all for its setting at the point where the River Lahn sweeps into the Rhine. Above the former is the only setpiece sight, the restored **Burg Lahneck** (guided tours daily Easter–Oct 10am–5pm; DM5), in whose grounds is the local **campsite** (☎02621/2765). There are also plenty of **hotels**, such as *Jung*, Bahnhofstr. 54 (☎02621/8001; ④); *Strassburger Hof*, Koblenzer Str. 2 (☎02621/96910; ④); and *Bock*, Westallee 11 (☎02621/2661; ⑤), all of which have **restaurants**. In the Kurpark, high above the Lahn at the extreme eastern edge of town, is *Hof Aspich*, one of the hottest *Szene* venues in the Rhineland, numbering among its attractions a *Hausbrauerei*, a large beer garden, and regular live music and cabaret performances. The **tourist office** (Mon–Fri 8am–5pm; April–Sept also Sat 10am–noon; ☎02621/914171) is in the Stadthallenpassage in the town centre.

From Lahnstein you can take the ferry (passengers only; if you're driving you'll have to go via the Koblenz road bridge) to the half-timbered village of **RHENS**, which preserves most of its medieval fortifications. The momentous-sounding **Königsstuhl** (Seat of Kings) on the heights above is a stone platform where the German Electors met from 1273 to 1400 to choose their king. In fact, like so many of the Rhine's "medieval" monuments, most of what can be seen today dates from as recently as 1842, inspired by the then fashionable vogue for resurrecting Germany's medieval past.

A detour up the Lahn

From Lahstein, it's well worth making a detour up the Lahn, a beautiful valley which provides a welcome escape from the tourist claustrophobia of the Rhine. Most of the river lies in Hesse, though the downstream stretch is in Rhineland-Palatinate.

The first town you come to is **BAD EMS**, a fashionable, elegant and very expensive spa, which still preserves much of the ambience that drew figures like King Wilhelm I of Prussia to take the waters. It was while resting here in July 1870 that Wilhelm received the letter from Napoleon III that sparked off the Franco-Prussian War. Just up the river is **Nassau**, cradle of the famous dynasty of the same name. In spite of its historical associations, there's little of interest left to see today. You're better pressing on to **DIEZ**, seat of one of the family offshoots. The town clusters at the foot of their highly distinctive medieval **Schloss**, an immensely tall building which looks more like a vast tower house. Nowadays, it has been refurbished as the local **youth hostel** (☎06432/2481; ✿). Also in Diez is the elegantly Baroque **Schloss Oranienstein** (guided tours Tues–Sun 9.30–11.30am & 2–4pm; DM2), the family home in more peaceful later years, decked out with lots of seventeenth- and eighteenth-century paintings and furniture. From here, it's only a few kilometres to the Hessian frontier and the episcopal city of Limburg (see p.372).

Koblenz

It's appropriate that the name of **KOBLENZ** derives from the Latin word for confluence, as it was the Romans who first recognized the favourable properties of the site at the point where the Mosel flows into the Rhine, establishing a settlement there in 14 AD. Nowadays, the town has become one of Germany's major tourist centres, profiting from its ready access to the two great river valleys and the hill ranges beyond. Koblenz itself polarizes opinion – some enjoy its relaxed, rather faded charm; others find it smug and boring. The connection with tourism actually has deep roots, as it was in Koblenz in 1823 that **Karl Baedeker** began publishing his famous series of guidebooks which aimed at saving travellers from having to depend on unreliable and extortionate local tour guides for information. Old editions of these (the one on *The Rhineland* itself is a good example) are still worth seeking out: their sententious prose evokes a vanished epoch, and their pull-out maps are wonderful to handle.

The town

The place to begin a tour of Koblenz is the **Deutsches Eck**, where the Mosel flows into the Rhine. In 1897, a colossal equestrian monument in the heroic taste of the time was erected here to Kaiser Wilhelm I. It was destroyed in World War II, but the base, itself a pompous structure with over a hundred steps, was rebuilt and piously dedicated to the unification of Germany. After much soul-searching, a copy of the statue was re-erected in 1993 in belated celebration of the achievement of this.

The **telephone code** for Koblenz is ☎0261

Close by is the finest building in the city, the Romanesque collegiate foundation of **St Kastor**, largely twelfth-century, whose imposing facade has twin towers with characteristic "bishop's mitre" roofs. A long-term project to restore the interior has left it looking wonderfully fresh. Look out for the elaborate **keystones** of the Gothic vault, especially the one showing the Madonna and Child in a boat. There's a good view of the church from the floral garden of the adjacent **Deutschherrenhaus** which now contains the **Ludwig-Museum** (Tues, Wed, Fri & Sat 11am–5pm, Thurs 11am–8pm, Sun 11am–6pm; DM5), with an important collection of (predominantly French) modern art.

The Rhine bank is today largely given over to tourist facilities; the curious old crane, the **Rheinkran**, which is now converted into a pricey restaurant, is the only thing to catch the eye. Only a few monuments of medieval Koblenz's centre, which bordered on the Mosel, remain; they're rather over-restored in the romantic image of old Germany, with the exterior walls painted in bright colours, but are undeniably picturesque. You come first of all to the **Deutscher Kaiser**, a sixteenth-century tower house which also is now a restaurant. Further on is the Florinsmarkt, with the Romanesque-Gothic **St Florin**, now a Protestant parish church, the **Schöffenhaus**, a pretty little orange building with corner turrets, and the **Altes Kaufhaus**. This last building now houses the **Mittelrhein-Museum** (Tues & Thurs–Sat 11am–5pm, Wed 11am–8pm, Sun 11am–6pm; DM5), a fairly miscellaneous collection of paintings, sculptures and antiquities. The ground floor has a few German Primitives, including an *Adoration of the Magi* by the Augsburg painter **Jörg Breu** which unashamedly plagiarizes a portrait by his fellow-citizen, Holbein the Elder, for the figure of one of the kings. Upstairs are many works by one of Germany's most accomplished Rococo painters, **Januarius Zick**, who eventually settled in Koblenz.

Further along the Mosel bank is the **Alte Burg**, altered to a Renaissance palace and now housing the municipal library, but originally constructed to defend the fourteenth-century **Balduinbrücke**. Turning away from the river, you come to **Münzplatz**, which still preserves the mint master's house. Also in the square is the mansion birthplace of the wily Habsburg statesman **Clemens von Metternich**, high priest of the theory (which was to dominate nineteenth-century politics) that the key to a peaceful Europe lay in maintaining a balance of power among the main states. His peak of influence came during his dominant hosting role at the Congress of Vienna in 1815, which laid down the structure of post-Napoleonic Europe; ironically, his native town was given to Prussia – arch-rival of his adopted Austria – as a result.

Down the pedestrian precinct at the intersection of Löhrstrasse and Markstrasse there's a fine grouping of four houses, each with ornamental oriel windows. Left from here is another large square, Plan, behind which are the exotic Baroque onion-shaped spires of the **Liebfrauenkirche**, a handsome if diffuse church with a galleried Romanesque nave and a Gothic chancel. Just beyond stands the **Rathaus**, incongruously housed in a cavernous former Jesuit college.

In the late eighteenth century, Koblenz was expanded to the south in the form of a planned Neoclassical town. The Archbishop-Electors of Trier moved their court here, centred on the huge **Schloss**; three years after its completion, the Elector fled in the wake of Napoleon's advance, never to return. The buildings were gutted during the last war and now serve as offices. A more lasting memento of the period is the stately **Theater** fronted by an obelisk on Deinhardplatz.

Ehrenbreitstein

Across the Rhine lies **EHRENBREITSTEIN**, with the original **Residenz** of the Electors, designed by Balthasar Neumann. Looming high above is the vast **Festung** – one of the largest fortresses in the world – with an impressive set of defences which the Prussians painstakingly and quite needlessly rebuilt over a ten-year period after Koblenz passed into their hands. It now contains the youth hostel and the **Landesmuseum** (daily mid-March to Nov 9am–12.30pm & 1–5pm; DM3). Even if you don't want to stay here, it's well worth the climb for the sake of the memorable panoramas of the city and its two great rivers. Access is possible (but expensive) by chairlift in season; otherwise, follow the main road along the shore of the Rhine until you come to a path which snakes upwards.

Schloss Stolzenfels

At Koblenz's southernmost extremity, reachable by any bus travelling down the left bank of the Rhine, is **Schloss Stolzenfels** (April–Sept Tues–Sun 9am–5pm; Oct, Nov & Jan–March Tues–Sun 10am–3.30pm; DM5), a Romantic-era fantasy designed by Karl Friedrich Schinkel to replace a thirteenth-century Burg which had gone up in smoke in 1688. The great Prussian architect let his imagination run riot, drawing inspiration not only from the old fortresses of the Rhineland – as evidenced by the main **Rittersaal** with its suits of armour and medieval weaponry – but from a variety of other historical sources, notably the Moorish palaces of Andalucia.

Practicalities

The **Hauptbahnhof** and **bus station** are side by side, to the southwest of the historical part of the city. Immediately opposite is the main **tourist office** (April, Oct & Nov Mon–Fri 9am–6pm, Sat & Sun 10am–6pm; May–Sept Mon–Fri 9am–8pm, Sat & Sun 10am–8pm; Nov–March Mon–Fri 9am–6pm; ☎31304). There's also a branch on the Rhine front at Konrad-Adenauer-Ufer (June–Sept Tues–Sun noon–6pm; ☎129 1630). Just to the south of this is the departure point of the **ferry** to Ehrenbreitstein; its Mosel counterpart runs in summer only from the pier west of Deutsches Eck.

Accommodation

As you'd expect, Koblenz offers a huge choice of accommodation, with **hotels** in every category, most of them competitively priced in terms of what they offer. The **youth hostel** (☎73737; ⚑) in Festung Ehrenbreitstein – buses #7, #8, #9 or #10 go closest – must rate as one of the most enticing in Germany. There's a **campsite** at Lützel, directly opposite Deutsches Eck (April to mid-Oct; ☎802489).

HOTELS AND PENSIONS

Brenner, Rizzastr. 20–22 (☎32060, fax 36278). Elegant, beautifully furnished hotel located between the Hauptbahnhof and the Altstadt. ⑦

Diehl's, Am Pfaffendorfer Tor 10, Ehrenbreitstein (☎97070, fax 970 7213). Koblenz's leading hotel is right by the Rhine, and commands wonderful views. Its facilities include thermal baths, a sauna and solarium, and there's a first-rate restaurant, *Rheinterrasse*. ⑦

Jan van Werth, Van-Werth-Str. 9 (☎36500, fax 36506). Good-value hotel between the Hauptbahnhof and Altstadt. Note that its basic single rooms cost less than half the price of any of the doubles. ④

Kleiner Riesen, Kaiserin-Augusta-Anlagen 18 (☎303460, fax 160725). Fine traditional hotel on the right-bank waterfront. ⑥

Kornpforte, Kornpfortstr. 11 (☎31174). Medium-range hotel with *Weinstube* in the heart of the Altstadt. ⑤

Mäckler, Helffensteinstr. 63–65, Ehrenbreitstein (☎73725). Pension offering some of the cheapest rooms in town. ①

Weinand, Weissernonnengasse 4–6 (☎32492, fax 38110). Budget hotel in the northwest of the Altstadt. ②

Zur Kaul, Helffensteinstr. 64, Ehrenbreitstein (☎75256, fax 76872). Another low-cost option in the right bank suburb. ②

Eating and drinking

If not one of the Rhineland's more renowned gastronomic centres, Koblenz still has a decent choice of places to eat and drink.

Historischer Weinkeller, Mehlgasse 16. Cosy wine bar-restaurant in a vaulted medieval cellar. Closed Mon.

Irish Pub, Burgstr. 7. Has all the main Irish beers on tap, and features live music on Mon and Wed evenings.

Königsbacher, An der Königsbach 8. Capacious restaurant in the premises of the eponymous brewery, located in the south of town on the road to Schloss Stolzenfels. It makes an excellent bitter-tasting *Pils*, and also has a very fruity *Kölsch* named *Richmodis*, which is made by its subsidiary in Cologne.

Loup de Meer, Neustadt 12. Small speciality fish restaurant, located just to the west of the Schloss. Open evenings only at the weekend.

Ratskeller, Am Plan 9. Typically reliable choice for *gutbürgerliche Küche*.

Salatgarten, Gymnasialstr. 14. Self-service vegetarian and wholefood restaurant. Closed Sun.

Stresemann, Rheinzollstr. 8. The bistro-style cooking here is among the most imaginative in town. Closed Tues (also Mon in winter).

Weindorf, Julius-Wegeler-Str. 2. A complex of four wine taverns, grouped together in the form of a village square. Although very tourist-orientated, it's a good place to sample the local *Riesling* and *Müller-Thurgau* vintages, and to eat typically Rhenish dishes. Closed all Nov.

Entertainment

The principal **cultural** venue is the aforementioned *Theater der Stadt Koblenz* on Deinhardplatz (☎129 2840), whose programme of plays, opera and other events put those of many larger cities to shame. Koblenz also boasts Germany's only specialist **comedy** venue in *Blaue Biwel*, Entenpful 9 (☎35577); English-language acts are featured occasionally. The two main **festivals** are Carnival and *Der Rhein in Flammen*; the latter takes place on the second Saturday in August, and features fireworks and bonfires.

The Rhine from Andernach to Bonn

Soon after leaving Koblenz, the Rhine gorge opens out, cutting between the ranges of the Eifel and Westerwald. If this stretch doesn't quite match the grandeur of the preceding section, it's impressive nonetheless and well worth following by either boat or train. With exceptions, it also has the benefit of being less touristy.

Andernach

ANDERNACH, which lies 16km down the Rhine from Koblenz, can trace its history back further than almost any other German town. It celebrated its two-thousandth anniversary in 1988, commemorating the foundation of a Roman base for the campaigns against the tribes on the eastern side of the Rhine. Subsequently Andernach became a Franconian royal seat, before passing to the control of the Archbishop-Electors of Cologne, serving as the southern border of their territory until the Napoleonic invasion. Nowadays, it's an odd hybrid, having a fair amount of industry, yet taking advantage of its situation and monuments to double as a holiday resort.

If you're travelling along the Rhine by boat, it's definitely worth breaking your journey for a couple of hours in order to walk round the thirteenth-century **Stadtmauer**, which was laid out on the Roman foundations. The walls survive largely intact, making a solid back for many later buildings, including a well-concealed row of houses. Extra defence on the southern stretch was provided by the **Burg**, the most important town castle in the Rhineland. Blown up by French troops in 1688, it has nevertheless survived, notably the later embellishments such as the **Pulverturm** and residential palace wing.

Round to the north, overlooking the river, is the **Rheintor**, whose inner gate has weather-worn statues illustrating the best-known local legend, that of the *Andernacher Bäckerjungen* (baker boys of Andernach), who saved the town from occupation by letting loose their bees on the invading army. The most picturesque feature of Andernach's fortifications, however, is the fifteenth-century **Runder Turm** (key available from the tourist office) overlooking the Rhine on the northern side of town, whose octagonal upper storeys give it an exotic, oddly Moorish air. Thankfully, the French siege guns failed to penetrate its thick walls, but the enormous dent they made can still be seen clearly. Continuing down the river bank, there's a remarkable sixteenth-century **crane** whose original wooden mechanism remained in service into the present century and is still in full working order.

Just to the west of the Runder Turm, the tall twin facade towers of the **Pfarrkirche Maria Himmelfahrt** rise majestically above the rest of the skyline. For the most part, it's an archetypal late Romanesque basilica with a pronounced Rhenish accent, though the northeastern belfry is in fact a survivor of the previous church on the site.

Andernach's main axis, Hochstrasse, runs from here to the Burg; about halfway down is the **Altes Rathaus**, occupying the site of the former ghetto. A **Mikwe** (Jewish bath) was recently discovered underneath the session room; to see it, ask for the key at the **tourist office** (see below). On the adjacent Läufstrasse is the Gothic **Christuskirche**, a former Minorite monastery with a curiously lopsided interior. A little further down the street is the **Haus von der Leyen**, a Renaissance patrician mansion that now houses the **Stadtmuseum** (Tues–Fri 10am–noon & 2–5pm, Sat & Sun 2–4pm; DM2). Lack of space means that only a small collection of antiquities is permanently on display, but the changing exhibitions (prominently featured on posters outside) are often surprisingly good.

Practicalities

Buses operate from Am Stadtgraben, the western range of the old wall. The **Bahnhof** is on Kurfürstendamm; to reach the centre, walk straight ahead, then turn right under the rail bridge. Andernach's **tourist office** is at Läufstr. 11 (Mon–Fri 8am–12.30pm & 1.30–5pm, Sat 9am–noon; ☎02632/922300).

In summer, the town is a popular overnight stop with tour coach operators; hence there are plenty of **hotels**, but many of these are often fully booked and anyway charge independent travellers inflated prices. Nonetheless, there are plenty of places worth trying, including *Römer*, Hochstr. 89 (☎02632/42209; ③); *Andernacher Hof*, Breite Str. 83 (☎02632/43175; ④); *Traube*, Konrad-Adenauer-Allee 14 (☎02632/96220; ⑤); *Alte Kanzlei*, Steinweg 30 (☎02632/96660; ⑦); and *Fischer*, Am Helmwartsturm 4–6 (☎02632/492047; ⑦). The last two on this list are also among the best places to **eat**; *Alte Kanzlei* offers a particularly attractive ambience in its vaulted cellar and garden courtyard.

Andernach hosts a number of **festivals**, including a medieval fair in the Burg (mid-July); *Die Tausenden Lichten* (The Thousand Lights), featuring fireworks and illuminations (first weekend in September); and, of course, Carnival.

Beyond Andernach

Immediately beyond Brohl, the train's second stop after Andernach, stands **Burg Rheineck**. This fortress, which was rebuilt in the nineteenth century, is no longer open to the public, but if you follow the path to the right, there's a belvedere commanding an impressive panorama. A further 3km on is **BAD BREISIG**, a popular spa and holiday resort, which makes a good base for exploring the area, thanks to a huge choice of accommodation in all categories, ranging from campsites via private **guesthouses** and riverside inns to luxury hotels.

From Bad Breisig, the rail line leaves the banks of the river for a spell, continuing to **SINZIG**, 6km away, which lies near the end of the valley of the Ahr. There's just one monument of note: the church of **St Peter**, one of the smallest but most original of the Romanesque basilicas of the Rhineland. Even more than usual, the impression is of a dream-like fantasy, an effect accentuated by the white and yellow paint covering the exterior walls. On the south side of the chancel is a chapel adorned with noble though fragmentary frescoes which are contemporary with the building, while the high altar has a brightly coloured late fifteenth-century *Passion Retable* from Cologne.

Remagen

Back on the Rhine, 4km north, is **REMAGEN**, a town famous for a **bridge** which – apart from its support towers – no longer exists. The towers on the Remagen side have been converted into the **Friedensmuseum** (daily March–Oct 10am–5pm; DM2.50), which chronicles the story of the bridge (see box below) by means of old photographs.

In the centre of town, the dominant building is the curious church of **St Peter und Paul**. At the turn of the century, it was decided that the original Romanesque-Gothic church was no longer sufficiently big for the town's expanding population; accordingly, a new church, imitating the style of the old but on a much larger scale, was tacked on to it at right angles. More directly appealing is the enigmatic **Pfarrhoftor**, a double gateway forming the entrance to the parish close. It's covered with carvings made by a Romanesque sculptor of limited technique but fertile imagination.

High above Remagen stands the mid-nineteenth-century **Apollinariskirche**, goal of a popular ten-day pilgrimage at the end of July. The church was built in tandem with the completion of the Dom in Cologne, and is a miniature version of it. Inside, the walls are covered with frescoes of the lives of Christ, the Virgin and Saint Apollinaris.

With its central location, Remagen is undoubtedly the best base for this part of the Rhine, and there's a **campsite** (☎02642/22222) right beside the river. The hotels beside the Bahnhof are geared to coach parties and are anyway best avoided, as thundering goods trains pass through all night. Far better to go for a room in a **private house** (②–③). For a full list, contact the **tourist office**, Kirchstr. 6 (Mon–Thurs 8.30am–noon & 2–4pm, Fri 8.30am–noon; ☎02642/22572).

Rolandseck

ROLANDSECK, a further 6km north, has now been absorbed by Remagen. The train station building is now designated the **Künstlerbahnhof** (daily 10am–5pm; DM2.50), housing a notable collection of works by Hans Arp, along with changing exhibitions of contemporary art. More sculptures by Arp and by Henry Moore can be seen for free on the lawn outside.

One of the most famous Rhine legends is closely associated with the vicinity of Rolandseck. In the middle of the Rhine, just beyond the village, is the island of

---

THE BRIDGE AT REMAGEN

Remagen's bridge was built during World War I to aid the movement of troops and supplies to the Western Front. On March 7, 1945, an advance regiment of the US Armoured Division reached this point, to find that the bridge – unlike all the others along the Rhine, Germany's most crucial natural defensive barrier – was still intact. The token Nazi force who had been left to guard it was quickly routed, enabling the Americans to establish a base on the opposite bank. Eisenhower declared the bridge to be "worth its weight in gold", while Hitler ordered the execution of four officers for their carelessness in failing to blow the bridge up. In retrospect, the importance of the Remagen episode seems exaggerated, as crossings were made by the Allies further up the Rhine the following week. Moreover, the bridge itself collapsed ten days later due to overloading, killing 28 American soldiers. However, it was symbolically a telling blow and has remained a popular subject for books, the best of which is Ken Hechler's *The Bridge at Remagen*.

Nonnenwerth, occupied by a former convent. On hearing news of the death of Roland (Charlemagne's nephew) in an ambush in northern Spain, his betrothed is alleged to have come here, taking her final vows the moment before the hero, miraculously recovered from his wounds, arrived to claim her. Stricken by grief, he built the **Rolandsbogen** fortress on the hill above in order to catch occasional glimpses of her. Whatever the veracity of the story, it's well worth climbing up to the ruin, which commands one of the most extensive views of this part of the Rhine, with Bonn and the Siebengebirge (see p.470 and p.477) immediately to the north.

THE EIFEL

Strictly speaking the mountains of the **Eifel** range – which are divided between the Rhineland-Palatinate and North Rhine-Westphalia – are little more than big hills. On the whole, they aren't desperately exciting, which probably accounts for the lack of mass tourism. However, in the part of the Eifel which lies in the Rhineland-Palatinate you'll find a gentle landscape of wooded hills and bare heathland, dotted with volcanic lakes and intersected by quiet, unspoiled valleys. The area is used to visitors, but most of them are Germans who spend their summer vacations abroad and come here for a second break in late spring or early autumn. This means that it's a good place to escape the crowds, particularly if you're otherwise concentrating on a nearby tourist area, such as the Rhine or Mosel.

The only part of the region which has completely succumbed to tourism is the **Ahr valley** in the northeast where truly spectacular scenery brings hundreds of thousands of visitors during a season that lasts from May until late October. Best-looking town outside the Ahr valley is **Mayen**, with its restored medieval centre and dramatic castles. Otherwise much of the Eifel has a slightly sleepy air, its life revolving round the seasonal influxes of visitors and people coming to the various spa towns or *Luftkurorte*.

The Ahr valley

The valley of the River Ahr rates as one of the most scenic corners of western Germany. The landscape and most of the towns in this valley, which cuts through from the **High Eifel** to join the Rhine just outside Remagen, form a real Brothers Grimm landscape of ruined castles, forests and vineyards. No effort has been spared when it comes to providing for mass tourism, and this is where the problems start. From May through to October all those idyllic little towns and villages are filled to overflowing with day-tripping German families, hikers, wine fans and British coach parties, and the only people who really benefit are the owners of tacky souvenir shops and the hotel keepers who rack up their prices.

The best thing to do is to visit the area out of season when you can absorb the atmosphere of the place without the crowds. There really is a lot to take in: the countryside is magnificent once you hit the upper reaches of the valley (particularly around **Altenahr**), and many of the towns and villages look like they've hardly changed in centuries. The area is best explored by taking the train up from Remagen; at first the valley seems flat and nondescript but gradually vineyards start to crowd up to the rail line and the sides of the valley become steeper.

Bad Neuenahr-Ahrweiler

First stop is **BAD NEUENAHR-AHRWEILER**, which threads its way along the Ahr for a few kilometres just before the valley becomes narrower and the spectacular stuff begins. It's really two towns which have grown into each other: Bad Neuenahr is fairly modern and commercially orientated while Ahrweiler is so impossibly old-fashioned that it looks like a film set.

Ahrweiler

The kernel of **AHRWEILER** dates back to the Middle Ages and seems wildly archaic with its narrow streets and half-timbered buildings. It's ringed by the **Stadtmauer,** built between the thirteenth and fifteenth centuries and still more or less intact despite numerous attempts to breach it during the Thirty Years' War. Four gateways survive, including the **Niedertor,** which leads into Niederhutstrasse, the town centre's main commercial street, which has plenty of tacky souvenir shops, along with delicatessens and wine merchants.

Niederhutstrasse runs into the broad Marktplatz, on the northern side of which is the thirteenth-century **Pfarrkirche St Laurentius.** Inside are fourteenth- and fifteenth-century frescoes and modern stained-glass windows, some of which have an almost Expressionist feel to them. At Altenbaustr. 3, just off the western end of Marktplatz, in a three-storey tower house which was originally built in the thirteenth century but partially remodelled in Baroque style, is the **Museum der Stadt** (Tues–Sun 10am–5pm; DM3). It contains objects relating to the town and the Ahr valley area, including some fine medieval sculptures and a section on local wine production methods through the centuries.

At the southern end of the centre the largest of the town gates, the **Ahrtor,** overlooks the River Ahr. From here you get a good view across to the **Ursulinenkloster Kalvarienberg,** which sits on the edge of town surrounded by vineyards. This imposing building, resembling a French château, now houses a convent and girls' school.

Ahrweiler's **Bahnhof** is conveniently located just a few minutes' walk from the centre of town. The **tourist office** is at Marktplatz 21 (late March to mid-Nov Mon–Fri 9am–6pm, Sat 10am–3pm, Sun 10.30am–4.30pm; rest of year Mon–Fri 8am–5pm, Sat 10am–1pm; ☎02641/977362). There's a fair provision of **private rooms** (①–③) and also many small **pensions,** including *Zur Erholung*, Schützenstr. 74 (☎02641/34936; ②); *Ippendorf*, Wolfgasse 7 (☎02641/34941; ②); and *Kronen*, Alveradisstr. 17 (☎02641/34202; ③). *Hohenzollern*, Silbergstr. 50 (☎02641/4268 or 9730; ⑤) on the west side of town is the best **hotel**. It also has a first-rate **restaurant,** though there are similarly good and much less expensive possibilities in the town centre, notably *Altes Zunfthaus*, Oberhutstr. 34, and *Eifelstube*, Ahrhutstr. 26. The **youth hostel** is at St-Pius-Str. 7 (☎02641/34924; ☎), about twenty minutes' walk from the Bahnhof along a well-signposted route. Ahrweiler's **campsite** is at Kalvarienbergstr. 1 (☎02641/35684), on the way out to the Ursulinenkloster.

Bad Neuenahr

Though less attractive than its sister town, **BAD NEUENAHR** has a couple of things worth seeing: the **Williborduskirche** on Schweizerstrasse, with its Romanesque west tower and the usual melange of architectural details, and the **Beethovenhaus** on Beethovenstrasse, a Baroque townhouse where the composer used to spend his holidays, probably to benefit from the town's thermal springs. Bad Neuenahr is still a well-known *Kurort*: the riverside **Kurgarten** (daily 7am–9.30pm; DM2.50) and the classically elegant **Thermal Badehaus** are survivors from an era when wealthy families from all over Europe came here to enjoy the waters and hothouse social life. Another big attraction is the **Spielbank** in Casinostrasse, the largest casino in Germany. The roulette wheels start rolling daily at 2pm (DM5 admission).

You'll find the **tourist office** at Hauptstr. 60 (late March to mid-Nov Mon–Fri 9am–6pm, Sat 10am–1pm, Sun 10.30am–4.30pm; ☎02641/977353), next door to the Bahnhof. Among the huge range of **hotels** on offer, try *Zum Ahrtal*, Sebastianstr. 68

(☎02641/26969; ③); *Zum Ännchen*, Hauptstr. 47 (☎02641/75000; ④); or *Griffels Goldener Anker*, Mittelstr. 14 (☎02641/8040; ⑦).

Altenahr

The next stop is **ALTENAHR**, a town which can only be described as picturesque and whose population seems to increase tenfold in the summer. It's horrendously clogged up then, but if you go off-season you could easily spend a few days here using the town as a base to explore the surrounding area. The landscape is magnificent – the valley is so narrow at this point it almost becomes a gorge and the town is situated on a tortuous bend in the river. If you follow the river eastwards out of town precipitous rock faces soar from the northern bank, and on the southern side steep forested slopes lead up to the craggy peaks of the **Voreifel**. By night, the whole place has an unearthly atmosphere.

In town there are plenty of suspiciously pristine half-timbered facades – and also plenty of souvenir shops and hotels. The best way to appreciate Altenahr's undeniable charms is to trek up to **Burg Are**, from whose ruined heights you get a tremendous view of the surrounding area. Burg Are itself was built around 1100 and the ruins have a romantic feel to them. Like most castles in this part of Germany it was destroyed by the French in 1690 after a nine-month siege. The whole town was once fortified but only a few remnants of the former wall and towers remain. There's also a Romanesque **Pfarrkirche** which, despite a few Gothic additions, retains very clear and simple lines.

In addition to the *Rotweinwanderweg*, there are fifteen signposted local **walking routes**. A number of paths lead up from the Bahnhof into the hills and to the nearby village of Altenburg. Look out for the **Teufelsloch**, a famous local landmark and viewpoint, where the elements have eroded a giant hole into the rock. From up here you gain a good view of the **Langfigtal** natural park and of the **Breite Ley**, a sheer volcanic rock formation which rises from the Ahr valley just outside town. There's also a chairlift which runs from the bottom of Seilbahnstrasse to the 330-metre-high **Ditschardhöhe**, with a café and good views.

Altenahr's **tourist office** is housed in the Bahnhof building (Mon–Fri 10am–noon & 3–5pm, Sat 10am–noon; ☎02643/8848). There are plenty of **private rooms** and small **pensions** (②), while a wide selection of **hotels** includes *Bahnhotel Hübel*, Altenburger Str. 3 (☎02643/1543; ③); *Gasthof Weiss*, Bahnhofstr. 36 (☎02643/8403; ③); and *Zur Post*, Brückenstr. 2 (☎02643/9310; ⑤). The local **youth hostel** (☎02643/1880; ❷) is about thirty minutes' walk out of town down the unlit Langfigtal. **Camping** facilities are available just outside town near Altenburg (☎02643/8503). The leading **wine restaurant** is *Schäferkarre*, Brückenstr. 29.

Adenau and the High Eifel

There are regular services (approximately one bus an hour) from Altenahr to **ADENAU** and the thirty-minute journey takes you through the upper reaches of the Ahr valley, via a succession of tiny villages, deep into the **High Eifel** (*Hohe Eifel*). Adenau is a pretty little tourist town straggling along the river valley, notable mainly for the fifteenth- and sixteenth-century half-timbered houses which surround its **Markt**. These are actually the genuine article, as the occasional sagging roof or slightly buckled facade shows, but they have been prettified for the tourists and now house the usual range of cafés, bars and shops. There's also a venerable Pfarrkirche here that dates from the eleventh century, but which was altered in the thirteenth century.

The **tourist office** is at Kirchstr. 15 (☎02691/30516). **Hotels** include *Poststübchen*, Hauptstr. 22 (☎02691/2589; ③); *Zum Wilden Schwein*, Hauptstr. 117 (☎02691/7061; ⑤); *Blaue Ecke*, in a sixteenth-century half-timbered house at Markt 4 (☎02691/2005; ⑤);

and *Landhaus Sonnenhof*, Auf dem Hirzenstein 1 (☎02691/7034; ⑥). All of these have **restaurants**, with that in *Blaue Ecke* being outstanding.

Nürburg and the Nürburgring

From Adenau, regular buses run to the **Nürburg**, a ruined castle which stands on one of the highest peaks in the Eifel range (678m). The Nürburg was originally the site of a Roman fortress but the ruins you see today are the remains of a twelfth-century fortress destroyed by French soldiers after a long siege in 1690. A few **pensions and hotels** lie in the eponymous nearby village, including *Am Tiergarten*, Kirchweg 4 (☎02691/92200; ④); and *Zur Burg*, Burgstr. 4 (☎02691/7575; ⑤).

Easily reached from the village itself is the famous **Nürburgring** race track. This is in two parts, much the larger being the northern loop, which was built between 1925 and 1927. This was long regarded as the ultimate test in Grand Prix motor racing; not only is it an exceptionally long circuit, travelling some 23km through the forested High Eifel, it incorporates a fearsomely fast 2km-long straight as well as numerous hills and bends. Jackie Stewart dubbed it "the green hell" and, following Niki Lauda's near-fatal crash in 1976, it was decided that it was too dangerous for Formula 1 races. Ever since, the German Grand Prix has been held at Hockenheim near Heidelberg. However, a new 5km-long southern loop was opened in 1984, and this is now used as the track for the Luxembourg Grand Prix. If you're travelling by car or motorbike you can take a spin round the northern loop yourself, at whatever speed you like and with no formalities other than paying the fee of DM17 per lap. For DM120 a professional racing driver will chauffeur a maximum of three passengers round this circuit in the so-called *Renntaxi*.

A new **Erlebnispark** is due to open alongside the track in May 1998; it will feature historic Mercedes vehicles from the now defunct museum, as well as driving simulators and other motoring-related entertainments. For up-to-date information on this, and on events in the Nürburgring, call ☎02691/302600.

Mayen and around

The first thing you should know about **MAYEN**, some 30km from Andernach at the end of the main Eifel rail line, is that it was almost completely flattened by the RAF on January 2, 1945 to prevent the Germans from using it as a staging post for troops during the Ardennes offensive. This will save you from disappointment when you find out that all its quaint and charming buildings date from the last forty years or so. The rebuilding programme has been carried out with a great deal of sensitivity and, apart from an ugly department store on the Marktplatz, no great architectural errors seem to have been made.

If you arrive by rail it's a five-minute bus ride from the **Westbahnhof** to the town centre. The bus will drop you off at the **Brückentor**, which, along with the **Obertor** on Boemundring at the other side of town, is all that remains of the once 1600-metre-long Stadtmauer. Walking up Marktstrasse towards the Marktplatz you pass the **Pfarrkirche St Clemens**, whose distinctive twisted steeple was caused by poor construction techniques and the influence of the weather. On Marktplatz itself is the Baroque **Altes Rathaus**, the only town centre building to survive the war just about intact.

From the other end of the square the thirteenth-century **Genoveveburg** glowers over the town. Nowadays it houses the **Eifeler Landschaftsmuseum** (mid-Feb to mid-Nov Tues–Sat 10am–12.30pm & 2–5pm, Sun 11am–5pm; DM6), where a range of Eifel-related exhibits takes you from the Stone Age to modern times. Look out for the before-and-after pictures showing the war damage inflicted on the town. About two-thirds of the **Herz-Jesu-Kirche**, which you can see from the battlements of the Genoveveburg, was destroyed: photographs inside record the destruction and reconstruction.

Close to Mayen is **Schloss Bürresheim** (April–Sept Tues–Sun 9am–6pm; Oct, Nov & Jan–March Tues–Sun 9am–5pm; DM5), which is the epitome of the German fairy-tale castle. It rises out of the wooded valley of the River Nette and is only about five minutes out of town by bus (leaving from the stop between Im Möhren and Wittbende on the Habsburgring). Begun as a fortress in 1220, it was turned into a residential castle during the sixteenth century, a change clearly reflected in its appearance, the grim stone walls of the original fortress being topped by more fanciful Renaissance turrets.

Mayen's **tourist office** (Mon–Fri 10am–12.30pm & 2–5pm; April–Oct also Sat 9.30am–12.30pm; ☎02651/88260) is in the Altes Rathaus. *Zum Alten Fritz*, Koblenzer Str. 56 (☎02651/43272; ②) is a good budget **hotel** with an excellent restaurant, while the most expensive place to stay is *Maifelder Hof*, Polcher Str. 74 (☎02651/96040; ⑥). The **youth hostel** is some way out of the town centre at Am Knüppchen 5 (☎02651/2355; ⚑); to get there walk down Göbelstrasse from Marktplatz, turn left onto Stehbachstrasse and then make an immediate right into Im Möhren and follow the road right up the steep hill.

Maria Laach

By far the most outstanding historical monument in the Eifel is the Benedictine monastery of **Maria Laach**, which lies in an isolated setting of forests, meadows and fields roughly 15km north of Mayen. Its name is derived from the adjacent **Laacher See**, which was formed by a volcanic cave-in, and which still has a primeval feeling to it. Bus #6032 links Maria Laach with the nearest train station at Niedermendig and with Mayen, while bus #6031 runs there from Andernach.

The **Klosterkirche** is a visual stunner, ranking as the most beautiful of all the great Romanesque churches of the Rhineland. Its sense of unity is all the more remarkable in that, although begun at the end of the eleventh century, it was not finished until well into the thirteenth century. One of its most distinctive features is its stonework – for the most part it's constructed from the local yellow-brown tufa, but dark basalt was used for architectural highlighting. Each end of the church is girded with an arrangement of three towers, presenting as varied and striking a silhouette as the Middle Ages ever produced.

Even more remarkable is the last part to be built, the **Paradise**, a courtyard placed in front of the building, enclosing the western choir. Apparently intended as a symbol of the innocence of the Garden of Eden, it's unique in Christian architecture, being suggestive of Islamic places of worship, an impression strengthened by the addition of the burbling Lions' Fountain in the middle. The capitals, showing a fabulous bestiary, were carved with a gossamer delicacy by a mason dubbed the Samson Master, who is also known to have worked at Andernach and Bonn.

After all this, the pure Romanesque sobriety of the interior comes as a surprise. However, the early Gothic **baldachin** at the high altar is again reminiscent of the art of Islam and is quite unlike any other such object in Europe. To see the **crypt**, the earliest part of the building, you have to join one of the regular guided tours (donation expected) conducted by the monks. It's worth catching one of the services to hear the Gregorian chant. Vespers are at 5.30pm, and finish in good time to catch the last bus.

The monastery has its own **hotel**, the *Seehotel Maria Laach* (☎02652/5840; ⑧) with an excellent restaurant, and there's a simple cafeteria alongside. You can also **camp** (☎02636/2485) on the shore of the Laacher See.

THE SAARLAND

The **Saarland**, taking its name from the River Saar which cuts through its length, is the poorest of the western German Länder, traditionally a big coal-mining area which is now suffering from a bad case of post-industrial malaise. It's always been a political football; much of it belonged to France up until 1815, and wrangles have continued into this century. After World War I the Saarland passed into League of Nations control, which effectively meant that the French took over, with the right to exploit local mines in compensation for damage done to their own mining industry during the war. In the January 1935 plebiscite ninety percent of Saarlanders voted for union with Nazi Germany. After World War II the Saar once again found itself in limbo, nominally autonomous but with the French government pushing for economic union. In November 1952 the population voted against reunion with Germany, but by January 1957 the increasing prosperity of the Federal Republic had convinced the Saarlanders that their future lay there, and they thus rejoined the fold – much to the chagrin of the French government.

Most Germans see the Saarland only from the vantage point of one of the various highways that criss-cross it; if you're driving through, it has to be said there aren't really many compelling reasons for getting out of your car, but if you happen to be in the area then there are a few interesting places and, away from the heavily industrialized areas, some pleasant gently rolling wooded countryside. The French have left a small linguistic legacy in the shape of the greeting *Salü* which replaces the normal *Guten Tag* here. Of late there's also been a marked French influence on local **cuisine**, traditionally always a poor man's fare, based on a thousand and one potato variations like *Hooriche* (raw potato rissoles).

Saarbrücken

The Land capital **SAARBRÜCKEN** is a sizeable and predominantly modern industrial city which is generally given a bad press. Nonetheless, it does have its attractions, notably a large array of handsome Baroque public buildings from its eighteenth-century heyday as a *Residenzstadt*, and - thanks in no small measure to the French connection - a distinguished culinary tradition.

The city

The city is bisected by the Saar, with the Altstadt lying on the south side of the river. Its centrepiece is Schlossplatz, with a Baroque **Schloss** designed by Friedrich Joachim Stengel, the prolific court architect to the House of Nassau-Saarbrücken. Badly damaged in World War II, it was remodelled in the early 1980s by Gottfried Böhm, who gave its main facade an unashamedly avant-garde appearance. The fifteenth-century **Schlosskirche** alongside contains a few tombs of the local princes.

Of the three museums on Schlossplatz, the most important is the **Museum für Vor- und Frühgeschichte** (Tues–Sat 9am–5pm, Sun 10am–6pm; free) in the former parliament building. It contains the findings from one of the most important archeological discoveries of the Celtic period, the intact contents of a princess's grave from around 400 BC. The **Historisches Museum** (Tues–Sun 10am–6pm; free) has permanent exhibitions on Saarland under the Third Reich and in the immediate postwar period, as well as temporary displays. On the top floor of the **Altes Rathaus**, another building by Stengel, is the **Abenteuermuseum** (Tues & Wed 9am–1pm, Thurs & Fri 3–7pm, first Sat of month 10am–2pm; DM3), which is devoted in roughly equal parts to the lives and cultures of "primitive" peoples and to the ego of its founder Heinz Rox-Schulz, who has spent most of his life travelling to far-flung corners of the world collecting and filming. Bizarre items from the collection include a 2000-year-old Peruvian mummy and some shrunken heads.

From Schlossplatz head down Schlossstrasse and turn right into Eisenbahnstrasse. On the right you'll see the plain white **Friedenskirche** (Peace Church) by Stengel, which has a startlingly austere interior, with just a single crucifix as decoration. Beyond is **Ludwigsplatz**, a masterly piece of late Baroque town planning which is regarded as Stengel's greatest achievement. Its focal point is the **Ludwigskirche**, a highly original design with an unorthodox tower placed over the opposite end of the building from the facade. The exterior, with its rich sculptural decoration, is unusually sumptuous for a Protestant church. Badly damaged in the war, it has been subject to painstaking restoration, though as yet only two of the four internal galleries have been rebuilt.

The **Deutschherrenkapelle** in Moltkestrasse to the west of the city centre is Saarbrücken's oldest building, dating back to the thirteenth century, although it has been frequently and radically altered over the centuries. At the eastern end of town, on St Arnualer Markt, is the **Stiftskirche St Arnual**, a solid early Gothic church topped by a Baroque tower. For five centuries it served as the main mausoleum of the House of Nassau-Saarbrücken, and contains around fifty tombs of members of the family. The most spectacular, both from the fifteenth century, are those of Count Johann III and Elizabeth von Lotharingen.

Crossing the **Alte Brücke** brings you to the north bank of the Saar. On the right is the **Staatstheater**, an angular, monumental building, nowadays used for musicals and drama, which is a good example of the kind of architectural thinking that went on in the Third Reich. Head up Saarstrasse to St Johanner Markt, an old town square with some elegant eighteenth-century houses and a Baroque fountain, all designed by Stengel. Nearby is the **Basilika St Johann**, another fine church by Stengel, this time in full Catholic pomp, with elaborate confessionals, balconies and high altar.

St Johanner Markt and Bahnhofstrasse to the northwest are where it's at in Saarbrücken – there are a few expensive shops, cafés and restaurants and a general sense that what money there is in the city tends to find its way here. A little to the south, at Bismarckstr. 11–19, is the **Moderne Galerie** (Tues–Sun 10am–6pm; DM3), a collection of nineteenth- and twentieth-century art which includes works by Rodin, Pissarro, Monet, Marc, Picasso and Beuys, among others. Opposite, at Karlstr. 1, is the **Alte Sammlung** (same times and ticket), with paintings, sculpture and decorative arts from the Middle Ages until the early nineteenth century.

Practicalities

Saarbrücken's **Hauptbahnhof** is at the northern end of the city centre. Within the station is a branch of the **tourist office** (Mon–Fri 9am–6pm, Sat 9am–3pm; ☎0681/36515). The head office is at Grossherzog-Friedrich-Str. 1 (Mon–Fri 8am–5pm; ☎0681/36901). For non-EU citizens, who may require visas to visit France, the **French consulate** is at Johannisstr. 2 (☎0681/30626). **Mitfahrzentrale** have an office at Rosenstr. 31 (☎0681/67981).

Accommodation

Hotels are almost uniformly geared to business visitors, and correspondingly expensive. *Schlosskrug*, Schmollerstr. 14 (☎0681/35448; ④) and *Atlantic*, Ursulinenstr. 59 (☎0681/31018; ④) are the cheapest with a central location; among the few other moderately priced alternatives are *Stadt Hamburg*, Bahnhofstr. 71–73 (☎0681/34692; ⑤), and *Madeleine*, Cecilienstr. 5 (☎0681/32228; ⑤). *Am Triller*, Trillerweg 57 (☎0681/580000; ⑧)) is the pick of the upmarket establishments.

There's a **youth hostel** at Meerwiesertalweg 31 (☎0681/33040; ☎), on the northeastern edge of town (bus #4, #15 or #16 from Bahnhofstrasse). The local **camping** facilities are at Am Spicherer Berg (☎0681/51780), a few kilometres south of Saarbrücken on the Franco-German border.

Eating, drinking and entertainment

There's a good range of places to eat and drink in town, and a lively nightlife, thanks in large part to the presence of a sizeable student population. The place to see and be seen in Saarbrücken is *Brasserie Fröschengasse*, Fröschengasse 18, while *Winzerstube d'Alsace*, Deutschherrenstr. 3, is the leading wine bar-restaurant, and *Zum Stiefel*, Am Stiefel 2, is an eighteenth-century *Gasthaus* serving excellent food as well as the products of its own *Hausbrauerei*. You'll get reasonably priced local dishes at *Bastei*, Saaruferstr. 16, on the south bank of the Saar. *Naturkost*, at the junction of Wilhelm-Heinrich-Strasse and Franz-Josef-Röder-Strasse, is the best bet for wholefood. At the *Kultur Café*, in the Stadtgalerie just off the St Johanner Markt, you can sit either outside, or surrounded by art on the second floor. The centre of the local **gay** scene (men and women) is *Big Ben* in Försterstrasse which is open most evenings. For **live jazz**, go to *Jazzkeller Giesskanne*, Am Steg 3.

The *Staatstheater*, Tbilisser Platz 1 (☎0681/30920) is the main **cultural** venue, presenting opera, operetta, dance, drama and concerts. One unusual event is the *Perspectives du Théâtre* **festival** of young French theatre, held every May, which usually throws up a few avant-garde offerings. There's also the *Max-Ophüls-Preis* film festival held every January.

Elsewhere in Saarland

Beyond Saarbrücken, the Saarland offers a major piece of nineteenth-century industrial heritage, a couple of Roman sites and a surprising amount of fine scenery, particularly along the banks of the Saar.

Völkingen

Improbable as it would have seemed only a few years ago, the industrial town of **VÖLKINGEN**, which lies just down the Saar from the Land capital, has been propelled to the status of a tourist attraction of international importance. The reason for this was UNESCO's decision in 1994 to include its redundant iron works, the **Alte Völkinger Hütte**, on the highly prestigious World Heritage List. Founded in 1873, the complex, which is centred on six huge blast furnaces, is of such vast and imposing scale that it has been described as a "cathedral of the Industrial Age". **Guided tours** (March–Nov Tues–Sun at 10am & 2pm; DM5) are run round the works, enabling you to step back into the not-so-distant heavy industrial past and see all the various phases of pig-iron production.

Mettlach and around

Continuing down the River Saar by road or rail will bring you to **METTLACH**, one of Saarland's prettier towns. The dominant monument is the Baroque **Abtei**, which is nowadays the headquartes of the ceramics firm Villeroy & Boch. Their visitors' centre, **Keravision** (Mon–Fri 9am–noon & 1–5pm, Sat 10am–1pm; free), features tableaux and explanatory material on the history of the company and of European ceramics. The more valuable treasures from the previous medieval abbey, including a triptych reliquary, can be seen in the **Pfarrkirche St Liutwin**. In the woods of the nearby park, whose entrance is marked by a neat Neoclassical fountain designed by Karl Friedrich Schinkel, is the octagonal **Alter Turm**, a tenth-century Romanesque mausoleum.

Reasonably priced **hotels** include *Zur Spitz*, Heinertstr. 5 (☎06864/581; ③), and *Zur Post*, Heinertstr. 17 (☎06864/557; ④). More upmarket options are *Zum Schwan*, Freiherr-von-Stein-Str. 34a (☎06864/7279; ⑥); and *Saarpark*, Bahnhofstr. 31 (☎06864/9200; ⑦). There are also plenty of rooms available in **private houses** (①–③) in the town and neighbouring villages; the **tourist office**, Freiherr-von-Stein-Str. 64 (☎06864/8384) has a complete list.

Around Mettlach

Bus #6300 runs from Mettlach to the village of **ORSHCOLZ** 7km west. From there, you can walk to **Cloef**, a viewpoint overlooking the Saarland's most celebrated beauty spot, the **Saarschleife**, a colossal loop in the River Saar which has created a narrow wooded peninsula. There's a **youth hostel** at Herbergstr. 1 (☎06868/270; ☎) in the village of Dreisbach to the west, served by bus #6300 from Mettlach.

The same bus goes to **NENNIG**, in the Mosel valley very close to the Luxembourg border, where there's an old **Schloss** and, more significantly, the remains of the **Römischer Mosaikfussboden** (April–Sept Tues–Sun 8.30–11.30am & 1–5.30pm; Oct, Nov & Jan–March 9–11.30am & 1–4pm; DM1). Along with the huge villa to which it belonged, this Roman floor mosaic was unearthed by a farmer in 1852 on the southeastern edge of the village. The mosaic originally formed part of the villa entrance hall and includes vivid and detailed depictions of gladiatorial combat.

Homburg

At the eastern end of the Land, 35km from Saarbrücken by road or rail, is **HOMBURG**. There's nothing much of interest in the town centre, but about ten minutes south by rail, just outside the incorporated village of **SCHWARZENACKER**, is the **Römisches Freilichtmuseum** (April–Nov Tues–Sun 9am–noon & 1–5pm; Dec–March Wed 9am–4.30pm, Sat & Sun noon–4.30pm; DM3), a big open-air museum on the site of an old Roman settlement which has been partly excavated and reconstructed. Also in the outskirts of Homburg are the **Schlossberghöhlen** (daily mid-Jan to mid-Dec 9am–noon & 1–5pm; DM3), a series of sandstone caves on twelve levels, covering 5km altogether. They were hollowed out over six centuries and at one time the sand from them was one of the area's main exports. During the seventeenth and eighteenth centuries, the caves were occupied by the French, who turned them into a frontier fortress, while in the last war they served as an air-raid shelter for the people of Homburg. Nearby there's a ruined **Schloss** set in gloomy wooded grounds.

Homburg's **tourist office** is at Am Forum 5 (☎06841/2066). There's a **youth hostel** at Sickingstr. 12 (☎06841/3679; ☎). The only budget **hotel** is *Brünnler*, Hauptstr. 8 (☎06841/294; ②) in the outlying village of Einöd south of Schwarzenacker and reachable by train, but there are three good upmarket places: *Stadt Homburg*, Ringstr. 80 (☎06841/1331; ⑦); *Schweizerstuben*, Kaiserstr. 72 (☎06841/92400; ⑦); and *Schlossberg* on Schlossberg-Höhenstrasse (☎06841/6660; ⑦).

travel details

Trains

Koblenz to: Andernach (hourly; 15min); Bingen (hourly; 1hr 10min); Boppard (hourly; 15min); Cologne (hourly; 1hr 50min); Rüdesheim (hourly; 1hr); Saarbrücken (8 daily; 2hr 25min).

Mainz to: Bonn (hourly; 1hr 15min); Cologne (hourly; 2hr 30min); Frankfurt (frequent; 2hr 30min); Idar-Oberstein (hourly; 1hr 10min); Karlsruhe (hourly; 1hr 5min); Koblenz (frequent; 50min); Saarbrücken (8 daily; 2hr 30min); Worms (every 30min; 40min).

Saarbrücken to: Cologne (5 daily; 3hr 30min); Koblenz (8 daily; 2hr 25min); Mainz (8 daily; 2hr 30min); Trier (5 daily; 1hr 5min).

CHAPTER FIVE

NORTH RHINE-WESTPHALIA

North Rhine-Westphalia (*Nordrhein-Westfalen*) is only the fourth largest of the Länder in terms of area, but has, with seventeen million inhabitants, by far the largest population. As its double-barrelled name suggests, it's historically two distinct provinces where separateness dates back to the very beginnings of German history, the North Rhineland having belonged to the Franks, while Westphalia marked the beginning of Saxon territory. With the industrialization process in the nineteenth century, any lingering distinction between the two became hopelessly blurred with the mushroom growth of a vast built-up area around the mineral-rich valley of the River Ruhr. This formed a clearly recognizable unit, yet was divided almost exactly in half by the traditional boundaries. After World War II, it was decided to preserve the economic integrity of the **Ruhrgebiet**, as the area came to be known, by uniting the two provinces.

Of the thirty-eight German cities registering a population of over 200,000, ten are in North Rhine and a further six in Westphalia. Many begin just as another ends, and the Ruhrgebiet is joined to a string of other cities stretching right to the southern border with Rhineland-Palatinate, making up the most densely populated area in Europe. In this conurbation, **Cologne** is by far the most outstanding city, managing to preserve much of the atmosphere and splendours of its long centuries as a free state, at times the most powerful in Germany. The Land's other city of top-class historical interest is **Aachen**, the original capital of the Holy Roman Empire. Next in line comes **Münster**, which would presumably be capital of Westphalia, if such a division still existed. As it is, the Land government meets in self-consciously cosmopolitan **Düsseldorf**, which inspires admiration and revulsion in roughly equal measure. At the southern end of the Land is **Bonn**, capital of the West German state for its forty-year existence, and still (for the time being) one of the national seats of government. Never suited for the role it was so casually given in 1949, it's a place all too easily maligned.

In spite of the stranglehold heavy industry has traditionally held over North Rhine-Westphalia, much of the landscape is rural, with agriculture and forestry making key contributions to the economy. The **Eifel** in the Rhineland, and the **Sauerland**, **Siegerland** and **Teutoburg Forest** in Westphalia all offer varied scenery, and are popular holiday spots with the Germans themselves, being such obvious antidotes to urban life. In these areas are some wonderful small towns – **Monschau**, **Bad Münstereifel**, **Soest** and **Lemgo** – which can stand comparison with any in Germany. Their counterparts along the Rhine have been scarred by war, but **Brühl** and **Xanten** are still particularly worth visiting.

Sobriety is the keynote of the province's architecture; new styles were slow to develop, and there was far less readiness to replace buildings simply because they were old-fashioned than was the case further south. There is thus a legacy of **Romanesque**

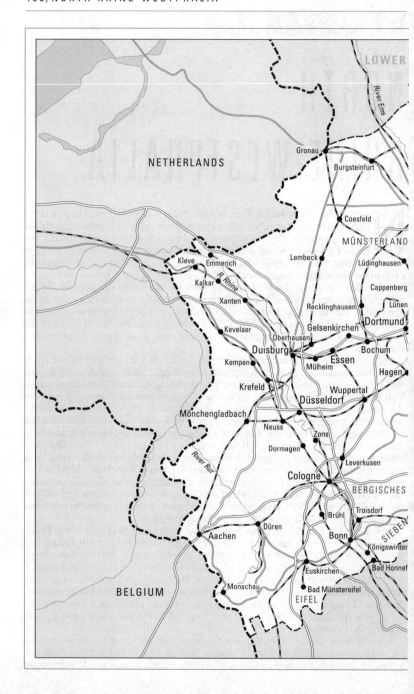

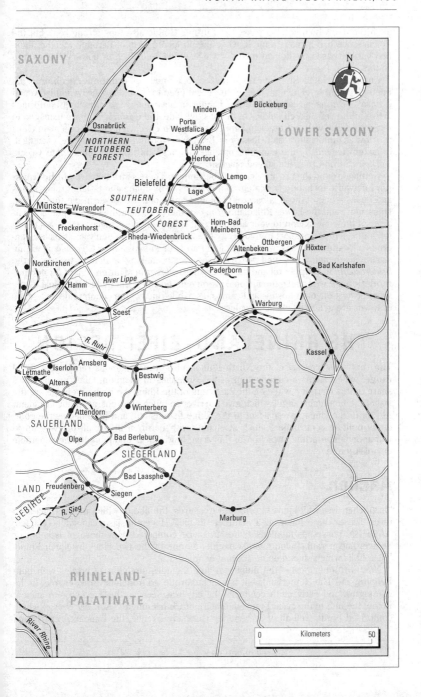

architecture which is unsurpassed in Europe. Gothic also took strong root, but the Renaissance barely made a mark, while the preferred form of Baroque was the dignified variety based on Roman models, which didn't lend itself to flowery Rococo offshoots.

Currently, North Rhine-Westphalia faces a number of **economic problems**. Its unemployment level is high, due to the recent need to scale down heavy industry, and it hasn't been as successful as other Länder in developing and attracting companies active in the new hi-tech fields. On the positive side, the *Gastarbeiter* have managed to integrate fairly well, with racism kept reasonably in check. The province's main cities are now as multicultural as Leicester or Bradford, Houston or Philadelphia, a fact tacitly acknowledged by the common practice of translating public notices into Greek, Turkish, Serbo-Croat, Italian and Spanish.

Getting around the province couldn't be simpler. There's an extensive **public transport** network, including two integrated systems of main-line and S-Bahn trains, trams and buses – one of these is based in Cologne and Bonn, the other in the Ruhrgebiet, Düsseldorf and the Lower Rhineland. You can therefore turn the claustrophobic character of the conurbation to your advantage: it's certainly never necessary to wait long for some form of transport from one city to another. Even the country areas have a generous allocation of buses, which are often hardly used by the locals. Transport enthusiasts, incidentally, will find two oddities worth making a detour to see – the *Schwebebahn* in **Wuppertal** and the *Wasserstrassenkreuz* in **Minden**. Prices for **accommodation** are well above the national average in the cities, but there's the usual extensive network of youth hostels and campsites, while rates in the countryside and smaller towns are generally excellent value.

THE RHINELAND–EIFEL REGION

The southwestern part of the North Rhineland is a mountainous region. The **Eifel range**, which forms a continuation of the Ardennes in Belgium, takes up the lion's share of this territory, while on the east bank of the Rhine the **Siebengebirge** are the last of the mountain ranges which give the river so much of its characteristic grandeur. At **Bonn**, the landscape adjacent to the Rhine flattens out, and here begins the enormous built-up conurbation which stretches, with hardly a break, all the way up to Dortmund. The prime attraction of this area, however, is undoubtedly the venerable city of **Aachen**.

Aachen

"In Aachen I saw all kinds of priceless treasures, the like of which no man has seen rarer," wrote Dürer following a visit there in 1560. His enthusiasm can still be echoed; **AACHEN** possesses fabulous riches fit to be compared with those of Istanbul or Venice, and it ranks, along with Cologne, as one of the two cities in North Rhine-Westphalia which should on no account be missed.

Now a frontier post – the municipal area includes stretches of border with both Belgium and The Netherlands – it has metamorphosed from a far grander role. In the late eighth and early ninth centuries the city was seen as the successor to ancient Rome, the hub of the great Frankish empire of **Charlemagne** (*Karl der Grosse*) which comprised pretty well all of present-day Germany, France, the Benelux, Austria and

The **telephone code** for Aachen is ☎0241

Switzerland, as well as much of Italy and part of northern Spain. In 794, after 26 years of almost constant campaigning, Charlemagne established Aachen as the main seat of his court. The choice was made partly for strategic reasons, but also because of the presence of hot springs, over which the Romans had first built thermal baths. Exercising in these waters was one of the emperor's favourite pastimes, and his contemporaries rated him a swimmer without peer. The **spa** has continually given the city prestige and visitors, but its political power was short-lived, lasting only a generation after Charlemagne's death.

Arrival, information and accommodation

Aachen's **Hauptbahnhof** is just south of the city centre and is the point of arrival for trains from the Ostend Channel ferry crossing. Some buses stop outside, but others – including those to Monschau – leave from the **bus station** at the coner of Peterstrasse and Kurhausstrasse. The **tourist office** occupies the *Atrium Elisenbrunnen* on Friedrich-Wilhelm-Platz (Mon–Fri 9am–6pm, Sat 9am–2pm; ☎180 2960). **Mitfahrzentrale** have an office at Roermonder Str. 4 (☎152011).

ACCOMMODATION PRICE CODES

All the pensions and hotels in this book have been graded according to the following price categories. The prices quoted are for the cheapest available double room, although many of the budget places will also have more expensive rooms. Youth hostels are graded under separate categories. See p.34 for more details.

① less than DM50	④ DM81–100	⑦ DM151–200
② DM51–65	⑤ DM101–125	⑧ DM201–250
③ DM66–80	⑥ DM126–150	⑨ more than DM250

There's a large concentration of **hotels** near the Hauptbahnhof, but most of the genuine budget options are a long way out. The **youth hostel** is also out of the centre, situated on a little hill in a suburban park to the southwest, at Maria-Theresia Allee 260 (☎71101; ☎); take bus #2 direction Preuswald from the Elisenbrunnen and alight at Brüsseler Ring or Ronheide. At the time of writing the **campsite** (May–Sept only) was located just to the northeast of the centre at Pass Str. 85 (☎158502), but it is likely to move in 1998.

Hotels

Benelux, Franzstr. 21–23 (☎22343, fax 22345). The most characterful of the upmarket city-centre hotels. ⑦

Brülls am Dom, Hühner Markt (☎31704, fax 404326). Medium-priced hotel with café-restaurant in the handiest of locations. ⑥

Burtscheider Markt, Burtscheider Markt 14–16 (☎600000, fax 600 0020). One of the city's best hotels – a true spa hotel with its own thermal baths. ⑦

Buschhausen, Adenauerallee 215 (☎60080, fax 602830). Hotel-restaurant in the south of Burtscheid, with a wide choice of rooms. ④

Drei Könige, Büchel 5 (☎48393, fax 36152). Superbly located just off the corner of the Markt. ⑤

Dura, Lagerhausstr. 5 (☎403135). Cheapest of the many hotels clustered around the Hauptbahnhof. ④

Eupener Hof, Krugenofen 63 (☎62035, fax 61390). Good middle-range hotel in Burtscheid. ⑤

Göbel, Trierer Str. 546 (☎523244, fax 564610). Some way out from the centre, 5km to the southeast, but a good budget option. Take bus #5, #15, #25, #35, #45, #55 or #65. ④

Hansa-Haus, Von-Coels-Str. 42 (☎551380). Located 5km east of the centre on the route of buses #12 and #22, this offers the cheapest rooms in Aachen. ③

Hesse am Marschiertor, Friedlandstr. 20 (☎34047, fax 470 5449). Good value, and also has a recommendable restaurant. ⑤

Marx, Hubertusstr. 33–35 (☎37541, fax 26705). Another fine middle-bracket choice, a little further west of the Hauptbahnhof. ⑤

The city centre

The historical centre of modern Aachen lies ten minutes from the Hauptbahnhof along Bahnhofstrasse and then left into Theaterstrasse. It's small and compact, and can comfortably be seen in a day, though you'll need longer to take in more than a few of the city's varied and excellent museums. Badly damaged in World War II, Aachen was also devastated by a terrible fire in 1656. This accounts for the unusually large number of Baroque buildings by north German standards; their restrained, classically derived style is a world away from the wild fantasies which were then all the rage in Bavaria.

The Dom

Thankfully, although hardly anything else remains from Charlemagne's time, Aachen retains its crowning jewel in the former **Pfalzkapelle** (palace chapel). Now forming the heart and soul of the present-day **Dom**, its presence is enshrined in the French name for the city, *Aix-la-Chapelle*. A ninth-century monk-chronicler, Notker the Stammerer, relates how skilled workmen were brought from many lands in order that this edifice should surpass any previously erected, and concluded that it was "built by human hands, yet with the inspiration of God". Charlemagne's courtier Einhard, who must have watched the building's construction, attributed its splendour to the emperor's religious devotion, and fills in details of the decoration – "gold and silver, with lamps, and with lattices and doors of solid bronze". He also explained that marble columns were brought from as far as Ravenna, on whose basilica of San Vitale the chapel was largely modelled; indeed, the Pope's letter authorizing Charlemagne to remove marbles and mosaics from the palace there still exists.

THE BUILDING

Even after such descriptions, you can't help being overwhelmed by the Dom's extraordinary symmetry, height and grandeur. Designed by **Odo von Metz**, it's an eight-sided dome, surrounded by a sixteen-sided ambulatory, above which is a two-tiered gallery with eight arcades of columns; the number eight is significant, representing perfection and harmony. The circumference of the octagon is 144 Carolingian feet – the cardinal number of the heavenly Jerusalem – and that of the outer polygon exactly twice that: an impeccable concord and order which are intended to symbolize Heaven. As a result of the cult of Charlemagne (he was canonized by an anti-pope in 1165), and the possession of the so-called Great Aachen Relics (allegedly the swaddling clothes and loin cloth of Christ, the gown of the Virgin and the garb of St John the Baptist), pilgrims poured into the city in such numbers that the building needed to be expanded. An airily high and narrow **Gothic chancel** was therefore added, modelled on the Sainte-Chapelle in Paris. Its original stained glass has been lost, but the replacements at least give the right effect. Also from this period is a series of two-storey chapels encircling the octagon.

THE FURNISHINGS

Some of the original furnishings survive: in the vestibule alone you can see the bronze doors with lions' heads mentioned by Einhard, along with a pinecone which seems to have been a waterspout, and an antique she-wolf. These are rather overshadowed by the costly embellishments with which Charlemagne's successors enhanced the Dom, making it positively drip with treasure. Adorning the main altar is the **Pala d'Oro**, an early eleventh-century altar front with ten embossed scenes of the Passion. Behind, and of similar date, is the **ambo**, a pulpit like no other, fashioned from gold-plated copper adorned with precious stones, reliefs of the Evangelists and ancient Egyptian ivories of profane subjects. Suspended from the dome by means of a mighty iron chain is the enormous twelfth-century **chandelier** given by Frederick Barbarossa. Regrettably, its weight quickly caused the mosaics to crack; those to be seen today are a nineteenth-century attempt at re-creating the effect of the originals. The gilded **shrine of Charlemagne** at the end of the chancel was finished in 1215, having been fifty years in the making. It contains the remains of the saint, who is depicted on the front, and also serves as a glorification of the Holy Roman Empire he founded, with portraits of his successors along the sides, instead of the normal biblical personages. The status accorded Charlemagne is further emphasized by the early fifteenth-century statue of him on the pier behind, the only outsider in a cycle of the Virgin and Apostles.

In the gallery is the **imperial throne**, a marble chair with a wooden seat approached by six steps, in the manner of that in Solomon's temple; from here the emperor had a grandstand view of all that was happening below. Although popularly believed to have belonged to Charlemagne, it now seems certain that it's at least a century later in date, perhaps made for the coronation of Otto I, which initiated the tradition of emperors being crowned at Aachen, a practice which lasted until the sixteenth century. In order to see the throne (with an added bonus of a different perspective on the Dom and its furnishings) you've no choice but to join a **guided tour**. These cost DM3 and leave from the **Schatzkammer**, which has its own entrance on Klostergasse; there are at least a couple a day, with hourly departures at the height of the season.

The Schatzkammer

The **Schatzkammer** (Mon 10am–1pm, Tues, Wed, Fri & Sat 10am–5/6pm, Thurs 10am–8pm, Sun 10.30am–5pm; DM5) is as much an essential sight as the Dom. Quite simply, it's the richest treasury in northern Europe, a dazzling feast for the eyes and an unashamed glorification of the wealth and power of the Church Triumphant. Prominent among its treasures is the greatest of all processional crucifixes, the late tenth-century **Lothair cross**, studded with jewels and bearing an antique cameo of the Emperor Augustus; the Crucifixion is modestly engraved on the reverse. From the beginning of the following century come a **holy water vessel**, carved from an elephant's tusk, and a **golden book cover** with an ivory of the Madonna and Child, which was made as an accessory to the Pala d'Oro in the decoration of the altar. A damaged **ivory diptych** is the only item from the time of Charlemagne, while the large **Roman sarcophagus** carved with a scene of the rape of Proserpine served as the emperor's improbable coffin for four hundred years.

The **base plates** of the great chandelier are delicately engraved with angels and scenes from the life of Christ. Among many superb fourteenth-century **reliquaries**, note the idealized portrait head of Charlemagne and the two shaped like Gothic chapels. Gifts from such devotees as Margaret of York and Louis of Hungary show the international extent of the Aachen cult. The astonishing vibrancy of the local goldsmith tradition down the centuries is proved by the sixteenth-century work of **Hans von Reutlingen**, which stands comparison with any of the older masterpieces.

The Rathaus

Charlemagne's palace once extended across the Katschhof, now lined with ugly modern buildings, to the site of the present **Rathaus**. Fronting the Markt, which boasts the finest of the medieval houses left in the city, its facade is lined with the figures of fifty Holy Roman Emperors – 31 of them crowned in Aachen. Above the entrance, Charlemagne shares a niche with Christ and Pope Leo III, who conducted his coronation ceremony in Rome on Christmas Day 800. Built in the fourteenth century on the palace foundations, and incorporating two of its **towers**, the Rathaus is a mix of attempts to restore its original Gothic form with the inevitable Baroque changes of later years. The best bit of the **interior** (daily 10am–1pm & 2–5pm, but liable to closure at any time for civic receptions; DM3) is the much-restored **Kaisersaal**. Here the Karlspreis (Charlemagne Prize) is awarded annually to the citizen who is deemed to have made the largest contribution to European unity. Five large frescoes by the

---

AACHEN'S FOUNTAINS

Seventeen fountains dot Aachen's streets. Most popular is the **Puppenbrunnen** (Dolls' Fountain), reached down Krämerstrasse; each doll – a rider, a market woman, a harlequin, a canon and a model – has moving limbs and represents a particular facet of Aachen life. In strong contrast is the stern Neoclassical solemnity of the **Elisenbrunnen**, a rotunda with two pavilions designed by Schinkel as the public drinking fountain, which lies due east. Plaques on the walls list the names of illustrious visitors to the springs, liberally augmented by many graffiti artists making their bid for immortality. The pervading smell is sulphuric, and the taste of the water – if you find its heat palatable – is hardly more appetizing.

Düsseldorf artist Alfred Rethel give a Romantic portrayal of scenes from Charlemagne's life, but your attention is more likely to be drawn by the crown jewels, dazzlingly displayed at one end. These are only reproductions, however; the originals have been kept in Vienna since the early nineteenth century, when they were commandeered by the Habsburgs (who had been hereditary holders of the title of Holy Roman Emperor for centuries) for their new role as Emperors of Austria.

The rest of the centre

Southeast of the Markt is another square, the Hühner Markt, where livestock was formerly sold. Here stands the **Couven-Museum** (Tues, Wed & Fri–Sun 10am–5pm, Thurs 10am–1pm; DM2), an elegant merchant-class home which has been named after a father and son team of architects who designed many of the city's Baroque buildings. It has been fitted out with mid-eighteenth- to mid-nineteenth-century furnishings gathered from houses of the Aachen-Liège region, giving an idea of the stylish if frivolous priorities of the local bourgeoisie. Look out for the complete pharmacy, a lavishly decorated first-floor living room with carved chimneypiece, and the huge Advent crib in the attic. Before the construction of modern facilities, the hub of Aachen's spa life was the **Altes Kurhaus**, an ornate late eighteenth-century building by the younger Couven, situated east of the Markt at Komphausbadstr. 19.

In a house on Pontstrasse, which leads north of the Markt, **Paul Julius von Reuter** established his famous news agency, using carrier pigeons to circulate the reports. To commemorate this, the **Internationales Zeitungsmuseum** (Tues–Fri 9.30am–1pm & 2.30–5pm, Sat 9.30am–1pm, May–Sept also Sun & Mon 2.30–5pm; free), with a collection of some 120,000 newspapers, has been established at no. 13 in the same street. An exhibition room has been set up to show by means of original editions how the press (German and English language examples dominate) reacted to great stories, from the 1848 revolutions via the two world wars to contemporary conflicts. If you're seriously interested, you can apply to see particular issues. At the end of Pontstrasse – which functions as the hub of the student nightlife scene – is the **Ponttor**, an awesome early fourteenth-century gateway which was formerly the strongest part of the city's fortification system. Of the ten other gates, the only survivior is the **Maschiertor** just to the west of the Hauptbahnhof.

At the eastern edge of the centre, at Wilhelmstr. 18, is the **Suermondt-Ludwig-Museum** (Tue, Thurs & Fri 11am–7pm, Wed 11am–9pm, Sat & Sun 11am–5pm; DM6 or DM10 combined ticket with the Ludwig Forum and other museums). It has an excellent collection of northern European medieval sculpture, with an extensive array of Pietàs, Madonnas and Passions; these are almost exclusively anonymous and predominantly folksy in style, though some, such as the large Lower Rhenish *St Peter Altar*, achieve a rather more developed artistic sense. Also of special note are the Baroque fancies of **Dietrich von Rath**, the city's last important goldsmith, and the sculptures and stained glass by **Ewald Mataré**, an Aachen artist best known for his role in creating new works for German cathedrals and churches in the period of their restoration following war damage. There are also a number of old masters, including notable works by Joos van Cleve, Cranach, Van Dyck, Ribera and Zurbarán.

The suburbs

One of Aachen's two spa quarters is centred on **Monheimsallee** to the northeast of the Altstadt. At no. 52 is the city's main thermal bathing hall, the **Kurbad Quellenhof** (daily 6am–10.30pm; from DM16), while the **Kurgarten** is the well-tended park you'd expect. However, Monheimsallee is best known for its **Casino** (daily 3pm–2am, Fri & Sat until 3am; minimum stake DM5 at the cheapest roulette table), housed in a Neoclassical building with a glitteringly modernized interior. Note that the management want only the better class of visitor, with full evening dress the normal attire. If you strike it lucky at the tables, the excellent restaurant provides a tempting outlet for your winnings.

Just south of the quarter, housed in a Bauhaus-style former umbrella factory building at Jülicher Str. 97–109, is the **Ludwig Forum für Internationale Kunst** (Tues & Thurs 10am–5pm, Wed & Fri 11am–8pm, Sat & Sun 11am–5pm; DM6). This is one of Germany's most vibrant centres for contemporary visual arts and while what's on display at any one time is obviously a lottery, all the big names of American painting and sculpture, including Roy Lichtenstein, Andy Warhol and Duane Hanson are well represented. Soviet and Eastern European art is another strength, with two large installations by the Ukrainian **Igor Kopytianskij** being particularly eye-catching. Also worth seeking out is a papier-mâché piece by a contemporary German-American sculptor, **Thomas Lanigan-Schmidt**, *A Rite of Passage – the Leprechaun*, which took eleven years to make; displayed alongside is his even more spectacular *Iconostasis*. **Jörg Immendorff**'s *Brandenburg Gate* is the highlight of an extensive representation of the German avant-garde.

About fifteen minutes' walk east of the Hauptbahnhof, at Bismarckstr. 68, is a moated medieval castle, **Burg Frankenberg** (Tues–Fri 10am–5pm, Sat & Sun 10am–1pm; DM2). The interior has been restored to house the local history museum; though mainly of parochial appeal, this has interesting models which attempt to re-create the likely original form of Charlemagne's palace. Ceramic products from Aachen are displayed in the tower. On the opposite side of the rail tracks is the suburb of **Burtscheid**, the second spa quarter, which has a distinctive skyline, thanks to a handsome pair of churches built on its heights by the elder Couven. Again, it features thermal bathing facilities and sedate areas of parkland.

Eating, drinking and nightlife

Many of the best places to eat and drink are found in and around the Markt, while the most animated district is the student quarter, centred on Pontstrasse.

Restaurants

Am Knipp, Bergdriesch 3. Finely appointed beer and wine restaurant in a seventeenth-century building in the north of the Altstadt. Closed Tues.

Da Salvatore, Bahnhofplatz 5. Upmarket Italian restaurant directly opposite the Hauptbahnhof.

Elisenbrunnen, Friedrich-Wilhelm-Platz 14. Offers traditional German cooking in the elegant surroundings of one of German's finest buildings.

Gala, Monheimsallee 44. The Casino's classy and very expensive restaurant; there's also a bistro here which is far less outrageously priced. Closed Sun & Mon.

Goldener Schwan, Markt 37. Typical *Gaststätte* occupying a fine old mansion with a Gothic facade.

Postwagen, Krämerstr. 2. Unquestionably Aachen's most famous pub-restaurant and a sight in itself, both for its cheerful Baroque exterior tacked onto the Rathaus and the cramped and irregular rooms within.

Ratskeller, Markt/Katschhof. House in the Rathaus cellars, this features more innovative cooking than most of its counterparts.

Tradition, Burtscheider Str. 11–13. Very highly regarded restaurant located just west of the Hauptbahnhof, featuring fish specialities and other international dishes. Closed Tues.

Zum Goldenen Einhorn, Markt 33. Has an enormous and inexpensive menu with Italian and Greek cuisine as well as German, the speciality being thin fillets of veal with a huge choice of sauces.

Zum Schiffgen, Hühner Markt 23. An ideal place for a sedate meal or *Kaffee und Kuchen*.

Bars and cafés

Atlantis, Pontstr. 141–9. Attached to the cinema of the same name, this popular student pub was decorated by two Berlin artists in an evocaton of the lost continent.

Frankfurt: Römer Platz

Frankfurt-am-Main

Vineyard in the Mosel valley

Kassel: sculpture,
Man Walking to the Sky

Limburg an der Lahn: the Dom

Burg Rheinstein at Bingen

The Lorelei overlooking the Rhine gorge at St Goarshausen

Düsseldorf: the Landhaus seen from the Fernsehturm

Monschau, the town centre

Cochem, on the River Mosel

Carnival in Düsseldorf

Cologne: the Dom

Café Liège, Aton-Kurz-Allee 4. Südstadt café with a wonderful range of Belgian chocolates and cakes. Closed Mon.

Domkeller, Hof 1. A genuine local, in spite of its location just off the Markt; always full, though it expands to the terrace outside in high summer.

Egmont, Pontstr. 1. French-style bistro featuring a range of live music including jazz, chansons, soul and funk as well as karaoke sessions.

Hauptquartier, Promenadenstr. 46. The city's most eccentric bar, a living testimony to the enduring popularity in Germany of all things punk.

Jakobshof, Stromgasse 31. Very trendy bar featuring live jazz and cabaret; does full meals. Closed Mon.

Labyrinth, Pontstr. 1. Labyrinthine student bar with huge tables and minimalist decor. Serves Greek-style food.

Leo van den Daele, Büchel 18. Historic wood-panelled café with exquisite furnishings. Renowned for its huge rice cakes, it's also the best place to sample *Printen*, a spiced gingerbread which is the city's main claim to culinary fame.

Meisenfrei, Boxgraben 138. This café has a bewildering choice of games to entertain you.

Molkerei, Pontstr. 141. Bright and cheerful during the day, but lacks atmosphere in the evening.

Tangente, Pontstr. 141. Sharing a terrace with *Molkerei*, this is an elegant daytime café which transforms itself into a lively bar frequented by Aachen's younger residents at night.

Discos and clubs

Aoxomoxoa, Reihstr, 15. A big favourite with the in-crowd, featuring both live and recorded music. Open 10pm–3am, 5am Fri & Sat, closed Sun.

B9, Blondelstr. 9. Aachen's top disco, with a bizarre range of music: funk on top of heavy metal via Europop to the jazz and soul played at the café next to the dance floor. Situated on the eastern side of town, and best visited after midnight when the schoolkids have cleared off.

Club Voltaire, Friedrichstr. 9. The only all-night joint worth mentioning; has a tiny dance floor, with music kept at conversation level. Open midnight–6am.

Odeon, Pontstr. 135. Very popular but rather poky disco in the student quarter.

Culture and festivals

The *Eurogress* centre next to the Casino at Monheimsallee 52 (☎91310) is where both rock and classical **concerts** are held. More highbrow culture is available at the *Theater Aachen* on Theaterplatz (☎478 4244); **drama** or **opera** is performed most evenings and standards are good – Herbert von Karajan first made his name as musical director here. *Grenzlandtheater* on Friedrich-Wilhelm-Platz (☎30060) offers modern fare, albeit with an emphasis on established playwrights.

The main **festivals** are Carnival, which is celebrated here with typical Rhenish enthusiasm; the *Karlspreis* in early May; and the *Europamarkt der Kunsthandwerker*, a handicrafts fair held on the first weekend of September. *CHIO*, an international jumping and riding tournament in late June or early July, is the main sporting event.

The Northern Eifel

The German section of the **Eifel** massif is divided by the Land boundary between North Rhine-Westphalia and Rhineland-Palatinate; the former's share consists mainly of the **Hohes Venn**, an extensive plateau of impervious rocks which stretches into Belgium. Variation in the scenery is provided by the River Rur, which cuts a deep, winding valley, and by the vegetation of gorse, broom and cotton grass. The area is poor in natural resources: no cities have ever developed, and the nineteenth century saw mass emigration, much of it to the United States. Nowadays, the principal industry is the provision of **activity holidays** – skiing in winter, hiking, angling and sailing in summer – punctuated by dead periods between the seasons.

Monschau

The Northern Eifel's other main draw is a series of well-preserved small towns, two of which rank among the finest in Germany. One of these is **MONSCHAU**, some 30km south of Aachen. It's only accessible by road, with slow but fairly frequent bus services; most of the Eifel rail lines have closed because of the high cost of maintenance and low usage levels, though excursion trains, often pulled by steam engines, run between Monschau and the Belgian town of Eupen on Sundays and holidays throughout the summer.

Monschau's main attraction is its dramatic setting deep in the Rur valley, with ruined fortresses – the **Burg** and the **Haller** (both with unrestricted access) – crowning two of the hills above. These offer some of the many superb **views** to be had in the area; others can be enjoyed from a belvedere just off the main road to Aachen, or from the commanding heights of the continuation of this road in the direction of Nideggen. The Burg, much the larger of the ruins, is the building from which Monschau developed. Its keep and gateway are Romanesque originals; the ring wall and parapets date from a strengthening of the defences in the fourteenth century, while the large **Eselsturm** (Asses' Tower), originally built in the same priod, was modified a couple of hundred years later, when the central **Palast** was added.

The lower part of Monschau is an almost completely preserved townscape, dominated by the magnificent **multi-storey mansions** lining the Rur, whose slate roofs are sometimes pierced by two tiers of dormer windows. Though half-timbering is used extensively, these houses aren't as old as they might appear – they date from Monschau's main period of prosperity, centred on cloth production, which followed the Thirty Years' War. The most ornate of all, the **Rotes Haus** (Red House; Good Friday–Nov 30 Tues–Sun entry at 10am, 11am, 2pm, 3pm & 4pm; DM5), adds a rare splash of colour to the town, which is otherwise so monochromatic that it seems to grow organically out of the landscape. Built by a merchant in the 1750s as a combined factory, office and house, it features a Rococo staircase with an elaborate iron railing, and is fully furnished in the same style. The nearby **Troistorff Haus** on Laufenstrasse, which is now used as municipal offices, is smaller, but has a fancier exterior and another fine stairway.

Practicalities

Monschau's **tourist office** (Mon–Wed 10am–4pm, Thurs & Fri 10am–6pm; Easter–Oct also Sat & Sun 11am–3pm) is at Stadtstr. 1 beside the main bridge.

Hotels are numerous and almost always good value. Right in the centre are *Eifeler Hof*, Stadtstr. 10 (☎02472/5046; ②); *Burghotel*, Laufenstr. 1 (☎02472/2332; ②); *Royal*, Stadtstr. 4–6 (☎02472/2033; ③); *Alt Montjoie*, Stadtstr. 18 (☎02472/3289; ③); and *Alte Herrlichkeit*, Stadtstr. 7 (☎02472/2120; ④). High above the town and commanding a wonderful view is *Hubertusklause*, Bergstr. 45 (☎02472/555036; ⑤).

There are two **youth hostels** in town, one located in the Palast (☎02472/2314; ⓐ) and the other at Hargardgasse 5 in Hargard (☎02472/2180; ⓐ), some 3km away. **Private houses** (①–②) with rooms to let, can be found mainly on Kirchstrasse, Laufenstrasse and Oberer Mühlenberg. There are **campsites** at Perlenau (☎02472/636) and at Grünentalstr. 36 in the adjoining village of Imgenbroich (☎02472/3931).

The **cafés** and **restaurants** which crowd the town centre are mostly of a high standard. All the hotels above have good restaurants, too, and the one at *Hubertusklause* is outstanding. Try the products of the local *Felsenkeller* brewery; its speciality is *Monschauer Zwickelbier*, a dark, cloudy, bottom-fermented beer rich in vitamin B.

Bad Münstereifel and around

BAD MÜNSTEREIFEL, at the extreme eastern edge of the Eifel at the dead end of a branch rail line, is easiest reached from Bonn. For all its concealed position, deep in the valley of the River Erft, it's a place of considerable character, rivalling Monschau in quality; though not so homogeneous, nor so picturesquely sited, its monuments are more enjoyable. Prominent among these is the thirteenth- to fourteenth-century **Stadtmauer**, which survives intact. Straight ahead from the Bahnhof is the formidable northern gate, the **Werther Tor**; the corresponding position to the south is guarded by the **Orchheimer Tor**. To the east and west, the fortifications rise high into the hills, giving extra protection to the town huddled along the banks of the river. On the eastern side are the **Burg** (the only ruined feature) and the **Johannistor**; the western front now forms the boundary of the **Kurgarten** with its spa facilities, and is defended on its southern corner by the **Heisterbacher Tor**. You can walk freely along this stretch of rampart, which offers wonderful views over the town and the surrounding foothills of the **Ahrgebirge** range (see p.448). For a wholly different perspective, it's worth following the footpath round the walls.

Münstereifel (minster in the Eifel) derives its name from the fact that the town developed from a Benedictine monastery; this was founded in 830 and quickly became a popular place of pilgrimage through possession of the relics of the Roman martyrs Chrysanthus and Daria. The present **Stiftskirche** (named after the saints, whose graves are in the crypt) is a magnificently severe twelfth-century Romanesque church, which dominates the skyline of the lower town. Across the Kirchplatz is the striking red facade of the **Rathaus**, which began life in the mid-fourteenth century as a guild house. On Langenhecke to the rear of the church is the **Heimatmuseum** (Tues, Thurs & Fri 9am–noon, Wed 9am–noon & 2–4pm, Sat & Sun 1–4pm; DM2). The building itself – once the home of a lay brother of the monastery – is more interesting than the local history displays inside. Dating back to 1167 and contemporary with the church, it's possibly the oldest intact house in Germany.

As well as these public buildings, Münstereifel offers one of the most satisfying townscapes in the region, enhanced by its rustic setting on the banks of the River Erft, which is never more than a stream; almost every street within the walls is worth exploring. Look out for the half-timbered mid-seventeenth-century **Haus Windeck** at Orchheimer Str. 23, the first floor of which is now a café. Also of interest is the seventeenth-century **Jesuitenkirche** facing the Markt, built in an anachronistic Gothic style.

Around Bad Münstereifel

The surrounding countryside is good for **hiking**; get a free tourist board brochure which outlines the best routes. The most popular excursion is to the world's largest **radio-telescope** situated just outside the hamlet of Effelsberg, 8km southeast. Visitors are only admitted in groups, but individuals can also join these; it's best to phone ahead (☎02257/30117; Tues–Sat at 10am, 11am, 1pm, 2pm, 3pm & 4pm; DM2).

Practicalities

Bad Münstereifel's **tourist office** is at Langenhecke 2 (Mon–Fri 9am–5pm, Sat 10am–noon & 2–4pm, Sun 10.30am–12.30pm; ☎02253/505182). Private houses with **rooms** (①–③) to let can be found all over town – just look out for the *Zimmer frei* signs. **Hotels** include the homely *Gästehaus Erftstiege*, Unnastr. 8–10 (☎02253/8900; ⑤) and *Wolfsschlucht*, Orchheimer Str. 19 (☎02253/92030; ⑥); both serve excellent buffet breakfasts, while the latter has a good, reasonably priced restaurant. There are also several spa hotels, notably *Waldhotel Brezing*, Am Quecken 7–10 (☎02253/4506; ⑤) and *Kur und Kongresshotel*, Nöthener Str. 10 (☎02253/54000; ⑦). The **youth hostel** is high in the hills about 2km east of town at Herbergsweg 1–5 (☎02253/7438; ✿) just before the village of Rodert, while the **campsite** is to the south on the banks of the Erft (☎02253/8282). There are plenty of reasonably priced places to **eat** and **drink**, particularly along the main Wertherstrasse. Watch out for set menus, which are often tremendous bargains; this is particularly true of the *Burg-Restaurant* in the castle ruins. Among the cafés, the long-established *Café am Salzmarkt*, Orchheimer Str. 2, stands out.

Bonn

The name of **BONN** is indissolubly associated with the West German state, having served as its capital from the time the country was set up in 1949 until the unification of 1990, when Berlin was restored to its former role. Although still a seat of government, it will lose that honour before the decade is out, and, in a colossal blow to the supreme self-confidence it has acquired, it's in grave danger of slipping back to its prewar obscurity. In some ways this is no more than it deserves, as it was the most unlikely and unloved of European capitals: just "A Small Town in Germany" according to the title of John le Carré's spy thriller, or "The Federal Village" in the condescending eyes of the inhabitants of grander German cities. Yet it is a historic town in its own right, chiefly renowned prior to its elevation as capital as the birthplace of **Ludwig van Beethoven**.

Arrival, information and accommodation

The **Hauptbahnhof** lies plumb in the middle of the city, the central pedestrian area opening out immediately before it. To the right is the **bus station**, whose local services, along with the trams (which become the U-Bahn in the city centre), form part of a system integrated with that of Cologne. As the attractions are well spaced out, it's better to buy tickets in blocks of four, or a 24-hour pass which costs DM11 for Bonn alone or DM12 including entrance to the city's main museums. In addition, a three-day pass is available, costing DM22. Also shared with Cologne is the **airport**, which is linked with the city by bus #670 at least every thirty minutes.

The **tourist office** (Mon–Fri 9am–6.30pm, Sat 9am–5pm, Sun 10am–2pm; ☎773466) is in the Cassius-Passage at Münsterstr. 20.

Accommodation

There are several good mid-range places right in the centre of Bonn, but beware that the top hotels charge grossly inflated rates. Those in Bad Godesberg are better value and are far more enticing places to stay. The city has a choice of two **youth hostels,** each among the most luxurious in Germany. **Camping** is possible all year round at Im Frankenkeller 49 (☎344949) in Mehlem on the banks of the Rhine south of Bad Godesberg.

THE CITY CENTRE

Beethoven, Rheingasse 26 (☎631411, fax 691629). Modern hotel situated right by the Rhine; ask for a room with a view of the river. Also has a good restaurant which serves bargain set meals. ⑥

Deutsches Haus, Kasernenstr. 19 (☎633777, fax 659055). Good-value hotel at the northwestern end of the Altstadt. Its restaurant is open weekday evenings only. ⑤

Mozart, Mozartstr. 1 (☎659071, fax 659075). On a quiet corner a few minutes' walk southwest of the Hauptbahnhof, this is among the best value in the centre. ⑤

The **telephone code** for Bonn is ☎0228

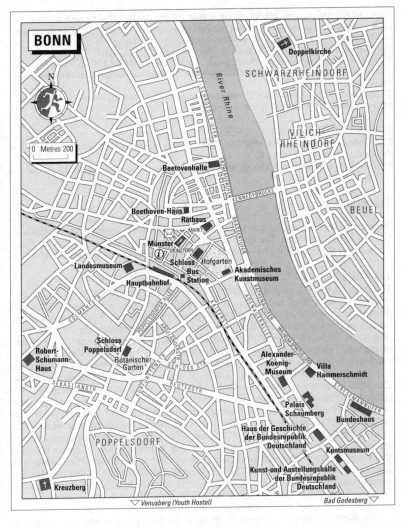

Savoy, Berliner Freiheit 17 (☎651356, fax 696899). At the northern end of the centre, not far from Kennedybrücke, with large, spacious rooms. ④

Sternhotel, Markt 8 (☎72670, fax 726 7125). Fine old hotel, right beside the Rathaus, run by the same family for a century. ⑦

Virneburg, Sandkaule 3a (☎636366). Basic budget hotel just north of the Altstadt. ②

BAD GODESBERG AND BEUEL

Damaskus, Goetheallee 9 (☎468771). One of the cheapest reasonable hotels in the city, this is located in the right-bank suburb of Beuel, close to the train station of the same name. ③

Eden, Am Kurpark 5a (☎957270, fax 362494). Classy hotel in Bad Godesberg's spa quarter. ⑦

Godesburg (☎316071, fax 311218). Modern hotel cunningly fitted into the ruins of the Burg, commanding a great view over the Rhine and the Siebengebirge. ⑦

Schlosshotel Kommende, Oberkasseler Str. 10 (☎440734, fax 44400). In the district of Ramersdorf in the southern part of Beuel (reached by U-Bahn #62, #66 or #68), this occupies a neo-Gothic Schloss of the Teutonic Knights, with beautiful furniture and antiques. Also has a top-notch Italian restaurant. ⑦

Wessel, Bonner Str. 22 (☎351230). Located in the northern part of Bad Godesberg, this is one of several reasonably priced small hotels in the spa town. ③

YOUTH HOSTELS

Bad Godesberg, Horionstr. 60 (☎317516). Take bus #615, leaving from the tram terminus beside the spa town's own train station. ☎

Venusberg, Haager Weg 42 (☎281200). Much the larger of the city's hostels, located in the suburb of Venusberg; take bus #621. ☎

The city

Present-day Bonn is actually a federation of a host of formerly separate communities on both banks of the Rhine. The main attractions are far more spread out than in many much larger German cities, meaning that it isn't a place easily appreciated in a hurry.

The Altstadt

The small Altstadt is now predominantly a pedestrianized shopping area centred on two spacious squares. That to the east is named after the huge Romanesque **Münster**, whose central octagonal tower with its soaring spire is the city's most prominent landmark. Inside, it's airy and pleasing, the sensitive proportions reinforcing the feel of massive space. Below the chancel is a fine crypt, while there's an impressively severe and monumental **cloister** adjoining the southern side. The pink Rococo **Rathaus** adds a touch of colour to the other square, the Markt, which still hosts a market each weekday.

A couple of minutes' walk north of here, at Bonngasse 20, is the **Beethoven-Haus** (Mon–Sat 10am–4/5pm, Sun 11am–4pm; DM8). This is one of the few old buildings in the centre to have escaped wartime devastation, and together with the more imposing house next door it contains an unfussy and intelligently presented museum dedicated to the great composer. Beethoven served his musical apprenticeship at the Electoral court of his home town, but left it for good at the age of 22, though this hasn't deterred Bonn from zealously building up the best collection of memorabilia of its favourite son. There's a bunch of uncomfortable portraits of the tormented genius (who was a reluctant sitter), along with manuscripts and correspondence. The three instruments with which he was associated as a professional performer are shown in the form of the console of the destroyed organ on which he played as a youth, his last piano, and his viola. Most poignant of all are the ear-trumpets which a friend made specially in order to combat his advancing deafness.

The Altstadt's second dominant building is the Baroque **Schloss**, an enormously long construction which was formerly the seat of the Archbishop-Electors of Cologne and is now used by the University. To the south, the Schloss is bounded by the open spaces of the Hofgarten, at whose far end is the **Akademisches Kunstmuseum** (Mon–Wed, Fri & Sun 10am–1pm, Thurs 10am–1pm & 4–6pm; DM1), housed in a Neoclassical pavilion designed by Schinkel. This has an eerie collection of casts of famous antique sculptures, originally made for the benefit of art students.

The Landesmuseum

Despite the advent of a brand-new museum quarter, the pick of Bonn's collections is still the **Landesmuseum** (Tues, Thurs & Fri 9am–5pm, Wed 9am–8pm, Sat & Sun

---

LUDWIG VAN BEETHOVEN (1770–1827)

No composer has ever made a greater impact on the history of music than **Ludwig van Beethoven**. The successor to the Viennese classical tradition of Haydn and Mozart, he developed the three great forms of the period – the symphony, the string quartet and the piano sonata – to their ultimate limits. His work reflects his libertarian concerns, and shows for the first time the ability of music to convey a humanitarian message without the aid of text, thus setting the scene for the Romantic composers of the next hundred years. From 1800, Beethoven had problems with his hearing, an affliction which was partly responsible for the transformations he wrought in orchestral sound; the menacing power of some of his symphonies was so different from anything previously composed that many contemporaries were – literally – physically scared of them. By the time he finished his *Ninth Symphony*, in which instrumental and choral music were woven into one for the very first time, he had become completely deaf, yet he continued to compose, notably five valedictory string quartets of awesome emotional intensity.

10am–5pm; DM4) at Colmantstr. 14–16 behind the Hauptbahnhof. Star exhibit is the **skull of Neanderthal Man**, found in a valley near Düsseldorf (see p.511), and calculated to be some 60,000 years old. Highlights of the important Roman department are the tomb of Marcus Caelius, a set of arcades from Aachen and a mosaic dedicated to the sun. The medieval section on the first floor includes the anguished sculpture known as the *Roettgen Pietà* and some lovely examples of the fifteenth-century Cologne School of painters. Look out for the delicate *Deposition* and *St Sebastian* by an anonymous artist who has been named **Master of the Bonn Diptych** as a result, and five panels by the painter known as **Master of the St Ursula Legend** after the dispersed series from which these came. Among later German paintings, a rare work by **Elsheimer**, *The Three Marys at the Sepulchre*, stands out.

Poppelsdorf and Kreuzberg

Also branching out from the Schloss is the kilometre-long avenue of chestnut trees which leads to **Poppelsdorf**, now a suburb of the city, where the Frenchman **Robert de Cotte**, who had undertaken modifications to the Schloss, was commissioned to build a second Electoral residence. The resulting **Schloss Poppelsdorf** follows an ingenious *trompe l'oeil* design, its circular courtyard concealed within a rectangular ground plan. Again, the palace is now occupied by University departments, the grounds serving as the **Botanischer Garten** (April–Sept Mon–Fri 9am–5pm, Sun 9am–1pm; Oct–March Mon–Fri 9am–4.30pm; free). For a sociological as well as architectural stroll, wander in the Südstadt, the streets immediately to the east, such as Schloss Strasse, Kurfürstenstrasse, Argelanderstrasse and Bismarckstrasse. These represent a remarkably complete picture of turn-of-the-century town planning for the better-off sections of the middle classes.

To the other side of Schloss Poppelsdorf at Sebastianstr. 182 is the **Robert-Schumann-Haus** (Mon & Fri 10am–noon & 4–7pm, Wed & Thurs 10am–noon & 3–6pm, Sun 10am–1pm; free), containing a collection of memorabilia of the Romantic composer. In spite of a blissful marriage to the pianist Clara Wieck, which inspired so many of his yearning, passionate song settings and virtuoso piano pieces, Schumann had a history of psychological instability, culminating in a complete mental breakdown and attempted suicide when he threw himself into the Rhine. At his own request, he spent the last two years of his life in Bonn confined to the sanatorium adjoining his house.

Continuing south from Poppelsdorf, a road leads uphill to the isolated pilgrimage church of **Kreuzberg**. The original seventeenth-century chapel was given the full Rococo treatment a hundred years later, including the addition of the Holy Steps, an imitation in the lavishly ornate style of Balthasar Neumann of those now in Rome on which Christ allegedly ascended to receive Pilate's judgment.

The Regierungsviertel

Bonn's **Regierungsviertel** (government quarter) can be reached either by following Reuterstrasse from Poppelsdorf, or by taking Adenauerallee from the Hofgarten: the distance is about the same. Saddled with its "temporary status", it was not custom-built, but utilized a series of existing structures. Ironically enough, work had just started on new buildings when the sudden fall of Communism in East Germany in 1989 shook the city out of its complacent assumption that it was going to be a long-term capital.

Both the **Villa Hammerschmidt** and the **Palais Schaumburg** are pompous Empire buildings from the last century, once private dwellings of the mega-rich but now the official residences of the Federal President and Chancellor respectively. You aren't allowed near them, never mind inside. Further south, the **Parliament buildings** are in the Bauhaus style of the 1930s. This time admission is possible, but only for groups by written appointment, though you can try joining a party who have booked to be shown around the **Bundesrat** (Upper House) – more trouble than it's worth, unless you're passionately keen on German politics. A better reason for coming is the wonderful **view** over the Rhine and the Siebengebirge on the opposite bank.

Planned as a fitting cultural accompaniment to the government quarter at a time when Bonn seemed set for an indefinite stint at the heart of German political life, the **Museumsmeile** (Museum Mile) on its western edge only came to fruition after national unification had been achieved, by which time it already seemed an anachronism. Of the four institutions along its route, only the **Alexander-Koenig-Museum** (Tues–Fri 9am–5pm, Sat 9am–12.30pm, Sun 9.30am–5pm; DM4) at Adenauerallee 160 existed

---

THE STRUGGLES TO BECOME CAPITAL

When Germany was finally unified through Prussian military might in 1871, **Berlin** became the first official and undisputed capital the country had ever had. The partition of Berlin after World War II meant that the city could no longer fulfil its role, though the eastern sector became the official capital of the GDR. Meanwhile **Bonn** – hitherto a provincial university town – was chosen as capital of the West German state. In a sense, this was a deliberately crass choice in line with the "provisional" nature of the new country (see "The Historical Framework" in *Contexts*). Konrad Adenauer, the first Chancellor, lived nearby and championed its cause as a matter of personal convenience, forming an unholy alliance with West Berlin representatives, who were desperate to thwart the claims of **Frankfurt** (the only other city considered for the role), astutely realizing that the latter might be powerful enough to deny Berlin's re-instatement as capital.

For all the swiftness of the unification process when it finally happened, four decades of national partition had made the name of Bonn virtually synonymous with that of the new, responsible face of Germany. Thus, although Berlin was confirmed as capital in 1990, Bonn fought to remain the seat of government. The campaign was vitriolic: the Bonn lobby contrasted its proven record at the heart of a prosperous, democratic and peace-loving country with Berlin's tainted history as the successive headquarters of a militaristic absolute monarchy, then Nazi and Communist totalitarian dictatorships; the huge costs of making the move were also cited, as was the fact that, now that the Eastern Territories were accepted as lost forever, Berlin's geographical position was no longer sufficiently central. In retaliation, Berlin's supporters rubbished Bonn as a backwater inappropriately sited for the great challenge of rebuilding the shattered economy and society of eastern Germany. Chancellor Helmut Kohl, like Adenauer a native of the Rhineland, surprisingly endorsed Berlin, which in June 1991 won a narrow majority in the deciding parliamentary vote.

prior to 1992. One of the best natural history collections in the country, its displays are laid out on four floors with a true Germanic thoroughness. Next in line, at no. 250 on the same boulevard, is the **Haus der Geschichte der Bundesrepublik Deutschland** (Tues–Sun 9am–7pm; free), which traces the political, cultural, social and economic history of the Federal Republic. To non-Germans, its emphases might seem ephemeral, though the presentations are greatly enlivened by the extensive use of archive film, including John F. Kennedy's famous "Ich bin ein Berliner" speech.

At the head of Friedrich-Ebert-Allee, the continuation of Adenauerallee, is the **Kunstmuseum** (Tues–Sun 10am–7pm; DM5), which contains the municipal gallery of modern art. Its main strength lies in its representation of the Expressionists, and in particular the brilliant **August Macke**, who spent part of his brief life in the city. The upper floor is devoted to the avant-garde, notably Joseph Beuys, Sigmar Polke and Anselm Kiefer. To the rear is the most attention-seeking of the three new museums, the **Kunst- und Ausstellungshalle der Bundesrepublik Deutschland** (Tues–Sun 10am–7pm; DM8), a space-age arts centre which can host up to five temporary exhibitions at one time. Already it has staged several blockbuster shows, including an ongoing series of loans from the great museums of the world, though the emphasis is firmly on diverse aspects of modern artistic creativity.

Bad Godesberg

When Bonn was officially expanded in 1969, it gobbled up a string of small villages, giving it a foothold on the eastern bank of the Rhine for the first time. It also annexed the old spa town of **BAD GODESBERG** (reached by U-Bahn #16 or #63, or main-line train) to the south, stretching its boundaries to the Land border. Bad Godesberg's character had already made it a favoured location for many of the diplomatic missions, who found its grandiose Empire-style villas just the sort of headquarters they were looking for. The town is also a famed conference centre, and has hosted at least two fateful events – the series of meetings between Chamberlain and Hitler in 1938, which paved the way for the Munich Agreement in which "peace in our time" was bought at Czechoslovakia's expense; and the 1959 conference of the Social Democrats, when the party, bidding to end a period of three decades in opposition, disavowed its earlier connections with Marxism, class warfare and anti-clericalism, and became part of the post-war consensus rooted in acceptance of the idea of a "social market economy".

Rearing high over the town is the **Godesburg**, the most northerly of the great series of castles crowning promontories above the Rhine, built in the thirteenth and fourteenth centuries by the archbishops of Cologne and blown up in 1583. Today it's chiefly a hotel (see p.472), but the cylindrical **keep** is still intact and can be ascended (April–Oct Wed–Sun 10am–6pm; DM0.50) for a panoramic **view**, including a distant glimpse of Cologne and the Siebengebirge. Views, indeed, are Bad Godesberg's major attraction; you'll find plenty more if you saunter down the **Rheinufer**, the promenade along the river bank. Otherwise, there are two spa parks in the town centre, separated by fashionable buildings, prominent among which is the late eighteenth-century **Redoute**, formerly the ballroom of the Electors, now a renowned function suite.

Schwarzrheindorf

The only one of Bonn's outer villages worth making a special detour to see is **SCHWARZRHEINDORF**, on the right bank of the Rhine to the extreme north, reached by bus #550 or #640. It boasts a relatively little-known but outstanding monument in the form of the **Doppelkirche**, a former manorial church. Built in the mid-twelfth century, this offers an intriguing insight into the social and religious preoccupations of the medieval world. The exterior cleverly disguises the fact that it encases two separate chapels, the upper reserved for the lord, the lower for the use of the labourers. Apart from its architectural idiosyncrasies, the church has rare Romanesque

fresco cycles. Turning on the light by the door reveals *The Vision of Ezekiel*, *The Transfiguration* and *The Crucifixion*, while upstairs the great visions of *The Apocalypse* were painted for their lordships' contemplation.

Eating, drinking and nightlife

Bonn has a fairly eclectic range of places to eat, its diplomatic status reflected in an unusually wide choice of **ethnic restaurants**. Most of the best bars are conveniently located in the Altstadt and the Südstadt. The city's nightlife is largely dependent on the University; out of term and at weekends the centre can resemble a ghost town come the evening.

Restaurants

Cassius Garten, Maximilianstr. 28d. Offers a mouth-watering choice of vegetarian food, which you pay for by weight. Closed Sun.

Don Quijote, Oxfordstr. 18. The most convenient of a surprising number of Spanish restaurants in the city. Evenings only.

Em Höttche, Markt 4. Good traditional *Gaststätte* in the handiest of locations.

Grand' Italia, Bischofsplatz 1. The best of the city's many Italian restaurants.

Im Bären, Acherstr. 1–3. Excellent *Gaststätte* owned by the local *Kurfürsten* brewery.

Marrakesch, Friesdorfer Str. 145, Bad Godesberg. Speciality Moroccan restaurant. Closed Wed.

Le Petit Poisson, Wilhelmstr. 23a. Expensive but very highly rated French restaurant, located just north of the Altstadt. Closed Sun.

Redüttchen, Kurfürstenallee 1, Bad Godesberg. *Gemütlich* little restaurant in the former gardener's house beside the Redoute.

Salvator, In der Sürst 5–7. A Bavarian-style beer hall-restaurant – something of an oddity for the Rhineland.

Stadthalle, Koblenzer Str. 80, Bad Godesberg. Traditional German food at reasonable prices in the eastern of the two spa parks.

Zur Lindenwirtin Aennchen, Aennchenplatz 2, Bad Godesberg. Historic student tavern with garden terrace, restored as an upmarket retaurant.

Zypern-Philoxenia, Clemens-August-Str. 34, Poppelsdorf. One of Germany's few specifically Cypriot restaurants; also features dishes from other Mediterranean countries.

Bars and cafés

Aktuell, Gerhard-von-Are-Str. 8. Best known as the favoured haunt of journalists, a profession represented in Bonn in force.

Bla, Bornheimer Str. 20. A garishly decorated meeting place of punk diehards.

Bonner Kaffeehaus, Remigiusplatz 5. Traditional café in the heart of the pedesrianized shopping area.

Brauhaus Bönnsch, Sterntorbrücke 4. *Hausbrauerei* producing a distinctive blond ale known as *Bönnsch*, which is served in a curious horn-shaped glass. Also does good-value meals.

Jazz Galerie, Oxfordstr. 24. Features live jazz sessions most evenings and a weekly jam session.

Köller, Heerstr. 1. Brasserie with a definite yuppyish appeal.

Namenlos, Bornheimer Str. 20. A less outlandish counterpart to the adjoining *Bla*, with minimalist decor.

Südstadt-Kneipe, Königstr. 9. Laid-back pub reflecting the civilized air of the Südstadt area. Offers a selection of reasonably priced cocktails and food to a background of good music.

Zebulon, Stockenstr. 19. A big favourite with arts students, particularly for breakfast.

Zur Kerze, Königstr. 25. Subtitled *Künstlerkeller* (Artists' Cellar), this popular bar is open till 5am. Bristling with alcoves and partitions, it's frequented by a mixed age range, and serves excellent (if fairly pricey) Italianate dishes.

Entertainment

To find out what's on in the fields of **theatre**, **concerts** and **exhibitions**, consult the fortnightly *Kulturkalender* produced by the tourist office. The monthly *De Schnüss* (DM3.50), available from newsagents, also gives listings for cinemas and live bands.

The Bonn highbrow cultural scene is good but by no means outstanding: top international musicians sometimes appear at the *Beethovenhalle*, Wachsbleiche 26 (☎631321), and the *Kammermusiksaal*, Bonngasse 24–26 (☎631321), while the *Oper* (which also hosts ballet) is at Am Boeslagerhof 1 (☎7281 or 773666). Among the theatres are *Euro Theater* at Mauspfad (☎652951) and *Haus der Springmaus*, Frangasse 8 (☎798081), which features cabaret.

The main alternative cultural centre is *Brotfabrik* at Kreuzstr. 16 (☎475424) in Beuel; it features exhibitions, cinema, readings and feminist events. *Pantheon* at Am Bundeskanzlerplatz (☎212521) in the government quarter is on the same lines, and also holds a disco at weekends, while *Biskuit-Halle* on Wesselwerke (☎257 1215) is the main venue for visiting live bands.

Listings

Airport ☎404 0012 for flight information.

Bookstores There's a wide selection in and around Am Hof (behind the Schloss).

Embassies *Australia*, Godesberger Allee 107, Bad Godesberg (☎81030); *Britain*, Friedrich-Ebert-Allee 77 (☎91670); *Canada*, Friedrich-Wilhelm-Str. 18 (☎5680); *Ireland*, Godesberger Allee 119, Bad Godesberg (☎376937); *New Zealand*, Bonn-Center, Am Bundeskanzlenplatz (☎228070); *US*, Deichmanns Aue 29, Bad Godesberg (☎3391).

Festivals Every year there's an international Beethoven festival in September. The main folklore event is the *Pützchensmarkt*, a colourful fair held annually on the first weekend of the same month in Beuel.

Markets Daily on the Markt; every third Sat of the month, there's a flea market on Rheinaue.

Mitfahrzentrale Herwarthstr. 11a (☎93030).

Post office The main post office is at Münsterplatz 17 with a poste restante service.

Rhine cruises These depart from Brassentufer just south of Kennedybrücke: *K-D Linie* (☎632134); *Bonner Personenschiffahrt* (☎636363).

The Siebengebirge

The **Siebengebirge** (Seven Mountains), on the eastern bank of the Rhine just before the Land boundary with Rhineland-Palatinate, rank among the river's most suggestively grand stretches, steeped in the lore of legend and literature. According to one story, the mountains were created by seven giants clearing the dirt from their shovels. They're also often regarded as the site of the most famous of the Grimms' fairy tales, *Snow White and the Seven Dwarfs*.

Despite the name, there are around thirty summits in this extinct volcanic range, which stretches for about 15km north to south and 5km east to west. From Bonn, six of the main peaks can be seen; the number seven, with its traditional mystical significance, applies only to those visible from a point further north. Of the group, **Drachenfels** (321m), **Wolkenburg** (325m) and **Lohrberg** (435m) are all of a mineral called trachyte; **Petersberg** (331m), **Nonnenstromberg** (336m) and **Grosser Ölberg** (461m) are of basalt, a later formation; while **Löwenburg** (455m) is of dolerite. For centuries, stone from these mountains was quarried to construct the great buildings of the Rhineland, notably the Dom in Cologne; this quarrying was brought to an end in 1889, when the whole area was designated as the first protected landscape in Germany. The

Siebengebirge are covered with thick woods, which means that views are very restricted most of the time, though all the more spectacular when you do reach a belvedere. This wasn't always so; old prints show the upper parts of the peaks free of trees, and generally crowned with a fortress.

The resorts

"One day suffices to explore the most interesting points in this district, unless the visit be for geological purposes," intoned last century's *Baedeker Guide*. This particular piece of advice still holds good, and the Siebengebirge make an easy outing from Bonn, to which they're connected by U-Bahn #66. Alternatively, you could base yourself at either **KÖNIGSWINTER** or **BAD HONNEF**. These two holiday resorts have avoided the fate of Bad Godesberg on the opposite bank of being swallowed up by the city. Königswinter has a relaxed, rather dated air. As befits a spa, Bad Honnef is more upmarket, preserving its Kurhaus in a fine park. It was the chosen residence of **Konrad Adenauer**, first Chancellor of the Federal Republic, whose home at no. 8c in the street named after him in the northern suburb of Rhöndorf is now a memorial **museum** (guided tours Tues–Sun 10am–4.30pm; free).

Hotel rooms in both towns are plentiful and, being geared to vacationing families, are generally good value; they're certainly worth considering as an alternative to paying Bonn's inflated prices. A full list is available from the regional **tourist office** at Drachenfelsstr. 9–11 in Königswinter (Easter–Oct Mon–Wed 10am–1.30pm & 2.30–5pm, Thurs 10am–1.30pm & 2.30–6pm, Sat 11am–1.30pm & 2.30–5pm; Nov–Easter Mon–Thurs 10am–1pm & 3–5pm, Fri 10am–1pm; ☎0244/889325). Bad Honnef has a **youth hostel** at Selhofer Str. 106 (☎02224/71300; ✿) at the very southern end of town, and a couple of **campsites**.

It's worth trying to time your visit to coincide with one of the numerous **festivals**, the most spectacular of which is *Der Rhein in Flammen*, a display of fireworks and illuminations held on the first Saturday in May; a week later, the cutting of the first crop of asparagus is celebrated. Bad Honnef's *Weinfest* is held on the first weekend in September; exactly a month later comes Königswinter's *Winzerfest*.

The mountains

Although the lowest of the mountains, **Drachenfels**, situated immediately behind Königswinter, is by far the most interesting, unfortunately it's also the most-climbed mountain in Europe, heavily tourist-orientated and even more heavily exploited. The rack rail line, built in 1883 using a system pioneered in Switzerland, is an ingenious piece of engineering, rising 220 metres over a total length of 1.5km. However, the fare (DM10 single, DM13 return)

KONRAD ADENAUER (1876–1967)

A local government stalwart of the Catholic Centre Party during the Weimar Republic, **Konrad Adenauer** seemed to be merely a stop-gap leader when he finally entered the national stage at the age of 73. In the event, his impeccable record as an anti-Nazi (he had been deposed as mayor of Cologne) and his moderate right-wing politics happened to be exactly in tune with the country's mood in the postwar period, and he remained in power for fourteen years, only retiring when his coalition partners made this a condition of their continued support. Adenauer's high reputation rests on his twin achievements of the "Economic Miracle" and the international rehabilitation of Germany, though there's little doubt that his inflexible attitude towards the Russians was a contributory factor in cementing the division of the nation into two hostile states.

is a bit of a a rip-off, the more so as the footpath is paved and makes for a steep but easy ascent. About a third of the way up is the **dragon's cave**, traditionally supposed to be the home of the fearsome monster slain by the hero **Siegfried**. By immediately immersing himself in its warm blood he gained a horny skin which would have rendered him invincible had a falling leaf not left a spot as vulnerable as Achilles' heel. From this legend comes the name of the wine, *Drachenblut* (dragon's blood), made from the grapes cultivated on these slopes, the most northerly vineyard in western Germany. It's best to pass by the cave, featuring a kitsch presentation of live reptiles and a model of the dragon, for which there's a stinging DM5 entrance fee. Your money is better spent on **Schloss Drachenburg** (guided tours Easter–Oct Tues–Sun 11am–6pm; DM3), which is a good example of the nineteenth-century German love of macabre Gothic fantasy. From the terrace there's a really spectacular **view**, which more than makes up for the tribulations en route. There's an even wider panorama from the Romanesque **Burg**, a ruin since the Thirty Years' War, at the summit of the mountain. Apart from being able to trace the Rhine's path both upstream and down, you can see over the Eifel to the west, and get a different perspective on the Siebengebirge themselves; on an even half-decent day, the spires of Cologne can also be distinguished.

Gimmicks are thankfully wholly absent in the rest of the mountains in the range, and a series of well-marked hiking trails enables you to choose your own route round. **Petersberg** is probably the best known; its summit is occupied by a grandiose luxury hotel (☎02233/7401; ⑨) often used for state visits, which was Chamberlain's base for his ill-fated talks with Hitler in Bad Godesberg. **Löwenburg** is allegedly haunted by a wild huntsman, doomed to an eternal chase as punishment for his cruelty when alive. **Grosser Ölberg** is the most enticing after Drachenfels, commanding the next best views. Although furthest from the Rhine of all the peaks, it has the advantage of being the highest, and of including panoramas over the Taunus to the east.

Kloster Heisterbach

From here, it's only a short descent to the area's sole great monument, the ruins of the early thirteenth-century Cistercian **Kloster Heisterbach**, built, like so many of this order's foundations, in the Transitional style between Romanesque and Gothic. One of the first priors, Caesarius, was a chronicler of legends, which he collected in the *Dialogus Miraculorum*. The most famous of these – which was retold by Henry Longfellow – concerns a monk who, while out for his daily walk, was meditating disbelievingly on the text of Psalm 90, "a thousand years in thy sight are but as yesterday"; on returning for vespers, he found that a whole century had elapsed since his departure. Heisterbach was pulled down at the beginning of the nineteenth century following the Napoleonic suppression, but the apse and its ambulatory were spared when the explosives failed to ignite. This tiny fragment had an impact on the Romantic imagination out of all proportion to its size; depictions of lonely, overgrown and crumbling abbeys set in wooded valleys, often illuminated by moonlight, became one of the favourite subjects of the movement's painters. Nowadays, the eighteenth-century monastic buildings are occupied by a convent of Augustinian nuns, who have built a modern church. They also run a café-restaurant, specializing in a huge choice of irresistible home-made gateaux.

Brühl

Midway between Bonn and Cologne, set inland from the Rhine, lies **BRÜHL**, a town which developed from a castle founded by the Archbishop-Electors in the thirteenth century. The eighteenth-century successor to this is the most sumptuous palace in the Rhineland, seemingly a little piece of Bavaria wafted mysteriously northwards. It makes the town one of the most interesting in the province, but the real reason two million people swarm here each summer is the hugely successful **Phantasialand** theme park.

The town

From an aesthetic point of view, the most notable part of Brühl is the huge park with two palaces – both on the UNESCO World Heritage list – stretching southeast of the pedestrianized town centre. The chief tourist attraction, Phantasialand, is at the southern fringe of Brühl, by the junction of the main roads to Trier and Aachen.

Schloss Augustusburg

In its own day Brühl's heart and soul, **Schloss Augustusburg** (guided tours lasting 1 hr; Feb–Nov Tues–Sun 9am–noon & 1.30–4pm; DM5) must have seemed as much of an extravaganza as Phantasialand does now. Such is its splendour that it's the favourite venue for state visits and the federal president's official binges; unfortunately, this means it's liable to unexpected periods of closure for up to three weeks at a time. It's very much a personal creation of the eighteenth-century Archbishop-Elector **Clemens August**, a member of the Bavarian Wittelsbach dynasty. From an early age, he had been earmarked for an ecclesiastical career in order to advance the family's power base. In this, he was brilliantly successful, though he showed no piety whatsoever, living a life of unashamedly pampered luxury and gaining a reputation as a womanizer – he was summoned to Rome by the pope to explain the presence of two particularly beautiful singers at his court, and his death came after he had danced the night away rather too energetically. He favoured Brühl as the seat of his court because of its ideal situation for his favourite hobby, falconry, and was determined to rebuild the medieval moated Schloss which had been destroyed by French troops in 1689.

Initially the design was in dignified Baroque by Johan Conrad Schlann: building was later entrusted to **François Cuvilliés**, who eliminated all features reminiscent of a fortress and transformed the complex into a pleasure palace facing a formal French-style garden. As the final *pièce de résistance*, the greatest architect of the day, **Balthasar Neumann**, was recruited to draw up plans for the ceremonial **staircase** – a fricassee of marble and stucco, crowned by a fresco glorifying the Virtues. The decorative scheme of this and the following Wachenhalle (Hall of Guards) and Musikzimmer (Music Room), which are almost equally sumptuous, is a complicated series of allegories in honour of the Wittelsbach dynasty.

The rest of the town centre

Adjoining the west front of the Schloss is the **Orangerie**; now housing a café-restaurant and an exhibition room, it forms a processional way to **St Maria zu den Engeln**. Built as a Franciscan monastery in the simplest form of Gothic, the church's interior was greatly pepped up for its new function as court chapel by the insertion of a lavish **high altar** – taking up the entire chancel – designed by Neumann. **Max Ernst**, the Dadaist and Surrealist painter, was born in Brühl, a fact commemorated by the **Max-Ernst-Kabinett** (Mon–Wed & Sun 2–5pm, Thurs 2–8pm; free) housed in his birthplace, a villa facing the northern wing of the Schloss. It has a few early oil paintings, but the bulk of the material is graphic work, displayed in a changing series of exhibitions.

Jagdschloss Falkenlust

Walking 2km east through the Schloss grounds takes you to the **Jagdschloss Falkenlust** (Feb–Nov Tues–Sun 9am–noon & 2–4pm; DM3.50), Clemens August's base for his falconry adventures, designed once again by Cuvilliés. It's intimate in scale, and this time you're allowed to explore it at your leisure. In the oval main Salon is a series of portraits of the Wittelsbachs in their hunting attire, but the most impressive rooms are the smallest – the **Lacquerkabinett**, reflecting the contemporary taste for chinoiserie, and the **Spiegelkabinett** directly above. Outside is the tiny **Kapelle**, a folly in imitation of a hermitage.

Phantasialand

Brühl's main draw nowadays is **Phantasialand** (daily April–Oct 9am–6pm; adults DM33, children under 1.20m free). It was the first amusement park in Europe to rival Disneyland and a clear example of how strong the transatlantic influence has become in Germany. Laid out on the site of an open-cast mine at the extreme southern end of town, it can be reached by regular **bus** services from Brühl's train station. Attractions range from re-creations of prewar Berlin, a Wild West town and China of a thousand years ago, through rides on a Viking ship, an overhead monorail, the world's largest roller-coaster and a mock-up of outer space. Be warned that even the park's owners admit that there are an uncomfortably large number of visitors on Sundays and throughout July and August.

Practicalities

The **tourist office** (Mon & Tues 7.30am–4pm, Wed 7.30am–2pm, Thurs 7.30am–6pm, Fri 7.30am–12.30pm; ☎02232/79345) is situated within the former monastic buildings of St Maria zu den Engeln. They keep a good list of private houses with **rooms** to let (②–③).

Alternatively, there are plenty of **hotels** in the town centre: these include *Kurfürst*, Kölnstr. 40 (☎02232/42239; ②), *Brühler Hof*, Uhlstr. 30 (☎02232/42711; ③) and *Clemens-August-Stube*, Römerstr. 86 (☎02232/27364; ④). Brühl's prices are generally so much lower than those in both Cologne and Bonn that it's worth considering as an alternative base – both cities can be reached quickly either by tram (from the town centre) or train (from the opposite side of the Schloss). Places to eat include *Brühler Schlosskeller*, Kölnstr. 74, and the aforementioned *Orangerie*, Schloss Str. 6, which functions as a café in the afternoon and a restaurant in the evening.

Concerts by top international musicians in the Schloss are the main cultural attraction, while October sees a **festival** of international puppet theatre.

COLOGNE (KÖLN)

Although now in the political shadow of the neighbouring upstarts of Bonn and Düsseldorf, **COLOGNE** stands as a colossus in the vast urban sprawl of the Rhine-Ruhr conurbation, being unquestionably one of the great German cities, and currently the fourth largest with a population which recently crept over the million mark. The huge Gothic **Dom** is the country's most visited monument, while its assemblage of Roman remains and medieval buildings is unsurpassed and the museums are bettered only by those in Berlin, Dresden and Munich. The annual **Carnival** in the early spring is one of Europe's major popular celebrations. The city also ranks high as a **beer** centre: there are 24 breweries (more than in any other city in the world), all producing the distinctive *Kölsch*.

Originally founded in 33 BC, Cologne quickly gained importance. It was the birthplace of Julia Agrippa, wife of the Emperor Claudius who in 50 AD raised it to the status of a colony (hence its name) with full rights as a **Roman city**. Subsequent development owed much to ecclesiastical affairs – a bishopric was founded in the fourth century and SS Severin, Gereon and Ursula were all martyred in the city; churches were soon dedicated to each and built over their graves. The **cult of Saint Ursula** was especially popular, being associated with the alleged death of her 11,000 virgin companions (the true figure was probably a more realistic eleven). In the twelfth century, Cologne forcibly acquired the relics of the Three Magi from Milan, thus increasing its standing as one of the greatest centres of **pilgrimage** in northern Europe.

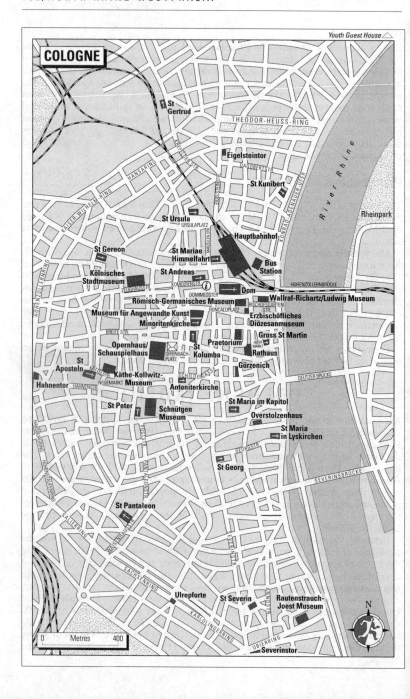

Youth Guest House △

COLOGNE

St Gertrud

THEODOR-HEUSS-RING

Eigelsteintor

DAGOBERTSTR.

St Kunibert

River Rhine

Rheinpark

St Ursula
URSULAPLATZ

St Gereon

St Mariae Himmelfahrt

Hauptbahnhof

Kölnisches Stadtmuseum

St Andreas

Bus Station

KOMÖDIENSTR.

Dom

HOHENZOLLERNBRÜCKE

Römisch-Germanisches Museum

DOMKLOSTER

Wallraf-Richartz/Ludwig Museum

Museum für Angewandte Kunst

RONCALLIPLATZ

BISCHOFSGARTEN-STR.

Erzbischöfliches Diözesanmuseum

Minoritenkirche

BREITE STR.

Praetorium

Gross St Martin
ALTER MARKT

Opernhaus/ Schauspielhaus

OFFENBACH-PLATZ

St Kolumba

Rathaus

Gürzenich

St Aposteln

MITTELSTR.

Käthe-Kollwitz-Museum
NEUMARKT

SCHILDERGASSE

Hahnentor
HAHNENSTR.

Antoniterkirche

DEUTZER BRÜCKE

St Peter

Schnütgen Museum

St Maria im Kapitol

Overstolzenhaus

St Maria in Lyskirchen

St Georg
GEORGSTR.

SEVERINSBRÜCKE

St Pantaleon

Ulrepforte

St Severin

Rautenstrauch-Joest Museum

N

0   Metres   400

KARLOLINGERRING

UBIERRING

Severinstor

The **telephone code** for Cologne is ☎0221

Medieval Cologne, a Free Imperial City with 150 churches, became enormously prosperous because of its strategic situation on the Rhine at the intersection of trade routes. The largest city in Germany, it was one of the great European centres of learning and boasted a distinctive school of painters. Decline inevitably set in, but something of a comeback was made in the eighteenth century with a recipe imported from Italy which involved distilling flower blossoms in almost pure alcohol. Although originally meant as an aphrodisiac, this was to achieve worldwide fame as a toilet water under the euphemism by which customers ordered it – *eau de Cologne*.

The modern city has reclaimed its old role as a major trade and business centre, and has also become Germany's radio and television metropolis. As a welcome contrast to the class-consciousness and frantic status-seeking of its neighbours, it has an openness about it similar to that of the city-states of Hamburg and Bremen. To this is added a general atmosphere of fun and irreverence more characteristic of the Mediterranean than Germany.

Arrival, information and getting around

The **Hauptbahnhof** is right in the centre of the city, immediately below the Dom. Moving on is never a problem as some thousand trains per day stop here. The **bus station** is directly behind, with international services on the lower tier. Cologne's **airport** is served by bus #170; there are departures approximately every twenty minutes, with a journey time of less than half an hour.

The **tourist office** is at Unter Fettenhennen 19, directly in front of the Dom (May–Oct Mon–Sat 8am–10.30pm, Sun & holidays 9am–10.30pm; Nov–April Mon–Sat 8am–9pm, Sun & holidays 9.30am–7pm; ☎221 3345). This is also the best place to try for a **hotel room**. They charge DM5 but you'll get the best advice and the pick of the bargains.

Cologne's **public transport** network uses a mixture of buses and trams; the latter become the U-Bahn around the centre. The system is shared with Bonn, and it's possible to take a stopping tram between the two cities – useful if you intend to leave from or arrive at somewhere which isn't central. Single ticket prices are high, making it better to invest in strips of four, or those valid for 24 hours (DM11), or three days (DM22).

Accommodation

Accommodation is plentiful, but it's scattered all over the city and mainly geared to the expense-account brigade attending the numerous trade fairs. This does mean, however, that some of the better **hotels** offer cut-price rates at slack times; even fifty per cent or more. The tourist office (see above) is the best place to start hunting, but if you prefer to look yourself, the cheapest options lie just beyond the fringes of the Altstadt. By far the largest concentration of accommodation is to the rear of the Hauptbahnhof, where you'll find several streets of very similar hotels, though prices can vary a great deal from one to the other, and even within individual establishments. There are also two **youth hostels** in the city and a good range of **campsites**.

Hotels and pensions

Altstadt, Salzgasse 7 (☎257 7851, fax 257 7853). On an alley not far from the Rhine, offering nicely furnished rooms and a sauna. ⑤

Antik-Hotel Bristol, Kaiser-Wilhelm-Ring 48 (☎120195, fax 131495). Quaintly appointed with old furniture and antiques; several of the rooms have four-poster beds. ⑦

Berg, Brandenburger Str. 6 (☎121124, fax 139 0011). One of a number of basic budget hotels immediately to the rear of the Hauptbahnhof. ④

Brandenburger Hof, Brandenburger Str. 2–4 (☎122889, fax 135304). Another of the hotels behind the Hauptbahnhof; this one has the advantage of its own little garden. ④

Cristall, Ursulaplatz 9–11 (☎16300, fax 163 0333). Fitted out in modern designer style and with a good location in a quiet quarter not far from the Hauptbahnhof. ⑧

DomBlick, Domstr. 28 (☎123742, fax 125736). Good-value hotel close to the Dom. ⑥

Dom-Hotel, Domkloster 2a (☎20240, fax 202 4444). Splendid nineteenth-century luxury hotel whose restaurant terrace offers a stunning view of the south side of the Dom. ⑨

Eden, Am Hof 18 (☎258 0491, fax 258 0495). Upmarket hotel next to the Wallraf-Richartz/Ludwig Museum. ⑦

Excelsior Hotel Ernst, Trankgasse 1–5 (☎2701, fax 135150). Cologne's top hotel for all the 130 years of its existence; ideally placed overlooking the north side of the Dom. ⑨

Gülich, Ursulaplatz 13–19 (☎120015, fax 120015). Middle-range hotel a few minutes' walk northwest of the Hauptbahnhof, which halves its prices at quiet times. ⑦

Im Kupferkessel, Probsteigasse 6 (☎135338, fax 125121). Renovated small hotel in the northwestern part of the Altstadt. ④

Im Wasserturm, Kaygasse 2a (☎20080, fax 200 8888). Designer hotel in a nineteenth-century water tower in the southeast part of the Altstadt. Its glass-topped eleventh-floor restaurant offers a view of the city. ⑨

Jansen, Richard-Wagner-Str. 18 (☎251875). Situated on the west side of the Altstadt, this is a small and frequently oversubscribed pension; excellent value. ③

Kirchner, Richard-Wagner-Str. 18 (☎252977). Another good pension located in the same building as the *Jansen*. ③

Das Kleine Stapelhäuschen, Fischmarkt 1–3 (☎257 7862, fax 257 4232). One of the most characterful hotels in the Altstadt, located in a pair of old houses at the corner of the square. Also has a cosy wine bar-restaurant. ⑤

Lindenhof, Lintgasse 7 (☎257 7771, fax 257 7771). Recommendable small hotel on an Altstadt alley. ④

Rhein-Hotel St Martin, Frankenwerft 31–33 (☎257 7955, fax 257 7875). Good medium-range hotel with a Rhine view. ④

Rossner, Jakordenstr. 19 (☎122703). The homeliest and best value of the hotels behind the Hauptbahnhof. ③

St Georg, Rolandstr. 61 (☎937 0200, fax 9370 2011). A small guesthouse to the south of the Ring, run by the Boy Scout offices. ④

Viktoria, Worringer Str. 23 (☎7204 4476, fax 727067). Fine turn-of-the-century hotel right beside the Rhine in the northern Altstadt. ⑧

Youth hostels

Jugendgästehaus Riehl, An der Schanz 14 (☎767081). Located in the northern suburb of Riehl, this youth guesthouse has modern spacious rooms with lockers and a bar: take U-Bahn #5, #16 or #18 from Dom/Hauptbahnhof, and alight at Boltensternstrasse. 🛏

Jugendherberge Deutz, Siegesstr. 5a (☎814711). The more central of the city's hostels, about a 15-min walk from the centre over the Hohenzollernbrücke, or just two blocks south of Deutz train station. It's rather dingy and claustrophobic, though it was the first hostel in Germany to take credit cards. 🛏

Campsites

Berger, Uferstr. 53a (☎392211). Located in the right bank suburb of Rodenkirchen by the Rodenkirchener Brücke and reached by U-Bahn #16 to Marienburg, then bus #130 from Marienburg. Open all year.

Städtischer Familienzeltplatz, Weidenweg (☎831966). In the suburb of Poll to the south of Deutz, this convenient campsite is reached by U-Bahn #16 to Marienburg, after which it's just a short walk across the Rodenkirchener Brücke. Open May to early Oct.

Waldbad, Peter-Baum-Weg (☎603315). Located in the extreme northeastern suburb of Dünnwald. Open all year.

The city

You don't need to walk very far to see the main attractions of Cologne – the **Dom** and the main **museums** are grouped conveniently together, with some of the traditional beer halls close by. Although most visitors venture no further, it would be a pity not to see something of the medieval **Altstadt**, which occupied an enormous area. Among the buildings to have survived are twelve Romanesque churches, much the finest collection anywhere. Don't expect to get more than a superficial impression in under two days, and a considerably longer period is needed to see everything. The best way to start your tour is to cross over to the right-bank suburb of Deutz – or at least to go some distance across either the Hohenzollernbrücke or the Deutzer Brücke – for the classic **view**, with the tall houses of the burghers lining the banks of the Rhine (crossed by no fewer than 8 bridges within the city boundaries), and the chunky Romanesque tower of Gross St Martin providing an ideal counterfoil to the soaring openwork steeples of the Dom.

The Dom

> ...it was the most beautiful of all the churches I have ever seen, or can imagine. If one could imagine the spirit of devotion embodied in any material form, it would be in such a building.

Lewis Carroll's gushing tribute is typical of the extravagant praise which has been heaped upon Cologne's **Dom**. One of the most massive Gothic buildings ever constructed, it dominates the city in every sense. Its size reflects its power and status as "queen and mother of all German churches", whose archbishop was one of the seven Electors of the Holy Roman Empire.

Today, pollution has made it hard to distinguish the medieval and nineteenth-century parts of the Dom, and the facade, of which you get a great uninterrupted view from the square in front, has an overwhelming, crushing power. Originally, the **spires** were, at 157m, the tallest structures in the world, but they were soon dwarfed by the Eiffel

---

THE HISTORY OF THE DOM

The history of the present building is an odd one, for, although the foundation stone was laid in 1248, the church was only completed in 1880. Most of what can be seen today was put up in two concentrated periods of activity separated by five centuries, yet in an almost identical architectural style. The impetus for the creation of a new cathedral came with the arrival of the alleged relics of the Magi and the subsequent increase in pilgrims. A spectacular **shrine** was commissioned to house the relics, begun in 1181 by **Nicholas of Verdun**, the greatest goldsmith of the day, and finished in 1220 by local craftsmen. What was then needed was a fitting palace to house this memorial to the kings. It was decided to adopt the ethereal new Gothic style of architecture for the cathedral, rather than the late Romanesque style still in vogue in the Rhineland, but to surpass earlier French models in size and splendour.

The chancel, designed by **Master Gerhard**, was completed in 1322, but thereafter the sheer ambitiousness of the plans began to take its toll. In 1560, the project was abandoned, with only the south tower and the lower parts of the nave and facade having been built. That might have been the end of the story, had it not been for the impact of the Romantic movement in the early nineteenth century, which led to a campaign for the completion of the cathedral, boosted by the discovery of two pieces of parchment which showed the medieval builders' designs for the facade. From 1842, in a remarkable act of homage from one age to another, the work was carried out in a style that would have been completely familiar to the original masons.

Tower and are no longer even the highest in Cologne. All the same, you need a fair bit of energy to climb up the south tower to the base of the steeple for a fine **panorama** over the city and the Rhine (daily 9am–4/5/6pm according to season; DM3).

The interior

Enter by the west door and your eye is immediately drawn down the great length of the building to the **high altar** with the shrine to the Magi, which illustrates the history of the world as described in the Bible, with Epiphany given due prominence. It's one of three artistic masterpieces to be found here; the others are in the chapels at the entrance to the ambulatory. On the north side is the ninth-century **Gero crucifix**, the most important monumental sculpture of its period. The corresponding chapel to the south has the greatest achievement of the fifteenth-century Cologne School of painters, the *Adoration of the Magi* triptych by **Stefan Lochner**. His refined, idealized style finds a perfect outlet in this truly gorgeous scene; the wings feature two of the Cologne martyrs, SS Ursula and Gereon, with their companions. Look out also for an elaborate sixteenth-century carved retable from Antwerp in the south transept, a colossal wooden *St Christopher* nearby, and (at the intersection of the north transept and the nave aisle) the fourteenth-century *Clares Altar*. The whole **chancel** is outstanding, preserving an unparalleled set of furnishings contemporary with the architecture – choir stalls; painted wooden panels; vibrant statues of Christ, the Virgin and the Apostles; and a delicate altar front. To penetrate beyond the barrier for a marginally better view of these, you have to take one of the **guided tours** which leave from the Dom Forum, the new visitor centre across from the facade. English language tours (DM6) start at 2.30pm every day except Saturday, when they begin at 10.30am.

Stained-glass windows are an essential component of a Gothic cathedral, and Cologne has a marvellously varied assemblage. The oldest, dating from 1260, is in the axis chapel of the ambulatory and is a "Bible" window, pairing New Testament scenes with a parallel from the Old Testament; another is two chapels to the south. In a wholly different, far more monumental style is the late Gothic glass on the north side of the nave, designed by some of the leading local painters. These in turn contrast well with the brilliantly coloured nineteenth-century Bavarian windows opposite, a gift from King Ludwig I towards the Dom's completion.

The Schatzkammer and Diözesanmuseum

The **Schatzkammer** (Mon–Sat 9am–4/5pm, Sun 12.30–4/5pm; DM3), currently housed in a chamber off the north transept, has a few lovely Ottonian manuscripts, as well as the usual arrays of ecclesiastical treasures. In 1998 it's due to be superseded by a larger **Dommuseum**, which will feature the sculptures which adorned the portal of the south tower, the only one dating from the medieval building period. Carved in the workshop of **Michael Parler**, they have been replaced *in situ* by faithful copies. Just outside, at Roncalliplatz 2, is the **Erzbischöfliches Diözesanmuseum** (10am–5pm, closed Thurs; free). A beautiful **Lochner**, *Madonna of the Violets*, forms the centrepiece, while in a glass case, and easily missed, is his little *Nativity*. Other highlights include an eleventh-century crucifix which bizarrely uses an antique lapis lazuli of a woman as the head; the *St Severin Medallion* with a portrait of the saint; and two priceless textiles – a sixth-century Syrian silk illustrating a hunt, discovered in the shrine of Saint Kunibert, and a Byzantine cloth embroidered with lions.

Museums around the Dom

Cologne's two most important museums are housed in ultra-modern buildings right beside the Dom; neither should be missed. Unless you have a student card (which allows half-price admission), it makes sense to invest in the DM20 *Museums Pass*, which allows continued entry to these and to all the other municipal collections on any two consecutive days, plus unlimited use of the public transport network on the first.

Wallraf-Richartz/Ludwig Museum

The **Wallraf-Richartz/Ludwig Museum** (Tues 10am–8pm, Wed–Fri 10am–6pm, Sat & Sun 11am–6pm; DM8) at Bischofsgartenstr. 1 houses the city's collection of paintings. On the first floor is the Wallraf-Richartz Museum of old masters, centred on the unique holdings of the fifteenth-century **Cologne School** (see "Painting and Graphics" in *Contexts*). Look out for the backdrop depictions of the medieval city, often featuring the unfinished Dom. **Stefan Lochner** is the most admired artist of the school, and his *Last Judgment* is a major work, enormously inventive in its detail, gentle and fantastic in its view. More typical of his style is the exquisite *Madonna of the Rose Bower*, his artistic swansong. From the preceding generation, the **Master of St Veronica** is the most accomplished painter, with two contrasting versions of the *Crucifixion*, one as delicately refined as an illuminated manuscript, the other with monumental figures. The best vignettes of Cologne are by the **Master of the Glorification of the Virgin** *(Meister der Verherrlichung Mariae)*, but the gems of the whole display are arguably the two large triptychs made for the Carthusians by the **Master of St Bartholomew**, who represented the final flowering of the school at the beginning of the sixteenth century. His figures are executed as if in imitation of sculpture and have a haunting, mystical quality.

Displayed alongside the Cologne masters are other German paintings, including a small **Dürer**, *Fifer and Drummer*, and several typical examples of **Cranach**. There are also a number of Flemish and Italian Primitives, among which a *Madonna and Child* by **Simone Martini** stands out. Grouped around the staircase are the largest works, including two canvases by **Rubens**, *Juno and Argus* and *Stigmatization of St Francis*. The latter was painted for the Capuchins of Cologne and is now hung back-to-back with *St Francis in the Porzincula Chapel* by **Murillo**, offering a fascinating comparison of treatment by two of the great masters of the Counter-Reformation.

The corridor and galleries beyond have a rich representation of seventeenth-century Dutch artists, including Hals, Ter Brugghen and Ruisdael, as well as what is probably the very last of **Rembrandt**'s great series of self-portraits, in which he depicted himself in the guise of a laughing philosopher (or perhaps the satirical painter Zeuxis) from ancient Greece. There's a comprehensive array of French painting from the seventeenth century to Impressionism, while the nineteenth-century German school is dominated by several examples of **Friedrich** and a large collection of the local artist **Wilhelm Leibl**, leader of the Realist movement.

THE LUDWIG MUSEUM

The Ludwig Museum of twentieth-century art occupies the remainder of the galleries, including all of the second floor. It's a shock to move from the fifteenth-century altarpieces and be confronted by Brillo boxes, Pepsi Cola and Campbell's Tomato Juice, the favourite subjects of **Andy Warhol**, which are the centrepiece of a notable display of Pop Art also including examples of Tom Wesselmann and Roy Lichtenstein. **Claes Oldenburg** is represented by *The Street,* which occupies a whole room. The many other eye-catching sculptures include the uncanny fibreglass creations of the Realists and **Ed Kienholz**'s *Portable War Memorial*, a devastating satire on his country's cultural values.

Among German works, there's a fine batch by **Kirchner**, notably a group portrait of *Die Brücke*; around it hang examples of these very painters. **Max Ernst** provided a similar memento of the Surrealists, including co-opted dead members, Raphael and Dostoyevsky. By the same artist is an iconoclastic ringing of the changes on the theme of the *Madonna and Child*; the furious mother administers a sound thrashing on the infant's buttocks while Ernst and friends look on. **Beckmann**, **Nolde** and **Kokoschka** are all strongly represented; look out for the latter's *View of Cologne*. There are three superb portraits by **Dix**, including one of himself, and a number of sculptures in various media by **Barlach**. Two rooms are devoted to **Picasso**, with sculptures and ceramics as well as paintings from most phases of his career. In contrast, there's only a single spectacular **Dalí**, *Perpignan Station*. Beside it hangs one of the most famous Surrealist canvases, *Presence of Mind* by **Magritte**. An impressive array of Russian paintings includes a large **Chagall**, *Moses Destroying the Tablets of the Law*.

The third museum in the premises, the **Agfa-Foto-Historama**, shows old photographic equipment and a changing selection of prints from the vast holdings of the famous company, whose headquarters are in nearby Leverkusen.

Römisch-Germanisches Museum

One of Germany's most important archeological collections, the **Römisch-Germanisches Museum** (Tues, Wed & Fri 10am–5pm, Thurs 10am–8pm, Sat & Sun 11am–5pm; DM5) at Roncalliplatz 4 is specially constructed around the star exhibit, the **Dionysos Mosaic**, excavated here in 1941. The finest work of its kind in northern Europe, it adorned the dining room of a patrician villa of about 200 AD. The mosaic is made from over a million pieces of limestone, ceramics and glass, covering an area of some 70 square metres, and depicts the inebriated Bacchus surrounded by dancers and satyrs. Its astonishing state of preservation is due to the protective covering it received from the burnt-out remains of the building falling on it when sacked by a Germanic tribe in the fourth century.

The other main item is the **tomb of Poblicius**, a veteran who had served in the Fifth Legion. Dating from about 40 AD, this is an even more recent discovery. It stands about 15m high and has been re-erected beside the mosaic, although considerably more restoration has been necessary.

Otherwise, the museum is arranged thematically. The collection of **glass** is reckoned to be unsurpassed anywhere in the world; it includes a tiny idealized portrait of Augustus Caesar made in 27 BC. From the second century, the Cologne workshops developed their own distinctive forms, with coloured serpentine threads used for decorative effects. This style culminated around 330 AD in the *diatreta* glass, decorated with a delicate network design. Perhaps of more general appeal is the dazzling array of **jewellery** on the first floor, most of which was found in Frankish graves.

The Altstadt and the Romanesque churches

The vast area that was medieval Cologne suffered grievous damage in the last war. Much of it was rebuilt as quickly as possible, but in the case of the churches, time was allowed in order to undertake faithful restoration projects, and these are still going on. What has been achieved is undoubtedly impressive – to realize this you only need to look at the photographs displayed in each church showing its state at the end of the war – although there's no denying that much has been irretrievably lost.

With that proviso, there's a lot to enjoy, and the twelve **Romanesque churches**, which range in date from the tenth to the thirteenth century, form one of the most coherent groups in a single architectural style to be found in any European city. The extraordinary **St Gereon** is the one that shouldn't be missed for its architecture, while **St Maria im Kapitol** has the finest furnishings, and **Gross St Martin** and **St Aposteln** have justifiably famous exteriors. The churches are generally open all day; some close at lunchtimes, which may last as long as noon till 3pm, though even then the vestibule may still be kept open. To avoid cultural indigestion, it's best to spread your exploration of the Altstadt over two or three days.

The east

For nearly six hundred years the tower of **Gross St Martin,** surrounded by four turrets, was the dominant feature of the Cologne skyline, not being usurped by the Dom's spires until last century. The rest of the church (formerly a monastery occupied by Benedictines from Scotland and Ireland) seems rather truncated for such a splendid adornment, although the interior has been returned to its simple original form. Such old houses as remain are in the streets nearby; seen at close quarters, it's rather obvious that many are recent reproductions.

A short distance beyond is the Alter Markt, one of three large squares in the heart of the city. From here, you can see the irregular octagonal tower of the **Rathaus** (Mon–Thurs 7.30am–4.45pm, Fri 7.30am–2pm; free), a building which is a real jumble of styles, yet with marvellous features. Its core is fourteenth-century Gothic; the following century the tower was added in a more flamboyant idiom, while in the 1570s a graceful loggia, a rare example of Renaissance architecture in the Rhineland, was provided as a frontispiece. Highlights of the interior include the **Hansa Saal** from the first building period, and the tower rooms with doorways of inlaid woods.

Just in front of the entrance to the Rathaus, a glass pyramid shelters the **Mikwe**, a Jewish ritual bath house dating from about 1160, the only remnant of the ghetto which was razed soon after the expulsion order of 1424. It's officially open on Sundays 11am–1pm, but from Monday to Friday you can ask for the key during office hours at the porter's desk in the Rathaus. More subterranean sights can be seen just a short distance away in the form of the foundations of the **Praetorium**, the Roman governor's palace, and the **Römischer Kanal**, a surprisingly elegant vaulted sewer some 100m long. The entrance to both of these is at Kleine Budengasse (Tues–Fri 10am–4pm, Sat & Sun 11am–4pm; DM3, but included on the *Museums Pass*).

Proceeding southwards, you pass the burnt-out **Alt St Alban**, left as a war memorial; the **Gürzenich**, a much-rebuilt Gothic festive hall, best known as the home of the Carnival balls; and the tower which is all that survives of **Klein St Martin**. Behind is **St Maria im Kapitol**, not seen to advantage from outside as it was built in a severe convent style and is now hemmed in by modern houses, but it possesses a majestic interior complete with a full circuit for processions around the aisles. Look out for the **wooden doors**, contemporary with the architecture and among the most precious works of their kind, depicting Christ's Nativity, Teachings and Passion. The church has a magnificent monumental Renaissance **rood screen**, while the **cloisters**, unusually placed adjoining the facade, are the only ones left in Cologne.

Continuing in a southerly direction, Rheingasse takes you to **Overstolzenhaus**, the finest mansion in the city, a step-gabled patrician home contemporary with the later Romanesque churches. A short walk from here is the sailors' church of **St Maria in Lyskirchen**; their *Schöne Madonna* of about 1420 is one of several fine works of art. The vaults are covered with thirteenth-century frescoes of scenes from the Old and New Testaments and lives of saints; they're seen to best effect if you climb the stairs to the gallery. From here, head up Grosse Witschgasse and Georgstrasse to **St Georg**, an eleventh-century pillared basilica which resembles early Christian churches. The westwork, added the following century, looks squat and stumpy from without, but is impressively spacious when you're inside.

The south

It's then a walk of some fifteen minutes due south to the **St Severin** quarter. The church itself is classified among the twelve Romanesque examples in Cologne, though only the twin-towered apse and part of the transept remain from that time, the rest being late Gothic. Now it's mainly of interest to archeology buffs, on account of the **Roman-Frankish graveyard** which has been found directly underneath; it can be visited on guided tours (Mon & Fri 4pm; free). Just beyond the church is the Severinstor, part of the medieval fortifications which were largely demolished last century when the Ring was built. A short walk to the east, at Ubierring 45, is the **Rautenstrauch-Joest Museum** (Tues–Fri 10am–4pm, Sat & Sun 11am–4pm; DM5). This large ethnological museum's particular strengths are Indo-China and Pre-Columbian America. West Africa, the Pacific and Indonesia are also well represented. There are often special exhibitions, and when these occur the *Museums Pass* isn't valid for even the permanent displays.

Following the ring road in a northwesterly direction, you pass the **Ulrepforte**, another turreted gateway. Further along, turn right at Waisenhausgasse for **St Pantaleon**, the oldest surviving church in the city, dating from the end of the tenth century. It's chiefly notable for its massive westwork with vestibule. Inside, there's an airy Flamboyant Gothic rood screen, crowned by a seventeenth-century organ in a Rococo case.

The west

North up Poststrasse and Peterstrasse is **St Peter**, a Gothic church with gleaming stained-glass windows. The magnificent *Crucifixion of St Peter*, painted by **Rubens** for the high altar, is now displayed in a chapel by the entrance. Next door is **St Cäcilien**, a Romanesque convent church which now houses the **Schnütgen Museum** (Tues, Thurs & Fri 10am–5pm, Wed 10am–8pm, Sat & Sun 11am–5pm; DM5), a collection of religious art (except paintings) of the Rhineland. There are some wonderful ivories, notably a diptych which belonged to Charlemagne and the comb of Saint Heribert. Major pieces of Romanesque sculpture include: the church's own tympanum, carved in a heavily antique style; the wooden *Crucifix* from St Georg; and the mysterious *Siegburg Madonna*. From the Gothic period the museum's most important possessions are the original carvings from the Dom's altar front and a polychrome console bust of a woman carved by a member of the Parler family.

Across the road and down Antongasse is the tiny Gothic **Antoniterkirche**, now a Protestant parish church, best known for housing one of the most famous of twentieth-century sculptures, **Barlach's** *Memorial Angel*. This is a cast made from the plaster of the original, which was created for the seven-hundredth anniversary of the Dom in Güstrow but destroyed in the perverse Nazi measures against "degenerate art". Around the church is the main shopping centre; the streets follow the same plan as their Roman predecessors, but almost all the buildings are modern. Up Herzogstrasse are the ruins of the Gothic **St Kolumba**, which wasn't restored after the war; instead Gottfried Böhm inserted a minute chapel within the shell in 1950.

Further down the same street is another Gothic church, the severe **Minoritenkirche**. It contains the tomb of John Duns Scotus, the Scots-born theologian who was the leading intellectual in early fourteenth-century Cologne. Ironically, he's the origin of the word "dunce": his defences of traditional religious orthodoxies so enraged his radical fellow-countrymen at the time of the Reformation that they used his name as a personification of stupidity. Alongside the church is the **Museum für Angewandte Kunst** (Tues & Thurs–Sun 11am–5pm, Wed 11am–8pm; DM5), a comprehensive array of applied art from the Middle Ages to the present day. The Jugendstil section is particularly impressive, though the incongruous highlight of the museum is an exquisite little panel of *The Nativity* by **Memling**. A short distance west of the Antoniterkirche lies Neumarkt. Housed in a bank at no. 18 is the **Käthe-Kollwitz-Museum** (Tues–Sun 10am–5pm; DM5). It has a large display of graphics and a few sculptures by Käthe Kollwitz, one of the leading female artists of this century. Her preference for black-and-white media helps give her work an enormous pathos, evident in her variation on the *Mother and Child* theme, and her denunciations of the follies and sufferings of war.

The far end of Neumarkt is dominated by the majestic early thirteenth-century apse of **St Aposteln** (Holy Apostles – an unusual dedication outside the Orthodox world). This is an archetypal Rhenish basilica with all the characteristic features – clover-leaf chancel with dwarf-gallery, central octagon with turrets and, above all, the great western tower with its "bishop's mitre" roof. Despite its apparently homogeneous design, building actually began in the eleventh century; the interior (closed Tues) is surprisingly plain. Nearby is another of the city gates, the **Hahnentor**, which resembles a castle's barbican.

The north

Due north of SS Aposteln is **St Gereon**, most idiosyncratic of the twelve Romanesque churches and a truly great building. Its kernel was an oval-shaped fourth-century chapel; in the eleventh and twelfth centuries a crypt, chancel and twin towers were added. Then, in the early thirteenth century, the Roman masonry was harnessed to form the basis of a magnificent four-storey decagon with ribbed dome vault, a work which has no parallel in European architecture. At this time, the adjoining baptistry was also built and adorned with frescoes. The decagon's interior seems more graceful and less massive than from outside; its modern stained glass is a controversial addition. In the crypt the original mosaic floor with Old Testament scenes is perserved.

From here, you can return towards the Dom, passing a fragment of Roman wall and the Zeughaus, which houses the **Kölnisches Stadtmuseum** (Tues 10am–8pm, Wed–Fri 10am–5pm, Sat & Sun 11am–5pm; DM5). This focuses on the history of local trade and industry, along with sections on Carnival and eau de Cologne. Some good models show the city's building development. A little further east, **St Andreas** has the **Maccabeus shrine**, a piece of early sixteenth-century craftsmanship, doubtless inspired by the Dom's shrine to the Magi. Another casket contains the relics of Saint Albertus Magnus, the thirteenth-century scholar who was the star teacher at Cologne's renowned Dominican College; his pupils there included Saint Thomas Aquinas, later to develop into the greatest philosopher of his time and arguably of the entire medieval period. A short way along Marzellenstrasse is the pink exterior of **St Mariae Himmelfahrt**, a seventeenth-century Jesuit foundation and Cologne's only Baroque building of note. Its galleried interior, which surprisingly employs the long-out-of-favour Gothic pointed arch, is lavishly decorated – unusual for the Rhineland, where Bavarian excesses never caught on.

A bit further down the same street, turn left into Ursulaplatz, where **St Ursula**, with its prominent sturdy tower, still retains some Romanesque features, along with Gothic and Baroque accretions. Unless you're squeamish, try to get hold of the sacristan, who will show you the **Goldene Kammer**, an ornate Baroque chamber gruesomely lined with reliquaries. He can be elusive, but should be available at the fixed times (Mon & Thurs–Sat 9am–noon & 1–5pm, Wed 9.30am–noon & 1–5pm). From here, the **Eigelsteintor**, another impressive survival of the medieval fortifications, is reached via the street of the same name. Dagobertstrasse then leads east to **St Kunibert**, the final

---

GREEN COLOGNE

Although there are few areas of green in the city centre, about a quarter of Cologne is given over to open spaces. Most popular is the **Rheinpark** in Deutz on the right bank of the Rhine, a legacy of large garden shows, with the Tanzbrunnen, round which concerts are held in summer. It's linked by the gondolas of the *Rheinseilbahn* (April–Oct daily 10am–6pm; DM6.50 single, DM9.50 return) over the Rhine to the **Flora- und Botanischer Garten** (summer 8am–9pm, winter 10am–dusk; free), near the **Zoo** and **Aquarium** (daily 9am–5/6pm; DM15). Other parks are in the far suburbs. To the south are the recreational *Volksgarten* and a forestry reserve at **Rodenkirchen** (daily 9am–4/6/8pm according to season) with trees, plants and shrubs from around the world. The right bank has nature reserves at **Dünnwald**, **Brück** and **Porz**, the last featuring birds of prey (daily April–Sept 9am–7pm, Oct–March 9am–5pm).

fling of the Romanesque in the early thirteenth century, completed just as work began on the Dom. It's also the last church to be restored following war damage, with the nave and massive westwork having only recently been joined up. Inside, note the stained-glass windows in the apse, which are contemporary with the architecture. On the piers of the transept are the two dramatic polychrome figures of an *Annunciation* group, an important piece of Gothic carving by **Conrad Kuyn**, master mason at the Dom in the early fifteenth century.

Outside the centre

If you want to stray beyond the confines of the Altstadt, Cologne's suburbs offer a wide choice of **parks** and some of the most exciting **modern architecture** in Germany. In every way, the dominant building outside the centre is the **Fernsehturm** (telecom-munications tower; daily 10am–10pm; DM4, including ascent by elevator to the viewing platform), in the Stadtgarten west of the Ring. Completed in 1980, at 243m it's consid-erably higher than the Dom, and it's definitely worth going up for the breathtaking views over the city and the Rhine. Very close by, within the Stadtgarten, is **Neu St Alban**, one of several highly praised modern churches in Cologne. Also near the Ring, but to the north, is **St Gertrud** on Krefelder Strasse, with an amazing tapering tower. It's the work of **Gottfried Böhm**, whose father **Dominikus** was a pioneer of radical church design in the inter-war period. An example of the latter's 1930s Expressionism is **St Engelbert**, a centrally planned building of eight identical concrete shells, located very near the Jugendgästehaus on Riehler Gürtel. His **St Maria Königin**, in the south-ern suburb of Marienburg, is one of the most accomplished of a new generation of churches built to serve the needs of the residential quarters then being built.

From the Hahnentor, Aachener Strasse runs in a dead-straight line westwards to the outer suburbs. Just beyond the Ring, a short walk down Universitätstrasse brings you to the **Museum für Ostasiatische Kunst** (Tues, Wed & Fri–Sun 11am–5pm, Thurs 11am–8pm; DM5). Devoted to the arts of China, Japan and Korea, this is yet another of Cologne's collections which has been given specially designed modern premises, appropriately enough by a Japanese architect and with a traditional Japanese garden. It's arranged thematically, with leaflets in English available on each topic.

Further along Aachener Strasse at no. 1328, in the suburb of Weiden, is the city's final important Roman monument, the **Grabkammer** (Tues–Thurs 10am–1pm, Fri 10am–5pm, Sat & Sun 1–5pm; DM1), a second-century burial chamber. It contains mar-ble busts of a couple and a young woman which are contemporary with the building, and a sarcophagus from the following century with carvings of the seasons.

Weiden lies about halfway along the route to **BRAUWEILER**, reached by regular bus services. The village clusters around the **Abteikirche**, built as a Benedictine monastery in the twelfth and thirteenth centuries. There are no fewer than six towers, and inside the pillars of the nave are capped by sensual figurative capitals. The serene stone retable in the south apse is one of the masterpieces of German Romanesque sculpture, depicting St Nicholas, the church's patron, in a gathering around the Madonna and Child.

Eating, drinking and nightlife

The gastronomy of Cologne is as distinctive and distinguished as that of any German city, with plenty of **local food specialities** in addition to the renowned *Kölsch* beer. With over three thousand restaurants, bars and cafés crammed into a relatively small area, there's certainly no shortage of choice, with the chic and trendy often standing cheek by jowl with the staid and traditional. A similarly wide-ranging cultural scene encompasses virtually every kind of theatre and music, and classical, jazz and rock fans are all well catered for.

Beer halls, restaurants and cafés

The great Cologne institutions for both **eating** and **drinking** are the **Brauhäuser** (or *Weetschaften*, as they're known in the local dialect). Most of these brewery-owned beer halls date from the turn of the century, though they claim a much longer pedigree; a few of them still brew their *Kölsch* in-house, though most have moved production to larger premises elsewhere in the city. Whilst smaller than their Munich counterparts, they have similarly cavernous interiors with sparse decor. They're staffed by horribly matey *Köbes*, who all year round keep up the Carnival tradition of making insulting and corny jokes. These pubs are often overrun with visiting businessmen and Dom-gawping tourists, but they're definitely worth sampling as they offer some of the cheapest food in the city, specializing in the local cuisine. Don't be misled by the dialect, however – *Halve Hahn* is not the half chicken you'd expect but a rye roll with cheese, while *Kölsche Kaviar* is less of a bargain than it appears when you realize it's a black pudding, again with rye bread.

Although itself marginally too far north for the cultivation of grapes, Cologne reflects its proximity to the Rhenish vineyards in the presence of a number of fine **Weinhäuser**. The city is amply endowed with **traditional cafés**, as well as a varied range of **ethnic restaurants**.

KÖLSCH

Kölsch beer is as much a piece of the local life of Cologne as the Dom or Carnival, and may only be produced in the breweries located in and around the city. It's clear, light, highly fermented and aromatically bitter, with a strong accentuation of hops. Invariably, it's served with a substantial head in a tall, thin glass (*Stange*) which holds only a fifth of a litre. This gives it a rather effete image among macho beer drinkers from elsewhere in Germany who tend to revile it, in contrast to the religious reverence it's accorded in Cologne.

Brauhäuser

Alt-Köln, Trinkgasse 7–9. This is a real one-off, its picturesque folly of an interior featuring a whole series of wooden alcoves and galleries which together represent a Romantic vision of a complex of old German taverns. The food is as good as the beer, and very reasonably priced for a place which gets an outsized share of tourists.

Brauhaus Sion, Unter Taschenmacher 5. Though close to the Dom, the sidestreet location means that locals rather than visitors form the bulk of the clientele here. Serves generous portions of *gutbürgerliche Küche*; its *Kölsch* is notable for its strong bouquet and dry finish.

Früh am Dom, Am Hof 12–14. The most visited of the *Brauhäuser*, partly because of its wonderful location opposite the Dom, partly because of its excellent food, and above all because of the prestige of its delicately fruity *Kölner Hofbräu*, a classic *Kölsch*.

Gaffel-Haus, Alter Markt 20. The *Kölsch* served here is the driest in Cologne; the food's pretty good too.

Haus Töller, Weyerstr. 96. Undoubtedly the cosiest of the *Brauhäuser*, occupying a fourteenth-century house in the southern Altstadt that was one of the first in Cologne to be built of stone. Meals are good value. Evenings only, closed Sun.

Küppers-Kölsch Brauhaus, Altenburger Str. 157. Situated way beyond the Südstadt (take tram #15 or #16), but definitely worth a special trip. As well as the beer garden and tavern, reconstructed to resemble those in the city centre, there's the added attraction of Cologne's **Brauerei-Museum** (guided tours hourly every Sat 11am–3pm), which includes a re-creation of an old brewery, complete with historic equipment.

Päffgen, Friesenstr. 64. This *Hausbrauerei* in the northwest Altstadt is the smallest brewery in Cologne, producing a *Kölsch* with a pleasingly hoppy finish. Also has a more centrally located branch at Heumarkt 62.

Peters Brauhaus, Mühlengasse 1. Though it looks as old as any of its competitors, this is a recent addition, housed in the palatial premises of the long-defunct *Zum Kranz*.

Sünner im Walfisch, Salzgasse 13. A newcomer, occupying a beautiful half-timbered seventeenth-century house moved here from its original location.

Zur Malzmühle, Heumarkt 6. Another *Hausbrauerei*, one whose name is reflected in the distinctly malty taste of its *Mühlenkölsch* and alcohol-free *Koch'sches Malzbier*.

Weinhäuser

Brungs, Marsplatz 3–5. Historic wine cellar in the heart of the Altstadt.

Kyffhäuser Keller, Kyffhäuser Str. 47. As recommendable a place as any in Cologne for a glass of wine, with over 40 varieties to choose from.

Ratskeller, Rathausplatz 1. Like its counterparts throughout the country, this cellar restaurant offers good food and wine at high but far from extortionate prices. It also has the bonus of a pleasant inner courtyard.

Cafés

Eigel, Brückenstr. 1–3. An enduringly favourite rendezvous point with city-centre shoppers.

Fassbender, Bazaar de Cologne, Mittelstrasse. The location in a big central shopping precinct may seem unpromising, but this café enjoys a high reputation for its pralines and other handmade chocolates.

Reichard, Untere Fettenhennen 11. Cologne's best-known bastion of *Kaffee und Kuchen*, an elegant salon profiting from its situation hard by the Dom.

Restaurants

Bei Barbara, Aachener Str. 22. Among the very few places in Germany serving authentic dishes from the country's Polish neighbour.

Daitokai, Kattenbug 2. Highly rated, if predictably expensive, Japanese restaurant. Closed Sun.

Em Krützche, Am Frankenturm 1–3. Historic *Gasthaus* which is probably Cologne's best traditional restaurant. Game and fish specialities.

Gourmet, Engelbertstr. 17. Offers an extreme form of *neue deutsche Küche* described as *bio-synergetische*.

Grande Milano, Hohenstaufenring 37. Arguably the best of a wide choice of Italian trattorias. Closed Sun.

Haxenhaus zum Rheingarten, Frankenwerft 19. Located right on the Rhine promenade, this specializes in pork and lamb knuckles and metre-long sausages.

Mandalay, Brüsseler Str. 53. Offers a rare chance to sample the little-known but delicious cuisine of Burma, which, logically enough, stands somewhere between that of India and China. Closed Tues.

Le Moissonier, Krefelder Str. 25. Fine and authentically French bistro. Closed Sun & Mon.

Pacifico's-Especial, Deutz-Neuhöffer-Str. 32. Extraordinarily popular Mexican cantina; the food is slightly adapted to suit the German palate, but is tasty nonetheless.

Sprössling, Mozartstr. 9. Good all-round veggie and wholefood specialist.

Tchang, Grosse Sandkaul 19. Perhaps the pick of Cologne's abundant supply of Chinese restaurants.

Zlata Praha, Salzgasse 1. Homely Bohemian cooking, with several excellent Czech and German beers on tap.

Zorba the Buddha, Brüsseler Str. 54. Along with the two discos (see p.496), this spacious vegetarian café stands as evidence of the long-standing high-profile presence of the Bhagwan in Cologne.

Bars and discos

There are four distinct quarters of Cologne with a recommendable concentration of nightspots. The most obvious is the area around Gross St Martin in the **Altstadt**; this tends to catch visiting tourists and businessmen, but the best places do manage to create their own distinctive atmosphere. Down the road from the University (in the southwestern part of the city), the **Quartier Lateng** is the place to mingle with the locals, even if it has lost its trendy edge. The **Südstadt**, or St Severin quarter, now has the most stylish bars and cafés, and the biggest crowds. For once, it pays to follow them – it's their sheer exuberance that makes the place. The more relaxed **Belgisches Viertel** (the streets around the Ring, just to the west of the centre) is nowhere near as packed or self-consciously trendy. The following is a selection of the best establishments within each quarter with recommendations for **breakfast**, often available until the afternoon.

Altstadt

Alter Wartesaal, Am Hauptbahnhof. A die-hard of the disco scene which has lost some of its freshness; music a mixture of Europop and Gothic.

Biermuseum, Buttermarkt 39. A favourite haunt with tourists and correspondingly pricey; there are 18 beers on tap.

Broadway Café, Ehrenstr. 11. At the entrance to the Broadway cinema; good breakfast from late morning onwards.

The Corkonian, Alter Markt 49. Large Irish pub serving Guinness and Kilkenny, often featuring live Irish music. Packed out, especially at weekends.

Kännchen, Am Bollwerk 13. Tiny traditional pub.

Kauri, Auf dem Rothenberg 11. Conveniently sited cellar bar with good selection of jazz, funk and blues; free entry but drinks are extortionate.

Papa Joe's Em Streckstrumpf, Buttermarkt 37. Germany's oldest jazz bar, this is a cosier, smaller, equally good version of *Klimperkasten*; invariably standing-room only, with music beginning at 8.30pm and special Sun sessions at 11am.

Papa Joe's Klimperkasten, Alter Markt 50. The deservedly popular place to go for traditional live jazz, which is belted out to an appreciative audience from 8pm onwards. Very expensive drinks but young clientele at weekends; more businessmen at other times.

Quartier Lateng

Café Central, Jülicher Str. 1. Stylish café which is one of the best places for breakfast; good selection of newspapers; outside tables in good weather.

Café Orlando, Engelbertstr. 9. Quiet café just off Zülpicherstrasse, offering breakfast and health food; 1950s decor with old jukebox.

Crimson, Zülpicher Str. 25. Good for food (especially breakfast) and cocktails; keeps a selection of newspapers and has occasional disco evenings.

Filmdose, Zülpicher Str. 39. One of the most original fun pubs in Cologne when busy (at weekends); otherwise a bit depressing. It has a tiny stage for cabaret and also shows films in English.

Gilberts Pinte, Engelbertstr. 1. Notorious student dive, home to 1000 *Stammtische*, but with plenty of atmosphere.

Luxor, Luxemburger Str. 40. Disco with a healthy mixture of black dance music and chart stuff; also a popular live venue. Free entry after 11pm.

Palä, Palanterstr. 12a. Backstreet café with a wide selection of ice creams and breakfasts.

Peppermint Lounge, Hohenstauffenring 23. One of the most popular late-nighters, springing into action around midnight; also good for a late breakfast.

Südstadt

Bi Pis Bistro, Rolandstr. 61. In the unlikely setting of the Boy Scout offices; older, left-wing clientele and regular poetry readings.

Chlodwig-Eck, Annostr. 1. Very trendy café-bar and restaurant.

Climax, Ubierring 18. A place to spot the in-crowd; very dark with ear-splitting music.

Kurfürstenhof, Kurfürstenstr. 1. Café-bar offering slads, sandwiches and hot specials.

Opera, Alteburger Str. 1. Huge, overlit barn of a place with very young punters queuing to get in at the weekends; good music and plenty of atmosphere.

Schröders, Alteburger Str. 11. Very chic; like a French brasserie with bright lights and mirrors.

Spielplatz, Ubierring 58. More in the style of a beer hall, with a lot more character than some of its newer counterparts.

Zaff, Ubierring 22. In the forefront of the Südstadt scene with good music under subdued lights.

Belgisches Viertel

Alabama, Antwerpener Str. 34. Cocktail bar cum American diner.

Alcazar, Bismarckstr. 39a. Snug and candlelit, with tasty if overpriced menu; somewhat older clientele.

Café Van Gogh, Bismarckstr. 44. Small and cosy artists' pub, totally unpretentious, yet with poetry readings, plays, cabaret and live music.

E.W.G., Aachener Str. 59. Chaotic pub packed out with students.

Micro Café, Venloer Str. 33. Tiny corner street café-bar.

Stadtgarten, Venloer Str. 40. Home of the *Kölner Jazzhaus Initiative*, so most of the jazz is modern and experimental; there's also a good restaurant.

Zorba the Buddha, Hohenzollernring 90. Disco with good selection of mainstream music. Dance floor sometimes clears at midnight so that the Bhagwan owners, decked from head to toe in red, can let rip with percussion instruments.

Zorba the Buddha die Kleine, Brabanter Str. 15. Smaller and quieter than the above, with older customers.

Entertainment

For music, theatre and film listings consult the billboards (which are found all over the city); the posters are changed weekly for the cinemas, every ten days for other entertainments. The tourist office publishes a comprehensive monthly programme, detailing important forthcoming events, *Köln-Monatsvorschau*, priced DM2. The best listings mags are *Stadt Revue* and *Kölner Illustrierte*, available from newsagents at DM5 each.

Music

Classical music performed to the highest international standards can be heard at the brand-new *Philharmonie* (☎2801) in the same building as the Wallraf-Richartz/Ludwig Museum on Bischofsgartenstrasse. There are two local symphony orchestras – the *Gürzenich* and *Westdeutscher Rundfunk*, the latter being attached to the national radio, whose headquarters are in Cologne. The radio studios were one of the pioneer centres of electronic music, being particularly associated with the work of Karlheinz Stockhausen, who is still a Cologne resident. As a contrast, look out for performances by *Musica Antiqua Köln*, Germany's leading specialist ensemble for Baroque music played on period instruments. The *Opernhaus* at Offenbachplatz (☎221 8400) is currently directed by the American James Conlon.

There are any number of free concerts in the churches; these are all listed in a monthly programme which you can pick up in the venues themselves. One regular series, featuring a seasonally appropriate Bach cantata, takes place at the Antoniterkirche on the first Sunday evening of each month.

Large-scale **pop concerts** and other shows attracting large audiences tend to be held at the *Sporthalle* (☎882031) in the Messegelände Deutz. The best places to hear **jazz** are the *Stadtgarten* and the two pubs called *Papa Joe's* (see p.495).

Theatre

The leading **theatre** is the *Schauspielhaus* on Offenbachplatz (☎221 8400); *Schlosserei* is part of the same complex, but with a more experimental programme. Alternatively, there are *Freie Kammerspiele*, Thebäerstr. 17 (☎510 3371), and the tiny *Theater der Keller* (☎318059), both of which offer classical and contemporary works. For mime and cabaret, try *Atelier Theater*, Roonstr. 78 (☎561591) and Die Machtwächter, Gertrudenstr. 24 (☎257 8360). The new *Musik Dom* beside the Hauptbahnhof on Breslauer Platz (☎530 2020) holds blockbuster musicals. Productions suitable for **kids** are held at *Comedia Colonia*, Löwengasse 7–9 (☎247670), *Kölner Künstler Theater*, Stamstr. 8 (☎510 7696) and *Kleine Komödie*, Turiner Str. 3 (☎122552). *Puppenspiele*, Eisenmarkt 2–4 (☎212095), has celebrated marionettes, but be warned that the unintelligible *Kölsch* dialect is used.

Carnival

While there's no doubt that Cologne is worth visiting at any season, by far the best time to come is during **Carnival**. It's celebrated here with a verve normally associated with Mediterranean countries, and is a useful corrective to the common misapprehension that the Germans are an excessively serious and respectful people. For the *drei tollen Tage* ("three crazy days"– Thursday, Sunday and Monday of Carnival week), life in the city comes to a complete stop and everyone, from punks to grannies, dons make-up and costume, taking to the streets as clown, fool, harlequin or historical personality.

The present highly organized festival (here always known as *Karneval*, as opposed to *Fasching* or *Fastnet* in southern Germany) dates back to 1823, but its true origins go back a lot further. In part it derives from a pagan exorcism of evil spirits in the transition from one season to another, and in part from a Christian tradition of periods of fasting, which were invariably preceded by counterbalancing periods of merriment. This latter factor governs the timetable of the festival, which has moveable dates; the climax occurs in the week preceding Ash Wednesday, immediately before the stringencies of Lent. However, the Carnival season actually begins as early as "the eleventh of the eleventh", ie November 11, a date which was seen as having a foolish significance. From then on, Cologne holds both costume balls and *Sitzungen* (sessions); at the latter, speeches are made in rhyming couplets in the local *Kölsch* dialect (incomprehensible to outsiders, but fairly close to Dutch).

The festivities

The real business begins with **Weiberfastnacht** on the Thursday prior to the seventh Sunday before Easter. A ceremony in the Alter Markt, starting at 10am, leads to the official inauguration of the festival with the handing over of the keys of the city by the mayor at 11.11am precisely to *Prinz Claus III*, who assumes command for the "three crazy days". Whereas in other cities he's aided by a princess, in Cologne he has two companions, the peasant *Bauer Knut* and the virgin *Jungfrau Karla*, who is played by a man and is emphatically not his betrothed. The fun can then begin in earnest; in repentance for the chauvinism of earlier centuries, this particular day is now given over to the supremacy of women, who are allowed to take the liberties of their choice. At 3pm there's the first of the great **processions**, beginning at Severinstor, based on the **legend of Jan and Griet**. The former was Jan von Werth, a seventeenth-century cavalry officer who saved the city from ruin in the Thirty Years' War. Griet was the Cologne girl who had spurned him, prompting him to assume a military career; they were not to meet again until she, as an ageing spinster, saw him enter the city as a general at the head of his troops. In the evening, the great series of **costume balls** begins, the most prestigious being those in the Gürzenich. However, there are plenty of spontaneous

---

HEINRICH BÖLL (1917–85)

Cologne and its Carnival form the setting for several novels and short stories by the local writer **Heinrich Böll**, notably *The Clown* and *The Lost Honour of Katharina Blum*, works which offer a trenchant examination of postwar West German society. Böll's earlier books, such as *And Where were You, Adam?* and *The Train was on Time*, give an equally penetrating analysis of the national psyche during World War II. His simple, direct style, refreshingly different from the intellectualization so often found in German literature, and the fearless way he bared the soul of his nation, brought him an international reputation as Germany's leading postwar writer – a status reflected in the award of the Nobel Prize for Literature in 1972. However, his work makes many Germans feel uncomfortable and even now, some years after his death, he has not yet been honoured with a memorial museum.

---

bouts of singing, dancing and boisterous conviviality in the streets and taverns as an authentic alternative.

For the next two days, the city returns to relative normality during daylight hours, although fancy dress is still much in evidence, and on the Saturday morning there's the **Funkenbiwack**, featuring the *Rote und Blaue Funken* (Red and Blue Sparks), men dressed up in eighteenth-century military outfits; they disobey every order – a symbol of Cologne's long tradition of anti-militarism. The celebrations come to a climax with the two big costumed processions with floats; on Sunday the **Schull- un Veedleszög**, largely featuring children, forms a prelude to the more spectacular **Rosenmontagzug** (Rose Monday Parade). The latter is unquestionably the highlight of the celebrations, a riot of colour featuring over 7000 people, half of them musicians, and 300 horses; and costing some DM1 million to mount. This is only partly due to the costumes; a dominant feature is the fact that 40 tons of sweets, 100,000 chocolates, 100,000 packets of popcorn and innumerable bunches of flowers and containers of eau de Cologne are hurled into the crowd. The first part of the procession is a pageant on the history of the city; then comes the satirical section in which local, national and international politicians appear in effigy; finally there's the gala in honour of the Cologne Carnival, with the spectacular retinues of the peasant, the virgin and the prince bringing up the rear. It's all done with a proper sense of Germanic thoroughness, taking all of four hours to pass by. After this, the festival runs down; there are numerous smaller parades in the suburbs on Shrove Tuesday, while the restaurants offer special fish menus on Ash Wednesday.

Carnival practicalities

Although the city gets jam-packed with visitors during Carnival time, many are day-trippers and there's no problem finding **accommodation**, but bear in mind that both youth hostels are likely to be full at the weekend. A greater difficulty comes in deciding **where to stand** during the processions; if you want the backdrop of the Dom, make sure you come several hours before they start (12.30pm on Sun, noon on Mon) and choose a position on the elevated terrace. Alternatively, go somewhere towards the beginning or end of the route (the tourist office provides free maps), where the crowds are thinner. You could consider renting one of the grandstand **seats**, positioned all along the course of the route; these are expensive for the Rose Monday Parade, but definitely good value at DM5 on the Sunday. Remember to keep well wrapped up; even when the weather is sunny, it's likely to be cold. Don't expect to do anything else during the "three crazy days"; all the museums and most of the shops are closed, and even the Dom's doors are firmly locked except for the occasional service. Above all, join in the fun; it isn't essential to get dressed up (though it helps), and don't hesitate to follow the crowds, usually congregated round a big drum – it's the impromptu events as much as the set pieces which make this such a great festival. Note that there's a special deal allowing unlimited travel on the public transport network between Weiberfastnacht and

Shrove Tuesday. For advance **tickets**, write to *Festkomitee des Kölner Karnevals*, Antwerpener Str. 55. **Dates** of forthcoming Rose Mondays are as follows: February 23, 1998; February 15, 1999; March 6, 2000; and February 26, 2001.

Listings

Airlines *British Airways*, Marzellenstr. 1 (☎135081); *Lufthansa*, Am Hof 30 (☎9254 9921).

Airport ☎404001 for flight information.

Bookstores The streets circling Neumarkt have a dense concentration of bookstores; try also around the Dom, on Komödienstrasse or the area around the University. Specially recommended is *Büchermarkt*, Ehrenstr. 4, which stocks a huge range of cut-price titles on the arts, including many in English.

Car rental *Avis*, Clemensstr. 29 (☎234333); *Condor*, Wilhelm-Mauser-Str. 53 (☎581055); *Europcar*, Christophstr. 24 (☎912 6010); *Hertz*, Bismarckstr. 19–21 (☎515084); also a number of offices at the airport.

Cultural institutes *Amerikahaus* at Apostelnkloster 13–15 (☎209010); *British Council* at Hahnenstr. 6 (☎206440).

Doctor ☎19292.

Festivals Everything else inevitably stands in the shade of Carnival (see previous pages). However, the Corpus Christi celebrations (variable date in May or June) are also impressive, featuring a barge procession along the Rhine, and another from the Dom through the streets of the Altstadt.

Markets The large squares in the Altstadt provide a fitting setting for frequent markets; there is a weekly one all day Fri in Alter Markt, and a flea market in the same location every third Sat. Special occasions are: the flower market in Alter Markt on weekends in late April and early May; the junk market in Neumarkt in mid-May and again in mid-Sept; the *Weinwoche* (actually nearer a fortnight) in Neumarkt in late May/early June; and the *Weihnachtsmarkt* in both locations throughout Advent.

Mitfahrzentrale Saarstr. 22 (☎19444); there's a women-only branch (along with a feminist book-store) at Moltkestr. 66 (☎523120).

Pharmacist ☎11500 for information on late-opening pharmacies.

Post office The main office with poste restante is at Breite Str. 6–62 (Mon–Fri 8am–8pm, Sat 8am–4pm).

Rhine cruises *K-D Linie* at Frankenwerft 15 (☎208 8318); *Köln-Tourist-Personenschiffahrt* at Konrad-Adenauer-Ufer (☎121600); *Colonia* at Anleger Hohenzollernbrücke (☎257 4225).

Shopping The pedestrian section of the Altstadt is the city's main shopping street. Eau de Cologne (*Kölnerwasser*) can be bought in innumerable stores. About 20 companies make the product: *Farina*, founded in 1709 and still in business today, is one of the original manufacturers; *Mülhens* is another firm with a long pedigree.

Sports The main outdoor ground is at Aachener Strasse in the western suburb of Müngersdorf; *FC Köln*, one of Germany's most successful football teams, play here, and there's an international athletics meeting in August or early Sept. An ice rink and swimming stadium are at Lentstr. 30 in Riehl, and a huge *Sporthalle* for indoor events is at Mülheimer Strasse in Deutz.

Travel agencies Many are to be found in the vicinity of the Dom, including *Thomas Cook* at Komödienstr. 7 (☎202080).

THE LOWER RHINELAND

The **Lower Rhineland** (*Niederrhein*) is the name given to the predominantly flat area north of Cologne; the great river thereafter offers no more dramatic scenery. Industrialization, though significant, is held in check most of the way up to **Düsseldorf**. Immediately beyond, however, begins the most developed industrial region in the world, consisting of the Ruhrgebiet (whose westernmost cities, such as Duisburg and Essen, overlap with this area) and the corresponding towns across the river, such as Krefeld and **Mönchengladbach**. After this, there's a dramatic change to a countryside very close in spirit to nearby Holland. There are no more cities, but a number of small historic towns, notably **Xanten** and **Kalkar**.

North from Cologne

Immediately north of Cologne, making for easy excursions from the city, are some exciting destinations. On the left bank of the Rhine are the medieval customs post of **Zons** and the monastery of **Knechtsteden**. On the right bank, the area known as the Bergisches Land is punctuated by the bleak manufacturing towns that put Germany at the forefront of industrial development in the nineteenth century. It retains much green countryside, however, now designated a *Naturpark*, and shelters the great monastic church of **Kloster Altenberg**.

Zons

The curious village of **ZONS** lies 25km downstream from Cologne. It's now part of the municipality of Dormagen, an industrial town of no interest in itself, and is some 3km east of the latter's Bahnhof, to which it's connected by regular bus services (#875 and #882).

In 1372 the Archbishop of Cologne, Friedrich von Saarwerden, decided to levy taxes on the profitable shipping route through his domain, and began the building of a walled town on the site of his predecessors' long-destroyed castle. For all Zons' history of bad luck – it's repeatedly been ravaged by fires and floods down the centuries – the original **Stadtbefestigung** remains largely intact. It ranks as one of the most important surviving examples of a medieval defensive system in Germany, though it now requires a bit of imagination to visualize the original setting, as silting means it's now some way back from the Rhine.

Zons is the sort of place you'd expect to be overrun by sightseeing coaches, but, on weekdays at least, it's remarkably quiet. You'll get the best views by walking around the outside of the circuit. Beginning at the bus stop, turn right and you come to the **Mühlenturm**, the upper section of which was converted into a windmill early in its history. From here, continue along the south side of the town, which has a double wall, the outer having been added for protection against flooding. At the corner are the ruins of **Schloss Friedestrom**, including the gateway, the chunky keep, and a courtyard which forms a fitting setting for open-air theatre and pageants (every Sun afternoon mid-June to mid-Sept; also other random days). The eastern wall has two cylindrical defensive towers, along with an octagonal watchtower; at its far corner is the **Rheinturm**, the medieval entrance to the town and the place where customs dues were collected. Three watching posts pierce the northern wall, which terminates in the battlemented **Krötschenturm**. In the town centre there's one more tower, the round **Juddeturm**, which served as both prison and look-out. Around the Rheinturm are the few old houses which have survived the natural disasters; everything else is Baroque or later. The handsome **Herrenhaus** contains the local museum (Tues–Fri 2–6pm, Sat & Sun 10am–12.30pm & 2–5pm; DM4), which mounts temporary exhibitions alongside its own collection of Jugendstil art.

Practicalities

Zons' **tourist office** (Mon, Wed & Fri 8.30am–noon, Tues 8.30am–noon & 2.15–4pm, Thurs 8.30am–noon & 2.15–5pm; ☎02133/3772) is at Schloss Str. 37 in the modern building behind the Juddeturm. **Hotels** include *Zum Feldtor*, Schloss Str. 40 (☎02133/5441; ⑤); *Schloss Destille*, Mauerstr. 26a (☎02133/47658; ⑤); and *Schloss Friedestrom*, Parkstr. 2 (☎01233/5030; ⑧). All of these have **restaurants**, and there are plenty of other places in town where you can have a full meal or a snack. There are two **campsites** at Stürzelberg 1km to the north – *Strandterrasse* (☎02106/71717) and *Pitt-Jupp* (☎02106/42210).

Throughout the summer, regular daily **boat trips** (☎02106/42149 or 42349) run to Benrath; there are very occasional sailings to Cologne.

Around Zons: Kloster Knechtsteden

Also within the municipality of Dormagen is the Romanesque **Kloster Knechtsteden**, built in the austere style favoured by its Premonstratensian founders, but enlivened by a central octagon flanked by twin towers. It stands in an isolated setting 3km west of the Bahnhof, connected by a frequent bus service (#876). As in the great imperial cathedrals, there's a choir at both ends of the building; the eastern one is a late Gothic replacement, while that to the west is adorned with mid-twelfth century **frescoes** showing *Christ as Pantocrator*, surrounded by angels and the Evangelical symbols, with portraits of the Apostles below. If you fancy a quiet night away from the cities, the *Klosterhof* (☎02106/80745; ③) just outside the monastery gate has rooms along with a bar-restaurant.

Kloster Altenberg

Set in isolation in a wooded valley of the River Dhün about 15km northeast of Cologne is **Kloster Altenberg**, popularly known as the **Bergischer Dom**. In spite of this nickname, it's not a cathedral but a monastery built by the Cistercians, whose rule prescribed secluded settings of this kind. In 1133 the Count of Berg moved his seat and donated his ancestral home, set on the hill above, to this reforming order of monks, who used the stones to construct their first church. What makes the present building, begun in 1255, particularly interesting is that it's contemporary with, and of similar stature to, the Dom in Cologne, only this time it was completed in just over a hundred years. In accordance with the austere Cistercian tradition there's no tower and little in the way of decoration. Nevertheless, it's still enormously photogenic, seeming to blend effortlessly into the landscape; the best view is from the hill to the east, where you see the choir with its corona of chapels (the earliest and finest feature) to best advantage.

Few buildings so perfectly encompass the basic tenets of the Gothic style: there are no grand gestures; everything is spacious, bright and harmonious, a visible manifestation of the order's quest for spiritual tranquillity. The chancel has wonderful original silvery-grey **stained-glass** windows which have geometric motifs only. This same type of glass, but with floral shapes, fills the big lights of the north transept, beaming down on the tombs of the Counts (later Dukes) of Berg. Relaxation of the normal Cistercian rejection of representational subjects is confined to the giant facade window, the largest in Germany: it depicts *The Heavenly Jerusalem* in predominantly golden tones, a particularly memorable sight when illuminated by the setting sun.

If you want to sample some of the atmosphere of rural peace, make sure you come on a weekday. On Sundays, Altenberg acts as a magnet for urban dwellers seeking their weekly retreat; a curiosity is that both Catholic and Protestant services are held. This was a condition laid down last century by the Prussian King Friedrich Wilhelm IV when he arranged for the church's repair and return to worship, after a period of disuse and decay following the Napoleonic suppression. Ask at *Küchenhof* (one of the bar-restaurants currently occupying the outbuildings) for the key to the early thirteenth-century **Markuskapelle**, the oldest surviving part of the complex.

The monastery can be reached in an hour from the centre of Cologne, if you strike lucky with connections: take U-Bahn #16 to Wiener Platz, then bus #434.

Wuppertal

WUPPERTAL stands at the northernmost end of the Bergisches Land group of industrial towns, and some 30km east of Düsseldorf. The overriding justification for a detour is to see its public transport system – little recommendation, you would think, but the **Schwebebahn** (hanging rail line), a monorail suspension system without wheels, is genuinely unique. Wuppertal didn't exist as such when the line was built between 1898 and 1900 to link the various towns strung along the valley of the River Wupper – **Barmen** and **Elberfeld** being the largest. These communities united in 1929, yet still preserve distinct identities; Wuppertal hasn't evolved a recognizable city centre.

THE SCHWEBEBAHN

The brainchild of **Carl Eugen Langen**, who failed to interest Berlin and Munich in his idea, the *Schwebebahn*, Wuppertal's creaking rail line, suspended on high and supported by 472 triangular girders, runs directly above the river between fifteen of its nineteen stations. It then passes over the main thoroughfares of Sonnborn and Oberwinkel to the west, leaving them permanently dank. The sleek orange and blue cars are fourth generation; at weekends in summer, one of the original models is run. This is the only gimmick associated with a genuine local facility which is both fast and efficient (services run every few minutes). Above all, it has proved the safest public transport system ever devised, never having seen a serious accident. Travel along the whole route for a complete picture of the town, and look out for the *Werther Brücke* station, which preserves its original Jugendstil decoration.

Elberfeld

The centre of **ELBERFELD** is a vast pedestrian shopping precinct. At Poststrasse 11, look out for the watchmaker's shop whose incredible display is trumped by its own **Uhrenmuseum** (Mon–Fri 4–6pm, Sat 10am–1pm; DM5). Here you can see over a thousand weird and wonderful timepieces, ranging from the earliest watch made in Germany to an eighteenth-century London fancy with an elephant and a rotating Chinese emperor's court.

Round the corner, at Turmhof 8, is the neo-Renaissance bulk of the former Rathaus, now containing the **Von-der-Heydt-Museum** (Tues, Wed & Fri–Sun 10am–5pm, Thurs 10am–9pm; DM6), one of the country's finest galleries of nineteenth- and twentieth-century art. Centrepiece of the display is a group of some two dozen canvases by a local man, **Hans von Marées**, whose pronounced intellectual approach, marked Italianate influence, and preference for a dark palette combine to make him one of Germany's most distinctive painters. Other artists particularly well represented are **Carl Spitzweg** (with five wonderfully humorous Biedermeier vignettes), **Max Beckmann** (notably self-portraits as a clown and as a World War I Red Cross worker), **Paula Modersohn-Becker** and **Alexej Jawlensky**, while individual highlights include **Kirchner's** *Women in the Street*, **Dix's** satirical *An die Schönheit*, and **Schlemmer's** *Twelve Figures in an Interior*. A good cross-section of French Impressionism is headed by a study for **Manet's** seminal *Déjeuner sur l'Herbe*.

Barmen

At Engelsstrasse in **BARMEN** is a collection of more marginal interest, the **Museum für Frühindustrialisierung** (Museum of Early Industry; Tues–Sun 10am–1pm &

3–5pm; DM3). In front stands the **Engels-Haus** (same times and ticket), an elegant late eighteenth-century building which belonged to a family of textile entrepreneurs. It now serves as a memorial to their celebrated black sheep **Friedrich Engels**, who was born nearby. As a young man, he was sent to England to work at the sister factory of *Ermen & Engels* in Manchester; there he became fascinated by the plight of the urban proletariat, and on his return to Barmen in 1845 wrote his celebrated *The Condition of the Working Class in England*. Soon afterwards, he began collaborating with Karl Marx, returning to work as a capitalist in Manchester in order to provide funds for their joint revolutionary writings. Though very much the junior partner in these, Engels always had a large input on matters concerning nationalities, diplomacy, the military and business practices – even in the books such as *Das Kapital* in which Marx appears as sole author.

Barmen really seems to relish its reputation as an anti-establishment town, as it was also the scene of the 1934 synod of the "Confessing Church", Protestant opponents of Hitler. At this meeting, the church declared its independence from state control, proclaiming itself the only true heir of the Lutheran tradition, in contrast to the bogus Reich Church most clergymen had been forced into joining. Its guiding force, **Pastor Martin Niemöller**, was later incarcerated in a concentration camp, but gained a reputation outside Germany as one of the most effective anti-Nazis, and survived to become a leading pacifist and international churchman after the war.

Practicalities

Wuppertal's **tourist office** (Mon–Fri 9am–6pm, Sat 9am–1pm; ☎0202/19433) is just across from the Hauptbahnhof in Elberfeld at Am Döppersberg beside the bus terminus. There's a **Mitfahrzentrale** office at Emilstr. 55 (☎0202/262 1443).

Hotels are scattered all over the city. Those in Elberfeld tend to be on the expensive side; options there include *Astor*, Schlossbleiche 4–6 (☎0202/450511; ⑥), and *Zur Post*, Poststr. 4 (☎0202/450131; ⑥). Barmen also has a number of budget places, including *Schulz*, Wittensteinstr. 223 (☎0202/597123; ④) and *CVJM-Gästehaus* on Bundeshöhe (☎0202/574226; ④) to the south, while the small *Villa Christina*, set in a park to the east of town at Richard-Strauss-Allee 18 (☎0202/621736; ⑦), is perhaps the most attractive place to stay in Wuppertal. The **youth hostel** is at Obere Lichtenplatzer Str. 70 (☎0202/552372; ⓑ), a few minutes' walk to the south of Barmen's train station.

Reasonably priced places to **eat** and **drink** can be found all over the city, especially in the large pedestrian precinct in the centre of Elberfeld; though the best traditional restaurant is probably *Zum Futterplatz*, south of Barmen's train station at Obere Lichtenplatzer Str. 102.

The *Schauspielhaus*, near the tourist office at Bundesallee 260 (☎0202/563 4444), presents plays and operas, but is best known for Pina Bausch's *Tanztheater*, by some way Germany's leading **modern dance** company.

Düsseldorf

DÜSSELDORF disputes with Hamburg and Stuttgart the right to be regarded as Germany's richest city, and in many ways is the paragon of the postwar face of the Federal Republic – orderly, prosperous and self-confident. Few places can have a name so inappropriate to their present status: the "village on the Düssel" is now a thriving Land capital of 600,000 inhabitants on both banks of the Rhine, crossed here by no fewer than six bridges. Since the war, it has developed a cosmopolitan and strangely un-European character. Never as industrialized as its neighbours in the Ruhr, Düsseldorf has concentrated on its role as the region's financial and

The **telephone code** for Düsseldorf is ☎0211

administrative centre, its skyline punctuated by the skyscrapers of innumerable multinational giants.

The extent to which you'll like or loathe Düsseldorf depends very much on your reaction to the way it has sold its soul to the corporate dream. If **luxury shops** are your scene, there are none more stylish between Paris and Berlin. The city likes to think of itself as Germany's leading fashion centre, with sartorial elegance and other displays of wealth serving as indicators of individual standing in its fiercely competitive high society. Even for a short visit, it's an expensive option, but there's no doubt that the **nightlife**, at least, is one of the most varied and enjoyable in the country.

Arrival, information and accommodation

The **Hauptbahnhof** is situated in the southeast part of the city centre; from here, the shopping streets begin to fan out. S-Bahn trains #7 and #21 leave at twenty-minute intervals for the **airport** to the north. Note that, unlike neighbouring cities, most of Düsseldorf's attractions are within walking distance of each other, so the DM10 24-hour ticket on the public transport network is really only of use if you specifically want to see the outlying suburbs. The **tourist office** (Mon–Fri 8.30am–6pm, Sat 9am–12.30pm; ☎172020) is on Konrad-Adenauer-Platz, directly facing the Hauptbahnhof.

It's best to check with the tourist office for any good **hotel** deals on offer, as accommodation is overwhelmingly geared to the business traveller, and prices are far above the national norm, even in the suburbs. Those in the vicinity of the Hauptbahnhof are as cheap as any. Faced with high prices, it's worth remembering that the **youth hostel** has single rooms as well as the normal dormitory facilities.

Hotels

Amsterdam, Stresemannstr. 20 (☎84058, fax 84050). Good medium-priced city-centre choice. ⑥

Breidenbacher Hof, Heinrich-Heine-Allee 36 (☎13030, fax 130 3830). Without a doubt, the pick of the city's luxury hotels, with an ideal situation just off Königsallee. Has three separate restaurants, all of them prestigious.

Bristol, Aderstr. 8 (☎370750, fax 373754). Surprisingly reasonable considering its location just south of the prestigious Königsallee. ④

CVJM, Graf-Adolf-Str.102 (☎172850, fax 361 3160). YMCA-run hotel by the Hauptbahnhof. Most of the bedrooms are grouped round an inner courtyard and are therefore well sheltered from street noise. ⑤

Diana, Jahnstr. 31 (☎375071, fax 364943). Popular, moderately priced hotel in a quiet street in the southern part of the centre. ③

Eden, Aderstr. 29–31 (☎38970, fax 389777). Among the best of the city's middle-range hotels, and one of the few in this category with a restaurant. ⑦

Haus Hillesheim, Jahnstr. 19 (☎371940, fax 386 8633). A few doors up from the *Diana*, with similar prices and facilities, plus a bar. ③

Komet, Bismarckstr. 93 (☎178790, fax 178 7950). A good medium-price recommendation in the city centre. ④

Manhattan, Graf-Adolf-Str. 39 (☎370244, fax 370247). Reasonably priced hotel right by the Hauptbahnhof and always full of young travellers. ④

Wurms, Scheurenstr. 23 (☎375001, fax 375003). Good medium-range hotel a few minutes' walk southwest of the Hauptbahnhof. ⑥

Youth hostel and campsites

Campingplatz Oberlörick, Niederkasseler Deich 305 (☎591401). Located on the left bank of the Rhine; take U-Bahn #76, #705 or #717 to Belsenplatz, then bus #828. April–Sept only.

Campingplatz Unterbacher See (☎899 2038). Düsseldorf's more tranquil campsite, at the eastern extremity of the city; take bus #781.

Jugendherberge und Jugendgästehaus Düsseldorf, Düsseldorfer Str. 1, Oberkassel (☎574041). From the Hauptbahnhof, take bus #835 or walk down Graf-Adolf-Strasse and continue in a straight line, crossing the Rheinkniebrücke; it's the first building on the other side. ⌂–⌂

The city centre

The **Altstadt**, close to the Rhine, reflects the meaning of Düsseldorf's name in its modest proportions. Never one of Germany's great cities from an architectural point of view, it's chiefly renowned today for its remarkable range of places of entertainment. Immediately to the east is a planned **green belt**, created by French landscape gardeners in the eighteenth and nineteenth centuries when Düsseldorf was a seat of the Electors Palatine, who succeeded the defunct line of the Dukes of Berg, the city's founders.

The Altstadt

Over 200 restaurants, beer halls, wine cellars, bistros, snack bars, jazz centres and discos are crammed into the small area of the Altstadt, which pulsates with activity day and night. This fact tends to overshadow the historical sights, but two very contrasting churches do catch the eye. **St Lambertus**, a fourteenth-century brick building in the

HEINRICH HEINE (1797–1856)

One of Germany's most celebrated and intriguing men of letters, Heinrich Heine modified the traditional Romantic themes of his day by using a biting sense of irony. The recurring image of the *Doppelgänger* in his work reflects his lifelong feeling of isolation – as a poet in a family of merchants, a Jew and Protestant convert among Catholics, a Francophile who eventually settled in Paris yet remained German at heart, and as a revolutionary familiar with Marxism who kept faith with the bourgeois liberal tradition. His early *Buch der Lieder* provided the dying Schubert with the texts for his last songs, and was to be a similar source of inspiration for subsequent composers, notably Schumann, Brahms and Wolf. Later, his *Reisebilder*, combining factual descriptions, poems and political comment, initiated a new and much-imitated form of travel writing.

hall church style, is easily recognizable because of its tall twisted spire, now ousted from its former physical and spiritual dominance over the city by the huge corporate skyscrapers. Inside, there's a graceful Gothic tabernacle, a fifteenth-century *Pietà*, and the spectacular late sixteenth-century marble and alabaster tomb of Duke Wilhelm V.

A short walk to the east is **St Andreas**, a Jesuit foundation of 1629 which is one of the chief reminders of the period when Düsseldorf was the seat of the Electors Palatine. Its galleried interior is ornately decorated with stucco; the **Mausoleum** (Mon–Fri 3–5.30pm) to the rear contains the surprisingly simple tin coffins of the Electors. The most famous and genuinely popular of these rulers was Johann Wilhelm II, better known as **Jan Wellem**, who ruled from 1679 to 1716. He's commemorated in the huge open area named after him in the heart of the city, and by a masterly equestrian statue (the work of his Italian court sculptor Gabriel de Grupello), erected during his own lifetime outside the Renaissance **Rathaus**. In the square immediately to the north is the **Schlossturm**, the only remnant of the old fortifications; it has been restored to house the **Schiffahrtmuseum** (Wed & Sat 2–6pm, Sun 11am–6pm; DM4), a small display of Rhineland navigation.

At Schulstr. 4, towards the southern end of the Altstadt, is the **Hetjens-Museum** (Tues & Thurs–Sat 2–6pm, Wed 2–8pm, Sun 11am–6pm; DM3), which boasts of being the only one in Germany entirely devoted to the art of ceramics. It's a tidy collection, albeit one mainly for aficionados. Düsseldorf's favourite son, the poet **Heinrich Heine** (see box above), is commemorated by a research institute and museum (Tue–Fri & Sun 11am–5pm, Sat 1–5pm; DM4) nearby at Bilkerstr. 14.

Overlooking the Rhine at the extreme southern end of the Altstadt is Peter Behrens' **Mannesmann-Gebäude**, a distinguished example of corporate architecture from the first decade of this century, but now dwarfed by the **Mannesmann-Haus**, the skyscraper which pioneered the postwar identification of Düsseldorf's appearance with the power of multinational companies. Nonetheless, the radio tower, the **Rheinturm**, built just to the south between 1979 and 1982, has now taken over as the city's highest building. You can ascend by high-speed lift to its observation platform (Mon–Fri 11am–11.30pm, Sat & Sun 10am–11.30pm; DM5.50) for an absolutely stunning view over the city and the Rhine. Alongside is the brand-new **Landtag**, the state parliament of North Rhine-Westphalia.

The museum quarter

Housed in an ultra-modern gallery in Grabbeplatz just north of St Andreas is the **Kunstsammlung Nordrhein–Westfalen** (Tues–Thurs, Sat & Sun 10am–6pm; Fri 10am–8pm; DM8). The genesis of this collection was a remarkable act of postwar contrition by the authorities. **Paul Klee**, the abstract painter, was a professor at the Düsseldorf Academy from 1930 until dismissed in the Nazi purges of 1933. In atonement for this, around ninety of his works were purchased from a private American source in 1960; shortly afterwards, a rapid acquisitions policy, of twentieth-century art only, was adopted. The Klee collection remains the obvious draw, although only about two-thirds of the works are on show at any one time. Even if you aren't attracted to this painter, there are many other highlights, such as one of **Picasso's** most famous representational works, *Two Sitting Women*; **Léger's** large *Adam and Eve*; **Kirchner's** *Negro Dance*; **Modigliani's** *Diego Rivera*; and self-portraits by **Kokoschka** and **Chagall**. Already the collection resembles a who's who of modern art, and it continues to grow.

The **Kunstmuseum** (Tues–Sun 11am–6pm; DM5), directly north of the Altstadt at Ehrenhof 5, has extensive displays on three floors. This could very nearly have been one of Europe's finest art galleries, as the Electors owned a marvellous array of paintings which followed the court to Munich in 1806 and soon formed one of the bases of the Alte Pinakothek. A **Rubens** masterpiece, an altarpiece of *The Assumption*, never made the journey because of its size; it now puts almost all the other old masters on the first floor completely in the shade. Among the few paintings not wholly outclassed are *Venus and Adonis* by the same painter; a *St Jerome* attributed to **Ribera**, and *St Francis in Meditation* by **Zurbarán**. Also on this floor is a series of powerful lithographs by **Otto Pankok** called *The Passion*, though in fact Christ's whole life is depicted. Their gloomy, highly charged emotionalism, with hateful mobs and angst-ridden victims, directly reflects the contemporary horrors of the Holocaust. Upstairs, there's a modern section which complements that in the Kunstsammlung, along with an extensive show of the nineteenth-century historical painters of the **Düsseldorf Academy**. Now long out of fashion, they suffer from failing to find a sense of inspiration to match their undoubted technical skill. More pleasing is the sparkling **glass** section on the ground floor, dominated by Art Nouveau and Art Deco pieces from Germany, France and America.

The Königsallee and Hofgarten

The city's main thoroughfare, the **Königsallee**, laid out at the beginning of the nineteenth century, was the culmination of the transformation of Düsseldorf by the Electors Palatine into a city of parks, ponds and canals. It's one of Germany's most famous streets and is chic rather than beautiful; down one side are banks and offices, with expensive stores, representing all the trendiest names in international designer-made goods, lining the other. People shop here with an incredibly self-conscious air; in antithesis to the intended effect, the prevailing hallmark is one of vulgarity, and it's appropriate that the architectural setting is so mediocre. Only the late Jugendstil **Kaufhaus** by the Viennese Joseph Maria Olbrich has any merits as a building, though it has suffered from an interior modernization. Diagonally opposite its rear entrance is **Wilhelm-Marx-Haus** erected in the 1920s, the earliest visible expression of Düsseldorf's infatuation with the New World,.

The largest of the parks is the **Hofgarten**, shaped like a great stiletto-heeled shoe, and now incongruously cut in several places by busy streets. Towering over it is the **Thyssen-Haus**, by far the most arresting of the corporate structures which so altered the city skyline in the 1950s, offering a fascinating play of light on its three huge silvery-green slabs. Beside it, the daring white curves of the **Schauspielhaus**, built in 1970, provide an effective counterpoint, as well as a reminder that, in this city, the public structures stand very much in the shadow of big business.

At the far end of the Hofgarten is **Schloss Jägerhof**, a Baroque palace which sustained severe damage in the last war. Its interior decorations have been refitted as the **Goethe-Museum** (Tues–Fri & Sun 11am–5pm, Sat 1–5pm; DM4), reckoned to be the best collection of memorabilia of the great poet and playwright after those in Frankfurt and Weimar. Unless you're an avid fan, the contents will seem fairly mundane, though it's worth glancing over the section on works of art inspired by his most celebrated drama, *Faust*. Just to the north of the Schloss is the city's finest modern church, **St Rochus**. Outside, it resembles a giant beehive; the interior is deliberately dark, in an attempt to re-create the old mysteries of religion.

Benrath

Of the towns which have been swallowed up by Düsseldorf, by far the most interesting is **BENRATH** to the south, best reached by S-Bahn #6. The **Schloss** (guided tours Tues–Sun 10am–4pm; DM7) and its park were commissioned by the Elector Carl Theodor (see p.308) in the mid-eighteenth century; the unusual harmony of the whole complex is due to the fact that the architect, the French-born **Nicholas de Pigage**, was also a landscape gardener. Its main block, in a style hovering between Rococo and Neoclassical, represents a very clever piece of *trompe l'oeil* construction – for all its seemingly small size, it contains eighty rooms. The tours take in the sumptuous reception and garden rooms on the ground floor, as well as some of the private apartments upstairs. Afterwards, you can stroll in the formal gardens and see the surviving building of the old palace.

Eating, drinking and nightlife

Walking through the Altstadt – "the longest bar in Europe" according to the tourist office – is an enjoyable activity in itself, especially on summer days when it's even more crowded than usual and virtually every pub and restaurant offers the opportunity for imbibing *al fresco*. **Eating** is one of the few things it's possible to do cheaply in Düsseldorf, thanks to the various ethnic communities. Cuisines on offer include Italian, Balkan, Spanish, Argentinian, various forms of Oriental, and fish specialities. By far the most popular **drink** is the distinctive local **Alt** beer, dark in colour and tending towards sweetness in some varieties, caused by the higher quantity of malt used than in lagers.

The heart of the Altstadt

This area is given over almost entirely to diverse places for eating and drinking, and is, unsurprisingly, by far the most popular with tourists.

Daitokai, Mutter-Ey-Str. 1. As Düsseldorf is the main European outpost of Japanese commerce, it's not surprising that the city is well endowed with Japanese restaurants, of which this is one of the very best.

Im Goldenen Kessel, Bolkerstr. 44. Flagship of the *Schumacher* brewery, renowned for its reasonably priced food.

Irish Pub, Hunsrückenstr. 13. Genuine reminder of Hibernia, owned and staffed by expatriates, and with a long-established tradition. Such is the current German mania for all things Irish that it now has several competitors, one of them just three doors away.

Pfannkuchenhaus, Bolkerstr. 55. Offers over 50 different varieties of pancakes, both savoury and sweet.

Schnabelewopski, Bolkerstr. 53. Literary café-bar housed in Heine's birthplace.

Tante Anna, Andreasstr. 2. Historic restaurant-cum-wine bar in a converted sixteenth-century chapel with 150 vintages to choose from.

Weisser Bär, Bolkerstr. 33. Popular pub with raucous music frequented by a curious mixture of young Düsseldorfers and young tourists, and staffed by relics of the '68 generation.

Zum Csikos, Andreasstr. 9. Highly rated but pricey Hungarian restaurant. Evenings only.

Zum Schlüssel, Bolkerstr. 45. *Hausbrauerei* which has spawned the much larger *Gatzweilers* brewery; products from both, as well as high quality local dishes, are available in the cavernous and well-patronized interior.

The northern Altstadt

You only need to move a few streets further north to escape from the tourists into an area preferred by locals.

Im Füchschen, Ratinger Str. 28. *Hausbrauerei* producing a relatively bitter *Alt*; also serves filling and inexpensive meals.

Im Goldenen Ring, Burgplatz 21. Traditional *Gaststätte* serving excellent food, including good value set meals.

Ratinger Hof, Ratinger Str. 10. Germany's first and most notorious punk bar lives on, frequented by diehards of the cult and blasting out ear-splitting music.

Schlosssturm, Mühlenstr. 2. Particularly enjoyable on fine days, offering a sheltered view over the Rhine from the cobbled square outside.

Zum Goldenen Einhorn, Ratinger Str. 18. An enduringly popular spot with the youth of the city, especially in summer when it opens its leafy little beer garden.

The southern Altstadt

This quarter is even more off the beaten tourist track and correspondingly laid-back. It's the best area if you're looking for live jazz.

Dr Jazz, Flingerstr. 11. Jazz hangout, with different bands each evening.

Front Page, Mannesmann-Ufer 9. Cosy piano bar.

The G@rden, Rathausufer 8. Internet café-bar, one of several modish hangouts along the waterfront.

Marktwirtschaft, Bernrather Str. 7. An excellent place to spend a quiet evening among the well-heeled youth of Düsseldorf.

Miles Smiles, Akademiestr. 6. Jazz bar which doubles as an Italian trattoria.

Zum Schiffchen, Hafenstr. 5. Traditional beer hall serving excellent food. Closed Sun.

Zum Uerige, Bergerstr. 1. A real drinking pub, this is among the most famous *Hausbrauerei* in all of Germany, producing the ultimate in *Alt* beer, plus a good *Weizen*. As a bonus, it has its own sausage kitchen, though only snacks are served.

Outside the Altstadt

To escape tourists altogether, you have to look a bit further afield. The first two bars listed here are tucked away in the shopping area between the Altstadt and the Hauptbahnhof; the others are on the left bank of the Rhine.

Café Bernstein, Oststr. 158. Stylish place for a nightcap, largely patronized by a distinctive Düsseldorf group – monied student couples.

Ferdinand Schumacher, Oststr. 123. *Hausbrauerei* which is the parent of *Im Goldenen Kessel* in the Altstadt.

DÜSSELDORF'S FESTIVALS

It's worth trying to time your visit to coincide with one of Düsseldorf's three main **popular festivals**. The **Carnival** celebrations (7 weeks before Easter) are ranked third in Germany, although those in nearby Cologne are the best of all. The celebrations are supposed to signify the end of winter; its beginning is heralded by **St Martin's Eve** on November 10, marked by an enormous procession of lantern-bearing children. In late July, the **Grosses Schützenfest** (riflemen's meeting) is an eight-day festival along the banks of the Rhine. Simultaneously, there's a huge funfair (claimed to be the largest of its type in the world) offering gut-churning rides on the Ferris wheel, the big dipper and other machines. The most celebrated local tradition is **cartwheeling** by local lads in the streets of the Altstadt. This is in honour of an urchin who saved the day when a wheel came loose on the popular Elector Palatine Jan Wellem's wedding coach, but the reason it survives is the less romantic one of extorting money from tourists. In spite of serving as an unofficial symbol of the city, you're unlikely to see any demonstrations out of season.

Sassafras, Düsseldorfer Str. 90. Café-bar with a youthful and unpretentious clientele.

ZAKK, Fichtenstr. 40. A bar with a difference, drawing visitors from neighbouring cities to its exhibitions, video showings and other arty events.

Clubs and discos

Bhaggy Disco, Graf-Adolf-Str. 55. Highly popular disco just a stone's throw from the Hauptbahnhof.

Soul Centre, Bolkerstr. 37. Of the two dozen discos in the Altstadt, one of only a couple deviating from playing standard modern fare.

Tor 3, Ronsdorfer Str. 143. South of the centre in the district of Bilk, this huge barn of a place is the city's leading disco. It has few concessions to comfort, but its customers are young, friendly and out to enjoy themselves with a vengeance.

Entertainment

Pop concerts and large-scale shows are staged at the *Philipshalle*, Siegburger Str. 15 (☎775057) in the southern district of Overbilk. There's also a strong local tradition in **classical music**. Both *Deutsche Oper am Rhein*, Heinrich-Heine-Allee 16a (☎890 8211), and the *Düsseldorfer Symphoniker* enjoy good provincial standing, even if present standards are short of the heyday last century when both Mendelssohn and Schumann did stints in charge of the city's musical affairs. The normal venue for concerts is the *Tonhalle*, a converted planetarium on Hofgartenufer (☎899 6123).

Choice in **theatre** is wide, with drama offered at the *Schauspielhaus*, Gustav-Grundgens-Platz 1 (☎369911), *Kammerspiele*, Jahnstr. 3 (☎378353), and *Theater an der Luegallee*, Luegallee 4 (☎572222). You'll find cabaret and satire at the bizarrely spelt *Kom(m)ödchen* on Kay-und-Lore-Lorentz-Platz (☎322333), with comedy programmes at *Komödie*, Steinstr. 23 (☎325151) and musicals at *Capitol*, Erkrather Str. 30 (☎73440). For **kids**, there are the *Puppentheater*, Heimholtzstr. 48 (☎372401), and the *Marionettentheater*, Bilkerstr. 7 (☎328432). Alternative theatre is presented by *Junges Theater in der Altstadt* (☎327210), based in a wing of Wilhelm-Marx-Haus at Kasernenstr. 6. Also in these premises is *Filminstitut Black Box*, most adventurous of the city's many **cinemas**.

Listings

Airlines *Aer Lingus*, Berliner Allee 38 (☎323 0231); *Air Canada*, Marienstr. 32 (☎162585); *British Airways*, Am Wehrhahn 2a (☎162161).

Airport 7km north of the city centre (☎421 2223 for flight information).

Consulates *British*, Yorckstr. 19 (☎94480); *Canadian*, Prinz-Georg-Str. 126 (☎172170).

Mitfahrzentralen Kruppstr. 102 (☎19444), Konrad-Adenauer-Platz 13 (☎376081).

Post office The main office is at Immermannstr. 1 with poste restante services.

Women's bookstore Becherstr. 2.

Neanderthal and Neuss

It's easy enough to escape the cosmopolitan atmosphere of central Düsseldorf, and a couple of contrasting destinations within and just outside the boundaries of the city make for good half-day trips.

Neanderthal

One of the slowest trains in Germany wends its way up the River Düssel to Mettmann, stopping at **NEANDERTHAL** en route. This valley and its hamlet are named after the seventeenth-century Protestant poet **Joachim Neander**, who liked to meditate there.

During his lifetime, the valley was a rugged canyon, not easily accessible; subsequently, the landscape was changed completely by limestone mining, and it was this that led to a sensational discovery which made Neanderthal famous. In 1856, workers dug up bones from the bottom of a cave; these were later identified as belonging to an earlier form of mankind than *homo sapiens*, one still bearing a slight facial resemblance to the ape. The term **Neanderthal Man** has since been used to describe the tribes of humans who were wiped out by the last Ice Age. A small **Neanderthalmuseum** (Tues–Sat 10am–5pm, Sun 11am–6pm; DM2) explains the living conditions of these hunting peoples; there are also a few prehistoric bones (though the original discovery is now in Bonn – see p.473), and hypothetical reconstructions of what the race looked like, including a model of Neanderthal Man wearing the clothes of 1980s city gent. The valley has a game reserve, including animals such as bison which haven't evolved much since prehistoric times, but the landscape around is now irretrievably ruined, and the Düssel – little more than a ditch in the city – is still nothing grander than a stream here.

Neuss

On the west bank of the Rhine, Düsseldorf's suburbs merge imperceptibly into **NEUSS**, officially a separate large industrial town with extensive dockyards; it's best reached by S-Bahn #8 or #11, as the fare is the same as for the trams. From the **Hauptbahnhof**, turn left and then left again into Krefelder Strasse, the start of the central shopping axis, which subsequently changes its name to Büchel, then Oberstrasse. About halfway down is the Markt, where you'll find the town's outstanding monument, the **Münster** or **St Quirinus**. It represents the apotheosis of the Rhineland Romanesque style, built in the early thirteenth century at a time when Gothic was established elsewhere. There's all the exuberance characteristic of the end of an era – blind arcades are employed in playful patterns, and the clover-leaf shape favoured by Rhenish architects is used in the design of the windows as well as in the plan of the chancel. The dome provides a touch of almost Oriental exoticism; together with its four turrets and the facade's belfry, it makes a memorable silhouette.

In complete contrast is the early twentieth-century **Dreikönigenkirche** to the south of the town centre at the junction of Jülicher Strasse and Dreikönigenstrasse. Following war damage, it was embellished with a wacky hanging vault by the father and son team of Dominikus and Gottfried Böhm. The church also has a complete set of stained-glass windows by the Dutch artist **Johan Thorn-Prikker**, one of the Jugendstil community based in Hagen; those in the chancel and transept are figurative and glow like jewels; the later geometric ones in the nave show his move to an abstract style. Neuss' only other building worth catching is the **Obertor** (part of the thirteenth-century fortifications), situated at the far end of the main shopping street. Along with a modern extension, it now houses the **Clemens-Sels-Museum** (Wed–Sun 11am–5pm; DM5), an average local collection with some surprises, such as paintings by the Pre-Raphaelites and French Symbolists.

Practicalities

The **tourist office** (Mon–Fri 9.30am–6.30pm, Sat 10am–2pm; ☎ 02131/273242) is in the *First Reisebüro*, Markt 4. There are plenty of **hotels**, ranging from *Mara*, Krefelder Str. 27 (☎02131/222280; ④) and *Haus Simrock*, Simrockstr. 1 (☎02131/42261; ⑤), to the luxurious *Swisshotel*, Rheinallee 1 (☎02131/153666; ⑨). There's also a **youth hostel**, close to the Rhine at Macherscheider Str. 113 (☎02101/39273; ⑧) in the suburb of Uedesheim. Good traditional **restaurants** include the seventeenth-century *Em Schwatte Päd*, Büchel 50, and *Vogthaus*, Münsterplatz 10; the much more expensive *An der Poz*, Oberstr. 10, is a well-regarded practitioner of *neue deutsche Küche*. Neuss's big festival is the **Shakespearefest**, held throughout June in a mock-up of the Globe Theatre, with performances of the Bard's plays in English and German.

Mönchengladbach

MÖNCHENGLADBACH, 30km west of Düsseldorf, is, like Bonn, an average-sized provincial town which has been catapulted to prominence since World War II. The new role for this old textile and machine manufacturing community is the rather less enviable one of serving as NATO's operations base for Northern and Central Europe, and as the head-quarters of the British Army on the Rhine. A purpose-built suburb, a real Little Britain, has been created at **Rheindahlen** to the west of the centre, reached by bus #7 or #17. Not only does English reign supreme as the language; everything, bar the buses and the use of the *Deutschmark* as currency, breathes the British way of life, as the colony does its utmost to forget that it's living on German soil. There are cricket and rugby pitches, halls for Scout and Brownie packs, Anglican and Presbyterian churches; the main thoroughfare is styled Queens Avenue, while the side streets tend to commemorate trees rather than deceased political leaders. However, the community is now very depleted as a result of the end of the Cold War, and is unlikely to survive much beyond the end of the millennium.

The town centre

Though not the most obvious destination unless you're visiting a friend or relative, Mönchengladbach does have some notable attractions, including the most audacious publicly owned art gallery in Germany, the **Museum Abteiberg** (Tues–Sun 10am–6pm; DM4), an ultra-modern building right in the heart of the old part of the town. Inaugurated in 1982, it was intended from its conception a decade earlier to be a major piece of modern architecture. An architect who is also an artist, the Viennese **Hans Hollein**, was chosen to see the project through, and the acquisitions policy has eschewed nearly all the century's best-known artists, and supported the avant-garde in a big way. **Joseph Beuys**, who first sprang to fame following an exhibition in Mönchengladbach, is copiously represented. Other artists include Lucio Fontana, Cy Twombly, Richard Sella, Sigmar Polke and Arman Fernandez. If you're keen on the iconoclastic and experimental nature of modern art, this museum warrants a special trip; but if you've even a suspicion of allergy, best keep well away.

Directly behind is the **Münster**, successor to the tenth-century Benedictine abbey from which the town derives its name (*Mönchen* means monks). The present building was erected throughout the thirteenth century, straddling the late Romanesque and early Gothic periods and culminates in the chancel by **Master Gerhard**, who was also master mason at the Dom in Cologne. Its central "Bible" window, pairing fourteen New Testament scenes with episodes from the Old Testament which were believed to antic-ipate them, is the only surviving piece of original glass. Notwithstanding the fact that three of the bottom panes have had to be replaced, it ranks as one of the loveliest in Germany. The **Schatzkammer** (Tues–Sat 2–4pm, Sun 2–6pm; DM2) displays the church's treasures, the most valuable of which is a twelfth-century portable altar from Cologne. You may have to ask to see the crypt and the sacristy: the former, unusually large for its time, is the oldest part of the church; the sacristy is a handsome Gothic room with delicately carved capitals and an amazingly well-preserved stone pavement.

Practicalities

Mönchengladbach's Hauptbahnhof is located fifteen minutes' walk from the old part of town: turn left at the exit and walk up Hindenburgstrasse, the main shopping street. The **tourist office** is in the *First Reisebüro* at Bismarckstr. 23–27, between the Hauptbahnhof and Alter Markt (Mon–Wed & Fri 9.30am–6.30pm, Thurs 9.30am–8pm, Sat 9.30am–1pm; ☎02161/22001).

Accommodation

Central hotels include *Gladbacher Hof*, diagonally opposite the Hauptbahnhof at Hindenburgstr. 233 (☎02161/22128; ④), and *Burgund*, a short distance to the west at Kaiserstr. 85 (☎02161/185970; ⑥). There's also a handy concentration in the suburb of Hardt (bus #13 or #23), including *HausFaassen*, Vorster Str. 233 (☎02161/559182; ②); *Kasteel-Scholl*, Vorster Str. 529 (☎02161/559694; ②); and *Lindenhof*, Vorster Str. 535 (☎02161/559340; ⑤), which also has a good restaurant.

Also in Hardt, but a further 1km south in the woods, is the **youth hostel** at Brahmsstr. 156 (☎02161/559512; ❽). Its location is less isolated than it might appear as the Rheindahlen garrison is situated close by.

Eating, drinking and nightlife

Mönchengladbach's best **restaurants** include *Haus Baues*, way to the west of the city centre at Bleichgrabenstr. 2, and the upmarket Italian *Michelangelo*, which is much more centrally placed at Lüpertzender Str. 133. At Alter Markt 21–22 is *Hannen Sudhaus*, the *Gaststätte* of the eponymous local brewery which specializes in dark *Alt* beer. Nearby, the steeply plunging Waldhausener Strasse is the epicentre of a fairly swinging nightlife, with a huge range of places of entertainment. Among them is *Dicker Turm*, a rebuilt tower which was formerly part of the fortifications; it now has snug little bars on three floors. At no. 89 on the same street, *Caspers am Grünewald* has a beer garden and a varied menu including many fish dishes.

Sport and festivals

Borussia Mönchengladbach gave the city an additional claim to fame in the 1970s when, most improbably, it supplanted Bayern München as Germany's leading **football** club for several seasons. They've now gone off the boil, but if you want to see them in action, their ground is at Bökelberg, north of the centre. Surprisingly, the favourite spectator sport is not soccer but horse-drawn wagon racing, a modern version of the Roman chariots, held at 6.30pm on Tuesdays at the Trabrennbahn stadium, An der Niersbrücke.

The list of **festivals** is headed by Carnival, which is unusual in featuring its main parade on Shrove Tuesday, meaning you can move on to it after the main celebrations have finished elsewhere.

Kempen and Kevelaer

Beyond Krefeld and the adjoining manufacturing town of Moers immediately to the north, the Lower Rhineland loses its urban nature and increasingly resembles the neighbouring Netherlands in character. This is true not only of the flat landscape and predominantly brick architecture, but also of the local dialect, which is the original Low German from which the Dutch language is derived.

Kempen

KEMPEN, 10km northwest of Krefeld, is the presumed birthplace of one of the best-selling writers of all time – not that **Thomas à Kempis** ever enjoyed fame or fortune during his life, or would have wanted to. A modest, retiring man, he spent seventy of his ninety years in the same Dutch Augustinian monastery, where he wrote *The Imitation of Christ*, a book whose influence on the Christian world is surpassed only by the Bible itself. An exhibition on Thomas à Kempis – including an example of the first Latin edition of his masterpiece, published in 1487, sixteen years after his death – is the centrepiece of the **Museum für Niederrheinische Sakaral Kunst** (Museum of

Lower Rhenish Sacred Art; Tues, Wed & Fri–Sun 11am–5pm, Thurs 11am–7pm; DM2), which occupies the old Franciscan Paterskirche and its monastic buildings in the town centre.

Nearby is the **Propsteikirche**, a bulky fourteenth-century Gothic church with a striking pink Romanesque tower. It's richly adorned with works of art collected during the town's heyday in the fifteenth and early sixteenth centuries: the three large altarpieces came from Antwerp while the tabernacle and Renaissance organ were made in Cologne. Elsewhere there remain a number of old houses, parts of the fortifications, and the medieval Burg, which was completely rebuilt last century in the Romantic manner.

Kempen's **train station** is immediately east of the town centre. The **tourist office** (Mon–Fri 9am–1pm & 2.30–6.30pm, Sat 10am–1pm; ☎02152/2407) is in the *Kempere Reisebüro*, Engerstr. 3. By far the best **restaurant** is *Et Kemp'sche Huus*, a reconstructed half-timbered house at Neustr. 31.

Kevelaer

KEVELAER, some 30km north on the main rail line to Kleve, is Germany's premier **place of pilgrimage**, drawing some 700,000 believers each year in a "season" lasting from May to October. Just before Christmas 1641, a local pedlar, Hendrick Busman, heard voices charging him to build a chapel on the site. Shortly after, his wife had a vision of the chapel containing the image of *The Blessed Virgin of Luxembourg* which she had seen carried by two soldiers; this picture had been attributed with healing properties during a plague in Luxembourg. Within six months, Busman had built a simple shrine with his own hands, in which the miraculous icon was placed; the cult quickly grew, and three years later the far more substantial **Kerzenkapelle** (Chapel of the Candles) was built alongside in an archaic Gothic style to house the pilgrims. A decade later, Busman's construction was replaced by the elaborate hexagonal **Gnadenkapelle** (Chapel of the Favours), in which the image is displayed facing the square outside. The fame of the pilgrimage spread so much in the nineteenth century that a vast neo-Gothic **Basilica** with a gaudily painted interior had to be built across the square to accommodate the crowds who flocked from all over the country.

No doubt it's a reflection of the Germanic nature that Kevelaer lacks the sheer, unadulterated bad taste that's the hallmark of other leading Marian shrines in Europe, such as Lourdes, Fátima and Knock. Unlike them, it can't really be recommended as worth seeing for shock value, which means you're unlikely to want to stay for long. Apart from the pilgrimage churches, the only other attraction is the **Niederrheinisches Museum für Volkskunde** (Lower Rhenish Museum of Folklore; Tues–Sun 10am–5pm; DM5), just a stone's throw away at Hauptstrasse 18. This contains a marvellous collection of toys from around the world, in addition to objects of local interest.

Kevelaer's **Bahnhof** is just east of the town centre. The **tourist office** (Mon–Thurs 7.30am–5.30pm, Fri 7.30am–12.30pm, Sat 10.30am–12.30pm; ☎02832/122151) is in the Rathaus, Peter-Plümpe-Platz 12. There's a **youth hostel** at Schravelen 50 (☎02832/8267; ❶); **hotels** are scattered all over town and, being geared to the pilgrim market, are mostly very reasonably priced (②–③).

Xanten

XANTEN, set just back from the Rhine some 45km north of Krefeld and 40km downstream from Duisburg, is one of the oldest settlements in Germany. In about 100 AD *Colonia Ulpia Traiana* was founded as a residential town (the only one in the Rhineland other than Cologne) in succession to the nearby garrison of Vetera, centre of operations for the campaign to subdue the eastern Germanic tribes. It in turn was abandoned with the collapse of the empire, and followed by a new community built immediately to the south around the graves of Christians martyred in the fourth century during the last wave of purges. The graves were popularly but implausibly believed to contain St Victor and members of the Thebian Legion; the name given to the town is a contraction of the Latin *Ad Sanctos Martyres* (To the Holy Martyrs). Writing at the end of the twelfth century, the anonymous poet of *The Nibelungenlied*, describing semi-mythical events centuries earlier, characterizes Xanten as "great", "splendid" and "far-famed", the birthplace and court of the invincible hero Siegfried, Lord of the Netherlands, Norway and the mysterious Nibelungland, home of the fantastic gold treasure of the Rhine which was to form the basis of the very different version of the legend unfolded in Wagner's epic *Ring* cycle 700 years later.

The town

Xanten is something of a Peter Pan, its current population of 16,000 little more than the probable size of the Roman town. It kept its medieval aspect until the last war, when it was badly bombed. Modern Xanten has successfully risen from the debris to appear once more as one of Germany's neatest country towns (the recipient of several prestigious conservation prizes), if one which is sometimes rather too crammed with day-trippers from the industrial hotbed to the south for its own good.

The Altstadt

The **Stadtbefestigung** survives in part, still defining the town's perimeter on the north and east sides. It's pierced by several towers, many of which have been converted into luxury flats, including the grandest of the group, the **Klever Tor**, whose double gateway formed the northwest entrance to the town. Just up Nordwall, the next tower underwent a more radical conversion in the eighteenth century, being reshaped to form a windmill. Immediately facing it is Brückstrasse, best preserved of the old streets.

Between here and the Markt is the church of **St Viktor**, popularly known as the **Dom**, though it's only the seat of a suffragan bishop. It lies cocooned in its own close or "Immunity", so named from its status as a haven from external laws and taxes. From afar, the massive facade dominates the town; it was the only part of the Romanesque church spared when a sober Gothic replacement was put up in the late thirteenth century. Subsequent builders tampered with it right up until 1525, by which time the towers had been heightened considerably. If you go around to the rear, you'll see a polychrome fifteenth-century statue to the Dom's patron saint, St Victor. Whether one of the ancient tombs discovered in the crypt excavations earlier this century is really his burial place is a matter resolved more by faith than cold logic. The five-aisled **interior** gives a rare opportunity of sampling the genuine, cluttered feel of a medieval church, thanks to the extraordinary range of objects it has preserved – expressive pier statues of saints, a rood screen, choir stalls, a hanging *Double Madonna*, stained-glass windows and a crowd of altars. Particularly notable are the four carved and painted late Gothic winged **retables** in the aisles, one from Antwerp and three from nearby Kalkar; finest is that on the south side, with scenes from the life of the Virgin springing from a pyrotechnic *Tree of Jesse* by Henrik Douverman. The same sculptor made the reliquary busts for the high altar, which also incorporates the twelfth-century shrine of St Victor.

In the southwest corner of the close is the **Regionalmuseum** (Tues–Fri 9/10am–5pm, Sat & Sun 11am–6pm; DM3), which serves as something of a repository for the Dom, with the treasury kept in the basement, and works of art no longer required for display on the ground floor. It also has extensive archeology and local history collections, but be warned that these are presented in an extremely didactic fashion, and that the most important finds from local excavations are housed in its parent

516/NORTH RHINE-WESTPHALIA

museum in Bonn. From here you can pass out into the **Markt**, something of a hotch-potch of styles, with houses ranging from Gothic to Rococo. At the far end, turn left down Karthaus, named after the former Charterhouse whose Baroque facade is the dominant feature of the street.

The Archäologischer Park

From here, continue along Rheinstrasse; across the main road is the site of *Colonia Ulpia Traiana*, now the **Archäologischer Park** (daily March–Nov 9am–6pm; Dec–Feb 10am–4pm; DM7, DM8 combind ticket with regional museum). Unlike many Roman towns in northern Europe, it was never built upon. That it subsequently disappeared is due to the fact that its stones were ideal building materials for later constructions, including the Dom. In the 1970s a proposal was made to develop the area into a recre-ation zone, but in return for sparing the site the authorities insisted that the excavations be given populist appeal. Thus, instead of merely uncovering ground plans, full-blood-ed conjectural reproductions of the main buildings of the town were attempted. The result is controversial to say the least, and purists will be horrified by the Disneyland touches. However, if you normally find archeological sites hamstrung by scholarly timidity, this will come as a revelation, giving a graphic picture of the true size and scale of a Roman town. Eventually, the aim is to go as far as re-creating the original riverside setting, which has now completely disappeared; at the moment, the **walls** with their massive fortifications, notably the **Hafentor** (Harbour Gate) at the very far end of the park, form the most impressive feature. Just inside the main entrance, an **inn** has been reconstructed; here the presentation goes outrageously over the top with toga-clad waiters serving the sort of meals it's alleged the Romans would have eaten. The **amphitheatre**, which is partly original, is now a venue for open-air theatrical perfor-mances; the **temple**, on the other hand, has been rebuilt only as a ruin.

Practicalities

The **Bahnhof**, terminus of a branch line from Duisburg, is only a few minutes' walk from the town centre via either Hagenbuschstrasse or Bahnhofstrasse. Services on the line northwards to Kleve are now replaced by buses, which leave from the forecourt. The **tourist office** (April–Sept Mon–Fri 9am–4.30pm, Sat & Sun 10am–4pm; Oct–March Mon–Thurs 9am–4pm, Fri 9am–noon, Sat & Sun 11am–2pm; ☎02801/772238) is located in the Rathaus, Karthaus 2. Here you can pick up an accom-modation list, which includes more than a dozen private houses with **rooms** (①–③) to let; you can choose a central location, or there are many in a more rural setting which are still within walking distance.

The least expensive of the **hotels**, all centrally situated, is *Galerie an de Marspoort*, Marsstr. 78 (☎02801/1057; ⑤), which doubles as an artists' gallery and pub. Alternatives are *Neumaier*, Orkstr. 19–21 (☎02801/71570; ⑤); *Nibelungen Hof*, Niederstr. 1 (☎02801/780; ⑤); *Hövelmann*, Markt 31–33 (☎02801/4081; ⑥); and the historic and luxurious *Van Bebber*, Klever Str. 12 (☎02801/6623; ⑦). The best **restau-rants** are in the last two hotels; there's also an inexpensive Balkan restaurant, *Dalmatien*, Markt 20. The town also has several good **cafés**, such as *Stadtcafé*, Markt 36–38, and *Café de Fries*, Kurfürstenstr. 8.

Kalkar (Calcar)

The little market town of **KALKAR** was built on a sandbank completely surrounded by an arm of the Rhine, but heavy silting has meant that it's now well inland. It lies mid-way between Xanten and Kleve, about 12km from either, and thanks to the presence of one of Germany's most remarkable churches, it rivals the former as the most interesting of the Lower Rhenish towns.

The town

The central **Markt** lost much of its character to wartime bombs, but some old houses have been restored to provide fitting company for the **Rathaus**, a brick building with a prominent octagonal turret. Behind, a step-gabled merchant's residence, connected by a modern extension to the oldest house in the town, contains the **Stadtmuseum** (Tues–Sun 10am–1pm & 2–5pm; DM2). This has an excellent collection of manuscripts and charters, along with the work of painters, most notably the Expressionist **Heinrich Nauen**, who lived in the town.

St Nicolai

None of this prepares you for the splendours of **St Nicolai**, built to the side of the Markt at the same time as the Rathaus. From the outside, it looks quite ordinary – a plain fifteenth-century brick building, enlivened only by its tall tower. The gleaming white interior (April–Oct Mon–Fri 10am–noon & 2–6pm, Sat 10am–noon & 2–4.45pm, Sun 2–4.45pm; Nov–March daily 2–4.45pm; DM1) is another matter altogether, bristling with such an astonishing array of **works of art** that it's now designated a "church-museum". It seems odd that what has never been more than a parish church in a town which has never been very large could have garnered such riches, but medieval Kalkar became wealthy through a cloth industry that used locally produced wool. The rich burghers showed their appreciation for this natural bounty by funding a school of woodcarving which flourished continuously for about a century from 1450, producing one great altarpiece after another, to illustrate the lives of Christ and the saints for the enlightenment of a largely illiterate congregation. Fifteen large retables and numerous other statues and paintings originally embellished the church; some were sold last century, but all the important pieces remain *in situ*.

It's worth taking time to examine the myriad details to be found in the big showpieces as all display an amazing level of technical virtuosity. **Henrik Douverman**, who made the *Altar of the Seven Sorrows of the Virgin* in the south apse, the *Double Madonna Candelabrum* in the middle of the nave and the superbly expressive *St Mary Magdalene* in the north aisle, has long been recognized as a highly individual artist, one who proved the continuing vitality of late Gothic forms well into the sixteenth century. However, many of his little-known predecessors, who were forced to submerge their artistic personalities in co-operative ventures, showed equal skill, nowhere more than in the crowded main *Passion Altar*, begun by the founder of the school, **Master Arnt**, and continued by **Ludwig Jupan**. These carvers were also responsible respectively for the *St George Altar* and the *Altar to the Virgin* fronting the entrance to the chancel. Painted panels were added to many of the retables to fill out the story; particularly fine are the colourful scenes on the *Passion Altar* by **Jan Joest**; the setting of *The Raising of Lazarus* is, incidentally, Kalkar's Markt.

Practicalities

Buses between Xanten and Kleve (which run hourly Mon–Fri, spasmodically on Sat and not at all on Sun) conveniently stop on the Markt. Though there's no **tourist office** as such, leaflets can be picked up at the *Stadtverwaltung*, Markt 20 (☎02824/131120) during normal working hours.

There are three **hotels**, all bang in the centre: *Siekmann*, Kesselstr. 32 (☎02824/2305; ④); *Seydlitz*, Markt 25 (☎02824/2053; ⑤); and *Zum Alten Handelshaus*, Markt 6 (☎02824/2252; ⑤). All have **restaurants**, though the best place to eat is the pricey *Ratskeller*, Markt 20. There's also a pleasant café-bar in an old windmill, the Kalkarer Mühle, just to the rear of the Stadtmuseum on Mühlensteg.

Just north of Kalkar is the **Wisseler See**, a natural lake which is a watersports centre; it also has a **campsite** (☎02824/6613).

Kleve (Cleves)

Unusually for the area, **KLEVE** is built on hills, dominated by a cliff (which gives the town its name) crowned by the **Schwanenburg** (Swan Castle), which is closely associated with the legend of Lohengrin, Knight of the Holy Grail. It was the seat of the once-powerful local dukes, whose dynastic aspirations reached a climax in 1539 with the marriage of Anne of Cleves to King Henry VIII of England – only to end in humiliation the following year. The town's frontier position made it a prime target for aerial bombardment during World War II, and all that remains of the old city are the main public buildings. These have lost much of their soul through heavy restoration, though a fine Baroque park and some notable works of art compensate. Kleve is linked to the commercial port of Emmerich, on the opposite bank of the Rhine, by the longest **suspension bridge** in Germany, an effortless structure spanning some 1300m.

The town

The present **Schwanenburg** dates from the fifteenth century, but has had so many subsequent alterations it's difficult to categorize its style. Nowadays, it serves as law courts and local government offices, but you can ascend the **tower** (April–Sept daily 11am–5pm; Nov–March Sat & Sun only same times; DM2), which also contains a small **Geologisches Museum**, for extensive views. Immediately opposite, the former stables house the town library, while behind is **St Mariae Himmelfahrt**, a large brick church similar to Kalkar's St Nicolai. In terms of artistic treasures, however, it's a poor relation, though its **high altar** was made by the star of the neighbouring town's school of woodcarving, Henrik Douverman. Little else remains of the old city, which has been transformed into a bland modern shopping centre.

Downhill at Kavarinerstr. 33 is **Haus Koekkoek** (Tues–Sun 10am–1pm & 2–5pm; DM2), the home of the Romantic artist Barent Koekkoek, many of whose works are on display. Also on show in the museum is a Book of Hours made in the workshop of the **Master of the Hours of Catherine of Cleves**, one of the most important illuminators of the late Middle Ages. The wonderful manuscript after which he's named became part of the transatlantic drain of works of art, and is now in the Pierpoint Morgan Library in New York. Another of the town's artists was **Joos van Cleve**, who settled in Antwerp, developing a style heavily indebted to the Italian Renaissance, but modified by a northern European brittleness. A *Male Portrait* by him has been placed on loan here by the federal government in order that his work may once more be seen in the place of his birth.

About 1km to the west via the street named after it is the **Tiergarten**, a terraced garden, laid out in 1656 in the Italian style by order of Johann Moritz of Nassau-Siegen, the erstwhile governor of Brazil. The garden features a rotunda, an amphitheatre, a canal and, as the centrepiece, a statue of Pallas Athenae by the Amsterdam sculptor, Artus Quellin. This is a copy, the original having been moved for preservation reasons to the nearby **Museum Kurhaus** (Tues–Sun 10am–6pm; DM6). Occupying the long-redundant spa buidings, this new museum is otherwise almost entirely devoted to modern art. It contains an important collection of works by the sculptor Ewald Mataré, as well as some spectacular installations such as *Plaza* by the Spaniard Juan Muñoz, with its super-realistic figures of Chinamen.

Practicalities

Kleve's **Bahnhof**, a dead end on the branch line from Krefeld, is a short walk east of the centre. There's no **tourist office** as such, but leaflets are available during working hours from the Rathaus at the corner of Minoritenstrasse and Kavarinerstrasse.

There are two moderately priced **hotels** in the centre: *Pension Heiligers*, Turmstr. 53 (☎02821/72480; ④) and *Zur Post*, Hagsche Str. 44 (☎02821/24579; ⑤); the latter's Balkan restaurant offers exceptionally good value lunches. In the middle price range, there's *Heek*, Lindenallee 37 (☎02821/72630; ⑦), while the top address is *Cleve,* north of the centre at Tichelstr. 11 (☎02821/7170; ⑦) which has an expensive restaurant, *Lohengrin*, plus a more moderately priced bistro. Kleve's **youth hostel** makes an inexpensive base for touring the Lower Rhineland, and is the only one, apart from Kevelaer, in the area. It's a fair way out though, at the top of a hill at St Annaberg 2 (☎02821/23671; 🖪); take bus #57. The nearest **campsite** is at Wisseler See to the south (see p.518).

Apart from the hotel **restaurants** above, it's worth knowing about *Altes Landhaus zur Münze*, Tiergartenstr. 68, which has a beer garden overlooking the park.

THE RUHRGEBIET

The **Ruhrgebiet** is the most heavily industrialized region in Europe, a sprawling conurbation stretching almost unbroken for some 65km east to west, and up to 30km north to south, in the middle of which is the traditional boundary between the Northern Rhineland and Westphalia. It takes its name from the River Ruhr, which flows right through the region to its confluence with the Rhine, and owes its extraordinary development to fabulously rich mineral deposits, often located close to the surface. The constituent towns, most of which were little more than villages until last century, do their best to preserve some kind of identity, but, apart from the fact that it's hard to determine where one ends and the other begins, they're mostly very similar in feel. Though certain cities are associated with a particular product or service (**Essen** and **Mülheim** with steel, **Gelsenkirchen** with coal, **Duisburg** with its docks, **Dortmund** with beer, **Bochum** with cars), each has a broad economic mix with heavy industry providing the lead.

On the face of things, it might seem you'd have to be out of your mind to want to come here, yet, once allowances are made for their less salubrious aspects, Dortmund and Essen, at least, can be enjoyed just like any other historic city. There's also no doubt that, although recent years have brought many problems to the Ruhrgebiet, caused by the worldwide need to scale down old industries, there has also been a vast improvement in the region's physical appearance. Only a fraction of the mines and factories which formerly blotted the landscape now survive; the redundant plants have been removed, often to be replaced by parkland. Moreover, the prosperity brought by industry has funded a **vibrant cultural scene** – Bochum is one of Germany's leading centres for theatre, while there is a highly diverse selection of art museums spread across the cities of the region.

The Ruhrgebiet has played a crucial role in modern German (and hence, world) history. Industrialization came for the most part after the area had fallen under the control of Prussia, the great predatory power of the nineteenth century. Weapons manufactured in the Ruhr helped win the battles which led to German unification; they also featured strongly in the arms race which led to World War I. Most ominously of all, it's doubtful if Hitler would ever have gained a truly national foothold, let alone come to power, had he not received the financial backing of many of the area's captains of industry.

Duisburg

With **DUISBURG**, separated from Düsseldorf by just a few kilometres of open countyside, the Ruhrgebiet begins with a vengeance. Until the early nineteenth century, this small walled town of about 5000 inhabitants had changed little since the great geographer Gerhard Mercator worked there in the sixteenth century. The Industrial Revolution saw it expand out of all recognition with the production of coal, iron and steel. Above all, it developed as a harbour for cargo, thanks to its key location at the point where the Ruhr enters the Rhine. It still ranks as the world's largest inland port, although recent years have seen a movement towards a post-industrial economy, with the closure of all but one of the seven pits, and steel production highly modernized. The city centre has been tidied up and largely given over to pedestrians, and a green belt has been created.

The city

Duisburg has little in the way of general attractions. The medieval city has almost completely disappeared: the **Salvatorkirche**, a rather ordinary large Gothic church where Mercator is buried, is virtually the only reminder of time past. It's not a place you're likely to want to stay in for long, and the only reason for coming at all is if you're interested in the river port or the museums.

The harbour

One of the oddball attractions of Duisburg is to take a **harbour cruise**; these run from April to October and cost DM12 for one hour, DM15 for two. Be warned that the views are a world away from the legendary landscapes further up the Rhine: coal tips, scrap heaps, gaunt warehouses and belching chimneys straight out of a Lowry painting are the order of the day. The two main departure points are the Schwanentor near the Salvatorkirche in the city centre (11am, 1pm & 3pm), and the Schifferbörse in the heart of the docklands at Ruhrort (12.15pm & 2.15pm). Bookings can be made at the offices at Harry-Epstein-Platz 10 (☎0203/604 4445). As a supplement, you can visit the **Museum der Deutschen Binnenschiffahrt** (Museum of German Inland Navigation), which is due to re-open in 1998 in a converted Jugendstil swimming pool at Apostelstr. 84 in Ruhrort, with an open-air section featuring historic vessels moored in the adjacent Eisenbahnhafen.

The Kultur- und Stadthistorisches Museum

The **Kultur- und Stadthistorisches Museum** (Tues & Thurs–Sat 10am–5pm, Wed 10am–4pm, Sun 11am–5pm; DM3) on Johannes-Corputius-Platz, housed in a former mill and warehouse, is for the most part of average interest only, with the usual archeology and local history exhibits, including a series of models on how the city has developed. These are completely outclassed by the (German only) display on the work of **Gerhard Mercator**, born in Flanders of German stock, who settled in Duisburg in 1552 and remained there until his death 42 years later. His most enduring legacy is the Mercator projection, still in use in a modified form today in both sea and air transport. It enabled maps to be drawn accurately on a flat surface and meant sailors could steer a course by plotting straight lines, instead of continually resorting to the compass. He was a prolific cartographer – several of his maps are shown – and it's from one of his collections that the term "atlas" has passed into use. The most eye-catching items here are the terrestrial globe of 1541 and its celestial counterpart of ten years later, works of art as much as science, whose beauty can be attributed to Mercator's early training in Antwerp as an engraver.

The Wilhelm-Lehmbruck-Museum

Modern art enthusiasts should overlook Duisburg's shortcomings in order to visit the **Wilhelm-Lehmbruck-Museum** (Tues–Sat 11am–5pm, Sun 10am–6pm; DM6), Germany's premier collection of twentieth-century sculpture, situated in the Immanuel-Kant-Park. Its centrepiece is the legacy of the sculptor **Lehmbruck** himself, born to a Duisburg mining family, who committed suicide in 1919 at the age of 38. There are many examples here of his classically beautiful portrait busts, but it's his more ambitious compositions of elongated, writhing figures, such as *The Fallen One* (*Der Gestürzte*), *Mother and Child*, *Kneeling Woman* (*Kniende*) and *The Brooder* (*Sinnende*), which make a more lasting impression. There's also work by the most prestigious international sculptors of the century – Rodin, Barlach, Giacometti, Henry Moore, Archipenko, Marini, Lipchitz, Arp and Naum Gabo. An attractive feature is the way artists chiefly famous as painters are represented by their much rarer sculptures – the Fauvist **Derain** abandons his usual bright palette in *The Twin*; the Surrealists **Dalí** and **Magritte** provide two of the most memorable pieces in *Head of Dante* and *L'Avenir des Statues*; while their colleague **Max Ernst**'s *Un Ami Empressé* and *Objet Mobile* are shown alongside two of his canvases. The most spectacular exhibits include **Joseph Beuys**' *End of the Twentieth Century* and **Duane Hanson**'s *Vietnam War Piece*, a devastating attack on the folly of the conflict, with a horrifyingly real depiction of five American soldiers dead and dying in the mud. In contrast, there's the light-hearted *Das Märchenrelief* by **Jean Tinguely**, which needs to be set in motion for full effect; ask an attendant.

Practicalities

The **Hauptbahnhof** is at the eastern end of the city centre, reached from Immanuel-Kant-Park by Friedrich-Wilhelm-Strasse. Turning right from here is the beginning of Königstrasse, the main shopping street, where at no. 53 you'll find the **tourist office** (Mon–Fri 9am–6pm, Sat 10am–1pm; ☎0203/283 2189).

Hotel rooms in the centre are relatively expensive: lowest rates are at *Zum Buchenbaum*, Hohe Str. 14 (☎0203/22847; ④); *Haus am Kantpark*, Gallenkampstr. 6 (☎0203/282 2890; ⑤); *Kalkmann*, Mülheimer Str. 65 (☎0203/331942; ⑤); and *Goldener Hahn*, Hohe Str. 26a (☎0203/20060; ⑤). Best value of the more expensive alternatives is *Haus Friedrichs*, Neudorfer Str. 33–35 (☎0203/355737; ⑥). Plenty of cheaper accommodation can be found in the suburbs; *Hof von Holland*, Bergiusstr. 46 (☎0203/81824; ③) in Ruhrort is worth trying. The **youth hostel**, Kalkweg 148 (☎0203/724164; ✿), is in the suburb of Wedau, near the recreation parks; take bus #934, #943 or #944.

The city's best **restaurants** are *Rôtisserie Laterne*, Mülheimer Str. 38, and the restaurant in the *Mercatorhalle* on König-Heinrich-Platz. For more moderately priced fare, try one of the new *Hausbrauereien*: *Brauhaus Schlacht 4/8*, which occupies a converted bank at Düsseldorfer Str. 21, or *Webster*, just north of Immanuel-Kant-Park at Dellplatz 13. Elsewhere, the obvious beer to sample is the locally produced *König Pils*, made in the largest brewery in Germany still in private hands. Concerts by the *Duisburger Sinfoniker*, among others, are held in the *Mercatorhalle* (☎0203/305050), while high-class **opera** and **drama** feature at the *Theater der Stadt Duisburg*, Neckarstr. 1 (☎0203/300 9100). The new *Musical Theater*, Plessingstr. 20 (☎0203/54444) hosts blockbuster musicals.

Essen

ESSEN is the largest city of the Ruhrgebiet, and the fifth in Germany, a sprawling conglomeration of some 700,000 people. For centuries it was a small town under the control of its convent's abbesses, but it sprang to prominence as the steel metropolis in the industrialization process last century, being effectively run by the most powerful of all

Germany's commercial dynasties, the **Krupp** family. Essen is proud of its heritage, boasting northern Europe's oldest parish church, largest synagogue and tallest town hall; indeed, the city's publicity manages to make it sound a very enticing destination. While that's a somewhat exaggerated claim, Essen does nevertheless have a handful of worthwhile attractions – it's one Ruhr city that definitely merits a day or more of anybody's time.

The city centre

The centre of Essen consists largely of an enormous shopping precinct. At the northeastern end are two dominant features of which the tourist office is wildly proud, though in truth neither is much of an asset. The domed **Alte Synagoge** (Tues–Sun 10am–6pm; free) is a neo-Moorish monstrosity from the early twentieth century, remarkable mainly for having outlasted the Third Reich; it now houses a documentary centre on the suffering of the Jews under the Nazis. The other building, the **Rathaus**, a 1970s skyscraper, doesn't rate as one of the gems of modern architecture either.

The Münster

In this setting, the **Münster** (or **Dom**) seems rather incongruous. A ninth-century foundation, it functioned as a collegiate church for aristocratic women until the Reformation. Since 1958, it has been the cathedral of a new diocese centred on the Ruhr. The west end is an eccentric tripartite eleventh-century structure apparently modelled on the Dom at Aachen; the rest of what must have been a magnificent building was destroyed by fire and replaced by a Gothic hall church. A stupendous collection of **treasures** by Ottonian craftsmen nonetheless makes the Münster a place of outstanding interest. Most prominent of these is the **Golden Madonna** of 965, the first known work of its kind. Housed in its own locked chapel beside the entrance to the crypt, it's highly venerated – at least as many people come to see it for devotional as for aesthetic reasons.

Also in the church is a large seven-branched candelabrum from about 1000, but the other star pieces are all in the **Schatzkammer**, housed in rooms off the south transept (Tues–Sun 10am–5pm; DM2). Here are four dazzling **processional crosses** of the tenth and eleventh centuries; a gospel book cover with scenes carved in ivory; the crown of Otto III; and many other priceless items. Joined to the front of the Münster by means of an atrium is the **Johanniskirche**, a miniature Gothic baptismal church containing a double-sided altarpiece by Barthel Bruyn; whether you see the Christmas or Easter scenes depends on the time of year.

Between the Münster and the Hauptbahnhof, on the second floor of Rathenaustr. 2, is the **Deutsches-Plakat-Museum** (Tues–Sun noon–8pm; DM2), a vast collection of artistic posters.

South of the centre

The main museum complex is at Goethestr. 41; to reach it, take Kruppstrasse westwards at the back of the Hauptbahnhof, turn left at Bismarckplatz into Bismarckstrasse and continue straight ahead. Here are two separate collections – the **Ruhrlandmuseum** and the **Museum Folkwang** (Tues, Wed & Fri–Sun 10am–6pm; Thurs 10am–9pm; combined ticket DM5). The former has the usual local displays, with geology on the ground floor, customs, folklore and industries upstairs. Far more enticing is the Folkwang Museum, one of Germany's top galleries of nineteenth- and twentieth-century art. Two rooms are devoted to the French Impressionists and their followers, including versions of **Monet's** favourite subjects, *Rouen Cathedral* and *Water Lilies*; an outstanding **Manet** *Fauré as Hamlet*; and four good examples each of **Gauguin** and **van Gogh**. In the German section, two works by **Friedrich** stand out among the Romantics, while there are examples of all the main figures of the present century, with **Nolde**, **Rohlfs** and **Kirchner** being particularly well represented; Kirchner's *Three Women in the Street* ranks as one of the key paintings in the development of the Expressionist movement. Unfortunately, restoration work means that none of these paintings is likely to be on show again until the end of 1998; in the meantime, the avant-garde section can be viewed.

Further south lies a surprising green belt. This begins with the **Gruga Park** (April–Sept 8am–midnight; Oct–March 9am–dusk; DM4), which incorporates the Botanical Gardens and large recreation areas. Beyond are extensive forests on both sides of the **Baldeneysee**, a long, narrow reservoir formed out of the River Ruhr. It's a popular leisure centre in summer, with watersports and walking trails. In this area are the grounds of the **Villa Hügel**, built for the **Krupp** family between 1868 and 1872, and serving as their home until 1945. You have to buy a ticket at the entrance to the park, just behind the S-Bahn station; it covers admission to both houses (Tues–Sun 10am–6pm; DM1.50). This idyllic setting gives little clue to the significance of the family, who personify many of the tragedies of modern German history, their genius for both engineering and organization being channelled into the most destructive of ends.

The smaller of the houses has a Technicolor PR-type presentation of the achievements of the corporation; upstairs, the family history of the Krupps is described, with the darker episodes carefully glossed over. In the large house, to which it's linked by a pavilion, you can wander at leisure around some of the forbidding, high-ceilinged, wood-panelled rooms, hung with tapestries and portraits of the leading lights of the day, including the Kaisers, who were close friends. Every so often (generally June–Oct in even-numbered years) there's a blockbuster international **loan exhibition** on a major artistic theme.

THE KRUPP DYNASTY

The industrialist **Alfred Krupp** (1812–87) brought the dynasty to national prominence 250 years after his ancestors had established themselves as Essen's foremost family. He was in some respects a model employer, pioneering sick pay, free medical treatment, pensions and retirement homes for his workers. On the other hand, he also had a paranoid obsession for inventing ever more deadly weapons; he has appropriately been dubbed "the father of modern warfare" and his field guns were largely responsible for Prussia's victory over France in 1871 which sealed the unity of Germany. His son Fritz gave a hard business edge to this policy, developing an unrelenting cycle of inventing new offensive weapons, followed by defences against them, only to make these superfluous by the creation of even more powerful means of attack. These were sold to all and sundry in the arms race which reached its inevitable conclusion in World War I, and ensured international honours and fabulous riches for the family to offset the disappointment of German defeat. The next head of the clan, Gustav Krupp von Bohlen, provided Hitler with essential funding; he and his son Alfried were also enthusiastic participators in the Holocaust, making extensive use of concentration camp labour in producing new weapons for the Nazi onslaught on world civilization. Both were sentenced as war criminals at Nürnberg, but the Americans later took pity, and Alfried once more assumed command of an organization which continued to grow spectacularly, with his own personal fortune estimated at one thousand million dollars. Eventually he stretched his interests too far; the family lost control of their empire in 1967, but their name lives on in the corporation which succeeded it. In 1997, this merged with its longtime bitter rival, Thyssen.

Werden

South of Hügel and connected by S-Bahn lies **WERDEN**, officially a suburb of Essen but still preserving its small-town atmosphere. It's built round the **Abteikirche St Liudger**, one of the last of the great series of Romanesque basilicas in the Rhineland, dating from the end of the twelfth century. The exterior is especially impressive, with its massive westwork and central octagon, while an oddity is that the crypt, where St Liudger is buried, is an extension of the chancel, rather than being its lower storey. In a building behind the church is the **Schatzkammer** (Tues–Sun 10am–noon & 3–5pm; DM2) containing many precious items, such as a fifth-century pyx, a ninth-century chalice, a bronze Romanesque crucifix and fragments of the saint's sarcophagus. Along Heckstrasse is the **Luciuskirche**, a daughter church of the abbey, but an even older building which is claimed as the earliest parish church in northern Europe still in existence. It's been restored to its original and simple tenth-century form.

Practicalities

Essen's **Hauptbahnhof** is situated bang in the city centre, only a couple of blocks south of the Münster. The **tourist office** (Mon–Fri 9am–5.30pm, Sat 10am–1pm; ☎235427 or 810 6081) is at Am Hauptbahnhof 2. **Mitfahrzentrale** is at Heinickestr. 33 (☎232423).

Essen's **public transport** system is comprehensive, embracing buses, trams (some of which become the U-Bahn for part of their route) and the S-Bahn. Given the size of the place, a 24-hour ticket can be a good investment as it doesn't take many journeys to cover the DM10 price.

Accommodation

The **youth hostel** (☎491163; ☎) is in Werden, at Pastoratsberg 2, a long way from the centre, but in a delightful location in the woods. To reach it, take the road passing uphill directly in front of the abbey, and carry straight on; it lies well above the houses. Also in Werden, but on the opposite side of the river near the S-Bahn station, is one of the three **campsites** (☎492978). The others aren't far away, being situated side by side on the south shore of the Baldeneysee in Fischlaken. A wide range of **hotels** can be found in all but the cheapest categories.

HOTELS

Europa, Hindenburgstr. 35 (☎232041, fax 232656). Mid-range hotel in the southwest of the city centre. ⑦

Handelshof, Am Hauptbahnhof 2 (☎17080, fax 170 8173). Fine old station hotel taken over and renovated by the *Mövenpick* chain. Its restaurant is quite reasonably priced. ⑨

Kessing, Hachestr. 30 (☎239988. fax 230289). Moderately priced, in a handy location just west of the Hauptbahnhof. ⑤

Lindenhof, Logenstr. 18 (☎233031, fax 234308). Budget place on the west side of the centre. ⑤

Luise, Dreilindenstr. 96 (☎239253, fax 200219). South of the centre, close to the Saalbau and not far from the Museum Folkwang. ⑤

Parkhaus Hügel, Freiherr-vom-Stein-Str. 209 (☎471091, fax 444207). Located right by Villa Hügel and boasting one of the very best restaurants in Essen. ⑦

Schloss Hugenpoet, August-Thyssen-Str. 51 (☎02054/12040, fax 02054/120450). This is, without doubt, the best place to stay in Essen, a magnificent *Wasserschloss* in the suburb of Kettwig immediately south of Werden, 11km from the city centre. Its restaurant has an extensive wine list. ⑨

Zum Deutschen Haus, Kastanienallee 16 (☎232989, fax 230692). In the northern part of the centre, with some of the least expensive rooms in the city. ④

Eating and drinking

Many of Essen's best **restaurants** are in the luxury hotels, but there are a few others worth seeking out.

Bahnhof Süd, Rellinghauser Str. 175. Located south of the city centre, this is a favourite with the student crowd. Has a beer garden in the summer and a reasonably priced menu.

Brauhaus Graf Beust, Kastanienallee 95. One of a small chain of *Hausbrauereien* in the Ruhrgebiet. Its standard products are the blond *Gruben Gold* and *Mulvany's*, an Irish-style stout, but it brews other beers seasonally and also offers wholesome German fare.

Franziskus Keller, I.-Weber-Str. 6. Crowded pub which has cheap daily specials. Evenings only.

Kockshusen, Pilgrimsteig 51. Located in the southeastern section suburb of Rellinghausen, this outstanding restaurant occupies a half-timbered building from the seventeenth century, and has a garden terrace.

La Fontaine, III Hagen 47. Among the best of the city's Italian restaurants, located just west of Münsterplatz.

Rüttenscheider Hausbrauerei, Girardetstr. 2. Another boutique brewery with restaurant, situated in the *Girardetshaus*, not far from the Gruga Park.

Entertainment

Pop concerts, musicals and other large-scale shows are held at the *Grugahalle*, at the northern end of the park at Norbertstr. 2 (☎724 4290). Twice or thrice a week, **live music** and **discos** feature at *Zeche Carl*, Wilhelm-Nieswandt-Allee 100, in the northern suburb of Altenessen. **Classical music** is performed in both the *Villa Hügel* (☎188 4837) and the *Saalbau*, south of the Hauptbahnhof at Huyssenallee 53 (☎221866); the *Essener Philharmonie* regularly perform at the latter. The *Aalto-Theater* behind at Rolandstr. 10 (☎81220) hosts opera and dance. **Drama** is performed at the *Grillo-Theater* on Theaterplatz (☎812 2200), variety at the *GOP Varieté-Theater*, Tottstr. 30 (☎247 9393), cabaret at *Satiricon* in the *Girardethaus*, Girardetstr. 2 (☎797539), block-buster musicals at the *Colosseum*, Altendorfer Sr. 1 (☎0180 5444) and celebrity shows at the *Theater in Rathaus* on Porscheplatz (☎245555).

Bochum

BOCHUM lies right at the heart of the Ruhrgebiet, sandwiched between the two giants of Essen and Dortmund, and marks the transition to the part of the area which is traditionally Westphalian. It boasts two of the best specialist **technical museums** on the achievements of Germany industry, but if these don't appeal, there's little else to justify a visit here, other than the remarkably vibrant **theatres**, which manage an improbable rivalry to the likes of Berlin and Munich. A pleasant if anonymous shopping area forms the centre, devoid of any sense of history bar the rather ghostly reminder provided by the **Propsteikirche**, a Gothic hall church now standing forlornly in its own grounds. In spite of the traditions in heavy industry, the leading employer is now the car plant of Opel, General Motors' European subsidiary.

The city

The 60m-high winding tower of the **Deutsches Bergbaumuseum** (German Mining Museum; Tues–Fri 8.30am–5.30pm, Sat & Sun 10am–4pm; DM6) is a dominant feature of the skyline. Established in 1930, this legitimately claims to be the most important collection of its kind in the world, and is both exhaustive and inventive in scope. Budget at least two hours for a visit, as the ticket includes a 45-minute conducted tour (Tues–Fri hourly departures, German only) around the demonstration pit in the bowels of the earth immediately below. It costs DM2 to ascend the tower.

Bochum's other main attraction is the **Eisenbahnmuseum** (Rail Museum; Wed & Fri 10am–5pm, Sun 10am–12.45pm; DM5.50), run by the national preservation society. Take the S-Bahn to Dalhausen, and turn left at the exit; it's then about 1.5km ahead. Some of the trains are in open yards, but most are grouped in two sheds. The first contains the locomotives themselves, with some real beauties, especially the oldest item, an imperious black and red monster from the 1920s. In the second hall are the passenger carriages, the comforts of the first class contrasting strongly with the hard benches in the third. Also here is an example of Deutsche Bundesbahn's most singular contribution to transport history, the *Schiene-Strasse-Bus*, a bizarre hybrid which looks like a bus but is also equipped with wheels for travelling along rails; it was widely used in forest areas until the late 1960s.

The **Museum Bochum** (Tues & Thurs–Sat 11am–5pm, Wed 11am–8pm, Sun 11am–6pm; DM5) is just round the corner from the Bergbaumuseum on Kortumstrasse. The displays here, mounted in a series of changing exhibitions, are devoted to post-1945 art only. There's a branch at **Wasserburg Kemnade**, a moated castle at the southeastern suburb of Hattingen (May–Oct Tues 9am–3pm, Wed–Fri 1–7pm, Sat & Sun 11am–6pm; Nov–April Wed–Fri 11am–5pm, Sat & Sun 10am–5pm; free). Although heavily restored, a couple of ornate chimneypieces remain, and there's a large collection of historical musical instruments. Adjacent is the **Bauernhausmuseum** (Farmhouse Museum) (same times, but May–Oct only; free).

Between here and the centre are the eye-catching futuristic buildings of the **Ruhr-Universität**, the largest of several institutions for technical education in the region. The **Botanischer Garten** is situated on the southern side (daily April–Sept 9am–6pm; Oct–March 9am–4pm; free), and the **Universitätsmuseum**, housed under the library (Tues–Fri noon–3pm, Sat & Sun 10am–6pm; free), has a collection of antiques, notably glass and sculptures, and some modern art.

Practicalities

Bochum's **Hauptbahnhof** is at the eastern end of the centre and the **tourist office** (Mon–Fri 9am–5.30pm, Sat 10am–1pm; ☎0234/13031) is in the front part of the station building. There's a **Mitfahrzentrale** office at Ferdinandstr. 20 (☎0234/37794).

Hotels with a central location include *Wiesmann*, Castroper Str. 191 (☎0234/591065; ④); *Sandkühler*, Flurstr. 1 (☎0234/581588; ④); *Oberste-Ufer*, Nordring 30 (☎0234/16712; ④); and *Plaza*, Hellweg 20 (☎0234/13085; ⑤). Bochum has no youth hostel, but those in Essen and Hagen are both within easy commuting range. The nearest **campsite** is by the north bank of the Ruhr in Hattingen (☎02324/80038).

There are abundant places to **eat** and **drink** in the city centre. Two local beers to try are *Vest* and *Fiege*; the *Stammhaus* of the latter brewery is at Bongardstr. 23, and is equally renowned for its food. *Mutter Wittig*, Bongardstr. 35, is another excellent traditional *Gaststätte*, while two establishments with a special ambience are *Altes Brauhaus Rietkökotter*, in a fine sixteenth-century house at Grosse Beckstr. 7, and *Luisenhof*, a Jugendstil bistro with beer garden at Luisenstr 14. *Oblomov*, Kurt-Schumacher-Platz 19, does cheap meals, while *Taufenbach*, Gerberstr. 19, is a *Hausbrauerei* which sometimes features live music. At Wasserburg Kemnade, there's a good restaurant in the castle itself.

Entertainment

Bochum has a high reputation for **theatre** with a renowned repertory company based at the *Schauspielhaus*, Königsallee 15 (☎0234/333142). Puppet shows and concerts by the *Bochumer Symphoniker*, a body of good provincial standing, are also held at this venue. The *Starlighthalle* on Stadionring (☎0234/507070) hosts large-scale spectaculars.

Tarm-Center, Rombacher Hütte 6–8 (☎0234/459070), a huge **disco** with nightly laser shows, is always packed, as is *Kulturzentrum Zeche*, Prinz-Regent-Str. 50 (☎0234/72003), which has weekly discos and regular rock, pop and jazz concerts. *Bahnhof Langendreer* at the extreme east end of town, is an alternative arts centre featuring music, theatre, cabaret and cinema. The city's main **festival** is *Bochum Total* in the second week of July.

Dortmund

The name of **DORTMUND** immediately brings **beer** to mind – it was first granted brewing rights in 1293, and even jealous rivals are forced to admit it's the national drink's number one city. Six top breweries are based here – *Kronen, Union, Ritter, Thier, Stifts* and *Actien* (*DAB*). Their chimneys form a distinctive feature of the skyline; those of *Union* are right in the centre. In all, six million hectolitres are produced annually, a total surpassed in world terms only by Milwaukee. Much of it is for export, which has led to the word being used to categorize certain types of beer.

Alone among Ruhr cities, Dortmund, now with a population of over 600,000, was important in the Middle Ages when it was an active member of the Hanseatic League. This helps give it a rounded and distinctive character which all its neighbours somehow lack. Provided you're prepared to overlook the obvious limitations of a place where wartime bombs wreaked horrendous damage and where heavy industry is prominent, it's an interesting and enjoyable city in which to spend a day or two.

> The **telephone code** for Dortmund is ☎0231

The city centre

The inner ring road, whose sections all bear the suffix "wall", follows the line of the vanished thirteenth-century fortifications and thus defines the perimeter of the medieval city. Only a fraction of this area was left standing after the war, and not a single secular building from the Hansa days remains. The four civic churches, however, survived the onslaught in a battered condition, and a painstaking restoration programme which lasted into the 1980s has returned them to their former state. Although they're now marooned in a modern shopping centre, the layout of the old streets and squares has been followed. None of the churches is architecturally outstanding, but their assem-

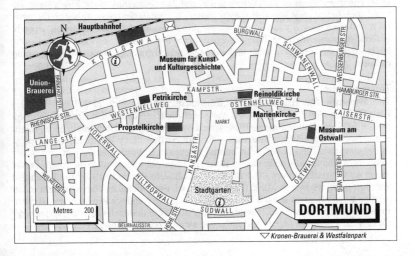

▽ *Kronen-Brauerei & Westfalenpark*

blage of Gothic art treasures justifies a visit to the city – if the beer isn't a sufficient draw.

The Petrikirche and the Propsteikirche

Directly facing the Hauptbahnhof is the **Petrikirche** (Tues–Fri 2–7pm, Sat 11am–2pm), boasting a colossal **Antwerp altar** from around 1520, which opens out to show expressively carved scenes of the Passion and Legend of the Cross, featuring no fewer than 633 separate figures. These can be seen between autumn and Whit; during the summer they're hidden behind the more modest painted section narrating the earlier part of Christ's life. A short walk down the central axis of Westenhellweg is the **Propsteikirche**, the one church retained by the Catholics when Dortmund embraced the Reformation. On the high altar is a colourful and crowded triptych from about 1490 by the Westphalian painter **Derick Baegert**, aided by his son **Jan**. Straddling the scenes of *The Holy Kinship*, *The Crucifixion* and *The Adoration of the Magi* is a view of a medieval town proudly girt with numerous towers and spires – the earliest-known depiction of Dortmund, and a poignant memorial to its long-lost splendours.

The Reinoldikirche and the Marienkirche

Continuing across Hansastrasse, Ostenhellweg leads to a large square overshadowed by the **Reinoldikirche**, named after the city's patron saint who was stoned to death in Cologne, whereupon his coffin is supposed to have rolled all the way to Dortmund under its own steam. He's depicted as a young knight in a superb fourteenth-century wooden statue guarding the entrance to the chancel; the corresponding but later figure of a richly attired emperor is almost certainly Charlemagne. Unfortunately the choir area is fenced off, so you can only admire its abundant furnishings at a distance.

Immediately opposite is the **Marienkirche**, the oldest of the churches, with a nave which is still largely Romanesque (Tues–Fri 10am–noon & 2–4pm, Sat 10am–1pm). Its two masterpieces of International Gothic painting are the city's finest works of art. The high altar triptych dates from around 1420 and is by **Conrad von Soest**, a Dortmund citizen in spite of his name, and as endearing a painter as Germany ever produced. These panels of *The Nativity*, *The Dormition of the Virgin* and *The Adoration of the Magi* show the uniquely graceful and delicate Soft Style (see "Painting and Graphics" in *Contexts*) at its greatest, even though all were truncated in order to fit into a Baroque altar. The inner wings of *The Annunciation* and *The Coronation of the Virgin* have suffered such heavy paint loss that they're generally kept under cover, although the caretaker will open them if you ask. In the nave, the *Berswordt Altar*, a Crucifixion triptych, is about 25 years earlier, but has survived in much better shape. See also the late Gothic stalls – their irreverent carvings include, appropriately enough, a man downing a mug of beer.

The museums

The **Museum für Kunst und Kulturgeschichte** (Museum of Art and Cultural History; Tues–Sun 10am–5pm; DM4), very near the Hauptbahnhof at Hansastr. 3, occupies an Art Deco building of the 1920s which was formerly a savings bank. Its highlight is a series of reassembled **interiors** – an eighteenth-century Westphalian pharmacy, the *Fliesensaal* (Tiled Room) with hunting scenes in Delft tiles, and a panelled music room from a bourgeois residence in Bremen. The most important of the rooms is *Der Raum als Gesamtkunstwerk* (The Room as a Complete Work of Art) by the Jugendstil architect-designer Joseph Maria Olbrich, in which every detail has been thought out in relation to its effect on the whole. Among the notable paintings is a stunning, sombre **Friedrich**, *Night on the Sea*. The archeology display is dominated by the *Dortmunder Goldschatz*, a hoard of fourth- and fifth-century gold coins found locally.

On the inner ring road is the **Museum am Ostwall** (Tues–Sun 10am–5pm; DM4), devoted to the municipal collection of modern art, with changing exhibitions on the ground floor. Upstairs is a comprehensive display of Expressionism, dominated by what's arguably **August Macke**'s masterpiece, *Grosser Zoologischer Garten*, which experiments with the new Cubist forms in an anachronistic triptych format. Experimental sculpture includes several works by **Jospeh Beuys**, but the most eye-catching is **Wolf Vostell**'s *Thermo-Elektronischer Kaugummi* of 1970. Occupying a whole gallery, this has 13,000 forks and spoons grouped behind two barbed wire fences, and – believe it or not – features 5000 pieces of chewing gum.

The **Mahn- und Gedenkstätte Steinwache** (Tues–Sun 10am–5pm; free), a short walk north of the Hauptbahnhof at Steinstr. 50, is a new museum housed in a building formerly used as a prison by the Gestapo. Between 1933 and 1945, thirty thousand opponents of the Nazi regime were detained here. Using original documents, photographs, personal effects and taped interviews, the exhibition comprehensively documents the rise of National Socialism, the resistance to it, and the brutal persecution of its opponents. Some of the rooms have been returned to their former state as prison cells, giving an added edge to the overall atmosphere.

Practicalities

Dortmund's **tourist office** (Mon–Fri 9am–6pm, Sat 9am–1pm; ☎502 5666) stands opposite the Hauptbahnhof at Königswall 20. There's a **Mitfahrzentrale** office at Grüne Str. 3 (☎822067).

Accommodation

There's a **campsite** at Syburger Dorfstr. 69 (☎774374) not far from the *Spielbank Hohensburg* casino; take bus #444. **Hotels** in every category can be found in the city centre.

Atlanta, Ostenhellweg 51 (☎557 0750, fax 586 0054). Moderately priced hotel on one of the main streets of the pedestrian precinct. ④

Carlton, Lütge-Brückstr. 5–7 (☎528030, fax 525020). Basic but fully acceptable budget hotel just a short walk from the Hauptbahnhof. ④

Cläre-Fritz, Reinoldstr. 6 (☎571523, fax 579623). Small pension facing the Reinoldikirche. ④

El Molino, Stiftstr. 5 (☎553130). Spanish restaurant-cum-hotel in a good central location. ④

Römischer Kaiser, Olpe 2 (☎543200, fax 574354). Part of the *Holiday Inn* chain, this is one of the best upmarket choices. Has a well-regarded restaurant offering budget menus. ⑨

Stadthotel Dortmund, Reinoldstr. 14 (☎571000, fax 577194). The best value of the city's medium-range hotels. ⑥

Eating and drinking

Inevitably, the **beer halls** are the focus for eating and drinking, and the city centre is ideal for a pub crawl. There's no need to move very far to sample the products of all the different breweries and the Markt makes the obvious place to begin.

Bass, Münsterstr. 95. Jazz bar with regular live performances. Also serves food, including many vegetarian options, and has a small beer garden. Closed Sat & Sun.

Brauhaus Kronen am Markt, Betenstr. 1. *Kronen* have had an uninterrupted presence on this spot since 1430, an even longer pedigree than the *Hofbräuhaus* in Munich. It currently has a *Hausbrauerei* which produces *Wenkers Utrüb*, a blond ale top-fermented with plenty of yeast sediment left in.

Brinkhoffs No. 1, Alter Markt. A flagship *Gaststätte* for the giant *Union* brewery, whose beers are milder, sweeter and maltier than those of its competitors.

Café Hemmer, Ostenhellweg 62. If hardly typical for Dortmund, this genteel salon is a good place for the archetypally German fare of *Kaffee und Kuchen*.

FZW, Neuer Graben 167. *Szene* bar with regular discos and live rock.

Holzknecht, Hohe Str. 5. Offers Swabian as well as Westphalian dishes, and *Stifts* beer.

Hövels Hausbrauerei, Hoher Wall 5. An offshoot of the *Thier* brewery, the main product line here is the deceptively named *Bitterbier*, a malty bronze-coloured brew; various seasonal beers are also produced. There's the bonus of a beer garden, while the food on offer is among the best in the city.

Pfefferkorn, Hoher Wall 38. Fine old *Gaststätte* of the *Union* brewery.

Zum Alten Markt, Alter Markt 3. Traditional Westphalian cooking and the full range of *Thier* beers, which include a very dry *Pils* as well as a typical *Export*.

Entertainment

Theatres include the *Schauspielhaus* and its *Studio* on Hiltropwall (☎163041), while the *Opernhaus* is at Platz der Alten Synagoge (☎163041). The huge *Westfalenhalle* (☎120 4666) southwest of the centre is used for **sports** and big shows such as **jazz** and **pop** concerts. *Live Station*, Am Hauptbahnhof (☎161783) presents **discos** and live music from Fridays to Sundays, while *Luna Varieté und Theater*, Harkortstr. 57a (☎773196) in the suburb of Hombruch, is the place for cabaret.

Hagen

Like nearby Wuppertal, **HAGEN** would be a characterless large town were it not for an imaginative and rather brilliant act of initiative around the turn of the present century. **Karl Ernst Osthaus**, a local industrialist and patron of the arts, was instrumental in persuading a group of talented international designers in the Art Nouveau style to come to Hagen. Prominent among them were the architects Peter Behrens of Hamburg, Henry van de Velde from Belgium and Mathiew Lauweriks from Holland, along with another Dutchman, the decorator Johan Thorn-Prikker. The artists' colony thus founded was a fitting successor to the one in Darmstadt, Germany's other main centre of **Jugendstil**, to which Behrens had also belonged. Nor were other styles shunned: the Expressionist painter Christian Rohlfs was summoned and stayed until he died in 1938, seventeen years after Osthaus' own premature death put an end to his ambitious plans for a complete garden city.

The town

Your first glimpse of Hagen's legacy comes at the **Hauptbahnhof**. Illuminating the exit is a large stained-glass window by Thorn-Prikker, an allegory entitled *The Obeisance of the Crafts before the Artist*. From the square in front, turn right and then follow Elberfelder Strasse straight ahead, eventually taking any of the small side streets to the right into the parallel Hochstrasse, where you'll find the **Karl-Ernst-Osthaus-Museum** (Tues, Wed & Fri–Sun 11am–6pm, Thurs 11am–8pm; free). The exterior is in the stolid end-of-century Wilhelmine style, but the interior, created a few years later by van de Velde, has all the sense of fantasy and romance characteristic of the best Art Nouveau. Originally this contained Osthaus' private art collection, the Folkwang Museum, which was hung in an unconventional thematic manner. After his death, it was sold *en bloc* by his heirs to the city of Essen, where it can still be seen. Since the acquisition of the building by the Hagen authorities in 1945, belated attempts have been made to re-create the original effect by acquiring works in line with Osthaus' tastes. There's a good representation of Expressionism and other twentieth-century German art, with several examples of **Rohlfs**, whose studio was housed here, along with works by **Macke** (*Women in Front of a Hat Shop*), **Dix** (the erotic *Artist and Muse*), **Kokoschka** (*The Actor Sommarunga*), Kirchner, Nolde, Beckmann and Schmidt-Rottluff.

To the east of the centre, reached by bus #522, is the projected garden suburb of **Hohenhagen**, of which only an incomplete crescent known as **Stirnband** was built. The nearer side of this consists of a row of houses by Lauweriks, homogeneous in style but each given its own identity. Still in private ownership, they are undoubtedly the ultimate residence within the Ruhrgebiet. Fronting the other entrance to the crescent is **Haus Cuno** by Behrens, now an academy of music. On weekdays it's worth sticking your head round the door to see the impressive stairwell. The rest of this street really forms a processional way to the vast **Hohenhof**, designed as Osthaus' own residence by van de Velde. This is one of the great achievements of the Art Nouveau movement, a dream home if ever there was one, and a building which seems to change dramatically from every angle of vision. Now owned by the city, it's a cultural centre, but the interior is generally only accessible on Saturdays between 2pm and 6pm. Try to come then to see the intricacies of its decorations, which include furniture designed by its architect, stained-glass windows by Thorn-Prikker and a huge canvas, *The Elect*, by the Swiss **Ferdinand Hodler**.

Hagen's other main attraction is the **Freilichtmuseum** (March–Oct Tues–Sun 9am–6pm; Nov Tues–Sun 9am–4.30pm; DM7) south of the city in Selbecke; take bus #507. Laid out in the valley of the Mäckingerbach, this marks the point where the industrial Ruhrgebiet gives way to the rural Sauerland. There are some 65 traditional buildings, but it differs from other museums of the same type in that the emphasis is technical, rather than social or architectural. Horny-handed old sons of toil demonstrate all kinds of historical equipment, ranging from machinery for producing iron and steel, through printing and papermaking, spinning, weaving and dyeing, to baking and mustard production; it's possible to buy many of the products made here. There's also a windmill near the entrance but, as it's some distance from the other buildings, check first for the times when it's going to be put into action. Just to walk round the site takes quite a while, and you need to budget at least three hours for a visit – longer if you want to see all the crafts demonstrated.

Practicalities

Hagen's **tourist office** (Mon–Thurs 8am–5pm, Fri 8am–1pm; ☎02331/207 3383) is in the Rathaus on Friedrich-Ebert-Platz. Given the fact that the sights of interest are so far apart, a day ticket on the **public transport** system, costing DM10, is worth considering. There's a **Mitfahrzentrale** office at Södingstr. 3 (☎02331/337555).

Within a stone's throw of the Hauptbahnhof are a couple of cheap **hotels**: *Bürgerkrug*, Werdestr. 2–4 (☎02331/26779; ②); and *Targan*, Hugo-Preuss-Str. 5 (☎02331/16863; ③). More upmarket are *Lex*, Elberfelder Str. 71 (☎02331/32030; ⑥); *Deutsches Haus*, Bahnhofstr. 35 (☎02331/210 5153; ⑦); *Central*, Dahlenkampstr. 2 (☎02331/16302; ⑦); and *Queens*, Wasserloses Tal 4 (☎02331/3910; ⑧).

The **youth hostel** is at Eppenhauser Str. 65a (☎02331/50254; ❷), just a few minutes' from Stirnband and reached by bus #522 or #523. Although there's no **campsite** within the city boundaries, the one at Syburg (see p.529) is only a few kilometres away, reached by bus #544.

The best **restaurant** is in the *Queens* hotel; cheaper alternatives are the *Ratskeller* on Friedrich-Ebert-Platz, and *Alt-Nürnberg*, Elbersufer 10. **Concerts** are held at the *Stadthalle* on Wasserloses Tal (☎02331/326513), while **drama**, **opera** and **ballet** all feature at the Jugenstil *Theater Hagen*, Elberfelder Str. 65 (☎02331/207 3218). For **live jazz**, go to *Tubakeller*, Hohenzollernstrasse 10; the pub above, *Spinne*, has a beer garden.

Recklinghausen

The northern part of the Ruhrgebiet, before the vast built-up area gives way to the open spaces of Münsterland, is known as the district of **Recklinghausen**, after its principal town. **RECKLINGHAUSEN** itself, though small-scale compared to the cities to the south, does its best to appear distinctive. Originally founded as a royal seat by Charlemagne, it was a Hanseatic city in the Middle Ages, dominated by blacksmiths and cloth merchants. There are no major surviving monuments, but you still get something of the feel of the old town amidst all the usual later accretions – certainly, there's more of a sense of continuous history here than is to be found anywhere else in the Ruhr.

The town centre

Streets in the centre still follow the old twisting and turning pattern and there are a number of half-timbered houses, some fragments of the city wall, and, as centrepiece, the **Petruskirche**, predominantly Gothic, but incorporating parts of its Romanesque predecessor as well as sundry modifications by subsequent builders. From the Baroque period, the **Engelsburg** on Augustinessenstrasse is a handsome mansion built round a courtyard. Round the corner on Geiststrasse is the **Gastkirche**, formerly an almshouse chapel, containing several striking altarpieces.

Recklinghausen's pride and joy, however, is its **Ikonmuseum** (Tues–Fri 10am–6pm, Sat & Sun 11am–5pm; DM5) at Am Kirchplatz beside the Petruskirche. This isn't just another example of the seemingly inexhaustible German capacity for creating museums on the most abstruse of subjects – it really is the finest collection of this simple yet haunting and powerful art form outside the Orthodox world. The star piece is the huge late sixteenth-century Russian *Calendar Icon of the Year*, a *tour de force* illustrating the main stories of the Bible, as well as portraying hundreds of saints, arranged according to their feast day. From the following century comes *The Credo*, executed using techniques reminiscent of Western manuscript illuminators, and a masterly *Enthroned Christ*, a signed work by the Cretan **Elias Moskos**. The earliest works, from the fifteenth-century Moscow and Novgorod schools, have perhaps the most overtly emotional appeal; among the finest are the symbolic *Christ the Unsleeping Eye* and *St Nicholas with Scenes from his Life*. In addition to over 400 icons displayed by subject, there are extensive collections on the decorative arts of the Orthodox and Coptic churches.

Practicalities

The **Hauptbahnhof** lies just to the east of the historic part of town. Recklinghausen has no **tourist office** as such, but you can pick up maps and leaflets at the Rathaus (☎02361/501551) during working hours; the museums also keep a stock.

The best budget **hotels** are *Kolpinghaus*, Herzogswall 38 (☎02361/22640; ③); and *Gasthof Albers*, Markt 3 (☎02361/23485; ⑤). If you've got more money to spend, head for *Barbarossa*, Löhrhof 8 (☎02361/25071; ⑦), or *Parkhotel Engelsburg*, Augustinessenstr. 10 (☎02361/2010; ⑧). Nearest **campsites** are at Haltern to the north – *Dülmener See*, (☎02594/2125), *Hoher Niemen* (☎02364/2511) and *Seegesellschaft Haltern* (☎02364/3360); the first two are open all year, the last April to September only.

For an animated **pub**, try *Hausbrauerei Boente*, Augustinessenstr. 4, where you can sample the products in a large beer garden. One of the best **restaurants** is *Altes Brauhaus*, just east of the centre at Dortmunder Str. 16.

Cultural life in Recklinghausen centres on the *Ruhrfestspiele*, a **festival** of concerts, plays, exhibitions and discussions held annually in May and June. The *Festspielhaus*, in the Stadtgarten to the west of the city centre, was opened in 1965 as the specially designed home for the festival.

WESTPHALIA

Westphalia (*Westfalen*) is named after one of the three main Saxon tribes, and by the early Middle Ages the term came to be used for all of Saxony west of the River Weser. Despite this long tradition as a definable part of Germany, it's never really been governed as a unit, and the boundaries have often been changed dramatically. The short-lived Kingdom of Westphalia, established by Napoleon for his brother Jérôme, consisted mostly of Hesse, while the present political division of the country has seen parts of the historic province transferred to Lower Saxony. Apart from the cities in the Ruhrgebiet which are traditionally Westphalian (including Dortmund, Recklinghausen, Gelsenkirchen, Hagen and Bochum), there are three distinct constituent parts – the fertile **Münsterland** plain to the north; the predominantly rural **Sauerland** and **Siegerland** to the south; and the depression to the east bounded by the vast stretch of the **Teutoburg Forest**. The last-named incorporates what was formerly one of the smallest states of the German Reich, the **Principality of Lippe**. Of the cities, the two largest, **Bielefeld** and **Münster**, could hardly be more different: the former is predominantly industrial whereas the latter is the epitome of middle-class prosperity. **Paderborn**, like Münster, is an important episcopal centre. However, many of the most memorable towns in the area – **Soest**, **Lemgo** and **Höxter** – are modest in size.

According to its tourist board, Westphalia is associated with "the solid and substantial things in life". In architecture, the characteristic features are moated castles, lofty hall churches and half-timbered farm buildings. Gastronomically, it's famous for hams, spit roasts, beer, schnapps and, above all, rye bread. Westphalia is an archetypal German province and a favourite holiday destination with the Germans themselves. In spite of a fair number of Britons visiting friends and family in the military bases, there's no more than a trickle of tourists from abroad.

Münster

Northern Westphalia is dominated by **MÜNSTER**, one of the most varied and enticing of the cities spread across the flat German plain. It has an unusually rich architectural

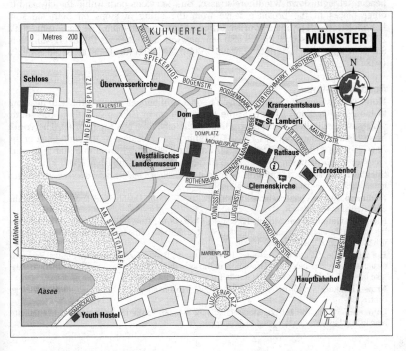

> The **telephone code** for Münster is 0251

heritage, including examples of all the main styles from Romanesque to Baroque. Industry has been confined to the peripheries, and the chic shops crowding the centre are an unabashed celebration of the affluent consumerism enjoyed by a population which is overwhelmingly middle-class. The University is among the largest in Germany; one consequence of this is that the city has come firmly under the rule of the bicycle. However, the dominant influence on Münster has been the Church, its very name – the equivalent of the English word "minster" – deriving from the evangelizing monastery of **St Liudger**, who was consecrated bishop in 805 as part of Charlemagne's policy of converting the Saxon tribes to Christianity. Apart from the years 1534–35 when it was taken over by the fanatical Anabaptist sect, it has remained intensely loyal to Roman Catholicism, even during the Third Reich, when the city's bishop, **Clemens August von Galen**, was one of the regime's most courageous and persistent opponents. In 1936, he organized a popular revolt which overturned an edict to remove crucifixes from school buildings – an apparently trivial incident, but one of the few occasions the Nazis gave in to domestic opponents. This defiance counted for nothing with the Allied bombing missions, which administered particularly brutal treatment on Münster, but the city recovered, adopting a much praised rebuilding programme.

Arrival and accommodation

The **Hauptbahnhof** is directly to the east of the city centre, which is reached by heading straight down Windthorststrasse. **Bus services** both within the city and to other places in the province leave from the string of stops on both sides of Bahnhofstrasse. The main **tourist office** (Mon–Fri 9am–6pm, Sat 9am–1pm; ☎492 2710) is at Klemensstr. 9; there's also a branch within the Rathaus (Mon–Fri 9am–5pm, Sat 9am–4pm, Sun 10am–1pm; ☎492 2724). **Mitfahrzentrale** is at Aegidiistr. 20a (☎19444).

Accommodation

Hotel rooms don't come cheap. If you're on a tight budget, you might like to head out to the concentration of hotels in the outlying town of Hiltrup directly to the south, which are generally less expensive than in the city; take bus #1, #6 or #9. The **youth hostel** is at Bismarckallee 31 (☎532470; ☎) in a good location by the right bank of the Aasee; buses #10 and #34 go closest. **Camping** is possible from mid-March to mid-October at Dorbaumstr. 35 (☎329312) in the northeastern suburb of Handorf.

Bockhorn, Bremer Str. 24 (☎65510). Somewhat old-fashioned budget hotel conveniently situated immediately to the rear of the Hauptbahnhof. ⑤

Feldmann, An der Clemenskirche 14 (☎43309, fax 414 4910). Quality hotel and restaurant at the eastern end of the Altstadt. ⑤

Haus von Guten Hirten, Mauritz Lindenweg 61 (☎37870, 374549). Church-run guesthouse offering some of the cheapest rooms in Münster. Situated 2km east of the Hauptbahnhof in the inner suburb of St Mauritz; bus #14 goes closest. ④

Hof zur Linde, Handorfer Werseufer 1 (☎32750, fax 328209). Classy hotel, part of the *Romantik* chain, in a seventeeth-century farmhouse in the suburb of Handorf, 7km northeast of the centre; take bus #10. It also has a top-class if rather pricey restaurant. ⑧

Krone, Hammer Str. 67 (☎ & fax 73868). Small, reasonably priced hotel just south of the city centre. ⑤

Lohmann, Mecklenbecker Str. 345 (☎71525, fax 714368). At the extreme southwest of the city, reached by bus #15, this is a good budget option. ③

Schloss Wilkinghege, Steinfurter Str. 374 (☎213045, fax 212898). Münster's top hotel occupies a sixteenth-century *Wasserschloss* in a landscaped park just off the B54 at the northwestern edge of the city. ⑨

Wienburg, Kanalstr 237 (☎29334, fax 294001). In a park 2km north of the Altstadt, reached by bus #9 or #17, with a renowned restaurant. ⑦

Windsor, Warendorfer Str. 177 (☎131330, fax 399 1610). Located east of the centre, reached by bus #2 or #10. Has a high-class Italian retaurant, *Il Cuchiaio d'Argento*. ⑦

Zum Schwan, Schillerstr. 27 (☎661166). Right behind the Hauptbahnhof with a *Bierstube* offering reasonably priced meals.

The city

Münster's population is swollen by the British and American soldiers whose bases ring the suburbs. They may be unpopular with the locals, but their justification for being there – the maintenance of the peace and balance of power in Europe – happens to be the historical role of which Münster is most proud. Most of the main sights are, as ever, in the Altstadt, but it's worth venturing out of the centre to the city's green belt, particularly to the southwest.

The Prinzipalmarkt

In the centre of the main street, the **Prinzipalmarkt**, stands the magnificent Gothic **Rathaus**, scene of the signing in 1648 of the **Peace of Westphalia**, which brought to an end the multitude of religious, constitutional and dynastic conflicts known as the Thirty Years' War. In honour of the treaty, the room where it was signed was renamed the **Friedensaal** (Peace Hall; Mon–Fri 9am–5pm, Sat 9am–4pm, Sun & holidays 10am–1pm; DM1.50); it's filled with exquisite carving and is the one part of the Rathaus generally open to the public. The 350th anniversary of the event will be marked by a full programme of exhibitions and other events through 1998.

Next door, the **Stadtweinhaus**, a Renaissance building with an abutting Italianate portico, has also been returned to its former splendour. The rest of what must once have been one of the most handsome main thoroughfares in Europe is rather more of a compromise. Alongside faithfully rebuilt houses are some which are mere approximations, while others are deliberately modern reinterpretations using the old motifs.

At the end of Prinzipalmarkt is **St Lamberti**, a good example of the spacious hall-church style characteristic of Westphalia. Its elegant openwork spire, one of the chief landmarks of the city, reflects the nineteenth-century German obsession with embellishing Gothic buildings. High up on the older part of the tower hang three wrought-iron cages; in them were displayed the bodies of the Anabaptist leader **Jan van Leyden** and his two principal lieutenants, following the crushing of their "Reich" by the Prince-bishop's army in 1535. Apart from insisting on adult baptism, this sect believed in the common ownership of property and in heeding the biblical injunction to be fruitful and multiply – the leader himself took no fewer than sixteen wives. The iconoclastic tendencies of the Anabaptists led them to destroy the beautiful sculptural decoration which was a key feature of the city's medieval churches; one of the rare examples left *in situ* is the elaborate *Tree of Jesse* over St Lamberti's south doorway. Facing the church's apse on Alter Steinweg is the **Krameramtshaus**, a late sixteenth-century building in the Dutch style which is the oldest guildhall to have survived; nowadays it serves as the main public library.

Domplatz

The vast **Domplatz**, on which markets are held on Wednesdays and Saturdays, is just a short walk from Prinzipalmarkt down either Domgasse or Michaelisplatz. Almost any point on the square offers a superb view of the huge thirteenth-century **Dom**, built in less than forty years in a style bridging the transition from Romanesque to Gothic. The only entrance is via the porch (or "Paradise"), which is adorned on the inside with statues of Christ and the Apostles dating from the very beginning of the building period the pier figure of St Paul, the Dom's patron, is from three hundred years later, the first of several subsequent additions to make up a full programme worthy of a Gate of Heaven, to which such doorways aspired.

The Dom's **interior** is highly unusual, the nave having just two bays of massive span It's jam-packed with sculptural memorials and other works of art. What really catches your eye is the **astronomical clock**, made in the 1530s, in the southern arm of the ambulatory. Based on the most precise mathematical calculations available at the time it shows the orbit of the planets and the movement of the fixed stars, as well as fulfilling the normal function of charting the course of the sun and the moon; the lowest section is a calendar. The leading Münster painter of the day, **Ludger tom Ring the Elder**, decorated the clock with the Evangelical symbols, delicate scenes of the Labours of the Months and a gallery of entranced spectators. If you brave the crowds at noon, you can hear the carillon and see the emergence of the Magi to pay tribute to the infant Christ.

At the far end of the cloisters the **Domkammer** (Tues–Sun 11am–4pm; DM1) houses the treasury. Pride of place goes to the eleventh-century gold reliquary of St Paul, studded with jewels a couple of hundred years later; other outstanding pieces are the thirteenth-century processional cross and fourteen bust-reliquaries of the prophets.

The Landesmuseum

The Domplatz, which also contains several Baroque mansions, serves as the city's museum centre. The **Westfälisches Landesmuseum** (Tues–Sun 10am–6pm; DM5) houses works of art of mostly Westphalian origin, but is of far more than parochial significance. On the ground floor is a really outstanding collection of **medieval sculpture** including the original statues from the Überwasserkirche (see below). The massive group of *Christ's Entry into Jerusalem* originally adorned the upper part of the Dom's facade, destroyed in the war, and is the work of **Hinrik Brabender**, a long-forgotten name who now appears as one of the most individual of the remarkable group of late Gothic German sculptors. Also by him is a series of Passion scenes made for the Domplatz; despite their weary appearance – the Anabaptists smashed them only a few years after they were made – the wonderful dignity and characterization of the figures can still be appreciated. Also on display are examples of the quite different art of his son **Johann Brabender**, who was fully Renaissance in style and happiest on a small scale, as in sensitive and delicate works such as *Calvary* from the Dom's rood screen and *Adam and Eve* from the Paradise.

Upstairs, the history of Westphalian painting is traced, beginning with the Soft Style of **Conrad von Soest** and the **Master of Warendorf** in the early fifteenth century. From the next generation is **Johann Koerbecke**, whose masterpiece, the *Marienfeld Altar*, contains background depictions of Münster. The Renaissance section is dominated by the diverse interests of the **tom Ring** family. Apart from the portraits for which they are best known, there are religious works by Hermann and pioneering still lifes by Ludger the Younger. On the second floor are two rooms of Expressionist paintings, with a good cross-section of the work of **Macke**.

The rest of the city

A short distance to the west of the Dom stands the **Liebfrauenkirche**, usually known as the **Überwasserkirche** (Church by the Water) since it stands beside the Aa, Münster's tiny river. Like St Lamberti, it's a fourteenth-century hall church, with a floridly decorated tower. Its superb sculptures proved particularly repugnant to the Anabaptists, who smashed and buried them; some 350 years later, they were dramatically rediscovered but were considered too fragile to return to their original location. From here, Frauenstrasse leads to Schlossplatz with the resplendent eighteenth-century **Schloss** of the Prince-bishops, its two side wings reaching out like embracing arms. The front facing the **Botanischer Garten** (daily 7.30am–5pm; free) is quite different, but the interior was completely destroyed in the war, and has been modernized for use by the University. Its architect, **Johann Conrad Schlaun**, was almost single-handedly responsible for making Münster the capital of north German Baroque, which was far more restrained than its southern counterpart. There are a couple of other buildings by him at the opposite end of the city centre, reached from the Rathaus by following Klemensstrasse. The **Erbdrostenhof**, a nobleman's mansion, again shows his talent for the grand manner and has survived in better shape than the Schloss. The circular **Clemenskirche**, immediately opposite, is his solution to the problem of building in a restricted space, and is richly decorated with a huge ceiling fresco.

Southwest from the centre

Heading southwest from the centre, the sausage-shaped **Aasee**, some 6km in circumference, is the most popular recreation area in the city, particularly at the weekend when the yachts and motorboats of prosperous locals crowd the water. At the lower end of the left bank is the **Mühlenhof**; though small, it's one of Germany's longest-established open-air museums (Mid-March–mid-Oct daily 10am–6pm; mid-Oct–mid-March Tues–Sat 1–4.30pm, Sun 11am–4.30pm; DM5; take bus #14). On a fine day, it's worth a plod round the twenty or so agricultural buildings from the province which have been re-erected here, the centrepieces being a trestle windmill of 1748 and an early seventeenth-century millhouse, fitted out with authentic furnishings.

Eating, drinking and nightlife

One of Münster's greatest attractions is its wonderful choice of **bars**, **cafés** and **restaurants**. The most obvious place to begin is around the Prinzipalmarkt, but an equally notable nightlife area is the **Kuhviertel** just beyond the Überwasserkirche; this is usually described as the Latin quarter, but students no longer predominate. Look out for the amazing range of **beers** – *Pils, Alt, Weizen, Malz, Leicht, Spezial* and the strong *Jubiläumsbier* – made by *Pinkus Müller*, although small, and the only one left in Münster, it's among the most highly regarded of all German breweries. *Alt*, whether from Pinkus or imported from Düsseldorf, is Münster's most popular drink and is generally mixed with syrup (*mit Schuss*) or with a punch of fresh raspberries and peaches (*Altbierbowle*).

Prinzipalmarkt and around

Altes Brauhaus Kiepenkerl, Spiekerhof 45. Named after the statue of the pedlar outside, this has a ground-floor beer hall and elegant upstairs café.

Bullenkopp, Alter Fischmarkt 24. Traditional *Gaststätte* still preserving its original nineteenth-century appearance. Serves many Münsterland specialities. Closed Sun.

Café Kleimann, Prinzipalmarkt 48. Occupying one of the finest of the old guild houses, it makes a cheaper alternative to *Feller Café Schucan* for *Kaffee und Kuchen*. Closed Sun.

Feller Café Schucan, Prinzipalmarkt 24–26. This pricey café serves delicious coffee and has an irresistible display of cakes. It attracts a varied clientele – students, businessmen and elderly women. Closed Sun.

Palmen Café, Aegidiimarkt 1. The best selection of teas in town. Closed Sun.

Stuhlmacher, Prinzipalmarkt 6. The city's most celebrated pub, it has a wide selection of beers, and is ideal for a spot of people-watching, particularly in the early evening. Its restaurant is expensive, however, and you can eat better elsewhere.

Kuhviertel

Cavete, Kreuzstr. 38. Popular bar with a young crowd, loud music and a selection of inexpensive pastas and puddings.

Das Blaue Haus, Kreuzstr. 16. A direct competitor of *Cavete* in every respect.

Fischbrathalle, Schlaunstr. 8. Fish restaurant which has been in existence since 1926. Lunchtimes only, closed Sun.

Pinkus Müller, Kreuzstr. 4–10. The brewery offers both a *Biergalerie* and a *Gaststätte*. The latter is decked out in traditional style; it fills up heavily from mid-evening – notably with members of the American community. Not the cheapest, but the best place in town for a traditional Westphalian meal. Closed Sun.

Ziege, Kreuzstr. 33. The smallest pub in Münster, with a truly *gemütlich* interior.

Elsewhere in the city

Altes Gasthaus Leve, Alter Steinweg 37. Gastronomically, the pick of the old-fashioned beer halls clustered along this street. Closed Mon.

Der Bunte Vogel, Alter Steinweg 41. Another beer hall, though a bit trendier than usual.

Café Vis a Vis, Hörsterstr. 11. Café-bar that's one of a number of popular meeting places in this street in the eastern part of the city centre.

Gambrinus, Königsstr. 34. Lively pub which does good-value schnitzels cooked in a score of different ways.

Kleines Restaurant im Oer'schen Hof, Königstr 42. Expensive restaurant serving top-notch French cuisine and fish specialities..

Kruse Baimken, Am Staatgraben 52. Located by the north bank of the Aasee, this is the place to come on a fine evening, when you may find close on a thousand people, including many of the beautiful set, relaxing in its beer garden.

Prütt Café, Bremer Str. 32. Vegetarian and wholefood specialist, situated just behind the Hauptbahnhof. Unusually for such institutions it stays open until late, and has its own little beer garden.

Torhaus, Mauritzstr. 27. Named after the Neoclassical guardhouse it occupies, this is the main local practitioner of *neue deutsche Küche*. Closed Mon & Tues.

Treibhaus, Steinfurter Str. 66. Less self-conscious alternative to *Kruse Baimken* further to the north; also does low-priced meals.

Villa Medici, Ostmarkstr. 15. Münster's best Italian restaurant. Closed Sun & Mon.

Clubs

Cascade, Berliner Platz 23. Offers different types of live music Fri & Sat from 10pm.

Elephant, Roggenmarkt 15. Situated in an arcade, this caters mainly for an older crowd.

Jovel Music Hall, Grevener Str. 91. Discos and live music Wed–Sat from 9pm. Under the same roof as *Internet Café Leeze*, which is open daily from 6pm.

Le Club, Roggenmarkt 11. In the basement of a clothes store, popular with young clubbers. Wed–Sat from 10pm.

Festivals and entertainment

The main **popular festival**, known as *Send*, is a fair held for five days at a stretch three times annually (March, June and Oct) in the Hindenburgplatz in front of the Schloss. Carnival is also celebrated, if not with the same gusto as in the Rhineland, while the *Lambertusfest*, beginning on September 17, is a festival for children. Münster's main **theatre** venue is the *Städtische Bühnen*, Neubrückenstr. 63 (☎590 9100); alternatives are *Wolfgang-Borchert-Theater*, Berliner Platz 23 (☎40019) and *Charivari*, Körnerstr. 3 (☎521500). The *Halle Münsterland*, Albertsloher Weg 32 (☎60466), to the south of the centre, hosts large-scale events.

Münsterland

Münsterland is the name given to the large tract of Westphalia stretching from the Rhine to the Teutoburg Forest, bounded by The Netherlands and Lower Saxony to the north, and by the Ruhrgebiet to the south. Its rich soils are agriculturally highly productive, and it remains predominantly rural, with no large towns other than the capital. Being almost unrelievedly flat, it's emphatically not a province you visit for scenery, but it boasts over fifty **historic castles** surrounded by tracts of water (known as *Wasserburgen*), the nearest the country comes to rivalling the French Loire châteaux.

The Wasserburgen

The local tourist offices are keen to promote the **Wasserburgen**, whose virtues they flaunt by means of irresistible photographic posters. However, there are pitfalls which you should be aware of, as it's easy to end up frustrated and disappointed. First, the vast majority of the castles remain private dwellings, generally still in the hands of old aristocratic families who are alive, well, and managing very nicely without the need of extra cash from prying outsiders. Few show much enthusiasm for the tourist board's initiatives; many castles can be seen from the outside only, and in some cases even that is kept out of bounds by the erection of large hedges and impenetrable gates. Secondly, the alluring posters are nearly all aerial views, and for good reason – from above the castles invariably look far more arresting than they do from the ground, where it's never possible to see the complete layout of the complex, and where your own photos often have to be made from very narrow angles. Thirdly, the interiors of those castles which are open for visits never measure up to the exteriors, where the umbilical relationship of the water to the buildings plays such an essential role.

Offputting as all this sounds, it should be stressed that the best of the castles, which are described below, are very much worth visiting and offer the easiest access. It definitely pays to be well organized; that way you can hope to see several in a day, as it's unlikely you'll need more than a couple of hours at any single one. Although there's a comprehensive local bus service, the timetabling isn't ideal for castle-crawling. If you don't have a car, consider **renting a bike**, available almost everywhere and at competitive prices. The most convenient place to go is the *Gepäckabfertigung* at Münster Hauptbahnhof, which charges DM10 per day, or DM6 if you're initially taking the bike on a train. Many other stations in the province offer the same deal, and plenty of private firms have daily rates of DM8 upwards. A full list is published in the tourist office's *Radwandern in Münsterland* brochure. An even handier companion is its *Gastgeberverzeichnis – Münsterland;* if you've a serious interest in the castles, this lists them all and tells you when and where you must write or phone in advance for an appointment. Münster itself is the obvious base to choose, as, although there are plenty of hotels and pensions in all the smaller towns, they're uniformly dull places come the evening. **Youth hostels** are unusually thin on the ground, and, like the more numerous **campsites**, are not in the best locations.

Around Münster

You don't need to venture far out of Münster for your first taste of these châteaux, as **Haus Rüschhaus** (guided tours March, April & Nov–mid-Dec Tues–Sun 11am–1pm & 2–4pm; May–Oct Tues–Sun 10am–1pm & 2.30–5.30pm; DM5) stands just beyond the end of the built-up area, and can be reached by bus #5. The present building was designed and built from 1745 to 1748 by **Johann Conrad Schlaun** as a summer house for himself. It's quite an eccentric little construction, mostly homely in feel, but with touches of Baroque swagger, as in the sloping roofline and the sweeping facade which in fact fronts a fully practical barn, integrated into the house as was the norm in traditional local farmsteads. The Italian Room, named after the capriccio scenes on the handmade wallpaper from Paris, provides the only decorative note in the house. Originally Schlaun's bedroom, it was transformed to its present state by later owners, the family of Germany's leading woman author of the nineteenth-century, **Annette von Droste-Hülshoff** (1797–1848), who lived here for twenty years from 1826, during which time she produced much of her finest work.

Best known for her charming poetic vignettes of nature, the writer spent the first three decades of her life in the original seat of her aristocratic family, **Haus Hülshoff** (daily mid-March–mid-Dec 9.30am–6pm; DM5). Buses #563 and #564 go there from Münster, or you can walk from Rüschhaus in about half an hour by continuing straight ahead and turning left down the footpath just past the highway junction; don't follow the road, which adds a considerable distance to the journey. This castle is a classic example of the Renaissance *Wasserburg* design, the outer barrier (*Vorburg*) being a severe, low-lying building with square corner towers, the inner building (*Hauptburg*) an airy L-shaped dwelling in the Dutch style, to which a neo-Gothic chapel was added last century. There's also an attractive park, recently re-created after old designs. The *Hauptburg* features a suite of six rooms authentically furnished in the early nineteenth-century style familiar to the poet.

Burgsteinfurt

The most varied **Schloss** in Münsterland is found in the town of **BURGSTEINFURT**, some 35km northwest of Münster, on the main rail line to Gronau. It's still the home of the Dukes of Bentheim, who introduced the Calvinist faith to northern Germany. Although the present incumbent is more generous with access than most private owners in the area, the organization of visits has been left in the hands of the **tourist office** based at the former Rathaus at Markt 2. Obviously, it's sensible to phone ahead (☎02551/1383) to find out when these are. It's a fascinating building, with all manner of fragments from diverse periods surviving in a ramshackle way, the courtyard alone serving as an encyclopedia of European architectural history. From the twelfth century there's a Romanesque double chapel, the lower of which remains in its simple original state, while the upper has been adapted according to Protestant tenets. On the left-hand side, a Renaissance wing was built, centred on a superb two-storey oriel window. To the south is the **Bagno**, a spacious public park, which offers good distant views of the castle.

Lembeck

LEMBECK, about 50km southwest of Burgsteinfurt, can be reached by train from there or from Münster via Coesfeld. The **Schloss**, set back from the village, is also still in private hands, but the fact that part of it is now a **hotel** (☎02369/7213; ⑤) means that access is easier than normal (guided tours daily mid-March–Oct every hour 10am–5pm; DM6.50). In spite of the impressive severity of the exterior, conforming to the old *Wasserburg* design, it seems to be the first in the province to have been built more for pleasure than defence, a fact suggested by the exuberant helmets on the towers and by the very obvious vulnerability of the rear, connected by a small causeway to the gardens. Just to the east of Lembeck is the **Naturpark Hohe Mark**, a protected area of gently sloping forests, a veritable oasis in the midst of so much flatness.

Lüdinghausen

There's a choice of bus or train from Münster to **LÜDINGHAUSEN**, 30km south; the buses are better, as the rail route is circuitous and the train station is a long way out. The moated castle named after the town itself has been too messed about down the years to be of much interest, but **Burg Vischering** at the northern boundary is the archetypal *Wasserburg*, as well as the only one wholly given over to tourism, being designated the **Münsterland-Museum** (Tues–Sun 10am–12.30pm & 1.30–4.30/5.30pm;

DM4). Its *Hauptburg*, horseshoe in shape, with a singular octagonal tower in the centre of the courtyard, was beautified around 1620 by the addition of the *Erker*, the abutting Renaissance section with an elegant oriel window. Directly facing this are the spreading branches of a trumpet tree, the most remarkable of several rare species planted in the grounds. As usual, the interiors are plain by comparison, but the *Rittersaal* with wooden beamed ceiling has been restored to good effect. There's an exhibition on life in the medieval castles of the region; other folklore displays, this time on the farms and the towns, are to be found in the *Vorburg*.

Nordkirchen

If you've only a day to spare on the castles, the best way to spend it is by combining a visit to Lüdinghausen and **NORDKIRCHEN**, 8km southeast. This redbrick giant is by far the largest and most spectacular **Schloss** of the group, a manifestation of the fantastic wealth of the **Plettenberg** dynasty of Prince-bishops, who decided to replace their old fortress with a palace in the French manner. Every tourist brochure refers to it as the "Westphalian Versailles", a nickname it has had since its conception in 1703, when it referred to the older and much smaller palace at Versailles, on which Nordkirchen was directly modelled.

The complex is on one island only (instead of the two normally required for a *Wasserburg*), and exhibits all the sense of order characteristic of the Age of Reason. It's almost completely symmetrical and is specially designed to produce a spectacular main vista, an effect achieved by breaking up the main block into sections and preceding them with long, narrow pavilions. Behind, there's a formal garden with Baroque sculptures. Nowadays, Nordkirchen belongs to the Land government, which has adapted it as a college for financial studies; consequently there's free access at all times, and what you can see from outside definitely justifies a visit. Official opportunities for viewing the **interior** aren't generous (guided tours Sat & Sun 2–5pm, usually on the hour; DM4). However, there are many private visits on weekdays throughout the summer, with which you're allowed to tag along; consult the list posted in the porter's office or, better still, phone ahead (☎02596/933402, mornings only). The rooms are less grandiose than you might imagine from outside, but have the full pomp of the Baroque in their rich stuccowork, ceiling paintings, wood panelling and plentiful furnishings.

There are no **buses** out of Nordkirchen on Sundays, and only one on Saturday afternoons (to Lüdinghausen), which entails taking the 2pm tour. The nearest station, on a line with a very restricted weekend service, is at Cappel, 5km east.

Cappenberg

CAPPENBERG, 12km south of Nordkirchen, stands just outside the industrial town of Lünen, which marks the beginning of the Ruhrgebiet. There's been a **Schloss** here since the ninth century; the present building is Baroque, and for many years it was home to the art treasures of Dortmund. With the creation of a new museum in the city, it has been freed to host temporary exhibitions of various kinds (Tues–Sun 10am–5pm; free). Far more significant is the **Stiftskirche** directly in front, founded by the brothers **Gottfried** and **Otto von Cappenberg** in atonement for the part they had played in helping Lothair of Saxony sack the city of Münster in 1121, destroying most of the Dom in the process. Their confessor, Norbert von Xanten, suggested that a fit form of repentance would be the establishment of a German headquarters for the Premonstratensian order he had recently founded in France. The plain architecture favoured by these monks, Romanesque with later Gothic additions, gives no hint of the riches within, which include two of the supreme masterpieces of German medieval art. Displayed in a safe in the south transept is the stunning **head-reliquary of Frederick Barbarossa**, the oldest surviving portrait of a German emperor made from life. Actually intended to contain a relic of St John the Evangelist, it's probably the work of an Aachen goldsmith of about 1160. In the choir is the early fourteenth-century **founders' memorial**, depicting them as rather jolly youths with virtually identical features clasping a model of the church. At around the same time, a tomb was made for the now-canonized Gottfried; it's kept in the south transept. Other important works of art are the polychrome Romanesque triumphal cross and the elaborately carved Gothic stalls (each of the misericords is worth looking at). Below the castle complex is a privately owned **Wildpark** offering various nature trails. A further 2km on, actually within Lünen, lies the artificial boating lake named **Cappenberger See**. There's a **youth hostel** (☎02306/53546; ☎) at Richard-Schirrmann-Weg on its northern shore.

Freckenhorst and Warendorf

FRECKENHORST, 25km east of Münster, and served by regular buses, also has an important Romanesque **Stiftskirche**. This time it's the architecture which is most striking, even if it's ruggedly impressive rather than beautiful. The massive solemn facade is particularly memorable, with two cylindrical corner towers huddling up against the great belfry. At the east end, a pair of square towers form a perfect counterpoint. In the crypt is the thirteenth-century **tomb of Geva**, a memorial to the woman who founded the original convent in the ninth century. The most important work of art is the **baptismal font**; the upper register is adorned with masterly carvings of scenes from the life of Christ, with fantastic animals below. On the walls around are paintings from a dismembered Soft Style retable of about 1430 by the **Master of Warendorf**.

Others from the same series can be seen in the Landesmuseum in Münster, but the central panel, a colourful *Calvary* surrounded by four other Passion scenes, remains in its original location, **St Laurentius** in **WARENDORF**, 3km north and with a direct rail link to the regional capital. This is a typical Westphalian hall church, which also has some fine sculptures, notably the three figures from the portal who have been moved just inside for protection, and the group of *St Peter, St Paul and a Canon* by Hinrik Brabender at the far end of the north aisle. The adjacent Markt is lined with old buildings, including the **Rathaus**, whose upper floors are open as a museum (Tues–Fri 3–5pm, Sat 10.30am–12.30pm, Sun 10.30am–12.30pm & 3–5pm; free).

Soest

About thirty minutes from Dortmund by train, **SOEST** was a city of similar importance at the time of the Hanseatic League. Nowadays it's a whole world away in spirit, ranking as one of Germany's most delightful towns, yet it could so easily have been incorporated into the Ruhr conurbation. This proximity to the industrial heartland led to Soest being heavily bombed during the war, but restoration has been so deft that the scars have healed completely and there's scarcely a street within the fortifications which doesn't live up to the tourist board image of Romantic Germany. All the main buildings were constructed from a local sandstone whose deep lime greens bestow a distinctive character on the town and are well offset against the many red-roofed and whitewashed half-timbered houses. The play of light on these surfaces produces such magical effects it's little wonder that Soest has nurtured more than its fair share of German artists.

The town

The town has never expanded much beyond its walls, which survive minus their battlements, and it preserves a medieval air and layout, with a varied group of churches and secular buildings.

The Wiesenkirche and Hohnekirche

Rising majestically above the northern part of the Altstadt are the twin spires of the Gothic **Wiesenkirche** (Our Lady of the Meadows). This is a key building in German architectural history, when the favoured but problematic hall church design finally acquired an elegance to match any other style of building. Although only a parish church, it's a cathedral in miniature, with an interior nothing short of stupendous. Slender unadorned piers thrust effortlessly up to the lofty vault, and the walls seem to be made of nothing but dazzlingly brilliant **stained glass**. These were inserted over a period ranging from just after the church's construction in the fourteenth century to the early sixteenth century, when money ran out before the south side could be glazed. The masterpiece of this assemblage, placed over the north portal, is from the final period, showing *The Last Supper* with a Westphalian menu of beer, ham and rye bread. As a bonus, the church houses a richly varied collection of works of art, including three large triptychs; that in the right-hand apse chapel was painted by **Heinrich Aldegraver**, a resident of Soest and one of Dürer's most accomplished followers.

On higher ground to the rear stands the **Hohnekirche** (Our Lady on the Hill). The same Protestant congregation owns both this and the Wiesenkirche, taking refuge in the cosier surroundings of this squat, box-like structure for the winter months. It's a Romanesque attempt of about a century earlier at creating a hall church. The rather plain result was, however, greatly enlivened by a sumptuous fresco decoration, much of which has survived. Also here are a couple of fine works of art in the *Passion Altar* by the late fifteenth-century Westphalian painter known as the Master of Liesborn, and the remarkable *Scheibenkreuz*, a four-metre-high triumphal cross from about 1200, adorned with delicate reliefs of the life of Christ.

The centre

The centre is soon reached from here by returning to Wiesenstrasse, continuing via an old water mill up Am Seel. Dominating the skyline is the noble tower of **St Patrokli**, generally (if inaccurately) referred to as the **Dom**. This forms part of a resplendent Romanesque westwork, which is so grandiose a frontage that the rest of the building comes as an anticlimax. The upper gallery houses the **Dommuseum** (currently closed for restoration), with the church treasure and some lovely stained glass, including precious twelfth-century examples.

Only a few yards in front stands the **Petrikirche**, towering over the square of the same name which also contains the **Rathaus**, the only significant Baroque addition to the city. Again with a westwork as its most notable feature, the Petrikirche is Romanesque with the addition of a Gothic chancel. On the third piers of the nave are two *Crucifixion* frescoes attributed to **Conrad von Soest**, a major figure of the fifteenth century, and one of the few early German masters known by name. An important painting probably by this artist, *St Nicholas Enthroned with SS Catherine, Barbara and the two Johns*, occupies the altar of the tiny Romanesque **Nicolaikapelle**, situated behind the east end of St Patrokli. In spite of an unprepossessing exterior, the inside of the chapel is a real gem, another variation on the hall-church theme, with rounded column shafts dividing the space into two equal aisles. It's generally locked (officially open 11am–noon on Tues, Wed, Fri & Sun); if so, ask for the key at the **Wilhelm-Morgner-Haus**, the local cultural centre based in a modern building directly in front (Mon–Sat 10am–noon & 3–5pm, Sun 10.30am–12.30pm; free). This is named after Soest's own Expressionist painter, whose short career overlapped with the presence in the city of two of the movement's leading lights, Christian Rohlfs and Emil Nolde. A number of Morgner's canvases can be seen on the first floor, revealing a versatile talent which was to end at the age of 26 on a Flanders battlefield. Also on view are a selection of Aldegraver's engravings, his favourite and most effective medium.

The rest of town

From here, follow Ulricher Strasse south, turning left into Burghofstrasse, and you'll come to a complex of buildings, including a rare Romanesque house and the **Burghof**, a sixteenth-century mansion now housing the local history museum (Tues–Sat 10am–noon & 3–5pm, Sun 11am–1pm; free). The main feature is the **Festsaal** on the ground floor, whose walls are covered with white stuccowork; the biblical subjects are original, the battle scenes and emperors skilful modern pastiches. Another small museum is housed in the **Osthofentor** (April–Sept Tues–Fri 2–4pm, Sat 11am–1pm, Sun 11am–1pm & 3–5pm; Oct–March Wed 2–4pm, Sun 11am–1pm; DM1), a stately Renaissance gateway which once formed the northeast entrance to the town, and a rare surviving adornment of the walls. The display here is mostly concerned with medieval warfare; what looks like a spectacular modern sculpture in the attic turns out to be a fancy arrangement of 25,000 crossbow bolts.

Practicalities

Both the **Hauptbahnhof** and the **bus station** are located just outside the northern stretch of the city walls. The **tourist office** (Mon–Wed & Fri 8.30am–12.30pm & 2–4.30pm, Thurs 8.30am–12.30pm & 2–5.30pm, Sat 9am–noon; ☎02921/103323) is at Am Seel 5.

Soest is at its liveliest during the five-day-long *Allerheiligenkirmes*, which is claimed as the biggest town centre **fair** in Europe; beginning on the Wednesday after All Saints' Day (Nov 1), it features a massive fairground, a horse market, and fireworks displays. Other local festivals include the *Bördetag* on a weekend in May and the *Gauklertag* on a Saturday in September.

Accommodation

Within the Altstadt is a broad range of **hotels** of which the best budget choices are: *Zum Amtsgericht*, Nöttenstr. 31 (☎02921/13303; ④); *Braustübl*, Thomästr. 53 (☎02921/4166; ④); and *Drei Kronen*, Jakobistr. 37–39 (☎02921/13665; ⑤). More upmarket places include *Stadt Soest*, Brüderstr. 50 (☎02921/1811; ⑥), and the wonderful old *Pilgrim-Haus*, Jakobistr. 75 (☎02921/1828; ⑦), Westphalia's oldest inn with an uninterrupted tradition dating back to the fourteenth century.

The **youth hostel**, Kaiser-Friedrich-Platz 2 (☎02921/16283; ❷), is just outside the southern section of the city wall. There's no **campsite**, but those around Möhnesee (see p.547) are just a few kilometres away and connected by regular bus services.

Eating and drinking

One consequence of the relentless flow of day-trippers from the Ruhr each weekend is an enormous choice of **restaurants** – over a hundred in all. Among the best are those in the last two hotels mentioned above. Almost equally enticing is the *Altes Gasthaus im Zuckerberg*, which occupies the oldest house in Westphalia at Höggenstr. 1. *Biermanns Restaurant*, Thomästr. 47, offers very expensive international dishes in designer premises; *Restaurant am Kattenturm*, Dasselwall 1, is of similar quality and more reasonably priced. *Brauhaus Zwiebel*, Ulrichstr. 24, is a *Hausbrauerei* producing both light and dark beers which gives Soest the brewery it until recently lacked. Many traditional **cafés** such as *Café Fromme*, Markt 1, and *Café am Dom*, Am Vreithof 2, provide a relaxed atmosphere for *Kaffee und Kuchen*; while *Haus Sauerland*, Filzenstr. 4, is a café-restaurant which has been run by the same family for two centuries.

The food you should on no account miss is Soest's own contribution to culinary history, the famed **Pumpernickel**, a strongly flavoured rye bread popular throughout

Germany at breakfast time. For the genuine article, go to *Wilhelm Haverland*; its factory at Markt 6 has been in operation since 1799, and you can choose from several different recipes in its side-street shop behind.

The Sauerland

The **Sauerland** forms an extensive part of eastern Westphalia, stretching from the eastern edge of the Ruhrgebiet across to the border with Hesse. Literally translated, the name means "Bitter Land", though it's unclear whether this comes from the fierce Saxon tribes who once inhabited the region and put up a doughty resistance to Charlemagne, or from the poor soils and hostile, rugged terrain. There's also the possibility that the name is a simple corruption of "South Land". It's rural, upland country, supposedly containing a thousand mountains; nowadays it serves as an obvious holiday and recreation area for the teeming millions who live in the nearby cities of the Rhine-Ruhr conurbation. The Sauerland's attractions are quintessentially German – above all, it's good **hiking** country, with nearly 12,000km of marked footpaths, and four nature parks fall wholly or largely within its boundaries. Dotted with rivers and artificial lakes, it's also one of the country's main centres for **angling** and **activity holidays**, such as surfing, rowing, canoeing, sailing and hang-gliding, while riding in covered wagons Wild-West style has also been made into a regional speciality. Much of the Sauerland is of a surprisingly Alpine character for a place so far north, and **winter sports** help to keep its tourist trade going all year round.

On the surface, the Sauerland is the mirror opposite of the Ruhrgebiet. However, though there are no major cities, there are many medium-sized industrial towns. **Beer** is a leading product – the soft local spring water is a crucial ingredient. As a result, many aficionados rate Sauerland brews superior even to those of nearby Dortmund. *Warsteiner*, dubbed "the queen of beers" for its delicate taste, is currently being heavily promoted abroad; *Veltins* is popular throughout Germany, while *Iserlohner* and *Hirsch* are also very fine. Sauerland water, moreover, plays a key role in the economy of the Ruhrgebiet, and the great **dams** of the region are key features of the German inland waterway system.

THE DAMBUSTERS

The importance of the Ruhr dams to the economy of the Third Reich was highlighted by the famous **"Dambusters"** episode of World War II (told in Paul Brickhill's book and in the popular film which, however, wasn't shot on location). At the time, these massive concrete structures would hardly have been grazed by existing explosives. In order to penetrate them, the inventor Barnes Wallis developed enormous ten-ton bombs which skipped across the water surface like a pebble, sinking behind the defensive nets and lodging themselves against the weakest point of the dams' walls. These "bouncing bombs" were dropped with devastating effect by the Lancasters of 617 Squadron, commanded by Wing Commander Guy Gibson, on May 17, 1943. Such havoc was caused by the ensuing flooding, which destroyed 123 factories, 25 bridges and 30 square kilometres of arable land, that it was estimated to have taken the equivalent of several months' work by 100,000 men to repair the damage – a telling blow to the whole Nazi war effort and a major propaganda coup. This, at any rate, is how the evidence has traditionally been presented. Latest research suggests that the claims were exaggerated, and that the Möhne dam, far from being wrecked, was eventually repaired. Fifty-six members of 617 Squadron were killed in the raid – "If only I'd known," Barnes Wallis said when he discovered the RAF losses, "I'd never have started this."

Märkisches Sauerland

Furthest to the west of the region is the **Märkisches Sauerland**, corresponding to the old Duchy of Mark. This is sometimes taken to include Hagen itself; more logically, it begins with the incorporated town of Hohenlimburg, where the continuously built-up land of the Ruhrgebiet first gives way to open countryside. A scenic rail line follows the course of the River Lenne and continues all the way south to Siegen. On the east bank is the Lennegebirge range, which forms part of the **Naturpark Homert**; to the west begins the **Naturpark Ebbegebirge**.

Altena

ALTENA, 25km from Hagen (see p.530), is the obvious star of the Sauerland towns, thanks to its superb setting deep in the valley, high above which is its massive **Burg**, one of the largest medieval castles in Germany. Begun in the twelfth century, the buildings were erected at intervals up to the sixteenth century. The central keep is strongly protected by an outer bailey and no fewer than three consecutive gateways. The complex inevitably crumbled with disuse, and there were plans last century to rebuild it in a phoney Romantic style. Fortunately these were never carried out, and the present condition of the castle is due to a drastic restoration in the 1900s.

The world's original youth hostel (see box below) has been ossified as one of several **museums** in the castle (Tues–Fri 9.30am–5pm, Sat & Sun 11am–6pm; inclusive ticket DM5). The day room is in the style of a traditional Westphalian farmstead; adjoining it is the area for groups, while downstairs is the spartan main dorm, its solid wooden bunks standing in triple tiers, and looking as if they could yet withstand many more years of service. Several of the rooms in the Burg have been restored in period style and equipped with impressive furniture. Highlights include the *Stadthalle* by the entrance, with its carved Renaissance chimneypiece; the Great Hall, with a notable collection of pewter; and the chapel, adorned with retables from Antwerp and Cologne, and a graceful fifteenth-century *Madonna and Child* made from Bamberg sandstone. Scattered throughout the rooms are important examples of **arms and armour**, reflecting the fact that the Sauerland was a major centre for their production.

There's a reasonable range of **hotels** including *Würschmidt am Markt*, Kirchstr. 43 (☎02352/22905; ③), *Bahnhofshotel*, Bahnhofstr. 33 (☎02352/22888; ③), and *Alte Linden*, Hauptstr. 38 (☎02352/71210; ⑥). In the outer bailey of the Burg is what's rather cheatingly called the world's oldest functioning **youth hostel** (☎02352/23522; ❷); its location makes it the most attractive place to stay in town, but, with only forty beds, it's regularly full.

THE BIRTH OF YOUTH HOSTELLING

In 1909, a teacher named **Richard Schirrmann** established the world's first-ever permanent **youth hostel** in the Burg at Altena, having previously operated from a schoolroom in town. Inspired by the simple idea of the need to provide low-cost accommodation for young travellers, Schirrmann's choice of Altena is explained by the fact that the countryside around is particularly good for hiking. In time, hundreds of hostels sprang up all over Germany, and have long been an established and important feature of national life. The idea was slow in catching on elsewhere (an international federation was only set up 20 years later), but eventually spread right around the world, to the gratitude of millions of travellers, not all of them young. Schirrmann's reward has been to have a plethora of streets named after him (usually the ones leading to the local hostel) – indeed, he's commemorated just as prolifically in western Germany as Marx and Lenin once were in the GDR.

Iserlohn and the Dechenhöhle

ISERLOHN, the Sauerland's largest town, can be reached from Altena by either bus or train. Still a centre of the iron industry, Iserlohn has a couple of moderately interesting churches, both with carved altars – Gothic **St Marien**, dominating the town from its hill, and the Romanesque **Bauernkirche**. Beside the latter is the **Stadtmuseum** (Tues, Wed & Fri–Sun 10am–5pm, Thurs 10am–7pm; free), housed in a ritzy Baroque mansion. The main local attraction, however, is the **Dechenhöhle** in the outlying village of Lethmathe, arguably the most outstanding of several **stalactite caves** in the Sauerland (guided tours April–Oct daily 9am–5pm; Nov, Dec, Feb & March daily 10am–4pm; DM5.50). Discovered last century when the rail line was being constructed, the geological formations are reckoned to be anything from 300 to 350 million years old. Inevitably, the chambers have been given nicknames according to the shapes they supposedly resemble. Particularly impressive are the *Baumkuchen*, with its single, tapering stem, and the *Kronleuchter*, so called for looking like an abstract version of the famous Romanesque crown-shaped chandeliers in Aachen, Hildesheim and Comburg.

There are plenty of **hotels** in all price categories ranging from *Haus Schäfer*, Friedrichstr. 84 (☎02371/60316; ④), to the rustic *Waldhotel Horn*, Seilerwaldstr. 10 (☎02371/9720; ⑧). A full list is available from the **tourist office** at Konrad-Adenauer-Ring 15 (☎02371/13233).

Nordsauerland

Soest is sometimes counted as part of the **Nordsauerland**, an area centred on a ten-kilometre-long artificial lake, the **Möhnesee**. The northern bank has been developed as a holiday resort area for angling and watersports, and there are **campsites** all along this shore. **Cruises** depart from Günne, Delecke and Körbecke from April to October. Between these first two villages is the famous **dam** which, though not the largest, was the prime target of the "Dambusters" (see p.545), due to its proximity to the industrial centres. Controlling the flow of the River Heve into the River Ruhr, it's 650m long and 40m high; when it was breached, 134 million tonnes of water gushed out into the countryside. Now long repaired, it's one of four footbridges interspersed at fairly regular intervals allowing you to cross over to the opposite bank of the lake. This has been left in its natural state, and a southerly arm, the **Hevesee**, is a protected area for birdlife. The **youth hostel** (☎02924/305; ⓕ) lies directly across from Körbecke. Immediately beyond is the beginning of the **Arnsberg Forest** *(Arnsberger Wald)*, an upland *Naturpark* of beech, birch and larch, which stretches for some 30km east to west, and up to 15km north to south.

Hochsauerland

The **Hochsauerland** is much the largest of the four districts, beginning immediately beyond the Arnsberg Forest and continuing east to the boundary with Hesse and south to the Siegerland. As its name suggests, it has the highest mountains in the area.

Arnsberg and around

ARNSBERG itself is traditionally considered the "capital" of the Sauerland, and is the administrative centre for the whole region. It's built on a spur of land on a bend of the River Ruhr, rising neatly upwards in tiers. The southern part of the old town is dominated by the **Propsteikirche**, a Gothic church with Baroque furnishings, beside which stands the ornate **Hirschberger Tor**, a rare example of north German Rococo. Beyond is the **Neumarkt**, lined with a series of Neoclassical buildings erected when the Prussians took the town following the Napoleonic Wars and made it the regional capital. Particularly notable is the **Auferstehungskirche** (Church of the Resurrection), designed by Schinckel. Numerous half-timbered houses line the streets of the heart of the town, while the **Sauerland–Museum** (Tues–Fri & Sun 10am–5pm, Sat 2–5pm; DM2) occupies the Renaissance **Landsberger Hof** at Alter Markt 26. Further uphill is the Schlossberg, with the ruins of the **Schloss**, which was destroyed in the Seven Years' War. It's the setting for the nine-day-long *Ruinenfest* in late May and early June.

Arnsberg's **tourist office** is at Neumarkt 6 (Mon–Fri 9am–noon & 2–4pm; May–Oct also Sat 10am–noon; ☎02931/4055) and they can advise on a good selection of **hotels**. Two of the best are *Zum Landsberger Hof,* Alter Markt 18 (☎02931/3318; ⑤), and *Menge,* Ruhrstr. 60 (☎02931/52520; ⑥), and both have high quality restaurants. There's a **youth hostel** at Rumbecker Höhe 1 (☎02931/10627; ☎) on the east side of town, by the Arnsberg Forest.

The **Sorpesee**, another artificial lake, lies 10km to the south of Arnsberg. Again, it's a centre for angling and watersports; cruises run from May to September, departing from **LANGSCHEID** on the northern shore. There are a string of **campsites** and a **youth hostel** (☎02935/1776; ☎) on the western bank. To the east and south of here is the bulk of the aforementioned **Naturpark Homert**; apart from its numerous trails, it's a good area for bird-watching, with some 450 resident species.

The Rothaargebirge

Further south is the **Naturpark Rothaargebirge** (Red-Haired Mountains), a range covered with conifers and deciduous woods, which separates the Sauerland from the Siegerland to the south. It's best known as winter-sports country; the main resort, **WINTERBERG**, can be reached by train from Arnsberg via a branch line from Bestwig. As well as the pistes, Winterberg has an indoor skating rink, and bobsleigh and toboggan runs, while international dog-sleigh races are held each January. The town stands at the foot of the **Kahler Asten**, which at 841m is the highest peak in the Sauerland; it's covered with snow for about a third of the year, and the average winter temperature is freezing point. You can ascend to an observation platform (DM1) for a huge panorama of the district. There's a **youth hostel** not far from the mountain in Astenberg (☎02981/2289; ☎). Winterberg itself has an abundant choice of **rooms** in private houses at only marginally higher rates, as well as **hotels** in all price categories. A full list is available from the **tourist office** (Mon–Fri 9am–5pm, Sat 10am–noon; ☎02981/92500) at Hauptstr. 1.

Südsauerland

At the heart of the **Südsauerland** is the largest of the reservoirs, the appropriately named **Biggesee**, which lies below the Ebbegebirge range. A branch of the main Hagen–Siegen rail line runs from Finnentrop down the western bank of the lake.

Attendorn

ATTENDORN, on the northern shore, is an old Hanseatic town. Its fourteenth-century **Altes Rathaus**, apart from being the only remaining secular structure of its period in the entire region, is a striking building, with elaborate gables on both its short ends, and an open lower storey which was intended to serve as a market hall. It now houses the **Kreisheimatmuseum** (Tues–Fri 9am–1pm & 3–5pm, Sat 9am–1pm, Sun 11am–1pm; DM2), which contains some fine examples of sacred art and a notable collection of tableaux of painted tin figurines. **St Johannes** is a fourteenth-century Gothic hall church incorporating the tower of its Romanesque predecessor. It's nicknamed the "cathedral of the Sauerland" due to its pre-eminence among the region's churches. Just to the north of town is the **Attahöhle** (guided tours April–Sept daily 9.30am–4.30pm; Oct, Feb & March daily 10.30am–4pm; Nov–Jan Tues–Sun 10.30am–4pm; DM8), a particularly impressive stalactite cave. To the east is **Burg Schnellenberg**, the largest of the few surviving hilltop castles in Westphalia, part of which has been rebuilt as a luxury hotel.

The **tourist office** is in the *Reisebüro am Rathaus* at Kölner Str. 12a (Mon–Fri 9am–6pm, Sat 10am–noon; ☎02722/64229). If you want to stay, there are plenty of **private rooms** (①–③). **Hotels** include *Rauch*, Wasserstr. 6 (☎02722/92420; ⑦), *Zur Post*, Niederste Str. 7 (☎02722/2465; ⑦) or, for real style, the *Burghotel* (☎02722/6940; ⑧) in the castle. There are two **campsites** just outside town.

Festivals include the best Carnival celebrations in the Sauerland, and various parades during Holy Week, while the first Saturday in August sees *Der Biggesee in Flammen* (The Biggesee in Flames), with fireworks and illuminations. **Cruises** are run on the lake between Easter and mid-October from both Attendorn and **OLPE**, the highly developed watersports resort on the southern bank, which is the terminus of the branch railway.

Siegerland-Wittgenstein

The Rothaargebirge range provides a horizontal dividing line separating the Sauerland from **Siegerland-Wittgenstein** to the south. This region is a somewhat bizarre mixture of a heavily industrialized valley (in many respects similar to South Wales) and a holiday resort area which, even more than the Sauerland, the Germans have reserved for themselves. It's a land of hills and mountains, cut right across the middle by the River Sieg which flows due west, entering the Rhine just north of Bonn.

Siegen

SIEGEN is the capital of this district and the only place within a radius of about 100km which can properly be called a city. Iron and steel production were the reasons for its development last century; relative isolation meant that its growth was checked, and even now its population is barely over 100,000. One of Siegen's main assets is its setting, rising from the banks of the river high into the hills above; this has recently been enhanced by the construction of a spectacular **viaduct** (the biggest in the country) which carries the A45 *Autobahn* – linking the Ruhrgebiet with Hesse – 104m above the Sieg.

The town

A curiosity of Siegen is that it has two castles originally belonging to the Nassau-Siegen family, one at the top of the town, the other a few hundred metres below. This is due to the fact that the line split in 1623 over continued support for the Reformation; thereafter, the Catholic branch lived in the **Oberes Schloss**. The original fortified Burg has been much modified down the centuries and isn't particularly picturesque, but its ramparts command the best views over the town, while the gardens, in honour of the dynasty's intermarriage with the Dutch house of Orange, are planted with 60,000 tulips.

Part of the building has been adapted to house the **Siegerland-Museum** (Tues–Sun 10am–5pm; DM4). This contains varied collections, including a realistic model of a mine 14 metres under the courtyard. There's also a display of memorabilia on the **Busch** brothers, a remarkable twentieth-century Siegen family whose anti-Nazism gave further impetus to their international careers. Adolf and Hermann founded the Busch Quartet with two friends; their 78rpm recordings, particularly of Beethoven, have never been surpassed in terms of interpretation, and many can still be bought in modern remasterings. They also blazed a pioneering trail by championing the playing of Baroque music by authentic-sized chamber groups, instead of in the souped-up arrangements which had been the norm for the previous century. Fritz Busch was a leading conductor who was prominent in the establishment of opera at Glyndebourne in southeast England, while Willi was one of Germany's best actors.

SIR PETER PAUL RUBENS (1577–1840)

Sir Peter Paul Rubens' father Jan, a Calvinist sympathizer, was forced to flee his native Antwerp, settling in Cologne, where he entered the service of Princess Anna of Saxony, second wife of William the Silent. Eventually he graduated from being her adviser and diplomatic agent to sharing her bed when her husband was at war. An untimely pregnancy led to his unmasking. Lucky to escape with his life, he was banished to Siegen, where the great painter was born in 1577. A year later, the family was allowed to return to Cologne; after Jan Rubens' death, they went back to Antwerp. Not only was the young artist quickly reconciled with Roman Catholicism, he was later one of the most ardent propagandists of the Counter-Reformation; he further went against his father in becoming a faithful diplomatic servant of the Spanish imperial power. A man who was almost indecently successful (he ran the equivalent of a picture factory, which churned out canvases by the hundred, all bearing the master's characteristic stamp even when he had contributed little to their actual execution), Rubens was an incorrigible social climber, a grovelling toady to all political and spiritual authority. Yet it's a measure of his greatness as an artist that these offputting traits don't seem to matter – his works can be enjoyed for their phenomenal technical skill, carefully planned design, glorious colours and unabashed *joie de vivre*.

However, the museum's main draw is its display on the art of **Peter Paul Rubens** (see box above) who, by a sheer fluke, can be counted a native of Siegen, though he was in no sense a German. His qualities are all present in a late masterpiece here: somewhat pompously named *The Victorious Hero Seizes the Opportunity for Peace*, it's an allegory featuring Perseus with the head of Medusa, Minerva, Abundance, Opportunity and Time. From a decade earlier, *Roman Charity* illustrates the legend of Cimon, who was saved from starving to death in prison by being breast-fed by his daughter Pero. There's also a haughty *Self-Portrait* from about the same time, and five more original works.

The **Unteres Schloss**, the seat of the Protestant line, originally occupied an abandoned Franciscan monastery. This was destroyed by fire in 1695 and replaced by the present extensive Baroque complex. It's now largely occupied by offices, but the royal crypt has survived. Between the two castles is the Markt, with the eighteenth-century Rathaus and the **Nikolaikirche**, one of the most distinctive of the extravagant series of late Romanesque churches founded in the Rhineland and around. The kernel of the building is a thirteenth-century galleried hexagon – the only example of this design in northern Europe. Two centuries later, the handsome red and white tower was added, forming a highly successful complement. Inside is a baptismal plate made in Peru, a legacy of the time when the Oranien-Nassau family, who used the Nikolaikirche as their court chapel, were playing an important role in the colonization of South America. Lower down the hill is the **Martinikirche**, the unremarkable late Gothic successor to one of the most important Ottonian churches in Germany, from which the mosaic pavement has been preserved.

Practicalities

The **tourist office** (Mon, Wed & Fri 8.30am–noon & 2–4pm, Thurs 8.30am–noon & 2–6pm; ☎0271/404 1316) is in the Rathaus, Markt 2; leaflets are also available at the pavilion immediately in front of the **Hauptbahnhof**. To reach the Altstadt from here, walk right through the pedestrian precinct and turn left uphill at the end.

The best budget **hotels** are *Schäfer*, Rosterstr. 111 (☎0271/338720; ④); *Gasthof Rörig*, Eintrachtstr. 9 (☎0271/331533; ④); *Gasthof Meier*, St-Johann-Str. 3 (☎0271/335066; ④); and *Bürger*, Marienborner Str. 132–136 (☎0271/62551; ③). More upmarket choices include *Berghotel Johanneshöhe*, which commands a grandstand view over Siegen from its hillside location on the west side of town at Wallhausenstr. 1 (☎0271/310008; ⑥), and *Queens*, which is south of the centre at Kampenstr. 83 (☎0271/50110; ⑨).

Siegen's top **restaurants** include those in the last two hotels, plus *Schloss-Stube* in the Oberes Schloss, and *Schwarzbrenner*, in an eighteenth-century house at Metzgerstr. 29. Local **beers** use the pure mountain water of the Siegerland; *Krombacher* is well known throughout Germany, whereas consumption of *Irle* and *Urzquell* is confined mainly to this district.

Freudenberg

FREUDENBERG, 11km northwest of Siegen, to which it's linked by very regular bus services, is an archetypal picture-postcard town which seems to feature on just about every German calendar. In 1660 the town was destroyed by fire for the second time in its two-hundred-year existence; the streets built thereafter as replacements have survived almost intact – row upon row of black and white half-timbered houses, whose steeply pitched slate roofs bear witness to the harshness of the winter climate. It's a popular recreation resort all year round, and has a couple of excellent **hotels**, both with restaurants: *Zum Alten Flecken*, Marktstr. 11 (☎02734/27680; ⑥) and *Zur Altstadt*, Orienstr. 41 (☎02734/4960; ⑦). There are also a few small **pensions** and **private rooms** (①–③); a full list is available from the tourist office (Mon–Fri 10am–4pm; ☎02734/43164) at Krottorfer Str. 25.

Wittgenstein

The former principality of **Wittgenstein**, nowadays administratively united with the Siegerland, features a string of holiday centres along the southern fringe of the Rothaargebirge. Snow can fall early in the winter – often before it arrives in the Alps – whereupon the towns are besieged by skiing parties. **BAD BERLEBURG** is the best-known resort, its spa facilities giving it a balancing pull in summer. It also has one of the few large-scale historical monuments in the region in its predominantly Baroque **Schloss** (guided tours May–Sept daily at 10.30am & 2.30pm; Oct–April Tues, Thurs & Sun at 2.30pm; DM3). From Erndtebrück, the starting point for the branch railway to Bad Berleburg, a different rail line goes to Marburg via **BAD LAASPHE**, another spa with half-timbered buildings reminiscent of Freudenberg. Its Schloss is still inhabited by the Wittgenstein family and may be viewed from the exterior only. All resorts have good **hiking** possibilities, while there is plentiful **accommodation** in all price categories.

Paderborn

The cathedral and market city of **PADERBORN** lies some 55km northeast of Soest, just before the North German plain gives way to the Teutoburg Forest. It's a characterful place, with a variety of archeological and artistic attractions to add to the geological curiosity from which it derives its name, meaning "source of the Pader". This, the country's shortest river at a mere 4km in length, rises in a park, the Paderquellgebiet, in the heart of the city. It's formed by the surfacing of more than two hundred warm springs, which pour out over 5000 litres of water per second. These originate as subterranean streams in the **Eggegebirge** range to the east; they're suddenly forced out into the open at this point by the abrupt change in topography from the plateau to a lowland whose soil contains an impermeable layer of marl.

The city

The **Paderquellgebiet**, right in the centre of the city, is an idyllic spot and makes the obvious place to begin any tour, offering as it does the best view of the city's two main churches – the twin-towered former **Abdinghof** monastery in the foreground, with the massive single steeple of the **Dom** rearing up behind.

The palaces

During postwar rebuilding of the city, the foundations of the **Carolingische Kaiserpfalz**, the site of Charlemagne's momentous meeting with Pope Leo III in 799 which led to the foundation of the Holy Roman Empire, were discovered just to the north of the Dom; they had been hidden from view since a fire destroyed the building in the year 1000. Soon it became the most exciting archeological site in the country, and was excavated in the 1960s, revealing the ground plan of a sizeable complex which included a King's Hall, a church, a monastery and courtyards. Also unearthed was an open-air throne, now under cover beneath the Dom's north portal; you can see it by peering in through the protective glass. To the rear was found the replacement **Ottonische Kaiserpfalz** (Tues–Sun 10am–6pm; DM2), dating from immediately after the 1000 fire and itself desecrated by another fire in 1165. This time the controversial decision was taken to go beyond a routine excavation, and to try and re-create its original form in as scholarly a manner as possible. In 1976 the palace made its belated reappearance, its pristine stonework making an odd contrast with the venerable status of the design. It now houses the regional archeology museum, but interest centres on the structure itself, as no original palaces from this epoch survive. The vestibule lies through a subsidiary building; to the right is the two-storey Ikenbergkapelle, while to the left is the Great Hall, which takes up the lion's share of the complex. Standing on its own near the entrance is the only authentic remnant of the palaces, the tiny **Bartholomäuskapelle**. As the very first hall church erected in Germany, it can claim to be the initiator of what was to become the pre-eminent national architectural form. Despite a glum exterior, it's very dapper inside, a classically inspired design of three aisles of rounded pillars crowned with flowery Corinthian capitals.

The Dom

In preparation for Pope Leo's visit, Charlemagne ordered the construction of a no-expense-spared church which was almost immediately raised to the status of a cathedral; ever since, the city's history has been dominated by its ecclesiastical role. The present **Dom** is a cavernous thirteenth-century Gothic hall church whose tower, slit by innumerable little windows, is a remnant of its Romanesque predecessor. It's entered by the southern porch (or "Paradise") whose portal is adorned with French-style figures. More refined carvings from a now vanished doorway can be seen on either side of the transept window; look out for the cartoon-like fables – a boar blowing a horn, a hare playing the fiddle, a crane removing a bone from a wolf's throat, and a fox dressed as a scholar to receive his diploma. Inside, the Dom resembles a museum of seventeenth-century heroic sculpture to the glory of the Prince-bishops, much of it by one of Germany's few Mannerists, **Heinrich Gröninger**. His masterpiece, almost facing you on entry, is the grandiose **monument to Dietrich von Fürstenberg**, complete with depictions of the buildings this bishop commissioned to transform the face of the city. The Dom's most enduring attraction returns to the animal theme and comes in the form of a puzzle, which you should try to work out in advance. Follow the signs marked *Hasenfenster* into the cloister garden; the tracery of one of the windows is the emblem of Paderborn, and a mason's trick which was celebrated in its day. This shows three hares running around in a circle, but, although each clearly has two ears of his own, it has only been necessary to carve one per creature.

The Markt

The south side of the Dom faces the open space of the vast Markt, lined with tall Baroque houses and the Romanesque **Gaukirche**. In this setting, the lead-plated glass palace which houses a couple of shops, a café and the **Erzbischöflisches Diözesanmuseum** (Tues–Sun 10am–6pm; DM4) creates a strident impact, the more so as it masks some of the wonderful views of the Dom. This brash modernist intrusion into the old city clearly had its supporters, as its architect was Gottfried Böhm, who immediately afterwards was asked to rebuild the Ottonian Kaiserpfalz. The interior, rising abruptly in tiers, is a cleverly thought-out design to provide a majestic setting for the museum. In the basement, the **Schatzkammer's** most valuable pieces are two inlaid reliquary cabinets, made for the Dom and the Adinghof in about 1100, and the Baroque shrine of Paderborn's patron, St Liborius. The Dom's old bells are invitingly displayed with hammers, allowing you to indulge in a bit of instant campanology. Upstairs, pride of place is rightly given to the *Imad Madonna*, a hierarchic mid-eleventh-century wooden statue named after its bishop donor.

The rest of the city

The remaining sights can be covered by means of a short circular walk. Following Schildern at the southwest corner of the Markt, you come to the city's most handsome building, the **Rathaus**, bedecked with arcades, gables and oriel windows, and fronted by a zappy facade. Erected in the early seventeenth century in the Weser Renaissance style, it was modelled on the patrician **Heisingsches Haus** just down the street. Up the hill from here is the **Jesuitenkolleg** from the end of the same century, whose church, like the one in Cologne, has a vast galleried interior with anachronistic Gothic pointed arches.

Further along Kamp is the sober **Dalheimer Hof** by the Westphalian Baroque architect, Johann Conrad Schlaun. Going back downhill along Kasseler Strasse, you see the Romanesque **Busdorfkirche**, whose main joy is its tiny cloister. A couple of minutes' walk down Heierstrasse, then left into Thisaut, is Hathumarstrasse, with the oldest remaining half-timbered house, **Adam-und-Eva-Haus**, now the local museum (Tues–Sun 10am–6pm; free). The most eye-catching exhibits are a couple of exquisite drawings of the city by Schlaun, and a display of engravings by **Heinrich Aldegraver**, a native of Paderborn who was one of Dürer's most faithful followers. From here, the Dom is back in view and only a few minutes' walk away.

Practicalities

The **Hauptbahnhof** is southwest of the centre; turn right at the exit and keep going straight. En route to the Markt you'll pass the **tourist office** at Marienplatz 2a (Mon–Fri 9.30am–6pm, Sat 9am–1pm; ☎05251/26461).

Centrally sited **hotels** include *Haus Irma*, Bachstr. 9 (☎05251/23342; ③); *Krawinkel*, Karlstr. 33 (☎05251/23663; ③); *Südhotel*, Borchener Str. 23 (☎05251/78005; ③); *Cherusker Hof*, Detmolder Str. 1 (☎05251/55534; ⑥); *Galerie Abdinghof*, Bachstr. 1a (☎05251/12240; ⑥); and *Arosa*, Westernmauer 38 (☎05251/1280; ⑨). For once, the **youth hostel** is conveniently sited just a few minutes' walk from the main attractions at Meinwerkstr. 16 (☎05251/22055; ❷), the continuation of Heierstrasse. The two **campsites** are both in the northern outreaches of the city – *Am Waldsee* at Husarenstr. 130 (☎05251/7372) and *Stauterrassen* at Auf der Thune 14 (☎05251/4504).

Among the best **restaurants** in the centre is that in the *Arosa* hotel. In addition, *Balthasar*, An der Alten Synagoge 1, presents genuinely creative cuisine, while the *Ratskeller* in the Rathaus offers both Westphalian dishes and *neue deutsche Küche*.

Pubs offering **live music** include *Tuba*, Kasseler Str. 26, *Das Treibhaus*, Detmolder Str. 21, and *Kukoz*, Tegelweg 3–5. Concerts, musicals, dance, opera and jazz are performed at the ultra-modern *PaderHalle,* Heiersmauer 45–51 (☎05251/25001). The main **popular festivals** occur in July, including a *Schützenfest* on the second weekend. There's also a beer week in October.

Bielefeld

BIELEFELD, some 35km north of Paderborn, clusters around the narrow middle strip of the Teutoburg Forest which runs right through the built-up areas. It's strongly reminiscent of the cities of the Ruhrgebiet in history, feel and appearance, and is the overwhelmingly dominant economic centre of eastern Westphalia. Founded in the thirteenth century by the Counts of Ravensberg, the town gained prosperity in the late Middle Ages through the linen trade. The nineteenth century saw a mushroom growth, due to the increased importance of this traditional industry, plus various new engineering products associated with it. Development was helped by the fact that nearby Minden, with a far more favourable geographical location, was preoccupied with its role as a garrison town.

The city

Right on the edge of the Teutoburg Forest, overlooking the southern end of the city centre, is Bielefeld's oldest building, the **Sparrenburg**, built between 1240 and 1250 as the seat of the Counts of Ravensberg and strengthened in the sixteenth and seventeenth centuries by massive bastions conforming to the latest theories about military architecture. The castle has a round **tower** (daily April–Oct 10am–6pm; DM1.20) which can be ascended for a panoramic view, and some 300m of underground **passageways** and **dungeons** (same times, but only accessible by joining a pre-booked group; DM1.50). In the courtyard is a statue to Margrave Friedrich Wilhelm of Brandenburg, the man who established Bielefeld's prosperity by introducing the *Leinenlegge*, a quality control for linen.

Below the Sparrenburg to the north is the so-called Neustadt (new town), grouped around the **Neustädter Marienkirche**, a handsome Gothic church built in the late thirteenth and early fourteenth centuries, and now standing, much in the manner of an English cathedral, in splendid isolation on a green. Its tall twin towers are crowned by unusually long and sharply pointed lead steeples; they look so venerable it's hard to believe they were devastated in an air-raid and had to be rebuilt almost from scratch. The church, which contains outstanding **works of art**, is kept locked; ring at the door of the halls directly in front for the caretaker. On the high altar is a masterpiece by the same Westphalian Soft Style artist who painted the *Berswordt Altar* in Dortmund. It shows the *Madonna and Child with Saints*, surrounded by a dozen small panels, mostly of scenes from Christ's life; the wings were cut up and sold last century, and are now in museums all over the world. A major but nameless fourteenth-century sculptor (whose works can also be seen in Cappenberg and Marburg) carved the frieze of apostles above the altar, which belonged to the former rood screen. He also created the magnificent **tomb** of Otto III von Ravensberg and Hedwig von Lippe, featuring a touching yet unsentimental portrayal of their previously deceased son. The other elaborate Ravensberg family monument is clearly modelled on this tomb, even though it was made over a century later.

On nearby Artur-Ladebeck-Strasse is the smooth red sandstone pile of the **Kunsthalle** (Tues, Wed, Fri–Sun 11am–6pm, Thurs 11am–9pm; DM5). The building itself, erected in the 1960s, was intended to be a significant addition to the city's heritage; it was designed by **Philip Johnson**, Mies van der Rohe's principal American follower, who was himself one of the leading lights in propagating the International Style in architecture. Most of the Expressionists are represented, with good examples of Beckmann, Kirchner, Nolde and Macke; there are sculptures by Rodin, Barlach, Archipenko, Lipchitz, Caro and Moore (some inside, others in the garden), and several rooms of European and American abstract painting.

What remains of the Altstadt is just a short walk from the Kunsthalle – turn right into Obernstrasse at the end of Artur-Ladebeck-Strasse. The Markt is lined by the patrician houses originally built by the most prosperous linen merchants. Oldest is the late Gothic **Crüwellhaus** of 1530; the others are in the cheerful Weser Renaissance style of the following century. Round the corner on Postgang is the Gothic **Altstädter Nicolaikirche**, which contains a spectacular sixteenth-century altar from Antwerp, featuring some 250 figures in the carved depictions of the Passion. Behind the church is the **Leineweber-Denkmal**, depicting a linen weaver with the traditional characteristics of a long pipe and walking stick.

Practicalities

The **Hauptbahnhof** is immediately to the north of the city centre; directly opposite in the Leinenmeisterhaus is the **tourist office** (Mon–Fri 9am–5.30pm, Sat 9am–1pm; ☎0521/178844). There's a second branch in the Neues Rathaus, on the eastern edge of the centre at Niederwall 23 (same hours; ☎0521/178899). The **Mitfahrzentrale** office is at Siegfriedstr. 46 (☎0521/130088).

Accommodation

A wide range of centrally sited **hotels** includes *Kaiser*, Schildescher Str. 47 (☎0521/61984; ②); *Wiegmann*, Kronenstr. 11 (☎0521/60471; ③); *Huning*, Kreuzstr. 9 (☎0521/62293; ④); *Stadt Bremen*, Bahnhofstr. 32 (☎0521/67088; ⑤); and in a forest setting *Waldhotel Brand's Busch*, Furtwänglerstr. 52 (☎0521/92110; ⑦). The tourist office can supply lists of generally cheaper alternatives in the suburbs (there's a whole clutch in Brackwede to the south), but you'd be better off looking for a room in a more congenial small town nearby, such as Lemgo (see p.559) or Detmold (see p.561).

Bielefeld's **youth hostel**, Oetzer Weg 25 (☎0521/22227; 🏠), is 4km south of the centre in an isolated location within the Teutoburg Forest; take U-Bahn #2 to its terminus, then bus #118, but note that the latter stops running soon after the evening rush hour. There are also two **campsites**, both on the edge of the forest, at Vogelweide 9 (☎0521/450336) and Campingstr. 23 (☎05203/445338).

Eating, drinking and entertainment

One of the city's best **restaurants** is *Sparrenburg* within the castle; another good choice is *Im Bültmannshof* in a fine half-timbered house at Kurt-Schumacher-Str. 17a.

The main **theatre** is the luxuriant Jugendstil *Stadttheater*, Niederwall 27 (☎0521/177077); drama is also performed at the *Theater am Alten Markt*

BIELEFELD'S FESTIVALS

If Bielefeld is rather thin on historic monuments, its numerous **popular festivals** provide a counterbalance. Best of these is the *Leineweber Markt* on the last weekend in May, which includes street theatre, jazz and rock concerts, as well as folklore displays. Open-air music of all kinds is played throughout the city during the summer, while every third Saturday from May to October sees a flea market; the location varies, but the Markt itself is regularly the venue. In mid-July, the *Sparrenburgfest* in the castle features tournaments and a medieval fair, while there's a week-long *Weinfest* in mid-September.

(☎0521/177077), while there's a *Puppenspiele* (puppet theatre) at Ravensberger Str. 12 (☎0521/66696). **Concerts** are given at *Rudolf-Oetker-Halle* on Stapenhorststrasse (☎0521/178899). Bielefeld's most original venue, however, is the *Alte Ravensberger Spinnerei*, east of Jahnplatz at Heeper Str. 37 (☎0521/516526), a grandiose nineteenth-century linen mill, worth seeing in its own right as a rare survivor of the sort of factory which once dotted large German industrial towns. Lovingly restored, it's now a cultural centre, featuring exhibitions, films and music recitals.

Minden

MINDEN's strategic importance, at an easily fordable point of the River Weser, 30km northeast of Bielefeld, has meant that military affairs have dominated its history: the old ramparts were converted into a full-blown fortress by the Swedes during the Thirty Years' War; it was the scene of a decisive battle in 1759 in which the British and Prussians defeated the French; and, during the Napoleonic Wars, it was equipped with the latest defensive systems as a leading Prussian frontier town, a role it retained until the unification of Germany in 1871. The city kept its historic appearance until the last war, when its strategic importance inevitably led to severe aerial bombardment.

The Wasserstrassenkreuz

Minden's role as a fortress meant it could not expand and industrialize, but its favourable geographical position led to its development as the hub of the German inland water transport system, and it's from this function that its main present-day attraction derives. In the northern part of the city, you'll find the **Wasserstrassenkreuz** (Waterway Junction) which is unique in Europe. The most eye-catching feature is the surrealistic **Kanalbrücke** (Canal Bridge), a 375-metre-long aquatic flyover built between 1911 and 1914; it allows the **Mittellandkanal** – which stretches right across north Germany, linking the Rhine with the Elbe – to pass directly over the Weser. The heart of the system is the fortress-like **Schachtschleuse** (Great Lock), which shifts 12,000 cubic metres of water while transferring ships from canal to river or vice versa in just seven minutes. Alongside is the exhibition hall (April–Oct Mon–Sat 9am–5pm, Sun 9am–6pm; DM1.50), which explains the layout and working of the Wasserstrassenkreuz by means of models and diagrams. A series of paths enable you to explore the area on foot, but it's far more fun to take a **cruise**. Run by the *Mindener Fahrgastschiffahrt* (☎0571/648 0800), these leave from the jetty immediately opposite the Schachtschleuse. There's a choice of fifty- and ninety-minute trips, costing DM8 and DM11 respectively. The former departs six times daily in the high season (mid-May to mid-Sept), and three times a day for the six weeks before and after these dates. Though the longer cruise is the more enticing, taking in a short stretch of the Weser as well as the harbour, it only runs once daily (Mon–Sat at 2pm in low season, 3pm in high season, Sun at 10.15am). It's also possible to sail for longer stretches up and down the Weser from here; check locally for details.

The rest of the city

The **Hauptbahnhof** is on the right side of the river; its situation, a good twenty minutes' walk from town, is explained by the fact that it was built as part of the Prussian fortifications. Along with the three small forts grouped in a semicircle around it, it's one of the few survivors of that period, as the citizens had no great love for their citadel, and dismantled it as soon as it was declared redundant.

The Altstadt is dominated by the **Dom**, whose massive westwork, with two subsidiary towers stuck like glue to the main belfry, is in the severest form of Romanesque.

The main body of the building, however, is a hall church, erected in the late thirteenth century in a pure early Gothic style; this has a light and airy feel, thanks to the huge windows decorated with highly elaborate tracery. On the south transept wall is a frieze of Apostles, the remnant of a former Romanesque rood screen; from the same period is the bronze *Minden Crucifix*, the Dom's most important work of art. However, the one currently displayed here is a copy; the original is in the **Domschatz** in the *Haus am Dom* opposite (Tues, Thurs, Sat & Sun 10am–noon; Wed & Fri 3–5pm; free). Among many other valuable items, note the gilded twelfth-century reliquary of St Peter.

Just beyond lies the Markt, whose north side is taken up by the **Rathaus**. Its lower storey, featuring an arcaded passageway, is contemporary with the Dom; the upper part is late Renaissance. Continuing up the steps from here takes you to the best-preserved part of the Altstadt, centred on Martinikirchhof. On this square are two survivors of the Prussian garrison buildings, the **Körnermagazin**, where weapons were stored, and the **Martinihaus**, which served as the bakery. Also here is the **Schwedenschänke**, used by the Swedish troops as their refectory during the Thirty Years' War. **St Martini** itself is the pick of Minden's gaunt and blackened parish churches, with a dignified interior housing notable furnishings – late Gothic stalls, Renaissance pulpit and wrought-iron font – and a magnificent organ, partly dating back to the sixteenth century.

Just off the square on Brüderstrasse is the **Alte Münze**, formerly the house of the master of the mint; today, it's a Greek restaurant. A rare example of Romanesque civil architecture, it owes its survival to the fact that it was subsequently embellished according to the tastes of the time (with a stepped gable in the Gothic period, and an oriel window in the Renaissance). Mansions in the characteristic Weser Renaissance style are dotted all over the quarter – the finest are on Bäckerstrasse, Am Scharn and Papenmarkt. The densest concentration, however, is on Ritterstrasse, where five houses have been adapted to contain the **Mindener Museum** (Tues–Fri 10am–1pm & 2.30–5pm, Sat 2.30–5pm, Sun 11am–6pm; free). Displayed in two courtyards are fragments of sculptural decoration from buildings such as these; see in particular a wonderful *Story of Samson*. Upstairs, along with the usual folklore displays, there's a room devoted to the **Battle of Minden**, a turning point in the Seven Years' War.

Practicalities

Minden's **tourist office** is at Grosser Domhof 3 (Mon–Fri 8am–1pm & 2–5pm, Sat 9am–1pm; ☎0571/89385).

If you want to spend the night in town, there are only a handful of central **hotels**. These include *Wappenkrug*, Marienstr. 121 (☎0571/45292; ③); *Altes Gasthaus Grotehof*, Wettiner Allee 14 (☎0571/54018; ⑥); *Stadthotel Kronprinz*, Friedrich-Wilhelm-Str. 1–3 (☎0571/934080; ⑦); and *Silke*, Fischerglacis 21 (☎0571/828070; ⑦). Other cheaper options tend to be far out – such as *Grashoff*, Bremer Str. 83 (☎0571/41834; ④), in the suburb of Todtenhausen, site of the Battle of Minden.

Among the best places to **eat** and **drink** are the *Ratskeller*, Markt 1, the vegetarian *Vita Table*, Simeonstr. 12, and the fish specialist *Zum Fishbäcker*, Obermarktstr. 34.

Lemgo

With its surprising vistas and architectural groupings, and the myriad delicate details on its buildings, **LEMGO**, 12km north of Detmold and 25km east of Bielefeld, would be a strong contender in any competition to find the prettiest town in northern Germany. It has escaped the ravages both of war and of mass tourism. Many of the buildings from its sixteenth-century Hanseatic heyday survive, and are now immaculately cared for, with the merchant class which built them from the profits of foreign trade now replaced by a mixture of retailers, wealthy commuters (over half the population works elsewhere) and public bodies.

The town

The Altstadt, though more extensive than might be expected from the present modest size of the town, is easily explored on foot, and the two main sights outside its boundaries are just a short walk away.

The Hexenbürgermeisterhaus

Breite Strasse, the main axis linking the southern part of town with the central Markt, is one of Lemgo's finest thoroughfares, dominated by the spectacular **Hexenbürgermeisterhaus** (Witches' Burgomaster House) at no. 19. The facade, with its elegantly tapering gables, its *Fall of Man* over the doorway and its two quite different oriel windows (something of a Lemgo speciality) adorned with the Seven Cardinal Virtues, ranks as one of the supreme masterpieces of the Weser Renaissance style. It was built in 1571, three years after the completion of the rest of the house, by a local man, **Hermann Wulf**. Originally commissioned by a merchant family, the house's present curious name derives from an occupant in a later, more mordant period, the notorious **Hermann Cothmann**. He was burgomaster of Lemgo at the height of the hysterical campaign against supposed witches between 1666 and 1681, apparently sentencing some ninety women to death.

Inside, an above average **Städtisches Museum** (Tues–Sun 10am–12.30pm & 1.30–5pm; DM1.50) appropriately includes a room devoted to gruesome instruments of torture, from the inquisition stool with its seat of protruding nails, through thumb and leg screws, to less brutal items such as the barrel which formed a moveable stocks. There is also an exhibition on a more enlightened Lemgo citizen of the same period, **Engelbert Kämpfer**. A pioneering traveller in Russia, Persia, Java and Japan, Kämpfer had de luxe accounts of his journeys printed and published in his native town, which was then a leading centre of book production.

The Marienkirche

Just off Breite Strasse down Stiftstrasse is the **Marienkirche**, the Gothic hall church of a convent which was suppressed when Lemgo went over to the Reformation. It has one of the richest musical traditions in Germany and there's a small international festival in the first week of June. The choir is celebrated, the **swallow's nest organ** even more so. Built between 1587 and 1613, initially by a Dutchman, and then by two brothers from Hamburg, it's rated amongst the sweetest-sounding instruments in Europe. If you aren't lucky enough to hear it, the woodwork is still an artistic treasure in its own right, although sadly stripped of its original bright polychromy. Also from the Renaissance is the **font**, the work of a local sculptor, **Georg Crossmann**, with unashamedly sensual figures of the Four Christian Virtues. Behind it are statues of the nobleman Otto Zur Lippe and his wife, masterpieces of late fourteenth-century funerary art.

The Markt and around

Beyond the end of Breite Strasse, past a fine series of gabled houses, you reach the **Wippermannsches Haus**, the only one of the great merchant buildings in the extravagant late Gothic style. Just a few paces away is the **Markt**, lined with a wealth of superb structures from the fourteenth century onwards. The **Rathaus** complex on the east side represents the changing building fashions in its photogenic jumble of arcades, pinnacles and gables. Its northern corner, the old **Apothekenerker**, is still used as a pharmacy, and has a magnificent oriel window. The gossamer carvings, again the work of Crossmann, include a frieze of ten famous scientists, while the columns of the upper windows show the Five Senses.

The south side of the square is fronted by the early seventeenth-century **Ballhaus**; beside it is the sixteenth-century **Zeughaus**, whose rear wall is painted in psychedelic zigzags. The stately Renaissance edifices on the west side are flanked by two prize-winning buildings from the 1970s, modernist, yet imbued with motifs from Lemgo's past, but perhaps rather too stridently self-confident. There can be no complaints, however, about the northern frontage of the square, which also forms part of Lemgo's central axis, Mittelstrasse. Appropriately, this is the street most evocative of the Hansa; half-timbering was used extensively, and some of the mansions have nicknames deriving from their decoration, such as **Planetenhaus** (House of the Planets) and **Sonnenuhrhaus** (Sundial House). The buildings to the right also have handsome backs, forming part of the close of the Gothic **Nikolaikirche**, whose twin towers were later varied by the addition of contrasting lead spires. Its interior, a characteristic hall design, has an assortment of works of art of various periods and styles, including another early Renaissance font by Crossmann.

The Junkerhaus and Schloss Brake

Continuing to the end of Mittelstrasse, then straight ahead down Bismarckstrasse to Hamelner Strasse, brings you to the remarkable **Junkerhaus** (Tues–Fri & Sun 10am–12.30pm & 1.30–5pm, Sat 10am–1pm; DM1.50). It's the obsessive single-handed creation of a totally eccentric local architect, painter and sculptor, **Karl Junker**, who was determined to bequeath his own vision of a dream house as a modern counterpart to the sixteenth-century mansions he knew so well. From the outside, it looks like the witch's cottage from *Hansel and Gretel*, while the interior is spookier than anything Hammer House of Horror ever produced; the sinuous woodcarvings are the stuff of nightmarish fantasies.

Returning down Hamelner Strasse, a sharp left into Pagenhelle before the start of Bismarckstrasse takes you to **Schloss Brake** (Tues–Sun 10am–6pm; DM4), a moated Renaissance palace of the Counts of Lippe, whose striking six-storey tower has a secret stairway leading to the most private apartments. The palace now houses a museum of the Weser Renaissance, with extensive collections of paintings, sculptures, furniture and *objets d'art*. In the grounds are two old mills, the **Schlossmühle** and the **Ölmühle**, together with the miller's house, now fitted out as the **Mühlenmuseum** (Tues–Sun 10am–12.30pm & 2–5pm; free).

Practicalities

Lemgo's **Bahnhof**, on a branch line from Bielefeld, is just to the south of the historic kernel of the city; **buses** operate from the bays in front. The **tourist office** is at Papenstr. 7 (Mon–Fri 9am–1pm & 2–5pm, Sat 10am–1pm; ☎05261/213347).

Centrally located **hotels** include *Bahnhofswaage*, Am Bahnhof (☎05261/3525; ④); *Hansa*, Breite Str. 14 (☎05261/94050; ⑥); *Lemgoer Hof*, Detmolder Weg 14 (☎05261/97670; ⑥); and the best in town, *Stadtpalais*, Papenstr. 24 (☎05261/94990; ⑦). There are also a few budget options a bit further out, including: *Zum Ilsetal*, Sommerhäuschenweg 45 (☎05261/5177; ③); and *Gasthof Zum Landsknecht*, Herforder Str. 177 (☎05261/68264; ③), whose restaurant specializes in Swiss-style dishes. There's no youth hostel, but the **campsite** *Alte Hansestadt Lemgo* (☎05261/14858) has a convenient riverside setting at Regentorstr. 106 between Schloss Brake and the Altstadt.

The Altstadt abounds with places to **eat** and **drink**, including most of the usual ethnic varieties and several classy cafés, but the best restaurants are that in the *Hotel Stadtpalais* (weekday evenings only) and the cosy *In der Neustadt*, Breite Str. 40.

Detmold and the Southern Teutoburg Forest

DETMOLD, capital of the former Lippe principality, makes the obvious base for seeing the varied attractions of the southern part of the **Teutoburg Forest** (*Teutoburger Wald*). If you're understandably baffled by the competing claims of Germany's innumerable forests, then this is one with a difference, adding extra natural, historical and artistic delights to the usual wooded trails.

The town

An old jingle, quoted ad infinitum in tourist brochures and on billboards all over town, describes Detmold as *eine wunderschöne Stadt*. That ranks as something of an exaggeration, but it's an agreeable place nonetheless, with a far more laid-back approach to life than is usual in Germany.

The centre

The largely pedestrianized historic area lies a short walk from the train station and bus station down to the left. Lange Strasse and the streets around, such as Bruchstrasse, Schülerstrasse, Krumme Strasse and Exterstrasse, are lined with large half-timbered **old houses**, interspersed with self-confident stone buildings of the Wilhelmine epoch. However, easily the most attractive street is the venerable and smaller-scale Adolfstrasse, running parallel to and east of Langestrasse.

North of the Markt is a green area centred on the **Residenzschloss** (guided tours daily April–Oct at 10am, 11am, noon, 2pm, 3pm, 4pm & 5pm; Nov–March at 10am, 11am, noon, 2pm, 3pm & 4pm; DM6), which is surrounded by water on three sides. The keep of the medieval fortress was incorporated into the present Renaissance structure, which was progressively shorn of its defensive features down the years. It remains in the possession of the descendants of the Counts (later Princes) of Lippe who built it. The interior is not what you'd expect from outside; its rooms were transformed in the eighteenth and nineteenth centuries according to the tastes of the time, but their most valuable adornment is a superb set of seventeenth-century Brussels tapestries of *The Life of Alexander the Great*, woven from cartoons made by the great French designer Charles Le Brun.

From here, the **Lippisches Landesmuseum** (Tues, Wed & Fri–Sun 10am–5pm, Thurs 10am–8pm; DM4) is reached down Ameide, to the rear of the Schloss. It's housed in two buildings, with natural history in one, archeology, local history and folklore in the other. The second building has a number of reconstituted period rooms, and displays on the history of fashion and on local agriculture, incorporating a rebuilt tithe barn and granary.

The Freilichtmuseum

The Landesmuseum makes a good prelude to the spectacular **Westfälisches Freilichtmuseum** (April–Oct Tues–Sun 9am–6pm; DM7), the most important open-air museum in Germany, which is being laid out at the southern side of the town; to reach it, go in a straight line down the Allee, the continuation of Lange Strasse. When complete (which will not be for several years) it will comprise 168 redundant original buildings from rural Westphalia; currently over ninety are in place. These are grouped together according to region, thus giving a clear picture of the different construction styles. As a centrepiece, there will be three complete simulated villages; other parts of the province are represented by a more modest selection, generally constructed round a large manor house. Apart from farmsteads and workshops of diverse kinds, you can see water mills and windmills, humble privys, wayside chapels and a complete school. The whole way of life associated with these buildings is preserved as well – thus the traditional crafts of weaving, spinning, pottery, milling and forging are demonstrated, farmyard animals are reared, and the gardens are planted to give a practical yield of vegetables. Several hours are needed to do justice to the museum; reasonably priced lunches are available at the eighteenth-century inn *Zum Wilden Mann* on the main street of the Paderborn village, less substantial fare at *Tiergartenkrug* near the Tecklenburg and Minden group of houses.

Practicalities

Detmold's **Bahnhof**, on the line between Bielefeld and the important junction of Altenbeken, is situated next to the **bus station** just a short walk from the centre of town. Turn left along Bahnhofstrasse, then right into Paulinenstrasse and you'll reach the historic area down to the left. The **tourist office** (Mon–Thurs 9am–noon & 1–5pm, Fri 9am–noon/4pm; April–Oct also Sat 9am–noon; ☎05231/977328) is located here in the Rathaus at Markt 5.

The tourist office has full lists of the extensive choice of **private rooms** and small **pensions** (①–③) available all over the surrounding area; there are only a couple in Detmold itself. Most of these are only practical if you've got your own transport. The cheapest **hotels** in town are the English-owned *Meier*, Bahnhofstr. 22 (☎05231/991844; ④) and its neighbour, *Brechmann*, Bahnhofstr. 9 (☎05231/25655; ⑤). In the middle range there's *Nadler*, Grabbestr. 4 (☎05231/92460; ⑥) whose *Café Stuck* serves good bistro-type meals. There are two excellent upmarket hotels in *Lippischer Hof*, Willy-Brandt-Platz 1 (☎05231/9360; ⑦) and *Detmolder Hof*, Lange Str. 19 (☎05231/99120; ⑦). Both of these have top-notch **restaurants**, though they're rivalled by *Speisekeller im Rosental* in the *Stadthalle*, Schlossplatz 7. There's a **youth hostel** at Schirrmannstr. 49 (☎05231/24739; ⓐ) right on the edge of town; from Paulinenstrasse, turn right into Freilingrathstrasse, then left into Brahmsstrasse, and follow its continuation, Schützenberg, to the end.

Around Detmold

Four of the **Teutoburg Forest**'s top sights are within 10km of Detmold; at a push, it's possible to see them all in a day, following a southerly route. Unless you've got your own transport, however, a fair amount of walking is necessary.

THE FIRST GERMAN HERO

Having served for three years in the Imperial army, **Arminius**, a warrior prince of the Cherusci tribe, originally allies of the Romans, became wise to the fact that, by stealthy means, the Germanic peoples were in danger of being subjugated in the same way as the Gauls. In 9 AD he inflicted a crushing defeat on the Roman army in the Teutoburg Forest, using techniques akin to modern guerilla warfare. He then tried to forge an alliance with the southern Germanic tribes, which might have spelt real disaster for the Empire, but was frustrated by their quisling leadership. Nevertheless, two more Roman campaigns to subdue Germania were repelled, leading them to abandon the attempt. The hero was murdered by his own in-laws in 21 AD and was forgotten for centuries, only to be rediscovered and eulogized by the Romantic movement, who saw him not only as a great liberator, but also (rather fancifully) as the first man with the vision of a united Germany, which was at long last to be achieved.

The Hermannsdenkmal

Firstly, there's what can be regarded as Germany's equivalent of the Statue of Liberty, the **Hermannsdenkmal** (daily April–Oct 9am–6.30pm; Nov–March 9.30am–4pm; DM2), situated on the **Grotenburg** to the southwest of the town; two buses go out daily (mid-May to mid-Sept only), or it can be reached on foot by gently ascending paths from the suburb of Hiddesen. The monument commemorates **Arminius** (or "Hermann", see box on previous page) and is as near as possible to the scene of his greatest victory. The completion of the project was entirely due to the single-minded dedication of the architect-sculptor **Ernst von Bandel**, who worked at it on and off from 1838 to 1875, according to the availability of funds. Resting on a colonnaded base, the monument is crowned with an idealized vision in copper of the hero brandishing his sword on high; the total height to the tip of the sword is 53m, and the figure weighs 76,865kg. From the platform there's a fine **view** over the whole range of the Teutoburg Forest.

The Vogel- und Blumenpark and Adlerwarte

Following Denkmalstrasse you descend in less than 2km to the first of two ornithological treats, the **Vogel- und Blumenpark** (Bird and Flower Park; daily variable date in March/April–Oct 9am–6pm; DM5) with over 2000 varieties from all over the world, from miniature hens hardly bigger than insects to the large South American nandu. Particularly impressive is the collection of parrots and cockatoos, sufficiently domesticated to be left uncaged.

From here, you can follow the footpath to the right and continue in a straight line to the **Adlerwarte** (Eagle Watch; daily April–Oct 8.30am–6pm; Nov–March 8.30am–dusk; DM6) in Berlebeck. This eyrie, commanding a fine panorama over the forest, serves as a breeding station and clinic for birds of prey, with around ninety of these magnificent creatures kept here permanently. Displayed on chains or in cages are all kinds of eagles – imperial, golden, prairie, sea, bald, martial, and the enormous and rare harpy – as well as falcons, hawks, kites, buzzards, vultures, condors, griffons and various breeds of owls. The site was specially chosen because of its suitability for **free flight**, and the demonstrations of this (11am & 2.30pm) are a memorable experience. There are three directions the bird can choose to ascend; it then glides out of sight for a while before returning to make a flawless swoop at the bait in the hand of the falconer, whose every movement it can follow from as far as 2km away.

The Externsteine

The **Externsteine**, a further 3km south just before the town of Horn-Bad Meinberg, is a jagged clump of sandstone rocks set by an artificial lake, a striking contrast to the wooded landscape to be found all around. It's one of Germany's most evocative sites, an enigmatic mixture of natural and man-made features, whose precise origin and significance has teased and baffled generations of scholars. Bus #782 passes nearby; a DM1.50 charge is levied when the caretaker is on duty, but access is always free in the evening.

Adorning the bulky rock at the far right is a magnificent large **twelfth-century relief** of *The Descent from the Cross*, which was carved on the spot, making it quite unlike any other known sculpture of the period. Although Romanesque in style, it's imbued with the hierarchical Byzantine spirit, one of the few German works of art, illuminated manuscripts apart, so influenced. Some limbs have been lost, but its state of preservation is otherwise remarkable. Directly below is a worn carving, probably representing Adam and Eve entwined around the serpent. To the side is a series of caves, now closed off; one of these bears an inscription saying it was consecrated as a chapel in 1115. There's also a stairway leading up to a viewing platform at the top. The next rock, fronted by an open-air pulpit, retains its natural peak, below which is a roofless chapel with a circular window exactly aligned to catch the sunrise on the summer solstice. It's too upright to accommodate a staircase, but you can ascend from the top of the stumpy rock to the left by means of a little bridge bent like a bow; from the ground it looks precarious, but it is totally secure. The fourth rock, bearing a plaque depicting the coat of arms of the Counts of Lippe, is again crowned with apparent danger, in this case a large stone which seems ready to fall down, but which is actually fastened with iron hooks, following the repeated failure of attempts to dislodge it.

Many are convinced that the Externsteine served as a centre of pagan worship; others maintain that the site's religious origins go back no further than the twelfth century, and that it's a re-creation of the Holy Places of Jerusalem, inspired by Crusaders' tales. What's known for sure is that it was an anchorite hermitage throughout medieval times, and that it then passed to the local counts, serving successively as a fortress, a pleasure palace and a prison, undergoing many alterations in the process, before being restored to its present form – assumed to be the original – early last century.

Höxter

HÖXTER, about 45km southeast of Detmold, is the easternmost town in Westphalia. Hameln (see pp.610), downstream along the River Weser and Bad Karlshafen (see pp.398), upstream, are just over the border in Lower Saxony and Hesse respectively. Höxter is principally of note for the venerable **Abtei Corvey**, though it also has a fine historic centre.

The town

The centre of Höxter is dominated by the twin towers of the red sandstone **Kilianikirche**, a Romanesque building clearly modelled on Corvey; inside is a Renaissance pulpit adorned with fine alabaster reliefs. Otherwise, the town is notable for the prevalence of **half-timbered houses**, which include the mid-sixteenth-century **Küsterhaus** facing the church. Beyond is the **Rathaus**, a late Renaissance structure from the following century, adorned with octagonal turret and oriel. It's rivalled in splendour by the earlier **Dechanei** (Deanery), an asymmetrical double house reached down Marktstrasse. Although it's the busiest street, Westerbachstrasse is astonishingly well preserved, offering a complete panorama of half-timbering down the centuries, from late Gothic (for example no. 43, *Haus Ohrmann*) to Neoclassical (for example no. 40). There's little doubt that the Renaissance buildings steal the show, particularly *Tilly Haus* (no. 33–37), *Corveyer Hof* (no. 29) and *Altes Brauhaus* (no. 28).

Abtei Corvey

The main claim on your attention is the once powerful **Abtei Corvey** (April–Oct daily 9am–6pm; DM4.50), just over 1km from the town centre, and reached by either following the river eastwards, or going in a straight line down Corbiestrasse. A ninth-century Carolingian foundation, it was a famous centre of scholarship, its greatest legacy being *The History of the Saxons*, written around 975 by the monk-chronicler **Widukind**. He gave the newly conquered barbarian race an appropriately grand origin in veterans of Alexander the Great's army, and vividly related their story right up to his own day. The **Abteikirche** (closed 1–2pm) actually retains the great westwork of the original building, one of the few pieces of architecture of this period to have survived anywhere in Europe. The towers and the gallery between them are twelfth-century modifications, but inside you can see the solemn entrance hall with the **Kaisersaal** above, surviving much as the early emperors would have known them, except that the organ now blocks the view downstairs. In any case, the church they looked down on was so badly ravaged in the Thirty Years' War that it had to be replaced by a completely new building, which

DEUTSCHLAND ÜBER ALLES

Hoffmann von Fallersleben is best known for what soon became the national anthem of a united Germany, *Das Lied der Deutschen*, set to Haydn's stately and spacious *Emperor's Hymn*. Its opening line *Deutschland, Deutschland über alles* became notorious under the Nazis, who were unaware that the melody was based on a Croatian folk song, and was thus part of the hated and "inferior" Slav culture. In reality, there's nothing sinister about the words, which are liberal in sentiment. What might seem to be an assertion of national superiority is actually a clarion call to abandon the petty feuding of the old states in favour of German unity. The third stanza was retained by the West German state as its national anthem, and recently there were moves to reinstate the first verse to celebrate the unification of the two Germanies. However, the frontiers delineated – "from the Maas to the Memel" – are very out of date: the latter is now in Lithuania with the entire length of Poland separating it from the nearest German territory.

dates from 1667 to 1671. Although normally described as Baroque, the architecture is Gothic in every respect, for all that this style was by then a total anachronism.

To the side of the church is the extensive complex of monastic buildings, built a generation later in the plain Baroque favoured in northern Germany. After the Napoleonic secularization it became a ducal **Schloss** and is now a museum. Temporary exhibitions are featured, and there are displays on folklore and local history, but you're likely to derive most pleasure simply from being allowed to roam loose through umpteen rooms. On the upper floor, the **Festsaal** forms an elegant setting for classical concerts by star international artists in May and June. In the adjacent rooms are displayed some of the 80,000 volumes from the abbey's famous library. From 1860 until his death fourteen years later, the poet **Heinrich August Hoffmann von Fallersleben** (see box above) served as their custodian, and there's an exhibition on his work. The *Schloss Restaurant* offers some of the best food in town, and is reasonably priced, provided you stick to the set menus.

Practicalities

The **Bahnhof** is surnamed Rathaus with good reason; it's just a stone's throw from the centre, right beside the River Weser. Services on this branch line are slow; a pleasant alternative (late April–early Oct only) is to travel to Hameln or Bad Karlshafen by **boat**; there's a departure point near the train station and another at Corvey. Höxter's **tourist office** is in the Rathaus, Weserstr. 11 (May–Sept Mon–Fri 8.30am–12.30pm & 2–6pm, Sat 10am–noon; Oct–April Mon–Fri 8.30am–12.30pm & 2–5pm; ☎05271/963431).

Hotels include *Zum Landsknecht*, Stummrigestr. 17 (☎05271/2477; ④), the aforementioned *Corveyer Hof*, Westerbachstr. 29 (☎05271/2272; ⑤), *Niedersachsen*, Möllinger Str. 4 (☎05271/6880; ⑥); and *Weserberghof*, Godelheimer Str. 16 (☎05271/97080; ⑧). A number of rooms are also available in **private houses** (①–③); the tourist office has a complete list. The **campsite** (☎05271/2589) has a good location on the right bank of the Weser opposite the town. Alternatively, there's a **youth hostel** at An der Wilhelmshöhe 59 (☎05271/2233; ⚑): from the far end of Westerbachstrasse, cross over to Gartenstrasse; after a couple of minutes' walk, turn left and follow the road to the end.

Höxter's best **restaurants** are in the last two hotels mentioned above. Other good places to eat and drink are the *Altes Brauhaus*, Westerbachstr. 28, which specializes in *vom heissen Stein* dishes; *Adam-und-Eva-Haus* on Stummrigestrasse, originally a Renaissance mansion; and *Strullenkrug* on Hennekenstrasse. The latter building is early nineteenth-century, but the site, with the largest beer garden in town, has a much longer tradition.

travel details

Trains

Bielefeld to: Cologne (every 30min; 1hr 30min); Detmold (hourly; 1hr 15min); Dortmund (every 30min; 40min); Hannover (frequent; 1hr 30min); Lemgo (hourly; 1hr).

Cologne to: Aachen (every 20min; 45min); Bielefeld (every 30min; 1hr 30min); Bonn (every 15min; 20min); Dortmund (frequent; 1hr 10min); Düsseldorf (frequent; 25min); Essen (frequent; 50min); Hagen (every 30min; 50min); Hannover (frequent; 2hr 50min); Münster (frequent; 1hr 45min); Siegen (hourly; 1hr 35min); Soest (hourly; 2hr 20min); Wuppertal (hourly; 30min).

Dortmund to: Aachen (hourly; 1hr 50min); Bielefeld (every 30min; 40min); Bochum (frequent; 10min); Cologne (frequent; 1hr 10min); Düsseldorf (frequent; 1hr); Essen (frequent; 25min); Hagen

(every 30min; 30min); Hannover (hourly; 2hr); Minden (hourly; 1hr 15min); Münster (hourly; 30min).

Düsseldorf to: Cologne (frequent; 25min); Dortmund (frequent; 1hr); Duisburg (frequent; 15min); Essen (frequent; 30min); Kleve (hourly; 1hr 25min); Mönchengladbach (frequent; 30min); Münster (frequent; 1hr 30min); Soest (4 daily; 1hr 20min); Wuppertal (every 30min; 40min).

Kleve to: Düsseldorf (hourly; 1hr 25min); Kalkar (hourly; 10min); Xanten (hourly; 40min).

Münster to: Bochum (frequent; 45min); Bremen (frequent; 1hr 15min); Cologne (frequent; 1hr 45min); Dortmund (hourly; 30min); Düsseldorf (every 30min; 1hr 20min); Essen (frequent; 55min); Hagen (hourly; 1hr 5min); Osnabrück (frequent; 25min); Wuppertal (hourly; 1hr 25min).

CHAPTER SIX

BREMEN AND LOWER SAXONY

he Land of **Lower Saxony** (*Niedersachsen*) only came into being in 1946, courtesy of the British military authorities. In forging this new province, the former **Kingdom of Hannover** – which had shared its ruler with Britain between 1714 and 1837, but which had later been subsumed into Prussia – was used as a basis. To it were added the two separate ex-duchies of **Braunschweig** and **Oldenburg**, plus the minute but hitherto seemingly indestructible principality of **Schaumburg-Lippe**. In spite of this diverse patchwork, the Land has strong historical antecedents, forming the approximate area inhabited by the Saxon tribes during the Roman period and the Dark Ages. In accordance with the general north–south divide, the Reformation took strong root in most of Lower Saxony.

Geographically, Lower Saxony is highly diverse. It contains much of Germany's sparse provision of **coastline** and **islands**, behind which stretches a flat landscape, at times below sea level. Further south is the monotonous stretch of the North German Plain, but this gives way to the **Lüneburg Heath** to the east, and to highland countryside further south, in the shape of the hilly region around the **River Weser** and the gentle wooded slopes of the **Harz** mountains. Although it is the second most extensive Land after Bavaria, it has a very low population density. None of its cities is as big as the old Hanseatic port of **Bremen**, an enclave within the province, but a Land in its own right, in continuation of its age-long tradition as a free state. Otherwise, there are just two cities with a population of over 200,000: the state capital, **Hannover**, which only came to prominence in the seventeenth century and is to be visited more for its museums and magnificent gardens than for its monuments: and the altogether more venerable **Braunschweig,** which still preserves considerable reminders of its halcyon period at the end of the twelfth century.

The province's smaller towns and cities present a fascinating contrast. **Hildesheim**, with its grandiloquent Romanesque architecture (revolutionary in its day, and of enormous influence throughout Europe), is the most outstanding from an artistic point of view. Nowhere is the mercantile heyday of the Hansa more vividly evoked than in **Lüneburg**, with its masterly brick Gothic showpieces. **Wolfenbüttel** is an early example of a planned town, and, with **Celle** and **Bückeburg**, is among the few places in Germany to be strongly marked by Italian-inspired Renaissance and Mannerist styles. Very different is the exuberantly ornate architecture of the archaic Weser Renaissance style, which reached its peak in and around the Pied Piper's stamping ground of **Hameln**. A mining town quite unlike any other in the world can be seen at **Goslar**, while **Göttingen** boasts one of Germany's most famous universities, and thus the liveliest nightlife in the province. **Einbeck**, home of *Bockbier*, is a reminder of the strength of the brewing tradition in these parts, and beer aficionados will find themselves spoilt for choice.

Getting around is seldom a problem, thanks to the usual efficient network of buses and trains. The only possible exceptions to this rule are in the Lüneburg Heath (in

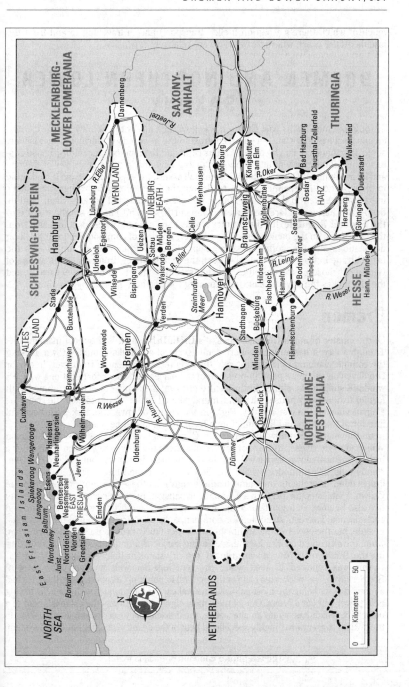

much of which there's a ban on fuelled transport) and in travelling to and from the islands off the coast, where ferry prices are relatively expensive.

BREMEN AND NORTHERN LOWER SAXONY

Throughout much of its past **Bremen** was governed not by the nobility, but by its merchants, as a free city state – a sharp contrast to the hundreds of German principalities, some tiny, that were run by feudal barons right into the nineteenth century. Those centuries of self-government and economic power have marked the character of the city and its inhabitants. There's a certain air of self-assuredness, superiority even, and pride in their political independence that marks out the Bremen people – a hangover that's inextricably linked to the town's **Hanseatic** past. Bremen still governs itself (and its deep-water harbour of **Bremerhaven**, 60km north; see p.577) as the **smallest state in the Federal Republic**. It's the country's oldest and second largest port too, safe from the North Sea on the banks of the River Weser. Imports of commodities from far-flung destinations – cotton, coffee, tobacco, tropical fruits and cereals – coupled with the export trade in wool and wood have been the foundation of Bremen's status as one of Germany's most prosperous cities. The hinterland is entirely within Lower Saxony, and the city makes the obvious base for exploring the northern part of this province.

Bremen

Of the cluster of north German cities, it's **BREMEN** which is the most manageable. Though a city, it has an atmosphere reminiscent of an English country town, lacking the commercial buzz of Hamburg, and the ugly redevelopment of Hannover. In one or two days you can get a good impression of the place: the former fortifications where a windmill still stands, almost in the centre of town; the Schnoorviertel, crammed with former fisher-family houses; the bold, mural-painted backs of houses near the river; the elegant villas of the last century. Right in the centre of town, the darkened, beautiful interior of the **Dom** and the sumptuous **Rathaus** shouldn't be missed.

In the eighth century the Emperor Charlemagne dispatched the Anglo-Saxon Willehad to the Weser to convert the Saxons there to Christianity. Seven years later a bishop of Bremen was appointed, and in 789 the first church was built where the Dom stands today. Two hundred years on, the city was granted free market status, giving independent merchants the same **trading rights** as those working on behalf of the Crown, a vital step for Bremen's economic expansion. By the eleventh century the city had also become an important centre for the Church, and over the centuries civic and ecclesiastical interests struggled for dominance. In 1358 Bremen joined the Hanseatic League, but the power of the archbishops was not finally broken until the Reformation, when the city opted for Protestantism. Having survived a virtual cessation of trade during the Thirty Years' War, it was granted free city status in 1646.

This was renewed in 1949 when Bremen, together with its deep-water port of Bremerhaven, was declared a Land of the Federal Republic of Germany. Since then, it's had a reputation for being the most politically radical part of the country, with the SPD having held power without a break. One of their most significant acts was the establishment of a university, which has set up an alternative, multi-disciplinary curriculum in opposition to the normal conservative, highly specialized bent of the country's higher education system.

The **telephone code** for Bremen is ☎0421

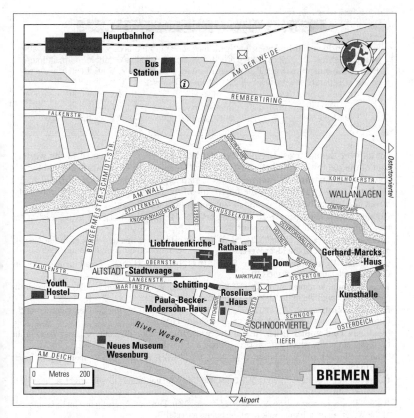

Map labels: Hauptbahnhof; Bus Station; AM DER WEIDE; REMBERTIRING; FALKENSTR.; CONTRESCARPE; KOHLHÖKERSTR.; Ostertorviertel; WALLANLAGEN; AM WALL; SPITZENKEIL; KNOCHENHAUERSTR.; SÖGESTR.; SCHÜSSELKORB; OSTERTORSWALLSTR.; VILLASTR.; CONTRESCARPE; BÜRGERMEISTER-SCHMIDT-STR.; Liebfrauenkirche; Rathaus; Dom; BÜCHTSTR.; Gerhard-Marcks-Haus; FAULENSTR.; OBERNSTR.; ALTSTADT; Stadtwaage; MARKTPLATZ; OSTERTOR; LANGENSTR.; Youth Hostel; MARTINISTR.; Schütting; Roselius-Haus; Kunsthalle; Paula-Becker-Modersohn-Haus; BÖTTCHERSTR.; BALGEBRÜCKSTR.; SCHNOOR; SCHNOORVIERTEL; OSTERDEICH; River Weser; TIEFER; AM DEICH; Neues Museum Wesenburg; 0 Metres 200; **BREMEN**; ▽ Airport

Arrival, information and accommodation

The **Hauptbahnhof** is just to the north of the city centre, and immediately outside stands the **tourist office** (Mon–Wed 9.30am–6.30pm, Thurs & Fri 9.30am–8pm, Sat & Sun 9.30am–4pm; ☎30800), best source of information for what's on in town, and with a room booking service. There's a second, smaller office at Liebfrauenkirchhof (same hours). From the Hauptbahnhof, getting to the old town is a simple matter of walking straight ahead and crossing the bridge over the Wall into the pedestrian zone.

The pivotal **tramline** is the #5, which starts from the airport, heads close to the Rathaus and Hauptbahnhof, and runs northwards parallel to the Bürgerpark. The *Bremen Kärtchen*, a **one-day go-anywhere ticket**, is available for DM8; this and other tickets may be bought at the booth outside the Hauptbahnhof. Bremen is flat and therefore ideal for exploring by **bike**, which you can rent right outside the Hauptbahnhof, on the left-hand side of the square as you come out. *Fahrrad Station* (Mon & Wed–Fri 10am–5pm; Sat & Sun in fine weather only 10am–noon & 5.30–6pm; ☎30114) charges DM15 per day; DM50 deposit on each bike.

Accommodation

The densest and most convenient cluster of **hotels** in the centre of town is near the Hauptbahnhof; not surprisingly, these are expensive. Budget accommodation is spread out all over the suburbs. Bremen's **youth hostel** is very well located in the western part of the old town at Kalkstr. 6 (☎171369; ⓑ) – take tram #6 or bus #26 – and there's a good central **campsite**, *Internationaler Campingplatz Freier Hansestadt Bremen*, Am Stadtwaldsee 1 (☎212002), on the north side of the Bürgerpark close to the university; buses #28 to Stadtwaldsee or #23 to the university go in the right direction.

Bremer Haus, Löningstr. 16–20 (☎32940; fax 329 4411). Located slightly to the east of the Hauptbahnhof, but still very convenient. ⑦

Enzensperger, Brautstr. 9 (☎503224, fax 507902). Located a few minutes' walk from the Altstadt, on the opposite side of the River Weser. ②

Gästehaus Peterswerder, Celler Str. 4 (☎447101, fax 447202). Small pension in the Ostertorviertel; book in advance. ③

Haus Bremen, Verdener Str. 47 (☎432720, fax 432 7222 or 494223). Good-quality pension ideally placed for the nightlife of the Ostertorviertel. ⑤

Heinisch, Wachmannstr. 26 (☎342925, fax 346 9946). Situated by the southeast corner of the Bürgerpark, about a 10min walk from the Hauptbahnhof. ⑤

Landhaus Louisenthal, Leher Heerstr. 105 (☎232076, fax 236716). Country house hotel in the northeast of the city which attracts large numbers of North American guests. ⑦

Schaper-Siedenburg, Bahnhofstr. 8 (☎30870, fax 308788). Another of the many quality hotels close to the Hauptbahnhof. ⑦

Überseehotel, Wachtstr. 27–29 (☎36010, fax 360 1555). An unbeatable location right at the edge of the Markt. ⑧

Walter, Buntentorsteinweg 86–88 (☎558027, fax 558029). Functional guesthouse on the south side of the Weser, about a 10min walk from the Schnoorviertel. ④

Weidmann, Am Schwarzen Meer 35 (☎ & fax 498 4455). Small pension in the Ostertorviertel, best booked well in advance. ④

Weltevreden, Am Dobben 62 (☎78015, fax 704091). Excellently located about halfway between the city centre and the Ostertorviertel, heart of Bremen's nightlife. ⑤

The city

Although more than half a million people live here, Bremen doesn't give the impression of being a large city – partly because the main area of historical interest is the **Altstadt**, on the Weser's northeast bank. The former fortification that surrounded it, the **Wall**, is now an area of green park, with a zigzagging moat forming a curve around the perimeter of the old city. To the east, the **Ostertorviertel** (known as *das Viertel* – "the Quarter") was the first part of the city to be built outside those city walls, and is today the liveliest part of town, the area to head for at night. North of the Hauptbahnhof, the **Bürgerpark** and **Schwachhausen** areas are worthy of a stroll for their many streets of villas, each discreetly advertising Bremen's turn-of-the-century wealth. The Bürgerpark is twice the size of London's Hyde Park, and apart from being beautiful in itself, contains old wartime bunkers too sturdy to be blown up, which have been decorated by local artists and now sport political murals.

Sögestrasse

Bremen's main shopping street is **Sögestrasse** (Sow Street), along which swine used to be driven to the market. A life-size bronze of pigs, a swineherd and his dog marks its beginning, but as a standard Euro-shopping precinct, it's not particularly inspiring. The single place worth stopping off for is Bremen's bastion of *Kaffee und Kuchen*, the *Café Knigge*, up on the right-hand side (see p.574). Just before Sögestrasse reaches the Markt is the **Liebfrauenkirche**, a lovely hall church with contrasting Romanesque and Gothic towers that's swathed by the flower market, with a number of booths around its walls – the flashy built-in sausage stand is the most incongruous.

The Markt

The **Markt** is relatively small and is dominated by the **Rathaus**, whose highly ornate **facade** – rich in mouldings, life-size figures and bas-reliefs, and with the undersides of its large rounded arches set with enormous "jewels" – is in Weser Renaissance style. It was added to the original Gothic structure between 1609 and 1612, two hundred years after the latter was first built. One of the most splendid of north Germany's buildings, it fortunately survived World War II unscathed. You can only visit the interior as part of a **guided tour** (Mon–Fri at 10am, 11am & noon, Sat & Sun 11am & noon; DM4), and it's worth it to see the extremes of Bremen's civic pride: rooms awash with gilded wallpaper and busy, ornate carving. Downstairs the **Ratskeller** is as usual pricey, but wine is served by the glass from the cellar's collection of six hundred vintages, some stored in the eighteenth-century barrels which double as partitions.

On the left as you face the Rathaus is a ten-metre-high stone **statue of Roland**, nephew of Charlemagne, who brandishes the sword of justice and carries a shield bearing the inscription (in the *Plattdeutsch* dialect): "Freedom do I give you openly". Erected by the burghers in 1404 as a symbol of Bremen's independence from its archbishop, he's the city's traditional protector; as long as Roland stands, they say, Bremen will remain free. Roland's pointy kneecaps were used as a medieval measurement-check by local housewives: the distance between the two is the exact length of one *Elle*, by which cloth was sold. In 1989 he was de-Nazified when a time-capsule placed there in 1938, and containing Nazi documents, was removed. Poor Roland now spends his time staring at the much-disputed modern facade of the **Haus der Bürgerschaft** (Parliament Building; guided tours Mon–Fri at 10am & 2.15pm; free), one of the ugliest edifices ever to disgrace a German town centre.

A happier postwar addition to the square is the bronze group of the **Bremen Town Band** by the local sculptor, Gerhard Marcks. Rising like a pyramid, it shows a cock standing on a cat standing on a dog standing on a donkey, and is an illustration of an old folk tale retold by the **Brothers Grimm**. In fact, this is the town band that never was: en route to the city, the animals arranged themselves in the way depicted and started to make music. In so doing, they frightened a group of robbers away from their hideout and took over the house for themselves, remaining there ever after.

The Dom

On a small rise beyond the Rathaus stands the twin-towered **Dom**, formerly the seat of one of medieval Germany's archbishops, but now a Protestant church. Any youngish men you see sweeping the steps are doing it because they have reached their thirtieth birthday without finding themselves a wife – this is the traditional penance (or, perhaps, a way of advertising their availability). The Dom itself has been restored recently, its brooding interior beautiful in architectural styles ranging from eleventh-century Romanesque to late Gothic. There are crypts at both ends of the building (one for the use of the emperor, the other for the archbishop), though that to the west had to be truncated when the huge twin-towered facade was erected in the thirteenth century. Just above the entrance is the early sixteenth-century **organ gallery**, adorned with statues, including Charlemagne and Willehad, by the Münster sculptor Hinrik Brabender. In the eastern crypt are more works of art, notably an eleventh-century *Enthroned Christ* and a magnificent thirteenth-century bronze **font**. At the southeastern corner is the **Dommuseum** (May–Oct Mon–Fri 10am–5pm, Sat 10am–noon, Sun 2–5pm; Nov–April Mon–Fri 1–4.30pm, Sat 10am–noon, Sun 2–5pm; DM3), which features restored vestments and other treasures found in ecclesiastical graves. Entered from outside is the **Bleikeller** (Easter Sat–Nov 1 only, Mon–Fri 10am–5pm, Sat 10am–noon, Sun 2–5pm; DM2), where lead for the roofing was stored. It was opened up a while ago, and some bodies, perfectly preserved due to the lack of air, were discovered. Unusually, it's open to visitors, the "mummies" providing a popular – if macabre – attraction. Finally, it's possible to ascend one of the **towers** (same hours May–Oct only; DM1) for a view over the Markt and the city.

Elsewhere on Marktplatz

Surviving buildings from Bremen's Hanseatic heyday are rare, but include the restored patrician houses lining much of the rest of the Marktplatz, and the **Schütting**, the ritzy, sixteenth-century Flemish-inspired mansion with contrasting gables, which was where the guild of merchants convened. Round the corner on Langenstrasse is the equally imposing, step-gabled **Stadtwaage**, the municipal office for weights and measures.

Off the south side of Marktplatz is a strange street which seems to combine elements of Gothic, Art Nouveau and fantasy: the **Böttcherstrasse** or Coopers' Street. Once a humble alleyway in which barrel-makers lived and worked, it was transformed in the 1920s by the Bremen magnate **Ludwig Roselius**, who made much of his fortune from *Kaffee Hag*, the first-ever decaffeinated coffee. He commissioned local avant-garde artists to effect the change. During the Nazi era, the whole street was to be demolished because it was considered corrupt art, but the charismatic Roselius persuaded the authorities to let it stand as a warning example, so to speak, of all that was considered bad in the arts.

The only old house in Böttcherstrasse is no. 6, a fourteenth-century step-gabled building with a sixteenth-century facade, that's now known as the **Roselius-Haus**. Roselius bought the property at the turn of the century, and converted it into a **museum** (Tues 11am–9pm, Wed–Sun 11am–6pm; DM10). Though it gives an interesting opportunity to see the interior of a Hanseatic merchant's house, its collection of medieval art and furniture is not especially well displayed; the best works are paintings by Cranach the Elder and the Younger and an alabaster statue of *St Barbara* by Riemenschneider. Adjoining is the **Paula-Becker-Modersohn-Haus** (same hours and same ticket valid), which contains a number of paintings by the artist, who lived and worked in the nearby village of Worpswede (see p.576).

The Schnoorviertel

Tucked away between the Dom and the river is a small, extraordinarily well-preserved area of medieval fisherfolks' houses known as the **Schnoorviertel**. Dating from the fifteenth century, this is Bremen's oldest surviving quarter. It's worth a wander through the small streets, far too narrow for modern traffic to pass, to see the variety of buildings and to get a feeling for the city's past. Predictably, in being preserved the area has been prettified and now houses pricey specialist shops selling antiques, crafts and toys. Thankfully, it still manages to be a residential area too, avoiding a gentrification that would have left it soulless.

The Kunsthalle

Just east of the Schnoorviertel at Am Wall 207 is the **Kunsthalle** (closed for reconstruction until spring 1998), one of the oldest municipal art galleries in Germany. The ground floor is mostly given over to changing displays of modern art, but also contains a Jugendstil room containing valuable collections of graphic art. Most of the outstanding group of watercolours by **Dürer** were for long thought to have been destroyed in the war, but are now known to have been confiscated by the Soviets as war booty; their future remains uncertain. Meanwhile a small panel of *St Onofrio* by this artist can be seen in the first room upstairs, along with **Altdorfer's** earliest surviving work, *The Nativity*, and several examples of **Cranach**. The adjacent galleries contain Dutch and Flemish paintings: *Noli Me Tangere* is a successful co-operative composition between **Rubens** (who painted the figures) and **Jan Brueghel** (who did everything else); there's also the striking full-length *Portrait of Duke Wolfgang Wilhelm of Pfalz-Neuburg* by **van Dyck**, and a *Portrait of a Man* attributed to **Rembrandt**. In the small cabinet rooms to the side are works by earlier European masters, notably Italians, of which the most important are *Madonna and Child* by **Masolino** (one of very few works by this artist to have left Italy) and *A Doctor* by **Moroni**.

However, the gallery's main draw is its superb array of nineteenth-century and early twentieth-century painting. Among the French School, there are five canvases by **Delacroix**, including *King Rodrigo*. A room is devoted to the Nabis: the most impressive works here are *Homage to Cézanne* by **Maurice Denis** and **Vuillard's** designs for the decoration of the former Champs Elysées Theatre. Other highlights are an important early **Monet**, *Camille*, and **Manet's** *Portrait of the Poet Zacharie Astruc*. Pick of the German works are **Beckmann's** *Apache Dance* and *Self-Portrait with Saxophone*, **Kirchner's** *Street Scene by Night,* and a comprehensive representation of the Worpswede colony, with some forty examples of **Paula Modersohn-Becker** on view around the landing.

Next door to the Kunsthalle is the **Gerhard-Marcks-Haus** (Tues–Sun 10am–6pm; DM6) which contains sculptures, drawings and watercolours by the artist. Apart from the monument to the Bremen Town Band, Marcks is best known for the bronze doors and other works of art he made for a number of German cathedrals and churches to replace those lost in the war.

Out of the centre

The **Focke-Museum** or **Landesmuseum** (Tues–Sun 10am–6pm; DM4) is unfortunately rather a long way from the centre of town at Schwachhauser-Heerstr. 240. Laid out in an imaginative and informative manner, this traces the history of Bremen and its port, and has a collection of decorative arts. Among the most important exhibits are the original statues of Charlemagne and the seven Electors from the Rathaus facade. If you're out this way, it's well worth continuing to the nearby **Botanischer Garten** which, in season, is ablaze with some eight hundred different species of rhododendrons and azaleas.

The latest addition to the city's cultural roster is the **Neues Museum Weserburg** (Tues–Fri 10am–6pm, Sat & Sun 11am–6pm; DM6), set up in a group of converted warehouses on the peninsula formed by the two arms of the Weser due south of the Altstadt. Devoted to art of the last thirty years only, it features extensive displays of most of the big guns, such as Warhol, Kienholz, Beuys, Fontana and Serra.

Eating, drinking and entertainment

In the gastronomic field, Bremen is renowned for its fish (particularly eel) specialities, best sampled in the *gemütlich* old restaurants of the Altstadt and Schnoorviertel. The city also has an excellently varied range of bistros and cafés. For drinking and nightlife, the place to head for is the Ostertorviertel, in particular along Ostertorsteinweg and in the short yard called Auf den Häfen, near the junction of Humboldtstrasse and Am Dobben. The best source of nightlife information is the tourist office, which has pamphlets listing events, and is the city's main ticket-booking agency. The monthly **listings magazines** *Bremer Blatt* and *Kursbuch* and the fortnightly *Prinz* are each around DM3, but a free magazine *Lokal Spezial* can be picked up in restaurants and cafés – useful for addresses rather than actual events. German-speakers staying longer might be interested in *Bremen bei Nacht* (DM5).

Restaurants

Alte Gilde, Ansgaritorstr. 24. In the vaulted cellar of a seventeenth-century house, this is a good place for full meals, whether fish or otherwise.

Deutsches Haus, Am Markt 1. Top-notch fish specialities served in a grand patrician house.

Flett, Böttcherstr. 3. In one of the fantasy houses in Bremen's most famous street (stained-glass windows and oriental carpets feature among the decor), this is another leading choice for fresh seafood dishes.

Friesenhof, Hinter dem Schütting 12. Excellent brewery-owned *Gaststätte*.

Kleiner Ratskeller, Hinter dem Schütting 11. Offers solid, reasonably priced *gutbürgerliche Küche* along with one of the best ranges of beer in town.

Ratskeller, Am Markt. The most celebrated example of a great national institution, this offers a wide range of dishes which are fairly pricey, though not exorbitantly so. According to an old statute, it cannot serve beer, but has an extraordinary wine list of over 600 vintages, some of them extremely rare.

Souterrain, Sielwall 50. Good, basic pizza place.

Bistros and cafés

Bistro Brasil, Ostertorsteinweg 83. Open all night, with a tropical atmosphere – at its best in the early hours of the morning.

Café Am Wall, Am Wall 164. Arty hangout with a good line in vegetarian food

Café Caruso, Friesenstr. 6–7. Offers a decent range of food and a friendly atmosphere.

Café Knigge, Sögestr. 44. Bremen's best (and best-known) traditional café.

Café Noir, Herdentorsteinweg 2. Open round the clock; near the Hauptbahnhof, so expect a very mixed crowd.

Kartoffelstube, Friedrich-Karl-Str. 11. Excellent for organic food, particularly the Swiss-style *Rösti*.

Sowieso Bistro, Schwachhauser-Heerstr. 281. Relaxed atmosphere and handy for light meals.

Vivaldi Café, Schwachhauser-Heerstr. 4. Highly popular and usually offering vegetarian dishes.

Bars

Bierakademie, Herdentorsteinweg 4. Hardened beer drinkers' watering hole: close to the Hauptbahnhof and open 24hr a day.

Brommy, Hemelinger Str. 7. One of the liveliest and most popular hangouts of the Ostertorviertel.

Gerken, Feldstr. 77. Another Ostertorviertel favourite.

Irish Pub, Stavendamm 16. A likely place to meet English-speakers: sells reasonably priced *Guinness* by the pint and has live folk music on Thurs.

Leierkasten, Pagentorner Heimweg. Tucked away between Staderstrasse and Friedrich-Karl-Strasse, this excellent pub has the bonus of a leafy beer garden.

Piano, Fehrfeld 64. Bustling bar in the Ostertorviertel.

Sewastopol, Am Schwarzen Meer. A Russian avant-garde interior, kitschly attired waitresses and an awe-inspiring list of vodkas are the off-beat attractions here.

Wüstestätte, Wüstestätte 11. Schnoorviertel cellar bar offering live jazz and blues.

BREMEN'S BEER

Bremen is one of Germany's most famous **beer cities** and the brewers' guild, founded in 1489, is the oldest in the country. It's the home of the internationally famous *Beck's*, one of the most heavily exported brews in the country, though it's a comparative newcomer, having existed for just over a century. *St Pauli Girl* is another brand well known abroad, but the products of *Haake-Beck* are the ones to go for in the city itself. They make both a filtered and an unfiltered *Pils* (the latter known as *Kräusen*), as well as the refreshing *Bremer Weisse*, which is usually sweetened with fruit syrup.

Discos and clubs

Delight, Unser Lieben Frauen Kirchhof. Plays disco pap to an older clientele than the other clubs. On arrival, a card is issued on which your drinks are marked; minimum charge on exit is DM12.

Lila Eule, Bernhardstr. 10. The best time to come is for the lively studenty night on Thursday.

Modernes, Neustadtwall. A cinema during the week and a disco at weekends, playing half-hour snatches of all sorts of mainstream music. Always busy and gets very hot, though there are periodic 5min breaks when the ceiling is opened for ventilation.

Römer, Fehrfeld 31. Caters mainly for lovers of dark indy-pop.

Music and theatre

Excellent concerts of **classical music** are regularly held in the *Stadthalle* behind the Hauptbahnhof at Auf der Bürgerweide (☎35051) and in various theatres. The city has recently become the permanent home of the *Deutsche Kammerphilharmonie*, an excellent chamber orchestra with plenty of young musicians. **Jazz** fans should head for the *Waldbühne* in the Bürgerpark for Sunday morning sessions, while the *Jazz Club Bremen* in the Tivoli building by the Hauptbahnhof has live concerts, mainly of traditional styles, on Fridays and Saturdays.

Bremen's main **theatres** are *Theater am Goetheplatz*, which hosts major dance performances, operas and musicals, and *Concordia*, Schwachhauser-Heerstr. 17, which specializes in modern and experimental works; ☎363 3333 for tickets for both. The *Bremen Shakespeare Company*, at the *Theater am Leibnizplatz* (☎500333), is the only company in Germany to have ten of Shakespeare's play in rep at any one time.

Listings

Bookstores *The Cosy Bookshop*, Dobbenweg 10 (Mon–Fri 3.30–6pm, Sat 10am–1pm; closed during school holidays; ☎703709), sells secondhand English-language books; swaps possible.

Car rental *Europcar* (☎170941).

Festivals Leading folklore events are the *Eiswette* on Jan 6 (Epiphany), and the *Freimarkt*, which begins with a procession in mid-Oct, and continues for a fortnight.

Gay line (☎704170).

Harbour cruises Departures April–Oct at 11.45am, 1.30pm and 3.15pm from *Martini–Anleger* (☎321229), through the pedestrian tunnel at the end of Böttcherstrasse. Tours last 75min and cost from DM13.

Markets Flea markets are held on Sat mornings on the north bank of the Weser from Wilhelm-Kaisen-Brücke and on Sun mornings on Bürgerweide.

Mitfahrzentrale Körnerwall 1 (☎72022 or 19440).

Post office The main post office is at the junction of An der Weide and Löningstrasse, beside the Hauptbahnhof, with poste restante services.

Sports *SV Werder Bremen* have been one of the most successful football teams in the country in recent seasons. They play at the *Weserstadion* in Osterdeich, on tram lines #2, #3 and #10; ☎498106 for fixtures and details. Indoor sporting events are held in the *Stadthalle*, just behind the Hauptbahnhof.

Women's centre (☎349573).

Around Bremen

If you're staying in Bremen and want a trip out, the most obvious places to head for are the port of **Bremerhaven**, the former artists' colony of **Worpswede**, and the old city of **Verden**, which is also a worthwhile stopoff if you're heading towards Hannover or the Lüneburg Heath.

Verden

The former episcopal seat of **VERDEN**, some 28km southeast of Bremen on the main rail line to Hannover, nowadays christens itself *Reiterstadt* in honour of its status as Germany's equestrian capital, the setting for seven **horse markets** each year, of which those in mid-April and mid-October, with their attendant festivals, are the most important.

The Altstadt

The compact **Altstadt** lies on the right bank of the River Aller. Much of it is now a bland pedestrianized shopping precinct, but towards the end of the latter is the impressive Gothic **Dom**. This imparts a surprising sense of unity, given that it was constructed over an unusually protracted period, and even then retains the tower and cloister of its Romanesque predecessor. The late thirteenth-century chancel is one of the earliest essays in the distinctively German hall-church style; although not finished until two hundred years later, the nave and transept dovetail perfectly with it.

In the shadow of the Dom is the Romanesque **Andreaskirche**, whose great treasure is the brass funerary slab – the oldest known example of its kind – of its founder Bishop Yso. Diagonally opposite is the **Deutsches Pferdemuseum** (Tues–Sun 9am–4pm; DM2), a rather serious institution with a huge collection of equine artefacts. Its valuable library is housed in the finest half-timbered house in the town, a couple of minutes' walk further west along the same street. At Untere Str. 13 just north of the Dom, another notable timber-framed construction, the early eighteenth-century **Domherrenhaus**, houses the **Historisches Museum** (Tues–Sun 10am–1pm & 3–5pm; DM3), with the expected archeology, folklore, handicraft and local history displays. Among the exhibits is a wooden spear which is believed to be the oldest hunting weapon ever discovered.The main building in the northern half of the Altstadt is the **Johanniskirche** on Ritterstrasse, a Romanesque brick basilica transformed into a Gothic hall church in the fifteenth century. It has well-restored cycles of medieval wall and ceiling frescoes and notable furnishings, including a relief of *The Last Judgment*.

Practicalities

Verden's **Hauptbahnhof** is situated east of the Altstadt. Between the two, at Ostertorstr. 7a, is the **tourist office** (May & late Oct Mon–Fri 8.30am–1pm & 2–6pm; June to mid-Oct Mon–Fri 8.30am–1pm & 2–6pm, Sat 10am–1pm; Nov–April Mon–Fri 8.30am–1pm & 2–5pm; ☎04231/12317 or 12323). The *Niedersachsenhalle*, scene of all the **equestrian events**, is situated in a park on the opposite side of the Hauptbahnhof from the town centre.

If you want to stay in the Altstadt, the only **hotels** are *Gasthaus zum Burgberg* (☎04231/2202; ⑤), just south of the Dom at Grüne Str. 36, and *Höltje*, Obere Str. 13 (☎04231/8920; ⑧). For budget prices you'll need to head out to the suburb of Eitze, at the southeastern extremity of town, where you'll find *Der Oelfkenhof*, Im Dicken Ort 17 (☎04231/62963; ③), and *Eitzer Hof*, Walsroder Str. 42 (☎04231/63004; ④). Verden's **youth hostel** (☎04231/61163; ⑧) is situated to the rear of the *Niedersachsenhalle*, at Saumurplatz 1.

Both the Altstadt hotels have fine **restaurants**, but the best food of all is served at *Pades*, Anita-Augspurg-Platz 7. Other less expensive places to eat and drink are *Am Rathaus*, Grosse Str. 46, which has *vom heissen Stein* dishes, and *Annes Café*, Alte Bergstr. 16, which serves breakfast until 5pm.

Worpswede

About 25km north of Bremen in the **Teufelsmoor** (the forbiddingly named "Devil's peat bog") is the intriguing village of **WORPSWEDE**. Back in the 1880s this was a simple farming village, where the inhabitants scraped together a living. The artists Fritz Mackensen and Otto Modersohn came here then, and over the next ten or so years Worpswede developed into an artists' colony, a movement run on roughly similar lines to the Pre-Raphaelites. The famous poet Rainer Maria Rilke was closely associated with them, as was his wife, Clara Westhoff. It was **Paula Becker**, who subsequently married Modersohn, who became the most significant of the set – her powerful, depressing pictures depicting the grim realities of peasant life, poverty and death stand out from the pretty, though comparatively facile, impressionistic scenes of the others.

Work by the first generation of Worpswede artists can be seen in a number of locations, notably the two main galleries in the heart of the village, the **Kunsthalle** (daily 10am–6pm; DM5) at Bergstr. 17 and the **Grosse Kunstschau** (daily 10am–6pm; DM5) round the corner at Lindenallee 3. The latter is among Worpswede's most significant buildings, one of several Expressionist masterpieces by Bernhard Hoetger. However, you're by no means limited to seeing the work of long-dead artists: the colony tradition is maintained to this day, and it's possible to visit – and, of course, to buy from – the workshops of a number of contemporary craftsmen.

Practicalities

Worpswede can be reached by bus #140 from Bremen's Hauptbahnhof; alternatively, there are infrequent boat services in summer. The village's own **tourist office** is at Bergstr. 13 (Mon–Fri 9am–1pm & 2–6pm; April–Oct also Sat, Sun & public holidays 10am–3pm; ☎04792/950121) and has details of a reasonable supply of **private rooms** (①–②) and small **pensions** (①–⑤). The most intriguing of these is the *Haus im Schluh* (☎04792/950061; ④), run by the descendants of Worpswede artist Heinrich Vogeler, whose work is on display here.

Worpswede has five **hotels**, each of which has its own distinctive character: *Gasthof Zum Hemberg*, Hembergstr. 28 (☎04792/1284; ④); *Haar*, Hembergstr. 13 (☎04792/93250; ⑤); and *Am Kunstcentrum*, Hans-am-Ende-Weg 4 (☎04792/9400; ⑥); *Waldhotel*, Hintern Berg 24 (☎04792/1273; ⑦); and *Eichenhof*, Ostendorfer Str. 13 (☎04792/2676; ⑨). There's a **youth hostel** a few minutes' walk west of the centre at Hammeweg 2 (☎04792/1360; ✿).

Among an enticing array of **cafés** (which generally also serve full meals), *Café Worpswede*, Lindenallee 1, housed in striking custom-designed premises by Hoetger, stands out, as does *Kaffeehaus Niedersachsen*, Am Thiergarten, which has original Worpswede furniture. The best **restaurants** are *Worpsweder Landhaus*, Findorffstr. 2, and those in the hotels *Am Kunstcentrum* and *Eichenhof*.

Bremerhaven

BREMERHAVEN is the Federal Republic's busiest fishing port, founded in 1827 as Bremen's deep-water harbour. The pride of the town is the **Deutsches Schiffahrtsmuseum** (National Museum of Navigation; Tues–Sun 10am–6pm; DM6) on Hans-Scharoun-Platz by the Alter Hafen, which lies between the modern commercial and fishing harbours. This traces the history of German sailing from prehistoric times to the present, and the star exhibit is a fourteenth-century Hanseatic log which was dredged up from the port of Bremen. Outside in the harbour is a wartime U-boat, the *Wilhelm Bauer* (April–Oct only; DM3 extra), the only one of its kind still in existence.

The other main attractions are in the immediate vicinity. Just to the south are the **Kunsthalle** (Tues–Fri 2–6pm, Sat & Sun 11am–1pm; DM2) which mounts temporary exhibitions of modern art, and the **Radarturm** (Radar Tower; April–Sept Tues–Sun 10am–1pm & 2–6pm; Oct–March Sun 10am–1pm & 2–5pm only; DM2) which commands a fine view over the harbours. To the north is the **Zoo am Meer** (daily 8am–5/7pm; DM4), which has an aquarium plus a number of animals with an aquatic connection.

Practicalities

Bremerhaven's **Hauptbahnhof** is at the eastern end of town, about 15 minutes' walk from the Alter Hafen. There are two **tourist offices**: at Van-Ronzelen-Str. 2 (Mon–Fri May–Oct 8am–6pm, Nov–Apr 8am–4pm; ☎0471/946460) and in the Columbus-Center, opposite the Schiffahrtsmuseum (Mon–Fri 9am–6pm, Sat 10am–1pm; ☎0471/43000). Ask at either of these about **private rooms** (①–③). There are plenty of **hotels**; those with a central location include *Elbinger Platz*, Georgstr. 2 (☎0471/924430; ③); *Geestemünde*, Am Klint 20 (☎0471/28800; ④); *Naber*, Theodor-Heuss-Platz 1 (☎0471/48770; ⑦); and *Haverkamp*, Prager Str. 34 (☎0471/48330; ⑥). The **youth hostel** is at Gauss Str. 54–56 (☎0471/590 2533; ✿–✿); take bus #2 or #6.

Pick of the town's fish speciality **restaurants** is *Natusch*, Am Fischbahnhof 1. A worthy rival is *Seute Deern*, a triple-masted barque in the Alter Hafen. Near the latter, at Van-Ronzelen-Str. 18, is *Koggen-Bräu*, a *Hausbrauerei*. Various harbour, river and sea **cruises** are available daily throughout the summer for around DM12; there are also sailings to Helgoland (see p.703).

Stade

Some 75km east of Bremerhaven, reachable by train via either Cuxhaven or Buxtehude, is the Elbe port of **STADE**. This old Hanseatic trading town, which was part of the Swedish Empire from 1645 to 1712, has flourished anew in recent decades, and its affluence has funded an ambitious restoration programme of its picturesque Altstadt of timber-framed brick houses, which is now in absolutely pristine shape; indeed, some would argue that it looks just a bit too polished for its own good,

The **Alter Hafen** at the northern end of the Altstadt functioned as a working port until 1966, but is nowadays an unashamedly showpiece area which has been regenerated by the introduction of museums, galleries, restaurants, cafés and bars where locals and tourists alike congregate. At the far end is the **Schwedenspeicher** (Swedish Warehouse; Tues–Fri 10am–5pm, Sat & Sun 10am–6pm; DM2 or DM3 inclusive ticket for all the town's museums), which contains a distinguished archeological collection plus local history displays. Of particular note are the four **Stade wheels**, which were part of a late Bronze Age cart from around 700 BC; each weighs around 12 kilos, making them the largest of the period yet discovered.

The town's finest mansions line the western side of the Alter Hafen, which is known as Wasser West. By far the most spectacular is the **Bürgermeister-Hintze-Haus**, with its showy Renaissance facade. It's now a commercial art gallery, the Galerie Fündling. Alongside is the **Goebenhaus**, named in honour of the Prussian general August von Goeben who was born there in 1816. A little further along, the **Kunsthaus** (same times as the Schwedenspeicher; DM2) displays a large number of works by the leading members of the original artists' colony at Worpswede (see p.576)

The central part of the Altstadt is dominated by the brick **Cosmaekirche**, which is Gothic in origin, though largely rebuilt after the disastrous town fire of 1659. From this period date the onion-shaped Baroque spire and a remarkable set of furnishings. These include a magnificent set of iron grilles, the high altar, the pulpit, the font, the chandeliers and the organ, which is in part an early work by the great Arp Schnitger. Regular recitals are held on it, including a Saturday morning series throughout the summer. The **Rathaus** alongside is likewise Baroque, only the cellars having escaped destruction in the town fire.

On **Die Insel**, a small island just west of the Altstadt, is the **Freilichtmuseum** (free access at all times), with a group of redundant rural buildings from the Altes Land, the fertile agricultural countryside around Stade. Its centrepiece is the **Altländer Haus** (May–Sept Tues–Sun 10am–1pm & 2–5pm; DM2), a large eighteenth-century farmstead.

Practicalities

Stade's **Bahnhof** lies a few minutes' walk south of the Altstadt. The **tourist office** (Mon–Fri 9am–6pm, Sat 9am–2pm; ☎04141/409170) is in the Zeughaus, a Swedish-era building which stands in the middle of the main square, Pferdemarkt. Here you can ask about **private rooms** (①–④); there's also a small centrally sited pension, *Fleetenieker*, Bäckerstr. 22 (☎04141/ 46655; ③). **Hotels** include *Zur Hanse*, Am Burggraben 4 (☎04141/44441; ⑤), *Am Fischmarkt*, Fischmarkt 2 (☎04141/44962; ⑤) and *Herzog Widukind*, Grosse Schmiedestr. 14 (☎04141/46096; ⑦).

The town's best **restaurant** is *Knechthausen*, which occupies a lovely old building with back courtyard at Bungenstr. 20; it's expensive but does good-value set lunches. Only marginally less enticing are the *Ratskeller* in the Gothic cellars of the Rathaus at Hökerstr. 10, and the *Insel-Restaurant*, a fine old half-timbered *Gasthaus* transported to the Freilichtmuseum. *Cave*, Wasser West 9, is a trendy wine bar and bistro, while there are plenty of good cafés, such as *Im Goebenhaus*, Wasser West 21, and *Altstadtcafé*, Hökerstr. 29. The main **festival** is the *Schwedenwoche*, usually held in the second week of June.

WESTERN LOWER SAXONY

This area takes in points west of Bremen, as far as the border with The Netherlands – much of it is agricultural land, and the main area of interest is **East Friesia** (*Ostfriesland*). Over the centuries the Friesians have resolutely avoided complete absorption by their German neighbours, retaining their own language and cultural identity. They inhabit a low-lying, fertile province that was prey to constant inundation by the sea; it was a miserable sort of existence, as **Pliny** observed around 50 AD:

Here a wretched race is found, inhabiting either the more elevated spots or artificial mounds where they pitch their cabins. When the waves cover the surrounding area they are like so many mariners on board a ship, and when again the tide recedes their condition is that of so many shipwrecked men.

Not surprisingly, the Friesians got pretty fed up with this sort of life, and as soon as the technology arrived began to build the dykes that have culminated in the sea-barrier that extends right round the coast from **Emden** to **Wilhelmshaven**.

East Friesia may have poor weather and interminably flat countryside, but it has spawned an ingenious tourist subculture taking advantage of the "bracing maritime climate . . . that regenerates the blood and nerves", while "a walk along the foreshore will provide natural inhalation treatment", as the local tourist brochure puts it. If you want more, you can pay for the privilege of being submerged in genuine North Sea mud in a number of large health spas, or join organized walks across the mud flats (the *Watt*) that encircle the coast – something you certainly shouldn't attempt on your own.

There are less esoteric alternatives: historic **towns** such as **Norden** and **Jever**; designated **nature reserves**; and two long-distance **footpaths** connecting Emden with Wilhelmshaven. The first follows the Ems–Jade canal, the second the coastline, taking the name of Klaus Störtebeker, a fifteenth-century Friesian pirate and Robin Hood-type character whose name is much lauded locally. The **East Friesian islands**, with their long sandy beaches, lie just off the coast and are immensely popular holiday resorts. Outside East Friesia the main attractions are two cities: the former ducal seat of **Oldenburg** and the old episcopal centre of **Osnabrück**, which is also a major rail junction.

Most inland **travel** can be done by bus, though it's worth noting that services can be sparse on Sundays. **Ferry** details are listed in the text, though services can be erratic, dependent on the time of year and North Sea tides.

Oldenburg

OLDENBURG, a junction on the two rail lines between Bremen and the North Sea ports, is a good place to break a journey for a few hours or an overnight stop, even if it hardly ranks as a major destination in its own right. It has enjoyed an eventful history. Having fallen under Danish rule for a century, it made a spectacular comeback in 1773 as the seat of the independent duchy of Oldenburg-Holstein-Gottorp, which kept its place on the map (latterly as a grand duchy and then as a free state) until it fell victim to Hitler's centralization policies. Nowadays the capital of the Weser–Ems region, it's a busy inland port, market and shopping centre which usually teems with people from the neighbouring countryside. Although it was only minimally damaged in World War II, Oldenburg looks surprisingly modern, almost all its older buildings having been swept away in a huge fire in 1676.

The city

Much of the moated Altstadt is a pedestrian precinct, with the main sights clustered together at the extreme southern end. Of these, the most important is the **Schloss**, an irregular horseshoe-shaped building begun in the early seventeenth century in a plain Renaissance style, but subsequently altered and enlarged. It now contains the **Landesmuseum für Kunst und Kulturgeschichte** (Tues–Fri 9am–5pm, Sat & Sun 10am–5pm; DM4), whose lure is a large collection of paintings and *objets d'art* set in period interiors. Particularly notable is the extensive array of the work of **Johann Heinrich Wilhelm Tischbein**, a friend of Goethe and the most accomplished member of one of Germany's best-known artistic dynasties. Duke Peter Friedrich Ludwig, an astute patron of the arts, brought him to the Oldenburg court in 1804, and he remained there for the last twenty-five years of his life. The large canvases, such as *Of Naked Men* and *Hector's Farewell to Andromache*, show his talent for the grand manner, but what really steals the show is the *Idyllen-Zyklus*, a cycle of 44 little mythological and pastoral scenes and landscapes, tree, bird and animal studies.

On the opposite side of Schlosswall is the **Schlossgarten**, originally a dairy and market garden for the court, but later remodelled into an English-style park. Nowadays, it also boasts hothouses, a rose garden and extensive patches of rhododendrons, and makes a good place to picnic or relax. Just across the moat on the corner of Elisabethstrasse and the Damm is a branch of the Landesmuseum, the **Augusteum** (same hours and ticket). It houses the modern parts of the collection: most of the leading Expressionists are represented, along with plenty of works by Franz Radzwill and other German Surrealists. Round the corner at Damm 40–44, the **Museum für Naturkunde und Vorgeschichte** (Tues–Thurs 9am–5pm, Fri 9am–3pm, Sat & Sun 10am–5pm; DM3) features natural history displays laid out in the manner of nineteenth-century curio cabinets. There are also archeological finds from prehistoric times to the early Middle Ages, the most eye-catching being the 2400-year-old corpses found in Lower Saxon peat bogs.

A couple of minutes' walk north of the Schloss, the Markt is dominated by the **Lambertikirche**, whose brick Gothic exterior has repeatedly been rebuilt, giving it an incongruously modern sheen. Its interior was competely transformed in the 1790s by order of Duke Peter Friedrich Ludwig into a Neoclassical rotunda based on the Pantheon in Rome. The overall effect is astonishing – rather like a Wedgwood vase turned inside out. Alongside are the **Altes Rathaus**, a Historicist fantasy borrowing freely from the vocabulary of the Gothic and Renaissance, and the early sixteenth-century **Haus Degode**, the oldest surviving house in the city.

Practicalities

It's easy to get disorientated when arriving at the **Hauptbahnhof**, which is about fifteen minutes' walk northeast of the Altstadt. Following Bahnhofstrasse straight ahead, then turning left into Gottorpstrasse will take you in the direction of the Schloss. The **tourist office** (Mon–Fri 9am–6pm, Sat 9am–1.30/6pm; ☎0441/15744) is at the extreme northwest corner of the Altstadt at Wallstr. 14. There's a **Mitfahrzentrale** office at Nadorster Str. 38 (☎0441/885656).

The best budget **hotels** are *Mandel*, just west of the Hauptbahnhof at 91er-Str. 2 (☎0441/25864; ③), *Harmonie*, southeast of the Schloss at Dragonerstr. 59 (☎0441/27704; ③); and *Hegeler*, north of the Altstadt at Donnerschweer Str. 27 (☎0441/87561; ④). If you want to be more in the centre, try *Posthalter*, Mottenstr. 13 (☎0441/25194; ⑥), or *Antares*, Am Staugraben 8 (☎0441/92250; ⑦). The tourist office also has details of a few **private rooms** (②–④), while the **youth hostel** is about ten minutes' walk north of the Altstadt at Alexanderstr. 65 (☎0441/87135; ⓗ).

For **food**, there's something to suit all tastes. *Seewolf*, Alexanderstr. 41, specializes in fish dishes; the *Fürsten- und Jugendstilsaal* in the Hauptbahnhof serves *gutbürgerliche Küche* in surprisingly elegant surroundings; *Steffmann*, Kurwickstr. 23, is a typical *Gaststätte*; *Le Journal*, Wallstr. 13, is an upmarket French-style bistro, while *Die Stube*, Achternstr. 63, caters for vegetarians. On Schlossplatz, there are a couple of contrasting cafés – the traditional *Schlosscafé* and the slightly idiosyncratic *Chaplin*, which also does light meals. If you're after a drink, there are plenty of **pubs** along Kurwickstrasse, or there's *Ulenspiegel*, Burgstr. 12, and *Hannenfass*, Baumgartenstr. 3, whose speciality is *Alt* beer, and which features live music on Wednesdays. Next door to the latter you'll find *Sunup's*, a disco-café-bar.

Oldenburg has plenty of **festivals**, including the *Hafenfest* on the weekend after Whitsun, the *Altstadtfest* on the last weekend in August, and the *Kramermarkt* for ten days in late September and early October. The main **theatre** and concert **venue** is the *Weser-Ems-Halle*, Europaplatz 12 (☎0441/80030).

Emden, Greetsiel and Borkum

The western gateway to East Friesia is the important seaport of **Emden**, which is easily accessible from Bremen or Oldenburg by train. Ferries run from here to **Borkum**, the first of the seven inhabited East Friesian islands, while the town's hinterland includes the peninsula of Krummhörn, whose main draw is the old fishing village of **Greetsiel**. Buses connect Greetsiel with Norden and Emden, though Sunday services are poor.

Emden

Despite its modest size, **EMDEN** is the principal town of East Friesia, and has been a trading centre since the days of Charlemagne. It was becalmed when the River Ems changed its course in the seventeenth century, and only revived some 300 years later with the digging of the Dortmund–Ems canal and the building of a new harbour. Heavily bombed in World War II, there's precious little of the old town left. Emden owes much of its present prosperity toVolkswagen, whose plant produces some 1000 cars per day.

The main historic monument is the former **Rathaus** at Am Delft in the centre of town, a Flemish Renaissance civic showpiece modelled directly on its Antwerp counterpart. Nowadays, it houses the **Ostfriesisches Landesmuseum** (April–Sept Mon–Fri 11am–1pm & 2–5pm, Sat 1–5pm, Sun 11am–5pm; Oct–March Tues–Fri

11am–1pm & 2–4pm, Sat 1–4pm, Sun 11am–4pm; DM5), which has a varied collection of items illustrating the history and culture of East Friesia, but which is notable mainly for the **Rüstkammer**, an arsenal containing one of the most impressive displays of sixteenth- and seventeenth-century arms and armour to be found anywhere in Europe.

Just outside, moored in the Ratsdelft canal, is the fireship *Deutsche Bucht*, which preserves its original machinery intact and is now open to the public as the **Museumsfeuerschiff** (April–Oct Mon–Fri 10am–1pm & 3–5pm, Sat & Sun 11am–1pm; DM2). On either side, and accessible with the same ticket, are the herring trawler *AE7* (same times) and the lifeboat *Georg Breusing* (daily April–Oct 10am–1pm & 3–5pm). The new **Bunkermuseum** (May–Oct Tues–Fri 11am–1pm & 3–5pm, Sat & Sun 11am–1pm; DM3) east of the canal on Holzsägerstrasse is the only one of its type in Germany. It occupies six storeys of an air-raid shelter and contains documentation on the city during the Third Reich. One other museum worth a look is the **Kunsthalle** (Tues 10am–8pm, Wed–Fri 10am–5pm, Sat & Sun 11am–5pm; DM9) on Hinter dem Rahmen in the northern part of the town centre, which concentrates on twentieth-century art, with a good Expressionist section.

Practicalities

Both the **Hauptbahnhof** and the **bus station** are on the west side of town, just a few minutes' walk from the centre. Emden's **tourist office** (May–Sept Mon–Fri 9am–6pm, Sat 10am–1pm; Sun 11am–1pm; Oct–April Mon–Fri 9am–1pm & 3–5.30pm, Sat 10am–1pm; ☎04921/97400), housed in a pavilion at Am Stadtgarten, can provide a list of **private rooms** (①–④). Among the **hotels** are *Haus Waage*, Hinne-Rhode-Str. 19 (☎04921/22600; ③); *Alt Emder Bürgerhaus*, Friedrich-Ebert-Str. 33 (☎04921/24241; ⑤); *Heerens*, Friedrich-Ebert-Str. 67 (☎04921/23740 or 23036; ⑥); *Deutsches Haus*, Neuer Markt 7 (☎04921/92760; ⑥); and *Goldener Adler*, Neutorstr. 5 (☎04921/92730; ⑥). All but the first of these has a **restaurant**. Other places to eat include two of the docked ships: the aforementioned *Deutsche Bucht* and *Nautilus* further south at Am Alten Binnenhafen. The **youth hostel** is at An der Kesselschleuse 5 (☎04921/23797; ❷) on the eastern outskirts, while there's a **campsite**, *Knock*, 8km west along the coast road. In summer, daily **harbour cruises** operate from in front of the Rathaus.

Greetsiel

The strip of agricultural land to the west of Emden, known as the **Krummhörn**, was reclaimed from the sea between the wars. Near its northern tip is the picturesque fishing village of **GREETSIEL**, a shrimp-fishing village since the fourteenth century, with cobbled streets, hump-backed bridges, windmills and teashops, but – in season – definitely not for those with a low bus-party tolerance.

There's plenty of accommodation for visitors, mainly in bed and breakfast arrangements, and the **tourist office** at Zur Hauner Hooge 15 (☎04926/91880) can arrange places to stay, though it gets difficult if you leave it too late in the day. The **youth hostel** is at Kleinbahnstr. 15 (☎04926/550; ❷), with **camping** fairly close by at Loquard (☎04927/595).

Don't miss *Is Teetied* opposite the church, an East Friesian style olde tea shoppe with many good things to eat. Friesians may account for less than one percent of the population, but they drink a third of the nation's tea. They like it strong, poured over special giant sugar crystals (*kluntjes*) and topped up with cream.

Borkum

The island of **Borkum** is the largest and most westerly of the East Friesian islands. A popular holiday spot, it has all the facilities of a resort, including a casino, an indoor swimming pool with sea water and artificial waves, a marina and long sandy beaches.

Despite the calm effected by a ban on cars during the tourist season, it has to be said that other islands are more appealing and more easily reached.

Ferries for Borkum leave from the harbour (*Aussenhafen*) just south of Emden four times daily in summer, twice daily in winter (journey takes 2hr 30min; return ticket DM47, DM25 for a day-trip, with a DM15 supplement for the catamaran, which takes 1hr). There are onward rail connections from the ferry terminal to Emden and other major German cities.

If you want to stay overnight, contact the **tourist office**, Goethestr. 1 (☎04922/841), in advance for accommodation, which ranges from private rooms to luxury **hotels**. There's also a **youth hostel** at Jann-Berghaus-Str. 63 (☎04922/579; ❷). It's possible to continue on to Holland from Borkum on a ferry sailing to the Dutch island of Eemshaven: tickets cost DM38 (DM21 for a day-trip). For further details call ☎04921/890722.

Norden

NORDEN, East Friesia's oldest town, lies some 30km north of Emden. A place with an individual if rather sleepy atmosphere, it's centred on a huge **Marktplatz**, half of which is grassed over and dominated by shady, mature trees, forming an odd (or at least unfamiliar) picture for this part of the world.

The square is dominated by the medieval **Ludgerikirche**, which was built between the thirteenth and fifteenth centuries, and the tall, narrow freestanding bell tower alongside. Pride of the church is its **organ**, made in the 1680s by north Germany's greatest exponent of the craft, Arp Schnitger. Recitals take place, among other times, on Wednesdays at 8pm from mid-June to mid-September. Along the paved part of the Marktplatz, on which markets are held on Mondays and Saturdays, are three Renaissance houses known as the **Drei Schwestern** (Three Sisters), and several other fine facades. Also on Marktplatz is the **Heimat- und Teemuseum** (March–Oct Tues–Sat 10am–4pm; DM4), which claims to be the first museum devoted to tea. It documents the history of the beverage in Europe, traces its cultural and commercial impact, and shows an array of porcelain and other accessories.

Practicalities

Norden's **tourist office** (Mon–Fri 8am–3pm, Sat 9am–1pm; ☎04931/98602) at Am Markt 24 can help find **private rooms** (①–④). There are plenty in town and all are excellent value. Good **hotels** include *Zur Post*, Am Markt 3 (☎04931/2787; ④), an "alternative" institution with a trendy café-bar; and *Reichshof*, Neuer Weg 53 (☎04931/1750; ⑤).

Choices for **eating** and **drinking** range from *Die Alte Backstube*, a traditional *Gaststätte* opposite the museum at Westerstr. 96, via *Vesuvio*, a reasonably priced Italian restaurant in the Schöninghsches Haus, a magnificent Renaissance building at Osterstr. 5, to *Die Borke*, Brummelkamp 1, the favoured hangout of local hippies.

Norddeich

Norden incorporates the seaside resort of **NORDDEICH**, which is just 2.5km away, ten minutes by bus from Marktplatz. **Ferries** run from here to the islands of Juist and Norderney, and trains – which arrive from Amsterdam and Copenhagen as well as a range of German cities – are timetabled to coincide with the boats, going right up to the jetty of **Norddeich-Mole**. Buses also link up with appropriate trains to take passengers to Nessmersiel, the ferry port for Baltrum.

You could, of course, stop off in Norddeich itself, but it's an ugly, rambling town with precious little to recommend it. Almost every house has **rooms** (②–④) to let (just look out for the *Zimmer frei* signs), but these are generally more expensive than in Norden.

The **youth hostel** is in the middle of the resort at Strandstr. 1 (☎04931/8064; **❷**), while the new *Nordsee* **campsite** (☎04931/8073) is situated by the sea dyke 1.5km west of town. Should you require further help, you'll find the **tourist office** at Dörper Weg 22 (July & Aug Mon–Sat 9am–5pm, Sun 10am–noon; rest of year Mon–Thurs 9am–5pm, Fri 8.30am–4pm, Sat 10am–4pm; ☎04931/986203).

The East Friesian Islands

The two most popular, attractive and accessible of the East Friesian islands, **Juist** and **Norderney**, are each a shortish ferry journey from Norddeich Mole. This proximity means it's worth considering visiting them on day-trips, rather than feeling bound to go over for an extended stay. If you do want accommodation, the islands are packed with hotels of all categories as well as holiday homes for self-catering, and the tourist offices are the best places to find out about vacancies.

The four easterly islands – **Baltrum**, **Langeoog**, **Spiekeroog** and **Wangerooge** – have none of the sophistication of their westerly neighbours, and are characterized by sandy beaches to the north and mud flats to the south, drab modern settlements with a suburban air, and nature reserves. All are connected by **bus** and **ferry** to Norden's Bahnhof in Norddeich (see p.583).

Juist

Depending on the tides, between one and three ferries leave Norddeich Mole for the island of **Juist** every day. The trip takes eighty minutes and costs DM30 for a day return, DM42 for a period return. Juist is a narrow strip of land 17km long and a few hundred yards wide. A sandy, dune-fringed beach extends the entire length of its northern shore and even on hot summer days privacy is not hard to find. The only **settlement** is halfway along the island near the ferry terminal. It's a rather drab suburban affair, but at least it's not dominated by high-rise hotels and, best of all, there are no cars. Criss-crossed by foot and cycle paths, Juist has the full range of tourist facilities, with dozens of bars and restaurants, a large covered swimming pool and a nature reserve (the "Bill").

Practicalities

Accommodation can be a little tricky in summer, but the **tourist office**, Friesenstr. 18 (May–Sept Mon–Sat 8.30am–noon & 3–5pm; Oct–April Mon–Sat 8.30am–noon; ☎04935/809222), is more than willing to help. In addition to scores of **pensions** (②–④) and **hotels** in all categories, there's a large **youth hostel** (March–Oct only) at Loogster Pad 20 (☎04935/1094; **❷**) with 400 beds and family rooms. **Camping** is not permitted anywhere on the island.

For details of sailings to local islands and the mainland a useful **travel agent** is *Reisebüro Kiesendahl*, Strandstr. 2 (☎04935/1096). Tours of the celebrated Juist **mud flats** and the protected wildlife areas are organized by *Wattführer Heino Behring* (☎04935/1443).

Norderney

According to the season, ferries make the fifty-minute journey from Norddeich Mole to **Norderney** between nine and thirteen times daily; a return – whether for one day or for a longer period – costs DM22.50. The rugged lifestyle of its islanders in the first half of last century was graphically described in the second part of Heinrich Heine's *Travel Pictures*, and also inspired his cycle of poems, *The North Sea*. Today, the reality is very different, as Norderney does its utmost to cater for all kinds of holidaymakers. In the summer the bars are packed with serious drinkers, middle-aged couples tuck into apple strudels, and gamblers fill the casino with no time to eat or drink. Meanwhile earnest joggers trot round the myriad footpaths, families sunbathe on the long sandy beach, pensioners take the cures and cyclists tour the nature reserve. If that's not enough, there are innumerable gourmet restaurants, a couple of small museums and the first-ever covered swimming pool to have sea water and artificial waves.

Slightly self-conscious, the town of **NORDERNEY** is the oldest bathing and health resort on the German North Sea coast, and was once a favourite royal holiday residence. The central square, with its manicured gardens, elegant cafés and Neoclassical buildings, has retained a certain nineteenth-century grace, though most of the town is a dull mixture of modern architectural styles. Its only surprise is a huge pyramid of stones piled up in the middle of an ordinary side street. This is in fact a monument to Kaiser Wilhelm I and his achievement of German unification: 61 stones marked with their state of origin.

Practicalities

The **tourist office** (Mon–Fri 9am–12.30pm & 2.30–6pm, March–Oct also Sat 10am–12.30pm & 2–4pm, Sun 10am–12.30pm; ☎04932/91850) is just off the main square at Bülowallee 5. It will find you a **room** in a pension or private house (②–④), or advise on **hotels**, of which there are many, particularly in the middle and upper ranges, though things get tight in high season.

There are two **youth hostels** (March–Oct only), which also fill up quickly in summer. The one at Südstr. 1 (☎04932/2451; 🏠) can be reached by bus from the ferry, or else by a 35-minute walk via Zum Fahranleger and Deichstrasse. The alternative at Am Dünensender 3 (☎04932/2574; 🏠) is way to the east of town, but has the advantage of attached **camping** facilities. There's another campsite, *Booken*, on the edge of town at Waldweg 2 (☎04932/448).

The easternmost islands

Just 5km long, **BALTRUM** is the smallest of the islands, with a quiet atmosphere thanks to a ban on cars. Three to six buses daily go from Norden's Bahnhof to the ferry port at Nessmersiel; they arrive in time for ferry departure, though crossings may be delayed in rough weather. Period returns cost DM36, though the DM24 day return allows plenty of time to explore the island. The **tourist office** (March–Oct Mon–Fri 8.30am–noon & 2.30–5pm; Nov–Feb Mon–Fri 9am–noon; ☎04939/8048) by the harbour can help find a **room** (①–④) or a **hotel**. Ask here for permission to use the sole **campsite**, at the edge of a nature reserve.

Regular buses leave Norden for Esens, where you have to change for the connections (3 to 5 daily) to the port of Bensersiel, the departure point for **LANGEOOG**, the next island to the east. The ferry costs DM34 return, or DM28 for a day return. It takes fifty minutes and synchronizes with the island's toytown rail line to the somewhat dull main settlement. Far more enticing is Langeoog's main attraction, the **nature reserve** at the eastern end of the island, home to a colony of seabirds. The **youth hostel** (April–Sept only; ☎04972/276; 🏠), pleasantly set behind the Melkhörn sand dunes some 3km to the east of the village, is the most atmospheric place to stay. It has a **campsite** attached. Otherwise, check the noticeboard outside the **tourist office** (April–Sept Mon–Sat 9am–7pm, Sun 10am–2pm; Oct–March Mon–Fri 9am–5pm; ☎04972/6930) at Hauptstr. 28 for the current **room** (②–④) and **hotel** vacancies.

Another bus leaves Esens for Neuharlingersiel, from where two to four ferries per day sail to **SPIEKEROOG**. Tickets for the fifty-minute journey cost DM36 return, or DM28 for a day return. This island has a rail line, and the oldest church on the islands, the late seventeenth-century **Inselkirche**. It contains wreckage from one of the ships of the Spanish Armada, wrecked off the nearby coast in 1588. Spiekeroog's **tourist office** (Mon–Fri 9am–noon & 2–4pm, Sat 9am–noon; ☎04976/91930) at Noorderpad 25 supplies the usual information on **rooms** (②–④) and **hotels**. There's also a **youth hostel**, open from mid-March until October, located within easy walking distance from the harbour at Bid' Utkiek 1 (☎04976/329; **⌀**).

The easternmost of the East Friesian islands, **WANGEROOGE**, is one of the most attractive of the group, boasting all the usual tourist facilities, a small museum in the old lighthouse, and several **bird sanctuaries**. It is reached via the port of Harle, which is linked to both Esens and Wilhelmshaven by bus, though a change may be necessary at the inland harbour of Carolinensiel. Tickets for the ferry crossing cost DM45. The main settlement is in the middle of the island, connected by rail to the ferry terminal. A branch line also goes to the western tip where you'll find the Westturm, a stone tower now housing the **youth hostel** (☎04469/439; **⌀**). As ever, the **tourist office** (April–Sept Mon–Sat 9am–noon & 2–5pm; Oct–March Mon–Fri 9am–noon; ☎04469/94880) on Strandpromenade can help with finding **rooms** (②–④) or a **hotel**.

Jever

Situated some 60km from both Oldenburg and Emden, modest little **JEVER** is the most attractive town in Friesia. For more than four centuries the capital of a minute aristocratic territory, it reached its apogee in the sixteenth century under the last of its noble rulers, the energetic and gifted **Fräulein Maria**, who give it city rights, had the fortifications built, founded a school, and commissioned several splendid works of art. Later, through marriage and conquest, Jever came under Russian, Dutch and French control, but it never developed into a place of significance, and remains something of a backwater to this day.

The town

Jever's dominant monument is the rather magnificent pink **Schloss** (March to mid-Jan Tues–Sun 10am–6pm; mid-June to mid-Sept also Mon 11am–5pm; DM4). Begun in the fifteenth century as a fortified castle, it was transformed by Fräulein Maria into a Renaissance palace. Highlight of the interior is the carved oak ceiling of the Audienzsaal, the work of the great Antwerp artist Cornelis Floris. It's sometimes possible to go up the tower for a fine view over the skyline and the Schlosspark.

The town centre to the north is laid out round two squares. Neuer Markt is dominated by the **Stadtkirche**, which has been burned down and rebuilt at least nine times in its nine-hundred-year history. It last had a fire in 1959, when over half of the church was destroyed and replaced with a contemporary design. The enormous **funerary monument** by Floris that Fräulein Maria commissioned in honour of her father somehow survived, and can be seen in the remains of the Baroque church, which is now integrated into the new building. A work of architecture as much as sculpture, it's particularly remarkable for the extraordinary variety of materials used – wood, marble, sandstone and clay.

A few blocks further north, at Elisabethufer 17, is the distinctive silhouette of the **Friesisches Brauhaus zu Jever** (guided tours April–Oct Mon–Fri at 9.30am, 10am & 10.30am; Nov–March Tues & Thurs at 10.30am; DM10), which is claimed as the most modern brewery in Germany. Its *Pils* enjoys cult status as the bitterest-tasting beer made in the country. Other products are the low-alcohol, low-calorie *Light* and the drolly named *Fun*, which is alcohol-free. The price of the tour includes not only a visit to the production lines and the museum, but also a presentation glass, which can be filled up twice, with a *Brezel* to ward off any hunger pangs.

Practicalities

Jever's **Bahnhof** is situated some distance southwest of the centre. The **tourist office** (May–Sept Mon–Fri 10am–6pm, Sat 10am–2pm, Sun 10am–noon; Oct–April Mon–Fri 9am–5pm, Sat 9am–1pm; ☎04461/71010) is at Alter Markt 18. Ask here about **private rooms** (①–③), which are in reasonable supply, both in the town itself and in the surrounding countryside.

There are several budget **hotels**: *Stöber*, just south of the Schloss at Hohnholzstr. 10 (☎04461/5580; ③); *Hennig*, Bahnhofstr. 32 (☎04461/3080; ③); *Schwarzer Adler*, Alter Markt 3 (☎04461/5532; ③); and *Weisses Haus*, Bahnhofstr. 20 (☎04461/6839; ④). The classiest hotel in town is *Friesen*, to the south of the centre at Harlinger Weg 1 (☎04461/2500; ⑥). There's a **youth hostel** (April–Oct only) at Mooshüttenweg 12 (☎04461/3590; ⓐ).

Among places to **eat** and **drink**, the historic *Haus der Getreuen* deserves special mention; it's the *Gaststätte* of the brewery, situated across from it at Schlachtstr. 1. Seasoned beer drinkers, however, might prefer the *Bier-Akademie*, Bahnhofstr. 44. Main **festivals** are the *Kiewittmarkt*, a spring market usually held at the end of March, and the *Altstadtfest* in mid-August.

Osnabrück

OSNABRÜCK, a major rail junction, on the main north–south and east–west lines, stands somewhat apart from the rest of Lower Saxony, at its extreme western end. Geographically and historically, it really belongs to Westphalia, and it has many parallels with Münster (see pp.533–538), which is just 55km to the south. Each city is now home to a British army base, and has a sizeable student population. Both owe their foundation to Charlemagne, and in the Middle Ages both were ruled by a Prince-bishop, and were important trading centres. Subsequently, they shared the hosting of the long negotiations – regarded as the birth of modern diplomatic practices – which led to the signing of the **Peace of Westphalia** in 1648, bringing the Thirty Years' War to an end. One curious agreement resulting from these talks was that Osnabrück was to be ruled in future by a Catholic and a Protestant bishop in turn. When the bishopric was secularized under Napoleon, the Hanoverians annexed its territories. After World War II, therefore, Osnabrück joined the rest of Hannover in the new province of Lower Saxony. Like Münster, Osnabrück will celebrate the 350th anniversary of the treaty with a year-long programme of special events.

Arrival, information and accommodation

Osnabrück's **Hauptbahnhof** is ten minutes' walk southeast of the city centre, which is reached by following Möserstrasse straight ahead, then crossing the River Hase. The **tourist office** (Mon–Fri 9.30am–6pm, Sat 9.30am–1pm; ☎323 2202) is just off the Markt at Krahnstr. 54, and **Mitfahrzentrale** is at Martinistr. 9 (☎42947).

Accommodation

Osnabrück has a good choice of **hotels** in all price categories. There's a **youth hostel** to the south of town at Iburger Str. 183a (☎54284; ⓐ); take bus #23 or #25 from Neumarkt, and alight at Kinderhospital. In addition, there are two **campsites** in the environs – *Niedersachsenhof* (☎77226) and *Attersee* (☎124147).

The **telephone code** for Osnabrück is ☎0541

HOTELS

Dom-Hotel, Kleine Domsfreiheit 5 (☎21554, fax 201739). Recommendable hotel right in the heart of the city. Also has a fine restaurant, though this is open Mon–Thurs evenings only. ⑤

Hohenzollern, Heinrich-Heine-Str. 17 (☎33170, fax 331 7351). Upmarket hotel close to the Hauptbahnhof on the way to the centre. ⑦

Jägerheim, Johannistorwall 19a (☎21635). Located on the southern inner ring road, this has the cheapest rooms in the city centre. ③

Kulmbacher Hof, Schlosswall 65–67 (☎35700, fax 357020). Another good middle-range hotel with restaurant on the southwestern section of the inner ring road. ⑦

Nord-Hotel, Hansastr. 31 (☎64133, fax 64122). Very good value hotel a short distance beyond the Bahnhof Hasetor at the northern end of the Altstadt. Its restaurant serves huge portions at amazingly low prices, especially at lunchtime. ③

Walhalla (see opposite), Bierstr. 24 (☎34910, fax 349 1144). Despite occupying a seventeenth-century timber-framed house, this is a modern hotel with all the amenities including sauna and solarium. Its restaurant is among the best in the city. ⑦

Welp, Natruper Str. 227 (☎913070, fax 913 0734). Good medium-priced hotel with restaurant located just to the northwest of the Altstadt. ⑤

The city

Much of the city is modern. Heavy damage was caused by bombing in World War II, and restoration has been less successful than in Münster. Some highly characterful streets and squares do remain, but it's a pity that more thought wasn't given to the planning of the bland shopping areas with which they're now intermingled.

The Dom

The **Dom** has a spacious setting in the middle of its own square in the heart of the city. Built in fits and starts between the twelfth and sixteenth centuries, its facade **towers** are a fascinating combination – the late Gothic one on the southern side is almost twice the width of its Romanesque neighbour. Inside, the Dom presents a pleasingly sober, predominantly Gothic appearance. Among a number of notable **works of art**, the early thirteenth-century bronze font and the exactly contemporary polychrome wood *Triumphal Cross* are outstanding. The latter's name is something of a misnomer, as Christ is here depicted as a pathetic, suffering, all-too-human figure. Wonderful gilded wrought-iron gates guard the entrance to the ambulatory, at the end of which is the *Margarethenaltar*, a limewood retable by the sculptor who also carved the *Madonna of the Rosary* in the north transept. The identity of this emotional artist, who was still working in the late Gothic style well into the sixteenth century, remains elusive: he's known simply as the **Master of Osnabrück**.

Further works by this carver can be seen in the **Diözesanmuseum** (Tues–Fri 10am–1pm & 3–5pm, Sat & Sun 11am–2pm; DM2), housed in rooms above the cloister. The most eye-catching item here, however, is the gilded *Kapitelkreuz*, made in the early eleventh century and studded with two pontifical rings, a couple of Roman cameos and a variety of coloured gems. The early seventeenth-century confessional, from a nearby convent, was made in the wake of the Tridentine reforms and is the earliest example in northern Europe of what was to become a very familiar structure.

The Markt

Just beyond the Dom is the other main square, the triangular-shaped **Markt**. Its colourful step-gabled mansions are modelled on the merchant houses of the Hanseatic ports, while in the centre there's a fountain which gushes with beer whenever there's a festival on. On the northern side of the square is the Gothic **Marienkirche**, which takes the hall-church design to its logical conclusion by omitting the transept. Inside are a fourteenth-century *Triumphal Cross*, a sixteenth-century *Passion Altar* from Antwerp and numerous tombs – including that of Justus Möser, whose researches into Westphalian folklore in the eighteenth century were to serve as a trail-blazer for the Romantic movement. You can climb the **tower** on Sundays (11.30am–1pm; DM2) for a view of the city. In the Stadtsbibliothek opposite there's a permanent exhibition **Remarque am Markt** (Tues–Fri 10am–1pm & 3–5pm, Sat 10am–1pm, first Sun in the month 11am–5pm; free), a documentary record of the career of the local author Erich Maria Remarque, whose novel *All Quiet on the Western Front* is the enduring German classic of World War I literature.

Closing the end of the Markt is the early sixteenth-century **Rathaus**, from whose steps the Peace of Westphalia was proclaimed. The present stairway dates from the nineteenth century, as do the large statues of German emperors, among which Kaiser Wilhelm I is lined up alongside his medieval predecessors. Inside, the wood-panelled **Friedensaal** (Mon–Fri 8am–6pm, Sat & Sun 10am–1pm; free) features generally glum portraits of the representatives of Sweden and the Protestant German principalities, who deliberated here while their Catholic counterparts met in Münster. Ask at the porter's desk to see the **Schatzkammer**, which contains valuable documents and treasury items. Star piece is the magnificent fourteenth-century *Kaiserpokal*, a goblet adorned with coloured glass and figurines.

The rest of the city
Facing the rear of the Rathaus on Bierstrasse is the pretty half-timbered frontage of Osnabrück's most famous inn, *Walhalla*, which features extensively in Erich Maria Remarque's *The Black Obelisk*, a novel describing the traumatic hyper-inflation of 1923. Most of Osnabrück's surviving **old houses** are nearby – on Marienstrasse, Hegerstrasse, Grosser Gildewartare, Krahnstrasse and Bierstrasse itself. The first three form a pedestrian precinct, where antique shops and bistros vie with each other for prominence. At the end of Bierstrasse is the former **Dominikanerkirche**, now a cultural centre which often features exhibitions of contemporary art. It also contains a weather-worn late Gothic statue of Charlemagne, the only survivor of the original cycle from the Rathaus facade. Beyond here, several fragments of the city wall can be seen round the ring road, including the Neoclassical **Heger Tor**, celebrating the victory at Waterloo.

Diagonally opposite is the **Kulturgeschichtliches Museum** (Tues–Fri 9am–5pm, Sat & Sun 10am–5pm; DM3). Dominating the archeology section are the spectacular Roman finds from nearby Kaltkriese, which is now known to be the site of their defeat by the Cherusci under Arminius in AD 9 (see p561). The local history collections are of interest for such fragments as the original medieval sculptures from the *Brautportal* of the Marienkirche. From the summer of 1998 a new extension will at last be able to show in its entirety the museum's large collection of works by the local Jewish artist **Felix Nussbaum**, a member of the *Neue Sachlichkeit* art movement, which rejected Expressionism in favour of a starkly realistic form of representation. He died in Auschwitz, aged forty, in 1944.

Continuing southwards along Heger-Tor-Wall, you soon see on the left the tall tower of the **Katharinenkirche**, a church broader than it is long. In the big square behind is Osnabrück's most original building, the **Leidenhof**. The sixteenth-century merchant owners converted their original fourteenth-century stone house into a miniature palace by the addition of a staircase tower and a new wing, whose facade resembles a gigantic cardboard cut-out. What really catches the attention, however, are the zigzags painted on the two Renaissance additions, making them look strangely modernistic. Opposite, set in its own fine park, is the huge yellow **Schloss** of the Prince-bishops. Built in Italianate Baroque style, it nowadays houses part of the university.

Eating and drinking

Osnabrück is a lively city come the evening, and is well endowed with places to **eat** and **drink**.

Alte Gaststätte Holling, Hasestr. 53. Nowadays more a pub than a restaurant, though it does light meals. Evenings only except Sat, when it is open lunchtime.

Filmkneipe 8 1/2, Hasestr. 71. Trendy bar attached to a cinema. Games can be hired, and there are changing monthly art exhibitions.

Grüner Jäger, An der Katharinen Kirche 1. Hugely popular student *Kneipe* with minimalist decor and a glass-roofed beer garden.

Hermann's, Domhof 7b. Bistro serving an international menu, with good value set lunches.

Pfannkuchenhaus, Lotter Str. 22. Specializes in wholemeal and buckwheat pancakes; also serves salads and pasta dishes. Evenings only except Sun, closed Mon.

Rampendahl, Hasestr. 35. *Hausbrauerei* which produces light and dark beer and a *Korn*. Also does full meals, including cheap set lunches.

Vital, Rosenplatz 23a. Vegetarian and wholefood restaurant (Mon–Fri 11.30am–7.30pm, Sat 11.30am–4pm).

EASTERN LOWER SAXONY

In the east of Lower Saxony, the landscape transforms itself from coastal plain to the rolling **Lüneburg Heath** (*Lüneburger Heide*), which contains the contrasting towns of **Lüneburg** and **Celle**, as well as several nature reserves. This extends eastwards to an area known as the **Wendland** that juts into the former GDR, and south towards the state capital of **Hannover** and the province's second city, **Braunschweig**. Continuing in a southerly direction, you soon come to more elevated land: **Hildesheim** stands in the foothills leading to the Harz, while there are fine rolling landscapes around **Hameln** in the valley of the River Weser further west.

Lüneburg

Of all the many medieval trading cities built by the Germans on and near the Baltic coast between Hamburg and Riga, only **LÜNEBURG** has survived virtually unscathed. It was all but ignored by the World War II bombing missions which destroyed so much of northern Germany, having by then declined into economic insignificance. Yet in the Middle Ages the city was immensely wealthy, profiting from the fact that it was (literally) built on **salt** – then a rare and essential commodity, almost worth its weight in gold. At its peak, the Lüneburg saltworks had two thousand employees, which probably made it the largest commercial enterprise in Europe. The city's magnificent brick buildings were funded from exports of the salt to Scandinavia, Burgundy, Poland and Russia, and the other trading links which ensued. Gabled facades, from Gothic to Baroque, still line the streets of the centre. Many have a pronounced tilt, as a result of subsidence caused by disused mines: the salt deposits haven't been worked since 1980, leaving the saline springs of the spa quarter as the only active reminder of a tradition dating back to the tenth century.

The town

Today, Lüneburg is far from being the museum piece it might appear. Its population almost doubled in 1945 as a result of an influx of refugees from the confiscated Eastern Territories, and it has again become a lively regional centre. The **Markt** is the focus of

The **telephone code** for Lüneburg is ☎04131

the town's commercial life, particularly on Wednesdays and Saturdays, when markets are held. In the middle of the square is a sixteenth-century bronze **fountain** with a statuette of the moon goddess Luna, after whom Lüneburg (which means "fortress of Luna") is somewhat improbably named.

The Rathaus

The grandiose **Rathaus** (guided tours May to mid-Oct Tues–Sun at 10am, 11am, noon, 2pm, 3pm & 4pm; mid-Oct to late April Tues–Sun at 10am, 11am, 2pm & 3pm; DM6) occupies the west side of the Markt. Its Baroque facade is a mere frontispiece to the largest and most impressive medieval town hall in Germany. The **Grosser Ratssaal**, the old council chamber, is the most famous part. Originally from the fourteenth century, it was embellished a hundred years later with richly traceried windows bearing stained-glass portraits of nine great heroes. Another century later, it received its impressive wall and ceiling decoration, which included a scene of *The Last Judgment* in honour of its new function as the court of justice. Other highlights include the tiny **Körkammer** where the burgomasters (4 of whom are depicted in the windows) were elected, and the **Fürstensaal**, the former dance hall, with its fifteenth-century candelabra made from stags' antlers, and seventeenth-century portraits of the local dukes. However, the finest room of all is the **Grosse Ratsstube**, which ranks as one of Germany's most important Renaissance interiors thanks to the pyrotechnic woodwork – benches, panelling and, most notably, the doorways – carved by Albert von Soest. At the end of the tour, you're allowed to linger over the municipal silverware, by far the finest collection in Germany. Unfortunately, what you see here are only replicas: the originals are now in the Kunstgewerbemuseum in Berlin.

Am Sande and St Johannis

Lüneburg's largest square is the elongated **Am Sande**, whose name reflects the fact that it was laid out on a sandy marsh. It lies almost due south of the Markt, and is reached along the partly pedestrianized Bäckerstrasse. On the way, take a peek inside the late sixteenth-century **Rathsapotheke**, whose orderly interior forms a perfect complement to the elaborate gable and portal outside. Am Sande itself has the finest group of burghers' mansions in town, illustrating the seemingly inexhaustible variations the local builders worked on the theme of the brick gable. The **Schwarzes Haus** (Black House) – so called from the colour of its glazed brickwork – is particularly impressive. Situated on the west side of the square, it was formerly an inn and brewery, and is now the seat of the local chamber of commerce.

The opposite end of Am Sande is closed off by the impressively large brick church of **St Johannis**. This was begun in the thirteenth century, but the tall tower (which leans a couple of metres out of true) was only erected in the early fifteenth century. The **organ** is celebrated – the case and some of the pipework are early eighteenth-century, but it incorporates much of its mid-sixteenth-century predecessor, one of the oldest instruments in the country. It can be heard briefly each Friday at 5.30pm; from July to October, longer recitals are given on Tuesdays at 8pm. Almost equally precious is the **high altar**, a co-operative work by several fifteenth-century artists from Hamburg and Lübeck. Its reverse side, illustrating the lives of SS John the Baptist, Cecilia, George and Ursula, was painted by Hinrik Funhof with a delicacy worthy of comparison with the great Flemish masters of the period. Two more notable retables are housed in the chapels to either side; look out also for the *Madonna and Child* candelabrum in the north aisle, which has a marked similarity to those in the Rathaus.

The museums

From the rear of St Johannis, follow the River Ilmenau south for a couple of minutes, and cross over by Wandrahmstrasse, on which stand an old mill and the **Museum für das Fürstentum Lüneburg** (Tues–Fri 10am–4pm, Sat & Sun 11am–5pm; DM4). This features a good collection of medieval artefacts, including the tomb of a local duke, along with the predictable folklore and local history displays. The most intriguing exhibit is a copy of the once-famous thirteenth-century map of the world from the nearby convent of Ebstorf, the original of which was destroyed in a bomb raid on Hannover.

Just off the western end of Am Sande, at Heiligengeiststr. 39, the **Kronen-Brauerei-Museum** (daily 10am–noon & 3–5pm; free) has been set up in the former premises of the only brewery left out of the eighty the town once had. A free English leaflet guides you round the four floors of equipment, enabling you to see every stage of the traditional beer-making process. The historic lobby and staircase of the front house are also open to view, and there's a permanent exhibition of old drinking vessels. You can end your tour in suitable style by enjoying the products of the modern brewery – the smooth *Lüneburger Pils* and the very dry *Moravia Pils* – in the beer hall, complete with garden.

Immediately to the rear, at Ritterstr. 10, is the **Ostpreussisches Landesmuseum** (Tues–Sun 10am–5pm; DM3), which owes its existence to Lüneburg's large influx of refugees from the Baltic state of East Prussia, which in prewar years was the most far-flung part of Germany. In 1945, it was divided horizontally along the middle, with the southerly half allocated to Poland (to whom the whole territory had once belonged), while the remainder, including the capital city of Königsberg (which was renamed Kaliningrad), was made a province of Russia. The museum illustrates East Prussian history from the German viewpoint, in the process showing why bitterness at the Russian annexation remains so acute.

The western quarters

At the edge of the Altstadt, several minutes' walk west of the Ostpreussisches Landesmuseum, is the site of the old saltworks. The surviving installations have been turned into the **Deutsches Salzmuseum** (Mon–Fri 9/10am–5pm, Sat & Sun 10am–5pm; DM4), which tells you everything you are ever likely to want to know about the extraction, history, geology and economics of salt. In addition, you get to see the city's sole surviving saltpan, which is put into production each day in summer at 3pm. Continuing southwards, you come to the **Kurzentrum**, a modern spa complex set in an extensive park. The **Salztherme** (Mon–Sat 10am–11pm, Sun 8am–9pm), a thermal bathing complex, forms the centrepiece (DM13 for 2 hours, DM18 for 4 hours, DM22 for a day ticket).

In the opposite direction from the Salzmuseum is **St Michael**, another brick Gothic hall church, and the original home of the celebrated *Goldene Tafel* treasures, which are now divided between the Kestner-Museum and Landesgalerie in Hannover (see p.604). It stands on J.S.-Bach-Platz, which is so named because the great composer was a pupil at the school established in the monastic buildings after secularization. From here, you can ascend **Kalkberg**, the low-lying hill to the west for a fine long-range view over Lüneburg and its surroundings. The best route back to the Markt is via Auf dem Meere, a street lined with old craftsmen's houses.

The Wasserviertel

Following Bardowicker Strasse north from the Markt, you come to the fifteenth-century parish church of **St Nicolai**, where the sailors and artisans used to worship,. which is noted for its vertiginous, star-vaulted interior. Its tower, a neo-Gothic replacement of the original, can be ascended in summer at 3pm daily (DM2) except Wednesdays, for a view over the city. The old port or **Wasserviertel** lies just to the east along Lüner Strasse. With its peaceful riverside setting, trees, bridges, mills and other imperious buildings, it's the most evocative spot in town, creating a picture about as far removed from a modern-day harbour as it is possible to imagine. Formerly a herring warehouse, the **Altes Kaufhaus** had to be rebuilt after a fire in 1959, but still has its cheery Baroque facade. Opposite is the **Alte Krane** (old crane), which received its present form in the 1790s, though it dates back at least as far as the fourteenth century.

Kloster Lüne

Kloster Lüne (guided tours April 1–Oct 15 Mon–Sat 10–12.30pm & 2.30–5pm, Sun 11.30am–5pm; DM5) lies 2km northeast of the Wasserviertel. The present complex dates largely from the late fourteenth and early fifteenth centuries, though the half-timbered outbuildings were added later. It became a Protestant convent at the Reformation, and has remained so to this day. Among the highlights of the tour are the church, with its intricately carved sixteenth-century altar and seventeenth-century organ; the frescoed winter refectory; the simple pre-Reformation cells, and their painted Baroque equivalents from centuries later. The new **Textilmuseum** (same times; DM5, combined ticket DM7) displays an astonishing collection of textiles, most of which were probably woven in the convent. Especially notable are the white embroideries from the thirteenth and fourtenth centuries, and the three huge, colourful tapestries from the early years of the sixteenth.

Practicalities

Lüneburg's **Hauptbahnhof** has two terminals facing each other across Bahnhofsplatz. The quickest way to reach the centre is to go north along Lüner Weg, then turn left into Lünertor Strasse; this brings you to the Wasserviertel. Alternatively, turn right at the southern end of Bahnhofsplatz into Altenbrückertor Strasse, which takes you straight to Am Sande. Under the Rathaus' front arches is the municipal **tourist office** (May–Sept Mon–Fri 9am–6pm, Sat & Sun 9am–1pm; Oct–April Mon–Fri 9am–1pm & 2–6pm, Sat 9am–1pm; ☎309593).

If you want to **rent a bike** to explore the area, go to *Laden 25* at Am Werder 25. Regular **cruises** on the River Ilmenau depart from the Wasserviertel; the office is at Im Wendischen Dorfe 3 (☎31016). Lüneburg's main **festivals** are the *Bachwoche* in June, devoted to music by J.S. Bach, and the *Stadtfest* in July.

Accommodation

There's a **youth hostel** at Saltauer Str. 133 (☎41864; ⚑) well to the south of town, best reached by bus #1. The **campsite**, *Rote Schleuse* (☎791500), is by the banks of the River Ilmenau even further south; catch a bus towards Deutschevern. Lüneburg has a reasonable number of **private rooms** (①–⑤); contact the tourist office for a list.

HOTELS

Alt-Lüneburger-Kutscherstube, Heiligengeiststr. 44 (☎441134). Small former coaching inn in the heart of the Altstadt. ⑤

Bergström, Bei der Lüner Mühle (☎3080, fax 308499). Part of the *Mövenpick* chain, Lüneburg's best hotel is beautifully situated in the Wasserviertel. ⑦

Bremer Hof, Lüner Str. 12–13 (☎2240, fax 224224). Characterful hotel in a former merchant's home; also has a good and not over-expensive restaurant. ⑦

Lübecker Hof, Lünertorstr. 12 (☎51420, fax 53952). Budget hotel just a stone's throw from the Hauptbahnhof. ③

Scheffler, Bardowicker Str. 7 (☎30080, fax 200820). Long-established hotel and restaurant in a seventeenth-century half-timbered house just off the Markt. ⑥

Stadt Hamburg, Am Sande 25 (☎44438, fax 404198). A quaintly old-fashioned hotel directly opposite St Johannis. Excellent value. ③

Zum Heidkrug, Am Berge 5 (☎31249, fax 37688). Middle-range hotel in a brick Gothic mansion. ⑥

Eating and drinking

Some of the best restaurants are in the hotels, especially *Bergström*, *Bremer Hof* and *Scheffler*, but there are plenty of other enticing places to eat and drink.

Camus, Am Sande 30. Does breakfasts until well into the afternoon, as well as pizzas cooked in a wood oven, meats grilled on lava stones, and various vegetarian and bistro-type dishes.

Dialog, Am Stintmarkt. One of a row of lively waterfront pubs which are particularly attractive in summer, when tables are placed outside.

Kloster-Krug, Am Domänenhof 1. *Gaststätte* in a sixteenth-century timber-framed building directly opposite Kloster Lüne.

Kronen-Brauhaus, Heiligengeiststr. 39. The beer hall-cum-restaurant of the local brewery, offering typical North German cuisine.

Ratskeller, Am Markt 1. In the cellars of the Rathaus, fairly pricey but with a more imaginative menu than most of its counterparts in other German cities.

Stadtcafé, Untere Schrangenstr. 4. Good traditional café in a fine old town house.

The Lüneburg Heath

Partly wooded, but mainly uncultivated open heathland, the **Lüneburg Heath** (*Lüneburger Heide*) between Lüneburg and Celle is grazed by large flocks of *Heidschnucken*, goaty-sheep descended from the Corsican *mouflon*. In late August the heather erupts in deep purple swathes, adding a mass of colour to the heath's otherwise subtle palette. Picturesque villages, with timber-and-brick houses and churches, are also dotted around, forming an idyllic backdrop for festivals, the annual coronation of the queen of the heath, and shepherds who still wear their traditional green outfits. It was here, on May 4, 1945, that Field Marshal Montgomery received the unconditional German surrender. British troops still exercise on the heath, though their presence has been much reduced in recent years. This is one part of Germany where a car or bike is a distinct advantage, as public transport to and within the area is fiddly, serving the northern part of the heath from Lüneburg, the southern from Celle.

The Naturschutzpark Lüneburger Heide

The **Naturschutzpark Lüneburger Heide** is a 200-square-kilometre nature reserve in the northwest of the region, where the heathland and villages are least changed. Motor traffic is forbidden in much of this park, but there are networks of footpaths and cycle paths (renting a bike is easy in most towns) and horse-riding is another possibility. Bees buzz over the heather, and the local honey is renowned – as are the potatoes, oddly enough. Places to stay (mostly at low rates) abound, so you can normally rely on finding **accommodation** as you go, particularly as most towns have a tourist office.

The gateway to the park is the town of **SOLTAU**, a junction of several minor rail lines, including one from Hannover and another from Uelzen on the main line from Lüneburg to Celle. Buses run to **UNDELOH**, an attractive village in the heart of the park which boasts a half-timbered church going back to the twelfth century, and which has some two dozen hotels and pensions. From Undeloh, you can walk 4km south to ultra-quaint **WILSEDE**, along a road closed to traffic. An old farmhouse, **Dat Ole Huss** (Tues–Sun 10am–5pm; DM2), has been opened as a museum illustrating the ways of the past. You can also climb up northern Germany's highest hill, the 169-metre **Wilseder Berg**, for all-round views of the heath. Because of their abundant accommodation, two other possible bases for exploring the area are the health resorts of **EGESTORF**, which lies just outside the western fringe of the park, and **BISPINGEN**, which is beyond the southern boundary. The latter is a particularly pretty village with a fourteenth-century church; it also has a youth hostel, at Töpinger Str. 42 (☎05194/2375; 🏠).

The Vogelpark Walsrode

The most popular destination in the Lüneburg Heath is **WALSRODE**, which lies on the direct rail line between Soltau and Hannover; it can be reached from Verden by bus, cycle path or by the very occasional excursion trains run on a privately owned rail line formerly used for the transportation of potash. The town itself is of scant appeal, but 3km north of the centre is the **Vogelpark Walsrode** (daily March–Oct 9am–7pm; DM16), with over 5000 indigenous and exotic birds representing some of the 850 different species on view in a beautifully manicured park which is the largest of its type in the world. There's a choice of three café-restaurants, and you can stay overnight at the *Parkhotel Luisenhöhe* (☎05161/2011; ⑦).

The southern heath

Down towards Celle, there's another protected area of landscape, the **Naturpark Südheide**. This has an extensive area of natural woodland, the Unterlüss Forest, which is crossed by marked hiking trails. The main base for the area is the recuperative health resort of **MÜDEN**, which has a **youth hostel** at Wiesenweg 32 (☎05053/225; ⑥), and plenty of cheap **pensions** (①–③). On the main road between Soltau and Celle, 16km southwest of Müden, is **BERGEN**. At Am Friedenplatz 7 in the town itself is a small **Freilichtmuseum** (Mon–Thurs 9.30am–noon & 3–5pm, Fri 9.30am–noon; DM2), which brings together a number of old farm buildings from throughout the region. However, the principal reason for many people to visit the southern part of the heath is grounded in more recent history: some 6km southwest, and reachable by Celle-bound buses, is the infamous **Konzentratsionslager Bergen-Belsen.**

Bergen-Belsen

Some 50,000 people died at **Bergen-Belsen**, many as a result of starvation and disease, or by the personal whim of the infamous camp commandant, Josef Kramer, the "Beast of Belsen". When the camp was liberated some 13,000 unburied bodies were found lying in heaps; many of the 30,000 survivors were on the point of death. The film made of the camp's liberation still appals: a number of Germans, who were forced to watch it and realize the atrocities that had been carried out in their name, subsequently committed suicide. In Britain the film was shown in every cinema in the country, revealing the horror of the "Final Solution" to the public for the first time. Nowadays it is a memorial run by the state office for political education. The buildings were destroyed at the end of the war by the British, for fear of a typhus outbreak, but the mass graves remain, and a visit to the site of such horror is deeply disturbing.

By car, the camp is 22km northwest of Celle on the B3; turn left when you reach Bergen. It's also reachable by turning off the main E4 route between Hannover and Hamburg at the Soltau-Süd junction. Local **buses** run fairly frequently from Bergen to the camp. There are also up to three direct services a day from Celle, making it a feasible excursion, albeit one that will take up most of the day. For this reason it may be better to spend the night in Bergen: there's plenty of accommodation, including **private rooms** (②–④) and **hotels** such as *Zum Schwan*, Bahnhofstr. 16 (☎05051/5151; ④) and *Kohlmann*, Lukenstr. 4–6 (☎05051/987690; ④).

Wienhausen

At the extreme southeastern edge of the Lüneburg heath, some 10km from Celle, to which it's connected by fairly regular buses, lies **WIENHAUSEN**, a village of half-timbered houses clustered around a remarkable **Kloster** (guided tours April to mid-Oct Mon–Sat at 10am, 11am, 2pm, 3pm, 4pm & 5pm, Sun at noon, 1pm, 2pm, 3pm, 4pm & 5pm; DM5). Founded in 1231 by Agnes von Meissen, daughter-in-law of Henry the Lion, the convent became Protestant at the Reformation, and is still in use today. The severity of the brick buildings stands in contrast to the walls of the nuns' chancel which are covered with a heavily restored cycle of fourteenth-century frescoes illustrating the life of Christ and the legend of the Holy Cross, along with secular subjects. In the centre of the chancel is a wooden *Holy Sepulchre*, complete with a figure of the dead Christ, which dates from the late thirteenth century.

The Kloster's most valuable treasures are its **tapestries**. Woven by the nuns in the fourteenth and fifteenth centuries, they rank among the greatest ever made. Also on view are some intriguing excavations, which include the implements used to weave the tapestries, and the spectacles worn by their creators. For conservation reasons, the display is only open to the public for two weeks immediately after Whitsun each year (when the entry charge is raised to DM8); check with the tourist office in Celle for the exact dates.

Celle

Despite being roughly the same size, having a closely connected history, and lying no more than 90km apart at opposite ends of the Lüneburg Heath, **CELLE** and Lüneburg seem to have come from different worlds. Celle has none of the massive brickwork public buildings which define the skyline of the Hanseatic trading cities of the north. For long a ducal *Residenzstadt*, it marks the transition to the timber-framed buildings so characteristic of central Germany. Like Lüneburg, it has been spared from serious war damage, and its centre retains whole streets of intact historic houses.

The town

The Schloss dominates the town, much as it has always done, and the streets of the Altstadt, which lies to the east, run towards it with a gesture of subservience. These contain Celle's other outstanding feature, an array of 480 **half-timbered buildings**, many of which have been adapted successfully to commercial use.

The Schloss

Originally built in the late thirteenth century, the **Schloss** (guided tours April–Oct Tues–Sun at 9am, 10am, 11am, noon, 1pm, 2pm, 3pm & 4pm; Nov–March Tues–Sun at 11am & 3pm; DM5) became the main residence of the Dukes of Braunschweig-Lüneburg in 1371, when the independently minded burghers of Lüneburg flexed their collective muscle and chucked out their feudal overlords. In 1530, the building was completely rebuilt in the Renaissance style and the present whitewashed exterior, with its idiosyncratic corner towers, decorative gable and lofty, confined courtyard, dates almost entirely from this period.

Sole survivor of the medieval castle, and the highlight of the tour, is the **Schlosskapelle**, which was cleverly incorporated into the southeastern tower facing the town, its pointed Gothic windows being the only giveaway as to its presence there. Its architectural simplicity was obscured in the second half of the sixteenth century by an integrated programme of Mannerist decoration that's still stunningly fresh and vibrant. The cycle of 76 paintings, commissioned from the Antwerp artist **Marten de Vos** (once an assistant to Tintoretto in Venice), forms a complete illustrated Bible, in accordance with the new Protestant doctrines. The two galleries are adorned with portrait sculptures of Old and New Testament figures, and wacky pendants of varying shapes and sizes hang from the vault. Both the pulpit, with beautiful reliefs of the Passion, and the organ, with painted shutters, are intrinsic parts of the scheme.

The **telephone code** for Celle is ☎05141

Early in the eighteenth century the Duchy of Lüneburg was reunited with Hannover (which had split off the previous century) when Sophie Dorothea, daughter of the last Duke of Lüneburg, married the future George I of Britain. Thereafter, Celle was no more than the second-string German residence of the Hanoverian dynasty, and a place where those who had fallen from grace could readily be dumped. In the 1770s the Schloss became home for a few years to an exiled queen, Caroline Mathilde of Denmark, who was banished following an indiscretion with a courtier. Her suite of rooms, the **Caroline-Mathilde-Räume**, contains a museum of the history of the Kingdom of Hannover (Tues–Sun 10am–4.30pm; DM4 including Bomann-Museum).

An especially pleasant way to sneak a look inside other parts of the Schloss is to go to a performance at the **Schlosstheater** – dating back to 1674, it's the oldest one in Germany to have a resident company. Concerts and plays are performed throughout the year, except during July and August. Tickets and information are available (mornings only) from the box office, currently at Schlossplatz 13 (☎22577) but likely to move to a new location. Unfortunately, you're unlikely to get near the handsome Baroque auditorium unless you're attending a performance.

The Altstadt

Every street in the Altstadt is a visual treat, and well worth including in a gentle stroll. The place to begin is Stechbahn (formerly a yard used for tournaments) which runs from the centre of Schlossplatz. Opposite the early sixteenth-century court pharmacy, the **Löwenapothek**, is the Gothic **Stadtkirche**, whose tower (April–Oct Tues–Sat 10am–noon & 3–4pm; DM2), which was added as recently as 1913, commands the best view of the town. A trumpeter plays a chorale from here at 6.30am and 6.30pm every day. The interior of the church was transformed in the late seventeenth century by the addition of the Italianate stuccowork and painted galleries, another complete illustrated Bible. A whole series of elaborate Gothic, Renaissance and Baroque **tombs** of the local dukes line the walls of the chancel. Behind the Stadtkirche is the **Rathaus**, whose fourteenth-century *Ratskeller* is the oldest restaurant in northern Germany. Most of the building, however, is in the carefree Weser Renaissance style, and is distinguished by two beautifully contrasted oriel windows: one at street level, the other an extension of a gable.

The most outstanding half-timbered house in Celle is the **Hoppener Haus** at the corner of Rundestrasse and Poststrasse. Built for a courtier in 1532, it's richly carved with allegorical figures, monsters, scrollwork and scenes of rural life. The oldest dated house, at Am Heiligen Kreuz 26, states that it was built in 1526, though Neue Str. 32 (originally fifteenth-century but with a Renaissance oriel) has the best claim to be regarded as the most venerable house in town. Look out for the corner of Nordwall and Bergstrasse, where someone built their home on top of a piece of the original city wall. Among later Baroque stone buildings is the **Stechinellihaus** on Grosser Plan, named after an influential Italian architect and courtier who lived in a house on this site.

The **Bomann-Museum** (Tues–Sun 10am–5pm; DM4), in a grandiose Jugendstil building at the corner of Schlossplatz and Stechbahn, is above average for a local collection. Its displays on regional trades, history and folklore feature several reconstructed farmhouses and (in the courtyard) a half-timbered house fully furnished in the Biedermeier style.

The rest of the town

Just outside the eastern edge of the Altstadt is the old ghetto, though the colourful Baroque half-timbered houses themselves hardly offer any clue to the area's former status. Within one of these houses, Im Kreise 24, is the **Synagoge** (Tues–Thurs 3–5pm, Fri 9–11am, Sun 11am–1pm). Its decoration was destroyed on *Kristallnacht*, but, most unusually, it wasn't burned down. After the war it was well restored, and it stands today as one of the very few historic Jewish temples left in Germany.

Not far from here, bounding the southern side of the Altstadt, is the **Französischer Garten** (French Garden), which was laid out in the seventeenth century and later adapted in the informal English manner. Beyond is the **Ludwigskirche**, a Neoclassical church built by local architects in close imitation of the style of Karl Friedrich Schinkel, who did so much to define the appearance of Berlin. The interior is a gem – a miniature, updated version of the columned basilicas of the Romans.

To the south, down Breite Strasse, is the **Niedersächsisches Landgestüt** (Lower Saxon Stud Farm), which was founded by King George II in 1735. It can be visited outside the season, when the 250 or so stallions are put out to stud (mid-July to mid-Feb Mon–Fri 8.30–11.30am & 3–4.30pm; free), but the best time to come is during the big autumn **festival**, the highlight of Celle's social calendar. Held on the last Sunday in September and the first in October (or, on occasions, the last two in Sept), plus the Wednesday preceding these, each programme lasts for three hours, and features a parade of the stallions, as well as a quadrille performed by coaches and ten.

Practicalities

Celle's **Hauptbahnhof** is ten minutes' walk west of the town centre along Bahnhofstrasse. The **tourist office** (May–mid-Oct Mon–Fri 9am–6pm, Sat 9am–1pm & 2–5pm; mid-Oct to April Mon–Fri 9am–5pm, Sat 10am–noon; ☎1212) is at Markt 6.

Accommodation

Celle has a particularly exciting range of **hotels**, many in wonderful old buildings. Alternatively, there's a **youth hostel** at Weghausstr. 2 (☎53208; 🏠); turn left on leaving the Hauptbahnhof and continue straight ahead for about 2km, or take bus #3 to Dorfstrasse. The **campsite**, *Silbersee* (☎31223), is in Vorwerk, a suburb at the northern end of town.

HOTELS

Am Landgestüt, Landgestütstr. 1 (☎217219, fax 23977). The cheapest hotel in Celle, with a decent location in a whitewashed house on a quiet street opposite the Landgestüt. ④

Am Stadtgraben, Fritzenwiese 20–22 (☎1091, fax 24082). Luxury small hotel in an early twentieth-century villa containing many antiques. ⑧

Celler Hof, Stechbahn 11 (☎28061, fax 201120). Modernized Baroque palace in the handiest of settings directly across from the Schloss. ⑦

Fürstenhof, Hannoversche Str. 55–56 (☎2010; fax 201120). Celle's most prestigious hotel occupies a seventeenth-century nobleman's palace a short distance south of the Altstadt. Its main restaurant, *Endtenfang*, is one of the best (and most expensive) in northern Germany; the *Kutscherstube* is altogether more affordable. ⑨

St Georg, St-Georg-Str. 25–27 (☎210513, fax 217725). Again in a seventeenth-century building, this time a half-timbered house at the eastern edge of the centre. ⑤

Schifferkrug, Speicherstr. 9 (☎7015, fax 6350). Medium-priced hotel with a particularly fine restaurant, midway between the Hauptbahnhof and the Schloss. ⑤

Utspann, Im Kreise 13 (☎92720, fax 927252). Yet another restored half-timbered house, this time in the old Jewish quarter, with good wine bar-restaurant. ⑧

Eating and drinking

As well as the restaurants in the hotels above, there are plenty of other good places to eat and drink in Celle.

Bier-Akademie, Weissen Wall 6. Traditional beer hall-cum-restaurant, with summer garden.

Café Kraatz, Piltzergasse 4–5. One of several good cafés in the Altstadt, particularly recommended for its cakes.

Café Kraemer, Stechbahn 7. Another fine coffee house, in a half-timbered building opposite the Stadtkirche.

Congress Union, Thaerplatz 1. Classy, municipally owned restaurant in a custom-built Jugendstil building with a winter garden. Bargain lunchtime menus and a mouth-watering cold table.

Hannen-Fass, Am Heiligen Kreuz 5. Perhaps the liveliest of the Altstadt pubs.

Ratskeller, Markt 14. Famous old cellar restaurant, among the best (and priciest) of its ilk in Germany.

Rissmann's Feinschmecker Treff, Am Heiligen Kreuz 33. Truly creative restaurant with fish and vegetarian cuisine, plus dishes featuring the distinctive sheep of Lüneburg Heath.

Hannover (Hanover)

At first, for some reason or other, Hanover strikes you as an uninteresting town, but it grows upon you. It is in reality two towns: a place of broad, modern, handsome streets and tasteful gardens, side by side with a sixteenth-century town, where old timbered houses overhang the narrow lanes; where through low arches one catches glimpses of cobbled courtyards, once often thronged, no doubt, with troops of horse, or blocked with lumbering coach and six, waiting its rich merchant owner and his fat placid frau . . .

Jerome K. Jerome, *Three Men on the Bummel*

Though written a century ago, this description of **HANNOVER** is still apposite. Initial impressions of this city are unlikely to be very promising, and despite having had the benefit of a long special relationship with Britain (see box on p.602) and having played an important part in European cultural history to boot, it hasn't generally been given a good press. Hannover was something of a late developer, only coming to the fore in the second half of the seventeenth century, and much of its best architecture belongs to the nineteenth and early twentieth centuries. Another oddity is the fact that Hannover's showpiece is not a great cathedral, palace or town hall, but a **series of gardens**. However, these are no ordinary gardens – they're among the most impressive in Europe, preserving their spectacular original Baroque features almost intact. Add this to a number of first-class **museums** and a vibrant cultural scene, and there's plenty in Hannover to keep you occupied for a couple of days.

The **telephone code** for Hannover is ☎0511

Arrival, information and accommodation

The **Hauptbahnhof** is right in the centre of town and to the rear lies the **bus station** for long-distance routes. Hannover's **airport** is 10km northwest of the city and is linked to the Hauptbahnhof by bus #60, two or three times an hour.

On Ernst-August-Platz, the square facing the Hauptbahnhof, is the **tourist office** (Mon–Fri 9am–6pm & Sat 9.30am–3pm; ☎30140). Among the brochures you can pick up is *The Red Thread*, a horribly chatty but very useful free booklet guiding visitors round the main sights via a painted red line which runs along the pavements, across roads and down subways.

EXPO 2000

From June 1 to October 31, 2000, Hannover will host EXPO 2000. Only the second World Fair in thirty years and the first ever staged in Germany, it will also be the first to utilize an existing trade fair site, namely the huge *Messegelände* in the southeast of the city, linked to the Hauptbahnhof by mainline train and by U-Bahn #8.

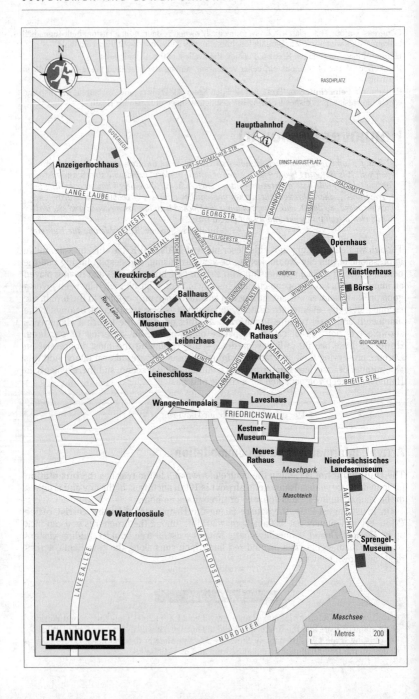

HANNOVER

N

RASCHPLATZ

Hauptbahnhof

ERNST-AUGUST-PLATZ

Anzeigerhochhaus

GOSERIEDE

KURT-SCHUMACHER-STR.

SCHILLERSTR.

BAHNHOFSTR.

LUISENSTR.

JOACHIMSTR.

LANGE LAUBE

GEORGSTR.

GOETHESTR.

AM MARSTALL

HEILIGERSTR.

IMBUSSTR.

KNOCHENHAUER STR.

SCHMIEDESTR.

GROSSE PACKHOF STR.

Opernhaus

Künstlerhaus

KRÖPCKE

WINDMÜHLENSTR.

RATHAUS

Börse

RATHAUSSTR.

Kreuzkirche

Ballhaus

SCHWINDERSTR.

GRUPENSTR.

Historisches Museum

Marktkirche

MARKT

Altes Rathaus

OSTERSTR.

BARINGSTR.

GEORGSPLATZ

River Leine

LEIBNIZUFER

KRAMERSTR.

Leibnizhaus

SCHLOSS STR.

LEINSTR.

Leineschloss

KARMARSCHSTR.

MARKTSTR.

Markthalle

BREITE STR.

Wangenheimpalais

Laveshaus

FRIEDRICHSWALL

Kestner-Museum

Neues Rathaus

Niedersächsisches Landesmuseum

Maschpark

Maschteich

AM MASCHPARK

Waterloosäule

WATERLOOSTR.

LAVESALLEE

Sprengel-Museum

Maschsee

NORDUFER

0   Metres   200

There are only two fares on the entire **public transport** network; nonetheless, it can be well worth investing in the DM7.50 24-hour pass or in the *HannoverCard*, which includes entry to all the museums and costs DM14 for one day, DM22 for three days. Some trams stop on Ernst-August-Platz, while others go underground to form the U-Bahn in the city centre, with stops at the Hauptbahnhof and Kröpcke. Among the features of the city centre are the tram stops decorated by contemporary artists.

Accommodation

As a flourishing centre of the lucrative trade fair industry (the April *Messe* is the largest in Europe), Hannover hoteliers can afford to charge fancy prices, though a few reasonably priced establishments do exist. The tourist office charges a stinging DM10 for its room-finding service.

HOTELS AND PENSIONS

Am Funkturm, Hallerstr. 34 (☎33980, fax 339 8111). One of the more reasonably priced upmarket options, situated a few minutes' walk from the rear of the Hauptbahnhof. Also has an excellent Italian restaurant, *Milano*. ⑥

Eden, Waldhausenstr. 30 (☎848310, fax 848 3144). Nicely furnished Südstadt villa serving good buffet breakfasts – one of the best bargains in Hannover. Take U-Bahn #1, #2 or #8 to Döhrener Tor. ④

Feuchers Lila Kranz, Berliner Allee 33 (☎858921, fax 854383). Although it has only five rooms, this is one of the city's best-known hotels, particularly for its restaurant, which offers creative local and international cooking and a huge wine list. ⑦

Flora, Heinrichstr. 36 (☎342334, fax 345899). Located about a 10min walk northeast of the Hauptbahnhof, this has some of the lowest rates in central Hannover. ⑤

Georgenhof, Herrenhaüser Kirchweg 20 (☎702244, fax 708559). Undoubtedly the most atmospheric place to stay in Hannover, this country house hotel in Herrenhausen, part of the *Romantik* chain, is set in its own private park. It has a nationally renowned and very expensive restaurant, *Stern*. ⑨

Gildehof, Joachimstr. 6 (☎15742, fax 306644). Medium-priced hotel with restaurant, just a stone's throw from the Hauptbahnhof. ⑥

Grand Hotel Mussman, Ernst-August-Platz 7 (☎36560, fax 365 6145). Fine old station hotel. ⑨

Indra, Schiffgraben 46 (☎810109, fax 852362). Small pension about a 10min walk east of the Hauptbahnhof. ④

Loccumer Hof, Kurt-Schumacher-Str. 16 (☎12640, fax 131192). Classy establishment with equally good restaurant, conveniently close to the Hauptbahnhof. ⑦

Reverey, Aegidiendamm 8 (☎883711, fax 883711). Medium-priced hotel just beyond the southeastern fringe of the Altstadt, handy for the Maschpark and the museums. ⑥

Schwab, Sedanstr. 20 (☎990 1610, fax 336 0004). One of the least expensive places in the central area, though the location, a 15min walk northeast of the Hauptbahnhof, is less than ideal. ④

HOSTELS

Jugendherberge Hannover, Ferdinand-Wilhelm-Fricke-Weg 1 (☎322941). Hannover's youth hostel is easy to get to: take U-Bahn #3 or #7 (direction Mühlenberg), and alight at Fischerhof, from where it's a 5min walk to the left over the bridge. Alongside is a campsite. ☎

Naturfreundehaus Stadtheim, Hermann-Bahlsen-Allee 8 (☎691493). A good location on the edge of the wooded Eilenriede park; take U-Bahn #3 (direction Lahe) or #7 (direction Fasanenkrug) to Spannhagenstrasse. Dorm beds for DM28.50, doubles for DM76.

The city centre

Hannover has had to reconstruct itself after being almost totally demolished by World War II bombing. The northern part of the city centre is a vast shopping area of mostly pedestrianized streets and arcades. Further south is the modest-sized Altstadt, beyond which is the inner ring road, the best museums and an attractive green belt.

HANOVERIAN HISTORY AND THE BRITISH CONNECTION

In the seventeenth century, the territories of the Welf House of Braunschweig-Lüneburg were split up, and a new duchy, clumsily named Braunschweig-Calenberg-Göttingen, came into being. This was commonly known as **Hannover**, after the old Hanseatic market and brewing town which was its principal city. A new summer residence for the court was slowly laid out at the village of Höringehusen, a few kilometres from Hannover's Altstadt.

Ernst August, who acceded to the duchy in 1679, was a man of high ambition. He charged Gottfried Wilhelm Leibniz, the great philosopher and scientist who served as librarian and historian to the Welfs for forty years, with the task of proving that the House was descended from the Italian Este family. The successful conclusion of this entitled the duke to claim a new Electorate in the Holy Roman Empire, which was formally bestowed in 1692. Even more significant was Ernst August's marriage to **Sophie von der Pfalz**, daughter of Elizabeth Stuart, the "Winter Queen" (see p.314). In 1701, the English parliament passed the Act of Settlement, in order to cut off the Catholic "Old Pretender" and his heirs and ensure the continuation of a Protestant monarchy. Sophie was named as next in line to the throne after Princess (later Queen) Anne. In the event, Sophie died just before Anne in 1714, and her son **Georg Ludwig** became King George I of Great Britain and Ireland. As well as a monarch, Britain gained one of the greatest composers of all time: anticipating the accession, the court director of music, **Georg Friedrich Händel**, was already well established in London by the time his employer took up residence.

Until 1837, Britain and Hannover shared the same ruler. At first, monarchs divided their residency between the territories (George I understandably so, as he never learned to speak English), but gradually they neglected their original seat. When William IV died without issue, however, the union came to an end. The exclusion of women from the succession in Hannover meant that another Ernst August ascended to its throne (since 1814 it had been a kingdom in its own right) whereas his niece Victoria became the British queen. This led to another bright period in Hannover's history, during which the city was transformed in Neoclassical style by the court architect, **Georg Ludwig Friedrich Laves**. In the event, it turned out to be a false dawn. During the Seven Weeks' War of 1866, the blind King Georg V opted to back neither Prussia nor Austria and the rampaging Prussian victors responded by driving him into exile and annexing his kingdom. Hannover thereafter remained part of Prussia until 1946, when the old duchy became the main component of the newly created Land of Lower Saxony, with the city itself reinstated as a provincial capital.

Around the Hauptbahnhof

The view on arrival at the Hauptbahnhof, to the north of the centre, isn't exactly prepossessing, with a bland pedestrian precinct stretching ahead. Underneath runs the **Passarelle**; mostly under cover, but with sections in the open air, it's meant to be a sort of subterranean bazaar-cum-piazza. While the prime sites at the flashy end are occupied by expensive shops, towards the station it predictably becomes seedier; many shop sites are empty, and walking through at night is a little disconcerting.

Standing at Hannover's most popular rendezvous, the *Café Kröpcke*, slap bang in the middle of the precinct, the most imposing building in view is the **Opernhaus**, a proud Neoclassical design which is arguably the finest of the city's Laves-designed showpieces. On Sophienstrasse, the yellow- and red-brick **Künstlerhaus**, originally a museum, is now a lively arts centre, while the neo-Renaissance **Ständehaus**, built as a guild-hall, houses the state treasury department. The **Börse** on Rathenaustrasse actually imitates the Tudor style – proof that British influence continued long after the end of the monarchical link.

If you're keen on modern architecture, make a detour along Georgstrasse to Goseriede to see the **Anzeigerhochhaus**. This newspaper office, made of brick-clad reinforced concrete and topped with a green copper dome, is an example of the 1920s

Expressionism of Fritz Höger. Even if it's hardly the skyscraper it purports to be, and is less dramatic than the same architect's Chilehaus in Hamburg, it's nonetheless an arresting, balanced and well thought-out design. The dome now houses the city's most adventurous cinema.

The Altstadt

A few minutes' walk south of the Anzeigerhochhaus are a few streets of rebuilt **half-timbered houses**. These convey something of the impression of the medieval town, which had already been much altered before the devastation of World War II. Its form is easier to imagine if you've seen nearby Celle, which is preserved almost intact. The first major building in their midst is the fourteenth-century **Kreuzkirche** where there's a *Passion Triptych* by Cranach at the high altar. One of the chapels is used by the local Serbian community, and is decorated with icons – a stark contrast with the Protestant sobriety of the rest of the church.

On Am Hohen Ufer to the south is the **Beginenturm**, the last surviving remnant of the city walls. It has been incorporated in the fabric of the modern building housing the **Historisches Museum** (Tues 10am–8pm, Wed–Fri 10am–4pm, Sat & Sun 10am–6pm; DM5), one of Germany's most imaginative local history museums. On the ground floor to the left are the four **state coaches** of the House of Hannover. These are still family property – even the gold carriage, adorned with Rococo paintings and carvings, which was made in London in 1783 and used for state openings of the Westminster parliament. Upstairs, there's a telling contrast to these limousines in the form of the *Hanomag*, a tiny two-seater convertible developed in 1928, a sort of trial run for the *Volkswagen* Beetle.

Just across the road is the **Ballhof**, a seventeenth-century half-timbered sports hall which is now the main repertory theatre. On nearby Holzmarkt (not its original location) the **Leibnizhaus** has been re-erected following its total destruction in the war. This magnificent Renaissance mansion was the home of **Gottfried Wilhelm Leibniz**. A historian by profession, Leibniz was active in a vast range of intellectual fields: he developed Pascal's calculating machine, arrived independently at the theory of differential calculus at the same time as Newton, charted the origins and migrations of mankind, and made enormous contributions to the disciplines of jurisprudence, philosophy, theology, geology and linguistics.

The Altstadt's dominant building is the fourteenth-century **Marktkirche**, one of the most southerly of the series of brick hall churches characteristic of the Baltic lands. Its bulky tower, terminating in a spire of unusual design, has long been the emblem of the city. Originally, it was meant to be much higher, but an old chronicle reports that it was finished off quickly because "the masons had become tired and sick in the purse". The unadorned interior walls are now closer to how the building originally looked than has been the case for some three hundred years. There's a noble carved *Passion Retable*, made around 1500, at the high altar; miraculously, the fourteenth- and fifteenth-century stained glass in the east windows has survived, and has recently been cleaned and restored. Across the square is the high-gabled fifteenth-century **Altes Rathaus**, whose elaborate brickwork is enlivened with colourful glazed tiles.

Friedrichswall and around

The line of the former city wall is now occupied by the inner ring road, forever seething with traffic. On Friederikenplatz stands the **Leineschloss**, which is now the Land parliament. Its dignified porticos, modelled on the temples of ancient Greece, were added by Laves, who carried out a thorough transformation of the original structure. Immediately to the east, two more buildings by him – the **Wangenheim-Palais** and the **Laveshaus** – stand side by side; the latter was his own home. Down Lavesallee is yet another of his works, the **Waterloosäule**, a triumphal column commemorating the part played by the Hanoverian troops in the final defeat of Napoleon.

Opposite the Laveshaus is the **Kestner-Museum** (Tues, Thurs & Fri 10am–4pm, Wed 10am–8pm, Sat & Sun 10am–6pm; DM3, free Wed). This compact decorative arts museum is named after its founder August Kestner, a Hanoverian diplomat in Rome. He was the son of Charlotte Buff, Goethe's first love and a central character in his novella *The Sufferings of Young Werther*. On the first floor, the medieval collection features treasures and textiles from Lower Saxon convents. Outstanding are surviving items from the *Goldene Tafel* of St Michael in Lüneburg, and the magnificent gilded bronze head-reliquary of an unknown saint, made around 1200 for Stift Fischbeck. The remaining galleries have an eclectic array of exhibits, ranging from Renaissance bronzes through eighteenth-century porcelain to a luxuriant selection of Art Nouveau *objets d'art* from America as well as Europe. Upstairs are examples of the ancient Greek, Etruscan, Roman and Cypriot civilizations, along with a more comprehensive Egyptian collection.

Next door is the **Neues Rathaus**, a gargantuan early twentieth-century Art Deco-cum-neo-Gothic fantasy, which is held into its marshy foundations by over 6000 piles of beechwood. It's definitely worth a peek inside; there are occasional guided tours but you can just wander round, up and down the spiral staircases. Between April and October (10am–12.45pm & 1.30–4.45pm; DM3) you can ascend to the dome for what are the best **views** of the city. However, the main attraction is the lift which takes you up – it follows an inclined path and is apparently one of only two in Europe like this. Look out for the models of Hannover at various stages of its history; the one of the bombed wartime city is a shocking record of the damage it suffered.

Directly behind the Neues Rathaus is the **Maschpark**, with a small artificial lake. Further on is a much larger man-made lake, the **Maschsee**, which serves as the locals' main playground. You can saunter down its tree-lined promenades, take a cruise on a pleasure steamer, or else rent a rowing boat or canoe.

The Niedersächsisches Landesmuseum

The **Niedersächsisches Landesmuseum** (Tues, Wed & Fri–Sun 10am–5pm, Thurs 10am–7pm; DM3, but likely to be wholly or partly closed until 1999) occupies stolid-looking premises facing the east side of the Maschpark. Its main draw is the Landesgalerie on the second floor, which has an excellent collection of paintings from the Middle Ages to the early twentieth century. On the left are two rooms of Primitives, of which the most notable is a *Passion Altar* by the first German artist known by name, **Master Bertram**. Most of the other works are by his anonymous Saxon contemporaries; particularly striking are *Two Scenes from the Life of St Paul* by a Hildesheim artist dubbed **Master of the Lambertikirche**, and the retables from which the **Master of the Golden Table** and the **Master of the Barfüsser Altar** get their names. In the following rooms, the star painting is an exquisite *Portrait of Philipp Melanchthon* by **Hans Holbein the Younger**, displayed alongside its lid, which is one of the few surviving examples of Holbein's skill as a decorative artist. Hanging beside it is a lurid *Luther on his Deathbed* by **Cranach**, and a small *Christ Carrying the Cross* attributed to **Dürer**. A decent display of Italian Renaissance work includes pictures by Botticelli, Raphael, Pontormo and Bronzino.

The large *Bacchus and Venus* by the Antwerp Mannerist **Bartholomeus Spranger** is an allegory illustrating an old proverb: "Wine and women bring two sorrows to life". It's one of the most imposing paintings created in the erotic style cultivated at the turn of the seventeeth century at the court of Emperor Rudolf II in Prague – and in the tiny neighbouring principality of Schaumburg-Lippe.

Pick of the seventeenth-century Flemish paintings are **Rubens'** *Madonna and Child*, **van Dyck**'s *A Gentleman of Santander, the Governor of Antwerp*, and *Men Bathing by Moonlight* by **Michael Sweerts**; the last, characteristically for the artist, is a highly original subject, with wonderful luminous effects. There's a good cross-section of the Dutch school, including one of **Rembrandt**'s rare excursions into nature painting, *Landscape* *with the Baptism of the Eunuch*, another masterly exposition of light and shade. Also of special note is *A Woman in Profile* by his most talented pupil, the short-lived **Carel Fabritius**.

A comprehensive array of the varied styles practised in nineteenth-century Germany includes a set of four small canvases illustrating *The Times of Day* by **Friedrich**; **Leibl**'s haunting *Peasant Girl*; several humorous paintings by Spitzweg; and numerous examples of the Impressionists Liebermann, Corinth and Slevogt. A specially dimmed room shows the giant cartoons made by the members of the **Nazarene Brotherhood** for the decoration of the Casa Bartholdy in Rome.

On the first floor of the museum, the **archeology** department has as its showpiece the bodies of prehistoric men preserved naturally in the peat bogs of Lower Saxony. The varied contents of several excavated graves are another highlight, along with an array of Bronze Age jewellery. On the same floor is a **natural history** section with a wide variety of stuffed animals and a full-scale reconstruction of a dinosaur, while downstairs there's an **aquarium** with live fish from round the world.

The Sprengel-Museum

Further down the road, on Kurt-Schwitters-Platz, is the **Sprengel-Museum** (Tues 10am–8pm, Wed–Sun 10am–6pm; DM7). Named after the chocolate magnate Bernhard Sprengel, whose gift of his private collection formed the basis of the museum, this ranks as one of the most exciting places in Germany in which to see modern art. Much of the display space is given over to changing exhibitions of photography, graphics and various experimental art forms, but there's also a first-rate permanent display of twentieth-century painting and sculpture.

Centrepiece of the museum is a huge range of the work of one of this century's most controversial and influential artists, Hannover's own **Kurt Schwitters**. His pleasing early landscapes and still lifes come as a surprise if you're only familiar with the famous Dadaist collages. The artist coined the term *Merz* to describe these, and set himself the target of creating a *Merzbau*, a work of art which would fill a house. Both completed versions of this were destroyed in the Nazi measures against "degenerate art", but an accurate reconstruction can be seen here.

Other highlights of the museum include a cross-section of **Picasso**'s work; complete rooms devoted to **Klee** and **Arp**; sculptures by Barlach and Henri Laurens; an updated *Prodigal Son* by **Beckmann**, along with self-portraits painted forty years apart; Surrealist paintings by Magritte, Tanguy and Ernst; and a huge range of Expressionists, with Munch, Nolde, Kirchner and Kokoschka all well represented.

Herrenhausen

The royal gardens of **Herrenhausen** (as Höringehusen came to be known) can be reached from the centre by U-Bahn #4 or #5. However, it's advisable to walk either there or back, as the route goes through two of the four gardens which make up the set. Before heading out, make sure you pick up the free tourist office leaflet which has an excellent plan of the complex.

The Welfengarten and the Georgengarten

Proceeding north from town along Nienburger Strasse, the least remarkable of the gardens – the **Welfengarten** – lies to the right, dominated by the huge neo-Gothic pile of the **Welfenpalais**, now occupied by the University. To the left, the dead-straight avenue of lime trees named Herrenhäuser Allee cuts through the **Georgengarten**. This is a *jardin anglais* of the type beloved by the Romantics, featuring trees arranged in an apparently natural setting, and an artificial lake, crossed by two graceful little bridges designed by Laves.

Also within this park is the Neoclassical **Georgenpalais**, home of the **Wilhelm-Busch-Museum** (Tues–Sat 10am–5pm, Sun 10am–6pm; DM6). Local people flock to the temporary exhibitions on the ground floor, which centre on the work of artists who have made a significant contribution to satirical expression – Daumier, Doré and Cruickshank have all been featured in recent years, as well as contemporary cartoonists. Upstairs, there's a permanent display on **Wilhelm Busch**, who lived and worked in Hannover last century. He was a capable painter of landscapes and genre scenes, but gained worldwide popularity through his illustrated books, notably *Max and Moritz*. In these, he invented what has become a stock vocabulary for strip-cartoonists, using patterns of oscillation to express movement, and conventional signs to depict each emotion.

The Grosser Garten

The Georgengarten was created as a foil to the magnificence of the formal **Grosser Garten** (daily 8am–4.30/8pm; DM3, free in winter), which is justifiably the city's pride and joy. It's best to time your visit to coincide with the playing of the **fountains** (May–Sept Mon–Fri 11am–noon & 3–4pm, Sat & Sun 10am–noon & 3–5pm) or when the **illuminations** are switched on (May–Sept Wed–Sun at dusk). Credit for the splendour of the layout goes to the Electress Sophie, who called them "my life", and her gardener, the Frenchman Martin Charbonnier, who transformed the modest garden into a spectacular showpiece which drew on elements of the French, Italian and Dutch traditions. Sadly the palace was totally destroyed by Allied bombing in the war, but the **Galerie**, a festive hall adorned with frothy frescoes of Virgil's *Aeneid*, and the **Orangerie** have survived.

Just inside the entrance gate is one of the most striking features, the **Gartentheater**. Temporary structures for music and drama were commonplace within royal gardens, but this one was permanent, featuring an auditorium in the form of an amphitheatre. The hornbeam hedges cleverly doubled as scenery and changing rooms, while a series of gilded statues on pedestals served as stage props. Plays by Molière and Racine, and music by Handel formed the staple repertoire of this theatre in its early days, and are still performed during the summer season. Immediately to the east is the **Grande Parterre**, whose eight sections are planted with geometric arrangements of flowers and shrubs. In front stands the Italianate **Grosse Kaskade**, belonging to the original garden, plus a sundial and grotto, while the maze is at the far end.

Behind the Grande Parterre is a modern embellishment: eight small plots have been laid out to illustrate different styles of landscape gardening down the centuries. Particularly notable is the **Renaissancegarten**, which reproduces a section of the now-vanished *Hortus Palatinus* in Heidelberg. West of here is the secluded **Boskettgarten**, used by courtiers for intrigues and romantic encounters. The rear section of the Grosser Garten consists of a series of radiating avenues bounded by hedges and trees, each ending at a fountain. As a centrepiece, there's the **Grosse Fontäne**, which spurts Europe's highest jet of water, at 82m.

The Berggarten and the Fürstenhaus

Across Herrenhäuser Strasse to the north of the Grosser Garten is the **Berggarten**, set up to tend rare and exotic plants. Its collection of orchids was considered the finest in Europe, and many are still cultivated in its hothouses. Behind these are a rock garden, a pergola garden and an iris garden; the last-named is in full bloom in April and May. Even more glorious is the central "Paradise" of rhododendrons. At the far end of the Berggarten stands the **Mausoleum** of the House of Hannover, a late work by Laves in the sternest Neoclassical manner. A graphic illustration of how the architect's style had developed is provided by the domed **Bibliothekspavilion** at the entrance, which he designed thirty years earlier in a carefree idiom still showing echoes of the Baroque.

Some compensation for the loss of the palace is provided by a number of courtly buildings to be found to the west along Herrenhäuser Strasse. The so-called **Fürstenhaus** (Tues–Sun 10am–5/6pm; DM5) has been adapted as a sort of museum of the House of Hannover. There's one striking room entirely covered by a panorama of a hunt, and some fine portraits, including likenesses of King George III and Queen Sophie Charlotte by both Thomas Gainsborough and Johann Zoffany.

Eating, drinking and nightlife

As you'd expect in such a cosmopolitan city, there's a huge choice of places to eat and drink, with the Altstadt and the streets around being the liveliest area at night. Hannover's **beer** tradition continues unabated: *Lindener Gilde*, the best-known local brewery, has operated uninterruptedly since 1546. Its main product, *Broyhan-Alt*, is named after the sixteenth-century Hannover man who allegedly invented export beer. The *Pils* of the rival *Herrenhausen* brewery is also worth seeking out. For a daytime snack or a quick lunch, the best place to head for is the *Markthalle* on Karmarschstrasse, where the stallholders sell a host of different kinds of ethnic cooking.

Restaurants

Altdeutsche Bierstube, Lärchenstr. 4. Hannover's best traditional *Gaststätte*, situated northeast of the Hauptbahnhof.

Hiller, Blumenstr. 3. Speciality vegetarian and wholefood place on the eastern edge of the city centre, with inexpensive set lunches. Closed Sun.

La Gamba, Goetheplatz 4. Long-established Spanish restaurant.

Mandarin-Pavillion, Marktstr. 45. One of the best Chinese restaurants in Germany; has bargain menus at lunchtimes.

Ratskeller, corner of Schmiedestrasse and Kobelinger Strasse. As dependable as you'd expect, with above average food for average prices.

St Petersburg, Berliner Allee 6. Russian and Eastern European specialities, just to the rear of the Hauptbahnhof.

Bars and cafés

Brauhaus Ernst August, Schmiedestr. 13. *Hausbrauerei* occupying the site of the original *Broyhan* brewery. One of the most popular spots in town, it serves reasonably priced meals and an excellent unfiltered *Pils*.

Hannen-Fass, Knochenhauerstr. 36. Hugely popular student bar which offers mountainous piles of cheap pub grub.

Klatsch, Limmerstr. 58. Café beside the Leinaustrasse stop on the route of tram #10, much favoured by alternative and arty types.

Kröpcke, Georgstr. 35. This famous café, now run by *Mövenpick*, is a real Hannover institution, one of its main landmarks.

Weinloch, Burgstr. 33. Liveliest of the several good pubs to be found in this street in the heart of the Altstadt.

Nightlife and entertainment

Hannover's best **discos** include the Bhagwan-run *Osho*, Raschplatz 7L; *Palo Palo*, Raschplatz 8a, which plays funk and soul; and the tiny *Casa Blanca*, Lister Meile 26a. For live jazz, head for the *Jazz-Club* on either Monday or Friday, which are devoted respectively to modern and traditional styles.

Many of the best **classical music** performances are to be heard in the Protestant churches; these are listed in a bi-monthly leaflet. The *Knabenchor Hannover* is currently at least as good as its famous Viennese counterpart; in spite of the name it generally performs with adult male voices as well as boys. Concerts by the *Staatsorchester* alternate with operas at the *Opernhaus,* Opernplatz 1 (☎368 1711).

The best places for **theatre** are the brand-new *Schauspielhaus*, Prinzenstr. 9 (☎321133) and the *Ballhof,* Ballhofstr. 5 (☎168 6142); other venues include *Theater am Aegi*, Aegidientorplatz 2 (☎989 3333) and *Landesbühne,* Bultstr. 7–9 (☎2828 2828). More experimental dramatic fare is offered at the *Künstlerhaus*, Sophienstr. 2 (☎343919), which also rivals the *Anzeigerhochhaus* for the best **cinema** programmes in town.

Listings

Airport ☎977 1223 for flight information.

British Consulate, Berliner Allee 5 (☎388 3808).

Festivals Hannover's *Schützenfest* (marksmen's festival) for 10 days in late June/early July is the most spectacular of the many held in northern Germany. It features processions with floats, fireworks and a considerable intake of alcohol, notably the *Lüttje-Lage*, in which you drink simultaneously from 2 glasses – one containing beer, the other schnapps – placed one inside the other.

Markets As well as the general markets on and around Am Markt, there's a flea market each Sat morning on Hohen Ufer.

Post office The main post office is beside the Hauptbahnhof on Ernst-August-Platz, with poste restante services.

Sports There's a huge *Sportpark* with indoor and outdoor stadiums and swimming pool on the west bank of the Maschsee.

Schaumburg

The tiny principality of **Schaumburg-Lippe** (formerly Holstein-Schaumburg) was one of the great survivors of imperial Germany. By skilful diplomacy it managed to avoid being swallowed up by unwelcome suitors, and kept its place on the map until 1946, when – shorn of its double-barrelled name – it became a part of Lower Saxony. Both of the towns which have served as its capital, **Stadthagen** and **Bückeburg**, lie on the main rail line between Hannover and Osnabrück. They're chiefly notable for having the finest Mannerist art and architecture on German soil, created by some of the same artists who worked at the famously eccentric court of Emperor Rudolf II in Prague.

Stadthagen

Situated some 45km west of Hannover, **STADTHAGEN** was the original capital of Schaumburg-Lippe, a role it regained after World War II. As an administrative as well as market centre, it's the more animated of the two towns, though it has less in the way of sights. The handsome Renaissance **Schloss** at the southern end of the town centre is now used as offices and can thus only be seen from outside. Focal point of the town is now the inevitable **Marktplatz**, which offers a palatial Renaissance Rathaus clearly modelled on the Schloss, several grandiose half-timbered burghers' houses and a deliberately over-the-top Rococo mansion.

Set in a close just off the square is **St Martini**, a rather gaunt Gothic hall church. This possesses an intricate fifteenth-century high altar and a Renaissance pulpit, but would be considered unremarkable were it not for the extraordinary seven-sided **Mausoleum** built onto the east end in the 1620s, in celebration of the promotion of the rulers of Schaumburg-Lippe from the rank of counts to princes of the Holy Roman Empire. The Dutchman **Adrian de Vries**, the most accomplished and least controversial of the imperial court artists of Prague, was commissioned to provide the sumptuous marble and bronze decorations. He responded with his masterpiece, the

Monument to Prince Ernst, which occupies centre-stage. This features a superbly vivacious scene of the Risen Christ surrounded by angels, lions and sleeping guards, as well as the family coats of arms and a medallion portrait of the prince.

Practicalities

Stadthagen's **Bahnhof** is at the northern end of town, a twenty-minute walk from the centre. The **tourist office** (Mon–Fri 9am–12.30pm & 2–5pm; ☎05721/7820) is just off Marktplatz at Rathauspassage 1.

The best of Stadthagen's selection of **hotels** are *Oelkrug,* Waldsstr. 2 (☎05721/76051; ⑥); *Gerber,* Echternstr. 14 (☎05721/9860; ⑥); *Zur Amtspforte*, Obernstr. 31 (☎05721/75746; ⑦); and *Parkhotel,* Büschingstr. 10 (☎05721/97270; ⑦). There are plenty of places to **eat** and **drink**: try the historic *Herrenhäuser* on Marktplatz, *Torschreiberhaus,* Krumme Str. 42, or the restaurant in *Zur Amtspforte,* which has a varied menu of Asian dishes.

Bückeburg

At the turn of the seventeenth century, the capital of Schaumburg-Lippe was moved 18km west to **BÜCKEBURG**, then a mere hamlet. This remains the seat of the former ruling family, who, like so many German aristocrats, are left with plenty of wealth and possessions as compensation for their loss of political power. It's worth bearing in mind that all the town's sights can be visited on Mondays – one of very few places in the country where this is so.

The Schloss

The **Schloss** stands in its own very extensive grounds at the edge of the town centre. On the bridge over the moat, look out for the two writhing bronzes of *Venus and Adonis* and *The Rape of Prosperine,* both the work of Adrian de Vries. In the courtyard, the wing facing you was rebuilt after a fire in the eighteenth century. Walk round to the right and you'll catch a glimpse of the resplendent Renaissance sections of the exterior, which were added to the original fourteenth-century tower-house in the mid-sixteenth century. Continuing onwards, you come to the sombre neo-Romanesque **Mausoleum** (daily April–Oct 10am–6pm; DM3), whose dome has what's apparently the largest mosaic in Germany.

Guided tours (daily 9am–noon & 1–5/6pm; DM7) of the Schloss itself take in the photogenic inner courtyard and the most imposing apartments. These are eclectic, to say the least, passing in quick succession from a grandiose Wilhelmine banqueting chamber with a huge Venetian-style fresco, through an intimate Rococo smoking room, to a Renaissance hall hung with superb Brussels tapestries. The **Schlosskapelle**, which was originally Gothic, was adapted in the Mannerist period for Protestant worship. As if to give the lie to the belief that the new faith was inimical to worldly beauty, it was decorated in the most extravagant manner possible. Every inch of the walls is covered with frescoes, and there's a complete set of gilded and carved furnishings. In the same period, the even more sumptuous **Goldener Saal** was built as a secular counterpart. Its doorway, rising to the full height of the room, is flanked by huge statues of Mars and Flora, with Mercury floating above in the company of cherubs and goddesses.

The town centre

The brothers Hans and Ebbert Wulf of Hildesheim, who had carried out the decoration of the Schlosskapelle and Goldener Saal, were afterwards commissioned to build Bückeburg's other focal building, the **Stadtkirche** (mid-April to mid-Oct Mon–Fri 10.30am–noon & 3–5pm, Sat 3–5pm; mid-Oct to mid-April Thurs & Sat 2–4pm), which lies at the top of the main Lange Strasse. This competes with Wolfenbüttel for the title of first full-scale Protestant church ever to be built. It's much the more unified building of the two, and is a real masterpiece of design, notwithstanding the Latin inscription running across the facade which declares that it is: "An Example of Piety, not of Architecture". Apart from its facade the exterior is a glum affair, but the **interior** is stunning. Massive Corinthian pillars shoot right up to the vault, and your eye is drawn to the gleaming gold case of the massive organ at the far end, at which Johann Christoph Friedrich Bach, son of J.S., presided for 45 years. In adapting the old hall-church formula to the Protestant emphasis on preaching, brightly painted galleries were added all round, and the **pulpit** placed in the centre. This pulpit is one of the most beautiful in the country, its base lined with gold-plated reliefs of the life of Christ. Even more impressive is Adrian de Vries' **font**, where the Holy Ghost, hooked up by wires, hovers above the Baptism of Christ.

Housed in a half-timbered house with a jarring modern extension on Sablé Platz, the pedestrian area between Lange Strasse and Bahnhofstrasse, is the **Hubschraubermuseum** (Helicopter Museum; daily 9am–5pm; DM5), apparently the only one of its kind in the world. A reminder of the proximity of the German and British military bases, it incorporates an educational display on vertical flight technique, and is well labelled in English. Following a section on the history of man's attempts to fly, there are dozens of original machines, representing all the famous names in helicopter design.

Practicalities

Bückeburg's **Bahnhof** lies at the northern end of town; it's a straight ten-minute walk down Bahnhofstrasse to the Schloss. The **tourist office** (Mon–Fri 8am–12.30pm & 2–5pm, Sat 9–11am; ☎05722/206181) is at Lange Str. 44. There's a good cross-section of **hotels** in the town centre: *Brauhaus*, Braustr. 1 (☎05722/4634; ④); *Bemfert*, Brauhausstr. 8 (☎05722/4721; ⑥); *Am Schlosstor*, Lange Str. 33 (☎05722/95120; ⑥); and *Ambiente*, Herminenstr. 11 (☎05722/1012; ⑦). The nearest **youth hostel** is at PortaWestfalica, two stops away on the train. There's also a **campsite** there and at **Doktorsee** (☎05751/2611) near Rinteln, some 10km south of Bückeburg. The best **restaurants** are the hotel *Ambiente* and the *Ratskeller* in the Rathaus directly opposite the Schloss gates; you'll get similarly good food at lower prices at the seventeenth-century *Zur Falle*, Lange Str. 13.

Hameln (Hamelin)

"A pleasanter spot you never spied" was how Robert Browning characterized the venerable town of **HAMELN**, situated on the River Weser 45km southwest of Hannover. His verse rendition of the **legend of the Pied Piper** has made the place one of the best-known towns in Germany as far as English-speaking people are concerned – and earned him the eternal gratitude of the local tourist board.

Inevitably, the Pied Piper legend – perhaps the most endurably fascinating of Germany's rich store of folktales – always looms large, which makes Hameln an ideal outing if you have kids. However, there are more serious attractions as well. Along with nearby Lemgo (see pp.557–559), it's the best place to see the distinctive **Weser Renaissance** style, a form of civil architecture which typically features large projecting bay windows, richly decorated gables ornamented with pyramids and scrollwork, ornamental fillets with coats of arms and inscriptions, and lavish grotesque carvings, many of which are appropriately dubbed *Neidköpfe* – "envious neighbours' heads". During the 1960s a comprehensive restoration programme was started, which has left Hameln looking in immaculate shape.

The **telephone code** for Hameln is ☎05151

THE PIED PIPER LEGEND

The **Pied Piper legend** was first chronicled in 1384, the exact centenary of when the event allegedly took place. A mysterious stranger dressed in a multicoloured coat appeared in Hameln and offered to rid the town of its plague of rats and mice. Upon promise of payment, he played on his pipe and lured the vermin to the Weser, where they all drowned. The ungrateful burghers reneged on the reward and sent the rat-catcher packing. He returned one Sunday morning when the adults were at church, dressed in a weird yellow and red huntsman's costume. This time it was the town's 130 children who answered the magnetic strains of his pipe, and they followed the stranger out of town and out of sight, apparently disappearing into a cavern, never to be seen again. The only children who were saved were a cripple and a deaf-mute.

Many **interpretations**, none of them conclusive, have been placed on this story. It may symbolize the plague epidemics that were a fact of life in medieval Europe – the term "children" of a town was often used in old chronicles as a synonym for "citizens". Alternatively, it's possible the piper was actually a land agent charged with finding settlers – the Count of Schaumburg had a plantation in Moravia, while there are communities in Transylvania which claim descent from the children of Hameln. Another plausible theory is that the events were linked to the disastrous Children's Crusade of 1212, when youngsters from all over Europe joined in an attempt to conquer the Holy Land from the Infidel by peace – something their seniors had failed to do by force. One of the two main leaders was a boy from Cologne called Nicolas, and it's quite likely that there were recruits to the cause from Hameln.

The town

For centuries Hameln was no more than a small milling and market town, which lay within a heavily fortified circular town wall. In the wake of the Thirty Years' War, its potential for growth was stunted by the strengthening of its defences by the Hanoverians, to the extent that it acquired the nickname of "the Gibraltar of the North". Napoleon ordered the demolition of the fortress so that the town could expand. The only surviving sections are two isolated medieval towers at the north end of town (the **Pulverturm** and the **Haspelmathsturm**) and the **Garnisonkirche**, now deconsecrated and used as a savings bank. It guards the entrance to **Osterstrasse**, the town's central axis – and one of Germany's finest streets.

Osterstrasse and the Markt

Facing the Garnisonkirche on the left is the **Rattenfängerhaus** (Rat-Catcher's House). Built for a local councillor at the beginning of the seventeenth century, its name is due solely to an inscription on the side wall documenting the legend. Its facade is one of the most original in Hameln, the delicacy of its ornamental details (which include plenty of "envious heads") standing in deliberate contrast to the massiveness of the overall design. The interior is only marginally less impressive; it now houses a restaurant (see p.613).

Further up the street to the right is the **Leisthaus**, built about fifteen years earlier for a merchant by the local mason Cord Tönnies. The statue of Lucretia in a niche above the oriel window offers a profane contrast to the figures of the Seven Christian Virtues on the frieze below, a juxtaposition of sacred and secular that is typical of the German Renaissance. In this case inspiration was obviously provided by the carvings on the timber supports of the sixteenth-century **Stiftsherrnhaus** next door, which feature the planetary deities along with the Apostles and other biblical personages.

The rest of the Stiftsherrnhaus, along with all of the Leisthaus, is given over to the **Museum Hameln** (Tues–Sun 10am–4.30pm; DM3). Among the collection of religious art on the first floor, the most striking items are a set of statues of the Apostles which formerly stood on the rood screen of the Münster, and the *Siebenlingsstein*. The latter commemorates another Hameln legend, that of the birth of septuplets to a local family in 1600. Though the parents and elder siblings are shown praying at the foot of a crucifix, there was again no happy ending, as all the babies died soon afterwards.

At the end of Osterstrasse is the huge **Hochzeithaus** (Wedding House), a festival hall erected in the early seventeenth century, whose main features are its high end gables and elaborate dormer windows, under each of which there is a doorway, which formerly led into a shop. On the side facing the Markt, a **carillon** has been installed. At 1.05pm, 3.35pm and 5.35pm each day, its figures enact the Piper's two visits to Hameln. Opposite is one of the most magnificent houses, the **Dempterhaus**, which was built a few years earlier for the burgomaster after whom it is named. The **Marktkirche** rather detracts from the scene; it was Hameln's only major loss to wartime air raids, and has been poorly rebuilt with smooth stones which clash with the remains of the original masonry.

The rest of the town

Among many fine buildings on Bäckerstrasse, which begins off the left-hand side of the Markt, two stand out. The Gothic **Löwenapotheke**, still in use as a pharmacy, illustrates that the Weser Renaissance style sprang from quite plain origins – the basic form is similar, but there's almost no decoration, apart from the hexagonal star on the gable, which was intended to ward off evil spirits. Further along is the **Rattenkrug**, built by Cord Tönnies a couple of decades before the broadly similar Leisthaus. Originally the home of a burgomaster, it has long served as a *Gaststätte*.

Halfway down Wendenstrasse, a fine narrow street opposite the Löwenapotheke, is the **Lückingsches Haus**, whose profuse carvings mark it out as the best example of the revival of half-timbering which occurred in the mid-seventeenth century. Also worth seeing is Alte Marktstrasse, which joins Bäckerstrasse by the Rattenkrug. Its most notable building is **Kurie Jerusalem**, a large half-timbered store from about 1500 which was long derelict, but has been magnificently restored as a play-centre (where kids can be left if you want to go sightseeing without them in tow). Further down stands the **Redenhof**, the only remaining nobleman's mansion in Hameln. Dating from the mid-sixteenth century, it's surprisingly plain in comparison with the contemporary houses of the prosperous burgher families.

At the end of Bäckerstrasse, overlooking the Weser, is the **Münster**, successor to a Benedictine monastery founded around 800. It's something of a mix of styles – the eleventh-century crypt and the squat octagonal lantern tower survive from a Romanesque basilica which was converted into a Gothic hall church from the thirteenth century onwards, the austere belfry only being added some two hundred years later. Inside, the raised chancel is the most striking feature.

Practicalities

Hameln's **Bahnhof** is situated well to the east of the centre, which is reached via Bahnhofstrasse and Diesterstrasse. The **tourist office** (May–Sept Mon–Fri 9am–1pm & 2–6pm, Sat 9.30am–12.30pm & 3–5pm, Sun 9.30am–12.30pm; Oct–April Mon–Fri 9am–1pm & 2–5pm; ☎202517) is in the Bürgergarten on Diensteralle just before the entrance to the old part of town. It has plenty of brochures in English, but the most useful is an index-folder in German with all sorts of helpful tips, even including the best times of day for photographing the main buildings. There is also a branch in the Hochzeithaus (mid-April to mid-Oct Tues–Fri 11am–2pm & 2.30–4.30pm, Sat & Sun 10am–2pm).

Accommodation

During the tourist season, it's a good idea to spend the night in Hameln; that way you can see the town before or after the day-trippers have come and gone. There are surprisingly few **hotels**, and they're not particularly cheap. The **youth hostel** is well placed about five minutes' walk north of the old town at Fischbecker Str. 33 (☎3425; **fi**), at the point where the Hamel (no more than a stream) flows into the Weser. On the latter's western bank is the **campsite** at Uferstr. 80 (☎61167), which is open all year round. There are around a score of private houses, including some in the Altstadt, with **rooms** to let (①–④). Some of the hotels occupy fine old buildings.

HOTELS

Altstadtwiege, Neue Marktstr. 10 (☎27854, fax 1045). Budget hotel and pub on a quiet Altstadt backstreet. ③

An der Altstadt, Diensterallee 16 (☎7591, fax 42025). Fine old hotel which has recently been modernized. ⑤

Christianenhof, Alte Marktstr. 18 (☎95080, fax 433 3611). Upmarket hotel in an old half-timbered building with sauna and swimming pool. ⑦

City, Neue Marktstr. 9 (☎7261, fax 45974). A marginally more expensive alternative to the *Altstadtwiege* next door. ④

Jugendstil, Wetterstr. 18 (☎95580, fax 955866). Part of the *Akzent* chain, this occupies a huge terraced house in the Jugendstil quarter of the city immediately north of the Altstadt. ⑥

Stadt Hameln, Münsterwall 2 (☎9010, fax 901333). The town's leading hotel, a palatial building with a modern extension. It has two restaurants, one on the terrace overlooking the river. ⑦

Zur Krone, Osterstr. 30 (☎7415 or 9070, fax 42632). Another upmarket hotel and restaurant, this time in a renovated half-timbered mansion on the main street. ⑦

Eating and drinking

Hameln is not a major gastronomic centre: it has few high quality restaurants other than those in the last two hotels listed above. Where it does score is in the range of highly distinctive eateries geared primarily to day-trippers and in many cases housed in premises which are sightseeing attractions in their own right.

Kaffeestuben, Wendenstr. 9. Coffee house in an old bakery. A good choice for *Kaffee und Kuchen*; also does light meals.

Kartoffelhaus, Kupferschmiedstr. 13. Potato-based dishes predominate in this restaurant in the Bürgerhaus, one of Hameln's most ornate timber-framed houses.

Klütturm, Auf der Klütberg. One of the town's very best restaurants, commanding a powerful view over the Weser valley from its hilltop position to the southwest.

Museums-Café, Osterstr. 8. Traditional café in the Stiftsherrnhaus, with outside tables in summer. Inevitably its speciality is called *Rattenfängertorte*.

Pfannkuchen, Hummenstr. 12. There are some 40 different pancakes – sweet and savoury, flour- or potato-based – on the menu in this cosy little restaurant in this delightful half-timbered house.

Rattenfängerhaus, Osterstr. 28. The cuisine here is predominantly *gutbürgerliche Küche*, though there are plenty of ice-cream based dishes if you don't want a full meal.

Entertainment

The Pied Piper legend is enacted in a **historical costume play** held in the town centre at noon every Sunday from mid-May to mid-September; performances last thirty minutes and are free. **Cruises** on the Weser (bear in mind that strong currents mean the upstream journeys are painfully slow) are run by *Oberweser Dampfschiffahrt* (☎22016), with departures from the jetty by the Münster; prices start at DM7.50 for an hour-long round trip.

The Weser country around Hameln

As a supplement to a visit to Hameln, it's well worth taking in some of the nearby sights in the Weser country. Three destinations in particular stand out; all are easy to reach, and needn't take up too much time. **Fischbeck** has an intriguing collegiate foundation,

Hämelschenburg one of Lower Saxony's most magnificent palaces, while **Bodenwerder** was the home town of Baron Münchhausen.

Fischbeck

Situated 8km north of Hameln and connected by buses #20, #25 and #26 (passenger trains no longer stop there), **FISCHBECK** is dominated by its **Stift**. This women's collegiate church was founded in 955, and has preserved an unbroken tradition ever since, having turned Protestant in the mid-sixteenth century. Today, five elderly canonesses keep up its charitable work, only taking their vows once they have retired from a professional career. One of their tasks is to show visitors round the complex; admission is by **guided tour** only (Easter to mid-Oct Tues & Fri 9am–11am & 2–4pm, Wed, Thurs, Sat & Sun 2–4pm; DM4). It's best to phone ahead first (☎05152/8603), or check at Hameln's tourist office, to ensure admission; ask for a tour in English – one of the guides is a fluent speaker.

The present church was built in the twelfth and early thirteenth centuries as a columned basilica. A drastic restoration at the turn of the century removed most of the Baroque accretions, but some additions remain – such as the wooden balconies from where the canonesses, in true aristocratic manner, observe the services. Architecturally the finest part of the Stift is the **crypt**, whose capitals are all carved in a different manner. The **cloister** is a Gothic structure, with the houses of the canonesses on its upper storey.

Fischbeck has several outstanding **works of art**, but there's only a copy of the most famous, a gilded head-reliquary of a saint; the original is now in the Kestner Museum in Hannover. Earlier this century, the long-lost polychrome wood *Statue of the Foundress Helmburg* was discovered and placed in the chancel. Made around 1300, it's an imaginary, idealized portrait, showing her as a young woman, instead of the elderly widow she was when she founded the Stift, a story illustrated in a late sixteenth-century tapestry in the south transept. On a wooden beam high above the end of the nave is a thirteenth-century *Triumphal Cross*, while beside the pulpit there's an extraordinary wooden *Seated Man of Sorrows* – carved around 1500, it radiates enormous pathos. According to legend, it was made for the Stift by an itinerant craftsman in gratitude for having been cured there of the plague.

Hämelschenburg

If Hameln has given you a taste for the Weser Renaissance, it's well worth travelling the 12km south to the tiny village of **HÄMELSCHENBURG**, whose **Schloss** (guided tours April–Oct Tues–Sun 10am–noon & 2–5pm; DM8) is arguably the most spectacular manifestation of the style. It was built between 1588 and 1613 for the Klencke family, in whose possession it still remains. The exterior, with its distinctive horseshoe shape, varied elevations and rich carvings, is particularly impressive. Inside are some splendid doorways and chimneypieces. On the main road below the complex is the former **Schlosskirche**, now the parish church. Erected in 1563, it was the first freestanding church ever built for Protestant worship. The furnishings include a Gothic lime-wood group of the *Garden of Paradise*. Unfortunately the church is only open on Sunday mornings or when a pre-booked tour is visiting.

Hämelschenburg can be reached by bus #40 from Hameln; this runs several times a day during the week, but services dry up mid-morning on Saturdays, necessitating a 2.5km walk to Emmern, which has a rail link as well as a much more frequent bus service to Hameln.

Bodenwerder

BODENWERDER, 25km downstream from Hameln, is a good choice of destination if you want to take a short cruise on the Weser; it can also be reached by bus #520. Its

BARON MÜNCHHAUSEN

The real-life **Karl Friedrich Hieronymous von Münchhausen** was an eighteenth-century soldier of fortune who fought for the Russians against the Turks, before retiring to his ancestral seat, where he regaled credulous listeners with monstrously boastful tales of his adventures. These came to the attention of **Rudolph Erich Raspe**, himself a real rogue, who embroidered the stories further and published them under the Baron's name in Britain. For all his failings, Raspe was highly talented – he had been a protégé of Leibniz in his native Hannover – and the book is stylishly written, perfectly capturing the understated manner of a boring old raconteur launching every few minutes into yet another totally implausible anecdote. The Baron's numerous adventures included stranger travels than even Gulliver's – he made two trips to the moon (one of them unintentional), a journey all the way through the earth's crust, and a voyage through a sea of milk to an island of cheese. In less far-flung parts, he shot a stag with a full-sized cherry tree between its antlers (thus obtaining haunch and sauce at the same time), served as a human cannonball in the war against the Turks, and single-handedly saved Gibraltar from falling into Spanish hands by tossing the enemy's 300 pieces of artillery into the sea. For all its spectacular special effects, Terry Gilliam's 1988 movie, *The Adventures of Baron Münchhausen*, is a leaden creation which flopped at the box office. Far more successful from an artistic point of view is the Goebbels-financed film of the same name – an incredibly futuristic wartime fantasy made in the UFA studios in Babelsberg.

name is synonymous with **Baron Münchhausen**, the King of Liars, who is one of Germany's most famous literary characters. Münchhausen's mansion, now the **Rathaus**, contains a small museum (daily April–Oct 10am–noon & 2–5pm; DM2) in his honour; its exhibits include the pistol with which he claimed to have shot down his charger from a church steeple. The ticket also gives admission to the **Heimatmuseum** (same times) next door, whose most notable exhibit is a fourteenth-century dugout canoe dredged up from the Weser. Outside is a fountain illustrating one of Münchhausen's most famous exploits – stopping to water his prize Lithuanian horse, he found that the liquid was pouring out of its body, the rear end having been shot off in battle. On the first Sunday of each month between May and September, some of Münchhausen's exploits are re-enacted.

The **tourist office** (Mon–Fri 9am–12.30pm & 2.30–6pm, Sat 9am–noon; ☎05533/40541) is in the *First Reisebüro*, Weserstr. 3. If you want to stay, there's an abundant range of **pensions** and **private rooms** (①–③), a **youth hostel** in the hills to the east of town on Richard-Schirrmann-Weg (☎05533/2685; ❶) and a **campsite** at An der Himmelspforte (☎05533/4938). **Hotels** are also good value, including: *Strandhotel zur Weser*, Homburgstr. 53 (☎05533/2064; ③); *Goldener Anker*, Weserstr. 13 (☎05533/2135; ④); and *Deutsches Haus*, Münchhausenplatz 4 (☎05533/3925; ⑤). The last has a particularly good **restaurant**, though it faces strong competition from Münchhausen Stube, Grosse Str. 5.

Hildesheim

HILDESHEIM, which lies 30km southeast of Hannover, stands unrivalled as Lower Saxony's premier city of art. Some of the finest buildings in all of Germany are to be found here, and its importance to European culture can hardly be exaggerated. During the eleventh-century Ottonian period, the **Romanesque style** – emerging hesitantly elsewhere – achieved a state of perfection here, not only in architecture, but in sculpture and painting as well. Five hundred years later, the city was adorned with a multitude of **half-timbered buildings** whose sheer artistry far surpasses those of any other German city.

Because of this legacy, old guides used to consider Hildesheim as one of the "must" cities of Germany. Just a month before the German surrender in 1945, however, Hildesheim was bombed and the consequent fire, fuelled by the wooden buildings, caused damage which even some exemplary restoration cannot disguise, and left the surviving monuments marooned among typically bland, functional modern developments. For decades, the city was a shadow of its former self, until it made an astonishing comeback in the 1980s. Fortified by commercial prosperity, the local council made the bold decision to re-create what had hitherto been regarded as irretrievably lost. A fillip was given by UNESCO's decision to list the two main churches, both of which had been shattered in the war, among the monuments of the world which must be protected at all costs.

Arrival, information and accommodation

The **Hauptbahnhof** is at the northern end of the city; the best way to reach the centre is to follow Bernwardstrasse, then Almstrasse, but be warned that these characterless shopping precincts make rather an inauspicious introduction. Tucked away behind the

The **telephone code** for Hildesheim is ☎05121

Marktplatz at Am Ratsbauhof is the **tourist office** (Mon–Fri 9am–6pm, Sat 9am–1pm; ☎15995). **Mitfahrzentrale** have an office at Annenstr. 15 (☎39051).

Accommodation

Hildesheim isn't well off for budget **hotels**, though there's plenty of choice in the middle and upper ranges. The nearest **campsite** is way to the east of town at Derneburg (☎05062/565). Unfortunately, the **youth hostel** isn't much more convenient; it occupies a rustic location high in the wooded hills above Moritzberg at Schirrmannweg 4 (☎42717; **⌿**), and is a good hour's walk from the centre. No bus goes anywhere near, though #1 and #4 will take you part of the way.

HOTELS AND PENSIONS

Bürgermeisterkapelle, Rathaustr. 8 (☎14021, fax 38813). Modern hotel with good restaurant situated right behind the Rathaus. ⑦

Forte, Markt 4 (☎3000, fax 300 0444). Luxury new hotel with restaurant, sauna and gym in a trio of reconstructed historic buildings. ⑧

Kurth, Küsthardtstr. 4 (☎32817). Small pension that's the only budget option in the Altstadt.

Marheinke, Peiner Landstr. 189 (☎ & fax 52667). *Gasthof* in the north of the city, reached by bus #1 to Alt Drispenstedt. ③

Meyer, Peiner Landstr. 185 (☎ 53179, fax 53107). A slightly more expensive alternative to the neighbouring *Marheinke*. ④

Parkhotel Berghölzchen, Am Berghölzchen 1 (☎9790, fax 979400). Upmarket hotel and restaurant up on the Moritzberg. ⑧

Zum Hagentor, Kardinal-Bertram-Str. 15 (☎35566, fax 14823). Mid-range city-centre hotel. ⑨

The city

Hildesheim's attractions are well spaced out, and cannot comfortably be covered in a single day. To help guide visitors from one monument to another, a trail of white roses has been painted on the streets; a detailed brochure describing this, the *Hildesheimer Rosenroute*, is available from the tourist office.

Marktplatz

In 1983 work began on resurrecting the picturesque jumble of buildings around the central **Marktplatz**, which has now re-emerged, following its almost complete destruction in the war, as Germany's most imposing market square. Only two of the buildings are original: the early Gothic **Rathaus** at the eastern end, which was only partially destroyed and hurriedly rebuilt, and the fifteenth-century **Tempelhaus** at the southeast corner, which somehow remained intact while all its neighbours collapsed. The most likely explanation for the latter's puzzling name and distinctive shape is that it was inspired by a Crusader's description of buildings he had seen in the Holy Land. Some softening of the rather spare, flat textures occurred with the addition of a late sixteenth-century oriel window bearing carvings of the Prodigal Son. Nowadays, the building houses a bookstore and the offices of the *Hildesheimer Allgemeine Zeitung*, the longest continually running daily newspaper in Germany. The Renaissance **Wedekindhaus** next door, the Baroque **Lüntzelhaus** and the part-Gothic, part-Baroque **Rolandstift** were restored by the local savings bank to serve as its headquarters. Directly opposite, Trusthouse Forte have rebuilt the mid-seventeenth-century inn known as the **Stadtschänke**, along with the aptly named **Rokokohaus** and the early sixteenth-century **Wollenwebergildehaus** (Wool Weavers' Guild House), to serve as their second hotel in Germany. The council themselves paid for a copy of the Renaissance **Marktbrunnen**, which is topped by a figure of a knight and has the municipal arms depicted on the basin.

As the culmination of the restoration project, the small **Bäckeramtshaus** (Bakers' Guildhall) of 1800 and the colossal early sixteenth-century **Knochenhaueramtshaus** (Butchers' Guildhall) on the west side of the square were re-created from scratch. The latter had earned for itself the title of "the most beautiful half-timbered house in the world", a title few would dispute on seeing its highly distinctive architecture and seemingly inexhaustible range of carvings on Christian, pagan and humorous subjects. Part of it now houses a restaurant, while the upper storeys contain the local history displays of the **Stadtgeschichtliches Museum** (Tues–Sun 10am–6pm; DM3).

St Michael

Hildesheim's supreme building, the mould-breaking church of **St Michael**, is about ten minutes' walk west of the Marktplatz, reached via Michaelisstrasse. Perched on a little hill and girded with six towers, it's not too fanciful to see it as a depiction of the heavenly Jerusalem. Originally a Benedictine monastery, St Michael's was very much a personal creation of **Bishop Bernward**. A confidant of Emperor Otto II and tutor to Otto III, this well-travelled, erudite man ruled the see of Hildesheim between 993 and 1022, and did much to foster the art and architecture of the city.

The nave forms the centrepiece of St Michael's meticulously thought-out design. An important innovation was the move away from the columned basilica of the Romans to a new system, subsequently known as the **Lower Saxon style**, whereby each bay is demarcated by a hefty square pillar, between which are placed two columns. These are topped by another new device, the cubiform capital, from which spring the arches, coloured in alternate white and red to impart a sense of rhythmic movement. The height of the roof is exactly twice the length of each bay of the nave. Shortly after Bernward was canonized in 1192, substantial embellishments were made in order that it should be a worthy resting place for his relics. Seven capitals were carved for the nave, and in the west transept a **choir screen** was erected; only part of this remains, yet its stucco carvings rank among the masterpieces of German sculpture.

An even more spectacular addition was the **ceiling**, which is one of only two Romanesque painted wooden ceilings to have survived. Fortunately, it had been removed for safety during World War II, and its fresh state of preservation is remarkable – three-quarters of its 1300 separate oak panels are original. Executed in the style of contemporary illuminated manuscripts, its programme is based on the imagery of the tree, a decision prompted by the fact that the church's most sacred relic was a piece of the Holy Cross. In the first main scene, Adam and Eve are shown beside the Tree of Knowledge. Next comes the sleeping Jesse, from whose loins springs the rod which passes through descendants such as David and Solomon before arriving at the Virgin Mary and Christ himself.

St Bernward's body is interred in a stone sarcophagus in the ground-level **crypt** at the western end of the building. This necessitated a rebuilding to accommodate a raised chancel, which impaired the previously perfect architectural unity of the church. The Catholics were allowed to retain the crypt when St Michael became Protestant at the Reformation. It's only open for Mass, but you can peek in by opening the door to the left of the choir screen. Another later addition was the Gothic **cloister** to the north of the church, of which only one wing survives.

The Dom

The **Dom**, which is set in its own close and reached via Burgstrasse, is a poor relation of St Michael's, but its hauntingly romantic cloister and superb art treasures convinced the UNESCO inspectors that it was an equally important piece of cultural heritage. The exterior is largely a fake, with prominent Gothic side chapels and a Romanesque facade and towers that are a modern guess at how the building might have looked before it was completely transformed in the Baroque epoch. Inside, the architecture has been restored to its original eleventh-century layout, a close adaptation of the forms pioneered at the great monastery fifty years before.

One of St Bernward's particular enthusiasms was the art of bronze-casting, and he established a foundry which was to flourish for centuries. Its first major product was a pair of **processional doors**, originally made for St Michael's, but moved a few years later to the Dom's main entrance, where they were installed on the inside. They tell the story of Adam and Eve on the left-hand side, and of Christ on the right. Soon afterwards, the craftsmen made the **triumphal column**, now in the southern transept. Rather more obviously inspired by Roman victory monuments, this illustrates the lives of Jesus and St John the Baptist in a manner akin to strip cartoons. Around 1065, the huge **wheel-shaped chandelier** was suspended from the vault of the nave. Mantled with alternate towers and gateways, it's yet another representation of the heavenly Jerusalem and was to serve as the prototype for the even more ornate candelabra in Aachen and Gross Comburg. In the baptismal chapel is the **font**; made in 1225, it rests on personifications of the four sacred rivers, while the basin and lid illustrate various biblical stories, mostly with a watery theme.

THE CLOISTER

The **cloister** (April–Oct Mon–Sat 9.30am–5pm, Sun noon–5pm; DM0.50) most unusually is built onto the transepts, forming a protective shield round the apse, on which grows the **thousand-year-old rosebush**, to which the legend of Hildesheim's foundation is inextricably tied. In 815, Ludwig the Pious, a son of Charlemagne, hung the royal chapel's relics of the Virgin on the tree while he was out hunting near *Hildwins Heim*. When he tried to remove them, they would not budge; taking this to be divine instruction, he decided to endow the mother church of a new diocese on the very spot. Whether this is really the original bush is disputed, but it's certainly many centuries old, and does seem to lead a charmed life – it burst into flower not long after the air-raid which had flattened most of the Dom itself, and has blossomed every year since. In the centre of the cloister garden is the **St-Annen-Kapelle**, a beautiful fourteenth-century miniaturization of a Gothic cathedral, with a set of gargoyles spouting from its walls. The sumptuous Renaissance **rood screen**, which fenced off the Dom's chancel until 1945, can be seen in the Antoniuskapelle off the cloister's southern walk.

THE DIÖZESANMUSEUM

Hildesheim's **Diözesanmuseum** (Tues–Sat 10am–5pm, Sun noon–5pm; DM4) contains one of the richest ecclesiastical treasuries in Germany. Among the highlights are several works dating from the time of St Bernward – the *Golden Madonna* (actually wooden but covered with gold leaf), a pair of candlesticks, and two crucifixes named after the bishop himself. Equally imposing are various twelfth-century pieces – the *Cross of Henry the Lion*, three shield-shaped crucifixes and a set of enamel plates. The eagle-lectern was made around the same time as the font, while the *Chalice of St Bernward*, though it has no real connection with the bishop, is an outstanding piece of goldsmith's work from around 1400.

The Roemer-Pelizaeus Museum and Andreasplatz

Adjoining the north side of the Dom's close is the old Franciscan monastery, which now contains the **Roemer-Pelizaeus Museum** (Tues–Sun 9am–4.30pm; DM3). Refreshingly different from the standard provincial museum, this hosts an international **loan exhibition** on a major archeological topic each year, when the opening times are extended and the admission raised to around DM10. What's on display is subject to change, but you're sure to be able to see part of the collection of **Egyptian antiquities**, which is one of the best in Europe and in itself enough to justify a visit to Hildesheim. The most famous exhibit is the white limestone funerary monument of Hem-iuni from

2530 BC. Other outstanding sculptures include statuettes of Amenophis III and Teje (parents of Akhenaton), a statue of the fearsome half-man, half-jackal Anubis (the god of death) and the reliefs from the tomb of Seschem-nefer IV. The museum's other main strengths include a comprehensive collection of Chinese porcelain and a varied array of exhibits from the Peru of the Incas.

Proceeding eastwards along Pfaffenstieg and Schuhstrasse, you see the church of **St Andreas** on the left. Within its exhilaratingly lofty Gothic interior, Luther's friend Johannes Bugenhagen converted the city to the Reformation. The church itself actually gained from the air raids – it was rebuilt according to the ambitious schemes of the original masons, which had never previously been fully put into effect. On the other hand, this hardly makes up for the almost complete loss of the square round the church, formerly regarded as a worthy rival to Marktplatz. For a fine view over the city, climb up the tall **tower** (March–Oct Mon–Sat 10am–5pm, Sun noon–6pm; Nov–Feb Sat & Sun noon–4pm; DM3).

The southern Altstadt

The southern part of Hildesheim was largely spared from war damage, and presents several streets of half-timbered houses as a reminder of what the whole of the old city once looked like. At the top end of Brühl, the nearest of these streets to the centre, the one surviving secular building from the time of St Bernward can be seen. Originally a fortified reception hall-cum-law court, it was converted into a collegiate foundation known as the **Kreuzkirche** in the late eleventh century, and now forms part of the otherwise Baroque parish church of the same name, making a truly odd combination. To the west of the southern section of Brühl runs the parallel Hinterer Brühl, an almost completely preserved old street. Look out for the early seventeenth-century **Wernesches-Haus**, with its allegorical depictions of the Virtues and Vices, and representations of historical personalities.

At the end of the street is **St Godehard**, a former Benedictine monastery church built in the mid-twelfth century to commemorate the recent canonization of the man who had succeeded St Bernward as Bishop of Hildesheim. Unusually well preserved, it boasts a pair of round towers on its facade, with a larger version of these over the transept. There is a delicate stucco relief over the north doorway showing Christ between St Godehard (holding a model of the church) and St Epiphanus. The interior proves the durability of the style pioneered at St Michael's, the only advance being the rich carvings on the capitals. The star piece of the church's rich treasury is a magnificent early twelfth-century psalter illuminated at the sister English monastery of St Albans; it is periodically kept here, but is also sometimes shown at the Diözesanmuseum.

East of St Godehard is another fine old street, Gelber Stern, among whose buildings is the mid-sixteenth-century **Haus des Waffenschieds**, the guild house of the armourers, decorated with carvings of the tools of the trade. At the end of the road, Lappenberg, which runs perpendicular to the south, has a complete row of craftsmen's homes. Nearby stands the **Kehrwiederturm**, the only surviving example of the gates which once surrounded the inner city. To the east is Kesslerstrasse, arguably the most imposing of the old streets, lined with impressive Renaissance and Baroque mansions. The largest and finest of these is the **Dompropstei** (Deanery) at no. 57, set in its own spacious yard. Just north of here is the **Lambertikirche**, which contains a lovely early fifteenth-century Soft Style retable painted by an unknown local master.

The suburbs

Another well-preserved old quarter is the **Moritzberg**, on a hill to the west of the city centre, and reached along Dammstrasse, Bergsteinweg and Bergstrasse. It's grouped round yet another Romanesque church, **St Mauritius**. Although dating from the second half of the eleventh century, this favoured the traditional format of a columned basilica, which is still evident despite the fact that the interior is now cloaked with Baroque decoration. The crypt and cloister, however, have been preserved in their original state. Unfortunately, there isn't much of a view from these heights; for that you have to go to the **Galgenberg**, at the opposite end of the city.

Eating, drinking and entertainment

Other than around Marktplatz, there's no obvious concentration of good places to eat and drink in Hildesheim, but there are plenty of possibilities dotted around the city which are well worth seeking out.

Hildesheimer Brauhaus, Speicherstr. 9. *Hausbrauerei* serving its own organically brewed *Pils*; also often features live music, for which there's a DM3 entry fee.

Krehla, Moritzstr. 9. Up on the Moritzberg; serves light meals, but is best known for its seven kinds of home-made fruit wines.

Kupferschmiede, Am Steinberg 6. In a secluded forest setting 5km south of town, this is one of the most famous restaurants in northern Germany, offering both *nouvelle cuisine* and hearty German fare. One for a splurge, although the set menus are far from extortionate; reservations (☎262351) recommended.

Ratskeller, Markt 1. Far less expensive than its counterparts in most other cities (there are cheap daily specials at lunchtimes) – yet it can rival any of them in quality.

Schlegels Weinstube, Am Steine 4–6. Cosy, highly atmospheric little wine bar-restaurant in a half-timbered sixteenth-century building directly opposite the Roemer-Pelizaeus Museum. Evenings only, closed Sun.

Schwejk, Osterstr. 16. Bohemian-style cooking and Czech beers are featured here; best at lunchtimes, when there are bargain menus.

Uwe's Fass, Andreas-Passage. Very popular bistro, with adjoining beer garden.

Entertainment

Jazz fans should head for Hildesheim at Whit weekend, when the *Jazz-Time* festival presents the whole gamut of styles, both in formal concerts and impromptu open-air events. The regular year-round venue for live jazz is *Bischofsmühle*, Dammstr. 32. All kinds of **music** are featured along with **drama** in the varied programmes of the *Stadttheater*, Theaterstrasse 6 (☎169351); there are also regular recitals and concerts in the Protestant churches.

Main **popular festivals** are the *Frühlingsfest* for nine days in March, the *Weinfest* for a week in mid-May, and the ubiquitous *Schützenfest* in mid-June.

Braunschweig (Brunswick)

Today **BRAUNSCHWEIG** is the epicentre of the most heavily industrialized part of Lower Saxony, but it preserves plenty of reminders of the far grander role it once played. During the twelfth century it was the chosen residence of **Henry the Lion** (*Heinrich der Löwe*), one of the most powerful princes in Europe, who commissioned innumerable monuments and works of art to grace his capital. Over the next few centuries the city became increasingly important as a commercial centre; its trade connections stretched into Russia, Scandinavia, Flanders and England, and the consequent wealth was put to use creating buildings worthy of the city's power and status. In the mid-eighteenth century Braunschweig had yet another brilliant period. The first technical university in the world, the *Collegium Carolinum*, was established here in 1745. When the local dukes took up residence again the following decade, having been absent for over three hundred years, their wonderful art treasures were put on public display and the city became a flourishing cultural centre.

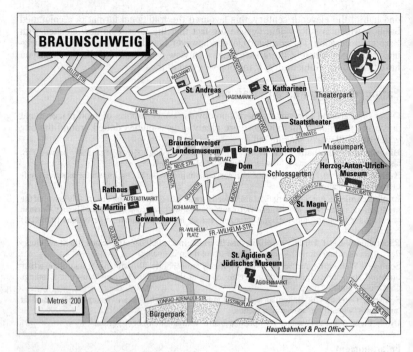

BRAUNSCHWEIG

St. Andreas
St. Katharinen
HAGENMARKT
Theaterpark
WOLLMARKT
CELLER STR.
WENDENSTR.
LANGE STR.
BOHLWEG
Staatstheater
STEINWEG
Braunschweiger
Landesmuseum
Burg Dankwarderode
Museumpark
BURGPLATZ
Dom
Herzog-Anton-Ulrich-Museum
NEUE STR.
Schlossgarten
GEORG ECKERT-STR.
MUSEUMSTR.
SCHÜTZENSTR.
SACKRING
MÜNZSTR.
MAGNITORWALL
Rathaus
ALTSTADTMARKT
KOHLMARKT
St. Magni
St. Martini
Gewandhaus
FR.-WILHELM-PLATZ
FR.-WILHELM-STR.
BÄLKERSTR.
St. Ägidien & Jüdisches Museum
ÄGIDIENMARKT
0 Metres 200
KONRAD-ADENAUER-STR.
LESSINGPLATZ
KURT-SCHUMACHER-STR.
Bürgerpark

Hauptbahnhof & Post Office▽

Arrival, information and accommodation

The **Hauptbahnhof** is some distance to the southeast of the centre. It's quite a walk, so it's best to take tram #1 or #5 to the "island" at the heart of the city. Braunschweig has two **tourist offices**: one is in the entrance hall of the Hauptbahnhof (Mon–Fri 8am–6pm, Sat 9am–noon; ☎79237); the other is housed in a pavilion on Bohlweg (Mon–Fri 9am–6pm, Sat 9.30am–noon; ☎46419). **Mitfahrzentrale** have an office at Bohlweg 42–43 (☎14041). The 24hr **public transport ticket** is good value at DM7.

Accommodation

Braunschweig has a good range of **hotels** to suit all budgets, with several enticing upmarket options. The **youth hostel** is at Salzdalumer Str. 170 (☎62268; ☎) to the south of the city, reached by bus #11 or #19 to Krankenhaus, and has a few single rooms in addition to dormitories.

HOTELS AND GUESTHOUSES

Café am Park, Wolfenbütteler Str. 67 (☎73079, fax 790906). Middle-range hotel about a 10min walk west of the Hauptbahnhof. ⑤

Deutsches Haus, Ruhfäutchenplatz 1 (☎1200, fax 120 0444). Fine old traditional hotel, part of the *Ringhotel* chain, at the corner of Burgplatz, to which it is linked by a picturesque "Bridge of Sighs". Its restaurant is good and reasonably priced. ⑧

Friedrich, Am Magnitor 5 (☎41728, fax 346777). Long-established *Gasthof* in the Magniviertel. It only has a few rooms, and is better-known for its wine bar-restaurant. ③

Ritter St Georg, Alte Knochenhauerstr. 12–13 (☎13039, fax 13038). Arguably the most attractive place to stay in the city, occupying its oldest half-timbered house dating back to 1346. The bedrooms

---

The **telephone code** for Braunschweig is ☎0532

---

are furnished in country house style; the high class, extremely expensive restaurant is beautifully appointed. ⑦

Simoné, Celler Str. 111 (☎577898, fax 574 3130). Budget hotel a short distance to the northwest of the Altstadt, not far from the terminus of tram #1. ③

Stadthotel Magnitor, Am Magnitor 1 (☎47130, fax 471 3499). Modern designer hotel in a fifteenth-century timber-framed building that was originally a storehouse. Its restaurant features both moderately priced and expensive dishes. ⑨

Wägener, Schleinitzstr. 18 (☎331281). Small guesthouse just over the water from the Altstadt. ④

The city

The historic heart of the city is still completely surrounded by water – a man-made system based on the two arms of the River Oker – and contains several distinct medieval districts, which were formerly governed separately. Each of these quarters was centred on a market square and usually had its own parish church. Severe bomb damage in World War II means that the old buildings are now interspersed with plenty of ugly modern shops and offices, but it's still possible to visualize the medieval layout.

Burgplatz

To look at the city in chronological order, the **Burgplatz** in the middle of the "island" is the place to start. It's full of memories of Henry the Lion (see box below), who was at the peak of his power at the time the square was laid out. In 1166, he commissioned the **Burglöwe** (Lion Monument) to form its centrepiece. Perched high on a pedestal, this bronze statue, which was originally gilded, was the first freestanding sculptural monument to be made since the days of the Romans. Even though it has been replaced twice, the lion still stands as a potent reminder of the long centuries of power enjoyed by the Welfs.

HENRY THE LION

Henry the Lion (1129/30–95) was born into the greatest of all dynastic feuds of the Middle Ages – that between his own family, the **Welfs**, and the **Hohenstaufens**, who then held a stranglehold on the office of Holy Roman Emperor. His father, Henry the Proud, had been a major loser in this conflict, having been divested of his titles of Duke of Saxony and Bavaria. By allying himself with his cousin, Emperor Frederick Barbarossa, "The Lion" quickly regained both duchies, and seemingly brought the feud to an end. His early career brought one success after another: he founded both the city of Munich and the port of Lübeck, and began the process of creating a strong Baltic state. However, he became too powerful for his own good, posing a threat to the feudal structure of the Holy Roman Empire. He fell out with Frederick over the price of his continued support of imperial policy in Italy and the Holy Land – his demand that the Free Imperial City of Goslar and its lucrative silver mines be made over to him was clearly excessive – and consequently was stripped of his titles and confined to his ancestral lands of Braunschweig-Lüneburg. The Welfs' feuding with the Hohenstaufens thereafter continued to bedevil medieval Germany – and dominated politics in Italy, where, under the names of the Guelphs and the Ghibellines, their followers championed the cause of papal and imperial power respectively. Nonetheless, the Welfs retained control over at least part of their heartland right up to the present century.

The Dom

In 1173 the **Dom** (daily 10am–1pm & 3–5pm) was begun, and was substantially complete before the end of the century. Its craggy, fortress-like external appearance (which seems to be another symbol of the power of the Welfs) is the prototype of a distinctive Braunschweig style, which was followed in all the other medieval churches of the city. Another feature copied throughout the city was the later insertion of a Gothic bell-gable between the two towers, which further increases the sense of the facade's massiveness.

The interior is far lighter in feel. This is partly due to the well-preserved Romanesque **frescoes**, dating from around 1220, which were hidden behind plaster for centuries. The portraits of saints in the nave, executed with the finesse of manuscript miniatures, are particularly fine. An even more crucial addition was the opening out of the north side of the Dom in the mid-fifteenth century by masons who seem to have been familiar with English Tudor architecture; the two new aisles are separated by a row of writhing **columns** which twist in alternate directions. On the end wall is the sole survivor of the previous cathedral which stood on this site, a Byzantine-inspired wooden *Crucifixion* signed by a certain Master Imerward. At the entrance to the choir a seven-branched **candelabrum**, donated by the founder, springs from a base of four crouching lions. In front is the limestone **tomb** of Henry the Lion and his second wife Matilda, daughter of Henry II of England. Memorials to other members of the Welf dynasty are housed in the crypt.

The rest of the square

Facing the Dom is Henry's castle, **Burg Dankwarderode** (Tues–Sun 10am–5pm; DM5 combined ticket with Herzog-Anton-Ulrich-Museum). Named in honour of the semi-mythical ninth-century founder of the city, it was constructed at the same time as the Dom. Its unusually complete appearance is mainly due to a nineteenth-century restoration, which follows the original form far more faithfully than most projects inspired by the Romantic reverence for the Middle Ages. Appropriately, it now houses a museum of medieval art and artefacts, of which the star attraction is the original of the Burglöwe. Other highlights include an eighth- or ninth-century walrus-tooth casket, the eleventh-century arm-reliquary of St Blasius (patron of the Dom), and the cloak of Otto IV, son of Henry the Lion – and the only Welf to become Holy Roman Emperor.

The Burgplatz used to be a courtyard in its truest sense – the houses that stood around its edge belonged to the courtiers. Two half-timbered sixteenth-century successors to these survive – the **Guildehaus** and the **Minsterialhof**, the latter now the seat of the local chamber of commerce. The Neoclassical mansion in the opposite corner of the square was originally a publishing house, but now accommodates the **Braunschweiger Landesmuseum** (Tues, Wed & Fri–Sun 10am–5pm, Thurs 10am–8pm; DM5 combined ticket with Jüdisches Museum). This contains local history displays on the Braunschweig region; in the entrance hall is the second version of the Burglöwe.

Altstadtmarkt

The other significant cluster of Braunschweig's past is found in and around the **Altstadtmarkt** to the west. A corner of this is taken up by the former **Rathaus**, which ranks as one of the most beautiful and original secular buildings in Germany. Consisting of two wings arranged in an L-shape, its present form dates back to the early fifteenth century, when the open upper arcades, with their flowing tracery and statues of the Welfs, were added. The graceful lead **Marienbrunnen** in the middle of the square was made around the same time; it's topped by a shrine-like structure with the Virgin and Child and the four Evangelists.

Opposite stands the **Gewandhaus** (Drapers' Hall), its grandeur reflecting the importance of the medieval tailors. The facade is a Dutch-influenced Renaissance composition of extraordinary elaborateness, whose gable, shaped like an equilateral triangle, is crowned by a figure of Justice. Alongside is the half-timbered seventeenth-century **Zollhaus**, once used by customs officials and the military. Also on the square is the Baroque **Stechinellihaus**, designed by the Italian court architect after whom it's named, who was also responsible for many buildings in Celle.

St Martini (Tues–Fri 10.30am–12.30pm, Sat 9am–noon), originally a twelfth-century basilica, stands at the far end of Altstadtmarkt. The finest and earliest of Braunschweig's parish churches, it follows the usual pattern of being modelled on the Dom, but was altered inside to form a spacious hall. It also gained some fine sculptures in the fourteenth century, notably the group of the Wise and Foolish Virgins on the north doorway. Another addition is the Gothic chapel dedicated to St Anne, housing a Renaissance pulpit that shows St Martin dividing his coat in order to clothe a beggar.

The other historic quarters

North of Burgplatz, reached via Casparistrasse or Bohlweg, is the old district of Hagen, centred on Hagenmarkt. Its fountain bears a nineteenth-century statue of Henry the Lion carrying a model of the church of **St Katharinen**, which he also founded. Closely modelled on the Dom, St Katharinen's interior was later transformed into a spacious Gothic hall church. The same is true of **St Andreas** further to the west, which was the parish church of the Neustadt district. Across from this church is the **Liberei**, a fifteenth-century library building which is the only example of Gothic brick architecture in the city. Further west, on Bäckerklimt, is the bronze **Eulenspiegelbrunnen**, commemorating the legendary jester Till Eulenspiegel (see box below). The owls and monkeys on the fountain represent the shapes into which he would work dough as an apprentice in a nearby bakery. The shop itself was bombed in 1944, but similar breads remain a local speciality to this day.

Raised above the old city on a slight hillock at its southern edge stands the former Benedictine monastery of **St Aegidien**, the only church in Braunschweig built in a pure Gothic style. Its handsome pulpit retains the original late Gothic reliefs by Hans Witten, a sculptor who was the equal of the more famous Riemenschneider and Stoss, but whose reputation suffers from the fact that most of his work is in remote Saxon towns. The monastic buildings now house the **Jüdisches Museum** (Tues & Thurs–Sun 10am–5pm, Wed 10am–8pm; DM5 combined ticket with Landesmuseum), which vividly illustrates German Jewish culture down the centuries. There's even a full-

---

TILL EULENSPIEGEL

One of Germany's most famous semi-historical characters, Till Eulenspiegel (the name means "Owl Mirror") was born of peasant stock in the village of Kneitlingen near Braunschweig around 1300. Disrespectful of all forms of authority and realizing the inherent foolishness of the human condition, he lived by his native wit, consistently putting points over on pompous aristocrats, merchants, churchmen and scholars with his practical jokes and punning sense of humour. Anecdotes about him were popular all over medieval Europe, and were first published in book form in the early sixteenth century. Oddly enough, it was not until 1995 that a complete and unbowdlerized English translation became available (see p.1029). His name has since been enshrined in the German word for tomfoolery (*Eulenspiegelei*) and the French name for a rogue or scoundrel (*espiègle*). He has also inspired two major works of art – a brilliant orchestral showpiece by Richard Strauss and an epic poem by a winner of the Nobel Prize for Literature, Gerhart Hauptmann.

scale reconstruction, complete with all the original fittings, of a Baroque synagogue dismantled earlier this century.

Braunschweig's other significant district is the Altewiek a few blocks further north. This is now usually known as the Magniviertel after the church of **St Magni** which forms its core. The few half-timbered streets in the city which completely escaped destruction in the air raids are found around here, and the semicircular group immediately behind the church and the blind alley called Herrendorftwerte, just to the east, are particularly evocative. This is also one of the liveliest areas at night, with a host of pubs and restaurants.

The Herzog-Anton-Ulrich-Museum

North of the Magniviertel, on Museumstrasse, is the **Herzog-Anton-Ulrich-Museum** (Tues & Thurs–Sun 10am–5pm, Wed 10am–8pm; DM5 combined ticket with Burg Dankwarderode). Of outstanding quality for a regional museum, it's particularly intriguing in that it reflects the personal artistic tastes of the duke after whom it's named, who was responsible for building it up some three hundred years ago. The collection was opened to the public in 1754, thus making it the first museum in Germany.

DUTCH AND FLEMISH PAINTING

In the first-floor picture gallery, pride of place goes to the Dutch school, and in particular to one of **Rembrandt's** most psychologically acute works, *A Family Group*. It was painted at the very end of his life, and shows his style at its most advanced and daring, with its loose brushwork supplemented by extensive use of the palette knife, its heavy chiaroscuro effects, and the informal arrangement of its subjects. Rembrandt's very personal vision of biblical stories is represented here by a tender nocturne of *The Risen Christ Appearing to Mary Magdalene*. The dramatic *Landscape with Thunderstorm*, bathed in warm golden hues, shows yet another side of his diverse genius.

Vermeer's *Girl with the Wineglass* displays a level of technical virtuosity fully equal to, but very different from, Rembrandt's. Probably executed with the help of a *camera obscura*, it captures the three-dimensional space of the interior to uncanny effect. Two other highlights of the Dutch collection include a subtly delicate late fifteenth-century portable altar known as the *Braunschweig Diptych*; and a sharply observed *Self-Portrait* by the country's leading sixteenth-century artist, **Lucas van Leyden**. Most of the specialist painters of the seventeenth century are represented; *The Marriage of Tobias and Sara* by **Jan Steen** and three landscapes by **Jacob van Ruisdael** are particularly notable. Among Flemish works of the same period are several pieces by **Rubens**, a fine **van Dyck** and a fetching **Teniers**, *The Alchemist's Workshop*.

GERMAN PAINTING

The most important of the German works on view in the gallery is the *Portrait of Cyriacus Kale* by **Holbein the Younger**. It was painted in London, where the Braunschweig-born sitter worked at the Hansa trading headquarters, as the inscription states. A strong representation of **Cranach** includes a lively workshop cycle of *The Labours of Hercules*, and a *Hercules and Omphale*. The latter is by Cranach's hand alone, as is the *Portrait of Albrecht von Brandenburg-Ansbach*, which depicts the cross-eyed Hohenzollern who had been Grand Master of the Teutonic Knights. By the time this picture was painted, Albrecht had converted to Protestantism, secularized his Order's holdings and become Duke of Prussia – events which were crucial in his family's ultimately successful drive to win leadership of the German nation. A delicate *Morning Landscape* by the short-lived **Elsheimer** rounds off this section.

Bremen: the Marktplatz (main square)

Sailing ships at Bremerhaven

Bremen: the Town Band statue in the Marktplatz

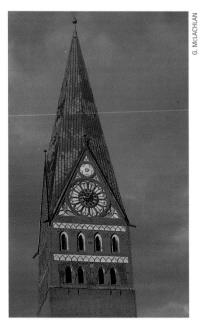

Lüneberg: the church of St Johannis

Lüneberg Heath

Hamburg: the Speicherstadt

Hameln: carving on the Stiftsherrnhaus

Celle: the Schloss

Hamburg: the Alsterarkaden

A squatted building in Hamburg

E. NÄGELE

The North Friesian island of Amrun

MICHAEL JENNER

Strandkörbe (beach shelters) at
Heringsdorf on the island of Usedom

G. McLACHLAN

Stralsund with Rügen Island in the
background

THE REST OF THE MUSEUM
Duke Anton Ulrich's taste in Italian painting seems to have been confined to the sixteenth-century Venetians and the bombastic artists of the Baroque. The most fascinating work is what's labelled a *Self-Portrait* by the mysterious father figure of Venice's Renaissance, **Giorgione**. One of the few surviving paintings widely accepted as genuine, it's probably a cut-down version of a *David with the Head of Goliath*. Important examples of the later Venetian Renaissance include works by Veronese, Tintoretto and Palma il Vecchio.

In the **decorative arts** section on the top floor Italy features rather more extensively, with a notable array of bronzes and porcelain, plus a valuable onyx vase from Mantua. Other particular strengths are Chinese lacquerwork, Limoges enamels, and jewellery, ceramics and furniture from all over Europe.

Eating and drinking

In addition to the excellent hotel restaurants mentioned above, Braunschweig has plenty of good places to eat and drink.

Restaurants
Brabanter Hof, Güldenstr. 77. Wonderful old *Gaststätte* serving some of the best food in town.

Brodocz, Stephanstr. 1. Vegetarian restaurant in a pretty half-timbered courtyard.

Datscha, Marstall 19. Inexpensive Russian speciality restaurant.

Gewandhauskeller, Altstadtmarkt 1. High quality restaurant in the Gothic cellars of the Gewandhaus. The menu includes several dishes in a dark sauce known as *Mumme*, named after a famous malt beer which was exported to England until the eighteenth century.

Mutter Habenicht, Papensteig 3. This candlelit *Gaststätte* with beer garden has been going strong for well over a century.

Schalander, Stobenstr. 12. Offers very moderately priced *gutbürgerliche Küche*.

Cafés and bars
Anders, Am Magnitor 7. Trendy bar in the Magniviertel.

Bassgeige, Bäckerklimt 11. Bar which holds regular live jazz sessions.

Café Emigré, Rosenhagen 3. French-style brasserie.

Café Voigt, Friedrich-Wilhelm-Platz 6. The pick of the traditional cafés.

Schadt's, Höhe 28. *Hausbrauerei*, which makes *Pils* and *Weizen* plus a seasonal *Märzen*; also serves full meals. There's a larger offshoot, *Zum Löwen*, at Waisenhausdamm 13.

Entertainment
Braunschweig has a strong **theatre** tradition; in the now demolished building on Hagenmarkt the first part of Goethe's *Faust* received its premiere in 1829. The building was replaced a few decades later by the *Staatstheater* (☎484 2800) on Am Theater (between Museumpark and Theaterpark), which remains the leading venue for opera and drama. Shows with an alternative slant are presented at *FreiBiZe*, an old waterworks in the Bürgerpark (☎470 2131).

Concerts of all kinds are held at the modern *Stadthalle* on Leonhardplatz (☎70770), not far from the Hauptbahnhof. There's a **festival** of modern chamber music each November, while the main annual folklore event is a medieval market held in Burgplatz in late May or early June.

Wolfenbüttel

Reached in just a few minutes from Braunschweig via the first state-owned rail line in Germany (opened in 1838), **WOLFENBÜTTEL** is a place which deserves to be far better known. One of the Welf duchies had its seat there from 1432 to 1754, and even today it preserves much of the layout and atmosphere of a ducal *Residenzstadt*. Indeed, it offers the most evocative example of the petty courts which once dotted the politically fragmented map of the Holy Roman Empire. When the local dukes moved back to Braunschweig, Wolfenbüttel seems to have fallen into a deep slumber. It came through World War II unscathed, and no fewer than 600 historic half-timbered houses survive, as well as plenty of large public buildings.

The city

Wolfenbüttel is the earliest example in Germany of a **planned town** – in fact, it evolved from several consecutive plans, all of whose outlines are still visible. At the western end is the spacious **Schlossplatz** with the main ducal showpieces, while beyond lies the **Alte Heinrichstadt**, the original centre. The subsequent planned suburbs lie further east.

The Schloss

On the western side of Schlossplatz is the huge, dazzlingly white **Schloss** (Tues–Sat 10am–5pm, Sun 10am–1pm; DM3). Apart from the moat and some re-used masonry, nothing remains of the medieval moated fortress, the present structure being a conflation of Renaissance and Baroque. The most distinguished feature is the Renaissance **tower**, whose unusual design includes a gabled clock-face on each side. It was built in the early seventeenth century by **Paul Francke**, who was responsible for many of the buildings in the first phases of the planning of Wolfenbüttel. This apart, the exterior of the Schloss dates from a century later and was designed by the highly inventive **Hermann Korb**.

The upper arcades of the Palladian-style inner **courtyard** were originally open, following normal Italian practice; however, they were filled in soon after, when the incompatibility of open arcades and northern weather became apparent. Round the back of the Schloss, a troupe of English actors under Thomas Sackville established themselves as the first permanent theatre company in Germany in 1590. This ushered in a golden era for the performing arts in Wolfenbüttel, but the opera house built there the following century has unfortunately not survived. The surprisingly modest **state apartments** give a good impression of how the dukes lived.

The Zeughaus and Herzog-August-Bibliothek

On the north side of Schlossplatz is the **Zeughaus**, again by Francke. Its cheerful crimson exterior, decorated with richly carved gables, hardly suggests its original function as an arsenal, whose cavernous lower floor once housed the biggest and most powerful cannons in Germany. Immediately behind is the grandest of Wolfenbüttel's half-timbered buildings, a huge mid-seventeenth-century storehouse.

Nowadays, the Zeughaus hosts temporary exhibitions from the pride of the town, the **Herzog-August-Bibliothek** (Tues–Fri 10am–4pm, Sat & Sun 10am–5pm; combined ticket DM6), whose headquarters are in the nineteenth-century pseudo-*palazzo* diagonally opposite. The Dukes of Braunschweig-Wolfenbüttel were true bibliophiles and by the mid-seventeenth century the scholarly August the Younger had built up the largest library in Europe, consisting of 130,000 volumes, all catalogued by himself. Several rooms of the main library have been laid out as a museum, with changing selections from its holdings of rare books, as well as other specialities such as Renaissance maps and globes and twentieth-century artists' sketchbooks. A strongroom holds a display on the library's greatest treasure, the **Gospel book of Henry the Lion** (see box opposite), but unfortunately the initial intention to put on permanent public display the original manuscript itself has not been honoured, though it is occasionally exhibited.

THE WORLD'S MOST EXPENSIVE BOOK

Arguably the most sumptuous manuscript produced in the Romanesque period, Henry the Lion's Evangelistary or **Gospel book** was commissioned around 1180 for use in the Dom in Braunschweig. Among its 24 beautifully coloured full-page miniatures is a scene showing Christ crowning Henry and his English wife Matilda; the saints in paradise include Thomas à Becket, recently murdered as a result of a misunderstood remark made by his friend Henry II, Matilda's father. Last century, the Welf family reacquired this heirloom, but sold it after World War II to a secretive private collector. In 1983, it was auctioned by Sotheby's in London; desperate to gain this key piece of their heritage, the Land government of Lower Saxony headed a consortium which splashed out £10 million, setting a world-record price for a work of art. It remains the most expensive book in the world.

The **Lessinghaus** (Tues–Fri 11am–5pm, Sat & Sun 10am–5pm; same tickets) in front of the Bibliothek was the official residence of the librarian. A triple-winged summer house, it was finished just three years before the dukes decided to abandon Wolfenbüttel as a residence. Its present name comes from the second famous holder of the librarian's post, the hugely influential playwright **Gotthold Ephraim Lessing**, who spent the last eleven years of his life there; a collection of memorabilia pays tribute to him. The main work from his Wolfenbüttel years is *Nathan the Wise*, a piece particularly interesting in the light of subsequent German history – its wholly admirable hero is a Jew.

Alte Heinrichstadt

East of Schlossplatz is the original late sixteenth-century planned town, the **Alte Heinrichstadt**. One of its focal points is the **Stadtmarkt**, a square lined with half-timbered buildings, in the centre of which is a bronze statue of Duke August the Younger, depicted leading his horse rather than riding it.

Off the north side of the square, on the street named after it, is the **Kanzlei** (Chancellery). Though somewhat messed about, it's notable as being the only surviving building by the Dutchman Hans Vredeman de Vries, the leading architectural theoretician of the Northern European Renaissance. The Kanzlei now houses the mildly interesting archeological section of the **Braunschweiges Museum** (Tues–Fri & Sun 10am–5pm; DM3). Almost all the other streets around here are worth walking along; look out for **Klein-Venedig** (Little Venice), so named because it fronts a canal.

The Hauptkirche

As a climax to the Alte Heinrichstadt, the **Hauptkirche** was begun in 1608 by Paul Francke; after two decades of restoration, it's now looking in pristine shape. Notwithstanding the dedication to *Beatae Mariae Virginis*, it was not only Lutheran from the outset, but was the first parish church to be built specifically for the Protestant faith (although Bückeburg's Stadtkirche, started three years later, was actually finished first). It's an extraordinary confection, mixing late Gothic, Renaissance and Mannerism, while the main portal – designed like a triumphal arch with statues of two of the dukes ensconced between Moses and Aaron below, and Christ at the summit – has all the swagger of the emergent Baroque style. On the long sides of the building are a series of profusely decorated gables, while on the facade and in the vestibule are hundreds of delicately carved reliefs of animals and demons.

The church's light and spacious **interior** (Tues–Fri 10am–12.30pm & 2–4/5pm, Sat 10am–12.30pm & 2–4pm) doubles as the ducal pantheon. Regular recitals are held on the early Baroque organ, first presided over by the composer **Michael Praetorius**, who is buried below. He's best known for his beguiling arrangements of over three hundred foot-tapping dance melodies, collectively known as *Terpsichore*.

The rest of the city

East of the Hauptkirche is the **Neue Heinrichstadt**, centred on the Holzmarkt; for the most part, its buildings faithfully follow the style of the earlier part of town. In the early eighteenth century, Hermann Korb finished off the square in an ingenious fashion by inserting the oval **Trinitatiskirche** (Tues 11am–1pm, Wed 11am–1pm & 2–4pm, Thurs 3–5pm Sat 11am–4pm) between the two redundant gateways at the far end, transforming the latter into a pair of towers for the church in the process.

Further east, across the Oker, a huge new town of manufacturing workshops called the **Juliusstadt** was once planned. However, it never got beyond a couple of streets. Instead, the far more modest craftsmen's suburb of **Augustadt** was laid out at the opposite end of Wolfenbüttel, to the west of the Schloss. Its houses are remarkably similar to those in the "better" part of town, and the half-timbered **Johanniskirche**, set beside its detached belfry in a shady green, brings a touch of rusticity to the quarter.

Practicalities

The **Bahnhof** is immediately south of the historic centre, on the opposite side of the River Oker. Wolfenbüttel's **tourist office** (Mon–Fri 9am–12.30pm & 2–4pm, April–Sept also Sat 9am–1pm; ☎05331/86487) is at Stadtmarkt 9.

Many of the **hotels** occupy interesting old buildings. North of the Altstadt the half-timbered *Forsthaus*, Neuer Weg 5 (☎05331/71711; ③) was for 30 years the holiday home of the cartoonist Wilhelm Busch. *Gasthof Kaltes Tal*, to the rear of the Bahnhof at Goslarsche Str. 56 (☎05331/43828; ④), is an inn first documented in the seventeenth century. *Kronprinz*, Bahnhofstr. 12 (☎05331/1265; ④) has an inner courtyard and a winter garden, while *Altes Haus*, Enge Str. 25 (☎05331/1362; ④) and *Bayrischer Hof*, Brauergildenstr. 5 (☎05331/5078; ⑤) both occupy timber-framed buildings in the Altstadt. The most luxurious hotel is the modern *Parkhotel Altes Kaffeehaus* just beyond the southeastern fringe of the centre at Harztorwall 18 (☎05331/8880; ⑦). There's a **campsite** (☎05331/298728) by the open-air swimming pool at the eastern side of town.

The best places to **eat** and **drink** are the restaurants of the hotels listed above, especially the *Historisches Weingrotte* in the *Parkhotel Altes Kaffeehaus*, a reconstruction of the once celebrated but long destroyed *Türkisches Kaffeehaus* of 1838. Main **festivals** are the open-air *Theaterfest* in June/July and the *Altstadtfest* in late August.

Königslutter and Wolfsburg

East of Braunschweig, on each of the two main rail routes into the former GDR, are a couple of very contrasting diversions, both well worth a visit. **Königslutter am Elm** is an adjunct to an imperial abbey, while **Wolfsburg** is the headquarters of one of Germany's most famous and successful enterprises, Volkswagen.

Königslutter am Elm

KÖNIGSLUTTER AM ELM lies some 20km away in the shadow of the beech forest of Elm. The one monument worth seeing here is the former **Abtei**, set at the opposite end of town from the Bahnhof. Founded by Emperor Lothar III in 1135, its earliest and finest parts were built by Romanesque masons from Lombardy. The small-scale and infinitely varied sculpture is an outstanding illustration of the thoughts and obsessions of the medieval

---

THE PEOPLE'S CAR

The impetus behind the setting-up of the **Volkswagen** company (which was initially state-owned) came directly from Hitler, who wanted a small, reliable car that anyone could afford to buy and run. It was Ferdinand Porsche – a name indelibly associated with vehicles aimed at the very opposite end of the market – who in 1936 provided the design for the distinctive little machine whose hallmarks were its sloping bonnet and its starting crank, and which popularly came to be known as the Beetle. Two years later, the factory was built; it was destroyed during the war, whereupon the story might well have ended.

In the event, Volkswagen became a fairy-tale postwar success, and one of the linchpins of West Germany's "economic miracle". The Beetle's cheapness and durability made it a huge export hit, and up to 20 million models were produced in a year. In 1961, 1.5 million small shareholders were given the chance to share in the profits when the government sold off its majority holding. However, the company ran into serious difficulties in the 1970s: no attempt had been made at diversification, and sales of the Beetle plummeted as increased general affluence led to a demand for more luxurious cars. To halt the decline, the drastic decision was taken to scrap the old faithful altogether (though it's still made under licence in Mexico), and to develop a new range of models, based on the more upmarket but still modest Golf. It was also decided to make extensive use of robots in the construction process. Finally, the CDU government, normally far less infatuated with privatization programmes than its Conservative counterpart in Britain, disposed of all its remaining shares in 1988. These measures have by and large been successful, even if the Midas-touch formula of the past is now accepted as having been lost for ever.

---

mind. It can be seen on the exterior of the apse, adorned with grotesque human masks, imaginary beasts and hunting scenes, and on the north doorway, whose twisted columns are guarded by menacing lions. It's also present in the north walk of the cloister, each of whose columns is of a different shape and design from any other. The interior of the church is covered with frescoes – an over-enthusiastic nineteenth-century attempt, admittedly using some rather ghostly traces as a starting point, to re-create the original appearance.

Wolfsburg

WOLFSBURG, 30km further north, is an archetypal company town. As late as the 1930s, it was a hamlet of 150 souls; nowadays 130,000 people live here, almost exactly half of them employees of the giant *Volkswagenwerk* (see box above). **Guided tours** of the factory are offered every weekday afternoon, generally at 1.30pm, but it's best to phone ahead first (☎05361/924270). The **Automuseum** (daily 10am–5pm; DM7.50), east of the Hauptbahnhof on the opposite side of the tracks at Dieselstrasse 35, displays around 90 different models produced in the course of the works' history, with examples by other German car makers. Other than this, the town boasts significant examples of modern architecture. Right in the heart of town is the **Kulturzentrum** by the internationally acclaimed Finnish architect Alvar Aalto. The adjacent **Kunstmuseum** (Tues 11am–8pm, Wed–Sun 11am–6pm; DM7) hosts permanent and temporary displays of modern art. Just to the southwest is the **Theater Wolfsburg**, a late work by one of Germany's leading twentieth-century designers, Hans Scharoun. About 1km south on Röntgenstrasse is Aalto's **Heilig-Geist-Kirche**.

SOUTHERN LOWER SAXONY

South of Wolfenbüttel, Lower Saxony's landscape soon makes a significant change to the gentle wooded slopes of the **Harz** mountain range. This was long a famous mining area, thanks to rich deposits of gold, silver and other less precious minerals, but these have, in the present century, become exhausted. At the edge of the mountains, the old imperial city of **Goslar** is the area's main draw, a place as evocative of medieval Germany as any you'll find. Nothing else within the Lower Saxon section of the Harz is of comparable quality, but just beyond the range are a number of impressive old half-timbered towns, such as **Einbeck**, the home of *Bockbier*, **Duderstadt** and **Hann. Münden**. As a complete contrast to these, there's the university city of **Göttingen**, which boasts the most exciting atmosphere of any town between Hannover and Frankfurt.

Goslar

The stereotype of a mining town immediately conjures up images of rows of grim identikit terraced houses paying obeisance to the gargantuan, satanic-looking machinery in whose shadow they lie. **GOSLAR**, which stands in an imposing location at the northern edge of the Harz, could not be more different. Admittedly, the mining here was always of a very superior nature – silver was discovered in the nearby six-hundred-metre-high **Rammelsberg** in the tenth century, and the town immediately prospered, soon becoming the "treasure chest of the Holy Roman Empire", and a favourite royal seat. As a Free Imperial City in the later Middle Ages, Goslar, though never very large, ranked as one of the most prosperous communities in Europe, with lead and zinc now added to the list of ready-to-hand mineral deposits. Despite two fires sweeping through the streets in 1800, much survives as a reminder of this heady epoch. The presence of a POW hospital during World War II spared it from Allied bombing, ensuring that the entire town now enjoys the status of a protected monument. With just cause too, as Goslar claims to have more **old houses** (over 1500, with 168 dating from before 1550) than any other town in Germany.

> The **telephone code** for Goslar is ☎05321

Arrival, information and accommodation

Goslar's **Bahnhof** and **bus station** are at the northern edge of the Altstadt, just across from the Neuwerkkirche. It's only about ten minutes' walk to Marktplatz, where you'll find the municipal **tourist office** at no. 7 (May–Oct Mon–Fri 9am–6pm, Sat 9.30am–5pm; Nov–April Mon–Fri 9am–5pm, Sat 9.30am–2pm; ☎28546).

Accommodation
There are more than two dozen **private houses** (①–④) with rooms to rent; a full list is available from the tourist office. If travelling in a group and intending to stay for at least three days, it can be an even better deal to rent a holiday home; most atmospheric are the luxury apartments in the *Burg Zwinger*, Thomasstr. 2 (☎41088 or 85135; ③). The **youth hostel**, Rammelsberger Str. 25 (☎22240; 🏠), is at the foot of the mine, not too far from the centre, but a long trek from the Bahnhof. Nearest **camping** is the well-equipped *Sennhütte*, Clausthaler Str. 28 (☎22502), in the Gose valley, along the B241 in the direction of Clausthal-Zellerfeld. Goslar is amply endowed with **hotels** and **guesthouses**, many of them in historic buildings.

HOTELS AND GUESTHOUSES

Der Achtermann, Rosentorstr. 20 (☎21002, fax 42748). Goslar's most prestigious hotel, diagonally opposite the Bahnhof, is a huge rambling complex of various dates, with thermal and steam baths, sauna, solarium and romantic old-style restaurant. ⑧

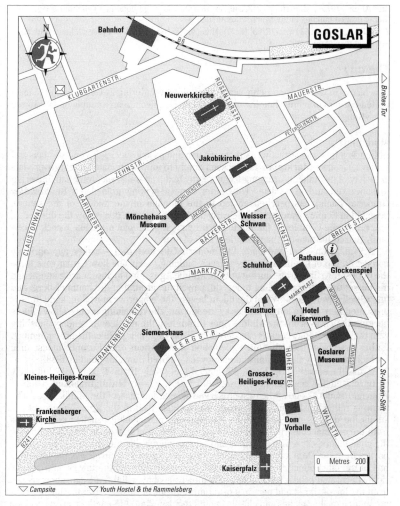

Map key labels: N, Bahnhof, B6, **GOSLAR**, KLUBGARTENSTR., Breites Tor, MAUERSTR., ROSENTORSTR., Neuwerkkirche, PETERSILIENSTR., Jakobikirche, ZEHNSTR., BÄRINGERSTR., SCHILDERSTR., JAKOBISTR., Mönchehaus Museum, Weisser Schwan, HOXENSTR., BREITE STR., CLAUSTORWALL, BÄCKERSTR., MÜNZSTR., MARKTSTR., Schuhhof, Rathaus, MARKTSTR., Glockenspiel, MARKTPLATZ, Brusttuch, Hotel Kaiserworth, WORTHSTR., FRANKENBERGER STR., Siemenshaus, BERGSTR., Goslarer Museum, KÖNIGSTR., St-Annen-Stift, Kleines-Heiliges-Kreuz, HOHER WEG, Grosses-Heiliges-Kreuz, Frankenberger Kirche, B241, Dom Vorhalle, WALLSTR., 0 Metres 200, Kaiserpfalz, ▽ Campsite, ▽ Youth Hostel & the Rammelsberg

Das Brusttuch, Hoher Weg 1 (☎22546). *Treff* chain hotel in a famous sixteenth-century patrician mansion with salacious carvings on its facade. Restaurant, *Weinstube* and large breakfast buffets. ⑦

Goldene Krone, Breite Str. 46 (☎34490, fax 344950). Very highly regarded hotel with restaurant in a half-timbered house at the northeastern end of the Altstadt. ④

Kaiserworth, Markt 3 (☎21111, fax 21114). Another of Goslar's best-known buildings, a 500-year-old guildhall with a 1000-year-old cistern, through which you pass to reach the bar, the *Dukatenkeller*. Also has a wine bar, gourmet restaurant and pavement café. ⑦

Möller, Schieferweg 6 (☎23098) One of the best bargains in Goslar, this guesthouse is in a large Jugendstil villa few minutes' walk west of the Bahnhof. The buffet breakfasts, with lots of home-made goodies, are remarkable. ③

Verhoeven, Hoher Weg 12 (☎23812, fax 46653). Guesthouse with café in a slate and half-timbered house overlooking the Kaiserpfalz. ③

Zur Alten Münze, Münzstr. 10 (☎22546, fax 18416). Mid-range hotel in a delightful 500-year-old timber-framed building in the heart of the Altstadt. ⑤
Zur Börse, Bergstr. 53 (☎22775, fax 18437). Hotel and restaurant in a 400-year-old house with characteristic rosette decorations. ④

The city

Few places in Germany so richly reward unguided wandering as Goslar, with the least visited corners often rivalling the obvious set pieces. Reckon on a couple of days to see everything.

Marktplatz

Although it hosts an attractive market with fish and pastry specialities on Tuesdays and Fridays, Goslar's **Marktplatz** is best seen empty to fully appreciate the gorgeous visual variety of its buildings, ranging from creamy-textured walls, via pretty half-timbering to sober red and grey slate. The rather comical-looking gold-plated **Reichsadler** (Imperial Eagle) sits perched on top of the fountain in the middle of the square. Sculpted in Romanesque style in the early thirteenth century, this is now the third copy, but, remaining completely faithful to the original, it still looks more like a cock uncertainly poised for take-off than a fearless bird of prey.

At 9am, noon, 3pm and 6pm, the modern **Glockenspiel** – rather appropriately housed on top of the municipal treasurer's building – explains how Goslar rose to be the richest town in Europe during the late Middle Ages. First to appear are a knight and his horse; the latter, according to legend, pawed the ground of the Rammelsberg, and uncovered silver traces. When the boom began, the emperors moved in, and Otto III is presented here with a lump of silver by the knight. The remaining groups show miners hacking their way from the Middle Ages through to the nineteenth century, finishing with their present-day counterparts proudly displaying their state-of-the-art equipment. Rather a sad twist, then, that due to depletion of the various ores, Europe's oldest mine – which had nearly three thousand employees – closed down for good in 1988.

Across the square is the **Rathaus** (guided tours daily 10am–4/5pm; DM3, but likely to be closed for restoration at least until 1999), whose **Huldigungssaal** (Hall of Homage) ranks as one of the best-preserved secular interiors of the Middle Ages. The name is rather misleading, as homage was actually paid in the great hall where the admission desk is now situated. Its gold-starred, marine-blue panelled ceiling dates from the original construction of the building in the latter half of the fifteenth century; the chandeliers, carved from antlers and carrying figures of the emperors, were transported from the Dom a few decades later. The Huldigungssaal itself was the assembly hall of the city council from 1500 onwards and later used for the town's archives. Its richly decorated panels, painted by an unknown artist over 400 years ago, show scenes from the life of Christ and portraits of various citizens of Goslar. Several valuable relics are hidden in altar niches and closets behind the panelling. Among them are a precious gold and silver tankard from the fifteenth century, elaborately embellished with mining and hunting scenes, and a facsimile of the **Goslarer Evangeliar** (Goslar Evangelistary), a thirteenth-century manuscript with exquisite Byzantine-inspired Romanesque miniature paintings. The **original Reichsadler** is also on view.

Opposite is the **Hotel Kaiserworth**, previously the guild house of tailors and clothmakers. Here Baroque and Gothic tumble down on top of Renaissance arches, while the frontage bears eight statues of German emperors, with a corbel depicting a naked man excreting a gold coin thrown in for good measure. Just behind the Rathaus is the **Marktkirche**, dedicated to the Roman martyrs SS Cosmas and Damian, patrons of the medical profession. The architecture, a mix of Romanesque and Gothic, with twin towers and rough-hewn masonry, is typical of Goslar. Inside, look out for the cycle of stained-glass windows illustrating the saints' lives, and the bronze baptismal **font** created by a local artist, Magnus Karsten, in 1573: just about every major biblical event is represented on it in magnificent detail.

The southwestern quarters

Goslar's **half-timbered** beauty begins in earnest in the streets behind the Marktkirche. The styles to look out for are Gothic, Renaissance and Baroque, many homes having two and sometimes all of these: Gothic pointed arches are transformed into three-stepped inlays, usually dull red, gold and olive green in colour; sombrely brilliant rosettes cartwheel across the rafters of the Renaissance houses, while gaudily coloured Baroque devils lie like flattened gargoyles bereft of their power in their prisons of beam.

The oldest houses lie in the Bergstrasse and Schreiberstrasse areas; the **Siemenshaus** (Tues & Thurs 9am–noon; free), which was built by a forefather of what is today one of Germany's largest suppliers of medical equipment, electrical appliances and armaments parts, is conveniently situated on the corner of both. Further down Schreiberstrasse, classic Gothic brick houses abound, the style exemplified by the early sixteenth century embodied at no. 10, with its lavishly decorated chimney passing through the two single-roomed storeys. From here, turn left into Frankenberger Strasse and continue down to Frankenberg Plan, on which stands the **Kleines-Heiliges-Kreuz**, set in spacious gardens where the old folk who retire there – and dozens of chickens – can amble about at their leisure.

Through the archway to the right, you can walk up to the **Frankenberger Kirche**, once the church favoured by miners for their weddings, which is situated in tranquil solitude on the little hill above. Built during the twelfth century as a Romanesque basilica, the later Gothic additions form part of the town's western ramparts. The gigantic Baroque carved wooden passion altar verges on pastiche and could easily dominate the place until you begin to take in a few other details. Towards the back of the church, two fierce lions stand facing each other to absorb the evil believed to have come from the west. Some faint thirteenth-century frescoes compete in vain for attention against an over-charged Baroque pulpit, and there's a strange *Triumphal Cross*, with a deathly-white Christ macabrely topped with a wig of the artist's own hair, a device used frequently in the Harz area.

On Peterstrasse immediately to the east are some of the most intriguing of the town's houses: the **Kuhhaus** (Cow House) at no. 27 is named after its previous function, while the **Kürbishaus** (Pumpkin House) at no. 23 is named after its shape. In the **Klauskapelle** to the right and the **Schmiedhaus** (Blacksmith's House) opposite, the miners would respectively pray and collect their sharpened tools before beginning their daily trek up to the Rammelsberg.

The Kaiserpfalz

Dominating a spacious park at the southern end of the Altstadt is the **Kaiserpfalz** (guided tours daily 10am–4/5pm; DM3.50). By far the largest and most important Romanesque royal palace to have survived anywhere in Europe, its exterior is still a potent symbol of the power and wealth enjoyed by Germany's medieval rulers. Built at the beginning of the eleventh century to be home to a succession of greedy emperors enticed by the riches hidden in the Rammelsberg behind it, the Kaiserpfalz continued to flourish for nearly 300 years, hosting important Imperial Diets and benefiting from Goslar's proximity to the crossroads of the two major trade routes of the Middle Ages – from Flanders to Magdeburg, and from Lübeck to Venice. A fire which gutted the palace in 1289 and a decline of interest around the same time by the emperors kept the building in a state of disrepair over the next few centuries, humbling it even to the point where it was used as a barn and stables during the seventeenth century. Kaiser Wilhelm I came to the rescue in 1868, paying for its reconstruction.

By present-day standards, the building seems over-restored. This is particularly true of the interior, where the vast **Reichsaal**, whose enormous arched window openings must have given birth to many a draughty Diet during the palace's heyday, was covered, floor to ceiling, with Romantic paintings. Various emperors are depicted being valiant (in battle), pious (distributing riches to the poor), conquering the earth and being blessed by heaven. On the southern side of the hall is the early twelfth-century **Ulrichskapelle**. This chapel, the most authentic part of the complex, is an ingenious piece of design: the ground plan is a Greek cross, but the upper storeys are shaped as a Byzantine-style octagon. In the centre stands the tomb of Emperor Heinrich III, though it contains only his heart: the rest of his body lies in Speyer.

Behind the palace, the *Goslar Warrior* by Henry Moore lies reclining with his shield on his toe; this is a legacy of the first of the annual prizes awarded by the city to a famous modern artist. Beyond it a pretty semi-walled rose garden, dotted about with firs and shady spreading trees, leads down to a small bridge, the Abzucht stream, and a stone-walled tower.

Hoher Weg

On the opposite side of the Kaiserpfalz, facing the Hoher Weg, the enormous car park stretching below you was once the site of the eleventh-century **Dom** – more accurately, the **Stiftskirche St Simeon und Judas** –pulled down in 1822 due to lack of funds for restoration. Only the **Vorhalle** with its facade of stucco statues survived. Behind the protective glass door is the original part-bronze **imperial throne**; it was used symbolically at the opening assembly of the Second Reich in Berlin in 1871. Other relics from the church are housed in the Goslarer Museum (see opposite). The Dom's stones are now embedded in any number of houses, having been sold at the time of demolition to townsfolk who subsequently built their homes with them.

Directly in front of the Dom, Hoher Weg leads down to the **Grosses-Heiliges-Kreuz** (daily 11am–4/5pm; free) at no. 7, one of the oldest hospices in Germany, dating back to 1254. It has recently been beautifully restored, and has been given a new lease of life as a handicrafts centre. The magnificent main hall hosts several markets a year, and several small shops have been set up in the ground-floor cells. Further down the street is the **Musikinstrumente- und Puppenmuseum** (daily 11am–5pm; DM4). On the first floor, an eclectic array of musical instruments from around the world features such oddities as a combined violin and trumpet, a cello with a keyboard, and a sub-contrabass lute. What is thought to be the oldest musical instrument in Germany, a recently unearthed hurdy-gurdy from around 1500, is also on view. The second floor has a collection of rare old dolls.

Goslar's most famous mansion, the sixteenth-century **Brusttuch**, lies at the bottom of Hoher Weg, almost opposite the Marktkirche. It's an outstanding example of the "Wild Man" style, whose theme of "natural" unbridled sexuality was a great favourite with German Renaissance artists and craftsmen. The beams of the top storey are crammed with satirical carvings of figures from medieval life, folklore, religion and mythology: mischievous cherubs firing arrows at angels, dignified ladies perched on top of goats, and a carelessly suggestive dairymaid churning the butter and squeezing her buttocks at the same time. Facing it across Marktstrasse is the **Bäckergildehaus** (Bakers' Guild House), a far more sober, yet equally imposing example of half-timbering.

The northern quarters

Immediately north of the Marktkirche is the **Schuhhof**, the site of the former shoemakers' guildhall and market. Fires over the centuries have ravaged one part of the square, but the surviving side has three- and four-storey half-timbered houses from the seventeenth century. Münzstrasse on its western side contains more architectural beauties, including a seventeenth-century coaching inn, the **Weisser Schwan** at no. 11, where the **Zinnfigurenmuseum** (Tin Figure Museum; daily 10am–5pm; DM4) depicts in miniature scenes from the history of Goslar and the Roman Empire.

At the end of the street, turn into Jakobistrasse, where, at no. 15, a Renaissance craftsman's house has been the subject of one of the most polished and professional pieces of restoration in Goslar. The **Mönchehaus Museum** (Tues–Sat 10am–1pm & 3–5pm, Sun 10am–1pm; free) lies just beyond, at the corner with Mönchestrasse. A black and white half-timbered sixteenth-century building, it's the curious home to Goslar's permanent modern art exhibition, featuring works by recipients of the city's annual prize. The contrast works amazingly well indoors, with de Koonings, Tinguelys and Vasarelys hanging amidst the oak beams. The effectiveness of the huge metal sculptures parked in the garden is more debatable, but it's good to see something in Goslar with an experimental touch.

On the square at the eastern end of Jakobistrasse is the Catholic parish church, the **Jakobikirche**. Only the west wing remains from the original Romanesque structure, which was rebuilt in Gothic style. Inside, there's a moving *Pietà* by the great but elusive early sixteenth-century sculptor, Hans Witten. North along Rosentorstrasse, the **Neuwerkkirche** (Mon–Fri 9.30–11.30am & 2.30–4.30pm, Sat 9.30am–11.30am) stands in a peaceful garden. It was built as a Cistercian convent church during the late twelfth and early thirteenth centuries; the most striking exterior features are the two polygonal towers, and the delicate late Romanesque carvings on the apse. Inside, there are works of art dating back to the period of construction, notably the choir screen and some rather clumsily retouched frescoes. The curious stone **handles** high up on the pillars of the nave are unique in the history of architecture and have a didactic purpose: those on the south have grotesque carvings and represent the temptations of the devil; the wreaths on the north symbolize the eternity for which the soul should strive.

The Abzucht and the Stadtbefestigung

From Marktplatz, south along Worthstrasse, a fairly successful attempt at an artists' quarter has been constructed along and around the banks of the **Abzucht**, the tiny stream that passes through the southern part of Goslar. On the corner of Abzuchtstrasse and Königstrasse is the **Goslarer Museum** (Tues–Sun 10am–4/5pm; DM3.50). This contains the usual local history displays, including a section on mining in the Rammelsberg. However, the collection is taken out of the ordinary by some superb treasures from the Dom, including a couple of stained-glass windows and the exotic *Krodoaltar* – which looks more as if it were fashioned deep in the heart of Africa than in eleventh-century Europe. The original **Goslarer Evangeliar** is also on view, though only the cover can be seen. Another highlight is the seventeenth-century laboratory of the **Ratsapotheke**.

The Abzucht bubbles along the cobbles to occasionally bump into one of the handful of rickety water mills still remaining of an original twenty-five; follow the red stones in the middle of the pathways to find the sites of the former mills, now replaced by houses. Look out for the **St-Annen-Stift** (Mon–Thurs 10am–noon & 3–5pm, Fri & Sat 10am–noon; knock at the door for entrance; free), a hospice dating from 1488, the oldest half-timbered building in Goslar. Inside, you can view the chapel with its medieval woodwork and seventeenth-century wall paintings.

From here, it's a short walk down St Annenhöhe to see the best-preserved parts of the **Stadtbefestigung**. It takes about two hours to walk the complete circuit, which is interspersed with many stretches of greenery. If pressed for time, go down Zingerwall to see the **Zwinger** (daily March 10am–4pm; April–Nov 15 10am–5pm; DM3), an ivy-covered, thick-walled tower once used by the town's artillery. It commands a fine view over Goslar and the Harz; there's also a display of medieval weapons and a restaurant. The most imposing part of the town's fortifications is the bulky ensemble of the **Breites Tor** at the northeasternmost corner, the sight of which alone must have been enough to scare off any would-be invaders.

The Rammelsberg

Of the various walks in the vicinity of Goslar, the most interesting is the geological trail round the **Rammelsberg** (ask at the tourist office for a leaflet). A more pressing reason for visiting the mountain which provided the city with its wealth is that a **Bergbaumuseum** (guided tours daily 9am–6pm; combined ticket DM12; take bus #C from the centre) has been set up in the famous mine. The visit begins in the hall-like changing room, now used as an exhibition explaining the historical background. Here you don a miner's overalls and helmet before descending into the bowels of the earth. Two separate tours, each lasting about an hour, are available. The first (individual tickets DM6) is a walk through the tunnels to see some of the old machinery, including the giant water wheels; the other (individual ticket DM9) is a ride on the underground railway to the part of the mine that was the last to be exploited.

Eating and drinking

Goslar's food and drink scene is geared to the fact that many of the town's visitors are taking a relaxing holiday – hence the presence of so many cafés. Many of the best restaurants are in the hotels (see pp.632–634).

Barock-Café Anders, Hoher Weg 4. Best place in town for *Kaffee und Kuchen*; there's a Baroque room upstairs and a garden at the back with a leafy vista of the Harz.

Bistro Filou, Worthstr. 10. Offers creative Gallic-style cooking.

Brauhaus Wolpertinger, Marstallstr. 1. This *Hausbrauerei*, serving one dark and two light beers, has revived Goslar's medieval brewing tradition after a long gap. It's one of several bars grouped round a courtyard which have collectively become the liveliest spot in town.

Butterhanne, Marktkirchhof 3. Located in a sixteenth-century hatmaker's shop, this café-restaurant specializes in home-made cakes and dishes using fresh game from the Harz.

Christall, Bäckerstr. 106. The long menu here features plenty of inventive vegetarian dishes.

Digeridoo, Hoher Weg 13. Australian theme bar and restaurant serving kangaroo steaks and *Foster*'s lager. Hugely popular with the locals.

Historisches Café, Markt 4. Another good choice for those with a sweet tooth, particularly when the weather is good and you can sit outside on the square.

Pupasch, Schilderstr. 4. Characterful old pub in a half-timbered building across from the Jakobikirche; claims to serve the best *Schmalzbrot* in the world.

Weisser Schwan, Münzstr. 11. Part of this famous old inn is given over to a Balkan grill-house that's a cut above the German norm.

Worthmühle, Worthstr. 4. Does excellent hot provincial cooking at very low prices.

The Harz mountains

Nowhere, other than in Berlin itself, was the reality of the postwar division of Germany more evident than in the **Harz** mountains (see map on p.839), the first barrier encountered by the icy winds which sweep across the North German Plain. A popular holiday destination since the nineteenth century, the Harz were divided right through the middle by the notorious barbed-wire frontier. Most roads came to a dead end, and adjacent villages were completely cut off from each other, often to the ruin of local economies. Despite the many changes which have occurred since the re-unification, the differences between the two sides of the Harz remain a vivid illustration of the effects of four decades of national division. For one thing, many of the towns on the Lower Saxon side were converted into modern resorts which are characterless in comparison with their eastern counterparts. For another, the mountain steam rail lines which are still such an attraction in the former GDR were closed down here and replaced by buses: the only trains left are those running along the northern and western fringes of the range.

The range has a climate which is euphemistically described as "bracing". Although this means that there's lots of rain and fog, with heavy snowfall in winter, it doesn't deter hordes of mainly elderly holidaymakers who have earned the region the derisive sobriquet *Rentnergebirge* (pensioners' mountains). Perhaps they're drawn by the relatively gentle slopes of the mountains ("the skiing here is for babies," according to another insult) which make the Harz ideal for healthy but undemanding **walking** holidays.

Clausthal-Zellerfeld

The most direct route into the Harz from Goslar will take you to **CLAUSTHAL-ZELLERFELD**, some 20km to the southwest. If you're driving, it's best to take time to admire the scenery: the direct B241 road winds and climbs its way through dense forest flanked by a number of small, hidden lakes. Buses tend to follow a more circuitous route via Hahnenklee, a big winter-sports resort built round a Scandinavian-style stave church from the first decade of the present century.

Two old towns merged into one, Clausthal-Zellerfeld is a characterful place where half-timbered houses are interspersed with those faced with coloured slate. It was the main mining centre of the Upper Harz, but the last pit shut down in 1931. The tradition is exhaustively documented in the excellent **Oberharzer Bergwerksmuseum** (daily 9am–5pm; DM6) at Bornhardtstr. 16 in Zellerfeld, the northern part of the double town. Included in the entrance fee is a tour through the life-sized model of a pit which has been erected in the garden; make sure you ask for the English-speaking guide, as the language used is very technical. You can wander at your leisure round the other mining buildings, which have been moved here from their original locations. Star piece is the *Pferdegaipel*, a shaft which was worked by horses and is the only one of its kind in Germany.

Clausthal clusters around the **Marktkirche**, the largest wooden church in central Europe. Built in the first half of the seventeenth century, its main body is of fir, while the tower is made of oak. Inside are notable furnishings, of which many, including the double gallery, the retable and pulpit, are also fashioned from wood. Across the street is the **Technische Universität**, Germany's most unlikely university, which grew out of the mining academy established here in the eighteenth century. Its **Mineraliensammlung** (Mon 2–5pm, Tues–Fri 9am–noon; free) is reckoned to be one of the largest and best collections of minerals in the world.

Practicalities

The **tourist office** is in the old train station building in the gulley between the towns at Bahnhofstr. 5a (Mon–Fri 9am–noon & 2–5pm, Sat 9am–noon; ☎05323/81024). Should you wish to linger they'll organize accommodation and, in winter, ski and sledge rental.

There are plenty of **private houses** with rooms to let (①–③). Hotels to try include *Kronprinz*, Goslarsche Str. 20 (☎05323/81088; ③), and *Lilienbrunner*, Markstr. 13 (☎05323/83523; ④), both in Zellerfeld. A generally wider choice in Clausthal ranges from *Pension Schindler*, An der Tillyschurze 18 (☎05323/1031; ②), to *Goldene Krone*, Am Kronenplatz 3 (☎05323/9300; ⑥), which also has the best restaurant.

The **youth hostel** is at the extreme eastern end of Clausthal at Altenauer Str. 55 (☎05323/2293; 🛏). One of the **campsites** is south of here at Lange Brüche 4 (☎05323/1300); another is at the northwestern fringe of Zellerfeld at Spiegeltaler Str. 31 (☎05323/81712).

The *Gaststätte* of the Bergwerksmuseum, which features game specialities, is an excellent place **to eat**, while the best **bar** is *Anno Tobak*, a student favourite at Osteroder Str. 4, diagonally opposite the Marktkirche.

Along the former border

The old border between East and West Germany has lost its barbed wire, and with it much of its fascination, but it remains well worth a visit for the scenery. The transport hub for the area is the plush spa of **BAD HARZBURG**, which has rail links to both Goslar (which is only 10min away) and Braunschweig. It also has plenty of accommodation to suit all pockets, from **private rooms** (①–③) to fine **hotels** such as *Parkblick*, Am Stadtpark 6 (☎05322/788499; ⑦); *Germania*, Berliner Platz 2 (☎05322/9500; ⑦) and *Braunschweiger Hof*, Herzog-Wilhelm-Str. 54 (☎05322/7880; ⑦).

The fifteen-kilometre hiking trail from Bad Harzburg to the crossroads hamlet of **TORFHAUS** used to be one of the most prized Cold War thrills, passing as it did right alongside the Iron Curtain. Even now, it has an eerie fascination, at least as long as the ghostly watchtowers remain as a blight on the landscape. Torfhaus, which can also be reached by bus, offers the best views of the celebrated **Brocken** (see p.855), rendezvous of the witches on *Walpurgisnacht* (April 30), a festival celebrated in all the towns in the Harz. The path from here was re-opened soon after the Berlin Wall came down, and makes an enticing alternative to the easier approach from Schierke. If you want to do some serious hiking in the area, Torfhaus' **youth hostel** (☎05320/242; ⓐ) makes an obvious base. A further 5km south, there's another crossroads at the **Oder-Teich**, an artificial lake made in the eighteenth century, where you can take a swim.

The western fringe

Along the western fringe of the Harz are a number of small historic towns – the most worthwhile being **Walkenried** and **Herzberg**. Each has at least one set-piece attraction to add to their proximity to the outstanding scenery.

Walkenried

WALKENRIED, at the extreme southwestern corner of the Harz, used to be another dead end, but was fortunate enough to have its rail link to Nordhausen in Thuringia restored even before German re-unification was formally achieved. This little health resort, arguably the most attractive on the western side of the Harz, has one of the area's few notable historic monuments – a Cistercian **Kloster** which was once among the most powerful in Germany. Built in the early thirteenth century in the Transitional style favoured by this order, the church is ruinous, though impressive fragments of the facade and one of the transepts remain to give an idea of its former grandeur. **Guided tours** (Easter–Sept Mon–Sat 10am–noon & 2–5pm, Sun noon–5pm; rest of year Sat & Sun only at 2pm & 3pm; DM3) are run round the monastic buildings, which have recently been restored to their original form. Highlights are the graceful north walk of the cloister, idiosyncratically divided into two aisles, and the former chapter house, now fitted out as the Protestant parish church.

The village is chock-a-block with **pensions** and private houses with **rooms** to let (①–②); a full list is available from the *Kurverwaltung*, Steinweg 4 (☎05525/357). There's also a **campsite** (☎05525/778) at the eastern fringe.

Herzberg

About 20km northwest via the rail line skirting the Harz is **HERZBERG**, one of the few places in the Harz not wholly given over to tourism – a fact reflected in the higher than normal accommodation prices. Overlooking the town is the **Welfenschloss** (April–Oct Tues–Fri 10am–1pm & 2–5pm, Sat & Sun 9.45am–1pm & 2–6pm; Nov–March Tues–Fri 11am–1pm & 2–4pm, Sat & Sun 11am–1pm & 2–5pm; DM2), a half-timbered seventeenth-century castle built in the "Wild Man" style seen in Goslar; inside is one of the tin-figure museums so beloved of the Germans. A lake in the town centre helps give the place a distinctive atmosphere.

Einbeck

EINBECK, which lies just to the west of the Harz, is something of a mecca for **beer** lovers, being the original home and the most authentic producer of Germany's famous strong brew, *Bockbier*. The town is almost equally well known for its half-timbered houses, characteristically painted in yellow, red, green and black – around 120 survive from the sixteenth century alone.

The town

The hub of life in Einbeck is the **Marktplatz**, which is surrounded by well-kept and obviously genuine sixteenth-century houses. Look out for the **Brodhaus** and the **Ratsapotheke,** which stand next door to each other like two superannuated old men opposite the **Ratswaage** (Weigh House) and the vaguely sinister-looking **Rathaus**. The Rathaus could well have served as a model for the witch's house in the Hansel and Gretel story, thanks to three low conical spires which sprout out of the stairwell and the two sharply contrasted oriel windows. Dominating the square from its central position is the **Marktkirche**, a box-like Gothic hall church with a striking red sandstone Baroque facade.

Immediately to the west lies **Tiedexer Strasse**, the most impressive street in town, with a gloriously picturesque ensemble of half-timbered houses. However, the finest house of all is no. 13 in **Marktstrasse**, whose whole facade is covered with intricate allegorical carvings, drawing on Christian and Classical themes. Another handsome street, Steinweg, leads north to another red sandstone Gothic church, the **Stiftskirche St Alexandri** (Mon–Fri 10am–noon). Its set of choir stalls, bearing the date of 1288, is the oldest in Germany, though the main treasure is a magnificent Romanesque chandelier. At Steinweg 11, a fine patrician mansion has been adapted to contain the local history collections of the **Städtisches Museum** (Tues–Fri 10am–noon & 3–5pm, Sat & Sun 10am–noon; DM3). The ticket also gives admission to the **Fahrradmuseum**

BOCKBIER

In the Middle Ages Einbeck boasted no fewer than seven hundred breweries – virtually all of which were tiny part-time operations run within the household. Many of the houses where beer was brewed can still be identified: two clues to look for are double doorways (one of which was used for rolling the barrels through), and dense groupings of dormer-like ventilation openings in the attic, where the raw ingredients were stored. Made from wheat and fermented from the top, what became known as *Einpöckisches Bier* was a strong brew designed for export, with fermentation taking place in the course of the journey to the customer. Its most famous historical appearance came at the Diet of Worms in 1521 when Luther used it to fortify himself during his heroic stand against the full might of the Empire and the papacy. In time, the drink became known as *Bockbier* (after a corruption of the town's name); it was introduced into the Hofbräuhaus in Munich, and has long been as popular in Bavaria as in Lower Saxony. Two crucial differences between the modern and old version are that it's now made from barley, and fermented from the bottom. Nowadays, the *Einbecker-Brauerei* is the only brewery left in the home town of this headily potent beer. It produces both light (*Hell*) and dark (*Dunkel*) varieties, as well as the special brown *Maibock*, available only in springtime. All of these have a smooth, dry and highly satisfying flavour. Curiously enough, locals tend to prefer its other, more conventional products: a *Brauherren-Pils* and a *Spezial*.

(same times), a short walk south of Marktplatz at Pupenstr. 1–3, a collection of bikes which has everything from the wooden-wheeled boneshakers of 1817 to the very latest racers. It's also worth taking a walk round the surviving sections of the **Stadtmauer**; much of the fortification network is intact and you can stroll along the massive earthworks which were constructed to increase the protection afforded by the wall itself.

Practicalities

Einbeck's **Bahnhof** is 4km from the centre in the castle-crowned village of Salzderhelden. **Buses** have replaced the former branch rail line into the town, but beware that these do not necessarily connect with the arrival and departure of trains. The **tourist office** is in the Rathaus (April–Sept Mon–Fri 9am–5.30pm, Sat 10am–1pm; Oct–March Mon–Thurs 9am–1pm & 2.30–5pm, Fri 9am–12.30pm; ☎05561/916121), Marktplatz 6–8.

Of the **hotels** with a central location, the most reasonably priced are *Zur Stadt Einbeck*, Benser Str. 27 (☎05561/4086; ④) and *Haus Joanna*, Bürgermeisterwall 8 (☎05561/93350; ④). For a bit more luxury, try *Der Schwann*, Tiedexer Str. 1 (☎05561/4609; ⑤), or *Gildehof*, Marktplatz 3 (☎05561/5026; ⑤). These also have the best **restaurants** in town – the former is the more expensive and is open evenings only – and are good places to sample the local beers. A good alternative in a wonderful fourteenth-century building is *Zum Brodhaus*, Marktplatz 13. There are also several elegant **cafés**, including the exquisitely furnished *Antik Café*, Tiedexer Str. 42–44.

Göttingen

GÖTTINGEN is positively metropolitan in contrast to the surrounding area. It owes its exciting, buzzing atmosphere to its large student population (30,000 out of a total populace of 130,000), who have made sure that the **nightlife** here almost has a big-city feel to it. In fact, a lot of students come to Göttingen after studying in Berlin, and they seem to have brought some of the latter's pace with them. Students here flirted briefly with the spirit of '68 but today they're more interested in patronizing the town's *Musikkneipen* and jazz clubs by night while studying for well-paid, secure careers during the day. Things quieten down a little outside term time – but there's usually something going on.

Arrival, information and accommodation

Göttingen's **Hauptbahnhof**, a major rail junction, lies just to the west of the centre, which is reached by going straight ahead via the underpass, then along Goetheallee. The main **tourist office** (April–Oct Mon–Fri 9.30am–6pm, Sat & Sun 10am–4pm; Nov–March Mon–Fri 9.30am–1pm & 2–6pm, Sat 10am–1pm; ☎54000) is on the first floor of the Altes Rathaus. There's another opposite the Hauptbahnhof at Berliner Str. 11 (Mon–Fri 10am–1pm & 2–5pm, Sat 10am–1pm; ☎56000). **Mitfahrzentrale**'s office is at Friedrichstr. 1 (☎0581/485988).

Accommodation

The **youth hostel** is 3km east of the centre at Habichtsweg 2 (☎57622; 🛏); take bus #18. Göttingen's centrally sited **hotels** tend to be on the pricey side, but there are plenty of bargains a bit further out.

The **telephone code** for Göttingen is ☎0551

Berliner Hof, Weender Landstr. 43 (☎383320, fax 383 3232). Moderately priced hotel, handily placed for the university. ④

Central, Jüdenstr. 12 (☎57157, fax 57105). The only hotel in the heart of the Altstadt. ⑤

Gebhards, Goetheallee 22–23 (☎49680, fax 496 8110). Göttingen's best hotel occupies a renovated eighteenth-century palace just across from the Hauptbahnhof on the way to the centre. Also has a fine restaurant. ⑦

Kasseler Hof, Rosdorfer Weg 26 (☎72081, fax 770 3429). Mid-range hotel a short distance south-west of the Altstadt. ⑤

Onkel Toms Hütte, Am Gewende 10–11 (☎72036, fax 770 0034). Very pleasant hotel with restaurant and beer garden in the southern outskirts, reached by bus #5 or #6. ⑤

Stadt Hannover, Goetheallee 21 (☎45957, fax 45470). Good quality hotel right alongside *Gebhards*. ⑥

Zum Schwan, Weender Landstr. 23 (☎383320, fax 383 3232). Small budget hotel close to the university. ③

The town

Most of Göttingen's sights are in the small Altstadt, particularly in and around the Markt. The famous University is spread out all over the town, though its most imposing buildings are found in the eastern part of the Altstadt, and around the green belt encircling the former fortifications.

GÖTTINGEN'S ACADEMIC TRADITION

Göttingen was a decayed market town when King George II of Great Britain, in his capacity as Elector of Hannover, founded the **University** in 1737. A free-thinking, liberal atmosphere was immediately promoted, in sharp contrast to the authoritarian traditions of Germany's other seats of learning. This enabled Göttingen to establish a high reputation very quickly, which it has maintained ever since. In its early days, it was particularly associated with poets, such as the group known as the *Göttinger Hain-Bund*, early Romantics who wrote on folklore, nature and homely themes, and **Gottfried August Bürger**, holder of the chair of aesthetics, whose ballads (especially *Leonore*, with its vivid image of Death) were enormously influential. The University's literary reputation continued in the nineteenth century with the appointment of the **Brothers Grimm** to professorships – while there Jacob wrote an exhaustive study, *Teutonic Mythology*, which was to inspire similar studies of national folklore all over Europe. Unfortunately, this tradition, along with Göttingen's liberal standing, was severely tarnished by the dismissal of the brothers and five colleagues in 1837 for failing to kowtow to the reactionary new constitution introduced into the Kingdom of Hannover.

Mathematics and science have, if anything, been even stronger academic specialities in Göttingen. In the eighteenth century, the leading figure was **Georg Christoph Lichtenberg**, who invented the prototype of the photocopying machine and the hot-air balloon. He was also a dedicated Anglophile and a brilliant satirical writer; his *Book of Aphorisms* (available in *Penguin Classics)* is a storehouse of worldly wisdom, whose clarity and precision puts all subsequent German philosophy to shame. Throughout the first half of the last century, **Carl-Friedrich Gauss** (the face on the DM10 note) dominated the University's intellectual life. His name is given to a unit of the field of magnetic intensity, and, in partnership with Wilhelm Weber, he invented the electromagnetic telegraph. In the next generation, the chemist **Friedrich Wöhler**, best known for his pioneering work with aluminium, preserved the University's position at the forefront of world science. The present century has seen a string of Nobel Prizes awarded to Göttingen professors. Since World War II, the town has been the headquarters of the fifty separate high-powered scientific research units of the **Max-Planck-Institut**, named in honour of the discoverer of quantum theory, who passed his last years here.

The Markt and around

The central Markt is dominated by the **Altes Rathaus**, a massive sandstone structure which has an almost Venetian feel to it, quite at odds with the half-timbered buildings nearby. Most of what you can see today dates back to the fourteenth and fifteenth centuries, when Göttingen was at the height of its commercial prosperity, but it was never completely finished, as resources had to be diverted to constructing the municipal fortifications. The only way of seeing much of the building is by taking a **guided tour** (Sun at 3pm; free). At other times, unless there's an exhibition on, you'll have to be content with viewing the medieval-looking frescoes and coats of arms painted on the inner walls; these are only a little over one hundred years old, having been commissioned by the authorities during the restoration of the building in the 1880s. When the weather is good the *Rathskeller* takes over part of the Markt and you can have a drink or a meal while looking at the **Gänseliesel**, "the most kissed girl in the world", a bronze statue of a goose-girl erected at the beginning of the century, to whom, according to tradition, the students must give a few smackers when they pass their finals.

Behind the Altes Rathaus is the **Johanniskirche** (daily May–Oct 11am–noon), a twin-towered fourteenth-century Gothic church. Theological students are allowed free accommodation in one of the **towers**, but they have to endure the sound of the bells from the other tower and miserable living conditions (no running water or WC), as well as granting admission on Saturdays between 2pm and 4pm to anyone wanting to climb up for a view of the town. Behind the church is the medieval **Johannesviertel**, more or less a slum district until the 1970s, when the city finally got round to tarting it up. At the point where Johanniskirchhof runs into Paulinerstrasse is the former **Paulinerkirche**, originally built by Dominican monks in 1331, which in 1529 was the scene of the first Lutheran church service in Göttingen. Used as the provisional home of the University when it first opened, the building now houses part of its library.

The rest of the town

Following the pedestrianized main street, Weender Strasse, north from the Markt brings you to the **Jakobikirche** (daily May–Oct 11am–1pm), another Gothic church, dominated this time by a single octagonal tower which was designed by an associate of the famous Parler dynasty of masons. From Judenstrasse at the back of the church, turn right into Ritterplan, where the only aristocratic mansion left in the town has been refurbished to house the **Städtisches Museum** (Tues–Fri 10am–5pm, Sat & Sun 10am–1pm; DM3). As you'd expect, this has a Göttingen bias, with a big collection of religious art and plenty of examples of locally produced glass and porcelain.

Finest of all the University buildings is the Neoclassical **Aula** on Wilhelmsplatz, a couple of blocks south of the Städtisches Museum and a similar distance east of the Markt; this graduation hall was built to celebrate the centenary of the University's foundation. Many of the departments have their own museum; unfortunately, these tend to be open only one day a week, or by appointment. One definitely worth trying to catch is the **Völkerkundliche Sammlung**, Theaterplatz 15 (Sun 10am–1pm; DM3), which includes part of the collection assembled by Captain Cook in the South Seas and a bizarre array of four hundred fertility symbols and mother-god effigies.

Anybody who knows anything about German history won't be able to resist the **Bismarckhäuschen** (Tues 10am–1pm, Thurs & Sat 3–5pm; DM1), a small tower on the southern edge of the town centre which forms part of the old city wall. In 1833 this was home to the seventeen-year-old **Otto von Bismarck**, then a student in the city. The man who later became the "Iron Chancellor" and who finally realized, by a mixture of brute force and astute politicking, the long-established ideal of a united Germany, was forced to live here, having been banned from the city centre for drunkenness and "misbehaviour of various kinds".

North along Angerstrasse is the **Marienkirche**, which stands on what used to be the boundary between the Altstadt and the so-called Neustadt, built as a rival town outside the original city walls by a local nobleman in an attempt to challenge the increasingly powerful burghers. The citizens' response to this threat was an astute one. They waited until the nobleman went bankrupt and then bought the Neustadt from him, incorporating it into Göttingen itself. The Marienkirche looks quite unecclesiastical, which probably has something to do with the fact that its bell tower used to be one of the gateways to the Neustadt; the street still passes through an archway cut in it.

Eating, drinking and entertainment

Above all, Göttingen is a city where you can enjoy yourself. There are dozens of cafés, bars and restaurants which, thanks to the large student contingent, tend to be high on atmosphere and low in cost.

Restaurants and historic student taverns

Junkerschänke, Barfüsserstr. 5. One of Göttingen's best restaurants, housed in a beautiful fifteenth-century half-timbered building; rather pricey, but worth it. Closed Mon.

Naturell, Lange-Geismar-Str. 40. Inventive vegetarian and wholefood restaurant (Mon–Fri 10.30am–7pm, Sat 10.30am–3pm).

Pfannkuchenhaus, Speckstr 10. A student favourite with a huge variety of sweet and savoury pancakes.

Rathskeller, Markt 9. Notwithstanding the anachronistic spelling, Göttingen's town hall restaurant is archetypal, with food to rival any in Germany.

Taormina, Groner-Tor-Str. 28. Recommended pizzeria which stays open until 1.30am.

Zum Altdeutschen, Prinzenstr. 16. Göttingen's most famous student tavern, even if these days its clientele seems to be dominated by tourists.

Zum Schwarzen Bären, Kurze Str. 12. Romantic *Gaststätte* dating back to the sixteenth century, complete with stained-glass windows and cosy little alcoves; the food is first class and fairly reasonable in price. Closed Sun evening & Mon.

Zum Szültenbürger, Prinzenstr. 7. Another celebrated student tavern, with basic dishes such as *Schmalzbrot* as an alternative to full meals.

Bars and cafés

Blue Note, Wilhelmsplatz 3. Slightly upmarket jazz/blues bar which seems to be favoured by medical and law students.

Chups, Kornmarkt 9. A chrome decor basement café, which, thanks to its cheap baguettes and live music in an animated atmosphere, is highly popular with undergraduates.

Cron & Lanz, Weender Str. 25. Celebrated traditional café with roof terrace – makes wonderful cakes, chocolate and marzipan.

Kaffeehaus Zindel, Kornmarkt 4. Popular coffee house which spills out onto the square in the summer.

KAZ-Keller, Hospitalstr 6. Trendy pub with beer garden; also does light meals.

Nörgelbuff, Groner Str. 23. Favourite haunt of the more bohemian members of the student community; features occasional live music and theatre.

Teehaus Klunje, Lange-Geismar-Str. 34. Has the best selection of teas in town.

Entertainment

Göttingen's main **cultural** venues are the *Deutsches Theater*, Theaterplatz 11 (☎496911), and the *Stadthalle*, Albaniplatz 2 (☎497 0020), which face each other across Theaterplatz, and the more experimental *Junges Theater*, Hospitalstr. 6 (☎55123). Each June, Göttingen celebrates the music of Handel in the *Händelfest*, one of Europe's best and most adventurous celebrations of the work of a single composer; many long-forgotten masterpieces have been dusted down here and successfully brought back into the repertoire.

Duderstadt

DUDERSTADT lies just over 30km east of Göttingen in the upper part of the remote **Eichsfeld** region. Most of this area became part of the GDR; in thanks for being spared this fate, Duderstadt styled itself the centre of *Die Goldene Mark* (The Golden Borderland). As a result of the success of Willi Brandt's *Ostpolitik*, the town was chosen as one of the places where the hitherto impenetrable border could be crossed.

The town

For much of its history, Duderstadt was an enclave belonging to the Archbishop-Electors of Mainz. The **half-timbered houses** (some 500 in all) have a unique subtlety which somehow stands out from that of all the other towns in the area. Typically, they're brightly coloured and decorated with carvings (including many impressive figures) and inscriptions, messages from the past which still have an uncanny vitality. The best examples are in **Hinterstrasse**, where there's a rich mix of architectural styles, reflecting phases in the town's history of partial destruction followed by intense reconstruction.

Duderstadt's central axis, **Marktstrasse**, widens to form a square at each end. Untermarkt to the west is dominated by the Protestant parish church of **St Servatius**, which was given a Jugendstil look inside after being burned out in 1915. On Obermarkt, its Catholic counterpart, **St Cyriakus**, is a handsome Gothic hall church with impressive Baroque furnishings inside, notably the tall candelabra with figures of angels, which are often carried on religious processions. Between the two churches is the **Rathaus** (Mon–Wed & Fri 9am–4.30pm, Thurs 9am–7pm, Sat & Sun 9.30am–12.30pm; April–Oct also Sat & Sun 2.30–4.30pm; DM2.50), whose thirteenth-century kernel can be appreciated from inside, though the exterior has been masked behind such superb embellishments as the late Gothic turrets and half-timbering, and the elaborate Renaissance balcony and stairwell. Outside the Rathaus stands the **Mariensäule**, a sandstone statue of the Virgin Mary set on top of a tall pillar whose base is flanked by palm trees, creating an incongruously Mediterranean atmosphere.

The other main sight is the **Westertorturm**, the original northwestern gateway to the town. Its high, narrow roof has, over the years, gradually turned on its own axis and taken on a characteristic spiral appearance. This makes the best point to begin a walk round the surviving parts of the fortifications, from where there are many surprising views of the town.

Practicalities

Duderstadt is not on a rail line, but there are frequent **bus** connections with Göttingen; some leave from the station below the Westertorturm, but others depart from Untermarkt. The **tourist office** is in the Rathaus, Marktstr. 66 (hours as above; ☎05527/841200), and this is the best place to ask about **private rooms** (①–③).

There are four **hotels** in the town centre: *Deutsches Haus*, Hinterstr. 29 (☎05527/4052; ④), *Zum Halben Mond*, Haberstr. 17–19 (☎05527/2698; ③), and *Budapest*, Marktstr. 99 (☎05527/3335; ④); all occupy half-timbered buildings. Top of the range is *Zum Löwen*, Marktstr. 30 (☎05527/3072; ⑨), in a splendid town palace. Each of these hotels has a **restaurant**: *Budapest* predictably offers Hungarian as well as German dishes, while *Zum Löwen* has the best kitchen in town, serving two restaurants, a cellar wine bar and a café with winter garden and terrace. Outside the hotels the best place to eat is the inevitable *Ratskeller*, Am Gropenmarkt.

The **youth hostel** at Adenauerring 23 (☎05527/98470; ❹) is brand-new and very comfortable. **Camping** facilities are available at *Campingplatz Forsthaus Nesselröder Warten* (☎05508/364) in Nesselröde, which lies on the Duderstadt–Göttingen road. Duderstadt's main local **festival** is the *Schützenfest* on the second weekend in July.

Hann. Münden

Playing the time-honoured game of listing the Seven Wonders of the World, the great German traveller-scholar Alexander von Humboldt – who had seen a fair bit of the globe for himself – listed **HANN. MÜNDEN** as ranking among the seven most beautifully sited towns. Even if this judgement seems tinged by excessive patriotism, there can be no doubt about the charm of the setting, below thickly wooded hills at the point where the **River Weser** is formed by the merging of the **Fulda** and **Werra**. The town's odd name, by the way, is the official contraction of "Hannoversch Münden", the name it assumed when it was part of the Kingdom of Hannover.

The town

Hann. Münden has even more **half-timbered houses** than Duderstadt – over 700 in all. Separated by some six centuries of history, they completely dominate the face of the town, and their main attraction lies in the effect of the overall ensemble – individually, they're less impressive than their counterparts elsewhere. Look out, however, for no. 34 on the main street, Lange Strasse. This was the home of the town's most celebrated citizen, **Johann Andreas Eisenbart**, an eighteenth-century doctor whose controversial medical techniques gained him a reputation as a miracle-worker. A statue of him stands outside, while his life is the subject of an open-air costume play held each Sunday between mid-May and the end of August.

Curiously enough, Hann. Münden's few set pieces are all of a more solid stone construction. The most impressive of these is the **Rathaus.** This dates back in part to the fourteenth century, but the side facing the Markt was rebuilt at the turn of the seventeenth century in the cheerful Weser Renaissance style by Georg Crossmann, the creator of many similar buildings in Lemgo. The facade is masterly, with the ornate gables, resplendent doorway and the obligatory two-storey oriel window all competing for pre-eminence. During working hours, the interior, including the elaborate main **Festsaal**, is freely accessible. Across Kirchplatz is **St Blasius** (May–Sept Mon–Fri 11am–12.30pm & 2–5pm, Sat 11am–12.30pm, Sun 2–6pm), an unusual-looking Gothic hall church with a hexagonal tower and a very steeply pitched roof of red slate. It contains a couple of masterpieces of late fourteenth-century bronzework in the font and the door of the sacrament niche.

The other major monument is the **Schloss** (Wed–Fri 10am–noon & 2.30–5pm, Sat 10am–noon & 2.30–4pm, Sun 10am–12.30pm; DM2), an L-shaped Renaissance palace overlooking the Werra from which one branch or other of the Welf family ruled the town for most of its history. It now houses the standard local history displays, but of more interest are the fresco cycles dating from soon after the time of the building's construction, among the few in Germany from this period. However, these can only be seen by taking the DM4 tour of the Rathaus and Schloss which departs from the former at 2.30pm on Fridays and Saturdays between mid-May and late September.

Behind the Schloss is the **Werrabrücke**, a bridge which dates back at least as far as the fourteenth century. From here, you can cross over to **Doktorwerder**, an island with a sculpture garden. Of the other islands around the confluence, the largest is

Unterer Tanzwerder, a popular recreation area. Here also are the landing stage for cruise boats, a swing bridge over the Fulda, and the **Weserstein**, a stone marking the birth of the great river at the point where, according to the rather trite inscription, "the Fulda and Werra kiss". Encircling the town centre are several towers, the remnants of the dismantled medieval **Stadtmauer**.

To appreciate the beauty of Hann. Münden's setting, and the harmonious layout of the town with its sea of red roofs, you really need to see it from above. One possibility is to cross over the Werrabrücke and follow the signs up to the **Weserliedanlage** belvedere. For a really magnificent bird's-eye view, at its best in the late afternoon or evening, cross the Fulda by the Pionierbrücke, and climb up to the nineteenth-century tower known as the **Tillyschanze** (daily 9am–dusk; DM1.50).

Practicalities

Hann. Münden lies on the express rail line between Göttingen and Kassel, 35km from the former, 23km from the latter. The **Bahnhof** is ten minutes' walk east of the town centre. The **tourist office** is in the Rathaus (May–Sept Mon–Fri 9am–1pm & 2–5pm, Sat 9am–1pm; Oct–April Mon–Thurs 9am–1pm & 2–4pm, Fri 9am–1pm; ☎05541/75313). After closing time, an information point is kept open daily until 8pm or 9pm according to season.

In addition to an abundant supply of **private rooms** (①–③), there are a couple of cheapish centrally sited **hotels**: *Gasthaus im Anker*, Bremer Schlagd 18 (☎05541/4923; ③) and *Rathausschänke*, Ziegelstr. 12 (☎05541/8866; ④). There is also a more upmarket option in *Schloss-Schänke*, Vor den Burg 3–5 (☎05541/70940; ⑦). Of the alternatives in the outskirts, the best and most convenient is *Schmucker Jäger*, on the left bank of the Fulda at Wilhelmshäuser Str. 45 (☎05541/8100; ④). The **youth hostel** is way to the north of town at Prof-Oelkers-Str. 10 (☎05541/8853; ❸), while you can **camp** at a handier location on an island in the River Fulda. All of the last three hotels have restaurants; the one in the *Schmucker Jäger* is probably the best. Alternatives include the *Ratskeller* in the Rathaus, which offers French-style cuisine, and the *Waldgaststätte* below the Tillyschanze. In summer, several daily **river cruises** leave from Unterer Tanzwerder; as well as local round trips, there are services downstream to Bad Karlshafen.

travel details

Trains

Bremen to: Bremerhaven (hourly; 50min); Emden (hourly; 2hr); Hannover (every 30min; 1hr); Norddeich (hourly; 2hr 50min); Oldenburg (every 30min; 35min); Osnabrück (hourly; 2hr).

Hannover to: Braunschweig (every 30min; 50min); Bremen (hourly; 1hr); Celle (every 20min; 25min); Einbeck (hourly; 1hr); Goslar (hourly; 1hr 20min); Göttingen (every 20min; 1hr); Hameln (hourly; 50min); Hann. Münden (hourly; 2hr); Hildesheim (every 20min; 25min); Lüneburg (every 30min; 1hr 20min), Wolfenbüttel (every 30min; 1hr 10min).

Ferries

Bensersiel to: Langeoog (3–5 daily; 50min).

Emden to: Borkum (summer 4 daily, winter 2 daily; 2hr 30min).

Harle to: Wangerooge (summer 2–3 daily, winter 1 daily; 1hr 10min).

Neuharlingersiel to: Spiekeroog (2–4 daily; 50min).

Norddeich Mole to: Juist (1–3 daily; 1hr 20min); Norderney (9–13 daily; 50min).

CHAPTER SEVEN

HAMBURG AND SCHLESWIG-HOLSTEIN

Jutting up between the Baltic and North Sea, and stretching as far as the Danish border, **Schleswig-Holstein** is the northernmost of Germany's Länder. It's about as far removed as is possible to imagine from the stereotyped image of the country — there are no mountains, cute fairy-tale towns or back-slapping dances, and a Bavarian would surely feel less at home than someone from Britain. Both geographically and culturally, Schleswig-Holstein might seem to belong more naturally to Scandinavia. Indeed, for most of its history it was quasi-independent, suspended nebulously between Germany and Denmark, and it was not until last century that the former finally achieved supremacy.

As the name suggests, Schleswig-Holstein was originally two separate territories, divided horizontally by the River Eider. The duchy of Schleswig was a fief of the Danish Crown, whereas Holstein was a county of the Holy Roman Empire. However, in 1386 the two came together under the same ruler, and in 1460 the king of Denmark was accepted as the perpetual overlord, even though this meant that the predominantly German-speaking Holstein had dual loyalties. Subsequently, the united duchy was partitioned among different branches of its ruling family, blurring the division between the two original component parts. This arrangement lasted until the nineteenth century when, under the impact of the nationalist fervour gripping Europe, both Denmark and the emerging German nation set their sights on absorbing at least "their" part of the territory. Because of the threat it posed to international peace and security, the so-called **Schleswig-Holstein Question** was a major preoccupation of chancelleries throughout the continent. The exasperation felt about finding a solution was summed up in 1864 by the British Prime Minister Lord Palmerston, who declared: "Schleswig-Holstein's history is so complicated that only three people have ever understood it. One of them, Prince Albert, is already dead. Another is myself, but I have already forgotten it all again. And the third is a Danish statesman, and it drove him mad."

The same year, the arch-manipulator of European power politics, the Prussian Chancellor **Otto von Bismarck**, solved the problem by his tried and trusted method of brute force. Precipitated into action by an ill-judged attempt to integrate Schleswig into Denmark, he formed an alliance with Austria which wrested the whole of the united duchy from all vestiges of Danish control, then picked an argument with his erstwhile ally to ensure it passed to Prussia and thence into the Second Reich established soon after. Following German defeat in World War I, the victorious Allies held a plebiscite in Schleswig which resulted in its northern half being returned to Denmark. These borders remain in force to this day.

One of the rare lasting legacies of the Third Reich has been the incorporation of **Lübeck** – a proud city-state for the previous seven centuries – into Schleswig-Holstein. One of only two places in the Land large enough to be regarded a city, its legacy of

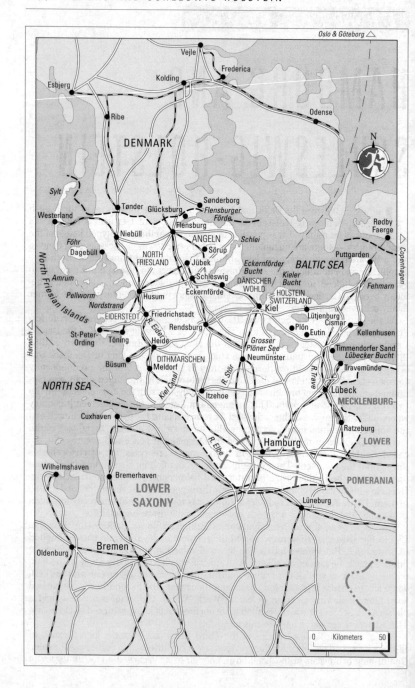

buildings from its heyday as Germany's premier mercantile port constitutes one of the country's most magnificent and distinctive monumental ensembles. In this, and many other respects, it totally overshadows the slightly larger city of **Kiel**, the somewhat surprising choice as capital of the modern Land and the starting point of the famous canal which bears its name. Stripped of its historic role as a seat of government, the lovely old town of **Schleswig**, which first came to prominence under the Vikings, has sunk into blissful obscurity. On the other hand, **Flensburg**, hard by the Danish border, remains a bustling port which has made a spectacularly successful adaptation of its well-preserved centre to modern needs.

North Friesland, Schleswig-Holstein's northwestern corner, has a reputation as Germany's bleakest region — a landscape of marshes and bogs whose few trees are contorted into strange shapes by the constant onshore winds, and which has to be protected by a network of dykes from the constant danger of encroachment by the North Sea. However, it's also one of the nation's favourite holiday areas, thanks to the archipelago off its coast. These have mile upon mile of beaches and a surprising amount of sunshine in summer; indeed **Sylt**, the largest of the islands, is normally the sunniest place in the country. The much gentler **Baltic coast**, characterized by a series of long, narrow inlets or fjords, is also popular with German holidaymakers, as is the lake district which lies just inland. A car or bike would be a definite asset for **travel** in the rural areas, though public transport links between the main centres are as comprehensive as elsewhere in Germany.

Hamburg, a Land in its own right, exists like an enclave in the south of the state. Firmly established as the nation's second city, its name is synonymous with the prostitution and sleaze of the infamous Reeperbahn. That's as much as many people care to know about the place, but it actually has plenty to offer – an extraordinary verdant setting among lakes, a sparkling nightlife, a vibrant cultural scene and a city centre made up of enjoyably contrasting and easily explorable neighbourhoods. It's possible to travel there directly by **ferry** from Harwich or Newcastle on the east coast of England, and a few days in the city coupled to a circular trip round Schleswig-Holstein would make a well-contained trip lasting about a fortnight.

HAMBURG

The River Elbe marks the southern border of Schleswig-Holstein, and 120km inland stands the port of **HAMBURG**. Exhilaratingly different from any other German city, Hamburg has always been a city-state, free to trade as it pleased, unencumbered by dukes and princes. Even now it officially bears the title of *Freie und Hansestadt:* "Free and Hanseatic City".

During World War II Hamburg was massively bombed by the Allies. As the first city that bombers flying from England would pass over on the North Sea route into central Germany, Hamburg was often attacked. But on July 28, 1943 it became the first city to suffer a **firestorm**, when the combination of high explosives and incendiary bombs turned 21 square kilometres of the centre into one huge conflagration, with winds the speed of hurricanes uprooting trees and sucking people into the inferno. On that night, over 42,000 civilians were killed.

Hamburg's wealth enabled it to recover quickly in the postwar years, and though today its reputation is tainted by tales of the red-light area, that's only a small part of what the city is about. It's a stylish media centre, a huge modern seaport, a scene of radical protest, and home of the latest generation of a long-standing merchant class. Unless you arrive at one of the coastal ports, Hamburg is also where you're likely to

---

The **telephone code** for Hamburg is ☎040

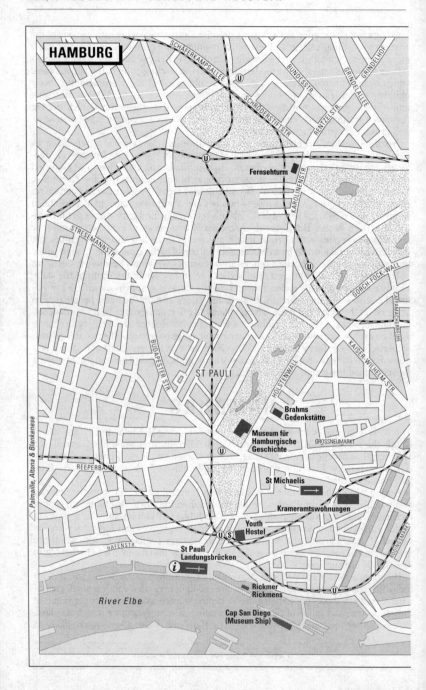

HAMBURG

SCHÄFERKAMPSALLEE

BUNDESSTR.

GRINDELHOF

GRINDELALLEE

SCHRÖDERSTIFTSTR.

RENTZELSTR.

KAROLINENSTR.

Fernsehturm

GORCH-FOCK-WALL

CAFAMACHEREIHE

STRESEMANNSTR.

KAISER-WILHELM-STR.

HOLSTENWALL

BUDAPESTER STR.

ST PAULI

Brahms
Gedenkstätte

Museum für
Hamburgische
Geschichte

GROSSNEUMARKT

REEPERBAHN

St Michaelis

Krameramtswohnungen

RODINGSMARKT

Palmaille, Altona & Blankenese

HAFENSTR.

Youth
Hostel

St Pauli
Landungsbrücken

Rickmer
Rickmens

River Elbe

Cap San Diego
(Museum Ship)

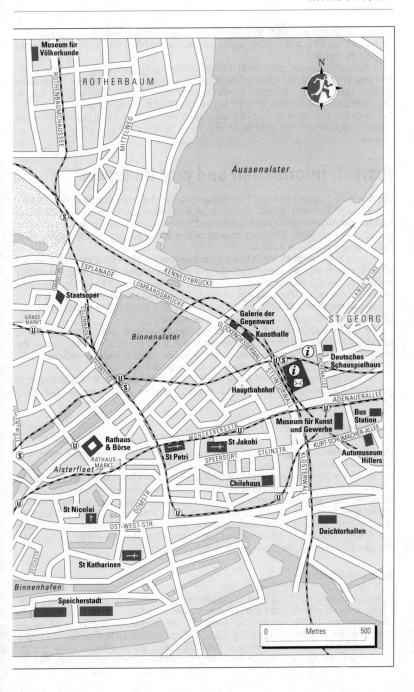

begin your travels around Schleswig-Holstein. Allow two or three days to explore the centre and suburbs, and as many nights as your pocket (and constitution) will stand to soak up its nightlife.

In spite of the vast proportions of the city's outline, only one third is actually built up. The rest is either parks, lakes or tree-lined canals – the city boasts that it has more bridges than Venice. To cycle around, you'd never believe you were in one of Germany's major industrial cities, the largest after Berlin. Municipal policy dictates that two thousand new trees have to be planted each year, and the result is a very pleasing effect, with almost every road lined with trees, keeping the city green and the air cleaner.

Arrival, information and city transport

Ferries from England arrive at Fischerhafen on Van-der-Smissen-Strasse from where buses run to Bahnhof Altona. Cruise ships from other countries dock at **St Pauli Landungsbrücken**, which has a U-Bahn and S-Bahn station attached, and is very close to the centre of town. There's a **tourist office** kiosk (daily 9.30am–5.30pm; ☎300 51200) between bridges 4 and 5.

Arriving at the **airport**, you'll find easy access into the city, either by taking the bus which connects with the Hauptbahnhof every twenty minutes, or by taking the slightly cheaper option of a municipal bus to Ohlsdorf, and then either a U- or S-Bahn to your required destination. If you want to book a hotel room immediately, you can go to terminal 2, where there's a free-phone service for all hotels listed on the information board there. Naturally they will be the more expensive hotels.

Arriving by **train**, you find yourself at the **Hauptbahnhof**, close to the city centre, and within walking distance of some cheap hotels, if not the youth hostels. Within the station, by the Kirchenallee exit, is the handiest of the **tourist offices** (daily 7am–11pm; ☎300 51201), which offers the full range of services.

The **bus station**, which has a wide range of international as well as local routes, is just to the southeast of the Hauptbahnhof, between Adenauerallee and Kurt-Schumacher-Allee.

City transport

Public transport around the city is quick and efficient by the integrated network of buses and U- and S-Bahn trains. Rather than buy normal tickets or day passes, it's much better value to invest in the **Hamburg-CARD**, which also gives free entry to the municipally owned museums plus substantial reductions on a number of other attractions, including lake and harbour cruises. Current prices are DM10.80 for a day ticket (which can be used from 6pm the day before) and DM21 for a three-day ticket valid from the first day until midnight on the last. Families or people travelling together can buy inclusive tickets: for one day, these cost DM12.50 for one adult plus three children, DM24 for five people of any age; for three days, DM25.50 and DM42.

Accommodation

In spite of a good variety of types of **accommodation**, it can be difficult to find somewhere easily affordable if you don't want to use the youth hostels or campsites. It's true that there are plenty of cheapish hotels in the St Georg quarter, next to the Hauptbahnhof, but the unsuspecting will as likely as not end up in a brothel: it's impossible to tell them apart from "normal" hotels. To avoid any possibility of this, pay the DM6 fee the tourist offices charge for making a reservation, or at least pick up their list of officially approved establishments. For budget accommodation, best bet is to ring the city's *Mitwohnzentralen* before you arrive. These offer an excellent service, being agencies that provide rooms in shared flats, and furnished or unfurnished apartments, both for short- and long-term stays.

Hotels

The main concentration of reasonably priced hotels is in the **St Georg quarter**, particularly around the Hauptbahnhof. Although this is sleazy in parts, especially along Steindamm, there are also areas which are quiet and residential.

St Georg

Alte Wache, Adenauerallee 21–27 (☎241291). Good-quality hotel close to the Hauptbahnhof. ⑧

Annenhof, Lange Reihe 23 (☎243426). A friendly small place to the east of the Hauptbahnhof run by a husband-and-wife team. ④

Fürst Bismarck, Kirchenallee 49 (☎280 1091). Another of the clutch of hotels right by the Hauptbahnhof. ⑦

Helga Schmidt, Holzdamm 14 (☎280 2119). Homely pension between the Hauptbahnhof and the Alster lakes. ⑥

Kieler Hof, Bremer Reihe 15 (☎243024). Basic budget hotel just east of the Hauptbahnhof. ③

Köhler, St-Georg-Str. 6 (☎249065). Perhaps the best deal in the Hauptbahnhof area; very small, so it's best to call ahead. ③

Kronprinz, Kirchenallee 46 (☎243258, fax 280 1097). Renowned for its restaurant, the top-notch *Schifferbörse*, though the accommodation is also of a high standard. ⑦

Lilienhof, Ernst-Merck-Str. 4 (☎241087). Decent if somewhat functional modern hotel by the Hauptbahnhof. ⑥

Nord, Bremer Reihe 22 (☎244693). Despite some very dubious neighbours, this hotel is respectable, and reasonably priced. ④

Sarah Petersen, Lange Reihe 88 (☎ & fax 249826). Small pension named after the artist who runs it. Has a certain celebrity status, so advance booking advisable. ⑤

Steens, Holzdamm 43 (☎244642, fax 280 3593). Charmingly located in a quiet, pretty corner of St Georg. ⑦

Terminus, Steindamm 5 (☎280 3144). Conveniently close to the Hauptbahnhof, and a regular choice for foreign budget travellers. ⑤

Elsewhere in the city

Alameda, Colonnaden 45 (☎344000, fax 343439). Located in the shopping area, just west of the Binnenalster. ⑥

Baseler Hof, Esplanade 11 (☎359060, fax 3590 6918). Very highly regarded hotel with a location equally handy for the city centre, the Univiertel and the Alster lakes. ⑨

Bei der Esplanade, Colonnaden 45 (☎342961). Occupies the upper floors of the same building as the *Alameda*, offering slightly cheaper rates. ⑤

Frauenhotel Hanseatin, Dragonerstall 11 (☎341345, fax 345825). Women-only hotel just west of the city centre, near the Gänsemarkt U-Bahn. ⑦

Sternschanze, Schanzenstr. 101 (☎433389). In the heart of the bohemian Schanzenviertel, and one of the best bargains in Hamburg. ③

Vier Jahreszeiten, Neuer Jungfernstieg 9–14 (☎34940, fax 349 4602). This top-notch luxury hotel beside the Binnenalster has been in business for a century. It is elegantly furnished with antiques, and some of the rooms overlook the lake. ⑨

Wedina, Gurlittstr. 23 (☎243011, fax 280 3894). Set on the southeastern edge of the Aussenalster, this recently renovated hotel with a garden and swimming pool is undoubtedly one of the best places to stay in central Hamburg. ⑥

Youth hostels

Hamburg has two **youth hostels**. Ignore any listings which name others, such as *Commodore* or *Mui* for example, since they only cater to organized groups and do not offer rooms to independent travellers.

Jugendgästehaus Horner Rennbahn, Rennbahnstr. 100 (☎651 1671), U-Bahn stop Horner Rennbahn. Slightly the more expensive of the two hostels, with marginally higher standards. Situated in a light, airy modern building next to the horse-race track in the eastern suburb of Horn, it's peaceful enough when there isn't a race on. There's a 1am curfew; breakfast is from 7 to 8.30am, and the staff will wake you up at 7.30am. ☎

Jugendherberge auf dem Stintfang, Alfred-Wegener-Weg 5 (☎313488), S- or U-Bahn stop Landungsbrücken. An excellent location, not just for the city's attractions, but also because it's perched on a steep incline above the port, with panoramic maritime views. The place is rather basic, with no extra facilities other than the day rooms. The hostel opens at 6.30am, breakfast is from 7 to 8.30am, to be out by 9am. There's also a 1am curfew. ☎

Mitwohnzentralen

Hamburg has two **Mitwohnzentralen**, providing the same service for similar fees: rooms will usually be around DM25 per night; apartment prices vary according to area and size, though the fee is normally worked out on the basis of one month's rent.

Home Company, Schulterblatt 112 (☎19445).

Mitwohnzentrale, Lobuschstr. 22 (☎391373 or 19430), S-Bahn stop Altona.

Camping

Most of Hamburg's **campsites** are located on the northwest edge of Greater Hamburg. Although they are most easily accessible by car, most are within reach of some form of public transport.

Anders, Kieler Str. 650 (☎570 4498). Fairly close to S-Bahn stop Schnelsen.

Buchholz, Kieler Str. 374 (☎540 4532). Near Eidelstedt station.

Campingplatz Blankenese, Falkensteiner Ufer 101 (☎812949). One of the largest and most beautiful of Hamburg's campsites, situated directly on the Elbe.

Ramcke, Kieler Str. 620 (☎570 5121). Near Eidelstedt station.

Schnelsen-Nord, Wunderbrunnen 2 (☎559 4225). Close to Stellingen station.

Spiederstadt, Poggenmühle 4 (☎324056). Very central, guarded park for motor homes.

The city

Central Hamburg is neatly recognizable on any map, as it's bordered by large roads which trace the original city's fortifications. It has a semicircular shape, with its base facing the River Elbe and Hamburg's massive **port**, while the rest of the city fans out around the centre's rounded contours. Bulging out to the northeast is the city's glamorous **Alster lake**, lined by some of the poshest quarters in town. To the west of the centre lie the quarters of **St Pauli** and **Altona**, and just north of these the **Univiertel** (University quarter), which together form the heartland of Hamburg's best nightlife. Finally, there are some famous **suburbs** worth visiting, chiefly Blankenese, Oevelgönne and Neuengamme. To get your bearings, there are excellent views from Hamburg's highest building, the **Fernsehturm** on Lagerstrasse (daily: summer 9am–11pm; winter 10am–10pm; DM6 including ascent by lift).

Most of the **centre** of Hamburg was consumed in a great fire in 1842: the flames ran out of control for several days, which is why you don't find many buildings dating from before that period. Add to that the British "Operation Gomorrah" in 1943, when half of the city was destroyed by bombs, and it's a wonder there's anything over fifty years old left to see at all. As it is, there are a great many nineteenth- and early twentieth-century buildings remaining, tucked in between prize-winning modern developments, and hidden within this central mêlée you'll also find the sole surviving seventeenth-century houses of the city.

The Altstadt

The centre arches in a great semicircle over the baseline of the Ost-West-Strasse, about 2km long. This semicircle is then loosely divided by the slanting Alsterfleet canal, which separates the original Altstadt quarter from the later Neustadt on the other side of the water. Most maps no longer record this difference, since nowadays they have melted into one. But the division is still useful for visitors to the city.

The oldest part of Hamburg is around the ruined tower of **St Nikolai**, formerly one of Germany's finest neo-Gothic churches, designed by Sir George Gilbert Scott, only to be flattened by his countrymen about a hundred years later. Today its blackened stump stands as an anti-war memorial. Close by is the **Trostbrücke**, which connected the old city with the Neustadt, the "new" quarters west of the Alsterfleet canal, which developed in the early Middle Ages. The two statues on the bridge are of St Ansgar, Hamburg's first archbishop, and Count Adolf III, founder of the new quarters and, more importantly for the city's future development, instrumental in the signing of the imperial decree which gave Hamburg the right to tax-free import of goods and transport of passengers from the sea to its port, 120km inland along the River Elbe. Thus the city's future as one of Europe's largest and most important commercial ports was sealed as early as the twelfth century. Today the bridge appears somewhat incongruous, surrounded as it is by modern office buildings.

Following the canal south, crossing the busy Ost-West-Strasse at Holzbrücke you'll find the remaining eighteenth-century merchant homes, with their grand facades facing the street and the red-brick, gabled backs facing the canal, where goods were directly hoicked into the merchant's attic store rooms. The most famous examples are the row of houses along the **Deichstrasse**, which is also where the Great Fire broke out. The best place to see the crooked backs of the houses is from the Hohe Brücke. Further east along Katharinenstrasse is the church of **St Katharinen**, much restored after war damage.

The Chilehaus and Historic Emigration Office

Heading northeast along the Dovenfleet, with the waterfront warehouses on your right, you come to the U-Bahn station Messberg, and directly opposite, the remarkable **Chilehaus**. Built with the traditional red bricks of north German architecture, this unconventional house was created in the early 1920s and remains one of the most original works of the period. It was designed by the Expressionist architect Fritz Höger, whose idea it was to mirror Hamburg's ocean-going ships in this large office block. As you wander around it – ideally from the other side of the road for the best views – you begin to recognize the contours of a great ship, the staggered balconies high above recalling the various decks, and the sharp corner of its eastern extremity representing a ship's bow. If the name seems incongruous, that's because it has nothing to do with the building, but recalls the country in which the architect originally made his fortune.

North American readers might care to know that nearby, at Steinstra. 7, is the **Historic Emigration Office** (Tues & Thurs 9.30am–5.30pm; ☎300 51282), which has the most comprehensive archives in existence of emigration to the New World. For the years 1850–1934, there are complete records of name, age, sex, occupation and place of origin of each and every one of the 5.8 million emigrants from all over Europe who departed from Hamburg. If you want to find your ancestors' records, all you need to know is the name and year of emigration, and the staff will conduct a search for a US$75 fee.

St Jakobi and St Petri

Across the Burchardsplatz and up the Mohlenhofstrasse is another of central Hamburg's five church towers, which traditionally characterize its skyline. This is **St Jakobi**, which contains the precious treasure of Arp Schnitger's seventeenth-century **organ**, considered a masterpiece of its time and still in frequent use. Unfortunately, postwar rebuilding did not attempt to re-create the original, so that the interior is in drab 1950s style, with only the outside recalling the building's former glory. The same can be said for all of the city's churches, with the glorious exception of St Michaelis.

Directly behind St Jakobi lies the **Mönckebergstrasse**, which is the main artery of the city's commercial shopping. Follow this street west, and you're heading to the hub of the city centre, which clusters around the grandiose Rathaus. On the way you pass **St Petri**, originally the oldest of the city's churches, believed to have its origin in an eleventh-century chapel. Destroyed in the Great Fire and then again in 1943, it nevertheless retains much of its nineteenth-century neo-Gothic architecture and, most famously, boasts Hamburg's oldest piece of craftwork: the fourteenth-century bronze **door-knocker** on the central western portal.

Around the Rathaus

A stone's throw away from here, the **Rathaus** sits heavily in all the boastful splendour of the German neo-Renaissance. Built to display the superior quality of Hamburg's civil parliament, there is something faintly self-conscious about the building's style. Perhaps they were trying a little too hard to create the proper symbolism, with both the city's patron saints and maritime images lined up alongside each other around its rooftop rim. When the city's parliament isn't in session, guided tours around its stately rooms offer an instructive view of Hamburg's uniquely glamorous municipal headquarters (tours in English and French hourly Mon–Thurs 10.15am–3.15pm, Fri–Sun 10.15am–1.15pm; in German every 30min Mon–Thurs 10am–3pm, Fri–Sun 10am–1pm; DM2).

In front of the Rathaus, the **Rathausmarkt** is usually teeming with tourists and shoppers alike, sampling goodies from the variety of stalls, while the elegant **Alsterarkarden** and its expensive stores lead out onto the **Binnenalster**, which is the petite forerunner of the larger **Aussenalster** lake, beyond the city centre. The arcades were built to echo those on Venice's Piazza San Marco, though it's pretty evident that a few arcades don't make up a Venetian square. If you're interested in seeing the **Börse**, Germany's first stock market and Hamburg's financial heart, then head along the arcades away from the lakes, and you'll soon find yourself round the back of the Rathaus on the Adolphsplatz. Founded in 1558, the stock market reflected the fact that Hamburg's cosmoplitan world of trade and commerce was bilingual, in those days commonly using both German and Dutch. The present building (guided tours Tues & Thurs 11am & noon; free) is a restored version of the Neoclassical one built in the mid-nineteenth century, and extended in the early part of this century.

The Neustadt

Turning away from the Rathaus and towards the Binnenalster, you cross the Reesendammbrücke, which has been there in some form or other since the thirteenth century. The present model was built in the 1840s, but in the early Middle Ages this was the site of a corn-mill, which dammed the River Alster's water to turn its wheel. From then onwards, there's always been a small lake here – the larger one beyond created a few hundred years later – and Hamburg's high society, then as now, delighted in promenading around its edges. The finest and most expensive promenade is traditionally the **Jungfernstieg**, named after the young women who used to twirl their umbrellas here. Head north, along the Neuer Jungfernstieg, and you'll find the splendid houses of the city's bankers and businessmen, as well as Hamburg's best address: the **Hotel Vier Jahreszeiten**. It boasts that it's the second best hotel in the world after one in Malaysia, and charges accordingly. The least expensive way to sample it is to go for a coffee in its lovely Biedermeier café.

If you're tempted by any of the **boat trips** offered along the Jungfernstieg, the best is undoubtedly the *Kanal-Fahrt* (daily end March to end April & end Sept to early Nov 9.45am, 12.45pm & 3.45pm; end April–end Sept 9.45am, 11.45am, 12.45pm, 2.45pm, 3.45pm & 5.45pm; lasts 2hr; DM19). This tour will take you round both the Alster lakes, and also along the River Alster itself, passing many of the city's finest villas and sailing clubs, and presenting a view of Hamburg otherwise impossible to see.

The Hanseviertel

The streets spreading out behind the Jungfernstieg, towards the Gänsemarkt and down Neuer Wall, Grosse Bleichen and ABC-Strasse, are collectively known as the **Hanseviertel**, an area of offices and the city's flashest shopping arcades. The city's renowned opera and ballet house, the **Staatsoper**, is on the Dammtorstrasse nearby.

Heading southwest from the Hanseviertel you enter a more residential area on the other side of Kaiser-Wilhelm-Strasse. Streets worth strolling along are Breiter Gang or Wexstrasse, where you'll not only find attractive houses, but also the odd bar or restaurant you might fancy. **Grossneumarkt**, in particular, is a favourite haunt for inner-city eating and drinking. Not far from here, the **Peterstrasse** is one of Hamburg's most beautiful streetscapes, a small stretch of completely restored eighteenth-century town houses, built in traditional red-brick style, with gabled tops tapering towards the sky. Walking along this street gives you an idea of what most of the city must once have looked like. If you're interested in musical heritage, the **Brahms Gedenkstätte** is here at Peterstr. 39 (Tues & Thurs 10am–1pm; DM3), and holds some documentation of the life and work of the composer, who was born in Hamburg and spent many unsuccessful years here.

Immediately to the west is Holstenwall, which marks the boundary between the Neustadt and St Pauli. At no. 24 the **Museum für Hamburgische Geschichte** (Tues–Sat 10am–5pm, Sun 10am–6pm; DM8) will tell you everything you could possibly want to know about Hamburg's origins and history, its people and times. There are meticulous miniaturized re-creations of historic quarters, and a large variety of model boats through the ages. An intriguing and unexpected section on the Reeperbahn dwells not on the commercial sex which makes it notorious these days, but on its original role as home to the ropemakers who supplied the giant ropes used by the port's ships.

St Michaelis

A few minutes' walk to the southeast stands Hamburg's city symbol and finest church: **St Michaelis**. Seated on a small hill, its copper-plated tower is visible from most parts of the city. The church was originally built between 1649 and 1661, but has burned down no less than three times since then: once after it was struck by lightning in the eighteenth century, again in 1906, and lastly in the World War II firebombing of the city. Happily, this is the one Hamburg church that has not only been rebuilt on the outside, but also on the interior, so that you can still marvel at its superb northern Baroque elegance. Inside, you find the typically Lutheran design, which directs the congregation's eyes not to the altar, but to the pulpit. The best bird's-eye view of the city is from the church tower **look-out platform**, at 82m (mid-March to Sept, Mon–Sat 9am–6pm, Sun 11am–6pm; Oct to mid-March Mon–Sat 10am–5pm, Sun 11am–5pm; DM4). The **vaults** are also worth a look; they contain the grave of the composer Carl Philipp Emanuel Bach, son of J.S. and pioneer of the symphonic form, and an exhibition about the history of the church. There is also a **multimedia show**, *Multivision Hamburg* (Thurs–Sun 12.30pm, 2.30pm & 3.30pm; DM5; combined ticket for all three DM9). If your German is up to it, this is an accessible introduction to the city's history and development, with many famous names and events portrayed with a vivid slide show, and suitably dramatic music – and even if you don't speak German, it makes an interesting moving picture gallery.

The Krameramtswohnungen

A rather touristy but nevertheless worthwhile visit is to the **Krameramtswohnungen**, Krayenkamp 10 (Tues–Sun 10am–5pm), round the corner from St Michaelis. This tiny backyard of seventeenth-century housing is the last remaining in the city. It was built as retirement homes for the widows of storekeepers, who were forbidden to carry on their husband's trade after his death and were housed here by the guild. They were still in use until the early 1960s, but now all but one of them has been turned into a trinket shop or art gallery. For DM2, you can squeeze inside the single house remaining in its original form.

The port: from Fischmarkt to Speicherstadt

The best time and place to begin an exploration of the length of Hamburg's harbour is to go to the **Fischmarkt**, not far from St Pauli Landungsbrücken, early on a Sunday morning. Between 5am and 10am (7–10am in winter), the former fishmarket hall and a large part of the waterfront around it are given over to a weekly circus of shopping and selling, where you can buy anything from fish to live ducks, potted palms, clothes or tacky trinkets. The bars and *Imbiss* stands in the vicinity open for the occasion, filled with shoppers and late-night survivors alike, all tucking into the sounds of early morning jazz and stall-holders bellowing out their wares. If you can make it, it's a spectacle worth seeing, though be prepared for crowds. By 10am, the market is supposed to end, in accordance with an old law that was to ensure trade didn't compete with Sunday church services. In fact, it lingers on for a good hour more, but many of the most colourful traders have sold out by then, no longer performing their crowd-drawing sales pitches.

The short stretch of waterfront road that connects the Fischmarkt with the Landungsbrücken is the infamous **Hafenstrasse**. Its occupied houses are hard to miss: the walls are covered with slogans and occasionally creative murals, many of the windows are smashed from past raids, and, depending on the state of siege, doors are barricaded and look-outs peer from top-floor windows. The houses stand on prime land, and have been the battleground between developers and squatters for some years now.

HAMBURG'S PORT

Hamburg's **port**, founded in the late twelfth century, was the making of the city. Today it's one of Europe's four major ports, and the world's largest depot for oriental carpets, as well as Germany's leading market for coffee, tea and spices from all over the world. Ever since Emperor Frederick Barbarossa granted free trade and a customs exemption for all goods brought in by ship in 1189, wealth and municipal status have been assured. These days, of course, the port's significance is tempered by the worldwide recession in ocean-going trade, as well as the decline in related industries such as shipbuilding. The authorities have tried to make their wharfs competitive by cutting labour and mechanizing the handling of containerized cargo, but the human cost of these measures has been great, and unemployment is higher here (and in the north generally) than in most other parts of the country.

The port's workforce has a history of powerful organization, and there were systemized strikes as early as the 1840s. In the 1880s came the longest strike the city has seen, when 18,000 harbour workers went out for ten weeks, in protest against the massive rehousing that was necessitated by the demolition of their homes to make way for the Speicherstadt, the port's tax-free warehouses. In the turmoil immediately following World War I, there was more action: a sailors' revolt in November 1918, two days after the one in Kiel. In 1923 came the **Hamburg uprising**, with fighting on the streets at the height of the postwar crisis of inflation and hunger. Today, the embattled Hafenstrasse is at the heart of present-day conflict with the authorities.

For the moment, things are quiet and tourists come to take pictures and gaze on the motley crew of inhabitants, something of an exotic attraction. But serious violence flares up at regular intervals, and in 1990 the city's authorities braced themselves for a final, semi-successful armed onslaught. If you want to find out more, you could venture into the collective kitchen, known as the *Volxküche*, or the intermittent cafés run in some of the houses.

Around the Landungsbrücken

Back down by the **Landungsbrücken**, many bridges lead to the floating pontoon lined with expensive *Imbiss* stands and restaurants, and there are plenty of boats offering hour-long **harbour tours** (*Hafenrundfahrten*) for about DM15, children half price. Make sure you go on one of the small ferries and not the large double-decker, since only the small ones take in the canals of the **Speicherstadt** as well as the port itself. If you want to see the hulls of mighty container ships close up, then this is the tour for you. **Tours in English** go from Brücke 1 between March and November, daily at 11.15am, DM15 (☎564523). For **alternative tours** highlighting environmental problems, phone ☎241031.

The distinctive green-hulled **Rickmer Rickmers** (daily 10am–6pm; DM6) is moored opposite the S-Bahn station. Built in 1896, this nineteenth-century three-masted, ocean-going barque had a history of international sailing before it was impounded by the British in 1916. They used it as part of their maritime war effort, and once World War I was over, gave it to the Portuguese. Eventually, some Hamburg businessmen found the boat mouldering away off the coast of Portugal, brought it back in 1987, restored it to its original beauty, and now it's regarded as one of the city's most important treasures. There's also a gourmet restaurant on board. A little to the east, at Überseebrücke, lies the **Cap San Diego** (daily 10am–6pm; DM6). This typical 1960s freighter is now an impressive museum. Visitors can walk all over the ship, from the engine room to the bridge, gaining a vivid impression of the sailors' living and working conditions. There's a restaurant on board here too.

A brisk fifteen minutes' walk further along the waterfront will take you to the separate world of the nineteenth-century **Speicherstadt**. The world's largest self-contained warehouse complex, complete with canals and cobblestone streets, it was built between 1885 and 1910 in the beautiful red-brick style of local architecture. Sacks of coffee can be seen piled high, thousands of oriental carpets lie rolled up, scents of teas and spices waft out of open doors, and men can be seen heaving goods by the traditional hooks used a hundred years ago. All the buildings are under protection, so there are no lifts or other machinery to assist present-day workers. Goods can be stored here over many years tax-free, until the merchant thinks he'll get the best price.

The Speicherstadt contains three unique museums: the **Gewürzmuseum** (Spice Museum; Tues–Sun 10am–5pm; DM4) at Am Sandtorka 32; the **Speicherstadtmuseum** (same times; DM4) at St Annenufer 2, with exhibits on the working life of the old warehouse quarter; and the **Zollmuseum** (same times; free), Alter Wandrahm 16, devoted to customs and smuggling.

The museum quarter

Hamburg's **museums** are scattered all over the city, but there's a handy concentration around the Hauptbahnhof, at the western fringe of the inner suburb of St Georg, including the **Kunsthalle,** the city's star museum.

The Kunsthalle

Immediately north of the Hauptbahnhof on Glockengiesserwall is the renowned **Kunsthalle** (Tues, Wed & Fri–Sun 10am–6pm, Thurs 10am–9pm; DM10). Its collection of paintings and sculpture ranges from medieval to contemporary, and is often augmented by special exhibitions, in which case there's a compulsory supplement to the entrance fee. Starting upstairs to the right with the earliest works, the collection is arranged in a broadly chronological fashion.

MEDIEVAL GERMAN PAINTING
One room is entirely devoted to three retables by **Master Bertram**. An important figure in German art, he was the country's first painter identifiable by name, and worked for most of his life in Hamburg. His masterpiece is the huge folding altar, mixing paintings and sculpture, which was made for St Petri. The panel showing *The Creation of the Birds and Beasts* is outstanding; the characterization of each creature is delightfully fresh, but a prophetic warning note is struck – already the polecat has attacked a sheep. In the next room is part of the dismembered *St Thomas à Becket Altar* by Bertram's successor, **Master Francke**. Painted for the league of merchants who traded with England, it's in a very different style – the figures are more monumental, the structure tauter, the mood more emotional. The most interesting work here from the Renaissance period is **Cranach**'s *The Three Electors of Saxony*. This uses the religious format of the triptych, with a continuous landscape background, in order to show the deceased dukes, Frederick the Wise and John the Fearless, alongside the then ruler, John Frederick the Magnanimous.

FLEMISH AND DUTCH PAINTING
The Flemish section begins with a tiny *House Altar* by **Isenbrandt** and the coolly beautiful *Mary Magdalene Playing the Lute* by the mysterious Antwerp painter dubbed **Master of the Female Half-Lengths** because of his preferred way of depicting his subjects. Also on view is a mature religious masterpiece by **van Dyck**, *The Adoration of the Shepherds*. Most of the specialist painters of seventeenth-century Holland are represented, but they're rather overshadowed by two examples of **Rembrandt**. *The Presentation in the Temple* is one of his earliest surviving works: he was only 21 when he painted it, yet

there's no sign of immaturity or lack of confidence. From five years later, when Rembrandt was established as a fashionable society portraitist, comes *Maurits Huyghens*.

SEVENTEENTH- AND EIGHTEENTH-CENTURY EUROPEAN PAINTING

Highlights among the display of seventeenth- and eighteenth-century European painting are: **Claude**'s *Dido and Aeneas at Carthage*; a pair of **Tiepolos**, *The Agony in the Garden* and *The Crowning with Thorns*; **Canaletto**'s *Capriccio with a View of Padua*; **Bellotto**'s *Ideal View with Palace Steps*; **Goya**'s *Don Tómas Pérez Estala*; and *The Creation of Eve* by the eccentric Swiss artist **Heinrich Füssli**, whose sensationalism makes a fascinating contrast with the paintings of Bertram from four hundred years earlier. There is one outstanding sculpture from this period – a bust of a cardinal by **Bernini**.

NINETEENTH- AND TWENTIETH-CENTURY GERMAN ART

The nineteenth-century German section is one of the museum's main strengths. Of a dozen works by **Caspar David Friedrich**, three rank among his most haunting and original creations. *Wanderer above the Mists* shows an isolated figure with his back to the viewer, contemplating an eternity of sky and clouds; overpowering and intimate at the same time, it stresses the awesome, unfathomable power of the natural world. This same theme is present to even greater effect in *Eismeer*, inspired by the voyages of polar exploration, which were then beginning, it depicts a ship half-submerged against a cracked iceberg. It also has political significance, since the picture symbolizes lost hopes after the 1848 Revolution. In contrast, *The First Snow of Winter* imparts a dimension of grandeur to a quite ordinary landscape scene.

Another German artist with a distinctive vision of the world was the short-lived **Philipp Otto Runge**, most of whose best work can be seen here. His most arresting images are portraits of children (usually his own). Chubby-cheeked, over life-size and bursting with energy, they're placed at eye level to face the viewer head-on. Very different, but equally effective, is the realist approach of **Wilhelm Leibl**, the German equivalent of Courbet. *Three Women at Church*, with its phenomenal detail, supersmooth texture and uncanny evocation of the rapt concentration of the subjects, is rightly considered his masterpiece.

The German Impressionists, **Max Liebermann** and **Lovis Corinth**, are each allocated a room, close to a choice collection of their French counterparts, including a version of **Manet**'s *Fauré as Hamlet* which is less finished but livelier than the one in Essen. Among the Expressionists, look out for two masterpieces by **Munch**: *Girls at the Seaside* and *Girls on the Bridge*. Pick of the usual range of twentieth-century paintings are **Otto Dix**'s *Der Krieg* triptych, a powerful anti-war statement, and **Paul Klee**'s translucent *Goldfish*, an abstract composition with a rare sense of poetry.

GALERIE DER GEGENWART

Directly adjacent to the main Kunsthalle rises the shining new modernist cube of the **Galerie der Gegenwart** (Gallery of Contemporary Art; same times and ticket). Opened in 1997, it is devoted to art from the 1960s to the present. Works by Andy Warhol, Joseph Beuys and Richard Serra can be found in the basement, surrounded by a chronology of artistic events. The first floor features young German artists; recent art from America, beginning with Bruce Nauman, can be found on the second; while the top floor is host to some of the stars of the German art world: Georg Baselitz, Gerhard Richter, Sigmar Polke and Markus Lüpertz.

The other museums

On Steintorplatz, facing the southern side of the Hauptbahnhof, is the **Museum für Kunst und Gewerbe** (Museum for Arts and Crafts; Tues, Wed & Fri–Sun 10am–6pm, Thurs 10am–9pm; DM8). This has excellent and well-displayed collections of applied

> ### MESSING ABOUT ON THE AUSSENALSTER
>
> Plenty of places **rent out sailing and rowing boats**. Nearest to the city centre, two out-fits operate outside the *Hotel Atlantic*, at An der Alster, which is on the southeastern side of the Aussenalster. On the northeastern side is *Kurt Bambauer* at *Café Hansa-Steg*, Schöne Aussicht 20a; and finally, at the northern tip of the Aussenalster, you'll find *Bobby Reich* at Fernsicht 2 (☎ 487824). Prices vary according to length of rental and how many people want to go in one boat, and your best bet is to check prices with the tourist office.

art, ranging from ancient Egypt, Greece and Rome right through to the present centu-ry. It's an ideal place to dip into various epochs and artistic styles, and find something you didn't know you liked. The Art Nouveau/Jugendstil collection is very extensive and is particularly memorable in that the museum pieces have been arranged to create complete rooms, so that you get an idea of how things looked in peoples' homes. Also impressive are the sections devoted to oriental art: there's an authentic room in which traditional Japanese tea ceremonies are held (advance booking recommended).

A further five minutes' walk south brings you to Altländer Strasse and the **Deichtorhallen** (Tues–Sun 11am–6pm; variable entrance charges), the former fruit and veg market halls. The original wrought-iron and glass structures were restored a few years ago as an important addition to the municipally owned stock of art galleries. There's no permanent show, but a challenging programme of travelling exhibitions, which are always worth checking on.

The Alster lakes and the river

The Alster lakes, in the heart of Hamburg, make up the main recreational area of the city. Whether with ice-skating in winter or sailing and boating in summer, the large **Aussenalster** is always a busy place, while the smaller **Binnenalster** is frequented mainly by commercial boats and pedestrians promenading around its shores. Together, the two lakes encompass an area of about 3 square kilometres with no fewer than nine thousand boats licensed to use them. Not surprisingly, there are times during the height of the summer season when the tourist boats can hardly squeeze through. The shoreline around both lakes is open to the public, and the footpaths along it are incor-porated into park landscapes.

To walk around the lakes would take about three hours, and take you past many of the city's finest villas, clubs and consulates, especially along the **western shore**, where the rich have traditionally built their lakeside homes. The areas known as **Rotherbaum** and **Harvestehude** are two of the most exclusive residential parts of Hamburg, and if you enjoy nineteenth-century and Jugendstil architecture, it's worth exploring some of the streets around here: especially those branching off from the Klosterstern, such as Harvestehuder Weg and its side streets. Around Pöseldorfer Weg and Milchstrasse, par-allel with Harvestehuder Weg, is an area known locally as **Pöseldorf**. This has become a particularly trendy and upmarket spot, where media types hang out in expensive cafés and pose in the similarly pricey restaurants. The **eastern shore** presents an equally well-heeled facade, but look beyond it and you soon find yourself in the sleazy streets of St Georg. Only further to the northeast does the surrounding area become respectably res-idential, gradually meeting up with the exclusive villas spilling over from Harvestehude.

Along the River Alster

The course of the **River Alster** stretches for a good 50km further, heading first north, through Hamburg's suburbs, and then twisting and turning its way westwards to

THE BEATLES IN HAMBURG

"I was raised in Liverpool, but I grew up in Hamburg."
John Lennon

Hamburg is inextricably bound up with the early career of the **Beatles**, who made five separate visits to the city between 1960 and 1962. During this period, they took up residence at four different clubs, and although these have long been closed, you can still see the original buildings in St Pauli. You'll get a good idea of the seedy environment the band found themselves in and you can visit all the sites in a matter of minutes as they are within a stone's throw of each other.

The fab five – John, Paul, George, bass player Stuart Sutcliffe and drummer Pete Best – first arrived in Hamburg on August 16, 1960. Thinking they were appearing at the *Kaiserkeller*, the lads were dismayed to find themselves booked at the *Indra* (Grosse Freiheit 34), a well-known strip club instead. They played four and a half hours a night every Tuesday to Friday and six hours every Saturday and Sunday. After seven weeks, the club was closed down, owing to complaints about the noise, and the group did make their debut at the *Kaiserkeller* (Grosse Freiheit 38) on October 4. Unfortunately, the next month, George was deported for being under-age at seventeen. The others decided to stay but a few days later both Paul and Pete were arrested and told to leave Hamburg for allegedly attempting to set fire to their lodgings at the back of the *Bambi Kino*, a small cinema at Paul-Roosen-Str. 33.

On their second visit, the Beatles were booked to play at the more prestigious *Top Ten Club* (Reeperbahn 136) and things started to pick up for them. Stuart wasn't so enchanted, however, and decided to leave the group. He'd already fallen in love with local photographer, **Astrid Kirchherr**, and decided to settle in Hamburg and concentrate on his painting. Tragically his artistic career was cut short – when the Beatles made their third visit to Hamburg on April 11, 1962, they were met by Astrid with the news that Stuart had died following a convulsion the day before. The band had little time to come to terms with the terrible news; their seven-week residence at the *Star Club* (Grosse Freiheit 39) started just two days later. Despite the traumatic circumstances, it became a popular venue with the group and on the two further visits they made to Hamburg later that year, it was to the *Star Club* that they returned.

The **influence of Hamburg** on the Beatles' musical career cannot be overstated. Bruno Koschmider, the owner of the *Indra*, was not impressed by the band's static performance and demanded they "make a show". Within weeks they had transformed their act, and began talking to the audience and fooling around on stage. The famous **Moptop haircut** was undoubtedly copied from the "mushroom" style (*Pilzkopf*) adopted by the *Exis*, Hamburg's young existentialists. Astrid Kirchherr first cut Stuart Sutcliffe's hair in this style and, despite initial reservations, the other Beatles soon followed suit. And it was in Hamburg in 1960 that the Beatles first met the drummer for Rory Storm and the Hurricanes – **Ringo Starr**.

Henstedt. There's a marked footpath (yellow triangles) that follows the course of the river, but the trip to Henstedt is not something you could manage in one day, unless you go by bike and are very energetic. However, for countrified bike excursions, you don't need to go too far out. The 18km stretch from the tip of the Aussenalster to the Wohldorf lock runs through shady park landscapes as well as past river scenes little changed for centuries. There's no need to retrace your route back into the city either, since public transport is available at various points. For example, the U-Bahn stops Ohlsdorf or Klein Borstel are not far from the Fuhlsbüttel lock; 6km further on is the Poppenbüttel S-Bahn stop; and not far from the Wohldorf lock is the Ohlstedt U-Bahn stop. Maps of the entire route are available from the tourist office, in the brochure entitled *Die Alster*.

St Pauli, Altona and Univiertel

Beginning along the shore of the River Elbe and curving northeast towards the base of the Aussenalster, the three quarters of St Pauli, Altona and Univiertel embrace the western curve of the city centre's traditional edge. **St Pauli** and **Altona** are the southernmost part, melting smoothly into each other, while the **Univiertel** sits compactly north of St Pauli. Collectively, they form the main stomping ground for night-time revellers of all kinds, and contain Hamburg's red-light district, home of the infamous **Reeperbahn**.

St Pauli

St Pauli, defined by the River Elbe, the Holstenstrasse towards Altona and the rail tracks to the north, is nearest to the city centre, and was originally home to Hamburg's sea-related trades and crafts. The **Reeperbahn**, for example, was where the rope-makers once lived; and the Grosse and Kleine Freiheit (Big Freedom and Little Freedom) are streets so-named not because of the live sex shows you see there today, but because in medieval times craftsmen were free to practise their trade here. To a large extent, St Pauli is a working-class, residential area to this day, with the sex industry confining itself to the very small area of the Reeperbahn and short streets running off either side, especially those leading towards the port.

Lately, St Pauli has been infiltrated by a new set of after-dark revellers, since many bars and clubs have been taken over by avant-garde theatre operators and entrepreneurs. In the middle of the Reeperbahn, for example, is one of the city's trendiest alternative cabaret and theatre bars, *Schmidt*. For detailed listings of local bars see pp.669–670.

Altona

Heading west, **Altona** follows directly on from St Pauli. Like its neighbour, it has its share of river, partly lined with industrial fish-processing plants, but also with the leafy environs of the **Palmaille** and **Elbchaussee**, grand avenues lined with nineteenth-century villas. Its western border is roughly defined by Fischersallee, while to the north it spreads almost as far as Fruchtallee. Although much of Altona is unremarkable for the visitor, it has had an interesting history. Originally a Danish settlement on the edges of German Hamburg, it has always been a haven of free-thinkers and religious tolerance. It was a place of racial tolerance too, and as maritime trade brought more and more foreigners to Hamburg, many chose to settle in Altona. A legacy of those times are the many excellent and cheap Portuguese restaurants near the harbour. In this century, Altona became a favoured home for the Turkish, Greek and Arabic "guestworkers" of the city, hence the many kebab shops and takeaway kiosks around Altona Bahnhof, especially along Ottenser Hauptstrasse. To find out more about the quarter's history, and in particular its Dutch heritage, the **Altonaer Museum** (Tues–Sun 10am–6pm; DM8), just south of the Bahnhof at Museumstr. 23, has displays on the entire region, concentrating on trades such as boat-building, farming, fishing and the many different crafts associated with ships and the sea.

Traditionally, Altona's residents were not much more upmarket than St Pauli's. But the developers have slowly been moving in on the beautiful but decaying nineteenth-century housing buildings, and certain areas are rapidly becoming rather chic with prices to match. One such street is the **Friedensallee**: this is still unremarkable at its northwestern end but stroll along the short stretch beginning near Altona station, and ritzy, neon-lit stores cluster among sophisticated restaurants and bars. However, it's not all super-cool around here. The nearby Barnerstrasse is home to one of the city's most favoured and enduring live music venues, the *Fabrik*.

The Schanzenviertel

Between here and the Univiertel to the northeast is another popular entertainments quarter, the **Schanzenviertel**. One of its main streets, **Schulterblatt** (near the Sternschanze S- and U-Bahn stop), is home to several popular student *Kneipen*, as well as excellent cheap restaurants. A very different atmosphere prevails around here, not so much trendy as relaxed and unpretentious. The **Schanzenstrasse**, which splits away from Schulterblatt, is also worth checking out, and for all bar and café listings, see pp.669–671.

The Univiertel

One U-Bahn stop further, to Schlump, and you're virtually in the **Univiertel**. The streets of most interest are **Grindelhof** and **Rentzelstrasse**: this is where you'll find the largest variety of reasonably priced restaurants and café-bars. Also here is the city's most popular "alternative" cinema, the *Abaton*, which has a large bar-restaurant upstairs, and is regularly packed. There's not much life except on these two streets, but for choice and variety it's the best place to be for relaxed eating and drinking, where dress code and image are of little significance.

Just beyond is the **Museum für Völkerkunde** (Tues, Wed & Fri–Sun 10am–6pm, Thurs 10am–9pm; DM7) at Rothenbaumchaussee 64. Here Hamburg's maritime associations with Africa, the South Pacific, the Americas and Russia are on display. It's particularly refreshing that the museum tries to avoid pandering to voyeuristic attitudes, by showing the cultures as present-day societies with present-day concerns, rather than as exotic curiosities. The effects of tourism on the Pacific is just one display that stimulates fresh attitudes.

The suburbs: Oevelgönne, Blankenese and Neuengamme

Expeditions to the edge of Hamburg take you to opposite ends of the spectrum: to the west are riverside Oevelgönne and Blankenese, with exquisitely restored fishermen's houses, which are now home to the very wealthy; and to the east, Neuengamme, site of one of the concentration camps that operated around the city during World War II, now a sobering museum.

Oevelgönne

Heading west along the Elbe, away from the city centre, a road and then a path lead first to **Oevelgönne** and then to Blankenese. Both were originally suburbs which housed fishermen and sea captains in beautiful, tiny houses. Today, these areas are among the most popular with the well-heeled, who pay silly prices to squeeze themselves into the "quaint" houses with wide views across the river. The route along the water is very pleasant, with plenty of sandy beaches along the way, and both can easily be visited within the space of a morning's relaxed cycling. Alternatively, catch a boat from St Pauli as far as Neumühlen, or one station further to Teufelsbrück, using the *HADAG Niederelbedienst* (the Lower Elbe boat service run by *HADAG* shipping), which will take your bicycle for a half-fare. Bus #112, from Altona Bahnhof, will also take you to Oevelgönne, or you can get the S-Bahn to Blankenese.

A particular attraction of Oevelgönne, worth a visit in its own right, is the **Museumshafen**, where around twenty old-time working boats are moored. Each one has been lovingly restored, from early twentieth-century fire brigade boats to nineteenth-century wooden fishing trawlers and double-masted freighters. It's a private museum, run by enthusiasts, who willingly show visitors around if they happen to be there. If nobody is around, you can still stop off at the *Flosscafé* (late June–early Aug only, daily 2–10pm), where a small exhibition describes the ecological problems of the Elbe resulting from industrial pollution. Less earnest and more upmarket is the café *Strandperle* on the beach, which is a favoured summertime hang-out among the "in-crowd". If your purse can stand the strain, there are also some excellent fish restaurants around here.

Blankenese

Blankenese, a twenty-minute cycle ride further along the river, is remarkable chiefly because it is situated on a small yet steep hill, a great rarity in this flat part of Germany. Long gone are the times when it was home to retired fishing folk, who watched the constant flow of ships sailing by. Now, villas squeeze tightly in alongside the older houses, and steep roads and stairway paths wind in among them. It's very picturesque, and down by the beach of beautiful white sand, refined cafés and restaurants cater to your every need. Nearby, there's also a fragrant park of ancient trees, now home to many deer. The woods conceal many cafés as well, notoriously hard to find – the *Witt Hüs* has music, a huge variety of teas and wonderful, wholesome cakes. It's at Elbchaussee 499a, but you'll need to ask directions.

Neuengamme

Neuengamme, the other side of Hamburg, on its eastern edge, is reached via the S-Bahn to Bergedorf, and then buses #227 or #327. The concentration camp **KZ-Gedenkstätte Neuengamme** (Tues–Fri 10am–5pm, Sat & Sun 10am–6pm; free) is now a political education centre, including an exhibition of photos and documents that re-creates the horrors of the past, recording the story of resistance. Hamburg's other concentration camp was at Fuhlsbüttel (near the airport), and some 50,000 people, including over 6000 Hamburg Jews, died in these two camps.

While in Bergedorf, you could look at its lovely thirteenth-century **Schloss**, (Tues–Thurs & Sat & Sun 10am–5pm; DM6) close to the S-Bahn. Originally surrounded by a moat, the gabled, red-brick castle was situated on an important medieval trade route, its role primarily tax-collecting rather than noble residence. Inside is a local museum, which concentrates on regional folklore and costumes, as well as traditional rural arts and crafts.

Eating, drinking and nightlife

When it comes to **eating and drinking** in Hamburg, it's always worth making your way out of the city centre. It is true that there are plenty of reasonable restaurants around the Grossneumarkt, but the choice and variety is just so much greater, and the prices lower, if you head to the nearby **Univiertel** or **Schanzenviertel**. For *Imbiss*-type food, the stalls in the St Georg area near the Hauptbahnhof offer cheap snacks, as do those in the Reeperbahn in St Pauli. Another place for quick snacks is the pedestrian area outside Altona Bahnhof.

Restaurants

There are two local specialities to try. *Aalsuppe*, generally made with plums and mixed vegetables as well as eels, is one of the most outstanding soups you'll encounter in Germany. *Labskaus*, a traditional sailor's dish, is more controversial, not to say indigestible; it's a hash which typically contains pickled corned beef, herring, beetroot, mashed potato, onions and gherkins, all topped with a fried egg. Otherwise the endless variety of fish dishes are the most typical meals around here.

Traditional Gaststätten

Traditional Hamburg restaurants are found throughout the city. From a choice of many, the following are always worth trying for traditional local dishes, as well as standard German fare.

Ahrberg, Strandweg 33. In Blankenese, down by the river. This is one of the city's best German/fish restaurants, with carp a speciality.

Alt Hamburger Aalspeicher, Deichstr. 43. The best place to sample *Aalsuppe*. It's not cheap, but is always excellent. Try to avoid the place during lunch hour when hordes of businessmen descend.

Anno 1750, Ost-West-Str. 47. Historic beer tavern known for its home-smoked eel. Closed Sun.

But'n Dammdoor, Mittelweg 27. Favoured by a number of prominent Hamburgers, but nevertheless offers great reasonably priced meals.

Fischerhaus, Fischmarkt 14. Offers no-nonsense fish dishes down by the Fischmarkt, not necessarily at cheap prices.

Franziskaner, Grosse Theaterstr. 9. A Bavarian-style beer hall and garden, a real rarity in these northerly climes. Closed Sun.

Nikolaikeller, Cremon 36. Supposedly the longest and best menu of herring dishes in Germany.

Old Commercial Room, Englische Planke 10. Touristy but well recommended and close to St Michaelis.

Ratsweinkeller, Grosse Johanisstr. 2. As is hinted by its longer-than-usual name, Hamburg's version of the inevitable town-hall cellar restaurant is posher – and better – than most. Closed Sun.

Other restaurants

A Hereford Beefstouw, Schopenstehl 32. Danish grill in a handsome old Baroque house.

Arkadasch, Grindelhof 17. Offers a large choice of Turkish dishes at very affordable prices.

At Nali, Rutschbahn 11. Turkish restaurant with a large menu and friendly atmosphere.

A Varinha, Karpfangerstr. 16. Excellent Portuguese restaurant; great food at great prices. Two people could easily share one of these tremendous portions.

Balutschi, Grinelallee 33. Pakistani food in authentic surroundings; leave your shoes at the door before sitting on the floor at one of the low tables.

Cuneo, Davidstr. 11. Long-established Italian, particularly recommendable for pasta dishes.

Deichgraf, Deichstr. 23. Not exclusively Italian, but very good-value pasta.

Goldene Oase, Eppendorfer Baum 34. Hamburg's most innovative vegetarian restaurant.

Matsumi, Colonnaden 96. Japanese restaurant with sushi and sashimi bars.

Medded, Bahrenfelder Chaussee 140. Egyptian food that's a bargain at the price.

Objektiv, Grindelhof 39. Luxurious snacks and small dishes for reasonable prices.

Peking Enten Haus, Rentzelstr. 48. As the name suggests, the house speciality is Peking duck: the poultry served is specially reared, and is prepared by chefs from the Chinese capital.

Sagres, Vorsetzen 42. One of the many Portuguese eating houses around the harbour, this is a homely place, popular with Portuguese dock workers – which means giant portions. Try the swordfish with paella.

Sala Thai, Brandsende 6. Thai restaurant featuring folk dancing on Wednesday evenings and specializing in seafood grills.

San Michele, Englische Planke 8. Classic Italian restaurant in the shadow of St Michaelis – the food is pricey but very good.

Shalimar, Dillstr. 16. Arguably the city's best Indian restaurant, specializing in Mughal cuisine.

Taipan, Alsterdorfer Str. 303. The one and only place in Germany where you can enjoy the delights of Mongolian barbecues. Evenings only, except at weekends; closed Mon.

Tre Fontane, Mundsburger Damm 45. Cosy and well-priced Italian; closed Tues.

Bars

Hamburg's **bars** regularly move in and out of favour, but the following make up the heart of the city's nightlife. These days it centres around the St Pauli area and many places don't open before 10pm. Popular student bars, which are drinking haunts as well as good for cheap meals, can be found in the **Univiertel** and the **Schanzenviertel**. In the former, Grindelhofstrasse, Rentzelstrasse and Grindelallee are particularly good streets to explore.

St Pauli

Blaue Nacht, Gerhardstr. 16. This is the one that started the trend into St Pauli in the mid-1980s. These days its popularity is waning, but it's not dead yet.

Casablanca, Beim Grünen Jäger 21. Excellent Mexican, Italian and German food (vegetarian too) at reasonable prices.

La Paloma, Gerhardstr. 2. Open 24hr, this is an intimate place mixing art on the walls with heavy drinking.

Mary Lou, Hans-Albers-Platz 3. Red lighting notwithstanding, a hangout favoured by the new set of St Pauli.

Molotow, Spielbudenplatz 5. Post-punk background music in this increasingly popular haunt.

Prinzenbar, Kastanienallee 20. Stuccoed angles and chandeliers are the setting for drinking, with good soul sounds as well as occasional live shows.

Tempelhof, Hamburger Berg 12. Very popular seedy bar, which retains its swivel chairs and lowered lights. Party troopers mix with red-light customers.

Schanzenviertel, Univiertel and Altona

Abaton, Grindelhof 14a, Univiertel. Has an innovative cinema attached, and is a large and noisy place that gets very busy with students at night.

Eisenstein, Friedensallee 5, Altona. Situated in an old factory, bare stone walls and a high ceiling are the setting for people to show just how important they are, or at least how good they are at looking like it. Excellent pizzas.

Erika's Eck, Sternstr. 98. The favoured haunt of late-night drinkers who work in the nearby slaughterhouse. Open until 3am, when it serves the largest and cheapest breakfast in the city.

Filmhaus, Friedensallee 7, Altona. Popular with creative types and media people. The interior is plain, with simple wooden tables and chairs comfortable enough for a whole night's drinking. The food is good, though the atmosphere gets very smoky.

Frank und Frei, Schanzenstr. 93. A big, slow-paced favourite with students.

Frauenkneipe, Stresemannstr. 60. Strictly women-only bar.

Gorki Park, Grindenallee 1 and Hans-Henny-Jahnn-Weg 69. Beer and Russian snacks and meals in a pseudo-Soviet ambience.

Kir, Max-Brauer-Allee 251. Friendly staff attend to serious posers.

Limerick, Gridenallee 18. Wonderful beer bar with wooden interior, offering good meals at good prices. Favourite with students.

PickenPack, Schulterblatt 3. A good place for an evening's unpretentious drinking, as well as filling meals.

Vienna, Fettstr. 2. Tries to create the atmosphere of a bistro-cum-sitting room.

Elsewhere in the city

Gröninger Braukeller, Ost-West-Str. 47. A city-centre *Hausbrauerei* that serves its own unfiltered dark malt beer; also does basic meals.

Souterrain, Papenhuder Str. 26. Popular, even though it is over on the eastern edge of the Aussenalster (nearest U-Bahn stop Mundsburg).

Cafés and café-bars

Most **café-bars** have food as well, most notably excellent breakfasts and snacks (expect to pay around DM8–12). Each reflects the area it's in: you can expect places like Pöseldorf to be pricey and full of yuppies, while the Univiertel and Schanzenviertel are more studenty; and Altona is unpretentious, with mixed crowds.

City centre

Café Oertel, Esplanade 29. One of the best choices for traditional *Kaffee und Kuchen*.

Café Schöne Aussichten, Gorch Fock Wall (in the park). An excellent summertime place, with tree-shaded terrace.

Gestern & Heute, Kaiser-Wilhelm-Str. 55. Legendary for the variety of its breakfasts, this place is open around the clock.

Loft, Grosse Bleichen 21 (in the Galleria). Exclusive daytime café for monied people.

GAY HAMBURG

Not surprisingly, Hamburg has a lively **gay scene**. Other than talking to people in bars and cafés, the best way to find out what's on is from the city's two gay publications, the magazine *Du und Ich* and the free sheet *Gay Express*, both available in most gay bars. Good starting points for **men** are: the *Café Gnosa* (see below); *Image*, Poststr. 39; and *Café Spund*, Mohlenhofstr. 3.

For **women**, the best place to find out what's on and where to go around town is probably the *Frauenbuchladen*, Bismarckstr. 98 (☎420 4748), which also runs a café. Other women's cafés, not necessarily exclusively lesbian, are *Café Meg Donna*, Grindelallee 43, *Frauenkneipe*, Stresemannstr. 60, and *Frauenkulturcafé*, now part of the *Frauenhotel Hanseatin* on Dragonerstall (see p.656). A **women-only disco** worth checking out is the *Camelot*, Hamburger Berg 12, in St Pauli.

St Georg

Café Gnosa, Lange Reihe 93. Lovely 1930s café with good food. Popular with the gay community.

Café Koppel, Koppel 66. Best known for its delicious chocolate cake; also serves vegetarian and wholefood dishes.

Café Urlaub, Lange Reihe 63. Breakfast and billiards.

Geel Haus, Koppel 76. One of the better places around here.

Max und Consorten, Spadenteich 7. Situated on a deceptively pretty square, whose trees shade daytime prostitutes.

Schanzenviertel, Univiertel and Altona

Café Backwahn, Grindelallee 148, Univiertel. Five different breakfasts from around DM8.

Café Stenzel, Schulterblatt 61, Schanzenviertel. A very mixed crowd frequent this pleasantly chaotic place.

Café Treibeis, Gausstr. 25, Altona. Alternative hangout, and a good place for weekend breakfasts.

Maybach, Heussweg 66, Altona. On the northern edges of the quarter, this has a beer garden too, a rarity in these parts.

Stradiwadi, Rentzelstr. 17, Univiertel. Relaxed café-theatre, with courtyard terrace round the back.

Nightlife and entertainment

Hamburg is a great city for live music, boasting just about the best jazz scene in Germany, and attracts a good range of visiting international bands. For the most up-to-date information on where to go, what's on and music venues of all kinds, consult the magazines *Szene Hamburg*, *Prinz* or *Oxmox*.

Discos

Grünspan, Grosse Freiheit 58. Long-established late-closing hard rock disco. Fri 9pm–7am, Sat 9pm–8am.

Kaiserkeller, Grosse Freiheit 36. Part of the *Grosse Freiheit* building, and one of the city's largest discos. DM4 admission includes a drink, open daily 9pm–4am.

Kazwo, Mittelweg 22. Popular with media types – a place to be seen. Tues–Sun 10pm onwards.

Madhouse, Valentinskamp 46a. Much the liveliest of the city's discos on weekdays.

Paparazzi, Stresemannstr. 206. Afro-Caribbean music Wed–Sun from 10pm – DM10 at weekends, cheaper in the week.

Live music venues

Birdland, Gärtnerstr. 122. Prestigious jazz venue; the music varies from avant-garde experimentation to trad Dixieland.

Cotton Club, Alter Steinweg. Traditional jazz club.

Dennis Swing Club, Papenhuderstr. 25. Jazz venue, though expect Dixieland rather than modern jazz.

Docks, Spielbudenplatz 19–20. Worth checking out, but the acoustics here are dodgy, and it can get very stuffy.

Fabrik, Barnerstr. 36. One of the longest-enduring live music venues in Hamburg, this place is always worth a visit.

Grosse Freiheit, Grosse Freiheit 36. The city's main venue for rock/contemporary live music, with big-name bands mostly playing at weekends. The admission charge depends on who's performing.

Logo, Grindelallee 5. Mainly English and American underground bands.

Markthalle, Klosterwall 9–12. Along with *Fabrik*, venue for better-known European bands.

Werkstatt 3, Nernstweg 32. Located in Altona, this is a centre for alternative projects which often acts as a stage for Third World bands. Fri and Sat evenings are tropical dance nights.

Classical music

Hamburg's musical tradition can match that of any city in the world. The present *Staatsoper* at Dammtorstr. 28 (☎351721 or 35680), not far from the famous but now vanished old building on the Gänsemarkt, once run by Telemann, is one of the top half-dozen **opera** houses in the world: Munich is its only German rival. In recent years, it has benefited from the inspired management of Rolf Liebermann. The **ballet** company attached to the house, run by the American John Neumeier, is also considered to be the best in the country at the moment. Lighter work is performed at the *Operettenhaus*, Spielbudenplatz 1 (☎311170), monopolized by the musical *Cats* for the last ten years.

There are three **orchestras** – the *Hamburger Philharmoniker*, the *Hamburger Symphoniker* and the *Norddeutscher-Rundfunk* (the house orchestra of the locally based national radio station). Of these the last-named has gained an unexpected international fame in recent years, particularly performing under its veteran conductor laureate Günter Wand – no orchestra can offer more definitive interpretations of the central German classics, such as the symphonies of Beethoven and Brahms. The main concert hall is the *Musikhalle*, Johannes-Brahms-Platz (☎346920). The *Monteverdi-Chor*, which excels in music of the Renaissance and Baroque eras, keeps up the city's choral tradition. It's also worth looking out for performances in the churches, especially St Jakobi.

Theatre

The *Deutsches Schauspielhaus* at Kirchenallee 39 (☎248713) is one of the country's leading **theatres**. It's the successor to the *Nationaltheater*, one of whose first employees was the great eighteenth-century playwright and critic Gotthold Ephraim Lessing.

Among the many venues for drama, some of the most renowned are: *Thalia-Theater* at Alstertor (☎328140); the *Hamburger Kammerspiele* at Hartungstr. 9 (☎441 9690); *Ernst-Deutsch-Theater*, Mundsburger Damm 60 (☎227 0140); and *Theater im Zimmer* at Alsterchaussee 30 (☎446539). For kids, there's the *Theater für Kinder*, Max-Brauer-Allee 76 (☎382538) or the *Puppentheater* at Reinbeker Weg 32 (☎720 3288). Plays in English are performed at the *English Theatre of Hamburg*, Lerchenfeld 14 (☎227 7089), while the *St-Pauli-Theater*, Spielbudenplatz 29 (☎314344) hosts musicals by British and American touring companies. *Hansa Theater*, Steindamm 17 (☎241414), presents old-fashioned variety and circus-type shows.

During the **summer open-air theatre festival** (usually in July), make sure you head for performances at the *Kampnagelfabrik* by the Barmbek S-Bahn stop. For the most interesting **cabaret** in the city, head for the *Schmidt*, Spielbudenplatz 24 (☎317 7880), on the Reeperbahn; *Ohnsorg-Theater*, Grosse Bleichen 23 (☎3508 0321), features plays in the local dialect.

Listings

Airport information ☎5075 2557 or 5075 2558.

American Express Rathausmarkt 5 (☎331141).

Brewery tours The famous *Holstenbrauerei*, Holstenstr. 224, has regular free tours (Mon–Wed 9.30am–1pm & Thurs 9.30am; 2hr; bookings ☎381010) which must be booked about three months in advance and are only for groups of three or more.

Car rental *Hertz* Kirchenallee 34–36 (☎280 1201); *Sixt Budget*, Hauptbahnhof (☎322419);*Topcar*, Gertrudenstr. 2 (☎335998).

Consulates *British*, Harvestehuder Weg 8a (☎448 0320); *Irish*, Feldbrunnenstr. 43 (☎4418 6213); *New Zealand*, Heimhuder Str. 56 (☎442 5550); *US*, Alsterufer 28 (☎411710).

Cultural Institutes *British Council* Rothenbaumchaussee 34 (☎446057).

Doctor ☎228022.

Festivals are by no means a Hamburg speciality, but the *Übersee Tag* on May 7 celebrates the founding of the port in 1189. A funfair, the *Dom*, is held on the Heiligengeistfeld, close to the St Pauli U-Bahn station, with separate spring, summer and autumn sessions.

Laundry *Wasch Center* chain, daily 6am–midnight at: Steilshooperstr. 317; Ohlsdorfer Str. 1–3; Mülenkamp 37; Hammer Landstr. 84; Pagenfelder Platz 5; Eppendorfer Weg 119; and Nobistor 34.

Mitfahrzentrale Lobuschstr. 22 (☎391721); Gotenstr. 19 (☎19444); Ernst-Merck-Str. 8 (☎19440).

Post office For the main post office with poste restante facilities, take the Kirchenallee exit out of the Hauptbahnhof.

Sports *Hamburger SV* are one of Germany's best football teams and play in the Volksparkstadion out in Altona. Sailing regattas are frequently held on the Aussenalster and there are various international events, such as a tennis championship in late May, and an equestrian event in early June.

Swimming The beautiful baths at Bismarckbad in Altona are the city's most luxurious, and have women-only days. For outdoor swimming the smaller lakes around Hamburg (such as the Grossensee, Mönchsteich and Bredenbeker Teich) are the best: getting to them is, however, tricky – ask at the tourist office for details.

Taxis ☎611061 or 292900.

Women's centre Schmilinskystr. 7 (☎245002).

Zoo *Hagenbecks Tierpark* (daily 9am–6pm or dusk; DM18) in the north of the city (take U-Bahn #2 to the station of the same name) is generally regarded as one of the world's leading zoos, pioneering the modern practice of simulating the animals' natural habitat, rather than keeping them caged up.

SCHLESWIG-HOLSTEIN

A land between two seas, **Schleswig-Holstein** is chiefly an agricultural region, with large areas of forest and moorland. There's little heavy industry, and only two major cities. **Kiel**, destroyed in the war and drably rebuilt, is the capital of the Land and seat of its only fully fledged university. For most of its history, it has lain in the shadow of **Lübeck**, once northern Europe's leading merchant city and the undoubted highlight of a visit to the province. Of the other towns, **Flensburg** is another highly atmospheric trading port, **Husum** is an attractive old fishing harbour, while **Schleswig**, the province's historic capital, is incongruously rich in treasures for a place so small.

Schleswig-Holstein has two very contrasting coastlines: the gently lapped and undulating **Baltic shore** and the flat, windblown **North Sea coast**, off which lie the **North Friesian islands**, providing a relaxing, if uneventful, break from the mainland. Hot tea and stiff alcohol are the traditional means of making the long, cold and dark winters pass. In summer, though, the landscape vibrates with blues and greens, the corn dotted with poppies and cornflowers, the fields burning with the bright yellow of rapeseed. It's beautiful countryside to meander through by any means, most perfectly by cycling, and along the coast frequent local boat services provide enjoyable alternatives. Many

---

BIKE RENTAL

It's worth knowing that **bikes** can be rented on a daily basis during summer months for about DM15 per day from the stations at Büsum, Flensburg, Meldorf, Niebüll and Schleswig. They are the perfect way to see the countryside of Schleswig-Holstein.

---

parts of the province, such as **Holstein Switzerland**, **Angeln** and **Dithmarschen**, have the added benefit of being well off any beaten tourist track.

The most obvious **route** to take, assuming that you're coming from and returning to Hamburg, is a circular one up the Baltic and down by the North Sea coast – though with so many ferries heading off to Scandanavia, it's also a good point for moving on.

Lübeck

In medieval times, **LÜBECK** was one of Europe's most important merchant cities and ports, dominating the highly lucrative trading routes along the Baltic. Although long over-shadowed by the North Sea harbours of Hamburg and Bremen, which replaced it as international seaports, the city proudly displays the magnificent architectural wealth of its merchant days – Germany's oldest town hall still in use, beautiful merchants' houses, fine Gothic brick-built churches, and quaint old charitable institutions – many of which employ a highly decorative form of brickwork. Indeed, Lübeck's leadership in the artistic sphere was as pronounced as it was in commerce, influencing the appearance of cities along the entire length of the northern European coast, from Amsterdam to Tallinn. The importance of Lübeck's heritage was given official recognition in 1987 by UNESCO's decision to place its entire Altstadt on the list of the world's most significant monuments – the first place in northern Europe to be so honoured. This award was not only a tribute to the past, but also to the skill and efficacy of modern German restoration techniques: the city was severely bombed in World War II, with a quarter of the centre completely destroyed, but what little evidence of this survives today has mostly been left as a deliberate reminder.

In the Cold War years, Lübeck was the only important city to be sited alongside the notorious barbed-wire frontier. Paradoxically, this stimulated a revival in its fortunes after a long period of decline. Nearly 100,000 refugees came to settle, not only from the lost Eastern Territories, but also from the GDR itself, before the frontier was finally sealed. Even if its days of glory are no more than a memory, it's still a vibrant city with a wide range of attractions which merits a visit of at least a couple of days.

Arrival, information and accommodation

The **Hauptbahnhof** lies just a few minutes' walk west of the Altstadt. Within the station itself is one of the **tourist offices** (Mon–Sat 9am–1pm & 3–6pm; ☎864675); there's another at Holstentor-Passage, Holstenstr. 20 (Mon–Fri 10.30am–6.30pm, Sat 10am–2pm, Sun 11am–1pm; ☎172300), and a third at Beckergrube 95 (Mon–Fri 8am–4pm; ☎122 8109). Almost immediately to the east is the **bus station**.

Accommodation
Hotels are clustered mainly around the Hauptbahnhof or within the Altstadt. There are very few rooms available in **private houses** (②–③), but it's still worth asking the tourist office about these, as some have enticing locations in the Altstadt. Lübeck is a

---

The **telephone code** for Lübeck is ☎0451

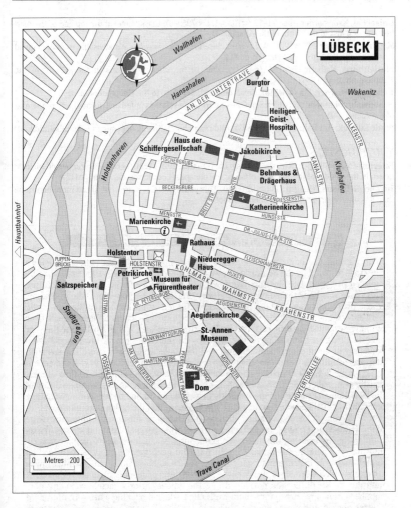

good place for budget travellers, with a choice of four places offering **dormitory** accommodation. The **campsite** is at Steinrader Damm 12 (☎893030) in the suburb of Schönböcken; take bus #7 or #8.

HOTELS

Alter Speicher, Beckergrube 91–93 (☎71045). A converted warehouse in the Altstadt fitted out with all the mod cons. ⑦

Altstadt, Fischergrube 52 (☎72083, fax 73778). Middle-range choice in the historic part of the city. ⑦

Am Dom, Dankwartsgrube 43 (☎702 0251). Reasonably priced option on a quiet street near the Dom. ⑥

Excelsior, Hansestr. 3 (☎88090). Located just beside the bus station, with large breakfast buffets a definite plus. ⑥

Jensen, Obertrave 4–5 (☎71646, fax 73386). In a modernized old mansion with a waterside view; also has a good restaurant. ⑦

Kaiserhof, Kronsforder Allee 11–13 (☎703301, fax 795083). Classy hotel at the top end of the market, situated just to the south of the Altstadt. ⑦

Koglin, Kottwitzstr. 39 (☎622432). Located close to the *Schönwald* – it's advisable to phone ahead before heading out here; take bus #4 or #14. ④

Marienburg, Katharinenstr. 41 (☎42512). One of the cheaper options in the vicinity of the Hauptbahnhof. ③

Petersen, Hansestr. 11a (☎84519). Small budget hotel close to the Hauptbahnhof. ③

Schönwald, Chasotstr. 25 (☎610580). One of the cheapest hotels in Lübeck, located well to the east of the Altstadt. ③

Stadt Lübeck, Am Bahnhof 21 (☎83883). Mid-range hotel directly opposite the Hauptbahnhof. ⑥

YOUTH HOSTELS

Interrail-Point-Sleep-In, Grosse Petersgrube 11 (☎71920). A YMCA hostel in a renovated historic house in the middle of the Altstadt, offering the cheapest beds in the city, from DM15.

Jugendgästehaus, Mengstr. 33 (☎702 0399). This youth hostel is more central and more luxurious than its counterpart at Am Gertrudenkirchhof. ☎

LÜBECK AND THE HANSEATIC LEAGUE

In the eleventh century, a small Wend settlement had been established at the point where the Trave is joined by the Schwartau. It was destroyed by a rival Slav tribe in 1138, to be replaced five years later by a trading town owing allegiance to the Counts of Holstein. This move was none too popular with **Henry the Lion**, the powerful Duke of Saxony, whose own economic situation was adversely affected by the success of the new Baltic port. After it had burned to the ground in 1157, he forced the count to hand the site over to him, re-establishing it as a city and harbour two years later, and as a bishopric the year after that. He gave it special privileges, whereby the merchants ran the town council independently of ducal control and administered their own system of justice. The so-called **statutes of Lübeck** were later adopted by over a hundred other Baltic towns, and set the trend for medieval German cities being far freer in outlook and atmosphere than the feudalistic principalities. In 1226 Lübeck was officially recognized as a Free Imperial City of the Holy Roman Empire and grew quickly in wealth and trading power. Within a century of its birth, it had become the richest city in Germany and the Baltic's premier port.

In 1243, Lübeck formed a trading alliance with Hamburg; this in time, under the name of the **Hanseatic League**, extended to nearly all other ports along the Baltic, as well as to inland cities such as Braunschweig, Lüneburg, Magdeburg and Cologne. A fairly informal grouping, it was initially inspired by the need for mutual protection against pirates, and as an instrument to settle disputes and squabbles among the member towns – matters which Germany's weak central authority was unable to influence. However, in time the Hanseatic League developed into the equivalent of a cartel, excluding nonmembers from any share in the lucrative Baltic trade and opening a network of trading centres abroad, the most important being in London, Bruges, Bergen and Novgorod. Lübeck was accepted as the leader and spokesman of the League, though it began to lose its supremacy to Danzig (now Gdańsk) in the latter half of the fifteenth century. Throughout the following century, the League itself declined, as valuable herring stocks diminished. The balance of power in Europe shifted, as the Dutch – with their superior vessels and forward-looking philosophy of free trade – began to bite deeply into the old monopoly, and as trading routes changed due to the discovery of the Americas and new shipping routes to the east. The Thirty Years' War, which drained energy and resources, and left the powerful nation-states of Sweden and the emergent Brandenburg-Prussia in control of much of the Baltic, finally killed it off. Down to just nine members, it met for the last time in Lübeck in 1669. However, Lübeck, along with Hamburg and Bremen, remained a significant port and trading centre. It was only in 1937 that it lost its status as a free city and was incorporated into Schleswig-Holstein.

Jugendherberge Gertrudenkirchhof, Am Gertrudenkirchhof 4 (☎33433). One of the city's two official youth hostels – go out of the Altstadt through the Burgtor, then bear left for about 200m. **☎** **Rucksackhotel Backpackers**, Kanalstr. 70 (☎706892). A privately owned hostel charging from DM21 for its dorms; also has doubles (DM75). It's located at the eastern edge of the Altstadt.

The Altstadt

Almost everything worth seeing in Lübeck is in the **Altstadt**, an egg-shaped island still surrounded by the water defences of the Trave and the city moat. Its streets, while not conforming to a pre-arranged plan, are nevertheless arranged very symmetrically, so it's easy to find your way around. For a general view of the magnificent skyline, walk northeast from the Hauptbahnhof to the Marienbrücke: better still, take one of the cruises round the harbour area (for details of these see "Listings" p.683).

The Holstentor, the Petrikirche and around

Entry to Lübeck was once through, but is now along, the side of, the **Holstentor** (Holstein Gate; April–Sept Tues–Sun 10am–5pm; Oct–March Tues–Sun 10am–4pm; DM4), whose two sturdy circular towers with turret roofs, joined by a gabled centre section, form the city's emblem. Built in 1477, it leans rather horrifyingly these days, but that shouldn't put you off calling in at its small historical museum, which provides a useful introduction to the city and Hanseatic history. On the waterfront to the right of the Holstentor is a row of lovely old gabled buildings, the **Salzspeicher** (salt warehouses). They were built in the sixteenth and seventeenth centuries to store precious salt, extracted in Lüneburg and destined for Scandinavia.

Straight ahead over the bridge and up Holstenstrasse, the first church on the right (just down a side street) is the Gothic **Petrikirche**, one of the many buildings to suffer during the massive Allied bombing of March 29, 1942. It no longer functions as a place of worship; instead, the whitewashed, five-aisled interior is put to use for changing exhibitions of contemporary art. A lift goes to the top of the **tower** (daily: mid-April to Sept 9am–6pm; Oct 1–6 9am–5pm; DM3.50), and Lübeck's centre is compact enough for this to be very useful for getting to grips with the layout of the city.

In the shadow of the church, at Kolk 16, is the **Museum für Puppentheater** (daily 10am–6pm; DM6), which claims to be the world's largest collection of puppet theatre material, with examples from all over Europe, Asia and Africa. Special matinees for kids are staged daily (except Mondays) at 3pm in the adjoining *Marionettentheater* (DM7); performances for adults are held on Fridays and Saturdays at 7.30pm (DM9–16). The next street along, **Grosse Petersgrube**, ranks as one of the finest in the city, with an impressive array of mansions showing all the different vernacular styles from Gothic to Neoclassical.

The Rathaus

Across Holstenstrasse from the Petrikirche is the Markt, two sides of which are occupied by the imposing **Rathaus**, which illustrates Lübeck's characteristic brickwork – with alternating rows of red unglazed and black glazed bricks – at its most inventive. The north wing, which dates from the mid-thirteenth century, has a high superstructure with spire-topped turrets and two huge holes to lessen wind resistance; its side facing the Markt was further enlivened by the addition of a Renaissance loggia made of very white-coloured stone from the city's old trading partner, the Swedish island of Gotland. At the turn of the fourteenth century, the east wing, with an arcade leading to Breite Strasse behind, was added. Its extension, the **Neue Gemach**, was begun around 1440 and is the finest part of all, providing a highly refined variation on the earlier theme of windbreaks and corner turrets, with the bonus of coats of arms embedded in the brickwork. On the Breite Strasse side, it was further embellished with an extremely elaborate stone staircase in the Dutch Renaissance style and an oriel window.

Guided tours (Mon–Fri at 11am, noon & 3pm; DM4) go round some of the interiors, though it has to be said that these don't quite match what you see from outside. The most notable rooms are the late Baroque **Audienzsaal**, with its allegorical paintings and Renaissance doorway, and the neo-Gothic **Bürgerschaft**. Leaving by the north side, you get a good view of the original thirteenth-century building, and can also see the **Kanzleigebäude**, the chancellery building tacked on in the fifteenth century.

The Marienkirche

Rearing up behind the north wing of the Rathaus is the city's largest and finest church, the **Marienkirche**. It's certain that the two buildings were intended to be seen as a coherent architectural group, as the Marienkirche was where the city's richest citizens worshipped – and they planned from the outset that it should overshadow the bishops' Dom not only by its prominent situation, but in its architectural splendour as well. Built at a leisurely pace between the early thirteenth and mid-fourteenth centuries, it's a tall, soaring building in the French Gothic style – but in brick, rather than stone, which gives it a very different and authentically German appearance. Its twin square **towers** are topped by spires to a height of 185m, while the nave is supported by flying buttresses that rise from the verdigris roofs of the side aisles. In the 1942 bombings the Marienkirche was severely damaged and burnt out – an exhibition inside shows photographs of the devastation and also of the restoration. Even more dramatically, the bells in the southern tower chapel have been left smashed on the ground, the way they fell during the bombing. War damage was a mixed blessing: the roof timbers and spires were destroyed, threatening the whole structure; both organs and many other items, including the chancel screen and much other fine woodwork, were lost. On the other hand, original Gothic **wall paintings** which had been covered for centuries were revealed and restored – indeed the entire interior was laid bare for a restoration to its original simplicity.

Today the interior is very light, with a feeling of great loftiness. Detail of the fine ribbing and vaulting is picked out against the pale grey chalk wash in the old terracotta and grey-green colours. All this makes a good backdrop for the church's **art treasures**. The fifteenth-century high altar, in front of which is a pretty fourteenth-century font, is of modest dimensions, but a number of impressive works, dating from the late fifteenth and early sixteenth centuries, can be seen in the ambulatory. These include a life-size carving of St John the Evangelist (unfortunately only partly restorable after war damage); a series of powerful Passion reliefs by the Münster sculptor Hinrik Brabender; and a beautiful locally made gilded tabernacle. In the axial chapel is a magnificent carved and painted altar from Antwerp in a gilded wood frame, depicting the life of the Virgin Mary, while in the Alenkapelle, the chapel adjoining the northern transept, is a grave slab of a merchant cast by Lübeck's greatest artist, Bernt Notke. Before leaving, have a look inside the **Briefkapelle** at the southwestern end of the nave, a masterly miniature church which is used by the congregation during the winter.

Mengstrasse and Breite Strasse

On the north side of the Marienkirche is **Mengstrasse**, which is lined with an impressive row of patrician houses. At no. 4 is the Baroque **Buddenbrookhaus** (daily 10am–5pm; DM5), which was where the famous literary brothers Heinrich and Thomas Mann (see box on p.679) grew up. Recently converted into a memorial museum in their honour it takes its name from the latter's youthful novel of mercantile life in the city. Further up the street, nos. 48 and 50 are together designated the **Schabbelhaus**, Lübeck's most famous – and most expensive – restaurant. Crammed full of antiques, it's one of several restaurants in the city regarded as sightseeing attractions in their own right.

THE MANN LITERARY DYNASTY

One of the giants of modern European literature, **Thomas Mann** (1875–1955) was equally adept at writing short stories and epic novels. He made his name with *Buddenbrooks*, the saga of a Lübeck merchant dynasty's decline. In *The Magic Mountain*, which won him the Nobel Prize, the inmates of a Swiss TB sanatorium present a microcosm of a sickened Europe sleepwalking towards World War I. Another favourite theme, the conflict between the artist and society, is superbly expressed in his most famous story, *Death in Venice*. Mann's opposition to Nazism, expressed in the story *Mario and the Magician*, led him to leave Germany voluntarily in 1933. He settled in the USA, where he wrote of biblical exile in the vast trilogy, *Joseph and his Brothers*. Mann's later works include *Doktor Faustus*, a terrifying allegory of Germany's pact with Nazism, in which the narrator – writing as Allied bombs reduce city after city to rubble – records the intellectual arrogance and descent into madness of his composer friend. Never really happy in the New World, Mann settled after the war in Switzerland, where he wrote his last works, including *The Confessions of Felix Krull, Confidence Man*, one of the German language's few comic novels.

Heinrich Mann (1871–1950) was initially preoccupied with similar themes, albeit with the addition of a good deal of erotic fantasy. However, he was given to more direct social and political comment than his soul-searching younger brother, and many of his novels are clear statements of his socialist views. His most famous work is his devastating attack on reactionary German pedagoguery, *Professor Unrat*, which was filmed as the Marlene Dietrich classic, *The Blue Angel*. Its scope was widened in his best novel, *Man of Straw*, which lays bare the true nature of the political and business ethics of the Second Reich.

Three of Thomas Mann's children became writers, and the short-lived **Klaus Mann** (1906–49) is increasingly regarded as a major literary figure in his own right. He tackled the Faust theme before his father in *Mephisto*, a thinly veiled attack on his former brother-in-law, an actor who sold out to the Nazis. His early work, *The Pious Dance*, is a graphic portrayal of the decadent homosexual underworld of Berlin in the days of the Weimar Republic.

Another of these is the **Café-Konditorei Niederegger**, facing the Rathaus across Breite Strasse, which is internationally famed for its vast displays of **marzipan**. This is the oddest hangover from the city's trading heyday: the confection was first produced in Lübeck in the Middle Ages from fine almonds imported from Italy. Herr Niederegger perfected the art in 1806, and this mind-boggling variety is the result of the uninterrupted continuation of his business. At the opposite, northern end of Breite Strasse are two impressive Renaissance halls – the **Haus der Kaufmannschaft**, the offices of the local chamber of commerce, and the **Haus der Schiffergesellschaft**, the former sea captains' guild house. The latter is another of the city's best-known restaurants, and is decked out inside with all sorts of seagoing paraphernalia; predictably, it's on the programme of every tour group.

Across the street stands the **Jakobikirche**, traditionally the parish church of the seafaring community. In comparison with the Marienkirche, it's modest in scale, the only obvious point of similarity being the Gothic wall paintings on its square pillars. Nonetheless, it's rich in works of art, the finest being the **Brömbse Altar** in the chapel to the right of the entrance, which features a carving of *The Crucifixion* by Hinrik Brabender and delicate little Flemish-style paintings. The carved oak **organ lofts** are also impressive; a beautifully worked spiral staircase leads up to the large Baroque organ in the west gallery, though its smaller counterpart in the transept, dating back in part to the fifteenth century, is the more precious instrument of the two.

Grosse Burgstrasse and Königstrasse

Guarding the extreme northern end of the Altstadt, but unlike the Holstentor still on the island itself, is the formidable-looking **Burgtor**, a square tower topped by a bell-shaped roof. The side buildings of the gateway were originally used for stabling the horses of people arriving in the city at this point. Behind it, in black and red Lübeck neo-Gothic style, is the **Versorgungsamt** – a town administration office of the 1890s.

Following Grosse Burgstrasse back towards the city centre, you come to the thirteenth-century **Heiligen-Geist-Hospital** (April–Sept Tues–Sun 10am–5pm; Oct–March Tues–Sun 10am–4pm; free), one of the earliest and best-preserved hospices of the medieval period, whose rhythmic facade is characterized by its gables and tall pepperpot turrets. Inside, the vaulted chapel is richly decorated with frescoes, retables and a Gothic rood screen bearing delicate paintings telling the story of St Elizabeth. The tiny chambers leading off the main hall were built in the nineteenth century as an improvement on the previous communal space which you can glimpse through the gateway; today the hospice is still used as a home for the elderly.

Königstrasse, the southern continuation of Grosse Burgstrasse, is dominated by stately mansions of the Baroque period and later. The **Gemeinnützige Gesellschaft** at no. 5 was another charitable institution; some of its elegant interiors are now used as a restaurant. Two patrician homes, the **Drägerhaus** at no. 9 and the **Behnhaus** at no. 11, have been combined to form the **Museum für Kunst und Kulturgeschichte** (Museum for Art and Cultural History; April–Sept Tues–Sun 10am–5pm; Oct–March 10am–4pm; DM5, free first Friday of the month). It's surprising to see how large these houses are inside, compared with the narrow street frontage; tax was once paid on a building's width rather than its overall size, which led to houses being built long and narrow. The Drägerhaus has impressive interiors with original nineteenth-century furniture, clocks, porcelain and other *objets d'art*, plus a room documenting the lives of the Mann brothers. A gallery of nineteenth- and early twentieth-century paintings occupies the Behnhaus. This includes a room devoted to Lübeck's own **Johann Friedrich Overbeck**, founder and guiding light of the influential Nazarene movement (see "Painting and Graphics" in *Contexts*). There's also a lovely *Coastal Landscape by Evening Light* by Friedrich, and fine examples of the Expressionists Kirchner and Munch.

At the corner of the next block is the **Katharinenkirche** (April–Sept Tues–Sun 10am–1pm & 2–5pm; free), formerly the church of a Franciscan convent – the city's only monastic foundation from the days of the Hansa to have survived intact. In the niches of the facade are nine life-size figures. The first three on the left (*Woman in the Wind, The Beggar* and *The Singer)* are by **Ernst Barlach**: he was commissioned to make the series in the early 1930s, but these were all he had completed by 1932, when his work was banned by the Nazis. The other six were added after the war by **Gerhard Marcks**: you can have a closer look at them in Schloss Gottorf in Schleswig, where another set of terracotta castings from the same moulds is exhibited. In due course, the entire convent will be open as a museum, but in the meantime you can view the inside of the church, whose main peculiarity is its two-storey chancel, the lower of which functioned as a crypt, even though it's at ground level. On the west wall is a large altarpiece of *The Raising of Lazarus* by **Tintoretto**, brought from Venice by a Lübeck merchant. Nearby stands a cast of Bernt Notke's masterpiece, a spectacular group of *St George and the Dragon*, the original of which is in Stockholm.

The eastern quarters

Down Glockengiesser Strasse to the side of the Katharinenkirche, you can step through what appear to be doors in the wall into two of Lübeck's finest courtyards, whose small almshouses were built by seventeenth-century benefactors. The **Füchtings-Hof** at no. 23 was built for the widows of sea captains and merchants; the slightly earlier **Glandorps-Gang** and **Glandorps-Hof** further down at no. 39 were intended for the widows of craftsmen. Another attractive example is the **Haasenhof**, a couple of blocks to the south at Dr-Julius-Leber-Str. 37. At the junction of this street with Königstrasse is the **Löwen-Apotheke**, the oldest remaining house in the city. Two groups of Gothic almshouses can be seen in streets further south – **Von-Höveln-Gang** at Wahmstr. 73–77 and **Dornes-Hof** at Schlumacher Str. 19.

Presiding over the quiet, village-like streets of the southeastern quarter (an area into which few tourists venture) is the handsome single tower of the **Aegidienkirche**, Lübeck's smallest parish church, whose congregation was made up of craftsmen, small-holders and the less affluent merchants. There was a strong musical tradition here, and the early Baroque organ can rival any in Lübeck. What really catches the eye, however, is the richly decorated Renaissance **choir gallery** which shuts off the chancel from the nave. A Protestant variant on the old Catholic idea of the rood screen, its very positioning emphasizes the importance of music in Lutheran worship, while its paintings interpret biblical stories in line with the doctrines of the new faith.

Round the corner, the **St-Annen-Museum** (April–Sept Tues–Sun 10am–5pm; Oct–March Tues–Sun 10am–4pm; DM5, free first Friday of the month) is housed in the surviving parts of the late Gothic St-Annen-Kloster, an Augustinian convent which burned down last century. It has a first-rate collection reflecting domestic, civic and religious art and history from the thirteenth to the eighteenth century. The star piece is the magnificent *Passion Triptych* which **Memling** painted for the Dom. There's also a room full of retables commissioned by the various guilds for their chapels; the finest, predictably enough, is that made for the artists' own Guild of St Luke, which has attractive paintings illustrating the life of their patron by the leading Lübeck master of the late fifteenth century, **Hermen Rode**. The courtyard, surrounded by very Dutch-looking buildings, is one of the most restful spots in the city; its garden contains many imposing monumental Baroque statues, including the original figures from the Puppenbrücke, the bridge leading from the Hauptbahnhof to the Holstentor.

The Dom

At the extreme southern end of the Altstadt is the only surviving reminder of Henry the Lion's city, the huge brick-built **Dom** (daily: summer 9am–6pm; winter 9am–3pm). It was completed in 1230, with its two 120-metre towers, as a Romanesque basilica. A couple of decades later, the pure early Gothic porch or "Paradise" was added on the south side to serve as the main entrance. Soon after, work began on replacing the original chancel with a spacious Gothic hall. The whitewashed interior is dominated by an enormous **triumphal cross**, the first important work of **Bernt Notke**, who was a celebrity throughout the Baltic lands in the late fifteenth and early sixteenth centuries. Probably a painter as well as a sculptor, he specialized in the grandiose, making highly original works to adorn churches in Denmark, Sweden and Estonia. This one is a complicated allegory on the salvation offered by the cross, which rests on an elaborate beamed structure bearing marvellously expressive figures of saints and angels. Notke was also responsible for the carvings on the **rood screen** behind, to which an astronomical clock was appended in the seventeenth century. Among the Dom's numerous other adornments, look out for the ornate Renaissance pulpit in the main nave, the fifteenth-century *Müllerkrone* candelabrum in the north aisle, the winged retables in the transept, and, in the chancel, the memorials to bishops and noblemen, which range from simple Gothic tombs to commemorative chapels in the swankiest Baroque.

Eating, drinking and entertainment

Lübeck's attractions are far from being only historical: the city is also a renowned gastronomic and musical centre, and there is plenty of nightlife. The tourist office publishes a free monthly brochure, *Lübeck Heute*, with details of current events.

Restaurants

You'll pass many of Lübeck's most prestigious restaurants – from the point of view of both food and setting – on a tour around the Altstadt. All are pricey, though less expensive menus are often available at lunchtimes. However, the city has plenty of cheaper alternatives, many of them of comparable quality.

Aubergine, Hüxstr. 57. Vegetarian and wholefood café-restaurant. Closed Sun.

Gemeinnützige Gesellschaft, Königstr. 5–7. A really classy restaurant, with beautifully furnished interiors plus a garden terrace. Closed Sun evening.

Historischer Weinkeller, Am Koberg. Wine bar-cum-restaurant in the cellars of the Heiligen-Geist-Hospital. Closed Tues.

Jever Stuben, An der Obertrave 11. Offers changing daily fish specials, and is particularly good value at lunchtime. Closed Mon.

Lübecker Hanse, Kolk 3–7. Housed in a beautiful old building by the Petrikirche, this excellent if pricey restaurant features French cuisine as well as German dishes. Mon–Fri only.

Ratskeller, Am Markt 13. This is the most innovative Ratskeller in Germany: in addition to excellent traditional dishes, they have a long vegetarian menu, and also brew their own naturally fermented beer, *Lübsch-Pils*.

Schabbelhaus, Mengstr. 48–50. Lübeck's most celebrated restaurant occupies a sixteenth-century merchant's house with courtyard. The food is outstanding but expensive.

Schiffergesellschaft, Breite Str. 2. Famous old seaman's tavern, often overrun by tour groups, but serves excellent food and is not unduly expensive. Closed Mon.

Schmidt's, Dr-Julius-Leber-Str. 60–62. Inexpensive café-restaurant in the heart of the student quarter, with a wide choice of dishes.

Stadtrestaurant, Im Hauptbahnhof. Despite its unpromising-looking setting on the first floor of the Hauptbahnhof, this serves food of a standard rivalling any of the city's most famous restaurants.

Tipasa, Schlumacher Str. 14. A great student favourite, run by Afghans and featuring a large, ever-changing and reasonably priced menu of bistro-type dishes, plus wonderful pizzas and bread. If you're pressed for time, it has a fast takeaway service next door.

Cafés and bars

Brauberger, Alfstr. 36. *Hausbrauerei* serving low-cost meals and its own unfiltered beer.

Café Amadeus, Königstr. 26. Good for rolls and salads – and for finding out what's on in town.

Café Belmondo, Am Bahnhof. A pleasant café with snacks, and a good place to wait for a train.

Café Niederegger, Breite Str. 89. The celebrated marzipan shop has an elegant backroom café, plus a first-floor dining room; there's a wide choice of breakfasts, plus good-value set lunches.

Charly Rivels Sohn, Glockengiesser Str. 91. Café-bar frequented by Lübeck's artistic set.

Engel, Engelsgrube 59. Music-bar in a street which is one of the liveliest in town come the evening.

Im Alten Zolln, Mühlenstr. 93. The most atmospheric of the city's traditional pubs; also does meals.

Discos

Body and Soul, Wahmstr. 28. As the name suggests, concentrates on soul music. Mon–Thurs & Sun 8pm–3am, Fri & Sat 8pm–4am.

Galaxis, Falkenstr. 45. Housed in a huge converted factory. Wed–Sat 7pm–1am.

Tiffany, Kreuzweg 5. Conveniently close to the Hauptbahnhof, this is for the real night owls. Mon–Thurs 8pm–3am, Fri–Sun 8pm–5am.

Culture

No German city is better known for its **organ recitals** – a tradition dating back to the early seventeenth century, when the Danish composer Diderik Buxtehude became one of the first musicians to achieve fame as a virtuoso solo instrumentalist, drawing huge crowds to his improvisatory recitals at the Marienkirche (see p.678). The Marienkirche's two modern organs (one of which is the biggest mechanical musical instrument in the world) are used alternately for recitals each Saturday at 6.30pm, while one or other of the Jakobikirche's historic organs is played on Saturdays at 5pm. Other **classical music** can be heard at the *Musikhochschule*, Grosse Petersgrube 17–29. The main **theatre** venue is *Bühnen der Hansestadt Lübeck*, Beckergrube 10–14.

Listings

Bike rental *Leihcycle,* Schwartauer Allee 39 (DM5 per day; ☎42660).

Car rental *Europcar,* Fackenburger Allee 32a (☎471035); *Sixt Budget,* Fackenburger Allee 56 (☎43966); *Autohansa* have an office in the Hauptbahnhof.

Cruises *KuFra Schiffahrtslinien* (☎26561 or 74489) offers cruises round the city and harbour, and to Travemünde, departing from Untertrave. *Lübecker Fahrgastschiff Manfred Quandt* (☎393734 or 73884) features the same destinations, plus the Elbe-Lübeck Canal and the Dassower See in Mecklenburg; all these depart from the Holstentorterrasse, whereas those to the Ratzeburger See leave from Moltkebrücke on the other side of the Altstadt. *Personenschiffahrt Reinhold Maiworm* (☎35455) leaves from the same location for the Ratzeburger See, with the option of continuing on to Ratzeburg itself.

Festivals Main events are: *Markt Anno Dazumal,* an old-time fair held in the Rathausmarkt for 10 days in May; a 2-week *Volksfest* in mid-July; and the *Altstadtfest* on the second weekend in Sept (even-numbered years only). The Advent celebrations are a cut above the norm, thanks to the setting of the *Kunsthandwerker-Weihnachtsmarkt* in the Heiligen-Geist-Hospital, and the fairyland displays of the *Weichnachtsmärchenwald* outside the Marienkirche.

Post offices are near the Hauptbahnhof (on the left as you come out) and in the Marktplatz by the Rathaus (with poste restante).

Around Lübeck

Within a short radius of Lübeck are a nicely contrasting series of destinations which make easy day-trips or overnight stops in their own right. These include the historic lakeside town of **Ratzeburg**, the upmarket beach resort of **Travemünde** and a fine stretch of coastline.

Ratzeburg

The wooded countryside south of Lübeck is punctuated by some forty lakes, the largest being the Ratzeburger See, through which the notorious border with the GDR used to run. Towards its southern end is the idyllic town of **RATZEBURG** itself, whose picturesque if vulnerable-looking Altstadt is built on a small island linked by causeways to the modern suburbs on either bank.

Towards the northern tip of the Altstadt is the **Dom** which, like Lübeck's, was founded by Henry the Lion. The main external features of this Romanesque brick basilica are its massive west tower and porticoed southern porch. Inside, the triumphal cross and choir stalls remain from the original furnishings. Of the many subsequent additions, pride of place goes to the stone **Passion altar** in the chancel, an outstanding example of the Westphalian Soft Style. Look out, too, for the many tomb slabs to local bishops and dukes.

Back towards the commercial centre, the **A. Paul-Weber-Museum** (Tues–Sun 10am–1pm & 2–5pm; DM3) at Domhof 5 displays the work of a satirical artist best known for his attacks on the Nazis. A few doors down at Domhof 12 is the **local history museum** (Tues–Sun 10am–1pm & 2–5pm; DM3). A few minutes' walk further south, the **Ernst-Barlach-Haus** (March–Nov Tues–Sun 10am–noon & 3–6pm; DM5) on Barlachplatz to the rear of the Markt commemorates an even more celebrated artistic opponent of the Third Reich, the sculptor who created the figures on the facade of Lübeck's Katharinenkirche. Barlach spent part of his youth in this house, which now contains examples of his wonderful Expressionist carvings and graphic work.

Practicalities

Ratzeburg's **Bahnhof**, on the line between Lübeck and Lüneburg, lies at the extreme western fringe of town. It's more convenient to make the 25-kilometre journey from Lübeck by **bus**, as this takes you right into the Altstadt.

The **tourist office** (May–Sept Mon–Thurs 9am–5pm, Fri 9am–6pm, Sat, Sun & holidays 10am–4pm; Oct–April Mon–Fri 9am–5pm; ☎04541/800080) is just to the west of the Altstadt at Schlosswiese 7. Here you can book **private rooms** (①–③); the other budget option is the **youth hostel** at Fischerstr. 20 (☎04541/3707; ❷), which has the benefit of an Altstadt setting with lakeward views.

Alternatively, there are a couple of small **pensions** on the western side of town: *Haus Betzinger*, Dermin 2a (☎04541/83430; ②), and *Inselblick*, Am Mühlengraben 26 (☎04541/5844; ③). The Altstadt has some first-rate **hotels**, notably *Wittler's*, Grosse Kreuzstr. 11 (☎04541/3204; ⑥), and *Der Seehof*, Lüneburger Damm 1–3 (☎04541/20551; ⑦).

The terrace **restaurant** at *Der Seehof* is the best place to eat in town. Another good choice is the sixteenth-century *Askanier-Keller*, Töpferstr. 1, which serves local specialities. Between May and September, 2hr **cruises** on the lake are run by *Personenschiffahrt Ratzeburger See*, Schlosswiese 6 (☎04541/891573; DM12).

Travemünde

Just to the north of Lübeck is **TRAVEMÜNDE**, the city's rather glamorous seaside resort. Go there in winter and you might find the odd playful seal on the fine sandy beach. In summer, though, Travemünde is hardly the place to go to get away from it all. The beach is packed full of busy *Strandkörbe* (hooded basket-seats rented out like deck chairs to keep off the breeze), sailing boats and windsurfers ply the water, and the fashionable **casino** makes fat profits (not least on its terrace, *the* place to sit for cool drinks and ice cream). The town itself is still quite attractive, but it is dominated by the shipping and fishing quays; this is the main port for ferries to and from Scandinavia. From the beach it's odd to watch large ships apparently sailing right onto land, whereas they are actually entering the mouth of the Trave. If you walk northwards up the beach, it eventually peters out and is replaced by cliffs, the Brodtener Ufer. This is the place to get a rare view of the Baltic from above sea level.

Practicalities

Travemünde has three stations on the branch line from Lübeck – the **Bahnhof Skandinavienkai** serves the ferries, the **Hafenbahnhof** the town centre and harbour, while the **Strandbahnhof** is close to the beach.

If you're tempted to stay over, the **tourist office** (daily 10am–5/6pm; ☎04502/80430) in the *Aqua Top* building at the southern end of the beach at Strandpromenade 1b can help find accommodation. At Mecklenburger Landstr. 36 is one of the cheaper **pensions** in town, *Siemer* (☎04502/2408; ⑤). Kaiserallee, immediately above the beach, is lined with a number of proud **hotels**, such as *Atlantic* at no. 2a (☎04502/75057; ⑤); *Sonnenklause* at no. 21 (☎04502/86130; ⑥); and *Strandperle* at no. 10 (☎04502/74249; ⑥). There is also a spa hotel, the *Kurhaus*, set in a fine park at Aussenallee 10 (☎04502/74002; ④). The **youth hostel** is across the Trave at Mecklenburger Landstr. 69 (open April–Oct; ☎04502/2576).

The coast: Travemünde to Kiel

Along the coast north of Travemünde are several resorts where the beaches are good, with fine sand, and camping facilities abound. **Timmendorfer Strand** is fairly elegant, in the style of Travemünde, but others, such as **Haffkrug**, are more like fishing villages still. By and large the beaches are narrow, and backed by thick pine forest – especially around **Kellenhusen.** Just inland from here is **Cismar**, whose thirteenth-century Benedictine Kloster has a church closely modelled on the Marienkirche in Lübeck. The rail line runs over a bridge to the island of **Fehmarn**, where ferries link Puttgarden with Scandinavia. The island is worth a small trip for its own sake: it has plenty of beaches and camping. West of Fehmarn you are in the **Kieler Bucht** (Kiel Bay). **Lütjenburg** makes a good stopover; it's very small and pretty, and you can visit the ancient burial ground (*Hünengrab*) nearby.

Kiel

The naval port of **KIEL**, Schleswig-Holstein's capital, lies some 90km northwest of Lübeck at the head of the Kieler Förde, a typical Baltic coast fjord (though nothing like as dramatic as the Norwegian variety). Long overshadowed by Lübeck, the city's fortunes soared with the opening in 1895 of what is still the world's biggest and busiest man-made shipping lane. This is always known in English as the **Kiel Canal**, though its German title of *Nord-Ostsee-Kanal* is a more accurate designation of its status as the link between the North Sea and the Baltic. In 1918, it was a mutiny by the sailors of Kiel which sparked off the German Revolution, which led to the abdication of the Kaiser and the birth of the Weimar Republic. As the main U-**boat centre** in World War II, it was a prime target for Allied bombing missions, and much of it subsequently had to be rebuilt from scratch. Consequently, there's not much point in looking for charm amid its sober 1950s three- and four-storey blocks: from a sightseeing point of view, Kiel is one of Germany's least rewarding cities. Nonetheless, it attracts hordes of visitors in the last week of June for the *Kieler Woche*, Germany's premier annual **regatta**.

The city

The dominant building of the centre of Kiel is the huge Jugendstil **Rathaus** (guided tours May–Sept Wed & Sun at 12.30pm; DM1) on Rathausstrasse, whose tower commands an extensive panorama of the city and its fjord. A few minutes' walk to the northeast is the Alter Markt, on which stands the **Nikolaikirche**, a Gothic church partially restored and remodernized following war damage. Inside are a few notable furnishings, such as a fourteenth-century font and a fifteenth-century altar and triumphal cross, while outside stands an imposing sculpture by Barlach, *Der Geistkämpfer* (literally, "The Fighter for the Spirit").

A few paces away, at Dänische Str. 19, the **Warleberger Hof**, one of the few surviving old mansions, now houses the **Stadtmuseum** (mid-April to mid-Oct daily 10am–6pm; rest of year Tues–Sun 10am–5pm; free), with changing exhibitions on the city's history. A little further along, set in gardens overlooking the promenade, is the exceedingly modest **Schloss**, part of which contains the **Stiftung Pommern** (Tues–Fri 10am–5pm, Sat & Sun 2–6pm; DM2), a collection of paintings which includes works by seventeenth-century Dutch masters as well as examples of German art from Romanticism to Impressionism.

The old fish market hall just opposite at Wall 65 has been adapted as the **Schiffahrtsmuseum** (mid-April to mid-Oct daily 10am–6pm; rest of year Tues–Sun 10am–5pm; free), documenting local maritime history. During the summer months, you can also look round the three sailing craft moored outside – the steamship *Bussard*, the lifeboat *Hindenburg* and the fireship *Kiel*. A few minutes' walk further north, at Düsternbrooker Weg 1, is the **Kunsthalle** (Tues & Thurs–Sun 10.30am–6pm, Wed 10.30am–8pm; DM6), which has a large array of predominantly modern art plus a collection of classical antiquities. At no. 20 on the same street, the **Aquarium im Institut für Meereskunde** (daily: April–Sept 9am–7pm; Oct–March 9am–5pm; DM2.50) is home to seals and large aquaria of Baltic fish.

The outskirts

The **Schleusen** (locks) at the eastern end of the Kiel Canal are among the most interesting parts of the waterway; to reach them, take bus #4 or #14 from the bus station to the terminus at Wik. There are raised platforms on both banks; to cross over to the northern side, walk west for a few minutes to catch one of the regular free ferries.

At **Molfsee**, some 6km southwest of the centre (take a bus bound for Flintbek), is what's arguably Kiel's most attractive corner, the **Freilichtmuseum** (April–June & mid-Sept to Oct Tues–Sun 9am–6pm; July to mid-Sept Mon–Sun 9am–6pm; Nov–March Sun & holidays 11am–4pm in fine weather only; DM7). Here around thirty sixteenth- to nineteenth-century farmsteads and barns from throughout Schleswig-Holstein have been reassembled in regional groups to give a comprehensive picture of rural life down the ages. A pottery, bakery, four mills, a forge and a dairy are all worked in the old ways, and their products are on sale. Many of the houses have tiny cabin beds in which whole families used to sleep: in winter they slept sitting up and huddled together against the cold.

Practicalities

Kiel's **Hauptbahnhof** and **bus station** are located together at the southern end of the central shopping area. Just opposite, at Sophienblatt 30, is the **tourist office** (May, Aug & Sept Mon–Sat 9am–6.30pm; June & July Mon–Sat 9am–6.30pm, Sun 9am–1pm; Oct–April Mon–Fri 9am–6.30pm, Sat 9am–1pm; ☎679100). **Mitfahrzentrale** have an office at Sophienblatt 54 (☎19440).

If you're intending to visit the outskirts, it makes sense to invest in the *Kieler Karte*, a runabout ticket on the **public transport** system: this costs DM12 for 24 hours, DM17 for three days, or DM27 for a week.

Accommodation

Bear in mind that accommodation is likely to be very difficult to come by during the *Kieler Woche* in June. Budget **hotels** are mostly in the distant outskirts, but two exceptions are *Schweriner Hof*, Königsweg 13 (☎61416; ②), and *Rendsburger Hof*, a couple of kilometres southwest of the centre at Rendsburger Landstr. 363 (☎690131; ③). On the other hand, there are plenty of medium- and upper-range establishments with convenient locations: try *Villa Ingeborg*, Goethestr. 7a (☎91557; ⑦); *Rabe's*, Ringstr. 30 (☎663070; ⑥); *City*, Wall 50 (☎91404; ⑥); *Berliner Hof*, Ringstr. 6 (☎66340; ⑦); or *Wiking*, Schützenwall 1–3 (☎673051; ⑨).

The **youth hostel** is not too far away from the centre of things at Johannesstr. 1 (☎731488; ⚑); take bus #4. However, the nearest **campsite**, *Falckenstein*, is in the far northern suburbs at Palisadenweg 171 (☎392078), and not a very practical option unless you've got your own transport.

Eating, drinking and entertainment

Kiel has a reasonable range of places to **eat** and **drink**. *Restaurant im Schloss*, Wall 80, is undoubtedly the best place for a full meal, while *Seeburg*, Düsternbrooker Weg 2, is a good café-restaurant handy for the museums and with the bonus of a view over the fjord. *Friesenhof* in the Rathaus is the ubiquitous *Ratskeller* masquerading under another name. There's also a *Hausbrauerei*, *Klosterhof* at Alter Markt 9, which also serves good-value food. *Oblomow*, at Hansastr. 82, does good cheap meals. Vegetarians should head for *Zauberlehrling*, Lutherstr. 24, although this also caters for carnivores.

The place to go for **live music** and to find out what's on is *Die Pumpe* at Hass Str. 22. Bergstrasse has a multi-storey **disco**, with different music on each floor and live bands at weekends. There's also an *Irish Pub* on this street, with another, *Wubbke*, at Holtenauer Str. 110.

In the summer, there are regular **cruises** round the harbour, across the Kieler Förde, and down the Kiel Canal. If you're tempted to move further afield, **ferries** run to various Danish destinations, as well as to Oslo and Göteborg.

Around Kiel

Within easy reach of Kiel are a wide variety of enticing destinations making good full or half-day trips; some of them are also possible stopovers on the way to or from Lübeck, Flensburg or Schleswig. Places to head for include the beach resorts of **Laboe** and **Eckernförde**, the lakes and palaces of **Holstein Switzerland**, and **Rendsburg**, where the most interesting features of the Kiel Canal can be seen.

Laboe

The Kieler Förde has a number of fine beaches, none better than that at **LABOE**, a popular resort some 18km from the city, reachable in well under an hour either by bus #54 or by one of the regular ferries which ply the inlet in summer. The waterfront is dominated by the celebrated 85-metre **Marine-Ehrenmal**, a memorial to sailors of all nationalities who died in the two world wars. Part of this now contains the **U-Boot-Museum** (daily: April 16–Oct 15 9.30am–6pm; Oct 16–April 15 9.30am–4pm; DM4.50), which tells you all you're likely to want to know about German submarines. As a supplement, you can visit **U-Boot 995** (same hours; DM3), which is moored alongside.

If you need to stop for the night, Laboe has plenty of **pensions** (②–③), plus an excellent **hotel**, *Seeterrassen*, Strandstr. 86 (☎04343/6070; ④). Full information about accommodation is available from the **tourist office**, Strandstr. 25 (May–Sept Mon–Fri 10am–noon & 1–4pm, Sat & Sun 10am–3.30pm; April & Oct daily 10am–2pm; Nov–March Mon–Fri 10am–2pm; ☎04343/427553).

Holstein Switzerland

The so-called **Holstein Switzerland** (*Holsteinische Schweiz*), which is crossed by the main road and rail routes between Kiel and Lübeck, has nothing resembling the Alps, so it presumably gets its nickname from the **lakes**, of which there are about 140 in all. Many of the towns in the area are designated *Kurorte*, being centres for health-related holidays, and offer all sorts of sports and leisure facilities. Round about, however, are many smaller and quieter places, linked by boat, footpaths and cycle tracks; as so often in Schleswig-Holstein, the bike is an ideal means of getting around.

PLÖN, 30km southeast of Kiel, is set on the largest of the lakes, the Grosser Plöner See. It was formerly the seat of the House of Sonderburg-Plön, one of the lines which ruled tracts of Schleswig-Holstein during its centuries of partition. The family's predominantly Baroque **Schloss** is now a school, though it's sometimes open for visits and concerts.

A further 15km east is **EUTIN**, which is again centred on a **Schloss** (closed for restoration until March 1998), set in a fine park with both French and English sections.

This began as a fortified castle of the Bishops of Lübeck, who were forbidden to reside within the boundaries of the city-state itself; later, it became one of the residences of the Dukes of Oldenburg. It has a distinguished collection of portraits, many by Goethe's friend **Johann Heinrich Wilhelm Tischbein**, who resided here as court painter for 21 years. In July and August, the *Sommerfest* features concerts in the Schloss of the work of **Carl Maria von Weber**, the founding father of musical Romanticism, who was born in Eutin in 1786.

The Dänischer Wohld and Eckernförde

There are two rail lines linking Kiel with Flensburg to the north. The first crosses the Kiel Canal immediately to the north of the city before passing through the area known as the **Dänischer Wohld**. The train stops at **Gettorf**, a good place to alight to explore some of the peaceful rural communities. There are cliffs, some quite high, along the coast (which is serviced only by buses), and the villages are not as developed for tourism as those along the Kieler Förde: try **Dänisch-Nienhof** for a stopover.

Eckernförde

Further on, about 30km from Kiel, the beach and health resort of **ECKERNFÖRDE** is at the head of the next major inlet, the Eckernförder Bucht. Despite having some typically bland modern *Kurzentrum* facilities tacked on, the old part of town is pretty enough, and the **Nikolaikirche** is worth looking into for its carved dark oak and beautifully painted choir ceiling and altar. The fifteenth-century **Rathaus** (July & Aug Mon 3–5pm, Tues–Sun 10am–5pm; rest of year Tues–Sat 3–5pm, Sun 10am–5pm; DM2) on Rathausmarkt is now a local history museum, mainly devoted to life earlier this century. There's a typical *Flüchtungszimmer* or refugee room, with an array of simple belongings and mementoes brought on a long odyssey from the east. It's a reminder that, just after the war, Schleswig-Holstein became the new home of many **refugees** who left behind most of their worldly goods and trekked for weeks or months to avoid having to live in the Soviet sector.

If you're looking for somewhere to stay, a full list of accommodation is available from the **tourist office**, Am Exer 1 (May 12–Aug 31 daily 8am–6pm; Sept 1–May 11 Mon–Fri 9am–noon & 1–5pm, Sat & Sun 10am–noon; ☎04351/71790). **Hotels** include *Park*, Preusserstr. 24 (☎04351/5411; ④); *Sandkrug*, Berliner Str. 146 (☎04351/41493; ⑤); *Seegarten*, Berliner Str. 73 (☎04351/5022; ⑤); and the super-luxurious *Stadthotel*, Am Exer 3 (☎04351/6044; ⑨). The **youth hostel**, towards the southern edge of town at Sehestedter Str. 27 (☎04351/2154; ❸), has views over the sea. Many of the best **eating** possibilities are concentrated around Frau-Clara-Strasse, though the top restaurant is definitely the *Ratskeller* in the Rathaus.

Rendsburg

The alternative rail line from Kiel to Flensburg first travels westwards for 35km to the garrison town of **RENDSBURG**. It's well worth going here for the ride alone, the last part of which is one of the most spectacular in Germany, as the rail line has to perform some extraordinary gymnastics in order to cope with crossing the Kiel Canal high enough for shipping to pass underneath, yet get back to ground level again for the Bahnhof in the town centre, only a few hundred metres ahead. The solution is ingenious – having traversed the bridge, the **Schwebefähre Hochbrücke**, the train descends via a gently sloping **loop**, which circles for a good 2km all the way round the inner suburb of Schleife. Bizarrely, this trip offers one of the best views of Rendsburg: when there's a train approaching in the opposite direction, the effect is positively surreal. Other impressive feats of transport engineering in town are the four-lane **road tunnel** taking road traffic beneath the canal, and Europe's longest **escalator**, which takes pedestrians down to it.

The main historic buildings are clustered together around the Altstädter Markt, a few minutes' walk north of the Bahnhof. Here the timber-framed sixteenth-century **Rathaus** is notable for the archway cut through it, allowing the street to pass underneath. Nearby is the brick **Marienkirche**, which dates back to the thirteenth century and is the oldest building in town.

In the opposite direction from the Bahnhof, at Prinzessinstr. 8, the handsome nineteenth-century **Synagoge** (Tues–Sat 11am–1pm & 4–6pm, Sun 3–6pm; DM2) has been restored to house a museum of Jewish life and culture. Just to the west is the spacious Paradeplatz, on which stands the late seventeenth-century **Christuskirche**, which was specially designed so that the garrison's entire contingent of two thousand men could all attend services at the same time.

Practicalities

Rendsburg's **tourist office** (Mon–Fri 10am–noon & 3–5pm; July & Aug also Sat 10am–noon; ☎04331/21120) is in the Rathaus. The only real budget accommodation in town is at the **youth hostel**, 1km west of the Altstadt at Rotenhöfer Weg 48 (☎04331/71205; ✆). There are, however, plenty of good **hotels**, such as *Roseneck*, Ostlandstr. 1 (☎04331/41129; ④); *Deutsche Eiche*, Herrenstr. 12 (☎04331/58020; ⑤); *Grüner Kranz*, Hollesenstr. 33 (☎04331/72366; ④); *Tüxen*, Lancasterstr. 44 (☎04331/26837; ⑦); and *Pelli-Hof*, a fine eighteenth-century mansion at Materialhofstr. 1 (☎04331/22216; ⑦).

Most of the best **restaurants** are in the hotels, but a cheaper alternative is *Niewarker* on Paradeplatz, a *Hausbrauerei* which makes both a bottom-fermented light beer and a top-fermented dark beer.

Schleswig

Though well off the tourist track, **SCHLESWIG**, which lies 25km north of Rendsburg, is worth going far out of your way to see. Nowadays an administrative centre with a sleepy, civil servant pace, it dozes gently on the banks of a beautiful fjord, the Schlei, and could easily trick you into thinking that nothing had ever happened there. It did, though – for three centuries from after around 800 the **Vikings**, whose trade routes stretched from the Black Sea to Greenland, had their main northern European trading centre here, the shortest crossing point between the Baltic and North Sea. Following their demise, the town was re-established on the opposite side of the Schlei. This subsequently became a Danish royal residence, and then, after the partition of Schleswig-Holstein in 1544, the seat of one of its lines, the Dukes of Gottorf. This illustrious history has bequeathed a marvellous legacy of monuments, making Schleswig one of the most outstanding small towns in all of Germany.

Arrival, information and accommodation

Schleswig's **Bahnhof** is over 1km south of Schloss Gottorf, and about 3km from the centre. Local buses #1 and #2 run to the **bus station**, which is located just to the north of the Altstadt. A couple of minutes' walk south of here, at Plessenstr. 7, is the **tourist office** (May–Sept Mon–Fri 9am–12.30pm & 1.30–5pm, Sat 9am–noon; Oct–April Mon–Thurs 9am–12.30pm & 1.30–5pm, Fri 9am–12.30pm; ☎24878).

The **telephone code** for Schleswig is ☎04621

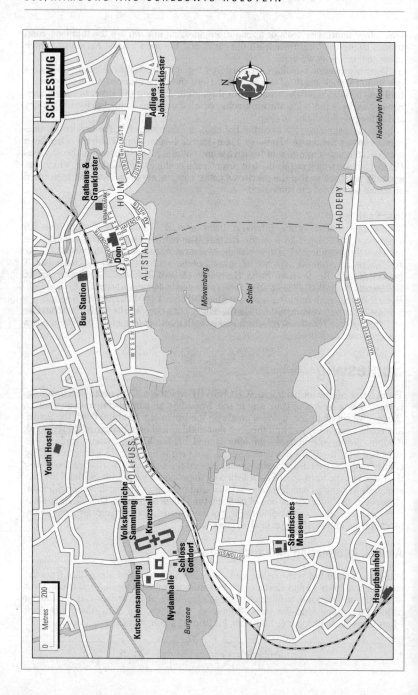

SCHLESWIG

Adliges Johanniskloster

Rathaus & Graukloster

RATHAUSMARKT

NORDERHOLMSTR

SÜDERHOLMSTR

HOLM

NORDERDOMSTR

SÜDERDOMSTR

HAFENSTR

AM HAFEN

Dom

ALTSTADT

Bus Station

WESENSTR

WESE DAMM

WESENSTR

Haddebyer Noor

HADDEBY

Schlei

Möwenberg

HADDEBYER CHAUSSEE

Youth Hostel

Volkskundliche Sammlung

Kreuzstall

LOLLFUSS

SCHLEISTR

Schloss Gottdorf

Städtisches Museum

GOTTORFSTR

Nydamhalle

Kutschensammlung

Burgsee

Hauptbahnhof

Metres 200

0

Accommodation

There is a full range of **hotels** on offer in Schleswig. The **youth hostel** is at Spielkoppel 1 (☎23893; 🏠): from the Bahnhof, take a bus as far as the Theater (ie before the bus station), then walk up the steps known as the Lollfusstreppe. There's a **campsite** (☎32450) at Haddeby, near the Wikinger Museum.

HOTELS

Matthiesen, Friedrichstr. 59 (☎32303). Good-value budget hotel, conveniently situated between the Bahnhof and Schloss Gottorf. ③

Olschewski, Hafenstr. 40 (☎25577, fax 22141). Overlooking the Schlei at the edge of the Altstadt, with the best restaurant in town. ⑥

Schleiblick, Hafengang 4 (☎23468 or 25987). The most atmospheric of the cheaper hotels, located in an old fishermen's house in the Altstadt. To book, it may be necessary to go to the *Friesenstube* restaurant on Fischbrückstrasse at the end of the same street. ②

Stadt Hamburg, Lollfuss 108 (☎9040). Between the Schloss and the Altstadt. ⑥

Strandhalle, Strandweg 2 (☎9090, fax 909100). The best address in town, alongside its own yachting marina just to the west of the Altstadt. ⑦

Waldhotel, Stampfmühle 1 (☎23288, fax 23289). Medium-range hotel to the rear of the Schloss. ⑥

Wikinger, Michaelisstr. 54 (☎25514). Bargain hotel in the area north of the bus station. ②

Zum Stadtfeld, Stadtfeld 2a (☎23947). Another bargain hotel to the north of the bus station. ②

The town

Despite a present-day population that barely tops the 25,000 mark, Schleswig possesses a sense of grandeur to match its past, not least in the way it sprawls over a large area. Its attractions are well spread out, meaning that it's a place not easily seen in a hurry, but all the sights are served by city buses.

The Dom

Schleswig's skyline, best viewed from across the Schlei, is dominated by the **Dom**, and in particular its oversized late nineteenth-century tower, which, close up, looks even more modern than it is, due to a re-facing of its brickwork in the 1950s. The main body of the building is essentially a Gothic hall church, though the imposing south **portal** and the transepts are Romanesque. Inside, the vaults of the latter, plus the triumphal arch of the choir, are covered with precious thirteenth-century **frescoes**, the most notable being *The Saviour of the Rainbow*. On the south wall is another of the Dom's early adornments, a lovely polychromed **retable** to the Three Magi, carved around 1400.

However, your attention is most likely to be drawn to the twelve-metre-high **Bordesholm altar** in the choir, one of Europe's most astonishing pieces of woodcarving. Carved from oak between 1514 and 1521, and originally commissioned for the Augustinian Kloster of Bordesholm south of Kiel, it shows some 400 figures on a background so delicate it resembles filigree. The Passion scenes appear to be based on woodcuts by Dürer, and are certainly the closest sculptural equivalent to the work of Germany's most famous artist. Yet the creator of this long-celebrated masterpiece, one **Hans Brüggemann** of Husum, remains a shadowy figure about whom little else is known, though one of his earlier works is the remarkable elongated **statue of St Christopher** by the transept entrance. Legend has it that the jealous monks of Bordesholm fed him with a potion which caused him to go blind, ensuring that he could never create an altar to rival their own.

In the northern ambulatory is the magnificent **tomb of King Friederick I**, carved in the 1550s by the Antwerp sculptor-architect **Cornelis Floris**. Its pure Renaissance style, with classically inspired Virtues and mourning angels bearing the reclining effigy of the deceased monarch, shows how tastes changed in the generation after

Brüggemann. Nearby hangs the **Kilmannseck altar**, an elaborate Baroque epitaph with an allegorical painting by the local painter **Jürgen Ovens**, a student of Rembrandt and the only German artist to take up the style of the great Dutch master. He was also responsible for *The Blue Madonna* on the pillar of the end bay of the nave.

The rest of the Altstadt and the Holm

Everything else in the Altstadt stands very much in the shade of the Dom. There are plenty of grand mansions of various dates, but the only other setpiece attraction is the **Graukloster** on Rathausmarkt immediately to the east. This former Franciscan monastery is the unlikely-looking headquarters of the local administration, and is linked to the **Rathaus** proper, a plain Neoclassical structure. You're free to wander around during working hours; at weekends, only the ground floor of the cloister is left open.

A couple of minutes' walk beyond the eastern end of the Altstadt brings you to the formerly separate fishing village of **Holm**, whose name (meaning "surrounded by water") reflects the fact that it was an island until 1935. These days, there are only some twenty fishermen still eking a living from the eel and herring catches of the Schlei, instead of the 300 or so in Holm's heyday. Nonetheless, the quarter preserves the appearance of a tightly knit community. The immaculately tended circular **cemetery**, with a rustic nineteenth-century chapel as its bull's-eye, provides the unexpected centrepiece. The houses around it are notable for their two-piece doorways (the so-called "chatting doors") and for their bay windows, which give views in three directions.

At the eastern edge of Holm is the fascinating **Adeliges St-Johannis-Kloster**, a one-time Benedictine convent which has been a Protestant collegiate foundation since the Reformation. The canonesses, who only come here on retirement from their normal careers, live in the splendid Baroque houses grouped round the courtyard. Call at the home of the prioress at no. 8, or, better still, phone in advance (☎24236), for a **guided tour** (DM1) round the complex, taking in the church, cloister and refectory.

Schloss Gottorf

On a little moated island in the Bergsee, a lake close to the head of the Schlei, about 1.5km west of the Altstadt, stands **Schloss Gottorf**, a truly regal palace whose facade, one of the finest achievements of northern European Renaissance architecture, masks what's actually an extremely disparate structure, incorporating older defensive features as well as many later additions. Together with its dependencies, it's home to the **Landesmuseen** (daily: March–Oct 9am–5pm; Nov–Feb 9.30am–4pm; DM7). Note that the ticket gives admission to six separate collections, which in total warrant a visit of several hours, and that it's best to avoid Mondays, when only some parts are open; take bus #1 or #2.

THE SCHLOSSMUSEUM

The **Schlossmuseum** in the Schloss itself contains a wide range of artefacts displayed chronologically in the building's finest interiors. At the entrance, the **Königshalle**, a stately Gothic hall, houses Gothic paintings and sculptures, though the finest pieces are in the small rooms beyond. These include a gorgeous *Nativity* by the Lübeck painter **Hermen Rode** and a small *Retable of the Holy Kinship* by **Brüggemann**; the latter postdates the Bordesholm altar, thereby suggesting that the story of the sculptor's blinding is a myth. Important later paintings are *Frederick the Wise* by **Cranach** and a wonderfully luminous *Cain and Abel* by **Johann Liss**. Passing through the re-erected interior of a seventeenth-century *Weinstube* from Lübeck, you come to a suite of rooms decorated in Baroque style, of which the finest, the **Blauer Saal** (Blue Room), makes an elegant backdrop for a number of canvases by **Ovens**. Beyond is the **Schlosskirche**, a perfectly preserved Renaissance gem complete with painted gallery, an ornate ducal oratory and a still-functioning sixteenth-century organ. Adjoining this is the most spectacular chamber of all, the main festive hall, known as the **Hirschsaal** because of the life-sized, startlingly realistic polychromed stuccos of deer on the walls. Finally, there's a first-class **folklore** collection upstairs, complete with a series of reconstructed interiors from rural houses.

THE REST OF THE COMPLEX

On the west side of the Schloss, the modern **Nydamhalle** is visually rather jarring, but its contents, which illustrate the pre- and early history of the region, are themselves sufficient reason for a visit to Schleswig. The major treasure is the huge **Nydamboot**, an oak rowing boat from around 350 AD. This is the single most important object to have survived from the era of the Germanic tribes who eventually came to form the German nation. There are other impressive sailing craft on show as well, including one from Roman times. Another highlight is the grisly display of *Moorleichen*, **peat-bog** corpses reckoned to be around two thousand years old. Most shocking are the facial expressions, ranging from the beatific look of one who seems to have died in peace, to the utter anguish of another, whose fate can only be imagined.

The **Kreuzstall**, a cross-shaped stables building on the other side of the Schloss, is home to a fine array of twentieth-century German art. On the ground floor, particular works to look out for are the second set of castings of the figures on the facade of the Katharinenkirche in Lübeck by **Gerhard Marcks** and the cartoons by **Kokoschka** for the destroyed mosaic he made for St Nikolai in Hamburg. Many of the other big names, such as Kirchner, Nolde, Macke, Rohlfs and Barlach are also well represented. Upstairs are more modern pieces, of which the most eye-catching are the brightly coloured set of 33 scenes by **Hap Grieshaber** illustrating Thomas Mann's biblical epic, *Joseph and his Brothers*.

The inclusive ticket also gives admission to the **Reithalle**, the riding hall immediately east of the Kreuzstall, where temporary exhibitions are held; the **Volkskundliche Sammlung**, a display on the history of local crafts and industries; and the **Kutschensammlung** (same times), a collection of old coaches kept in the building behind the Nydamhalle.

The Städtisches Museum

Just south of Schloss Gottorf runs Friedrichstrasse, the main thoroughfare of the suburb on the opposite side of the Schlei. It's predominantly modern, but has a few older survivals, notably **Von Günderotscher Hof**, an intact seventeenth- and eighteenth-century manor house with dependencies, grouped round a courtyard. The main building now contains the **Städtisches Museum** (Tues–Sun 10am–5pm; DM3), whose disparate exhibits include finds from the recent excavations of the Altstadt, an overview of local history which includes a surprisingly extensive and candid documentation of life during the Third Reich, and an excellent collection of historic children's toys. Periodically, demonstrations are held in the **Druckerei**, which has a complete hand-composing room with old typesetting and printing equipment.

Haithabu

Haithabu, the site of the original Viking settlement, is about 4km from the Altstadt by road. It can be reached by any bus going in the direction of Kiel, but in summer there's the far more atmospheric option of reaching it by a small boat across the Schlei which leaves the Stadthafen just south of the Dom. The earthwork ramparts of the otherwise vanished town have survived, and the extensive excavations yielded by the site are now kept in the **Wikinger Museum** (April–Oct daily 9am–5pm; Nov–March Tues–Sun

10am–4pm; DM4), a bold modern design constructed, Viking-fashion, like a series of upturned boats. The main discovery has been a **longship**, now partially reconstructed to its original state and exhibited alongside models illustrating how it was built. Elsewhere, there are informative displays (English translations are available) on all aspects of Viking life; look out in particular for some wonderful jewellery and for the runic stones, one of which is engraved with a lurid orange script.

Eating, drinking and entertainment

Other than the hotels, good places to **eat** and **drink** include the fish specialist *Zur Schleimöwe* at Süderholmstr. 8 in Holm; *Senatorenkroog*, Rathausmarkt 9–10, offering upmarket *gutbürgerliche Küche*; and *Café Ringelnatz* on Fischbrückstrasse between the Dom and Holm, which serves good-value food, teas and beer in a series of intimate little rooms, each quite different from the other.

Bikes and **boats** can both be rented at the Stadthafen during the summer months, when various companies also run **cruises** on the Schlei. The **folklore** tradition of Holm continues in the *Holmer Beliebung* held two weeks after Whitsun and featuring processions, music, and a ball in which the minuet and fandango are performed; another big annual event is the *Twiebakken-Regatta* in late August.

Flensburg

There's a quite astonishing contrast in feel between Schleswig and its larger near neighbour **FLENSBURG**, a bustling commercial port and border town just over 30km to the north. Once the richest mercantile city under the Danish Crown, Flensburg has continued to prosper in spite of having lost much of its hinterland to Denmark in the wake of the 1920 plebiscite, when it opted to remain part of Germany. Standing at the head of the gentle Flensburger Förde, the town has expanded from its original waterside location up into the hills on either side of the inlet. Until a decade or so ago, it looked rather scruffy, but its Altstadt, which was surprisingly little touched by war, has gradually been restored to pristine shape as a result of an extremely imaginative urban regeneration programme.

The town

Flensburg's pride and joy is its central axis, a pedestrian precinct successively known as Holm, Grosse Strasse and Norderstrasse, which stretches for well over a kilometre along the entire length of the Altstadt from the Südermarkt to the Nordertor. Along its length are a series of **Höfe**, former merchants' courtyards (see box opposite). These have no counterpart anywhere else in Germany, and are illuminating documents of social history, as well as the main contributory factor to the town's indubitably distinctive appearance.

The Südermarkt, on which markets are held on Wednesdays and Saturdays, is dominated by the **Nikolaikirche**, whose massive late sixteenth-century steeple, a very tardy example of Gothic, had to be reconstructed last century following fire damage. The rest of the building, which is in the traditional hall-church style, belongs to an earlier phase of Gothic. Inside, the most important adornment is the Renaissance **organ**, the largest in Schleswig-Holstein, which preserves its original case, a loving piece of

The **telephone code** for Flensburg is ☎0461

THE FLENSBURG HÖFE

Most of Flensburg's courtyards are laid out according to a clear pattern. Facing the main street is the showpiece home of the merchant, with his offices often incorporated as well. The two side wings typically have the stables and workshops where the imported raw materials were turned into finished products, while the far end is normally closed off by a large warehouse building with an entrance gateway and crane. For obvious reasons of convenience, most of these back directly onto the harbour, which is only one block to the east. Therefore, the western side of Flensburg's main axis was left to those of lesser means and was populated mainly by craftsmen, whose modest houses stand in stark contrast to the courtyards directly opposite.

craftsmanship by the sculptor Heinrich Ringerinck, who probably also made the pulpit. Also of note is the late fifteenth-century bronze **font** with its picturesque Baroque canopy.

Proceeding up Holm, look out for nos. 19–21, a courtyard dating back to the sixteenth century, and for house no. 10 opposite, which has a well-restored facade. At the back of no. 24 on Grosse Strasse is the **Westindienspeicher** (West Indies Warehouse), a late eighteenth-century "skyscraper" which stands as a reminder of the importance of the rum and sugar trade to the local economy. Like many of the other historic buildings it has, following restoration, been converted into a mixture of offices and apartments. On the left-hand side further up Grosse Strasse is the **Heiliggeistkirche**, a fourteenth-century chapel which has been the main place of worship of the local Danish-speaking community since 1588.

Just beyond is Nordermarkt, on which stands the **Neptunbrunnen**, which gushes out the famous spring water used for rum-making. Also here is the **Marienkirche**, a Gothic hall church with impressive frescoes from about 1400 in its northern aisle and a fine set of Renaissance furnishings – altar, pulpit and font. Alongside are the **Schrangen**, covered arcades where traders' stalls have stood since the sixteenth century. Kompagniestrasse goes down to the right to the **Kompagnietor**, the former mariners' guildhall, where a plaque reveals something of the northern mercantile philosophy that behaving justly will, with the help of God, always bring large profits.

Continuing onwards, the **Künstlerhof** at no. 22 Norderstrasse is a courtyard of half-timbered houses which have been restored as artists' studios. The central axis terminates at the **Nordertor**, a step-gabled Renaissance gateway which has become the symbol of the town. It bears the coats of arms of both Flensburg and King Christian IV of Denmark.

Facing the harbour at Schiffbrücke 39, only a couple of minutes' walk from Nordertor, a warehouse which was still in use as late as the 1970s has been adapted to contain the **Schiffahrts- und Rum-Museum** (Tues–Sat 10am–5pm, Sun 10am–1pm; DM2). The main part of this is devoted to the history of the port and its trade, including many fetching models of ships made by sailors. In the basement, a new section focuses on the local rum business; at the last count, there were 58 different varieties being produced in Flensburg.

Returning to Norderstrasse, the stone stairway known as the Marientreppe leads up some 150 steps to the **Schlosswall**, the site of the former castle, from where there's a good view across the harbour to the opposite and traditionally less salubrious side of town. Also on the heights, a bit further south on Lutherplatz, and reached via Rathausstrasse from the junction of Grosse Strasse and Holm, is the vast neo-Renaissance bulk of the **Städtisches Museum** (Tues–Sat 10am–5pm, Sun 10am–1pm; DM2). Its displays include some fine medieval artefacts, a series of interiors from rural farmsteads, and a collection of watercolours by Emil Nolde.

Finally, it's worth crossing eastwards from Südermarkt to reach the oldest part of the town, grouped round the **Johanniskirche**, a rustic little twelfth-century church. Viewed from inside, the building almost seems to sag under the weight of its wacky sixteenth-century vault, which is covered with what is, for the most part, a decidedly unecclesiastical decorative fresco scheme.

Practicalities

Flensburg's **Hauptbahnhof** is about fifteen minutes' walk due south of the centre; the **bus station** is south of the harbour, on the opposite side of the busy Süderhofenden from the Altstadt. The **tourist office** (Mon–Fri 9am–1pm & 3–6pm; ☎23090) is centrally located at Norderstr. 6 and there's a **Mitfahrzentrale** on St-Jürgen-Platz (☎17961).

Accommodation

There are plenty of **private rooms** (①–③) on offer, but these may be less convenient than one of the cheaper **hotels** such as *Pension Ziesemer*, right beside the bus station at Wilhelmstr. 2 (☎25164; ③). Along the main axis are a couple of other reasonably priced options in historic buildings: *Stadt Hamburg*, Grosse Str. 59 (☎12611; ③); and *Flensborg-Hus*, Norderstr. 76 (☎26105; ③). The upper end of the market is well served by *Am Rathaus*, Rote Str. 32–34 (☎17333; ⑥); *Am Wasserturm*, Blasberg 13 (☎315 0600; ⑦); *Flensburger Hof*, Süderhofenden 38 (☎141990; ⑦); and *Bel Air*, Norderhofenden 6–9 (☎84110; ⑧). Well to the northeast of town, reached by Glücksburg-bound buses, is the **youth hostel**, Fichtestr. 16 (☎37742; ❷).

Eating, drinking and entertainment

The Altstadt has a nicely varied selection of places to **eat** and **drink**. Liveliest place is *Hansens*, Grosse Str. 83, which includes a tramcar among its furnishings and has changing hot and cold buffets, but is mainly of note as a *Hausbrauerei* brewing its own *Pils* and *Alt*. This marks a bold challenge to the renowned *Flensburger Pilsener* of the town's main brewery, which holds sway in most of the other bars and restaurants – and is something of a cult drink in Berlin.

Das Kleine Restaurant, Grosse Str. 73, has a varied menu including good pastas and salads, while the *Vegetarisches-Vollwert Restaurant*, Marienstr. 29, is, as its name suggests, a vegetarian and wholefood specialist. *Alt-Flensburger Haus*, Norderstr. 8, occupies one of the town's finest mansions; while *Borgerforeningen*, Holm 17, serves arguably the best meals of all. The *Galerie-Musikkneipe*, Holm 66, features live bands and food, and *Kunstwerk*, Norderstr. 107–109, is the best café-bar, serving breakfast until well into the afternoon.

A varied programme of **drama** and **music** is held at the *Landestheater*, Nordergraben 2–6 (☎141000). To find out **what's on** here and elsewhere, pick up the monthly *Flensburger Programm* from the tourist office, or the alternative magazine called *Hallimasch*.

Boat trips are run by *Förde-Reederei*, Norderhofenden 20 (☎8640, tickets ☎27686).

Around Flensburg

The obvious excursion from Flensburg is to nearby **Glücksburg**, whose Schloss is among the finest in Schleswig-Holstein. A little further afield is **Angeln**, with its impressive old village churches, while to the west, **Niebüll** is gateway to the North Friesian islands and home to two notable art collections.

Glücksburg

A few kilometres along the fjord from the end of the built-up part of Flensburg lies **GLÜCKSBURG**, a fairly typical little *Kurort* offering parks, beaches, forest walks and a first-rate sea-water swimming pool. It also has a late sixteenth-century **Schloss** (April & Oct Tues–Sun 11am–4pm; May–Sept daily 10am–5pm; Nov Sat & Sun 11am–4pm; Dec–March Sat & Sun noon–3pm; DM4), which is still the seat of the Sonderburg-Glücksburg line of the Schleswig-Holstein duchy. Set in a small lake, it now looks a little austere – it was shorn last century of its original decoration, which closely resembled the ebullient Weser Renaissance style – but is nonetheless impressive, especially when floodlit. Unusually, it is constructed not on the normal wooden piles, but on a massive granite base sunk into the bed of the lake. Its interior is equally singular, with each floor featuring a long central hallway with four rooms leading off on either side and a further room in each of the corner turrets. The decoration of the **Schlosskapelle** is a classic example of Lutheran Baroque, while the festive rooms have a marvellous array of **tapestries** and **leather wall hangings**.

Angeln

The land to the east of the rail line between Flensburg and Schleswig is **Angeln**, home of the Angles who came to Britain in the fifth century. They must have felt at home there as Angeln's slightly hilly landscape, with clusters of woodland and fields divided by hedgerows and pocked with marshes is far more reminiscent of England than of most of Germany. The larger villages here have some unimpressive modern buildings, but in the smaller hamlets, and along the lanes, you come across plenty of **traditional farmhouses**. Unique to Angeln are the **early churches** built of enormous blocks of granite – the oldest, with a thirteenth-century font, is in **SÖRUP**, roughly 20km south and east of Flensburg. Husby, Norderbrarup, Eggebek, Munkbrarup, Oeversee and Struxdorf all have thirteenth-century Romanesque churches too. Many small areas are designated nature reserves, such as the peat bog of **Satrupholmer Moor**. The **Torsberger Moor** is the site of major archeological finds of early Germanic settlements, though the best place to find out more and actually see anything of this is in the Schloss Gottorf museum in Schleswig.

Getting around this area is not exactly straightforward: trains will take you from Flensburg to Sörup and on either to Schleswig or via Süderbrarup to Eckernförde. Buses, however, are notoriously rare. The best way to explore the countryside is under your own steam – rent a bike in Flensburg or Schleswig and you can explore the coastline (beaches and campsites all the way along) as well as the villages with their Danish-sounding names. Flensburg tourist office (see opposite) has a cycle map called *Rad- und Wanderwege*, indicating touring routes in this area. Most of the roads are pretty quiet, and there are some special routes, such as the old rail line from Tarp to Süderbrarup.

Niebüll

A one-horse town in Schleswig-Holstein's farthest-flung northwest corner isn't top of anyone's list of places to visit, but **NIEBÜLL**, which lies in the bleak North Friesian landscape 40km west of Flensburg, has one or two surprises. First, it's from here that the train runs across that thin strip of land to the island of Sylt. Secondly, there are two terrific museums dedicated to artists who fell foul of the Third Reich – Emil Nolde and, less famously, Richard Haizmann.

The **Richard-Haizmann-Museum** (April–Oct Mon–Fri 10am–noon & 1–4.30pm, Sat 10am–noon; Dec & Jan Mon–Fri 1–4.30pm, Sat 10am–noon; DM3) in the Rathaus on Rathausplatz is dedicated to the artist's sculpture, pottery and pictures. Haizmann was exiled to Schleswig-Holstein in what was termed "inner emigration" following the banning of his work by the Nazis. Some of it had been displayed in the famous 1930s Berlin exhibition of so-called degenerate art and was subsequently destroyed. Haizmann's work bears the influence of oriental and African art, and is beautifully displayed in a museum created by the curator and the artist's widow, who struggled for many years to open a museum, achieving her ambition only days before her death.

Elsewhere in the town centre, the only place of interest is the **Friesisches Heimatmuseum** (daily June–Sept 2–6pm; DM2) at Osterweg 76, an old farmhouse decked out in seventeeth-century style.

The Nolde-Museum

The **Nolde-Museum** (March–Oct Tues–Sun 10am–6pm; Nov 10am–5pm; DM5) stands alone in the countryside at **SEEBÜLL** (about 5km from Niebüll) in the house and gallery that Emil Nolde built in the 1950s. These were the years when Nolde could be acknowledged again after his work had been condemned by the Nazis. A novel by post-war author Siegfried Lenz, *The German Lesson*, has as a main character an artist, painting in secret during the war, who was based on Nolde. The museum can be very full in summer, but if you are there on a quiet day you may have the luxury of enjoying Nolde's vibrant colours on your own. His Expressionistic paintings have some brutal themes; the brilliant flower and landscape series are simpler, but powerful nonetheless. In accordance with Nolde's wishes, the shop sells books and postcards, but no reproductions. A bus runs out to the museum from Niebüll, and the way is clearly signposted if you are travelling by car or bike.

Practicalities

The **tourist office** (☎04661/60190) is in the Rathaus. You can ask here about **private rooms** (①–③), though the town's **hotels** are all quite reasonably priced. The best choices are *Insel-Pension*, Gotteskoogstr. 4 (☎04661/2145; ④); *Zum Morgenstern*, Deezbüller Str. 70 (☎04661/4204; ④); *Zur Alten Schmiede*, Hauptstr. 27 (☎04661/4218; ④); and *Stadt Tonder*, Hauptstr. 70 (☎04661/96600; ⑤). There's also a **youth hostel** at Deezbülldeich 2 (☎04661/8762; ❷).

Whereas there are ample trains passing through on the Hamburg–Sylt line, note that the cross-country route to Flensburg is serviced only by buses.

INTO DENMARK

From both Flensburg and Niebüll (see above) it's very easy to get across the border into **Denmark**. Boats run regularly from Flensburg to Sønderborg, and there are regular bus connections. It's definitely worth making a short trip by bus from either Flensburg or Niebüll to **TØNDER**, the oldest market town in Denmark, first mentioned in the twelfth century. The semicircular old town has at its heart the lovely **Kristikirk**, with **small gabled houses** round about. Some, such as in the Uldgade, are so tiny you can touch the roof. On the last weekend of August Tønder hosts a large international **jazz and blues festival**, but all through the summer there are music performances in the market place. The extremely helpful **tourist office** (they speak excellent English – proof that you're in Scandinavia) is at Ostergade 2a (☎721220), right in the centre of the old town.

The North Friesian Islands

The **North Friesian Islands** lie scattered off the coast, storm-battered for centuries and until recently the home of a small population of fisherfolk and farmers eking out a fragile existence. Today tourism is by far the biggest source of income. The land is so flat directly offshore that the sea retreats to reveal large areas of mud flat – the **Watt** –

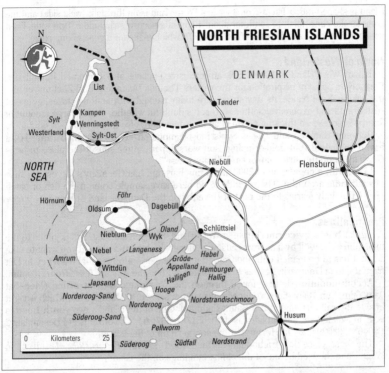

which have their own sensitive ecosystem, including masses of birdlife. The main islands are **Föhr**, **Amrum** and **Sylt**, which, although little more than a strip of land running north–south, is touristically the most developed and sophisticated. They are all family holiday centres, with holiday homes and riding, tennis and windsurfing facilities. In season, all are likely to be very busy.

Sylt

Sylt is an altogether different kettle of fish from the other homely islands. It's a favourite among monied Germans, who visit to mix business with pleasure and impress their guests with second homes in the sun. As a result, the island is heavily populated during the major holidays (including Christmas and Easter), and prices for both eating out and accommodation can be high. Such is the demand for **rooms**, which are available in all price categories here, that unless you have booked a couple of months in advance – regardless of when you visit – you could be unlucky. To add to complications, there's no central tourist office – each resort on the island has its own agency.

Westerland

WESTERLAND is Sylt's main town and the hub for bus and train connections. It's considered rather chic and glamorous: a place to dress up for an evening in the **casino** on Andreas-Nilsen-Strasse rather than stomp around in boots. Outside of Westerland the island is quieter (though full of holiday houses). Above all there's plenty of **fine sandy beach** here. The island is shaped rather like a T on its side – Westerland is on the stalk (west side) and the cross-stroke runs north to south for about 40km in a narrow strip, under 1km wide, lined with beaches, dunes and small cliffs (*Rotes Kliff*) which make for a good hiking route.

North of Westerland

North of Westerland is **KAMPEN**, an exclusive enclave of 650 monied inhabitants. Formerly a place of inspiration for the writers Thomas Mann and Carl Zuckmayer and the painter Emil Nolde, its tiny streets are today packed with antique stores, gourmet restaurants and expensive clothes stores. It's doubtful whether such a large amount of luxury is spread so thick on so small an area anywhere else in Germany.

Between Kampen and List is Sylt's most famous stretch of beach, **Buhne 16**, a haven for naked (but gold-dripping) sun worshippers. After sunset the place to be is *Gogärtchen* on the strip known as "Whiskystrasse".

LIST, with a population of 2000 and a tiny harbour, has Germany's largest expanse of sand dune around it. There's little to do here save sample some fresh fish or catch one of the daily ferries to the port of Havenby on the Danish island of Rømø.

Practicalities

A regular **bus service** runs between Westerland, Kampen and List. Sylt is joined to the mainland at Niebüll by a narrow causeway along which **trains** run – if you want to take a car, it has to be loaded onto the train first. A cheaper option is to take a **ferry** to List from Rømø in Denmark. Ferries to the islands of Föhr and Amrum leave from Hörnum.

Accommodation is best found through the Westerland **tourist office** (Mon–Sat 9am–6pm, Sun 10am–6pm, reduced hours out of season; ☎04651/9988), which is right beside the rail terminal at Am Bandesbahnhof. One of the island's two **youth hostels** is in an isolated setting outside List (☎04651/870397; ☎). The other is at Friesenplatz 2 (☎04651/880294; ☎) in Hörnum at the southern tip of the island.

The best place for traditional German **food** is *Alte Friesenstube*, Gaadt 4, in Westerland, housed in one of the oldest buildings on the island.

Föhr

Föhr is Sylt's nearest neighbour, but quite different in character. Outside of a few bars and cafés nightlife is non-existent, and accommodation is reasonably easy to come by. Ferries from Dagebüll on the mainland arrive at **WYK**, the island's main town. It's a peaceful old place with a thirteenth-century church, a harbour and precious little else. Depending on finances you can either take a **taxi** for around DM15 and go for a one-hour ride around the island (try the taxi office at Birkenweg 11, or call ☎04681/3705 for more details on this), or **rent a bike** (from one of the numerous shops displaying a *Fahrrad Verleih* sign; around DM15 per week). First place to cycle to should be the village of **NIEBLUM** to the west, an exceptionally quaint and picturesque place of old gabled and thatched cottages along cobbled streets, with a thirteenth-century church. Listen to the local dialect: a mixture of Plattdeutsch, Hochdeutsch and Friesian, which is itself a mix of Danish, Dutch and English.

There's a **campsite** and a **youth hostel** in Wyk at Fehrstieg 41 (☎04681/2355; ☎). Other accommodation can be arranged via the **tourist office** (☎04681/3053) at Hafenstr. 23.

Amrum

Amrum is a less exciting prospect than the previous islands. Ferries land at the town of **WITTDÜN**, where, if you're not careful, you'll find yourself stuck since ferries and local buses aren't synchronized. The village has a one-horse feel, though you can rent bikes and there's a **tourist office** (☎04682/19433) at Mittelstr. 34. on the edge of the harbour car park. Walks, beaches, sea birds and sports are the order of the day here, and the bracing breeze becomes quite enjoyable in the end. Most visitors book into **hotels** and bed and breakfasts for a week or more, so it is easiest to ask the tourist office about vacancies – in season they may be hard to come by. The **youth hostel** (☎04682/2010; ⌂) is at Mittelstr. 1.

It is possible – tides permitting and only under the supervision of an experienced guide – to **walk across the Watt** from Amrum to Föhr. For more information and details of tours, contact the *Schutzstation Wattenmeer* in Hörnum on Sylt (Tues–Sun 10am–noon & 3–5pm; ☎04651/881093).

The Halligen

Smaller, and almost at sea level, is another, distinct group of undyked islands – the **Halligen**. These last remnants of land are scarcely above sea level; as you approach them by ship all you see are a few houses apparently sitting on the waves. Once you set foot on dry land you discover that these houses are built on specially constructed hummocks that stay dry when the rest of the land is washed over by winter storms. The land is really good only for grazing sheep, and bed and breakfast is a major source of income for the Hallig inhabitants nowadays. Even more than on the mainland, few young people are interested in staying on to maintain old ways of life, and the Halligen seem set for a slow but sure period of decline.

The islands

The main Halligen are inhabited, but the tiny **Hallig Habel** is a nature reserve, with just one family present in summer; the even smaller **Norderoog** is a **bird breeding sanctuary**, and also just has a summertime warden. The main islands, **Nordstrand** and **Pellworm** (together with Hamburger Hallig and Nordstrandischmoor), used to form a larger island known as **Alt-Nordstrand**, or just Strand, with five quays and some fifty-nine churches and chapels – a major settlement in its time. A tidal wave in 1634 created today's geography. Nordstrand is now connected to the mainland by a narrow causeway, as are Nordstrandischmoor and Hamburger Hallig; the latter has become a virtual peninsula because of silting up on both sides of its link with the mainland. Hallig Langeness is similarly connected to Hallig Oland, which in turn has a mainland connection.

Pellworm and Hallig Hooge, however, are reached by peak-season **ferries** running from Dagebüll and Schlüttsiel (run by *WDR* lines) and from Nordstrand (*Kurt Paulsen*). **Pellworm,** to the southeast of Amrum, has thirteenth- and seventeenth-century churches bearing witness to its history, and hardly anything else. Its future may be anticipated by a huge **solar collector** (it's one of Germany's sunniest places, which bodes well for visitors), generating 280,000 kilowatt hours per year. A small **Wattmuseum** holds the former local postman's lifetime collection of finds from the Watt. The **tourist office** is at Uthlandestr. 1 (☎04844/04844).

All the tourist offices and some train stations have leaflets and posters with details of ferries. It doesn't take long to look round a Hallig – so unless you feel like communing with wind and water, the few hours between boats may be all the time you want to spend there.

Husum and around

HUSUM, some 40km south of Niebüll and 35km west of Schleswig, is by far the most attractive town in North Friesland. Its character is defined by the small harbour right in the centre, which must have given welcome shelter to generations of fishermen returning from the perils of the North Sea. As a town, it's a mixture of small-scale grandeur and workaday simplicity, filled with fishy smells that waft in from the harbour, and with a sufficient smattering of interesting buildings to catch the imagination. In summer, it serves as the main jumping-off point for the Halligen islands and for Helgoland (see opposite), though it's at its picturesque best during the springtime bloom.

Husum is perhaps best known in association with the name of **Theodor Storm**, a nineteenth-century novelist, poet and civil figure (it was he who gave the town its rather unfair title *Die graue Stadt am Meer* — "the grey town by the sea") who was especially active in Schleswig-Holstein's struggle to remain out of the clutches of the expansionist state of Prussia. His name crops up all over the town: you may even find yourself staying in the hotel or youth hostel named after him.

The town

The main axis of the town centre is the broad **Gross Strasse**, which opens out into the **Markt**. Both of these are lined with large houses, mainly eighteenth- and nineteenth-century (though there are one or two beautiful seventeenth-century gabled buildings reminiscent of Lübeck), most of which have stores on the ground floor. Here too is the step-gabled fourteenth-century **Herrenhaus**, the oldest building in town, albeit with sandstone pillars and a doorway added in the seventeenth and eighteenth centuries. On the north side of the square stands the seventeenth-century **Rathaus**.

Turning northwards from here, you come to the Schlossgang, a narrow walkway leading past small houses, a couple of cafés and craft-giftshops to the **Schloss** (April–Oct Tues–Sun 11am–5pm; DM5). Over to the left, the **Torhaus**, the former gatehouse, is actually more attractive than the main building. It has retained some ornate Renaissance features, whereas the Schloss itself, built at the same time, underwent extensive later modifications, giving it a Baroque interior with fine sandstone and alabaster fireplaces. The **Schlosspark**, which contains a memorial to Theodor Storm, turns into a great sea of mauve crocuses in spring. These were originally planted in the Middle Ages by monks who had a monastery on the site.

About 100m south of Gross Strasse is the **Schiffbrücke**, an inner harbour busy with fishing boats; it's also the place where the ferry takes shelter in winter. One famous catch landed here is *Husumer Krabben* – not crabs, confusingly, but tasty little brown shrimps. They're found in abundance on local menus, especially in the form of *Husumer Krabbensuppe*, a soup that often comes topped with whipped cream. In summer, there's a shrimp stall on Hafenstrasse, towards the outer harbour, selling the freshly boiled catch.

Up Wasserreihe, the narrow street to the right, is the **Theodor-Storm-Haus** (April–Oct Tues–Fri 10am–noon & 2–5pm, Mon, Sat & Sun 2–5pm; Nov–March Tues, Thurs & Sat 2pm–5pm; DM3), the home of the writer between 1866 and 1880, when he was at the height of his career. With many original documents, and as the headquarters of the Theodor Storm society, it's obviously chiefly of interest to his fans. However, the house is worth catching as an example of nineteenth-century middle-class lifestyle in this area, as the rooms still have original furnishings. Storm's wood-panelled study, where he produced about twenty of his novels, has a display of correspondence with the Russian novelist Turgenev and other literary figures. The Wasserreihe itself is a characterful street, with several typical fisherfolk houses.

A couple of blocks further north, at Nordhusumer Str. 13, is the **Ostenfelder Bauernhaus** (April–Oct Tues–Sun 10am–noon & 2–5pm; DM3), a reconstructed seventeenth-century farmhouse. At the southern end of the town centre, in the Nissenhaus at Herzog-Adolf-Str. 25, is the **Nordfriesisches Museum** (April–Oct daily 10am–5pm; Nov–March 10am–4pm, closed Sat; DM5). This was founded in the early 1930s by local-boy-made-good Ludwig Nissen, who amassed a fortune in the United States. It's especially good on the geological background of the area, flood control and town history.

Practicalities

Both the **Bahnhof** and the **bus station** are just a short walk from the town centre, which is reached via Herzog-Adolf-Strasse. The **tourist office** (June to mid-Sept Mon–Wed 10am–6pm, Thurs & Fri 10am–8pm, Sat 10am–1pm; rest of year Mon–Thurs 8am–noon & 2–4.30pm, Fri 8am–noon & 2–3pm; ☎04841/898730) is in the Altes Rathaus, Gross Str. 27.

At the tourist office you can pick up the extensive list of **private rooms** (①–②). There's a good range of **hotels** in every category. At the lower end are *Rödekrog*, Wilhelmstr. 10 (☎04841/3771; ②), and *Wohlert*, Markt 30 (☎04841/2229; ⑤). In the medium range, *Zur Grauen Stadt am Meer*, overlooking the harbour at Schiffbrücke 8–9 (☎04841/89320; ⑤), is a lovely place, with an excellent restaurant serving local fish specialities. An alternative in this range is *Osterkrug*, Osterende 56 (☎04841/2885; ⑤), while the upper end of the market is well served by the inevitably named *Theodor Storm*, Neustadt 60 (☎04841/3085; ⑧); the latter's restaurant has hot and cold buffets every day, plus its own *Hausbrauerei*.

Husum's **youth hostel** is at the far northwestern end of town at Schöbuller Str. 34 (☎04841/2714; ⚑) and the **campsite** is well located right by the beach to the west of the centre at Dockkoog (☎04841/61911).

Quite apart from the hotels, Husum is well off for places to **eat** and **drink**. *Dragseth's Gasthof* at Zingel 11, a sixteenth-century house with a small gallery and teashop, offers a good selection of food including vegetarian dishes. *Anna*, in the basement of Stadtpassage, Schiffbrücke 16, also does good vegetarian (as well as other) food. *Friesenkroog*, Kleikuhle 6, has a fine selection of fresh fish. *Café Schöneck* at Schiffbrücke, whose rooms are crammed with old Friesian furniture, has good soups, a vast array of warming alcoholic drinks, and Danish pastries far surpassing those normally found south of the border. *Husumer Speicher*, a converted warehouse at Hafenstr. 17, is the local place for **live music** and entertainment.

Ferries to Helgoland (DM49) leave from the Eidersperrwerk; those to the Halligen (upwards of DM16) leave from Nordstrand. There's a bus link (included in the cost of the ticket) to both terminals from Husum Aussenhafen; information is available from *Schiffsmakler Schmidt* (☎04841/2014). There's also a bus from the Bahnhof to the island of Nordstrand.

Helgoland (Heligoland)

Husum is the most obvious starting point for visiting Germany's most isolated corner, the red limestone island of **Helgoland** which stands on its own in the North Sea, 70km from the mouth of the Elbe. Alternative sailings are from Bremerhaven, Cuxhaven and Wilhelmshaven; there are daily crossings between April and October, less frequent at other times. Expect to pay around DM70 for a period return from any of these ports; day tickets are also available for about DM55, but these are of limited use as they only allow about four hours on the island – roughly the same time as it takes to get there.

Once an important naval base and coaling station, Helgoland was long occupied by the British, and only came into German hands in 1890, when it was swapped for Zanzibar. Bombarded during World War II, its inhabitants were forcibly evacuated in 1947, and the remaining fortifications were blown up. For five years it served as a bombing target for the RAF, until finally returned to Germany in 1952. Reconstruction began immediately and Helgoland has become a popular holiday resort with all the usual facilities, plus the added advantage of duty-free status. The craggy cliffs are certainly dramatic, though whether they are special enough to warrant the time and expense of getting here is a moot point.

If you do decide to come, it would be best to contact the **tourist office** (☎04725/81430) in advance for accommodation. Alternatively, you could book directly with the **youth hostel** (☎04725/341; **⚑**), which is open from April to October, and situated only a short walk from the harbour.

Eiderstedt and Friedrichstadt

Southwest of Husum and directly north of the Eider estuary is the peninsula (*Halbinsel*) of **Eiderstedt**. Tönning and St Peter Ording, its two little harbour towns, are not spectacular, but are possible bases for exploring the countryside. **TÖNNING**, for instance, is right by the Katinger Watt, while **ST-PETER-ORDING** has 12km of beaches, backed by forest and dunes. Both towns have extensive camping facilities.

FRIEDRICHSTADT, 15km south of Husum, is certainly worth a look – a small corner of Holland apparently transported to North Friesland. It was built in the 1620s by Dutch settlers with the encouragement of Duke Friedrich III, who rather hoped it would develop into a major commercial town. It didn't, but the town, complete with its canals and bridges, remains a gem of Dutch Renaissance architecture in an unlikely setting.

Dithmarschen

The region encircled by the waters of the North Sea, the Eider, the Kiel Canal and the Elbe, is known as **Dithmarschen**. Dyking of the area began around the fifth century AD, and doubtless the long struggle to protect the land they worked from the ravages of the sea made the local peasantry especially defensive of their property. In the thirteenth century, they expelled their feudal overlords and founded an independent peasant's republic. The nobility never returned, and Dithmarschen gained a reputation for being an individualistic stronghold.

Dithmarschen is covered by a network of some 1500km of **cycle paths**, so you can tour away from the traffic, which is in any case light. This is by far the best means of exploration, though the Husum to Hamburg rail line passes through the main towns. Coming here from Lower Saxony, incidentally, you can bypass Hamburg by crossing the Elbe by ferry from Wischhafen (just north of Stade) to Glückstadt.

Heide

The market town of **HEIDE**, 25km south of Friedrichstadt, is nowadays the Dithmarschen "capital", and is particularly proud that its vast central **Markt** is the largest open square in all of Germany. North of the pedestrian precinct, the dominant landmark is the idiosyncratic **Wasserturm** erected at the beginning of the century, near which are some ancient stones which mark a burial ground from 2600 BC. Also in the vicinity, at Brahmsstr. 8, is the **Museum für Dithmarscher Vorgeschichte und Heider Heimatmuseum** (April–Sept Tues–Fri 9am–noon & 2–5pm, Sun 10am–5pm; Oct–March Tues–Fri 2–5pm, Sun 10am–noon & 2–5pm; free), which documents the archeology and history of the region.

Heide's **tourist office** (July & Aug Mon–Fri 8am–6pm, Sat 10am–noon; Sept–June Mon–Thurs 8am–4pm, Fri 8am–noon; ☎0481/685 0117) is in the Rathaus, just off the Markt at Postelweg 1. **Hotels** include *Kotthaus*, Rüsdorfer Str. 3 (☎0481/850980; ⑦). There are also plenty of **private houses** (①–③) with rooms to rent, while the **youth hostel** is a couple of blocks west of the Wasserturm at Poststr. 4 (☎0481/71575; **⚑**).

Büsum and the coast

About 20km west of Heide by road or rail is the seaside town of **BÜSUM**, which has good beaches with accommodation to suit all pockets, but it's a fairly staid family resort. Better are the far less busy stretches of sand running from the north of town all the way to the Eider. This whole coast is dyked, and the mouth of the Eider – between Husum and Büsum – has been barred·against tidal floods (which used to rush 100km inland) by a massive barrier, the **Eidersperrwerk**. You can cross this by road, towards Tönning and St Peter Ording. It's also worth knowing that in summer ferries ply between Büsum and the island of Helgoland.

Meldorf

MELDORF, 12km south of Heide on the rail line to Hamburg, was the capital of the Dithmarschen peasants' republic, and the first town in the area to have a church, in 826. On the site of that building now stands the **Johanniskirche** – which is thirteenth-century, but heavily remodelled, particularly on the exterior, last century. Also in town, at Bütjestr. 2–4, is the **Landesmuseum** (Easter–Oct Tues–Fri 9am–4.30pm, Sat & Sun 11am–4pm; Nov–Easter Tues–Fri 9am–4pm, Sat & Sun 11am–4pm; DM4), which has displays on the folklore of Dithmarschen as well as models showing how the dyking and drainage process works.

travel details

Trains

Hamburg to: Flensburg (every 2hr; 1hr 45min); Husum (hourly; 2hr); Kiel (hourly; 1hr 15min); Lübeck (hourly; 40min); Rendsburg (every 2hr; 1hr 10min); Schleswig (every 2hr; 1hr 30min).

Kiel to: Flensburg (hourly; 1hr 10min); Husum (hourly; 1hr 30min); Lübeck (hourly; 1hr 10min); Rendsburg (hourly; 30min); Schleswig (hourly; 50min).

Ferries

Dagebüll to: Amrum (winter 5 daily, summer 8 daily; 2hr); Föhr (winter 7 daily, summer 10 daily; 45min).

Hamburg to: Harwich (every 2 days; 20hr 30min); Newcastle Tynemouth (May to early Sept; every 4 days; 24hr).

Nordstrand to: Pellworm (winter 3–5 daily, summer 5–7 daily; 35–40min).

Schlüttsiel to: Amrum (1 daily; 2hr 30min); Hallig Hooge (summer 2 daily; winter very irregular; 1hr 15min); Hallig Langeness (same times and boat as to Hallig Hooge; 1hr 50min).

CHAPTER EIGHT

MECKLENBURG-LOWER POMERANIA

Mecklenburg-Lower Pomerania (*Mecklenburg-Vorpommern*) is eastern Germany's maritime province. The tideless Baltic Sea laps at the slim coastline of some 370km, while the rivers Elbe and Oder form natural borders to the west and east; to the south is a spacious lakeland which is the most thinly populated part of Germany. The Land is something of a compromise creation, most of its territory once belonging to two separate grand duchies; the remainder is the German rump (not deemed to be viable as a Land in its own right) of the ancient and much-disputed province of Pomerania, the greater part of which was ceded to Poland in 1945.

From **Wismar**, the incongruously large-scale medieval townscape at the western end of the province, the coastal landscape gradually changes from flat indented shores to the windswept dunes behind **Rostock**, the chief port and largest city. Further east, within the surviving German part of Pomerania, is **Stralsund**, whose grand Hanseatic buildings look across a narrow channel to **Rügen**, Germany's largest island, characterized by dramatic landscapes of battered headlands and chalky cliffs rising steeply from the sea. Beyond here, the coast curves southeastwards via the university city of Greifswald and the Pomeranian ducal capital of **Wolgast** towards the sandy island of **Usedom** and the Polish border. During the summer the coast is overrun by holiday-makers, but for the rest of the year the region returns to a peaceful emptiness, and a Sunday afternoon atmosphere descends on even the larger towns.

Inland, the great **Mecklenburg Lake Plateau** tilts gently south, with few major towns disturbing the rural landscape before Berlin, about 300km away. This, eastern Germany's granary, is a real backwater and has changed relatively little since debt-enslaved peasants worked the land for their aristocratic masters. The GDR era left a surprisingly small mark around here, mainly manifesting itself in the shape of ugly apartment buildings next to villages. The greatest change is only now unfolding, as western-style tourism discovers the potential of this quietly scenic part of the country. For the moment, however, it remains a beautiful land of innumerable lakes and ancient forests almost untouched by human habitation.

The Land capital and former ducal residence of **Schwerin** in the northwest seems disproportionately sophisticated and elegant in such a rustic region. It escaped the ravages of wartime bombs – its Baroque and Neoclassical architecture is romantically faded but not derelict as in so many other places. Not far southwest lies **Ludwigslust**, a fascinating planned town which was temporarily the Schwerin dukes' main seat in the eighteenth century. A little further northeast, picturesque **Güstrow**, another former ducal seat, makes an ideal base for exploring the lakes. **Neubrandenburg**, at the eastern edge of the lake district, retains a spectacular medieval defensive system, while nearby **Neustrelitz** is a Baroque town specially built to serve as capital of the smaller of the two Mecklenburg duchies.

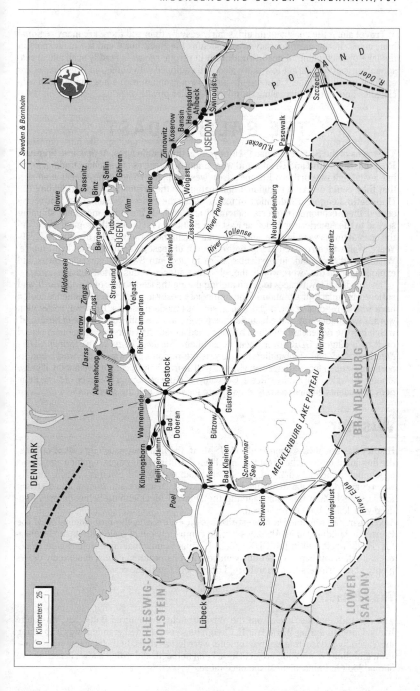

Travel along the coast and inland is fairly easy by train and there are many regional bus routes. In the more touristy areas, such as the Baltic coast and the main spots in the lake district, plentiful **accommodation** in private rooms is readily available at reasonable prices. The larger towns are also well equipped with hotels, and new places are opening up all the time. Camping shouldn't be a problem with a large number of official sites and an ever-increasing number of smaller private ones.

THE BALTIC COAST

The towns of the Baltic coast had their heyday in the Middle Ages. At that time **Wismar**, **Rostock**, **Stralsund** and **Greifswald** were important centres of merchant trading, forming a vital link on northern Europe's east–west shipping routes. They became so rich that they could override traditional domination by the aristocracy, instead joining the **Hanseatic League**, a federation of towns along the entire German coast that represented their economic interests nationally and abroad. But once merchant shipping spread to the Americas and the Far East, the Baltic Sea routes lost their importance and the coastal towns went into decline. The final nail in the coffin was the disastrous Thirty Years' War, which resulted in this entire stretch of coast going to the Swedish Empire. Wismar and Stralsund, in particular, were turned into Swedish garrison towns and exploited for all they were worth, though little evidence of this period remains today.

The medieval townscapes took a battering during the later stages of World War II, and suffered from lack of attention in the immediate postwar years, when aesthetics took a back seat to rehousing the population in soulless modern estates. However, restoration work is well under way in the historic showpieces, and the entire city centre of Stralsund, which has the richest architectural heritage, had already had a preservation order placed on it by a diligent GDR government department. Rostock, home to the former GDR's merchant navy and shipbuilding industry, is the region's gateway to the world, and its port is now open for passenger services as well as freight traffic. Like Greifswald, it's also among the oldest university cities in Germany, and the continued presence of large numbers of students ensures a lively atmosphere for at least half the year.

Wismar

History has not always been kind to **WISMAR**, the first Hanseatic city east of Lübeck, the dominant force in the great trading alliance. During the League's golden age, it was a rich and influential port, but after it was taken over by the Swedes in 1648, the city was regarded as a vital defensive bulwark against Denmark and turned into a strong fortress. In 1803, it was mortgaged to the Duke of Mecklenburg-Schwerin on a hundred-year lease, but not reclaimed.

Wismar has remained a modest-sized town ever since, the monumentality of the Hanseatic buildings in its Altstadt seeming completely out of scale with its modern status. Badly neglected in the GDR epoch, Wismar is now making a determined comeback: it takes tourism very seriously indeed, and its beautiful centre deservedly draws plenty of day-trippers from Hamburg, Lübeck and the Baltic resorts.

The Altstadt

The **Altstadt**, set just back from the Wismarbucht, a sheltered Baltic bay, was quite badly damaged during World War II, though its sense of faded grandeur was if anything increased by the fact that key monuments were left as ruins. In the past few years, however, ambitious restoration projects have been initiated, and within a few years the town should look in immaculate shape once more.

Marktplatz and around

The hundred-square-metre **Marktplatz**, one of the largest in Germany, has regained its commercial function since the fall of Communism. Showpiece of the square, though sometimes rather obscured by all the stalls, is the **Wasserkunst**, a domed wrought-iron pavilion in the Dutch Renaissance style which shelters the municipal well, the town's only source of drinking water until 1897. Opposite is a mansion misleadingly known as the **Alter Schwede**: the oldest surviving house in town, dating back to 1380, it's a fine example of the brick Gothic architecture typical of the Baltic. In contrast to the gabled east and south sides of the square, the northern end is dominated by the slate-blue of the Neoclassical **Rathaus**.

Standing forlorn in the middle of the Marienkirchhof, the next square to the west, is the disembodied tower of the **Marienkirche**, the rest of which was destroyed in the war; sadly, this seems to be the one building accepted as being past meaningful restoration. At the square's southeastern corner is the **Archdiakonat**, a fine example of black and red brickwork from the fifteenth century.

Kellerstrasse leads west to Wismar's most distinctive building, the **Fürstenhof**, a mid-sixteenth-century palace constructed in a Baltic adaptation of the Italian Renaissance style. It's adorned with beautiful friezes: the lower is of limestone and depicts the Trojan War on the street facade, the story of the Prodigal Son on the court-yard side; the upper is of terracotta and has portrait medallions of personalities of the day intermingled with heroes of the Classical world. The magnificent portal bears the coat of arms of the Mecklenburg dukes.

Beyond is the hefty torso of the **Georgenkirche**, Wismar's largest church, a highly decorative example of Gothic brickwork which, in the days of the Hansa, was the place of worship of the craftsmen and tradesfolk. Left as a roofless shell in 1945, it's current-ly the subject of the town's most ambitious restoration project, with the aim of recon-structing it completely.

North of Marktplatz

On Lübsche Strasse, a block north of Marktplatz, the **Heiligen-Geist-Spital** (daily 11am–noon & 2–3pm; free), ranks second to Lübeck's as the best-preserved old hospi-tal in Germany. Originally fifteenth-century Gothic, it was partially remodelled a couple of hundred years later in late Renaissance style. The most notable feature from the lat-ter period is the painted wooden ceiling of the church, whose medallions illustrate Old Testament scenes. Look out also for some notable older furnishings, including a pair of processional candelabra and a regal stone group of the Adoration of the Magi.

Further north, the Altstadt is bisected by the **Grube**, the oldest landscaped canal in any German city, and lined with recently restored buildings. On its southern bank, alongside Schweinsbrücke, is the **Schabbellhaus** (May–Sept Tues–Sun 10am–8pm; Oct–April Tues, Wed & Fri–Sun 10am–4.30pm, Thurs 10am–6pm; DM3), a ritzy man-sion in the Dutch Renaissance style built as the home and workplace of a local brewer and town councillor. Today, it contains an excellent museum on the history of Wismar. There's a gory section on medieval torture, with the grisliest exhibit being two shriv-elled human hands preserved in a bowl. These came from a murder victim and were used to confront the perpetrator in court – an accusing finger from the grave, so to speak, successfully used to extract a confession. Other, more aesthetic, highlights are the bronze doorknocker from the Georgenkirche, the drinking horn of the wool weavers' guild and the original figures from the Wasserkunst. A small archeology department features the so-called Wismar Horn from 1200 BC.

Directly opposite stands the **Nikolaikirche**, the only one of the three brick Gothic churches to remain intact in 1945. As with Marktplatz, its monumental proportions seem highly exaggerated for this small town: indeed, its dizzying 37-metre-high interi-or makes it the tallest church in the whole of the former GDR. The lofty sense of space conveyed is undoubtedly the most memorable feature, though there are a few fine works of art, notably in the chapel beside the sacristy, which has a fourteenth-century bronze font and the fifteenth-century retable of the mariners' guild.

Just to the northwest is the **Wassertor**, the only one of the five medieval gateways to have survived. It guarded the entrance to the harbour, the **Alter Hafen**, which these days still buzzes with fishing boats.

Practicalities

Wismar's **Hauptbahnhof** lies just outside the northeastern confines of the Altstadt. The extent to which the town takes tourism seriously is reflected in the unusually long opening hours of the **tourist office** in the Stadthaus, Am Markt 11 (daily 9am–6pm; ☎03841/282958).

Some **private rooms** (①–③) are available, and there's a **youth hostel** 8km west at Haus no. 21 (☎038428/362; ⓪) in the village of Beckerwitz, which can be reached by bus. More convenient are a couple of Altstadt **pensions**: *Chez Fasan*, Bodemutterstr. 19 (☎03841/213425; ③) and *Gästehaus Wismaria*, Bohrstr. 10 (☎03841/645 7524; ③). Similarly central are several quality medium- and upper-range **hotels**: *Reingard*, Weberstr. 18 (☎03841/284972 or 213495; ④); *Altes Brauhaus*, Lübsche Str. 33 (☎03841/283223; ⑥); *Alter Speicher*, Bohrstr. 12 (☎03841/211746; ⑥); and *Stadt Hamburg*, Am Markt 24–25 (☎03841/2390; ⑦).

The **restaurants** of the last two hotels are among the best in town. Other places to eat and drink include *Alter Schwede*, Am Markt 22, which lives up to its name by offering Swedish as well as German cuisine; the historic *Zum Weinberg*, Hinter dem Rathaus 3; and the fish specialists *Seehase*, Altböterstr. 6, and *Hanse Keller*, Lübsche Str. 24. A good choice for *Kaffee und Kuchen* is *Caféhaus 15*, Lübsche Str. 15, while *Brauhaus am Lohberg*, Lohberg 15, is a new *Hausbrauerei*.

You'll find the nearest stretch of reasonable Baltic **beach** on the island of **Poel**, about 10km north of town. Its best section is at Schwarzer Busch – but don't expect too much, as it's only a very thin strip of land that gets very crowded. Local buses regularly run over the causeway to Poel; in summer there are also ferries, which sail from Alter Hafen, passing the bird sanctuary on the isle of Walfisch en route. There's a **campsite**, *Timmendorf* (☎038422/844), on Poel, one of several in Wismar's immediate vicinity.

ACCOMMODATION PRICE CODES

All the pensions and hotels in this book have been graded according to the following price categories. The prices quoted are for the cheapest available double room, although many of the budget places will also have more expensive rooms. Youth hostels are graded under separate categories. See p.34 for more details.

① less than DM50	④ DM81–100	⑦ DM151–200
② DM51–65	⑤ DM101–125	⑧ DM201–250
③ DM66–80	⑥ DM126–150	⑨ more than DM250

Bad Doberan and the beach resorts

Between Wismar and Rostock lie a number of holiday resorts which have begun to reclaim the prestigious status they held before the GDR brought them firmly downmarket. Prominent among these, and an excellent touring base for the whole region, is the spa town of **Bad Doberan**, which lies 50km northeast of Wismar and 17km west of Rostock. It now forms a joint municipality with nearby **Heiligendamm**, the oldest seaside resort in Germany, while just to the west is an even bigger beachcomber's paradise, **Kühlungsborn**. An added attraction is that the three towns are linked by one of eastern Germany's celebrated narrow-gauge rail lines.

Bad Doberan

BAD DOBERAN, the one-time summer residence of the Grand Dukes of Mecklenburg-Schwerin, began life as an adjunct to one of the country's most powerful Cistercian monasteries. Of this, the **Münster** (April–June, Sept & Oct Tues–Sun 9am–4.30pm; July & Aug daily 9am–4.30pm; Nov–March Tues–Sun 9am–3pm; DM2), the former monastic church, still survives at the eastern edge of the centre. It incorporates a fragment of the original Romanesque building, but is otherwise a peerless example of the brick Gothic architecture characteristic of the Baltic lands. Although the graceful pillars and vaulting provide the most imposing features of the interior, there are a number of impressive adornments, including the winged fourteenth-century high altar and the tall tabernacle. Just to the northeast of the church is a curious octagonal structure in a similar style; known as the **Beinhaus**, it used to serve as an ossuary.

To the west, the **Kamp**, formerly a common, was transformed into an English-style park when Doberan came into favour with the Schwerin court. On the east side of August-Bebel-Strasse, which bisects the park from north to south, are a number of grand Empire buildings from the same period, among them the ducal **Palais**, which was recently transformed into the opulent *Kurhotel* (see below). Amid the greenery to the west are two whimsical garden pavilions in the Chinese style: the smaller **Roter Pavillon** is a commercial art gallery, while the larger **Weisser Pavillon** is a café.

Northwest of here lies **Goethestrasse**, a street of eighteenth- and nineteenth-century mansions now under reconstruction following decades of shameful neglect. The *Molli*, the **narrow-gauge railway** linking Bad Doberan with the two coastal resorts, begins its fifteen-kilometre journey by running right along the middle of this street before chugging through a forest nature reserve towards the nearby beaches.

Practicalities

Bad Doberan's **Bahnhof** is located at the southern end of the town centre. The **tourist office** at Goethestr. 1 (May–Sept Mon–Fri 9am–6pm, Sat 10am–4pm; Oct–April Mon & Wed–Fri 9am–5pm, Tues 9am–6pm; ☎038203/2154) has plenty of **private rooms** (①–③) on its books. Another budget option is the **youth hostel** on the western side of town at Am Tempelberg (☎038203/2439; ②).

There's also a **pension**, *Am Fuchsberg*, Am Fuchsberg 7 (☎038203/3474; ④). The only **hotel** as such is the *Kurhotel*, August-Bebel-Str. 2 (☎038203/3036; ⑦); this has the best **restaurant** in town, though the *Ratskeller*, August-Bebel-Str. 3, is a reliable and cheaper alternative.

Heiligendamm and Kühlungsborn

The first main stop on the *Molli* is **HEILIGENDAMM**, a grand remnant of Germany's aristocratic past. Founded in 1793 by Duke Friedrich Franz I, this was the first place in Germany where the well-heeled came to enjoy the newly fashionable pastime of swimming in the sea. Throughout the GDR period, its palatial white buildings served as holiday homes for manual workers, but these are gradually being restored as hotels and sanatoria. Currently, choice in **accommodation** lies between *Pension Hildebrandt*, Seedeichstr. 18 (☎038203/2996; ⑤), which also administers the *Ostsee* holiday bungalow site; and the plush *Residenzhotel*, Prof-Dr-Vogel-Str. 16–18 (☎038203/4620; ⑦).

For a bit more life and bustle, continue to the *Molli*'s terminus of **KÜHLUNGSBORN**, one of the Baltic's largest holiday resorts. Here there are dozens of **hotels**, particularly along the seafront. Many are in elegant Wilhelmine and Jugendstil buildings; among the most attractive are the jointly run *Rheingold* and *Schloss am Meer*, Tannenstr. 7/8 (both ☎038293/7226 or 85300; ④ and ⑤ respectively); *Villa Verdi*, Str. des Friedens 26 (☎038293/8570; ⑥); *Villa Patricia*, Str. des Friedens 2 (☎038293/8540; ⑥); and *Neptun*, Strandstr. 37 (☎038293/630; ⑥). There's also a **youth hostel** at Dünenstr. 4 (☎038293/270; ☎). Further information about accommodation can be had from the **tourist office**, Poststr. 20 (☎038293/6620).

Rostock

ROSTOCK is well served by ferry routes, but approaching by boat you'd never guess you were heading for the German Baltic's largest port. Instead, the little fishing village of Warnemünde presents its sandy beach, and tugs are the largest boats around. However, you then swing round to the River Warnow's wide estuary, with its vast deep-sea port; Rostock itself stands a few kilometres further down, on the southern riverbank. It presents an intriguing architectural mix – medieval and 1950s architecture in the centre, nineteenth-century villas in the suburb of Steintor-Vorstadt, and modern housing estates for the rest.

The city has had a tough time coming to terms with the consequences of German unification, which brought to a speedy end its postwar role as the shipbuilding metropolis of the Communist bloc, resulting in mass unemployment. A vicious neo-Nazi attack on an immigrants' hostel in 1992, which was captured on film and broadcast round the world, has brought it a notoriety it will find hard to shake off.

The **telephone code** for Rostock is ☎0381

The Altstadt

If you're heading into town from the Hauptbahnhof, you pass fading villas on Rosa-Luxemburg-Strasse before entering the medieval sector via the **Steintor**, one of three surviving gates of the old fortifications. **Neuer Markt** is the city's main square, where the fifteenth-century Gothic **Rathaus**, which had a Baroque facade slapped on it in the eighteenth century, stands opposite slim, gabled Renaissance houses. The area between here and the Warnow was all but razed by wartime bombs, and almost everything you see now has been built during the last forty years. **Lange Strasse** was intended to be the showpiece of socialist rebuilding, but its only notable quality is its size: overwide, and lined by large red-brick buildings, it dwarfs the people and cars below.

The Marienkirche

Just northwest of Neuer Markt is the Altstadt's overwhelmingly dominant monument, the **Marienkirche** (Mon–Sat 10am–5pm, Sun 11.15am–noon; DM2), a late Gothic church built with the red bricks characteristic of north German architecture. It was intended to rival its counterpart in Lübeck, but the nave collapsed, leaving only two bays extant, and a long hall transept had to be added to stabilize the structure. The result is a building of strange yet striking proportions, both inside and out. From the **tower** there's a fine view over the city.

Among the furnishings, look out for the Baroque **organ** and the late thirteenth-century bronze **font**. But the prize feature of this church is the **astronomical clock**, the only one of its kind left in Europe. Originally made in 1472, it's been running continuously since 1643, when it was modernized in accordance with the latest state of scientific knowledge. Its upper clockface is divided into 24 hours, as well as rings showing monthly star signs and the work associated with each one. The lower, older face consists of thirteen concentric circles showing time and planetary movements.

West of Neuer Markt

Kröpeliner Strasse cuts through the pedestrianized heart of the city to the west of Neuer Markt. Look out for the **Spitalpfarrhaus** at no. 82, the finest brick gabled Gothic house remaining in the city; formerly belonging to the medieval hospital, it's now the public library. Beyond lies **Universitätsplatz**, where people loll around the Brunnen der Lebensfreude (Fountain of Happiness), playing music and drinking, surrounded by market stalls and open-air cafés. Around here are the main buildings of the University, founded in 1419, the first in northern Germany. Although nothing remains from this period – most of the structures are examples of the varied but heavy-handed Historicist tastes of last century – there's a fine **Barocksaal** on the east side of the square, which is regularly used as a concert hall. Across from it is the **Blücherdenkmal**, erected in 1819 immediately after the death of the city's most illustrious son, the Prussian Field Marshal Gebhard Leberecht von Blücher. Both the statue and the bas-reliefs were carved by the great Berlin Neoclassical sculptor Johann Gottfried Schadow; the latter depict Blücher's most important victories, among them Waterloo.

Just to the west of Universitätsplatz is the **Kloster zum Heiligen Kreuz**, a former Cistercian monastery which has been refurbished to house the **Kulturhistorisches Museum** (Tues–Sun 9am–5pm; DM4). Its ground-floor exhibits include eighteenth-century trunks and fourteenth- and fifteenth-century religious artefacts and retables. The rest of the museum has paintings from the coastal school of painters. On the first floor are works from both before and after World War II from the artists' colony in nearby Ahrenshoop (see p.716). The second floor covers the late nineteenth- and early twentieth-century period, during which Ahrenshoop was first "discovered".

The southern fortifications

At the end of Kröpeliner Strasse stands the **Kröpeliner Tor** (Wed–Sun 9am–5pm; DM4), the most impressive of the city's gateways. Its lower part dates back to the late thirteenth century, while the more elegant upper storey was added around 1400. Inside is the local history museum. From here, you walk southeastwards through the landscaped Wallangen, laid out alongside a well-preserved segment of the medieval walls. Between here and the previously mentioned Steintor is a rose garden, while immediately to the east of the latter is another surviving section of wall, including the **Kuhtor**, the oldest of the gates.

A couple of minutes' walk south of the Steintor, at August-Bebel-Str. 1, the **Schiffahrtsmuseum** (Tues–Sun 9am–5pm; DM4) is mainly concerned with the region's seafaring history. It contains collections of model boats and sailing craft from the days of the Hanseatic League to the battleships of Kaiser Wilhelm II.

East of Neuer Markt

The eastern sector of town is perched on a hill a little apart from the rest. The twisting cobbled streets of this old working-class neighbourhood display the names of many former trades like leather-dyeing, fishing and milking. Less honourable occupations get a look in too – Diebstrasse means "thief street". The **Petrikirche** on the Alter Markt is a wonderfully peaceful spot. Its tall spire, by which ships would navigate their way to harbour, was blown off during the war, and now only a stump remains. Nonetheless, you can go up to the platform (May–Sept Mon–Fri 9am–noon & 2–5pm, Sat & Sun 11am–5pm; DM2.50, DM3 by lift) for a fine view of the Warnow. The last important part of the fortifications stretches southwards from here almost as far as the Kuhtor.

The outskirts

WARNEMÜNDE, now Rostock's seaside suburb but still preserving the distinctive feel of a separate town, is best reached by S-Bahn. Unlike the rest of the city, it has profited enormously from the demise of the GDR, and has undergone a spectacular visual transformation, with many of its villas returned to their nineteenth-century splendour. On either side of the picturesque old harbour, **Alter Strom**, small fishermen's houses stand sideways to the sea to avoid biting winds, and along the seafront a boulevard stretches for about a kilometre, with cafés on one side and a white sandy beach on the other. It's not exactly St Tropez – the ugly *Hotel Neptun*, a five-star monstrosity built to obtain hard currency from westerners, disfigures the far end of the seafront – but it's still one of the country's favourite holiday spots. For a view over the harbour, climb up the hundred-year-old **Leuchtturm** (daily May–Sept 10am–7pm; DM3). If you'd like to see what the old fishermen's homes looked like inside, there's a doll's house of a **Heimatmuseum** at Theodor-Körner-Str. 31 (April–Sept Wed–Sun 10am–6pm; Oct–March Wed–Sun 9am–5pm; DM3).

Between Warnemünde and the centre of Rostock, the **Schiffbaumuseum** (Tues–Sun 9am–5pm; DM4) is on an old merchant navy ship, known as the *Friedensschiff*, moored about a kilometre east of S-Bahn stop Lütten-Klein. Walking around the ship's engine room is the best feature unless you're fascinated by the history of shipbuilding and the tools and parts of the trade.

Practicalities

The **Hauptbahnhof** is situated well to the south of the Altstadt, and connected to the town centre by trams #11 or #12. **Ferries** (including catamarans and jetfoils) dock at the **Überseehafen** on the right bank of the Warnow by the S-Bahn terminus Seehafen-Nord, and at the **Fährhafen** beside Warnemünde's Bahnhof. There are services to and from Wismar, Travemünde, Trelleborg in Sweden and Gedser or Bornholm in Denmark. Harbour **cruises** depart from Alter Strom in Warnemünde, or from the Stadthafen on the west side of the city centre.

The main **tourist office** is just north of Lange Strasse at Schnickmannstr. 13–14 (May–Sept Mon–Fri 10am–6pm, Sat & Sun 10am–2.30pm; Oct–April Mon–Fri 10am–5pm, Sat 10am–2.30pm; ☎19433 or 49799). There's another in Warnemünde at Heinrich-Heine-Str. 17 (June–Aug Mon–Fri 10am–5pm, Sat 10am–2pm; Sept–May Mon–Fri 10am–4pm; ☎51142). **Mitfahrzentrale** is at Am Kabutzenhof 21 (☎493 4438).

Accommodation

Accommodation in **private homes** (①–④) is plentiful in Warnemünde and the coastal villages between Rostock and Bad Doberan, but the tourist office does have some city-centre rooms on its books. There's a **youth hostel** in the same old ship as the Schiffbaumuseum; take the S-Bahn to Lütten-Klein (☎716202; ✿). Another is at Parkstr. 46 (☎548 1700; ✿) in Warnemünde.

Rostock is the one town in the province where **hotels** abound, but those in the centre are geared to business visitors and priced accordingly; Warnemünde is an altogether happier hunting ground for anyone on a budget.

HOTELS AND PENSIONS

Am Alten Strom, Am Strom 60, Warnemünde (☎52581, fax 52581). Large hotel with a picturesque location by the old harbour. ⑥

Am Bahnhof, Konrad-Adenauer-Platz 1 (☎36331; fax 493 4679). Medium-range hotel directly opposite the Hauptbahnhof. ⑥

An der Stadthalle, Platz der Freundschaft 3 (☎405200, fax 405 2062). Box-like hotel to the rear of the Hauptbahnhof. ⑥

Bellevue, Seestr. 8, Warnemünde (☎54333, fax 543 3444). Good old-fashioned seaside hotel with balconies directly facing the beach. ⑦

Mecklenburger Hof, August-Bebel-Str. 111 (☎492 2301, fax 492 2303). City-centre hotel run in tandem with a fish restaurant, *Gastmahl des Meeres*. ⑥

Neptun, Seestr. 19, Warnemünde (☎7770, fax 54023). This hotel enjoys a certain notoriety, both because of its GDR origins and its over-prominent position. Now run by the *Arkona* chain, it nonetheless retains its status as one of the most luxurious addresses on the entire Baltic coast. ⑨

Nordland, Steinstr. 7 (☎492 3706, fax 492 2285). Another good central choice; has a reasonably priced restaurant. ⑦

Ramada, Schwaansche Str. 6 (☎49700, fax 497 0700). Although part of the eponymous chain, this is the grandest and most characterful of the city centre hotels. It has a relatively quiet Altstadt setting and one of Rostock's best restaurants. ⑧

Zum Alten Strom, Alexandrinenstr. 128, Warnemünde (☎51616, fax 51617). One of a number of moderately priced pensions in the heart of Warnemünde. ④

Zur Brücke, Alexandrinenstr. 35, Warnemünde (☎52448, fax 52448). Another budget option on the same street as the above. ④

Eating and drinking

As you'd expect, Rostock's main strength in the food and drink field lies in the many fish restaurants, though there are plenty of other recommendable establishments as well.

Am Windspiel, Schnickmannstr. 7. Hip hangout which puts on regular art exhibitions.

Fischerklause, Am Strom 123, Warnemünde. Speciality fish restaurant located right by the harbour where the catch is landed.

Gartenlaube, Anastasiastr. 24, Warnemünde. One of the city's best and most inventive restaurants.

Il Ristorante, Am Strom 107, Warnemünde. Excellent but pricey Italian restaurant overlooking the harbour. Evenings only.

Lord Nelson, Am Kabutzenhof. Rostock's best fish restaurant is located on the fifth floor of the Portcenter, a large harbour building a short distance west of the Altstadt.

Ratskeller, Neuer Markt 1. Typically reliable choice for *gutbürgerliche Küche*.

Studentenkeller, Universitätsplatz. The best-known student rendezvous, functioning as a café in the daytime and a bar with live music and discos in the evening.

Zur Kogge, Wokrenterstr. 27. Historic seamen's tavern that's cosy in an obvious, tourist-catering sort of way.

Culture and festivals

Rostock's main **cultural** venue is the *Volkstheater*, Doberaner Str. 134/5 (☎2440), which puts on a varied programme of drama, opera and ballet, plus orchestral concerts by the *Norddeutsche Philharmonie*. Local **festivals** tend to be dominated by the nautical theme: these include the *Warnemünder Woche* in early July and the *Hanse Sail* in early August.

Fischland, Darss and Zingst

Seen on a map, the peninsula of **Fischland**, **Darss** and **Zingst** looks like a crooked finger hooking itself around the mainland coast midway between Rostock and Stralsund. Bounded to the north by the Baltic and to the south by a series of shallow bays or *Bodden*, this isolated area makes a good destination either as a day-trip or overnight stop. Like the whole Baltic coast, the peninsula gets crowded, but isn't invaded in summer in the same way that the holiday islands of Rügen and Usedom are – probably because the beaches are less sandy, the scenery a little more rugged and communications sparser.

Fischland

The isthmus of **Fischland** is the most rewarding part of this area. From Rostock travel by rail to Ribnitz-Damgarten, from where buses cover the whole area. First stop is **WUSTROW**, a sleepy little settlement overlooking the **Saaler Bodden**. Just past the village entrance it's worth climbing the tower of the **Dorfkirche**, built on the remnants of Slavonic defences, which offers expansive views of the whole island (if the doors are locked the key is available from the parish house in the first street on the right after the church itself). Otherwise simply wander the streets taking in the reed-roofed houses, an architectural characteristic of the area. There's a small **tourist office** at Sandstr. 10 (☎038220/251), and from the village's small harbour behind the church a cruise-boat plies the *Bodden* chain.

Ahrenshoop

North from Wustrow the windswept cliffs of the **Hohes Ufer** lead to the quiet resort of **AHRENSHOOP**, which developed into an artists' colony at the turn of the century. Eventually artistic overpopulation and the realization that the area only offered a limited number of themes led to the painters decamping in search of new inspiration. However, the tradition has revived, and exhibitions can be seen in the village's four commercial **galleries**: *Kunstkaten*, Strandweg 1, *Bunte Stube*, Dorfstr. 24, *Dünenhaus*, Am Schifferberg, and *Kunsthaus Guttenberg*, Feldweg 3. The local beach, just 100m north of Dorfstrasse, is narrow and a little stony, protected from the Baltic waves by a series of groynes.

Ahrenshoop's **tourist office** is in the small *Kurverwaltung* building, Kirchnersgang 3 (Mon, Wed & Fri 9am–4pm; Tues & Thurs 9am–noon, Sat & Sun in summer 9am–3pm; ☎038220/234). *Charlottenhof*, Grenzweg 3 (☎038220/302; ②) is a good budget **pension**; among the **hotels** are *Möwe*, Schifferberg 16–17 (☎038220/6080; ⑤); *Café Namenlos*, Schifferberg 2 (☎038220/6060; ⑤); and *Haus am Meer*, Dorfstr. 37

(☎038220/80816; ⑥). Apart from the hotels, the best place for **eating and drinking** is the *Café Buhne*, Grenzweg 12, an arty place overlooking the sea at the head of the Hohes Ufer – the food, which includes fish specialities, is excellent. **Bike rental** is available from *Reiner Gielow*, Dorfstr. 21.

Darss

Darss, which marks the traditional transition from Mecklenburg to Pomerania, is a heavily forested area, jutting out into the sea north of Fischland. Much of it lies within the **Nationalpark Vorpommersche Boddenlandschaft**, which stretches via Darss to the west coast of Rügen. From Ahrenshoop the main road snakes around the edge of the Darss forest, passing through the traditional fishing villages of Born and Wieck.

Prerow

About 3km northeast of Wieck is the resort of **PREROW**, a little place protected from the Baltic by a line of sand dunes. Prerow doesn't really have a centre, it just straggles along two streets, Strandstrasse and Waldstrasse, which lead off Wiecker Weg, the main road into town. The **beach** is about 300m north of Waldstrasse along Im Schuning, its "entrance" marked by a cluster of cafés and kiosks.

Other attractions are the **Darss-Museum**, Waldstr. 48 (daily May–Sept 9am–5pm; Oct 9am–4pm; DM2), devoted to the history of Darss and the seafaring past of its people, and the eighteenth-century **Seemannskirche** (Seamen's Church) on the Zingst road heading west out of town. This simple church has a surprisingly elaborate Baroque altar, and its graveyard is littered with simple monuments that form a sociological history in stone. As with other villages on the peninsula, wandering the side streets can be rewarding with lots of unusual architectural features (colourfully painted doors, carved window frames and ornate weathercocks) adorning the reedbedecked wooden houses. From Prerow there are a number of walking possibilities: a woodland path marked by posts with horizontal red lines leads from Bernsteinerweg (opposite Küsters Allee) on the northwest corner of town through the woods to **Darsser Ort** headland with its isolated lighthouse, while another path traverses the sand dunes west of town in the direction of Zingst.

Prerow's **tourist office** is at Gemeindeplatz 1 (Mon–Fri 10am–6pm; ☎038233/551 or 6100). If you want to stay, there are a few **pensions**, including *Voss*, Villenstr. 6 (☎038233/370; ②); and *Haus Wiesenau*, Grüne Str. 37 (☎038233/787; ④). The leading **hotel** is *Waldschlösschen*, Bernsteinweg 4 (☎038233/6170; ⑦), which is also the best place for a meal. You can rent **bikes** at Bebelstr. 37.

Zingst

The village of **ZINGST**, just over 5km east of Prerow, is notable mainly for its **beach**, which stretches for 10km, with fine yellow sand, backed by high dunes. Otherwise, the only set-piece attraction is the **Heimatmuseum** (mid-May to Sept Tues–Sat 9am–noon & 1–4pm; rest of year same hours Tues, Fri & Sat only; DM2), in a sea captain's house at Strandstr. 19. The wooded eastern end of Zingst is home to numerous rare plants and birds, and at the end of the road there's a small exhibition house hidden away in the woods behind the car park.

Zingst's **tourist office** at Klosterstr. 21 (☎038232/231) has information on the whole region and can arrange **accommodation**. **Hotels** include *Boddenhus*, Hafenstr. 9 (☎038232/713; ⑥) and *Am Strand*, Birkenstr. 21 (☎038232/600; ⑦), both of which have restaurants. There's also a **youth hostel**, Glebe 14 (☎038232/465; ❶).

Stralsund

Pomerania's westernmost city is **STRALSUND**, which lies 70km along the coast from Rostock. It's far more provincial than its neighbour, but is also far more attractive, and is undoubtedly one of the best places to stay along the coast, particularly as it's possible to make day-trips to the holiday island of Rügen (see p.726), to which it's linked by a causeway carrying both road and rail traffic. First impressions of the city don't flatter, as it's ringed by horrid concrete suburbs, but the Altstadt, despite four decades of neglect under the GDR, is wonderfully evocative of its Hanseatic past, preserving a wealth of outstanding buildings. Life in Stralsund has always been tied closely to the fisheries trade: the German Baltic's main fishing fleet is based here, and the local shipyard specializes in building trawlers and the enormous fish-processing ships that work the North and South Atlantic. These activities help to ensure that the town is in no danger of mothballing into a museum piece.

The Altstadt

The Altstadt stands on what is almost an island, with the sea and two natural ponds – the **Frankenteich** and the **Kneiper Teich** – forming a kind of moat. The skyline, framed by the towers of the great brick Gothic churches, is best seen from the southern shore of the willow-lined Frankenteich. As Stralsund was one of only a handful of places the GDR authorities placed under a total protection order, there remains a wonderful legacy of Gothic architecture from the Hansa days, and Baroque from the two centuries of Swedish rule.

The Marienkirche

Crossing the isthmus via Tribseer Damm, Tribseer Strasse leads to Neuer Markt, one of the two town squares. Here stands Stralsund's largest church, the late fourteenth-century **Marienkirche**, the main local rallying point for opposition groups during the *Wende*. It's a good idea to start your tour by ascending the original medieval wooden staircase of its single **tower** (Mon–Sat 10am–4/5pm, Sun 11.30am–4/5pm; DM2), part of a massive westwork which has undergone repeated alterations down the centuries. From the top, there's a marvellous view of the medieval townscape, as well as of Rügen a couple of hundred metres across the straits.

The scrubbed interior of the church is notable for its vertiginous elevation; the most spectacular vaults are in the narthex, which are fashioned into a dazzling variety of star shapes. Of the many Baroque adornments, pride of place goes to the **organ**, one of the most celebrated in the country, which was made by the Lübeck master, Friedrich Stellwagen, in the 1650s. During the summer months, it can normally be heard at 11am each day, except on Thursdays, when there's a full-scale recital at 8pm on alternate weeks.

The central streets

On Mönchstrasse just north of Neuer Markt, the **Katharinenkloster**, the former Dominican monastery, has been converted to contain the city's two main museums. The church itself contains what has long been the most popular sightseeing attraction in the whole of the former GDR, the **Deutsches Museum für Meereskunde und Fischerei** (May, June, Sept & Oct daily 10am–5pm; July & Aug Mon–Thurs 9am–6pm,

The **telephone code** for Stralsund is ☎03831

Fri–Sun 10am–5pm; Nov–April Tues–Sun 10am–5pm; DM7). Much loved by kids, but also a serious scientific institute, it focuses on all aspects of life under the sea. On the ground floor is an aquarium full of all kinds of tropical fish, while the upper floors focus on evolution and on the fishing trade. The most spectacular exhibit is the skeleton of a finback whale washed up on Rügen in 1825.

Next door, occupying the conventual buildings, is the **Kulturhistorisches Museum** (Tues–Sun 10am–5pm; DM4). Its medieval artefacts are beautifully displayed in a series of elegant Gothic halls, but unfortunately only facsimiles are on view of the glittering hoard of tenth-century treasure dug up on the nearby island of Hiddensee. Another highlight is the wonderful collection of eighteenth- and nineteenth-century dolls' houses and other children's toys. On Böttcherstrasse immediately to the south, the museum has opened an extension in a splendidly grand old warehouse or **Speicher** (same hours and ticket); this is devoted to the folklore, costumes and lifestyle of the rural communities of the Baltic coast.

At the end of the same street is the **Jacobikirche**, the youngest of the three brick Gothic parish churches; it's under restoration and isn't open for visits. From here, follow Jacobiturmstrasse north to **Badenstrasse**, Stralsund's finest street, lined with mansions ranging in style from Gothic to Neoclassical.

The Alter Markt and the Nikolaikirche

Towards the northern end of the Altstadt is the **Alter Markt**, the original main square, one clearly modelled on its Lübeck counterpart. The focal point is the **Rathaus**, whose showpiece late fourteenth-century facade, crafted from delicately glazed bricks and bristling with fantastical gables, ranks as one of the greatest masterpieces of Gothic civil architecture. Very different in style is the Baroque southern portal on Ossenreyerstrasse, which bears the royal coat of arms of Sweden. Another important legacy of Stralsund's era as a Swedish town is the **Commandanten-Hus** at no. 14 on Alter Markt, the mansion of the local governor. It stands in stark contrast to the city's finest Gothic house, the **Wulflamhaus** at no. 5, named after the mayor who commissioned it as his residence.

Behind the Rathaus is the **Nikolaikirche**, which was built virtually in tandem with it. In design, above all in its twin towers (one of which is now capped by a Baroque helmet and spire), it's clearly modelled on the Marienkirche in Lübeck, which pioneered the Hanseatic format of pairing the main civic church with the town hall. Inside are a number of outstanding furnishings, including two **high altars** – the one in the choir itself is a carved Passion retable made around 1500, while that in front of the screen is a frilly Baroque creation designed by the great Berlin sculptor, Andreas Schlüter. The **astronomical clock** in the ambulatory is dated 1394 and is thus one of the oldest in Europe. However, the most intriguing adornment is the **Novgorod stall** in the southern aisle, named after the Russian city which was the easternmost outpost of the Hanseatic League. Its reliefs depict Russians hunting for animal skins, and taking honey and wax from bees, products which they then sell to a German merchant.

The rest of the Altstadt

To the north and west of the Alter Markt are **Fährstrasse**, **Schillstrasse** and **Mühlenstrasse**, which together contain many of Stralsund's finest medieval town houses. Mühlenstr. 3 is particularly worth seeking out: as it's now an exhibition hall, you can go inside and see the interior of this typical Hanseatic trader's residence. There are no partitioning walls, only three open-plan levels, which were used as combined living and storage quarters. At the southern end of the same street is the **Kütertor**, one of two surviving city gates. From here, it's worth following the course of the old fortifications, passing along the shore of the Kneiper Teich, then continuing via the **Kneiper Tor** to the **Johanniskloster** (mid-May to mid-Oct Tues–Sun 10am–6pm;

DM3). Although this former Franciscan monastery was badly damaged in the war, some parts still survive, including the remarkable **Räucherboden** (Smokehouse) and the Baroque **Bibliothek** (Library). The ruined church serves as an occasional open-air theatre.

Practicalities

From the **Hauptbahnhof**, the Tribseer Damm traverses the isthmus leading directly into the Altstadt. There are regular **ferry** services across to Altefähr on Rügen, and three a day in summer to Hiddensee; these are all run by *Weisse Flotte*, Fährstr. 16 (☎268116). The same company runs harbour cruises (DM8) twice daily from May to September.

Stralsund's **tourist office** is opposite the Rathaus at Ossenreyerstr. 1–2 (May 1 to Oct 15 Mon–Fri 9am–7pm, Sat & Sun 9am–2pm; Oct 16 to April 30 Mon–Fri 10am–6pm, Sat 10am–2pm; ☎24690). It's well worth investing in the *Touristenpass* (DM19 in summer, DM15 in winter), which gives entry to all the museums plus a variety of other attractions.

Accommodation

Plenty of **private rooms** (②–③) are available at the tourist office (☎246969 for advance reservations), but these tend to be booked out well in advance in mid-summer. There are two **youth hostels** – one has an ideal position in a half-timbered building with a courtyard at Am Kütertor 1 (☎292160; 🏠), the other is 8km from the Altstadt in the seaside suburb of Devin at Strandstr. 21 (☎270358; 🏠); take bus #3. The middle and upper levels of the **hotel** market are well served, but there are only a few small **pensions** to cater for the budget end.

HOTELS AND PENSIONS

Haus am Rügendamm, Reiferbahn 29 (☎295051, fax 295053). Large and somewhat institutional concrete box aimed mainly at tour groups, though its individual rates are among the least expensive in the city. ⑤

Herwig's, Heilgeiststr. 50 (☎293954 or 26680, fax 266823). Medium-range hotel with an atmospheric cellar restaurant. ⑥

Im Grünen, Rostocker Chaussee 28a (☎494868, fax 494868). Capacious pension offering some of the cheapest rooms in town. The drawback is its suburban location, 3km southwest of the centre. ③

Klabautermann, Am Querkanal 2 (☎293628, fax 280612). Small hotel directly overlooking the harbour. ⑤

Norddeutscher Hof, Neuer Markt 22 (☎293161, fax 293161). Pleasant hotel in the very heart of the Altstadt. ⑥

Regenbogen, Richtenberger Chaussee 2a (☎497674, fax 494846). This pension is one of the rare budget options. It's situated in the Tribseer Vorstadt, a 10min walk west of the Hauptbahnhof. ③

Royal Am Bahnhof, Tribseer Damm 4 (☎295268, fax 292650). Palatial station hotel with a very reasonably priced restaurant, *Esprit*. ⑦

Stralsund, Heinrich-Heine-Ring 105 (☎3670 or 390330, fax 367111). Located in the Kneiper Vorstadt, 2km north of the centre. Its restaurant, *Herwig's*, is among the best in Stralsund. ⑤

Eating and drinking

Many of the fine old buildings in Stralsund's Altstadt have been taken over for gastronomic purposes. Some of the best restaurants are in the hotels listed above.

Café Lütt, Alter Markt 12. Good traditional coffee house.

Galerie Café Art, Badenstr. 44. Artists' café, serving light meals and staging regular exhibitions. Closed Sun.

Nur Fisch, Heilgeiststr. 92. Inexpensive fish specialist (Mon–Wed & Fri 10am–6pm, Thurs 10am–7pm, Sat 11am–2pm).

Scheelehaus, Fährstr. 23. One of Stralsund's best restaurants, this occupies a lovely gabled Gothic mansion and has a grand hall-like dining room.

Speicher-Café, Katharinenberg 34. Popular youthful hangout in a converted warehouse. Often has live music or discos in the evening.

Torschliesserhaus, Am Kütertor 1. Trendy bar next door to the youth hostel which does bistro-type food.

Wulfcronas Bier- und Weinstube, Heilgeiststr. 30. Period-piece bar which still looks much as it did when it was founded in the heady days of the Weimar Republic. Closed Sun.

Zur Kogge, Tribseer Str. 26. Has a traditional *Gaststätte* on the ground floor and a bar-disco in the basement.

Culture and festivals

The main **cultural** venue is the *Theater Stralsund* on Olaf-Palme-Platz (☎295491). Stralsund has been quick to launch or reinstate a number of **festivals** since the demise of the GDR. These include the *Stralsunder Segelwoche* in July, a regatta round Rügen and Hiddensee; and the *Wallensteintage* for several days around July 24, a commemoration of the city's successful defence during the Thirty Years' War against the siege mounted by the Imperial forces of Alfred von Wallenstein.

Greifswald

GREIFSWALD, the final member of the province's quartet of old Hanseatic trading cities, lies 30km south of Stralsund on the fast rail line to Berlin. Founded in the thirteenth century by the Cistercian monks of Kloster Eldena, which now lies within the boundaries of the modern municipality, it became the seat of a university in 1456, and retains a distinct academic atmosphere to this day.

The Altstadt

In contrast to its Hanseatic neighbours, the Altstadt of Greifswald lies 3km inland from the Baltic. Both in terms of individual monuments and overall appearance, it seems rather small-scale in comparison with the others. Substantial parts of the **Stadtbefestigung** which ringed the original town survive intact, and the area around them has been transformed into a shady promenade.

Greifswald's skyline was immortalized in a number of paintings by the town's favourite son, the Romantic artist Caspar David Friedrich. The dominant building, then as now, is the **Dom**, a typical example of Gothic brickwork, which lies close to the middle of the Altstadt. Its most remarkable feature is the mighty **tower** (May–Sept Mon–Fri 10am–4pm, Sat 10am–2pm, Sun 11am–noon; DM2), whose four turrets, octagonal upper storeys and onion-domed Baroque spire combine to produce a memorable silhouette. A medieval wooden staircase leads to the **viewing platform**, which commands a fine panorama over the Altstadt to the Baltic. The Dom's interior was given a romanticized neo-Gothic remodelling last century, with most of the walls covered with a coat of whitewash. However, a precious series of **frescoes**, painted around 1400 in the manner of manuscript illuminations, still adorn some of the south side chapels.

Diagonally opposite the west front of the Dom are the buildings of the **Ernst-Moritz-Arendt-Universität**. Most of these are in the bloated Historicist styles of the nineteenth century, but the main block is a fine example of the dignified Baroque so characteristic of northern Germany. Its **Aula** is a fittingly splendid graduation hall, but unfortunately neither this nor other parts of the complex – such as the graffiti-covered student prison, which is reminiscent of its renowned counterpart in Heidelberg – are as yet regular tourist sights, so it's pot luck whether you find anything open.

A couple of minutes' walk to the east of the Dom is the **Markt**, a bustling square lined with a variety of well-restored buildings. Principal among these is the **Rathaus**, originally Gothic, but nowadays with a rather composite appearance as the result of various alterations.

On Brüggstrasse just to the north, the **Marienkirche** is the town's oldest surviving church, unmissable with its distinctive square tower. It lacks a chancel, a fact which gives it striking dimensions, both inside and out. Look out for the humorous frescoes in the entrance hall, and for the Renaissance pulpit with its portraits of the Reformers Luther, Melanchthon and Bugenhagen. Finally, the **Museum der Stadt** (July & Aug Mon & Tues 1–6pm, Wed–Sun 10am–6pm; rest of year Wed–Sun 10am–6pm; DM3), occupying the former Franciscan monastery just off the southeastern corner of the Markt on Theodor-Pyl-Strasse, is devoted to the history of the town and its university. High point is the section on Caspar David Friedrich, which includes a couple of original oil paintings plus drawings.

Wieck and Eldena

Greifswald's most famous sights are not in the centre, but in two incorporated villages by the River Ryck (which also forms the northern boundary of the Altstadt), just before it disgorges itself into the Baltic. They can be reached by bus #40 from the Hauptbahnhof or from Wolgaster Strasse immediately beyond the eastern boundary of the Altstadt.

WIECK is a fishing village of the active rather than tourist variety, as the smell of herring wafting from the harbour testifies. Here the river is traversed by the photogenic **Hubbrücke**, a Dutch-style wooden drawbridge recently restored to pristine condition in celebration of its centenary. On the northern side of the river, take a stroll along Dorfstrasse, where there are a number of old fishermen's cottages.

A few minutes' walk south of Wieck is **ELDENA**, whose ruined **Kloster**, directly facing Wolgaster Strasse, was home to a wealthy Cistercian congregation which exercised an enormous influence on the surrounding area. It was a favourite subject of Caspar David Friedrich, and thus became at least the indirect inspiration for the vogue depictions of lonely, overgrown and crumbling monasteries in secluded settings produced by so many painters of the Romantic movement. Founded in the twelfth century by Danish monks, the Kloster was destroyed by Swedish soldiers, who carted off most of its bricks as building material. Only skeletal remains survive, but the arched doorways and empty windows of the ruin are undeniably romantic, and, more prosaically, make a good spot for a picnic.

Practicalities

Greifswald's **Hauptbahnhof** lies immediately below the southwestern corner of the Stadtbefestigung, only a few minutes' walk from the Dom. A block east of the Markt, at Schuhhagen 22, is the **tourist office** (May–Sept Mon–Fri 10am–6pm, Sat 9am–noon; Oct–April Mon–Fri 9am–5pm; ☎03834/3460).

There are a fair number of **private rooms** (①–③) available. In Wieck there's also an inexpensive **pension**, *Schipp in*, Am Hafen 3 (☎03834/840026; ③), plus several **hotels**, including *Maria*, Dorfstr. 45 (☎03834/841426; ⑤); *Zur Fähre*, Fährweg 2 (☎03834/840049; ⑥); and *Ryckhotel*, Rosenstr. 17b (☎03834/83300; ⑥). Among the options in the town centre are *Möller*, Hans-Fallada-Str. 4 (☎03834/502229; ⑤); *Am Dom*, Lange Str. 44 (☎03834/79750; ⑤); and *Kronprinz*, Lange Str. 22 (☎03834/7900; ⑦).

All the hotels listed above have **restaurants**. *Alter Speicher*, Rossmühlenstr. 25, is another good choice for dining, while *Zur Hütte*, Am Markt 12, does everything from

Kaffee und Kuchen to light meals, and *Zum Alten Fritz*, Am Markt 13, is a new *Hausbrauerei* with beer garden.

Wolgast

The relaxed little harbour town of **WOLGAST** lies 24km southeast of Greifswald on the southern shore of the Peene Strom, the narrow sound separating the German mainland and the holiday island of Usedom. Best viewed as a stopover of a few hours en route to Usedom, Wolgast was for centuries a residence of the dukes of Lower Pomerania, developing into an important trade centre during the eighteenth and nineteenth centuries. Much of its old fabric survives in the network of narrow streets that slope down to the harbour from the central square, and the town remains important as a port with a large working shipyard.

The town

On the main square, **Rathausplatz**, is the pretty little **Rathaus**, with a fluid Baroque facade which looks almost like an upturned boat. A fountain in front is decorated with scenes depicting the town's history. Also on the square is Wolgast's oldest secular building, the half-timbered **Kaffeemühle** ("Coffee Grinder") – so called because of its distinctive shape. It now houses the **Stadt- und Kreismuseum** (June–Aug Tues–Fri 10am–6pm, Sat & Sun 10am–2pm; Sept–May Tues–Fri 10am–5pm, Sat 10am–2pm; DM5), a local history museum which also includes a small section on the development of the V2 at nearby Peenemünde (see p.724), plus changing exhibitions by local artists.

Wolgast's main sight is the nearby **Petrikirche**, a huge, angular Gothic structure whose tall **tower** (mid-May to mid-Sept Mon–Sat 10.30am–noon & 1.30–3pm, Sun 1.30–3pm; DM3) dominates the town's skyline. It was the court church of the Dukes of Lower Pomerania and is the last resting place of nine of them. The most notable interior decorative feature is the action-packed *Totentanz* (Dance of Death) frieze, depicting Death in various guises from soldier to well-dressed noblewoman.

On Kronwiekstrasse overlooking the harbour is the **Philipp-Otto-Runge-Haus** (June–Aug Tues–Fri 10am–6pm, Sat & Sun 10am–2pm; Sept–May Tues–Fri 10am–5pm, Sat 10am–2pm; DM6), the recently restored birthplace of the eponymous artist, an important figure in the early Romantic school and contemporary of Caspar David Friedrich. A large number of his graphic works are on view. To the north of the harbour is a bridge leading across to **Schlossinsel**, a small island between the mainland and Usedom which was once the site of Wolgast's castle. From here, the Brücke der Freundschaft spans the sound across to Usedom.

Practicalities

Wolgast's **Hauptbahnhof** is at the southwestern edge of town, but it's better to alight at **Wolgast-Hafen**, the harbour stop (not all trains travel direct to Wolgast, some require a change at Züssow). If you're travelling on to Usedom, note that trains do not run between Wolgast-Hafen and **Wolgast-Fähre** on the island itself, though it only takes five minutes to walk between the two. The **tourist office** (June–Aug Mon–Fri 9am–6pm, Sat 10am–2pm; Sept–May Mon–Fri 9am–5pm; ☎03836/600118 or 251215) in the Kaffeemühle at Rathausplatz 6 can book **private rooms** (①–③) in the town or in Usedom.

Otherwise, there are a few **pensions**, including *Peene-Ufer*, Badstubenstr. 24 (☎03836/206698; ⑤) and *Kirchstein*, Schützenstr. 25 (☎03836/27220; ⑤), plus one **hotel**, *Zur Insel*, Str. der Freundschaft 54 (☎03836/261077; ⑤).

For **eating** and **drinking**, the *Ratskeller* in the Rathaus is excellent, and, most unusually, offers Italian as well as German cuisine. Best choice for *Kaffee und Kuchen* is *Café Biedenweg*, Lange Str. 15.

Usedom

Directly north of Wolgast, **Usedom** is Germany's second largest island. It has some fine beaches but is very much in the shadow of Rügen as a Baltic holiday destination, lacking the latter's variety of landscape. Fifty kilometres in length and at times only a kilometre wide, the island has a random shape, like the pattern of spilled water, and is separated from the mainland by the Peene Strom, which, though little more than a narrow channel for most of its length, expands suddenly and takes a big bite out of the southern shore as the **Achter Wasser** bay. At its eastern end Usedom is abruptly cut off by the border with Poland, leaving a tiny sliver of its area, including the port of Świnoujście (formerly German Swinemünde), in Polish hands.

Before the war Usedom was the haunt of Europe's rich and its resorts ranked among Germany's most fashionable. In the GDR period, it catered primarily to working-class holidaymakers, but since the *Wende* it has gradually moved upmarket again, with many of the grand old Wilhelmine hotels having undergone expensive refurbishments. Much fine Baltic shorefront architecture, and some of the ambience that drew the prewar glitterati, can be experienced in the trio of resorts – **Bansin**, **Heringsdorf** and **Ahlbeck** – which are collectively styled the *Kaiserbäder*. The finest stretch of beach is at **Koserow**, while the most significant historical site is the Nazi rocket research station at **Peenemünde**, where Werner von Braun developed the V2. As everywhere on the Baltic coast, there's little chance of being able to find a room in July or August without booking in advance. Public transport is good: a railway runs along the entire length of the island, with a link to Wolgast, and there are also buses serving the main destinations. Usedom is fairly flat and so well suited to cycling, although the volume of car traffic in summer is heavy.

Zinnowitz and Koserow

Leaving all this and heading southeast leads you to a string of seaside towns. First up after rejoining the main road, and connected by bus and train to Wolgast and Peenemünde, is **ZINNOWITZ**, Usedom's largest resort, which has a 2km-long beach and a wide promenade. Many of its grandiose-looking **hotels** were converted into factory and trade union holiday centres during the GDR period, but those currently open to the general public include *Kastanienhof*, Ahlbecker Str. 14 (☎038377/40904; ④); *Dünenschloss*, Neue Sandstr. 27 (☎038377/40811; ⑤) and *Parkhotel Am Glienberg*, Glienbergweg 10 (☎038377/720; ⑦). Private rooms (①–③) can be booked at the **tourist office** (Mon–Fri 9am–noon & 2–5pm, Sat 2–5pm; ☎038377/42220) at Möwenstr. 1. There's a **campsite**, *Pommernland* (☎038377/40348), just off the main road on the northern edge of town.

Koserow

Continuing by bus or train, **KOSEROW** lies a few kilometres to the east. At first sight this village of modern houses straggling along the road seems to have little to offer. However, beyond the pine-covered slope rising above it is a wonderful stretch of sandy beach backed by low cliffs. If you're contemplating spending any time on Usedom, Koserow makes an excellent base; there's virtually nothing to see here, but the beach (nudist for substantial stretches) has a delightfully secluded feel, and the volume of visitors, though heavy, is not unbearable.

The **tourist office** is at Hauptstr. 34 (May–Sept Mon–Fri 9am–noon & 2–6pm, Sat & Sun 9am–noon; reduced hours the rest of the year; ☎038375/20231), and you can book **private rooms** here (①–②). Other options include a **pension**, *Herkules*, Karlstr. 9 (☎038375/20143; ⑤) and a **hotel**, *Hanse-Kogge*, Hauptstr. 22 (☎038375/2600; ⑥). There's also a handy **campsite** at Hauptstr. 15 (☎038375/359).

For **eating and drinking** try *Kelchs*, Karlstr. 9, which does decent fish dishes. At the other end of town, at the foot of the sixty-metre Streckelberg (Usedom's highest elevation), is *Zum Streckelberg*, good for a post-beach ice cream or beer. Koserow's **bike rental** facilities are at *Fahrrad Ortmann*, Meinholdstr. 34, en route to the Streckelberg.

Bansin, Heringsdorf and Ahlbeck

Fifteen kilometres down the main road from Koserow, the resorts of Bansin, Heringsdorf and Ahlbeck (all served by bus and rail line) merge into one another in rapid succession, though despite the blurring of the boundaries between them each town retains its separate identity.

Bansin

BANSIN is very much a family holiday destination with an excellent, but inevitably crowded, sandy beach. There's otherwise not much to detain you, though Seestrasse, the town's main drag, running from station to beach, is lined by impressive turn-of-the-century houses in brilliant white with wrought-iron balconies. The street terminates at a small square with a clock which marks the main entrance to the beach.

The **tourist office** (May–Sept Mon–Fri 9am–noon & 1–6pm, Sat & Sun 9am–noon; Oct–April Mon–Thurs 9am–noon & 1–4pm, Fri 9am–noon; ☎038378/29433), where you can book **private rooms** (①–③), is at Waldstr. 5c. There are plenty of **hotels** in all price ranges including *Villa Ingeborg*, Bergstr. 25–26 (☎038378/29247; ④); *Zur Post*, Seestr. 5 (☎038378/560; ⑦); and *Strandhotel Atlantic*, Strandpromenade 18 (☎038378/605; ⑧). The **restaurants** of the hotels are the best places for full meals.

Heringsdorf

Best of the resort triumvirate is **HERINGSDORF**, which retains something of its pre-war atmosphere to complement its near-impeccable looks. Described by Baedeker as "the most fashionable of the Baltic sea-bathing places", Heringsdorf is the oldest resort on Usedom and at one time enjoyed international fame, attracting aristocratic and wealthy holidaymakers from all over Europe, despite its rather unprepossessing name – "Herring Village" – a leftover from its origins as a small fishing port.

The centre of Heringsdorf is **Platz des Friedens**, reached by following Friedenstrasse from the Bahnhof. The town's architecture is mostly in the familiar Baltic-resort style of abundant white facades and attractive balconies, though Platz des Friedens is disfigured by an enormous residential/shopping complex.

The new **Seebrücke** is the longest in Germany, its imposing dimensions being a direct tribute to its celebrated predecessor, which was demolished by the Communists. Heading west, the **Strandpromenade**, decked out with well-regimented flowerbeds, leads past the **Kunstpavillon**, an odd structure looking like a futurist bandstand enclosed by glass, that plays host to temporary art exhibitions.

At the western end of Strandpromenade, a sharp left into Strandstrasse, followed by a right turn, leads you into Maxim-Gorki-Strasse. Here, at no. 13, is the **Maxim-Gorki-Gedenkstätte** (daily 9am–noon & 1–4pm; DM2), a small museum devoted to Maxim Gorky and the time he spent in Heringsdorf in 1922. It's housed in the former *Pension Irmgard*, where the author stayed, a period in which he wrote the autobiographical volume *My Universities*. Returning to Platz des Friedens via Badstrasse and Kulmstrasse offers a chance to appreciate Heringsdorf at its best; quiet leafy streets straggle up a hill, flanked by small villas with flaking facades set in little gardens.

The **tourist office** (July & Aug Mon–Fri 9am–6pm, Sat & Sun 9am–1pm; reduced hours out of season; ☎038378/2451) is on the Seebrücke. There are plenty of **private rooms** (①–③), though there will be almost no chance of finding one during high season. Inexpensive **pensions** include *Sommerheim*, Grenzstr. 2 (☎038378/32215; ②) and *Diekelmann*, Schulstr. 5 (☎038378/22744; ④). Most **hotels** are of high quality and consequently expensive; among the most attractive are *Wald und See*, Rudolf-Breitscheid-Str. 8 (☎038378/31416; ⑥); *Stadt Berlin*, Bülowstr. 15 (☎038378/22304; ⑦); *Weisses Schloss*, Rudolf-Breitscheid-Str. 3 (☎038378/31984; ⑦); and *Oasis*, Puschkinstr. 10 (☎038378/2650; ⑦).

All these hotels have **restaurants**; other possibilities for **eating and drinking** are *Zur Klause*, Strandstr. 6, which does a reasonable selection of inexpensive dishes, or the *Terrassencafé*, Kulmstr. 29, with a good view of the sea.

Ahlbeck

AHLBECK is another good-looking town with some ornate villas and grand hotels, and there's a pleasant promenade and sandy beach. Its **Seebrücke**, which is graced with four corner towers, is by far the most picturesque on the island.

The **tourist office** (July & Aug Mon–Thurs 9am–6pm, Fri 9am–8pm, Sat & Sun 10am–4pm; reduced hours out of season; ☎038378/24415) is at Dünenstr. 45. There's the usual supply of **private rooms** (①–③) and plenty of **hotels** in all categories including *Ostseestrand*, Neue Str. 4 (☎038378/28381; ③); *Ostseehotel*, Dünenstr. 41 (☎038378/600; ⑥); *Villa Augusta Viktoria*, Bismarckstr. 1 (☎038378/2410; ⑦); *Ostende*, Dünenstr. 24 (☎038378/510; ⑧); and *Ahlbecker Hof*, Dünenstr. 47 (☎038378/620; ⑧).

RÜGEN

Rügen is Germany's largest island and has been a favourite summer destination since bathing first became fashionable during the nineteenth century. Its long, sandy beaches and airy forests make it an ideal family holiday destination and even in GDR days Rügen drew over a million visitors a year. Today the area is trying hard to adapt an overburdened infrastructure to an ever-increasing volume of tourists. **Accommodation** is virtually unobtainable during the months of July and August without advance booking, and you may well consider visiting off-season. Rügen is particularly atmospheric and empty in winter when the Baltic often freezes over to create an eerie ice-scape.

Geographical divisions split the island into four distinct areas: **South Rügen** with the best, and most heavily populated, stretches of beach; **Jasmund** with its forested national park and chalk cliffs overlooking the Baltic; windswept **Wittow** in the north; and **West Rügen**, a gentle landscape of farmland and woods.

West Rügen is also home to the island of **Hiddensee**, an isolated strip of land a few kilometres offshore with a landscape of surprising contrasts and an idyllic, car-free atmosphere. Also not to be missed are wind-battered **Kap Arkona** at the northeastern corner of Wittow with its Schinkel-designed lighthouse and, nearby, the secluded fishing village of **Vitt**. Equally spectacular are the **Stubbenkammer** cliffs, the most famous of Jasmund's chalk faces. Of Rügen's towns, the main places to head for are in South Rügen: **Binz** and **Sellin** are archetypal faded resorts with tree-lined boulevards and grandiose but often crumbling villas, many of which are now in use as hotels, while **Putbus** is, in effect, a giant Neoclassical folly built during the early 1800s to the greater glory of a local prince. Island capital **Bergen** provides the nearest there is to an urban atmosphere, while **Sassnitz** in Jasmund is a bustling port offering ferry services to Sweden and the Danish island of Bornholm.

Island transport

Getting to Rügen poses no problems as the island is linked to Stralsund by a causeway which takes both road and rail traffic. The quickest approach is by **train** – there are very frequent services on the line from Stralsund to Sassnitz via Bergen, a fair number of which originate in Berlin or even further afield. There's a regular local **bus** link between Stralsund and Altefähr on Rügen's southern coast, a route also served by ferries which leave at approximately two-hour intervals.

Island **transport links** are fairly good, with various branch rail lines leading from the main line on the eastern half of the island, and bus links to more out-of-the-way destinations. Travelling around the island is considerably easier if you have your own car; cycling is a possibility but Rügen is hilly and roads are often potholed or cobbled.

South Rügen

South Rügen offers a relaxing landscape of fields and woods, but the main attraction is its kilometres of fine beach. The best stretches start in **Binz** and run northwards, with further strands between the resorts of **Sellin** and **Thiessow**. Island capital **Bergen** isn't really a resort, but is a communications junction most visitors will pass through at least once. **Putbus**, the other main inland town and starting point of the island's narrow-gauge rail line, is well worth a visit, as is the nearby harbour village of **Lauterbach** from where cruises run to the nature-reserve isle of **Vilm**.

Bergen

Rügen's capital **BERGEN** is a small market town and hub of the island's communications. It's built on a pronounced incline, at the top of which is the **Marienkirche**. This church, originally Romanesque but with substantial Gothic additions, is the oldest on the island, dating back to the days when its inhabitants were Slavs. Embedded in its western wall is a **Slavonic gravestone**, blurrily depicting a bearded man; inside are some fine but faded old frescoes.

Immediately below is the central Markt. Heading northwest from here along Vieschstrasse, past a memorial to the victims of the Nazis, brings you to Bergen's only other sight, the **Ernst-Moritz-Arndt-Turm** (May–Oct daily 10am–6pm; Nov–April Mon–Fri 10am–4pm, Sat & Sun 10am–5pm; DM2). This red-brick viewing tower set on top of a pimply hill offers views of surrounding tree tops and not much else, while the interior contains a cursory display about Ernst Moritz Arndt, a locally born writer and German patriot active during the Napoleonic Wars.

The **Bahnhof** is at the southern edge of town, with the **bus station** a couple of minutes' walk to the north along Friedenstrasse. Bergen's **tourist office** is at Markt 11 (mid-May to mid-Oct Mon–Fri 10am–8pm, Sat 10am–2pm; mid-Oct to mid-May Mon–Fri 10am–6pm; ☎03838/811206). It might be worth enquiring about **private rooms** (②–③) here if you're stuck for accommodation, though even Bergen fills up during the summer. Another possibility is the *Ratskeller*, Markt 27 (☎03838/23112; ⑥), which is a **hotel** as well as one of the town's most reliable **restaurants**.

Putbus

About 8km south of Bergen by rail or bus is the little town of **PUTBUS**, built as a planned Neoclassical *Residenzstadt* by local aristocrat Prince Wilhelm Malte during the early nineteenth century. Under the GDR it fell into a decaying melancholic state, but is now staging a recovery. With its attractive layout and architecture, based on plans originally drawn up by Karl Friedrich Schinkel, it's the artistic highlight of Rügen.

The town

Heart of it all is the **Circus**, a large roundel with a plain pillar at its centre commemorating the founding of the town. Around are grand houses with peeling facades, most of which have been converted into apartments and defaced by satellite dishes. Alleestrasse runs southwest from the Circus past the **Theater**, the only one on Rügen. Its flamboyant exterior, bedecked with an exaggerated portico and pseudo-Classical friezes showing poets, lyre-players and assorted muses, belies its present status as a venue for light classical concerts and farces. Next to it is the **Marktplatz**, ringed by stolid nineteenth-century buildings, with a monument at its centre commemorating Prussia's military triumphs over Austria, Denmark and France.

On the other side of Alleestrasse, the **Schlosspark** is bisected from north to south by the chestnut-tree-lined Kastanienallee. The Schloss itself was demolished in 1962, just before a visit to the area by Walter Ulbricht, the then GDR leader. Allegedly, the local party bosses hoped to score points with the SED top brass by eradicating this symbol of the feudal past. Fortunately some fine-looking ancillary buildings remain, and the leafy lanes of the park and the banks of the **Schwanenteich**, a small lake with adjacent ruined stables, make for good strolling. At the western end is the

Christuskirche, which has been the parish church for the past century, but was built fifty years before as the dining room, games room and ballroom for visitors on recuperative holidays. Towards the eastern end of the park (just off Kastanienallee) is the **Orangerie**, once a winter refuge for exotic plants from the park, and now housing exhibition rooms.

Lauterbach

Some 3km southeast of Putbus, and still within its municipality, is the small fishing and sailing harbour of **LAUTERBACH**. It's the terminus of the branch rail line from Bergen, and is also served by buses from the Circus. Lauterbach was chosen as the site of Wilhelm Malte's very own purpose-built resort, and his opulent colonnaded Neoclassical **Badehaus** still stands on the eastern outskirts. The large wooded park behind it is the beginning of a pleasant coastal walking route. For the less energetic, Lauterbach also has a decent **restaurant** in the shape of the *Hafenklause*, Am Hafen/Dorfstr. 1, which does reasonably priced fish dishes.

Vilm

Lauterbach is the starting point for boat trips around the island of **Vilm**, which was inaccessible to the public during the GDR period. Then, its designation as a nature reserve served mainly to camouflage its role as an exclusive holiday island for the SED hierarchy (revelations in the press about "Erich Honecker's private island" served further to discredit the SED chief after his fall from power). Vilm was opened to the public after the *Wende* but then closed again, since it was felt that indigenous rare animal and plant species were being harmed by the renewed tourist traffic. Access was then reinstated, albeit on a strictly limited basis, and most cruises simply circumnavigate the island. To find out about whether there's any possibility of making a landing, contact *Fahrgastreederei Lenz,* Alleestr. 9 (☎038301/61896) in Putbus or the *Agentur Rolf Kempe* (see below).

Practicalities

Putbus' **tourist office** (July & Aug Mon–Fri 8am–noon & 1–6pm; rest of year Mon & Wed–Fri 8am–noon & 1–4pm, Tues 8am–noon & 1–6pm; ☎038301/431) is at August-Bebel-Str. 1. Another useful contact for accommodation and other services is the privately run *Agentur Rolf Kempe*, Bahnhofstr. 2 (Mon–Fri 9am–6pm, Sat 10am–2/4pm; ☎038301/60513).

Although there are a fair number of **private rooms** (②–③), currently the only **hotel** is *Koos*, Bahnhofstr. 7 (☎038301/278; ⑥). For **eating and drinking**, the *Rosencafé*, on the eastern side of Kastanienallee, serves Italian dishes, while the *Kurhaus* at the western end of Alleestrasse has a good German menu; both have terraces which are good in summer if you've doused yourself with mosquito repellent. Another possibility is the *Jägerhütte*, just beyond the Tierpark in the Schlosspark, which specializes in game.

Putbus is a terminus for the *Rasender Roland*, a **narrow-gauge steam rail line** that runs from here to Binz, Sellin and Göhren, the main resorts on Rügen's southeastern coast (see "travel details" on p.748). The **Bahnhof** is at the eastern edge of town, downhill from the Circus.

Binz and around

In common with the rest of the Baltic coast, Rügen's main beach resorts preface their names with the official designation *Ostseebad*. Biggest of these is **BINZ**, which lies 14km east of Putbus by road or the narrow-gauge rail line. It's been in business since the days of the Kaisers and retains much of its nineteenth-century atmosphere. The town's tree-shaded streets are lined by solid mansions with wrought-iron balconies and fancy gables. These houses were originally built as holiday residences for wealthy families, and most were confiscated by the GDR government for use as workers' rest homes. They have since been sold off for conversion into hotels and apartments, ventures which promise to be lucrative, given the heavy volume of summer visitors.

Binz has two **train stations** – the Bahnhof Binz-Ost for the *Rasender Roland* is southwest of the centre, while the Bahnhof for the branch rail line up the coast (which connects with the main line between Bergen and Sassnitz) is to the north. From the former, Bahnhofstrasse leads down into **Hauptstrasse**, the town's main shopping street. At the end of Hauptstrasse is Binz's apparently endless sandy **beach**, scattered with *Strandkörbe*. Nearby stands the impeccably grand **Kurhaus**, whose terrace looks out over the Baltic.

The beach stretches north for about 10km to the cranes of Neu Mukran, while in the opposite direction it curves southeast for a kilometre or so before disappearing at the foot of tree-covered cliffs. At the southern end of the beach a sewage-polluted stream flows into the sea and notices warn that it's advisable to avoid swimming for at least 50m either side of it. From here, a path leads through the cliff-top woods to the headland viewpoints of **Silvitzer Ort** and **Granitzer Ort**.

Practicalities

Binz's **tourist office** (Mon–Fri 9am–6pm, Sat 9am–noon; ☎038393/37421) is at Heinrich-Heine-Str. 7, though it might be better to head for the branch at Schillerstr. 15 (Mon–Fri 9am–6pm, Sat & Sun 9am–3pm, reduced hours out of season; ☎038393/2782) which deals with **private rooms** (①–③).

Most of the **hotels** have recently been refurbished and are consequently on the pricey side. In the town centre are *Granitz*, Bahnhofstr. 2 (☎038393/32479; ⑤) and *Central,* Hauptstr. 13 (☎038393/347; ⑥). There are more options down by the seafront, with *Haus Schwanebeck*, Margaretenstr. 18 (☎038393/2013; ⑤) and *Binzer Hof*, Lottumstr. 15 (☎038393/2326; ⑥) both just a block away from the beach. Directly on the Strandpromenade are most of the top addresses, including *Am Strand* at no. 17 (☎038393/350; ⑤); *Rugard Strandhotel* at no. 59 (☎038393/360; ⑦); *Villa Salve* at no. 41 (☎038393/2223; ⑧); and *Strandhotel Lissek* at no. 33 (☎038393/3810; ⑧).

The **youth hostel** is at Strandpromenade 35 (☎038393/32597; ⑨), while the **campsite** (☎038393/5141) is just north of town at Prora in the woods between the main road and the beach.

Eating and drinking won't be a problem here – in addition to the excellent food served in all the hotels listed above, there are plenty of restaurants and cafés. The best restaurants are the fish specialist *Poseidon*, Lottumstr. 1; *Dünenhaus*, Strandpromenade 23, which has a pleasant terrace; and *Grand*, Strandpromenade 22, which does game and fish dishes. Binz has the only real **nightlife** possibilities on Rügen – *Im Goldenen Löwe*, Hauptstr. 23, has a disco until 3am and a *Nachtbar* that stays open until 6am.

Jagdschloss Granitz and Lancken-Granitz

The **Jagdschloss Granitz** (May–Sept daily 9am–5.30pm; Oct–April Tues–Sun 9am–4pm; DM4.50), another Wilhelm Malte folly, built on top of the 107-metre Tempelberg, makes a good inland excursion from Binz; take the narrow-gauge rail line to *Haltepunkt Jagdschloss*. Again designed by Schinkel, it's in the heavily romanticized neo-Gothic style the great architect favoured for his fantasy castles. Within, a vertiginous cast-iron staircase leads up the viewing tower to a prospect of Binz and the Jasmunder Bodden freshwater lake to the west, and the island of Vilm. The Jagdschloss also houses a small hunting museum, plus portraits of Malte's ancestors.

Older vestiges of the past can be found near the village of **LANCKEN-GRANITZ** (reached by taking the narrow-gauge rail line to *Haltepunkt Granitz* and walking south for about 1km, or by direct bus from Binz). Turn right at the signpost marked

Ziegensteine at the southwestern edge of the village; after about 1km there's a car park from where a path leads across the fields to a number of prehistoric grave sites. The first, under a massive oak tree, dates back to 2300 BC and consists of two huge stone slabs laid over uprights to create a grave chamber. Nearby are a couple of similar but less well-defined examples, and the surrounding fields and woods hide a number of grave mounds and indeterminate piles of stone.

Sellin

About 4km east of Lancken-Granitz, and reached by a narrow-gauge rail connection from *Haltepunkt Granitz* or by bus, is **SELLIN**, another fine example of turn-of-the-century holidaymaking grandeur. The main street here is the dignified **Wilhelmstrasse** (from the Bahnhof follow Ostbahnstrasse and then turn left into Granitzer Strasse), which slopes up in some style to the top of low cliffs overlooking the beach. The street is lined by wonderful late nineteenth-century edifices, many of which are in use as hotels and pensions. Steps lead down to the beach, which, though littered with *Strandkörbe*, is marginally less crowded than that at Binz.

Practicalities

The **tourist office** is at Warmbadstr. 4 (Mon–Fri 9am–5pm, Sat 10am–noon; ☎038303/293). Also in Sellin, at August-Bebel-Str. 12 (☎038303/1470), you'll find the tourist office for the whole island of Rügen.

There's a wide range of family **pensions** such as *Ingeborg*, Wilhelmstr. 18 (☎038303/291; ③); *Haus Lottum*, Wilhelmstr. 32 (☎038303/941; ③); *Seeschloss*, Am Hochufer 7 (☎038303/666; ③); and *Tatjana*, Wilhelmstr. 28 (☎038303/1450; ④). *Tatjana* also has a Russian restaurant and tearoom. **Hotels** include *Villa Subklew*, Warmbadstr. 1 (☎038303/342; ⑤), and *Bernstein*, Hochuferpromenade 8 (☎038303/1717; ⑦).

Sellin also boasts one of the ex-GDR's premier luxury hotel complexes, the *Cliff Hotel*, Siedlung am Wald 22a (☎038303/181010; ⑨). Here, party bosses enjoyed holidays in style, taking full advantage of their own tennis courts, cinema and private beach (served by an elevator); there are also eight bars, restaurants and cafés to choose from.

Outside the hotels, Sellin's **eating and drinking** possibilities could be better, but try *Berliner Hof*, Granitzer Str. 48, open all day for everything from breakfast to evening meals.

Göhren and the Mönchgut peninsula

Rügen's southeastern extremity is the **Mönchgut**, a jagged, three-pronged peninsula of gentle hills and sheltered bays. Straddling an exposed headland on the east coast is the windswept little resort of **GÖHREN**. The **Bahnhof** (southern terminus of the *Rasender Roland*) is close to the seafront. Just offshore is the **Buskam**, a glacier-deposited rock, once used as an altar by the Slav inhabitants of the island. The name is derived from the old Slavonic *bogis kamien*, meaning "God's Stone", and it's the biggest of Rügen's many *Findlinge* – rocks left by the passage of Ice-Age glaciers.

In town the only attractions are a few museums. At the junction of Strandstrasse and Poststrasse you'll find the **Mönchguter Museum** (June & Sept Tues–Sun 10am–5pm; July & Aug daily 10am–6pm; Oct–May Tues–Sun 10am–4pm; DM3), a mildly diverting display of local folk costumes and material about the development of tourism and other indigenous industries like fishing and piloting. A few doors down on the same street is the **Museumshof** (same times; DM3), essentially an old barn crammed with diverse and improbable-looking agricultural implements. There's another museum, the **Rookhus** (May–Oct Tues–Sun 10am–4/5pm; DM3), a seventeenth-century fishing cottage, on the road to Lobbe. Just out of town, off the main road in the dunes of the southern beach, is the **Museumsschiff Luise** (same hours and price as the Rookhus), an old beached freighter.

Göhren's **tourist office** is at Schulstr. 8 (Mon–Thurs 8am–6pm, Fri 8am–12.30pm & 4–6pm, Sat & Sun 10am–noon & 4–6pm, reduced hours out of season; ☎038308/25910). In addition to **private rooms** (②–③), there are a couple of cheap **pensions**: *Ilona*, Schmiedestr. 4 (☎038308/2280; ④); and *Seerose*, Carlstr. 13 (☎038308/2339; ④). Among the **hotels** are *Waldperle*, Carlstr. 6 (☎038308/5400; ⑤); *Nordperd*, Nordperdstr. 11 (☎038308/70; ⑤); *Albatros*, Ulmenallee 5 (☎038308/5430; ⑦); and *Waldhotel*, Waldstr. 7 (☎038308/25387; ⑦). The **campsite** (April–Oct; ☎038308/2122) is hidden away in the woods a stone's throw from the sea, just northeast of the Bahnhof; with a capacity of four thousand, it's the largest on the island and can get overrun in high season.

Eating and drinking possibilities include *Kaiser's Hofkneipe*, Waldstr. 11, and *Zur Muschel Bar* on Strandweg, again specializing in fish.

Down the peninsula

South of Göhren, sandy beaches fringed with stones run all the way to the southern end of the peninsula. However, the presence of a massive **campsite** (Easter–Sept; ☎038308/2314) just south of Lobbe and innumerable holiday homes, mostly still associated with factories and concerns all over the ex-GDR, means that these are often vastly oversubscribed. One way of escaping the crowds is to take a left turn off the main road about a kilometre south of Lobbe, and make for the tiny, one-street village of **GROSS ZICKER**. A path beyond the car park at the western end of the settlement ends at a stretch of isolated, sandy beach which, though popular, seems empty after the crowds on the eastern beaches. From Gross Zicker there's also access to the 66-metre **Bakenburg**, the Mönchgut's highest point, with correspondingly good views.

Thiessow and around

At the southern end of the Mönchgut, the low-lying village of **THIESSOW** lives mainly from fishing, with a little tourism on the side. Local seamen also act as pilots for vessels sailing through the shallows separating Rügen from the mainland. To reach the nearest stretch of beach, cut through the woods just north of the village. Though there are no hotels, about three dozen private houses (①–③) on Hauptstrasse and Strandstrasse have **rooms** to rent. There's a **campsite** just west of the main road on the way into town (closed Nov to mid-Dec; ☎038308/8226). The *Strandcafé* on the northern beach does excellent ice cream, while *Mönchguter Fischerklause*, towards the southern end of the village at Hauptstr. 69, has good fish dishes.

The absolute end of the road is the village of **KLEIN ZICKER**, just under 2km west of Thiessow. Crammed into the space at the foot of a hill on an odd blob of land sticking out into the sea, the place is a mecca for watersports enthusiasts, particularly surfers.

Jasmund

Rügen's most striking scenery is to be found in **Jasmund**, an area of undulating woods and fields jutting out into the Baltic on the island's northeastern shore. The celebrated white cliffs of **Stubbenkammer** have become Rügen's unofficial symbol, partly because of the romanticized paintings of Caspar David Friedrich. Running back from the coast is the forested pocket of **Stubnitz**, where easy walking routes criss-cross a woodland landscape more reminiscent of Europe's centre than its northern coast. Jasmund's only major town, **Sassnitz**, is the departure point for ferries to Denmark and Sweden.

Sassnitz

The large port of **SASSNITZ** is the terminus of Rügen's main rail line. Before World War II, Sassnitz was the most popular seaside resort in Rügen, but during the GDR epoch this function played second fiddle to the fish-processing industry. Now, the crumbling old villas are gradually being restored as hotels and guesthouses, and tourism looks set to regain its prominent role within the local economy.

Hotels include *Villa Aegir*, Mittelstr. 5 (☎038392/33002 or 33024; ⑤); *Rügen-Hotel*, Seestr. 1 (☎038392/53100; ⑥) *Waterkant*, Walterstr. 3 (☎038392/50844; ⑥); *Gastmahl des Meeres*, Strandpromenade 2 (☎038392/5170; ⑦); and *Kurhotel Sassnitz*, Hauptstr. 1 (☎038392/530; ⑦). The **tourist office** (April–Oct Mon–Fri 8am–7pm, Sat & Sun 3–7pm; Nov–March Mon–Fri 8am–5pm; ☎038392/5160) is in the aforementioned *Rügen-Hotel*, the big concrete box dominating the townscape; it offers the usual booking service for **private rooms** (②–③).

Gastmahl des Meeres is primarily a fish **restaurant**, whose main rival is *Zur Mole* next door. Another good place to eat is *Köpi-Eck*, Hauptstr. 26.

Ferries run regularly from Sassnitz to the Danish island of Bornholm and the Swedish port of Trelleborg; there are also **cruises** up the coast, giving a sea view of the famous cliffs to the north.

Stubbenkammer and around

Unless Scandinavia-bound, your best bet is to leave Sassnitz behind and head for the area's real attractions, the **Stubbenkammer** chalk cliffs of the coast, and the surrounding **Stubnitz** forest, all within the **Nationalpark Jasmund**. There are two ways to do this. The most obvious option is to head direct to Stubbenkammer by bus, a pleasant hilly ride through the woods. The alternative is to follow the coastal path from the northern end of Sassnitz; allow at least 3 hours for this. Mostly it's a cliff-top walk, but occasionally the route dips down into steep-sided stream valleys. The *Gaststätte Waldhalle*, a few kilometres beyond the edge of Sassnitz, is a handy place to interrupt your journey. Adjacent is the **Wissower Klinken**, first of the really large chalk blocks, best appreciated from the cliff-top viewpoint on the **Ernst-Moritz-Arndt-Sicht**, just to the north.

Kleine Stubbenkammer and the Königstuhl

The path continues for several kilometres to the **Kleine Stubbenkammer** with the best views of the mighty **Königstuhl**, a vast pinnacle of chalk standing free from the main cliff face. Königstuhl means "king's seat", and legend has it that in days of yore whoever could climb the seaward side of the 117-metre cliff would become king of Rügen and occupy a stone throne at the top. These days the place swarms with visitors, most of whom choose an easier means of access via the narrow footbridge (DM2) from the car park at the head of the road from Sassnitz. The view from the Königstuhl is, inevitably, splendid though you may have to fight for a space by the rail at the summit. The lines of parked cars along the approach road usually stretch back for several kilometres and the army of day-trippers is served by a *Gaststätte*, a couple of *Imbiss* stands and souvenir shops. From the Königstuhl footbridge a precipitous path meanders down to the beach, which stinks and is strewn with seaweed. The last couple of metres are descended by ladder.

The Herthasee

Shortly before the Königstuhl, a track branches off into the forest from the main road. A path leads from this junction to the mysterious **Herthasee**, a dark lily-bedecked pool hidden in the woods, said to have been the bathing place of the Germanic goddess Hertha, who rewarded the efforts of local farmers with rich harvests. According to the tale, after bathing Hertha would drown her mortal servants, and their spirits gather on the shore each night. North of the Herthasee is the **Herthaburg,** a small hill with a large stone block nearby, which is thought to have served Rügen's early Slav inhabitants as a sacrificial altar.

Glowe

At the western end of Jasmund is **GLOWE**, distinguished by the transmitting masts of Radio Rügen, broadcasting mainly for the benefit of ships at sea and monitoring distress frequencies in the Baltic. Glowe is the gateway to the **Schaabe**, a sandy isthmus planted with Scots pine, separating the Grosser Jasmunder Bodden from the sea, with superb beaches along the Baltic side. In addition to **private rooms** (②–③), there are two excellent **hotels**: *Alt Glowe*, Hauptstr. 37a (☎038302/53059; ⑤) and *Meeresblick*, Hauptstr. 128 (☎038302/53050; ⑥). Both of these have fine **restaurants**, though there's also a renowned fish specialist, *Fischerhus*, Hauptstr. 53.

Wittow

Wittow is Rügen's northern extremity, wind-battered and sparsely populated, with the headland of **Kap Arkona** and the hidden village of **Vitt** as its main tourist pulls. The area has some decent stretches of beach but these tend to be more exposed and generally less hospitable than those elsewhere on the island. Fish figures highly on local menus and is well worth sampling.

Breege-Juliusruh and Altenkirchen

Wittow begins at the western end of the Schaabe with the twin village of **BREEGE-JULIUSRUH,** reached by bus from Stubbenkammer and Glowe. Largely given over to holiday camps, the only real reason to stop here is to take advantage of the beaches, a continuation of the Schaabe strands to the south. With your own transport, Breege, overlooking the Breeger Bodden inlet, is just about worth a quick diversion from the main road to look at the thatched *Kapitänshäuser,* eighteenth- and nineteenth-century fisher houses lining the main street, and to stop off for a bite at the *Fischerstube,* a fish speciality place (eels mainly – grilled, jellied and in soup) on the harbour. If you want to stay, choice is between *Gasthof zum Breeger Bodden,* Dorfstr. 55 (☎038391/538; ④) and *Am Wasser,* Dorfstr. 79 (☎038391/4020; ⑤).

En route from Breege-Juliusruh to Kap Arkona you'll pass the village of **ALTENKIRCHEN,** whose thirteenth-century **Pfarrkirche** is one of the most venerable churches on the whole Baltic coast, richly decorated with thirteenth-century frescoes, only uncovered during the late 1960s.

Kap Arkona

At the northern end of Wittow is **Kap Arkona,** whose cliff-top lighthouses and Slavonic fort draw streams of visitors. Buses run from Altenkirchen to **PUTGARTEN,** an inoffensive little place from where the Kap Arkona lighthouses are clearly visible.

Just north of the village is a large parking lot for visitors to the cape. Here also is the **tourist office** (daily 10/11am–5/7pm according to season; ☎038391/4190), which can help find **private rooms** (②–③) in the area. The **Neuer Leuchtturm** (New Lighthouse), dating from the turn of the century and looking very business-like with its orange and black stripes, is the first to assert itself. Moving closer, the **Alter Leuchtturm** (Old Lighthouse), designed by the ubiquitous Schinkel in 1826, doesn't really look much like a lighthouse at all, but this three-storey red-brick building, with its inset windows and verdigris-dusted dome, does justice to its creator.

The **seafood kiosk** just below the last leg of the approach road to Kap Arkona does excellent herring and fried potatoes with beer, soft drinks or coffee to wash it all down.

Vitt

It might be better, though, to save your appetite for a visit to the village of **VITT**, which has one of the island's best *Gaststätten*. This small fishing port lies hidden in the trees about a kilometre southeast of Putgarten at the end of a rudimentary concrete road. The best approach is to walk from Kap Arkona, although multi-seated horse-drawn carriages run to and from Putgarten (signs at the beginning of the road from Putgarten forbid cars, but there's a car park near the entrance to the village). Also at the village entrance is the small thatched **Dorfkapelle** with an octagonal ground plan (the hand of Schinkel once again). The interior is almost bare with only naive wall paintings of fishing-village life as decoration. From the chapel a path leads down into a small valley and the village itself, a cluster of improbably well-preserved and unspoiled thatched cottages. Vitt survives almost unchanged since the nineteenth century, seemingly oblivious to the tourists who flock here to wonder at its unique atmosphere, which owes much to the absence of cars, supermarkets and other facets of modern life. Throughout the GDR period it was a much sought-after holiday address, particularly among artists and writers: its popularity is increasing every year, though it hasn't attracted any grandiose development schemes – so far. Vitt's **beach** is stony and not particularly attractive, but it's quiet, the water is fairly clean and there's not a *Strandkorb* in sight.

Practicalities

Vitt's justly famous *Gasthof zum Goldenen Anker* is one of the best **restaurants** around, serving up wonderful fish and seafood dishes (particularly eel). Inside it's intimate and a model of *Gemütlichkeit*, while outside you can sit on benches in good weather.

The chances of finding somewhere **to stay** in Vitt are practically nil, at least in summer. There are no pensions or hotels; what few rooms do exist are privately rented, usually to long-standing regular visitors, but should you wish to try your luck head for the small craft shop run by Käthe Graf at Vitt no. 8, who may be able to find you accommodation. **Rowing boats** can be rented from the small harbour or you can let a local sea dog do the work for you in a motorboat.

Hiddensee

Another artist's holiday destination of long standing is the idyllic car-free island of **Hiddensee**, a sixteen-kilometre-long finger of land that stands like a barrage between Rügen and the Baltic. Always classed as part of Rügen, it's among its most appealing corners and the only real tourist draw in **West Rügen**.

Hiddensee experiences a heavy volume of visitors, but with a little leg-work or pedalling it's not difficult to escape the crowds. Despite its small size, the island has a startling variety of landscapes. The northern **Dornbusch** area is a plug of high ground topped by scrubby fields and sandy woods, while the central part of the island, focusing on the **Dünenheide**, is low-lying heath, giving way to a tapering strip of ever-shifting sand dunes called **Gellen**. Hiddensee has only a few thousand inhabitants, most of whom are concentrated in the villages of **Kloster**, **Vitte** and **Neuendorf**, though these numbers swell considerably during the summer. Kloster is easily the most appealing of the Hiddensee villages, and the best way to explore the rest of the island is to rent a bike here (around DM10 per day) and pedal your way around. Though most visitors come to Hiddensee as day-trippers, the relatively small number of available beds means that, as elsewhere on Rügen, it's impossible to find somewhere to stay on Hiddensee during July and August.

From the thirteenth century onwards life on Hiddensee was dominated by the Cistercian order of monks, who, while the island's lay inhabitants plundered grounded ships, were not averse to mixing it with mainland fishermen for the prize of exclusive rights to the island's waters. The Reformation ended all that and the island later passed into Swedish hands until Prussia took over in 1815. Not to be left out of the general nineteenth-century tourism boom, Hiddensee used its superior natural charms to lure a better class of visitor, and the island attracted its share of artists and writers.

Getting there

The best approach to Hiddensee is via the small port of **SCHAPRODE** on Rügen's western shore, which can be reached by bus from Bergen. Most visitors pass straight through this little village en route to the jetty for Hiddensee-bound boats. If you find yourself with time to kill, have a look in the late Romanesque **Dorfkirche**, a red-brick thirteenth-century church with a richly decorated pulpit and altarpiece that are strongly reminiscent of south German Baroque.

Ferries from Schaprode are run by *Weisse Flotte*, whose office at Fährstr. 16 in Stralsund (☎03831/268116) is the contact for up-to-the-minute information. The first departure from Schaprode is at 7am or 7.15am; the last return service departs from Hiddensee at 5.45pm or 6.45pm, according to season. From mid-April until late September, there are five direct departures to Neuendorf, eleven to Vitte and four to Kloster, with a further three going to Kloster via one of the other two ports. Frequencies are slightly, but not significantly reduced out of season. Single journeys cost DM10 to any of the three, returns DM17.50. A further DM10 is levied for transporting a bike.

The same company runs either two or three services daily from Stralsund, according to season; all call at both Neuendorf and Vitte, and some continue on to Kloster. Prices are DM13 single, DM22–26 return, with an extra DM10 for bikes. From May to September inclusive, there are two or three ferries per day from Breege to Vitte, costing DM18 return, with DM8 for bikes. Further information about these is available from Dorfstr. 103, or from *Arkona Reederei*, Bahnhofstr. 19 in Sassnitz (☎038392/22455).

Kloster

Hiddensee's most popular destination is the little town of **KLOSTER**, straddling the northern end of the island. It's incredibly unspoilt, and is at its best when the daytime crowds have disappeared. There's easy access from the village to the west coast of the island which basically forms an eight-kilometre-long beach.

From the small harbour where ferries from the mainland dock a lane leads into Kloster. A left turn at the village pond leads along Hauptstrasse, the nearest thing the town has to a main street. To the north of Hauptstrasse is the **Inselkirche** (Island Church), in whose graveyard **Gerhart Hauptmann** (1862–1946) is buried. Hauptmann, one of the many writers and artists who moved to Rügen in the nineteenth century, belonged to the Naturalist movement of the 1880s, and his dramas focused mainly on the lives and struggles of ordinary people. The realism of his most famous play *Vor Sonnenaufgang* (Before Sunrise), a "social drama" dealing with the human impact of industrialization, caused a sensation at its premiere, and though his earlier works remain his most famous Hauptmann's influence on modern German drama has been extensive. Signposts point the way to the **Gerhart-Hauptmann-Gedenkstätte** (daily April–Oct 10am–5pm; Nov–March 11am–4pm; DM3), the writer's former home, which is also known more picturesquely as *Haus Seedorn*. It's now packed with photos, manuscripts and theatre posters, though some of the rooms have been left as they were when the playwright lived and worked in them.

A little further along Hauptstrasse, just before the beach, is the **Museum der Insel Hiddensee** (daily April 20–Nov 30 10am–4pm; DM4), the island museum, packed with archeological bits and pieces and ceramics. The **beach**, protected by blocks of rock, can be windswept and wave-battered, but on a good day it's perfect, and if you're willing to walk you can soon leave your fellow visitors behind as the sands stretch south for a good 8km. To the north the beach rounds a headland, continuing for several kilometres at the base of the steepish cliffs of the Dornbusch.

Practicalities

The most obvious **accommodation** possibilities in Kloster are *Haus Wieseneck*, Kirchweg 18 (☎038300/316; ③–④) and *Hitthim*, Hafenweg 8 (☎038300/208; ⑤–⑦), which also has a good fish restaurant. For **bike rental** try *Fahrradverleih Gerhard Wannewitz*, Leuchtturmweg 5, reached by heading straight on at the village pond rather than turning left.

The Dornbusch

The gentle hills of the **Dornbusch** area to the north of Kloster are the most appealing part of the Hiddensee and dominated by a lighthouse that warns ships of the island's presence. It's a good region to explore by bike: take the road north to the minuscule hamlet of **GRIEBEN**, where *Zum Enddorn* (☎038300/304; ⑥) and its large garden entice thirsty cyclists. A little further along is *Hella's Eiscafé*, an ice-cream place in a thatched cottage. From the "main" road – in reality a crudely concreted track – there are a couple of turnings in the direction of the **Leuchtturm**, reached after a steep climb, but worth the effort for the excellent views of the island. Adjacent to the lighthouse is a military installation and signs warn of the risk of being shot if you approach.

Skirting the edge of the nearby woods leads to a clearing and *Zum Klausner* (☎038300/215; ④), one of the island's best eating and drinking places with outside tables during summer. In addition to its own double rooms, it also has rustic-looking twin-bedded bungalows for rent. From here a steep path leads back down into Kloster.

Vitte and Neuendorf

A kilometre or so south of Kloster is **VITTE**, Hiddensee's biggest settlement and a kind of island capital. Despite this there's not much here, local builders having been less than discriminating in their efforts, though the **Blaue Scheune**, an old fisher-house painted completely blue, is worth a look for occasional art exhibitions. The **tourist office** (for the whole island) is at Norderende 162 (☎038300/64226). There are several **hotels**, including *Godewind*, Süderende 53 (☎038300/2351; ④); *Zum Hiddenseer*, Wiesenweg 22 (☎038300/419; ⑥); and *Post Hiddensee*, Wiesenweg 26 (☎038300/6430; ⑦). *Zum Hiddenseer* has the best **restaurant** on the island. **Bike rental** is available from *Fahrradverleih Ludwig Müller* near the *Kaufhalle* supermarket opposite the harbour.

South of Vitte is the **Dünenheide**, an area of heathland which is at its best in August when the abundant heather blooms purple. A road leads across it via the *Heiderose*, a pleasant *Gaststätte* and good point to take a breather. Looked after by the *Gaststätte* management are a group of holiday **bungalows** (☎038300/214; ③) in the woods between the road and the Baltic.

Neuendorf

Southernmost of the island's three villages is **NEUENDORF**, a quiet little place which makes a good starting point for wandering the **Gellen**, a sandy spit jutting out south towards the mainland. For crowd-haters, this is the island's most peaceful part. On the western shore, just south of Neuendorf, is a bathing beach, though on the Gellen itself you're restricted to marked paths as the whole area is a nature reserve.

Accommodation is currently pretty much limited to the *Hotel am Meer* (☎038300/201; ⑥), a GDR-era luxury hotel with a swanky restaurant. An alternative place for drinks and light snacks is the *Strandcafé*. For **bike rental** enquire at the *Freizeitcenter Neuendorf*, Neuendorf no. 20.

THE MECKLENBURG LAKE DISTRICT

The **Mecklenburg Lake District** represents one of Germany's last great unspoiled areas of natural beauty. Here, in a landscape of endless fields dotted by innumerable lakes and criss-crossed by quiet country lanes, life is still dominated by the agricultural calendar rather than the tourist season. The area stretches roughly 100km between **Schwerin** and **Neubrandenburg** on its west to east axis, and 80km north to south. In all, there are about 650 lakes in the region, of which the Müritzsee and the Schweriner See are the largest. Many of the hitherto undisturbed lakeshores are home to unique wildlife, though these habitats are now being disturbed by the rush to turn the larger lakes into watersports resorts.

Schwerin used to be the capital of the larger of the two Mecklenburg duchies and the city retains some of its old air with its lakeside Schloss and grandiose municipal architecture. Until the early nineteenth century it was a centre of *Junker* life – the landowning elite of the era dividing their time between here and Berlin while their serfs worked the great land-holdings. Not far south is picturesque **Ludwigslust**, a complete courtly town built in the eighteenth century as the new home of the Schwerin dukes. Another destination is **Güstrow**, a noted artistic centre and gateway to a chain of lakes. At the eastern end of this region are the towns of Neubrandenburg and **Neustrelitz**. The former lost most of its original architecture under a hail of bombs, with only the magnificent medieval wall and gates surviving, while the latter, despite a well-preserved Baroque centre, is struggling to find a way out of the GDR era.

Having your own **transport** makes exploration immeasurably easier, as the public transport network is limited. **Accommodation**, on the other hand, shouldn't be a problem: private rooms are readily available in many of the lakeside villages, and larger towns have a reasonable complement of hotels. **Campers** are well catered for with plenty of established sites and new ones opening all the time.

Schwerin

SCHWERIN, situated amid a chain of lakes 30km south of Wismar and 65km east of Lübeck, is the Land capital of the new province of Mecklenburg-Lower Pomerania. Revelling in its role, it has become one of the ex-GDR's most go-ahead cities, and is undoubtedly among the most rewarding to visit, helped enormously by the fact that it is relatively unencumbered with Communist-era eyesores.

Founded in 1160 by Henry the Lion (see p.623), Schwerin is the oldest town in the province, though little remains of its early heritage. Its glory period began in 1837, when Grand Duke Paul Friedrich of Mecklenburg-Schwerin decided to demote Ludwigslust to a secondary residence and to reinstate his dynasty's original base as the main seat of his court. This led to the creation of a monumental nineteenth-century

The **telephone code** for Schwerin is ☎0385

cityscape which remains largely extant to this day; a vibrant cultural life was also introduced then, and has been of significance ever since.

The city

Water is an omnipresent feature of Schwerin: the city is built around no fewer than ten lakes (the largest being the **Schweriner See** to the east), while the constituent parts of the centre – the Altstadt, the Baroque Schelfstadt, and the nineteenth-century Paulusstadt – each border a different side of the pond known as the **Pfaffenteich**. A stay of at least two days is required in order to cover all the sights, which are spread over a wide geographical area.

The Dom

The only significant medieval building left in Schwerin is the **Dom**, whose massive bulk rises high above the rest of the centre. It was one of four cathedrals founded by Henry the Lion, but, unlike the others, was completely rebuilt a century later in Gothic style. The **tower** (Mon–Fri 11am–noon & 2–3pm, Sat 11am–noon & 2–4pm, Sun noon–3pm; DM1), which was only added last century, gives a great view over the city.

Inside, the architectural details are picked out in orange and green against a whitewashed background. The most remarkable furnishing is the gilded fifteenth-century **triumphal cross**, a work of enormous poignancy and pathos brought here after the war from the destroyed Marienkirche in Wismar. It rather overshadows the beautiful but undersized **high altar** below, carved later the same century in a Lübeck workshop. In the north transept are some splendid brasses in honour of fourteenth-century bishops, while a varied range of **funerary monuments** to aristocrats can be seen in the ambulatory and its chapels. Particularly outstanding are those to Helena von der Pfalz by the great Nürnberg bronze-founder Peter Vischer, and to Duke Christopher of Mecklenburg and his consort Elizabeth of Sweden.

The central streets

To the rear of the Dom is the **Markt**, the hub of the city's commercial life. On its eastern side, the mock-Tudor facade of the **Rathaus** is typical of the city's nineteenth-century architecture. Altogether grander, the **Neues Gebäude** on the north side, an imperious Neoclassical building with a columned portico, is currently used for temporary art exhibitions. Most of the rest of the Altstadt is a pedestrianized shopping centre with a fair number of surviving half-timbered houses.

Far more atmospheric, the **Schelfstadt** immediately to the northeast was founded at the beginning of the eighteenth century but not integrated into Schwerin until well over a hundred years later. Though still a bit rundown-looking, it has street after street of old houses, and is a good place for strolling at leisure. At the heart of the quarter is the **Schelfkirche**, a Baroque parish church with a strikingly emphatic cruciform design, including entrance portals on each wing. Across the Pfaffenteich are the straight-laced buildings of the **Paulusstadt**, the most notable being the huge **Arsenal**, which again mimics the architectural tastes of Tudor England.

Directly east of the Markt, Grosser Moor leads down towards the Schweriner See. At no. 38 on this street is the **Historisches Museum** (Tues–Sun 10am–6pm; DM2), currently offering temporary exhibitions on the history of the city. With luck, you'll be able to see the much-prized aerial photographs of Schwerin shot during the Third Reich.

The Staatliches Museum

At the foot of Grosser Moor, on a square named Alter Garten, stands the stern Neoclassical premises of Schwerin's pride and joy, the **Staatliches Museum** (Tues–Sun 10am–5/6pm; DM7). One of Germany's most engaging art galleries, it's imbued with a pronounced collector's instinct, this being a legacy of the tastes of the local ducal family which was responsible for most of the acquisitions. The displays on the main floor begin with a section on early German painting, including official portraits by **Cranach** of Luther and his wife Katharina von Bora and of King Ferdinand, the brother of Emperor Charles V. However, most of the rest of the floor space is given over to a marvellous array of works illustrating the full diversity of the art of seventeenth-century Holland. **Hals** is represented by an enchanting pair of roundels of laughing boys, while there are several examples of the highly polished genre scenes of Rembrandt's collaborator **Gerrit Dou**, plus a rare masterpiece, *The Guard*, by his most talented pupil, the short-lived **Carel Fabritius**. Another painter who died very young, the animal specialist **Paulus Potter**, is represented by some of his best works, notably *The Milkmaid*. **Ter Brugghen**'s *St Peter Liberated from Prison* is one of the finest examples of Dutch Tenebrism, while the same artist's *Flautist* and *Violinist* are perceptive character studies.

One gallery is devoted to still-life specialists, including a number of canvases by the Haarlem artist **Jan de Heem**. Equally fascinating are the compositions of the little-known **Otto Marseus van Schrick**, which typically feature reptiles or butterflies among the flowers and fruit. At the opposite end of the building, there's a selection of the museum's copious holdings of the works of **Jean-Baptiste Oudry**, court painter to King Louis XV of France; these include several of his familiar hunting scenes and trophies, though the keenly observed animal studies, such as *The Antelope* and *The Leopard*, make a more lasting impression. In the same room is a magnificent full-length portrait of a British queen, the former Princess Charlotte of Mecklenburg-Strelitz, by **Gainsborough**.

The Schloss and its gardens

A few paces south of here, a bridge leads over to Schwerin's vast neo-Renaissance apparition of a **Schloss** (Tues–Sun 10am–5/6pm; DM6), which occupies the same site as Henry the Lion's original castle, an island in the Schweriner See. Gloriously over the top, it was modelled on the famous château of Chambord in France's Loire valley. Plans were originally drawn up by the Dresden architect Gottfried Semper, though only the main tower was built according to his plans. The rest is the work of two pupils of Schinkel, Georg Adolph Demmler and Friedrich August Stüler, who between them were responsible for most of Schwerin's showpiece nineteenth-century buildings.

On the first floor, highlights are the wood-panelled **Speisezimmer** and the circular **Teezimmer** next door, with its ornate white stuccowork. Upstairs, the **Ahnengalerie** is hung with (mostly imaginary) portraits of all the Mecklenburg dukes, while the gilded **Thronsaal**, like the Schloss itself, is of a scale and splendour more appropriate for a powerful kingdom than a tiny duchy. There's also a gallery devoted to local painters, of whom the most notable are **Carl Malchin**, with his evocative nineteenth-century landscapes, and **Erich Venzmer**, who specialized in stark views of sodden Mecklenburg flatlands.

The remainder of the island is occupied by the **Burggarten**, a fine example of nineteenth-century landscape gardening. It makes a fascinating comparison with the much larger **Schlossgarten** to the south, which is in the formal Baroque style, and features a set of statues (now replaced by copies) of Classical gods by the great sculptor of Baroque Dresden, Balthasar Permoser. At the far end, about fifteen minutes' walk from the Schloss, is the **Schleifmühle** (Easter to early Nov Tues–Sun 9am–5pm; DM2). This half-timbered water mill, the only one of its kind in Europe still in full working order, dates back to 1705 but was rebuilt fifty years later for grinding down the precious stones needed to make the furnishings for the Mecklenburg palaces. The actual process, which is painfully slow but highly effective, is demonstrated to visitors.

The Schweriner See

No trip to Schwerin is complete without a **cruise** on the **Schweriner See**: this is the only way of seeing the city's skyline to best effect. Boats, run by *Weisse Flotte* (☎581 1596), depart from the jetty on the north side of the Schloss. From April until October, round trips (DM12.50 for 1hr, DM18 for 2hr) run every day, leaving every half an hour at the height of summer. A good alternative is the ferry service which runs back and forth from May to October down the lake to the beach at **Zippendorf** (DM2.40) and the idyllic island nature reserve of **Kaninchenwerder** (DM4.80).

Set back from the lake at Crivitzer Landstr. 13 in the suburb of Muess, a twenty-minute walk east of Zippendorf, is the **Mecklenburgisches Volkskundemuseum** (May–Oct Tues–Sun 10am–6pm; DM2), an open-air museum featuring eighteenth- and nineteenth-century buildings brought here from all over rural Mecklenburg.

Practicalities

Schwerin's **Hauptbahnhof** is in the Paulusstadt, two blocks west of the Pfaffenteich, and a ten-minute walk from the Altstadt. The **tourist office** is at Am Markt 11 (Mon–Fri 10am–6pm, Sat 10am–2/6pm; ☎592 5212).

Accommodation

A fair number of **private rooms** (③–④) are available via the tourist office. The **youth hostel** is in a lakeside setting at Waldschulenweg 3 (☎213005; 🏠); bus #15 wll take you most of the way, though it's better to take the ferry to the jetty at Zippendorf, from where it's only a few minutes' walk northwards. Along the banks of the Schweriner See are a number of **campsites**, the most convenient being *Seehof* (☎512540) in the village of the same name just north of the city.

There are now plenty of **hotels**: most of those in the centre are a bit overpriced for what they offer, though at least this means there's seldom any problem getting a room. Schwerin is one city where it's certainly worth considering staying in the suburbs, where there are a number of enticing establishments in attractive surroundings.

HOTELS

Am Hauptbahnhof, Grunthalplatz 11–12 (☎565702, fax 557 4296). One of a group of hotels on the square directly facing the Hauptbahnhof. ④

An den Linden, Franz-Mehring-Str. 26 (☎512084, fax 512281). The most appealing of the centrally sited hotels, occupying a late Neoclassical building. The facilities include a sauna and a winter garden. ⑥

Arte, Dorfstr. 6, Krebsförden (☎63450, fax 634 5100). Occupies a recently converted brick farmstead in a southern suburb, close to the Ostorfer See. Its restaurant, *Fontane*, serves high-quality local dishes. ⑦

Hospiz am Pfaffenteich, Gauss Str. 19 (☎565606, fax 569612). Pleasant medium-range establishment in the Schelfstadt, overlooking the Pfaffenteich. ⑥

Reichshof, Grunthalplatz 15–17 (☎565798, fax 565798). The cheapest of the cluster of hotels by the Hauptbahnhof. Its Chinese restaurant, *Canton*, offers good-value set lunches. ④

Seehotel Frankenhorst, Frankenhorst 5, Frankenhorst (☎555071, fax 555073). Located in a lovely landscaped park at the northern tip of the Ziegelsee, in the far north of the city. The restaurant, *Bootshaus*, has a terrace overlooking the lake. ⑥

Strandhotel, Am Strand 13, Zippendorf (☎213053, fax 200 2202). Hotel with café-restaurant named after the small beach it overlooks. ⑤

Zur Guten Quelle, Schusterstr. 12 (☎565985, fax 565985). Small hotel with restaurant in a half-timbered building in the heart of the city. ⑥

Zur Muesser Bucht, Muesser Bucht 1, Muess (☎644500, fax 644 5044). Reasonably priced lakeside hotel with restaurant and beer garden in the far southeast of the city. ⑤

Zur Traube, Ferdinand-Schultz-Str. 20 (☎512417, fax 512417). One of the rare budget options, located on a quiet street just east of the Schelfstadt, and not far from the Schloss. Its *Gaststätte* is a popular "local". ④

Eating, drinking and entertainment

The centre of Schwerin is well endowed with good places to **eat** and **drink**, with wine bars being a particular strength of the local gastronomic scene.

Alt Schweriner Schankstuben, Schlachtermarkt 9. Good traditional wine restaurant.

Gastmahl des Meeres, Grosser Moor 5. The main fish specialist.

Gewölbe-Restaurant, Am Markt 1. *Gaststätte* offering typical examples of *gutbürgerliche Küche*.

Jagdhaus, Güstrower Str. 109. Excellent speciality game restaurant, located at the northern fringe of the built-up part of the city.

Schlosscafé, Lennéstr. 1. Good place for *Kaffee und Kuchen*, located in the Schloss itself.

Schlossgartenpavillon, Am Kreuzkanal. Café-restaurant in the grounds of the Schloss.

Weinhaus Uhle, Schusterstr. 15. Schwerin's best restaurant is a superemely elegant wine bar housed in fine Rococo premises.

Zum Goldenen Reiter, Puschkinstr. 44. Offers an eclectic menu of international dishes.

Entertainment

The liveliest **nightspots** are on Wittenberger Strasse, where you'll find the bar-discos *Charivary* (at no. 50) and *Phillies* (at no. 51). Highbrow cultural events, including drama, opera and concerts, are staged in the main **theatre**, the *Mecklenburgisches Staatstheater*, opposite the Staatliches Museum at Alter Garten (☎530 0126). In summer, however, the courtyard of the Schloss is often used instead.

Ludwigslust

Thirty-five kilometres south of Schwerin is **LUDWIGSLUST**, founded in 1756 on the site of a hunting lodge as the residence of the local dukes, remaining as such until 1837, when the court moved back to the original capital. In accordance with the taste of the time, it's a planned town with a generous complement of green spaces, and it remains almost completely intact. Under the GDR regime, Ludwigslust's all-too-obvious feudalist overtones meant that it was allowed to fall into decay, but an enormous amount of reconstruction work has already been carried out, and the whole town should soon be in immaculate shape. As such, it makes a fascinating contrast with Neustrelitz, its direct counterpart in the other former Mecklenburg duchy.

The town

The story of the construction of Ludwigslust is dogged by a yawning gap between the ambition of its rulers and the finances available to them. This meant that all kinds of cost-cutting measures were adopted, the most immediately obvious being the use of plain, ordinary bricks for the construction of almost all the buildings.

The outsized **Schloss** (Tues–Sun 10am–5/6pm; DM5) in the heart of the town, which was not even begun until 16 years after Ludwigslust's foundation, provides the clearest evidence of the crafty measures taken to skimp on money. Outwardly, it looks very imposing indeed, its show frontage revealing the first stirrings of Neoclassicism while retaining the full pomp of late Baroque. However, the resplendent stonework is a facade in both senses of the word, masking the brickwork from which the palace is actually built. An even cleverer trick is played in the **Goldener Saal**, the main reception hall of the interior. Glittering with mirrors and gilt, adorned with golden vases, columns and figures of cherubs, it makes a stunning setting for concerts. Almost everything, however, is fashioned from a form of papier-mâché known as *Ludwigsluster Carton*, which was specially developed here to produce such trompe l'oeil effects. The rest of the interior, which served as the home of the deposed ducal family until it was appropriated in 1945, subsequently suffered from the depredations of the Red Army and its use as offices. However, a number of smaller rooms have also been restored and refurnished in period style.

To the north and west stretches the enormous **Schlosspark**, a masterly exercise in English-style landscaping by the ubiquitous Peter Joseph Lenné. Its varied delights include a canal, fountains, cascades, a beautiful stone bridge, two Neoclassical mausolea, a neo-Gothic chapel, a grotto, and a bizarre funeral monument to a horse.

South of the Schloss is a large oval-shaped green, down the sides of which are the modest little cottages built for the estate workers. Another, this time rectangular, area of greenery separates the axial road from the second main focal point of the town, the **Stadtkirche**. Designed, like the Schloss and most of the rest of Ludwigslust, by the local architect Johann Joachim Busch, it ranks as one of the most distinctive and unexpected Protestant churches in Germany. The monumental facade is like a great Classical Roman temple, though the rest of the exterior is completely plain. Inside, everything is pure theatre, from the ornate ducal loft at one end to the vast mural of *The Adoration of the Shepherds* at the other. In the latter, the church's organ, most of which is hidden from view, appears to be played by one of the angels in the heavenly apparition above.

Practicalities

Ludwigslust's **Bahnhof**, which is on the main line between Schwerin and Stendal in Saxony-Anhalt, lies at the far northern end of town, a fifteen-minute walk from the centre. The **tourist office** (Mon–Fri 10am–12.30pm & 1.30–4pm; ☎03874/29076) is diagonally opposite the Schloss at Schlossfreiheit 8. Here you can book **private rooms** (②–③), which are in reasonable supply and noticeably cheaper than in Schwerin. There's also a small **pension**, *Schwarzenberg*, Am Seminargarten 4 (☎03874/22438; ③).

The local **hotels**, however, are fairly pricey, though this is justified by the refurbishments all have undergone. Between the Bahnhof and the centre, good choices are *Park*, Kanalstr. 19 (☎03874/22015; ⑤); *Stadt Hamburg*, Letzte Str. 4–6 (☎03874/4150; ⑤); and *Erbprinz*, Schweriner Str. 38 (☎03874/47174; ⑦). In the heart of town, occupying a ritzy mansion at Schloss Str. 15, *Landhotel de Weimar* (☎03874/4180; ⑦) is the best and most expensive of the lot. All of these hotels have recommendable restaurants.

Güstrow

About 60km northeast of Schwerin lies **GÜSTROW**, formerly the capital of one of the Mecklenburg duchies, which was for a short time ruled by the mercurial and inscrutable military genius Alfred von Wallenstein, supreme commander of the Imperial forces in the Thirty Years' War. When the ruling house died out in 1695, however, it was reduced to the status of a second-string residence of the Dukes of Mecklenburg-Schwerin, and has remained pretty provincial ever since, a fact which enabled it to escape the attentions of wartime bombers.

Before the war it was the home and workplace of **Ernst Barlach**, the greatest German sculptor of the twentieth century, and the important collections of his work here are a prime tourist draw. Güstrow is also the birthplace of **Uwe Johnson**, a GDR author who went into exile in 1959 following conflict with the authorities. His novels deal with the psychological shock of Germany's division and the development of fear and distrust on opposite sides of the border between the two states.

The town

Mostly pedestrianized, the **Altstadt** is still the heart of the modern town. Its predominantly eighteenth- and nineteenth-century buildings are in better shape than most in the former GDR, and retain many original features such as brass shop signs and elaborately carved doors. Güstrow's other highlight is the gorgeous surrounding countryside, with easy access to lakes such as the Inselsee and Sumpfsee on the outskirts of the town, and the much larger Krakower See to the south.

The Altstadt

The central Markt is built up in the middle on the central European model, with the secular and the sacred, in the shape of the Baroque **Rathaus** and Gothic **Pfarrkirche**, given equal billing centre-stage. The church contains a marvellous array of furnishings, dominated by a really magnificent early sixteenth-century **high altar** made in Brussels. When open, it shows delicately carved and polychromed oak scenes of the Passion by the sculptor Jan Borman; when closed, the brightly coloured paintings of the life of the Virgin by Barent van Orley, court painter to the Habsburgs, are on view.

A couple of blocks away, at the southern end of the Altstadt, is the huge sixteenth-century **Schloss** (Tues–Sun 9/10am–5/6pm; DM5). From the outside, it's one of the most impressive Renaissance palaces anywhere in Germany, providing a classic example of how Italianate forms could be ever so subtly modelled to suit these more northerly climes. Unfortunately, it fell into disrepair on the demise of the local duchy, and was only regularly used again in 1811 when Napoleon's troops set up a field hospital here on their way to Russia. The Nazis transformed it into a prison, destroying much of what was left of the furniture and decor. Nonetheless, some fine original interiors remain, notably in the south wing. There's also a decent representation of German, Italian and Dutch art of the sixteenth century.

Hidden away unassumingly at the southwestern corner of the Altstadt is the **Dom**, another brick Gothic church which was first a collegiate foundation, then the court chapel, rather than the cathedral its name would suggest. The architecture is almost totally overshadowed by some extraordinary furnishings, which include a gilded high altar by the fifteenth-century Hamburg carver Hinrik Bornemann, and a vibrant series of Apostles on the pillars of the nave by the sixteenth-century Lübeck sculptor, Claus Berg. Even more arresting are the Renaissance **funerary monuments** in the choir by the Dutchman Philipp Brandin. Look out in particular for the two largest – to the Dom's founder Heinrich Borwins II, and to the sculptor's patron Duke Ulrich with his two wives – each of which has an elaborate armorial background. In the northern aisle of the nave are three **Barlach sculptures**, including the famous *Flying Angel*, which is suspended above an ornate Renaissance grille. The original of this, a memorial to the dead of World War I, was melted down in 1938 as part of the Nazi measures against "degenerate art". Fortunately, a cast had previously been taken, enabling the work to be re-created after the war.

The Barlach museums

The stature of Ernst Barlach continues to rise, and few would now dispute his right to be regarded among the century's most significant artists. His bronzes and woodcarvings, borrowing techniques from the medieval and Renaissance German masters, show a warm humanity and a haunting sense of pathos; he also carried his Expressionism over into other media, being a fine graphic artist and an accomplished playwright. There are two museums in Güstrow devoted to him; between them they contain the largest collection of his work in existence.

The museum in the **Gertrudenkapelle** (Tues–Sun 10/11am–5pm; DM3), a little Gothic chapel set in its own grounds just over the ring road from the northwestern side of the Altstadt, is the obvious destination, particularly if you're pressed for time, as it contains original versions of many of his finest works. The **Atelierhaus** (same hours; DM3), Barlach's house and workshop, lies in the narrow strip of land between the Inselsee and the wooded Heidberg; it's about 4km south of the Altstadt, and can be reached by bus #4. Here you can see the sculptures left unfinished at his death in 1938, along with casts of his other work in a variety of different media.

Practicalities

Güstrow's **Bahnhof**, which has regular services on the lines to Schwerin, Rostock and Neubrandenburg, is five minutes' walk from the northern end of the Altstadt. The **tourist office** (Mon–Fri 9am–6pm, Sat 9.30am–1pm, May–Sept also Sun 9.30am–1pm; ☎03843/681023) is at Domstr. 9.

Plenty of **private rooms** (①–③) are available at the tourist office. The new **youth hostel** is near the Barlach Atelierhaus at Heidberg 33 (☎03843/840044; ❶). There's now a good selection of centrally sited **hotels**: *Villa Camenz*, Lange Stege 13 (☎03843/214993; ③); *Rubis*, Schweriner Str. 89 (☎03843/69380; ⑤); *Am Güstrower Schloss*, Schlossberg 1 (☎03843/7670; ⑤); *Altstadt*, Baustr. 8–10 (☎03843/686003; ⑥); and *Stadt Güstrow*, Pferdemarkt 58 (☎03843/7800; ⑦).

The **restaurant** of the last-named is rivalled for the title of best in town by *Barlach-Stuben*, Hageböcker Str. 9, which features typical Mecklenburg dishes. Reliable alternatives include the *Ratskeller*, Markt 10, and *Marktkrug*, Markt 14, while *Dill und Petersilie*, Schloss Str. 1, offers fish and game specialities. The best place for *Kaffee und Kuchen* is the long-established *Café Küpper*, Domstr. 15.

Güstrow's main **cultural** venue is the Neoclassical *Ernst-Barlach-Theater* on Franz-Parr-Platz (☎03843/684146). **Festivals** include the *Stadtfest* in June, the *Schlossfest* in July, and the *Inselseefest* on the first weekend of August.

Neubrandenburg

At the eastern end of the Mecklenburg lake district, about 75km southeast of Güstrow and 100km south of Stralsund, is **NEUBRANDENBURG**, an important rail junction, especially for routes into Poland. Like so many places in the former GDR, it offers the dichotomy of historic monuments of the highest class co-existing with the most painful of eyesores. As the main sights can be seen in a few hours, it's best viewed as a stopoff en route to or from the Baltic coast or the lakes to the west.

The Altstadt

Neubrandenburg was founded in 1248 by Margrave Johann I of Brandenburg (hence its name), but was incorporated into Mecklenburg early the following century. From this period dates the extraordinary 2.5-kilometre-long **Stadtmauer** – one of the most impressive municipal fortification systems anywhere in Europe – encircling the Altstadt. Miraculously, it came through World War II virtually intact, though the rest of the town was almost completely destroyed. Subsequently, the Altstadt was filled with the concrete architecture beloved of the GDR regime, with a fifteen-storey cultural centre placed smack in the middle.

To appreciate the Stadtmauer to the full, you need to walk round it twice – once on the inside, once on the outside. It's pierced by four colossal gateways, whose patterned brickwork is of a scale or delicacy more in keeping with a great civic church or town hall than a defensive system. Earliest of these is the **Friedländer Tor**, the northeastern entrance to the town, which has inner and outer gateways linked by a stretch of fortified wall, plus a semicircular tower, known as the *Zinger*, as a first line of defence. Today it's a café and commercial art gallery. Only slightly less formidable-looking is the **Treptower Tor** (Tues–Fri 9am–5pm, Sat & Sun 1–5pm; DM2) on the western side of town, which now houses the local archeology museum. The most elaborately decorative brickwork of all is found on the southern gateway, the **Stargarder Tor**, whose inner face is adorned with nine enigmatic, highly stylized female figures. Eight more statues in the same vein can be seen on the **Neues Tor** to the east, which is distinguished by enormous finger-shaped gables. Another curiosity of Neubrandenburg is the presence of 26 (out of an original total of 56) half-timbered houses, known as **Wiekhäuser**, which are conversions of the bastions built directly onto the Stadtmauer. Not surprisingly, they're the most sought-after properties in town; several are now craft shops.

Two large brick Gothic churches are the only set-piece attractions within the walls. The modest architecture of the **Johanniskirche** at the northern end of the Altstadt is a reflection of its original function as a Franciscan monastery: the church itself is now a Protestant parish, while the refectory is used as local government offices. Altogether grander is the **Marienkirche** a few minutes' walk to the south, which forms a clear ecclesiastical counterpart to the four gateways. Grievously damaged in the war, it's only now being restored, and is due to re-open as a concert hall in time for the town's 750th anniversary in 1998.

Practicalities

Neubrandenburg's **Bahnhof** is just beyond the northern confines of the Altstadt, separated from it only by the width of Friedrich-Engels-Ring, which follows the perimeter of the Stadtmauer. The **tourist office** (Mon–Fri 9am–5/6pm, Sat & Sun 10am–2pm; ☎0395/19433), which is right in the heart of the Altstadt at Marktplatz 1, can arrange **private rooms** (②–③).

A fair number of **hotels** can be found just outside the perimeters of the Stadtmauer. These include *Jahnke*, Rostocker Str. 12 (☎0395/581700; ⑤); *St Georg*, St Georg 6 (☎0395/544 3788; ⑥); *Borchert*, Friedrich-Engels-Ring 40 (☎0395/582 2607; ⑤); *Weinert*, Ziegelbergstr. 23 (☎0395/581230; ⑥); and *Andersen*, Grosse Krauthöfer Str. 1 (☎0395/5560; ⑥). There's also a **youth hostel**, situated about 1.5km northeast of the Altstadt at Ihlenfeldstr. 73 (☎0395/422 5801; 🛉).

Choices for **eating** and **drinking** are surprisingly wide, with the finest food being served at *Fritz Reuter,* at Friedländer Str. 2a in the Altstadt. Other restaurants with a cosy atmosphere are *Wiekhaus 45* and *Mudder-Schulten-Stuben*, both on 4-Ringstrasse; and *Gasthaus zur Lohmühle*, Am Stargarder Tor 4, a converted mill with a wine and beer garden.

Neustrelitz

About 35km south of Neubrandenburg by road or rail is the odd town of **NEUSTRE-LITZ**, which was founded in 1732 as the custom-built capital of Mecklenburg-Strelitz, the smaller of the two duchies into which Mecklenburg was divided in 1701. First impressions are good – streets of sober Baroque buildings radiate out from a central square to striking effect, and the town slopes down towards the tree-lined shores of the Zierker See. However, it soon becomes evident that Neustrelitz is one of those places struggling to adapt to the realities of the new Germany, and despite some recent improvements is clearly still suffering from post-GDR malaise. This is a great shame, as Neustrelitz is a fascinating example of a planned *Residenzstadt* built to a strict geometric plan around a small hunting lodge transformed into a grand ducal palace. Though it benefited initially from its position on trade routes between the coast and Berlin, it never rose above sleepy backwater status, as the absence of significant post-eighteenth-century development testifies.

Neustrelitz benefits from its setting between the two constituent parts of the **Müritz Nationalpark**, which was established a few years ago to protect a section of the Mecklenburg Lake District which is particularly rich in flora (especially orchids) and bird life. Much the larger of the two parts lies immediately west of town, and stretches all the way to the eastern bank of the Müritzsee.

The town

The focal point of the town is the central **Markt**, which is a perfect square measuring 120 metres on each side. For several years after the *Wende*, a huge Soviet war memorial stood in the grassy area in the middle. Although it has now been removed, the square has not yet followed the normal eastern German pattern of being reclaimed for commerce. The one set piece now left is the Baroque **Stadtkirche**, which was built according to plans drawn up by a doctor in the service of one of the local dukes.

From the Markt, the streets radiate outwards in eight directions. Head down Schloss Strasse to the **Schlosspark**, a lakeside ornamental garden laid out in the English style by the great Berlin landscape gardener, Peter Joseph Lenné. The Schloss itself was destroyed in 1945 and no traces now remain, though its **Orangerie**, built in 1755 as a winter home for plants, still survives. Its previously bare interior was transformed in the 1840s by two more leading lights of the Berlin art world — the architect Karl Friedrich Schinkel and the sculptor Christian Daniel Rauch. Together they created three highly ornate interiors for festive purposes, each dominated by a particular colour scheme and decorated in a pseudo-Pompeiian style. Recently, these served respectively as a concert room, a café and a restaurant, though the building is currently closed for restoration.

Schinkel was also responsible for the design of the nearby **Schlosskirche**, which shows all the idiosyncrasies of his very personal and visionary neo-Gothic manner. At the northwestern end of the Schlosspark, just past the small Neoclassical **Tempel**, the **Zierker See** begins. Its shores are wonderful for strolling; you can also **rent boats**, and there are **cruises** during the summer months.

Practicalities

Neustrelitz's **Bahnhof** is only about ten minutes' walk from the Markt along Strelitzer Strasse. The **tourist office** (Mon–Fri 9am–noon & 1–4.30/5pm; ☎03981/253119) is at Markt 1.

Chances are that you won't want to stay overnight, but there are plenty of **private rooms** (②–③) available here, plus several **hotels** which are generally better value than normal by eastern German standards. These include *Zur Klause*, Strelitzer Str. 53 (☎03981/200570; ③); *Haegert*, Zierker Str. 44 (☎03981/200305; ③); *Pinus*, Ernst-Moritz-Arndt-Str. 55 (☎03981/445350; ⑤); *Schlossgarten*, Tiergartenstr. 15 (☎03981/245000; ⑤); and *Park*, Karbe-Wagner-Str. 59 (☎03981/443600; ⑦).

Each of the hotels lised above, except *Pinus*, has a **restaurant**. An alternative place for a meal is the *Inselgaststätte Helgoland*, on an islet linked to the shore by a footbridge; it's near the town's harbour area, just north of the Schlosspark.

travel details

Trains

Bergen to: Lauterbach (via Putbus: 9 daily; 40min); Lietzow (for Binz: 12 daily; 10min); Sassnitz (10 daily; 45min).

Greifswald to: Berlin (13 daily; 2hr 30min); Stralsund (frequent; 25min); Wolgast (change at Züssow: 11 daily; 25min).

Lietzow to: Binz (12 daily; 20min).

Neubrandenburg to: Berlin (10 daily; 2hr 10min); Güstrow (8 daily; 2hr); Neustrelitz (17 daily; 45min); Stralsund (10 daily; 1hr 50min).

Neustrelitz to: Berlin (frequent; 1hr 30min); Neubrandenburg (frequent; 45min); Rostock (13 daily; 1hr 40min); Stralsund (10 daily; 2hr 30min).

Putbus to: Göhren (*Rasender Roland* narrow-gauge line via Binz, Jagdschloss Granitz, Sellin and Baabe; 9 daily; 1hr 10min).

Rostock to: Bad Doberan (16 daily; 25min); Berlin (12 daily; 3hr); Güstrow (frequent; 40min); Magdeburg (9 daily; 4hr); Neubrandenburg (13 daily; 2hr 30min); Neustrelitz (13 daily; 2hr); Sassnitz (15 daily; 1hr); Schwerin (12 daily; 1hr 15min); Stralsund (15 daily; 1hr 20min);

Warnemünde (frequent; 25min); Wismar (11 daily; 1hr 45min).

Sassnitz to: Rostock (via Bergen: 2 daily; 3hr 30min); Stralsund (via Bergen: 11 daily; 1hr).

Schwerin to: Berlin (7 daily; 3hr); Bützow (for Güstrow; 12 daily; 1hr); Ludwigslust (hourly; 30min); Magdeburg (6 daily; 3hr); Rostock (15 daily; 2hr 30min); Wismar (11 daily; 1hr).

Stralsund to: Berlin (17 daily; 4hr 30min); Neubrandenburg (10 daily; 1hr 50min); Neustrelitz (7 daily; 2hr 30min); Rostock (15 daily; 1hr 20min); Sassnitz (10 daily; 1hr 10min).

Wismar to: Rostock (12 daily; 1hr 45min); Schwerin (12 daily; 1hr).

Wolgast to: Ahlbeck (12 daily; 1hr 30min); Züssow (for Greifswald and Stralsund; 10 daily; 30min).

Ferries

Stralsund to: Kloster (9 daily; 1hr 30min); Vitte (6 daily; 45min).

Warnemünde to: Gedser (6 daily; 2hr); Travemünde (daily; 9hr); Wismar (daily; 5hr).

CHAPTER NINE

BERLIN AND BRANDENBURG

Berlin is like no other city in Germany, or, indeed, the world. For over a century its political climate has either mirrored or determined what has happened in the rest of Europe. Heart of the Prussian kingdom, economic and cultural centre of the Weimar Republic, and, in the final days of Nazi Germany, the headquarters of Hitler's Third Reich, Berlin is a weather vane of European history. After the war, the world's two most powerful military systems stood face to face here, sharing the spoils of a city for years split by that most tangible object of the East–West divide, the Berlin Wall. As the Wall fell in November 1989, Berlin was once again pushed to the forefront of world events. It's this weight of history, the sense of living in a hothouse where all the dilemmas of contemporary Europe are nurtured, that gives Berlin its excitement and troubling fascination.

It was, of course, **World War II** that defined the shape of today's city. A seventh of all the buildings destroyed in Germany were in Berlin, Allied and Soviet bombing razing 92 percent of all the stores, houses and industry here. At the end of the war, the city was split into French, American, British and Soviet sectors, according to the agreement at the Yalta Conference. The Allies took the western part of the city, traditionally an area of bars, hotels and shops fanning out from the Kurfürstendamm and the Tiergarten park. The Soviet zone contained what remained of the pompous civic buildings, churches and grand museums around Unter den Linden. After the building of **the Wall** in 1961, which sealed the Soviet sector and consolidated its position as capital of the young German Democratic Republic, the divided sections of the city developed in different ways. The authorities in the West had a policy of demolition and rebuilding; the East restored wherever possible, preserving some of the nineteenth-century buildings that had once made Berlin magnificent.

Though Berlin is impossible to understand without some knowledge of its history, it is easy to enjoy. For years its isolation in the middle of the GDR meant that **western Berlin** had a pressure-cooker mentality. This, combined with the fact that a large and youthful contingent came here to drop out or involve itself in alternative lifestyles, created a vivacious **nightlife** and a sense of exhausted excitement on the streets.

Now that the Wall has gone, the two Germanys are unified and the city has won the role of German capital, Berlin seems less sure of its identity. The border, once so rigidly defined, has faded away, and the change from west to east passes unnoticed. But, essentially, Berlin is still very much a city of two separate parts, **eastern Berlin** forming a strange twin to its western neighbour. Here, on the streets and in the factories and housing estates, you'll see constant reminders of a discarded social experiment – one whose traces the new authorities are urgently trying to erase.

The postwar schizophrenia that marred the city has quickly vanished, but **unification** seems destined to leave behind its own damage: the huge subsidies that the west-

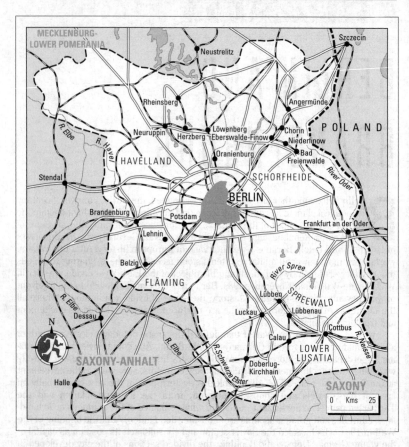

ern sector received, along with the massive social support schemes that the former GDR granted its citizens, have been completely removed, causing unprecedented unemployment and the flight of big companies from the city. In many cases, unification has left former East Berliners in the role of second-class citizens to their western counterparts, while the Turkish guestworkers and their East German counterparts, migrants from Vietnam and African nations that used to have "fraternal" relations with the GDR, are increasingly subject to attack by neo-Nazi thugs. But in the final analysis no amount of facts and figures, economics or history can really explain the place; only by seeing it for yourself can you attempt some understanding.

Inevitably, **the pace of change** in Berlin, particularly the eastern part of the city, means that certain sections of this chapter are going to be out of date even as you read them, such as the speed of transformation. Bars, restaurants and (especially) clubs open and close weekly, and though this can be annoying it adds to the city's excitement.

One great advantage of unification is that, for the first time since the 1930s, the area around Berlin and the newly designated Land of **Brandenburg** can easily be visited. **Potsdam** and the magnificent palace of Sanssouci is the obvious day-trip, and the city of **Brandenburg** itself has its attractions, as does the lake- and forest-strewn countryside. It's important to visit now, since the "lost-in-time" feel of some of the small towns and villages, like **Neuruppin**, will soon be gone for ever.

BERLIN

The division of **BERLIN** into zones of occupation in 1945, although seemingly arbitrary, followed exisiting local government boundaries, and the dual profile which emerged was by no means solely a product of the Cold War. In his famous interwar collection of short stories, *Goodbye to Berlin*, Christopher Isherwood wrote:

> *Berlin is a city with two centres – the cluster of expensive hotels, bars, cinemas, shops around the Memorial Church, a sparkling nucleus of light, like a sham diamond, in the shabby twilight of the town; and the self-conscious civic centre of buildings around the Unter den Linden, carefully arranged.*

The latter, the political and cultural core of the Imperial German capital, duly became the heart of East Berlin and of the GDR, while the former quickly adapted itself to the makeshift role of city centre of the stranded enclave that was West Berlin.

Because it occupies a vast geographical area, one interrupted by a plethora of parks, forests and lakes, Berlin is not a place that is appreciated easily or quickly. Some of the most rewarding attractions are in the most far-flung corners; the **museums** are magnificent; choice in **theatre, music** and **nightlife** is so wide as to be bewildering; while the era of division means that the reunited city still has two of almost everything.

Arrival and information

Most scheduled and charter flights arrive at **Tegel airport**, from where frequent #109 buses run directly to the Bahnhof Zoologischer Garten (**Zoo Station**) in the city centre (journey time 25–40min; DM3.60). Alternatively, take the #109 bus to Jakob-Kaiser-Platz U-Bahn and transfer to the U-Bahn system (the bus ticket is valid for the U-Bahn journey: see p.754). Taxis cover the distance in half the time and cost around DM35 to Zoo Station. Many domestic flights land at **Tempelhof**, much nearer the city centre. Bus #119 takes you to Zoo Station in ten to twenty minutes, or U-Bahn line #6 is a short walk away; change at Stadtmitte for Zoo Station. Take time to have a look at the airport buildings – though some of them predate the Nazi era, the main building is a classic example of Fascist architecture.

Schönefeld has been chosen to replace Tegel as the city's main international airport; for the moment, though, you'll probably land there if arriving from a central or Eastern European destination. To reach town from Schönefeld, take bus #171 either to S-Bahnhof Flughafen Schönefeld, where S-Bahn line #9 provides a link to the city centre (via Hauptbahnhof, Alexanderplatz, Friedrichstrasse and Zoo Station), or continue on the #171 to Rudow U-Bahn station and take line #7 into town. Journey time is around forty minutes and costs DM3.60.

Berlin has four main **train stations**: trains from the north and west generally arrive at the **Zoo Station** or **Friedrichstrasse;** those from the south and east at **Lichtenberg** or **Hauptbahnhof**. All these stations are connected to the U- and S-Bahn network. International **buses** mostly stop at the central bus station, west of the centre near the Funkturm; regular #149 buses or the U-Bahn from Kaiserdamm station link it to the city centre, in about fifteen minutes.

The **telephone code** for Berlin is ☎030

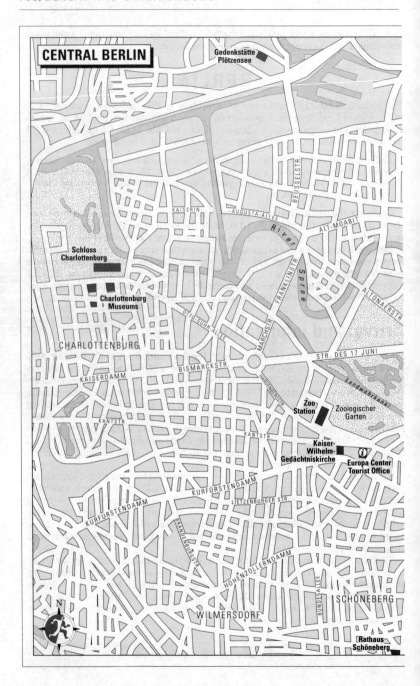

CENTRAL BERLIN

Gedenkstätte
Plötzensee

BEUSELSTR.

KAISERIN-

AUGUSTA-ALLEE

ALT-MOABIT

River Spree

FRANKLINSTR.

ALTONAERSTR.

Schloss
Charlottenburg

Charlottenburg
Museums

OTTO-SUHR-ALLEE

MARCHSTR.

STR. DES 17 JUNI

CHARLOTTENBURG

Landwehrkanal

KAISERDAMM

BISMARCKSTR.

HARDENBERGSTR.

KANTSTR.

Zoo
Station

Zoologischer
Garten

KANTSTR.

Kaiser-
Wilhelm-
Gedächtniskirche

Europa Center
Tourist Office

KURFÜRSTENDAMM

LIETZENBURGER STR.

KURFÜRSTENDAMM

BRANDENBURGSTR.

HOHENZOLLERNDAMM

BUNDESALLEE

SCHÖNEBERG

N

WILMERSDORF

Rathaus
Schöneberg

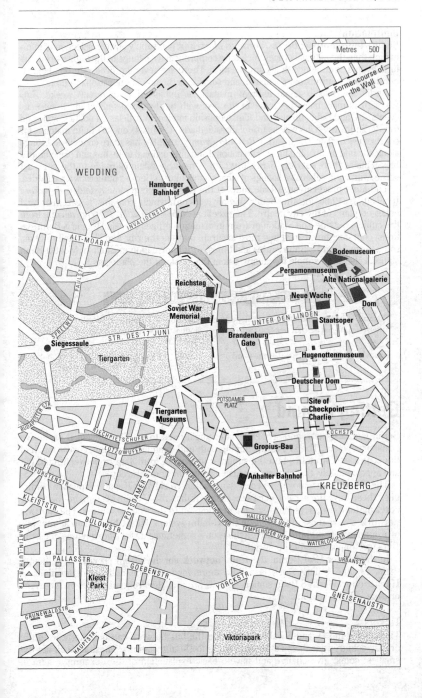

0 Metres 500

Former course of the Wall

WEDDING

Hamburger Bahnhof

INVALIDENSTR.

ALT-MOABIT

PAULSTR.

Bodemuseum

Pergamonmuseum
Alte Nationalgalerie

Reichstag

Neue Wache

Soviet War
Memorial

Dom

Staatsoper

UNTER DEN LINDEN

SPREEWEG

Brandenburg
Gate

STR. DES 17 JUNI

Siegessaule

Hugenottenmuseum

Tiergarten

Deutscher Dom

POTSDAMER
PLATZ

BUDAP.STR.

Site of
Checkpoint
Charlie

Tiergarten
Museums

REICHPIETSCHUFER

KOCHSTR.

LUTZOWUFER

SCHÖNEBERGER

Gropius-Bau

REICHPIETSCHUFER

KURFÜRSTENSTR.

POTSDAMER STR.

Anhalter Bahnhof

KLEISTSTR.

KREUZBERG

BULOWSTR.

LANDWEHRKANAL

MARTIN-LUTHER-STR.

HALLESCHES UFER

TEMPELHOFER UFER

WATERLOOUFER

PALLASSTR.

GOEBENSTR.

URBANSTR.

Kleist
Park

YORCKSTR.

GRUNEWALDSTR.

GNEISENAUSTR.

HAUPTSTR.

Viktoriapark

Information

Berlin's **tourist office**, *Berlin Tourismus Marketing*, can supply a wider selection of information than the national offices, including comprehensive listings of the higher-brow cultural events, and help with accommodation. There are several offices (see box below), but the best, in terms of information and service, is the one in the Europa Center.

Berlin has two essential **listings** magazines, published on alternate weeks. *Zitty* (DM3.50) is marginally the better of the two, with day-by-day details of gigs, concerts, events, TV and radio, theatre and film, alongside intelligent articles on politics, style and the Berlin in-crowd, as well as useful classified ads. *Tip* (DM4) doesn't quite match it for conciseness or flair. The monthly *Berlin Programm* (DM2.80) has more condensed listings alongside info on opening times, and national and international train, bus and plane timetables. Finally, there's *Artery Berlin* (DM3.50), a monthly bilingual guide to the city's art scene, with comprehensive listings of what's happening in Berlin's numerous art galleries.

The most practical large-scale **map** of the city is the ingeniously folded *Falk Plan* (DM9.80, DM12.80 for the better, bigger version) which contains a gazetteer and enlarged plans of the city centre. The excellent *Nahverkehrsatlas* (DM7), available from the cubicle outside Zoo Station or from information offices at major U- and S-Bahn stations, contains the clearest and most accurate maps of the city, and also details all bus, tram, ferry, U- and S-Bahn routes and times, with information in English. Most U-Bahn stations also have simple free maps; ask at the kiosk on the platform.

BERLIN'S TOURIST OFFICES

Europa Center, entrance on Budapester Strasse (Mon–Sat 8am–10pm, Sun 9am–9pm; ☎250025).

Brandenburg Gate (daily 9.30am–6pm).

Info-Point Dresdner Bank, Unter den Linden 17 (Mon–Fri 8.30am–2pm; Tues & Thurs 3.30–6pm as well).

Tegel airport, main hall (Mon–Sat 8am–11pm, Sun 9am–9pm; ☎4101 3426).

Getting around

Berlin is a large city, and sooner or later you'll need to use its efficient if expensive transport system. The **U-Bahn**, running both under- and overground, covers much of the centre and stretches into the suburbs; trains run from 4am to between midnight and approximately 12.30am, an hour later on Friday and Saturday.

The **S-Bahn** system was severely damaged in World War II, and renovation continues. These days the service is far less frequent than the U-Bahn system, but better for covering long distances fast – say for heading out to the Wannsee lakes. The city **bus network** covers most of the gaps in the U-Bahn system. **Night buses** run at intervals of around twenty minutes, although the routes sometimes differ from daytime ones; the *BVG* (see opposite) will supply a map.

In the former East Berlin, the **tram network** survives from prewar days, though thankfully the rolling stock is a little more modern. The main tram terminus is **Hackescher Markt** S-Bahn station. Tickets are available from machines on the trams or from U-Bahn stations.

Tickets

Tickets for the U- and S-Bahn system and the bus network can be bought from the orange-coloured machines at the entrances to U-Bahn stations. These take all but the smallest coins, give change and have a basic explanation of the ticketing system in

English. Though it's tempting to ride without a ticket, be warned that plain-clothes inspectors frequently cruise the lines (particularly at the beginning of the month), meting out on-the-spot fines of DM60 for those without a valid ticket or pass.

Single tickets (*Einzelfahrschein Normaltarif*) common to all the systems cost DM3.60, and allow you to travel in any two of the three tariff areas; they're valid for two hours, enabling you to transfer across the three networks to continue your journey, and to return within that time on a different route. An *Einzelfahrschein Kurzstreckentarif*, or short-trip ticket, costs DM2.50 and allows you to travel up to three train or six bus stops (no return journeys). If you're intending to use the system frequently it's better to buy a **day ticket** (*Tageskarte*) for DM7.50 from any U-Bahn station or the *BVG* office on Grunewaldestrasse, next to Kleistpark U-Bahn station (Mon–Fri 8am–3pm). You can also buy a weekly ticket (*Wochenkarte*) for DM40, or a monthly ticket (*Monatskarte*) for DM93: these allow unlimited travel on the entire system and obviously can represent a considerable saving.

Accommodation

Since the fall of the Wall, interest in Berlin has dramatically worsened the chance of getting an inexpensive room. It's essential to book as far ahead as possible to be guaranteed accommodation, particularly at the budget places on the western side of the city. Remember, too, that the city's hotels fill completely during important trade fairs and festivals, and at Easter and Christmas. The majority of affordable accommodation is in the western section of the city, and it's easiest to look for a room there.

Compared to the *Mitwohnzentralen*, most other forms of accommodation seem overpriced or inconvenient. The **tourist office** in the Europa Center (with other offices elsewhere see opposite) offers a hotel and pension **booking service** for DM3, though their options, especially in the high season, are limited to mid-range and upmarket places. The tourist office also provides an advance booking service: phone or fax *Berlin Tourismus Marketing* (☎250025, fax 2500 2424), stating the length of your stay and how much you're prepared to spend.

Otherwise, your chances of finding somewhere directly are good, if you're prepared to phone around and wear out some shoe leather. Summer weekends are the most problematic periods, and if you're arriving on a Friday night any time from June to August it makes sense to have at least the first few days' accommodation booked in a hotel if you haven't been able to reserve a room from the *Mitwohnzentralen*. The tourist office's leaflets *Tips für Jungendliche* and *Berlin Hotelverzeichnis* (also available from German National Tourist Offices abroad) have useful lists of hotels and pensions.

Mitwohnzentralen

Easily the best way of finding a place to stay is by contacting one of the *Mitwohnzentralen* organizations. The shortest period of time a *Mitwohnzentrale* will

ACCOMMODATION PRICE CODES

All the pensions and hotels in this book have been graded according to the following price categories. The prices quoted are for the cheapest available double room, although many of the budget places will also have more expensive rooms. Youth hostels are graded under separate categories. See p.34 for more details.

① less than DM50	④ DM81–100	⑦ DM151–200
② DM51–65	⑤ DM101–125	⑧ DM201–250
③ DM66–80	⑥ DM126–150	⑨ more than DM250

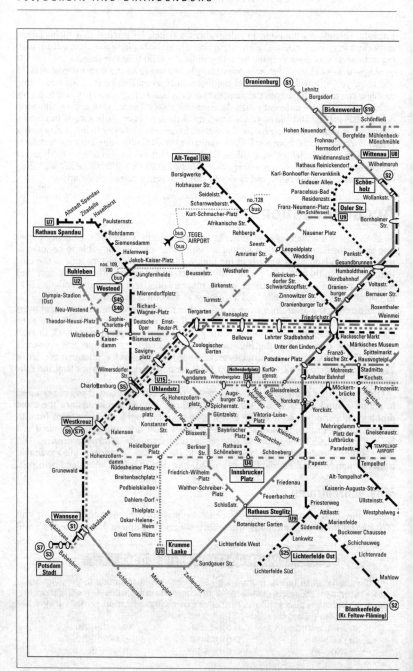

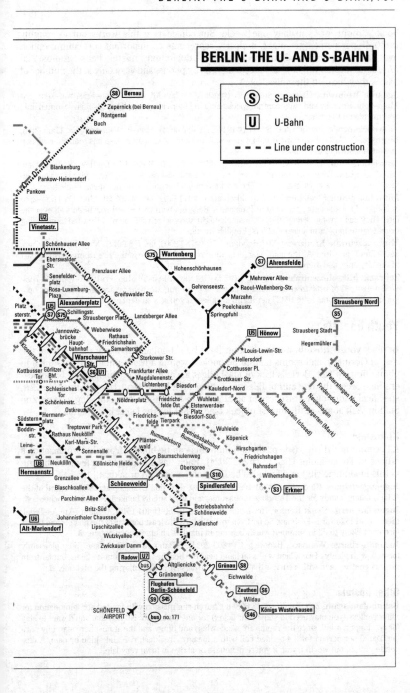

book a room for is usually one week. But considering this works out to roughly DM30–45 per person per night, it clearly represents an important cost-cutting option over anything other than the cheapest dormitory hostel beds. Almost all *Mitwohnzentralen* will take advance bookings by phone, and vary only in the number of places they have on their files.

Agentur Wohnwitz, Holsteinischestr. 55 (☎861 8222, fax 861 8272). Mon–Fri 10am–7pm, Sat 11am–2pm. Friendly and fairly central, specializing in inner-city rooms. They also have women-only apartments on their lists.

Mitwohnzentrale, Joachimstaer Str. 17 (☎19445, fax 882 6694). Mon–Fri 9am–6pm, Sat 11am–2pm. Biggest of the *Mitwohnzentralen*, and an easy walk from the Zoo Station. Also has rooms for women in women-only apartments.

Mitwohnagentur Atlas, Boxhagener Str. 13 (☎2949 0063). If all else fails try this Friedrichshain-based company. They have rooms all over the city (DM20–30 per person) but advise that you contact them at least a week in advance. The staff are rather abrupt and do not speak English.

Mitwohnagentur Streicher, Immanuelkirchstr. 8 (☎441 6622, fax 441 6623). Mon–Fri 11am–2pm & 3–6pm. Friendly agency located in Prenzlauer Berg but with rooms and apartments all over the city. They can arrange everything from single-night stays in private rooms (from DM45 including breakfast) to long-term apartment lets. English spoken.

Mitwohnzentrale Kreuzberg, Mehringdamm 72 (☎786 2003, fax 785 0614). Mon–Fri 10am–7pm, Sat & Sun 11am–4pm. As the name suggests, their rooms tend to be in the Kreuzberg/eastern part of the city only, and therefore cheaper.

Zeitraum Mitwohnzentrale, Horstweg 7 (☎325 6181, fax 321 9546). Mon–Fri 10am–1pm & 3–7pm. Well-organized *Mitwohnzentrale* that specializes in providing inexpensive accommodation for budget travellers. Rooms from DM25 per night, even less if you're a student and book ahead.

Youth hostels

Berlin's **youth hostels** are used extensively by school and sporting parties from the rest of Germany, and rooms tend to be booked well in advance: hence it's essential to phone first. In fact, Berlin's lack of low-budget accommodation suitable for backpackers has forced the city authorities into setting up a **large tent**, *Übernachtung im Zelt*, specifically for young travellers in an attempt to keep them from dossing around Zoo Station. Ask at any of the tourist offices (see p.754) for the latest information.

HI hostels

All require an HI card (see p.35), although this can be bought from the organization's offices in Tempelhofer Ufer 32 (☎262 3024). Each has a midnight curfew (frustrating in this insomniac city) and includes bedding and a spartan breakfast.

Jugendgästehaus, Kluckstr. 3 (☎261 1097). Bus #129, direction Oranienplatz. Most central of the IYHF hostels, handy for the Tiergarten museums, and very solidly booked. 9am–noon lockout. 🛏

Jugendherberge Ernst Reuter, Hermsdorfer Damm 48–50 (☎404 1610). U-Bahn #6 to Alt-Tegel, then bus #125 towards Frohnau. So far from town that it's the least popular of the hostels and therefore least likely to fill in summer; worth bearing in mind as an emergency option. 🛏

Jugendherberge Wannsee, Badeweg 1 (☎803 2034). S-Bahn #3 to Nikolassee. Very pleasantly located, with plenty of woodland walks on hand near the beaches of the Wannsee lakes, but far from the city centre – and with a curfew that renders it useless if you're enjoying the nightlife. 🛏

Other hostels

Bahnhofsmission, Zoo Station (☎313 8088). Church-run mission with limited accommodation for rail travellers (you may need to show your ticket) for one night only. No risk that you'd want to stay for any longer, mind, since the rooms are windowless and dingy and the atmosphere starchily puritan. DM20 per person for a 4-bedded cell with a meagre breakfast; rise and shine by 6am. A desperate option, but worth trying if you're penniless or arrive in town very late.

Jugendgästehaus am Zoo, Hardenbergstr. 9a (☎312 9410, fax 3125 5030). Zoologischer Garten U- and S-Bahn. Excellent location, extremely popular. Singles DM47, doubles DM85, four people in a room DM35. No curfew.

Jugendgästehaus Deutsche Schreberjugend, Franz-Künstler-Str. 10 (☎615 1007, fax 614 6339). U-Bahn line #1 to Hallesches Tor. Easy access to hot spots in both eastern and western areas of the city. Doubles or triples DM37, including breakfast. No curfew.

Studentenhotel Berlin, Meininger Str. 10 (☎784 6720, fax 788 1523). Buses #104 or #146 or U-Bahn line #4 to Rathaus Schöneberg. Dormitory accommodation at the relaxed edge of the city's action. Doubles DM41 per person, including breakfast. No curfew; key deposit DM20.

Hotels and pensions

All but the cheapest places include an as-much-as-you-can-eat breakfast in the price. The best choice of mid-range places is in the western part of the city around Kurfürstendamm and Savignyplatz, extending into the district of Charlottenburg.

The West End

Alpenland, Carmerstr. 8 (☎312 9370, fax 313 8444). Well situated and a good choice at the lower end of this price group. ⑤

Am Lehninerplatz, Damaschkestr. 4 (☎323 5100, fax 323 9359). Youth hostel-type atmosphere bang in the middle of good nightlife. Dormitory-style rooms for DM45 per person as well as single and double rooms. ⑤

Artemisia, Brandenburgischestr. 18 (☎873 8905, fax 861 8653). The first women-only hotel in the city. Dormitory-type accommodation in a 3-bedded room, DM73 per person, as well as singles and doubles. Fills up quickly, so it's advisable to book in advance. ⑦

Bogota, Schlüterstr. 45 (☎881 5001, fax 883 5887). Pleasant luxury at sensible prices. ⑤

Bregenz, Bregenzer Str. 5 (☎881 4307). A small family-run set-up only a 10min walk from the Ku'damm. Children are welcome. ④

Charlot, Giesebrechtstr. 17 (☎323 4051, fax 324 0819). Neatly restored, efficiently run hotel near Adenauerplatz. Excellent value for money. ⑤

Cortina, Kantstr. 140 (☎313 9059, fax 312 7396). Reasonable rooms in a good area – one that's ideal for exploring the West End and Savignyplatz. ⑤

Dittberner, Wielandstr. 26 (☎884 6950, fax 885 4046). Old-fashioned finery in comfortable surroundings and at affordable prices. ⑥

Hansablick, Flotowstr. 6 (☎390 4800, fax 392 6937). A short hop from the Tiergarten, this is one of the few "alternative" hotels in town, being run by a collective; breakfast included. ⑦

Imperator, Meinekestr. 5 (☎881 4181 or 882 5185). Good-value, central, intimate hotel, situated on one of the most friendly streets in the city. Breakfast not included. ⑤

Meineke, Meinekestr. 10 (☎882 811). Typical Berlin hotel with an amiable atmosphere, about a minute's walk from the Ku'damm. ⑧

Pariser Eck, Pariser Str. 19 (☎881 2145 or 883 6335, fax 883 6335). Adequate lodgings in a pleasant, leafy back street. A 10min walk from the Ku'damm and with some classy cafés nearby. ④

Mitte

Aacron, Friedrichstr. 124 (☎282 9352, fax 280 8057). About as central as you're likely to get at this price. The rooms are spartan but bearable. ⑤

Märkischer Hof, Linienstr. 133 (☎282 7155, fax 282 4331). Centrally located a stone's throw from Oranienburger Strasse and within easy strolling distance of the Unter den Linden. Comfortable rooms with TV, minibar etc. Most have shower and WC. ⑦

Merkur, Torstr. 156 (☎282 8297, fax 282 7765). Fairly comfortable rooms within easy walking distance of city centre attractions and local nightlife. Most rooms have showers. ⑤

Novalis, Novalisstr. 5 (☎282 4008, fax 283 3781). Quiet, small hotel not far from Oranienburger Tor S-Bahn station. Rooms have shower and WC. ⑦

Kreuzberg

Kreuzberg, Grossbeerenstr. 64 (☎251 1362). Close to Kreuzberg hill at the smarter end of that neighbourhood. ④

Südwest, Yorckstr. 80 (☎785 8033). Dreary part of town, but close to Kreuzberg hill and an area that's buzzing at night. ⑤

Transit, Hagelberger Str. 53–54 (☎785 5051, fax 785 9619). Not quite as daunting as the name suggests, and well located: it lies in the quieter streets to the north of Viktoriapark, but is a stone's throw from Kreuzberg's nightlife and action. ③

Prenzlauer Berg

Hotel Greifswald, Greifswalder Str. 211 (☎442 7888, fax 442 7898). Located in an unnotable neighbourhood, but not far from Alexanderplatz and the nightlife along Oranienburger Strasse. ⑦

Kastanienhof, Kastanienallee 65/66 (☎443 050, fax 443 05111). Well-appointed rooms at reasonable prices. Away from the centre of things but handy for the nightlife of Prenzlauer Berg. ⑦

Campsites

None of western Berlin's four **campsites** is close to the centre; however, they're all inexpensive (prices are a uniform DM7 per tent plus DM9 per person per night), well run and, with one exception, open year-round. "The Tent" is a new addition to the city's accommodation options, in response to Berlin's lack of low-budget choices for young backpackers.

Camping Dreilinden, Albrechts Teerofen (☎805 1201). From Oskar-Helene-Heim U-Bahn, take a #118 bus in the direction of Kohlhasenbrück. Open March 1–Oct 31. Two and a half kilometres from the nearest bus stop, this site is inadvisable unless you have transport. Free showers and a small restaurant.

Camping Kladow, Krampnitzer Weg 111–117 (☎365 2797). U-Bahn to Rathaus Spandau, then #134 bus to Kladow; at the southern end of Kladower Damm change to bus #234, get off when the bus swings off Krampnitzer Weg and walk to the end of the road. Friendly campsite with the best facilities, including a free crèche, bar, restaurant, shop and showers (DM0.50). Six-week maximum stay.

Camping Kohlhasenbrück, Neue Kreis Str. 36 (☎805 1737). Closest of all the Berlin sites – take bus #118 in the direction of Drewitz. Facilities include a restaurant, showers and laundry room.

Camping Krossinsee, Wernsdorfer Str. 45 (☎675 8687, fax 675 9150). The only site in the erstwhile GDR, *Krossinsee* is pleasantly located in the woods just outside the southeastern suburb of Schmöckwitz, and offers easy access to local lakes. From S-Bahnhof Grünau, take tram #68 to Schmöckwitz; here, catch bus #463 to camp site.

Übernachtung im Zelt (Jugendcamp Fliesstal), Waidmannsluster Damm/Ziekowstrasse (☎791 3040). "The Tent" is open July 1–Aug 31 and you'll be provided with a sleeping mat and blanket. Only those aged between 14 and 26 (which you will be asked to prove) are admitted. The Tent is a 35min journey from Friedrichstrasse U-Bahnhof. First take U-Bahn #6 direction Alt-Tegel to the end of the line; it's then a short hop on bus #222 direction Alt-Lübars. Basic facilities; DM10 per night.

Western Berlin

Until November 1989, the **western areas of Berlin** formed the distinct and artificially created city of West Berlin, a pocket of western capitalism kept alive by interested parties in the centre of Soviet-occupied territory. Today, western Berlin has the appearance of a badly patched-up skeleton, and even in the flashiest sections of the new centre, around the **Kaiser-Wilhelm-Gedächtniskirche**, it still seems half-built. The points of interest are, almost without exception, sombre: the **Reichstag**, looming symbol of the war years; the scant remains of the **Wall**, facet of its aftermath; and several

museums which openly and intelligently try to make sense of twentieth-century German history. The brighter side is that this isn't the only face of modern western Berlin. By night the city changes, awakening into a **nightlife** that's among the best in Europe – the bars here are by turn raucous, shady, stylish and promiscuous, the discos and clubs blasting their stuff well into the early hours; restaurants are excellent, cheap and of unequalled variety.

Culturally, this part of the city has enjoyed the advantage of massive subsidies from Bonn and has a legacy of great **art collections**. About a third of western Berlin is either forest or park. In the centre, **Schloss Charlottenburg** and its gardens are a great place to loll away a summer afternoon, and, on the city's western outskirts, the **Havel lakes** and the **Grunewald forest** have a lush, relaxed attraction that's the perfect antidote to the city's excesses.

Zoo Station, the Kurfürstendamm and the Tiergarten

Whether you come by train, coach or bus from Tegel airport, chances are you'll arrive at Bahnhof Zoologischer Garten – **Zoo Station**. Perched high above the street, and with views across to the Zoo, the train station is an exciting place to end a journey, conjuring memories of prewar steam trains under its glassy roof. At street level, though, it's an unkempt and conspicuously lavatorial-smelling spot that's not a place to linger. By day, but chiefly by night, it's the meeting place for the city's drunks and dope pushers, but has been much cleaned up since a few years back when it was a marketplace for heroin dealing and child prostitution.

The Kurfürstendamm

Step out east from Zoo Station and you're in the centre of the city's maelstrom of bright lights, traffic and high-rise buildings. A short walk south and you're at the eastern end of the **Kurfürstendamm** (known as the **Ku'damm**), a 3.5-kilometre strip of ritzy shops, cinemas, bars and cafés that zeros in on the centre like the spoke of a broken wheel. The great landmark here, the one that's on all the postcards, is the **Kaiser-Wilhelm-Gedächtniskirche**, built at the end of the last century and destroyed by British bombing in November 1943. Left as a reminder, it's a strangely effective memorial, the broken tower providing a hint of the old city. Adjacent, a new **chapel** contains the tender *Stalingrad Madonna*, while the blue glass campanile at the back has gained the local nickname of the "Lipstick" or the "Soul-Silo".

The area around the church acts as a focal point for western Berlin's punks and down-and-outs, who threaten the well-heeled Ku'damm shoppers with demands for cash. It's a menacing, unfriendly spot and **Breitscheidplatz**, the square behind, isn't much better, a dingy concrete slab usually filled with skateboarders and street musicians. This area marks the beginning of Tauentzienstrasse, with the **Europa Center**, a huge shopping centre that contains the *Berlin Tourismus Marketing* (tourist office), a bland, generic mall built in the 1960s as a capitalist showcase for West Berlin, complete with a huge Mercedes-Benz symbol on the top. Further down Tauentzienstrasse is the *KaDeWe*, an abbreviation of the German for "the Department Store of the West", and which all Berliners will tell you is the largest store in Europe. This it isn't, though it's still an impressive statement of the city's standard of living.

There's little to do on the Ku'damm other than spend money, and there's only one cultural attraction, the **Käthe-Kollwitz-Museum** at Fasanenstr. 24 (11am–6pm; closed Tues; DM6; buses #109, #119 or #219). The drawings and prints of Käthe Kollwitz are among the most moving to be found from the first half of this century. Born in 1867, she lived for almost all her life in Prenzlauer Berg in the eastern part of the city, where her work evolved a radical left-wing perspective. Following the death of her son in

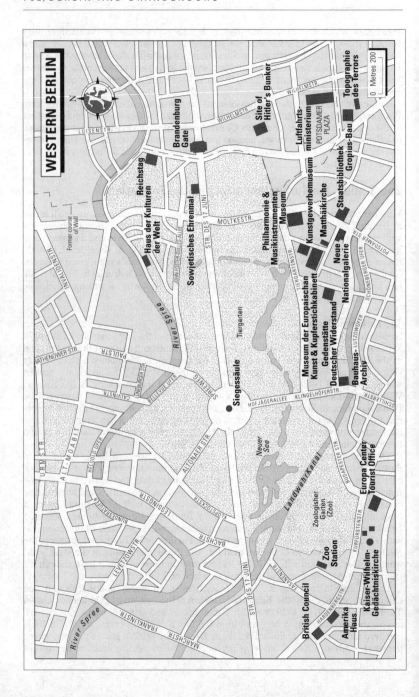

WESTERN BERLIN

N

0 Metres 200

Site of Hitler's Bunker

Brandenburg Gate

Reichstag

Haus der Kulturen der Welt

Sowjetisches Ehrenmal

Former course of Wall

WILHELMSTR.

WILHELMSTR.

LUISENSTR.

Luftfahrts-ministerium

POTSDAMER PLAZA

Topographie des Terrors

Gropius-Bau

Staatsbibliothek

Matthäikirche

Kunstgewerbemuseum

Philharmonie & Musikinstrumenten Museum

Neue Nationalgalerie

Museum der Europaischen Kunst & Kupferstichkabinett

Gedenstätte Deutscher Widerstand

Bauhaus-Archiv

MOLTKESTR.

STR. DES 17 JUNI

JOHN-FOSTER-DULLES-ALLEE

River Spree

INVALIDENSTR.

RATHENOWER STR.

PAULSTR.

LÜBBENER STR.

CALVINSTR.

BELLEVUE UFER

Tiergarten

SPREEWEG

Siegessäule

HOFJÄGERALLEE

KLINGELHÖFERSTR.

TIERGARTENSTR.

SCHÖNEBERGER UFER

LÜTZOWUFER

POTSDAMER STR.

SCHILLSTR.

Neuer See

Landwehrkanal

Europa Center Tourist Office

ALTONAER STR.

KLOPSTOCKSTR.

URMSTR.

ALT-MOABIT

HELGOLD UFER

BUNDESRAUFER UFER

LESSINGSTR.

BACHSTR.

LEVETZOWSTR.

Zoologischer Garten (Zoo)

BUDAPESTER STR.

KURFÜRSTENSTR.

Zoo Station

Kaiser-Wilhelm-Gedächtniskirche

British Council

Amerika Haus

HARDENBERGSTR.

JEBENSTR.

STR. DES 17 JUNI

River Spree

FRANKLINSTR.

MÄRCHSTR.

World War I, her woodcuts, lithographs and prints became explicitly pacifist, often dwelling on the theme of mother and child. When her grandson was killed in World War II her work became even sadder and more poignant. The museum's collection of her work makes it possible to trace its development, culminating in the tragic sculptures on the top floor.

By the time you reach **Adenauerplatz**, the slick showrooms of the Ku'damm have died out and the bars become affordable; although the clientele tends towards brash kids and sloshed squaddies, it's not a bad starting point for an evening's boozing. Best of all for eating, drinking and nightlife, though, is the squashed rectangle of streets south and west of Zoo Station, focusing on **Savignyplatz** (see p.792).

The Zoologischer Garten and the Tiergarten

Back in the centre, the **Zoologischer Garten** (daily 9am–sunset, 9pm at the latest; DM11, Aquarium DM11, combined ticket DM18, kids half-price) forms the beginning of the **Tiergarten**, a restful expanse of woodland and lakes originally laid out under Elector Friedrich III as a hunting ground and destroyed during the Battle of Berlin in 1945 – though so successful has been its replanting that these days it's hard to tell. The Zoo is beautifully landscaped, with surprising views of the city, and the animal enclosures have been sensitively constructed. You can wander through the Tiergarten tracing the course of the **Landwehrkanal**, an inland waterway off the River Spree. Near the Corneliusbrücke a small, odd sculpture commemorates the radical leader **Rosa Luxemburg**. In 1918, along with fellow revolutionary Karl Liebknecht, she declared a new Socialist Republic in Berlin along the lines of Soviet Russia. The pair were kidnapped by members of the First Cavalry Guards: Liebknecht was shot while "attempting to escape", Luxemburg was knocked unconscious and shot, her body dumped in the Landwehrkanal at this point.

The broad avenue that cuts through the Tiergarten is the **Strasse des 17 Juni**, its name commemorating the day in 1953 when workers in the East rose in revolt against the occupying Soviet powers, demanding free elections, the removal of all borders separating the two Germanys, and freedom for political prisoners. Soviet forces quickly mobilized, and between two and four hundred people died. The authorities also ordered the execution of twenty-one East Berliners and eighteen Soviet soldiers – for "moral capitulation to the demonstrators". At the centre of the avenue is the **Siegessäule** (Mon 1–6pm, Tues–Sun 9am–6pm; DM2; bus #100, #187 or #341), the victory column celebrating Prussia's military victories. It was shifted to this spot from what is today's Platz der Republik on Hitler's orders in 1938. Though the boulevard approaches exaggerate its size, it's still an eye-catching monument: 67m high and topped with a gilded winged victory that symbolically faces France. The view from the top is one of Berlin's best – the Brandenburg Gate announcing the grandly restored streets of eastern Berlin, the Reichstag standing like a gnarled protector at the edge of the park. Have a look, too, at the mosaics at the column's base, which show the unification of the German peoples and incidents from the Franco-Prussian War: they were removed after 1945 and taken to Paris, only to be returned when the lust for war spoils had subsided.

From the Reichstag to Checkpoint Charlie

Strasse des 17 Juni comes to an end at the Brandenburg Gate, but it's better to start a little further north – at the Reichstag. The building was seriously damaged by fire in 1933, an event Hitler used as a pretext for his assumption of power.

The Reichstag – and the legacy of the Wall

Built in the late nineteenth century to house the German parliament, the **Reichstag** today seems lost in a sea of irony. Inscribed with the words *Dem Deutschen Volke* (To the German People), the former symbol of national unity for years stood hard by the border that underlined its division. It's not difficult to imagine the scenes the building has witnessed; in November 1918 the German Republic was declared from a balcony here, while Karl Liebknecht was proclaiming a Socialist Republic in eastern Berlin – and cementing his and Rosa Luxemburg's fate. The Reichstag is currently undergoing major renovations to prepare it to house once again – and for the first time since 1933 – united Germany's parliament. The revamped building, its original interior completely gutted, will sport a new glass dome designed by British architect Sir Norman Foster. The new Reichstag will be not be open until at least 1999, but it's worth a visit to check out the progress, both of the building itself and the surrounding area, where a huge new government quarter is being created more or less from scratch.

Immediately behind the Reichstag, it's now only just possible to make out the course of the **Berlin Wall**, which for 28 years divided the city. To the right of the entrance, a series of plaques marks the names (where known) of those killed trying to swim to the West across the nearby River Spree. Erected overnight on August 13, 1961, to cordon off the Soviet sector and corral the British, American and French sectors of the city inside the GDR, the Wall underlined the city's schizophrenia and marked its *raison d'être* – the "stabilization of the impossible". Late in 1989 the East German government, spurred by *glasnost* and confronted by a tense domestic climate, realized it could keep the impossible stable no longer. Travel restrictions for East German citizens were lifted on November 9, 1989 – effectively, the Wall had ceased to matter, and pictures of Berliners East and West hacking away at the detested symbol filled newspapers and TV bulletins around the world. Now the Wall has vanished, and the few sections of it that remain are protected from tourist chisels by barbed wire and by its official status as an "historic landmark".

The Brandenburg Gate

Head south from the Reichstag by the edge of the Tiergarten and you follow the former course of the Wall down to the **Brandenburg Gate** (Brandenburger Tor), another Berlin building dense with meaning and historical associations. Originally built as a city gate-cum-triumphal arch in 1791 and modelled by its architect, Carl Gotthard Langhans, on the Propylaea in Athens, it became, like the Reichstag later, a symbol of German unity, looking out to the Siegessäule and guarding the leafy passage of Unter den Linden, the continuation of what is now Strasse des 17 Juni, in eastern Berlin. In 1806 Napoleon marched under the arch and took home with him the **Quadriga**, the horse-drawn chariot atop the Gate. It was returned a few years later, and the revolutionaries of 1848 and 1918 met under its gilded form. Later the Gate was a rallying point for Nazi torch-lit marches. After the building of the Wall placed the Gate in the Eastern sector, nearby observation posts became the place for visiting politicians to secure a handy photo-opportunity – the view was apparently emotive enough to reduce Margaret Thatcher to tears in 1987. With the opening of a border crossing here just before Christmas 1989, the East–West axis of the city was symbolically recreated and the post-Wall mood of eagerness for unification was strengthened. Yet, despite all the recent joy, it's easy enough to see why some, mindful of historical precedent, still view the Gate with a frisson of unease.

Walk through the Gate and you're in what used to be East Germany, with all the attractions of Unter den Linden lying before you (see p.778), but before continuing cross to the north side of Strasse des 17 Juni for a look at the **Sowjetisches Ehrenmal** (Soviet War Memorial) to the Red Army troops who died in the Battle of Berlin. Built from the marble of Hitler's destroyed Berlin HQ, the Reich's Chancellery, it's flanked by two tanks that were supposedly the first to reach the city.

THE WALL

After the war, Berlin was split between its conquerors, as Stalin, Roosevelt and Churchill had agreed at Yalta. Each sector was administered by the relevant country, and was supposed to exist peacefully with its neighbour under a unified city council. But almost from the outset, antagonism between the Soviet and other sectors was high. Only three years after the war ended the Soviet forces closed down the land access corridors to the city from the Federal Republic, in what became known as the **Berlin Blockade**. It was successfully overcome by a massive Western **airlift** of food and supplies that lasted nearly a year. This, followed by the 1953 uprising, large-scale cross-border emigration (between 1949 and 1961, the year the Wall was built, over 3 million East Germans fled to the Federal Republic – almost a fifth of the population) and innumerable "incidents", led to the building of what was known in the GDR as the "anti-Fascist protection wall".

When the four powers were deciding on sectors, one of the parish maps of Greater Berlin of 1920 was used to delineate them: the Wall followed the Soviet sector boundary implacably, cutting through houses, across squares and rivers with its own cool illogicality. One oddity about the Wall was that it was actually built a few metres inside GDR territory; the West Berlin authorities therefore had little control over the **graffiti** that covered it like a static New York subway car. The Wall was an ever-changing mixture of colours and slogans, with the occasional burst of bitterness: "*My friends are dying behind you*"; humour: "*Last one out please turn off the lights*"; "*Why not jump over and join the Party?*"; and stupidity: "*We shoulda nuked 'em in '45*".

Over the years, at least eighty people were **killed** endeavouring to cross the Wall. Initial escape attempts were straightforward and often successful – hollowing out furniture, ramming checkpoint barriers and simple disguise brought many people over. However, the authorities quickly rose to the challenge, and would-be escapees became more resourceful, digging tunnels, constructing gliders and one-man submarines, building their own hot-air balloons. By the time the Wall came down, every escape method conceivable seemed to have been used – even down to passing through Checkpoint Charlie in the stomach of a pantomime cow – and those who were desperate to get out of the GDR preferred the long wait and complications of applying to leave officially to the risk of being gunned down by a border guard. The guards, known as *Grepos*, were under instructions to shoot anyone attempting to scale the Wall, and to shoot accurately: any guard suspected of deliberately missing was court-martialled, and his family could expect severe harassment from the authorities.

When the end came, it happened so quickly that Berliners East and West seemed not to believe it, but within days of the announcement that citizens of the GDR were free to travel, enterprising characters were renting out hammers and chisels so that souvenir hunters could take home their own chip of the Wall. Today, especially in the city centre, it's often hard to tell exactly where the Wall ran: odd juxtapositions of dereliction against modernity, or an unexpected swathe of erstwhile "death strip" are in many cases all that's left of one of the most hated borders the world ever knew.

Around Potsdamer Platz

The stretch of land south of the Brandenburg Gate on the eastern edge of the Tiergarten is now the scene of the continent's largest construction site. **Potsdamer Platz** was once the heart of Berlin and a prewar hub of the city's transport and nightlife. It was made desolate by wartime bombing, and for fifty years after the war remained wasteland. The Berlin Wall wrapped around it and incorporated the once busy quarter into the death strip, ensuring that it would remain undeveloped.

When the Wall came down, Potsdamer Platz instantly became prime real estate. The city sold parcels to Mercedes-Benz and Sony (for a song, according to critics), who are now erecting immense corporate headquarters. The construction of this huge development has turned Potsdamer Platz into an unbelievable thicket of towering cranes, heavy machinery and scaffolding.

Proud of all this rebuilding, the city has erected a bright red information centre and viewing platform called the **Info Box** (Fri–Wed 9am–7pm, Thurs until 9pm; free) on the southern side of the site. The exhibition inside, basically an extensive advertisement that shows, with lots of big screens, computers and architectural models, how wonderful the area will be in the future, is not very interesting, but a trip to the **viewing platform** above (DM2) is worthwhile. From there you can see, in addition to the beehive of construction activity, the site of Hitler's bunker on the near side of the 1980s housing project on the eastern edge of the Platz. This is where the Führer spent his last days, issuing meaningless orders as the Battle of Berlin raged above. Here he married Eva Braun and wrote his final testament: he personally was responsible for nothing, he had been betrayed by the German people, who had proved unequal to his leadership and deserved the future he could now envisage ahead of them. On April 30, 1945, he shot himself, his body hurriedly burned by loyal officers. In the wrangles after the war to prove his death, the Soviet Army apparently came up with Hitler's teeth, which they had managed to retrieve from the charred remains and have verified by the Führer's dentist.

Soon the site of the bunker will be covered by office buildings, and the city, much to the relief of many, will have one less reminder of its sordid past.

South and east from Potsdamer Platz

Wending your way through the construction site and crossing south you come across one of the few remaining stretches of the **Berlin Wall**. Now protected from souvenir hunters, it's illegal to chip a bit off. Wall shards are rather hard to come by these days. Be warned that the pieces sold on the street by the Brandenburg Gate and Checkpoint Charlie are not authentic.

South and east of Potsdamer Platz, the woodland of the Tiergarten falls away and you enter a semi-desolate area that has never really recovered from 1945 devastation. A magnificently restored exception is the **Martin-Gropius-Bau** at Stresemannstr. 110 (Tues–Sun 10am–8pm; main collections DM6, though times and prices for temporary exhibitions vary; bus #248 or #341), now the city's main site for large, prestigious exhibitions. Also contained in the building are the main sections of the **Jüdisches Museum** (Tues–Sun 10am–8pm), with rotating exhibitions and large collections of German applied and fine art. Its small café is a useful stopping-off point and necessary pick-me-up before tackling an adjacent exhibition, **The Topography of Terror** (Tues–Sun 10am–6pm; free). This is housed in a newly built structure a little way from the Gropius-Bau, for nothing is left of the buildings that once stood here. Formerly known as Prinz-Albrecht-Strasse, Niederkirchenstrasse was the base of the Gestapo, the SS and Reich Security offices. In buildings along here Himmler planned the Final Solution, the deportation and genocide of European Jews, and organized the Gestapo, the feared secret police. The exhibition is housed in what were once the cellars of the Gestapo headquarters, where important prisoners were interrogated and tortured. Though the photos here tell their own story, you'll need the English translation (DM2) or the glossy guidebook (DM10) for the main text of the exhibits.

Checkpoint Charlie

The wasteland behind the Gropius-Bau is currently in the initial stages of redevelopment to provide new, larger facilities for the Topography of Terror museum. Until this opens there's nothing to detain you, and it's a ten-minute walk (or #129 bus ride) down Wilhelmstrasse and Kochstrasse to **Friedrichstrasse**, once one of the city's great streets, packed with cafés and shops, now a dusty avenue in the initial stages of revival. **Checkpoint Charlie**, an allied military post and one of Berlin's more celebrated landmarks, stood in Friedrichstrasse until July 1990, when it was declared redundant and removed, probably to be reassembled in a west German museum. The building lent its name informally to the adjacent GDR border crossing which, with its dramatic "YOU ARE NOW LEAVING THE AMERICAN SECTOR" signs and unsmiling border guards, used to be the archetypal movie-style Iron Curtain crossing.

Tangible evidence of the trauma the Wall caused is still on hand at the **Haus am Checkpoint Charlie** at Friedrichstr. 44 (daily 9am–10pm; DM7.50; nearest U-Bahn Kochstrasse or bus #129), which tells the history of the Wall in photos of escape tunnels, and with the converted cars and home-made aircraft by which people attempted, succeeded, and sometimes tragically failed to break through the border. Films document the stories of some of the eighty people killed by the East German border guards, and there's a section on human rights behind the Iron Curtain, but it's a scruffy, rather dated collection. For more details, pick up a copy of It Happened at the Wall or Berlin – from Frontline Town to the Bridge of Europe, both on sale here.

Walk a little down Kochstrasse and you'll see a high-rise building marked "**Axel Springer Verlag**". The late Axel Springer, extreme right-wing newspaper and publishing magnate (the newspaper Bild was his most notorious creation), deliberately had his offices built here, right next to the border, as an act of provocation towards the GDR authorities.

The Tiergarten Museum Complex

To the west of Potsdamer Platz, the **Tiergarten Complex** (also known as the Kulturforum) is a recently built mixture of museums and cultural forums that could easily fill several days. The jewel of the complex is the **Gemäldegalerie**, newly built to house a world-class collection of paintings until recently divided between museums in east and west Berlin. Bus #142 or #148 from the centre will bring you to the Tiergarten.

The Gemäldegalerie

The new **Gemäldegalerie** (Picture Gallery; Tues–Fri 9am–5pm; Sat & Sun 10am–5pm; DM8, concessions DM4, free first Sun of each month) houses a stupendous collection of early European paintings. Originally part of the prewar Kaiser-Friedrich-Museum, the paintings were stored in various places throughout the city for safekeeping during World War II, with the result that after the division of Berlin the collection was split between the Bode Museum in the east and the Dahlem museum complex in the west. As of summer 1998, some 900 paintings – reunited for the first time in 50 years – can be viewed in this new custom-built gallery.

Arranged in chronological order, and subdivided by region, the gallery covers the early medieval to late eighteenth-century periods, the section of early Netherlandish painting and later Dutch and Flemish works being the most authoritative.

The exhibitions begin on the north side of the building, past the rotunda, with **German paintings of the Middle Ages and Renaissance**. Here can be found the large and crude Passion Altar of 1437, made in the workshop of the great Ulm sculptor **Hans Multscher**, an ancient precursor of Expressionist painting. There's an interesting contrast with Solomon before the Queen of Sheba, painted in the same year by **Conrad Witz**, who was far more subtle in his aim of developing German painting away from its hitherto idealized forms.

These apart, the best works here are by **Altdorfer**, one of the first fully realized German landscape painters, and **Dürer** – a marvellous group of portraits. By **Holbein the Younger** are five superbly observed portraits, the most celebrated of which is The Danzig Merchant Georg Gisze – its still-life background is a real tour de force of artistic virtuosity. Among the many works by **Cranach** are the tongue-in-cheek The Fountain of Youth, where old women emerge from the miraculous bath as fresh young girls whereas the men are rejuvenated merely by association, and his free reinterpretation of Bosch's famous triptych The Garden of Earthly Delights.

Following the German medieval and Renaissance rooms are the **Netherlandish** sections, which reveal the contrast between German and Netherlandish treatments of religious subjects: almost always, the German works are darker and more crudely drawn. The sophistication and urbanity of the Netherlandish painters is brilliantly exemplified in the work of the artist credited with the creation of European realism, **Jan van Eyck**: his beautifully lit *Madonna in the Church* is crammed with architectural details. **Petrus Christus** may have been a pupil of Van Eyck, and certainly knew his work, as *The Virgin and Child with St Barbara and a Carthusian Monk* reveals: in the background are tiny Flemish houses and street scenes, the artist carefully locating the event in his native Bruges.

Also to be found are some works of **Rogier van der Weyden**, which show the development of the Eyckian technique to a warmer, much more emotional treatment of religious subjects in works like his *Bladelin Altarpiece*. Two other major paintings nearby are both by **Hugo van der Goes**: The *Adoration of the Shepherds* (painted when the artist was in the first throes of madness) and *The Adoration of the Magi* – also known as the *Monforte Altarpiece*. The collection then moves into the sixteenth century and the works of Jan Gossaert, Quentin Massys and **Pieter Brueghel the Elder**, whose *Netherlandish Proverbs* is an amusing, if hard-to-grasp, illustration of over a hundred sixteenth-century proverbs and maxims.

The next section reveals the gallery's second strength, its **Dutch** and **Flemish** collections. This contains large portraits by **Van Dyck** and the fleshy canvases of **Rubens**, as well as a fine group of Dutch interiors. The paintings of **Vermeer** are the most easily identifiable: *Man and Woman Drinking Wine* uses his usual technique of placing furniture obliquely in the centre of the canvas, the scene illuminated by window light. Other rooms trace the development of Dutch art through the works of Maes, Terborch, Dou, Jan Steen and Frans Hals.

The high point of this section, hung in a large octagonal room, are the paintings of **Rembrandt**, perhaps the largest collection of his work in the world. Recently, his most famous picture here, *The Man in the Golden Helmet*, was proved to be the work of his studio rather than the artist himself, though this does little to detract from the elegance and power of the portrait. Following this room are paintings of French artists, and English portraits of the eighteenth century.

The galleries on the museum's southern side contain Italian painting, beginning with the **Italian Renaissance** and concluding with Venetian painters of the eighteenth century. This collection is particularly strong on works from the Florentine Renaissance: **Fra Filippo Lippi**'s *The Adoration in the Forest* is rightly one of the most admired of all the paintings of the period. Another much-prized work is the gorgeously colourful *Adoration of the Magi* by the rarely seen **Domenico Veneziano**, which perfectly captures the full regal splendour of the subject. There's work here, too, by Giotto, Correggio, Verrocchio, Masaccio. Mantegna, Raphael and Titian, and, most importantly by **Botticelli**, whose *Virgin and Child with the Two St Johns, Portrait of a Young Woman* and *St Sebastian* are among the highlights of this section.

Other noteworthy painters to be found in the museum include Goya, Caravaggio (*Cupid Victorious*, heavy with symbolism and homo-eroticism), Poussin (the important *Self-Portrait)*, Claude and Canaletto.

The Kupferstichkabinett and the Staatsbibliothek

Next door to the Gemäldegalerie is the **Kupferstichkabinett** (Engravings Cabinet; Tues–Fri 9am–5pm, Sat & Sun 10am–5pm; DM4, free first Sun of each month), displaying its holdings – which include drawings and watercolours as well as all types of graphic work – in a series of rotating exhibitions. The reunion of the two parts of the collection has been of particular significance with regard to its most celebrated possession, Botticelli's illustrated version of Dante's *Divine Comedy*. During the years of partition,

27 of the drawings were held in Dahlem in the west, 57 on Museumsinsel in the east, with political considerations making it impossible to exhibit them together.

The **Staatsbibliothek** (Mon–Fri 9am–9pm, Sat 9am–5pm; free access), across Potsdamer Strasse from the other buildings, has over three and a half million books, occasional exhibitions, a small concert hall, a cheapish café and a wide selection of British newspapers. The final building to be designed by Hans Scharoun, the *Staabi*'s most recent claim to fame came when it was used as an important backdrop in Wim Wenders' poetic film elegy to the city, *Wings of Desire*.

The Neue Nationalgalerie

Far and away the finest building in the Tiergarten is the **Neue Nationalgalerie**, Potsdamer Str. 50 (Tues–Fri 9am–5pm, Sat & Sun 10am–5pm; DM4, free first Sun of each month), a black-rimmed glass box that seems almost suspended above the ground, its clarity of line and detail having all the intelligent simplicity of the Parthenon. Designed by Mies van der Rohe in 1965, the upper section is used for temporary exhibits, often of contemporary art, while the underground galleries contain paintings from the beginning of the twentieth century onwards. Many, though by no means all, of the works are German, including portraits and Berlin cityscapes of **Grosz** and **Dix**. **Kirchner** spent time in Berlin before World War I, and his *Potsdamer Platz* dates from 1914. A good cross-section of work by other Expressionists is also featured. There's also work by Miró, Karel Appel, Jasper Johns and Francis Bacon: a fine, easily assimilated collection.

The Philharmonie and around

North of the Nationalgalerie the **Matthäikirche** stands in lonely isolation on a blitzed landscape that now forms a car park for the **Philharmonie**, home of the Berlin Philharmonic, and until he retired and subsequently died in 1989, its renowned conductor Herbert von Karajan. Looking at the gold-clad ugliness of the building, designed in the 1960s by Hans Scharoun, it's easy to see how it got its nickname among Berliners of "Karajan's circus". Should you wish to reserve a ticket, the box office is open Monday to Friday from 3.30 to 6pm, Saturday and Sunday 11am to 2pm (☎254880 or 2548 8132). The chances of getting a seat for major concerts under the orchestra's present conductor, Claudio Abbado, are slim unless you've booked months in advance, but it's worth trying your luck for other performances under guest conductors.

Continuing the musical theme, the **Musikinstrumenten Museum** (Tues–Fri 9am–5pm, Sat & Sun 10am–5pm; DM4, free first Sun of each month) at Tiergartenstr. 1, just below the Philharmonie, comes as something of a disappointment. Its collection of (mostly European) keyboards, wind and string instruments from the fifteenth century to the present day is comprehensive and impressively laid out, and the pre-recorded tapes give a taste of the weird and wonderful sounds the instruments make.

The **Kunstgewerbemuseum** (Museum of Applied Arts; Tues–Fri 9am–5pm, Sat & Sun 10am–5pm; DM4, free first Sun of each month), at Matthäikirchplatz 10, is an encyclopedic but seldom dull collection of European arts and crafts. The top floor contains wonderful Renaissance, Baroque and Rococo silver and ceramics, along with Jugendstil and Art Deco objects, particularly furniture. The first floor holds the Middle Ages to Early Renaissance collections, with some sumptuous gold pieces. The highlights, though, are Lüneburg's municipal silver and the treasures of churches such as Braunschweig's Dom, Basel's Münster and Enger's Stiftskirche. In the basement is a small but great assembly of Bauhaus furniture and a display of the evolution of product design.

Kreuzberg

The area directly south and east of the Martin-Gropius-Bau is **Kreuzberg**, famed for its large immigrant community and self-styled "alternative" inhabitants, nightlife and goings-on. Effectively there are two Kreuzbergs: the **west**, the area bounded by Friedrichstrasse, Viktoriapark and Südstern, is a richer, fancier, more sedate neighbour than the **east**, which is still sometimes referred to as SO 36 after its old postal code. East Kreuzberg is western Berlin's "happening" quarter, a mix of punks and old hippies, and the place to hang out and hit the really raucous nightspots, names like *Trash* and *Bronx* giving you an idea of the atmosphere. Though there's precious little in the way of things to see, it is, in many ways, the city's liveliest neighbourhood – however, the new "in" areas around Öranienburger Strasse (see p.787) are vying for the title.

West Kreuzberg

It's only a short walk south, cutting down Stresemannstrasse, from the Gropius-Bau to the remains of the **Anhalter Bahnhof**, a sad reminder of misguided civic action that some would term civic vandalism. The Anhalter Bahnhof was once one of the city's (and Europe's) great rail termini, forming Berlin's gateway to the south. Completed in 1870, it received only mild damage during the war and was left roofless but substantial in 1945. Despite attempts to preserve it as a future museum building, it was blown up in 1952 – essentially because someone had put in a good offer for the bricks. Now only a fragment of the facade stands, giving a hint at past glories. The patch of land that the station once covered is today a park, and, though there's nothing to see save the paths of the old rail tracks at the far end, it's an oddly atmospheric spot.

A brisk walk east from here, through streets levelled during wartime bombing, takes you to another Kreuzberg high spot, the **Berlin-Museum** at Lindenstr. 14, which attempts to show the history and development of the city through paintings, prints and crafts. However, the museum will unfortunately be closed until 1998 for major work. Its best exhibits are from this century, particularly the collections of wartime posters and kids' toys, and Klaus Richter's portraits of Hitler and Göring. Next door, a striking, aluminium-clad annexe by post-modernist Daniel Libeskind is being built to hold the **Jüdisches Museum** (Jewish Museum). Slated to open at the end of 1998, the museum will chronicle the history and destruction of Berlin's once vibrant Jewish community. Until then, temporary exhibitions at the Martin-Gropius-Bau (see p.766) reveal some of the city's Judaica holdings. More whimsically – and the reason most people come here – there's a mock-up of an old Berlin bar, the *Alt-Berliner Weissbierstube*, which serves a traditional Berlin buffet – distinguished by being very heavy on pork – washed down with pale beer. You'll have to wait until late 1998 to enjoy it, though – it will reopen at the same time as the Berlin-Museum.

An alternative and easier approach to the area is to catch the U-Bahn to Möckernbrücke station on line #1, an enjoyable above-ground ride through old warehouses and towering postwar redevelopment. A little further on, at Trebbiner Str. 9, is the **Deutsches Technikmuseum Berlin** (German Technology Museum; Tues–Fri 9am–5.30pm, Sat & Sun 10am–6pm; DM5; bus #129 and #248), one of the city's most entertaining museums and a button-pushers' and kids' delight. The technology section has plenty of experiments, antiquated machinery and computers to play with, alongside some elegant old cars and planes. The transport museum, a collection of ancient steam trains and carriages, is even more impressive, the polished behemoths brought to rest in what was once a workshop of the old Anhalter Bahnhof.

Reaching the **Viktoriapark** (the "Kreuzberg", as it's popularly known) from here means a half-hour's walk, retracing your steps to the U-Bahn and heading south down Grossbeerenstrasse. On the slopes of a hill, the park is one of the city's most likeable, a relaxed ramble of trees and green space with a pretty brook running down the middle, and on summer afternoons there's no better place to stretch out and relax. To one side is the *Golgotha Café* and disco, packed on summer evenings. On another side is what claims to be Germany's northernmost vineyard; and atop the hill is the **Befreiungsdenkmal** (a neo-Gothic cross) from which Kreuzberg gets its name, designed by Schinkel to commemorate the Napoleonic Wars. The view is a good one, too, made all the more pleasant by the wafting aromas from the *Schultheiss* brewery on the southern slopes. The well-restored streets that side the hill, along with Yorckstrasse to the north, have a scattering of sedate cafés. Between Hagelbergerstrasse and Yorckstrasse, **Riehmer's Hofgarten** is an impressive turn-of-the-century bourgeois residential block, though the modern steel and glass Yorck cinema doesn't fit well in the ensemble.

South and east of the Viktoriapark, the housing fades away to the flatlands containing **Tempelhof Airport**. Much enlarged by the Nazis (it was once the world's largest airport), it's still possible to see the Nazi eagles that decorate the buildings. Today it's used mainly for short-haul domestic flights, after 40 years as a US air base. It was here that the Allies flew in supplies to beat the Berlin Blockade of 1948 to 1949 – an act that was to strengthen anti-Soviet feeling among West Berliners and increase the popularity of the occupying forces. At the height of the fifteen-month airlift a plane landed every minute, and the **Luftbrückendenkmal**, a memorial at the entrance to the airport symbolizing the three air corridors used, commemorates the seventy airmen and eight ground crew who died in crashes while attempting to land. The memorial represents half a bridge: the other half, "joined by air", is in Frankfurt.

East Kreuzberg: "SO 36"

Despite its reputation as a hotbed of radical protest and alternative lifestyles (a leftover from the days when West Germany's disaffected youth came to Berlin, since those living in the city were exempt from military service), you don't need any interest in revolution or city machinations to enjoy the eastern part of Kreuzberg. The **nightlife** here is among the city's wildest, and it's an enjoyable area to wander through by day, stopping off at one of the innumerable Turkish snack bars for a kebab, breakfasting on a 9am vodka-and-beer special at a café, or just taking in the feel of the place – which is much like an Istanbul market in an Eastern bloc housing development.

Catching U-Bahn line #1 to **Kottbusser Tor** or **Schlesisches Tor** stations is a good introduction to Kreuzberg. The area around Kottbusser Tor is typical: a scruffy, earthy shambles of Turkish street vendors and cafés. Cutting through Dresdener Strasse, past the Babylon cinema, takes you to Kreuzberg's main strip, **Oranienstrasse**, which from Moritzplatz east is lined with café-bars, art galleries and clothes shops, and in a way forms an "alternative" Kurfürstendamm. Stop off at any of the bars along here for a taste of what the locals call a *Szene* place – somewhere that's in and happening.

The Landwehrkanal runs south of Oranienstrasse, and below that the broad path of Hasenheide-Gneisenaustrasse marks the transition from east to west Kreuzberg. Around the Südstern (which has a convenient U-Bahn station) is another clutch of café-bars, and Gneisenaustrasse has some good restaurants; but the flavour of east Kreuzberg has gone, and things feel (and are) a lot tamer.

Schöneberg and around

Like Kreuzberg, **Schöneberg** was once a separate suburb, one that was swallowed up by Greater Berlin as the city expanded in the late eighteenth and nineteenth centuries. Blown to pieces during the war, it's now a mostly middle-class residential area, stretching below the Tiergarten and sandwiched between Kreuzberg to the east and Wilmersdorf to the west. Things to see are few, but what is here is both fascinating and moving.

Schöneberg officially begins south of Kurfürstenstrasse, but just north of the Landwehrkanal, on the edge of Tiergarten at Klingelhöferstr. 13–14, is the **Bauhaus-Archiv** (10am–5pm; closed Tues; DM5, free Mon; bus #129 to Lützowplatz). The Bauhaus school of design, crafts and architecture was founded in 1919 in Weimar (see p.879) by Walter Gropius. It moved to Dessau in 1925 (see p.859) and then to Berlin, to be closed by the Nazis in 1933. The influence of Bauhaus has been tremendous, and you get some idea of this in the small collection here. There's work too by Kandinsky, Moholy-Nagy, Schlemmer and Klee, each of whom worked at the Bauhaus. The building, incidentally, was designed by Gropius himself.

Around Nollendorfplatz

Back in the middle of Potsdamer Strasse, it's a short detour west to **Nollendorfplatz** which, on its southern side, holds the proto-Deco **Metropol disco** (see p.797). Nearby, at Nollendorfstr. 17, is the building in which **Christopher Isherwood** lived during his years in prewar Berlin, a time that was to be elegantly recounted in perhaps the most famous collection of stories about the city ever written – *Goodbye to Berlin*.

Schöneberg has since been reborn as a fancy, even chic neighbourhood; the would-be Isherwoods of the moment hang out in East Kreuzberg, or more likely, in Prenzlauer Berg in eastern Berlin. At night, this part of Schöneberg, particularly the area around **Winterfeldtplatz**, is a good one for eating and especially drinking: tidily bohemian, less sniffy than Savignyplatz, and much more middle-of-the-road than East Kreuzberg. On Wednesday and Saturday mornings the square holds an excellent general **market**.

Rathaus Schöneberg

Schöneberg's most famous attraction actually has the least to see: the **Rathaus Schöneberg** on Martin-Luther-Strasse, the penultimate stop on U-Bahn line #4. Built just before World War I, the Rathaus became the seat of the West Berlin parliament and senate after the last war, and it was outside here in 1963 that **John F. Kennedy** made his celebrated "Ich bin ein Berliner" speech on the Cold War political situation, just a few months after the Cuban missile crisis. What the president didn't realize as he read from his phonetically written text was that he had actually said "I am a doughnut", since *Berliner* is the name given in west Germany to those cakes. ("Ich bin Berliner" would have expressed his meaning more idiomatically.) So popular has this subtext become that the city's souvenir shops sell little plastic doughnuts bearing the historic words. The day after Kennedy was assassinated, the square in front of the Rathaus was given his name – a move apparently instigated by the city's students, among whom the president was highly popular.

If you've time and interest you can climb the Rathaus tower (Mon–Fri 8am–4pm) and see the replica **Liberty bell** donated to the city by the US in 1950, though it's more pleasant, and certainly less strenuous, to take a stroll in the small **Volkspark**, a thin ribbon of greenery that runs west from here.

Charlottenburg: the Schloss and museums

The district of **Charlottenburg** stretches north and west of the centre of town, reaching as far as the forests of the Grunewald. To the west it contains a number of things worth seeing (see p.777), but far and away the most significant target, one that needs a day at least to cover, is the **Schloss Charlottenburg and Museum complex** on Spandauer Damm. The buses which run nearest are #110 and #145; the closest U-Bahn station is Richard-Wagner-Platz.

Schloss Charlottenburg

Schloss Charlottenburg (Tues–Fri 9am–5pm, Sat & Sun 10am–5pm) comes as a surprise after the unrelieved modernity of the city streets. Commissioned as a country house by the future Queen Sophie Charlotte in 1695 (she also gave her name to the district), the Schloss was expanded and added to throughout the eighteenth and early nineteenth centuries to provide a summer residence for the Prussian kings, the master builder Karl Friedrich Schinkel providing the final touches. Approaching the sandy elaborateness of the Schloss at the main courtyard, you're confronted with Andreas Schlüter's **statue of Friedrich Wilhelm**, the Great Elector, cast as a single piece in 1700. To see the Schloss's central section, which includes the restored residential quarters, you're obliged to go on the conducted tour that's in German only, which makes it worth buying the detailed (English) guidebook before you start. The tour is a traipse through increasingly sumptuous chambers and bedrooms, filled with gilt and carving. Most eye-catching are the **Porzellanzimmer**, packed to the ceiling with china, and the **chapel**, which includes a portrait of Sophie Charlotte as the Virgin ascending to heaven.

It's just as well to remember that much of the Schloss is in fact a fake, a reconstruction of the former buildings following wartime damage. This is most apparent in the **Knobelsdorff-Flügel**, to the right of the Schloss entrance as you face it; the upper rooms, such as the Rococo *Goldene Galerie* are too breathlessly perfect, the result of intensive restoration. Better is the adjacent *Weisser Saal*, whose destroyed eighteenth-century ceiling painting has been replaced by a witty contemporary paraphrase. Next door, the *Konzertzimmer* contains a superb collection of works by **Watteau**, including two of his greatest paintings, *The Embarcation for Cythera* and *The Shop Sign*.

Galerie der Romantik and Museum für Vor- und Frühgeschichte

Downstairs, the Knobelsdorff Wing currently contains the **Galerie der Romantik** (same hours as the Schloss; DM4, free first Sun of each month), a collection of nineteenth-century paintings from the German Romantic masters, and the Classical and Biedermeier movements, that will eventually be transplanted to a planned extension of the Neue Nationalgalerie in the Tiergarten. Most dramatic are the works of **Caspar David Friedrich**, all of which express a powerful elemental and religious approach to landscape, particularly *Morning in the Riesengebirge* and *The Watzmann*.

This room also contains works by **Karl Friedrich Schinkel**, the architect responsible for the war memorial in Kreuzberg and, more notably, the Neoclassical designs of the Altes Museum and many other buildings standing today in eastern Berlin. His paintings are meticulously drawn Gothic fantasies, often with sea settings. *Gothic Church on a Seaside Bluff* is the most moodily dramatic. Look out for the topographical paintings of **Eduard Gaertner**, which show the Berlin of the early nineteenth century and reveal just how good a restoration job has been made of Unter den Linden.

The western wing of the Schloss once sided an **Orangerie** (much depleted after the war) and the gallery there now houses major exhibitions. Also in the west wing is the **Museum für Vor- und Frühgeschichte** (Museum of Pre- and Early History; same hours as the Schloss; DM4, free first Sun of each month), an odd collection mixing archeological finds from the Berlin area with excavations from the Near East including copies of the famous treasures from Troy which vanished in World War II and recently turned up in Russia.

The gardens

If this isn't to your taste, there are few better ways to idle away a morning in Berlin than to explore the **Schloss Gardens** (open daily, till 9pm in summer). Laid out in the French style in 1697, the gardens were transformed into an English-style landscaped park in the early nineteenth century; after severe damage in the war, they were mostly restored to their Baroque form. Right beside the eastern end of the Schloss is the **Schinkel-Pavillon**, an Italianate villa built by Schinkel as a retreat for King Friedrich Wilhelm III. Inside are a number of paintings and drawings by the great architect plus Gaertner's most spectacular composition, the hexagonal *Panorama from the Friedrichswerdersche Kirche*, showing Berlin at its most salubrious. Towards the north-eastern corner of the park is the **Belvedere** (same hours and entrance), a tea house designed by Carl Gotthard Langhans of Brandenburg Gate fame, now containing a museum of Berlin porcelain. On the western side of the gardens a long, tree-lined avenue leads to the hushed and shadowy **Mausoleum** (April–Oct Tues–Fri 10am–5pm) where Friedrich Wilhelm III is buried alongside his queen, Luise, his sarcophagus making him seem a good deal younger than his seventy years. Later burials here include Kaiser Wilhelm I, looking every inch a Prussian king.

Ägyptisches Museum and Sammlung Berggruen

Though you could spend an idle morning wandering around the Schloss and its gardens, just across the way a group of excellent museums beckons. Best of these is the **Ägyptisches Museum** at Schloss Str. 70 (Tues–Fri 9am–5pm, Sat & Sun 10am–5pm; DM8, free first Sun of each month), the result of innumerable German excavations in Egypt from the early part of the century. The museum's pride and joy is the *Bust of Nefertiti* on the ground floor, a treasure that has become a symbol for the city as a cultural capital. There's no questioning its beauty – the queen has a perfect bone structure and gracefully sculpted lips – and the history of the piece is equally interesting. Created around 1350 BC, the bust probably never left the studio in Akhetaten in which it was housed, acting as a model for other portraits of the queen (its use as a model explains why the left eye was never drawn in). When the studio was deserted, the bust was left there, to be discovered some 3000 years later in 1912. Elsewhere in the museum, atmospheric lighting focuses attention on the exhibits, which are of a uniformly high standard. Look out for the expressionistic, almost futuristic *Berlin Green Head* of the Ptolemaic period, and the *Kalabsha Monumental Gate*, given by the Egyptian government in 1973.

Across Schloss Strasse is the recently opened **Sammlung Berggruen** (Berggruen collection; same hours; DM8, free first Sun of each month). This small but outstanding collection – some 70 works in all – focuses on the development of modern art from Cézanne through Picasso, Klee and Giacometti to the present day. Just south, the **Bröhan-Museum** (Tues–Sun 10am–6pm; DM5) houses a great collection of Art Deco and Jugendstil ceramics and furniture, laid out in period rooms dedicated to a particular designer and hung with contemporary paintings.

Continuing westwards, Charlottenburg breaks out into open country and forest, with the Olympic stadium and tower the main draws (see p.776).

The western suburbs

While there's more than enough to detain you in the centre, the western **suburbs** hold a disparate group of attractions of considerable historical interest. Once you're out of the claustrophobic city, the verdant countryside and lakes come as a surprise, a reminder of Berlin's position in *Mitteleuropa* – and of the fact that one third of the city is greenery and parkland. Thanks to the efficient U- and S-Bahn system it's possible to reach Berlin's western edges in under three-quarters of an hour.

Dahlem: The Museum Complex

The suburb of **Dahlem** lies to the southwest of central Berlin in the district of Zehlendorf, a neat village-like enclave that feels a world away from the techno-flash city centre. Mostly residential, it's home to the Free University, the better-off bourgeoisie and a group of museums that are among the best in Europe. Housed in a large building, the **Museen Dahlem** (Tues–Fri 9am–5pm, Sat & Sun 10am–5pm; DM4, free first Sun of each month) can be overpowering if you try and do too much too quickly and it's well worth a couple of trips out here. The **ethnographic sections** are worth a visit in their own right: rich and extensive collections from Asia, and the Pacific and South Sea islands of Melanesia and Polynesia, imaginatively and strikingly laid out. In particular, look out for the group of sailing boats from the South Sea Islands, dramatically lit and eminently touchable. Other collections within the museum include **Islamic**, **Asian**, **East Asian** and **Indian art**. The last includes one of the most valuable treasures in Berlin – a sensational collection of fifth- to eleventh-century **Buddhist cave paintings** from the Silk Road trade route. To reach the museums, take U-Bahn line #1 to Dahlem-Dorf and follow the signs; the main block is on Arnimallee.

The Gedenkstätte Plötzensee

Berlin sometimes has the feel of a city that has tried, unsuccessfully, to sweep its past under the carpet of the present. When concrete reminders of the Third Reich can be seen, their presence in today's postwar city becomes all the more powerful. Nowhere is this more true than in the buildings where the Nazi powers brought dissidents and political opponents for imprisonment and execution – the **Gedenkstätte Plötzensee** (Plötzensee Prison Memorial; March–Sept 8am–6pm; Oct & Feb 8.30am–5.30pm; Nov & Jan 8.30am–4.30pm; Dec 8.30am–4pm; free).

Plötzensee stands in the northwest of the city, on the border between the boroughs of Charlottenburg and Wedding. To get there, take bus #123 from Tiergarten S-Bahn station to the beginning of Saatwinkler Damm (ask for the "Gedenkstätte Plötzensee" stop) and walk away from the canal along the wall-sided path of Hüttigpfad.

The former prison buildings have now been refurbished as a juvenile detention centre, and the memorial consists of the buildings where the **executions** took place. Over 2500 people were hanged or guillotined here between 1933 and 1945, usually those sentenced in the Supreme Court of Justice in the city. Following the July Bomb Plot, 89 of the 200 people condemned were executed here in the space of a few days: Hitler ordered the hangings to be carried out with piano wire, so that the victims would slowly strangle rather than die from broken necks. Each execution was recorded on film and subsequently screened in the Reich's Chancellery. Many of those murdered were only vaguely connected to the conspirators; several died simply because they were relatives. Today the execution chamber has been restored to its wartime condition: on occasion, victims were hanged eight at a time, and the hanging beam, complete with hooks, still stands. Though decked with wreaths and flowers, the atmosphere in the chamber is chilling, and as a further reminder of Nazi atrocities an urn in the courtyard contains soil from each of the concentration camps.

The Funkturm, Olympia-Stadion and beyond

Reaching the **Funkturm**, the skeletal transmission mast that lies to the west of Charlottenburg, is an easy matter of catching U-Bahn line #2 to Kaiserdamm, or bus #149, or #219 from Zoo Station. Since being built in 1928 as a radio and TV transmitter, it has been popular with Berliners for the toe-curling views from its 138-metre observation platform (daily 10am–11pm; DM6). With the aluminium-clad monolith of the **Internationales Congress Centrum** immediately below, it's possible to look out across newly restored S-Bahn tracks to the gleaming city in the distance – a sight equally mesmerizing at night.

The **Deutsches Rundfunk-Museum** (German Museum of Radio and Broadcasting; 10am–5pm, closed Tues; DM3) is housed in a former studio to one side of the tower. Tracing the development of radios, record players and televisions from the beginning of broadcasting in Germany in 1923 until World War II, it's as much a history of design as technology, made all the more entertaining by a scattering of period rooms and a mock-up of the first-ever German radio studio.

To reach the Olympia-Stadion from here, catch the #2 U-Bahn three stops westwards to the station of the same name. From there, it's a fifteen-minute signposted walk to the stadium itself.

The Olympia-Stadion

Built for the 1936 Olympic Games, the **Olympia-Stadion** (9am–sunset; DM1) is one of the few Nazi buildings left intact in the city, and remains very much in use. Whatever your feelings about it, it's still impressive, the huge Neoclassical space a deliberate rejection of the modernist architecture then prevalent elsewhere.

If you cut south and west around the stadium, down the road named after Jesse Owens, and take a right onto Passenheimer Strasse, you reach the **Glockenturm** or bell tower (daily April–Oct 9am–6pm; DM4). Rebuilt after wartime damage, it's chiefly interesting for the stupendous **view** it gives, not only over the stadium but also north to the natural amphitheatre that forms the **Waldbühne**, an open-air concert site (see p.797), and across the beginnings of the Grunewald to the south. Central here is **Teufelsberg** (Devil's Mountain), a massive mound that's topped with a faintly terrifying fairy-tale castle that was formerly a US signals and radar base. The mountain itself is artificial: at the end of the war, the mass of debris that was once Berlin was carted to several sites around the city. Beneath the poplars, maples and ski runs lies the old Berlin, about 25 million cubic metres of it, presumably awaiting the attention of some future archeologist. In the meantime, it's popular as a place for weekend kite flying, and skiing and tobogganing in winter.

THE 1936 OLYMPICS

Hitler used the international attention the **1936 Olympics** attracted to show the "New Order" in Germany in the best possible light. Anti-Semitic propaganda and posters were suppressed in the city, German half-Jewish athletes were allowed to compete, and when the Olympic flame was relayed from Athens, the newsreels and the world saw the road lined with thousands wearing swastikas and waving Nazi flags. To the outside world, it seemed that the new Germany was rich, content and firmly behind the Führer.

Though the Games themselves were stage-managed with considerable brilliance – a fact recorded in Leni Riefenstahl's poetic and frighteningly beautiful film of the events, *Olympia* – not everything went according to official National Socialist doctrine. Black American athletes did supremely well in the games, **Jesse Owens** alone winning four gold medals, disproving the Nazi theory that blacks were "subhuman" and the Aryan race all-powerful. But eventually Germany won the most gold, silver and bronze medals (there's a memorial at the western end of the stadium), and the games were deemed a great success.

Spandau

Spandau, situated on the confluence of the Spree and Havel rivers, about 10km as the crow flies northwest of the city centre, is Berlin's oldest suburb – it was granted a town charter in 1232, and managed to escape the worst of the wartime bombing, preserving its ancient moated fort, the Zitadelle. But the word Spandau immediately brings to mind the name of its jail's most famous – indeed in later years only – prisoner, **Rudolf Hess**, Hitler's former deputy who flew to Scotland in 1941 on a bizarre peace mission, and who hanged himself here in 1989.

However, there's little connection between Hess and Spandau itself. The jail, 3km away on Wilhelmstrasse, was demolished shortly after Hess died to make way for a supermarket for the British armed forces, and the chief reason to come here today is to escape the city centre, wander Spandau's village-like streets, and to visit the explorable, if not totally engrossing, **Zitadelle** at Strasse am Juliusturm (Tues–Fri 9am–5pm, Sat & Sun 10am–5pm; DM1.50), a fort established in the twelfth century to defend the town. The Zitadelle has a small *Heimatmuseum*, a pricey *bürgerlich* restaurant and the **Juliusturm**, from which there's a good view over the ramshackle Zitadelle interior and the surrounding countryside. If nothing else, it's a pleasant spot to picnic away a hot summer's day.

Other than this, **Spandau town**, a ten-minute walk from here, is of minor interest, at its best around its church (where there's a good *Konditorei*), in the playful sculptures of its modern marketplace, and in the recently restored street called **Kolk** (turn right off Am Juliusturm opposite Breite Strasse). To get to Spandau from the city centre, take U-Bahn line #7 to the Zitadelle station – or to Altstadt Spandau station then doubling back to the Zitadelle, or bus #133. It's also possible to catch **boats** from Spandau to Tegel, Wannsee and elsewhere; see below for details.

The Grunewald, Havel and Wannsee

Few people associate Berlin with walks through dense woodland or swimming from crowded beaches, though that's just what the **Grunewald** forests and beaches on the **Havel** lakes have to offer. The Grunewald is 32 square kilometres of mixed woodland that lies between the suburbs of Dahlem and Wilmersdorf and the Havel lakes to the west; it's popular with Berliners for its bracing air and walks. Seventy percent of the Grunewald was cut down in the postwar years for fuel, and subsequent replanting has replaced pine and birch with oak and ash, making it all the more popular.

One possible starting point is the **Jagdschloss Grunewald** (May 10–Oct 12 Tues–Sun 10am–5pm; Oct 13–May 9 Sat & Sun only 10am–4pm; DM2.50), a royal hunting lodge built in the sixteenth century and enlarged by Friedrichs I and II. Today it's a museum, housing old furniture and Dutch and German painting, including works by Cranach the Elder and Rubens. To reach the Jagdschloss, take bus #115 from Fehrbelliner Platz U-Bahn to the stop at Pücklerstrasse and head west down that street into the forest. Near the Pücklerstrasse stop, you'll find the **Brücke-Museum** at Bussardsteig 9 (11am–5pm; closed Tues; DM7), a collection of works by the group known as *Die Brücke* ("The Bridge") who worked in Dresden and Berlin from 1905 to 1913, and whose work was later banned by the Nazis. The big names are Kirchner, Heckel and Schmidt-Rottluff, who painted Expressionist cityscapes and had considerable influence over later artists.

An alternative approach to the Grunewald, and with the added attraction of beginning at a strip of **beaches**, is to take the #1 or #3 S-Bahn to Nikolasee station from where it's a ten-minute walk or a quick bus ride to **Strandbad Wannsee**, a kilometre-long strip of pale sand that's the largest inland beach in Europe, and one that's packed as soon as the sun comes out. From here it's easy to wander into the forests, or, more adventurously, catch one of several **ferries** that leave a little way from the S-Bahn station (ask there for directions). It's possible to sail to Potsdam, Spandau, Kladow, across the lake (your S-Bahn ticket is valid; otherwise DM3.60) or to the **Pfaueninsel** (Peacock Island; daily April & Sept 8am–6pm; May–Aug 8am–8pm; March & Oct 9am–5pm; Nov–Feb 10am–4pm; ferry DM2), whose attractions include a picturesque folly of a **Schloss** (guided tours April–Sept Tues–Sun 10am–5pm; Oct Tues–Sun

10am–4pm; DM4). No cars are allowed on the island (nor are dogs, ghetto-blasters or smoking), which has been designated a conservation zone and is home to a flock of peacocks.

Eastern Berlin

It's no surprise that, despite the rapid pace of change since reunification, the **eastern part of Berlin** retains a distinct identity. For nearly 41 years it was the official capital of the German Democratic Republic, one of eastern Europe's staunchest Communist regimes, suffering from a badly decayed infrastructure and an economy that was virtually closed down. Yet, in many ways this part of the city, encompassing the district of Mitte, *is* Berlin, home of its historic heart. It was the showpiece of Hohenzollern Berlin, capital of Brandenburg-Prussia and later the German Empire, and today the area is the site of Berlin's most imposing monuments.

East Berlin developed along very different lines from West Berlin. After the war, as American aid flooded into West Berlin, the East Berliners watched the Russians dismantle and ship east practically everything that was still in working order – even whole factories. Despite this they managed to rebuild their skeletal city with little outside help, preserving much more of its historic identity than did their counterparts in West Berlin.

The most atmospheric approach to eastern Berlin starts under the city's most celebrated symbol, the **Brandenburg Gate** (see p.764), and leads up the stately boulevard of **Unter den Linden** to the **Museumsinsel**, island home to eastern Berlin's leading museums. However, to gain a true impression of this part of the city, it's important to get away from the well-trodden sight-seeing routes and head for the outlying parts such as **Prenzlauer Berg** or **Oranienburger Strasse**, at the heart of Berlin's former Jewish quarter, which have become the centre of a vibrant nightlife and arts scene.

Unter den Linden

The **Unter den Linden** is Berlin's grandest boulevard, rolling east from the Brandenburg Gate towards Alexanderplatz. Once the main east–west axis of Imperial Berlin and site of many of the city's foreign embassies, Unter den Linden, meaning "beneath the lime trees", was named after the lime trees that line its central island. The present generation of trees dates from the period of postwar planting. During the GDR era it was effectively a grandiose blind alley cut off from Charlottenburger Chaussee (today Strasse des 17 Juni), its prewar continuation leading to the city's west end, by the sterile white concrete of the Berlin Wall. Since 1989, however, Unter den Linden has been revitalized, reassuming its role as one of the city's most important streets. Expensive stores have opened and strolling tourists compete for pavement space with business people and civil servants from the various Federal ministries that have opened here in preparation for the full transfer of government from Bonn, scheduled for completion early next century. A few hundred metres beyond the Brandenburg Gate is the Friedrichstrasse intersection. Before the war this was one of the busiest crossroads in the city, a focal point for cafés and hotels. Like most of the rest of Weimar Berlin it vanished in the debris of the war, and remains a shadow of its former self.

A couple of hundred metres beyond here is an equestrian **monument to Frederick the Great**, the enlightened despot who laid the foundations of Prussian power. After the war the statue of "Der alte Fritz", as the king was popularly known, was removed from Unter den Linden, and only restored to its city centre site in 1980 after a long exile in Potsdam.

This monument is the vanguard of a whole host of historic buildings, restored over the last 45 years or so from the postwar rubble. On the left-hand side of the street is the

Humboldt Universität, a restrained Neoclassical building from 1748. Alumni of the university include Karl Marx, Friedrich Engels and Karl Liebknecht. The philologists Jacob and Wilhelm Grimm (better known as the Brothers Grimm) and Albert Einstein are some of the better-known former staff members.

Around Bebelplatz

Directly opposite the university is **Bebelplatz**, formerly Opernplatz, the scene on May 11, 1933 of the infamous *Buchverbrennung*, the burning of books that conflicted with Nazi ideology. Thousands of books went up in smoke, including the works of "un-German" authors like Erich Maria Remarque, Thomas Mann, Heinrich Mann and Erich Kästner, along with volumes by countless foreign writers. Perhaps the most fitting comment on this episode was made with accidental foresight by Heinrich Heine during the previous century: "Where they start by burning books, they'll end by burning people." If you go to the middle of Bebelplatz and look through the glass pane set in the ground, you can see an intriguing monument to the book-burning, "The Empty Library", set underneath the square.

On the western side of Bebelplatz is the **Alte Bibliothek**, a former royal library known colloquially as the **Kommode** (chest of drawers), thanks to its curved Baroque facade. Lenin spent some time here poring over dusty tomes while waiting for the Russian Revolution, and, despite the fact that only the building's facade survived the war, it's been immaculately restored. On the east side of the square, the Neoclassical **Deutsche Staatsoper** by Georg von Knobelsdorff, looking a little plain opposite the Kommode, was designed as Berlin's first theatre. Like virtually everything else around here it has been totally reconstructed and is now eastern Berlin's leading opera house (see p.797).

Just behind is another Knobelsdorff creation, the **St Hedwigs-Kathedrale**, which was built for the city's Catholics in 1747 and is still in use. Reduced to a shell on March 2, 1943, the cathedral was not reconstructed until 1963, a restoration that left it with a modernized interior. Just east of the Deutsche Staatsoper is the **Kronprinzenpalais**. Originally built in 1663 and given a Baroque face-lift in 1732, this became a leading venue for modern art exhibitions in 1919. In 1933 the Nazis closed it, declaring hundreds of Expressionist and contemporary works housed in it to be examples of "*entartete Kunst*" or "degenerate art". One wing of the palace is now home to a couple of pricey restaurants and the genteel Operncafé (see p.794).

Karl Friedrich Schinkel (1781–1841) was the architect who, more than anyone, gave nineteenth-century Berlin its distinctive stamp, and his **Friedrichwerdersche Kirche**, at Am Werderschen Markt, now houses the **Schinkel-Museum** (Tues–Sun 9am–5pm; DM4, free first Sun of each month). Here, a permanent exhibition in the church's upper gallery gives a full rundown of Schinkel's designs, setting his work in the context of the times. Schinkel's great work, the **Neue Wache**, can be found opposite the Deutsche Staatsoper. Resembling a stylized Roman temple, it was built as a sort of Neoclassical police station for the royal watch, and served as a guardhouse until 1918. In 1931 it was converted into a memorial to the military dead of World War I, and in 1960 the GDR government extended this concept to include those killed by the Nazis, dedicating the building as a "Memorial to the Victims of Fascism and Militarism". These days it serves as the Central Memorial of the Federal Republic of Germany housing the tombs of an unknown soldier and an unknown concentration camp victim. Above these is a statue, depicting a mother clutching her dying son, dedicated to the "victims of war and tyranny".

Next door, housed in Berlin's finest Baroque building, the old Prussian Arsenal or **Zeughaus**, is the **Deutsches Historisches Museum** (10am–6pm, closed Wed; free). The museum's permanent exhibition, "Pictures and Objects from German History", is an engrossing if cursory presentation, well worth a visit. A concise guide in English

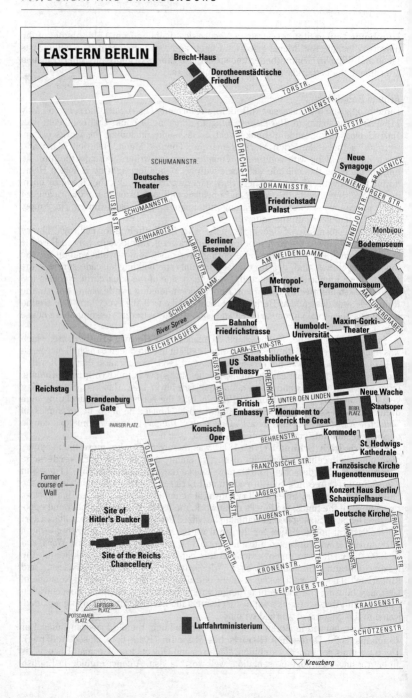

EASTERN BERLIN

Brecht-Haus

Dorotheenstädtische Friedhof

TORSTR.

LINIENSTR.

FRIEDRICHSTR.

AUGUSTSTR.

SCHUMANNSTR.

Neue Synagoge

KRAUSNICK

Deutsches Theater

ORANIENBURGER STR.

JOHANNISSTR.

Friedrichstadt Palast

MONBIJOUSTR.

SCHUMANNSTR.

Monbijou-

REINHARDTST

Bodemuseum

LUISENSTR.

Berliner Ensemble

ALBRECHTSTR.

AM WEIDENDAMM

AM KUPFERGRABEN

Metropol-Theater

Pergamonmuseum

SCHIFFBAUERDAMM

River Spree

Bahnhof Friedrichstrasse

REICHSTAGUFER

Humboldt-Universität

Maxim-Gorki-Theater

CLARA-ZETKIN-STR.

NEUSTADT KIRCHSTR.

US Embassy

Staatsbibliothek

FRIEDRICHSTR.

Reichstag

Neue Wache

UNTER DEN LINDEN

Brandenburg Gate

British Embassy

Monument to Frederick the Great

BEBEL PLATZ

Staatsoper

PARISER PLATZ

Komische Oper

Kommode

BEHRENSTR.

St. Hedwigs-Kathedrale

TOLERANZSTR.

Former course of Wall

FRANZÖSISCHE STR.

Französische Kirche Hugenottenmuseum

GLINKASTR.

JÄGERSTR.

Konzert Haus Berlin/ Schauspielhaus

Site of Hitler's Bunker

TAUBENSTR.

Deutsche Kirche

MAUERSTR.

CHARLOTTENSTR.

MARKGRAFENSTR.

JERUSALEMER STR

Site of the Reichs Chancellery

KRONENSTR.

LEIPZIGER STR.

LEIPZIGER PLATZ

KRAUSENSTR.

POTSDAMER PLATZ

Luftfahrtministerium

SCHÜTZENSTR.

▽ *Kreuzberg*

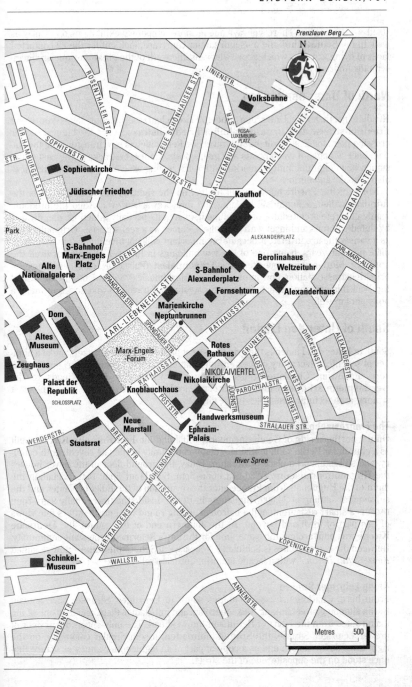

(DM9.80) is available. There's always one or more temporary exhibitions on display as well. In the **Schlüterhof**, the museum's inner courtyard, look out for the 22 contorted faces of dying warriors which adorn the walls, the work of the great Baroque architect-sculptor Andreas Schlüter.

North of Unter den Linden

Heading north at the Unter den Linden/Friedrichstrasse junction takes you along **Friedrichstrasse** itself towards **Bahnhof Friedrichstrasse**, once the biggest border crossing point for East Berlin-bound travellers. Renovation is now transforming the station, once a tangle of checkpoints and guard posts. Under the tracks to the east of the station is a delightful antique market with a fascinating assemblage of of old art, jewellery, books and curios.

North of the Friedrichstrasse rail bridge, on the right, at Friedrichstr. 101 is the **Admiralspalast**, a Jugendstil building and rare prewar survivor. Amid the predominantly concrete architecture of the immediate area its partially gilded facade, divided by fluted columns and inset with bas-reliefs, comes as a real surprise. Originally built as a variety theatre in 1910, it became an important political meeting hall in the immediate postwar years, being one of the few buildings in the area to have survived the bombing. More or less opposite is the **Tränenpalast** (Palace of Tears), an annexe of Friedrichstrasse station, now in use as a theatrical/musical venue. Until the demise of the Wall this was the departure point for westbound travellers and scene of many a poignant farewell.

South of Unter den Linden

South of Unter den Linden is the grid-like street pattern of Friedrichstadt, one of a number of seventeenth-century city extensions that took Berlin beyond its original walled core. Following Charlottenstrasse south from Unter den Linden leads to the **Gendarmenmarkt**, an historic cluster of restored buildings that forms one of the most striking architectural ensembles in the city.

The Französische Kirche
On the northern side of Gendarmenmarkt you'll find the **Französische Kirche**, built as a church for Berlin's influential Huguenot community in the late seventeenth century, and still in use as a place of worship. Today, the ground floor of the tower houses the **Hugenottenmuseum** (Wed–Sat noon–5pm, Sun 11am–5pm; DM2), detailing the flight of the Huguenots from France after the revocation of the Edict of Nantes and the subsequent settling of 20,000 Huguenots in Berlin. Inside the tower (daily 9am–7pm; DM3) is a smart restaurant, and a balcony running round the outside offers fine views of this part of town and beyond. At the southern end of the square, the **Deutsche Kirche** was built around the same time for the city's Reformed Protestant community. Between the two churches is Schinkel's Neoclassical **Schauspielhaus** – now renamed *Konzerthaus Berlin* – with a facade featuring intricate relief-work.

Along Leipziger Strasse
From here, Charlottenstrasse continues south to **Leipziger Strasse**, once a main Berlin shopping street linking Alexanderplatz and Potsdamer Platz, and now one of the main routes from the heart of Berlin and the west end. The only apparent survivor of prewar Leipziger Strasse, the **Spittelkolonnaden**, a semicircular colonnade on the right towards its eastern end, is a copy of part of an eighteenth-century structure that once stood on the opposite side of the street.

At the western end of Leipziger Strasse is Göring's **Luftfahrtministerium** (Air Ministry), a forbidding structure with a fortress-like air. Göring promised Berliners that not a single bomb would fall on the city during the war; if this were to happen, the Reichsmarshal said, he would change his name to Meyer – a common Jewish surname. Ironically, the Air Ministry was one of the few buildings to emerge more or less unscathed from the bombing and Red Army shelling. After the establishment of the GDR it became the SED regime's *Haus der Ministerien* (House of Ministries), and was the venue for a mass demonstration on June 16, 1953, a prelude to a general but short-lived uprising against the Communist government the next day. It's planned to house the finance ministry here when the national government finally makes the move from Bonn.

Beyond the former Air Ministry, Leipziger Strasse runs into **Potsdamer Platz**, reopened to traffic in the aftermath of November 9, 1989. A huge business development, which will include corporate headquarters for Mercedes-Benz and Sony, has turned the Platz into an immense building site.

The Museumsinsel and around

At the eastern end of Unter den Linden the Schinkel-designed **Schlossbrücke** spans the Spree. The classical statues which line each side of the bridge represent scenes from ancient Greek mythology, and earned the bridge the popular epithet of *Puppenbrücke* or "Puppet Bridge". The bridge leads onto **Schlossplatz** (formerly Marx-Engels-Platz), once the site of the **Berliner Schloss**, the old Imperial Palace, the remains of which were demolished after the war. Schlossplatz marks the mid-point of a city-centre island, whose northwestern part, extending peninsula-like from the square, is known as the **Museumsinsel** (**Museum Island**), location of the best of eastern Berlin's **museums**. Your main problem will be finding enough time to see everything: your best bet is to pick out one collection in particular rather than trying to cram them all into a single day.

THE MUSEUMSINSEL: PRICES AND OPENING DAYS

Entry to the Museumsinsel museums is, apart from the Altes Museum and Pergamonmuseum, a uniform DM4 (free first Sun in each month). The DM8 ticket to the Pergamonmuseum allows you entry on the same day to all the other museums on the Museuminsel. Note that all the museums are closed on Monday.

The Palast der Republik and around

Much of the space occupied by the former Schloss ended up as a car park for the **Palast der Republik**, which was built on the southeastern side of Schlossplatz during the early 1970s to house the *Volkskammer*, the GDR's parliament. The huge angular building with its bronzed, reflecting windows was completed in less than a thousand days, and was a source of great pride to the Honecker regime. The interior is a masterpiece of tastelessness and the hundreds of lamps hanging from the ceiling of the main foyer explain its nickname, *Erichs Lampenladen* – "Erich's lamp shop". Shortly before reunification an asbestos hazard was discovered in the building, and in October 1990 it was shut down indefinitely. Current speculation in the city suggests that it may well soon suffer the same fate as the Schloss.

On the southern side of Schlossplatz is the former GDR **Staatsrat**, an early 1960s building enhanced by the inclusion in its facade of the royal palace **balcony** from which Karl Liebknecht proclaimed the German revolution in 1918. Immediately to the east of the Staatsrat is the **Neue Marstall**, an unimaginatively extravagant turn-of-the-century construction, built to house the hundreds of coaches and horses used to ferry the royal household around the city. These days the ground floor is in use as an exhibition hall.

The Pergamonmuseum

The **Pergamonmuseum** (Tues–Sun 9am–5pm; DM8, free first Sun in each month) is a massive structure, built in the early part of this century to house the treasure trove of the German archeologists who were busy plundering the ancient world. The museum is divided into four sections, the most important of which, the **Department of Antiquities**, contains the **Pergamon Altar**: a huge structure dedicated to Zeus and Athena, dating from 180 to 160 BC, which was unearthed in Turkey and brought to Berlin in 1903. The **frieze** shows a battle between the gods and giants, and it's a tremendously forceful piece of work, the powerfully depicted figures writhing in a mass of sinew and muscle. The section also contains other pieces of Hellenistic architecture (albeit on a smaller scale), including a **market gate** from the Turkish town of Miletus and various examples of Greek sculpture.

The **Western Asian Section** has items going back four thousand years to Babylonian times, including the enormous **Ishtar Gate**, the **Processional Way** and the facade of the **Throne Room** from Babylon, all of which date from the reign of Nebuchadnezzar II in the sixth century BC. While it's impossible not to be awed by the size and remarkable state of preservation of the deep blue enamelled bricks of the Babylon finds, it's as well to remember that much of what you see is a mock-up, built around the original finds.

The museum's **Islamic Section** contains the facade of a Jordanian **Prince's Palace** at Mshatta from 743 AD, presented to Kaiser Wilhelm II by the Sultan of Turkey, as well as a host of smaller but no less impressive exhibits from Arabia and Persia. Finally, the **East Asian Collection** has a large collection of ceramics, lacquer work and jade, spanning four thousand years.

The Altes Museum

Directly to the north of Schlossplatz is the **Altes Museum** (Tues–Sun 10am–5pm; price varies depending on exhibition, rotunda free), perhaps Schinkel's most impressive surviving work and now home to large-scale international-loan art exhibitions on artistic or archeological themes. Make sure you see the interior of the ground floor, a rotunda modelled on the Pantheon in Rome to house a collection of Classical statues.

The Neues Museum and Alte Nationalgalerie

Just behind the Altes Museum is the **Neues Museum**, a war ruin until a few years ago and now being put to rights to house the Bodemuseum's Egyptian section and the Ancient and Early History collection from the Antikensammlung in Charlottenburg (see p.773). The restoration process is a fairly gradual one and not expected to be complete before the turn of the century.

While the Alte Nationalgalerie (see opposite) is being renovated, highlights from its collection of nineteenth-century art can be seen here on a rotating basis. Particularly noteworthy are several works of the "German Romans", mid-nineteenth-century artists such as **Anselm Feuerbach** and **Arnold Böcklin**, who spent much of their working lives in Italy. Böcklin's mortality-obsessed Romanticism is particularly eye-catching; his best-known paintings, including *The Isle of the Dead* and *Self-Portrait with Death Playing the Fiddle*, have a distinctive melancholy grandeur. The broad canvases of **Adoph von Menzel** strike a rather different note. Though he was chiefly known during his lifetime for his detailed depictions of court life under Frederick the Great, it's his interpretations of Berlin on the verge of the industrial age, such as *The Iron Foundry* and *The Berlin–Potsdam Railway*, that make more interesting viewing today. Also on hand are a handful of Impressionist and post-Impressionist works by Degas, Monet, Van Gogh, and Cézanne.

One floor below is a new permanent installation of objects from the **Antikensammlung**, small sculpture and pottery from the city's famed Greek and Roman collections. The holdings of Greek vases is considered to be among the finest in the world.

Next door, just north of Bodestrasse, is the **Alte Nationalgalerie**, which normally displays the nineteenth-century section of Berlin's state art collection. It's currently undergoing renovations and will not reopen until 2001: meanwhile a selection of its works can be seen at the Altes Museum (see opposite). It's worth taking a peek at the building, though, a grandiose interpretation of a Corinthian temple, built in 1876 and placed atop a huge pediment fronted by a statue of its royal patron, Friedrich Wilhelm IV. Subtle it's not. There's a pleasant little lawn in front punctuated by several sculptures, including *Centaur and Nymph* by Reinhold Begas, dating from around 1888, and Louis Tuaillon's 1895 *Amazon*.

The Bodemuseum

At the northeastern tip of the Museumsinsel is the **Bodemuseum**, also presently closed (until the end of 2000) as part of the large-scale renovation and reorganization of Berlin's collections. When restored, the impressive neo-Baroque building will house the **Skulpturensammlung**, an excellent, chiefly German collection of sculpture that is particularly authoritative in its sections detailing the Middle Ages, including work by the masters Tilman Riemenschneider, Nicolaus Gerhaert, Michael Erhart and Hans Multscher. Also finding a home here will be the **Museum für Spätantike und Byzantinische Kunst**, with an extensive range of objects, mainly religious, from the pre-medieval eastern Mediterranean. Later on, sometime around 2004, it is planned that the Aegyptisches Museum (see p.774), with its famous *Bust of Nefertiti*, will end up here as well.

Alexanderplatz and around

Alexanderplatz, dominated by the huge TV tower and furnished almost exclusively in concrete, is an unmistakable product of old East Germany. During East Berlin's forty-year existence, while the Unter den Linden was allowed to represent the glories of Berlin past, Alexanderplatz and its environs were meant to reflect the glories of a modern socialist capital city. How much longer this uncompromising reminder of the recent past will endure is questionable, as extensive redevelopment plans for the area have already been drawn up. To get to "Alex" from the Museumsinsel, head up the shopping strip of **Karl-Liebknecht-Strasse**, to the right of which lies the **Marx-Engels Forum**, a severely well-ordered park, with a lumpen bronze representation of the founders of Marxism at its heart.

The Rotes Rathaus and the Marienkirche

Beyond here, across Spandauer Strasse, is a large open space on which stands the **Neptunbrunnen**, a fountain incorporating statues of Neptune and his courtiers. Across Rathausstrasse, to the southeast of the fountain, stands the **Rotes Rathaus** or Red Town Hall, seat of the united Berlin city government since October 1991. It's a grandiose, almost Venetian-looking building, which has lost some of its impact now that it's been hemmed in by new buildings. From the Rathaus the pedestrianized Rathausstrasse leads past a series of tawdry shops and cafés, legacy of the old regime's efforts to jazz up the city centre, to Alexanderplatz.

To the north of the Neptunbrunnen is the **Marienkirche**, Berlin's oldest parish church. The nave dates back to about 1270, and the interior is an excellent place to escape the increasingly frenetic street life of the area. Look out, too, for the fifteenth-century *Totentanz*, a 22-metre frieze showing the Dance of Death, and a magnificent decorative pulpit by Schlüter.

The Fernsehturm

The Marienkirche, like every other building in the vicinity, is overshadowed by the gigantic **Fernsehturm** or TV tower (daily 9am–1am; DM8) that dominates the eastern Berlin skyline like a displaced satellite sitting atop a huge factory chimney. The 365-metre tower was completed in 1969 and does have a couple of positive features: it makes a good orientation point, and there's a tremendous view (40km on a rare clear day, although the summit is often shrouded in cloud) from the observation platform.

Above the observation platform is the *Tele-Café*, whose main attraction is that it turns on its own axis a couple of times every hour. When the sun shines on the globe of the tower, the reflected light forms a cross visible even in western Berlin, much to the reported chagrin of the old authorities and amusement of Berliners, who call it the "pope's revenge".

Alexanderplatz

Immediately northeast of the Fernsehturm is **S-Bahnhof Alexanderplatz**, a good point from which to catch trains out to the eastern suburbs, and around which myriad *Imbiss* stands and street stalls have sprung up since unification.

On the other side of the tracks is Alexanderplatz itself, named after the Russian Czar Alexander I and made famous by Alfred Döblin's novel of life in the Weimar era, *Berlin Alexanderplatz*. This windswept pedestrianized plaza has figured prominently in the city's history. In 1848 it was barricaded by revolutionaries, and during the revolution of 1918 sailors occupied the Alexanderplatz police headquarters and freed the prisoners held there. More recently, Alexanderplatz was the focal point of the million-strong city-wide **demonstration** of November 4, 1989, which formed a prelude to the events of November 9. Hundreds of thousands of people crammed into the square to hear opposition leaders speak. Veteran writer Stefan Heym summed up the mood in his speech to the crowd: "Power belongs not to one, not to a few, not to the Party and not to the state. The whole people must have a share."

Alexanderplatz presents a bleak prospect and there's little apparent reason to hang around. The only structures that stand out architecturally amid the surrounding high-rises are the **Alexanderhaus** and **Berolinahaus**, at the western end of the square adjacent to the S-Bahn tracks. These functional prewar survivors were constructed during the 1930s to designs by Peter Behrens, the architect whose ideas influenced the founders of the Bauhaus.

The Nikolaiviertel and around

Slightly to the southwest of the Rotes Rathaus lies the **Nikolaiviertel**, a recent development that attempts to re-create the old prewar heart of Berlin on the site of the city's medieval core, which was razed overnight on June 16, 1944. The Nikolaiviertel consists partly of exact replicas of historic Berlin buildings which didn't make it through to the postwar era, such as *Zum Nussbaum* (see p.794), a convincing enough re-creation of a celebrated sixteenth-century *Gaststätte,* and partly of stylized buildings not based on anything in particular, but striving for an "old Berlin" feel.

At the centre of it all is the Gothic **Nikolaikirche** (Tues–Sun 10am–6pm; DM3), a thirteenth-century church, restored to its twin-towered prewar glory. It now houses an exhibition about medieval Berlin. Nearby, at Poststr. 23, is the **Knoblauchhaus** (Tues–Sun 10am–6pm; DM2), built in 1759. On Mühlendamm you'll find the rebuilt Rococo **Ephraim-Palais** (Tues–Sun 10am–6pm; DM3), devoted to the art of Berlin from the seventeenth century to the beginning of the nineteenth.

North from Bahnhof Friedrichstrasse

From the station, Friedrichstrasse itself runs north across the River Spree over the wrought-iron **Weidendammbrücke**. Immediately to the left on Bertolt-Brecht-Platz is the **Berliner Ensemble** theatre (see p.798), generally thought of as Berlin's Brecht theatre, complete with statue of the man himself in front. After spending much of the Nazi era in American exile, Brecht returned in 1949 with his wife, Helene Weigel, to take over direction of the theatre, marking his return by painting a still-visible red cross through the coat of arms on the royal box. Today the theatre is undergoing something of an artistic revival after many years churning out lacklustre productions of Brecht's work.

A little way to the north along Friedrichstrasse is **Oranienburger Tor**. Roughly opposite here is the **Dorotheenstädtischer Friedhof** (8am–sunset), a VIP cemetery, which contains the graves of Bertolt Brecht and Helene Weigel, the author Heinrich Mann, John Heartfield (the Dada luminary and interwar photomontage exponent), the philosopher Georg Hegel, whose ideas influenced Marx, and Berlin's great Neoclassical architect Karl Friedrich Schinkel. There are guided tours most days – check the sign at the entrance for details. Just beyond the cemetery is the **Brecht-Haus**, Chausseestr. 125 (guided tours Tues, Wed & Fri 10–11.30am, Thurs 10am–noon & 5–6.30pm, Sat 9.30am–1.30pm; DM4), Brecht's last home and workplace. It now houses a Bertolt Brecht archive and has half-hourly guided tours of the rooms where the playwright worked and lived. Helene Weigel lived here until her death in 1971, and a small collection of artefacts commemorates her life.

Oranienburger Strasse

Altogether more lively is **Oranienburger Strasse**, running southeast from Oranienburger Tor. One of Berlin's seedier red-light districts by night, since the *Wende* Oranienburger Strasse has become a major bar/café-crawling strip with a host of stylish watering holes both here and on the surrounding streets. The revitalization of Oranienburger Strasse began with *Tacheles*, a collective of young international artists who took over a big, derelict building on the southern side of the street just beyond the Oranienburger Tor junction. The exterior is usually festooned with works-in-progress, and the building has become home and workplace to an ever-changing band of alternative artists, kindred spirits and hangers-on. Inside, the building, which looks like a bomb site, houses a café/bar (see p.794) and regular gigs and events take place here.

The presence of the grand **Neue Synagoge** halfway down Oranienburger Strasse is a reminder that this area was, before the war, Berlin's main Jewish quarter. Inaugurated in the presence of Bismarck in 1866, the synagogue was burned out on *Kristallnacht*, the night of November 9–10, 1938, when the Nazis unleashed an all-out pogrom on Germany's Jewish community. Further damaged by bombing during the war it stood derelict for many years, a silent reminder of the savagery of Nazi rule. Restoration, which began during GDR days, is now complete and the gilded dome of the building is once again a Berlin landmark.

The Jüdischer Friedhof and the Sophienkirche

At the eastern end of Oranienburger Strasse, turn left into Grosse Hamburger Strasse, where on the immediate right you'll see the location of the **Jüdischer Friedhof**, Berlin's oldest Jewish cemetery, established in 1672, and the site of the first Jewish old people's home to be founded in the city. A memorial tablet and a sculpted group of harrowed-looking figures representing concentration camp victims mark the spot. The Nazis used the building, destroyed in the war, as a detention centre for Jews from the city, and 55,000 people were held here before being shipped off to the camps. The open space behind is the site of the cemetery itself which was destroyed by the Gestapo in

1943; their desecration involved digging a trench, which they shored up with grave-stones, through the site.

Continuing along the street, past turn-of-the-century neo-Baroque apartment buildings with shrapnel-pitted facades, brings you to the entrance gateway of the **Sophienkirche** on the right-hand side. This church, dating back to 1712, is one of the city's finest Baroque buildings, and the only central Berlin church to survive the war more or less undamaged.

The eastern districts

The eastern *Bezirke* or districts of Berlin are still noticeably different from those in the western part of the city. Generally less affluent and more run-down, it's here that you'll see the most visible reminders of the city's long division. Despite numerous restoration and renovation projects, many areas still have that air of crumbling neglect that characterized the old GDR. The tenements of **Prenzlauer Berg**, a part working-class, part bohemian district that fans out northeast of the city centre, have long been a centre of "alternative" culture and lifestyles. This area is also home to the best cafés, bars and nightlife in the eastern part of the city. With enough time, it's worth heading out to **Treptow** and its massive Soviet war memorial and riverside parks.

Prenzlauer Berg

One eastern *Bezirk* that should on no account be missed is **Prenzlauer Berg**. This run-down working-class district radiates out from the northeastern edge of the city centre in a network of tenement-lined cobbled streets divided by a series of major traffic arteries. Before the *Wende*, Prenzlauer Berg, like Kreuzberg in West Berlin, enjoyed a big influx of "alternative" lifestyle adherents and artists who chose this district to live on the edge of established GDR society. Since the events of late 1989, large numbers of west Berliners have come here, hoping to re-create the counter-culture *Szene* that thrived in the west a decade ago. This, coupled with the opening of numerous new cafés and galleries, has turned Prenzlauer Berg into one of the most exciting parts of the city. Although much of the area retains an authentically gritty ambience, extensive renovation projects are doing much to sanitize the area. This process actually began at the tail end of the GDR era when the authorities restored Husemannstrasse to its stuccoed, pastel-painted, turn-of-the-century glory.

The quickest way to **get to Prenzlauer Berg** is to take the U-Bahn from Alexanderplatz and head for either Eberswalder Strasse or Schönhauser Allee U-Bahn stations. For a more atmospheric approach take tram #1 from Am Kupfergraben, or tram #53 from Hackescher Markt.

Schönhauser Allee is Prenzlauer Berg's main drag and cuts through **Senefelder Platz**. A stone's throw from here is the **Jüdischer Friedhof**, Prenzlauer Berg's Jewish cemetery (Mon–Thurs 10am–4pm, Fri 10am–1pm; male visitors are requested to keep their heads covered), just to the right of Schönhauser Allee. Over 20,000 people are buried here, but shortly before the end of the war the gravestones were smashed into the ground, and much renovation work has gone into what you see today.

Beyond the junction of Schönhauser Allee, Danziger Strasse, Kastanienallee and Eberswalder Strasse, **Schönhauser Allee** assumes its true identity as an old-fashioned shopping street with cobbles and narrow shop facades. Just to the southeast of Schönhauser Allee U-Bahn station, at the intersection of Stargarder Strasse and Greifenhagener Strasse, is the **Gethsemene Kirche**, which was an important focal point for reformist activities during the summer 1989 exodus from the GDR. These days, however, it's in the maze of run-down streets east of Schönhauser Allee that Prenzlauer Berg's real attractions lie. Here you'll find some of the best cafés and bars in the eastern part of Berlin (see p.794); the area is best explored by turning into Sredzkistrasse from Schönhauser Allee.

A left turn from Sredzkistrasse into Knaackstrasse leads you to the **Kulturbrauerei** at Knaackstr. 97. This former brewery has been transformed into a cultural centre with a decidedly alternative slant. Passing through the entrance, you'll discover an inner courtyard of clubs, galleries and studios amid artefacts of the original brewery. There's almost always something cultural, political – or just plain fun – going on.

Retracing your path down Knaackstrasse and past Sredzkistrasse leads to **Kollwitzplatz**, named after the artist **Käthe Kollwitz**, who lived in nearby Weissenburgerstrasse (now called Kollwitzstrasse) from 1891 to 1943. An unflattering statue of the artist sits in the little park at the centre of the square. Her work embraced political and pacifist themes and can be best appreciated in the Käthe-Kollwitz-Museum in western Berlin (see p.761). Since 1989 a number of new bars have opened on and in the immediate vicinity of Kollwitzplatz (see p.794).

Treptow – the Sowjetisches Ehrenmal

The main reason to come to **Treptow** is to see the huge and sobering **Sowjetisches Ehrenmal**, Berlin's main Soviet war memorial. Standing in the **Treptower Park**, a well-known interwar assembly point for revolutionary workers about to embark on demonstrations, it commemorates the Soviet soldiers killed during the Battle of Berlin in April and May 1945, and is burial place to 5000 of the Soviet Union's estimated 305,000 casualties during the Battle of Berlin. To get there, take the S-Bahn to Treptower Park station: from here it's just a few hundred metres to the memorial's arched entrance on the south side of Puschkin Allee. A little way to the south of the entrance is a sculpture of a grieving woman representing the Motherland, to the left of which a broad concourse slopes upwards towards a viewing point flanked by two vast triangles of red granite, fashioned from stone bought from Sweden by the Nazis to furnish Berlin with projected victory monuments. From the viewing point the vista is dominated by a vast symbolic statue, a typically Soviet piece of gigantism fashioned out of marble from Hitler's Chancellery. Over 11m high and set on top of a hill, it shows an idealized Russian soldier clutching a saved child and resting his sword on a shattered swastika. Inside the plinth is a memorial crypt with a mosaic in true Socialist Realism style, showing Soviet citizens honouring the dead. In the long sunken park area which leads up to the statue are the mass graves of the Red Army troops, lined by sculpted frescoes of stylized scenes from the Great Patriotic War.

Eating and drinking

Nowhere is more than a stone's throw from a **bar** in the western part of the city. Just about every street corner has a small *Kneipe*, ranging from lugubrious beer-swilling holes to slick, upscale hangouts for Berlin's night people. You'll find that most bars stay open later than elsewhere in Germany: it's quite feasible to drink around the clock here, the result of a law that requires bars to close only for an hour a day for cleaning. Over on the eastern side, things aren't quite so lively – here the new cafés and bars springing up along Oranienburger Strasse and in Prenzlauer Berg are the places to head for.

The city's compressed, cosmopolitan nature means that the range of **restaurants** in the west is wider than in any other German city: indeed, the national cuisine takes a back seat to Greek, Turkish, Balkan, Indian and Italian food, and plenty of places exist where a meal costs under DM15. Almost all the better bars serve food, too, and this can be a bargain – though beware the most chic places, where that interesting-looking item on the menu turns out to be a plate of asparagus tips for DM25. Food in the eastern parts of the city has been improving rapidly, and in lively neighbourhoods such as Mitte and Prenzlauer Berg equals what's on offer on the western side.

Eating

You can spend as much or as little as you like on **food** in Berlin; it's one item, at least, that won't break the bank. Don't forget that many of Berlin's **bars** (see pp.792–795) can be excellent (and inexpensive) choices for food, especially breakfast, which may be served till afternoon – or later.

Snacks

Cheapest way of warding off hunger pangs is to use the small **Imbiss** snack stands found on many street corners, where for a few marks you can fill up on *Currywurst* and chips. Many butchers' shops sell meaty snacks at low prices, and around Zoo Station are any number of budget-priced burger bars and pizzerias.

For something a bit more substantial but not that much more expensive, try any one of four sit-down **Imbiss restaurants**, which charge between DM5 and DM12 a meal, or, at lunchtime, either of the city's **mensas**, officially for German students only but usually open to anyone who fits that general description, and always to those with *ISIC* cards.

Ashoka-Imbiss, Grolmanstr. 51, off Savignyplatz. Daily 11am–2am. About the best of the lot, dishing up good portions of tremendous-bargain Indian food. Vegetarian options.

Einhorn, Mommsenstr. 2, and Wittenbergplatz 5. Vegetarian wholefood at its best, in a friendly and relaxed atmosphere – though it's standing only and closes at 6.30pm weekdays, 4pm on Sat.

Ernst-Reuter-Platz Mensa, Ernst-Reuter-Platz. Mon–Fri 11.15am–2.30pm. Small mensa of the nearby Technical University, with limited choice of meals. *ISIC* required.

Konnopke, Schönhauser Allee/Kastanienallee, Prenzlauer Berg. Beneath the S-Bahn, a Prenzlauer Berg legend that serves the best *Currywurst* in the city. Open Mon–Fri 5am–7pm, Sat & Sun 6am–6pm.

Mensa of the Free University, Habelschwerdter Allee, at the junction with Thiel Allee (nearest U-Bahn #1 to Dahlem-Dorf). Mon–Fri noon–2pm. Only worth considering if you're spending the day at the Dahlem museums. *ISIC* advisable.

Nachtigall Imbiss, Ohlauerstr. 10. Arab specialities including the delicious *Schaurma kebab* – lamb and hummus in pitta bread. Good salads for vegetarians.

TU Mensa, Hardenbergstr. 34. Mon–Fri 11.15am–2.30pm. Here you buy your meal ticket before getting your food. Inferior quality to the Free University mensa, but much more central.

Restaurants

AMERICAN

Jimmy's Diner, Pariser Str. 41 (☎882 3141). American-style diner housed in an old dining carriage shipped from the USA. Popular with the under-30s crowd, who visit for chilled American beer and real hamburgers. Open till 3am, 5am at weekends.

CHINESE, INDIAN AND SOUTHEAST ASIAN

Bengwan Solo, Kaiserin-Augusta-Allee 1 (☎345 2772). Charming Indonesian restaurant tucked away in an area otherwise devoid of any real eating opportunities. Meals are plentiful and highly spiced, with a good range of choices for vegetarians. Make a reservation, especially at weekends.

Edd's Thailändisches Restaurant, Goebenstr. 20–21 (☎215 5294). Huge portions of Thai food make this a popular place and one of Berlin's better Thai restaurants. Booking advised.

India-Haus, Feurigstr. 38. Solid quality Schöneberg Indian, with first-rate veggie options.

India-Palace, Leibnizstr. 35. Incredible variety and low prices.

Mao Thai, Wörther Str. 30, Prenzlauer Berg (☎441 9261). Despite being rather pricey, this place is a welcome addition to the Prenzlauer Berg restaurant scene. Booking advisable.

Ostwind, Husemannstr. 13 (☎441 5951). Delicate and unusual country Chinese offerings. Booking advisable at weekends.

Tuk-Tuk, Grossgörschenstr. 2 (☎781 1588). Amiable Indonesian near Kleistpark U-Bahn. Enquire about the heat of your dish before ordering. Booking advisable.

FRENCH AND ITALIAN

Aroma, Hochkirchstr. 8 (☎782 5821). Well above average, inexpensive Italian with photo gallery and Italian films on Tues evenings. One of the best places to eat in east Schöneberg, it's advisable to book after 8pm.

Borchardt, Französische Str. 47. Elegant French dining for the chic and well-heeled.

Canto Maggio, Alte Schönhauser Str. 4, Mitte. A smart Scheunenviertel Italian, run by Italians and serving excellent value pizzas.

Cour Carrée, Savignyplatz 5. Deservedly popular French restaurant with *fin-de-siècle* decor and garden seating.

XII Apostoli, Georgenstr. 177–180 (☎201 0222). Kitschy religious decor adorns this capacious Italian restaurant, known for its huge and wonderful pizzas. The kitchen closes at ten, but if you like the sacred atmosphere and generally well-heeled patrons, you can retire to the adjoining piano bar.

Französischer Hof, Jägerstr. 36, Mitte (☎204 3570). French and German specialities in plush surroundings overlooking the Gendarmenmarkt.

Osteria No.1, Kreuzbergstr. 71 (☎786 9162). Classy, inexpensive and therefore highly popular Italian restaurant run by a fun Italian collective.

GERMAN AND AUSTRIAN

Austria, Bergmannstr. 30 (☎694 4440). Delicious Austrian classics in warm, woody rooms reminiscent of a hunting lodge. Portions fit for a woodsman. Bookings advisable.

Ermeler Haus, Am Märkischen Ufer 10, Mitte. In the *Raabediele*, an unpretentious basement, traditional German dishes are served in folksy surroundings, while on the first floor there's a pricier wine restaurant.

Exil, Paul-Lincke-Ufer 44 (☎612 7037). Popular with the Kreuzberg arts crowd for its attractive site next to the canal and its moderate to expensive Viennese food. Something of a bohemian meeting place. Booking advisable.

Florian, Grolmanstr. 52. Leading light of the new German cuisine movement in Berlin, this is as much a place to be seen in as to eat. The food, similar to French *nouvelle cuisine*, is light, flavourful – and expensive.

Keller Restaurant im Brecht Haus, Chausseestr. 125, Mitte (☎282 3843). A cellar restaurant decorated with Brecht memorabilia in the basement of Brecht's old house. Viennese specialities supposedly dreamed up by Brecht's wife, Helen Weigel, make this a very popular place. Worth booking.

Restauration 1900, Husemannstr. 1, Prenzlauer Berg. Imaginative *neue deutsche Küche*.

Tegernseer Tönnchen, Berliner Str. 1184. Bavarian cuisine – which means enormous dishes of *Wursts* and *Schnitzels* washed down with pitchers of beer. Excellent value.

MEXICAN AND LATIN AMERICAN

Brazil, Gormannstr. 22, Mitte. Dishes from Brazil, Chile and Mexico. Attracts arty types who don't seem put off by the chaotic service.

Carib, Motzstr. 30. Classical Caribbean cuisine, friendly service, lethal rum cocktails.

El Parron, Carmerstr. 17. Solid Latin American food, and good fun when patrons leave their tables to tango.

La Estancia, Bundesallee 45. Very good value for money Latin American restaurant, patronized mainly by environmentally and politically conscious Berliners.

Lone Star Taqueria, Bergmannstr. 11. Casual and convivial Mexican joint. Authentic food and frozen margaritas by the pitcher.

Patio, Görlitzer Str. 32. Popular Mexican with all the usual staples. When it's good it's very good, but it has a reputation for erratic standards.

Tres Kilos, Marheinekeplatz 3 (☎693 6044). An upmarket Tex-Mex place just by the Marheinekeplatz covered market, and popular with the bright young things who've taken over the Chamissoplatz neighbourhood. Brain-stewing cocktails.

MIDDLE EASTERN

Am Nil, Kaiserdamm 114 (near Sophie-Charlotte-Platz). Moderately priced Egyptian, easy-going service.

Der Ägypter, Kantstr. 26. Egyptian falafel-type meals. Spicy, filling and an adventurous alternative to the safe bets around Savignyplatz. Good vegetarian selections.

Merhaba, Hasenheide 39. Highly rated Turkish restaurant that's usually packed with locals. A selection of the starters here can be more interesting than a main course.

Sondo, Husemannstr. 10, Prenzlauer Berg (☎442 0724). Refined Anatolian cuisine.

VEGETARIAN AND OTHER

Abendmahl, Muskauerstr. 9 (☎612 5179). Congenial atmosphere, excellent veggie (but including fish) dishes and reasonable prices make it one of the most enjoyable places to eat in the city.

Arche Noah, Fasanenstr. 79. Tucked inside the Jewish Community Centre, serving wonderful kosher delights in a good atmosphere.

Art of Greens, Mittenwalder Str. 51. Not only meatless, but alcohol-free and non-smoking as well. Creative dishes with a Southeast Asian touch.

Oren, Oranienburger Str. 28 (☎282 8228). Next door to the Oranienburger Strasse synagogue, offering tasty vegetarian dishes in a stylish interior. At its best in the summer, when you can eat outside in the courtyard. Fills quickly.

Thürnägel, Gneisenaustr. 57 (☎691 4800). Small, smart, convivial place in west Kreuzberg. Booking necessary at weekends.

Drinking

Though it's fun enough to dive into any bar that takes your fancy, western Berlin has three focal points for drinking, each with enough bars to tackle through the course of an evening, and each with a subtly differing character. Those **around Savignyplatz** are the haunt of the city's conspicuous good-timers; **Kreuzberg** drinkers include political activists, punks and the Turkish community, in a mix that forms this area's appeal. The area **around Nollendorfplatz and Winterfeldtplatz** is the territory of sped-out all-nighters and the pushing-on-forty crew. Elsewhere in **Schöneberg** bars are on the whole more mixed and more relaxed. Unless you're into pissed businessmen, avoid the Ku'damm and the rip-off joints around the Europa Center.

On the eastern side, the **Scheunenviertel** is the city's nocturnal melting pot attracting people from all over Berlin and from well outside the city. **Prenzlauer Berg** drinkers are a mixed crowd, part tourists and part locals. Elsewhere in Mitte, there are places worth dropping in on while sight-seeing, and the atmosphere is generally quieter if you want to escape the wildness of the Scheunenviertel.

Berlin **drink specialities** include *Berliner Weisse*, a watery top-fermented wheat beer that's traditionally pepped up by adding a shot of fruity syrup or *Schuss*. Ask for it *mit grün* and you get a dash of woodruff, creating a greeny brew with a strong herby taste; *mit rot* is a raspberry-flavoured kiddy drink that works wonders at breakfast time.

Savignyplatz and around

Dralles, Schlüterstr. 69. Notably more expensive than other bars in the area, this is the place to see and be seen: the 1950s decor is chic and understated, the clientele aspire likewise. Go beautiful and loaded, or not at all.

Rosalinde, Knesebeckstr. 16. Upmarket café with an unusual variety of breakfasts: their Fitness Frühstück (muesli, fresh fruit and nuts) does the trick after a rough night out, and there's hot food until 2am.

Schwarzes Café, Kantstr. 148. Kantstrasse's best hangout for the young and chic, with a relaxed atmosphere, good music and food. Although perhaps dating, still a classic Berlin bar (open Wed–Sun 24hr, Mon until 3am, Tues from noon).

Shell, Knesebeckstr. 22. The archetypal Berlin posing parlour, the air thick with the sipping of Perrier and the rustle of carefully organized Filofaxes. Slick, starchy and self-consciously superior. Vegetarian food.

Zillemarkt, Bleibtreustr. 48. Wonderful if shabby bar that attempts a *fin-de-siècle* feel. Unpretentious and fun, and a good place to start Savignyplatz explorations – it's by the S-Bahn. Serves breakfast till 6pm.

Zwiebelfisch, Savignyplatz 7. Corner bar for would-be arty/intellectual types. Lots of jazz and earnest debate. Good cheap grub.

Kreuzberg

Bierhimmel, Oranienstr. 181. The back room is fitted out as a plush Fifties cocktail bar; one of the most intimate and comfortable drinking spots in town.

Homo-Bar (aka *Oranienbar*), Oranienstr. 168. Famed Kreuzberg watering hole, which despite the name is by no means solely a gay bar. The interior is half-plastered (as are most of the clientele), giving it a sort of post-nuclear chic.

Milchbar, Manteuffelstr. 41. Typical late-night meeting place of black-clad *Szene* groupies. One of the more "in" spots of Kreuzberg – though it's hard to figure out why.

Wunderbar, Körtestr. 38. Large and animated bar with pool room and youthful, varied customers. Essential for the first drink of the evening when arriving at Südstern U-Bahn, just across the street.

Around Nollendorfplatz and Winterfeldtplatz

Bar am Lützowplatz, Lützowplatz 7. Distinguished in having the longest bar in the city, this also has Berlin's best selection of whiskies (63) and a superb range of moderately priced cocktails. A dangerously great bar.

Café Einstein, Kurfürstenstr. 58. Housed in a seemingly ancient mansion, this is about as close as you'll get to the ambience of the prewar Berlin *Kaffeehaus*, with international newpapers and breakfast served till 2pm. Occasional live music plus a good garden. Expensive.

Café M, Goltzstr. 34. Though littered with tatty plastic chairs and precious little else, *M* is Berlin's most favoured rendezvous for self-styled creative types and the conventionally unconventional. The cool thing to drink is *Flensburger Pils*, from the bottle.

Slumberland, Goltzstr. 24. The gimmicks here are sand on the floor and a tropical theme. Laid-back, likeable, and one of the better bars of this area.

Schöneberg

Estoril, Vorbergstr. 11. A favourite Schöneberg bar that serves good tapas with drinks.

Pinguin Club, Wartburgstr. 54. Tiny and cheerful bar with 1950–60s America supplying its theme and background music.

Zoulou Club, Hauptstr. 5. Compact, little-known bar packed after 11pm with local Schönebergers. Rather wonderful, in a low-key sort of way.

Elsewhere in western Berlin

Blisse 14, Blissestr. 14. Café-bar designed especially, but not exclusively, for disabled people. A good meeting place.

Café Adler, Friedrichstr. 206. Small café whose popularity came from the fact that it is next to the site of the Checkpoint Charlie border crossing. Serves breakfasts and meals.

Café Hardenberg, Hardenbergstr. 10. Large, old-fashioned café with excellent and cheap food that draws in local students. Recommended.

E&M Leydicke, Mansteinstr. 4. Claims to be the oldest *Kneipe* in western Berlin and, though some of the decorations look suspiciously recent, it does have the feel of an old-fashioned bar. Geared towards tourists.

Klo, Leibnitzstr. 57. This one you'll love or hate. A theme bar based on or around things lavatorial (drinks are served in urine sample bottles). If you share the German fascination for anything related to potties and peeing you'll probably wet yourself laughing; otherwise it's pricey and a bit tacky. Entry DM0.25.

Kumpelnest 3000, Lützowstr. 23. Carpeted walls and a mock-Baroque effect attract a rough-and-ready crew of under-30s to this erstwhile brothel. Gets going around 2am. Fine fun, and the best place in the area.

Saftladen Wilmersdorf, Wegenerstr. 1. When the booze gets too much for you this could be the place: it specializes in alcohol-free drinks, some of which are quite inventive.

Scheunenviertel

Assel, Oranienburger Str. 61. A simply furnished cellar bar attracting students and passing tourists. Carefully maintained bohemian ambience and cheap food.

Hackbarths, Auguststr. 49a. Dominated by a huge triangular bar that seems to fill the whole place, this bar attracts a very mixed crowd, but one more interested in having a good time than posing. The food, particularly the breakfasts, is recommended too.

Obst & Gemüse, Oranienburger Str. 48. An invariably crowded and chaotic bar opposite the *Tacheles* alternative arts emporium. Lots of attitude from staff and customers alike.

Silberstein, Oranienburger Str. 27. Usually packed to the gills with Oranienburger Strasse party people, and celebrated for its weird welded chairs. Club nights are a regular feature ranging from house to dub.

VEB OZ, Auguststr. 92. A kind of East German theme bar serving *Berliner Pilsener*, a former Eastern brew that's still selling well. The decor includes a Trabant turned into a bench and various other bits of GDR ephemera.

Zapata, Oranienburger Str. 54–56. Part of the *Tacheles* multimedia extravaganza. Not quite as chaotic as it was but still a major hangout for *Szene* tourists and fans of Berlin's alternative arts scene.

Zosch, Tucholskystr. 30. A dark, sloppy and comfortable place drawing a crowd of local punks and squatters.

Prenzlauer Berg

Anita Wronski, Knaackstr. 26–28. Epitomizing the new breed of Prenzlauer Berg cafés, this lively place spread out over a couple of floors attracts a mixed crowd of locals and tourists. Not a bad place to start the evening.

Bla-Bla, Sredzkistr. 19a. Laid-back atmosphere and service. Sink down into the deep, comfortable sofas amid the flea market decor and take it easy.

Kommandantur, Knaackstr. 20. Something of a veteran in the neighbourhood, it still packs a crowd at weekends.

Krähe, Kollwitzstr. 84. Irreproachably tasteful with its pastel walls and post-designer candlesticks.

Pasternak, Knaackstr. 22–24. Popular with the hip-tourist contingent. Russian specialities served.

Titanic, Winsstr. 30. A laid-back friendly bar, a bit off the beaten track but worth seeking out.

Westphal, Kollwitzstr. 63. One of the first places to open up after the Wall came down, its rough-hewn chic attracts a slightly po-faced *Szene* crowd.

Elsewhere in Mitte

Broker's Bier Börse, Schiffbauerdamm 8. A slick, well-polished bar where the prices of the large selection of beers fluctuate with the stock market. The gimmick has proved popular.

Operncafé, Opernpalais, Unter den Linden 5. In a former royal palace, this elegant café is a deliberate attempt to evoke the atmosphere of *fin-de-siècle* Berlin. Coffee and amazing cakes.

Zum Nussbaum, Am Nussbaum/Probstrasse. In the heart of the Nikolaiviertel and overshadowed by the Nikolaikirche, this is a convincing replica of a prewar *Kneipe*.

Zur letzten Instanz, Waisenstr. 14–16. One of the city's oldest *Gaststätten* with a wonderful old-fashioned interior including a classic tiled oven. There's also a beer garden and traditional dishes are served, such as herring specialities. Closed Sun.

Gay men's bars

The most concentrated area of gay men's bars is between Wittenbergplatz and Nollendorfplatz, south of Kleiststrasse. For more detailed listings, pick up a copy of either *Siegessäule* or *Berlin von Hinten*, available from most bars.

Anderes Ufer, Hauptstr. 157. Quiet Schöneberg café-bar favoured by students and alternative types. Women welcomed. Serves breakfasts.

Blue Boy Bar, Eisenacher Str. 3a. Tiny, convivial and relaxed bar, far less raucous than many that surround it.

Fledermaus, Joachimstaler Str. 14. Bar and coffee shop popular with tourists as well as locals; one of the city's most relaxing gay bars.

Hafen, Motzstrasse 19; adjacent to *Tom's Bar*. One of the main cruising bars in the city. Always packed, open till late.

Tom's Bar, Motzstr. 19. Dark, sweaty and wicked cruising bar with a large back room.

Zufall, Pfalzburger Str. 10a. Mixed gay bar: ring the bell to gain admission. Open till late.

Women's cafés and bars

Many of Berlin's women-only bars have a strong lesbian following, though straight women are welcome everywhere.

Begine, Potsdamer Str. 139 (women only). Stylishly decorated bar-bistro/gallery with limited choice of inexpensive food.

Café Seldenfaden, Dircksenstr. 47. A non-alcoholic café tucked away by the S-Bahn tracks in Mitte. Tues–Sun 11am–8.30pm.

Dinelo, Vorbergstr. 10. Restaurant attracting lesbians of all ages and varied styles. Tues–Sun 6pm–midnight.

Pour Elle, Kalckreuthstr. 10 (closed Mon; women only except Tues). Intimate disco-bar frequented by the straighter sort of (generally older) lesbian. Expensive.

Music and nightlife

Since the time of the Weimar Republic, and even through the lean postwar years, Berlin has had a reputation for having some of the best – and steamiest – **nightlife** in Europe, an image fuelled by the cartoons of George Grosz and films like *Cabaret*. Today, Berlin is still a city that wakes up when others are going to sleep, with some energetic nightclubs and one of Europe's great orchestras. Perhaps inevitably, it's in the western parts of the city that you'll find the most exciting nightlife: venues cover a breadth of tastes, and are rarely expensive. **Clubs and discos** range from slick hangouts for the trendy to dingy, uninviting punk dives. As ever, it's the tension the city seems to generate that gives the nightlife its colour.

Berlin's reputation as a leader of the avant-garde is reflected in the number of small, often experimental **theatre groups** working here. The scene is an active one, though bear in mind that many theatre companies take a break in July and August. **Classical**

TICKET OFFICES

Ticket offices or *Theaterkassen* are usually the easiest way of buying tickets for all major music, theatre and dance events, although they charge a hefty commission (up to 17 percent) on the ticket price.

Berlin Ticket, Potsdamer Str. 96 (☎2308 8230).

Box office, Nollendorfplatz 7 (☎215 5463).

Europa Center, Tauentzienstr. 9 (☎264 1138).

KaDeWe, Tauentzienstr. 21 (☎217 7754).

Kant-Kasse, Krumme Str. 55 (☎313 4554).

Karstadt, Schloss Str. 7–10 (☎792 2800).

Theaterkasse Centrum, Meinekestr. 25 (☎882 7611).

Ticket Hotline (☎809 9090). Credit card bookings only.

Wertheim, Kurfürstendamm 231 (☎882 2500).

Wildbad-Kiosk, Rankestr. 1 (☎881 4507).

music has long been dominated by the world-class Berlin Philharmonic, though other orchestras play in the city, and several museums and historic buildings often host chamber concerts and recitals. Vanishing subsidies have cast a shadow over the theatres, orchestras and opera houses in the city, though it's likely that the big name venues (like the Berliner Ensemble and Deutsches Theater) will weather current storms.

Two of the city's venues are unclassifiable: the *Waldbühne* is a large outdoor amphitheatre on the Hollywood Bowl model, just west of the Olympic Stadium. It presents everything from opera to movies to hard rock – unbeatable in summer. The *Tempodrom*, two tents in the Tiergarten, hosts concerts and circuses in the larger tent, cabaret and more intimate performances in the smaller.

Discos and clubs

Berlin's discos are smaller, cheaper and less exclusive than their counterparts in London or New York – and fewer in number. It doesn't take much to work out that the places along the Ku'damm are tourist rip-offs: the real all-night sweats take place in Kreuzberg and Prenzlauer Berg, where glitz is out and post-punk cool in. Don't bother turning up until midnight at the earliest, since few places get going much before then. Admission is often free – when you do pay, it shouldn't be much more than DM10. Like most cities, Berlin's turnover in nightspots is rapid: expect the following listings to have changed at least slightly by the time you arrive.

90°, Dennewitzstr. 37. Practically an institution and still hip. Soul, house and funk. Thurs–Sat from 11pm.

Delicious Doughnuts, Rosenthaler Strasse/Auguststrasse, Mitte. A place for would-be beautiful party people to groove to Acid jazz and funk beats. 10pm onwards. Closed Mon.

Dunckerclub, Dunckerstr. 64, Prenzlauer Berg. Indie, industrial and unashamedly gothic sounds.

E-Werk, Wilhelmstr. 43, Mitte. Rave lives on in this former power station in the shadow of the Treuhand Air Ministry building. Currently, the in place for trance, house and techno. Fri–Sun 11pm onwards.

Q-Club, Pücklerstr. 34. A tiny basement packed with funk and house fans. Fri–Sat from 10pm.

Sophienclub, Sophienstr. 6, Mitte. Different nights cover soul, funk, house and indie. Daily 9pm onwards.

Tacheles, Oranienburger Str. 54–56, Mitte. Chaotic club nights in the Theatersaal, mostly of a dance persuasion but with much multi-media weirdness thrown in. Fri 10pm onwards.

Tresor, Leipziger Str. 126a, Mitte. A key player in the Berlin dance scene since 1990 and still going strong. Trouser-shaking techno in the cellar and slightly mellower house and hip-hop beats upstairs. Fri & Sat midnight onwards.

Live music

The way to find out exactly what's on and where is to look in the listings magazines *Tip* and *Zitty*, in *Berlin Programm*, or on the innumerable flyposters about town. Remember that many bars and cafés often have live music.

Major venues

The following are the sort of places you can expect to find international supergroups playing. Book well in advance for anything even vaguely popular. Invariably you can't buy tickets from the places themselves but need to go to one of the ticket agencies (see p.795).

Alte TU-Mensa, Hardenbergstr. 35 (☎311 2233). Part of the Technical University.

Deutschlandhalle, Messedamm 26 (☎30380). Part of the Congress Centre west of the city.

ICC Berlin, Messedamm (☎30380). Vast, soulless hall for trade fairs that often hosts gigs.

Tränenpalast, Reichstagsufer 17 (☎238 6211). A former waiting room on the border between East and West, the "Palace of Tears" now hosts visiting mid-level bands.

Waldbühne, corner of Glockenturmstrasse and Passenheimer Strasse (☎2308 8230). Open-air spot in a natural amphitheatre near the Olympic stadium that features movies, bands, classical concerts and other diverse entertainments. Great fun on summer evenings, but arrive early as it gets crowded.

Contemporary

Huxley's, Hasenheide 108–114 (☎627 9320). Popular, reasonably famous bands in solid surroundings.

Knaack, Greifswalderstr. 224, Prenzlauer Berg. Mostly local rock bands you're unlikely to have heard of, plus the odd visiting band you probably won't have heard of either.

K.O.B., Potsdamer Str. 157. A pub in a (now legally) squatted house which on weekdays hosts interesting groups at low prices (DM5). R&B, jazz and psychedelic sounds play here, but the favourites are local anarcho- and fun-punk bands.

Metropol, Nollendorfplatz 5 (☎216 4122). Well-known, if not mega, names play frequently in this large dance space.

Pfefferberg, Schönhauser Allee 176 (☎449 6534). A dressed-down club heavy on roots and reggae.

Tempodrom, near the *Haus der Kulturen der Welt* on John-Foster-Dulles-Allee (☎394 4045). Two tents, the larger hosting contemporary bands of middling fame.

The Loft, part of the *Metropol*, Nollendorfplatz 5 (☎786 5023). Features a whole range of independent artists, with a view to innovation and introducing new music.

Jazz, folk and blues

A-Trane, Bleibtreustr. 1 (☎313 2550). One of the city's best jazz venues, featuring name bands in a comfortable room.

Blues Café, Körnerstr. 11 (☎261 3698). Hiding away in a small street off Potsdamer Strasse, this low-profile café is the place to head for if you like your blues pure and original.

Flöz, Nassauische Str. 37 (☎861 1000). Basement club that's the meeting point for Berlin's jazz musicians and a testing ground for the city's new bands. Also offers occasional salsa and cabaret. Can be wild.

Franz, Schönhauser Allee 36–39, Prenzlauer Berg (☎442 8203). Heavy on jazz and blues but with regular reggae, latin and rock gigs too. They claim to put on 365 concerts a year.

Junction Bar, Gneisenaustr. 18 (☎694 6602). A small and good-natured basement club featuring local talent ranging from jazz to funk to folk.

Podewil, Klosterstr. 68, Mitte (☎247496). Mostly jazz, but with world music and occasional classical concerts.

Quasimodo, Kantstr. 12a (☎312 8086). Berlin's best jazz spot, with daily programmes starting at 10pm. A high quality mix of international stars and up-and-coming names. Small with good atmosphere.

Classical

Deutsche Oper, Bismarckstr. 34 (☎341 0249). As well as opera and ballet, there are good classical concerts here.

Komische Oper, Behrenstr. 55–57 (box office at Unter den Linden 41; ☎220 2603). An ensemble company, without the star soloists of the other two opera houses.

Konzerthaus Berlin, Schauspielhaus am Gendarmenmarkt, Gendarmenmarkt 2 (☎209 09201). This striking building is home to both the *Berliner Sinfonie-Orchester* and the *Deutsches Sinfonie-Orchester*, and also plays host to visiting orchestras. Orchestras perform in the Grosser Konzertsaal, while the smaller Kammermusiksaal is for chamber music. Box office Mon–Sat noon–8pm, Sun noon–4pm.

Philharmonie, Kemperplatz, Matthäikirchestr. 1 (☎2548 8132). For years classical music in Berlin meant one man and one orchestra: Herbert von Karajan and the *Berliner Philharmoniker*. Since his death in 1989 the orchestra has retained its popularity under new conductor Claudio Abbado, and tickets are extremely difficult to get. Call the box office as far in advance as possible Mon–Fri 3.30–6pm, Sat & Sun 11am–2pm.

Staatsoper, Unter den Linden 7, Mitte. (☎2035 4555). Excellent operatic productions under the direction of Daniel Barenboim. Box office Mon–Fri 10am–6pm, Sat & Sun 2–6pm.

Urania, An der Urania 17 (☎218 9091). A wide-ranging programme and reasonably priced seats.

Theatre

Sad to say, the mainstream **civic and private theatres** in Berlin are on the whole dull, unadventurous and expensive – and though it's often possible to cut costs by buying student standby tickets, you'll find little in English save for the work of small, roving theatre groups. However, the city is still a major venue for **experimental work**, and if your German is up to it a number of groups are worth the ticket price; check under "Off-Theater" in *Tip* or *Zitty* for up-to-the-minute listings.

Civic and private theatres

Berliner Ensemble, Bertolt-Brecht-Platz 1, Mitte (box office ☎282 3160). Fomerly lacklustre Brecht theatre now undergoing something of a revival. Box office Mon–Sat 11am–6pm, Sun 3–6pm.

Deutsches Theater, Schumannstr. 13a, Mitte (☎2844 1225). One of the best in Berlin with an extensive repertoire of classic modern works. Invariably sold out. Also includes a second theatre the *Kammerspiele des Deutschen Theaters*, and the experimental *Baracke* nearby.

Die Distel, Friedrichstr. 101, in the Admiralspalast (☎204 4704). An heir to Berlin's legendary inter-war cabaret tradition, this cabaret now addresses the issues raised by life in a united Germany.

Friends of the Italian Opera, Fidicinstr. 40 (☎691 1211). Kreuzberg theatre hosting English-language performances.

Schaubühne am Lehniner Platz, Kurfürstendamm 153 (☎890023). State-of-the-art equipped theatre that hosts performances of the classics and some experimental pieces.

Theater des Westens, Kantstr. 12 (☎882 2888). Musicals and light opera, the occasional Broadway-style show. Beautiful turn-of-the-century building, often sold out.

Theater Zerbrochener Fenster, Fidicinstr. 3 (☎691 1211). Another Kreuzberg venue hosting English-language theatre.

Experimental and free theatre groups

bat studiotheater, Belforter Str. 15, Prenzlauer Berg (☎442 7996). Originally a workers' and students' theatre, this one can usually be relied on to come up with challenging experimental offerings including theatre-student graduation productions. Box office daily 9am–4pm.

Theater O.N., Kollwitzstr. 53, Prenzlauer Berg (☎440 9214). Small alternative theatre that somehow manages to survive, putting on its own productions and playing host to visiting companies.

UFA-Fabrik, Viktoriastr. 13 (☎752 5030). The most famous, and most efficiently run, cultural factory, with just about every aspect of the performing arts on offer. The UFA-Fabrik acts as an umbrella group for all kinds of performance – theatre, dance, music and film – and it's always worth checking out what's on.

Varieté Chamäleon, Rosenthaler Str. 40–41, Mitte (☎282 7118). Cabaret and variety theatre. Check out the *Mitternachtshow* at midnight on Friday and Saturday.

Listings

Airline offices *Air France*, Europa Center (☎264 7440); *British Airways*, Europa Center (☎691021); *Delta*, Europa Center (☎230 9400); *Lufthansa*, Kurfürstendamm 220 (☎887588).

Airports Schönefeld (☎6091 5166), Tegel (☎4101 2306), Tempelhof (☎6951 2288).

Bike rental Available from several shops, though not at the train station. *Fahrradstation*, Möckernstr. 92 (☎216 9177) is a good choice offering bikes from DM18 per day, DM70 per week.

Bookstores Best selection of English paperbacks and books on the city can be found at *Kiepert*, Hardenbergstr. 4–5, and the *British Book Shop*, Mauerstr. 83–84.

Car rental *Ass Rent a Car*, Albrechtstr. 117 (☎792 0015) and *Allround*, Kaiser-Friedrich-Str. 86(☎342 5091) are among the city's cheapest. International firms have offices at Tegel airport and are listed in the phone book.

Cultural Centres *Amerika Haus*, Hardenbergstr. 22–24 (Tues–Fri 2–5pm; ☎310 0010); *British Council*, Hardenbergstr. 20, first floor (Mon, Wed & Fri noon–6pm, Tues & Thurs noon–7pm).

Dentist ☎8900 4333.

Disabled travel It comes as no surprise to hear that facilities in the western part of the city are better than those in the east. Most of the major western museums have wheelchair access, as do many other public buildings. The full colour U- and S-Bahn map also indicates which stations are accessible by wheelchair.

Doctor ☎310031.

Embassies *Britain*, Unter den Linden 32 (☎201840); *Canada*, Friedrichstr. 95 (☎261 1161); *Ireland*, Ernst-Reuter-Platz 10 (☎3480 0822); *USA* (consulate), Clayallee 170 (☎832 4087).

Exchange facilities The exchange at the main entrance to the Zoo Station (Mon–Sat 8am–9pm, Sun 10am–6pm) will cash travellers' cheques and give cash advances on major credit cards, though subject to a minimum of DM200.

Laundry Dahlmannstr. 17 (Mon–Fri 9am–1pm & 3–6pm); Hauptstr. 151 (7.30am–10.30pm); Uhlandstr. 53 (6.30am–10.30pm). Other addresses are listed under *Wäschereien* in the *Yellow Pages*.

Mitfahrzentralen Bergmannstr. 57 (☎693 6095); Kurfürstendamm 227 (☎882 7606); *Mitfahrzentrale am Zoo*, U2 platform direction Vinetastrasse; *Frauenmitfahrzentrale*, Potsdamer Str. 139 (☎215 3165). Many more listings can be found in *Tip* and *Zitty* magazines.

Pharmacies Prescriptions can be filled at any *Apotheke*; outside normal hours a notice on the door of any *Apotheke* indicates the nearest one open. Otherwise try *Europa-Apotheke*, Tauentzienstr. 9 (☎261 4142); 9am–8pm daily.

Post office Handiest is at Zoo Station (Mon–Fri 8am–6pm, Sat 8am–noon), with one counter open until midnight. This is also the place for poste restante facilities: Postamt Bahnhof Zoo, 10623 Berlin.

Taxis congregate outside *KaDeWe*, on Savignyplatz and by the Zoo Station in the west; and in the east at the northern entrance to Friedrichstrasse station, at the *Centrum* department store, entrances to Alexanderplatz S-Bahn station and the *Forum Hotel* nearby, and at the *Hotel Adlon* on the Unter den Linden. Or call ☎ 210101 or 261026.

Travel agents *Flugbörse*, Windscheidtstr. 22 (☎323 7097) and Nollendorfstr. 28 (☎216 3061). Youth and student travel specialists: *STATravel*, Goethestr. 73 (☎311 0950).

Women's centre Stresemannstr. 40 (☎251 2828). Friendly and well-organized help and information centre that offers advice on a wide range of subjects.

BRANDENBURG

Brandenburg is geographically the largest of Germany's five new Länder, though it has a very low population density, largely because it is shorn of Berlin, its epicentre and traditional capital, which is now a Land in its own right. The province was founded as a margraviate or frontier district by **Albert the Bear** (*Albrecht der Bär*) in 1157 from land bequeathed to him by a Pribislav-Heinrich, a Slav king who had converted to Christianity. Its importance to the predatory German nation's desire for eastward expansion was recognized by its Margrave being designated one of the seven Electors of the Holy Roman Empire. In 1415, this title was bestowed on the **Hohenzollern** family, and from then until 1918 the fortunes of the two became inextricably linked, with Brandenburg being the heartland of the expansionist military state of Brandenburg-Prussia, whose name was shortened to Prussia in 1701.

The Brandenburg landscape consists of undulating farmland and sandy forests which are unexceptional but by no means unattractive. In lieu of Berlin, the old royal residence of **Potsdam** on its outskirts has taken over as Land capital, and its outstanding group of Baroque palaces is the province's prime draw. West of here lies the long-overshadowed city of **Brandenburg** which, despite the ravages of war and pollution, preserves an important medieval heritage. The only other major towns, **Frankfurt an der Oder** and **Cottbus**, are similarly scarred, though the latter has the good fortune to lie close to the province's one area of outstanding natural beauty, the water-strewn **Spreewald**, which is still inhabited by the Sorbs, Germany's only indigenous Slav minority.

Travel throughout the province is easy, thanks to the continued survival of an extensive public transport network. Most places make easy day-trips from Berlin – which is fortunate, as tourist facilities often remain rudimentary.

Potsdam

"The first fine day should be devoted to Potsdam, without which a complete impression of Berlin can scarcely be obtained," claims the prewar *Baedeker*, a nod to the fact that **POTSDAM**, although not officially part of Berlin, was the natural completion of the Hohenzollern city, forming a unity with Charlottenburg and the old centre along the Unter den Linden. Potsdam is a dazzling triumph of man over nature – the swampy marshland of the Havel and its lakes having been transformed into a glorious planned townscape replete with palaces, parks and gardens. The main complex is **Park Sanssouci**, but there are two other important areas of landscaped greenery in the shape of the **Neuer Garten** and **Park Babelsberg**. Potsdam's **Altstadt**, notwithstanding grievous losses in the war, is itself a magnificent Baroque and Neoclassical town.

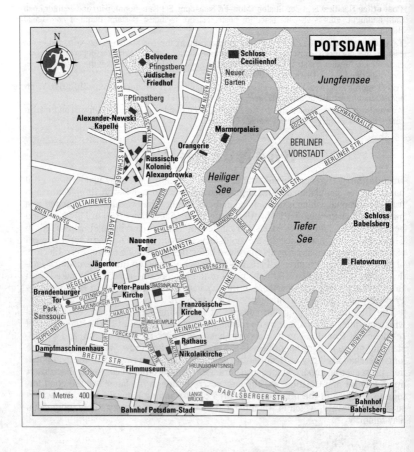

> The **telephone code** for Potsdam is ☎0331

Despite the fact that it lay just to the southwest of Berlin, until 1990 it was difficult to reach Potsdam: visa regulations made visiting a complicated affair and many people left it off their itineraries. Since the withering away of the border, however, the town has enjoyed an enormous influx of visitors from the west, and you'll find that you need at least three days to take everything in.

Arrival, information and accommodation

There are excellent transport links from Berlin to Potsdam. Bus #116 runs from S-Bahnhof Wannsee to the Glienicker Brücke, where you can pick up tram #93 to Platz der Einheit, Potsdam's central square and traffic hub.

Otherwise, S-Bahns #3 and #7 link Berlin city centre to **Potsdam Stadt station**, from where it's only a few minutes' walk north over the Lange Brücke and along Friedrich-Ebert-Strasse to Platz der Einheit. From the station bus #695 takes you to the grounds of Schloss Sanssouci, a short distance from the Orangerie. Alternatively take a taxi (DM20) or rent a bike (DM15) from the station forecourt. A more atmospheric approach is provided by the twice-daily *Weisse Flotte* sailings from Wannsee (see p.777). Most trains from cities outside Berlin stop at the **Hauptbahnhof**, 2km due south of the western end of Park Sanssouci.

Just south of Platz der Einheit is Potsdam's **tourist information office**, at Friedrich-Ebert-Str. 5 (Mon–Fri 9am–8pm, Sat 10am–6pm, Sun 10am–4pm; ☎291100). It's well equipped with maps, and books rooms in private accommodation.

Accommodation

With so much to see, it's a good idea to stay in Potsdam, but accommodation is scarce when the summer crowds descend. If you're on a tight budget the best bet is to book a **private room** (②–③) through the tourist office at Friedrich-Ebert-Str. 5 (see above). Potsdam also has a couple of **campsites**. For information, call at the tourist information office (☎291100) where they'll be able to direct you to the nearest available space.

HOTELS

Am Jägertor, Hegelallee 11 (☎4243 9650). The best option in central Potsdam. ⑤

art'otel potsdam, Zeppelinstr. 136 (☎98150). A bright, splashy new luxury hotel, part of which occupies a historic building. ⑧

POTSDAM – SOME RECENT HISTORY

Under the Hohenzollerns the small village of Potsdam became a royal residence and garrison town, roles that it enjoyed right up until the abdication of Kaiser Wilhelm II in 1918. World War II left Potsdam badly damaged and 4000 people were killed in the bombing raid of April 14, 1945, which left the town centre in ruins and destroyed many fine Baroque buildings. Immediately after the war, Potsdam was chosen by the victorious Allies as venue for a **conference** where, on August 2, 1945, the division of Germany and Europe was confirmed. Subsequently, under the SED regime, it was decided to demolish the ruins of much of the old town and undertake extensive modern building programmes in pursuit of a "new, socialist Potsdam". These account for the ugly eastern half of the town centre and, although attempts were made to preserve the architectural integrity of the town during the 1980s, the Communists always felt ill at ease with its historical role and imperial associations. With the opening of the border in 1989, Potsdam's links with the rest of Berlin were once again revived, and the last Soviet troops left in summer 1994.

Babelsberg, Stahndorfer Str. 68 (☎749010). A value-for-money old-fashioned hotel on the Babelsberg side of the Havel. ③

Schloss Cecilienhof, Im Neuen Garten (☎37050, fax 292498). Housed in a wing of Schloss Cecilienhof, this is the place to be if you want to stay in luxury in Potsdam. ⑧

Zum Hummer, Im Park Babelsberg 2 (☎619549). A good-value place pleasantly located in Babelsberg Park. ④

The Altstadt

Platz der Einheit makes a good starting point for any exploration of the town, although only a few non-concrete buildings survive in its immediate vicinity, hinting at a world long since vanished. The fancy-looking building at the southeast corner of the square is a neo-Baroque **post office**, to the immediate north of which stood the synagogue until it was wrecked on *Kristallnacht*, and later completely demolished – a plaque marks the spot. From the post office, Am Kanal and **Am Alten Markt** lead to the **Nikolaikirche**. This stately, domed building, its Neoclassical lines at odds with its surroundings, was originally built according to plans drawn up by Schinkel, and the impact of its exterior is echoed within – the walls are decorated with paintings of New Testament scenes and the effect of the dome is, if anything, more impressive than from the outside.

Diagonally opposite the Nikolaikirche is another survivor, Potsdam's former **Rathaus**, which was built in Palladian style during the mid-eighteenth century. Until 1875 the circular Rathaus tower served as town jail; it lost its town hall function in 1885, and was taken over by a bank, which remained there until the bombs came. Under the old authorities the building became a *Kulturhaus* or arts centre, a role it retains. Inside you'll find a theatre, a couple of galleries and a number of cafés.

East of the Platz der Einheit only a few ailing eighteenth-century town houses survive on Am Kanal, although this area is the oldest part of Potsdam. South of here lies the **Freundschaft Insel**, a leafy mid-Havel island which makes a good place to take a break from street-pounding, with its ornamental garden, café and boats for rent.

West of Platz der Einheit

Slightly more tangible vestiges of old Potsdam survive in a few of the streets west of Wilhelmsplatz. **Yorckstrasse** boasts a number of fine – albeit slightly run-down – **Baroque houses**, as does **Wilhelm-Staab-Strasse**. The **Neuer Markt** quarter just to the south of Yorckstrasse also has a couple of good-looking survivors, including some improbably grand eighteenth-century coaching stables with an entrance in the form of a triumphal arch, which are now home to a haulage firm. At Am Neuen Markt 1 is the **Kabinetthaus**, a small palace which was the birthplace of Friedrich Wilhelm II, the only member of the Hohenzollern family actually born in Potsdam.

The Marstall and around

A little to the northwest across Breite Strasse is the former palace **Marstall** or royal stables, the oldest town centre survivor. Originally built as an orangery, it was prettified by Knobelsdorff in the eighteenth century. Today the Marstall houses Potsdam's **Filmmuseum** (Tues–Fri 10am–5pm, Sat & Sun 10am–6pm; DM4). Drawing on material from the UFA studios in nearby Babelsberg (later DEFA, the GDR state film company; see p.810), the museum presents both a technical and an artistic history of German film from 1895 to 1980, with some particularly fascinating material concerning the genres of the immediate postwar period. There's a vaguely hands-on feel, with a few visitor-operated bioscopes and numerous screens playing clips. The museum **cinema** is the best in Potsdam, and there's also a good café.

To the west of the Marstall, it's worth making a quick detour down **Kiezstrasse**, where a number of eighteenth-century Rococo houses have been beautifully restored, including no. 4 which houses *Der Froschkasten*, one of Potsdam's better bars. The nearby high-rises on the Neustädter Havebucht hide in their midst the **Dampfmaschinenhaus** (guided tours Sat & Sun 10am–noon & 1–5pm only; DM4), probably the most imaginative pump house in the world. At first sight it looks like a mosque, with a chimney in the shape of a minaret. The Moorish forms are also present in the interior, though much of the space is taken up by a giant steam engine which was recently electrified.

The Barock-Viertel

North of the Platz der Einheit, the area bounded by Schopenhauerstrasse, Hegelallee, Hebbelstrasse and Charlottenstrasse is Potsdam's **Barock-Viertel** (Baroque Quarter), built between 1732 and 1742 on the orders of Friedrich Wilhelm I. At the southeastern corner of **Bassinplatz** is the **Französische Kirche**, completed according to plans by Knobelsdorff in 1753, in imitation of the Pantheon in Rome, a recurring theme of the period. At its western end, Bassinplatz is graced by the nineteenth-century **Peter-Pauls-Kirche**, with a replica of the campanile of San Zeno Maggiore in Verona.

The ornate Baroque houses, built with slight variations in detail to avoid monotony, lie to the west of here on and around **Brandenburger Strasse**, Potsdam's pedestrianized main shopping street. The whole quarter was intended as a settlement for tradespeople in the then rapidly expanding town. To the north and west of the Barock-Viertel are two of Potsdam's three surviving town gates – the **Jägertor** or "Hunter's Gate" (at the end of Lindenstrasse), and the **Brandenburger Tor** (at the western end of Brandenburger Strasse), a triumphal arch of 1733 which has a playfulness lacking in its Berlin namesake.

The Holländisches Viertel

Just to the north of Bassinplatz is the **Holländisches Viertel** or Dutch Quarter, the best-known and most appealing part of Friedrich Wilhelm I's town extension. In the area bounded by Gutenbergstrasse, Kurfürstenstrasse, Friedrich-Ebert-Strasse and Hebbelstrasse are 134 gabled red-brick houses put up by Dutch builders for the immigrants from Holland who were invited to work in Potsdam by the king. In fact, not that many Dutch took up the invitation, and many of those who did returned home when the promised employment dried up following Friedrich Wilhelm's death. A disturbingly large number of the houses look derelict, but some excellent restored examples can be found along Mittelstrasse, particularly at the junction with Benkertstrasse, many already functioning as trendy boutiques. Immediately north of the quarter is the colossal **Nauener Tor**, the last of the city gates, built in the 1750s as the first German building in the English Gothick style.

Park Sanssouci

Park Sanssouci, Frederick the Great's fabled retreat, stretches out for 2km west of the town centre, and its gardens and palaces are what draw most visitors to Potsdam. In 1744 Frederick ordered the construction of a residence where he would be able to live "without cares" – *"sans souci"* in the French spoken in court. The task was entrusted to the architect Georg von Knobelsdorff who had already proved himself on other projects in the town and in Berlin. **Schloss Sanssouci**, on a hill overlooking the town, was completed in the year that work began, while extensive parklands to the west – the **Rehgarten** – were laid out over the following five years. As a finishing touch Frederick ordered the construction of the **Neues Palais** at the western end of the park to mark the end of the Seven Years' War. Over the following 150 years or so, numerous additions were made, including the **Orangerie** and the laying of Jubiläumsstrasse (now known as Maulbeerallee) just south of the Orangerie in 1913. The park is at its best in spring when the trees are in leaf and the flowers in bloom, but these days it's all too often overrun by visitors. To avoid the crowds, visit on a weekday, preferably outside summer, when you'll be better able to appreciate the place.

Schloss Sanssouci

To approach **Schloss Sanssouci** as Frederick the Great might have done, make for the eighteenth-century **Obelisk** on Schopenhauerstrasse that marks the main entrance to the park. Beyond, Hauptallee runs through the ornate Knobelsdorff-designed **Obelisk-Portal** – two clusters of pillars flanked by the goddesses Flora and Pomona – to the **Grosse Fontäne**, the biggest of the park's many fountains, just to the north. The approach to the Schloss itself leads up through terraced ranks of vines which are among the northernmost in Germany.

Frederick had very definite ideas about what he wanted and worked closely with Knobelsdorff on the design of his palace, which was to be a place where the king, who had no great love for his capital Berlin or his wife Elizabeth Christine, could escape both. It's a surprisingly modest one-storey Baroque affair, looking out over the vine terraces towards the high-rises of the Neustädter Havelbucht. Frederick loved the Schloss so much that he intended to be buried here and had a tomb excavated for himself in front of the eastern wing, near the graves of his Italian greyhounds, animals whose company he preferred to that of human beings during the last, increasingly eccentric years of his life. When he died, however, his nephew Friedrich Wilhelm II had him interred in the now-demolished Garnisonkirche in Potsdam itself, next to the father Frederick hated. Towards the end of World War II, the remains of Frederick and his father were exhumed and eventually taken to Burg Hohenzollern in Swabia for safe-keeping from the approaching Soviet army. Only in 1991, after unification, were the remains returned and buried in Frederick's preferred site.

Inside, the Schloss is a frenzy of Rococo, spread through the twelve rooms where Frederick lived and entertained his guests – a process which usually entailed quarrelling and arguing with them. The most eye-catching rooms are the opulent **Marmorsaal** (Marble Hall) and the **Konzertzimmer** (Concert Room), where the flute-playing king had eminent musicians play his own works on concert evenings. Frederick's favourite haunt was his **library** where, surrounded by his two thousand volumes – mainly French translations of the classics and a sprinkling of contemporary French writings – he could oversee the work on his tomb. One of Frederick's most celebrated house guests was **Voltaire** who lived here from 1750 to 1753, acting as a kind of private tutor to the king, finally leaving when he'd had enough of Frederick's bizarre behaviour. In revenge Frederick ordered that Voltaire's former room be decorated with carvings of apes and parrots.

The **Damenflügel**, the west wing of the Schloss (mid-May to mid-Oct Sat & Sun only 10am–5pm; DM3), was added in 1840, and its thirteen rooms housed ladies and gentlemen of the court. Nearby on the terrace is a wrought-iron summer house protecting a weather-beaten copy of a Classical statue, while just to the south an eighteenth-century sculpture of Cleopatra looks over the graves of Frederick's horses.

SCHLOSS SANSSOUCI – TICKETS AND OPENING HOURS

It is essential to arrive early in the day as tickets, which cost DM10, must be bought in advance for a set guided tour later in the day. At weekends and in summer, they sell out quickly. The Schloss is open April–October 9am–5pm; February & March 9am–4pm; November–January 9am–3pm; closed 12.30–1pm.

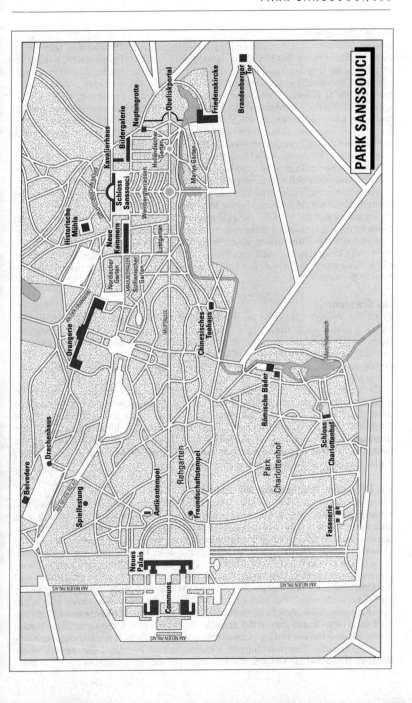

Around the Schloss

West of Schloss Sanssouci, overlooking the ornamental **Holländischer Garten** or Dutch Garden, is the **Bildergalerie** (mid-May to mid-Oct Tues–Sun 10am–noon & 12.30–5pm; DM4), a restrained Baroque creation that was the first building in Europe to be erected specifically as a museum. The collection's most famous work is Caravaggio's *Incredulity of St Thomas*. There's also a wonderful *Supper at Emmaus* by his Dutch follower, Ter Brugghen. Rubens and Van Dyck are both extensively represented; the most important works by the former are *St Jerome in his Study* and *The Four Evangelists*; by the latter are portraits of members of the British court, plus a couple of mythological works, *Rinaldo and Armida* and *Venus in Vulcan's Workshop*.

On the opposite side of the Schloss, from a point near the Cleopatra statue, steps lead down to the **Neue Kammern** (mid-May to mid-Oct Tues–Sun 10am–5pm; closed rest of year; DM4), the architectural twin of the Bildergalerie, originally used as an orangery and later as a guest house. Frederick was prepared to go to some lengths to achieve the desired carefree rural ambience for Sanssouci and retained an old wooden windmill as an ornament just north of the Neue Kammern. Four years after his death, this was replaced by a rustic-looking stone construction, the **Historische Mühle**, which is now a restaurant. The **Ruinenberg**, rising to the north of Schloss Sanssouci, looks like a cluster of Classical ruins, but in fact these fragments are artificial, designed to render a little more interesting a reservoir built during the eighteenth century to feed the fountains in the park.

The Orangerie

From the western corner of the Sizilianischer Garten, **Maulbeerallee** (Mulberry Alley), a road open to traffic, cuts through the park to the ascent to the **Orangerie** (open for special exhibitions only; DM5). A series of terraces with curved retaining walls sporting waterspouts in the shape of lions' heads leads up to the sandy-coloured Italian Renaissance-style structure, whose slightly down-at-heel appearance lends it added character.

The western wing of the building is still used for its original purpose, as a refuge for tropical plants in winter, and during the summer it's possible to ascend the western tower, from where there are great views of the Neues Palais and depressing vistas of Potsdam's high-rises to the east. The Orangerie also houses a gallery, the **Raphaelsaal**, with copies of Raphael's most famous masterpieces. Part of the Orangerie is given over to private apartments, occupied by members of the park staff – which must be just about the best addresses in Potsdam.

The Belvedere, Drachenhaus and around

From the western wing of the Orangerie, the arrow-straight, lime tree-lined **Krimlindenallee** leads up towards a ruined Rococo **Belvedere**, the last building to be built under Frederick the Great. It was the sole building in the whole park to suffer war damage and has only recently been restored. A couple of hundred metres short of the Belvedere a path branches off to the left, leading to the **Drachenhaus**, a one-time vintner's house built in the style of a Chinese pagoda for the small vineyard nearby. Today there's a genteel café inside, an ideal point to interrupt your wanderings. Southwest of the Drachenhaus a pathway leads across the park to the **Spielfestung**, the toy fort to end all toy forts, which was built for the sons of Wilhelm II and even armed with miniature Krupp cannons. Returning to the path, follow it to the **Antikentempel**, originally built in 1768 to house part of the art collection of Frederick the Great. This domed rotunda is now the last resting place of a number of members of the Hohenzollern family, including the Empress Auguste Victoria, and of Hermine, the woman whom Wilhelm II married in exile and who was known as the "Last Empress".

The Neues Palais

To the west through the trees rises the **Neues Palais** (April–Oct 9am–12.45pm & 1.15–5pm; Feb & March closes 4pm; Nov–Jan closes 3pm; DM8), another massive Rococo extravaganza from Frederick the Great's time, built between 1763 and 1769 to reaffirm the might of Prussia and its king after the Seven Years' War. At the centre of the palace is a huge green-weathered dome, topped by a gilded crown. The edges of the roof are lined with statues, which were specially mass-produced by a team of sculptors.

Visits inside the palace are guided in the winter, but not in summer. The highlights of the interior are the amazing encrusted entrance hall, the *Grottensaal* and the *Marmorsaal*, directly above, which is the main festive hall. The southern wing (which these days houses a small café) contains Frederick's apartments and the theatre where the king enjoyed Italian opera and French plays. A francophile to the point of near mania, Frederick believed that the Germans were philistines incapable of producing great art. The last imperial resident of the Neues Palais was Kaiser Wilhelm II, who packed sixty train carriages with the contents of the palace when he and his family fled in November 1918, following the revolution and abdication. Across the courtyard behind the Neues Palais are the **Communs**, a couple of pointless Rococo fantasies joined by a curved colonnade. They look grandiose, but their purpose was mundane: they were built for the serving and maintenance staff of the Palais.

The Rehgarten and Charlottenhof

From the Neues Palais, Ökonomieweg leads east through the **Rehgarten** or Deer Garden, former court hunting ground, where you'll find the **Chinesisches Teehaus** (mid-May to mid-Oct Sat–Thurs 9am–noon & 12.30–5pm; DM2), a kind of Rococo pagoda housing a small museum of Chinese and Meissen porcelain and surrounded by eerily lifelike statues of oriental figures. A path to the south leads over a bridge past a small farm building to the **Römischer Bäder** (mid-May to mid-Oct Fri–Wed 10am–noon & 12.30–5pm; DM7.50 includes entry to Schloss Charlottenhof), built by Schinkel and Ludwig Persius in convincing imitation of a Roman villa. To the south, set in the broad expanse of rough parkland, **Charlottenhof**, is **Schloss Charlottenhof** (mid-May to mid-Oct Thurs–Tues 10am–12.30pm & 1–5pm; DM7.50 includes entry to Römisher Bäder), a Roman-style building designed by Schinkel and Persius for Friedrich IV. Its interior is impressive: the hallway is bathed in blue light filtered through coloured glass decorated with stars, a prelude to the **Kupferstichzimmer**, whose walls are covered in copies of Italian Renaissance paintings.

The Grüner Gitter and around

At the southwestern corner of Sanssouci is the **Grüner Gitter** or Green Gateway entrance to the grounds, where there's an **information kiosk**. Immediately to the north of this entrance way is the Italianate **Friedenskirche**, designed by Persius for Friedrich Wilhelm IV and completed in 1850. With its 39-metre campanile and lakeside setting it conjures up the southern European atmosphere that Friedrich Wilhelm was striving to create when he ordered the construction of the church using the San Clemente basilica in Rome as a model. The entire design of the church is determined by the magnificent apse mosaic from Murano, the only intact Byzantine mosaic north of the Alps. Adjoining the church is a domed Hohenzollern mausoleum containing the tombs of Friedrich Wilhelm IV, Friedrich III and their wives.

North of the centre

Heading north from the Nauener Tor along Friedrich-Ebert-Strasse will bring you to some of Potsdam's most fascinating, yet least-known, corners. The beginnings are inauspicious – on the left is a mid-nineteenth-century Italianate villa, once the house of a royal gardener, behind which lie the former district headquarters of the *Stasi*, while the neo-Baroque affair to the north is a turn-of-the-century local government office.

Alexandrowka and the Alexander-Newski-Kapelle

However, after about fifteen minutes' walking you'll reach **Alexandrowka**, a settlement of Russian-style wooden houses, built for a group of Russian military musicians who found themselves marooned here after the Napoleonic Wars. Its incongruity makes it one of the most intriguing sights in town, a collection of two-storey dwellings with steeply pitched roofs, laid out in the form of a St Andrew's cross. In 1826, Friedrich Wilhelm III gave the order that houses should be built for these men and their families. Eight houses were built on the arms of the cross, four more at the semicircular linking roads at each end, with an overseer's residence in the middle. The names of the original occupants and subsequent inhabitants (a few of them descendants of the Russians, even today) are carved into the house fronts. Some of the oldest inscriptions are in Cyrillic script.

Directly to the north of the settlement is the **Kapelle des heiligen Alexander Newski**, a church built for the Russians in 1829, set on top of the closely wooded Kapellenberg hill. Access is either by scrambling up the hillside, or via a track branching to the right off Nedlitzer Strasse which leads to a rudimentary car park. The chapel is a compact building in pink stucco edged with white, topped by a central onion-domed tower, with smaller domes at each corner. The chapel is usually accessible at weekends, but if there's anyone about during the week it's often possible to take a look round. The interior is festooned with icons, many of them gifts from the Czarina Alexandra, who started life as Princess Charlotte of Prussia. The priest's wife oversees a little stall selling replica icons and holy medals, and often plays Russian Orthodox choir tapes which enhance the already ethereal effect.

The Pfingstberg

Immediately to the north of the Kapellenberg is the wooded **Pfingstberg**, another little-known Potsdam curiosity which, like the Russian settlement and the Kapellenberg, is undergoing a process of gradual rediscovery. At the foot of the hill is the walled **Jüdischer Friedhof** or Jewish cemetery. Officially, only organized visits are possible (every Sunday at 10am – you can enquire at the tourist information office in town for details), but it's easy enough to gain access to the overgrown graveyard via the numerous gaps in the wall. The cemetery was given by the town to Potsdam's growing Jewish population in 1763 – until then they had to bury their dead in Berlin. As recently as 1933 the Jewish community of Potsdam numbered several hundred, of whom just two returned after the war. The forgotten state of the cemetery stands today as a symbol of their fate: the wall has been patched in haphazard fashion and a few attempts have been made to keep the weeds at bay. It's in urgent need of restoration, for which the authorities have promised to make money available.

From the cemetery the path leads on up the hill to the ruined nineteenth-century **Belvedere**, a vast and improbable-looking edifice, built to plans drawn up from Friedrich Wilhelm IV's sketches of the folly-like castles constructed in Italy during the Renaissance. Its walkways and towers give great views of Potsdam itself, and of the landscape north as far as Spandau and Charlottenburg, and west as far as the town of Brandenburg. Unfortunately, it's almost impossible to enjoy them today. Although virtually undamaged by the war, the belvedere was allowed to collapse into ruin by the pre-*Wende* city authorities, because (according to some Potsdamers) it afforded such good views of the border and West Berlin. Just to the southeast of the belvedere is the **Pomonatempel**, Schinkel's first-ever finished building, a neat, Neoclassical temple fronted by a portico, constructed in 1800 when he was a nineteen-year-old student of architecture.

The Neuer Garten and around

To the east of the Pfingstberg is the **Neuer Garten**, another large park complex, which includes Schloss Cecilienhof, venue of the Potsdam conference. The main entrance is at the eastern end of Alleestrasse, beyond which a road snakes through the park. A couple of hundred metres east of the road, overlooking the Heiliger See, is the **Marmorpalais** (Marble Palace; Mon–Fri 10am–6pm, Wed until 8pm; DM10 includes entry to the Orangerie in Neuer Garten and Schloss Charlottenburg in Berlin), built for Friedrich Wilhelm II who died a premature death here in 1797, allegedly as a result of his dissolute lifestyle. Until 1990 it was home to the GDR's main military museum; it has recently been restored to an approximation of its original royal condition, and is now open to the public.

Schloss Cecilienhof

Towards the end of the road through the wooded grounds of the Neuer Garten is **Schloss Cecilienhof** (Tues–Sun 9am–5pm; DM8), which looks like a mock-Elizabethan stately mansion transplanted from the English Home Counties. Building work on this "English-style" palace, the last to be commissioned by the Hohenzollern family, began in 1913 and was completed in 1917, the war evidently having done nothing to change the architectural style. Cecilienhof would only rate a mention in passing, were it not for the fact that the **Potsdam Conference**, confirming the decisions made about the post-war European order earlier that year at Yalta, was held here from July 17 to August 2, 1945. The conference was as much symbolic as anything else, providing a chance for Truman, Stalin and Churchill (replaced mid-conference by Clement Attlee) to show the world that they had truly won the war by meeting in the heart of the ruined Reich.

Centre of attraction within is the **Konferenzsaal**, or conference chamber, where the Allied delegates worked out the details of the division of Europe and which resembles the assembly hall of a minor public school. Everything has been left pretty much as it was in 1945, with the huge round table specially made in Moscow for the conference still in place, despite the fact that on July 27, 1990, there was an arson attack on the hall. The fire brigade arrived within a few minutes and extinguished the fire, but not before considerable damage had been done. A remarkably quick restoration job has left few traces of what happened. It's still not known who was responsible for the attack, but local *Faschos* – neo-fascists – are thought to be the most likely culprits.

It's also possible to visit the delegates' work-rooms furnished in varying degrees of chintziness. The study of the Soviet delegation is about the most tasteless, but the British room (with a bronze stag at bay in the fireplace and furniture that looks like it was bought as a job lot from a defunct presbytery) comes a close second. Cecilienhof has been used as a hotel since 1960 (see p.802) and there's an expensive restaurant which is also only for the deep of pocket (see p.811).

Berliner Vorstadt

On the opposite shore of the Heiliger See to the Neuer Garten is the **Berliner Vorstadt**, formerly an elegant Potsdam suburb, whose crumbling villas were given over to various Party and social institutions under the SED regime. Here, too, were numerous Imperial army barracks, housing elite units like the Garde du Corps and Hussars. At the end of Berliner Strasse, leading back to Berlin, is the **Glienicker Brücke**, the famous spy-swap bridge which inspired many a Cold War film scene. Here in 1962 U-2 pilot Gary Powers was traded for a Soviet agent, while more recently in 1986 Jewish dissident Anatoly Scharansky was freed into the West by the Soviet authorities in an early manifestation of Gorbachev's *glasnost*. The bridge was reopened to normal traffic at the beginning of 1990, and today there are few reminders of the era when people living in the immediate vicinity needed special permits simply to come and go from their own homes.

Babelsberg

On the eastern bank of the Havel is the town of **BABELSBERG**, now officially part of Potsdam. Crossing the Lange Brücke from Potsdam, it's hard not to notice a square tower rising up out of the trees atop the **Brauhausberg** on the Babelsberg side. This is the former local SED headquarters or *Kreml* (Kremlin), to give it its local nickname. Originally built as a military college at the turn of the century, it later served as a state archive building – a dark oval patch on the side of the tower marks where the SED symbol used to be.

The Telegrafenberg and the Einsteinturm

Like Potsdam, Babelsberg has a few secrets ripe for rediscovery. Above the Lange Brücke, Albert-Einstein-Strasse leads up onto the **Telegrafenberg**. In the late nineteenth century an astronomical **observatory** was built here, but much more striking is the nearby **Einsteinturm**, a twenty-metre-high observatory tower designed by Erich Mendelsohn in 1920. The most remarkable modern building in the Potsdam area, this Expressionist tower looks like an element from a Dalí dreamscape. Experiments testing the theory of relativity were carried out here in the presence of Einstein.

On the eastern side of the Telegrafenberg are a couple of musts for cemetery fans: the **Neuer Friedhof**, laid out in 1866 according to plans drawn up by the architect Lenné and, below it on the other side of Heinrich-Mann-Allee, the eighteenth-century **Alter Friedhof** with its classical mausoleum and overgrown monuments.

Park Babelsberg

Potsdam's third major landscape garden is the often-overlooked **Park Babelsberg**, accessible on foot from the centre of Babelsberg, or from the Berlin side of the Glienicker Brücke. Its focal point is **Schloss Babelsberg** (Tues–Sun 10am–5pm; DM4), a Romantic extravaganza inspired by Windsor Castle and designed by Schinkel for the future Kaiser Wilhelm I. The main room is the huge octagon at the back; this served as the dance hall and has a spectacular vault covered with heroic frescoes. Also in the park are several smaller buildings, including the **Flatowturm**, a guest house and lookout tower in mock-medieval style; the **Matrosenhaus**, a gabled dwelling for the crew of the royal boats; and the **Gerichtslaube**, the original Gothic court house and town hall of Berlin, brought here in 1872 after the completion of the Rotes Rathaus.

The Babelsberg studios

At the eastern end of town, served by buses #601, #603, #690 and #692 from the centre, are the **Babelsberg film studios**, August-Bebel-Str. 26–53, entrance on Grossbeeren Strasse (daily March–Oct 10am–6pm; DM25, concessions DM18), a huge complex, originally founded in 1917. As the UFA film studios during the 1920s this was the heart of the German film industry, rivalling Hollywood as a centre of cinematic innovation. Films produced during the heyday of UFA included Robert Wiene's Expressionist masterpiece *Das Cabinet des Dr Caligari* (The Cabinet of Dr Caligari), Fritz Lang's *Metropolis* and *Der Blaue Engel* (The Blue Angel) starring the young Marlene Dietrich. Under the Nazis the anti-Semitic *Jud Süss* was filmed here in 1940, followed a few years later by the special-effect-laden colour epic *Münchhausen*. Later, as the DEFA studios, it was the heavily subsidized centre of the GDR film industry, which didn't last much longer than the GDR itself after the *Wende*. These days Babelsberg has reinvented itself as the "Film Experience Park", and visitors can wander through the costume and props departments and watch technicians going through the motions of shooting film scenes for their benefit. It's also possible to visit the hangar-like studio where Fritz Lang may have filmed *Metropolis* (no one is quite sure of the location) and admire a reproduction of his futuristic set. It takes several hours to see round the whole site and makes a good day-trip in itself.

Eating, drinking and nightlife

Eating and drinking pose few problems in Potsdam. There's a reasonable array of **restaurants**, and most places are pleasant enough, though few would gain any stars in a gourmet's guide to the Berlin area. In town the major and most convenient concentration of possibilities is along Brandenburger Strasse, although it pays to go a little further afield.

Restaurants

Hafthorn, Friedrich-Ebert-Strasse 90 (☎280 0820). Large and lively restaurant offering Swabian specialities for surprisingly little money.

Kleines Schloss, Park Babelsberg (☎705156). A lakeside place worth investigating for standard German dishes. Daily 11am–9pm.

Luise Restaurant, Luisenplatz 6 (☎292797). Mid-priced German and continental food in casual surroundings. The perfect place to eat before tackling Sanssouci just up the road.

Hotel Schloss Cecilienhof in Schloss Cecilienhof (☎37050). The poshest and, not surprisingly, most expensive restaurant in Potsdam. Similar dishes were allegedly served up to Churchill, Stalin and Truman during the Potsdam conference, but the high prices do not always guarantee the quality of the food.

Terrassenrestaurant Minsk, Max-Planck-Str. 10, am Brauhausberg (☎239636). This ugly-looking modern establishment on the Babelsberg side of the Havel serves surprisingly good Belarusian cuisine. Clear views across to Potsdam are an additional attraction.

Cafés and bars

Babette, Brandenburger Str. 71 (☎291648). The centre of Potsdam's thriving café scene. Open 10am–7pm, until 8pm Sun, Mon & Tues. Also open as a cocktail bar Wed–Sun until 1am.

Café im Filmmuseum, Schloss Str. 1 (☎270 2041). One of Potsdam's best cafés, and a good place to take a break after visiting the museum.

Froschkasten, Kiezstr. 4 (☎291315). One of the best and oldest bars in Potsdam, a *Kneipe* that also serves good food.

Im Drachenhaus, Maulbeerallee (☎291594). A pleasant and genteel little café in the grounds of Schloss Sanssouci itself, housed in a pagoda-style building once used by royal vintners.

Matschkes Galerie Café, Alleestrasse10 (☎270 1210). A quiet, leafy courtyard provides a wonderfully restful spot to enjoy authentic Russian cuisine.

Die Rebe, Feuerbachstr. 1 (☎964847). A very pleasant wine-*Kneipe* serving food, just southwest of the Brandenburg Gate. It's open until midnight but closed Sun and Mon.

Nightlife

For **nightlife** the best bets are, as usual, the former *FDJ* clubhouses. Best of these is the *Lindenpark*, Stahndorfer Str. 76–78 (☎747970), over in Babelsberg, with regular "alternative" discos and live bands, usually of a thrashy nature. *Fabrik*, Gutenbergstr. 105, is also an alternative venue for gigs and events, and *Waschhaus*, Schiffbauergasse 1 (☎271 5626), just off Berliner Strasse on the way into town from the Glienicker Brücke, stages dance-music-oriented, ravey events. For German-speakers the *Hans-Otto-Theater*, Am Alten Markt (☎275710), is Potsdam's main theatre with a programme worth investigating. The town also boasts a cabaret, the *Kabarett am Obelisk*, Schopenhauerstr. 27 (☎291069).

Listings

Bike rental *Fahrrad Bels*, Röhrenstr. 4. Mon–Fri 10–6pm, Sat 9am–2pm.

Boat rental on the Freundschaftsinsel, and at Grosse Fischer 11 (☎619026).

Boat trips *Weisse Flotte*, Lange Brücke (☎275 9210). Tickets and information May–Sept daily 8–11am & 11.30am–5.45pm; April & Oct daily 10am–3.30pm. Regular sailings to Wannsee, Caputh, Werder, Ferch and Templin.

Car rental *Babelsberger Autovermietung*, Babelsberger Str. 29 (☎270 3700); *Ahrens & Merkle*, Grünstr. 25 (☎707713).

Police Henning-von-Treskow-Str. 9–13 (☎28302).

Post office Main post office is at Am Kanal 16–18 (☎380).

Taxis ☎292231. Taxi ranks at Am Bassinplatz, the Hauptbahnhof, Potsdam-West and Drewitz S-Bahn stations, Rathaus Babelsberg and Friedrich-Wolf-Strasse.

Womens' centre *Frauenzentrum*, Zeppelinstr. 189 (☎291475), with café on Fri and Sat.

Brandenburg and around

BRANDENBURG, the city from which the province takes its name, lies on the main Berlin–Hannover rail line just over 30km west of Potsdam. For all its illustrious past – it was founded by the Slavs in the sixth century, made the seat of a precarious missionary German bishopric in the tenth century, before becoming the capital of the margraviate established by Albert the Bear in 1157 – its recent history has been a catalogue of misfortunes. These began when the Nazis chose it as the site of a concentration camp; future GDR dictator Erich Honecker served twelve years there, and among those murdered were 10,000 victims of a compulsory euthanasia programme for the mentally handicapped. The Nazis turned Brandenburg's industry – hitherto based on the production of bikes and motor vehicles – over to military purposes, ensuring the city was a prime target of Allied bombers. It was further damaged by the Red Army in 1945, when the defenders mounted a futile last-ditch resistance. After the war, the Communists made it the metropolis for the steel industry their dogma demanded; as a result, the medieval skyline was disfigured by the addition of sixteen smoking chimneys (four of which found their way onto the municipal coat of arms) and drab apartment buildings to accommodate its workers. Many historic buildings were left as ruins, while others rotted under the impact of some of the worst air pollution in Europe.

Yet Brandenburg still has much to offer. It's one of the most beautifully sited cities in Germany, occupying three islands, the **Neustadt**, the **Altstadt** and the **Dominsel**, at a point where the broad course of the Havel fashions a wondrous lake-strewn landscape. The city's surviving monuments represent north German brick architecture at its most inventive. One of five cities in the former GDR chosen for comprehensive restoration projects, it will hopefully re-emerge before long as the attractive place it once was.

The Neustadt

Closest to the Hauptbahnhof, the first of the three island quarters is the **Neustadt** or New Town. It's new only in a relative sense, having been founded as the commercial quarter at the end of the twelfth century, a generation after the previously Slav Altstadt had been re-established as a German town. Despite conspicuous gaps left by the war, its narrow streets retain much of their old feel. The first building in view is the cylindrical **Steintor**, one of four surviving gateways out of the ten the two settlements once possessed. In summer, it's open for special exhibitions on the city's history. Northeast of here is the **Paulikloster**, a thirteenth-century Dominican monastery left in ruins during World War II, though some reconstruction work has been carried out since the *Wende*.

Right in the middle of the island is the Neustädtischer Markt, now returned to its age-old role as a market square. It's dominated by the **Katharinenkirche**, a Gothic pile from the turn of the fifteenth century. Outside, the walls are crammed with spouting gargoyles and frilly gables tacked on for purely decorative effect, with the varied colouring and positioning of the bricks helping to transform the surface effects yet further. The fantastical interior design tends to overshadow the church's treasures, which include a finely carved fifteenth-century altar and a fourteenth-century stained-glass window in the choir which was fortuitously removed from the Paulikloster in 1942.

The Altstadt

Hauptstrasse runs northwestwards over the Havel into the **Altstadt**, which occupies only a small portion of a much larger island. Immediately over the river is the **Johanniskirche**, another brick Gothic church still remaining – for the time being, at least – in the burnt-out state it was left in at the end of the war. Further along, at Hauptstr. 96, is the **Freyhaus** (Tues–Fri 9am–5pm, Sat & Sun 10am–5pm; DM1.50), a Baroque mansion which now houses the district museum. This array of local ephemera is more interesting than you might expect, particularly the displays on the archeology of the Havelland, the graphic art section and a fascinating toy collection.

At the end of Hauptstrasse, Plauer Strasse leads north to the Altstädtischer Markt, over which looms the fourteenth-century **Altstädtisches Rathaus**, whose facade is topped with an unusual stepped gable. In front of it stands a mighty five-metre-high **statue of Roland**, medieval symbol of Brandenburg's status as a market town. He previously stood guard in front of the Neustädtisches Rathaus opposite the Katharinenkirche, but was brought here after its destruction in World War II.

Continuing northwards, you come to the parish church of the Altstadt, the **Gotthardtkirche**. Its facade is in the austere Romanesque style of the Premonstratensian monks, but behind it stands a light and airy Gothic hall church erected in the fifteenth century. Inside, look out for the thirteenth-century font and the lovely Burgundian tapestry showing the hunting of the unicorn. On the square facing the church is the **Schulhaus**, a half-timbered former school building from the sixteenth century.

The Dominsel

The **Dominsel**, the smallest of the three islands on which the historic quarters of Brandenburg are built, escaped the worst of the bombing and is by far the most visually pleasing part of town. From the Gotthardtkirche, you have to approach it circuitously via yet another island, occupied mainly by sports fields, to the north; there's a more direct approach along Mühlendamm from the Neustädtischer Markt. Taking the latter approach, the first monument you come to is the **Petrikapelle**, a thirteenth-century chapel given a spectacular interior transformation three hundred years later, with the addition of the intricate late Gothic cellular vault resting on hexagonal pillars.

The Dom

The **Dom** (closed for restoration, but due to re-open summer 1998) was begun around 1165 as a Romanesque basilica, and slowly converted to Gothic in the fourteenth and fifteenth centuries, though many parts of the old structure were retained, notably the arcades of the nave. The most atmospheric part is the **crypt**, where you can see the poignant original triumphal cross, supplanted *in situ* by a more monumental Gothic group. Even more eye-catching are the **capitals**, whose carvings of fabulous beasts and eerie half-human creatures show the vivid flights of imagination of which the medieval mind was capable. A contrastingly sombre note is struck by a series of metal plates, each accompanied by an appropriate biblical quotation, commemorating local clergymen murdered by the Nazis. It's a fitting reminder of the high-profile political role the Dom has played, most recently during the *Wende* of 1989 when the church was regularly filled for recitals given on the magnificent Baroque **organ**, attracting large financial donations for the democratic cause in the process.

In the south transept is a beautifully carved and painted **Bohemian altar** from around 1375, whose radiantly joyous saints mark a refreshing change from the anguished figures normally found in religious art. This was originally the high altar, but it was displaced in favour of a large retable brought here when Kloster Lehnin (see below) was secularized after the Reformation. In front of the latter stands a delicately modelled fourteenth-century **font**, with scenes from the childhood of Christ on its basin, and more fantastic animals on the base. On the north side of the choir, look out for the appropriately named **Bunte Kapelle** (Painted Chapel), another survivor from the Romanesque period.

The **Dommuseum** (May–Oct Mon, Tues & Thurs–Sat 10am–6pm, Wed 10am–noon, Sun 11am–4pm; Oct–April Mon–Sat 10am–4pm, Sun 11am–4pm; DM3) occupies the conventual buildings of the Premonstratensian collegiate foundation which moved here from the Gotthardtkirche. There's a superb array of medieval textiles, including a *Hungertuch* of 1290, made to cover the altar during Lent. Even finer is the collection of manuscripts, of which the star piece is the **Brandenburg Evangelistary**, a sumptuous late Romanesque gospel book adorned with colourful miniatures. The original is displayed with one page open; a facsimile of the whole book is kept for examination at leisure.

Practicalities

Brandenburg's **tourist office** is at Hauptstr. 51 (Mon–Wed & Fri 9am–7pm, Thurs 9am–8pm, Sat 10am–2/4pm; ☎03381/19433) and can, as usual, arrange **private rooms** (①–③). There are also a few small **pensions**, some with a central location, such as *Zum Birnbaum*, Mittelstr. 1 (☎03381/52750; ④); and *Engel*, Grosse Gartenstr. 37 (☎03381/200393; ④).

As yet there are only a handful of **hotels** within the city: *Am Stadion*, Thüringer Str. 250 (☎03381/369525 or 524005; ④); *Gerono*, Magdeburger Str. 12 (☎03381/34090; ④); *City*, Grosse Gartenstr. 2 (☎03381/522692; ⑤); *Am St Gotthard*, Mühlentorstr. 56 (☎03381/52900; ⑥); and *Sorat*, Altstädtischer Markt 1 (☎03381/5970; ⑧). If you're looking for budget accommodation, the **youth hostel** is at Hevellerstr. 7 (☎03381/521040; ⑫) on the Dominsel. There are a number of **campsites** on the lakes around the city: most convenient is *Die Malge* (☎03381/663134) on the Breitlingsee, which also has bungalows for rent. Two more can be found on the nearby islands; yet another, the *Margaretenhof* (☎03381/403227), is on the peninsula jutting into the Plauensee.

For **eating** and **drinking**, the last three hotels listed above all have recommendable restaurants. Otherwise, by far the best bet is the *Ratskeller* in the Altstädtisches Rathaus. The *Stadtcafé*, Hauptstr. 26–28, is typical of the vogue for trendy western-style cafés in the ex-GDR, but isn't bad for all that. **Cruises** (DM10 for a 2hr round trip), run by *Bollmann Flotte* (☎03381/223959), depart from Salzhofufer, located on the Altstadt side of the river.

Lehnin

About 20km southeast of Brandenburg, and equally accessible from Potsdam, the time-warped village of **LEHNIN** clusters round its huge **Kloster** (May–Oct Mon–Sat 9am–5pm, Sun 11am–5pm; DM3), which was founded in 1180 by Cistercian monks on what was then a swampy marsh deep in a forest populated mainly by heathen and hostile Slavs. Despite many vicissitudes, the **Klosterkirche** survives intact and offers a graphic illustration of the way the Romanesque style of the east end, the first part to be built, had given way to Gothic by the time the building was completed in 1260. Although the simple majesty of the elevation is the most impressive feature, there are also a few notable works of art, including a Romanesque triumphal cross and the tomb slab of Margrave Otto IV, son-in-law of Emperor Rudolf von Habsburg, the founder of medieval Europe's most powerful dynasty. Within the monastic complex is a **guest-**

house (☎03382/7686; ⑤); the village also has a good **hotel** with restaurant, *Markgraf*, Friedensstr. 13 (☎03382/700604; ⑤).

Oranienburg

About 20km northwest out of Berlin at the terminus of S-Bahn #1 is **ORANIENBURG**, a drab-looking place, home to little more than moribund industry and a nondescript Schloss. The one thing that sets Oranienburg apart from dozens of other towns around the capital is a monument that recalls the grimmest chapter in German history – **Sachsenhausen concentration camp**.

Sachsenhausen Concentration Camp

The camp, officially known as the **Nationale Mahn- und Gedenkstätte Sachsenhausen** (April–Sept Tues–Sun 8am–6pm; Oct–March Tues–Sun 8.30am–4.30pm; free) is in the northern suburb of Sachsenhausen. It's reached from S-Bahnhof Oranienburg by bus #273. A tree-lined road leads to a **museum** devoted to resistance to the Nazis. Just north of here is **Turm A**, the gatehouse entrance to the camp proper with a stretch of the original electrified camp fence running either side of it.

THE HISTORY OF SACHSENHAUSEN CAMP

Opened as a memorial on April 23, 1961 by the GDR government, **Sachsenhausen Concentration Camp** is an inevitably sobering place: as the official guidebook puts it, "Every footstep of this earth is soaked with the blood and death-sweat of tens of thousands of martyrs from many different nations". The camp was originally opened in July 1936 (replacing an earlier ad hoc camp housed in a local brewery from 1933 to 1935) as a *Schutzhaftlager* or "Protective Custody Camp", specifically to house opponents of the Nazi regime – mainly Communists, Socialists and trade unionists. New categories of prisoner were added with every year of Nazi rule: people convicted of "anti-social" behaviour, homosexuals and finally Jews, of whom 6000 were brought to Sachsenhausen after the brutal *Kristallnacht* attacks of November 9–10, 1938. The war years saw thousands of new internees arrive from the occupied countries and the beginning of organized mass murder, as opposed to the relatively arbitrary killings and executions of the 1930s.

At the end of the war the SS evacuated the camp, moving 33,000 prisoners north towards the Baltic where it was intended to herd them aboard boats which would then be sunk. Known as the **Todesmarsch** (Death March), this pitiless forced march across northern Germany claimed the lives of 6000 prisoners, most of whom died by the roadside (today plaques across the region commemorate them). Fortunately the survivors fell into Allied hands before the SS could put the final stage of their plan into effect. A further 3000 prisoners, most of them only barely alive, were found in the camp hospital when the liberating Soviet army arrived at Sachsenhausen on April 22, 1945.

In August 1945 the MVD, the military branch of the Soviet secret police, reopened Sachsenhausen as **MVD Special Camp No. 7**. Originally for war criminals, former Nazis and *Wehrmacht* officers, it gradually filled with people who were simply opponents of the occupying regime including, after 1946, large numbers of Social Democrats who had protested about the forced merger of their party with the Communist Party. Among all these prisoners were a few who had previously been interned here by the Nazis. By the time the camp was finally closed on March 10, 1950, about 60,000 prisoners had passed through, of whom some 20,000 died, mainly of hunger and lung diseases. In a recent postscript to this episode, mass graves containing the bodies of Germans executed by the MVD were unearthed in nearby woods in the spring of 1990.

Beyond Turm A is the **Apellplatz** or parade ground, where the prisoners were gathered for roll call and often kept standing for hours on end or forced to witness executions on the camp **gallows**. Behind the gallows, in four semicircular rows, were the **barrack buildings**, originally intended to hold 130 prisoners in cramped conditions but each filled by the end of the war with up to 500 men. Only three now remain: one now houses the camp **museum**, and the left-hand one is a memorial hall and **cinema** where a film about life in the camp is shown every hour, on the hour. The positions of the other barracks are marked with granite blocks. Beyond them is an open space leading to the stylized camp **memorial**.

Many of the victims commemorated by the memorial died nearby at **Station Z**, where the Germans turned the process of executing Soviet prisoners of war into an almost industrial one, dispatching tens of thousands of men with shots to the back of the neck. At the opposite side of the camp are two surviving barrack blocks used to house **Jewish inmates**, with a special exhibition devoted to their sufferings. Just beyond here are **cells** where prominent prisoners, mainly workers' leaders and patriots from the occupied countries, were held in isolation, usually pending execution. One of the inmates best known to posterity is the anti-Nazi cleric, **Pastor Martin Niemöller**, who was one of the few to survive incarceration here.

Neuruppin

Reached easily by road or rail from Oranienburg, the lakeside town of **NEURUPPIN** is the birthplace of the writer Theodor Fontane and the architect Karl Friedrich Schinkel. It's a predominantly eighteenth-century town, whose historic centre is all the more appreciable for being slightly faded.

The town

The town is laid out on a grid-like pattern around three large squares: a result of carefully planned reconstruction following a great fire in 1787. From the **Hauptbahnhof** access to the town is via Bahnhofstrasse, which leads into Schinkelstrasse and ends at the large square of **Kirchplatz** on which sits the **Pfarrkirche St Marien**, a tatty-looking Baroque-influenced church from the early nineteenth century. Karl Friedrich Schinkel's father was superintendent of the Pfarrkirche's predecessor and, behind the church, is the **Schinkel-Denkmal**, a monument to his famous son. Schinkel was born in 1781 and lived in Neuruppin through the time of the great fire and rebuilding, something that may have influenced his later choice of profession. In his adolescence he was sent to school in Berlin, and, having studied architecture, entered the Prussian civil service as a surveyor, later rising to take overall control of the Prussian building office. The mark he left on Berlin is tremendous. He completely transformed the old capital, doing much to give the city its predominantly Neoclassical feel, best exemplified by buildings along and around the Unter den Linden like the Neue Wache and the Altes Museum. Lesser works by the architect crop up all over north Germany, and there seems to be hardly a town in the region untouched by his hand.

Not far from the Schinkel monument is the **Fontanehaus**, the pharmacy with a stone lion above its doorway at Karl-Marx-Str. 84, which was the birthplace of Neuruppin's other famous son, the author Theodor Fontane – though these days there's little about the building to betray its past.

A few steps along Karl-Marx-Strasse from the Fontanehaus is Neuruppin's Neoclassical **Gymnasium**, the school attended by both Schinkel and Fontane, now containing a commercial art gallery. A similarly grandiose edifice is the **Heimatmuseum** (Tues–Fri 10am–5pm, Sat & Sun 10am–4pm; DM2) at August-Bebel-Str. 14–15. This building was one of the first in Germany to be erected specifically as a museum (the

THEODORE FONTANE 1818–98

Fontane was born in Neuruppin in 1819 to a couple of Huguenot descent. Before publishing his first work he was employed as a pharmaceutical dispenser, later serving as a war correspondent during the Austro-Prussian War of 1866 and the Franco-Prussian War of 1870–71. He wrote a couple of books describing his war experiences and four volumes about his travels in the Mark of Brandenburg, plus two others on his visits to Scotland and England. His career as a writer of fiction did not begin until the age of 57 when he began the Napoleonic epic *Before the Storm*. He subsequently published a further seventeen novels, mostly with a contemporary setting, which collectively stand as the summit of late nineteenth-century German literature. His best-known work is *Effi Briest*, published in 1895, the story of an upper-class Prussian woman drawn into an adulterous affair with predictably tragic consequences. Fontane, by his sympathetic portrayal of the protagonists, turns what could easily have become a rather trite reworking of the *Madame Bovary* story into a thinly veiled critique of the inflexible social mores of Prussian society of the time and their devastating effect on the individual.

Bildergalerie in Potsdam came first) and contains, naturally enough, extensive material about Neuruppin and its surroundings, as well as sections devoted to Schinkel and Fontane. Just behind the Heimatmuseum is the **Tempelgarten**, a park where Frederick the Great often retreated from his duties as commander of a local army regiment, after being sent here as a young Crown Prince by his father. The park is named after its circular Neoclassical temple, the first work of the architect Georg von Knobelsdorff. Towards the southwestern end of Karl-Marx-Strasse is **Ernst-Thälmann-Platz**, a bleak parade ground previously known as Königsplatz, around which large numbers of attractive Baroque buildings survive. At the very end of the street is the **Fontane-Denkmal**, a bronze statue of Fontane surveying the main road into town.

A few hundred metres south of Karl-Marx-Strasse lies **Seeufer**, a broad lakeside promenade on the shores of the **Ruppiner See**, the lake that threads south of town for about 10km. Overlooking Seeufer, the spire of the thirteenth-century **Klosterkirche** (April–Oct 11am–4pm) offers clear views of the lake and town.

Practicalities

Neuruppin's **tourist office** at August-Bebel-Str. 15 (Mon–Fri 9am–6pm, Sat 10am–2pm; ☎03391/2345) can arrange accommodation in any of the dozens of **private houses** (①–③) with rooms for rent. There's also a reasonable choice of **hotels**: *Berliner Hof*, Karl-Marx-Str. 96 (☎03391/2939; ④); *Ruppiner Spiesegaststätte*, August-Babel-Str. 36–37 ☎03391/2944; ④); *Märkischer Hof*, Karl-Marx-Str. 51–52 (☎03391/2801; ④); *Zum alten Siechenhospital*, Siechenstr. 4 ☎03391/398844; ⑤); and *Altes Kasino*, Seeufer 11 ☎03391/3059; ⑤). Most of the hotels have their own **restaurants**; otherwise try *Fehrbelliner Hof*, Karl-Marx-Str. 63 or *Café Huth*, Karl-Marx-Str. 85.

Between May and September, **cruises** are run on the Ruppiner See, departing from Seeufer.

Rheinsberg

About 20km northeast of Neuruppin, and the dead-end terminus of a branch rail line from Herzberg to the east, is **RHEINSBERG**, a small resort at the southern tip of a network of lakes dotted with campsites and watersports facilities. It's a pleasant, predominantly eighteenth-century town, best known for its associations with Frederick the

Great, mouldering quietly on the shore of the Grienericksee, the southernmost end of the Rheinsberger See.

The main sight is the lakeside **Schloss** (Feb & March Tues–Sun 10am–4.45pm; April–Oct Tues–Sun 9.30am–4.45pm; Nov–Jan Tues–Sun 10am–3.45pm; DM5), a three-winged building in smudged white at the southwestern edge of the centre. An earlier building on the same site was the residence of Frederick the Great from 1736 until he acceded to the throne in 1740. He spent his time in Rheinsberg in the study of science and art, later claiming it as the happiest period of his life. His favourite architect, Georg Wenzeslaus von Knobelsdorff, was commissioned to design the present structure as a palace for Frederick's younger brother Heinrich, who spent sixty years there, enjoying the company of attractive young men and redesigning the gardens. Highlight of the Schloss' interior is an allegorical ceiling painting *Day Drives Away the Night*. This shows a barn owl (representing the unloved "Soldier King", Friedrich Wilhelm I) retreating in the wake of the advance of Aurora (Frederick and/or Heinrich).

Part of the Schloss is designated as a memorial to the Berlin writer **Kurt Tucholsky** (1890–1935), who immortalized the town in *Rheinsberg – A Picture Book for Lovers*, a tender, ironic idyll about two sweethearts paying a weekend visit. It's very untypical of the author's output as a whole, which is mostly made up of short, devastatingly witty satires. Like his nineteenth-century precursor Heinrich Heine, Tucholsky was a Jew who abandoned Judaism and became a vociferous critic of Germany's Jewish community, yet who never really adopted an alternative faith or value system. With the advent of Nazism, he fled to Denmark, where he took his own life.

The **Schlosspark** is dotted with a number of odd monuments including, just to the west of the Schloss itself, the red-brick **Pyramide** to Prince Heinrich. Near the lakeshore is one of his own creations, the strange **Steingrotte**, a grotto containing a jumble of urns and statue pediments. The **Obelisk** on the opposite shore to the Schloss celebrates the Prussian generals who fell in the Seven Years' War.

Practicalities

Rheinsberg's **tourist office** is in the Kavalierhaus on the Markt (Mon–Sat 10am–4pm, Sun 10am–2pm; ☎033931/2059). For **eating and drinking**, try one of the collection of places around the Markt. Best of the lot is the *Deutsches Haus* at Seestr. 13, an excellent restaurant incorporating a *Kaffee und Kuchen* café, but the *Ratskeller*, Markt 1, is also worth investigating. Also on Seestrasse, the lakeside *Café Seepavillon* is good, and there's a reasonable *Gaststätte*, *Goldener Anker* at Karl-Marx-Str. 25, the street running parallel to the lake from the northeast corner of the Markt.

As far as accommodation goes, there are plenty of good-value **private rooms** (①-②). The only **hotel** is *Goldener Stern*, just east of the Schloss at Mühlenstr. 4 (☎033931/2179; ④), but there are also a couple of **pensions**: *Zu den Vier Jahreszeiten*, Rhinstr. 4 (☎033931/2424; ④); and *Am Rheinsberger Schlosspark*, Fontaneplatz 2a (☎033931/39271; ⑤). There are **campsites** at the Warenthiner Ablage and Prinzenstrand on the southern shore of the lake.

The Schorfheide

The largest area of protected landscape anywhere in Germany is the **Schorfheide** to the northeast of Berlin, which occupies a total of almost 1300 square kilometres. Nearly half of this is forest; there are also some 250 lakes, plus moorland, wetland and farmland. Although the Schorfheide is distinctive enough to have gained inclusion on the UNESCO list of World Biosphere Reserves, it's better known for its set-piece attractions, which include the magnificent ruined Kloster at **Chorin** and what is surely the most visually impressive technical monument in the country, the Schiffshebewerk at **Niederfinow**. These are easily combined in a day-trip from Berlin by train, though when travelling between the two it's necessary to change at Eberswalde-Finow, a rather nondescript industrial town 50km from the capital. Should you wish to stay over, the best base is **Bad Freienwalde**, a once-prestigious spa at the southeastern corner of the region.

Chorin

Sixty kilometres from Berlin, on the main rail line to the Polish city of Szczecin, is the tiny village of **CHORIN**. Alight at Bahnhof Kloster Chorin, the first of the two train stations, to see the evocatively ruined Cistercian **Kloster** (daily mid-March to Oct 9am–6pm; Nov to mid-March 9am–4pm; DM3), which, in accordance with the ideals of its founders, is set in a secluded setting in the middle of the woods by a small lake, the Amtssee. To reach it, walk all the way through the village, bearing right, then follow the forest path. Established on this site in 1273, it was constructed over the following sixty years, and is an example of Gothic brick architecture at its most daringly inventive. Last century, Schinkel carried out major structural repairs on the long-abandoned monastery, then in danger of collapse. Both the church and the monastic quarters are substantially intact, though the former now gapingly opens out directly onto the cloister – helping create a much expanded auditorium for the **concerts** which are regularly held throughout the summer months. Architecturally, the finest feature is the highly idiosyncratic **facade**, the last part of the church to be built. A dazzling exercise in patterned brickwork, it contrasts sharply but effectively with the solemn grandeur of the structure behind. Also of special note are the gabled **Brauhaus** (brewery) by the entrance and the **Küche** (kitchen) to its rear.

There are two **hotels** in Chorin: *Landgasthaus Zur Kroneiche*, Bahnhofstr. 1 (☎033366/280; ④) and *Haus Chorin*, Neue Klosterallee 10 (☎033366/447; ⑤). Both of these have **restaurants**; an alternative is *Alte Klosterschänke*, Am Amt 9.

Niederfinow and the Schiffshebewerk

Ten kilometres east of the Eberswalde rail junction, at **NIEDERFINOW**, is one of the area's more unexpected sights, the **Schiffshebewerk**, a barge-lift of titanic proportions on the Havel–Oder canal. It can be reached by bus from Niederfinow Bahnhof, although it's a pleasant enough walk of only a couple of kilometres (cross the bridge near the station and head north).

The Schiffshebewerk is used to transport barges from the western upland section of the canal down into the Oder valley and vice versa, replacing an antiquated system of locks. It was opened in 1934, and at the time of its construction was the largest structure of its kind in the world: 94m long, 27m wide and an amazing 60m high. Subsequently it became an important staging post on the canal network linking Germany and Poland, reducing the time taken to lower and raise vessels from several painstaking hours to about fifteen minutes. The lift is basically an enormous steel trough capable of accommodating a thousand-tonne barge, raised and lowered by an electric-powered system of counterweights, within a casing of steel girders.

For a closer look at how it works, follow the crowds up the steps on the western side of the road. These will bring you to the upper canal level and a walkway that runs around the outside of the barge-lift (daily 9am–7pm or dusk; DM3, although this is often waived). The structure attracts its fair share of visitors and there's a large car park with souvenir shop and *Imbiss* stands in the shadow of its massive girders. If you want something more substantial to eat or drink, head back along the main road towards the Bahnhof, where there are a couple of *Gaststätten* and a plush new hotel, *Am Schiffshebewerk* (☎033362/70099; ⑤).

Bad Freienwalde

Another 10km east, a couple of stops on the rail line to Frankfurt an der Oder, lies **BAD FREIENWALDE**, a spa resort on the edge of the Oder marshes which was much patronized by the Hohenzollern dynasty from the time of the Great Elector onwards. The centre, based on the perpendicular axes of Karl-Marx-Strasse, which sweeps uphill from the Bahnhof, and Hauptstrasse, has a market town feel. The dominant monument is the brick Gothic **Nikolaikirche**, which contains a rich array of furnishings from various epochs. Just to the south, at Uchtenhagenstr. 2, is the **Oberlandmuseum** (Tues–Fri 9am–noon & 2–5pm, March–Oct also Sun 10am–noon & 1.30–4.30pm; DM2), which has the usual local archeological finds and an interesting section about the reclamation of the Oderbruch.

Hauptstrasse leads to the Lenné-designed **Schlosspark**, which spreads along the slopes of the hill beyond. The Neoclassical **Schloss** (Wed–Fri 9am–noon & 2–5pm, Sat & Sun 1–5pm; DM2) was designed by the Berlin architect David Gilly, the teacher of Schinkel, as a widow's residence for Queen Friederike Luise of Prussia. It's now a memorial to Walter Rathenau, foreign minister during the early years of the Weimar Republic, who was assassinated in 1922. The exhibits focus on his diverse talents as a businessman, writer and artist as well as politician. Alongside stands the **Teehäuschen**, an engaging pavilion surrounded by an open loggia, which was formerly the setting for theatre and concerts as well as tea ceremonies.

Also by Lenné is the restful **Kurpark** at the southern end of town. Focal point of this is the **Moor-Badeanstalt**, a spa complex still much frequented by rheumatism sufferers. At the fringe of the park is the original guest house for patients, the so-called **Landhaus**, a handsome Neoclassical structure by Carl Gotthard Langhans, architect of Berlin's Brandenburg Gate.

Bad Freienwalde's **tourist office** is at Karl-Marx-Str. 25 (Mon–Fri 9am–5pm, Sat 9am–noon; ☎03344/3402) and you can book **private rooms** (①–②) here. Other than the sanatoria there's only one **pension**, *Schulz*, Sonnenburger Str. 12 (☎03344/2521; ③), and one **hotel**, *Gasthaus Zum Löwen*, Hauptstr. 41 (☎03344/41660; ⑤). The latter also has a **restaurant**, which provides a fitting rivalry to the *Schlossgaststätte* in the terrace of the Schloss. The **youth hostel** occupies a secluded setting at Hammerthal 3 (☎03344/3875; ⓐ), 3km west of the town centre.

Frankfurt an der Oder

Some 70km southeast of Bad Freienwalde, and 90km east of Berlin, lies the border town of **FRANKFURT AN DER ODER**. Like so many communities along the course of the River Oder, it was split in two in 1945, with the Altstadt on the west bank remaining in German hands, while the east bank suburb became the Polish town of Słubice. As Frankfurt was almost totally destroyed during the war, it's mainly of interest as a stopover point on journeys to and from Poland. Nonetheless, it's a place with a long and distinguished history, dating back to the thirteenth century, when German merchants founded a settlement and built a wooden bridge over the Oder. Subsequently, the town developed as an important trade centre.

The town

Today the **Marktplatz** remains the focal point of the centre. Its open, empty feel is the consequence of wartime devastation, whose effects are shockingly brought home by the state of the **Marienkirche** on its southern side. This, the biggest of all Germany's brick Gothic hall churches, was reduced to a roofless ruin following a bomb raid,

---

HEINRICH VON KLEIST (1777–1811)

Born into an old Prussian military family, **Heinrich von Kleist** began his career as a soldier, but resigned his commission and adopted a wandering lifestyle. Depite taking his own life at the age of 34 in a bizarre suicide pact with a woman dying of cancer, he bequeathed an astonishingly varied body of literature, which speaks more forcefully to the modern reader than that of any other great German writer of his time. His plays range from *The Broken Jug*, a comedy in which a crooked village judge tries a case in which he is the real culprit, via *Penthesilea*, a tragi-comic mythological spoof, to *Prince Frederick of Homburg*, in which Prussia's Great Elector appears as Justice and Mercy personified. In contrast to the emotional tone of the plays, Kleist's short stories are narrated with detached objectivity. Often set in exotic locations, they characteristically feature dramatic twists of plot, with scenes of lyrical intensity alternating with episodes of savage brutality.

---

although restoration work has been in progress since the demise of the GDR. Directly opposite, forming a deliberate juxtaposition of the sacred and secular, is the **Rathaus**, another exercise in virtuoso brickwork, which ranks among the most impressive town halls in Germany.

Between Marktplatz and the river is the **Kleist-Museum** (Tues–Sun 11am–5pm; DM2.50), which is devoted to the life and works of the town's favourite son, the dramatist and short story writer **Heinrich von Kleist** (see box). At C.-P.-E.-Bach-Str. 11 is the **Bezirkmuseum Viadrina** (Tues–Sun 11am–5pm; DM1), a grandiose Prussian *Junker* house containing displays on the history of Frankfurt and the surrounding region.

Further north, beyond the bridge to Poland, is the **Konzerthalle C.P.E. Bach**, the main concert hall of a town with a strong musical tradition, as is reflected by the presence of the academy alongside. The building, an intact Gothic hall church, is named in honour of Carl Philipp Emmanuel Bach – son of J.S. and one of the most bizarrely idiosyncratic composers of musical history – who spent part of his life in the town. Finally, at the southern end of the Altstadt, the curious two-storey **Gertaudkirche** (Mon–Fri 10am–noon; DM1.50) contains the treasures formerly kept in the Marienkirche, including two outstanding fourteenth-century pieces: a tall candelabra and a font adorned with 44 reliefs of Old and New Testament scenes.

Practicalities

Frankfurt's **Hauptbahnhof**, itself a border crossing point, occupies an elevated position about ten minutes' walk southwest of the Altstadt. The **tourist office** (Mon–Fri 10am–noon & 12.30–6pm, Sat 10am–noon; ☎0335/325216) lies just west of Marktplatz at Karl-Marx-Str. 8a.

Though there's no particular reason to stay over, you can book **private rooms** (②-④) at the tourist office. There are three **hotels** in the town centre: *Gallus*, Fürstenwalder Str. 47 (☎0335/56150; ④); *Zur Alten Oder*, Fischerstr. 32 (☎0335/556220; ⑤) and *Frankfurter Hof*, Logenstr. 2 (☎0335/55360; ⑤). All of these have **restaurants**, though the best place to eat is the *Ratskeller* in the historic cellars of the Rathaus, which includes vegetarian dishes on its menu.

The Spreewald

The **Spreewald**, a unique forest area bisected by the River Spree, which lies 100km southeast of Berlin, is by far the most beautiful landscape in the Land of Brandenburg, although its atmosphere can be marred by the sheer volume of visitors. It falls into two parts: the **Unterspreewald** and **Oberspreewald**, north and south of the town of **Lübben** respectively. Although the Unterspreewald, east of Schlepzig, is pleasant enough, the real attraction is the Oberspreewald, a 500-square-kilometre area of deciduous woodland. The woods, which are broken up in places by land given over to market gardening – the cucumbers produced here are renowned – are watered by 300 channels (fed by the River Spree) known as *Fliesse*, and criss-crossed by man-made canals, creating an environment that Theodor Fontane described as "Venice as it might have been 1500 years ago".

Most of the local populace are Slavic **Sorbs** (also known as **Wends**; see opposite) with their own language and traditions, and Sorbish street signs add more than a hint of exotica to an already unusual region. Unfortunately, the Spreewald was discovered a long time ago and tourists flock here in unbelievable numbers during the summer, overrunning the local *Gaststätten* and block-booking seats on the **punts** that ferry visitors around the area (motorized craft are banned), charging on average DM4–5 per hour for trips which can last from anything between ninety minutes and ten hours. Nevertheless, the Spreewald really does live up to tourist-brochure hyperbole. **Walking** is just as good a way of getting around as taking a punt, but it's essential to get hold of the local *Wanderkarte*, as it's all too easy to get lost or disorientated. The provision of **accommodation** has mushroomed since the *Wende*, but if visiting in summer it's still advisable to book in advance.

Lübben (Lubin)

LÜBBEN (easily reached by rail from Berlin) is the first major town in the Spreewald and from its harbour it's possible to take punt trips into both the Unter- and Oberspreewald. The town also has a **Schloss** and a sixteenth-century church, the **Paul-Gerhardt-Kirche**, which is named in honour of the religious poet buried there. At the **tourist office**, Lindenstr. 14 (Mon–Fri 9am–6pm, Sat 10am–4pm, Sun 10am–noon; reduced hours out of season; ☎03546/3090), you can ask about **private rooms** (②–③). There are also several small **pensions**, the most convenient being *Am Markt*, Hauptstr. 5 (☎03546/4576; ③). **Hotels** include *Spreeblick*, Gübbener Str. 53 (☎03546/8312; ④); and *Stephanshof*, Lehnigksberger Weg 1 (☎03546/27210; ⑤). The local **youth hostel** is 3.5km from the centre at Zum Wendenfürsten 8 (☎03546/3046; ❷). Both the hotels mentioned above have good **restaurants**, though the best place to eat is the *Historischer Weinkeller*, Von-Houwald-Damm 14.

Lübbenau (Lubnjow)

Perhaps a better starting point for exploring the Oberspreewald is the slightly larger town of **LÜBBENAU**, a 15km train journey southeast of Lübben. It gets incredibly crowded, though, giving the impression that all of the one million visitors who come here each year are passing through at once. Lübbenau's origins are also Slavonic, and it was defended by a wooden wall, later destroyed by the Germans who built a castle here. The original castle was in turn replaced by the Neoclassical **Schloss** visible today, which was built just after the Napoleonic Wars by Count Lynar. The Lynar family owned much of the area until 1945, when their castle was turned into a school; they returned to claim their seat after the *Wende*, converting it into a hotel. In a Baroque building near the Schloss is the **Spreewaldmuseum** (April–Oct Tues–Sun 10am–5/6pm; DM3), which details the history of the town and area.

Punt trips run from either of the **harbours**, the Grosser Hafen and Kleiner Hafen. It's best to be there as early as possible (around 8–8.30am) as there are bound to be very heavy crowds during the tourist season. The **tourist office** at Ehm-Welk-Str. 15

THE SORBS

A West Slav tribe whose language resembles both Czech and Slovak, the **Sorbs** have lived throughout their history in the province known as **Lusatia** (*Lausitz*), which still maintains a tenuous position on maps of Germany. In the fifteenth century it was divided into Upper Lusatia (*Oberlausitz*) and Lower Lusatia (*Niederlausitz*): the former is now in Saxony; the latter (of which the Spreewald forms the northern part) is in Brandenburg. As many as a hundred thousand Sorbs still live throughout the region. There were nationalist stirrings in the nineteenth century, leading in 1912 to the formation of the *Domowina* (a word equivalent to the German *Heimat* or "homeland", a cultural and political organization which is still the main vehicle for Sorbist aspirations.

They were particularly persecuted under the Nazis when Göring proposed expelling them to turn the Spreewald into a gigantic game hunting park stocked with elk and bison. Things improved under the GDR, when the Sorbs were allowed a degree of cultural autonomy, with their language given equal status with German. However, they were mercilessly exploited for tourist purposes: their vivid costumes and popular **festivals** added a much-needed dash of colour to that grey puritan land. The latter include the *Vogelhochzeit* (Marriage of the Birds) on January 25, Carnival, horseback Easter processions and, on April 30, the *Hexenbrennen*, a variant of the witches' *Walpurgisnacht*.

(Mon–Fri 9am–6pm, Sat & Sun 10am–6pm; reduced hours out of season; ☎03222/3668) can advise on **private rooms** (②–④). Among many **pensions** are *Höhn*, Dammstr. 38 (☎03222/45722; ③); and *Zum Brauhaus*, Brauhausgasse 2 (☎03222/2126; ③–④). There are also four **hotels**: *Lübbenauer Hof*, Ehm-Welk-Str. 20 (☎03222/83162; ⑥); *Turm*, Nach Stottof 1 (☎03222/89100; ⑦); *Spreewaldeck*, Dammstr. 31 (☎03222/89010; ⑦); and *Schloss Lübbenau*, Schlossbezirk 6 (☎03222/8730; ⑦). For **eating and drinking**, try any of the hotels or *Zum grünen Strand der Spree*, a reasonable though often packed *Gaststätte*.

Lehde (Ledy)

One way to escape the crowds is to walk (rather than take a punt) to the incorporated village of **LEHDE**, which will take about thirty minutes. Until 1931 the village could only be reached by water transport or by crossing the ice of the frozen channels in winter. Lehde's **Freilandmuseum** (daily April–Sept 10am–6pm; Oct 10am–5pm; DM3) is packed with information about the area's history and customs. Farmhouses typical of the region have been brought here from other parts of the Spreewald and you can see how they were constructed: the foundations were built on large stones which in turn rested on timber poles driven deep into the marshy ground. Inside, examples of furniture (look out for the large beds designed to accommodate a whole family) and household objects offer an impression of how the Sorbish populace lived during the last century.

Good places to **eat** in Lehde are *Café Venedig* or *Zum Fröhlichen Hecht*. If you don't mind paying much more than you would for similar facilities in Lübbenau, there are a couple of **pensions** where you can stay: *Hirschwinkel* (☎03222/899950; ⑤) and *Quappenschänke* (☎03222/899960; ⑤).

Cottbus (Chośebuz)

At the southern end of the Spreewald stands **COTTBUS**, formerly the capital of one of the three *Bezirke* into which Brandenburg was divided in GDR days. It has a long industrial tradition, the twin pillars of the local economy being the textile industry, established by Dutch settlers in the Middle Ages and later developed by Huguenot refugees, and coal mining, which was the chief cause of the city's rapid growth last century.

Because of this pedigree, Cottbus was seen by the Communists as something of a role model for the rest of the country, though its mixture of crumbling old tenements and Stalinist-style apartment buildings was not one that many others found attractive. Since the *Wende*, however, the city has done much to make itself more appealing, and has added a new dimension to its existence by becoming the seat of a technical university.

The town

The heart of the town is the **Altmarkt**, which is lined with an impressive series of Baroque mansions, dating from immediately after one of the many disastrous fires which have ravaged the town. At no. 24 is the **Löwenapotheke** (guided tours Tues–Fri 11am & 2pm, Sat & Sun 2pm & 3pm; DM4), a pharmacy which has functioned continuously since 1573 and contains a number of historic interiors. A block to the south, at Mühlenstr. 12, is the **Wendisches Museum** (Tues–Fri 8.30am–5pm, Sat & Sun 2–6pm; DM4), which has extensive displays on the history and culture of the Sorbs. Just north of Altmarkt is the Gothic **Klosterkirche**, whose tower is, most unusually, placed at the east end. A later and more visually impressive Gothic church, the **Oberkirche**, stands northeast of the Altmarkt. Its high altar, fashioned in marble, wood, alabaster and sandstone, is a hymn to late Renaissance extravagance.

Between here and the Spree is the **Münzturm**, where the town's first coins were minted. It's one of three towers surviving from the old fortifications: the others are the **Lindenpforte**, through which the path from the Stadtpromenade to the Altstadt leads, and the **Spremberger Turm**, at the far end of Spremberger Strasse, which goes south from the Altmarkt. On Schillerplatz, just outside the confines of the Altstadt, is the impressively large Jugendstil **Staatstheater**.

Cottbus' star attraction, however, is **Schloss Branitz** (Tues–Sun 10am–5/6pm; DM3.50) at the southeastern edge of town. This was the custom-built seat of one of the great characters of nineteenth-century Germany, Prince Hermann of Pückler-Muskau, who was the worthy successor to Lenné as landscape gardener to the Prussian court, as well as a writer, world traveller, and landowning aristocrat in his own right. The Schloss itself, designed by the Dresden architect Gottfried Semper in a tardy Baroque idiom, contains displays on the life of the prince, who himself designed the wonderful **Schlosspark**. This features a whimsical series of buildings, including a pergola, grandiose stables in the English neo-Gothic style, and, at the western end, a curious series of mock-Egyptian pyramids, one of which serves as his own mausoleum.

Practicalities

The **Hauptbahnhof** is situated well to the southwest of the centre in a particularly unsalubrious neighbourhood, so it's worth taking tram #1 to Stadtpromenade, then walking east along Marktstrasse to the Altmarkt. The **tourist office** is at the western edge of the city centre at Karl-Marx-Str. 68 (Mon–Fri 9am–6pm, Sat & Sun 9/9.30am–12.30/1pm; ☎0355/24254).

As an overnight stop, Cottbus is less enticing than the smaller towns of the Spreewald, but if you want to stay, **private rooms** (②–④) can be booked via a special number at the tourist office (☎0355/24255). There are also plenty of **pensions**, among which *Aarian*, Karlstr. 22a (☎0355/791229; ④) is conveniently central, while *Café Pücklerstube*, Menzelstr. 4 (☎0355/715731; ⑤) is close to the Schlosspark. Among the many **hotels** are *Zum Schwan*, Bahnhofstr. 57 (☎0355/78200 or 795335; ⑤); *Zur Sonne*, Taubenstr. 7–8 (☎0355/791910; ⑥); and *Ostrow*, Wassenstr. 4 (☎0355/780080; ⑥). There's also a **youth hostel**, occupying an old half-timbered house at Klosterplatz 2 (☎0355/22558; ❸). The choice of **restaurants** and **cafés** is also good. *Wendisches Café*, August-Bebel-Str. 82, serves Sorb dishes; *Promenadeneck*, Stadtpromenade 17, does regional specialities; *Paulaner Bräu*, Sandower Str. 57, is a Bavarian-style beer hall; while *Café Altmarkt*, Altmarkt 10, is best for *Kaffee und Kuchen*. **Nightlife** possibilities include *Stadtwächter*, a cosy tavern in an old watchman's house attached to the Stadtmauer; *Zum Nachtschwärmer*, Stadtpromenade 10, an Irish pub offering exotic food; and *Clou Nachtbar*, Oberkirchplatz 10, a bar with a dance floor. The *Staatstheater Cottbus*, Schillerplatz 1 (☎0355/782 4152) presents a varied programme of **theatre** and **music**.

travel details

Berlin-Hauptbahnhof to: Dessau (6 daily; 2hr 15min); Dresden (hourly; 2hr 30min).

Berlin-Lichtenberg to: Cottbus (5 daily; 1hr 45min); Leipzig (10 daily; 2hr 20min); Lübbenau (5 daily; 1hr 10min).

Berlin-Zoologischer Garten to: Brandenburg (frequent; 1hr 30min); Hamburg (8 daily; 3hr 30min); Hannover (12 daily; 4hr 25min); Munich (8 daily; 7hr 20min); Potsdam (frequent; 50min).

CHAPTER TEN

SAXONY-ANHALT

A fter the fall of the GDR, there was much talk about the reinstatement of the five "historic" Länder in the east. In the case of **Saxony-Anhalt** (*Sachsen-Anhalt*), the description was a complete misnomer: the province had first come into existence, courtesy of the Soviet military authorities, in 1947. Five years later it was abolished in line with the GDR's policy of concentrating power in the centre. Despite its dubious pedigree, there was genuine popular demand that this somewhat artificial Land should be revived, and it has duly taken its place on the new political map of the country.

The **"Saxony"** in the Land's title is a throwback to the old Prussian province of that name. It came into existence after the 1815 Congress of Vienna forced the Kingdom of Saxony to cede about half of its territories as a punishment for having supported Napoleon; these were then united with a number of secularized bishoprics Prussia had acquired after the Thirty Years' War. **Anhalt** was a duchy founded by descendants of Albert the Bear, the first Margrave of Brandenburg. For centuries it was splintered into a number of petty principalities; these finally united in 1863, and the province served as a constituent state of Germany up to World War II.

Given its diverse make-up, it's hardly surprising that Saxony-Anhalt is the most varied of the new German Länder. The northernmost tract is the **Altmark**, the first piece of Slav territory taken over by the Germans in the great drive to the east they launched in the early medieval period. It's a varied landscape, with stretches of heath and sandy marshes in addition to farmland. The **River Elbe** defines its eastern border; the same river washes the **Börde**, the plain to the south. This has some of Germany's richest and most productive soils, though the otherwise monotonous agricultural countryside is punctuated by **Magdeburg**, one of only two major cities in the Land and its new capital.

Continuing southwards, the **Harz**, Germany's northernmost mountain chain, is approached via gentle foothills. Thickly covered with forests, the Harz proper is by far the best-known part of the Land. The home of the *Walpurgisnacht* legend, it's archetypally German in character, containing some outstanding scenery plus a clutch of well-preserved old towns. Beyond here, eastern Germany's largest area of heavy industry can be found in and around **Halle**, the Land's largest city, and **Dessau**, the historical capital of Anhalt. Further up the valley of the **Saale**, at the southern end of the province, the scenery becomes more rustic, the towns smaller.

Because the early history of the territories which make up Saxony-Anhalt is closely associated with missionary activity towards heathen Slavs, the Land is unusually rich in medieval cathedrals and monasteries. The archbishops' Dom in Magdeburg ranks among the finest in all of Germany, yet its counterparts (all demoted to parish churches long ago) in **Halberstadt**, **Havelberg**, **Merseburg** and especially **Naumburg** are worthy rivals. For all the impact these had on the history of Germany, their influence pales beside that of **Wittenberg**, the little university town from where Martin Luther launched the Protestant Reformation. Two other modest-sized places, **Quedlinburg** and **Tangermünde**, had short spells as the capital of Germany; each retains a striking medieval appearance, and respectively has some of the best half-timbered and brick architecture to be found in the country.

Travel throughout the region presents few problems; the transport network itself is one of the main draws of the Harz, which retains the most comprehensive network of

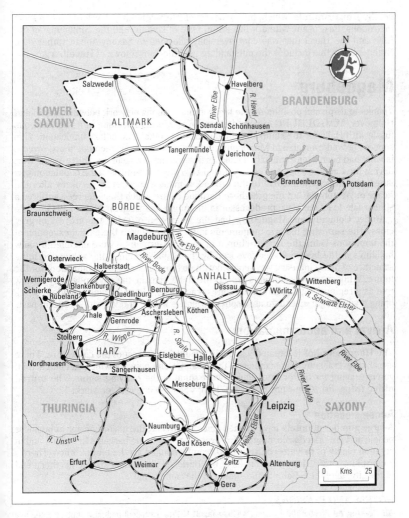

narrow-gauge steam rail lines to be found anywhere in Europe. The popularity of this with foreigners in GDR days is one reason the tourist facilities are so much better here than anywhere else in the Land.

THE ELBE-HAVEL REGION

The highlights of northern Saxony-Anhalt are thinly spread. In the Börde, **Magdeburg** is the only destination of note; as well as its Dom, it boasts a range of historical and technical monuments. The Altmark's chief town, **Stendal**, has reclaimed its role as a bustling market centre, though its monuments are rather overshadowed by those of nearby **Tangermünde**, which, but for a twist of fate, might have developed into a great metropolis. East of the Altmark lies a thin strip of land around the confluence of the Elbe and the Havel that was controversially allocated to Saxony-Anhalt rather than Brandenburg; this includes the outstanding yet little-known town of **Havelberg**.

Magdeburg

Thanks to its pivotal position on the key communications network between Berlin and Hannover, **MAGDEBURG** received strong West German backing in its acrimonious tussle with Halle for the status of capital of Saxony-Anhalt just before unification. This support proved crucial; had Magdeburg lost out, it would have been one more reverse in what had been a long run of bad luck. Its first calamity came in the Thirty Years' War: during the Catholic siege and occupation of 1631, over two-thirds of the population perished, and the city was burnt to the ground. It made a spectacular recovery after the Peace of Westphalia, but the grandiose Baroque centre which then emerged suffered a similar fate to its medieval predecessor in the Anglo-American air raids of 1945.

Under Communism, Magdeburg had the reputation of being the greyest of grey cities. The surviving historic monuments in the centre – with the partial exception of the imperious Dom, the largest church in eastern Germany – were engulfed by new buildings in the brutalist style favoured by the Stalinist regime; the antiquated infrastructure of heavy industry was retained with no thought for the environment or for the future. While many unsalubrious aspects inevitably remain, the city, buoyed by its new role as a regional capital, has undergone an astonishingly swift transformation, developing a vibrant get-up-and-go atmosphere which is wholly at odds with its recent past.

Arrival and accommodation

The **Hauptbahnhof** is situated just a few minutes' walk west of the city centre. There are also several suburban stations on the small S-Bahn network which can be useful if you're staying far out or intending to visit some of the outlying sights. The **tourist office** (Mon–Fri 10am–6pm, Sat 10am–1pm; ☎540 4903) is at Alter Markt 12.

Accommodation

A large number of **hotels** have opened since the *Wende*; the majority cater to business people and are priced accordingly. However, there are some bargains to be had, and in addition plenty of **private rooms** (③–④) can be booked via the tourist office. There's a **campsite** (☎503244) on the banks of the Barleber See at the extreme northern end of the city; take the S-Bahn to the station of the same name.

HOTELS AND PENSIONS

Alt Prester, Alt Prester 102, Prester (☎81930, fax 819 3118). Excellent mid-range hotel located in a southeastern suburb on the right bank of the Elbe. Its inexpensive restaurant with beer garden is a popular excursion destination with locals. ⑥

Am Theater, Erzberger Str. 9 (☎5616 3901, fax 543 4796). Huge GDR-era concrete box offering both basic and well-appointed rooms. ⑤

Eberlein, Letzlinger Str. 6 (☎561 7397). Budget pension in the Neustadt, near the S-Bahn station of the same name, and within walking distance of the centre. ④

Herrenkrug, Herrenkrugstr. 194 (☎850800, fax 850 8501). Magdeburg's most prestigious hotel occupies a mansion located in an Elbe-side park designed by the doyen of German landscape gar-

The **telephone code** for Magdeburg is ☎0391

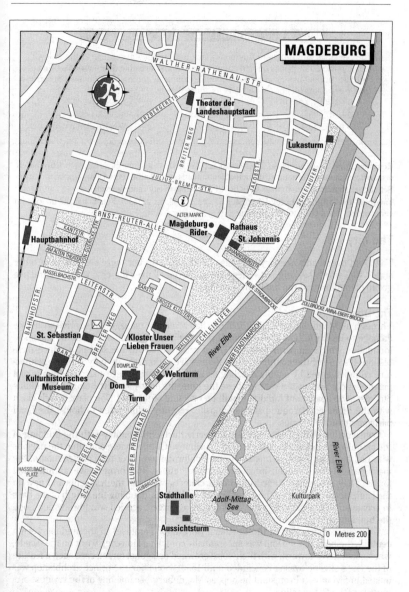

deners, Peter Joseph Lenné. Its two restaurants, *Eiskeller* (evenings only, closed Sun & Mon) and *Die Saison* (which has original Jugendstil decor), are among the very best in the city. ⑨

Löwenhof, Halberstädter Chaussee 19 (☎631 3576, fax 631 3583). Medium-priced hotel with restaurant located just beyond the southern end of the city centre. ⑤

Ratswaage, Ratswaageplatz 1–4 (☎59260, fax 561 9615). Luxury hotel with restaurant, part of the *Upstalboom* chain, located on the square immediately north of Alter Markt. ⑨

ACCOMMODATION PRICE CODES

All the pensions and hotels in this book have been graded according to the following price categories. The prices quoted are for the cheapest available double room, although many of the budget places will also have more expensive rooms. Youth hostels are graded under separate categories. See p.34 for more details.

① less than DM50	④ DM81–100	⑦ DM151–200
② DM51–65	⑤ DM101–125	⑧ DM201–250
③ DM66–80	⑥ DM126–150	⑨ more than DM250

Residenz Joop, Jean-Burger-Str. 16 (☎62620, fax 626 2100). One of the city's most attractive hotels, occupying a nineteenth-century villa, about ten minutes' walk south of the Dom. ⑧
Schröder, Matthissonstr. 4 (☎733 6813 or 721 5431). Small city centre pension. ④
Tagungs- und Bildungshotel, Lorenzweg 57 (☎251 5065, fax 223430). Functional and no-frills yet very modern hotel close to the city centre. ④

The city

The Dom overshadows everything else in Magdeburg, but there's a variety of other sights well worth seeking out. These are scattered all over the city, with an attractive group on and around the banks of the Elbe.

The Dom

Through all Magdeburg's trials, the **Dom** has somehow managed to survive with little damage to its fabric. The present building is the immediate successor to the monastic foundation which Emperor Otto the Great raised in 962 to the seat of a prince-archbishop. It's one of the country's most impressive cathedrals, its lofty Gothic architecture complemented by a truly dazzling array of sculpture. There's also the bonus of a picturesquely landscaped setting above the Elbe, the only sour note being the insidious Stalinist-style apartment buildings built on one side of the vast Domplatz, which clash with the dignified Baroque palaces opposite, recently refurbished to house the Land parliament and ministries.

Construction of the Dom began in the early thirteenth century with the building of the ambulatory and its chapels in a pure if primitive Gothic style. Soon after, the masons who had built the Swabian monastery of Maulbronn took over the construction of the main part of the chancel, introducing more refined and progressive architectural forms. They in turn were succeeded by architects who built the transepts and nave in the High Gothic manner of the great French cathedrals, doubling the length of the bays to create an impression of space, and designing large traceried windows which flood the building with light.

With the construction of the northern **porch** (or Paradise) in the mid-fourteenth century, the body of the Dom was substantially complete. However, work on the facade, whose distinctive **towers**, with their spire-crowned octagonal turrets, are such a feature of the city's skyline, wasn't concluded until 1520. Soon after, the prince-archbishop was ousted in favour of a Protestant bishop, as Magdeburg became one of the stoutest promoters of the Reformation.

THE SCULPTURES
Were it a museum of sculpture, the Magdeburg Dom, with its range of masterpieces from Romanesque to modern, would be regarded as the best in Germany. The chapels of the ambulatory, whose capitals are inventively carved with depictions of fabulous

beasts, luxuriant foliage and contorted human heads, contain a number of notable **tombs**. Oldest of these are the bronze monuments to two twelfth-century archbishops. There's also a touching stone memorial to a fourteenth-century successor to these, Otto of Hesse, the great-grandson of St Elisabeth, and a highly elaborate Flamboyant Gothic cenotaph belatedly honouring Empress Edith, wife of Otto the Great.

The last-named contrasts with the plain, box-like tomb of the emperor himself, which sits in solemn grandeur in the middle of the choir. Also surviving from his original cathedral are the beautiful coloured **marble columns** from Ravenna, which were re-used to support the statues of saints placed high up between the piers of the tribune gallery. These figures, together with the unique little scenes in the niches below, belong to the period in the mid-thirteenth century when the Magdeburg workshop, along with its counterparts in Bamberg and Naumburg, was producing some of the greatest sculpture of the Middle Ages. The most arresting figure made here is the **statue of St Maurice**, placed on a pedestal on the south side of the choir; although now truncated, the masterly originality of what was probably the first representation of a black man in Western art is still very apparent. Only marginally less fine are the companion figure of St Catherine, the Dom's other patron, and the Annunciation group at the chancel entrance.

A more substantial production of the earlier Magdeburg sculptors is the **portal** of the Paradise, which features superbly dramatic portrayals of the Wise and Foolish Virgins, and the enlightened Church and the blindfolded Synagogue, along with a tympanum of the Death of the Virgin. Just indoors, in the northern transept, is a masterpiece of twentieth-century sculpture, the haunting *Monument to the Victims of World War I* by **Ernst Barlach**. It forms a surprisingly effective counterfoil to the idealized beauty of the late thirteenth-century *Madonna and Child*, once believed to have miracle-working powers, in the other transept.

THE CHAPELS

The most intriguing feature of the interior is the freestanding **sixteen-sided chapel** in the nave, whose original function is an enigma. It contains thirteenth-century statues of a seated royal couple, leading to speculation that it's another memorial to Otto the Great and Edith, though it's more likely to be an allegorical representation of Christ as ruler of the world, with the Church as his bride. Finally, under the tower is the **memorial chapel to Archbishop Ernst**, whose decision to honour himself in such a way has meant that the Dom's main entrance has been blocked up for the past five centuries, an act of megalomania partially mitigated by the sheer magnificence of the tomb, cast by the great bronze-founder of Renaissance Nürnberg, Peter Vischer the Elder.

The Kulturhistorisches Museum

A couple of minutes' walk west of the Dom, at Otto-von-Guericke-Str. 68–73, is the **Kulturhistorisches Museum** (Tues, Wed & Fri–Sun 10am–6pm, Thurs 10am–8pm; DM2). The star exhibit here, housed right by the entrance, is the original of the **Magdeburg Rider** (*Magdeburger Reiter*), a secular product of the mid-thirteenth-century Dom workshop, which disputes with its Bamberg counterpart the right to be regarded as the first equestrian statue since Classical antiquity. This time, it's quite likely that the mounted figure is an idealized portrait of Otto the Great, accompanied by two maidens. The museum's other displays are pretty eclectic, ranging from an important archeology section to local history, arts and crafts; its collection of paintings, including works by Cranach and Friedrich, is sadly depleted as a result of losses in World War II.

St Sebastian and the Kloster Unser Lieben Frauen

Immediately north of the museum is the former monastic church of **St Sebastian**, itself a cathedral nowadays, being the seat of the local Catholic bishop. Outwardly unprepossessing, it has a light late Gothic interior, with slender, twisting columns.

Magdeburg's oldest surviving building, the **Kloster Unser Lieben Frauen** (Tues, Wed & Fri–Sun 10am–6pm, Thurs 10am–8pm; DM3), lies just beyond the northern end of Domplatz. Badly damaged during the war, this severe-looking former Premonstratensian monastery has been patiently restored to serve as a museum and cultural centre. The **Klosterkirche**, now the city's main concert hall, has a highly unusual interior, the original Romanesque forms having been clad with Gothic overlay and vaulting at around the same time as work began on the Dom. However, the most impressive part of the monastery is the **cloister**, and in particular its picturesque well chapel, nicknamed the *Tonsur*. Housed in the conventual buildings is a nationally owned collection of **small sculptures**, divided into a medieval section of mostly anonymous devotional works and a more extensive gallery of modern pieces, with examples of Rodin, Barlach and Lehmbruck, plus examples of the Socialist Realism fostered by the GDR state.

The Alter Markt

Ten minutes' walk to the north, the **Alter Markt** has regained since the fall of Communism its former role as the hub of day-to-day trading activity, with small-time hawkers frequenting it and the streets nearby. Sadly, the square itself is a shadow of its former self, with only the Baroque **Rathaus** restored to its prewar state. Fragments from burnt-out buildings have been stuck up on the side wall of the tourist office as a reminder of past splendours, while a bronze replica of the Magdeburg Rider has been set up under the Baroque canopy which once housed the original. There are also memorials to Otto von Guericke (see below) and Till Eulenspiegel, while the Gothic hall church of **St Johannis** rears up behind; burnt out in 1945, the shell was made into a war memorial. The post-unification fever for overturning decisions made in the Communist epoch means that it's likely to be rebuilt, though there has been considerable controversy about this. For the time being, you can climb the southern **tower** (Wed–Sun 10am–6pm; DM1) for a view over the city.

Along the River Elbe

From 1680, when it was incorporated into Brandenburg-Prussia, until just before World War I, Magdeburg was one of the most strongly fortified cities in Germany. Fragments of the Prussian-built **Festungsanlagen** can be seen all along the banks of the Elbe; the most impressive bits are those incorporating parts of the medieval city walls, which include the two towers immediately to the rear of the Dom and the section north of St Johannis. The latter terminates at the **Lukasturm** (Wed–Sun 10am–6pm; DM1), a brick-built fifteenth-century tower now housing a special display on the inventions of **Otto von Guericke**, inventor of the "Magdeburg hemispheres" that first demonstrated the power of the vacuum in the seveteenth century.

For a better perspective on these, it's well worth crossing over to the **Kulturpark Rotehorn**, a large park laid out in the 1920s between two branches of the Elbe, utilizing a smaller central arm as a boating area. Overlooking the main course of the Elbe towards the southern end of the park, across from the striking **Pferdetor** (a row of columns topped by stylized sculptures of horses), is the Bauhaus-influenced **Aussichtsturm** (Tues–Sun 10am–6pm; DM1), which you can ascend by lift for a fine panoramic view. Moored in the river just outside is the **SS Württemberg** (daily 10am–4pm; DM1.50), a paddle steamer built at the beginning of the century, which has been preserved as a reminder of the sort of vessels used at the time Elbe shipping was at its peak; it also houses a decent restaurant. Immediately north is the city's most remarkable industrial monument, the **Hubbrücke**. This was built in the 1840s as a rail bridge on the line to Potsdam and was equipped with a turning central mechanism to allow ships to pass through. Some fifty years later, it was converted into a lift bridge, before being transformed to its present appearance in the 1930s.

Eating, drinking and nightlife

Even if Magdeburg still lags well behind comparable western German cities in the gastronomic field, it's relatively well off by ex-GDR standards. It's also among the few eastern cities with much of a reputation left for beer-making – the *Diamant-Brauerei*, housed in splendid castellated mock-Gothic premises just north of the Neustadt S-Bahn station, was one of the few breweries allowed to maintain a diverse product line.

Restaurants

Bötelstube, Alter Markt 11. Basic but serviceable *Gaststätte* which offers the cheapest full meals available in the city centre.

Damm-Mühle, Alt Prester 1, Prester. Cosy restaurant on three floors of a converted mill in the southeast of the city. Closed Mon.

Deneckes Kartoffelhaus, Otto-von-Guericke-Str. 57. As its name implies, this specializes in all kinds of potato-based dishes. Closed Sun.

Pannenkoekenhuis, Sternstr. 29. Serves inexpensive savoury and sweet pancakes.

Ratskeller, Alter Markt 13. Historic restaurant under the Rathaus, with similar standards and prices to its western counterparts.

Savarin, Breiter Weg 226. Rivals the restaurants in the *Hotel Herrenkrug* (see p.828) as the best in Magdeburg. Closed Sun.

SS Württemberg, Heinrich-Heine-Platz. Restaurant located in Magdeburg's museum ship. Daily except Tues from 2pm or 3pm.

Zum Paulaner, Einsteinstr. 13b. New eastern outpost of the eponymous Bavarian brewery, serving typically hearty food.

Cafés and bars

Café am Dom, Breiter Weg 214. Trendy café-bar and popular rendezvous point.

Café Lilliput, Breiter Weg 180. Small café-bar in one of the city's few remaining Baroque mansions.

Exlibris, Weitlingstr. 1a. Bar featuring regular live music, discos and film nights. Closed Tues & Wed.

Mausefalle, Breiter Weg 224. Popular student pub.

Entertainment

The main **theatre**, with a varied programme of drama, opera, operetta and ballet, is the *Theater der Landeshauptstadt*, Universitätsplatz 13 (☎551835); other venues include the cabaret *Kugelblitze*, Breiter Weg 200 (☎543 3956) and the *Städtisches Puppentheater*, Warschauer Str. 25 (☎42429). Magdeburg's chief **concert** venue is the Kloster Unser Lieben Frauen (☎541 4722), which regularly features the works of the most prolific composer of all time, the Magdeburg-born **Georg Philipp Telemann**.

Stendal

STENDAL, which lies 60km north of Magdeburg, is an important rail junction on the main route to the Baltic with the second-string line between Berlin and Hannover. It has maintained its historic role as the main town of the Altmark, and, despite its modest size, is positively cosmopolitan in comparison with the rest of this rural backwater.

The town

The Altstadt comprises a surprisingly large proportion of the present-day town and retains two surviving gateways. The **Tangermünder Tor**, on Bahnhofstrasse in the southern Altstadt, has a stone lower storey dating back to the town's thirteenth-century origins; the upper part, with its characteristically fancy brickwork, is from a hundred years later. Just across the street, occupying the former Katharinenkloster, is the **Altmärkisches Museum** (Tues–Fri 10am–noon & 2–5pm, Sat & Sun 1–5pm; DM5), which documents the history of Stendal and the Altmark region, and includes a collection of medieval religious art.

The Stiftskirche St Nikolaus

Set, in the manner of many an English cathedral, in splendid isolation in the spacious green to the west of here is the **Stiftskirche St Nikolaus**, popularly if inaccurately known as the **Dom** (May–Sept daily 10am–noon & 3–5pm; Oct–April Mon–Fri 1–2pm only). It's the largest of the town's medieval churches – which display a remarkable degree of similarity with one another, reducing the favoured north German format of the brick hall church to the barest essentials, with fortress-like towers and a minimum of surface decoration. A rare touch of extravagance, however, was allowed in the north transept, with its elaborate gable and bricks patterned into a false rose window and six-sided stars.

Pride of the interior is what's arguably the most impressive set of **stained-glass windows** in Germany – 23 in all, each dating from the fifty-year period in the middle of the fifteenth century when the church itself was erected. The twelve windows in the choir use sombre colours in a deliberate attempt to create a mystical atmosphere in the holiest part of the building; those in the nave and transepts, in contrast, sparkle like jewels. Of similar vintage are the **choir stalls**, whose misericords are vivid illustrations of the humour of the day. Also of special note are the **reliefs** of the life of Christ on the back of the rood screen, masterly Romanesque carvings retained from the church which previously stood on the spot.

The Markt

From the north side of the Dom, follow Am Dom to the east, then turn right into Hallstrasse, which eventually leads to the central **Markt**. Guarding the picturesquely gabled Renaissance **Rathaus** is a weather-worn statue of Roland, almost as big as its celebrated counterpart in Bremen. However, it's only a replica of the sixteenth-century original, which was destroyed by a hurricane in 1972. Rising up behind the Rathaus is the main parish church, the **Marienkirche** (May–Oct Mon–Sat 10am–noon & 3–5pm, Sun 2–4pm), whose similarities with the Dom even extend to having Romanesque carvings adorning the Gothic rood screen. However, the main treasure is the painstakingly reconstructed sixteenth-century **astronomical clock**. It's set underneath the organ gallery, whose frieze of paintings of the life of Christ, along with part of the instrument itself, are from the same epoch.

The northern Altstadt

Breite Strasse leads north from here to the oldest quarter of town, which is dominated by the **Jacobikirche** (if shut, get the key from the parish house at the back of the close). This church has another magnificent array of stained glass in the chancel; this time some of the windows date back to the fourteenth century. At the end of Breite Strasse, Altes Dorf leads west to the symbol of the city, the **Uenglinger Tor** (May–Sept Sat & Sun 10am–noon & 2–4pm; DM2). Incredible as it seems, this lovingly crafted masterpiece of fifteenth-century patterned brickwork was built for a purely defensive role; nowadays it provides something of an obstacle for traffic – as well as the best view of the town.

Just south of here, at Winckelmannstr. 36, the **Winckelmann Museum** (Tues–Sun 10am–noon & 1–5pm; DM5) has been set up in the half-timbered house where Johann Joachim Winckelmann, connoisseur and art historian, the son of the local shoemaker, was born in 1717. The rooms are devoted to displays on the life and work of the man whose writings, based on exhaustive research during a twelve-year stay in Rome, set the study of archeology and art history on a rigorous scientific footing and provided the most potent stimulus for the great flowering of German classicism in Weimar.

Practicalities

The **Hauptbahnhof** is situated just beyond the southern edge of the Altstadt. Stendal's **tourist office** (Mon–Fri 8.30am–noon & 12.30–5pm; May–Sept also Sat 9.30am–3pm; ☎03931/216186) is opposite the Rathaus at Kornmarkt 8.

As yet, choice of accommodation remains somewhat limited. The few **hotels** with a central location are *Postamt* 3, Hallstr. 64 (☎03931/213511; ⑥); *Altstadt*, Breite Str. 60 (☎03931/69890; ⑦); and *Am Bahnhof*, Bahnhofstr. 30 (☎03931/715548; ⑦). **Private rooms** (②–③) are in short supply and the nearest **campsite** (☎039321/2249) is 10km to the northeast in the hamlet of Wischer.

The best **restaurant** is the *Ratskeller*, in the vaulted former merchants' hall under the Rathaus; another good choice is *Altstadt-Bierstube*, Mittelstr. 6.

Tangermünde and around

Towns languishing in centuries-long decay are a common enough feature of the Mediterranean lands, but are a rarity in Germany. **TANGERMÜNDE**, which lies at the confluence of the rivers Tanger and Havel 10km southeast of Stendal, is an exception – and a truly spectacular exception at that. When Charles IV, King of Bohemia and the most astute and successful Holy Roman Emperor of the later medieval period, acquired the Margraviate of Brandenburg in 1373, he chose this prosperous market town, a midway point on the trade routes between the Baltic and central Europe, as the second-string royal residence to Prague. Tangermünde's planned development into a national capital received a setback with the emperor's death five years later, though it continued to prosper for another hundred years, whereupon its star rapidly waned. At the beginning of the present century, it became the Altmark's only industrial centre other than Stendal. The GDR regime's ideology kept it in a time warp, its skyline presenting an endearing juxtaposition of magnificent but crumbling medieval brick buildings and outdated factories.

The fortifications

Tangermünde's **Stadtmauer** is one of the most complete and impressive municipal defences to have survived in Germany. The north side, the first you see if you arrive in town by public transport, has been laid out as a park and is relatively unforbidding, save for the bleak cylindrical **Schrotturm** which guards the northwestern corner. Altogether more arresting is the **Neustädter Tor** on the west side. Its elaborately patterned tower is a stylistic twin of the Uenglinger Tor in Stendal and was the work of the same builders; in addition, there's a sturdy barbican, adorned with coats of arms.

The defences were particularly strong along the harbour side, in case of attack from the river; to see them to best advantage, it's well worth crossing over to the rustic pathway laid out on the opposite bank. Towards the far end of this section is another fine gateway, the **Elbtor**; the part-brick, part-timber extension suspended above its archway on the side facing the town was the home of the watchman. Subsequent expansion of the town has partially obscured the eastern side of the walls, though the oldest gateway, the **Hünendorfer Tor**, survives as a marker at the opposite end of Lange Strasse from the Neustädter Tor.

Charles IV's **Burg** was built overlooking the Elbe just outside the confines of the Stadtmauer. It was successively occupied by the Danes and the Imperialists during the Thirty Years' War, and was all but destroyed in 1640 during an ultimately successful siege by the Swedes. At the beginning of the present century, the ruins were made into a shady public park, to which there's free access at all times. In addition to the main gateway and two very picturesque towers, the **Kanzlei**, which formerly served as a festive hall, survives, albeit in desperate need of restoration.

The town centre

Set in its own close just to the east of the Hünendorfer Tor is the fourteenth-century **Stephanskirche**, whose mighty westwork looks more like a fortress than any of the far more decorative towers of the fortification system. Most of the rest of the exterior is equally austere, though there are occasional deft touches, such as the patterned double doorway. The hall interior, with its graceful pillars, is altogether lighter in feel. After its conversion to Protestant worship, it gained a number of intriguing adornments, including a Baroque altar which has an unusual depiction of Christ in the guise of the Lion of Judea. The early seventeenth-century **organ** is by one of the greatest ever masters of the craft, the Hamburg builder Hans Scherer, and is especially valuable for being his only instrument to have survived relatively intact. Recitals are held at 4.30pm on Saturdays from mid-May to late October.

Tangermünde's other set piece is the **Rathaus** (Tues–Sun 10am–5pm; DM2), built on the central Markt in the 1430s, the period when the town was at its commercial peak. Its fantastical eastern facade, bristling with pinnacles and gables, and pierced by ornate open and false rose windows, is one of the great pieces of secular Gothic architecture. The vaulted basement is given over to a small museum of local history; you can also see the two upstairs halls, the **Festsaal** and the **Standesamt**, upon request.

Close to the harbour, the streets are cobblestoned and still medieval in aspect. In the centre, on the other hand, are large numbers of **half-timbered houses** from the seventeenth and eighteenth centuries, some with elaborate doorways. The reason for this new building activity was that much of Tangermünde was destroyed by fire in 1617; a woman by the name of Grete Minde was made the scapegoat and burned as a witch. Over 250 years later, she became the eponymous heroine of a novel by Theodor Fontane, who used the incident to write one of his many powerful indictments of the moral injustices suffered by women.

Practicalities

Tangermünde is linked to Stendal by a branch rail line and by buses, which alternate at approximately two-hour intervals throughout the day; both arrive and depart from the **Bahnhof**, which is a couple of blocks north of the Altstadt. The **tourist office** (April–Oct Mon–Fri 10am–6pm, Sat & Sun 11am–4pm; Nov–March Mon–Fri 10am–5pm, Sat 1–4pm; ☎039322/3710) is at Marktstr. 13. Here you can book **private rooms** (①–③) of which the town has a reasonable number.

There are also a couple of **pensions**: *Am Schrotturm*, Lindenstr. 5 (☎039322/2497; ③); and *Altmarkperle*, Arneburger Str. 37 (☎039322/2344; ③). Three **hotels** can be found on Lange Strasse: *Utescher* at no. 5 (☎039322/2401; ④); *Stars Inn* at no. 47 (☎039322/9870; ④); and *Schwarzer Adler* at no. 52 (☎039322/2391 or 450805; ⑥). South of the centre, there's one more option, *Genschmar*, Luisenstr. 38 (☎039322/3348; ⑤).

For a good **meal** try the restaurant in *Schwarzer Adler*, or else *Galerie Ludwig*, Stendaler Str. 54; *Zur Post*, Lange Str. 4; *Zur Palme*, Lange Str. 70; or the *Störtebeker*, which occupies a ship moored outside the Burg. *Reederei Kaiser* (☎039322 421 8162) run a variety of **cruises**, mostly short round trips, but also weekly sailings to both Magdeburg and Havelberg.

Jerichow

JERICHOW, 8km southeast of Tangermünde, is strictly speaking outside the Altmark, the Elbe having formed the natural eastern border of the old province. Its biblical-sounding name seems a fitting reflection of its role as an important missionary centre in the early Middle Ages, though in fact this is pure coincidence, being a slight corruption of the title of the Slav settlement which preceded it. At the northern end of the village is the huge **Klosterkirche** (guided tours April–June, Sept & Oct Mon–Fri at 2pm, Sat & Sun at 11am & 2pm; July & Aug daily at 11am & 2pm; DM2). It's the oldest significant building in the area, its typically plain brick architecture Romanesque in style with a few later Gothic touches like the twin towers. Highlight of the interior is the **crypt** underneath the choir, whose columns bear immaculately carved stone capitals. The separately run **Klostermuseum** (April–Oct daily 10am–5pm; Nov–March Tues–Fri 10am–noon & 1–4pm; DM2), in the attractive monastic buildings grouped round the cloister, displays important archeological finds from the cloister garden along with documentation on the history of the monastery.

Havelberg

HAVELBERG, which lies just shy of the confluence of the Havel with the Elbe some 45km north of Jerichow, is another medieval gem as yet barely touched by overzealous restoration, or by the invasion of foreign visitors. Founded in 968 by Otto the Great as a missionary bishopric, in what was then heathen Slav territory, it proved impossible to defend and was abandoned for nearly a century and a half before being resettled by Premonstratensian monks. The town subsequently became a fishing port, even managing to establish a monopoly on fish sales on the Hamburg–Berlin trading route. When it fell to Brandenburg-Prussia after the Thirty Years' War, it was developed into a major shipbuilding centre.

The town

Dominating the town from its hillside location above the north bank of the Havel, the **Dom** is no more than a Protestant parish church nowadays. The lower part of its gaunt, fortress-like **westwork** probably belongs to the original Ottonian cathedral, which the Premonstratensians restored and expanded in the twelfth century. This building in turn was ravaged by fire a hundred years later; the subsequent reconstruction features Gothic vaulting and false arcades superimposed on the Romanesque framework. Also from this period are the monumental *Triumphal Cross*, the choir stalls and the three large column-shaped candelabra.

However, the most imposing work of art in the Dom is the fourteenth-century **choir screen**, which ranks among the masterpieces of monumental German sculpture. In the manner of a poor man's Bible, it bears statues of saints and twenty large reliefs illustrating the Passion of Christ, carved by a workshop familiar with both the Soft Style of Prague and the more realistic Netherlandish masters. The refined spirituality of the most accomplished of the sculptors contrasts sharply with the boisterous and patently anti-Semitic approach of one of his colleagues, who favoured an expressionistic idiom, with exaggerated mannerisms and facial contortions. Contemporary with the screen are two **stained-glass windows** at the end of the northern aisle, unusual grisailles with depictions of vine, acorn and ivy leaves.

Adjoining the south side of the Dom is a complex of part-Romanesque, part-Gothic brick monastic buildings, which bear more than a passing resemblance to their counterparts in Jerichow. The upper storeys now contain the **Prignitz-Museum** (Wed–Sun 10am–noon & 1–5/6pm; DM2), which details the history of Havelberg and the vicinity from prehistoric times to the nineteenth century. Clustered around the Dom's close are a number of formerly dependent buildings such as the school, the deanery and the houses of the canons; these are now put to an imaginative variety of uses, ranging from the local police headquarters to a small clothing factory.

At the foot of the Dom's hill is the **Annenkapelle**, a small octagonal Gothic brick chapel with a strikingly pointed roof. From here, the Steintorbrücke leads to the compact little **Altstadt**, which occupies an island in the Havel; an alternative approach is by the Dombrücke, directly below the Dom. Crooked old houses once occupied by fisherfolk and farmers line the banks of the river; even today, smallholdings and market gardening are clearly in evidence. The main attraction of the Altstadt is its constantly changing range of watery panoramic views. However, it's well worth walking all round the tightly packed little streets: look out for the late fourteenth-century **Beguinenhaus**, whose portal has a lintel of *The Crucifixion* carved in a similar style to the Dom's choir screen. Towering above the rest of the island is the Gothic **Stadtkirche St Laurentius**, whose vivid ceiling frescoes were recently discovered when the wooden vaulting which had concealed them for over a century was removed.

Practicalities

Havelberg is no longer on a rail line, but there's a reasonable **bus** link with Stendal via Tangermünde; the best place to alight or embark is at the stop by the Annenkapelle.

The sole **hotel** is *Am Schmokenberg*, Schönberger Weg 6 (☎039387/89177; ⑤). Otherwise, there are a few small **pensions**, including *Elb-Havel*, Genthiner Str. 5 (☎039387/89379; ②) and plenty of **private rooms** (①–③). Bookings can be made at the **tourist office** (Mon–Fri 9am–6pm, Sat 10am–3pm; ☎039387/19433 or 88224), Salzmarkt 1. The town's best **restaurants** are the one in *Am Schmokenberg*, plus *Güldene Pfanne*, Lehmkule 2, and *Harmonie*, Hinter der Kirche 3.

On the first weekend in September, Havelberg takes on a wholly different appearance with the arrival of over 100,000 visitors – most of whom end up camping or sleeping in their cars – for the *Pferdemarkt*, one of the biggest **festivals** in the former GDR. As its name suggests, it was originally a horse market, but now spawns a flea market in which anything and everything is bought and sold, a handicrafts bazaar, a giant funfair, sports events, dancing and beer tents.

THE HARZ REGION

The **Harz** mountains were formerly divided right through the middle by the notorious barbed wire frontier separating the two German states. Uniquely, comparisons between the two were, the border itself apart, almost entirely in the East's favour – it inherited the best of the scenery, several gorgeous unspoiled old towns and an extensive network of **narrow-gauge steam rail lines**. Until the 1970s, it was almost impossible for Westerners to stay, though it was one of the main holiday areas for East Germans themselves, with a vast provision of trade-union holiday homes. Restrictions were subsequently relaxed, because the growing number of train buffs wanting to visit was seen as a useful source of hard currency. Since the fall of the Wall, the Harz has become one of the most desirable areas in the east in which to travel, not least because the tourist facilities are better and more extensive than almost anywhere else.

In the foothills of the Harz are the impressive old cathedral city of **Halberstadt** and the half-timbered towns of **Osterwieck** and **Quedlinburg**, both of which have comprehensive preservation orders. Similarly protected are **Blankenberg** and **Wernigerode** on the edge of the mountains, and **Stolberg** in the very heart of the range. Wernigerode is also the starting point of the *Harzquerbahn*, the longest of the narrow-gauge rail lines; the other important line, the *Selketalbahn*, leaves from

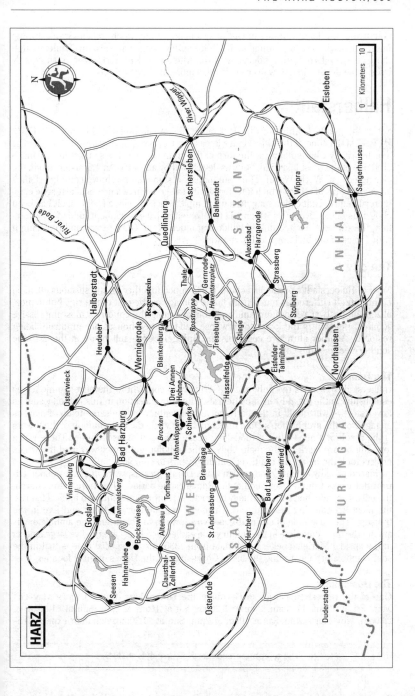

N

0 Kilometers 10

Eisleben

River Wipper

Sangerhausen

Aschersleben

Wippra

SAXONY-

Ballenstedt

Quedlinburg

ANHALT

River Bode

Harzgerode

Alexisbad

Thale

Gernrode

Strassberg

Halberstadt

Hexentanzplatz

Rosstrappe

Stolberg

Heudeber

Regenstein

Treseburg

Stiege

Wernigerode

Blankenburg

Eisfelder
Talmühle

Nordhausen

Osterwieck

Drei Annen
Hohne

Hasselfelde

Brocken

Schierke

Hohneklippen

Bad Harzburg

Braunlage

Vienenburg

Torfhaus

LOWER

Bad Lauterberg

Rammelsberg

Altenau

St Andreasberg

Walkenried

THURINGIA

Goslar

SAXONY

Bockswiese

Herzberg

Hahnenklee

Clausthal-
Zellerfeld

Seesen

Osterode

Duderstadt

HARZ

Gernrode, a village with one of Germany's most distinctive churches. Scenically, the finest landscapes are to be found in the **Bode valley**, particularly around **Thale**, though the legendary **Brocken**, rendezvous of the witches on *Walpurgisnacht*, is an equally irresistible destination, now accessible once more by the *Brockenbahn*.

Halberstadt

Set in the gentle foothills of the Harz, about 55km southwest of Magdeburg, **HAL-BERSTADT** is one of the oldest cities in eastern Germany, having been established as a bishopric by Charlemagne at the turn of the ninth century. It also used to be considered one of the most beautiful, but was devastated by an Anglo-American air raid in the closing days of World War II. The Communists restored some showpieces, but demolished the ruins of others which interfered with the creation of a new Stalinist-style commercial centre. Unification may herald a complete face-lift: since Halberstadt has been chosen as one of five cities which will receive extensive government funds for restoration, there's been excited talk of bulldozing much of the GDR legacy and replacing it with copies of old buildings lost in the war.

The city

Most of Halberstadt's prime attractions are grouped together on the spacious elliptical **Domplatz**. It suffered as much from bomb damage as the rest of the city, but monopolized the postwar restoration funds and ranks among the country's most impressive squares. Below it is the lower town whose half-timbered houses are gradually being restored. Another attractive corner is the **Spiegelsberge** hill range at the extreme southern edge of the city.

The Dom

Halberstadt's **Dom** is the only one in Germany to conform to the pure Gothic forms established in the great French cathedrals. The only exception to this is the facade: its lower storeys were built in the early thirteenth century by the same team of masons engaged on the archbishop's Dom in Magdeburg, while the current look of the towers is the result of a neo-Gothic remodelling at the very end of last century. There was a long lull before work on the main body of the building got under way, and the whole project took the better part of three hundred years to complete.

Placed proudly atop its rood screen is the Dom's greatest work of art, a wooden **triumphal cross** from the very end of the Romanesque period. Elsewhere in the church, the pillars are adorned with unusually characterful **statues** of saints and biblical figures, the most eye-catching being the unashamedly sensual pair of Adam and Eve in the transept. The ensemble of **stained-glass windows** in the choir and the ambulatory is among the most complete in the country; the earliest and finest are the five large lancets in the apsidal Marienkapelle, which date from 1330. Also of special note is that in the south ambulatory illustrating the life of Charlemagne, the Dom's original founder.

The Domschatz

One of the richest treasuries in Germany, the **Domschatz** (guided tours May–Oct Mon–Fri at 10am, 11.30am, 2pm & 3.30pm, Sat at 10am & 2pm, Sun at 11.30am & 2.30pm; Nov–April Mon–Sat at 10am & 2pm, Sun at 11.30am; donation expected) is

---

The **telephone code** for Halberstadt is ☎03941

housed in the cloister and its dependencies; entrance is via the doorway on the southeast side. The most valuable items are the textiles, and in particular three twelfth-century **tapestries** which are among the oldest in existence. One tells the story of the patriarch Abraham, another is dedicated to the Apostles, while the third shows Charlemagne with philosophers of Classical antiquity. From the same period are two outstanding pieces of **woodcarving** – *The Seated Madonna*, which was probably made in the same workshop as the great triumphal cross, and a cupboard painted with a depiction of *The Visitation*. The **treasury** items include the fourth-century *Consular Diptych* from Rome and the Byzantine *Weihbrotschale*, a magnificent gilded silver dish for consecrated bread which was brought here by a crusader. Also included on the tour is a visit to the **Kapitelsaal**, the only surviving part of the Romanesque Dom.

The Kurien

The two long sides of Domplatz are lined with the **Kurien**, the houses of the members of the Dom chapter. Oldest of these is the **Dompropstei**, the elegant Renaissance mansion in the middle of the south side, which marries two very disparate styles in its Italianate arcaded lower storey and archetypally German half-timbered upperwork.

A similar architectural mix is found in the **Gleimhaus** (Mon–Fri 9am–4/5pm, Sat & Sun 10am–4pm; DM5 including admissions to the museums below) at the far northeast corner of the square. It was the home of the eighteenth-century poet **Johann Wilhelm Ludwig Gleim**, who served as secretary to the Dom for 56 years, and has been preserved as one of the earliest – and best – literary museums in the country. A prolific letter-writer, he maintained contact with almost all the great and good in the German society of his day. To celebrate his range of contacts, he hit upon the idea of creating a **Freundschaftstempel** (Temple of Friendship), commissioning 150 portraits, which are hung throughout the first-floor rooms.

Next door, the stately Baroque **Domdechanei** is now a medical school. The slightly more modest palace next door houses the **Städtisches Museum** (Tues–Fri 9am–5pm, Sat & Sun 10am–5pm; DM5 inclusive ticket), which documents the history of the town, including material on the buildings lost in the bombings. However, the exhibits in the main building are overshadowed by those in the garden extension, the **Heineanum** (same hours and ticket). Greeting you on entry are two spectacular dinosaur skeletons, thought to be up to 220 million years old, found during excavations in the town. The rest of the collection is devoted to ornithology, with stuffed birds of the Harz region on the ground floor and an international display upstairs.

The Liebfrauenkirche

Forming a counterbalance to the Dom at the western end of Domplatz is the Romanesque **Liebfrauenkirche**, formerly an Augustinian monastery. The main feature of the exterior is the roofline, with the two octagonal towers with pointed spires at the east end forming a contrast with the pair of "bishops' mitres" on the facade. Despite the dilapidated appearance of the interior, it's worth coming when it's open in order to see two more products of the school of sculptors active here in the early thirteenth century. Suspended on high is another **triumphal cross**, with a youthful-looking Christ in a strikingly Classical pose. Even more impressive is the **choir screen**, a rare work in stucco which still preserves its original polychromy; it features realistic portraits of Christ, the Virgin and the Apostles, plus decorative friezes carved with a gossamer sense of delicacy. Look out also for the Barbarakapelle, whose walls are covered with a cycle of late fourteenth-century frescoes.

Set in an idiosyncratic position in front of the church, the Gothic **cloister** (Mon–Fri 9am–4pm; free) has been made into a small open-air museum, with decorative fragments from some of the many half-timbered houses destroyed in 1945. Adjoining it to the south is the **Petershof**, the massive former bishops' palace, entered via a handsome Renaissance portal.

The rest of the centre

The **lower town** (*Unterstadt*) on the north side of Domplatz has a confusingly mazy layout, with some of the streets following quasi-circular routes. This quarter, which has most of the surviving **half-timbered houses**, fell into shocking disrepair in the 1970s, eventually taking on the appearance of a ghost town as the inhabitants were evacuated to ugly new apartment buildings nearby. Soon after the revolution, private citizens began buying up the properties, and some have already been turned into dream homes. A few showpieces had previously been restored by the GDR state, prominent among them being the mansion at Voigtei 48. Its courtyard wing, now the **Museum Bürgerlicher Wohnkultur um 1900** (Museum of Middle-Class Living Conditions around 1900; Tues–Sun 10am–4pm; same ticket as other museums), formerly the home of a wealthy burgher family, was bequeathed to the city as a time capsule of life at the turn of the century.

Another half-timbered building well worth seeking out is the **Johanniskirche**, which lies in a peaceful garden just off Westendorf, the busy street immediately to the south of Domplatz. This rustic-looking church, built for a Protestant congregation at the end of the Thirty Years' War, has a disarmingly artless appearance from the outside, with its barn-like roof and stumpy detached belfry. Inside, however, it's surprisingly dapper, the coffered ceiling, galleries and pulpit all finely carved in late Renaissance style.

To the east of Domplatz lies the old market quarter. With the exception of the severe Gothic **Martinikirche**, what was left of its two old squares was bulldozed after the war in favour of a windswept piazza which had no apparent function until the recent return of open-air markets. The Martinikirche itself was the local rallying-point during the *Wende* of 1989 – an appropriate choice, as it had been built by the citizens as a deliberate statement of civic pride in opposition to the prince-bishops' Dom across the road. Indeed, the two towers, linked by a look-out gallery, were a key part of the city's defences, with the huge fifteenth-century **statue of Roland** underneath as a good luck charm. In the interior, which is open in summer for art exhibitions, look out for the elaborate Renaissance pulpit and the early fourteenth-century bronze **font**, resting on symbolic representations of the four rivers of Paradise and adorned with brightly coloured scenes from the life of Jesus.

The Spiegelsberge

At the southern edge of the city, reached by tram #1 or #2, is the range of hills known as the **Spiegelsberge**. Following a visit to the famous gardens of Wörlitz, the poet Gleim had the idea of creating something similar in Halberstadt. The result was the construction here of a number of follies which, while falling short of their great model, nevertheless make for a pleasing diversion. Centrepiece of the complex is the **Jagdschloss**, now a restaurant (see opposite). Ask to see inside the cellars, whose Renaissance doorway and great vat – the second largest in Germany – were brought here from the former country house of the defunct bishopric. Other attractions include a mausoleum, a grotto, a memorial column and the **Belvedere**, an observation tower (free access) built against a romanticized rocky backdrop, which commands a fine distant view of the city.

Practicalities

Halberstadt's **Hauptbahnhof** is situated well to the east of the centre; best take tram #1 or #2 as the walk is boring. There are also a couple of suburban stations, including one for Spiegelsberge. The **bus station** is about midway between the Hauptbahnhof and the Markt., while the **tourist office** is situated just north of Domplatz at Düsterngraben 3 (Mon–Fri 9am–1pm & 2–6pm, Sat 10am–1pm; ☎551815).

Accommodation

There's now a reasonable choice of **hotels** and **pensions**, thanks to the opening of a number of new establishments. Otherwise, you should be able to find a **private room** (②–④) via the tourist office. The **campsite** (☎24596) is on the right bank of the Halberstädter See at the northeastern edge of the city, and within easy walking distance of the Hauptbahnhof.

HOTELS AND PENSIONS

Abtshof, Abtshof 27a (☎68830, fax 688368). This new hotel in a half-timbered Altstadt house offers really excellent value at the price asked. ④

Am Grudenberg, Grudenberg 10 (☎69120, fax 691269). Another recent venture, this is again in a half-timbered building, and includes a sauna and fitness room among its facilities. ⑤

Antares, Sternstr. 6 (☎600250, fax 600249). Brand-new, custom-built business-class hotel with restaurant in the west of town. ⑥

Assauer, Bergstr. 11 (☎27000, fax 605288). Pension located a short distance southwest of the Altstadt. ③

Halberstädter Hof, Trillgasse 10 (☎27080, fax 26189). High class hotel and restaurant in a renovated half-timbered building. ⑦

Harsleber Hof, Kirchstr. 1, Harsleben (☎603257). This pension with restaurant occupies a three-hundred-year-old farmstead 1km southeast of Halberstadt; take bus #11. ③

Heimliche Liebe, Robert-Koch-Str. 25 (☎442393, fax 442393). Small pension with restaurant, just to the southeast of the Altstadt. ④

Parkhotel Unter den Linden, Klamrothstr. 2 (☎600077, fax 600078). Halberstadt's top hotel, now part of the *Romantik* chain, occupies a villa built according to the principles of the British Arts and Crafts movement. Its restaurant is also the best in town. ⑧

Eating and drinking

As with the hotels, the gastronomic situation has shown marked improvement over the past few years.

Alt Halberstadt, Voigtei 17–19. Café-restaurant with beer garden offering local speciality dishes. Closed Mon.

Alt Westendorfer Hanse Haus, Westendorf 16. Large complex of eateries including a bistro, a café, a beer bar and a cellar restaurant which offers "medieval" dishes.

Am Kühlinger Tor, Kühlingerstr. 24. Good traditional *Gaststätte*.

Galerie Café 1580, Lichtengraben 15. Recommendable place for *Kaffee und Kuchen*, with the bonus of exhibitions of contemporary art on the walls.

Jagdschloss Spiegelsberge, Spiegelsberge. This café-restaurant in a historic hunting lodge is the obvious place for a meal or a snack when visiting the Spiegelsberge. Open 10am–6pm, closed Thurs.

Kreuzgang, Domplatz 5. The eclectic menu here includes plenty of vegetarian dishes.

Museumscafé, Domplatz 36. Pleasant café with garden which offers inexpensive light meals.

Osterwieck

The entire town centre of **OSTERWIECK**, which lies between two arms of the River Ilm 25km northwest of Halberstadt, is under a protection order, and with good reason: it has some four hundred historic **half-timbered houses**, many of them of outstanding quality. It's an archetypal example of a place stuck in a time warp: the number of inhabitants has remained virtually unchanged for hundreds of years, despite extensive industrialization last century, which saw the town become a leading centre for the manufacture of gloves. The GDR's penchant for outdated technology has left it as a wonderful period piece, but one consequence of this was that many of the houses were allowed to fall into a terrible state of decay – a situation that is now gradually being remedied.

On the small central Markt, the **Altes Rathaus** (Tues–Thurs 10am–noon & 1–4pm, Sun 10am–2pm; DM1) has been converted into a museum of the town's history; it also serves as the nearest thing to a local tourist office and keeps the keys to the **Stephanikirche** (otherwise Sat & Sun 2–4pm only) in the close behind. The church's fortress-like facade, crafted from rough stonework, dates from the first half of the twelfth century, with the steeples added four hundred years later. The main body of the church is built in a florid late Gothic style, its vault bearing elaborate keystones showing the crests of prosperous local families. Among the diverse furnishings are a Romanesque font, a Renaissance pulpit and many fine epitaphs.

Two of the finest half-timbered houses are on the L-shaped Schultenstrasse, which wends its way round the back of the Markt. The **Alte Voigtei** at no. 3 started a local trend for having a frieze of coloured rosettes for decoration, while the **Eulenspiegelhaus** at no. 8 is the best example of those favouring a richer decoration, with lots of small, symbolic carvings. Kapellenstrasse, the main street into town from the east, has another fine group; no. 4 here is the oldest in Osterwieck, dating back to 1480. Following Hagen north from here, you come to one of the largest of the buildings, the **Hospital St Bartholmäus**. The other main set piece is the **Bunter Hof**, a huge manor on Rössingstrasse at the southeastern end of the old town, but this is in a bad state of disrepair.

Practicalities

Osterwieck is on a **branch rail line**; change at Heudeber if coming from Halberstadt. There are actually two stations, one to the east of the centre, the other (the terminus) to the north. Between the former and the Markt is the **bus station**, a halt on the Halberstadt–Goslar route, and with other services into the Harz.

Accommodation options are limited to one **hotel**, *Waldhaus*, 1km north of the centre at Am Fallstein 1 (☎039421/72232; ⑤), and the odd **private house** (②–③). Apart from the aforementioned *Waldhaus*, the best place to **eat** is the *Ratsweinstube* on the Markt.

Quedlinburg

QUEDLINBURG, 14km southeast of Halberstadt, is one of the most remarkable places in all of Germany – over 1600 of its buildings are listed as being of historic interest, and the entire town has been declared a World Heritage Site by UNESCO. Although the big set pieces are all hewn out of a whitish sandstone which has taken on a grey patina, the town's character is defined by the **half-timbered houses** which line almost all its streets. The full diversity of this quintessentially German architectural form is on view, with examples ranging from the fourteenth to the nineteenth century. Thankfully, the GDR authorities saw Quedlinburg as a great national asset. The factories the state's dogma deemed essential were confined to the outskirts and have caused only a modest degree of pollution. This has helped to ensure that Quedlinburg is the ideal combination of a genuine, living community in a stunning visual setting, which has avoided the fate – suffered by so many of its western German counterparts – of becoming over-reliant on tourism.

The **telephone code** for Quedlinburg is ☎03946

The town

The original medieval layout of the town is preserved intact: the River Bode divides the Altstadt, the merchants' quarter on the right bank, from the Neustadt, where the small-holders lived, while at the southern end of the former are the two hills where monastic life was centred.

Quedlinburg owes its distinctive silhouette to the buildings on the **Burgberg**, the larger of the two hills at the southern end of town. In the early part of the tenth century this became the headquarters of the German nation when the expansionist drive to the east was begun by the Saxon king, **Henry the Fowler** (*Heinrich der Vogler*). He built a palace here, which on several occasions hosted meetings of the Imperial Diet. On his death in 936, his widow **Mathilde** established a collegiate foundation for aristocratic women, which survived until the Napoleonic suppression. Its abbesses effectively controlled the town which grew up in the valley below; when it attempted to assert municipal independence by joining the Hanseatic League in the fifteenth century, the abbesses succeeded in re-establishing ecclesiastical dominance – hence the reason Quedlinburg never developed into a major city.

The Schloss

The present **Schloss** complex on the Burgberg is predominantly Renaissance, though the plain exterior walls below the frilly gables are evidence of the original defensive function. Access from the town is via the Torbau, a much-modified medieval gateway, beyond which are a number of half-timbered service buildings and a terrace commanding a sweeping view.

Apart from the Stiftskirche, the two main buildings on the courtyard are the **Residenzbau**, the palace of the abbesses, and the L-shaped **Wohntrakt**, which contained the apartments of the other canonesses, the kitchen, bakery, pharmacy and workshops. The former now contains the **Schlossmuseum** (May–Sept Tues–Sun 10am–6pm; Oct–April Tues–Sun 9am–5pm; DM5), a rambling, old-fashioned display which ranges through Ice Age fossils, a hoard of Bronze Age treasure and a comprehensive array of medieval instruments of torture, to regional costumes and sections on the history of the town. However, the main attraction is being able to wander through the building itself, whose rooms are surprisingly modest – even in the elegantly furnished Baroque extension which replaced a redundant part of the fortifications.

The Stiftskirche St Servatius

The **Stiftskirche St Servatius** (Tues–Sat 10am–4/5pm, Sun noon–4/5pm; DM5) is the eleventh- and twelfth-century successor to Mathilde's original church. Apart from the twin towers, which are nineteenth-century pastiches, and the Gothic apse, it's a very pure example of Romanesque architecture. The **capitals**, together with the friezes above, provide the only decoration; carved with supreme delicacy by Lombard craftsmen, they show animal, plant and geometric motifs. Another fine group can be seen in the **crypt**, the last resting place of Henry and Mathilde. Their plain sarcophagi are overshadowed by those of the abbesses, which are placed upright against the south wall, a position which helps endow the life-size effigies with a Byzantine sense of hierarchy.

In the northern transept is the fabulous **Schatzkammer**, now intact once more, following the return in 1993 of a number of long-lost items which turned out to have been pilfered by the American lieutenant put in charge of their safety in 1945. The glittering twelfth-century reliquary of the church's patron, St Servatius, is outstanding, with its vibrant ivory carvings of the Apostles and its encrusted diamonds and enamels. The gilded casket dedicated to St Catherine, though more orthodox, is equally beautiful.

Another highlight is an early thirteenth-century bridal chest, decorated with 31 different coats of arms, which rank as the earliest surviving heraldic symbols in Germany. Of the recently returned pieces, the finest are two gospel books and the so-called comb of Heinrich I, an elaborate ivory creation perhaps dating back as far as the seventh century. Housed in the transept opposite is the church's most valuable treasure, the oldest **tapestry** north of the Alps; woven around 1200, it shows the marriage of Mercury to Philology, the Queen of Knowledge.

The Klopstockhaus and neighbouring museums

At no. 12 on Schlossberg, the street of half-timbered houses below the Schloss, is the **Klopstockhaus** (May–Sept Tues–Sun 10am–6pm; Oct–April Tues–Sun 9am–5pm; DM2.50), the boyhood home of the eighteenth-century poet **Friedrich Gottlieb Klopstock**. Founder of the classicizing tendency in German literature, Klopstock self-consciously regarded himself as a Christian Homer, devoting much of his life to the composition of a huge twenty-part epic, *The Messiah*; he also wrote odes on typical enlightenment themes such as man and nature, the fatherland, peace and liberty. Though his reputation is somewhat in eclipse, his verses have gained a wide audience through Mahler's settings, notably in the hugely popular *Resurrection Symphony*. The museum also contains memorabilia of two other influential Quedlinburgers of the same epoch: **Dorothea Christiana Erxleben**, the first German woman to gain the title of doctor, in 1754, and **Johann Christoph GuthsMuths**, the founding father of school gymnastics – and thus the unwitting begetter of the somewhat sinister role sport has played in German society, from Prussian militarism via the Nazis to the GDR.

To the rear of here, in a heavy turn-of-the-century building at Finkenherd 5a, is the **Lyonel-Feininger-Galerie** (Tues–Sun 10am–noon & 1–6pm; DM3), devoted to the German-American Cubist, a key member of staff of the Bauhaus during its Weimar and Dessau periods. A large selection of his woodcuts, engravings, lithographs, drawings and watercolours are on display in specially dimmed galleries; there are also a few oil paintings, including an early *Self-Portrait*.

A couple of minutes' walk northwest of here, on the bank of an arm of the Bode at Wordgasse 3, is the **Fachwerkmuseum Ständerbau** (May–Sept Mon–Wed & Fri–Sun 10am–5pm; DM2.50). The building itself, which probably dates from the early fourteenth century, is the earliest surviving timber-framed house in Germany and a good 150 years older than any other in Quedlinburg. Inside, the displays illustrate how the different styles of half-timbering evolved.

The Markt and around

The spacious triangular **Markt** was the subject in the 1970s of the sort of thorough restoration programme characteristic of western Germany. The buildings are a varied mix – no. 5 and nos. 13/14 were the sixteenth-century guild houses of the weavers and tanners respectively; the music school at no. 2 occupies a large Baroque palace, while the Neoclassical *Zum Bär* is a celebrated hotel whose reputation is tainted because of *Stasi* patronage. At the far end stands the **Rathaus** (guided tours Mon–Fri at 1.30pm; DM2.50), most of which, including the graceful portal, is Renaissance. Outside the Rathaus is a puny-looking **statue of Roland**, erected as a symbol of municipal independence when Quedlinburg was a member of the Hansa – and removed as soon as the abbesses re-established full authority.

To the rear of the Rathaus, and set in an unusual semicircular close, is the **Marktkirche St Benedikti**. Its fortress-like facade shows the transition from Romanesque to early Gothic; the rest of the structure was rebuilt at the end of the Gothic period. Entrance is via the Kalandskapelle on the north side, whose walls are hung with Renaissance memorials to local dignitaries. The main body of the church is of particular interest for the furnishings dating from after its conversion to Protestant worship, in particular the Mannerist wooden pulpit and the sober Baroque high altar. A more effusive form of Baroque was employed in the burial chapel of the Gebhardt family, which stands outside the church.

Breite Strasse, the long street leading north from here, has some superb half-timbered buildings, notably no. 33, which is Gothic, and no. 39, the Renaissance **Gildehaus zur Rose**, which is generally regarded as the most beautiful house in Quedlinburg. East of here, at Klink 11, is the **Freihaus**, another outstanding Renaissance mansion of almost palatial dimensions.

The Neustadt

Across the Bode from the Freihaus is Steinweg, the main east–west axis of the Neustadt, with the best examples of half-timbering to be found in the quarter. Particularly notable are the Baroque **Zur Goldenen Sonne** at no. 11, which has been immaculately restored and returned to its historic role as a hotel (see p.848), and the late Renaissance **Zur Börse** at no. 23, which boasts an ingenious corner oriel. Due south of here, on Hinter der Mauer, are the best-preserved fragments of the **Stadtmauer**, including a couple of watchtowers.

The **Nikolaikirche**, the Gothic parish church of the Neustadt, is principally of note for its wonderful setting in the middle of a close of truly monumental grandeur. Outwardly, the two towers, one somewhat broader than the other, tend to overwhelm the rest of the building, an impression confirmed by the squat appearance of the hall interior, whose most notable furnishings are the elaborately Baroque high altar and pulpit and a touchingly naive statue of St Godehard.

The Münzenberg and the Wippertikirche

The **Münzenberg**, the hill just to the west of the Burgberg, was formerly crowned by a convent founded in Quedlinburg's tenth-century heyday. This was dissolved at the Reformation, whereupon a community of artisans, minstrels and travelling folk settled here, re-using its stones in the construction of their modest little houses. Even now, the quarter has an engagingly quiet, run-down feeling, and the view of the Burgberg from here alone justifies the trek up.

In the valley to the south, a large cemetery has grown up around the **Wippertikirche** (guided tours daily May–Oct at 11am; DM2.50), a former monastic church whose simple architecture rather resembles that of a barn – which is exactly the function it performed throughout most of last century. Its crypt dates back to the tenth century and is the only surviving monument from Quedlinburg's period as the German capital, while the Romanesque north portal, with its exquisite columns and weather-worn carvings, was brought here from the destroyed convent on the Münzenberg.

Practicalities

Quedlinburg's **Bahnhof** and **bus station** are side by side to the east of town. The Neustadt lies just over the Bode, while the Altstadt is a ten-minute walk away straight ahead along Bahnhofstrasse, then left into August-Wolf-Strasse. However, the most atmospheric approach to the town is to follow the Bode upstream towards the Burgberg; many picturesque panoramic views open up en route. The **tourist office** (March, April & Oct Mon–Fri 9am–6pm, Sat & Sun 10am–3pm; May–Sept Mon–Fri 9am–8pm, Sat & Sun 9am–6pm; Nov–Feb Mon–Fri 9am–5pm; ☎905622) is at Markt 2.

Accommodation

There's a plentiful supply of **private rooms** (①–③) on the tourist office books. The town has no hostel or campsite, but now has a good stock of **hotels**, many in fine old buildings.

HOTELS AND PENSIONS

Am Brühl, Billungstr. 11 (☎96180, fax 961 8246). Classy hotel in a historic building which was formerly a barn, then a spirits factory. Appropriately, a home-made liqueur, *Harzgeist*, can be ordered in its *Weinstube* (closed Sun), one of the best restaurants in town. ⑦

Am Dippeplatz, Breite Str. 16 (☎705022, fax 705022). Moderately priced hotel in the heart of town. ⑤

Quedlinburger Hof, Harzweg 1 (☎2276, fax 2276). Long-established hotel located by the Bahnhof. ⑥

Theophano, Markt 13–14 (☎96300, fax 963036). Offers an absolutely ideal location, nicely furnished rooms, and a fine vaulted *Weinkeller* which serves some of the best food in Quedlinburg. ⑥

Villa Klara, Am Schiffbleek 11a (☎705295, fax 705294). Bargain-priced pension, well located just below the Schlossberg. ④

Zum Bär, Markt 8–9 (☎7770, fax 700268). This eighteenth-century inn was for long the top address in town, and was the only place Westerners were allowed to stay in GDR days. It then suffered a huge slump in its reputation because of its *Stasi* connections, but is now making a comeback. ⑥

Zur Goldenen Sonne, Steinweg 10–11 (☎96250, fax 962530). Occupies a magnificent example of Baroque half-timbering, complete with oriel window and saddle roof. The restaurant serves reasonably priced specialities of the Harz. ⑥

Zum Schloss, Mühlenstr. 22 (☎3333, fax 707484). Small hotel with restaurant in a seventeenth-century half-timbered building by the Stiftskirche. ⑦

Eating and drinking

It's a measure of Quedlinburg's tourist appeal that the choice of places to **eat** and **drink** has always been wide by eastern German standards.

Am Finkenherd, Schlossberg 15. Good traditional coffee house.

Boulevard-Café, Markt 1. Another option for *Kaffee und Kuchen*, particularly recommendable in summer, when tables are placed out on the square.

Brauhaus Lüdde, Blasiistr. 14. This was one of the first home-brew pubs to open in the former GDR. It makes a *Pils* and an *Alt* as well as various seasonal beers, and also serves full meals.

Buntes Lamm, Schmale Str. 1a. Pricey wine bar-cum-restaurant in one of the Altstadt's few ugly buildings. Closed Mon.

Münzenberger Klause, Pölle 22. Fine traditional *Gaststätte*. Closed Thurs.

Ratskeller, Markt 1. Offers really splendid *gutbürgerliche Küche*, and as such is a worthy rival to any of the hotel restaurants. Closed Wed.

Schlosskrug, Schlossberg 1. Restaurant with a handy location in the Schloss complex. Closed Mon, and at 8pm on other days.

Word-Haus, Im Wasserwinkel 4. Occupying an example of nineteenth-century half-timbering, this serves regional specialities and has a good wine list.

Gernrode and the Selke valley

The recuperative health resort of **GERNRODE**, situated 9km south of Quedlinburg on the fringe of the Harz mountains, clusters round one of Germany's oldest and most remarkable churches. For the most part it's a somnolent little place – except around the Bahnhof to the north of the town proper, where the shed and freight yards of the *Selketalbahn*, the oldest **narrow-gauge steam rail line** in the region, stand directly opposite the main line.

Gernrode's history goes back to the mid-tenth century, when a women's collegiate church, the **Stiftskirche St Cyriakus** (guided tours daily at 3pm, otherwise only variably open), was founded. This is substantially the same building as the one which can be seen today, with the exception of the west choir and towers and the double-storey cloister, all of which were added a couple of hundred years later. By far the best preserved of any church of its date, it exhibits most of the characteristics associated with Romanesque, the first original architectural style indigenous to northern Europe. The nave's triforium gallery was the first ever built north of the Alps, and suggests a certain

The **Selketalbahn**, the narrow-gauge rail line which runs the 35km between Gernrode and Stiege, is named after the peaceful valley of the **River Selke**, which defines part of its route. Gernrode itself does not lie in the valley, which is reached by the most atmospheric part of the journey, a steep climb past a couple of secluded lakes, then through wooded countryside unpenetrated by roads. Built in 1887, the line is plied by a number of antique locomotives, among them a *Mallet* of 1897, the oldest still-functioning train in Germany; unfortunately, (relatively) modern diesels have been introduced as well. Alone among eastern Germany's nine surviving narrow-gauge passenger lines, freight carriages are attached – proof that this is no tourist trap.

The River Selke is reached at Mägdesprung, 10km south of Gernrode. A couple of stops further on is **ALEXISBAD**, a curious little resort whose spa buildings are an illustration of the Romantic movement's infatuation with chinoiserie. From here there's a three-kilometre branch line (served by 6 trains a day) to **HARZGERODE**. For several decades this town was the capital of a minute principality of the House of Anhalt – hence the late Renaissance Schloss, which, with the half-timbered Rathaus and the slate-towered Marienkirche, gives the place an air of grandeur wholly inconsistent with its size.

Three trains a day go all the way to **STIEGE**, where the link with the *Harzquerbahn* (see p.853), which fell into disuse after World War II, was reinstated in 1984. Here you can choose between continuing on the two through trains to the *Harzquerbahn*'s southern terminus at Nordhausen; going as far as Eisfelder Talmühle, then changing to the service north to Wernigerode; taking the five-kilometre-long branch line to Hasselfelde; or returning with the train to its shed in Gernrode.

Byzantine influence – a connection explained by the fact that the dowager Empress Theophanu, a native of Greece, was then living in Quedlinburg. Another innovation pioneered at Gernrode – alternating columns and pillars – became a hallmark of churches throughout the Saxon lands.

In the southern aisle stands a **Holy Sepulchre**, the oldest German reproduction of Christ's tomb in Jerusalem, which probably dates back to the late eleventh century. Unfortunately, it's somewhat mutilated, but the high quality of its carvings can still be seen on two of its sides, one showing Jesus appearing to Mary Magdalene after the Resurrection, the other with a wonderfully delicate frieze – a sort of carved version of an illuminated manuscript – featuring prophets, fantastic animals, foliage and a decorative border. Other highlights of the interior are the retouched frescoes in the east choir, the twelfth-century font and the late Gothic monument in honour of Margrave Gero.

The survival of the steam rail line ensured a steady stream of foreign visitors in GDR days, but, as they were forced to stay elsewhere, tourist facilities are underdeveloped in comparison with other parts of the Harz. Now, however, there are a couple of **hotels**: *Gasthof zum Bären*, Marktstr. 13 (☎039485/76040; ⑤) and *Panoramahotel Stubenberg*, Stubenberg 1 (☎039485/61186; ⑤), plus a fair number of **private rooms** (①–③) bookable via the **tourist office**, Marktstr. 20 (☎039485/478).

The Bode valley

Before reaching Quedlinburg, the **River Bode** travels a mazy route right through the Harz mountains. Not only is it, at 169km, the longest river in the range, it also offers by far the most beautiful scenery the region has to offer, seen at its best under the menacingly dramatic skies the uncertain climate so often brings – making it easy to understand why such a rich store of supernatural folklore has grown up in association. The Bode has stirred the imagination of the literati to an extent unmatched by any other beauty spot in the country: Goethe, Herder, Klopstock, Eichendorff, Heine and Fontane all sang its praises.

Thale and around

German unification has meant that **THALE**, which lies right on the edge of the Harz 10km southwest of Quedlinburg, must look to tourism for its future, as its ironworks – the bedrock of the local economy for over five hundred years – was a casualty of the GDR's failure to invest in modern plant and machinery. The town itself is of scant interest, the only monument of note being the **Wendhusenturm**, a tower house (perhaps dating back as far as the tenth century) in the old quarter north of the Bode. However, the surroundings are marvellous; with 150km of marked trails in the vicinity, Thale is unquestionably one of the best **hiking** bases in eastern Germany. Nor should the unenergetic be put off: the best of the scenery starts to unfold just beyond the Friedenspark, the park across from the Bahnhof, terminus of a branch line from Quedlinburg.

Hexentanzplatz and Rosstrappe

Guarding the southern entrance to Thale are two rocky crags, both known to have been sites of pagan worship, and commanding superb views over the valley and beyond. On the right bank, 454m above the valley, is the vertiginous **Hexentanzplatz** (Witches' Dancing Place), so named because it was where the local witches supposedly had their initial rendezvous on *Walpurgisnacht* (see p.855), before flying off to the main celebration on the Brocken. The lazy way to reach it is by **cable car** (DM5 single, DM8 return); the station for this is on the opposite side of the Bode, just over the bridge at the end of Friedenspark. There's also a road up from the southeastern end of Thale, plus several pathways, quickest and most convenient being the steps of the *Hexenstiege*, which lead to the belvedere via the **Harzer Bergtheater**, a fine natural amphitheatre where plays are staged regularly during the summer months. Alongside is the **Walpurgishalle** (daily May–Sept 9am–5pm; Oct–April 9am–1pm; DM3), an exhibition hall with displays on the *Walpurgisnacht* legend.

Directly across the river, at a height of 437m, is the **Rosstrappe** (Horse's Clip-Clops). There were once plans to make a direct transport link with the Hexentanzplatz, but instead a **chair lift** was built just north of the valley terminus of the cable car (DM4 single, DM6 return). Alternative ways up are the looping main road from the centre of Thale, and a walking trail, the *Präsidentenweg*. From the plateau-like summit, you can descend to a curious group of rocks poised directly above the river; here can be seen a natural indentation closely resembling that of a horse's hoof. According to legend, this was made by the mighty steed being ridden by a princess called Brunnhilde, who was being chased through the Harz by a lustful knight by name of Bodo. Coming to this point, she spurred her mount on to make a successful leap across to Hexentanzplatz. Bodo, however, plunged into the chasm, where he was turned into a hound, compelled forever to guard the crown of Brunnhilde which had fallen into the river in her wake.

Up the valley

The classic walk from Thale is the 10km route along a path (identified by signs marked with blue triangles) which closely follows the course of the Bode; contrary to what you'd expect, the views from the valley floor surpass those from the heights. If you don't want to walk the whole way, the best of the scenery can be seen in the first 3km, around the **Teufelsbrücke** (Devil's Bridge), from where you can make a detour up to the Rosstrappe via a belvedere-punctuated trail named the *Schurre*. Beyond the Teufelsbrücke, the main path climbs high above the river, affording wonderful views back to the Rosstrappe and of the spectacular **Bodekessel** below, a gorge in which steep granite cliffs rise directly from the foaming waters with their angry whirlpools. You then descend to a more placid landscape, which is chiefly notable for its richly varied flora and fauna. Orchids, daphnes, Turk's-cap lilies and hart's-tongues are among the plants here; some of the trees are hundreds of years old, while the large numbers of waterfowl make this stretch a magnet for bird-watchers.

TRESEBURG, the terminus of the walk, is a scattered village of grand houses picturesquely spaced out along the banks of the Bode, with a very ruinous castle crowning the hill above. It's beginning to develop its potential as a resort, with guesthouses and holiday homes springing up, though it's being upstaged in this by **ALTENBRAK**, a somewhat larger village 4km upstream, which has taken to the new opportunities afforded by tourism like a duck to water.

Practicalities

Thale's **tourist office** (Jan–April, Sept, Oct & Dec Mon–Fri 9am–5pm; May–Aug Mon–Fri 9am–6pm, Sat 10am–3pm; Nov Mon–Fri 9am–4pm; ☎03947/2597) is in the pavilion directly facing the Bahnhof at Rathausstr. 1. Here you can get a list of the numerous **private houses** (①–③) with rooms to rent. **Pensions** include *Kleiner Ritter*, Markt 2 (☎03947/2570; ③); *Schröder*, Karl-Marx-Str. 10 (☎03947/2392; ③); and *Am Steinbach*, Poststr. 9 (☎03947/63883; ④). There are **hotels** on the summits of the two mountains: *Berghotel Rosstrappe* (☎03947/3011; ④) and *Berghotel Hexentanzplatz* (☎03947/2212; ⑥). The **youth hostel** (☎03947/2881; ✿) occupies an ideal position for a hiking centre, on the right bank of the Bode just beyond the *Hexenstiege*.

Restaurants can be found in the hotels, as well as around the Bode on the early stages of the path to Treseburg.

Rübeland and around

A few kilometres upstream from Altenbrak, the waters of the Bode and its tributaries have been harnessed to create an eight-kilometre-long reservoir, the **Rappbodetalsperre**, whose hilly eastern bank is another attractive walking area. The large dam at the northern end, built in the 1950s, was one of the GDR's proudest technological achievements, particularly as various prewar projects to build it had come to nought. A much smaller second reservoir, the **Talsperre Wendefurth**, was built in the 1960s, principally as a protection against flooding.

RÜBELAND, another old iron-smelting town, lies a couple of kilometres northwest of here, clustering round a remarkable group of stalactite caves. Oldest of these, formed some 600,000 years ago, is the **Baumannshöhle** (guided tours daily 9.30am–3.30/5.45pm; DM7). It was inhabited by prehistoric bears, some of whose skeletons, which are between 20,000 and 40,000 years old, are on display; much later, Stone Age peoples also made it their home. Discovered in the early sixteenth century, the Baumannshöhle already had the status of a famous tourist attraction when Goethe paid three visits here in the last quarter of the eighteenth century. In his honour, the magnificent natural auditorium at the heart of the complex has been named the Goethesaal, and is occasionally used as a theatre.

If anything, the stalactite formations are even finer in the only other cave open to the public, the triple-tiered **Hermannshöhle** (same hours; DM7). Although this lies directly opposite, its existence remained unknown until a workman engaged on the construction of the main road stumbled across it last century. A far more diverse range of skeletons of prehistoric mammals has been found here, while thirteen sorts of salamander still inhabit its underground lake. From the Hermannshöhle, you can walk up to Rübeland's only other attraction, the ruined **Burg Birkenfeld**, from where there's a fine panoramic view over the region.

Rübeland can be reached by regular **buses** from Thale and the other villages of the Bode valley. It also lies on a branch **rail line** from Halberstadt via Blankenburg; the Bahnhof is right beside the entrance to the Baumannshöhle.

Blankenburg and around

BLANKENBURG, which lies on the edge of the Harz, 10km northeast of Rübeland and 13km west of Quedlinburg, is a quiet spa and residential town, which, at the turn of the seventeenth century, briefly found itself at the forefront of European power politics. In 1690, Ludwig Rudolf, a younger son of the Welf House of Braunschweig-Wolfenbüttel, made Blankenburg into the resplendent capital of a new principality. He also brought off an amazing double dynastic coup by marrying one of his daughters to the future Holy Roman Emperor Charles VI, and another to the son of Czar Peter the Great of Russia. Four decades later, he inherited his family's main duchy – and relegated the town he had himself built up to a second-string residence.

Despite the brevity of its period of glory, Blankenburg acquired two Baroque palaces. The smaller and prettier of these is the **Kleines Schloss** (Tues–Sat 10am–5pm, Sun 2–5pm; DM2) just east of the centre, which houses a better-than-average local museum. Its curvaceous northern facade overlooks a fine French-style formal garden, in which stand an over-the-top grotto dedicated to Neptune and a copy of the celebrated Burglöwe (Lion Monument) of Braunschweig.

From here, Marktstrasse leads west to the Renaissance **Rathaus**, above whose door are the coats of arms of both Blankenburg and Braunschweig. Steps lead up to the **Bartholomäuskirche**, a Gothic hall church restored through the munificence of the Welfs as a sweetener to their demand for the return of their palaces. East of here, Burgstrasse is lined with seventeenth-century **half-timbered houses**; others can be seen in the streets west of the Rathaus, though most are in a sadly dilapidated condition. At the very top of the town is the main **Schloss**, which is likewise in poor repair, though the monumental majesty of its courtyard is still evident.

Just to the north of the historic part of town is the **spa quarter**, centred on two large areas of greenery, the Kurpark and the Thiepark. At the edge of the latter is the **Teufelsbad**, which offers a wide range of facilities, the speciality of the house being mud baths.

Practicalities

Blankenburg lies on the rail line from Halberstadt to Rübeland; the **Bahnhof** and **bus station** are both at the northern end of town. The **tourist office** (Mon–Fri 9am–6pm; May–Oct also Sat 9am–noon; ☎03944/2898) is right in the centre at Tränkestr. 1.

There are dozens of **private rooms** (②–③) for rent. Similar rates are available at a couple of **pensions** – *Wegner*, Friedrich-August-Str. 2 (☎03944/3075; ③), and *Klaus*, Lindestr. 12 (☎03944/364142; ③). An excellent range of upmarket choices includes *An der Teufelsmauer*, Timmenröder Str. 2 (☎03944/364100; ⑤), and *Kurhotel Fürstenhof*, Mauerstr. 9 (☎03944/90440; ⑥).

Around Blankenburg

Blankenburg, being set in particularly attractive surroundings, makes a good walking base. From a scenic point of view, the best excursion is the four-kilometre circular path which leads southeast from the Kleines Schloss to the **Teufelsmauer** (Devil's Wall), a row of huge, heavily fissured sandstone boulders believed to have been formed some

90 million years ago. Near the beginning of the circuit are the **Grossvaterfelsen** (Grandfather Rocks), from where there's a wonderful view over the town.

Another walking trail leads 3km north from the Bahnhof to the fascinating labyrinthine ruins of **Burg Regenstein** (May–Oct daily 9am–6pm; Nov–April Wed–Sun 9am–4pm; DM3). The original twelfth-century Romanesque castle, partly carved out of the living rock, was the first seat of the local counts. It was badly damaged in feudal wars against the combined might of the Bishop of Halberstadt, the Count of Wernigerode and the burghers of Quedlinburg, who joined together to prevent Blankenburg establishing regional dominance. In 1670, the castle was taken over by the Prussians, although it lay outside the boundaries of their state; they enlarged the old fortifications to create a modern military stronghold.

Wernigerode and around

Known as "the colourful town in the Harz" because of the kaleidoscopic paintwork on its half-timbered buildings, **WERNIGERODE** has by far the most animated atmosphere to be found in the region. In part, this is due to the fact that it's no stranger to

THE HARZQUERBAHN

The **Harzquerbahn**, undoubtedly one of Europe's most memorable rail lines, travels the 60.5km between Wernigerode and Nordhausen in Thuringia. Up to five trains per day make the complete trip; many others cover shorter stretches. Most of the locomotives used are steam trains built in the 1950s, but diesels, to the horror of purists, were introduced in 1988. A *Mallet* of 1898 – the same year as the line was inaugurated – is brought out of storage for occasional excursion trips, for which advance booking is necessary. Although the *Harzquerbahn* has been something of a tourist attraction since its inception, it has always been used for the movement of goods, as well as providing a genuine public transport service to the villages in the remotest part of the Harz. It accounts for nearly half the length of the surviving narrow-gauge network in the region; since the link with the *Selketalbahn* (see p.849) was re-established in 1984, it has been possible to travel along the whole system, apart from the short branch lines, in the course of a single day.

The first stop, *Westerntor*, a station designed by Fritz Höger, architect of notable Expressionist buildings in Hamburg and Hannover, is located just outside the eponymous medieval gateway at the western end of the Altstadt; it's a handy place to pick up the train if you don't want to trail down to the Hauptbahnhof. There are two more stations within Wernigerode itself, before the train passes through its only tunnel in the course of its exhilarating climb – maintaining an almost constant one in thirty gradient – to its highest point at **DREI ANNEN HOHNE**. Here is the junction with the *Brockenbahn* (see p.856); it's also the place to alight if you want to follow the 10km trail up the other main mountain in the area, the Hohneklippen (908m).

The *Harzquerbahn* then descends to the villages of **ELEND** and **SORGE**, whose names ("Misery" and "Sorrow") seemed particularly appropriate in GDR days, when they found themselves right up against the notorious frontier between the two Germanys. Indeed, the train used to travel within a few metres of the electrified barbed wire on this stretch, and guards kept a wary eye on passengers' behaviour. Only the markings on the trees now indicate where the border used to be. After climbing again to the little resort of **BEN-NECKENSTEIN**, the train begins its rapid descent to **Nordhausen**. The junction with the *Selketalbahn* is at **EISFELDER TALMÜHLE**, which is just over the boundary with Thuringia. At around 6.30pm each day, three passenger steam trains travelling in different directions have to wait for each other here, before proceeding in their separate directions – a sight which can no longer be seen anywhere else in the world.

international tourism – in GDR days, it was the only place in the Harz where Westerners were encouraged to stay. This led to an influx of steam-train buffs from all over the world, who came to ride the *Harzquerbahn*, the longest and most scenic **narrow-gauge rail line** in the country. Wernigerode is its northern terminus, and the sight of antiquated locomotives puffing their way through the streets before beginning their ascent into the mountains remains the most enduring image of a town plentifully endowed with picturesque corners.

The town

The town clusters along the valleys of the Holtemme and Zillerbach, with the Altstadt lying just to the east of their confluence. From the streets of the Altstadt, the striking silhouette of the Schloss, perched high on a hill at the southern end of town, can often be seen looming in the background. Immediately beyond the Schloss, the thickly wooded slopes of the Harz mountains begin to unfold, and even within the boundaries of the town there are marked walking trails which give a good idea of the characteristic scenery and vegetation of the range.

The Altstadt

Wernigerode's pride and joy is the **Rathaus** on Marktplatz, a building of stridently pictorial qualities that could belong in no country but Germany. The bright orange facade, with sharply pointed lead steeples sprouting from resplendent double-storey oriels, represents the final phase of Gothic in the mid-sixteenth century. This formed part of an ingenious building programme whereby the Rathaus was crafted out of two existing structures – the former theatre-cum-gymnasium which forms the core, and the municipal weigh house to the south west. The exterior of the latter, with its painted corbels of saints and Carnival characters, can be seen by walking down Klintgasse.

On the western side of the Markt is the **Gothisches Haus**, another richly decorated building, originally the home of a wealthy fifteenth-century burgher family. Since the middle of last century, it has been a restaurant, and latterly a hotel as well. At no. 5 on Klintgasse is the **Teichmühle**, a seventeenth-century mill popularly known, for obvious reasons, as "The Leaning House of Wernigerode". The Neoclassical mansion at no. 10 on the same street houses the **Harzmuseum** (Mon–Sat 10am–4/5pm; DM3), which features displays on the town's half-timbered houses and their construction, as well as on the history, geology, flora, fauna and industries of the Harz region.

Just south of here is the **Silvestrikirche**, the parish church of the Altstadt, but far more remarkable than the church itself is its peaceful close, the **Oberkirchhof**, which is lined with a beautiful and varied group of houses that range from two to four hundred years old. Particularly outstanding is no. 13, the **Gadenstedtsches Haus**, a late Gothic half-timbered construction to which was added a spectacularly protruding upper-storey oriel in High Renaissance style.

On Kochstrasse, at the southernmost end of the Altstadt, can be seen the more modest dwellings of the local craftsmen. Notwithstanding its three storeys, no. 43 is the smallest house in town; sandwiched between the low-ceilinged kitchen and minute attic bedroom is the "main" level, consisting of a single room with a floor space of just 10 square metres. Another street worth seeking out is **Hinterstrasse**, a block north of the Markt, which has the oldest houses in town, some of which date back to the 1400s.

Much the most imposing street, however, is **Breite Strasse**, the pedestrianized main shopping thoroughfare leading east from the Markt. Despite some losses in a 1944 air raid, it preserves an almost uninterrupted array of high-quality vernacular architecture. Oldest house is the late sixteenth-century merchant's residence at no. 4, which was given an improbable but effective Jugendstil interior refit as a Viennese-style café. Even more eye-catching is the **Krummelsches Haus** at no. 72, whose half-timbering is all but obscured by the exuberant Baroque carvings which cover almost all its facade. At no. 95 is the **Krell'sche Schmiede** (Wed, Thurs, Sat & Sun 1–5pm, Fri 10am–3pm; DM3), decorated with horseshoes and a horse's head to indicate its function as a smithy – which it remains today, an uninterrupted tradition dating back over three hundred years.

The Schloss

The **Schloss** (May–Oct daily 10am–6pm, Nov Sat & Sun 10am–6pm; Dec–April Tues–Sun 10am–6pm; DM7), a Romantic fantasy which almost completely replaced the original fortress, was the brainchild of Count Otto of Stolberg-Wernigerode, one of Bismarck's closest cronies. Although the architecture is pseudo-Gothic and Renaissance in style, there's nothing fake about the furnishings, which include valuable pieces ranging from the thirteenth to the nineteenth centuries, many of them brought from the former count's first-string residence of Stolberg.

Especially notable are two works in the chapel – an embroidery dedicated to St Mary Magdalene woven around 1250 and the late fifteenth-century retable carved by Ulrich Mair. The other big attraction is the **view** over Wernigerode and the Harz from the ramparts.

Practicalities

Wernigerode's **Hauptbahnhof** – which, in addition to being the terminus of the *Harzquerbahn*, has mainline services to Magdeburg via Halberstadt – lies about fifteen minutes' walk north of the town centre. Alongside is the **bus station**. The **tourist office** (Mon–Fri 9am–5/6pm, Sat & Sun 10am–3pm; ☎03943/633035) is at Nicolaiplatz 1. There's the usual **private room** (①–③) booking service, though this has competition from agencies at Hinterstr. 24 (daily 10am–7.30pm; ☎03943/606000) and at Burgberg 9a (Mon–Fri 11am–7pm, Sat & Sun 11am–3pm; ☎03943/54590).

Among many good-value **pensions** are *Oberbeck*, Hilleborchstr. 4 (☎03943/632662; ③); *Zur Neuen Quelle*, Friedrichstr. 129 (☎03943/632725; ④); *Hasseröder Hof*, Amtsfeldstr. 33a (☎03943/632506; ⑤); and *Harzkrone*, Nöschenröder Str. 42–46 (☎03943/23256; ⑤). There's a wide choice of **hotels**, mostly in grand half-timbered buildings, including *Zur Tanne*, Breite Str. 57–59 (☎03943/632554; ④); *Schossblick*, Burgstr. 58 (☎03943/632004; ⑥); *Zur Post*, Marktstr. 17 (☎03943/69040; ⑥); *Weisser Hirsch*, Am Markt 5 (☎03943/602020; ⑦); and *Gothisches Haus*, Am Markt 2 (☎03943/6750; ⑦). Wernigerode's **youth hostel** is at Friedrichstr. 53 (☎03943/32061; ✿).

All the recommended hotels have **restaurants**, though they face strong competition from the *Ratskeller* under the Rathaus, which is as good as any in eastern Germany. *Café Wien*, Breite Str. 4, is the obvious place to go for ice cream or coffee. Wernigerode's *Hasseröder* **beer** ranks fairly high by eastern standards; its premium product is called *Pilsator*.

The town has a number of **festivals**, including the *Weintage* towards the end of May, the *Rathausfest* in late June and the *Schützenfest* in mid-July.

The Brocken

Southwest of Wernigerode is the celebrated peak of the **Brocken** (1142m), meeting place of the witches on *Walpurgisnacht* (April 30), an event vividly described in the first part of Goethe's *Faust*. The legend seems to have arisen at least partly as a result of the so-called "spectre of Brocken" – when the sun is low, it casts magnified silhouettes from the peak onto clouds hanging around the lower neighbouring mountains. *Walpurgisnacht* is somewhat oddly named after St Walburga, an eighth-century

English-born missionary whose name is evoked as a protection against evil spirits; however, it seems she gained this role through her name having been confused with that of Waldborg, the pagan goddess of fertility.

Throughout the entire history of the GDR, the Brocken's mystique was increased by the fact that it was a restricted military area used for border surveillance activities, with Westerners forbidden to come anywhere near it. Such is its impact on the German consciousness, however, that it was made accessible to walkers within a month of the fall of the Berlin Wall. Soon afterwards work began on restoring the *Brockenbahn*, a narrow-gauge branch line of the *Harzquerbahn*, and the full 19km of this, from Drei Annen Hohne to the summit of the mountain, is now back in operation. Near the terminus, the **Brockenmuseum** (daily 10am–4pm; DM2.50) has displays on the geology, history and legends of the peak.

Of the many other paths up the mountain, the most atmospheric is that from Torfhaus (see p.640), which offers the best views of the peak. Another favourite hiking base is **SCHIERKE** which has a station on the *Brockenbahn* line, and which can also be reached from Wernigerode in about forty minutes by bus. This resort village is amply endowed with **places to stay**, including several converted state holiday homes. A full list is available from the **tourist office** at Brockenstr. 10 (Mon–Fri 9am–noon & 1.30–4.30pm, Sat 10am–noon; ☎039455/310).

Stolberg

It's not without justification that **STOLBERG** styles itself as "the pearl of the southern Harz", as this former county capital occupies a secluded setting bestriding beautiful hills and valleys. Although a centre for silver, iron and copper mining for much of its history, it's had the status of a *Kurort* since 1945. Formerly it used this as a prefix to distinguish it from other towns of the same name, but, just before the *Wende* of 1989, this was replaced with the designation "Thomas-Müntzer-Stadt", in celebration of the five-hundreth anniversary of the birth here of the most radical figure of the Reformation period. Müntzer's leadership of the Peasants' War of 1525 was regarded by the GDR authorities as the first precursor of Communist rule, and he came close to rivalling Marx in the state's roll call of heroes.

The town

At first sight, the painted sundial seems to be the only remarkable feature of the half-timbered **Rathaus** on the Markt. A closer inspection shows that it's actually a real architectural curiosity – there are no interior stairways, access to each upper storey only being possible from the steps which serve as the public footpath up the hill. Formerly, there was a second peculiarity, in that the number of windows equalled the number of weeks in the year and the number of panes equalled the number of days in the year, but these tidy calculations have been spoiled by subsequent remodelling.

At the top of the steps is the gaunt late Gothic church of **St Martini**, where, at the height of the Peasants' War, Luther – who regarded Müntzer as a dangerous upstart liable to undo all the achievements of the Reformation – dared to come to preach against the town's famous son. At the top of the hill is the part-Renaissance, part-Baroque **Schloss**, which is currently being converted into a luxury hotel.

The town's finest houses can be seen along Niedergasse, which leads south from the Markt. Best of all is the brightly coloured **Alte Münze** (Tues–Sat 10am–12.30pm & 1–5pm, Sun 10am–12.30pm & 1.30–5pm; DM2) at no. 19. Inside, you can see a reconstruction, complete with original equipment, of the workshop of the mint formerly housed here; there are also sections on the other craft industries and on mining. The top floor is a memorial to Müntzer: the four sixteenth-century console figures are all that remain of the house on this street where he was born, which was destroyed by fire last century. Finally, while all the hills around which Stolberg is built offer fine views, the best of the town itself are from the belvedere known as the **Lutherbuche**, almost due west of the Markt.

Stolberg is an excellent hiking centre, with a wide variety of marked trails in the vicinity. The most popular destination is the **Josefskreuz** (daily 10am–7pm or dusk if earlier; DM2), 6km to the northeast. This huge iron double cross was erected at the end of last century to replace its Schinkel-designed wooden predecessor, which had been destroyed by lightning. You can ascend the platform for a sweeping panoramic view stretching from the Brocken to the Kyffhäuser; there's also a *Gaststätte* (same hours) offering full meals or snacks.

Practicalities

Full information about walks is available from the **tourist office** (Mon–Fri 9am–12.30pm & 1–6pm; ☎034654/454) at Markt 2. Here you can also book a room in a **private house** (①–③), of which the town has an abundant supply.

Stolberg also has several attractive hotels, all of which are very good value considering their quality: *Zum Kanzler*, Markt 8 (☎034654/205; ④); *Stolberger Hof*, Markt 6 (☎034654/320; ⑤); *Weisses Ross*, Rittergasse 5 (☎034654/403 or 600; ⑤); and *Zum Bürgergarten*, Thyratal 1 (☎034654/401; ⑤). All these also have reasonably priced **restaurants**, with the last-named perhaps having the edge on the others. An even cheaper alternative is the *Ratskeller* on the ground floor of the Rathaus.

Note that trains from the **Bahnhof**, at the southern end of town, only go southwards into Thuringia, but that there are good **bus** connections from here – and from the stop on the Markt – to other towns in the Harz.

THE ELBE-SAALE REGION

As in the north of Saxony-Anhalt, the main tourist draws in the south of the province are found in the basin of the Elbe and one of its major tributaries, in this case the Saale. Of the old Anhalt princely capitals, **Bernburg** is particularly attractive, while **Köthen**, despite pollution, also has its points. **Dessau**, on the other hand, was devastated in the war, but is worth a visit for its wonderful heritage of Bauhaus architecture; it's also the hub of an eighteenth-century scheme of landscaped gardens which reached its climax at nearby **Wörlitz**. Not far from here is **Wittenberg**, the unlikely-looking university town which, during its spell as the capital of Saxony, was the main setting for the Reformation. **Halle** is principally of note as a major city which still evokes the nation's vanished prewar existence; nearby **Merseburg** preserves reminders of its time as a missionary bishopric, though its Dom is overshadowed by that of **Naumburg** further up the Saale, which lies close to the river's most picturesque stretch around **Bad Kösen**.

Bernburg and Köthen

Until it was finally united in 1863, with Dessau as its capital, Anhalt had had an almost continuous history of political fragmentation, with each branch of the same family ruling a tinpot principality from its own *Residenzstadt*. Apart from Dessau itself (the only one which developed into a city), **Bernburg** and **Köthen** both served as courtly towns for extended periods and preserve reminders of their heady days – which contrast sharply with their present provincial status.

Bernburg

By far the most attractive of the Anhalt capitals is **BERNBURG**, which spreads across both banks of the River Saale, just east of the Harz range and about 30km south of Magdeburg. The town was extraordinarily quick at shaking itself free from the decades of neglect in which it was plunged during the GDR epoch: shortly after unification, all the streets were renamed and glossy brochures were produced trumpeting its claims as an enticing tourist destination.

A curiosity of Bernburg is that it's a place whose centre has shifted. The **Talstadt**, or lower town, on the north bank of the Saale is the oldest part: here are a couple of Gothic churches and a spacious but incongruously quiet Marktplatz lined with Renaissance and Baroque houses. Far more memorable than any of these, however, is the **waterfront**, where a lock and several museum-piece mills make a picturesque foreground to the wonderful view of the **Bergstadt**, or upper town, on the opposite bank.

Completely dominating the Bergstadt, which has become the modern commercial centre, is the **Schloss**, by origin a medieval fortress but converted into a magnificent Renaissance palace in the mid-sixteenth century. It has a richly varied skyline of towers, turrets and gables, with the defensive features of the old castle softened with decorative adornments. The courtyard is also impressive, particularly the showpiece northern facade with its two double-storey oriels adorned with colourful carvings, grotesque heads and heraldic emblems. A small part of the complex houses the **Schlossmuseum** (Tues 9am–1pm & 2–6pm, Wed & Thurs 9am–1pm & 2–4.30pm, Fri 9am–1pm, Sat & Sun 10am–1pm & 2–5pm; DM3), with the expected archeology and local history displays, plus an extensive section on the local mills. There's also a surprisingly good lapidary department, with sculptures from the Romanesque period onwards: look out for the relief portraits, which formerly decorated the exterior of the Schloss, of seven princes of the Reformation period. On summer weekends, you can ascend the Romanesque keep, the **Eulenspiegelturm**, for a panorama over the town and the valley.

Practicalities

Bernburg's **Bahnhof** is at the eastern end of the Bergstadt, while the **bus station** is right in the centre. The **tourist office** (Mon–Fri 9am–6pm; ☎03471/372030) is at Rheineplatz 1a. Between March and October, you can take a **cruise** on the Saale from the landing stage below the Schloss; the boats sail from here as far as Halle.

In addition to the **private rooms** (①–③) which can be booked at the tourist office, there's a selection of rather expensive **hotel** options, including *Kammerhof*, Breite Str. 62 (☎03471/353945; ⑤); *Ulmer Spatz*, Heinrich-Zille-Str. 2 (☎03471/24021; ⑥); *City*, Lindenstr. 1c (☎03471/22170; ⑥); and *Askania*, Breite Str. 2–3 (☎03471/3540; ⑦).

The **youth hostel** is to the west of the Talstadt at Krumbholzallee 2 (☎03471/25167; ⑪) and a **campsite** at the extreme southwestern edge of town at Am Stadtbad (☎03471/22334).

Bernburg's best **restaurants** are *Alter Markt,* Markt 26, in the Talstadt and the *Haus des Handwerks,* Karlsplatz 34, in the Bergstadt.

Köthen

KÖTHEN, which lies 20km east of Bernburg, is a blackened town standing at the northern end of the notorious industrial region centred on Halle. Despite its present appearance, it's a place of considerable interest, holding an honoured place in musical history as a result of **Johann Sebastian Bach**'s period of service as court *Kapellmeister* from 1717 to 1723, and an equally distinguished position in the field of ornithology as the home town of the German Audubon, **Johann Friedrich Naumann**, whose work is commemorated in a gem of a museum.

Like all the town's historic buildings, the outsized **Schloss** at the northern end of the town centre is hard to appreciate because of its thick coat of grime. Its southern wing, the **Ludwigsbau**, was built in Renaissance style at the turn of the seventeenth century, when the principality of Anhalt-Köthen was first established. It's undergoing a desperately needed restoration programme at the moment, though the chapel, now the **Bachsaal**, and the throne room, the **Spiegelsaal**, are regularly used for concerts and can be viewed if you ask at either the reception or the tourist office. There are plans to establish a Bach museum in due course, in recognition of the special place the Köthen period occupies in his career. Freed of the commitment of producing a continuous stream of church music, he wrote here a host of instrumental masterpieces, including the *Brandenburg Concertos*, the first part of *The Well-Tempered Clavier*, and the extraordinary works for solo violin and cello which occupy unique places in the repertoire of their respective instruments.

Across the courtyard, the Neoclassical **Ferdinandsbau**, erected by the last ruler of Anhalt-Köthen, houses the **Naumann-Museum** (Tues–Fri 9am–4.30pm, Sun 10am–noon & 2–5pm; DM3). A series of Biedermeier display cabinets contain the collection of stuffed birds instituted by the great nineteenth-century ornithologist, one of the pioneers of taxidermy and author of a definitive thirteen-volume study of the bird life of Germany. Naumann was a highly talented artist who made all the illustrations for his publications, and the highlight of the museum is a display of original watercolours which served as the basis for these.

On Springstrasse, to the west of the Schloss, is another Neoclassical building, the **Marienkirche**, which Duke Ferdinand erected to mark his conversion to Catholicism; it stands in the strongest possible contrast to the gaunt Gothic **Jacobskirche** used by the Protestants, which dominates the central Marktplatz. On Museumsgasse, a block south of here, is the **Historisches Museum** (Wed 9am–noon & 2–5pm, Sat 2–5pm, Sun 10am–noon & 2–5pm; DM3), a fusty array of local ephemera which includes, pending the restoration of the Schloss, a large collection of Bach memorabilia.

Practicalities

Köthen's **Bahnhof**, an important junction offering good connections to Magdeburg, Halle and Dessau, is about ten minutes' walk east of the centre. The **tourist office** (Mon–Fri 9am–12.30pm & 1.30–5pm, April–Sept also Sat 10am–2pm; ☎03496/216217) is at Hallesche Str. 10.

Apart from a fair provision of **private rooms** (②–③), there are numerous **pensions** such as *Feldner*, Hallesche Str. 53–54 (☎03496/213613; ③); *Zum Ausspann*, Georgstr. 9 (☎03496/213177; ③); and *City*, Magdeburger Str. 41–42 (☎03496/40340; ⑤). There are also three **hotels**: *Stadt Köthen*, Friedrich-Ebert-Str. 22 (☎03496/556106; ③); *Zum Rüdesheimer*, Friedrich-Ebert-Str. 48 (☎03496/213026; ④); and *Anhalt*, Ludwigstr. 53 (☎03496/550011; ⑥). The **restaurant** of the last-named, which specializes in Italianate dishes, is the best in town. Otherwise, try either *Troika*, Holzmarkt 8, or the *Ratskeller* in the Rathaus on Marktplatz.

Dessau

DESSAU, the former capital of Anhalt, lies 60km southeast of Magdeburg. These days, it's a bleak industrial city which has suffered from all the worst aspects of modern Germany – with post-unification blight the latest sorry episode in a list which began with horrendous wartime damage followed by drab Stalinist rebuilding. All of which is a pity, as Dessau had previously maintained a highly distinguished cultural tradition. In the late eighteenth century, its pastoral-type setting between the Elbe and Mulde rivers was put to full use in its transformation into a garden city, with parks and palaces laid out all around its environs. Even more significantly, it was home to the **Bauhaus**, the most influential architecture and design movement of the twentieth century, during its most exciting and innovative period between 1925 and 1932. The survival of a large number of buildings from this time means that Dessau is a place no modern architecture buff should miss.

The city

There are plenty of delights to be found amid the prefabricated concrete jungles – but this requires time and patience given that the sights are very scattered. Curiously the city centre is fairly low on sights, but there are important clusters of Bauhaus buildings in both the northern and southern quarters, plus several lovely areas of greenery.

The Bauhausgebäude and around

The **Bauhausgebäude**, one of the classic buildings of modern times, stands just west of the Hauptbahnhof on Gropiusallee, and can be reached in about five minutes from the rear exit via Schwabestrasse and Bauhausstrasse. A striking-looking structure even today, it was a sensation when the Bauhaus director, **Walter Gropius**, designed it in 1925 as the new custom-built headquarters for the school on its move here from Weimar (see p.883). Built according to the very latest methods around a steel and concrete skeleton with much use of light-admitting glass, it was the forerunner of architectural styles that would not come into their own until the 1950s and 1960s. There are actually three interconnected structures – one with the classrooms, a second with the workshops, the third the student residence. Following a comprehensive restoration programme in the 1970s (the Bauhausgebäude was damaged in World War II and not properly restored), an art and design college was re-established here, so there's unrestricted access to much of the building. The workshop wing – whose starkly Cubist appearance has inspired countless buildings around the world – also houses the **Bauhausmuseum** (Tues–Sun 10am–5pm; DM4). This contains an enormous collection of furniture, ceramics, graphics and photographs detailing the work done here, with background information about the Germany of the 1920s.

Ten minutes' walk north of the Bauhausgebäude itself, at the beginning of Ebertallee, are the **Meisterhäuser**, a collection of seven houses built for the senior staff of the school. Gropius, who was again responsible for the design, lived in the first house in the scheme, which was later occupied in turn by the subsequent directors, Hannes Meyer and Mies van der Rohe; the others were the homes of Moholy-Nagy, Feininger, Muche, Schlemmer, Kandinsky and Klee. These angular buildings were revolutionary for 1926, though the passing of years and familiarity with styles of architecture derived from Gropius and others lessens their impact today. The **Feiningerhaus** is now home to the **Kurt-Weill-Zentrum** (Tues 2–4pm, Thurs 10am–noon, Sat 2–5pm; DM3), a display on the work of the Dessau-born composer. Best known for *The Threepenny Opera* and other collaborations with Bertolt Brecht, Weill was one of the twentieth century's most versatile and distinctive musicians, whose legacy ranges from symphonies to Broadway musicals. About fifteen minutes' walk north of here, overlooking a horseshoe bend in the Elbe, is the **Kornhaus**, a restaurant-cum-dance hall by Carl Fieger, one of Gropius' assistants. With the fine views over the river from its terrace, it makes a good spot for a relaxing break from sight-seeing.

The Georgium

Immediately to the northwest of the Hauptbahnhof is the **Georgium**, the most accessible of the eighteenth-century parks to be found in and around the city. At its heart stands the modest-sized and graceful Neoclassical **Schloss Georgium** (Tues–Sun 10am–5pm; DM5). The collection of old masters inside includes works by Cranach, Rubens, Hals and Dou; there are also a large number of official portraits of members of the ruling house, many by J. F. A. Tischbein. It's worth walking through the shady park itself, which is dotted with pools and artificial ruins. At its eastern end, just across Georgenallee, is the **Lehrpark**, planted with 125 different kinds of tree and home to numerous semi-captive small animals.

The city centre

Taking a stroll through the centre of Dessau, you could be forgiven for thinking that the bombing occurred only a few years ago, such is the desolate impression made by the concrete efforts of the rebuilders. The few surviving old buildings are the **Stadtbibliothek**, which lies just north of Schlossplatz, and, on the square itself, the turn-of-the-century **Rathaus** and the ruined **Marienkirche**. After unification, it was decided to rebuild the latter, the most southerly of the brick Gothic churches so characteristic of northern Germany, and work is now well under way, with the tower already in place. However, the **Schloss** itself is probably too far gone for any kind of meaningful restoration: the fragment known as the Johannbau is all that remains of what must once have been a splendid Renaissance palace.

A few minutes' walk west of here, on August-Bebel-Platz, is Gropius' **Arbeitsamt**, an employment office designed at the end of the 1920s, nowadays a health centre. The building consists of a semicircular hall, well lit by glass skylights, joined to a two-storey administration building. It was built to achieve maximum efficiency, serving job-seekers as quickly as possible – something that was to become an urgent necessity after the start of the Depression in 1929.

Törten

A few kilometres south of town, reached by tram #1 from the Hauptbahnhof or a centre to Damaschkestrasse, is the suburb of **Törten**, a purpose-built settlement designed under the direction of Gropius to provide decent living conditions for Dessau's working-class population. The earliest buildings include the large **Konsumgebäude** in the middle of the scheme and the rows of houses along Klein Ring, Mittel Ring and Doppel Reihe; a second phase, constructed to designs by Hannes Meyer, added the **Laubenganghäuser**, the monumental apartment buildings on Peterholzstrasse. Unfortunately, the Bauhaus buildings are now somewhat engulfed by later developments. Nevertheless, fans of the school should definitely come out here to see two of its finest products – the austere, appropriately named **Stahlhaus** (Steel House) by Georg Muche, and the futuristic **Haus Fieger**, built by Carl Fieger as his own home. Both are among the detached houses standing in their own gardens at the southern end of Südstrasse.

Schloss Mosigkau and the Luisium

There are a couple of other worthwhile palace-garden complexes in the outer fringes of Dessau. The more important of the two is **Schloss Mosigkau** (guided tours April & Oct Tues–Sun 10am–5pm; May–Sept Tues–Sun 10am–6pm; Nov–March Tues–Fri 10am–4pm, Sat & Sun 11am–4pm; DM5), set in the western suburb of the same name, and reached by bus #D or #L or mainline train. Designed by Georg von Knobelsdorff, court architect to Frederick the Great, it contains a fine array of *objets d'art* and seventeenth-century Dutch and Flemish paintings, star piece being Van Dyck's *Portrait of Wilhelm II of Oranien-Nassau*. The **Luisium**, at the northeastern extremity of the city near the terminus of bus #G, is an English-style park with fake ruins, grottoes, sculptures and an Italianate villa – a pleasure to stroll through on summer afternoons.

Practicalities

Dessau's **tourist office** is at Friedrich-Naumann-Str. 12 (Mon–Fri 10am–6pm, Sat 9am–noon; ☎0340/214661). As ever, you can book here for a **private room** (②–④).

Alternatively, there are several **pensions**: *Nord*, Kantstr. 2 (☎0340/212318; ③); *Bürgerhaus*, Mendelssohnstr. 43 (☎0340/220 4528; ④); and *An der Sieben Säulen*, Ebertallee 66 (☎0340/619620; ⑥). The main central **hotels** are *Astron*, Zerbster Str. 29 (☎0340/25140; ⑦); and *Steigenberger Avance* on Friedensplatz (☎0340/25150; ⑧), which is decked out in Bauhaus style. An enticing alternative to these is *Zum Kleinen Prinzen*, Erich-Weinert-Str. 16 (☎0340/517071; ⑥) in Mosigkau.

Dessau also has a **youth hostel** at Waldkaterweg 11 (☎0340/619452; ⓑ); take bus #K from the Hauptbahnhof for four stops. The **campsite** is at An der Adria 1 (☎0340/216 0945) in the eastern lakeside suburb of Mildensee, reached by bus #B or #G.

For **eating** and **drinking**, Dessau is relatively well off in comparison with most eastern German towns of its size. Good choices for a full sit-down meal are *Dessauer Bierstuben*, Hobuschgasse 2, and *Restaurant am Museum*, Franzstr. 90, with the *Ratskeller* in the Rathaus a more than acceptable alternative. If you're out visiting Törten, make a short detour south to *Jägerklause*, Alte Leipziger Str. 76, a restaurant specializing in game dishes which is open daily till late evening. The aforementioned *Kornhaus*, Kornhausstr. 146, is the obvious destination if visiting the Bauhaus buildings. In the Bauhausgebäude itself, there's a café serving coffee, cakes and snacks; while the *Teehäuschen* in the Stadtpark at the western edge of the city centre is a teahouse which also serves full meals.

Wörlitz

WÖRLITZ, which lies 18km east of Dessau, seems a world away in spirit: there's no sign of industrial blight here, just a quiet rural village destined to prosper as one of eastern Germany's greatest tourist magnets. For that, it can thank Leopold Friedrich Franz of Anhalt-Dessau, an enlightened despot who commissioned Friedrich Wilhelm von Erdmannsdorff, Anhalt's court architect, to upgrade his family's old hunting seat into the crowning showpiece of the principality's group of landscaped gardens. The **village** itself contains a number of buildings by Erdmannsdorff, including the central Markt with the Rathaus, a brewery and a farm.

The Schlosspark

The **Schlosspark** seems to grow seamlessly out of the village of Wörlitz, an embryonic relationship inspired by the then revolutionary intention that the public should be free to enjoy the park at all times – hence the lack of entrance barriers. The layout of the park, with its carefully planned axes and perspectives, was strongly influenced by the spirit of the Age of Reason and the theoretical writings of Rousseau and Winckelmann. It's a very conscious act of homage to England, then in the first throes of the Industrial Revolution, which had made a great impression on both Prince Leopold and Erdmannsdorff when they travelled there together. In particular, it copies the very English idea of a country house with a working estate, a concept then completely foreign to Germany, where the aristocracy retained a far greater degree of feudalistic political power and hence generally resided in urban palaces, creating gardens for purely private recreational use.

The Schloss

To further emphasize the narrowing of the gap between rulers and ruled, the pristine white **Schloss** (guided tours April & Oct Mon 1–4.30pm, Tues–Sun 10am–4pm;

May–Sept daily 10am–6pm; DM5) was built right beside the village, at the edge rather than the middle of the park. Strongly influenced by the neo-Palladian stately homes of England, it marked the German debut of Neoclassicism. Inside, there's none of the bombast normally found in German palaces; instead, everything is on an intimate scale. There are a number of impressive antique statues, the most important being the *Amazon of Wörlitz*, a Roman copy of a lost Greek original. Pick of a choice group of old master paintings is Rubens' *Alexander the Great Crowning Roxana*.

The gardens

To the rear of the Schloss is the elliptical **Wörlitzer See**, the largest of the park's four lakes, which are interconnected by means of canals. It's overlooked by the circular **Synagoge**, which, in a sad reversal of the original ideals of Wörlitz, had its interior burnt out on *Kristallnacht*. To reach the main gardens you have to take a ferry over the lake from here, but you can avoid the expense by making a detour east to the least visited but perhaps the most attractive part of the park. At the **Grotto der Egeria**, which stands opposite the **Stein**, an island with a number of fake Roman ruins, the path swings north, passing over a miniature version of the Industrial Revolution's symbol, the Iron Bridge in Shropshire, to the lakeside **Pantheon**, a mini-version of its great Roman counterpart.

West of here, on the northern shore of the Wörlitzer See, the central **Schochs Garten** is dotted with mock-classical statues, urns and sarcophagi, plus temples to Flora and Venus. The wider Historicist sympathies marking the beginnings of Romanticism are shown by the inexhaustible types of **bridges** – chain, swing, stepped, floating and arched being just some of the varieties. An even clearer indication of this trend comes with the second of the palaces, the **Gotisches Haus** (guided tours as for Schloss; DM4), which presents a somewhat squat, dreamlike vision of the long-neglected Gothic style. The interior furnishings cunningly mix the genuine and the pastiche; among the former are a roomful of paintings by Cranach. At the southernmost end of the park are a number of islands. Largest of these is **Neumarks Garten**, which features a labyrinth, a pergola, a library and an exhibition building.

Practicalities

To see Wörlitz properly, you really need the best part of a day: it takes several hours just to walk round the entire length of the park – and there are surprises in even the most far-flung corners. If possible, avoid weekends and holidays, when an uncomfortably large number of people throng the immediate vicinity of the Schloss. Unfortunately, the most atmospheric way to approach the village – on the *Wörlitzer Eisenbahn*, a **train** which leaves from its own station just north of Dessau's Hauptbahnhof – is only possible on Wednesdays, Saturdays and Sundays between Easter and October; two return journeys are made each day, and historic locomotives are sometimes used. Otherwise, there's a very regular **bus** link with Dessau and a somewhat less frequent one with Wittenberg.

The **tourist office** (April–Oct Mon–Fri 9am–6pm, Sat & Sun 9am–noon & 12.30–6pm; Nov–March Mon–Wed & Fri 9am–4pm, Thurs 9am–6pm; ☎034905/19433 or 20216) is at Neuer Wall 103, just south of the park. There are more than a dozen **private houses** (②–③) in the village with rooms to rent. Additionally, there are three very fine **hotels**: *Parkhotel*, Erdmannsdorffstr. 62 (☎034905/20322; ⑥); *Zum Stein*, Erdmannsdorffstr. 228 (☎034905/500; ⑥); and *Wörlitzer Hof*, Markt 96 (☎034905/20242; ⑥). All of these have restaurants and beer gardens.

Wittenberg

It's seems hard to believe such a small and unassuming town as **WITTENBERG**, which lies 35km east of Dessau on the main Berlin–Halle rail line, played a pivotal role in the history of Europe. Although the capital of Electoral Saxony, it stretched for no more than 1.5km along a sandbank on the north side of the Elbe and had a population of just 2500 at the time when **Martin Luther** – the man whose impact on German society and culture has arguably been more profound and long-lasting than that of any other individual – formulated his 95 theses attacking the corrupt trade in indulgences and so launched the Protestant Reformation.

Nowadays bearing the official designation of "Lutherstadt Wittenberg", the town retains its historic core and, though slightly run-down by western standards, is positively gleaming in comparison with most places in the former GDR, due to the comprehensive restoration programme carried out in 1983 to mark the five-hundredth anniversary of Luther's birth. This had been preceded by a stealthy political rehabilitation of the reformer, hitherto regarded as a great historical villain for his opposition to the Peasants' War of 1525.

The town

All Wittenberg's sights are within the confines of the Altstadt. Although the university at which Luther taught was shut down in 1815 and incorporated into that of Halle, there has been a renewal of academic life revolving around a theology faculty which is a leading centre of Protestant thought.

Lutherhalle and around

At no. 54 on Wittenberg's main street, Collegienstrasse, is the **Augusteum**, the former medical faculty building of the University. On the southern side of its courtyard stands the **Lutherhalle** (April–Sept Tues–Sun 9am–6pm; Oct–March Tues–Sun 10am–5pm; DM6), which was originally the Augustinian monastery that Luther entered on arriving in Wittenberg. When this dissolved at the beginning of the Reformation, it was given to him as his home; he and his family occupied a few rooms, with the rest serving as a hall of residence for students. Entry is via the ornate **Katharinenportal**, a birthday gift to Luther from his wife, the former Cistercian nun Katharina von Bora, in 1540.

A display on the ground floor relates the history of the building itself, and in the former monks' refectory (now an occasional concert hall) an exhibition chronicles the career of one of Luther's immediate circle, **Lucas Cranach the Elder**. Court painter to the Electors of Saxony, Cranach had an astonishingly successful career, not only as an artist, but as a local businessman and politician, and was for several years mayor of the town. His role as chief pictorial propagandist for the Reformation is illustrated by his didactic depiction of *The Ten Commandments* which forms the centrepiece of the display. Eleven carefully laid-out rooms on the first floor take the visitor through Luther's life and work, with the aid of contemporary paintings, excerpts from his writings and numerous items of Lutherabilia. Particularly intriguing is the **Lutherstube**, the part of the building Luther and his family lived in, complete with ornate Renaissance tiled oven and faded seventeenth-century wall decorations. The second floor is devoted to Luther's role as a translator of the Bible, work which played an important role in the development of written German.

At the eastern end of Collegienstrasse is the **Luthereiche**, an oak planted on the exact spot where, in December 1520, Luther burned the papal bull threatening him with excommunication if he failed to retract his views.

LUTHER'S 95 THESES

Luther, then an Augustinian monk, came to give philosophy lectures in 1508 at the University of Wittenberg, settling permanently in the town three years later, whereupon he was appointed to the chair of biblical studies and quickly established a reputation as its star teacher. The subsequent course of the Reform movement was directed by Luther and his associates from Wittenberg, earning it the nickname of "the Protestant Rome".

The issue which finally triggered the Reformation was the trade in **indulgences**, a blatantly corrupt practice used by the Church for raising revenues. Their purchase enabled the buyer to gain some form of remission of sin. Many of the great medieval cathedrals were largely funded from this racket; ironically enough, Wittenberg University was itself financially dependent on cash raised from indulgences sold at the Schlosskirche on All Saints' Day each year.

Luther's theses were conceived in reaction against the campaign mounted in 1517 by the most renowned and skilful indulgence salesman, the Dominican monk **Johann Tetzel**. One of the main beneficiaries was the luxury-loving Pope Leo X, who required extra money for the rebuilding of St Peter's in Rome. Luther was incensed on two counts – from a political point of view he saw his beloved Germany being bled dry by Italian popes; and from the perspective of a devout monk he regarded the whole trade as outright blasphemy. In formulating his theses, he mounted an audacious attack on both these fronts; by pinning them to the door of the Schlosskirche, he was following the accepted practice for initiating a scholarly dispute. The matter at first seemed a monkish quarrel and Tetzel retaliated by formulating 122 antitheses. However, Luther's theses were translated into German, and gained immediate and powerful popular support. He broadened his attack on indulgences to a more general repudiation of the religious and political status quo. Within a couple of years, Luther was regarded as the veritable champion of the nation - the "German Hercules".

The Melanchthonhaus

A couple of doors down from the Lutherhaus at Collegienstr. 60 is the **Melanchthonhaus** (April–Sept Tues–Sun 9am–6pm; Oct–March Tues–Sun 10am–5pm; DM2), a Renaissance residence with a gable that resembles fingers rising above an outstretched palm. It commemorates the career of Luther's closest lieutenant and the greatest scholar of the Reformation period, **Philipp Schwarzerd**, who is generally known as **Melanchthon**. He came to Wittenberg as professor of Greek in 1519, when aged just 21, and soon found himself caught up in the dramatic events which had begun there two years previously. Though he lacked Luther's self-assuredness, he possessed a sharper intellect and was primarily responsible for the precise articulation of the new Protestant doctrines: the Augsburg Confession, the definitive statement of the Lutheran faith, is chiefly his work.

Upstairs, Melanchthon's apartments have been re-created using cleverly aged furniture – even the woodworm is fake, reproduced by means of shotgun blasts. Along the ground-floor corridor is an exhibition devoted to the history of Wittenberg, including the mummified hand of a woman broken on a wheel before the Rathaus in 1728 for poisoning her four step-children.

The Marktplatz

Collegienstrasse terminates at the **Marktplatz**, which preserves a number of Renaissance mansions, among them the pharmacy owned by Cranach and the **Rathaus**, an august, white gabled building with a red-tiled roof. Its richly decorated portal, adorned with allegorical figures, completes the picture of sixteenth-century grandeur, and provides a suitable backdrop for **monuments to Luther and**

Melanchthon. That to Luther was erected in 1821, with a statue by the great Berlin Neoclassical sculptor Johann Gottfried Schadow topped with a cage-like canopy designed by Schinkel. The similarly styled Melanchthon memorial was not added until 1860.

Rising high above the row of houses at the eastern end of Marktplatz is the **Stadtkirche St Marien**. This twin-towered Gothic church is Wittenberg's oldest surviving building; the choir dates back to around 1300, though work on the rest went on until 1470, while the distinctive octagonal turrets were only added after the Reformation. Luther often preached from its pulpit; he was married there in 1525, while each of his six children were baptized in the church's magnificent late Gothic **font**, which was made by Hermann Vischer, founder of the renowned Nürnberg dynasty of bronze-casters. The church's walls are hung with a splendid series of carved and painted **epitaphs**, the finest being that to Lucas Cranach the Younger. However, the most eye-catching decorative feature is the large and complex **Reformation altar** by Cranach the Elder. In the central scene of *The Last Supper*, Luther is shown as the disciple receiving the cup; in the predella he preaches on the theme of the crucified Christ; while other leading figures of the Reformation, including Melanchthon and the Elector, Frederick the Wise, are featured on the wings.

The Schlosskirche and Residenzschloss

Schloss Strasse leads west from Marktplatz to the far end of the historic part of town, and the **Schlosskirche** (Sun & Mon 2–4/5pm, Tues–Sat 9/10am–noon & 2–4/5pm), late Gothic by origin, but extensively remodelled last century. The famous wooden **doors** where Luther nailed his theses on October 31, 1517 were destroyed during the Seven Years' War; their heavy bronze replacements were installed in 1858 to commemorate the 375th anniversary of Luther's birth, and have the Latin texts of the 95 theses inscribed on them. More or less opposite the doorway of the church are the simple tombs of Luther and Melanchthon. The rest of the interior is a riot of statues, reliefs, portraits and epitaphs of local worthies. Look out for the bronze epitaph to Frederick the Wise, and the pair of large alabaster statues of the same Elector and his heir, John the Steadfast. You can also ascend the **tower** (Mon–Fri 2–4pm, Sat & Sun 10am–noon & 2–4pm; DM1) for a view over the town.

The Schlosskirche forms part of the **Residenzschloss**, though this once-resplendent Renaissance palace is but a shadow of its former self, having been repeatedly ravaged by fire and war. These days, it houses a youth hostel, reached via an unusual exterior staircase in the western wing. The same wing is also home to the **Museum für Natur- und Völkerkunde** (Tues–Sun 9am–5pm; DM2), which has natural history and ethnography collections.

Practicalities

Wittenberg's **Hauptbahnhof** is a few minutes' walk east of the Altstadt. The **tourist office** is at Schlossplatz 2 (Mon–Fri 9am–6pm, Sat 10am–2pm, Sun 11am–3pm; ☎03491/414848 or 498610). They can fix you up with **private rooms** (②–③).

Budget rates are also available at a number of **pensions**, some of which are in the Altstadt: *Gloeckner-Stift*, Fleischerstr. 17 (☎03491/410707; ②); *An der Stadtkirche*, Mittelstr. 7 (☎03491/419361; ③); *Central*, Mittelstr. 20 (☎03491/411572; ④); and *Zur Elbe*, Elbstr. 4a (☎03491/419024; ④). Wittenberg also has a good choice of **hotels**; those with a convenient location are *Am Alten Anker*, Dessauer Str. 286 (☎03491/62000; ④); *Klabautermann*, Dessauer Str. 93 (☎03491/662149; ④); *Am Schwanenteich*, Töpferstr. 1 (☎03491/411034; ⑤); *Art*, Puschkinstr. 15 (☎03491/401241; ⑥); and *Park Inn*, Neustr. 7–10 (☎03491/4610; ⑦). It's worth knowing that the **youth hostel**, with its enticing location in the Residenzschloss (☎03491/403255; ✿), has double rooms.

STEVE BENBOW

Berlin: the Berliner Dom and the Fernsehturm

PETER WILSON

A squat in eastern Berlin

Berlin: viewing platform, Potsdamer Platz

Berlin: the newly-restorted synagogue, Oranienburger Strasse

Berlin: construction work on the Reichstag

Dessau: the Bauhaus

The Wartburg, Thuringia

Berlin: the new Kulturforum in the Tiergarten

Potsdam: Schloss Sanssouci

Weimar: the Schloss

The Oberweissbacher Bergbahn at Obstfelderschmiede, Thuringia

Dresden: the Hofkirche and Schloss

Dresden: one of the Baroque atlantes in the Zwinger

The *Park Inn* has the best **restaurant** in the Altstadt. Other options include *Haus des Handwerks*, Collegienstr. 53a, which offers tasty no-nonsense Teutonic cuisine at reasonable prices; the swanky *Schlosskeller*, Schlossplatz 1; and the gimmicky *Schlossfreiheit* at Coswiger Str. 24 just off the Markt.

Halle

When the Land of Saxony-Anhalt was created in 1947, the old market and salt-producing city of **HALLE** was chosen as capital. It recommended itself to the authorities on account of its position at the heart of one of eastern Germany's largest industrial belts and its distinguished Socialist pedigree. Communist favour, however, proved a severe disadvantage when it competed with Magdeburg to become capital of the resurrected Land in 1990. In compensation, it became the Land's largest city by the incorporation of Halle-Neustadt (the most important new town built during the GDR period) on the opposite side of the Saale. Relatively little damaged in World War II, Halle ranks, along with Erfurt, as the German city most reminiscent of its prewar self. It has been racked by pollution, but still contains enough of interest to warrant a visit of a day or two.

Arrival and accommodation

Halle's **Hauptbahnhof** is just beyond the southeastern edge of the city centre. The **tourist office** (Mon, Tues, Thurs & Fri 9am–6pm, Wed 10am–6pm, Sat 9am–1pm; April–Sept also Sun 10am–2pm; ☎202 3340) is in the Roter Turm on Marktplatz.

Accommodation

Private rooms (③–④) can be booked via the tourist office's special phone number (☎202 8371). The **youth hostel** occupies a Jugendstil villa in the northern part of the Uni–Viertel at August-Bebel-Str. 48a (☎03451/24716; 🏠). A dramatic increase in the number of **hotels** in the past few years means that the middle and upper ranges are very well served, whereas budget choices are still quite scarce.

HOTELS AND PENSIONS

Am Alten Markt, Schmeerstr. 3 (☎521 1411, fax 523 2956). Centrally located pension in a recently renovated nineteenth-century tenement. ⑤

Am Ratshof, Rathausstr. 14 (☎202 5632, fax 202 1296). Small Altstadt hotel where you start the day with a buffet served in a vaulted Gothic room. ⑥

Apart, Kohlschütterstr. 5 (☎52950, fax 525 9200). Located midway between the city centre and Giebichenstein, this is the most luxurious of several new hotels set up in Jugendstil buildings, with a sauna, solarium and whirlpool among the facilities. ⑤

Bergschänke, Heidestr. 1, Nietleben (☎647453, fax 805 7653). Moderately priced hotel on the edge of the heathland in the northwestern outskirts of Halle, not far from the S-Bahn terminus of Dölau. ④

Kaffeehaus Sasse, Geiststr. 22 (☎233380, fax 36355). New venture in a renovated Jugendstil apartment block just north of the centre. ⑥

Martha-Haus, Adam–Kuckhoff-Str. 5–8 (☎51080, fax 510 8515). Run under the auspices of the Protestant churches, this immaculate hotel occupies a handsome old house in a quiet central street. ⑦

Phantasie, Burgstr. 6 (☎522 6788). Pension with restaurant, situated just a stone's throw from Burg Giebichenstein. ④

Saaletal, Fischerweg 3, Lettin (☎550 8618, fax 550 8618). One of the cheapest places to stay in the city, this pension lies 7km north of the centre on the roue of bus #21. ③

The **telephone code** for Halle is ☎0345

GEORGE FRIDERIC HANDEL (1685–1759)

The career of the man born as Georg Friedrich Händel differs starkly from that of any previous German musician. Unattracted by the musician's normal, very provincial existence as *Kapellmeister* to a court, or *Kantor* in a large church (roles which occupied his close contemporary J.S. Bach throughout his entire life), Handel embarked on a dazzling peripatetic career as a virtuoso keyboard player and composer. Notwithstanding his devout Protestant faith, he was lionized during his long sojourn in Italy, and successfully blended the showy Italianate forms with solid German counterpoint into a unique musical language of his own. On his return to Germany, he had a spell as musical director to the court at Hannover.

Anticipating the succession of his patron to the British throne, he moved to London, where he stayed for the rest of his life. There he found his true spiritual home – he abandoned his previously footloose existence altogether, changing both his name and nationality – and entered his most productive creative phase, in which his favoured format increasingly became oratorios set to English texts. Of these, the sublime *Messiah* has become one of the great set pieces of Protestant culture, whose annual performance is a ritual performed by choirs, both amateur and professional, all round the world.

Schweizer Hof, Waisenhausring 15 (☎202 6392, fax 503068). Among the most characterful of the upmarket hotels in the centre. Its restaurant is one of the best in the city. ⑦

Zum Kleinen Sandberg, Kleiner Sandberg 5 (☎202 3173, fax 202 5488). Hotel with restaurant in a half-timbered Altstadt house. ⑥

The city

A cross-section of Halle can be seen in the fifteen minutes it takes to walk to the central Marktplatz from the **Hauptbahnhof**. You're first confronted with a monumental Stalinist-style square-cum-highway intersection, complete with the one hotel Westerners were allowed to stay in during GDR days. Crossing via the pedestrian underpass, you come to the **Leipziger Tor**, the sole surviving medieval gateway; this guards the inner ring road, whose course follows that of the fortifications, of which only fragments survive. Ahead is the pedestrianized Leipziger Strasse, lined with grandiose Wilhelmine buildings; since the *Wende*, this has adopted the character of a typical main shopping street.

The Marktplatz

Halle's **Marktplatz**, which is surveyed by a pensive statue of the city's favourite son, the composer **George Frideric Handel** (see box), immediately impresses by virtue of its monumental dimensions and its many-towered skyline. Unfortunately, the Marktplatz's beauty is impaired by mass of tram rails and cables. A far less excusable eyesore is the gallery, now housing the tourist office, which was added in the 1970s to the **Roter Turm** (Red Tower), a freestanding late Gothic belfry topped by an engagingly fantastical spire with little corner turrets. Outside is a **statue of Roland**, an eighteenth-century stone copy of the wooden original, erected when Halle was a member of the Hansa as an assertion of the city's desire for independence from its feudal overlords, the Magdeburg archbishops.

The **Marktkirche Unser Lieben Frauen** (Mon, Tues & Thurs–Sat 10am–noon & 3–6pm, Wed 3–6pm, Sun 11am–noon) opposite is a real oddity. It owes its existence to Cardinal Albrecht von Brandenburg, Archbishop of Magdeburg and Mainz, who planned to turn Halle into a showpiece Catholic city to spearhead a counter-attack on the Wittenberg-led Reformation. The Hausmannstürme to the east and the Blaue

Türme (Blue Towers) to the west once belonged to two different Romanesque churches, which were demolished in 1529; the two pairs of towers were then linked up by a
brand-new hall church in the Flamboyant Gothic style. An unknown follower of
Cranach, dubbed the Master of Annaberg, painted its **high altar**, which immodestly
features a large portrait of Cardinal Albrecht flanked by SS Mary Magdalene, John the
Evangelist and Catherine; he also turns up at the far right of the predella in the group
of saints adoring the Madonna and Child. A few years after the Marktkirche was completed, Halle adopted the Reformation; the church was then converted to Protestant
use. A later adornment was the tiny Baroque **organ**, on which Handel received lessons;
it can be heard on Tuesdays and Thursdays at 4.30pm.

The small Renaissance palace at no. 13 on the square, the **Marktschlösschen**,
houses a collection of historical instruments (Wed–Sun 1.30–5.30pm; DM2); the rest is
a gallery featuring changing exhibitions of contemporary art.

The northern Altstadt

Immediately north of Marktplatz is a maze of run-down but nonetheless evocative old
streets. At Grosse Nikolaistr. 5 is the **Händelhaus** (Mon–Wed & Fri–Sun
9.30am–5.30pm, Thurs 9.30am–7pm; DM4, free Thurs), the large Baroque mansion
where the great composer was born. It contains extensive documentation on his life
and times, and you can listen to many of Handel's most famous works.

A couple of minutes' walk west of the Händelhaus is the **Dom**. Originally, this was
part of a Dominican monastery, and the basic structure employs the simple, unadorned
forms favoured by preaching orders of monks. Its present eccentric appearance, however, is largely due to a remodelling commissioned by Cardinal Albrecht, who took it
over to serve as his court church. A curious gabled upper storey in brick, one of the
earliest Renaissance constructions in central Germany, was tacked onto the old building; the entrance portal and interior staircase are also in this style. Most of the lavish
interior decorations have been dispersed, though seventeen over-life-sized **statues of
saints** by Peter Schroh remain *in situ*. A later Baroque transformation, carried out after
the Dom became a Protestant parish church, brought the high altar and the organ, at
which Handel presided as a teenager.

On the south side of the Dom is the **Neue Residenz**, a Tuscan-style *palazzo* which
the cardinal hoped to develop into the Catholic answer to Wittenberg University, but
which, in a neat twist of fate, is used by the institution now known as the Martin-Luther-
Universität Halle-Wittenberg. Part of the building is given over to the
Geiseltalmuseum (Mon–Fri 9am–noon & 1–5pm; free), a fascinating collection of fossils, reckoned to be fifty million years old, found perfectly preserved in the brown coal
region of the Geisel valley just south of the city.

A couple of blocks north of the Dom is the **Moritzburg**, constructed as a citadel
against the rebellious burghers by Archbishop Ernst at the end of the fifteenth century, but converted into a palace a generation later under Cardinal Albrecht. It now contains the main student club and a satirical cabaret, while the south and west wings
house the **Staatliche Galerie** (Tues 11am–8.30pm, Wed–Fri 10am–5pm, Sat & Sun
10am–6pm; DM5, free Tues). In its vaulted cellars is a good decorative arts section, the
most notable pieces being statues from demolished buildings. Elsewhere, the emphasis is on painting and sculpture of the nineteenth and twentieth centuries: Klimt,
Kirchner, Marc, Munch, Beckmann and Barlach are among those represented.

The southern Altstadt

From the Marktplatz, Schmeerstrasse leads to the **Alter Markt**, the elongated original
square with the **Eselbrunnen** (Donkey Fountain) in the centre, which was used for
markets until supplanted by its much larger successor. **Rannische Strasse**, which
leads south from the intersection of Schmeerstrasse and Alter Markt, boasts a superb

array of Renaissance, Baroque and Rococo mansions, among which nos. 10, 17, 20 and 21 are particularly outstanding.

Beyond the western end of Alter Markt is the fifteenth-century **Moritzkirche**, the Catholic parish church. From outside, it presents an austere picture, an appearance accentuated by the fact that it's built directly onto one of the surviving sections of the medieval walls. The hall interior, in contrast, is light and spacious, with elaborate star and network vaults and limpid sculptures by Conrad von Einbeck, the church's master mason; these include a poignant *Man of Sorrows* and a sharply characterized *Bust of a Man*, traditionally assumed to be a self-portrait.

Outside the Altstadt

Among the varied attractions outside the confines of the Altstadt is the old saltworks, now the **Technisches Halloren- und Salinenmuseum** (Tues–Sun 10am–4/5pm; DM3). It's set on an island formed by two arms of the Saale, and is about ten minutes' walk from either the Moritzkirche or the Neue Residenz, with the tall brick chimney which rises above the half-timbered buildings providing a useful pointer. If you come on a Sunday, you can see the last surviving saltpan being used to produce an excellent coarse-grained salt – which is on sale at the shop. At other times, you'll have to be content with seeing the machinery and the associated historical documentation.

On the fringes of the ring road are a couple of historical curiosities well worth seeking out. East of the Moritzkirche are the **Franckesche Stiftungen** (Tues–Sun 10am–5pm; DM5), a complex of buildings, forming a virtual miniature township, founded at the end of the seventeenth century by the pedagogue August Hermann Franck as an orphanage, school and charitable instution. The main building, an immensely long Baroque structure, contains a vast library and an extraordinary array of artefacts used for teaching purposes. Ten minutes' walk northeast of here, beyond the Leipziger Tor, is the **Stadtgottesacker**, a cemetery founded by Cardinal Albrecht, which was converted by Nickel Hoffmann into an elaborate galleried necropolis in the manner of the Campo Santo in Pisa.

To the north of the city centre, at Richard-Wagner-Str. 9, is the **Landesmuseum für Vorgeschichte** (Tues 9am–7pm, Wed–Fri 9am–5pm, Sat & Sun 10am–6pm; DM3), which contains an important collection of Stone, Bronze and Iron Age artefacts found in the Halle area. To get to the museum, it's best to take tram #7, which continues on to **Burg Giebichenstein** (also served by tram #8 from the centre). There are actually two castles here, both of which were destroyed in the Thirty Years' War. The lower, or **Unterburg**, was first constructed in the tenth century under King Henry the Fowler, although the oldest surviving portions are mid-fifteenth-century. It was rebuilt in the Baroque period, and now serves as a school of arts and crafts. The fourteenth-century **Oberburg** (April 1 to Sept 14 Tues–Fri 9am–6pm, Sat & Sun 9am–6.30pm, Sept 15 to Oct 31 Tues–Sun 10am–5pm; DM2), perched on the cliff above, has been left in an appropriately ruinous and overgrown state, but it's worth climbing for the sake of the sweeping view over the Saale valley. **Cruises** on the river depart daily in summer from the landing stage immediately below the castle.

Eating, drinking and entertainment

Halle has developed into one of the best places in the former GDR for **food** and **drink**, and has by far the liveliest nightlife in Saxony-Anhalt.

Restaurants

Gildenhaus St Niklaus, Grosse Nikolaistr. 9–11. Traditional *Gaststätte* whose menu includes dishes made according to old recipes of the local saltworkers.

Holly Marie's, Ankerstr. 3c. New and absolutely genuine American restaurant, with adjoining bar and bistro, the latter adorned with huge paintings.

Mönchshof, Talamtstr. 6. Directly overlooking the Marktkirche, this is generally agreed to be Halle's best restaurant, yet is quite moderately priced. Closed Sun.

Wirtshaus Alt Halle, Kleine Ulrichstr. 32–33. Cosy *Gaststätte* in a sixteenth-century timber-framed building which offers many local specialities. Evenings only, closed Fri.

Yak & Yeti, Grosse Gosenstr. 32. An unexpected oddity – a Tibetan speciality restaurant. Evenings only, but also has a daytime coffee shop at Hansering-Passage 10.

Zum Mohr, Burgstr. 72. Historic inn below Burg Giebichenstein; it serves fine traditional dishes and has a summer beer garden.

Bars and café-bars

Café Nöö, Grosse Klausstr. 11. Café-bar much patronized by the alternative set; serves light meals and sometimes features live music.

Kaffeeschuppen, Kleine Ulrichstr. 11. *Szene* café-bar whose clientele includes artists, students and foreign construction workers.

Objekt 5, Seebener Str. 5. Student bar with live music and other artistic events.

Pierrot, Grosser Sandberg 10. Bar-disco at the forefront of the local gay scene.

Weiberwirtschaft, Harz 1. Feminist café-bar.

Zur Apotheke, Mühlberg 4a. Popular theme bar, decked out with all sorts of pharmaceutical paraphenalia.

Entertainment

Among the trendiest **nightspots** are the *Studentenclub Turm* in the Moritzburg (free admission with student ID) and *Capitol*, Lauchstädter Str. 1a.

The main **theatre** venues are the *Opernhaus*, Universitätsring 24 (☎202 6458), which features opera and dance, and the *neues theater*, Grosse Ulrichstr. 50 (☎512 5949), which presents wide-ranging dramatic fare. There's also a *Puppentheater* at Mühlweg 12 and a satirical cabaret, *Die Kiebitzensteiner*, in the Moritzburg (both ☎202 4962).

Concerts are held in the Händelhaus (☎500900) and in the *Konzerthalle Ulrichskirche*, a deconsecrated Gothic church at Kleine Brauhausstr. 26 (☎202 8936).

Festivals include the *Händel-Festspiele* in June, featuring the music of Handel; the *Lanternenfest* on the last weekend of August; and the *Drachenfest* in October.

Merseburg

MERSEBURG, the most venerable of the towns in the region, was a favourite royal seat in the tenth century but is now a virtual suburb of Halle. It has the misfortune to be sandwiched between two giant chemical plants, *Buna-Werke* and *Leuna-Werke*; these are nowadays operating at a very reduced capacity, but their incessant burning of lignite throughout the GDR period has left the historic monuments badly scarred. Nonetheless, the upper town still retains its arresting medieval skyline, which is seen to best advantage from the bridge spanning the Saale.

The town

Set high above the river, the **Dom** (Mon–Sat 9am–noon & 1–4/6pm; Sun 1–4/6pm; DM6) was founded as a missionary bishopric in the early eleventh century, though only the crypt survives from this time. Of the thirteenth-century Transitional-style rebuilding there remain the choir, transepts and westwork, whose pair of octagonal towers contrasts well with their cylindrical counterparts at the east end. A Flamboyant Gothic hall nave was substituted in the sixteenth century.

The most eye-catching furnishings are the **funerary monuments**. Look out in particular for the hauntingly hierarchical bronze memorial in the choir to the eleventh-century royal pretender Rudolf of Swabia, and the Renaissance epitaph in the north transept, cast by Hermann Vischer of Nürnberg, to Bishop Thilo von Trotha. A chapel in the cloisters houses the mid-thirteenth-century memorial to the knight Hermann von Hagen, carved with a sense of characterization clearly inspired by the famous workshop of nearby Naumburg.

Adjoining the north side of the Dom is the stately **Schloss**, originally the residence of the prince-bishops, later of the secular dukes. Its wings range in style from Flamboyant Gothic to Baroque, though Renaissance predominates, with the superb portal and oriel being the most distinguishing features. The peace of the courtyard is constantly disturbed by the squawkings of the caged **raven**, the latest in a line dating back to the late fifteenth century. Its presence is explained by the fact that, when Bishop Thilo von Trotha's most precious ring was stolen, an innocent man was charged with the crime, tried and executed. After his death, the missing ring was found in a raven's nest, whereupon the guilty bird was imprisoned in a cage for the rest of its life, with its sin ever after being visited on a member of the same species. Most of the Schloss is used as offices, but a small part contains the **Kulturhistorisches Museum** (Tues–Sun 9am–5pm; DM2), with the standard archeology and local history displays.

Practicalities

Merseburg's **Bahnhof** lies at the western edge of the town centre. The **tourist office** (Mon–Fri 9am–1pm & 2–6pm, Sat 10am–4pm; ☎03461/214170) is at Burgstr. 5. There are several budget **pensions** on the opposite side of the Bahnhof from the centre: *Leisner*, Klobikauer Str. 58 (☎03461/210695; ③); *Elisa*, August-Bebel-Str. 23 (☎03461/202435; ③); *Am Park*, Gutenbergstr. 18 (☎03461/215472; ③); and *Luise*, Gutenbergstr. 4 (☎03461/213429; ④). Centrally sited **hotels** include *C'est la Vie*, König-Heinrich-Str. 47–49 (☎03461/204420; ⑥); and *Dessauer Hof*, Dammstr. 2–4 (☎03461/21145; ⑥). The best **restaurant** is the *Ratskeller*, Ölgrube 1.

Naumburg

Before the war, **NAUMBURG**, which is set on heights overlooking the Saale valley 20km upstream from Merseburg, was considered one of Germany's most beautiful and distinctive towns, thanks mainly to its peerless Dom, which dominates the skyline and shows medieval architecture and sculpture at their highest peak. Although it suffered minimal bomb damage, Naumburg fell off tourist itineraries in the GDR period and became the headquarters of a large Soviet garrison. Since the *Wende* the town has made giant steps in scraping off the grime which had smothered its buildings and is well on the way to reappearing at its best.

The Dom

Naumburg's **Dom** is among the country's greatest buildings, above all for its wondrous sculptural decoration. In 1027, the prince-bishopric of Zeitz was transferred 29km north-west to Naumburg, which had been founded at the beginning of the century as a fortress by Margrave Ekkehardt I of Meissen. By the beginning of the thirteenth century, the town had prospered as a market centre, and it was decided to replace the original cathedral with a spectacular new structure – the present **Dom** (April–Sept Mon–Sat 8am–noon & 1–6pm, Sun noon–6pm; March & Oct Mon–Sat 9am–noon & 1–5pm, Sun noon–5pm; Nov–Feb Mon–Sat 9am–noon & 1–4pm, Sun noon–4pm; DM6). Yet, although it was built as one of Germany's showpiece cathedrals, with choirs at both ends of the building to emphasize its imperial status and a monastery-like range of ancillary buildings, it's been no more than a Protestant parish church since 1564, when the bishopric was suppressed following the reign of the first and last Lutheran incumbent.

Because the Dom was built at a time of rapidly changing architectural tastes, it exhibits a variety of different yet compatible styles – despite having been substantially completed in the relatively short period of fifty years. The original masons began by erecting the **east choir**, complete with its almost oriental-looking **towers**, according to florid late Romanesque principles; the cupolas added in the Baroque period further add to the exotic appearance. The transepts and the nave are Transitional in approach, whereas the marvellously harmonious **west choir**, with its polygonal apse (a replica of which was added to the east choir the following century), adopts the pure High Gothic of the great French cathedrals. Nonetheless, its towers help give it a distinctively German accent, though only the northern one dates back to this time. Its stylistic twin was added, in accordance with the original plans, at the end of last century, as a result of the Romantic movement's frenzied enthusiasm for all things Gothic which inspired the belated completion of so many important German churches.

The west choir

Pride of the interior is the assemblage of sculptures in the west choir, which rank among the all-time masterpieces of the art. They were carved by a workshop led by the so-called **Master of Naumburg**, by far the most idiosyncratic and original of all the masons who created the great European cathedrals: his ideas and techniques were at least 150 years ahead of their time, anticipating both the Renaissance and the Reformation. Though it's reasonable to suppose that he was a German, he was trained in France, after which he worked at the Dom in Mainz, where a few fragmentary carvings by him can still be seen.

The polychrome **rood screen**, illustrating the Passion, is unlike anything previously found in religious art. Each of the life-sized figures of the crucified Christ, the Virgin and St John radiates an enormous sense of suffering and pathos – but recognizably human, not other-worldly. On the upper frieze, the small scenes unfold like a great drama, with plenty of anecdotal detail and a wonderfully rhythmic sense of movement imparted in the gestures and groupings of the figures. Sadly, the last two of these were destroyed by fire, and replaced by Baroque pastiches, whose feebleness serves to emphasize the Master's genius. Plants, flowers and fruits are featured on a second frieze, and on the capitals and keystones; carved with a matchless sensitivity, these are the earliest botanically accurate depictions in western art.

Very different from the rood screen, but recognizably the product of the same humanistic mind, are the twelve large **statues of the founders**, again still preserving much of their original colouring, which are placed on pedestals within the west choir. The granting of such prominent positions of honour to lay personages was, to say the least, unusual, but what is even more remarkable is that each is given a highly distinctive and noble characterization. Particularly outstanding are the imperiously serene couple **Ekkehardt II and Uta**, who stand together on the first pillar on the north side of the apse; they've become the most famous statues in the country, symbolizing the Germans' own romantic view of their chivalrous medieval past.

The east choir

Inevitably, the east choir is overshadowed by the west, though it's equally well preserved. It also has a **rood screen** – this is the only medieval church in Europe to have two – in this case a simple Romanesque structure adorned with a cycle of retouched frescoes. Ascending to the intimate **high choir**, with its elaborate late Gothic stalls, its fourteenth-century high altar and its gleaming stained-glass windows, is like eaves-dropping on the past, as it can hardly have changed in centuries. Here also are two more works from the celebrated sculptural workshop – the statue of a deacon and the tomb of Bishop Dietrich II.

The rest of the town

Everything else in town is very much overshadowed by the Dom, though most of the Altstadt is quietly attractive. Steinweg and its continuation Herrenstrasse – each of which has its fair share of fine houses – lead eastwards from the Dom. At the end of the latter is the **Museumseck** (Tues–Fri 1–6pm, Sat 10am–1pm & 2–5pm, Sun 2–6pm; free), the local history museum. Its most outstanding possession is the *Ratrinkhorn*, the elegant late fourteenth-century municipal drinking horn.

Immediately round the corner is the central **Markt**. Dominating the square is the **Rathaus**, late Gothic by origin but remodelled in Renaissance style in the sixteenth century, when it received the huge curved gables which clearly served as a model for other mansions in the city. The Mannerist portal, a later addition, strikes a supremely self-confident note, but the building's most endearing feature is the polychrome capital at the northeastern corner, showing two dogs fighting over a bone – this symbolizes the conflict between the ruling prince-bishops and the increasingly self-confident burghers. Of the other houses on the Markt, the most imposing are the **Schlösschen** at no. 6, which was built for the one Protestant bishop, and the **Alte Residenz** at no.7, three houses knocked together to serve as the temporary palace for Duke Moritz of Saxony while he waited for Schloss Moritzburg outside Dresden to be completed.

Rising behind the south side of the Markt is the curiously elongated **Stadtkirche St Wenzel**, which was the burghers' answer to the prince-bishop's Dom. In the Baroque period, this late Gothic church was given an interior face-lift, including the provision of an organ, highly praised by Bach, built by Zacharias Hildebrand, a pupil of the great Silbermann. Also of note are two paintings by **Cranach** – *The Adoration of the Magi* and *Christ Blessing Children*. The single **tower** (April–Oct Wed–Sun 10am–6pm; DM2, but liable to be closed for restoration until 1999), which was deliberately built higher than those of the Dom, commands a magnificent panorama over the city and the Saale valley.

More fine mansions can be seen on Jacobstrasse, which leads eastwards from the Markt. Also well worth seeing is the **Marientor** at the northeastern edge of the inner ring road. This double gateway, one of the best-preserved in the country, is the only significant reminder of the fifteenth-century fortifications which, on this evidence, must have presented a formidable obstacle to would-be invaders. In summer, the courtyard is used as a puppet theatre. At the southeastern edge of the Altstadt, at Weingarten 18, is the **Nietzsche-Haus** (Tues–Fri 2–5pm, Sat & Sun 10am–4pm; DM3), the philosopher's home throughout his childhood and youth. Nietzsche was one of the GDR's all-time bogeymen, and it was not until well after the *Wende* that the house was restored to serve as a memorial museum.

Practicalities

Naumburg's **Hauptbahnhof**, which has good rail links with Halle, Leipzig and Weimar, is below and northwest of the historic centre, which is reached by heading along Bahnhofstrasse, then up Bergstrasse. The **tourist office** (March–Oct Mon–Fri 10am–1pm & 2–6pm, Sat 10am–4pm; Nov–Feb Mon–Fri 10am–4pm, Sat 10am–2pm; ☎03445/201617) is at Markt 6.

A huge improvement in the local accommodation provision has occurred in the past few years. In addition to **private rooms** (①–③), there are a number of small **pensions**:

Hentschel, Lindenhof 16 (☎03445/201230; ③); *St Othmar*, Othmarsplatz 7 (☎03445/201213; ③); *Zum Alten Krug*, Lindenring 44 (☎03445/200406; ⑤); and *Caféhaus Kattler*, Lindenring 36–37 (☎03445/202823; ⑤). There's also a good range of hotels: *Deutscher Hof*, Franz-Ludwig-Rasch-Str. 10 (☎03445/702734 or 706134; ④); *St Marien*, Marienstr. 12 (☎03445/201522 or 201558; ④); *Siedlungsklause*, Friedrich-Nietzsche-Str. 21 (☎03445/71790; ⑤); *Zur Alten Schmiede*, Lindenring 36 (☎03445/24360; ⑤); and *Stadt Aachen*, Markt 11 (☎03445/247; ⑦). The **youth hostel** is way to the south of the centre at Am Tennisplatz 9 (☎03445/703422; ⓐ).

With the exception of *St Marien*, all the hotels listed above have **restaurants**, with *Carolus Magnus* in *Stadt Aachen* perhaps having the edge over the others. However, it faces strong competition from the *Ratskeller* in the Rathaus, Markt 1, and *Zum Alten Stadtgefängnis*, Mühlgasse 18.

Bad Kösen and around

By far the best base for exploring the Saale region is the spa town of **BAD KÖSEN**, which lies in the most beautiful part of the valley, 7km upstream from Naumburg, and one stop away by train. It's a quiet and restful place to stay, with a wide choice of accommodation; it also has the advantage of having excellent transport connections into the neighbouring provinces of Saxony and Thuringia – Leipzig, Jena, Weimar and Erfurt can all be reached within an hour or so.

The town

Bad Kösen presents a rare case of the GDR state's penchant for outdated technology being a cause for thanks rather than criticism. The side of town on the southern bank of the Saale is dominated by an extraordinary set of very primitive-looking wooden structures erected in 1730 for the extraction and production of **salt**, which survived in full working order until 1945, when they were electrified. There are four separate parts to the system. Right by the river is the **Wasserrad** or water wheel. From here, the **Kunstgestänge**, a double set of drill stems, travels to the **Soleschacht**, a well dug to a depth of 175m for the extraction of brine. The Kunstgestänge then continues up the hill to the huge 320-metre-long **Gradierwerk**, where the salt was crystallized. When the town became a spa in the middle of last century, the Gradierwerk doubled as part of the cure facilities, because of its unusually healthy air.

Overlooking the Wasserrad is the **Romanisches Haus** (May–Sept Tues–Fri 10am–noon & 1–5pm, Sat & Sun 10am–5pm; Oct–April Tues–Fri 9am–noon & 1–4pm, Sat & Sun 9am–4pm; DM4), which dates back to about 1140 and is thus the oldest surviving house in central Germany. It now contains a small museum, with displays on the history of local salt production, plus carved fragments from, and documentary material about, the Cistercian monastery of Kloster Pforta 3km to the south of the town. Also on this side of the river is the **Loreleypromenade**, which is well worth walking along for views over the town and the river. On the opposite bank is the shady **Kurpark**, in which you'll find exotic trees, floral gardens and the Neoclassical spa buildings.

Rudelsburg and Burg Saaleck

From the landing pier by the Kurpark, you can take a motorboat cruise (DM4 single, DM7 return) up the Saale to two feudal castles which both date back to the twelfth century. You're deposited below the first and larger of the two, the **Rudelsburg**, which was sacked by the citizens of Naumburg in 1348 and subsequently rebuilt. Although ruinous, a great deal of masonry survives, and the layout of the defensive Vorburg and residential Kernburg is still obvious. The latter now contains a restaurant, open daily

10am–6pm, when there's free and unrestricted access to the castle, though you're expected to make a DM1 donation if you want to climb the keep, which commands a superb view over the valley.

It's only a few minutes' walk to **Burg Saaleck** (May to mid-Oct Wed–Sun 9am–5pm; DM1), of which only the two keeps and the lower sections of the curtain wall remain. One of the keeps can be ascended for a view of the valley with the Rudelsburg in the picture. The other was the hiding place of the men who assassinated the German foreign minister, Walther Rathenau, in 1922. It now contains a display on the background to that event, which brought home the strength and determination of the anti-democratic forces ranged against the infant Weimar Republic.

Practicalities

Bad Kösen's **Bahnhof** is at the southern end of the Kurpark; the main bus stop lies slightly to the west. The **tourist office** (Mon–Fri 9am–7pm, Sat & Sun 10am–6pm; ☎034463/28289) is on Loreleypromenade. They have a long list of **private houses** (①–③) with rooms to let.

Centrally sited **hotels** (which are also the best places to eat and drink) include *Loreley*, Loreleypromenade 8 (☎034463/28788; ④); *Zum Wehrdamm*, Loreleypromenade 3 (☎034463/28405; ④); *Schöne Aussicht*, Ilskeweg 1 (☎034463/27367; ⑤); and *Villa Ilske*, Ilskeweg 2(☎034463/27363; ⑤). The last two command fine views over the valley, though best of all is from *Berghotel Wilhelmsburg*, Eckartsbergaer Str. 20 (☎034463/27679; ⑤), 2.5km to the northwest.

There's also a **youth hostel** at Bergstr. 3 (☎034463/27597) and a **campsite** (☎034463/27674) on the south bank of the Saale at the western edge of town.

travel details

Trains

Dessau to: Bernburg (frequent; 1 hr); Köthen (frequent; 30min); Wittenberg (frequent; 30min).

Halberstadt to: Blankenburg (frequent; 30min); Quedlinburg (frequent; 30min); Thale (frequent; 45min); Wernigerode (frequent; 40min).

Halle to: Dessau (frequent; 45min); Halberstadt (8 daily; 1hr 45min); Merseburg (frequent; 15min); Naumburg (12 daily; 30min); Wittenberg (frequent; 45min).

Magdeburg to: Dessau (frequent; 1hr 45min); Halberstadt (hourly; 1hr 15min); Halle (frequent; 1hr 30min); Köthen (frequent; 1hr); Stendal (frequent; 1hr).

CHAPTER ELEVEN

THURINGIA

O f all the Länder, east or west, it's **Thuringia** (*Thüringen*) which comes nearest to encapsulating the nation's soul – and to providing an insight into the Germany of old, which elsewhere has largely been swept away by one or other of the dramatic events of the twentieth century. In many ways, it stands apart from the other eastern provinces – for one thing, it has been German since the Dark Ages, rather than land won from Slavs; for another, it suffers relatively little from industrial blight, thanks to being predominantly rural in character, with a vast forest accounting for a considerable proportion of its area.

Despite having been one of the five original provinces of early medieval Germany, Thuringia became defunct as a political entity in the thirteenth century. Most of it fell to the powerful **House of Wettin**, who amalgamated it with their Saxon holdings; smaller tracts were held by the dynasties of **Schwarzburg** and **Reuss**. In the sixteenth century, the Wettin possessions began to fragment into a series of tiny duchies (identified in English by the prefix "Saxe-"), while Schwarzburg and Reuss were also partitioned. Despite many subsequent amalgamations, there were still eight separate Thuringian principalities among the 25 states which came together to form the Second Reich in 1871. It took German defeat in World War I to bring this rather feudalistic situation to an end: the aristocracy was forced to follow the Kaiser's lead in resigning political power. Thuringia made a phoenix-like return to the map, having managed to preserve a definite regional identity throughout this long history of political fragmentation.

The most visible expression of Thuringia's past is the unparalleled number of **castles** and **palaces**, many of which turned what would otherwise have been villages into proud capital cities, and which should now help ensure that the Land has a secure future in the tourism stakes. Yet these are by no means always empty expressions of the vanity of Ruritanian princes – some of the courts were vibrant cultural centres which have made an impact on the nation out of all proportion to their size. Indeed, **Weimar** was the main driving force behind the German Enlightenment, and its overall contribution to the country's development far surpasses that of most of its major cities. Nearby **Jena** has maintained a strong academic tradition, particularly in the sciences, while **Eisenach**, which likewise belonged to the same duchy for a considerable period, has also made a huge mark on the national consciousness.

The capital of modern Thuringia is **Erfurt**. Although its population is less than a quarter of a million, it's by far the largest city in the province and a place very different from the former courtly towns, the well-preserved historic core evoking its past as a major episcopal centre. Walled **Mühlhausen** is, if anything, even more suggestive of the Middle Ages, while **Schmalkalden** offers plenty of reminders of its heyday during the Renaissance and Reformation. In contrast, **Gera**, the province's second city, has shrugged off its past as a *Residenzstadt* to become a bustling modern community; of the other princely capitals, **Altenburg** and **Gotha** have (in common with Weimar, Jena and Eisenach) become medium-sized towns, whereas all the others remain engagingly provincial. In terms of scenery, the attractions are fairly low-key, though the **Thuringian Forest** has its fair share of beauty spots, as does the valley of the **Saale** at its far end, while at the far north of the province are the **Kyffhäuser**, a miniature mountain chain.

Travel in Thuringia is rendered particularly easy by the small distances separating most of the major attractions; at a pinch, it would even be possible to cover much of the

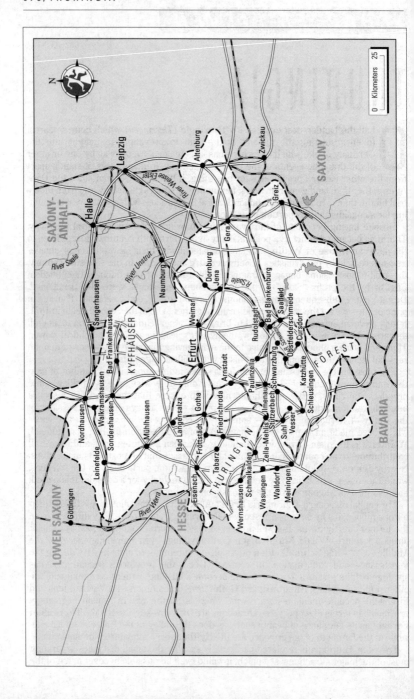

province from a single centrally sited base, such as Weimar, Erfurt or Gotha. Tourist **facilities** are, on the whole, much better than average for eastern Germany; this is particularly true of the Thuringian Forest, which has a glut of accommodation, though it also applies to the main towns, which are used to a heavy volume of visitors.

CENTRAL THURINGIA

The central part of Thuringia, in which lie four outstanding historic cities, is the part most tourists come to see. It's also the most easily assimilated – only 80km separates **Weimar**, which lies just beyond the Saxony-Anhalt border, from **Eisenach**, near the former East–West German frontier. The two are linked by one of eastern Germany's main express rail lines; en route are **Erfurt** and **Gotha**.

Weimar

If Heidelberg is the German city foreigners are most prone to drool over, then **WEIMAR** is the one the Germans themselves hold dearest. Despite its modest size, its role in the development of national culture is unmatched. Above all, it was here that the German Enlightenment had its most brilliant flowering, when it was home to the writers Friedrich Schiller, Johann Gottfried Herder, Christoph-Martin Wieland, and, most significantly, **Johann Wolfgang von Goethe** (see box on p.884), whose name is commemorated all over the town. Prior to this, Weimar's roll call of famous citizens had included Lucas Cranach and J.S. Bach; it would later number Franz Liszt, Richard Strauss, Friedrich Nietzsche and the architects and designers of the Bauhaus school. Later, the name of Weimar became synonymous with the republic established after defeat in World War I, which marked the birth of German democracy. Its inglorious failure, culminating fifteen years later with the Nazis gaining power by largely legal means, brought a sad twist to the town's cultural reputation, as it was the birthplace of the Hitler Youth movement and the site of one of the most notorious concentration camps.

Arrival, information and accommodation

Weimar's **Hauptbahnhof** is well to the north of the main sights. From here, Carl-August-Allee leads straight ahead to Theaterplatz; to get to the Schloss, turn left at the first main junction into Friedenstrasse, then right into Jakobstrasse. The **tourist office** (March–Oct Mon–Fri 9am–6pm, Sat 9am–4pm, Sun 10am–4pm; Nov–Feb Mon–Fri 9am–6pm, Sat 9am–1pm; ☎24000) is in the Stadthaus at Markt 10. It is well worth investing in the DM25 *Weimar Card*, which is valid for three consecutive days and gives unlimited travel on the town's buses as well as admission to most (though not all) of the museums and sights.

Accommodation

You can book **private rooms** (②–④) at the tourist office. The plentiful provision of these is a real boon, given that there's a shortage of budget **hotels** (although there are now plenty of options in the middle and upper ranges).

Weimar has no fewer than three **youth hostels**. Closest to the centre is that at Humboldtstr. 17 (☎8507 7792; ✿). There's another near the Hauptbahnhof at Carl-August-Allee 13 (☎850 0490; ✿), and the last is 5km south, near the route of bus #8 at Zum Wilden Graben 12 (☎850750; ✿).

The **telephone code** for Weimar is ☎03643

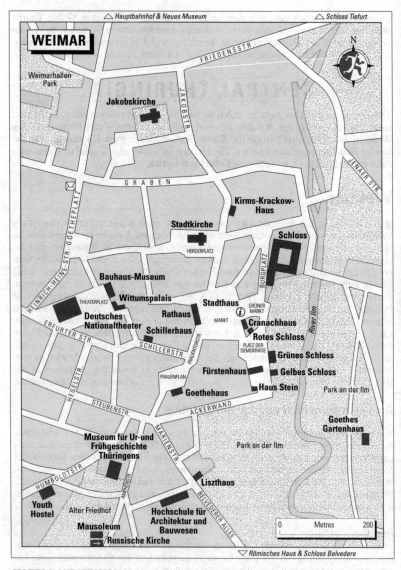

△ *Hauptbahnhof & Neues Museum*　　　　△ *Schloss Tiefurt*

WEIMAR

FRIEDENSSTR.

Weimarhallen Park

JAKOBSTR.

Jakobskirche

GRABEN

HEINRICH-HEINE-STR.

GOETHEPLATZ

Kirms-Krackow-Haus

Stadtkirche

HERDERPLATZ

Schloss

BURGPLATZ

JENAER STR.

Bauhaus-Museum

THEATERPLATZ

Wittumspalais

Deutsches Nationaltheater

Rathaus

Stadthaus

GRÜNER MARKT

ERFURTER STR.

Schillerhaus

MARKT

Cranachhaus

Rotes Schloss

River Ilm

SCHILLERSTR.

FRAUENTORSTR.

PLATZ DER DEMOKRATIE

Grünes Schloss

HEGELSTR.

FRAUENPLAN

Fürstenhaus

Gelbes Schloss

STEUBENSTR.

Goethehaus

Haus Stein

ACKERWAND

Park an der Ilm

Park an der Ilm

Goethes Gartenhaus

Museum für Ur-und Frühgeschichte Thüringens

MARIENSTR.

HUMBOLDTSTR.

AMPFERSTR.

Liszthaus

Youth Hostel

Alter Friedhof

Hochschule für Architektur und Bauwesen

BELVEDERER ALLEE

Mausoleum

Russische Kirche

0　　Metres　　200

▽ *Römisches Haus & Schloss Belvedere*

HOTELS AND PENSIONS

Alt Weimar, Prellerstr. 2 (☎86190, fax 861910). Characterful hotel and restaurant at the southern edge of the centre. ⑦

Am Berkaer Bahnhof, Peter-Cornelius-Str. 7 (☎202010). Small pension located just north of the suburban station after which it is named, reached by bus #3 from Goetheplatz. ③

Amalienhof, Amalienstr. 2 (☎5490, fax 549100). Church-affiliated hotel occupying an Enlightenment-era palace. ⑦

Dorotheenhof, Dorotheenhof 1 (☎4590, fax 459200). Located in the suburb of Schöndorf, 4km

ACCOMMODATION PRICE CODES

All the pensions and hotels in this book have been graded according to the following price categories. The prices quoted are for the cheapest available double room, although many of the budget places will also have more expensive rooms. Youth hostels are graded under separate categories. See p.34 for more details.

① less than DM50   ④ DM81–100   ⑦ DM151–200
② DM51–65   ⑤ DM101–125   ⑧ DM201–250
③ DM66–80   ⑥ DM126–150   ⑨ more than DM250

north of the centre on the route of bus #7, this was formerly the manor house of a cavalry officer, set in its own park. ⑦

Elephant, Markt 19 (☎8020, fax 65310). Weimar's most famous hotel dates back to 1696, but the interior is predominantly Art Deco. It has a gourmet restaurant, *Anna Amalia*, plus the surprisingly affordable *Elephantenkeller* and *Franz-Liszt-Bistro*. ⑨

Hainfels, Belvederer Allee 65 (☎850116, fax 850118). Pension cum café-restaurant at the extreme south of town, not far from Schloss Belvedere; take bus #12. ③

InterCity, Carl-August-Allee 17 (☎2340, fax 234444). Recently modernized mid-nineteenth-century hotel, complete with winter garden restaurant, directly opposite the Hauptbahnhof. ⑦

Liszt, Lisztstr. 1–3 (☎54080, fax 540830). A good mid-range choice in a quiet area just south of the centre. ⑥

Savina, Meyerstr. 60, (☎86690, fax 866911). Pension situated a few minutes' walk south of the Hauptbahnhof. ④

Thüringen, Brennerstr. 42 (☎3675, fax 3676). Medium-price hotel and restaurant diagonally opposite the Hauptbahnhof. ⑥

The town

If you aren't interested in its literary and artistic associations, Weimar can seem a dull and provincial sort of place. But its great merit is that it uncannily preserves both the appearance and atmosphere of its heyday as the most influential of the hundreds of capitals of pint-sized independent states which once littered the map of Germany. A rather tatty place in GDR days, it is now undergoing a frantic programme of restoration in preparation for 1999, when it will celebrate the 250th anniversary of Goethe's birth and serve as European City of Culture.

The Schloss

Set by the River Ilm at the eastern edge of the town centre, Weimar's **Schloss** (Tues–Sun 10am–6pm; DM6) is of a size more appropriate for ruling a great empire than a duchy whose population never rose much above 100,000. The complex is mostly in the Neoclassical style typical of the town: only the tall tower and the portal at the southwest corner remain of the original Renaissance palace of John Frederick the Magnanimous of Saxony, who established Weimar as the capital of the truncated duchy in 1547 following the loss of Wittenberg in the Schmalkaldic Wars.

On the ground floor is a collection of old masters, dominated by important examples of the **Cranach** family, who followed the erstwhile Elector here from Wittenberg. Pick of the works by Lucas the Elder are *Luther as Junker Jörg* (showing him in the disguise he adopted when in hiding at the Wartburg), *John Frederick the Magnanimous and Sybille von Cleve* (a pair of official bridal portraits), *Samson and the Lion*, and the erotically suggestive *Age of Silver*, illustrating the favourite Renaissance theme of a battle between "wild men". Other highlights are **Dürer**'s *Hans and Elspeth Tucher* (a pair of portraits of a prominent Nürnberg patrician couple), and a typically idiosyncratic canvas by his pupil **Baldung**, *The Sacrifice of Marcus Civitius*.

Upstairs, some fine original interiors can be seen, of which the most distinctive are the huge main **Festsaal** and the **Falkengalerie** (Falcon Gallery). Also here are seventeenth-century Dutch school still lifes and German painting from the Age of Enlightenment to the present day: look out for **Friedrich**'s haunting *Tomb of Hutten* and **Moritz von Schwind**'s colourful *Seven Ravens*, and for works by the Swiss **Arnold Böcklin** and **Christian Rohlfs**, one of Germany's most accomplished Impressionists.

Herderplatz, Jakobstrasse and beyond

Just west of the Schloss on Herderplatz is the **Stadtkirche St Peter und Paul** (May–Sept Mon–Sat 10am–noon & 2–4pm, Sun 11am–noon & 2–3pm; Oct–April Mon–Sat 11am–noon & 2–3pm, Sun 2–3pm), a much-remodelled Gothic church usually known as the **Herderkirche** in honour of the poet, folklorist and literary theorist who was its chief pastor for three decades. Inside, the eye is drawn to the large **triptych** at the high altar, which is usually described as the artistic swan song of the elder Cranach, but was almost certainly painted as a memorial by his son, as it features the aged painter and his friend Luther as the main spectators at a Crucifixion scene arranged as a propaganda statement of the new Protestant doctrine of salvation. On the wings, John Frederick can be seen in the company of his wife and children. Also in the choir are a number of elaborate **tombstones**, including that of the elder Cranach and members of the ducal family; Herder is commemorated by a plain tablet under the organ loft.

Up Jakobsstrasse at the northeast corner of the square is the **Kirms-Krackow-Haus**. This used to contain a museum devoted to Herder, but is due to re-open in late 1998 as a literary centre with a regular programme of events.. This mansion belonged to a rich bourgeois family and preserves a suite of rooms furnished according to early nineteenth-century taste. Its courtyard of wooden galleries is particularly characteristic of the domestic architecture favoured in Weimar's glory days.

Further up the street is the **Jakobskirche**, a plain Baroque church with a Neoclassical interior. In 1806, it was the scene of the wedding of Goethe to Christiane Vulpius, with whom he had been living for eighteen years in a relationship that had scandalized many influential figures in Weimar society. Christiane lies buried in the peaceful cemetery surrounding the church, as does Cranach, whose original tombstone has been replaced here by a copy.

Further north on Carl-August-Allee, the long-derelict Grossherzogliches Museum is being renovated to house the **Neues Museum**. This will exhibit German and international contempoary art, and is due to open in 1999.

The Markt and the Platz der Demokratie

South of Herderplatz is the **Markt**, lined by an unusually disparate jumble of buildings. Most eye-catching is the green and white gabled **Stadthaus** on the eastern side. Beside it is the **Cranachhaus**, where the artist spent his final years; directly opposite stands the neo-Gothic **Rathaus**. On the south side is the **Hotel Elephant**, the setting for all but the last chapter of Thomas Mann's novel about the town in Goethe's day, *Lotte in Weimar*. The historic inn was much favoured by Hitler, and it was just about the only place Westerners were allowed to stay during the GDR period, when it swarmed with *Stasi* agents; subsequently it has reclaimed its former position as one of Germany's leading hotels. Adjoining it are two more old hostelries and the **Bachstube**, where the composer lived during his years as leader of the court orchestra and organist from 1708 to 1717. This ended with a month-long imprisonment, following his fury at being passed over for the musical directorship, whereupon he left for a new position at the much smaller court of Köthen.

Beyond is an even larger square, the **Platz der Demokratie**, lined by a colourful series of palaces, over which an equestrian statue of Grand Duke Carl August presides. On the north side is the **Rotes Schloss** (Red Palace), a Renaissance building with Neoclassical additions, while to the south the grand Baroque **Fürstenhaus** is where Goethe was received on his arrival in Weimar. It now houses the Liszt-Hochschule, a prestigious academy of music. The east side of the square is closed by the **Grünes Schloss** (Green Palace; April–Oct Mon–Sat 11am–12.30pm; DM2). The finest of the group, it contains the **Herzogin-Anna-Amalia-Bibliothek**, one of the most important collections of German literature in the world. If you ask at the reception, you can see the exquisite central **Rokokosaal**. Beside it stands the more modest **Gelbes Schloss** (Yellow Palace), while further south is the **Haus Stein**, the former ducal stables, which the stablemaster, Baron Friedrich von Stein, converted into a house. His wife Charlotte was Goethe's first great Weimar love, notwithstanding the fact that she was seven years the poet's senior and the mother of seven children.

Schillerstrasse and Theaterplatz

Schillerstrasse snakes away from the southwest corner of the Markt to the **Schillerhaus** (9am–4/5pm, closed Tues; DM6), the home of Friedrich Schiller for the last three years of his life, following his resignation of his academic chair at Jena. Here he wrote his last two dramas on great historical personalities, *The Maid of Orleans* (the story of Joan of Arc) and *William Tell*; and the rooms are furnished as he knew them. The modern extension behind contains the **Schillermuseum**, with extensive documentation on his life and work; it is due to re-open in 1999.

Beyond lies **Theaterplatz**, in the centre of which is a large monument to Goethe and Schiller. The **Deutsches Nationaltheater** on the west side of the square was founded and directed by Goethe, though the present building, for all its stern Neoclassical appearance, is a pastiche, the facade from the beginning of the present century, the rest from a rebuilding necessitated by its almost complete destruction in World War II. Apart from having seen the premieres of many of the greatest plays in the German language, the theatre was also the venue for the National Assembly's sittings in 1919 and saw the adoption of the constitution of the Weimar Republic.

Opposite is the **Wittumspalais** (Tues–Sun 9am–noon & 1–4/5pm; DM6), a large Baroque palace built as the retirement home of Regentess Anna Amalia, Weimar's great patron of the arts. Even as a dowager duchess, she continued to play a leading role in the town's intellectual life, organizing "Round Table" sessions here at which Goethe presided each Friday. The interiors are among the finest in Weimar, with the main **Festsaal** a design based on Goethe's ideas. There's also a large array of mementos of Christoph-Martin Wieland, now a rather neglected figure, but then regarded as the leading theoretician of the Enlightenment, as well as a major poet and philosopher.

Also on the square is the Kunsthalle, which has been converted to house the **Bauhaus-Museum** (Tues–Sun 10am–6pm; DM5). The main gallery displays works produced by artists of the Bauhaus during its early yars in Weimar. One of the two small rooms is devoted to its forerunner, the Belgian Art Nouveau architect Henry van de Velde's Kunstgewerbeschule, founded in 1900 in an attempt to revive Weimar as a major artistic centre. The other room documents the successor to the Bauhaus, Otto Barting's Staatliche Bauhochschule.

The Goethe museums

On Frauenplan south of the Markt is the excellent **Goethewohnhaus und Nationalmuseum** (Tues–Sun 9am–4/5pm; DM8). As its name suggests, it's in two parts. The more rewarding of these is the large Baroque mansion where the titan of German literature resided for some fifty years until his death in 1832. It's been preserved exactly as he knew it, and still has a lived-in feel to it, particularly the study with the desk where he sat dictating works to his secretary (he only composed poems with his own hand), and the little chamber where he died. In the adjoining museum (currently closed but due to re-open in 1999), the full range and versatility of his achievement is chronicled with typically Teutonic attention to detail.

JOHANN WOLFGANG VON GOETHE (1748–1832)

Often regarded as the last of the great universal geniuses, **Johann Wolfgang von Goethe** produced a vast and diverse literary output – ranging from lyric to philosophic poetry, via comic and tragic dramas, to novels, short stories, travelogues, artistic criticism and scientific tracts – even though he was never truly a full-time writer. Despite his youth, he had already gained a European-wide literary reputation before his appointment to the Weimar court, thanks largely to the epistolary novel *The Sorrows of Young Werther*. His first decade in Weimar furnished him with a broad range of practical experience which he would later put to full use, but it left him little time for writing. By undertaking a long Italian sojourn in 1786, his creative spark was rekindled, though the play *Torquato Tasso* is a thinly veiled exposition of the frustration he felt at having to operate in the environment of a small court. His major prose work, *Wilhelm Meister*, is a cycle of six novels written over a period of five decades which, in common with much of his output, is a close reflection of his own personal development. A similarly protracted process attended the writing of his supreme masterpiece, the two-part drama *Faust*, completed just before his death, which symbolically examines the nature of Western man, his errors and ultimate salvation. The reverence accorded Goethe in Germany, and the academic industry which has grown up around him, is almost as extensive as that surrounding Shakespeare in the English-speaking world.

The Südstadt

Most of the remaining sights are found in the **Südstadt**, the southern part of town. From the Goethewohnhaus, continue down Marienstrasse to the **Liszthaus** (Tues–Sun 9am–1pm & 2–4/5pm; DM4), the garden house of the great Austro-Hungarian composer Franz Liszt. His move to Weimar in 1848, where he spent eleven years as director of the local orchestra and opera company, marked a sea change in his career away from his earlier preoccupation with barnstorming virtuoso piano music towards richly scored programmatic orchestral pieces – the most ambitious being the Goethe-inspired *Faust Symphony* – which in turn cast a strong spell over his son-in-law, Richard Wagner. Despite leaving in a huff over the town's narrow-minded tastes, he returned in 1869, staying at this house for each of the remaining seventeen summers of his life.

A couple of minutes' walk to the west down Geschwister-Scholl-Strasse is Henry van de Velde's custom-built home for the Kunstgewerbeschule, the **Hochschule für Architektur und Bauwesen**. In 1919, Walter Gropius established the original **Bauhaus** – which was to have such a profound impact on the subsequent course of modern architecture and design throughout the world – in this college. However, it only remained here for six years before its move, prompted by hostility from reactionary elements in the town, to the more liberal climate at Dessau. The building still functions as an art college (one recently raised to university status), and isn't a regular tourist sight, though you're free to wander in and look at any exhibitions that may be on.

Further to the west, at Amalienstr. 6, is the **Museum für Ur- und Frühgeschichte Thüringens** (Museum of Ancient and Early Thuringian History; Mon–Fri 9am–5pm, Sat & Sun 10am–1pm & 2–5pm; DM3), the most important archeological museum in the province. It charts the history and prehistory of the area from the Stone Age to the Thuringian tribes of the early medieval period. Highlights include Bronze Age jewellery from Schwarza, imaginatively displayed on reconstructed period dresses; the contents of a Germanic princess's grave unearthed at Hassleben; and the spectacular hoard of jewellery from the time of the fifth-century Thuringian kingdom found at nearby Ossmanstedt.

Immediately south of here is the **Alter Friedhof** (Old Cemetery), complete with a poignant array of carved tombstones and a Neoclassical **Mausoleum** (daily 9am–1pm & 2–4/5pm; DM4). Originally, this was intended for the Grand Ducal family, but it now has the tombs of Goethe and Schiller as well, following Carl August's decision that he wanted to be buried beside the two brightest stars of his court – though this necessitated re-interring the latter's corpse. Built onto the rear of the Mausoleum is the tiny **Russische Kirche**, built for the Grand Duchess Maria Pavlova, daughter-in-law of Carl August, who insisted on remaining loyal to the Orthodox faith of the Russian royal family to which she belonged.

Further to the southwest, at Humboldtstr. 36, is the Villa Silberblick, where the philosopher Friedrich Nietzsche, by then mentally ill, spent the last three years of his life. His sister commissioned Henry van de Velde to remodel the ground floor as a memorial and study centre, the **Nietzsche-Archiv** (Tues–Sun 1–5pm; DM4). This has recently re-opened, having been closed by the GDR authorities who used the villa as an official guest house.

The Park an der Ilm

The **Park an der Ilm** is a large English-style park, complete with ruined follies, a statue of Shakespeare and a cemetery for Soviet soldiers killed in World War II, stretching southwards on both sides of the Ilm from the Schloss to the southern edge of town. Almost due east of the Liszthaus, though on the opposite bank, is **Goethes Gartenhaus** (9am–noon & 1–4/5pm, closed Tues; DM4), where the writer stayed when he first came to Weimar; later, it served as his summer retreat. It has recently been the subject of a drastic and highly controversial restoration, which has led to the banishment of all the furniture which had been acquired since Goethe's time, leaving the interiors looking very bare. Further south and back on the west side of the Ilm is the Neoclassical ducal summer house, known as the **Römisches Haus**, which is adorned with mock-Pompeiian murals. It is being restored and will re-open in 1999.

Schloss Belvedere and Schloss Tiefurt

At the extreme south edge of town, reached by bus #12, is the full-blown summer palace, **Schloss Belvedere** (April–Oct Tues–Sun 10am–6pm; DM5). Its light and airy Rococo style and its collections of porcelain form a refreshing contrast to the Neoclassical solemnity of so much of the town. The **Orangerie** (April–Oct Tues–Sun 10am–1pm & 2–6pm; DM1) contains a dozen historic coaches which served the Weimar court, while the surroundings were transformed under Goethe's supervision into another park in the English manner.

Schloss Tiefurt (March–Oct Tues–Sun 9am–5pm; Nov–Feb Wed–Sun 9am–4pm; DM6), situated northeast of the town centre and reached by bus #3 or #4, is a far more modest palace, more like a small manor house in fact. It was created for the Dowager Duchess Anna Amalia, who transferred her "Round Table" meetings here during the summer months. Again, there's a fine park with plenty of small follies and retreats.

Buchenwald

The **Konzentrationslager Buchenwald** (May–Sept Tues–Sun 9.45am–6pm; Oct–April Tues–Sun 8.45am–5pm; free) is situated to the north of Weimar on the Ettersberg heights, and can be reached by bus #6, which runs hourly from the Hauptbahnhof. Over 240,000 prisoners were incarcerated in this concentration camp, with 56,000 dying here from starvation, torture and disease; but despite the high number of deaths – averaging 200 a day – Buchenwald was never an extermination camp. Among the prisoners killed here was the interwar leader of the German Communist Party, **Ernst Thälmann**. This gave the place a special significance for the GDR authorities, but the official state propaganda was tarnished by the discovery in 1990 of mass graves in the nearby woods, which provided conclusive proof that the Soviets used the camp after the war to round up and eliminate former Nazis, and other political opponents. A documentary centre on the history of the camp has been set up in the former storehouse. The crematorium, disinfection chambers and prisoners' canteen are the other main buildings which may be visited.

Eating and drinking

Many of Weimar's best **restaurants** are in the hotels (see p.880), though there are plenty of good alternatives.

Felsenkeller, Humboldtstr. 37. Thuringia's first *Hausbrauerei*, set among the villas of the Südstadt, brews light and dark beers known as *Deinhardt* and also serves reasonably priced meals.

Frauentor, Schillerstr. 2. Serves both *Kaffee und Kuchen* and bistro-type meals.

Gastmahl des Meeres, Obere Schlossgasse 3. Fish specialist currently in temporary premises – in due course it will move back to its original home at Herderplatz 16.

Ratskeller, Markt 10. Typically German cellar restaurant, though it's opposite rather than underneath the Rathaus.

Residenz-Café, Grüner Markt 4. Coffee house with a 150-year-old tradition; a good choice for breakfast.

Sommers Weinstuben, Humboldtstr. 2. Wine bar-cum-restaurant which has been run by the same family, save for a short interregnum during the GDR period, for five generations. It's decked out in nineteenth-century style and has a small garden to the rear.

Theater-Café, Theaterplatz 1a. Offers late breakfasts, vegetarian and *vom heissen Stein* dishes, with regular live music sessions.

Zum Weissen Schwan, Frauentorstr. 23. Historic *Gasthaus* that's generally agreed to be the best restaurant in Weimar. Fairly pricey, but not excessively so, with the game dishes particularly recommendable.

Entertainment

The liveliest **nightspot** is the *Studentenklub Kasseturm*, Goetheplatz 1, which is no longer exclusively for students. Weimar's main **theatre** venue is the *Deutsches Nationaltheater*, Theaterplatz 2 (☎7550), which regularly features plays by Goethe and Schiller alongside touring productions and cabaret, as well as opera and concerts.

Festivals include the *Bachtage* at the end of March, the *Liszttage* in October and the *Zwiebelmarkt* (Onion Market) on the second weekend of October.

Erfurt

Of all Germany's large cities, it's the Thuringian capital of **ERFURT**, which lies 20km west of Weimar, that's most redolent of its prewar self. Although it lost several important monuments in the air raids of 1944 and 1945, the damage to the overall historic fabric was relatively slight, while the many streets of stately turn-of-the-century stores were saved by the Communist interregnum from the developers who would have demolished them had the city lain on the other side of the Iron Curtain.

In 1970, Erfurt was the scene of the meeting between West German Chancellor Willy Brandt and East German Premier Willi Stoph which marked the beginning of the former's **Ostpolitik** and the end of the GDR's status as an international pariah. During the *Wende*, the city again provided a national lead by being the first place where the *Stasi* offices were stormed, thus preventing the destruction of incriminating files. Erfurt celebrated its 1250th birthday in 1992 with a year-long programme of events. The culmination was the re-establishment of the **University**, which was founded in 1392; it was once one of the largest and most prestigious in northern Europe, numbering Martin Luther among its graduates, but had been dormant since the Prussians suppressed it in 1816.

Arrival, information and accommodation

Erfurt's **Hauptbahnhof** is situated at the southeastern corner of the city centre. One of the two **tourist offices** (Mon–Fri 9am–6pm, Sat 10am–1pm; ☎562 6267) is at Schlösserstr. 44; the other is at Krämerbrücke 3 (Mon–Fri 10am–6pm, Sat 10am–4pm, Sun 10am–1pm; ☎562 3436). At either of these you can buy the DM25 *Erfurt Card*, which gives three consecutive days of travel on the local trams and buses, plus entry to all the municipally owned museums and sights.

The **telephone code** for Erfurt is ☎0361

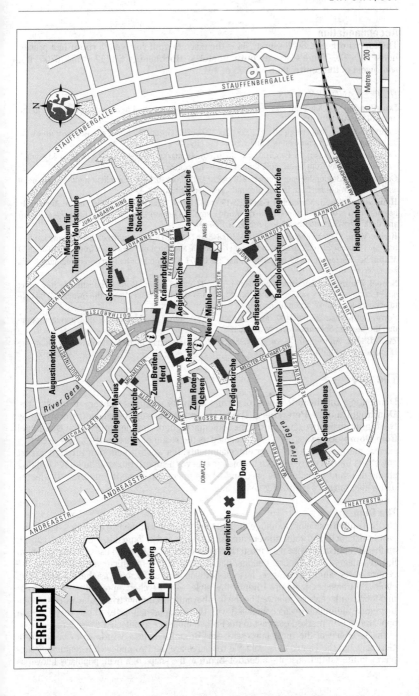

ERFURT

Metres
0   200

Museum für Thüringer Volkskunde
Haus zum Stockfisch
Kaufmannskirche
Reglerkirche
Angermuseum
Schottenkirche
STAUFFENBERGALLEE
JURI-GAGARIN-RING
JOHANNESSTR.
METIENBERGSTR.
Krämerbrücke
WENGEMARKT
Aegidienkirche
ANGER
Barfüsserkirche
Bartholomäusturm
BAHNHOFSTR.
SCHLOSSERSTR.
Neue Mühle
Augustinerkloster
Hauptbahnhof
AUGUSTINERSTR.
GOTHADISTR.
JOHANNESSTR.
River Gera
Zum Breiten Herd
Rathaus
MICHAELSSTR.
Collegium Maius
Michaeliskirche
FISCHMARKT
Zum Roten Ochsen
Predigerkirche
MEISTER-ECKHARTSTR.
Statthalterei
REGIERUNGSSTR.
River Gera
WALKSTROM
Schauspielhaus
MICHAELSSTR.
GROSSE ARCHE
MARKTSTR.
ANDREASSTR.
DOMPLATZ
ANDREASSTR.
Dom
Severikirche
Petersberg
THEATERSTR.
JURI-GAGARIN-RING
BAHNHOFSTR.
BAHNHOFSVORPLATZ
STAUFFENBERGALLEE
N

Accommodation

The tourist office at Schlösserstr. 44 is the place to go if you want a **room** in a private house (②–④). There's also a **youth hostel** at Hochheimer Str. 12 (☎562 6705; 🏠), southwest of the centre; take tram #5 or #51.

HOTELS AND PENSIONS

Don Camillo, Michaelisstr. 29 (☎642 2923). Small pension attached to an Italian restaurant in the heart of the Altstadt. ⑤

Erfurtblick, Nibelungenweg 20 (☎220660, fax 220 6620). Green belt hotel, reached by tram #1. As its name suggests, it commands a fine view of the city. ⑥

Excelsior, Bahnhofstr. 35 (☎56700, fax 567 0100). Upmarket modern hotel behind a Jugendstil facade on the way from the Hauptbahnhof to the city centre. ⑦

Gartenstadt, Binderslebener Landstr. 212 (☎210 4512, fax 210 4513). Excellent middle-range hotel and restaurant not far from the *ega* grounds, reached by tram #1. ⑥

Haus zum Pfauen, Marbacher Gasse 12–13 (☎643 8099). Characterful old inn in the Altstadt. In its courtyard is what is claimed to be the world's smallest brewery, which makes light (*Pfauenbräu*) and dark (*Der Schluntz*) beers to a recipe of 1587. ④

Kleine Villa, Theo-Neubauer-Str. 19 (☎642 1484, fax 561 3357). Pension which, as its name implies, occupies a small villa. It's located in the inner suburbs, about ten minutes' walk from the Altstadt. ⑤

Malluche, Kartäuserstr. 32 (☎225 4251, fax 222 0787). Pension in a half-timbered Jugendstil villa not far from the centre. ⑤

Scheel Zimmervermietung, Paulinzeller Weg 23 (☎413 3838). Homely guesthouse in a quiet street in the southern suburbs; take tram #3 or #6 to Blücherstrasse. If full, the owner will be able to arrange alternative accommodation. ④

Sorat, Gotthardstr. 27 (☎67400, fax 674 0444). New designer hotel built alongside, and incorporating, the historic *Schwanenkeller* restaurant. ⑧

Zum Bären, Andreasstr. 26 (☎562 8698, fax 562 8698). Small high-class hotel overlooking the Domplatz; good buffet breakfasts. ⑦

The city

Dominating the historic heart of Erfurt from its western side are two hills, the **Domhügel** and the **Petersberg**. The former is the city's episcopal centre, crowned by two highly distinctive churches. A monumental flight of steps leads up to the Domhügel from **Domplatz**, a vast open space formed as the result of a fire in 1813, now used as a site for markets, fairs and other entertainments. It's worth wandering through almost any street in the centre of Erfurt, which preserves a superb range of buildings evoking all the different periods of its past, and whose open, expansive layout offers the bonus of a whole range of surprising vistas.

The Dom

On the southern side of Domhügel is the **Dom**, the larger of the two churches. The lower parts of its north and south **towers** are Romanesque and belonged to the previous church on the site, but otherwise it's a masterly Gothic construction which uses its sloping site to full advantage. From the first building period at the end of the thirteenth century are the central tower, and the massive, fortress-like substructure known as the **Kavaten**. The choir and transepts, in a pure High Gothic style, were perched on top of the latter in the mid-fourteenth century, followed by the flamboyantly decorative **triangular porch**. A century later, the building was completed with the spacious hall nave, whose very German appearance is in marked contrast to the French influence manifested elsewhere.

Inside is one of the most impressive sets of **stained-glass windows** to be found in Germany, but the Dom's most valuable treasures are the two mid-twelfth-century masterpieces in the south transept – a **candelabrum** in the shape of a man, popularly known as

Wolfram, and the stucco **altar** of *The Enthroned Madonna with Saints*. Among the adornments of the nave are a small altar of *The Madonna and Child with SS Catherine and Barbara* by **Cranach**, and the tomb of the supposedly bigamous Count of Gleichen and his wives (see p.908). The central tower houses the *Gloriosa*, the largest bell cast during the Middle Ages. In 1997, to celebrate its 500th anniversary, guided tours (May–Oct Mon–Sat 9am–4pm, Sun 1–4pm; DM4) to see it were introduced, and it's hoped to continue these in future years.

The Severikirche

Alongside the Dom is the **Severikirche**, whose distinctive triple-towered east end, sheltering a disarmingly small choir, acts as a perfect foil to its neighbour. The five-aisled hall nave has an impressively lofty feeling considering its relatively modest size. It contains the monumental **tomb of St Severus**, carved out of a soft pink sandstone by a sensitive mid-fourteenth-century sculptor, now dubbed the Master of St Severus, who also made the statue of the saint over the entrance doorway. Both of the other important furnishings – **the alabaster relief** of *St Michael* on the south wall, and the **font** with its spectacular fifteen-metre-high canopy – date from the year 1467.

The Petersberg

Behind the Domhügel is a much larger hill, the **Petersberg**, which lies off the well-worn tourist trail. It was likewise once a centre of religious life, as the site of a Benedictine abbey, the **Peterskirche**, which five times hosted the Imperial Reichstag in the days of Emperor Frederick Barbarossa. This still stands, but what was once the outstanding creation of the Romanesque period in Thuringia is now a sorry sight, having been ruined by its change of status under Prussian rule to a gunpowder magazine. The church is cocooned within the **Zitadelle**, one of the finest surviving examples of Baroque military architecture anywhere in Europe. As a bonus, there's a wonderful view over the city, with the spires on the Domhügel in the foreground.

Marktstrasse and the Fischmarkt

Marktstrasse, which leads eastwards from Domplatz, was once on the trade route that linked Frankfurt and Leipzig with the Russian city of Novgorod. These days, it seems a tad narrow for a major thoroughfare, particularly given the greatly increased volume of traffic since the *Wende*. It's worth making detours off it south down Grosse Arche, and north along Allerheiligenstrasse. At no. 11 on the latter is one of the city's finest houses, **Zum Roten Stern**, the late Gothic home, complete with oriel window, of one of the city's many distinguished printers.

Given that it was trade and commerce which made Erfurt rich in the Middle Ages, the central **Fischmarkt** is of unassuming dimensions. The statue of Roland in the middle was built as a symbol of defiance against the feudal overlords, the Archbishop-Electors of Mainz, though Erfurt never managed to gain the status of a Free Imperial City. On the north side of the square is a showy Renaissance mansion, **Zum Breiten Herd**, which rivals the less demonstrative, more classically balanced **Zum Roten Ochsen** (Wed & Fri–Sun 10am–6pm, Thurs 10am–10pm; DM3) on the west side for the title of best building on the square. The latter is now a gallery, often featuring major temporary exhibitions of modern art. The bulky **Rathaus** is nineteenth-century, and primarily of note for the heroically Romantic fresco cycles inside, depicting scenes from the lives of legendary and historical figures with a Thuringian connection.

The Krämerbrücke

Just east of Fischmarkt is Erfurt's most singular sight, the **Krämerbrücke**, which adds a welcome dash of colour to a city which, for all its grandeur, can appear rather monochrome. Walking along, you have the illusion of entering a narrow medieval alley; the fact that this is actually a bridge lined with shops in the manner of the Ponte Vecchio in Florence is concealed at street level and only becomes obvious if you go down to the banks of the River Gera. The Krämerbrücke is known to have existed in the early twelfth century, but the history of the present structure begins with the stone rebuilding of 1325. In the Middle Ages, there were over sixty little shops on it, mostly associated with the trade in silk, spices, sugar and paper; their larger half-timbered replacements currently number thirty-two and contain a mixture of boutiques, antique dealers and commercial art galleries. House no. 20 has been designated the **Brückenhausmuseum** (Tues–Sun 10am–6pm; DM2) with displays documenting the history of the bridge. The far end of the Krämerbrücke is framed by the **Aegidienkirche**, a small upstairs church used by a German Methodist congregation. Its **tower** (variable opening times; DM2) commands a marvellous view over the city.

Michaelisstrasse

Just before the western end of the Krämerbrücke, the **Michaelisstrasse** – the heart of the old University quarter, but now one of the quietest parts of the city – stretches northwards. Just off it is Waagegasse, a picturesque alley lined with sixteenth- and seventeenth-century storehouses. At the junction with Allerheiligenstrasse is the **Michaeliskirche**, an early Gothic church which was the main place of worship of the academic community. Its Renaissance high altar doubles as a memorial to a local councillor, while the **Dreifaltigkeitskapelle**, added at the turn of the sixteenth century, boasts a prominent oriel window, an embellishment rarely found in ecclesiastical architecture. The galleried courtyard is one of the most peaceful spots in Erfurt.

Across the street is the imposing Flamboyant Gothic portal of the **Collegium Majus**; the rest of this, the main University building, was a casualty of World War II bombs. However, its outstanding collection of old manuscripts, the **Amploniana**, survived and is now kept in the nineteenth-century science library behind.

East of the River Gera

Across the river is the **Augustinerkloster** (guided tours April–Oct Tues–Sat at 10am, 11am, noon, 2pm, 3pm & 4pm; Nov–March Tues–Sat at 10am, noon & 2pm; DM4.50), the monastery where Luther lived between 1505 and 1511, first as a novice, then as a monk and priest. The complex was badly damaged in the war and has only been partially restored. A visit to a reconstruction of Luther's cell forms part of the tour, which also includes the cloister and the typically austere church, now used by Protestants. It's enlivened by some of Erfurt's most beautiful stained-glass windows, including one depicting the life of the order's founder, St Augustine.

A few blocks to the south, not far from the eastern end of Krämerbrücke, is the **Schottenkirche** (Scottish Church), so called from the nationality of the monks who lived here in the Middle Ages. The Baroque facade masks a simple pillar basilica which is one of the few Romanesque buildings left in Erfurt.

To the east is the north–south Johannesstrasse, the longest street in the Altstadt, lined with some of its most impressive Renaissance mansions. Particularly striking is the **Haus zum Stockfisch** at no. 169, which has a rusticated facade reminiscent of an Italian *palazzo*, with a carving of a dried cod above the door which gives the house its name. The interior now contains the local history displays of the **Stadtmuseum** (Tues–Thurs & Sun 10am–5pm, Fri 10am–1pm, Sat 1–5pm; DM3). Further east, the Juri-Gagarin-Ring marks the boundary of the medieval city. Across it, at no. 140a, is the sixteenth-century **Hospital**, now housing the **Museum für Thüringer Volkskunde** (Tues–Thurs & Sun 10am–5pm, Fri 10am–1pm, Sat 1–5pm; DM3), a folklore collection focusing on the province's traditional lifestyles (re-created in a number of interiors), festivals, costumes, crafts and industries.

Anger and around

Johannesstrasse terminates at the **Kaufmannskirche** (Merchants' Church), with a memorial to Luther outside. This also marks the beginning of **Anger**, which starts off as a square but continues westwards as one of the main shopping streets, lined with the most opulent mansions in the city. It's worth making a short detour down Bahnhofstrasse to see the **Reglerkirche** (Mon–Fri 10am–noon), another Augustinian collegiate church, whose high altar is the best of the large carved and painted retables which were an Erfurt speciality in the fifteenth century.

Straddling Bahnhofstrasse and Anger is an ornate Baroque palace built as a weigh house and repository. It's now the **Angermuseum** (Tues & Thurs–Sun 10am–5pm, Wed 10am–8pm; DM3), an excellent collection of fine and decorative arts. The highlight is the medieval section, which features the painted shields which formerly adorned the ceiling of the demolished fourteenth-century Rathaus, and several works – a *Crucifixion*, a *Pietà* and a *St Michael* – by the Master of St Severus. From the Renaissance period are paintings by Cranach and Baldung, while the usual range of nineteenth- and twentieth-century German paintings is supplemented by a chamber frescoed by the Expressionist Erich Heckel.

Further down Anger, you pass the **Bartholomäusturm** (Tues–Thurs & Sun 10am–1pm & 2–5pm, Fri 10am–1pm, Sat 1–5pm; DM2), the only surviving part of the court church of the Counts of Gleichen. At the far end of the street, there's a fork; the northern branch, Regierungsstrasse, leads to the **Statthalterei**, a magnificent Baroque palace built by Maximilian von Welsch, court architect to the Archbishops of Mainz, to serve as the headquarters of the city's government. A room on the first floor was the scene in 1808 of one of history's famous meetings – that between Goethe and Napoleon, who conversed knowledgeably about the former's plays.

The Barfüsserkirche and the Predigerkirche

Just north of here is the **Barfüsserkirche** (Tues & Thurs–Sun 10am–5pm, Wed 10am–8pm; DM3, free on Wed), a vast, austere Franciscan monastery church which was the most serious casualty of World War II bombs. Its nave has been left as a shell, but the choir has been restored to house a small branch of the Angermuseum's medieval collection. The stained-glass windows, which include a depiction of the life of St Francis, have been restored to their original position; some of them date back to the early thirteenth century.

On the other side of the river is the **Predigerkirche**, formerly the Dominican monastery but since the Reformation the city's main Protestant church. Its exterior takes plainness to an extreme, but the interior is a masterpiece of spacial harmony in the purest Gothic style, and has preserved its layout and furnishings intact. The church was constructed in the thirteenth century when Master Eckhart, Germany's most celebrated mystic, was a monk there; he later became prior and vicar of Thuringia, in spite of holding pantheistic beliefs which many regarded as heresy. On the **rood screen**, which you can ascend for a rare aerial view, is a beautiful mid-fourteenth-century group of *The Annunciation*; the niches of the **choir screen** behind shelter a number of works of the same date. Elsewhere in the church are many elaborate epitaphs, a fifteenth-century carved and painted high altar and some lovely thirteenth-century stained glass made up of floral motifs.

To the rear of the church at Schlösserstr. 25a is the **Neue Mühle** (guided tours hourly Tues–Thurs & Sun 10am–5pm, Fri 10am–1pm, Sat 1–5pm; DM3), the last still-functioning water mill in the city.

Cyriaksburg

For the past three decades, the ample grounds of the **Cyriaksburg** (daily April–Sept 9am–6pm; Oct–March 10am–4pm; DM4), a castle southwest of the city centre at the terminus of tram #2, have been given over to the **Internationale Gartenbauausstellung** (commonly known as *ega*), a vast garden show. It's best visited in spring, when the eye-swimming plantations of flowers are in full bloom. However, there are plenty of other attractions, notably the **Gartenbaumuseum** (daily Easter–Sept 11am–5pm; included in entrance ticket) in the Cyriaksburg itself, which traces the history of gardening. There are also several restaurants, exhibition halls, a look-out tower and hothouses displaying orchids, cacti and other tropical plants.

Eating and drinking

Under Communism, Erfurt had a noticeable shortage of places to **eat** and **drink**, but the situation is improving every year.

Ampolonius Burse, Michaelisstr. 40. One of several café-restaurants that have sprung up in the university quarter.

Bärenkeller, Andreasstr. 26. Offers Thuringian specialities and *vom heissen Stein* dishes.

Caponniere, Cyriaksburg. A good wine bar-cum-restaurant; take tram #2. (Evenings only, except Thurs).

Gildehaus, Fischmarkt 13. The best restaurant in Erfurt, housed in the neo-Renaissance extension to *Zum Breiten Herd*, with a small beer garden to the rear.

Grafik-Café Zimmerman, Kürschnergasse 8. Artists' café adjoining a print gallery. Closed Mon.

Haus zur Güldenen Sonne, Michaelisstr. 37. Historic *Gasthaus* in the university district..

Kaffeemühle, Schlösserstr. 25a. Café in the Neue Mühle, with riverside garden. (Open till 1am, closed Mon).

Kleines Café, Anger 19–20. Good choice for breakfast or *Kaffee und Kuchen*.

Rathaus-Arkade, Fischmarkt 1. Smart new restaurant in the ground floor of the Rathaus.

Suppengrün, Regierungstr. 20. Vegetarian and wholefood restaurant. Open Mon–Fri 9am–6pm, Sat 10am–2pm.

Entertainment

Erfurt's main **theatre** is the *Schauspielhaus* on Klostergang; its box office is at Dalbergsweg 2 (☎223 3155). For the forseeable future, it is likely to host opera and concerts as much as drama, the *Opernhaus* having been condemned as a fire hazard and beyond repair. *Theater die Schotte*, Schottenstr. 7 (☎643 1722) is the other venue for straight plays, while the *Waldspeicher* on Grosse Arche, whose box office is at Domplatz 18 (☎598 2924) features cabaret and puppet shows. The principal **festival**, the *Kramerbrückenfest*, takes place in the latter part of June and features a medieval market and all kinds of music.

CLUBS AND LIVE MUSIC

Jazzkeller, Anger 28–29. The city's premier jazz venue (Thurs at 8pm).

Museumskeller, Juri-Gagarin-Ring 140a. Features live bands (Fri & Sat at 10.30pm), and the rest of the time is a hip-hop club.

Rotplombe, corner of Schlüterstr./Amploniusstr. Live music bar (usually Wed–Sat from 8pm).

Studentenclub Engelsburg, Allerheiligenstr. 20. The liveliest dance club in the city.

Gotha

GOTHA, which lies 25km west of Erfurt, is a handsome market town and main gateway to the popular holiday area of the Thuringian Forest. In the English-speaking world, it is indelibly associated with the **House of Saxe-Coburg-Gotha**, the name of the British royal family until they changed it to Windsor for patriotic reasons at the outbreak of World War I. The end of the war saw the dissolution of this united duchy, with the citizens of Coburg plumping for union with Bavaria rather than joining all the region's other petty states in the revived province of Thuringia. Gotha also holds an honoured place in the pantheon of the German left, as it was here in 1875 that the Socialist Workers' Party of Germany – renamed the **Social Democratic Party** fifteen years later, and still one of the country's main political forces – was formed.

The town

Almost the whole of the southern half of central Gotha is taken up by the **Schlosspark**, whose spacious effect is slightly marred by being divided by two main thoroughfares – through the middle by Parkallee, and down the eastern fringe by Friedrichstrasse. **Schloss Friedenstein**, which lies towards the northwestern end, is a U-shaped palace with massive square corner towers, built in sober early Baroque style. After the park, the rest of Gotha is for the most part an anti-climax, though the Hauptmarkt is a highly original square.

The Schlossmuseum

The historical apartments and art collections of the Schloss Friedenstein are together designated the **Schlossmuseum** (Tues–Sun 9am–5pm; DM8 or DM10 for inclusive tickets covering all the museums in the Schlosspark). Despite the plain exterior, it's highly elaborate inside, forming a visual encyclopedia of changing tastes in interior design, ranging from the heavy Baroque stuccowork of the main **Festsaal** to the **Dichter-Zimmer** (Poets' Chamber), adorned with Romantic landscapes, including **Friedrich**'s *Cross in the Mountains*, a variant of one of his favourite themes. The **Kunstkammer** is a typical princely curio cabinet, whose dazzling if slightly frivolous treasures include a gilded elephant by the great Dresden goldsmith Dinglinger.

The picture gallery's star attraction is the hauntingly enigmatic *Pair of Lovers*, the most important of the few surviving paintings by the great but mysterious Rhenish draughtsman dubbed the **Master of the Housebook**. No less striking are the little boxwood figures of *Adam and Eve* by **Conrad Meit**, which rank among the greatest carvings of the German Renaissance. A marvellous group of works by **Cranach** includes several known to be by the master's own hand, rather than the more usual products of his workshop. *The Adoration of the Magi* is the masterpiece of his middle period, while a rare self-portrait of the artist can be seen at the far left corner of *Judith at the Table of Holofernes*, a story continued in the companion *Death of Holofernes*. A diptych of *The Fall and Salvation of Man* is a complicated tract illustrating the theological teachings of Melanchthon. Another, albeit far less sophisticated work inspired by the new Protestant doctrines, is a folding altar painted by **Heinrich Füllmaurer** with 157 scenes full of anecdotal details on German life of the day. There's also an array of paintings from the Low Countries; look out for a brilliant pair of **Rubens** sketches for the ceiling of the Jesuit church in Antwerp.

The rest of the Schloss

The southwest tower of the Schloss contains the **Ekhof-Theater** (same hours as the Schlossmuseum; DM3, but part of inclusive ticket), a perfectly preserved Baroque gem, which is still in regular use. It's named in honour of Conrad Ekhof, a theatrical reformer who between 1774 and 1778 directed here the first company in Germany staffed by fully professional actors. Upstairs is the **Regionalmuseum** (same hours; DM3), with the usual local history displays.

At the northwestern end of the complex, the **Schlosskirche** is only open for services. The **Pagenhaus** (Pages' House) at the opposite end now contains the **Kartographisches Museum** (same hours as the Schlossmuseum; DM3), which is claimed as the first and only map museum in the world. Its presence here is explained by Gotha's long tradition as a cartographic centre, with a still-functioning publishing house first established in 1785. If you're at all interested in the subject, it's a fascinating display, with examples ranging from Mercator's maps of Crete and Cyprus up to the prestige GDR world atlas of 1981.

Around the Schlosspark

Facing the Schloss across Parkallee is a heavy neo-Renaissance pile built to house the Kunstkammer, but now containing the **Museum der Natur** (same hours as the Schlossmuseum; DM4). Should you be intending to visit the Thuringian Forest, it's worth coming here to see the displays on its flora and fauna – including creatures such as the wolf and the lynx now extinct there. In addition, there's a section on the *Thüringer Waldbahn*, the forest tramway (see p.900). Elsewhere in the southern half of the Schlosspark are a large boating lake and the **Dorischer Tempel**, designed by Friedrich Wilhelm von Erdmannsdorff, creator of the gardens of Wörlitz. East of Schloss Friedenstein is the so-called **Teeschlösschen**, a folly, long used as a kindergarten, built in imitation of an English church. Beyond are the two pavilions of the **Orangerie**, one of which is a library, the other a café.

The rest of the town

The **Hauptmarkt** is an interesting feature of the town. Not only is it built on a pronounced incline, which sweeps majestically up to Schloss Friedenstein, but it also features the Renaissance **Rathaus** standing in splendid isolation in the middle. Also on the square are a Baroque fountain and a number of colourful houses, among them the **Lucas-Cranach-Haus** at the top end, which is known to have belonged to the painter, though the facade is much later. From here, Lucas-Cranach-Strasse leads to the Rococo **Frankenbergsches Gartenhaus**, which stands in its own pretty courtyard down a little alley.

A few minutes' walk southwest of the Hauptmarkt, at Cosmarstr. 10, is the **Haus Tivoli**, where the Socialist Workers' Party of Germany was founded in 1875. In the past, it was open as a memorial, though it posed something of a problem for the Communist authorities, as Marx had bitterly opposed the new party, which he regarded as a sellout; indeed, his scathing *Critique of the Gotha Programme* was rated by Lenin as one of his three seminal texts.

Practicalities

Gotha's **Hauptbahnhof** is at the southern end of town and trams #1, #2 and #4 will all take you in the direction of the centre; the last of these is actually the *Thüringer Waldbahn*. The **tourist office** is situated west of the Hauptmarkt at Blumenbachstr. 1–3 (Mon–Fri 9am–6pm, Sat 9am–noon; ☎03621/854036) and, as ever, can book **private rooms** (②–④) for you.

There are plenty of **pensions**, some of them near the town centre including *Am Schloss*, Bergallee 3a (☎03621/8555 3206; ③), *Gaa*, Kleine Fahnenstr. 6 (☎03621/755890; ③) and the much larger *Regina*, Schwabhäuser Str. 4 (☎03621/408020; ④). The most conveniently sited **hotels** include *St Gambrin*, Schwabhäuser Str. 47 (☎03621/30900; ⑥), which also has a fish speciality restaurant; and *Waldbahn*, Bahnhofstr. 16 (☎03621/2340; ⑦) whose amenities include a sauna, solarium, beer garden and reasonably priced restaurant. At the far eastern side of town, *Landhaus*, Salzgitterstr. 76 (☎03621/36490; ⑤) is a renovated half-timbered farm building tastefully furnished in country style.

The **youth hostel** is handily located just east of the Schlosspark and north of the Hauptbahnhof at Mozartstr. 1 (☎03621/54008; 🏠).

Gotha's top **restaurant** is the *Pagenhaus* in the Schloss. Alternatives include the reasonably priced *Tanne*, Burgeraue 3, the historic *Weinschänke*, Gartenstr. 28, and the *Ratskeller* in the Rathaus. The wackily decorated *Firlefansz*, Klosterstr. 5, serves Swiss-style dishes and is well worth a visit. The best traditional café is *Loesche*, Buttermarkt 6.

Eisenach

EISENACH, 28km west of Gotha, grew up as an appendage to the **Wartburg**, the original seat of the Landgraves of Thuringia, which overlooks it from the fringe of the Thuringian Forest to the south. Though foreigners may prefer the fantasy creations of King Ludwig II of Bavaria, the Wartburg's rich historical associations make it the castle the Germans themselves most treasure, and its proximity to the hated postwar border has made it something of a symbol of the newly united nation.

The town

For all its modest size, Eisenach is so rich in monuments and museums that it warrants an unhurried visit. It's best to proceed systematically southwards, perhaps leaving the Wartburg, the undoubted climax, for a second day.

The fortifications

From the Hauptbahnhof, it's only a couple of minutes' walk along Bahnhofstrasse to the **Nikolaitor**, a massive gateway erected in the second half of the twelfth century. Above its arch are two sculptures, one presumed to be of Ludwig I, founder of the Ludowingian dynasty which first ruled Thuringia, the other the province's heraldic lion. A few decades later, the **Nikolaikirche** was built directly onto the Nikolaitor to serve both as a parish church and as a convent for Benedictine nuns. One other significant section of the **Stadtmauer**, including a couple of towers, survives; it can be seen at the northern end of town, just beyond Jakobsplan.

The Markt

Heading diagonally across Karlsplatz brings you to Karlstrasse, leading to the bright orange **Rathaus**, many times rebuilt, which faces onto the Markt. On the north side of the square is the **Stadtschloss**, a compact Rococo palace begun in 1741 as the second residence of the newly united House of Saxe-Weimar-Eisenach. Previously the elegant interiors housed a museum of Thuringian decorative arts, but at present the building is closed indefinitely.

In the middle of the Markt stands the **Georgenkirche**, cathedral of the Protestant diocese of Thuringia. It is the late Gothic successor to the church where Landgrave Ludwig IV married the Hungarian princess now known as St Elisabeth (see also pp.376–377) in 1221, and where Luther, whose mother was a native of the town, sang as a choirboy. Soon after its construction, it was adapted to the needs of Protestant worship, notably by the erection of the tiered galleries. J.S. Bach was baptized here in 1685; and the church maintained its reputation as a place of destiny by being a key meeting place of opposition groups in the *Wende* of 1989. On the walls are a number of fourteenth-century carved epitaphs commemorating the Ludowingian rulers. Outside is the mid-sixteenth-century **Marktbrunnen**, showing the church's patron, St George, in his familiar dragon-slayer role.

The **telephone code** for Eisenach is ☎03691

The Thüringer Museum

Just off the eastern side of the Markt is the **Predigerkirche**, built in the simple and austere Gothic style favoured by the Dominicans whose monastery church it was. For nearly a century it has been home to the **Thüringer Museum** (Tues–Sun 9am–5pm; DM5), an outstanding collection of wood sculpture, an art form in which Thuringia excelled throughout the Middle Ages. The earliest pieces are from the twelfth century, and include a *St John the Evangelist* of enormous tragic pathos, and range through a whole series of *Madonnas*, *Pietàs* and *Crucifixions* from the various phases of Gothic, to the large winged altars produced in Erfurt and Saalfeld in the years immediately before the Reformation. However, the most intriguing exhibit is the thirteenth-century **statue of Heinrich Raspe**, carved under the realist influence of the Naumburg School. As the crown on his head indicates, Raspe, the brother-in-law of St Elisabeth, usurped the German throne, though he was subsequently accorded the status of an "anti-king". He was also the last Landgrave of Thuringia, his death without issue leading to a war which saw the end of the province as a unit.

The Lutherhaus and the Bachhaus

Off the southwestern corner of the Markt is Lutherplatz, on which stands the **Lutherhaus** (May–Sept daily 9am–5pm; Oct–April Mon–Sat 9am–5pm, Sun 2–5pm; DM5), in actual fact the home of the Cotta family, with whom Luther boarded as a schoolboy. The present house, predominantly a half-timbered structure of the sixteenth and eighteenth centuries, encloses the original, which preserves the two rooms used by the famous lodger. Inside are displays on his two periods in Eisenach, plus a large collection of Reformation books and other archive material.

A few minutes' walk south of the Lutherhaus is Frauenplan, with the **Bachhaus** (April–Sept Mon noon–5.45pm, Tues–Sun 9am–5.45pm; Oct–March Mon 1–4.45pm, Tues–Sun 9am–4.45pm; DM5), a large Baroque house presumed to be the birthplace of J.S. Bach. Inside, an attempt has been made at re-creating the sort of bourgeois interi-

---

JOHANN SEBASTIAN BACH (1685–1750)

Despite the fact that popular imagination has turned Mozart into the supreme composer touched by a flawless genius, most practising musicians would, if pressed, be far more likely to accord this honour to **Johann Sebastian Bach**. The most remarkable feature of his career was its sheer provinciality. Born into a long-standing Thuringian musical family, he followed their tradition of salaried employment, serving as a church organist in Arnstadt and Mühlhausen, and as a court musician in Weimar and Köthen, before spending the last 27 years of his life as *Kantor* in Leipzig. Bach's vast output includes well over two hundred cantatas, the entire kernel of the organist's repertoire, and most of the greatest music written for solo violin, cello and harpsichord. Although associated primarily with music of intense spirituality – of which the heart-rending *St Matthew Passion* is the supreme expression – Bach was a peerless practitioner of dance rhythms, as the *Orchestral Suites* show, and even adept at humorous effects, as in the *Coffee Cantata*.

Strangely, his reputation during his lifetime was based primarily on his prowess as a virtuoso performer. Few contemporaries appreciated the unique genius of his music, which, because it brought the Baroque age to a glorious climax rather than breaking new ground, was quickly forgotten after his death, not to be revived until Mendelssohn exhumed it a century later. Bach ensured the continuity of the family musical tradition by fathering twenty children, of whom at least two, the waywardly eccentric Carl Philipp Emmanuel and the elegantly refined Johann Christian, who brought the *galant* style to London, deserve to be considered as important composers in their own right.

ors typical of the composer's childhood. There's also extensive documention on his career and a valuable collection of historical musical instruments. To round off the visit, it's worth waiting for one of the demonstrations given by a member of staff, who puts a harpsichord, clavichord and chamber organ through their paces in performances of short pieces by Bach.

Elsewhere in the centre

Just east of the Bachhaus is Marienstrasse, where at no. 45 is the **Goldener Löwe** (Mon–Fri 9am–4pm; free), the former inn where August Bebel and Wilhelm Liebknecht set up their revolutionary socialist party in 1869, only to amalgamate it with its more moderate rival six years later in Gotha. Unlike most such memorial museums, it has re-opened following a period of closure after the *Wende*. At the end of Marienstrasse, Reuterweg leads west to the **Reutervilla** (Tues–Sun 10am–5pm; DM4), home of the nineteenth-century Low German writer Fritz Reuter, and still furnished as he knew it. Of more general appeal is the huge array of Wagner memorabilia, including his death mask. These were bought to commemorate the composer's sojourn in Eisenach, where he came to find inspiration for his opera *Tannhäuser*, which is set in and around the Wartburg, fusing into an imaginary, romanticized whole two true episodes from the castle's history.

Housed in temporary premises in the savings bank building at Rennbahn 6–8, a short walk west of the Hauptbahnhof on the opposite side of the tracks from the town centre, is the **Automobilbaumuseum** (Tues–Sun 9am–5pm; DM4). This collection of historic vehicles celebrates Eisenach's tradition, dating back to 1898, as a leading centre of the German car industry. One of the earliest exhibits, the *Dixi*, was capable of the then mind-boggling speed of 60km per hour – it initiated a reputation for quality products which continued with the flashy BMW sports cars of the 1930s. From the postwar period are examples of the different versions of the Wartburg, the flagship of GDR car production. Unlike the ridiculous Trabant, with which it was often unfairly bracketed, it was a respectable motor – and like the Rolls-Royce, one of very few which had the body fitted to the chassis by hand. To local dismay, the factory, which lay immediately behind the bank, was closed down as unprofitable in 1991, though many of the workers were able to find alternative employment with BMW and Opel, who have both set up plants here. On the site, it is hoped to build a new museum that will be capable of displaying the entire collection instead of just the small selection currently on display.

The Wartburg

From the Reutervilla, it's a steep thirty-minute ramble through the woods to the **Wartburg** (March–Oct daily 8.30am–6pm; Nov–Feb 9am–5pm; DM6, or DM10 including tour of the Palas) – a far more atmospheric approach than the circuitous main road. If at all possible, avoid visiting at weekends or holiday periods, and arrive first thing: tourism here has soared since the *Wende*, often approaching bursting point.

Given its richly varied history, it's perhaps appropriate that the Wartburg is a melange of several different epochs, unfolding like a great picture book of German architecture. The oldest and most imposing part is the late twelfth-century **Palas** at the left-hand end of the second courtyard, one of Europe's few surviving examples of a Romanesque palace. A number of structures – including the **Torhalle** between the courtyards, the cross-crowned **Bergfried** or keep and the **Neue Kemenate** adjoining the Palas – were added in Romantic style last century, when the whole castle was given a thorough, albeit over-enthusiastic, restoration. The entrance ticket entitles you to climb the **Südturm**, from where there's a good view over the complex – and of the dense tracts of the Thuringian Forest.

THE HISTORY OF THE WARTBURG

The Wartburg was founded by Count Ludwig I in 1067. His descendants, promoted to the status of Landgraves, presided over a cultured court, patronizing some of the greatest **Minnesänger** (German troubadours), including Wolfram von Eschenbach, who wrote part of his epic *Parzifal* here, and Walter von der Vogelweide, the finest lyric poet of the day.

The most significant event in the Wartburg's history began in May 1521 when **Martin Luther**, having been declared an outlaw by the Diet of Worms, was kidnapped by order of Elector Frederick the Wise and taken to this safe haven. During his ten-month stay, the hitherto tonsured and clean-shaven monk disguised himself under a head of hair and beard, passing as a minor landowner by name of *Junker Jörg* (Farmer George). In a frenzy of activity, he translated the New Testament from Erasmus' Greek into the vernacular language spoken by the people of his day, so creating the foundations of modern written German.

In 1817 the Wartburg was the rallying place of the **Burschenschaften**, idealistically minded students protesting at the continued division of Germany, even after the Congress of Vienna, into a host of tinpot principalities.

The Palas

To see beyond the interiors of the Palas, you have to take a **guided tour** (departure approximately every 15min; April–Oct 9am–4.30pm; Nov–March 9.30am–3.30pm). In all the Palas has around two hundred carved **capitals**, a third of them original, highly stylized masterpieces of late Romanesque carving. The finest are those on the central columns which are a distinguishing feature of most of the rooms, including the fourteenth-century **Burgkapelle**. To the modern eye, it's a matter of regret that there are so many Romantic embellishments, though these are often beautiful works in their own right, notably the three fresco cycles by **Moritz von Schwind** illustrating the life of St Elisabeth, the Minnesänger contest and the history of the castle. Rather more over the top are the Jugendstil mosaics in the saint's bedroom, and the colossal coffered vault of the main **Festsaal**, where the Burschenschaften met.

The museums

The museum in the Neue Kemenate is largely devoted to artefacts from around the time of the Reformation, including paintings, sculptures, weapons, furniture and tapestries. Among several works by **Cranach**, look out for the pendants of *Hans and Margarete Luther*, the parents of the great reformer.

From here, you cross the courtyard to the beamed interior of the Wehrgang (sentry walk), which leads round to the **Lutherstube**, the simple wood-panelled room where the German translation of the Bible was made. In the glass case is a copy of the original *Lutherbibel*, while on the walls hang portraits of Luther and Melanchthon, plus an engraving of Luther as *Junker Jörg*, all by Cranach. There was once a blot on the wall by the stove which, according to tradition, was made when Luther threw an inkpot at an apparition of the Devil, but souvenir hunters chipped away at it so much that there's now nothing but a hole going right through to the bare masonry.

Practicalities

Eisenach's **tourist office** (Mon 10am–12.30pm & 1.15–6pm, Tues–Fri 9am–12.30pm & 1.15–6pm, Sat 10am–2pm; ☎670260) is at Markt 2. There is also a separate information centre for the Wartburg in the town centre at Schlossberg 2 (Mon–Fri 9am–5pm,

April–Oct also Sat 9am–4pm; ☎77072). The main **festivals** are the folkloric *Sommergewinn* on the Saturday three weeks before Easter, and the concerts of the *Thüringer Bachtage* around Easter. A varied **cultural programme** is presented all year round at the *Thüringer Landestheater*, Theaterplatz 4–7 (☎2560).

Accommodation

Eisenach has two **youth hostels**: one at Mariental 24 (☎203613; 🛏), on a road which branches off Wartburger Allee; the other closer to the centre at Bornstr. 7 (☎732012; 🛏). There is the usual supply of **private rooms** (②–④) bookable via the tourist office. The town also has a wide range of **hotels** and **pensions**, including many in fine old buildings.

HOTELS AND PENSIONS

Auf der Wartburg (☎ & fax 5111). Luxury hotel with restaurant in the Wartburg itself. ⑨

Burgfried, Marienstr. 60 (☎214221, fax 214224). Good old-fashioned hotel in a large villa at the southern edge of the centre. ⑥

Haus Hainstein, Am Hainstein (☎2420, fax 242109). Church-run hotel with café-restaurant in the green belt directly below the Wartburg. ⑤

Kaiserhof, Wartburgallee 2 (☎0213513, fax 203653). The top hotel in the town centre, run by the *Romantik* chain. Has two restaurants – the *Weinrestaurant Trumschänke* is archetypically Thuringian, whereas *Der Zwinger* is in the style of a Bavarian *Bierkeller*. ⑦

St Peter, Am Petersberg 7 (☎890401, fax 72830). Small pension in the southern part of town. ④

Schlosshotel, Markt 20 (☎214260, fax 214259). New hotel in the converted buildings of the former Franziskanerkloster; also has a good wine bar/restaurant. ⑦

Sophienaue, Mariental 40 (☎711000, fax 711030). Eisenach's oldest hotel, in a secluded location below the Wartburg with direct access to some fine walking trails. ⑦

Storchenturm, Georgenstr. 43 (☎215250). New *Gasthof* tucked away in a courtyard behind its street address, with plain but exceptionally good-value rooms and a restaurant in a renovated barn. ③

Villa Anna, Fritz-Koch-Str. 12 (☎23950, fax 239530). Charming small hotel in a nineteenth-century villa with tasteful modern furnishings in the southern part of town. ⑥

Villa Kesselring, Hainweg 32 (☎ & fax 732049). Occupies an extravagant Romantic-era villa in a very quiet setting just south of the centre, near one of the paths up to the Wartburg. ④

Eating and drinking

Many of the best restaurants and cafés are in the hotels listed above, but there are plenty of others elsewhere.

Alt Eisenach, Karlstr. 51. Offers Thuringian specialities plus *Kaffee und Kuchen*.

Alt Nürnberg, Marienstr. 7. Spacious restaurant serving typical *gutbürgerliche Küche*. Look out for the elaborate murals in its *Musikkeller*.

Brauhaus Rheinischer Hof, Clemensstr. 15. *Hausbrauerei* located immediately to the rear of the Hauptbahnhof. Makes both light and dark beers, and serves full meals.

Brunnenkeller, Markt 10. Restaurant in the historic cellars of the Stadtschloss.

Café Moritz, Bahnhofstr. 7. Long-established café, complete with summer terrace.

Lackner, Johannisstr. 22. Another traditional café, good for breakfast though it also does full meals.

Residenzkeller, corner of Esplanade and Markt. Cosy little restaurant with a shady beer garden.

SOUTHWESTERN THURINGIA

The **Thuringian Forest** (*Thüringer Wald*), a typical central European highland area of densely wooded hills and valleys, covers almost the entire southwestern part of the province. In GDR days, it rivalled the Baltic coast as the main national holiday area, and its resorts had the advantage that they could function all year round, thanks to the suitable conditions for skiing and other winter sports. However, it's as a hiking area that the forest is best known, and it offers some of Germany's finest walks, notably in the countryside around **Friedrichroda**, **Suhl** and **Ilmenau**. Nor are the attractions purely scenic; there are several fine historic towns, including **Schmalkalden** in the heart of the forest, and **Meiningen** and **Arnstadt** on its fringes. Because of the nature of the terrain, communications can be difficult, yet public transport services are as excellent as ever.

Friedrichroda and around

It isn't necessary to stray far from Thuringia's central belt in order to see some of the best of the forest, as nowhere was more popular or developed during the GDR era than the area centred on **FRIEDRICHRODA**, just 20km from Gotha. Thanks to the super-abundance of cheap accommodation possibilities, this makes an excellent place for either a quiet break or some serious hiking – the only way to see the best of the forest.

Friedrichroda can be reached by the branch rail line from Fröttstädt, on the main line between Eisenach and Gotha. However, the best approach is by the **forest tramway**, the *Thüringer Waldbahn*, which runs from Gotha Hauptbahnhof to an interchange at the small industrial town of Waltershausen, whereupon it climbs steeply up to Friedrichroda before veering westwards to its terminus at the neighbouring resort of Tabarz. It's painfully slow – the timetable suggestion of an hour for the complete 23-kilometre journey is invariably an underestimate – but it's the easiest way to see the scenery in comfort. Before the war, rural tramways were a common feature of Germany: now the only other remaining is a much shorter one in Saxon Switzerland.

On leaving Friedrichroda, the *Waldbahn* stops outside the Thuringian Forest's most important natural curiosity, the **Marienglashöhle** (guided tours daily 9am–4/5pm; DM6). This is the largest crystalline cave in Europe, complete with underwater lake; its name comes from the fact that, in times past, its products were used for making jewels to adorn statues of the Virgin Mary. The most pleasant part of Friedrichroda itself is the northern **Reinhardsbrunn** suburb, which has its own station and *Waldbahn* stop. Here an English-style park has been laid out around the medieval monastery which was converted last century in grand neo-Gothic style into a **Schloss**, now the area's top hotel.

Hikes around Friedrichroda

By far the most popular hike in the area is the ascent of the Thuringian Forest's third highest and best-known peak, the **Grosser Inselberg** (916m), which lies just to the southwest of Tabarz. Unfortunately, the summit itself is disfigured by an ugly TV tower and a number of other buildings, including a couple of restaurants and a **youth hostel** (☎036840/2551; ☻). In compensation, there's a truly sweeping view, which is often given added drama by fickle microclimatic conditions. It isn't necessary to expend much energy getting to the top – taking the Friedrichroda to Brotterode bus to the *Grenzwiese* stop leaves only a short walk up. The same place marks the convergence of several other trails; among these is the **Rennsteig** (see box opposite), one of Germany's oldest and finest long-distance wilderness footpaths.

Another recommended area for walks is the vicinity of **FINSTERBERGEN**, a small resort 4km southeast of Friedrichroda. Its name means "Dark Mountains", and the forest around here is unusually dense and seen at its best under lowering skies. The village itself is attractive, with an unassuming-looking **Dorfkirche** whose interior, complete with double galleries, painted ceiling and organ, is a perfectly preserved example of the rustic interpretation of the Baroque style.

THE RENNSTEIG

The 168-kilometre-long **Rennsteig** cuts right through the heart of the Thuringian Forest, from Hörschel, west of Eisenachall, all the way to Blankenstein by the border with the Czech Republic. In the Dark Ages, it served as the frontier between the Thuringians and the Franks; later, it was used to demarcate the limits of the province's petty principalities, and a number of boundary stones, some dating back as far as the sixteenth century, survive as a reminder of this. When hiking became a popular pastime last century, the Rennsteig was laid out as a marked footpath, identified by signs bearing a large R. Five or six days is the normal time needed for the complete walk. Hostels, campsites and refuges lie directly on the trail, though there are also plenty of resorts on the way – Brotterode, Oberhof, Neustadt, Neuhaus and Steinbach – which make obvious places for an overnight stop. If you don't want to do the complete route, plenty of small sections make for satisfying walks in their own right.

Practicalities

If you want help in finding accommodation in Friedrichroda, the **tourist office** is in the *Kurverwaltung*, Marktstr. 13–15 (☎03623/304575). There are dozens of **private rooms** (①–③), while **hotels** include *Im Grund*, Im Grund 3 (☎03623/304 5883; ⑤), and the *Schlosshotel* in Reinhardsbrunn (☎03623/304253, fax 304251; ⑥). There's also a **youth hostel** at Waldstr. 25 (☎03623/4410; ❶).

Schmalkalden

Some of the buses which pass the Grosser Inselberg continue south to the lively market town of **SCHMALKALDEN**, 18km southwest of Friedrichroda. The town's name is associated above all with the Reformation, in which it played a key role; the Schmalkaldic League, formed here in 1531, was an alliance of Protestant princes and Free Imperial Cities determined to protect their independence against the renewed threat of a re-imposition of centralized political and religious authority posed by Emperor Charles V. The Schmalkaldic Wars, which broke out just after Luther's death in 1546, led to a disastrous defeat for the Protestants and the occupation of Wittenberg, but they staged such a spirited recovery that by 1555 their aim of a decentralized Germany with each state free to choose its own religion had been enshrined in the Peace of Augsburg.

The town

The Altmarkt is dominated by the **Stadtkirche St Georg** (May–Oct Mon–Sat 10am–noon & 2–4pm), a late Gothic hall church whose clock face shows Death claiming a young girl. Among the many notable old houses are the half-timbered **Lutherhaus** on Luthermarkt (formerly the potters' market), where the reformer stayed during his visits to the town; the **Heiliggrabesbehausung**, a huge sixteenth-century tenement on Weidebrunner Gasse; and the **Hessenhof** on Neumarkt. Preserved under the last-named is a Romanesque cellar with some of the oldest secular frescoes in Europe, depicting scenes from *The Iwein Saga* by the troubadour Hartmann von der Aue.

Schloss Wilhelmsburg

Standing proudly on its hill at the eastern end of town is the whitewashed **Schloss Wilhelmsburg** (Feb–Oct Tues–Sun 9am–5pm, Nov–Jan Tues–Sun 10am–4pm; DM4), built in the 1580s as a summer residence and hunting seat for the Landgraves of Hesse-Kassel, who had recently won complete control of the town. One of the best-preserved Renaissance palaces in Germany, its interior now houses exhibits outlining the town's complicated history, but these are overshadowed by the reception rooms themselves, most of which have elaborate coffered ceilings and huge decorative wall paintings. Particularly outstanding is the **Riesensaal** (Hall of Giants), with Landgrave Wilhelm intruding among the portraits of Old Testament and mythological heroes.

However, the most striking and significant part of the building is the **Schlosskirche**, the earliest surviving church to adhere faithfully to the design tenets of Protestantism. Taking up most of one wing, the only clue to its presence from outside is the small tower. Inside, each of the three tiers has, grouped vertically one above the other, the three essential props of Protestant worship – the plain marble altar table, here resting on the four Evangelical symbols; the pulpit, whose basin is carved with a depiction of Pentecost; and the organ, which is adorned with painted shutters (and is still in fine working order, being regularly used during concerts). Otherwise, the rich stucco vault provides the only extravagant touch.

Practicalities

Schmalkalden's **tourist office** (April–Oct Mon–Fri 9am–1pm & 2–5pm, Sat 10am–1pm & 2–5pm; Nov–March Mon–Fri 9am–1pm & 2–5pm, Sat 10am–1pm; ☎03683/403182) is at Mohrengasse 2. Plenty of **private rooms** (①–③) can be booked there.

There are two **hotels** in the centre: *Noblesse*, Rötweg 8 (☎03683/88301; ⑤), and *Stadthotel Patrizier*, Weidebrunner Gasse 9 (☎03683/604514; ⑦), which has two restaurants, the *Thüringer Stube* and the gourmet *Feinschmecker*, the latter open evenings only. There are a couple of enticing alternatives in the outskirts: *Jägerklause*, Pfaffenbach 45 (☎03683/600143; ④); and *Henneberger Haus* on Notstrasse (☎03683/604041; ⑦); both have good restaurants. Apart from the hotels, by far the best **place to eat** is the *Ratskeller*, Altmarkt 2.

Meiningen and around

On the banks of the River Werra at the extreme southwestern corner of the Thuringian Forest, some 25km from Schmalkalden, lies **MEININGEN**, an old ducal capital with a very distinctive tradition in the performing arts. In the latter half of last century, under the enterprising rule of Duke Georg II, it became one of Germany's leading centres for both theatre and music, with a resident orchestra, the *Meininger Hofkapelle*, which was among the most celebrated in the world, and one of the first to undertake global concert tours.

The town

Today Meiningen is a purely provincial town with a population of little more than 25,000, but it's an agreeable place with beautiful surroundings and an interesting Schloss, and warrants a stay of a day or two.

Schloss Elisabethenburg

Meiningen's dominant building is **Schloss Elisabethenburg** (May–Sept Tues–Sun 10am–6pm; Oct–April Tues–Sun 10am–4.45pm; DM6), which stands in its own park at the northern end of the Altstadt, this combined area being separated from the rest of the town by a narrow canal system linked to the Werra. The Schloss was built in the late seventeenth century, immediately after the foundation of the duchy of Saxe-Meiningen, and is in the plainest possible Baroque style; indeed its geometric austerity seems strangely anticipatory of the Bauhaus, with the red-and-white colour scheme providing one of the few surface distractions. However, its ground plan is highly unusual, featuring an enclosed courtyard as a result of the addition of the so-called *Rundbau* (Round Building) to the orthodox palace format.

Most of the **interiors** were remodelled according to the Historicist tastes of Duke Georg, and evoke the whole gamut of European architectural styles. They house three separate permanent exhibitions. That devoted to the fine arts includes notable examples of Gothic wood sculpture, plus an eclectic display of old masters whose star piece is *Lot and his Daughters* by Ribera. The other two collections focus on local achievement in music and theatre. There are displays on the *Hofkapelle's* music directors, who included Hans von Bülow — one of the first virtuoso conductors — and the composers Richard Strauss and Max Reger. Perhaps of more general appeal is the theatre exhibition, which features some spectacular stage sets plus a number of sketches for costume designs by Duke Georg himself.

One of the few original interiors to have survived is the ornate **Hessensaal** on the top storey of the central tower – it now houses the museum café (open from 1pm). The only other Baroque interior which can be visited is the former **Schlosskirche** (same hours as the Schloss; DM0.50) in the southern wing, which has been converted, albeit with the retention of all its furnishings, into a concert hall.

The rest of the town

Just across from the entrance to the Schloss, at Burggasse 22, is one of the town's finest half-timbered constructions, the **Baumbachhaus** (same times and ticket as the Schloss, otherwise DM2). This houses a small museum on literary figures who have stayed in or near the town, among them Schiller and Jean Paul; the latter was the most popular and influential German novelist of the late eighteenth and early nineteenth centuries.

A few minutes' walk south, in the very heart of the Altstadt, is the spacious rectangular Markt. It's dominated by the **Stadtkirche St Marien** whose eccentrically fantastical twin spires help create a memorable silhouette. Although by origin late Gothic, the church's present appearance, both inside and out, is yet another manifestation of the artistic tastes of Duke Georg.

East of the Altstadt is Bernhardstrasse, a stately boulevard lined with several imposing buildings, notably the **Meininger Theater**. Despite its uncompromising Neoclassicism, above all in the porticoed facade, it only dates from the first decade of the present century, and is a replacement for its fire-damaged predecessor. It retains the services of a full-sized orchestra, now re-christened the *Orchester des Meininger Theaters*, and presents ambitious programmes of music, opera, ballet and drama (☎03693/451222). Behind is the town's second important park, the Englischer Garten.

Practicalities

Meiningen's **Bahnhof** directly overlooks the Englischer Garten, and is just a few minutes' walk from the centre. The **tourist office** (April–Oct Mon–Fri 9am–6pm, Sat 10am–3pm; Nov–March Mon–Fri 9am–5pm; ☎03693/44650) at Bernhardstr. 6 performs the usual booking service for **private rooms** (②–③), which are fairly numerous. Additionally, there are several small **pensions**, including *Zum Bratwurstglöckle*, Untere Kaplaneistr. 8 (☎03693/476528; ③), *Pelzer*, Georgstr. 8 (☎03693/44210; ④) and *Sonnengarten*, Gartenstr. 14 (☎03693/829961; ④).

Town-centre **hotels** include *An der Kapelle*, Anton-Ulrich-Str. 19 (☎03693/44920; ⑤); *Im Kaiserpark*, Günter-Raphael-Str. 9 (☎03693/471816; ⑥); and *Sächsischer Hof*, Georgstr. 1 (☎03693/4570; ⑦). However, the best place to stay has to be the newly renovated *Schloss Landsberg*, a medieval castle rebuilt last century in neo-Gothic style; it's situated 4km northwest of the centre at Landsberger Str. 150 (☎03693/502352; ⑦).

The best places to **eat** and **drink** are the hotels (all those listed have recommendable restaurants), or there's the *Schlossgaststätte* in the *Rundbau* of the Schloss, which offers Hungarian as well as traditional German dishes.

Walldorf and Wasungen

Immediately north of Meiningen, the first two stops on the rail line to Eisenach are a couple of contrasting small towns which are both well worth a visit. First up is **WALL-DORF**, from where there's a fine view of the aforementioned Schloss Landsberg. At the western edge of town are the **Sandstein- und Märchenhöhle** (guided tours daily March–May, Sept & Oct 9am–5pm; June–Aug 9am–6pm; DM5), a series of stalactite caves which have been made specially attractive for kids by being fitted out with three dozen scenes illustrating fairy tales and sagas. Nearby, set atop a rock, is the highly idiosyncratic **Kirchenburg**, a plain Renaissance church erected within the ruins of a twelfth-century fortress.

WASUNGEN, a few kilometres beyond, was one of the rare towns the GDR authorities placed under a total preservation order. Rightly so, as this is a distinctive little place, tightly packed in the restricted area between the Werra and the hills above. Its run-down appearance only adds to the charm, and the backstreet alleys present an undisturbed medieval picture. There are many outstanding half-timbered buildings, typically with a lower storey of stone, two of the best examples being the **Rathaus** and the **Damenstift**, both on the main street. High above the town, commanding a grandstand view over the Thuringian Forest, is **Burg Marienluft**, a ruined medieval castle whose later outbuildings house a **hotel** (☎036941/780; ⑤) and restaurant.

Suhl and around

About 30km northeast of Meiningen, on the mazy rail and road routes to Erfurt, lies **SUHL**, the largest town within the Thuringian Forest, and one primarily of note for offering easy access to some of its finest scenery. However, it also has a certain curiosity value as a place which was heavily moulded in the GDR image. In 1951, it was chosen as the capital of one of the fifteen *Bezirke* into which the country was divided; thereafter, its population grew rapidly, and it was developed according to the "Socialist" method of planning, with the tiny historic centre ringed by skyscraper-lined boulevards, with suburbs of massive concrete apartment buildings which look wholly incongruous in their surroundings.

The main attraction in Suhl itself is the **Waffenmuseum** (April–Oct Tues–Sun 9am–5pm; Nov–March Tues–Sat 9am–4pm, Sun 10am–4pm; DM4), housed in the Malzhaus, an impressively long half-timbered construction on Friedrich-König-Strasse on the northern fringe of the Altstadt. This celebrates Suhl's pre-eminence in weapons manufacture. In the sixteenth century, the town established itself as the armaments-producing capital of Europe, and the industry remains an important local employer to this day, specializing in hunting and sporting guns. Given that shooting was a favourite pastime among the GDR leadership, it's not too fanciful to see this being the reason they lavished their favours on Suhl. The museum offers a typically comprehensive documentary history of local production, with plenty of examples from other manufacturing centres for comparison.

The best vantage point within the town boundaries is the **Domberg** to the north: it's accessible by car, but is otherwise a long and steep walk through the forest. At the top are a *Gaststätte* (closed Wed) and an outlook tower, which is freely open during the summer months.

Practicalities

Suhl's **Hauptbahnhof**, at the rear of which is the **bus station**, is at the western end of the town centre; it's about ten minutes' walk to Marktplatz. The **tourist office** (Mon–Fri 10am–6pm, Sat 10am–4pm, Sun 10am–2pm; ☎03681/720052) is located in the Congress Centrum, Friedrich-König-Str. 42.

There's a wide provision of **private rooms** (①–③) in the town and its surroundings, while *Am Markt*, Pfarrstr. 20 (☎03681/39750; ④), is a conveniently central pension. **Hotels** include *Simson-Villa*, Dombergsweg 7 (☎03681/22483; ⑤), and the GDR-era showpieces, *Stadt Suhl*, Bahnhofstr. 25 (☎03681/5940; ⑥), and the all-too-prominent *Ringberg* (now part of the *Holiday Inn* chain), occupying a commanding hilltop position above the town, about 7km east by road, at Ringberg 10 (☎03681/3890; ⑦).

Choice for **eating** and **drinking** is surprisingly good. The best restaurant – apart from those in the hotels – is the *Ratskeller* in the beautiful sixteenth-century Rathaus of the formerly separate town of Heinrichs, now a western suburb. In the centre of Suhl itself, *Tivoli*, Rimbachstr. 4, does Italian and German cuisine equally well, while *Gastmahl des Meeres*, Steinweg 15, offers the expected fish dishes.

The Vesser valley

The best hiking area around Suhl lies to the east; the easiest means of access is to take any Ilmenau-bound bus for about 10km to the *Wegscheide* stop, which marks the convergence of several marked trails. Of these, the most popular is that following the entire course of the **Vesser valley**, a lovely and undemanding thirteen-kilometre walk. It's 1km from the *Wegscheide* to the source of the river, reached by following the signs marked *Vesserquelle*. The Vesser initially tumbles gently downhill through the trees before cutting across open meadows to **VESSER**, a sleepy village grouped around a half-timbered Pfarrkirche. Hitherto no more than a stream, its character changes rapidly in its lower stage, as it cleaves a deep valley through the forest. The trail ends with the Vesser's confluence with the Breitenbach at the village of the same name, from where it's 1km to St Kilian, which has rail and bus links with Suhl.

Schleusingen

Rather than return directly from St Kilian to Suhl, it's worth continuing a further 6km south to **SCHLEUSINGEN**, the terminus of the branch rail line, and also the starting point for a line to Ilmenau. This little town is dominated by one of the most outwardly imposing castles in Thuringia, **Schloss Bertholdsburg** (May–Sept Tues–Fri 9am–5pm, Sat & Sun 10am–6pm; Oct–April Tues–Sun 9am–5pm; DM3.50). The seat of the Counts of Henneberg, this dates back to the thirteenth century, but was rebuilt three hundred years later, with some picturesque half-timbered sections, in a hybrid late Gothic and Renaissance style. Most of the interior is given over to a museum on the geology and natural history of the region, though the last room is covered with impressive monochrome trompe l'oeil paintings made around 1600. Additionally, you can climb the tower for a view over the town and the Thuringian Forest.

Ilmenau and the Goethe trail

The old glass-making and procelain-producing town of **ILMENAU** lies on the River Ilm some 30km northeast of Suhl by a circuitous road, and also has a direct rail link with both Schleusingen and Arnstadt. It's a place with an unexpectedly youthful presence, being the seat of several colleges, including the recently founded Technical University. However, its name is associated above all with **Goethe**, who declared it to be a place where he was always happy. His administrative work on behalf of the Duchy of Saxe-Weimar meant that he was a regular visitor. The main reason for visiting Ilmenau is to walk one of Germany's best-known **footpaths**, *Auf Goethes Spuren*. While primarily of interest to literary buffs, it also offers an excellent overview of the scenery of the Thuringian Forest, and along the route are several excellent country *Gaststätten* offering wholesome German cooking. The starting point for this is the **Amtshaus** (daily May–Oct 9am–noon & 1–4.30pm; Nov–April 10am–noon & 1–4pm; DM2), the administrative building at the top end of the Markt. This contains a small museum with period interiors containing mementoes of Goethe, who lived and worked there during his sorties to the town, and examples of local porcelain.

Practicalities

Ilmenau has two stations – the **Hauptbahnhof** is east of the town centre and marginally closer to the Markt than the **Bad-Bahnhof** to the south. The latter is more useful if you want to take the direct trail to the Kickelhahn. It's also closer to the **tourist office** (Mon–Fri 9am–6pm, Sat 9am–noon; ☎03677/202358), which is just over the Ilm at Lindenstr. 12.

You can book **private rooms** (①–③) at the tourist office. There are also a few small **pensions**, including *Melanie*, just south of the Bad-Bahnhof at Heinrich-Heine-Str. 3 (☎03677/670145; ③). There's also one budget **hotel**, *Zum Elephant*, right in the heart of town at Marktstr. 16 (☎03677/202441; ③). The alternatives, all much more expensive, are *Tanne*, Lindenstr. 38 (☎03677/6590; ⑤); *Zur Sonne*, Am Markt 3

THE GOETHE TRAIL

The famous footpath, *Auf Goethes Spuren* (In Goethe's Footsteps), takes in a number of places connected with the poet in the course of an 18.5-kilometre route from Ilmenau. The terrain is fairly demanding, with many steep uphill stretches; allowing for regular sight-seeing stops, it's likely to take up a full day. It's very well signposted by means of a G monogram copied from Goethe's own handwriting.

From the Markt in the centre of Ilmenau, the route travels westwards to the village of Manebach, from where it ascends to the celebrated **Kickelhahn** (861m), which can also be reached directly by a much shorter path from the southern end of Ilmenau. On this mountain are an outlook tower, which commands an extensive panorama over Ilmenau and the Thuringian Forest, and a replica of the long-destroyed **Goethehäuschen**, the little wooden hideaway, where the poet composed one of his most quoted poems, *The Wayfarer's Night Song II*.

About fifteen minutes' walk further along the route is the **Jagdhaus Gabelbach** (Wed–Sun 9am–noon & 1–4/5pm; DM4), a hunting lodge containing a museum devoted to Goethe's studies in natural history, a subject which preoccupied him during his visits to this region.

From here, the trail continues south to its terminus at the village of **STÜTZERBACH**, where the **Goethehaus** (Wed–Sun 9am–noon & 1–4/5pm; DM4) preserves rooms where Goethe stayed and worked, and also features displays on the local glass industry.

(☎03677/888777; ⑥); *Lindenhof*, Lindenstr. 7–11 (☎03677/6590; ⑤) and *Ilmenauer Hof*, Erfurterstr. 38 (☎03677/677 7610; ⑥). All but the last of these have a restaurant. Also worth considering is the *Berghotel Gabelbach*, situated 2km from the town near the Jagdhaus at Waldstr. 23a (☎03677/566; ⑤). The **youth hostel** is in the southeastern part of town at Am Stollen 49 (☎03677/202413; 🏠).

Arnstadt and around

First documented in 704, **ARNSTADT**, which lies just beyond the fringes of the Thuringian Forest, 22km north of Ilmenau and 18km southwest of Erfurt, has the best claim to be regarded as the oldest town in eastern Germany. Its well-preserved historic centre of narrow alleys and half-timbered houses evokes the sort of timeless provincial air that has all but vanished from the western Länder and may not last for much longer here. It also has the advantage of being surrounded by a typically Germanic landscape of woods and hills, with three castles steeped in rich legends within easy distance.

The town

Arnstadt's layout is characteristic of the feudal pattern of Thuringia with the princely palace occupying a green area at the edge of the town centre. The best times to visit are during Arnstadt's **musical festivals**, the *Bachtage* at the end of March and the *Orgelsommer* in June and July.

The Neues Palais
The tower and a few other scanty remains of the sixteenth-century Schloss Neideck – the original seat of the House of Schwarzburg-Arnstadt – stand in the Stadtpark at the end of Bahnhofstrasse. Before the old Schloss fell into disrepair, a second palace, the **Neues Palais** (May–Sept Tues–Sun 8.30am–noon & 1–4.30pm; Oct–April Tues–Sun 9.30am–4pm; DM3.50), was built to the south in the early eighteenth century. Its main attraction is **Mon Plaisir**, a collection of over 400 dolls arranged into 82 scenes, depicting the life of all social classes of the day. This is far more profound than it at first appears – far from being intended as playthings for children, these scenes were commissioned over half a century by Princess Augusta Dorothea as a serious artistic enterprise. As well as the figures, the clothes, utensils and furniture are all precisely crafted, and are a valuable documentary source on social conditions in the period. The palace is also renowned for its seventeenth- and eighteenth-century china, some of which is ingeniously displayed on gilded tables in the **Spiegelkabinett**, but this is closed indefinitely for restoration.

The Markt and around
A few minutes' walk to the west is the Markt, where the Renaissance **Rathaus** springs a surprise in its uncompromising imitation of Dutch-style architecture. The church opposite was once known as the Neue Kirche. In 1703, the eighteen-year-old J.S. Bach gained his first major professional appointment as organist here; as a result, it's now officially called the **Bachkirche**, and the organ on which he played still survives. Unfortunately, the Arnstadt congregation failed to appreciate his genius as either a composer or performer and, stung by criticism of his revolutionary improvisatory style, he left four years later for Mühlhausen. The Bach theme is taken up in the Renaissance-Baroque **Haus zum Palmbaum** (Mon–Fri 8.30am–12.30pm & 1–5pm, Sat & Sun 9.30am–5pm; DM4) at Markt 3, which contains the local history museum. Among the memorabilia of the composer, the most striking is the original console of his organ, which had to be removed when the instrument's action was modernized.

Beyond the far end of the Markt is the **Liebfrauenkirche**, whose architecture, and in particular the two magnificent west towers, is loosely based on the Dom in Naumburg. The chapel on the north side of the choir served as the mausoleum of the Counts of Schwarzburg and contains the beautiful double **tomb** of Günther XXV and his wife Elisabeth, thought to have been carved in the famous workshop of Peter Parler in Prague. Also of note are the **stained-glass** windows in the nave aisles, and the **high altar** of *The Coronation of the Virgin*, a fine example of fifteenth-century Thuringian woodcarving. Alongside the church is one of the town's oldest half-timbered houses, the **Alte Mühle**, which began life as the corn mill of a convent.

Practicalities

Arnstadt's **Hauptbahnhof** is situated at the northern end of town, and you'll find the **tourist office** (Mon–Fri 9am–6pm, Sat 9am–noon; ☎03628/602049) in the Haus zum Palmbaum, Markt 3.

As well as the **private rooms** (①–③) which can be booked at the tourist office, there are **hotels** to suit most pockets. At the budget end of the scale are the *Goldene Sonne*, Ried 3 (☎03628/602776; ④), and *Riedschenke*, Vor dem Riedtor 6 (☎03628/602374; ④). For more luxury, head for *Krone*, Am Bahnhof 8 (☎03628/77060; ⑤), *Mon Plaisir*, Lessingstr. 21 (☎03628/739111; ⑤), or *Anders*, Gehrener Str. 22 (☎03628/3620; ⑤).

As well as those in the hotels, good **restaurants** include *Zum Goldenen Adler*, Markt 12, and *Ratsklause*, Ledermarkt 3.

The Drei Gleichen

To the northwest of Arnstadt, in the direction of Gotha, stand three hilltop castles known as the **Drei Gleichen** (Three Alike). This nickname has its origins in a thirteenth-century legend, which maintains that all three were hit by a shot from a single cannon ball, whereupon they appeared on the skyline as three smouldering pyres. In reality, however, the three were and are totally dissimilar in appearance.

Closest to Arnstadt is the **Wachsenburg**, which is just outside Holzhausen, 5km away and served by bus. This Romanesque-Gothic fortress, barely visible from below because of its densely wooded slopes, was restored to an approximation of its medieval form in the GDR period as a luxury **hotel** and restaurant (☎03628/74240, fax 742488; ⑤). It was much favoured by Erich Honecker and his SED cronies as a base for their hunting jaunts in the region. From here, it's an easy half-hour walk northwest to the **Mühlburg** (March–Oct Mon–Thurs 10am–5pm, Sat & Sun 10am–6pm; DM2), which is known to have existed back in the eighth century. However, the present ruins, which are very scanty apart from the tower, are about five hundred years younger than this. The adjacent village of **MÜHLBERG** is also worth a quick look – its **Dorfkirche** is a Baroque period piece, with the original painted galleries, altar, organ and other furnishings all as they were when the church was first built.

The final castle, **Burg Gleichen** (Jan & Feb Sat & Sun 9am–5pm, March, Nov & Dec daily 9am–5pm, April–Oct daily 9am–6pm; DM3.50), is a couple of kilometres further north, and a similar distance south of Wandersleben, where you can pick up a train back to Arnstadt, or on to Erfurt or Gotha. It's the most rewarding of the three to visit, preserving picturesque remains of the early medieval fortress plus its Renaissance residence. Associated with the castle is the legend (inspired by the tomb in Erfurt's Dom) of one of its counts, Ernst III. Taken prisoner during the Crusades, he became a slave of the Turkish sultan, but was saved from captivity by the latter's daughter, who fell in love with him and converted to Christianity. As he already had a wife, he had to obtain special dispensation from the pope to enter into a bigamous marriage with her, to which his first wife, glad to have her husband released, readily consented. The two wives agreed to live together as sisters; the valley below the fortress has ever since been known as Freudenthal (Vale of Joy) in honour of this happy solution.

Paulinzella

From Arnstadt, there's a slow but scenic rail line which goes along the eastern fringe of the Thuringian Forest to Saalfeld. If travelling this way, it's worth stopping off at the village of **PAULINZELLA**, about halfway along. Here you can see one of Germany's most imposing ruins, a large Romanesque **Kloster** of the reform movement initiated at Hirsau in the Black Forest, which in turn was influenced by that of Cluny in Burgundy, the most powerful monastery of the Middle Ages. Despite its roofless state, the church is a substantial torso, its massive portal being especially impressive. To find out about the Kloster's history and former appearance, visit the **Zinsboden** (daily May–Sept 9am–noon & 1–5pm; DM1), a half-timbered medieval store resting on an older stone base, standing just to the west.

NORTHERN THURINGIA

The northern part of Thuringia is, in comparison with the central belt, little touched by tourism. Here are two towns, **Mühlhausen** and **Nordhausen**, which went against the regional grain in the medieval period by functioning as city-states. Though Nordhausen is now a shadow of its former self, the centre of Mühlhausen looks much as it has done for centuries. The other main draws in the north are the often-overlooked princely seat of **Sondershausen** and the hills of the **Kyffhäuser** range.

Mühlhausen

Even within Thuringia, there are few places which conjure up the past so vividly as **MÜHLHAUSEN**, which dates back at least as far as Charlemagne. Its historic core has almost completely intact medieval walls, inside which is a maze of alleys lined with half-

---

THOMAS MÜNTZER AND THE PEASANTS' WAR

By far the most controversial, not to say sinister, figure of the Reformation, **Thomas Müntzer** has a significance far beyond the distorted one promoted by the GDR – he can be regarded as the father of all the myriad forms of sectarian Protestantism which retain such an influence to this day. As vitriolic about Luther (whom be dismissed as "Dr Pussyfoot" and "Dr Easychair") as about Catholicism, Müntzer believed that the Bible had to be reinterpreted by a second Daniel (needless to say, himself) who would lead the elect in a crusade against the ungodly. His electrifying preaching gained him a huge popular following, but his bloodthirsty message so alarmed the authorities of Electoral Saxony that he was expelled from the territory.

On his appointment at Mühlhausen, he hitched his cause to that of the peasants who were already in revolt against their feudal masters over their economic plight. In reality, Müntzer was primarily interested in them for religious reasons, though he was the only leading churchman of the day who understood that faith among the common people was not nourished by starvation. Incensed by Müntzer's actions, Luther was inspired to write a pamphlet condemning the peasants, and backed the princely armies which crushed his rival's untrained forces at Frankenhausen. Müntzer was captured in the battle and brought back to Mühlhausen, where he was tried, tortured and executed.

timbered houses and six Gothic churches, with a further four standing just outside the fortifications. As a Free Imperial City throughout the Middle Ages, Mühlhausen was a rare island of independence in this part of the country, which explains why it became the headquarters of the ill-fated Peasants' War of 1525, led by the town's firebrand pastor, **Thomas Müntzer** (see box on p.909). To the GDR authorities, this was the first great social revolution in German history; accordingly, Müntzer became one of the state's supreme heroes, regarded as a Moses-like precursor of Marx. In 1975, to mark the 450th anniversary of the event, the town was officially renamed "Thomas-Müntzer-Stadt-Mühlhausen", and two of the churches were made over as memorials to him. The latter have survived the post-*Wende* re-evaluations, though the town's forename has been discarded.

The town

The best introduction to Mühlhausen is to walk all the way round the outside of the 2.7-kilometre-long **Stadtmauer**, which still preserves six towers and two gateways. It's at its most impressive around the main western entrance, the **Inneres Frauentor**. Here a small section has been opened to the public, enabling you to go along part of the sentry walk and ascend the **Rabenturm** (May–Oct Tues–Sun 10am–4pm; DM2).

On Holzstrasse, the northern of the two streets leading to the centre, you pass the thirteenth-century **Hospital** and a number of fine houses, of which the most notable is no. 1, which began life as the town house of Kloster Zella before becoming a post office in the period of the Thurn and Taxis monopoly. Herrenstrasse to the south also has fine buildings, though the parish house at the far end is a replacement of the one where Müntzer lived, which was destroyed by fire.

Both streets terminate at the **Marienkirche** (daily 10am–4.30pm; DM3), where Müntzer served as pastor during the three fateful months he lived in Mühlhausen. The church itself has a distinctive triple-towered **facade** in which the massive Flamboyant Gothic central tower, crowned with a bravura nineteenth-century steeple, is flanked by its two modest counterparts, one late Romanesque, the other early Gothic. No less idiosyncratic is the **south portal**: although some of its original statuary – carved by the Parler school of Prague – was destroyed as a result of the iconoclasm fomented by Müntzer, the balcony with the peering figures of Emperor Charles IV, Empress Elisabeth and two courtiers survives intact. Inside, the most impressive feature is the soaring architecture of the five-aisled hall nave with its elaborate vault. The **furnishings** include a number of fine retables (the high altar to the Virgin Mary was made during the brief return to Catholicism following Müntzer's demise), and the grand white *Ratsstuhl*, where councillors sat during services.

Following Ratsstrasse south from here brings you to the **Rathaus** (Sat & Sun 10am–5pm; DM1) complex, which dates back to about 1300 but which grew in size to such an extent down the centuries that it straddles the street, with the two parts linked by a covered passageway. In the **Ratsstube**, adorned with Gothic wall paintings, Müntzer held his daily *Ewig Rat* (Perpetual Council); the **Archiv**, with its complete set of Renaissance furniture and documents pertaining to Mühlhausen's period as a city-state, is also worth a look.

A couple of blocks south on Kornmarkt is the **Barfüsserkirche** (Tues–Sun 10am–4pm; DM2), a barn-like former Franciscan monastery church given over to a museum on the Peasants' War. Further south on Johann-Sebastian-Platz is the **Divi-Blasii-Kirche**, a former church of the Teutonic Knights, whose place in musical history is assured as a result of the year Bach spent there as organist following his departure from Arnstadt. Its twin towers are a good illustration of the way late Romanesque passed seamlessly into Gothic: the rest of the building is, like the Marienkirche, a four-teenth-century hall church.

Practicalities

Mühlhausen's **Bahnhof**, which has regular services to both Gotha and Erfurt, is three blocks beyond the easternmost part of the Stadtmauer. The **tourist office** (Mon–Fri 9am–5pm; May–Oct also Sat 10am–noon; ☎03601/452335) is at Ratsstr. 20; there's a separate phone number (☎03601/452320) for booking **private rooms** (①–③).

The **youth hostel** is in the outskirts of town at Auf den Tonberg 1 (☎03601/813318; ④). There are many **pensions**, some of them centrally located, such as *Schilling*, Erfurterstr. 30 (☎03601/812883; ②); *Höfler*, Kuttelgasse 23 (☎03601/446 9909; ③); and *Adams*, Allerheiligengasse 2 (☎03601/442418; ④). **Hotels** include *Gasthof Bundschuh*, Jüdenstr. 43 (☎03601/46230; ④); *Stadt Mühlhausen*, Untermarkt 18 (☎03601/4550; ⑤); *An der Stadtmauer*, Breitenstr. 5 (☎03601/46500; ⑤); *Ammerscher Bahnhof*, Ammerstr. 83–85 (☎03601/873132; ⑥); *Mirage*, Karl-Marx-Str. 9 (☎03601/440 7750; ⑥); and *Brauhaus Zum Löwen*, Kornmarkt 3 (☎03601/4710; ⑥).

There's a surprisingly good choice of **restaurants**; among the best is *Zum Nachbarn*, just east of the Marienkirche at Steinweg 65, which specializes in poultry dishes. Strong competition comes from several of the hotel restaurants, particularly *Brauhaus Zum Löwen*, which brews its own beer, and *An der Stadtmauer*.

Mühlhausen was one of the few places in the GDR which kept up much of a tradition in **festivals**, of which the most important is the *Kirmes*, a fair held at the end of August.

Nordhausen

NORDHAUSEN lies just to the south of the Harz mountains, at the fringe of the fertile plain known as the *Goldene Aue* (Golden Meadow), about 45km northeast of Mühlhausen. It's predominantly an industrial town, best known for its production of spirits (a mouth-burning *Korn* has been made here since the early sixteenth century) and tobacco (especially *Kautabak*, or "chewing tobacco"). Unfortunately, this rather overshadows its historical role as a former Free Imperial City, the more so as a large number of monuments were destroyed in 1945, during the severest bombing raid carried out on any Thuringian town.

Nonetheless, there are a few sights well worth stopping to see if you happen to find yourself here – Nordhausen is the southern terminus of the narrow-gauge steam rail line through the Harz, the *Harzquerbahn* (see p.853), and also has the only functioning train connection with the Lower Saxon side of the range.

The town

The **Stadtmauer** was among the monuments damaged in the war, though 1.5km of the circuit still remain, the most impressive section being the set of double fortifications around Jüdenstrasse, about halfway up the hill between the Hauptbahnhof and the Markt. Following the wall northwards, you can see the **Finkenburg**, one of the oldest and finest of the few half-timbered houses spared by the bombs, at An der Wassertreppe. East of here is the Markt, whose late Renaissance **Rathaus**, outside which stands the inevitable statue of Roland, was rebuilt from wartime ruins.

Further up, the skyline is dominated by the so-called **Dom**, more correctly the **Kloster zum Heiligen Kreuz**, the successor to a nunnery founded by Empress Mathilde in 963. The present church is an architectural jumble – the towers, the cloister and the crypt are Romanesque, the choir early Gothic, the lofty hall nave Flamboyant Gothic. Inside, the finest feature is the group of six late thirteenth-century statues in the choir, clearly modelled on their counterparts in Naumburg.

The Konzentrationslager Mittelbau-Dora

In 1943, a subsidiary concentration camp of Buchenwald, under the name of **Dora**, was set up at the foot of the Kohnstein at the northernmost fringe of Nordhausen. The following year, renamed **Mittelbau**, it became a full-blown camp in its own right. 60,000 prisoners from twenty-one different countries were interned here, engaged on the secret production of V1 and V2 missiles, working underground in a network of tunnels and caverns. Nearly a third of them died here; in their honour, the site has been turned into a **memorial** (daily April–Sept 10am–6pm; Oct–March 10am–4pm; free), with documentary displays on the conditions they suffered. The easiest way to get here is to take the *Harzquerbahn* to **Krimderode**, then follow the main road round to the west.

Practicalities

Nordhausen's **Hauptbahnhof** lies south of the Altstadt, on the opposite side of the River Zorge; the *Harzquerbahn*'s terminus, misleadingly designated *Nordhausen-Nord*, is just across Bahnhofsplatz. The **tourist office** (Mon–Fri 7am–7pm, Sat & Sun 9am–5pm; ☎03631/629151) at Bahnhofstr. 3a can book **private rooms** (①–③).

The town has few **hotels**, the best being *Zur Sonne*, Hallesche Str. 8 (☎03631/48938; ④); *Avenu*, Hallesche Str. 13 (☎03631/602060; ⑤); and *Handelshof*, Bahnhofstr. 13 (☎03631/6250; ⑥). There's also a **youth hostel** at Johannes-Kleinspehn-Str. 1 (☎03631/8587; ②) in the suburb of Salza, just behind the Bahnhof of the same name, the first stop on the mainline route north.

Nordhausen doesn't score highly for **eating** and **drinking**, but try *Café Altstadt*, Kranichstr. 19, or the *Ratskeller*, Markt 1. The main local **festival** is the *Rolandfest* on the second weekend in June.

Sondershausen

SONDERSHAUSEN, which lies 20km south of Nordhausen in a pretty setting in the valley cut by the River Wipper between two groups of wooded hills, the Hainleite and the Windleite, is a place which deserves to be far better known. Formerly the capital of the county of Schwarzburg, and later of the principality of Schwarzburg-Sondershausen, its main attraction is one of the courtly towns so characteristic of Thuringia. However, it's far less soporific than most of its counterparts. The huge winding tower (now preserved as a technical monument) which greets you on arrival at the Hauptbahnhof is a reminder that Sondershausen has for centuries been a major centre of potash production, while the historic heart of the town has regained its former role as a market and trading centre.

The town

A typically oversized **Schloss** (Tues–Sun 10am–4/5pm; DM4) is Sondershausen's overwhelmingly dominant building. It can be approached from the west via its rustic park, or from the Markt by the monumental steps to the side of the Neoclassical guardhouse, the Alte Wache. The north wing dates back to the sixteenth century, while the seventeenth century saw the beginning of a massive extension programme, including the addition of a Baroque tower and south wing. A late Rococo palace, subsequently modified in Neoclassical style, was then added at an angle of 45 degrees to the original, creating an almost triangular courtyard.

The wonderfully eclectic **interior**, graphically conjures up the real-life fantasy world of a petty German court. In the original palace is the most individual chamber, the

Mannerist **Wendelstein**, which boasts a dazzlingly brilliant stucco vault showing the Elements, the Seasons, the Virtues, putti and mythological characters. The main reception room is the Baroque **Riesensaal** (Giants' Hall), so called from the sixteen over-life-sized statues of Classical deities; it also boasts a superb coffered vault with ornate stucco trophies and paintings illustrating Ovid's *Metamorphoses*. If, as is probable, this is closed for repairs, there's the compensation of being able to see its recently restored Rococo counterpart, the turquoise **Festsaal**, whose vault continues the antique theme with the story of Jupiter and Calypso. Two other highlights are the **Liebhabertheater** (Conoisseurs' Theatre), a Biedermeier gem which is one of the smallest theatres in Germany, and the gilded **state coach**.

In the park west of the Schloss is the **Karussel** or **Achteckiges Haus**, a tall, eccentric-looking octagon with interior galleries and a fresco of *The Triumph of Venus*. Built at the beginning of the eighteenth century to serve as the main venue for court entertainments, it's occasionally used for concerts by the *Loh-Orchester*.

The Hainleite

It's well worth taking a walk in the **Hainleite**, the hills to the south of Sondershausen; they're best reached by following Possenallee straight ahead from the town centre. From here, it's an easy ascent to the **Rondell**, a belvedere commanding a fine view of the valley. A couple of kilometres further south brings you to the **Jagdschloss zum Possen**, the former hunting lodge of the court, which is now a recuperative centre with a wildlife park alongside. There's also a tall half-timbered **Aussichtsturm** (daily 10am–6pm; DM1) dating from the very end of the eighteenth century, which you can climb for the most extensive panorama of the whole region.

Practicalities

Sondershausen's **Hauptbahnhof** is about fifteen minutes' walk west of the centre; the *Haltepunkt Sondershausen-Süd* below the Hainleite is actually slightly nearer the Markt and the Schloss. The **tourist office** (Mon–Fri 9am–12.30pm & 1.30–5pm, Sat 9–11am; ☎03632/788111) is in the Alte Wache, Markt 9.

There are plenty of **private rooms** (①–③) for rent in Sondershausen. Alternatively, there are a few **pensions**: *Zur Sonne*, Conrad-Röntgen-Str. 11 (☎03632/602486; ②); *Schweizer Haus*, Im Loh 1a (☎03632/601111; ③); and *Haus Waldheim*, Erfurter Str. 29 (☎03632/758779; ⑤). The only **hotel** as such is *Thüringer Hof*, Hauptstr. 30–32 (☎03632/6560, fax 65611; ⑤). The best **restaurants** are the one in *Thüringer Hof*, the *Ratskeller*, Markt 7, and the *Schlossrestaurant* in the Schloss.

The Kyffhäuser

The **Kyffhäuser**, a small group of wooded sandstone mountains, form a virtual southern continuation of the Harz, which they closely resemble – except for the fact that they're virtually uninhabited. Despite their modest dimensions – they occupy less than 60 square kilometres, while the peaks are all under 500m – they have a grandeur that belies their actual size. In addition, they hold a special place in the national consciousness, being the seat of one of the great Imperial castles of early medieval Germany and the place where, according to legend, Emperor Frederick Barbarossa (the country's real-life counterpart of King Arthur) lies slumbering, awaiting his second coming. For the GDR state, the Kyffhäuser had the additional allure of being where the first German revolution, the Peasants' War of 1525, came to its untimely end.

Bad Frankenhausen

The gateway to the Kyffhäuser, and the obvious base for a visit, is the small spa town of **BAD FRANKENHAUSEN**, which lies at their southern edge, 20km east of Sondershausen, just below the **Schlachtberg** (Battle Hill) where Thomas Müntzer's peasant army was routed by vastly superior forces loyal to the nation's rulers.

In the late sixteenth century, Frankenhausen became the capital of one of the four counties into which Schwarzburg was divided, an event which necessitated the building of the modest little **Schloss** (Tues–Sun 10am–5pm; DM3) at the southern end of the old quarter, about five minutes' walk from the Bahnhof. It's now a museum devoted to the Kyffhäuser region, with displays on its flora, fauna, archeology, history, arts and crafts, with the highlight being a diorama of the battle of 1525.

Just north of the Schloss is the Markt, with a Neoclassical Rathaus; from here, Kräme, a pedestrianized shopping street, leads to **Anger**, the spacious main square, which boasts a few half-timbered houses. Uphill lies the best-preserved section of the thirteenth-century fortification system, centred on the impressive **Hausmannsturm**.

The Bauernkriegs-Panorama

Much further up, crowning the top of the Schlachtberg, is the white rotunda housing one of Germany's newest yet already somewhat anachronistic tourist attractions, the **Bauernkriegs-Panorama** (guided tours April–June & Sept Tues–Sun 10am–6pm; July & Aug Mon 1–6pm, Tues–Sun 10am–6pm; Oct–March Tues–Sun 10am–5pm; DM10). Claimed as the largest painting in the world, this huge, vividly coloured panoramic picture of the battle was unveiled in 1989 to celebrate Müntzer's five-hundredth anniversary, and the fortieth birthday of the GDR.

Begun twelve years previously, it was commissioned as a co-operative work by a team of artists, on the model of the many nineteenth-century panoramic battle pictures, a once-popular art form which, until then, seemed to have been killed off by the cinema. As work progressed, the Leipzig professor **Werner Tübke** assumed an increasingly dominant role, eventually taking over the project completely. Over seventy percent of the painting is by him, with much of the rest being detail provided by specialists. Both politically and artistically the end result is controversial, though neither critical derision nor the inflated entrance fee deters the crowds who flock here, often queuing for hours during the main holiday periods because of the restricted admissions policy.

Practicalities

The **tourist office** (May–Sept Mon–Fri 9am–6pm, Sat 10am–3pm, Sun 10am–noon; Oct–April Mon–Fri 9am–5pm, Sat 10am–noon; ☎034671/71716) is at Anger 14, the oldest half-timbered house in town. You can book a **private room** (①–③) here, though they're easy enough to find on your own if you look for the *Zimmer frei* signs.

For a bit more luxury, there are several good **hotels** – *Grabenmühle*, Am Wellgraben 1 (☎034671/79882; ④); *Bellevue*, Goethestr. 13 (☎034671/306; ⑥); *Reichental*, Rottleber Str. 4 (☎034671/680; ⑦); and *Residence Frankenburg*, Am Schlachtberg 3 (☎034671/750; ⑦). All of these also have reasonable **restaurants**. There's a **youth hostel** at Bahnhofstr. 6 (☎034671/2018; 🏠).

The mountains

The Kyffhäuser are combed with marked walking trails, and it's easy enough to devise your own circular routes. Easiest hike is to the **Barbarossahöhle** (guided tours daily 9am–5/6pm; DM5), 5km to the west and just north of Rottleben, the next stop on the rail line to Sondershausen. Discovered during mining operations last century – whereupon it immediately became coupled to the Barbarossa legend – this is, with a total length of 800m, one of Europe's largest gypsum caves, featuring some amazing vaults and tiny lakes with crystal-clear waters.

For the more energetic, there's a ten-kilometre path from Bad Frankenhausen which travels right through the heart of the Kyffhäuser to its highest summit, the **Kulpenberg** (477m). If you want a yet more extensive view, you can go up its **Fernsehturm** (television tower; daily April–Sept 10am–5pm; Oct–March 10am–4pm) to the café and observation platform.

A few kilometres east of here, and linked by a direct trail to Bad Frankenhausen, is the **Kyffhäuserdenkmal** (daily May–Sept 9am–7pm; Oct–April 9am–5pm; DM5). This Historicist monstrosity, which commands another sweeping view over the region, was erected at the end of the nineteenth century in honour of the recently deceased Kaiser Wilhelm I, the first emperor of the Second Reich and thus the man seen as something of a reincarnation of Frederick Barbarossa, an early champion of German unity. In order to build it, a substantial portion of the surviving fragments of the upper fortress of the famous Romanesque **Reichsburg**, one of the strongholds of the Hohenstaufen emperors, had to be demolished – an act of vandalism uncharacteristic of the time. Thankfully, the ruins of the lower fortress, including a well some 176m deep, survive to give an idea of the scale and appearance of the original.

EASTERN THURINGIA

The easternmost part of Thuringia has a natural border in the form of the middle reaches of the valley of the River Saale, on whose banks lie the university city of **Jena**, and the former courtly towns of **Rudolstadt** and **Saalfeld**. Further east lies **Gera**, capital of one of the old principalities of Reuss, while jutting into Saxony, and only recently returned to its traditional Thuringian homeland, is a strip of territory centred on **Altenburg**.

Jena and around

JENA, which is just 20km southeast of Weimar, lies at the point where the Saale valley is at its grandest, surrounded by red sandstone and chalk hills, which have a climate mild enough for the growing of vines. The **University** is among the most famous in Germany; founded in 1558 with the help of Melanchthon, it was closely associated with the great flowering of Classicism in Weimar, to which Jena then belonged, following its own short-lived period as capital of an independent duchy. In the nineteenth century, it played a leading role in scientific research, and was closely associated with the world-renowned optics company, the Carl-Zeiss-Stiftung, whose works are still a prominent feature of the skyline.

Sadly, the city was exceptionally badly bombed in World War II and still bears the scars of this. Nevertheless, there's still plenty to see – particularly if you are at all of a scientific bent – while the atmosphere is the liveliest, and the choice in eating, drinking and nightlife by far the best in Thuringia.

Arrival and accommodation

Jena has two main stations, though the **Westbahnhof** to the southwest of the centre is increasingly being overshadowed by the **Saalbahnhof** to the north. Slow trains also

The **telephone code** for Jena is ☎03641

stop at the **Paradiesbahnhof**, which is at the southern fringe of the centre; slightly to the north of here is the **bus station**.

The **tourist office** (Mon–Fri 9am–6pm, Sat 9am–2pm; ☎58630 or 19433) is at Holzmarkt 8. Here you can buy the *JenaCard*, which is valid for three consecutive days' travel on the buses and trams, plus entry to all the museums and the Zeiss-Planetarium.

Accommodation

Private rooms (②–④) can be booked, as usual, at the tourist office. There's an unofficial **youth hostel**, *Internationales Jugendgästehaus IB Jena*, Am Herrenberge 3 (☎6870), in the suburb of Lichtenhain southwest of the centre; it costs DM34 for the first night; DM24 thereafter. **Hotels** and **pensions** are scattered all over the city, with something to suit all pockets.

HOTELS AND PENSIONS

Am Saalestrand, Wenigenjenaer Ufer 15 (☎445572, fax 890050). Small pension run as an adjunct to a Balkan restaurant, *Adria Grill*. ④

Esplanade, Carl-Zeiss-Platz 4 (☎8000, fax 800150). Jena's most prestigious hotel, part of the exclusive *Goethe-Galerie* shopping centre. Its restaurant *Rotunda* occupies a hexagonal tower with a panorama terrace. ⑧

Jembo Park, Rudolstädter Str. 93 (☎6850, fax 685299). Thuringia's first motel, located on the B88 just a short distance north of Bahnhof Göschwitz, 4km south of the centre. Has bungalows as well as hotel rooms, a restaurant and an English-style pub. ⑤

Jenaer Hof, Bachstr. 24 (☎443855, fax 443866). Small hotel in a Jugendstil building right in the city centre. ④

Kerzel, Lutherstr. 38 (☎44307, fax 406113). Good value pension just west of the centre. ③

Schwarzer Bär, Lutherplatz 2 (☎4060, fax 406113). Hotel with a tradition dating back some 500 years at the northwestern corner of the Altstadt, not far from the Saalbahnhof. Its restaurant is very reasonably priced. ⑥

Thüringer Hof, Westbahnhofstr. 8 (☎29290, fax 292999). Budget hotel near the Westbahnhof. ④

Zur Noll, Oberlauengasse 19 (☎ and fax 441566). *Gasthof* in the very heart of the Altstadt, with restaurant, beer garden and exhibition gallery. Often hosts different types of live music. ⑤

Zur Schweiz, Quergasse 15 (☎449355, fax 449354). Another good central *Gasthof*, with a particularly recommendable restaurant. ⑥

Zur Weintraube, Rudolstädter Str. 70 (☎695770, fax 606583). Eighteenth-century inn on the B88 in the suburb of Winzerla, 3km south of the centre. Its excellent, moderately priced restaurant offers many Thuringian specialities. ⑤

The city

Given its size, Jena's attractions are fairly spread out. However, most of what you're likely to want to see is concentrated in a few easily assimilated areas and can be covered comfortably on foot.

Eichplatz

Dominating the centre of Jena from the middle of the spacious Eichplatz, dwarfing even the Carl Zeiss buildings just to the west, is the **Universitätshochhaus**, a 120-metre-high cylindrical tower inaugurated in 1972. Though by no means the worst example of the GDR school of brutalist architecture, it's distinctly unloved locally: irreverent students were quick to dub it *Phallus Jenensis*, and this has since passed into the cruder vernacular form of *Jenaer Pimmel* (Jena's Willie). If the building has a saving grace, it's the view from the café at the top – just walk in and take the lift up.

In order to build the tower, many of the surviving historical buildings on Eichplatz and the streets around had to be razed, and it was only as a result of a protest campaign that the original University, the **Collegium Jenense**, which stands just to the south on Collegienstrasse, was spared. Originally a Dominican monastery, it's a marvellously ramshackle array of bits and pieces from various epochs, which evoke the cloistered tranquillity of academe. The most arresting feature is the bravura Renaissance carving in the courtyard of the coat of arms of the Ernestine line of the House of Wettin, the University's original patrons. Just east of the Collegium is the ruined **Anatometurm**, one of the three towers surviving from the fourteenth-century fortification system.

The Markt and around

Separating Eichplatz from the much smaller Markt is the **Rathaus**, a simple Gothic structure crowned with a miniature Baroque belfry housing the *Schnapphans*, a mechanism which strikes the hours. In the middle of the square stands the **statue of Hannfried**, this being the nickname given locally to the University's founder, John Frederick the Magnanimous.

Such few old houses as Jena possesses can be found mostly on the Markt itself and in the two alleys, Oberlauengasse and Unterlauengasse, immediately to the east. The finest of these, at Markt 7, is now the **Stadtmuseum Göhre** (Tues & Thurs–Sun 10am–5pm, Wed 10am–6pm; DM5). It contains displays on local arts and crafts, wine-making, religious art, the so-called "Seven Wonders of Jena" and the history of the University (including a reproduction of the Studentenkarzer or prison with its characteristic graffiti). There's also a reconstruction of a nineteenth-century café if you need a bit of light refreshment.

Despite its name, Unterm Markt, which stretches to the west, is a street rather than a square. At no. 12a is the large Baroque mansion which was formerly the home of Johann Gottlieb Fichte, one of a host of renowned philosophers (Hegel, Schelling, the Schlegels and the Humboldts were others) based in Jena during the Romantic period. Now designated the **Romantikerhaus** (March–Nov Tues & Thurs–Sat 10am–1pm & 2–5pm, Wed 10am–1pm & 2–6pm; DM5), it's decked out with period furnishings, and also has a small art gallery.

The Stadtkirche and around

Behind the Markt rises the Gothic **Stadtkirche St Michael** (May–Sept Mon–Fri 10am–5.30pm, Sat 10am–2pm). Outside, the main features are the *Brautportal* (Bridal Doorway) on the south side, and the remarkable street passageway under the chancel, the best-known of the "Seven Wonders", the more so as there's not the slightest hint of its presence in the brightly painted hall interior, whose light and lofty feel is achieved by means of slender pillars which shoot directly up to the vault. The church's most celebrated treasure is the original bronze **tombstone of Luther** – with a full-length portrait cast from designs provided by Cranach – on the north wall. It was brought here for safekeeping because of the threat of desecration from the Imperial forces occupying Wittenberg, but was never returned.

From the Stadtkirche, Johanniskirche leads west along the northern side of Eichplatz; no. 12, the **Haus zur Rosen**, is a Baroque mansion whose cellars contain a renowned student club. At the end of the street is the **Johannistor**, the only gateway remaining from the city's fortifications; just to the north is the most impressive of the surviving towers, the battlemented **Pulverturm**.

The Botanischer Garten

Across Goetheallee is the **Botanischer Garten** (daily 9am–5/6pm; DM2), which was first created for growing medicinal herbs; it was then turned into a pleasure park before assuming its current function, which is primarily one of scientific research. The **Inspektorhaus** on the street side was designed by Goethe and was his favourite residence during his many sojourns in Jena, which he found to be a more amenable working environment than Weimar. Here he completed many of his literary projects; he also undertook a great deal of scientific research and produced the rather odd work he himself considered his masterpiece, *The Theory of Colours*. Part of the building is now designated the **Goethe Gedenkstätte** (mid-April to mid-Oct Wed–Fri 10am–noon & 1–4pm, Sat & Sun 11am–4pm; free) and contains memorabilia of his stays here.

On the eastern fringe of the garden is the domed **Zeiss-Planetarium**, which, when it was built in 1925, was the first such structure in the world. Now as then, it utilizes the technology of the Carl Zeiss works; there are several sessions each day, costing DM6–8, except Mondays. There are occasional showings in English for groups, so it would also be worth checking here or at the tourist office to see if any are scheduled.

The Carl-Zeiss-Stiftung

The factory buildings of the **Carl-Zeiss-Stiftung**, mostly dating from the first two decades of this century, stand immediately to the west of Eichplatz; among them is a tower which is claimed as Germany's earliest skyscraper. **Carl Zeiss** was a mechanic who established himself in Jena in 1846, and attempted to develop microscopes of improved optical performance. Having failed to make the desired progress within twenty years, he formed what proved to be a spectacularly fruitful partnership with the physicist **Ernst Abbe**. Their company soon became the world leader in the field of optics, and has maintained this position ever since, though its post-1945 history was sullied by the existence of rival companies in the two Germanys, which have recently come together again.

The **Optisches Museum** (Tues–Fri 10am–5pm, Sat 1–4.30pm, Sun 9.30am–1pm; DM8) on Carl-Zeiss-Platz is in two parts. In the first, there's a re-creation of the 1866 workshop of Zeiss and Abbe; the second contains a huge collection of historic spectacles, microscopes, telescopes and other instruments. Outside stands the imposing **memorial** to Abbe, a shrine-like construction by Henry van de Velde, inside which are four bronze reliefs of working-class life by Constantin Meunier.

Ernst-Haeckel-Haus and the Schiller-Gedenkstätte

A few minutes' walk to the south is Ernst-Haeckel-Strasse, where, at the corner with Berggasse, is the **Ernst-Haeckel-Haus** (guided tours Tues–Fri at 8.30am, 10am, 11.30am, 2pm & 3.30pm, Sat at 8.30am, 10am, 11am & 2pm; DM2). Haeckel, the leading Continental protagonist of Darwin's theories of evolution, dominated intellectual life at Jena around the turn of the century. He was also a talented artist, and his watercolour landscapes are the highlight of the displays in the villa where he lived. Just to the south, at Am Paradiesbahnhof, is the **Phyletisches Museum** (daily 9am–4pm; DM1), which Haeckel founded in 1907. It's a natural history collection with a difference, concentrating on how each species developed.

For a time Haeckel lived in the house at Schillergässchen 2, which is now the **Schiller-Gedenkstätte** (Tues–Fri 10am–noon & 1–4pm, Sat 11am–4pm; DM2) in honour of a previous occupant, the poet and dramatist **Friedrich Schiller**, after whom the University is now named. As professor of history, he lived in Jena for ten years, the longest he spent in any one place. The conditions in which he worked have been lovingly re-created; particularly evocative is the upstairs room in the garden pavilion, his favourite work place.

Eating, drinking and nightlife

Undoubtedly one of the prime attractions of Jena is its wide variety of places to eat, drink and socialize; indeed, within the former GDR it offers a better choice than almost anywhere outside the three largest cities.

Restaurants, bars and cafés

Alt Jena, Markt 10. Bavarian-style beer hall-cum-restaurant of *Augustinerbräu*.

Café Immergrün, Fürstengraben 30. Café serving vegetarian and wholefood meals.

Fiddler's Green, Sophienstr 10. The local Irish pub, often with live music. Daily 5pm–1am.

Fuchsturm, Turmgasse 26. Traditional *Gaststätte* in a tower on top of the Hausberg, a hill on the west side of the Saale. Closes 10pm during the week, midnight on Sat, 7pm on Sun.

Grüner Baum zur Nachtigall, Cospeda. Historic *Gaststätte* in the westerly village of Cospeda; take bus #16 to the end of Erfurter Strasse, then climb up to the village. Wed–Fri & Sun 4–11pm, Sat 11am–midnight.

Johannis, Johannisstr. 11. Trendy cocktail bar-cum-disco. Mon–Sat 9pm–4am.

Marktmühle, Saalstr. 23. Pub with a good selection of whiskies, plus Irish and English beers.

Rosenkeller, Johannisstr. 13. By far the most popular student club, set in cavernous cellars. Often features live music; even out of term, it has an animated atmosphere. Free admission with student ID, otherwise you'll have to pay DM2–4 to get in.

Saaltor, Saalstr. 8. Thuringia's first-ever Chinese restaurant; the food is reasonably authentic, and the set lunches are exceptional value.

Zum Roten Hirsch, Holzmarkt 10. Serves cheap but decent food, with a fast lunchtime service.

Dornburg

The one unmissable excursion from Jena is to **DORNBURG**, 15km down the Saale. From the Bahnhof, it's a steep twenty-minute climb up to the three palaces lining the terrace which has been laid out on a precipitous ninety-metre-high rock perched directly above the valley, of which there's a stunning view. Entry to the park is by the **Renaissanceschloss** (April–Oct Tues–Sun 9am–noon & 1–5pm; Nov & Jan–March Wed–Sun 9am–4pm; DM2) at the southern end, a grand country house with frilly gables and prominent stair turret. Built at the turn of the seventeenth century by a high official of the Duchy of Saxe-Weimar, this was one of Goethe's favourite retreats. The three rooms he used are furnished and decorated according to the tastes of Weimar Classicism, and contrast strongly with the splendours of the **Kaminzimmer**, the one chamber to have survived in something like its original form.

The **Rokokoschloss** (same times; DM4) in the middle of the terrace was commissioned as a summer retreat for the Weimar dukes; it's decorated with stuccowork, porcelain and period furniture, though the show is stolen by the magnificent garden. Beyond it is the **Altes Schloss**, by origin an Imperial fortress of the Romanesque period, though most of what you see today dates from the mid-fifteenth century, when it belonged to the Electors of Saxony. At the moment, it's used as an old folks' home, so you have to be satisfied with seeing it from the outside.

Rudolstadt and the Schwarza valley

Some 40km upstream from Jena is **RUDOLSTADT**, set in a picturesque stretch of wooded and hilly countryside, near the point where the Saale is joined by the **River Schwarza**, which cuts a particularly beautiful valley to the southwest. For three and a half centuries it was the capital of the county, later principality, of Schwarzburg-Rudolstadt, then, for the decade before its abolition after World War I, of the united province of Schwarzburg, and it still preserves both the authentic appearance and the languid atmosphere of a rural county town.

Schloss Heidecksburg

Perched high on a hill above Rudolstadt is the vast bulk of **Schloss Heidecksburg** (Tues–Sun 10am–6pm; DM6). The previous Renaissance Schloss was so badly damaged by fire in 1735 that Friedrich Anton, who also wanted to celebrate his earlier promotion from count to a fully fledged prince of the Holy Roman Empire, decided to commission an extravagant new building in the Dresden Rococo style. In lieu of the great Pöppelmann, who was too ill to accept, the plans were drawn up by the most talented Dresden architect of the next generation, Johann Christoph Knöffel, while the work was completed by another native of that city, Gottfried Heinrich Krohne.

The former Schlosskapelle in the west wing has been stripped of all religious connotations and now houses a collection of porcelain, much of it of local manufacture. This is the departure point for the **guided tours** round the ornate state apartments. Highlights are the galleried main **Festsaal**, with its huge ceiling fresco of Mount Olympus, the gorgeous **Spiegelkabinett**, with its striking inlaid floor and mock oriental touches, and the highly original **Bänderzimmer**, whose medallion portraits give a foretaste of the forthcoming Neoclassical style. At the end of the tour, you're free to wander round the art gallery at leisure; the star piece is Friedrich's brooding *Morning Mist in the Mountains*. The north wing of the Schloss, which still preserves the brightly painted double Renaissance portal with statues of the Virtues, now houses the **Schlossmuseum**. On the ground floor is a particularly outstanding arsenal, containing weapons from the fifteenth to the nineteenth centuries. The upstairs displays on local history are more prosaic, but include the *Schwarzenburger Willkomm*, a fine piece of late sixteenth-century goldsmithery.

The town

In the town itself, the main building is the **Stadtkirche St Andreas** (Mon–Fri 8am–4pm) at its eastern end, which in its own way evokes the local courtly tradition as vividly as the Schloss itself. By origin an unexceptional Gothic hall church, it was progressively beautified down the years to create the present sumptuous effect. From the Renaissance period are the fantastical portal with its fake door knockers and resplendent coat of arms, and the monumental marble and alabaster epitaph to the Schönefeld family on the end wall of the nave. A burst of creative activity after the Thirty Years' War brought a host of Baroque embellishments, including the eccentric sculptures of angels suspended from the vault, plus the princes' loft and burial chamber, the pulpit and the organ.

Rudolstadt's only other attraction is the **Volkskundemuseum Thüringer Bauernhäuser** (Wed–Sun 9am–noon & 1–4/5pm; DM2) in the Stadtpark to the rear of the Bahnhof. One of Germany's oldest open-air museums, this brings together two redundant farmhouses from the region, complete with their furnishings. The larger, standing alongside its original barn, dates back to the 1660s; the other, which is a few decades younger, houses a complete village apothecary's shop.

Practicalities

Rudolstadt's **tourist office** (Mon–Fri 9am–6pm, Sat 9am–noon; ☎03672/424543) is at Marktstr. 57; there's the usual booking service for **private rooms** (①–③). As yet, there are only a few **hotels**, including *Grey*, Schloss Str. 40 (☎03672/422755; ④); *Weiss*, Schwarzburgerstr. 31 (☎03672/353120; ④); *Zur Pilsener Schenke*, Mörlaer Str. 8 (☎03672/422343; ④); and *Thüringer Hof*, Bahnhofsgasse 3 (☎03672/412422; ③–⑤). Overlooking Rudolstadt, some 3km to the southeast, is the *Panoramahotel Marienturm*, Marienturm 1 (☎03672/43270; ④). The best **restaurants** are in the hotels, notably *Grey*, *Thüringer Hof* and *Marienturm*; otherwise try *Adler*, Markt 17. Rudolstadt's main **festival** is the *Tanz- und Folkfest* in July.

The Schwarza valley

The **Schwarza valley** is at its most imposing in the ten-kilometre canyon between Bad Blankenburg and Schwarzburg, the original seat of the princely dynasty. This stretch also has an exceptionally rich indigenous flora, including Turk's-cap lilies, columbines, akelei and liverworts. Although there's a road linking the two towns, you really need to follow the footpath, which is liberally endowed with belvederes, to appreciate the landscape to the full. The wonderfully scenic rail line, the *Schwarzatalbahn* from Rudolstadt, does not follow the Schwarza at this point, instead travelling along its tributary, the Rottenbach, to the town of the same name, a junction on the line to Arnstadt. From Schwarzburg, however, it hugs the bank of the Schwarza all the way along the remaining 20km of its route to the terminus at Katzhütte.

About halfway along this last stage is **OBSTFELDERSCHMIEDE**, the valley station of one of Germany's great transport curiosities, the *Oberweissbacher Bergbahn*. This is the world's steepest **cable rail line** on which normal carriages can run: it ascends 323m in the 1.4-kilometre-long track to **LICHTENHAIN**, a journey which takes eighteen minutes. At the summit, passengers transfer to a tiny diesel train, which takes a further eight minutes to cover the journey through meadows to **CURSDORF**, a pretty resort village of slate-faced houses.

Saalfeld

The old mining town of **SAALFELD**, 10km south of Rudolstadt, marks the transition between the middle and upper parts of the Saale valley; beyond lie the Schiefergebirge (Slate Mountains), now a popular recreational area of wooded hills and artificial lakes with watersports facilities. Saalfeld itself has reclaimed its former status as a tourist resort – apart from its value as an excursion base, it possesses one of Germany's most strangely beautiful natural wonders and has a historic centre which will look very striking once it has been tidied up.

The town

The Hauptbahnhof lies on the east bank of the Saale; Bahnhofstrasse leads over the two arms of the river to the **Saaltor**, one of three surviving medieval gateways. From here, there's a choice of routes. The right-hand fork, Puschkinstrasse, follows the former course of the fortifications past two more gates, beyond which lies the largest remaining stretch of the walls. Saalstrasse, to the left, leads straight to the Markt, but it's worth making a small detour to the south up Am Hügel to see the Renaissance **Schlösschen Kitzerstein** (now the music school), with its stylized, Dutch-looking gable, and the ruins of the **Hoher Schwarm**, a feudal castle of the type characteristic of the Saale.

At the southeastern corner of the Markt, returned once more to its original function, is the pristine white **Rathaus**. It's a quintessential building of the German Renaissance with its lingering Gothic feel, its protruding stairwell, its prominent gables and its two strongly contrasted oriel windows. Opposite is the partially Romanesque **Marktapotheke**, which dates back to the town's twelfth-century origins, though it's been altered repeatedly down the centuries.

Towering above the northern side of the Markt, and fronting Blankenburger Strasse, the pedestrianized main shopping street, is the Gothic **Johanniskirche**. Its exterior is richly decorated with late fourteenth-century sculptures of the Parler school; the west portal tympanum of *The Last Judgment* is particularly fine. The most startling feature of the hall interior is the bright red colouring of the vault – a symbolical reference to the blood of Christ. It reaches its climax in the elaborate network design in the chancel, which is painted with a recently uncovered vision of the path to Heaven.

Up Brudergasse is the former Franciscan monastery, now housing the **Thüringer Heimatmuseum** (Tues–Fri 8am–noon & 1–4pm, Sat & Sun 9.30am–noon & 1–5pm; DM2), a good-quality regional collection featuring displays on mining, folklore and arts and crafts, the highlight being examples of the local Gothic school of woodcarvers.

Between 1680 and 1735, Saalfeld was capital of the duchy of Saxe-Saalfeld, which was then assumed into Saxe-Coburg. The inevitable legacy of this period is a large Baroque **Schloss**, situated a few minutes' walk north of the confines of the Altstadt along Schloss Strasse, then right into Schlossberg. It's now used by the municipality as offices, but you can wander in and have a look round, particularly at the showpiece staircase; ask to see the ornate Schlosskapelle, which is regularly used for concerts in summer. Extravagantly decorated with stuccowork and trompe l'oeil frescoes, its unorthodox design features an irregular octagon within a rectangular ground plan.

The Feengrotten

The **Feengrotten** (Fairy Grottoes; guided tours Jan 20–Nov 20 daily 9am–5pm; Nov 21–Dec 19 Sat & Sun 10am–3pm; Dec 20–Jan 19 daily 10am–3pm; DM7), Saalfeld's chief attraction, lie about 1.5km southwest of the town centre, and can be reached by bus #13. Geologically formed 400 million years ago, the present astonishing appearance of this site is the result of a fluke caused by the interaction of natural and human forces. From the mid-sixteenth century, there was a mine here, which was exploited for its alum slate and vitriol. This functioned until the 1840s, when it was run down and closed as stocks moved towards exhaustion and demand from the chemical industry slumped. In 1910, waters rich in mineral resources were found pouring out of the abandoned mine; an investigation of its interior revealed that oxidization had turned the galleries into a natural drip-water cave, with stalactites and stalagmites formed from iron phosphate, and the walls cloaked in an astonishing kaleidoscope of colours. Artificial lighting further enhances the effect, seen at its best in the *Märchendom* (fairy-tale cathedral), also known as the *Gralburg* (Holy Grail castle) because of its uncanny resemblance to a Wagnerian theatre set.

Practicalities

Saalfeld's **tourist office** (Mon–Fri 9am–6pm, Sat 9am–noon; ☎03671/33950) is at Blankenburger Str. 4. There are plenty of **private rooms** (①–③) available.

In the town centre there are a couple of small, budget **hotels**, *Weltrich,* Saalstr. 44 (☎03671/2732; ③) and *Fisherman's Friend*, Sonneberger Str. 44 (☎03671/530612; ④). More upmarket options are *Tanne*, Saalstr. 37 (☎03671/8260; ⑤); *Am Hohen Schwarm,* Schwarmgasse 18 (☎03671/2884; ⑤); and *Anker*, Markt 25–26 (☎03671/5990; ⑤). A good-value alternative in the outskirts is *Asterra*, high above the town to the east at Sperberhölzchen 34 (☎03671/517440; ④). Its **restaurant** serves innovative local specialities. The best place to eat, however, has to be *Zum Güldenen Gans*, a historic cellar restaurant in the *Anker* hotel.

Gera

Thuringia's second largest city is **GERA**, which lies 45km east of Jena in the hilly countryside of the Weisse Elster valley. For nearly four centuries it was the capital of one of Germany's smallest states, the junior of the two Reuss principalities. However, it's totally different from the province's other courtly residences, being predominantly an industrial town, with a long tradition in the production of textiles and musical instruments. Indeed, during the Second Reich it was one of the richest places in Germany, and the multitude of industrialists' villas which can still be seen in its inner suburbs are a reminder of this heady epoch. Despite heavy wartime damage, it's a surprisingly agreeable place, generally recognized as being the one and only town in the GDR where postwar planning was carried out with sensitivity and good taste. The result is a lively city which offers a balanced mixture of old and new.

The city

Gera's compact historical centre lies on a gentle incline about fifteen minutes' walk southeast of the Hauptbahnhof. Its exemplary preservation is marred only by the loss of the huge Baroque palace of the Reuss princes which stood above. This was damaged by bombs in the last days of the war and subsequently razed by the Communists, though may yet make a phoenix-like return.

The Altstadt

At the heart of the Altstadt is the **Markt**, whose good looks compensate for its modest dimensions. In the centre burbles the **Simsonbrunnen**, showing the Old Testament hero Samson wrestling with the lion; this is a modern replica of the water-worn late seventeenth-century original. The whitewashed Renaissance **Rathaus**, the town's finest building, stands proudly to the northeastern corner. Designed by Nicol Gromann, the Saxon court architect, it boasts a dignified off-centre octagonal tower and a riotously decorative portal with busts, grotesque figures, inscriptions and brightly painted coats of arms. A similar style can be seen on the oriel of the **Stadt-Apotheke** at the opposite end of the square; apart from heraldic motifs, its carvings show the Apostles and the Four Seasons. Kleine Kirchstrasse leads to a vast open square, Zentraler Platz, whose handsome red Baroque palace standing in splendid isolation was once the town orphanage. Nowadays it houses the local history displays of the **Stadtmuseum** (10am–5pm, closed Fri; DM4).

Uphill from the Markt, Grosse Kirchstrasse – which is lined with a number of fine mansions, now mostly stores – leads to the **Salvatorkirche**, a large Baroque church with Jugendstil furnishings perched at the top of a monumental stairway. On its northern side stands the **Schreiberhaus**, the late seventeenth-century mansion of a rich merchant. It is now the **Museum für Naturkunde** (Tues–Sun 10am–5pm; DM4), with displays on the natural history and geology of the Gera region, including the skeleton of a prehistoric rhinoceros. The interior itself is at least as good a reason for a visit, however. At the back of the house is the entrance to the town's most unusual attraction, the **Geraer Höhle** (guided tours Mon–Fri at 11am & 3pm, Sat at 2pm & 3pm, Sun at 10am, 11am, 2pm & 3pm; DM4), a network of caverns and tunnels used in the seventeenth and eighteenth centuries as workshops, and as a place where home-brewed beer could mature in cool conditions.

The western quarters

To the rear of the Hauptbahnhof is the **Bühnen der Stadt**, the Jugendstil municipal theatre. It overlooks the Küchengarten, a pleasant park at whose far end stands the Rococo **Orangerie** (Tues 1–8pm, Wed–Fri 10am–5pm, Sat & Sun 10am–6pm; DM2). Inside is a collection of paintings and sculptures from the Middle Ages to the present day. On Mohrenplatz, just to the west over the Weisse Elster, is the **Otto-Dix-Haus** (Tues–Fri 10am–5pm, Sat & Sun 10am–6pm; DM4 or DM6 for a combined ticket that includes the Orangerie), birthplace of one of the most highly regarded German artists of the present century, the leading light of the *Neue Sachlichkeit* movement. In addition to a huge number of drawings and graphics, displayed in rotation, there are a couple of dozen canvases, the pick of which is *St Christopher*, an allegorical work inspired by the emigration from Germany under the Nazis. Apart from the Markt, this is the finest square in Gera, dominated by the Romanesque-Gothic **Marienkirche**.

Schlossbergstrasse leads up from here to the site of **Schloss Osterstein**, now occupied by a terrace café-restaurant The restored Romanesque **tower** survives from the original castle, and on the afternoons of summer weekends and holidays it may be ascended (DM1) for a view over the town.

Practicalities

Gera's **tourist office** (Mon–Fri 8am–8pm, Sat 8am–4pm; ☎0365/619301) is a short walk from the Hauptbahnhof at Ernst-Tolle-Str. 14. There is a good selection of **hotels** in Gera. At the budget end of the scale, there's *Burgkeller*, Schuhgasse 2 (☎0365/838 1691; ④), while the best mid-range establishment is *An der Elster*, Südstr. 12 (☎0365/710 6161; ⑥). The most characterful of the upmarket places are *Galerie*, Leibnizstr. 21 (☎0365/20150; ⑦), in the western suburb of Untermhaus, which – as its name implies – incorporates an art gallery, and the centrally located and beautifully furnished *Schillerhöhe*, Schillerstr. 9 (☎0365/839880; ⑦).

The best **restaurant** for traditional Thuringian dishes is *Ritterhof*, Rittergasse 6, while *Paulaner Keller*, Clara-Zetkin-Str. 14, represents the burgeoning Bavarian influence. An eclectic range of ethnic eateries includes the Bulgarian *Trajika*, Altenburger Str. 16, and the Tunisian *El Kantaoui*, Leipziger Str. 3, while *Royal*, Sorge 19, offers French as well as local cuisine.

The main **theatre** venue is the Jugendstil *Bühnen der Stadt* (☎0365/827 9105) on Küchengartenallee to the rear of the Hauptbahnhof. There's also a *Puppentheater* on Gustav-Henning-Platz (☎0365/24707), and a satirical cabaret, *Fettnäppchen*, in the cellars of the Rathaus (☎0365/23131).

Altenburg

ALTENBURG, 40km northeast of Gera, dubs itself *Skatstadt* in honour of the fact that *skat*, Germany's most popular card game, has both its main production centre and governing headquarters here. Its name is relatively little-known abroad, though it's one of the most worthwhile of Thuringia's old courtly towns. Lying in the easternmost part of the Land, close to the borders with both Saxony and Saxony-Anhalt, Altenburg makes an excellent base for forays into three provinces; alternatively, it can be used as a stopover if travelling on the main rail route south from Leipzig.

The town

Although the town centre of Altenburg is pleasant enough, it's totally overshadowed by the two main attractions – the Schloss which overlooks it from the north, and the unexpectedly rich Lindenau-Museum further to the northeast.

The Lindenau-Museum

From the Hauptbahnhof at the northern end of town, the rusticated neo-Renaissance *palazzo* containing the **Lindenau-Museum** (Tues–Sun 10am–6pm; DM3) can be seen facing you from the Schlosspark at the far end of Wettinerstrasse. Its cosmopolitan displays, originating in the private collections of Bernhard von Lindenau, a nineteenth-century statesman and Italophile, are a world away from those normally found in small German towns. On the ground floor, an important group of Greek and Roman vases are kept in one wing, changing selections of modern art in the other. Upstairs, the old masters department includes choice examples of Gothic and Renaissance paintings from Florence and Siena. Small panels from dispersed polyptychs predominate – look out for a rare pair by **Masaccio** of *The Agony in the Garden* and *St Jerome in the Desert*, and for **Fra Angelico's** exquisite *Three Dominican Monks* and *St Francis' Trial by Fire*. Of the larger works, the star pieces are *Catherina Sforza as St Catherine* by **Botticelli**, *St Helena* and the *Blessed Filippo Benizzi* by **Perugino**, and a tondo of *The Holy Family* by **Beccafumi**.

The Schloss

The vast hilltop **Schloss** complex, which features just about every European architectural style, has to be entered from the southern end of its park. Despite its long spell as a ducal residence, it still preserves part of its medieval defences, among which the round tower known as the **Flasche**, built into the northern walls, dates back as far as the eleventh century. Nearby is a freestanding tower of uncertain vintage, the **Hausmannsturm** (Tues–Sun 10am–4pm; DM1), which can be ascended for a fine view over the Schloss and the town. Across the courtyard, in the centre of which is a Mannerist fountain to Neptune, lies the main palace block, now designated the **Schloss- und Spielkarten Museum** (Tues–Sun 9am–5pm; DM5). Predictably, the main emphasis is on the history of playing cards throughout the last five centuries, and in particular of *skat*. Other highlights are a display of medieval weapons, and Bernhard von Lindenau's collections of oriental and Meissen porcelain.

From the museum, **guided tours** are run round the state apartments of the Schloss, which are slowly being restored. They're a surprising mixture: the **Goldsaal** is elegantly Baroque, while the main **Festsaal** is a nineteenth-century Historicist extravaganza in red, white and gold, with frothy ceiling frescoes by the Munich Romantic artist Karl Mossdorf depicting stories from Apuleius' *The Golden Ass*. It's occasionally used for concerts, as is the more intimate **Bachsaal**, an early twentieth-century pastiche of its fire-destroyed Renaissance predecessor.

Included in the tour is a visit to the sumptuous **Schlosskirche**. This is otherwise only open for services and for the summer weekend recitals on the eighteenth-century **organ**. The church itself is predominantly late Gothic, with a magnificent star vault. However, the general appearance owes much to a mid-seventeenth-century interior transformation, which added the ducal loft at the west end, the galleries with their statues of saints and Old Testament figures, and the theatrical high altar.

The rest of the town

The townscape south of the Schloss is dominated by the **Rote Spitze** (Red Points), the two brick towers of a twelfth-century Augustinian collegiate church. To the west, across the busy Wallstrasse, lies the old merchant quarter, centred on two squares. Much the larger of these, the Weibermarkt, has become the modern commercial heart of town. It's overlooked by the handsome Renaissance **Rathaus**, with its dignified portal and showpiece corner oriel. Further north is the Alter Markt, with the Baroque **Seckendorff'sche Palais** and a turn-of-the-century fountain that honours the game of *skat*. Just off the square is the main parish church, the **Bartholmäikirche** (Mon, Fri & Sat 10am–4pm, Tues & Thurs 10am–5pm), whose kernel is Gothic, but whose most notable features are the tapering octagonal Renaissance tower and the graceful little Romanesque crypt.

Practicalities

Altenburg's **tourist office** (Mon 9am–3pm, Tues, Wed & Fri 9am–5pm, Thurs 9am–6pm, Sat 9am–1pm; ☎03447/19433 or 594174) is at Moritzstr. 21, with the entrance on Kornmarkt. You can ask here for **private rooms** (②–③), which are in plentiful supply, and small **pensions** (②–④). A few rooms are also available at the local Irish pub, *Dubliner*, Rosa-Luxemburg-Str. 2 (☎03447/500500; ③).

The town has a good cross-section of **hotels**; in the budget category there are *Europäischer Hof*, Wettinerstr. 21 (☎03447/56740, fax 567488; ③); *Treppengasse*, Treppengasse 5 (☎03447/313549, fax 313559; ④); and *Wettiner Hof*, Johann-Sebastian-Bach-Str. 11 (☎03447/313532, fax 504936; ④). More upmarket choices are *Am Rossplan*, Rossplan 8 (☎03447/56610, fax 566161; 5) and *Parkhotel*, August-Bebel-Str. 16–17 (☎03447/5830, fax 583444; ⑤).

All except the last of the hotels have a **restaurant**; apart from these, the best place to eat is the *Ratskeller* in the Rathaus, Markt 1. Altenburg manages to maintain an ambitious **cultural** programme centred on the *Landestheater*, Theaterplatz 19 (☎03447/585161) below the Schloss.

travel details

Trains

Erfurt to: Arnstadt (frequent; 25min); Eisenach (frequent; 1hr); Gera (11 daily; 2hr); Gotha (frequent; 30min); Jena (frequent; 45min); Meiningen (14 daily; 2hr 30min); Mühlhausen (11 daily; 1hr); Nordhausen (10 daily; 1hr 30min); Sondershausen (10 daily; 1hr 30min/2hr); Suhl (14 daily; 2hr); Weimar (frequent; 15min).

Gera to: Saalfeld (frequent; 1hr 15min/2hr).

Gotha to: Friedrichroda (frequent; 35min); Mühlhausen (frequent; 1hr).

Jena to: Gera (frequent; 1hr); Rudolstadt (frequent; 1hr); Saalfeld (frequent; 1hr 20min); Weimar (frequent; 30min).

CHAPTER TWELVE

SAXONY

Saxony (*Sachsen*) is the most enigmatic of Germany's Länder. Its identity appears very secure and well defined, yet it has only the most nebulous connection with the tribes and territories after which it's named. Seemingly so archetypally German, it occupies land which originally belonged to the Slavs, while much of its scenery has more in common with the neighbouring Czech Republic than anywhere in Germany, and many of its towns bear the distinctive central European hallmark of a diversity of cultural influences. Other than Berlin, all three of the ex-GDR's largest cities are here, yet the Land is politically by far the most right-wing in all of Germany. Whereas at least two of the major cities should slot into the new economic framework without too much disruption, other parts of Saxony seem to belong to a bygone age, trying to maintain the same industries that have supported them for centuries. The list of contradictions seems endless.

Like Thuringia, Saxony's history is closely tied to that of the **Wettin** family, whose original early medieval power base was as **Margraves of Meissen**, charged with securing the Holy Roman Empire's eastern frontier and pushing it deeper into Slav territory to the east and south. The name of "Saxony" only came to be associated with the territory when it became the heartland of the **Albertine** line of the dynasty, which gained the prized Electorate in the Holy Roman Empire in 1547 and thereafter built up a strong, centralized state. They also gained the crown of Poland on three separate occasions, but failed to make it a hereditary possession. Compensation came in 1806, when Napoleon proclaimed Saxony a **kingdom** in its own right; a heavy price had to be paid for this nine years later, when Prussia made huge territorial annexations, although the royal status was retained until 1918.

Dresden, the capital since the foundation of the Albertine line in 1485, is nowadays chiefly associated with the terrible Anglo-American bomb raid of 1945 which obliterated one of Europe's greatest artistic and cultural centres. Its remarkable comeback has gathered pace since the *Wende*, the ultimate aim being to return it to its former appearance. The similarly sized city of **Leipzig** is basking in the glory of having provided the leadership of the revolution which overthrew totalitarian rule. **Chemnitz**, wallowing in industrial filth, is a place only the most dedicated of travellers will include on their itinerary, but is of special interest for the remarkable insights it offers into the preoccupations of the GDR period. The one other place large enough to be regarded as a city is **Zwickau**, whose attraction of a well-preserved centre is overshadowed by a reputation as home of the infamous *Trabi* car.

Of the smaller towns, the undoubted star is **Meissen**, the original political heart of the region, and the place where the first European porcelain was manufactured. **Freiberg** and **Annaberg-Buchholz** are the most notable of the mining towns which reached the height of their prosperity in the sixteenth century, a period commemorated in the dazzlingly rich interiors of their churches. **Bautzen** is the main cultural centre of the Sorbs, the Slav people who have remained in the area throughout a millennium of German rule, while **Görlitz** is another place with a richly diverse historical tradition. **Torgau** is best known to English-speaking people for its wartime connections, though it's the little town of **Colditz** which brings back the most vivid memories of that era. **Saxon Switzerland**,

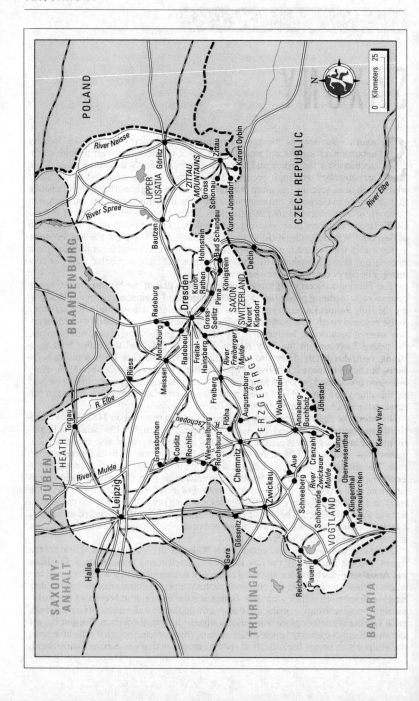

the rocky and wooded countryside round the Elbe south of Dresden, is deservedly the best-known scenic part of the Land, though the raw mountain landscapes around **Zittau** and in the **Erzgebirge** range have their attractions, as does the somewhat gentler scenery of the **Vogtland** further west.

Travel throughout the area presents few problems; a comprehensive rail network includes numerous narrow-gauge lines, some of which have only recently been put back into operation. For **accommodation**, the multitude of private houses recently opened up for tourism often offer a valuable lifeline as several towns are noticeably short of hotels.

WESTERN SAXONY

The northwestern part of Saxony is a flat plain, with nothing of interest other than the vibrant city of **Leipzig**. Bounding it on the east is a beautiful but little-known valley, that of the **Zwickauer Mulde**, which is dotted with a number of enticing little towns, among them **Colditz**, home of the famous prisoner-of-war camp. Upstream, **Zwickau** itself, along with the large industrial city of **Chemnitz** and the old mining town of **Freiberg** to the east, stands in the foothills of the **Erzgebirge**, a windswept highland region whose mineral wealth was responsible for such former boom towns as **Schneeberg** and **Annaberg**. To the extreme southwest lies the plateau of the **Vogtland**, an area of spa resorts and craft industries centred on the lace-making town of **Plauen**.

Leipzig

Pictures from **LEIPZIG** filled the world's television screens in the autumn of 1989, as the GDR's second city assumed leadership of the *Wende*, the peaceful revolution that toppled the Communist dictatorship and ushered in the elections which led to national unification a year later. Having traditionally been one of Germany's most dynamic cities, it was perhaps inevitable that Leipzig was the place where the frustration of GDR citizens about their postwar lot reached breaking point. Its **trade fairs** (the only ones in Europe with an uninterrupted tradition dating back to the Middle Ages) remained of importance during the Communist interregnum: for all the difficulties the authorities had in squaring these with their ideology, the lure of promoting and developing the GDR as the economic success story of Eastern Europe, with Leipzig as its commercial heart, proved too difficult to resist. This did mean, however, that the city never suffered the sense of isolation from outside influences experienced by so many places behind the Iron Curtain.

The **telephone code** for Leipzig is ☎0341

In Goethe's *Faust*, Leipzig is described as "Little Paris". That was always an exaggeration – it has never been considered one of Germany's more visually appealing cities – and seems even less so now. Not only did Leipzig suffer horrendous wartime damage; the Communist years have bequeathed a legacy of eyesores and pollution, added to an inappropriate economic infrastructure which will now be even more dependent on trade fair business for a secure future. Nonetheless, the general appearance of the city has improved enormously since the *Wende*, and it remains an important cultural centre, particularly in the field of **music**, where the great tradition of Bach, Mendelssohn, Schumann and Wagner is jealously maintained.

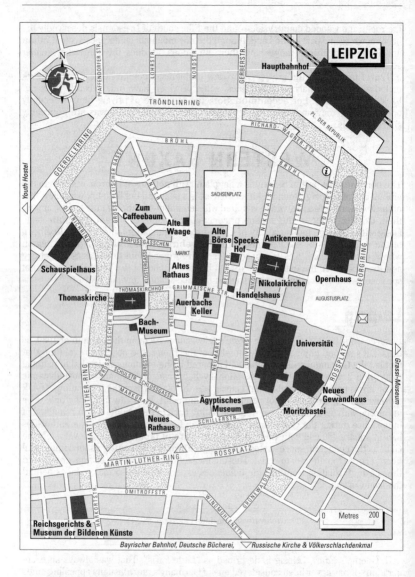

Bayerischer Bahnhof, Deutsche Bücherei, ▽ *Russische Kirche & Völkerschlachdenkmal*

Arrival, information and accommodation

Leipzig's **airport** is the most important in the former GDR, and is linked to the Hauptbahnhof by buses which run approximately every thirty minutes. The vast **Hauptbahnhof** is at the northeastern end of the Ring (ring road), which encircles the Altstadt; a few local services, particularly from Zwickau, use the **Bayerischer Bahnhof**, which is a few minutes' walk south of the Ring.

ACCOMMODATION PRICE CODES

All the pensions and hotels in this book have been graded according to the following price categories. The prices quoted are for the cheapest available double room, although many of the budget places will also have more expensive rooms. Youth hostels are graded under separate categories. See p.34 for more details.

① less than DM50	④ DM81–100	⑦ DM151–200
② DM51–65	⑤ DM101–125	⑧ DM201–250
③ DM66–80	⑥ DM126–150	⑨ more than DM250

Leipzig's main **tourist office** is at Richard-Wagner-Str. 1 (Mon–Fri 9am–7pm, Sat & Sun 9.30am–2pm; ☎710 4260). There's also a branch at the airport (Mon–Fri 7am–9pm, Sat & Sun 9am–6pm; ☎224 1156). It's well worth investing in the **Leipzig Card** (DM9.90 for a day, DM21 for 3 days), which covers all public transport in the city, and gives reduced entry prices to the museums.

Accommodation

Leipzig is exceptionally well endowed with **hotels** geared to expense-account travellers and priced accordingly; these are scattered all over the city, with only a minority in the centre. There's also a much smaller provision of accommodation in small hotels and **pensions**, which are likewise spread over the entire urban area. The tourist office can book **private rooms** (③–⑤) for a DM10 fee; note that the trade fair business means that prices for most of these are higher than might be expected for the facilities on offer.

Alternative budget options include the **youth hostels** at Käthe-Kollwitz-Str. 64–66 (☎470530; ▣), west of the centre (take tram #1, #2 or #8), and at Gustav-Esche-Str. 4 (☎461 1114; ▣), way to the northwest (reached by trams #10 or #28). Note that both of these are slated for closure in the near future, though at least one replacement is planned. Near the latter hostel is the **campsite** (☎465 1600), which also has bungalows to rent – by far the cheapest option if you're travelling in a group.

HOTELS AND PENSIONS

Am Zoo, Pfaffendorfer Str. 23 (☎960 2432, fax 960 2432). Small pension situated a few minutes' walk north of the Ring. ⑥

Continental, Georgiring 13 (☎12940, fax 129 4999). The most reasonably priced of the cluster of high-rise hotels around the Hauptbahnhof. ⑥

De Saxe, Gohliser Str. 25 (☎59380, fax 593 8299). Well-regarded hotel, part of the *Akzent* chain, located just north of the Zoo; take tram #6 to Menckestrasse. It has a gourmet restaurant and a somewhat less expensive bistro. ⑦

Deutscher Hof, Waldstr. 31 (☎71100, fax 711 0222). Fine old hotel just to the southwest of the Ring. There are two restaurants, both open evenings only, the smaller a cosy cellar, the larger with Jugendstil decor. ⑦

Fürstenhof, Tröndlinring 8 (☎1400, fax 140 3700). Leipzig's top address is a late eighteenth-century patrician palace transformed internally when it became a hotel a century later. Long dormant, it has recently been restored at enormous expense by the *Kempinski* chain, with the addition of modern facilities, including a fitness centre. There's also a top-notch restaurant. ⑨

Haus Ingeborg, Nordstr. 58 (☎960 3143, fax 564 9871). Small budget hotel just north of the Ring, and about a 10min walk west of the Hauptbahnhof. ④

Lindenau, Georg-Schwarz-Str. 33, Lindenau (☎448 0310, fax 448 0300). Capacious hotel named after the western suburb – reached by S-Bahn or by tram #5, #13 or #15 – where it is located. The facilities include a sauna and solarium, as well as a restaurant (evenings only). ⑦

Merseburger Hof, Merseburger Str. 107, Lindenau. Located in the same suburb as the above, this is slightly less luxurious, but also has a fitness centre, as well as a restaurant with beer garden. ⑥

Parkhotel SeaSide, Richard-Wagner-Str. 7 (☎98520, fax 985 2750). Art Deco hotel directly facing the Hauptbahnhof, recently refurbished to a very high standard. Its main restaurant, *Orient Express*, is open evenings only, though the less expensive *Nikolai-Bistro* is also open for lunch. ⑨

prima, Dresdner Str. 82 (☎688 3481). A medium-sized pension directly on the main eastbound road, about 2km from the Ring; take tram #2, #4, #6 or #20 to Reudnitz Strassenbahnhof. ④

Ratskeller Plagwitz, Weissenfelser Str. 10, Plagwitz (☎479 6035, fax 479 6055). Fine traditional hotel and restaurant in an eastern suburb which can be reached by S-Bahn or tram #2. ⑦

Weisses Ross, Ross Str. 20 (☎960 5951). Small budget hotel just south of the Ring run in conjunction with a traditional *Gaststätte* which is open weekdays only. ④

The city

Leipzig is easy to get to grips with: the historic buildings lie mostly within the Altstadt, whose boundaries are defined by the Ring, with the main museums lying just outside. The only sights beyond immediate walking distance are conveniently grouped near to each other southwest of the centre.

The Hauptbahnhof and the Ring

The **Hauptbahnhof** is a masterpiece of early twentieth-century rail architecture and deserves to be considered one of the main sights of Leipzig. It's the largest dead-end passenger station in the world and covers a site formerly occupied by four small terminals. A curiosity is that it has two entrance halls and two levels, as until centralization was introduced under the Third Reich, the Prussian and Saxon authorities each ran their own half of the station as a separate concern.

The **Ring**, now busy with a far heavier volume of traffic than it had in GDR days, is familiar from news footage as the place where the famous Monday demonstrations against totalitarian abuses of power took place. It's therefore particularly appropriate that the **Runde Ecke** (Wed–Sun 2–6pm; free), the former *Stasi* headquarters building at Dittrichring 24, now contains a permanent exhibition on the organization entitled *Macht und Banalität* (Power and Banality). As well as documentary material, you can see examples of the different types of surveillance equipment used, as well as massive piles of confiscated mail.

The Nikolaikirche and the Alte Nikolaischule

Following Nikolaistrasse (the street immediately facing the Hauptbahnhof's entrance) due southwards brings you to the **Nikolaikirche**, one of the two main civic churches, and one which has gained an honoured place in the national consciousness. Not only was it the local key rallying point during the *Wende*, but the Monday meetings and prayers which had been held there since 1982 entitle it to be considered as the true fountainhead of the revolution. Although a sombre medieval structure from outside, the church's interior is a real eye-opener, thanks to an audacious late eighteenth-century transformation which flirts between Rococo and Neoclassical. The double-galleried nave is particularly striking: its coffered vault is supported by fluted Corinthian columns with capitals sprouting out in the shape of palm trees.

Opposite the church is its former school, the **Alte Nikolaischule**. It's now used by the University, with one floor given over to the **Antikenmuseum** (Tues–Thurs, Sat & Sun 10am–5pm; DM2), an important collection of Classical antiquities only recently returned to public view after several decades of closure. The main highlights are a fine array of Attic vases and the so-called *Leipzig Alexander*, a marble head of Alexander the Great carved in Roman-occupied Egypt around 150 BC.

The Altes Rathaus

A couple of blocks to the west of the Nikolaikirche is the open space of the Markt, whose eastern side is entirely occupied by the city's finest building, the **Altes Rathaus**

(Tues–Fri 10am–6pm, Sat & Sun 10am–4pm; DM4). Designed by **Hieronymous Lotter**, it's in the grandest German Renaissance style, with elaborate gables, an assymmetrical clock tower – and the longest inscription to be found on any building in the world. The ground floor retains its traditional function as a covered walkway with shops; the upper storeys, long abandoned as the town hall, now house the local history museum. However, the main reason for going in is to see the 53-metre-long **Festsaal** on the first floor, with its ornate chimneypieces and haughty full-length portraits of the local mayors and Saxon Electors. Upstairs, there's a room of memorabilia of **Felix Mendelssohn-Bartholdy**, who spent the last twelve years of his life in the city. In addition to his compositional activities, he directed the *Gewandhausorchester*, founded the Conservatory, and was responsible for reviving the long-forgotten music of his great predecessor J.S. Bach.

The historic trade fair buildings
On the north side of the square is another handsome public building by Lotter, the old weigh house or **Alte Waage**; only its sundial-crowned facade was restored following its destruction in the war. A survivor of the Baroque period is **Barthels Hof**, just off the west side of the square. This is the only extant example of the courtyards where trading used to take place – a distinctive feature is that it also opens out onto Kleine Fischergasse behind, in order that carriages bearing goods for sale did not have to turn. As the trade fair grew in the early years of this century, many historic buildings nearby were demolished to make way for the functional modern structures which now predominate, a fate the Altes Rathaus escaped through the casting vote of the mayor. Another survivor is the **Alte Börse** (Old Exchange), the joyous little Baroque building immediately to its rear.

The historic shopping malls and taverns
Another distinctive legacy of Leipzig's commercial tradition is the presence of a number of covered shopping malls, of which the largest is the partially modernized **Specks Hof**, entered from Reichsstrasse, a block to the east of the Markt. A better-preserved example is the **Mädler-Passage** at the head of Grimmaische Strasse, just off the Markt's southeastern corner. Tucked away underneath its boutiques is **Auerbachs Keller**, a sixteenth-century tavern which is the setting for the famous scene in Goethe's *Faust* when Mephistopheles tricked the local topers with optical illusions before vanishing into the air on a barrel. This, along with other scenes from the play, is depicted in the murals now adorning the cellar.

Following Barfussgässchen off the western side of the Markt brings you to Kleine Fleischergasse and Leipzig's other celebrated refreshment house, the Baroque **Zum Kaffeebaum**. Leipzig was one of the main centres of the craze for coffee which followed the Turkish invasion of central Europe in the late seventeenth century, a theme satirized by Bach in the *Coffee Cantata*. The café has been closed off and on for several years, but should be re-opening – you can at least see the carving above the doorway, which shows a Turk reclining under a coffee tree, proffering a cup of the beverage to a small cherub.

The Thomaskirche and the Bachmuseum
Klostergasse leads southwards from here to the **Thomaskirche**, the senior of the two big civic churches, and the place where **Johann Sebastian Bach** (see also p.896) served as *Kantor* for the last 27 years of his life, composing a vast body of choral works for use in its services. Originally part of an Augustinian monastery, the church is predominantly Gothic but has been repeatedly altered down the centuries. The main features of the interior are the galleries added by Hieronymous Lotter, in line with the

Protestant emphasis on preaching; the Gothic winged altarpiece; the Renaissance font; and the many elaborate epitaphs. However, the most remarkable feature of the church is its musical tradition, and its **choir**, the *Thomanerchor*, which Bach once directed, can usually be heard on Fridays at 6pm, Saturdays at 3pm and at the Sunday service at 9.30am.

Outside the church is a **monument to Bach**. Across from it, at Thomaskirchhof 16, the **Bosehaus** contains a concert hall, a satirical cabaret and the **Bachmuseum** (daily 10am–5pm; DM4), which has an extensive show of mementos of the great composer, along with a collection of musical instruments of his time.

Augustusplatz and the University quarter

East of the Markt is a vast square, returned to its old name of Augustusplatz, which serves as the main focus of both academic and musical life in the city. On its northern side is the **Opernhaus**, whose sombre pseudo-Neoclassical form recalls the architecture of the Third Reich, though it was actually built under Communism. Very different is the **Neues Gewandhaus** opposite, an avant-garde building inaugurated in 1981 as the new home of the famous *Gewandhausorchester*, the oldest and largest orchestra in the world – and still one of the best, the tradition of Felix Mendelssohn, Arthur Nikisch, Wilhelm Furtwängler and Bruno Walter having been maintained by Kurt Masur for the quarter century prior to his retirement in 1997.

Rising high up from the centre of the square is the 34-storey **Universitätshochhaus**, begun in 1968 as a prestige project of the then dictator of the GDR, Walter Ulbricht, a native of Leipzig. In order to build this new home for the University, which was founded back in 1409, a number of historic buildings were demolished, including the Universitätskirche. Only a Schinkel-designed gateway on the west side remains, looking hopelessly forlorn against the skyscraper, which is shaped to resemble an open book. By far the best thing about the latter is the view from the top, which can only be reached by lift, though this is not always accessible to the general public. The **Moritzbastei** to the rear, another Lotter creation, is the only surviving part of the fortifications, and has found a new lease of life as the focal point of the student social scene.

To the west, at Schillerstr. 6, the **Ägyptisches Museum** (Tues–Sat 1–5pm, Sun 10am–1pm; DM3) has a surprisingly good collection of Egyptian antiquities from nineteenth-century excavations by University archeologists. At the end of Schillerstrasse is Burgplatz, on which stands the **Neues Rathaus**, a turn-of-the-century monstrosity, which uses elements of just about every European architectural style, even incorporating a "Bridge of Sighs" to link the main building to its extension.

The Reichsgerichts and the Museum der Bildenen Künste

South across the Ring is Georgi-Dimitroff-Platz and the supreme court of prewar Germany, the **Reichsgerichts**, a bulky neo-Renaissance palace. The opulent main courtroom and its ancillary chambers on the first floor were the setting for the famous trial on the Reichstag fire – the event which served as a pretext for the Nazis' clampdown on the activities of their political opponents. During the trial, one of those accused of starting the fire, Georgi Dimitroff, the Bulgarian head of the Communist International, completely outwitted Hermann Göring, the chief prosecutor. This was celebrated with relish in GDR days, when the building served as a museum. However, preparations are well under way to return to judicial use, which means it will probably not be readily accessible again.

This development means that the **Museum der Bildenen Künste** (Tues & Thurs–Sun 9am–5pm, Wed 1–9.30pm; DM5), an eclectic collection of paintings from the Middle Ages to the present century, is being forced to vacate the premises. Work has not yet begun on its new custom-built home on Sachsenplatz, but from 1998 at least part of the collection should be temporarily on view in the Handelskammer on Grimmaische Strasse. The museum has some fine early German works, notably a *Man of Sorrows* by Hamburg's **Master Francke** and an erotic allegory, *The Magic of Love*, by an unknown Lower Rhenish painter. There are also a few outstanding Netherlandish panels of the same period, among which *The Visitation* by **Rogier van der Weyden** and *The Institution of the Rosary*, attributed to the very rare **Geertgen tot Sint Jans**, stand out. German painting of the Renaissance is dominated by several examples of **Cranach**, among which *Nymph at the Well* is outstanding, and **Baldung**, whose *Seven Ages of Woman* is one of his most inspired compositions. Highlights of a broad range of seventeenth-century works from across Europe are *The Mulatto* by **Hals**, *The Miracle of St Walburga* by **Rubens** and *The Annunciation* by **Murillo**. From a strong display of Romantic painting, *The Steps of Life* by **Friedrich**, the marvellously comic *The Knight Kuno von Falkenstein* by **Moritz von Schwind**, and the celebrated *Isle of the Dead* by **Böcklin** stand out. Finally, there are a large number of works by the versatile Leipzig artist **Max Klinger**, who was equally proficient at painting, engraving and sculpture, and who is increasingly coming to be seen as a figure of some stature.

The Grassi-Museum

From Augustusplatz, crossing the Ring and following Grimmaisch Steinweg eastwards brings you to Johannisplatz and the **Grassi-Museum**, a vast Bauhaus complex. It still has not recovered fully from extensive war damage, though two of the three separate museums (DM10 combined ticket) contained within are reasonably complete. The **Musikinstrumentenmuseum** (Tues–Sat 10am–5pm, Sun 10am–1pm; DM5), entered from Täubchenweg to the north, houses the University's collection of historical musical instruments; the keyboards are particularly notable, and sometimes used for recitals. On the left side of the interior courtyard is the **Museum für Völkerkunde** (Tues–Fri 10am–5.30pm, Sat & Sun 10am–4pm; DM5), whose ethnology displays range across Russia and the other states of the former Soviet Union, Africa (including a distinguished group of sculptures from Benin), China, India, Australia and the South Seas.

Across from it is the **Museum für Kunsthandwerk** (Tues & Thurs–Sun 10am–6pm, Wed 10am–8pm; DM4). This is one of Europe's finest collections of decorative arts, though only a small part is on view. The exhibits range from a Carolingian ivory of St Michael to the products of the Bauhaus. Particular highlights are several Renaissance goldsmiths' pieces from the municipal treasure, the *Leipziger Ratsschatz*; the ivory, bronze, copper and wood *Triumph of the Cross* by the Dresden Baroque sculptor Balthasar Permoser; the gem cabinet from the Stadtbibliothek; and a group of sketches for Meissen chinoiserie.

South of the centre

Rail buffs should make the trek south of the Altstadt to see the **Bayerischer Bahnhof**, the oldest functioning train station in Europe. The grand Neoclassical structure erected in the 1840s was virtually flattened during World War II, and only the facade has been restored. Just a handful of services still run from here, suggesting it's kept open principally for the sake of preserving its record.

A few other worthwhile sights lie south of here on the route of tram #21; they can also be reached by tram #15 from elsewhere. On Deutscher Platz is the **Deutsche Bücherei**, the largest German-language library in the world. Part of it is given over to the **Deutsches Buch- und Schriftmuseum** (Mon–Sat 9am–4pm; free), which traces the history of books during the past 5000 years. Just to the east is the **Russische Kirche**, a striking pastiche of the churches of Novgorod, decorated inside with original eighteenth-century icons. It was built in 1913 to commemorate the 22,000 Russian soldiers who died in the **Battle of the Nations** a hundred years previously.

The actual site of this conflict, in which the Russians combined with the Prussians, Austrians and Swedes to defeat Napoleon, lies just to the south, on the opposite side of the trade fair site. Thereafter, the French dictator was banished to exile in Elba. A colossal and tasteless monument, known as the **Völkerschlachtdenkmal** (daily May–Oct 10am–5pm; Nov–April 9am–4pm; DM5), was erected to commemorate the centenary of the victory; it can be ascended for an extensive if unexciting view over the city and the flat countryside around.

Eating and drinking

Leipzig rivals most western German cities in its choices for eating and drinking, offering a wide range of traditional German taverns, ethnic restaurants, cafés and bars. Many of the best places are conveniently close to the Markt.

Restaurants

Apels Garten, Kolonnadenstr. 2. Although moderately priced, this is one of the very best restaurants in Leipzig. Featured on the menu are several dishes made according to recipes from the *Leipziger Kochbuch* of 1706. Closed Sun evening.

Auerbachs Keller, Mädlerpassage, Grimmaische Str. 2–4. This restaurant's fame makes it a must, and the food served is of high quality. Except when there's a fair on, there's seldom any problem getting a table in either the cavernous main cellar, or in the smaller dining room on the other side of the stairway.

Barthels Hof, Hainstr. 1. Restaurant and wine bar in a celebrated old courtyard. The house specialities are the *Eintopf* dishes, which are available as either starters or main courses.

Gasthaus des Meeres, Pfaffendorfer Str. 1. Speciality fish restaurant. Closed Sun evening.

Kubanische Speisebar Varadero, Barfussgässchen 8. Popular and genuine Cuban restaurant specializing in grills and cocktails.

Medici, Nikolaikirchhof 5. The city's leading Italian restaurant.

Paulaner-Palais, Klostergasse 3. Post-*Wende* venture by the eponymous Munich brewery which has already established itself amongst the top restaurants in town. On Fri evenings, there's an eat-as-much-as-you-can fish buffet.

Ratskeller, Lotterstr. 1. Typically reliable cellar restaurant in the Neues Rathaus; because of its situation well away from the Markt, it's less than usually prone to be full of tourists. Closed Sun evening.

Stadtpfeiffer, Augustusplatz 8. Highly rated, rather pricey restaurant of the *Neues Gewandhaus*. Closed Sun.

Thüringer Hof, Burgstr. 19. Sixteenth-century *Gaststätte* with rambling layout of rooms and a glass-covered inner courtyard that's the best-value choice for a hearty German meal.

Zill's Tunnel, Barfussgässchen 9. Self-consciously smart restaurant, with a beer hall downstairs, a wine bar upstairs. Food relatively pricey and often erratic.

Zur Neuberin, Grosse Fleischergasse 2. Cosy wine bar-restaurant on four floors of a fifteenth-century timber-framed house. Evenings only, closed Sun.

Cafés and bars

Anker, Knopstr. 1. Functions as a youth café 4–8pm, then as a bar-disco. Closed Sat & Sun.

Boomerang, Waldstr. 29. Australian theme bar, serving wines, beers and rum from Down Under.

Café am Brühl, Richard-Wagner-Platz 1. Olde-worlde café housed in an elegant Rococo mansion.

Café Art, Wächterstr. 11. As the name suggests, this café-bar is a favourite with the arty set.

Café Vis à Vis, Rudolf-Breitscheid-Str. 33. Café-bar with a predominantly youthful clientele; open round the clock.

Dr Schreber's Kneipe, Aachener Str. 7. Has a large beer beer garden, and also serves meals, including plenty of vegetarian dishes.

Gosenschenke, Menckestr. 5. Historic *Gaststube* with beer garden to the north of the city centre. It has revived production of *Gose*, a wheat beer similar in character to the Belgian *Gueuze*.

Kaffeehaus Riquet, Schumachergässchen 1. Viennese-style coffee house and wine cellar recently established in a wacky old shop building.

Kultur-Café, Nikolaikirchhof 1. Offers breakfast from 10am, regular live music sessions in the evening.

Moritzbastei, Universitätstr. 9. Complex of student clubs, bars and a disco which offers a choice of live entertainments most evenings.

Podium, Naschmarkt 1–3. One of several Irish pubs to have sprung up in the city since the *Wende*.

Spizz, Markt 9. Live music bar, with jazz the most regular feature.

Culture

Though you'll need to have a good command of German to understand what's being said, the city's **cabaret** tradition is worth catching. Among the many venues, the best-known are *Academixer*, Kupfergasse 6 (☎960 4848), *Pfeffermühle*, Thomaskirchhof 16 (☎960 3253), *Funzel*, Nikolaistr. 12–14 (☎960 3232), *Leipziger Brettl*, Grosse Fleischergasse 13 (☎961 3547), and *Gohglmohsch*, Markt 9 (☎961 5111). Leipzig's leading **theatre** is the *Schauspielhaus*, Bosestr. 1 (☎126 8168), which concentrates on dramatic classics, while *Neue Szene*, Gottschedstr. 16 (☎980 4842), focuses on modern plays and other contemporary art forms. The *Theater der Jungen Welt*, Lindenauer Markt 21 (☎477 2990) stages performances for children and young people.

In the field of **music**, the Thomaskirche continues its role with regular organ recitals and choral concerts (by the *Thomanerchor* and others), to which there's often free aDMission. The *Gewandhausorchester* is renowned for the clean, beautifully balanced sound it produces; the *MDR Sinfonieorchester* is also of good standing, while the associated *MDR Chor* is one of Europe's best large mixed-voiced choirs. The main venue for major **concerts** is the *Neues Gewandhaus*, Augustusplatz 8 (☎127 0280), while performances by small ensembles are held at the *Bosehaus*, Thomaskirchhof 16 (☎964410). **Operas** are staged at the *Opernhaus*, Augustusplatz 12 (☎126 1261), operettas and musical comedy at *Musikalische Komödie*, Dreilindenstr. 30 (☎483 5115). A venue with true curiosity value is the *Völkerschlachtdenkmal* (☎878 0471), whose own choir performs regular concerts under quite extraordinary acoustic conditions: the echo lasts up to twenty seconds.

Listings

Airport information ☎2240.

Car rental *Avis*, in *Hotel Mercure*, Augustusplatz 5–6 (☎214 6891); *Europcar InterRent*, in Hauptbahnhof Westhalle (☎211 3884); *Hertz*, in *Maritim Hotel Astoria*, Willy-Brandt-Platz 2 (☎128 4701); *Sixt*, in *Hotel Inter-Continental*, Gerberstr. 15 (☎988 1149). All these companies also have offices at the airport.

Consulate *US*, Wilhelm-Seyfferth-Str. 4 (☎213 8420).

Cultural Institute *British Council*, Lumumbustr. 11–13 (☎564 7154).

Festivals The *Ostermesse* on the Markt is a nine-day-long Easter market; the *Bachfest* around the same time celebrates the music of J.S. Bach; the *Leipziger Kulturwochen* in the first half of Oct offers a varied programme of concerts; the *Lachmesse* in mid-Oct is a festival of humour and satire centred on the cabaret venues listed above; the *Dokfest* in mid-Nov features documentaries and short films.

Mitfahrzentrale Rudolf-Breitscheid-Str. 39 (☎19440 or 211 4222).

Post office The main post office is at Augustusplatz 1 with poste restante service.

Women's centre Braustr. 17 (☎213 0030).

Torgau

TORGAU, a former residence of the Saxon Electors, stands on the banks of the Elbe 50km to the northeast of Leipzig; it can be reached in an hour or less by the regular trains on the fast line to Cottbus. Beside the road bridge is a memorial commemorating the fact that it was at this spot, in the closing days of World War II, that the advancing Soviet and American armies finally met up.

Before the war, Torgau hosted one of Germany's biggest **folk festivals**, the biennial *Auszugfest*, which combined a horseback procession in sixteenth-century costume with a marksmen's fair. This was revived in May 1994, and will hopefully become re-established on a regular basis. There's also the annual *Elbe Day* on April 25, commemorating the meeting of the American and Soviet forces and featuring Dixieland performers from around the world.

The town

The town centre is built on a cliff high above the river, and centred on a typically spacious Markt with a handsome Renaissance **Rathaus**. Directly overlooking the river is the **Marienkirche**, a Gothic church containing the tombstone of Katharina von Bora, wife of Luther, who died in the town, and a panel of *The Fourteen Helpers in Need* by Cranach. This was part of his early masterpiece, *The Holy Kinship*, now in the Städel in Frankfurt.

Schloss Hartenfels

Frederick the Wise, the man of power who made the Reformation possible, was born in **Schloss Hartenfels**, the large castle which dominates the town. It dates back to the tenth century, but in its present form is predominantly a residential palace; entry is over a moat with a bear pit, into which brown bears have been reintroduced. The **Albrechtsbau** at the southeastern corner is one of the earliest Renaissance buildings in Germany; its **tower** (Tues–Sun 9.30am–noon & 1–4pm; DM1) can be ascended for a fine view over the town and the complex. An altogether grander style is present in the **Johann-Friedrich-Bau** which forms the east wing of the courtyard, and its exterior spiral staircase, the *Grosse Wendelstein*, is the Schloss's most arresting feature.

Part of the north wing is given over to the **Kreismuseum** (Tues–Sun 9.30am–noon & 1–4.30pm; DM2), which houses a collection of medieval arms and armour, together with displays on the history of the town. Far more intriguing is the **Schlosskapelle** alongside, which was consecrated by Luther in 1544, and thus has the best (though disputed) claim to be regarded as the first building designed specifically for Protestant worship. In line with the ideals of the Reformation, the architecture is plain and simple, adopting a rectangular format with no apse. The galleries introduced here became a standard feature of Protestant buildings, while the elaborate vaulting was also favoured in early Lutheran churches.

Practicalities

Torgau's **Bahnhof** is ten minutes' walk northwest of the centre. The **tourist office** (April–Sept Mon–Fri 10am–6pm, Sat & Sun 11am–4pm; Oct–March Mon–Fri 10am–5pm; ☎03421/712571) is at Schloss Str. 11, and you can book **private rooms** (②–③) here.

Additionally, there are a few **pensions**: *Haus am Stadtpark*, north of the centre at Reditzer Weg 1 (☎03421/903432; ③); *Zum Eisbären*, southwest of the centre at

Lassallestr. 1 (☎03421/708450; ③); and *Am Markt*, Bäckerstr. 12 (☎03421/711379, fax 712528; ④). The town's three **hotels** are *Torgauer Brauhof*, in the north of town at Warschauer Str. 7 (☎03421/73000; ⑤); *Goldener Anker*, Markt 6 (☎03421/903874; ⑥), and *Central*, Friedrichplatz 8 (☎03421/710026; ⑤).

All these hotels have **restaurants**. Alternatively, try *Restaurant im Kulturhaus*, Rosa-Luxemburg-Str. 16; the cosy little *Bärenschenke*, Schloss Str. 25; and the inevitable *Ratskeller*, Markt 1.

Colditz and the Zwickauer Mulde valley

Mention the name of **COLDITZ** to most Germans and you're likely to be met with a blank stare. This is the one place in the country that, because of **Oflag IVC**, the wartime maximum security camp for prisoners of war, is far better known abroad than at home. The main reason for this is that the GDR regime, embarrassed about the fact that the camp had been on their territory and unable to make any pro-Communist propaganda out of it (as they could with the concentration camps, where many of their own number had been incarcerated), chose to suppress its very existence. No references to it could be found in the official English-language guide to the country, while the 64-page German booklet on the town gave it just one sentence. Although a fair number of English-speaking visitors used to travel the 48km south from Leipzig out of curiosity, they were unable to visit the site of the camp, which reverted to its prewar status as a psychiatric hospital, while Colditz itself went back to being a sleepy rural community. Since the *Wende*, there has been a positive encouragement of visitors and a willingness to make a dispassionate examination of the past.

The town

On its own merits, Colditz is a surprisingly pretty town in attractive surroundings: add in the wartime connection and it's easy to see why the potential for tourism is very real. The streets, laid out on a ramshackle old pattern, are full of historic half-timbered houses, while the main **Markt** is a highly distinctive sloping cobblestoned square. At the top stands a handsome gabled **Rathaus** in the ebullient style of the German Renaissance.

The Schloss

From the foot of Marktplatz, there's a great view of the huge **Schloss** (guided tours Tues–Sun 10am–4pm; DM6), the former Oflag IVC, which completely dominates the town from its cliff-top site. There's been a fortress here since the eleventh century, which came into the possession of the Wettins, the Saxon ruling house, in 1404. In the middle of the following century, Elector August rebuilt it as a Renaissance palace, though retaining its medieval format of defensive *Vorburg* protecting the main *Hauptburg*. The magnificent armorial decoration above the second gateway shows his own coat of arms, alongside that of his wife.

Under Augustus the Strong (see p.960), the Schloss was used as a hunting lodge, but it was abandoned by later Saxon rulers in favour of more modern palaces. In 1800, it became the local poorhouse, later becoming one of Germany's first psychiatric hospitals. It was specially chosen in World War II as the place to house men who had escaped from less secure confinements and subsequently been recaptured, and for *Prominenten*, prisoners who were specially prized because of their high rank or important connections.

Currently, its future is uncertain. The Land government moved out the psychiatric patients and put it up for sale in 1994, hoping to find a foreign buyer prepared to turn it into a hotel or conference centre but have subsequently assumed responsibility for its

---

OFLAG IVC

Schloss Colditz was chosen as the site of **Oflag IVC**, the Third Reich's most secure prisoner-of-war camp, principally because of its geographical position – it was 700km to any border not controlled by the Nazis. The nature of the castle itself, with its secure medieval defences and situation above a small, isolated town, was another factor. **Major Pat Reid**, who wrote a trilogy of books about his Colditz experiences, recorded his initial impression of it as "beautiful, serene, majestic and yet forbidding enough to make our hearts sink into our boots". According to the Nazi authorities, Colditz castle was impossible to escape from, but in all, 31 men performed the feat, aided by the fact that the main qualification for being sentenced to the castle – that of having attempted to escape before – gave the prisoners a rich fund of experience and ingenuity, which they gladly pooled.

In 1941, **Peter Allan** became the first Briton to escape, by hiding in a sack which was taken away in a delivery van; however, on reaching Vienna, he was recaptured and sent back. Following a number of successful getaways by French prisoners, **Airey Neave** (who later led the campaign to make Margaret Thatcher the Conservative Party leader, five years before he was blown up by the IRA) made the first of the eleven British "home-runs" early in 1942, dressed in the uniform of a German officer; Reid was among the others who accomplished the feat that same year. The latter's books are the best source for an insight into life in the camp; for a completely different perspective, see *Colditz – the German Story* by Reinhold Eggers, the official in charge of security.

---

restoration, opening the **tower** as a documentary exhibition centre. The exhibits include a large number of photographs taken during World War II plus a fascinating display of some of the ingenious devices the prisoners used in planning their escapes, including a typewriter which could be taken to pieces to prevent its discovery, a razor transformed into a saw and a home-made sewing machine, along with false identification papers and German banknotes. You can also see inside the galleried chapel and descend to the 44-metre-long **tunnel** which the French prisoners dug over an eight-month period. They intended this to be the means of a mass escape, but it was discovered before it could be used.

To join one of the tours, go first to the **Städtisches Museum** (same hours and ticket), which occupies a fine Baroque house at Tiergartenstr. 1, just uphill from the church near the entrance to the Schloss.

Practicalities

Colditz lies on a minor rail line; to get there from Leipzig, it's normally necessary to change at Grossbothen, though there's a direct bus service as an alternative. The **tourist office** is at An der Kirche 1 (Mon–Fri 9am–5pm; ☎034381/43519). Accommodation options are limited – there's a **youth hostel** just below the Schloss at Haingasse 42 (☎034381/43335; ➊); a few **private rooms** (➁–➂); a **pension**, *Zur Alten Stadtmauer*, Am Graben 5–7 (☎034381/43179; ➃); and, at the edge of town, a **hotel**, *Waldhaus*, Lausicker Str. 60 (☎034381/43371; ➂). In the village of Zschadrass a couple of kilometres to the northeast is another hotel – *Gildehof Zschadrass*, Hauptstr. 4 (☎034381/8020; ➂). The best places to **eat** and **drink** are the *Schloss-Café* (a traditional *Gaststätte*, in spite of its name) and the *Marktstübl*, both on the Markt, and *Ponydiele*, Schulstr. 15.

The Zwickauer Mulde valley

Upstream along the **Zwickauer Mulde** from Colditz lies a really lovely secluded valley, which is often surprisingly deep, considering the modest scale of the river itself.

Along its banks are several outstandingly picturesque towns and villages, all linked by a scenic rail line.

Rochlitz

ROCHLITZ, 11km upstream from Colditz, is a junction of three rail lines. From the Bahnhof at the northern end, the line along the Zwickauer Mulde departs from the river's snaking course to run right down the length of the town, passing over a viaduct before traversing the river. At this point, there's briefly a dramatic view of the large fifteenth- and sixteenth-century **Schloss** (Tues–Sun 10am–4pm; DM3), the former headquarters of the local counts, with its picturesque silhouette of church-like towers and palace buildings with huge sloping roofs. It's in a poor state of repair and is currently the subject of a long-term restoration project. However, you can visit the small museum of local history and climb one of the towers for a view over the valley. The town centre, with its two market squares, has recaptured its old county town atmosphere and is worth a quick stroll. Varied perspectives on the Schloss can be had from the pedestrian footbridge, and from the hills above, which are dotted with marked trails.

Sassnitzer Weg leads up from the footbridge to the **youth hostel** (☎03737/42131; 🛉). There are also two reasonably priced **hotels**, *Bayrische Bierstube*, Markt 23 (☎03737/42220; ④), and *Goldener Löwe*, Markt 3 (☎03737/42438; ④), plus a plentiful number of **private rooms** (①–③) – look out for *Zimmer frei* signs.

Wechselburg

Set high above the valley a further 9km south is **WECHSELBURG**, formerly one of the seats of another aristocratic dynasty, the Counts of Schönburg. In contrast to Rochlitz, it's a quiet village sleeping in rural obscurity, with its Renaissance **Schloss** now functioning as a children's home.

The other dominant monument is the Romanesque **Stiftskirche**, which, in line with the faith of the former aristocratic masters, is Catholic – one of the few such historic churches in eastern Germany. Its extraordinary **rood screen**, made around 1235, is a masterpiece of both architecture and sculpture. One of the most remarkable things about it is that it was reassembled a couple of decades ago; for the previous three hundred years, its constituent parts were scattered throughout the building: the section above the archway, with its relief of Christ in Majesty, served as the pulpit. The six niche figures of Old Testament characters – particularly the large statue of Melchizedek to the far right – and the triumphal cross group at the summit, are brilliant bits of carving. Look out also for the **tomb** of the founders, Count Dedo and his wife Mechthila.

Rochsburg

Another 8km upstream is **ROCHSBURG**, entered via a spectacular double viaduct over the river. The village is, if anything, even more soporific than Wechselburg, and is similarly set on lofty heights. It takes its name from the **Rochsburg** (Tues–Sun 9am–noon & 1–4/5pm; DM3) whose silhouette rears up proudly above the wooded slopes. Originally built as a feudal castle by an offshoot of the Counts of Rochlitz, it was acquired by the Schönburgs in the sixteenth century and skilfully transformed, after a fire, into the present Renaissance palace, which has the best of both worlds by retaining many of the old defensive features. The interiors, though fairly low-key, have some impressive doorways and Renaissance furniture. One wing is now a **youth hostel** (☎037383/6503; 🛉).

Zwickau

ZWICKAU, Saxony's fourth largest city, is a major rail junction and gateway to both the rural areas in the south of the province, the Vogtland and the Erzgebirge. It's about

90km south of Leipzig, and can be reached directly by express services via the Thuringian town of Altenburg, or more picturesquely by the line along the Zwickauer Mulde. For the foreseeable future, Zwickau's name will be irrevocably associated with the *Trabant* (popularly known as the *Trabi*), the wretched but now rather celebrated "people's car" of the GDR, which was manufactured here. However, in spite of its industrial tradition, it's an agreeable city of broad parks, with a historic centre which came through World War II almost entirely unscathed.

The city

Zwickau grew up as a market town trading in minerals mined in the Erzgebirge. Its medieval core, the **Altstadt**, occupies a roughly circular area inside the busy inner ring road, Dr-Friedrichs-Ring, with the Zwickauer Mulde forming a second boundary to the east. Because of earlier wars, only a few monuments from the Middle Ages remain; instead, there's a varied assemblage, with plenty of grand nineteenth- and early twentieth-century offices and stores. Largely pedestrianized, it's quickly developing into a modern commercial city centre on the western German model.

Between the Altstadt and the Hauptbahnhof to the west is the extensive **Stadtpark**, which provides welcome peace in the middle of the city. It's centred on a huge artificial boating lake; other attractions are an open-air theatre, a music pavilion and an aviary, though it's fun enough just to wander through and watch the locals at play.

The Hauptmarkt

At the southwestern corner of the central Hauptmarkt is the **Robert-Schumann-Haus** (Tues–Sat 10am–5pm; DM5), birthplace of German music's purest Romantic spirit. It documents all phases of his career, from his early days as a virtuoso pianist in Leipzig (which were brought to an end after his fingers were damaged in a hand-stretching machine), to his sad final years, during which he was racked by mental instability. There's similarly extensive material on his devoted wife, **Clara Wieck**, who inspired his vast outpourings of passionate, heart-on-sleeve piano pieces and songs. As the leading pianist of her day and an accomplished composer in a style derived from her husband's, she was herself a substantial figure.

In the middle of the south side of the square is the **Rathaus**, whose showy facade masks a medieval structure. Further along is the Renaissance **Gewandhaus**, built in the early sixteenth century as the market hall and guild house of the drapers. Now serving as the town's main theatre, its most notable feature is the amazing five-tiered gable.

The Marienkirche

Just off the western side of Hauptmarkt is the main civic church, the **Marienkirche** (now designated as the **Dom**, though it's never been a cathedral). Its decorative late Gothic hall-church format, and the profusion of furnishings from the same period, are typical of the Erzgebirge region. Many of the present sumptuous exterior adornments, including the large south porch with its depiction of the Wise and Foolish Virgins, and the now very blackened figures on the buttresses, were only added a century ago in a flush of Romantic over-enthusiasm. The **tower**, whose lead helmet with double cupola is a Baroque embellishment, can be ascended for a view over the Hauptmarkt and the city (entry from inside the church Mon–Fri at 3.30pm; DM1.50).

Inside, the main adornment is the magnificent **high altar**, made in the Nürnberg workshop of **Michael Wolgemut**, the teacher of Dürer. It can be opened to reveal any of three sections, though only one of these is visible at a time. Normally the carved part, with life-size gilded figures of the Madonna and Child surrounded by eight female saints, is on view, but the cycles of paintings illustrating the Nativity and the Passion are shown during their respective seasons. Also in the chancel is a **Holy Sepulchre**, carved in filigree style in the manner of a Flamboyant Gothic chapel, and adorned with figures of sleeping knights. The other work of art of special note is the *Pietà* in a north aisle chapel, the masterpiece of **Peter Breuer**, a local man who is one of the brilliant group of German sculptors straddling the late Gothic and early Renaissance eras.

The rest of the Altstadt

Just south of the Marienkirche, on the triangular site formed by the pointed intersection of Domhof and Münzstrasse, is Zwickau's most eccentric building, the **Schiffchen-Haus**, a late fifteenth-century house shaped like the prow of a ship. The Altstadt's remaining sights are all north of the Hauptmarkt. The semicircular Nicolaistrasse loops round via the back of the **Pulverturm** (Powder Tower), the only remaining part of the city walls, to the **Katharinenkirche**, another late Gothic hall church, which formerly belonged to a Benedictine monastery. Inside are a high altar made in Cranach's workshop and a statue of *The Risen Christ* by Breuer. Opposite is the Renaissance **Posthalterei**, which was built as the home of a wealthy cloth manufacturer and merchant, later serving as a coaching house, before becoming a top-class restaurant. At the extreme northern end of the Altstadt is an even grander Renaissance structure, **Schloss Osterstein**. Formerly a residence of the Electors of Saxony, it's currently under restoration with the aim of converting it into a luxury hotel and conference centre. Alongside is the late fifteenth-century **Kornhaus**, one of the largest and oldest grain stores in the country.

The rest of the city

About ten minutes' walk north of the Stadtpark, along Crimmitschauer Strasse, is Lessingstrasse, on which stands the **Städtisches Museum** (Tues–Fri 9am–5pm, Sat & Sun 10am–5pm; DM3), a rambling, old-fashioned collection in a specially designed domed building from the end of the Jugendstil epoch. Its exhibits range from medieval sculpture, including a triptych and a *Crucifixion* by Breuer, via displays of locally produced porcelain and official portraits of the Saxon Electors, to the minerals and mining history of the Erzgebirge.

From here, it's just a short walk north to the **Automobilmuseum August Horch** at Walter-Rathenau-Str. 51 (Tues–Thurs 9am–noon & 2–5pm, Sat & Sun 10am–5pm; DM3), which celebrates Zwickau's role as a leading centre of car production. As the exhibits show, the *Trabi* (see box on p.944) was the unworthy and improbable inheritor of a distinguished tradition dating back via the prewar Audi to the Horch factory of 1904. Another ten minutes' walk to the northeast brings you to Leipziger Strasse, the city's north–south arterial road. At no. 182, set in a small park by the Zwickauer Mulde, is **Neue Welt** (New World), a Jugendstil complex built for concerts and dances. Part of it now houses a restaurant; a door on the north side is usually kept open, allowing you to peek in at the ornate main hall.

Practicalities

Zwickau's **Hauptbahnhof** is about fifteen minutes' walk west of the Hauptmarkt. The **tourist office** (Mon–Fri 9am–6pm, Sat 9am–noon; ☎0375/293713 or 835770) is right in the heart of town at Hauptstr. 6, and can arrange **private rooms** (②–④).

Although there's no hostel, there's a trio of **hotels**, *Beherbergungsgewerbe Kretzschmar*, offering basic rooms at rock-bottom rates; two lie north of the centre at Alexanderstr. 7 (☎0375/215410; ①) and Leipziger Str. 240 (☎0375/204 0140; ①), the other to the west at Hilfegottesschachtstr. 3b (☎0375/301400; ①). More salubrious options include

---

THE TRABI

Because it is now a common sight on western German streets (from which it was previously banned on environmental grounds), the *Trabi* has, perversely, become the most potent symbol of the unification of Germany. The first version of the Communist answer to the *Volkswagen* was first built in 1955 in the former Horch and Audi works; two years later, it was put into mass production under the name of Trabant. Three million vehicles were subsequently manufactured, repeating the original formula almost exactly, apart from a few changes introduced in 1964. With its plastic bodywork and two-cylinder, two-stroke engine, the *Trabi* was hopelessly antiquated even in its early days. It was also a major contributor to the GDR's pollution, belching out five times as much carbon monoxide and nine times as much hydrocarbon as the average Western car. Though it was the cheapest and most readily available car in the GDR, it wasn't easy to obtain – twelve years was about the normal waiting time. Its lawnmower-like noise was an omnipresent feature on GDR streets, while it's the only car ever built capable of coming off the worse in a collision with a pedestrian.

The most popular of the many *Trabi* jokes – the suggestion that you could double its value by filling it up with petrol – suddenly came true in the summer of 1989, when East Germans escaping to the west via Hungary gladly exchanged their *Trabis* for the price of the petrol in its tank. Production ended in 1990, when Volkswagen moved back to Zwickau, but the *Trabi* will be a familiar sight for a while yet, as its one strong point was its remarkable longevity.

Sachsenring, Leipziger Str. 160 (☎0375/26251; ⑤); *Zum Uhu*, Bahnhofstr. 51 (☎0375/295044; ⑥); *Merkur*, Bahnhofstr. 58 (☎0375/294286; ⑥); and *Park Eckersbach*, northeast of the Altstadt near the terminus of tram #1 at Trillerplatz 1 (☎0375/475572; ⑦).

The last of these has an inexpensive **restaurant** with beer garden, while *Zum Uhu* has a strong line in game dishes. In the Altstadt, the best places for a full meal are *Posthalterei*, Katharinenstr. 27, *Goldener Anker*, Hauptmarkt 6, and *Zur Grünhainer Kapelle*, Peter-Breuer-Str. 3. The *Ringkaffee*, Dr-Friedrichs-Ring 21a, is also recommended – in spite of its name, it's a traditional *Gaststätte*. There are also plenty of traditional **cafés** if it's coffee and cake or ice cream you're after; *Engelmann* on Hauptstrasse is particularly popular with locals.

The Vogtland

The southwesternmost part of Saxony is known as the **Vogtland**, a name which has lingered on from the Middle Ages, when it was governed on behalf of the Holy Roman Emperor by administrators known as Vogts. For the most part, the Vogtland is a high plateau, but the scenery is far from being monotonous – it's cut by many rivers and streams which often cleave surprisingly deep valleys. Since medieval times, it has been one of Germany's main centres of textile production; a strong handicrafts tradition, and in particular the making of musical instruments, has also been maintained in the villages. The Vogtland has long been a popular holiday destination, with a couple of spas at the very southern tip of the region and a clutch of resorts offering both winter and summer facilities further east.

Plauen

PLAUEN is the only major town in the Vogtland, lying 48km southwest of Zwickau. The journey there via a stretch of the Leipzig–Nürnberg rail line is one of Germany's most spectacular train rides – the viaducts, and in particular the triple-tiered **Göltzschtalbrücke** just beyond Mylau, are triumphs of mid-nineteenth-century engineering. Although Plauen itself was devastated in World War II, with much of its centre rebuilt in an uncompromisingly modern style, it has many attractive features, not least its imposing setting in the hills above the Weisse Elster and Syra rivers, and the profusion of Jugendstil houses scattered all over the town. Each June, Plauen hosts a major **popular festival**, the *Spitzenfest*.

The town

At the heart of Plauen is the Alter Markt, now revived as an outdoor market. On its northern side is the **Altes Rathaus**, dwarfed by its monstrous early twentieth-century replacement behind. The facade facing the square is a handsome building, complete with curly gables, a resplendent clock and a balcony with a double stairway. The ground floor still preserves an elegant Gothic hallway, which, together with the adjoining rooms, is home to the **Museale Abteilung Plauener Spitze** (Mon–Fri 10am–5pm; Sat 9am–2pm; DM1.50). This traces the history and production methods of **Plauen lace**, with plenty of examples of the town's most celebrated product.

Southeast of Alter Markt is the **Johanniskirche**, fronted by the twin Romanesque towers of the original building, which are now capped with Baroque cupolas. The rest of the structure is a hall church of the 1550s, one of the last major buildings in Germany to be built in the Gothic style. By this time the Reformation had been adopted in Plauen, so it was constructed with the Renaissance galleries characteristic of Lutheran churches. An expressive winged altar stands in the choir.

East across the broad expanse of Syrastrasse is the **Schloss** of the Vogts; apart from the Roter Turm (Red Tower), which survives intact, it has been left as a ruin following its destruction in World War II. From here, you can descend to the Weisse Elster, which can be crossed on foot via the **Alte Elsterbrücke**, a bridge known to date back at least as far as the thirteenth century. Uphill from the Schloss, the **Nonnenturm** (Nuns' Tower) is the only remaining part of the medieval fortifications, now standing forlorn in the large open square created during postwar reconstruction of the town. Just to the west is the **Lutherkirche**, which has a late fifteenth-century retable from Erfurt with emotional carvings of scenes from the Passion.

Plauen's most imposing street is **Nobelstrasse**, a block west of the Markt. Here three adjacent merchants' houses of the late eighteenth century have been converted to contain the **Vogtland-Museum** (Tues–Sun 10am–4pm; DM1.50), which documents the folklore, arts, crafts and history of the region, but is mainly of interest for a captivating series of period interiors, some re-created, others original to the buildings themselves. Among the latter is the very French-looking **Festsaal**, decorated in the full-blown Louis XVI style, whose rich stuccowork includes wall panels symbolizing the months of the year.

West of here is the **Friedensbrücke** over the Syra, which was the world's largest arched stone bridge at the time of its construction at the beginning of the century, a distinction it kept until 1945. An equally impressive technical monument is the **Syratalbrücke** further to the west, which the Upper Vogtland railway crosses on its journey south towards the Czech border.

Practicalities

Plauen has two train stations, each for separate lines. The **Oberer Bahnhof** at the top of the town, reached from the centre straight along Bahnhofstrasse, is on the Leipzig–Nürnberg route, and is the start of the line to the Czech city of Plzeň via the Upper Vogtland. The **Unterer Bahnhof**, on the south bank of the Weisse Elster, has services along that valley to the Thuringian towns of Greiz and Gera. Plauen's **tourist**

office (Mon–Fri 9am–6pm, Sat 9–noon; ☎03741/291 1027) in the Rathaus, Unterer Graben 1, can book the usual range of **private rooms** (①–③).

Additionally, there are a number of good-value small **pensions**, such as *Fritsche*, Fritz-Reuter-Str. 9 (☎03741/526000; ②); *Lochbauer*, Pfaffengutstr. 30 (☎03741/526641; ③); and *Fischer*, Thiergartner Weg 81 (☎03741/227720; ③). Plauen's **hotels** include *Echo*, Alte Pausaer Str. 169 (☎03741/522101; ④); *Heinz*, Jössnitzer Str. 112 (☎03741/525822; ⑤); *Alexandra*, Bahnhofstr. 17 (☎03741/221414; ⑥); *Parkhotel*, Rädelstr. 18 (☎03741/20060; ⑦); and *Am Theater*, Theaterstr. 7 (☎03741/121100; ⑦). There's also a **youth hostel** at Reusaer Waldhaus 1 (☎03741/431881; ❷).

The best **restaurants** are in the hotels listed above. Otherwise, try *Roma*, Oberer Steinweg 8, which offers Italian food and wines. Just to the south, at Alter Teich 9, is the *Malzhaus*, an eighteenth-century maltings which is now a lively bar and arts centre.

The Musikwinkel

During the Counter-Reformation, large numbers of Bohemian Protestants escaped into Saxony, settling in a cluster of villages now collectively known as the **Musikwinkel** (Music Corner), because of their long tradition for handmade musical instruments. The main centre for this is **MARKNEUKIRCHEN**, where around two hundred different kinds of instruments are made. A huge array of historical examples – not only from here, but also from around the world – are on display in a small Baroque palace, the **Paulusschlössel** (Tues–Sun 9am–5pm; DM2). Markneukirchen can be reached by bus; it also lies 3km west of Siebenbrunn, the first stop on a branch rail line running west from Adorf, the first station north of Bad Elster. This line terminates at **KLINGENTHAL**, itself one of the instrument-producing towns, although it's now much better known as a major winter-sports resort.

The Erzgebirge

The **Erzgebirge** (Iron Ore Mountains) occupy most of southern Saxony, stretching from the Vogtland to just before the Elbe. They take their name from the rich mineral deposits found there in the Middle Ages. These were of crucial importance to the wealth of the Saxon state and in turn to its high-profile political role within the Holy Roman Empire. As the mines became exhausted, the inhabitants turned to cottage industries, notably lace-making, woodcarving and the production of children's toys.

The landscapes of the Erzgebirge are stark and often bleak, while the climate is decidedly raw – these conditions are exacerbated by the fact that much of the range is an environmental disaster area. In particular, a huge percentage of its trees are suffering from *Waldsterben* as a result of smog blown here from lignite-burning factories in the Czech Republic. Despite this, the Erzgebirge is a popular tourist area, both in summer and winter – this being a rare part of Germany where snow is virtually guaranteed. Another plus is that it's one of the few parts of eastern Germany which has retained much of a tradition in **popular festivals**; it also has a couple of historic towns which are well worth a detour in their own right.

Schneeberg

The old silver-mining town of **SCHNEEBERG** lies on a ridge high above the valley of the Zwickauer Mulde, 18km southeast of Zwickau. It's rich in old traditions and is particularly worth visiting during the run-up to Christmas, when there are a whole series of events, including the *Fest des Lichtes und der Freude* (Festival of Light and Joy) in the second week of Advent. At this time, the town (in common with others in the region) is decorated with huge illuminated wooden pyramids adorned with figures of miners. Another big annual event is the *Streittag* on July 22, featuring a costumed procession of mining guilds.

Focal point of most of Schneeberg's festivities is the sixteenth-century **Stadtkirche St Wolfgang** at the top of the town. Outwardly plain, it has a highly original hall interior whose galleries, most unusually, go all the way round the church, including the chancel. The suspiciously fresh look the church has is due to the fact that its restoration following destruction in the closing days of World War II was only recently completed. The main treasure is the huge *Passion Altar*, a mature masterpiece by **Cranach**.

Down on the **Markt** is an assemblage of handsome Baroque, Rococo and Neoclassical mansions. Just off the western side, on Obere Zobelgasse, the **Museum für Bergmännische Volkskunst** (Tues–Thurs, Sat & Sun 9am–12.30pm & 1–5pm, Fri 1–5pm; DM4) illustrates the crafts and costumes of the local miners.

Practicalities

Schneeberg is one of the few places of any size in the former GDR to have lost its rail link – the nearest station is in the adjacent town of Aue, which lies across the valley, but there are regular **bus** connections with Zwickau, departing from just off the Markt.

The **tourist office** is in the Rathaus, Markt 1 (Mon–Fri 9am–6pm, Sat 9am–1pm, Sun 10am–1pm; ☎03772/19433 or 22347). Here you can book **private rooms** (①–③), which are in plentiful supply. There are also a couple of small **pensions**: *Drei Tannen*, Eibenstocker Str. 3 (☎03772/28479; ②), and *Sabine*, Hartensteiner Str. 13 (☎03772/21036; ③). The only **hotel** as such is the luxury *Berghotel Steiger*, high above town at Am Mühlberg (☎03772/22674; ⑦). This also has a good and not too expensive restaurant; otherwise the best place to **eat** is the *Ratskeller* in the Rathaus.

Annaberg-Buchholz

In the early sixteenth century, the largest town in Saxony was **ANNABERG**, which grew up alongside the range's richest silver mines. It's now the northern half of a double town set high above both sides of the Sehma valley and in the lee of the commanding heights of the Pöhlberg, 35km east of Schneeberg and 30km south of Chemnitz. Although nowadays very provincial in feel, it remains the undoubted star of the Erzgebirge, possessing the finest artistic and technical monuments in the region. Annaberg is also host to the biggest **festival** in the Erzgebirge, the *Rät*, which has been going since 1520, and begins on the Saturday after Trinity Sunday (May–June).

The town

Occupying the dominant position in town, the **Stadtkirche St Annen** was erected during the town's short-lived heyday in the first quarter of the sixteenth century. Crafted from rough masonry, the exterior's only feature of note is the tower, shaped like the keep of a castle with an octagonal superstructure; the rest is little more than a shell covering one of Germany's most dazzlingly brilliant interiors. Ribs spring in all directions from the slender columns, forming an intricate star vault adorned with fancy keystones and elaborate little carved figures.

The rich and colourful furnishings are contemporary with the architecture. There are two masterpieces by **Hans Witten**, whose reputation has suffered from the fact that most of his work is found in the relative obscurity of the Erzgebirge region. The **Schöne Pforte** (Beautiful Doorway) at the facade end of the northern aisle shows the Holy Trinity adored by the angelic host, with SS Francis and Clare looking on. Witten's **font** is another extraordinary creation, strangely foreshadowing the productions of Fabergé. Both the **pulpit** and the **gallery** were carved by his colleague Franz

---

THE NARROW-GAUGE RAILWAYS OF THE ERZGEBIRGE

There are no fewer than four narrow-gauge rail lines in the Erzgebirge, two of which have functioned continuously since they were built in the late nineteenth century. The *Erzgebirgsbahn*, opened in 1897, was the last such railway to be built in Germany. Its 17.4km route links Cranzahl with Kurort Oberwiesenthal, and did much to stimulate the development of the latter's tourist industry. In the course of its journey, it climbs 238 metres, passing through the valleys of the Sehma and Pöhlbach before traversing a 110-metre-long iron viaduct shortly before reaching its terminus.

The *Osterzgebirgsbahn* (also known as the*Weisseritztalbahn* after the river whose valley it follows) is the longest-running narrow-gauge service in Germany, having been in operation since 1883. It begins at Freital-Hainsberg, on the main line between Freiberg and Dresden. From there, it skirts the eastern edge of the Erzgebirge all the way to its terminus at **KURORT KIPSDORF**, 26km away. This unassuming little health resort has by far the largest narrow-gauge station in Germany, a sight in itself with its eight running lines. However, the highlight of the journey comes 5km before at **SCHMIEDEBURG**, where the train passes high above the village on a stone viaduct.

Until it was closed and dismantled in 1984, the *Pressnitztalbahn* was considered by rail buffs to be the most enjoyable of all eastern Germany's narrow-gauge railways. Beginning at **WOLKENSTEIN**, on the main line between Annaberg-Buchholz and Flöha, it climbed 293 metres and crossed 52 bridges in the course of its 23km-long journey south along the River Pressnitz to **JÖHSTADT** on the Czech border. Since the *Wende*, the final 4km of this line have been reinstated, and a further section will be re-opened in due course.

Finally, at **SCHÖNHEIDE** in the southwest of the Erzgebirge, a short stretch of narrow-gauge railway – one which formerly serviced nearly fifty different commercial enterprises – has been put back into operation, and there are plans to re-lay the entire route.

Maidburg; the latter forms an illustrated Bible in one hundred scenes. The **high altar**, by the Augsburg sculptor Adolf Daucher, shows the Tree of Jesse, its cool Renaissance poise standing in contrast to the late Gothic sumptuousness of the other works.

Just across from the Stadtkirche, at Grosse Kirchgasse 16, is the **Erzgebirgsmuseum** (Tues–Sun 10am–5pm; DM4), which has some fine displays on the folk art of the region. There's also a roomful of medieval sculptures, plus sections on mining and the guilds.

In the valley below the town is the **Frohnauer Hammer** (guided tours daily 9–11.45am & 1–4pm; DM4). The visit has three separate parts, beginning with the hammer mill itself, the only one of its kind left in Europe. In the fifteenth century it was a grain mill with four millstones, but was rebuilt at the turn of the seventeenth century for iron and copper production, worked by three huge hammers which each weigh nearly six hundredweight. After this has been demonstrated, you cross over the road to see another collection of local crafts, before touring the Baroque **Herrenhaus**, the half-timbered mansion of the mill owner.

Practicalities

Annaberg-Buchholz has three train stations, the most useful being the **Unterer Bahnhof**, which lies about ten minutes' walk east of the Frohnauer Hammer, and immediately below the town centre. The **bus station** is at the western end of the upper part of town.

Among the centrally sited accommodation options are a **pension**, *Clärchen*, Buchholzer Str. 21 (☎03733/24955; ③); and three **hotels**: *Alt Annaberg*, Farbegasse 4 (☎03733/27252 or 18310; ③); *Goldene Sonne*, Adam-Ries-Str. 11 (☎03733/22183; ⑤); and *Wilder Mann*, Markt 13 (☎03733/1440; ⑥). Down in the valley, choice is between

Gasthof Zur Schmiede, Sehmatalstr. 8 (☎03733/23019; ④) and *Parkhotel Waldschlösschen*, Waldschlösschenpark 1 (☎03733/64581; ⑥). As usual, there are plenty of **private rooms** (①–③), though these are often inconveniently situated; they can be booked at the **tourist office** (Mon–Fri 9am–6pm, Sat 10am–noon; ☎03733/425139) in the Rathaus, Markt 1.

The best **restaurants** are in the hotels, with *Waldschlösschen* (in particular) and *Goldene Sonne* leading the way. Other possibilities are the *Ratskeller* in the Rathaus and the *Frohnauer Hammer* in the Herrenhaus.

Kurort Oberwiesenthal

The main resort in the Erzgebirge is **KURORT OBERWIESENTHAL**, which lies hard by the Czech border, 27km south of Annaberg. It's most easily reached by bus, but it's far more fun to take a mainline train to Cranzahl, then transfer to the narrow-gauge *Erzgebirgsbahn* (see box opposite), which terminates in the very centre of the village. If you want **to stay**, there should be no problem in finding accommodation – in addition to the big Alpine-style hotels, geared mainly to the skiing market (and priced accordingly), practically every other house seems to have rooms (①–③) to let.

Oberwiesenthal, itself the highest village in the former GDR, stands at the foot of its highest mountain, the **Fichtelberg** (1214m). A fairly straight hiking path leads to the summit, or you can ascend in five minutes by cable car, which costs DM5 single, DM6 return. Even by the standards of the Erzgebirge, the Fichtelberg has a depressing climate – it's said to have fog on an average of 270 days each year and storms on 150 days. On the rare clear days, the view is extensive, but, because the whole range is so high above sea level, the individual peaks have little sense of grandeur.

Chemnitz and around

When the GDR authorities looked for a place to be renamed in honour of Karl Marx, their choice fell on **CHEMNITZ** (pronounced "Kemnitz"), their fourth largest city, set in the northern foothills of the Erzgebirge, at a pivotal point on the main communications network between Zwickau and Dresden. Thus, between 1953 and 1990, the city became "Karl-Marx-Stadt", with its real name expunged altogether – though the West Germans insisted on retaining it as a suffix. As a city which was rebuilt after the war in a deliberately Soviet-influenced style, Chemnitz has a special curiosity value. In GDR days, its broad boulevards, with their creaking trams and Stalinist-style high-rise offices and tenements, looked and felt quite unnervingly like Russia rather than Germany, and the illusion to some extent persists, despite the heavy volume of traffic.

The **telephone code** for Chemnitz is ☎0371

The city centre

Chemnitz's main north–south axis is Strasse der Nationen. Towards its southern end is the **Versteinerter Wald**, the remains of a petrified forest, with tree stumps reckoned to be 250 million years old. Behind stands the huge pile of the **König-Albert-Museumsbau**, which contains two separate collections. Much the more interesting is the **Städtische Kunstsammlungen** (Tues, Thurs, Sat & Sun 11am–5pm, Wed 11am–7.30pm, Fri noon–5pm; DM4), which features a large number of works by the local painter Karl Schmidt-Rottluff, the most abstract member of the *Die Brücke* group of Expressionists; the furnishings from a Jugendstil villa, Haus Esche, designed by Henry van de Velde (it's aimed to restore the original house as a museum in due course); and several galleries of twentieth-century art. The **Museum für Naturkunde** (Tues, Thurs & Fri 9am–noon & 2–5pm, Wed 9am–noon & 2–7.30pm, Sat & Sun 11am–5pm; DM4 or DM6 combined ticket) is mainly of note for its explanatory displays on the Versteinerter Wald.

Turning right at the next junction, previously Karl-Marx-Allee, now Brückenstrasse, you come to the huge Soviet-made **bronze head of Karl Marx**, behind which stands a plaque bearing his famous dictum, "Working men of all countries, unite!", in several languages. After the *Wende*, there were plans to tear these monuments down, but it's been decided to retain them as a reminder of the "culture" of the GDR years. Across the road is a park containing the Stadthalle and the **Roter Turm** (Red Tower), a survivor from the medieval city wall.

Further south the Markt, the only olde-worlde corner of Chemnitz, is once more the scene of market stalls. The whitewashed **Altes Rathaus** is entered via a portal bearing statues of Judith and Lucretia. Behind is the **Hoher Turm** (High Tower) and the turn-of-the-century Neues Rathaus. This incorporates a few Jugendstil features, but a better example of the style is the facade which was added to the Gothic **Jakobikirche** alongside. The house at no. 20, with its frilly Rococo facade, seems something of an anomaly in this city, though all the more welcome for that.

At the far northern end of the centre is a park centred on a large artificial lake, the Schlossteich. On the hill above is the **Schlosskirche**, a late Gothic hall church with a stumpy neo-Gothic tower, incorporating some of the masonry from a former twelfth-century monastery. Inside are two masterpieces by **Hans Witten** – a typically idiosyncratic carved group of *Christ at the Column* at the high altar, and the church's original north portal, carved with the help of Franz Maidburg, which now stands against the south wall. This has a tympanum showing the Holy Trinity, along with carvings of the church's founders, Emperor Lothar and Empress Richenza.

A Renaissance **Schloss** for the Electors of Saxony supplanted the former monastic buildings. In commemoration of the five-hundredth anniversary of the birth of Georgius Agricola, Chemnitz's favourite son and four times burgomaster, and an early pioneer in the sciences of mineralogy and metallurgy, it was recently restored to serve as home to the local history displays of the **Museum für Stadtgeschichte** (May–Sept Tues–Sun 11am–5pm; Oct–April Tues–Fri 11am–4pm, Sat & Sun 11am–5pm; DM4).

Outside the centre

In the far north of Chemnitz, standing in a disarmingly rustic setting in open fields and served by bus #40, is the **Stiftskirche Ebersdorf** (if shut, get the key from the parish house at the back of the close). This was a popular pilgrimage spot in the late Middle Ages, the goal being the beautiful Marienkapelle, the star-vaulted chapel on the south side. The whole interior bristles with works of art, notably of the late Gothic period, including several by Witten – a *Crucifixion*, statues of an angel and a deacon, and the tomb of Dietrich von Harras, which bears a startlingly realistic effigy of the dead knight.

At the western extremity of the city, reached by tram #3, is the **Schaubergwerk Felsendome Rabenstein** (guided tours Mon 10am–4pm, Wed–Sun 9am–6pm; DM5), an underground limestone quarry where the atmospheric conditions since the cessation of mining have caused the walls to take on subtly luminous effects. Alongside is the former limekiln, a half-timbered eighteenth-century structure which has an exhibition outlining the history of the works. About twenty minutes' walk west of here, connected to the city centre by bus #47, is **Burg Rabenstein** (Tues–Sun 9am–noon &

1–6pm; DM2), the tower and residential block of a large feudal castle, the rest of which has disappeared. Inside are a few Renaissance murals, and a display of *objets d'art*.

Practicalities

Chemnitz's **bus station** lies just off the western side of Strasse der Nationen, while the **Hauptbahnhof** is a block to the east. The **tourist office** (Mon–Fri 9am–6pm, Sat 9am–noon; ☎19433) is in the *Stadthalle*, Rathausstr. 1.

You can book **private rooms** (③–④) at the tourist office or at *Röder Zimmerservice* (Mon–Thurs 10.30am–8pm, Fri 10am–6pm; ☎216 6736), whose kiosk is in the taxi rank outside the Hauptbahnhof. **Hotels** are geared almost exclusively to business visitors. Those with a central location include *Europa*, Str. der Nationen 56 (☎681129; ⑥); *Elisenhof*, Mühlenstr. 102 (☎471690; ⑥); *Sächsischer Hof*, Brühl 26 (☎461480; ⑤); and *Chemnitzer Hof*, which occupies an original Bauhaus building of the 1920s at Theaterplatz 4 (☎6840; ⑧). In the suburbs, by far the most attractive place to stay is *Burghotel Rabenstein*, Grünaer Str. 2 (☎856502; ⑦). Chemnitz's **youth hostel** is out in the southeastern suburbs, at Augustusburger Str. 369 (☎71331; 👜) – take bus #T245, or tram #1 or #6 to the terminus and then walk the remaining 1.5km. The **campsite** is at Thomas-Müntzer-Höhe 10, just north of Burg Rabenstein.

Each of the last three hotels listed above has an excellent **restaurant**; another good choice is *Metropolitan*, An der Alten Post 1. Vegetarians should head for *Café Henrie* in the basement of the *Umweltzentrum*, Henriettenstr. 5. There are homely *Gaststätten* outside both the Schaubergwerk Felsendome and Burg Rabenstein.

Chemnitz maintains a lively **cultural** scene, with concerts at the *Luxorpalast*, Hartmannstr. 11 (☎690490), operas at the *Opernhaus*, Theaterplatz 2 (☎488 4671), plays at the *Schauspielhaus* in the Park der Opfer des Faschismus (☎488 4315), and puppet shows at the *Puppentheater*, Hartmannstr. 5 (☎644 6751).

Augustusburg

The most obvious excursion from Chemnitz is to the village of **AUGUSTUSBURG** 14km to the east. Augustusburg clusters below its cliff-top Renaissance **Schloss** (April–Oct daily 10am–7pm; Nov–March Mon–Fri 10am–5pm, Sat & Sun 10am–5.30pm; separate tickets required for each section), built as the hunting lodge of the Saxon Electors by the Leipzig architect, Hieronymous Lotter, though its colossal dimensions suggest an altogether grander function.

Thirty-minute **guided tours** (DM2.50) take you to the **Brunnenhaus**, a deep well still preserving its original wooden machinery, and the **Schlosskapelle**, a beautiful galleried Renaissance chapel, which is among the earliest buildings designed specifically for Lutheran worship. The latter features a tiny historic organ on which recitals are occasionally given, an altarpiece by Cranach the Younger showing the Elector Augustus and his wife with fourteen children, and a pulpit adorned with paintings of scenes from the life of Christ by the same artist. An hour-long version of the tour (DM5) includes a visit to the **Küchenhaus**, which again has impressive historic equipment; here a film on the history of the Schloss is shown.

Other parts of the Schloss including the **tower** (DM1) can be visited independently. The **Hasenhaus** (DM3) has a museum on the fauna of the Erzgebirge region, but is mainly of note for the rooms themselves, adorned with monumental trompe l'oeil murals, including the humorous depictions of hares in the guise of humans which give the wing its name. Within the Küchenhaus is the **Motorradmuseum** (DM5), Germany's most impressive museum of bicycles and motorbikes, with a collection ranging from a *Laurin-Klement* from the end of last century, through the many productions of *NSU* to the latest roadsters. The **Marstall** (DM2.50) or stables houses the

Kutschenmuseum, a collection of historic coaches including those used by the postal services. Finally, the **Adler- und Falkenhof** (DM6) has a wide variety of birds of prey, some of which take part in the free-flight demonstrations (April–Sept Tues–Fri at 11am & 3pm, Sat & Sun at 11am, 3pm & 5pm; March & Oct Tues–Sun at 11am & 3pm; Nov–Feb Sat & Sun at 2pm only).

To get to Augustusburg, alight at Erdmannsdorf, on the main rail line between Chemnitz and Annaberg-Buchholz; from here a **funicular** (*Drahtseilbahn*), ascends directly to the Schloss. There's a really top-notch **restaurant**, the *Augustuskeller* (closed Sun evening and Mon) within the Schloss, which also houses a **youth hostel** (☎037291/20256; ②). The village has three **hotels**: *Morgensonne*, Morgensternstr. 2 (☎037291/20508; ④); *Ferienhotel Augustusburg*, Waldstr. 16 (☎037291/20810; ④); and *Café Friedrich*, Hans-Planer-Str. 1 (☎037291/6666; ④).

Freiberg

Exactly halfway along the eighty-kilometre-long rail line between Chemnitz and Dresden is **FREIBERG**, whose town centre looks, by eastern German standards, startlingly immaculate. Somehow the town came through World War II completely undamaged, and thereafter its long history as a mining community so endeared it to the GDR authorities that they had all the historic buildings cleaned and spruced up in the 1980s. The mining tradition is enshrined in the town's name, "Free Mountain", which is a reference to a twelfth-century Imperial decree allowing anyone to come to the area to prospect for minerals and keep all the proceeds. In 1765, the Bergakademie, the world's first college of mining, was founded here; now raised to university status, it's a centre of metallurgical training and research of international repute, imparting a degree of sophistication to what might otherwise now be a very provincial town indeed.

The town

Freiberg is centred on two market squares, Obermarkt and Untermarkt. From the outside the most remarkable feature is the assemblage of old buildings, but the overall highlight is the interior of the Dom, the town's principal monument.

The Dom

The **Dom** (guided tours May–Oct Mon–Sat at 10am, 11am, 2pm, 3pm & 4pm, Sun at 11am, 2pm, 3pm & 4pm; Nov–April Mon–Sat at 11am, 2pm & 3pm, Sun at 11am, 2pm, 3pm & 4pm; DM3), as the Marienkirche is officially designated despite never having been a bishop's seat, is outwardly unassuming and doesn't even have a prominent position, being stuck at the back of the lower of the two main squares, the Untermarkt. However, in sheer richness and variety of interior decoration (a legacy of the patronage of the Saxon Electors, and of the wealth brought by the mines), it's unsurpassed by any of the country's cathedrals.

Two important survivors of the original building, destroyed by fire in the late fifteenth century, were incorporated in the airily light hall church that replaced it. One is the **Goldene Pforte** (Golden Doorway – a reference to its original gilding), which formed the main entrance, but is now placed on the south side. Dating from the 1230s, it's one of the few German counterparts of the great figure portals characteristic of the Gothic cathedrals of France; it's a symbolical vision of a heavenly paradise, centred on a tympanum showing *The Adoration of the Magi*. Similar in date, though still Romanesque in spirit, is the anguished **triumphal cross** group placed high up on a beam above the entrance to the choir. Below it is an early example of a Protestant **high**

altar; painted by a follower of Cranach, it incorporates suitably modest-sized figures of a host of local burghers as spectators at the Last Supper.

In the nave, your eye is drawn to the extraordinary writhing, twisting forms of the most precious adornment from the time of the church's construction, the **Tulpenkanzel** (Tulip Pulpit) by **Hans Witten**. Even judged against his own prodigious originality, it's a singular work, being an allegory of the Church as the flower in the garden of God. Resting at the foot is the figure of a local miner in the guise of Daniel in the lion's den, a theme developed in the second pulpit alongside, accordingly known as the **Bergmannskanzel** (Miners' Pulpit), which was made just over a century later. The chancel was transformed to serve as the **mausoleum** of the Albertine line of the House of Wettin. The huge tomb of the Elector Moritz occupies centre stage, though the double memorial to two princesses by Balthasar Permoser, the Baroque sculptor of Dresden, is no less imposing. Another addition from this period is the **ducal loft** on the north side of the nave, designed by the Dresden architect Pöppelmann.

However, the church's most significant Baroque adornments are the two **organs**, both the work of **Gottfried Silbermann**, a friend of Bach and one of the first manufacturers of pianos. The ringing, silvery tones of the larger of these, which many organists regard as the greatest instrument ever made, can be heard at the recitals held each Thursday from May to October at 8pm. This is also the best time to visit the Dom, as you're then able to look round at leisure.

The rest of the town

At the corner of Am Dom and Untermarkt, a number of late Gothic houses have been knocked together to contain the **Stadt- und Bergbaumuseum** (Tues–Sun 10am–5pm; DM4), which explains the history of mining in the area in a surprisingly illuminating way, with plenty of large-scale models. Untermarkt itself has a fine assemblage of mansions, including examples of Gothic, Renaissance and Baroque, as does Kirchgasse, the western continuation of Am Dom. If you want to pursue the mineralogical connection, visit the **Mineralogische Sammlung der Bergakademie** (Wed–Fri 9am–noon & 1–4pm, Sat 9am–4pm; free), just off the northwestern corner of Untermarkt at Brenhausgasse 14, which has a valuable collection drawn from all round the world.

A block to the north, at the edge of the historic part of town, is **Schloss Freudenstein**, a much-restored Renaissance palace of the Saxon Electors; there's free access to the courtyard, but otherwise nothing much to see. From here Burgstrasse, which is lined with a number of superb Renaissance and Baroque houses, leads to the harmonious-looking main square, the **Obermarkt**, where local youths loll around the central fountain with its statue of Emperor Otto the Rich, the town's founder. The late Gothic **Rathaus** stands on the east side, with the (for once) separate **Ratskeller**, entered via a handsome Renaissance portal, to the north. Just to the west of Obermarkt, set in its own peaceful close, is the Gothic **Petrikirche**, proud possessor of another Silbermann organ.

Practicalities

Freiberg's **Hauptbahnhof** is located about fifteen minutes' walk south of Obermarkt, while the **bus station** is about halfway between the two, just before the inner ring road. The **tourist office** (Mon–Fri 9am–6pm, Sat 9am–noon; ☎03731/23602) at Burgstr. 1 offers the usual booking service for **private rooms** (①–④).

There are also plenty of inexpensive **pensions**; those with a central location include *Gemeiner*, Schöne Gasse 6 (☎03731/356794; ③); *Heidi*, Lange Str. 46 (☎03731/34681; ④); and *Bräustübel*, Donatsgasse 3 (☎03731/26480; ④). The town is also well supplied with characterful **hotels**. *Gasthof Brauhof*, Körnerstr. 2 (☎03731/23281; ④) is a particular bargain; it serves excellent meals and also has a beer garden. *Mauk'sches Gut*,

Hornstr. 20 (☎03731/33978; ④) occupies an old farmstead just outside the Altstadt; *Am Obermarkt*, Waisenhausstr. 2 (☎03731/34361; ⑤) has an ideal location plus a fine café and cellar restaurant; *Alekto*, Am Bahnhof 3 (☎03731/7940; ⑦) is a grand station hotel with a distinguished Italian restaurant; while *Silberhof*, Silberhofstr. 1 (☎03731/23970 or 247271; ⑦) occupies a Jugendstil mansion on a quiet inner suburban street.

Apart from the hotels, good **restaurants** include the *Ratskeller*, Obermarkt 16; *Zum Alten Brennmeister*, Kesselgasse 30, a specialist in game dishes; and the wine bars *Weinstube St Nikolai*, Kesselgasse 24, and *Weinhaus Blasius*, Burgstr. 26. Also recommended is a long-established **café**, *Hartmann*, Peterstr. 1.

A varied programme of **music** and **drama** is presented at the late eighteenth-century *Mittelsächsisches Theater*, Borngasse 3 (☎03731/358234). The main **festival** is the *Bergstadtfest* in late June, a celebration of local mining tradition.

EASTERN SAXONY

In GDR days, the eastern part of Saxony was jokingly referred to as the "Valley of the Clueless", on the grounds that most of the area, unlike everywhere else in the country, was unable to receive West German television and hence unable to hear a non-Communist view of the outside world. The end of the Erzgebirge range is marked here by the valley of the **River Elbe**, one of the most beautiful parts of Germany, particularly the area immediately before the Czech border known as **Saxon Switzerland**. Downstream lies the state capital of **Dresden** which, despite its wartime losses, still has some of Europe's greatest buildings, museums and theatres. The former capital of **Meissen**, a short distance beyond, is also one of eastern Germany's most attractive towns, preserving its medieval appearance almost intact.

To the east is **Upper Lusatia** (*Oberlausitz*), one of the two main homelands of the Sorbs, the original Slav inhabitants of the region (see p.823). It's had a turbulent history, having frequently changed hands, though the two finest towns, **Bautzen** and **Görlitz**, along with **Zittau**, the gateway to the mountain region to the south, all came through the last war with relatively little damage.

Dresden

The name of **DRESDEN** stands alongside Hiroshima as a symbol of the horrendously destructive consequences of modern warfare. What was generally regarded as Germany's most beautiful large city – the "Baroque Florence" – survived World War II largely unscathed until the night of February 13 and 14, 1945. Then, in a matter of hours, it was reduced to a smouldering heap of ruins in the most savage **saturation bombing** ever mounted by the British and American air forces against civilian targets (see box on p.956). At least 35,000 people died – though the total may have been considerably higher (according to one estimate, by as much as 100,000), as the city was packed with refugees fleeing from the advancing Red Army. With this background, it's all the more remarkable that Dresden has adapted to the economic framework of the re-united Germany better than anywhere else in the former GDR. Like Berlin, it's an exciting place to be in at the moment: be prepared for striking visual changes as the post-Communist authorities put into effect their new policy of restoring all the historic buildings left as ruins.

By origin a Slav fishing village, Dresden stood in the shadow of nearby Meissen until it was made capital of the Albertine line of the House of Wettin in 1485. Its glory period came in the early eighteenth century, when the Elector **Augustus the Strong** gathered round him a brilliant group of artists and architects who transformed the city

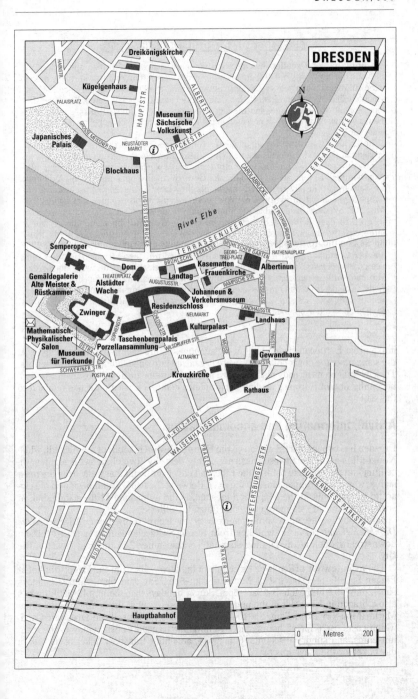

DRESDEN

Dreikönigskirche

Kügelgenhaus

HAINSTR.

HAUPTSTR.

ALBERTSTR.

PALAISPLATZ

GROSSE MEISSNER STR.

Museum für
Sächsische
Volkskunst

N

Japanisches
Palais

NEUSTÄDTER
MARKT

KÖPCKESTR.

TERRASSENUFER

Blockhaus

CAROLABRÜCKE

ST. PETERSBURGER STR.

AUGUSTUSBRÜCKE

River Elbe

TERRASSENUFER

Semperoper

BRÜHLSCHE TERRASSE

BRÜHLSCHER GARTEN

RATHENAUPLATZ

Dom

THEATERPLATZ

BRÜHLSCHE

GEORG-
TREU-PLATZ

Gemäldegalerie
Alte Meister &
Rüstkammer

Alstädter
Wache

AUGUSTUSSTR.

Landtag

Kasematten
Frauenkirche

Albertinun

SCHIESSGASSE

Zwinger

SOPHIENSTR.

SCHLOSS STR.

Residenzschloss

Johanneun &
Verkehrsmuseum

RAMPISCHE STR.

LANDHAUSSTR.

Mathematisch-
Physikalischer
Salon

NEUMARKT

Landhaus

RINGSTR.

Museum
für Tierkunde

OSTRA-ALLEE

Taschenbergpalais
Porzellansammlung

Kulturpalast

WILSDRUFFER STR.

WEISSE

SCHWERINER STR.

ALTMARKT

Gewandhaus

KREUZSTR.

POSTPLATZ

Kreuzkirche

Rathaus

DR.-KÜLZ-RING

WAISENHAUSSTR.

PRAGER STR.

ST. PETERSBURGER STR.

BÜRGERWIESE PARKSTR.

BUDAPESTER STR.

PRAGER STR.

Hauptbahnhof

0   Metres   200

THE BOMBING OF DRESDEN

The **bombing of Dresden** has attracted far more criticism of British and American methods during World War II than any other event – even though it was in reality merely the culmination of a deliberately destructive bombing policy, operational since 1940, in which civilian targets and historic buildings were regarded as fair game. However, the sheer extent of the damage, and the fact that thousands of innocent people who were themselves victims of Nazism perished in the raids, put it in a different class from all previous such attacks.

The greatest tragedy of Dresden is that it remains unclear exactly why the raids were carried out at all. The genesis seems to have been a nebulous decision taken in 1944 to carry out a saturation raid on some city (none was specified) which had hitherto not been bombed, as a means of breaking the German resolve once and for all. Although the Soviets specifically requested this tactic, they later distanced themselves from it completely, using it during the Cold War period as a useful propaganda tool against the West. (They were responsible for the casualty estimate of 135,000, which is now believed to have been a deliberate exaggeration.) Winston Churchill, who certainly authorized the attack, also tried to feign ignorance almost immediately afterwards, leaving most of the opprobrium to fall on **Sir Arthur Harris**, the controversial head of Bomber Command. After the war, Harris was denied the peerage which all other service chiefs received, and was shunned by the British establishment, while his forces, who had suffered appalling casualties throughout the war, were refused a campaign medal. The posthumous reassessment of his reputation, culminating in the decision to honour him with a statue in central London, drew widespread official protests from Dresden and other bombed cities.

into a great European capital built in a distinctive, highly decorative Baroque style. At the same time, the court collections were organized into outstanding public **museums**. The city built on its already distinguished musical tradition during the Romantic period, becoming one of Europe's leading performance centres, a position it has retained to this day.

Arrival, information and accommodation

Dresden has two main train stations – the **Hauptbahnhof** is south of the Altstadt, while **Neustadt** is at the northwestern corner of the "new city" (which in fact is eighteenth-century) on the opposite bank of the Elbe, and only slightly further away from the main sights, which are grouped close to the river. Between the two, located beside an old cigarette factory built in the shape of a mosque, is the unmanned **Mitte** station, but, in spite of its name, it's no more convenient than the others.

Undoubtedly the most atmospheric way to arrive is by **boat**. All *Sächsische Dampfschiffahrt* services, whether from Saxon Switzerland upstream or Meissen downstream, dock at the landing stage at Terrassenufer 2 in the very heart of the city.

The main **tourist office** is just a couple of minutes' walk from the Hauptbahnhof at Prager Str. 10–11 (March–Oct Mon–Fri 9am–8pm, Sat 9am–6pm, Sun & holidays 9am–2pm; Nov–Feb Mon–Sat 9am–6pm, Sun & holidays 9am–2pm; ☎491920); there's also a branch in Neustadt in the underground passageway at the southern side of the Markt (Mon–Fri 10am–6pm, Sat 10–2pm; ☎804 3539). Both sell the **Dresden Card**, which costs DM26 for 48 hours, and covers public transport costs, entry to the main museums, and sundry discounts. Otherwise, a 24-hour transport ticket costs DM8, a day ticket for the museums DM12.

Accommodation

Nowhere is the recent revitalization of Dresden more manifest than in the improvement in its stock of **hotels**, which can rival that of any German city, at least in the middle and upper ranges. Any deficiency at the budget end of the market is remedied by small suburban **pensions** and a plentiful supply of **private rooms** (②–④), which can be booked at either tourist office or the independently run *Zentraler Zimmernachweis* (daily 1–7pm; ☎471 6121) just inside the entrance to the Hauptbahnhof. Dresden has three **youth hostels** and there are several campsites in the area, although only two are within the city boundaries.

HOTELS AND PENSIONS

Am Birkenhain, Barbarastr. 76, Pieschen (☎85140, fax 851 4100). Moderately priced hotel with restaurant in a green area northwest of Neustadt, close to the S-Bahn station Pieschen. ⑥

art' otel, Ostra-Allee 33 (☎49220, fax 492 2777). Trendy new venture whose distinctively arty appearance is the joint work of a local painter and a Milanese designer. Its restaurant, *Factory*, serves high-quality Californian-style food. ⑧

Bastei, Prager Strasse (☎4856 6661). One of a trio of huge GDR-era concrete boxes (the others are *Königstein* and *Lilienstein*) on this street, all now part of the *ibis* chain. They're worth trying for their geographical convenience and for the special deals which are often available; with over 400 beds in each, there's seldom a problem getting a room. ⑤

Bellevue, Grosse Meissner Str. 15 (☎81200, fax 812 0609). Before the *Wende*, this modern hotel incorporating a Baroque palace was Dresden's flagship address. Despite losing this status, it still offers the advantage of a marvellous Neustadt location right by the Elbe, and has a true curiosity in its Polynesian speciality restaurant, *Buri-Buri*. ⑨

Bülow Residenz, Rähnitzgasse 19 (☎80030, fax 800 3100). Exclusive hotel in a renovated Baroque palace in Neustadt with a handsome interior courtyard. The restaurant, open evenings only, is one of the best and most expensive in the city. ⑨

Gewandhaus, Ringstr. 1 (☎49490, fax 494 9490). Occupying the former cloth hall, this was a medium-range hotel in GDR days, but has just been refurbished to five-star standard by the *Radisson* chain. ⑨

Glasewald, Berggasse 27, Hellerau (☎890 2524, fax 890 2527). Hotel in a rustic wooded setting at the extreme northern end of the city, not far from the terminus of tram #8. ④

Hotelschiff Florentina, Terrassenufer (☎459 0169, fax 459 5036). This hotel-ship moored in the Elbe just east of the Carolabrücke is one of the least expensive city-centre options. ⑥

Loschwitz, Grundstr. 40 (☎268 7785). Bargain-priced pension in the valley between the *Standseilbahn* and the *Bergschwebebahn*. ④

Martha Hospiz, Nieritzstr. 11 (☎81760, fax 817 6222). Turn-of-the-century church-affiliated Neustadt hotel modernized to a high standard. Its cellar houses the *Kartoffelkeller*, where potato-based dishes predominate. ⑦

Pillnitzer Elbblick, Pillnitz. Söbrigener Str. 2 (☎261 0942, fax 261 0952). Small hotel at the far southeastern edge of the city. Its high-quality restaurant is the obvious place to break for a meal when visiting the nearby Schloss. ⑥

Schloss Eckberg, Bautzener Str. 134 (☎80990, fax 809 9199). English-style neo-Gothic stately home set in its own lovely park high above the north bank of the Elbe, linked to the centre by tram #11. ⑦

Schöne Aussicht, Krügerstr. 1, Loschwitz (☎268 3305, fax 268 3305). Olde-worlde hotel of the type normally found in German villages than in major cities, located just above the upper station of the *Bergschwebebahn*. It has a really excellent, reasonably priced restaurant, complete with terrace beer garden. ⑦

Stadt Rendsburg, Kamenzer Str. 1 (☎804 1551, fax 802 2586). Located in a well-preserved late nineteenth-century district in the north of Neustadt, this has some very basic rooms as well as others of a higher standard. ④

Taschenberg-Palais, Taschenberg 3 (☎49120, fax 491 2812). This magnificent palace alongside the Residenzschloss was built by Augustus the Strong for one of his mistresses, Countess Kosel. Left as a burnt-out shell for four decades, it has been restored according to the original plans by the *Kempinski* chain and is now easily the best hotel in town, with every conceivable luxury including swimming pool, sauna and solarium. Surprisingly, its *Paulaner* restaurant is moderately priced, and is an ideal place for lunch. ⑨

Villa Emma, Stechgrundstr. 2, Weisser Hirsch (☎374810, fax 374 8118). Beautifully restored Jugenstil villa in Dresden's poshest suburb, reached by tram #11. It also has a high-quality and fairly expensive restaurant. ⑧

Wenotel, Schachthofring 24 (☎49760, fax 497 6100). Located a short distance northwest of the Altstadt, this hotel offers modern standards and facilities at a relatively low cost. Although large, it has double rooms only, with only a small discount for single occupancy. ⑤

Zur Pillnitzer Schlossfähre, Hosterwitzer Str. 22, Kleinzschachwitz (☎201 9588, fax 201 9557). Budget pension at the extreme southeastern edge of the city, close to the terminus of trams #9 and #14, and the ferry to Schloss Pillnitz from which it takes its name. ④

YOUTH HOSTELS AND CAMPSITES

Jugendgästehaus, Maternistr. 22 (☎492620). Large new hostel in a tower block just a few minutes' walk southwest of the main Altstadt sights. ⌂

Jugendherberge, Hübnerstr. 11 (☎471 0667). Located just to the south of the Hauptbahnhof. ⌂

Jugendherberge Oberloschwitz, Sierksstr. 33, Loschwitz (☎36672). Located a short distance from the upper terminus of the *Bergschwebebahn*, and also on the route of bus #84, which connects with trams #1 and #6 at Schillerplatz. ⌂

Campingplatz Mockritz, Boderitzer Str. 30, Mockritz (☎471 8226). Has bungalows to rent as an alternative to pitching a tent. Take bus #76 from the Hauptbahnhof.

Campingplatz Wostra, Triekestr. 100, Kleinzschachwitz (☎223 1903). Situated on the banks of the Elbe, south of the terminus of trams #9 and #14. Also has bungalows to rent.

The city centre

Central Dresden consists of two distinct districts, the Altstadt and the Neustadt, which lie south and north of the Elbe respectively. The former contains the lion's share of sights, but both have Baroque masterpieces from the city's golden age. Both also have plenty of Communist-era concrete buildings.

The southern Altstadt

If you arrive at the Hauptbahnhof, you see the worst of modern Dresden first, as the **Prager Strasse**, which leads to the historic part of the city, is an example of Stalinist town planning on the grand scale – a spacious pedestrian precinct containing the standard cocktail of high-rise luxury hotels, public offices, box-like apartment, soulless cafés and restaurants catering mainly for organized tour groups, with a few fountains and statues thrown in for relief. It was here that masses of people congregated in October 1989, hoping to be able to jump aboard the special trains laid on for the East Germans who had sought refuge in the West German embassy in Prague.

At the far end, beyond the inner ring road, is the **Altmarkt**, which was much extended after its wartime destruction; the only building of note which remains is the **Kreuzkirche**, the Protestant cathedral. The present structure mixes a Baroque body with a Neoclassical **tower** (April–Sept Mon, Tues, Thurs & Fri 10am–6pm, Wed & Sat 10am–5pm; Oct–March Mon–Sat 10am–4pm; DM2) and a modernized interior impressive in its starkness and loftiness. On Saturdays at 6pm and at the 9.30am Sunday service you can usually hear the *Kreuzchor*, one of the world's leading church choirs, which specializes in performances of the seventeenth-century Dresden composer Heinrich Schütz, father figure of Germany's rich musical tradition.

Behind stands the heavy bulk of the **Rathaus**, built early this century in a lumbering Historicist style complete with a belfry which rises well above that of the church.

Further east is the late eighteenth-century **Gewandhaus**, the old cloth hall, which has been transformed into a hotel. Across the wide Wilsdruffer Strasse from here is the contemporaneous **Landhaus**, home to the local history collections of the **Stadtmuseum** (10am–6pm, closed Fri; DM3), which are presented in a far more interesting manner than usual.

The Zwinger

North of Wilsdruffer Strasse lies the palace quarter. At its western end is the great glory of Baroque Dresden, the joyous pleasure palace known as the **Zwinger**, built for festivals and tournaments. It was badly damaged in the war, but quickly rebuilt and is now once more the subject of a major restoration programme. The building was designed by **Matthaeus Daniel Pöppelmann**, one of the most original architects Germany ever produced, and the plan he chose here is appropriately daring: a vast open space with fountains surrounded by a single-storey gallery linking two-storey pavilions, and entered from exuberantly grandiose gateways. The effect is further enhanced by the marvellously expressive decoration by the sculptor **Balthasar Permoser**, though much of this has had to be replaced by copies. Unfortunately, the northern wing was never built because funds ran out.

The main entry to the courtyard is via the **Kronentor**, which guards the moat on the western side; shaped like a triumphal arch, it takes its name from the huge carving of the Polish royal crown which stands on top. An alternative way in is via the **Glockenspielpavillon** at the southwest corner, which has a carillon of forty bells crafted out of Meissen porcelain. At the opposite end of the courtyard is the most beautiful pavilion, the lantern-shaped **Wallpavillon**, astride which rises a heroic figure of Hercules carrying the world on his shoulders. Behind it is the **Nymphenbad**, an elaborate sculptured fountain which ranks as Permoser's most ornate creation.

The Zwinger contains several **museums**. Beautifully displayed in the southeastern pavilion, entered from Sophienstrasse, is the **Porzellansammlung** (10am–6pm, closed Thurs; DM3). Products from the famous Meissen factory are featured extensively, making a fascinating comparison with examples drawn from the two-thousand-year-old history of Chinese porcelain manufacture. A small natural history display, the **Tierkundemuseum** (July & Aug daily 10am–5pm; rest of year Tues–Sun 9am–4pm; DM2), is housed in the southern gallery. The southwestern pavilion is known as the **Mathematisch-Physikalischer Salon** (9.30am–5pm, closed Thurs; DM3), which is a good deal more interesting than it sounds, offering a fascinating array of old globes, clocks and scientific instruments.

The Rüstkammer

The open space on the north side of the Zwinger was filled by the **Semperbau**, which is named in honour of its architect Gottfried Semper, who was responsible for many of the city's finest nineteenth-century buildings. Exhibited in an elegant columned hall on its ground floor is a selection of pieces from the Saxon armoury or **Rüstkammer** (Tues-Sun 10am–6pm; DM3), which has a really magnificent collection of historic arms and armour from around the world. The focal point of the display is a dazzling Renaissance suit of armour for a man and a horse, adorned with engravings of scenes of the Labour of Hercules and the Trojan War, which was made in Antwerp in the 1560s by Eliseus Libaerts. Other highlights include the sword commissioned by Duke Moritz of Saxony to celebrate his promotion to the rank of Elector; the tournament armour of Elector August; tiny suits of armour made for the children of the court; the coronation robes of Augustus the Strong (see box overleaf); and various ornate artefacts used in the pageants held in the Zwinger.

AUGUSTUS THE STRONG (1670–1733)

The irony behind Dresden's magnificent Baroque heritage is that it was commissioned by, and for the greater glory of, **Augustus the Strong** (*August der Starke*), who, even by the standards of the Age of Absolutism, was an exceptionally loathsome character. He came to power in 1694 as Elector Friedrich August I of Saxony, and three years later won the contest to become King of Poland, assuming the title Augustus II. As if to disprove the false maxim that religion and politics do not mix, Augustus converted to Catholicism in order to qualify for the latter election, thus reversing the stance of his ancestors who had backed Luther against the papacy and the empire, in the process strengthening their own political position. His nickname derives partly from his great physical strength – he could allegedly break a horseshoe with his bare hands – but mainly from his sexual prowess, which is said to have included the siring of a child for each day of the year. This may have been a scurrilous exaggeration put about by his estranged wife, a member of the Hohenzollern family, but he certainly did keep a bevy of regular mistresses, many of them prominent figures in their own right, such as Countess Aurora of Königsmark, abbess of the Imperial convent in Quedlinburg. But if he was popular in bed, Augustus was an inept political operator, whose reign was an unmitigated disaster for Poland, which plummeted from its position as Europe's premier military power to being a client state of Russia, a position from which, it could be argued, it has only recently managed to escape. Deposed by the Poles in 1706, he was reinstated with Russian help four years later, but was no more than a puppet ruler for the remaining 23 years of his reign. Saxony also suffered financially by being tied to an old nation in terminal decline – but in compensation gained a gloriously beautiful capital.

The Gemäldegalerie Alte Meister

The **Gemäldegalerie Alte Meister** (Tues–Sun 10am–6pm; DM7) is also within the Semper building, except for the early Netherlandish and German paintings, which are displayed in an interconnected chamber in the Baroque Zwinger. Although it has had almost no additions made to it in the past century, the collection of old masters built up by the Saxon Electors still ranks among the dozen best in the world.

ITALIAN PAINTINGS

The Gemäldegalerie contains some of the most familiar of all Italian Renaissance paintings, of which the star is **Raphael's** *Sistine Madonna*, a wondrous vision of the Virgin and Child among the clouds, adored by SS Sixtus (who bears the features of the warrior pope Julius II) and Barbara. Almost equally celebrated is the *Holy Night* by **Correggio**, which interprets one of the most ubiquitous artistic subjects in a completely fresh manner, stressing the nocturnal element ignored by so many other painters. The *Sleeping Venus* by **Giorgione** is one of the most sensual nudes of western art, and among the few paintings almost universally accepted as being by this short-lived father figure of the Venetian Renaissance. It's documented as having been unfinished at the time of his death by plague and was completed by his friend **Titian**, who is represented here by several of his own finest works, including *Young Woman with a Fan* and the deeply psychological *Christ and the Pharisees*. Among several typically resplendent works by **Veronese** is one of his famous banquet scenes, *The Marriage at Cana*, while **Tintoretto** is represented with a diverse group of works, the most memorable being the vividly sketched *St Michael*.

Antonello da Messina's *St Sebastian* is a composition of startling audacity, using an unorthodox low vantage point and incorporating plenty of anecdotal detail in the background, to which the eye is irresistibly drawn. Other Renaissance works to look out for are the sumptuous depiction of *The Annunciation* by the rare Ferrarese painter

Francesco del Cossa; the disarmingly simple *Portrait of a Boy* by **Pinturicchio**; and the consciously theatrical *Scenes from the Life of St Zenobius* by **Botticelli**. A distinguished group of seventeenth-century Italian pictures includes **Carracci**'s *The Genius of Fame* and **Guercino**'s arresting *Ecstasy of St Francis*. However, the gems are the series of the Parables – including many rarely depicted scenes – which rank as the masterpieces of the short-lived **Domenico Feti**; the wonderfully simple *Parable of the Lost Coin* is particularly memorable. From the eighteenth century, the brilliantly detailed views of Dresden, then at its most resplendent, by the court painter **Bernardo Bellotto** (often known as Canaletto, after his more celebrated uncle) particularly merit attention, not least for the poignance they have acquired since the wartime destruction of the city. Several of his views of Pirna are also on show.

GERMAN PAINTINGS
Among the German pictures are two masterpieces by **Holbein the Younger** – *Thomas and John Godsalve* presents, in its unusual diagonal poses, a successful solution to the particularly tricky art of the double portrait, while *Le Sieur de Morette* is executed with stunning virtuosity of technique. Very different is the almost abstract style apparent in the pendants *Duke Henry the Pious* and *Duchess Anna of Mecklenburg* by **Cranach**, which are among the earliest full-length portraits ever painted. The same artist's *Martyrdom of St Catherine* was painted for the Schlosskirche in Wittenberg, as was the so-called *Dresden Altarpiece* by **Dürer**, who is also represented by *Portrait of a Young Man*. Among later paintings, there's a striking *Rape of Prosperine* by **Josef Heintz**, a Swiss Mannerist who worked at the Imperial court in Prague, and a large number of works by the highly influential Neoclassicist **Anton Raffael Mengs** and other painters of the Dresden school.

PAINTINGS OF OTHER SCHOOLS
The Gemäldegalerie has few early Netherlandish works, but the *Madonna and Child* triptych by **van Eyck**, executed with a miniature-like precision, is unquestionably one of its supreme treasures. Pick of the many works by **Rubens** is *Bathsheba Receiving King David's Letter*, a subject which provided him with an excuse to paint a suggestive portrait of his youthful second wife. **Van Dyck** is represented by one of the variants of his *The Three Children of King Charles I*, and by a superbly characterized *Man in Armour*. The most famous of the **Rembrandt** canvases here is *Self-Portrait with Saskia*, in which he somewhat enigmatically shows himself with his new and clearly not overjoyous wife in the guise of the Prodigal Son carousing in an inn. His interpretation of *The Rape of Ganymede* is also highly unconventional – instead of showing the handsome young boy being carried off to become the cupbearer to the gods by the jealous Jupiter disguised as an eagle, he chose to depict an infant being dragged by his shirt tail, stricken with fear and urinating in desperation. There are two canvases by **Vermeer** – *Girl Reading a Letter* is a typical work, set by a window, and concentrating on the subtle play of light and shade, while the painting known as *The Procuress* is a mysterious composition whose exact meaning is unclear.

Among the French paintings, **Poussin**'s vivacious mythological scenes, such as *The Kingdom of Flora* and *Pan and Syrinx*, make a fascinating contrast with the cooly classical approach favoured by **Claude** in works like *Landscape with Acis and Galatea*. In the eighteenth-century section, **Watteau**'s frilly *Conversation in a Park* stands out, though the pastels of the Swiss painter **Liotard**, and in particular *The Chocolate Girl*, are among the most popular with visitors to the gallery. The Spanish section is modest, but shows no fall-off in quality, with **El Greco**'s *Christ Healing the Blind* (which actually dates from his Venetian years), **Ribera**'s *St Agnes in Prison* and **Zurbarán**'s *St Bonaventure Kneeling before the Papal Crown* being particularly outstanding.

The Residenzschloss

Across from the Zwinger is the colossal main palace of the Electors and kings of Saxony, the predominantly Renaissance **Residenzschloss** (Tues–Sun 10am–5pm; DM5). This was horribly destroyed in the war, and, although the GDR authorities paid lip service to the ideal of restoring it, in practice they did little more than employ two or three workmen to ensure that the ruins, which were kept fenced off, remained upright. The rebuilding programme now under way is a massive task, which will cost an estimated DM500 million: even the projected completion date of 2006 (the city's 800th anniversary) seems optimistic. In the meantime, you can climb the **Hausmannsturm** for a view over the complex and beyond, and see an illuminating exhibition on the history of the building. At some point in the next few years the famous Grünes Gewölbe treasures (see opposite) will be returned to their original location in the **Spiegelzimmern** (Mirror Rooms), which miraculously survived the bombing.

The Hofkirche

At the end of this street is the **Hofkirche** (now the **Dom**), the largest church in Saxony. It was commissioned by Friedrich August II, the only legitimate son of Augustus the Strong, who succeeded him as Elector of Saxony and, after a short interregnum, as King of Poland as well. To emphasize its Catholic allegiance in what was otherwise a staunchly Protestant province, the Italian architect Gaetano Chiaveri was imported to draw up plans. He responded with a highly original design, featuring advancing and receding walls topped by numerous theatrical statues, the whole rounded off with a flourish by an elegant campanile. The gleaming white interior has an elliptical central space surrounded by large chapels. Some of these are normally fenced off; to see them, and the crypt with its tombs of members of the Wettin dynasty, you have to take a **guided tour** (Mon–Thurs at 11am & 2pm, Fri & Sat at 1pm & 2pm, Sun at 1pm; donation expected).

At the **high altar** is a large canvas of *The Ascension* by Anton Raffael Mengs, who had been appointed court artist in Madrid by the time he finished the work. The side altar of *The Immaculate Conception* and *The Dream of Joseph* are by the same artist. Balthasar Permoser made the wonderfully frilly limewood **pulpit**, which was later given an extravagant canopy; he also made the marble font, and the huge statues of SS Ambrose and Augustine under the gallery. The immaculately voiced **organ** (on which recitals are given on summer Saturdays at 4pm) is the artistic testament of the doyen of the craft, Gottfried Silbermann.

Theaterplatz

Facing the Hofkirche across Theaterplatz is the **Italienisches Dörfchen** (Italian Village), whose name recalls that it was the site of the huts of the Italian masons who built the church. Following its recent immaculate restoration, it houses a trio of restaurants (see p.966). Opposite is the plush **Sächsische Staatsoper**, now usually known as the **Semperoper** in honour of its architect. Its tradition is second to none, having seen the premieres of Wagner's *The Flying Dutchman* and *Tannhäuser* and Richard Strauss' *Elektra*, *Salome* and *Der Rosenkavalier*. **Guided tours** (DM8) of the interior take place throughout the year, except for two months in mid-summer; check the noticeboard for details. Tickets for performances are hard to come by – the box office for this and other musical events is in the **Altstädter Wache**, a sternly Neoclassical guard house designed by Schinkel.

The Johanneum, the Frauenkirche and the Kasamatten

Augustusstrasse snakes southeast from the Hofkirche between the **Landtag**, the parliament building, and the back of the **Johanneum**, the former stables. Along the wall of the latter can be seen a huge turn-of-the-century Meissen porcelain frieze, the *Fürstenzug*, showing a procession of all the ruling members of the Wettin dynasty. On the other side of the complex is the **Lange Gang** (Long Walk), an arcaded late sixteenth-century courtyard in Florentine Renaissance style, and the **Schöne Pforte** (Beautiful Gateway). Part of the building is given over to the **Verkehrsmuseum** (Transport Museum; Tues–Sun 10am–5pm; DM4), with exhibits ranging from trams to aeroplanes.

The entrance to the museum is on Neumarkt, which was formerly dominated by the **Frauenkirche**, a domed church by Georg Bähr, the most talented Dresden Baroque architect after Pöppelmann. One of the finest ever built for Protestant worship, it was designed as both a foil and rival to the Hofkirche. As it was reduced to a heap of rubble in the war with only a fragment of wall left standing, the Communists decided to leave it in this condition as a permanent war memorial. It became the focus for annual peace meetings to mark the anniversary of the wartime bomb raids, and was an important rallying point during the *Wende*. After a fierce controversy, the decision was taken in 1991 to rebuild it completely, and work is now well under way.

North of Neumarkt, a spacious promenade, the Brühlsche Terrasse, runs along the bank of the Elbe. Here are the **Kasamatten** (guided tours daily 10am–5/6pm; DM6), the underground sections of the municipal fortification system, which were built in the mid-sixteenth century according to the most advanced principles of Renaissance military architecture.

The Albertinum

Also on Brühlsche Terrasse is the **Albertinum** (10am–6pm, closed Thurs; DM7), which houses many of Dresden's most celebrated art treasures, grouped in several collections.

THE GEMÄLDEGALERIE NEUE MEISTER

The **Gemäldegalerie Neue Meister** contains nineteenth- and twentieth-century paintings and sculpture. It begins with German Romantic paintings, among which the dozen or so canvases by **Friedrich** stand out. These include one of his most famous and haunting works, *The Cross in the Mountains*, a purely secular subject framed to resemble an altarpiece and originally used as such in a private chapel. The Saxon **Ludwig Richter**, better known as a book illustrator, is well represented, while the Biedermeier style is seen at its best in the humorous compositions of **Spitzweg**. Realist masterpieces include several striking works by **Menzel**, but the portraits – including **Lenbach's** *Paul Heyse* (the Nobel Prize-winning writer) and *Wilhelm Busch* (the cartoonist), and **Leibl's** *Baron von Stauffenberg* – steal the show. Works by most of the French Impressionists and their German contemporaries, including Liebermann and Corinth, precede a section devoted to the Expressionist artists of the *Die Brücke* group, which was founded in Dresden. Of the later pictures, look out for two pacifist works in an anachronistic triptych format: *War* by **Otto Dix** and the Bosch-like *The Thousand Year Reich* by **Hans Grundig**, a local artist who spent four years in a concentration camp.

THE GRÜNES GEWÖLBE

The Albertinum's other museums are centred on the famous **Grünes Gewölbe** or Green Vault. This dazzling array of treasury items, one of the richest in the world, was formerly shown in the Spiegelzimmern of the Residenzschloss, and it's intended to return them there in due course, although the display cabinets here make a good stab at re-creating the original effect. After a few medieval works, the collection really gets into its stride with the elaborate creations of sixteenth-century Nürnberg goldsmiths. However, the most fetching works are the Rococo fancies specially made by Augustus the Strong's court jeweller, **Johann Melchior Dinglinger**. His *Court of Delhi on the Birthday of the Great Moghul* is a real *tour de force*, featuring 137 gilded and enamelled figures studded with 3000 diamonds, emeralds, rubies and pearls. He and his brothers, together with a host of apprentices, worked on this for seven years; its glorification of an absolute monarch is a thinly veiled allegory praising the Saxon Electors themselves. Many of Dinglinger's smaller pieces were made in collaboration with Balthasar Permoser – the pick of these are the riotously ornate *Bath of Diana* and the *Moor with a Basket of Emeralds*. By Permoser himself are a number of dainty little ivories, notably the *Hottentot Couple*.

With the same entry ticket you also get to see the **Münzkabinett** with its displays of coins and medallions, and the **Skulpturensammlung**, which is particularly strong on the Classical period, with Roman copies of lost Greek originals.

The Neustadt

The Neustadt across the Elbe was a planned Baroque town, and its layout is still obvious, even if few of the original buildings survive. In the centre of the Markt rises the **Goldener Reiter**, a gilded equestrian statue of Augustus the Strong. The only Baroque building to have been rebuilt here is the **Blockhaus**, a guardhouse designed by Zacharias Longuelune, a Frenchman who worked closely with Pöppelmann. Just to the east of the square, on Köpckestrasse, is the seventeenth-century **Jägerhaus**, now housing the **Museum für Sächsische Volkskunst** (Tues–Sun 10am–6pm; DM3), a collection of folklore objects from throughout Saxony.

The Neustadt's central axis, Hauptstrasse, is a pedestrian precinct lined with a host of restaurants and cafés. It's something of a compromise between the old and the new. Although it in some ways resembles Prager Strasse, a number of Baroque houses have been preserved, among them the **Kügelgenhaus** at no. 13, now decked out with early nineteenth-century furnishings as the **Museum zur Dresdner Frühromantik** (Wed–Sun 10am–6pm; DM3). Beyond stands the Neustadt's parish church, the **Dreikönigskirche**, which was designed by Pöppelmann and built by Georg Bähr. Only recently restored following war damage, it is currently home to the huge carved Renaissance frieze of *The Dance of Death* which formerly adorned a gateway to the Residenzschloss.

In the park overlooking the Elbe is the most esoteric creation of Dresden Baroque, the **Japanisches Palais**, in which most of the city's leading architects had a hand. It now contains the **Landesmuseum für Vorgeschichte** (Tues–Sun 10am–5pm; DM4), a turgid archeological museum, but you don't have to pay to see the courtyard, a fantasy inspired by the eighteenth-century infatuation with chinoiserie.

Another whimsical attraction is **Pfund's Molkerei** at Bautzener Str. 79 at the eastern end of Neustadt. Long derelict, its tiled Jugendstil decoration, a mixture of grotesque motifs and picture-book scenes, has been lovingly restored, and its claim to be regarded as "the most beautiful dairy shop in the world" is surely justified. It sells a marvellous selection of cheeses from around the world, and makes a good spot for lunch - whether in the stand-up section in the shop itself, or in the café-restaurant upstairs (see p.967).

The outskirts

In stark contrast to the centre, some of the suburbs of Dresden sustained very little damage in the 1945 air raids. Although off the beaten tourist track, they contain some of the city's most rewarding sights, and are well worth a day of anyone's time.

The villa quarters

During Dresden's period as capital of the Kingdom of Saxony, it grew to be Germany's fourth largest city, with a population far in excess of its present-day level. In the process, it spawned a whole series of new suburbs, the most prosperous of which consisted largely of exclusive custom-built **villas** commissioned by the most affluent members of society. Collectively they form an important and distinctive feature of the cityscape; although many have fallen into decay, others have been restored and some now serve as hotels and restaurants (see p.958 and p.967).

The densest and most architecturally distinguished group of villas is to be found in **Blasewitz** on the left bank of the Elbe 3km east of the centre; as a result, the entire district has been given the status of a protected monument. To get there, take tram #1 from the Altstadt, or tram #6 from Neustadt. One of Germany's most famous bridges, the so-called **Blaues Wunder** (Blue Wonder) links Blasewitz with **Loschwitz**, a villa suburb on the opposite side of the river. Opened in 1893 after a two-year construction period, this steel suspension bridge was a revolutionary design for its day, and was subsequently much imitated.

In Loschwitz there are two impressive transport curiosities from the time of the Second Reich; it costs DM3 for a single ticket for either, though they're free with the *Dresden Card*, and half-price with the 24-hour public transport ticket. Just up from the Blaues Wunder is the valley station of the **Drahtseilbahn**, a funicular railway which runs to the former spa of **Weisser Hirsch**. Instituted in 1895, the funicular was given a thorough overhaul and modernization in preparation for its centenary. A couple of minutes' walk to the south is the rather less orthodox **Bergschwebebahn** (Hanging Mountain Railway), which ascends to Oberloschwitz, the upper part of the quarter. It was put into operation in 1901, and thus postdates its much larger counterpart in Wuppertal, though it was the first of its type in the world built to negotiate a gradient.

At Grundstr. 26, in the valley between the *Drahtseilbahn* and the *Bergschwebebahn*, is one of the most spectacular villas, the **Leonhardi-Museum** (Tues–Fri 2–6pm, Sat & Sun 10am–6pm; DM1.50). This mock-medieval mansion was the home and studio of Edouard Leonhardi, a landscape painter of the late Romantic period who was a professor at the Dresden Academy. Several of his huge, luxuriantly detailed canvases are on view; regular exhibitions of the work of contemporary artists are also featured. A stone's throw south of the *Bergschwebebahn* station is Loschwitz's parish church, now known as the **Georg-Bähr-Kirche** in honour of its architect. Left as a shell after the war, it has recently been rebuilt, with work still continuing on the decoration of the interior.

Schloss Pillnitz

Schloss Pillnitz, which lies up the Elbe at the extreme edge of the city boundary, is a Pöppelmann creation inspired by the mystique of the Orient. He built two separate summer palaces: the **Wasserpalais** (late April–Oct 9.30am–5.30pm, closed Tues; DM3) directly above the river contains a museum of applied arts; the **Bergpalais** (late April–Oct Tues–Sun 9.30am–5.30pm; DM3) across the courtyard is an almost exact replica, although this time you get to see round the apartments. However, what you can see inside is of small account in comparison with the exteriors, whose main inspiration seems to have been the palaces of Moghul India, despite the painted Chinese scenes under the eaves. Between the two palaces is a formal garden, while the **Neues Schloss** at the far end is a Neoclassical replacement for its burnt-out Renaissance predecessor, which Pöppelmann retained as the focus of his design. In addition, there's a fine park laid out according to the aristocratic tastes of the time, with sections in both the English and Chinese styles.

Pillnitz can be reached from Blasewitz or Loschwitz by bus #85, or from the city centre by taking tram #9 or #14 to the terminus at Kleinzschachwitz, then crossing the Elbe by ferry. More enjoyably, it's a stop on the route of the *Sächsische Dampfschiffahrt* cruise ships which sail from the Terrassenufer in the heart of the city down into Saxon Switzerland.

Eating, drinking and nightlife

When looking for somewhere to eat or drink in Dresden, it's worth bearing in mind that places in Neustadt generally offer better value than the more tourist-oriented establishments close to the main sights. One of the most adventurous nightlife scenes in the former GDR is concentrated in the fringes of Neustadt, though this is still overshadowed by more highbrow cultural offerings, for which the city has a world-class reputation.

Restaurants, cafés and bars

There's now a good range of eating possibilities in both the Altstadt and the Neustadt, as well as several worthwhile destinations in the suburbs, some of which lie conveniently close to sight-seeing attractions. See also the hotels section (pp.957–8) for many of the city's best restaurants.

ALTSTADT

Café Schinkelwache, Theaterplatz 1. Coffee house occupying part of the Altstädter Wache. In summer, when tables are put out on the square, some of Dresden's finest views can be enjoyed while imbibing.

Fischgalerie, Maxstr. 2. High quality, very expensive fish speciality restaurant whose decor is inspired by aquatic themes. Closed Sun, open evenings only Mon & Sat.

Haus Altmarkt, Wilsdruffer Str. 19–21. This huge complex, with the typically German cellar restaurant plus 4 separate cafés and bars, remains the city's most popular venue.

Italienisches Dörfchen, Theaterplatz 3. This historic building with a terrace overlooking the Elbe has been refurbished to house three restaurants. The *Kurfürstenzimmer* and *Weinzimmer* are pricey but not excessively so; *Erlwein* is one of the best and most expensive places to eat in the city.

Kahnaletto, Terrassenufer. Drolly named bar-restaurant situated in one of the ships moored in the Elbe.

Kulturpalast, Schloss Str. 2. Classy second-floor restaurant, serving both local and international dishes, in the main arts centre.

Mandarin, Gewandhausstr. 5. Dresden's best Chinese restaurant, tucked away on a quiet square behind the Gewandhaus.

Maximius, Maxstr. 5. Art Deco-style café-restaurant with beer garden. It has an international menu, and is open continuously 9am-3am.

Ratskeller, Dr-Kulz-Ring 19. Cavernous cellar restaurant decorated in the German Romantic manner, serving typically hearty fare.

Schauspielhaus, Ostra-Allee 2. Theatre restaurant with traditional Saxon and Bohemian cooking.

Semperoper, Theaterplatz 2. Modern, expensive restaurant and bar right beside the opera house.

Szeged, Wilsdruffer Str. 4. The local Hungarian restaurant.

NEUSTADT

Am Thor, Hauptstr. 35. Small *Gaststätte* serving good draught beer and tasty food, with changing daily specials.

barracuda, Jordanstr. 8. Dresden's main vegetarian restaurant. It has a summertime beer garden shaded by apple trees, and sometimes features live music.

Café Kästner, Alaunstr. 1. *Szene* café-bar named in honour of Erich Kästner, author of the children's classic *Emil and the Detectives*, who was born nearby.

Kö 5, Königstr. 5. *Gutbürgerliche Küche* is served in several tastefully furnished rooms of this recently restored Baroque building with a pretty inner courtyard.

König Albert, Königstr. 26. Upmarket restaurant with a truly international menu. Closed Sat lunchtime and Sun.

Kügelgenhaus, Hauptstr. 13. Atmospheric café-cum-restaurant, housed in a Baroque building with a beer cellar.

La Vie en Rose, Alaunstr. 64. French-style café and bistro with Jugendstil decor.

Narrenhäusel 7 Schwaben, Grosse Meissner Str. 3. Spacious restaurant specializing in Swabian dishes.

Pfund's, Bautzener Str. 79. Although a new venture, this aims to re-create the appearance and atmosphere of a prewar Dresden coffee house. Some of the items on the menu come from the famous dairy shop downstairs (see p.964).

Plantwirtschaft, Louisenstr. 20. Has one of Dresden's largest and most popular beer gardens.

Raskolnikov, Böhmische Str. 34. One of the city's trendiest watering holes, offering Russian food and a large selection of vodkas in minimalist surroundings. Evenings only.

Reiter In, Schnitzer Str. 36. Student bar with a handsome tiled fireplace and cheap beer.

ELSEWHERE IN THE CITY

Brauhaus Watzke, Kötzschenbroder Str. 1, Mickten. Lamplit *Hausbrauerei*, which makes an unfiltered *Pils*, in the cellars of a late nineteenth-century ballroom. Its beer garden commands a fine view up the Elbe to the Altstadt, from which it can be reached by tram #4 or #5.

Linie 6, Schaufuss Str. 24, Blasewitz. Award-winning theme bar containing a host of paraphenalia associated with tramcars. Its cellar, inevitably named *U6*, hosts late-nite cabaret sessions Thurs-Sat. As you'd expect, it lies on the route of tram #6 (and #4 and #10 as well); the nearest stop is Ludwig-Hartmann-Strasse.

Schillergarten, Schillerplatz 9, Blasewitz. Nineteenth-century half-timbered restaurant right beside the Blaues Wunder, with a winter garden directly overlooking the river.

Villa Marie, Fährgässchen 1, Blasewitz. Located opposite *Schillergarten*, this Italian-inspired villa appropriately houses a restaurant specializing in Tuscan cuisine.

Zur Eule, Grundstr. 100, Loschwitz. Historic *Gasthaus*, serving typical Saxon dishes, with a tradition dating back to 1378.

Discos and clubs

Bärenzwinger, Brühlscher Garten. Student club with a varied nightly programme of discos, films, folk music, jazz and dancing.

Down Town, Katharinenstr. 11–13. Disco which plays a varied daily mixture of indie, soul, rap and funk. Upstairs is a rock bar, *Groove Station*.

Jazzclub Tonne, Am Brauhaus 3. The main jazz venue in the city. Live music on Fri, Sat and Sun at 8.30pm.

Scheune, Alaunstr. 36–40. Arts centre in Neustadt with live music, theatre and a cinema. Its café serves Indian food, including plenty of vegetarian dishes, and has a beer garden.

Yenidze, Weisseritzstr. 3. Disco in one of Dresden's most prominent landmarks, the Moorish-style former cigarette factory beside Bahnhof Mitte.

Theatre and classical music

Dresden has a lively drama and music scene with two world-famous symphony **orchestras**, the *Staatskapelle Dresden* and the *Dresdner Philharmonie*, plus an excellent chamber-sized body, the *Virtuosi Saxoniae*. Tickets for the *Staatsoper* and *Schauspielhaus* are available from the booking office in the Altstädter Wache on Theaterplatz (☎491 1705); unsold tickets can be bought at the venue immediately before each performance. It's also well worth checking up on the regular musical events in the city's churches.

Dresdner Brettl, Maternistr. 17 (☎496 9450). Cabaret venue.

Komödie, Freiberger Str. 39 (☎866410). Venue for blockbuster musicals, housed in the new World Trade Centre building.

Kulturpalast, northern end of Altmarkt (☎486 6250). A large arts centre often used for classical concerts.

Puppentheater, Leipziger Str. 220 (☎840640). Puppet show theatre.

Schauspielhaus, Ostra-Allee 3 (☎491 3555). The city's main venue for classical drama.

Staatsoper, Theaterplatz 2 (☎491 1705). Opera and orchestral concerts in one of the city's finest buildings.

Staatsoperette, Pirnaer Landstr. 131 (☎207 9929). Dresden's home of operetta, located in the southeast of the city. Take tram #6, #9, #12 or #14 to Altleuben.

theater 50, Clara-Zetkin-Str. 44 (☎495 4123). Fifty-seater theatre presenting avant-garde shows.

Theater Junge Generation, Meissner Landstr. 4 (☎421 4567). Children's and youth theatre.

Listings

Boats *Sächsische Dampfschiffahrt*, Hertha-Lindner-Str. 10 (☎866090). Services depart from Terrassenufer to Saxon Switzerland and Meissen.

Car rental *Europcar*, Liebstädter Str. 5. (☎254640); *Hertz*, in *Maritim Hotel Bellevue*, Grosse Meissner Str. 15 (☎502 3890); *Sixt*, Pieschener Allee 14 (☎495 4105).

Festivals In mid-April there's a film festival, centred on the celebrated *Rundkino* on Prager Strasse. A big jazz event, the *International Dixieland Festival*, is held each May/June; around the same time, there's a classical music event, the *Dresdner Musikfestspiele*.

Mitfahrzentralen Antonstr. 41 (☎804 5275), Königstr. 10 (☎502 2230).

Post office The main office is at Am Queckbrunnen 1 with poste restante service.

Women's centre Angelikastr. 1 (☎804 1470).

Around Dresden

Two undamaged examples of the work of the great Baroque architects of Dresden can be seen just outside the city boundaries in **Moritzburg** and **Gross-Sedlitz**. Both of these make enjoyable half-day outings; as a bonus, the journey to the former can be an experience in itself.

Moritzburg

The small village of **MORITZBURG**, 15km north of Dresden, is connected with the Hauptbahnhof by bus #326, but it's far more fun to take the **narrow-gauge railway**, the *Lössnitztalbahn*. This starts from the Ostbahnhof at Radebeul, on the S-Bahn line between Dresden-Neustadt and Meissen, and takes about an hour to cover the 17km to its terminus at Radeburg. No fewer than seventeen bridges are crossed in the course of the journey along the Lössnitz valley, which is mostly a pastoral landscape with fields, meadows and ponds; Moritzburg is about halfway along.

At the edge of the village is the **Schloss** (March & Nov Tues–Sun 10am–4.30pm; April Tues–Sun 10am–5.30pm; May–Oct daily 10am–5.30pm; Dec Tues–Sun 10am–4pm; DM7). It was founded as a hunting lodge in 1542 by Duke Moritz of Saxony, but was almost completely rebuilt in the 1720s for Augustus the Strong using designs provided by Pöppelmann – only the Schlosskapelle (an addition of the 1660s), the corner towers and foundations were retained. A large artifical lake, fashioned out of several small ponds, was created round the Schloss, giving it an appearance akin to the great French châteaux of the Loire. Like them, the interior doesn't quite match the exterior, though there are some fine rooms, notably the **Audienzsaal** with its grand mythological paintings, the **Zimmer mit Damenbildnissen**, featuring portraits of court beauties (including some of Augustus' mistresses) and the **Speisesaal**, which was used both as a dining room and a theatre and is adorned with a large number of hunting trophies.

It's also worth taking a stroll in the vast English-style **Schlosspark**. Towards its western end is the **Fasanenschlösschen** (April–Oct Tues–Sun 9.30am–4pm; DM1), a small gaming lodge of the 1780s, which is now given over to a collection of stuffed birds. Nearby, at the side of the lake, are two follies – the **Mole** (pier) and the **Leuchtturm** (lighthouse).

Between the wars, Moritzburg was the main home of the Wettin family, who had recently been stripped of royal status. In 1944, Prince Ernst Heinrich invited the great Berlin sculptress and graphic artist Käthe Kollwitz, whose home had been bombed, to settle at at Meissner Str. 7 in the village, and she spent the last year of her life there. Now designated the **Käthe-Kollwitz-Gedenkstätte** (April–Oct Tues–Fri 11am–5pm, Sat & Sun 10am–5pm; Nov–March Tues–Fri noon–3pm, Sat & Sun 11am–4pm; DM3.50), it contains displays of her work.

Practicalities

Moritzburg's **tourist office** (April–Oct Mon–Fri 9am–6pm, Sat & Sun noon–4pm; Nov–March Mon–Fri 10am–4pm; ☎035207/85410) is at Schlossallee 3b. In addition to **private rooms** (①–②), there's a pension, *Schlossallee*, Schlossallee 35 (☎035207/81690; ⑤) and several **hotels**, including *Eisenberger Hof*, Kötzschenbrodaer Str. 8 (☎035207/81673; ⑥); *Landhaus*, Schlossallee 37 (☎035207/81602; ⑦); and *Waldschänke*, an eighteenth-century hostelry in a wooded setting off Grosse Fasanenstrasse (☎035207/81489; ⑦). All of these have fine **restaurants**, with the last-named being the most renowned.

Gross-Sedlitz

A short walk from the S-Bahn station of **GROSS-SEDLITZ**, on the line linking Dresden with Saxon Switzerland, is the **Barock-Garten** (daily April–Sept 7am–8pm; Oct–March 8am–6pm; DM2), a masterpiece of landscape gardening by Pöppelmann and two of his closest associates, Zacharias Longuelune and Johann Christoph Knöffel. Modelled on the gardens of Versailles, it contains a small palace, the **Friedrichschlösschen**, plus two orangeries, and a double staircase with fountains known as **Stille Musik**. Statues from the workshop of Balthasar Permoser are placed throughout the formally arranged gardens, which are in bloom for much of the year. In summer, open-air concerts are often held.

Meissen

Regular S-Bahn trains take around 45 minutes to cover the 25km between Dresden and **MEISSEN**, although you can also take the slow scenic route by boat down the Elbe. Meissen is associated in most people's minds with "Dresden china", yet the famous porcelain factory is only one of the attractions of this photogenic and unspoiled old city. In total contrast to Dresden, it came through World War II almost unscathed; it suffered quite badly from pollution under the GDR, but is already being cleaned up, having been one of five towns selected to receive special Federal restoration grants.

> The **telephone code** for Meissen is ☎03521

Arrival, information and accommodation

Meissen's **Hauptbahnhof** is on the right bank of the Elbe directly across the river from the city centre. The **tourist office** (April–Oct Mon–Fri 10am–6pm, Sat & Sun 10am–3pm; Nov–March Mon–Fri 10am–5pm, Sat 10am–3pm; ☎454470) is at Markt 3.

Accommodation

Following several years of total flux in the accommodation situation, Meissen now has a decent number of **pensions** and **hotels** in most price categories, as well as **private** rooms (②–⑤) bookable via the tourist offfice. There's also a **youth hostel** on a hillside south of the Altstadt at Wilsdruffer Str. 28 (☎453065; 🏠).

HOTELS AND PENSIONS

Burkhardt, Neugasse 29 (☎458198, fax 458197). Pension with an ideal location in the heart of the Altstadt. ④

Goldgrund, Goldgrund 14 (☎47930, fax 479344). Fine medium-range hotel in a very quiet woodland setting at the southern edge of town, a few minutes' walk from the Staatliche Porzellan-Manufaktur. ⑥

Im Kleinen Haus, Leinewebergasse 3 (☎453018, fax 451090). Small pension in a half-timbered Altstadt house. ③

Landhaus Nassau, Nassauweg 1 (☎738160, fax 738169). Good-value hotel and restaurant set at the edge of a nature reserve at the extreme eastern edge of town, reached by bus #D. ④

Parkhotel Pannonia, Hafenstr. 27–31 (☎72250, fax 722904). Meissen's leading hotel occupies a large Jugendstil villa in a park by the right bank of the Elbe. Its facilities include a fine restaurant, a summer terrace and a whirlpool. ⑦

Ross, Grossenhainer Str. 9 (☎7510, fax 751999). Grand, recently refurbished late nineteenth-century hotel with restaurant close to the Bahnhof. ⑥

Schweizerhaus, Rauhentalstr. 1 (☎457162, fax 457162). Pension with restaurant in a half-timbered chalet opposite the Staatliche Porzellan-Manufaktur. ④

Tagungszentrum Domherrenhof, Freiheit 10 (☎460941, fax 460949). A small hotel occupies part of this former canons' residence. Its café-restaurant has a summer terrace which commands a wonderful view over the Altstadt to the Burgberg. ⑥

The city

Never having grown into a major city, Meissen is compact and ideal for exploration on foot. Even from afar, its feudal layout is apparent, with the houses of the **Bürgerstadt** clustered in the valley under the **Burgberg**, which is crowned by the buildings of the joint rulers, the margrave and the bishop. The city centre lies on the left bank of the Elbe, but it is from the right bank (where you will arrive if you come by train) that the strategic significance of the site can be appreciated more easily. You're also rewarded with the best of the many breathtaking panoramas the town has to offer.

The Albrechtsburg

Centrepiece of all the views is the commandingly sited **Albrechtsburg** (daily Feb–Dec 10am–5/6pm; DM6). This isn't the original castle of the Margraves of Meissen, but a late fifteenth-century replacement commissioned by Elector Ernst of Saxony and his brother Duke Albrecht, who jointly ruled the combined Wettin territories. It retains the medieval requirement for a military fortress, but combines this, for the first time in Germany, with the new demands of Renaissance princes for a residential palace. It's the masterpiece of one of the most prolific and accomplished builders of the time, **Arnold von Westfalen**. To appreciate the ingenuity of his design, it really needs to be viewed from afar: that way, you can see how the architect was forced to use the contours of the rocky, sloping site, solving the problem by building in huge blocks of six storeys, the first two being essentially to support the superstructure. While work was under way, the heirs of the two brothers split into two hostile factions, with Meissen becoming the seat of the Albertines, the junior of the two lines. Soon after completion, the court decamped to Dresden, leaving the Albrechtsburg as something of a white elephant. In 1710, it was given a wholly new function as the headquarters of the original porcelain factory, the first in Europe.

As it stands directly above the valley, the Albrechtsburg has to be approached from the rear, where it's guarded by a bridge and gateway leading into a vast courtyard. The under-use of the palace largely explains the somewhat bare feeling of most of its **interior**, which over-enthusiastic nineteenth-century Romantic painters tried to liven up by adding cycles of heroic historical frescoes, with decidedly dubious consequences. Nonetheless, it's worth paying to go inside just to see the truly spectacular, almost crazy, **vaulting**, which was something of a speciality of Arnold von Westfalen. There's a seemingly inexhaustible range of variations, those with deep pyramidal niches between their ribs being the most original. The other highlight of the visit is the ascent of the beautiful **external staircase**, the *Grosser Wendelstein*, the main feature of the castle's courtyard exterior. Housed in the last few rooms on the visitors' circuit is the medieval section of the state sculptural collection, the rest of which is in Dresden.

The Dom

Cocooned within the Albrechtsburg courtyard is the **Dom** (daily April–Oct 9am–5.30/6pm; Nov–March 9am–4pm; DM3.50), along with its subsidiary buildings, such as the bishop's palace and the houses of the canons, most of which have been altered repeatedly down the years. For the most part, the Dom itself is a pure High Gothic structure, begun in the mid-thirteenth century by the same masonic workshop that had built the famous west choir in Naumburg, though the relative decline in quality suggests that its director, the so-called Master of Naumburg, had died in the interim. However, the somewhat eccentric facade long remained unfinished: Arnold von Westfalen added the third storey in Flamboyant Gothic style, but the florid openwork spires, which soar above the rest of Meissen's skyline, only date from the early 1900s.

Entry is via the **Fürstenkapelle**, which was tacked onto the facade in the fifteenth century to serve as a mausoleum for members of the Wettin family. It contains a number of resplendent bronze memorials, sometimes using designs by Dürer and Cranach. The richly sculptured **portal** behind was made the previous century as the main entrance to the Dom; its archway is cleverly used as a frame for the depiction of Christ in Majesty. Just to the right of here is the **Georgenkapelle**, the private memorial chapel of Duke George the Bearded, entered via a strikingly Italianate Renaissance doorway. At the far end of the south nave aisle is the **Achteckbau** (Octagon); it opens directly outside, and contains three fine statues by the Naumburg carvers.

The same men were also responsible for the **rood screen**, except for its Flamboyant upper storey, added in the sixteenth century as a choir gallery; and for the statues of the founders and patron saints in the choir. The central **stained-glass window**, showing Old and New Testament scenes in pairs, dates back to the thirteenth century, while *The Adoration of the Magi* **triptych** is by an unknown Netherlandish painter of the turn of the sixteenth century. From here you can exit via the **cloister**, off which is the **Magdalenenkapelle**, where the original statues of the south portal have been brought for conservation reasons.

The Bürgerstadt

The Bürgerstadt is laid out as a series of twisting and meandering streets between the Burgberg and the Elbe. More impressive as an ensemble than for any outstanding highlights, it's ideal for an aimless stroll. Centrepiece is the Markt, dominated by the **Rathaus**, in which the dying flickers of Flamboyant Gothic are fused with the new spirit of the Renaissance. At no. 8 on the square is the *Fachgeschäft*, the porcelain factory's shop, which is well worth a visit even if you aren't intending to buy. Next door, at no. 9, the *Küfertheke*, is one of the places where you can try local wines.

On its own small square to the side is the Flamboyant Gothic **Frauenkirche** (daily May–Oct 10am–12.30pm & 1–4pm), whose carillon, with the first bells in the world to be fashioned from porcelain, can be heard six times daily. The pride of the interior is the retable of *The Coronation of the Virgin*, made around 1500, while the **tower** (same hours; DM2) commands a superb view over the city and the Elbe. On the terrace above the church is the celebrated **Gasthaus Vincenz Richter**, an old half-timbered tavern which preserves an early eighteenth-century wine press. The wines served here have the reputation of being the best in eastern Germany, though that's less of a claim than it might appear, as the area around is the only significant part of the former GDR with a climate mild enough for growing grapes.

The Staatliche Porzellan-Manufaktur Meissen

The **Staatliche Porzellan-Manufaktur Meissen** lies about 1.5km south of the Markt, and is easiest reached by going down Fleischer Gasse, then continuing straight along Neugasse; it also lies close to the S-Bahn terminus, Meissen–Triebischtal. This is the latest factory to manufacture "Dresden china", whose invention had truly bizarre origins. Augustus the Strong imprisoned the alchemist **Johann Friedrich Böttger** in Festung Königstein in Saxon Switzerland, charging him with what was then believed to be a feasible task, the production of gold. Instead, he invented the first true European porcelain, according to a formula which remains a jealously guarded secret – its products are identified by the trademark of crossed blue swords.

Guided tours (daily 9am–noon & 1–5pm; DM7 or DM10 combined ticket with Schauhalle) are run round the workshops, enabling you to see all the different stages of the production process. Be aware that this is on the itinerary of just about every tour group visiting eastern Germany and in summer you can be faced with a horrendous wait unless you arrive early. No such problems beset the **Schauhalle** (daily 9am–5pm; DM7), which in any event is of far more immediate appeal, showing how the style of the factory has developed from the beginning to the present day. Highlight is the display of the gloriously over-the-top Rococo fripperies created by the most talented artist employed here, **Joachim Kaendler**.

If you're walking between the town centre and the factory, it's worth stopping off at the **Nikolaikirche** (May–Sept Tues–Thurs & Sun 2–4pm), a little Romanesque church set in the Stadtpark. Inside, forming a poignant memorial to the fallen of World War I, are the largest porcelain figures ever made, two groups of mothers with children, each of which is 2.5m high and 300kg in weight.

Eating and drinking

Few ex-GDR towns are as well equipped gastronomically as Meissen, whose wine bar-restaurants represent its main strength in this field.

Bahrmanns Brauereikeller, Webergasse 2. Large cellar restaurant, warmed by a huge open fire, in the nineteenth-century premises of a former brewery.

Café Schönitz, Neugasse 22. French-style café-bistro which often features live music.

Café Zieger, Rote Stufen 5. Traditional coffee house which has been run by the same family for over 150 years. Its speciality is a puff pastry known as the *Meissner Fummel*.

Domkeller, Domplatz 9. Meissen's oldest restaurant, with a tradition dating back to 1520. It serves Saxon specialities and has a terrace offering a fine view over the town.

Monasterium, Freiheit 13. New restaurant in the chapel and cloisters of the former Kloster St Afra. Open 11am–5pm, closed Wed.

Probierestube der Sächsischen Winzergenossenschaft, Bennoweg 9. Historic wine restaurant in the northeast of town, offering local dishes served on Meissen porcelain, and regular sampling sessions. Evenings only.

Vincenz Richter, An der Frauenkirche 12. This sixteenth-century *Weinschänke* is one of the essential sights of Meissen. Although the menu is short, the food served is arguably the best in town. Open Tues–Fri 4–11pm, Sat 3pm–midnight, Sun noon–6pm.

Zur Seemannsruhe, Uferstr. 12. Restaurant in a late sixteeenth-century house directly on the left bank of the Elbe offering Bohemian cuisine and a variety of fish dishes.

Saxon Switzerland

The area between Dresden and the Czech border 50km south is popularly known as **Saxon Switzerland** (*Sächsische Schweiz*), though this nickname, first coined by artists of the Romantic movement, is misleading. The landscape, far from looking Swiss, is archetypally Middle European, with the meandering **River Elbe** cutting a grand valley through dense forests interrupted by outcrops of rock welded into truly fantastic shapes. There's no better **hiking** country in all of Germany, and some walking is essential if you want to see the best of the scenery. If pressed for time, the S-Bahn line down the left bank offers a good overview of the region, and, even on a day-trip from Dresden, it should be possible to combine this with a visit to a couple of the main set-piece attractions. A good alternative is to take a **cruise** with the *Sächsische Dampfschiffahrt* ships: there are two or three departures daily from Dresden throughout the season (see p.968). However, given that there's abundant and inexpensive **accommodation** in all the resorts mentioned below, it would be a pity not to stay for a few days.

Pirna

PIRNA, 17km south of Dresden Hauptbahnhof, is the gateway to Saxon Switzerland. Untouched in World War II, this old market town is currently being spruced up in line with its new role as a major tourist centre. Set on a hill overlooking the town is **Schloss Sonnenstein**, now mainly used as offices, though it does have a terrace restaurant. The central **Markt** is lined with a variety of handsome mansions, while the Rathaus stands on its own in the middle of the square.

Between the Schloss and the Markt is the **Stadtkirche St Marien**, a Flamboyant Gothic hall church similar to those in the Erzgebirge region, with all interest concentrated inside. Here, it's the stupendous star and network **vaulting** that steals the show – at times the ribs erupt into audacious flights of fancy, notably in the chancel, where they take on the form of a tree trunk. A curiosity of the church's building history is that it was begun at the turn of the sixteenth century as a Catholic parish church, but was appropriated for Protestant use before its completion. This change was immediately given visible expression in the painted decoration which was added to the vault: two of the Evangelists are depicted with the features of Luther and Melanchthon.

Practicalities

The **tourist office** (Mon & Tues 9am–3pm, Wed–Fri 9am–5pm; May–Sept also Sat 10am–noon; ☎03501/528497) is north of the Markt at no. 31 on the main shopping street, Dohnaische Strasse. Here you can book **private rooms** (①–③) in the town, and in other places in Saxon Switzerland.

A wide range of **hotels** includes *Weisse Taube*, Arthur-Thiermann-Str. 58 (☎03501/524120; ③); *Schwarzer Adler*, Dohnaischer Platz 2 (☎03501/528610; ④); *Zur Post*, Liebstädter Str. 30 (☎03501/5500; ④); *Sächsicher Hof*, Gartenstr. 21 (☎03501/447551; ⑤); and, both situated in old buildings, *Pirna'scher Hof*, Am Markt 4 (☎03501/44380; ⑤); and *Deutsches Haus*, Niedere Burgstr. 1 (☎03501/443440; ⑦).

There's also a **youth hostel**, situated on the opposite side of the Elbe from the centre at Birkwitzer Str. 51 (☎03501/527316; ❶). The best **restaurants** are in the last three hotels listed above.

Kurort Rathen and Hohnstein

If you're visiting Saxon Switzerland on a day-trip, one place you should definitely make for is **KURORT RATHEN**, a small health resort on the east bank of the Elbe, linked by regular ferries to its Bahnhof, which is 12km and three stops on from Pirna. Should you want to stay, there are ample accommodation possibilities on both sides of the river, including plenty of **private rooms** (①–③) and a **youth hostel** at Niederrathen 3 (☎035024/70425; ❷). The best hotel is *Erbgericht* (☎035034/70454; ⑥) with a terrace overlooking the Elbe.

High above the village, about thirty minutes' walk away, is the **Bastei**. Even the unfortunate siting of the GDR-era *Berghotel* (☎035024/70406; ⑥) cannot detract from the grandeur of this natural belvedere of strangely shaped rocks, which is not only astonishing in itself – seemingly fashioned by some great divine sculptor – but also commands really stunning views, both over the Elbe and into the forest. As a bonus, there are the ruins of **Felsenburg Neurathen**, a thirteenth-century castle ingeniously juxtaposed among the rocks. Lower down, the setting has been put to a more peaceful use by the creation of a spectacular open-air theatre.

Another walk well worth making is the hour-long trail along the *Knotenweg* to **HOHNSTEIN**, the most picturesque of the villages set away from the riverside, with a hilly site which affords a wide range of perspectives. The **Schloss** (free access to courtyard; interiors daily March–Oct 9am–5pm; DM2), itself a fine vantage point, houses a particularly attractive **youth hostel** (☎035975/202; ❷). There are a number of fine Baroque buildings on and around the Markt, notably the Georg-Bähr-Kirche, a rustic-looking church named in honour of its architect, one of the key figures of Dresden Baroque.

Königstein

From Rathen, the train follows the loops of the Elbe round to the small country town of **KÖNIGSTEIN**, 6km away. It's of no interest in itself, but the colossal fortress above, **Festung Königstein** (May–Sept 9am–8pm; Oct 9am–6pm; Nov–April 9am–5pm; DM7), rivals the Bastei as the most impressive sight in Saxon Switzerland. It takes a steep climb of thirty or forty minutes to reach it, though a tourist "train" has been introduced for the benefit of the better-heeled visitors who now visit the region. Once a virtually impregnable frontier post of the Saxon state, the fortress was continually strengthened right up until the Napoleonic period, so that it forms a virtual encyclopedia of changing defensive techniques. Long before this, it had ceased to have much strategic value, and its main function was as Saxony's most secure prison. Johann Friedrich Böttger, the inventor of Meissen porcelain, was incarcerated here by Augustus the Strong; the same fate later befell the nineteenth-century Socialist leader August Bebel, and a number of prominent anti-Nazis. It also proved a secure home in World War II for the movable art treasures of Dresden. The most remarkable structure is the sixteenth-century **Tiefer Brunnen** (Deep Well), which is 152m deep and took a group of miners from Freiberg six years to dig. Also of note are the cellars, the barracks and the two arsenals, both containing an array of historic weapons. However, there's no doubt that the view – even finer than that from the Bastei – is the prime draw.

To see Königstein itself at reasonably close range, there's a choice of vantage points – the **Pfaffenstein** to the south, or the **Lilienstein** on the opposite side of the Elbe. Ferries run across to the latter from Königstein; it's then a walk of about an hour to the summit.

In town, there are plenty of **private rooms** (①–③) bookable via the **tourist office**, just off the central Markt at Schreiberberg 2 (Mon, Tues, Thurs & Fri 9am–5.30pm, Wed 1–5.30pm; April–Oct also Sat 9am–noon; ☎035021/68261). There's a small centrally sited **guest house**, *Schrägers*, Kirchgasse 1 (☎035021/68352; ③), plus three **hotels** in the outskirts: *Vogelsberg*, Elbhäuser Weg 20 (☎035021/68232; ④); *Panoramahotel Lilienstein*, Ebenheit 7 (☎035021/530; ⑤); and *Lindenhof*, Gohrischer Str. 2 (☎035021/68243; ⑥).

Bad Schandau and around

Next stop, a further 5km on, is the spa of **BAD SCHANDAU**, the chief resort of the area and a wonderful base for hikes. It's also the border post, having swallowed up all the villages before the frontier. The best view over the area is from the tall platform tower of the iron lift or **Personenaufzug** (daily dawn–dusk; DM2) which was built at the southern end of town in 1904. Also worth a quick look is the **Johanniskirche** just off the Markt, a Gothic church remodelled in the Baroque period, which contains two notable Renaissance furnishings in the pulpit and the high altar.

From the park in the centre of Bad Schandau, the *Kirnitzschtalbahn*, one of only two surviving examples of the once-ubiquitous **rural tramways**, creaks along the banks of the River Kirnitzsch to the **Lichtenhainer Wasserfall** 7km northeast. (If driving along this stretch, take extra care, as the tram travels on the main road most of the time, making overtaking extremely hazardous.) From the terminus, where there's a restaurant, it's a gentle uphill signposted walk to the **Kuhstall** (Cow Stall), one of Saxon Switzerland's most picturesque rock groupings and a fine vantage point over the wooded countryside away from the Elbe. Overlooking the river, a couple of hours' walk from here or Bad Schandau, are the **Schrammsteine**, the most extended group of rock formations in the area and a favourite haunt of daredevil climbing enthusiasts.

Practicalities

Bad Schandau's **tourist office** at Markt 8 (April–Sept Mon–Fri 9am–noon & 1–5pm, Sat 9am–noon; Oct–March Mon, Tues, Thurs & Fri 9am–noon & 1–5pm; ☎035022/42412) provides the normal booking service for **private rooms** (①–③).

There are a couple of homely **pensions** in *Kopprasch's Bierstübl*, Kirchstr. 10 (☎035022/42566; ③); and *Café Menge*, Badallee 12 (☎035022/42827; ④). The town has many fine **hotels**, such as *Zum Roten Haus*, Marktstr. 10 (☎035022/42343; ④); *Lindenhof*, Rudolf-Sendig-Str. 11 (☎035022/4890; ⑤); *Parkhotel*, Rudolf-Sendig-Str. 12 (☎035022/42505; ⑤); and *Elbhotel*, An der Elbe 2 (☎035022/42506; ⑥). All of these have **restaurants**. There's a **campsite** at Ostrauer Mühle on the Kirnitzsch (☎035022/42742) and a **youth hostel** at Rudi-Hempel-Str. 14 (☎035022/42408; ⑪) in the village of Ostrau.

Bautzen (Budyšin)

Some 60km east of Dresden is **BAUTZEN**, the cultural capital of the Sorbs, Germany's only indigenous Slav minority, whose homeland is divided between Upper Lusatia in Saxony and Lower Lusatia in Brandenburg (see p.823). They settled in this area as far back as the sixth century, and have remained ever since; the bilingual signs, and the two official forms of the city's name, impart a touch of exoticism, though in Bautzen itself (as opposed to some of the outlying villages) you're unlikely to hear the language spoken in the streets. Bautzen is potentially a really beautiful town: it occupies a compact site high above the still young River Spree, which looks wild and untamed, although it's harnessed to form a reservoir immediately beyond the northern suburbs.

The city

The silhouette of Bautzen, dotted with towers of all shapes and sizes, looks magnificent when seen from a distance. Closer up, it's not quite so impressive, the GDR period having bequeathed a legacy of pollution and tattiness which will take years to clean up.

The central streets

A good way to begin your tour is by climbing the **Reichenturm** (daily April–Oct 10am–5pm; DM1), which lies at the top end of Kornmarkt at the eastern edge of the Altstadt. The original defensive tower dates back to the late fifteenth century, and was subsequently adorned with a relief portrait of Bautzen's then overlord, Emperor Rudolf II, ruler of the famously degenerate court at Prague. When an over-large Baroque lantern was added in the early eighteenth century, a pronounced tilt immediately occurred – hence the nickname of "the leaning tower of Bautzen". After World War II there were plans to demolish it for safety reasons, but it was decided to secure the foundations instead. From the top, you get a good overview of the layout of the town.

The busy pedestrianized **Reichenstrasse**, lined with Baroque houses built after one of the many fires that have ravaged the town throughout its history, leads from the Reichenturm to the **Hauptmarkt**, where markets are held on Tuesdays, Thursdays and Saturdays. This is separated from a second market square, Fleischmarkt, by the **Rathaus**, a Classically-inspired Baroque building whose most pleasing feature is the tall tower, Gothic by origin, but neatly remodelled to harmonize with the rest of the structure. Opposite is the **Gewandhaus**, a neo-Renaissance replacement of the old trading hall and weigh house, whose handsome vaulted cellars, now the *Ratskeller* restaurant, survive underneath.

Fleischmarkt's top end is closed by the very parochial-looking **Dom** (March–May & Nov Mon–Sat 10am–noon & 1–3pm; June–Oct Mon–Sat 10am–noon & 1–5pm; Dec–Feb Mon–Fri 11am–1pm), whose late Gothic architecture reduces the hall church to its simplest format. It's chiefly of note for two peculiarities. First, as can be seen from the outside, but is far more noticeable within, the body of the church is built with a very pronounced curve, possibly symbolic of the body of Christ on the cross, but more likely due to the restrictions of the site. The second curiosity is that this is a *Simultankirche*, one used by Protestants and Catholics alike. Immediately the Reformation was introduced, it was divided in two, the Catholics taking the choir and the Protestants the nave, a situation that persists to this day, with only a small iron barrier separating the two congregations. The very different set of furnishings immediately betray which part you're in; the Catholics have the star piece in the large *Crucifixion* by Balthasar Permoser, a donation from the sculptor himself.

To the rear of the Dom is the **Domstift**, a triple-winged Baroque palace entered via a cheerful gateway adorned with statues inspired by Counter-Reformation theology. Inside, the ecclesiastical treasures of the **Domschatzkammer** (Mon–Fri 10am–noon & 1–4pm; free) are on view. All around this area are twisting little alleys of peeling houses which are marvellously evocative of days gone by, but desperately in need of restoration.

Along the fortifications

The Reichenturm also makes a good jumping-off point for a walk round the fortifications, of which many portions survive. Immediately to the north is the **Wendischer Turm**, whose name signifies that it presided over the quarter where the Wends (the alternative name for the Sorbs) lived. Long used as a prison, it was saved from demolition through the ingenuity of Gottfried Semper, who incorporated it into the castellated **Kaserne** (barracks) he was commissioned to build on the site. This rather wonderful neo-Gothic fantasy itself became redundant, but has found a new lease of life as municipal offices.

The L-shaped alley known as Gickelsberg leads from here to the **Schülerturm**, beyond which is Am Zwinger, a rustic-looking potholed road leading west past the **Gerberbastei** (now the youth hostel) to the **Nikolaiturm**. Alongside the latter is the **Nikolaikirche**, once the church of the Catholic Sorbs, but a ruin since its destruction in the Thirty Years' War. It's a peaceful spot, now used as a cemetery, commanding a fine view over the Spree.

An even better vantage point is the terrace of **Schloss Ortenburg** further west. The present castle, replacing a much earlier stronghold of the Margraves of Meissen, was erected in the late fifteenth century by order of Matthis Corvinus, King of Hungary and Bohemia, who is depicted seated between crown-bearing angels in the nine-metre-high memorial on the entrance gateway. Later additions include the playful Renaissance gables and the plain Baroque wing now housing the **Sorbisches Museum** (daily 10am–12.30pm & 1–4/5pm; DM3), documenting the festivals, costumes and literature of the Sorbs. If you've got time to spare, it's well worth descending to the Spree and crossing the footbridge to a belvedere offering a view of the Schloss and the town.

Following Osterweg southwards, you pass the **Mühlenturm** en route to the **Michaeliskirche**, the parish church of the Sorb Protestants, which forms a picturesque corner in conjunction with the **Alte Wasserkunst** (daily April–Oct 10am–5pm; DM1), a mid-sixteenth-century water tower which was operational until 1963. Inside is a small museum outlining the technical particulars of its machinery, while the viewing platform at the top offers yet another outlook on the valley. On the bank of the Spree below is the **Hexenhäuschen** (Witches' House), the only old fisherman's house to have withstood all the fires which destroyed its counterparts – the belief that the inhabitants must therefore have been possessed of magical powers led to its present nickname. Finally, the wonderful full-frontal view of Bautzen that appears in all the tourist brochures can be seen for real by walking a short distance south to **Friedensbrücke**.

Practicalities

The **Hauptbahnhof** is about fifteen minutes' walk south of the Altstadt, which is reached via Bahnhofstrasse and Karl-Marx-Strasse. Bautzen's **tourist office** (Mon–Fri 9am–6pm, Sat 10am–noon; May–Oct also Sun 10am–noon; ☎03591/42016) is at Hauptmarkt 1. There's a reasonable number of **private rooms** (①-③) on their books. Other budget possibilities are the **youth hostel**, Am Zwinger 1 (☎03591/44045; ❶), and the **campsite** (☎03591/41113), which is situated by a reservoir to the north of town.

Additionally, there are several conveniently sited **pensions**, such as *Fischer*, Löhrstr. 19 (☎03591/607185; ③); *Lausitz*, Bahnhofstr. 16 (☎03591/37810; ⑤); and *Le Petit*, Steinstr. 35 (☎03591/43598; ⑤). Centrally located **hotels** include *Spree*, Fischergasse 6 (☎03591/45060; ⑤); *Alte Gerberei*, Uferweg 1 (☎03591/301011; ⑤); *Schloss-Schänke*, Burgplatz 5 (☎03591/304990; ⑤); and *Goldener Adler*, Hauptmarkt 4 (☎03591/48660; ⑦).

Each of the hotels listed above has a **restaurant**. For more exotic fare, head to either of the Sorb restaurants: *Sorbisches Café*, Postplatz 2, or *Wjelbik*, Kornstr. 7. Another oddity is *Kaniga*, just east of the Reichenturm at Kurt-Pchalek-Str. 1, whose entire menu consists of different sorts of rabbit dishes. Both Italian and German fare is served at the *Ratskeller*, Innere Lauenstr. 1.

The *Deutsch–Sorbisches Volkstheater*, Seminarstr. 12 (☎03591/5840), is the only bilingual **theatre** in the country, with performances in Sorb alternating with German.

Zittau and the Zittau mountains

Some 65km from Bautzen, near the meeting point of the frontiers with the Czech Republic and Poland at the extreme southeastern corner of Saxony, is the town of **ZITTAU**. Despite its industrial infrastructure, it's a well-preserved historic town, but is best known as the gateway to a wooded upland area, the **Zittau mountains**

(*Zittauer Gebirge*). The wild scenery, characterized by dramatic rock formations, is a reminder that the region was once part of the old kingdom of Bohemia, with Zittau itself having been founded in the early thirteenth century by one of its monarchs, Otakar I.

The town

Zittau's Altstadt is a circular area bounded by green boulevards which have replaced the dismantled fortifications. With its spacious squares and innumerable fountains, it has a vaguely Mediterranean look to it, which seems more than a little incongruous, given its volatile central European climate.

The central Markt features a fountain dedicated to Mars, an old pharmacy, and a number of Baroque and Rococo mansions. To the east, it merges seamlessly with Rathausplatz, dominated by the **Rathaus** itself, a Schinkel-designed reinterpretation of an Italian Renaissance *palazzo*. Beyond lies Neustadt, an enormous elongated open space. It has no fewer than three fountains: from south to north these respectively depict the Good Samaritan, Hercules and a group of swans. The **Marstall** in the middle of the square was originally a sixteenth-century warehouse for storing salt, but was transformed into stables a couple of centuries later, when the colossal mansard roof was added.

To the north of the Markt is the **Johanniskirche**, whose present sombre Neoclassical aspect, with a grand facade and a high, flat-ceilinged interior, is due to plans provided by Schinkel. Its **tower** (May–Oct Mon–Fri noon–6pm, Sat & Sun 1–6pm; DM2) commands a fine view over the town. Across from the church stands the oldest of the town's surviving houses, the sixteenth-century **Dornspachhaus**, named after the burgomaster who lived there.

Further to the northeast is Klosterplatz, named after the Franciscan monastery that now houses the **Stadtmuseum** (Tues & Thurs 10am–noon & 1–4pm, Wed 10am–noon & 1–6pm, Fri 10am–1pm, Sat 2–4pm, Sun 10am–noon & 2–5pm; DM3). The cellars, with an intact drinking well and a frightening display of torture instruments, are the highlight of the displays. On the same square are the town's finest fountain, the **Grüner Born**, which shelters under an imposing wrought-iron canopy, and a gabled Renaissance mansion, the **Heffterhaus**.

At the extreme northeastern edge of the Altstadt is the **Kreuzkirche**, a fine example of the distinctive Bohemian Gothic style. It has been earmarked as the new home of the town's greatest artistic treasures, two **Lenten embroideries** which, until their recent restoration, had not been on public view for over sixty years. Woven for the medieval Johanniskirche, the larger dates from 1472 and forms a complete illustrated Bible with ninety different scenes; the smaller was made 101 years later.

Practicalities

The **Hauptbahnhof** lies due north of the centre, and Bahnhofstrasse and Bautzener Strasse will lead you towards the Markt via the Johanniskirche. Zittau's **tourist office** (Mon–Fri 8am–6pm, Sat 9am–1pm, Sun 10am–1pm; ☎03583/752137) is in the Rathaus, Markt 1. They can find you a **private room** (①-②) here or in a nearby village.

Alternatively, there are several **hotels**, including *Gasthof Bergschlösschen*, Kummersberg 8 (☎03583/510717; ④); *Riedel*, Friedensstr. 23 (☎03583/6860; ⑤); *Linden*, Christian-Keimann-Str. 34 (☎03583/5520; ⑤); *Dresdner Hof*, Äussere Oybiner Str. 9 (☎03583/57300; ⑥); *Schwarzer Bär*, Ottokarplatz 12 (☎03583/5510; ⑥).

Each of these hotels has a reasonably priced **restaurant**. Other places to eat are *Klosterstübl*, Johannisstr. 4; *Stadtkrug*, Markt 8; *Zum Schwaben*, Innere Weberstr. 11; and *Gewandhauskeller*, Rathausplatz 14.

Into the Zittau mountains by steam train

Most visitors to Zittau come to ride the *Bimmelbahn*, a **narrow-gauge steam rail line** which travels from the Hauptbahnhof into the mountains to the south. This was earmarked for closure a few months before the *Wende*, as a seam of lignite, the GDR's favourite but most environmentally damaging fuel, was discovered in the area. National unification has won it a reprieve.

Kurort Oybin and Kurort Jonsdorf

After 9km, there's a fork in the *Bimmelbahn* at Bertsdorf; one part of the train continues a further 3km south to **KURORT OYBIN**, a quiet little health resort centred on the **Bergkirche**, a perfectly preserved example of Baroque at its most rustic. Towering above the village is **Berg Oybin** (daily May–Aug 9am–6pm; Sept–April 9am–4pm; DM4), on which stand a ruined castle and monastery founded by Emperor Charles IV in his capacity as King of Bohemia, and built by masons of the great Parler workshop of Prague, but destroyed by lightning in the sixteenth century. A great deal of the monastic church still survives; given its semi-overgrown appearance and theatrical backdrop, it's hardly surprising that it was a favourite subject with painters of the Romantic movement.

The other section of the *Bimmelbahn* branches 4km southwest from Bertsdorf to **KURORT JONSDORF**. It's far less attractive than its neighbour but has a pretty open-air theatre, and is an equally good base for **hiking** in the range, which is peppered with marked trails. Westerners were unable to stay in either resort during GDR days; now there's a wide choice of accommodation in each, ranging from luxury **hotels** (⑤–⑦) via plenty of **private rooms** (①–②) to Jonsdorf's **youth hostel** at Hainstr. 14 (☎035844/70220; ⚑).

Gross Schönau

The lovely town of **GROSS SCHÖNAU** lies in the valley of the River Mandau immediately below the Zittau mountains; it's about 9km northwest of Jonsdorf and can be reached by mainline train from Zittau. For centuries, weaving was the foundation of the local economy, with the production of damask a speciality. A surprisingly entertaining **Damask- und Heimatmuseum** (May–Oct Tues–Sun 9am–noon & 2–5pm; Nov–April Mon–Fri 9am–4pm; DM2) has been set up in the early nineteenth-century mansion of a factory owner overlooking the river at Schenaustr. 3. In addition to demonstrations of the old looms (with explanations in English on request), you can also see displays on the folklore of the region.

Gross Schönau has a fine ensemble of historic houses, including the best examples of a vernacular style of building peculiar to Upper Lusatia, a hybrid between half-timbering and wood panelling known as an *Umgebindehaus*. The *Gaststätte* next to the museum is a recommendable place to **eat**. **Private rooms** (①–②) are particularly cheap here, while the only **campsite** (☎035841/2493) in the Zittau mountains is located by an artificial lake a couple of kilometres out of town on the road to Jonsdorf.

Görlitz

GÖRLITZ, the largest town of Upper Lusatia and Germany's easternmost point, lies 45km east of Bautzen and 34km north of Zittau. Travelling by train from the latter has a certain curiosity value: the line threads its way along the Neisse valley, skipping from one bank to the other and therefore in and out of Poland. One of the consequences of the Oder–Neisse border was that Görlitz found itself divided between two countries – the historic part of the city lies on the west bank and therefore remained German, while the suburbs opposite became the Polish town of Zgorzelec.

Perhaps that's an appropriate fate for a true central European city which doesn't easily fit into any nationalist framework. Slav by origin, Görlitz has been dominated by Germans since the thirteenth century, but belonged to Bohemia for much of its history; it fell to Saxony in the Thirty Years' War, but following its annexation by Prussia in 1815, was incorporated into Silesia. It now stands as one of the few reminders of a province that the Germans have finally accepted is lost to them forever.

The city

Wartime damage to Görlitz, whose ensemble of Renaissance and Baroque houses is unsurpassed in Germany, was minimal. The Communist authorities put the entire city centre under a preservation order; thus, though it has suffered badly from pollution, it will no doubt soon be restored to its original beauty.

Marienplatz and Demianiplatz

Marienplatz at the southern end of the Altstadt is dominated by the very blackened **Frauenkirche**, the late Gothic church of the former hospital and poorhouse, whose most notable feature is the double portal topped by an Annunciation group. Close by is the **Karstadt-Warenhaus**, a large Jugendstil department store which survives as an intact period piece, both in its statue-lined exterior, and in its steel-framed galleried interior. Just to the north, the **Dicker Turm** (Fat Tower) is a cylindrical structure of the early fourteenth century, adorned with a prominent sandstone relief of Görlitz's coat of arms and crowned by a graceful Renaissance cupola.

Following either of the alleys to the left, you come to Demianiplatz, the first in a row of three squares at the heart of the town. On the south side is the Neoclassical **Theater**, now named in honour of Gerhard Hauptmann, the Nobel Prize-winning Realist writer. His intense early drama *The Weavers*, set against the background of a heroic but inevitably futile mid-nineteenth-century uprising by the Silesian weavers against the mill owners, was a theatrical sensation, gaining its reputation as the first "Socialist" play by having a collective rather than a single hero.

The west side of the square is framed by the **Kaisertrutz** (May–Oct Tues–Sun 10am–5pm; DM2), a circular double bastion from the middle of last century, encasing its fifteenth-century predecessor. Inside is part of the local museum, including sections on medieval religious art, Upper Lusatian painters of the last two centuries and the history of the city, though the curious building is itself the main attraction. The original formed a defensive pair with the tall **Reichenbacher Turm** (same hours, DM2) opposite, whose lower storey, culminating in the sentry gallery, dates back to the fourteenth century. The cylindrical upper section was added a hundred years later, and the whole finally topped off with a Baroque turret. A collection of arms and armour is housed inside; you can also climb to the summit for a fine view over the city.

Obermarkt and Untermarkt

Demianiplatz opens out to the east into the long oblong **Obermarkt**, the main market square, which is lined with a colourful array of Baroque houses. At the northeastern corner stands the **Dreifaltigkeitskirche**, formerly the church of a Franciscan monastery. Its splendidly musty interior has several fine late Gothic furnishings, including a set of richly carved choir stalls, a touching *Holy Sepulchre* and a carved retable to the Virgin. Underneath the **Mönch** (Monk), as the church's tall, curiously thin-looking tower is popularly known, is the **Kunstbrunnen**, a Renaissance figure bearing the arms of Electoral Saxony. Bruderstrasse, which prolongs the Obermarkt to the east, is lined with some of the town's finest mansions, including the **Schönhof** at no. 8, the work of Wendel Roskopf, the leading local architect of the Renaissance period.

Downhill is the **Untermarkt**, one of Germany's most imposing squares, which is built up in the middle, on the normal central European model. Best of the many mansions are nos. 2–5, late Gothic and early Renaissance, along the south side, which are collectively known as the **Lange Laube**. They belonged to the richest merchants and officials, and characteristically have bright vaulted entrance halls. It's particularly worth peeking into no. 5, whose original murals have survived. Also of special note are the Renaissance **Ratsapotheke** at no. 24, with its elaborate sundial; the **Flüsterbogen** (Whispering Arch) at no. 22; the large **Waage** (Weigh House) in the central block; and the early Baroque **Alte Börse**, the merchant's hall.

The **Städtisches Museum** (Tues–Sun 10am–5pm; DM3) occupies a Baroque mansion just off the east side of Untermarkt at Neiss Str. 30. It displays fine and decorative arts from the Renaissance to Biedermeier, along with material on Upper Lusatian folklore, and documentation on **Jakob Böhme**, the city's most distinguished son, the man regarded as both the first true German philosopher and the last of the medieval mystics and alchemists. Alongside at no. 29 is one of Görlitz's most unusual buildings, the **Biblisches Haus**; it dates from about 1570 and is adorned with little reliefs of scenes from the Old and New Testaments – a sure sign that the Reformation had taken root here, as religious depictions had hitherto been banned from secular buildings. Peterstrasse, which leads north from Untermarkt, is another impressive street; take a look inside no. 14, whose amazing stairway seems to defy gravity.

The northern quarters

At the end of Peterstrasse is the **Peterskirche**, a five-aisled Flamboyant Gothic hall church with whitewashed exterior walls, a sturdy pair of towers crowned by fantastical nineteenth-century steeples, and a crypt which is itself of church-like dimensions. To the south side, the thirteenth-century **Renthaus** is the oldest house in the city; the terrace beyond preserves remnants of the former walls and commands a view over the Neisse to Poland. A few minutes' walk to the northeast lies the **Nikolaifriedhof**, a hillside cemetery with many elaborate tombstones, including that of Jakob Böhme.

East along Steinweg, you come to Görlitz's most intriguing sight, the **Heiliges Grab** (guided tours Wed, Sat & Sun at 11.30am, otherwise enquire at tourist office; donation expected). The only complete (and reasonably authentic) medieval reproduction of the Holy Places of Jerusalem, it was built by Georg Emmerich, a rich young citizen of Görlitz. He went on pilgrimage to the Holy Land, where he made plans of the biblical sites which he commissioned Conrad Pflüger, the architect of the Peterskirche, to build on a site meant to resemble the Garden of Gethsemane. You first visit the **Kapelle zum Heiligen Kreuz**, a two-storey chapel whose crypt is named in honour of Adam, the upper part after Golgotha, symbolizing the tradition that Christ was crucified on the site of Adam's grave. Alongside is the tiny **Salbhaus**, behind whose wrought-iron gates is a sculpture of the Virgin Mary lamenting over Jesus' dead body. Finally comes the **Grabkapelle**, which is of special interest as being a far more accurate, if miniaturized, version of the original, than its much-altered counterpart in Jerusalem. It's an elegant building in its own right; particularly outstanding is the turret, a skilful fusion of European and Middle Eastern architecture.

Practicalities

The **Hauptbahnhof** lies southwest of the Altstadt, and it's only a ten-minute walk straight ahead to Marienplatz from here. Görlitz's **tourist office** (Mon–Fri 10am–6pm,

Sat 10am–4pm, Sun 10am–1pm; ☎03581/47570) occupies a handsome Baroque mansion at Obermarkt 29. They have plenty of **private rooms** (②–③) on offer.

There are also several inexpensive **pensions**, including three with a central location: *Lisakowski*, Landeskronstr. 23 (☎03581/400539; ④); *Drehscheibe*, Landeskronstr. 26 (☎03581/314149; ④); and *Haus Wiesbaden*, Schulstr. 7 (☎03581/406847; ④). A good spread of **hotels** can likewise be found in the heart of town: *Goldener Engel*, Hugo-Keller-Str. 1 (☎03581/403337; ⑤); *Hansa*, opposite the Hauptbahnhof at Berliner Str. 33–34 (☎03581/406301; ⑦); *Zum Klötzelmönch*, which occupies a Baroque palace at Fleischerstr. 3 (☎03581/47580; ⑦); and *Sorat*, in a Jugendstil mansion at Struvestr. 1 (☎03581/406577; ⑦). In the Südstadt, on the opposite side of the rail tracks from the city centre, are two more grand hotels: *Zum Grafen Zeppelin*, Jauernicker Str. 15–16 (☎03581/405212; ⑥); and *Silesia*, Biesnitzer Str. 11 (☎03581/48100; ⑥). Also in this area is the **youth hostel**, which occupies a spectacular Jugendstil villa at Goethestr. 17 (☎03581/406510; ✿); note that it has rooms which can be let as doubles or triples.

Restaurants can be found in all the hotels listed above, with *Goldener Strauss* in the *Sorat* being perhaps the pick of the bunch. Other good places to eat and drink are the traditional *Destille*, Nikolaistr. 6, the *Bulgarischer Keller* on Konsulplatz, and the fish specialist *Gastmahl des Meeres*, Struvestr. 2.

The main **cultural** venues are the aforementioned *Theater*, Demianiplatz 2 (☎03581/474747), which puts on a varied programme of drama, ballet, opera and musicals, and the *Stadthalle*, Am Stadtpark 1 (☎03581/47500), where concerts are held.

travel details

Trains

Dresden to: Bad Schandau (every 30min; 1hr); Bautzen (hourly; 1hr); Chemnitz (hourly; 1hr 30min); Freiberg (every 30min; 50min); Görlitz (hourly; 2hr); Leipzig (hourly; 2hr); Meissen (every 30 min; 45min); Pirna (every 30min; 30min); Zittau (10 daily; 2hr).

Chemnitz to: Annaberg-Buchholz (10 daily; 2hr); Freiberg (every 30 min; 50min); Rochlitz (5 daily; 1hr 15min); Zwickau (hourly; 1hr).

Görlitz to: Bautzen (hourly; 1hr); Zittau (10 daily; 1hr).

Leipzig to: Chemnitz (15 daily; 1hr 30min/2hr); Colditz (10 daily; 1hr 20min); Plauen (15 daily; 2hr); Rochlitz (10 daily; 1hr 40min); Torgau (frequent; 1hr); Zwickau (hourly; 1hr 30min).

Zwickau to: Plauen (hourly; 1hr).

CONTEXTS

THE HISTORICAL FRAMEWORK

To think of a continuous German history is impossible, since there was no single nation called Germany until 1871, and even then it was not strictly speaking a country, but an empire made up of a number of sovereign states. Nevertheless, a recognizable German culture can be traced through the history of a large and disparate group of territories and traditions.

THE BEGINNINGS

From around the eighth century BC, the bulk of present-day Germany was inhabited by **Celtic peoples**, who established the first permanent settlements. Warlike, nomadic Germanic tribes gradually appeared further north and began pushing their way into the Celtic lands. Their loose structure later made them awkward opponents to the expanding **Roman Empire**, which decided to use the natural boundaries of the rivers Rhine and Danube as the limit of their territory: attempts to push eastwards were finally abandoned after a crushing defeat in the Teutoburg Forest in 9 AD.

A number of towns founded by the Romans – Trier, Regensburg, Augsburg, Mainz and Cologne – were to be the main bases of urban settlement for the next millennium. **Christianity** was introduced under Emperor Constantine, and a bishopric (the first north of the Alps) was established in Trier in 314.

At the beginning of the fifth century Germany was overrun by the Huns, an action which precipitated the indigenous Saxons into invading England. Gradually the **Franks**, who had been based in what is now Belgium, began to assert themselves over the other Germanic peoples, particularly towards the end of the fifth century under King Clovis, who established the **Merovingian** dynasty and built up a powerful Rhenish state. In time, the Merovingians were supplanted by their former henchmen, the **Carolingians**, with the help of papal support. The new dynasty was bent on expansion, and saw the benefits of involving the Church in its plans. Missionaries – the most influential of whom was the English-born Saint Boniface – were recruited to undertake mass conversion campaigns among rival tribes.

Under **Charlemagne**, who succeeded to the throne in 768, the fortunes of the Franks went from strength to strength. A series of campaigns saw them stretch their power base from the North Sea to Rome, and from the Pyrenees to the River Elbe. In the context of Western Europe, only Britain plus the southern parts of Spain and Italy lay beyond their control. A power-sharing structure for Europe, in which the pope and the king of the Germans would be the dominant forces, was agreed. On Christmas Day 800, Charlemagne was anointed emperor in Rome, giving him the official status of heir to the Caesars. Though the name was only coined much later, this brought into existence the concept of the **Holy Roman Empire**, which was to last for the next thousand years. This gave the German king considerable power over Italian internal affairs, while the Church's influence in matters of state was similarly assured.

When Charlemagne died, however, the empire began to crack because of its very size. In 843, by the **Treaty of Verdun**, it was split into a Germanic Eastern Europe and a Latin Western Europe, thus sharply delineating the French and Germans for the first time. The first king of the newly formed German eastern empire was **Ludwig the German**. Under his rule the Germanic people became more closely defined, with a specific culture of their own – still with many disparate regions but recognizably made up of the same peoples. When the last of Charlemagne's descendants died in 911, rulership passed to the Saxon King Henry the Fowler, bringing the Carolingian era to an end.

THE BUILDING OF A NEW EMPIRE

In the mid-tenth century the second Saxon monarch, **Otto the Great**, was faced with the problem of the growing power of the hereditary duchies which posed a threat to the unity of the empire. In order to curb this, he strengthened his alliance with the papacy. The Church was given grants of land, coupled with temporal powers of jurisdiction over them, thus creating the basis for subsequent ecclesiastical dominance over much of the country by a series of prince-bishoprics. In 962, he was crowned **Holy Roman Emperor**, firmly establishing himself as the main ruler in the Christian world. In many respects, this marks a second foundation of the curious dichotomy that characterized the Holy Roman Empire; from then on, only kings of Germany could gain the title of Roman Emperor, and it was only the pope who could grant this title.

Following a series of bitter **power struggles** between the papacy and the emperors, imperial interference in Church affairs was severely curtailed. So too was the centralized power of the emperor, as the nobility were released by the pope from their vows of allegiance to any secular authority. They soon made their own demands, the most important of which was that emperors should no longer be hereditary rulers, but elected by a council of princes.

By the twelfth century, most of the powerful **dynasties** which were to dominate German politics at both local and national level for hundreds of years to come had appeared. There was an intense feud between the two most powerful, the **Hohenstaufens** and **Welfs**, which was to continue for centuries, particularly in Italy. The Hohenstaufens, until they died out, managed to keep the upper hand, holding on to the office of Holy Roman Emperor for well over a century. **Frederick Barbarossa**, best known as an enthusiastic Crusader in the Holy Land, was their most successful ruler.

By the mid-thirteenth century the nation's boundaries began to be pushed increasingly eastwards, following a policy begun by Otto the Great. Impetus for this came from many sources, being particularly associated with the **Knights of the Teutonic Order**, who turned their attentions towards the Christianization of Eastern Europe. By the early fourteenth century, they had conquered much of the Baltic (notably the area known as Prussia) and repopulated the land with German peasants. Subsequently, they grew rich on their control of the highly profitable grain trade.

THE MIDDLE AGES

In the fourteenth century, a number of significant changes were made to the structure of the Holy Roman Empire. The **Golden Bull** of 1356 finally established the method for choosing the monarch. This fixed the electoral college at the traditional number of seven, with three **Electors** drawn from the ecclesiastical sphere (the Archbishops of Cologne, Mainz and Trier) and four from different ranks of the nobility (the King of Bohemia, the Duke of Saxony, the Margrave of Brandenburg and the Count Palatine of the Rhine).

From then on, these seven princes were tremendously powerful grandees – they had the right to construct castles, mint their own coinage, impose tolls and act as judges in all disputes, with no right of appeal. Oddly enough, the title of emperor almost invariably went to a candidate outside this group. Increasingly, it was conferred on a member of the **Habsburg** dynasty, who had built up Austria into the most powerful of the German states.

The Church's residual power over internal German affairs was killed off by the **Great Schism** of 1378–1417, when rival popes held court in Rome and Avignon. By this time, the social structure was undergoing changes that had far-reaching effects. The most important was the growth of **towns** at strategic points and along important trading routes. Initially, these were under patrician control. However, merchants and craftsmen organized themselves into guilds which gradually wrested control of civic life and laid the foundations for a capitalist economy.

Most important towns gained the status of **Free Imperial City**, which meant they were independent city-states, responsible only to the emperor. Their prosperity was greatly enhanced by the ruinous Hundred Years' War between France and England, which enabled them to snap up diverted trade to and from the Mediterranean. Though in many ways in competition with each other, the leadership of the towns realized they also had common cause. This led to the foundation of various trading and defence leagues. Of particular importance was the north German **Hanseatic League**, founded in Lübeck, which successfully combated piracy, and led not only to German economic domination of the Baltic and North Sea, but to increased political power as well, with the establishment of German communities in Scandinavia and all along the opposite coast as far as Estonia.

The **bubonic plague** swept Europe in the fourteenth century, wiping out a quarter of the German population. In all probability, the plague was introduced by merchants returning from Asia, but a different scapegoat had to be found, and the **Jews**, who lived in segregated settlements around the towns, readily fitted the bill. Jews had lived in Europe since the tenth century, but their place had never been an easy one, with their close-knit and separate communities giving rise to popular suspicion and prejudice. Excluded from guilds and trades, they took up the only occupation forbidden to Christians: money-lending – a service that did nothing to endear them to the locals. **Pogroms** therefore frequently occurred.

The fifteenth century saw the Habsburgs establish themselves firmly as the driving force in high politics, holding on to the office of Holy Roman Emperor from 1432 until its abolition nearly four hundred years later. **Maximilian I** acceded to the title in 1493, and embarked on a policy of making his family the most powerful not just in Germany, but in all of Europe. His own wedding to Mary of Burgundy gained him The Netherlands; a series of astute dynastic marriages involving his relatives led to Spain, Hungary and Bohemia all coming under Habsburg control. However, he antagonized the members of the Swiss Confederation, which broke away from the empire to become a separate state in 1499.

THE REFORMATION AND AFTER

In order to cash in on popular fear, the Church demanded money from the faithful to ensure salvation of their souls, and a lucrative trade in **indulgences** was established, whereby people could buy absolution of their sins. Bishops across the land acted as agents, and the papal coffers filled up to finance the building of St Peter's in Rome and many other great sacred buildings. Discontent with the Church was particularly widespread in Germany, given the Church's dual role within society and the fact that territories under the control of religious office-holders tended to be particularly harshly run. Thus it was hardly surprising that it was here that the full-frontal assault on the Church's traditional powers began.

The attack was led by a man of burning religious convictions, the Augustinian monk **Martin Luther**, who had been appointed Professor of Theology at the University of Wittenberg. Believing that the Church was corrupt and had lost its way totally, Luther focused his attentions on the problem of **salvation**, finding in the Bible that Man justifies himself by faith alone. This meant that he could play no part in his own salvation; therefore the trade in indulgences was a total fraud. On the eve of All Saints' Day, 1517, he nailed his **95 theses** to the door of the Schlosskirche in Wittenberg. This was in fact the normal way of inviting academic discussion, but it was seen as a deliberately provocative act and is now considered the official **beginning of the Reformation**.

In time Luther widened his attack, denouncing the centralized power of the pope, the privileged position of priests as intercessors between God and the faithful, and the doctrine of transubstantiation, which maintained that the bread and wine used in the sacrament of the Eucharist physically turned into Christ's body and blood.

However, Luther's arguments might have had as little impact as any other scholarly dispute, or led to his immediate execution as a heretic, had not the curious power structure in Germany dealt him an amazing piece of good fortune. The death of Maximilian I in 1519 led to a bizarre **European-wide power struggle** for the crown of the Holy Roman Empire. Francis I of France decided to stake a claim for the title, in order to stop the unhealthy concentration of power which would ensue if victory went to the Habsburg candidate, Charles I of Spain. In order to stop this interference from abroad, the pope had to keep the Electors sweet, even suggesting one of their number, Luther's patron Elector Frederick the Wise of Saxony, as a compromise candidate.

After much bribery by the two main contenders, the Spanish king won the election unanimously and took office as Emperor Charles

V. However, he immediately became embroiled in a war with France. As a result, the powerful princes of the Holy Roman Empire seized this chance to establish a far greater degree of independence. Many of them saw the religious struggle as a convenient cloak for their ambitions. Luther was excommunicated in 1520, but still had the right, as a citizen of the empire, to have a hearing before an Imperial Diet. This was hastily convened at Worms the following year, and, though Luther was branded an outlaw and his books were ordered to be burned, he was given a safe haven at the Wartburg castle in Thuringia, under the protection of Elector Frederick. There he **translated the Bible into German**, thus making it accessible to the common man for the first time; this work is also seen as the foundation stone of the modern German language.

Luther's ideas spread like wildfire throughout society, greatly aided by the fact that books could now be produced cheaply and quickly, thanks to the printing revolution launched by the German inventor **Johannes Gutenberg** during the previous century. They found a ready market among the oppressed classes, who took the attacks on Church authority as invitations to attack authority in general.

This formed one of the causes of the **Peasants' War** of 1524–25, which brought wholesale destruction of monasteries and castles. Poorly armed, organized and led, it was brutally crushed by the princely armies. To the dismay of the rebels, Luther aligned himself on the side of worldly authority, arguing that it was God's will that there should be different strata in society; equality was only for the hereafter. Thus, the Reformation progressed as a revolution controlled from above, setting the tone for German history for centuries to come.

In 1529, the representatives of six principalities and fourteen Free Imperial Cities which supported Luther met at Speyer, where the name **Protestant** came to be used for the first time. The following year, Charles V convened a Diet at Augsburg in an attempt to defuse the growing crisis. However, he was confronted by a closely argued definition of the Reformers' position, thereafter known as the **Confession of Augsburg**, which was drawn up by Luther's indispensible sidekick, the brilliant scholar Philipp Melanchthon. This set the seal not only on the division of the Western Church, but also on the effective division of Germany into a plethora of small states.

So many states had joined the Protestant cause by 1555 that Charles V had to admit defeat, abdicating in order to retire to a Spanish monastery. He was succeeded by his brother Ferdinand, who almost immediately signed the **Peace of Augsburg**, a historic agreement that institutionalized religious tolerance, leaving the decision as to the form of religion practised in each state firmly in the hands of its secular rulers. Though a measure of considerable significance, it was in effect a carve-up between the Catholics and Lutherans at the expense of more radical Protestant groups.

THE STRUGGLE FOR RELIGIOUS SUPREMACY

After Luther's death in 1546, the Catholics began to make something of a comeback after the reforms thrashed out at the Council of Trent launched the **Counter-Reformation**. Radical Protestantism was also given a fillip by Melanchthon's shift away from central Lutheran doctrines to more extreme solutions. Inevitably, one of the political goals of Protestantism was to gain control of the imperial electoral college, and oust the Catholic Habsburgs from their long tradition of pre-eminence.

Bavaria's annexation of the predominantly Protestant free city of Donauwörth in 1608 led to the formation of the **Protestant Union**, an armed alliance under the leadership of the Palatinate. The **Catholic League** was set up in opposition by the Bavarians the following year, meaning that there was now a straight division of the country into two hostile camps. Meanwhile, the way central authority in Germany had collapsed was cruelly exposed by the weak 36-year reign of Rudolf II, who chose to govern from Prague, at the very fringe of the empire. There he presided over a bizarre court filled with astrologers and alchemists, until his growing insanity led to his deposition in 1611.

As it happened, this same city was to see the beginning of the great trial of strength between the two faiths. In 1618, the youthful Count Palatine Friedrich V usurped the crown of Bohemia, which itself was an elected office, thus seemingly ensuring a Protestant majority in the next imperial election. Unfortunately for him, he lost both his titles a year later, and had by then set in train the complicated series of religious and dynastic conflicts commonly known as the **Thirty Years' War**.

Much of the German countryside was laid waste, towns were pillaged, and there was mass rape and slaughter, at the end of which the total population of the country may have been reduced by as much as a third. Initially, the Catholic League, commanded by the brutal Johann Tilly, held the upper hand, but first Denmark, then Sweden intervened, fearing for both their independence and their Protestant faith. The Swedes, led by King Gustavus II Adolphus, had their greatest moment of triumph on the European stage, defeating Tilly and over-running the country, thus rising to the rank of a major power. Spain intervened on behalf of its Habsburg cousins, while Catholic France sup-ported the Protestants, on the grounds that their faith was a lesser evil than the threatened Habsburg hegemony.

From 1643, concerted attempts were made to end the war, with the Catholics meeting in Münster, the Protestants in Osnabrück. The negotiations are generally seen as the begin-nings of modern diplomacy; they culminated five years later in the signing of the **Peace of Westphalia**. While the ending of the messy conflicts was a major achievement in itself, for Germany the peace treaty was as disastrous as the war itself; the Holy Roman Empire was killed off in all but name, with the emperor reduced to a figurehead.

Real power was diffused among a **plethora of states**, numbering some 300 principalities, plus over 1000 other territories, some of them minute – a system which could hardly have been better designed to waste resources and stunt economic and political development. Germany ceased to be a factor of importance on the European stage.

THE RISE OF PRUSSIA

In the course of the late seventeenth and eigh-teenth century, almost all the petty German princes adopted an **absolutist** system of gov-ernment, based on the divine right of rulers. They spent a vast amount of their revenue build-ing palaces on a scale out of all proportion to their needs, to create at least the visual pre-tence that they were mighty monarchs. Only a few managed to rise above the general level of mediocrity; one of these was the House of Welf, which made an astonishing comeback after cen-turies of confinement to its Lower Saxon heart-lands. As a result of clever politicking, the **Hanoverian** branch of the family gained the British crown in 1714 and maintained a royal union until 1837.

Within the Holy Roman Empire itself, **Austria** at first maintained her dominance, with the Habsburgs holding on to the imperial title, for what it was worth. The country received a severe jolt when the Turks reached the gates of Vienna in 1683, but after the enemy was beaten back, the way was cleared for Austria to build up an empire in the Balkans. As German-speak-ing influence spread eastwards, so the western flank became vulnerable. The **French**, like the Romans before them, saw the Rhine as the nat-ural limit of their territory. They formally annexed Alsace and Strasbourg in 1681, then laid claim to the Palatinate in a series of bloody campaigns between 1688 and 1697.

By then, a new power had arisen in north-eastern Germany in the shape of **Brandenburg-Prussia**. In 1415, the old fron-tier district of Brandenburg was given to the ambitious **Hohenzollern** family, whose attempts to gain power at the heart of the empire had met with no success. Since 1525, the family had also held the Baltic territory known as Prussia, which lay outside the Holy Roman Empire and thus was not subject to any of its rules. One of these forbade princes from promoting themselves to royal titles: in 1701, Friedrich III defied this with impunity by having himself crowned as King of Prussia. The Habsburgs duly turned a blind eye to this in order to gain Hohenzollern support in the **War of the Spanish Succession**, which broke out as a result of rival Austrian and French claimants for the throne of Spain.

Throughout the eighteenth century, Prussia was built up as a strongly centralized state, based in Berlin. There was a tight administra-tive structure, but it became associated above all with **militarism**. It was a second Sparta, described with some justification as not a state with an army, but an army with a state: at times, two-thirds of national revenue was spent on the military. The other dominant force in society was the **Junker** class, landowners who ran huge estates in which the labourers were treat-ed as little more than serfs.

Prussia's rise to the rank of a major European power was achieved under **Frederick the**

Great, who came to the throne in 1740. A Francophile and epitome of the enlightened despot, Frederick softened his country's rough-hewn image by introducing a few liberal reforms at home, and developed a cultured courtly life. However, his main concern was expansion by military force, and he used an old Brandenburg claim on Silesia to extract that territory from Austria. In revenge, the Habsburgs launched the Seven Years' War in 1756, thereby hoping to annihilate Prussia as a potential rival; in this, they had the full military backing of the two other great continental powers, France and Russia, whereas Frederick had only the tacit support of Britain and Hannover to fall back on.

Within three years, the highly rated Prussian troops seemed to have overreached themselves. They were given an unexpected reprieve when the Austrians and Russians fell out; new recruits were thrown into the conflict, eventually achieving an incredible turn-around in fortunes, in the process establishing Prussia as a force of the first rank. By annexing much of Poland in the partition of 1772, Frederick achieved his aim of establishing a north German version of Austria.

THE NAPOLEONIC PERIOD AND ITS AFTERMATH

Ironically, the first steps towards unifying Germany came as a result of the expansionist aims of revolutionary France. By the War of the First Coalition of 1792–97, the left bank of the Rhine fell under French control. However, it was only with the advent of the dictator **Napoleon Bonaparte** that radical changes were made. Following the defeat of Austria in 1802 in the War of the Second Coalition (in which Prussia tactfully remained aloof), he decided to completely re-order the German map, which he rightly saw as anachronistic. All but a handful of the free cities, and every single one of the ecclesiastical territories, were stripped of their independence, which in many cases went back five or six centuries.

Napoleon created a series of buffer states: Bavaria, Württemberg and Saxony were raised to the rank of kingdoms, while Baden and Hesse-Darmstadt became Grand Duchies. In 1806, during the War of the Third Coalition, the Holy Roman Empire was officially abolished with the Habsburgs consoling themselves for suffering yet another defeat by promoting themselves from Archdukes to Emperors of Austria, deciding thereafter to concentrate their energies on preserving their Balkan lands. Gradually the German satellite states began to remove economic, religious and servile restrictions, developing into societies which were liberal by German standards.

The same year, Prussia suffered a series of humiliating defeats; Berlin was occupied and the country forced to sign away half its territory and population. Thereafter, it was made to mend its ways: serfdom was abolished, and its cities were allowed to develop their own municipal government. In the event, Prussia's humiliation was short-lived, and it soared in international prestige as a result of its key role at the **Battle of Waterloo** in 1815, when Napoleon's over-ambitious plans for the total subjugation of Europe were finally put to rest.

The **Congress of Vienna**, which met the same year to determine the structure of post-Napoleonic Europe, established Prussian dominance in German affairs. Westphalia and the Rhineland were added to its territories, meaning that it now stretched all the way from the French border to the River Memel, interrupted only by a few enclaves. Otherwise, much of the Napoleonic reorganization of the Holy Roman Empire was ratified, leaving 39 independent states: still far too many, but a major step forward nonetheless. A German Confederation was established, with each state represented in the Frankfurt-based Diet, which, however, had no effective power.

TOWARDS GERMAN UNIFICATION

Whereas the main political forces in German society in the aftermath of the Congress of Vienna were still staunchly conservative, the accelerating **Industrial Revolution** was resulting in radical economic and social changes. This closely followed the British lead, but profited by learning from the pioneering country's mistakes. The first German railway was established in 1835, and industrial production advanced in leaps and bounds. Thanks to its rich mineral deposits, the dominant centre for industry was the Rhine-Ruhr area, which had recently been allocated to Prussia. In 1834, Prussia's increasingly dominant role within the German nation was underlined by the establishment of a Customs union, known as the **Zollverein**.

The Industrial Revolution led to a whole **new social order**, with wage-earning workers and an emergent bourgeoisie. Both groups were quick to agitate for their interests – the workers for better working conditions and the bourgeoisie for political representation. Meanwhile the large peasantry was still living in abject poverty and under almost feudal conditions, which pressed hard during the failed harvests of the late 1840s. Social unrest was inevitable, and violence erupted both in the countryside and the cities, causing ever more reactionary policies from the land-owning elite with the political power.

In 1848, there were uprisings all over Europe. This forced the Prussian king to allow elections to the **National Assembly** in Frankfurt, thereby hoping to nip republican and socialist aspirations in the bud. For the first time, an opportunity was presented to found a liberal tradition in the country, but it was completely muffed. The bourgeois members of the Assembly were much too keen to establish the new-found status of their own social groups to attempt any far-reaching political reforms, and they certainly posed no threat to the existing order. Thus, when armed rebellions broke out in 1849, the National Assembly was exposed as an ineffective talking shop, easily disbanded in the face of the revolutionary emergency. Any steps towards constitutional rule were wiped out by the combined forces of the Prussian army and battalions from other German kingdoms and principalities.

The 1850s saw political stagnation, but the increasing success of the Industrial Revolution meant that the creation of a single internal German market, preferably accompanied by a political union, was of paramount importance. By now, Prussia had manoeuvred herself into a position of such power that she was the only possible agent for enforcing such a change.

In 1862, **King Wilhelm I** chose as Chancellor the career diplomat **Otto von Bismarck**, a member of the Junker class who had already gained a reputation as an operator of a rare sharpness. In order to win over the Prussian liberals, Bismarck backed the concept of universal male suffrage. He also played the nationalist card immediately: seeing that the Chancellor was bent on creating a united Germany, the liberals muted their opposition and backed his plans for a thorough modernization of the army.

In 1864, Bismarck lured Austria into supporting him in a war against Denmark to recapture the lost duchies of Schleswig and Holstein. Having achieved an easy victory, he then provoked a disagreement over the spoils: the result was the **Seven Weeks' War** of 1866, in which the superior Prussian weapons and organization achieved a crushing victory. Not only was Austria forced out of Germany's affairs, but those states which had remained neutral, including Hannover and Hesse-Kassel, were incorporated into Prussia. The German Confederation was dissolved, to be replaced by one covering the north of the country only, which was totally under Prussian domination.

To complete the jigsaw, Bismarck still needed to woo the southern states. His tactic was an original one: to provoke a war against the old enemy, France. In 1870, having carefully prepared the diplomatic ground to ensure that no other power would intervene to support the French, he goaded them by proposing that a Hohenzollern should succeed to the vacant throne of Spain. The French emperor, Napoleon III, managed to force the Prussians to withdraw, but foolishly sent a telegram asking for an apology. Bismarck doctored this to make it seem worse than it was, giving the excuse to begin the **Franco-Prussian War**.

By January 1871, the Prussian field guns had helped chalk up yet another easy victory. A united German empire, which once more included the long-disputed provinces of Alsace and Lorraine, was proclaimed in Versailles. King Wilhelm I of Prussia was the inevitable choice as Kaiser; four other monarchs were among the rulers who were henceforth subjugated to him. The new empire became known as the Second Reich, in honour of the fact that it had revived the German imperial tradition after a gap of 65 years.

THE SECOND REICH

In his domestic policy for the united Germany, Bismarck indulged in a series of **liberal reforms**. Uniform systems of law, administration and currency were introduced, an imperial bank was set up, restrictions on trade and movement of labour were lifted, and cities were given municipal autonomy.

By such measures, Bismarck aimed to control the opposition parties in the Reichstag, and to keep power in the hands of the elite. The darker side of his nature came out in the Kulturkampf, which aimed at curbing the power of the Catholic Church, whose power and influence was anathema to the Protestant aristocracy of Prussia. However, this met with spirited opposition, which led to Bismarck making a rare retreat, though not until he had exacted his price: the Catholics were forced to support protectionist agricultural measures, designed to subsidize the large, outdated Junker estates. By then, a formidable new opposition had arisen in the shape of the **Social Democratic Party** (SPD), founded in 1875. In order to take the wind out of its sails, Bismarck introduced a system of welfare benefits for workers, a system belatedly copied in many other industrialized countries.

Bismarck's **foreign policy** involved a complicated set of jugglings. He set up the Dreikaiserbund, an alliance of the three great imperial powers of Germany, Austria and Russia; indulged in a Mediterranean naval alliance with Britain in order to check Russian designs on the Balkans; yet initiated a bit of colonial rivalry with the British.

Bismarck's awesome reputation for political sure-footedness meant that Germany's internal and external stability seemed completely safe in his hands. However, Friedrich III, who succeeded his father Wilhelm I in 1888, died after only a few months on the throne. His son, **Wilhelm II**, was a firm believer in the divine right of kings. He was of a generation which did not feel beholden to Bismarck, and strongly disliked the veteran politician. Two years later, he removed the Chancellor from office – a move compared to dropping the pilot from a ship – and thereafter relied on a series of ineffective kowtowing men to lead his government.

Britain, which had hitherto been a natural ally of Germany as a result of dynastic ties and mutual suspicion of France, was increasingly seen as the main rival. A notorious telegram sent by the Kaiser in support of the Boers in 1896 signalled the beginning of a severe deterioration in relations between the two countries. This was fuelled by an **arms race**, affecting all of Europe, in which the Krupp armaments factory played a crucial role. Nowhere was the attempt to establish supremacy more evident than in the naval sphere, where the Germans set out to usurp Britain's long period of supremacy, achieving parity by 1909.

By this time, the major powers of Europe were divided into **two nervous alliances**. Bismarck's successors failed to maintain his two-faced foreign policy. As a result, Germany was bound up once more with Austria, whose eastern empire was tottering under the nationalist aspirations of the many ethnic groups contained within it; Italy was a somewhat reluctant partner. Ranged against them were France and Russia, drawn together by mutual fear of the ever-increasing power of the German-speaking countries. Britain, maintaining her time-honoured policy of trying to preserve an effective balance of power in Europe, was increasingly drawn towards the latter alliance.

WORLD WAR I

Everybody expected that war would come sooner or later, and master strategies were carefully planned. The Germans developed the **first-strike theory**, which envisaged a quick knock-out blow against both France and Russia, as a prelude to a tougher struggle against the more formidable British. Public opinion in the country was easily won over by the bogus theory that the Fatherland was under threat from the "iron ring" which surrounded it. Even the Social Democrats were persuaded of the necessity and desirability of a war.

The spark which lit the inferno happened to come in **Austria's unwieldy empire**. In 1914, the crown prince, Archduke Franz Ferdinand, was assassinated in Sarajevo by a Bosnian nationalist. Austria sent the independent neighbouring state of Serbia a threatening ultimatum, although no connection between the Serbian government and the conspirators was ever proved. This inevitably provoked the Russians, who had an agreement to protect their fellow Slavs from any threat. The German generals saw this as a golden opportunity to put their first-strike theory into operation. As soon as the Russians mobilized, German troops were sent to attack France. The quickest route was through Belgium, thus violating its neutrality, which was guaranteed by Britain. So fast did events move that the Kaiser sent a telegram ordering withdrawal, but this was ignored. **World War I** was thus under way.

The German High Command believed the French would capitulate within six weeks, the Russians within six months. They were soon proved hopelessly wrong, and found themselves with what they had been most anxious to avoid – a war on two fronts. Even then, they could hardly have anticipated the Armageddon which was unleashed. After rapidly advancing towards Paris, they were forced to retreat at the first Battle of the Marne in September, and dig **trenches** all across northern France and Belgium. This gave rise to a wholly new form of warfare, with casualties quite unlike any that had previously been known. In 1916, an attempt to exhaust the French at the four-month-long Battle of Verdun proved to be self-defeating, and the same year the British proved their continued mastery of the seas at the Battle of Jutland.

As a result of these setbacks, the Kaiser handed over effective military and political power to the dual leadership of Field Marshal **Paul von Hindenburg**, and his quartermaster-general, **Erich Ludendorff**; though the latter was nominally the junior partner, he became the effective dictator of the country. In January 1917, it was decided to introduce unrestricted submarine warfare. This was a complete disaster, its barbarity prompting the United States to enter the war. A reprieve was gained as a result of the revolution in Russia that autumn, which ended the fighting on the eastern front. This allowed the Germans to transfer large numbers of troops to the west, break through the Allied lines in February 1918, and advance deep into France.

THE END OF THE WAR; FAILURE OF THE GERMAN REVOLUTION

The euphoria of this triumph soon faded, however: the German lines became hopelessly overextended; captured Allied supply dumps showed the German troops how poorly provisioned they were by comparison; many soldiers from the east had acquired Communist views and were agitating against the war; and American troops were at last beginning to arrive in substantial numbers. On August 8, 1918 – the "Black Day of the German Army" – the Allies broke the German offensive and turned it into a rout. Finally convinced that the war was lost, Ludendorff looked about for ways to minimize the High Command's loss of face. He seized on the idea of letting a parliamentary government handle the **peace negotiations**; it would be likely to secure more lenient terms, and would also be a useful scapegoat in the

event of a harsh treaty. Furthermore, it would help counteract the far more horrifying alternative of a Bolshevik-style revolution, an only too real prospect once the German people realized the extent to which their leaders had been deceiving them.

Accordingly, he persuaded the Kaiser to appoint the liberal monarchist **Prince Max von Baden** as Chancellor. A full parliamentary democracy was proclaimed; the cabinet was drawn from the ranks of the Reichstag, with Social Democrats included for the first time. On October 3, Prince Max sued for peace. Ludendorff, sensing that the Allies were going to drive a hard bargain, subsequently resigned; Hindenburg offered to do likewise, but was allowed to remain at his post.

Towards the end of the month, Admiral Scheer decided to mount a futile last-ditch offensive; his crews mutinied, refusing to lay down their lives so unnecessarily. This revolt spread throughout northern Germany and might well have developed into the full-scale revolution Ludendorff had been conniving to avert, had it not been for the bitter **division of the political left-wing** into three factions.

The SPD had previously split into two separate parties over the war; the pacifist group, the USPD, was now frustrated by the tepid nature of their erstwhile colleagues' socialism, which embraced constitutional monarchy and a bourgeois social order. In turn, their politics were seen as too tame by the Spartakist League, a Marxist group who aimed to follow the example of their Russian mentors by seizing power in Berlin. **Friedrich Ebert**, leader of the SPD, decided to forestall them by calling a general strike to demand the Kaiser's abdication. Prince Max took matters into his own hands by announcing this without the monarch's consent, and then himself resigned in favour of Ebert. Matters were still delicately poised with the news that **Karl Liebknecht** of the Spartakists intended to proclaim the establishment of a socialist republic on November 9.

In order to wrest the initiative, Ebert's lieutenant **Philipp Scheidemann** made an impromptu declaration of a free German Republic from the Reichstag balcony, thus bringing the regime of the Kaisers to an abrupt end. Two days later, an armistice was signed, as Ebert realized that either a collapse of military discipline, or the spread of Bolshevism, would lead to an Allied invasion. As part of his plans, he made a pact with the High Command, which provided him with an army to protect the state against internal left-wing opponents, but at the price of allowing it almost complete autonomy.

This policy paid immediate dividends for him, as the military was used to crush an attempted revolution by the Spartakists in January, a last-ditch attempt at a Communist seizure of power before the elections for the new National Assembly later in the month. The brutal behaviour of the army – Liebknecht and his co-leader Rosa Luxemburg were among those murdered – was to have disastrous long-term consequences for the fledgling republic, which should have made a purging of the anti-democratic and war-crazed officer class one of its most urgent priorities.

THE WEIMAR REPUBLIC

The elections confirmed the SPD as the new political leaders of the country, with 38 percent of the vote; as a result, Ebert was made President, with Scheidemann as Chancellor. Initially, **Weimar**, the small country town which had seen the most glorious flowering of the German Enlightenment, was chosen as the seat of government in preference to Berlin, which was tinged by its monarchical and militaristic associations.

A **new constitution** was drawn up, hailed as the most liberal and progressive in the world. While on the surface an admirable document, this constitution was hopelessly idealistic for a people so unfamiliar with democratic practice and responsibilities. No attempt was made to outlaw parties hostile to the system; this opened the way for savage attacks on the republic by extremists at both ends of the political spectrum. The use of proportional representation, without any qualifying minimum percentage of the total vote, favoured a plethora of parties promoting sectional interests. This meant that the Weimar governments were all unwieldy coalitions, whose average life was about eight months, and which often pursued contradictory policies in different ministries.

Two months before the constitution was ratified in July 1919, Germany had been forced to accede to the **Treaty of Versailles**. In contrast to the Habsburg Empire, which was broken up into a series of successor states, German territorial integrity was largely preserved, but the losses were painful ones – the industrially productive Saarland and Alsace-Lorraine went to France, while the resurrected country of Poland was given Upper Silesia plus a corridor to the sea, which left East Prussia cut off from the rest of the country. All overseas colonies were confiscated, the Rhineland was declared a demilitarized zone, the navy limited to six light battleships, and the army to 100,000 men with conscription prohibited. Germany and her allies were found guilty of having started the war, and, as a result, were landed with an enormous **reparations bill**, which would have taken over half a century to pay.

In all, this amounted to a pretty stiff settlement, albeit one considerably less harsh than the Germans had recently enforced on the Russians at Brest-Litovsk. So incensed were the military leaders with this humiliating diktat that they toyed with the idea of resuming hostilities. As this was not a feasible option, they contented themselves with inventing the **"stab in the back" legend**, maintaining that the army, undefeated in the field, had been betrayed by unscrupulous politicians – a preposterous distortion accepted all too easily by gullible sections of the public.

The treaty spelled the beginning of the end for the Social Democratic republic. Scheidemann immediately resigned as Chancellor, and, following gains by the two political extremes in the 1920 elections under the new constitution, the party, though still the largest in the Reichstag, withdrew from government altogether, leaving power in the hands of minority administrations drawn from liberal and moderate conservative parties. Right-wing extremism flourished in a series of political murders and attempted putsches, which were barely punished by a judiciary which rivalled the army in its contempt for the republic.

The reparations bill crippled the economy, to the extent that payments began to be withheld. This gave the French the excuse to occupy the Ruhr in 1923; they were met by a policy of passive resistance. As no work was done, galloping **inflation** – the most catastrophic ever known in world history – quickly ensued, causing the ruin of the entire middle class as the currency became utterly worthless. The Weimar Republic seemed irretrievably doomed, but it made an astonishing comeback, largely due to the political skills of the new Chancellor, **Gustav**

Stresemann. He was an unlikely saviour, an old-fashioned conservative who had begun his career as Ludendorff's mouthpiece in the Reichstag, and whose precise commitment to the republic is still disputed. A supreme pragmatist, he realized the danger of economic collapse and the futility of confrontation with the Allies. Therefore he ended passive resistance and negotiated huge American loans to rebuild the economy. This was so successful that by October 1924 money had regained its former value; (nearly) full employment and general prosperity soon followed.

Although Stresemann's government broke up long before these effects were felt, he subsequently served as foreign minister for six years in a variety of coalitions, achieving **Germany's rehabilitation on the world stage**. By the 1925 Locarno Pact, he gained *rapprochement* with France and guarantees that there could be no further threat of foreign occupation. Reparation payments were scaled down, and further American aid given. It seemed that the republic was set for a secure future, even if the political immaturity of the German people was still apparent, most notably in the presidential election of 1925. This was won by the 78-year-old Hindenburg, a wily operator basking in an undeserved military reputation, vocal exponent of the "stab in the back" legend, and an embarrassing reminder of times past.

THE RISE OF NAZISM

The **National Socialist German Workers' Party** was founded in 1918 by a locksmith by the name of Anton Drexler, but only gained momentum when he was ousted three years later by **Adolf Hitler**, a failed artist and ex-corporal from Austria. It was a rag-bag group of fanatics and misfits whose views, as the party name suggests, were an odd mixture of the extreme right and left. They modelled their organization on the Communists and the Italian Fascisti, adopting their own uniform and slogans, and developing a private army, the brown-shirted **SA** (*Sturmabteilung*, or "Storm Troopers"). Such limited success as the party enjoyed was at first confined to Bavaria, where a botched attempt at a putsch was made in 1923; following this, Hitler was arrested and convicted of high treason.

The leniency shown by the judiciary to right-wing opponents of the republic — aided by the fact that he had involved Ludendorff in the plot — meant that Hitler only served nine months in prison, during which he set out his ideology and political programme in his autobiography, *Mein Kampf*. This consists of verbose rantings and ravings, drawing from all the nastiest and most reactionary theories of the day, but is an important source, as it sets out unequivocally what Hitler genuinely believed, and was to serve as his blueprint for power.

Racism forms the keynote: the so-called Aryans were the earth's rightful masters, while inferior peoples such as the Slavs were fit only to serve them. All ills could ultimately be laid at the door of the Jews, who were stealthily conspiring for world dominance. The German *Volk* had been betrayed by socialism, democracy and the traitors who had signed the Versailles Treaty. A new German Reich must be created under the direction of an all-powerful *Führer*, uniting with Austria and gaining living space (*Lebensraum*) to the east; to this end, France had to be subdued and Russia crushed.

Sales of the book — in spite of its ready captive market in the ranks of the party faithful — failed to reach 10,000 in the first year, and declined steadily for the next five. Nazi representation in the Reichstag also decreased from twenty-five in 1924 to just twelve after the 1928 elections, making it the ninth and smallest party, and one widely regarded as something of a joke. Only the extraordinarily mesmeric personality of Hitler held it together; having learnt from past mistakes, he was now determined to gain power by strictly legal means.

Stresemann died in October 1929, exhausted by overwork and by persecution from his former right-wing allies. Three weeks later came the **Wall Street crash** in America, whose repercussions swiftly destroyed the new German order he had created. Wholesale withdrawal of credit — on which the economy was totally dependent — led to another bout of escalating unemployment and inflation, to which there was no ready-made solution, as there had been in 1923. The coalition partners quarrelled over what measures to take; as a result, the SPD, who had only recently returned to government following eight years voluntarily out of office, once more abdicated the responsibility of leadership. A minority government was set up under the centrist **Heinrich Brüning**; frustrated by having to rely on rule by presidential decree, he took a gamble by asking Hindenburg to dissolve the Reichstag.

The elections, held in September 1930, offered a golden opportunity for the political extremes, with their formulas for righting all wrongs. The Nazi rise was meteoric, taking even Hitler by surprise – they gained 6.4 million votes and became the second largest party. This support was overwhelmingly from the disaffected ranks of the unemployed (particularly the young) and the ruined petty bourgeoisie. Though a significant breakthrough, it was far from being a decisive one, and there was still no inevitability about the Nazi triumph, which was only achieved because of the **short-sightedness and greed of the traditional right wing**.

In Hitler, they at last found their Kaiser-substitute, a man who could give them the broad mass of support they could not otherwise muster and who would return Germany to its traditions of hierarchical authoritarian rule at home and military glory abroad. Leading figures in industry and politics latched onto Hitler and gave him respectability; by acting as his financiers and power brokers, they believed they would be able to control his excesses. Nazi coffers were swelled by contributions from many of the giant corporations, following a lead given some years before by the steel magnate Fritz Thyssen. The army began to abandon its role above party politics, overlooking its earlier aversion to the paramilitary SA.

Hitler offered a clue as to the naivety of these hopes by standing against the revered Hindenburg in the 1932 presidential election, only just managing to secure German citizenship in time to be eligible. The desperate straits into which the republic had fallen were shown by the fact that the ancient soldier, teetering on the verge of senility, was supported by the SPD and all the other democratic parties, who abstained from fielding a candidate of their own in the belief that there was no other way of beating Hitler.

In the event, Hindenburg only just failed to obtain an outright majority on the first ballot, and comfortably won the second, with the Communists trailing a very poor third. Fresh hope was provided by the remarkable success of Chancellor Brüning, still dependent on presidential decree, who was developing into a worthy successor to Stresemann. His sensible economic programme alleviated the worst hard-

ships, and he was on the verge of pulling off a tremendous double success in foreign affairs, with the end of reparations and the return of Germany's right to equality of armaments in sight. An attempt at reforming the outdated pattern of land ownership proved to be Brüning's undoing; the aristocracy howled with rage at this alleged crypto-Bolshevism, and Hindenburg was left with no alternative but to ditch him.

That marked the last attempt to make the republic work; power passed to a small coterie of traditional conservatives close to the president, who bear the final responsibility for Hitler's assumption of power. The next two Chancellors – the bumbling intriguer **Franz von Papen** and the far more astute fixer **General Kurt von Schleicher**, who had elaborate plans for using Hitler and then destroying him – had no taste for democracy, and were content to play courtier-style politics.

Two elections held in 1932 were inconclusive; in the first, following a campaign of mass terror by the SA, the Nazis gained nearly fourteen million votes and became the largest party, but were still well short of a majority. As Hindenburg's hand-picked cabinet failed to secure the support of the Reichstag, new elections had to be called; these saw the Nazis lose two million votes, as the party's true aims and methods became clearer. However, having been toppled by von Schleicher, it was von Papen – a figure seemingly escaped from a comic opera, now at centre-stage in one of the world's greatest-ever tragedies – who entered into a disastrous plot with Hitler which brought the end of the republic.

Von Papen persuaded Hindenburg to make Hitler Chancellor, with himself as deputy, of a coalition able to command a Reichstag majority. As the Nazis would only be given two other cabinet seats, von Papen assumed that he would retain the real control for himself. Hitler was therefore sworn in on January 30, 1933, having achieved with ease his objective of coming to power by constitutional means.

THE THIRD REICH

Once in power, **Hitler acted swiftly to make his position absolute**; he had no intention of being beholden to anyone, least of all a fool and political amateur such as von Papen. New elections were arranged for March; this time, the Nazis had the advantage of being able to use the full apparatus of the state to back up their campaign of terror. In this, they were greatly aided by the fact that **Hermann Göring**, one of the Nazis in the cabinet, was Prussian minister of the interior and thus in control of the police.

On the night of February 27, the **Reichstag** was burned down; a simple-minded Dutch Communist was arrested for this, though the fire was almost certainly the work of the Nazis themselves. At any rate, it gave them the excuse to force Hindenburg into declaring a state of emergency. Thereafter, opponents could be gagged legally, and Communists persecuted. The Nazis duly were elected with over seventeen million votes, just short of an absolute majority.

An **Enabling Bill** was laid before the Reichstag, which was effectively asked to vote itself out of existence. By the arrest of the Communist deputies and some of the SPD, and the support of the traditional right, Hitler was only just short of the two-thirds majority he needed to abolish the Weimar Republic quite legally. The SPD salvaged some self-respect by refusing to accede to this, but the Catholic Centrists failed to repeat their act of defiance against Bismarck, meekly supporting the measure in return for minor concessions.

Now officially the country's dictator, Hitler immediately put into effect the remainder of his **policy of co-ordination** (*Gleichschaltung*), by which society was completely Nazified. With breathtaking speed, every institution surrendered. The Länder were stripped of their powers, making Germany a centralized state for the first time. All political parties except the Nazis were forced to dissolve, and free trade unions were banned. Purges were carried out in the police, judiciary and professions, to ensure that each was in the control of party loyalists.

Many of the vicious features for which Nazism became notorious soon made their appearance. **Jews were ostracized and persecuted**; their businesses were boycotted and they were banned from the professions; two years later, they were stripped of citizenship and forbidden to marry Germans. Fifty or so **concentration camps** were set up for political opponents, who were sadistically tortured and often cold-bloodedly murdered. Conformity was ensured by networks of informers under the control of the secret police, the **Gestapo**. The educational system was perverted in order to indoctrinate the great "truths" of Nazi ideology.

Recognizing the importance of controlling young minds at all times, membership of the **Hitler Youth** and League of Young German Women was made compulsory. Cultural life virtually collapsed, as "degenerate" forms of expression were suppressed. These ranged from virtually all modern art to books and plays with a liberal or socialist slant; it even affected music, as the performance of works by composers with Jewish blood was outlawed. Soon the main threat to the regime lay within the Nazi Party itself, with the original socialist wing, backed by the SA, pressing for a second revolution.

On June 30, 1934, the **"Night of the Long Knives"**, hundreds of potential Nazi opponents were assassinated, notably the leading leftwinger Gregor Strasser and the SA chief Ernst Röhm. The SA was stripped of its powers and put under the control of **Heinrich Himmler**'s blackshirted **SS** (*Schutzstaffel*), originally no more than Hitler's bodyguard. This measure also had the benefit of laying to rest the one remaining threat, that of intervention by the army; with their potential usurpers out of the way, they quickly came to terms with Nazism. When Hindenburg died a few weeks later, Hitler combined the offices of President and Chancellor into that of an all-powerful *Führer*, a measure he had ratified by a plebiscite in which he was endorsed by ninety percent of those eligible to vote.

The genuine **popular support** Hitler enjoyed is one of the most striking and disturbing features of what became known as the Third Reich, the successor to the empires of Charlemagne and Bismarck. Although many of the most talented people, especially in the arts and sciences, fled the country, and many others tenaciously defied it from within, the level of opposition was negligible.

However, there's no doubt that the economic policies Hitler pursued were popular on both sides of industry. Full employment was restored, and, although industrial and agricultural workers were effectively reduced to the status of serfs, there was no question of starvation or total financial ruin. Business leaders were pleased for a different reason – when it came to profits, the totalitarian state stopped short of its normal all-embracing function.

One by one, the terms of Versailles were breached – reparation payments were stopped, the formerly secret rearmament was stepped up and made open, with conscription reintroduced; the Rhineland was re-occupied; and Austria was forced into becoming part of the Reich. The German-speaking people in the Sudetenland part of Czechoslovakia, who had never previously been a source of discontent, were used as an excuse to begin the policy of *Lebensraum*; the matter escalated into an international crisis in 1938, in which the British and French made a humiliating climbdown by an agreement signed at Munich, in which they sacrificed Czech territorial integrity for what they believed would be world peace.

Hitler was encouraged by this show of weakness to launch one of his most cherished ambitions the following year – the elimination of Poland. It's probable he believed there would be a similar collapse of will by the western powers, the more so as he first pulled off the spectacular coup of signing a non-aggression pact with his ultimate enemy, the Soviet Union, thus ensuring there would not be a war on two fronts. However, this was a miscalculation; two days after the invasion began on September 1, Britain and France, realizing that the earlier promises of an end to German expansion in Eastern Europe were a sham, decided to honour their treaty obligations. Thus **World War II** began.

WORLD WAR II

At first, the war went well for the Nazis, aided by the fact that Germany was the only country properly prepared, by reason of the massive arms build-up that it had semi-secretly been instigating since 1930. Poland was routed and the Low Countries soon fell, leading to the British evacuation from Dunkirk in May 1940. Within a month, France had signed an armistice, and a puppet government was installed. A quick invasion would probably then have accounted for Britain, but Hitler delayed in favour of an aerial bombardment in which the Luftwaffe was repulsed by the RAF. Rather than prolong this approach, German sights turned eastwards again. The Balkans were subdued, and in June 1941 plans were hatched for the largest military operation in history – the invasion of the Soviet Union. This period also marks the beginnings of the worst **concentration camps**, in which Nazi racial theories were put fully into practice. Inmates from the conquered territories were used as slave labour, and horrendous experiments in

the name of Nazi "science" were carried out, followed by an attempt at the "final solution" of the Jewish "problem". Over six million (about a third of the population of world Jewry) perished as a result; a similar number of other "undesirable" peoples were massacred in addition.

On December 7, 1941 Hitler's Japanese allies (courted in the hope they would attack the USSR from the east) attacked Pearl Harbor, an action which almost immediately **brought the USA into the war**, the very reverse of German intentions. In any event, Nazi Germany had hopelessly overreached itself; defeats in North Africa in 1942 were followed by **the turning-point at Stalingrad** (today's Volgograd/Tsaritsyn) the following year when the Russian winter and the vast size of the country combined, not for the first time, to repulse a foreign invader. German losses rivalled those sustained in World War I, and a crushing blow was dealt to morale, as this ranked as the most disastrous defeat in the country's military history.

THE DEFEAT OF NAZISM

From then onwards, the story is one of Nazi retreat on all fronts. A **German resistance movement** sprang up under the leadership of senior army officers. Various attempts were made to assassinate Hitler, and he had several extraordinary escapes, most notably in the carefully hatched plot of July 20, 1944, when a planted bomb killed several people sitting alongside him. Yet, bad luck apart, the conspiratorial groups were handicapped by their excessive concern to secure in advance lenient terms for a defeated but democratic Germany; they also had no firm base of popular support, nor a detailed plan of campaign for what to do once Hitler had been killed.

As it turned out, the country's ultimate collapse was drawn out, and did not occur before all major German cities and innumerable small towns had been ruthlessly bombed. Eventually, the Allies occupied the entire country; on April 30, 1945, marooned in his Berlin bunker, Hitler committed suicide, so bringing the "thousand-year Reich" to an inglorious end.

THE DIVISION OF GERMANY

The Allied powers, determined not to repeat the mistakes of Versailles, now had to decide **what**

to do with Germany. At Potsdam in August, the country was partitioned into four zones of occupation, corresponding to an agreement made earlier in the year at Yalta when the war was still in progress; Berlin was similarly divided. The eastern frontier of Germany was redrawn at the Oder–Neisse line, meaning that East Prussia and most of Pomerania and Silesia passed to Poland, in compensation for territory annexed by the Soviet Union.

Initially, there was a great deal of co-operation amongst the Allies. All the leading Nazis who had survived were brought to **trial in Nürnberg** for war crimes or crimes against humanity, and the civil service was purged of the movement's sympathizers. Relief measures were taken against the terrible famine sweeping the country, refugees from the former Eastern Territories were given help to begin a new life, and the first steps were made towards rebuilding destroyed cities and the shattered economy.

Germany's internal **political life** was relaunched under the leadership of prominent anti-Nazis. The right of the spectrum was occupied by a new and moderate party, the **Christian Democrats** (CDU). Left-wing politics were still marred by the legacy of bad blood between the SPD and the Communists. In the Russian zone, the SPD took the lead in forming a new group, the **Socialist Unity Party** (SED), which was intended to be Marxist but not Marxist-Leninist; the Communists only tagged along under Russian pressure after the poor showing of the party in the Austrian elections. This new grouping was not repeated in the other zones.

Inevitably, **strains developed among the Allies**; the zones began to develop in different ways, mirroring the societies of their conquerors. Frustrated by Russian stalling, the Western powers began a currency reform in their zones in 1948, soon extended to West Berlin. This gesture was regarded as highly provocative by the Soviets, who retaliated by cutting off western access to the divided city in the **Berlin Blockade**. Another world war could have ensued, but the beleaguered western zones were saved by the success of **air lifts** bringing essential supplies, forcing the Russians to abandon the blockade within a year.

By this time, two different societies were emerging on German soil: the Russians enforced massive nationalization and collectivization; in contrast, the Western powers allowed even those industrialists most associated with the Nazis, such as Thyssen and the Krupps, to return to their businesses with minimal punishment. Rocked by the independent line taken by Tito in Yugoslavia, the Russians transformed the SED into a Soviet-style party led by a Politburo into which the erstwhile SPD members were trapped, while a Parliamentary Council was set up in the west to draft a new constitution. The logical conclusion of these events – the creation of two rival states – soon followed. In May 1949, the three western zones amalgamated to form the **German Federal Republic**; four months later, the Russians launched their territory as the **German Democratic Republic**.

THE FEDERAL REPUBLIC

Like the Weimar Republic, the new West German state was founded on **liberal democratic principles**, only this time the constitution was much tighter. The power of the President was sharply reduced, giving him a role not unlike that of the British monarch. A true federal structure was created, in which the Länder were given considerable powers over all areas of policy except defence, foreign affairs and currency control. Proportional representation was retained, but with a five percent qualifying minimum, and elections were fixed for every four years. A constitutional court was established to guarantee civil and political liberties, and anti-democratic parties were outlawed.

Konrad Adenauer became the first Chancellor following elections in which his Christian Democrats emerged as the largest party, though far short of a majority. Aged 73 and with no experience of national politics – he had been mayor of Cologne until removed by the Nazis – he bore the look of a temporary leader, though as an elder statesman with an untainted past he fitted the precise needs of the time exactly.

In the event, the evening of his career was a prolonged one; he remained in power for fourteen years, during which time he developed an aura of indispensability at home and appeared as a figure of substance abroad. Much of this success was due to the **"Economic Miracle"** masterminded by **Ludwig Erhard**, in which the wrecked economy made a spectacular recovery, with high-quality products fuelling an export boom. An annual growth rate of eight percent was achieved; within a decade West Germany ranked as the most prosperous major European country. In many ways, this was due simply to disciplined hard work by the bulk of the population, but it was also aided by the fact that a fresh start had to be made. Industry was relaunched with the most modern equipment, and in a sensible atmosphere of partnership between management and just seventeen large trade unions which eliminated the class-based fear and inter-union rivalry which continued to dog other countries. Erhard also promoted the concept of the 'social-market economy', giving due emphasis to the development of a welfare state.

In foreign affairs, priority was given to **ending the long era of enmity with France**; the two countries formed the European Coal and Steel Pact in 1951, serving as a prelude to the creation of the European Economic Community six years later. The Federal Republic's integration into the Western alliance was cemented by admission to **NATO**, and the adoption of a hard-nosed attitude towards the Soviet Union and her satellites.

By the **Hallstein Doctrine**, the Federal Republic claimed to be the legitimate voice of all Germany, arguing that it was the only part properly constituted. Not only did it fail to recognize the GDR, it successfully ostracized its neighbour by refusing to establish diplomatic relations with any country who did.

THE GERMAN DEMOCRATIC REPUBLIC

Meanwhile the inappropriately styled German Democratic Republic rapidly evolved a **centralized system of government on the Soviet model**. The Christian Democratic and Liberal parties were forcibly subordinated to the SED, and two further bourgeois groups were created from above. Elections were still held, but a single list of candidates was drawn up which the voters had to accept *en bloc*. The only method of protest was to reject it outright, which had to be done publicly, making it a dangerous as well as a futile gesture. Police, education and management of the economy were all put under SED control. Real power was centralized in the hands of party secretary **Walter Ulbricht**, a hard-line Stalinist who had spent almost the

entire Nazi period ensconced in the Soviet Union.

At first, the Russians were ambivalent about their rump state. They administered punitive reparations, stripping it of much of its industry and shipping valuable plants and machinery to the Soviet Union; they were worried about the GDR's long-term viability and may even have been prepared to sacrifice it altogether in their own defensive interests. Stalin was on record as saying in 1944, "Communism fits Germany as a saddle fits a cow", and it's doubtful if he was ever particularly keen on a separate GDR. In 1952, he made **an offer to establish a unified and neutral Germany on a democratic basis**, which was rejected out of hand in the West as mere bluff.

The **GDR began life unpromisingly**, exploited by its parent, having no historical or economic rationale, unloved by the vast majority of its populace, thousands of whom emigrated to the West, and seemingly wanted only by its leaders who had had power handed to them on a plate. A second industrial revolution had to be launched, simply to meet reparation commitments; the existing infrastructure included very little heavy industry (which was now developed apace, though more for ideological reasons than out of necessity), and was now deprived of access to its commercial hinterland. The pressure of this caused the first revolt in the Soviet satellite states, a series of **workers' strikes** in 1953, put down by Russian tanks. The following year, reparations were ended and the country began to develop as a key member of the bloc, becoming one of the founder members of the **Warsaw Pact**.

In spite of many problems – access to Western markets was hindered by the lack of a convertible currency, trade with the Soviet Union was conducted on unfavourable terms, and imbalances were caused by the ideological imperative to give massive subsidies to basic necessities – the 1950s saw an **economic recovery** which in its own way was as extraordinary as West Germany's. Once again, the people showed their legendary ability to adapt to any kind of regime; they were in any event now well attuned to totalitarian life. If West Germans felt a sense of superiority in their far more advanced lifestyle, the comparison was hardly a fair one – they had received munificence from their conquerors, not retribution;

they had also started with the enormous benefit of being in possession of the Ruhr and other
areas of rich natural resources and advanced
industry. At the 1958 Party Congress, Ulbricht
was rash enough to predict that, within a few
years, the country would have overtaken its
neighbour in terms of per capita income, thus
proving the inherent superiority of the
Communist system.

THE BERLIN WALL

This optimism proved short-lived, as the late
1950s saw the beginning of a period of
**unprecedented West German prosperity
and expansion**. A shortage of labour meant
that workers had to be imported; the unskilled
labourers tended to come from Turkey, Greece,
Yugoslavia, Italy and Spain. For the better-qual-
ified positions, industry looked to East Germany
and a flood of **emigration** started.

Quickly realizing that he could not afford to
lose so many professionals, engineers, intellectuals and craftsmen, Ulbricht was forced into
drastic action. The loophole was the western
sector of Berlin; if it could be sealed off, the
problem would disappear. Having failed at a
second attempt to make the Allies evacuate the
city, Ulbricht persuaded the Soviets of the
necessity of constructing the **Berlin Wall**,
erected on August 13, 1961. It was immediately patrolled by armed guards under instructions
to shoot to kill, and the main boundaries of the
country were also greatly strengthened. A visual and moral affront to humanity, it was justified
as the "Anti-Fascist Protection Wall", a label it
retained until its demolition.

In the Federal Republic, Adenauer was finally forced into retirement in 1963, to be succeeded by Erhard, who proved far less successful as
the country's leader than he had been as economic guru. The liberal Free Democrats (FDP),
who had served as the CDU's junior coalition
partners for all but a short period of the Federal
Republic's history, went into opposition in 1966.
A **"Grand Coalition"** was established with the
SPD, who thus returned to government for the
first time since 1930. To rid itself of its tarnished
image, the party had undergone a substantial
reform (or sell-out, according to many) at its
1959 conference, disavowing its roots in
Marxism and class conflict and its traditional
anti-clericalism, embracing instead the CDU's
"social-market economy", but with a stronger

emphasis on the social side of the equation.

The Chancellor, the CDU's Kurt Georg
Kiesinger, was remarkable mainly for being a
reformed Nazi – a rather uncomfortable indica-
tor as to how far West Germans were prepared
to forget the past. It was hardly surprising that
the period of the Grand Coalition saw the first
simmerings of disenchantment with the cosy
form of consensus politics which had dominated the country's postwar history, with the
Communists re-formed as a counterweight to
the neo-Nazi NPD; neither party, however,
gained much of a following. More serious were
the beginnings of what has since become a persistent feature of West German life, **extra-parliamentary opposition**. This first came to the
fore with the 1968 student revolt under Rudi
Dutschke. Grievances initially centred on unsat-
isfactory conditions in the universities but
spread to wider discontent with society and the
new materialistic culture.

OSTPOLITIK

A more positive feature of the Grand Coalition
was the rise of **Willi Brandt**, the dynamic
leader of the SPD, who assumed the foreign
affairs portfolio. A former Resistance journalist,
he had been mayor of West Berlin throughout
the period of crisis leading up to the building of
the Wall, and was determined to take a new
tack on the problem. His **Ostpolitik** began in
earnest, helped by a general thawing of the
Cold War, when he became Chancellor in 1969,
at the head of a SPD–FDP coalition, itself something of a mould-breaker. Treaties were signed
with the Soviet Union and Poland in 1970, recognizing the validity of the Oder–Neisse line;
West Berlin's special status was guaranteed by
the Four Power Agreement the following year;
and in 1972 a Basic Treaty was signed between
the two Germanys which at last normalized
relations.

This stopped short of full diplomatic recognition of the GDR, but the Federal Republic recognized its frontiers and separate existence, aban-
doning the Hallstein Doctrine. In return, West
Germans were allowed to visit family and
friends over the border, though movement the
other way was confined to pensioners and the
disabled. One consequence of Ostpolitik was
the **fall of Ulbricht** in 1971; he wanted to drive
a harder bargain than suited the Soviets, who
were in any case tired of his constant lectures

to them on ideological purity. His replacement was **Erich Honecker**, who, although regarded as a comparative liberal, had first come to prominence as construction supremo of the Berlin Wall.

With the mirage of reunification now cleared, the two German societies were able to continue developing in their separate ways. **The GDR began to clarify and modify its image**; in 1974, the country was given yet another new constitution, which omitted previous references to overcoming the division of Germany, and stated the country was "forever and irrevocably" allied with the USSR. The GDR was characterized as a "developed socialist society", in which different divisions existed. This had the twin benefits of justifying both the inequality which was still clearly manifest (though less extreme than in the West) and the continued leadership role of the SED – along with all the attendant privileges for its elite.

To counterbalance this, a "**social contract**" was made with the population, which curbed arbitrary use of police powers, effectively meaning that only active dissidents were persecuted. Honecker cultivated an avuncular image for himself which came as a refreshing change after the austere authoritarianism of his predecessor. **Sports** – or at least those with a high profile in the Olympic Games, such as athletics, swimming and skiing – were increasingly used as the chief means of gaining international prestige, and the results proved stunningly successful, catapulting the country to the dizzy heights of the improbable third "super-power" in these events. **Economic performance** became ever more impressive, and was easily the best in the Soviet bloc; full employment was preserved as much out of necessity as principle. However, in comparison with West Germany the economic mix looked hopelessly outdated, and the average earner was little more than half as well off in real terms, with the gap widening rather than narrowing. As well as all the old problems, there were frequent shortages (often caused by sudden opportunities to sell stocks to gain hard currency) and a lack of consumer goods for which the demand was growing apace.

Boosted by the success of both his Ostpolitik and his welfare programmes, Brandt led his coalition to victory in 1972, with the SPD winning more votes than the CDU for the first (and,

as yet, only) time. In view of the reconciliatory nature of his approach to the GDR, it was ironical that Brandt's downfall occurred two years later as a result of the unmasking of one of his closest aides as an East German spy.

Staying on in the influential role as SPD chairman (until 1987, when another scandal, this time over a bizarre choice of a young CDU-sympathizing Greek woman as party spokesperson, caused his retirement), Brandt was succeeded by **Helmut Schmidt**, an able pragmatist who increasingly came to be seen as something of a right-winger, though this was in part due to the nature of the problems he faced. The quadrupling of OPEC oil prices in 1974, and the stagnation in world trade which ensued, posed particular difficulties for the export-led and growth-geared German economy. These were tackled more successfully than in most countries, but **unemployment** became an issue for the first time since Hitler.

Extra-parliamentary opposition had by now taken on a fearsome and anarchic character. In the early 1970s, there had been a spate of kidnappings and armed bank robberies by the Baader-Meinhof gang. These had no sooner been quelled than there arose a far more organized and ruthless offshoot, the **Red Army Faction**, who assassinated a number of public figures. The turning point in the government's campaign against them came with the hijacking of a *Lufthansa* plane in 1977, and a threat to kill the hostages if the remaining members of the gang were not released from prison.

On personal instructions from Schmidt – on which he was prepared to stake his chancellorship – the aircraft was successfully stormed; within three years, most of the terrorist leaders had been arrested and imprisoned. Peaceful extra-parliamentary opposition proved to be a far more potent significance. This was inspired above all by fears that divided Germany would serve as the stage for a future nuclear war. NATO's 1979 decision to install medium-range American nuclear missiles in West Germany was a particular source of protest, but there was also **increased general concern about the environment**, especially pollution of the beloved forests.

These issues then served as a focus for the many who were dissatisfied with a society which had become over-competitive and too obsessed with consumerism, and out of an amorphous collection of pressure groups active in these areas the **Green Party** was born. Schmidt's backing of the bases alienated the SPD's left wing, but he was still able to lead his coalition to victory in 1980. In this he was aided by the CDU's recurrent leadership problem, which reached its nadir at this point with the fielding of **Franz-Josef Strauss**, who had last held federal office under Adenauer, as Chancellor-candidate. Long-standing leader of the CSU, the separate and exclusively Bavarian counterpart of the CDU, this blatant careerist and strident right-winger unsurprisingly proved to be a major electoral liability.

THE 1980s

Despite this lifeline, the long period of SPD domination was coming to an end. Schmidt's tough economic policies under the influence of another round of drastic oil price increases further widened the party's divisions, leading the FDP to lose confidence and withdraw from the government in September 1982. The CDU, now revived under **Helmut Kohl**, gambled on a "constructive vote of no confidence" – the only way round the fixed-term parliaments enshrined in the constitution. Having won this, they formed a new government with the FDP and called for fresh elections. Fears that the FDP would fail to surmount the five percent threshold (having damaged themselves by their rather dubious stance) proved unfounded, and Kohl was able to continue as before.

Kohl was something of a departure, the first German leader drawn from a generation too young to have Nazi associations of any kind. He has remained in power ever since, unexpectedly seeing Germany through its biggest upheaval since World War II.

Initially, his government was rather unexciting, cutting back on the state's very modest role in economic intervention, but making **further strides in Ostpolitik**. Since Brandt, this had become low-key, and depended very much on the climate of superpower relations. The new developments were in many cases cynical – massive **interest-free loans** were given to the GDR in return for allowing greater numbers of its citizens to emigrate, and football-style transfer fees were paid for its political prisoners.

Honecker was keen to **set the seal of legitimacy on the GDR** by paying an official visit to the Federal Republic; two attempts were abandoned in the face of Soviet pressure before he finally made it in September 1987. It was the high point of his career and seemed to provide its justification as, amid much publicity, he was received in a way just below that for a head of state.

As the 1980s drew to a close the **West German political scene** settled down into a straight left/right division with the well-entrenched CDU/FDP ruling coalition lined up against the SPD and Greens. The Greens, however, demonstrated an unexpected staying power, and a new generation of SPD leaders, most notably Oskar Lafontaine, seemed to be advocating the creation of an effective red–green alliance as the left's only way forward. At the other end of the political scale was the emergence of a new far-right group, the **Republicans**, who made worrying advances at local level, notably in West Berlin.

In **East Germany** things remained static, much to the dismay of large sections of the populace who had hoped that the reformist policies promoted by **Mikhail Gorbachev** in the Soviet Union might eventually filter down to their own leadership. The ageing SED hierarchy remained solidly in place and, despite some easing of travel restrictions, public dissent was not tolerated.

As Gorbachev's *glasnost* and *perestroika* transformed Soviet political life, the GDR regime found it necessary to **insulate its citizens from the mood of reform in the east**; the Soviet magazine *Sputnik* was banned, and a number of Russian-language films examining the Stalin and Brezhnev periods were accused of "distorting history" and withdrawn from circulation. An implacable Erich Honecker declared that the Berlin Wall, that most potent symbol of the SED's increasingly isolated stance, would stand for another fifty or a hundred years if necessary, "to protect our republic from robbers".

For many individuals in the GDR, **leaving the country** seemed to be the only way forward. One option sought by increasing numbers of people was legal emigration, a soul-destroying process dogged by bureaucratic obstruction. Others, more desperate, attempted to **escape to the West** across the country's heavily guarded borders.

1989 – DIE WENDE

1989 ranks as the most significant year in German history since 1945. In the space of twelve months a complete and unforeseeable transformation (what Germans call *die Wende*) occurred. It was reform in another country that provided the initial impetus for the incredible events of 1989. On May 2, 1989, the Hungarian authorities began taking down the barbed wire along their border with Austria, creating **a hole in the Iron Curtain**. Many East Germans, aware that visa laws making travel to Hungary more difficult would come into force in the autumn, headed south for their holidays.

By August about 200 East Germans were **crossing into Austria every night**, and on August 19, 700 people surged across the frontier in broad daylight unhindered by the Hungarian border guards. By this stage about 20,000 refugee East Germans were being housed in the West German embassy in Budapest and in Hungarian holiday camps, awaiting their chance to leave for the West. On September 10 the Hungarian government finally **gave the East Germans leave to depart**. Forbidden to travel to Hungary, would-be refugees now made for Prague, swamping the West German embassy. On September 30 they too were allowed to leave, the result of a special deal announced by West German foreign minister Hans-Dietrich Genscher.

In the GDR **opposition groups** such as Neues Forum were starting to emerge. Popular unrest came to a head at the **October 7** celebration of the fortieth anniversary of the GDR. Guest Mikhail Gorbachev stressed the need for dialogue and openness to new ideas, while Erich Honecker responded with a clichéd speech praising the status quo. A vainglorious official parade of military hardware was followed by angry **demonstrations** which were brutally suppressed by the police. There were also demonstrations in Leipzig and Dresden, and open popular unrest spread across the country over the following weeks despite widespread fears of an armed crackdown by the authorities. The expected violence never materialized and on October 18 Erich Honecker was suddenly replaced by **Egon Krenz**, his long-time heir apparent, a man widely regarded as a neo-Stalinist hardliner.

To everyone's surprise Krenz **expressed a desire for dialogue** with opposition groups. The exodus of GDR citizens continued but there was now a feeling that change might be possible. On November 4 one million people gathered in the centre of East Berlin, in **the biggest anti-Communist demonstration** since the workers' uprising of 1953. Three days later most of the old government resigned and **Hans Modrow**, the former Dresden SED chief, a man regarded as a liberal, was appointed Prime Minister. By now 200,000 East Germans had left the GDR since the start of the year.

The **opening of the Berlin Wall** was announced almost casually. On the evening of Thursday, November 9, Berlin party boss Günter Schabowski told a press conference that East German citizens were free to leave the GDR with valid exit visas which were henceforth to be issued without delay. Events immediately took on a momentum of their own. TV stations broadcast the announcement and citizens began heading for the nearest border crossings. All along the frontier border guards began letting through the masses, and people on both sides of the city flocked to the Wall. Huge crowds converged on the Brandenburg Gate where an impromptu street party broke out celebrating an event that many Germans had never imagined they would see. Over the days that followed **East Germans poured across the border**: 2,700,000 exit visas were issued in the first weekend after the Wall was opened, and the two Germanys rediscovered each other at breakneck speed.

The writing was now on the wall for the Communists and the GDR. On December 1 the East German parliament passed a motion ending the leading role of the SED and **free elections were promised** for the following May. The SED changed their name, becoming the supposedly voter-friendly PDS - Partei Demokratische Sozialismus or "Democratic Socialist Party". A more significant event for the future of Germany was Chancellor Helmut Kohl's visit to Dresden on December 19 when he declared to cheering crowds that his ultimate goal was a **united Germany**.

THE 1990s

With the new decade things progressed rapidly. The GDR elections, brought forward to March 18, resulted in a **victory for a right-wing alliance dominated by the CDU** under Lothar de Mazière. This really represented a victory for Chancellor Helmut Kohl, the self-proclaimed champion of reunification.

Almost immediately the new East German government set about dissolving the GDR. An agreement with the West Germans about **economic union** was hammered out and put into effect on July 1. The next step was to work out a formula for political reunification. This was effectively left to Helmut Kohl and Mikhail Gorbachev (who at this stage still had the final say); between them during a July summit in the Caucasus, they worked out a mutually acceptable agreement which was quickly rubber-stamped by the GDR parliament.

October 3, 1990 was the date of **German reunification**, an event which did not see a repeat of earlier celebrations. For many people in the east, dazed by the rapid economic collapse of the GDR and subsequent social dislocation, reunification seemed to offer little, other than the prospect of unemployment and uncertainty. Nonetheless, Kohl remained determinedly upbeat, maintaining that no German would lose out as a result of unification. His opportunistic masterminding of events meant that the SPD was forced into making penny-pinching complaints about costs, thereby inviting the charge that it was not up to dealing with the great historical challenge facing the nation. Now that the two states had formally merged, Kohl's fast-track approach to a fully integrated economy and society offered no more risks than the slower methods advocated by his opponents, and it was therefore no surprise that the **CDU-led coalition scored a landslide victory** in the first united German elections, held in December 1990.

The rosy picture painted by Kohl of the country's economic prospects was not mere optimistic posturing. He rashly calculated that an initial spending spree would be unleashed in the east as a result of the introduction of the Deutschmark, and that the natural capacity of Germans to work hard, coupled with the fact that a large percentage of women in the former GDR were in gainful employment, would thereafter fuel a major boom which would spread to the west as well.

The essential weakness in this prognosis was that it failed to anticipate the speed and totality of the collapse of the Soviet Union in the wake of its satellites. This spelt absolute **ruin for whole sectors of the economy of the former GDR**, which were suddenly left without markets for their products. Worse, the logistics of central planning meant that entire towns, dependent on a single industry, found themselves facing a desperate future, with half or more of the local population out of work at a single stroke.

Not only did the government's standing plummet in the east, it also nose-dived in the west when vastly unpopular **tax increases** were introduced in 1991 for the specific purpose of funding the unification process. The CDU paid the electoral penalty in the state elections in the Rhineland-Palatinate soon afterwards, losing to the SPD what had always been considered a sure-fire stronghold, the place where Chancellor Kohl had built his original power base. Similar humiliations befell the party in subsequent elections in other Länder.

One of the beneficiaries of the government's discomfiture was the **far right**, which had hitherto failed to make much of an impact on postwar Germany. Playing heavily on the political immaturity of the eastern German electorate, and on the fears and resentments building up in the west, the far right, in the shape of the outwardly respectable Republican Party, made some unexpectedly strong showings in these local elections, leading many at home and abroad to voice fears that Germany might yet again embrace Nazism.

The far right concentrated on the issues of **unemployment and immigration**, making a direct and largely bogus connection between the two. Violent racist attacks on foreigners, sometimes resulting in deaths, soon became commonplace, particularly in the former GDR, where a number of shocking incidents of mob hatred were captured on film and broadcast round the world. The official response to this was a review of Germany's exceptionally liberal immigration laws, introduced as an atonement for the crimes of the Third Reich, and these were eventually repealed in 1993.

While the government was widely condemned for what looked like a weak-kneed reaction to the problem of racist violence, it was also possible to see its response as a pragmatic one to a situation that was otherwise in danger of getting out of hand, particularly when political refugees from the disintegrating Yugoslavia started to arrive in force to swell the ranks of the mainly economic refugees from the former Soviet bloc. It certainly seemed to help put the advance of the far right firmly into reverse, though it failed to touch on a key issue of race relations – the lack of citizenship rights of the large *Gastarbeiter* population, which now includes an entire generation who were born in Germany and have lived their whole lives there.

By 1992, it was clear that the economy was in **recession**. Defeat for the CDU in the fixed-term general elections set for October 1994 looked inevitable, but the SDP's massive lead in the opinion polls was gradually whittled away by its seemingly perennial crisis over its choice of Chancellor-candidate, while an economic upturn rallied CDU support. Meanwhile, the PDS profited from the renewed sympathy for reformed Communists expressed throughout Eastern Europe. Kohl's biggest worry was the very real prospect that his coalition partners in the FDP would fail to get the five percent of votes necessary to gain parliamentary representation – a scenario which would virtually ensure the accession of some form of left-wing coalition. In the event, the FDP achieved the qualifying minimum with a bit to spare, and the **Kohl government continued in office**, albeit with its majority slashed to just ten seats.

Kohl's fourth term in office was dominated by the drive towards **European Monetary Union**, for which he lobbied energetically in the face of the misgivings of many of Germany's European partners. After announcing that the 1998 election would mark his retirement, he changed his mind and decided to run for an unprecedented fifth term. But his prospects of re-election were shadowed by the state of the economy. The austerity measures demanded by the need to meet the convergence criteria for EMU exacerbated problems that remained unsolved in the wake of reunification. By late 1997 the Deutschmark was at its lowest for decades, while **unemployment** had reached almost 5 million – its highest since 1933. And, despite widespread western jealousy about the extent of publicly funded investment in the former GDR, it was in the east that unemployment hit hardest.

There remain massive tasks ahead. **Berlin**'s reinstatement as seat of government as well as official capital, agreed by a narrow Bundestag majority in 1991, will in itself cause a major upheaval; the lower house is due to move from Bonn in 1999, with all functions transferred by 2003. Despite the boost this will give to the east, it will clearly be a long while before the two parts of the country really do look and feel like one.

PAINTING AND GRAPHICS

Germany's artistic history is marked more by solid and sustained achievement than by the more usual pattern of pre-eminence followed by decline. As in Italy, the fragmentation of the nation into a multitude of tiny states led to the development of many important centres of art, often of a very distinctive character.

The country's geographical position has meant that it has been a melting pot for influences from Italy, France and the Low Countries, although, with several notable exceptions, the work of German painters never managed to gain the same international esteem. This, however, is mainly because the vast majority of German paintings have remained within the German-speaking countries, a consequence of the fact that many of the petty princes were great art collectors, and also because of the Romantic movement, which fostered a sense of awareness of the national heritage. As a result, important **museums** existed all over the country by the mid-nineteenth century.

German **graphic work**, being by its nature for dissemination, is perhaps more immediately familiar; the stark contrasts enforced by the media of woodcut, engraving and etching obviously proved temperamentally ideal for the country's artists, whose legacy in these fields far surpasses that of anywhere else in Europe.

German painting has its roots in the ninth-century Carolingian epoch. **Illuminated manuscripts** were created in the scriptoria of the court and the monasteries; these typically featured vibrant figures in flowing draperies, charged with movement and set in elaborate architectural surrounds. This art form was refined and developed in the subsequent Ottonian period, most notably in Trier, which in the late tenth century boasted the first great German artist in an illuminator now dubbed **Master of the Registrum Gregorii**. A number of manuscripts by him have been identified; they show a new, more plastic style based on an understanding of Classical antiquity, solving the problems of space and form which baffled all the other illuminators of the time. He built up a highly influential fund of forms which was imitated in the other great places of book production – Fulda, Hildesheim and Bavaria – although there were also more conservative centres, particularly those on the island of the Reichenau, favouring an expressive linear form.

Fresco cycles were the other chief form of painting, and were often more closely related to the art of the book than might be supposed from the contrasting nature of the two forms. One of the best early examples to have survived is again from Trier; probably dating from the end of the ninth century, it originally adorned the crypt of St Maximin, but has been removed to the Bischöfliches Museum. From the following century, there is an important cycle still *in situ* at St Georg in Oberzell on the Reichenau, along with one in the Andreaskirche in Fulda. Belonging more obviously to international Romanesque currents are the later fresco cycles of the Lower Rhineland and Regensburg. The former – St Gereon in Cologne, Schwarzrheindorf and Knechtsteden – are all influenced by Byzantine concepts of form, style and iconography; regrettably, their quality has been impaired by over-enthusiastic nineteenth-century restorers who indulged in far too much speculative retouching.

Later Romanesque illuminated manuscripts tend to follow rather than develop the Ottonian forms, although there was something of a revival in the late twelfth century, with such de luxe products as the *Gospels of Henry the Lion*, now in Wolfenbüttel. Roughly contemporary is a survival which is unique of its kind, the painted **wooden ceiling** illustrating the *Tree of Jesse* which adorns the vault of St Michael in Hildesheim.

THE EARLY GOTHIC PERIOD

The earliest Gothic **panel paintings** to have survived in Germany date from around 1300. Throughout the fourteenth century, religious themes retained their monopoly, and the most active workshops were in Cologne and Westphalia. The former was the dominant city of medieval Germany, and maintained its own strong and characteristic traditions right up until the early sixteenth century, assimilating varied foreign influences yet remaining rooted in tradition. Painting there was based on a strict **guild system**, which imposed stiff tests of skill on would-be applicants and even stipulated the quality of materials which had to be employed. Among the most important productions of this school in the fourteenth century were the monumental paintings on the backs of the Dom's stalls, the *Clares Altar*, again in the Dom, and some very ruinous frescoes for the Rathaus which have been attributed to a somewhat legendary figure named **Master Wilhelm**.

The first German artist about whom much information has survived is **Master Bertram** (c.1345–1415), a Westphalian who worked in Hamburg. He seems to have been influenced by the art of Bohemia, which was part of the Holy Roman Empire, and was far in advance of fourteenth-century Germany in terms of the achievements of its painters. Bertram favoured narrative cycles of little panels grouped round pieces of sculpture; his major work is the *Grabow Altar* of 1379 in Hamburg, which displays prodigious and original imaginative powers, particularly in the charming scenes of the Creation. From about a decade later is the *Passion Altar* in Hannover, while the *Buxtehude Altar*, again in Hamburg, is from ten years later; both are remarkably consistent in style.

Another Westphalian was the **Master of the Berswordt Altar** (active late fourteenth century), named after a triptych still *in situ* in the Marienkirche in Dortmund; he also painted a polyptych for the Neustädter Marienkirche in Bielefeld. The influence of French and Burgundian manuscripts is apparent, and he was an early representative of the courtly and idealized International Gothic style which was to spread all over Europe. In Germany, this is usually referred to as the **Soft Style**, and is found in sculpture as well as painting. Its greatest exponent was **Conrad von Soest** (active c.1394–1422), one of the most immediately appealing of all German painters, who may even have been the son of the previous artist. His panels are refined and beautiful, executed in glowing colours and including a fair amount of amusing anecdotal detail. The late high altar triptych of the Marienkirche in his native Dortmund shows his art at its peak, but is sadly truncated. The triptych in Bad Wildungen, however, has survived in remarkable shape. Another major painter in this style was **Master Francke** (active c.1405–25), who succeeded Bertram in Hamburg and could conceivably have been his pupil; his reputation rests largely on the *St Thomas à Becket Altar* which was commissioned by the local merchants who traded with England. Also active at this time were the **Master of the Virgin of Benediktbeuern** in Bavaria and various artists in Lower Saxony, most of whose works are now in Hannover.

THE FIFTEENTH-CENTURY COLOGNE SCHOOL

The entire fifteenth century was an outstandingly brilliant artistic period for Cologne. Although the artists still mostly remain anonymous, their styles became far more contrasted than in former times, and art historians have been able to group bodies of work under pseudonyms based on the names of their major masterpieces, which are now mostly housed in the city's Wallraf-Richartz Museum, or in the Alte Pinakothek in Munich. As well as large-scale commissions to adorn the plethora of churches and monasteries, there's increasing evidence of the burgeoning of the merchant class in the number of small altarpieces (obviously intended for private devotion) which have survived. The symbolic depiction of the Madonna and Child in the Garden of Paradise was enduringly popular; another vogue subject (the two were sometimes combined) was the Holy Kinship, depicting the extended family of Christ. First to develop a distinctive style was the **Master of St Veronica** (active c.1400–20), named after *St Veronica with the Sudarium*, now in Munich. The monumental faces in this work, mirrored elsewhere in his output, give evidence of influence from

Bohemia, but that he had also understood the lessons of Burgundian miniatures is proved by the crowded *Calvary* in Cologne. His workshop may have been taken over after his death by the **Master of St Lawrence** (active c.1415–30), whose main work is a retable made for the demolished church of St Lorenz, parts of which survive in the museums of Cologne and Nürnberg.

These artists were surpassed by **Stefan Lochner** (c.1400–51), a Swabian who settled in the city and perfectly assimilated its traditions, along with innovations from Flanders. His soft, gentle and painstakingly detailed panels are among the peaks of the entire International Gothic movement, and he appears to have been something of a celebrity, which accounts for his name surviving the oblivion into which his rivals have plunged. His masterpiece is the *Epiphany* triptych now in Cologne's Dom, originally painted for the Rathaus, a far more monumental work than was usual in Cologne. It has been criticized for a failure to characterize the figures, but that is to miss the point – Lochner's art is quite consciously ethereal in spirit. If anything, the later *Presentation in the Temple*, now in Darmstadt, is even more sumptuous, while his last work, *Madonna of the Rose Bower* in Cologne, takes the art of the small altar to a level beyond which it could not progress. Even with gruesome subjects, such as *Last Judgment* in Cologne and its reverse, *Martyrdoms of the Apostles*, now in Frankfurt, Lochner did not depart from his essential gentleness, always drawing the optimistic lesson from the subject; if that can be counted as a failing, his extraordinary inventive powers amply compensate.

The following generation moved away from static and decorative effects to a lively narrative style, clearly modelled on the great contemporary Netherlanders. Rogier van der Weyden's late *St Columba* triptych (now in Munich) was painted for a church in Cologne, and must have made an enormous impact, although the more rounded and less emotional style of Dieric Bouts is the obvious source for the leading artist of the group, the **Master of the Life of the Virgin** (active c.1460–85), so named from a cycle of eight panels, seven of which are also now in Munich. He displays all the qualities of a great storyteller, the figures strongly drawn and richly clad, standing out in sharp relief from the background, with plenty of subsidiary anec-

dotal detail including exquisite still lifes. This artist's later work includes portraits of merchants, which mark the end of the ecclesiastical monopoly over art. Three other painters closely associated with him are the **Master of the Lyversberg Passion**, the **Master of the St George Legend** and the **Master of the Bonn Diptych**; they may even have shared the same studio. Slightly later is the **Master of the Glorification of the Virgin** (active c.1475–95) who is less overtly Flemish in spirit; his backgrounds include accurate depictions of Cologne and its surrounding countryside.

Among the final generation of Cologne painters, the **Master of the Holy Kinship** (c.1450–1515) takes his name from the most spectacular version ever painted of the favourite Cologne subject, which shows acquaintance with the very latest Flemish innovations; otherwise, he seems to have been more adept on a smaller scale, his larger canvases betraying the use of inexperienced assistants. His contemporary, the **Master of the St Ursula Legend** (active c.1490–1505), developed the narrative tradition in a now dispersed series, partly preserved in the museums of Cologne, Bonn and Nürnberg. This artist displays far more interest in integrating the backgrounds with the action, and his handling of space and perspective shows a sizeable advance, while his technique of rapid brushstrokes is quite different from the smooth layered approach of his predecessors. He influenced the **Master of St Severin** (active c.1490–1510), a prolific and uneven painter, with whom he probably shared a studio.

Ultimately, the Cologne School simply burned itself out, but it did come to a fitting climax with the **Master of the St Bartholomew Altar** (active c.1470–1510), whose highly idiosyncratic compositions display all the sense of freedom and mannerism which so often characterize the final fling of an artistic style. He was trained in Utrecht and may have been Dutch; at first he worked as a manuscript illuminator. His earlier panels are rather hesitant, but by about 1495 he was painting with ever-increasing confidence, using bright, enamel-type colours. Invariably his figures are executed as if in imitation of sculpture, and some of his paintings, such as the eponymous work in Munich and the *Crucifixion* triptych in Cologne, appear as trompe l'oeil versions of carved retables. Even more bizarre are canvases such as the *St Thomas Altar* in Cologne, where the highly realistic figures are made to float quite illogically in space.

GOTHIC ELSEWHERE IN GERMANY

In the early fifteenth century, Cologne unquestionably held the artistic lead in Germany; a gorgeous *Garden of Paradise* preserved in Frankfurt by an unknown Upper Rhenish master from about 1420 is a clear case of the hegemony this style enjoyed. The equally beautiful *Ortenberg Altar* in Darmstadt, painted the following decade by an anonymous Middle Rhenish artist, is likewise imbued with the idealized forms characteristic of Cologne, though it has a greater sense of monumentality.

As the century wore on, however, it was Swabian painters who pioneered moves towards more realistic forms, and thus paved the way to the Renaissance. First of these was **Lucas Moser**, probably a stained-glass designer by training, whose sole known work is the outside of the triptych still *in situ* in Tiefenbronn, dated 1431. Although the execution is still very soft and beautiful, an attempt is made at diminishing perspectives, while the water in the sea has both ripples and reflections. Very different is the *Wurzach Altar* of six years later, now in Berlin, which was made in the workshop of the great Ulm sculptor **Hans Multscher** (c.1400–67), though it's unresolved as to whether it was executed by the master himself, or by an unknown assistant who specialized in the painting side of the business. The figures in these Passion scenes are made deliberately crude, with exaggerated theatrical gestures, and seem to have been modelled on real-life peasants; they are about as far away from the contemporary work of Lochner as it is possible to get.

A far more refined realist painter was **Conrad Witz** (c.1400–46) of Rottweil, who spent his working life in Switzerland. His surviving legacy consists of about twenty panels taken from three separate retables; Basel and Geneva have the best examples, but others are in Berlin and Nürnberg. In them, he successfully resolved the new realism with traditional forms and grappled with such problems as perspective and movement. His figures have a sculptural quality and are treated as masses, not as means of portrayal; the rich and luminous colours employed are also an important feature. Most enduring of all was his contribution to landscape painting, being the first to introduce topographically accurate views of scenery, as opposed to cities, into his pictures. Witz's influence is discernible in the few surviving works of the **Master of the Darmstadt Passion**, who was active mid-century in the Middle Rhine region. **Friedrich Herlin** (c.1435–1499) of Nördlingen, who painted grave, severe figures, was another to follow his example; he in turn was succeeded by **Bartholomäus Zeitblom** (c.1455–1520) of Ulm.

Among Bavarian painters of this period, the **Master of the Tegernsee Altar** (active c.1430–50) was somewhat archaic in style but capable of highly dramatic effects, notably the curious *Crucifixion* in his native Munich, which is set within elaborate Gothic architecture. Also working in this city was the **Master of the Polling Panels** (active c.1434–50), who retained the International Gothic style, whilst injecting it with a dose of realism. In the same period, Nürnberg boasted the **Master of the Imhoff Altar** and the **Master of the Tucher Altar**; the latter's work is characterized by strongly drawn thick-set figures, prominent still lifes, and attempts at perspective. They were succeeded by **Hans Pleydenwurff** (c.1420–72), who showed a thorough knowledge of Netherlandish artists such as Bouts in colour, figure modelling and background cityscapes, often with small subsidiary scenes; he was also a notable portraitist. After his death, his workshop was taken over by **Michael Wolgemut** (1434–1519). **Rueland Frueauf** (c.1440–1507) founded the Danube School of painting in Passau and Salzburg; although few works by him survive, the *Man of Sorrows* in Munich is an arresting masterpiece, achieved by great economy of means. His son of the same name (c.1470–1545) carried on his style.

The late Gothic period also saw something of a revival in Westphalia. In Münster, **Johann Koerbecke** (active 1446–90) gave a more forceful treatment to facial expression than his Cologne contemporaries. A sensitive touch is revealed in the work of the **Master of Liesborn** (active late fifteenth century); whilst **Derick Baegert** (c.1440–1515) imbued his paintings with a rugged dramatic quality.

Jan Joest of Kalkar (c.1455–1519) submerged himself in the art of the nearby

Netherlands; he appears to have had a remarkable career, travelling as far afield as Spain, where he painted a retable for Palencia Cathedral which remains *in situ*. Two north German practitioners of the new Netherlandish-influenced realism were **Hinrik Funhof** (c. 1435–85), whose masterpiece is in St Johannis in Lüneburg, and Lübeck's **Hermen Rode** (active 1485–1504).

THE RISE OF GRAPHIC ARTS

Gutenberg's printing revolution sounded the death knell for illuminated manuscripts and gave an enormous stimulus to the black-and-white arts, with the traditional woodcut being followed by the new techniques of line engraving and drypoint, which appeared in the 1440s. At first, the forms were dominated by obscure figures from the Mainz area – the two pioneers were the so-called **Master of the Playing Cards**, whose reputation rests on an elaborate card deck, and **Master ES**, among whose creations is a fantastic alphabet. Another engraver known only by his initials is **Master LCZ** of Bamberg, by whom some expressive panels also survive.

A more rounded personality appears in the **Master of the Housebook** (active c.1470–1500), around whom a sizeable body of work has been gathered; many attempts have been made to equate him with **Erhard Reuwich**, who executed a series of woodcuts for a book on a journey to the Holy Land. His pseudonym derives from an extraordinary book of drawings in a private collection; it was the manual of a master of munitions at a princely court, and contains elaborate astrological groupings as well as scenes of warfare. Even finer are his delicate drypoints, which depict with both humanity and humour the everyday life of the time, from the fashions and fantasies of the small courts to the earthy pastimes of the peasantry. The draughtsman's technique is also evident in the linear form of his few paintings, which include two retables, one in Mainz, the other dispersed in the museums of Freiburg, Berlin and Frankfurt.

An equally great but very different graphic artist was **Martin Schongauer** (c.1450–91) of Colmar, which was then very much a German city. He has always been a revered figure, as he marks the transition from the late Gothic to the Renaissance, and is thus the founding father of

the short but glorious period when the German visual arts reached the highest peaks of their achievement. Over a hundred surviving engravings show his successful fusion of realism and expressionism from northern artists with the exotic interests and technical innovations of space, form and perspective which characterize the Italian Renaissance. They were to serve as a model and an inspiration to the succeeding generation, who increasingly came to realize that the print was an important new democratic art form closely in tune with the spirit of the age, with potential for reaching a far wider public than had ever been possible before. Schongauer's surviving paintings are tantalizingly few but always of very high quality – they include the large *Madonna of the Rose Bush* in his native city, some damaged frescoes of *The Last Judgment* in nearby Breisach, and several little panels of *The Nativity*, the finest of which is in Berlin.

THE TRIUMPH OF THE RENAISSANCE

The most dominant personality in the history of German art was **Albrecht Dürer** (1471–1528), who trained under Wolgemut in his native Nürnberg. Dürer was a true man of the Renaissance, gaining a broad range of experiences in antithesis to the painstaking workshop traditions which were the lot of the medieval artist. He undertook travels to Italy, Switzerland, Alsace and the Low Countries, assimilating their traditions, and gained mastery in all artistic media, yet also found time to write and engage in mathematical and scientific research as well as to be involved in the Reformation, ending up excommunicated for Lutheran sympathies. Surprisingly, canvas painting does not always show Dürer at his best – he was at times rather conservative in his earlier religious panels, but increased in confidence with time, as can be seen in his valedictory *Four Apostles* in Munich. His portraits from life, however, are almost uniformly superb, laying bare the soul of the subject in penetrating psychological observations, as in *Jacob Muffel* and *Hieronymus Holzschuher*, both now in Berlin. With the woodcut, Dürer was in a class of his own; while still in his twenties he created an *Apocalypse* series of quite menacing power and profound imagination, which he printed and published himself. This was followed by two *Passion* series, a lovely *Life of the*

Virgin and the stupendous *Triumphal Arch* commissioned by the Emperor Maximilian; he also made many memorable engravings, often deeply overlaid with symbolic meaning. Dürer was also the first artist to realize the possibilities of watercolour, executing beautiful landscapes, plant and animal studies. The originals of these are now rarely exhibited for conservation reasons, yet such works as *Young Hare* and *Blade of Grass* rank among the most familiar images in Renaissance art.

In Munich, the Polish-born **Jan Polack** (active c.1480–1519) painted mannered altarpieces featuring emotional figures clad in swirling draperies, along with portraits more obviously imbued with the new Renaissance outlook. A far more significant artistic centre was Augsburg, seat of the Habsburg court. **Hans Holbein the Elder** (c.1465–1524) showed increasing Renaissance influence in his prolific output of retables, although he was never entirely able to free himself from the old forms. His brother-in-law **Hans Burgkmair** (1473–1531) was more successful, benefiting from a spell as Schongauer's assistant; he particularly delighted in the most luxuriant Italianate features, which he skilfully synthesized into his altars. This decorative talent was given full rein by Emperor Maximilian I, who commissioned him to supervise the overall programme of the huge series of woodcuts of his *Triumphal Procession*; many of the leading German artists, including Dürer, contributed, although the success of the project was due to the relish shown by Burgkmair. **Jörg Breu** (c.1475–1537) was another fine retable painter resident in the city, while **Bernhardin Strigel** (c.1460–1528) served as court portraitist. Strigel developed family groups as an independent art form.

By far the greatest painter Augsburg produced was **Hans Holbein the Younger** (1497/8–1543), but he left while still in his teens, and spent the rest of his career in Switzerland and England. He first settled in Basel (which retains by far the best collection of his art), where he was enormously productive in all kinds of media – portraits, altarpieces, decorative schemes of many types (now mostly lost) and woodcuts, including the celebrated *Dance of Death*. One of his masterpieces from this period, and one of the few works by him actually in Germany, is the *Madonna of Burgomaster Mayer* in Darmstadt Schloss, which combines sharply characterized portraits and a devotional theme. He subsequently concentrated almost exclusively on portraiture, developing a cool, detached style based on absolute technical mastery, and frequently incorporating amazingly precise still lifes based on the paraphernalia of the sitter's occupation; *The Danzig Merchant Georg Gisze*, now in Berlin, is an outstanding example. On his second visit to England, he became court painter to Henry VIII, and left a haunting series of drawings of that magnificent but tragic circle, though sadly few of the finished paintings have been preserved.

Lucas Cranach the Elder (1472–1553) was the earliest great Saxon painter. The first thirty years of his life are obscure; he is first known as a mature artist playing a dominant role in the Danube School, painting portraits and religious scenes set in lush and suggestively beautiful verdant landscapes. His masterpiece of this period is *The Three Crosses* in Munich, which uses a blatantly eccentric vantage point in order to emphasize the artist's technical control. Whereas these works have consistently been admired, Cranach's long second phase at Wittenberg in the service of the Electors of Saxony is far more controversial. He ran the equivalent of a picture factory, often repeating the same subjects ad infinitum with only minor variations; the style is mannered with imperfections in drawing and subjects placed in wholly unrealistic relationships. Yet these were surely deliberate traits by a great humorist and individualist, whose sinuous nudes and erotic mythological scenes added a dimension to German painting which had previously been lacking. He seems to have invented the full-length portrait as a genre, and excelled at characterization. As a personal friend of Luther and Melanchthon, he created the definitive images of the leaders of the Reformation and made propaganda woodcuts on their behalf, but was not averse to accepting traditional commissions from the Catholics as well. His son **Lucas Cranach the Younger** (1515–86) took over the workshop and continued its tradition faithfully.

Albrecht Altdorfer (c.1480–1538) of Regensburg became the leading master of the Danube School; his luxuriant landscape backgrounds assume even greater significance than with Cranach, and at times the ostensible subject is quite unimportant, as with *St George and the*

Dragon in Munich. Fantastic buildings also feature in several of his works, reflecting the fact that he was also a practising architect. When the figures do matter, they are integrated with their surroundings and given highly expressive tendencies, achieved by deliberate anatomical imprecisions and exaggerated gestures. Light is often an important feature, with unnaturally colourful effects; unorthodox aerial perspectives further distinguish his paintings. The largest group of Altdorfer's work, in which all these features appear, is still mostly *in situ* in the Austrian monastery of St Florian. However, his masterpiece is the *Battle of Darius and Alexander* in Munich; commissioned as part of a war series, each by different artists, it makes all the others look like the work of bumbling amateurs. The actual battle is depicted with all the skill of a miniaturist, yet it is set within a spectacular cosmic perspective in what ranks as one of the most formidable displays of sheer pyrotechnics in the history of painting. His chief follower was **Wolf Huber** (c.1490–1553) of Passau, who was rather more restrained in his effects.

The extreme tendency towards expression in German painting is found in the work of the painter known as **Grünewald**, although his real name was **Mathis Gothardt-Neithardt** (c.1470/5–1528), who is almost a direct opposite of Dürer. Fully proficient in the new Renaissance developments of space and perspective, he used them as mere adjuncts to his sense of drama; he was also the only great German artist of his time who seems to have had no interest in the print. Even in an early work such as *The Mocking of Christ* in Munich, Grünewald's emotional power is evident. No artist ever painted Passion scenes with anything like the same harrowing intensity, in the words of the nineteenth-century French novelist Huysmans, "he promptly strikes you dumb with the fearsome nightmare of a Calvary". His huge folding polyptych, the *Isenheim Altar*, represents the majority of his surviving work. Though its panels are of uneven quality, its moods – ranging from a tender *Madonna and Child* to the blazing triumphant glory of *The Resurrection* – are of such variety that it deserves its reputation as the ultimate masterpiece of German painting; ironically, its Colmar home is now French territory.

Grünewald's art is so individual and overpowering that he had no successors. However,

Jerg Ratgeb (c.1480–1526) must have come under his influence as his few works – fresco cycles in Frankfurt and Maulbronn, and the *Herrenberg Altar* in Stuttgart – have an even rawer expressiveness, which might have developed had he not been quartered for his leading role in the Peasants' War.

Of the younger generation of Renaissance artists, by far the most interesting is **Hans Baldung Grien** (1484/5–1545), a flawed genius who studied under Dürer and eventually settled in Strasbourg. Colour and volume play a large part in his pictures, but his fascination with the bizarre is the most obvious recurring element, with moralistic fantasies being among his finest works. Baldung's main religious works are two altars for the Freiburg Münster, but there is no concentration of his output, which is now spread among many museums. The late engravings such as *Wild Horses* and *Bewitched Stable Boy* are quite unlike the work of any other artist, and arguably rank as his greatest achievements.

Hans Süss von Kulmbach (c.1480–1522) and **Hans Leonard Schäuffelein** (c.1483–1539/40) were loyal followers of Dürer's example, but their productions ultimately lack his inspired touch; the specialist engravers, the brothers **Hans Sebald Beham** (1500–50) and **Barthel Beham** (1502–40), and the Westphalian **Heinrich Aldegraver** (1502–60) were arguably more successful at capturing his spirit. The **Master of Messkirch** (active c.1430–45) added a personal expressive sense to the Düreresque idiom.

The early sixteenth century also saw a mushrooming of talented provincial portraitists who were able to satisfy the ever-increasing demand from the rising middle classes; they often painted religious and mythological subjects as well, but with less success. In Nürnberg, **Georg Pencz** (c.1500–50), possibly another pupil of Dürer, was strongly influenced by Venetian models. Augsburg at this time had **Cristoph Amberger** (c.1500–61/2), who was more associated with the court, and **Ulrich Apt** (c.1460–1532). The works of Frankfurt's **Conrad Faber von Creuznach** (c.1500–53) are particularly felicitous, with the sitters placed against landscapes reminiscent of the Danube School; he also executed a magnificent woodcut of the siege of his home city. **Barthel Bruyn** (1492/3–1555) was the first Cologne painter to break away from two centuries of tradition; in spite of several diverse influences, the city's great heritage seems to have made little impression on his art. In Münster, **Ludger tom Ring the Elder** (1496–1547) founded a dynasty which specialized in slightly crude portraits and altars for both Protestant and Catholic use. His style was continued by his sons **Hermann tom Ring** (1521–96) and **Ludger tom Ring the Younger** (1522–84); the latter seems to have been the first German artist to treat still life as an independent form.

MANNERISM AND THE EARLY BAROQUE

Mannerism is already evident in the work of the generation after Dürer, but only appears in a full-blooded way with **Hans von Aachen** (1552–1616), who particularly excelled at sensual mythological subjects, and who played a leading role in the highly distinctive erotic style fostered at the court of Emperor Rudolf II in Prague. **Johann Rottenhammer** (1564–1625) travelled extensively in Italy, before returning to his native Augsburg. He came under the spell of Paolo Veronese's huge decorative works filled with figures; his response was to reduce such compositions onto little copper panels, adding an extra degree of luminosity into the landscapes.

This highly skilled technique was developed by his pupil, **Adam Elsheimer** (1578–1610), who settled in Rome and achieved a remarkable synthesis of diverse influences which gives his works a stature that belies their small size. Elsheimer drew on Altdorfer's heritage in creating a union between the subjects and nature, which Rottenhammer left as rather disparate features. He also seemed to share the earlier master's genius for light effects, and was particularly adept at night scenes and at strong contrasts of brightness and shadow derived from Caravaggio. A slow and deliberate worker, his early death meant that his legacy is numerically modest, but it was to influence such contrasting great successors as Rubens, Rembrandt and Claude. The largest assemblage of his work is *Altar of the Holy Cross*, whose panels have been painstakingly reassembled over the years in his native Frankfurt; many of his best paintings are in Britain, due to the esteem in which he was held by the aristocrats of the Grand Tour.

Unfortunately, there was no great German successor, although his style was continued with varying success long after his death by **Johann König** (1586–1642). Elsheimer's influence is also evident in the legacy of **Gottfried Wals** (c.1595–1638), best known as the teacher of Claude, but a distinctive artist in his own right, specializing in small copper roundels of landscapes with figures bathed in light.

The other main German painter of the early seventeenth century, **Johann Liss** (1597–1629), was constantly on the move, leaving his native Holstein for the Low Countries and then Italy, absorbing their diverse traditions. One vein of his work, the small arcadian landscapes, reveals the impact of Elsheimer or at least his Roman followers, but his best canvases are far more monumental in scale, swaggering in the full pomp characteristic of the new Baroque age. These religious and mythological scenes, sometimes featuring sumptuous banquets, are executed with fluid brushwork in daringly unorthodox colours.

Liss was also to occupy a premature grave, and it seems as if German painting in the seventeenth century was to be jinxed, in contrast to its richness and diversity in this period over the rest of Europe. The Thirty Years' War, which so exhausted and preoccupied the country, acted as a massive restraint on artistic activity at the time, but was to fuel a long-standing vogue for depictions of battles and genre scenes of military life evidenced in the work of **Matthias Scheits** (c.1630–1700) and **Georg Philip Rugendas** (1666–1742), though these tend to follow the decorative Dutch manner, rather than convey the true horrors the country suffered. An increased religious fervour as a result of the war is mirrored in the emotional cycles of canvases and frescoes by the Catholic convert **Michael Willmann** (1630–1706), the best of which are in the monasteries in Silesia (now part of Poland).

The Moravian-born **Georg Flegel** (1566–1638) was the first German artist to specialize exclusively in still life, initiating a vogue for this genre in his adopted home city of Frankfurt. Equally precise and detached, the works of the last major Frankfurt master of still life, **Abraham Mignon** (1640–79), are altogether lusher in effect, typically showing ripe fruit and flowers in full bloom. Other specialist painters of the period include **Wolfgang Heimbach** (c.1613–78), a deaf-mute who created small scenes of middle-class life and used nocturnal lighting to good effect; and the animal artists **Carl Andreas Ruthart** (c.1630–73) and **Philipp Peter Roos** (1655–1706).

Far more versatile than any of these was **Johann Friedrich Schönfeld** (1609–84), whose output is rather uneven due to an excessive number of changes of style in response to the diversity he encountered on his Italian travels. His best paintings are colourful history scenes with elaborate backgrounds, painted under the influence of the classically derived compositions of Poussin which held sway in Rome, but tempered by the more light-hearted Neapolitan approach. The only German artist to fall under the spell of Rembrandt was **Jürgen Ovens** (1623–78), who spent part of his career in Amsterdam in the circle of the great Dutch master, before returning to his native Schleswig-Holstein, where he produced portraits and history scenes in his teacher's most Baroque vein.

However, the most significant art works produced in mid-seventeenth-century Germany were the detailed engravings of towns, known as *Topographia Germaniae*, started by **Matthäus Merian** (1593–1650), and continued by his sons. In due course, the appearances of some 2000 German communities – a unique pictorial record – were preserved for posterity.

LATE BAROQUE, ROCOCO AND NEOCLASSICISM

The best late Baroque German painting is not to be found in any museum, but on the walls of the ornate pilgrimage churches of Bavaria and Baden-Württemberg. These buildings, which aimed at fusing all the visual arts into a coherent synthesis, are among the most original creations in the country. Their rich interior decoration formed an intrinsic part of the architecture from the outset, and was often the work of the same masters.

One of the most accomplished of these was **Cosmas Damian Asam** (1686–1739), who formed a team with his sculptor brother, Egid Quirin Asam. At first they decorated existing churches, such as the Dom in Freising, but later moved on to undertaking the entire programme themselves. They trained in Rome and remained loyal to its dignified High Baroque, rather than to the more frivolous Rococo derivatives favoured by their fellow countrymen. C.D.

Asam's ceiling frescoes fall into two separate categories – the trick device of diminishing perspective in the manner of the Italian Jesuit Andrea Pozzo, and a more conventional spatial format of open heavens.

Johann Baptist Zimmerman (1680–1758), in contrast, is fully Rococo; he did not design buildings himself, but enjoyed a particularly close relationship with two of the leading architects of the time, François Cuvilliés, with whom he collaborated on the Munich Residenz and Schloss Nymphenburg; and his own younger brother Dominikus, with whom he worked at Steinhausen and the Wieskirche. Two other major fresco painters were **Johann Georg Bergmüller** (1688–1762) and **Matthäus Günther** (1705–88), who successively directed the Augsburg Academy.

By this time, Prussia had arisen as a major power in European affairs, and was by far the dominant German state. Frederick the Great was a major patron of the arts, but he was also a Francophile whose court painter was the Parisian-born **Antoine Pesne** (1683–1757). This artist was commissioned to paint allegorical and mythological decorative schemes for the royal palaces, but his realistic portraits, very much in the French manner of the time with rich colours and subtle lighting effects, were more successful and ultimately highly influential, serving as the model for later Berlin artists. His most important pupil was **Bernhard Rode** (1725–97), who was also involved in the work on the palaces, but who is seen at his best in quietly observed genre scenes. For the last period of his life, he directed the Berlin Academy, one of several founded in the major cities in order to foster a theoretical approach to painting. Another of this circle was **Daniel Nikolaus Chodowiecki** (1726–1801), although his talent was best suited to vignette etchings, mostly to illustrate books. A later Berlin artist, **Asmus Jakob Carstens** (1754–98) was also at his finest in black and white media, executing large chalk cartoons of Classical subjects.

One of the guiding lights of the movement was **Anton Raffael Mengs** (1728–79), son of the court painter in Dresden, who had ruthlessly prepared him for artistic fame from a very early age. Mengs was to have an amazingly successful career in Germany, Italy and particularly Spain. He was a key theorist and guru of the new Neoclassicism; his works are enormously skilful technically, but emotionally cold. The Swiss-born **Anton Graff** (1736–1835) was also a leading academic portraitist in Dresden. This same city was home to a succession of landscape painters throughout the century, whose work foreshadows the far more arresting compositions of the Romantics; **Johann Alexander Thiele** (1685–1752) was the first and most accomplished of these.

A strict Neoclassical style was adopted at the Kassel Academy under **Johann Heinrich Tischbein** (1722–89). This was modified by his nephews **Johann Friedrich August Tischbein** (1750–1812) and **Johann Heinrich Wilhelm Tischbein** (1751–1829), who introduced the greater warmth found in English and French works of the time, though both remained loyal academicians. The latter's *Goethe in the Campagna* in Frankfurt is the most celebrated work of the dynasty.

Another family of painters had as by far its most accomplished member **Januarius Zick** (1730–97), who turned his back on his academic training. He was a theatrical but effective frescoist in the grand manner, as can be seen in the cycles in Wiblingen and Bruchsal. In contrast, his canvases are often of modest size, achieving an original synthesis of the light effects often found in Rembrandt's deeply intimate small-scale works with the airy Rococo grace of Watteau.

ROMANTICISM

The Romantic movement, a reaction against the rigidity of Neoclassicism but with the same Roman roots, was particularly strong in Germany; the rich outpourings of music and literature make it one of the supreme high points in the country's cultural history. Although there was not the same depth of talent in painting, the haunting and highly original landscapes of **Caspar David Friedrich** (1774–1840) form a fitting visual counterpart to the works of the great poets and composers of the time. Friedrich created a new spiritual way of looking at the scenery: it was always the immensity and majesty of Nature that he sought to convey, often using the technique of enormously long perspectives. Unlike his great predecessor Altdorfer, he did not stress the unity of man and landscape, but rather the unconquerable power of the latter. Where figures are introduced, they

are typically seen from the back, contemplating the wonders before them; in the more common absence of humans, the evidence of Man's presence tends to stress his fragility and ephemeral status – as in the famous *Eismeer* in Hamburg, or the many scenes with Classical temples and Gothic abbeys – in comparison with the omnipotent changelessness of the surroundings.

The influence of Friedrich's way of looking can sometimes be detected in the canvases of **Karl Friedrich Schinkel** (1781–1841), who was forced by financial considerations to turn to painting, where he abandoned the Neoclassicism of his buildings in favour of vast panoramas and architectural fantasies. **Leo von Klenze** (1794–1864), the other great architect of German Neoclassicism, was likewise a gifted occasional painter, producing romanticized views of the ruins of Greece and Rome. More orthodox followers of Friedrich include **Carl Gustav Carus** (1787–1869) and **Ernst Ferdinand Oehme** (1797–1855).

Philipp Otto Runge (1777–1810) might have developed into Friedrich's figurative counterpart had he lived longer. He had enormously grandiose ideas, aiming to recover the lost harmony of the universe through the symbolism of colours and numbers, and began a project called *The Times of Day*, of four panels over 8m in height, which he aimed to instal in a specially designed building in which poetry and music would be performed. That he managed to persuade Goethe to co-operate in this suggests that there was genuine substance to this apparently utopian dream, but it was never executed and only studies survive, leaving Runge's reputation to rest largely on his portraits, particularly the oversized ones depicting children.

Johann Friedrich Overbeck (1789–1869) was another Romantic with original convictions, settling in Rome where he founded the **Nazarene Brotherhood** of painters who lived like monks in a deconsecrated monastery. They produced two large co-operative fresco cycles: *The Story of Joseph*, now in the Nationalgalerie in Berlin, and another, still *in situ*, of scenes taken from Italian Renaissance literature. These detailed works emphasized theme and content at the expense of form.

Whereas Overbeck remained in Italy, his collaborators **Peter von Cornelius** (1783–1867), **Philipp Veit** (1793–1877), **Julius Schnorr von**

Carolsfeld (1794–1872) and **Wilhelm Schadow** (1788–1862) returned to Germany where they pursued careers in the academies. Cornelius had spells in charge of the two most dominant, Düsseldorf and Munich, and aimed to establish a tradition of monumental historical painting to rival the great frescoes of Italy. Although both influential and genuinely popular in its day, this style of painting has, since the turn of the present century, attracted nothing but critical scorn, appearing as an empty display of bombastics. It can still be seen all over the country, often desecrating the walls of great medieval buildings; among the better efforts are the cycles by **Alfred Rethel** (1816–59) in the Aachen Rathaus and by the Austrian-born **Moritz von Schwind** (1804–71) in Karlsruhe's Kunsthalle, and the Wartburg near Eisenach. The latter was the most refined illustrator of the Romantic view of the German Middle Ages, whose ethos he captured in numerous beautifully coloured and detailed canvases. **Ferdinand Olivier** (1785–1841) painted narrative canvases in the Nazarene style, as well as more conventional Romantic landscapes.

Standing somewhat apart are the expansive, open-ended fresco views painted in Munich by Ludwig I's court artist **Carl Rottmann** (1797–1850). Other Munich artists took the grand academic manner to its most extreme. Prominent among them were **Wilhelm von Kaulbach** (1805–76), a pupil of Cornelius, who produced monumental designs for the decoration of the Neue Pinakothek, and **Karl von Piloty** (1826–86), whose huge, highly theatrical history paintings were intended to evoke patriotic sentiment.

Romanticism in one form or another flourished throughout the nineteenth century. The brothers **Andreas Achenbach** (1815–1910) and **Oswald Achenbach** (1827–1905) continued in Friedrich's manner; the former was particularly successful at evocative northern scenery, whereas the latter added popular scenes to his pictures. **Karl Blechen** (1798–1840) also began in this style, but his later works, following a visit to Paris, became more consciously realist. **Anselm Feuerbach** (1829–80) pursued a heavily Italianate form of Romanticism in his portraits and densely crowded mythological scenes. There is a highly personal mixture of the Neoclassical and Romantic in **Hans von Marées** (1837–87), who achieved his masterpiece in his one commission for monumental frescoes, the Aquarium in Naples. For long out of critical favour, his canvases have recently begun to attract a great deal of interest. The inconsistent **Hans Thoma** (1839–1924) tried many styles in his time; the Romantic views of the Black Forest are by far the most successful.

OTHER NINETEENTH-CENTURY STYLES

Although many different trends were current in nineteenth-century German painting, none of them can match the vitality of the best Romantic work. A style which was largely confined to the country and its immediate neighbours from about 1815 to 1848 was Biedermeierstil, a bourgeois-inspired Classicism which drew on the pleasant aspects of living. **Carl Spitzweg** (1808–85) was its principal exponent; his homely pictures of the middle classes are injected with a touch of humour mocking the complacency that was all too apparent. **Franz Krüger** (1797–1857) chronicled Berlin life of the time in a more straight-laced vein, particularly in his ceremonial scenes and architectural views; **Eduard Gaertner** (1801–77) executed more felicitous topographical views of Berlin, while the Prussian court painter **Carl Graeb** (1816–84) produced exquisitely detailed little works of the same city and of the palaces and gardens of nearby Potsdam. Though he sometimes worked in the Düsseldorf academic manner, **Georg Friedrich Kersting** (1785–1847) was at his best in small-scale interiors, in which he showed his interest in everyday objects and activities as matters of beauty in their own right. The Dresden artist **Ludwig Richter** (1804–83) was a fine landscape painter, but again his true métier lay in a quite different field, in this case illustrations of legends for children's books. His pupil **Edouard Leonhardi** (1825–1905) specialized in highly detailed, meticulously executed forest scenes.

In contrast to this movement, there was a continued demand for official portraitists; one of the most accomplished was **Franz von Lenbach** (1836–1904), who painted Bismarck eighty times. **Franz Xaver Winterhalter** (1805–73) had the most dazzling career of all, progressing round all the main European courts, leaving behind unremittingly flattering portrayals of smug monarchs.

In the Realist tradition, Germany lagged behind France, although the versatile **Adolf von Menzel** (1815–1905), who also executed portraits and history scenes in the grand manner, was one of the first to portray the Industrial Revolution and its effects. **Wilhelm Trübner** (1851–1917) was another to undertake this mix of subjects. The best examples of this style were to come from **Wilhelm Leibl** (1844–1900), who aimed to re-create the technical skill of the old masters. To this end he conducted such experiments as reviving tempera to create an enamel-like surface, and painting with the attention to detail of a miniaturist, as in *Three Women in Church* in Hamburg. Much of his finest work was done in the 1870s, when he lived in rural Bavaria, and used peasants as real-life models.

Impressionism was very slow to catch on, and never seems to have suited the German temperament, but three artists who adopted it at some point in their careers were **Max Liebermann** (1847–1935), who originally favoured the sombre colours of the French Barbizon School and the Realists; **Lovis Corinth** (1858–1925), whose best works are the late landscapes executed in cold colours; and **Max Slevogt** (1868–1932), who was also a book illustrator and, late in life, a painter of monumental frescoes. Liebermann was the leading figure in the Berlin section of the **Secession movement** which began in the 1890s; this was a reaction by the avant-garde against the stultifying power wielded by the academies. The earlier Munich group was dominated by **Franz von Stuck** (1863–1928), an artist of violent mythological scenes, humorous drawings and large-scale decorative work. Based in the artistic backwater of Leipzig, the painter, sculptor and engraver **Max Klinger** (1857–1920) cut a somewhat solitary figure; although his output is very uneven in quality, he was capable, particularly in his graphic work, of real emotional power.

The most successful of several artists' colonies was that at Worpswede near Bremen, which was founded by **Fritz Mackensen** (1866–1953) in 1889. It survives to this day, though much of the best work done there was in its early years, when Mackensen and his friends **Otto Modersohn** (1856–1943), and **Hans am Ende** (1864–1918) produced a stream of canvases illustrating the bleakness of the local landscape and the harshness of life for its inhabitants.

EXPRESSIONISM

Much as the early part of the nineteenth century saw the dominance of Romanticism in German painting, so the first decades of this century came under the sway of Expressionism, a new and largely indigenous style, which aimed to root modern painting firmly in the tradition of the old German masters, and to establish it on an equal footing with France, for some time the dominant force in world art. Because of the entrenched power of existing interests, artists found they had to bind themselves into **groups** in order to make an impact; the early history of Expressionism is particularly associated with two of these.

Although its members were younger, **Die Brücke** (The Bridge) was first to be founded, in 1905. Its initial personnel, **Ernst Ludwig Kirchner** (1880–1938), **Erich Heckel** (1883–1970) and **Karl Schmidt-Rottluff** (1884–1976), were architectural students in Dresden who felt constrained by the inability of their subject to capture the immediate freshness of inspiration. Consequently, they turned to painting, in which none had much experience; they were shortly joined by **Max Pechstein** (1881–1955) and **Otto Müller** (1874–1930). They valued colour as a component in its own right, and later strove to enhance its surface effect as well. Their devotion to the country's artistic heritage was shown in the emphasis they placed on feeling, and on their revival of the woodcut as a valid alternative to oils.

The group moved to Berlin, where they turned away from their original preoccupation with landscapes to the depiction of city life. Kirchner developed into the leader and best artist of the group. *Three Women in the Street*, now in Essen, is a key work; its strong sense of line shows the impact made by the arts of primitive peoples, then being appreciated in Europe for the first time. The group broke up in 1913, and thereafter each artist pursued an independent career. Kirchner turned to decorative design in the 1920s, working on embroideries and tapestries; his later paintings show a stronger sense of abstraction. Heckel's work is closest to Kirchner's, though he was later to add a greater sense of realism to his pictures. Pechstein, at the time regarded as the most important Expressionist of all, has since suffered a slump in reputation; he was the most loyal to naturalistic representation and thus stands furthest removed from the path followed by Schmidt-Rottluff. Gypsy culture features strongly in Müller's work; he seems to have felt a genuine affinity with it, and spent much of the 1920s travelling among Balkan communities.

The second group of artists was **Der Blaue Reiter** (The Blue Rider), a strongly intellectual movement originating in Munich which aimed at uniting all the arts. Its name is taken from its magazine, which appeared only once (in 1912); it was very loosely structured and far more diverse than *Die Brücke*, with the lead being taken by two contrasting artistic personalities. The Russian-born **Wassily Kandinsky** (1866–1944) was a pioneer of pure abstraction, using fluid and soft forms, but strong and vibrant colours; he was also a noted writer and used words as the starting points for his images. **Franz Marc** (1880–1916), on the other hand, always retained at least a partial form of representation in his compositions. He was devoted to nature, and animals are a recurrent theme in his art; he regarded them as noble and uncorrupted, the complete antithesis to Man. At first they appear detached in the foreground; from 1913, when he adopted more abstract methods, they are more closely integrated with their surroundings. Geometry was always important to Marc, and he favoured prismatic colours, to which he attached a mystical significance. His development was cut short by the outbreak of war, and he died in combat.

This fate also befell an even younger member of the group, **August Macke** (1887–1914). Although Macke was clearly influenced by the new Cubist movement, his works are always representational, and he ranks as the most poetic and gentle of all the Expressionists. The figures are unmistakeable; slim and column-like, they glide across the picture surface, taking their Sunday stroll in the park, or indulging in a bit of window-shopping. More often than not, they wear a hat, which serves to distinguish them, as their facial features are never included. Strong colours are used, but they are never strident; they rather add to the happy and relaxed atmosphere.

Paul Klee (1879–1940), born in Switzerland but having German nationality as well, was the fourth main member of the group. He never concerned himself with any of the social, political or psychological problems of the age, but preferred to construct his own abstract language in which he aimed to recapture the mystery and magic of the universe. To this end, he developed a series of fractured and fragmented forms – arcs, forks and bars – which were usually painted black against a coloured background. In the 1920s, when they worked at the Bauhaus, he and Kandinsky formed *Die Blauen Vier* (The Blue Four) as a successor to *Der Blaue Reiter*.

The other members were **Alexej Jawlensky** (1864–1941), also of Russian birth, who specialized in characterful portrait heads; and **Lyonel Feininger** (1871–1956), who was born and died in New York, but who can be regarded as the most loyal German Cubist, being most notable for his architectural and marine scenes. Russian influence is apparent in the paintings of **Heinrich Campendonk** (1889–1957), the youngest member of *Der Blaue Reiter*, although his preferred medium was the woodcut.

A number of Expressionists unattached to either group were active in the Rhine-Ruhr area, where Macke also spent much of his life. Throughout a very long career, **Christian Rohlfs** (1849–1938) tried many different styles; he clearly came under the influence of the Impressionists but never fully adopted their manner. His true artistic personality did not emerge until his Expressionist phase, particularly the architectural paintings he made in Soest and Erfurt, and the very late flower pieces. Rohlfs clearly inspired **Wilhelm Morgner** (1891–1917), another war casualty. **Heinrich Nauen** (1880–1940) was one of several Expressionists who were quite overt about following French leads, in his case Matisse and the Fauves, whose bright colours form an important feature of his hybrid style.

Fauvism, particularly the Classically-inspired works of Derain, was also important to **Carl Hofer** (1878–1955). Primitive art as filtered through Gauguin made a strong impression on **Paula Modersohn-Becker** (1876–1907), the most talented artist of the colony at Worpswede. Whether or not she is really an Expressionist is debatable, as she did not concern herself with drama or emotions, though her favourite *Mother and Child* theme has achieved a certain poignancy as she later died in childbirth.

The most individualistic Expressionist of all, even though he had a spell as a member of *Die Brücke*, was **Emil Hansen** (1867–1956), generally called **Nolde** after his birthplace. In his depictions of the rugged North Sea coastline that was his home, he can be regarded as the successor to Friedrich. However, there's no sense of romance in Nolde's landscapes, which convey the harsh and forbidding nature of the terrain and its climate, emphasized in the way he captured its special colours and light effects by means of rich, strong and violently contrasting tones. Flowers and garden scenes provide a lighter note, but he also revived the somewhat lost art of religious painting, in which he aimed to recreate something of the intensity of Grünewald, along with the simple devotion he found in primitive art.

Ludwig Meidner (1884–1966) was dubbed the most Expressionist of the Expressionists, as a result of the powerful apocalyptic visions he painted before the war, which stand at the opposite extreme to the primitive trends in the movement. The union of all the arts sought by so many found its best individual manifestation in the work of **Ernst Barlach** (1870–1938). Primarily a sculptor, he was also a talented graphic artist, illustrating his own plays and travel writings. Another sculptor, **Käthe Kollwitz** (1867–1945) achieved great emotional power in her pacifist woodcuts, engravings and lithographs of wartime horrors.

OTHER TWENTIETH-CENTURY MOVEMENTS

Expressionism, in spite of its dominance, does not by any means cover the entire richness of German art in the early part of this century. The nihilistic Dada movement, which grew up during the war, included **Kurt Schwitters** (1887–1948), who took the concept of non-art to its extreme, experimenting with collages incorporating pieces of torn-up paper before moving on to using rubbish as his basic component. He dubbed his art *Merz* after the letters from one of the pieces of paper he used, and intended his life's work to be a huge composition which would fill a house, but the first two completed versions were destroyed, and his last attempt, in exile in England, was unfinished at his death. **Hannah Höch** (1889–1978) and the Austrian-born **Raoul Hausmann** (1886–1944) were two rather milder Dadaists.

George Grosz (1893–1959) also began in this style, but his later works were more representational. A committed Communist, he was a savage satirist, particularly in his humorous drawings, ruthlessly attacking the corrupt and decadent vested interests of the Weimar Republic. Ironically, he was entranced by America and emigrated there just before the Nazi rise to power. Another prominent Dadaist and left-winger was **John Heartfield** (1891–1968), who adopted an anglicized form of his original name, Helmut Herzfeld, in protest at German xenophobia. Best known as the inventor of the photomontage, which he used to devastating effect to attack the Nazis from his exile in Czechoslovakia and Britain, he settled in the GDR after World War II, where his work, in the service of the state, lost much of its sharpness.

Inevitably, there grew a tendency which stood in polar opposition to Expressionism: *Neue Sachlichkeit* (New Objectivity), a term first used in 1923 to describe trends already apparent. This can be thought of as an updated form of realism, which aimed at depicting subjects in a straightforward and detailed way. Some of Grosz's work belongs to this style, but its finest practitioner was **Otto Dix** (1891–1969), who had been profoundly affected by the war. This formed a persistent subject of his work, although he used it to depict Man's suffering as opposed to any directly political overtone. He aimed to recapture the actual technique of the old masters, and his portraits show larger-than-life characters under a rich sheen of paint. In spite of the overt eroticism of many of his canvases, he was also drawn to the Passion, on which he placed a humanitarian and allegorical interpretation.

The former Dadaist **Christian Schad** (1894–1982) represents a more extreme form of Dix's style, with many explicit scenes drawn from the bohemian world he himself inhabited; **Rudolf Schlichter** (1890–1955) had similar preoccupations. In contrast, there was a romantically inclined wing of this movement, exemplified by **Georg Schrimpf** (1898–1938). The Jewish artist **Felix Nussbaum** (1900–1944), another member of *Neue Sachlichkeit*, is best known for his sombre late works depicting the Auschwitz concentration camp where he died.

Max Beckmann (1884–1950) defies classification, lying somewhere between Expressionism and *Neue Sachlichkeit*. He believed it was the artist's duty to express Man's spiritual condition. To this end, he used the self-portrait as a means of expressing his changing reaction to world events, making himself appear in different guises, whether as clown, convict, king or hero. The symbolism associated with Carnival and the circus is a recurring theme in his work, as are the use of gesture to reveal character and the manipulation of space. To express opposition to the Nazis, he took to the anachronistic format of the triptych.

Max Ernst (1891–1976) was another who began as a Dadaist, producing first collages and then frottages. However, he is best known as one of the leading Surrealist painters, a style he turned to on its foundation in 1924, and for which his early interest in psychology and the creative works of the mentally ill made him most suitable. To what extent he can be considered a German artist is debatable, as he left his native country in 1922, taking first American then French nationality. The most accomplished Surrealist who can definitely be classed as German is **Edgar Ende** (1901–66), whose compositions are directly comparable with those of the Italian Giorgio de Chirico. **Wolfgang Lettl** (b. 1919) keeps the tradition alive in a distinctive manner, in which humour is very much to the forefront.

Oskar Schlemmer (1888–1943) was one of the most varied German painters of the century, touched by seemingly every style; he also practised both decorative and functional art. Among the practitioners of abstraction following Kandinsky and Klee, **Willi Baumeister** (1889–1955), **Ernst Wilhelm Nay** (1902–68) and **Alfred Wolfgang Schulze** (1913–51), better known as **Wols**, acquired the greatest reputations.

Apart from Heartfield, leading luminaries of the GDR artistic establishment in its early years included **Otto Nagel** (1894–1967), who had established his reputation before the war as a chronicler of proletarian life in Berlin, and Dresden's **Hans Grundig** (1901–58), whose powerful visionary images show an obvious debt to medieval and Renaissance predecessors. For most of its life, however, the state fostered a particularly sterile form of Socialist Realism as the only acceptable form of artistic activity; artists who rebelled against this, such as **Roger Loewig** (b.1930), faced persecution and eventual expulsion. Few products of the state-sponsored style are likely to survive much longer on public display unless as mere historical curiosities. An exception, however, is the most spectacular commission granted by the regime, the controversial *Panorama* in Bad Frankenhausen in honour of the Peasants' War, painted by Leipzig professor **Werner Tübke** (b. 1929).

In the postwar Federal Republic, avant-garde artistic activity flourished, thanks to generous subsidy levels by all tiers of government. How many of the painters whose work currently lines the walls of the country's many museums of modern art will prove to be of lasting significance remains a moot point. Among those who have gained international standing, **Georg Baselitz** (b.1940) paints figuratively but groups the different components of his works in a deliberately arbitrary way. **Sigmar Polke** (b.1941) can be seen as something of a disciple of Dadaism in the objects he tacks on to his canvases, mirroring his interest in German society's obsession with kitsch. **Anselm Kiefer** (b.1945) has been concerned with the German psyche in its historical context, focusing on gestures, symbols and myths. **Jörg Immendorff** (b.1945) and **Bernd Koberling** (b.1938) have taken an overtly left-wing political stance in their work, with ecological themes also being associated with the latter.

BOOKS

Publishers are detailed below in the form of British publisher/American publisher, where both exist. University Press is abbreviated to UP and Oxford University Press to OUP.

Heinrich Heine *Deutschland: A Winter's Tale* (Angel; also included in the *Complete Poems*). This magisterial verse travelogue describes Heine's journey from exile in Paris to his family home in Hamburg. It's full of insight into the places he passed through, and contains devastating exposés of mid-nineteenth-century German society. *The Harz Journey* (*Selected Prose*, Penguin) is one of the author's *Travel Pictures* – much imitated travelogues featuring inserted poems within the narrative.

Patrick Leigh Fermor *A Time of Gifts* (Penguin). The author set out to walk from Rotterdam to Constantinople in 1933, travelling along the Rhine and Danube valleys en route. Written up forty years later in luscious, hyper-refined prose, it presents the fresh sense of youthful discovery distilled through considerable subsequent learning and reflection. Prewar Germany is shown suffering from all the schizophrenic influences of the era, yet the country's enduring beauty is also captured.

Claudio Magris *Danube* (Harvill). Absorbing, searching exploration of the great river and the places along it from the Black Forest to the Black Sea, mixing travelogue with all manner of scholarly diversions; not the easiest of reads, but rewards the effort.

Mark Twain *A Tramp Abroad* (Century Hutchinson/Hippocrene). The early, German-based part of this book, particularly the descriptions of Heidelberg, show Twain on top form, by turns humorous and evocative. There's an over-the-top appendix entitled "The Awful German Language", which mercilessly pillories the over-complexity of "this fearsome tongue".

Roland Bainton *Here I Stand* (Lion/NAL). The best and liveliest biography of Martin Luther, one of the undisputed titans of European history.

Geoffrey Barraclough *Origins of Modern Germany* (Blackwell/Norton). The most easily digestible general introduction to the country's history, tackling the medieval period better than any more specialized book.

Volker Berghahn *Germany and the Approach of War in 1914* (Macmillan/St Martin's Press). An instructive general picture of Germany before World War I. It chronicles the political, economic and social pressures, and succeeds in giving plausible explanations for the apparently inevitable.

Owen Chadwick *The Reformation* (Penguin). Traces the German origins of the biggest-ever rupture in the fabric of the Church, and follows their impact on the rest of Europe.

Einhard and Notker the Stammerer *Two Lives of Charlemagne* (Penguin). Einhard was a leading courtier in the service of the founder of the Holy Roman Empire, and provided a beautifully written, all-too-short biography of his master. Written a century later, Notker's book is a series of monkish anecdotes, many no doubt apocryphal, which help flesh out the overall portrait of Charlemagne.

Mary Fulbrook *A Concise History of Germany* (Cambridge UP). "Concise" is the key word for this post-unification history, whose brevity is simultaneously its strength and its weakness.

Friedrich Heer *The Holy Roman Empire* (Phoenix). Comprehensive account of the thousand-year history of the First German Reich.

Golo Mann *The History of Germany Since 1787* (Pimlico). Written by the son of Thomas Mann, this comprehensive study traces not only the politics but also the intellectual and cultural currents of the period.

Nancy Mitford *Frederick the Great* (Penguin). Lively biography of the man who brought

Prussia to the forefront of German affairs, and to a place among the great powers of Europe.

Detlev Pleukert *The Weimar Republic* (Penguin). Trenchant dissection of the endlessly fascinating but fundamentally flawed state – until recently the only experiment at a united and democratic German nation – which survived for just fourteen years.

Tacitus *The Germania* (Penguin). Brilliant series of concise analyses of each of the warlike Germanic tribes, which are often compared favourably with the author's native Rome. Some of the observations about German character are startlingly prophetic.

A.J.P. Taylor *Bismarck: The Man and the Statesman* (Penguin/Random House). Britain's most controversial historian here provides a typically stirring portrait of the ruthless schemer who forged (reluctantly, in the author's view) the nineteenth-century unification of Germany.

Veronica (C.V.) Wedgwood *The Thirty Years War* (Methuen/Routledge). Easily the most accomplished book on the series of conflicts which devastated the country and divided the continent in the first half of the seventeenth century.

Andrew Wheatcroft *The Habsburgs* (Penguin). Wide-ranging history of the extraordinary dynasty which not only dominated German affairs for several centuries, but controlled much of the rest of Europe as well.

NAZISM AND WORLD WAR II

Alan Bullock *Hitler: A Study in Tyranny* (Penguin). Ever since it was published, this scholarly yet highly readable tome has ranked as the classic biography of the failed Austrian artist and discharged army corporal whose evil genius fooled a nation and caused the deaths of millions.

Joachim Fest *The Face of the Third Reich* (Penguin). Mainly of interest for its biographies of the men surrounding the Führer – Göring, Goebbels, Hess, Himmler, Speer et al.

Klaus P. Fischer *Nazi Germany* (Constable). Offers a well-balanced general history of the Third Reich and its origins.

Daniel Jonah Goldhagen *Hitler's Willing Executioners* (Abacus). One of the most important recent contributions to the history of the

Third Reich, this controversial tome sets out to prove that guilt for the implementation of the Holocaust lies with a far broader constituency than the Nazi elite.

Adolf Hitler *Table Talk* (OUP/AMS Press). Hitler in his own words: Martin Bormann, one of his inner circle, recorded the dictator's pronouncements at meetings between 1941 and 1944. The early *Mein Kampf* (Pimlico/Noontide), a series of rambling, irrational and hysterical outbursts on every subject under the sun, is also of interest, as it genuinely constituted Hitler's blueprint for power.

Claudia Koonz *Mothers in the Fatherland* (Methuen/St Martin's Press). Perceptive study of the role of women in Nazi Germany. Includes a rare and revealing interview with the chief of Hitler's Women's Bureau, Gertrud Scholtz-Klink.

William Shirer *The Rise and Fall of the Third Reich* (Mandarin/Simon & Schuster). This makes a perfect complement to Bullock's book: Shirer was an American journalist stationed in Germany during the Nazi period. Notwithstanding the inordinate length and excessive journalese, this book is full of insights and is ideal for dipping into, with the help of its exhaustive index.

Albert Speer *Inside the Third Reich* (Phoenix). Candid review of the Nazi legacy by the only senior figure who repented of his involvement.

James Taylor and Warren Shaw *A Dictionary of the Third Reich* (Grafton/Pharos). The handiest reference book of the period.

Hugh Trevor-Roper *The Last Days of Hitler* (Macmillan). A brilliant reconstruction of the closing chapter of the Third Reich, set in the Berlin Bunker. Trevor-Roper subsequently marred his reputation as the doyen of British historians by authenticating the forged *Hitler Diaries*, which have themselves been the subject of several books.

POSTWAR SOCIETY AND POLITICS

John Ardagh *Germany and the Germans* (Penguin/Harper & Collins). The most comprehensive English-language characterization of the country and its people, taking into account its history, politics and psyche, and covering almost every aspect of national life, newly revised after unification. Its approach is always lively, yet remains scrupulously unbiased.

David Childs *The GDR – Moscow's German Ally* (Unwin Hyman). The best book on the GDR period, fully revised the year before the *Wende*, when the regime still seemed fully secure. Obviously now dated, but still of considerable interest for its detailed descriptions and explanations.

W.A. Coupe *Germany Through the Looking-Glass* (Berg). The author presents the period 1945–1986 via a collection of German political cartoons, adding his own analysis of the issues in each case. Opinionated and subjective, the book introduces German humour and a German view of the country's postwar development.

Ian Derbyshire *Politics in Germany* (Chambers). Survey of the German political scene, with the *Wende* and the subsequent elections fully documented.

Stuart Parkes *Understanding Contemporary Germany* (Routledge). Sympathetic examination – with a broadly optimistic conclusion – of the political, economic and social structures of post-unification Germany.

Peter Schneider *The Germany Comedy* (I. B. Tauris/Farrar, Straus & Giroux). Discussion of the myriad problems caused by unification, with many wry descriptions and observations of the bizarre contradictions and anomalies that ensued.

Günther Wallraff *Lowest of the Low* (Methuen/Freundlich). In 1983, Wallraff spent two years labouring among Turkish and other immigrant workers, finding out about the underside of German affluence. The book was a political bombshell when it came out, painting a picture of exploitation and malpractice rarely discussed in Germany. Unfortunately, it now seems that the author was guilty of fabricating some of the evidence, thus diminishing its long-term impact. *The Undesirable Journalist* (Pluto Press) is a collection of short but similarly shocking pieces exposing some of the nastier aspects of the country's postwar prosperity.

Alan Watson *The Germans – Who are they now?* (Mandarin). A guide to German identity and the way it is shaping for the future. Each of the eight chapters attempts to provide an answer to one strand of the question posed in the title.

GERMANY IN ENGLISH FICTION

Elizabeth von Arnim *Elizabeth and her German Garden* (Virago), *Elizabeth in Rügen* (Virago). Although billed as novels, these are effectively autobiographical works by Katherine Mansfield's cousin, an Australian who married a German aristocrat and went to live in his Pomeranian estates.

Sybille Bedford *A Legacy* (Picador). Semi-autobiographical novel about two German families – one Berlin, Jewish and mercantile, the other rural, Catholic and aristocratic – improbably united by marriage. Full of sparkling dialogue and richly comic episodes.

Erskine Childers *The Riddle of the Sands* (Wordsworth). Set against the background of the Great Naval Race in the run-up to World War I, this is generally regarded as the first modern spy novel. The authentic descriptions of the Friesian islands give it a strong local colour.

Daniel Defoe *Memoirs of a Cavalier* (OUP). The first half of this novel is set in the Germany of the Thirty Years' War, and offers vivid descriptions of some of the key battles: indeed the book is so lifelike that Defoe was able to pass it off as a true autobiography of a soldier of fortune.

Thomas de Quincey *Klosterheim* (Woodbridge Press). The only novel by the celebrated opium eater, this spooky Gothic fantasy again uses the backdrop of the Thirty Years' War, but (in contrast to Defoe) is told from the point of view of the Catholic side.

Richard Hughes *The Fox in the Attic*, *The Wooden Shepherdess* (Harvill). The most taciturn of writers, Hughes established an enormous literary reputation on a handful of works, including these first two parts of an unfinished trilogy about an Anglo-German family in the years following World War I. Focusing heavily on the fatal attraction of the Nazis, each mixes fictional episodes with vivid descriptions of real-life events, including Hitler's Beer Hall Putsch and the Night of the Long Knives.

Christopher Isherwood *Mr Norris Changes Trains*, *Goodbye to Berlin* (Methuen/New Directions). Set in the decadent atmosphere of the Weimar Republic, these stories brilliantly evoke the period and bring to life some classic Berlin characters. They subsequently formed the basis of the films *I Am a Camera* and the later remake *Cabaret*. See also *Christopher and his Kind* (Methuen), a fairly dire autobiographical product of the author's declining years which is nonetheless of interest for describing the true-life events and people on which the stories were based.

Jerome K. Jerome *Three Men on the Bummel* (Penguin). Sequel to the (deservedly) more famous *Three Men in a Boat*, this features the same trio of feckless English travellers taking a cycling holiday through Germany at the turn of the century. The second half of the book features plenty of entertaining anecdotes, with opinions bandied about on every conceivable subject. *Diary of a Pilgrimage* (Alan Sutton) is an account of the same author's visit to see the Oberammergau Passion Play.

John Le Carré *A Small Town in Germany* (Coronet). Vintage spy novel set in 1960s Bonn. The then recently built Berlin Wall is the setting for both the beginning and ending of *The Spy Who Came in from the Cold* (Coronet), Le Carré's best-known Cold War fiction.

Katherine Mansfield *In a German Pension* (Penguin). One of the author's earliest works, this is a collection of short stories set in early twentieth-century Bavaria. Funny but often acerbic too.

Robert Muller *The World That Summer* (Sceptre). A beautifully written novel based on the author's own experience as a half-Jewish boy growing up in Hamburg during the Third Reich, with all the inevitable conflicts that involved.

Rudolph Erich Raspe *The Adventures of Baron Münchausen* (Dedalus/Hippocrene). The outrageously exaggerated humorous exploits of the real-life Baron Münchhausen were embroidered yet further by Raspe and first published in English. Copies with the classic nineteenth-century engravings of Gustave Doré can often be found in remainder and secondhand shops.

Stephen Spender *The Temple* (Faber & Faber). Set in Hamburg and the Rhineland during the Weimar Republic years, this makes a fascinating comparison with the closely related works of Isherwood, who is actually one of the main characters. Because of its explicit homosexuality, it could not be published at the time, and remained in draft manuscript until a few years ago.

Anthony Trollope *Linda Tressel* (OUP). One of the Victorian master novelist's shorter full-length works, a powerful psychological study, set against the backdrop of Nürnberg, of the crushing of a young woman's spirit by her bigoted aunt.

GERMAN FICTION CLASSICS

Theodor Fontane *Before the Storm* (OUP). Set in Prussia during the period of the Napoleonic Wars, this epic is by some way the greatest German historical novel of the second half of the nineteenth century, dealing with the conflict between patriotism and liberty. The much shorter *Effi Briest* (Penguin) focuses on adultery in the context of the social mores of the age. *Cécile* (Angel) likewise deals with moral dilemmas and ends tragically, while *Two Novellas* (Penguin) demonstrate the author's mastery of the small-scale.

Johann Wolfgang von Goethe *The Sorrows of Young Werther* (Penguin/Random House). An early epistolary novella, treating the theme of suicide for the first time ever. *Wilhelm Meister: The Years of Apprenticeship* (John Calder/Riverrun Press) and *Wilhelm Meister: The Years of Travel* (John Calder/Riverrun Press) is a huge, episodic and partly autobiographical cycle of novels. *Tales for Transformation* (City Lights) is a series of short stories, showing Goethe's interest in the supernatural.

Johann Jacob Christoffel von Grimmelshausen *Simplicius Simplicissimus* (Dedalus/University Press of America). This massive, brilliantly witty semi-autobiographical novel is one of the high points of seventeenth-century European literature. Set against the uncertainties of the Thirty Years' War, it charts the story of its hero from boyhood to middle age.

Gerhart Hauptmann *Lineman Thiel and Other Stories* (Angel/Ungar). These three remarkable stories, written towards the end of last century, anticipate Freud in their psychological penetration, and the techniques of the cinema in their use of strong visual symbols.

Johann Peter Hebel *The Treasure Chest* (Penguin). A wonderful collection of moral tales, anecdotes, jokes, reports of of murders, disasters and mysteries, all originally written for inclusion in a popular religious almanac.

Ernst Theodor Amadeus Hoffmann *Tales of Hoffmann* (Penguin), *The Best Tales of Hoffmann* (Dover). These selections of work by the schizophrenic master of fantasy and the macabre overlap slightly, but each features only one of his two greatest masterpieces; *Penguin* has *Mademoiselle de Scudéry*, the world's first detective story, while *Dover* includes the nightmarish allegory, *The Golden Pot*, in Thomas Carlyle's inspired translation.

Heinrich von Kleist *The Marquise of O and Other Stories* (Penguin). Like Hoffmann, who was only one year older, Kleist was one of the all-time greats of short story writing. His eight tales range in length from three to one hundred pages, but they're all equally compelling.

Frank G. Ryder (ed.) *German Romantic Stories* (Continuum). A marvellous anthology which includes three of the classic novellas of German Romanticism: *Memoirs of a Good-for-Nothing* by Joseph von Eichendorff; *Undine* by Friedrich de la Motte Fouqué and *The Strange Story of Peter Schlemihl* by Adelbert von Chamisso.

Jeffrey L. Sammons (ed.) *German Novellas of Realism* (Continuum). Another fine collection, including two exquisite prose idylls by writers better known as poets: *The Jew's Beech* by Annette von Droste-Hülshoff and *Mozart on the Way to Prague* by Eduard Mörike.

Theodor Storm *The Dykemaster* (Angel). Powerful short novel, set against the bleak western coastline of Schleswig-Holstein, about the inventor of a new type of dyke who is demonized by the self-centred community which opposes him.

TWENTIETH-CENTURY GERMAN FICTION

Heinrich Böll *The Lost Honour of Katharina Blum* (Minerva/McGraw Hill). Winner of the Nobel Prize for Literature in 1972, Heinrich Böll is the most popular postwar German novelist – at least with non-Germans. Certainly his books are accessible and always on contentious topics. This is the harrowing story of a young woman whose life is ruined by the combined effects of a gutter-press campaign and her accidental involvement with a wanted terrorist. *The Clown* (Marion Boyars/McGraw Hill) again uses the backdrop of Cologne for a more detailed critique of modern German society. *And Where*

Were You, Adam? (Minerva/McGraw Hill) is set in 1944, chronicling the effect of war and Nazism on ordinary German people.

Wolfgang Borchert *The Man Outside* (Marion Boyars). As well as the play which gives the volume its title, this includes most of the short stories of the first important new author to emerge from Germany after the war – one whose career lasted for just two years before his untimely death.

Bertolt Brecht *The Threepenny Novel* (Penguin). Brecht's only novel, a much-expanded version of the *Opera*, is a disaster. The joke underpinning the book has worn thin after about three chapters, but the author ploughs on relentlessly through a further 300 pages. On the other hand, many of the collected *Short Stories* (Methuen/Routledge) are highly entertaining, proving that this side of his output has been unfairly neglected.

Alfred Döblin *Berlin-Alexanderplatz* (Ungar). A prominent socialist intellectual during the Weimar period, Döblin went into exile shortly after the banning of his books in 1933. *Berlin-Alexanderplatz* is his weightiest and most durable achievement, an unrelenting epic of the city's underclass.

Hans Fallada *Little Man, What Now?* (Libris/Academy Chicago Publishers). A once-famous but now unjustly neglected masterpiece, describing with style, humour and tenderness the story of a young couple struggling against the spiralling inflation of the final Weimar years. The German psyche on the eve of the Nazi takeover is captured and distilled more effectively than in any history book.

Hubert Fichte *The Orphanage* (Serpent's Tail). Powerful, heavily symbolic novel exploring the themes of sex, identity and the intellectual roots of Nazism through a World War II story of a half-Jewish boy moved from his Protestant grandparents' home to a Catholic orphanage.

Günter Grass *From the Diary of a Snail* (Picador/Harcourt Brace), *The Flounder* (Picador/Harcourt Brace), *The Tin Drum* (Picador/Random House). Grass is one of Germany's best-known postwar novelists, concerned to analyse and come to terms with his country's awful recent heritage. His highly political novels are all studies of the German character, concentrating on how Nazism found a foothold among ordinary Germans, on postwar guilt, but also on postwar materialism and spiritual poverty.

Hermann Hesse *Narziss and Goldmund* (Penguin/Bantam). A beautifully polished novel, set in medieval Germany and narrated in the picaresque vein, about two monks, one a dedicated scholar, the other a wanderer, artist and lover. *Steppenwolf* (Penguin/Bantam) is a bizarre fantasy about schizophrenia, while *The Glass Bead Game* (Picador/Henry Holb) is a monumental utopian novel, set in a future where an elite group develops a game which resolves the world's conflicts.

Georg Heym *The Thief and Other Stories* (Libris). These seven Expressionist stories, notable for their rich imagery and relentlessly grim subject matter, comprise the entire prose output of the author, who was already a well-established poet at the time of his death in a skating accident at the age of 25.

Gert Hofmann *The Parable of the Blind* (Minerva/Fromm), *Our Conquest* (Minerva). Hofmann was a latecomer to fiction, but quickly established himself among the most original contemporary German writers. The first of these is an imaginative rendering of the story behind Bruegel's enigmatic painting; the other offers a child's-eye view of the aftermath of defeat in World War II.

Ernst Jünger *The Glass Bees* (Noonday Press), *Eumeswill* (Quartet), *Aladdin's Problem* (Quartet). Jünger is the most controversial German writer of the century, mainly because, although never a Nazi, he was an avowed right-winger who willingly served as a soldier in World War II. His novels belong to the genre of utopian fiction and are multi-layered in approach, offering critiques which can be taken to apply to Germany in particular or modern society in general.

Wolfgang Koeppen *Pigeons on the Grass* (Holmes & Meier). A collage-like novel describing through a score of different characters the events in a single day in an occupied German city after World War II. It's part of an informal trilogy which also includes *Death in Rome* (Penguin), a ruthless dissection of the various component parts of the German soul as manifested through four members of the same family, each of whom personifies one of its key elements.

Siegfried Lenz *The German Lesson* (New Directions). A classic German novel about World War II, focusing on the clashes between a father and son, and between duty and personal loyalty. *The Lightship* (Methuen) examines similar themes in a very different setting.

Heinrich Mann *Man of Straw* (Penguin). The best novel by Thomas Mann's more politically committed elder brother, here analysing the corrupt nature of political and business life under the Second Reich.

Klaus Mann *The Pious Dance* (Gay Men's Press), *Mephisto* (Penguin). The erotic novels of Thomas Mann's son were long banned; he now appears as a remarkable individual voice in his own right. His vivid descriptions of the Berlin underworld in the former strongly influenced Isherwood, while *Mephisto* is a striking *roman à clef* about an actor who sells his soul to the Nazi party.

Thomas Mann *The Magic Mountain* (Minerva/Random House). Generally considered the author's masterpiece, this is a weighty novel of ideas discussing love, death, politics and war through a collection of characters in a Swiss sanatorium, whose sickness mirrors that of European society as a whole. *Buddenbrooks* (Minerva/Random House) is the story of a merchant dynasty in the author's native Lübeck; *Confessions of Felix Krull, Confidence Man* (Minerva/Random House) is the great comic novel of German literature; *Lotte in Weimar* (Minerva/Random House) is a brilliant evocation of Weimar in the era of Goethe; while *Doctor Faustus* (Minerva/Random House) updates the Faust legend through the story of a twentieth-century German composer.

Erich Maria Remarque *All Quiet on the Western Front* (Picador/Fawcett). The classic German novel of World War I, focusing on the traumatic impact of the conflict on the life of an ordinary soldier.

Herbert Rosendorfer *The Architect of Ruins* (Dedalus). This, the first and best novel of one of Germany's most admired contemporary writers, is an amusing, dreamlike work consisting of a series of stories within stories. *The Night of the Amazons* (Minerva) is a black comedy about Nazi Germany, while *Stephanie* (Dedalus) narrates a German housewife's trips back in time to her previous existence as an eighteenth-century Spanish duchess.

Peter Schneider *The Wall Jumper* (Allison & Busby/Pantheon). A series of vignettes about the Berlin Wall: about those who crossed it (in both directions), and about the two different states of mind it induced. Although billed as fiction, much of it is clearly autobiographical and factual, albeit larded with a few hoaxes.

W.G. Sebald *The Emigrants* (Harvill). Billed as a work of fiction – notwithstanding the inclusion of numerous old photographs as evidence of its factual basis – this is a haunting lament for the vanished Jewish culture of Germany, illustrated through the lives of four exiles.

Anna Seghers *The Seventh Cross* (Monthly Review Press). Now rather a neglected figure, the author was one of the literary stalwarts of the GDR. This, her best-known novel, is a stirring wartime adventure story about a Communist on the run from the Nazi prison camps.

Kurt Tucholsky *Germany? Germany!* (Carcanet). A reader drawn from the writings of the sharpest German satirist of the century. The outrageously witty monologues of the complacent Jewish businessman Herr Wendriner are chillingly prophetic.

Jakob Wassermann *Caspar Hauser* (Penguin). A masterly exposition of the theme of innocence betrayed, this novel is the finest of the many books inspired by the true story of the famous foundling.

Christa Wolf *A Model Childhood* (Virago/Farrar, Straus & Giroux). The author gained a reputation for literary integrity, despite her loyalty to the GDR. This book is a fictionalized account of her own youth in Bavaria in the 1930s, providing an excellent portrait of a child's confrontation with Nazi ideas and the shattering disillusionment that came from facing the truth as an adult.

POETRY

Anon *Carmina Burana* (Penguin). A wonderful collection of (originally) dog-Latin songs and poems from thirteenth-century Bavaria. In spite of their monastic origin, the texts are often bawdy and erotic. Many were used by Carl Orff in his choral showpiece named after the manuscript.

Bertolt Brecht *Poems* (Eyre Methuen/ Routledge, Chapman and Hall). Brecht's poems have worn far better than his plays. They sound even more inspired when heard in the musical settings provided by Kurt Weill and the more ideologically inspired Paul Dessau and Hans Eisler. Many recordings are available of these – the best are by Lotte Lenya (CBS), Ute Lempe (Decca) and, in English, Robyn Archer (EMI).

Leonard Forster (ed.) *The Penguin Book of German Verse* (Penguin). Best of the anthologies, representing all the big names (and many more) from the eighth century to the present day, with folk songs, ballads and chorales added for good measure.

Johann Wolfgang von Goethe *Selected Poems* (John Calder/Princeton UP), *Selected Verse* (Penguin), *Epigrams and Poems* (Anvil). Varied anthologies drawn from Goethe's prodigious output. *Roman Elegies and The Diary* (Libris) couples two of Goethe's most accessible poetic works.

Heinrich Heine *Complete Poems* (OUP/Gordon Press), *Selected Verse* (Penguin). Heine's works, with their strong rhythms and dramatic, acerbic thrusts, translate far better into English than those of any of his contemporaries; he was also the favourite poet of the great Romantic composers.

Friedrich Hölderlin *Selected Verse* (Anvil). Hölderlin's poetry, with its classical metres and vivid imagery, is notoriously difficult to translate, but this anthology makes a successful stab at the thankless task. Another selection (Chicago UP) also includes some of the very different lyric poetry of Eduard Mörike.

Novalis (Georg Philipp von Hardenberg) *Hymns to the Night* (Enitharmon). Fine new translation of, accompanied by an illuminating essay on, the great mystic masterpiece of German Romanticism.

DRAMA

Bertolt Brecht *Plays* (Eyre Methuen/Random House). Brecht's short but fruitful collaboration during the Weimar Republic with the composer Kurt Weill – *The Threepenny Opera*, *The Rise and Fall of the City of Mahagonny* and *The Seven Deadly Sins* – show him on top form, though the music is an essential component in these works. Of his other plays, the "parables" – *The Caucasian Chalk Circle* and *The Good Woman of Setzuan* – are generally more successful than those with a more overtly political tone.

Georg Büchner *Complete Plays* (Penguin). Büchner died in 1837 at the age of 23. Two of his three plays are masterpieces – *Danton's Death* is a political statement about the French Revolution, while the astonishing unfinished *Woyzeck*, a tragedy based on the life of an insignificant soldier, must be the tersest drama ever written, with not a word wasted in the telling. This anthology also includes his only major prose work, the unfinished novella *Lenz*.

Johann Wolfgang von Goethe *Faust Part One* (Penguin/OUP), *Faust Part Two* (Penguin/OUP). Goethe made the completion of this vast drama – which examines the entire gamut of preoccupations of European civilization – the major task of his life, and he duly finished it just before his death, having worked at it for around sixty years. All his other important works for the stage are collected together in *Early Verse Drama and Prose Plays* (Princeton UP) and *Verse Plays and Epics* (Princeton UP).

Georg Kaiser *Plays Vol. 1*, *Plays Vol. 2* (John Calder/Riverrun). These contain a selection of the vast output of the leading dramatist of the Expressionist movement, typically using very stark language and stressing ideas at the expense of characterization – the players are typically denoted by their worldly function, rather than their name. Another piece by Kaiser features in *Seven Expressionist Plays* (John Calder/Riverrun), which also contains works by two dramatists better known as artists – Ernst Barlach and Oskar Kokoschka.

Heinrich von Kleist *Five Plays* (Yale UP). Ranges over Kleist's varied output, from German theatre's finest comedy, *The Broken Jug*, to the patriotic drama, *Prince Frederick of Homburg*.

Gotthold Ephraim Lessing *Nathan the Wise, Minna von Barnhelm and Other Plays* (Continuum). The first of these plays is unusual in German literature in having a Jew as the hero; the second is one of German theatre's earliest examples of middle-class comedy, using contemporary eighteenth-century events as a backdrop.

Friedrich Schiller *The Robbers, Wallenstein* (Penguin). This pairs an early *Sturm und Drang* drama (which established him as the leader of that movement) with one of his later historical plays, set against the background of the Thirty Years' War. *William Tell* (Chicago UP) is the playwright's last work.

Martin Walser *Rabbit Race Detour* (Marion Boyars). Walser is a writer critical of postwar German society and its ambivalent attitude to Nazism.

Ottmar Weiss and Alois Daisenberger *Oberammergau: A Passion Play* (Dedalus). A complete translation of the classic nineteenth-century text of the play.

LEGENDS AND FOLKLORE

Anon *The Nibelungenlied* (Penguin). Germany's greatest epic was written around 1200 by an unknown Danubian poet; the story varies greatly from Wagner's *Ring*, which draws equally heavily on Nordic sources of the legend. It's here given a highly entertaining prose translation.

Anon *Till Eulenspiegel* (OUP). This new translation is the first complete and uncensored English version of the adventures of Germany's most famous folk hero, the roguish jester who fought pomposity in all its many manifestations.

Francis G. Gentry (ed.) *German Medieval Tales* (Continuum). Includes most of the best-known German legends with a medieval origin, notably the *Historia and Tale of Doctor Johannes Faustus*, which became one of European literature's most fertile sources.

Jakob and Wilhelm Grimm *Complete Grimm's Tales* (Gollancz/Doubleday). The world's most famous collection of folk tales, meticulously researched by the Brothers Grimm, has stories to appeal to all age ranges. A selection of the tales (Penguin) has the ingenious idea of rendering some of them in Scots and Irish, thus capturing something of the dialect flavour of the originals, which is otherwise lost in translation.

Jennifer Russ *German Festivals* (Oswald Wolff/Ungar). Rather a pity it's not a bit longer, but this book provides useful background information on all the main annual folklore celebrations.

Frank G. Ryder (ed.) *German Literary Fairy Tales* (Continuum). An anthology of elaborate reworkings of folk tales made by Goethe, Novalis, Eichendorff, Mörike, Storm and others.

Lewis Spence *Germany – Myths and Legends* (Bracken). Narrates the rich store of legends associated with the Rhine, arranged in the form of a journey down the great river.

Gottfried von Strassburg *Tristan* (Penguin), **Wolfram von Eschenbach** *Parzifal* (Penguin/Random House) are two more epic masterpieces from early thirteenth-century Germany, both based on the Grail legends.

THE ARTS

Peter Adam *The Arts of the Third Reich* (Thames & Hudson). Engrossing and well-written account of the officially approved state art of Nazi Germany – a subject that for many years has been ignored or deliberately made inaccessible. Includes over three hundred illustrations, many reproduced for the first time since the war.

Jost Amman *The Book of Trades* (Dover). The 114 woodcuts illustrate the trades and crafts practised in early sixteenth-century Germany; each is accompanied by a poem by the most famous of the *Meistersinger*, Hans Sachs.

Michael Baxendall *The Limewood Sculptors of Renaissance Germany* (Yale UP). Examines the work of Tilman Riemenschneider, Veit Stoss, and many other lesser-known artists in their social and political context. A lavish series of photographs accompanies the text.

Wolf-Dieter Dube *The Expressionists* (Thames & Hudson). A general introduction to Germany's most distinctive contribution to twentieth-century art.

Albrecht Dürer *The Complete Woodcuts* (Dover), *The Complete Etchings, Engravings and Drypoints* (Dover). These two books enable you to own, at minimal cost, a complete set of the graphic work of one of the world's greatest-ever masters of the art. The book of woodcuts is particularly recommended.

William Vaughan *German Romantic Painting* (Yale UP). A good introduction to many of Germany's best nineteenth-century artists.

Frank Whiteford *Bauhaus* (Thames & Hudson). Introduction to the twentieth century's most influential art and design movement, tracing its development during its early years in Weimar, Dessau and Berlin.

GUIDE BOOKS

Karl Baedeker *The Rhineland, Northern Germany, Southern Germany, Berlin* (Baedeker). The old Baedekers, all out of print, are still indispensible classics. They covered a Germany which was considerably more extensive than today, stretching all across Poland into Russia and Lithuania. Look out for the editions dating from the early years of the present century, immensely learned and full of now-untenable opinions. The glossy, modern successors to these (Automobile Association) are not in the same class.

Grant Bourne and Sabine Kröner-Bourne *Walking in the Bavarian Alps* (Cicerone). New and much-needed hiking guide to Germany's most spectacular scenic region.

Jack Holland and John Gawthrop *The Rough Guide to Berlin* (Rough Guides). Companion volume to the book you're holding, this gives the full lowdown on the sights, culture and nightlife of one of Europe's most exciting cities. Essential reading for those bound for the city.

Bob Larson *Your Swabian Neighbours* (Schwaben International Verlag). Written by a US Army liaison officer and long-time resident of the semi-mythical part of southern Germany known as Swabia, this book is very American and error-prone in places, but is nonetheless a highly entertaining and remarkably candid account of a fascinating part of the country.

Graham Lees *Good Beer Guide to Munich and Bavaria* (CAMRA). Impressively wide-ranging guide to the myriad brews of the world's premier beer region, and to the best places to sample them.

Gordon McLachlan *Berlin* (Odyssey). Predominantly a cultural guide, lavishly illustrated with both archive and commissioned photographs. The main text is accompanied by a wide selection of literary excerpts. *Germany's Romantic Road* (Cicerone) is a detailed guide, with special reference to walkers and cyclists, to the country's most popular tourist route.

Fleur and Colin Speakman *Walking in the Black Forest* (Cicerone), *King Ludwig Way* (Cicerone), *Walking in the Harz Mountains* (Cicerone). Three guides for specific hikes in Germany.

George Wood *The Visitor's Guide to the Black Forest* (Visitor's Guides). A specific guide for hiking or motoring round one of Germany's most beautiful – and touristed – areas; unfortunately, a bit short on detail.

LANGUAGE

German is a very complex language and you can't hope to master it in a short time. As English was a compulsory subject in the West German school curriculum, many people have some familiarity with it, which eases communication a great deal. English is now compulsory in schools throughout Germany.

Nonetheless, a smattering of German does help, especially in out-of-the-way rural areas, or in the former East, where Russian was more commonly taught in schools. Also, given the long-standing and continued presence of American and British forces who make little effort to integrate into local communities or learn German, people are particularly sensitive to presumptuous English-speakers. On the other hand, most will be delighted to practise their English on you once you've stumbled through your German introduction. In the former East Germany, a phrase-book knowledge of German is essential.

Should you be interested in **studying the language** during your stay, the best places to enrol in are the *Goethe-Instituten*, which can be found in most major cities. The German Tourist Board or local information offices have all relevant addresses.

PRONUNCIATION

English-speakers find the complexities of German grammar hard to handle, but **pronunciation** isn't as daunting as it might first appear. Individual syllables are generally pronounced as they're printed – the trick is learning how to place the stresses in the notoriously lengthy German words.

VOWELS AND UMLAUTS

a as in f**a**ther
e as in d**ay** or as in w**e**t
i as in l**ee**k
o as in b**o**ttom or as in r**o**se
u as in b**oo**t
ä is a combination of a and e, sometimes pronounced like **e** in b**e**t (eg Länder) and sometimes like **ai** in p**ai**d (eg spät)
ö is a combination of o and e, like the French eu
ü is a combination of u and e, like tr**ue**, only sharper in sound

VOWEL COMBINATIONS

ai as in l**ie**
au as in h**ou**se
ie as in fr**ee**
ei as in h**ei**ght
eu as in **oi**l

CONSONANTS

Consonants are pronounced as they are written, with no silent letters. The differences from English are:
r is given a dry throaty sound, similar to French
j pronounced similar to an English y
s pronounced similar to, but slightly softer than an English z
v pronounced somewhere between f and v
w pronounced same way as English v
z pronounced ts
The German letter ß, the *Scharfes S*, usually replaces ss in a word: pronunciation is identical.

CONSONANT COMBINATIONS

ch is a strong back-of-the-throat sound as in the Scottish loch
sp (at the start of a word) is pronounced shp
st (at the start of a word) is pronounced sht

GENDER

German words can be one of three genders: masculine, feminine or neuter. Unfortunately, the designation of these can appear very illogical: for example, a train is masculine, a cat (even a tomcat) is feminine, and a girl is neuter. Each has its own definite article (respectively *der*, *die*, *das*); as with qualifying adjectives, these decline according to the case used.

GERMAN WORDS AND PHRASES

BASICS

Ja, nein	yes, no	*Gross, klein*	large, small
Bitte	please/ you're welcome	*Mehr, weniger*	more, less
Bitte schön	a more polite form of *Bitte*	*Wenig*	a little
Danke, Danke schön	thank you, thank you very much	*Viel*	a lot
		Billig, teuer	cheap, expensive
Wo, wann, warum?	where, when, why?	*Gut, schlecht*	good, bad
Wieviel?	how much?	*Heiss, kalt*	hot, cold
Hier, da	here, there	*Mit, ohne*	with, without
Geöffnet, offen, auf	all mean "open"	*Rechts*	right
Geschlossen, zu	both mean "closed"	*Links*	left
Da drüben	over there	*Geradeaus*	straight ahead
Dieses	this one	*Oben*	above
Jenes	that one	*Unten*	below

GREETINGS AND TIMES

Guten Morgen	Good morning	*Übermorgen*	The day after tomorrow
Guten Abend	Good evening	*Tag*	Day
Guten Tag	Good day	*Nacht*	Night
Grüss Gott	Good day (in southern Germany)	*Mittag*	Midday
		Mitternacht	Midnight
Gute Nacht	Good night	*Drei Uhr*	Three o'clock
Wie geht es Ihnen?	How are you? (polite)	*Viertel nach drei*	Quarter past three
Wie geht es dir?	How are you? (informal)	*Halb vier*	Half past three (ie half to four)
Lass mich in Ruhe	Leave me alone		
Hau ab	Get lost	*Viertei vor vier*	Quarter to four
Geh weg	Go away	*Woche*	Week
Auf wiedersehen	Goodbye	*Wochenende*	Weekend
Tschüs	Goodbye (informal)	*Monat*	Month
Jetzt, später	Now, later	*Jahr*	Year
Früher	Earlier	*Am Vormittag/ Vormittags*	In the morning
Heute	Today		
Gestern	Yesterday	*Am Nachmittag/ Nachmittags*	In the afternoon
Morgen	Tomorrow		
Vorgestern	The day before yesterday	*Am Abend*	In the evening

DAYS, MONTHS AND DATES

Montag	Monday	*März*	March	*Herbst*	Autumn
Dienstag	Tuesday	*April*	April	*Winter*	Winter
Mittwoch	Wednesday	*Mai*	May	*Ferien*	holidays
Donnerstag	Thursday	*Juni*	June	*Feiertag*	bank holiday
Freitag	Friday	*Juli*	July	*Montag,*	Monday, the
Samstag	Saturday	*August*	August	*der erste*	first of April
Sonnabend	Saturday (in northern Germany)	*September*	September	*April*	
		Oktober	October	*Der zweite*	the second of
		November	November	*April*	April
Sonntag	Sunday	*Dezember*	December	*Der dritte*	the third of April
Januar	January	*Frühling*	Spring	*April*	
Februar	February	*Sommer*	Summer		

QUESTIONS AND REQUESTS

All enquiries should be prefaced with the phrase *Entschuldigen Sie bitte* (Excuse me, please). Note that *Sie* is the polite form of address to be used with everyone except close friends, though young people and students often don't bother with it. The older generation will certainly be offended if you address them with the familiar *Du*, as will all officials.

Sprechen Sie Englisch?	Do you speak English?	*Sind die Plätze noch frei?*	Are these seats taken?
Ich spreche kein Deutsch	I don't speak German	*Die Rechnung bitte*	The bill please
Sprechen Sie bitte langsamer	Please speak more slowly	*Ist der Tisch frei?*	Is that table free?
Ich verstehe nicht	I don't understand	*Die Speisekarte bitte*	The menu please
Ich verstehe	I understand	*Fräulein...!*	Waitress...! (for attention)
Wie sagt man das auf Deutsch?	How do you say that in German?	*Herr Ober...!*	Waiter...! (for attention)
Können Sie mir sagen wo... ist?	Can you tell me where... is?	*Haben Sie etwas billigeres?*	Have you got something cheaper?
Wo ist...?	Where is...?	*Haben Sie Zimmer frei?*	Are there rooms available?
Wie komme ich nach...?	How do I get to (a town)?	*Wo sind die Toiletten bitte?*	Where are the toilets?
Wie komme ich zur/zum...	How do I get to (a building, place)?	*Ich hätte gern dieses*	I'd like that one
Wieviel kostet das?	How much does that cost?	*Ich hätte gern ein Zimmer für zwei*	I'd like a room for two
Wann fährt der nächste Zug?	When does the next train leave?	*Ich hätte gern ein Einzelzimmer*	I'd like a single room
Um wieviel Uhr?	At what time?	*Hat es Dusche, Bad, Toilette...?*	Does it have a shower, bath, toilet...?
Wieviel Uhr ist es?	What time is it?		

SOME SIGNS

Damen/Frauen	Women's toilets	*Notausgang*	Emergency exit
Herren/Männer	Men's toilets	*Baustelle*	Building works
Eingang	Entrance	*Ampel*	Traffic light
Ausgang	Exit	*Krankenhaus*	Hospital
Ankunft	Arrival	*Polizei*	Police
Abfahrt	Departure	*Nicht rauchen*	No smoking
Ausstellung	Exhibition	*Kein Eingang*	No entrance
Autobahn	Motorway	*Drücken*	Push
Auffahrt	Motorway entrance	*Ziehen*	Pull
Ausfahrt	Motorway exit	*Frei*	Vacant
Geschwindigkeits- begrenzung	Speed limit	*Besetzt*	Occupied
		Verboten	Prohibited
Umleitung	Diversion	*Zoll*	Customs
Achtung!	Attention!	*Kasse*	Cash desk
Vorsicht!	Beware!	*Grenzübergang*	Border crossing

NUMBERS

1	*eins*	10	*zehn*	19	*neunzehn*	60	*sechzig*
2	*zwei, zwo*	11	*elf*	20	*zwanzig*	70	*siebzig*
3	*drei*	12	*zwölf*	21	*ein-und- zwanzig*	80	*achtzig*
4	*vier*	13	*dreizehn*			90	*neunzig*
5	*fünf*	14	*vierzehn*	22	*zwei-und- zwanzig*	100	*hundert*
6	*sechs*	15	*fünfzehn*			1000	*tausend*
7	*sieben*	16	*sechszehn*	30	*dreissig*	1992	*neunzehn- hundert-zwei- und-neunzig*
8	*acht*	17	*siebzehn*	40	*vierzig*		
9	*neun*	18	*achtzehn*	50	*fünfzig*		

GLOSSARIES

ART AND ARCHITECTURE

AISLE part of church to the side of the nave.

AMBULATORY passage round the back of the altar, in continuation of the aisles.

APSE vaulted termination of the east (altar) end of a church.

ART DECO geometrical style of art and architecture prevalent in 1930s.

ART NOUVEAU sinuous, highly stylized form of architecture and interior design; in Germany, mostly dates from period 1900–15 and is known as Jugendstil.

BALDACHIN canopy over an altar or tomb.

BAROQUE expansive, exuberant architectural style of the seventeenth and early eighteenth centuries, characterized by ornate decoration, complex spatial arrangements and grand vistas. The term is also applied to the sumptuous style of painting of the same period.

BASILICA church in which nave is higher than the aisles.

BAUHAUS plain, functional style of architecture and design, originating in early twentieth-century Germany.

BIEDERMEIERSTIL simple, bourgeois style of painting and decoration practised throughout first half of the nineteenth century.

CAPITAL top of a column, usually sculpted.

CHANCEL part of the church in which altar is placed; normally at east end, though some German churches also have one at the west.

CHOIR part of church in which service is sung, usually beside the altar.

CRYPT underground part of a church.

EXPRESSIONISM emotional style of painting, concentrating on line and colour, extensively practised in early twentieth-century Germany; term is also used for related architecture of the same period.

FRESCO mural painting applied to wet plaster, so that colours immediately soak into the wall.

GOTHIC architectural style with an emphasis on verticality, characterized by pointed arch, ribbed vault and flying buttress; introduced to Germany around 1235, surviving in an increas-

ingly decorative form until well into the sixteenth century. The term is also used for paintings of this period.

GRISAILLE painting executed entirely in monochrome.

HALF-TIMBERED style of building in which the walls have a framework of timber interspersed with either bricks or plaster.

HALL CHURCH (*Hallenkirche*) church design much favoured in Germany, in which all vaults are of approximately equal height.

LAVABO well-house in a cloister.

MANNERISM deliberately mannered style of late Renaissance art and architecture.

MODELLO small version of a large picture, usually painted for the patron's approval.

NAVE main body of a church, generally forming the western part.

NEOCLASSICAL late eighteenth- and early nineteenth-century style of art and architecture returning to Classical models as a reaction against Baroque and Rococo excesses.

ORIEL projecting bay window.

PARADISE (*Paradies*) richly sculpted porch forming the entrance to some cathedrals.

POLYPTYCH carved or painted altarpiece on several joined panels.

PREDELLA lowest part of an altarpiece, with scenes much smaller than in main sections.

RENAISSANCE Italian-originated movement in art and architecture, inspired by the rediscovery of Classical ideals.

RETABLE altarpiece.

ROCOCO highly florid, light and graceful eighteenth-century style of architecture, painting and interior design, forming the last phase of Baroque.

ROMANESQUE solid architectural style of late tenth to mid-thirteenth centuries, characterized by round-headed arches and a penchant for horizontality and geometrical precision. The term is also used for paintings of this period.

ROMANTICISM late eighteenth- and early nineteenth-century movement, particularly strong in Germany, rooted in adulation of the natural world and rediscovery of the achievements of the Middle Ages.

ROOD SCREEN screen dividing nave from chancel (thus separating laity and clergy), originally bearing a rood (crucifix).

SOFT STYLE (*Weicher Stil*) delicate style of painting and sculpture pioneered in fourteenth-century Bohemia, which dominated German art to the mid-fifteenth century.

STUCCO plaster used for decorative effects.

TABERNACLE a freestanding canopy or ornamental recess designed to contain the Holy Sacrament.

TRANSEPT arm of a cross-shaped church, placed at ninety degrees to nave and chancel.

TRANSITIONAL architectural style between Romanesque and Gothic in which the basic shapes of the older style were modified by the use of such new forms as the pointed arch and ribbed vault.

TRIPTYCH carved or painted altarpiece on three panels.

TROMPE L'OEIL painting designed to fool the viewer into believing it is three-dimensional.

TYMPANUM sculptured panel above a doorway.

WESER RENAISSANCE archaic, highly elaborate style of secular Renaissance architecture cultivated in and around the Weser valley in Hesse, Lower Saxony and Westphalia.

WESTWORK (*Westwerk*) grandiose frontage found on many German medieval churches, traditionally reserved for the use of the emperor and his retinue.

GERMAN TERMS

ABTEI abbey.

ALTSTADT old part of a city.

AUSKUNFT information.

AUSLÄNDER foreigner; the word has come to be a pejorative term for any non-white non-German.

AUSSTELLUNG exhibition.

AUSWEIS identity document.

BAD spa (before the name of a town), bath.

BAHNHOF station.

BAU building.

BEFESTIGUNG fortification.

BERG mountain, hill.

BERGBAHN funicular.

BIBLIOTHEK library.

BRÜCKE bridge.

BRUNNEN fountain, well.

BUNDESKANZLER Federal Chancellor (Prime Minister).

BUNDESRAT Upper House of German Parliament.

BUNDESTAG Lower House of German Parliament.

BURG castle, fortress.

BÜRGERMEISTER mayor.

CAROLINGIAN (*Karolingisch*) dynasty founded by Charles Martel in the early eighth century which ruled Germany until last quarter of ninth century. The term is particularly associated with the reign of Charlemagne (768–814).

DENKMAL memorial.

DIET Parliament of Holy Roman Empire.

DOM cathedral.

DONAU River Danube.

DORF village.

EASTERN TERRITORIES (*Ostgebiete*) lands to the east of the Oder–Neisse line, occupied by German-speaking peoples since the Middle Ages, but forcibly evacuated, and allocated to Poland and the Soviet Union after World War II.

EINBAHNSTRASSE one-way street.

ELECTOR (*Kurfürst*) sacred or secular prince with a vote in the elections to choose the Holy Roman Emperor. There were seven for most of the medieval period, with three more added later.

EVANGELISCHE KIRCHE federation of Protestant churches, both Lutheran and Reformed.

FACHWERKHAUS half-timbered house.

FASCHING name given to Carnival, especially in Bavaria.

FASTNET name given to Carnival, especially in Baden-Württemberg.

FEIERTAG holiday.

FEST festival.

FESTUNG fortress.

FLUGHAFEN airport.

FLUSS river.

FRANCONIA (*Franken*) historical province of central Germany, stretching as far west as Mainz; name later became associated only with the eastern portion of this territory, most of which is now incorporated in Bavaria.

FREE IMPERIAL CITY (*Freiereichstadt*) independent city-state within the Holy Roman Empire.

FREIHERR baron.

FREMDENZIMMER room for short-term let.

FÜRST prince.

FUSSGÄNGERZONE pedestrian area.

GASSE alley.

GASTARBEITER (guest worker) anyone who comes to Germany to do menial work.

GASTHAUS, GASTHOF guesthouse, inn.

GEDENKSTÄTTE memorial museum.

GEMÄLDE painting.

GEMÜTLICH snug or cosy.

GRAF count.

GRÜNEN, DIE (The Greens) political party formed from environmental and anti-nuclear groups.

HABSBURG the most powerful family in medieval Germany, operating a base in Austria. They held the office of Holy Roman Emperor from 1452 to 1806, and by marriage, war and diplomacy acquired territories all over Europe.

HAFEN harbour, port.

HANSEATIC LEAGUE (*Hansebund*) medieval trading alliance of Baltic and Rhineland cities, numbering about one hundred at its fifteenth-century peak. Slowly died out in the seventeenth century with competition from Baltic nation-states and rise of Brandenburg-Prussia.

HAUPTBAHNHOF main train station in a city.

HAUPTBURG central, residential part of a castle.

HAUPTSTRASSE main street.

HEIDE heath.

HEIMAT homeland; often given a mystical significance and used emotively in connection with Germans displaced from the Eastern Territories.

HERZOG duke.

HOF court, courtyard, mansion.

HOHENSTAUFEN Swabian dynasty who held office of Holy Roman Emperor from 1138 to 1254.

HOHENZOLLERN dynasty of Swabian origin, who became Margrave-Electors of Brandenburg in 1415, and slowly built up their territorial base. In the nineteenth century they ousted the Habsburgs from their pre-eminent place in German affairs, forging the Second Reich in 1871 and serving as its emperors until 1918.

HÖHLE cave.

HOLY ROMAN EMPIRE (*Heiliges Römisches Reich*) title used to describe the First German Reich, established in 800. Despite its weak structure, it survived until 1806, when the ruling Habsburgs, in response to the Napoleonic threat, began building up a more solid empire from their Austrian base.

INSEL island.

JAGDSCHLOSS hunting lodge.

JUGENDHERBERGE youth hostel.

JUGENDSTIL German version of Art Nouveau.

JUNKER Prussian landowning class.

KAISER emperor.

KAMMER room, chamber.

KAPELLE chapel.

KARNEVAL term used for Carnival, especially in Rhineland.

KAUFHAUS department store.

KINO cinema.

KIRCHE church.

KLOSTER monastery, convent.

KÖNIG king.

KREUZGANG cloister.

KUNST art.

KURHAUS assembly rooms (in a spa).

KURORT health resort.

KURVERWALTUNG reception building in spa resorts.

LAND (pl. **LÄNDER**) name given to the constituent states of the Federal Republic; first introduced in Weimar Republic.

LANDGRAVE (Landgraf) count in charge of a large province.

LEUCHTTURM lighthouse.

MARGRAVE (Markgraf) count in charge of a Mark ("March"; later "Margraviate"), a frontier district established at the time of Charlemagne.

MARKT market, market square.

MAUER wall.

MEER sea or lake.

MEROVINGIAN Frankish dynasty established by Clovis in 481; ruled until the early eighth century.

MIKWE Jewish ritual bath.

MÜNSTER minster, large church.

NATURPARK area of protected countryside.

NEUES FORUM umbrella group for political opposition organizations within the former GDR.

ODER–NEISSE LINE eastern limit of German territory set by victorious Allies in 1945.

OSTPOLITIK West German policy of détente towards the GDR.

OTTONIAN (*Ottonisch*) epoch of Otto I and his two eponymous successors. Term is used in connection with the early Romanesque art forms pioneered in this and the subsequent Salian epoch (mid-tenth to mid-eleventh century).

PALAS, PALAST residential part of a castle.

PALATINATE (*Pfalz*) territory ruled by the Count Palatine, a high-ranking imperial official. The present Land is only the western part of the historical province, whose original centre is now part of Baden-Württemberg.

PFARRKIRCHE parish church.

PLATZ square.

PRINZ prince; since 1918, used in a less grandiose way as a courtesy title for aristocrats in place of the plethora of now-defunct titles.

PRUSSIA (*Preussen*) originally, an eastern Baltic territory (now divided between Poland and the Russian Federation). It was acquired in 1525 by the Hohenzollerns who merged it with their own possessions to form Brandenburg-Prussia (later shortened to Prussia); this took the lead in forging the unity of Germany, and was thereafter its dominant province. The name was abolished after World War II because of its monarchical and militaristic connotations.

QUITTUNG official receipt.

RASTPLATZ picnic area.

RATHAUS town hall.

RATSKELLER cellars below the Rathaus, invariably used as a restaurant serving *gutbürgerliche Küche*.

REICH empire.

REISEBÜRO travel agency.

RESIDENZ palace.

RESIDENZSTADT courtly town.

RITTER knight.

ROMANTISCHE STRASSE ("Romantic Road") scenic road in Bavaria and Baden-Württemberg, running between Würzburg and Füssen.

RUNDGANG way round.

SAAL hall.

SALIAN dynasty of Holy Roman Emperors, 1024–1125.

SAMMLUNG collection.

SÄULE column.

S-BAHN commuter railway network operating in and around conurbations.

SCHATZKAMMER treasury.

SCHICKIE or **SCHICKIE-MICKIE** yuppie.

SCHLOSS castle, palace (equivalent of French château).

SEE lake.

SEEBRÜCKE pier.

SEILBAHN cable car.

SESSELBAHN chair lift.

STADT town, city.

STAMMTISCH table in a pub or restaurant reserved for regular customers.

STASI (*Staatssicherheitsdienst*) former "State Security Service" or secret police of the GDR.

STAUFIAN pertaining to the epoch of the Hohenstaufen.

STIFTSKIRCHE collegiate church.

STIFTUNG foundation.

STRAND beach.

STRANDKORB wicker beach chair with hood.

STRASSENBAHN tram.

SWABIA (*Schwaben*) name used for the south-western part of Germany from the eleventh century onwards; after the ruling Hohenstaufen dynasty died out, became politically fragmented.

SZENE trendy bar or club.

TAL valley.

TALSPERRE dam.

TANKSTELLE petrol station.

TOR gate, gateway.

TRABI conversational shorthand for the now-famous Trabant, East Germany's two-cylinder, two-stroke car.

TURM tower.

U-BAHN network of underground trains or trams.

VERKEHRSAMT, **VERKEHRSVEREIN** tourist office.

VIERTEL quarter, district.

VOLK people, folk; given mystical associations by Hitler.

VORBURG outer, defensive part of a castle.

VORSTADT suburb.

WALD forest.

WALDSTERBEN ("dying forest syndrome") term used to describe the environmental pollution which has decimated Germany's forests.

WALLFAHRT pilgrimage.

WASSERBURG castle surrounded by a moat.

WECHSEL exchange.

WEIMAR REPUBLIC (*Weimarische Republik*) parliamentary democracy established in 1918 which collapsed with Hitler's assumption of power in 1933.

WEINGUT wine-producing estate.

WELF dynastic rivals of Hohenstaufens in Germany and Italy. Descendants became Electors of Hannover, and subsequently Kings of Great Britain.

WENDE literally "turning point" – the term used to describe the events of November 1989 and after.

WETTIN dynasty chiefly responsible for pushing Germany's frontiers eastwards from the tenth century, becoming Electors of Saxony in 1423 and ruling the province and the Thuringian principalities until 1918. The Saxe-Coburg line provided monarchs for several countries; renamed as Windsor, it is the current British royal family.

WIES field, meadow.

WILHELMINE (*Wilhelminisch*) pertaining to the epoch of the Second Reich (1871–1918).

WITTELSBACH dynasty which ruled Bavaria from 1180 to 1918; a branch held the Palatinate Electorate, while the family often held several bishoprics, notably the Archbishop-Electorate of Cologne.

ZEITSCHRIFT magazine.

ZEITUNG newspaper.

ZEUGHAUS arsenal.

ZIMMER room.

ACRONYMS

BRD (*Bundesrepublik Deutschlands*) official name of West German state (1949–90) and of the unified Germany since 1990.

CDU (*Christlich Demokratische Union*) ruling Christian Democratic Party.

CSU (*Christlich Soziale Union*) Bavarian-only counterpart of CDU, generally more right-wing in outlook.

DB (*Deutsche Bahn, formerly Deutsche Bundesbahn*) national rail company retaining the logo of its West German predecessor under a modified name.

DDR (*Deutsche Demokratische Republik*) the Communist East German state, 1949–90.

FDP (*Freie Demokratische Partei*) Free Democratic Party.

GDR (German Democratic Republic) English version of DDR.

NSDAP (*National Sozialistische Deutsche Arbeiterpartei*, "National Socialist German Workers' Party") official name for the Nazis, totalitarian rulers of Germany in the Third Reich, 1933–45.

PDS (*Partei Demokratische Sozialismus*) repackaged former SED.

SED (*Sozialistische Einheitspartei Deutschlands*) Socialist Unity Party of Germany, the permanent governing party of the GDR, formed in 1946 as a union of the SPD and Communists in the Russian zone of occupation.

SPD (*Sozialdemokratische Partei Deutschlands*) Social Democratic Party.

ZOB (*Zentral-Omnibus-Bahnhof*) main bus station.

INDEX

Stay in touch with us!

**ROUGH*NEWS* is Rough Guides' free newsletter.
In four issues a year we give you news, travel
issues, music reviews, readers' letters and the
latest dispatches from authors on the road.**

I would like to receive ROUGH*NEWS*: please put me on your free mailing list.

NAME . . . .

ADDRESS . . . .

Please clip or photocopy and send to: Rough Guides, 62–70 Shorts Gardens, London WC2H 9AB,
England or Rough Guides, 375 Hudson Street, New York, NY 10014, USA.

**HOSTELLING
INTERNATIONAL**

The last word in accommodation

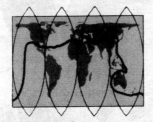

the perfect getaway vehicle

low-price holiday car rental.

rent a car from holiday autos and you'll give yourself real freedom to explore your holiday destination. with great-value, fully-inclusive rates in over 4,000 locations worldwide, wherever you're escaping to, we're there to make sure you get excellent prices and superb service.

what's more, you can book now with complete confidence. our £5 undercut* ensures that you are guaranteed the best value for money in holiday destinations right around the globe.

drive away with a great deal, call holiday autos now on **0990 300 400** and quote ref RG.

holiday autos
miles ahead